WESTERN LITERATURE IN A WORLD CONTEXT

✤

Volume Two
The Enlightenment through the Present

WESTERN LITERATURE IN A WORLD CONTEXT

Volume Two

The Enlightenment through the Present

Paul Davis
Gary Harrison
David M. Johnson
Patricia Clark Smith
John F. Crawford

THE UNIVERSITY OF NEW MEXICO

ST. MARTIN'S PRESS

NEW YORK

Editor: Nancy Lyman
Development editor: Sylvia L. Weber
Manager, publishing services: Emily Berleth
Publishing services associate: Kalea Chapman
Project management: Publication Services
  (*Copy editor,* Carol Anne Peschke;
  Production supervisor, Heather Raak TenHuisen;
  Production coordinators, Rick Dudley and Jeff Topham)
Production manager: Patricia Ollague
Text design: Anna George
Cover design: Carolyn Joseph

Library of Congress Catalog Card Number: 92-62768

Manufactured in the United States of America.
987
fedc

For information, write:
St. Martin's Press, Inc.
175 Fifth Avenue
New York, NY 10010

ISBN: 0-312-08125-1

ACKNOWLEDGMENTS

Molière, "Tartuffe," translated by Richard Wilbur. Copyright © 1963, 1962, 1961 and renewed 1991, 1990, 1989 by Richard Wilbur. Reprinted with the permission of Harcourt Brace & Company. CAUTION: Professionals and amateurs are hereby warned that this translation, being fully protected under the laws of the United States of America, the British Commonwealth, including the Dominion of Canada, and all other countries which are signatories to the Universal Copyright Convention and the International Copyright Union, is subject to royalty. All rights, including professional, amateur, motion picture, recitation, lecturing, public reading, radio broadcasting, and television, are strictly reserved. Particular emphasis is laid on the question of readings, permission for which must be secured from the author's agent in writing. Inquiries on professional rights (except for amateur rights) should be addressed to Curtis Brown, Ltd., 10 Astor Place, New York, NY 10003; inquiries on translation rights should be addressed to Harcourt Brace & Company, Permissions Department, Orlando, FL 32887. The amateur acting rights of TARTUFFE are controlled exclusively by the Dramatists Play Service, Inc., 440 Park Avenue South, New York, NY 10016. No amateur performance of the play may be given without obtaining in advance the written permission of the Dramatists Play Service, Inc., and paying the requisite fee.

PREFACE

PLACING WESTERN LITERATURE IN A WORLD CONTEXT

As our title suggests, this anthology places the great works of Western literature into the broader context of world literature. We group key works of Western and world literature around a set of core stories in order to allow teachers and students to compare how different cultures treat similar themes and issues. In our experience, this thematic approach to the literature of Western and non-Western traditions helps students to synthesize an otherwise unwieldy array of diverse texts and traditions in the two-semester or three-quarter sequence of most Western literature, world literature, or humanities courses.

For the past five years, we have been developing and team-teaching a new humanities course at the University of New Mexico, and it is from this experience that *Western Literature in a World Context* has come. We set out to develop a world literature course reflecting recent reevaluations of the Western tradition and its literary canon. We wanted a reading list that included works from all parts of the world—from Asia, the Middle East, Africa, Latin America, and native America, as well as the areas usually represented in world literature courses. We also wanted to study these works as more than aesthetic masterpieces; we hoped to investigate the ways in which literary works contributed to our tradition, our values, and our place in history. As we articulated these goals into a course syllabus, the great works of the Western tradition continued to hold their central place in our canon, but they entered into a dialogue with works from outside the West and with each other.

This ongoing dialogue made clear that great writings do not speak with a single voice and that the Western tradition is pluralistic and has been enriched throughout its history by its encounters with the literature and cultures of the world. By representing the diversity of our contemporary cultural situation, *Western Literature in a World Context* invites students and teachers to take part in the conversation about the formation of value and meaning in a global community. We think that our thematic and historical approach helps students appreciate the multitude of forms, styles, and themes in world literature, and enables them to draw from their readings the important features of European and non-European literary history.

ORGANIZATION

Our anthology is divided into the six periods usually studied in Western and world literature courses. The subtitle of each part indicates an important motif that is examined in the Western literature of the period:

- The Ancient World: The Heroic Ideal and the Rise of Patriarchy
- The Middle Ages: The Pilgrimage of Life
- The Renaissance: Power and Discovery
- The Enlightenment: Reason and Sensibility
- The Nineteenth Century: The Romantic Self and Social Reality
- The Twentieth Century: The Modern Age and the Emerging World Culture

The works from each period are grouped into four chronologically arranged sections:

- **Representative Texts** begin each part with a sampling of Western works that explore an issue of prevailing interest during the period.
- **Western Texts**, the largest section within the chronological structure, includes works from the Euro-American tradition. Many of these selections are familiar classics, but we also include a number of newcomers to the canon, many by women and minority writers.
- **The World Context** section that follows includes texts from outside the Western tradition—from Asia, the Middle East, Latin America, Africa, and native America. These are grouped chronologically by nationality.
- **Background Texts**, the final section, features philosophical and social commentaries and other historical documents that exemplify the intellectual milieu of the period.

In two periods, this organization varies. The representative and Western texts for The Ancient World include two forebears of European literature, Graeco-Roman and Judeo-Christian, or biblical, writings. For The Twentieth Century, when many writers see themselves as addressing a global rather than a regional or national audience, we have removed the distinction between Western literature and the world context in order to suggest the emergence of a literature that transcends such a division. Instead, we present chronological sections, Modernist Texts from the earlier half of the century and Contemporary Texts of the post–World War II era.

Representative Texts

The representative texts for each part introduce important stories or themes that characterize the period and that have ongoing significance in our cultural history. Our introductions to each period and our headnotes to the representative texts emphasize what we believe to be the predominant stories or themes, but they also suggest other ways to approach these multifaceted works.

In Volume One, the classical part emphasizes the rise of the heroic ideal and the early formation of patriarchy with Homer's *Iliad* and *Odyssey* and with Genesis. Beginning with St. Augustine's *Confessions* and Dante's *The Divine Comedy,* the medieval part emphasizes the spiritual and literary motif of the pilgrimage of life. Petrarch's "Ascent of Mount Ventoux" and selections from the *Canzoniere* and Marlowe's *Doctor Faustus* present different perspectives on the Renaissance celebration of human power and the mastery of nature. In Volume Two, Voltaire's *Candide* and Rousseau's *Confessions* set up an Enlightenment dialogue about reason and sensibility. For the nineteenth century, Goethe's *Faust* and Brontë's *Wuthering Heights* introduce the entangled impulses of romanticism and realism. Finally, in the twentieth century, with Conrad's *Heart of Darkness* and Achebe's *Things Fall Apart,* we take up the importance of storytelling as a way to construct meaning, discover purpose, and define identity. As is obvious from the canonical nature of the texts we have chosen, instructors and students have much leeway here and may choose to treat these representative texts chronologically or use them to evince themes other than those we emphasize.

Western Texts

The other works of Western literature for each period, ordered chronologically by the author's birthdate (or presumed date of composition), further develop, challenge, and elaborate on the themes and stories in the representative texts. Many of these works are established classics, such as Sophocles' *Antigone,* Chaucer's *The Canterbury Tales,* Machiavelli's *The Prince,* Molière's *Tartuffe,* Ibsen's *A Doll's House,* and Kafka's *The Metamorphosis.* We also include many works that expand the traditional Western canon and show the rich diversity of literary and cultural traditions within the West, such as Christine de Pizan's *Book of the City of Ladies,* Marguerite de Navarre's *Heptameron,* Mary Rowlandson's *Narrative of the Captivity and Restoration of Mrs. Mary Rowlandson,* Harriet Jacobs's *Incidents in the Life of a Slave Girl,* and the poems of Anna Akhmatova. We have chosen these works for their literary merit and their commentary on ideas and historical developments within Western culture. In Volume Two, we include some major texts by African-American, Hispanic, and native American writers that offer opportunities to rethink the traditional boundaries of Western culture.

The World Context

The selections in The World Context sections are historically contemporary with the Western texts and often represent masterworks of the literary traditions from which they come. Whenever possible, we have included non-Western texts that raise issues and themes relevant to those raised by the Western texts. Setting up a dialogue between the Western and non-Western worlds, these works sometimes complement and sometimes challenge the assumptions of the Western texts, thereby allowing us to reconsider the meaning and values of our tradition. We match the classical texts of Greece and Rome, for example, with texts from the ancient wisdom traditions of China and India. Lao Tzu's poems in the *Tao Te Ching* and the parables of Chuang Tzu and the Buddha represent ways of being in the world that are very different from the heroic model found in Homer and the Greek tragedians; similarly, Tagore's Srivilas and Goethe's Faust gain wisdom through suffering, but the nature of their suffering is very different.

Background Texts

The philosophical, historical, and cultural documents in the background texts make it easier to place the literary works into their broader historical and cultural environments. In the background texts for the Middle Ages, for example, we include a selection from Capellanus's *Art of Courtly Love* to provide a context for the love poetry included among Western texts. In the nineteenth century, we include Madame de Staël on Napoleon, Marx and Engels on the class struggle, Darwin on the struggle for existence, and Nietzsche on the superman, all of which reflect on the transformation of ideas about the self and its place in society.

PEDAGOGY

Our **introductions to each period** and our **headnotes to the selections** set the works in their literary, historical, and cultural contexts. The part introductions begin with **time lines** that show concurrent events in history and politics; science, culture, and technology; and literature. The narrative elaborates on these events and discusses the major theme that appears in works throughout the period. We have included **maps** and time lines to assist the reader in placing the selections in their geographical and chronological context. The headnotes describe the lives and works of the authors; we also include lists of additional readings about the period and individual authors to provide guides for further study.

We have prepared an **instructor's manual** entitled *Teaching Western Literature in a World Context*. This manual provides information to supplement the headnotes in the text and includes questions for discussion and writing for each author in the Western Texts and World Context sections. Many of these questions involve comparisons of readings, often readings from different periods. We have also developed projects designed to elicit the reader's creative response to the selections.

Although we have emphasized certain stories and themes in our anthology, instructors and students using this book will inevitably take other approaches to the literature, discuss other themes, see other connections between the Western and non-Western texts, and perhaps even find other unifying stories within each period. Moreover, the users of this anthology may identify other works in world literature that they can use to supplement or replace some of our selections. We welcome your comments and suggestions.

A NOTE ON TRANSLATIONS

We have set clarity and accessibility as the two key principles guiding our selection of translations. In many cases, our aim to use texts that are both precise and teachable led us to what have become standards in the canon of translations, such as Robert Fitzgerald's *Iliad*, Theodore Morrison's *Canterbury Tales*, Edward Seidensticker's *Tale of Genji*, and Earl Miner's *Narrow Road through the Provinces*. We have also used such outstanding recent works as Allen Mandelbaum's *Odyssey*, Stephen Mitchell's poems of Rilke, and Miguel León-Portilla's translations of Nahuatl poetry. In some cases, our translators are themselves distinguished poets whose treatment of their originals captures their poetic quality; among these we include John Ciardi's *Divine Comedy*, Thomas Kinsella's *Exile of the Sons of Uisliu*, Richard Wilbur's *Tartuffe*, and Judith Hemschemeyer's poems of Anna Akhmatova. On occasion, as in the King James version of the Bible, we have chosen older translations of high literary quality that have influenced later writers so that students can hear or identify literary allusions in later works.

ACKNOWLEDGMENTS

This project began in a team-taught, multicultural "great books" course at the University of New Mexico in the mid-1980s. That course, developed initially with a grant from the National Endowment for the Humanities, sought to broaden the traditional canon of Western literature and incorporate works from outside the Western tradition. The grant gave us time to develop the course and supported the luxury of team-teaching, which enabled us to discuss daily the course syllabus and our teaching strategies. Joseph B. Zavadil was a member of that committee, a member of the teaching team in its first years, and one of the editors who began to design this anthology. He died in May 1992, before we had gotten very far into the making of the book. We hope that Joe's spirit—his courage, wit, scholarship, and humanity, and his zest for living and for teaching, especially undergraduate teaching—lives on in this book.

An anthology of world literature from ancient times to the present is necessarily selective. Our selection attempts to provide our readers with a collection of writings that both epitomize the time and place of their origin and stand out as works of literary value. To help us meet these goals, we consulted colleagues who teach Western and world literature courses and specialists in the periods and places represented. We would like to express our appreciation to the following reviewers for their advice:

Ruth Albrecht, Lane Community College; Barbara Apstein, Bridgewater State College; Lillian Baggett, Union University; Michael Bright, Eastern Kentucky University; Gary Brodsky, Northeastern Illinois University; Jewel Spears Brooker, Eckerd College; Joe R. Christopher, Tarleton State University; William Combs, Western Michigan University; William Crisman, Pennsylvania State University at Altoona; Frances Ferguson, Johns Hopkins University; David Ferris, Yale University; Raymond-Jean Frontain, University of Central Arkansas; Sarah Webster Goodwin, Skidmore College; Robert H. Grimes, California University of Pennsylvania; John Hagge, Iowa State University; Spencer Hall, Rhode Island College; Jim Hauser, William Paterson College; Ann Rosalind Jones, Smith College; James P. Kain, Neumann College; Marianne E. Kalinke, University of Illinois at Urbana–Champaign; Diane M. Kammeyer, Anoka–Ramsey Community College; Carol Owens Lewis, Trident Technical College; Herbert Lindenberger, Stanford University; Jack Miller, Normandale Community College; Kostas Myrsiades, West Chester University of Pennsylvania; William F. Naufftus, Winthrop University; Elizabeth Otten, Northeast Missouri State University; Ernest R. Pinson, Union University; William Bowman Piper, Rice University; Victoria Price, Lamar University; Julie Rodakowski, Rochester Community College; Shirley Samuels, Cornell University; Carole Slade, Columbia University; David Spurr, University of Illinois at Chicago; Johnny E. Tolliver, Delaware State University; Faye P. Whitaker, Iowa State University; and Katherine H. Wilson, University of Georgia.

No book of this size happens without critical and supportive friends and advisors. We want foremost to thank our families for their patience and support over the past four years or more, during which this book occupied so much of our and their time: Mary, Kate, Ben, and Josh Davis; Marlys, Miranda, and Jeremy Harrison; Mona, Peter, Sarah, and Maia Johnson; Caleb and Josh Smith; and Patricia Zavadil. Thanks also to the support we have had from the Department of English at the University of New Mexico and to our colleagues at UNM and its branches, especially

Patricia and Rudolfo Anaya, Gail Baker, Lee Bartlett, Helen Damico, Michael Fischer, Cheryl Fresch, Gene Frumkin, Barry Gaines, Janet Gaines, Patrick Gallacher, Erlinda Gonzales-Berry, Minrose Gwin, Elizabeth Hadas, Harmony Hammond, Joy Harjo, Michael Hogan, Ted Jojola, David Jones, Enrique Lamadrid, Tony and Teresa Marquez, Wanda Martin, David McPherson, Vera Norwood, Louis Owens, Mary Power, V. B. Price, Diana Rebolledo, Patricia Risso, Diana Robin, Ruth Salvaggio, Paul Schmidt, Warren Smith, Hector Torres, Howard Tuttle, Marta Weigle, Mary Bess Whidden, Peter White, Barbara and Hugh Witemeyer, and Carolyn Woodward.

Among our UNM graduate students, Anna Carew-Miller, Janice Gould, Jefferson Voorhees, John Martinez Weston, Nora Yazzie-Hunter, and especially Anne Grigsby, who served one year as our graduate research assistant, have helped us with their suggestions and interest. Colleagues and supporters at UNM–Valencia Campus include Rigo Chavez, Michelle LeBeau, Richard Melzer, Kaye Reeves, Nancee Ryan, and Debra Venable. Thanks especially to Pat Lockhart, Margaret Shinn, and the support staff in the English Department at UNM for their administrative and technical assistance.

People at other institutions have generously shared with us their ideas: Janet Adelman, University of California at Berkeley; Paula Gunn Allen, UCLA; John Bale, Carol and Mark Gilbertson-Muggli, and Harland Nelson, all at Luther College; Reed Dasenbrock and Kevin McIlvoy, New Mexico State University; Frances Gillmor, the University of Arizona; Robert Hanning, Columbia University; Linda Hogan, the University of Colorado; Judith Kroll, the University of Texas; E. A. Mares, the University of North Texas; Bob Martin, Haskell Indian Junior College; William McGlothing, West Texas State College; Janice Monk, Southwest Institute for Research on Women at the University of Arizona; Thomas Richards, Harvard University; and Luci Tapahonso, University of Kansas. William Woods of Wichita State University and the late Dennis Jones of Luther College both were perceptive NEH evaluators of the course from which the anthology grew.

For particular advice and encouragement, thanks to Nancy Abbey, Barbara Beyers, John Bierhorst, Richard Bodner, Rita Clark, Meinrad Craighead, Thomas Cummings, Bernadette Devine, Norah Flatley, Nancy Gage, Rose Hansen, Martha Heard, Jay Koch, Lucy Lippard, Robert Lloyd, Carolyn Meyer, Patricia Nelson, Janice Northerns, Jonathan Price, John Randall, Margaret Randall, Susan Rennie, Clayton Rich, June and Michael Romero, Mimi Wheatwind, Jill T. Williams, James Wimsatt, Margaret Wimsatt, Lenore Wolfe, and Diane Wolkstein.

A profound thanks also to our undergraduate students in the Western literature course we have been teaching since 1985 in all its incarnations at UNM and UNM–Valencia. Their questions and insights have helped round out the perspectives on literature and the world context presented in this book.

For her keen interest in our project, her helpful suggestions about the tables of contents and selection of maps, and her overall guidance over the course of preparing this first edition, we want to thank especially our development editor at St. Martin's Press, Sylvia Weber. Nancy Lyman, our acquisitions editor, has been gracious with her advice, encouragement, and support. We are particularly indebted to Emily Berleth, manager of publishing services at St. Martin's, who, with publishing services associate Kalea Chapman, painstakingly saw the book through press with careful attention and patience. Others at St. Martin's who have contributed to our book include Steven Kutz, who edited the instructor's manual, and Cheryl Friedman, Mark Gallaher, Joyce Hinnefeld, and Cathy Pusateri, who first supported our project. We thank Anna George for the attractive design that effectively reinforces the organization of the text. We appreciate the editorial and technical assistance of Rick Dudley and Jeff Topham, the production coordinators at Publication Services; Heather Raak TenHuisen, production supervisor; Carol Anne Peschke, copy editor; Dan Niles and Buddy Ritchie, technical typesetters; and Richard Bunk, artist, who handled the many problems that inevitably arise in preparing a first edition of this proportion. A special thanks to Frederick T. Courtright, who coordinated the permissions contracts for us, and without whose assistance we would not have been able to include some of the outstanding editions we have here. Finally, we also appreciate the assistance of the many people—editorial assistants and copy editors—who worked behind the scenes at St. Martin's and at Publication Services for their hand in bringing this work to light.

CONTENTS

THE ENLIGHTENMENT
Reason and Sensibility
1

THE NINETEENTH CENTURY
The Romantic Self and Social Reality
529

THE TWENTIETH CENTURY
The Modern Age and the Emerging World Culture
1345

WESTERN
LITERATURE
IN A WORLD
CONTEXT

Volume Two
The Enlightenment
through the Present

THE ENLIGHTENMENT

❧

Reason

and

Sensibility

TIME LINE FOR THE ENLIGHTENMENT

Date	History and Politics
1600–1650	1603 Tokugawa Ieyasu establishes Shogunate at Edo; begins Tokugawa period.
	1614 Ieyasu decrees that all foreigners must leave Japan and all Japanese Christians renounce their faith.
1650–1660	1652 Dutch found Cape Town.
	1656 Dutch begin trade with China.
	1657 Great Fire destroys Edo, Japan.
	1659 Aurangzeb succeeds Shah Jahan as Mongul emperor in India.
1660–1670	1660 Charles II; Restoration of Stuart monarchy in England.
	1662 K'ang-hsi (second emperor of Manchu dynasty) begins reign in China.
1670–1680	
1680–1690	1680 Tsunayoshi becomes Shogun in Japan.
	1682 La Salle claims Mississippi Basin for Louis XIV.
	1685 Louis XIV revokes Edict of Nantes; absolute monarchy in France; K'ang-hsi opens Chinese ports to foreigners.
	1688 Glorious Revolution in England; James II deposed; William and Mary crowned.
1690–1700	
1700–1710	1701–1714 War of Spanish Succession.
	1709 Ienobu new Shogun in Japan.
1710–1720	1713 Peace of Utrecht; French domination of Europe ends.
	1714 Ahmed Bey becomes ruler of Tripoli and founds Karamanli dynasty.
	1715 Death of Louis XIV; Louis XV crowned King of France.
	1716 Yoshimune Shogun in Japan.

Science, Culture, and Technology

Literature

1622 de Gournay, *On the Equality of Men and Women.*

1628–1630 Ahmad al-Maqqari, *Gust of Fragrance (Nafh al-Tib).*

1640 Hsu Kwan-ch'i, *Encyclopedia of Agriculture (Yo Lu Ch'üan Shu).*

1637 Descartes, *Discourse on Method.*

1661 John Eliot translates New Testament into Algonquin.

1664 Molière, *Tartuffe.*

1662 Royal Society founded in London.

1667 Milton, *Paradise Lost.*

1675 Chrestien Le Clercq arrives in Canada.

1677 Racine, *Phaedra;* Spinoza, *Ethics.*

1678 La Fayette, *The Princess of Clèves.*

1682 Rowlandson, *Narrative of the Captivity and Restoration of Mrs. Mary Rowlandson.*

1687 Newton, *Principia Mathematica.*

1688 Genroku period in Japan; beginnings of Kabuki theater.

1690 John Locke, *Treatises of Civil Government & Essay Concerning Human Understanding.*

1692 Astell, *A Serious Proposal to the Ladies.*

1704 Newton, *Opticks.*

1702 Bashō, *Narrow Road through the Provinces.*

1706 Excavations of Pompeii and Herculaneum begin.

1703 Chikamatsu, *Love Suicides at Sonezaki.*

1710 Handel musical director to George I.

1710 Leibniz, *Theodicy*

1711 Addison & Steele, *The Spectator.*

1714 Pope, *The Rape of the Lock.*

1719 Defoe, *Robinson Crusoe.*

(Continued on next page)

TIME LINE FOR THE ENLIGHTENMENT (Continued)

Date	History and Politics
1720–1730	
	1727 George II crowned King of England.
1730–1740	
1740–1750	1740 Frederick the Great assumes control of Prussia; Maria Theresa head of Hapsburg empire.
	1740–1745 Frederick the Great defeats Austria.
	1745 Ieharu becomes Shogun in Japan.
1750–1760	1755 Lisbon Earthquake kills 30,000 people.
	1756–1763 Seven Years' War; massacre in Black Hole of Calcutta.
	1757 Sidi Mohammed begins rule in Morocco.
1760–1770	1760 George III crowned King of England.
	1763 End of Seven Years' War: France loses colonies.
	1766 Ali Bey becomes ruler of Egypt; proclaims independence of Turks.
1770–1780	1775–1783 American War of Independence.
	1776 Declaration of Independence.
1780–1790	
	1783 Treaty of Paris; U.S. recognized as an independent nation.
	1789 Storming of the Bastille; French Revolution begins; George Washington becomes first U.S. president.

Science, Culture, and Technology

Literature

1720 Mammoth *History of Japan,* begun by Tokugawa Mitsukuni, completed; Yoshimune lifts restrictions on study of Western thought in Japan.

1729 J. S. Bach, *St. Matthew Passion.*

1733 Flying shuttle patented.

1739 David Hume, *Treatise of Human Nature.*

1744 Hogarth, *Marriage à la Mode.*

1748 Montesquieu, *Spirit of the Laws.*

1749 Buffon, *Natural History.*

1751 Benjamin Franklin invents lightning rod.

1755 Samuel Johnson's *Dictionary.*

1759 Haydn, *First Symphony.*

1762 Rousseau, *Social Contract* and *Émile;* Gluck's *Orfeo ed Euridice* performed in Venice.

1764 Beccaria, *On Crimes and Punishments.*

1767-1769 Bougainville sails around the world.

1769 James Watt patents steam engine.

1770 James Hargreaves patents spinning jenny; Gainsborough, *The Blue Boy.*

1776 Adam Smith, *Wealth of Nations.*

1777 Haydn, *C-Major Symphony.*

1781 Immanuel Kant, *Critique of Pure Reason.*

1785 Charles Wilkins publishes first European (English) translation of *Bhagavad Gita.*

1787–1788 Mozart, *Don Giovanni;* the last three symphonies.

1788 Joseph Banks founds the African Association.

1789 Mozart, *Cosi Fan Tutte.*

1721 Chikamatsu, *Love Suicides at Amijima.*

1726 Swift, *Gulliver's Travels.*

1728 John Gay, *The Beggar's Opera.*

1731 Abbé Prévost, *Manon Lescaut.*

1733–1758 Franklin, *Poor Richard's Almanack.*

1733–1734 Pope, *An Essay on Man.*

1740 Samuel Richardson, *Pamela.*

1748 Richardson, *Clarissa.*

1751–1772 Diderot, *Encyclopédie.*

1759 Voltaire, *Candide.*

1761 Rousseau, *Julie, or The New Heloise.*

1763 Montagu, *The Turkish Letters.*

1771 Franklin begins *Autobiography.*

1776 Jefferson, *The Declaration of Independence.*

1779 Lessing, *Nathan the Wise.*

1781–1788 Rousseau, *Confessions.*

1789 Equiano, *The Interesting Narrative of the Life of Olaudah Equiano, or Gustavus Vassa the African.*

(Continued on next page)

INTRODUCTION

IN EPISTLE II OF *An Essay on Man* (1733–1734), Alexander Pope describes human nature as a "Chaos of Thought and Passion." Like other thinkers of his generation, Pope strove to find a balance between these two complementary, but often contradictory, forces. Although Pope wrote during the Age of Enlightenment, a term that emphasizes the characteristic faith of this era in the ability of reason to set the world aright, writers from Francis Bacon to Jean-Jacques Rousseau saw humanity as an arena in which reason and passion struggled for control. The sometimes unruly human passions often challenged the great work of reason that characterizes the age; an awareness that passion, if unrestrained, could undo the most well-reasoned project always tempered the promise of a utopia stemming from intellectual, social, and moral progress. As Pope's *Essay* cautioned:

> Man's superior part
> Unchecked may rise, and climb from art to art;
> But when his own great work is but begun,
> What Reason weaves, by Passion is undone.

Although some writers such as François–Marie Arouet de Voltaire (our first representative writer for the Enlightenment) may have emphasized the powers of reason, whereas writers such as Rousseau (our second representative writer) emphasized those of passion, the chaos of thought and passion figures prominently in almost all works of the period.

The Enlightenment faith in the ability of empirical science, rationalism, and philosophy to resolve the problems of human society intensified the worldliness and secularism begun during the Renaissance. Without completely abandoning the idea of a God, the Enlightenment redefined God's relationship to the world and to human beings. For writers such as Voltaire, Rousseau, Thomas Jefferson, and Benjamin Franklin, God was the maker of a great clock that, once completed, ran independently of its maker according to the perfect principles and laws embodied in its design. Through rational investigation and empirical observation of themselves and their world, these thinkers believed that human beings could discover the natural laws that governed their world and so make it a better place, free from tyranny, violence, and instability. Of course, some writers, the Baron D'Holbach among them, carried these deistic ideas further; taking God out of the picture altogether, they argued that nature alone should be the guide for social and moral practices. Thus, from this faith in reason was born the idea of progress, an idea that involved an increasing emphasis upon the separation of the Church from secular matters, an increasing demand for political justice and civil liberty, and an increasing desire for personal freedoms.

Science, Culture, and Technology	Literature
	1791 Le Clercq, *Nouvelle Relation de Gaspesia*.
1793 Invention of cotton gin.	1792 Wollstonecraft, *A Vindication of the Rights of Woman*.
	1796 Diderot, *Supplement to the Voyage of Bougainville*.

Although significant differences obtain between the forms of governments throughout Europe during the Enlightenment period, the eighteenth century was overall a period of relative peace and stability that promoted economic growth and trade. The flourishing of empirical science led to important discoveries, such as James Watt's steam engine, and to advances in mining, farming, and textile production. As a result of these changes, Europe saw a dramatic increase in population and, especially in England, the consolidation of what we now call the middle class. Artists and writers began to direct more attention to the tastes and concerns of this new group of literate consumers of their work. As a result, new forms of music, art, and literature emerged. Throughout Europe, the arts shifted their focus from the court and country house of the nobility and aristocracy to the salon and coffeehouse of the bourgeoisie.

THE AGE OF ENLIGHTENMENT

Scholars have drawn up various historical boundaries for the Enlightenment, but it is fair to say that the era falls roughly between two spectacular and terrifying events: the beheading of Charles I of England in 1649, during the English Civil Wars, and the beheading of Louis XVI of France in 1793, during the French Revolution. Throughout much of the seventeenth century, Europe was in a state of turmoil. The Thirty Years' War (1618–1648), which began as a conflict between Protestant and Catholic interests in the Holy Roman Empire, spread fighting and confusion to all of Europe and heightened religious factionalism in many states. After this war, Spain lost its hold as the leading power of Europe, yielding its stature to England and France, whose attempts to gain the edge over one another led to increased tension between them.

Both England and France witnessed internal conflict in the seventeenth century. For England, that conflict culminated in the English Civil War (1642–1660); for France, in peasant uprisings and the Fronde (1648–1653), a series of attempts on the part of discontented nobles and members of the Parlement of Paris to limit the powers of the monarch. But these events had totally different outcomes. In England, royal power was restricted, the landed gentry and merchant class gained more control over government, and the country entered a period of economic growth; in France, royal power was strengthened, the disillusioned nobles were silenced, and, with no one to limit royal expenditures, France entered a period of economic decline. Nonetheless, both countries temporarily brought to an end their long-standing social and political divisions, and Europe as a whole entered the eighteenth century with a sense of political and social stability, especially after 1714 when the Peace of Utrecht ended the War of the Spanish Succession and initiated a period of relative calm and prosperity in Europe.

The period from the Peace of Utrecht in 1713 to the beginning of the French Revolution in 1789 has been called the age of absolutism and empire. Between these events, monarchy still prevailed in Europe and the landed aristocrats were the most important brokers of power, even in England, where the doctrine of divine right had been abandoned in the Glorious Revolution of 1688, which established a constitutional monarchy and placed clear restrictions on royal power. The spirit of the age did catch on with some European monarchs, such as Catherine the Great of Russia, Frederick the Great of Prussia, and Maria Theresa and her son Joseph II of Austria, who earned the name "enlightened despots." Although these rulers, in Frederick's phrase, assented to be considered the "first servant[s] of the people" and although some, such as Joseph II, took steps toward religious toleration and freedom for their serfs, the enlightened despots generally failed to follow through with the modest reforms they delighted in discussing with the *philosophes* they invited to their courts. Nonetheless, in various degrees each ruler limited the special privileges of the aristocracy, showed more interest than before in the common citizenry, promoted economic diversity, and, importantly, supported the arts and sciences. Only Spain and Italy kept their borders closed from the spread of Enlightenment ideals; Germany, at this time a palatinate of more than 300 states ruled by self-interested dukes, also stifled the spread of Enlightenment ideals. The exception to the rule in Germany was Karl August of Weimar, whose ardent patronage of the arts drew one of the leading figures of the German Enlightenment, Johann Wolfgang von Goethe. Whereas France under Louis XV and Louis XVI continued its policy of absolute despotism throughout the eighteenth century, the pressures for reform brought on by its intellectual leaders and inspired by the American Revolution of 1775–1781 finally reached a bloody conclusion in the French Revolution. Indeed, America was the place where the intellectual ideals of political liberty, individual freedom, religious toleration, and social welfare seemed to all of Europe to be succeeding. Beginning with the storming of the Bastille in 1789, the French people finally brought down Louis XVI, secured for the middle classes a share of power, and began—regrettably with little success—to rebuild their society under the guiding lamp of Reason, now idolized as a secular god.

Although wars between rival countries such as France and England and Prussia and Austria continued to break out in the eighteenth century, it was a period of relative peace. Some countries, especially England, France, Prussia, and Russia, experienced significant growth in population and the rapid acceleration of commerce. Fully recovered from the Civil War of the last century, England in particular experienced economic growth and political stability that enabled it to accelerate the pace of its empire building. Thus England expanded its colonial holdings in the West Indies, North America, Africa, and India, so that its empire eventually surpassed those of France, Holland, and Spain. Empire building also led to intense competition between France and Britain that culminated in a series of wars, beginning with King William's War, from 1689 to 1697, and ending with the Seven Years' War, from 1756 to 1763. The last war finally led to victory for England, which acquired important territories in America and gained control over French interests in India. By expanding its foothold in India, Britain placed itself strategically to further trade with other parts of Asia and effectively blocked hopes for a Mogul empire in India.

Profits from colonies supplied up to one third of the wealth of European nations during this period. Ironically, perhaps, at the same time Adam Smith's *Wealth of Nations* (1776) argued in favor of private enterprise, free markets, and laissez-faire, the tremendous growth of European economies came primarily from mercantile practices such as the strict regulation of trade, tariffs, and commercial restrictions that ensured international trade would serve state interests first and private interests second. Still, some venturing

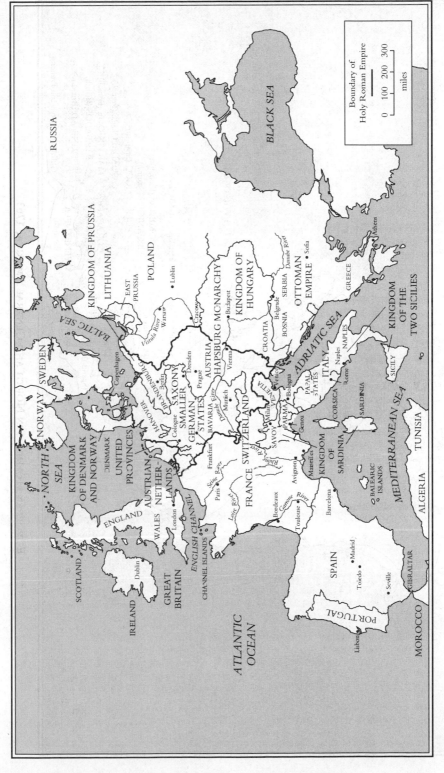

EUROPE IN 1740

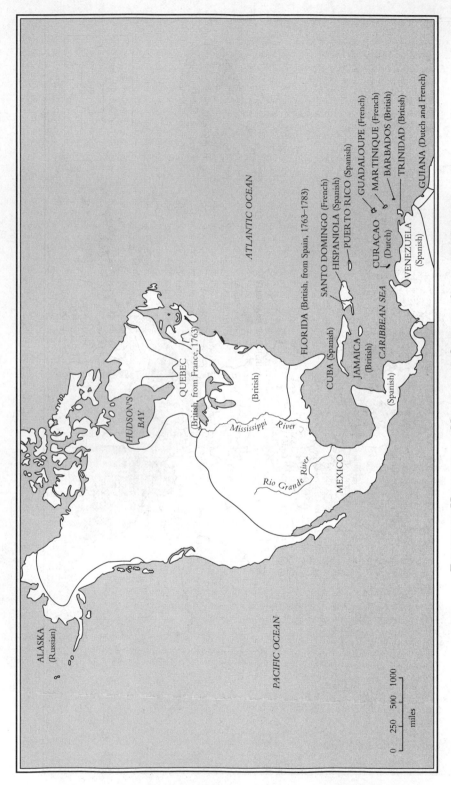

EUROPEAN HOLDINGS IN NORTH AND CENTRAL AMERICA, 1763

aristocrats, merchants, plantation owners, and certain manufacturers acquired vast private fortunes. Because trade with the colonies centered around labor-intensive crops such as tobacco, sugar, coffee, and cotton, many European fortunes were built upon the brutal foundation of slavery. About 12 million slaves were put to work on plantations, and it has been estimated that three times more men, women, and children died from disease or mistreatment en route to the colonies in squalid slave ships. Thus, the building of empires led to a depletion of the African population and an African diaspora that would have a profound impact on world history and culture over the next two centuries. Olaudah Equiano's *The Interesting Narrative of the Life of Olaudah Equiano, or Gustavus Vassa the African* (1789), included in the World Context section, records the experience of one of the more fortunate of these African slaves.

This economic involvement in the Orient stimulated Europeans' curiosity and desire for products and ideas from China and India. While philosophers such as Voltaire (1694–1778) and Schopenhauer (1788–1860) expressed admiration for Confucianism and Hinduism, respectively, the Swedish botanist Linnaeus (1707–1778) sent his students to China to collect specimens of its plant life. Moreover, fashionable aristocrats and the newly rich bourgeoisie were decorating their estates after the example of the Chinese in a fit of "Chinoiserie." Although some shrewd imitators made fortunes off of the ephemeral taste for Chinese furnishings, porcelains, and gardens, the import of tea from China and coffee from the colonies actually made lasting transformations in the social habits of Europeans.

The influence of the Orient upon Europe was primarily one-way, for both China and Japan were wary of the possible contamination of their cultures from foreign influence. Eighteenth-century Chinese and Japanese astronomers did take into consideration the ideas of Copernicus and Galileo, introduced to them by Jesuit missionaries who had been in China since the sixteenth century, but both countries developed isolationist policies that limited the influence of Europe. China, which will be discussed in more detail in the head-notes to the World Context section, was experiencing a period of stability and prosperity under the Ch'ing dynasty, which dated from the invasion of the Manchus in 1644.

Like its European counterparts, Japan in the eighteenth century was also in the midst of a period of relative calm after a period of chaotic civil wars. These wars between rival lords were ended around 1603 when Tokugawa Ieyasu set up a military government, the Shogunate, which led to increased nationalism and prosperity over the next 200 years. In 1624 and 1638, respectively, Spanish and Portuguese traders were ousted from Japan, leaving open foreign trade only to the Dutch and the Chinese, whose activities were highly regulated. In the eighteenth century, Japan saw the rise of its middle class and growth in the size and numbers of its cities. Japan had a strong merchant class under the control of a feudal aristocracy, although the rise in wealth among merchants enabled a few to buy their way up in social status, especially in the later eighteenth and early nineteenth centuries. In addition, Japan under the Tokugawa rulers emphasized order and tradition. Thus, the Tokugawa shoguns promoted Confucianism, with its emphasis upon duty and order, throughout Japan. Japan remained effectively isolated from the rest of the world until after 1853 when Commodore Perry forcibly opened its doors, giving way to the Meiji era, which began in 1868. The seat of the emperor, who had only nominal power during the Tokugawa era, now moved from Kyoto to Edo (now Tokyo), the capital city, and the new emperor removed the obstacles to the exchange of foreign goods and ideas.

ENLIGHTENMENT PHILOSOPHY AND CULTURE

The intellectual legacy of the Enlightenment still permeates Western thought. Inspired by the great intellectual achievements of the seventeenth century, such as Francis Bacon's *Novum Organum* (1620), René Descartes's *Discourse on Method* (1637), Isaac

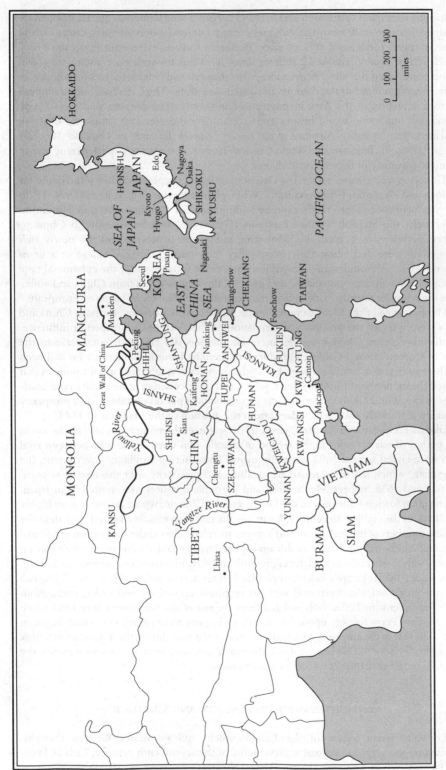

CH'ING DYNASTY CHINA AND TOKUGAWA JAPAN, c.1700

Newton's *Principia Mathematica* (1687), and John Locke's *Essay Concerning Human Understanding* (1690), Enlightenment thinkers set out by means of reason and direct observation to discover the fundamental laws governing nature, humanity, and society. The critical and experimental tendencies of the Enlightenment led to a pervasive critique of the status quo, reflected in literature by satire; in philosophy and religion by empiricism, rationalism, and sometimes skepticism; and in politics by reform and ultimately revolution. The French philosopher d'Alembert described the critical spirit of his age as an intensive philosophical ferment, that "spreading through nature in all directions like a river which has burst its dams...has swept with a sort of violence everything along with it which stood in its way...."

Although many key writers such as Molière, Pope, and even Voltaire had royalist sympathies and launched their satires upon human folly in order to uphold conservative causes, the flood of philosophical thought, including theirs, ultimately called into question received dogma in science, philosophy, law, and politics. The authority of the Church, the divine right of kings, and the privilege of the aristocracy trembled under the scrutinizing gaze of the *philosophes*—the name given to thinkers such as Voltaire, Diderot, and Montesquieu in France; David Hume and Adam Smith in England; Gotthold Ephraim Lessing and Immanuel Kant in Germany; and Thomas Jefferson and Benjamin Franklin in America. Kant's *What Is the Enlightenment* (1784) contains one of the most famous definitions of enlightenment, which he describes as "man's release from his self-incurred tutelage. Tutelage is man's inability to make use of his understanding without direction from another." In the Horatian motto, *sapere aude*—dare to know—Kant found the principle upon which hinged Western philosophy in the eighteenth century: Dare to reason independently and question authority, even if it means toppling the very foundations of culture and society, even if it results—as it did for Voltaire, Diderot, Rousseau, and other *philosophes*—in imprisonment or exile.

Though deemed iconoclasts and rebels, Enlightenment thinkers hoped by means of their critique to rebuild society; still, these independent thinkers disagreed about whether the present system needed simply to be set aright or to be struck down and started again from scratch. Writers such as Molière and Pope, for example, valued order and tradition, turning their criticism primarily to the emptiness, corruption, and hypocrisy that had seeped into the old institutions of church and state. Voltaire and Swift, the two most biting critics of the age, used their works to express moral outrage at the pervasive folly of human beings and the evil in the world that had corroded the political and moral authority of once-respected institutions. Voltaire praised what he called the "happy mixture" of commoners, lords, and king in England, and thereby distanced himself from any direct attack upon monarchy. Moreover, although he advocated religious tolerance and despised the sectarianism that had led to religious wars in his country and elsewhere, he stopped short of atheism. Even Rousseau looked back to ancient Sparta as a model for his ideal society in *The Discourse on Inequality* (1755) and *The Social Contract* (1762). Thus, if the "age of criticism," as Kant called it, involved the application of rational thought, empirical observation, and sensibility to correct the errors of the present and to construct a better, more just, and more humane world, operating in better harmony with the laws of nature, it did not present a single and consistent view of what it meant to follow those laws.

If, as Newton had shown, simple, regular, and universal laws governed the diversity in the natural world, surely careful study similarly could reveal simple and general laws to govern human nature and institutions. The delineation of such laws was the project of David Hume's *A Treatise of Human Nature* (1739–1740), in which the Scottish philosopher attempted to "introduce the experimental method of reasoning into moral subjects," to paraphrase the subtitle of his treatise. By discovering laws governing the "moral subjects" such as knowledge, belief, the passions, justice, and goodness, human beings could learn to live together more harmoniously and perhaps even experience unlimited progress.

Although many *philosophes,* such as Voltaire, had doubts about how far such progress could go, by the end of the eighteenth century the Marquis de Condorcet's *Sketch for a Historical Picture of the Progress of the Human Mind* (1793) claimed "that the perfectibility of man is truly indefinite; and that the progress of this perfectibility . . . has no other limit than the duration of the globe upon which nature has cast us."

Writing in the midst of the frenzied promise of the French Revolution, Condorcet shows more optimism than many of his predecessors who recognized that although reason could enable us to discover the operable truths about nature and society, some truths were beyond the reach of study, experiment, and thought. In 1690, John Locke warned in his *Essay Concerning Human Understanding,* "Our business here is not to know all things, but those which concern our conduct"—an idea most memorably revisited in Alexander Pope's *Essay on Man:* "Know then thyself, presume not God to scan; / The proper study of mankind is man." Thus, metaphysical speculation and the high rationalism of Descartes were tempered during the eighteenth century by an increasing emphasis upon practical reason, common sense, and moral philosophy.

The business of living, of course, involves more than just making rational choices and exercising judgment, for passion, as Pope cautioned, always threatens to undo what reason weaves. Although Locke, Adam Smith, and David Hume, among others, had seriously studied the role of the passions in human affairs, the writer who more than any other concerned himself with feeling was Jean-Jacques Rousseau. Rousseau takes a complex and contradictory stand both within and against the principles of the Enlightenment. The critical temper and progressivism of his important *Discourses* and *The Social Contract* link Rousseau directly to the Enlightenment, whereas the image he creates of himself as a "man of feeling" in his *Confessions* (1781–1788) and *Reveries of a Solitary Walker* (1782) anticipates the romanticism of the next generation. Rousseau recognized that human beings could never return to the state of nature that his works appear to glorify, but his works abound in descriptions of nature, celebrate the natural innocence of the child, and attest to his desire to create a civilization in which all human beings could be free to think and to feel deeply. Thinking into his own heart and into the heart of society, Rousseau shifts the emphasis of the Enlightenment onto human feeling in general, and onto his own feelings in particular. Whereas Voltaire, Pope, Swift, Diderot, Montesquieu, and others had sought to promote through the corrosive acids of satire a more humane and just society that acted in accordance with the tenets of reason, Rousseau found the seat of that humanity and justice in the record of his own life, in the history of the growth of his own reason and feeling. Thus Rousseau brings out the dialectical play between reason and sensibility, the chaos of thought and passion, that permeates the Age of Enlightenment.

Thought and feeling elide also in the art and music of the period, and the changes in style and form in painting and music roughly follow the shift in emphasis from reason to sensibility, from aristocratic to middle-class taste and culture, that characterizes the literature. Although painting, music, and literature during this era were called the "sister arts," terms such as *baroque, rococo,* and *classical* that critics use to describe the broader movements in the art, architecture, and music do not cross over well to literature. The baroque style, which flourished from 1600 to about 1725, emphasizes dramatic force and emotion, sometimes associated with the Counter-Reformation and sometimes with the consolidation of power and the rise of absolutism. The dynamic sense of power, the emotional appeal, the complexity of design, and the allusion to classical motifs found in the baroque style appear in the paintings of Peter Paul Rubens (1577–1640) and Diego Velázquez (1599–1660); the sculpture and architectural designs of Gianlorenzo Bernini (1598–1680); and in the music of Johann Sebastian Bach (1685–1750) and George Frideric Handel (1685–1759). The Palace of Versailles designed by Louis Le Vau and Jules Hardoun-Mansart stands as one of the great monuments of baroque architecture in France and symbolizes the immense power and wealth of Louis XIV, for whom it was built. The gardens at Versailles, designed by André Le Notre, reflect in their geometric symmetry and proportional regularity the power of the French monarchy in the late seventeenth century. As we approach the reign of Louis XV, who took the French throne upon the Sun King's death in 1715, the grandeur and power of the baroque gives way to a more refined and elegant style that partly reflects the court's emphasis upon polished manners, delicate wit, and epicureanism. Among the rococo painters are Antoine Watteau (1684–1721) and Jean-Honoré Fragonard (1732–1806); the latter's painting *The Swing* (1766) epitomizes the delicacy, frivolity, and sensuality that typifies the French rococo—a style still very much aimed at aristocratic taste.

Although England had its own version of baroque architecture in St. Paul's Cathedral designed by Christopher Wren (1632–1723) and in the commanding facade and colonnade of Blenheim Palace designed by Sir John Vanbrugh (1664–1726), English aristocrats preferred the more modest but precise classicism of Palladian architecture, which reflected classical order and balance in a form less spectacular—and more in keeping with English principles of limited monarchy and liberty—than the ornate and grandiose baroque. Thomas Jefferson's designs for his house at Monticello demonstrate nicely the compact simplicity and effortless balance of the Palladian style. The landed gentry in England decorated the walls of their Palladian-style country houses with portraits by such painters as Thomas Gainsborough (1727–1788), Joshua Reynolds (1723–1792), and George Romney (1734–1802); their American cousins put up portraits and historical paintings by Benjamin West (1738–1820) and John Singleton Copley (1738–1815). In England, however, where the middle classes advanced apace, William Hogarth (1697–1764) rose to popularity by painting and engraving satiric and moralistic series, such as *A Harlot's Progress* (1732) and *Marriage à la Mode* (1744); these series, very much like the novel, whose narrative art Hogarth's series closely imitate, displayed the values of the middle classes and, like the sentimental novels, showed virtue rewarded and vice punished.

Finally, composers and musicians, both professional and amateur, flourished during the Enlightenment, which witnessed sweeping changes in form, style, and even instrumenta-tion, as the arrival of the versatile piano led to the demise of the harpsichord. Moreover, as a middle-class audience arose, public theaters were built and the musician and composer were freed, like their literary contemporaries, from the constraints of aristocratic patronage. Composers such as Johann Sebastian Bach (1685–1750), Alessandro Scarlatti (1660–1725), George Frideric Handel (1685–1759), and Antonio Vivaldi (1678–1741) perfected new musical forms such as the fugue, the cantata, the oratorio, and the concerto, respectively. As opera moved into the eighteenth century, the elaborate *opera seria* gave way to the *opera buffa* and the *opera comique,* which tempered the aristocratic pretensions of the earlier operatic forms and drew upon popular musical styles. In particular, Christoph Willibald von Gluck's *Orfeo ed Euridice* (1762) challenged the conventions of baroque opera and emphasized simplicity, plot, and character development over the lavish display of musical virtuosity. Music also passed through a rococo phase, and in the late eighteenth century moved into the heyday of what we now call the classical period, typified by some of the greatest names in the history of symphonic music: Joseph Haydn (1732–1809), Wolfgang Amadeus Mozart (1756–1791), and Ludwig van Beethoven (1770–1827).

ENLIGHTENMENT LITERATURE

European literature in the first part of the eighteenth century imitated classical models and placed high emphasis upon conventional form, public purpose, and urbane wit; in the latter part of the century, many writers placed greater stress upon innovation, the private, and feeling. It is important to keep in mind, however, that these polarities are not absolute. The poetry of Alexander Pope, for example, takes liberties with and even parodies the classical conventions it invokes. *The Rape of the Lock* uses epic machinery to describe a relatively trivial affair (at least in his view), in which a tribe of ethereal creatures, the Sylphs, perform the supernatural functions that the gods perform in the epic. The literature of the earlier period is often called neoclassical because it frequently alludes to classical literature and mythology and emphasizes classical values such as order, balance, and decorum. Moreover, it displays a certain civic- or public-mindedness, reflected particularly in its urban settings and its urbane humor.

Key words for the neoclassical literary artist were *decorum* and *wit*. Decorum indicated a kind of natural ease in style and the perfect balance between form and expression; wit indicated an inventiveness tempered by good judgment, so that the work would convey with a kind of transparent inevitability the general truths that neoclassical artists prized. In couplets from *An Essay on Criticism* (1711), Alexander Pope gives the quintessential definition: "True wit is Nature to advantage dressed, / What oft was thought, but ne'er so well expressed; / Something whose truth convinced at sight we find, / That gives us back the image of our mind" (II. 297–300). Nonetheless, it is important to remember that cultures that praise order and decorum call attention to their opposites, and beneath the polished surfaces of neoclassical works the prince of misrule threatens always to break out: There is always, as in the case of the Princesse de Clèves, an inner desire threatening to contradict the publicly accepted gallantry; always, as in Pope's *The Rape of the Lock* (1714), a rake to threaten the precarious delicacy of Belinda's world; always, as in Swift's *Gulliver's Travels* (1726), a Yahoo to disturb the all-too-perfect universe of the Houyhnhnms.

Just as Newton discovered general laws and a grand order in the cosmos, so too the poet wanted to discover general, natural laws of the mind and art. In the works of Augustan Age poets such as Horace and Virgil, the neoclassical writers found rules governing their art that they believed to be equivalent to natural laws. To quote from Pope's *Essay on Criticism*, "Those rules of old discovered, not devised, / Are Nature still, but nature methodized" (I. 88–89). In drama, these rules were characterized by the "unities" of time, place, and action derived in part from Aristotle's *Poetics*. Neoclassical dramatists, especially Jean Racine (1639–1699) in France, limited heroic tragedies to a single action, place, and time, while eliciting powerful emotion and complex psychological struggle. In accordance with the principle of decorum, writers developed an elevated and formal poetic diction suited for high and serious subjects often drawn from, and almost always alluding to, classical and biblical history and mythology. Eventually, poetic diction stiffened into a set of stock "epithets" against which romantic poets such as Wordsworth would argue for a plainer, more honest, and more colloquial language. The greatest neoclassical writers, of course, saw such rules as flexible parameters within which they could exercise imaginative range rather than as prescriptions to follow by the book. The one precept that all writers agreed upon was drawn from Horace, who had said that all art and literature should both please and instruct.

Given the preeminence of the aristocracy throughout the century in France and Germany and through most of the century in England, much early eighteenth-century literature, such as Madame de La Fayette's *The Princess of Clèves* (1678) or Pope's *The Rape of the Lock,* focuses on the manners of the elite, powerful, and wealthy. Here decorum is translated into duty, and novels and poetry alike inquired into just what were the proper manners and responsibilities of gentlemen and gentlewomen, even as they explored the awakening of private sensibility and sexual awareness. Because aristocrats conducted their lives in the full light of the public eye, novelists in particular began to explore the conflicts and contradictions between public expectations and private desires. Despite the differences between their culture and the genres in which they wrote, the works of Pope and Madame de La Fayette emphasize the values of moral responsibility, duty, and order even when, as in the case of de La Fayette's novel, the exercise of those responsibilities leads to unhappiness.

As populations rose in Europe and as standards of living and literacy grew, the importance of the middle classes and the possibilities for social rising (or falling) more and more dominated the attention of writers. As wealthy merchant families united through marriage with the families of traditional landed aristocrats, the boundaries between social groups became more permeable, and the question of one's identity became more complex because it was open to expanded horizons. The widely held belief that human nature was the same in all places and at all times began to be shaken, as we can see in Diderot's *Supplement to the Voyage of Bougainville* (written 1772) and especially in Rousseau's *Confessions*. With the advance of literacy and greater leisure and spending power among the middle classes emerged a publishing industry and new literary forms, most notably the novel. These new literary forms addressed the need for a literature that could define middle-class responsibilities, clarify their rather unstable identity, and portray the emotional crises and shifting of people, especially women, whose position in society was particularly precarious and did not fit aristocratic models of classical tragedy and romance. Thus, by the middle of the century, many writers focused more upon the manners of the "middling orders," as they were called in England. Decorum and urbane wit had to make room for the burgeoning taste for the expressive, meditative, and spontaneous. Practical guides to manners flourished in the popular press, as the growing number of middle-class readers sought to elevate themselves both economically and socially. No writer during this period better represents this practical side of the Enlightenment than Benjamin Franklin, whose *Autobiography* (written 1771–1790) could serve as a guide to what Samuel Johnson called "the business of living," a business that, for Johnson and others, was plagued with great difficulty, injustice, and downright gloom.

By the middle of the eighteenth century, the conventions of reason and tradition had grown somewhat stifling, and the critical temper of the early Enlightenment now was infused with a renewed spirit of feeling. In England, Edmund Burke's *A Philosophical Enquiry into Our Ideas of the Sublime and the Beautiful* (1757) attempted systematically to explain the intellectual and physiological mechanisms of the passions and the origins of aesthetic taste. Already in Samuel Richardson's *Pamela* (1740) the novel had begun to analyze states of mind and high feeling in an atmosphere charged with moral sentiment. Particularly popular throughout his native England and the Continent, Richardson's novels explored the relationships between men and women, focusing primarily, as in *Pamela* and *Clarissa* (1748), upon the conflict between a virtuous woman who represents solid middle-class values and an aristocratic lord who preys upon her innocence. Like Richardson's novels, Rousseau's *The New Heloise* (1761) played upon the passions and reinforced the morality of the middle class by portraying the thwarted love between young Saint-Preux and Julie, who keeps her virtue intact by choking her passion for her lover and remaining faithful to her husband.

The novel stands out as the preeminent literary form of the later eighteenth century to which women writers such as Frances Burney (1752–1840) and Anne Radcliffe (1764–1823) made significant contributions. The formal possibilities of the novel were exploited by Laurence Sterne's masterful *The Life and Opinions of Tristram Shandy* (1759–1767), which in its comic subversion of plot and its contrived accidents and digressions deliberately manipulates the reader's expectations for a good realistic story and anticipates the stream-of-consciousness techniques of modernist novels. Alongside the novel, however, other forms in this "age of prose" were popular, including the satirical tale, the travelogue, letters, and the popular and philosophical essay. Mary Rowlandson's *Narrative of the Captivity and Restoration of Mrs. Mary Rowlandson* (1682) is the earliest of the captivity narratives that were popular in America in the late seventeenth and eighteenth century. Set on the colonial frontier, this autobiographical tale takes the form of a spiritual trial. Olaudah Equiano's *The Interesting Narrative of the Life of Olaudah Equiano, or Gustavus Vassa the African* (1789), one of the earliest slave narratives, offers a unique hybrid of autobiographical writing and the European travelogue. The travelogue, an account of a journey often to exotic lands, often took an epistolary form, as in Lady Mary Wortley Montagu's *Turkish Letters* (1763). Poetry continued to be important in the later part of the eighteenth century, but it turned its gaze inward and abandoned its satiric engagement with urban life for a reflective meditation on the virtues of country life.

Japanese literature flourished during the seventeenth and eighteenth centuries as a result of the peace and economic stability during the Tokugawa period. Poets such as Matsuo Bashō (1644–1694) and Taniguchi Buson (1715–1783), masters of the *haiku;* novelists such as Saikaku (1663–1742), one of the greatest Japanese novelists since Murasaki; and playwrights such as Chikamatsu Monzaemon (1653–1724) and Ki No Kaion (1663–1742), whose dramas focused upon contemporary life, were major figures in the literary revival of the seventeenth and eighteenth centuries in Japan. Because of the country's isolation from non-Japanese influences, the literature of the Tokugawa period (1600–1867) was profoundly indigenous in theme and style, but that native focus allowed writers to nuance the traditional forms. Moreover, some writers became interested in the "floating world," the lives of the burgeoning middle classes in the great cities such as Osaka, Kyoto, and Edo, the capital. This interest in the merchant classes and their courtesans is particularly notable in the plays of Chikamatsu, one of the first writers in the world to focus upon the domestic and personal tragedies of the common people.

The emphasis upon an indigenous literary tradition appears in the writing of Bashō and his many disciples. Bashō's artistic sensibility evolved from his studies of the Japanese and Chinese classics, but his work is remarkable for its innovation upon conventional forms, especially in the art of *haibun,* linked verse and prose, in which he describes his sojourns through the countryside to sacred shrines and places far from the floating world of the cities. Although the literary renaissance of the Tokugawa era declined after 1800, the two writers we include here represent two of the greatest talents writing at the height of this period in two very distinctive genres. The next period of innovation and change takes place in Japan during the Meiji period (1868–1912), when the physical and intellectual borders once again opened up to world influences and when the great controversy over Western influence on Japanese culture fostered another deep examination of its oldest traditions.

CANDIDE AND THE CONFESSIONS

The two works that we offer here as representative Western texts, Voltaire's *Candide* (1759) and Rousseau's *Confessions,* embody both the critical and the utopian aspects of Enlightenment thought while they display the difference between the public and private orientations of the early and late century. Moreover, each text modulates between biting criticism and utopian desire: In short, both works aim to expand the horizons of European consciousness and to transform European society. In both *Candide* and *Confessions,* we see the two sides of the structure of contrasts inherent to most utopian narratives: the dissatisfaction with the present order of things that leads to a biting critique of *the world as it is;* and the desire for positive change that leads to an imaginative but reasoned projection of *the world as it could be.* Voltaire's novella emphasizes the folly and hypocrisy of European custom and culture, and Rousseau's autobiography emphasizes the inherent potential for Europeans to redeem themselves from that folly and free themselves from the prison house of custom.

The acid bath of Voltaire's satire cuts through the finished surfaces of European moral and religious hypocrisy, exposing a malicious society of self-interested scoundrels who stoop to the most brutal means to preserve their own wealth, property, and social position, and who are willing to ignore the genuine suffering of the thousands of wretches who fall victim to their barbarism. Candide is kicked and tricked around much of the known world, partly by accident and partly by his willful search for his Lady Cunegund, an embodiment of his desire to find the ideal woman. This errant tour symbolizes Candide's constantly interrupted and diverted quest for happiness. From his native Westphalia, Candide finds himself sometimes stumbling in slavery and sometimes running with good fortune along a highway riddled with detours that takes him to Lisbon, Paraguay, the famed paradise El Dorado, Constantinople, Surinam, and Paris. Having learned from his tutor Pangloss that "all is for the best," Candide strives to overcome a succession of his own misfortunes and scrapes with death, learns the miserable tales of those he encounters, and samples a variety of philosophies from those who have found unique and often ridiculous ways to cope with the brutal forces of nature and society.

Voltaire uses *Candide* to scoff at those like Leibniz who build metaphysical castles in the air and ignore or excuse the harsh actualities of life. Candide's misfortunes subvert and invalidate Pangloss's blind optimism. Although Candide often stubbornly clings to that metaphysic amid the most brutal experiences, he finally abandons his Panglossianism. Yet he does not abandon Pangloss himself, thereby suggesting that Candide has learned to accept the world despite its faults and showing that at least in his small society there is a place for sympathy and human kindness. Although he embodies in part the revolt of the *philosophes* against abstract systems of thought and their outrage at hypocrisy and corruption in the world, Candide also shows us the importance of resilience in the face of nearly devastating accidents and defeats and the possibility in such a world for humane principles. Thus, he ends his life reconciled, not resigned, to human and worldly realities. *Candide*'s concluding vision of a world in which each person cultivates his or her own garden may hardly seem to project the image of a new Garden of Eden, but it does suggest the practical, this-worldly emphasis of Enlightenment thought that earned Voltaire the tribute of many later writers and *philosophes*.

If Voltaire remains short on utopian renewal and long on social critique, Rousseau tips the balance the other way. Rousseau criticizes the institutions that he believed led people astray and suggests that European civilization created such pervasive artificiality and deception that no one could escape its corruption. Criticizing the Enlightenment project itself, Rousseau refused to accept the title *philosophe*, for he suspected that even the critical philosophy of his peers had been corrupted in the customhouse of European civilization and was itself implicated in the very problems it hoped to solve. By virtue of the very independence of his thought, Rousseau symbolizes the greatest of Enlightenment figures: the free thinker who bows down before no authority other than his or her own. To quote Rousseau on his own work: "Whence could the painter and apologist of human nature have taken his model, if not from his own heart? He has described this nature just as he felt it within himself.... In a word, it was necessary that one man should paint his own portrait to show us, in this manner, the natural man." At the same time, Rousseau's doctrine of the natural goodness and perfectibility of human beings returns us to that great Enlightenment search for the true nature of men, women, and society and the doctrine of natural law.

To avoid the corrupting influence of civilized society, Rousseau turned to the "natural man" latent within us all. In the self-exploration of the *Confessions,* Rousseau internalizes the "extraordinary journey" of the utopian narratives, and converts the extraordinary voyage to a new land of striking contrasts into a sentimental journey to the heart of all human projects and social organization—human nature itself. Rather than test the laws of nature in the exotic laboratories of island paradises, as in Diderot's *Supplement to the Voyage of Bougainville,* Rousseau in the *Confessions* conducts his experiments in the familiar laboratory of his own heart, which he rather audaciously believes is representative of everyone's experience and feeling. Although Rousseau, like his fellow *philosophes,* celebrates reason, he adds with vigorous emphasis that emotions must assist reason to achieve its goal: a person of independent judgment, living in a state of equality and free submission to the general will that constitutes the good society of the social contract. That vision of thinking and feeling individuals working together in a democratic community is the closest we come in Rousseau's thinking to the realization of utopia, to the perfection of human beings and their society in a world that bars them from returning to a presocial Golden Age. For Rousseau, because there is no turning back to a state of nature, human beings have no choice but to go forward, always seeking, but inevitably falling short of, the best of all possible worlds.

SUGGESTED READINGS

For a readable history of the age, see Isser Woloch's *Eighteenth-Century Europe: Tradition and Progress 1715–1789* (1982). One of the best studies of Enlightenment philosophy as a whole remains Peter Gay's *The Enlightenment: An Interpretation,* 2 vols. (1969). Paul Hazard's two studies, *The European Mind, 1680–1715* (1953) and *European Thought in the Eighteenth Century* (1954), translated by J. L. May, remain useful surveys. Donald Greene's *The Age of Exuberance* (1970) offers a critical view of the intellectual and literary history. For perspectives on the Enlightenment in England and France, respectively, see Harold Nicolson's *The Age of Reason: The Eighteenth Century* (1960), and Lester Crocker's *An Age of Crisis: Man and the World in Eighteenth-Century Literature* (1959). Ian Watt's *The Rise of the Novel* (1957) still serves as a useful introduction to the development of the novel as a literary form, but it should be supplemented by Michael McKeon's *Origins of the English Novel* (1987) and Nancy Armstrong's *Desire and Domestic Fiction: A Political History of the Novel* (1987). More specialized studies include Roger Chartier's *The Cultural Origins of the French Revolution* (1991), Roy Porter's *English Society in the Eighteenth Century* (1982), and Marilyn Williamson's *Raising Their Voices, 1650–1750* (1990), which discusses the development of women's writing in this period. *Aspects of the Eighteenth Century* (1965), edited by Earl R. Wasserman, is a good collection of essays on many aspects of eighteenth-century culture, and *The New 18th Century: Theory, Politics, English Literature* (1987), edited by Felicity Nussbaum and Laura Brown, contains many fine essays on literary culture in England.

REPRESENTATIVE TEXTS

FRANÇOIS-MARIE AROUET DE VOLTAIRE
[1694–1778]

During the French Revolution, more than ten years after his death, Voltaire's bones were transported to Paris in a hearse that had inscribed upon it: "Poet, philosopher, historian, he gave wings to the human intelligence; he prepared us for freedom." More than any other single person of the eighteenth century, Voltaire epitomizes in the breadth of his intellectual endeavors the Age of Enlightenment, which put its faith in human reason and a rational universe, championed human rights, and believed that reason could chart a common-sense path for improving the human condition. Voltaire was not an originator of new ideas, but he took hold of the liberal ideas of his time—such as John Locke's theories about equality and human rights, Isaac Newton's natural philosophy, and English Deism—and became the propagandist for these ideas in France and eventually throughout Europe. He captured the spirit of the times and was its popularizer, applying Enlightenment ideas to the social and political events of his day.

He wrote, he lectured, and he acted in his own plays; he argued, he criticized, he satirized his intellectual and political adversaries; he was persecuted and jailed, and he fled persecution and traveled throughout Europe. For more than sixty years he was an outspoken critic of French society and the spokesperson of his historical era, and for most of his life he was a refugee from his own country.

Although he gave considerable thought to the ideal conditions of human existence, his primary efforts were directed at removing the obstacles to progress by analyzing them and holding them up to scorn or ridicule. The institutions of government and religion, with their goals of dominance and control, were prime candidates for Voltaire's barbed pen. In Voltaire's Europe, the Roman Catholic Church wielded enormous power and the French government grew top-heavy with kings, nobles, and abused privileges.

Voltaire believed in the open exchange of ideas, and therefore deplored any political or religious agency that sought to shelter ignorance and superstition in order to deceive and manipulate its followers. At the end of his life, Voltaire became almost obsessed with the belief that humans needed to be freed from the authority of the Church and from centuries of theological doctrines that prevented people from acting rationally and sensibly.

LIFE

The facts of Voltaire's life are a testimony to his lifelong desire to put ideas into action and to the power of his foes, who tried to silence Voltaire's extraordinary voice. Voltaire was born Francois-Marie Arouet in a prosperous bourgeois family. Voltaire was introduced at an early age to Deism by his godfather, the Abbé de Châteauneuf. Deism was the belief that a rational deity created the world and left the running of it to natural laws, much as a watchmaker makes a watch to run on its own. He embraced Deism for his entire life, and it became the basis from which he launched his unending attacks on Christianity. He was given a solid classical education at a famous Jesuit school, College Louis-le-Grand. While in his teens he steered away from his father's law profession, and instead became involved with various social factions in Paris, where he wrote libelous poems for which he was briefly jailed and exiled. At twenty-three, he adopted the pen name of "Voltaire," the exact meaning of which is unknown. His first serious literary efforts were in the theater; his play Oedipe (1718) was a financial success. In it the main culprit is God, who becomes responsible for the crimes of Oedipus and Jocasta. A popular epic poem, Le Henriade, celebrated Henry IV as a champion of religious tolerance in the sixteenth century.

In 1725, Voltaire's life took a sharp turn. He was insulted by the chevalier de Rohan; Voltaire returned the insult and was beaten up by Rohan's hired thugs, in full view of aristocrats whom Voltaire had previously thought of as his friends. He challenged Rohan to a duel, but on the appointed day was arrested, jailed, and exiled to England for almost three years, from 1726 to 1729. He was so impressed by English tolerance in the areas of religion and speech that he learned to speak and read English and became friends with Alexander Pope, Jonathan Swift, and William Congreve. Access to the English court was provided by Sir Robert Walpole, an important English statesman, and Lord Bolingbroke, a friend of writers and a gentleman philosopher. Voltaire also became acquainted with the writings and ideas of Shakespeare, Bacon, Locke, and Newton, and with the English parliamentary system.

On the basis of his experiences in England, he wrote Philosophical Letters or Letters Concerning the English Nation, published in 1734; while complimenting English ways, it indirectly criticized the abuses of French institutions. The book was condemned, copies of it were burned, and a warrant was issued for Voltaire's arrest. This time Voltaire was prepared for the attack; financially secure, he took up residence with Emilie de Breteuil, marquise du Châtelet, at the château of Cirey, situated in the independent duchy of Lorraine. At this refuge, Voltaire wrote plays and essays, experimented with physics in a laboratory, and supported the development of iron foundries.

For several years Frederick the Great of Prussia had been trying to entice Voltaire to his court in Potsdam, where he was creating a royal environment for art and ideas. Voltaire joined him, but this alliance of two extremely headstrong men was doomed to failure. Voltaire was not cut from diplomatic cloth and soon was embroiled in intrigues and social power plays. The finale came when Maupertuis, the president of the Academy of Berlin, had the philosopher König dismissed from the Academy. Frederick backed Maupertuis and Voltaire took König's side, eventually publishing a lampoon of Maupertuis, his *Diatribe of Doctor Akaia* (1752). Apparently, Voltaire obtained permission to publish this work under false pretenses by deceiving the touchy Frederick about the documents he was actually signing. Frederick burned the work and had Voltaire arrested.

Having been denied a residence in France, Voltaire at sixty years of age bought a country house on the border between Geneva and France, along with several other houses in nearby jurisdictions, so as never to be without a refuge in case of persecution. At this house called *Les Délices* (The Delights), along with his niece and mistress, Madame Denis, he established his own literary "court," along with a private theater where his plays were performed. Geneva, however, had a ban against theater of any kind, and again Voltaire's freedoms were threatened. He persuaded a friend, d'Alembert, to criticize Geneva's prohibition against theater in his article on Geneva in the *Encyclopédie*; Jean-Jacques Rousseau, the most famous citizen of Geneva, answered this article and Voltaire in his important *Letter to d'Alembert* (1758), which defended Geneva's ban on theater.

Voltaire again had to move and he bought Ferney, a large estate just inside the border of France, but fronting on Lake Geneva. As the patriarch of Ferney, Voltaire experimented with a model agricultural community. He provided supplementary employment by developing a stone quarry; he built factories for manufacturing tiles, stockings, watches, and leather goods. He started schools and promoted fair wages and equitable taxes. He actively defended victims of civil injustice. In one case, he rescued a young noblewoman from a convent and established her in his household, nicknaming her "Belle et Bonne." He eventually matched her with the Marquis of Villette. At his houses, he entertained the most illustrious scientists, philosophers, and artists of his time.

In February 1778, after an absence of twenty-eight years, Voltaire returned to Paris, where he was celebrated by the Académie Française, local and foreign dignitaries, and crowds of chanting Parisians. When he died ten weeks later on May 30, he was denied burial by Christian authorities, and was secretly interred at the abbey of Scellieres in Champagne.

WORK

Voltaire's literary output was enormous, amounting to over 135 volumes in a modern French edition. He wrote dozens of plays and novels. His several histories focused on important political figures. A book on the philosophy of history, the *Essay on the Manners and the Spirit of Nations* (1756), stretched the domain of history to include prebiblical and oriental civilizations. A blizzard of essays and pamphlets attacked the corruption of his era and were often published under various pen names. His lucid writing style and biting wit, however, readily identified the true author of the pieces.

After 1760, his dislike of Christianity was constant and wholehearted. In a letter to him, Diderot addressed him as his "sublime, honorable and dear Anti-Christ." Voltaire's *Philosophical Dictionary* (1764) was a culminating diatribe against conventional religion that simultaneously delineated his own brand of Deism. Under the heading of "religion,"

Voltaire discusses a deity that is a product of Copernicus and Newton rather than the Bible:

> Last night I was meditating; I was absorbed in the contemplation of nature, admiring the immensity, the courses, the relations of those infinite globes, which are above the admiration of the vulgar.
>
> I admired still more the intelligence that presides over this vast machinery. I said to myself: A man must be blind not to be impressed by this spectacle; he must be stupid not to recognize its author; he must be mad not to adore him. What tribute of adoration ought I to render him? Should not this tribute be the same throughout the extent of space, since the same Supreme Power reigns equally in all that extent?
>
> Does not a thinking being, inhabiting a star of the Milky Way, owe him the same homage as the thinking being on this little globe where we are? Light is the same to the dog-star as to us; mortality, too, must be the same....

The *Philosophical Dictionary* was immediately burned and condemned by both Protestant and Catholic authorities.

The works that have brought Voltaire most of his fame since the eighteenth century are his philosophical tales, especially *Zadig* (1748) and *Candide* (1759). Voltaire writes didactic fiction; that is, he is always interested in teaching, in using his plot and characters to develop arguments about contemporary issues. He does not intend to create well-rounded characters. He is less interested in the aesthetics of writing fiction than in the clarity of intellectual discussion. Generally, his technique is to express his opinions through the guises of various characters from history or mythology; a character might represent a particular philosophy. His plots using oriental characters and settings are mirrors continually reflecting back on Europe or France.

Like others of his stories, *Candide* was first published under a pseudonym. It quickly became a best-seller, going through forty editions during Voltaire's lifetime. Candide, whose very name suggests openness, is a naïve optimist who has been educated by an impractical philosopher, Pangloss, whose name indicates a simplification of all experience. With his belief that all is for the best in the best of all possible worlds, Pangloss represents the ivory tower philosopher for whom theories are radically disconnected from reality. In Chapter Five, Candide, wounded and dying from the Lisbon earthquake, urgently begs for some wine and oil. Deaf to his request, Pangloss speculates: "This concussion of the earth is no new thing... the city of Lima in South America, experienced the same last year; the same cause, the same effects; there is certainly a vein of sulphur all the way underground from Lima to Lisbon." Unheeded, Candide loses consciousness.

It would seem that Voltaire's primary target via the character of Pangloss is the philosopher Leibniz, who used a complex metaphysical argument to claim that this world is the best of all possible worlds on the grounds that the universe was created by a God whose plans are perfect. It has been suggested that Voltaire is also satirizing Christian Wolff (1679–1754), a German mathematician and philosopher who expressed the optimism and confidence of the age by writing a book titled *Reasonable Thoughts on God, the World, and the Soul of Man, Also on Things in General*. In fact, Voltaire is actually ridiculing any simplistic explanation for the complexities of experience, any universal principle that is applied unquestioningly to every situation. In particular he satirizes any religious belief that accounts for human disasters such as the Lisbon earthquake by reference to an ultimate good or a beneficent Providence. Although evil might be justified as some form of good or a mystery in God's ultimate plan, Voltaire prefers to link evil to human choice and weakness. The Lisbon earthquake of 1755 produced suffering that optimists had difficulty explaining away. Irrespective of theology, the innocent suffer: in hospitals, in homes, and on the streets. Voltaire's real enemy is complacency, any attitude or theory that seems content with the present state of affairs. No particular Christian denomination, whether Protestant or Catholic, is safe from Voltaire's scorn.

In one adventure after another, Candide is exposed to the treachery and immorality, the greed and lust just below the surface of political officials, military commanders, and religious professionals. The short chapters and wide range of experiences keep *Candide* entertaining and engaging. When Candide and his valet Cacambo finally arrive in the famed utopia of El Dorado, they discover it to be boring; naturally they find a common-sense religion, to which Cacambo remarks, "What! ... have you no monks among you to dispute, to govern, to intrigue, and to burn people who are not of the same opinion with themselves?" In Candide's search for situations that would confound Pangloss's philosophy, he finally meets Martin, a thoroughgoing pessimist who is a foil to Pangloss. Steering a philosophical course between them, Candide arrives in Constantinople and is rejoined by his former comrades, including his beloved Lady Cunegund. Candide's adjustments to all the changes in their respective lives leads to conclusions about living the simple life, neither optimistic nor pessimistic. He proposes a practical, modest realism; the importance of work is summed up in the enigmatic dictum, "We must take care of our garden."

Voltaire was not a pessimist, given to hopelessness and despair. He certainly believed in the possibility of change; if humans could free themselves from the narrow blinders of traditional religion and from the influence of corrupt public officials, progress toward a better world would be possible. In the meantime, "we must take care of our garden," a statement that has been much debated ever since *Candide*. Is Voltaire suggesting that we should retreat from involvement in the world and simply tend to our private desires and needs? Or is his emphasis on working in those areas of our lives that might bear fruit, and abandoning abstract theorizing and faddish philosophies? It is consistent with Voltaire's role as an intellectual gadfly that he would leave the ultimate resolutions to issues of personal morality and social responsibility to his readers.

SUGGESTED READINGS

Biographies of Voltaire include Theodore Besterman's *Voltaire*, 3rd ed. (1976), Henry N. Brailsford's *Voltaire* (1935), and Ira O. Wade's *The Intellectual Development of Voltaire* (1969). A recent translation of *Candide* with informative commentary is Peter Gay's *Candide* (1963). Additional commentary can be found in Peter Gay's *Voltaire's Politics: The Poet as Realist* (1959) and Ira O. Wade's *Voltaire and "Candide": A Study in the Fusion of History, Art, and Philosophy* (1959).

Candide

Translated by Tobias Smollett; revised by William F. Fleming

CHAPTER 1

How Candide Was Brought Up in a Magnificent Castle and How He Was Driven Thence

In the country of Westphalia,[1] in the castle of the most noble baron of Thunder-ten-tronckh, lived a youth whom nature had endowed with a most sweet disposition. His face was the true index of his mind. He had a solid judgment joined to the most unaffected simplicity; and hence, I presume, he had his name of Candide. The old servants of the house suspected him to have been the son of the baron's sister, by a very good sort of a gentleman of the neighborhood, whom that young lady refused to marry, because he could produce no more than threescore and eleven quarterings

---

[1]A region in western Germany.

in his arms; the rest of the genealogical tree belonging to the family having been lost through the injuries of time.

The baron was one of the most powerful lords in Westphalia; for his castle had not only a gate, but even windows; and his great hall was hung with tapestry. He used to hunt with his mastiffs and spaniels instead of greyhounds; his groom served him for huntsman; and the parson of the parish officiated as his grand almoner. He was called My Lord by all his people, and he never told a story but every one laughed at it.

My lady baroness weighed three hundred and fifty pounds, consequently was a person of no small consideration; and then she did the honors of the house with a dignity that commanded universal respect. Her daughter was about seventeen years of age, fresh colored, comely, plump, and desirable. The baron's son seemed to be a youth in every respect worthy of the father he sprung from. Pangloss,[2] the preceptor, was the oracle of the family, and little Candide listened to his instructions with all the simplicity natural to his age and disposition.

Master Pangloss taught the metaphysico-theologo-cosmolo-nigology. He could prove to admiration that there is no effect without a cause; and, that in this best of all possible worlds, the baron's castle was the most magnificent of all castles, and my lady the best of all possible baronesses.[3]

It is demonstrable, said he, that all things cannot be otherwise than as they are; for as all things have been created for some end, they must necessarily be created for the best end. Observe, for instance, the nose is formed for spectacles, therefore we wear spectacles. The legs are visibly designed for stockings, accordingly we wear stockings. Stones were made to be hewn, and to construct castles, therefore My Lord has a magnificent castle; for the greatest baron in the province ought to be the best lodged. Swine were intended to be eaten, therefore we eat pork all the year round: and they, who assert that everything is *right*, do not express themselves correctly; they should say that everything is *best*.

Candide listened attentively, and believed implicitly; for he thought Miss Cunegund excessively handsome, though he never had the courage to tell her so. He concluded that next to the happiness of being baron of Thunder-ten-tronckh, the next was that of being Miss Cunegund, the next that of seeing her every day, and the last that of hearing the doctrine of Master Pangloss, the greatest philosopher of the whole province, and consequently of the whole world.

One day when Miss Cunegund went to take a walk in a little neighboring wood which was called a park, she saw, through the bushes, the sage Doctor Pangloss giving a lecture in experimental philosophy to her mother's chambermaid, a little brown wench, very pretty, and very tractable. As Miss Cunegund had a great disposition for the sciences, she observed with the utmost attention the experiments, which were repeated before her eyes; she perfectly well understood the force of the doctor's reasoning upon causes and effects. She retired greatly flurried, quite pensive and filled with the desire of knowledge, imagining that she might be a *sufficing reason* for young Candide, and he for her.

On her way back she happened to meet the young man; she blushed, he blushed also; she wished him a good morning in a flattering tone, he returned the salute, without knowing what he said. The next day, as they were rising from dinner, Cunegund and Candide slipped behind the screen. The miss dropped her handkerchief, the young man picked it up. She innocently took hold of his hand, and he as innocently kissed hers with a warmth, a sensibility, a grace—all very

---

[2]"All tongue" (from Greek).
[3]Simplified echoes of Leibniz's philosophy.

particular; their lips met; their eyes sparkled; their knees trembled; their hands strayed. The baron chanced to come by; he beheld the cause and effect, and, without hesitation, saluted Candide with some notable kicks on the breech, and drove him out of doors. The lovely Miss Cunegund fainted away, and, as soon as she came to herself, the baroness boxed her ears. Thus a general consternation was spread over this most magnificent and most agreeable of all possible castles.

CHAPTER 2

What Befell Candide among the Bulgarians

Candide, thus driven out of this terrestrial paradise, rambled a long time without knowing where he went; sometimes he raised his eyes, all bedewed with tears, towards heaven, and sometimes he cast a melancholy look towards the magnificent castle, where dwelt the fairest of young baronesses. He laid himself down to sleep in a furrow, heartbroken, and supperless. The snow fell in great flakes, and, in the morning when he awoke, he was almost frozen to death; however, he made shift to crawl to the next town, which was called Wald-berghoff-trarbk-dikdorff, without a penny in his pocket, and half dead with hunger and fatigue. He took up his stand at the door of an inn. He had not been long there, before two men dressed in blue, fixed their eyes steadfastly upon him.[4] "Faith, comrade," said one of them to the other, "yonder is a well made young fellow, and of the right size." Upon which they made up to Candide, and with the greatest civility and politeness invited him to dine with them. "Gentlemen," replied Candide, with a most engaging modesty, "you do me much honor, but upon my word I have no money." "Money, sir!" said one of the blues to him, "young persons of your appearance and merit never pay anything; why, are you not five feet five inches high?" "Yes, gentlemen, that is really my size," replied he, with a low bow. "Come then, sir, sit down along with us; we will not only pay your reckoning, but will never suffer such a clever young fellow as you to want money. Men were born to assist one another." "You are perfectly right, gentlemen," said Candide, "this is precisely the doctrine of Master Pangloss; and I am convinced that everything is for the best." His generous companions next entreated him to accept of a few crowns, which he readily complied with, at the same time offering them his note for the payment, which they refused, and sat down to table. "Have you not a great affection for—" "O yes! I have a great affection for the lovely Miss Cunegund." "May be so," replied one of the blues, "but that is not the question! We ask you whether you have not a great affection for the king of the Bulgarians?" "For the king of the Bulgarians?" said Candide, "oh Lord! not at all, why I never saw him in my life." "Is it possible! oh, he is a most charming king! Come, we must drink his health." "With all my heart, gentlemen," says Candide, and off he tossed his glass. "Bravo!" cry the blues; "you are now the support, the defender, the hero of the Bulgarians; your fortune is made; you are in the high road to glory." So saying, they handcuffed him, and carried him away to the regiment. There he was made to wheel about to the right, to the left, to draw his rammer, to return his rammer, to present, to fire, to march, and they gave him thirty blows with a cane; the next day he performed his exercise a little better, and they gave him but twenty; the day following he came off with ten, and was looked upon as a young fellow of surprising genius by all his comrades.

Candide was struck with amazement, and could not for the soul of him conceive how he came to be a hero. One fine spring morning, he took it into his head to

---

[4] Prussian recruiting officers.

take a walk, and he marched straight forward, conceiving it to be a privilege of the human species, as well as of the brute creation, to make use of their legs how and when they pleased. He had not gone above two leagues when he was overtaken by four other heroes, six feet high, who bound him neck and heels, and carried him to a dungeon. A court-martial sat upon him, and he was asked which he liked better, to run the gauntlet six and thirty times through the whole regiment, or to have his brains blown out with a dozen musket-balls? In vain did he remonstrate to them that the human will is free, and that he chose neither; they obliged him to make a choice, and he determined, in virtue of that divine gift called free will, to run the gauntlet six and thirty times. He had gone through his discipline twice, and the regiment being composed of 2,000 men, they composed for him exactly 4,000 strokes, which laid bare all his muscles and nerves from the nape of his neck to his stern. As they were preparing to make him set out the third time our young hero, unable to support it any longer, begged as a favor that they would be so obliging as to shoot him through the head; the favor being granted, a bandage was tied over his eyes, and he was made to kneel down. At that very instant, his Bulgarian majesty happening to pass by made a stop, and inquired into the delinquent's crime, and being a prince of great penetration, he found, from what he heard of Candide, that he was a young metaphysician, entirely ignorant of the world; and therefore, out of his great clemency, he condescended to pardon him, for which his name will be celebrated in every journal, and in every age. A skillful surgeon made a cure of the flagellated Candide in three weeks by means of emollient unguents prescribed by Dioscorides.[5] His sores were now skinned over and he was able to march, when the king of the Bulgarians gave battle to the king of the Avars.[6]

CHAPTER 3

How Candide Escaped from the Bulgarians, and What Befell Him Afterwards

Never was anything so gallant, so well accoutred, so brilliant, and so finely disposed as the two armies. The trumpets, fifes, hautboys, drums, and cannon made such harmony as never was heard in hell itself. The entertainment began by a discharge of cannon, which, in the twinkling of an eye, laid flat about 6,000 men on each side. The musket bullets swept away, out of the best of all possible worlds, nine or ten thousand scoundrels that infested its surface. The bayonet was the next sufficient reason of the deaths of several thousands. The whole might amount to thirty thousand souls. Candide trembled like a philosopher, and concealed himself as well as he could during this heroic butchery.

At length, while the two kings were causing *Te Deums* to be sung in their camps, Candide took a resolution to go and reason somewhere else upon causes and effects. After passing over heaps of dead or dying men, the first place he came to was a neighboring village, in the Avarian territories, which had been burned to the ground by the Bulgarians, agreeably to the laws of war. Here lay a number of old men covered with wounds, who beheld their wives dying with their throats cut, and hugging their children to their breasts, all stained with blood. There several young virgins, whose bodies had been ripped open, after they had satisfied the natural necessities of the Bulgarian heroes, breathed their last; while others, half burned in the flames, begged to be despatched out of the world. The ground about them was covered with the brains, arms, and legs of dead men.

---

[5]First century C.E.
[6]A Scythian tribe.

Candide made all the haste he could to another village, which belonged to the Bulgarians, and there he found the heroic Avars had enacted the same tragedy. Thence continuing to walk over palpitating limbs, or through ruined buildings, at length he arrived beyond the theatre of war, with a little provision in his budget, and Miss Cunegund's image in his heart. When he arrived in Holland his provision failed him; but having heard that the inhabitants of that country were all rich and Christians, he made himself sure of being treated by them in the same manner as at the baron's castle, before he had been driven thence through the power of Miss Cunegund's bright eyes.

He asked charity of several grave-looking people, who one and all answered him, that if he continued to follow this trade they would have him sent to the house of correction, where he should be taught to get his bread.

He next addressed himself to a person who had just come from haranguing a numerous assembly for a whole hour on the subject of charity. The orator, squinting at him under his broad-brimmed hat, asked him sternly, what brought him thither and whether he was for the good old cause? "Sir," said Candide, in a submissive manner, "I conceive there can be no effect without a cause; everything is necessarily concatenated and arranged for the best. It was necessary that I should be banished from the presence of Miss Cunegund; that I should afterwards run the gauntlet; and it is necessary I should beg my bread, till I am able to get it: all this could not have been otherwise." "Hark ye, friend," said the orator, "do you hold the pope to be Antichrist?" "Truly, I never heard anything about it," said Candide, "but whether he is or not, I am in want of something to eat." "Thou deservest not to eat or to drink," replied the orator, "wretch, monster, that thou art! hence! avoid my sight, nor ever come near me again while thou livest." The orator's wife happened to put her head out of the window at that instant, when, seeing a man who doubted whether the pope was Antichrist, she discharged upon his head a utensil full of water. Good heavens, to what excess does religious zeal transport womankind!

A man who had never been christened, an honest anabaptist named James, was witness to the cruel and ignominious treatment showed to one of his brethren, to a rational, two-footed, unfledged being. Moved with pity he carried him to his own house, caused him to be cleaned, gave him meat and drink, and made him a present of two florins, at the same time proposing to instruct him in his own trade of weaving Persian silks, which are fabricated in Holland. Candide, penetrated with so much goodness, threw himself at his feet, crying, "Now I am convinced that my Master Pangloss told me truth when he said that everything was for the best in this world; for I am infinitely more affected with your extraordinary generosity than with the inhumanity of that gentleman in the black cloak, and his wife." The next day, as Candide was walking out, he met a beggar all covered with scabs, his eyes sunk in his head, the end of his nose eaten off, his mouth drawn on one side, his teeth as black as a cloak, snuffling and coughing most violently, and every time he attempted to spit out dropped a tooth.

CHAPTER 4

How Candide Found His Old Master Pangloss Again and What Happened to Him

Candide, divided between compassion and horror, but giving way to the former, bestowed on this shocking figure the two florins which the honest anabaptist, James, had just before given to him. The spectre looked at him very earnestly, shed tears and threw his arms about his neck. Candide started back aghast. "Alas!" said the one wretch to the other, "don't you know your dear Pangloss?" "What do I hear? Is it you, my dear master! you I behold in this piteous plight? What dreadful misfortune has befallen you? What has made you leave the most magnificent and delightful of all castles? What has become of Miss Cunegund, the mirror of young ladies, and nature's masterpiece?" "Oh Lord!" cried Pangloss, "I am so weak I cannot stand," upon which Candide instantly led him to the anabaptist's stable, and procured him something to eat. As soon as Pangloss had a little refreshed himself, Candide began to repeat his inquiries concerning Miss Cunegund. "She is dead," replied the other. "Dead!" cried Candide, and immediately fainted away; his friend restored him by the help of a little bad vinegar, which he found by chance in the stable. Candide opened his eyes, and again repeated: "Dead! is Miss Cunegund dead? Ah, where is the best of worlds now? But of what illness did she die? Was it of grief on seeing her father kick me out of his magnificent castle?" "No," replied Pangloss, "her body was ripped open by the Bulgarian soldiers, after they had subjected her to as much cruelty as a damsel could survive; they knocked the baron, her father, on the head for attempting to defend her; my lady, her mother, was cut in pieces; my poor pupil was served just in the same manner as his sister, and as for the castle, they have not left one stone upon another; they have destroyed all the ducks, and the sheep, the barns, and the trees; but we have had our revenge, for the Avars have done the very same thing in a neighboring barony, which belonged to a Bulgarian lord."

At hearing this, Candide fainted away a second time, but, having come to himself again, he said all that it became him to say; he inquired into the cause and effect, as well as into the sufficing reason that had reduced Pangloss to so miserable a condition. "Alas," replied the preceptor, "it was love; love, the comfort of the human species; love, the preserver of the universe; the soul of all sensible beings; love! tender love!" "Alas," cried Candide, "I have had some knowledge of love myself, this sovereign of hearts, this soul of souls; yet it never cost me more than a kiss and twenty kicks on the backside. But how could this beautiful cause produce in you so hideous an effect?"

Pangloss made answer in these terms: "O my dear Candide, you must remember Pacquette, that pretty wench, who waited on our noble baroness; in her arms I tasted the pleasures of paradise, which produced these hell-torments with which you see me devoured. She was infected with an ailment, and perhaps has since died of it; she received this present of a learned cordelier, who derived it from the fountain head; he was indebted for it to an old countess, who had it of a captain of horse, who had it of a marchioness, who had it of a page, the page had it of a Jesuit, who, during his novitiate, had it in a direct line from one of the fellow-adventurers of Christopher Columbus; for my part I shall give it to nobody, I am a dying man."

"O sage Pangloss," cried Candide, "what a strange genealogy is this! Is not the devil the root of it?" "Not at all," replied the great man, "it was a thing unavoidable, a necessary ingredient in the best of worlds; for if Columbus had not caught in an island in America this disease, which contaminates the source of generation, and frequently impedes propagation itself, and is evidently opposed to the great end of nature, we should have had neither chocolate nor cochineal. It is also to be observed, that, even to the present time, in this continent of ours, this malady, like our religious controversies, is peculiar to ourselves. The Turks, the Indians, the Persians, the Chinese, the Siamese, and the Japanese are entirely unacquainted with it; but there is a sufficing reason for them to know it in a few centuries. In the meantime, it is making prodigious havoc among us, especially in those armies composed of well-disciplined hirelings, who determine the fate of nations; for we may safely affirm, that, when an army of thirty thousand men engages another equal in size, there are about twenty thousand infected with syphilis on each side."

"Very surprising, indeed," said Candide, "but you must get cured." "Lord help me, how can I?" said Pangloss; "my dear friend, I have not a penny in the world; and you know one cannot be bled or have a clyster without money."

This last speech had its effect on Candide; he flew to the charitable anabaptist, James; he flung himself at his feet, and gave him so striking a picture of the miserable condition of his friend that the good man without any further hesitation agreed to take Doctor Pangloss into his house, and to pay for his cure. The cure was effected with only the loss of one eye and an ear. As he wrote a good hand, and understood accounts tolerably well, the anabaptist made him his bookkeeper. At the expiration of two months, being obliged by some mercantile affairs to go to Lisbon he took the two philosophers with him in the same ship; Pangloss, during the course of the voyage, explained to him how everything was so constituted that it could not be better. James did not quite agree with him on this point: "Men," said he, "must, in some things, have deviated from their original innocence; for they were not born wolves, and yet they worry one another like those beasts of prey. God never gave them twenty-four pounders nor bayonets, and yet they have made cannon and bayonets to destroy one another. To this account I might add not only bankruptcies, but the law which seizes on the effects of bankrupts, only to cheat the creditors." "All this was indispensably necessary," replied the one-eyed doctor, "for private misfortunes are public benefits; so that the more private misfortunes there are, the greater is the general good." While he was arguing in this manner, the sky was overcast, the winds blew from the four quarters of the compass, and the ship was assailed by a most terrible tempest, within sight of the port of Lisbon.

CHAPTER 5

A Tempest, a Shipwreck, an Earthquake;
and What Else Befell Dr. Pangloss, Candide, and James the Anabaptist

One-half of the passengers, weakened and half-dead with the inconceivable anxiety and sickness which the rolling of a vessel at sea occasions through the whole human frame, were lost to all sense of the danger that surrounded them. The others made loud outcries, or betook themselves to their prayers; the sails were blown into shreds, and the masts were brought by the board. The vessel was a total wreck. Every one was busily employed, but nobody could be either heard or obeyed. The anabaptist, being upon deck, lent a helping hand as well as the rest, when a brutish sailor gave him a blow and laid him speechless; but, with the violence of the blow the tar himself tumbled headforemost overboard, and fell upon a piece of the broken mast, which he immediately grasped. Honest James, forgetting the injury he had so lately received from him, flew to his assistance, and, with great difficulty, hauled him in again, but, in the attempt, was, by a sudden jerk of the ship, thrown overboard himself, in sight of the very fellow whom he had risked his life to save, and who took not the least notice of him in this distress. Candide, who beheld all that passed and saw his benefactor one moment rising above water, and the next swallowed up by the merciless waves, was preparing to jump after him, but was prevented by the philosopher Pangloss, who demonstrated to him that the roadstead of Lisbon had been made on purpose for the anabaptist to be drowned there. While he was proving his argument *a priori*, the ship foundered, and the whole crew perished, except Pangloss, Candide, and the sailor who had been the means of drowning the good anabaptist. The villain swam ashore; but Pangloss and Candide reached the land upon a plank.

As soon as they had recovered from their surprise and fatigue they walked towards Lisbon; with what little money they had left they thought to save themselves from starving after having escaped drowning.

Scarcely had they ceased to lament the loss of their benefactor and set foot in the city, when they perceived that the earth trembled under their feet, and the sea, swelling and foaming in the harbor, was dashing in pieces the vessels that were riding at anchor. Large sheets of flames and cinders covered the streets and public places; the houses tottered, and were tumbled topsy-turvy even to their foundations, which were themselves destroyed, and thirty thousand inhabitants of both sexes, young and old, were buried beneath the ruins.[7] The sailor, whistling and swearing, cried, "Damn it, there's something to be got here." "What can be the *sufficing reason* of this phenomenon?" said Pangloss. "It is certainly the day of judgment," said Candide. The sailor, defying death in the pursuit of plunder, rushed into the midst of the ruin, where he found some money, with which he got drunk, and, after he had slept himself sober he purchased the favors of the first good-natured wench that came in his way, amidst the ruins of demolished houses and the groans of half-buried and expiring persons. Pangloss pulled him by the sleeve; "Friend," said he, "this is not right, you trespass against the *universal reason*, and have mistaken your time." "Death and zounds!" answered the other, "I am a sailor and was born at Batavia, and have trampled four times upon the crucifix in as many voyages to Japan; you have come to a good hand with your *universal reason*."

In the meantime, Candide, who had been wounded by some pieces of stone that fell from the houses, lay stretched in the street, almost covered with rubbish. "For God's sake," said he to Pangloss, "get me a little wine and oil! I am dying." "This concussion of the earth is no new thing," said Pangloss, "the city of Lima in South America, experienced the same last year; the same cause, the same effects; there is certainly a vein of sulphur all the way underground from Lima to Lisbon." "Nothing is more probable," said Candide; "but for the love of God a little oil and wine." "Probable!" replied the philosopher, "I maintain that the thing is demonstrable." Candide fainted away, and Pangloss fetched him some water from a neighboring spring.

The next day, in searching among the ruins, they found some eatables with which they repaired their exhausted strength. After this they assisted the inhabitants in relieving the distressed and wounded. Some, whom they had humanely assisted, gave them as good a dinner as could be expected under such terrible circumstances. The repast, indeed, was mournful, and the company moistened their bread with their tears; but Pangloss endeavored to comfort them under this affliction by affirming that things could not be otherwise than they were: "For," said he, "all this is for the very best end, for if there is a volcano at Lisbon it could be in no other spot; and it is impossible but things should be as they are, for everything is for the best."

By the side of the preceptor sat a little man dressed in black, who was one of the *familiars* of the Inquisition. This person, taking him up with great complaisance, said, "Possibly, my good sir, you do not believe in original sin; for, if everything is best, there could have been no such thing as the fall or punishment of man."

"I humbly ask your excellency's pardon," answered Pangloss, still more politely; "for the fall of man and the curse consequent thereupon necessarily entered into the system of the best of worlds." "That is as much as to say, sir," rejoined the *familiar,* "you do not believe in free will." "Your excellency will be so good as to excuse me," said Pangloss, "free will is consistent with absolute necessity; for it was necessary we should be free, for in that the will—"

Pangloss was in the midst of his proposition, when the inquisitor beckoned to his attendant to help him to a glass of port wine.

---

[7] The great Lisbon earthquake of 1755.

CHAPTER 6

How the Portuguese Made a Superb Auto-da-fé to Prevent Any Future Earthquakes,
and How Candide Underwent Public Flagellation

After the earthquake, which had destroyed three-fourths of the city of Lisbon, the sages of that country could think of no means more effectual to preserve the kingdom from utter ruin than to entertain the people with an *auto-da-fé,*[8] it having been decided by the University of Coimbra, that the burning of a few people alive by a slow fire, and with great ceremony, is an infallible preventive of earthquakes.

In consequence thereof they had seized on a Biscayan for marrying his godmother, and on two Portuguese for taking out the bacon of a larded pullet they were eating; after dinner they came and secured Doctor Pangloss, and his pupil Candide, the one for speaking his mind, and the other for seeming to approve what he had said. They were conducted to separate apartments, extremely cool, where they were never incommoded with the sun. Eight days afterwards they were each dressed in a *sanbenito,* and their heads were adorned with paper mitres.[9] The mitre and *sanbenito* worn by Candide were painted with flames reversed and with devils that had neither tails nor claws; but Doctor Pangloss's devils had both tails and claws, and his flames were upright. In these habits they marched in procession, and heard a very pathetic sermon, which was followed by an anthem, accompanied by bagpipes. Candide was flogged to some tune, while the anthem was being sung; the Biscayan and the two men who would not eat bacon were burned, and Pangloss was hanged, which is not a common custom at these solemnities. The same day there was another earthquake, which made most dreadful havoc.

Candide, amazed, terrified, confounded, astonished, all bloody, and trembling from head to foot, said to himself, "If this is the best of all possible worlds, what are the others? If I had only been whipped, I could have put up with it, as I did among the Bulgarians; but, oh my dear Pangloss! my beloved master! thou greatest of philosophers! that ever I should live to see thee hanged, without knowing for what! O my dear anabaptist, thou best of men, that it should be thy fate to be drowned in the very harbor! O Miss Cunegund, you mirror of young ladies! that it should be your fate to have your body ripped open!"

He was making the best of his way from the place where he had been preached to, whipped, absolved and blessed, when he was accosted by an old woman, who said to him: "Take courage, child, and follow me."

CHAPTER 7

How the Old Woman Took Care of Candide, and How He Found the Object of His Love

Candide followed the old woman, though without taking courage, to a decayed house, where she gave him a pot of pomatum to anoint his sores, showed him a very neat bed, with a suit of clothes hanging by it; and set victuals and drink before him. "There," said she, "eat, drink, and sleep, and may our blessed lady of Atocha, and the great St. Anthony of Padua, and the illustrious St. James of Compostella,

---

[8] Literally, "act of faith"; the burning of heretics.
[9] Yellow capes and imitation bishop miters.

take you under their protection. I shall be back to-morrow." Candide struck with amazement at what he had seen, at what he had suffered, and still more with the charity of the old woman, would have shown his acknowledgment by kissing her hand. "It is not my hand you ought to kiss," said the old woman; "I shall be back to-morrow. Anoint your back, eat, and take your rest."

Candide, notwithstanding so many disasters, ate and slept. The next morning, the old woman brought him his breakfast; examined his back, and rubbed it herself with another ointment. She returned at the proper time, and brought him his dinner; and at night, she visited him again with his supper. The next day she observed the same ceremonies. "Who are you?" said Candide to her. "Who has inspired you with so much goodness? What return can I make you for this charitable assistance?" The good old beldame kept a profound silence. In the evening she returned, but without his supper; "Come along with me," said she, "but do not speak a word." She took him by the arm, and walked with him about a quarter of a mile into the country, till they came to a lonely house surrounded with moats and gardens. The old conductress knocked at a little door, which was immediately opened, and she showed him up a pair of back stairs, into a small, but richly furnished apartment. There she made him sit down on a brocaded sofa, shut the door upon him, and left him. Candide thought himself in a trance; he looked upon his whole life, hitherto, as a frightful dream, and the present moment as a very agreeable one.

The old woman soon returned, supporting, with great difficulty, a young lady, who appeared scarce able to stand. She was of a majestic mien and stature, her dress was rich, and glittering with diamonds, and her face was covered with a veil. "Take off that veil," said the old woman to Candide. The young man approached, and, with a trembling hand, took off her veil. What a happy moment! What surprise! He thought he beheld Miss Cunegund; he did behold her—it was she herself. His strength failed him, he could not utter a word, he fell at her feet. Cunegund fainted upon the sofa. The old woman bedewed them with spirits; they recovered—they began to speak. At first they could express themselves only in broken accents; their questions and answers were alternately interrupted with sighs, tears, and exclamations. The old woman desired them to make less noise, and after this prudent admonition left them together. "Good heavens!" cried Candide, "is it you? Is it Miss Cunegund I behold, and alive? Do I find you again in Portugal? then you have not been ravished? they did not rip open your body, as the philosopher Pangloss informed me?" "Indeed but they did," replied Miss Cunegund; "but these two accidents do not always prove mortal." "But were your father and mother killed?" "Alas!" answered she, "it is but too true!" and she wept. "And your brother?" "And my brother also." "And how came you into Portugal? And how did you know of my being here? And by what strange adventure did you contrive to have me brought into this house? And how——" "I will tell you all," replied the lady, "but first you must acquaint me with all that has befallen you since the innocent kiss you gave me, and the rude kicking you received in consequence of it."

Candide, with the greatest submission, prepared to obey the commands of his fair mistress; and though he was still filled with amazement, though his voice was low and tremulous, though his back pained him, yet he gave her a most ingenuous account of everything that had befallen him, since the moment of their separation. Cunegund, with her eyes uplifted to heaven, shed tears when he related the death of the good anabaptist James, and of Pangloss; after which she thus related her adventures to Candide, who lost not one syllable she uttered, and seemed to devour her with his eyes all the time she was speaking.

CHAPTER 8

Cunegund's Story

"I was in bed, and fast asleep, when it pleased heaven to send the Bulgarians to our delightful castle of Thunder-ten-tronckh, where they murdered my father and brother, and cut my mother in pieces. A tall Bulgarian soldier, six feet high, perceiving that I had fainted away at this sight, attempted to ravish me; the operation brought me to my senses. I cried, I struggled, I bit, I scratched, I would have torn the tall Bulgarian's eyes out, not knowing that what had happened at my father's castle was a customary thing. The brutal soldier, enraged at my resistance, gave me a wound in my left leg with his hanger, the mark of which I still carry." "Methinks I long to see it," said Candide, with all imaginable simplicity. "You shall," said Cunegund, "but let me proceed." "Pray do," replied Candide.

She continued. "A Bulgarian captain came in, and saw me weltering in my blood, and the soldier still as busy as if no one had been present. The officer, enraged at the fellow's want of respect to him, killed him with one stroke of his sabre as he lay upon me. This captain took care of me, had me cured, and carried me as a prisoner of war to his quarters. I washed what little linen he possessed, and cooked his victuals: he was very fond of me, that was certain; neither can I deny that he was well made, and had a soft, white skin, but he was very stupid, and knew nothing of philosophy: it might plainly be perceived that he had not been educated under Doctor Pangloss. In three months, having gambled away all his money, and having grown tired of me, he sold me to a Jew, named Don Issachar, who traded in Holland and Portugal, and was passionately fond of women. This Jew showed me great kindness, in hopes of gaining my favors; but he never could prevail on me to yield. A modest woman may be once ravished; but her virtue is greatly strengthened thereby. In order to make sure of me, he brought me to this country-house you now see. I had hitherto believed that nothing could equal the beauty of the castle of Thunder-ten-tronckh; but I found I was mistaken.

"The grand inquisitor saw me one day at mass, ogled me all the time of service, and when it was over, sent to let me know he wanted to speak with me about some private business. I was conducted to his palace, where I told him all my story; he represented to me how much it was beneath a person of my birth to belong to a circumcised Israelite. He caused a proposal to be made to Don Issachar, that he should resign me to his lordship. Don Issachar, being the court banker, and a man of credit, was not easy to be prevailed upon. His lordship threatened him with an *auto-da-fé;* in short, my Jew was frightened into a compromise, and it was agreed between them, that the house and myself should belong to both in common; that the Jew should have Monday, Wednesday, and the Sabbath to himself; and the inquisitor the other four days of the week. This agreement has subsisted almost six months; but not without several contests, whether the space from Saturday night to Sunday morning belonged to the old or the new law. For my part, I have hitherto withstood them both, and truly I believe this is the very reason why they are both so fond of me.

"At length to turn aside the scourge of earthquakes, and to intimidate Don Issachar, my lord inquisitor was pleased to celebrate an *auto-da-fé.* He did me the honor to invite me to the ceremony. I had a very good seat; and refreshments of all kinds were offered the ladies between mass and the execution. I was dreadfully shocked at the burning of the two Jews, and the honest Biscayan who married his godmother; but how great was my surprise, my consternation, and concern, when I beheld a figure so like Pangloss, dressed in a *sanbenito* and mitre! I rubbed my eyes, I looked at him attentively. I saw him hanged, and I fainted away: scarce had I recovered my senses, when I saw you stripped of clothing; this was the height of horror, grief, and despair. I must confess to you for a truth, that your skin is whiter and more blooming than that of the Bulgarian captain. This spectacle worked me up to a pitch of distraction. I screamed out, and would have said, 'hold, barbarians!' but my voice failed me; and indeed my cries would have signified nothing. After you had been severely whipped, how is it possible, I said to myself, that the lovely Candide and the sage Pangloss should be at Lisbon, the one to receive a hundred lashes, and the other to be hanged by order of my lord inquisitor, of whom I am so great a favorite? Pangloss deceived me most cruelly, in saying that everything is for the best.

"Thus agitated and perplexed, now distracted and lost, now half dead with grief, I revolved in my mind the murder of my father, mother, and brother, committed before my eyes; the insolence of the rascally Bulgarian soldier; the wound he gave me in the groin; my servitude; my being a cook-wench to my Bulgarian captain; my subjection to the hateful Jew, and my cruel inquisitor; the hanging of Doctor Pangloss; the *Miserere* sung while you were being whipped; and particularly the kiss I gave you behind the screen, the last day I ever beheld you. I returned thanks to God for having brought you to the place where I was, after so many trials. I charged the old woman who attends me to bring you hither as soon as was convenient. She has punctually executed my orders, and I now enjoy the inexpressible satisfaction of seeing you, hearing you, and speaking to you. But you must certainly be half-dead with hunger; I myself have a great inclination to eat, and so let us sit down to supper."

Upon this the two lovers immediately placed themselves at table, and, after having supped, they returned to seat themselves again on the magnificent sofa already mentioned, where they were in amorous dalliance, when Señor Don Issachar, one of the masters of the house, entered unexpectedly; it was the Sabbath day, and he came to enjoy his privilege, and sigh forth his passion at the feet of the fair Cunegund.

CHAPTER 9

What Happened to Cunegund, Candide, the Grand Inquisitor, and the Jew

This same Issachar was the most choleric little Hebrew that had ever been in Israel since the captivity of Babylon. "What," said he, "thou Galilean slut? the inquisitor was not enough for thee, but this rascal must come in for a share with me?" In uttering these words, he drew out a long poniard, which he always carried about him, and never dreaming that his adversary had any arms, he attacked him most furiously; but our honest Westphalian had received from the old woman a handsome sword with the suit of clothes. Candide drew his rapier, and though he was very gentle and sweet-tempered, he laid the Israelite dead on the floor at the fair Cunegund's feet.

"Holy Virgin!" cried she, "what will become of us? A man killed in my apartment! If the peace-officers come, we are undone." "Had not Pangloss been hanged," replied Candide, "he would have given us most excellent advice, in this emergency; for he was a profound philosopher. But, since he is not here, let us consult the old woman." She was very sensible, and was beginning to give her advice, when another door opened on a sudden. It was now one o'clock in the morning, and of course the beginning of Sunday, which, by agreement, fell to the lot of my lord inquisitor. Entering he discovers the flagellated Candide with his drawn sword in his hand, a dead body stretched on the floor, Cunegund frightened out of her wits, and the old woman giving advice.

At that very moment, a sudden thought came into Candide's head. If this holy man, thought he, should call assistance, I shall most undoubtedly be consigned to the flames, and Miss Cunegund may perhaps meet with no better treatment: besides, he was the cause of my being so cruelly whipped; he is my rival; and as I have now begun to dip my hands in blood, I will kill away, for there is no time to hesitate. This whole train of reasoning was clear and instantaneous; so that, without giving time to the inquisitor to recover from his surprise, he ran him through the body, and laid him by the side of the Jew. "Here's another fine piece of work!" cried Cunegund. "Now there can be no mercy for us, we are excommunicated; our last hour is come. But how could you, who are of so mild a temper, dispatch a Jew and an inquisitor in two minutes' time?" "Beautiful maiden," answered Candide, "when a man is in love, is jealous, and has been flogged by the Inquisition, he becomes lost to all reflection."

The old woman then put in her word: "There are three Andalusian horses in the stable, with as many bridles and saddles; let the brave Candide get them ready: madam has a parcel of moidores and jewels, let us mount immediately, though I have lost one of nature's cushions; let us set out for Cadiz; it is the finest weather in the world, and there is great pleasure in travelling in the cool of the night."

Candide, without any further hesitation, saddled the three horses; and Miss Cunegund, the old woman, and he, set out, and travelled thirty miles without once halting. While they were making the best of their way, the Holy Brotherhood entered the house. My lord, the inquisitor, was interred in a magnificent manner, and master Issachar's body was thrown upon a dunghill.

Candide, Cunegund, and the old woman, had by this time reached the little town of Avacena, in the midst of the mountains of Sierra Morena, and were engaged in the following conversation in an inn, where they had taken up their quarters.

CHAPTER 10

In What Distress Candide, Cunegund, and the Old Woman Arrive at Cadiz,
and of Their Embarkation

"Who could it be that has robbed me of my moidores and jewels?" exclaimed Miss Cunegund, all bathed in tears. "How shall we live? What shall we do? Where shall I find inquisitors and Jews who can give me more?" "Alas!" said the old woman, "I have a shrewd suspicion of a reverend father cordelier, who lay last night in the same inn with us at Badajoz; God forbid I should condemn any one wrongfully, but he came into our room twice, and he set off in the morning long before us." "Alas!" said Candide, "Pangloss has often demonstrated to me that the goods of this world are common to all men, and that everyone has an equal right to the enjoyment of them; but, according to these principles, the cordelier ought to have left us enough to carry us to the end of our journey. Have you nothing at all left, my dear Miss Cunegund?" "Not a maravedi," replied she. "What is to be done then?" said Candide. "Sell one of the horses," replied the old woman, "I will get up behind Miss Cunegund, though I have only one cushion to ride on, and we shall reach Cadiz."

In the same inn there was a Benedictine friar, who bought the horse very cheap. Candide, Cunegund, and the old woman, after passing through Lucina, Chellas, and Letrixa, arrived at length at Cadiz. A fleet was then getting ready, and troops were assembling in order to induce the reverend fathers, Jesuits of Paraguay, who were accused of having excited one of the Indian tribes in the neighborhood of the town of the Holy Sacrament, to revolt against the kings of Spain and Portugal. Candide, having been in the Bulgarian service, performed the military exercise of that nation before the general of this little army with so intrepid an air, and with such agility and expedition, that he received the command of a company of foot. Being now made a captain, he embarked with Miss Cunegund, the old woman, two valets, and the two Andalusian horses, which had belonged to the grand inquisitor of Portugal.

During their voyage they amused themselves with many profound reasonings on poor Pangloss's philosophy. "We are now going into another world, and surely it must be there that everything is for the best; for I must confess that we have had some little reason to complain of what passes in ours, both as to the physical and moral part. Though I have a sincere love for you," said Miss Cunegund, "yet I still shudder at the reflection of what I have seen and experienced." "All will be well," replied Candide, "the sea of this new world is already better than our European seas: it is smoother, and the winds blow more regularly." "God grant it," said Cunegund, "but I have met with such terrible treatment in this world that I have almost lost all hopes of a better one." "What murmuring and complaining is here indeed!" cried the old woman: "If you had suffered half of what I have, there might be some reason for it." Miss Cunegund could scarce refrain from laughing at the good old woman, and thought it droll enough to pretend to a greater share of misfortunes than her own. "Alas! my good dame," said she, "unless you had been ravished by two Bulgarians, had received two deep wounds in your belly, had seen two of your own castles demolished, had lost two fathers, and two mothers, and seen both of them barbarously murdered before your eyes, and to sum up all, had two lovers whipped at an *auto-da-fé*, I cannot see how you could be more unfortunate than I. Add to this, though born a baroness, and bearing seventy-two quarterings, I have been reduced to the station of a cook-wench." "Miss," replied the old woman, "you do not know my family as yet; but if I were to show you my posteriors, you would not talk in this manner, but suspend your judgment." This speech raised a high curiosity in Candide and Cunegund; and the old woman continued as follows:

CHAPTER 11

The History of the Old Woman

"I have not always been blear-eyed. My nose did not always touch my chin; nor was I always a servant. You must know that I am the daughter of Pope Urban X, and of the princess of Palestrina.[10] To the age of fourteen I was brought up in a castle, compared with which all the castles of the German barons would not have been fit for stabling, and one of my robes would have bought half the province of Westphalia. I grew up, and improved in beauty, wit, and every graceful accomplishment; and in the midst of pleasures, homage, and the highest expectations. I already began to inspire the men with love. My breast began to take its right form, and such a breast! white, firm, and formed like that of Venus of Medici; my eyebrows were as black as jet, and as for my eyes, they darted flames and eclipsed the lustre of the stars, as I was told by the poets of our part of the world. My maids, when they dressed and

---

[10]The following is allegedly by Voltaire: "Note the author's extreme discretion! So far there has been no pope named Urban X; he is afraid to ascribe a bastard daughter to a known pope. What circumspection! What delicacy of conscience!"

undressed me, used to fall into an ecstasy in viewing me before and behind: and all the men longed to be in their places.

"I was contracted in marriage to a sovereign prince of Massa Carara. Such a prince! as handsome as myself, sweet-tempered, agreeable, witty, and in love with me over head and ears. I loved him, too, as our sex generally do for the first time, with rapture, transport, and idolatry. The nuptials were prepared with surprising pomp and magnificence; the ceremony was attended with feasts, carousals, and burlettas: all Italy composed sonnets in my praise, though not one of them was tolerable. I was on the point of reaching the summit of bliss, when an old marchioness, who had been mistress to the prince, my husband, invited him to drink chocolate. In less than two hours after he returned from the visit, he died of most terrible convulsions. But this is a mere trifle. My mother, distracted to the highest degree, and yet less afflicted than I, determined to absent herself for some time from so fatal a place. As she had a very fine estate in the neighborhood of Gaeta,[11] we embarked on board a galley, which was gilded like the high altar of St. Peter's, at Rome. In our passage we were boarded by a Sallee rover. Our men defended themselves like true pope's soldiers; they flung themselves upon their knees, laid down their arms, and begged the corsair to give them absolution in articulo mortis.[12]

"The Moors presently stripped us as bare as ever we were born. My mother, my maids of honor, and myself, were served all in the same manner. It is amazing how quick these gentry are at undressing people. But what surprised me most was, that they made a rude sort of surgical examination of parts of the body which are sacred to the functions of nature. I thought it a very strange kind of ceremony; for thus we are generally apt to judge of things when we have not seen the world. I afterwards learned that it was to discover if we had any diamonds concealed. This practice has been established since time immemorial among those civilized nations that scour the seas. I was informed that the religious knights of Malta never fail to make this search whenever any Moors of either sex fall into their hands. It is a part of the law of nations, from which they never deviate.

"I need not tell you how great a hardship it was for a young princess and her mother to be made slaves and carried to Morocco. You may easily imagine what we must have suffered on board a corsair. My mother was still extremely handsome, our maids of honor, and even our common waiting-women, had more charms than were to be found in all Africa. As to myself, I was enchanting; I was beauty itself, and then I had my virginity. But alas! I did not retain it long; this precious flower, which had been reserved for the lovely prince of Massa Carara, was cropped by the captain of the Moorish vessel, who was a hideous negro, and thought he did me infinite honor. Indeed, both the princess of Palestrina and myself must have had very strong constitutions to undergo all the hardships and violences we suffered before our arrival at Morocco. But I will not detain you any longer with such common things; they are hardly worth mentioning.

"Upon our arrival at Morocco we found that kingdom deluged with blood. Fifty sons of the emperor Muley Ishmael[13] were each at the head of a party. This produced fifty civil wars of blacks against blacks, of tawnies against tawnies, and of mulattoes against mulattoes. In short, the whole empire was one continued scene of carnage.

"No sooner were we landed than a party of blacks, of a contrary faction to that of my captain, came to rob him of his booty. Next to the money and jewels, we

[11]Between Rome and Naples.
[12]"At the point of death."
[13]Sultan of Morocco who died in 1727.

were the most valuable things he had. I witnessed on this occasion such a battle as you never beheld in your cold European climates. The northern nations have not that fermentation in their blood, nor that raging lust for women that is so common in Africa. The natives of Europe seem to have their veins filled with milk only; but fire and vitriol circulate in those of the inhabitants of Mount Atlas and the neighboring provinces. They fought with the fury of the lions, tigers, and serpents of their country, to decide who should have us. A Moor seized my mother by the right arm, while my captain's lieutenant held her by the left; another Moor laid hold of her by the right leg, and one of our corsairs held her by the other. In this manner almost all of our women were dragged by four soldiers. My captain kept me concealed behind him, and with his drawn scimitar cut down everyone who opposed him; at length I saw all our Italian women and my mother mangled and torn in pieces by the monsters who contended for them. The captives, my companions, the Moors who took us, the soldiers, the sailors, the blacks, the whites, the mulattoes, and lastly, my captain himself, were all slain, and I remained alone expiring upon a heap of dead bodies. Similar barbarous scenes were transacted every day over the whole country, which is of three hundred leagues in extent, and yet they never missed the five stated times of prayer enjoined by their prophet Mahomet.

"I disengaged myself with great difficulty from such a heap of corpses, and made a shift to crawl to a large orange-tree that stood on the bank of a neighboring rivulet, where I fell down exhausted with fatigue, and overwhelmed with horror, despair, and hunger. My senses being overpowered, I fell asleep, or rather seemed to be in a trance. Thus I lay in a state of weakness and insensibility between life and death, when I felt myself pressed by something that moved up and down upon my body. This brought me to myself. I opened my eyes, and saw a pretty fair-faced man, who sighed and muttered these words between his teeth, *O che sciagura d'essere senza coglioni!*[14]

CHAPTER 12

The Adventures of the Old Woman Continued

"Astonished and delighted to hear my native language, and no less surprised at the young man's words, I told him that there were far greater misfortunes in the world than what he complained of. And to convince him of it, I gave him a short history of the horrible disasters that had befallen me; and as soon as I had finished, fell into a swoon again. He carried me in his arms to a neighboring cottage, where he had me put to bed, procured me something to eat, waited on me with the greatest attention, comforted me, caressed me, told me that he had never seen anything so perfectly beautiful as myself, and that he had never so much regretted the loss of what no one could restore to him. 'I was born at Naples,' said he, 'where they make eunuchs of thousands of children every year; some die of the operation; some acquire voices far beyond the most tuneful of your ladies; and others are sent to govern states and empires. I underwent this operation very successfully, and was one of the singers in the princess of Palestrina's chapel.' 'How,' cried I, 'in my mother's chapel!' 'The princess of Palestrina, your mother!' cried he, bursting into a flood of tears. 'Is it possible you should be the beautiful young princess whom I had the care of bringing up till she was six years old, and who at that tender age

---

[14]"O, what a misfortune to be without testicles!"

promised to be as fair as I now behold you?' 'I am the same,' I replied. 'My mother lies about a hundred yards from here cut in pieces and buried under a heap of dead bodies.'

"I then related to him all that had befallen me, and he in return acquainted me with all his adventures, and how he had been sent to the court of the king of Morocco by a Christian prince to conclude a treaty with that monarch; in consequence of which he was to be furnished with military stores, and ships to enable him to destroy the commerce of other Christian governments. 'I have executed my commission,' said the eunuch; 'I am going to take ship at Ceuta, and I'll take you along with me to Italy. *Ma che sciagura d'essere senza coglioni!'*

"I thanked him with tears of joy, but, instead of taking me with him into Italy, he carried me to Algiers, and sold me to the dey of that province. I had not been long a slave when the plague, which had made the tour of Africa, Asia, and Europe, broke out at Algiers with redoubled fury. You have seen an earthquake; but tell me, Miss, have you ever had the plague?"

"Never," answered the young baroness.

"If you had ever had it," continued the old woman, "you would own an earthquake was a trifle to it. It is very common in Africa; I was seized with it. Figure to yourself the distressed condition of the daughter of a pope, only fifteen years old, and who in less than three months had felt the miseries of poverty and slavery; had been debauched almost every day; had beheld her mother cut into four quarters; had experienced the scourges of famine and war; and was now dying of the plague at Algiers. I did not, however, die of it; but my eunuch, and the dey, and almost the whole seraglio of Algiers, were swept off.

"As soon as the first fury of this dreadful pestilence was over, a sale was made of the dey's slaves. I was purchased by a merchant who carried me to Tunis. This man sold me to another merchant, who sold me again to another at Tripoli; from Tripoli I was sold to Alexandria, from Alexandria to Smyrna, and from Smyrna to Constantinople. After many changes, I at length became the property of an aga of the janissaries, who, soon after I came into his possession, was ordered away to the defence of Azoff,[15] then besieged by the Russians.

"The aga, being very fond of women, took his whole seraglio with him, and lodged us in a small fort, with two black eunuchs and twenty soldiers for our guard. Our army made a great slaughter among the Russians; but they soon returned us the compliment. Azoff was taken by storm, and the enemy spared neither age, sex, nor condition, but put all to the sword, and laid the city in ashes. Our little fort alone held out; they resolved to reduce us by famine. The twenty janissaries, who were left to defend it, had bound themselves by an oath never to surrender the place. Being reduced to the extremity of famine, they found themselves obliged to kill our two eunuchs, and eat them rather than violate their oath. But this horrible repast soon failing them, they next determined to devour the women.

"We had a very pious and humane man, who gave them a most excellent sermon on this occasion, exhorting them not to kill us all at once; 'Cut off only one of the steaks of each of those ladies,' said he, 'and you will fare extremely well; if you are under the necessity of having recourse to the same expedient again, you will find the like supply a few days hence. Heaven will approve of so charitable an action, and work your deliverance.'

---

[15] Near the mouth of the Don.

"By the force of this eloquence he easily persuaded them, and all of us underwent the operation. The man applied the same balsam as they do to children after circumcision. We were all ready to give up the ghost.

"The janissaries had scarcely time to finish the repast with which we had supplied them, when the Russians attacked the place by means of flat-bottomed boats, and not a single janissary escaped. The Russians paid no regard to the condition we were in; but there are French surgeons in all parts of the world, and one of them took us under his care, and cured us. I shall never forget, while I live, that as soon as my wounds were perfectly healed he made me certain proposals. In general, he desired us all to be of a good cheer, assuring us that the like had happened in many sieges; and that it was perfectly agreeable to the laws of war.

"As soon as my companions were in a condition to walk, they were sent to Moscow. As for me, I fell to the lot of a boyard, who put me to work in his garden, and gave me twenty lashes a day. But this nobleman having about two years afterwards been broken alive upon the wheel, with about thirty others, for some court intrigues, I took advantage of the event, and made my escape. I travelled over a great part of Russia. I was a long time an innkeeper's servant at Riga, then at Rostock, Wismar, Leipsic, Cassel, Utrecht, Leyden, The Hague, and Rotterdam: I have grown old in misery and disgrace, living with only one buttock, and having in perpetual remembrance that I am a pope's daughter. I have been a hundred times upon the point of killing myself, but still I was fond of life. This ridiculous weakness is, perhaps, one of the dangerous principles implanted in our nature. For what can be more absurd than to persist in carrying a burden of which we wish to be eased? to detest, and yet to strive to preserve our existence? In a word, to caress the serpent that devours us, and hug him close to our bosoms till he has gnawed into our hearts?

"In the different countries which it has been my fate to traverse, and at the many inns where I have been a servant, I have observed a prodigious number of people who held their existence in abhorrence, and yet I never knew more than twelve who voluntarily put an end to their misery; namely, three negroes, four Englishmen, as many Genevese, and a German professor, named Robek.[16] My last place was with the Jew, Don Issachar, who placed me near your person, my fair lady; to whose fortunes I have attached myself, and have been more concerned with your adventures than with my own. I should never have even mentioned the latter to you, had you not a little piqued me on the head of sufferings; and if it were not customary to tell stories on board a ship in order to pass away the time. In short, my dear Miss, I have a great deal of knowledge and experience in the world, therefore take my advice: divert yourself, and prevail upon each passenger to tell his story, and if there is one of them all that has not cursed his existence many times, and said to himself over and over again that he was the most wretched of mortals, I give you leave to throw me head-foremost into the sea."

CHAPTER 13

How Candide Was Obliged to Leave the Fair Cunegund and the Old Woman

The fair Cunegund, being thus made acquainted with the history of the old woman's life and adventures, paid her all the respect and civility due to a person of her rank and merit. She very readily acceded to her proposal of engaging the

---

[16]Johann Robeck (1672–1739), an advocate of suicide.

passengers to relate their adventures in their turns, and was at length, as well as Candide, compelled to acknowledge that the old woman was in the right. "It is a thousand pities," said Candide, "that the sage Pangloss should have been hanged contrary to the custom of an *auto-da-fé*, for he would have given us a most admirable lecture on the moral and physical evil which overspreads the earth and sea; and I think I should have courage enough to presume to offer (with all due respect) some few objections."

While everyone was reciting his adventures, the ship continued her way, and at length arrived at Buenos Ayres, where Cunegund, Captain Candide, and the old woman, landed and went to wait upon the governor Don Fernando d'Ibaraa y Figueora y Mascarenes y Lampourdos y Souza. This nobleman carried himself with a haughtiness suitable to a person who bore so many names. He spoke with the most noble disdain to everyone, carried his nose so high, strained his voice to such a pitch, assumed so imperious an air, and stalked with so much loftiness and pride, that everyone who had the honor of conversing with him was violently tempted to bastinade his excellency. He was immoderately fond of women, and Miss Cunegund appeared in his eyes a paragon of beauty. The first thing he did was to ask her if she was not the captain's wife. The air with which he made this demand alarmed Candide, who did not dare to say he was married to her, because indeed he was not; neither did he venture to say she was his sister, because she was not: and though a lie of this nature proved of great service to one of the ancients, and might possibly be useful to some of the moderns, yet the purity of his heart would not permit him to violate the truth. "Miss Cunegund," replied he, "is to do me the honor to marry me, and we humbly beseech your excellency to condescend to grace the ceremony with your presence."

Don Fernando d'Ibaraa y Figueora y Mascarenes y Lampourdos y Souza, twirling his mustachio, and putting on a sarcastic smile, ordered Captain Candide to go and review his company. The gentle Candide obeyed, and the governor was left with Miss Cunegund. He made her a strong declaration of love, protesting that he was ready to give her his hand in the face of the church, or otherwise, as should appear most agreeable to a young lady of her prodigious beauty. Cunegund desired leave to retire a quarter of an hour to consult the old woman, and determine how she should proceed.

The old woman gave her the following counsel: "Miss, you have seventy-two quarterings in your arms, it is true, but you have not a penny to bless yourself with: it is your own fault if you do not become the wife of one of the greatest noblemen in South America, with an exceeding fine mustachio. What business have you to pride yourself upon an unshaken constancy? You have been outraged by a Bulgarian soldier; a Jew and an inquisitor have both tasted of your favors. People take advantage of misfortunes. I must confess, were I in your place, I should, without the least scruple, give my hand to the governor, and thereby make the fortune of the brave Captain Candide." While the old woman was thus haranguing, with all the prudence that old age and experience furnish, a small bark entered the harbor, in which was an alcayde and his alguazils. Matters had fallen out as follows:

The old woman rightly guessed that the cordelier with the long sleeves, was the person who had taken Miss Cunegund's money and jewels, while they and Candide were at Badajoz, in their flight from Lisbon. This same friar attempted to sell some of the diamonds to a jeweller, who presently knew them to have belonged to the grand inquisitor, and stopped them. The cordelier, before he was hanged, acknowledged that he had stolen them, and described the persons, and the road they had taken. The flight of Cunegund and Candide was already the town-talk. They sent in pursuit of them to Cadiz; and the vessel which had been sent to make the greater despatch, had now reached the port of Buenos Ayres. A report was spread that an alcayde was going to land, and that he was in pursuit of the murderers of my lord, the inquisitor. The sage old woman immediately saw what was to be done. "You cannot run away," said she to Cunegund, "but you have nothing to fear; it was not you who killed my lord inquisitor: besides, as the governor is in love with you, he will not suffer you to be ill-treated; therefore stand your ground." Then hurrying away to Candide, she said: "Be gone hence this instant, or you will be burned alive." Candide found there was no time to be lost; but how could he part from Cunegund, and whither must he fly for shelter?

CHAPTER 14

The Reception Candide and Cacambo Met with among the Jesuits in Paraguay

Candide had brought with him from Cadiz such a footman as one often meets with on the coasts of Spain and in the colonies. He was the fourth part of a Spaniard, of a mongrel breed, and born in Tucuman. He had successively gone through the profession of a singing boy, sexton, sailor, monk, peddler, soldier, and lackey. His name was Cacambo; he had a great affection for his master, because his master was a very good man. He immediately saddled the two Andalusian horses. "Come, my good master, let us follow the old woman's advice, and make all the haste we can from this place without staying to look behind us." Candide burst into a flood of tears: "O, my dear Cunegund, must I then be compelled to quit you just as the governor was going to honor us with his presence at our wedding! Cunegund, so long lost and found again, what will now become of you?" "Lord!" said Cacambo, "she must do as well as she can; women are never at a loss. God takes care of them, and so let us make the best of our way." "But whither wilt thou carry me? where can we go? what can we do without Cunegund?" cried the disconsolate Candide. "By St. James of Compostella," said Cacambo, "you were going to fight against the Jesuits of Paraguay; now let us go and fight for them; I know the road perfectly well; I'll conduct you to their kingdom; they will be delighted with a captain that understands the Bulgarian drill; you will certainly make a prodigious fortune. If we cannot succeed in this world we may in another. It is a great pleasure to see new objects and perform new exploits."

"Then you have been in Paraguay?" asked Candide. "Ay, marry, I have," replied Cacambo; "I was a scout in the college of the Assumption, and am as well acquainted with the new government of Los Padres as I am with the streets of Cadiz. Oh, it is an admirable government, that is most certain! The kingdom is at present upwards of three hundred leagues in diameter, and divided into thirty provinces; the fathers there are masters of everything, and the people have no money at all; this you must allow is the masterpiece of justice and reason. For my part, I see nothing so divine as the good fathers, who wage war in this part of the world against the troops of Spain and Portugal, at the same time that they hear the confessions of those very princes in Europe; who kill Spaniards in America and send them to heaven at Madrid. This pleases me exceedingly, but let us push forward; you are going to see the happiest and most fortunate of all mortals. How charmed will those fathers be to hear that a captain who understands the Bulgarian military drill is coming among them."

As soon as they reached the first barrier, Cacambo called to the advance guard, and told them that a captain wanted to speak to my lord, the general. Notice was given to the main guard, and immediately a Paraguayan officer ran to throw himself at the feet of the commandant to impart this news to him. Candide and Cacambo were immediately disarmed, and their two Andalusian horses were seized. The two strangers were conducted between two files of musketeers, the commandant was at the further end with a three-cornered cap on his head, his gown tucked up, a sword by his side, and a half-pike in his hand; he made a sign, and instantly four-and-twenty soldiers drew up round the newcomers. A sergeant told them that they must wait, the commandant could not speak to them; and that the reverend father provincial did not suffer any Spaniard to open his mouth but in his presence, or to stay above three hours in the province. "And where is the reverend father provincial?" said Cacambo. "He has just come from mass and is at the parade," replied the sergeant, "and in about three hours' time you may possibly have the honor to kiss his spurs." "But," said Cacambo, "the captain, who, as well as myself, is perishing of hunger, is no Spaniard, but a German; therefore, pray, might we not be permitted to break our fast till we can be introduced to his reverence?"

The sergeant immediately went and acquainted the commandant with what he heard. "God be praised," said the reverend commandant, "since he is a German I will hear what he has to say; let him be brought to my arbor."

Immediately they conducted Candide to a beautiful pavilion adorned with a colonnade of green marble, spotted with yellow, and with an intertexture of vines, which served as a kind of cage for parrots, humming-birds, guinea-hens, and all other curious kinds of birds. An excellent breakfast was provided in vessels of gold; and while the Paraguayans were eating coarse Indian corn out of wooden dishes in the open air, and exposed to the burning heat of the sun, the reverend father commandant retired to his cool arbor.

He was a very handsome young man, round-faced, fair, and fresh-colored, his eyebrows were finely arched, he had a piercing eye, the tips of his ears were red, his lips vermilion, and he had a bold and commanding air; but such a boldness as neither resembled that of a Spaniard nor of a Jesuit. He ordered Candide and Cacambo to have their arms restored to them, together with their two Andalusian horses. Cacambo gave the poor beasts some oats to eat close by the arbor, keeping a strict eye upon them all the while for fear of surprise.

Candide having kissed the hem of the commandant's robe, they sat down to table. "It seems you are a German," said the Jesuit to him in that language. "Yes, reverend father," answered Candide. As they pronounced these words they looked at each other with great amazement and with an emotion that neither could conceal.

"From what part of Germany do you come?" said the Jesuit.

"From the dirty province of Westphalia," answered Candide. "I was born in the castle of Thunder-ten-tronckh."

"Oh heavens! is it possible?" said the commandant.

"What a miracle!" cried Candide.

"Can it be you?" said the commandant.

On this they both drew a few steps backwards, then running into each other's arms, embraced, and wept profusely. "Is it you then, reverend father? You are the brother of the fair Miss Cunegund? You that was slain by the Bulgarians! You the baron's son! You a Jesuit in Paraguay! I must confess this is a strange world we live in. O Pangloss! Pangloss! what joy would this have given you if you had not been hanged."

The commandant dismissed the negro slaves, and the Paraguayans who presented them with liquor in crystal goblets. He returned thanks to God and St. Ignatius a thousand times; he clasped Candide in his arms, and both their faces were bathed in tears. "You will be more surprised, more affected, more transported," said Candide, "when I tell you that Miss Cunegund, your sister, whose belly was supposed to have been ripped open, is in perfect health."

"Where?"

"In your neighborhood, with the governor of Buenos Ayres; and I myself was going to fight against you." Every word they uttered during this long conversation was productive of some new matter of astonishment. Their souls fluttered on their tongues, listened in their ears, and sparkled in their eyes. Like true Germans, they continued a long while at table, waiting for the reverend father; and the commandant spoke to his dear Candide as follows:

CHAPTER 15

How Candide Killed the Brother of His Dear Cunegund

"Never while I live shall I lose the remembrance of that horrible day on which I saw my father and mother barbarously butchered before my eyes, and my sister ravished. When the Bulgarians retired we searched in vain for my dear sister. She was nowhere to be found; but the bodies of my father, mother, and myself, with two servant maids and three little boys, all of whom had been murdered by the remorseless enemy, were thrown into a cart to be buried in a chapel belonging to the Jesuits, within two leagues of our family seat. A Jesuit sprinkled us with some holy water, which was confounded salty, and a few drops of it went into my eyes; the father perceived that my eyelids stirred a little; he put his hand upon my breast and felt my heart beat; upon which he gave me proper assistance, and at the end of three weeks I was perfectly recovered. You know, my dear Candide, I was very handsome; I became still more so, and the reverend father Croust, superior of that house, took a great fancy to me; he gave me the habit of the order, and some years afterwards I was sent to Rome. Our general stood in need of new recruits of young German Jesuits. The sovereigns of Paraguay admit of as few Spanish Jesuits as possible; they prefer those of other nations, as being more obedient to command. The reverend father-general looked upon me as a proper person to work in that vineyard. I set out in company with a Polander and a Tyrolese. Upon my arrival I was honored with a subdeaconship and a lieutenancy. Now I am colonel and priest. We shall give a warm reception to the king of Spain's troops; I can assure you they will be well excommunicated and beaten. Providence has sent you hither to assist us. But is it true that my dear sister Cunegund is in the neighborhood with the governor of Buenos Ayres?"

Candide swore that nothing could be more true; and the tears began again to trickle down their cheeks. The baron knew no end of embracing Candide, he called him his brother, his deliverer.

"Perhaps," said he, "my dear Candide, we shall be fortunate enough to enter the town, sword in hand, and recover my sister Cunegund."

"Ah! that would crown my wishes," replied Candide; "for I intended to marry her; and I hope I shall still be able to effect it."

"Insolent fellow!" cried the baron. "You! you have the impudence to marry my sister, who bears seventy-two quarterings! really, I think you have an insufferable degree of assurance to dare so much as to mention such an audacious design to me."

Candide, thunderstruck at the oddness of this speech, answered: "Reverend father, all the quarterings in the world are of no signification. I have delivered your sister from a Jew and an inquisitor; she is under many obligations to me, and she is resolved to give me her hand. My master, Pangloss, always told me that mankind are by nature equal. Therefore, you may depend upon it that I will marry your sister."

"We shall see to that, villain!" said the Jesuit baron of Thunder-ten-tronckh, and struck him across the face with the flat side of his sword. Candide in an instant drew his rapier and plunged it up to the hilt in the Jesuit's body; but in pulling it out reeking hot, he burst into tears.

"Good God!" cried he, "I have killed my old master, my friend, my brother-in-law; I am the best man in the world, and yet I have already killed three men; and of these three two were priests."

Cacambo, who was standing sentry near the door of the arbor, instantly ran up.

"Nothing remains," said his master, "but to sell our lives as dearly as possible; they will undoubtedly look into the arbor; we must die sword in hand."

Cacambo, who had seen many of this kind of adventures, was not discouraged. He stripped the baron of his Jesuit's habit and put it upon Candide, then gave him the dead man's three-cornered cap and made him mount on horseback. All this was done as quick as thought.

"Gallop, master," cried Cacambo; "everybody will take you for a Jesuit going to give orders; and we shall have passed the frontiers before they will be able to overtake us." He flew as he spoke these words, crying out aloud in Spanish, "Make way; make way for the reverend father-colonel."

CHAPTER 16

What Happened to Our Two Travellers with Two Girls, Two Monkeys, and the Savages, Called Oreillons

Candide and his valet had already passed the frontiers before it was known that the German Jesuit was dead. The wary Cacambo had taken care to fill his wallet with bread, chocolate, some ham, some fruit, and a few bottles of wine. They penetrated with their Andalusian horses into a strange country, where they could discover no beaten path. At length a beautiful meadow, intersected with purling rills, opened to their view. Cacambo proposed to his master to take some nourishment, and he set him an example.

"How can you desire me to feast upon ham, when I have killed the baron's son and am doomed never more to see the beautiful Cunegund? What will it avail me to prolong a wretched life that must be spent far from her in remorse and despair? And then what will the journal of Trévoux[17] say?" was Candide's reply.

While he was making these reflections he still continued eating. The sun was now on the point of setting when the ears of our two wanderers were assailed with cries which seemed to be uttered by a female voice. They could not tell whether these were cries of grief or of joy; however, they instantly started up, full of that inquietude and apprehension which a strange place naturally inspires. The cries proceeded from two young women who were tripping disrobed along the mead, while two monkeys followed close at their heels biting at their limbs. Candide was touched with compassion; he had learned to shoot while he was among the Bulgarians, and he could hit a filbert in a hedge without touching a leaf. Accordingly he took up his double-barrelled Spanish gun, pulled the trigger, and laid the two monkeys lifeless on the ground.

"God be praised, my dear Cacambo, I have rescued two poor girls from a most perilous situation; if I have committed a sin in killing an inquisitor and a Jesuit, I have made ample amends by saving the lives of these two distressed damsels. Who knows but they may be young ladies of a good family, and that the assistance I have been so happy to give them may procure us great advantage in this country?"

---

[17] A Jesuit journal that had attacked Voltaire.

He was about to continue when he felt himself struck speechless at seeing the two girls embracing the dead bodies of the monkeys in the tenderest manner, bathing their wounds with their tears, and rending the air with the most doleful lamentations.

"Really," said he to Cacambo, "I should not have expected to see such a prodigious share of good nature."

"Master," replied the knowing valet, "you have made a precious piece of work of it; do you know that you have killed the lovers of these two ladies?"

"Their lovers! Cacambo, you are jesting! It cannot be! I can never believe it."

"Dear sir," replied Cacambo, "you are surprised at everything; why should you think it so strange that there should be a country where monkeys insinuate themselves into the good graces of the ladies? They are the fourth part of a man as I am the fourth part of a Spaniard."

"Alas!" replied Candide, "I remember to have heard my master Pangloss say that such accidents as these frequently came to pass in former times, and that these commixtures are productive of centaurs, fauns, and satyrs; and that many of the ancients had seen such monsters; but I looked upon the whole as fabulous."

"Now you are convinced," said Cacambo, "that it is very true, and you see what use is made of those creatures by persons who have not had a proper education; all I am afraid of is that these same ladies may play us some ugly trick."

These judicious reflections operated so far on Candide as to make him quit the meadow and strike into a thicket. There he and Cacambo supped, and after heartily cursing the grand inquisitor, the governor of Buenos Ayres, and the baron, they fell asleep on the ground. When they awoke they were surprised to find that they could not move; the reason was that the Oreillons who inhabit that country, and to whom the ladies had given information of these two strangers, had bound them with cords made of the bark of trees. They saw themselves surrounded by fifty naked Oreillons armed with bows and arrows, clubs, and hatchets of flint; some were making a fire under a large cauldron; and others were preparing spits, crying out one and all, "A Jesuit! a Jesuit! we shall be revenged; we shall have excellent cheer; let us eat this Jesuit; let us eat him up."

"I told you, master," cried Cacambo, mournfully, "that these two wenches would play us some scurvy trick."

Candide, seeing the cauldron and the spits, cried out, "I suppose they are going either to boil or roast us. Ah! what would Pangloss say if he were to see how pure nature is formed? Everything is right; it may be so; but I confess it is something hard to be bereft of dear Miss Cunegund, and to be spitted like a rabbit by these barbarous Oreillons."

Cacambo, who never lost his presence of mind in distress, said to the disconsolate Candide: "Do not despair; I understand a little of the jargon of these people; I will speak to them."

"Ay, pray do," said Candide, "and be sure you make them sensible of the horrid barbarity of boiling and roasting human creatures, and how little of Christianity there is in such practices."

"Gentlemen," said Cacambo, "you think perhaps you are going to feast upon a Jesuit; if so, it is mighty well; nothing can be more agreeable to justice than thus to treat your enemies. Indeed the law of nature teaches us to kill our neighbor, and accordingly we find this practised all over the world; and if we do not indulge ourselves in eating human flesh, it is because we have much better fare; but for your parts, who have not such resources as we, it is certainly much better judged to feast upon your enemies than to throw their bodies to the fowls of the air; and thus lose all the fruits of your victory. But surely, gentlemen, you would not choose to eat your friends. You imagine you are going to roast a Jesuit, whereas my master is your friend, your defender, and you are going to spit the very man who has been destroying your enemies; as to myself, I am your countryman; this gentleman is my master, and so far from being a Jesuit, give me leave to tell you he has very lately killed one of that order, whose spoils he now wears, and which have probably occasioned your mistake. To convince you of the truth of what I say, take the habit he has on and carry it to the first barrier of the Jesuits' kingdom, and inquire whether my master did not kill one of their officers. There will be little or no time lost by this, and you may still reserve our bodies in your power to feast on if you should find what we have told you to be false. But, on the contrary, if you find it to be true, I am persuaded you are too well acquainted with the principles of the laws of society, humanity, and justice, not to use us courteously, and suffer us to depart unhurt."

This speech appeared very reasonable to the Oreillons; they deputed two of their people with all expedition to inquire into the truth of this affair, who acquitted themselves of their commission like men of sense, and soon returned with good tidings for our distressed adventurers. Upon this they were loosed, and those who were so lately going to roast and boil them now showed them all sorts of civilities; offered them girls, gave them refreshments, and reconducted them to the confines of their country, crying before them all the way, in token of joy: "He is no Jesuit, he is no Jesuit."

Candide could not help admiring the cause of his deliverance. "What men! what manners!" cried he; "if I had not fortunately run my sword up to the hilt in the body of Miss Cunegund's brother, I should have certainly been eaten alive. But, after all, pure nature is an excellent thing; since these people, instead of eating me, showed me a thousand civilities as soon as they knew I was not a Jesuit."

CHAPTER 17

Candide and His Valet Arrive in the Country of El Dorado—What They Saw There

When they got to the frontiers of the Oreillons, "You see," said Cacambo to Candide, "this hemisphere is not better than the other; now take my advice and let us return to Europe by the shortest way possible."

"But how can we get back?" said Candide; "and whither shall we go? To my own country? The Bulgarians and the Avars are laying that waste with fire and sword; or shall we go to Portugal? There I shall be burned; and if we abide here we are every moment in danger of being spitted. But how can I bring myself to quit that part of the world where my dear Miss Cunegund has her residence?"

"Let us return towards Cayenne," said Cacambo; "there we shall meet with some Frenchmen; for you know those gentry ramble all over the world; perhaps they will assist us, and God will look with pity on our distress."

It was not so easy to get to Cayenne. They knew pretty nearly whereabouts it lay; but the mountains, rivers, precipices, robbers, savages, were dreadful obstacles in the way. Their horses died with fatigue and their provisions were at an end. They subsisted a whole month on wild fruit, till at length they came to a little river bordered with cocoa trees; the sight of which at once revived their drooping spirits and furnished nourishment for their enfeebled bodies.

Cacambo, who was always giving as good advice as the old woman herself, said to Candide: "You see there is no holding out any longer; we have travelled enough on foot. I spy an empty canoe near the river side; let us fill it with cocoanuts, get into it, and go down with the stream; a river always leads to some inhabited place. If we do not meet with agreeable things, we shall at least meet with something new."

"Agreed," replied Candide; "let us recommend ourselves to Providence."

They rowed a few leagues down the river, the banks of which were in some places covered with flowers; in others barren; in some parts smooth and level, and in others steep and rugged. The stream widened as they went further on, till at length it passed under one of the frightful rocks, whose summits seemed to reach the clouds. Here our two travellers had the courage to commit themselves to the stream, which, contracting in this part, hurried them along with a dreadful noise and rapidity. At the end of four-and-twenty hours they saw daylight again; but their canoe was dashed to pieces against the rocks. They were obliged to creep along, from rock to rock, for the space of a league, till at length a spacious plain presented itself to their sight. This place was bounded by a chain of inaccessible mountains. The country appeared cultivated equally for pleasure and to produce the necessaries of life. The useful and agreeable were here equally blended. The roads were covered, or rather adorned, with carriages formed of glittering materials, in which were men and women of a surprising beauty, drawn with great rapidity by red sheep of a very large size; which far surpassed the finest coursers of Andalusia, Tetuan, or Mecquinez.

"Here is a country, however," said Candide, "preferable to Westphalia."

He and Cacambo landed near the first village they saw, at the entrance of which they perceived some children covered with tattered garments of the richest brocade, playing at quoits. Our two inhabitants of the other hemisphere amused themselves greatly with what they saw. The quoits were large, round pieces, yellow, red, and green, which cast a most glorious lustre. Our travellers picked some of them up, and they proved to be gold, emeralds, rubies, and diamonds; the least of which would have been the greatest ornament to the superb throne of the Great Mogul.

"Without doubt," said Cacambo, "those children must be the king's sons that are playing at quoits." As he was uttering these words the schoolmaster of the village appeared, who came to call the children to school.

"There," said Candide, "is the preceptor of the royal family."

The little ragamuffins immediately quitted their diversion, leaving the quoits on the ground with all their other playthings. Candide gathered them up, ran to the schoolmaster, and, with a most respectful bow, presented them to him, giving him to understand by signs that their royal highnesses had forgot their gold and precious stones. The schoolmaster, with a smile, flung them upon the ground, then examining Candide from head to foot with an air of admiration, he turned his back and went on his way.

Our travellers took care, however, to gather up the gold, the rubies, and the emeralds.

"Where are we?" cried Candide. "The king's children in this country must have an excellent education, since they are taught to show such a contempt for gold and precious stones."

Cacambo was as much surprised as his master. They then drew near the first house in the village, which was built after the manner of a European palace. There was a crowd of people about the door, and a still greater number in the house. The sound of the most delightful instruments of music was heard, and the most agreeable smell came from the kitchen. Cacambo went up to the door and heard those within talking in the Peruvian language, which was his mother tongue; for every one knows that Cacambo was born in a village of Tucuman, where no other language is spoken.

"I will be your interpreter here," said he to Candide. "Let us go in; this is an eating-house."

Immediately two waiters and two servant-girls, dressed in cloth of gold, and their hair braided with ribbons of tissue, accosted the strangers and invited them to sit down to the ordinary. Their dinner consisted of four dishes of different soups, each garnished with two young paroquets, a large dish of bouillé that weighed two hundred weight, two roasted monkeys of a delicious flavor, three hundred humming-birds in one dish, and six hundred fly-birds in another; some excellent ragouts, delicate tarts, and the whole served up in dishes of rock-crystal. Several sorts of liquors, extracted from the sugar-cane, were handed about by the servants who attended.

Most of the company were chapmen and wagoners, all extremely polite; they asked Cacambo a few questions with the utmost discretion and circumspection; and replied to his in a most obliging and satisfactory manner.

As soon as dinner was over, both Candide and Cacambo thought they should pay very handsomely for their entertainment by laying down two of those large gold pieces which they had picked off the ground; but the landlord and landlady burst into a fit of laughing and held their sides for some time. When the fit was over, "Gentlemen," said the landlord, "I plainly perceive you are strangers, and such we are not accustomed to charge; pardon us, therefore, for laughing when you offered us the common pebbles of our highways for payment of your reckoning. To be sure, you have none of the coin of this kingdom; but there is no necessity of having any money at all to dine in this house. All the inns, which are established for the convenience of those who carry on the trade of this nation, are maintained by the government. You have found but very indifferent entertainment here, because this is only a poor village; but in almost every other of these public houses you will meet with a reception worthy of persons of your merit." Cacambo explained the whole of this speech of the landlord to Candide, who listened to it with the same astonishment with which his friend communicated it.

"What sort of a country is this," said the one to the other, "that is unknown to all the world; and in which Nature has everywhere so different an appearance to what she has in ours? Possibly this is that part of the globe where everything is right, for there must certainly be some such place. And, for all that Master Pangloss could say, I often perceived that things went very ill in Westphalia."

CHAPTER 18

What They Saw in the Country of El Dorado

Cacambo vented all his curiosity upon his landlord by a thousand different questions; the honest man answered him thus: "I am very ignorant, sir, but I am contented with my ignorance; however, we have in this neighborhood an old man retired from court, who is the most learned and communicative person in the whole kingdom." He then conducted Cacambo to the old man; Candide acted now only a second character, and attended his valet. They entered a very plain house, for the door was nothing but silver, and the ceiling was only of beaten gold, but wrought in such elegant taste as to vie with the richest. The antechamber, indeed, was only incrusted with rubies and emeralds; but the order in which everything was disposed made amends for this great simplicity.

The old man received the strangers on his sofa, which was stuffed with humming-birds' feathers; and ordered his servants to present them with liquors in golden goblets, after which he satisfied their curiosity in the following terms:

"I am now one hundred and seventy-two years old, and I learned of my late father, who was equerry to the king, the amazing revolutions of Peru, to which he had been an eye-witness. This kingdom is the ancient patrimony of the Incas, who very imprudently quitted it to conquer another part of the world, and were at length conquered and destroyed themselves by the Spaniards.

"Those princes of their family who remained in their native country acted more wisely. They ordained, with the consent of their whole nation, that none of the inhabitants of our little kingdom should ever quit it; and to this wise ordinance we owe the preservation of our innocence and happiness. The Spaniards had some confused notion of this country, to which they gave the name of *El Dorado*,[18] and Sir Walter Raleigh, an Englishman, actually came very near it about three hundred years ago; but the inaccessible rocks and precipices with which our country is surrounded on all sides, has hitherto secured us from the rapacious fury of the people of Europe, who have an unaccountable fondness for the pebbles and dirt of our land, for the sake of which they would murder us all to the very last man."

The conversation lasted some time and turned chiefly on the form of government, their manners, their women, their public diversions, and the arts. At length, Candide, who had always had a taste for metaphysics, asked whether the people of that country had any religion.

The old man reddened a little at this question.

"Can you doubt it?" said he; "do you take us for wretches lost to all sense of gratitude?"

Cacambo asked in a respectful manner what was the established religion of El Dorado. The old man blushed again, and said: "Can there be two religions, then? Ours, I apprehend, is the religion of the whole world; we worship God from morning till night."

"Do you worship but one God?" said Cacambo, who still acted as the interpreter of Candide's doubts.

"Certainly," said the old man; "there are not two, nor three, nor four Gods. I must confess the people of your world ask very extraordinary questions."

However, Candide could not refrain from making many more inquiries of the old man; he wanted to know in what manner they prayed to God in El Dorado.

"We do not pray to him at all," said the reverend sage; "we have nothing to ask of Him, He has given us all we want, and we give Him thanks incessantly." Candide had a curiosity to see some of their priests, and desired Cacambo to ask the old man where they were. At which he smiling said:

"My friends, we are all of us priests; the king and all the heads of families sing solemn hymns of thanksgiving every morning, accompanied by five or six thousand musicians."

"What!" said Cacambo, "have you no monks among you to dispute, to govern, to intrigue, and to burn people who are not of the same opinion with themselves?"

"Do you take us for fools?" said the old man. "Here we are all of one opinion, and know not what you mean by your monks."

During the whole of this discourse Candide was in raptures, and he said to himself, "What a prodigious difference is there between this place and Westphalia; and this house and the baron's castle. Ah, Master Pangloss! had you ever seen El Dorado, you would no longer have maintained that the castle of Thunder-ten-tronckh was the finest of all possible edifices; there is nothing like seeing the world, that's certain."

This long conversation being ended, the old man ordered six sheep to be harnessed and put to the coach, and sent twelve of his servants to escort the travellers to court.

"Excuse me," said he, "for not waiting on you in person, my age deprives me of that honor. The king will receive you in such a manner that you will have no reason

---

[18]A legendary land of gold.

to complain; and doubtless you will make a proper allowance for the customs of the country if they should not happen altogether to please you."

Candide and Cacambo got into the coach, the six sheep flew, and, in less than a quarter of an hour, they arrived at the king's palace, which was situated at the further end of the capital. At the entrance was a portal two hundred and twenty feet high and one hundred wide; but it is impossible for words to express the materials of which it was built. The reader, however, will readily conceive that they must have a prodigious superiority over the pebbles and sand, which we call gold and precious stones.

Twenty beautiful young virgins in waiting received Candide and Cacambo on their alighting from the coach, conducted them to the bath and clad them in robes woven of the down of humming-birds; after which they were introduced by the great officers of the crown of both sexes to the king's apartment, between two files of musicians, each file consisting of a thousand, agreeable to the custom of the country. When they drew near to the presence-chamber, Cacambo asked one of the officers in what manner they were to pay their obeisance to his majesty; whether it was the custom to fall upon their knees, or to prostrate themselves upon the ground; whether they were to put their hands upon their heads, or behind their backs; whether they were to lick the dust off the floor; in short, what was the ceremony usual on such occasions.

"The custom," said the great officer, "is to embrace the king and kiss him on each cheek."

Candide and Cacambo accordingly threw their arms round his majesty's neck, who received them in the most gracious manner imaginable, and very politely asked them to sup with him.

While supper was preparing orders were given to show them the city, where they saw public structures that reared their lofty heads to the clouds; the market-places decorated with a thousand columns; fountains of spring water, besides others of rose water, and of liquors drawn from the sugar-cane, incessantly flowing in the great squares; which were paved with a kind of precious stones that emitted an odor like that of cloves and cinnamon. Candide asked to see the high court of justice, the parliament; but was answered that they had none in that country, being utter strangers to lawsuits. He then inquired if they had any prisons; they replied none. But what gave him at once the greatest surprise and pleasure was the palace of sciences, where he saw a gallery two thousand feet long, filled with the various apparatus in mathematics and natural philosophy.

After having spent the whole afternoon in seeing only about the thousandth part of the city, they were brought back to the king's palace. Candide sat down at the table with his majesty, his valet Cacambo, and several ladies of the court. Never was entertainment more elegant, nor could any one possibly show more wit than his majesty displayed while they were at supper. Cacambo explained all the king's *bons mots* to Candide, and, although they were translated, they still appeared to be *bons mots*. Of all the things that surprised Candide, this was not the least. They spent a whole month in this hospitable place, during which time Candide was continually saying to Cacambo:

"I own, my friend, once more, that the castle where I was born is a mere nothing in comparison to the place where we now are; but still Miss Cunegund is not here, and you yourself have doubtless some fair one in Europe for whom you sigh. If we remain here we shall only be as others are; whereas, if we return to our own world with only a dozen of El Dorado sheep, loaded with the pebbles of this country, we shall be richer than all the kings in Europe; we shall no longer need to stand in awe of the inquisitors; and we may easily recover Miss Cunegund."

This speech was perfectly agreeable to Cacambo. A fondness for roving, for making a figure in their own country, and for boasting of what they had seen in their travels, was so powerful in our two wanderers that they resolved to be no longer happy; and demanded permission of the king to quit the country.

"You are about to do a rash and silly action," said the king. "I am sensible my kingdom is an inconsiderable spot; but when people are tolerably at their ease in any place, I should think it would be to their interest to remain there. Most assuredly, I have no right to detain you, or any strangers, against your wills; this is an act of tyranny to which our manners and our laws are equally repugnant; all men are by nature free; you have therefore an undoubted liberty to depart whenever you please, but you will have many and great difficulties to encounter in passing the frontiers. It is impossible to ascend that rapid river which runs under high and vaulted rocks, and by which you were conveyed hither by a kind of miracle. The mountains by which my kingdom are hemmed in on all sides, are ten thousand feet high, and perfectly perpendicular; they are above ten leagues across, and the descent from them is one continued precipice. However, since you are determined to leave us, I will immediately give orders to the superintendent of my carriages to cause one to be made that will convey you very safely. When they have conducted you to the back of the mountains, nobody can attend you farther; for my subjects have made a vow never to quit the kingdom, and they are too prudent to break it. Ask me whatever else you please."

"All we shall ask of your majesty," said Cacambo, "is only a few sheep laden with provisions, pebbles, and the clay of your country."

The king smiled at the request, and said: "I cannot imagine what pleasure you Europeans find in our yellow clay; but take away as much of it as you will, and much good may it do you."

He immediately gave orders to his engineers to make a machine to hoist these two extraordinary men out of the kingdom. Three thousand good machinists went to work and finished it in about fifteen days, and it did not cost more than twenty millions sterling of that country's money. Candide and Cacambo were placed on this machine, and they took with them two large red sheep, bridled and saddled, to ride upon, when they got on the other side of the mountains; twenty others to serve as sumpters for carrying provisions; thirty laden with presents of whatever was most curious in the country, and fifty with gold, diamonds, and other precious stones. The king, at parting with our two adventurers, embraced them with the greatest cordiality.

It was a curious sight to behold the manner of their setting off, and the ingenious method by which they and their sheep were hoisted to the top of the mountains. The machinists and engineers took leave of them as soon as they had conveyed them to a place of safety, and Candide was wholly occupied with the thoughts of presenting his sheep to Miss Cunegund.

"Now," cried he, "thanks to heaven, we have more than sufficient to pay the governor of Buenos Ayres for Miss Cunegund, if she is redeemable. Let us make the best of our way to Cayenne, where we will take shipping and then we may at leisure think of what kingdom we shall purchase with our riches."

CHAPTER 19

What Happened to Them at Surinam, and How Candide Became Acquainted with Martin

Our travellers' first day's journey was very pleasant; they were elated with the prospect of possessing more riches than were to be found in Europe, Asia, and Africa together. Candide, in amorous transports, cut the name of Miss Cunegund on almost every tree he came to. The second day two of their sheep sunk in a morass, and were swallowed up with their lading; two more died of fatigue; some few days afterwards seven or eight perished with hunger in a desert, and others, at different times, tumbled down precipices, or were otherwise lost, so that, after travelling about a hundred days they had only two sheep left of the hundred and two they brought with them from El Dorado. Said Candide to Cacambo:

"You see, my dear friend, how perishable the riches of this world are; there is nothing solid but virtue."

"Very true," said Cacambo, "but we have still two sheep remaining, with more treasure than ever the king of Spain will be possessed of; and I espy a town at a distance, which I take to be Surinam, a town belonging to the Dutch. We are now at the end of our troubles, and at the beginning of happiness."

As they drew near the town they saw a negro stretched on the ground with only one half of his habit, which was a kind of linen frock; for the poor man had lost his left leg and his right hand.

"Good God," said Candide in Dutch, "what dost thou here, friend, in this deplorable condition?"

"I am waiting for my master, Mynheer Vanderdendur, the famous trader," answered the negro.

"Was it Mynheer Vanderdendur that used you in this cruel manner?"

"Yes, sir," said the negro; "it is the custom here. They give a linen garment twice a year, and that is all our covering. When we labor in the sugar works, and the mill happens to snatch hold of a finger, they instantly chop off our hand; and when we attempt to run away, they cut off a leg. Both these cases have happened to me, and it is at this expense that you eat sugar in Europe; and yet when my mother sold me for ten patacoons on the coast of Guinea, she said to me, 'My dear child, bless our fetiches; adore them forever; they will make thee live happy; thou hast the honor to be a slave to our lords the whites, by which thou wilt make the fortune of us thy parents.' Alas! I know not whether I have made their fortunes; but they have not made mine: dogs, monkeys, and parrots are a thousand times less wretched than I. The Dutch fetiches who converted me tell me every Sunday that the blacks and whites are all children of one father, whom they call Adam. As for me, I do not understand anything of genealogies; but if what these preachers say is true, we are all second cousins; and you must allow that it is impossible to be worse treated by our relations than we are."

"O Pangloss!" cried out Candide, "such horrid doings never entered thy imagination. Here is an end of the matter; I find myself, after all, obliged to renounce thy Optimism."

"Optimism," said Cacambo, "what is that?"

"Alas!" replied Candide, "it is the obstinacy of maintaining that everything is best when it is worst." And so saying he turned his eyes towards the poor negro, and shed a flood of tears; and in this weeping mood he entered the town of Surinam.

Immediately upon their arrival our travellers inquired if there was any vessel in the harbor which they might send to Buenos Ayres. The person they addressed themselves to happened to be the master of a Spanish bark, who offered to agree with them on moderate terms, and appointed them a meeting at a public house. Thither Candide and his faithful Cacambo went to wait for him, taking with them their two sheep.

Candide, who was all frankness and sincerity, made an ingenuous recital of his adventures to the Spaniard, declaring to him at the same time his resolution of carrying off Miss Cunegund from the governor of Buenos Ayres.

"O ho!" said the shipmaster, "if that is the case, get whom you please to carry you to Buenos Ayres; for my part, I wash my hands of the affair. It would prove

a hanging matter to us all. The fair Cunegund is the governor's favorite mistress."
These words were like a clap of thunder to Candide; he wept bitterly for a long
time, and, taking Cacambo aside, he said to him, "I'll tell you, my dear friend, what
you must do. We have each of us in our pockets to the value of five or six millions in
diamonds; you are cleverer at these matters than I; you must go to Buenos Ayres and
bring off Miss Cunegund. If the governor makes any difficulty give him a million;
if he holds out, give him two; as you have not killed an inquisitor, they will have
no suspicion of you. I'll fit out another ship and go to Venice, where I will wait for
you. Venice is a free country, where we shall have nothing to fear from Bulgarians,
Avars, Jews, or Inquisitors."

Cacambo greatly applauded this wise resolution. He was inconsolable at the
thoughts of parting with so good a master, who treated him more like an intimate
friend than a servant; but the pleasure of being able to do him a service soon got
the better of his sorrow. They embraced each other with a flood of tears. Candide
charged him not to forget the old woman. Cacambo set out the same day. This
Cacambo was a very honest fellow.

Candide continued some days longer at Surinam, waiting for any captain to
carry him and his two remaining sheep to Italy. He hired domestics, and purchased
many things necessary for a long voyage; at length Mynheer Vanderdendur, skipper
of a large Dutch vessel, came and offered his service.

"What will you have," said Candide, "to carry me, my servants, my baggage,
and these two sheep you see here, directly to Venice?"

The skipper asked ten thousand piastres, and Candide agreed to his demand
without hesitation.

"Ho, ho!" said the cunning Vanderdendur to himself, "this stranger must be very
rich; he agrees to give me ten thousand piastres without hesitation." Returning
a little while after he tells Candide that upon second consideration he could not
undertake the voyage for less than twenty thousand. "Very well; you shall have
them," said Candide.

"Zounds!" said the skipper to himself, "this man agrees to pay twenty thousand
piastres with as much ease as ten." Accordingly he goes back again, and tells him
roundly that he will not carry him to Venice for less than thirty thousand piastres.

"Then you shall have thirty thousand," said Candide.

"Odso!" said the Dutchman once more to himself, "thirty thousand piastres seem
a trifle to this man. Those sheep must certainly be laden with an immense treasure.
I'll e'en stop here and ask no more; but make him pay down the thirty thousand
piastres, and then we may see what is to be done farther." Candide sold two small
diamonds, the least of which was worth more than all the skipper asked. He paid
him beforehand, the two sheep were put on board, and Candide followed in a small
boat to join the vessel in the road. The skipper took advantage of his opportunity,
hoisted sail, and put out to sea with a favorable wind. Candide, confounded and
amazed, soon lost sight of the ship. "Alas!" said he, "this is a trick like those in our
old world!"

He returned back to the shore overwhelmed with grief; and, indeed, he had lost
what would have made the fortune of twenty monarchs.

Straightway upon his landing he applied to the Dutch magistrate; being transported with passion he thundered at the door, which being opened, he went in, told
his case, and talked a little louder than was necessary. The magistrate began with
fining him ten thousand piastres for his petulance, and then listened very patiently
to what he had to say, promised to examine into the affair on the skipper's return,
and ordered him to pay ten thousand piastres more for the fees of the court.

This treatment put Candide out of all patience; it is true, he had suffered
misfortunes a thousand times more grievous, but the cool insolence of the judge,

and the villainy of the skipper raised his choler and threw him into a deep melancholy. The villainy of mankind presented itself to his mind in all its deformity, and his soul was a prey to the most gloomy ideas. After some time, hearing that the captain of a French ship was ready to set sail for Bordeaux, as he had no more sheep loaded with diamonds to put on board, he hired the cabin at the usual price; and made it known in the town that he would pay the passage and board of any honest man who would give him his company during the voyage; besides making him a present of ten thousand piastres, on condition that such person was the most dissatisfied with his condition, and the most unfortunate in the whole province.

Upon this there appeared such a crowd of candidates that a large fleet could not have contained them. Candide, willing to choose from among those who appeared most likely to answer his intention, selected twenty, who seemed to him the most sociable, and who all pretended to merit the preference. He invited them to his inn, and promised to treat them with a supper, on condition that every man should bind himself by an oath to relate his own history; declaring at the same time, that he would make choice of that person who should appear to him the most deserving of compassion, and the most justly dissatisfied with his condition in life; and that he would make a present to the rest.

This extraordinary assembly continued sitting till four in the morning. Candide, while he was listening to their adventures, called to mind what the old woman had said to him in their voyage to Buenos Ayres, and the wager she had laid that there was not a person on board the ship but had met with great misfortunes. Every story he heard put him in mind of Pangloss.

"My old master," said he, "would be confoundedly put to it to demonstrate his favorite system. Would he were here! Certainly if everything is for the best, it is in El Dorado, and not in the other parts of the world."

At length he determined in favor of a poor scholar, who had labored ten years for the booksellers at Amsterdam: being of opinion that no employment could be more detestable.

This scholar, who was in fact a very honest man, had been robbed by his wife, beaten by his son, and forsaken by his daughter, who had run away with a Portuguese. He had been likewise deprived of a small employment on which he subsisted, and he was persecuted by the clergy of Surinam, who took him for a Socinian.[19] It must be acknowledged that the other competitors were, at least, as wretched as he; but Candide was in hopes that the company of a man of letters would relieve the tediousness of the voyage. All the other candidates complained that Candide had done them great injustice, but he stopped their mouths by a present of a hundred piastres to each.

CHAPTER 20

What Befell Candide and Martin on Their Passage

The old philosopher, whose name was Martin, took shipping with Candide for Bordeaux. Both had seen and suffered a great deal, and had the ship been going from Surinam to Japan round the Cape of Good Hope, they could have found sufficient entertainment for each other during the whole voyage, in discoursing upon moral and natural evil.

---

[19]Socinianism was a religious doctrine that advocated reason and challenged mysteries such as the Trinity and the Virgin Birth.

Candide, however, had one advantage over Martin: he lived in the pleasing hopes of seeing Miss Cunegund once more; whereas, the poor philosopher had nothing to hope for; besides, Candide had money and jewels, and, notwithstanding he had lost a hundred red sheep laden with the greatest treasure outside of El Dorado, and though he still smarted from the reflection of the Dutch skipper's knavery, yet when he considered what he had still left, and repeated the name of Cunegund, especially after meal times, he inclined to Pangloss's doctrine.

"And pray," said he to Martin, "what is your opinion of the whole of this system? what notion have you of moral and natural evil?"

"Sir," replied Martin, "our priest accused me of being a Socinian; but the real truth is, I am a Manichæan."[20]

"Nay, now you are jesting," said Candide; "there are no Manichæans existing at present in the world."

"And yet I am one," said Martin; "but I cannot help it. I cannot for the soul of me think otherwise."

"Surely the devil must be in you," said Candide.

"He concerns himself so much," replied Martin, "in the affairs of this world that it is very probable he may be in me as well as everywhere else; but I must confess, when I cast my eye on this globe, or rather globule, I cannot help thinking that God has abandoned it to some malignant being. I always except El Dorado. I scarce ever knew a city that did not wish the destruction of its neighboring city; nor a family that did not desire to exterminate some other family. The poor in all parts of the world bear an inveterate hatred to the rich, even while they creep and cringe to them; and the rich treat the poor like sheep, whose wool and flesh they barter for money; a million of regimented assassins traverse Europe from one end to the other, to get their bread by regular depredation and murder, because it is the most gentlemanlike profession. Even in those cities which seem to enjoy the blessings of peace, and where the arts flourish, the inhabitants are devoured with envy, care, and inquietudes, which are greater plagues than any experienced in a town besieged. Private chagrins are still more dreadful than public calamities. In a word," concluded the philosopher, "I have seen and suffered so much that I am a Manichæan."

"And yet there is some good in the world," replied Candide.

"May be so," said Martin, "but it has escaped my knowledge."

While they were deeply engaged in this dispute they heard the report of cannon, which redoubled every moment. Each took out his glass, and they spied two ships warmly engaged at the distance of about three miles. The wind brought them both so near the French ship that those on board her had the pleasure of seeing the fight with great ease. After several smart broadsides the one gave the other a shot between wind and water which sunk her outright. Then could Candide and Martin plainly perceive a hundred men on the deck of the vessel which was sinking, who, with hands uplifted to heaven, sent forth piercing cries, and were in a moment swallowed up by the waves.

"Well," said Martin, "you now see in what manner mankind treat one another."

"It is certain," said Candide, "that there is something diabolical in this affair." As he was speaking thus he spied something of a shining red hue, which swam close to the vessel. The boat was hoisted out to see what it might be, when it proved to be one of his sheep. Candide felt more joy at the recovery of this one animal than he did grief when he lost the other hundred, though laden with the large diamonds of El Dorado.

---

[20]Founded by Mani (third century C.E.), Manichæans believed that life was a struggle between the forces of light and dark.

The French captain quickly perceived that the victorious ship belonged to the crown of Spain; that the other was a Dutch pirate, and the very same captain who had robbed Candide. The immense riches which this villain had amassed, were buried with him in the deep, and only this one sheep saved out of the whole.

"You see," said Candide to Martin, "that vice is sometimes punished; this villain, the Dutch skipper, has met with the fate he deserved."

"Very true," said Martin, "but why should the passengers be doomed also to destruction? God has punished the knave, and the devil has drowned the rest."

The French and Spanish ships continued their cruise, and Candide and Martin their conversation. They disputed fourteen days successively, at the end of which they were just as far advanced as the first moment they began. However, they had the satisfaction of disputing, of communicating their ideas, and of mutually comforting each other. Candide embraced his sheep with transport.

"Since I have found thee again," said he, "I may possibly find my Cunegund once more."

CHAPTER 21

Candide and Martin, While Thus Reasoning with Each Other, Draw Near to the Coast of France

At length they descried the coast of France, when Candide said to Martin, "Pray Mr. Martin, were you ever in France?"

"Yes, sir," said Martin, "I have been in several provinces of that kingdom. In some, one-half of the people are fools and madmen; in some, they are too artful; in others, again, they are, in general, either very good-natured or very brutal; while in others, they affect to be witty, and in all, their ruling passion is love, the next is slander, and the last is to talk nonsense."

"But, pray, Mr. Martin, were you ever in Paris?"

"Yes, sir, I have been in that city, and it is a place that contains the several species just described; it is a chaos, a confused multitude, where everyone seeks for pleasure without being able to find it; at least, as far as I have observed during my short stay in that city. At my arrival I was robbed of all I had in the world by pickpockets and sharpers, at the fair of St. Germain. I was taken up myself for a robber, and confined in prison a whole week; after which I hired myself as corrector to a press, in order to get a little money towards defraying my expenses back to Holland on foot. I knew the whole tribe of scribblers, malcontents, and fanatics. It is said the people of that city are very polite; I believe they may be."

"For my part, I have no curiosity to see France," said Candide; "you may easily conceive, my friend, that after spending a month in El Dorado, I can desire to behold nothing upon earth but Miss Cunegund; I am going to wait for her at Venice. I intend to pass through France, on my way to Italy. Will you not bear me company?" "With all my heart," said Martin; "they say Venice is agreeable to none but noble Venetians; but that, nevertheless, strangers are well received there when they have plenty of money; now I have none, but you have, therefore I will attend you wherever you please." "Now we are upon this subject," said Candide, "do you think that the earth was originally sea, as we read in that great book which belongs to the captain of the ship?" "I believe nothing of it," replied Martin, "any more than I do of the many other chimeras which have been related to us for some time past." "But then, to what end," said Candide, "was the world formed?" "To make us mad," said Martin. "Are you not surprised," contin- ued Candide, "at the love which the two girls in the country of the Oreillons had for

those two monkeys?—You know I have told you the story." "Surprised?" replied Martin, "not in the least; I see nothing strange in this passion. I have seen so many extraordinary things that there is nothing extraordinary to me now." "Do you think," said Candide, "that mankind always massacred one another as they do now? were they always guilty of lies, fraud, treachery, ingratitude, inconstancy, envy, ambition, and cruelty? were they always thieves, fools, cowards, gluttons, drunkards, misers, calumniators, debauchees, fanatics, and hypocrites?" "Do you believe," said Martin, "that hawks have always been accustomed to eat pigeons when they came in their way?" "Doubtless," said Candide. "Well then," replied Martin, "if hawks have always had the same nature, why should you pretend that mankind change theirs?" "Oh," said Candide, "there is a great deal of difference; for free will—"
and reasoning thus they arrived at Bordeaux.

CHAPTER 22

What Happened to Candide and Martin in France

Candide staid no longer at Bordeaux than was necessary to dispose of a few of the pebbles he had brought from El Dorado, and to provide himself with a post-chaise for two persons, for he could no longer stir a step without his philosopher Martin. The only thing that gave him concern was the being obliged to leave his sheep behind him, which he intrusted to the care of the academy of sciences at Bordeaux, who proposed, as a prize subject for the year, to prove why the wool of this sheep was red; and the prize was adjudged to a northern sage, who demonstrated by A *plus* B, *minus* C, divided by Z, that the sheep must necessarily be red, and die of the mange.

In the meantime, all the travellers whom Candide met with in the inns, or on the road, told him to a man, that they were going to Paris. This general eagerness gave him likewise a great desire to see this capital; and it was not much out of his way to Venice.

He entered the city by the suburbs of St. Marceau, and thought himself in one of the vilest hamlets in all Westphalia.

Candide had not been long at his inn, before he was seized with a slight disorder, owing to the fatigue he had undergone. As he wore a diamond of an enormous size on his finger and had among the rest of his equipage a strong box that seemed very weighty, he soon found himself between two physicians, whom he had not sent for, a number of intimate friends whom he had never seen, and who would not quit his bedside, and two women devotees, who were very careful in providing him hot broths.

"I remember," said Martin to him, "that the first time I came to Paris I was likewise taken ill; I was very poor, and accordingly I had neither friends, nurses, nor physicians, and yet I did very well."

However, by dint of purging and bleeding, Candide's disorder became very serious. The priest of the parish came with all imaginable politeness to desire a note of him, payable to the bearer in the other world.[21] Candide refused to comply with his request; but the two devotees assured him that it was a new fashion. Candide replied, that he was not one that followed the fashion. Martin was for throwing the priest out of the window. The clerk swore Candide should not have Christian burial. Martin swore in his turn that he would bury the clerk alive if

---

[21] In the middle of the eighteenth century in Paris, it was necessary to have a document certifying that one was not a Jansenist in order to receive extreme unction.

he continued to plague them any longer. The dispute grew warm; Martin took him by the shoulders and turned him out of the room, which gave great scandal, and occasioned a *procès-verbal*.

Candide recovered, and till he was in a condition to go abroad had a great deal of good company to pass the evenings with him in his chamber. They played deep. Candide was surprised to find he could never turn a trick; and Martin was not at all surprised at the matter.

Among those who did him the honors of the place was a little spruce abbé of Périgord, one of those insinuating, busy, fawning, impudent, necessary fellows, that lay wait for strangers on their arrival, tell them all the scandal of the town, and offer to minister to their pleasures at various prices. This man conducted Candide and Martin to the playhouse; they were acting a new tragedy. Candide found himself placed near a cluster of wits: this, however, did not prevent him from shedding tears at some parts of the piece which were most affecting, and best acted. One of these talkers said to him between the acts, "You are greatly to blame to shed tears; that actress plays horribly, and the man that plays with her still worse, and the piece itself is still more execrable than the representation. The author does not understand a word of Arabic, and yet he has laid his scene in Arabia, and what is more, he is a fellow who does not believe in innate ideas. To-morrow I will bring you a score of pamphlets that have been written against him." "Pray, sir," said Candide to the abbé, "how many theatrical pieces have you in France?" "Five or six thousand," replied the abbé. "Indeed! that is a great number," said Candide, "but how many good ones may there be?" "About fifteen or sixteen." "Oh! that is a great number," said Martin.

Candide was greatly taken with an actress, who performed the part of Queen Elizabeth in a dull kind of tragedy that is played sometimes. "That actress," said he to Martin, "pleases me greatly; she has some sort of resemblance to Miss Cunegund. I should be very glad to pay my respects to her." The abbé of Périgord offered his service to introduce him to her at her own house. Candide, who was brought up in Germany, desired to know what might be the ceremonial used on those occasions, and how a queen of England was treated in France. "There is a necessary distinction to be observed in these matters," said the abbé. "In a country town we take them to a tavern; here in Paris, they are treated with great respect during their life time, provided they are handsome, and when they die we throw their bodies upon a dunghill." "How?" said Candide, "throw a queen's body upon a dunghill!" "The gentleman is quite right," said Martin, "he tells you nothing but the truth. I happened to be at Paris when Miss Monimia made her exit, as one may say, out of this world into another. She was refused what they call here the rites of sepulture; that is to say, she was denied the privilege of rotting in a churchyard by the side of all the beggars in the parish. They buried her at the corner of Burgundy street, which must certainly have shocked her extremely, as she had very exalted notions of things." "This is acting very impolitely," said Candide. "Lord!" said Martin, "what can be said to it? it is the way of these people. Figure to yourself all the contradictions, all the inconsistencies possible, and you may meet with them in the government, the courts of justice, the churches, and the public spectacles of this odd nation." "Is it true," said Candide, "that the people of Paris are always laughing?" "Yes," replied the abbé, "but it is with anger in their hearts; they express all their complaints by loud bursts of laughter, and commit the most detestable crimes with a smile on their faces."

"Who was that great overgrown beast," said Candide, "who spoke so ill to me of the piece with which I was so much affected, and of the players who gave me so much pleasure?" "A very good-for-nothing sort of a man I assure you," answered the abbé, "one who gets his livelihood by abusing every new book and play that is written or performed; he dislikes much to see any one meet with success, like eunuchs, who detest every one that possesses those powers they are deprived of; he is one of those vipers in literature who nourish themselves with their own venom; a pamphlet-monger." "A pamphlet-monger!" said Candide, "what is that?" "Why, a pamphlet-monger," replied the abbé, "is a writer of pamphlets—a fool."[22]

Candide, Martin, and the abbé of Périgord argued thus on the staircase, while they stood to see the people go out of the playhouse. "Though I am very anxious to see Miss Cunegund again," said Candide, "yet I have a great inclination to sup with Miss Clairon,[23] for I am really much taken with her."

The abbé was not a person to show his face at this lady's house, which was frequented by none but the best company. "She is engaged this evening," said he, "but I will do myself the honor to introduce you to a lady of quality of my acquaintance, at whose house you will see as much of the manners of Paris as if you had lived here for forty years."

Candide, who was naturally curious, suffered himself to be conducted to this lady's house, which was in the suburbs of St. Honoré. The company was engaged at basset; twelve melancholy punters held each in his hand a small pack of cards, the corners of which were doubled down, and were so many registers of their ill fortune. A profound silence reigned throughout the assembly, a pallid dread had taken possession of the countenances of the punters, and restless inquietude stretched every muscle of the face of him who kept the bank; and the lady of the house, who was seated next to him, observed with lynx's eyes every play made, and noted those who tallied,[24] and made them undouble their cards with a severe exactness, though mixed with a politeness, which she thought necessary not to frighten away her customers. This lady assumed the title of marchioness of Parolignac.[25] Her daughter, a girl of about fifteen years of age, was one of the punters, and took care to give her mamma a hint, by signs, when any one of the players attempted to repair the rigor of their ill fortune by a little innocent deception. The company were thus occupied when Candide, Martin, and the abbé made their entrance; not a creature rose to salute them, or indeed took the least notice of them, being wholly intent upon the business in hand. "Ah!" said Candide, "my lady baroness of Thunder-ten-tronckh would have behaved more civilly."

However, the abbé whispered in the ear of the marchioness, who half raising herself from her seat, honored Candide with a gracious smile, and gave Martin a nod of her head, with an air of inexpressible dignity. She then ordered a seat for Candide, and desired him to make one of their party at play; he did so, and in a few deals lost near a thousand pieces; after which they supped very elegantly, and every one was surprised at seeing Candide lose so much money without appearing to be the least disturbed at it. The servants in waiting said to each other, "This is certainly some English lord."

The supper was like most others of its kind in Paris. At first every one was silent; then followed a few confused murmurs, and afterwards several insipid jokes passed and repassed, with false reports, false reasonings, a little politics, and a great deal of scandal. The conversation then turned upon the new productions in literature.

---

[22]Fréron, a popular journalist who had attacked Voltaire's plays.
[23]Claire Leris (1723–1803), a famous French actress.
[24]Players dog-eared cards to indicate they wished to increase their winnings without the risk of losing.
[25]She is clever at cards; *paroli* is an illegal doubling of one's bet.

"Pray," said the abbé, "good folks, have you seen the romance written by the Sieur Gauchat, doctor of divinity?" "Yes," answered one of the company, "but I had not patience to go through it. The town is pestered with a swarm of impertinent productions, but this of Dr. Gauchat's outdoes them all. In short, I was so cursedly tired of reading this vile stuff that I even resolved to come here, and make a party at basset." "But what say you to the archdeacon T——'s[26] miscellaneous collection," said the abbé. "Oh my God!" cried the marchioness of Parolignac, "never mention the tedious creature! only think what pains he is at to tell one things that all the world knows; and how he labors an argument that is hardly worth the slightest consideration! how absurdly he makes use of other people's wit! how miserably he mangles what he has pilfered from them! The man makes me quite sick! A few pages of the good archdeacon are enough in conscience to satisfy any one."

There was at the table a person of learning and taste, who supported what the marchioness had advanced. They next began to talk of tragedies. The lady desired to know how it came about that there were several tragedies, which still continued to be played, though they would not bear reading? The man of taste explained very clearly how a piece may be in some manner interesting without having a grain of merit. He showed, in a few words, that it is not sufficient to throw together a few incidents that are to be met with in every romance, and that to dazzle the spectator the thoughts should be new, without being far-fetched; frequently sublime, but always natural; the author should have a thorough knowledge of the human heart and make it speak properly; he should be a complete poet, without showing an affectation of it in any of the characters of his piece; he should be a perfect master of his language, speak it with all its purity, and with the utmost harmony, and yet so as not to make the sense a slave to the rhyme. "Whoever," added he, "neglects any one of these rules, though he may write two or three tragedies with tolerable success, will never be reckoned in the number of good authors. There are very few good tragedies; some are idyls, in very well-written and harmonious dialogue; and others a chain of political reasonings that set one asleep, or else pompous and high-flown amplifications, that disgust rather than please. Others again are the ravings of a madman, in an uncouth style, unmeaning flights, or long apostrophes to the deities, for want of knowing how to address mankind; in a word a collection of false maxims and dull commonplace."

Candide listened to this discourse with great attention, and conceived a high opinion of the person who delivered it; and as the marchioness had taken care to place him near her side, he took the liberty to whisper her softly in the ear and ask who this person was that spoke so well. "He is a man of letters," replied her ladyship, "who never plays, and whom the abbé brings with him to my house sometimes to spend an evening. He is a great judge of writing, especially in tragedy; he has composed one himself, which was damned, and has written a book that was never seen out of his bookseller's shop, excepting only one copy, which he sent me with a dedication, to which he had prefixed my name." "Oh the great man," cried Candide, "he is a second Pangloss."

Then turning towards him, "Sir," said he, "you are doubtless of opinion that everything is for the best in the physical and moral world, and that nothing could be otherwise than it is?" "I, sir!" replied the man of letters, "I think no such thing, I assure you; I find that all in this world is set the wrong end uppermost. No one knows what is his rank, his office, nor what he does, nor what he should do. With the exception of our evenings, which we generally pass tolerably merrily, the

---

[26] Abbé Trublet, a rival of Voltaire's.

rest of our time is spent in idle disputes and quarrels, Jansenists against Molinists, the parliament against the Church, and one armed body of men against another; courtier against courtier, husband against wife, and relations against relations. In short, this world is nothing but one continued scene of civil war."

"Yes," said Candide, "and I have seen worse than all that; and yet a learned man, who had the misfortune to be hanged, taught me that everything was marvellously well, and that these evils you are speaking of were only so many shades in a beautiful picture." "Your hempen sage," said Martin, "laughed at you; these shades, as you call them, are most horrible blemishes." "The men make these blemishes," rejoined Candide, "and they cannot do otherwise." "Then it is not their fault," added Martin. The greatest part of the gamesters, who did not understand a syllable of this discourse, amused themselves with drinking, while Martin reasoned with the learned gentleman; and Candide entertained the lady of the house with a part of his adventures.

After supper the marchioness conducted Candide into her dressing-room, and made him sit down under a canopy. "Well," said she, "are you still so violently fond of Miss Cunegund of Thunder-ten-tronckh?" "Yes, madam," replied Candide. The marchioness said to him with a tender smile, "You answer me like a young man born in Westphalia; a Frenchman would have said, 'It is true, madam, I had a great passion for Miss Cunegund; but since I have seen you, I fear I can no longer love her as I did.' " "Alas! madam," replied Candide, "I will make you what answer you please." "You fell in love with her, I find, in stooping to pick up her handkerchief which she had dropped; you shall pick up my garter." "With all my heart, madam," said Candide, and he picked it up. "But you must tie it on again," said the lady. Candide tied it on again. "Look ye, young man," said the marchioness, "you are a stranger; I make some of my lovers here in Paris languish for me a whole fortnight; but I surrender to you at first sight, because I am willing to do the honors of my country to a young Westphalian." The fair one having cast her eye on two very large diamonds that were upon the young stranger's finger, praised them in so earnest a manner that they were in an instant transferred from his finger to hers.

As Candide was going home with the abbé he felt some qualms of conscience for having been guilty of infidelity to Miss Cunegund. The abbé took part with him in his uneasiness; he had but an inconsiderable share in the thousand pieces Candide had lost at play, and the two diamonds which had been in a manner extorted from him; and therefore very prudently designed to make the most he could of his new acquaintance, which chance had thrown in his way. He talked much of Miss Cunegund, and Candide assured him that he would heartily ask pardon of that fair one for his infidelity to her, when he saw her at Venice.

The abbé redoubled his civilities and seemed to interest himself warmly in everything that Candide said, did, or seemed inclined to do.

"And so, sir, you have an engagement at Venice?" "Yes, Monsieur l'Abbé," answered Candide, "I must absolutely wait upon Miss Cunegund," and then the pleasure he took in talking about the object he loved, led him insensibly to relate, according to custom, part of his adventures with that illustrious Westphalian beauty.

"I fancy," said the abbé, "Miss Cunegund has a great deal of wit, and that her letters must be very entertaining." "I have never received any from her," said Candide; "for you are to consider that, being expelled from the castle upon her account, I could not write to her, especially as soon after my departure I heard she was dead; but thank God I found afterwards she was living. I left her again after this, and now I have sent a messenger to her near two thousand leagues from here, and wait here for his return with an answer from her."

The artful abbé let not a word of all this escape him, though he seemed to be musing upon something else. He soon took his leave of the two adventurers, after having embraced them with the greatest cordiality. The next morning, almost as soon as his eyes were open, Candide received the following billet:

"My Dearest Lover—I have been ill in this city these eight days. I have heard of your arrival, and should fly to your arms were I able to stir. I was informed of your being on the way hither at Bordeaux, where I left the faithful Cacambo, and the old woman, who will soon follow me. The governor of Buenos Ayres has taken everything from me but your heart, which I still retain. Come to me immediately on the receipt of this. Your presence will either give me new life, or kill me with the pleasure."

At the receipt of this charming, this unexpected letter, Candide felt the utmost transports of joy; though, on the other hand, the indisposition of his beloved Miss Cunegund overwhelmed him with grief. Distracted between these two passions he took his gold and his diamonds, and procured a person to conduct him and Martin to the house where Miss Cunegund lodged. Upon entering the room he felt his limbs tremble, his heart flutter, his tongue falter; he attempted to undraw the curtain, and called for a light to the bedside. "Lord, sir," cried a maid servant, who was waiting in the room, "take care what you do, Miss cannot bear the least light," and so saying she pulled the curtain close again. "Cunegund! my dear Cunegund!" cried Candide, bathed in tears, "how do you do? If you cannot bear the light, speak to me at least." "Alas! she cannot speak," said the maid. The sick lady then put a plump hand out of the bed and Candide first bathed it with tears, then filled it with diamonds, leaving a purse of gold upon the easy chair.

In the midst of his transports came an officer into the room, followed by the abbé, and a file of musketeers. "There," said he, "are the two suspected foreigners;" at the same time he ordered them to be seized and carried to prison. "Travellers are not treated in this manner in the country of El Dorado," said Candide. "I am more of a Manichæan now than ever," said Martin. "But pray, good sir, where are you going to carry us?" said Candide. "To a dungeon, my dear sir," replied the officer.

When Martin had a little recovered himself, so as to form a cool judgment of what had passed, he plainly perceived that the person who had acted the part of Miss Cunegund was a cheat; that the abbé of Périgord was a sharper who had imposed upon the honest simplicity of Candide, and the officer was a knave, whom they might easily get rid of.

Candide following the advice of his friend Martin, and burning with impatience to see the real Miss Cunegund, rather than be obliged to appear at a court of justice, proposed to the officer to make him a present of three small diamonds, each of them worth three thousand pistoles. "Ah, sir," said this understrapper of justice, "had you committed ever so much villainy, this would render you the honestest man living, in my eyes. Three diamonds worth three thousand pistoles! why, my dear sir, so far from carrying you to jail, I would lose my life to serve you. There are orders for stopping all strangers; but leave it to me, I have a brother at Dieppe, in Normandy; I myself will conduct you thither, and if you have a diamond left to give him he will take as much care of you as I myself should."

"But why," said Candide, "do they stop all strangers?" The abbé of Périgord made answer that it was because a poor devil of the country of Artois[27] heard somebody tell foolish stories, and this induced him to commit a parricide; not such a one as that in the month of May, 1610, but such as that in the month of

---

[27] The beggar was Robert-Francis Damiens, who tried to assassinate Louis XV in 1757.

December, in the year 1594, and such as many that have been perpetrated in other months and years, by other poor devils who had heard foolish stories.

The officer then exclaimed to them what the abbé meant. "Horrid monsters," exclaimed Candide, "is it possible that such scenes should pass among a people who are perpetually singing and dancing? Is there no flying this abominable country immediately, this execrable kingdom where monkeys provoke tigers? I have seen bears in my country, but men I have beheld nowhere but in El Dorado. In the name of God, sir," said he to the officer, "do me the kindness to conduct me to Venice, where I am to wait for Miss Cunegund." "Really, sir," replied the officer, "I cannot possibly wait on you farther than Lower Normandy." So saying, he ordered Candide's irons to be struck off, acknowledged himself mistaken, and sent his followers about their business, after which he conducted Candide and Martin to Dieppe, and left them to the care of his brother. There happened just then to be a small Dutch ship in the harbor. The Norman, whom the other three diamonds had converted into the most obliging, serviceable being that ever breathed, took care to see Candide and his attendants safe on board this vessel, that was just ready to sail for Portsmouth in England. This was not the nearest way to Venice, indeed, but Candide thought himself escaped out of hell, and did not, in the least, doubt but he should quickly find an opportunity of resuming his voyage to Venice.

CHAPTER 23

Candide and Martin Touch upon the English Coast—What They See There

"Ah Pangloss! Pangloss! ah Martin! Martin! ah my dear Miss Cunegund! what sort of a world is this?" Thus exclaimed Candide as soon as he got on board the Dutch ship. "Why something very foolish, and very abominable," said Martin. "You are acquainted with England," said Candide; "are they as great fools in that country as in France?" "Yes, but in a different manner," answered Martin. "You know that these two nations are at war about a few acres of barren land in the neighborhood of Canada, and that they have expended much greater sums in the contest than all Canada is worth. To say exactly whether there are a greater number fit to be inhabitants of a madhouse in the one country than the other, exceeds the limits of my imperfect capacity; I know in general that the people we are going to visit are of a very dark and gloomy disposition."

As they were chatting thus together they arrived at Portsmouth. The shore on each side the harbor was lined with a multitude of people, whose eyes were steadfastly fixed on a lusty man who was kneeling down on the deck of one of the men-of-war, with something tied before his eyes. Opposite to this personage stood four soldiers, each of whom shot three bullets into his skull, with all the composure imaginable; and when it was done, the whole company went away perfectly well satisfied. "What the devil is all this for?" said Candide, "and what demon, or foe of mankind, lords it thus tyrannically over the world?" He then asked who was that lusty man who had been sent out of the world with so much ceremony, and he received for answer, that it was an admiral.[28] "And pray why do you put your admiral to death?" "Because he did not put a sufficient number of his fellow-creatures to death. You must know, he had an engagement with a French admiral, and it has been proved against him that he was not near enough to his antagonist." "But," replied Candide, "the French admiral must have been as far from him." "There is no doubt of that; but in this

---

[28] After being defeated by the French fleet, Admiral John Byng was executed in 1757.

country it is found requisite, now and then, to put an admiral to death, in order to encourage the others to fight."

Candide was so shocked at what he saw and heard, that he would not set foot on shore, but made a bargain with the Dutch skipper (were he even to rob him like the captain of Surinam) to carry him directly to Venice.

The skipper was ready in two days. They sailed along the coast of France, and passed within sight of Lisbon, at which Candide trembled. From thence they proceeded to the Straits, entered the Mediterranean, and at length arrived at Venice. "God be praised," said Candide, embracing Martin, "this is the place where I am to behold my beloved Cunegund once again. I can confide in Cacambo, like another self. All is well, all very well, all as well as possible."

CHAPTER 24

Of Pacquette and Friar Giroflée

Upon their arrival at Venice Candide went in search of Cacambo at every inn and coffee-house, and among all the ladies of pleasure, but could hear nothing of him. He sent every day to inquire what ships were in, still no news of Cacambo. "It is strange," said he to Martin, "very strange that I should have had time to sail from Surinam to Bordeaux; to travel thence to Paris, to Dieppe, to Portsmouth; to sail along the coast of Portugal and Spain, and up the Mediterranean to spend some months at Venice; and that my lovely Cunegund should not have arrived. Instead of her, I only met with a Parisian impostor, and a rascally abbé of Périgord. Cunegund is actually dead, and I have nothing to do but follow her. Alas! how much better would it have been for me to have remained in the paradise of El Dorado than to have returned to this cursed Europe! You are in the right, my dear Martin; you are certainly in the right; all is misery and deceit."

He fell into a deep melancholy, and neither went to the opera then in vogue, nor partook of any of the diversions of the carnival; nay, he even slighted the fair sex. Martin said to him, "Upon my word, I think you are very simple to imagine that a rascally valet, with five or six millions in his pocket, would go in search of your mistress to the further end of the world, and bring her to Venice to meet you. If he finds her he will take her for himself; if he does not, he will take another. Let me advise you to forget your valet Cacambo, and your Mistress Cunegund." Martin's speech was not the most consolatory to the dejected Candide. His melancholy increased, and Martin never ceased trying to prove to him that there is very little virtue or happiness in this world; except, perhaps, in El Dorado, where hardly anybody can gain admittance.

While they were disputing on this important subject, and still expecting Miss Cunegund, Candide perceived a young Theatin friar in St. Mark's Place, with a girl under his arm. The Theatin looked fresh-colored, plump, and vigorous; his eyes sparkled; his air and gait were bold and lofty. The girl was pretty, and was singing a song; and every now and then gave her Theatin an amorous ogle and wantonly pinched his ruddy cheeks. "You will at least allow," said Candide to Martin, "that these two are happy. Hitherto I have met with none but unfortunate people in the whole habitable globe, except in El Dorado; but as to this couple, I would venture to lay a wager they are happy." "Done!" said Martin, "they are not what you imagine." "Well, we have only to ask them to dine with us," said Candide, "and you will see whether I am mistaken or not."

Thereupon he accosted them, and with great politeness invited them to his inn to eat some macaroni, with Lombard partridges and caviare, and to drink a bottle of Montepulciano, Lacryma Christi, Cyprus, and Samos wine. The girl blushed;

the Theatin accepted the invitation and she followed him, eyeing Candide every now and then with a mixture of surprise and confusion, while the tears stole down her cheeks. No sooner did she enter his apartment than she cried out. "How, Mr. Candide, have you quite forgot your Pacquette? do you not know her again?" Candide had not regarded her with any degree of attention before, being wholly occupied with the thoughts of his dear Cunegund. "Ah! is it you, child? was it you that reduced Doctor Pangloss to that fine condition I saw him in?"

"Alas! sir," answered Pacquette, "it was I, indeed. I find you are acquainted with everything; and I have been informed of all the misfortunes that happened to the whole family of my lady baroness and the fair Cunegund. But I can safely swear to you that my lot was no less deplorable; I was innocence itself when you saw me last. A cordelier, who was my confessor, easily seduced me; the consequences proved terrible. I was obliged to leave the castle some time after the baron kicked you out from there; and if a famous surgeon had not taken compassion on me, I had been a dead woman. Gratitude obliged me to live with him some time as a mistress; his wife, who was a very devil for jealousy, beat me unmercifully every day. Oh! she was a perfect fury. The doctor himself was the most ugly of all mortals, and I the most wretched creature existing, to be continually beaten for a man whom I did not love. You are sensible, sir, how dangerous it was for an ill-natured woman to be married to a physician. Incensed at the behavior of his wife, he one day gave her so affectionate a remedy for a slight cold she had caught that she died in less than two hours in most dreadful convulsions. Her relations prosecuted the husband, who was obliged to fly, and I was sent to prison. My innocence would not have saved me, if I had not been tolerably handsome. The judge gave me my liberty on condition he should succeed the doctor. However, I was soon supplanted by a rival, turned off without a farthing, and obliged to continue the abominable trade which you men think so pleasing, but which to us unhappy creatures is the most dreadful of all sufferings. At length I came to follow the business at Venice. Ah! sir, did you but know what it is to be obliged to receive every visitor; old tradesmen, counsellors, monks, watermen, and abbés; to be exposed to all their insolence and abuse; to be often necessitated to borrow a petticoat, only that it may be taken up by some disagreeable wretch; to be robbed by one gallant of what we get from another; to be subject to the extortions of civil magistrates; and to have forever before one's eyes the prospect of old age, a hospital, or a dunghill, you would conclude that I am one of the most unhappy wretches breathing."

Thus did Pacquette unbosom herself to honest Candide in his closet, in the presence of Martin, who took occasion to say to him, "You see I have half won the wager already."

Friar Giroflée was all this time in the parlor refreshing himself with a glass or two of wine till dinner was ready. "But," said Candide to Pacquette, "you looked so gay and contented, when I met you, you sang and caressed the Theatin with so much fondness, that I absolutely thought you as happy as you say you are now miserable." "Ah! dear sir," said Pacquette, "this is one of the miseries of the trade; yesterday I was stripped and beaten by an officer; yet to-day I must appear good humored and gay to please a friar."

Candide was convinced and acknowledged that Martin was in the right. They sat down to table with Pacquette and the Theatin; the entertainment was agreeable, and towards the end they began to converse together with some freedom. "Father," said Candide to the friar, "you seem to me to enjoy a state of happiness that even kings might envy; joy and health are painted in your countenance. You have a pretty wench to divert you; and you seem to be perfectly well contented with your condition as a Theatin."

"Faith, sir," said Friar Giroflée, "I wish with all my soul the Theatins were every one of them at the bottom of the sea. I have been tempted a thousand times to set fire to the convent and go and turn Turk. My parents obliged me, at the age of fifteen, to put on this detestable habit only to increase the fortune of an elder brother of mine, whom God confound! Jealousy, discord, and fury, reside in our convent. It is true I have preached often paltry sermons, by which I have got a little money, part of which the prior robs me of, and the remainder helps to pay my girls; but, at night, when I go hence to my convent, I am ready to dash my brains against the walls of the dormitory; and this is the case with all the rest of our fraternity."

Martin, turning towards Candide, with his usual indifference, said, "Well, what think you now? have I won the wager entirely?" Candide gave two thousand piastres to Pacquette, and a thousand to Friar Giroflée, saying, "I will answer that this will make them happy." "I am not of your opinion," said Martin, "perhaps this money will only make them wretched." "Be that as it may," said Candide, "one thing comforts me; I see that one often meets with those whom one never expected to see again; so that, perhaps, as I have found my red sheep and Pacquette, I may be lucky enough to find Miss Cunegund also." "I wish," said Martin, "she one day may make you happy; but I doubt it much." "You lack faith," said Candide. "It is because," said Martin, "I have seen the world."

"Observe those gondoliers," said Candide, "are they not perpetually singing?" "You do not see them," answered Martin, "at home with their wives and brats. The doge has his chagrin, gondoliers theirs. Nevertheless, in the main, I look upon the gondolier's life as preferable to that of the doge; but the difference is so trifling that it is not worth the trouble of examining into."

"I have heard great talk," said Candide, "of the Senator Pococuranté,[29] who lives in that fine house at the Brenta, where, they say, he entertains foreigners in the most polite manner." "They pretend this man is a perfect stranger to uneasiness. I should be glad to see so extraordinary a being," said Martin. Candide thereupon sent a messenger to Seignor Pococuranté, desiring permission to wait on him the next day.

CHAPTER 25

Candide and Martin Pay a Visit to Seignor Pococuranté, a Noble Venetian

Candide and his friend Martin went in a gondola on the Brenta, and arrived at the palace of the noble Pococuranté. The gardens were laid out in elegant taste, and adorned with fine marble statues; his palace was built after the most approved rules of architecture. The master of the house, who was a man of affairs, and very rich, received our two travellers with great politeness, but without much ceremony, which somewhat disconcerted Candide, but was not at all displeasing to Martin.

As soon as they were seated, two very pretty girls, neatly dressed, brought in chocolate, which was extremely well prepared. Candide could not help making encomiums upon their beauty and graceful carriage. "The creatures are well enough," said the senator; "I amuse myself with them sometimes, for I am heartily tired of the women of the town, their coquetry, their jealousy, their quarrels, their humors, their meannesses, their pride, and their folly; I am weary of making sonnets, or of paying for sonnets to be made on them; but after all, these two girls begin to grow very indifferent to me."

---

[29]"Caring little."

After having refreshed himself, Candide walked into a large gallery, where he was struck with the sight of a fine collection of paintings. "Pray," said Candide, "by what master are the two first of these?" "They are by Raphael," answered the senator. "I gave a great deal of money for them seven years ago, purely out of curiosity, as they were said to be the finest pieces in Italy; but I cannot say they please me: the coloring is dark and heavy; the figures do not swell nor come out enough; and the drapery is bad. In short, notwithstanding the encomiums lavished upon them, they are not, in my opinion, a true representation of nature. I approve of no paintings save those wherein I think I behold nature herself; and there are few, if any, of that kind to be met with. I have what is called a fine collection, but I take no manner of delight in it."

While dinner was being prepared Pococuranté ordered a concert. Candide praised the music to the skies. "This noise," said the noble Venetian, "may amuse one for a little time, but if it were to last above half an hour, it would grow tiresome to everybody, though perhaps no one would care to own it. Music has become the art of executing what is difficult; now, whatever is difficult cannot be long pleasing.

"I believe I might take more pleasure in an opera, if they had not made such a monster of that species of dramatic entertainment as perfectly shocks me; and I am amazed how people can bear to see wretched tragedies set to music; where the scenes are contrived for no other purpose than to lug in, as it were by the ears, three or four ridiculous songs, to give a favorite actress an opportunity of exhibiting her pipe. Let who will die away in raptures at the trills of a eunuch quavering the majestic part of Cæsar or Cato, and strutting in a foolish manner upon the stage, but for my part I have long ago renounced these paltry entertainments, which constitute the glory of modern Italy, and are so dearly purchased by crowned heads." Candide opposed these sentiments; but he did it in a discreet manner; as for Martin, he was entirely of the old senator's opinion.

Dinner being served they sat down to table, and, after a hearty repast, returned to the library. Candide, observing Homer richly bound, commended the noble Venetian's taste. "This," said he, "is a book that was once the delight of the great Pangloss, the best philosopher in Germany." "Homer is no favorite of mine," answered Pococuranté, coolly; "I was made to believe once that I took a pleasure in reading him; but his continual repetitions of battles have all such a resemblance with each other; his gods that are forever in haste and bustle, without ever doing anything; his Helen, who is the cause of the war, and yet hardly acts in the whole performance; his Troy, that holds out so long, without being taken: in short, all these things together make the poem very insipid to me. I have asked some learned men, whether they are not in reality as much tired as myself with reading this poet: those who spoke ingenuously, assured me that he had made them fall asleep, and yet that they could not well avoid giving him a place in their libraries; but that it was merely as they would do an antique, or those rusty medals which are kept only for curiosity, and are of no manner of use in commerce."

"But your excellency does not surely form the same opinion of Virgil?" said Candide. "Why, I grant," replied Pococuranté, "that the second, third, fourth, and sixth books of his 'Æneid' are excellent; but as for his pious Æneas, his strong Cloanthus, his friendly Achates, his boy Ascanius, his silly king Latinus, his ill-bred Amata, his insipid Lavinia, and some other characters much in the same strain, I think there cannot in nature be anything more flat and disagreeable. I must confess I prefer Tasso far beyond him; nay, even that sleepy tale-teller Ariosto."

"May I take the liberty to ask if you do not experience great pleasure from reading Horace?" said Candide. "There are maxims in this writer," replied Pococuranté, "whence a man of the world may reap some benefit; and the short measure of the verse makes them more easily to be retained in the memory. But I see nothing extraordinary in his journey to Brundusium, and his account of his bad dinner; nor in his dirty, low quarrel between one Rupillius, whose words, as he expresses it, were full of poisonous filth; and another, whose language was dipped in vinegar. His indelicate verses against old women and witches have frequently given me great offence: nor can I discover the great merit of his telling his friend Mæcenas, that if he will but rank him in the class of lyric poets, his lofty head shall touch the stars. Ignorant readers are apt to judge a writer by his reputation. For my part, I read only to please myself. I like nothing but what makes for my purpose." Candide, who had been brought up with a notion of never making use of his own judgment, was astonished at what he heard; but Martin found there was a good deal of reason in the senator's remarks.

"O! here is a Tully," said Candide; "this great man I fancy you are never tired of reading?" "Indeed I never read him at all," replied Pococuranté. "What is it to me whether he pleads for Rabirius or Cluentius? I try causes enough myself. I had once some liking for his philosophical works; but when I found he doubted everything, I thought I knew as much as himself, and had no need of a guide to learn ignorance."

"Ha!" cried Martin, "here are fourscore volumes of the memoirs of the Academy of Sciences; perhaps there may be something curious and valuable in this collection." "Yes," answered Pococuranté; "so there might if any one of these compilers of this rubbish had only invented the art of pin-making: but all these volumes are filled with mere chimerical systems, without one single article conducive to real utility."

"I see a prodigious number of plays," said Candide, "in Italian, Spanish, and French." "Yes," replied the Venetian; "there are I think three thousand, and not three dozen of them good for anything. As to those huge volumes of divinity, and those enormous collections of sermons, they are not all together worth one single page in Seneca; and I fancy you will readily believe that neither myself, nor anyone else, ever looks into them."

Martin, perceiving some shelves filled with English books, said to the senator: "I fancy that a republican must be highly delighted with those books, which are most of them written with a noble spirit of freedom." "It is noble to write as we think," said Pococuranté; "it is the privilege of humanity. Throughout Italy we write only what we do not think; and the present inhabitants of the country of the Cæsars and Antonines dare not acquire a single idea without the permission of a Dominican father. I should be enamored of the spirit of the English nation, did it not utterly frustrate the good effects it would produce by passion and the spirit of party."

Candide, seeing a Milton, asked the senator if he did not think that author a great man. "Who?" said Pococuranté sharply; "that barbarian who writes a tedious commentary in ten books of rumbling verse, on the first chapter of Genesis? that slovenly imitator of the Greeks, who disfigures the creation, by making the Messiah take a pair of compasses from heaven's armory to plan the world; whereas Moses represented the Deity as producing the whole universe by his *fiat?* Can I think you have any esteem for a writer who has spoiled Tasso's hell and the devil; who transforms Lucifer sometimes into a toad, and at others into a pygmy; who makes him say the same thing over again a hundred times; who metamorphoses him into a school-divine; and who, by an absurdly serious imitation of Ariosto's comic invention of firearms, represents the devils and angels cannoning each other in heaven? Neither I nor any other Italian can possibly take pleasure in such melancholy reveries; but the marriage of Sin and Death, and snakes issuing from the womb of the former, are enough to make any person sick that is not lost to all sense of delicacy. This obscene, whimsical, and disagreeable poem met with the neglect it deserved at its first publication; and I only treat the author now as he was treated in his own country by his contemporaries."

Candide was sensibly grieved at this speech, as he had a great respect for Homer, and was fond of Milton. "Alas!" said he softly to Martin, "I am afraid this man holds our German poets in great contempt." "There would be no such great harm in that," said Martin. "O what a surprising man!" said Candide, still to himself; "what a prodigious genius is this Pococuranté! nothing can please him."

After finishing their survey of the library, they went down into the garden, when Candide commended the several beauties that offered themselves to his view. "I know nothing upon earth laid out in such bad taste," said Pococuranté; "everything about it is childish and trifling; but I shall have another laid out to-morrow upon a nobler plan."

As soon as our two travellers had taken leave of his excellency, "Well," said Candide to Martin, "I hope you will own that this man is the happiest of all mortals, for he is above everything he possesses." "But do you not see," answered Martin, "that he likewise dislikes everything he possesses? It was an observation of Plato, long since, that those are not the best stomachs that reject, without distinction, all sorts of ailments." "True," said Candide, "but still there must certainly be a pleasure in criticising everything, and in perceiving faults where others think they see beauties." "That is," replied Martin, "there is a pleasure in having no pleasure." "Well, well," said Candide, "I find that I shall be the only happy man at last, when I am blessed with the sight of my dear Cunegund." "It is good to hope," said Martin.

In the meanwhile, days and weeks passed away, and no news of Cacambo. Candide was so overwhelmed with grief, that he did not reflect on the behavior of Pacquette and Friar Giroflée, who never stayed to return him thanks for the presents he had so generously made them.

CHAPTER 26

Candide and Martin Sup with Six Sharpers—Who They Were

One evening as Candide, with his attendant Martin, was going to sit down to supper with some foreigners who lodged in the same inn where they had taken up their quarters, a man with a face the color of soot came behind him, and taking him by the arm, said, "Hold yourself in readiness to go along with us; be sure you do not fail." Upon this, turning about to see from whom these words came, he beheld Cacambo. Nothing but the sight of Miss Cunegund could have given him greater joy and surprise. He was almost beside himself. After embracing this dear friend, "Cunegund!" said he, "Cunegund is come with you doubtless! Where, where is she? Carry me to her this instant, that I may die with joy in her presence." "Cunegund is not here," answered Cacambo; "she is in Constantinople." "Good heavens! in Constantinople! but no matter if she were in China, I would fly thither. Quick, quick, dear Cacambo, let us be gone." "Soft and fair," said Cacambo, "stay till you have supped. I cannot at present stay to say anything more to you; I am a slave, and my master waits for me; I must go and attend him at table: but mum! say not a word, only get your supper, and hold yourself in readiness."

Candide, divided between joy and grief, charmed to have thus met with his faithful agent again, and surprised to hear he was a slave, his heart palpitating, his senses confused, but full of the hopes of recovering his dear Cunegund, sat down to table with Martin, who beheld all these scenes with great unconcern, and with six strangers, who had come to spend the carnival at Venice.

Cacambo waited at table upon one of those strangers. When supper was nearly over, he drew near to his master, and whispered in his ear, "Sire, your majesty may go when you please; the ship is ready"; and so saying he left the room. The guests, surprised at what they had heard, looked at each other without speaking a word;

when another servant drawing near to his master, in like manner said, "Sire, your majesty's post-chaise is at Padua, and the bark is ready." The master made him a sign, and he instantly withdrew. The company all stared at each other again, and the general astonishment was increased. A third servant then approached another of the strangers, and said, "Sire, if your majesty will be advised by me, you will not make any longer stay in this place; I will go and get everything ready"; and instantly disappeared.

Candide and Martin then took it for granted that this was some of the diversions of the carnival, and that these were characters in masquerade. Then a fourth domestic said to the fourth stranger, "Your majesty may set off when you please;" saying which, he went away like the rest. A fifth valet said the same to a fifth master. But the sixth domestic spoke in a different style to the person on whom he waited, and who sat near to Candide. "Troth, sir," said he, "they will trust your majesty no longer, nor myself neither; and we may both of us chance to be sent to jail this very night; and therefore I shall take care of myself, and so adieu." The servants all being gone, the six strangers, with Candide and Martin, remained in a profound silence. At length Candide broke it by saying, "Gentlemen, this is a very singular joke upon my word; how came you all to be kings? For my own part I own frankly, that neither my friend Martin here, nor myself, have any claim to royalty."

Cacambo's master then began, with great gravity, to deliver himself thus in Italian. "I am not joking in the least, my name is Achmet III. I was grand seignor for many years; I dethroned my brother, my nephew dethroned me, my viziers lost their heads, and I am condemned to end my days in the old seraglio. My nephew, the Grand Sultan Mahomet, gives me permission to travel sometimes for my health, and I am come to spend the carnival at Venice."

A young man who sat by Achmet, spoke next, and said: "My name is Ivan. I was once emperor of all the Russias, but was dethroned in my cradle. My parents were confined, and I was brought up in a prison, yet I am sometimes allowed to travel, though always with persons to keep a guard over me, and I am come to spend the carnival at Venice."

The third said: "I am Charles Edward, king of England; my father has renounced his right to the throne in my favor. I have fought in defence of my rights, and near a thousand of my friends have had their hearts taken out of their bodies alive and thrown in their faces. I have myself been confined in a prison. I am going to Rome to visit the king my father, who was dethroned as well as myself; and my grandfather and I have come to spend the carnival at Venice."

The fourth spoke thus: "I am the king of Poland; the fortune of war has stripped me of my hereditary dominions. My father experienced the same vicissitudes of fate. I resign myself to the will of Providence, in the same manner as Sultan Achmet, the Emperor Ivan, and King Charles Edward, whom God long preserve; and I have come to spend the carnival at Venice."

The fifth said: "I am king of Poland also. I have twice lost my kingdom; but Providence has given me other dominions, where I have done more good than all the Sarmatian kings put together were ever able to do on the banks of the Vistula; I resign myself likewise to Providence; and have come to spend the carnival at Venice."

It now came to the sixth monarch's turn to speak: "Gentlemen," said he, "I am not so great a prince as the rest of you, it is true, but I am, however, a crowned head. I am Theodore, elected king of Corsica. I have had the title of majesty, and am now hardly treated with common civility. I have coined money, and am not now worth a single ducat. I have had two secretaries, and am now without a valet. I was once seated on a throne, and since that have lain upon a truss of straw, in a common jail in London, and I very much fear I shall meet with the same fate here in Venice, where I came, like your majesties, to divert myself at the carnival."

The other five kings listened to this speech with great attention; it excited their compassion; each of them made the unhappy Theodore a present of twenty sequins, and Candide gave him a diamond, worth just a hundred times that sum. "Who can this private person be," said the five princes to one another, "who is able to give, and has actually given, a hundred times as much as any of us?"

Just as they rose from table, in came four serene highnesses, who had also been stripped of their territories by the fortune of war, and had come to spend the remainder of the carnival at Venice. Candide took no manner of notice of them; for his thoughts were wholly employed on his voyage to Constantinople, where he intended to go in search of his lovely Miss Cunegund.

CHAPTER 27

Candide's Voyage to Constantinople

The trusty Cacambo had already engaged the captain of the Turkish ship that was to carry Sultan Achmet back to Constantinople, to take Candide and Martin on board. Accordingly they both embarked, after paying their obeisance to his miserable highness. As they were going on board, Candide said to Martin, "You see we supped in company with six dethroned kings, and to one of them I gave charity. Perhaps there may be a great many other princes still more unfortunate. For my part I have lost only a hundred sheep, and am now going to fly to the arms of my charming Miss Cunegund. My dear Martin, I must insist on it, that Pangloss was in the right. All is for the best." "I wish it may be," said Martin. "But this was an odd adventure we met with at Venice. I do not think there ever was an instance before of six dethroned monarchs supping together at a public inn." "This is not more extraordinary," said Martin, "than most of what has happened to us. It is a very common thing for kings to be dethroned; and as for our having the honor to sup with six of them, it is a mere accident, not deserving our attention."

As soon as Candide set his foot on board the vessel, he flew to his old friend and valet Cacambo; and throwing his arms about his neck, embraced him with transports of joy. "Well," said he, "what news of Miss Cunegund? Does she still continue the paragon of beauty? Does she love me still? How does she do? You have, doubtless, purchased a superb palace for her at Constantinople."

"My dear master," replied Cacambo, "Miss Cunegund washes dishes on the banks of the Propontis, in the house of a prince who has very few to wash. She is at present a slave in the family of an ancient sovereign named Ragotsky,[30] whom the grand Turk allows three crowns a day to maintain him in his exile; but the most melancholy circumstance of all is, that she is turned horribly ugly." "Ugly or handsome," said Candide, "I am a man of honor; and, as such, am obliged to love her still. But how could she possibly have been reduced to so abject a condition, when I sent five or six millions to her by you?" "Lord bless me," said Cacambo, "was not I obliged to give two millions to Seignor Don Fernando d'Ibaraa y Figueora y Mascarenes y Lampourdos y Souza, the governor of Buenos Ayres, for liberty to take Miss Cunegund away with me? and then did not a brave fellow of a pirate gallantly strip us of all the rest? And then did not this same pirate carry us with him

---

[30]Francis Leopold Rakoczy, king of Transylvania in the eighteenth century.

to Cape Matapan, to Milo, to Nicaria, to Samos, to Petra, to the Dardanelles, to Marmora, to Scutari? Miss Cunegund and the old woman are now servants to the prince I have told you of; and I myself am slave to the dethroned sultan." "What a chain of shocking accidents!" exclaimed Candide. "But after all, I have still some diamonds left, with which I can easily procure Miss Cunegund's liberty. It is a pity though she is grown so ugly."

Then turning to Martin, "What think you, friend," said he, "whose condition is most to be pitied, the Emperor Achmet's, the Emperor Ivan's, King Charles Edward's, or mine?" "Faith, I cannot resolve your question," said Martin, "unless I had been in the breasts of you all." "Ah!" cried Candide, "was Pangloss here now, he would have known, and satisfied me at once." "I know not," said Martin, "in what balance your Pangloss could have weighed the misfortunes of mankind, and have set a just estimation on their sufferings. All that I pretend to know of the matter is that there are millions of men on the earth, whose conditions are a hundred times more pitiable than those of King Charles Edward, the Emperor Ivan, or Sultan Achmet." "Why, that may be," answered Candide.

In a few days they reached the Bosphorus; and the first thing Candide did was to pay a high ransom for Cacambo; then, without losing time, he and his companions went on board a galley, in order to search for his Cunegund on the banks of the Propontis, notwithstanding she was grown so ugly.

There were two slaves among the crew of the galley, who rowed very ill, and to whose bare backs the master of the vessel frequently applied a lash. Candide, from natural sympathy, looked at these two slaves more attentively than at any of the rest, and drew near them with an eye of pity. Their features, though greatly disfigured, appeared to him to bear a strong resemblance with those of Pangloss and the unhappy baron Jesuit, Miss Cunegund's brother. This idea affected him with grief and compassion: he examined them more attentively than before. "In troth," said he, turning to Martin, "if I had not seen my master Pangloss fairly hanged, and had not myself been unlucky enough to run the baron through the body, I should absolutely think those two rowers were the men."

No sooner had Candide uttered the names of the baron and Pangloss, than the two slaves gave a great cry, ceased rowing, and let fall their oars out of their hands. The master of the vessel, seeing this, ran up to them, and redoubled the discipline of the lash. "Hold, hold," cried Candide, "I will give you what money you shall ask for these two persons." "Good heavens! it is Candide," said one of the men. "Candide!" cried the other. "Do I dream," said Candide, "or am I awake? Am I actually on board this galley? Is this my lord baron, whom I killed? and that my master Pangloss, whom I saw hanged before my face?"

"It is I! it is I!" cried they both together. "What! is this your great philosopher?" said Martin. "My dear sir," said Candide to the master of the galley, "how much do you ask for the ransom of the baron of Thunder-ten-tronckh, who is one of the first barons of the empire, and of Mr. Pangloss, the most profound metaphysician in Germany?" "Why, then, Christian cur," replied the Turkish captain, "since these two dogs of Christian slaves are barons and metaphysicians, who no doubt are of high rank in their own country, thou shalt give me fifty thousand sequins." "You shall have them, sir; carry me back as quick as thought to Constantinople, and you shall receive the money immediately—No! carry me first to Miss Cunegund." The captain, upon Candide's first proposal, had already tacked about, and he made the crew ply their oars so effectually, that the vessel flew through the water, quicker than a bird cleaves the air.

Candide bestowed a thousand embraces on the baron and Pangloss. "And so then, my dear baron, I did not kill you? and you, my dear Pangloss, are come to life again after your hanging? But how came you slaves on board a Turkish galley?" "And is it true that my dear sister is in this country?" said the baron. "Yes," said Cacambo. "And do I once again behold my dear Candide?" said Pangloss. Candide presented Martin and Cacambo to them; they embraced each other, and all spoke together. The galley flew like lightning, and soon they were got back to port. Candide instantly sent for a Jew, to whom he sold for fifty thousand sequins a diamond richly worth one hundred thousand, though the fellow swore to him all the time by Father Abraham that he gave him the most he could possibly afford. He no sooner got the money into his hands, than he paid it down for the ransom of the baron and Pangloss. The latter flung himself at the feet of his deliverer, and bathed him with his tears: the former thanked him with a gracious nod, and promised to return him the money the first opportunity. "But is it possible," said he, "that my sister should be in Turkey?" "Nothing is more possible," answered Cacambo, "for she scours the dishes in the house of a Transylvanian prince." Candide sent directly for two Jews, and sold more diamonds to them; and then he set out with his companions in another galley, to deliver Miss Cunegund from slavery.

CHAPTER 28

What Befell Candide, Cunegund, Pangloss, Martin, etc.

"Pardon," said Candide to the baron; "once more let me entreat your pardon, reverend father, for running you through the body." "Say no more about it," replied the baron; "I was a little too hasty I must own; but as you seem to be desirous to know by what accident I came to be a slave on board the galley where you saw me, I will inform you. After I had been cured of the wound you gave me, by the college apothecary, I was attacked and carried off by a party of Spanish troops, who clapped me in prison in Buenos Ayres, at the very time my sister was setting out from there. I asked leave to return to Rome, to the general of my order, who appointed me chaplain to the French ambassador at Constantinople. I had not been a week in my new office, when I happened to meet one evening with a young Icoglan, extremely handsome and well made. The weather was very hot; the young man had an inclination to bathe. I took the opportunity to bathe likewise. I did not know it was a crime for a Christian to be found naked in company with a young Turk. A cadi ordered me to receive a hundred blows on the soles of my feet, and sent me to the galleys. I do not believe that there was ever an act of more flagrant injustice. But I would fain know how my sister came to be a scullion to a Transylvanian prince, who has taken refuge among the Turks?"

"But how happens it that I behold you again, my dear Pangloss?" said Candide. "It is true," answered Pangloss, "you saw me hanged, though I ought properly to have been burned; but you may remember, that it rained extremely hard when they were going to roast me. The storm was so violent that they found it impossible to light the fire; so they hanged me because they could do no better. A surgeon purchased my body, carried it home, and prepared to dissect me. He began by making a crucial incision from my navel to the clavicle. It is impossible for anyone to have been more lamely hanged than I had been. The executioner was a subdeacon, and knew how to burn people very well, but as for hanging, he was a novice at it, being quite out of practice; the cord being wet, and not slipping properly, the noose did not join. In short, I still continued to breathe; the crucial incision made me scream to such a degree, that my surgeon fell flat upon his back; and imagining it was the devil he was dissecting, ran away, and in his fright tumbled down stairs. His wife hearing the noise, flew from the next room, and seeing me stretched upon the table with my crucial incision, was still more terrified than her husband, and fell upon him. When they had a little recovered themselves, I heard her say to her husband, 'My dear, how could you think of dissecting a heretic? Don't you know that the devil is always in them? I'll run directly to a priest to come and drive the evil spirit out.' I trembled from head to foot at hearing her talk in this manner, and exerted what little strength I had left to cry out, 'Have mercy on me!' At length the Portuguese barber took courage, sewed up my wound, and his wife nursed me; and I was upon my legs in a fortnight's time. The barber got me a place to be lackey to a knight of Malta, who was going to Venice; but finding my master had no money to pay me my wages, I entered into the service of a Venetian merchant, and went with him to Constantinople.

"One day I happened to enter a mosque, where I saw no one but an old man and a very pretty young female devotee, who was telling her beads; her neck was quite bare, and in her bosom she had a beautiful nosegay of tulips, roses, anemones, ranunculuses, hyacinths, and auriculas; she let fall her nosegay. I ran immediately to take it up, and presented it to her with a most respectful bow. I was so long in delivering it that the imam began to be angry; and, perceiving I was a Christian, he cried out for help; they carried me before the cadi, who ordered me to receive one hundred bastinadoes, and sent me to the galleys. I was chained in the very galley and to the very same bench with the baron. On board the galley there were four young men belonging to Marseilles, five Neapolitan priests, and two monks of Corfu, who told us that the like adventures happened every day. The baron pretended that he had been worse used than myself; and I insisted that there was far less harm in taking up a nosegay, and putting it into a woman's bosom, than to be found stark naked with a young Icoglan. We were continually whipped, and received twenty lashes a day with a heavy thong, when the concatenation of sublunary events brought you on board our galley to ransom us from slavery."

"Well, my dear Pangloss," said Candide to him, "when you were hanged, dissected, whipped, and tugging at the oar, did you continue to think that everything in this world happens for the best?" "I have always abided by my first opinion," answered Pangloss; "for, after all, I am a philosopher, and it would not become me to retract my sentiments; especially as Leibnitz could not be in the wrong: and that pre-established harmony is the finest thing in the world, as well as a *plenum* and the *materia subtilis*."

CHAPTER 29

In What Manner Candide Found Miss Cunegund and the Old Woman Again

While Candide, the baron, Pangloss, Martin, and Cacambo, were relating their several adventures, and reasoning on the contingent or non-contingent events of this world; on causes and effects; on moral and physical evil; on free will and necessity; and on the consolation that may be felt by a person when a slave and chained to an oar in a Turkish galley, they arrived at the house of the Transylvanian prince on the coasts of the Propontis. The first objects they beheld there, were Miss Cunegund and the old woman, who were hanging some tablecloths on a line to dry.

The baron turned pale at the sight. Even the tender Candide, that affectionate lover, upon seeing his fair Cunegund all sunburnt, with blear eyes, a withered neck, wrinkled face and arms, all covered with a red scurf, started back with horror; but, recovering himself, he advanced towards her out of good manners. She embraced Candide and her brother; they embraced the old woman, and Candide ransomed them both.

There was a small farm in the neighborhood, which the old woman proposed to Candide to make shift with till the company should meet with a more favorable destiny. Cunegund, not knowing that she was grown ugly, as no one had informed her of it, reminded Candide of his promise in so peremptory a manner, that the simple lad did not dare to refuse her; he then acquainted the baron that he was going to marry his sister. "I will never suffer," said the baron, "my sister to be guilty of an action so derogatory to her birth and family; nor will I bear this insolence on your part: no, I never will be reproached that my nephews are not qualified for the first ecclesiastical dignities in Germany; nor shall a sister of mine ever be the wife of any person below the rank of a baron of the empire." Cunegund flung herself at her brother's feet, and bedewed them with her tears; but he still continued inflexible. "Thou foolish fellow," said Candide, "have I not delivered thee from the galleys, paid thy ransom, and thy sister's, too, who was a scullion, and is very ugly, and yet condescend to marry her? and shalt thou pretend to oppose the match! If I were to listen only to the dictates of my anger, I should kill thee again." "Thou mayest kill me again," said the baron; "but thou shalt not marry my sister while I am living."

CHAPTER 30

Conclusion

Candide had, in truth, no great inclination to marry Miss Cunegund; but the extreme impertinence of the baron determined him to conclude the match; and Cunegund pressed him so warmly, that he could not recant. He consulted Pangloss, Martin, and the faithful Cacambo. Pangloss composed a fine memorial, by which he proved that the baron had no right over his sister; and that she might, according to all the laws of the empire, marry Candide with the left hand. Martin concluded to throw the baron into the sea; Cacambo decided that he must be delivered to the Turkish captain and sent to the galleys; after which he should be conveyed by the first ship to the father-general at Rome. This advice was found to be good; the old woman approved of it, and not a syllable was said to his sister; the business was executed for a little money; and they had the pleasure of tricking a Jesuit, and punishing the pride of a German baron.

It was altogether natural to imagine, that after undergoing so many disasters, Candide, married to his mistress and living with the philosopher Pangloss, the philosopher Martin, the prudent Cacambo, and the old woman, having besides brought home so many diamonds from the country of the ancient Incas, would lead the most agreeable life in the world. But he had been so robbed by the Jews, that he had nothing left but his little farm; his wife, every day growing more and more ugly, became headstrong and insupportable; the old woman was infirm, and more ill-natured yet than Cunegund. Cacambo, who worked in the garden, and carried the produce of it to sell at Constantinople, was above his labor, and cursed his fate. Pangloss despaired of making a figure in any of the German universities. And as to Martin, he was firmly persuaded that a person is equally ill-situated everywhere. He took things with patience. Candide, Martin, and Pangloss, disputed sometimes about metaphysics and morality. Boats were often seen passing under the windows of the farm laden with effendis, bashaws, and cadis, that were going into banishment to Lemnos, Mytilene and Erzerum. And other cadis, bashaws, and effendis, were seen coming back to succeed the place of the exiles, and were driven out in their turns. They saw several heads curiously stuck upon poles, and carried as presents to the sublime porte. Such sights gave occasion to frequent dissertations; and when no disputes were in progress, the irksomeness was so excessive that the old woman ventured one day to tell them, "I would be glad to know which is worst, to be ravished a hundred times by negro pirates, to have one buttock cut off, to run the gauntlet among the Bulgarians, to be whipped and hanged at an *auto-da-fé*, to be dissected, to be chained to an oar in a galley; and, in short, to experience all the miseries through which every one of us hath passed, or to remain here doing nothing?" "This," said Candide, "is a grand question."

This discourse gave birth to new reflections, and Martin especially concluded that man was born to live in the convulsions of disquiet, or in the lethargy of idleness. Though Candide did not absolutely agree to this, yet he did not determine anything on that head. Pangloss avowed that he had undergone dreadful sufferings; but having once maintained that everything went on as well as possible, he still maintained it, and at the same time believed nothing of it.

There was one thing which more than ever confirmed Martin in his detestable principles, made Candide hesitate, and embarrassed Pangloss, which was the arrival of Pacquette and Brother Giroflée one day at their farm. This couple had been in the utmost distress; they had very speedily made away with their three thousand piastres; they had parted, been reconciled; quarrelled again, been thrown into prison; had made their escape, and at last Brother Giroflée had turned Turk. Pacquette still continued to follow her trade; but she got little or nothing by it. "I foresaw very well," said Martin to Candide, "that your presents would soon be squandered, and only make them more miserable. You and Cacambo have spent millions of piastres, and yet you are not more happy than Brother Giroflée and Pacquette." "Ah!" said Pangloss to Pacquette, "it is heaven that has brought you here among us, my poor child! Do you know that you have cost me the tip of my nose, one eye, and one ear? What a handsome shape is here! and what is this world!" This new adventure engaged them more deeply than ever in philosophical disputations.

In the neighborhood lived a famous dervish who passed for the best philosopher in Turkey; they went to consult him: Pangloss, who was their spokesman, addressed him thus: "Master, we come to entreat you to tell us why so strange an animal as man has been formed?"

"Why do you trouble your head about it?" said the dervish; "is it any business of yours?" "But, my reverend father," said Candide, "there is a horrible deal of evil on the earth." "What signifies it," said the dervish, "whether there is evil or good? When his highness sends a ship to Egypt does he trouble his head whether the rats in the vessel are at their ease or not?" "What must then be done?" said Pangloss. "Be silent," answered the dervish. "I flattered myself," replied Pangloss, "to have reasoned a little with you on the causes and effects, on the best of possible worlds, the origin of evil, the nature of the soul, and a pre-established harmony." At these words the dervish shut the door in their faces.

During this conversation, news was spread abroad that two viziers of the bench and the mufti had just been strangled at Constantinople, and several of their friends empaled. This catastrophe made a great noise for some hours. Pangloss, Candide, and Martin, as they were returning to the little farm, met with a good-looking old man, who was taking the air at his door, under an alcove formed of the boughs of orange-trees. Pangloss, who was as inquisitive as he was disputative, asked him what was the name of the mufti who was lately strangled. "I cannot tell," answered the good old man; "I never knew the name of any mufti, or vizier breathing. I am entirely ignorant of the event you speak of; I presume that in general such as are concerned in public affairs sometimes come to a miserable end; and that they deserve it: but I never inquire what is doing at Constantinople; I am contented with sending thither the produce of my garden, which I cultivate with my own hands." After saying these words, he invited the strangers to come into his house.

His two daughters and two sons presented them with divers sorts of sherbet of their own making; besides caymac, heightened with the peels of candied citrons, oranges, lemons, pineapples, pistachio nuts, and Mocha coffee unadulterated with the bad coffee of Batavia or the American islands. After which the two daughters of this good Mussulman perfumed the beards of Candide, Pangloss, and Martin.

"You must certainly have a vast estate," said Candide to the Turk; who replied, "I have no more than twenty acres of ground, the whole of which I cultivate myself with the help of my children; and our labor keeps off from us three great evils—idleness, vice, and want."

Candide, as he was returning home, made profound reflections on the Turk's discourse. "This good old man," said he to Pangloss and Martin, "appears to me to have chosen for himself a lot much preferable to that of the six kings with whom we had the honor to sup." "Human grandeur," said Pangloss, "is very dangerous, if we believe the testimonies of almost all philosophers; for we find Eglon, king of Moab, was assassinated by Aod; Absalom was hanged by the hair of his head, and run through with three darts; King Nadab, son of Jeroboam, was slain by Baaza; King Ela by Zimri; Okosias by Jehu; Athaliah by Jehoiada; the kings Jehooiakim, Jeconiah, and Zedekiah, were led into captivity: I need not tell you what was the fate of Crœsus, Astyages, Darius, Dionysius of Syracuse, Pyrrhus, Perseus, Hannibal, Jugurtha, Ariovistus, Cæsar, Pompey, Nero, Otho, Vitellius, Domitian, Richard II. of England, Edward II., Henry VI., Richard III., Mary Stuart, Charles I., the three Henrys of France, and the emperor Henry IV." "Neither need you tell me," said Candide, "that we must take care of our garden." "You are in the right," said Pangloss; "for when man was put into the garden of Eden, it was with an intent to dress it: and this proves that man was not born to be idle." "Work then without disputing," said Martin; "it is the only way to render life supportable."

The little society, one and all, entered into this laudable design; and set themselves to exert their different talents. The little piece of ground yielded them a plentiful crop. Cunegund indeed was very ugly, but she became an excellent hand at pastry-work; Pacquette embroidered; the old woman had the care of the linen. There was none, down to Brother Giroflée, but did some service; he was a very good carpenter, and became an honest man. Pangloss used now and then to say to Candide, "There is a concatenation of all events in the best of possible worlds; for, in short, had you not been kicked out of a fine castle for the love of Miss Cunegund; had you not been put into the Inquisition; had you not travelled over America on foot; had you not run the baron through the body; and had you not lost all your sheep, which you brought from the good country of El Dorado, you would not have been here to eat preserved citrons and pistachio nuts." "Excellently observed," answered Candide; "but let us take care of our garden."

JEAN-JACQUES ROUSSEAU
[1712–1778]

In an age of philosophical skepticism and critical inquiry, an age that searched the globe for universal principles that govern human nature, an age of the great *Encyclopédie* project that attempted to categorize and define everything that was known and everything that had recently been invented, it is perhaps surprising to recall that one of the most important figures of the age would be remembered for turning the attention of Europe to the neglected realm of human feeling. Often considered a precursor to, and certainly one of the greatest influences upon, the European romantic movement, Jean-Jacques Rousseau rediscovered (if not reinvented) the inner life for an era preoccupied with exterior accomplishments and achievements. The *Confessions*, written between 1765 and 1770 but posthumously published from 1781 to 1788, records his tortuous journey into the depths of his very being, his pilgrimage to the childhood origins of the self. For Lord Byron, the great English romantic poet, Rousseau was the "apostle of affliction" who "threw / Enchantment over passion, and from woe / Wrung overwhelming eloquence" (*Childe Harold* III, Canto 77). In a tribute to Rousseau in *The Triumph of Life*, another English poet, Percy Shelley, claims that Rousseau revived the Socratic doctrine of *gnothi seauton*, to know thyself, for an age of giants such as Voltaire and Napoleon who respectively could master the intellect or the world, but not the human heart. Madame de Staël, the great French woman of letters, writes that Rousseau "grew passionate through thinking." In recording these thoughts about sentiment and feeling, this watchmaker's son from Geneva exerted an influence on Western thought that still informs our discussions of art, literature, politics, society, and human nature.

LIFE

For a writer of such influence upon Western thought, the self-taught Rousseau had admirably humble beginnings, in keeping perhaps with the romantic doctrine of simplicity that his work helped to promote. He was born in Geneva in 1712, the son of Isaac Rousseau, a watchmaker who was exiled when Jean-Jacques was ten years old, and Susanne Bernard, who died a few days after his birth. His father introduced Jean-Jacques very early to contemporary novels and the classics gleaned from his home library, and to this reading Rousseau attributes the birth of his intensity of feeling: "In a short time I acquired . . . not only extreme facility in reading and understanding what I read, but a knowledge of the passions that was unique in a child of my age. I had no idea of things in themselves, although all the feelings of actual life were already known to me. I had conceived nothing, but felt everything." Upon Isaac's exile, father and son were separated and Jean-Jacques moved in with his uncle, who set him up as an engraver's apprentice. After three unhappy years, in March 1728 the young man rather impulsively left Geneva, beginning a brief period of vagabondage through Switzerland, Savoy, Italy, and France, taking up jobs ranging from footman to tutor.

Ending up eventually in Turin, Rousseau converted to Catholicism and moved in with thirty-year-old Madame de Warens, with whom he lived at Chambery and her country house at Les Charmettes until 1742. During these years Rousseau continued his self-education, keeping extensive notes on a wide range of subjects, including science, mathematics, astronomy, and music. In 1742 Rousseau left for Paris, where he found the patronage of Madame Dupin, among others; fell in love with Therese Levasseur (among others), a laundress whom he would eventually marry; met Diderot and d'Alembert, the editors of the *Encyclopédie*; and took up his writing with greater earnest. In 1750 he earned a prize from the Academy of Dijon for his *Discourse on the Sciences and Arts*, and began making a name for himself as the writer of plays and operas, especially *The Village Soothsayer,* performed first in 1752. The next decade saw from the pen of the "Citizen of Geneva," as he sometimes called himself, a succession of important philosophical treatises, works of criticism and fiction: *Discourse on Inequality* (1755), *Discourse on Political Economy* (1755), the *Letter to d'Alembert on Spectacles* (1758), *Julie, or the New Heloise* (1761), *The Social Contract* (1762), and *Émile* (1762). On June 9, 1762, the Parlement of Paris issued a warrant for Rousseau's arrest and ten days later the Advisory Council of Geneva burned and banned both *Émile* and *The Social Contract.* Rousseau's demand in these works for individual liberties, his indictment of government and European civilization for inevitably corrupting the innate goodness of human beings, and his ideas for political reform had exceeded the tolerance of those in power. As Rousseau wrote in the first sentence of *Émile*, "God makes all things good; man meddles with them and they become evil."

For the remainder of his life, Rousseau was, in his words, a *promeneur solitaire*—a solitary walker. His flight from Paris only began a pattern of persecution and expulsion that took him across Europe—from Motiers, a territory in Prussia, to the Isle of Saint-Pierre; back to Paris, where he assumed various aliases; to England upon the invitation of the philosopher David Hume; and finally back to Paris, where he was allowed to remain from 1770 until his death in 1778, even though the order for his arrest was not rescinded. In his last years he completed his autobiography and wrote the moving and troubled *Reveries of a Solitary Walker* (1782), in which he attempts to vindicate his life and work to posterity. The latter, in particular, is a record of the isolation and alienation brought on by years of persecution and hostile criticism. In a plaintive tone, he begins the *Reveries* with a lament that summarizes his experience at the hands of his contemporaries:

> The most sociable and loving of men has with one accord been cast out by all the rest. With all the ingenuity of hate they have sought out the cruellest torture for my sensitive soul, and have violently broken all the threads that bound me to them. I would have loved my fellow-men in spite of themselves. It was only by ceasing to be human that they could forfeit my affection. So now they are strangers and foreigners to me; they no longer exist for me, since such is their will. But I, detached as I am from them and from the whole world, what am I? This must now be the object of my inquiry.

WORK

Many of Rousseau's ideas have become a part of that intellectual and aesthetic complex we call romanticism, including his central concern for the individual, whose potentials and ideals may be tainted or stifled by social custom, his belief in the basic goodness of human beings, and the perfectibility or at least correctability of society by means of nonrestrictive methods of education (although his views on the education of women seem unworthy of his higher ideals). Rousseau's attention to the inner life of human beings, his celebration of childhood innocence, his contemplative communication with nature, and the high value he places on feeling anticipated and influenced European romantic writers who revolted against the empirical and materialist tendencies of mainstream Enlightenment thought and poetics. Hence writers such as Goethe, Madame de Staël, Chateaubriand, Wordsworth, Pushkin, Byron, and Proust followed Rousseau's footsteps along an inner path in search of a self that could transcend or escape from the constraints imposed upon it by the social bustle of the busy world.

Nonetheless, Rousseau is not without his critics, and for good reason. As Mary Wollstonecraft pointed out, Rousseau's ideals of virtue and principles of justice and egalitarianism were often compromised and contradicted in his own practices. In the words of her *A Vindication of the Rights of Woman,* in which she justly attacks Rousseau for his retrograde views on the education of women, "had Rousseau mounted one step higher in his investigation [of the principles of society], or could his eye have pierced through the foggy atmosphere which he almost disdained to breathe, his active mind would have darted forward to contemplate the perfection of man in the establishment of true civilization, instead of taking his ferocious flight back to the night of sensual ignorance." Samuel Johnson thought him a "bad man," and his work has been blamed for the transformation of manners in the sometimes affected "sensibility" of the late eighteenth century, as well as for the French Revolution. Even his detractors, however, acknowledge his genius and the value of his principles if not his earthbound practices. What is certain is that Rousseau's writings led him—and continue to lead us—on a sentimental journey to the very center of the human heart.

The *Confessions*

Rousseau attempted many times to answer the question he posed in the *Reveries*, "What am I?," but nowhere more exhaustively than in the *Confessions*, where he systematically reflects upon the origins of his own subjectivity. Madame de Staël may have summed up Rousseau's design for the *Confessions* best in her *Letters on Rousseau* (1788), where she speculates, "I think he wrote his memoirs to shine as a historian rather than as the hero of his story. He cared about the portrait rather than the face. He observed himself and painted himself as if he had been his own model: I am convinced that his primary wish was to make himself a good likeness." Appealing to the reader to trust his honesty, Rousseau presents himself in the opening paragraphs of his work as an impartial recorder of his life, leaving the judgment up to others: "I have shown myself as I was: mean and contemptible, good, highminded and sublime, according as I was one or the other. I have unveiled my inmost self even as Thou hast seen it, O Eternal Being. Gather round me the countless host of my fellow-men; let them hear my confessions, lament for my unworthiness, and blush for my imperfections."

Readers may be wary of taking Rousseau at his word, for not all critics agree with Madame de Staël about his honesty or verisimilitude. Indeed, it often seems that like Benjamin Franklin, Rousseau intends his portrait to draw the reader's sympathy for even his more egregious faults, of which there is no short supply in his history. More unabashedly, consistently, and explicitly than Franklin's *Autobiography*, the *Confessions* parades before its readers a succession of errors, misfortunes, and misdeeds. Ironically, perhaps, Rousseau presents these faults to show that he is at heart a man of virtue and sensitivity, that truth and goodness are woven into the very fabric of his being. So far as the actual details of incidents along his life's way, Rousseau admits to imprecision; but he argues that he is more at pains to present a record of his feelings than an account of events. At the beginning of Book 7, which opens Part II of the *Confessions*, Rousseau explains that his inner life is what concerns him most:

> I have only one faithful guide upon which I can depend; the chain of the feelings which have marked the development of my being, and which will remind me of the succession of events, which have been either the cause or the effect of these feelings. I find it easy to forget my misfortunes, but I cannot forget my faults, still less my virtuous feelings, the recollection of which is too precious ever to be effaced from my heart. I may omit or transpose facts, I may make mistakes in dates, but I cannot be deceived in regard to what I have felt or what my feelings have prompted me to do; and this is the chief subject under discussion. The real object of my Confessions is, to contribute to an accurate knowledge of my inner being in all the different situations of my life. What I have promised to relate, is the history of my soul; I need no other memoirs in order to write it faithfully; it is sufficient for me to enter again into my inner self as I have hitherto done.

Although many readers note a certain disingenuousness in the autobiography, Rousseau's *Confessions* introduced to the Age of Enlightenment the "man of feeling," a person who attempts to bring the mind into balance with the heart through self-reflection, acts of compassion, and an appreciation of the delicate interplay of emotion involved in human relationships. Yet, like Molière, Alexander Pope, Jonathan Swift, and other Enlightenment writers who satirize the affectation and hypocrisy of their age, Rousseau distinguishes between true feeling and artificial manners. A key concept in his work is *amour propre*, which designates the love of social approval. Governed by *amour propre*, a person loses touch with his or her true self, for his or her actions and manners are oriented toward winning the approval and respect of others. Thus, marking a transition between the Enlightenment and the age of romanticism, Rousseau seeks in the *Confessions* and other writings to achieve a kind of transparency of the self, to express the true rather than the false self. The *Confessions* in particular purport to be the "artless" record of the life and feelings of a man who was essentially honest and innately good, despite the faults and errors that clutter the course of his life. In this regard, Rousseau's *Confessions* may be usefully compared with St. Augustine's; but where Augustine attributes his essential goodness and salvation to the grace of God, Rousseau finds the source of his goodness in human nature itself.

SUGGESTED READINGS

Among the many biographies of Rousseau, the three most important are Maurice Cranston's *The Noble Savage: Jean-Jacques Rousseau* (1991), Jean Guehenno's *Jean-Jacques* (1948–1952), and Frances Winwar's *Jean-Jacques Rousseau: Conscience of an Era* (1961). For a useful general study of Rousseau's works consult Ronald Grimsley's *Jean-Jacques Rousseau* (1983); Judith Shklar focuses primarily upon the political and social treatises in *Men and Citizens: A Study of Rousseau's Social Theory* (1969); Jean Starobinski's *Jean-Jacques Rousseau: Transparency and Obstruction* (1971; trans. 1988) offers an intriguing analysis of Rousseau's attempt to find a means of true expression in the *Confessions* and the *Reveries*, among other works; Huntington Williams discusses the *Confessions* in his *Rousseau and Romantic Autobiography* (1983).

Confessions

Translator anonymous

BOOK 1

[1712–1719]

I am commencing an undertaking, hitherto without precedent, and which will never find an imitator. I desire to set before my fellows the likeness of a man in all the truth of nature, and that man will be myself.

Myself alone! I know the feelings of my heart, and I know men. I am not made like any of those I have seen; I venture to believe that I am not made like any of those who are in existence. If I am not better, at least I am different. Whether Nature has acted rightly or wrongly in destroying the mould in which she cast me, can only be decided after I have been read.

Let the trumpet of the Day of Judgment sound when it will, I will present myself before the Sovereign Judge with this book in my hand. I will say boldly: "This is what I have done, what I have thought, what I was. I have told the good and the bad with equal frankness. I have neither omitted anything bad, nor interpolated anything good. If I have occasionally made use of some immaterial embellishments, this has only been in order to fill a gap caused by lack of memory. I may have assumed the truth of that which I knew might have been true, never of that which I knew to be false. I have shown myself as I was: mean and contemptible, good, highminded and sublime, according as I was one or the other. I have unveiled my inmost self even as Thou hast seen it, O Eternal Being. Gather round me the countless host of my fellow-men; let them hear my confessions, lament for my unworthiness, and blush for my imperfections. Then let each of them in turn reveal, with the same frankness, the secrets of his heart at the foot of the Throne, and say, if he dare, *'I was better than that man!'*"

I was born at Geneva, in the year 1712, and was the son of Isaac Rousseau and Susanne Bernard, citizens. The distribution of a very moderate inheritance amongst fifteen children had reduced my father's portion almost to nothing; and his only means of livelihood was his trade of watchmaker, in which he was really very clever.

My mother, a daughter of the Protestant minister Bernard, was better off. She was clever and beautiful, and my father had found difficulty in obtaining her hand. Their affection for each other had commenced almost as soon as they were born. When only eight years old, they walked every evening upon the Treille;[1] at ten, they were inseparable. Sympathy and union of soul strengthened in them the feeling produced by intimacy. Both, naturally full of tender sensibility, only waited for the moment when they should find the same disposition in another—or, rather, this moment waited for them, and each abandoned his heart to the first which opened to receive it. Destiny, which appeared to oppose their passion, only encouraged it. The young lover, unable to obtain possession of his mistress, was consumed by grief. She advised him to travel, and endeavour to forget her. He travelled, but without result, and returned more in love than ever. He found her whom he loved still faithful and true. After this trial of affection, nothing was left for them but to love each other all their lives. This they swore to do, and Heaven blessed their oath.

Gabriel Bernard, my mother's brother, fell in love with one of my father's sisters, who only consented to accept the hand of the brother, on condition that her own brother married the sister. Love arranged everything, and the two marriages took place on the same day. Thus my uncle became the husband of my aunt, and their children were doubly my first cousins. At the end of a year, a child was born to both, after which they were again obliged to separate.

My uncle Bernard was an engineer. He took service in the Empire and in Hungary, under Prince Eugène.[2] He distinguished himself at the siege and battle of Belgrade. My father, after the birth of my only brother, set out for Constantinople, whither he was summoned to undertake the post of watchmaker to the Sultan. During his absence, my mother's beauty, intellect and talents gained for her the devotion of numerous admirers. M. de la Closure, the French Resident, was one of the most eager to offer his. His passion must have been great, for, thirty years later, I saw him greatly affected when speaking to me of her. To enable her to resist such advances, my mother had more than her virtue: she loved her husband tenderly. She pressed him to return; he left all, and returned. I was the unhappy fruit of this return. Ten months later I was born, a weak and ailing child; I cost my mother her life, and my birth was the first of my misfortunes.

I have never heard how my father bore this loss, but I know that he was inconsolable. He believed that he saw his wife again in me, without being able to forget that it was I who had robbed him of her; he never embraced me without my perceiving, by his sighs and the convulsive manner in which he clasped me to his breast, that a bitter regret was mingled with his caresses, which were on that account only the more tender. When he said to me, "Jean Jacques, let us talk of your mother," I used to answer, "Well, then, my father, we will weep!"—and this word alone was sufficient to move him to tears. "Ah!" said he, with a sigh, "give her back to me, console me for her loss, fill the void which she has left in my soul. Should I love you as I do, if you were only my son?" Forty years after he had lost her, he died in the arms of a second wife, but the name of the first was on his lips and her image at the bottom of his heart.

Such were the authors of my existence. Of all the gifts which Heaven had bestowed upon them, a sensitive heart is the only one they bequeathed to me; it had been the source of their happiness, but for me it proved the source of all the misfortunes of my life.

---

[1] A popular walk or promenade in Geneva.

[2] The Austrian empire; Eugène was an Austrian general who served in the wars against Turkey.

I was brought into the world in an almost dying condition; little hope was entertained of saving my life. I carried within me the germs of a complaint which the course of time has strengthened, and which at times allows me a respite only to make me suffer more cruelly in another manner. One of my father's sisters, an amiable and virtuous young woman, took such care of me that she saved my life. At this moment, while I am writing, she is still alive, at the age of eighty, nursing a husband younger than herself, but exhausted by excessive drinking. Dear aunt,[3] I forgive you for having preserved my life; and I deeply regret that, at the end of your days, I am unable to repay the tender care which you lavished upon me at the beginning of my own. My dear old nurse Jacqueline is also still alive, healthy and robust. The hands which opened my eyes at my birth will be able to close them for me at my death.

I felt before I thought: this is the common lot of humanity. I experienced it more than others. I do not know what I did until I was five or six years old. I do not know how I learned to read; I only remember my earliest reading, and the effect it had upon me; from that time I date my uninterrupted self-consciousness. My mother had left some romances behind her, which my father and I began to read after supper. At first it was only a question of practising me in reading by the aid of amusing books; but soon the interest became so lively, that we used to read in turns without stopping, and spent whole nights in this occupation. We were unable to leave off until the volume was finished. Sometimes, my father, hearing the swallows begin to twitter in the early morning, would say, quite ashamed, "Let us go to bed; I am more of a child than yourself."

In a short time I acquired, by this dangerous method, not only extreme facility in reading and understanding what I read, but a knowledge of the passions that was unique in a child of my age. I had no idea of things in themselves, although all the feelings of actual life were already known to me. I had conceived nothing, but felt everything. These confused emotions which I felt one after the other, certainly did not warp the reasoning powers which I did not as yet possess; but they shaped them in me of a peculiar stamp, and gave me odd and romantic notions of human life, of which experience and reflection have never been able wholly to cure me.

[1719–1723]

The romances came to an end in the summer of 1719. The following winter brought us something different. My mother's library being exhausted, we had recourse to the share of her father's which had fallen to us. Luckily, there were some good books in it; in fact, it could hardly have been otherwise, for the library had been collected by a minister, who was even a learned man according to the fashion of the day, and was at the same time a man of taste and intellect. The "History of the Empire and the Church," by Le Sueur; Bossuet's "Treatise upon Universal History"; Plutarch's "Lives of Famous Men"; Nani's "History of Venice"; Ovid's "Metamorphoses"; La Bruyère; Fontenelle's "Worlds"; his "Dialogues of the Dead"; and some volumes of Molière—all these were brought over into my father's room, and I read to him out of them while he worked. I conceived a taste for them that was rare and perhaps unique at my age. Plutarch, especially, became my favourite author. The pleasure I took in reading him over and over again cured me a little of my taste for romance, and I soon preferred Agesilaus, Brutus, and Aristides

---

[3]Madame Gonçeru, to whom Rousseau paid a small stipend.

to Orondates, Artamenes, and Juba.[4] This interesting reading, and the conversations between my father and myself to which it gave rise, formed in me the free and republican spirit, the proud and indomitable character unable to endure slavery or servitude, which has tormented me throughout my life in situations the least fitted to afford it scope. Unceasingly occupied with thoughts of Rome and Athens, living as it were amongst their great men, myself by birth the citizen of a republic and the son of a father whose patriotism was his strongest passion, I was fired by his example; I believed myself a Greek or a Roman; I lost my identity in that of the individual whose life I was reading; the recitals of the qualities of endurance and intrepidity which arrested my attention made my eyes glisten and strengthened my voice. One day, while I was relating the history of Scaevola[5] at table, those present were alarmed to see me come forward and hold my hand over a chafing-dish, to illustrate his action.

I had a brother seven years older than myself, who was learning my father's trade. The excessive affection which was lavished upon myself caused him to be somewhat neglected, which treatment I cannot approve of. His education felt the consequences of this neglect. He took to evil courses before he was old enough to be a regular profligate. He was put with another master, from whom he was continually running away, as he had done from home. I hardly ever saw him; I can scarcely say that I knew him; but I never ceased to love him tenderly, and he loved me as much as a vagabond can love anything. I remember that, on one occasion, when my father was chastising him harshly and in anger, I threw myself impetuously between them and embraced him closely. In this manner I covered his body with mine, and received the blows which were aimed at him; I so obstinately maintained my position that at last my father was obliged to leave off, being either disarmed by my cries and tears, or afraid of hurting me more than him. At last, my brother turned out so badly that he ran away and disappeared altogether. Sometime afterwards we heard that he was in Germany. He never once wrote to us. From that time nothing more has been heard of him, and thus I have remained an only son.

If this poor boy was carelessly brought up, this was not the case with his brother; the children of kings could not be more carefully looked after than I was during my early years—worshipped by all around me, and, which is far less common, treated as a beloved, never as a spoiled child. Till I left my father's house, I was never once allowed to run about the streets by myself with the other children; in my case no one ever had to satisfy or check any of those fantastic whims which are attributed to Nature, but are all in reality the result of education. I had the faults of my age: I was a chatterbox, a glutton, and, sometimes, a liar. I would have stolen fruits, bonbons, or eatables; but I have never found pleasure in doing harm or damage, in accusing others, or in tormenting poor dumb animals. I remember, however, that I once made water in a saucepan belonging to one of our neighbours, Madame Clot, while she was at church. I declare that, even now, the recollection of this makes me laugh, because Madame Clot, a good woman in other respects, was the most confirmed old grumbler I have ever known. Such is the brief and true story of all my childish offences.

How could I become wicked, when I had nothing but examples of gentleness before my eyes, and none around me but the best people in the world? My father, my aunt, my nurse, my relations, our friends, our neighbours, all who surrounded

---

[4]Agesilaus, Brutus, and Aristides appear in Plutarch's *Lives* (c. 100 C.E.); the last three are heroes from popular romances.

[5]The legendary Roman hero; when about to be executed for attempting to kill the Etruscan chief Lars Porsena, who was attacking Rome, Scaevola (which means "left-handed") held his right hand in fire to show his determination. The chief was so impressed that he withdrew his forces from Rome.

me, did not, it is true, obey me, but they loved me; and I loved them in return. My wishes were so little excited and so little opposed, that it did not occur to me to have any. I can swear that, until I served under a master, I never knew what a fancy was. Except during the time I spent in reading or writing in my father's company, or when my nurse took me for a walk, I was always with my aunt, sitting or standing by her side, watching her at her embroidery or listening to her singing; and I was content. Her cheerfulness, her gentleness and her pleasant face have stamped so deep and lively an impression on my mind that I can still see her manner, look, and attitude; I remember her affectionate language: I could describe what clothes she wore and how her head was dressed, not forgetting the two little curls of black hair on her temples, which she wore in accordance with the fashion of the time.

I am convinced that it is to her I owe the taste, or rather passion, for music, which only became fully developed in me a long time afterwards. She knew a prodigious number of tunes and songs which she used to sing in a very thin, gentle voice. This excellent woman's cheerfulness of soul banished dreaminess and melancholy from herself and all around her. The attraction which her singing possessed for me was so great, that not only have several of her songs always remained in my memory, but even now, when I have lost her, and as I grew older, many of them, totally forgotten since the days of my childhood, return to my mind with inexpressible charm. Would anyone believe that I, an old dotard, eaten up by cares and troubles, sometime find myself weeping like a child, when I mumble one of those little airs in a voice already broken and trembling? One of them, especially, has come back to me completely, as far as the tune is concerned; the second half of the words, however, has obstinately resisted all my efforts to recall it, although I have an indistinct recollection of the rhymes. Here is the beginning, and all that I can remember of the rest:

> Tircis, I dare not listen
> To your pipe
> Under the elm;
> For already in our village
> People have begun to talk.
>
> . . . to engage
> . . . with a shepherd
> . . . without danger
> And always the thorn is with the rose.[6]

I ask, where is the affecting charm which my heart finds in this song? it is a whim, which I am quite unable to understand; but, be that as it may, it is absolutely impossible for me to sing it through without being interrupted by my tears. I have intended, times without number, to write to Paris to make inquiries concerning the remainder of the words, in case anyone should happen to know them; but I am almost certain that the pleasure which I feel in recalling the air would partly disappear, if it should be proved that others besides my poor aunt Susan have sung it.

Such were my earliest emotions on my entry into life; thus began to form or display itself in me that heart at once so proud and tender, that character so effeminate but yet indomitable, which, ever wavering between timidity and courage, weakness and self-control, has throughout my life made me inconsistent, and has caused abstinence and enjoyment, pleasure and prudence equally to elude my grasp.

This course of education was interrupted by an accident, the consequences of which have exercised an influence upon the remainder of my life. My father had

---

[6]Rousseau's text deliberately leaves out the sixth line of this popular song: "It is dangerous for a heart."

a quarrel with a captain in the French army, named Gautier, who was connected with some of the members of the Common Council. This Gautier, a cowardly and insolent fellow (whose nose happened to bleed during the affray), in order to avenge himself, accused my father of having drawn his sword within the city walls. My father, whom they wanted to send to prison, persisted that, in accordance with the law, the accuser ought to be imprisoned as well as himself. Being unable to have his way in this, he preferred to quit Geneva and expatriate himself for the rest of his life, than to give way on a point in which honour and liberty appeared to him to be compromised.

I remained under the care of my uncle Bernard, who was at the time employed upon the fortifications of Geneva. His eldest daughter was dead, but he had a son of the same age as myself. We were sent together to Bossey,[7] to board with the Protestant minister Lambercier, in order to learn, together with Latin, all the sorry trash which is included under the name of education.

Two years spent in the village in some degree softened my Roman roughness and made me a child again. At Geneva, where no tasks were imposed upon me, I loved reading and study, which were almost my only amusements; at Bossey, my tasks made me love the games which formed a break in them. The country was so new to me, that my enjoyment of it never palled. I conceived so lively an affection for it, that it has never since died out. The remembrance of the happy days I have spent there filled me with regretful longing for its pleasures, at all periods of my life, until the day which has brought me back to it. M. Lambercier was a very intelligent person, who, without neglecting our education, never imposed excessive tasks upon us. The fact that, in spite of my dislike of restraint, I have never recalled my hours of study with any feeling of disgust—and also that, even if I did not learn much from him, I learnt without difficulty what I did learn and never forgot it—is sufficient proof that his system of instruction was a good one.

The simplicity of this country life was of inestimable value to me, in that it opened my heart to friendship. Up to that time I had only known lofty but imaginary sentiments. The habit of living peacefully together with my cousin Bernard drew us together in tender bonds of union. In a short time, my feelings towards him became more affectionate than those with which I had regarded my brother, and they have never been effaced. He was a tall, lanky, weakly boy, as gentle in disposition as he was feeble in body, who never abused the preference which was shown to him in the house as the son of my guardian. Our tasks, our amusements, our tastes were the same: we were alone, we were of the same age, each of us needed a companion: separation was to us, in a manner, annihilation. Although we had few opportunities of proving our mutual attachment, it was very great; not only were we unable to live an instant apart, but we did not imagine it possible that we could ever be separated. Being, both of us, ready to yield to tenderness, and docile, provided compulsion was not used, we always agreed in everything. If, in the presence of those who looked after us, he had some advantage over me in consequence of the favour with which they regarded him, when we were alone I had an advantage over him which restored the equilibrium. When we were saying our lessons, I prompted him if he hesitated; when I had finished my exercise, I helped him with his; and in our amusements, my more active mind always led the way. In short, our two characters harmonised so well, and the friendship which united us was so sincere, that, in the five years and more, during which, whether at Bossey or Geneva, we were almost inseparable, although I confess that we often fought, it was never necessary

---

[7] A village three miles from Geneva.

to separate us, none of our quarrels ever lasted longer than a quarter of an hour, and neither of us ever made any accusation against the other. These observations are, if you will, childish, but they furnish an example which, since the time that there have been children, is perhaps unique.

The life which I led at Bossey suited me so well that, had it only lasted longer, it would have completely decided my character. Tender, affectionate and gentle feelings formed its foundation. I believe that no individual of our species was naturally more free from vanity than myself. I raised myself by fits and starts to lofty flights, but immediately fell down again into my natural languor. My liveliest desire was to be loved by all who came near me. I was of a gentle disposition; my cousin and our guardians were the same. During two whole years I was neither the witness nor the victim of any violent feeling. Everything nourished in my heart those tendencies which it received from Nature. I knew no higher happiness than to see all the world satisfied with me and with everything. I shall never forget how, if I happened to hesitate when saying my catechism in church, nothing troubled me more than to observe signs of restlessness and dissatisfaction on Mademoiselle Lambercier's face. That alone troubled me more than the disgrace of failing in public, which, nevertheless, affected me greatly: for, although little susceptible to praise, I felt shame keenly; and I may say here that the thought of Mademoiselle's reproaches caused me less uneasiness than the fear of offending her.

When it was necessary, however, neither she nor her brother were wanting in severity; but, since this severity was nearly always just, and never passionate, it pained me without making me insubordinate. Failure to please grieved me more than punishment, and signs of dissatisfaction hurt me more than corporal chastisement. It is somewhat embarrassing to explain myself more clearly, but, nevertheless, I must do so. How differently would one deal with youth, if one could more clearly see the remote effects of the usual method of treatment, which is employed always without discrimination, frequently without discretion! The important lesson which may be drawn from an example as common as it is fatal makes me decide to mention it.

As Mademoiselle Lambercier had the affection of a mother for us, she also exercised the authority of one, and sometimes carried it so far as to inflict upon us the punishment of children when we had deserved it. For some time she was content with threats, and this threat of a punishment that was quite new to me appeared very terrible; but, after it had been carried out, I found the reality less terrible than the expectation; and, what was still more strange, this chastisement made me still more devoted to her who had inflicted it. It needed all the strength of this devotion and all my natural docility to keep myself from doing something which would have deservedly brought upon me a repetition of it; for I had found in the pain, even in the disgrace, a mixture of sensuality which had left me less afraid than desirous of experiencing it again from the same hand. No doubt some precocious sexual instinct was mingled with this feeling, for the same chastisement inflicted by her brother would not have seemed to me at all pleasant. But, considering his disposition, there was little cause to fear the substitution; and if I kept myself from deserving punishment, it was solely for fear of displeasing Mademoiselle Lambercier; for, so great is the power exercised over me by kindness, even by that which is due to the senses, that it has always controlled the latter in my heart.

The repetition of the offence, which I avoided without being afraid of it, occurred without any fault of mine, that is to say, of my will, and I may say that I profited by it without any qualm of conscience. But this second time was also the last; for Mademoiselle Lambercier, who had no doubt noticed something which convinced her that the punishment did not have the desired effect, declared that it tired her too much, and that she would abandon it. Until then we had slept in her room, sometimes even in her bed during the winter. Two days afterwards we were put to sleep in another room, and from that time I had the honour, which I would gladly have dispensed with, of being treated by her as a big boy.

Who would believe that this childish punishment, inflicted upon me when only eight years old by a young woman of thirty, disposed of my tastes, my desires, my passions, and my own self for the remainder of my life, and that in a manner exactly contrary to that which should have been the natural result? When my feelings were once inflamed, my desires so went astray that, limited to what I had already felt, they did not trouble themselves to look for anything else. In spite of my hot blood, which has been inflamed with sensuality almost from my birth, I kept myself free from every taint until the age when the coldest and most sluggish temperaments begin to develop. In torments for a long time, without knowing why, I devoured with burning glances all the pretty women I met; my imagination unceasingly recalled them to me, only to make use of them in my own fashion, and to make of them so many Mlles. Lambercier.

Even after I had reached years of maturity, this curious taste, always abiding with me and carried to depravity and even frenzy, preserved my morality, which it might naturally have been expected to destroy. If ever a bringing-up was chaste and modest, assuredly mine was. My three aunts were not only models of propriety, but reserved to a degree which has long since been unknown amongst women. My father, a man of pleasure, but a gallant of the old school, never said a word, even in the presence of women whom he loved more than others, which would have brought a blush to a maiden's cheek; and the respect due to children has never been so much insisted upon as in my family and in my presence. In this respect I found M. Lambercier equally careful; and an excellent servant was dismissed for having used a somewhat too free expression in our presence. Until I was a young man, I not only had no distinct idea of the union of the sexes, but the confused notion which I had regarding it never presented itself to me except in a hateful and disgusting form. For common prostitutes I felt a loathing which has never been effaced: the sight of a profligate always filled me with contempt, even with affright. My horror of debauchery became thus pronounced ever since the day when, walking to Little Sacconex[8] by a hollow way, I saw on both sides holes in the ground, where I was told that these creatures carried on their intercourse. The thought of the one always brought back to my mind the copulation of dogs, and the bare recollection was sufficient to disgust me.

This tendency of my bringing-up, in itself adapted to delay the first outbreaks of an inflammable temperament, was assisted, as I have already said, by the direction which the first indications of sensuality took in my case. Only busying my imagination with what I had actually felt, in spite of most uncomfortable effervescence of blood, I only knew how to turn my desires in the direction of that kind of pleasure with which I was acquainted, without ever going as far as that which had been made hateful to me, and which, without my having the least suspicion of it, was so closely related to the other. In my foolish fancies, in my erotic frenzies, in the extravagant acts to which they sometimes led me, I had recourse in my imagination to the assistance of the other sex, without ever thinking that it was serviceable for any purpose than that for which I was burning to make use of it.

In this manner, then, in spite of an ardent, lascivious and precocious temperament, I passed the age of puberty without desiring, even without knowing of any other

---

[8] A village near Geneva.

sensual pleasures than those of which Mademoiselle Lambercier had most innocently given me the idea; and when, in course of time, I became a man, that which should have destroyed me again preserved me. My old childish taste, instead of disappearing, became so associated with the other, that I could never banish it from the desires kindled by my senses; and this madness, joined to my natural shyness, has always made me very unenterprising with women, for want of courage to say all or power to do all. The kind of enjoyment, of which the other was only for me the final consummation, could neither be appropriated by him who longed for it, nor guessed by her who was able to bestow it. Thus I have spent my life in idle longing, without saying a word, in the presence of those whom I loved most. Too bashful to declare my taste, I at least satisfied it in situations which had reference to it and kept up the idea of it. To lie at the feet of an imperious mistress, to obey her commands, to ask her forgiveness—this was for me a sweet enjoyment; and, the more my lively imagination heated my blood, the more I presented the appearance of a bashful lover. It may be easily imagined that this manner of making love does not lead to very speedy results, and is not very dangerous to the virtue of those who are its object. For this reason I have rarely possessed, but have none the less enjoyed myself in my own way—that is to say, in imagination. Thus it has happened that my senses, in harmony with my timid disposition and my romantic spirit, have kept my sentiments pure and my morals blameless, owing to the very tastes which, combined with a little more impudence, might have plunged me into the most brutal sensuality.

I have taken the first and most difficult step in the dark and dirty labyrinth of my confessions. It is easier to admit that which is criminal than that which is ridiculous and makes a man feel ashamed. Henceforth I am sure of myself; after having ventured to say so much, I can shrink from nothing. One may judge what such confessions have cost me, from the fact that, during the whole course of my life, I have never dared to declare my folly to those whom I loved with the frenzy of a passion which deprived me of sight and hearing, which robbed me of my senses and caused me to tremble all over with a convulsive movement. I have never brought myself, even when on most intimate terms, to ask women to grant me the only favour of all which was wanting. This never happened to me but once—in my childhood, with a girl of my own age; even then, it was she who first proposed it.

While thus going back to the first traces of my inner life, I find elements which sometimes appear incompatible, and yet have united in order to produce with vigour a simple and uniform effect; and I find others which, although apparently the same, have formed combinations so different, owing to the co-operation of certain circumstances, that one would never imagine that these elements were in any way connected. Who, for instance, would believe that one of the most powerful movements of my soul was tempered in the same spring from which a stream of sensuality and effeminacy has entered my blood? Without leaving the subject of which I have just spoken, I shall produce by means of it a very different impression.

One day I was learning my lesson by myself in the room next to the kitchen. The servant had put Mademoiselle Lambercier's combs in front of the fire-place to dry. When she came back to fetch them, she found one with a whole row of teeth broken. Who was to blame for the damage? No one except myself had entered the room. On being questioned, I denied that I had touched the comb. M. and Mademoiselle Lambercier both began to admonish, to press, and to threaten me; I obstinately persisted in my denial; but the evidence was too strong, and outweighed all my protestations, although it was the first time that I had been found to lie so boldly. The matter was regarded as serious, as in fact it deserved to be. The mischievousness, the falsehood, the obstinacy appeared equally deserving of punishment; but this time it was not by Mademoiselle Lambercier that chastisement was inflicted. My uncle Bernard was written to, and he came. My poor cousin was accused of another equally grave offence; we were involved in the same punishment. It was terrible. Had they wished to look for the remedy in the evil itself and to deaden for ever my depraved senses, they could not have set to work better, and for a long time my senses left me undisturbed.

They could not draw from me the desired confession. Although I was several times brought up before them and reduced to a pitiable condition, I remained unshaken. I would have endured death, and made up my mind to do so. Force was obliged to yield to the diabolical obstinacy of a child—as they called my firmness. At last I emerged from this cruel trial, utterly broken, but triumphant.

It is now nearly fifty years since this incident took place, and I have no fear of being punished again for the same thing. Well, then, I declare in the sight of heaven that I was innocent of the offence, that I neither broke nor touched the comb, that I never went near the fire-place, and had never even thought of doing so. It would be useless to ask me how the damage was done: I do not know, and I cannot understand; all that I know for certain is, that I had nothing to do with it.

Imagine a child, shy and obedient in ordinary life, but fiery, proud, and unruly in his passions: a child who had always been led by the voice of reason and always treated with gentleness, justice, and consideration, who had not even a notion of injustice, and who for the first time becomes acquainted with so terrible an example of it on the part of the very people whom he most loves and respects! What an upset of ideas! what a disturbance of feelings! what revolution in his heart, in his brain, in the whole of his little intellectual and moral being! Imagine all this, I say, if possible. As for myself, I feel incapable of disentangling and following up the least trace of what then took place within me.

I had not yet sense enough to feel how much appearances were against me, and to put myself in the place of the others. I kept to my own place, and all that I felt was the harshness of a frightful punishment for an offence which I had not committed. The bodily pain, although severe, I felt but little: all I felt was indignation, rage, despair. My cousin, whose case was almost the same, and who had been punished for an involuntary mistake as if it had been a premeditated act, following my example, flew into a rage, and worked himself up to the same pitch of excitement as myself. Both in the same bed, we embraced each other with convulsive transports: we felt suffocated; and when at length our young hearts, somewhat relieved, were able to vent their wrath, we sat upright in bed and began to shout, times without number, with all our might: *Carnifex! carnifex! carnifex!*[9]

While I write these words, I feel that my pulse beats faster; those moments will always be present to me though I should live a hundred thousand years. That first feeling of violence and injustice has remained so deeply graven on my soul, that all the ideas connected with it bring back to me my first emotion; and this feeling, which, in its origin, had reference only to myself, has become so strong in itself and so completely detached from all personal interest, that, when I see or hear of any act of injustice—whoever is the victim of it, and wherever it is committed—my heart kindles with rage, as if the effect of it recoiled upon myself. When I read of the cruelties of a ferocious tyrant, the crafty atrocities of a rascally priest, I would gladly set out to plunge a dagger into the heart of such wretches, although I had to die for it a hundred times. I have often put myself in a perspiration, pursuing or stoning a cock, a cow, a dog, or any animal which I saw tormenting another merely because

---

[9]Executioner or torturer (Latin).

it felt itself the stronger. This impulse may be natural to me, and I believe that it is; but the profound impression left upon me by the first injustice I suffered was too long and too strongly connected with it, not to have greatly strengthened it.

With the above incident the tranquillity of my childish life was over. From that moment I ceased to enjoy a pure happiness, and even at the present day I feel that the recollection of the charms of my childhood ceases there. We remained a few months longer at Bossey. We were there, as the first man is represented to us—still in the earthly paradise, but we no longer enjoyed it; in appearance our condition was the same, in reality it was quite a different manner of existence. Attachment, respect, intimacy, and confidence no longer united pupils and guides: we no longer regarded them as gods, who were able to read in our hearts; we became less ashamed of doing wrong and more afraid of being accused; we began to dissemble, to be insubordinate, to lie. All the vices of our age corrupted our innocence and threw a veil of ugliness over our amusements. Even the country lost in our eyes that charm of gentleness and simplicity which goes to the heart. It appeared to us lonely and sombre: it seemed as it were covered with a veil which concealed its beauties from our eyes. We ceased to cultivate our little gardens, our plants, our flowers. We no longer scratched up the ground gently, or cried with joy when we saw the seed which we had sown beginning to sprout. We were disgusted with the life, and others were disgusted with us; my uncle took us away, and we separated from M. and Mademoiselle Lambercier, having had enough of each other, and feeling but little regret at the separation.

Nearly thirty years have passed since I left Bossey, without my recalling to mind my stay there with any connected and pleasurable recollections; but, now that I have passed the prime of life and am approaching old age, I feel these same recollections springing up again while others disappear; they stamp themselves upon my memory with features, the charm and strength of which increase daily, as if, feeling life already slipping away, I were endeavouring to grasp it again by its commencement. The most trifling incidents of that time please me, simply because they belong to that period. I remember all the details of place, persons, and time. I see the maid or the manservant busy in the room, a swallow darting through the window, a fly settling on my hand while I was saying my lesson: I see the whole arrangement of the room in which we used to live; M. Lambercier's study on the right, a copperplate engraving of all the Popes, a barometer, a large almanack hanging on the wall, the raspberry bushes which, growing in a garden situated on very high ground facing the back of the house, shaded the window and sometimes forced their way through it. I am quite aware that the reader does not want to know all this; but I am bound to tell him. Why have I not the courage to relate to him in like manner all the trifling anecdotes of that happy time, which still make me tremble with joy when I recall them? Five or six in particular—but let us make a bargain. I will let you off five, but I wish to tell you one, only one, provided that you will permit me to tell it in as much detail as possible, in order to prolong my enjoyment.

If I only had your pleasure in view, I might choose the story of Mademoiselle Lambercier's backside, which, owing to an unfortunate somersault at the bottom of the meadow, was exhibited in full view to the King of Sardinia, who happened to be passing by; but that of the walnut-tree on the terrace is more amusing for me who took an active part in it, whereas I was merely a spectator of the somersault; besides, I declare that I found absolutely nothing to laugh at in an accident which, although comic in itself, alarmed me for the safety of a person whom I loved as a mother and, perhaps, even more.

Now, O curious readers of the important history of the walnut-tree on the terrace, listen to the horrible tragedy, and keep from shuddering if you can!

Outside the gate of the court, on the left of the entrance, there was a terrace, where we often went to sit in the afternoon. As it was entirely unprotected from the sun, M. Lambercier had a walnut-tree planted there. The process of planting was carried out with the greatest solemnity. The two boarders were its godfathers; and, while the hole was being filled up, we each of us held the tree with one hand and sang songs of triumph. In order to water it, a kind of basin was made round the foot. Every day, eager spectators of this watering, my cousin and I became more strongly convinced, as was natural, that it was a finer thing to plant a tree on a terrace than a flag upon a breach, and we resolved to win this glory for ourselves without sharing it with anyone.

With this object, we proceeded to cut a slip from a young willow, and planted it on the terrace, at a distance of about eight or ten feet from the august walnut-tree. We did not forget to dig a similar trench round our tree; the difficulty was how to fill it, for the water came from some distance, and we were not allowed to run and fetch it. However, it was absolutely necessary to have some for our willow. For a few days, we had recourse to all kinds of devices to get some, and we succeeded so well that we saw it bud and put forth little leaves, the growth of which we measured every hour, convinced that, although not yet a foot high, it would soon afford us a shade.

As our tree so completely claimed our attention that we were quite incapable of attending to or learning anything else, and were in a sort of delirium: as our guardians, not knowing what was the matter with us, kept a tighter hand upon us, we saw the fatal moment approaching when we should be without water, and were inconsolable at the thought of seeing our tree perish from drought. At length necessity, the mother of invention, suggested to us how to save ourselves from grief and the tree from certain death; this was, to make a channel underground, which should secretly conduct part of the water intended for the walnut-tree to our willow. This undertaking was at first unsuccessful, in spite of the eagerness with which it was carried out. We had made the incline so clumsily that the water did not run at all. The earth fell in and stopped up the channel; the entrance was filled with mud; everything went wrong. But nothing disheartened us: *Labor omnia vincit improbus.*[10] We dug our basin deeper, in order to allow the water to run; we cut some bottoms of boxes into small narrow planks, some of which were laid flat, one after the other, and others set up on both sides of these at an angle, thus forming a triangular canal for our conduit. At the entrance we stuck small pieces of wood, some little distance apart, which, forming a kind of grating or lattice-work, kept back the mud and stones, without stopping the passage of the water. We carefully covered our work with well-trodden earth; and when all was ready, we awaited, in the greatest excitement of hope and fear, the time of watering. After centuries of waiting, the hour at length arrived; M. Lambercier came as usual to assist at the operation, during which we both kept behind him, in order to conceal our tree, to which very luckily he turned his back.

No sooner had the first pail of water been poured out, than we saw some of it running into our basin. At this sight, our prudence deserted us: we began to utter cries of joy which made M. Lambercier turn round; this was a pity, for he took great delight in seeing how good the soil of the walnut-tree was, and how greedily it absorbed the water. Astonished at seeing it distribute itself into two basins, he cried out in his turn, looked, perceived the trick, ordered a pickaxe to be brought, and, with one blow, broke off two or three pieces from our planks; then, crying

---

[10]"Tenacious work overcomes all difficulties" (Virgil, *Georgics* I).

loudly, "An aqueduct, an aqueduct!" he dealt merciless blows in every direction, each of which went straight to our hearts. In a moment planks, conduit, basin, willow, everything was destroyed and uprooted, without his having uttered a single word, during this terrible work of destruction, except the exclamation which he incessantly repeated. "An aqueduct!" he cried, while demolishing everything, "an aqueduct, an aqueduct!"

It will naturally be imagined that the adventure turned out badly for the little architects: that would be a mistake: it was all over. M. Lambercier never uttered a single word of reproach, or looked upon us with displeasure, and said nothing more about it; shortly afterwards, we even heard him laughing loudly with his sister, for his laughter could be heard a long way off; and what was still more astonishing, when the first fright was over, we ourselves were not much troubled about the matter. We planted another tree somewhere else, and often reminded ourselves of the disaster that overtook the first, by repeating with emphasis, "An aqueduct, an aqueduct!" Hitherto I had had intermittent attacks of pride, when I was Aristides or Brutus; then it was that I felt the first well-defined promptings of vanity. To have been able to construct an aqueduct with our own hands, to have put a cutting in competition with a large tree, appeared to me the height of glory. At ten years of age I was a better judge on this point than Cæsar at thirty.

The thought of this walnut-tree and the little history connected with it has remained so vivid in my memory, or returned to it, that one of the plans which gave me the greatest pleasure, on my journey to Geneva, in 1754, was to go to Bossey and revisit the memorials of my boyish amusements, above all, the dear walnut-tree, which by that time must have been a third of a century old; but I was so continually occupied, so little my own master, that I could never find the moment to afford myself this satisfaction. There is little prospect of the opportunity ever occurring again; yet the wish has not disappeared with the hope; and I am almost certain that, if ever I should return to those beloved spots and find my dear walnut-tree still alive, I should water it with my tears.

After my return to Geneva, I lived for two or three years[11] with my uncle, waiting until my friends had decided what was to be done with me. As he intended his own son to be an engineer, he made him learn a little drawing and taught him the elements of Euclid.[12] I learned these subjects together with him, and acquired a taste for them, especially for drawing. In the meantime, it was debated whether I should be a watchmaker, an attorney, or a minister. My own preference was for the last, for preaching seemed to me to be a very fine thing; but the small income from my mother's property, which had to be divided between my brother and myself, was not sufficient to allow me to prosecute my studies. As, considering my age at that time, there was no immediate need to decide, I remained for the present with my uncle, making little use of my time and, in addition, as was only fair, paying a tolerably large sum for my board. My uncle, a man of pleasure like my father, was unable, like him, to tie himself down to his duties, and troubled himself little enough about us. My aunt was somewhat of a pietist, and preferred to sing psalms rather than attend to our education. We were allowed almost absolute freedom, which we never abused. Always inseparable, we were quite contented with our own society; and, having no temptation to make companions of the street boys of our own age, we learned none of the dissolute habits into which idleness might have led us. I am

---

[11]Rousseau actually lived with his uncle for less than a year; this is only one of the many details in the autobiography that are inaccurate.

[12]Third-century Greek mathematician, whose *Elements* established many of the principles of geometry.

even wrong in saying that we were idle, for we were never less so in our lives; and the most fortunate thing was, that all the ways of amusing ourselves, with which we successively became infatuated, kept us together busy in the house, without our being even tempted to go out into the street. We made cages, flutes, shuttlecocks, drums, houses, squirts, and cross-bows. We spoilt my good old grandfather's tools in trying to make watches as he did. We had a special taste for wasting paper, drawing, painting in water-colours, illuminating, and spoiling colours. An Italian showman, named Gamba-Corta, came to Geneva; we went to see him once and never wanted to go again. But he had a marionette-show, and we proceeded to make marionettes; his marionettes played comedies and we composed comedies for ours. For want of a squeaker, we imitated Punch's voice in our throat, in order to play the charming comedies, which our poor and kind relations had the patience to sit and listen to. But, my uncle Bernard having one day read aloud in the family circle a very fine sermon which he had composed himself, we abandoned comedy and began to write sermons. These details are not very interesting, I confess, but they show how exceedingly well-conducted our early education must have been, seeing that we, almost masters of our time and ourselves at so tender an age, were so little tempted to abuse our opportunities. We had so little need of making companions, that we even neglected the chances of doing so. When we went for a walk, we looked at their amusements as we passed by without the slightest desire, or even the idea of taking part in them. Our friendship so completely filled our hearts, that it was enough for us to be together to make the simplest amusements a delight.

Being thus inseparable, we began to attract attention: the more so as, my cousin being very tall while I was very short, we made an oddly-assorted couple. His long, slim figure, his little face like a boiled apple, his gentle manner, and his slovenly walk excited the children's ridicule. In the *patois* of the district he was nicknamed Barna Bredanna,[13] and, directly we went out, we heard nothing but "Barna Bredanna!" all round us. He endured it more quietly than I did: I lost my temper and wanted to fight. This was just what the little rascals desired. I fought and was beaten. My poor cousin helped me as well as he could; but he was weak, and a single blow of the fist knocked him down. Then I became furious. However, although I received blows in abundance, I was not the real object of attack, but Barna Bredanna; but my obstinate anger made matters so much worse, that, in future, we only ventured to go out during school-hours, for fear of being hooted and followed.

Behold me already a redresser of wrongs! In order to be a regular Paladin[14] I only wanted a lady; I had two. From time to time I went to see my father at Nyon, a little town in the Vaud country, where he had settled. He was very much liked, and his son felt the effects of his popularity. During the short time I stayed with him, friends vied with each other in making me welcome. A certain Madame de Vulson, especially, bestowed a thousand caresses upon me, and, to crown all, her daughter took me for her lover. It is easy to understand the meaning of a lover eleven years old for a girl of twenty-two. But all these roguish young women are so ready to put little puppets in front in order to hide larger ones, or to tempt them with the idea of an amusement which they know how to render attractive! As for myself, I saw no incongruity between us and took the matter seriously; I abandoned myself with all my heart, or rather with all my head—for it was only in that part of me that I was in love, although madly—and my transports, excitement and frenzy produced scenes enough to make anyone split his sides with laughing.

---

[13] A "bridled donkey."

[14] A chivalric hero from the twelfth-century *Song of Roland*.

I am acquainted with two very distinct and very real kinds of love, which have scarcely anything in common, although both are very fervent, and which both differ from tender friendship. The whole course of my life has been divided between these two kinds of love, essentially so different, and I have even felt them both at the same time; for instance, at the time of which I am speaking, while I took possession of Mademoiselle de Vulson so openly and so tyrannically that I could not endure that any man should approach her, I had several meetings, brief but lively, with a certain little Mademoiselle Goton, in which she deigned to play the schoolmistress, and that was all; but this all, which was really all for me, seemed to me the height of happiness; and, already feeling the value of the mystery, although I only knew how to make use of it as a child, I paid Mademoiselle de Vulson, who had scarcely any suspicion of it, in the same coin, for the assiduity with which she made use of me to conceal other amours. But, to my great regret, my secret was discovered, or not so well kept on the part of my little schoolmistress as on my own; we were soon separated; and, some time afterwards, on my return to Geneva, while passing through Coutance, I heard some little girls cry, in an undertone, "Goton tic-tac Rousseau!"[15]

This little Mademoiselle Goton was really a singular person. Without being pretty, she had a face which was not easy to forget, and which I still recall to mind, often too tenderly for an old fool. Neither her form, nor her manner, nor, above all, her eyes were in keeping with her age. She had a proud and commanding air, which suited her part admirably, and which in fact had suggested the first idea of it to us. But the oddest thing about her was a mixture of impudence and reserve which it was difficult to comprehend. She took the greatest liberties with me, but never allowed me to take any with her. She treated me just like a child, which makes me believe, either that she was no longer one herself, or that, on the contrary, she was still childish enough to see nothing but an amusement in the danger to which she exposed herself.

I belonged entirely, so to say, to each of these two persons, and so completely, that, when I was with one, I never thought of the other. In other respects, there was not the slightest similarity between the feelings with which they inspired me. I could have spent all my life with Mademoiselle de Vulson, without ever thinking of leaving her; but, when I approached her, my joy was tranquil and free from emotion. I loved her above all in fashionable society; the witty sallies, railleries, and even the petty jealousies attracted and interested me; I felt a pride and glory in the marks of preference she bestowed upon me in the presence of grown-up rivals whom she appeared to treat with disdain. I was tormented, but I loved the torment. The applause, encouragement, and laughter warmed and inspirited me. I had fits of passion and broke out into audacious sallies. In society, I was transported with love; in a *tête-à-tête* I should have been constrained, cold, perhaps wearied. However, I felt a real tenderness for her; I suffered when she was ill; I would have given my own health to restore her own, and, observe! I knew very well from experience the meaning of illness and health. When absent from her, I thought of her and missed her; when I was by her side, her caresses reached my heart—not my senses. I was intimate with her with impunity; my imagination demanded no more than she granted; yet I could not have endured to see her do even as much for others. I loved her as a brother, but I was as jealous of her as a lover.

I should have been as jealous of Mademoiselle Goton as a Turk, a madman, or a tiger, if I had once imagined that she could accord the same treatment to another as

---

[15]Coutance is a district in Geneva where Rousseau's family lived after 1718; "tic tac": Goton is in love with, or comes to blows with, Rousseau.

to myself; for even that was a favour which I had to ask on my knees. I approached Mademoiselle de Vulson with lively pleasure, but without emotion; whereas, if I only saw Mademoiselle Goton, I saw nothing else, all my senses were bewildered. With the former I was familiar without familiarity; while on the contrary, in the presence of the latter, I was as bashful as I was excited, even in the midst of our greatest familiarities. I believe that, if I had remained with her long, I should have died; the throbbings of my heart would have suffocated me. I was equally afraid of displeasing either; but I was more attentive to the one and more obedient to the other. Nothing in the world would have made me annoy Mademoiselle de Vulson; but if Mademoiselle Goton had ordered me to throw myself into the flames, I believe I should have obeyed her immediately.

My amour, or rather my meetings, with the latter, continued only for a short time—happily for both of us. Although my relations with Mademoiselle de Vulson had not the same danger, they were not without their catastrophe, after they had lasted a little longer. The end of all such connections should always be somewhat romantic, and furnish occasion for exclamations of sorrow. Although my connection with Mademoiselle de Vulson was less lively, it was perhaps closer. We never separated without tears, and it is remarkable into what an overwhelming void I felt myself plunged as soon as I had left her. I could speak and think of nothing but her; my regret was genuine and lively; but I believe that, at bottom, this heroic regret was not felt altogether for her, and that, without my perceiving it, the amusements, of which she was the centre, played their part in it. To moderate the pangs of absence, we wrote letters to each other, pathetic enough to melt the heart of a stone. At last I triumphed; she could endure it no longer, and came to Geneva to see me. This time my head was completely turned; I was drunk and mad during the two days she remained. When she left I wanted to throw myself in the water after her, and the air resounded with my screams. Eight days afterwards she sent me some bonbons and gloves, which I should have considered a great compliment, if I had not learnt at the same time that she was married, and that the visit with which she had been pleased to honour me was really made in order to buy her wedding-dress. I will not attempt to describe my fury; it may be imagined. In my noble rage I swore that I would never see the faithless one again, being unable to imagine a more terrible punishment for her. She did not, however, die of it; for, twenty years afterwards, when on a visit to my father, while rowing with him on the lake, I asked who the ladies were whom I saw in a boat not far from ours. "What!" said my father with a smile, "does not your heart tell you? it is your old love, Mademoiselle de Vulson that was, now Madame Cristin." I started at the almost forgotten name, but I told the boatmen to change their course. Although I had a fine opportunity of avenging myself at that moment, I did not think it worth while to perjure myself and to renew a quarrel, twenty years old, with a woman of forty.

[1723–1728]

Thus the most valuable time of my boyhood was wasted in follies, before my future career had been decided upon. After long deliberation as to the bent of my natural inclination, a profession was determined upon for which I had the least taste; I was put with M. Masseron, the town clerk, in order to learn, under his tuition, the useful trade of a *fee-grabber*.[16] This nickname was extremely distasteful to me; the hope of gaining a number of crowns in a somewhat sordid business by no means flattered my pride; the occupation itself appeared to me wearisome and unendurable; the constant application, the feeling of servitude

---

[16] A lawyer.

completed my dislike, and I never entered the office without a feeling of horror, which daily increased in intensity. M. Masseron, on his part, was ill-satisfied with me, and treated me with contempt; he continually reproached me with my dullness and stupidity, dinning into my ears every day that my uncle had told him that I knew something, whereas, in reality, I knew nothing; that he had promised him a sharp lad, and had given him a jackass. At last I was dismissed from the office in disgrace as being utterly incapable, and M. Masseron's clerks declared that I was good for nothing except to handle a file.

My calling being thus settled, I was apprenticed, not, however, to a watchmaker, but to an engraver. The contempt with which I had been treated by M. Masseron had made me very humble, and I obeyed without a murmur. My new master, M. Ducommun, was a rough and violent young man, who in a short time succeeded in tarnishing all the brightness of my childhood, stupefying my loving and lively nature, and reducing me, in mind as well as in position, to a real state of apprenticeship. My Latin, my antiquities, my history, were all for a long time forgotten; I did not even remember that there had ever been any Romans in the world. My father, when I went to see him, no longer found in me his idol; for the ladies I was no longer the gallant Jean Jacques; and I felt so certain myself that the Lamberciers would not have recognised their pupil in me, that I was ashamed to pay them a visit, and have never seen them since. The vilest tastes, the lowest street-blackguardism took the place of my simple amusements and effaced even the remembrance of them. I must, in spite of a most upright training, have had a great propensity to degenerate; for the change took place with great rapidity, without the least trouble, and never did so precocious a Cæsar so rapidly become a Laridon.[17]

The trade in itself was not disagreeable to me; I had a decided taste for drawing; the handling of a graving-tool amused me; and as the claims upon the skill of a watchmaker's engraver were limited, I hoped to attain perfection. I should, perhaps, have done so, had not my master's brutality and excessive restraint disgusted me with my work. I stole some of my working hours to devote to similar occupations, but which had for me the charm of freedom. I engraved medals for an order of knighthood for myself and my companions. My master surprised me at this contraband occupation, and gave me a sound thrashing, declaring that I was training for a coiner, because our medals bore the arms of the Republic. I can swear that I had no idea at all of bad, and only a very faint one of good, money. I knew better how the Roman As[18] was made than our three-sou pieces.

My master's tyranny at length made the work, of which I should have been very fond, altogether unbearable, and filled me with vices which I should otherwise have hated, such as lying, idleness and thieving. The recollection of the alteration produced in me by that period of my life has taught me, better than anything else, the difference between filial dependence and abject servitude. Naturally shy and timid, no fault was more foreign to my disposition than impudence; but I had enjoyed an honourable liberty, which hitherto had only been gradually restrained, and at length disappeared altogether. I was bold with my father, unrestrained with M. Lambercier, and modest with my uncle; I became timid with my master, and from that moment I was a lost child. Accustomed to perfect equality in my intercourse with my superiors, knowing no pleasure which was not within my reach, seeing no dish of which I could not have a share, having no desire which I could not have openly expressed, and carrying my heart upon my lips—it is easy to judge what I was bound to become, in a house in which I did not venture to open

---

[17] A degenerate dog, from La Fontaine's *Fables* (1668 f.).
[18] A Roman unit of monetary measure.

my mouth, where I was obliged to leave the table before the meal was half over, and the room as soon as I had nothing more to do there; where, incessantly fettered to my work, I saw only objects of enjoyment for others and of privation for myself; where the sight of the liberty enjoyed by my master and companions increased the weight of my servitude; where, in disputes about matters as to which I was best informed, I did not venture to open my mouth; where, in short, everything that I saw became for my heart an object of longing, simply because I was deprived of all. From that time my ease of manner, my gaiety, the happy expressions which, in former times, when I had done something wrong, had gained me immunity from punishment—all were gone. I cannot help laughing when I remember how, one evening, at my father's house, having been sent to bed without any supper for some piece of roguery, I passed through the kitchen with my melancholy piece of bread, and, seeing the joint turning on the spit, sniffed at it. All the household was standing round the hearth, and, in passing, I was obliged to say good-night to everybody. When I had gone the round, I winked at the joint, which looked so nice and smelt so good, and could not help bowing to it as well, and saying in a mournful voice, "Good-night, roast beef!" This naïve sally amused them so much that they made me stop to supper. Perhaps it might have had the same effect with my master, but I am sure that it would never have occurred to me, and that I should not have had the courage, to say it in his presence.

In this manner I learnt to covet in silence, to dissemble, to lie, and, lastly, to steal—an idea which, up to that time, had never even entered my mind, and of which since then I have never been able to cure myself completely. Covetousness and weakness always lead in that direction. This explains why all servants are rogues, and why all apprentices ought to be; but the latter, in a peaceful state of equality, where all that they see is within their reach, lose, as they grow up, this disgraceful propensity. Not having had the same advantages, I have not been able to reap the same benefits.

It is nearly always good, but badly-directed principles, that make a child take the first step towards evil. In spite of continual privations and temptations, I had been more than a year with my master without being able to make up my mind to take anything, even eatables. My first theft was a matter of obliging some one else, but it opened the door to others, the motive of which was not so praiseworthy.

My master had a journeyman, named M. Verrat, whose house was in the neighbourhood, and had a garden some way off which produced very fine asparagus. M. Verrat, who was not too well supplied with money, conceived the idea of stealing some of his mother's young asparagus and selling it in order to provide himself with two or three good breakfasts. As he was unwilling to run the risk himself, and was not very active, he selected me for the expedition. After some preliminary cajoleries, which the more easily succeeded with me as I did not see their aim, he proposed it to me as an idea that had struck him on the spur of the moment. I strongly opposed it; he persisted. I have never been able to resist flattery: I gave in. I went every morning to gather a crop of the finest asparagus, and carried it to the Molard, where some good woman, who saw that I had just stolen it, told me so to my face in order to get it cheaper. In my fright I took whatever she chose to offer me, and took it to Verrat. The amount was immediately converted into a breakfast, of which I was the purveyor, and which he shared with another companion; I myself was quite satisfied with a few scraps, and never even touched their wine.

This little arrangement continued several days, without its even occurring to me to rob the robber, and to levy my tithe of the proceeds of M. Verrat's asparagus. I performed my part in the transaction with the greatest loyalty; my only motive was to please him who prompted me to carry it out. And yet, if I had been caught, what blows, abuse, and cruel treatment should I have had to endure, while the wretch, who would have been sure to give me the lie, would have been believed on his word, and I should have suffered double punishment for having had the impudence to accuse him, seeing that he was a journeyman, while I was only an apprentice! So true it is that, in every condition of life, the strong man who is guilty saves himself at the expense of the innocent who is weak.

In this manner I learned that stealing was not so terrible a thing as I had imagined, and I soon knew how to make such good use of my discovery, that nothing I desired, if it was within my reach, was safe from me. I was not absolutely ill-fed, and abstinence was only rendered difficult to me from seeing that my master observed it so ill himself. The custom of sending young people from the table when the most appetising dishes are brought on appears to me admirably adapted to make them gluttons as well as thieves. In a short time I became both the one and the other; and, as a rule, I came off very well; occasionally, when I was caught, very badly.

I shudder, and at the same time laugh, when I remember an apple-hunt which cost me dear. These apples were at the bottom of a store-room, which was lighted from the kitchen by means of a high grating. One day, when I was alone in the house, I climbed upon the kneading-trough, in order to look at the precious fruit in the garden of the Hesperides,[19] which was out of my reach. I went to fetch the spit to see if I could touch the apples; it was too short. To make it longer, I tied on to it another little spit which was used for small game, for my master was very fond of sport. I thrust several times without success; at last, to my great delight, I felt that I had secured an apple. I pulled very gently; the apple was close to the grating; I was ready to catch hold of it. But who can describe my grief, when I found that it was too large to pass through the bars? How many expedients I tried, to get it through! I had to find supports to keep the spit in its place, a knife long enough to divide the apple, a lath to hold it up. At last I managed to divide it, and hoped to be able to pull the pieces towards me one after the other; but no sooner were they separated than they both fell into the store-room. Compassionate reader, share my affliction!

I by no means lost courage; but I had lost considerable time. I was afraid of being surprised. I put off a more lucky attempt till the following day, and returned to my work as quietly as if I had done nothing, without thinking of the two tell-tale witnesses in the store-room.

The next day, finding the opportunity favourable, I made a fresh attempt. I climbed upon my stool, lengthened the spit, adjusted it, and was ready to make a lunge.... but, unfortunately, the dragon was not asleep; all at once the door of the store-room opened, my master came out, folded his arms, looked at me, and said, "Courage!" .... the pen falls from my hand.

In consequence of continuous ill-treatment I soon became less sensitive to it, and regarded it as a kind of compensation for theft, which gave me the right to continue the latter. Instead of looking back and considering the punishment, I looked forward and thought of revenge. I considered that, if I were beaten as a rogue, I was entitled to behave like one. I found that stealing and a flogging went together, and constituted a sort of bargain, and that, if I performed my part, I could safely leave my master to carry out his own. With this idea, I began to steal more quietly than before. I said to myself: "What will be the result? I shall be flogged. Never mind; I am made to be flogged."

I am fond of eating, but am not greedy; I am sensual, but not a gourmand; too many other tastes prevent that. I have never troubled myself about my food

---

[19]In Greek mythology, the nymphs who guarded a tree of golden apples.

except when my heart has been unoccupied: and that has so seldom been the case during my life that I have scarcely had time to think about dainties. For this reason I did not long confine my thievish propensities to eatables, but soon extended them to everything which tempted me; and, if I did not become a regular thief, it was because I have never been much tempted by money. Leading out of the common workshop was a private room belonging to my master, the door of which I found means to open and shut without being noticed. There I laid under contribution his best tools, drawings, proofs—in fact, everything which attracted me and which he purposely kept out of my reach. At bottom, these thefts were quite innocent, being only committed to serve him; but I was transported with joy at having these trifles in my power; I thought that I was robbing him of his talent together with its productions. Besides, I found boxes containing gold and silver filings, little trinkets, valuables and coins. When I had four or five sous in my pocket, I thought I was rich; and yet, far from touching anything of what I found there, I do not even remember that I ever cast longing eyes upon it. I looked upon it with more affright than pleasure. I believe that this horror of stealing money and valuables was in great part the result of my bringing-up. With it were combined secret thoughts of disgrace, prison, punishment and the gallows, which would have made me shudder if I had been tempted; whereas my tricks only appeared to me in the light of pieces of mischief, and in fact were nothing else. They could lead to nothing but a sound flogging from my master, and I prepared myself for that beforehand.

But, I repeat, I never felt sufficient longing to need to control myself; I had nothing to contend with. A single sheet of fine drawing-paper tempted me more than money enough to buy a ream of it. This singularity is connected with one of the peculiarities of my character; it has exercised such great influence upon my conduct that it is worth while to explain it.

I am a man of very strong passions, and, while I am stirred by them, nothing can equal my impetuosity; I forget all discretion, all feelings of respect, fear and decency; I am cynical, impudent, violent and fearless; no feeling of shame keeps me back, no danger frightens me; with the exception of the single object which occupies my thoughts, the universe is nothing to me. But all this lasts only for a moment, and the following moment plunges me into complete annihilation. In my calmer moments I am indolence and timidity itself; everything frightens and discourages me; a fly, buzzing past, alarms me; a word which I have to say, a gesture which I have to make, terrifies my idleness; fear and shame overpower me to such an extent that I would gladly hide myself from the sight of my fellow-creatures. If I have to act, I do not know what to do; if I have to speak, I do not know what to say; if anyone looks at me, I am put out of countenance. When I am strongly moved I sometimes know how to find the right words, but in ordinary conversation I can find absolutely nothing, and my condition is unbearable for the simple reason that I am obliged to speak.

Add to this, that none of my prevailing tastes centre in things that can be bought. I want nothing but unadulterated pleasures, and money poisons all. For instance, I am fond of the pleasures of the table; but, as I cannot endure either the constraint of good society or the drunkenness of the tavern, I can only enjoy them with a friend; alone, I cannot do so, for my imagination then occupies itself with other things, and eating affords me no pleasure. If my heated blood longs for women, my excited heart longs still more for affection. Women who could be bought for money would lose for me all their charms; I even doubt whether it would be in me to make use of them. I find it the same with all pleasures within my reach; unless they cost me nothing, I find them insipid. I only love those enjoyments which belong to no one but the first man who knows how to enjoy them.

Money has never appeared to me as valuable as it is generally considered. More than that, it has never even appeared to me particularly convenient. It is good for nothing in itself; it has to be changed before it can be enjoyed; one is obliged to buy, to bargain, to be often cheated, to pay dearly, to be badly served. I should like something which is good in quality; with my money I am sure to get it bad. If I pay a high price for a fresh egg, it is stale; for a nice piece of fruit, it is unripe; for a girl, she is spoilt. I am fond of good wine, but where am I to get it? At a wine merchant's? Whatever I do, he is sure to poison me. If I really wish to be well served, what trouble and embarrassment it entails! I must have friends, correspondents, give commissions, write, go backwards and forwards, wait, and in the end be often deceived! What trouble with my money! my fear of it is greater than my fondness for good wine.

Times without number, during my apprenticeship and afterwards, I have gone out with the intention of buying some delicacy. Coming to a pastrycook's shop, I notice some women at the counter; I think I can already see them laughing amongst themselves at the little glutton. I go to a fruiterer's; I eye the fine pears; their smell tempts me. Two or three young people close by me look at me; a man who knows me is standing in front of his shop; I see a girl approaching in the distance: is it the housemaid? My short-sightedness causes all kinds of illusions. I take all the passers-by for acquaintances; everywhere I am intimidated, restrained by some obstacle; my desire increases with my shame, and at last I return home like a fool, consumed with longing, having in my pocket the means of satisfying it, and yet not having had the courage to buy anything.

I should enter into the most insipid details if, in relating how my money was spent by myself or others, I were to describe the embarrassment, the shame, the repugnance, the inconvenience, the annoyances of all kinds which I have always experienced. In proportion as the reader, following the course of my life, becomes acquainted with my real temperament, he will understand all this, without my taking the trouble to tell him.

This being understood, it will be easy to comprehend one of my apparent inconsistencies—the union of an almost sordid avarice with the greatest contempt for money. It is a piece of furniture in which I find so little convenience, that it never enters my mind to long for it when I have not got it, and that, when I have got it, I keep it for a long time without spending it, for want of knowing how to make use of it in a way to please myself; but if a convenient and agreeable opportunity presents itself, I make such good use of it that my purse is empty before I know it. Besides this, one need not expect to find in me that curious characteristic of misers—that of spending for the sake of ostentation; on the contrary, I spend in secret for the sake of enjoyment; far from glorying in my expenditure, I conceal it. I feel so strongly that money is of no use to me, that I am almost ashamed to have any, still more to make use of it. If I had ever had an income sufficient to live comfortably upon, I am certain that I should never have been tempted to be a miser. I should have spent it all, without attempting to increase it; but my precarious circumstances make me careful. I worship freedom; I abhor restraint, trouble, dependence. As long as the money in my purse lasts, it assures my independence; it relieves me of the trouble of finding expedients to replenish it, a necessity which always inspired me with dread; but the fear of seeing it exhausted makes me hoard it carefully. The money which a man possesses is the instrument of freedom; that which we eagerly pursue is the instrument of slavery. Therefore I hold fast to that which I have, and desire nothing.

My disinterestedness is, therefore, nothing but idleness; the pleasure of possession is not worth the trouble of acquisition. In like manner, my extravagance is nothing but idleness; when the opportunity of spending agreeably presents itself, it cannot be too profitably employed. Money tempts me less than things, because between money and the possession of the desired object there is always an intermediary, whereas between the thing itself and the enjoyment of it there is none. If I see the thing, it tempts me; if I only see the means of gaining possession of it, it does not. For this reason I have committed thefts, and even now I sometimes pilfer trifles which tempt me, and which I prefer to take rather than to ask for; but neither when a child nor a grown-up man do I ever remember to have robbed anyone of a farthing, except on one occasion, fifteen years ago, when I stole seven *livres* ten *sous*. The incident is worth recording, for it contains a most extraordinary mixture of folly and impudence, which I should have found difficulty in believing if it concerned anyone but myself.

It took place at Paris. I was walking with M. de Franceuil in the Palais-Royal about five o'clock. He pulled out his watch, looked at it, and said: "Let us go to the Opera." I agreed; we went. He took two tickets for the amphitheatre, gave me one, and went on in front with the other. I followed him; he went in. Entering after him, I found the door blocked. I looked, and seeing everybody standing up, thought it would be easy to lose myself in the crowd, or at any rate to make M. de Franceuil believe that I had lost myself. I went out, took back my check, then my money, and went off, without thinking that as soon as I had reached the door everybody had taken their seats, and that M. de Franceuil clearly saw that I was no longer there.

As nothing was ever more foreign to my disposition than such behaviour, I mention it in order to show that there are moments of semi-delirium during which men must not be judged by their actions. I did not exactly want to steal the money, I wanted to steal the employment of it; the less of a theft it was, the greater its disgracefulness.

I should never finish these details if I were to follow all the paths along which, during my apprenticeship, I descended from the sublimity of heroism to the depths of worthlessness. And yet, although I adopted the vices of my position, I could not altogether acquire a taste for them. I wearied of the amusements of my companions; and when excessive restraint had rendered work unendurable to me, I grew tired of everything. This renewed my taste for reading, which I had for some time lost. This reading, for which I stole time from my work, became a new offence which brought new punishment upon me. The taste for it, provoked by constraint, became a passion, and soon a regular madness. La Tribu, a well-known lender of books, provided me with all kinds of literature. Good or bad, all were alike to me; I had no choice, and read everything with equal avidity. I read at the work-table, I read on my errands, I read in the wardrobe, and forgot myself for hours together; my head became giddy with reading; I could do nothing else. My master watched me, surprised me, beat me, took away my books. How many volumes were torn, burnt, and thrown out of the window! how many works were left in odd volumes in La Tribu's stock! When I had no more money to pay her, I gave her my shirts, neckties and clothes; my three sous of pocket-money were regularly taken to her every Sunday.

Well, then, I shall be told, money had become necessary to me. That is true; but it was not until my passion for reading had deprived me of all activity. Completely devoted to my new hobby, I did nothing but read, and no longer stole. Here again is one of my characteristic peculiarities. In the midst of a certain attachment to any manner of life, a mere trifle distracts me, alters me, rivets my attention, and finally becomes a passion. Then everything is forgotten; I no longer think of anything except the new object which engrosses my attention. My heart beat with impatience to turn over the leaves of the new book which I had in my pocket; I pulled it out as soon as I was alone, and thought no more of rummaging my master's work-room. I can hardly believe that I should have stolen even if I had had more expensive tastes. Limited to the present, it was not in my way to make preparations in this manner for the future. La Tribu gave me credit, the payments on account were small, and, as soon as I had my book in my pocket, I forgot everything else. The money which came to me honestly passed in the same manner into the hands of this woman; and, when she pressed me, nothing was easier to dispose of than my own property. It required too much foresight to steal in advance, and I was not even tempted to steal in order to pay.

In consequence of quarrels, blows, and secret and ill-chosen reading, my disposition became savage and taciturn; my mind became altogether perverted, and I lived like a misanthrope. However, if my good taste did not keep me from silly and insipid books, my good fortune preserved me from such as were filthy and licentious; not that La Tribu, a woman in all respects most accommodating, would have made any scruple about lending them to me; but, in order to increase their importance, she always mentioned them to me with an air of mystery which had just the effect of making me refuse them, as much from disgust as from shame; and chance aided my modest disposition so well, that I was more than thirty years old before I set eyes upon any of those dangerous books which a fine lady finds inconvenient because they can only be read with one hand.

In less than a year I exhausted La Tribu's little stock, and want of occupation, during my spare time, became painful to me. I had been cured of my childish and knavish propensities by my passion for reading, and even by the books I read, which, although ill-chosen and frequently bad, filled my heart with nobler sentiments than those with which my sphere of life had inspired me. Disgusted with everything that was within my reach, and feeling that everything which might have tempted me was too far removed from me, I saw nothing possible which might have flattered my heart. My excited senses had long clamoured for an enjoyment, the object of which I could not even imagine. I was as far removed from actual enjoyment as if I had been sexless; and, already fully developed and sensitive, I sometimes thought of my crazes, but saw nothing beyond them. In this strange situation, my restless imagination entered upon an occupation which saved me from myself and calmed my growing sensuality. This consisted in feeding myself upon the situations which had interested me in the course of my reading, in recalling them, in varying them, in combining them, in making them so truly my own that I became one of the persons who filled my imagination, and always saw myself in the situations most agreeable to my taste; and that, finally, the fictitious state in which I succeeded in putting myself made me forget my actual state with which I was so dissatisfied. This love of imaginary objects, and the readiness with which I occupied myself with them, ended by disgusting me with everything around me, and decided that liking for solitude which has never left me. In the sequel we shall see more than once the curious effects of this disposition, apparently so gloomy and misanthropic, but which is really due to a too affectionate, too loving and too tender heart, which, being unable to find any in existence resembling it, is obliged to nourish itself with fancies. For the present, it is sufficient for me to have defined the origin and first cause of a propensity which has modified all my passions, and which, restraining them by means of themselves, has always made me slow to act, owing to my excessive impetuosity in desire.

In this manner I reached my sixteenth year, restless, dissatisfied with myself and everything, without any of the tastes of my condition of life, without any of the pleasures of my age, consumed by desires of the object of which I was ignorant, weeping without any cause for tears, sighing without knowing why—in short, tenderly caressing my chimeras, since I saw nothing around me which counterbalanced them. On Sundays, my fellow-apprentices came to fetch me after service to go and amuse myself with them. I would gladly have escaped from them if I had been able; but, once engaged in their amusements, I became more excited and went further than any of them; it was as difficult to set me going as to stop me. Such was always my disposition. During our walks outside the city I always went further than any of them without thinking about my return, unless others thought of it for me. Twice I was caught: the gates were shut before I could get back. The next day I was treated as may be imagined; the second time I was promised such a reception if it ever happened again, that I resolved not to run the risk of it; yet this third time, so dreaded, came to pass. My watchfulness was rendered useless by a confounded Captain Minutoli, who always shut the gate at which he was on guard half-an-hour before the others. I was returning with two companions. About half a league from the city I heard the retreat sounded: I doubled my pace: I heard the tattoo[20] beat, and ran with all my might. I arrived out of breath and bathed in perspiration; my heart beat; from a distance I saw the soldiers at their posts; I rushed up and cried out with a voice half-choked. It was too late! Twenty paces from the outposts, I saw the first bridge raised. I shuddered when I saw those terrible horns rising in the air—a sinister and fatal omen of the destiny which that moment was opening for me.

In the first violence of my grief I threw myself on the *glacis*[21] and bit the ground. My companions, laughing at their misfortune, immediately made up their minds what to do. I did the same, but my resolution was different from theirs. On the spot I swore never to return to my master; and the next morning, when they entered the city after the gates were opened, I said good-bye to them for ever, only begging them secretly to inform my cousin Bernard of the resolution I had taken, and of the place where he might be able to see me once more.

After I had entered upon my apprenticeship I saw less of him. For some time we used to meet on Sunday, but gradually each of us adopted other habits, and we saw one another less frequently. I am convinced that his mother had much to do with this change. He was a child of the upper city; I, a poor apprentice, was only a child of Saint-Gervais.[22] In spite of our relationship, there was no longer any equality between us; it was derogatory to him to associate with me. However, relations were not entirely broken off between us, and, as he was a good-natured lad, he sometimes followed the dictates of his heart instead of his mother's instructions. When he was informed of my resolution, he hastened to me, not to try and dissuade me from it or to share it, but to lessen the inconveniences of my flight by some small presents, since my own resources could not take me very far. Amongst other things he gave me a small sword, which had taken my fancy exceedingly, and which I carried as far as Turin, where necessity obliged me to dispose of it, and where, as the saying is, I passed it through my body. The more I have since reflected upon the manner in which he behaved towards me at this critical moment, the more I have felt convinced that he followed the instructions of his mother, and perhaps of his father; for it is inconceivable that, left to himself, he would not have made some effort to keep me back, or would not have been tempted to follow; but, no! he rather encouraged me in my plan than tried to dissuade me; and, when he saw me quite

---

[20] A signal, sounded before taps, to call soldiers to their barracks for the night.

[21] The slope in front of the city walls.

[22] Bernard lived in the more fashionable part of Geneva; Rousseau lived in the Saint-Gervais, the poorer part.

determined, he left me without shedding many tears. We have never corresponded or seen each other since. It is a pity: his character was essentially good; we were made to love each other.

Before I abandon myself to the fatality of my lot, allow me to turn my eyes for a moment upon the destiny which, in the nature of things, would have awaited me if I had fallen into the hands of a better master. Nothing was more suitable to my disposition or better adapted to make me happy than the quiet and obscure lot of a respectable artisan, especially of a certain class such as that of the engravers of Geneva. Such a position, sufficiently lucrative to afford a comfortable livelihood, but not sufficiently so to lead to fortune, would have limited my ambition for the rest of my days, and, leaving me an honourable leisure to cultivate modest tastes, would have confined me within my own sphere, without offering me the means of getting out of it. My imaginative powers were rich enough to beautify all callings with their chimeras, and strong enough to transport me, so to speak, at will from one to another; so it would have been immaterial to me in what position I actually found myself. It could not have been so far from the place where I was to my first castle in the air, that I could not have taken up my abode there without any difficulty. From this alone it followed that the simplest vocation, that which involved the least trouble and anxiety, that which allowed the greatest mental freedom, was the one which suited me best: and that was exactly my own. I should have passed a peaceful and quiet life, such as my disposition required, in the bosom of my religion, my country, my family and my friends, in the monotony of a profession that suited my taste, and in a society after my own heart. I should have been a good Christian, a good citizen, a good father of a family, a good friend, a good workman, a good man in every relation of life. I should have loved my position in life, perhaps honoured it; and, having spent a life—simple, indeed, and obscure, but calm and serene—I should have died peacefully in the bosom of my family. Though, doubtless, soon forgotten, I should at least have been regretted as long as anyone remembered me.

Instead of that—what picture am I going to draw? Let us not anticipate the sorrows of my life; I shall occupy my readers more than enough with this melancholy subject.

WESTERN TEXTS

JEAN-BAPTISTE POQUELIN MOLIÈRE
[1622–1673]

Originally named Jean-Baptiste Poquelin, this French dramatist adopted the stage name of Molière and became famous for comedies that satirize the follies of human nature while amusing his audiences. He recognized the power of theater to expose the disguises people wear and the deceptions they practice in their private and public lives.

During the seventeenth century, French society was changing. A rigid hierarchy of social classes was being challenged by the rise of a commercial population, which was questioning the power and privilege of the upper classes and the validity of the monarchy. While science and philosophy were examining the basic principles of physical reality, social critics and artists were analyzing social roles and institutions. To all appearances, science was making astonishing strides in discovering and describing a rational universe, but human society, despite its hopes and pretensions, seemed to linger behind. It was easier to formulate a new law of physics than to eradicate a basic fault of human nature, such as greed. Molière used the full resources of French theater to expose the gap between ideal and real by creating comedies that poke fun at hypocrisy, greed, affectation, zealotry, and immoderation.

LIFE

Molière, the son of a well-to-do upholsterer at court, was in line to inherit his father's position as *tapissier ordinaire du roi* and enjoy a comfortable life. He received a fine education at College de Clermont, a Jesuit college, and practiced law for a short time. In 1643 he drastically changed careers by becoming one of nine founders of an acting company in Paris, the *Illustre Théâtre*. Taking the name of Molière for the first time, he devoted the rest of his life to theater—writing, directing, staging, and producing plays. Although theater was very popular with the general public, the acting profession itself was condemned by the clergy; in fact, an actor was automatically excommunicated by the Church and denied Christian burial unless a renunciation of his chosen career was forthcoming before death.

Molière's new company was a total failure, at least financially; twice he ended up in jail for debts. As a result, Molière made a wise decision and retreated to the countryside where he learned the organizational nuts and bolts of successful theater by touring the back roads and provinces of France. For thirteen years he served an apprenticeship in the various practical and artistic responsibilities of a theatrical company. He also turned his attention from tragedies to comedies—his true calling.

In 1658 Molière returned to Paris, found favor with the court through Louis XIV's brother, "Monsieur," and had an undisputable hit with *Les Précieuses ridicules* (*The High-Brow Young Ladies,* 1659). From then on he enjoyed huge success and the patronage of the king. The titles of his masterpieces constitute a list of the kinds of people Molière subjected to satire and ridicule. *L'École des femmes* (*School for Wives,* 1662) examines the insecurities of courtship. *Don Juan* (1665) picks up the theme of the playboy and explores intimate relationships. *The Misanthrope* (1666) shows the shortsightedness of a self-righteous intellectual. *L'Avare* (*The Miser,* 1668), as the title says, satirizes lust for money. *Le Bourgeois gentilhomme* (*The Would-Be Gentleman,* 1670) turns on the aspiring middle classes and *Les Femmes savantes* (*The Learned Ladies,* 1672) attacks educated women. In his last play, *Le Malade imaginaire* (*The Hypochondriac,* 1673), Molière depicts a hypochondriac at the mercy of the medical profession, a subject that grew out of his personal experiences during the last years of his life. Molière weathered the uncertainties of live theater and the maintenance of an acting company by writing a large number of plays himself. One of his editors, René Bray, estimates that in a fourteen-year period, 1660–1673, Molière wrote thirty-one plays. In all, his company performed ninety-three of Molière's plays.

Molière died in 1673, a few hours after having acted the title role in *Le Malade imaginaire*. Priests were not allowed to bring the last rites to him, so Molière did not have the opportunity to renounce his profession. A Christian burial was denied him until his widow and friends persuaded the king to intervene with the Archbishop. It was only then that one of France's greatest playwrights was buried, after dark, in the Cemetery Saint-Joseph on February 21. One can only wonder how Molière would have staged such a convoluted scenario. Molière understood the potential role of theater in the transformation of society. In the Preface to *Tartuffe*, he explains why he chose religious hypocrisy for ridicule in that play and why the instrument of satire is so effective:

If the function of comedy is to correct men's vices, I do not see why any should be exempt. Such a condition in our society would be much more dangerous than the thing itself; and we have seen that the theater is admirably suited to provide correction. The most forceful lines of a serious moral statement are usually less powerful than those of satire; and nothing will reform most men better than the depiction of their faults. It is a vigorous blow to vices to expose them to public laughter.

WORK

The attack on religious hypocrisy in *Tartuffe* (1664) raised the feathers of both clergy and laity, especially a secret society called the Company of the Blessed Sacrament, and the play was banned from public view by the king. In defending his play, Molière attributed the censorship to the very hypocrites he was satirizing and commented on them in the preface to the first edition of *Tartuffe* (1669).

> This is a comedy about which a great deal of fuss has been made and it has long been persecuted. The people it makes fun of have certainly shown [by keeping his play off the stage for nearly five years] that they command more influence in France than any of those I have been concerned with before. Noblemen, pretentious women, cuckolds, and doctors have all submitted to being put on the stage and pretended to be as amused as everyone else at the way I portrayed them, but the hypocrites would not stand for a joke.

Molière's defense is not entirely correct because there were those who felt that his attacks on excessive or false piety might somehow also blemish the reputations of the truly pious. Molière had to rewrite the play twice before it met with a large success in 1669.

The character Tartuffe is a pious hypocrite who weasels his way into the household of a rather shallow, credulous man named Orgon. Using religious puffery and flattery, Tartuffe eventually persuades Orgon to relinquish his daughter's hand, while making passes at Orgon's wife. The play becomes even more complicated and potentially damaging when Tartuffe replaces Orgon's son as the inheritor of Orgon's estate. Incredible as it seems, moral arbiters were actually placed in people's homes by the Church to reform the family's practices, so Molière was cutting close to institutional reality with his portrayal. Although Orgon seems decent enough, he is gullible and incapable of delving beneath the false masks worn by Tartuffe.

One of the persistent themes in this play is how private life with its passions and ambiguities can conflict with an orderly code of behavior in the public sphere. Marriage is a convenient arrangement for showing the discrepancies between public gestures and private needs, especially with the explosive power of sexuality. Although the women in the play clearly reveal the subordinate roles of women in French society of the time, two of them nevertheless have strong, intelligent roles to play. The servant Dorine not only provides humor with her outrageous tongue, she often articulates a sensible explanation for activities in the play. Orgon's wife, Elmire, is clever enough to ensnare Tartuffe in his own lust.

Underneath the laughter and wit in *Tartuffe* there is a persistent faith in common sense and the individual; with the unmasking of human foibles comes the person who, irrespective of social rank, is able to sort out the excesses of human nature and pursue a path of moderation and caring companionship. It is Orgon's brother-in-law, Cléante, who consistently articulates this common-sense point of view and an ethic of moderation; his rational commentaries reflect an Enlightenment perspective, tying Molière to the conventional wisdom of his times:

> Ah, Brother, man's a strangely fashioned creature
> Who seldom is content to follow Nature,

> But recklessly pursues his inclination
> Beyond the narrow bounds of moderation,
> And often, by transgressing Reason's laws,
> Perverts a lofty aim or noble cause.

Early in the play Orgon is incapable of appreciating the good sense behind Cléante's words, but through sad experiences and the timely intervention of the king at the end of the play, Orgon triumphs, and his daughter is promised to the appropriate suitor. Although the conclusion of the play indirectly raises questions about the patriarchal system that made Tartuffe's escapades possible, Orgon will "give Valère, whose love has proven so true, / The wedded happiness which is his due." Certainly the best ending for a comedy.

SUGGESTED READINGS

Informative biographies are provided in T. Mantzius's *Molière* (1908) and Hallam Walker's *Molière* (1990). General criticisms of Molière's works, as well as specific analysis of *Tartuffe*, can be found in Lionel Gossman's *Men and Masks: A Study of Molière* (1963), J. D. Hubert's *Molière and the Company of Intellect* (1962), Wyndham Lewis's *Molière: The Comic Mask* (1959), and Gertrude Mander's *Molière* (1973).

Tartuffe

Translated by Richard Wilbur

MME. PERNELLE, *Orgon's mother*
ORGON, *Elmire's husband*
ELMIRE, *Orgon's wife*
DAMIS, *Orgon's son, Elmire's stepson*
MARIANE,   *Orgon's daughter, Elmire's
   stepdaughter, in love with Valère*
VALÈRE, *in love with Mariane*

CLÉANTE, *Orgon's brother-in-law*
TARTUFFE, *a hypocrite*
DORINE, *Mariane's lady's-maid*
M. LOYAL, *a bailiff*
A POLICE OFFICER
FLIPOTE, *Mme. Pernelle's maid*

THE SCENE THROUGHOUT: ORGON*'s house in Paris*

ACT I

Scene 1

MADAME PERNELLE:
   Come, come, Flipote; it's time I left this place.
ELMIRE:
   I can't keep up, you walk at such a pace.
MADAME PERNELLE:
   Don't trouble, child; no need to show me out.
   It's not your manners I'm concerned about.
ELMIRE:
   We merely pay you the respect we owe.
   But, Mother, why this hurry? Must you go?
MADAME PERNELLE:
   I must. This house appalls me. No one in it
   Will pay attention for a single minute.
   Children, I take my leave much vexed in spirit.

I offer good advice, but you won't hear it.   10
You all break in and chatter on and on.
It's like a madhouse with the keeper gone.

DORINE:
    If...

MADAME PERNELLE:
        Girl, you talk too much, and I'm afraid
You're far too saucy for a lady's-maid.
You push in everywhere and have your say.

DAMIS:
    But...

MADAME PERNELLE:
        You, boy, grow more foolish every day.
To think my grandson should be such a dunce!
I've said a hundred times, if I've said it once,
That if you keep the course on which you've started,
You'll leave your worthy father broken-hearted.   20

MARIANE:
    I think...

MADAME PERNELLE:
        And you, his sister, seem so pure,
So shy, so innocent, and so demure.
But you know what they say about still waters.
I pity parents with secretive daughters.

ELMIRE:
    Now, Mother...

MADAME PERNELLE:
        And as for you, child, let me add
That your behavior is extremely bad,
And a poor example for these children, too.
Their dear, dead mother did far better than you.
You're much too free with money, and I'm distressed
To see you so elaborately dressed.   30
When it's one's husband that one aims to please,
One has no need of costly fripperies.

CLÉANTE:
    Oh, Madame, really...

MADAME PERNELLE:
        You are her brother, Sir,
And I respect and love you; yet if I were
My son, this lady's good and pious spouse,
I wouldn't make you welcome in my house.
You're full of worldly counsels which, I fear,
Aren't suitable for decent folk to hear.
I've spoken bluntly, Sir; but it behooves us
Not to mince words when righteous fervor moves us.   40

DAMIS:
    Your man Tartuffe is full of holy speeches...

MADAME PERNELLE:
    And practises precisely what he preaches.
He's a fine man, and should be listened to.
I will not hear him mocked by fools like you.

DAMIS:

    Good God! Do you expect me to submit
    To the tyranny of that carping hypocrite?
    Must we forgo all joys and satisfactions
    Because that bigot censures all our actions?

DORINE:

    To hear him talk—and he talks all the time—
    There's nothing one can do that's not a crime.   50
    He rails at everything, your dear Tartuffe.

MADAME PERNELLE:

    Whatever he reproves deserves reproof.
    He's out to save your souls, and all of you
    Must love him, as my son would have you do.

DAMIS:

    Ah no, Grandmother, I could never take
    To such a rascal, even for my father's sake.
    That's how I feel, and I shall not dissemble.
    His every action makes me seethe and tremble
    With helpless anger, and I have no doubt
    That he and I will shortly have it out.   60

DORINE:

    Surely it is a shame and a disgrace
    To see this man usurp the master's place—
    To see this beggar who, when first he came,
    Had not a shoe or shoestring to his name
    So far forget himself that he behaves
    As if the house were his, and we his slaves.

MADAME PERNELLE:

    Well, mark my words, your souls would fare far better
    If you obeyed his precepts to the letter.

DORINE:

    You see him as a saint. I'm far less awed;
    In fact, I see right through him. He's a fraud.   70

MADAME PERNELLE:

    Nonsense.

DORINE:

           His man Laurent's the same, or worse;
    I'd not trust either with a penny purse.

MADAME PERNELLE:

    I can't say what his servant's morals may be;
    His own great goodness I can guarantee.
    You all regard him with distaste and fear
    Because he tells you what you're loath to hear,
    Condemns your sins, points out your moral flaws,
    And humbly strives to further Heaven's cause.

DORINE:

    If sin is all that bothers him, why is it
    He's so upset when folk drop in to visit?   80
    Is Heaven so outraged by a social call
    That he must prophesy against us all?
    I'll tell you what I think: if you ask me,
    He's jealous of my mistress' company.

MADAME PERNELLE:

    Rubbish! [*to* ELMIRE] He's not alone, child, in complaining

    Of all your promiscuous entertaining.

    Why, the whole neighborhood's upset, I know,

    By all these carriages that come and go,

    With crowds of guests parading in and out

    And noisy servants loitering about.   90

    In all of this, I'm sure there's nothing vicious;

    But why give people cause to be suspicious?

CLÉANTE:

    They need no cause; they'll talk in any case.

    Madam, this world would be a joyless place

    If, fearing what malicious tongues might say,

    We locked our doors and turned our friends away.

    And even if one did so dreary a thing,

    D'you think those tongues would cease their chattering?

    One can't fight slander; it's a losing battle;

    Let us instead ignore their tittle-tattle.   100

    Let's strive to live by conscience's clear decrees,

    And let the gossips gossip as they please.

DORINE:

    If there is talk against us, I know the source:

    It's Daphne and her little husband, of course.

    Those who have greatest cause for guilt and shame

    Are quickest to besmirch a neighbor's name.

    When there's a chance for libel, they never miss it;

    When something can be made to seem illicit

    They're off at once to spread the joyous news,

    Adding to fact what fantasies they choose.   110

    By talking up their neighbor's indiscretions

    They seek to camouflage their own transgressions,

    Hoping that others' innocent affairs

    Will lend a hue of innocence to theirs,

    Or that their own black guilt will come to seem

    Part of a general shady color-scheme.

MADAME PERNELLE:

    All that is quite irrelevant. I doubt

    That anyone's more virtuous and devout

    Than dear Orante; and I'm informed that she

    Condemns your mode of life most vehemently.   120

DORINE:

    Oh, yes, she's strict, devout, and has no taint

    Of worldliness; in short, she seems a saint.

    But it was time which taught her that disguise;

    She's thus because she can't be otherwise.

    So long as her attractions could enthrall,

    She flounced and flirted and enjoyed it all,

    But now that they're no longer what they were

    She quits a world which fast is quitting her,

    And wears a veil of virtue to conceal

    Her bankrupt beauty and her lost appeal.   130

    That's what becomes of old coquettes today:

Distressed when all their lovers fall away,
They see no recourse but to play the prude,
And so confer a style on solitude.
Thereafter, they're severe with everyone,
Condemning all our actions, pardoning none,
And claiming to be pure, austere, and zealous
When, if the truth were known, they're merely jealous,
And cannot bear to see another know
The pleasures time has forced them to forgo.   140

MADAME PERNELLE [*initially to* ELMIRE]:
That sort of talk is what you like to hear,
Therefore you'd have us all keep still, my dear,
While Madam rattles on the livelong day.
Nevertheless, I mean to have my say.
I tell you that you're blest to have Tartuffe
Dwelling, as my son's guest, beneath this roof;
That Heaven has sent him to forestall its wrath
By leading you, once more, to the true path;
That all he reprehends is reprehensible,
And that you'd better heed him, and be sensible.   150
These visits, balls, and parties in which you revel
Are nothing but inventions of the Devil.
One never hears a word that's edifying:
Nothing but chaff and foolishness and lying,
As well as vicious gossip in which one's neighbor
Is cut to bits with epee, foil, and saber.
People of sense are driven half-insane
At such affairs, where noise and folly reign
And reputations perish thick and fast.
As a wise preacher said on Sunday last,   160
Parties are Towers of Babylon, because
The guests all babble on with never a pause;
And then he told a story which, I think . . .
[*To* CLÉANTE] I heard that laugh, Sir, and I saw that wink!
Go find your silly friends and laugh some more!
Enough; I'm going; don't show me to the door.
I leave this household much dismayed and vexed;
I cannot say when I shall see you next.
[*Slapping* FLIPOTE] Wake up, don't stand there gaping into space!
I'll slap some sense into that stupid face.   170
Move, move, you slut.

Scene 2

CLÉANTE:
                I think I'll stay behind;
I want no further pieces of her mind.
How that old lady . . .

DORINE:
                Oh, what wouldn't she say
If she could hear you speak of her that way!
She'd thank you for the *lady,* but I'm sure
She'd find the *old* a little premature.

CLÉANTE:
  My, what a scene she made, and what a din!
  And how this man Tartuffe has taken her in!
DORINE:
  Yes, but her son is even worse deceived;
  His folly must be seen to be believed.   10
  In the late troubles, he played an able part
  And served his king with wise and loyal heart,
  But he's quite lost his senses since he fell
  Beneath Tartuffe's infatuating spell.
  He calls him brother, and loves him as his life,
  Preferring him to mother, child, or wife.
  In him and him alone will he confide;
  He's made him his confessor and his guide;
  He pets and pampers him with love more tender
  Than any pretty mistress could engender,   20
  Gives him the place of honor when they dine,
  Delights to see him gorging like a swine,
  Stuffs him with dainties till his guts distend,
  And when he belches, cries "God bless you, friend!"
  In short, he's mad; he worships him; he dotes;
  His deeds he marvels at, his words he quotes,
  Thinking each act a miracle, each word
  Oracular as those that Moses heard.
  Tartuffe, much pleased to find so easy a victim,
  Has in a hundred ways beguiled and tricked him,   30
  Milked him of money, and with his permission
  Established here a sort of Inquisition.
  Even Laurent, his lackey, dares to give
  Us arrogant advice on how to live;
  He sermonizes us in thundering tones
  And confiscates our ribbons and colognes.
  Last week he tore a kerchief into pieces
  Because he found it pressed in a *Life of Jesus:*
  He said it was a sin to juxtapose
  Unholy vanities and holy prose.   40

Scene 3

ELMIRE [*to* CLÉANTE]:
  You did well not to follow; she stood in the door
  And said *verbatim* all she'd said before.
  I saw my husband coming. I think I'd best
  Go upstairs now, and take a little rest.
CLÉANTE:
  I'll wait and greet him here; then I must go.
  I've really only time to say hello.
DAMIS:
  Sound him about my sister's wedding, please.
  I think Tartuffe's against it, and that he's
  Been urging Father to withdraw his blessing.
  As you well know, I'd find that most distressing.   10
  Unless my sister and Valère can marry,

My hopes to wed *his* sister will miscarry,
And I'm determined...

DORINE:

He's coming.

Scene 4

ORGON:

Ah, Brother, good-day.

CLÉANTE:

Well, welcome back. I'm sorry I can't stay.
How was the country? Blooming, I trust, and green?

ORGON:

Excuse me, Brother; just one moment.
[*To* DORINE]   Dorine...
[*To* CLÉANTE] To put my mind at rest, I always learn
The household news the moment I return.
[*To* DORINE] Has all been well, these two days I've been gone?
How are the family? What's been going on?

DORINE:

Your wife, two days ago, had a bad fever,
And a fierce headache which refused to leave her.   10

ORGON:

Ah. And Tartuffe?

DORINE:

Tartuffe? Why, he's round and red,
Bursting with health, and excellently fed.

ORGON:

Poor fellow!

DORINE:

That night, the mistress was unable
To take a single bite at the dinner-table.
Her headache-pains, she said, were simply hellish.

ORGON:

Ah. And Tartuffe?

DORINE:

He ate his meal with relish,
And zealously devoured in her presence
A leg of mutton and a brace of pheasants.

ORGON:

Poor fellow!

DORINE:

Well, the pains continued strong,
And so she tossed and tossed the whole night long,   20
Now icy-cold, now burning like a flame.
We sat beside her bed till morning came.

ORGON:

Ah. And Tartuffe?

DORINE:

Why, having eaten, he rose
And sought his room, already in a doze,
Got into his warm bed, and snored away
In perfect peace until the break of day.

ORGON:
  Poor fellow!
DORINE:
                  After much ado, we talked her
  Into dispatching someone for the doctor.
  He bled her, and the fever quickly fell.
ORGON:
  Ah. And Tartuffe?
DORINE:
                      He bore it very well.   30
  To keep his cheerfulness at any cost,
  And make up for the blood *Madame* had lost,
  He drank, at lunch, four beakers full of port.
ORGON:
  Poor fellow!
DORINE:
                  Both are doing well, in short.
  I'll go and tell *Madame* that you've expressed
  Keen sympathy and anxious interest.

                            Scene 5

CLÉANTE:
  That girl was laughing in your face, and though
  I've no wish to offend you, even so
  I'm bound to say that she had some excuse.
  How can you possibly be such a goose?
  Are you so dazed by this man's hocus-pocus
  That all the world, save him, is out of focus?
  You've given him clothing, shelter, food, and care;
  Why must you also...
ORGON:
                  Brother, stop right there.
  You do not know the man of whom you speak.
CLÉANTE:
  I grant you that. But my judgment's not so weak   10
  That I can't tell, by his effect on others...
ORGON:
  Ah, when you meet him, you two will be like brothers!
  There's been no loftier soul since time began.
  He is a man who...a man who...an excellent man.
  To keep his precepts is to be reborn,
  And view this dunghill of a world with scorn.
  Yes, thanks to him I'm a changed man indeed.
  Under his tutelage my soul's been freed
  From earthly loves, and every human tie:
  My mother, children, brother, and wife could die,   20
  And I'd not feel a single moment's pain.
CLÉANTE:
  That's a fine sentiment, Brother; most humane.
ORGON:
  Oh, had you seen Tartuffe as I first knew him,
  Your heart, like mine, would have surrendered to him.

He used to come into our church each day
And humbly kneel nearby, and start to pray.
He'd draw the eyes of everybody there
By the deep fervor of his heartfelt prayer;
He'd sigh and weep, and sometimes with a sound
Of rapture he would bend and kiss the ground;   30
And when I rose to go, he'd run before
To offer me holy-water at the door.
His serving-man, no less devout than he,
Informed me of his master's poverty;
I gave him gifts, but in his humbleness
He'd beg me every time to give him less.
"Oh, that's too much," he'd cry, "too much by twice!
I don't deserve it. The half, Sir, would suffice."
And when I wouldn't take it back, he'd share
Half of it with the poor, right then and there.   40
At length, Heaven prompted me to take him in
To dwell with us, and free our souls from sin.
He guides our lives, and to protect my honor
Stays by my wife, and keeps an eye upon her;
He tells me whom she sees, and all she does,
And seems more jealous than I ever was!
And how austere he is! Why, he can detect
A mortal sin where you would least suspect;
In smallest trifles, he's extremely strict.
Last week, his conscience was severely pricked   50
Because, while praying, he had caught a flea
And killed it, so he felt, too wrathfully.
CLÉANTE:
Good God, man! Have you lost your common sense—
Or is this all some joke at my expense?
How can you stand there and in all sobriety . . .
ORGON:
Brother, your language savors of impiety.
Too much free-thinking's made your faith unsteady,
And as I've warned you many times already,
'Twill get you into trouble before you're through.
CLÉANTE:
So I've been told before by dupes like you: 60
Being blind, you'd have all others blind as well;
The clear-eyed man you call an infidel,
And he who sees through humbug and pretense
Is charged, by you, with want of reverence.
Spare me your warnings, Brother; I have no fear
Of speaking out, for you and Heaven to hear,
Against affected zeal and pious knavery.
There's true and false in piety, as in bravery,
And just as those whose courage shines the most
In battle, are the least inclined to boast,   70
So those whose hearts are truly pure and lowly
Don't make a flashy show of being holy.
There's a vast difference, so it seems to me,
Between true piety and hypocrisy:

How do you fail to see it, may I ask?
Is not a face quite different from a mask?
Cannot sincerity and cunning art,
Reality and semblance, be told apart?
Are scarecrows just like men, and do you hold
That a false coin is just as good as gold?   80
Ah, Brother, man's a strangely fashioned creature
Who seldom is content to follow Nature,
But recklessly pursues his inclination
Beyond the narrow bounds of moderation,
And often, by transgressing Reason's laws,
Perverts a lofty aim or noble cause.
A passing observation, but it applies.
ORGON:
    I see, dear Brother, that you're profoundly wise;
    You harbor all the insight of the age.
    You are our one clear mind, our only sage,   90
    The era's oracle, its Cato too,
    And all mankind are fools compared to you.
CLÉANTE:
    Brother, I don't pretend to be a sage,
    Nor have I all the wisdom of the age.
    There's just one insight I would dare to claim:
    I know that true and false are not the same;
    And just as there is nothing I more revere
    Than a soul whose faith is steadfast and sincere,
    Nothing that I more cherish and admire
    Than honest zeal and true religious fire,   100
    So there is nothing that I find more base
    Than specious piety's dishonest face—
    Than these bold mountebanks, these histrios
    Whose impious mummeries and hollow shows
    Exploit our love of Heaven, and make a jest
    Of all that men think holiest and best;
    These calculating souls who offer prayers
    Not to their Maker, but as public wares,
    And seek to buy respect and reputation
    With lifted eyes and sighs of exaltation;   110
    These charlatans, I say, whose pilgrim souls
    Proceed, by way of Heaven, toward earthly goals,
    Who weep and pray and swindle and extort,
    Who preach the monkish life, but haunt the court,
    Who make their zeal the partner of their vice—
    Such men are vengeful, sly, and cold as ice,
    And when there is an enemy to defame
    They cloak their spite in fair religion's name,
    Their private spleen and malice being made
    To seem a high and virtuous crusade,   120
    Until, to mankind's reverent applause,
    They crucify their foe in Heaven's cause.
    Such knaves are all too common; yet, for the wise,
    True piety isn't hard to recognize,
    And, happily, these present times provide us

With bright examples to instruct and guide us.
Consider Ariston and Périandre;
Look at Oronte, Alcidamas, Clitandre;
Their virtue is acknowledged; who could doubt it?
But you won't hear them beat the drum about it.   130
They're never ostentatious, never vain,
And their religion's moderate and humane;
It's not their way to criticize and chide:
They think censoriousness a mark of pride,
And therefore, letting others preach and rave,
They show, by deeds, how Christians should behave.
They think no evil of their fellow man,
But judge of him as kindly as they can.
They don't intrigue and wangle and conspire;
To lead a good life is their one desire;   140
The sinner wakes no rancorous hate in them;
It is the sin alone which they condemn;
Nor do they try to show a fiercer zeal
For Heaven's cause than Heaven itself could feel.
These men I honor, these men I advocate
As models for us all to emulate.
Your man is not their sort at all, I fear:
And, while your praise of him is quite sincere,
I think that you've been dreadfully deluded.
ORGON:
Now then, dear Brother, is your speech concluded?   150
CLÉANTE:
Why, yes.
ORGON:
                    Your servant, Sir. [*He turns to go.*]
CLÉANTE:
                        No, Brother; wait.
There's one more matter. You agreed of late
That young Valère might have your daughter's hand.
ORGON:
I did.
CLÉANTE:
        And set the date, I understand.
ORGON:
Quite so.
CLÉANTE:
        You've now postponed it; is that true?
ORGON:
No doubt.
CLÉANTE:
        The match no longer pleases you?
ORGON:
Who knows?
CLÉANTE:
        D'you mean to go back on your word?
ORGON:
I won't say that.

CLÉANTE:

                Has anything occurred
Which might entitle you to break your pledge?

ORGON:

    Perhaps.

CLÉANTE:

                Why must you hem, and haw, and hedge?   160
The boy asked me to sound you in this affair...

ORGON:

    It's been a pleasure.

CLÉANTE:

                But what shall I tell Valère?

ORGON:

    Whatever you like.

CLÉANTE:

                But what have you decided?
What are your plans?

ORGON:

                I plan, Sir, to be guided
By Heaven's will.

CLÉANTE:

                Come, Brother, don't talk rot.
You've given Valère your word; will you keep it, or not?

ORGON:

    Good day.

CLÉANTE:

                This looks like poor Valère's undoing;
I'll go and warn him that there's trouble brewing.

ACT II

Scene 1

ORGON:

    Mariane.

MARIANE:

            Yes, Father?

ORGON:

                A word with you; come here.

MARIANE:

    What are you looking for?

ORGON [*peering into a small closet*]:

                Eavesdroppers, dear.
I'm making sure we shan't be overheard.
Someone in there could catch our every word.
Ah, good, we're safe. Now, Mariane, my child,
You're a sweet girl who's tractable and mild,
Whom I hold dear, and think most highly of.

MARIANE:

I'm deeply grateful, Father, for your love.

ORGON:

That's well said, Daughter; and you can repay me
If, in all things, you'll cheerfully obey me.   10

MARIANE:
  To please you, Sir, is what delights me best.
ORGON:
  Good, good. Now, what d'you think of Tartuffe, our guest?
MARIANE:
  I, Sir?
ORGON:
              Yes. Weigh your answer; think it through.
MARIANE:
  Oh, dear. I'll say whatever you wish me to.
ORGON:
  That's wisely said, my Daughter. Say of him, then,
  That he's the very worthiest of men,
  And that you're fond of him, and would rejoice
  In being his wife, if that should be my choice.
  Well?
MARIANE:
          What?
ORGON:
                What's that?
MARIANE:
                            I...
ORGON:
                                  Well?
MARIANE:
                                        Forgive me, pray.
ORGON:
  Did you not hear me?
MARIANE:
                      Of *whom,* Sir, must I say   20
  That I am fond of him, and would rejoice
  In being his wife, if that should be your choice?
ORGON:
  Why, of Tartuffe.
MARIANE:
                    But, Father, that's false, you know.
  Why would you have me say what isn't so?
ORGON:
  Because I am resolved it shall be true.
  That it's my wish should be enough for you.
MARIANE:
  You can't mean, Father...
ORGON:
                            Yes, Tartuffe shall be
  Allied by marriage to this family,
  And he's to be your husband, is that clear?
  It's a father's privilege...   30

Scene 2
ORGON [*to* DORINE]:
                      What are you doing in here?
  Is curiosity so fierce a passion

With you, that you must eavesdrop in this fashion?
DORINE:
    There's lately been a rumor going about—
    Based on some hunch or chance remark, no doubt—
    That you mean Mariane to wed Tartuffe.
    I've laughed it off, of course, as just a spoof.
ORGON:
    You find it so incredible?
DORINE:
                     Yes, I do.
    I won't accept that story, even from you.
ORGON:
    Well, you'll believe it when the thing is done.   10
DORINE:
    Yes, yes, of course. Go on and have your fun.
ORGON:
    I've never been more serious in my life.
DORINE:
    Ha!
ORGON:
        Daughter, I mean it; you're to be his wife.
DORINE:
    No, don't believe your father; it's all a hoax.
ORGON:
    See here, young woman...
DORINE:
               Come, Sir, no more jokes;
    You can't fool us.
ORGON:
          How dare you talk that way?
DORINE:
    All right, then: we believe you, sad to say.
    But how a man like you, who looks so wise
    And wears a moustache of such splendid size,
    Can be so foolish as to...
ORGON:
            Silence, please!   20
    My girl, you take too many liberties.
    I'm master here, as you must not forget.
DORINE:
    Do let's discuss this calmly; don't be upset.
    You can't be serious, Sir, about this plan.
    What should that bigot want with Mariane?
    Praying and fasting ought to keep him busy.
    And then, in terms of wealth and rank, what is he?
    Why should a man of poverty like you
    Pick out a beggar son-in-law?
ORGON:
            That will do.
    Speak of his poverty with reverence.   30
    His is a pure and saintly indigence
    Which far transcends all worldly pride and pelf.

He lost his fortune, as he says himself,
Because he cared for Heaven alone, and so
Was careless of his interests here below.
I mean to get him out of his present straits
And help him to recover his estates—
Which, in his part of the world, have no small fame.
Poor though he is, he's a gentleman just the same.

DORINE:
Yes, so he tells us; and, Sir, it seems to me   40
Such pride goes very ill with piety.
A man whose spirit spurns this dungy earth
Ought not to brag of lands and noble birth;
Such worldly arrogance will hardly square
With meek devotion and the life of prayer.
. . . But this reproach, I see, has drawn a blank;
Let's speak, then, of his person, not his rank.
Doesn't it seem to you a trifle grim
To give a girl like her to a man like him?
When two are so ill-suited, can't you see   50
What the sad consequence is bound to be?
A young girl's virtue is imperilled, Sir,
When such a marriage is imposed on her;
For if one's bridegroom isn't to one's taste,
It's hardly an inducement to be chaste,
And many a man with horns upon his brow
Has made his wife the thing that she is now.
It's hard to be a faithful wife, in short,
To certain husbands of a certain sort,
And he who gives his daughter to a man she hates
Must answer for her sins at Heaven's gates.   60
Think, Sir, before you play so risky a role.

ORGON:
This servant-girl presumes to save my soul!

DORINE:
You would do well to ponder what I've said.

ORGON:
Daughter, we'll disregard this dunderhead.
Just trust your father's judgment. Oh, I'm aware
That I once promised you to young Valère;
But now I hear he gambles, which greatly shocks me;
What's more, I've doubts about his orthodoxy.
His visits to church, I note, are very few.   70

DORINE:
Would you have him go at the same hours as you,
And kneel nearby, to be sure of being seen?

ORGON:
I can dispense with such remarks, Dorine.
[To MARIANE] Tartuffe, however, is sure of Heaven's blessing,
And that's the only treasure worth possessing.
This match will bring you joys beyond all measure;
Your cup will overflow with every pleasure;
You two will interchange your faithful loves

Like two sweet cherubs, or two turtle-doves.
No harsh word shall be heard, no frown be seen,   80
And he shall make you happy as a queen.
DORINE:
And she'll make him a cuckold, just wait and see.
ORGON:
What language!
DORINE:
                          Oh, he's a man of destiny;
He's *made* for horns, and what the stars demand
Your daughter's virtue surely can't withstand.
ORGON:
Don't interrupt me further. Why can't you learn
That certain things are none of your concern?
DORINE:
It's for your own sake that I interfere.
    [*She repeatedly interrupts* ORGON *just as he is turning to speak to his daughter.*]
ORGON:
Most kind of you. Now, hold your tongue, d'you hear?
DORINE:
If I didn't love you ...
ORGON:
                          Spare me your affection.   90
DORINE:
I love you, Sir, in spite of your objection.
ORGON:
Blast!
DORINE:
          I can't bear, Sir, for your honor's sake,
To let you make this ludicrous mistake.
ORGON:
You mean to go on talking?
DORINE:
                          If I didn't protest
This sinful marriage, my conscience couldn't rest.
ORGON:
If you don't hold your tongue, you little shrew ...
DORINE:
What, lost your temper? A pious man like you?
ORGON:
Yes! Yes! You talk and talk. I'm maddened by it.
Once and for all, I tell you to be quiet.
DORINE:
Well, I'll be quiet. But I'll be thinking hard.   100
ORGON:
Think all you like, but you had better guard
That saucy tongue of yours, or I'll ...
    [*Turning back to* MARIANE]   Now, child,
I've weighed this matter fully.
DORINE [*aside*]:
                          It drives me wild
That I can't speak.

[ORGON *turns his head, and she is silent.*]

ORGON:

      Tartuffe is no young dandy,

But, still, his person...

DORINE [*aside*]:

       Is as sweet as candy.

ORGON:

Is such that, even if you shouldn't care

For his other merits...

    [*He turns and stands facing* DORINE, *arms crossed.*]

DORINE [*aside*]:

       They'll make a lovely pair.

If I were she, no man would marry me

Against my inclination, and go scot-free.

He'd learn, before the wedding-day was over,

How readily a wife can find a lover.   110

ORGON [*to* DORINE]:

It seems you treat my orders as a joke.

DORINE:

Why, what's the matter? 'Twas not to you I spoke.

ORGON:

What *were* you doing?

DORINE:

     Talking to myself, that's all.

ORGON:

Ah! [*aside*] One more bit of impudence and gall,

And I shall give her a good slap in the face.

    [*He puts himself in position to slap her;* DORINE,

    whenever he glances at her, stands immobile and silent.]

Daughter, you shall accept, and with good grace,

The husband I've selected... Your wedding-day...

[*To* DORINE] Why don't you talk to yourself?

DORINE:

       I've nothing to say.

ORGON:

Come, just one word.

DORINE:

     No thank you, Sir. I pass.   120

ORGON:

Come, speak; I'm waiting.

DORINE:

     I'd not be such an ass.

ORGON [*turning to* MARIANE]:

In short, dear Daughter, I mean to be obeyed,

And you must bow to the sound choice I've made.

DORINE [*moving away*]:

I'd not wed such a monster, even in jest.

    [ORGON *attempts to slap her, but misses.*]

ORGON:

Daughter, that maid of yours is a thorough pest;

She makes me sinfully annoyed and nettled.

I can't speak further; my nerves are too unsettled.

She's so upset me by her insolent talk,
I'll calm myself by going for a walk.

Scene 3

DORINE [*returning*]:
    Well, have you lost your tongue, girl? Must I play
    Your part, and say the lines you ought to say?
    Faced with a fate so hideous and absurd,
    Can you not utter one dissenting word?
MARIANE:
    What good would it do? A father's power is great.
DORINE:
    Resist him now, or it will be too late.
MARIANE:
    But...
DORINE:
        Tell him one cannot love at a father's whim;
    That you shall marry for yourself, not him;
    That since it's you who are to be the bride,
    It's you, not he, who must be satisfied;   10
    And that if his Tartuffe is so sublime,
    He's free to marry him at any time.
MARIANE:
    I've bowed so long to Father's strict control,
    I couldn't oppose him now, to save my soul.
DORINE:
    Come, come, Mariane. Do listen to reason, won't you?
    Valère has asked your hand. Do you love him, or don't you?
MARIANE:
    Oh, how unjust of you! What can you mean
    By asking such a question, dear Dorine?
    You know the depth of my affection for him;
    I've told you a hundred times how I adore him.   20
DORINE:
    I don't believe in everything I hear;
    Who knows if your professions were sincere?
MARIANE:
    They were, Dorine, and you do me wrong to doubt it;
    Heaven knows that I've been all too frank about it.
DORINE:
    You love him, then?
MARIANE:
        Oh, more than I can express.
DORINE:
    And he, I take it, cares for you no less?
MARIANE:
    I think so.
DORINE:
        And you both, with equal fire,
    Burn to be married?
MARIANE:
        That is our one desire.

DORINE:
> What of Tartuffe, then? What of your father's plan?

MARIANE:
> I'll kill myself, if I'm forced to wed that man.   30

DORINE:
> I hadn't thought of that recourse. How splendid!
> Just die, and all your troubles will be ended!
> A fine solution. Oh, it maddens me
> To hear you talk in that self-pitying key.

MARIANE:
> Dorine, how harsh you are! It's most unfair.
> You have no sympathy for my despair.

DORINE:
> I've none at all for people who talk drivel
> And, faced with difficulties, whine and snivel.

MARIANE:
> No doubt I'm timid, but it would be wrong...

DORINE:
> True love requires a heart that's firm and strong.   40

MARIANE:
> I'm strong in my affection for Valère,
> But coping with my father is his affair.

DORINE:
> But if your father's brain has grown so cracked
> Over his dear Tartuffe that he can retract
> His blessing, though your wedding-day was named,
> It's surely not Valère who's to be blamed.

MARIANE:
> If I defied my father, as you suggest,
> Would it not seem unmaidenly, at best?
> Shall I defend my love at the expense
> Of brazenness and disobedience?   50
> Shall I parade my heart's desires, and flaunt...

DORINE:
> No, I ask nothing of you. Clearly you want
> To be Madame Tartuffe, and I feel bound
> Not to oppose a wish so very sound.
> What right have I to criticize the match?
> Indeed, my dear, the man is a brilliant catch.
> Monsieur Tartuffe! Now, there's a man of weight!
> Yes, yes, Monsieur Tartuffe, I'm bound to state,
> Is quite a person; that's not to be denied;
> 'Twill be no little thing to be his bride.   60
> The world already rings with his renown;
> He's a great noble—in his native town;
> His ears are red, he has a pink complexion,
> And all in all, he'll suit you to perfection.

MARIANE:
> Dear God!

DORINE:
>   Oh, how triumphant you will feel
> At having caught a husband so ideal!

MARIANE:
> Oh, do stop teasing, and use your cleverness
> To get me out of this appalling mess.
> Advise me, and I'll do whatever you say.

DORINE:
> Ah no, a dutiful daughter must obey   70
> Her father, even if he weds her to an ape.
> You've a bright future; why struggle to escape?
> Tartuffe will take you back where his family lives,
> To a small town aswarm with relatives—
> Uncles and cousins whom you'll be charmed to meet.
> You'll be received at once by the elite,
> Calling upon the bailiff's wife, no less—
> Even, perhaps, upon the mayoress,
> Who'll sit you down in the *best* kitchen chair.
> Then, once a year, you'll dance at the village fair   80
> To the drone of bagpipes—two of them, in fact—
> And see a puppet-show, or an animal act.
> Your husband...

MARIANE:
>   Oh, you turn my blood to ice!
> Stop torturing me, and give me your advice.

DORINE [*threatening to go*]:
> Your servant, Madam.

MARIANE:
>   Dorine, I beg of you...

DORINE:
> No, you deserve it; this marriage must go through.

MARIANE:
> Dorine!

DORINE:
>   No.

MARIANE:
>   Not Tartuffe! You know I think him...

DORINE:
> Tartuffe's your cup of tea, and you shall drink him.

MARIANE:
> I've always told you everything, and relied...

DORINE:
> No. You deserve to be tartuffified.   90

MARIANE:
> Well, since you mock me and refuse to care,
> I'll henceforth seek my solace in despair:
> Despair shall be my counsellor and friend,
> And help me bring my sorrows to an end.
>   [*She starts to leave.*]

DORINE:
> There now, come back; my anger has subsided.
> You do deserve some pity, I've decided.

MARIANE:
> Dorine, if Father makes me undergo
> This dreadful martyrdom, I'll die, I know.

DORINE:
Don't fret; it won't be difficult to discover
Some plan of action . . . But here's Valère, your lover.   100

Scene 4

VALÈRE:
Madame, I've just received some wondrous news
Regarding which I'd like to hear your views.
MARIANE:
What news?
VALÈRE:
You're marrying Tartuffe.
MARIANE:
I find
That Father does have such a match in mind.
VALÈRE:
Your father, Madam . . .
MARIANE:
. . . has just this minute said
That it's Tartuffe he wishes me to wed.
VALÈRE:
Can he be serious?
MARIANE:
Oh, indeed he can;
He's clearly set his heart upon the plan.
VALÈRE:
And what position do you propose to take, Madam?
MARIANE:
Why—I don't know.
VALÈRE:
For heaven's sake—   10
You don't know?
MARIANE:
No.
VALÈRE:
Well, well!
MARIANE:
Advise me, do.
VALÈRE:
Marry the man. That's my advice to you.
MARIANE:
That's your advice?
VALÈRE:
Yes.
MARIANE:
Truly?
VALÈRE:
Oh, absolutely.
You couldn't choose more wisely, more astutely.
MARIANE:
Thanks for this counsel; I'll follow it, of course.

VALÈRE:
Do, do; I'm sure 'twill cost you no remorse.
MARIANE:
To give it didn't cause your heart to break.
VALÈRE:
I gave it, Madam, only for your sake.
MARIANE:
And it's for your sake that I take it, Sir.
DORINE [*withdrawing to the rear of the stage*]:
Let's see which fool will prove the stubborner.   20
VALÈRE:
So! I am nothing to you, and it was flat
Deception when you . . .
MARIANE:
                              Please, enough of that.
You've told me plainly that I should agree
To wed the man my father's chosen for me,
And since you've designed to counsel me so wisely,
I promise, Sir, to do as you advise me.
VALÈRE:
Ah, no, 'twas not by me that you were swayed.
No, your decision was already made;
Though now, to save appearances, you protest
That you're betraying me at my behest.   30
MARIANE:
Just as you say.
VALÈRE:
                    Quite so. And I now see
That you were never truly in love with me.
MARIANE:
Alas, you're free to think so if you choose.
VALÈRE:
I choose to think so, and here's a bit of news:
You've spurned my hand, but I know where to turn
For kinder treatment, as you shall quickly learn.
MARIANE:
I'm sure you do. Your noble qualities
Inspire affection . . .
VALÈRE:
                          Forget my qualities, please.
They don't inspire you overmuch, I find.
But there's another lady I have in mind   40
Whose sweet and generous nature will not scorn
To compensate me for the loss I've borne.
MARIANE:
I'm no great loss, and I'm sure that you'll transfer
Your heart quite painlessly from me to her.
VALÈRE:
I'll do my best to take it in my stride.
The pain I feel at being cast aside
Time and forgetfulness may put an end to.
Or if I can't forget, I shall pretend to.

No self-respecting person is expected
To go on loving once he's been rejected.   50
MARIANE:
Now, that's a fine, high-minded sentiment.
VALÈRE:
One to which any sane man would assent.
Would you prefer it if I pined away
In hopeless passion till my dying day?
Am I to yield you to a rival's arms
And not console myself with other charms?
MARIANE:
Go then: console yourself; don't hesitate.
I wish you to; indeed, I cannot wait.
VALÈRE:
You wish me to?
MARIANE:
                          Yes.
VALÈRE:
                                    That's the final straw.
Madam, farewell. Your wish shall be my law.   60
                    [*He starts to leave, and then returns: this repeatedly.*]
MARIANE:
Splendid.
VALÈRE [*coming back again*]:
              This breach, remember, is of your making;
It's you who've driven me to the step I'm taking.
MARIANE:
Of course.
VALÈRE [*coming back again*]:
                    Remember, too, that I am merely
Following your example.
MARIANE:
                                I see that clearly.
VALÈRE:
Enough. I'll go and do your bidding, then.
MARIANE:
Good.
VALÈRE [*coming back again*]:
              You shall never see my face again.
MARIANE:
Excellent.
VALÈRE [*walking to the door, then turning about*]:
                    Yes?
MARIANE:
                          What?
VALÈRE:
                                What's that? What did you say?
MARIANE:
Nothing. You're dreaming.
VALÈRE:
                                Ah. Well, I'm on my way.
Farewell, *Madame.*
                    [*He moves slowly away.*]

MARIANE:
  Farewell.
DORINE [*to* MARIANE]:
        If you ask me,
  Both of you are as mad as mad can be.
  Do stop this nonsense, now. I've only let you
  Squabble so long to see where it would get you.
  Whoa there, Monsieur Valère!
      [*She goes and seizes* VALÈRE *by the arm; he makes a great show of resistance.*]
VALÈRE:
                    What's this, Dorine?
DORINE:
  Come here.
VALÈRE:
          No, no, my heart's too full of spleen.
  Don't hold me back; her wish must be obeyed.
DORINE:
  Stop!
VALÈRE:
        It's too late now; my decision's made.
DORINE:
  Oh, pooh!
MARIANE [*aside*]:
          He hates the sight of me, that's plain.
  I'll go, and so deliver him from pain.
DORINE [*leaving* VALÈRE, *running after* MARIANE]:
  And now *you* run away! Come back.
MARIANE:
                      No, no.
  Nothing you say will keep me here. Let go!
VALÈRE [*aside*]:
  She cannot bear my presence, I perceive.
  To spare her further torment, I shall leave.
DORINE [*leaving* MARIANE, *running after* VALÈRE]:
  Again! You'll not escape, Sir; don't you try it.
  Come here, you two. Stop fussing, and be quiet.
      [*She takes* VALÈRE *by the hand, then* MARIANE, *and draws them together.*]
VALÈRE [*to* DORINE]:
  What do you want of me?
MARIANE [*to* DORINE]:
                What is the point of this?
DORINE:
  We're going to have a little armistice.
  [*To* VALÈRE] Now weren't you silly to get so overheated?
VALÈRE:
  Didn't you see how badly I was treated?
DORINE [*to* MARIANE]:
  Aren't you a simpleton, to have lost your head?
MARIANE:
  Didn't you hear the hateful things he said?
DORINE [*to* VALÈRE]:
  You're both great fools. Her sole desire, Valère,
  Is to be yours in marriage. To that I'll swear.

70

80

90

[*To* MARIANE] He loves you only, and he wants no wife
But you, Mariane. On that I'll stake my life.
MARIANE [*to* VALÈRE]:
Then why you advised me so, I cannot see.
VALÈRE [*to* MARIANE]:
On such a question, why ask advice of *me?*
DORINE:
Oh, you're impossible. Give me your hands, you two.
[*To* VALÈRE] Yours first.
VALÈRE [*giving* DORINE *his hand*]:
                        But why?
DORINE [*to* MARIANE]:
                        And now a hand from you.
MARIANE [*also giving* DORINE *her hand*]:
What are you doing?
DORINE:
                There: a perfect fit.
You suit each other better than you'll admit.   100
    [VALÈRE *and* MARIANE *hold hands for some time without looking at each other.*]
VALÈRE [*turning toward* MARIANE]:
Ah, come, don't be so haughty. Give a man
A look of kindness, won't you, Mariane?
                [MARIANE *turns toward* VALÈRE *and smiles.*]
DORINE:
I tell you, lovers are completely mad!
VALÈRE [*to* MARIANE]:
Now come, confess that you were very bad
To hurt my feelings as you did just now.
I have a just complaint, you must allow.
MARIANE:
You must allow that you were most unpleasant...
DORINE:
Let's table that discussion for the present;
Your father has a plan which must be stopped.
MARIANE:
Advise us, then; what means must we adopt?   110
DORINE:
We'll use all manner of means, and all at once.
[*To* MARIANE] Your father's addled; he's acting like a dunce.
Therefore you'd better humor the old fossil.
Pretend to yield to him, be sweet and docile,
And then postpone, as often as necessary,
The day on which you have agreed to marry.
You'll thus gain time, and time will turn the trick.
Sometimes, for instance, you'll be taken sick,
And that will seem good reason for delay;
Or some bad omen will make you change the day—   120
You'll dream of muddy water, or you'll pass
A dead man's hearse, or break a looking-glass.
If all else fails, no man can marry you
Unless you take his ring and say "I do."
But now, let's separate. If they should find
Us talking here, our plot might be divined.

[*To* VALÈRE] Go to your friends, and tell them what's occurred,
And have them urge her father to keep his word.
Meanwhile, we'll stir her brother into action,
And get Elmire, as well, to join our faction.   130
Good-bye.

VALÈRE [*to* MARIANE]:
           Though each of us will do his best,
It's your true heart on which my hopes shall rest.

MARIANE [*to* VALÈRE]:
Regardless of what Father may decide,
None but Valère shall claim me as his bride.

VALÈRE:
Oh, how those words content me! Come what will...

DORINE:
Oh, lovers, lovers! Their tongues are never still.
Be off, now.

VALÈRE [*turning to go, then turning back*]:
           One last word...

DORINE:
                No time to chat:
You leave by this door; and *you* leave by that.
[DORINE *pushes them, by the shoulders, toward opposing doors.*]

ACT III

Scene 1

DAMIS:
May lightning strike me even as I speak,
May all men call me cowardly and weak,
If any fear or scruple holds me back
From settling things, at once, with that great quack!

DORINE:
Now, don't give way to violent emotion.
Your father's merely talked about this notion,
And words and deeds are far from being one.
Much that is talked about is left undone.

DAMIS:
No, I must stop that scoundrel's machinations;
I'll go and tell him off; I'm out of patience.   10

DORINE:
Do calm down and be practical. I had rather
My mistress dealt with him—and with your father.
She has some influence with Tartuffe, I've noted.
He hangs upon her words, seems most devoted,
And may, indeed, be smitten by her charm.
Pray Heaven it's true! 'Twould do our cause no harm.
She sent for him, just now, to sound him out
On this affair you're so incensed about;
She'll find out where he stands, and tell him, too,
What dreadful strife and trouble will ensue   20
If he lends countenance to your father's plan.
I couldn't get in to see him, but his man

Says that he's almost finished with his prayers.
Go, now. I'll catch him when he comes downstairs.
DAMIS:
  I want to hear this conference, and I will.
DORINE:
  No, they must be alone.
DAMIS:
                    Oh, I'll keep still.
DORINE:
  Not you. I know your temper. You'd start a brawl,
  And shout and stamp your foot and spoil it all.
  Go on.
DAMIS:
         I won't; I have a perfect right...
DORINE:
  Lord, you're a nuisance! He's coming; get out of sight.   30
     [DAMIS *conceals himself in a closet at the rear of the stage.*]

Scene 2

TARTUFFE [*observing* DORINE, *and calling to his manservant offstage*]:
  Hang up my hair-shirt, put my scourge in place,
  And pray, Laurent, for Heaven's perpetual grace.
  I'm going to the prison now, to share
  My last two coins with the poor wretches there.
DORINE [*aside*]:
  Dear God, what affectation! What a fake!
TARTUFFE:
  You wished to see me?
DORINE:
               Yes...
TARTUFFE [*taking a handkerchief from his pocket*]:
                    For mercy's sake,
  Please take this handkerchief, before you speak.
DORINE:
  What?
TARTUFFE:
        Cover that bosom, girl. The flesh is weak,
  And unclean thoughts are difficult to control.
  Such sights as that can undermine the soul.   10
DORINE:
  Your soul, it seems, has very poor defenses,
  And flesh makes quite an impact on your senses.
  It's strange that you're so easily excited;
  My own desires are not so soon ignited,
  And if I saw you naked as a beast,
  Not all your hide would tempt me in the least.
TARTUFFE:
  Girl, speak more modestly; unless you do,
  I shall be forced to take my leave of you.
DORINE:
  Oh, no, it's I who must be on my way;

I've just one little message to convey.
Madame is coming down, and begs you, Sir,
To wait and have a word or two with her.

TARTUFFE:
Gladly.

DORINE [*aside*]:
    That had a softening effect!
I think my guess about him was correct.

TARTUFFE:
Will she be long?

DORINE:
      No: that's her step I hear.
Ah, here she is, and I shall disappear.

        Scene 3

TARTUFFE:
May Heaven, whose infinite goodness we adore,
Preserve your body and soul forevermore,
And bless your days, and answer thus the plea
Of one who is its humblest votary.

ELMIRE:
I thank you for that pious wish. But please,
Do take a chair and let's be more at ease.
        [*They sit down.*]

TARTUFFE:
I trust that you are once more well and strong?

ELMIRE:
Oh, yes: the fever didn't last for long.

TARTUFFE:
My prayers are too unworthy, I am sure,
To have gained from Heaven this most gracious cure;
But lately, Madam, my every supplication
Has had for object your recuperation.

ELMIRE:
You shouldn't have troubled so. I don't deserve it.

TARTUFFE:
Your health is priceless, Madam, and to preserve it
I'd gladly give my own, in all sincerity.

ELMIRE:
Sir, you outdo us all in Christian charity.
You've been most kind. I count myself your debtor.

TARTUFFE:
'Twas nothing, Madam. I long to serve you better.

ELMIRE:
There's a private matter I'm anxious to discuss.
I'm glad there's no one here to hinder us.

TARTUFFE:
I too am glad; it floods my heart with bliss
To find myself alone with you like this.
For just this chance I've prayed with all my power—
But prayed in vain, until this happy hour.

ELMIRE:

    This won't take long, Sir, and I hope you'll be
    Entirely frank and unconstrained with me.

TARTUFFE:

    Indeed, there's nothing I had rather do
    Than bare my inmost heart and soul to you.
    First, let me say that what remarks I've made
    About the constant visits you are paid   30
    Were prompted not by any mean emotion,
    But rather by a pure and deep devotion,
    A fervent zeal...

ELMIRE:

                  No need for explanation.
    Your sole concern, I'm sure, was my salvation.

TARTUFFE [*taking* ELMIRE's *hand and pressing her fingertips*]:

    Quite so; and such great fervor do I feel...

ELMIRE:

    Ooh! Please! You're pinching!

TARTUFFE:

                  'Twas from excess of zeal.
    I never meant to cause you pain, I swear.
    I'd rather...

           [*He places his hand on* ELMIRE's *knee.*]

ELMIRE:

    What can your hand be doing there?

TARTUFFE:

    Feeling your gown; what soft, fine-woven stuff!

ELMIRE:

    Please, I'm extremely ticklish. That's enough.   40

        [*She draws her chair away;* TARTUFFE *pulls his after her.*]

TARTUFFE [*fondling the lace collar of her gown*]:

    My, my what lovely lacework on your dress!
    The workmanship's miraculous, no less.
    I've not seen anything to equal it.

ELMIRE:

    Yes, quite. But let's talk business for a bit.
    They say my husband means to break his word
    And give his daughter to you, Sir. Had you heard?

TARTUFFE:

    He did once mention it. But I confess
    I dream of quite a different happiness.
    It's elsewhere, Madam, that my eyes discern
    The promise of that bliss for which I yearn.   50

ELMIRE:

    I see: you care for nothing here below.

TARTUFFE:

    Ah, well—my heart's not made of stone, you know.

ELMIRE:

    All your desires mount heavenward, I'm sure,
    In scorn of all that's earthly and impure.

TARTUFFE:

    A love of heavenly beauty does not preclude

A proper love for earthly pulchritude;
Our senses are quite rightly captivated
By perfect works our Maker has created.
Some glory clings to all that Heaven has made;
In you, all Heaven's marvels are displayed.   60
On that fair face, such beauties have been lavished,
The eyes are dazzled and the heart is ravished;
How could I look on you, O flawless creature,
And not adore the Author of all Nature,
Feeling a love both passionate and pure
For you, his triumph of self-portraiture?
At first, I trembled lest that love should be
A subtle snare that Hell had laid for me;
I vowed to flee the sight of you, eschewing
A rapture that might prove my soul's undoing;   70
But soon, fair being, I became aware
That my deep passion could be made to square
With rectitude, and with my bounden duty.
I thereupon surrendered to your beauty.
It is, I know, presumptuous on my part
To bring you this poor offering of my heart,
And it is not my merit, Heaven knows,
But your compassion on which my hopes repose.
You are my peace, my solace, my salvation;
On you depends my bliss—or desolation;   80
I bide your judgment and, as you think best,
I shall be either miserable or blest.

ELMIRE:
Your declaration is most gallant, Sir,
But don't you think it's out of character?
You'd have done better to restrain your passion
And think before you spoke in such a fashion.
It ill becomes a pious man like you...

TARTUFFE:
I may be pious, but I'm human too:
With your celestial charms before his eyes,
A man has not the power to be wise.   90
I know such words sound strangely, coming from me,
But I'm no angel, nor was meant to be,
And if you blame my passion, you must needs
Reproach as well the charms on which it feeds.
Your loveliness I had no sooner seen
Than you became my soul's unrivalled queen;
Before your seraph glance, divinely sweet,
My heart's defenses crumbled in defeat,
And nothing fasting, prayer, or tears might do
Could stay my spirit from adoring you.   100
My eyes, my sighs have told you in the past
What now my lips make bold to say at last,
And if, in your great goodness, you will deign
To look upon your slave, and ease his pain,—
If, in compassion for my soul's distress,

You'll stoop to comfort my unworthiness,
I'll raise to you, in thanks for that sweet manna,
An endless hymn, an infinite hosanna.
With me, of course, there need be no anxiety,
No fear of scandal or of notoriety.   110
These young court gallants, whom all the ladies fancy,
Are vain in speech, in action rash and chancy;
When they succeed in love, the world soon knows it;
No favor's granted them but they disclose it
And by the looseness of their tongues profane
The very altar where their hearts have lain.
Men of my sort, however, love discreetly,
And one may trust our reticence completely.
My keen concern for my good name insures
The absolute security of yours;   120
In short, I offer you, my dear Elmire,
Love without scandal, pleasure without fear.

ELMIRE:
I've heard your well-turned speeches to the end,
And what you urge I clearly apprehend.
Aren't you afraid that I may take a notion
To tell my husband of your warm devotion,
And that, supposing he were duly told,
His feelings toward you might grow rather cold?

TARTUFFE:
I know, dear lady, that your exceeding charity
Will lead your heart to pardon my temerity;   130
That you'll excuse my violent affection
As human weakness, human imperfection;
And that—O fairest!—you will bear in mind
That I'm but flesh and blood, and am not blind.

ELMIRE:
Some women might do otherwise, perhaps,
But I shall be discreet about your lapse;
I'll tell my husband nothing of what's occurred
If, in return, you'll give your solemn word
To advocate as forcefully as you can
The marriage of Valère and Mariane,   140
Renouncing all desire to dispossess
Another of his rightful happiness,
And...

Scene 4

DAMIS [*emerging from the closet where he has been hiding*]:
          No! We'll not hush up this vile affair;
I heard it all inside that closet there,
Where Heaven, in order to confound the pride
Of this great rascal, prompted me to hide.
Ah, now I have my long-awaited chance
To punish his deceit and arrogance,
And give my father clear and shocking proof

Of the black character of his dear Tartuffe.
ELMIRE:
    Ah no, Damis; I'll be content if he
    Will study to deserve my leniency.   10
    I've promised silence—don't make me break my word;
    To make a scandal would be too absurd.
    Good wives laugh off such trifles, and forget them;
    Why should they tell their husbands, and upset them?
DAMIS:
    You have your reasons for taking such a course,
    And I have reasons, too, of equal force.
    To spare him now would be insanely wrong.
    I've swallowed my just wrath for far too long
    And watched this insolent bigot bringing strife
    And bitterness into our family life.   20
    Too long he's meddled in my father's affairs,
    Thwarting my marriage-hopes, and poor Valère's.
    It's high time that my father was undeceived,
    And now I've proof that can't be disbelieved—
    Proof that was furnished me by Heaven above.
    It's too good not to take advantage of.
    This is my chance, and I deserve to lose it
    If, for one moment, I hesitate to use it.
ELMIRE:
    Damis...
DAMIS:
            No, I must do what I think right.
    Madam, my heart is bursting with delight,   30
    And, say whatever you will, I'll not consent
    To lose the sweet revenge on which I'm bent.
    I'll settle matters without more ado;
    And here, most opportunely, is my cue.

Scene 5

DAMIS:
    Father, I'm glad you've joined us. Let us advise you
    Of some fresh news which doubtless will surprise you.
    You've just now been repaid with interest
    For all your loving-kindness to our guest.
    He's proved his warm and grateful feelings toward you;
    It's with a pair of horns he would reward you.
    Yes, I surprised him with your wife, and heard
    His whole adulterous offer, every word.
    She, with her all too gentle disposition,
    Would not have told you of his proposition;   10
    But I shall not make terms with brazen lechery,
    And feel that not to tell you would be treachery.
ELMIRE:
    And I hold that one's husband's peace of mind
    Should not be spoilt by tattle of this kind.
    One's honor doesn't require it: to be proficient
    In keeping men at bay is quite sufficient.

These are my sentiments, and I wish, Damis,
That you had heeded me and held your peace.

Scene 6

ORGON:

Can it be true, this dreadful thing I hear?

TARTUFFE:

Yes, Brother, I'm a wicked man, I fear:
A wretched sinner, all depraved and twisted,
The greatest villain that has ever existed.
My life's one heap of crimes, which grows each minute;
There's naught but foulness and corruption in it;
And I perceive that Heaven, outraged by me,
Has chosen this occasion to mortify me.
Charge me with any deed you wish to name;
I'll not defend myself, but take the blame.
Believe what you are told, and drive Tartuffe
Like some base criminal from beneath your roof;
Yes, drive me hence, and with a parting curse:
I shan't protest, for I deserve far worse.   10

ORGON [*to* DAMIS]:

Ah, you deceitful boy, how dare you try
To stain his purity with so foul a lie?

DAMIS:

What! Are you taken in by such a bluff?
Did you not hear . . . ?

ORGON:

                Enough, you rogue, enough!

TARTUFFE:

Ah, Brother, let him speak: you're being unjust.
Believe his story; the boy deserves your trust.   20
Why, after all, should you have faith in me?
How can you know what I might do, or be?
Is it on my good actions that you base
Your favor? Do you trust my pious face?
Ah, no, don't be deceived by hollow shows;
I'm far, alas, from being what men suppose;
Though the world takes me for a man of worth,
I'm truly the most worthless man on earth.
[*To* DAMIS] Yes, my dear son, speak out now: call me the chief
Of sinners, a wretch, a murderer, a thief;   30
Load me with all the names men most abhor;
I'll not complain; I've earned them all, and more;
I'll kneel here while you pour them on my head
As a just punishment for the life I've led.

ORGON [*to* TARTUFFE]:

This is too much, dear Brother.
[*To* DAMIS]   Have you no heart?

DAMIS:

Are you so hoodwinked by this rascal's art . . . ?

ORGON:

   Be still, you monster.

   [*To* TARTUFFE]   Brother, I pray you, rise.

   [*To* DAMIS] Villain!

DAMIS:

               But...

ORGON:

                    Silence!

DAMIS:

                         Can't you realize...?

ORGON:

   Just one word more, and I'll tear you limb from limb.

TARTUFFE:

   In God's name, Brother, don't be harsh with him.   40

   I'd rather far be tortured at the stake

   Than see him bear one scratch for my poor sake.

ORGON [*to* DAMIS]:

   Ingrate!

TARTUFFE:

            If I must beg you, on bended knee,

   To pardon him...

ORGON [*falling to his knees, addressing* TARTUFFE]:

                  Such goodness cannot be!

   [*To* DAMIS] Now, *there's* true charity!

DAMIS:

                    What, you...?

ORGON:

                                Villain, be still!

   I know your motives; I know you wish him ill:

   Yes, all of you—wife, children, servants, all—

   Conspire against him and desire his fall,

   Employing every shameful trick you can

   To alienate me from this saintly man.

   Ah, but the more you seek to drive him away,   50

   The more I'll do to keep him. Without delay,

   I'll spite this household and confound its pride

   By giving him my daughter as his bride.

DAMIS:

   You're going to force her to accept his hand?

ORGON:

   Yes, and this very night, d'you understand?

   I shall defy you all, and make it clear

   That I'm the one who gives the orders here.

   Come, wretch, kneel down and clasp his blessed feet,

   And ask his pardon for your black deceit.   60

DAMIS:

   I ask that swindler's pardon? Why, I'd rather...

ORGON:

   So! You insult him, and defy your father!

   A stick! A stick! [*to* TARTUFFE] No, no—release me, do.

   [*To* DAMIS] Out of my house this minute! Be off with you,

And never dare set foot in it again.

DAMIS:

Well, I shall go, but...

ORGON:

                   Well, go quickly, then.

I disinherit you; an empty purse

Is all you'll get from me—except my curse!

Scene 7

ORGON:

How he blasphemed your goodness! What a son!

TARTUFFE:

Forgive him, Lord, as I've already done.

[*To* ORGON] You can't know how it hurts when someone tries

To blacken me in my dear Brother's eyes.

ORGON:

Ahh!

TARTUFFE:

      The mere thought of such ingratitude

Plunges my soul into so dark a mood...

Such horror grips my heart...I gasp for breath,

And cannot speak, and feel myself near death.

ORGON [*He runs, in tears, to the door through which he has just driven his son.*]:

You blackguard! Why did I spare you? Why did I not

Break you in little pieces on the spot?

Compose yourself, and don't be hurt, dear friend.   10

TARTUFFE:

These scenes, these dreadful quarrels, have got to end.

I've much upset your household, and I perceive

That the best thing will be for me to leave.

ORGON:

What are you saying!

TARTUFFE:

             They're all against me here;

They'd have you think me false and insincere.

ORGON:

Ah, what of that? Have I ceased believing in you?

TARTUFFE:

Their adverse talk will certainly continue,

And charges which you now repudiate

You may find credible at a later date.   20

ORGON:

No, Brother, never.

TARTUFFE:

            Brother, a wife can sway

Her husband's mind in many a subtle way.

ORGON:

No, no.

TARTUFFE:

          To leave at once is the solution;

Thus only can I end their persecution.

ORGON:

No, no, I'll not allow it; you shall remain.

TARTUFFE:

Ah, well; 'twill mean much martyrdom and pain,
But if you wish it . . .

ORGON:

               Ah!

TARTUFFE:

               Enough; so be it.
But one thing must be settled, as I see it.
For your dear honor, and for our friendship's sake,
There's one precaution I feel bound to take.   30
I shall avoid your wife, and keep away . . .

ORGON:

No, you shall not, whatever they may say.
It pleases me to vex them, and for spite
I'd have them see you with her day and night.
What's more, I'm going to drive them to despair
By making you my only son and heir;
This very day, I'll give to you alone
Clear deed and title to everything I own.
A dear, good friend and son-in-law-to-be
Is more than wife, or child, or kin to me.   40
Will you accept my offer, dearest son?

TARTUFFE:

In all things, let the will of Heaven be done.

ORGON:

Poor fellow! Come, we'll go draw up the deed.
Then let them burst with disappointed greed!

ACT IV

Scene 1

CLÉANTE:

Yes, all the town's discussing it, and truly,
Their comments do not flatter you unduly.
I'm glad we've met, Sir, and I'll give my view
Of this sad matter in a word or two.
As for who's guilty, that I shan't discuss;
Let's say it was Damis who caused the fuss;
Assuming, then, that you have been ill-used
By young Damis, and groundlessly accused,
Ought not a Christian to forgive, and ought
He not to stifle every vengeful thought?   10
Should you stand by and watch a father make
His only son an exile for your sake?
Again I tell you frankly, be advised:
The whole town, high and low, is scandalized;
This quarrel must be mended, and my advice is
Not to push matters to a further crisis.

No, sacrifice your wrath to God above,
And help Damis regain his father's love.
TARTUFFE:
Alas, for my part I should take great joy
In doing so. I've nothing against the boy.   20
I pardon all, I harbor no resentment;
To serve him would afford me much contentment.
But Heaven's interest will not have it so:
If he comes back, then I shall have to go.
After his conduct—so extreme, so vicious—
Our further intercourse would look suspicious.
God knows what people would think! Why, they'd describe
My goodness to him as a sort of bribe;
They'd say that out of guilt I made pretense
Of loving-kindness and benevolence—   30
That, fearing my accuser's tongue, I strove
To buy his silence with a show of love.
CLÉANTE:
Your reasoning is badly warped and stretched,
And these excuses, Sir, are most far-fetched.
Why put yourself in charge of Heaven's cause?
Does Heaven need our help to enforce its laws?
Leave vengeance to the Lord, Sir; while we live,
Our duty's not to punish, but forgive;
And what the Lord commands, we should obey
Without regard to what the world may say.   40
What! Shall the fear of being misunderstood
Prevent our doing what is right and good?
No, no; let's simply do what Heaven ordains,
And let no other thoughts perplex our brains.
TARTUFFE:
Again, Sir, let me say that I've forgiven
Damis, and thus obeyed the laws of Heaven;
But I am not commanded by the Bible
To live with one who smears my name with libel.
CLÉANTE:
Were you commanded, Sir, to indulge the whim
Of poor Orgon, and to encourage him   50
In suddenly transferring to your name
A large estate to which you have no claim?
TARTUFFE:
'Twould never occur to those who know me best
To think I acted from self-interest.
The treasures of this world I quite despise;
Their specious glitter does not charm my eyes;
And if I have resigned myself to taking
The gift which my dear Brother insists on making,
I do so only, as he well understands,
Lest so much wealth fall into wicked hands,   60
Lest those to whom it might descend in time
Turn it to purposes of sin and crime,
And not, as I shall do, make use of it
For Heaven's glory and mankind's benefit.

CLÉANTE:
>Forget these trumped-up fears. Your argument
>Is one the rightful heir might well resent;
>It *is* a moral burden to inherit
>Such wealth, but give Damis a chance to bear it.
>And would it not be worse to be accused
>Of swindling, than to see that wealth misused?
>I'm shocked that you allowed Orgon to broach
>This matter, and that you feel no self-reproach;
>Does true religion teach that lawful heirs
>May freely be deprived of what is theirs?
>And if the Lord has told you in your heart
>That you and young Damis must dwell apart,
>Would it not be the decent thing to beat
>A generous and honorable retreat,
>Rather than let the son of the house be sent,
>For your convenience, into banishment?
>Sir, if you wish to prove the honesty
>Of your intentions . . .

70

80

TARTUFFE:
>   Sir, it is half-past three.
>I've certain pious duties to attend to,
>And hope my prompt departure won't offend you.

CLÉANTE [*alone*]:
>Damn.

Scene 2

DORINE:
>   Stay, Sir, and help Mariane, for Heaven's sake!
>She's suffering so, I fear her heart will break.
>Her father's plan to marry her off tonight
>Has put the poor child in a desperate plight.
>I hear him coming. Let's stand together, now,
>And see if we can't change his mind, somehow,
>About this match we all deplore and fear.

Scene 3

ORGON:
>Hah! Glad to find you all assembled here.
>[*To* MARIANE] This contract, child, contains your happiness,
>And what it says I think your heart can guess.

MARIANE [*falling to her knees*]:
>Sir, by that Heaven which sees me here distressed,
>And by whatever else can move your breast,
>Do not employ a father's power, I pray you,
>To crush my heart and force it to obey you,
>Nor by your harsh commands oppress me so
>That I'll begrudge the duty which I owe—
>And do not so embitter and enslave me
>That I shall hate the very life you gave me.
>If my sweet hopes must perish, if you refuse
>To give me to the one I've dared to choose,
>Spare me at least—I beg you, I implore—

10

The pain of wedding one whom I abhor;
And do not, by a heartless use of force,
Drive me to contemplate some desperate course.
ORGON [*feeling himself touched by her*]:
  Be firm, my soul. No human weakness, now.
MARIANE:
  I don't resent your love for him. Allow
  Your heart free rein, Sir; give him your property,   20
  And if that's not enough, take mine from me;
  He's welcome to my money; take it, do,
  But don't, I pray, include my person too.
  Spare me, I beg you; and let me end the tale
  Of my sad days behind a convent veil.
ORGON:
  A convent! Hah! When crossed in their amours,
  All lovesick girls have had the same thought as yours.
  Get up! The more you loathe the man, and dread him,
  The more ennobling it will be to wed him.
  Marry Tartuffe, and mortify your flesh!   30
  Enough; don't start that whimpering afresh.
DORINE:
  But why . . . ?
ORGON:
                  Be still, there. Speak when you're spoken to.
  Not one more bit of impudence out of you.
CLÉANTE:
  If I may offer a word of counsel here . . .
ORGON:
  Brother, in counseling you have no peer;
  All your advice is forceful, sound, and clever;
  I don't propose to follow it, however.
ELMIRE [*to* ORGON]:
  I am amazed, and don't know what to say;
  Your blindness simply takes my breath away.
  You are indeed bewitched, to take no warning   40
  From our account of what occurred this morning.
ORGON:
  Madam, I know a few plain facts, and one
  Is that you're partial to my rascal son;
  Hence, when he sought to make Tartuffe the victim
  Of a base lie, you dared not contradict him.
  Ah, but you underplayed your part, my pet;
  You should have looked more angry, more upset.
ELMIRE:
  When men make overtures, must we reply
  With righteous anger and a battle-cry?
  Must we turn back their amorous advances
  With sharp reproaches and with fiery glances?   50
  Myself, I find such offers merely amusing,
  And make no scenes and fusses in refusing;
  My taste is for good-natured rectitude,
  And I dislike the savage sort of prude
  Who guards her virtue with her teeth and claws,

And tears men's eyes out for the slightest cause:
The Lord preserve me from such honor as that,
Which bites and scratches like an alley-cat!
I've found that a polite and cool rebuff   60
Discourages a lover quite enough.

ORGON:
I know the facts, and I shall not be shaken.

ELMIRE:
I marvel at your power to be mistaken.
Would it, I wonder, carry weight with you
If I could *show* you that our tale was true?

ORGON:
Show me?

ELMIRE:
        Yes.

ORGON:
           Rot.

ELMIRE:
              Come, what if I found a way
To make you see the facts as plain as day?

ORGON:
Nonsense.

ELMIRE:
           Do answer me; don't be absurd.
I'm not now asking you to trust our word.
Suppose that from some hiding-place in here   70
You learned the whole sad truth by eye and ear—
What would you say of your good friend, after that?

ORGON:
Why, I'd say . . . nothing, by Jehoshaphat!
It can't be true.

ELMIRE:
            You've been too long deceived,
And I'm quite tired of being disbelieved.
Come now: let's put my statements to the test,
And you shall see the truth made manifest.

ORGON:
I'll take that challenge. Now do your uttermost.
We'll see how you make good your empty boast.

ELMIRE [*to* DORINE]:
Send him to me.

DORINE:
           He's crafty; it may be hard   80
To catch the cunning scoundrel off his guard.

ELMIRE:
No, amorous men are gullible. Their conceit
So blinds them that they're never hard to cheat.
Have him come down. [*to* CLÉANTE *and* MARIANE] Please leave us, for a bit.

Scene 4

ELMIRE:
Pull up this table, and get under it.

ORGON:
  What?
ELMIRE:
      It's essential that you be well-hidden.
ORGON:
  Why there?
ELMIRE:
        Oh, Heavens! Just do as you are bidden.
  I have my plans; we'll soon see how they fare.
  Under the table, now; and once you're there,
  Take care that you are neither seen nor heard.
ORGON:
  Well, I'll indulge you, since I gave my word
  To see you through this infantile charade.
ELMIRE:
  Once it is over, you'll be glad we played.
  [*To her husband, who is now under the table*] I'm going to act quite strangely,
      now, and you   10
  Must not be shocked at anything I do.
  Whatever I may say, you must excuse
  As part of that deceit I'm forced to use.
  I shall employ sweet speeches in the task
  Of making that impostor drop his mask;
  I'll give encouragement to his bold desires,
  And furnish fuel to his amorous fires.
  Since it's for your sake, and for his destruction,
  That I shall seem to yield to his seduction,
  I'll gladly stop whenever you decide   20
  That all your doubts are fully satisfied.
  I'll count on you, as soon as you have seen
  What sort of man he is, to intervene,
  And not expose me to his odious lust
  One moment longer than you feel you must.
  Remember: you're to save me from my plight
  Whenever . . . He's coming! Hush! Keep out of sight!

                            Scene 5
TARTUFFE:
  You wish to have a word with me, I'm told.
ELMIRE:
  Yes. I've a little secret to unfold.
  Before I speak, however, it would be wise
  To close that door, and look about for spies.
            [TARTUFFE *goes to the door, closes it, and returns.*]
  The very last thing that must happen now
  Is a repetition of this morning's row.
  I've never been so badly caught off guard.
  Oh, how I feared for you! You saw how hard
  I tried to make that troublesome Damis
  Control his dreadful temper, and hold his peace.   10
  In my confusion, I didn't have the sense
  Simply to contradict his evidence;
  But as it happened, that was for the best,

And all has worked out in our interest.
This storm has only bettered your position;
My husband doesn't have the least suspicion,
And now, in mockery of those who do,
He bids me be continually with you.
And that is why, quite fearless of reproof,
I now can be alone with my Tartuffe,   20
And why my heart—perhaps too quick to yield—
Feels free to let its passion be revealed.

TARTUFFE:
  Madam, your words confuse me. Not long ago,
  You spoke in quite a different style, you know.

ELMIRE:
  Ah, Sir, if that refusal made you smart,
  It's little that you know of woman's heart,
  Or what that heart is trying to convey
  When it resists in such a feeble way!
  Always, at first, our modesty prevents
  The frank avowal of tender sentiments;   30
  However high the passion which inflames us,
  Still, to confess its power somehow shames us.
  Thus we reluct, at first, yet in a tone
  Which tells you that our heart is overthrown,
  That what our lips deny, our pulse confesses,
  And that, in time, all noes will turn to yesses.
  I fear my words are all too frank and free,
  And a poor proof of woman's modesty;
  But since I'm started, tell me, if you will—
  Would I have tried to make Damis be still,   40
  Would I have listened, calm and unoffended,
  Until your lengthy offer of love was ended,
  And been so very mild in my reaction,
  Had your sweet words not given me satisfaction?
  And when I tried to force you to undo
  The marriage-plans my husband has in view,
  What did my urgent pleading signify
  If not that I admired you, and that I
  Deplored the thought that someone else might own
  Part of a heart I wished for mine alone?   50

TARTUFFE:
  Madam, no happiness is so complete
  As when, from lips we love, come words so sweet;
  Their nectar floods my every sense, and drains
  In honeyed rivulets through all my veins.
  To please you is my joy, my only goal;
  Your love is the restorer of my soul;
  And yet I must beg leave, now, to confess
  Some lingering doubts as to my happiness.
  Might this not be a trick? Might not the catch
  Be that you wish me to break off the match   60
  With Mariane, and so have feigned to love me?
  I shan't quite trust your fond opinion of me
  Until the feelings you've expressed so sweetly

Are demonstrated somewhat more concretely,
And you have shown, by certain kind concessions,
That I may put my faith in your professions.

ELMIRE [*She coughs, to warn her husband.*]:
Why be in such a hurry? Must my heart
Exhaust its bounty at the very start?
To make that sweet admission cost me dear,
But you'll not be content, it would appear,   70
Unless my store of favors is disbursed
To the last farthing, and at the very first.

TARTUFFE:
The less we merit, the less we dare to hope,
And with our doubts, mere words can never cope.
We trust no promised bliss till we receive it;
Not till a joy is ours can we believe it.
I, who so little merit your esteem,
Can't credit this fulfillment of my dream,
And shan't believe it, Madam, until I savor
Some palpable assurance of your favor.   80

ELMIRE:
My, how tyrannical your love can be,
And how it flusters and perplexes me!
How furiously you take one's heart in hand,
And make your every wish a fierce command!
Come, must you hound and harry me to death?
Will you not give me time to catch my breath?
Can it be right to press me with such force,
Give me no quarter, show me no remorse,
And take advantage, by your stern insistence,
Of the fond feelings which weaken my resistance?   90

TARTUFFE:
Well, if you look with favor upon my love,
Why, then, begrudge me some clear proof thereof?

ELMIRE:
But how can I consent without offense
To Heaven, toward which you feel such reverence?

TARTUFFE:
If Heaven is all that holds you back, don't worry.
I can remove that hindrance in a hurry.
Nothing of that sort need obstruct our path.

ELMIRE:
Must one not be afraid of Heaven's wrath?

TARTUFFE:
Madam, forget such fears, and be my pupil,
And I shall teach you how to conquer scruple.   100
Some joys, it's true, are wrong in Heaven's eyes;
Yet Heaven is not averse to compromise;
There is a science, lately formulated,
Whereby one's conscience may be liberated,
And any wrongful act you care to mention
May be redeemed by purity of intention.
I'll teach you, Madam, the secrets of that science;
Meanwhile, just place on me your full reliance.

Assuage my keen desires, and feel no dread:
The sin, if any, shall be on my head.   110

> [ELMIRE *coughs, this time more loudly.*]

You've a bad cough.

ELMIRE:

> Yes, yes. It's bad indeed.

TARTUFFE [*producing a little paper bag*]:
A bit of licorice may be what you need.

ELMIRE:
No, I've a stubborn cold, it seems. I'm sure it
Will take much more than licorice to cure it.

TARTUFFE:
How aggravating.

ELMIRE:

> Oh, more than I can say.

TARTUFFE:
If you're still troubled, think of things this way:
No one shall know our joys, save us alone,
And there's no evil till the act is known;
It's scandal, Madam, which makes it an offense,
And it's no sin to sin in confidence.   120

ELMIRE [*having coughed once more*]:
Well, clearly I must do as you require,
And yield to your importunate desire.
It is apparent, now, that nothing less
Will satisfy you, and so I acquiesce.
To go so far is much against my will;
I'm vexed that it should come to this; but still,
Since you are so determined on it, since you
Will not allow mere language to convince you,
And since you ask for concrete evidence, I
See nothing for it, now, but to comply.   130
If this is sinful, if I'm wrong to do it,
So much the worse for him who drove me to it.
The fault can surely not be charged to me.

TARTUFFE:
Madam, the fault is mine, if fault there be,
And ...

ELMIRE:

> Open the door a little, and peek out;
I wouldn't want my husband poking about.

TARTUFFE:
Why worry about that man? Each day he grows
More gullible; one can lead him by the nose.
To find us here would fill him with delight,
And if he saw the worst, he'd doubt his sight.   140

ELMIRE:
Nevertheless, do step out for a minute
Into the hall, and see that no one's in it.

Scene 6

ORGON [*coming out from under the table*]:
That man's a perfect monster, I must admit!

I'm simply stunned. I can't get over it.

ELMIRE:

What, coming out so soon? How premature!
Get back in hiding, and wait until you're sure.
Stay till the end, and be convinced completely;
We mustn't stop till things are proved concretely.

ORGON:

Hell never harbored anything so vicious!

ELMIRE:

Tut, don't be hasty. Try to be judicious.
Wait, and be certain that there's no mistake.
No jumping to conclusions, for Heaven's sake!   10

> [*She places* ORGON *behind her, as* TARTUFFE *re-enters.*]

Scene 7

TARTUFFE [*not seeing* ORGON]:

Madam, all things have worked out to perfection;
I've given the neighboring rooms a full inspection;
No one's about; and now I may at last...

ORGON [*intercepting him*]:

Hold on, my passionate fellow, not so fast!
I should advise a little more restraint.
Well, so you thought you'd fool me, my dear saint!
How soon you wearied of the saintly life—
Wedding my daughter, and coveting my wife!
I've long suspected you, and had a feeling
That soon I'd catch you at your double-dealing.   10
Just now, you've given me evidence galore;
It's quite enough; I have no wish for more.

ELMIRE [*to* TARTUFFE]:

I'm sorry to have treated you so slyly,
But circumstances forced me to be wily.

TARTUFFE:

Brother, you can't think...

ORGON:

                              No more talk from you;
Just leave this household, without more ado.

TARTUFFE:

What I intended...

ORGON:

                    That seems fairly clear.
Spare me your falsehoods and get out of here.

TARTUFFE:

No, I'm the master, and you're the one to go!
This house belongs to me, I'll have you know,   20
And I shall show you that you can't hurt *me*
By this contemptible conspiracy,
That those who cross me know not what they do,
And that I've means to expose and punish you,
Avenge offended Heaven, and make you grieve
That ever you dared order me to leave.

Scene 8

ELMIRE:
   What was the point of all that angry chatter?
ORGON:
   Dear God, I'm worried. This is no laughing matter.
ELMIRE:
   How so?
ORGON:
   I fear I understood his drift.
   I'm much disturbed about that deed of gift.
ELMIRE:
   You gave him . . . ?
ORGON:
   Yes, it's all been drawn and signed.
   But one thing more is weighing on my mind.
ELMIRE:
   What's that?
ORGON:
   I'll tell you; but first let's see if there's
   A certain strong-box in his room upstairs.

Act V

Scene 1

CLÉANTE:
   Where are you going so fast?
ORGON:
   God knows!
CLÉANTE:
   Then wait;
   Let's have a conference, and deliberate
   On how this situation's to be met.
ORGON:
   That strong-box has me utterly upset;
   This is the worst of many, many shocks.
CLÉANTE:
   Is there some fearful mystery in that box?
ORGON:
   My poor friend Argas brought that box to me
   With his own hands, in utmost secrecy;
   'Twas on the very morning of his flight.
   It's full of papers which, if they came to light,
   Would ruin him—or such is my impression.
CLÉANTE:
   Then why did you let it out of your possession?
ORGON:
   Those papers vexed my conscience, and it seemed best
   To ask the counsel of my pious guest.
   The cunning scoundrel got me to agree
   To leave the strong-box in his custody,
   So that, in case of an investigation,

10

I could employ a slight equivocation
And swear I didn't have it, and thereby,
At no expense to conscience, tell a lie.   20
CLÉANTE:
It looks to me as if you're out on a limb.
Trusting him with that box, and offering him
That deed of gift, were actions of a kind
Which scarcely indicate a prudent mind.
With two such weapons, he has the upper hand,
And since you're vulnerable, as matters stand,
You erred once more in bringing him to bay.
You should have acted in some subtler way.
ORGON:
Just think of it: behind that fervent face,
A heart so wicked, and a soul so base!   30
I took him in, a hungry beggar, and then . . .
Enough, by God! I'm through with pious men:
Henceforth I'll hate the whole false brotherhood,
And persecute them worse than Satan could.
CLÉANTE:
Ah, there you go—extravagant as ever!
Why can you not be rational? You never
Manage to take the middle course, it seems,
But jump, instead, between absurd extremes.
You've recognized your recent grave mistake
In falling victim to a pious fake;   40
Now, to correct that error, must you embrace
An even greater error in its place,
And judge our worthy neighbors as a whole
By what you've learned of one corrupted soul?
Come, just because one rascal made you swallow
A show of zeal which turned out to be hollow,
Shall you conclude that all men are deceivers,
And that, today, there are no true believers?
Let atheists make that foolish inference;
Learn to distinguish virtue from pretense,   50
Be cautious in bestowing admiration,
And cultivate a sober moderation.
Don't humor fraud, but also don't asperse
True piety; the latter fault is worse,
And it is best to err, if err one must,
As you have done, upon the side of trust.

Scene 2

DAMIS:
Father, I hear that scoundrel's uttered threats
Against you; that he pridefully forgets
How, in his need, he was befriended by you,
And means to use your gifts to crucify you.
ORGON:
It's true, my boy. I'm too distressed for tears.

DAMIS:
    Leave it to me, Sir; let me trim his ears.
    Faced with such insolence, we must not waver.
    I shall rejoice in doing you the favor
    Of cutting short his life, and your distress.
CLÉANTE:
    What a display of young hotheadedness!   10
    Do learn to moderate your fits of rage.
    In this just kingdom, this enlightened age,
    One does not settle things by violence.

Scene 3

MADAME PERNELLE:
    I hear strange tales of very strange events.
ORGON:
    Yes, strange events which these two eyes beheld.
    The man's ingratitude is unparalleled.
    I save a wretched pauper from starvation,
    House him, and treat him like a blood relation,
    Shower him every day with my largesse,
    Give him my daughter, and all that I possess;
    And meanwhile the unconscionable knave
    Tries to induce my wife to misbehave;
    And not content with such extreme rascality,   10
    Now threatens me with my own liberality,
    And aims, by taking base advantage of
    The gifts I gave him out of Christian love,
    To drive me from my house, a ruined man,
    And make me end a pauper, as he began.
DORINE:
    Poor fellow!
MADAME PERNELLE:
                No, my son, I'll never bring
    Myself to think him guilty of such a thing.
ORGON:
    How's that?
MADAME PERNELLE:
                The righteous always were maligned.
ORGON:
    Speak clearly, Mother. Say what's on your mind.
MADAME PERNELLE:
    I mean that I can smell a rat, my dear.   20
    You know how everybody hates him, here.
ORGON:
    That has no bearing on the case at all.
MADAME PERNELLE:
    I told you a hundred times, when you were small,
    That virtue in this world is hated ever;
    Malicious men may die, but malice never.
ORGON:
    No doubt that's true, but how does it apply?

MADAME PERNELLE:
They've turned you against him by a clever lie.
ORGON:
I've told you, I was there and saw it done.
MADAME PERNELLE:
Ah, slanderers will stop at nothing, Son.
ORGON:
Mother, I'll lose my temper... For the last time,   30
I tell you I was witness to the crime.
MADAME PERNELLE:
The tongues of spite are busy night and noon,
And to their venom no man is immune.
ORGON:
You're talking nonsense. Can't you realize
I saw it; saw it; saw it with my eyes?
Saw, do you understand me? Must I shout it
Into your ears before you'll cease to doubt it?
MADAME PERNELLE:
Appearances can deceive, my son. Dear me,
We cannot always judge by what we see.
ORGON:
Drat! Drat!
MADAME PERNELLE:
                    One often interprets things awry;   40
Good can seem evil to a suspicious eye.
ORGON:
Was I to see his pawing at Elmire
As an act of charity?
MADAME PERNELLE:
                    Till his guilt is clear,
A man deserves the benefit of the doubt.
You should have waited, to see how things turned out.
ORGON:
Great God in Heaven, what more proof did I need?
Was I to sit there, watching, until he'd...
You drive me to the brink of impropriety.
MADAME PERNELLE:
No, no, a man of such surpassing piety
Could not do such a thing. You cannot shake me.   50
I don't believe it, and you shall not make me.
ORGON:
You vex me so that, if you weren't my mother,
I'd say to you... some dreadful thing or other.
DORINE:
It's your turn now, Sir, not to be listened to;
You'd not trust us, and now she won't trust you.
CLÉANTE:
My friends, we're wasting time which should be spent
In facing up to our predicament.
I fear that scoundrel's threats weren't made in sport.
DAMIS:
Do you think he'd have the nerve to go to court?

ELMIRE:
> I'm sure he won't: they'd find it all too crude   60
> A case of swindling and ingratitude.

CLÉANTE:
> Don't be too sure. He won't be at a loss
> To give his claims a high and righteous gloss;
> And clever rogues with far less valid cause
> Have trapped their victims in a web of laws.
> I say again that to antagonize
> A man so strongly armed was most unwise.

ORGON:
> I know it; but the man's appalling cheek
> Outraged me so, I couldn't control my pique.

CLÉANTE:
> I wish to Heaven that we could devise   70
> Some truce between you, or some compromise.

ELMIRE:
> If I had known what cards he held, I'd not
> Have roused his anger by my little plot.

ORGON [*to* DORINE, *as* M. LOYAL *enters*]:
> What is that fellow looking for? Who is he?
> Go talk to him—and tell him that I'm busy.

Scene 4

MONSIEUR LOYAL:
> Good day, dear sister. Kindly let me see
> Your master.

DORINE:
>   He's involved with company,
> And cannot be disturbed just now, I fear.

MONSIEUR LOYAL:
> I hate to intrude; but what has brought me here
> Will not disturb your master, in any event.
> Indeed, my news will make him most content.

DORINE:
> Your name?

MONSIEUR LOYAL:
>   Just say that I bring greetings from
> Monsieur Tartuffe, on whose behalf I've come.

DORINE [*to* ORGON]:
> Sir, he's a very gracious man, and bears
> A message from Tartuffe, which, he declares,   10
> Will make you most content.

CLÉANTE:
>   Upon my word,
> I think this man had best be seen, and heard.

ORGON:
> Perhaps he has some settlement to suggest.
> How shall I treat him? What manner would be best?

CLÉANTE:
> Control your anger, and if he should mention
> Some fair adjustment, give him your full attention.

MONSIEUR LOYAL:

    Good health to you, good Sir. May Heaven confound

    Your enemies, and may your joys abound.

ORGON [*aside, to* CLÉANTE]:

    A gentle salutation: it confirms

    My guess that he is here to offer terms.   20

MONSIEUR LOYAL:

    I've always held your family most dear;

    I served your father, Sir, for many a year.

ORGON:

    Sir, I must ask your pardon; to my shame,

    I cannot now recall your face or name.

MONSIEUR LOYAL:

    Loyal's my name; I come from Normandy,

    And I'm a bailiff, in all modesty.

    For forty years, praise God, it's been my boast

    To serve with honor in that vital post,

    And I am here, Sir, if you will permit

    The liberty, to serve you with this writ...   30

ORGON:

    To—*what?*

MONSIEUR LOYAL:

    Now, please, Sir, let us have no friction:

    It's nothing but an order of eviction.

    You are to move your goods and family out

    And make way for new occupants, without

    Deferment or delay, and give the keys...

ORGON:

    I? Leave this house?

MONSIEUR LOYAL:

             Why yes, Sir, if you please.

    This house, Sir, from the cellar to the roof,

    Belongs now to the good Monsieur Tartuffe,

    And he is lord and master of your estate

    By virtue of a deed of present date,

    Drawn in due form, with clearest legal phrasing...   40

DAMIS:

    Your insolence is utterly amazing!

MONSIEUR LOYAL:

    Young man, my business here is not with you,

    But with your wise and temperate father, who,

    Like every worthy citizen, stands in awe

    Of justice, and would never obstruct the law.

ORGON:

    But...

MONSIEUR LOYAL:

        Not for a million, Sir, would you rebel

    Against authority; I know that well.

    You'll not make trouble, Sir, or interfere

    With the execution of my duties here.   50

DAMIS:

    Someone may execute a smart tattoo

    On that black jacket of yours, before you're through.

MONSIEUR LOYAL:
  Sir, bid your son be silent. I'd much regret
  Having to mention such a nasty threat
  Of violence, in writing my report.
DORINE [*aside*]:
  This man Loyal's a most disloyal sort!
MONSIEUR LOYAL:
  I love all men of upright character,
  And when I agreed to serve these papers, Sir,
  It was your feelings that I had in mind.
  I couldn't bear to see the case assigned   60
  To someone else, who might esteem you less
  And so subject you to unpleasantness.
ORGON:
  What's more unpleasant than telling a man to leave
  His house and home?
MONSIEUR LOYAL:
                    You'd like a short reprieve?
  If you desire it, Sir, I shall not press you,
  But wait until tomorrow to dispossess you.
  Splendid. I'll come and spend the night here, then,
  Most quietly, with half a score of men.
  For form's sake, you might bring me, just before
  You go to bed, the keys to the front door.   70
  My men, I promise, will be on their best
  Behavior, and will not disturb your rest.
  But bright and early, Sir, you must be quick
  And move out all your furniture, every stick:
  The men I've chosen are both young and strong,
  And with their help it shouldn't take you long.
  In short, I'll make things pleasant and convenient,
  And since I'm being so extremely lenient,
  Please show me, Sir, a like consideration,
  And give me your entire cooperation.   80
ORGON [*aside*]:
  I may be all but bankrupt, but I vow
  I'd give a hundred louis, here and now,
  Just for the pleasure of landing one good clout
  Right on the end of that complacent snout.
CLÉANTE:
  Careful; don't make things worse.
DAMIS:
                              My bootsole itches
  To give that beggar a good kick in the breeches.
DORINE:
  Monsieur Loyal, I'd love to hear the whack
  Of a stout stick across your fine broad back.
MONSIEUR LOYAL:
  Take care: a woman too may go to jail if
  She uses threatening language to a bailiff.   90
CLÉANTE:
  Enough, enough, Sir. This must not go on.
  Give me that paper, please, and then begone.

MONSIEUR LOYAL:
   Well, *au revoir*. God give you all good cheer!
ORGON:
   May God confound you, and him who sent you here!

Scene 5

ORGON:
   Now, Mother, was I right or not? This writ
   Should change your notion of Tartuffe a bit.
   Do you perceive his villainy at last?
MADAME PERNELLE:
   I'm thunderstruck. I'm utterly aghast.
DORINE:
   Oh, come, be fair. You mustn't take offense
   At this new proof of his benevolence.
   He's acting out of selfless love, I know.
   Material things enslave the soul, and so
   He kindly has arranged your liberation
   From all that might endanger your salvation.   10
ORGON:
   Will you not ever hold your tongue, you dunce?
CLÉANTE:
   Come, you must take some action, and at once.
ELMIRE:
   Go tell the world of the low trick he's tried.
   The deed of gift is surely nullified
   By such behavior, and public rage will not
   Permit the wretch to carry out his plot.

Scene 6

VALÈRE:
   Sir, though I hate to bring you more bad news,
   Such is the danger that I cannot choose.
   A friend who is extremely close to me
   And knows my interest in your family
   Has, for my sake, presumed to violate
   The secrecy that's due to things of state,
   And sends me word that you are in a plight
   From which your one salvation lies in flight.
   That scoundrel who's imposed upon you so
   Denounced you to the King an hour ago   10
   And, as supporting evidence, displayed
   The strong-box of a certain renegade
   Whose secret papers, so he testified,
   You had disloyally agreed to hide.
   I don't know just what charges may be pressed,
   But there's a warrant out for your arrest;
   Tartuffe has been instructed, furthermore,
   To guide the arresting officer to your door.
CLÉANTE:
   He's clearly done this to facilitate

His seizure of your house and your estate.   20
ORGON:
   That man, I must say, is a vicious beast!
VALÈRE:
   Quick, Sir; you mustn't tarry in the least.
   My carriage is outside, to take you hence;
   This thousand louis should cover all expense.
   Let's lose no time, or you shall be undone;
   The sole defense, in this case, is to run.
   I shall go with you all the way, and place you
   In a safe refuge to which they'll never trace you.
ORGON:
   Alas, dear boy, I wish that I could show you
   My gratitude for everything I owe you.   30
   But now is not the time; I pray the Lord
   That I may live to give you your reward.
   Farewell, my dears; be careful...
CLÉANTE:
                              Brother, hurry.
   We shall take care of things; you needn't worry.

Scene 7
TARTUFFE:
   Gently, Sir, gently; stay right where you are.
   No need for haste; your lodging isn't far.
   You're off to prison, by order of the Prince.
ORGON:
   This is the crowning blow, you wretch; and since
   It means my total ruin and defeat,
   Your villainy is now at last complete.
TARTUFFE:
   You needn't try to provoke me; it's no use.
   Those who serve Heaven must expect abuse.
CLÉANTE:
   You are indeed most patient, sweet, and blameless.
DORINE:
   How he exploits the name of Heaven! It's shameless.   10
TARTUFFE:
   Your taunts and mockeries are all for naught;
   To do my duty is my only thought.
MARIANE:
   Your love of duty is most meritorious,
   And what you've done is little short of glorious.
TARTUFFE:
   All deeds are glorious, Madam, which obey
   The sovereign prince who sent me here today.
ORGON:
   I rescued you when you were destitute;
   Have you forgotten that, you thankless brute?
TARTUFFE:
   No, no, I well remember everything;
   But my first duty is to serve my King.   20

That obligation is so paramount
That other claims, beside it, do not count;
And for it I would sacrifice my wife,
My family, my friend, or my own life.

ELMIRE:

Hypocrite!

DORINE:

All that we most revere, he uses
To cloak his plots and camouflage his ruses.

CLÉANTE:

If it is true that you are animated
By pure and loyal zeal, as you have stated,
Why was this zeal not roused until you'd sought
To make Orgon a cuckold, and been caught?   30
Why weren't you moved to give your evidence
Until your outraged host had driven you hence?
I shan't say that the gift of all his treasure
Ought to have damped your zeal in any measure;
But if he is a traitor, as you declare,
How could you condescend to be his heir?

TARTUFFE [to the OFFICER]:

Sir, spare me all this clamor; it's growing shrill.
Please carry out your orders, if you will.

OFFICER:

Yes, I've delayed too long, Sir. Thank you kindly.
You're just the proper person to remind me.   40
Come, you are off to join the other boarders
In the King's prison, according to his orders.

TARTUFFE:

Who? I, Sir?

OFFICER:

Yes.

TARTUFFE:

To prison? This can't be true!

OFFICER:

I owe an explanation, but not to you.
[To ORGON] Sir, all is well; rest easy, and be grateful.
We serve a Prince to whom all sham is hateful,
A Prince who sees into our inmost hearts,
And can't be fooled by any trickster's arts.
His royal soul, though generous and human,
Views all things with discernment and acumen;   50
His sovereign reason is not lightly swayed,
And all his judgments are discreetly weighed.
He honors righteous men of every kind,
And yet his zeal for virtue is not blind,
Nor does his love of piety numb his wits
And make him tolerant of hypocrites.
'Twas hardly likely that this man could cozen
A King who's foiled such liars by the dozen.
With one keen glance, the King perceived the whole
Perverseness and corruption of his soul,   60

And thus high Heaven's justice was displayed:
Betraying you, the rogue stood self-betrayed.
The King soon recognized Tartuffe as one
Notorious by another name, who'd done
So many vicious crimes that one could fill
Ten volumes with them, and be writing still.
But to be brief: our sovereign was appalled
By this man's treachery toward you, which he called
The last, worst villainy of a vile career,
And bade me follow the impostor here   70
To see how gross his impudence could be,
And force him to restore your property.
Your private papers, by the King's command,
I hereby seize and give into your hand.
The King, by royal order, invalidates
The deed which gave this rascal your estates,
And pardons, furthermore, your grave offense
In harboring an exile's documents.
By these decrees, our Prince rewards you for
Your loyal deeds in the late civil war,   80
And shows how heartfelt is his satisfaction
In recompensing any worthy action,
How much he prizes merit, and how he makes
More of men's virtues than of their mistakes.

DORINE:
Heaven be praised!

MADAME PERNELLE:
           I breathe again, at last.

ELMIRE:
We're safe.

MARIANE:
        I can't believe the danger's past.

ORGON [*to* TARTUFFE]:
Well, traitor, now you see...

CLÉANTE:
             Ah, Brother, please,
Let's not descend to such indignities.
Leave the poor wretch to his unhappy fate,
And don't say anything to aggravate   90
His present woes; but rather hope that he
Will soon embrace an honest piety,
And mend his ways, and by a true repentance
Move our just King to moderate his sentence.
Meanwhile, go kneel before your sovereign's throne
And thank him for the mercies he has shown.

ORGON:
Well said: let's go at once and, gladly kneeling,
Express the gratitude which all are feeling.
Then, when that first great duty has been done,
We'll turn with pleasure to a second one,   100
And give Valère, whose love has proven so true,
The wedded happiness which is his due.

MARIE DE LA VERGNE DE LA FAYETTE
[1634–1693]

The Princess of Clèves has been described as the first French novel and the first psychological novel in Western literature. Although these characterizations exaggerate, they are close enough to the truth to suggest the extraordinary importance of Madame de La Fayette's short novel, published in 1678. It was a work that redirected the course of French literature and defined the direction of the novel.

The concise narrative and plain style of *The Princess of Clèves* reduced the story to its essentials and established an ideal of classical restraint. Its realism and its historical accuracy made it an intriguing account of the French court in the mid-sixteenth century, but indirectly it was also a picture of court life in Madame de La Fayette's own time, during the opulent and spectacular reign of the Sun King, Louis XIV. The focus on individual characters and their motives and on the inner life of its heroine departed from the conventional stereotypes of earlier romances and adventure stories. Even if it did not pursue this individualistic impulse to the revolutionary conclusions that would be reached a century later, *The Princess of Clèves* explored in depth a conflict central to the Enlightenment between duty and desire, public responsibility and private passion, reason and emotion.

LIFE

Born in Paris in 1634, Marie-Madeleine Pioche de La Vergne was the daughter of a family on the fringes of the French court. Her father, a military engineer, died when she was fifteen, and when her mother remarried, to the Chevalier Renaud-René de Sévigné, new opportunities opened for Marie-Madeleine. She moved into the inner circles of the court and became a lady-in-waiting to Anne of Austria, the widowed queen of Louis XIII. She also became a close friend of her stepfather's niece, the Marquise de Sévigné, whose letters to her daughter would become one of the classics of French literature. The two women remained friends for life, sharing court gossip, discussing ideas and issues of the day, and consulting and advising one another. Marie-Madeleine's first published work, a portrait of Madame de Sévigné (1659), began her literary career. At this time she also met the widow of Charles I of England, Henriette-Marie of France, who had escaped to France after the king's execution in 1649 with her daughter, Henriette d'Angleterre, taking up residence at the Convent of the Visitation in Chaillot. The daughter became one of Marie-Madeleine's close friends and later, after she married the brother of Louis XIV, she became Madame de La Fayette's sponsor at court. She would also be the subject of one of Madame de La Fayette's literary works, a *History of Henriette of England*. At the Convent of the Visitation, Marie-Madeleine also met her future sister-in-law, the abbess Louise-Angélique de La Fayette.

Her marriage with François, Comte de La Fayette, was an arranged union. Her substantial dowry helped with his financial difficulties; his much higher social position enabled her to rise considerably in the world. He was thirty-nine and a widower and she only twenty-one when they married in 1655, and although she spent several years on her husband's estates in Auvergne, a mountainous region in central France, Madame de La Fayette was not happy so far from Paris. She returned to the capital to give birth to her two sons, Louis in 1658 and Renaud-Armand in 1659, and when her husband returned to Auvergne in 1661, she remained in Paris. There was no bitterness in the separation, but it was continued for the rest of her married life. She took care of her husband's lawsuits in

Paris, settling the financial encumbrances on his estates shortly before his death. He spent his time in the country, occasionally visiting his wife in Paris, where she reestablished her place at court, developed friendships with other writers and thinkers, and became the center of one of the most famous salons.

Under Louis XIV, the Sun King, whose seventy-two-year reign (1643-1715) is the longest in European history, France reached heights of absolutism and ceremony. Louis asserted, "I am the state," and at least one of his subjects remarked that living in the presence of the Sun King was like living in the presence of God. "My dominant passion," Louis declared, "is certainly the love of glory," and in the ceremony and grandeur of his court, and of his palaces and gardens at Versailles, Louis lived out this passion. To be part of this splendid court gave Madame de La Fayette direct and personal knowledge of the power of the king's presence, of the ceremonial order and glory he imposed, and of the secrets behind the glittering surfaces in a world of intrigue, shifting alliances, and suppressed passions.

Among Madame de La Fayette's literary colleagues, La Rochefoucauld was the most important. The skeptical and cynical writer, famous for his *Maxims* (1664), regularly attended her salon, collaborated with her on some of her writings, and was her closest friend for many years. His death in 1680 and her husband's death in 1683 left Madame de La Fayette alone and depressed during the last decade of her life. She died in Paris in 1693.

WORK

Nearly all of Madame de La Fayette's works center on the life of the court. Her first novel, *The Princess of Montpensier* (1662), is set in the court of Charles IX (1560–1574), and, like *The Princess of Clèves,* it recounts the secret love affair of a woman caught in an arranged marriage. *Zaïde* (1670–1671), written with La Rochefoucauld and Jean-Regnauld de Segrais, differs from her other works. A long and rambling romance set in ninth-century Spain, it tells love stories, but it has none of the psychological analysis found in her *nouvelles.* Her masterpiece, *The Princess of Clèves* (1678), published anonymously like the rest of her work, once again set its love story in the past, in the court of Henry II in the 1550s. Three works published after her death—a novel, *The Comtesse de Tende* (1724), and two histories, *History of Henriette of England* (1720) and *Memoirs of the Court of France During the Years 1688 and 1689* (1731)—are all based on the life of the court.

The Princess of Clèves was controversial when it first appeared in 1678. She called the book an *histoire,* a word in French that means both *history* and *story,* and the mixture of fact and fiction in the novel disturbed many readers. All of the figures in the novel from the court of Henry II, who reigned from 1547 to 1559, are historically accurate. The king, his mistress Diane de Poitiers, the queen, and the nobles and ladies of the court, including the representatives of the three most prominent aristocratic families, the houses of Bourbon, Guise, and Montmorency, are all historical figures. Even Jacques, the Prince of Clèves, and the Duke of Nemours are historical persons, although Madame de La Fayette changed their lives to fit her fiction. Only the Princesse, her marriage, and her love story are invented. The accuracy of the history made it difficult to separate fiction from fact and gave authority to the love story. The carefully observed and recorded details of courtly life made the emotions of the love story seem equally real. Even such implausible events as the princess's confession to her husband took on an aspect of truth because of the detailed historical context in which they were set.

The implicit parallel between the historical Henry II and the splendid court of Louis XIV also contributed to the believability of the novel. Even if Madame de La Fayette did not link specific persons from the past with figures from her own time, *The Princess of*

Clèves fed the fascination with the glittering life at Versailles and the gossip about Louis's court seemed to be confirmed in the pages of the novel.

The description of the court with its intrigues and love affairs that opens *The Princess of Clèves* sets a context for the whole novel. The court is not as grand or as orderly as it appears from the outside. To be initiated into the court is to become aware of the difference between the surface of things and the hidden realities beneath. Outward appearances show a world that operates by the rules of established hierarchy and order, rules of duty and obligation. But behind the scenes passion challenges authority, emotion upsets order, love overcomes duty. As we share the princess's growth in awareness, from her initial naïveté, to her acceptance of the arranged marriage, and then to her awakening to love and passion, we are made aware of the gulf between external appearances and suppressed truths.

The distance between appearance and reality in the novel enabled Madame de La Fayette to explore the conflict between love and duty, a theme that engaged many writers of her time. As the princess learns the manners of the court, she learns how to control her public behavior and to suppress her private emotion. The public life of the court, like the discourse of rational people, conformed to certain agreed-upon rules. Flirtation was acceptable; passion was not. Allowing private emotion to govern public behavior would threaten not only the princess's marriage, but because she is part of the court, it would threaten the very stability of the state. Her duty is not simply a form of self-denial; it is an assertion of her commitment to a rational social order.

Nevertheless, the personal denial is very strong. Madame de La Fayette's interior view of her heroine leaves no doubt of the intensity of her passion or of her private wishes. Rousseau might have said of her, as he did of Madame de Warens, "instead of listening to her heart, which gave her good counsel, she listened to her reason, which gave her bad." Rousseau and Madame de La Fayette are obsessed with the same struggle, the conflict between reason and emotion, public duty and private desire, even if they come out on opposite sides of the issue. Both writers recognize the strength of the case that can be made on either side.

The Princess of Clèves traces the princess's learning of the gulf between appearance and reality, a theme central to the novel as a literary form, but it does not provide a predictably realistic or comic resolution to her story. The princess does not learn about the world and accept the option of living a double life, a realistic solution to her dilemma. Nor does she take the comic way out, celebrating her husband's convenient demise by accepting Nemours's proposal. Neither of these resolutions affirms her inner need to reconcile love with duty, her inner passion with the established order of things. Madame de La Fayette wrote about the conflict between love and duty as a way of exploring the depths of her character's personality. We know from her inner view of the princess's youthful innocence when she first attends the court and of the docility with which she accepts the arranged marriage with Clèves. We discover love when she is surprised by it and we share her temptation and agony over Nemours. So convincing is the presentation of the princess's inner life that we, like many of the novel's original readers, are surprised when she confesses to her husband that she loves another man. The novel prompted a vigorous debate in the seventeenth century over whether her confession was believable or reasonable. But we may be even more surprised when, after the death of her husband, the princess rejects Nemours's proposal. Why, we ask, does the princess reject this solution to her dilemma? Is she too fastidiously loyal to the memory of her husband? Guilty for her psychological collusion in his death? Afraid of her own passionate attraction to Nemours? Afraid that her passion will be lost in a marriage to him? Unwilling to accept a facile resolution to the conflict between love and duty that does not resolve the underlying issues? That the novel can raise these possibilities and more is a measure of its richness and of the depth of its psychological analysis.

SUGGESTED READINGS

No recent biography has replaced Lilian Rhea's *The Life and Times of Marie-Madeleine, Countess of La Fayette* (1908). Among the useful introductions to Madame de La Fayette's work are Stirling Haig's *Madame de Lafayette* (1970), Janet Raitt's *Madame de Lafayette and "La Princesse de Clèves"* (1971), Peggy Kamf's "A Mother's Will: *The Princess de Clèves*" in *Fictions of Feminine Desire* (1982), and J. W. Scott's *Madame de La Fayette: "La Princesse de Clèves"* (1983).

The Princess of Clèves

Translated by Mildred Sarah Greene

BOOK 1

Magnificence and gallantry had never appeared in France with such brilliance as in the last years of the reign of Henry II.[1] This Prince was gallant, handsome, and amorous. Although his passion for Diane de Poitiers, the Duchesse de Valentinois,[2] had begun more than twenty years ago, it was no less intense, nor did he give her less dazzling tokens of it.

As the King excelled in all physical exercises, he spent most of his time at them. Every day there were hunting parties, tennis matches, ballets, tilting at the ring, or similar amusements. The colors and the insignia of the Duchesse de Valentinois were seen everywhere, and she herself appeared as richly dressed as her grand-daughter, Mademoiselle de La Marck, who was then of marriageable age. The Queen's[3] presence authorized the Duchesse's. Although the Queen was no longer in her first youth, she was beautiful: she loved grandeur, magnificence, and pleasure. The King had married her when he was still the Duc d'Orleans, and had an elder brother who died at Tournon[4]—a Prince whose birth and fine qualities made him an honourable successor to his father, King Francis I.

The ambitious temperament of the Queen made ruling a great pleasure to her. She did not seem to mind the King's attachment to the Duchesse de Valentinois, and she never displayed any jealousy towards her. But she was capable of such profound dissimulation that it was difficult to judge her feelings. In any case, policy demanded that she keep the Duchesse closely attached to herself, since this also insured the attachment of the King. He enjoyed the company of women, even of those he did not love. Every day he stayed at the Queen's apartment at the hour when she was holding court, where could be found the handsomest and most attractive of both sexes. A Court never had so many beautiful women and such amazingly handsome men. It seemed that nature took pleasure in endowing the noblest Princesses and Princes with her most striking gifts.

---

[1] Henri II (1519–1559) reigned from 1547 to 1559. The main action of the novel takes place in the last years of Henri's reign, between 1557 and 1559.

[2] Diane de Poitiers (1499–1566), the most famous of the ladies at Henri's court, was formerly the mistress to Henri's father, François I. She became Henri's mistress when he was still the Dauphin, even though she was twenty years older than the future king. She remained his mistress throughout his reign. After Henri's death in 1559, Diane de Poitiers was dispatched from the court by Henri's surviving queen.

[3] Henri's queen was the Florentine commoner Catherine de Médicis (1519–1589), daughter of Lorenzo de' Medici.

[4] François de Valois's death in 1539 cleared the way for Henri to become king.

Madame Elizabeth de France,[5] who was later to be the Queen of Spain, was beginning to display that sparkling wit and incomparable beauty which were later to be so unfortunate for her. Mary Stuart, the Queen of Scotland,[6] who had just married the Dauphin, and who was called the Reine Dauphine, was perfection itself both in mind and body. She had been brought up at the French Court, and had absorbed all of its refinement. She was born with such a taste for all the most beautiful things that, despite her extreme youth, she was a connoisseur and appreciated them better than anyone. The Queen, her mother-in-law, and Madame,[7] the King's sister, also enjoyed poetry, drama, and music. The taste that King Francis I had had for poetry and *belles lettres* still reigned in France, and since his son, the King, enjoyed outdoor exercises, all the pleasures were to be found at Court. But what made this Court beautiful and majestic, was the great number of Princes and nobles of an extraordinarily striking merit. Those whom I am going to name were, each in his different way, the adornment and wonder of their century.

The King of Navarre[8] commanded everyone's respect by the grandeur of his rank and character. He excelled in war, and the Duc de Guise's[9] admiration for him caused the Duc at times to leave his post as general to fight at his side in the most dangerous places as a simple soldier. It is also true that this Duc had shown such admirable valor and was so successful in battle that there was no great captain who could avoid being envious of him. His valor was sustained by all the other fine character traits. He had a vast and profound understanding, a noble and elevated soul, and an equal capacity for war and for politics. The Cardinal de Lorraine, his brother, was born with a limitless ambition, an alert intelligence, and an admirable eloquence. He had acquired a profound knowledge that he used to make himself prominent in defending the Catholic Church, which, at that time, was coming under attack. The Chevalier de Guise who was later called the Grand Prior, was a Prince beloved by everyone. He was handsome, witty, adroit, and had a valor known throughout Europe. The Prince de Condé had a grand and lofty soul in a small body, scarcely favored by nature, and was so amusing that even the most beautiful women fell in love with him. The Duc de Nevers,[10] who had covered himself with glory in war and who had held important positions, although a little advanced in age, was the delight of the Court. He had three very attractive sons. The second, who was called the Prince de Clèves, was worthy of upholding his family's name. He was brave and magnanimous and had a prudence that is rarely found in

---

[5]Elizabeth de France (1545–1568) married Philip II of Spain and became Queen of Spain in 1559. Her death was rumored to be the result of poisoning by Philip because of her love for her stepson, Don Carlos.

[6]Mary Queen of Scots married François de Valois, Henri's son. He became François II in 1559.

[7]"Madame" was Marguerite de France, the Duchesse de Berry.

[8]Antoine de Bourbon, Duc de Vendôme, succeeded to the rule of Navarre in 1555 when he married Marguerite d'Angoulême. Their son would become Henri IV of France in 1589.

[9]The Maison de Guise, the Maison de Bourbon, and the Maison de Montmorency were the three most powerful families in the court of Henri II. François de Lorraine, Duc de Guise (1519–1563), Charles de Guise, Cardinal de Lorraine (c. 1525–1574), and François de Lorraine, the Chevalier de Guise (1534–1563) are the three brothers described here. In the religious wars between the Protestant Huguenots, led by Louis de Bourbon, the powerful Prince de Condé (1530–1569), and the Catholics, the Guises were the leaders on the Catholic side. Peace was restored between the Protestant Bourbons and the Catholic Guises in 1589 when a Bourbon, Henry IV, became king.

[10]François de Clèves, Duc de Nevers (1516–1562) was a figure Madame de La Fayette found in the records of the period. Some accounts give him only two sons, suggesting that she invented the third, but other accounts list a son, Jacques, who would have been only a boy of fourteen in 1558, the time of the novel.

youth. The Vidame de Chartres,[11] descended from the ancient house of Vendôme, a name which even the Princes of blood were not too proud to bear, was equally distinguished in war and in courtly manners. He was handsome, had a genteel face, was valiant, brave, and generous. All these good qualities were evident and striking. In fact, he alone was worthy of comparison with the Duc de Nemours,[12] if anyone could be compared with him.

But Nemours was a masterpiece of nature! His least remarkable quality was that of all men in the world he was the handsomest. What elevated him above all the others was an incomparable valor and agreeableness in his wit, expression, and conduct which could be found in him alone. He had a gaiety which was equally pleasing to men and to women, an extraordinary skill in all sports, a manner of dressing which was always followed, but which could never be imitated, and finally a personal air which attracted everyone's attention wherever he went. There was not a woman of the Court who was not flattered to have him devoted to her. Few of those to whom he paid attention could boast of having resisted him, and several for whom he had never shown any affection could not help being in love with him. He had so much sweetness and such a disposition for gallantry, that he could not neglect those who tried to please him. Thus he had several mistresses, but it was difficult to tell which one he really loved. He was often seen with the Reine Dauphine. Her beauty and sweetness, the effort she took to please everyone, and the special favor she showed the Duc, made everyone think he set his cap for her.

The Reine Dauphine's uncles, the Ducs de Guise, had greatly profited in rank and importance by her marriage. Their ambition made them aspire to equal the Princes of blood and to share in the power of the Connétable de Montmorency.[13] To a great extent, the King trusted the Connétable with the management of his affairs and treated the Duc de Guise and the Maréchal de Saint André[14] as his favorite companions. But the King was never so happy to bestow favors and bounty on his courtiers as when they were recommended by the Duchesse de Valentinois. Although she was no longer young and beautiful, she ruled the King with such absolute control that one could say that she was mistress of his person and of the State. The King had always loved the Connétable, and, as soon as he began to rule, he recalled him from that exile into which Francis I had sent him.

The Court was divided between the Ducs de Guise and the Connétable, who was supported by the Princes of blood. Both parties had always dreamed of winning the support of the Duchesse de Valentinois. The Duc d'Aumale, the Duc de Guise's brother, had married one of her daughters. The Connétable aspired to a similar relationship. He was not content to have married his oldest son to Madame Diane, the daughter of the King and of a Piedmontese, who went into a convent as soon as the baby was born. There were many obstacles to this marriage because of the promises that his son had made to one of the Queen's maids of honor, Mademoiselle de Piennes. Although the King arranged matters with extreme tact and kindness, the Connétable could not feel secure unless he were assured of the support of the Duchesse de Valentinois, and unless he separated her from the Ducs de Guise, whose power began to alarm her.

---

[11] François de Vendôme, Prince de Chabanois, Vidame de Chartres (1524–1562).

[12] Although Jacques de Savoie, Duc de Nemours (1531–1615) was a historical figure, Madame de La Fayette invented much of the story about him in the novel.

[13] Anne de Montmorency (1493–1567) was the chief administrator of the government.

[14] The Maréchal de Saint André, an officer of the court, was Jacques d'Albon.

The Duchesse de Valentinois had delayed as much as possible the Dauphin's marriage to the Queen of Scotland. This young Queen's beauty and quick wit as well as the prestige which her marriage gave to the Ducs de Guise were almost more than the Duchesse could bear. She particularly disliked the Cardinal de Lorraine, who had spoken to her harshly and even sarcastically. She saw that he had taken the Queen's side. Thus the Connétable found her disposed to enter into an alliance with him by the marriage of her grand-daughter, Mademoiselle de La Marck, with his second son, Monsieur d'Anville, who was to succeed to his power under Charles IX. The Connétable did not think that he would find objections to the marriage in Monsieur d'Anville's mind as he had found in the Connétable de Montmorency's. But the reasons were not less important, although they had remained hidden up until this time. Monsieur d'Anville was desperately in love with the Reine Dauphine, and, although his passion was hopeless, he could not take on an engagement which would divide his attentions.

The Maréchal de Saint-André was the only one of the Court who did not take sides. He was a personal favorite. The King had loved him from the time that he was Dauphin. Since then, he had made him Maréchal de France at an age when it was most unusual to receive any honors at all. The King's favor gave him a brilliance which was sustained by his character, by his personal charm, by the taste of his table and furniture, and by the greatest splendor that had ever been seen by an individual. The King's generosity allowed such an extravagance. The King was absolutely prodigal to those he loved. His character was not perfect, but he had several fine qualities, and above all, a liking and understanding of warfare. He had also been very successful, and except for San Quentin,[15] his reign had been a succession of victories. He had won in person the battle of Renti. He had conquered the Piedmont, driven the English from France, and brought an end to the good fortunes of the Emperor, Charles V,[16] before the city of Metz, which Charles had besieged with all the forces of the Empire and of Spain. Nevertheless, as the misfortune of San Quentin had diminished the hope of our conquests, and as the fortunes of war seemed to be divided between the two Kings, they found themselves inevitably disposed to peace.

The Dowager Duchesse de Lorraine had begun to make overtures at the time of the Dauphin's marriage, and ever since, there had been secret negotiations going on. Finally, Cercamps, in the Artois country, was chosen for the place where they could assemble. The Cardinal de Lorraine, the Connétable de Montmorency, and the Maréchal de Saint-André represented the King. The Duc d'Albe and the Prince d'Orange were for Philippe II. And the Duc and Duchesse de Lorraine were the mediators. The principal conditions were the marriage of Madame Elizabeth de France with Don Carlos, heir to the throne of Spain, and that of Madame, the King's sister, with the Duc de Savoye.

The King, however, remained at the front, and there he received the news of the death of Mary Tudor, the Queen of England.[17] He sent Comte Randan to Elizabeth on her succession to the throne. She received him gladly because her claims were so insecure that it was advantageous for her to be recognized by the King. The Comte found her informed about the French Court and the personalities of those

---

[15]The Spanish defeated the French at Saint-Quentin in 1557.

[16]Charles V (1500–1558) was monarch of Spain, the Low Countries, the Archduchy of Austria, and the kingdom of Naples, as well as Emperor of the Holy Roman Empire. In 1557, Charles abdicated and retired to a monastery, leaving his throne to his son Philip II (1527–1598), who won the battle of Saint-Quentin.

[17]Mary I of England died in 1558, leaving the throne to her half-sister, Elizabeth I.

who composed it. Above all, he found that she knew so much about the Duc de Nemours, and she spoke to him so often of the Duc and with such eagerness, that when the Comte de Randan returned and was giving an account of his voyage to the King, he told him that there was not anything that the Duc de Nemours could not expect from the Queen, and that he did not doubt that she would be willing to marry him. The King spoke of it to the Duc the same evening, making the Comte de Randan repeat to him his conversations with Elizabeth, and advised him to attempt this great match.

At first the Duc de Nemours thought that the King was joking with him, but as he saw that he was serious, he said, "At least, sir, if I embarked on such a fantastic enterprise on your advice and in your Majesty's service, I urge you to keep the secret for me until I am justified by success. Otherwise it will appear that I am so full of vanity as to claim that a Queen who has never set eyes on me, is so much in love with me that she wishes to marry me."

The King agreed. He promised to speak only to the Connétable about the plan, and even considered secrecy necessary to its success. The Comte de Randan advised the Duc de Nemours to go to England as a mere visitor, but the Duc could not bring himself to do that. He sent Lignerolles, who was a clever young man and a favorite of his, to assess the sentiments of the Queen and to begin some sort of courtship of her. While awaiting the outcome of this trip, he went to see the Duc de Savoy, who was then at Brussels with the King of Spain. The death of Mary of England caused great obstacles to the peace at Cercamps. The assembly broke up at the end of November, and the King returned to Paris.

Now there appeared a beauty at Court who attracted the attention of everyone. It could be said that she was a perfect beauty, since she caused a sensation in a place where lovely women were the rule of the day. She belonged to the same family as the Vidame de Chartres, and was one of the greatest heiresses in France. Her father had died young, and had left her to be brought up by her mother, Madame de Chartres, whose nobility, virtue, and character were extraordinary. After she lost her husband, she spent several years without returning to Court. During this absence, she devoted herself to her daughter's education. She not only cultivated her intellect and beauty, but she also sought to give her virtue and to make her lovable. Most mothers think that to protect their daughters from love affairs, it is enough not to mention them. But Madame de Chartres had different ideas. She often described love affairs to her daughter, pointing out their charms, in order to make her more readily understand their dangers. She told her of men's inability to be sincere, of their deceits, of their infidelities. She described the unhappiness that love affairs caused. On the other hand, she made her see what tranquility filled the life of a good woman, and how much virtue gave brilliance and stature to a person of beauty and birth. But she also made her see how difficult it was to preserve this virtue except by an extreme distrust of herself and by taking great care to attach herself to the only happiness of a woman—which is to love her husband and to be loved by him.

This girl was one of the greatest heiresses in France, and, although she was extremely young, several matches had already been proposed for her. But Madame de Chartres, who was extremely proud, did not find any of them worthy of her daughter, and decided that, since she was in her sixteenth year, she would bring her to Court. When she arrived, the Vidame de Chartres was the first to visit her. He was astonished, as well he might be, by his niece's extraordinary beauty. The whiteness of her skin and her blond hair gave her a glamour which was unparalleled. All her features were regular, and her face and figure were full of grace and charm.

The day after her arrival, Mademoiselle de Chartres went to choose some jewels at the shop of an Italian jeweller who traded throughout the world. This man had come from Florence with the Queen, and had become so enriched by his trade, that he lived more like a nobleman than a merchant. While she was there, the Prince de Clèves arrived. He was so surprised at her beauty that he could not hide his astonishment. She could not help blushing to see the effect she had on him. She composed herself, however, without paying any more attention to the Prince's behaviour than was demanded by ordinary civility to a man of such quality. The Prince de Clèves looked at her with admiration, unable to imagine who this beautiful young woman, as yet unknown to him, could be. He saw by her air and by all her retinue that she was of the highest rank. Her youth made him believe that she was unmarried. But since he did not see her mother, and since the Italian jeweller, who did not know her, called her Madame, he did not know what to think. He continued to look at her with astonishment. But he saw that, in contrast with other young people who like to see the effect of their beauty on others, his glances embarrassed her. He felt that he was hastening her departure, and, in fact, she left quite promptly. The Prince de Clèves consoled himself in losing sight of her with the hope of finding out who she was. But he was very surprised when he discovered that no one knew who she was. He remained so touched with her beauty and with the modest air that he noticed in all her actions—it could be said that at that moment he fell in love with her.

That evening, he went to Madame, the King's sister. Madame was of great importance because of the influence she had over the King. Her influence was so great that the King, in making peace, consented to give up the Piedmont so that she could marry the Duc de Savoye. Although she had hoped to marry all her life, she never wanted to marry anyone but a sovereign ruler, and for this reason, she had refused the King of Navarre when he was still the Duc de Vendôme. She had always hoped to marry the Duc de Savoye and kept alive her feelings for him ever since she had seen him at Nice at the interview between King Francis I and Pope Paul III. Since she was very witty and had a great discernment for art, she attracted the finest people. There were certain hours when the whole Court was with her. The Prince de Clèves went there as usual. He was so full of the charm and beauty of Mademoiselle de Chartres that he could not speak of anything else. He told his adventure to everyone, and never tired of praising this person whom he had seen and whom he did not know. Madame told him that there was not any such person as he described, because, if there were, everyone would have known of her. Madame de Dampierre, her maid of honor, who was a friend of Madame de Chartres, overheard this conversation and whispered to Madame that it must have been Mademoiselle de Chartres whom the Prince de Clèves had seen. So Madame turned towards him and told him that if he would return the next day, she would arrange for him to meet this beauty who interested him so much.

Accordingly, the next day, Mademoiselle de Chartres made her first appearance. She was received by the Queens with all the kindness imaginable, and with such an admiration by everyone that nothing but praises were heard on every side. She accepted her praises with such a noble modesty that it appeared that she had not even heard them, or at least that she was not impressed by them. Next she went to Madame, the King's sister, who, after praising her beauty, told her the astonishment she had caused the Prince de Clèves.

The Prince entered a moment later. "Come," she said to him, "see if I didn't keep my promise, and if, in showing you Mademoiselle de Chartres, I'm not showing you that beauty you were looking for. Thank me, at least, because I've told her how much you admire her."

The Prince de Clèves felt a great joy to see that this young person, whom he had found so attractive, was as well born as she was beautiful. He went over to her and begged her never to forget that he was the first to admire her and that, without even knowing her name, he had felt for her all the respect and esteem that were due her.

The Chevalier de Guise and he, who were friends, left Madame's together. At first they praised Mademoiselle de Chartres highly. Then they discovered that they were praising her too much, and they stopped telling each other what they thought of her. But in the following days, whenever they met, they could not help talking about her. Indeed, this new beauty was, for a long time, the subject of all the conversations at Court. The Queen praised her highly and was extremely kind to her. The Reine Dauphine made her one of her favorites and begged Madame de Chartres to bring her to Court often. The King's daughters sent for her presence at all their entertainments. In fact, she was loved and admired by the whole Court. The great exception was the Duchesse de Valentinois—not because she thought her beauty diminished hers, since she had learned from long experience that she had nothing to fear from the King—but because she had such a hatred for the Vidame de Chartres. She had hoped to get him on her side through marriage with one of her daughters, but he had attached himself to the Queen. Therefore she could not regard favorably a lady who bore his name and whom he seemed to care for so much.

The Prince de Clèves was now passionately in love with Mademoiselle de Chartres, and ardently wished to marry her. But he feared that Madame de Chartres would be too proud to give her daughter to a man who was not the eldest of his house. However, his family was so important, and his eldest brother, the Comte d'Eu, had just married a person so close to the royal family that it was the timidity of love rather than real obstacles which made the Prince de Clèves fearful.[18] He had a great number of rivals. The most formidable seemed to be the Chevalier de Guise because of his birth, his merit and the royal favor which his family enjoyed.

The Chevalier de Guise fell in love with Mademoiselle de Chartres the first day he saw her. He and the Prince de Clèves perceived each other's feelings for the lady; their rivalry caused a coolness between them, so that they were never able to clarify the situation to each other. The Prince de Clèves' good fortune of being the first to see Mademoiselle de Chartres, appeared to him a happy omen and seemed to give him some advantage over his rivals. But he foresaw that his father, the Duc de Nevers, would cause difficulties. The Duc de Nevers was closely allied to the Duchesse de Valentinois. Since she was an enemy of the Vidame, he was not very likely to allow his son to think of marrying the Vidame's niece.

Madame de Chartres, who had worked so hard to inspire virtue in her daughter, did not relax her attention in a place where the many dangerous examples made her precautions more necessary than ever. Ambition and gallantry were the soul of the Court, and absorbed the men and the women equally. There were so many factions and so many different intrigues, and the women played such a large part in them, that Love was always mixed with politics and politics with Love. No one was either tranquil or indifferent, bored or lazy. People were always busy trying to better their positions by flattering or helping or hindering somebody else. The occupations of the day were pleasure and intrigue. The ladies attached themselves to the Queen, the Reine Dauphine, the Queen of Navarre, Madame, the King's sister, or the Duchesse de Valentinois, according to taste, interest or whim. Those past their first

---

[18]The historical François de Clèves, Comte d'Eu, did not marry until 1561.

youth or those who professed an austere virtue, were attached to the Queen. Those who were younger and sought pleasure and love affairs paid their court to the Reine Dauphine. The Queen of Navarre had her favorites. She was young and she had power over the King, her husband. He was attached to the Connétable, and because of that, had much influence. Madame, the King's sister, was still beautiful and attracted several ladies to her. The Duchesse de Valentinois could attract all she wished. But she liked few women, and except for a few intimate friends, whose characters suited her, she received only on those days when it amused her to hold a court like the Queen's.

All these different cabals vied with each other constantly, while the ladies who composed them also had their jealousies among themselves either for favor or for lovers. Thus the interests of grandeur and status were often mixed up with other less important, but not less passionately disputed issues. Therefore, there was a kind of subtle agitation without confusion in this Court which made it very agreeable, but also very dangerous for a young person. Madame de Chartres saw this danger, and her great task was to find means to protect her daughter against it. She asked her, not as a mother, but as a friend, to confide in her all the flattering things that were said to her, and she promised her guidance and support in those matters which were always embarrassing to the young.

The Chevalier de Guise made his feelings and intentions towards Mademoiselle de Chartres so obvious that everyone knew them. Nevertheless, he saw only the impossibility of what he desired. He knew that he was not a suitable match for Mademoiselle de Chartres, since he had little means to support his rank. He also knew that his brothers would not approve of his marrying, for fear of the reduction of power which the marriage of younger sons usually brought to noble families. The Cardinal de Lorraine soon made him see that he was not mistaken. He condemned his brother's attachment to Mademoiselle de Chartres, but he did not tell him the real reasons. The Cardinal had a hatred for the Vidame which remained secret at the time, but which came out later. He proclaimed so publicly how much he was opposed to the idea that Madame de Chartres was extremely offended. She took great pains to make the Cardinal de Lorraine see that he had nothing to fear from her, and that she was not thinking of such a marriage. The Vidame pursued the same conduct. He was even more annoyed than Madame de Chartres at the Cardinal de Lorraine's attitude because he knew the reasons for it better.

The Prince de Clèves had not given any less public indications of his passion than had the Chevalier de Guise. The Duc de Nevers learned of this attachment with chagrin. He thought, however, that he had only to speak to his son to make him change his mind. But he was very surprised to find in him a very firm intention to marry Mademoiselle de Chartres. He found fault with this decision. He became angry and concealed his anger so little that the Court, and even Madame de Chartres, soon knew of it. She had not doubted that the Duc de Nevers would regard the marriage of her daughter to his son as an advantage; she was really astonished that the houses of Clèves and of Guise feared rather than desired an alliance with her. Anger made her think of finding a match for her daughter which would place her above those who considered themselves superior to her. After examining all the possibilities, she came upon the eldest son of the Duc de Montpensier. He was still unmarried and was the greatest match at Court. Madame de Chartres was very clever; she was aided by the Vidame who was held in great esteem, and her daughter was in fact a desirable match. Madame de Chartres acted so skillfully that it appeared as if the Duc de Montpensier desired this marriage, and as if there would be no difficulties.

But the Vidame knew that Monsieur d'Anville, as well as being a friend of the Prince de Montpensier, was passionately in love with the Reine Dauphine. He decided to use the Reine Dauphine's influence over Monsieur d'Anville to further Madame de Chartres' cause with the King and with the Prince de Montpensier. He thus spoke to the Reine Dauphine about this, and she joyfully undertook a project in which there was a chance of elevating someone she loved so much. She said this to the Vidame, and assured him that, even though she was well aware that her undertaking would be displeasing to her uncle, the Cardinal de Lorraine, she would be happy to overlook this consideration because he had always taken the Queen's side against her.

Romantic young ladies are always pleased to be given an excuse to talk to those who love them. As soon as the Vidame had left the Reine Dauphine, she ordered Chastelart, who was a favorite of Monsieur d'Anville, and knew that Monsieur d'Anville was in love with her, to tell him to be at the Queen's reception that evening. Chastelart received the command with delight. This gentleman was descended from the house of Dauphiné. Although his family was good, he had improved his position beyond what his birth had warranted by his character and wit. He was accepted and treated with kindness by all the great nobles of the Court, and through the favor of the house of Montmorency, he had become particularly attached to Monsieur d'Anville. He was handsome, skillful in all sorts of sports; he sang agreeably, wrote verse, and had a gallant and passionate spirit which pleased Monsieur d'Anville so much that he confided in him his love for the Reine Dauphine. Unfortunately, Chastelart's role as confidante to Monsieur d'Anville put him in the Reine Dauphine's society, and by seeing her often, he began his ill-fated passion for her which destroyed his reason and ultimately cost him his life.[19]

Monsieur d'Anville did not fail to go to the Queen's that evening. He was pleased that the Reine Dauphine had chosen him to work for something he so much desired. He promised to obey her orders exactly. But, since the Duchesse de Valentinois had been warned of the plans for this marriage, she worked against it, and turned the King against it to such an extent, that when Monsieur d'Anville spoke to him of the proposal, he told him how much he disapproved of it, and even commanded him to say so to the Prince de Montpensier. It is easy to understand how disappointed Madame de Chartres was at the collapse of something she so much desired. This misfortune put her enemies in a much better position and damaged her daughter's prospects of marriage.

It was a great relief for the Reine Dauphine to reveal to Mademoiselle de Chartres the unhappiness she felt at not being able to help her. "You see that my power is very limited. The Queen and the Duchesse hate me so much that it's not very difficult for them or for their followers to stand in the way of everything I want. Although I've always tried to please them, they hate me also because of the Queen my mother,[20] who formerly made them suspicious and caused them some jealousy. The King was in love with her before he was in love with the Duchesse de Valentinois. In the years of his marriage, which were childless, he thought of divorcing the Queen in order to marry my mother, even though he now loved the Duchesse de Valentinois. She, fearful that he would marry a woman he had already loved, and whose beauty and wit could diminish her own, joined forces

---

[19]After the death of François II, Chastelart, who had fallen in love with Mary Stuart, returned to Scotland with her. He was executed when he was found hiding in her bedchamber.

[20]Marie de Lorraine, daughter of the Duc de Guise, was, by her second husband, James V of Scotland, the mother of Mary Stuart.

with the Connétable. The Connétable didn't want the King to marry a sister of the Guises. They told the late King their feelings, and, although he mortally hated the Duchesse de Valentinois, as much as he loved the Queen, he worked with them to prevent the King from divorcing her. In order to remove my mother from the King's thoughts completely, they married her to the King of Scotland, whose first wife had been Madame Magdeleine, the King's sister. They arranged this marriage because it was easy to conclude, but in doing so, they broke their promise to the King of England, who ardently wished to marry her. This nearly caused a rupture between the two Kings. Henry VIII never got over not having married my mother. Whenever other French princesses were proposed to him, he always said they could never replace the one whom they had deprived him of. My mother was certainly a great beauty. It is really remarkable that when she was the widow of the Duc de Longueville, three Kings wished to marry her. Misfortune married her to the least important of them and put her in a country where there were only difficulties. It is said that I resemble her in her unfortunate fate. Whatever happiness seems in store for me, I don't think that I shall enjoy it."

Mademoiselle de Chartres told the Queen that these presentiments were so ill-founded that she wouldn't keep them for long and that she shouldn't doubt that her future happiness would fulfill all her expectations.[21]

After this, no one dared to think of Mademoiselle de Chartres. Either they feared displeasing the King, or they feared that they could not compete with someone who desired a Prince of blood. The Prince de Clèves was not deterred by any of these considerations. The death of his father, the Duc de Nevers, which occurred at this time, freed him to follow his own inclinations. As soon as the proprieties of mourning were over, he thought only of marrying Mademoiselle de Chartres. He felt lucky to be making his proposal at a time when recent events had driven away all the other suitors. He was almost certain that he would not be refused. What clouded his happiness was the fear of not being attractive to her. He would have preferred the possibility of pleasing her to the certainty of marrying her without being loved by her.

He had felt some jealousy on account of the Chevalier de Guise, but this was founded on the Chevalier's character rather than on Mademoiselle de Chartres' conduct. Therefore he longed to find out whether she approved of his suit. Since he saw her only at the Queens' or at the assemblies, it was difficult to have a private conversation with her. But he found the means to talk with her, and he told her of his love and of his plans for the future with all the respect imaginable. He begged her to tell him what her feelings for him were. He told her that his love for her was such that he would always be unhappy if she married him only from a sense of duty to her mother's wishes.

Since Mademoiselle de Chartres had a very fine and noble heart, she was touched with gratitude by the Prince de Clèves' proposal. This gratitude lent an air of sweetness to her answers to him, which was enough to give hope to a man as deeply in love as the Prince. Thus he flattered himself that he had the match he so much desired. Mademoiselle de Chartres repeated this conversation to her mother, who told her that the Prince de Clèves was a person of such grandeur and worth, and that he displayed such wisdom for his age, that if she wished to marry him, she would gladly consent to it. Mademoiselle de Chartres replied that she had noticed

---

[21]When Mary's husband, François II, died in 1560 after only one year on the throne, she returned to Scotland, but she was forced to abdicate in 1568. She fled to England, where she was imprisoned and beheaded by her cousin, Queen Elizabeth I.

the same good qualities. She said that she would marry him with less aversion than another, but that she didn't feel any physical attraction to him. The next morning marriage proposals were made to Madame de Chartres; she consented to them. She had no fear that in giving the Prince de Clèves to her daughter as a husband, she was, perhaps, marrying her to a man she could not love. The articles were drawn up. The King was notified, and the marriage was announced.

The Prince de Clèves was happy without being entirely satisfied. He saw very painfully that Mademoiselle de Chartres' feelings did not exceed those of esteem and respect. He could not even flatter himself that she hid more gratifying ones, since their social relationship would have allowed her to reveal them without injuring her extreme sense of modesty.

Hardly a day passed without his complaining to her. "Is it possible," he said, "that I cannot be happy in marrying you? However, it's true that I am not. You feel only a sort of kindness for me that can never satisfy me. You have no longing, no anxiety, no impatience. You are no more moved by my passion than you would be by a devotion to your fortune rather than to your personal charms."

"You're unjust in your complaints," she answered him. "I don't know what you could wish beyond what I do. It seems to me that propriety won't allow me to do more."

"It's true," he replied, "that you give certain indications that would make me happy if there were anything behind them. But, instead of propriety inhibiting you, it's propriety alone that makes you act as you do. I affect neither your passions nor your heart, and my presence neither pleases nor disturbs you."

"How can you doubt," she said, "that I'm not happy to see you? As for emotion, I blush so often when I see you, that you cannot doubt that your presence affects me."

"I'm not deceived by your blushing," he replied. "It reflects your modesty, and not the movement of your heart; I only take such pleasure from it as I may."

Mademoiselle de Chartres was non-plussed; these distinctions were beyond her comprehension. The Prince de Clèves saw only too well how impossible it was for her to have the feelings that could satisfy him, since it appeared that she did not even understand them.

The Chevalier de Guise came back from a journey a few days before the wedding. Although he had seen so many insurmountable obstacles to his marrying Mademoiselle de Chartres that he knew that he could not succeed, he felt saddened to see her become another man's wife. This sadness did not stifle his passion, and he was as much in love with her as ever. Mademoiselle de Chartres was not unaware of the Chevalier's feelings for her. Now that he had returned, he let her know that she was the cause of his sad demeanor. He was so good and so charming that she could not make him unhappy without feeling some pity for him. She did feel some, but she did not allow this pity to lead to other feelings, and she told her mother of the pain that the Chevalier's affection caused her.

Madame de Chartres admired her daughter's sincerity, and she admired it with reason. Never had a person possessed such sincerity and showed it so naturally. But she was surprised that her daughter's heart was not touched, and even more so, when she realized that the Prince de Clèves had not affected her daughter any more than her other suitors. This was why Madame de Chartres took great care to attach her daughter to her husband and to make her understand what she owed him for having loved her before he even knew who she was, and for proving his love by preferring her to all other matches at a time when no one else dared to think of her.

The marriage was performed. The ceremony was held at the Louvre.[22] In the evening, the King and the Queen with all the Court came to a magnificent supper party at Madame de Chartres'. The Chevalier de Guise did not dare to be conspicuous by his absence from the ceremony, but he could not conceal his sadness.

The Prince de Clèves did not discover that Mademoiselle de Chartres had changed her feelings in changing her name. As a husband, he had more privileges, but no greater place in his wife's heart. Thus, being her husband, he did not cease to be her lover, having always something to desire beyond what he possessed. Although she lived perfectly honorably with him, he was not entirely happy. He maintained a violent passion for her which clouded his joy. Jealousy played no part in this unhappiness. Never was there a husband less inclined to be jealous, and never was there a wife less likely to make him so. She was, however, exposed to the atmosphere of the Court. Every day she went to the Queens and to Madame. All the young attractive men saw her at home and at the Duc de Nevers', her brother-in-law's, whose house was open to everyone. But she had an air which imposed such respect and seemed so far removed from flirtation that even the Maréchal de Saint-André, bold as he was, and supported by the King's favor, was attracted by her beauty without daring to reveal anything but courteous attentiveness to her. Several others had the same feelings about her, so that with Madame de Chartres' concern for her daughter's reputation, as well as her own natural goodness, Madame de Clèves appeared to be the kind of woman who was unattainable.

While the Duchesse de Lorraine was working for the peace, she was also negotiating the marriage of her son, the Duc de Lorraine. It was concluded, and the bride was Madame Claude de France, the second daughter of the King. The wedding was set for the month of February. While the Duc de Nemours remained at Brussels, he was entirely absorbed with his plans for England. He received and sent messengers continually. His hopes rose daily, and finally Lignerolles sent word to him that he must appear and finish in person what his planning had so well begun. He received the news with as much joy as was possible for a man who saw himself raised to a throne on the basis of his reputation alone. His mind became unconsciously accustomed to the grandeur of his destiny. The difficulties had been erased from his imagination, and instead of considering the marriage an undertaking which could not possibly succeed, as he had at first, he no longer saw any obstacles.

The Duc de Nemours went to Paris quickly to give all the necessary orders for a magnificent retinue, so that he might appear in England with a splendor equal to his undertaking. Then he hastened to Court to attend the marriage of the Duc de Lorraine. He arrived the night before the betrothals. The same evening he went to report to the King the state of his plans and receive orders for what remained to be done. Then he called on the two Queens. Madame de Clèves was not there, so she never saw him and did not know that he had arrived. She had heard everyone speak of the Duc as the most attractive and most charming gentleman of the Court. Above all, the Reine Dauphine had spoken of him so often and in such a manner that she was curious and even impatient to see him.

Madame de Clèves spent the whole day of the betrothals at home, dressing so that she might appear at the ball in the evening and at the royal festival to be held at the Louvre. When she arrived, everyone admired her beauty, attire, and jewels. The ball began, and while she was dancing with the Chevalier de Guise, there was quite a stir at the door as if someone were coming in and people were making way for him. Madame de Clèves finished dancing. As she was looking around for someone

---

[22]A royal residence, not a museum, at the time of the novel.

to dance with, the King called to her to take the one who had just arrived as a partner. She turned around and saw a man who was striding over some chairs to arrive at the dance floor, and who she thought could only be the Duc de Nemours. The Duc was so attractive that it was difficult not to be startled in seeing him for the first time, especially that evening, when the care he had taken in dressing had made him even more striking. But it was also difficult to see Madame de Clèves for the first time without feeling a great astonishment.

The Duc de Nemours was so struck with her beauty that when he approached her, and she curtsied to him, he could not hide his admiration. The King and the Queen reminded each other that these two had never been introduced. They found it rather strange to see the Duc and the Princesse dancing together without knowing each other. They called the Duc and the Princesse over when they had finished dancing, without giving them a chance to talk with anyone else, and asked them if they did not wish to be introduced, or whether they had guessed who each other was.

"For myself, Madame, there's no doubt. But, since Madame de Clèves hasn't the same reasons for knowing who I am as I have for recognizing her, I would appreciate it if your Majesty would be kind enough to tell her my name."

"I think," said the Reine Dauphine, "that she knows your name as well as you know hers."

"I assure you," answered Madame de Clèves, who appeared a little embarrassed, "that I can't guess as well as you think I can."

"You can guess very well," replied the Reine Dauphine, "and there's even something flattering to the Duc de Nemours in not wishing to admit that you knew him without ever having seen him."

The Queen interrupted the conversation to say that the ball must go on. The Duc de Nemours took the Reine Dauphine as a partner. She was a perfect beauty and had appeared so in the eyes of the Duc de Nemours before he went to Flanders. But all evening he had eyes only for Madame de Clèves.

The Chevalier de Guise, who still adored her, was standing near her, and felt great unhappiness at what had just happened. He took it as an evil omen that fortune destined the Duc de Nemours to fall in love with Madame de Clèves. Whether she revealed some emotion in her face, or whether jealousy made the Chevalier de Guise see through her façade, he thought that she was affected by the sight of the Duc, and he could not help telling her that the Duc de Nemours was indeed fortunate to make her acquaintance in so romantic and extraordinary a manner.

Madame de Clèves went home; her mind was so filled with all that had happened at the ball that, although it was very late, she went into her mother's room to tell her about it. She praised the Duc de Nemours to her with a certain air that caused Madame de Chartres to have the same suspicions about her as had the Chevalier de Guise.

The next morning the wedding took place. There Madame de Clèves saw the Duc de Nemours behave with so admirable a grace and dignity that she was even more astonished. In the days that followed, she saw him at the Reine Dauphine's, watched him play tennis with the King, saw him tilt at the ring, and heard him talk. But she always noticed that he so far surpassed all the others in personality and charm, and made himself so much the master of conversation wherever he went, that in a very short time, she fell deeply in love with him. The Duc de Nemours' violent attraction to her gave him that sweetness and liveliness which newly awakened love always inspires, so that he was even more charming than usual. Thus, meeting each other often, and seeing in each other the most desirable at Court, it was natural for them to be delighted with each other's company.

The Duchesse de Valentinois was present at all the pleasure parties, and the King showed her the same attentiveness and courtesy as he had at the beginning of his passion. Madame de Clèves—who was at an age when she could not believe that a woman past twenty-five years could be loved—watched the King's devotion to the Duchesse de Valentinois with astonishment. After all, she was a grandmother who had just married off her grand-daughter.

She spoke of it often to Madame de Chartres. "Is it possible, Madame," she asked her, "that the King could be in love with her so long? How could he be devoted to a woman who was much older than he, who had been his father's mistress, and who, as I've been told, has been the mistress of several others?"

"It's true," she replied, "that neither the integrity nor the faithfulness of the Duchesse de Valentinois caused the King to fall in love with her and kept his love alive. For this reason, his passion is less excusable. For if this woman had youth and beauty as well as family, and if she had the merit of never having loved before, and if she had loved the King completely faithfully, and only for himself, without any concern for grandeur or fortune, and without using her power except for the King's benefit, it would be difficult not to praise his deep devotion to her."

"If I didn't fear," continued Madame de Chartres, "that you would say of me what is said of all women of my age, that they like to tell stories of their youth, I would tell you of the beginning of the King's passion for the Duchesse de Valentinois, and several other events in the Court of the late King which have much to do with present circumstances."

"Far from accusing you of repeating old stories," replied Madame de Clèves, "I complain that you haven't instructed me enough on present events and that you haven't taught me enough about the various interests and intrigues of the Court. I'm so entirely ignorant of them that a few days ago I thought that the Connétable was on good terms with the Queen."

"Your opinion is quite the reverse of the truth," replied Madame de Chartres. "The Queen hates the Connétable, and if she had some power, he would be only too aware of it. She knows that he has told the King several times that of all his children, the only ones who resemble him are the illegitimate ones."

"I would never have suspected that hatred," interrupted Madame de Clèves, "after seeing the care the Queen took to write to the Connétable while he was in prison, the joy she pretended on his return, and the fact that she always calls him 'comrade,' as the King does."

"If you judge on appearances in this place," replied Madame de Chartres, "you will always be deceived. What appears is practically never the truth."

"But to return to the Duchesse de Valentinois. You know that she is called Diane de Poitiers. Her family is very illustrious. She descends from the ancient Ducs d'Aquitaine. Her grandmother was the illegitimate daughter of Louis XI. In fact there is nothing but greatness in her lineage. Saint-Valier, her father, found himself involved in the affair of the Connétable de Bourbon, of whom you have heard talk. He was condemned to be beheaded and was led to the scaffold. His daughter, whose beauty was admirable, and who had already pleased the late King, managed so well (I don't know by what means) that she obtained her father's life. He was informed of his pardon as he awaited his death-stroke. But he was so overcome with fear, that he lost consciousness and died a few days later. His daughter appeared at Court as the King's mistress. The King's journey to Italy and his imprisonment there interrupted his love affair.[23] When he returned from Spain and when Madame, the

---

[23] In 1525, François I was defeated and imprisoned by Emperor Charles V at Pavia in Italy.

Queen Regent, went ahead of him to Bayonne, she took with her all her maids of honour. Among them was Mademoiselle de Pisseleau, who became the Duchesse d'Estampes. The King fell in love with her. She was inferior in birth, in wit and in beauty to the Duchesse de Valentinois, and she was superior to her only in the advantage of her extreme youth. I've heard it said that she was born the day that the Duchesse de Valentinois was married. But malice and not truth was responsible for that rumor. For unless I'm mistaken, the Duchesse de Valentinois married Monsieur de Brézé, Grand Sénéschal of Normandy, at the same time that the King fell in love with the Duchesse d'Estampes. There has never been such a violent hatred as existed between these two women. The Duchesse de Valentinois could not forgive the Duchesse d'Estampes for taking away from her the title of the King's mistress. The Duchesse d'Estampes was extremely jealous of the Duchesse de Valentinois because the King kept up a relationship with her. The King was not completely faithful to his mistresses. There was always one who had the title and honor. But the ladies who were called "the little band" shared him in turn. The loss of his son, the Dauphin, who died at Tournon and who was believed to have been poisoned, caused him great pain. He did not have the same affection or liking for his second son who is ruling now. He did not think he was brave enough or lively enough. He complained about this one day to the Duchesse de Valentinois. She told the King that to make the Dauphin more lively and pleasing, she would make him fall in love with her. She succeeded, as you see. This passion has lasted for more than twenty years without being changed by time or obstacles.

"The late King opposed it at first, either because he was still enough in love with the Duchesse de Valentinois to be jealous, or because he was influenced by the Duchesse d'Estampes who despaired over the fact that the Dauphin was devoted to her enemy. Whatever the reason, it is obvious that the King viewed his son's passion with an anger and chagrin that he did not hesitate to reveal. His son feared neither his anger nor his hatred, and nothing could interfere with his devotion to the Duchesse de Valentinois. The King simply had to allow it. This opposition to his wishes made the King more alienated from the Dauphin and made him even more devoted to his third son, the Duc d'Orleans, who was well-built, handsome, and full of ambition. His impetuous youthfulness needed to be tempered, but he would have made a noble prince if his character had been ripened by age.

"The Dauphin's status as eldest and the Duc d'Orleans' favor with the King caused a rivalry between them which went as far as hatred. The rivalry had begun in their childhood and was still maintained. When the Emperor passed through France, he gave his complete support to the Duc d'Orleans in preference to the Dauphin, who resented it so much that when the Emperor was at Chantilly, he wanted to have the Connétable arrest the Emperor without awaiting the King's order. He did not want to. Later the King blamed the Connétable for not following his son's advice, and when the Connétable was removed from Court, this reason played a large part.

"The division between the two brothers gave the Duchesse d'Estampes the idea of depending on the Duc d'Orleans to support her with the King against the Duchesse de Valentinois. She succeeded in her plan. Without being in love with her, the Duc d'Orleans entered into her projects no less than the Dauphin undertook those of the Duchesse de Valentinois. Thus were formed two cabales in the Court, such as you can imagine. But these intrigues were not limited to the contentions of women.

"The Emperor, who had maintained his friendship with the Duc d'Orleans, had offered to give him the Duchy of Milan several times. In the propositions that were made for the peace, he gave him hopes of handing over to him the seventeen provinces and of marrying him to his daughter. The Dauphin wished neither the peace nor the marriage. He used the Connétable, whom he had always loved, to make the King see how important it was not to give his successor a brother as powerful as the Duc d'Orleans would be with the alliance of the Emperor and the seventeen provinces. The Connétable was even more inclined to agree with the sentiments of the Dauphin, because, by this means, he hoped to oppose the plans of the Duchesse d'Estampes. She was his declared enemy and ardently wished the advancement of the Duc d'Orleans.

"The Dauphin now commanded the King's army in Champagne and would have reduced the Emperor's army to such weakness that it would have perished completely were it not for the Duchesse d'Estampes. Fearing that too great advantages on our side would make us refuse the peace and the Emperor's alliance with the Duc d'Orleans, she had the enemy secretly warned to surprise Espernay and Chateau-Thierry, which were full of provisions. They did so, and by this means, saved their army.

"The Duchesse d'Estampes did not enjoy the success of her treachery for long. Shortly afterwards, the Duc d'Orleans died at Farmoutier of some contagious disease. He loved one of the most beautiful women of the Court and was loved by her. I can't tell you her name because she has lived with such discretion since then, and she has concealed her feelings for the Duc so carefully, that she deserves to have her reputation preserved. By accident, she received news of her husband's death on the same day that she heard of the Duc d'Orleans' death, and, without having to restrain her grief, she used this pretext as an excuse to hide her genuine affliction.

"The King barely survived his son, the Duc d'Orleans. He died two years afterwards. He recommended that the Dauphin use the Cardinal de Tournon and the Admiral d'Annebault, and did not speak of the Connétable, who was relegated to Chantilly at that time. The first thing that the Dauphin did as King, however, was to recall the Connétable and give him the management of his affairs.

"The Duchesse d'Estampes was sent away and received all the punishment that she could expect from such a powerful enemy. The Duchesse de Valentinois was fully revenged on the Duchesse d'Estampes and on all of those who had displeased her. Her influence over the King's opinions appeared more absolute now than when he was the Dauphin. For more than twelve years of the King's reign, she has been the absolute mistress of everything. She disposes of his offices and appointments. She has had the Cardinal de Tournon, Chancellor Olivier, and Villeroy banished. Those who wished to enlighten the King on her conduct have perished in the attempt. The Comte de Taix, who was the grand master of the artillery, did not like her and could not help talking about her love affairs, especially about the one with the Comte de Brissac. The King was already jealous of him. Nevertheless, the Duchesse managed so well that the Comte de Taix was disgraced and relieved of his post. Further, and this is most unbelievable: the Duchesse had the post given to the Comte de Brissac and later had him made Maréchal de France. The King's jealousy, however, increased, so that he could not bear to have him stay at Court. But jealousy, which is bitter and violent in others, is sweet and tempered in him because of his extreme deference to his mistress. Thus he did not dare to remove his rival except with the excuse of giving him the government of the Piedmont. The Comte de Brissac remained there several years. He returned last winter supposedly to ask for troops and the other equipment necessary for the army he commanded. His desire to see the Duchesse de Valentinois again and his fear of being forgotten played an important part in his return. The King received him very coldly. The Ducs de Guise, who did not like him, but who did not dare to reveal their dislike because of the Duchesse de Valentinois, made use of the Vidame de Chartres, who was his declared enemy, to see to it that he did not obtain anything he came for. This frustration was not difficult to carry out. The King hated him, and his presence made the King so anxious that the Comte de Brissac had to return without bringing back anything from his journey, except perhaps for reviving in the Duchesse de Valentinois' heart the feelings that absence had begun to lessen. There were several other persons who might have made the King jealous. But either he did not know about them, or he did not care to complain about them.

"I don't know, my daughter," said Madame de Chartres, "but what you will discover is that I've told you about events you don't really care to know about."

"I'm very far from making such a complaint," said Madame de Clèves, "and if I didn't fear imposing on you, I would ask about several other details of which I'm unaware."

The Duc de Nemours' passion for Madame de Clèves was so violent at first that he lost any desire for and even memory of all the other ladies that he had loved and with whom he had kept up a correspondence during his absence. He did not even take the trouble to find excuses for breaking with them. He was too impatient to listen to their complaints or to answer their reproaches. The Reine Dauphine, for whom he had quite strong feelings, could not hold his heart against Madame de Clèves. His impatience for the English expedition began to cool, and he did not even press with his usual ardor for the things that were necessary for his departure. He often went to the Reine Dauphine's apartments because Madame de Clèves could usually be found there. He had no objections to allowing the Court to think what it wished of his attachment to the Reine Dauphine. Madame de Clèves seemed to him to be such a great prize that he preferred to be remiss in showing her the marks of his passion, rather than to risk revealing his love in public. He did not even mention it to the Vidame de Chartres, his intimate friend, from whom he hid nothing. He decided upon such scrupulous conduct and followed it so carefully that no one but the Chevalier de Guise suspected his love for Madame de Clèves. Even she would have had difficulty in knowing it herself if the attraction she felt for him had not given her a particular sensitivity to his actions so that she could not doubt his feelings for her.

Madame de Clèves did not have the same desire to tell her mother what she thought about the Duc as she did to tell her about her other admirers. Without having a firm intention to hide her feelings, she simply did not discuss them. But Madame de Chartres saw only too well the attraction that her daughter felt for the Duc. This knowledge gave her much pain. She well understood the danger for a vulnerable young woman to be loved by a man like the Duc de Nemours. She was completely confirmed in her suspicions of her daughter's feelings by something which occurred a few days later.

The Maréchal de Saint-André, who sought all kinds of occasions to display his grandeur, begged the King on the excuse of showing him his house, which had just been finished, to do him the honor of having supper at his home with the Queens. The Maréchal was also eager to show off to Madame de Clèves his extraordinary hospitality which went as far as extravagance.

Several days before the one chosen for the supper, the young King was weak in health, was not feeling well and had not seen anyone. His wife, the Reine Dauphine, spent the whole day with him. Since he was feeling better in the evening, he allowed all the people of rank who were in his antechamber to come in. The Reine Dauphine returned to her apartments. There, among several other ladies who were her closest friends, she found Madame de Clèves.

That evening, as it was already late and she was not yet dressed, the Reine Dauphine did not go to the Queen's apartment. She sent word to her that she would not see her, and had her jewels brought so that she could choose some for the Maréchal de Saint-André's ball, and give some to Madame de Clèves. While the ladies were busy with their jewels, the Prince de Condé arrived. His rank gave him free access everywhere. The Reine Dauphine said that he had probably just come from her husband's the young King's apartment, and asked what was going on there.

"Madame, they're arguing with the Duc de Nemours," he replied. "He's defending his side of the argument he's supporting with such warmth that it must be his own. I think that he must have some mistress who worries him when she goes to a ball because he finds it so upsetting for a lover to see the person he loves there."

"How's that!" replied the Reine Dauphine. "The Duc de Nemours doesn't want his mistress to go to a ball? I could believe that husbands wouldn't wish their wives to go. But, as for lovers—I wouldn't have believed that they could have such thoughts."

"The Duc de Nemours," replied the Prince de Condé, "says that a ball is the most intolerable for lovers, whether they are loved or not. He says that if they are loved, they have the frustration of not receiving any attention for several days. He says that there isn't a woman whose concern for her costume will not prevent her from thinking of her lover. These ladies are completely concerned with their dresses, and this concern is for everyone and not just for those they love. When they are at a ball, they wish to please everyone who looks at them, and when they are successful in their beauty, they experience a happiness in which their lover doesn't play the largest part. He also said that a lover who isn't loved, suffers even more to see his mistress at a ball. The more she is admired in public, the more unhappy he is not to be loved. He always fears that her beauty will cause another flame to start, which will be more fortunate than his own. Thus the Duc de Nemours considers that there is no suffering equal to seeing one's mistress at a ball, unless it is to know that she is present when one cannot be there oneself."

Madame de Clèves pretended not to hear what the Prince de Condé was saying. But she listened with attention. She perceived easily what part she played in the opinion that the Duc de Nemours supported. Above all, she understood what he was saying about the inconvenience of not being at a ball where his mistress would be, because he would not be at the Maréchal de Saint-André's ball, since the King was sending him ahead to meet the Duc de Ferrare.

The Reine Dauphine laughed with the Prince de Condé, and did not approve of the Duc de Nemours' opinion.

"There's only one occasion, Madame," said the Prince de Condé, "when the Duc de Nemours would allow his mistress to go to a ball. That is when he gives it. He said that last year he gave one for your Majesty. He felt that his mistress did him a favor in coming, although she seemed only to follow you there. He said that it always makes a lover grateful when a mistress takes part in a festival he gives. He said, too, that it is pleasing for a lover when a mistress sees him the host of an entertainment where the whole Court is present, and when she sees him acquit himself well in doing the honors."

"The Duc de Nemours is right," said the Reine Dauphine, smiling, "to approve his mistress's going to a ball. There were so many ladies to whom he gave that title, that if they all didn't come, there would be few people at the ball."

As soon as the Prince de Condé began to describe the Duc de Nemours' attitude towards a ball, Madame de Clèves felt a great reluctance to go to the Maréchal de Saint-André's. She easily agreed that it was not necessary to visit the house of a man who showed a preference for her, and it would be very easy to use decorum as an excuse to avoid doing something which would be upsetting to the Duc de

Nemours. Nevertheless, she took home the jewelry which the Reine Dauphine had given her. In the evening, when she showed it to her mother, however, she told her that she would not wear it. She said that the Maréchal de Saint-André took so much trouble to make her see that he liked her, that she didn't doubt that he wanted her to play a role in the entertainment he was giving for the King. She also feared that under the pretext of honoring the King, he would pay her some attentions that would be embarrassing to her.

Madame de Chartres opposed her daughter's opinion for quite a while. But, seeing that she was determined, she gave in. She told her that she must pretend to be ill to have an excuse for not going, because the real reasons that prevented her from going would never be approved of, and it was important that they not even be suspected. Madame de Clèves consented voluntarily to spend several days at home in order not to attend a social function from which the Duc de Nemours would be absent. He left without having the pleasure of knowing that she would not attend.

He returned the morning after the ball. He knew that she was not there. But, as he did not know that the conversation at the Reine Dauphine's had been repeated in front of her, he was far from believing that he was fortunate enough to be the one who prevented her from going. The next morning, when he was at the Queen's and was talking to the Reine Dauphine, Madame de Chartres and Madame de Clèves arrived and approached the Reine Dauphine. Madame de Clèves was dressed a bit carelessly, as if she had been ill, but her demeanor did not correspond with her costume.

"There you are so beautiful," said the Reine Dauphine, "that I can't believe you were ill. In telling you the Duc de Nemours' opinion on a ball, I think that the Prince de Condé has persuaded you that you would be doing the Maréchal de Saint-André a favor if you went to his house, and it is that which has prevented you from going."

Madame de Clèves blushed because the Reine Dauphine guessed the truth so well and because she was revealing it in front of the Duc de Nemours. Madame de Chartres saw in a flash why her daughter had not wished to go to the ball. To prevent the Duc de Nemours from knowing as well as she, she spoke with a conviction that seemed based on the truth.

She said to the Reine Dauphine, "I assure you that your Majesty does my daughter more honor than she deserves. She was truly ill, but I think that if I hadn't prevented her, she would not have hesitated to follow you and to show herself, changed as she was, to have the pleasure of seeing all the extraordinary entertainment yesterday evening."

The Reine Dauphine believed what Madame de Chartres said. The Duc de Nemours was happy to perceive the appearance of truth in her conversation. But Madame de Clèves' blush made him suspect that what the Reine Dauphine had said was not entirely removed from the truth. Madame de Clèves was unhappy at first because the Duc de Nemours had reason to believe that he was the one who had prevented her from going to the Maréchal de Saint-André's ball. But then she felt a kind of annoyance that her mother had completely deprived him of that idea.

Although the assembly at Cercamps had broken up, the negotiations for peace still continued so that by the end of February the delegates reassembled at Câteau Cambrésis.[24] The same delegates returned; but the Maréchal de Saint-André's absence rid the Duc de Nemours of his most formidable rival, rather by the care

---

[24]The Treaty of Câteau-Cambrésis (1559) ended a sixty-year struggle between France and Spain over control of Italy.

that the Maréchal took in observing those who approached Madame de Clèves than by any progress he could make in her affections.

Madame de Chartres did not wish to let her daughter know that she was aware of her feelings for the Duc because she did not wish to prejudice her against the uncomplimentary things she had to say about him. She spoke of his many love affairs and mixed in some poisoned praises on the great wisdom he showed in not really being able to fall in love and in not taking his relationships with women seriously.

"It is thought," she added, "that he has a great passion for the Reine Dauphine. Even I see that he goes to her apartments often, and I counsel you to avoid talking with him as much as possible, particularly in private. Since the Reine Dauphine treats you as she does, it will be said that you are their confidante, and you know how disagreeable that reputation can be. I think that if this rumor continues, you should spend less time in the Reine Dauphine's apartments so as not to become involved in her love affairs."

Madame de Clèves had never heard any gossip about the Duc de Nemours and the Reine Dauphine. She was so surprised at what her mother had just said, and felt so deceived about the Duc's feelings that her facial expression changed. Madame de Chartres noticed this change. At that moment some visitors arrived. Madame de Clèves went home and closed herself in her room.

In thinking over what her mother had just said, she could not express the sadness she felt in recognizing the emotions she had for the Duc de Nemours. She now saw that the feelings she had for him were those that the Prince de Clèves had so much desired. She reflected on how shameful it was to have these feelings for another than for a husband who deserved them so much. She felt hurt and embarrassed by the fear that the Duc de Nemours was only making use of her as a pretext to see the Reine Dauphine, and this thought made her decide to admit to Madame de Chartres all that she had not yet told her.

The next morning she went into her mother's room to discuss things with her, but she found that Madame de Chartres had a little fever so that she did not wish to talk. The illness appeared so slight, however, that Madame de Clèves did not hesitate to go to the Reine Dauphine's apartment after dinner. The Reine Dauphine was in her room with two or three ladies who were her closest friends.

"We were talking about the Duc de Nemours," said the Reine Dauphine when she saw her, "and we were amazed at how changed he is since his return from Brussels. Even before he went, he had an infinite number of mistresses. This showed a lack of taste in him, for he was equally attentive to those with good reputations and those without them. Since his return, he pays attention neither to one type nor to the other. There has never been such a great change in his personality, and even I find that he is less cheerful than usual."

Madame de Clèves did not answer. She was filled with shame at the idea that she would have taken all that was said about the change in the Duc's temperament as proof of his passion for her if she had not been undeceived. She felt a certain bitterness against the Reine Dauphine for appearing to be astonished at something for which she knew the causes better than anyone.

She could not help revealing some of her feelings, and, as the other ladies moved away, she went up to the Reine Dauphine and whispered to her, "Is it for my benefit that you have just been talking, and do you wish to hide from me the fact that you are the one who has made the Duc de Nemours change his conduct?"

"You are unjust," said the Reine Dauphine. "You know that I have nothing to hide from you. It's true that before the Duc de Nemours went to Brussels, he had the intention, I think, of letting me know that he was fond of me. But since his return, it seems to me that he doesn't even remember the things he said. I admit that I'm very curious to know who has made him change, and it will be a strange thing if I can't figure it out," she added. "The Vidame de Chartres is in love with a lady over whom I have a certain amount of influence. Through her I will try to find out what has caused this great change."

The Reine Dauphine spoke with an air that convinced Madame de Clèves. She discovered in spite of herself that she was calmer and happier than she had ever been before.

When she returned to her mother, she realized that her mother was much worse than when she had left her. The fever had doubled, and in the following days it rose so that it became apparent that the illness would be a serious one. Madame de Clèves was extremely upset. She never left her mother's room. The Prince de Clèves spent almost all his days with her, both because of his concern for Madame de Chartres, and to prevent his wife from abandoning herself to her sadness. But he also loved having the pleasure of seeing his wife: his passion had not diminished.

The Duc de Nemours, who always showed a great friendship for the Prince de Clèves, did not hesitate to do so on his return from Brussels. During Madame de Chartres' illness, the Duc figured out ways of seeing Madame de Clèves several times, as he pretended to call for her husband to take him for a walk. He even came looking for him at hours when he knew he would not be there. Under the pretext of waiting for him, he remained in Madame de Chartres' antechamber where there were always several noble people. Madame de Clèves came and went often, but her anxiety did not make her appear any less beautiful to the Duc de Nemours. He made her see how concerned he was with her distress, and he spoke to her about it with such a sweet and submissive air that he easily convinced her that he was not in love with the Reine Dauphine.

She could not help being troubled at the sight of him, and yet she felt pleasure in seeing him. But when she did not see him anymore, and when she thought that the emotions she felt when she was with him were the beginnings of a passion, she thought that she almost hated him because her attraction to him was almost too painful to bear.

Madame de Chartres became considerably worse so that the doctors began to despair for her life. She heard the doctors inform her about her danger with a courage that equalled her virtue and piety. When the doctors had left, she made everyone leave the room, and she called Madame de Clèves to her.

"We must part, my daughter," she said, as she stretched out her hand to her. "The danger I leave you in and the great need you have for me increases the sadness I feel in leaving you. You are in love with the Duc de Nemours. I don't ask you to admit it to me. I can no longer make use of your sincerity to guide you. I've been aware of your feelings for a very long time, but I didn't wish to call them to your attention for fear of accentuating them in you. You are only too aware of them now. You are on the edge of a precipice. Great efforts and violent measures are necessary to restrain you. Think of what you owe your husband. Think of what you owe yourself, and remember that you are going to lose that reputation you have acquired and which I so much desired for you. Have the strength and the courage, my daughter, to retire from the Court. Get your husband to take you away. Don't fear to take the most violent and difficult measures no matter how extreme they may appear to you at first. They will be easier in the long run than the misfortunes of a love affair. If other reasons than your sense of duty could make you do as I wish, remember that if anything could happen to trouble the peace I hope for in leaving this world, it would be to see you fall like other women. If this misfortune should happen, however, I accept death with joy in order not to be its witness."

Madame de Clèves burst into tears as she held her mother's hand, and she held it pressed in both of hers.

Feeling herself moved, Madame de Chartres said, "Farewell, my child. Let's end a conversation that is too painful for both of us. If you can, remember all that I've told you."

Without wishing to speak any longer, she turned aside with these words, and asked her daughter to call her maids. Madame de Clèves left her mother's room in a state not difficult to imagine. Madame de Chartres thought only of preparing herself for death. She lived two days longer; during this time she did not wish to see her daughter again—the only person in the world to whom she was devoted.

Madame de Clèves was terribly distressed. Her husband never left her. As soon as Madame de Chartres passed away, he took his wife to the country in order to remove her from a place which could only increase her sorrow. No one had ever seen such grief as hers. Although tenderness and gratitude played a large part in it, her great need for her mother to protect her against the Duc de Nemours did not allow her any other feelings. She was unhappy to be abandoned at a time when she was so little in control of her emotions and when she needed so much to have someone to comfort her and to give her strength. The Prince de Clèves protected her so tenderly that she wished more fervently than ever not to be remiss in her duty to him. She gave him more friendship and tenderness than she ever had shown before. She did not wish him to leave her. It seemed to her that by keeping him with her, he would protect her against the Duc de Nemours.

The Duc came to see the Prince de Clèves in the country. He also tried to pay a visit to Madame de Clèves, but she did not want to see him. Because she knew that she could not help finding him lovable, she decided not to see him and to avoid all opportunities which depended on her for doing so.

The Prince de Clèves went to Paris to visit the Court and promised his wife that he would return the next day. But he did not return until the day after.

"I waited for you all day yesterday," said Madame de Clèves when he arrived, "and I must criticize you for not coming back when you promised. You know that if I were able to feel a new grief at this moment, it would be to mourn the death of Madame de Tournon, which I heard about this morning. I would have been touched even if I had not known her. It's always sad when a young and beautiful woman dies in a few days. But, beyond that, she was one of the people who pleased me the most in the world, and who seemed to be as wise as she was good."

"I'm very sorry that I didn't return yesterday," said the Prince de Clèves, "but there was an unhappy man who needed me so much to console him that I couldn't leave him. As for Madame de Tournon, I advise you not to waste your tears on her if you consider her a woman worthy of your esteem."

"You astonish me," replied Madame de Clèves. "I've heard you say several times that there wasn't a woman at Court whom you admired more."

"It's true," he replied. "But women are so difficult to understand that when I see them all, I feel so lucky to have you that I can't help marvelling at my good fortune."

"You praise me beyond my worth," replied Madame de Clèves, sighing. "You haven't had time yet to test my worthiness of you. Tell me, I beg you, what has happened to disillusion you about Madame de Tournon?"

"I've known about her for a long time," he replied, "and I knew that she loved the Comte de Sancerre whom she promised to marry."

"I can't believe," interrupted Madame de Clèves, "that after the extraordinary aversion to marriage which Madame de Tournon has shown all during her widowhood, after the public declarations she has made that she would never remarry, she has encouraged Sancerre to think that she would marry him."

"If she had encouraged only him," replied the Prince de Clèves, "it would not be so surprising, but what is truly amazing is that she encouraged Estouteville at the same time. I will tell you the whole story."

BOOK 2

"You know about the friendship that has always existed between Sancerre and me," continued the Prince de Clèves. "Nevertheless, he fell in love with Madame de Tournon about two years ago, and hid it from me, as he did from the rest of the world, with so much care that I never suspected it. Madame de Tournon appeared still inconsolable for her husband's death and lived in an austere retirement. Sancerre's sister was the only person that Madame de Tournon saw, and it was at her house that Sancerre fell in love with her.

"One evening when there was supposed to be a play at the Louvre, and while they were waiting for the King and the Duchesse de Valentinois in order to begin, word was sent that the Duchesse was ill and that the King would not come. Everyone thought that the Duchesse de Valentinois' illness was some quarrel with the King. We knew how jealous he was of the Maréchal de Brissac during his stay at Court; it was now several days since the Maréchal had returned to the Piedmont, and we could not imagine what was causing this little quarrel.

"As I was talking about it with Sancerre, Monsieur d'Anville arrived and whispered to me that the King was in a state of anger and distress that was pitiful. In a reconciliation which was made several days ago between him and the Duchesse de Valentinois after their quarrels about the Maréchal de Brissac, the King had given the Duchesse a ring and asked her to wear it. While she was getting dressed to come to the comedy, he noticed that she was not wearing the ring and asked for her reasons. She appeared astonished not to have it, and she inquired of her ladies in waiting, who, either by accident, or because they were not told what to say, replied that they had not seen it for four or five days.

" 'This was precisely the time of the Maréchal de Brissac's departure,' continued Monsieur d'Anville. 'The King did not doubt that she gave it to him as a farewell present. This thought revived all the jealousy which was not yet extinguished so that the King flew into a rage and reproached her a thousand times. He has just returned to his own apartments and is very upset, but I don't know whether it's because he thinks that the Duchesse has sacrificed his ring, or whether he fears having reproached her too severely.' As soon as Monsieur d'Anville finished telling me this news, I went directly to Sancerre to inform him of it. I told it to him as a secret which had just been confided to me and which I forbade him to speak of.

"The next morning fairly early I went to see my sister-in-law. I found Madame de Tournon sitting at her bedside. She did not like the Duchesse de Valentinois, and she knew that my sister-in-law was not in the habit of praising her either. Sancerre had been to see her after leaving the play and had told her about the quarrel between the King and the Duchesse; Madame de Tournon had just told my sister-in-law about it, without knowing or without reflecting that I was the one who had told her lover the story.

"As soon as I appeared at my sister-in-law's, she said to Madame de Tournon that I could be trusted with what she had just said, and without waiting for Madame de Tournon's permission, she told me word for word all that I had told Sancerre the evening before. You can imagine how astonished I was. I looked at Madame de Tournon who appeared a little embarrassed to me. Her discomfort made me suspicious as I had told no one but Sancerre, and he had left me at the end of the play without giving me a reason. I remembered having heard him praise Madame de Tournon very highly. All these things opened my eyes, and I had no difficulty in realizing that he was having a love affair with her and had gone to see her as soon as he had left me.

"I was so annoyed that he was keeping this love affair from me that I said several things to Madame de Tournon which must have made her realize how unwise she had been. I escorted her to her carriage, and, as I parted from her, I assured her that I envied the good fortune of whoever it was that had told her about the King's quarrel with the Duchesse de Valentinois.

"I immediately went to find Sancerre. I reproached him harshly; I told him that I knew about his passion for Madame de Tournon, without telling him how I discovered it. He was forced to admit it to me. I then told him how I had found out, and he told me all about his love affair. He admitted to me that although he was a younger son and was far from being considered a good match, she nevertheless had decided to marry him. No one could be more surprised than I was. I told Sancerre to hasten his marriage since he could expect anything from a woman who was hypocritical enough to have acted such a role in public. He replied that she was truly distraught until her love for him had cured her, and that she did not want people to know how suddenly she had recovered. He gave me several other reasons for her conduct which made me see how much he was in love with her. He assured me that he would obtain her consent to my knowledge of their love-affair, since she herself had let me in on the secret. He did gain her consent, although with some difficulty, and after that I was very much in their confidence.

"I've never seen a woman so open and so delightful with her lover. But all the same I was shocked that she still pretended to be heartbroken. Sancerre was so much in love with her and so content with the way she treated him that he did not dare urge her to hasten their marriage for fear that she would think that he loved her for her money rather than for herself. All the same, he did speak to her about it, and she appeared determined to marry him. She even began to leave the seclusion in which she lived and to make her appearance in the world. She went to my sister-in-law's at a time of day when some of the courtiers were there. Sancerre rarely went there, but those who attended every evening and who saw her often, found her very charming.

"A little while after she had begun to abandon her solitary life, Sancerre thought that her love for him had begun to cool. He spoke to me of it several times without my being able to find any justification for his complaints. But, finally, when he told me that instead of wishing to solemnize their marriage, she seemed to be hesitating, I began to think that he was right to be anxious. I replied to him that if Madame de Tournon's love, after having lasted for two years, seemed to cool, he should not be surprised, and that he must not complain if her love was not strong enough to make her marry him, even if it had not lessened. This marriage, I told him, would do him no good as far as society was concerned, because it was a bad match for her, and also because it would injure her reputation. Under the circumstances, I thought that all he could hope for was that she would remain faithful to him without holding out any false hopes. I also told him that if she did not have the strength to marry him, or if she admitted to him that she loved someone else, he should not get angry at her or complain, but must respect her and be grateful to her.

"I told him that I was giving him much the same advice as I would accept for myself because sincerity so moves me that I believe that if my mistress or even my wife admitted to me that she loved another man, I would be unhappy without being bitter; I would put aside the role of lover or husband to advise and pity her."

These words made Madame de Clèves blush, since she found in them a certain similarity to her own state of mind. She was so surprised and so troubled by them that it took her a long time to recover her self-possession.

The Prince de Clèves went on with his story: "Sancerre talked to Madame de Tournon as I had advised him. But she reassured him so carefully and appeared so offended by his suspicions that she entirely removed them. It is true that she postponed their marriage until after a trip he had to take which would be quite long. But she conducted herself so well until his departure and appeared so unhappy when he left, that I believed, as he did, that she truly loved him. He left about three months ago. During his absence I saw little of Madame de Tournon. I was so taken up with you that I only knew that he was supposed to return soon.

"The day before yesterday when I arrived in Paris I learned of her death. I immediately sent word to find out how he was. I was told that he had arrived the day before, the very day of Madame de Tournon's death. I went to see him immediately, knowing quite well the state in which I would find him. But his affliction surpassed anything I could imagine. I've never seen a grief so deep and so tender. He threw himself into my arms from the moment he saw me and burst into tears. 'I'll never see her again,' he told me. 'I'll never see her again. She's dead! I wasn't worthy of her, but I'll soon follow her!'

"After that, he was quiet. Then he would repeat from time to time, 'She's dead. I'll never see her again!' He went on with his cries and lamentations and seemed like one out of his mind with grief. He told me that he had received very few letters from her while he was absent, but that he wasn't surprised because he knew how much she disliked trusting anyone with her letters. He didn't doubt that she would marry him when he returned. He thought of her as the most lovable and most faithful person in the world. He believed that he had been tenderly loved by her and had lost her at the moment when he had hoped to belong to her forever. All these thoughts plunged him into such a violent grief that he seemed completely overcome. I admit that I couldn't help being touched by the whole situation. At last I had to leave him to go and see the King, but I promised him that I would soon return.

"When I returned as I had promised, imagine my surprise when I found him in a totally different mood from that in which I had left him. He was standing in the middle of his room with a furious expression on his face, striding up and down and then coming to a full stop, like one out of his mind. 'Come, come,' he said to me. 'Come and see the most despairing man in the world. I'm a thousand times more unhappy than I was before. What I've just learned about Madame de Tournon is worse than her death.'

"I thought that his grief had entirely maddened him. I could not imagine anything worse than the death of an adoring mistress whom one loved. I told him that if he controlled his grief, I could understand it and sympathize with him, but that I could not console him for a grief that allowed him to go out of his mind with despair. 'I only wish I were mad,' he cried, 'or dead! Madame de Tournon has been unfaithful to me. I discovered her infidelity the day after I learned of her death—at a time when my soul was filled with the most intense grief and tender love that one has ever felt, at a time when her memory was enshrined in my heart as perfection, perfection towards me. Now I find that I was mistaken, that she has betrayed me. Meanwhile I suffer her death as if she had been faithful and her infidelity as if she were still alive. If I had learned of her betrayal before her death, jealousy and anger would have hardened me against the sorrow of her loss. But now my state of mind is such that I can neither be consoled nor hate her.'

"You can imagine how surprised I was at Sancerre's words. I asked how he had found out what he had just told me. He said that a minute after I left his chamber, Estouteville, who was a close friend of his, but who didn't know anything about his love for Madame de Tournon, came to see him. As soon as he sat down, he burst into tears. He begged Sancerre's pardon for having kept from him the secret he was going to tell him. He implored his sympathy, since he was going to open his heart to him, and said that Sancerre saw in front of him the man whom Madame de Tournon's death had afflicted more than anyone in the world.

" 'Her name,' continued Sancerre, 'so surprised me that although my first instinct was to tell him that I was more upset than he, I was too amazed to speak. Estouteville went on talking. He told me that he had been in love with her for six months, that he had always wanted to tell me, but that she had expressly forbidden him to do so with such authority that he hadn't dared to disobey her. It seems that they had fallen in love simultaneously. They had hidden their passion from everyone; he was never seen by the members of the Court at her house. His was the pleasure of consoling her for her husband's death. And, finally, he was supposed to marry her just at the time that she died. But she had persuaded her father to command her to marry Estouteville, so that this marriage, which was really a love match, would appear to be an act of filial duty and obedience on the part of one who had always seemed averse to remarriage.

" 'As Estouteville went on talking,' said Sancerre, 'I couldn't help believing in his words, because I found a certain coincidence between the time that he said that he had begun to love Madame de Tournon and that when I myself began to notice a change in her. But a moment later I thought that he was a liar or a dreamer! I nearly said so to him; then I felt that I should clarify the facts. I questioned him, letting him see that I wasn't quite convinced. Finally, when I had done all I could to assure myself of my unhappiness, he asked me if I would recognize Madame de Tournon's handwriting. He laid four letters and her portrait on my bed. Just then my brother came in. Estouteville, whose face was covered with tears, had to leave in order not to be seen. He said that he would return that evening to pick up what he had left me. I hurried my brother out of the room on the pretext of illness because I was so impatient to see the letters that Estouteville had left me, hoping to find there something that would fail to convince me of everything Estouteville had said. Alas! What did I find? What tenderness! What protestations! What promises of marriage! What letters! She had never written anything like that to me! Thus,' he said, 'I feel at once the sadness of her death and that of her betrayal. They are two sorrows which have often been compared, but never felt simultaneously by the same person. I must confess to my shame that I grieve more for her death than for her faithlessness. I can't seem to find her guilty enough to accept her death. If she still lived, I would have the pleasure of reproaching her and avenging myself in making her know that I was aware of her infidelity. But I will never see her again,' he repeated, 'I will never see her again. This is the worst of all evils. I would be happy to bring her back to life at the expense of my own. What a wish! If she returned, she would live for Estouteville. How happy I was yesterday!' he cried, 'How happy! I was the saddest man in the world, but at least there was some reason to my sadness. I felt a certain sweetness in thinking that I could never be consoled. But today all my feelings are unreal. I pay the same tribute of grief to a false love that I would to a true one. I can neither hate her memory, nor love it. I can neither console myself, nor can I actually grieve for her. At least,' he said, turning to me suddenly, 'see to it, I beg of you, that I never see Estouteville again. Estouteville! His very name horrifies me. I well know that I cannot blame him. It's my fault for having hidden my love for Madame de Tournon. If he had known about it, he wouldn't have sought her out. She wouldn't have been unfaithful to me. He sought me out to confide his grief in me. I pity him, alas! with reason,' he cried. 'He loved Madame de Tournon! He was loved by her, and he will never see her again. But I know that I can't help hating him. Again, I implore you to see to it that I don't see him any more.'

"Sancerre began to cry again, to miss Madame de Tournon, to talk to her and to say the tenderest things in the world to her, passing from hatred to complaints, to reproaches, and to imprecations against her. Since I saw him in such a violent state, I knew that I needed someone to help me calm him down. I sent for his brother whom I had just left at the King's. I went to talk to him in the antechamber before he entered; I told him the state of mind that Sancerre was in. We gave orders that Estouteville wasn't to be admitted, and we spent a good part of the night attempting to make him see reason. This morning I found him more afflicted than ever. His brother has remained with him, and I've returned to you."

"No one could be more surprised than I am," said Madame de Clèves. "I believed Madame de Tournon incapable of deceitful love."

"No one could have carried cleverness and dissimulation further than she did," replied the Prince de Clèves. "Note that when Sancerre thought that her feelings towards him had changed, he was right, and she had begun to love Estouteville. She said to Estouteville that he consoled her for the death of her husband and that he was the reason why she had left her retirement; it appeared to Sancerre that it was because we had decided that she should no longer be so heartbroken. She made Estouteville value the secrecy of their relationship and made him appear to be obliged to marry her by her father's orders, if he cared for her reputation. All this was planned in order to abandon Sancerre without giving him reason to complain. I must return," continued the Prince de Clèves, "in order to see this unfortunate man, and I think you must return to Paris also. It's almost time for you to see the world and to receive all those condolences which you know you can't avoid."

Madame de Clèves consented to return to Paris and went back the next morning. She felt calmer about the Duc de Nemours than she had before. All that Madame de Chartres had said to her on her deathbed, and the grief she felt at her mother's death, had suppressed her feelings for the Duc so that she thought she had entirely overcome them.

The very same evening that she arrived in Paris, the Reine Dauphine came to see her. After showing her how deeply she sympathized with her grief, she said, in order to distract her from her sad thoughts, that she would tell her all that had happened at Court in her absence. She then revealed several secrets.

"But what I most wanted to tell you," she added, "is that it is certain that the Duc de Nemours is passionately in love, and that his most intimate friends not only are not in his confidence, but can't seem to guess who the person can be. What is more, this love seems strong enough to make him ignore or even abandon his hopes for a crown."

The Reine Dauphine then told her everything that had happened about England. "I've learned what I'm about to tell you," she continued, "from Monsieur d'Anville. He told me this morning that the King sent for the Duc de Nemours yesterday evening about some letters from Lignerolles who asks to return, and who wrote to the King that he can no longer make excuses for the Duc de Nemours' delays to the Queen of England. He says that she is beginning to be offended, but that, although she has made no positive commitment, she has said enough to make the Duc's voyage worthwhile. The King read this letter to the Duc de Nemours, who, instead of taking it seriously, as he had in the beginning, only laughed and joked and made fun of Lignerolles' hopes. He said that all of Europe would condemn his imprudence if he dared to go to England as a suitor to the Queen without being assured of success. 'It seems to me,' he added, 'that I would be choosing a very bad time to make this voyage just as the King of Spain is putting forth such efforts to marry this Queen.[25] He wouldn't be a very formidable rival in a love affair, but I don't think that your Majesty would want me to dispute a marriage with him.'

" 'In this case I would certainly advise it,' replied the King. 'But you won't have anything to dispute with him. I know that he has other thoughts. And even if he didn't, Queen Mary was too unhappy with the yoke of Spain for her sister to wish it back again or to be dazzled by the splendor of uniting so many kingdoms together.' 'Even if she couldn't be dazzled,' replied the Duc de Nemours, 'it appears that she would like to be happy in love. She has loved Milord Courtenay for several years. Queen Mary also loved him and would have married him with the consent of all of England except that she knew that the youth and beauty of her sister Elizabeth attracted him more than the hope of reigning. Your Majesty knows that her violent jealousies finally led her to put them both in prison and then to exile Milord Courtenay and finally made her decide to marry the King of Spain. I think that Elizabeth, now that she is on the throne, will soon recall this Milord and that she will choose a man whom she has loved, who is very attractive, and who has suffered so much for her, rather than another whom she has never seen.'

" 'I would agree with you,' replied the King, 'if Courtenay still lived. But I learned a few days ago that he died in Padua where he was exiled. Well, I can see,' he added, in leaving the Duc de Nemours, 'that we shall have to arrange your marriage, as we did the Dauphin's, by sending ambassadors to marry you to the Queen of England.'

"Monsieur d'Anville and the Vidame de Chartres, who were at the King's with the Duc de Nemours, are persuaded that it is love which has so conquered him and which has changed his mind about so great an undertaking. The Vidame, who is closer to him than anyone, has said to Madame de Martigues that the Duc is so changed that he is no longer recognizable. What surprises him even more is that there do not seem to be any secret communications, nor any hours when he disappears, so that it seems that he has no understanding with the woman he loves. What seems most unlike the Duc de Nemours is to see him love a woman who doesn't return his passion."

What poison for Madame de Clèves was the Reine Dauphine's conversation! How could she help but recognize herself as the person whose name was unknown? And how could she help but be overcome with gratitude and tenderness in learning from an unbiased source that this Duc, who already touched her heart, hid his passion from all the world, and, for love of her, neglected his hopes for a crown? It is impossible to describe her feelings and the turmoil that was aroused in her soul. If the Reine Dauphine had watched her carefully, she would have easily noticed that Madame de Clèves was not indifferent to the things which had just been told to her, but as the Reine Dauphine had no suspicion of the truth, she went on talking without thinking about it.

---

[25] After the death of Queen Mary in 1558, her husband, Philip II of Spain, proposed marriage to Queen Elizabeth and was refused.

"Monsieur d'Anville," she added, "who, as I've just explained to you, told me all I know, believes that I'm more informed on the subject than he is. He has such a high opinion of my charms that he's persuaded that I am the only person who could cause such a change in the Duc de Nemours."

These last words caused a different kind of agitation in Madame de Clèves than she had felt before. She replied, "I would easily be of Monsieur d'Anville's opinion. There is a good deal of truth in it. Of course, it would require nothing less than a Princesse like you to make him scorn the Queen of England."

The Reine Dauphine answered, "I would admit it to you if I knew it, and I would know it if it were true. Love is never hidden from those who cause it. They are the first to recognize it. The Duc de Nemours has been only slightly attentive to me, but there is a tremendous difference between the way he acts now and the way he acted before. I can assure you that I am not the cause for his indifference towards the Crown of England."

"I forget everything when I'm with you," said the Reine Dauphine, "and I've just remembered that I have to go and visit Madame Elizabeth. You know that a peace is almost concluded, but you probably don't know that the King of Spain refuses to sign the articles of peace except on the condition that he, instead of his son, Don Carlos, be allowed to marry Madame Elizabeth. The King has had great difficulty in making up his mind. Finally he has agreed to it, and he has just gone to announce the news to Madame Elizabeth. I think that she will be inconsolable. It cannot possibly make her happy to marry a man of the King of Spain's age and temperament, particularly since she is young and beautiful and was attracted to Don Carlos without ever having met him. I don't know whether the King will find her as obedient as he hopes. He has asked me to go and see her because he knows that she loves me and he thinks that I will have some influence over her. After that, I have to pay an entirely different kind of visit. I'm going to rejoice with Madame, the Sister of the King. Everything is arranged for her marriage with the Duc de Savoye. He will be here in a short time. Never has a Princesse of her age had such complete joy in marrying. The Court is going to be more crowded and more resplendent than it has ever been, and despite your grief, you must come and help us make the foreigners realize that our beauties are not to be despised."

After these words, the Reine Dauphine left Madame de Clèves, and the next morning Madame Elizabeth's marriage was known by everyone. On the following days the King and the Queens went to see Madame de Clèves. The Duc de Nemours, who had awaited her return with extreme impatience, and who ardently wished to talk with her alone, wanted to visit her at an hour when everyone would leave and probably no one would return. He succeeded in his plan, arriving at a time when the guests were leaving.

Madame de Clèves was on her bed. It was very warm, and the sight of the Duc de Nemours gave her a high color which did not make her appear any less beautiful. He sat facing her, full of that fear and timidity which true love causes. He remained silent for a long time without being able to speak. Madame de Clèves felt no less overcome with emotion, so that they were both silent for a very long time. Finally the Duc de Nemours began to speak. He sympathized with her grief. Madame de Clèves was quite content to continue speaking on this subject. She spoke for a long time about the grief she felt. Finally she said that when time had diminished the violence of her sorrow, it would leave such an impression on her heart that her temperament would be changed.

"Great afflictions and violent passions," replied the Duc de Nemours, "make great changes in one's soul. I've noticed this in myself since I returned from Flanders.

Many people have noticed this change in me, and the Reine Dauphine even spoke to me of it yesterday."

"It's true," replied Madame de Clèves, "that she has noticed it. I think I've heard her speak about it."

"I'm not sorry, Madame, that she realized it," replied the Duc de Nemours. "But I wish that she were not the only one to notice it. Sometimes a man doesn't dare to reveal his feelings to the woman he loves except by the most indirect means. Even though he isn't brave enough to show it, he would at least wish his beloved to see that he doesn't wish to be loved by anyone else. He would wish her to know that there is no beauty, whatever her rank might be, whom he would not regard with indifference, and that there is no crown that would be worth the price of never seeing her again. A woman usually judges her lover's passion by the pains he takes to seek her out and to please her, but none of this is particularly difficult if she is at all lovable. What is truly difficult is never to abandon oneself to the pleasure of following one's beloved, to avoid her for fear of revealing to the public and also to her the feelings he has for her. And what marks a genuine attachment is to become entirely different from what one was before, to no longer seek ambition or pleasure after having devoted all one's life to the pursuit of one or the other."

Madame de Clèves easily understood that these words were meant for her. She thought that she ought to reply to him and not let him go on talking. She also thought that she should not listen to these words, or give any indication that she took them as referring to her. She thought that it was her duty to speak, and not to speak. The Duc de Nemours' conversation equally pleased and offended her. In it she found the confirmation of everything that the Reine Dauphine had made her suspect. She discovered in his words something chivalrous and respectful, but she also found in them something brazen and a little bit too open. The attraction that she felt for him agitated her so much that she was no longer mistress of herself. The most veiled references of a man whom one finds attractive cause more agitation than the most open declarations of one whom one does not care for. Thus she did not answer him, and the Duc de Nemours, who became aware of her silence, might have drawn the most favorable implications from it, if the Prince de Clèves' arrival had not ended the visit and the conversation.

The Prince de Clèves came to tell his wife the most recent news of Sancerre. But she did not have much curiosity to hear the rest of this adventure. She was so preoccupied with what had just happened that she could barely hide her mental distraction. When she was at liberty to think it over, she realized that she had deceived herself in believing that she was merely indifferent to the Duc de Nemours. What he had just told her made as complete an impression on her heart as he could have wished and entirely convinced her of his love. The Duc's actions agreed so well with his words that the Princesse felt very little doubt about them. She did not flatter herself any longer with the hope of not loving him; she merely desired to give him no indication of her feelings. This was a very difficult decision, the pains of which she had already experienced. She knew that the only way to succeed was to avoid the Duc's presence. As her mourning gave her an excuse to lead an existence which was more retired than usual, she used this pretext not to visit the places where he could see her. She was in very deep sorrow. Her mother's death appeared to be the cause, and no further reason was sought.

The Duc de Nemours was in despair not to be able to see her anymore. Knowing that he would not find her at any assembly or at any of the Court's entertainments, he could not decide to appear there himself. He pretended to have a great passion for hunting, and he made up hunting parties on the same days that the Queens held their assemblies. A slight illness provided him for a long time with an excuse to stay home so that he could avoid visiting those places where he knew that he would not find Madame de Clèves.

The Prince de Clèves became ill at about the same time. Madame de Clèves did not leave his room during his illness, but when he was better and began to receive company, she found that she could not remain because the Duc de Nemours, on the pretext that he was still weak from his own illness, spent a good part of the day there. Nevertheless, she did not have the strength to leave the first few times he arrived. It was too long a time since she had seen him to be able to make up her mind not to see him again. The Duc found the means of making her understand by conversation that seemed to be directed towards everybody, but which was really aimed at her because it related to what he had said to her in private, that he went hunting in order to daydream and that he no longer went to the assemblies because he knew he would not find her there.

Not without doing extreme violence to her feelings, she finally carried out her resolution to leave her husband's room when the Duc was there. He was well aware that she was avoiding him, and was deeply affected by it. At first the Prince de Clèves did not pay any attention to his wife's conduct, but finally he realized that she did not wish to be in his room when he had company. He spoke to her about it, and she replied that she did not think it was proper to spend every evening with the youngest people at Court. She begged him to approve of her leading a more retired life than she had been accustomed to when her mother's virtuous presence had allowed her to conduct herself in a manner which was difficult for a young woman of her age to maintain on her own.

The Prince de Clèves, who usually displayed great sweetness and indulgence towards his wife, did not show any on this occasion. He said that there was absolutely no possibility of her changing her conduct. She was tempted to tell him that there was a rumor at Court that the Duc de Nemours was in love with her, but she did not have the strength to utter his name. She also felt ashamed to use a false argument and to hide the truth from a man who admired her so much.

Several days later, the King was at the Queen's at the time she held her court. They were discussing horoscopes and predictions. Opinions were divided about how much faith one should have in them. The Queen had a good deal of faith in them. She felt that after so many things had occurred which had been predicted, it couldn't be doubted that there was some truth in this science. Others maintained that among the infinite number of predictions, the few that came true indicated that it was only a matter of chance.

"I used to have a good deal of curiosity about the future," said the King. "But I have been told so many things that were false, and so few that were true, that I have become convinced that one can't really know anything for certain. Several years ago there was a man who had a great reputation in astrology. Everyone went to see him, and I went like the others, but without telling him who I was. I took along the Duc de Guise and Monsieur d'Escars. I had them go in first. But the astrologer addressed me first as if he knew that I was their master. Perhaps he recognized me. Nevertheless he told me something that could not apply to me even if he knew me. He predicted that I would be killed in a duel. He then said that the Duc de Guise would be killed from behind, and that Monsieur d'Escars would have his head kicked in by a horse. The Duc de Guise was very angry at this prediction, as if it accused him of running away. Monsieur d'Escars was hardly pleased to discover that he would come to such an unfortunate end. Thus we all left, very unhappy with the astrologer. I don't know what will happen to the Duc de Guise and Monsieur d'Escars, but it seems very unlikely that I will be killed in a duel. We have just made peace with the King of Spain. And even if we hadn't, I doubt that we would have fought a duel, or that I would have challenged him as my father, the King of Spain, called out Charles V."

After hearing what had been predicted for the King, those who had supported astrology, abandoned their point of view, agreeing that it really could not be believed.

"As far as I'm concerned," said the Duc de Nemours, "I'm the last person in the world who can believe in it." Turning to Madame de Clèves who stood near by, he whispered, "It has been predicted that I will be made happy by the sweetness of the person in the world for whom I feel the most violent and most respectful love. So, Madame, you can well imagine if I dare to believe in such predictions."

The Reine Dauphine, who thought that the Duc de Nemours had spoken aloud what he had merely whispered, and that it was some false prediction that had been made to him, asked what he was saying to Madame de Clèves. If he had had less presence of mind, he would have been surprised by this question.

But he answered without hesitating, "I was telling her, Madame," he replied, "that it was predicted that I would be raised to such a high fortune that I would not even dare aspire to it."

"If you were made that prediction," replied the Reine Dauphine, smiling and thinking about the English affair, "I counsel you not to decry astrology, but to find reasons for supporting it."

Madame de Clèves clearly understood what the Reine Dauphine meant, but she also understood that the fortune to which the Duc de Nemours referred had nothing to do with being King of England.

As it was now quite a long time since her mother's death, Madame de Clèves had begun to appear in the world and to take her place at Court as she used to do. She saw the Duc de Nemours at the Reine Dauphine's. She saw him at the Prince de Clèves', where he came with other young men of his age in order not to be noticed. But, whenever she saw him, she felt a certain agitation which he easily perceived. However hard she tried not to catch his eye, and to talk less to him than to others, from her very first actions when she was in his presence, the Duc realized that she was not indifferent to him. A less penetrating man might not have been aware of it, but he had already been loved so many times that it was difficult for him not to know when someone loved him. He saw only too well that the Chevalier de Guise was his rival, and the Chevalier knew that the Duc de Nemours was his. He was the only man in the Court who had unravelled the truth. His own interest made him more perceptive than others. The knowledge of each other's feelings gave these men a certain bitterness which appeared everywhere. Without exploding, they always took opposite sides. They were rivals at tilting, at jousting, or at any of the King's entertainments, and their rivalry was so great that it could not be hidden.

The English affair was very much in Madame de Clèves' mind. It seemed to her that the Duc de Nemours could no longer hold out against the King's advice, nor against the demands of Lignerolles. She saw with some concern that this envoy had not returned, and she awaited his return with impatience. If she could have followed his movements she would have been informed about the state of this affair. But the same feelings which made her curious obliged her to conceal her curiosity, so that she merely inquired about the beauty, the talent, and the character of Queen Elizabeth. One of her portraits was brought to the King, and Madame de Clèves found it more beautiful than she had hoped. She could not help remarking that it must flatter the Queen.

"I don't believe it," replied the Reine Dauphine, who was present. "This Queen has a reputation for being beautiful and for being more talented than most. I know only too well that she has been held up to me as an example for most of my life.

She must be charming if she is like her mother, Anne Boleyn. Never was there a woman so attractive in every way. I've heard that she was singularly animated and full of character, and that she did not at all resemble the other English beauties."

"It seems to me also," replied Madame de Clèves, "that I've heard the rumor that Anne Boleyn was born in France."

"Those who think so are mistaken," replied the Reine Dauphine. "I will tell you her story in a few words. She came from a good English family. Henry VIII was in love with her sister and her mother, and it was even suspected that she was his daughter. She came here with Henry VII's sister, who married King Louis XII. After the death of her husband, this Princesse, who was young and flirtatious, was reluctant to leave the French Court. But Anne Boleyn, who had the same feelings as her mistress, couldn't resolve to leave it at all. The late King was in love with her, and she stayed on as Lady in Waiting to Queen Claude. This Queen died, and Madame Marguerite, the King's sister, Duchesse d'Alençon, and later Queen of Navarre, whose stories you have read, took her into her household. There she became interested in the new religion. Then she returned to England and charmed everyone. She had French manners which are always pleasing to other countries. She sang well; she danced admirably. She was made Lady in Waiting to Queen Catherine of Aragon, and King Henry VIII fell madly in love with her.

"Cardinal Wolsey, his favorite and his Prime Minister, had had hopes of the papacy and not satisfied with the Emperor, who did not support him in his claims, he decided to get revenge on him by uniting the King of England with the King of France. He influenced Henry VIII to believe that his marriage with the Emperor's aunt[26] was nul and void and proposed that he marry the Duchesse d'Alençon, whose husband had just died. Anne Boleyn, who was ambitious, looked at this divorce as a way of elevating herself to the throne. She began by impressing the English King with Luther's religion and got our late King to favor Henry's divorce at Rome in the hopes of his marrying the Duchesse d'Alençon. Cardinal Wolsey got Henry to send him to France to negotiate this affair under the pretext of attending to other business. But Henry VIII was so opposed to the match, that he sent orders to Wolsey at Calais not even to mention the marriage.

"On his return from France, Cardinal Wolsey was received with honors worthy of the King himself. Never did a favorite carry pride and vanity to such extremes. He arranged an interview between the two Kings which took place at Boulogne. Francis I offered his hand to Henry VIII, who did not wish to take it. They entertained each other in turn with extraordinary magnificence, and they gave each other suits like those that they had had made for themselves. I remember hearing that the suit which the late King sent to the King of England was of crimson satin, decorated with triangles of pearls and diamonds, and that the robe was of white velvet trimmed with gold. After spending several days at Boulogne, they went to Calais. Anne Boleyn was lodged at Henry VIII's with the Queen's suite, and Francis I gave her the same presents and rendered her the same honors as if Anne herself had been Queen. Finally, after loving her for nine years, Henry married her without waiting for the dissolution of his first marriage, for which he had been petitioning Rome for a long time. The Pope excommunicated him immediately, and Henry was so angry that he declared himself Head of the Church and carried all of England with him into that unfortunate change of religion in which you now see it.

"Anne Boleyn did not enjoy her glory for long. For, just as she thought herself secure because of Catherine of Aragon's death, one day when she was seated with

---

[26]Catherine of Aragon (1485–1536), aunt of Charles V.

all of the Court watching the Vicomte de Rochefort her brother tilting at the ring, the King was so suddenly struck with jealousy that he left the match and went to London where he gave orders to arrest the Queen, the Vicomte de Rochefort, and several others whom he believed were her lovers or confidantes. Although his jealousy had seemed to have been born in a moment, it had really been brewing for a long time and had been inflamed by the Vicomtesse de Rochefort who could not bear the relationship between her husband and the Queen and made the King think that it was a criminal passion. Besides this, the King was already in love with Jane Seymour and was only looking for a way to get rid of Anne Boleyn. Within less than three weeks he had this Queen and her brother tried and executed and married Jane Seymour. Then there were several wives whom he repudiated or had killed, and among others was Catherine Howard, to whom the Comtesse de Rochefort was the confidante. She had her head cut off along with Catherine. Thus she was punished for the crimes of which she had accused Anne Boleyn. And Henry VIII died, having become enormously fat . . ."

All the ladies who were present at the Reine Dauphine's narration thanked her for teaching them so well about the English Court, and among them was Madame de Clèves, who could not help asking a few more questions about Queen Elizabeth.

The Reine Dauphine was having miniatures made of all the beautiful ladies at Court to send them to the Queen, her mother. The day that Madame de Clèves' was finished, the Reine Dauphine came to spend the evening with her after dinner. The Duc de Nemours did not fail to appear. He never let slip an opportunity to see Madame de Clèves without letting it appear that he was seeking her out. She was so beautiful that particular day that he would have fallen in love with her all over again. But he did not dare to watch her too closely while her hair was being combed out for fear that the pleasure he had in gazing at her would be noticed too much. The Reine Dauphine asked the Prince de Clèves for a miniature that he had of his wife in order to compare it with the one that was just being finished. Everyone gave their opinion of one or the other, and Madame de Clèves asked the painter to fix something in the coiffure of the one that had just been brought. In order to do so, the painter took the portrait out of the box it was in and, after working on it, put it back on the table.

For a long time the Duc de Nemours had wanted a portrait of Madame de Clèves. When he saw the one belonging to the Prince de Clèves, he could not resist the desire to take it away from a husband whom he believed was tenderly loved. And he thought that of all the people who were in the same place, he would not be suspected any more than anyone else.

The Reine Dauphine was sitting on the bed whispering to Madame de Clèves, who was standing in front of her. Madame de Clèves could see through one of the curtains which was not quite closed. The Duc de Nemours, his back against the table, was at the foot of the bed, and she saw, without turning her head, that he skillfully took something off the table. She did not doubt that it was her portrait, and she was so upset that the Reine Dauphine noticed that she was not listening and asked out loud what she was looking at. The Duc de Nemours turned around at these words. He met Madame de Clèves' eyes that were fastened on him, and he thought that she might well have seen what he had just done.

Madame de Clèves was more than a little embarrassed. It would have been reasonable for her to ask for her portrait. But in asking for it publicly she would let everyone know his feelings for her, and to ask him for it in private would be almost to invite him to speak of his love. Finally, she decided that it would be better to let him have the portrait. She was happy to do him a favor when she could do it without letting him know it. The Duc de Nemours, who noticed her embarrassment and who practically guessed the cause, went up to her and whispered, "If you've noticed what I've dared to do, be kind, Madame, and ignore it. I don't ask any more." And after these words, he left without waiting for her answer.

The Reine Dauphine left to go walking, followed by all of her ladies. The Duc de Nemours closed himself up in his room, unable to bear in public the happiness of having a portrait of Madame de Clèves. He was enjoying all the most tender feelings that love can bring, loving the most adorable person in the Court, and making her return his love in spite of herself. And, despite all of her efforts to conceal it, he saw the kind of hesitancy and shyness that love causes in very young people.

That evening the portrait was looked for everywhere. As the case in which it belonged was found, no one suspected that the portrait had been stolen, and it was believed that it had fallen down by accident. The Prince de Clèves was very upset at the loss, but after it had been looked for in vain, he said to his wife teasingly that she must have a secret lover to whom she had given the portrait or who had taken it—for who but a lover would be content with a portrait without its case?

These words, although jokingly spoken, made a deep impression on Madame de Clèves. She felt very remorseful. Reflecting on her violent attraction for the Duc de Nemours, she discovered that she was no longer mistress of her words or of her facial expressions. She thought that Lignerolles had returned, that she need no longer fear the English affair, and that she could not suspect the Reine Dauphine. Thus, she felt that she had no defense against the Duc de Nemours except by fleeing. But, as she was not mistress enough of herself to be able to flee, she found herself in extreme difficulty, and almost ready to fall into what she considered the worst misfortune—letting the Duc de Nemours see the attraction that she felt for him. She remembered all that her mother had told her when she died and the advice she had given her to take all kinds of precautions, however difficult, rather than become involved in a love affair. She remembered what the Prince de Clèves had told her about sincerity when he was speaking of Madame de Tournon. It seemed to her that she ought to confess to him the attraction she felt for the Duc de Nemours. She thought about this for a very long time. Then she was astonished to have had such a mad idea, and fell back into the difficulty of not knowing what to do.

The peace was signed. And after much reluctance, Madame Elizabeth decided to obey the King, her father. The Duc d'Albe was named to come and marry her in the name of the Catholic King; he was expected soon. The Duc de Savoye, who was supposed to marry Madame, the King's sister, was expected, and the marriages were to be celebrated at the same time. The King could only think about celebrating these marriages with such entertainments as would show off the skill and magnificence of his Court. All the most wonderful plays and ballets were proposed, but the King did not consider these entertainments spectacular enough. He decided to have a tournament open to foreigners, where the people of Paris would be the spectators. All the princes and young nobles took up the King's idea with delight, and particularly the Duc de Ferrare, the Duc de Guise, and the Duc de Nemours, who surpassed all the others in this kind of sport. The King chose all three to be with him the four champions of the tournament.

It was proclaimed throughout the realm that in the city of Paris on the fifteenth of June, his very Christian Majesty and the Prince Alphonse d'Este, Duc de Ferrare, François de Lorraine, Duc de Guise, and Jacques de Savoie, Duc de Nemours, would hold an open tournament against all challengers. The first combat would be on horseback in the lists, with double armour, to break four lances, and one for the ladies; the second combat with swords, one to one, or two to two, at the discretion of the judges; the third combat on foot, three thrusts of the pikes and six hits with the swords, and the champions would furnish the lances, the swords and the pikes at the choice of the challengers. Whoever struck his horse in the combat was to be put out of the lists. There would be four judges of the field to give orders for the combat and to determine the prizes to be given to those combatants who broke the most lances and performed the best. All the challengers, whether French or foreign, would be obliged to come and strike one, or more, if they chose, from the coats of arms which would be hung by the steps at the end of the lists. There they would find a herald of arms who would enroll them according to their rank and according to the shields they had touched. The combatants were to send a gentleman to hang up their shields and their arms three days before the beginning of the tournament, or else they would not be admitted without leave of the champions.

A great list was set up near the Bastille, which stretched from the Chateau de Tournelles across the street of St. Antoine as far as the Royal stables. There were two sides of scaffolding and amphitheatres with covered boxes which formed a kind of gallery, very attractive to look at, and capable of holding a great many people. All the princes and nobles were completely preoccupied with ordering the accoutrements which would make them appear the most splendid and with gallantly adding to their cyphers and emblems something appropriate for the ladies they loved.

A few days before the Duc d'Albe's arrival, the King played tennis with the Duc de Nemours, the Chevalier de Guise and the Vidame de Chartres. The Queens went to see them play, followed by all of their ladies, and, among others, Madame de Clèves. After the match was finished, as they were leaving the tennis game, Chastelart went up to the Reine Dauphine and said to her that by chance he had gotten hold of a love-letter that had fallen from the Duc de Nemours' pocket. The Reine Dauphine, who was always curious about the Duc, asked Chastelart to give it to her. She took it and followed the Queen, her mother-in-law, who was going out with the King to watch them work on the lists. After they had been there awhile, the King had some horses brought in that he had recently acquired. Although they were not yet broken in, he insisted upon mounting them, giving one to each of his companions. The King and the Duc de Nemours found themselves on the two most fiery, who wanted to hurl themselves on each other. For fear of hurting the King, the Duc de Nemours pulled his horse back against a pillar of the stable with such violence that the shock made him fall down. Everyone ran to him and thought that he was severely wounded. Madame de Clèves thought that his injury was worse than the others. The feeling that she had for him gave her an apprehension and an agitation that she could not hide. She went up to him with the Queens, and her expression was so changed that even someone less interested than the Chevalier de Guise would have perceived it. But he recognized it easily and gave more attention to Madame de Clèves' state of mind than he did to the Duc de Nemours. The blow that the Duc had given himself stunned him so that he remained for a long time leaning his head against those who were holding him up. When he raised it, he first saw Madame de Clèves; on her face was revealed the pity that she felt for him, and he looked at her in such a way that she could well understand how deeply he was touched by it. He then thanked the Queens for their kindness to him and apologized for his condition in front of them. The King ordered him to go and rest.

After recovering from the fright she had had, Madame de Clèves soon reflected on the signs she had given of it. The Chevalier de Guise did not leave her very long in the hope that no one had noticed them. Giving her his hand to lead her from the lists, he said, "I'm more to be pitied than the Duc de Nemours, Madame. Pardon me if I depart from the profound respect with which I've always treated you in letting you know the deep sorrow I feel at what I've just seen. It is the first time that I've been brave enough to talk to you, and it will also be the last. Death, or at least an eternal absence will remove me from the place where I can no longer live since I've lost the sad consolation of believing that all those who dare to look at you are as unfortunate as I."

Madame de Clèves responded with only a few confused words, as if she had not understood the significance of what the Chevalier de Guise had said. At another time she would have been offended that he had talked of his feelings towards her. But at that moment she was only saddened in realizing that he had perceived her feelings for the Duc de Nemours.

The Chevalier de Guise was so convinced and so overcome with sadness from the day that he saw the expression on Madame de Clèves' face that he decided never again to think of being loved by her. But to give up that hope, which appeared so difficult and glorious, he needed some other great project in which to become involved. Again, he considered the taking of Rhodes, a project to which he had already given some thought. When death took him out of this world in the flower of his youth and at a time when he had acquired a reputation for being one of the greatest princes of his age, the only regret that he showed was in not having executed such a fine resolution, whose success he believed to be infallible because of all the cares he had taken in planning it.

In leaving the lists, Madame de Clèves went to the Queen's, but her mind was very preoccupied with what had just happened. The Duc de Nemours came soon afterwards, magnificently dressed, like one who had not experienced the accident that had just happened to him. He appeared even more cheerful than usual, and the joy that he felt because of what he thought he had seen made him appear even more attractive. Everyone was surprised when he came in, and there was not anyone who did not ask how he felt, except Madame de Clèves, who stayed near the chimney, pretending not to have seen him. The King came in, and seeing him among the others, called him over to tell about his accident.

The Duc de Nemours passed close to Madame de Clèves and whispered to her, "Today I received signs of your pity, Madame. But, it is not of that alone that I am the most worthy."

Madame de Clèves had not doubted that the Duc had noticed her feeling for him, and these words made her see that she was not mistaken. It had made her very unhappy to see that she had not been mistress enough of her feelings to hide them from the Chevalier de Guise. She was also unhappy that the Duc de Nemours knew them, but this sadness was mixed with a certain kind of sweetness.

The Reine Dauphine, who was extremely impatient to know what was in the letter that Chastelart had given her, went up to Madame de Clèves, and said, "Go and read the letter. It is addressed to the Duc de Nemours, and from all appearances, it must be from that mistress for whom he has left all others. If you can't read it now, keep it, and come to me when I go to bed to return it to me and tell me if you recognize the handwriting." After these words, the Reine Dauphine left Madame de Clèves so astonished and trembling so much that it was quite a while before she could leave the place. As the impatience and agitation that she felt would not permit her to stay at Court, she went home before her usual hour of retirement. She held the letter in a hand that trembled. Her thoughts were all confused so that nothing was clear to her. She felt an unbearable unhappiness that she had never known before or even dreamed of. As soon as she was in her sitting room, she opened the letter and found the following:

Letter

I have loved you too much to let you think that the change which you see in me is the effect of my fickleness, and I want to let you know that your unfaithfulness is the cause. You are very surprised that I should speak to you of your unfaithfulness since you have hidden it from me with so much skill, and I have taken so much care to hide from you the fact that I knew about it. I am surprised that I could prevent you from noticing that I knew. Nobody has ever suffered as I do. I thought that you were violently in love with me, as I was with you. At the time that I let you see my feelings completely, I learned that you were deceiving me, that you loved another, and that apparently you were sacrificing me to the new mistress. I realized it the day of the tilting. That was why I did not attend. I pretended to be ill in order to hide my unhappiness, but I became actually ill, as my body could not bear such a violent shock. When I began to feel better, I pretended still to be ill, so as not to have to see you or write to you. I wanted time to make up my mind how to behave with you. I made up and abandoned the same resolutions twenty times. But finally I decided that you did not deserve to see my unhappiness, and I decided to hide it from you. I wanted to wound your pride by making you think that my passion was dying of itself, so that the value of what you were sacrificing would be lessened. I did not want you to have the pleasure of using my love as an ornament to make you more attractive. I decided to write you cool and nonchalant letters so that the person to whom you showed them would think that you were no longer loved. I did not want her to have the pleasure of knowing that she had triumphed over me, nor did I wish to increase her triumph by my despair and reproaches. Then I thought that merely to break with you would not punish you enough, and that you would be only slightly wounded if I ceased to love you when you no longer loved me. No. I felt that you would have to love me, if you were to feel the unhappiness of not being loved which I so cruelly felt. I thought that if anything could reawaken the feelings you had for me, it would be to make you see that my feelings were dead; but to reveal this change to you by seeming to hide it as if I did not have the strength to admit it to you.

This is what I finally decided. But how difficult to resolve, and when I saw you again it seemed almost impossible to put into action! I was ready to burst into tears and reproaches a thousand times. But the state of my health, which was still poor, enabled me to hide my turmoil and affliction from you. Then I was supported by the pleasure of deceiving you as you had deceived me. Nevertheless, I did myself such violence in speaking to you and writing to you that I loved you, that you soon saw that I had not planned on your seeing that my feelings were changed. You were hurt. You complained about it. I tried to reassure you, but my manner was so forced that you were soon persuaded that I did not love you anymore. Thus I had accomplished all that I had intended. The strangeness of your heart made you come back to me just as I was leaving you. I had all the joy that revenge can give. It seemed to me that you loved me more than you had ever loved me before, while I had let you see that I did not love you anymore. I had reason to believe that the one for whom you left me had been abandoned. I was also persuaded that you had not told her about me. But your return and your discretion could not make up for your fickleness. Once your heart has been divided between me and another, once you have deceived me, there is no more pleasure in being loved by you as I thought I deserved to be. So I have made this resolution which surprises you so much—never to see you again.

Madame de Clèves read and re-read this letter several times without being aware of what she read. She only saw that the Duc de Nemours did not love her as she thought he did, and that he had loved others whom he had deceived as he was deceiving her. What a discovery for a person of her temperament, who loved violently and who had just given signs of it to a person whom she deemed unworthy of her love, and to another to whom she had been rude on his account! Never had she felt such sharp and intense pain! She felt that all the events of the day aggravated her affliction and that she might not have cared that the Duc de Nemours had loved another if she had not just given him indications that she loved him. But she was deceiving herself. And this affliction which she found so insupportable was jealousy with all the horrors that could accompany it! From this letter, she saw that the Duc de Nemours had been having a love-affair for a long time. She felt that the person who had written the letter was intelligent and good; she seemed to her to be worthy of being loved. She found in her more courage and more control than she had had in hiding her feelings from the Duc de Nemours. From the last words of the letter, she saw that this person believed that she was loved. Madame de Clèves thought that the discretion which the Duc had displayed towards her and with which she had been so touched, could perhaps only be the result of the love that he felt for this other person whom he did not want to displease. Finally, she tortured herself with everything that could augment her despair. What reproaches she made against herself! What reflections on the advice her mother had given her! How she repented not having the strength to oppose the Prince de Clèves about retiring from the social world, or not having carried out her idea of admitting to him her attraction to the Duc de Nemours! She felt that it would have been better to admit it to a husband whose goodness she knew, and to whose advantage it was to hide it, than to let it be seen by a man who was unworthy of her, who was deceiving her, and, who, for all she knew, was sacrificing her to another, who only wished to be loved out of a sense of pride or vanity. Thus she felt that all the evils that could happen to her and all the excesses that she could bear were nothing compared with letting the Duc de Nemours see that she loved him when she knew that he loved another. All that consoled her after this recognition was her belief that she had nothing further to fear from herself, that she was entirely cured of her attraction to the Duc.

She forgot the Reine Dauphine's order to return at bedtime. She went to bed and pretended to be ill so that when the Prince de Clèves returned from the King's, he was told that she was asleep. But she was far from the calmness which leads to sleepiness. She spent the night torturing herself and re-reading the letter that had fallen into her hands.

Madame de Clèves was not the only person whose sleep was troubled by this letter. Not the Duc de Nemours, but the Vidame de Chartres, who had actually lost the letter, was extremely upset. He had spent the whole evening with the Duc de Guise, who had given a fine supper party for the Duc de Ferrare, his brother-in-law, and all the young people of the Court. It so happened that at supper the conversation turned to love letters. The Vidame de Chartres said that he had with him one of the finest love-letters that had ever been written. He was urged to show it; he refused. The Duc de Nemours claimed that he did not have any, that he was speaking only out of vanity. The Vidame de Chartres replied that he was testing his discretion to its utmost, but that, nevertheless, he would not show them the letter, but that he would read passages so that they could realize that few men received such letters. Just as he went to take out the letter, he could not find it. He looked for it everywhere. They teased him about it, but he appeared so upset that they stopped discussing it with him. He left earlier than the others and went home impatiently to see if he had not left the missing letter there. As he was still looking for it, a first footman of the Queen came to see him to tell him that the Vicomtesse d'Uzès thought he should be warned that they were gossiping about him at the Queen's. A love-letter had fallen from his pocket while he was playing tennis. They were bandying about a good deal of what was in the letter. The Queen had shown a great curiosity to see it; she had sent for it by one of her footmen, but he replied that he had given it to Chastelart.

The first footman then said other things to the Vidame de Chartres which made him very upset. He left at once to go and see a gentleman who was a close friend of Chastelart's. The Vidame got the gentleman out of bed, although it was a strange hour to ask for letters, without even revealing to him who wanted the letter or who had lost it. Chastelart, who had made up his mind that the letter belonged to the Duc de Nemours, and that the Duc was in love with the Reine Dauphine, did not doubt that it was he who wanted the letter back. He replied, with a malicious joy, that he had given the letter to the Reine Dauphine. The friend went back to the

Vidame de Chartres with this reply. It augmented the anxiety that he already felt and added new worries to it. After being undecided for a long time about what he ought to do, he decided that the Duc de Nemours was the only one who could help him to get out of his difficulty.

He went to his house and came into his bedroom just as dawn was breaking. The Duc was sleeping peacefully; what he had seen the day before of Madame de Clèves had given him only pleasant thoughts. He was surprised to be awakened by the Vidame de Chartres. He asked if he had come to wake him from his sleep out of revenge for what he had said to him during supper. The Vidame showed by the expression on his face that only a very serious reason could have brought him there.

He said, "I've come to confide in you the most important affair of my life. I know well that you won't be grateful to me, since I'm telling you about it at a time when I need your help. And I also know that I would have lost your esteem if I had revealed to you what I'm going to tell you without it's being absolutely necessary. That letter that I was talking about yesterday fell out of my pocket. It is extremely important to me that no one know that it was addressed to me. It was seen by lots of people who were at the tennis game yesterday. You were there also; and I beg and implore you to say that it was you who lost the letter."

"In making such a proposition," replied the Duc de Nemours, smiling, "you must think that I don't have a mistress; you must imagine that no one would be upset in being allowed to think that I receive such letters."

"I beg of you," said the Vidame de Chartres, "to listen to me seriously. If you have a mistress, which I don't doubt, although I don't know who she is, it will be easy for you to justify yourself; I will give you incontestable proofs. Even if you can't justify yourself with her, it will only cost you a slight disagreement. But as for me, by this adventure, I will dishonor a person who has loved me passionately, and who is one of the finest women in the world. And besides, I will draw upon myself an implacable hatred which will cost me my fortune and perhaps something else too."

"I can't understand everything you're telling me," said the Duc de Nemours, "but you are making me understand that the rumors which have circulated about the interest which a great Princesse takes in you are not completely false."

"They are not indeed," replied the Vidame de Chartres. "But I wish to God that they were. Then I wouldn't find myself in the difficult situation that I'm in. But I must tell you everything that has happened, so that you can see everything that I have to fear.

"Ever since I've been at the Court, the Queen has treated me with much distinction and favor, and she let me know that she was favorably disposed towards me. Nevertheless, there was nothing that I could put my finger on, and I never dreamed of having any other feelings for her but those of respect. In fact, at the time, I was very much in love with Madame de Thémines. One would only have to look at her to realize that it would be easy to be very much in love with her if one's love were returned, as mine was. About two years ago now, when the Court was at Fontainebleau, I found myself in conversation with the Queen two or three times when there were very few people around. It seemed that she was pleased with my wit, and that she was interested in everything I said. One day, among other things, we began to talk about people who could be trusted. I said that there was no one whom I could trust completely. I found that I always had regrets when I confided in someone, and that I knew many things about which I never spoke. The Queen said that this raised me in her esteem, because she had not found anybody in France who could keep a secret. She found this very annoying because she did not have the pleasure of confiding in anyone. It was a necessary thing in life, particularly for someone of her rank, to have a person in whom she could confide. On the following days she returned several times to the same topic of conversation. She told me some rather confidential things that were happening. Finally, it seemed to me that she wanted to learn some of my secrets, and that she wanted to confide hers in me. This idea made me fond of her; I was touched by her singling me out, and I paid more attention to her than I usually did. One evening when the King and all the ladies went horseback riding in the forest, and she did not wish to go because she was not feeling well, I stayed with her. She walked down to the edge of the lake and left her equerries so that she could walk more freely. After she had walked around a few times she came up to me and ordered me to follow her. 'I want to talk to you,' she said, 'and you will see by what I'm going to tell you that I am your friend.' With these words, she stopped and looked at me earnestly. 'You are in love,' she continued, 'and because you don't confide in anyone, you think that your love isn't known. But it is known, and even by those people who are concerned. You are watched. The places where you meet your mistress are known. There is a plan to surprise you there. I don't know who she is, and I won't ask you. I only wish to protect you from the dangers into which you can fall.'

"Now, just see, I beg of you, what a trap the Queen was setting for me, and how difficult it was not to fall into it. She wanted to know if I was in love. She would not ask me if I was, and she did not want me to have the idea that she was talking to me out of curiosity or design. She simply wanted to make me feel that she was acting for my own good. However, I soon got to the bottom of it all. I was in love with Madame de Thémines. But, although she loved me, I wasn't fortunate enough to have a particular place in which to see her where I might not fear being discovered. So I saw that it was not of her that the Queen was speaking. I also knew that I was carrying on a love affair with another woman less beautiful but also less virtuous than Madame de Thémines, and that it was not impossible that the place where I met her had been found out. But, since I did not care very much for her, it was easy for me to protect myself from danger by not seeing her. Thus I decided to admit nothing to the Queen; on the contrary, to assure her that I had long abandoned the desire of making myself loved by women, even where I had hopes of being successful, because I found almost all of them unworthy of the attachment of a man of integrity, and that it would take something above the level of such women to involve me.

" 'You're not answering me sincerely,' said the Queen. 'I know that the opposite of what you tell me is true. The manner in which I've been speaking to you obliges you not to hide anything from me. I want us to be friends,' she continued, 'but, in giving you this honor, I cannot be ignorant of your attachments. See if you wish to pay the price of telling me about them. I give you two days to think it over. But after that time, think about what you tell me, and remember, that if afterwards I find that you've deceived me, I will not forgive you for as long as I live.'

"The Queen left me after saying these words, without waiting for my response. You can imagine that my mind was filled with what she had just said to me. The two days that she gave me to think it over didn't appear too long to make such a decision. I saw that she wanted to know whether I was in love, and that she wished that I wasn't. I saw the consequences of the part that I had to play. My vanity was more than a little flattered by the thought of a special relationship with the Queen, and a Queen who was still physically very attractive. On the other hand, I loved Madame de Thémines, and although I had been somewhat unfaithful to her with this other woman, about whom I've told you, I couldn't resolve to break with her. I also saw the peril to which I exposed myself in deceiving the Queen, and how difficult it would be to deceive her. Nevertheless, I couldn't decide to refuse what fortune offered me. I decided to take a chance on what my bad conduct could cost me. I broke with this woman whose affair could be found out, and I hoped to hide the one I was having with Madame de Thémines.

"At the end of the two days that the Queen gave me, as I went into the room where she was holding her court, she asked me aloud and with a seriousness which surprised me, 'Have you thought about that business I asked you to, and found out the truth of it?'

"'Yes, Madame,' I answered her. 'And it is as I told your Majesty.' 'Come this evening, at an hour I will write down,' she replied. 'And I will finish giving you my instructions.' I made a deep bow, without answering, and made sure to be there at the hour that she had indicated. I found her in the gallery with her secretary and one of her ladies. As soon as she saw me, she came to me and led me to the end of the gallery. 'Ah!' she said to me, after having thought about it well. 'You still have nothing to tell me? I should think that after the way I've treated you, you would be sincere with me.' 'It's exactly as I've told you, Madame. I have nothing to tell you. And I swear to your Majesty with all the respect that I owe you, that I am not in love with any woman in the Court.'

"'I believe you because I wish to,' replied the Queen. 'And I wish to because I want you to be completely devoted to me. It would be impossible for me to be content with your friendship if you were in love. Lovers are not to be trusted. Their discretion cannot be depended upon. They are too distracted and too divided, and their mistresses naturally come first. This would not agree at all with the manner in which I want you to become devoted to me. Remember that it's on your word that you are not in love that I'm choosing you to give you all of my confidence. Remember that I want you to be completely devoted to me. You must have no friend, either male or female, of whom I do not approve. Your only occupation must be to please me. You will not lose anything thereby. I will watch over your affairs with more care than you would. And whatever I do for you, I will consider myself well repaid, if I find in you everything that I wish. I have chosen to confide in you all of my frustrations, and to aid me in smoothing them over. You can judge that they are not minor. I pretend not to mind the King's attachment to the Duchesse de Valentinois, but I find it unbearable. She rules the King; she deceives him; she despises me, and all my servants are on her side. My daughter-in-law, the Reine Dauphine, proud of her own beauty and of her uncles' importance, pays no allegiance to me. The Connétable de Montmorency is master of the King and of the Kingdom. He hates me and has given me indications of his hatred that I can't forget. The Maréchal de Saint-André is a bold young favorite who doesn't treat me any better than the others. The story of my unhappy life must make you feel sorry for me. Until now I haven't dared to confide in any one, but I trust you. See to it that I do not regret it, and be my only consolation.' The Queen's eyes were red as she finished speaking. I was so touched at the faith that she showed in me that I almost threw myself at her feet. Since then I've been completely in her confidence. She does nothing without consulting me. And our liaison has lasted until this day."

BOOK 3

"Now, however preoccupied I was because of my new understanding with the Queen, I clung to Madame de Thémines with an attachment that I couldn't overcome. It seemed to me that her love for me had cooled, but instead of being wise and using her change of heart to get over my feelings for her, my love redoubled and I behaved so badly that the Queen became aware of my attachment. Jealousy is natural to people of her country,[27] and perhaps the Queen had feelings for me that were stronger than she realized herself. But finally the rumor that I was in love gave her such great anxiety and distress that I thought I was completely lost as far as she was concerned. At last I was able to reassure her by being very attentive to her, by extreme submissiveness and by swearing false oaths. But I would never have been able to deceive her for long if the change in Madame de Thémines hadn't detached me from her in spite of myself. She made me realize that she didn't love me anymore and I was so convinced of this fact that I was forced not to bother her any more, and to leave her in peace.

"Sometime afterwards she wrote me this letter which I've lost. Through it I learned that she knew about the relationship I had with that other woman whom I mentioned to you and that this was the reason for her change of heart. Because my feelings were no longer divided, the Queen was quite happy with me. But since the feelings I had for her were not such as to make me incapable of any other attachment, and since love cannot be commanded at will, I fell in love with Madame de Martigues. I had already felt some attraction for her when she was a Villemontais and lady in waiting to the Reine Dauphine. I have reason to believe that she doesn't hate me. She is pleased with the discretion with which I treat her, although she doesn't understand all the reasons for it. The Queen has no suspicion about this affair, but she is concerned about another, which is scarcely less upsetting to her. Since Madame de Martigues is always at the Reine Dauphine's, I go there more often than usual. The Queen imagines that I'm in love with the Reine Dauphine. Her rank, which is equal to the Queen's, and her youth and beauty, which surpass the Queen's, have caused a jealousy which amounts to madness and a hatred against her daughter-in-law that she can't hide. The Cardinal de Lorraine, who has seemed for a long time to be aspiring to the Queen's favor, and who saw me occupying a position that he would like to fill, is looking into the differences between the Queen and the Reine Dauphine under the pretext of reconciling the two women. I don't doubt that he has discovered the true reason for the Queen's anger, and that he will do me all sorts of harm without letting it appear that he has any intention of hurting me. This is the state of affairs at the moment I'm speaking to you. Imagine the effect that could be produced by the letter which I've lost and which I was unfortunate enough to put into my pocket in order to return it to Madame de Thémines! If the Queen sees the letter, she will know I was deceiving her, and at almost the same time that I was being untrue to her with Madame de Thémines, I was being false to Madame de Thémines with another woman. Imagine what kind of an opinion she will have of me, and if she will ever believe in me again. If she doesn't actually see the letter, what will I say to her? She knows that it is in the Reine Dauphine's hands. She will think that Chastelart has recognized the Reine Dauphine's handwriting and that the letter is from her. She will imagine that she is perhaps the woman whose jealousy is mentioned. Finally, there is nothing that she may not think, and there is nothing that I cannot fear from her thoughts. Add to this that I deeply care about Madame de Martigues, that the Reine Dauphine will show her the letter, and that she will think that it was written recently. Thus I will be equally embroiled with the woman I most love and the woman I most fear. You do see now why I beg you to say that the letter is yours, and to go and get it from the Reine Dauphine."

"I see only too well," said the Duc de Nemours, "that nobody could be in greater difficulty than you are, but I must admit that you deserve it. I've been accused of

---

[27]Catherine was Italian.

being an unfaithful lover and of carrying on several love affairs at once, but you have outdone me to such a degree that I wouldn't dare even to imagine the things that you have undertaken. Could you imagine that you could continue your relationship with Madame de Thémines at the same time as you were involving yourself with the Queen? And did you hope to have an understanding with the Queen and at the same time deceive her? She is Italian and the Queen, and consequently full of jealousy, suspicion and pride. When your good luck rather than your careful conduct relieved you of one entanglement, you took on another. Did you imagine that in the midst of the Court you could love Madame de Martigues without the Queen's noticing it? You should have tried to wipe out the shame she must have felt at having taken the first step. She has a violent passion for you. You are too discreet to tell me about it, and I'm too discreet to ask. At all events, she loves you, she is suspicious, and the facts are all against you."

"Are you going to overwhelm me with reprimands?" interrupted the Vidame de Chartres. "Shouldn't your own experience make you treat my mistakes a little more indulgently? I'm willing to agree with you that I'm wrong, but just think about it. I beg you to extricate me from the difficult situation I'm in. It seems to me that you must see the Reine Dauphine as soon as she is awake and ask her to return the letter to you as though you had lost it."

"I've already told you," replied the Duc de Nemours, "that the proposition you've made to me is a little bit extraordinary, and because of my interests I find it very hard to carry out. But beyond that, if the letter was supposed to have fallen from your pocket, it seems to me that it's going to be very difficult to persuade anybody it fell out of mine."

"I thought I had already informed you," replied the Vidame de Chartres, "that the Reine Dauphine was told it fell from your pocket."

"What?" replied the Duc de Nemours sharply, seeing in an instant the evil effects this misapprehension would have on Madame de Clèves. "Somebody told the Reine Dauphine the letter fell out of my pocket?"

"Yes," replied the Vidame de Chartres. "Somebody told her so. The mistake was made because several of the Queen's valets were in the rooms adjoining the tennis courts; they had gone there to look for our clothes. At the time the letter dropped, the valets picked it up and began reading it aloud. Some thought that it belonged to you, and others thought that it belonged to me. Chastelart, who picked it up and whom I've just seen to ask if he would give it back to me, said that he had given it to the Reine Dauphine, telling her that it was your letter. Those who have talked to the Queen about it have said that it was mine. Thus you can easily see how much I want to extricate myself from this embarrassing situation."

The Duc de Nemours had always been fond of the Vidame de Chartres, and the fact that he was related to Madame de Clèves made him even dearer. Nevertheless, the Duc could not resolve to take a chance on her hearing about the letter in connection with him. He began to ponder the situation very seriously, and the Vidame de Chartres, guessing what was on his mind, said, "I see only too well that you fear getting into difficulties with your mistress. Even if you wanted me to believe that it was none other than the Reine Dauphine, Monsieur d'Anville displays so little jealousy towards you that I would wonder about it. But whatever the situation is, it's not fair for you to sacrifice your peace of mind to mine. I very much want to give you the means of letting the one you love know that the letter was addressed to me and not to you. Here is a note from Madame d'Amboise, Madame de Thémines' friend, to whom she confided all that she felt about me. In this note she asks me to return her friend's letter which I have lost. My name is on the note; what is inside will prove without a doubt that the letter she is asking me for is the one that has been found. I put this note into your hands, and I consent to your showing it to your mistress in order to justify yourself to her. But promise me that you won't lose a minute, and you will go this very morning to see the Reine Dauphine."

The Duc de Nemours promised the Vidame de Chartres that he would do so and took Madame d'Amboise's note. Nevertheless, his plan was not to see the Reine Dauphine, because he had something much more urgent to do. He did not doubt that the Reine Dauphine had already spoken about the letter to Madame de Clèves, and he could not bear the fact that the one he loved so dearly could believe that he was attached to someone else.

He went to see Madame de Clèves as soon as he thought she was awake, and he sent a message in to her that he would not ask for the honor of seeing her at such an unusual hour if a matter of extreme importance did not require it. Madame de Clèves was still in bed, very upset by all the thoughts which had angered her during the night. She was extremely surprised when she was told that the Duc de Nemours wanted to see her. The anger she felt caused her not to hesitate in answering that she was ill and could not talk to him.

The Duc was not hurt at her refusal. A display of anger at a time when she must feel jealous could not be a bad sign. He went to the Prince de Clèves' apartment and told him that he had just called on his wife and was particularly sorry that she could not see him because he had something very important to tell her about the Vidame de Chartres. He soon made the Prince de Clèves understand the urgency of the situation, and at that very same moment, the Prince de Clèves led him to Madame de Clèves' room. If she had not been in the shadows, she would have had difficulty in concealing her agitation and astonishment at seeing the Duc de Nemours enter her room, escorted by her husband. The Prince de Clèves told her that it was a question of a letter, that her help was needed in the interests of the Vidame de Chartres, that she must decide with the Duc de Nemours what had to be done, and that he himself had to go to see the King who had just sent for him.

The Duc de Nemours stayed behind with Madame de Clèves, as he had wished. "I have come to ask you, Madame," he said to her, "if the Reine Dauphine hasn't spoken to you about a letter which Chastelart put in her hands yesterday."

"She said something to me about it," replied Madame de Clèves. "But I don't see what the letter has to do with my uncle, and I assure you that he isn't mentioned in the letter."

"It's true, Madame," replied the Duc de Nemours, "that he isn't mentioned in it. Nevertheless it's addressed to him and it's very important that you get it back from the Reine Dauphine."

Madame de Clèves replied, "I don't understand why he should mind the letter's being seen, and why his name should be used to get it back."

"If you will listen to me for a few minutes," replied the Duc de Nemours, "I will soon be able to explain everything to you, and I will even tell you some very important things about the Vidame de Chartres that I wouldn't even have your husband know if I hadn't needed his help in order to have the privilege of seeing you."

"I think that anything you have to tell me will be useless," replied Madame de Clèves in a rather sharp tone. "It would be better for you to go and see the Reine Dauphine and tell her the great interest you take in this letter, since she was told that the letter was yours."

The sharpness which the Duc de Nemours saw in Madame de Clèves' manner gave him so much pleasure that he did not hasten to justify himself.

"I don't know, Madame," he replied, "what could have been said to the Reine Dauphine, but the letter hasn't anything to do with me. It was written to the Vidame de Chartres."

"I believe you," replied Madame de Clèves, "but the Reine Dauphine has been told quite the opposite, and she may find it difficult to believe that the Vidame de Chartres' letter would fall out of your pockets. So, unless you have some reason, which I don't understand, for hiding the truth from the Reine Dauphine, I suggest that you admit everything to her."

"I haven't anything to admit," he replied. "The letter wasn't addressed to me, and if there were anyone I wished to convince of the truth, it wouldn't be the Reine Dauphine. But let that be as it may. Since the Vidame de Chartres' fortune is at stake, allow me to tell you a few things that I think you ought to know."

Madame de Clèves showed by her silence that she was ready to listen to the Duc de Nemours, and he told her as succinctly as possible all that he had learned from the Vidame de Chartres. Although he related some sensational events, Madame de Clèves listened with such great coldness that it appeared that either she did not believe that they happened or else she was not interested in them. Her attitude did not change until the Duc de Nemours told her about Madame d'Amboise's note which was addressed to the Vidame de Chartres and which was proof of all that he had said. Since Madame de Clèves knew that this lady was a friend of Madame de Thémines, she found some truth in what the Duc de Nemours was saying. This made her think that perhaps the letter was not addressed to him after all. Suddenly her coldness began to melt. The Duc de Nemours, after having read to her the note which proved his justification, gave it to her for her to read, saying that she might recognize the handwriting. She could not help taking the letter and examining the outside to see if it was addressed to the Vidame de Chartres, and she could not help reading the whole letter to see whether or not the letter that was asked for was the one she had in her hands. The Duc de Nemours said all he could to persuade her; and as one is easily persuaded of a truth one wants to believe in, Madame de Clèves was convinced that the Duc de Nemours had no part in the letter.

She now began to discuss the whole matter with him—the embarrassment and danger of the Vidame de Chartres, the irresponsibility of his behaviour. She began to consider ways of helping him. She was astonished at the behaviour of the Queen. She admitted to the Duc de Nemours that she had the letter. Finally, because she believed in his innocence so entirely, she took part with an open and tranquil attitude in the same kinds of discussions she had formerly scorned. She and the Duc agreed that they should not return the letter to the Reine Dauphine for fear that she would show it to Madame de Martigues. Madame de Martigues knew Madame de Thémines' handwriting, and because of her interest in the Vidame de Chartres, she would easily guess that it was addressed to him. They also decided that it was not necessary to relate to the Reine Dauphine all the things that concerned her mother-in-law, the Queen. Under the pretext that she was protecting her uncle, Madame de Clèves readily agreed to keep all the secrets that the Duc de Nemours confided in her.

The Duc de Nemours did not spend all his time talking about the Vidame de Chartres' interests. In fact the freedom he found in talking with Madame de Clèves gave him a courage to express himself that he had never felt before. Suddenly they were interrupted by a messenger from the Reine Dauphine, asking Madame de Clèves to appear immediately. The Duc de Nemours had to retire. He went to find the Vidame de Chartres in order to tell him that he had thought it best to talk with his niece, Madame de Clèves, instead of going straight to the Reine Dauphine. He was not at a loss for reasons to make the Vidame approve of what he had done and to make him hope that all would turn out well.

Meanwhile, Madame de Clèves got dressed as quickly as possible to go and see the Reine Dauphine. She had scarcely appeared in her room when the Reine Dauphine came up to her and whispered, "I've been waiting for you for two hours, and never in my life have I been so embarrassed in my attempts to conceal the truth as I was this morning. The Queen has heard gossip about the letter I gave you yesterday. She thinks that the Vidame de Chartres dropped it. You know that she takes a great interest in him. She's had everybody looking for that letter, and she even sent to Chastelart to ask him for it. They came to ask me about it, on the pretext that it was a charming example of letter-writing and that the Queen wanted to see it. I didn't dare say that you had it. I was afraid that she would think that I gave it to you because of your uncle, the Vidame de Chartres, and that there was some kind of understanding between him and me. I've already noticed that she suffers terribly whenever he comes to see me. So I said to her that the letter was in the pocket of the dress that I was wearing yesterday and that whoever had the key to my wardrobe room had gone out. Hurry up and give me the letter so that I can send it to her, but first I must read it to see if I can recognize the handwriting."

Madame de Clèves, more embarrassed than she had thought she would be, replied, "I don't know what you're going to do; for the Prince de Clèves, to whom I've just given it to read, has returned it to the Duc de Nemours, who came early this morning to ask to have it back. The Prince de Clèves was imprudent enough to admit that he had it, and he also had the weakness to give in to the Duc de Nemours' requests."

"You have put me in the most embarrassing situation that I've ever been in," replied the Reine Dauphine. "You shouldn't have given the letter back to the Duc de Nemours. Since I was the one who gave it to you, you shouldn't have given it to him without my permission. What do you think I'm going to say to the Queen, and what's she going to think? She will imagine, quite naturally, that the letter concerns me, and that there is something going on between the Vidame and me. Nobody will ever be able to persuade her that the letter belongs to the Duc de Nemours."

"I'm terribly sorry to have caused you so much embarrassment," replied Madam de Clèves. "I had no idea how important it was, but it's the Prince de Clèves' fault, and not mine."

"It's yours," replied the Reine Dauphine, "to have given it to him. There isn't a woman in the world except you who tells her husband everything she knows."

"I admit I was wrong," replied Madame de Clèves. "But let's think about how to right the wrong instead of finding fault with each other."

"Don't you remember at least a little bit of what was in the letter?" asked the Reine Dauphine.

"Yes, Madame," she replied. "I remember having read it several times."

"If that's so," replied the Reine Dauphine, "you must immediately go and have it written out in an unknown handwriting. I will send it to the Queen. She will not show it to anyone who has already seen it. And if she does so, I will swear that it's the letter that Chastelart gave me, and he won't dare to contradict me."

Madame de Clèves agreed to this project all the more willingly since it involved sending for the Duc de Nemours to see the letter again so that they might copy it word for word, imitating the handwriting as carefully as possible so that the Queen would be completely deceived. As soon as Madame de Clèves was home, she told her husband about the Reine Dauphine's embarrassment and begged him to send for the Duc de Nemours. He was sent for, and he came right away. Madame de Clèves repeated to him what she had already told her husband, and asked him for the letter, but the Duc de Nemours replied that he had already given it back to the Vidame de Chartres. The Vidame was so happy to see it again and to be out of danger that he immediately sent it to Madame de Thémines' friend. Madame de Clèves found herself in a new difficulty. Finally, after consulting together, she and the Duc decided to write out the letter from memory.

They closed themselves in to work, gave orders that they would not receive anyone, and sent back the Duc de Nemours' attendants. This air of mystery and secrecy was not without a certain charm for the Duc de Nemours and even for Madame de Clèves. Her husband's presence and the fact that everything was in the interests of the Vidame de Chartres quieted her conscience. She felt only the pleasure of seeing the Duc de Nemours. She experienced a kind of happiness without qualms that she had never known before. Her joy made her more lively and playful than she had ever appeared to the Duc de Nemours so that his love for her redoubled. As he had never enjoyed himself so much before, his spirits soared. When Madame de Clèves began to think seriously about the letter that had to be written, the Duc de Nemours failed to take her seriously and help her. Instead, he only interrupted her to tease her and pay her compliments. Madame de Clèves joined in the spirit of gaiety so that they were closeted a very long time, and the Reine Dauphine had to send word to them twice before the letter was half finished.

The Duc de Nemours was so happy to spend his time agreeably that he forgot the interests of his friend. Madame de Clèves was far from bored, and she too forgot her uncle's interests. Finally, by four o'clock the letter was barely finished. It was so badly written, and the handwriting so little resembled the handwriting they were supposed to be copying, that the Queen could hardly fail to guess the truth. In fact, she was not deceived no matter how hard they tried to persuade her that the letter belonged to the Duc de Nemours. She remained convinced, not only that the letter belonged to the Vidame de Chartres, but that the Reine Dauphine had some part in it and that there was an understanding between her and the Vidame. This thought so increased the Queen's hatred for the Reine Dauphine that she refused to pardon her and persecuted her until the day that she was forced to leave France.

As for the Vidame de Chartres, he was ruined as far as the Queen was concerned. Perhaps it was because the Cardinal de Lorraine already had tremendous influence over her. Perhaps it was because the incident of the letter, in revealing to her that she was deceived, helped her in unravelling other infidelities that the Vidame had committed. Anyway, he was never able to make it up with her again. Their liaison was broken off, and she completed his ruin at the time of the conspiracy of Amboise in which he had become involved.[28]

After they had sent the letter to the Reine Dauphine, the Prince de Clèves and the Duc de Nemours went out, leaving the Princesse alone.

Now that her spirits were no longer sustained by the presence of the one she loved, she came to her senses, and began to reflect with some astonishment on the extraordinary difference between her present state of mind and that of the previous evening. She saw herself as she had been—bitter and cold towards the Duc de Nemours when she had thought that Madame de Thémines' letter had been addressed to him, and then, what calm and sweetness had succeeded the bitterness when the Duc de Nemours had convinced her that the letter had nothing to do with him. When she thought that the day before she had reproached herself as if she had been a criminal because she had let him see a certain solicitude in her, which

---

[28] In 1560, a plot by the Protestant Huguenots to capture François II in the town of Amboise failed. The conspirators were caught and executed.

was really no more than ordinary compassion, and that now by her bitterness she had let him know she was jealous in a way that only lovers are jealous, she could hardly recognize herself.

Then she went on to think that the Duc de Nemours was completely aware that she knew of his love, that in spite of this knowledge, she not only failed to alter her behaviour towards him, but on the contrary, she had never acted more responsive to him in the presence of her husband. In fact, she had made the Prince de Clèves send for the Duc de Nemours so that she could spend an entire afternoon with him alone. She felt that she had an understanding with the Duc de Nemours, that she was deceiving her husband, who of all the men in the world least deserved to be deceived. She felt ashamed of herself, and unhappy to appear unworthy in the eyes of her lover. But what seemed to her the most unbearable was the memory of her state of mind during the night and the agony that she had suffered when she thought that the Duc de Nemours was being unfaithful to her and that he loved someone else.

Until that moment she had been unaware of the terrible anxiety which could be caused by suspicion and jealousy. She had only thought of preventing herself from loving the Duc de Nemours and she had not yet begun to fear that he might love another. Although the suspicions that the letter had aroused in her were erased, they opened her eyes about the possibilities of being deceived and gave her a taste of mistrust and jealousy that she had never known before. She was astonished that she had never before recognized how unlikely it was that a man like the Duc de Nemours, who had always displayed such fickleness towards the ladies, would be capable of a sincere and lasting attachment. She realized that it would be impossible for her to be satisfied with his love.

"But even if I could be," she said to herself, "what do I wish to do with it? Do I wish to respond to it? Do I wish to become involved in a love affair? Do I wish to fail the Prince de Clèves? Do I wish to fail myself? Finally, do I wish to expose myself to the cruel remorse and the deadly sorrows that follow in the wake of love? I am conquered and overcome by an attraction which carries me away in spite of myself. All my resolutions are in vain. I thought yesterday all that I am thinking today, but what I do today is the contrary of yesterday's resolutions. I must tear myself away from the Duc de Nemours' presence. I must go to the country. However strange my journey may seem, I must go and see if the Prince de Clèves insists on preventing me, or on knowing my reasons. Perhaps I shall have to hurt him and myself also by telling him." She decided upon this resolution and stayed at home all evening without going to find out from the Reine Dauphine what had happened to the forged letter of the Vidame de Chartres.

When the Prince de Clèves returned, she told him that she wanted to go to the country, that she felt ill and that she needed fresh air. The Prince de Clèves, to whom she appeared radiant, and who could not be persuaded that there was much the matter with her, at first made fun of the journey she suggested. He said that she must be forgetting the marriages of the princesses and the great tournament. She had not too much time to see about her clothes, he said, if she was to appear with the same magnificence as the other ladies. None of these reasons made her change her mind, however, and she begged her husband to let her go to Colomiers while he was at Compiègne with the King. Colomiers was a beautiful house which they were building with much care about a day's journey from Paris. The Prince de Clèves consented. She went, not intending to return very soon, and the King left for Compiègne where he was planning to stay for only a few days.

The Duc de Nemours was very sorry not to have seen Madame de Clèves again since that delightful afternoon he had spent with her which had so much raised his hopes. He felt an impatience to see her again which gave him no rest, so that when the King returned to Paris, he decided to visit his sister, Madame de Mercœur, who lived in the country quite close to Colomiers. Thinking that they might go together to visit Madame de Clèves, the Duc de Nemours invited the Vidame de Chartres to go with him—an invitation which he readily accepted.

Madame de Mercœur was delighted to receive them, and she only thought about how to amuse them in the country. While they were out stag hunting, the Duc de Nemours got lost in the forest, and when he was asking about the way back, he learned that he was very close to Colomiers. At the word, "Colomiers," he set off at a full gallop in the direction that was pointed out to him without thinking about what he would do when he got there. When he reached the forest he rode at random along well-kept bridle paths which he thought would lead to the house. At the end of these paths he found a pavilion which consisted of a large room adjoining two smaller ones. One of these opened out on a flower garden, which was only separated from the forest by a fence; the other looked down a great avenue into the park. He went into the pavilion, where he would have lingered, admiring its beauty, if he had not seen the Prince and Princesse de Clèves, accompanied by a great number of servants coming up the avenue. As he had not expected to find the Prince de Clèves here, since he had left him with the King, his first thought was to hide himself. He went into the little room that looked out on the flower garden with the idea of leaving by a gate that opened onto the forest. But, seeing that the Princesse de Clèves and her husband were sitting down in front of the pavilion, while their servants stayed in the park, unable to get to him without going through the place where the Prince and the Princesse were, he could not resist the curiosity of seeing the Princesse and overhearing her conversation with her husband, who made him more jealous than any of his other rivals.

He heard the Prince de Clèves say to his wife, "But why don't you wish to return to Paris? Who is keeping you in the country? For a long time now you have had a taste for solitude which surprises and upsets me because it keeps us apart. I find that you are more depressed than usual, and I'm afraid that you are worried about something."

"No, I don't have anything in particular on my mind," she replied, with some embarrassment. "But there is always so much going on at Court and there are always so many people at our house, that it is impossible not to be mentally and physically exhausted. I need some peace and quiet."

"Peace and quiet," he replied, "are hardly fitting for a young person of your age. Neither your life at home nor at Court is so tiring, and I'm frightened to think that you like being apart from me."

"You do me a great injustice to think that," she replied, with steadily rising embarrassment. "But I beg you to let me stay here. If you could stay with me, I would be even happier, provided that you would stay alone and that you didn't need to be surrounded by such a large crowd of people who never leave us alone."

"Ah, Madame," cried the Prince de Clèves, "your words and your manner imply that you have reasons for wishing to be alone which I don't know about and which I beg you to tell me."

For a long time, he went on urging her to tell him the reasons without any success, while she refused in a manner that aroused his curiosity further. She sat silent with her eyes lowered.

Finally, she looked at him and said, "Don't force me to confess to you something which I haven't the strength to confess, although I've often thought of doing so. Only consider whether it's prudent for a young woman of my age, who must be mistress of her own conduct, to be exposed to the temptations of the Court?"

"What do you want me to think? I wouldn't dare tell you what your words suggest to me for fear of shocking you, Madame!" cried the Prince de Clèves.

Madame de Clèves did not answer, and her silence confirmed his suspicions.

"You don't say anything," he replied, "which is as good as telling me that there are some reasons for my suspicions."

"Alas," she replied, throwing herself on her knees, "I'm going to make a confession such as no woman has ever made to her husband before. But the innocence of my motives and my actions gives me the strength to do it. It's true that I have good reasons for leaving the Court. I want to avoid the dangers into which young women of my age sometimes fall. I've never shown any weakness, nor would I fear showing any, if you would allow me to retire from the Court, or if I still had Madame de Chartres to guide me. However extreme the measures I'm taking, I undertake them with joy in order to remain worthy of your respect and esteem. If I have any thoughts which displease you, I beg your pardon a thousand times. At least my actions won't displease you. Remember that in order to do what I'm doing, I must have more tenderness and respect for my husband than any wife has ever shown before. Guide me, have pity on me, and love me, still, if you can."

During this conversation, the Prince de Clèves was sitting with his head buried in his hands, so beside himself with grief that he did not even think about helping his wife to rise. When she stopped talking, he looked down at her, and saw her on her knees, her face all covered with tears, and looking so beautiful that he thought he would die of grief.

Kissing her, he lifted her up to her feet, and said, "Madame, you must pity me too. I deserve it. Forgive me if in the first moments of a grief as violent as mine I didn't respond as I should have to such sincerity as yours. But, at the same time that you seem to me more worthy of esteem and admiration than any woman in the world, I feel that I am the most unhappy man who has ever lived. I've loved you from the first moment that I saw you. Neither your early indifference nor our married life together has cooled my passion. I'm still in love with you. I haven't been able to make you love me. Now I see that you fear loving another. Who is this lucky man who makes you afraid? How long has he attracted you? How has he found the way to your heart that I could not find? At first, I felt some consolation in the thought that no one could move you. But now, another has done what I could not do. At the same time as I feel the jealousy of a lover, I feel that of a husband. But it's impossible to suffer a husband's jealousy after you have behaved with such sincerity. It's too noble not to make me feel completely secure. Even as your lover, it consoles me. Your confidence in me and your sincerity are priceless. You have enough faith in me to believe that I won't abuse your trust. You're right, Madame. I won't abuse it, nor will I love you the less for it. You cause my unhappiness by giving me the greatest proof of fidelity that a wife has ever given her husband. But finish your story, Madame. Tell me who it is you wish to avoid."

"I beg you not to ask me," she replied. "I've resolved not to tell you, and I don't think it would be prudent to name him."

"Never fear, Madame," said the Prince de Clèves. "I know too much of the world not to realize that a man's friendship for the husband cannot prevent him from loving the wife. One must hate such a person, but one cannot complain. So, once again, Madame, I beg you to tell me what I want to know."

"You can't make me do that," she replied. "I have the strength to be silent when I think that my duty demands it. My confession was not inspired by weakness, for it required more strength to tell you the truth than to hide it."

The Duc de Nemours did not miss a word of this conversation. What Madame de Clèves had just said did not make him any less jealous than her husband. He was so madly in love with her that he thought everyone else had similar feelings. He imagined that he had more rivals than in fact he had, and he searched his memory to figure out whom Madame de Clèves could possibly be talking about. He had thought on several occasions that he was not unattractive to her, but he made this judgment on the basis of such trivialities that he could not imagine that he could have awakened in her a passion violent enough to make her take such a desperate remedy. He was so carried away that he hardly knew what was happening, and he could not forgive the Prince de Clèves for not urging his wife more strongly to reveal the man's name.

The Prince de Clèves made every effort to find out who the man was. After he had urged her without success, the Princesse said, "It seems to me that you should be content with my sincerity. Don't ask me anymore, and don't let me regret what I've just done. Be satisfied with the assurance I've given you that my actions have never revealed my feelings, that nothing has ever been said to me which could offend me."

"Madame," the Prince de Clèves burst out, "I can't believe you. I remember how embarrassed you were the day your portrait was lost. You have given it away, Madame. You have given away the portrait that was so dear to me and that was mine by right. You haven't been able to hide your feelings. You are in love. It is known. Your virtue alone has so far been your guarantee."

"Is it possible," cried the Princesse, "that you can think there is some deception in a confession like mine, which I have made of my own free will? You must believe me. I've paid very dearly for the trust I have in you. Believe me, that I never gave away my portrait. It's true that I saw it taken, but I didn't want it known for fear of letting the person who took it speak to me in a manner which up to that time no one has dared to use."

"Then, how do you know this person loves you?" asked the Prince de Clèves. "What marks of passion has he given you?"

"Spare me the pain," she replied, "of telling you all the little details which I'm ashamed even to have noticed, since they convince me only too well of my weakness."

"You are right, Madame. It's not fair of me to ask you," said the Prince de Clèves. "Refuse to answer me whenever I ask about such things. But don't be offended with me for asking you."

Just then several servants who had been waiting in the bridle paths came to tell the Prince de Clèves that a gentleman had come with a message from the King, ordering him to be in Paris that evening. The Prince de Clèves had to leave, and could say no more to his wife except that he urged her to be in Paris the next morning, and implored her to believe that, although he was very troubled, he still felt a tenderness and esteem for her that ought to satisfy her.

When the Prince de Clèves had left, and Madame de Clèves was alone, she considered what she had just done, and she was so horrified at it that she could hardly believe it was true. She felt that she had deprived herself of her husband's love and esteem and that she had opened an abyss from which she would never be able to escape. She wondered why she had undertaken anything so dangerous, and she discovered that she had done it without really intending to. The singularity of such a confession, for which she could discover no precedent, made her see all the dangers.

But when she began to think that this measure, however extreme it was, was the only one which could defend her against the Duc de Nemours, she felt that she could not blame herself, and that she had not taken too great a risk. She spent the night full of indecision, worry and fear, but finally calm returned to her spirit.

She even felt a certain sweetness in giving this proof of fidelity to a husband who deserved it so much, and who had shown how much he loved and esteemed her by the way in which he received her confession.

Meanwhile, the Duc de Nemours left the place where he had overheard the conversation which affected him so deeply, and plunged back into the forest. What Madame de Clèves had said about her portrait had revived him by revealing to him that he was the man whom she did not hate. At first he gave himself up to this joy, but it did not last long when he reflected that by the very incident which revealed to him that he had touched Madame de Clèves' heart, he learned that not only would she never give him any token of her love, but that it would be impossible for him to involve in a love affair a woman who took such extreme measures to avoid it. Nevertheless, he felt a certain pleasure in having reduced her to this extremity, and also felt a kind of glory in having won the love of a woman so different from the rest of her sex. He felt at once extremely happy and vastly unhappy. Night overtook him in the forest, and he had great difficulty finding the road back to Madame de Mercœur. He arrived at daybreak. He was quite embarrassed to explain what had kept him. He got out of this as best he could and returned to Paris with the Vidame de Chartres the same day.

The Duc de Nemours was so full of his passion and so overcome by what he had heard that he committed the not unusual indiscretion of talking in general terms and of retelling his own adventures, using borrowed names. As they were returning to Paris, the Duc de Nemours turned the conversation to the subject of love. He exaggerated the pleasures of being in love with a woman who deserved to be loved. He spoke of the strange effects of love, and finally, not being able to keep to himself his astonishment at Madame de Clèves' confession, he recounted it to the Vidame de Chartres, without naming her, and without saying that he was involved in the story. But he told the tale with such warm admiration that the Vidame de Chartres easily suspected that the Duc de Nemours was involved in the story. He strongly urged the Duc to admit this to him. He said to him that he had known for a long time that the Duc was deeply in love with somebody, and that there was some injustice in keeping this from a man who had entrusted him with his life's secret. The Duc de Nemours was too much in love to admit his passion. He had always hidden it from the Vidame de Chartres, although he loved him more than any man at the Court. He replied that one of his friends had told him this story, that he had promised not to talk about it, and he begged the Vidame de Chartres to keep this secret. The Vidame de Chartres assured him that he would not talk about it. Nevertheless, the Duc de Nemours repented having told him so much.

Meanwhile, the Prince de Clèves, his heart pierced with a mortal sorrow, went to see the King. Never had a husband felt such a violent passion for his wife and never had he admired her so much. What he had just learned did not lessen his esteem, but he felt a different kind of respect for her than he had felt before. He was deeply preoccupied with trying to find out whom she was in love with. The Duc de Nemours came to mind first because he was the most attractive at Court; then he thought of the Chevalier de Guise and the Maréchal de Saint-André, both of whom had hoped to please her and had paid a great deal of attention to her. Thus he decided that it must be one of the three, and stopped guessing. He arrived at the Louvre and the King led him into his study and told him that he had chosen him to accompany Madame Elizabeth to Spain. The King believed that no one could fulfill this responsibility better than he, and that no one could do more honor to France than the Princesse de Clèves. The Prince de Clèves accepted the honor of this choice as he should, and even saw in it an opportunity to take his wife away from the Court without making any apparent change in her way of life. But the time of this departure was too far distant to remedy his present difficulties. He wrote at once to Madame de Clèves, informing her of what the King had just told him, and repeated that he insisted upon her returning to Paris.

She came as he had commanded, and when they saw each other, they were overcome by an extraordinary sadness.

The Prince de Clèves spoke to her as the most honorable man in the world and the most worthy of what she had just done, "I'm not at all worried about your conduct. You are stronger and more virtuous than you think. Nor am I afraid of the future. I'm just unhappy to see that you have for someone else the feelings you couldn't have for me."

"I don't know what to answer you," she said. "I'm dying of shame to be discussing it with you. I beg you to spare me these cruel conversations. Tell me what to do. See to it that no one comes to visit me—that's all I ask of you. But realize that I can't talk about something which makes me feel so unworthy of you and of myself."

"You are right," he replied. "I'm abusing your sweet disposition and your confidence. But also you must have some compassion for the emotional state I'm in. Remember that whatever you may have revealed to me, you are hiding from me a name which arouses in me an unbearable curiosity. I'm not going to ask you to satisfy my curiosity, but I can't help telling you that the man I must envy must be the Maréchal de Saint-André, the Duc de Nemours, or the Chevalier de Guise."

Madame de Clèves blushed and said, "I'm not going to tell you anything, nor will my responses allay or confirm your suspicions. But if you try to find out by watching me, you will make me so nervous that everyone will know about it. In God's name," she continued, "find some way, on the pretext of some illness, to see to it that nobody visits me."

"No, Madame, it would soon be known that the reason was invented, and more than that, I want to trust you. This is the course both my mind and my heart counsel me to take. In the state of mind you're in, by giving you complete liberty, I give you stricter limits than I could ever prescribe."

The Prince de Clèves was not mistaken. The confidence he showed in his wife strengthened her even more against the Duc de Nemours and made her take stricter resolutions than any her husband could have imposed. She went to the Louvre and she went to the Reine Dauphine's, as was her custom, but she avoided the company of the Duc de Nemours and avoided his glances so carefully that she practically deprived him of all the joy he had in believing himself loved by her. He only saw in her actions indications to the contrary. He even began to think that he had dreamed the whole episode. There seemed so little likelihood of its having happened. The only evidence which reassured him was Madame de Clèves' apparent sadness, no matter how hard she tried to hide it. Perhaps all the glances and the sweet words in the world would not have increased the Duc de Nemours' love for her so much as her austere conduct.

One evening when the Prince and Princesse de Clèves were at the Queen's, a rumor was overheard that the King would name another high prince of the Court to accompany Madame Elizabeth to Spain. The Prince de Clèves had his eyes on his wife while they added that it would probably be the Chevalier de Guise or the Maréchal de Saint-André. He noticed that she was not affected by either of these two names, nor by the proposition that they accompany her on the voyage. This made him think that it was not one of these whose presence she feared. Wishing to clarify his suspicions, he went into the Queen's room where the King was. After staying there for a little while, he returned to his wife and whispered to her that it would be the Duc de Nemours who would go with them to Spain.

The Duc de Nemours' name and the thought of being exposed to his looks in her husband's presence during every day of a long voyage caused Madame de Clèves an anxiety which she could not hide.

Wishing to give another excuse for her feelings, she said to her husband, "It's a very unfortunate choice for you. He will share all the honors, and it seems to me that you ought to try to arrange to have someone else chosen in his place."

The Prince de Clèves replied, "It isn't his honors that make you fear the Duc de Nemours' coming with me. You are upset because of something else. Your dejection tells me what another woman's joy would have told me. But fear not. What I've just told you is not the truth. I invented it to assure myself of something I've suspected for a long time."

With these words, he left the room. He could see that his wife was very embarrassed, and he did not wish to agitate her further by his presence.

The Duc de Nemours entered the room at this moment and immediately noticed Madame de Clèves' state of mind. He went up to her and whispered that out of respect for her he did not dare ask her why she was more preoccupied than usual. The Duc de Nemours' voice made her come out of her reverie.

She looked at him, and without hearing what he said to her, full of her own thoughts and of the fear that her husband would see him near her, she said to him, "In God's name, leave me alone!"

"For heaven's sake, Madame," he replied, "I leave you alone only too much. What are you complaining about? I don't dare talk to you. I don't dare look at you. I tremble to go near you. How have I deserved your reproach? And why do you make it seem as if I've caused the dejection I see you in?"

Madame de Clèves was very angry with herself to have given the Duc de Nemours an opportunity to speak to her more plainly than he had ever spoken in his life. She left him without answering and went home more upset than she had ever been. Her husband easily perceived her increased agitation. He saw that she feared his speaking to her about what had just happened. He followed her into her room, which she had just entered.

"Don't avoid me, Madame," he said to her. "I don't want to say anything to you that will displease you. I want to ask your pardon for the surprise I've given you just now. I'm punished enough for what I've just learned. Of all men, the Duc de Nemours is the one that I fear the most. I see the danger you're in. You must control yourself for your own sake, and if possible, for love of me. I don't ask this of you as a husband, but as a man whose entire happiness depends upon you, and who has a more tender and violent passion for you than the one your heart prefers."

The Prince de Clèves nearly broke down at these last words. His wife was overcome, and bursting into tears, she embraced him with a tenderness and sadness which put him in a similar state of mind. They remained silent for a long time without saying anything and separated without having the strength to speak to each other.

The preparations for Madame Elizabeth's wedding were completed. The Duc d'Albe arrived to marry her.[29] He was received with all the magnificence and all the ceremony that were proper for such an occasion. To meet him the King sent the Prince de Condé, the Cardinals de Lorraine and de Guise, the Ducs de Lorraine, de Ferrare, d'Aumale, de Bouillon, de Guise and de Nemours, accompanied by several gentlemen and their pages dressed in livery. The King himself awaited the Duc d'Albe at the first gate of the Louvre with two hundred gentlemen in waiting,

---

[29] As Philip's representative.

headed by the Connétable. When the Duc approached the King, he would have embraced his knees, but the King would not let him and made him walk beside him to the Queen's apartment and then to Madame Elizabeth's, to whom the Duc d'Albe brought a magnificent present from his master. Then he went to the apartment of Madame Marguerite, the King's sister, to whom he conveyed the compliments of the Duc de Savoye and assured her that he would be there in a few days. Large receptions were given at the Louvre to show the Duc d'Albe and the Prince d'Orange, who accompanied him, the beauties of the Court.

Madame de Clèves did not dare to stay at home, much as she would have liked to, for fear of displeasing her husband, who absolutely commanded her to go. What made him even more determined was the absence of the Duc de Nemours. He had gone to meet the Duc de Savoye, and after the Duc de Savoye had arrived, he had to stay near him to help him with all the preparations for the marriage ceremonies. Therefore, Madame de Clèves did not meet the Duc de Nemours as often as usual, and this gave her some peace of mind.

The Vidame de Chartres did not forget his conversation with the Duc de Nemours. He made up his mind that the adventure which the Duc de Nemours had told him about was his own. The Vidame de Chartres watched him so closely that he would probably have figured it out if the arrival of the Duc d'Albe and the Duc de Savoye had not interrupted the Court routine, which prevented him from watching Nemours closely enough. The desire to get more information, or rather the natural inclination to tell everything to the person one loves, made him describe to Madame de Martigues the extraordinary behaviour of the young woman who had confessed to her husband her love for another man. He assured her that it was the Duc de Nemours who had inspired this violent passion, and he begged her to watch him closely. Madame de Martigues was very interested in what the Vidame had told her, and the curiosity she had always felt about the Reine Dauphine's relationship with the Duc de Nemours made her more anxious than ever to figure out this adventure.

A few days before the one chosen for the wedding, the Reine Dauphine gave a supper party for her father-in-law, the King, and the Duchesse de Valentinois. Madame de Clèves, who had been busy getting dressed, went to the Louvre a little later than usual. On the way she met a gentleman whom the Reine Dauphine had sent to come and get her. As Madame de Clèves entered the Reine Dauphine's room, she called to her from the bed where she was, that she had been waiting for her very impatiently.

Madame de Clèves answered that she did not know if she ought to thank her for this eagerness because it was probably caused by something other than a desire to see her.

"You are right," answered the Reine Dauphine, "but nevertheless, you ought to be grateful, for I have a story to tell you that I'm sure you will find fascinating."

Madame de Clèves knelt down by her bed, and luckily for her, her face was hidden from the light.

"You know," said the Reine Dauphine, "the desire we have always had to discover the cause for the change in the Duc de Nemours. I think I know it, and it is something which will surprise you very much. He is madly in love with one of the most beautiful women in the Court, and she loves him too."

These words, which Madame de Clèves could not imagine applied to herself, since no one knew that she loved the Duc de Nemours, upset her very much, but she managed to say, "I don't see anything extraordinary in that, considering the Duc de Nemours' age and how handsome he is."

"It's not that which is so surprising," answered the Reine Dauphine. "But you must know that this woman who loves the Duc de Nemours has never revealed her love to him, and her fear that she might give in to her passion has made her confess her predicament to her husband so that he would take her away from the Court. And it was the Duc de Nemours himself who told this story."

If Madame de Clèves began by feeling hurt because she thought that she had no part in this story, the last words of the Reine Dauphine made her despair because she realized that it concerned her only too much. She could not answer, and remained with her head on the bed while the Reine Dauphine continued talking, so preoccupied with what she was saying that she did not notice Madame de Clèves' embarrassment.

When Madame de Clèves felt a little calmer, she said, "That story doesn't seem very likely to me. I would like to know from whom you learned it."

"It was from Madame de Martigues who learned it from the Vidame de Chartres. You know he's in love with her, and he confided it to her as if it were a secret he learned from the Duc de Nemours himself. The Duc de Nemours didn't reveal the lady's name, nor did he admit that he was the one she loved, but the Vidame de Chartres doesn't doubt that it's he."

As the Reine Dauphine finished these words, someone approached her bed. Madame de Clèves was turned in such a way that she did not see who it was.

But she did not doubt who it was when the Reine Dauphine cried with an air of gaiety and surprise, "There he is himself! I'm going to ask him all about it."

Madame de Clèves knew that it was the Duc de Nemours. And without turning towards him, she threw herself upon the Reine Dauphine and whispered to her that she must not talk about this adventure that he had confided to the Vidame de Chartres, for fear of causing a quarrel between them. But the Reine Dauphine only laughed and said that Madame was too careful. She turned towards the Duc de Nemours, who was already dressed for the party.

Speaking with that charm which was always so natural to him, he said, "Madame, I think that I can guess without too much boldness that you were talking about me when I came into the room, and that you wanted to ask me about something to which Madame de Clèves objected."

"That's true," replied the Reine Dauphine, "but I'm not going to give in to her the way I usually do. I want to know if a story that's been told to me, is true, and if you're not the one who loves and is loved by a lady of the Court, who carefully hides her feelings from you, but has admitted them to her husband."

It is impossible to imagine Madame de Clèves' agitation and embarrassment. If death could have appeared at this moment to rescue her from her predicament, she would have welcomed it gratefully. But the Duc de Nemours was, if it were possible to be so, even more embarrassed. These words of the Reine Dauphine, who he believed was fond of him, in the presence of Madame de Clèves, in whom she had the greatest confidence, and who also had the most in her, confused him so much that he could not control his facial expression. The embarrassment he realized he had caused Madame de Clèves and the thought that he now had given her a reason to hate him, upset him so much that he could not answer.

Noticing his extreme embarrassment, the Reine Dauphine said to Madame de Clèves, "Look at him! Look at him! See if it isn't his own story!"

Meanwhile, the Duc de Nemours, recovering from his first shock, and seeing the importance of extricating himself from such a compromising situation, suddenly regained his composure and said, "I swear to you, Madame, that no one could be more surprised and upset than I am at the Vidame de Chartres' infidelity in repeating the story of one of my friends that I confided in him. I know how to get my revenge," he continued smiling, which practically removed the Reine Dauphine's suspicions. "He has confided in me things that are quite important to him. But I don't know, Madame," he continued, "why you do me the honor of involving me in this affair. The Vidame could not have said it was my story, since I told him the opposite. It would be possible to describe me as a man in love, but I don't think it would be possible for you to describe me as a man who was loved!"

The Duc was very happy to say something to her which pertained to the way he had felt about her formerly in order to divert her thoughts from the present. She thought she understood him. But, without replying, she continued to tease him.

"I'm very troubled," he continued, "about my friend and the just reproaches he will make to me for having repeated something which was dearer to him than life itself. He only told me half of it, however. He didn't tell me the name of the woman he loved. I only know that of all the men in the world, he is the most loving, and the most to be pitied."

"Why is he to be pitied," asked the Reine Dauphine, "if he is beloved?"

"Do you really think he is, Madame?" asked the Duc de Nemours. "Do you think that a woman who was genuinely in love would admit it to her husband? This woman doesn't know anything about love, and probably feels for him only a kind of gratitude for the devotion he has for her. My friend can't flatter himself with any hope. But however unhappy he might be, he feels at least happy to have made the lady fear to love him, and he wouldn't change places with the luckiest lover in the world."

"Your friend's passion is easily satisfied," said the Reine Dauphine, "and I am beginning to think that you are not talking about yourself. Indeed, it wouldn't be difficult to agree with Madame de Clèves that this adventure didn't happen at all."

"In fact, I can't believe that it did happen," said Madame de Clèves, who up until that time had remained silent. "And if it could have happened, how could it have become known? It doesn't seem as if a wife who was capable of such a confession would have the weakness to tell about it. Certainly her husband would not have revealed it either, or he would be unworthy of his wife's behaviour."

The Duc de Nemours, seeing that Madame de Clèves felt some suspicions about her husband, was only too anxious to increase them. He knew that the Prince was the most formidable rival he had to overcome. "Jealousy," he replied, "as well as curiosity to know more than he had been told, can even cause a husband to be imprudent."

By now Madame de Clèves had reached the end of her strength, and not being able to carry on the conversation any longer, was just about to say that she was ill, when, luckily for her, the Duchesse de Valentinois came in to tell the Reine Dauphine that the King would be there. The Reine Dauphine went into her dressing room to get ready.

As Madame de Clèves was about to follow her, the Duc de Nemours went up to her and said, "I would give my life to talk to you for a moment, but of all the most important things I have to say to you, the most pressing is that if I said anything which seemed to suggest that the Reine Dauphine played a part, I did it for reasons which have nothing to do with her."

Madame de Clèves acted as if she had not heard the Duc de Nemours. She left without glancing at him, and followed the King who had just appeared. As there was a large crowd of people there, she got her foot entangled in her dress, and she stumbled. She used this as an excuse to leave a place where she did not have the strength to stay, and pretending that she could not stand, she went home.

The Prince de Clèves went to the Louvre and was astonished not to find his wife there. He was told about her accident, and he went home immediately to find out what happened to her. He found her in bed, but he discovered that there was not too much the matter with her. When he had stayed with her awhile, he realized that she was so very unhappy that it surprised him.

"What's the matter with you, Madame?" he asked her. "It seems to me that there is something the matter with you other than what you are complaining about."

"I've been more unhappy than I've ever been," she said. "How have you repaid the extraordinary trust I've been foolish enough to place in you? Don't I deserve your keeping my secret? And if I don't deserve it, shouldn't your own interests cause you to keep it? I suppose your curiosity to know the person's name which I didn't tell you impelled you to try and find it out. Did your curiosity have to force you to an imprudence so cruel that the consequences would be as bad as possible? The whole story has come out. It's been told to me by one who has no idea that I am the principal person involved in it."

"What are you saying, Madame?" he asked. "Are you accusing me of having repeated what passed between you and me? Are you telling me that it is known? I am not going to justify myself. You wouldn't believe me if I did. You must have taken as yours a story that was told about somebody else."

"Oh my dear sir," she replied, "there isn't anybody else in the world with a story like mine! No other woman would be capable of such a thing! Nobody could have imagined or invented it. Nobody else but me has ever had such a thought. The Reine Dauphine just told me the whole adventure. She learned it from the Vidame de Chartres, and he got it from the Duc de Nemours."

"The Duc de Nemours!" cried the Prince de Clèves, with an expression that marked the depths of despair. "The Duc de Nemours knows that you love him, and that I know it?"

"You're always talking about the Duc de Nemours rather than anybody else," replied Madame de Clèves. "I've told you that I won't confirm your suspicions. I don't know whether the Duc de Nemours knows the part I played in this adventure, or whether you've given him the other part, but he has told it to the Vidame de Chartres as if he had learned it from one of his friends who didn't name the lady involved. It must be that the Duc de Nemours' friend is also your friend, in whom you confided to try to learn more."

"Is there a friend in the world to whom one would tell such a story?" asked the Prince de Clèves. "And would a person clarify his suspicions at the price of telling someone a secret that he would rather keep from himself? Think, Madame, to whom you're talking. Is it very likely that I am the kind of a person who would let such a secret escape? All by yourself, you haven't been able to bear the situation you find yourself in, and so you have sought some kind of comfort in confiding in a friend who has betrayed you."

"Stop blaming me," she cried, "and don't be so harsh as to accuse me of a fault that you have committed. How can you suspect me? Because I was capable of talking to you, do you think I was capable of talking to anyone else?"

The confession that Madame de Clèves had made to her husband was such a great indication of her sincerity, and she so strongly denied having spoken to anyone else, that the Prince de Clèves did not know what to think. On the one hand, he was sure that he had not said anything. It was something which could not be guessed. The confession was known, so it must have been revealed by one of them. But what made him the most unhappy was to realize that the secret was out, and that soon everybody would know it.

Madame de Clèves thought practically the same thing. She considered it equally impossible that her husband had talked or that he had said nothing. What the Duc de Nemours had mentioned about curiosity making a husband imprudent agreed so well with the Prince de Clèves' state of mind that she could not believe that the story was told by accident. This likelihood made her believe that her husband had abused the confidence she had placed in him. Each of them was so preoccupied that it was a long time before they spoke to each other. They did not break their silence except to say the same things to each other that they had already said. Thus they remained more altered and more estranged in mind and heart than they had ever been before.

It is not difficult to imagine what kind of night each of them spent. The Prince de Clèves had exhausted his endurance in suffering the unhappiness of seeing his wife, whom he adored, in love with someone else. He could bear it no more. Indeed, he thought that he should not have to tolerate something which so wounded his honor and his reputation. He no longer knew what to think of his wife. He no longer knew what he ought to ask her to do, nor how he should behave himself. Everywhere he saw precipices and chasms. Finally, after much worry and indecision, since the trip to Spain was imminent, he decided not to do anything which would attract attention to his unhappy state. He went to find Madame de Clèves to tell her that there was no point in attempting to find out who had given away their secret, but rather she must act as if it were a fable in which she played no part. It was up to her to persuade the Duc de Nemours and the others of this by treating him with the severity and coldness she owed a man who openly dared to show her that he loved her. This way she would easily discourage the idea that she was attracted to him. Also she must not worry about what he thought of her, since ultimately, if she did not reveal any weakness, all these ideas would disappear of themselves. Above all, she must attend the Louvre and the receptions as usual.

With these words, the Prince de Clèves left his wife without waiting for her answer. She found much sense in what he said, and the anger she felt against the Duc de Nemours made her believe that she would also find these orders easy to carry out. But it seemed very difficult to be present at all the marriage ceremonies with a calm face and a free spirit. However, since she had been chosen above several other princesses to carry the Reine Dauphine's train at Madame Elizabeth's wedding, she could not refuse without causing a good deal of talk and speculation about her reasons. So she resolved to exert herself and make a tremendous effort. But she took the rest of the day to get ready and to abandon herself to all the worries that were bothering her. She closed herself in her room and decided that of all the evils she suffered, the worst was to have something to complain about in the Duc de Nemours' conduct, and not to be able to find any way of justifying him. She did not doubt that he had told the story to the Vidame de Chartres—he had admitted as much. And neither did she doubt from the way in which he talked that the adventure involved her. How could she excuse such great carelessness? And what had happened to the Duc's extreme discretion that had impressed her so much?

He was discreet, she decided, as long as he thought he had nothing to hope for, but once he had even an uncertain hope of happiness, he was no longer discreet. He could not imagine being loved without wanting someone to know it. He guessed that he was loved without knowing it. He said all that he could say. I never admitted that he was the one I loved. He suspected it and let his suspicions be known. If he had been sure, he would not have acted in the same way. I was wrong to believe that any man in the world could hide something that flattered his vanity. However, it was for this man whom I believed so different from all the rest, that I have appeared like other women, I, who was always so different from them. I have lost the love and esteem of the husband who used to constitute my entire happiness. I will soon be looked at by everyone as a woman who has an irresponsible and violent passion. He for whom I have this passion is not unaware of it. Yet it was to avoid these misfortunes that I have risked all my peace of mind and even my life.

These sad thoughts were followed by a torrent of tears. But however much she was overcome by sorrow, she felt that she would have the strength to support it if she could be satisfied with the Duc de Nemours' behaviour.

The Duc was not in a calmer frame of mind. The indiscretion he had committed in speaking to the Vidame de Chartres and the cruel consequences of his behaviour caused him terrible unhappiness. He could not think of the terrible embarrassment, anxiety and sorrow he had caused Madame de Clèves without being overcome with remorse. He was inconsolable to have mentioned to her things about this episode which, though romantic in themselves, now appeared to him gross and impolite since they implied that he knew her to be a woman with a violent passion and that he was the object of that passion. All that he desired was to have a conversation with her, but he found that he feared it more than he desired it.

"What would I say to her?" he asked himself. "Shall I show her even more clearly what I have already revealed to her? Shall I let her know that I am aware of her love, I who haven't dared to tell her that I love her? Shall I begin to speak openly of my love, so that I will appear like a man who is sure of his hopes? Can I even think of approaching her when I'm afraid that the mere sight of me will embarrass her? How can I justify myself? I have no excuse. I am unworthy of being looked at by Madame de Clèves, and I cannot hope that she will ever look at me again. Through my own fault I have given her the best means of defending herself against me, which she might never have found by herself. Through my own indiscretion, I have lost the happiness and the honor of being loved by the best and loveliest woman in the world. But I would not mind losing that happiness if I had not caused her to be hurt. I regret more deeply at this point the suffering I have caused her than my loss of reputation in her eyes."

The Duc de Nemours spent a long time blaming himself and thinking about these things. All the time he desired to speak with Madame de Clèves. He thought about how he could arrange this. He thought about writing to her. But finally he decided that after the mistakes he had committed, and considering the humor she must be in, the best thing was to show her by his humility and by his silence his profound respect. He decided to make her see that he would not even dare to approach her until the moment, the occasion, and even perhaps the attraction she felt for him, gave him an opportunity to speak to her. He decided not to reproach the Vidame de Chartres for his treachery for fear of confirming his suspicions.

The betrothals of Madame Elizabeth which were celebrated the next day, and the marriage which took place the day after, so absorbed the Court that Madame de Clèves and the Duc de Nemours were easily able to hide their sadness and anxiety. The Reine Dauphine only spoke in passing to Madame de Clèves of the conversation they had had with the Duc de Nemours, and the Prince de Clèves pretended not to talk with his wife about what had happened, so that she did not feel as embarrassed as she expected to be.

The engagement took place at the Louvre, and after the banquet and the ball, the whole royal household, as was the custom, went to sleep at Evêché, at the Bishop's palace, which was near the Louvre. In the morning, the Duc d'Albe, who was always very simply dressed, put on a coat of gold cloth, mingled with red, gold and black, all covered with precious stones, and on his head he wore a crown. The Prince d'Orange, also dressed magnificently with his liveried servants, and all the Spaniards, followed by their servants, went to call for the Duc d'Albe, where he was staying at the Hotel de Villeroy, and left, marching four abreast, to the Bishop's palace. As soon as they arrived, they went in order to the Church. The King led Madame Elizabeth, who also wore a crown, and her train was carried by the Mademoiselles de Montpensier and de Longueville. Then marched the Queen without a crown. After her came the Reine Dauphine, the King's sister, Madame de Lorraine, and the Queen of Navarre, their trains carried by the princesses. The Queens and the princesses all had their maids of honor magnificently dressed in the same colors that they wore, so that one could recognize the maids of honor by the colors of their dresses. They mounted the platform set up in the church and the wedding ceremony was performed. Then they returned to dine at the Bishop's palace, and at five o'clock they left to go to the royal palace, where the banquet was held to which the members of Parliament, the Sovereign Courts, and the city officials were invited. The King, the Queens, the princes and princesses ate at a marble table in the great hall of the palace, the Duc d'Albe seated next to the new Queen of Spain. Below the marble table, at the King's right hand, was a table for the ambassadors, the archbishops, and the knights of the order. On the other side was a table for the members of the Parliament.

The Duc de Guise, dressed in a coat of gold frieze, served the King as grand chamberlain. The Prince de Condé was steward of the household, and the Duc de Nemours was cupbearer. After the tables were cleared, the ball began. It was interrupted by ballets and theatrical tableaux. It began again, and finally, after midnight, the King and all the Court returned to the Louvre. No matter how sad Madame de Clèves was, she only appeared to everyone else and especially to the Duc de Nemours as extraordinarily beautiful. He did not dare to talk with her, although the confusion of the ceremonies gave him several opportunities. But he appeared so dejected and so respectfully aloof, that she found it difficult to blame him, even though he said nothing to justify himself. He behaved in the same manner during the following days, and his behaviour had the same effect on Madame de Clèves' heart.

Finally, the day of the tournament arrived. The Queens went into the galleries and onto the platforms assigned to them. The four champions appeared at the end of the lists, with a number of horses and men in livery, making the most magnificent spectacle that had ever been seen in France.

The King always had the same colors—black and white—which he wore in honor of Madame de Valentinois, who was a widow. The Duc de Ferrare and all of his train wore yellow and red. The Duc de Guise appeared in carnation and white, and at first everyone wondered why he wore these colors, but they remembered that these were the colors of a beautiful young woman whom he loved before she was married, and whom he still loved, although he did not dare to show it. The Duc de Nemours wore yellow and black, and no one knew why. It was not very hard for Madame de Clèves to guess. She remembered having said in front of him that she loved yellow, and that she was sorry to be blonde, because she could not wear it. The Duc de Nemours thought that he could wear this color without committing any indiscretion, since Madame de Clèves never wore this color, and no one would think it was hers.

Never has there been such skill as was displayed by the four champions. Although the King was the best horseman of his realm, it was hard to know to whom to give the advantage. The Duc de Nemours displayed a grace in all his actions which would have made him favored in less interested eyes than those of Madame de Clèves. As soon as she saw him appear at the end of the lists, she felt an extraordinary emotion, and at every contest he won, she had difficulty concealing her joy.

On the evening when all the tournaments were over and everybody was ready to retire, to the misfortune of the realm, the King wished to break another lance. He directed the Comte de Montgomery, who was extremely skillful, to enter the lists. The Comte begged the King to forget about it, and gave all the excuses he could think of; but the King became angry and said that he absolutely insisted on fighting. The Queen sent word to the King, begging him not to fight, saying that he had already done so well that he ought to be satisfied, and asking him to return to her. He replied that it was for love of her that he was going to fight and entered the barrier. Again, she sent the Duc de Savoye to beg him for a second time to return to her, but it was useless. He charged, the lances were broken, and a splinter from the Comte de Montgomery's lance lodged in the King's eye. The King fell down; his equerries and Monsieur de Montmorency, one of the judges, ran to him. They were astonished that the King could be so badly wounded, but the King was very calm. He said that he was only slightly wounded and that he pardoned the Comte de Montgomery. One can imagine the agitation and affliction caused by such an unfortunate accident on a day destined for joy. As soon as the King was put to bed, the surgeons visited him and found that his wound was quite serious. At that moment the Connétable remembered the prediction that had been made about the King, that he would be killed in a single combat, and he did not doubt that the prediction would come true.

The King of Spain, now at Brussels, heard of the accident, and sent his doctor, who was a man of great reputation. But he too thought the King's condition was desperate.

A Court so divided, and so full of opposing interests, could be in no slight state of agitation on the night of such a momentous event. Nevertheless, all the undercurrents were hidden, and people seemed to be concerned only with the King's health. The Queens, the princes and the princesses practically never left the King's antechamber.

Madame de Clèves knew that she should be there. But, she knew that if she saw the Duc de Nemours there, she would not be able to hide from her husband the agitation he caused her, and she also recognized that the mere presence of the Duc would justify him in her eyes and destroy all of her resolutions, so she decided to feign illness. The Court was too busy to notice her behaviour or to guess whether her illness was genuine or false. Her husband was the only one who knew the truth, but she did not mind his knowing. Thus she remained at home, little concerned with the great changes that were being prepared. Full of her own reflections, she had all the freedom in the world to abandon herself to them.

Everyone was at the King's. The Prince de Clèves came and went at various hours to tell her of the news. He treated her as he had always treated her, except that when they were alone, he treated her a little more coldly and a bit less openly. He never mentioned what had happened, and she did not have the strength to discuss it, nor did she think it wise to reopen that conversation.

The Duc de Nemours, who had expected to find a few minutes to talk with Madame de Clèves, was very surprised and even upset not to have even the pleasure of seeing her. The King became so much worse that on the seventh day the doctors despaired of his life. He faced his imminent death with amazing calmness, which was all the more extraordinary since he was losing his life by an unfortunate accident, so that he died in the flower of his youth, happy, adored by his people, and loved by his mistress whom he loved to distraction. The night before his death, he had his sister, Madame, married to the Duc de Savoye privately without any ceremony. One can imagine the Duchesse de Valentinois' state of mind. The Queen would not let her visit the King, and sent to demand from her the King's seals and the crown jewels that she had in her possession.

The Duchesse de Valentinois asked if the King was dead, and when she was told that he was not, she said, "Then I have no master, and no one can force me to return what he entrusted to me."

As soon as the King died at the Chateau of Tournelles, the Duc de Ferrare, the Duc de Guise and the Duc de Nemours accompanied the Queen Mother, the new King, and his wife, who had been the Reine Dauphine. The Duc de Nemours was leading the Queen Mother, but as they began to walk, she told the new Queen, her daughter-in-law, that she must go first. It was easily apparent that there was more bitterness than courtesy in this compliment.

BOOK 4

The Cardinal de Lorraine's influence over the Queen was now complete, and the Vidame de Chartres was quite out of favor. He did not mind this as much as he might have, finding consolation in his love for Madame de Martigues and his love of liberty. During the ten days of the King's illness, the Cardinal de Lorraine had time to make his plans to convince the Queen to make decisions which would further them. Thus, as soon as the King was dead, the Queen ordered the Connétable de Montmorency to remain at Tournelles near the body of the King, to perform the customary ceremonies. This assignment kept him away from the center of activities and removed his liberty of action. He sent a courier to the King of Navarre to make him hasten to him so that together they might oppose the growing power of the Guises. The Duc de Guise was given command of the army, and the Cardinal de Lorraine was put in charge of finance. The Duchesse de Valentinois was sent away from the Court, and the Cardinal de Tournon, the openly declared enemy of the Connétable, and the Chancellor Olivier, the declared enemy of the Duchesse de Valentinois, were recalled. Thus the aspect of the Court was entirely changed. The Duc de Guise carried the King's mantle at the funeral ceremonies, exactly as if he had been a Prince of blood. He and his brother had complete mastery over the Court, both because of the Cardinal's influence over the Queen, and because the Queen thought that she could dismiss them if they gave her difficulties, but that she could not depose the Connétable, who was supported by the Princes of blood.

When the mourning ceremonies were over, the Connétable went to the Louvre and was very coldly received by the King. He wished to talk with him alone, but the King called in the Ducs de Guise, and said to the Connétable in front of them that he would advise him to retire, that the control of finances and the command of the army had been disposed of, and that he would call on him if he had need of his services. He was received even more coldly by the Queen Dowager than he was by the King. She even reproached him for having told the late King that his children did not resemble him.

The King of Navarre arrived and was not treated any better. The Prince de Condé, less patient than his brother, complained loudly; but his complaints were useless. He was removed from the Court under the pretext of sending him to Flanders to sign the ratification of the peace treaty. The King of Navarre was shown a forged letter from the King of Spain which accused him of having designs on his territory. This made him fearful of losing his lands and made him decide that he had better go back to Béarn. The Queen furnished him with the means to do so, putting Madame Elizabeth in his charge and making him go ahead of her. Thus no one remained at Court who could balance the power of the Guises.

Although the Prince de Clèves was displeased not to be accompanying Madame Elizabeth, he could not complain because of the exalted rank of the substitute. But it was less for the honor that the mission would have brought him that he regretted it than for the opportunity it would have permitted him for removing his wife from the Court without his appearing to wish it.

A few days after the King's death, it was decided to go to Rheims for the Coronation. As soon as this journey was discussed, Madame de Clèves, who had been staying home, pretending to be ill, begged her husband to permit her not to follow the Court and to allow her to go to Colomiers for a change of air and to care for her health. He answered her that he really did not want to find out whether or not it was her health which made her unwilling to take the journey, but he consented. It was not difficult for him to agree to something which he had already decided himself. However high an opinion he had of his wife's virtue, he was well aware of the prudence of not wishing to expose her any longer to the sight of the man she loved.

The Duc de Nemours soon found out that Madame de Clèves would not follow the Court. He could not bear to leave without seeing her. The eve of the departure, he went to see her as late as propriety would allow, in order to find her alone. Luck favored his plan. As he entered the courtyard, he found Madame de Nevers and Madame de Martigues, who were just leaving, and who said that they had left her alone. He went up the stairs with an agitation and confusion which could only be compared with Madame de Clèves' when she heard that the Duc de Nemours was waiting to see her.

The fear that he would speak to her of his passion, the apprehension that she would respond too favorably, the anxiety that this visit could cause her husband, the pain of giving him an account of the visit and hiding all these things from him, flashed into her mind in a moment and upset her so much that she decided to avoid the one thing in the world that she most desired. She sent one of her maids to the Duc de Nemours, who was in the antechamber, to tell him that she had just taken ill and that she was terribly sorry not to be able to accept the honor he wished to do her.

What sadness for the Duc de Nemours not to see Madame de Clèves, and not to see her because she did not wish him to! He left the next morning, having nothing further to hope. He had not said anything to her since that conversation at the Reine Dauphine's, and he had reason to believe that he had destroyed his own hopes by talking to the Vidame de Chartres. Thus, as he departed, his sadness was deeply tinged with bitterness.

As soon as Madame de Clèves had recovered a bit from the agitation caused by the thought of a visit from the Duc de Nemours, all the reasons that she had made up for refusing him disappeared. She even thought that she had made a mistake, and if she had dared, or if there had still been time, she would have recalled him.

Upon leaving her, Madame de Nevers and Madame de Martigues went to the Reine Dauphine's. The Prince de Clèves was still there. The Reine Dauphine asked them where they had been. They said they had just come from Madame de Clèves', where they had spent part of the afternoon with lots of people, but only the Duc de Nemours was still there when they left. These words, which seemed quite harmless to them, were not so for the Prince de Clèves. Although he must have realized that the Duc de Nemours often had occasions to talk to his wife, the thought that he was with her, that he was with her alone, and that he could speak to her of his love, appeared at that moment something so new and so unbearable, that he felt more jealousy than he had ever felt before. It was impossible for him to stay at the Reine Dauphine's any longer. He went home, not knowing why he did so, or even whether he intended to interrupt the Duc de Nemours. As soon as he approached the house, he looked to see if the Duc were still there. He felt relieved to see that he was not, and was happy to think that he could not have stayed very long. Then he began to think that perhaps it was not of the Duc de Nemours that he ought to be jealous, and although he really did not doubt it, he began to question it. But so many things convinced him of it, that he did not remain for very long in the uncertainty he desired.

He went immediately to his wife's room, and after talking to her for a while about unimportant things, he could not help asking her what she had done and whom she had seen. She gave him an account of her afternoon. When he saw that she did not name the Duc de Nemours, he asked her, trembling with emotion, if that was all whom she had seen, in order to give her a chance to name the Duc and not cause him the sadness of knowing that she was not being candid with him.

As she had not seen the Duc, she did not name him. The Prince de Clèves then spoke in a voice that revealed his suffering. "And Monsieur de Nemours?" he said. "Haven't you seen him? Or have you forgotten him?"

"I didn't see him, in fact," she replied. "I fell ill and I sent one of my maids to make excuses."

"You were ill only for him," questioned the Prince de Clèves, "since you saw everybody else? Why make these distinctions for the Duc de Nemours? Why don't you act towards him as you do towards anybody else? Why do you have to fear seeing him? Why do you show him that you take advantage of the influence his passion gives you over him? How could you dare to refuse him when you know very well that he could distinguish between your severity and mere incivility? But why do you need to be severe with him? From someone like you, Madame, any attention is a favor except indifference."

"However suspicious you might be of the Duc de Nemours, I couldn't believe you would reproach me for not having seen him," replied Madame de Clèves.

"I do reproach you," he replied, "and with reason. Why don't you see him if he hasn't said anything to you? But Madame, he *has* spoken to you. If his silence alone had been the only indication of his passion, it would not have made such a great impression on you. You haven't been able to tell me the whole truth. You are hiding the greater part of it. You have even regretted the little you have told me and you haven't the strength to continue. I'm more unhappy than I thought—the most unhappy of all men. You are my wife. I love you as my mistress, and I see you in love with another. This other man is the most charming of the Court, and he sees you every day. He knows that you love him. Ah! I thought that you could overcome your passion for him! I must have lost my senses to believe that this could be possible."

"I don't know if you were wrong to approve of behaviour as extraordinary as mine," replied Madame de Clèves sadly. "But I don't know if I was wrong in believing that you would treat me justly."

"Don't doubt it, Madame," replied the Prince de Clèves. "You were wrong! You have expected from me things as impossible as I have expected from you. How could you imagine that I could be reasonable? Have you forgotten that I'm madly in love with you and that I'm your husband? Either of these two could make me go to extremes. What couldn't the two together do? Alas, how they affect me! I have violent and uncertain feelings of which I'm no longer the master. I don't feel worthy of you. You don't seem worthy of me. I adore you. I hate you. I offend you. I ask your forgiveness. I admire you. I'm ashamed of admiring you. Finally, there is nothing calm nor reasonable in me. I don't know how I've existed since you spoke to me at Colomiers and since the day that you learned from the Reine Dauphine that your story was known. I haven't been able to figure out how it became known, nor what passed between you and the Duc de Nemours on the subject. You never explain anything to me, and I never ask you for any explanations. I only ask you to remember that you have made me the most unhappy man in the world."

With these words, the Prince de Clèves left his wife's room, and departed the next morning without seeing her again. But he wrote her a letter full of sadness, sincerity and sweetness. She wrote him a very touching response, full of assurances about her past and future conduct. Since these assurances were based on the truth, and she really meant them, the letter made an impression on the Prince de Clèves and made him feel calmer. Moreover, the Duc de Nemours was with the King, and the Prince de Clèves had some peace of mind in knowing that he was no longer in the same place as Madame de Clèves. Every time that Madame de Clèves talked to her husband, the devotion he revealed, the courtesy he showed her, the friendship she felt for her husband and which she owed him, made an impression on her heart which weakened the idea of the Duc de Nemours. But this was only for a time. Then the idea of him would return more persistent and vivid than ever.

The first days after the Duc's departure, she barely felt his absence. Then she missed him cruelly. Since the beginning of her love for him, not a day had passed that she did not fear or hope to meet him, and she suffered to think that even chance could not bring about their meeting.

She went to Colomiers. In preparing to leave, she was careful to take with her the large paintings which she had had copied from the originals ordered by Madame de Valentinois for her beautiful house at Annet. Among these pictures were those depicting the remarkable events that occurred during the reign of the King. There was, among others, the siege of Metz and very life-like portraits of all those who had distinguished themselves there. The Duc de Nemours was one of these, and this was perhaps why Madame de Clèves had the idea of bringing these portraits.

Madame de Martigues, who had not been able to leave with the Court, promised to spend a few days at Colomiers. The fact that they were both in favor with the Queen had not caused any jealousy between them, and they were friends although they did not confide all their feelings to one another. Madame de Clèves knew that Madame de Martigues loved the Vidame, but Madame de Martigues did not know that Madame de Clèves loved the Duc de Nemours nor that she was loved by him. The fact that she was the Vidame's niece made Madame de Clèves dearer to Madame de Martigues. Madame de Clèves also liked Madame de Martigues as one who was in love also, and, at that, with an intimate friend of her beloved.

Madame de Martigues went to Colomiers as she had promised, and found Madame de Clèves leading a very solitary life. In fact she even attempted to be left completely alone, and she spent her evenings in the garden without the company of her servants. She went into the pavilion where the Duc de Nemours had overheard her, and she went into the room which opened onto the garden, while her maids and servants remained apart, only coming in to see her if she called them. Madame de Martigues had never seen Colomiers. She was surprised at all the beauties she found there and particularly at the charm of the pavilion, in which she and Madame de Clèves spent all their evenings. These two young women, both passionately in love, alone at night in the most beautiful place in the world, found their conversation never came to an end. Although they did not confide in each other, they found great pleasure in talking to each other. Madame de Martigues would not have been able to leave Colomiers, if in leaving, she were not going to be in a place where the Vidame was. She left for Chambord, where the Court was now being held.

The Coronation was performed at Rheims by the Cardinal de Lorraine, and the plans were to spend the rest of the summer at Chambord, which was newly built. The Queen displayed great joy in seeing Madame de Martigues again, and, after giving several indications of this, asked for news about Madame de Clèves and what she was doing in the country. The Duc de Nemours and the Prince de Clèves were in the Queen's room at this time. Madame de Martigues, who had found Colomiers delightful, told all about its beauties and dwelt especially on the description of the forest pavilion and the pleasure which Madame de Clèves took in walking alone there during part of the evening. The Duc de Nemours, who knew the place well enough to imagine what Madame de Martigues was saying, thought that it was possible to see Madame de Clèves without being seen by her.

He asked Madame de Martigues several questions to clarify for himself the situation, and the Prince de Clèves, who had been watching the Duc de Nemours all the time that Madame de Martigues was talking, thought that he saw at that moment the thoughts that were passing through his mind. The questions the Duc asked confirmed his suspicions, so that he did not doubt that he planned to visit his wife. He was not mistaken in these suspicions. The Duc de Nemours was so taken with this idea that, after spending the night in thinking of ways to execute this plan, he asked the King's permission the very next morning to go to Paris on some pretext he invented.

The Prince de Clèves did not doubt the object of his journey. But he decided to make certain of his wife's conduct and not to remain in this cruel uncertainty. He wished to leave at the same time as the Duc de Nemours and find out for himself, from some hiding place, what success the journey would have. But, fearing that his departure would appear extraordinary and that the Duc de Nemours, being warned, would take other measures, he decided to trust one of his gentlemen whose loyalty and sincerity he knew. He described his difficulties to him, but also told him of Madame de Clèves' virtuous conduct up to that time, and ordered him to follow the Duc de Nemours, to observe him closely, to see whether he went to Colomiers and whether he entered the forest garden at night.

The gentleman, who was well-suited to such an errand, acquitted himself with all the exactitude imaginable. He followed the Duc de Nemours to the village about half a league from Colomiers, where the Duc stopped, he thought, no doubt, to wait for the night. The gentleman did not think it was necessary to wait also. He skirted the village and went into the forest to a place where he guessed the Duc de Nemours would pass. He was not at all mistaken in what he had guessed. As soon as night fell, he heard footsteps, and although it was dark, he easily recognized the Duc de Nemours. He saw him walk around the garden as if to see if he heard anyone and to find a place where he could most easily enter. The fence was very high, and there was another one beyond that to stop people from coming in, so it was quite difficult to get through. Nevertheless, the Duc de Nemours succeeded. As soon as he was in the garden, he had no difficulty in figuring out where Madame de Clèves was. He saw many lights in the little room—all its windows were wide open—and gliding along the fence, he approached with an agitation and emotion which is easy to imagine. He hid behind one of the windows which served as a door to see what Madame de Clèves was doing. He saw that she was alone, but he saw her looking so beautiful that he could scarcely restrain the rapture which the sight of her gave him. It was warm, and she had nothing on her head and shoulders but her hair, which hung loose. She lay on a daybed with a table in front of her, where there were several baskets full of ribbons. She chose some, and the Duc de Nemours noticed that they were the same colours that he wore at the tournament. He saw that she was making them into bows on a very unusual malacca cane, that he had carried some time ago and then given to his sister, from whom Madame de Clèves had taken it, pretending that she did not know that it belonged to the Duc de Nemours. After finishing her work with a grace and sweetness that reflected in her face the state of her heart, she took up a candlestick and went up to a big table which was opposite a picture of the siege of Metz, where there was a portrait of the Duc de Nemours. She sat down and began to look at this portrait with an attention and a reverie that passion alone could give her.

How to express the Duc de Nemours' feelings at this moment? To be seeing in the middle of the night in the most beautiful place in the world, a person whom he adored, to be seeing her without her knowing that he was looking at her, to see her completely occupied with things to do with him and with the passion she hid from him? This was something which has never been experienced or imagined by any other lover.

The Duc was so beside himself that he remained motionless in looking at Madame de Clèves without thinking that these moments were precious to him. When he had recovered a little, he thought that he ought to wait and talk to her when she came into the garden. He thought that he could do so with more safety because she would be quite a distance from her maids. However, upon seeing that she remained in the little room, he decided to enter. When he wished to carry out his decision, what difficulties he had! What fear of displeasing her! What fear of changing the expression on a face that had reflected so much sweetness to one full of severity and anger! He decided that he was foolish not to have paid Madame de Clèves a formal visit, but to have attempted to see her without being seen. He realized all that he had not thought of before. It seemed to him an extravagant boldness to surprise in the middle of the night a person to whom he had not yet declared his love. He thought that he could not expect her to wish to listen to him, that she would quite rightly be angry because of the dangers he exposed her to, and the accidents which might happen. All his courage abandoned him. Several times he was tempted to decide to return without being seen. Urged on, however, by the desire to see her, and reassured by the hopes that everything he had seen had given him, he advanced a few steps, but with so much difficulty that a scarf he was wearing got caught in the window and made a noise. Madame de Clèves turned her head. Whether it was because her mind was so full of this Duc, or whether it was because he stood in enough light to be seen, she thought it was he. Without hesitating or once looking towards him, she went to the place where her maids were staying. She was so upset when she entered that she was forced to hide her confusion by saying she was ill. She also said this to occupy her servants and to give the Duc de Nemours time to leave. When she had time to reflect, she thought that she had deceived herself and that it was merely an effect of her imagination to have thought that she had seen the Duc de Nemours. She knew that he was at Chambord, and she could not persuade herself that he had undertaken so hazardous a journey. Several times she had the desire to go back to the little room and see if there was anyone in the garden. Perhaps she wished as much as she feared to find the Duc de Nemours there. But, finally, reason and prudence triumphed over all her other feelings, and she felt that it was better to remain in the doubt she was in than to take a chance on clearing it up. It took her a long time to decide to leave a place where the Duc was perhaps so near. Thus it was almost daylight when she returned to the Chateau.

The Duc de Nemours remained in the garden as long as he saw the light. He had not given up all hope of seeing Madame de Clèves again, although he was convinced that she had recognized him and that she had stayed inside in order to avoid him. But, seeing that the doors were being closed, he decided that he had nothing further to hope. He went to remount his horse very close to the place where the Prince de Clèves' gentleman was waiting. This gentleman followed him as far as the same village he had left the previous evening. The Duc de Nemours decided to spend the whole day there with the idea of returning at night to Colomiers to see if Madame de Clèves had the cruelty to flee from him or not to let herself be seen at all. Although he felt a certain joy in having found her so full of thoughts of him, he was, nevertheless, very upset that she had taken the very instinctive step of fleeing from him.

No one has ever felt such tender and violent passion as did the Duc. He wandered under the willows along a little stream that ran behind the house where he was staying. He went as far away as possible so as not to be seen by anyone. He gave himself up to the ecstasies of his love, and his heart was so full that he could not help shedding some tears. But these tears were not merely the tears of sadness—they were mixed with that sweetness and charm only caused by love.

He began to recall all of Madame de Clèves' actions since he had first fallen in love with her. What proper and modest severity she had always shown him, although she loved him! "For, after all, she *does* love me," he said. "She loves me.

I don't doubt it. The finest pledges and the greatest favours are not such genuine indications as those I have seen. Yet I am treated with the same severity as if I were hated. I had thought that time would do its work. I now have nothing more to hope from that. I see her constantly defend herself against me and against herself. If I weren't loved, I could hope to please, but I please, I'm loved, and that love is hidden from me. What have I thus to hope for, and what change can I expect in my destiny? What? Am I to be loved by the most adorable person in the world and feel that excess of love that arises from the first knowledge of being loved only to suffer the torment of knowing that I'm rebuffed? Let me see that you love me, beautiful Princesse," he cried. "Let me see your feelings, so I can learn them from you once in my life; then I allow you to take up again, forever, that same severity with which you overwhelm me. At least look at me with those same eyes with which you looked at my portrait the other night. How can you have looked at it with such sweetness and have fled from me with so much severity? What do you fear? Why does my love seem so frightening to you? You love me and you hide it from me uselessly. You yourself have given me involuntary indications of it. I'm aware of my happiness. Let me enjoy it and stop making me unhappy." He began again, "Can I be loved by Madame de Clèves, and can I be unhappy? How beautiful she was last night! How could I resist the impulse to throw myself at her feet? If I had done so, I might have prevented her fleeing from me. My respect would have reassured her. But perhaps she didn't recognize me. I'm making myself suffer more than I ought to. Perhaps the sight of a man at such an extraordinary hour would have frightened her."

The Duc de Nemours was preoccupied with these thoughts. He awaited nightfall with impatience, and when it came, he again took the road to Colomiers. The Prince de Clèves' gentleman, who had disguised himself so as not to be noticed, followed him as far as he had the preceding evening and saw him enter the same garden. The Duc soon saw that Madame de Clèves did not wish to take a chance on his trying to see her again. All the doors were shut. He turned every way to see if he could see some lights, but it was useless.

Madame de Clèves, not doubting that the Duc de Nemours would return, had stayed in her room. She had feared that she would not always have the strength to flee from him, and she did not wish to take the risk of speaking to him in a manner that would be so little consistent with her conduct up to this point.

Although the Duc de Nemours did not have any hope of seeing her, he could not make up his mind to leave so early a place where she was accustomed to be. He spent the whole night in the garden and found at least some consolation in seeing the same things that she looked at every day. The sun had risen before he thought of leaving, but finally the fear of being discovered obliged him to go away.

It was impossible for him to leave the place entirely without seeing Madame de Clèves, so he went to see Madame de Mercœur who was then at her house near Colomiers.

She was extremely surprised at her brother's arrival. He invented an excuse for his journey, reasonable enough to deceive her, and finally managed his plan so cleverly that he got Madame de Mercœur herself to propose a visit to Madame de Clèves. This plan was executed the very next day when the Duc de Nemours said that he would leave her at Colomiers to return in all haste to the King. He gave her this idea of parting at Colomiers so that she would leave first. In this way, he would have an infallible opportunity to speak to Madame de Clèves.

When they arrived, they walked along the broad path which bordered the terrace. The sight of the Duc de Nemours caused her no slight agitation and left her no longer in any doubt that it was he whom she had seen in the garden the night before. This certainty made her a little bit angry because of the boldness and imprudence she found in such an undertaking. The Duc noticed the coldness of her expression, which caused him a certain sadness. They conversed on various topics, and, despite everything, he managed to appear so clever, so full of respect and admiration for Madame de Clèves, that he was able to dissipate, in spite of her, some of the coldness she had felt at first.

When he thought that she was reassured about her first fears, he showed an extreme curiosity to see the pavilion in the forest. He spoke of it as the most agreeable place in the world and described it so exactly that Madame de Mercœur said that he must have been there several times to be so completely aware of all its beauties.

"I don't think the Duc de Nemours has ever entered it," replied Madame de Clèves. "It has only recently been finished."

"I was there, not so very long ago," replied the Duc de Nemours, looking at her, "and I don't know whether I ought to be happy that you have forgotten that you saw me." Madame de Mercœur, who was looking at the beauties of the garden, did not pay any attention to what her brother was saying.

Madame de Clèves blushed and, lowering her eyes without looking at the Duc de Nemours, said, "I don't remember seeing you. If you were there, you were there without my knowing it."

"It's true, Madame," replied the Duc de Nemours, "that I was there without your orders. There I passed the sweetest and cruellest moment of my life."

Madame de Clèves understood only too well what the Duc was saying, but she did not reply. She was thinking about how to prevent Madame de Mercœur from going into the little room because the Duc de Nemours' portrait was there, and she did not want her to see it. She managed so well that time passed without their knowing it, and Madame de Mercœur talked of returning. But when Madame de Clèves saw that the Duc de Nemours and his sister were not leaving together, she knew only too well what she would be exposed to. She found herself in the same predicament she was in in Paris, and she took the same attitude. The fear that this visit would only be a confirmation of her husband's suspicions was not a small factor in her decision. In order to avoid the Duc de Nemours' being alone with her, she said to Madame de Mercœur that she would accompany her to the edge of the forest, and she ordered her carriage to follow her. The Duc's sorrow at always finding the same severity in Madame de Clèves was so violent that he turned pale in a moment. Madame de Mercœur asked him if he was ill. But he looked at Madame de Clèves without anyone's knowing it, and he looked at her in such a way that it was very apparent to her that his only illness was his despair. However, he had to let them leave without daring to follow them, and after what he had said, he could not return with his sister. Thus he returned to Paris and left from there the very next morning.

The Prince de Clèves' gentleman had been observing him continuously. He also returned to Paris, and, as he saw the Duc de Nemours leave for Chambord, he took the post coach to arrive before him and give an account of his journey. His master awaited his return as for something which would determine the unhappiness of his entire life.

As soon as he saw him, he judged by his face and not by his silence that he had nothing but unfortunate things to tell him. He remained for some time overcome with unhappiness; he lowered his head without being able to talk. Finally, he motioned to him to leave.

"Go on," he said. "I see what you have to tell me, but I haven't the strength to listen to it."

"I've nothing to tell you," replied the gentleman, "on which conclusive evidence can be based. It's true that on two nights in a row, the Duc de Nemours entered the garden in the forest and that the day after, he was at Colomiers with Madame de Mercœur."

"That's enough," replied the Prince de Clèves. "That's enough," he said, again motioning to him to retire. "I don't need any more explanations."

The gentleman was forced to leave his master abandoned to his despair. There was never, perhaps, a more violent depression. Few men with the courage of the Prince de Clèves, and as deeply in love as he was, have experienced at the same time the sadness caused by the infidelity of a mistress and the shame of being deceived by one's wife.

The Prince de Clèves could not resist being overcome by his sorrow. He suffered a fever that very night, and it came on with such suddenness that his illness was immediately considered very serious. Madame de Clèves was informed. She came in haste. When she arrived, his condition worsened. She found something so cold and so icy in his manner towards her that she was extremely surprised and hurt. It even seemed to her that he could hardly bear her taking care of him, but then she thought this was, perhaps, an effect of his illness.

As soon as she was at Blois, where the Court was assembled, the Duc de Nemours could not help being joyful at knowing she was near him. He tried to see her, and every day he went to the Prince de Clèves' on the pretext of finding out how he was. But this was useless. Madame de Clèves never left her husband's room, and was terribly upset about the condition she found him in. The Duc de Nemours was in despair that she was so unhappy. He knew only too well how much this affliction would reinforce the affection she felt for the Prince de Clèves, and how much this affection would be a dangerous diversion from her love for him. This feeling caused much chagrin for a while, but the seriousness of the Prince de Clèves' illness opened up new hopes. He saw that Madame de Clèves would perhaps be free to follow her own inclinations and that he would be able to find lasting happiness in the future. He could not bear this thought, so great were the feelings of agitation and ecstasy which it caused him. Therefore, he put these thoughts out of his mind, so that he would not be too unhappy if his hopes were disappointed.

In the meantime, the Prince de Clèves was almost given up by his doctors. One of the last days of his illness, after he had spent a very bad night, he said in the morning that he would like to rest. Madame de Clèves remained alone with him in his room. It seemed to her that instead of resting, he was very anxious. She came close to him and knelt in front of his bed, her face all covered with tears. The Prince de Clèves had decided not to reveal the violent anger he felt against her. But the care she took of him and the affliction that sometimes seemed so genuine and sometimes seemed indications of dissimulation and betrayal, aroused in him such unhappy and conflicting feelings that he could not keep them to himself. "You weep many tears, Madame, for a death that you are causing and about which you cannot be as unhappy as you make it appear." He continued in a voice weakened by sickness and sorrow, "I'm no longer in a position to reproach you, but I'm dying of the cruel displeasure you have caused me. Was such an extraordinary avowal as your talking to me at Colomiers necessary if it was going to be so little adhered to? Why enlighten me about the passion you had for the Duc de Nemours if your virtue wasn't going to be strong enough to resist it? I loved you so much that I would have been willing to be deceived—I admit this to my shame. I've longed for the false serenity from which you took me. Why didn't you leave me in that tranquil blindness that so many husbands enjoy? Perhaps for my entire life I would have been unaware that you loved the Duc de Nemours. I'm dying, but know that you make death pleasant. After the esteem and tenderness I felt for you were removed, life would be horrible to me. What would I do with life if I had to spend it with a woman I loved so much and who has cruelly deceived me, or if I had to live apart from this woman, and burst out openly into those recriminations which are so foreign to my nature and to my love for you? It has been far beyond what you've seen in me. I've hidden the greater part of it from you so as not to bother you or cause you to lose your esteem for me by conduct unsuitable to a husband. After all, I deserved your love. Also, I'm dying without regret since I couldn't win your heart and no longer wish it. Goodbye, Madame. Some day you'll miss a man who loved you with such a genuine and legitimate passion. You'll feel the chagrin that sensitive people feel in these involvements. You'll recognize the difference between being loved as I've loved you, and being loved by those who, in showing you passion, only want the honor of seducing you. But my death will leave you at liberty, and you can make the Duc de Nemours happy without feeling guilty. What does it matter, what happens when I'm no longer here? Why must I have the weakness even to think about it?"

Madame de Clèves was so far from imagining that her husband could be suspicious of her that she listened to all these words without understanding them, and without having any other idea except that he was reproaching her for loving the Duc de Nemours.

Finally, suddenly emerging from her blindness, she cried, "I, guilty? Even the thought of it is unknown to me! The most austere virtue could not inspire any other conduct than what I have pursued, nor have I participated in any action of which I would not wish you to be the witness."

"Would you have wished me to witness those nights you spent with the Duc de Nemours in the forest garden?" asked the Prince de Clèves, looking at her with disdain. "Is it of you that I'm talking when I speak of a woman spending nights with a man?"

"No, Monsieur," she replied. "No. It's not of me you're speaking. I have not spent any nights or moments with the Duc de Nemours. He's never seen me alone. I've never allowed it or listened to it. I'll swear all kinds of oaths about it."

"Don't say anymore," interrupted the Prince de Clèves. "False oaths or a confession would make me equally unhappy."

Madame de Clèves could not reply. Her tears and her sorrow prevented her speaking. Finally, making an effort, she said to him, "Look at me. Listen to me. If I were the only one concerned, I would suffer these reproaches, but your life is at stake. Listen to me for your own sake. It's impossible that with so much truth on my side, I cannot persuade you of my innocence."

"I wish to God you could persuade me," he cried. "But what can you say? The Duc de Nemours hasn't been at Colomiers with his sister? And he didn't spend the preceding two nights with you in the forest garden?"

"If that's my crime," she replied, "it's easy for me to justify myself. I don't ask you to believe me, but believe your servants and find out whether I went into the forest garden the night before the Duc de Nemours came to Colomiers, and whether the night before that I didn't leave two hours earlier than I was accustomed to do."

Then she told him how she thought she had heard someone in the garden. She admitted to him that she thought it was the Duc de Nemours. She spoke with such conviction, and the truth is so persuasive even when it's unlikely, that the Prince de Clèves was almost convinced of her innocence.

"I don't know if I ought to let myself go on believing in you," he said to her. "I feel so close to death that I don't want to know anything that will make me hang onto life. You have enlightened me too late. But it will always be a comfort to me to carry with me the idea that you were worthy of the respect I have always had for you. I beg you also to give me the consolation of knowing that my memory will be dear to you, and that if it had been up to you, you would have had the feelings for me that you have had for another."

He wanted to go on, but weakness deprived him of speech. Madame de Clèves called in the doctors. They found him almost lifeless. However, he lingered a few days and then died with an admirable fortitude.

Madame de Clèves fell into such a violent state of grief that she nearly lost her mind. The Queen, concerned about her, came to see her and put her in a convent without her being aware of it. When she no longer felt her sadness quite so sharply, her sister-in-law brought her back to Paris. When she began to have the strength to be aware of what was going on around her, and realized what a husband she had lost, that she was the cause of his death, and that his death was caused by her love for another, she felt an indescribable loathing for herself and for the Duc de Nemours.

At first, the Duc did not dare to pay her any more attention than the occasion demanded. He knew Madame de Clèves well enough to know that an early pressing of his suit would be distasteful to her. But what he learned later showed him that he would have to maintain this same conduct for a long time.

A servant of his told him that the Prince de Clèves' gentleman, who was his intimate friend, had spoken to him in his sadness over losing his master, and had said that the Duc de Nemours' trip to Colomiers had been the cause of his death. The Duc de Nemours was extremely surprised at this story, but, after thinking about it, he guessed part of the truth. He knew only too well what Madame de Clèves' feelings would be and how estranged she would be from him if she thought that her husband's illness was caused by jealousy. He realized that he should not even remind her of his name just now, and painful as he found this course of action, he followed it.

He made a trip to Paris, but he could not prevent himself from going to her door to find out about her. He was told that she was seeing no one and that she had even given orders not to be told about those who came to call on her. Perhaps these exact orders were given with the Duc de Nemours in mind, so that she would not hear about him. The Duc was too much in love to be able to live completely deprived of the sight of Madame de Clèves. He decided to find the means, however difficult they might be, to rectify a situation that seemed unbearable to him.

This Princesse's grief went beyond reason. Her husband's dying, and dying because of her, with so much tenderness for her, was never far from her mind. Repeatedly she called to mind everything that she owed him. She felt criminal not to have loved him as he had loved her, as if such a thing were in her power. Her only consolation could be found in realizing that she would miss him as much as he deserved, and that for the rest of her life she would act in a manner that would have pleased him if he had lived.

She wondered several times how the Prince de Clèves came to know that the Duc de Nemours had been at Colomiers. She did not suspect that the Duc had told him, and it was even indifferent to her whether he had or not—she felt so cured and so far removed from the passion she had felt for him. But she was intensely grieved to realize that he was the cause of her husband's death, and she remembered painfully the fear that the Prince de Clèves had revealed to her, as he was dying, that she would marry the Duc de Nemours. But all these sorrows were overshadowed by the loss of her husband, and she was not conscious of any other.

After several months had gone by, she came out of her state of violent affliction and passed into one of sadness and languor. Madame de Martigues made a trip to Paris, and during her stay there she visited her often. She entertained her with chatter about the Court and about all that went on there. Although Madame de Clèves did not seem particularly interested, Madame de Martigues went on talking just to divert her. She gave her news of the Vidame, of the Duc de Guise, and of all the others who were known for their personal qualities as well as for their deeds.

"As for the Duc de Nemours," she said, "I don't know if business has taken the place of gallantry in his heart, but he is much less cheerful than he used to be. He seems to avoid all feminine society, and often takes trips to Paris. I think he's here now."

The Duc de Nemours' name surprised Madame de Clèves and made her blush. She changed the subject, and Madame de Martigues did not seem to be aware of her agitation.

The next morning, the Princesse de Clèves, who wanted to occupy herself in a manner suitable to her newly widowed state, went nearby to a man who made things of silk in a very distinctive style. She intended to have something like them made for herself. When she had been shown some material, she saw the door of a room where she thought there was more and asked to have it opened. The master replied that he did not have the key, and that it was used by a man who came there several times a day to draw the beautiful houses and gardens to be seen from his windows.

"He's the handsomest man in the world," he added. "He doesn't look like the kind of man who has to work for his living. Every time he comes here, I see him look at the houses and gardens, but I never see him work."

Madame de Clèves listened to this discourse with rapt attention. What Madame de Martigues had said about the Duc de Nemours' often coming to Paris connected itself in her imagination with this handsome young man who visited a place close to her, and gave her the idea that it must be the Duc de Nemours, and a Duc de Nemours determined to see her. This produced a kind of agitation in her for which she hardly knew the cause. She went to the windows to see what they looked out on. She noticed that they looked out on the whole garden and the front of her apartment. And, when she was in her room, she easily noticed the window where she had been told this man came. The thought that this was the Duc de Nemours completely changed her state of mind. She no longer found herself in the sort of sad peacefulness that she had begun to enjoy. Instead, she felt anxious and agitated. Finally, not being able to contain herself, she left to take the air in a garden outside the suburbs where she thought she could be alone. Upon arrival, she thought that she had not been mistaken. She did not see any trace of anyone, and she walked around for quite a while.

After crossing a little wood, she noticed at the end of an alley in a more secluded corner of the garden, a kind of shelter open on all sides. To this she directed her steps. As she approached, she saw a man who seemed deep in reverie, lying on one of the benches. She recognized the Duc de Nemours. This sight stopped her short, but her servants who were following her made some noise, which woke the Duc de Nemours out of his reverie. Without noticing who made the noise he had heard, he got up from his place to avoid the people who were coming towards him and turned down another path, making such a deep bow that it even prevented him from seeing the people he was saluting.

If he had known whom he was avoiding, with what ardor he would have turned back in his tracks! But he continued to follow the path, and Madame de Clèves saw him leave by a gate behind which his carriage was waiting.

What effect this sight produced in a moment on Madame de Clèves' emotions! What dormant passion was relit in her heart and with what violence! She went and sat down in the same place which the Duc de Nemours had just left. She stayed there as if overcome. The Duc presented himself to her mind as the most lovable man in the world, loving her for so long with a passion full of respect and fidelity, scorning everything for her sake, respecting her sorrow, dreaming of seeing her without thinking of being seen, leaving the Court, in which he took such delight, to go and watch the walls which enclosed her, coming to day-dream about her in a place where he could not hope to meet her. Finally, he was a man worthy of being loved for his faithfulness alone, a man to whom she was so violently attracted that she would have loved him even if he had not loved her. But more than that, he was a man of elevated social position, suitable to her own. No more duty, no more virtue need stand in the way of her feelings. All the obstacles were removed, and nothing remained of their past except the Duc de Nemours' love for her and hers for him.

All these ideas were new to the Princesse de Clèves. Her affliction over the Prince de Clèves' death had occupied her too much to think about them. The presence of the Duc de Nemours made them crowd into her mind. But when her mind was preoccupied with him, and when she remembered also that this same man whom she regarded as free to marry her, was the one whom she had loved during her husband's lifetime, and who caused his death, whom her husband, even as he had been dying, had been afraid she would marry, her sense of virtue was so shocked that she scarcely felt less guilty in marrying the Duc de Nemours than she had in loving him during her husband's lifetime. She gave herself up to these reflections so contrary to her happiness. She strengthened them with reasons concerning her peace of mind and the troubles she foresaw in marrying him. Finally, after remaining in the same place for two hours, she returned home, persuaded that she must avoid the sight of him as something completely opposed to her duty.

But this persuasion, which was a manifestation of her reason and virtue, did not involve her heart. It remained attached to the Duc de Nemours with a violence which kept her in a state of mind which invited compassion, and which left her no peace. She spent one of the cruellest nights she had ever spent. The next morning her first act was to go and see if there was anyone at the window which looked out on hers. She went there and saw the Duc de Nemours. This sight surprised her, and she retired with such swiftness that the Duc realized he had been recognized. He had often wished to be, ever since his passion had forced him to find the means of seeing Madame de Clèves. And when he did not hope to have this pleasure, he went to dream of her in the same garden where she had found him.

Finally, worn out with such an unhappy and uncertain situation, he decided to do something which would clarify his position. "What should I wait for?" he said to himself. "I've known for a long time that she loves me. She's free. She no longer has her duty to oppose me with. Why limit myself to seeing her without being seen and without talking to her? Can love have so completely taken away my sense and my courage as to make me act differently in this relationship than in former love affairs? I had to respect Madame de Clèves' grief, but I have respected it too long. I have given her the time in which to stifle her love for me."

After these reflections, he thought about finding a way to see Madame de Clèves. He believed that nothing now obliged him to hide his passion from the Vidame de Chartres. He decided to talk to him and tell him about his intention concerning his niece.

At that time the Vidame was in Paris. Everyone had come to put retinues and outfits in order, so as to follow the King, who was to escort the Queen to Spain. The Duc de Nemours went to the Vidame and made a sincere confession of all that he had hidden from him until then, except for Madame de Clèves' state of mind, about which he did not wish to appear knowledgeable.

The Vidame listened to everything he said with much joy and assured him that without knowing his feelings, he had often thought that ever since Madame de Clèves was widowed, she was the only person worthy of him. The Duc de Nemours begged the Vidame to give him the means of speaking to her and discovering her intentions.

The Vidame proposed to take him to her house, but the Duc de Nemours thought that she would be displeased, since she had not received any visitors yet. They decided that the Vidame de Chartres ought to invite her to his house on some pretext, and that the Duc de Nemours ought to arrive by a secret staircase so as not to be seen by anyone. The plan was carried out as they had decided. Madame de Clèves arrived. The Vidame went to receive her and led her into a large study at the end of his apartment. A little while later the Duc de Nemours entered as if by chance. Madame de Clèves was extremely surprised to see him. She blushed and tried to hide her discomfort. The Vidame talked for a while about different things. Then he left on the pretext of having some order to give. He asked Madame de Clèves to act as hostess and said he would return in a few moments.

One cannot express the Duc de Nemours' and Madame de Clèves' feelings at being left alone to talk for the first time. They remained for a long while without saying anything to each other.

Then the Duc de Nemours broke the silence, "Will you forgive the Vidame de Chartres, Madame, for giving me the opportunity to see and speak with you, since you have always so cruelly deprived me of it?"

"I ought not to forgive him," she replied, "for ignoring my situation and the dangers to which he is exposing my reputation."

As she spoke these words, she attempted to move away, but the Duc de Nemours stopped her, saying, "Don't fear anything, Madame. No one knows I'm here. There's no danger to fear. Listen to me, Madame, listen to me—if not out of kindness to me, then at least out of love for yourself, and to save yourself from the extravagances to which I might be carried by a passion I can no longer control."

For the first time, Madame de Clèves gave way to the feelings she had for the Duc de Nemours. Looking at him with eyes full of sweetness and charm, she said, "But what do you hope from the favor you ask of me? You would perhaps repent receiving it, and I would doubtless regret giving it to you. You deserve a happier destiny than you have had thus far and than you can expect in the future unless you look for it elsewhere."

"I, Madame," he said. "Look for happiness elsewhere? And is there any happiness but to be loved by you? Although I have never spoken to you, I cannot believe that you're unaware of my love, or that you can fail to recognize it as the truest and most ardent that could ever be! How has it been tested by proofs that are unknown to you? How much have you tested it by your own severity?"

"Since you wish me to talk to you, and since I'm resolved to do so," replied Madame de Clèves, sitting down, "I'll do so with a sincerity that is rarely found in women. I'll not deny that I've seen the attachment that you feel for me. Perhaps you would not believe me if I said so. I'll now admit not only that I've seen it, but that I've recognized it in the light you would have wished me to."

"And if you have seen it, Madame," he interrupted, "is it possible that you were not touched by it? And do I dare to ask if it has not made some impression on your heart?"

"You ought to be able to judge that by my conduct," she replied. "But I would like to know what you have thought of it."

"I would have to be in a happier state of mind to dare to tell you," he replied. "And my future has too little to do with what I would say to you. All that I can say, Madame, is that I have ardently wished that you had not confessed to the Prince de

Clèves what you hid from me and that you had hidden from him what you let me see."

Blushing, she asked, "How did you find out that I confessed anything to the Prince de Clèves?"

"I found out through you, Madame," he replied. "But to pardon me for my boldness in overhearing you, try to remember whether or not I have taken advantage of what I have heard, whether my hopes have increased on account of it, or whether I have been any bolder in speaking to you?"

He began to tell her how he had overheard her conversation with the Prince de Clèves. But she interrupted him before he had finished. "Don't tell me anymore," she said, "I now see where you have learned everything. You already made it only too clear at the Reine Dauphine's, who learned the adventure from someone you had confided in."

The Duc de Nemours then informed her how the whole thing had happened.

"Don't make any more excuses," she said. "I forgave you long ago without your giving me any reasons. But since you heard from me what I intended to keep from you for my entire lifetime, I admit that you have inspired feelings in me that I wasn't aware of before I saw you. In fact, I had so little knowledge of them that they surprised me at first and increased the agitation that is always present in such circumstances. I confess this to you now with less shame because, at this time, I can do so without guilt, and because you are aware that my conduct has never been guided by my feelings."

"Believe me," said the Duc de Nemours, throwing himself at her feet, "that I feel as if I were dying of joy."

"I'm not telling you anything that you didn't know only too well before," she replied, smiling.

"Ah, Madame," he answered, "what a difference there is between finding it out by chance and learning it from you because you wish me to know it!"

"It's true," she said, "that I want you to know it and I take a certain pleasure in telling it to you. I don't even know whether I'm revealing it more for my own sake or for yours. For, when all is said and done, this confession will have no consequences, since I am resolved to follow the strictest rules my duty has ever prescribed."

"You mustn't think of duty," replied the Duc. "It no longer binds you. You're free. If I dared, I would even tell you that it depends on you to act in such a way that someday your duty will oblige you to cherish the feelings you have for me."

"My duty," she answered, "forbids me ever to think of any man, and least of all of you, for reasons which are unknown to you."

"Perhaps they are," he replied, "but they're not the real reasons. I think I know that the Prince de Clèves thought I was luckier than I was. He imagined that you had approved of the extremes my love forced me to undertake without your consent."

"Don't talk to me any more about that episode," she said to him. "I can't bear the thought of it. I'm ashamed of it, and I'm terribly unhappy because the consequences have been so fatal. It's too true that you caused the Prince de Clèves' death. Your inconsiderate conduct aroused suspicions in him which cost him his life, as much as if you had deprived him of it in a duel. Imagine what I would have to do if you had both gone to such extremes and the same misfortune had happened! I know that it isn't the same thing in the eyes of the world, but in mine there's no difference, since I know that he's dead because of you, and that on my account."

"Ah, Madame," said the Duc de Nemours, "what phantom of duty do you raise against my happiness? Shall a vain and groundless idea prevent you from making a man happy to whom you are attracted? I had hopes of spending my life with you. My destiny would have allowed me to love the most estimable woman in the world. Have I not seen in her everything that would make an adorable mistress? She would not have been untouched by my love, and I would have discovered in her conduct all that could be desired in a wife. After all, you are perhaps the only woman who combines these two qualities to such a degree. All those who marry the women who have been their mistresses, fear that they will be to others what they have been to them. But with you there is nothing to fear. No matter how carefully one scrutinizes your behaviour, one finds only new reasons for admiration. Have I anticipated such great happiness only to have you raise obstacles? Ah, Madame, you forget that you have chosen me above all others. Or rather, perhaps you did not. You have made a mistake, and I have flattered myself."

"You haven't flattered yourself," she replied. "The reasons for my duty would probably not appear so strong to me, if I had not chosen you as you suspect. This is what makes me fear that marrying you can lead only to unhappiness."

"I have nothing to answer you," he replied, "when you tell me that you fear unhappiness. But I must admit that after all you have been so good as to tell me, I didn't expect to discover such a cruel reason."

"But it's so far from being uncomplimentary to you," replied Madame de Clèves, "that I even have great difficulty in making you understand what I mean."

"Alas! Madame," he responded, "how can you fear flattering me too much after what you have just said?"

"I wish to continue speaking to you as sincerely as I began," she went on, "and without using all the reserve and delicacy which is proper to a first conversation. But I beg you to listen to me without interrupting.

"At least I owe to your love the slight recompense of not hiding my feelings from you and of letting you see them exactly as they are. This will probably be the only time in my life that I allow myself the freedom of telling you what I feel. But I blush to admit to you that the certainty of your not always loving me as you now do, appears such a dreadful misfortune to me, that even if I were not moved by insurmountable reasons of duty, I doubt that I could decide to face such unhappiness. I know that you are free, that I am also, and that no one perhaps would blame us if we decided to spend the rest of our days together. But do men maintain their passion in eternal relationships? Can I expect a miracle in my favor, and can I put myself in a position to see the certain end of a love which constitutes my entire happiness? Perhaps the Prince de Clèves was the only man in the world who could maintain love in marriage. My destiny did not allow me to enjoy such happiness, and perhaps his love lasted only because I could not respond to it. But I would not have the same means of keeping your love; for I think it was the obstacles that caused your constancy. You found enough difficulties to challenge you to overcome them. At the same time, my involuntary actions and the things you found out by chance gave you enough hope not to become discouraged."

"Really," said the Duc de Nemours, "I can't keep silent any longer. You're too unfair to me. You make me see only too clearly how far removed you are from being influenced in my favor."

"I confess," she admitted, "that my passions may lead me but they can never blind me. Nothing can prevent my knowing that you are a born seducer, endowed with every charm to make you successful in love affairs. You have had several affairs, and you will have more. I would no longer constitute your happiness. I would see you become to another what you have been to me. I would be mortally unhappy, defenceless as I am against the pangs of jealousy. I've revealed too much to hide from you the fact that I've experienced this jealousy already. Indeed, I suffered it terribly the evening when the Queen handed me Madame de Thémines' letter, saying that it was supposed to be addressed to you. From this experience, I've learned that jealousy is the worst of all evils. Because of vanity, or through choice, all women wish to be involved with you. There are few who are not attracted to you. My observation makes me believe that there are few whom you cannot win. I would always imagine you loving or being loved, and I would not often be mistaken. Then there would be nothing for me to do but suffer. I would not even dare to complain. One can reproach a lover, but can one reproach a husband when one's only complaint is that he no longer loves? Even if I could accustom myself to this kind of unhappiness, could I get used to the fact that I would always imagine the Prince de Clèves' accusing you of his death, reproaching me for having loved you and for marrying you, and making me feel the difference between his love and yours? It's impossible to vanquish such overpowering reasons. I have to remain in my present state and maintain my resolution never to leave it."

"Ah! but do you think you're strong enough?" asked the Duc de Nemours. "Do you think that you can maintain your resolutions against a man who adores you and who is lucky enough to be attractive to you? To resist someone who loves you and whom you love is more difficult than you know. You have succeeded so far by an austere and unparalleled virtue. But this virtue is no longer an obstacle to your feelings, and I hope that you will succumb to them in spite of yourself."

"I know that there's nothing more difficult than what I'm undertaking," replied Madame de Clèves. "I distrust my strength in the midst of my reasons. What I think I owe to the Prince de Clèves' memory would be weak were it not sustained by a concern for my peace of mind. And my peace of mind must be strengthened by my sense of duty. But, although I distrust my own strength, I doubt that I shall ever vanquish my scruples, nor do I think I will ever overcome my love for you. It will make me unhappy, and I must not allow myself to see you, no matter how much pain it costs me. I beg you by all the power I have over you, not to seek another opportunity to see me. I'm in a state of mind that makes me feel guilty about something that could be permitted at another time. Propriety itself forbids further conversation between us."

The Duc de Nemours threw himself at her feet and abandoned himself to all the sorrow with which he was agitated. With his words and with his tears, he made Madame de Clèves see that he loved her with the most intense and tender passion a human heart has ever felt.

Madame de Clèves' heart was not untouched by his passion. Looking at the Duc de Nemours with her eyes full of tears, she cried, "Why must I accuse you of the Prince de Clèves' death? Why couldn't I have first met you when I was free? Or why didn't I meet you before I was engaged? Why does fate separate us with such insurmountable obstacles?"

"There aren't any obstacles," replied the Duc. "You alone oppose my happiness. You impose upon yourself a principle which neither reason nor virtue demands."

"It's true," she answered. "I'm sacrificing much to a duty which exists only in my imagination. Wait and see what will happen in time. The Prince de Clèves has just died, and the sadness of this event is too recent for me to think clearly and distinctly. Meanwhile, have some pleasure in knowing that you have made a woman love you who would never have loved anyone, if she had not met you. Believe me that the feelings I have for you will last forever, and that no matter what becomes of me, they will remain unchanged. Farewell," she said. "This is a conversation that makes me ashamed. Tell the Vidame about it. I consent to it—I beg it of you."

Saying these words, she went out of the room. The Duc de Nemours was unable to restrain her. On her way out, she found the Vidame de Chartres in the next room. He saw her looking so upset that he did not dare speak to her. He put her in her carriage without saying a word. When he went back to see the Duc de Nemours, he found him so full of joy, sadness, astonishment, and admiration—in fact of all the feelings which belong to a passion full of fear and hope—that he was practically incapable of reason. It took the Vidame a long time to get the Duc de Nemours calm enough to repeat his conversation with Madame de Clèves. But he finally did so. Not being in love with Madame de Clèves, the Vidame felt hardly less admiration for her virtue, spirit, and worth than did the Duc de Nemours himself. They discussed what the Duc could expect in the future. Despite all the fears which his love aroused in him, the Duc agreed with the Vidame that Madame de Clèves could not possibly keep the resolutions she had taken. They agreed, nevertheless, that they must follow her orders, so that people would not notice his attachment to her, and to prevent the possibility that, out of fear that it would be said she had loved him during her husband's lifetime, she would take a course of action which she might later feel obliged to maintain.

The Duc de Nemours resolved to follow the King. It was a journey he could not avoid anyway. He decided to leave without even attempting to catch a glimpse of Madame de Clèves from the place where he had previously watched her. He asked the Vidame to speak to her in his favor. What an infinite number of reasons did he give him to persuade her to overcome her scruples! After all this discussion, much of the night had passed before the Duc de Nemours thought of leaving the Vidame in peace.

Madame de Clèves was in no state of mind to find any peace either. It was so unusual for her to depart from the restraint she had always imposed upon herself—to allow someone to tell her he loved her and to admit that she loved him—that she hardly recognized herself. She was astonished at what she had done. She repented it—she was happy about it—all her feelings were full of love and anguish. She considered once again the reasons for her duty which put obstacles in the way of her happiness. She was saddened to find them so strong, and she repented having explained them so clearly to the Duc de Nemours. Although the idea of marrying him had occurred to her as soon as she had seen him in the garden, it had not made the same impression on her as the conversation she had just had with him. At times it was difficult for her to believe that she would be unhappy in marrying him. She would have liked to believe that she was mistaken—that there was no basis for past scruples or future fears. At other moments, reason and duty revealed to her so many things to the contrary that she was rapidly brought to the resolution never to remarry and never again to see the Duc de Nemours. But this resolution did violence to a heart as deeply touched as was hers, and as recently given over to the charms of love. Finally, to calm herself down a bit, she decided that she need not yet force herself to take such a decisive step. Propriety itself gave her a certain amount of time to make up her mind. But she resolved to remain firm in her decision not to have any further correspondence with the Duc de Nemours.

The Vidame came to see her and pleaded the Duc's case with great spirit and earnestness. He could not make her change her conduct nor what she imposed upon the Duc de Nemours. She said that she intended to remain as she was. She knew that this intention was difficult to carry out, but she hoped to have the strength to do so. She made him see how completely she was convinced of the opinion that the Duc de Nemours caused her husband's death, and how strongly she was persuaded that she would be acting contrary to her duty if she married him. Therefore the Vidame was afraid that it would be very difficult to change her mind. However, he did not reveal his fears to the Duc, but rather in repeating his conversation with Madame de Clèves, he left the Duc with all the hopes that a man who is beloved can reasonably have.

They left the next morning and went to rejoin the King. At the request of the Duc de Nemours, the Vidame wrote to Madame de Clèves. In the second letter from the Vidame to her which followed swiftly on the first, the Duc penned some sentences in his own handwriting. But Madame de Clèves was determined to keep the rules she had imposed on herself, and fearing the accidents that could happen to correspondence, she instructed the Vidame not to write about the Duc de Nemours or she would refuse to receive his letters. Her commands were so definite that even the Duc begged the Vidame not to mention him.

The Court was to escort the Queen of Spain as far as Poitou. During this absence, Madame de Clèves remained by herself. The further she was removed from the Duc de Nemours and everything that could remind her of him, the more she cherished the memory of the Prince de Clèves. Her reasons for not marrying the Duc de Nemours seemed strong as far as her duty was concerned and insurmountable for her peace of mind. The likelihood of the Duc's ceasing to love her and the evils of jealousy which appeared inevitable, showed her the certain unhappiness to which she would be subjecting herself in such a marriage. But she also recognized the impossibility of resisting the most charming man in the world, who loved and was loved by her, especially as neither virtue nor propriety required her to do so. She decided that only absence and distance from him could give her some strength. She discovered that she needed this distance not only to maintain her resolution not to marry him, but also to prevent herself from seeing the Duc de Nemours. She decided to take a rather long trip to spend the time that propriety required her to live in retirement. Her large estate in the Pyrenées seemed to her the best place she could choose. She left a few days before the Court returned. Before leaving, she wrote to the Vidame, asking that no one seek news of her or write to her.

The Duc de Nemours was as afflicted by this journey as another man would have been by the death of his mistress. The thought of being deprived of the sight of her, after having just had the pleasure of seeing her moved by his love, caused him great unhappiness. In the meantime he could only grieve, but his grief augmented considerably. Madame de Clèves, whose mind had been so agitated, fell into a serious illness as soon as she reached home. When the news reached the Court, the Duc de Nemours was inconsolable. In his sorrow and despair he went to extravagant extremes. The Vidame had great difficulty preventing him from revealing his feelings in public. He had equal difficulty in restraining him from going to find out about her himself. The Vidame's close relationship to Madame de Clèves and his devotion to her, permitted him to send messengers and find out about her. Finally, they learned that she was out of danger. But she remained in a languishing illness which left little hope for her life.

Such a long and close view of death made Madame de Clèves view the things of this life in quite a different light than she had seen them when she had been healthy. The inevitability of death, to which she felt herself so close, taught her to detach herself from everything, and the length of her illness made this detachment a habit. When she recovered from her illness, she discovered, nevertheless, that the image of the Duc de Nemours had still not been banished from her heart. But, to defend herself against him, she called to her aid all the reasons she believed she had for never marrying him. A tremendous struggle took place within her. Finally, she overcame the remains of her love which had been weakened by her illness. Thoughts of death recalled the memory of the Prince de Clèves. This memory, which was in harmony with her own sense of duty, impressed itself forcefully upon her heart. The passions and involvements of the world appeared to her as they do to those who have a distant and detached view of them.

Her health, which remained quite weakened, enabled her to maintain her decision. But, fearing the effects of chance on the sincerest intentions, she did not wish to risk destroying her own, nor did she wish to risk returning to the place where the man she loved, lived. She retired to a convent on the pretext of needing a change of air, without letting it appear that she had definitely intended to renounce the Court.

As soon as the Duc de Nemours received the news, he felt the seriousness of her retreat and recognized its importance. At that moment, he realized that he had nothing more to hope. This presentiment, however, did not prevent him from trying everything to make Madame de Clèves return. He had the Queen write to her. He had the Vidame write to her and visit her, but all in vain. The Vidame saw her. She did not admit that she had made up her mind, but he guessed that she would never return. Finally, the Duc de Nemours went to see her himself on the pretext of taking the baths. She was extremely upset and surprised to learn of his arrival. She sent him word by a worthy person whom she loved, that she wished him to understand if she did not expose herself to the dangers of seeing him, and of destroying by his presence the sentiments which she felt she ought to keep. She wanted him to know that to give way to her feelings would be fatal to her duty and to her peace of mind. She was so indifferent to all the other things in the world that she had renounced them forever and was thinking only of the next life. She only wished to see him in the same state of mind.

The Duc de Nemours thought that he would die of grief in the presence of the person who told him this. He begged her twenty times to return to Madame de Clèves and arrange for him to see her. But this person told him that Madame de Clèves had not only forbidden her to bring any message from him, but had even requested her not to repeat their conversation. Finally, the Duc had to depart. He was as overcome with sorrow as a man could be who had lost all his hopes of seeing again the woman he loved with the most violent, the most natural, and the best deserved passion.

But he did not let himself get discouraged. He did everything he could to make her change her mind. At last, when many years had passed, time and absence softened his sorrow and extinguished his passion. Madam de Clèves gave no indication of returning. She spent part of each year in the convent and the rest at home, but in a retreat and in occupations more holy than those of the strictest convents. Her life, which was quite short, left examples of inimitable virtue.

MARY ROWLANDSON
[C. 1635–C. 1711]

Mary White Rowlandson gave her account of her captivity among the Wampanoag Indians a title that makes clear her purpose in writing: *The Sovereignty and Goodness of God, Together with the Faithfulness of His Promises Displayed; Being a Narrative of the Captivity and Restoration of Mrs. Mary Rowlandson*. A lively combination of Christian testimony and harrowing true adventure tale, the narrative sold briskly into the late nineteenth century and became the model for hundreds of captivity narratives to follow, but the text fascinates readers today for quite different reasons than Rowlandson intended. It is an early personal account written from the European and female perspective of a close encounter between white and American Indian people; moreover, the encounter mostly happens not among the lanes and houses of the white settlements, but on the native American ground of forest and swamp. The *Narrative* suggests some of the disjunctions between American Indian and European values. Rowlandson herself is a member of a community that conceives of itself as striving to become a Christian utopian settlement. In Rowlandson's Massachusetts, women are expected not to call attention to themselves; despite the community's belief in Christian charity, it is very much a capitalist society. Rowlandson is forcibly snatched into an enemy society where feisty behavior in women is rewarded, where women are accorded high status and may even be leaders, and where the sharing of all goods among the group is an absolute ethic. The *Narrative* reflects Rowlandson's struggles to accommodate these facts of life among the Wampanoag.

LIFE

We know very little about Mary White Rowlandson beyond what she tells us in her narrative. The daughter of a wealthy Puritan landowner named John White, she was born about 1635 in England, and probably was brought to Salem, Massachusetts, as a child. John White became one of the founders of the town of Lancaster, and around 1656 Mary married Joseph Rowlandson, the first minister of that town. We know of four children born to the couple; the death of the youngest during the events of 1676 is described in the *Narrative*. After her ransom from captivity, Mary Rowlandson moved with her husband to Wethersfield, Connecticut, where records show she was given a pension after his death in 1678. She probably lived until about 1711. Although the *Narrative* was not printed until 1682, it was probably composed soon after the events, and with Mr. Rowlandson's encouragement; it was originally bound with an accompanying sermon by him.

WORK

Rowlandson's story belongs to the tradition of Puritan spiritual autobiography. In the words of John Winthrop, the governor of Massachusetts Bay Colony, the New England Puritans were about the business of founding "a City on a Hill," a Christian utopian community intended to be a sort of earthly head start on the New Jerusalem promised in *Revelations*. Like Eden and like the old Jerusalem, the utopia in Massachusetts was threatened. When Puritans wrote in their journals of walking abroad in the New England forests and catching a whiff of brimstone, they were not being metaphorical; many believed that the native peoples were "imps," agents of the devil, and that the forest beyond their cleared fields was the province of the Prince of Darkness. In keeping with their sense of themselves as a chosen people under siege, Puritans practiced a rigorous self-examination of both their private lives and the histories of their communities. They produced vast numbers of diaries, journals, spiritual autobiographies, and histories, for they were zealous to monitor their own conduct and to search their own stories for signs of God's providence at work—and for signs of Satan's inroads as well. Such is Rowlandson's understanding of autobiography and of New England history; this was the sort of narrative she aimed to write, one that principally revealed God's chastising or merciful hand in events.

The origins of the raids and captivities recounted in the *Narrative* predate the White and Rowlandson family presence in Massachusetts. In the 1620s, the great Wampanoag chief Massasoit had generously aided the first English colonists; Massasoit figures in sentimental First Thanksgiving pageants as the quintessential friendly Indian chief. By 1676, Massasoit and most of the original Plymouth Plantation settlers were dead, and their descendants were engaged in a more hard-eyed and desperate confrontation. Massasoit's son, the young

Wampanoag chief Metacomet, who had been given the English name of Philip by the colonists, had come to see that it was not possible to deal with the English on equal terms. He understood that if his people lost their land base to the rapidly expanding English settlements, it would mean the end of the Wampanoag way of life. Metacomet forged an alliance among the leaders of Algonquin-speaking tribes in Massachusetts and Rhode Island, principally with his former sister-in-law Weetamoo, leader of the Rhode Island Pocasset tribe, the woman into whose service Mary Rowlandson would be given during her captivity. Benjamin Church, the great colonial military strategist, called Weetamoo "next after Philip in the making of this war." During the winter of 1675-1676, the Algonquin resistance movement nearly succeeded in routing the English colonists from American shores. Metacomet's forces attacked many white towns, including Lancaster, which they set afire on February 20, 1676, when Rowlandson was captured; Rowlandson gives a different date because she is using the Julian calendar.

There is a conflict in the narrative between the sort of story Rowlandson believes she ought to tell and the story she feels compelled to tell. In her independent behavior during her captivity and in the act of writing for publication about her adventures, she is doing something extraordinary in her society. She is a woman giving public testimony, and she ought to be doing so only to glorify God. But she cannot contain the proud note in her voice as she recounts how she recovers from the trauma of her capture and the death of her baby and how she creates for herself an economic and social niche, which she is able to do because the Wampanoag admire her clever needlework and her resolute spirit. Rowlandson understandably thinks of her captors as instruments of Satan, but as the narrative progresses we begin to discern their humanity through her words. Even at the beginning of the trek, when she is almost mad with shock and grief at the death of her baby, we see the Wampanoag with considerable psychological skill persuade her to leave the dead child behind and turn her attention back to the necessary business of wilderness survival. Toward the end of her narrative, although she struggles to shape her adventures into the story of a Christian soul sustained by God while in the clutches of evil, she feels obligated to report that among these "savages" she has witnessed no sexual violence, and that she has seen no one, native or captive, starve among them because they share with one another whatever food they have.

Rowlandson comes genuinely to admire Metacomet, and she praises other American Indian people for their endurance or their charity, but she simply cannot stand her "mistress" Weetamoo, whom she is rather loosely obligated to serve. We know from Benjamin Church's account and from Algonquin speakers' oral tradition of Weetamoo's beauty, her delight in finery, her pride of bearing, her skill at leading whole groups of children and elders stealthily through enemy lines to safety, of the loving regard in which people of many tribes held her. Rowlandson has no way to conceptualize Weetamoo's actual high status within the group as a chief in her own right; she can only see Weetamoo as a "proud hussy." Weetamoo galls Rowlandson not only because they are temporarily set against each other as captive and mistress. Weetamoo's beauty and sexuality, her ornate dress, her air of authority, the attributes her own people value in her because they augment their collective spiritual power—all these are as alien to Rowlandson as the eating of horse hooves and acorns. But many white women who experienced captivity from the sixteenth through the nineteenth centuries came to wish for themselves the degree of freedom and independence American Indian women enjoyed. As Benjamin Franklin himself pointed out, one great problem faced by European colonists was that captured women and children—although not usually grown men—once they had spent some time with American Indians, often declined to be ransomed or, if ransomed, would "take the first good Opportunity of escaping again into the Woods, from whence there is no reclaiming them."

The Algonquin resistance did not last for very long after Rowlandson's release in May of 1676. By late summer, both Weetamoo and Metacomet were dead, their heads impaled upon poles in the Taunton stockade. We are fortunate to have this glimpse of three extraordinary people—Metacomet, Weetamoo, and Rowlandson herself—at this crux in their lives. The *Narrative* does not, perhaps, teach readers of today a great deal about the operations of Providence, as Rowlandson intended, but it does reveal a lot about two very different cultures in mortal conflict, and about the human relationships that may be established even under such desperate circumstances.

SUGGESTED READINGS

Russell Bourne's *The Red King's Rebellion; Racial Politics in New England, 1675–1676* (1990) is a good account of Metacomet's war and the events surrounding it. Annette Kolodny, in *The Land Before Her: Fantasy and Experience of the American Frontiers, 1630– 1860* (1984), gives a fascinating feminist critical and historical reading of captivity narratives by women.

Narrative of the Captivity and Restoration of Mrs. Mary Rowlandson

On the tenth of February 1675[1] came the Indians with great numbers upon Lancaster. Their first coming was about sunrising. Hearing the noise of some guns, we looked out; several houses were burning and the smoke ascending to heaven. There were five persons taken in one house; the father and the mother and a sucking child, they knocked on the head; the other two they took and carried away alive. There were two others, who, being out of their garrison upon some occasion, were set upon; one was knocked on the head, the other escaped. Another there was who running along was shot and wounded and fell down; he begged of them his life, promising them money (as they told me), but they would not hearken to him but knocked him in [the] head, stripped him naked, and split open his bowels. Another, seeing many of the Indians about his barn, ventured and went out, but was quickly shot down. There were three others belonging to the same garrison who were killed; the Indians, getting up upon the roof of the barn, had advantage to shoot down upon them over their fortification. Thus these murderous wretches went on, burning and destroying before them.

At length they came and beset our own house, and quickly it was the dolefullest day that ever mine eyes saw. The house stood upon the edge of a hill. Some of the Indians got behind the hill, others into the barn, and others behind anything that could shelter them; from all which places they shot against the house so that the bullets seemed to fly like hail; and quickly they wounded one man among us, then another, and then a third. About two hours (according to my observation in that amazing time) they had been about the house before they prevailed to fire it (which they did with flax and hemp which they brought out of the barn, and there being no defense about the house, only two flankers[2] at two opposite corners and one of

---

[1] 1676, by our present calendar.
[2] Fortifications.

them not finished). They fired it once, and one ventured out and quenched it, but they quickly fired it again, and that took.

Now is that dreadful hour come that I have often heard of (in time of war as it was the case of others), but now mine eyes see it. Some in our house were fighting for their lives, others wallowing in their blood, the house on fire over our heads, and the bloody heathen ready to knock us on the head if we stirred out. Now might we hear mothers and children crying out for themselves and one another, "Lord, what shall we do?" Then I took my children (and one of my sisters, hers) to go forth and leave the house, but as soon as we came to the door and appeared, the Indians shot so thick that the bullets rattled against the house as if one had taken an handful of stones and threw them, so that we were fain to give back. We had six stout dogs belonging to our garrison, but none of them would stir, although another time, if any Indian had come to the door, they were ready to fly upon him and tear him down. The Lord hereby would make us the more to acknowledge His hand and to see that our help is always in Him. But out we must go, the fire increasing and coming along behind us roaring, and the Indians gaping before us with their guns, spears, and hatchets to devour us. No sooner were we out of the house, but my brother-in-law (being before wounded, in defending the house, in or near the throat) fell down dead; whereat the Indians scornfully shouted, hallooed, and were presently upon him, stripping off his clothes. The bullets flying thick, one went through my side, and the same (as would seem) through the bowels and hand of my dear child in my arms. One of my elder sister's children, named William, had then his leg broken, which the Indians perceiving, they knocked him on the head. Thus were we butchered by those merciless heathen, standing amazed, with the blood running down to our heels.

My eldest sister being yet in the house and seeing those woeful sights, the infidels hailing mothers one way and children another and some wallowing in their blood, and her elder son telling her that her son William was dead and myself was wounded, she said, "And, Lord, let me die with them." Which was no sooner said, but she was struck with a bullet and fell down dead over the threshold. I hope she is reaping the fruit of her good labors, being faithful to the service of God in her place. In her younger years she lay under much trouble upon spiritual accounts till it pleased God to make that precious scripture take hold of her heart, 2 Cor. 12:9, "And he said unto me, my grace is sufficient for thee." More than twenty years after I have heard her tell how sweet and comfortable that place was to her. But to return: the Indians laid hold of us, pulling me one way and the children another, and said, "Come go along with us." I told them they would kill me. They answered, if I were willing to go along with them they would not hurt me.

Oh, the doleful sight that now was to behold at this house! "Come, behold the works of the Lord, what desolation He has made in the earth."[3] Of thirty-seven persons who were in this one house, none escaped either present death or a bitter captivity save only one, who might say as he, Job 1:15, "And I only am escaped alone to tell the news." There were twelve killed, some shot, some stabbed with their spears, some knocked down with their hatchets. When we are in prosperity, oh, the little that we think of such dreadful sights, and to see our dear friends and relations lie bleeding out their heart-blood upon the ground! There was one who was chopped into the head with a hatchet and stripped naked, and yet was crawling up and down. It is a solemn sight to see so many Christians lying in their blood,

---

[3] Psalm 46:8.

some here and some there, like a company of sheep torn by wolves, all of them stripped naked by a company of hell-hounds, roaring, singing, ranting and insulting, as if they would have torn our very hearts out. Yet the Lord by his almighty power preserved a number of us from death, for there were twenty-four of us taken alive and carried captive.

I had often before this said that if the Indians should come I should choose rather to be killed by them than taken alive, but when it came to the trial, my mind changed; their glittering weapons so daunted my spirit that I chose rather to go along with those (as I may say) ravenous beasts than that moment to end my days. And that I may the better declare what happened to me during that grievous captivity, I shall particularly speak of the several removes[4] we had up and down the wilderness.

THE FIRST REMOVE

Now away we must go with those barbarous creatures with our bodies wounded and bleeding and our hearts no less than our bodies. About a mile we went that night up upon a hill within sight of the town where they intended to lodge. There was hard by a vacant house (deserted by the English before, for fear of the Indians). I asked them whether I might not lodge in the house that night, to which they answered, "What, will you love English men still?" This was the dolefullest night that ever my eyes saw. Oh, the roaring and singing and dancing and yelling of those black creatures in the night, which made the place a lively resemblance of hell. And as miserable was the waste that was there made of horses, cattle, sheep, swine, calves, lambs, roasting pigs, and fowl (which they had plundered in the town), some roasting, some lying and burning, and some boiling to feed our merciless enemies, who were joyful enough though we were disconsolate. To add to the dolefulness of the former day and the dismalness of the present night, my thoughts ran upon my losses and sad bereaved condition. All was gone: my husband gone (at least separated from me, he being in the Bay,[5] and to add to my grief, the Indians told me they would kill him as he came homeward), my children gone, my relations and friends gone, our house and home and all our comforts within door and without, all was gone except my life, and I knew not but the next moment that might go too. There remained nothing to me but one poor wounded babe, and it seemed at present worse than death that it was in such a pitiful condition bespeaking compassion, and I had no refreshing for it nor suitable things to revive it. Little do many think what is the savageness and brutishness of this barbarous enemy, ay, even those that seem to profess more than others among them when the English have fallen into their hands.

Those seven that were killed at Lancaster the summer before upon a Sabbath day and the one that was afterward killed upon a week day were slain and mangled in a barbarous manner by one-eye John and Marlborough's praying Indians which Capt. Mosely brought to Boston, as the Indians told me.[6]

---

[4]A remove is a journey; metaphorically, she means to emphasize that she is being removed further and further from the center of Christianity and Euro-American civilization.

[5]Boston, the capital of Massachusetts Bay Colony. Rowlandson's husband had gone there to ask for reinforcements for the defense of Lancaster.

[6]Praying Indians were those who were counted by the colonists as Christian converts. Many of them renounced the faith and joined the American Indian forces during King Philip's War.

THE SECOND REMOVE[7]

But now, the next morning, I must turn my back upon the town and travel with them into the vast and desolate wilderness, I knew not whither. It is not my tongue or pen can express the sorrows of my heart and bitterness of my spirit that I had at this departure, but God was with me in a wonderful manner, carrying me along and bearing up my spirit that it did not quite fail. One of the Indians carried my poor wounded babe upon a horse; it went moaning all along, "I shall die, I shall die." I went on foot after it with sorrow that cannot be expressed. At length I took it off the horse and carried it in my arms till my strength failed, and I fell down with it. Then they set me upon a horse with my wounded child in my lap. And there being no furniture[8] upon the horse['s] back, as we were going down a steep hill, we both fell over the horse's head, at which they like inhuman creatures laughed and rejoiced to see it, though I thought we should there have ended our days, as overcome with so many difficulties. But the Lord renewed my strength still and carried me along that I might see more of His power; yea, so much that I could never have thought of had I not experienced it.

After this it quickly began to snow, and when night came on, they stopped. And now down I must sit in the snow by a little fire and a few boughs behind me, with my sick child in my lap and calling much for water, being now (through the wound) fallen into a violent fever. My own wound also [was] growing so stiff that I could scarce sit down or rise up; yet so it must be that I must sit all this cold winter night upon the cold, snowy ground with my sick child in my arms, looking that every hour would be the last of its life, and having no Christian friend near me either to comfort or help me. Oh, I may see the wonderful power of God that my spirit did not utterly sink under my affliction! Still the Lord upheld me with His gracious and merciful spirit, and we were both alive to see the light of the next morning.

THE THIRD REMOVE[9]

The morning being come, they prepared to go on their way. One of the Indians got up upon a horse, and they set me up behind him with my poor sick babe in my lap. A very wearisome and tedious day I had of it, what with my own wound and my child's being so exceedingly sick in a lamentable condition with her wound. It may be easily judged what a poor feeble condition we were in, there being not the least crumb of refreshing that came within either of our mouths from Wednesday night to Saturday night except only a little cold water. This day in the afternoon, about an hour by sun, we came to the place where they intended, *viz.* an Indian town called Wenimesset, nor[th]ward of Quabaug. When we were come, oh, the number of pagans (now merciless enemies) that there came about me that I may say as David, Psal. 27:13, "I had fainted, unless I had believed," etc. The next day was the Sabbath. I then remembered how careless I had been of God's holy time, how many Sabbaths I had lost and misspent and how evilly I had walked in God's sight, which lay so close unto my spirit that it was easy for me to see how righteous it was with God to cut the thread of my life and cast me out of His presence forever. Yet

---

[7] To Princeton, Massachusetts.
[8] Saddle.
[9] To a place near New Braintree, Massachusetts. Rowlandson was held here February 12–27.

the Lord still showed mercy to me and upheld me, and as He wounded me with one hand, so He healed me with the other.

This day there came to me one Robert Pepper (a man belonging to Roxbury), who was taken in Captain Beers his fight and had been now a considerable time with the Indians and up with them almost as far as Albany to see King Philip, as he told me, and was now very lately come into these parts. Hearing, I say, that I was in this Indian town, he obtained leave to come and see me. He told me he himself was wounded in the leg at Captain Beers his fight and was not able some time to go, but, as they carried him, and as he took oaken leaves and laid to his wound, and through the blessing of God, he was able to travel again. Then I took oaken leaves and laid to my side, and, with the blessing of God, it cured me also. Yet before the cure was wrought, I may say, as it is in Psal. 38:5, 6, "My wounds stink and are corrupt, I am troubled, I am bowed down greatly, I go mourning all the day long." I sat much alone with a poor wounded child in my lap, which moaned night and day, having nothing to revive the body or cheer the spirits of her, but instead of that sometimes one Indian would come and tell me one hour that, "Your master will knock your child in the head." And then a second, and then a third, "Your master will quickly knock your child in the head."

This was the comfort I had from them. "Miserable comforters are ye all," as he said.[10] Thus nine days I sat upon my knees with my babe in my lap till my flesh was raw again; my child being even ready to depart this sorrowful world, they bade me carry it out to another wigwam (I suppose because they would not be troubled with such spectacles), whither I went with a heavy heart, and down I sat with the picture of death in my lap. About two hours in the night my sweet babe like a lamb departed this life on Feb. 18, 1675, it being about six years and five months old. It was nine days from the first wounding in this miserable condition without any refreshing of one nature or other except a little cold water. I cannot but take notice how at another time I could not bear to be in the room where any dead person was, but now the case is changed; I must and could lie down by my dead babe side by side all the night after. I have thought since of the wonderful goodness of God to me in preserving me in the use of my reason and senses in that distressed time, that I did not use wicked and violent means to end my own miserable life.

In the morning, when they understood that my child was dead, they sent for me home to my master's wigwam. (By my master in this writing must be understood Quanopin, who was a sagamore and married [to] King Philip's wife's sister,[11] not that he first took me, but I was sold to him by another Narragansett Indian, who took me when first I came out of the garrison.) I went to take up my dead child in my arms to carry it with me, but they bid me let it alone. There was no resisting, but go I must and leave it. When I had been at my master's wigwam, I took the first opportunity I could get to go look after my dead child. When I came, I asked them what they had done with it. Then they told me it was upon the hill. Then they went and showed me where it was, where I saw the ground was newly digged, and there they told me they had buried it. There I left that child in the wilderness and must commit it and myself also in this wilderness condition to Him who is above all.

God having taken away this dear child, I went to see my daughter Mary, who was at this same Indian town at a wigwam not very far off, though we had little liberty or opportunity to see one another. She was about ten years old and taken

---

[10]"He" is Job, in Job 16:2.

[11]Quanopin or Quinnapin was married to Weetamoo, Philip's sister-in-law by a previous marriage. Weetamoo was herself the respected leader of the Pocassets. *Sagamore* is the Algonquin term for a subordinate chief.

from the door at first by a praying Indian and afterward sold for a gun. When I came in sight, she would fall a-weeping, at which they were provoked and would not let me come near her, but bade me be gone, which was a heart-cutting word to me. I had one child dead, another in the wilderness I knew not where; the third they would not let me come near to. "Me," as he said, "have ye bereaved of my children, Joseph is not, and Simeon is not, and ye will take Benjamin also, all these things are against me."[12] I could not sit still in this condition, but kept walking from one place to another. And as I was going along, my heart was even overwhelmed with the thoughts of my condition and that I should have children and a nation which I knew not ruled over them. Whereupon I earnestly entreated the Lord that He would consider my low estate and show me a token for good, and if it were His blessed will, some sign and hope of some relief.

And indeed quickly the Lord answered in some measure my poor prayers; for, as I was going up and down mourning and lamenting my condition, my son [Joseph] came to me and asked me how I did. I had not seen him before since the destruction of the town, and I knew not where he was till I was informed by himself that he was amongst a smaller parcel of Indians whose place was about six miles off. With tears in his eyes he asked me whether his sister Sarah was dead and told me he had seen his sister Mary and prayed me that I would not be troubled in reference to himself. The occasion of his coming to see me at this time was this: there was, as I said, about six miles from us a small plantation of Indians, where it seems he had been during his captivity, and at this time there were some forces of the Indians gathered out of our company and some also from them (among whom was my son's master) to go to assault and burn Medfield.[13] In this time of the absence of his master his dame brought him to see me. I took this to be some gracious answer to my earnest and unfeigned desire.

The next day, *viz.* to this, the Indians returned from Medfield (all the company, for those that belonged to the other small company came through the town that now we were at). But before they came to us, oh, the outrageous roaring and whooping that there was! They began their din about a mile before they came to us. By their noise and whooping they signified how many they had destroyed, which was at that time twenty-three. Those that were with us at home were gathered together as soon as they heard the whooping, and every time that the other went over their number, these at home gave [such] a shout that the very earth rung again. And thus they continued till those that had been upon the expedition were come up to the sagamore's wigwam. And then, oh, the hideous insulting and triumphing that there was over some Englishmen's scalps that they had taken (as their manner is) and brought with them!

I cannot but take notice of the wonderful mercy of God to me in those afflictions in sending me a Bible. One of the Indians that came from Medfield fight [who] had brought some plunder came to me and asked me if I would have a Bible; he had got one in his basket. I was glad of it and asked him whether he thought the Indians would let me read. He answered, "Yes." So I took the Bible, and in that melancholy time it came into my mind to read first the 28 chapter of Deut., which I did, and when I had read it, my dark heart wrought on this manner, that there was no mercy for me, that the blessings were gone and the curses come in their room, and that I had lost my opportunity. But the Lord helped me still to go on reading till I came to chapter 30, the seven first verses, where I found there was mercy promised again if we would return to him by repentance, and, though we

---

[12] Genesis 42:36.
[13] Medfield was attacked on February 21, 1676.

were scattered from one end of the earth to the other, yet the Lord would gather us together and turn all those curses upon our enemies. I do not desire to live to forget this scripture and what comfort it was to me.

Now the Indians began to talk of removing from this place, some one way and some another. There were now besides myself nine English captives in this place, all of them children except one woman. I got an opportunity to go and take my leave of them, they being to go one way and I another; I asked them whether they were earnest with God for deliverance. They told me they did as they were able, and it was some comfort to me that the Lord stirred up children to look to Him. The woman, *viz.* Goodwife[14] Joslin, told me she should never see me again and that she could find in her heart to run away; I wished her not to run away by any means, for we were near thirty miles from any English town and she very big with child and had but one week to reckon and another child in her arms, two years old, and bad rivers there were to go over, and we were feeble with our poor and coarse entertainment. I had my Bible with me; I pulled it out and asked her whether she would read. We opened the Bible and lighted on Psalm 27, in which psalm we especially took notice of that *ver. ult.,* "Wait on the Lord, be of good courage, and He shall strengthen thine heart, wait I say on the Lord."

THE FOURTH REMOVE[15]

And now I must part with that little company I had. Here I parted from my daughter Mary (whom I never saw again till I saw her in Dorchester, returned from captivity) and from four little cousins and neighbors, some of which I never saw afterward. The Lord only knows the end of them. Amongst them also was that poor woman before mentioned, who came to a sad end, as some of the company told me in my travel. She, having much grief upon her spirit about her miserable condition, being so near her time, she would be often asking the Indians to let her go home; they, not being willing to that and yet vexed with her importunity, gathered a great company together about her and stripped her naked and set her in the midst of them. And when they had sung and danced about her (in their hellish manner) as long as they pleased, they knocked her on [the] head and the child in her arms with her. When they had done that, they made a fire and put them both into it and told the other children that were with them that if they attempted to go home they would serve them in like manner. The children said she did not shed one tear, but prayed all the while. But to return to my own journey, we traveled about half a day or little more and came to a desolate place in the wilderness where there were no wigwams or inhabitants before; we came about the middle of the afternoon to this place, cold and wet, and snowy, and hungry, and weary, and no refreshing for man but the cold ground to sit on and our poor Indian cheer.

Heartaching thoughts here I had about my poor children, who were scattered up and down among the wild beasts of the forest. My head was light and dizzy (either through hunger or hard lodging or trouble or all together), my knees feeble, my body raw by sitting double night and day, that I cannot express to man the affliction that lay upon my spirit, but the Lord helped me at that time to express it to Himself. I opened my Bible to read, and the Lord brought that precious scripture to me, Jer. 31:16, "Thus saith the Lord, 'Refrain thy voice from weeping and thine eyes from tears, for thy work shall be rewarded, and they shall come again from the land of

---

[14] *Goodwife* is analogous to the modern *Mrs.*

[15] To Petersham, Massachusetts, where Rowlandson stayed from February 28 to March 3.

the enemy.'" This was a sweet cordial to me when I was ready to faint; many and many a time have I sat down and wept sweetly over this scripture. At this place we continued about four days.

THE FIFTH REMOVE[16]

The occasion (as I thought) of their moving at this time was the English army, it being near and following them. For they went as if they had gone for their lives for some considerable way, and then they made a stop and chose some of their stoutest men and sent them back to hold the English army in play whilst the rest escaped. And then, like Jehu,[17] they marched on furiously with their old and with their young; some carried their old decrepit mothers; some carried one and some another. Four of them carried a great Indian upon a bier, but, going through a thick wood with him, they were hindered and could make no haste; whereupon they took him upon their backs and carried him, one at a time, till they came to Bacquaug River. Upon a Friday a little after noon we came to this river. When all the company was come up and were gathered together, I thought to count the number of them, but they were so many and, being somewhat in motion, it was beyond my skill. In this travel, because of my wound, I was somewhat favored in my load; I carried only my knitting work and two quarts of parched meal. Being very faint, I asked my mistress to give me one spoonful of the meal, but she would not give me a taste. They quickly fell to cutting dry trees to make rafts to carry them over the river, and soon my turn came to go over. By the advantage of some brush which they had laid upon the raft to sit upon, I did not wet my foot (when many of themselves at the other end were mid-leg deep) which cannot be but acknowledged as a favor of God to my weakened body, it being a very cold time. I was not before acquainted with such kind of doings or dangers. "When thou passeth through the waters, I will be with thee, and through the rivers they shall not overflow thee," Isai. 43:2. A certain number of us got over the river that night, but it was the night after the Sabbath before all the company was got over. On the Saturday they boiled an old horse's leg which they had got, and so we drank of the broth as soon as they thought it was ready, and when it was almost all gone, they filled it up again.

The first week of my being among them I hardly ate anything; the second week, I found my stomach grow very faint for want of something; and yet it was very hard to get down their filthy trash. But the third week, though I could think how formerly my stomach would turn against this or that and I could starve and die before I could eat such things, yet they were sweet and savory to my taste. I was at this time knitting a pair of white cotton stockings for my mistress and had not yet wrought upon a Sabbath day. When the Sabbath came, they bade me go to work; I told them it was the Sabbath day and desired them to let me rest and told them I would do as much more tomorrow, to which they answered me they would break my face. And here I cannot but take notice of the strange providence of God in preserving the heathen. They were many hundreds, old and young, some sick and some lame, many had papooses at their backs. The greatest number at this time with us were squaws, and they traveled with all they had, bag and baggage, and yet they got over this river aforesaid. And on Monday they set their wigwams on fire, and away they went. On that very day came the English army after them to this river and saw the smoke of their wigwams, and yet this river put a stop to them. God

---

[16]To Orange, Massachusetts, March 3–5.
[17]Jehu drove "furiously" in II Kings 9:20.

did not give them courage or activity to go over after us; we were not ready for so great a mercy as victory and deliverance. If we had been, God would have found out a way for the English to have passed this river, as well as for the Indians with their squaws and children and all their luggage. "Oh that my people had hearkened to me, and Israel had walked in my ways, I should soon have subdued their enemies and turned my hand against their adversaries," Psal. 81:13, 14.

THE SIXTH REMOVE[18]

On Monday (as I said) they set their wigwams on fire and went away. It was a cold morning, and before us there was a great brook with ice on it; some waded through it up to the knees and higher, but others went till they came to a beaver dam, and I amongst them, where through the good providence of God I did not wet my foot. I went along that day mourning and lamenting, leaving farther my own country and traveling into the vast and howling wilderness, and I understood something of Lot's wife's temptation when she looked back.[19] We came that day to a great swamp by the side of which we took up our lodging that night. When I came to the brow of the hill that looked toward the swamp, I thought we had been come to a great Indian town (though there were none but our own company). The Indians were as thick as the trees: it seemed as if there had been a thousand hatchets going at once. If one looked before one, there was nothing but Indians, and behind one nothing but Indians, and so on either hand, I myself in the midst, and no Christian soul near me, and yet how hath the Lord preserved me in safety. Oh, the experience that I have had of the goodness of God to me and mine!

THE SEVENTH REMOVE[20]

After a restless and hungry night there, we had a wearisome time of it the next day. The swamp by which we lay was, as it were, a deep dungeon and an exceeding high and steep hill before it. Before I got to the top of the hill, I thought my heart and legs and all would have broken and failed me. . . . What through faintness and soreness of body, it was a grievous day of travel to me. As we went along, I saw a place where English cattle had been. That was comfort to me, such as it was. Quickly after that we came to an English path, which so took with me that I thought I could have freely laid down and died. That day, a little after noon, we came to Squakeag, where the Indians quickly spread themselves over the deserted English fields, gleaning what they could find; some picked up ears of wheat that were crickled[21] down; some found ears of Indian corn; some found groundnuts, and others sheaves of wheat that were frozen together in the shock, and went to threshing of them out. Myself got two ears of Indian corn, and whilst I did but turn my back, one of them was stolen from me, which much troubled me. There came an Indian to them at that time with a basket of horse liver. I asked him to give me a piece. "What," says he, "can you eat horse liver?" I told him I would try if he would give a piece, which he did, and I laid it on the coals to roast, but before it was half ready they got half of it away from me, so that I was fain to take

---

[18]To Northfield, Massachusetts.
[19]Lot's wife was transformed into a pillar of salt when she looked wistfully back at her home as she left the wicked city of Sodom in Genesis 19:26.
[20]Near Northfield.
[21]Crushed.

the rest and eat it as it was with the blood about my mouth, and yet a savory bit it was to me: "For to the hungry soul every bitter thing is sweet."[22] A solemn sight methought it was to see fields of wheat and Indian corn forsaken and spoiled and the remainders of them to be food for our merciless enemies. That night we had a mess of wheat for our supper.

THE EIGHTH REMOVE[23]

On the morrow morning we must go over the river, i.e. Connecticut, to meet with King Philip. Two canoesful they had carried over; the next turn I myself was to go, but as my foot was upon the canoe to step in, there was a sudden outcry among them, and I must step back. And instead of going over the river, I must go four or five miles up the river farther northward. Some of the Indians ran one way and some another. The cause of this rout was, as I thought, their espying some English scouts who were thereabout. In this travel up the river about noon the company made a stop and sat down, some to eat and others to rest them. As I sat amongst them musing of things past, my son, Joseph, unexpectedly came to me. We asked of each other's welfare, bemoaning our doleful condition and the change that had come upon us. We had husband and father, and children, and sisters, and friends, and relations, and house, and home, and many comforts of this life, but now we may say as Job, "Naked came I out of my mother's womb, and naked shall I return. The Lord gave, and the Lord hath taken away, blessed be the name of the Lord."[24] I asked him whether he would read; he told me he earnestly desired it. I gave him my Bible, and he lighted upon that comfortable scripture, Psal. 118:17, 18, "I shall not die but live and declare the works of the Lord: the Lord hath chastened me sore, yet he hath not given me over to death." "Look here, Mother," says he, "did you read this?" And here I may take occasion to mention one principal ground of my setting forth these lines: even as the psalmist says, to declare the works of the Lord and His wonderful power in carrying us along, preserving us in the wilderness while under the enemy's hand and returning of us in safety again, and His goodness in bringing to my hand so many comfortable and suitable scriptures in my distress.

But to return, we traveled on till night, and in the morning we must go over the river to Philip's crew. When I was in the canoe, I could not but be amazed at the numerous crew of pagans that were on the bank on the other side. When I came ashore, they gathered all about me, I sitting alone in the midst. I observed they asked one another questions and laughed and rejoiced over their gains and victories. Then my heart began to fail and I fell a-weeping, which was the first time to my remembrance that I wept before them. Although I had met with so much affliction and my heart was many times ready to break, yet could I not shed one tear in their sight, but rather had been all this while in a maze and like one astonished. But now I may say as Psal. 137:1, "By the rivers of Babylon there we sat down; yea, we wept when we remembered Zion." There one of them asked me why I wept; I could hardly tell what to say, yet I answered they would kill me. "No," said he, "none will hurt you." Then came one of them and gave me two spoonfuls of meal to comfort me, and another gave me half a pint of peas, which was more worth than many bushels at another time. Then I went to see King Philip. He bade me come in and sit down and asked me whether I would smoke it (a usual compliment nowadays among saints and sinners), but this no way suited me. For though I had formerly used tobacco, yet I had left it ever since I was first taken. It seems to be a bait

---

[22] Proverbs 27:7.   [23] To South Vernon, Vermont.   [24] Job 1:21.

the devil lays to make men lose their precious time. I remember with shame how formerly when I had taken two or three pipes I was presently ready for another, such a bewitching thing it is. But I thank God He has now given me power over it; surely there are many who may be better employed than to lie sucking a stinking tobacco pipe.

Now the Indians gather their forces to go against Northampton. Overnight one went about yelling and hooting to give notice of the design, whereupon they fell to boiling of groundnuts and parching of corn (as many as had it) for their provision, and in the morning away they went. During my abode in this place Philip spoke to me to make a shirt for his boy, which I did, for which he gave me a shilling. I offered the money to my master, but he bade me keep it, and with it I bought a piece of horseflesh. Afterwards he asked me to make a cap for his boy, for which he invited me to dinner. I went, and he gave me a pancake about as big as two fingers; it was made of parched wheat, beaten and fried in bear's grease, but I thought I never tasted pleasanter meat in my life. There was a squaw who spoke to me to make a shirt for her *sannup*[25] for which she gave me a piece of bear. Another asked me to knit a pair of stockings, for which she gave me a quart of peas. I boiled my peas and bear together and invited my master and mistress to dinner, but the proud gossip,[26] because I served them both in one dish, would eat nothing except one bit that he gave her upon the point of his knife.

Hearing that my son was come to this place, I went to see him and found him lying flat upon the ground. I asked him how he could sleep so. He answered me that he was not asleep but at prayer and lay so that they might not observe what he was doing. I pray God he may remember these things now he is returned in safety. At this place (the sun now getting higher), what with the beams and heat of the sun and the smoke of the wigwams, I thought I should have been blind. I could scarce discern one wigwam from another. There was here one Mary Thurston of Medfield, who, seeing how it was with me, lent a hat to wear; but as soon as I was gone, the squaw who owned that Mary Thurston came running after me and got it away again. Here was the squaw that gave me one spoonful of meal. I put it in my pocket to keep it safe, yet notwithstanding, somebody stole it, but put five Indian corns in the room of it,[27] which corns were the greatest provision I had in my travel for one day.

The Indians, returning from Northampton, brought with them some horses, and sheep, and other things which they had taken. I desired them that they would carry me to Albany upon one of those horses and sell me for powder, for so they had sometimes discoursed. I was utterly hopeless of getting home on foot the way that I came. I could hardly bear to think of the many weary steps I had taken to come to this place.

THE NINTH REMOVE[28]

But instead of going either to Albany or homeward, we must go five miles up the river and then go over it. Here we abode awhile. Here lived a sorry Indian who spoke to me to make him a shirt. When I had done it, he would pay me noth-

---

[25]Husband.

[26]Wife. Weetamoo may be observing a menstrual taboo or other sort of taboo pertaining to wartime here.

[27]In place of it.

[28]To a camp near Keene, New Hampshire.

ing. But he living by the riverside where I often went to fetch water, I would often be putting of him in mind and calling for my pay; at last he told me, if I would make another shirt for a papoose not yet born, he would give me a knife, which he did when I had done it. I carried the knife in, and my master asked me to give it him, and I was not a little glad that I had anything that they would accept of and be pleased with. When we were at this place, my master's maid came home; she had been gone three weeks into the Narragansett country to fetch corn where they had stored up some in the ground. She brought home about a peck and [a] half of corn. This was about the time that their great captain, Naananto, was killed in the Narragansett country. My son being now about a mile from me, I asked liberty to go and see him; they bade me go, and away I went. But quickly [I] lost myself, traveling over hills and through swamps, and could not find the way to him. And I cannot but admire at the wonderful power and goodness of God to me in that though I was gone from home and met with all sorts of Indians, and those I had no knowledge of, and there being no Christian soul near me, yet not one of them offered the least imaginable miscarriage to me.

I turned homeward again and met with my master; he showed me the way to my son. When I came to him, I found him not well, and withall he had a boil on his side which much troubled him. We bemoaned one another awhile, as the Lord helped us, and then I returned again. When I was returned, I found myself as unsatisfied as I was before. I went up and down mourning and lamenting, and my spirit was ready to sink with the thoughts of my poor children. My son was ill, and I could not but think of his mournful looks, and no Christian friend was near him to do any office of love for him either for soul or body. And my poor girl, I know not where she was nor whether she was sick or well, or alive or dead. I repaired under these thoughts to my Bible (my great comfort in that time) and that scripture came to my hand, "Cast thy burden upon the Lord, and He shall sustain thee," Psal. 55:22.

But I was fain to go and look after something to satisfy my hunger, and going among the wigwams, I went into one and there found a squaw who showed herself very kind to me and gave me a piece of bear. I put it into my pocket and came home, but could not find an opportunity to broil it for fear they would get it from me, and there it lay all that day and night in my stinking pocket. In the morning I went to the same squaw, who had a kettle of groundnuts boiling; I asked her to let me boil my piece of bear in her kettle, which she did and gave me some groundnuts to eat with it, and I cannot but think how pleasant it was to me. I have sometime seen bear baked very handsomely among the English, and some like it, but the thoughts that it was bear made me tremble, but now that was savory to me that one would think was enough to turn the stomach of a brute creature.

One bitter cold day I could find no room to sit down before the fire. I went out and could not tell what to do, but I went into another wigwam where they were also sitting around the fire, but the squaw laid a skin for me, bid me sit down, gave me some groundnuts, bade me come again, and told me they would buy me if they were able, and yet these were strangers to me that I never saw before.

THE TENTH REMOVE

That day a small part of the company removed about three-quarters of a mile, intending further the next day. When they came to the place where they intended to lodge and had pitched their wigwams, being hungry, I went again back to the place we were before at to get something to eat, being encouraged by the squaw's kindness who bade me come again when I was there. There came an Indian to look after me, who, when he had found me, kicked me all along. I went home and found venison roasting that night, but they would not give me one bit of it. Sometimes I met with favor and sometimes with nothing but frowns.

THE ELEVENTH REMOVE[29]

The next day in the morning they took their travel, intending a day's journey up the river. I took my load at my back, and quickly we came to wade over the river and passed over tiresome and wearisome hills. One hill was so steep that I was fain to creep up upon my knees and to hold by the twigs and bushes to keep myself from falling backward. My head also was so light that I usually reeled as I went, but I hope all these wearisome steps that I have taken are but a forewarning of me to the heavenly rest. "I know, O Lord, that Thy judgments are right, and that Thou in faithfulness hast afflicted me," Psal. 119:71 [actually 75].

THE TWELFTH REMOVE

It was upon a Sabbath-day morning that they prepared for their travel. This morning I asked my master whether he would sell me to my husband; he answered me *nux*,[30] which did much rejoice my spirit. My mistress, before we went, was gone to the burial of a papoose, and, returning, she found me sitting and reading in my Bible. She snatched it hastily out of my hand and threw it out of doors; I ran out and catched it up and put it into my pocket and never let her see it afterward. Then they packed up their things to be gone and gave me my load. I complained it was too heavy, whereupon she gave me a slap in the face and bade me go. I lifted up my heart to God, hoping the redemption was not far off, and the rather because their insolency grew worse and worse.

But the thoughts of my going homeward (for so we bent our course) much cheered my spirit and made my burden seem light and almost nothing at all. But (to my amazement and great perplexity) the scale was soon turned, for when we had gone a little way, on a sudden my mistress gives out. She would go no further but turn back again and said I must go back again with her. And she called her *sannup* and would have had him gone back also, but he would not, but said he would go on and come to us again in three days. My spirit was upon this, I confess, very impatient and almost outrageous. I thought I could as well have died as went back; I cannot declare the trouble that I was in about it, but yet back again I must go. As soon as I had an opportunity, I took my Bible to read, and that quieting scripture came to my hand, Psal. 46:10, "Be still and know that I am God," which stilled my spirit for the present. But a sore time of trial, I concluded, I had to go through, my master being gone, who seemed to me the best friend that I had of an Indian both in cold and hunger, and quickly so it proved. Down I sat with my heart as full as it could hold, and yet so hungry that I could not sit neither. But, going out to see what I could find and walking among the trees, I found six acorns and two chestnuts, which were some refreshment to me. Towards night I gathered me some sticks for my own comfort that I might not lie a-cold, but when we came to lie

---

[29]Near Chesterfield, New Hampshire.   [30]Yes.

down they bade me go out and lie somewhere else, for they had company (they said) come in more than their own. I told them I could not tell where to go; they bade me go look. I told them if I went to another wigwam they would be angry and send me home again. Then one of the company drew his sword and told me he would run me through if I did not go presently. Then was I fain to stoop to this rude fellow and to go out in the night, I knew not whither. Mine eyes have seen that fellow afterwards, walking up and down Boston under the appearance of a friend-Indian, and several others of the like cut.

I went to one wigwam, and they told me they had no room. Then I went to another, and they said the same; at last an old Indian bade me come to him, and his squaw gave me some groundnuts; she gave me also something to lay under my head, and a good fire we had. And through the good providence of God I had a comfortable lodging that night. In the morning another Indian bade me come at night, and he would give me six groundnuts, which I did. We were at this place and time about two miles from Connecticut River. We went in the morning to gather groundnuts, to the river, and went back again that night. I went with a good load at my back (for they, when they went though but a little way, would carry all their trumpery with them); I told them the skin was off my back, but I had no other comforting answer from them than this, that it would be no matter if my head were off too.

THE THIRTEENTH REMOVE[31]

Instead of going toward the Bay, which was that I desired, I must go with them five or six miles down the river into a mighty thicket of brush, where we abode almost a fortnight. Here one asked me to make a shirt for her papoose, for which she gave me a mess of broth which was thickened with meal made of the bark of a tree, and to make it the better she had put into it about a handful of peas and a few roasted groundnuts. I had not seen my son a pretty while, and here was an Indian of whom I made inquiry after him and asked him when he saw him. He answered me that such a time his master roasted him and that himself did eat a piece of him as big as his two fingers and that he was very good meat. But the Lord upheld my spirit under this discouragement, and I considered their horrible addictedness to lying and that there is not one of them that makes the least conscience of speaking of truth. In this place on a cold night as I lay by the fire, I removed a stick that kept the heat from me; a squaw moved it down again, at which I looked up, and she threw a handful of ashes in mine eyes. I thought I should have been quite blinded and have never seen more, but lying down, the water run out of my eyes and carried the dirt with it, that by the morning I recovered my sight again. Yet upon this and the like occasions I hope it is not too much to say with Job, "Have pity upon me, have pity upon me, oh, ye my friends, for the hand of the Lord has touched me."[32]

And here I cannot but remember how many times sitting in their wigwams and musing on things past I should suddenly leap up and run out as if I had been at home, forgetting where I was and what my condition was. But when I was without and saw nothing but wilderness and woods and a company of barbarous heathens, my mind quickly returned to me, which made me think of that spoken concerning

---

[31] To Hinsdale, New Hampshire.   [32] Job 19:21.

Samson, who said, "I will go out and shake myself as at other times, but he wist not that the Lord was departed from him."[33]

About this time I began to think that all my hopes of restoration would come to nothing. I thought of the English army and hoped for their coming and being taken by them, but that failed. I hoped to be carried to Albany as the Indians had discoursed before, but that failed also. I thought of being sold to my husband, as my master spake, but instead of that my master himself was gone and I left behind, so that my spirit was now quite ready to sink. I asked them to let me go out and pick up some sticks, that I might get alone and pour out my heart unto the Lord. Then also I took my Bible to read, but I found no comfort here neither, which many times I was wont to find. So easy a thing it is with God to dry up the streams of scripture-comfort from us. Yet I can say that in all my sorrows and afflictions God did not leave me to have my impatience work towards Himself, as if His ways were unrighteous. But I knew that He laid upon me less than I deserved. Afterward, before this doleful time ended with me, I was turning the leaves of my Bible and the Lord brought to me some scriptures, which did a little revive me, as that Isai. 55:8, " 'For my thoughts are not your thoughts, neither are your ways my ways,' saith the Lord." And also that Psal. 37:5, "Commit thy way unto the Lord, trust also in Him, and He shall bring it to pass."

About this time they came yelping from Hadley, where they had killed three Englishmen and brought one captive with them, *viz*. Thomas Read. They all gathered about the poor man, asking him many questions. I desired also to go and see him, and when I came he was crying bitterly, supposing they would quickly kill him. Whereupon I asked one of them whether they intended to kill him; he answered me they would not. He being a little cheered with that, I asked him about the welfare of my husband; he told me he saw him such a time in the Bay, and he was well but very melancholy. By which I certainly understood (though I suspected it before) that whatsoever the Indians told me respecting him was vanity and lies. Some of them told me he was dead, and they had killed him. Some said he was married again, and that the governor wished him to marry and told him he should have his choice, and that all persuaded [him] I was dead. So like were these barbarous creatures to him who was a liar from the beginning.[34]

As I was sitting once in the wigwam here, Philip's maid came in with the child in her arms and asked me to give her a piece of my apron to make a flap for it. I told her I would not. Then my mistress bade me give it, but still I said no. The maid told me if I would not give her a piece she would tear a piece off it. I told her I would tear her coat then; with that my mistress rises up and takes up a stick big enough to have killed me and struck me with it, but I stepped out, and she struck the stick into the mat of the wigwam. But while she was pulling of it out, I ran to the maid and gave her all my apron, and so that storm went over.

Hearing that my son was come to this place, I went to see him and told him his father was well but very melancholy. He told me he was as much grieved for his father as for himself; I wondered at his speech, for I thought I had enough upon my spirit in reference to myself to make me mindless of my husband and everyone else, they being safe among their friends. He told me also that a while before his master, together with other Indians, were going to the French for powder, but by the way the Mohawks met with them and killed four of their company, which made the rest turn back again, for which I desire that myself and he may bless the Lord. For

---

[33]Judges 16:20.   [34]Satan.

it might have been worse with him had he been sold to the French than it proved to be in remaining with the Indians.

I went to see an English youth in this place, one John Gilbert of Springfield. I found him lying without doors upon the ground; I asked him how he did. He told me he was very sick of a flux with eating so much blood. They had turned him out of the wigwam and with him an Indian papoose almost dead (whose parents had been killed) in a bitter cold day without fire or clothes. The young man himself had nothing on but his shirt and waistcoat. This sight was enough to melt a heart of flint. There they lay quivering in the cold, the youth [curled] round like a dog, the papoose stretched out with his eyes, nose, and mouth full of dirt and yet alive and groaning. I advised John to go and get to some fire; he told me he could not stand, but I persuaded him still, lest he should lie there and die. And with much ado I got him to a fire and went myself home. As soon as I was got home, his master's daughter came after me to know what I had done with the Englishman; I told her I had got him to a fire in such a place. Now had I need to pray Paul's prayer, 2 Thess. 3:2, "That we may be delivered from unreasonable and wicked men." For her satisfaction I went along with her and brought her to him, but before I got home again, it was noised about that I was running away and getting the English youth along with me, that as soon as I came in they began to rant and domineer, asking me where I had been, and what I had been doing, and saying they would knock him on the head. I told them I had been seeing the English youth and that I would not run away. They told me I lied, and taking up a hatchet, they came to me and said they would knock me down if I stirred out again and so confined me to the wigwam. Now may I say with David, 2 Sam. 24:14, "I am in a great strait." If I keep in, I must die with hunger, and if I go out, I must be knocked in [the] head. This distressed condition held that day and half the next. And then the Lord remembered me, whose mercies are great.

Then came an Indian to me with a pair of stockings that were too big for him, and he would have me ravel them out and knit them fit for him. I showed myself willing and bid him ask my mistress if I might go along with him a little way; she said yes, I might, but I was not a little refreshed with that news that I had my liberty again. Then I went along with him, and he gave me some roasted groundnuts, which did again revive my feeble stomach.

Being got out of her sight, I had time and liberty again to look into my Bible, which was my guide by day and my pillow by night. Now that comfortable scripture presented itself to me, Isa. 54:7, "For a small moment have I forsaken thee, but with great mercies I will gather thee." Thus the Lord carried me along from one time to another and made good to me this precious promise and many others. Then my son came to see me, and I asked his master to let him stay awhile with me that I might comb his head and look over him, for he was almost overcome with lice. He told me when I had done that he was very hungry, but I had nothing to relieve him, but bid him go into the wigwams as he went along and see if he could get anything among them, which he did. And it seems [he] tarried a little too long, for his master was angry with him and beat him, and then sold him. Then he came running to tell me he had a new master, and that he had given him some groundnuts already. Then I went along with him to his new master, who told me he loved him and he should not want. So his master carried him away, and I never saw him afterward till I saw him at Pascataqua in Portsmouth.

That night they bade me go out of the wigwam again. My mistress's papoose was sick, and it died that night, and there was one benefit in it—that there was more room. I went to a wigwam, and they bade me come in and gave me a skin to lie upon and a mess of venison and groundnuts, which was a choice dish among them. On the morrow they buried the papoose, and afterward, both morning and evening, there came a company to mourn and howl with her, though I confess I could not much condole with them. Many sorrowful days I had in this place, often getting alone "like a crane, or a swallow, so did I chatter; I did mourn as a dove, mine eyes fail with looking upward. Oh, Lord, I am oppressed; undertake for me," Isai. 38:14. I could tell the Lord as Hezekiah, ver. 3, "Remember now, O Lord, I beseech Thee, how I have walked before Thee in truth."[35]

Now had I time to examine all my ways. My conscience did not accuse me of unrighteousness toward one or other, yet I saw how in my walk with God I had been a careless creature. As David said, "Against Thee, Thee only, have I sinned," and I might say with the poor publican, "God be merciful unto me a sinner."[36] On the Sabbath days I could look upon the sun and think how people were going to the house of God to have their souls refreshed and then home and their bodies also, but I was destitute of both and might say as the poor prodigal, "He would fain have filled his belly with the husks that the swine did eat, and no man gave unto him," Luke 15:16. For I must say with him, "Father I have sinned against heaven and in thy sight," ver. 21. I remembered how on the night before and after the Sabbath, when my family was about me and relations and neighbors with us, we could pray and sing, and then refresh our bodies with the good creatures of God, and then have a comfortable bed to lie down on. But instead of all this I had only a little swill for the body and then like a swine must lie down on the ground. I cannot express to man the sorrow that lay upon my spirit; the Lord knows it. Yet that comfortable scripture would often come to my mind, "For a small moment have I forsaken thee, but with great mercies will I gather thee."[37]

THE FOURTEENTH REMOVE[38]

Now must we pack up and be gone from this thicket, bending our course toward the Bay towns, I have nothing to eat by the way this day but a few crumbs of cake that an Indian gave my girl the same day we were taken. She gave it me, and I put it in my pocket; there it lay till it was so moldy (for want of good baking) that one could not tell what it was made of; it fell all to crumbs and grew so dry and hard that it was like little flints, and this refreshed me many times when I was ready to faint. It was in my thoughts when I put it into my mouth that if ever I returned I would tell the world what a blessing the Lord gave to such mean food. As we went along, they killed a deer with a young one in her; they gave me a piece of the fawn, and it was so young and tender that one might eat the bones as well as the flesh, and yet I thought it very good. When night came on, we sat down. It rained, but they quickly got up a bark wigwam, where I lay dry that night. I looked out in the morning, and many of them had laid in the rain all night, [which] I saw by their reeking. Thus the Lord dealt mercifully with me many times, and I fared better than many of them. In the morning they took the blood of the deer and put it into the paunch and so boiled it; I could eat nothing of that, though they ate it sweetly. And yet they were so nice[39] in other things that when I had fetched

---

[35] Isaiah 38:3.
[36] Psalm 51:4; Luke 18:13.
[37] Isaiah 57:7.
[38] Removes fourteen through nineteen retrace the previous route. Rowlandson travels a total distance of about one hundred and fifty miles.
[39] Fussy.

water and had put the dish I dipped the water with into the kettle of water which I brought, they would say they would knock me down, for they said it was a sluttish trick.

THE FIFTEENTH REMOVE

We went on our travel. I having got one handful of groundnuts for my support that day, they gave me my load, and I went on cheerfully (with the thoughts of going homeward), having my burden more on my back than my spirit. We came to Baquaug River again that day, near which we abode a few days. Sometimes one of them would give me a pipe, another a little tobacco, another a little salt, which I would change for a little victuals. I cannot but think what a wolfish appetite persons have in a starving condition, for many times when they gave me that which was hot, I was so greedy that I should burn my mouth that it would trouble me hours after, and yet I should quickly do the same again. And after I was thoroughly hungry, I was never again satisfied. For though sometimes it fell out that I got enough and did eat till I could eat no more, yet I was as unsatisfied as I was when I began. And now could I see that scripture verified (there being many scriptures which we do not take notice of or understand till we are afflicted), Mic. 6:14, "Thou shalt eat and not be satisfied." Now might I see more than ever before the miseries that sin hath brought upon us. Many times I should be ready to run out against the heathen, but the scripture would quiet me again, Amos 3:6, "Shall there be evil in the city, and the Lord hath not done it?" The Lord help me to make a right improvement of His word and that I might learn that great lesson, Mic. 6:8, 9, "He hath showed thee (Oh Man) what is good, and what doth the Lord require of thee, but to do justly and love mercy and walk humbly with thy God? Hear ye the rod and who hath appointed it."

THE SIXTEENTH REMOVE

We began this remove with wading over Baquaug River; the water was up to the knees and the stream very swift and so cold that I thought it would have cut me in sunder. I was so weak and feeble that I reeled as I went along and thought there I must end my days at last after my bearing and getting through so many difficulties. The Indians stood laughing to see me staggering along, but in my distress the Lord gave me experience of the truth and goodness of that promise, Isai. 43:2, "When thou passest through the waters, I will be with thee, and through the rivers, they shall not overflow thee." Then I sat down to put on my stockings and shoes with the tears running down mine eyes and many sorrowful thoughts in my heart, but I got up to go along with them. Quickly there came up to us an Indian who informed them that I must go to Wachuset to my master, for there was a letter come from the council to the sagamores about redeeming the captives and that there would be another in fourteen days and that I must be there ready. My heart was so heavy before that I could scarce speak or go in the path and yet now so light that I could run. My strength seemed to come again and recruit my feeble knees and aching heart, yet it pleased them to go but one mile that night, and there we stayed two days. In that time came a company of Indians to us, near thirty, all on horseback. My heart skipped within me, thinking they had been Englishmen at the first sight of them, for they were dressed in English apparel, with hats, white neckcloths, and sashes about their waists, and ribbons upon their shoulders, but when they came near there was a vast difference between the lovely faces of Christians and the foul looks of those heathens which much dampened my spirit again.

The Seventeenth Remove

A comfortable remove it was to me because of my hopes. They gave me a pack, and along we went cheerfully, but quickly my will proved more than my strength. Having little or no refreshing, my strength failed me, and my spirits were almost quite gone. Now may I say with David, Psal. 119:22, 23, 24, "I am poor and needy, and my heart is wounded within me. I am gone like the shadow when it declineth: I am tossed up and down like the locust; my knees are weak through fasting, and my flesh faileth of fatness."

At night we came to an Indian town, and the Indians sat down by a wigwam discoursing, but I was almost spent and could scarce speak. I laid down my load and went into the wigwam, and there sat an Indian boiling of horses' feet (they being wont to eat the flesh first, and when the feet were old and dried and they had nothing else, they would cut off the feet and use them). I asked him to give me a little of his broth or water they were boiling in; he took a dish and gave me one spoonful of samp and bid me take as much of the broth as I would. Then I put some of the hot water to the samp and drank it up and my spirit came again. He gave me also a piece of the rough or ridding[40] of the small guts, and I broiled it on the coals; and now may I say with Jonathan, "See, I pray you, how mine eyes have been enlightened because I tasted a little of this honey," I Sam. 14:29. Now is my spirit revived again; though means be never so inconsiderable, yet if the Lord bestow His blessing upon them, they shall refresh both soul and body.

The Eighteenth Remove

We took up our packs and along we went, but a wearisome day I had of it. As we went along I saw an Englishman stripped naked and lying dead upon the ground, but knew not who it was. Then we came to another Indian town where we stayed all night. In this town there were four English children, captives, and one of them my own sister's. I went to see how she did, and she was well, considering her captive condition. I would have tarried that night with her, but they that owned her would not suffer it. Then I went into another wigwam, where they were boiling corn and beans, which was a lovely sight to see, but I could not get a taste thereof. Then I went to another wigwam, where there were two of the English children. The squaw was boiling horses' feet; then she cut me off a little piece and gave one of the English children a piece also. Being very hungry, I had quickly eat up mine, but the child could not bite it, it was so tough and sinewy, but lay sucking, gnawing, chewing, and slabbering of it in the mouth and hand. Then I took it of the child and ate it myself, and savory it was to my taste. Then I may say [as] Job, chap. 6:7, "The things that my soul refused to touch are as my sorrowful meat." Thus the Lord made that pleasant and refreshing which another time would have been an abomination. Then I went home to my mistress' wigwam, and they told me I disgraced my master with begging, and if I did so anymore they would knock me in [the] head. I told them they had as good knock me in [the] head as starve me to death.

---

[40]Trimmed-off scrap.

THE NINETEENTH REMOVE

They said when we went out that we must travel to Wachuset this day. But a bitter weary day I had of it, traveling now three days together without resting any day between. At last, after many weary steps, I saw Wachuset Hills, but many miles off. Then we came to a great swamp, through which we traveled up to the knees in mud and water, which was heavy going to one tired before. Being almost spent, I thought I should have sunk down at last and never got out, but I may say, as in Psal. 94:18, "When my foot slipped, Thy mercy, O Lord, held me up." Going along, having indeed my life but little spirit, Philip, who was in the company, came up and took me by the hand and said, "Two weeks more and you shall be mistress again." I asked him if he spake true. He answered, "Yes, and quickly you shall come to your master again, who has been gone from us three weeks." After many weary steps we came to Wachuset, where he was, and glad I was to see him. He asked me when I washed me. I told him not this month. Then he fetched me some water himself and bid me wash and gave me the glass to see how I looked and bid his squaw give me something to eat. So she gave me a mess of beans and meat and a little groundnut cake. I was wonderfully revived with this favor showed me, Psal. 106:46, "He made them also to be pitied of all those that carried them captives."

My master had three squaws, living sometimes with one and sometimes with another one. This old squaw at whose wigwam I was, my master had been [with] those three weeks. Another was Weetamoo, with whom I had lived and served all this while. A severe and proud dame she was, bestowing every day in dressing herself neat as much time as any of the gentry of the land, powdering her hair and painting her face, going with necklaces, with jewels in her ears, and bracelets upon her hands. When she had dressed herself, her work was to make girdles of wampum and beads. The third squaw was a younger one, by whom he had two papooses. By that time I was refreshed by the old squaw with whom my master was, Weetamoo's maid came to call me home, at which I fell a-weeping. Then the old squaw told me, to encourage me, that if I wanted victuals I should come to her, and that I should lie there in her wigwam. Then I went with the maid and quickly came again and lodged there. The squaw laid a mat under me and a good rug over me; the first time I had any such kindness showed me. I understood that Weetamoo thought that if she should let me go and serve with the old squaw, she would be in danger to lose not only my service but the redemption pay also. And I was not a little glad to hear this, being raised in my hopes that in God's due time there would be an end of this sorrowful hour. Then came an Indian and asked me to knit him three pairs of stockings, for which I had a hat and a silk handkerchief. Then another asked me to make her a shift, for which she gave me an apron.

Then came Tom and Peter with the second letter from the council about the captives. Though they were Indians, I got them by the hand and burst out into tears; my heart was so full that I could not speak to them, but recovering myself, I asked them how my husband did and all my friends and acquaintances. They said they [were] all very well, but melancholy. They brought me two biscuits and a pound of tobacco. The tobacco I quickly gave away; when it was all gone, one asked me to give him a pipe of tobacco. I told him it was all gone. Then began he to rant and threaten. I told him when my husband came I would give some. "Hang [the] rogue," says he, "I will knock out his brains if he comes here." And then again in the same breath they would say that if there should come a hundred without guns they would do them no hurt, so unstable and like madmen they were, so that fearing the worst, I durst not send to my husband though there were some thoughts of his coming to redeem and fetch me, not knowing what might follow. For there was little more trust to them than to the master they served.

When the letter was come, the sagamores met to consult about the captives and called me to them to inquire how much my husband would give to redeem me. When I came, I sat down among them as I was wont to do, as their manner is. Then they bade me stand up and said they were the General Court.[41] They bid me speak what I thought he would give. Now knowing that all we had was destroyed by the Indians, I was in a great strait. I thought if I should speak of but a little, it would be slighted and hinder the matter; if of a great sum, I knew not where it would be procured. Yet at a venture, I said twenty pounds, yet desired them to take less; but they would not hear of that, but sent that message to Boston that for twenty pounds I should be redeemed. It was a praying Indian that wrote their letter for them. There was another praying Indian who told me that he had a brother that would not eat horse; his conscience was so tender and scrupulous (though as large as hell for the destruction of poor Christians). Then he said he read that scripture to him, 2 Kings, 6:25, "There was a famine in Samaria, and behold they besieged it, until an ass's head was sold for fourscore pieces of silver, and the fourth part of a kab of doves' dung for five pieces of silver." He expounded this place to his brother and showed him that it was lawful to eat that in a famine which is not at another time. "And now," says he, "he will eat horse with any Indian of them all."

There was another praying Indian who, when he had done all the mischief that he could, betrayed his own father into the English hands thereby to purchase his own life. Another praying Indian was at Sudbury fight, though, as he deserved, he was afterward hanged for it. There was another praying Indian so wicked and cruel as to wear a string about his neck strung with Christians' fingers. Another praying Indian, when they went to Sudbury fight, went with them and his squaw also with him with her papoose at her back.

Before they went to that fight, they got a company together to pow-wow; the manner was as followeth. There was one that kneeled upon a deerskin with the company round him in a ring, who kneeled, and striking upon the ground with their hands and with sticks, and muttering or humming with their mouths; besides him who kneeled in the ring, there also stood one with a gun in his hand. Then he on the deerskin made a speech, and all manifested assent to it, and so they did many times together. Then they bade him with the gun go out of the ring, which he did, but when he was out, they called him in again. But he seemed to make a stand; then they called the more earnestly till he returned again. Then they all sang. Then they gave him two guns, in either hand one. And so he on the deerskin began again, and at the end of every sentence in his speaking, they all assented, humming or muttering with their mouths and striking upon the ground with their hands. Then they bade him with the two guns go out of the ring again, which he did a little way. Then they called him in again, but he made a stand; so they called him with greater earnestness, but he stood reeling and wavering as if he knew not whether he should stand or fall or which way to go. Then they called him with exceeding great vehemency, all of them, one and another. After a little while he turned in, staggering as he went, with his arms stretched out, in either hand a gun. As soon as he came in, they all sang and rejoiced exceedingly awhile. And then he upon the deerskin made another speech, unto which they all assented in a rejoicing manner, and so they ended their business and forthwith went to Sudbury fight.

To my thinking they went without any scruple but that they should prosper and gain the victory. And they went out not so rejoicing, but they came home with

---

[41] Massachusetts Bay Colony's highest judicial and legislative body.

as great a victory, for they said they had killed two captains and almost an hundred men. One Englishman they brought along with them; and he said it was too true, for they had made sad work at Sudbury, as indeed it proved. Yet they came home without that rejoicing and triumphing over their victory which they were wont to show at other times but rather like dogs (as they say) which have lost their ears. Yet I could not perceive that it was for their own loss of men. They said they had not lost but above five or six, and I missed none except in one wigwam. When they went, they acted as if the devil had told them that they should gain the victory, and now they acted as if the devil had told them they should have a fall. Whither it were so or no, I cannot tell, but so it proved, for quickly they began to fall and so held on that summer till they came to utter ruin.

They came home on a Sabbath day, and the powwow that kneeled upon the deerskin came home (I may say without abuse) as black as the devil. When my master came home, he came to me and bid me make a shirt for his papoose of a holland lace pillowbeer.[42] About that time there came an Indian to me and bid me come to his wigwam at night, and he would give me some pork and groundnuts, which I did. And as I was eating, another Indian said to me, "He seems to be your good friend, but he killed two Englishmen at Sudbury, and there lie their clothes behind you." I looked behind me, and there I saw bloody clothes with bullet holes in them, yet the Lord suffered not this wretch to do me any hurt. Yea, instead of that, he many times refreshed me; five or six times did he and his squaw refresh my feeble carcass. If I went to their wigwam at any time, they would always give me something, and yet they were strangers that I never saw before. Another squaw gave me a piece of fresh pork and a little salt with it and lent me her pan to fry it in, and I cannot but remember what a sweet, pleasant and delightful relish that bit had to me to this day. So little do we prize common mercies when we have them to the full.

THE TWENTIETH REMOVE[43]

It was their usual manner to remove when they had done any mischief, lest they should be found out, and so they did at this time. We went about three or four miles, and there they built a great wigwam big enough to hold a hundred Indians, which they did in preparation to a great day of dancing. They would say now amongst themselves that the governor would be so angry for his loss at Sudbury that he would send no more about the captives, which made me grieve and tremble. My sister being not far from the place where we now were, and hearing that I was here, desired her master to let her come and see me, and he was willing to it and would go with her. But she, being ready before him, told him she would go before and was come within a mile or two of the place. Then he overtook her and began to rant as if he had been mad and made her go back again in the rain so that I never saw her till I saw her in Charlestown. But the Lord requited many of their ill doings, for this Indian, her master, was hanged afterward at Boston.

The Indians now began to come from all quarters, against their merry dancing day. Among some of them came one Goodwife Kettle. I told her my heart was so heavy that it was ready to break. "So is mine, too," said she. But yet [she] said, "I hope we shall hear some good news shortly." I could hear how earnestly my sister desired to see me, and I as earnestly desired to see her, and yet neither of us could

---

[42]Pillowcase.
[43]To the vicinity of Princeton, Massachusetts, from April 28 to May 2.

get an opportunity. My daughter was also now about a mile off, and I had not seen her in nine or ten weeks as I had not seen my sister since our first taking. I earnestly desired them to let me go and see them; yea, I entreated, begged, and persuaded them but to let me see my daughter, and yet so hardhearted were they that they would not suffer it. They made use of their tyrannical power whilst they had it, but through the Lord's wonderful mercy their time was now but short.

On a Sabbath day, the sun being about an hour high in the afternoon, came Mr. John Hoar (the council permitting him and his own forward spirit inclining him) together with the two forementioned Indians, Tom and Peter, with their third letter from the council. When they came near, I was abroad; though I saw them not, they presently called me in and bade me sit down and not stir. Then they catched up their guns and away they ran as if an enemy had been at hand, and the guns went off apace. I manifested some great trouble, and they asked me what was the matter. I told them I thought they had killed the Englishman (for they had in the meantime informed me that an Englishman was come). They said, "No." They shot over his horse and under, and before his horse, and they pushed him this way and that way at their pleasure, showing what they could do. Then they let them come to their wigwams. I begged of them to let me see the Englishman, but they would not; but there was I fain to sit their pleasure. When they had talked their fill with him, they suffered me to go to him. We asked each other of our welfare, and how my husband did and all my friends. He told me they were all well and would be glad to see me. Amongst other things which my husband sent me, there came a pound of tobacco, which I sold for nine shillings in money, for many of the Indians for want of tobacco smoked hemlock and ground ivy. It was a great mistake in any who thought I sent for tobacco, for through the favor of God that desire was overcome.

I now asked them whether I should go home with Mr. Hoar. They answered, "No," one and another of them. And it being night, we lay down with that answer. In the morning Mr. Hoar invited the sagamores to dinner, but when we went to get it ready, we found that they had stolen the greatest part of the provision Mr. Hoar had brought out of his bags in the night. And we may see the wonderful power of God in that one passage in that when there was such a great number of the Indians together and so greedy of a little good food and no English there but Mr. Hoar and myself, that there they did not knock us in the head and take what he had, there being not only some provision but also trading cloth, a part of the twenty pounds agreed upon. But instead of doing us any mischief, they seemed to be ashamed of the fact and said it were some *matchit*[44] Indian that did it. Oh, that we could believe that there is nothing too hard for God! God showed His power over the heathen in this as He did over the hungry lions when Daniel was cast into the den.[45] Mr. Hoar called them betime to dinner, but they ate very little, they being so busy in dressing themselves and getting ready for their dance, which was carried on by eight of them—four men and four squaws, my master and mistress being two. He was dressed in his Holland shirt with great laces sewed at the tail of it; he had his silver buttons, his white stockings, his garters were hung round with shillings, and he had girdles of wampum upon his head and shoulders. She had a kersey coat[46] and [was] covered with girdles of wampum from the loins upward; her arms from her elbows to her hands were covered with bracelets; there were

---

[44]Bad.

[45]Daniel 6:16–23.

[46]Wool petticoat. As war chiefs, Quinnapin and Weetamoo stage a ritual dance and a giveaway ceremony to garner power for their enterprise.

handfuls of necklaces about her neck and several sorts of jewels in her ears. She had fine red stockings and white shoes, her hair powdered and face painted red that was always before black. And all the dancers were after the same manner. There were two others singing and knocking on a kettle for their music. They kept hopping up and down one after another with a kettle of water in the midst, standing warm upon some embers, to drink of when they were dry. They held on till it was almost night, throwing out wampum to the standers by.

At night I asked them again if I should go home. They all as one said no except my husband would come for me. When we were lain down, my master went out of the wigwam, and by and by sent in an Indian called James the Printer, who told Mr. Hoar that my master would let me go home tomorrow if he would let him have one pint of liquors. Then Mr. Hoar called his own Indians, Tom and Peter, and bid them go and see whether he would promise it before them three, and if he would, he should have it, which he did, and he had it. Then Philip, smelling the business, called me to him and asked me what I would give him to tell me some good news and speak a good word for me. I told him I could not tell what to give him. I would [give] anything I had and asked him what he would have. He said two coats and twenty shillings in money and half a bushel of seed corn and some tobacco. I thanked him for his love, but I knew the good news as well as the crafty fox.

My master, after he had had his drink, quickly came ranting into the wigwam again and called for Mr. Hoar, drinking to him and saying he was a good man. And then again he would say, "Hang [the] rogue." Being almost drunk, he would drink to him, and yet presently say he should be hanged. Then he called for me. I trembled to hear him, yet I was fain to go to him, and he drank to me, showing no incivility. He was the first Indian I saw drunk all the while that I was amongst them. At last his squaw ran out, and he after her round the wigwam, with his money jingling at his knees, but she escaped him. But having an old squaw, he ran to her, and so through the Lord's mercy, we were no more troubled that night.

Yet I had not a comfortable night's rest, for I think I can say I did not sleep for three nights together. The night before the letter came from the council I could not rest, I was so full of fears and troubles, God many times leaving us most in the dark when deliverance is nearest. Yea, at this time I could not rest night nor day. The next night I was overjoyed, Mr. Hoar being come and that with such good tidings. The third night I was even swallowed up with the thoughts of things, *viz.* that ever I should go home again and that I must go, leaving my children behind me in the wilderness, so that sleep was now almost departed from mine eyes.

On Tuesday morning they called their General Court (as they call it) to consult and determine whether I should go home or no. And they all as one man did seemingly consent to it that I should go home, except Philip, who would not come among them.

But before I go any further, I would take leave to mention a few remarkable passages of providence which I took special notice of in my afflicted time.

1. Of the fair opportunity lost in the long march, a little after the fort fight, when our English army was so numerous, and in pursuit of the enemy, and so near as to take several and destroy them, and the enemy in such distress for food that our men might track them by their rooting in the earth for groundnuts while they were flying for their lives. I say that then our army should want provision and be forced to leave their pursuit and return homeward. And the very next week the enemy came upon our town like bears bereft of their whelps or so many ravenous wolves, rending us and our lambs to death. But what shall I say? God seemed to leave His people to themselves and order all things for His own holy ends. "Shall there be evil in the city and the Lord hath not done it? They are not grieved for the affliction

of Joseph, therefore shall they go captive with the first that go captive."[47] It is the Lord's doing, and it should be marvelous in our eyes.

2. I cannot but remember how the Indians derided the slowness and dullness of the English army in its setting out. For after the desolations at Lancaster and Medfield, as I went along with them, they asked me when I thought the English would come after them. I told them I could not tell. It may be they will come in May, said they. Thus did they scoff at us, as if the English would be a quarter of a year getting ready.

3. Which also I have hinted before: when the English army with new supplies were sent forth to pursue after the enemy, and they, understanding it, fled before them till they came to Baquaug River where they forthwith went over safely, that the river should be impassable to the English. I can but admire to see the wonderful providence of God in preserving the heathen for further affliction to our poor country. They could go in great numbers over, but the English must stop. God had an overruling hand in all those things.

4. It was thought if their corn were cut down they would starve and die with hunger, and all their corn that could be found was destroyed, and they driven from that little they had in store into the woods in the midst of winter. And yet how to admiration did the Lord preserve them for His holy ends and the destruction of many still amongst the English! Strangely did the Lord provide for them that I did not see (all the time I was among them) one man, woman, or child die with hunger. Though many times they would eat that that a hog or dog would hardly touch, yet by that God strengthened them to be a scourge to His people.

The chief and commonest food was groundnuts. They eat also nuts and acorns, artichokes, lily roots, groundbeans, and several other weeds and roots that I know not.

They would pick up old bones and cut them to pieces at the joints, and if they were full of worms and maggots, they would scald them over the fire to make the vermin come out and then boil them and drink up the liquor and then beat the great ends of them in a mortar and so eat them. They would eat horses' guts and ears, and all sorts of wild birds which they could catch; also bear, venison, beaver, tortoise, frogs, squirrels, dogs, skunks, rattlesnakes, yea, the very bark of trees, besides all sorts of creatures and provision which they plundered from the English. I can but stand in admiration to see the wonderful power of God in providing for such a vast number of our enemies in the wilderness, where there was nothing to be seen but from hand to mouth. Many times in a morning the generality of them would eat up all they had and yet have some further supply against they wanted. It is said, Psal. 81:13, 14, "Oh, that My people had hearkened to Me, and Israel had walked in My ways; I should soon have subdued their enemies and turned My hand against their adversaries." But now our perverse and evil carriages in the sight of the Lord have so offended Him that instead of turning His hand against them the Lord feeds and nourishes them up to be a scourge to the whole land.

5. Another thing that I would observe is the strange providence of God in turning things about when the Indians [were] at the highest and the English at the lowest. I was with the enemy eleven weeks and five days, and not one week passed without the fury of the enemy and some desolation by fire and sword upon one place or other. They mourned (with their black faces) for their own losses, yet triumphed and rejoiced in their inhuman and many times devilish cruelty to the English. They would boast much of their victories, saying that in two hours' time they had destroyed such a captain and his company at such a place, and such a captain and his company in such a place, and such a captain and his company

---

[47] Amos 3:6, 6:7.

in such a place, and boast how many towns they had destroyed; and then scoff and say they had done them a good turn to send them to heaven so soon. Again they would say this summer that they would knock all the rogues in the head, or drive them into the sea, or make them fly the country, thinking surely Agag-like, "The bitterness of death is past."[48] Now the heathen begins to think all is their own, and the poor Christians' hopes to fail (as to man), and now their eyes are more to God, and their hearts sigh heavenward and to say in good earnest, "Help Lord, or we perish." When the Lord had brought His people to this that they saw no help in anything but Himself, then He takes the quarrel into His own hand, and though they [the Indians] had made a pit in their own imaginations as deep as hell for the Christians that summer, yet the Lord hurled themselves into it. And the Lord had not so many ways before to preserve them, but now He hath as many to destroy them.

But to return again to my going home, where we may see a remarkable change of providence. At first they were all against it except my husband would come for me, but afterwards they assented to it and seemed much to rejoice in it. Some asked me to send them some bread, others some tobacco, others shaking me by the hand, offering me a hood and scarf to ride in, not one moving hand or tongue against it. Thus hath the Lord answered my poor desire and the many earnest requests of others put up unto God for me. In my travels an Indian came to me and told me if I were willing, he and his squaw would run away and go home along with me. I told him no. I was not willing to run away, but desired to wait God's time that I might go home quietly and without fear. And now God hath granted me my desire. O, the wonderful power of God that I have seen and the experience that I have had! I have been in the midst of those roaring lions and savage bears that feared neither God nor man nor the devil, by night and day, alone and in company, sleeping all sorts together, and yet not one of them ever offered me the least abuse of unchastity to me in word or action. Though some are ready to say I speak it for my own credit, I speak it in the presence of God and to His glory. God's power is as great now and as sufficient to save as when He preserved Daniel in the lion's den or the three children in the fiery furnace.[49] I may well say as his Psal. 107:12, "Oh, give thanks unto the Lord for He is good, for His mercy endureth forever." Let the redeemed of the Lord say so whom He hath redeemed from the hand of the enemy, especially that I should come away in the midst of so many hundreds of enemies quietly and peaceably and not a dog moving his tongue.

So I took my leave of them, and in coming along my heart melted into tears more than all the while I was with them, and I was almost swallowed up with the thoughts that ever I should go home again. About the sun going down, Mr. Hoar, myself, and the two Indians came to Lancaster, and a solemn sight it was to me. There had I lived many comfortable years amongst my relations and neighbors, and now not one Christian to be seen nor one house left standing. We went on to a farmhouse that was yet standing, where we lay all night, and a comfortable lodging we had, though nothing but straw to lie on. The Lord preserved us in safety that night and raised us up again in the morning and carried us along, that before noon we came to Concord. Now was I full of joy and yet not without sorrow—joy to see such a lovely sight, so many Christians together and some of them my neighbors. There I met with my brother [Josiah White] and my brother-in-law [Henry Kerley], who asked me if I knew where his wife was. Poor heart! He had helped to bury her and knew it not, she being shot down [when] the house was partly burned so that those who were at Boston at the desolation of the town and came back afterward

---

[48] I Samuel 15.   [49] Daniel 3:13–30.

and buried the dead did not know her. Yet I was not without sorrow to think how many were looking and longing, and my own children amongst the rest, to enjoy that deliverance that I had now received, and I did not know whether ever I should see them again.

Being recruited with food and raiment, we went to Boston that day, where I met with my dear husband, but the thoughts of our dear children, one being dead and the others we could not tell where, abated our comfort each to other. I was not before so much hemmed in with the merciless and cruel heathen but now as much with pitiful, tenderhearted, and compassionate Christians. In that poor and distressed and beggarly condition I was received in, I was kindly entertained in several houses; so much love I received from several (some of whom I knew and others I knew not) that I am not capable to declare it. But the Lord knows them all by name. The Lord reward them sevenfold into their bosoms of His spirituals for their temporals.[50]

The twenty pounds, the price of my redemption, was raised by some Boston gentlemen and Mrs. Usher, whose bounty and religious charity I would not forget to make mention of. Then Mr. Thomas Shepard of Charlestown received us into his house, where we continued eleven weeks, and a father and mother they were to us. And many more tenderhearted friends we met with in that place. We were now in the midst of love, yet not without much and frequent heaviness of heart for our poor children and other relations who were still in affliction. The week following after my coming in, the governor and council sent forth to the Indians again, and that not without success, for they brought in my sister and Goodwife Kettle.

Their not knowing where our children were was a sore trial to us still, and yet we were not without secret hopes that we should see them again. That which was dead lay heavier upon my spirit than those which were alive and amongst the heathen, thinking how it suffered with its wounds and I was no way able to relieve it, and how it was buried by the heathen in the wilderness from among all Christians. We were hurried up and down in our thoughts; sometimes we should hear a report that they were gone this way, and sometimes that, and that they were come in in this place or that. We kept inquiring and listening to hear concerning them, but no certain news as yet. About this time the council had ordered a day of public thanksgiving, though I thought I had still cause of mourning, and, being unsettled in our minds, we thought we would ride toward the eastward to see if we could hear anything concerning our children. And as we were riding along (God is the wise disposer of all things), between Ipswich and Rowly we met with Mr. William Hubbard, who told us that our son Joseph was come in to Major Waldren's, and another with him which was my sister's son. I asked him how he knew it. He said the major himself told him so.

So along we went till we came to Newbury, and, their minister being absent, they desired my husband to preach the thanksgiving for them, but he was not willing to stay there that night but would go over to Salisbury to hear further and come again in the morning, which he did and preached there that day. At night when he had done, one came and told him that his daughter was come in at Providence. Here was mercy on both hands. Now hath God fulfilled that precious scripture which was such a comfort to me in my distressed condition. When my heart was ready to sink into the earth (my children being gone I could not tell whither), and my knees trembled under me, and I was walking through the valley of the shadow of death, then the Lord brought and now has fulfilled that reviving word unto me. Thus saith the Lord, "Refrain thy voice from weeping, and thine eyes from tears,

---

[50]Worldly goods.

for thy work shall be rewarded," saith the Lord, "and they shall come again from the land of the enemy."[51]

Now we were between them, the one on the east and the other on the west. Our son being nearest, we went to him first to Portsmouth, where we met with him and with the major also, who told us he had done what he could but could not redeem him under seven pounds, which the good people thereabouts were pleased to pay. The Lord reward the major and all the rest, though unknown to me, for their labor of love. My sister's son was redeemed for four pounds, which the council gave order for the payment of. Having now received one of our children, we hastened toward the other; going back through Newbury, my husband preached there on the Sabbath day, for which they rewarded him manyfold.

On Monday we came to Charlestown, where we heard that the governor of Rhode Island had sent over for our daughter to take care of her, being now within his jurisdiction, which should not pass without our acknowledgments. But she being nearer Rehoboth than Rhode Island, Mr. Newman went over and took care of her and brought her to his own house. And the goodness of God was admirable to us in our low estate in that he raised up [com]passionate friends on every side to us when we had nothing to recompense any for their love. The Indians were now gone that way, that it was apprehended dangerous to go to her; but the carts which carried provision to the English army, being guarded, brought her with them to Dorchester, where we received her safe. Blessed be the Lord for it, for great is His power, and He can do whatsoever seemeth Him good.

Her coming in was after this manner. She was traveling one day with the Indians with her basket at her back; the company of Indians were got before her and gone out of sight, all except one squaw. She followed the squaw till night, and then both of them lay down, having nothing over them but the heavens and under them but the earth. Thus she traveled three days together, not knowing whither she was going, having nothing to eat or drink but water and green hirtleberries. At last they came into Providence, where she was kindly entertained by several of that town. The Indians often said that I should never have her under twenty pounds. But now the Lord hath brought her in upon free cost and given her to me the second time. The Lord make us a blessing indeed, each to others. Now have I seen that scripture also fulfilled, Deut. 30:4, 7: "If any of thine be driven out to the outmost parts of heaven, from thence will the Lord thy God gather thee, and from thence will He fetch thee. . . . And the Lord thy God will put all these curses upon thine enemies, and on them which hate thee, which persecuted thee." Thus hath the Lord brought me and mine out of that horrible pit and hath set us in the midst of tenderhearted and compassionate Christians. It is the desire of my soul that we may walk worthy of the mercies received and which we are receiving.

Our family being now gathered together (those of us that were living), the South Church in Boston hired an house for us. Then we removed from Mr. Shepard's, those cordial friends, and went to Boston, where we continued about three-quarters of a year. Still the Lord went along with us and provided graciously for us. I thought it somewhat strange to set up housekeeping with bare walls, but as Solomon says, "Money answers all things,"[52] and that we had through the benevolence of Christian friends, some in this town and some in that and others, and some from England, that in a little time we might look and see the house furnished with love. The Lord hath been exceeding good to us in our low estate in that when we had neither house nor home nor other necessaries, the Lord so moved the hearts of these and those towards us that we wanted neither food nor raiment for ourselves or ours,

---

[51]Jeremiah 31:16.   [52]Ecclesiastes 10:19.

Prov. 18:24, "There is a friend which sticketh closer than a brother." And how many such friends have we found and now living amongst! And truly such a friend have we found him to be unto us in whose house we lived, *viz.* Mr. James Whitcomb, a friend unto us near hand and afar off.

I can remember the time when I used to sleep quietly without workings in my thoughts whole nights together, but now it is other ways with me. When all are fast about me and no eye open but His who ever waketh, my thoughts are upon things past, upon the awful dispensation of the Lord toward us, upon His wonderful power and might in carrying of us through so many difficulties, in returning us in safety and suffering none to hurt us. I remember in the night season how the other day I was in the midst of thousands of enemies and nothing but death before me. It [was] then hard work to persuade myself that ever I should be satisfied with bread again. But now we are fed with the finest of the wheat, and, as I may say, with honey out of the rock. Instead of the husk, we have the fatted calf.[53] The thoughts of these things in the particulars of them, and of the love and goodness of God towards us, make it true of me what David said of himself, Psal. 6:5 [actually 6:6]. "I watered my couch with my tears." Oh, the wonderful power of God that mine eyes have seen, affording matter enough for my thoughts to run in, that when others are sleeping mine eyes are weeping!

I have seen the extreme vanity of this world. One hour I have been in health and wealth, wanting nothing, but the next hour in sickness and wounds and death, having nothing but sorrow and affliction. Before I knew what affliction meant, I was ready sometimes to wish for it. When I lived in prosperity, having the comforts of the world about me, my relations by me, my heart cheerful, and taking little care for anything, and yet seeing many whom I preferred before myself under many trials and afflictions, in sickness, weakness, poverty, losses, crosses, and cares of the world, I should be sometimes jealous lest I should have my portion in this life, and that scripture would come to mind, Heb. 12:6, "For whom the Lord loveth he chasteneth and scourgeth every son whom He receiveth." But now I see the Lord had His time to scourge and chasten me. The portion of some is to have their afflictions by drops, now one drop and then another, but the dregs of the cup, the wine of astonishment, like a sweeping rain that leaveth no food, did the Lord prepare to be my portion. Affliction I wanted and affliction I had, full measure (I thought) pressed down and running over. Yet I see when God calls a person to anything and through never so many difficulties, yet He is fully able to carry them through and make them see and say they have been gainers thereby. And I hope I can say in some measure, as David did, "It is good for me that I have been afflicted."[54]

The Lord hath showed me the vanity of these outward things. That they are the vanity of vanities and vexation of spirit, that they are but a shadow, a blast, a bubble, and things of no continuance. That we must rely on God himself and our whole dependence must be upon Him. If trouble from smaller matters begin to arise in me, I have something at hand to check myself with and say, why am I troubled? It was but the other day that if I had had the world I would have given it for my freedom or to have been a servant to a Christian. I have learned to look beyond present and smaller troubles and to be quieted under them, as Moses said, Exod. 14:13, "Stand still and see the salvation of the Lord."

[53] Psalm 81:16; Luke 15:23.
[54] Psalm 119:71.

JONATHAN SWIFT
[1667–1745]

Satire was the most characteristic literary genre of the Enlightenment, especially in England and in France, and Jonathan Swift was its most powerful and notorious practitioner. *Gulliver's Travels*, his major work, was instantly popular upon its publication in 1726, and it has remained throughout the world one of the most widely read books of European origin. Because of his authorship of this book, whose views of humanity are by turns hilarious, disgusting, and terrifying, from his own time to the present Swift has often been called a misanthrope, even a madman. Readers who have previously met with Swift only in expurgated versions of the book telling of a kindly traveler stranded in a Disneyesque land of miniature people and knee-high palaces are often shocked by the real text of *Gulliver's Travels*. Although his targets sometimes include recognizable individuals and particular religious or political parties, his most potent satire is directed almost unrelentingly at humanity itself, in all its physical and moral ugliness. As he explained in a letter to his great friend Alexander Pope,

> I have ever hated all nations, professions, and communities, and all my love is toward individuals: for instance I hate the tribe of lawyers, but I love Counsellor Such-a-one, Judge Such-a-one; for so with physicians, . . . soldiers, English, Scotch, French, and the rest. But principally I hate and detest that animal called man, although I heartily love John, Peter, Thomas, and so forth.

The stinging accuracy with which Swift depicts the grossness, folly, and wickedness of humanity in general is much harder for many readers to take than partisan satire; while reading Swift, no one can remain quite secure in his or her own virtue and dignity for very long at a stretch.

LIFE

Swift was born in Dublin in 1667 to a recently widowed mother. Both of his parents were conservative English people living in Ireland. Thus, Swift was born into a colonial heritage that had been been oppressing the Irish ever since the twelfth century, when Pope Adrian granted overlordship of Ireland to Henry II of England. By Swift's time, the Protestant English had been functioning for centuries as Roman Catholic Ireland's rulers and absentee landlords.

The fatherless boy was helped by a paternal uncle to an education, first at Kilkenny School and then at Trinity College, Dublin. Shortly after his graduation, while Swift was still casting about trying to determine a career, there came a period of great political upheaval when James II first abdicated the British throne and then unsuccessfully attempted to invade Ireland, hoping to restore himself to power from a base there. In the confusion, like many Anglo-Irish, Swift fled to England, where between 1689 and 1699 he was taken in by his relative Sir William Temple.

Temple was a sophisticated retired diplomat, and to be a member of his household was in itself a further political and intellectual education for the young man. While at Temple's, Swift took orders in the Anglican church, although this initially seems to have been a practical move rather than a response to a passionate calling. In other ways, he seriously began to discover his real tastes, talents, and vocations. He read widely in politics, philosophy, and literature; he made friends with the leading wits, poets, and intellectuals of his day, among them Alexander Pope, John Gay, Joseph Addison, and the Tory ministers Oxford and Bolingbroke. He undertook the education of Temple's steward's young daughter Esther Johnson, who became his lifelong friend, perhaps his lover or even his wife, in a relationship whose nature remained a secret between the two of them. The letters and poems between Swift and his "Stella" are testaments to their lifelong playful, loving devotion to each other.

In the 1690s, Swift also began to come into his full powers as a writer, producing *The Battle of the Books* and *A Tale of a Tub*, both published in 1704. *The Battle of the Books* attacks corruption in educational and intellectual circles, defending classical writers against the moderns. In this satire, Swift describes the classical writers as modest bees who work earnestly to make honey and the beeswax used in candles, thus supplying civilization with both "sweetness and light." The modern writer, in contrast, is a bloated spider, utterly self-involved, spinning "nothing but dirt" out of his own entrails. *A Tale of a Tub* in part satirizes religious fanaticism from both Puritan and High Church extremes. Here, Swift depicts Christianity as a simple serviceable coat. High Church people, unable to value simplicity, decorate the honest garment with all sorts of gilded frippery and furbelows, and make faddish alterations until the garment becomes nearly unrecognizable; in their turn, rabid reformers angrily rip out the new seams and tear off all adornments, nearly destroying the fabric of the poor coat entirely. Rereading *A Tale of a Tub* as an old man, Swift exclaimed, "God, I had genius then!" It was clear from both of these early works that, like many satirists, Swift would put that genius into the service of conservative viewpoints; while he savagely critiques the status quo, he takes an equally acid view of radical attempts at reform and the waste and devastation they are likely to bring about.

In 1699, Swift's English idyll ended when he returned to Ireland as chaplain to the Lord Justice, although he still cherished hopes of a post back in England. Like most Anglo-Irish, Swift regarded it as a penance to live in what he called "wretched Dublin in miserable Ireland"; warmth, light, laughter, and civilization lay across the Irish Sea in England. From this point on, he seems to have become deeply committed to his double vocation as clergyman and writer. He served and defended the Anglican church with fierce devotion, and continued to write brilliant political and religious satires, often for the Tory ministers Bolingbroke and Oxford. Instead of the English bishopric he hoped for, in 1713 he was given the deanship at Dublin's St. Patrick's Cathedral. Britain's Tory government soon fell from power, weakening the influence of Swift's friends, and he resigned himself to spending the remainder of his life in Ireland.

Despite his own feelings about living in Ireland, Swift won the enduring respect of Irish people for two brilliant satirical pieces. *The Drapier Letters* (1724) purports to be correspondence from a humble Dublin draper; the letters take aim at England's corrupt move to devalue Irish coinage when Ireland was already in a severe depression. The Crown offered a reward for the name of the author of the anonymous *Letters*, but although Swift's authorship was widely known, no one betrayed him. *A Modest Proposal* (1729), a satire on the many cold-blooded or impractical "projects" devised by British outsiders to solve the woes of the Irish economy, was published five years later. In this outrageous satire, Swift's persona, a social scientist, recommends in his sweetly reasonable voice that the dual problems of Irish famine and Irish overpopulation could be solved by the simple expedient of breeding, raising, butchering, and eating Irish babies. In the end, he seems to suggest that he has been driven mad by the utter failure of humane and rational solutions he has proposed in the past to the Irish and their absentee landlords.

Swift's life darkened toward its end as he became more grievously afflicted by Ménière's syndrome, from which he apparently suffered most of his life; the neurological condition is marked by increasing deafness, vertigo, and nausea. Esther Johnson, his beloved friend, died in 1728. By 1732, Swift's ailments caused him to resign his duties as dean, although he remained mentally sound. Gradually, old friends deserted him, and in 1742, after he suffered a paralytic stroke that left him mute, guardians were appointed to manage his affairs. He died in 1745. The epitaph Swift composed for himself in Latin was well translated by his countryman William Butler Yeats:

> Swift has sailed into his rest.
> Savage indignation there
> Cannot lacerate his breast.
> Imitate him if you dare,
> World-besotted traveller, he
> Served human liberty.

WORK

Travels into Several Remote Nations of the World (1726), supposedly penned by one "Lemuel Gulliver, first a surgeon and then a captain of several Ships," is Swift's greatest work, and it is one of the richest, most challenging texts in the English language. Its surface is so simple and fascinating that children enjoy it; its depths are so complex and slippery that critics have been fighting about it ever since its appearance. Lemuel Gulliver (from *gull*, an easily duped person) throughout is portrayed as a decent, occasionally resourceful fellow who, like Voltaire's Candide, is not terribly bright and is apt to accept uncritically what he's told. Gulliver undertakes four voyages in the course of the *Travels*; we present here a portion of the third and all of the fourth. On Gulliver's first voyage, he is shipwrecked on the shores of the Lilliputians, who initially appear to be an enchantingly tiny and delicate people; their smallness in other regards—their overly dainty manners, their petty politics, and their narrow-mindedness—reveals itself, but only very partially and gradually, to Gulliver, who will be accused by his Lilliputian enemies of such offenses as urinating in public (which he does in order to put out a raging fire in the palace) and of committing adultery with the six-inch-tall wife of the Lilliputian Secretary of the Treasury.

His second voyage lands Gulliver among the Brobdingnagians, giants whose blunt speech and physical grossness disgust him; thanks to the accident of proportion, Brobdingnagian warts and pimples appear the size of boulders to the fastidious Gulliver. But these giants prove to be as large hearted and broad-minded as they are physically big. Gulliver finds himself in the awkward position of defending English government and European mores and culture to their thoughtful king, who can only shake his head at the inhumane, petty, and wasteful practices he hears described, ranging from the customs of court preferment to the horrors of warfare.

The third voyage is largely a satire upon "projectors" like those whom Bacon so enthusiastically describes in *The New Atlantis*. At the Grand Academy of Lagado, the theory-maddened projectors do not care that their social, linguistic, and scientific experiments are impractical or destructive; the experiment is all.

The final voyage is the most troubling. It takes Gulliver to the country of the Houyhnhnms, the supremely rational horses, with their nasty-tempered draft-animals, the human-looking Yahoos. Houyhnhnm society is inarguably in some ways an improvement over European ones. Free as it is from all dissent, shock, excess, greed, pride, and grief, it is a sort of utopia, but like *Candide*'s El Dorado, it is paradoxically an imperfect one, in that normal human beings would have a difficult time submitting to a lifetime of Houyhnhnmland's bland conformity. The upper-class equine citizens graze together in unending amiability, conversing about the virtues of friendship and benevolence. Their lives are supported by the work of their own Houyhnhnm servant-class. Those with white, sorrel, and gray coats are adjudged to be "naturally" the inferiors of bay, black, and dapple-gray Houyhnhnms, and all accept the distinction; there are no rebels here. The catch is that, for good or ill, human beings are not Houyhnhnms: They possess feelings as well as reason. If a life of perfect rationalism means a life without conflict, it also means a life without joy or love, or art, or most things that seem to define for us the best of the human condition. The Houyhnhnms cannot be a symbol for moderate or well-balanced men and women, for they are devoid of all but the mildest ripples of emotions, and they have no imaginations. They cannot, for example, extend themselves to see that the Gulliver who stands before them actually is an exception to the rule, a rational Yahoo. They dwell in an insipid middle state of being that is not really a human possibility at all.

The Yahoos disturb most readers of *Gulliver's Travels*. These creatures, very likely descended from a marooned human couple, are all passion and gross sensuality. They are lazy, filthy, lustful, greedy, and aggressive. (They are, in fact, very like contemporary English notions of the Irish, who were caricatured as brawny, stupid, dirty, oversexed simians; part of what Swift is describing is the relationship between colonizer and colonized.) The Houyhnhnms claim Yahoos lack reason and the ability to learn; luckily, they also lack the technology of European people to pursue their aggressive impulses, and can only scratch, bite, and lob excrement at their foes. Yet some of their practices seem alarmingly like European ones. Yahoo females flirt with males with whom they have no intention of mating. Yahoos hoard pretty rocks and fight over them; often, one Yahoo acts as go-between when two others are involved in such a dispute and makes off with the treasure himself in lawyerlike fashion. Yahoos, like human beings, are subject to causeless fits of melancholy and depression, and, unlike any other animals except human beings, Yahoos initially frighten or repel all other creatures in their vicinity. They are unmistakably degenerate versions of human beings, though just how degenerated Swift intended them to seem is not clear.

Gulliver, always easily impressed, is totally won to the horses' way of life, and desperately disassociates himself from the Yahoos. His voice takes on a whinnying note and his gait is a modified trot, in imitation of his masters. He has become a servile toady among the rational equines, thinking of himself and the Houyhnhnms as Us, the Yahoos as Them. Exiled from the land, he embarks in a boat caulked with Yahoo tallow whose sails are fashioned from tanned Yahoo skins, and he troubles himself no more than the Houyhnhnms about Yahoo genocide. Later, he is disgusted by the very sight of the generous captain who rescues him, and once back home he is only by degrees able to bear the company of his own family, preferring to be with his carriage horses. Perhaps the final indictment is that people are capable of such mad egotism as Gulliver displays at the end, sitting smug and deluded in his darkened stable.

At the heart of the book lies the question, What does it mean to be a human being? Swift, unlike the Deists of his age, is certainly not on the optimistic side of this question, and he is certainly at some distance from the misanthropic Gulliver, but exactly where he himself would place humanity on the scale between Houyhnhnm and Yahoo is not at all clear. Readers take passionate—and very different—positions on that vexing question.

SUGGESTED READINGS

A good critical biography of Swift is David Nokes's *Jonathan Swift; A Hypocrite Reversed* (1985). Frank Brady's *Twentieth Century Interpretations of Gulliver's Travels* (1968) is a compendium of critical essays on that work.

Gulliver's Travels

PART III.

A VOYAGE TO LAPUTA, BALNIBARBI, GLUBBDUBDRIB, LUGGNAGG, AND JAPAN

Chapter 5

The Author permitted to see the Grand Academy of Lagado.[1] *The Academy
largely described. The Arts wherein the professors employ themselves.*

This Academy is not an entire single building, but a continuation of several
houses on both sides of a street, which growing waste was purchased and applied to
that use.

I was received very kindly by the Warden, and went for many days to the
Academy. Every room hath in it one or more projectors, and I believe I could not
be in fewer than five hundred rooms.

The first man I saw was of a meagre aspect, with sooty hands and face, his hair
and beard long, ragged and singed in several places. His clothes, shirt, and skin,
were all of the same colour. He had been eight years upon a project for extracting
sun-beams out of cucumbers, which were to be put into vials hermetically sealed,
and let out to warm the air in raw inclement summers. He told me, he did not
doubt, in eight years more, he should be able to supply the Governor's gardens
with sunshine at a reasonable rate; but he complained that his stock was low, and
entreated me to give him something as an encouragement to ingenuity, especially
since this had been a very dear season for cucumbers. I made him a small present,
for my lord had furnished me with money on purpose, because he knew their
practice of begging from all who go to see them.

I went into another chamber, but was ready to hasten back, being almost
overcome with a horrible stink. My conductor pressed me forward, conjuring me
in a whisper to give no offence, which would be highly resented, and therefore I
durst not so much as stop my nose. The projector of this cell was the most ancient
student of the Academy; his face and beard were of a pale yellow; his hands and
clothes daubed over with filth. When I was presented to him, he gave me a close
embrace (a compliment I could well have excused). His employment from his first
coming into the Academy, was an operation to reduce human excrement to its
original food, by separating the several parts, removing the tincture which it receives
from the gall, making the odour exhale, and scumming off the saliva. He had a
weekly allowance from the society, of a vessel filled with human ordure, about the
bigness of a Bristol barrel.

I saw another at work to calcine ice into gunpowder, who likewise showed me
a treatise he had written concerning the malleability of fire, which he intended to
publish.

There was a most ingenious architect who had contrived a new method
for building houses, by beginning at the roof, and working downwards to the
foundation, which he justified to me by the like practice of those two prudent
insects, the bee and the spider.

There was a man born blind, who had several apprentices in his own condition:
their employment was to mix colours for painters, which their master taught them

---

[1] The account of the Academy of Lagado satirizes the Royal Society of London, founded in 1662 to
advance knowledge.

to distinguish by feeling and smelling. It was indeed my misfortune to find them at that time not very perfect in their lessons, and the professor himself happened to be generally mistaken: this artist is much encouraged and esteemed by the whole fraternity.

In another apartment I was highly pleased with a projector, who had found a device for ploughing the ground with hogs, to save the charges of ploughs, cattle, and labour. The method is this: in an acre of ground you bury, at six inches distance and eight deep, a quantity of acorns, dates, chestnuts, and other mast or vegetables whereof these animals are fondest; then you drive six hundred or more of them into the field, where in a few days they will root up the whole ground in search of their food, and make it fit for sowing, at the same time manuring it with their dung. It is true, upon experiment they found the charge and trouble very great, and they had little or no crop. However, it is not doubted that this invention may be capable of great improvement.

I went into another room, where the walls and ceiling were all hung round with cobwebs, except a narrow passage for the artist to go in and out. At my entrance he called aloud to me not to disturb his webs. He lamented the fatal mistake the world had been so long in of using silk-worms, while we had such plenty of domestic insects, who infinitely excelled the former, because they understood how to weave as well as spin. And he proposed farther, that by employing spiders, the charge of dying silks should be wholly saved, whereof I was fully convinced when he showed me a vast number of flies most beautifully coloured, wherewith he fed his spiders, assuring us, that the webs would take a tincture from them; and as he had them in all hues, he hoped to fit everybody's fancy, as soon as he could find proper food for the flies, of certain gums, oils, and other glutinous matter to give a strength and consistence to the threads.

There was an astronomer who had undertaken to place a sun-dial upon the great weathercock on the town-house, by adjusting the annual and diurnal motions of the earth and sun, so as to answer and coincide with all accidental turnings by the wind.

I was complaining of a small fit of colic, upon which my conductor led me into a room, where a great physician resided, who was famous for curing that disease by contrary operations from the same instrument. He had a large pair of bellows with a long slender muzzle of ivory. This he conveyed eight inches up the anus, and drawing in the wind, he affirmed he could make the guts as lank as a dried bladder. But when the disease was more stubborn and violent, he let in the muzzle while the bellows were full of wind, which he discharged into the body of the patient, then withdrew the instrument to replenish it, clapping his thumb strongly against the orifice of the fundament; and this being repeated three or four times, the adventitious wind would rush out, bringing the noxious along with it (like water put into a pump), and the patient recover. I saw him try both experiments upon a dog, but could not discern any effect from the former. After the latter, the animal was ready to burst, and made so violent a discharge, as was very offensive to me and my companions. The dog died on the spot, and we left the doctor endeavouring to recover him by the same operation.

I visited many other apartments, but shall not trouble my reader with all the curiosities I observed, being studious of brevity.

I had hitherto seen only one side of the Academy, the other being appropriated to the advancers of speculative learning, of whom I shall say something when I have mentioned one illustrious person more, who is called among them *the universal artist*. He told us he had been thirty years employing his thoughts for the improvement of human life. He had two large rooms full of wonderful curiosities, and fifty men at work. Some were condensing air into a dry tangible substance, by extracting the nitre, and letting the aqueous or fluid particles percolate; others softening marble for pillows and pincushions; other petrifying the hoofs of a living horse to preserve them from foundering. The artist himself was at that time busy upon two great designs; the first, to sow land with chaff, wherein he affirmed the true seminal virtue to be contained, as he demonstrated by several experiments which I was not skilful enough to comprehend. The other was, by a certain composition of gums, minerals, and vegetables outwardly applied, to prevent the growth of wool upon two young lambs; and he hoped in a reasonable time to propagate the breed of naked sheep all over the kingdom.

We crossed a walk to the other part of the Academy, where, as I have already said, the projectors in speculative learning resided.

The first professor I saw was in a very large room, with forty pupils about him. After salutation, observing me to look earnestly upon a frame, which took up the greatest part of both the length and breadth of the room, he said perhaps I might wonder to see him employed in a project for improving speculative knowledge by practical and mechanical operations. But the world would soon be sensible of its usefulness, and he flattered himself that a more noble exalted thought never sprang in any other man's head. Every one knew how laborious the usual method is of attaining to arts and sciences; whereas, by his contrivance, the most ignorant person at a reasonable charge, and with a little bodily labour, may write books in philosophy, poetry, politics, law, mathematics, and theology, without the least assistance from genius or study. He then led me to the frame, about the sides whereof all his pupils stood in ranks. It was twenty foot square, placed in the middle of the room. The superficies[2] was composed of several bits of wood, about the bigness of a die, but some larger than others. They were all linked together by slender wires. These bits of wood were covered on every square with paper pasted on them, and on these papers were written all the words of their language, in their several moods, tenses, and declensions, but without any order. The professor then desired me to observe, for he was going to set his engine at work. The pupils at his command took each of them hold of an iron handle, whereof there were forty fixed round the edges of the frame, and giving them a sudden turn, the whole disposition[3] of the words was entirely changed. He then commanded six and thirty of the lads to read the several lines softly as they appeared upon the frame; and where they found three or four words together that might make part of a sentence, they dictated to the four remaining boys who were scribes. This work was repeated three or four times, and at every turn the engine was so contrived, that the words shifted into new places, as the square bits of wood moved upside down.

Six hours a day the young students were employed in this labour, and the professor showed me several volumes in large folio already collected, of broken sentences, which he intended to piece together, and out of those rich materials to give the world a complete body of all arts and sciences; which, however, might be still improved, and much expedited, if the public would raise a fund for making and employing five hundred such frames in Lagado, and oblige the managers to contribute in common their several collections.

He assured me, that this invention had employed all his thoughts from his youth, that he had emptied the whole vocabulary into his frame, and made the strictest

---

[2]Surface.
[3]Arrangement.

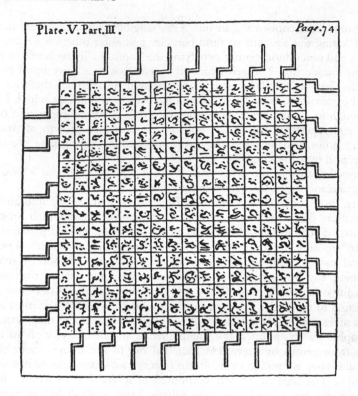

Plate.V. Part.III.　　　　　　　　Page.74.

computation of the general proportion there is in books between the numbers of particles, nouns, and verbs, and other parts of speech.

I made my humblest acknowledgment to this illustrious person for his great communicativeness, and promised if ever I had the good fortune to return to my native country, that I would do him justice, as the sole inventor of this wonderful machine; the form and contrivance of which I desired leave to delineate upon paper, as in the figure here annexed. I told him, although it were the custom of our learned in Europe to steal inventions from each other, who had thereby at least this advantage, that it became a controversy which was the right owner, yet I would take such caution, that he should have the honour entire without a rival.

We next went to the school of languages, where three professors sat in consultation upon improving that of their own country.

The first project was to shorten discourse by cutting polysyllables into one, and leaving out verbs and participles, because in reality all things imaginable are but nouns.

The other project was a scheme for entirely abolishing all words whatsoever; and this was urged as a great advantage in point of health as well as brevity. For it is plain, that every word we speak is in some degree a diminution of our lungs by corrosion, and consequently contributes to the shortening of our lives. An expedient was therefore offered, that since words are only names for *things*, it would be more convenient for all men to carry about them such things as were necessary to express the particular business they are to discourse on. And this invention would certainly have taken place, to the great ease as well as health of the subject, if the women, in conjunction with the vulgar and illiterate, had not threatened to raise a rebellion, unless they might be allowed the liberty to speak with their tongues, after the manner of their ancestors; such constant irreconcilable enemies to science are the common people. However, many of the most learned and wise adhere to the new scheme of expressing themselves by things, which hath only this inconvenience attending it, that if a man's business be very great, and of various kinds, he must be obliged in proportion to carry a greater bundle of things upon his back, unless he can afford one or two strong servants to attend him. I have often beheld two of those sages almost sinking under the weight of their packs, like pedlars among us; who, when they met in the streets, would lay down their loads, open their sacks, and hold conversation for an hour together; then put up their implements, help each other to resume their burthens, and take their leave.

But for short conversations a man may carry implements in his pockets and under his arms, enough to supply him, and in his house he cannot be at a loss. Therefore the room where company meet who practice this art, is full of all things ready at hand, requisite to furnish matter for this kind of artificial converse.

Another great advantage proposed by this invention, was that it would serve as an universal language to be understood in all civilised nations, whose goods and utensils are generally of the same kind, or nearly resembling, so that their uses might easily be comprehended. And thus ambassadors would be qualified to treat with foreign princes or ministers of state, to whose tongues they were utter strangers.

I was at the mathematical school, where the master taught his pupils after a method scarce imaginable to us in Europe. The proposition and demonstration were fairly written on a thin wafer, with ink composed of a cephalic tincture.[4] This the student was to swallow upon a fasting stomach, and for three days following eat nothing but bread and water. As the wafer digested, the tincture mounted to his brain, bearing the proposition along with it. But the success hath not hitherto been answerable, partly by some error in the *quantum*[5] or composition, and partly by the perverseness of lads, to whom this bolus[6] is so nauseous, that they generally steal aside, and discharge it upwards before it can operate; neither have they been yet persuaded to use so long an abstinence as the prescription requires.

PART IV.
A VOYAGE TO THE COUNTRY OF THE HOUYHNHNMS[7]

Chapter 1

The Author sets out as Captain of a ship. His men conspire against him, confine him a long time to his cabin, set him on shore in an unknown land. He travels up into the country. The Yahoos, a strange sort of animal, described. The Author meets two Houyhnhnms.

I continued at home with my wife and children about five months in a very happy condition, if I could have learned the lesson of knowing when I was well. I left my poor wife big with child, and accepted an advantageous offer made me to be Captain of the *Adventurer,* a stout merchantman of 350 tons: for I understood navigation well, and being grown weary of a surgeon's employment at sea, which

---

[4] A dye that is drawn toward the brain when injected.
[5] Amount.
[6] A pill.
[7] The name, pronounced *Hwin'ims*, is meant to sound like the neigh of a horse.

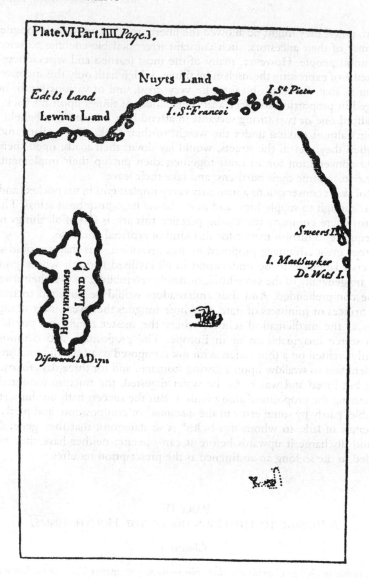

Plate.VI.Part.IIII.Page.].

Nuyts Land

Edels Land

Lewins Land

I. S.ᵗFrancoi

I. Sᵗ Pieter

Sweers I

I. Maetsuyker
De Witt I.

HOUTKINKSNIS LAND

Discovered. AD 1711

however I could exercise upon occasion, I took a skilful young man of that calling, one Robert Purefoy, into my ship. We set sail from Portsmouth upon the seventh day of September, 1710; on the fourteenth we met with Captain Pocock of Bristol, at Teneriffe,[8] who was going to the bay of Campechy,[9] to cut logwood. On the sixteenth, he was parted from us by a storm; I heard since my return, that his ship foundered, and none escaped but one cabin boy. He was an honest man, and a good sailor, but a little too positive in his own opinions, which was the cause of his

---

[8]One of the Canary Islands.
[9]In the Gulf of Mexico.

destruction, as it hath been of several others. For if he had followed my advice, he might have been safe at home with his family at this time, as well as myself.

I had several men died in my ship of calentures,[10] so that I was forced to get recruits out of Barbadoes, and the Leeward Islands, where I touched by the direction of the merchants who employed me, which I had soon too much cause to repent: for I found afterwards that most of them had been buccaneers. I had fifty hands on board, and my orders were, that I should trade with the Indians in the South-Sea, and make what discoveries I could. These rogues whom I had picked up debauched my other men, and they all formed a conspiracy to seize the ship and secure me; which they did one morning, rushing into my cabin, and binding me hand and foot, threatening to throw me overboard, if I offered to stir. I told them, I was their prisoner, and would submit. This they made me swear to do, and then they unbound me, only fastening one of my legs with a chain near my bed, and placed a sentry at my door with his piece charged, who was commanded to shoot me dead, if I attempted my liberty. They sent me down victuals and drink, and took the government of the ship to themselves. Their design was to turn pirates, and plunder the Spaniards, which they could not do, till they got more men. But first they resolved to sell the goods in the ship, and then go to Madagascar for recruits, several among them having died since my confinement. They sailed many weeks, and traded with the Indians, but I knew not what course they took, being kept a close prisoner in my cabin, and expecting nothing less than to be murdered, as they often threatened me.

Upon the ninth day of May, 1711, one James Welch came down to my cabin; and said he had orders from the Captain to get me ashore. I expostulated with him, but in vain; neither would he so much as tell me who their new Captain was. They forced me into the longboat, letting me put on my best suit of clothes, which were as good as new, and a small bundle of linen, but no arms except my hanger; and they were so civil as not to search my pockets, into which I conveyed what money I had, with some other little necessaries. They rowed about a league, and then set me down on a strand. I desired them to tell me what country it was. They all swore, they knew no more than myself, but said, that the Captain (as they called him) was resolved, after they had sold the lading, to get rid of me in the first place where they could discover land. They pushed off immediately, advising me to make haste, for fear of being overtaken by the tide, and so bade me farewell.

In this desolate condition I advanced forward, and soon got upon firm ground, where I sat down on a bank to rest myself, and consider what I had best to do. When I was a little refreshed, I went up into the country, resolving to deliver myself to the first savages I should meet, and purchase my life from them by some bracelets, glass rings, and other toys which sailors usually provide themselves with in those voyages, and whereof I had some about me. The land was divided by long rows of trees, not regularly planted, but naturally growing; there was great plenty of grass, and several fields of oats. I walked very circumspectly for fear of being surprised, or suddenly shot with an arrow from behind or on either side. I fell into a beaten road, where I saw many tracks of human feet, and some of cows, but most of horses. At last I beheld several animals in a field, and one or two of the same kind sitting in trees. Their shape was very singular, and deformed, which a little discomposed me, so that I lay down behind a thicket to observe them better. Some of them coming forward near the place where I lay, gave me an opportunity of distinctly marking

---

[10] A tropical fever.

their form. Their heads and breasts were covered with a thick hair, some frizzled and others lank; they had beards like goats, and a long ridge of hair down their backs and the fore parts of their legs and feet, but the rest of their bodies were bare, so that I might see their skins, which were of a brown buff colour. They had no tails, nor any hair at all on their buttocks, except about the anus; which, I presume, nature had placed there to defend them as they sat on the ground; for this posture they used, as well as lying down, and often stood on their hind feet. They climbed high trees, as nimbly as a squirrel, for they had strong extended claws before and behind, terminating in sharp points, and hooked. They would often spring, and bound, and leap with prodigious agility. The females were not so large as the males; they had long lank hair on their heads, but none on their faces, nor any thing more than a sort of down on the rest of their bodies, except about the anus, and pudenda. Their dugs hung between their fore-feet, and often reached almost to the ground as they walked. The hair of both sexes was of several colours, brown, red, black, and yellow. Upon the whole, I never beheld in all my travels so disagreeable an animal, nor one against which I naturally conceived so strong an antipathy. So that thinking I had seen enough, full of contempt and aversion, I got up and pursued the beaten road, hoping it might direct me to the cabin of some Indian. I had not got far when I met one of these creatures full in my way, and coming up directly to me. The ugly monster, when he saw me, distorted several ways every feature of his visage, and stared as at an object he had never seen before; then approaching nearer, lifted up his fore-paw, whether out of curiosity or mischief, I could not tell. But I drew my hanger, and gave him a good blow with the flat side of it, for I durst not strike with the edge, fearing the inhabitants might be provoked against me, if they should come to know, that I had killed or maimed any of their cattle. When the beast felt the smart, he drew back, and roared so loud, that a herd of at least forty came flocking about me from the next field, howling and making odious faces; but I ran to the body of a tree, and leaning my back against it, kept them off by waving my hanger. Several of this cursed brood getting hold of the branches behind, leapt up into the tree, from whence they began to discharge their excrements on my head; however, I escaped pretty well, by sticking close to the stem of the tree, but was almost stifled with the filth, which fell about me on every side.

In the midst of this distress, I observed them all to run away on a sudden as fast as they could, at which I ventured to leave the tree, and pursue the road, wondering what it was that could put them into this fright. But looking on my left hand, I saw a horse walking softly in the field; which my persecutors having sooner discovered, was the cause of their flight. The horse started a little when he came near me, but soon recovering himself, looked full in my face with manifest tokens of wonder: he viewed my hands and feet, walking round me several times. I would have pursued my journey, but he placed himself directly in the way, yet looking with a very mild aspect, never offering the least violence. We stood gazing at each other for some time; at last I took the boldness to reach my hand towards his neck, with a design to stroke it, using the common style and whistle of jockeys when they are going to handle a strange horse. But this animal seeming to receive my civilities with disdain, shook his head, and bent his brows, softly raising up his right fore-foot to remove my hand. Then he neighed three or four times, but in so different a cadence, that I almost began to think he was speaking to himself in some language of his own.

While he and I were thus employed, another horse came up; who applying himself to the first in a very formal manner, they gently struck each other's right hoof before, neighing several times by turns, and varying the sound, which seemed to be almost articulate. They went some paces off, as if it were to confer together,

The mare soon after my entrance, rose from her mat, and coming up close, after having nicely observed my hands and face, gave me a most contemptuous look; then turning to the horse, I heard the word *Yahoo* often repeated betwixt them; the meaning of which word I could not then comprehend, although it were the first I had learned to pronounce; but I was soon better informed, to my everlasting mortification: for the horse beckoning to me with his head, and repeating the word *Hhuun, Hhuun,* as he did upon the road, which I understood was to attend him, led me out into a kind of court, where was another building at some distance from the house. Here we entered, and I saw three of those detestable creatures, whom I first met after my landing, feeding upon roots, and the flesh of some animals, which I afterwards found to be that of asses and dogs, and now and then a cow dead by accident or disease. They were all tied by the neck with strong withes, fastened to a beam; they held their food between the claws of their fore-feet, and tore it with their teeth.

The master horse ordered a sorrel nag, one of his servants, to untie the largest of these animals, and take him into the yard. The beast and I were brought close together, and our countenances diligently compared, both by master and servant, who thereupon repeated several times the word *Yahoo.* My horror and astonishment are not to be described, when I observed, in this abominable animal, a perfect human figure: the face of it indeed was flat and broad, the nose depressed, the lips large, and the mouth wide. But these differences are common to all savage nations, where the lineaments of the countenance are distorted by the natives suffering their infants to lie grovelling on the earth, or by carrying them on their backs, nuzzling with their face against the mother's shoulders. The fore-feet of the *Yahoo* differed from my hands in nothing else but the length of the nails, the coarseness and brownness of the palms, and the hairiness on the backs. There was the same resemblance between our feet, with the same differences, which I knew very well, though the horses did not, because of my shoes and stockings; the same in every part of our bodies, except as to hairiness and colour, which I have already described.

The great difficulty that seemed to stick with the two horses, was, to see the rest of my body so very different from that of a *Yahoo*, for which I was obliged to my clothes, whereof they had no conception. The sorrel nag offered me a root, which he held (after their manner, as we shall describe in its proper place) between his hoof and pastern; I took it in my hand, and having smelt it, returned it to him again as civilly as I could. He brought out of the *Yahoo's* kennel a piece of ass's flesh, but it smelt so offensively that I turned from it with loathing: he then threw it to the *Yahoo*, by whom it was greedily devoured. He afterwards showed me a wisp of hay, and a fetlock full of oats; but I shook my head, to signify, that neither of these were food for me. And indeed, I now apprehended that I must absolutely starve, if I did not get to some of my own species; for as to those filthy *Yahoos*, although there were few greater lovers of mankind, at that time, than myself, yet I confess I never saw any sensitive being so detestable on all accounts; and the more I came near them, the more hateful they grew, while I stayed in that country. This the master horse observed by my behaviour, and therefore sent the *Yahoo* back to his kennel. He then put his fore-hoof to his mouth, at which I was much surprised, although he did it with ease, and with a motion that appeared perfectly natural, and made other signs to know what I would eat; but I could not return him such an answer as he was able to apprehend; and if he had understood me, I did not see how it was possible to contrive any way for finding myself nourishment. While we were thus engaged, I observed a cow passing by, whereupon I pointed to her, and expressed a desire to let me go and milk her. This had its effect; for he led me back into the house, and ordered a mare-servant to open a room, where a good store of milk lay in earthen and wooden vessels, after a very orderly and cleanly manner. She gave me a large bowl full, of which I drank very heartily, and found myself well refreshed.

About noon I saw coming towards the house a kind of vehicle, drawn like a sledge by four *Yahoos*. There was in it an old steed, who seemed to be of quality; he alighted with his hind-feet forward, having by accident got a hurt in his left fore-foot. He came to dine with our horse, who received him with great civility. They dined in the best room, and had oats boiled in milk for the second course, which the old horse eat warm, but the rest cold. Their mangers were placed circular in the middle of the room, and divided into several partitions, round which they sat on their haunches upon bosses of straw. In the middle was a large rack with angles answering to every partition of the manger; so that each horse and mare eat their own hay, and their own mash of oats and milk, with much decency and regularity. The behaviour of the young colt and foal appeared very modest, and that of the master and mistress extremely cheerful and complaisant to their guest. The gray ordered me to stand by him, and much discourse passed between him and his friend concerning me, as I found by the stranger's often looking on me, and the frequent repetition of the word *Yahoo*.

I happened to wear my gloves, which the master gray observing, seemed perplexed, discovering signs of wonder what I had done to my fore-feet; he put his hoof three or four times to them, as if he would signify, that I should reduce them to their former shape, which I presently did, pulling off both my gloves, and putting them into my pocket. This occasioned farther talk, and I saw the company was pleased with my behaviour, whereof I soon found the good effects. I was ordered to speak the few words I understood, and while they were at dinner, the master taught me the names for oats, milk, fire, water, and some others; which I could readily pronounce after him, having from my youth a great facility in learning languages.

When dinner was done, the master horse took me aside, and by signs and words made me understand the concern that he was in, that I had nothing to eat. Oats in their tongue are called *hlunnh*. This word I pronounced two or three times; for although I had refused them at first, yet upon second thoughts, I considered that I could contrive to make of them a kind of bread, which might be sufficient with milk to keep me alive, till I could make my escape to some other country, and to creatures of my own species. The horse immediately ordered a white mare-servant of his family to bring me a good quantity of oats in a sort of wooden tray. These I heated before the fire as well as I could, and rubbed them till the husks came off, which I made a shift to winnow from the grain; I ground and beat them between two stones, then took water, and made them into a paste or cake, which I toasted at the fire, and ate warm with milk. It was at first a very insipid diet, though common enough in many parts of Europe, but grew tolerable by time; and having been often reduced to hard fare in my life, this was not the first experiment I had made how easily nature is satisfied. And I cannot but observe, that I never had one hour's sickness, while I stayed in this island. 'Tis true, I sometimes made a shift to catch a rabbit, or bird, by springes[11] made of *Yahoos'* hairs, and I often gathered wholesome herbs, which I boiled, and eat as salads with my bread, and now and then, for a rarity, I made a little butter, and drank the whey. I was at first at a great loss for salt; but custom soon reconciled the want of it; and I am confident that the frequent use

---

[11] Snares.

of salt among us is an effect of luxury, and was first introduced only as a provocative to drink; except where it is necessary for preserving of flesh in long voyages, or in places remote from great markets. For we observe no animal to be fond of it but man: and as to myself, when I left this country, it was a great while before I could endure the taste of it in anything that I eat.

This is enough to say upon the subject of my diet, wherewith other travellers fill their books, as if the readers were personally concerned whether we fared well or ill. However, it was necessary to mention this matter, lest the world should think it impossible that I could find sustenance for three years in such a country, and among such inhabitants.

When it grew towards evening, the master horse ordered a place for me to lodge in; it was but six yards from the house, and separated from the stable of the *Yahoos*. Here I got some straw, and covering myself with my own clothes, slept very sound. But I was in a short time better accommodated, as the reader shall know hereafter, when I come to treat more particularly about my way of living.

Chapter 3

The Author studious to learn the language, the Houyhnhnm *his master assists in teaching him. The language described. Several* Houyhnhnms *of quality come out of curiosity to see the Author. He gives his master a short account of his voyage.*

My principal endeavour was to learn the language, which my master (for so I shall henceforth call him), and his children, and every servant of his house, were desirous to teach me. For they looked upon it as a prodigy that a brute animal should discover such marks of a rational creature. I pointed to every thing, and enquired the name of it, which I wrote down in my journal-book when I was alone, and corrected my bad accent by desiring those of the family to pronounce it often. In this employment, a sorrel nag, one of the under servants, was very ready to assist me.

In speaking, they pronounce through the nose and throat, and their language approaches nearest to the High-Dutch, or German, of any I know in Europe; but is much more graceful and significant. The Emperor Charles V. made almost the same observation, when he said, that if he were to speak to his horse, it should be in High-Dutch.

The curiosity and impatience of my master were so great, that he spent many hours of his leisure to instruct me. He was convinced (as he afterwards told me) that I must be a *Yahoo*, but my teachableness, civility, and cleanliness, astonished him; which were qualities altogether so opposite to those animals. He was most perplexed about my clothes, reasoning sometimes with himself, whether they were a part of my body: for I never pulled them off till the family were asleep, and got them on before they waked in the morning. My master was eager to learn from whence I came, how I acquired those appearances of reason, which I discovered in all my actions, and to know my story from my own mouth, which he hoped he should soon do by the great proficiency I made in learning and pronouncing their words and sentences. To help my memory, I formed all I learned into the English alphabet, and writ the words down with the translations. This last, after some time, I ventured to do in my master's presence. It cost me much trouble to explain to him what I was doing; for the inhabitants have not the least idea of books or literature.

In about ten weeks time I was able to understand most of his questions, and in three months could give him some tolerable answers. He was extremely curious to know from what part of the country I came, and how I was taught to imitate a rational creature, because the *Yahoos* (whom he saw I exactly resembled in my head, hands, and face, that were only visible), with some appearance of cunning, and the strongest disposition to mischief, were observed to be the most unteachable of all brutes. I answered, that I came over the sea from a far place, with many others of my own kind, in a great hollow vessel made of the bodies of trees. That my companions forced me to land on this coast, and then left me to shift for myself. It was with some difficulty, and by the help of many signs, that I brought him to understand me. He replied, that I must needs be mistaken, or that I *said the thing which was not*. (For they have no word in their language to express lying or falsehood.) He knew it was impossible that there could be a country beyond the sea, or that a parcel of brutes could move a wooden vessel whither they pleased upon water. He was sure no *Houyhnhnm* alive could make such a vessel, nor would trust *Yahoos* to manage it.

The word *Houyhnhnm*, in their tongue, signifies a *horse*, and in its etymology, *the perfection of nature*. I told my master, that I was at a loss for expression, but would improve as fast as I could; and hoped in a short time I should be able to tell him wonders: he was pleased to direct his own mare, his colt and foal, and the servants of the family, to take all opportunities of instructing me, and every day for two or three hours, he was at the same pains himself. Several horses and mares of quality in the neighbourhood came often to our house upon the report spread of a wonderful *Yahoo*, that could speak like a *Houyhnhnm*, and seemed in his words and actions to discover some glimmerings of reason. These delighted to converse with me: they put many questions, and received such answers as I was able to return. By all these advantages, I made so great a progress, that in five months from my arrival I understood whatever was spoke, and could express myself tolerably well.

The *Houyhnhnms* who came to visit my master, out of a design of seeing and talking with me, could hardly believe me to be a right *Yahoo*, because my body had a different covering from others of my kind. They were astonished to observe me without the usual hair or skin, except on my head, face, and hands; but I discovered that secret to my master, upon an accident, which happened about a fortnight before.

I have already told the reader, that every night when the family were gone to bed, it was my custom to strip and cover myself with my clothes: it happened one morning early, that my master sent for me, by the sorrel nag, who was his valet; when he came, I was fast asleep, my clothes fallen off on one side, and my shirt above my waist. I awaked at the noise he made, and observed him to deliver his message in some disorder; after which he went to my master, and in a great fright gave him a very confused account of what he had seen. This I presently discovered; for going as soon as I was dressed, to pay my attendance upon his Honour, he asked me the meaning of what his servant had reported, that I was not the same thing when I slept as I appeared to be at other times; that his valet assured him, some part of me was white, some yellow, at least not so white, and some brown.

I had hitherto concealed the secret of my dress, in order to distinguish myself, as much as possible, from that cursed race of *Yahoos*; but now I found it in vain to do so any longer. Besides, I considered that my clothes and shoes would soon wear out, which already were in a declining condition, and must be supplied by some contrivance from the hides of *Yahoos* or other brutes; whereby the whole secret would be known. I therefore told my master, that in the country from whence I came, those of my kind always covered their bodies with the hairs of certain animals prepared by art, as well for decency as to avoid the inclemencies of air, both hot and cold; of which, as to my own person, I would give him immediate conviction, if he pleased to command me: only desiring his excuse, if I did not expose those parts that nature taught us to conceal. He said my discourse was all very strange, but especially the last part; for he could not understand why nature should teach us to conceal what nature had given. That neither himself nor family were ashamed of any parts of their bodies; but however I might do as I pleased. Whereupon, I first unbuttoned my coat, and pulled it off. I did the same with my waistcoat; I drew off my shoes, stockings, and breeches. I let my shirt down to my waist, and drew up the bottom, fastening it like a girdle about my middle to hide my nakedness.

My master observed the whole performance with great signs of curiosity and admiration. He took up all my clothes in his pastern, one piece after another, and examined them diligently; he then stroked my body very gently, and looked round me several times, after which he said, it was plain that I must be a perfect *Yahoo;* but that I differed very much from the rest of my species, in the softness, and whiteness, and smoothness of my skin, my want of hair in several parts of my body, the shape and shortness of my claws behind and before, and my affectation of walking continually on my two hinder feet. He desired to see no more, and gave me leave to put on my clothes again, for I was shuddering with cold.

I expressed my uneasiness at his giving me so often the appellation of *Yahoo,* an odious animal, for which I had so utter a hatred and contempt. I begged he would forbear applying that word to me, and take the same order in his family, and among his friends whom he suffered to see me. I requested likewise, that the secret of my having a false covering to my body might be known to none but himself, at least as long as my present clothing should last; for as to what the sorrel nag his valet had observed, his Honour might command him to conceal it.

All this my master very graciously consented to, and thus the secret was kept till my clothes began to wear out, which I was forced to supply by several contrivances, that shall hereafter be mentioned. In the meantime, he desired I would go on with my utmost diligence to learn their language, because he was more astonished at my capacity for speech and reason, than at the figure of my body, whether it were covered or no; adding, that he waited with some impatience to hear the wonders which I promised to tell him.

From thenceforward he doubled the pains he had been at to instruct me; he brought me into all company, and made them treat me with civility, because, as he told them, privately, this would put me into good humour, and make me more diverting.

Every day when I waited on him, beside the trouble he was at in teaching, he would ask me several questions concerning myself, which I answered as well as I could; and by these means he had already received some general ideas, though very imperfect. It would be tedious to relate the several steps by which I advanced to a more regular conversation: but the first account I gave of myself in any order and length, was to this purpose:

That I came from a very far country, as I already had attempted to tell him, with about fifty more of my own species; that we travelled upon the seas, in a great hollow vessel made of wood, and larger than his Honour's house. I described the ship to him in the best terms I could, and explained by the help of my handkerchief displayed, how it was driven forward by the wind. That upon a quarrel among us, I was set on shore on this coast, where I walked forward without knowing whither, till he delivered me from the persecution of those execrable *Yahoos.* He asked me, who made the ship, and how it was possible that the *Houyhnhnms* of my country would leave it to the management of brutes? My answer was, that I durst proceed no further in my relation, unless he would give me his word and honour that he would not be offended, and then I would tell him the wonders I had so often promised. He agreed; and I went on by assuring him, that the ship was made by creatures like myself, who in all the countries I had travelled, as well as in my own, were the only governing, rational animals; and that upon my arrival hither, I was as much astonished to see the *Houyhnhnms* act like rational beings, as he or his friends could be in finding some marks of reason in a creature he was pleased to call a *Yahoo*, to which I owned my resemblance in every part, but could not account for their degenerate and brutal nature. I said farther, that if good fortune ever restored me to my native country, to relate my travels hither, as I resolved to do, every body would believe that I *said the thing which was not*; that I invented the story out of my own head; and with all possible respect to himself, his family and friends, and under his promise of not being offended, our countrymen would hardly think it probable, that a *Houyhnhnm* should be the presiding creature of a nation, and a *Yahoo* the brute.

Chapter 4

The Houyhnhnms' *notion of truth and falsehood. The Author's discourse disapproved by his master. The Author gives a more particular account of himself, and the accidents of his voyage.*

My master heard me with great appearances of uneasiness in his countenance, because *doubting*, or *not believing*, are so little known in this country, that the inhabitants cannot tell how to behave themselves under such circumstances. And I remember in frequent discourses with my master concerning the nature of manhood, in other parts of the world, having occasion to talk of *lying* and *false representation*, it was with much difficulty that he comprehended what I meant, although he had otherwise a most acute judgment. For he argued thus: that the use of speech was to make us understand one another, and to receive information of facts; now if any one *said the thing which was not*, these ends were defeated; because I cannot properly be said to understand him; and I am so far from receiving information, that he leaves me worse than in ignorance, for I am led to believe a thing black when it is white, and short when it is long. And these were all the notions he had concerning that faculty of *lying*, so perfectly well understood, and so universally practised, among human creatures.

To return from this digression; when I asserted that the *Yahoos* were the only governing animals in my country, which my master said was altogether past his conception, he desired to know, whether we had *Houyhnhnms* among us, and what was their employment: I told him, we had great numbers, that in summer they grazed in the fields, and in winter were kept in houses, with hay and oats, where *Yahoo* servants were employed to rub their skins smooth, comb their manes, pick their feet, serve them with food, and make their beds. I understand you well, said my master, it is now very plain, from all you have spoken, that whatever share of reason the *Yahoos* pretend to, the *Houyhnhnms* are your masters; I heartily wish our *Yahoos* would be so tractable. I begged his Honour would please to excuse me from proceeding any farther, because I was very certain that the account he expected from me would be highly displeasing. But he insisted in commanding me to let him know the best and the worst: I told him, he should be obeyed. I owned, that the *Houyhnhnms* among us, whom we called horses, were the most generous and comely animals we had, that they excelled in strength and swiftness; and when they belonged to persons of quality, employed in travelling, racing, or drawing chariots, they were treated with much kindness and care, till they fell into diseases, or became foundered in the feet; and then they were sold, and used to all kind of drudgery till they died; after which their skins were stripped and sold for what they were worth, and their bodies left to be devoured by dogs and birds of prey. But the common race of horses had not so good fortune, being kept by farmers and carriers, and other mean people, who put them to greater labour, and fed them worse. I described, as well as I could, our way of riding, the shape and use of a bridle, a saddle, a spur, and a whip, of harness and wheels. I added, that we fastened plates of a certain hard substance called iron at the bottom of their feet, to preserve their hoofs from being broken by the stony ways on which we often travelled.

My master, after some expressions of great indignation, wondered how we dared to venture upon a *Houyhnhnm's* back, for he was sure, that the weakest servant in his house would be able to shake off the strongest *Yahoo*, or by lying down, and rolling on his back, squeeze the brute to death. I answered, that our horses were trained up from three or four years old to the several uses we intended them for; that if any of them proved intolerably vicious, they were employed for carriages; that they were severely beaten while they were young for any mischievous tricks; that the males, designed for common use of riding or draught, were generally castrated about two years after their birth, to take down their spirits, and make them more tame and gentle; that they were indeed sensible of rewards and punishments; but his Honour would please to consider, that they had not the least tincture of reason any more than the *Yahoos* in this country.

It put me to the pains of many circumlocutions to give my master a right idea of what I spoke; for their language doth not abound in variety of words, because their wants and passions are fewer than among us. But it is impossible to express his noble resentment at our savage treatment of the *Houyhnhnm* race, particularly after I had explained the manner and use of castrating horses among us, to hinder them from propagating their kind, and to render them more servile. He said, if it were possible there could be any country where *Yahoos* alone were endued with reason, they certainly must be the governing animal, because reason will in time always prevail against brutal strength. But, considering the frame of our bodies, and especially of mine, he thought no creature of equal bulk was so ill contrived, for employing that reason in the common offices of life; whereupon he desired to know whether those among whom I lived resembled me or the *Yahoos* of his country. I assured him, that I was as well shaped as most of my age; but the younger and the females were much more soft and tender, and the skins of the latter generally as white as milk. He said, I differed indeed from other *Yahoos*, being much more cleanly, and not altogether so deformed, but, in point of real advantage, he thought I differed for the worse. That my nails were of no use either to my fore or hinder-feet; as to my fore-feet, he could not properly call them by that name, for he never observed me to walk upon them; that they were too soft to bear the ground; that I generally went with them uncovered, neither was the covering I sometimes wore on them, of the same shape, or so strong as that on my feet behind. That I could not walk with any security, for if either of my hinder-feet slipped, I must inevitably fall. He then began to find fault with other parts of my body, the flatness of my face, the prominence of my nose, my eyes placed directly in front, so that I could not look on either side without turning my head: that I was not able to feed myself, without lifting one of my fore-feet to my mouth: and therefore nature had placed those joints to answer that necessity. He knew not what could be the use of those several clefts and divisions in my feet behind; these were too soft to bear the hardness and sharpness of stones without a covering made from the skin of some other brute; that my whole body wanted a fence against heat and cold, which I was forced to put on and off every day with tediousness and trouble. And lastly, that he observed every animal in this country naturally to abhor the *Yahoos*, whom the weaker avoided, and the stronger drove from them. So that supposing us to have the gift of reason, he could not see how it were possible to cure that natural antipathy which every creature discovered against us; nor consequently, how we could tame and render them serviceable. However, he would (as he said) debate the matter no farther, because he was more desirous to know my own story, the country where I was born, and the several actions and events of my life before I came hither.

I assured him, how extremely desirous I was that he should be satisfied on every point; but I doubted much, whether it would be possible for me to explain myself on several subjects whereof his Honour could have no conception, because I saw nothing in his country to which I could resemble them. That, however, I would do my best, and strive to express myself by similitudes, humbly desiring his assistance when I wanted proper words; which he was pleased to promise me.

I said, my birth was of honest parents in an island called England, which was remote from this country, as many days' journey as the strongest of his Honour's servants could travel in the annual course of the sun. That I was bred a surgeon, whose trade it is to cure wounds and hurts in the body, got by accident or violence; that my country was governed by a female man, whom we called a Queen. That I left it to get riches, whereby I might maintain myself and family when I should return. That, in my last voyage, I was commander of the ship, and had about fifty *Yahoos* under me, many of which died at sea, and I was forced to supply them by others picked out from several nations. That our ship was twice in danger of being sunk; the first time by a great storm, and the second, by striking against a rock. Here my master interposed, by asking me, how I could persuade strangers out of different countries to venture with me, after the losses I had sustained, and the hazards I had run. I said, they were fellows of desperate fortunes, forced to fly from the places of their birth, on account of their poverty or their crimes. Some were undone by lawsuits; others spent all they had in drinking, whoring, and gaming; others fled for treason; many for murder, theft, poisoning, robbery, perjury, forgery, coining false money, for committing rapes or sodomy, for flying from their colours, or deserting to the enemy, and most of them had broken prison; none of these durst return to their native countries for fear of being hanged, or of starving in a jail; and therefore were under the necessity of seeking a livelihood in other places.

During this discourse, my master was pleased to interrupt me several times; I had made use of many circumlocutions in describing to him the nature of the several crimes for which most of our crew had been forced to fly their country. This labour took up several days' conversation, before he was able to comprehend me. He was wholly at a loss to know what could be the use or necessity of practising those vices. To clear up which I endeavoured to give some ideas of the desire of power and riches, of the terrible effects of lust, intemperance, malice, and envy. All this I was forced to define and describe by putting of cases, and making of suppositions. After which, like one whose imagination was struck with something never seen or heard of before, he would lift up his eyes with amazement and indignation. Power, government, war, law, punishment, and a thousand other things had no terms, wherein that language could express them, which made the difficulty almost insuperable to give my master any conception of what I meant. But being of an excellent understanding, much improved by contemplation and converse, he at last arrived at a competent knowledge of what human nature in our parts of the world is capable to perform, and desired I would give him some particular account of that land which we call Europe, but especially of my own country.

Chapter 5

The Author, at his master's commands, informs him of the state of England. *The causes of war among the princes of* Europe. *The Author begins to explain the* English *constitution.*

The reader may please to observe, that the following extract of many conversations I had with my master, contains a summary of the most material points, which were discoursed at several times for above two years; his Honour often desiring fuller satisfaction as I farther improved in the *Houyhnhnm* tongue. I laid before him, as well as I could, the whole state of Europe; I discoursed of trade and manufactures, of arts and sciences; and the answers I gave to all the questions he made, as they arose upon several subjects, were a fund of conversation not to be exhausted. But I shall here only set down the substance of what passed between us concerning my own country, reducing it into order as well as I can, without any regard to time or other circumstances, while I strictly adhere to truth. My only concern is, that I shall hardly be able to do justice to my master's arguments and expressions, which must needs suffer by my want of capacity, as well as by a translation into our barbarous English.

In obedience, therefore, to his Honour's commands, I related to him the Revolution under the Prince of Orange; the long war with France entered into by the said prince, and renewed by his successor, the present Queen, wherein the greatest powers of Christendom were engaged, and which still continued: I computed at his request, that about a million of *Yahoos* might have been killed in the whole progress of it; and perhaps a hundred or more cities taken, and thrice as many ships burnt or sunk.[12]

He asked me what were the usual causes or motives that made one country go to war with another. I answered they were innumerable; but I should only mention a few of the chief. Sometimes the ambition of princes, who never think they have land or people enough to govern; sometimes the corruption of ministers, who engage their master in a war in order to stifle or divert the clamour of the subjects against their evil administration. Difference in opinions hath cost many millions of lives: for instance, whether flesh be bread, or bread be flesh; whether the juice of a certain berry be blood or wine; whether whistling be a vice or a virtue; whether it be better to kiss a post, or throw it into the fire; what is the best colour for a coat, whether black, white, red, or gray; and whether it should be long or short, narrow or wide, dirty or clean; with many more.[13] Neither are any wars so furious and bloody, or of so long continuance, as those occasioned by difference in opinion, especially if it be in things indifferent.

Sometimes the quarrel between two princes is to decide which of them shall dispossess a third of his dominions, where neither of them pretend to any right. Sometimes one prince quarrelleth with another, for fear the other should quarrel with him. Sometimes a war is entered upon, because the enemy is too strong, and sometimes because he is too weak. Sometimes our neighbours want the things which we have, or have the things which we want; and we both fight, till they

---

[12]Gulliver disingenuously describes to his master the "Glorious Revolution" of 1688 that ousted the English James II, and the War of the Spanish Succession, which occupied the decade between 1703 and 1713.

[13]Gulliver alludes to a number of religious doctrines and practices disputed hotly by Christians since the Reformation. He refers specifically here to transubstantiation, to the use of crucifixes and music in worship, and to the wearing of ecclesiastical robes.

take ours or give us theirs. It is a very justifiable cause of a war to invade a country after the people have been wasted by famine, destroyed by pestilence, or embroiled by factions among themselves. It is justifiable to enter into war against our nearest ally, when one of his towns lies convenient for us, or a territory of land, that would render our dominions round and complete. If a prince sends forces into a nation, where the people are poor and ignorant, he may lawfully put half of them to death, and make slaves of the rest, in order to civilize and reduce them from their barbarous way of living. It is a very kingly, honourable, and frequent practice, when one prince desires the assistance of another to secure him against an invasion, that the assistant, when he hath driven out the invader, should seize on the dominions himself, and kill, imprison, or banish the prince he came to relieve. Alliance by blood or marriage is a frequent cause of war between princes; and the nearer the kindred is, the greater is their disposition to quarrel: poor nations are hungry, and rich nations are proud; and pride and hunger will ever be at variance. For these reasons, the trade of a soldier is held the most honourable of all others; because a soldier is a *Yahoo* hired to kill in cold blood as many of his own species, who have never offended him, as possibly he can.

There is likewise a kind of beggarly princes in Europe, not able to make war by themselves, who hire out their troops to richer nations, for so much a day to each man; of which they keep three fourths to themselves, and it is the best part of their maintenance; such are those in Germany and other northern parts of Europe.

What you have told me (said my master), upon the subject of war, does indeed discover most admirably the effects of that reason you pretend to: however, it is happy that the shame is greater than the danger; and that nature hath left you utterly uncapable of doing much mischief.

For your mouths lying flat with your faces, you can hardly bite each other to any purpose, unless by consent. Then as to the claws upon your feet before and behind, they are so short and tender, that one of our *Yahoos* would drive a dozen of yours before him. And therefore in recounting the numbers of those who have been killed in battle, I cannot but think that you have *said the thing which is not*.

I could not forbear shaking my head, and smiling a little at his ignorance. And being no stranger to the art of war, I gave him a description of cannons, culverins, muskets, carabines, pistols, bullets, powder, swords, bayonets, battles, sieges, retreats, attacks, undermines, countermines, bombardments, sea fights; ships sunk with a thousand men, twenty thousand killed on each side; dying groans, limbs flying in the air, smoke, noise, confusion, trampling to death under horses' feet; flight, pursuit, victory; fields strewed with carcases left for food to dogs, and wolves, and birds of prey; plundering, stripping, ravishing, burning and destroying. And to set forth the valour of my own dear countrymen, I assured him, that I had seen them blow up a hundred enemies at once in a siege, and as many in a ship, and beheld the dead bodies come down in pieces from the clouds, to the great diversion of the spectators.

I was going on to more particulars, when my master commanded me silence. He said, whoever understood the nature of *Yahoos* might easily believe it possible for so vile an animal to be capable of every action I had named, if their strength and cunning equalled their malice. But as my discourse had increased his abhorrence of the whole species, so he found it gave him a disturbance in his mind, to which he was wholly a stranger before. He thought his ears being used to such abominable words, might by degrees admit them with less detestation. That although he hated the *Yahoos* of this country, yet he no more blamed them for their odious qualities, than he did a *gnnayh* (a bird of prey) for its cruelty, or a sharp stone for cutting his hoof. But when a creature pretending to reason could be capable of such enormities, he dreaded lest the corruption of that faculty might be worse than brutality itself. He seemed therefore confident, that instead of reason, we were only possessed of some quality fitted to increase our natural vices; as the reflection from a troubled stream returns the image of an ill-shapen body, not only larger, but more distorted.

He added, that he had heard too much upon the subject of war, both in this, and some former discourses. There was another point which a little perplexed him at present. I had informed him, that some of our crew left their country on account of being ruined by *Law*; that I had already explained the meaning of the word; but he was at a loss how it should come to pass, that the law which was intended for every man's preservation, should be any man's ruin. Therefore he desired to be farther satisfied what I meant by law, and the dispensers thereof, according to the present practice in my own country; because he thought nature and reason were sufficient guides for a reasonable animal, as we pretended to be, in showing us what we ought to do, and what to avoid.

I assured his Honour, that law was a science wherein I had not much conversed, further than by employing advocates, in vain, upon some injustices that had been done me; however, I would give him all the satisfaction I was able.

I said, there was a society of men among us, bred up from their youth in the art of proving by words multiplied for the purpose, that white is black, and black is white, according as they are paid. To this society all the rest of the people are slaves. For example, if my neighbour hath a mind to my cow, he hires a lawyer to prove that he ought to have my cow from me. I must then hire another to defend my right, it being against all rules of law that any man should be allowed to speak for himself. Now in this case, I, who am the right owner, lie under two great disadvantages. First, my lawyer, being practised almost from his cradle in defending falsehood, is quite out of his element when he would be an advocate for justice, which as an office unnatural, he always attempts with great awkwardness, if not with ill-will. The second disadvantage is, that my lawyer must proceed with great caution, or else he will be reprimanded by the judges, and abhorred by his brethren, as one that would lessen the practice of the law. And therefore I have but two methods to preserve my cow. The first is, to gain over my adversary's lawyer with a double fee; who will then betray his client, by insinuating that he hath justice on his side. The second way is for my lawyer to make my cause appear as unjust as he can, by allowing the cow to belong to my adversary; and this, if it be skilfully done, will certainly bespeak the favour of the bench.

Now, your Honour is to know, that these judges are persons appointed to decide all controversies of property, as well as for the trial of criminals, and picked out from the most dexterous lawyers, who are grown old or lazy, and having been biassed all their lives against truth and equity, are under such a fatal necessity of favouring fraud, perjury, and oppression, that I have known several of them refuse a large bribe from the side where justice lay, rather than injure the faculty,[14] by doing any thing unbecoming their nature or their office.

It is a maxim among these lawyers, that whatever hath been done before, may legally be done again: and therefore they take special care to record all the decisions formerly made against common justice, and the general reason of mankind. These, under the name of *precedents*, they produce as authorities, to justify the most iniquitous opinions; and the judges never fail of directing accordingly.

In pleading, they studiously avoid entering into the merits of the cause; but are loud, violent, and tedious in dwelling upon all circumstances which are not to the

---

[14]Profession.

purpose. For instance, in the case already mentioned: they never desire to know what claim or title my adversary hath to my cow; but whether the said cow were red or black; her horns long or short; whether the field I graze her in be round or square; whether she was milked at home or abroad; what diseases she is subject to, and the like; after which they consult precedents, adjourn the cause from time to time, and in ten, twenty, or thirty years, come to an issue.

It is likewise to be observed, that this society hath a peculiar cant and jargon of their own, that no other mortal can understand, and wherein all their laws are written, which they take special care to multiply; whereby they have wholly confounded the very essence of truth and falsehood, of right and wrong; so that it will take thirty years to decide whether the field left me by my ancestors for six generations belongs to me, or to a stranger three hundred miles off.

In the trial of persons accused for crimes against the state, the method is much more short and commendable: the judge first sends to sound the disposition of those in power, after which he can easily hang or save the criminal, strictly preserving all due forms of law.

Here my master interposing, said it was a pity, that creatures endowed with such prodigious abilities of mind as these lawyers, by the description I gave of them, must certainly be, were not rather encouraged to be instructors of others in wisdom and knowledge. In answer to which, I assured his Honour, that in all points out of their own trade, they were usually the most ignorant and stupid generation among us, the most despicable in common conversation, avowed enemies to all knowledge and learning, and equally disposed to pervert the general reason of mankind in every other subject of discourse, as in that of their own profession.

Chapter 6

A continuation of the state of England. *The character*
of a first or chief minister of state in European *courts.*

My master was yet wholly at a loss to understand what motives could incite this race of lawyers to perplex, disquiet, and weary themselves, and engage in a confederacy of injustice, merely for the sake of injuring their fellow-animals; neither could he comprehend what I meant in saying they did it for hire. Whereupon I was at much pains to describe to him the use of money, the materials it was made of, and the value of the metals; that when a *Yahoo* had got a great store of this precious substance, he was able to purchase whatever he had a mind to; the finest clothing, the noblest houses, great tracts of land, the most costly meats and drinks, and have his choice of the most beautiful females. Therefore since money alone was able to perform all these feats, our *Yahoos* thought they could never have enough of it to spend or to save, as they found themselves inclined from their natural bent either to profusion or avarice. That the rich man enjoyed the fruit of the poor man's labour, and the latter were a thousand to one in proportion to the former. That the bulk of our people were forced to live miserably, by labouring every day for small wages to make a few live plentifully. I enlarged myself much on these and many other particulars to the same purpose; but his Honour was still to seek,[15] for he went upon a supposition that all animals had a title to their share in the productions of the earth, and especially those who presided over the rest. Therefore he desired I would let him know, what these costly meats were, and how any of us happened to want them. Whereupon I enumerated as many sorts as came into my head, with the various methods of dressing them, which could not be done without sending

---

[15] Still did not understand.

vessels by sea to every part of the world, as well for liquors to drink, as for sauces, and innumerable other conveniences. I assured him, that this whole globe of earth must be at least three times gone round, before one of our better female *Yahoos* could get her breakfast, or a cup to put it in. He said, that must needs be a miserable country which cannot furnish food for its own inhabitants. But what he chiefly wondered at, was how such vast tracts of ground as I described should be wholly without fresh water, and the people put to the necessity of sending over the sea for drink. I replied, that England (the dear place of my nativity) was computed to produce three times the quantity of food, more than its inhabitants are able to consume, as well as liquors extracted from grain, or pressed out of the fruit of certain trees, which made excellent drink, and the same proportion in every other convenience of life. But, in order to feed the luxury and intemperance of the males, and the vanity of the females, we sent away the greatest part of our necessary things to other countries, from whence in return we brought the materials of diseases, folly, and vice, to spend among ourselves. Hence it follows of necessity, that vast numbers of our people are compelled to seek their livelihood by begging, robbing, stealing, cheating, pimping, forswearing, flattering, suborning, forging, gaming, lying, fawning, hectoring, voting, scribbling, star-gazing, poisoning, whoring, canting, libelling, free-thinking, and the like occupations: every one of which terms, I was at much pains to make him understand.

That wine was not imported among us from foreign countries, to supply the want of water or other drinks, but because it was a sort of liquid which made us merry, by putting us out of our senses; diverted all melancholy thoughts, begat wild extravagant imaginations in the brain, raised our hopes, and banished our fears, suspended every office of reason for a time, and deprived us of the use of our limbs, till we fell into a profound sleep; although it must be confessed, that we always awaked sick and dispirited, and that the use of this liquor filled us with diseases, which made our lives uncomfortable and short.

But beside all this, the bulk of our people supported themselves by furnishing the necessities or conveniences of life to the rich, and to each other. For instance, when I am at home and dressed as I ought to be, I carry on my body the workmanship of an hundred tradesmen; the building and furniture of my house employ as many more, and five times the number to adorn my wife.

I was going on to tell him of another sort of people, who get their livelihood by attending the sick, having upon some occasions informed his Honour that many of my crew had died of diseases. But here it was with the utmost difficulty, that I brought him to apprehend what I meant. He could easily conceive, that a *Houyhnhnm* grew weak and heavy a few days before his death, or by some accident might hurt a limb. But that nature, who works all things to perfection, should suffer any pains to breed in our bodies, he thought impossible, and desired to know the reason of so unaccountable an evil. I told him, we fed on a thousand things which operated contrary to each other; that we eat when we were not hungry, and drank without the provocation of thirst; that we sat whole nights drinking strong liquors without eating a bit, which disposed us to sloth, inflamed our bodies, and precipitated or prevented digestion. That prostitute female *Yahoos* acquired a certain malady, which bred rottenness in the bones of those who fell into their embraces; that this and many other diseases were propagated from father to son, so that great numbers came into the world with complicated maladies upon them; that it would be endless to give him a catalogue of all diseases incident to human bodies; for they would not be fewer than five or six hundred, spread over every limb and joint; in short, every part, external and intestine, having diseases appropriated to each. To remedy which, there was a sort of people bred up among us, in the profession or pretence of curing the sick. And because I had some skill in the faculty, I would in gratitude to his Honour, let him know the whole mystery and method by which they proceed.

Their fundamental is, that all diseases arise from repletion, from whence they conclude, that a great evacuation of the body is necessary, either through the natural passage, or upwards at the mouth. Their next business is, from herbs, minerals, gums, oils, shells, salts, juices, seaweed, excrements, barks of trees, serpents, toads, frogs, spiders, dead men's flesh and bones, birds, beasts, and fishes, to form a composition for smell and taste the most abominable, nauseous, and detestable, they can possibly contrive, which the stomach immediately rejects with loathing; and this they call a vomit; or else from the same store-house, with some other poisonous additions, they command us to take in at the orifice above or below (just as the physician then happens to be disposed) a medicine equally annoying and disgustful to the bowels; which relaxing the belly, drives down all before it, and this they call a purge, or a clyster. For nature (as the physicians allege) having intended the superior anterior orifice only for the intromission of solids and liquids, and the inferior posterior for ejection, these artists ingeniously considering that in all diseases nature is forced out of her seat, therefore to replace her in it, the body must be treated in a manner directly contrary, by interchanging the use of each orifice; forcing solids and liquids in at the anus, and making evacuations at the mouth.

But, besides real diseases, we are subject to many that are only imaginary, for which the physicians have invented imaginary cures; these have their several names, and so have the drugs that are proper for them, and with these our female *Yahoos* are always infested.

One great excellency in this tribe is their skill at prognostics, wherein they seldom fail; their predictions in real diseases, when they rise to any degree of malignity, generally portending death, which is always in their power, when recovery is not: and therefore, upon any unexpected signs of amendment, after they have pronounced their sentence, rather than be accused as false prophets, they know how to approve[16] their sagacity to the world by a seasonable dose.

They are likewise of special use to husbands and wives, who are grown weary of their mates; to eldest sons, to great ministers of state, and often to princes.

I had formerly upon occasion discoursed with my master upon the nature of government in general, and particularly of our own excellent constitution, deservedly the wonder and envy of the whole world. But having here accidentally mentioned a minister of state, he commanded me some time after to inform him, what species of *Yahoo* I particularly meant by that appellation.

I told him, that a First or Chief Minister of State, who was the person I intended to describe, was a creature wholly exempt from joy and grief, love and hatred, pity and anger; at least made use of no other passions but a violent desire of wealth, power, and titles; that he applies his words to all uses, except to the indication of his mind; that he never tells a truth, but with an intent that you should take it for a lie; nor a lie, but with a design that you should take it for a truth; that those he speaks worst of behind their backs, are in the surest way of preferment; and whenever he begins to praise you to others or to yourself, you are from that day forlorn. The worst mark you can receive is a promise, especially when it is confirmed with an oath; after which every wise man retires, and gives over all hopes.

There are three methods by which a man may rise to be chief minister: the first is, by knowing how with prudence to dispose of a wife, a daughter, or a sister:

---

[16]Prove.

the second, by betraying or undermining his predecessor: and the third is, by a furious zeal in public assemblies against the corruptions of the court. But a wise prince would rather choose to employ those who practise the last of these methods; because such zealots prove always the most obsequious and subservient to the will and passions of their master. That these ministers having all employments at their disposal, preserve themselves in power, by bribing the majority of a senate or great council; and at last, by an expedient called an Act of Indemnity (whereof I described the nature to him) they secure themselves from after-reckonings, and retire from the public, laden with the spoils of the nation.[17]

The palace of a chief minister is a seminary to breed up others in his own trade: the pages, lackeys, and porters, by imitating their master, become ministers of state in their several districts, and learn to excel in the three principal ingredients, of insolence, lying, and bribery. Accordingly, they have a subaltern court paid to them by persons of the best rank, and sometimes by the force of dexterity and impudence, arrive through several gradations to be successors to their lord.

He is usually governed by a decayed wench, or favourite footman, who are the tunnels through which all graces are conveyed, and may properly be called, in the last resort, the governors of the kingdom.

One day in discourse my master, having heard me mention the nobility of my country, was pleased to make me a compliment which I could not pretend to deserve: that he was sure I must have been born of some noble family, because I far exceeded in shape, colour, and cleanliness, all the *Yahoos* of his nation, although I seemed to fail in strength and agility, which must be imputed to my different way of living from those other brutes; and besides, I was not only endowed with the faculty of speech, but likewise with some rudiments of reason, to a degree, that with all his acquaintance I passed for a prodigy.

He made me observe, that among the *Houyhnhnms*, the white, the sorrel, and the iron-gray, were not so exactly shaped as the bay, the dapple-gray, and the black; nor born with equal talents of the mind, or a capacity to improve them; and therefore continued always in the condition of servants, without ever aspiring to match out of their own race, which in that country would be reckoned monstrous and unnatural.

I made his Honour my most humble acknowledgments for the good opinion he was pleased to conceive of me; but assured him at the same time, that my birth was of the lower sort, having been born of plain honest parents, who were just able to give me a tolerable education; that nobility among us was altogether a different thing from the idea he had of it; that our young noblemen are bred from their childhood in idleness and luxury; that as soon as years will permit, they consume their vigour, and contract odious diseases among lewd females; and when their fortunes are almost ruined, they marry some woman of mean birth, disagreeable person, and unsound constitution, merely for the sake of money, whom they hate and despise. That the productions of such marriages are generally scrofulous, ricketty, or deformed children; by which means the family seldom continues above three generations, unless the wife takes care to provide a healthy father among her neighbours or domestics, in order to improve and continue the breed. That a weak diseased body, a meagre countenance, and sallow complexion, are the true marks of noble blood; and a healthy robust appearance is so disgraceful in a man of quality, that the world concludes his real father to have been a groom or a coachman. The imperfections of his mind run parallel with those of his body, being a composition of spleen, dullness, ignorance, caprice, sensuality, and pride.

---

[17] The Act provides immunity to statesmen who have unknowingly violated a law.

Without the consent of this illustrious body, no law can be enacted, repealed, or altered; and these have the decision of all our possessions without appeal.

Chapter 7

The Author's great love of his native country. His master's observations upon the constitution and administration of England, as described by the Author, with parallel cases and comparisons. His master's observations upon human nature.

The reader may be disposed to wonder how I could prevail on myself to give so free a representation of my own species, among a race of mortals who are already too apt to conceive the vilest opinion of human kind, from that entire congruity betwixt me and their *Yahoos.* But I must freely confess, that the many virtues of those excellent quadrupeds placed in opposite view to human corruptions, had so far opened my eyes and enlarged my understanding, that I began to view the actions and passions of man in a very different light, and to think the honour of my own kind not worth managing; which, besides, it was impossible for me to do before a person of so acute a judgment as my master, who daily convinced me of a thousand faults in myself, whereof I had not the least perception before, and which with us would never be numbered even among human infirmities. I had likewise learned from his example an utter detestation of all falsehood or disguise; and truth appeared so amiable to me, that I determined upon sacrificing every thing to it.

Let me deal so candidly with the reader, as to confess, that there was yet a much stronger motive for the freedom I took in my representation of things. I had not been a year in this country, before I contracted such a love and veneration for the inhabitants, that I entered on a firm resolution never to return to human kind, but to pass the rest of my life among these admirable *Houyhnhnms* in the contemplation and practice of every virtue; where I could have no example or incitement to vice. But it was decreed by fortune, my perpetual enemy, that so great a felicity should not fall to my share. However, it is now some comfort to reflect, that in what I said of my countrymen, I extenuated their faults as much as I durst before so strict an examiner, and upon every article gave as favourable a turn as the matter would bear. For, indeed, who is there alive that will not be swayed by his bias and partiality to the place of his birth?

I have related the substance of several conversations I had with my master, during the greatest part of the time I had the honour to be in his service, but have indeed for brevity sake omitted much more than is here set down.

When I had answered all his questions, and his curiosity seemed to be fully satisfied; he sent for me one morning early, and commanding me to sit down at some distance (an honour which he had never before conferred upon me), he said, he had been very seriously considering my whole story, as far as it related both to myself and my country; that he looked upon us as a sort of animals to whose share, by what accident he could not conjecture, some small pittance of reason had fallen, whereof we made no other use than by its assistance to aggravate our natural corruptions, and to acquire new ones, which nature had not given us. That we disarmed ourselves of the few abilities she had bestowed, had been very successful in multiplying our original wants, and seemed to spend our whole lives in vain endeavours to supply them by our own inventions. That as to myself, was manifest I had neither the strength or agility of a common *Yahoo;* that I walked infirmly on my hinder feet; had found out a contrivance to make my claws of no use or defence, and to remove the hair from my chin, which was intended as a shelter from the sun and the weather. Lastly, that I could neither run with speed, nor climb trees like my brethren (as he called them) the *Yahoos* in this country.

That our institutions of government and law were plainly owing to our gross defects in reason, and by consequence, in virtue; because reason alone is sufficient to govern a rational creature; which was therefore a character we had no pretence to challenge, even from the account I had given of my own people; although he manifestly perceived, that in order to favour them, I had concealed many particulars, and often *said the thing which was not.*

He was the more confirmed in this opinion, because he observed, that as I agreed in every feature of my body with other *Yahoos*, except where it was to my real disadvantage in point of strength, speed and activity, the shortness of my claws, and some other particulars where nature had no part; so from the representation I had given him of our lives, our manners, and our actions, he found as near a resemblance in the disposition of our minds. He said the *Yahoos* were known to hate one another more than they did any different species of animals; and the reason usually assigned was the odiousness of their own shapes, which all could see in the rest, but not in themselves. He had therefore begun to think it not unwise in us to cover our bodies, and by that invention conceal many of our own deformities from each other, which would else be hardly supportable. But he now found he had been mistaken, and that the dissensions of those brutes in his country were owing to the same cause with ours, as I had described them. For if (said he), you throw among five *Yahoos* as much food as would be sufficient for fifty, they will, instead of eating peaceably, fall together by the ears, each single one impatient to have all to itself; and therefore a servant was usually employed to stand by while they were feeding abroad, and those kept at home were tied at a distance from each other: that if a cow died of age or accident, before a *Houyhnhnm* could secure it for his own *Yahoos*, those in the neighbourhood would come in herds to seize it, and then would ensue such a battle as I had described, with terrible wounds made by their claws on both sides, although they seldom were able to kill one another, for want of such convenient instruments of death as we had invented. At other times the like battles have been fought between the *Yahoos* of several neighbourhoods without any visible cause; those of one district watching all opportunities to surprise the next before they are prepared. But if they find their project hath miscarried, they return home, and, for want of enemies, engage in what I call a civil war among themselves.

That in some fields of his country, there are certain shining stones of several colours, whereof the *Yahoos* are violently fond, and when part of these stones is fixed in the earth, as it sometimes happeneth, they will dig with their claws for whole days to get them out, then carry them away, and hide them by heaps in their kennels; but still looking round with great caution, for fear their comrades should find out their treasure. My master said, he could never discover the reason of this unnatural appetite, or how these stones could be of any use to a *Yahoo;* but now he believed it might proceed from the same principle of avarice which I had ascribed to mankind: that he had once, by way of experiment, privately removed a heap of these stones from the place where one of his *Yahoos* had buried it: whereupon, the sordid animal missing his treasure, by his loud lamenting brought the whole herd to the place, there miserably howled, then fell to biting and tearing the rest, began to pine away, would neither eat, nor sleep, nor work, till he ordered a servant privately to convey the stones into the same hole, and hide them as before; which when his *Yahoo* had found, he presently recovered his spirits and good humour, but took good care to remove them to a better hiding place, and hath ever since been a very serviceable brute.

My master farther assured me, which I also observed myself, that in the fields where the shining stones abound, the fiercest and most frequent battles are fought, occasioned by perpetual inroads of the neighbouring *Yahoos*.

He said, it was common when two *Yahoos* discovered such a stone in a field, and were contending which of them should be the proprietor, a third would take the advantage, and carry it away from them both; which my master would needs contend to have some kind of resemblance with our suits at law; wherein I thought it for our credit not to undeceive him; since the decision he mentioned was much more equitable than many decrees among us; because the plaintiff and defendant there lost nothing beside the stone they contended for, whereas our courts of equity would never have dismissed the cause while either of them had any thing left.

My master continuing his discourse, said, there was nothing that rendered the *Yahoos* more odious than their undistinguishing appetite to devour every thing that came in their way, whether herbs, roots, berries, the corrupted flesh of animals, or all mingled together: and it was peculiar in their temper, that they were fonder of what they could get by rapine or stealth at a greater distance, than much better food provided for them at home. If their prey held out, they would eat till they were ready to burst, after which nature had pointed out to them a certain root that gave them a general evacuation.

There was also another kind of root very juicy, but somewhat rare and difficult to be found, which the *Yahoos* sought for with much eagerness, and would suck it with great delight; and it produced in them the same effects that wine hath upon us. It would make them sometimes hug, and sometimes tear one another; they would howl and grin, and chatter, and reel, and tumble, and then fall asleep in the mud.

I did indeed observe, that the *Yahoos* were the only animals in this country subject to any diseases; which, however, were much fewer than horses have among us, and contracted not by any ill treatment they meet with, but by the nastiness and greediness of that sordid brute. Neither has their language any more than a general appellation for those maladies, which is borrowed from the name of the beast, and called *Hnea-Yahoo*, or *Yahoo's evil*, and the cure prescribed is a mixture of their own dung and urine forcibly put down the *Yahoo's* throat. This I have since often known to have been taken with success, and do freely recommend it to my countrymen, for the public good, as an admirable specific against all diseases produced by repletion.

As to learning, government, arts, manufactures, and the like, my master confessed he could find little or no resemblance between the *Yahoos* of that country and those in ours. For he only meant to observe what parity there was in our natures. He had heard indeed some curious *Houyhnhnms* observe, that in most herds there was a sort of ruling *Yahoo* (as among us there is generally some leading or principal stag in a pack), who was always more deformed in body, and mischievous in disposition, than any of the rest. That this leader had usually a favourite as like himself as he could get, whose employment was to lick his master's feet and posteriors, and drive the female *Yahoos* to his kennel; for which he was now and then rewarded with a piece of ass's flesh. This favourite is hated by the whole herd, and therefore to protect himself, keeps always near the person of his leader. He usually continues in office till a worse can be found; but the very moment he is discarded, his successor, at the head of all the *Yahoos* in that district, young and old, male and female, come in a body, and discharge their excrements upon him from head to foot. But how far this might be applicable to our courts and favourites, and ministers of state, my master said I could best determine.

I durst make no return to this malicious insinuation, which debased human understanding below the sagacity of a common hound, who has judgment enough to distinguish and follow the cry of the ablest dog in the pack, without being ever mistaken.

My master told me, there were some qualities remarkable in the *Yahoos*, which he had not observed me to mention, or at least very slightly, in the accounts I had given him of human kind. He said, those animals, like other brutes, had their females in common; but in this they differed, that the she-*Yahoo* would admit the male while she was pregnant; and that the hees would quarrel and fight with the females as fiercely as with each other. Both which practices were such degrees of infamous brutality, that no other sensitive creature ever arrived at.

Another thing he wondered at in the *Yahoos,* was their strange disposition to nastiness and dirt, whereas there appears to be a natural love of cleanliness in all other animals. As to the two former accusations, I was glad to let them pass without any reply, because I had not a word to offer upon them in defence of my species, which otherwise I certainly had done from my own inclinations. But I could have easily vindicated human kind from the imputation of singularity upon the last article, if there had been any swine in that country (as unluckily for me there were not), which although it may be a sweeter quadruped than a *Yahoo,* cannot I humbly conceive in justice pretend to more cleanliness; and so his Honour himself must have owned, if he had seen their filthy way of feeding, and their custom of wallowing and sleeping in the mud.

My master likewise mentioned another quality which his servants had discovered in several *Yahoos,* and to him was wholly unaccountable. He said, a fancy would sometimes take a *Yahoo* to retire into a corner, to lie down and howl, and groan, and spurn away all that came near him, although he were young and fat, wanted neither food nor water; nor did the servants imagine what could possibly ail him. And the only remedy they found was to set him to hard work, after which he would infallibly come to himself. To this I was silent out of partiality to my own kind; yet here I could plainly discover the true seeds of spleen, which only seizeth on the lazy, the luxurious, and the rich; who, if they were forced to undergo the same regimen, I would undertake for the cure.

His Honour had further observed, that a female *Yahoo* would often stand behind a bank or bush, to gaze on the young males passing by, and then appear, and hide, using many antic gestures and grimaces, at which time it was observed, that she had a most offensive smell; and when any of the males advanced, would slowly retire, looking often back, and with a counterfeit show of fear, run off into some convenient place where she knew the male would follow her.

At other times if a female stranger came among them, three or four of her own sex would get about her, and stare and chatter, and grin, and smell her all over; and then turn off with gestures that seemed to express contempt and disdain.

Perhaps my master might refine a little in these speculations, which he had drawn from what he observed himself, or had been told him by others; however, I could not reflect without some amazement, and much sorrow, that the rudiments of lewdness, coquetry, censure, and scandal, should have place by instinct in womankind.

I expected every moment, that my master would accuse the *Yahoos* of those unnatural appetites in both sexes, so common among us. But nature, it seems, hath not been so expert a school-mistress; and these politer pleasures are entirely the productions of art and reason, on our side of the globe.

Chapter 8

The Author relates several particulars of the Yahoos. *The great virtues of the* Houyhnhnms. *The education and exercise of their youth. Their general assembly.*

As I ought to have understood human nature much better than I supposed it possible for my master to do, so it was easy to apply the character he gave of the *Yahoos* to myself and my countrymen; and I believed I could yet make farther discoveries from my own observation. I therefore often begged his favour to let me go among the herds of *Yahoos* in the neighbourhood, to which he always very graciously consented, being perfectly convinced that the hatred I bore those brutes would never suffer me to be corrupted by them; and his Honour ordered one of his servants, a strong sorrel nag, very honest and good-natured, to be my guard, without whose protection I durst not undertake such adventures. For I have already told the reader how much I was pestered by those odious animals upon my first arrival. And I afterwards failed very narrowly three or four times of falling into their clutches, when I happened to stray at any distance without my hanger. And I have reason to believe they had some imagination that I was of their own species, which I often assisted myself, by stripping up my sleeves, and showing my naked arms and breast in their sight, when my protector was with me. At which times they would approach as near as they durst, and imitate my actions after the manner of monkeys, but ever with great signs of hatred; as a tame jackdaw with cap and stockings is always persecuted by the wild ones, when he happens to be got among them.

They are prodigiously nimble from their infancy; however, I once caught a young male of three years old, and endeavoured by all marks of tenderness to make it quiet; but the little imp fell a squalling, and scratching, and biting with such violence, that I was forced to let it go; and it was high time, for a whole troop of old ones came about us at the noise, but finding the cub was safe (for away it ran), and my sorrel nag being by, they durst not venture near us. I observed the young animal's flesh to smell very rank, and the stink was somewhat between a weasel and a fox, but much more disagreeable. I forgot another circumstance (and perhaps I might have the reader's pardon if it were wholly omitted), that while I held the odious vermin in my hands, it voided its filthy excrements of a yellow liquid substance, all over my clothes; but by good fortune there was a small brook hard by, where I washed myself as clean as I could; although I durst not come into my master's presence, until I were sufficiently aired.

By what I could discover, the *Yahoos* appear to be the most unteachable of all animals, their capacities never reaching higher than to draw or carry burdens. Yet I am of opinion, this defect ariseth chiefly from a perverse, restive disposition. For they are cunning, malicious, treacherous, and revengeful. They are strong and hardy, but of a cowardly spirit, and by consequence, insolent, abject, and cruel. It is observed, that the red-haired of both sexes are more libidinous and mischievous than the rest, whom yet they much exceed in strength and activity.

The *Houyhnhnms* keep the *Yahoos* for present use in huts not far from the house; but the rest are sent abroad to certain fields, where they dig up roots, eat several kinds of herbs, and search about for carrion, or sometimes catch weasels and *luhimuhs* (a sort of wild rat), which they greedily devour. Nature hath taught them to dig deep holes with their nails on the side of a rising ground, wherein they lie by themselves; only the kennels of the females are larger, sufficient to hold two or three cubs.

They swim from their infancy like frogs, and are able to continue long under water, where they often take fish, which the females carry home to their young. And upon this occasion, I hope the reader will pardon my relating an odd adventure.

Being one day abroad with my protector the sorrel nag, and the weather exceeding hot, I entreated him to let me bathe in a river that was near. He consented, and I immediately stripped myself stark naked, and went down softly into the stream. It happened that a young female *Yahoo*, standing behind a bank, saw the whole proceeding, and inflamed by desire, as the nag and I conjectured, came running with all speed, and leaped into the water, within five yards of the place where I bathed. I was never in my life so terribly frighted; the nag was grazing at some distance, not suspecting any harm. She embraced me after a most fulsome manner; I roared as loud as I could, and the nag came galloping towards me, whereupon she quitted her grasp, with the utmost reluctancy, and leaped upon the opposite bank, where she stood gazing and howling all the time I was putting on my clothes.

This was matter of diversion to my master and his family, as well as of mortification to myself. For now I could no longer deny that I was a real *Yahoo* in every limb and feature, since the females had a natural propensity to me, as one of their own species. Neither was the hair of this brute of a red colour (which might have been some excuse for an appetite a little irregular), but black as a sloe, and her countenance did not make an appearance altogether so hideous as the rest of the kind; for, I think, she could not be above eleven years old.

Having lived three years in this country, the reader I suppose will expect, that I should, like other travellers, give him some account of the manners and customs of its inhabitants, which it was indeed my principal study to learn.

As these noble *Houyhnhnms* are endowed by nature with a general disposition to all virtues, and have no conceptions or ideas of what is evil in a rational creature, so their grand maxim is, to cultivate reason, and to be wholly governed by it. Neither is reason among them a point problematical as with us, where men can argue with plausibility on both sides of the question; but strikes you with immediate conviction; as it must needs do where it is not mingled, obscured, or discoloured by passion and interest. I remember it was with extreme difficulty that I could bring my master to understand the meaning of the word *opinion,* or how a point could be disputable; because reason taught us to affirm or deny only where we are certain; and beyond our knowledge we cannot do either. So that controversies, wranglings, disputes, and positiveness in false or dubious propositions, are evils unknown among the *Houyhnhnms.* In the like manner when I used to explain to him our several systems of natural philosophy, he would laugh that a creature pretending to reason, should value itself upon the knowledge of other people's conjectures, and in things, where that knowledge, if it were certain, could be of no use. Wherein he agreed entirely with the sentiments of Socrates, as Plato delivers them; which I mention as the highest honour I can do that prince of philosophers. I have often since reflected what destruction such a doctrine would make in the libraries of Europe; and how many paths to fame would be then shut up in the learned world.

Friendship and benevolence are the two principal virtues among the *Houyhnhnms*; and these not confined to particular objects, but universal to the whole race. For a stranger from the remotest part is equally treated with the nearest neighbour, and wherever he goes, looks upon himself as at home. They preserve decency and civility in the highest degrees, but are altogether ignorant of ceremony. They have no fondness for their colts or foals, but the care they take in educating them proceeds entirely from the dictates of reason. And I observed my master to show the same affection to his neighbour's issue that he had for his own. They will have it that nature teaches them to love the whole species, and it is reason only that maketh a distinction of persons, where there is a superior degree of virtue.

When the matron *Houyhnhnms* have produced one of each sex, they no longer accompany with their consorts, except they lose one of their issue by some casualty, which very seldom happens; but in such a case they meet again, or when the like accident befalls a person whose wife is past bearing, some other couple bestow him one of their own colts, and then go together again till the mother is pregnant. This caution is necessary to prevent the country from being overburthened with numbers. But the race of inferior *Houyhnhnms* bred up to be servants is not so strictly limited upon this article; these are allowed to produce three of each sex, to be domestics in the noble families.

In their marriages they are exactly careful to choose such colours as will not make any disagreeable mixture in the breed. Strength is chiefly valued in the male, and comeliness in the female; not upon the account of love, but to preserve the race from degenerating; for where a female happens to excel in strength, a consort is chosen with regard to comeliness. Courtship, love, presents, jointures, settlements, have no place in their thoughts; or terms whereby to express them in their language. The young couple meet and are joined, merely because it is the determination of their parents and friends: it is what they see done every day, and they look upon it as one of the necessary actions of a reasonable being. But the violation of marriage, or any other unchastity, was never heard of: and the married pair pass their lives with the same friendship, and mutual benevolence that they bear to all others of the same species, who come in their way; without jealousy, fondness, quarrelling, or discontent.

In educating the youth of both sexes, their method is admirable, and highly deserves our imitation. These are not suffered to taste a grain of oats, except upon certain days, till eighteen years old; nor milk, but very rarely; and in summer they graze two hours in the morning, and as many in the evening, which their parents likewise observe; but the servants are not allowed above half that time, and a great part of their grass is brought home, which they eat at the most convenient hours, when they can be best spared from work.

Temperance, industry, exercise, and cleanliness, are the lessons equally enjoined to the young ones of both sexes: and my master thought it monstrous in us to give the females a different kind of education from the males, except in some articles of domestic management; whereby as he truly observed, one half of our natives were good for nothing but bringing children into the world: and to trust the care of our children to such useless animals, he said, was yet a greater instance of brutality.

But the *Houyhnhnms* train up their youth to strength, speed, and hardiness, by exercising them in running races up and down steep hills, and over hard stony grounds; and when they are all in a sweat, they are ordered to leap over head and ears into a pond or a river. Four times a year the youth of a certain district meet to show their proficiency in running and leaping, and other feats of strength and agility; where the victor is rewarded with a song made in his or her praise. On this festival the servants drive a herd of *Yahoos* into the field, laden with hay, and oats, and milk, for a repast to the *Houyhnhnms*; after which, these brutes are immediately driven back again, for fear of being noisome to the assembly.

Every fourth year, at the vernal equinox, there is a representative council of the whole nation, which meets in a plain about twenty miles from our house, and continues about five or six days. Here they enquire into the state and condition of the several districts; whether they abound or be deficient in hay or oats, or cows or *Yahoos*. And wherever there is any want (which is but seldom), it is immediately supplied by unanimous consent and contribution. Here likewise the regulation of children is settled: as for instance, if a *Houyhnhnm* hath two males, he changeth one of them with another that hath two females; and when a child hath been lost by any casualty, where the mother is past breeding, it is determined what family in the district shall breed another to supply the loss.

Chapter 9

A grand debate at the general assembly of the Houyhnhnms, *and how it was determined. The learning of the* Houyhnhnms. *Their buildings. Their manner of burials. The defectiveness of their language.*

One of these grand assemblies was held in my time, about three months before my departure, whither my master went as the representative of our district. In this council was resumed their old debate, and indeed, the only debate which ever happened in that country; whereof my master after his return gave me a very particular account.

The question to be debated was, whether the *Yahoos* should be exterminated from the face of the earth. One of the members for the affirmative offered several arguments of great strength and weight, alleging, that as the *Yahoos* were the most filthy, noisome, and deformed animal which nature ever produced, so they were the most restive and indocible, mischievous and malicious: they would privately suck the teats of the *Houyhnhnms*' cows, kill and devour their cats, trample down their oats and grass, if they were not continually watched, and commit a thousand other extravagancies. He took notice of a general tradition, that *Yahoos* had not been always in that country; but, that many ages ago, two of these brutes appeared together upon a mountain; whether produced by the heat of the sun upon corrupted mud and slime, or from the ooze and froth of the sea, was never known. That these *Yahoos* engendered, and their brood in a short time grew so numerous as to over-run and infest the whole nation. That the *Houyhnhnms* to get rid of this evil, made a general hunting, and at last enclosed the whole herd; and destroying the elder, every *Houyhnhnm* kept two young ones in a kennel, and brought them to such a degree of tameness, as an animal so savage by nature can be capable of acquiring; using them for draught and carriage. That there seemed to be much truth in this tradition, and that those creatures could not be *Ylnhniamshy* (or *aborigines* of the land), because of the violent hatred the *Houyhnhnms*, as well as all other animals, bore them; which although their evil disposition sufficiently deserved, could never have arrived at so high a degree, if they had been aborigines, or else they would have long since been rooted out. That the inhabitants taking a fancy to use the service of the *Yahoos*, had very imprudently neglected to cultivate the breed of asses, which were a comely animal, easily kept, more tame and orderly, without any offensive smell, strong enough for labour, although they yield to the other in agility of body; and if their braying be no agreeable sound, it is far preferable to the horrible howlings of the *Yahoos*.

Several others declared their sentiments to the same purpose, when my master proposed an expedient to the assembly, whereof he had indeed borrowed the hint from me. He approved of the tradition mentioned by the honourable member, who spoke before, and affirmed, that the two *Yahoos* said to be first seen among them, had been driven thither over the sea; that coming to land, and being forsaken by their companions, they retired to the mountains, and degenerating by degrees, became in process of time, much more savage than those of their own species in the country from whence these two originals came. The reason of this assertion was, that he had now in his possession a certain wonderful *Yahoo* (meaning myself), which most of them had heard of, and many of them had seen. He then related to them, how he first found me; that my body was all covered with an artificial composure of the skins and hairs of other animals; that I spoke in a language of my own, and had thoroughly learned theirs: that I had related to him the accidents which brought me thither: that when he saw me without my covering, I was an exact *Yahoo* in every part, only of a whiter colour, less hairy, and with shorter claws. He added, how I had endeavoured to persuade him, that in my own and other countries the *Yahoos* acted as the governing, rational animal, and held the *Houyhnhnms* in servitude: that he observed in me all the qualities of a *Yahoo*, only a little more civilized by some tincture of reason, which however was in a degree as far inferior to the *Houyhnhnm* race, as the *Yahoos* of their country were to me: that, among other things, I mentioned a custom we had of castrating *Houyhnhnms* when they were young, in order to render them tame; that the operation was easy and safe; that it was no shame to learn wisdom from brutes, as industry is taught by the ant, and building by the swallow. (For so I translate the word *lyhannh*, although it be a much larger fowl.) That this invention might be practised upon the younger *Yahoos* here, which, besides rendering them tractable and fitter for use, would in an age put an end to the whole species without destroying life. That in the mean time the *Houyhnhnms* should be exhorted to cultivate the breed of asses, which, as they are in all respects more valuable brutes, so they have this advantage, to be fit for service at five years old, which the others are not till twelve.

This was all my master thought fit to tell me at that time, of what passed in the grand council. But he was pleased to conceal one particular, which related personally to myself, whereof I soon felt the unhappy effect, as the reader will know in its proper place, and from whence I date all the succeeding misfortunes of my life.

The *Houyhnhnms* have no letters, and consequently their knowledge is all traditional. But there happening few events of any moment among a people so well united, naturally disposed to every virtue, wholly governed by reason, and cut off from all commerce with other nations, the historical part is easily preserved without burthening their memories. I have already observed, that they are subject to no diseases, and therefore can have no need of physicians. However, they have excellent medicines composed of herbs, to cure accidental bruises and cuts in the pastern or frog of the foot by sharp stones, as well as other maims and hurts in the several parts of the body.

They calculate the year by the revolution of the sun and moon, but use no subdivision into weeks. They are well enough acquainted with the motions of those two luminaries, and understand the nature of eclipses; and this is the utmost progress of their astronomy.

In poetry they must be allowed to excel all other mortals; wherein the justness of their similes, and the minuteness, as well as exactness of their descriptions, are indeed inimitable. Their verses abound very much in both of these, and usually contain either some exalted notions of friendship and benevolence, or the praises of those who were victors in races, and other bodily exercises. Their buildings, although very rude and simple, are not inconvenient, but well contrived to defend them from all injuries of cold and heat. They have a kind of tree, which at forty years old loosens in the root, and falls with the first storm: it grows very straight, and being pointed like stakes with a sharp stone (for the *Houyhnhnms* know not the use of iron), they stick them erect in the ground about ten inches asunder, and then weave in oat-straw, or sometimes wattles betwixt them. The roof is made after the same manner, and so are the doors.

The *Houyhnhnms* use the hollow part between the pastern and the hoof of their fore-feet, as we do our hands, and this with greater dexterity than I could at first imagine. I have seen a white mare of our family thread a needle (which I lent her on purpose) with that joint. They milk their cows, reap their oats, and do all the work which requires hands, in the same manner. They have a kind of hard flints, which by grinding against other stones, they form into instruments, that serve instead of wedges, axes, and hammers. With tools made of these flints, they likewise cut their hay, and reap their oats, which there groweth naturally in several fields: the *Yahoos* draw home the sheaves in carriages, and the servants tread them in certain covered huts, to get out the grain, which is kept in stores. They make a rude kind of earthen and wooden vessels, and bake the former in the sun.

If they can avoid casualties, they die only of old age, and are buried in the obscurest places that can be found, their friends and relations expressing neither joy nor grief at their departure; nor does the dying person discover the least regret that he is leaving the world, any more than if he were upon returning home from a visit to one of his neighbours. I remember my master having once made an appointment with a friend and his family to come to his house upon some affair of importance; on the day fixed, the mistress and her two children came very late; she made two excuses, first for her husband, who, as she said, happened that very morning to *shnuwnh*. The word is strongly expressive in their language, but not easily rendered into English; it signifies, *to retire to his first mother*. Her excuse for not coming sooner was, that her husband dying late in the morning, she was a good while consulting her servants about a convenient place where his body should be laid; and I observed she behaved herself at our house as cheerfully as the rest. She died about three months after.

They live generally to seventy or seventy-five years, very seldom to fourscore: some weeks before their death they feel a gradual decay, but without pain. During this time they are much visited by their friends, because they cannot go abroad with their usual ease and satisfaction. However, about ten days before their death, which they seldom fail in computing, they return the visits that have been made them by those who are nearest in the neighbourhood, being carried in a convenient sledge drawn by *Yahoos*; which vehicle they use, not only upon this occasion, but when they grow old, upon long journeys, or when they are lamed by any accident. And therefore when the dying *Houyhnhnms* return those visits, they take a solemn leave of their friends, as if they were going to some remote part of the country, where they designed to pass the rest of their lives.

I know not whether it may be worth observing, that the *Houyhnhnms* have no word in their language to express any thing that is evil, except what they borrow from the deformities or ill qualities of the *Yahoos*. Thus they denote the folly of a servant, an omission of a child, a stone that cuts their feet, a continuance of foul or unseasonable weather, and the like, by adding to each the epithet of *Yahoo*. For instance, *Hhnm Yahoo, Whnaholm Yahoo, Ynlhmndwihlma Yahoo*, and an ill-contrived house *Ynholmhnmrohlnw Yahoo*.

I could with great pleasure enlarge further upon the manners and virtues of this excellent people; but intending in a short time to publish a volume by itself expressly upon that subject, I refer the reader thither. And in the mean time, proceed to relate my own sad catastrophe.

Chapter 10

The Author's economy, and happy life among the Houyhnhnms. *His great improvement in virtue, by conversing with them. Their conversations. The Author has notice given him by his master that he must depart from the country. He falls into a swoon for grief, but submits. He contrives and finishes a canoe, by the help of a fellow-servant, and puts to sea at a venture.*

I had settled my little economy to my own heart's content. My master had ordered a room to be made for me after their manner, about six yards from the house; the sides and floors of which I plastered with clay, and covered with rush-mats of my own contriving; I had beaten hemp, which there grows wild, and made of it a sort of ticking: this I filled with the feathers of several birds I had taken with springes made of *Yahoos'* hairs, and were excellent food. I had worked two chairs with my knife, the sorrel nag helping me in the grosser and more laborious part. When my clothes were worn to rags, I made myself others with the skins of rabbits, and of a certain beautiful animal about the same size, called *nnuhnoh*, the skin of which is covered with a fine down. Of these I likewise made very tolerable stockings. I soled my shoes with wood which I cut from a tree, and fitted to the upper leather, and when this was worn out, I supplied it with the skins of *Yahoos* dried in the sun. I often got honey out of hollow trees, which I mingled with water, or eat with my bread. No man could more verify the truth of these two maxims, *That nature is very easily satisfied*; and *That necessity is the mother of invention*. I enjoyed perfect health of body, and tranquillity of mind; I did not feel the treachery of inconstancy of a friend, nor the injuries of a secret or open enemy. I had no occasion of bribing, flattering or pimping, to procure the favour of any great man or of his minion. I wanted no fence against fraud or oppression; here was neither physician to destroy my body, nor lawyer to ruin my fortune; no informer to watch my words and actions, or forge accusations against me for hire: here were no gibers, censurers, backbiters, pickpockets, highwaymen, house-breakers, attorneys, bawds, buffoons, gamesters, politicians, wits, splenetics, tedious talkers, controvertists, ravishers, murderers, robbers, virtuosos; no leaders or followers of party and faction; no encouragers to vice, by seducement or examples; no dungeon, axes, gibbets, whipping-posts, or pillories; no cheating shopkeepers or mechanics; no pride, vanity, or affectation; no fops, bullies, drunkards, strolling whores, or poxes; no ranting, lewd, expensive wives; no stupid, proud pedants; no importunate, overbearing, quarrelsome, noisy, roaring, empty, conceited, swearing companions; no scoundrels, raised from the dust for the sake of their vices, or nobility thrown into it on account of their virtues; no lords, fiddlers, judges, or dancing-masters.

I had the favour of being admitted to several *Houyhnhnms*, who came to visit or dine with my master; where his Honour graciously suffered me to wait in the room, and listen to their discourse. Both he and his company would often descend to ask me questions, and receive my answers. I had also sometimes the honour of attending my master in his visits to others. I never presumed to speak, except in answer to a question; and then I did it with inward regret, because it was a loss of so much time for improving myself: but I was infinitely delighted with the station of an humble auditor in such conversations, where nothing passed but what was useful, expressed in the fewest and most significant words; where (as I have already said) the greatest decency was observed, without the least degree of ceremony; where no person spoke without being pleased himself, and pleasing his companions; where there was no interruption, tediousness, heat, or difference of sentiments. They have a notion, that when people are met together, a short silence doth much improve conversation: this I found to be true; for during those little intermissions of talk, new ideas would arise in their thoughts, which very much enlivened the discourse. Their subjects are generally on friendship and benevolence, or order and economy; sometimes upon the visible operations of nature, or ancient traditions; upon the bounds and limits of virtue; upon the unerring rules of reason, or upon some determinations to be taken at the next great assembly; and often upon the various excellencies of poetry. I may add, without vanity, that my presence often gave them sufficient matter for discourse, because it afforded my master an occasion of letting his friends into the history of me and my country, upon which they were all pleased to descant in a manner not very advantageous to human kind; and for that reason I shall not repeat what they said: only I may be allowed to observe, that his Honour, to my great admiration, appeared to understand the nature of *Yahoos* much better than myself. He went through all our vices and follies, and discovered many which I had never mentioned to him, by only supposing what qualities a *Yahoo* of their country, with a small proportion of reason, might be capable of exerting; and concluded, with too much probability, how vile as well as miserable such a creature must be.

I freely confess, that all the little knowledge I have of any value, was acquired by the lectures I received from my master, and from hearing the discourses of him and his friends; to which I should be prouder to listen, than to dictate to the greatest and wisest assembly in Europe. I admired the strength, comeliness, and speed of the inhabitants; and such a constellation of virtues in such amiable persons produced in me the highest veneration. At first, indeed, I did not feel that natural awe which the

Yahoos and all other animals bear towards them; but it grew upon me by degrees, much sooner than I imagined, and was mingled with a respectful love and gratitude, that they would condescend to distinguish me from the rest of my species.

When I thought of my family, my friends, my countrymen, or human race in general, I considered them as they really were, *Yahoos* in shape and disposition, perhaps a little more civilized, and qualified with the gift of speech, but making no other use of reason, than to improve and multiply those vices, whereof their brethren in this country had only the share that nature allotted them. When I happened to behold the reflection of my own form in a lake or fountain, I turned away my face in horror and detestation of myself, and could better endure the sight of a common *Yahoo*, than of my own person. By conversing with the *Houyhnhnms*, and looking upon them with delight, I fell to imitate their gait and gesture, which is now grown into a habit, and my friends often tell me in a blunt way, that *I trot like a horse*; which, however, I take for a great compliment. Neither shall I disown, that in speaking I am apt to fall into the voice and manner of the *Houyhnhnms*, and hear myself ridiculed on that account without the least mortification.

In the midst of all this happiness, and when I looked upon myself to be fully settled for life, my master sent for me one morning a little earlier than his usual hour. I observed by his countenance that he was in some perplexity, and at a loss how to begin what he had to speak. After a short silence, he told me, he did not know how I would take what he was going to say; that in the last general assembly, when the affair of the *Yahoos* was entered upon, the representatives had taken offence at his keeping a *Yahoo* (meaning myself) in his family more like a *Houyhnhnm* than a brute animal. That he was known frequently to converse with me, as if he could receive some advantage or pleasure in my company; that such a practice was not agreeable to reason or nature, or a thing ever heard of before among them. The assembly did therefore exhort him, either to employ me like the rest of my species, or command me to swim back to the place from whence I came. That the first of these expedients was utterly rejected by all the *Houyhnhnms* who had ever seen me at his house or their own, for they alleged, that because I had some rudiments of reason, added to the natural pravity of those animals, it was to be feared, I might be able to seduce them into the woody and mountainous parts of the country, and bring them in troops by night to destroy the *Houyhnhnms'* cattle, as being naturally of the ravenous kind, and averse from labour.

My master added, that he was daily pressed by the *Houyhnhnms* of the neighbourhood to have the assembly's exhortation executed, which he could not put off much longer. He doubted it would be impossible for me to swim to another country, and therefore wished I would contrive some sort of vehicle resembling those I had described to him, that might carry me on the sea; in which work I should have the assistance of his own servants, as well as those of his neighbours. He concluded, that for his own part, he could have been content to keep me in his service as long as I lived; because he found I had cured myself of some bad habits and dispositions, by endeavouring, as far as my inferior nature was capable, to imitate the *Houyhnhnms*.

I should here observe to the reader, that a decree of the general assembly in this country is expressed by the word *hnheoayn*, which signifies an exhortation, as near as I can render it; for they have no conception how a rational creature can be compelled, but only advised, or exhorted; because no person can disobey reason, without giving up his claim to be a rational creature.

I was struck with the utmost grief and despair at my master's discourse; and being unable to support the agonies I was under, I fell into a swoon at his feet; when I came to myself, he told me, that he concluded I had been dead (for little better than conjecture, yet I resolved to steer my course eastward, hoping to reach the south-west coast of New Holland, and perhaps some such island as I desired, lying westward of it. The wind was full west, and by six in the evening I computed I had gone eastward at least eighteen leagues, when I spied a very small island about half a league off, which I soon reached. It was nothing but a rock with one creek,[20] naturally arched by the force of tempests. Here I put in my canoe, and climbing up a part of the rock, I could plainly discover land to the east, extending from south to north. I lay all night in my canoe; and repeating my voyage early in the morning, I arrived in seven hours to the south-east point of New Holland. This confirmed me in the opinion I have long entertained, that the maps and charts place this country at least three degrees more to the east than it really is; which thought I communicated many years ago to my worthy friend Mr. Herman Moll, and gave him my reasons for it, although he hath rather chosen to follow other authors.

I saw no inhabitants in the place where I landed, and being unarmed, I was afraid of venturing far into the country. I found some shellfish on the shore, and eat them raw, not daring to kindle a fire, for fear of being discovered by the natives. I continued three days feeding on oysters and limpets, to save my own provisions; and I fortunately found a brook of excellent water, which gave me great relief.

On the fourth day, venturing out early a little too far, I saw twenty or thirty natives upon a height, not above five hundred yards from me. They were stark naked, men, women, and children round a fire, as I could discover by the smoke. One of them spied me, and gave notice to the rest; five of them advanced towards me, leaving the women and children at the fire. I made what haste I could to the shore, and getting into my canoe, shoved off: the savages observing me retreat, ran after me; and before I could get far enough into the sea, discharged an arrow, which wounded me deeply on the inside of my left knee (I shall carry the mark to my grave). I apprehended the arrow might be poisoned, and paddling out of the reach of their darts (being a calm day), I made a shift to suck the wound, and dress it as well as I could.

I was at a loss what to do, for I durst not return to the same landing-place, but stood to the north, and was forced to paddle; for the wind, though very gentle, was against me, blowing north-west. As I was looking about for a secure landing-place, I saw a sail to the north-north-east, which appearing every minute more visible, I was in some doubt whether I should wait for them or no; but at last my detestation of the *Yahoo* race prevailed, and turning my canoe, I sailed and paddled together to the south, and got into the same creek from whence I set out in the morning, choosing rather to trust myself among these barbarians, than live with European *Yahoos*. I drew up my canoe as close as I could to the shore, and hid myself behind a stone by the little brook, which, as I have already said, was excellent water.

The ship came within half a league of this creek, and sent her long boat with vessels to take in fresh water (for the place it seems was very well known), but I did not observe it till the boat was almost on shore, and it was too late to seek another hiding-place. The seamen at their landing observed my canoe, and rummaging it all over, easily conjectured that the owner could not be far off. Four of them well armed searched every cranny and lurking-hole, till at last they found me flat on my face behind the stone. They gazed awhile in admiration at my strange uncouth dress; my coat made of skins, my wooden-soled shoes, and my furred stockings; from whence, however, they concluded I was not a native of the place, who all

---

[20]Bay or sheltered cove.

the most accomplished *Houyhnhnms*. I write without any view towards profit or praise. I never suffer a word to pass that may look like reflection, or possibly give the least offence even to those who are most ready to take it. So that I hope I may with justice pronounce myself an author perfectly blameless, against whom the tribes of answerers, considerers, observers, reflecters, detecters, remarkers, will never be able to find matter for exercising their talents.

I confess, it was whispered to me, that I was bound in duty as a subject of England, to have given in a memorial to a Secretary of State, at my first coming over; because, whatever lands are discovered by a subject, belong to the Crown. But I doubt whether our conquests in the countries I treat of, would be as easy as those of Ferdinando Cortez over the naked Americans. The *Lilliputians* I think, are hardly worth the charge of a fleet and army to reduce them; and I question whether it might be prudent or safe to attempt the *Brobdingnagians*; or whether an English army would be much at their ease with the Flying Island over their heads. The *Houyhnhnms*, indeed, appear not to be so well prepared for war, a science to which they are perfect strangers, and especially against missive weapons. However, supposing myself to be a minister of state, I could never give my advice for invading them. Their prudence, unanimity, unacquaintedness with fear, and their love of their country, would amply supply all defects in the military art. Imagine twenty thousand of them breaking into the midst of an European army, confounding the ranks, overturning the carriages, battering the warriors' faces into mummy[24] by terrible yerks[25] from their hinder hoofs; for they would well deserve the character given to Augustus: *Recalcitrat undique tutus.*[26] But instead of proposals for conquering that magnanimous nation, I rather wish they were in a capacity or disposition to send a sufficient number of their inhabitants for civilizing Europe, by teaching us the first principles of honour, justice, truth, temperance, public spirit, fortitude, chastity, friendship, benevolence, and fidelity. The names of all which virtues are still retained among us in most languages and are to be met with in modern as well as ancient authors; which I am able to assert from my own small reading.

But I had another reason which made me less forward to enlarge his Majesty's dominions by my discoveries. To say the truth, I had conceived a few scruples with relation to the distributive justice of princes upon these occasions. For instance, a crew of pirates are driven by a storm they know not whither; at length a boy discovers land from the topmast; they go on shore to rob and plunder; they see an harmless people, are entertained with kindness, they give the country a new name, they take formal possession of it for their king, they set up a rotten plank or a stone for a memorial, they murder two or three dozen of the natives, bring away a couple more by force for a sample, return home, and get their pardon. Here commences a new dominion acquired with a title by *divine right*. Ships are sent with the first opportunity; the natives driven out or destroyed, their princes tortured to discover their gold; a free licence given to all acts of inhumanity and lust, the earth reeking with the blood of its inhabitants: and this execrable crew of butchers employed in so pious an expedition, is a *modern colony* sent to convert and civilize an idolatrous and barbarous people.

But this description, I confess, doth by no means affect the British nation, who may be an example to the whole world for their wisdom, care, and justice in planting colonies; their liberal endowments for the advancement of religion and

---

[24]Into powder; the modern equivalent would be "into a pulp."
[25]Kicks.
[26]Horace, *Satires* 2:1:20; "He kicks backward, guarding himself at every point."

learning; their choice of devout and able pastors to propagate Christianity; their caution in stocking their provinces with people of sober lives and conversations from this the mother kingdom; their strict regard to the distribution of justice, in supplying the civil administration through all their colonies with officers of the greatest abilities, utter strangers to corruption; and to crown all, by sending the most vigilant and virtuous governors, who have no other views than the happiness of the people over whom they preside, and the honour of the King their master.

But, as those countries which I have described do not appear to have any desire of being conquered, and enslaved, murdered or driven out by colonies; nor abound either in gold, silver, sugar, or tobacco; I did humbly conceive, they were by no means proper objects of our zeal, our valour, or our interest. However, if those whom it more concerns think fit to be of another opinion, I am ready to depose, when I shall be lawfully called, that no European did ever visit these countries before me. I mean, if the inhabitants ought to be believed; unless a dispute may arise about the two *Yahoos*, said to have been seen many ages ago on a mountain in *Houyhnhnm-land*.

But, as to the formality of taking possession in my Sovereign's name, it never came once into my thoughts; and if it had, yet as my affairs then stood, I should perhaps in point of prudence and self-preservation, have put it off to a better opportunity.

Having thus answered the only objection that can ever be raised against me as a traveller, I here take a final leave of all my courteous readers, and return to enjoy my own speculations in my little garden at Redriff, to apply those excellent lessons of virtue which I learned among the *Houyhnhnms*; to instruct the *Yahoos* of my own family as far as I shall find them docible animals; to behold my figure often in a glass, and thus if possible habituate myself by time to tolerate the sight of a human creature: to lament the brutality of *Houyhnhnms* in my own country, but always treat their persons with respect, for the sake of my noble master, his family, his friends, and the whole *Houyhnhnm* race, whom these of ours have the honour to resemble in all their lineaments, however their intellectuals came to degenerate.

I began last week to permit my wife to sit at dinner with me, at the farthest end of a long table; and to answer (but with the utmost brevity) the few questions I asked her. Yet the smell of a *Yahoo* continuing very offensive, I always keep my nose well stopped with rue, lavender, or tobacco leaves. And although it be hard for a man late in life to remove old habits, I am not altogether out of hopes in some time to suffer a neighbour *Yahoo* in my company, without the apprehensions I am yet under of his teeth or his claws.

My reconcilement to the *Yahoo*-kind in general might not be so difficult, if they would be content with those vices and follies only which nature hath entitled them to. I am not in the least provoked at the sight of a lawyer, a pickpocket, a colonel, a fool, a lord, a gamester, a politician, a whore-master, a physician, an evidence, a suborner, an attorney, a traitor, or the like; this is all according to the due course of things: but when I behold a lump of deformity, and diseases both in body and mind, smitten with *pride*, it immediately breaks all the measures of my patience; neither shall I be ever able to comprehend how such an animal and such a vice could tally together. The wise and virtuous *Houyhnhnms*, who abound in all excellencies that can adorn a rational creature, have no name for this vice in their language, which hath no terms to express any thing that is evil, except those whereby they describe the detestable qualities of their *Yahoos*, among which they were not able to distinguish this of pride, for want of thoroughly understanding human nature, as it showeth itself in other countries, where that animal presides. But I, who had more experience, could plainly observe some rudiments of it among the wild *Yahoos*.

But the *Houyhnhnms,* who live under the government of reason, are no more proud of the good qualities they possess, than I should be for not wanting a leg or an arm, which no man in his wits would boast of, although he must be miserable without them. I dwell the longer upon this subject from the desire I have to make the society of an English *Yahoo* by any means not insupportable; and therefore I here entreat those who have any tincture of this absurd vice, that they will not presume to come in my sight.

ALEXANDER POPE
[1688–1744]

By 1737, the British poet Alexander Pope, physically impaired from childhood and nearing fifty, was already arranging and collating his poetry and his vast correspondence for final editions, as though he sensed his life were nearing its end. (He would, in fact, die at fifty-six.) In the midst of worsening physical ailments and the somber task of readying his work for posterity, Pope presented the Prince of Wales, with whom he had maintained a wary friendship, a puppy from his Great Dane Bounce's new litter, together with a collar engraved with a couplet:

> I am his Highness' Dog at Kew;
> Pray tell me Sir, whose Dog are you?

Minor verse, to be sure, but in a number of ways it embodies Pope's work and times. First, there is the completely social context of the couplet, designed to be read and reacted to by unwary people fawning over the royal puppy, with their reactions observed by others in the know; Pope's poetry grows out of and flourishes within an intensely gossipy and self-conscious aristocratic society. Secondly, there is the economy of the couplet itself, small enough to fit upon a dog collar, packing into its neat repetition of the word *dog* a great deal of comment about those who fawn, those who follow, those who are owned. Pope is matchless for his compressed subtlety, his ability to manipulate sound to convey thought. And finally, there is the darkness just beneath the surface of the playful gesture. Dogs proverbially have pure hearts and remain loyal even toward abusive owners. But how many people had compromised all their human morality and judgment there amid the Prince's wide lawns and splendid halls, in return for a good dinner or some preferment at court?

In his own time, Pope was mocked, despised, and reviled for his work, his opinions, and his body, cruelly misshapen and weakened by tuberculosis of the spine. But he was also regarded as *the* poet among poets, *the* heir of the spirit of Western European poetry, *the* British writer against whom others must be measured. Physical deformities were fair game for satirists in Pope's day, and vicious caricatures of the dwarfed and hunchbacked poet were popularly circulated, showing Pope's head grotesquely topping the body of a spider or a monkey. At the same time, it became fashionable to paint and sculpt him nobly posed as the head of dignified and idealized full-body portraits of Homer, Virgil, Dante, Chaucer, Petrarch, and other forebears of the grand tradition of European literature.

The literary ancestors whose traditions Pope most consciously sought to make new in his own "Neo-Augustan Age" were classical authors. Horace is his model for the *Moral Essays,* where in easy, colloquial language he takes on the excesses and shortcomings of women, or landscape gardeners, or the moneyed aristocracy. Lucretius' *De Rerum Natura* inspired Pope and his contemporaries to attempt in verse the presentation of complex philosophical ideas, as Pope does in his *Essay on Man.* Above all, the epic poets echo constantly in Pope's poetry. His thorough knowledge of Homeric and Virgilian scope and music becomes transmuted in his own brilliant mock epics *The Rape of the Lock* and *The Dunciad,* where contemporary people's petty affairs are depicted surrounded by epic panoply partly to underscore their vapidity and tawdriness. The pedantic scholar Colley Cibber, the principal butt of *The Dunciad,* builds a pyre of the writings he has been unable to sell in honor of the goddess Dulness, but in the nick of time she stops him from setting these treasures afire and whisks him off to her sordid palace amid the flea-markets of London in order to proclaim him her own dear heir. Other goddesses and their favorite sons in the great epics come to mind—Thetis and Achilles, Athene and Odysseus, Venus and Aeneas—with a terrible difference. It was not only Pope's technical mastery of rhyme and rhythm and his ability to catch the particular satiric spirit of the times for which he was celebrated; he seems to have given his contemporaries confidence that this new Augustan Age was indeed a legitimate and powerful extension of a great classical tradition that valued sense, treasured knowledge, and mocked folly.

LIFE

Pope was born in 1688 into a well-to-do Catholic linen merchant's family in London, a fiercely anti-Catholic city where the Roman Catholic pontiff was still often burned in effigy. In 1711 the Pope family moved to a small farm in Windsor Forest, some thirty miles from London, where other Catholic families sought relief from persecution. Pope's passion for country scenes and gardening began here in this gentle landscape. His experience of both the natural world and school were limited by his fragile health; his tubercular, hunched spine halted his growth at four feet six inches, and he was racked by fierce headaches and respiratory problems all his life. But the little boy's mind was remarkable. He avidly read English, French, and Latin poetry, and his father encouraged him to write verses of his own.

Pope's Catholicism barred him from the Universities, but he was determined to venture beyond his pious and overprotective household. In 1705 he gained a ready education by walking boldly into Will's Coffeehouse in London, where the famous writers of the older generation still gathered. Pope struck the old guard as an odd country bumpkin, but they recognized his genius, and by 1709 he could boast of his first published poems, imitations of Virgil's *Eclogues.*

In 1711 the audacious newcomer brought out his *Essay on Criticism,* a long tour de force of a poem in which he dispensed literary criticism and wickedly satirized a number of his less brilliant elders along the way. At twenty-three Pope was already famous and controversial, and in the next few years, between 1712 and 1714, he produced *The Rape of the Lock,* his brilliant mock-heroic account of a feud among society belles and beaux. In that same year, Pope began spending time with a new set of extraordinary friends, mostly Tory and literary, whom he would keep for life, among them Jonathan Swift and John Gay. Together they devised the character of a droning pedant named Martinus Scriblerus, for whom they gleefully invented a vast body of memoirs and correspondence. Swift and Pope, especially, spurred each other's genius, but the circle of friends, many of whom held political offices, were scattered when Queen Anne died and the Tory government fell.

Pope next embarked on the absorbing and profitable task of rendering Homer's *Iliad* into English, a five-year project. In 1719, a year after his father's death, Pope and his mother moved to a villa at Twickenham, on whose five acres he would exercise his passion for landscape gardening. He built a rustic grotto and outfitted it with a system of lamps and mirrors, enabling him to project on small surfaces in tiny "moving images" the outer world of river traffic on the Thames, much as he captured the social world of his England in the miniature frame of the heroic couplet. Here at Twickenham he delighted to entertain his friends, including a number of strong and intellectual women such as Martha Blount, with whom he had an enduring friendship.

After his early and fast-paced start, the years between 1719 and 1728 were a sort of hiatus in Pope's career, largely filled with editing Shakespeare, translating the classics, and landscape gardening. But in 1728 came the *The Dunciad,* a dark mock epic in which Pope took on not merely *dunces,* his personal literary enemies, but everything that seemed to him to embody the petty corruption, shoddy art, and slippage of standards that might quietly erode an entire culture. In 1743, a burlesque variorum scholarly edition of the revised poem was offered to the public, complete with full names of the indignant dunces whom it satirized.

Pope's poetry now turned increasingly to moral and philosophical subjects such as are found in the *Essay on Man.* Still, Pope never left off writing satire; *The Dunciad,* in particular, kept appearing in ever more elaborate editions, and Pope remained a prolific writer to the end. He died of asthma on May 30, 1744, after receiving the last rites of the Church.

WORK

The selections we present here show different sides of Pope's range and temperament. The *Essay on Man* (1733–1734) is aimed at defending God and the universe from the charges of randomness; Pope wants to continue Milton's task of justifying the ways of God to man, but in this more secular age he will do it without any explicit Christian reference. This section from the Third Epistle of the *Essay* celebrates a cohesive principle of interdependence among all the living and inanimate entities in the universe. Pope sees the Great Chain of Being not merely as a hierarchical arrangement of creation, but as a "chain of love." Though Pope derives his argument from many older sources, there is an oddly modern-sounding ecological edge as he declares that creation is not solely designed for the good of human beings, and calls attention to God's care for all living things.

The Rape of the Lock is a more lighthearted matter, but genuine moral and social issues underlie the delightful, shimmering surface of this mock epic, a form beloved by Enlightenment satirists for its ability to show up triviality and pettiness by presenting silly actions as heroic conflicts surrounded with Homeric, Virgilian, and Miltonic panoply. The poem grew out of a real incident, a feud that started between two prominent Roman Catholic families when Robert Lord Petre sneaked up on the young beauty Arabella Fermor and cut off a lock of her hair as a trophy. Pope did not know either party, but John Caryll, a mutual friend who believed the Catholic minority was embattled enough without internal disputes, begged Pope to write a poem that would "laugh them together." Pope obligingly produced first a short version in 1712. Two years later, he added the features for which the poem is now mainly celebrated: the "machinery" of the attendant spirits, the sylphs and gnomes he derived from Rosicrucian belief, as well as from classical gods and Miltonic angels; the delicious account of Belinda's elaborate toilet; the long section in which the war between the sexes is recounted in terms of the realistic hands of a game of cards called ombre; and the obligatory journey to the underworld that lies at the heart of most epics, Umbriel's visit to the surreal Cave of Spleen. Later still, Pope added Clarissa's wise but ill-timed and disregarded words about the need for common sense and good humor.

The poem's action occupies a day, as the belle Belinda groggily arises, forgets the dream-warning her attendant sylph whispers about some dire event impending, and arrays herself like Achilles for the particular battles that await her—not only card games and gossip, but the real dangers of predatory beaux, rivals, and a social world where the only real choices are marriage and spinsterhood, either of which may be losing hands, as Pope well knows. Belinda travels by barge to Hampton Court, where she wins a card game, but loses a lock of her hair to the scissors of the Baron. Although this seems the slightest of occasions for a full-scale war, Pope manages at once to lightly mock the participants and to imply something darker than a temporarily ruined hairdo. It is not thoughtlessly that he calls this

The Rape of the Lock. In mythology, the shearing of hair is often connected to shame and loss of personal power, and this poem is shot through with references to virginity, one of the few talismanic powers young women hold in this male-dominated society, but it is a talisman that becomes worthless if it is defended too well for too long. Virginity, or "honor," can be variously guarded, locked away, yielded up, lost, traded off, or forcibly taken. We may laugh at the epic solemnity summoned up to describe an adolescent prank visited by a lovestruck beau upon a spoiled belle, but we are conscious that at some level there has been a personal violation, and that what is partly being fought over is the right to call one's body one's own. It does not really matter that Belinda's own dedication to chastity is somewhat questionable; it is true she might weep with identical grief were she to "stain her honor, or her new brocade." Nonetheless, at the heart of the poem, there is an uncomfortable feeling of a social engine more dire than any pair of silver workbasket scissors closing in upon Belinda. She may choose to be of "good humor" and go along with the world of courtship and marriage preordained for her, or she can be a "prude," and find herself in the dreadful Cave of Spleen, the fate of women who rigidly deny their sexuality, transmuted into a hysterical bottle crying piteously for a cork.

Needless to say, these are not especially wide-ranging options. In the climactic mock-epic battle, the women apparently win, but neither side really does, for the lock, like innocence, is not restorable, nor is it retainable as a trophy of male aggression, the gods in this case having enshrined Belinda's tresses in the skies as a new comet. Of course, it is Pope himself who contrives this ending, immortalizing Arabella Fermor's lock and making a work of art out of a personal squabble he knew of second-hand. In *The Rape of the Lock* he evokes with equal measures of irony and affection the fragile beauty of the young aristocrats whom he personally knew, and the shadows he could see gathering just beyond the shimmer of their charmed lives.

SUGGESTED READINGS

Alexander Pope: A Life, by Maynard Mack (1985), is a detailed and entertaining biography containing fine readings of the major poems. W. K. Wimsatt's essay "One Relation of Rhyme to Reason" in *The Verbal Icon* (1954) is a brilliant exposition of Pope's manipulation of sound to fit sense in his poetry. *Alexander Pope* by Laura Brown (1985) rereads Pope in the light of recent literary theory.

The Rape of the Lock

Nolueram, Belinda, tuos violare capillos;
Sed juvat, hoc precibus me tribuisse tuis.
—MARTIAL *[Epigrams xii. 84]*[1]

TO MRS. ARABELLA FERMOR

Madam,
It will be in vain to deny that I have some regard for this piece, since I dedicate it to You. Yet you may bear me witness, it was intended only to divert a few young

---

[1] "I did not wish, Belinda, to do violence to your locks, but I am pleased to have granted this to your prayers." This epigraph from the poet Martial implies that Arabella Fermor had asked Pope to publish the poem.

Ladies, who have good sense and good humour enough to laugh not only at their sex's little unguarded follies, but at their own. But as it was communicated with the air of a Secret, it soon found its way into the world. An imperfect copy having been offered to a Bookseller, you had the good nature for my sake to consent to the publication of one more correct: This I was forced to, before I had executed half my design, for the Machinery was entirely wanting to complete it.

The Machinery, Madam, is a term invented by the Critics, to signify that part which the Deities, Angels, or Dæmons are made to act in a Poem: For the ancient Poets are in one respect like many modern Ladies: let an action be never so trivial in itself, they always make it appear of the utmost importance. These Machines I determined to raise on a very new and odd foundation, the Rosicrucian doctrine of Spirits.[2]

I know how disagreeable it is to make use of hard words before a Lady; but 'tis so much the concern of a Poet to have his works understood, and particularly by your Sex, that you must give me leave to explain two or three difficult terms.

The Rosicrucians are a people I must bring you acquainted with. The best account I know of them is in a French book called *Le Comte de Gabalis*,[3] which both in its title and size is so like a Novel, that many of the Fair Sex have read it for one by mistake. According to these Gentlemen, the four Elements are inhabited by Spirits, which they call Sylphs, Gnomes, Nymphs, and Salamanders. The Gnomes or Dæmons of Earth delight in mischief; but the Sylphs, whose habitation is in the Air, are the best-conditioned creatures imaginable. For they say, any mortals may enjoy the most intimate familiarities with these gentle Spirits, upon a condition very easy to all true Adepts, an inviolate preservation of Chastity.

As to the following Cantos, all the passages of them are as fabulous as the Vision at the beginning, or the Transformation at the end; (except the loss of your Hair, which I always mention with reverence). The Human persons are as fictitious as the Airy ones; and the character of Belinda, as it is now managed, resembles you in nothing but in Beauty.

If this Poem had as many Graces as there are in your Person, or in your Mind, yet I could never hope it should pass through the world half so Uncensured as You have done. But let its fortune be what it will, mine is happy enough, to have given me this occasion of assuring you that I am, with the truest esteem,

Madam,

Your most obedient, Humble Servant,

A. Pope

CANTO 1

What dire offence from amorous causes springs,
What mighty contests rise from trivial things,
I sing—This verse to CARYLL,[4] Muse! is due:
This, even Belinda may vouchsafe to view:
Slight is the subject, but not so the praise,
If She inspire, and He approve my lays.

---

[2]The seventeenth-century Rosicrucian system of mystic philosophy borrowed from a number of older occult traditions. Pope apparently learned what Rosicrucian lore he knew from a contemporary manual put out by the society.

[3]The author was the Abbé de Montfauçon de Villars; the book appeared in 1670.

[4]John Caryll, the unofficial leader of well-born Roman Catholic families in Pope's circle, had urged him to write something that would soothe both families and "laugh them together."

Say what strange motive, Goddess! could compel
A well-bred Lord t' assault a gentle Belle?
O say what stranger cause, yet unexplored,
Could make a gentle Belle reject a Lord?
In tasks so bold, can little men engage,   10
And in soft bosoms dwells such mighty Rage?
    Sol through white curtains shot a timorous ray,
And oped those eyes that must eclipse the day:
Now lap dogs give themselves the rousing shake,
And sleepless lovers, just at twelve, awake:
Thrice rung the bell, the slipper knocked the ground,
And the pressed watch returned a silver sound.⁵
Belinda still her downy pillow prest,
Her guardian SYLPH prolonged the balmy rest: 20
'Twas He had summoned to her silent bed
The morning dream that hovered o'er her head;
A Youth more glittering than a Birth-night Beau,⁶
(That even in slumber caused her cheek to glow)
Seemed to her ear his winning lips to lay,
And thus in whispers said, or seemed to say.
    Fairest of mortals, thou distinguished care
Of thousand bright Inhabitants of Air!
If e'er one Vision touched thy infant thought,
Of all the Nurse and all the Priest have taught;   30
Of airy Elves by moonlight shadows seen,
The silver token, and the circled green,⁷
Or virgins visited by Angel powers,
With golden crowns and wreaths of heavenly flowers;
Hear and believe! thy own importance know,
Nor bound thy narrow views to things below.
Some secret truths, from learnèd pride concealed,
To Maids alone and Children are revealed:
What though no credit doubting Wits may give?
The Fair and Innocent shall still believe.   40
Know, then, unnumbered Spirits round thee fly,
The light Militia of the lower sky:
These, though unseen, are ever on the wing,
Hang o'er the Box, and hover round the Ring.⁸
Think what an equipage thou hast in Air,
And view with scorn two Pages and a Chair.⁹
As now your own, our beings were of old,
And once enclosed in Woman's beauteous mould;

---

⁵Belinda thumps on the floor with her slipper to summon her maid; her watch rings the hour and the quarter when she presses its stem.

⁶On the birthday of the reigning British sovereign, people dressed elegantly.

⁷The "little people," spirits who go by various names, would sometimes leave a silver coin in thanks for a gift (such as a bowl of cream) or to reward an industrious servant; the fairy ring, an especially lush circle of grass that grows in connection with a certain underground fungus, marks the places where they dance.

⁸Theater boxes, and the driving circle or Ring in Hyde Park, where the upper classes rode in their carriages to see and be seen.

⁹A sedan chair.

Thence, by a soft transition, we repair
From earthly Vehicles to these of air.   50
Think not, when Woman's transient breath is fled,
That all her vanities at once are dead;
Succeeding vanities she still regards,
And though she plays no more, o'erlooks the cards.
Her joy in gilded Chariots, when alive,
And love of Ombre,[10] after death survive.
For when the Fair in all their pride expire,
To their first Elements[11] their Souls retire:
The Sprites of fiery Termagants in Flame
Mount up, and take a Salamander's name.   60
Soft yielding minds to Water glide away,
And sip, with Nymphs, their elemental Tea.
The graver Prude sinks downward to a Gnome,
In search of mischief still on Earth to roam.
The light Coquettes in Sylphs aloft repair,
And sport and flutter in the fields of Air.
   Know further yet; whoever fair and chaste
Rejects mankind, is by some Sylph embraced:
For Spirits, freed from mortal laws, with ease
Assume what sexes and what shapes they please.   70
What guards the purity of melting Maids,
In courtly balls, and midnight masquerades,
Safe from the treacherous friend, the daring spark,
The glance by day, the whisper in the dark,
When kind occasion prompts their warm desires,
When music softens, and when dancing fires?
'Tis but their Sylph, the wise Celestials know,
Though Honour is the word with Men below.
   Some nymphs there are, too conscious of their face,
For life predestined to the Gnomes' embrace.   80
These swell their prospects and exalt their pride,
When offers are disdained, and love denied:
Then gay Ideas[12] crowd the vacant brain,
While Peers, and Dukes, and all their sweeping train,
And Garters, Stars, and Coronets appear,[13]
And in soft sounds, Your Grace salutes their ear.
'Tis these that early taint the female soul,
Instruct the eyes of young Coquettes to roll,
Teach Infant cheeks a bidden blush to know,
And little hearts to flutter at a Beau.   90

---

[10] A card game; see note 30.

[11] The four elements of which all matter was thought to be composed are Earth, Air, Fire, and Water. One of these elements was thought to predominate in each human being, determining personality and physical constitution. In Pope's scheme, the souls of women who have died transmigrate into spirits appropriate to their ruling element. Because salamanders—amphibians that often hide beneath loose bark—were sometimes seen escaping from blazing wood, they were believed to dwell in fire, and their name was given to a species of fire spirit.

[12] Flashy images.

[13] Symbols of the nobility.

Oft, when the world imagine women stray,
The Sylphs through mystic mazes guide their way,
Through all the giddy circle they pursue,
And old impertinence expel by new.
What tender maid but must a victim fall
To one man's treat, but for another's ball?
When Florio speaks what virgin could withstand,
If gentle Damon did not squeeze her hand?
With varying vanities, from every part,
They shift the moving Toyshop of their heart;   100
Where wigs with wigs, with sword-knots sword-knots strive,
Beaux banish beaux, and coaches coaches drive.
This erring mortals Levity may call;
Oh blind to truth! the Sylphs contrive it all.
    Of these am I, who thy protection claim,
A watchful sprite, and Ariel is my name.
Late, as I ranged the crystal wilds of air,
In the clear Mirror of thy ruling Star
I saw, alas! some dread event impend,
Ere to the main this morning sun descend,   110
But heaven reveals not what, or how, or where:
Warned by the Sylph, oh pious maid, beware!
This to disclose is all thy guardian can:
Beware of all, but most beware of Man!
    He said; when Shock,[14] who thought she slept too long,
Leaped up, and waked his mistress with his tongue.
'Twas then, Belinda, if report say true,
Thy eyes first opened on a Billet-doux;
Wounds, Charm, and Ardors were no sooner read,
But all the Vision vanished from thy head.   120
    And now, unveiled, the Toilet stands displayed,
Each silver Vase in mystic order laid.
First, robed in white, the Nymph intent adores,
With head uncovered, the Cosmetic powers.
A heavenly image in the glass appears,
To that she bends, to that her eyes she rears;
Th' inferior Priestess, at her altar's side,
Trembling, begins the sacred rites of Pride.
Unnumbered treasures ope at once, and here
The various offerings of the world appear;   130
From each she nicely culls with curious toil,
And decks the Goddess with the glittering spoil.
This casket India's glowing gems unlocks,
And all Arabia breathes from yonder box.
The Tortoise here and Elephant unite,
Transformed to combs, the speckled, and the white.[15]
Here files of pins extend their shining rows,
Puffs, Powders, Patches,[16] Bibles, Billet-doux.

---

[14] Belinda's dog. A "shock" was a small, long-haired poodle, a fashionable breed of lapdog.
[15] Tortoiseshell and ivory were popular materials for fancy combs and brushes.
[16] It was the fashion among both men and women to wear patches of court plaster for beauty marks.

Now awful Beauty puts on all its arms;
The fair each moment rises in her charms, 140
Repairs her smiles, awakens every grace,
And calls forth all the wonders of her face;
Sees by degrees a purer blush arise,
And keener lightnings quicken in her eyes.
The busy Sylphs surround their darling care,
These set the head, and those divide the hair,
Some fold the sleeve, whilst others plait the gown;
And Betty's[17] praised for labours not her own.

CANTO 2

Not with more glories, in th' etherial plain,
The Sun first rises o'er the purpled main,
Than, issuing forth, the rival of his beams
Launched on the bosom of the silver Thames.
Fair Nymphs, and well-dressed Youths around her shone,
But every eye was fixed on her alone.
On her white breast a sparkling Cross she wore,
Which Jews might kiss, and Infidels adore.
Her lively looks a sprightly mind disclose,
Quick as her eyes, and as unfixed as those: 10
Favours to none, to all she smiles extends;
Oft she rejects, but never once offends.
Bright as the sun, her eyes the gazers strike,
And, like the sun, they shine on all alike.
Yet graceful ease, and sweetness void of pride,
Might hide her faults, if Belles had faults to hide:
If to her share some female errors fall,
Look on her face, and you'll forget 'em all.
    This Nymph, to the destruction of mankind,
Nourished two Locks, which graceful hung behind 20
In equal curls, and well conspired to deck
With shining ringlets the smooth ivory neck.
Love in these labyrinths his slaves detains,
And mighty hearts are held in slender chains.
With hairy springes[18] we the birds betray,
Slight lines of hair surprise the finny prey,
Fair tresses man's imperial race ensnare,
And beauty draws us with a single hair.
    Th' adventurous Baron the bright locks admired;
He saw, he wished, and to the prize aspired. 30
Resolved to win, he meditates the way,
By force to ravish, or by fraud betray;
For when success a Lover's toil attends,
Few ask, if fraud or force attained his ends.

---

[17]A generic name for a maid; Betty is Belinda's "inferior priestess" at the dressing-table altar.
[18]Snares to entrap birds and small animals, sometimes made of braided horsehair.

For this, ere Phœbus rose, he had implored
Propitious heaven, and every power adored,
But chiefly Love—to Love an Altar built,
Of twelve vast French Romances, neatly gilt.
There lay three garters, half a pair of gloves;
And all the trophies of his former loves;
With tender Billets-doux he lights the pyre,
And breathes three amorous sighs to raise the fire.
Then prostrate falls, and begs with ardent eyes
Soon to obtain, and long possess the prize:
The powers gave ear, and granted half his prayer,
The rest, the winds dispersed in empty air.

   But now secure the painted vessel glides,
The sunbeams trembling on the floating tides:
While melting music steals upon the sky,
And softened sounds along the waters die;
Smooth flow the waves, the Zephyrs gently play,
Belinda smiled, and all the world was gay.
All but the Sylph—with careful thoughts opprest,
Th' impending woe sat heavy on his breast.
He summons strait his Denizens of air;
The lucid squadrons round the sails repair:
Soft o'er the shrouds aërial whispers breathe,
That seemed but Zephyrs to the train beneath.
Some to the sun their insect wings unfold,
Waft on the breeze, or sink in clouds of gold;
Transparent forms, too fine for mortal sight,
Their fluid bodies half dissolved in light,
Loose to the wind their airy garments flew,
Thin glittering textures of the filmy dew,
Dipped in the richest tincture of the skies,
Where light disports in ever-mingling dyes,
While every beam new transient colours flings,
Colours that change whene'er they wave their wings.
Amid the circle, on the gilded mast,
Superior by the head, was Ariel placed;
His purple pinions opening to the sun,
He raised his azure wand, and thus begun.

   Ye Sylphs and Sylphids, to your chief give ear!
Fays, Fairies, Genii, Elves, and Dæmons, hear!
Ye know the spheres and various tasks assigned
By laws eternal to th' aërial kind.
Some in the fields of purest Æther play,
And bask and whiten in the blaze of day.
Some guide the course of wandering orbs on high,
Or roll the planets through the boundless sky.
Some less refined, beneath the moon's pale light
Pursue the stars that shoot athwart the night,
Or suck the mists in grosser air below,
Or dip their pinions in the painted bow,
Or brew fierce tempests on the wintry main,

40

50

60

70

80

Or o'er the glebe[19] distil the kindly rain.
Others on earth o'er human race preside,
Watch all their ways, and all their actions guide:
Of these the chief the care of Nations own,
And guard with Arms divine the British Throne.   90
    Our humbler province is to tend the Fair,
Not a less pleasing, though less glorious care;
To save the powder from too rude a gale,
Nor let th' imprisoned essences exhale;[20]
To draw fresh colours from the vernal flowers;
To steal from rainbows e'er they drop in showers
A brighter wash;[21] to curl their waving hairs,
Assist their blushes, and inspire their airs;
Nay oft, in dreams, invention we bestow,
To change a Flounce, or add a Furbelow.   100
    This day, black Omens threat the brightest Fair
That e'er deserved a watchful spirit's care;
Some dire disaster, or by force, or slight;
But what, or where, the fates have wrapped in night.
Whether the nymph shall break Diana's law,[22]
Or some frail China jar receive a flaw;
Or stain her honour, or her new brocade;
Forget her prayers, or miss a masquerade;
Or lose her heart, or necklace, at a ball;
Or whether Heaven has doomed that Shock must fall.   110
Haste, then, ye spirits! to your charge repair:
The fluttering fan be Zephyretta's care;
The drops to thee, Brillante, we consign;
And, Momentilla, let the watch be thine;
Do thou, Crispissa, tend her favorite Lock;[23]
Ariel himself shall be the guard of Shock.
    To fifty chosen Sylphs, of special note,
We trust th' important charge, the Petticoat:
Oft have we known that sevenfold fence to fail,
Though stiff with hoops, and armed with ribs of whale;   120
Form a strong line about the silver bound,
And guard the wide circumference around.
    Whatever spirit, careless of his charge,
His post neglects, or leaves the fair at large,
Shall feel sharp vengeance soon o'ertake his sins,
Be stopped in vials, or transfixed with pins;
Or plunged in lakes of bitter washes lie,
Or wedged whole ages in a bodkin's eye:[24]

---

[19] Field under cultivation.

[20] Nor allow perfume to evaporate.

[21] Cosmetic lotion.

[22] Diana was the Roman goddess of virginity and chastity.

[23] The sylphs' names are appropriate to their duties: Brillante would be in charge of drops, probably containing digitalis, to dilate the pupils and make Belinda's eyes seem larger and brighter; "Crispissa" suggests curliness.

[24] A blunt needle used to weave ribbon through eyelets.

Gums and Pomatums[25] shall his flight restrain,
While clogged he beats his silken wings in vain;
Or Alum styptics[26] with contracting power
Shrink his thin essence like a rivelled[27] flower:
Or, as Ixion fixed, the wretch shall feel
The giddy motion of the whirling Mill,[28]
In fumes of burning Chocolate shall glow,
And tremble at the sea that froths below!
  He spoke; the spirits from the sails descend;
Some, orb in orb, around the nymph extend;
Some thrid the mazy ringlets of her hair;
Some hang upon the pendants of her ear;
With beating hearts the dire event they wait,
Anxious, and trembling for the birth of Fate.

130

140

CANTO 3

Close by those meads, for ever crowned with flowers,
Where Thames with pride surveys his rising towers,
There stands a structure of majestic frame,
Which from the neighboring Hampton takes its name.[29]
Here Britain's statesmen oft the fall foredoom
Of foreign Tyrants, and of Nymphs at home;
Here thou, great ANNA! whom three realms obey,
Dost sometimes counsel take—and sometimes Tea.
  Hither the heroes and the nymphs resort,
To taste awhile the pleasures of a Court;
In various talk th' instructive hours they past,
Who gave the ball, or paid the visit last;
One speaks the glory of the British Queen,
And one describes a charming Indian screen;
A third interprets motions, looks, and eyes;
At every word a reputation dies.
Snuff, or the fan, supply each pause of chat,
With singing, laughing, ogling, *and all that.*
  Meanwhile, declining from the noon of day,
The sun obliquely shoots his burning ray;
The hungry Judges soon the sentence sign,
And wretches hang that jurymen may dine;
The merchant from th' Exchange returns in peace,
And the long labours of the Toilet cease.
Belinda now, whom thirst of fame invites,
Burns to encounter two adventurous Knights,

10

20

---

[25]Perfumed hair ointments.
[26]Styptics contract tissue to shrink pores or check bleeding.
[27]Withered.
[28]Ixion was punished in Hades by being bound to a revolving wheel; the erring sylph will be tied to a mill for grinding coffee or cocoa beans.
[29]The royal palace, Hampton Court, situated on the Thames about fifteen miles from London.

At Ombre[30] singly to decide their doom;
And swells her breast with conquests yet to come.
Straight the three bands prepare in arms to join,
Each band the number of the sacred nine.   30
Soon as she spreads her hand, th' aërial guard
Descend, and sit on each important card:
First Ariel perched upon a Matadore,
Then each, according to the rank they bore;
For Sylphs, yet mindful of their ancient race,
Are, as when women, wondrous fond of place.

    Behold, four Kings in majesty revered,
With hoary whiskers and a forky beard;
And four fair Queens whose hands sustain a flower,
Th' expressive emblem of their softer power;   40
Four Knaves in garbs succinct,[31] a trusty band,
Caps on their heads, and halberts[32] in their hand;
And particoloured troops, a shining train,
Draw forth to combat on the velvet plain.

    The skilful Nymph reviews her force with care:
Let Spades be trumps! she said, and trumps they were.

    Now move to war her sable Matadores,
In show like leaders of the swarthy Moors.
Spadillio first, unconquerable Lord!
Led off two captive trumps, and swept the board.   50
As many more Manillio forced to yield,
And marched a victor from the verdant field.
Him Basto followed, but his fate more hard
Gained but one trump and one Plebeian card.
With his broad sabre next, a chief in years,
The hoary Majesty of Spades appears,
Puts forth one manly leg, to sight revealed,
The rest, his many-coloured robe concealed.
The rebel Knave, who dares his prince engage,
Proves the just victim of his royal rage.   60
Even mighty Pam,[33] that Kings and Queens o'erthrew
And mowed down armies in the fights of Lu,
Sad chance of war! now destitute of aid,
Falls undistinguished by the victor Spade!

    Thus far both armies to Belinda yield;
Now to the Baron fate inclines the field.
His warlike Amazon her host invades,
Th' imperial consort of the crown of Spades.

---

[30] Ombre, the game played by Belinda, the Baron, and another beau, originated in Spain. Pope describes exactly a quite plausible succession of play. The player who gets the bid is called the ombre, and she names trumps and must take more tricks than the stronger of her two opponents. When spades are trumps in ombre, the "Matadores," the high cards, in order of descending value, are "Spadillio," the ace of spades; "Manillio," the deuce of spades; and "Basto," the ace of clubs. Belinda wins steadily until the next-to-the-last trick, which the Baron takes, but she recoups on the final trick.

[31] Girded up.

[32] A renaissance weapon combining an ax and a lance.

[33] The jack of clubs, the highest card in the game of loo.

The Club's black Tyrant first her victim died
Spite of his haughty mien, and barbarous pride: 70
What boots the regal circle on his head,
His giant limbs, in state unwieldy spread;
That long behind he trails his pompous robe,
And, of all monarchs, only grasps the globe?
    The Baron now his Diamonds pours apace;
Th' embroidered King who shows but half his face,
And his refulgent Queen, with powers combined
Of broken troops an easy conquest find.
Clubs, Diamonds, Hearts, in wild disorder seen,
With throngs promiscuous strew the level green.   80
Thus when dispersed a routed army runs,
Of Asia's troops, and Afric's sable sons,
With like confusion different nations fly,
Of various habit, and of various dye,
The pierced battalions disunited fall,
In heaps on heaps; one fate o'erwhelms them all.
    The Knave of Diamonds tries his wily arts,
And wins (oh shameful chance!) the Queen of Hearts.
At this, the blood the virgin's cheek forsook,
A livid paleness spreads o'er all her look;   90
She sees, and trembles at th' approaching ill,
Just in the jaws of ruin, and Codille.[34]
And now (as oft in some distempered State)
On one nice Trick depends the general fate.
An Ace of Hearts steps forth: The King unseen
Lurked in her hand, and mourned his captive Queen:
He springs to vengeance with an eager pace,
And falls like thunder on the prostrate Ace.
The nymph exulting fills with shouts the sky;
The walls, the woods, and long canals reply.   100
    Oh thoughtless mortals! ever blind to fate,
Too soon dejected, and too soon elate.
Sudden, these honours shall be snatched away,
And cursed for ever this victorious day.
    For lo! the board with cups and spoons is crowned,
The berries crackle, and the mill turns round;[35]
On shining Altars of Japan[36] they raise
The silver lamp; the fiery spirits blaze:
From silver spouts the grateful liquors glide,
While China's earth receives the smoking tide:[37]   110
At once they gratify their scent and taste,
And frequent cups prolong the rich repast.
Straight hover round the Fair her airy band;
Some, as she sipped, the fuming liquor fanned,

---

[34]Losing a hand of cards.
[35]Beans are roasted and ground as the elaborate rites of preparing and drinking coffee begin.
[36]Coffee is being brewed on small lacquered tables.
[37]The coffee is poured into cups of Chinese porcelain.

Some o'er her lap their careful plumes displayed,
Trembling, and conscious of the rich brocade.
Coffee, (which makes the politician wise,
And see through all things with his half-shut eyes)
Sent up in vapours to the Baron's brain
New stratagems, the radiant Lock to gain.   120
Ah cease, rash youth! desist ere 'tis too late,
Fear the just Gods, and think of Scylla's Fate![38]
Changed to a bird, and sent to flit in air,
She dearly pays for Nisus' injured hair!
   But when to mischief mortals bend their will,
How soon they find fit instruments of ill!
Just then, Clarissa drew with tempting grace
A two-edged weapon from her shining case:
So Ladies in Romance assist their Knight,
Present the spear, and arm him for the fight.   130
He takes the gift with reverence, and extends
The little engine on his fingers' ends;
This just behind Belinda's neck he spread,
As o'er the fragrant steams she bends her head.
Swift to the Lock a thousand Sprites repair,
A thousand wings, by turns, blow back the hair;
And thrice they twitched the diamond in her ear;
Thrice she looked back, and thrice the foe drew near.
Just in that instant, anxious Ariel sought
The close recesses of the Virgin's thought;   140
As on the nosegay in her breast reclined,
He watched th' Ideas rising in her mind,
Sudden he viewed, in spite of all her art,
An earthly Lover lurking at her heart.
Amazed, confused, he found his power expired,
Resigned to fate, and with a sigh retired.
   The Peer now spreads the glittering Forfex[39] wide,
T' enclose the Lock; now joins it, to divide.
Even then, before the fatal engine closed,
A wretched Sylph too fondly interposed;   150
Fate urged the shears, and cut the Sylph in twain,
(But airy substance soon unites again)
The meeting points the sacred hair dissever
From the fair head, for ever, and for ever!
   Then flashed the living lightning from her eyes,
And screams of horror rend th' affrighted skies.
Not louder shrieks to pitying heaven are cast,
When husbands, or when lap dogs breathe their last;
Or when rich China vessels fallen from high,
In glittering dust, and painted fragments lie!   160
   Let wreaths of triumph now my temples twine,
(The Victor cried) the glorious Prize is mine!

---

[38]Scylla—not the sea monster of Scylla and Charybdis—was turned into a shore bird in punishment for
cutting the lock of her father's hair that magically protected him from harm.
[39]Scissors.

While fish in streams, or birds delight in air,
Or in a coach and six the British Fair,
As long as Atalantis shall be read,[40]
Or the small pillow grace a Lady's bed,
While visits shall be paid on solemn days,
When numerous wax-lights in bright order blaze,
While nymphs take treats, or assignations give,
So long my honour, name, and praise shall live!   170
What Time would spare, from Steel receives its date,
And monuments, like men, submit to fate!
Steel could the labour of the Gods destroy,
And strike to dust th' imperial towers of Troy;
Steel could the works of mortal pride confound,
And hew triumphal arches to the ground.
What wonder then, fair nymph! thy hairs should feel,
The conquering force of unresisted steel?

CANTO 4

But anxious cares the pensive nymph oppressed,
And secret passions laboured in her breast.
Not youthful kings in battle seized alive,
Not scornful virgins who their charms survive,
Not ardent lovers robbed of all their bliss,
Not ancient ladies when refused a kiss,
Not tyrants fierce that unrepenting die,
Not Cynthia when her manteau's[41] pinned awry,
E'er felt such rage, resentment, and despair,
As thou, sad Virgin! for thy ravished Hair.   10
    For, that sad moment, when the Sylphs withdrew,
And Ariel weeping from Belinda flew,
Umbriel, a dusky, melancholy sprite,
As ever sullied the fair face of light,
Down to the central earth, his proper scene,
Repaired to search the gloomy Cave of Spleen.[42]
    Swift on his sooty pinions flits the Gnome,
And in a vapour reached the dismal dome.
No cheerful breeze this sullen region knows,
The dreaded East is all the wind that blows.   20
Here in a grotto, sheltered close from air,
And screened in shades from day's detested glare,
She sighs for ever on her pensive bed,
Pain at her side, and Megrim[43] at her head.
    Two handmaids wait the throne: alike in place,
But differing far in figure and in face.
Here stood Ill Nature like an ancient maid,

---

[40] A 1709 novel by a Mrs. Manley that presented, in thin disguise, many current scandals.
[41] Negligée.
[42] Ill temper.
[43] Migraine headache; at times, simply low spirits.

Her wrinkled form in black and white arrayed;
With store of prayers, for mornings, nights, and noons,
Her hand is filled; her bosom with lampoons.   30
   There Affectation, with a sickly mien,
Shows in her cheek the roses of eighteen,
Practised to lisp, and hang the head aside,
Faints into airs, and languishes with pride,
On the rich quilt sinks with becoming woe,
Wrapped in a gown, for sickness, and for show.
The fair ones feel such maladies as these,
When each new nightdress gives a new disease.
   A constant Vapour[44] o'er the palace flies;
Strange phantoms rising as the mists arise;   40
Dreadful, as hermit's dreams in haunted shades,
Or bright, as visions of expiring maids.
Now glaring fiends, and snakes on rolling spires,[45]
Pale spectres, gaping tombs, and purple fires:
Now lakes of liquid gold, Elysian scenes,
And crystal domes, and Angels in machines.[46]
   Unnumbered throngs on every side are seen,
Of bodies changed to various forms by Spleen.
Here living Teapots stand, one arm held out,
One bent; the handle this, and that the spout: 50
A Pipkin there, like Homer's Tripod walks;[47]
Here sighs a Jar, and there a Goose Pie talks;
Men prove with child, as powerful fancy works,
And maids turned bottles, call aloud for corks.
   Safe passed the Gnome through this fantastic band,
A branch of healing Spleenwort[48] in his hand.
Then thus addressed the power: "Hail, wayward Queen!
Who rule the sex to fifty from fifteen:
Parent of vapours and of female wit,
Who give th' hysteric, or poetic fit,   60
On various tempers act by various ways,
Make some take physic, others scribble plays;
Who cause the proud their visits to delay,
And send the godly in a pet to pray.
A nymph there is, that all thy power disdains,
And thousands more in equal mirth maintains.
But oh! if e'er thy Gnome could spoil a grace,
Or raise a pimple on a beauteous face,
Like Citron waters[49] matrons' cheeks inflame,
Or change complexions at a losing game;   70

---

[44]"The vapors" was a catchall term used to indicate hypochondria, depression, and moodiness, especially in women.
[45]Coils.
[46]Stage machinery used to hoist aloft actors representing winged gods, angels, etc.
[47]See Homer's *Iliad* 18, 373–377, where Vulcan has created three-legged stool robots; here, the animated object is an earthen pot.
[48]An herb that renders the bearer immune to spleen. Pope is alluding to Aeneas' golden bough that enables him to pass unharmed through the underworld in the sixth book of Virgil's *Aeneid*.
[49]Brandy in which citrus peel has been steeped.

If e'er with airy horns[50] I planted heads,
Or rumpled petticoats, or tumbled beds,
Or caused suspicion when no soul was rude,
Or discomposed the headdress of a Prude,
Or e'er to costive lap dog gave disease,
Which not the tears of brightest eyes could ease:
Hear me, and touch Belinda with chagrin,
That single act gives half the world the spleen."
　　The Goddess with a discontented air
Seems to reject him, though she grants his prayer. 　　　　80
A wondrous Bag with both her hands she binds,
Like that where once Ulysses held the winds;[51]
There she collects the force of female lungs,
Sighs, sobs, and passions, and the war of tongues.
A Vial next she fills with fainting fears,
Soft sorrows, melting griefs, and flowing tears.
The Gnome rejoicing bears her gifts away,
Spreads his black wings, and slowly mounts to day.
　　Sunk in Thalestris'[52] arms the nymph he found,
Her eyes dejected and her hair unbound. 　　　　　　　　90
Full o'er their heads the swelling bag he rent,
And all the Furies issued at the vent.
Belinda burns with more than mortal ire,
And fierce Thalestris fans the rising fire.
"O wretched maid!" she spread her hands, and cried,
(While Hampton's echoes, "Wretched maid!" replied)
"Was it for this you took such constant care
The bodkin, comb, and essence to prepare?
For this your locks in paper durance bound,
For this with torturing irons wreathed around? 　　　　100
For this with fillets strained your tender head,
And bravely bore the double loads of lead?[53]
Gods! shall the ravisher display your hair,
While the Fops envy, and the Ladies stare!
Honour forbid! at whose unrivalled shrine
Ease, pleasure, virtue, all our sex resign.
Methinks already I your tears survey,
Already hear the horrid things they say,
Already see you a degraded toast,
And all your honour in a whisper lost! 　　　　　　　　110
How shall I, then, your helpless fame defend?
'Twill then be infamy to seem your friend!
And shall this prize, th' inestimable prize,
Exposed through crystal to the gazing eyes,
And heightened by the diamond's circling rays,
On that rapacious hand for ever blaze?

---

[50]Horns symbolize the cuckold whose wife has cheated on him. Umbriel is speaking of "airy"—imaginary—horns on men who wrongly suspect their wives of infidelity thanks to his mischief.
[51]See *Odyssey* 10.19 ff., where Aeolus hands Odysseus a bag containing all the ill winds that might blow him off course.
[52]The name is taken from a queen of the Amazons.
[53]The leaden frames around which fashionable high-piled hairdos were shaped.

Sooner shall grass in Hyde Park Circus grow,
And wits take lodgings in the sound of Bow;[54]
Sooner let earth, air, sea, to Chaos fall,
Men, monkeys, lap dogs, parrots, perish all!"   120
  She said; then raging to Sir Plume repairs,[55]
And bids her Beau demand the precious hairs:
(Sir Plume of amber snuffbox justly vain,
And the nice conduct of a clouded cane)
With earnest eyes, and round unthinking face,
He first the snuffbox opened, then the case,
And thus broke out—"My Lord, why, what the devil?
Z—ds![56] damn the lock! 'fore Gad, you must be civil!
Plague on't! 'tis past a jest—nay, prithee, pox!
Give her the hair"—he spoke, and rapped his box.   130
  "It grieves me much" (replied the Peer again)
"Who speaks so well should ever speak in vain.
But by this Lock, this sacred Lock I swear,
(Which never more shall join its parted hair;
Which never more its honours shall renew,
Clipped from the lovely head where late it grew)
That while my nostrils draw the vital air,
This hand, which won it, shall for ever wear."
He spoke, and speaking, in proud triumph spread
The long-contended honours of her head.   140
  But Umbriel, hateful Gnome! forbears not so;
He breaks the Vial whence the sorrows flow.
Then see! the nymph in beauteous grief appears,
Her eyes half languishing, half drowned in tears;
On her heaved bosom hung her drooping head,
Which, with a sigh, she raised; and thus she said.
  "For ever cursed be this detested day,
Which snatched my best, my favorite curl away!
Happy! ah ten times happy had I been,
If Hampton Court these eyes had never seen!   150
Yet am not I the first mistaken maid,
By love of Courts to numerous ills betrayed.
Oh had I rather unadmired remained
In some lone isle, or distant Northern land;
Where the gilt Chariot never marks the way,
Where none learn Ombre, none e'er taste Bohea![57]
There kept my charms concealed from mortal eye,
Like roses, that in deserts bloom and die.
What moved my mind with youthful Lords to roam?
O had I stayed, and said my prayers at home!   160
'Twas this, the morning omens seemed to tell,
Thrice from my trembling hand the patch box fell;[58]

---

[54] Within hearing of the bells of the church of St. Mary-le-Bow in the Cockney district of London, where no fashionable person would deign to live.
[55] Goes.
[56] Zounds; an old curse that is a contraction of "God's wounds," alluding to the passion of Christ.
[57] An expensive tea.
[58] A box to contain the court plaster both men and women pasted on their faces as beauty marks.

The tottering China shook without a wind,
Nay, Poll[59] sat mute, and Shock was most unkind!
A Sylph too warned me of the threats of fate,
In mystic visions, now believed too late!
See the poor remnants of these slighted hairs!
My hands shall rend what even thy rapine spares:
These in two sable ringlets taught to break,
Once gave new beauties to the snowy neck;   170
The sister lock now sits uncouth, alone,
And in its fellow's fate foresees its own;
Uncurled it hangs, the fatal shears demands,
And tempts once more, thy sacrilegious hands.
Oh hadst thou, cruel! been content to seize
Hairs less in sight, or any hairs but these!"

CANTO 5

She said: the pitying audience melt in tears.
But Fate and Jove had stopped the Baron's ears.
In vain Thalestris with reproach assails,
For who can move when fair Belinda fails?
Not half so fixed the Trojan could remain,
While Anna begged and Dido raged in vain.[60]
Then grave Clarissa graceful waved her fan;
Silence ensued, and thus the nymph began.
    "Say why are Beauties praised and honoured most,
The wise man's passion, and the vain man's toast?   10
Why decked with all that land and sea afford,
Why Angels called, and Angel-like adored?
Why round our coaches crowd the white-gloved Beaux,
Why bows the side-box from its inmost rows;
How vain are all these glories, all our pains,
Unless good sense preserve what beauty gains:
That men may say, when we the front-box grace,
'Behold the first in virtue as in face!'
Oh! if to dance all night, and dress all day,
Charmed the smallpox, or chased old age away;   20
Who would not scorn what housewife's cares produce,
Or who would learn one earthly thing of use?
To patch, nay ogle, might become a Saint,
Nor could it sure be such a sin to paint.
But since, alas! frail beauty must decay,
Curled or uncurled, since Locks will turn to grey;
Since painted, or not painted, all shall fade,
And she who scorns a man, must die a maid;
What then remains but well our power to use,
And keep good humour still whate'er we lose?   30

---

[59]Belinda's parrot.
[60]In Virgil's *Aeneid*, Aeneas forsakes his lover Dido despite her fury and her sister Anna's attempts to intervene.

And trust me, dear! good humour can prevail,
When airs, and flights, and screams, and scolding fail.
Beauties in vain their pretty eyes may roll;
Charms strike the sight, but merit wins the soul."
   So spoke the Dame, but no applause ensued;
Belinda frowned, Thalestris called her Prude.
"To arms, to arms!" the fierce Virago cries,
And swift as lightning to the combat flies.
All side in parties, and begin th' attack;
Fans clap, silks rustle, and tough whalebones crack;   40
Heroes' and Heroines' shouts confusedly rise,
And bass and treble voices strike the skies.
No common weapons in their hands are found,
Like Gods they fight, nor dread a mortal wound.
   So when bold Homer makes the Gods engage,
And heavenly breasts with human passions rage;
'Gainst Pallas, Mars; Latona, Hermes arms;
And all Olympus rings with loud alarms:
Jove's thunder roars, heaven trembles all around,
Blue Neptune storms, the bellowing deeps resound: 50
Earth shakes her nodding towers, the ground gives way,
And the pale ghosts start at the flash of day!
   Triumphant Umbriel on a sconce's[61] height
Clapped his glad wings, and sat to view the fight:
Propped on their bodkin spears, the Sprites survey
The growing combat, or assist the fray.
   While through the press enraged Thalestris flies,
And scatters death around from both her eyes,
A Beau and Witling[62] perished in the throng,
One died in metaphor, and one in song.   60
"O cruel nymph! a living death I bear,"
Cried Dapperwit, and sunk beside his chair.
A mournful glance Sir Fopling upwards cast,
"Those eyes are made so killing"—was his last.
Thus on Mæander's flowery margin lies
Th' expiring Swan, and as he sings he dies.
   When bold Sir Plume had drawn Clarissa down,
Chloe stepped in, and killed him with a frown;
She smiled to see the doughty hero slain,
But, at her smile, the Beau revived again.   70
   Now Jove suspends his golden scales in air,
Weighs the Men's wits against the Lady's hair;
The doubtful beam long nods from side to side;
At length the wits mount up, the hairs subside.
   See, fierce Belinda on the Baron flies,
With more than usual lightning in her eyes:
Nor feared the Chief th' unequal fight to try,
Who sought no more than on his foe to die.

---

[61] A candlestick bolted to the wall.
[62] One who feebly attempts to be a wit.

But this bold Lord with manly strength endued,
She with one finger and a thumb subdued: 80
Just where the breath of life his nostrils drew,
A charge of Snuff the wily virgin threw;
The Gnomes direct, to every atom just,
The pungent grains of titillating dust.
Sudden with starting tears each eye o'erflows,
And the high dome re-echoes to his nose.
  Now meet thy fate, incensed Belinda cried,
And drew a deadly bodkin from her side.
(The same, his ancient personage to deck,
Her great great grandsire wore about his neck,   90
In three seal rings; which after, melted down,
Formed a vast buckle for his widow's gown:
Her infant grandame's whistle next it grew,
The bells she jingled, and the whistle blew;
Then in a bodkin graced her mother's hairs,
Which long she wore, and now Belinda wears.)
  "Boast not my fall" (he cried) "insulting foe!
Thou by some other shalt be laid as low.
Nor think, to die dejects my lofty mind:
All that I dread is leaving you behind!   100
Rather than so, ah let me still survive,
And burn in Cupid's flames—but burn alive."
  "Restore the Lock!" she cries; and all around
"Restore the Lock!" the vaulted roofs rebound.
Not fierce Othello in so loud a strain
Roared for the handkerchief that caused his pain.[63]
But see how oft ambitious aims are crossed,
And chiefs contend till all the prize is lost!
The Lock, obtained with guilt, and kept with pain,
In every place is sought, but sought in vain: 110
With such a prize no mortal must be blest,
So heaven decrees! with heaven who can contest?
  Some thought it mounted to the Lunar sphere,
Since all things lost on earth are treasured there.
There Heroes' wits are kept in ponderous vases,
And beaux' in snuffboxes and tweezer cases.
There broken vows and deathbed alms are found,
And lovers' hearts with ends of riband bound,
The courtier's promises, and sick man's prayers,
The smiles of harlots, and the tears of heirs,   120
Cages for gnats, and chains to yoke a flea,
Dried butterflies, and tomes of casuistry.
  But trust the Muse—she saw it upward rise,
Though marked by none but quick, poetic eyes:
(So Rome's great founder to the heavens withdrew,
To Proculus alone confessed in view)[64]

---

[63] In Shakespeare's *Othello* 3.4, Desdemona's embroidered handkerchief is falsely produced as evidence that she has cuckolded Othello.
[64] Romulus, one of the legendary founders of Rome, is said to have been transported to heaven by a storm cloud while reviewing his troops.

A sudden Star, it shot through liquid air,
And drew behind a radiant trail of hair.
Not Berenice's Locks first rose so bright,[65]
The heavens bespangling with dishevelled light.   130
The Sylphs behold it kindling as it flies,
And pleased pursue its progress through the skies.
  This the Beau monde shall from the Mall[66] survey,
And hail with music its propitious ray.
This the blest Lover shall for Venus take,
And send up vows from Rosamonda's lake.[67]
This Partridge[68] soon shall view in cloudless skies,
When next he looks through Galileo's eyes;
And hence th' egregious wizard shall foredoom
The fate of Louis, and the fall of Rome.   140
  Then cease, bright Nymph! to mourn thy ravished hair,
Which adds new glory to the shining sphere!
Not all the tresses that fair head can boast,
Shall draw such envy as the Lock you lost.
For, after all the murders of your eye,
When, after millions slain, yourself shall die;
When those fair suns shall set, as set they must,
And all those tresses shall be laid in dust,
This Lock, the Muse shall consecrate to fame,
And midst the stars inscribe Belinda's name.   150

FROM

An Essay on Man

[TO HENRY ST. JOHN, LORD BOLINGBROKE]

Epistle 3

Argument: Of the Nature and State of Man with respect to Society

I. The whole Universe one system of Society. Nothing made wholly for *itself*, nor yet wholly for *another*. The happiness of *Animals* mutual. II. *Reason* or *Instinct* operate alike to the good of each Individual. *Reason* or *Instinct* operate also to Society, in all animals. III. How far *Society* carried by Instinct. How much farther by Reason. IV. Of that which is called the *State of Nature*. Reason instructed by Instinct in the invention of *Arts*, and in the Forms of *Society*. V. Origin of Political Societies. Origin of Monarchy. Patriarchal government. VI. Origin of true Religion and Government, from the same principle, of Love. Origin of Superstition and

---

[65]Berenice, the wife of Ptolemy III, sacrificed a lock of her hair to ensure her husband's safe return from battle. After it disappeared from the altar, a court astronomer found that it had been transformed into a new constellation.

[66]A popular walkway for fashionable strollers in St. James Park, London.

[67]Another feature of St. James Park, proverbially frequented by the lovelorn.

[68]A contemporary astrologer whom Pope and others enjoyed satirizing; "Galileo's eyes" would be a telescope.

Tyranny, from the same principle, of Fear. The Influence of Self-love operating to the *social* and *public* Good. Restoration of true Religion and Government on their first principle. Mixed Government. Various Forms of each, and the true end of all.

Here then we rest: "The Universal Cause
Acts to one end, but acts by various laws."
In all the madness of superfluous health,
The trim of pride, the impudence of wealth,
Let this great truth be present night and day;
But most be present, if we preach or pray.
  I. Look round our World; behold the chain of Love
Combining all below and all above.
See plastic Nature working to this end,
The single atoms each to other tend,   10
Attract, attracted to, the next in place
Formed and impelled its neighbour to embrace.
See Matter next, with various life endued,
Press to one centre still, the general Good.
See dying vegetables life sustain,
See life dissolving vegetate again:
All forms that perish other forms supply,
(By turns we catch the vital breath, and die)
Like bubbles on the sea of Matter born,
They rise, they break, and to that sea return.   20
Nothing is foreign: Parts relate to whole;
One all-extending, all-preserving Soul
Connects each being, greatest with the least;
Made Beast in aid of Man, and Man of Beast;
All served, all serving: nothing stands alone;
The chain holds on, and where it ends, unknown.
  Has God, thou fool! worked solely for thy good,
Thy joy, thy pastime, thy attire, thy food?
Who for thy table feeds the wanton fawn,
For him as kindly spread the flowery lawn: 30
Is it for thee the lark ascends and sings?
Joy tunes his voice, joy elevates his wings.
Is it for thee the linnet pours his throat?
Loves of his own and raptures swell the note.
The bounding steed you pompously bestride,
Shares with his lord the pleasure and the pride.
Is thine alone the seed that strews the plain?
The birds of heaven shall vindicate their grain.
Thine the full harvest of the golden year?
Part pays, and justly, the deserving steer: 40
The hog, that ploughs not nor obeys thy call,
Lives on the labours of this lord of all.
  Know, Nature's children all divide her care;
The fur that warms a monarch, warmed a bear.
While Man exclaims, "See all things for my use!"
"See man for mine!" replies a pampered goose:
And just as short of reason He must fall,
Who thinks all made for one, not one for all.

BENJAMIN FRANKLIN
[1706–1790]

The young printer Benjamin Franklin wrote a witty mock epitaph for himself that suggested the sort of optimistic and secularized Christianity he subscribed to, and anticipated the revisionist way he would write his own autobiography more than forty years later:

> The Body of
> B. Franklin, Printer
> (Like the Cover of an old Book
> Its Contents torn out
> And strip of its Lettering & Gilding),
> Lies here, Food for Worms.
> But the Work shall not be lost;
> For it will, (as he believ'd) appear once more,
> In a new and more elegant Edition
> Revised and corrected
> By the Author.

For generations of U.S. citizens, Benjamin Franklin's engaging *Autobiography* (1771–1790) demonstrated in a very satisfying, practical manner the hopeful doctrines of the Enlightenment. Franklin had come out of a poor and overcrowded candlemaker's household to become a printer, a successful businessman, an inventor, and a statesman who toward the end of his life helped to frame the Constitution and negotiate the treaty with Great Britain that ended the American Revolutionary War. An American boy, then, might be born into poverty among mean-spirited people, but with discipline, hard work, decent morals, and the occasional help of friends and Providence, he could make of himself anything he wished. This doctrine, though much tarnished by hard-working people's actual experience, continues to be an article of faith in the United States.

LIFE

Franklin was born in Boston in 1706, the thirteenth of fifteen children of Josiah and Abiah Franklin. His parents sent him to Boston Grammar School, intending to educate him for the ministry; when money ran short, he was taken out of school and put to work in the family trade. But it was plain to see how deeply this bright boy detested cutting wicks and dipping molds, and when Benjamin was twelve, his father apprenticed him to another of his sons, his elder half-brother James, a Boston printer and newspaper publisher. The printshop and newspaper proved a far more congenial business for Franklin, and soon, writing under the pen name of Silence Dogood, a sharp-tongued and opinionated widow, Franklin began sneaking essays into his brother's paper addressing a wide range of subjects. Speaking as Silence, the young Franklin mocked hoopskirts and other fashionable affectations, berated drunkards and religious hypocrites, and advocated the education of women. When James was briefly jailed for printing in his *New-England Courant* charges of incompetence against the government of Massachusetts, Franklin, at sixteen, managed the paper. For a time after James was freed, he was forbidden to publish the *Courant* except under government scrutiny, and young Benjamin became the nominal publisher of the paper.

Franklin's situation was not happy, despite all he was learning in his apprenticeship about printing and politics. There was a fierce sibling rivalry between the brothers; Franklin claimed James often beat him, and the more the younger brother gained in experience and competence, the more he longed for independence. In 1723 Franklin ran away from his apprenticeship, a criminal act in those times, and made his way to Philadelphia, where he worked as a printer, with an interlude in England in a London printing house. After he returned to Philadelphia, he prospered steadily through the very industry, temperance, and frugality he recommended to others; by the age of twenty-four he owned his own paper, and he soon began publishing the annual *Poor Richard's Almanack* (1733–1758). Almanacs were best-sellers in the American colonies; the present-day *Old Farmer's Almanac* is a continuing example of the genre. These little books were crammed full of astrological information, jokes, mini-essays, and weather predictions, tables charting the phases of the moon and the tides, and, above all, pithy advice about how to get ahead in this world. Very soon, *Poor Richard's Almanack* was outselling all its competitors. Its maxims still ring familiar to us, for Franklin's aphorisms were wittier and more prettily phrased than those of other almanac writers: there are no gains without pains; to be intimate with a foolish friend is like going to bed with a razor; a penny saved is a penny earned; a small leak will sink a great ship.

Franklin was able to retire at forty-two from the printing business thanks to the best-selling *Almanacks,* his *Pennsylvania Gazette,* and his thriving printshop, but his days both before and after retirement were filled with projects and public service. One of his most winning characteristics all his life was his open-minded curiosity about how nature and human nature worked; on a stormy seasick Atlantic crossing, he passed the time noting how the mussels attached to the heaving hull of his ship reacted to their alternate wetting and drying. He invented the Franklin stove, the lightning rod, and bifocal spectacles, and he devised literally hair-raising experiments with kites and keys and voltaic batteries that helped prove that the lightning of thunderstorms was indeed electrical. He conceived of public libraries and volunteer fire departments, and started the American Philosophical Society and the University of Pennsylvania. He served in many public posts, including a period as Indian Commissioner of Pennsylvania during the 1750s. From his diplomatic dealings with members of the Iroquois League, Franklin came to admire the detailed workings of the Iroquois' Great Law of Peace, the system of representative government combined with tribal sovereignty that had for centuries enabled Iroquoian peoples of different tribes to work together amiably. In 1754, when delegates from the thirteen North American British colonies met to explore the possibilities of union at the Albany Congress, the plan for a unified government Franklin proposed borrowed heavily from the Iroquoian system; although his plan was rejected, a version of it was eventually incorporated into the United States Constitution in 1787.

WORK

Franklin's part in the shaping of the young nation was indispensable. He helped to frame not only the Constitution, but the Declaration of Independence (1776); he tirelessly pursued diplomatic missions during the Revolutionary War; and he negotiated the Treaty of Paris (1783), the document that recognized the United States as a sovereign nation. He died in 1790, at eighty-four, at home in Philadelphia, after decades spent largely abroad in England and France.

Like most autobiographers, Franklin simplified his own complex life in order to make it appear to follow a rational pattern of development. By concentrating on his early years, he demonstrated clearly how industry and common sense could help a young man to rise above his less disciplined peers. Seen through the mellow distance of memory—Franklin was sixty-five when he began writing the *Autobiography*—his early years seem quite definitively shaped. His youth is a book with a coherent plot line and some few "errata"—the printer's jargon for misprints, a word Franklin uses in the *Autobiography* to mean moral shortcomings and errors of judgment—that his printer's hand itches to correct. He presents himself as a down-to-earth and good-natured Enlightenment boy-hero, and on the whole he authentically seems to have been just that. But what Franklin omits to mention, whether it be suppressed "errata" or simple everyday circumstances, interests historians almost as much as what he chooses to tell.

Over the two centuries since the *Autobiography* was written, we have become accustomed to an increasingly personal and confessional style of autobiography, one that shares information about private life and inner feelings with the reader. Given that fact, it is still unsettling to find Franklin's wife, Deborah Read, figuring in the book mainly as a spectator to the poverty and adolescent awkwardness he will soon overcome; when he first lands in Philadelphia, he buys three "great puffy rolls" and strolls down the street, eating one and carrying the others tucked beneath his arms, while his future wife looks on in amusement. In an episode omitted from our selection, he allows his initial courtship of Deborah to lapse, but joins with her three years later in a common-law marriage, after she has been abused and abandoned by her first husband. But almost no mention is made of the considerable part she played in Franklin's household and business affairs during the first half of his life.

Similarly, although Franklin addresses the first part of the *Autobiography* to his illegitimate son William (who was the governor of New Jersey), he omits almost all mention of his other children except for the death of one child by smallpox, which he takes as an occasion to urge parents to practice immunization. This omission seems particularly hard in the case of his favorite daughter, Sally, the only legitimate child who survived into adulthood, who served her father through much of his life as helpmate and hostess.

Moreover, the *Autobiography* leaves us with the impression of a profoundly American Benjamin Franklin. In fact, we know from other writings that Franklin felt himself almost as much British as American, and actively worked to stay abroad as much as possible. None of these things figure into the *Autobiography* to complicate the picture of the earnest and energetic young man tackling his own life as an ongoing improvement project, complete with a handy chart upon which to record his progress in Order, Industry, Temperance, and other virtues valued by the Protestant work ethic.

For many modern readers, Franklin's saving grace is a sly and self-deprecating wit that keeps him a wonderfully human figure. Wittiness, like compassion and joy and any number of other human possibilities, does not figure on Franklin's prim chart of virtues, but wit marks Franklin every bit as much as his industry and his inventiveness. This is the man who, after a long disquisition upon how he increased his daily output of virtuous behavior, remarks that he has come to see that perfection invites hatred, and tells the story of the farmer who sheepishly admits he prefers a speckled ax to a brightly polished one.

SUGGESTED READINGS

Ronald W. Clark's *Benjamin Franklin: A Biography* (1983) and Claude-Anne Lopez and Eugenia Herbert's *The Private Franklin: The Man and His Family* (1975) are good accounts of Franklin's life and works. N. Fiering's "Benjamin Franklin and the Way to Virtue" in *The American Quarterly*, Summer 1978, looks closely at Franklin's self-improvement ethic.

FROM

Autobiography

Twyford, at the Bishop
of St. Asaph's, 1771

Dear Son,

I have ever had a pleasure in obtaining any little anecdotes of my ancestors. You may remember the enquiries I made among the remains of my relations when you were with me in England and the journey I undertook for that purpose. Imagining it may be equally agreeable to you to know the circumstances of *my* life—many of which you are yet unacquainted with—and expecting a week's uninterrupted leisure in my present country retirement, I sit down to write them for you. Besides, there are some other inducements that excite me to this undertaking. From the poverty and obscurity in which I was born and in which I passed my earliest years, I have raised myself to a state of affluence and some degree of celebrity in the world. As constant good fortune has accompanied me even to an advanced period of life, my posterity will perhaps be desirous of learning the means, which I employed, and which, thanks to Providence, so well succeeded with me. They may also deem them fit to be imitated, should any of them find themselves in similar circumstances. That good fortune, when I reflected on it, which is frequently the case, has induced me sometimes to say that were it left to my choice, I should have no objection to go over the same life from its beginning to the end, only asking the advantage authors have of correcting in a second edition some faults of the first. So would I also wish to change some incidents of it for others more favourable. Notwithstanding, if this condition were denied, I should still accept the offer. But as this repetition is not to be expected, that which resembles most living one's life over again, seems to be to recall all the circumstances of it; and, to render this remembrance more durable, to record them in writing. In thus employing myself I shall yield to the inclination so natural to old men of talking of themselves and their own actions, and I shall indulge it, without being tiresome to those who, from respect to my age, might conceive themselves obliged to listen to me, since they will be always free to read me or not. And lastly (I may as well confess it, as the denial of it would be believed by nobody) I shall perhaps not a little gratify my own vanity. Indeed, I never heard or saw the introductory words, "Without Vanity I may say," etc., but some vain thing immediately followed. Most people dislike vanity in others whatever share they have of it themselves, but I give it fair quarter wherever I meet with it, being persuaded that it is often productive of good to the possessor and to others who are within his sphere of action. And therefore, in many cases it would not be altogether absurd if a man were to thank God for his vanity among the other comforts of life.

And now I speak of thanking God, I desire with all humility to acknowledge that I owe the mentioned happiness of my past life to his divine providence, which led me to the means I used and gave them success. My belief of this induces me to *hope,* though I must not *presume,* that the same goodness will still be exercised towards me in continuing that happiness or in enabling me to bear a fatal reverse, which I may experience as others have done—the complexion of my future fortune being known to him only, and in whose power it is to bless to us even our afflictions....

My elder brothers were all put apprentices to different trades. I was put to the grammar school at eight years of age, my father intending to devote me as the tithe of his sons to the service of the church. My early readiness in learning to read (which must have been very early, as I do not remember when I could not read) and the opinion of all his friends that I should certainly make a good scholar, encouraged him in this purpose of his. My uncle Benjamin, too, approved of it and proposed to give me all his shorthand volumes of sermons to set up with, if I would learn his shorthand. I continued, however, at the grammar school rather less than a year, though in that time I had risen gradually from the middle of the class of that year to be at the head of the same class, and was removed into the next class, whence I was to be placed in the third at the end of the year. But my father, burdened with a numerous family, was unable without inconvenience to support the expence of a college education, considering, moreover, as he said to one of his friends in my presence, the little encouragement that line of life afforded to those educated for it.

He gave up his first intentions, took me from the grammar school, and sent me to a school for writing and arithmetic kept by a then famous man, Mr. Geo. Brownell. He was a skillful master, and successful in his profession, employing the mildest and most encouraging methods. Under him I learned to write a good hand pretty soon, but I failed in the arithmetic and made no progress in it. At ten years old, I was taken home to help my father in his business, which was that of a tallow chandler and soap boiler—a business he was not bred to but had assumed on his arrival in New England, because he found his dyeing trade, being in little request, would not maintain his family. Accordingly, I was employed in cutting wick for the candles, filling the molds for cast candles, attending the shop, going of errands, etc.

I disliked the trade and had a strong inclination to go to sea, but my father declared against it; however, living near the water, I was much in it and on it. I learned early to swim well and to manage boats; and when embarked with other boys, I was commonly allowed to govern, especially in any case of difficulty; and upon other occasions I was generally the leader among the boys and sometimes led them into scrapes, of which I will mention one instance as it shows an early projecting public spirit, tho' not then justly conducted.

There was a salt marsh that bounded part of the mill pond, on the edge of which at high water, we used to stand to fish for minnows. By much trampling we had made it a mere quagmire. My proposal was to build a wharf there for us to stand upon, and I showed my comrades a large heap of stones which were intended for a new house near the marsh and which would very well suit our purpose. Accordingly, in the evening when the workmen were gone home, I assembled a number of my play-fellows, and we worked diligently like so many emmets,[1] sometimes two or three to a stone, 'till we brought them all to make our little wharf. The next morning the workmen were surprised at missing the stones, which had formed our wharf; enquiry was made after the authors of this transfer; we were discovered, complained of; several of us were corrected by our fathers, and tho' I demonstrated the utility of our work, mine convinced me that that which was not honest could not be truly useful.

I suppose you may like to know what kind of man my father was. He had an excellent constitution, was of middle stature, but well set and very strong. He was ingenious, could draw prettily, was skilled a little in music; his voice was sonorous and agreeable, so that when he played Psalm tunes on his violin and sung withal as he sometimes did in an evening after the business of the day was over, it was extremely agreeable to hear. He had some knowledge of mechanics, too, and on occasion was very handy with other tradesmen's tools. But his great excellence was a sound understanding and a solid judgment in prudential matters, both in private and public affairs. It is true he was never employed in the latter, the numerous family he had to educate and the straitness of his circumstances keeping him close to his trade; but I remember well his being frequently visited by leading men who consulted him for his opinion in affairs of the town or of the church he belonged to, and who showed a good deal of respect for his judgment and advice. He was also much consulted by private persons about their affairs when any difficulty occurred, and frequently chosen an arbitrator between contending parties. At his table he liked to have, as often as he could, some sensible friend or neighbour to converse with, and always took care to start some ingenious or useful topic for discourse which might tend to improve the minds of his children. By this means he turned our attention to what was good, just, and prudent in the conduct of life; and little

---

[1] Ants.

or no notice was ever taken of what related to the victuals on the table—whether it was well or ill dressed, in or out of season, of good or bad flavour, preferable or inferior to this or that other thing of the kind; so that I was brought up in such a perfect inattention to those matters as to be quite indifferent what kind of food was set before me, and so unobservant of it, that to this day I can scarce tell a few hours after dinner of what dishes it consisted. This has been a great convenience to me in travelling, where my companions have been sometimes very unhappy for want of a suitable gratification of their more delicate, because better instructed, tastes and appetites.

My mother had likewise an excellent constitution. She suckled all her ten children. I never knew either my father or mother to have any sickness but that of which they died, he at eighty-nine and she at eighty-five years of age. They lie buried together at Boston, where I some years since placed a marble stone over their grave with this inscription:

Josiah Franklin
And Abiah his wife
Lie here interred.
They lived lovingly together in wedlock
Fifty-five years.
Without an estate or any gainful employment,
By constant labour and industry,
With God's blessing,
They maintained a large family
Comfortably;
And brought up thirteen children,
And seven grandchildren
Reputably.
From this instance, Reader,
Be encouraged to diligence in thy calling,
And distrust not Providence.
He was a pious and prudent man,
She a discreet and virtuous woman.
Their youngest son,
In filial regard to their memory,
Places this stone.
J. F. born 1655—Died 1744—AEtat. 89.
A. F. born 1667—Died 1752——85.

By my rambling digressions I perceive myself to be grown old. I used to write more methodically. But one does not dress for private company as for a public ball. Perhaps 'tis only negligence.

To return: I continued thus employed in my father's business for two years, that is, till I was twelve years old; and my brother John, who was bred to that business, having left my father, married and set up for himself at Rhode Island, there was every appearance that I was destined to supply his place and be a tallow chandler. But my dislike to the trade continuing, my father had apprehensions that if he did not put me to one more agreeable, I should break loose and go to sea, as my brother Josiah had done, to his great vexation. In consequence he sometimes took me to walk with him and see joiners, bricklayers, turners, braziers, etc., at their work that he might observe my inclination and endeavour to fix it on some trade that would keep me on land. It has ever since been a pleasure to me to see good workmen handle their tools; and it has been useful to me to have learned so much by it as to be able to do little jobs myself in my house, when a workman could not read-ily be got, and to construct little machines for my experiments when the intention of making these was warm in my mind. My father determined at last for the cutler's trade, and placed me for some days on trial with Samuel, son of my uncle Benjamin, who was bred to that trade in London and had just established him in Boston. But the sum he exacted as a fee for my apprenticeship displeased my father, and I was taken home again.

From my infancy I was passionately fond of reading, and all the little money that came into my hands was laid out in the purchasing of books. I was very fond of voyages. My first acquisition was Bunyan's works in separate little volumes. I afterwards sold them to enable me to buy R. Burton's historical collections; they were small chapmen's[2] books and cheap, forty or fifty in all. My father's little library consisted chiefly of books in polemic divinity, most of which I read. I have since often regretted that at a time when I had such a thirst for knowledge, more proper books had not fallen in my way, since it was now resolved I should not be bred to divinity. There was among them Plutarch's *Lives,* in which I read abundantly, and I still think that time spent to great advantage. There was also a book of Defoe's called an *Essay on Projects* and another of Dr. Mather's called *Essays to do Good,* which perhaps gave me a turn of thinking that had an influence on some of the principal future events of my life.

This bookish inclination at length determined my father to make me a printer, though he had already one son (James) of that profession. In 1717 my brother, James, returned from England with a press and letters to set up his business in Boston. I liked it much better than that of my father, but still had a hankering for the sea. To prevent the apprehended effect of such an inclination, my father was impatient to have me bound[3] to my brother. I stood out some time, but at last was persuaded and signed the indenture, when I was yet but twelve years old. I was to serve as apprentice till I was twenty-one years of age, only I was to be allowed journeyman's wages during the last year. In a little time I made a great progress in the business and became a useful hand to my brother. I now had access to better books. An acquaintance with the apprentices of booksellers enabled me sometimes to borrow a small one, which I was careful to return soon and clean. Often I sat up in my room reading the greatest part of the night, when the book was borrowed in the evening and to be returned early in the morning, lest it should be found missing or wanted.

After some time a merchant, an ingenious, sensible man, Mr. Matthew Adams, who had a pretty collection of books and who frequented our printing house, took notice of me, invited me to see his library, and very kindly proposed to lend me such books as I chose to read. I now took a fancy to poetry and made some little pieces. My brother, supposing it might turn to account, encouraged me and induced me to compose two occasional ballads. One was called the "Lighthouse Tragedy," and contained an account of the shipwreck of Capt. Worthilake with his two daughters; the other was a "Sailor's Song on the Taking of the Famous *Teach,* or Blackbeard, the Pirate." They were wretched stuff, in street ballad style; and when they were printed, he sent me about the town to sell them. The first sold prodigiously, the event being recent and having made a great noise. This success flattered my vanity, but my father discouraged me by ridiculing my performances and telling me verse-makers were generally beggars. Thus I escaped being a poet and probably a very bad one. But as prose writing has been of great use to me in the course of my life and was a principal means of my advancement, I shall tell you

---

[2]Peddler's cheap copy.
[3]Apprenticed.

how in such a situation I acquired what little ability I may be supposed to have in that way.

There was another bookish lad in the town, John Collins by name, with whom I was intimately acquainted. We sometimes disputed, and very fond we were of argument, and very desirous of confuting one another—which disputatious turn, by the way, is apt to become a very bad habit, making people often extremely disagreeable in company, by the contradiction that is necessary to bring it into practice; and thence besides souring and spoiling the conversation, it is productive of disgusts and perhaps enmities where you may have occasion for friendship. I had caught it by reading my father's books of dispute on religion. Persons of good sense, I have since observed, seldom fall into it, except lawyers, university men, and men of all sorts who have been bred at Edinburgh. A question was once somehow or other started between Collins and me on the propriety of educating the female sex in learning and their abilities for study. He was of opinion that it was improper and that they were naturally unequal to it. I took the contrary side, perhaps a little for dispute sake. He was naturally more eloquent, having a greater plenty of words, and sometimes, as I thought, I was vanquished more by his fluency than by the strength of his reasons. As we parted without settling the point and were not to see one another again for some time, I sat down to put my arguments in writing, which I copied fair and sent to him. He answered and I replied. Three or four letters on a side had passed, when my father happened to find my papers and read them. Without entering into the subject in dispute, he took occasion to talk with me about my manner of writing, observed that though I had the advantage of my antagonist in correct spelling and pointing[4] (which I owed to the printing house) I fell far short in elegance of expression, in method, and in perspicuity—of which he convinced me by several instances. I saw the justice of his remarks and thence grew more attentive to my manner of writing, and determined to endeavour to improve my style.

About this time I met with an odd volume of the *Spectator*.[5] It was the third. I had never before seen any of them. I bought it, read it over and over, and was much delighted with it. I thought the writing excellent and wished if possible to imitate it. With that view, I took some of the papers, and making short hints of the sentiment in each sentence, laid them by a few days, and then without looking at the book, tried to complete the papers again by expressing each hinted sentiment at length and as fully as it had been expressed before, in any suitable words that should occur to me. Then I compared my *Spectator* with the original, discovered some of my faults, and corrected them. But I found I wanted a stock of words or a readiness in recollecting and using them, which I thought I should have acquired before that time if I had gone on making verses; since the continual search for words of the same import but of different length to suit the measure, or of different sound for the rhyme would have laid me under a constant necessity of searching for variety, and also have tended to fix that variety in my mind, and make me master of it. Therefore I took some of the tales in the *Spectator* and turned them into verse, and after a time, when I had pretty well forgotten the prose, turned them back again. I also sometimes jumbled my collections of hints into confusion, and after some weeks endeavoured to reduce them into the best order before I began to form the full sentences and complete the paper. This was to teach me method in the

---

[4] Punctuation.

[5] *The Spectator* was an English literary daily paper featuring essays by Joseph Addison (1672–1719) and Richard Steele (1672–1729).

arrangement of the thoughts. By comparing my work afterwards with the original, I discovered many faults and corrected them; but I sometimes had the pleasure of fancying that in certain particulars of small import I had been lucky enough to improve the method or the language, and this encouraged me to think that I might possibly in time come to be a tolerable English writer, of which I was extremely ambitious.

The time I allotted for these exercises and for reading, was at night after work, or before it began in the morning, or on Sundays, when I contrived to be in the printing house alone, avoiding as much as I could the common attendance on public worship which my father used to exact of me, when I was under his care—and which, indeed, I still thought a duty, though I could not, as it seemed to me, afford the time to practise it.

When about sixteen years of age I happened to meet with a book written by one Tryon, recommending a vegetable diet. I determined to go into it. My brother, being yet unmarried, did not keep house but boarded himself and his apprentices in another family. My refusing to eat flesh occasioned an inconveniency, and I was frequently chid for my singularity. I made myself acquainted with Tryon's manner of preparing some of his dishes, such as boiling potatoes or rice, making hasty pudding,[6] and a few others; and then proposed to my brother that if he would give me weekly half the money he paid for my board, I would board myself. He instantly agreed to it, and I presently found that I could save half what he paid me. This was an additional fund for buying of books. But I had another advantage in it. My brother and the rest going from the printing house to their meals, I remained there alone, and dispatching presently my light repast (which often was no more than a biscuit or a slice of bread, a handful of raisins or a tart from the pastry cook's, and a glass of water) had the rest of the time till their return for study, in which I made the greater progress from that greater clearness of head and quicker apprehension which generally attend temperance in eating and drinking. Now it was that being on some occasion made ashamed of my ignorance in figures, which I had twice failed in learning when at school, I took Cocker's book of arithmetic, and went through the whole by myself with the greatest ease. I also read Seller's and Sturmy's book on navigation and became acquainted with the little geometry it contains, but I never proceeded far in that science. I read about this time Locke *On Human Understanding,* and *The Art of Thinking* by Messrs. du Port Royal.

While I was intent on improving my language, I met with an English grammar (I think it was Greenwood's) at the end of which there were two little sketches on the arts of rhetoric and logic, the latter finishing with a dispute in the Socratic method. And soon after I procured Xenophon's *Memorable Things of Socrates,* wherein there are many examples of the same method. I was charmed with it, adopted it, dropped my abrupt contradiction and positive argumentation, and put on the humble enquirer. And being then, from reading Shaftsbury and Collins,[7] made a doubter, as I already was in many points of our religious doctrines, I found this method the safest for myself and very embarrassing to those against whom I used it; therefore, I took a delight in it, practised it continually, and grew very artful and expert in drawing people, even of superior knowledge, into concessions the consequences of which they did not foresee, entangling them in difficulties out of which they could not extricate themselves, and so obtaining victories that neither myself nor

---

[6]Pudding made of sweetened cornmeal mush.

[7]*Characteristics of Men, Manners, Opinions, and Times* (1711), by Anthony Ashley Cooper, the Earl of Shaftsbury (1671–1713), and *A Discourse of Free Thinking* (1713), by Anthony Collins (1676–1729).

my cause always deserved. I continued this method some few years but gradually left it, retaining only the habit of expressing myself in terms of modest diffidence, never using when I advance anything that may possibly be disputed the words, "certainly," "undoubtedly," or any other that give the air of positiveness to an opinion; but rather say, "I conceive or apprehend a thing to be so or so," "It appears to me," or "I should think it so or so, for such and such reasons," or "I imagine it to be so," or "It is so if I am not mistaken." This habit, I believe, has been of great advantage to me when I have had occasion to inculcate my opinions and persuade men into measures that I have been from time to time engaged in promoting. And as the chief ends of conversation are to *inform*, or to *be informed*, to please or to *persuade*, I wish well-meaning and sensible men would not lessen their power of doing good by a positive, assuming manner that seldom fails to disgust, tends to create opposition, and to defeat every one of those purposes for which speech was given to us. In fact, if you wish to instruct others, a positive, dogmatical manner in advancing your sentiments may provoke contradiction and prevent a candid attention. If you desire instruction and improvement from the knowledge of others, you should not at the same time express yourself as firmly fixed in your present opinions; modest and sensible men, who do not love disputation, will probably leave you undisturbed in the possession of your error. In adopting such a manner you can seldom expect to please your hearers, or to persuade those whose concurrence you desire. . . .

My brother had in 1720 or '21 begun to print a newspaper. It was the second that appeared in America and was called *The New England Courant*.[8] The only one before it was *The Boston Newsletter*. I remember his being dissuaded by some of his friends from the undertaking as not likely to succeed, one newspaper being in their judgment enough for America. At this time, 1771, there are not less than five-and-twenty. He went on, however, with the undertaking; I was employed to carry the papers to the customers, after having worked in composing the types and printing off the sheets. He had some ingenious men among his friends who amused themselves by writing little pieces for this paper, which gained it credit and made it more in demand; and these gentlemen often visited us. Hearing their conversations and their accounts of the approbation their papers were received with, I was excited to try my hand among them. But being still a boy and suspecting that my brother would object to printing anything of mine in his paper if he knew it to be mine, I contrived to disguise my hand; and writing an anonymous paper, I put it at night under the door of the printing house. It was found in the morning and communicated to his writing friends when they called in as usual. They read it, commented on it in my hearing, and I had the exquisite pleasure of finding it met with their approbation, and that in their different guesses at the author, none were named but men of some character among us for learning and ingenuity. I suppose now that I was rather lucky in my judges and that perhaps they were not really so very good as I then believed them to be. Encouraged, however, by this attempt, I wrote and sent in the same way to the press several other pieces, which were equally approved, and I kept my secret till my small fund of sense for such performances was pretty well exhausted, and then I discovered it,[9] when I began to be considered a little more by my brother's acquaintance. However, that did not quite please him as he thought that it tended to make me too vain.

This might be one occasion of the differences we began to have about this time. Though a brother, he considered himself as my master and me as his apprentice, and

---

[8] It was actually the fifth such publication, but most earlier ones only lasted for a single issue.
[9] Revealed it.

accordingly expected the same services from me as he would from another; while I thought he degraded me too much in some he required of me, who from a brother expected more indulgence. Our disputes were often brought before our father, and I fancy I was either generally in the right or else a better pleader, because the judgment was generally in my favour. But my brother was passionate and had often beaten me, which I took extremely amiss. I fancy his harsh and tyrannical treatment of me might be a means of impressing me with that aversion to arbitrary power that has stuck to me through my whole life. Thinking my apprenticeship very tedious, I was continually wishing for some opportunity of shortening it, which at length offered in a manner unexpected.

One of the pieces in our newspaper on some political point which I have now forgotten, gave offence to the Assembly. He was taken up, censured, and imprisoned for a month by the Speaker's warrant, I suppose because he would not discover the author. I, too, was taken up and examined before the Council; but though I did not give them any satisfaction, they contented themselves with admonishing me and dismissed me, considering me, perhaps, as an apprentice who was bound to keep his master's secrets. During my brother's confinement, which I resented a good deal notwithstanding our private differences, I had the management of the paper, and I made bold to give our rulers some rubs in it, which my brother took very kindly, while others began to consider me in an unfavourable light as a young genius that had a turn for libelling and satire. My brother's discharge was accompanied with an order from the House (a very odd one) that "James Franklin should no longer print the paper called the *New England Courant.*" There was a consultation held in our printing house amongst his friends in this conjuncture. Some proposed to elude the order by changing the name of the paper; but my brother seeing inconveniences in that, it was finally concluded on as a better way to let it be printed for the future under the name of "Benjamin Franklin"; and to avoid the censure of the Assembly that might fall on him as still printing it by his apprentice, the contrivance was that my old indenture should be returned to me with a full discharge on the back of it, to show in case of necessity; but to secure to him the benefit of my service, I should sign new indentures for the remainder of the term, which were to be kept private. A very flimsy scheme it was, but, however, it was immediately executed, and the paper went on accordingly under my name for several months. At length a fresh difference arising between my brother and me, I took upon me to assert my freedom, presuming that he would not venture to produce the new indentures. It was not fair in me to take this advantage, and this I therefore reckon one of the first errata[10] of my life. But the unfairness of it weighed little with me, when under the impressions of resentment for the blows his passion too often urged him to bestow upon me, though he was otherwise not an ill-natured man. Perhaps I was too saucy and provoking.

When he found I would leave him, he took care to prevent my getting employment in any other printing house of the town by going round and speaking to every master, who accordingly refused to give me work. I then thought of going to New York as the nearest place where there was a printer; and I was the rather inclined to leave Boston when I reflected that I had already made myself a little obnoxious to the governing party; and from the arbitrary proceedings of the Assembly in my brother's case, it was likely I might if I stayed soon bring myself into

---

[10]Latin for *errors*; the word is used for mistakes in general, but in this text and in modern English it is especially used to mean printers' errors. Franklin represents himself as the aging printer, and metaphorically as the typesetter of the text of his own life, who wants to acknowledge, if not correct, the *errata* of his youth; see Introduction.

scrapes, and further that my indiscreet disputations about religion began to make me pointed at with horror by good people as an infidel or atheist. I determined on the point, but my father now siding with my brother, I was sensible that if I attempted to go openly, means would be used to prevent me. My friend Collins therefore undertook to manage my flight. He agreed with the captain of a New York sloop for my passage, under pretence of my being a young man of his acquaintance that had had an intrigue with a girl of bad character, whose parents would compel me to marry her and therefore I could not appear or come away publicly. I sold some of my books to raise a little money, was taken on board the sloop privately, had a fair wind, and in three days found myself at New York, near three hundred miles from my home, at the age of seventeen, without the least recommendation to or knowledge of any person in the place, and with very little money in my pocket.

The inclination I had had for the sea was by this time done away, or I might now have gratified it. But having another profession and conceiving myself a pretty good workman, I offered my services to the printer of the place, old Mr. Wm. Bradford (who had been the first printer in Pennsylvania, but had removed thence in consequence of a quarrel with the Governor, Geo. Keith). He could give me no employment, having little to do and hands enough already. "But," says he, "my son at Philadelphia has lately lost his principal hand, Aquila Rose, by death. If you go thither I believe he may employ you."

Philadelphia was a hundred miles farther. I set out, however, in a boat for Amboy, leaving my chest and things to follow me round by sea. In crossing the bay we met with a squall that tore our rotten sails to pieces, prevented our getting into the kill,[11] and drove us upon Long Island. In our way a drunken Dutchman, who was a passenger, too, fell overboard; when he was sinking, I reached through the water to his shock pate[12] and drew him up so that we got him in again. His ducking sobered him a little, and he went to sleep, taking first out of his pocket a book which he desired I would dry for him. It proved to be my old favourite author Bunyan's *Pilgrim's Progress* in Dutch, finely printed on good paper with copper cuts, a dress better than I had ever seen it wear in its own language. I have since found that it has been translated into most of the languages of Europe, and suppose it has been more generally read than any other book except, perhaps, the Bible. Honest John was the first that I know of who mixes narration and dialogue, a method of writing very engaging to the reader, who in the most interesting parts finds himself, as it were, admitted into the company and present at the conversation. Defoe has imitated him successfully in his *Robinson Crusoe,* in his *Moll Flanders,* and other pieces; and Richardson has done the same in his *Pamela,* etc.

On approaching the island, we found it was in a place where there could be no landing, there being a great surf on the stony beach. So we dropped anchor and swung out our cable towards the shore. Some people came down to the water edge and hallooed to us, as we did to them, but the wind was so high and the surf so loud that we could not understand each other. There were some canoes on the shore, and we made signs and called to them to fetch us, but they either did not comprehend us or thought it impracticable, so they went off. Night approaching, we had no remedy but to have patience till the wind abated, and in the meantime the boatman and I concluded to sleep if we could, and so we crowded into the scuttle with the Dutchman who was still wet, and the spray breaking over the head of our boat leaked through to us, so that we were soon almost as wet as he.

---

[11] The channel separating Staten Island from New Jersey.
[12] A bushy outcrop of hair.

In this manner we lay all night with very little rest; but the wind abating the next day, we made a shift to reach Amboy before night, having been thirty hours on the water without victuals or any drink but a bottle of filthy rum, the water we sailed on being salt.

In the evening I found myself very feverish and went to bed; but having read somewhere that cold water drank plentifully was good for a fever, I followed the prescription, sweat plentifully most of the night, my fever left me, and in the morning crossing the ferry, I proceeded on my journey on foot, having fifty miles to Burlington, where I was told I should find boats that would carry me the rest of the way to Philadelphia.

It rained very hard all the day, I was thoroughly soaked and by noon a good deal tired, so I stopped at a poor inn, where I stayed all night, beginning now to wish I had never left home. I made so miserable a figure, too, that I found by the questions asked me I was suspected to be some runaway servant, and in danger of being taken up on that suspicion. However, I proceeded the next day, and got in the evening to an inn within eight or ten miles of Burlington, kept by one Dr. Brown.

He entered into conversation with me while I took some refreshment and, finding I had read a little, became very sociable and friendly. Our acquaintance continued all the rest of his life. He had been, I imagine, an itinerant doctor, for there was no town in England or any country in Europe of which he could not give a very particular account. He had some letters and was ingenious, but he was an infidel and wickedly undertook some years after to travesty the Bible in doggerel verse as Cotton had done with Virgil.[13] By this means he set many of the facts in a very ridiculous light and might have done mischief with weak minds if his work had been published, but it never was. At his house I lay that night, and the next morning reached Burlington, but had the mortification to find that the regular boats were gone a little before and no other expected to go before Tuesday, this being Saturday. Wherefore, I returned to an old woman in the town of whom I had bought some gingerbread to eat on the water and asked her advice; she invited me to lodge at her house till a passage by water should offer; and being tired with my foot travelling, I accepted the invitation. Understanding I was a printer, she would have had me remain in that town and follow my business, being ignorant of the stock necessary to begin with. She was very hospitable, gave me a dinner of ox cheek with great goodwill, accepting only of a pot of ale in return. And I thought myself fixed till Tuesday should come. However, walking in the evening by the side of the river, a boat came by, which I found was going towards Philadelphia with several people in her. They took me in, and as there was no wind, we rowed all the way; and about midnight, not having yet seen the city, some of the company were confident we must have passed it and would row no farther; the others knew not where we were, so we put towards the shore, got into a creek, landed near an old fence, with the rails of which we made a fire, the night being cold in October, and there we remained till daylight. Then one of the company knew the place to be Cooper's Creek, a little above Philadelphia, which we saw as soon as we got out of the creek, and arrived there about eight or nine o'clock, on the Sunday morning and landed at the Market Street wharf.

I have been the more particular in this description of my journey, and shall be so of my first entry into that city, that you may in your mind compare such unlikely beginnings with the figure I have since made there. I was in my working dress, my

---

[13]Charles Cotton (1630–1687), an English poet, satirized the Roman poet Virgil in his *Scarronides; On the First Book of Virgil Travestied* (1664).

best clothes being to come round by sea. I was dirty from my journey; my pockets were stuffed out with shirts and stockings; I knew no soul, nor where to look for lodging. Fatigued with walking, rowing, and want of sleep, I was very hungry, and my whole stock of cash consisted of a Dutch dollar and about a shilling in copper coin, which I gave to the boatmen for my passage. At first they refused it on account of my having rowed, but I insisted on their taking it. A man is sometimes more generous when he has little money than when he has plenty, perhaps through fear of being thought to have but little. I walked towards the top of the street, gazing about till near Market Street, where I met a boy with bread. I have often made a meal of dry bread, and inquiring where he had bought it, I went immediately to the baker's he directed me to. I asked for biscuit, meaning such as we had in Boston, but that sort, it seems, was not made in Philadelphia. I then asked for a threepenny loaf and was told they had none such. Not knowing the different prices nor the names of the different sorts of any bread, I told him to give me three pennyworth of any sort. He gave me accordingly three great puffy rolls. I was surprized at the quantity but took it, and having no room in my pockets, walked off with a roll under each arm and eating the other. Thus I went up Market Street as far as Fourth Street, passing by the door of Mr. Read, my future wife's father, when she, standing at the door, saw me, and thought I made—as I certainly did—a most awkward, ridiculous appearance. Then I turned and went down Chestnut Street and part of Walnut Street, eating my roll all the way, and coming round, found myself again at Market Street wharf near the boat I came in, to which I went for a draught of the river water, and being filled with one of my rolls, gave the other two to a woman and her child that came down the river in the boat with us and were waiting to go farther. Thus refreshed, I walked again up the street, which by this time had many clean dressed people in it who were all walking the same way; I joined them, and thereby was led into the great meetinghouse of the Quakers near the market. I sat down among them, and after looking round awhile and hearing nothing said, being very drowsy through labour and want of rest the preceding night, I fell fast asleep and continued so till the meeting broke up, when someone was kind enough to rouse me. This was therefore the first house I was in or slept in, in Philadelphia.

I then walked down again towards the river and looking in the faces of everyone, I met a young Quaker man whose countenance pleased me, and accosting him requested he would tell me where a stranger could get a lodging. We were then near the Sign of the Three Mariners. "Here," says he, "is a house where they receive strangers, but it is not a reputable one; if thee wilt walk with me, I'll show thee a better one." He conducted me to the Crooked Billet in Water Street. There I got a dinner. And while I was eating, several sly questions were asked me, as from my youth and appearance I was suspected of being a runaway. After dinner my sleepiness returned; and being shown to a bed, I lay down without undressing and slept till six in the evening, when I was called to supper. I went to bed again very early and slept soundly till next morning. Then I dressed myself as neat as I could, and went to Andrew Bradford, the printer's. I found in the shop the old man his father, whom I had seen at New York, and who travelling on horseback, had got to Philadelphia before me. He introduced me to his son, who received me civilly, gave me a breakfast, but told me he did not at present want a hand, being lately supplied with one. But there was another printer in town lately set up, one Keimer, who perhaps might employ me; if not, I should be welcome to lodge at his house, and he would give me a little work to do now and then till fuller business should offer.

The old gentleman said he would go with me to the new printer. And when we found him, "Neighbour," says Bradford, "I have brought to see you a young man of your business; perhaps you may want such a one." He asked me a few questions, put a composing stick in my hand to see how I worked, and then said he would employ me soon, though he had just then nothing for me to do. And taking old Bradford, whom he had never seen before, to be one of the townspeople that had a good will for him, entered into a conversation on his present undertaking and prospects; while Bradford, not discovering that he was the other printer's father, on Keimer's saying he expected soon to get the greatest part of the business into his own hands, drew him on by artful questions and starting little doubts to explain all his views, what influence he relied on, and in what manner he intended to proceed. I, who stood by and heard all, saw immediately that one of them was a crafty old sophister, and the other a true novice. Bradford left me with Keimer, who was greatly surprized when I told him who the old man was.

Keimer's printing house, I found, consisted of an old damaged press and a small worn-out fount of English types, which he was then using himself, composing an elegy on Aquila Rose, before-mentioned, an ingenious young man of excellent character, much respected in the town, secretary to the Assembly, and a pretty poet. Keimer made verses, too, but very indifferently. He could not be said to write them, for his method was to compose them in the types directly out of his head; so there being no copy but one pair of cases,[14] and the elegy probably requiring all the letter, no one could help him. I endeavoured to put his press (which he had not yet used, and of which he understood nothing) into order fit to be worked with; and promising to come and print off his elegy as soon as he should have got it ready, I returned to Bradford's, who gave me a little job to do for the present, and there I lodged and dieted. A few days after Keimer sent for me to print off the elegy. And now he had got another pair of cases, and a pamphlet to reprint, on which he set me to work.

These two printers I found poorly qualified for their business. Bradford had not been bred to it and was very illiterate; and Keimer, though something of a scholar, was a mere compositor, knowing nothing of presswork. He had been one of the French prophets[15] and could act their enthusiastic agitations. At this time he did not profess any particular religion, but something of all on occasion, was very ignorant of the world, and had—as I afterwards found—a good deal of the knave in his composition. He did not like my lodging at Bradford's while I worked with him. He had a house, indeed, but without furniture, so he could not lodge me; but he got me a lodging at Mr. Read's, before-mentioned, who was the owner of his house. And my chest and clothes being come by this time, I made rather a more respectable appearance in the eyes of Miss Read than I had done when she first happened to see me eating my roll in the street.

. . . It was about this time I conceived the bold and arduous project of arriving at moral perfection. I wished to live without committing any fault at any time; I would conquer all that either natural inclination, custom, or company might lead me into. As I knew, or thought I knew, what was right and wrong, I did not see why I might not *always* do the one and avoid the other. But I soon found I had undertaken a task of more difficulty than I had imagined. While my attention was taken up and care employed in guarding against one fault, I was often surprized by another. Habit took the advantage of inattention. Inclination was sometimes too strong for reason. I concluded at length that the mere speculative conviction that it was our interest to be completely virtuous was not sufficient to prevent our slipping, and that the contrary habits must be broken and good ones acquired and established

---

[14]Printers' trays holding both uppercase and lowercase type.
[15]French Protestant refugees, who practiced a charismatic form of worship.

before we can have any dependence on a steady, uniform rectitude of conduct. For this purpose I therefore contrived the following method.

In the various enumerations of the moral virtues I had met with in my reading, I found the catalogue more or less numerous, as different writers included more or fewer ideas under the same name. Temperance, for example, was by some confined to eating and drinking, while by others it was extended to mean the moderating every other pleasure, appetite, inclination, or passion—bodily or mental, even to our avarice and ambition. I proposed to myself, for the sake of clearness, to use rather more names with fewer ideas annexed to each than a few names with more ideas; and I included under thirteen names of virtues all that at that time occurred to me as necessary or desirable, and annexed to each a short precept which fully expressed the extent I gave to its meaning.

These names of virtues with their precepts were

1. Temperance—Eat not to dulness. Drink not to elevation.

2. Silence—Speak not but what may benefit others or yourself. Avoid trifling conversation.

3. Order—Let all your things have their places. Let each part of your business have its time.

4. Resolution—Resolve to perform what you ought. Perform without fail what you resolve.

5. Frugality—Make no expence but to do good to others or yourself; i.e., waste nothing.

6. Industry—Lose no time. Be always employed in something useful. Cut off all unnecessary actions.

7. Sincerity—Use no hurtful deceit. Think innocently and justly; and, if you speak, speak accordingly.

8. Justice—Wrong none by doing injuries or omitting the benefits that are your duty.

9. Moderation—Avoid extremes. Forbear resenting injuries so much as you think they deserve.

10. Cleanliness—Tolerate no uncleanness in body, clothes or habitation.

11. Tranquillity—Be not disturbed at trifles or at accidents common or unavoidable.

12. Chastity—Rarely use venery but for health or offspring—never to dulness, weakness, or the injury of your own or another's peace or reputation.

13. Humility—Imitate Jesus and Socrates.

My intention being to acquire the *habitude* of all these virtues, I judged it would be well not to distract my attention by attempting the whole at once but to fix it on one of them at a time, and when I should be master of that, then to proceed to another, and so on till I should have gone thro' the thirteen. And as the previous acquisition of some might facilitate the acquisition of certain others, I arranged them with that view as they stand above. *Temperance* first, as it tends to procure that coolness and clearness of head which is so necessary where constant vigilance was to be kept up, and guard maintained, against the unremitting attraction of ancient habits, and the force of perpetual temptations. This being acquired and established, *Silence* would be more easy, and my desire being to gain knowledge at the same time that I improved in virtue, and considering that in conversation it was obtained rather by the use of the ear than of the tongue, and therefore wishing to break a habit I was getting into of prattling, punning, and joking, which only made me acceptable to trifling company, I gave *Silence* the second place. This and the next, *Order,* I expected would allow me more time for attending to my project and my studies. *Resolution,* once become habitual, would keep me firm in my endeavours to obtain all the subsequent virtues; *Frugality* and *Industry,* freeing me from my remaining debt and, producing affluence and independence, would make more easy the practice of *Sincerity* and *Justice,* etc., etc. Conceiving then that agreeable to the advice of Pythagoras in his golden verses, daily examination would be necessary, I contrived the following method for conducting that examination.

I made a little book in which I allotted a page for each of the virtues. I ruled each page with red ink so as to have seven columns, one for each day of the week, marking each column with a letter for the day. I crossed these columns with thirteen red lines, marking the beginning of each line with the first letter of one of the virtues, on which line and in its proper column I might mark by a little black spot every fault I found upon examination to have been committed respecting that virtue upon that day.

I determined to give a week's strict attention to each of the virtues successively. Thus in the first week my great guard was to avoid even the least offence against temperance, leaving the other virtues to their ordinary chance, only marking every evening the faults of the day. Thus if in the first week I could keep my first line marked "T." clear of spots, I supposed the habit of that virtue so much strengthened and its opposite weakened that I might venture extending my attention to include the next, and for the following week keep both lines clear of spots. Proceeding thus to the last, I could go thro' a course complete in thirteen weeks, and four courses in a year. And like him who, having a garden to weed, does not attempt to eradicate all the bad herbs at once, which would exceed his reach and his strength, but works on one of the beds at a time, and having accomplished the first, proceeds to a second; so I should have (I hoped) the encouraging pleasure of seeing on my pages the progress I made in virtue by clearing successively my lines of their spots, till in the end by a number of courses, I should be happy in viewing a clean book after a thirteen weeks' daily examination.

This my little book had for its motto these lines from Addison's *Cato;*

> Here will I hold: if there is a power above us,
> (And that there is, all Nature cries aloud
> Thro' all her works) he must delight in virtue,
> And that which he delights in must be happy.

Another from Cicero,

> *O vitae philosophia dux! O virtutum indagatrix, expultrixque vitiorum! Unus dies bene et ex preceptis tuis actus, peccanti immortalitati est anteponendus.*[16]

Another from the proverbs of Solomon speaking of wisdom or virtue;

> Length of days is in her right hand, and in her left hand riches and honours; her ways are ways of pleasantness, and all her paths are peace (III, 16, 17).

---

[16]Cicero (106–43 B.C.E.) was a Roman philosopher and orator; the passage Franklin partially quotes from the *Tuscan Disputations* reads in full, "O Philosophy, guide of life! O you, who discover virtues and expel vice!... One day well lived according to your precepts is better than an eternity of sin."

FORM OF THE PAGES

	S	M	T	W	T	F	S
TEMPERANCE							
Eat not to dulness. *Drink not to elevation.*							
T							
S	√√	√		√		√	
O	√	√	√		√	√	√
R	√	√				√	
F		√			√		
I			√				
S							
J							
M							
Cl.							
T							
Ch							
H							

And conceiving God to be the fountain of wisdom, I thought it right and necessary to solicit his assistance for obtaining it; to this end I formed the following little prayer, which was prefixed to my tables of examination, for daily use.

O powerful Goodness, bountiful Father, merciful Guide! Increase in me that wisdom which discovers my truest interests; strengthen my resolutions to perform what that wisdom dictates. Accept my kind offices to thy other children, as the only return in my power for thy continual favours to me.

I used also sometimes a little prayer which I took from Thomson's *Poems;* viz.,

Father of light and life, thou Good supreme,
Oh, teach me what is good, teach me thy self!
Save me from folly, vanity and vice,
From every low pursuit, and fill my soul

With knowledge, conscious peace, and virtue pure,
Sacred, substantial, never-fading bliss![17]

The precept of *Order* requiring that *every part of my business should have its allotted time,* one page in my little book contained the following scheme of employment for the twenty-four hours of a natural day.

I entered upon the execution of this plan for self-examination and continued it with occasional intermissions for some time. I was surprized to find myself so much fuller of faults than I had imagined, but I had the satisfaction of seeing them diminish. To avoid the trouble of renewing now and then my little book, which by scraping out the marks on the paper of old faults to make room for new ones

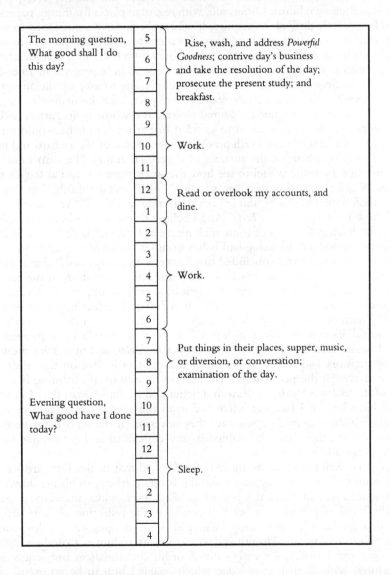

The morning question, What good shall I do this day?	5	Rise, wash, and address *Powerful Goodness*; contrive day's business and take the resolution of the day; prosecute the present study; and breakfast.
	6	
	7	
	8	
	9	Work.
	10	
	11	
	12	Read or overlook my accounts, and dine.
	1	
	2	
	3	
	4	Work.
	5	
	6	
	7	Put things in their places, supper, music, or diversion, or conversation; examination of the day.
	8	
	9	
Evening question, What good have I done today?	10	
	11	
	12	
	1	Sleep.
	2	
	3	
	4	

---

[17]From the long poem *The Seasons* (1726), by James Thompson (1700–1748); the passage Franklin quotes is from "Winter," 218–223.

in a new course became full of holes, I transferred my tables and precepts to the ivory leaves of a memorandum book on which the lines were drawn with red ink that made a durable stain, and on those lines I marked my faults with a black lead pencil, which marks I could easily wipe out with a wet sponge. After a while I went thro' one course only in a year, and afterwards only one in several years, till at length I omitted them entirely, being employed in voyages and business abroad with a multiplicity of affairs that interfered; but I always carried my little book with me. My scheme of *Order* gave me the most trouble, and I found that tho' it might be practicable where a man's business was such as to leave him the disposition of his time, that of a journeyman printer for instance, it was not possible to be exactly observed by a master, who must mix with the world and often receive people of business at their own hours. Order, too, with regard to places for things, papers, etc., I found extremely difficult to acquire. I had not been early accustomed to *method,* and having an exceeding good memory, I was not so sensible of the inconvenience attending want of method. This article therefore cost me so much painful attention, and my faults in it vexed me so much, and I made so little progress in amendment and had such frequent relapses, that I was almost ready to give up the attempt and content myself with a faulty character in that respect. Like the man who in buying an ax of a smith my neighbour, desired to have the whole of its surface as bright as the edge; the smith consented to grind it bright for him if he would turn the wheel. He turned while the smith pressed the broad face of the ax hard and heavily on the stone, which made the turning of it very fatiguing. The man came every now and then from the wheel to see how the work went on; and at length would take his ax as it was, without further grinding. "No," says the smith, "turn on, turn on; we shall have it bright by and by; as yet 'tis only speckled." "Yes," says the man, "*but I think I like a speckled ax best.*" And I believe this may have been the case with many who having, for want of some such means as I employed, found the difficulty of obtaining good and breaking bad habits in other points of vice and virtue, have given up the struggle and concluded that "a speckled ax was best." For something that pretended to be reason was every now and then suggesting to me that such extreme nicety as I exacted of myself might be a kind of foppery in morals, which if it were known would make me ridiculous; that a perfect character might be attended with the inconvenience of being envied and hated; and that a benevolent man should allow a few faults in himself, to keep his friends in countenance. In truth, I found myself incorrigible with respect to *Order;* and now I am grown old and my memory bad, I feel very sensibly the want of it. But on the whole, tho' I never arrived at the perfection I had been so ambitious of obtaining but fell far short of it, yet I was by the endeavour a better and a happier man than I otherwise should have been if I had not attempted it; as those who aim at perfect writing by imitating the engraved copies, tho' they never reach the wished-for excellence of those copies, their hand is mended by the endeavour and is tolerable while it continues fair and legible.

It may be well my posterity should be informed that to this little artifice, with the blessing of God, their ancestor owed the constant felicity of his life down to his seventy-ninth year, in which this is written. What reverses may attend the remainder is in the hand of providence; but if they arrive, the reflection on past happiness enjoyed ought to help his bearing them with more resignation. To *Temperance* he ascribes his long-continued health and what is still left to him of a good constitution; to *Industry* and *Frugality,* the early easiness of his circumstances and acquisition of his fortune, with all that knowledge which enabled him to be an useful citizen and obtained for him some degree of reputation among the learned. To *Sincerity* and *Justice,* the confidence of his country and the honourable employs it conferred upon him; and to the joint influence of the whole mass of the virtues, even in the imperfect state he was able to acquire them, all that evenness of temper and that cheerfulness in conversation which makes his company still sought for and agreeable even to his younger acquaintance. I hope, therefore, that some of my descendants may follow the example and reap the benefit.

It will be remarked that, tho' my scheme was not wholly without religion, there was in it no mark of any of the distinguishing tenets of any particular sect. I had purposely avoided them; for being fully persuaded of the utility and excellency of my method, and that it might be serviceable to people in all religions, and intending sometime or other to publish it, I would not have anything in it that should prejudice anyone of any sect against it. I purposed writing a little comment on each virtue, in which I would have shown the advantages of possessing it and the mischiefs attending its opposite vice; I should have called my book *The Art of Virtue* because it would have shown the means and manner of obtaining virtue, which would have distinguished it from the mere exhortation to be good, that does not instruct and indicate the means, but is like the apostle's man of verbal charity, who only, without showing to the naked and hungry how or where they might get clothes or victuals, exhorted them to be fed and clothed (*James* II: 15, 16).

But it so happened that my intention of writing and publishing this comment was never fulfilled. I did, indeed, from time to time put down short hints of the sentiments, reasonings, etc., to be made use of in it, some of which I have still by me; but the necessary close attention to private business in the earlier part of life and public business since, have occasioned my postponing it. For it being connected in my mind with *a great and extensive project* that required the whole man to execute, and which an unforeseen succession of employs prevented my attending to, it has hitherto remained unfinished.

In this piece it was my design to explain and enforce this doctrine: That vicious actions are not hurtful because they are forbidden, but forbidden because they are hurtful, the nature of man alone considered; that it was therefore everyone's interest to be virtuous who wished to be happy even in this world. And I should from this circumstance, there being always in the world a number of rich merchants, nobility, states, and princes who have need of honest instruments for the management of their affairs, and such being so rare have endeavoured to convince young persons, that no qualities are so likely to make a poor man's fortune as those of probity and integrity.

My list of virtues contained at first but twelve. But a Quaker friend having kindly informed me that I was generally thought proud, that my pride showed itself frequently in conversation, that I was not content with being in the right when discussing any point, but was overbearing and rather insolent—of which he convinced me by mentioning several instances—I determined endeavouring to cure myself if I could of this vice or folly among the rest, and I added *Humility* to my list, giving an extensive meaning to the word. I cannot boast of much success in acquiring the *reality* of this virtue, but I had a good deal with regard to the *appearance* of it. I made it a rule to forbear all direct contradiction to the sentiments of others and all positive assertion of my own. I even forbade myself agreeable to the old laws of our Junto, the use of every word or expression in the language that imported[18] a fixed opinion, such as "certainly," "undoubtedly," etc.; and I adopted instead of them, "I conceive," "I apprehend," or "I imagine" a thing to be so or so, or "It so appears to me at present." When another asserted something that I

---

[18]Implied.

thought an error, I denied myself the pleasure of contradicting him abruptly and of showing immediately some absurdity in his proposition; and in answering I began by observing that in certain cases or circumstances his opinion would be right, but that in the present case there "appeared" or "seemed to me" some difference, etc. I soon found the advantage of this change in my manners: The conversations I engaged in went on more pleasantly; the modest way in which I proposed my opinions procured them a readier reception and less contradiction; I had less mortification when I was found to be in the wrong, and I more easily prevailed with others to give up their mistakes and join with me when I happened to be in the right. And this mode, which I at first put on with some violence to natural inclination, became at length so easy and so habitual to me that perhaps for these fifty years past no one has ever heard a dogmatical expression escape me. And to this habit (after my character of integrity) I think it principally owing that I had early so much weight with my fellow citizens when I proposed new institutions or alterations in the old, and so much influence in public councils when I became a member. For I was but a bad speaker, never eloquent, subject to much hesitation in my choice of words, hardly correct in language, and yet I generally carried my point.

In reality there is perhaps no one of our natural passions so hard to subdue as *pride;* disguise it, struggle with it, beat it down, stifle it, mortify it as much as one pleases, it is still alive and will every now and then peep out and show itself. You will see it perhaps in this history. For even if I could conceive that I had completely overcome it, I should probably be proud of my humility.

DENIS DIDEROT
[1713–1784]

Perhaps more than Voltaire and Rousseau, whose names come to mind when one thinks of the *philosophes,* Denis Diderot embodied the spirit of the Enlightenment—in both its empirical approach to nature and its critical attention to society and humanity. Diderot wrote fiction, plays, and criticism, and under his direction the thirty-eight-volume *Encyclopédie,* a compendium of articles on science, mathematics, literature, art, technology, history, and society, was completed. A reflection of Diderot's own critical spirit, the *Encyclopédie* was intended to bring under the scrutinizing eye of reason all that could be explained and understood in and about the universe. The *Encyclopédie* eschewed the objects of metaphysics, with its focus on the spiritual realm and the nature of God, because they lay outside the bounds of reason and were therefore suspect; consequently, this collective work constituted a major critique of the Church, whose doctrines rested upon faith or, in the language of the *philosophes,* superstition. Moreover, in its essays on politics and society, the *Encyclopédie* criticized the inequities of absolute monarchy and the frivolity and arbitrary authority of the aristocracy, and hence won many enemies from the state and its official supporters. Embodying the spirit of unflagging inquiry and the dissemination of knowledge that typifies the Enlightenment, Diderot nonetheless clandestinely completed the *Encyclopédie,* even after it was suppressed by the authorities in 1759.

LIFE

Denis Diderot was born on October 5, 1713, in the Champagne region north of Dijon, in France. The son of a cutler, Diderot received his education in Jesuit schools, and made his way in 1729 to Paris, where he completed his master of arts degree in

1732, began to prepare for a career in law, and started to support himself by tutoring, translating, and hack writing. In 1743 he married Anne-Toinette Champion, a seamstress, to whom he remained attached despite differences of temperament and Diderot's penchant for romantic affairs. Supporting himself primarily by translating English works such as Shaftesbury's *Inquiry Concerning Virtue or Merit* and Robert James's *Medical Dictionary*, Diderot managed to write a number of works, including an anonymously published novel, *Les Bijoux indiscrets* (1748), eventually getting himself arrested for his *Letter to the Blind* (1749). By this time, Diderot was working on the *Encyclopédie*, bringing out the first two volumes by January 1752, which led to further accusations and threats of arrest. When the Parlement of Paris finally banned the *Encyclopédie* in 1759, and after a decisive and bitter disagreement with Rousseau, Diderot wavered in his confidence in the project. Nonetheless, Diderot continued his work, supported in part by Sophie Volland, with whom he had fallen in love shortly before, and by his new friends Friedrich Grimm and Baron d'Holbach. Because of Grimm's association with Madame d'Epinay's salon and Holbach's own philosophical circle, Diderot kept at the center of new thinking, saw the *Encyclopédie* through to completion, and had a burst of creative energy in the 1770s, when he wrote some of his greatest works, *Rameau's Nephew* (not published until 1823), *The Dream of d'Alembert* (1769), and the *Supplement to the Voyage of Bougainville*, which was completed in 1772 but not published until more than twenty years later.

Partly to raise money for his daughter's dowry and partly because the contract on the *Encyclopédie* had run out, Diderot decided to sell his library to Catherine II of Russia. Under her offer, Diderot was free to use the books, and she paid in handsome installments that supported him until his death. In 1773, he undertook an arduous journey to Russia in order to visit Catherine, one of the so-called enlightened despots, about whom he had mixed feelings, which can be detected in his *Memoirs for Catherine II* and his *Observations on the Nakaz*, which he wrote upon his return to France. He spent much of his last years contributing to Guillaume Raynal's *History of the Two Indies*, and writing a commentary on Seneca. He died in July 1784, uttering on his deathbed, "The first step toward philosophy is disbelief."

WORK

Although generally thought of as a philosopher, Diderot wrote novels, plays, some journalistic pieces, translations, art criticism, and even mathematical treatises. Diderot's broad range of interests was characteristic of the group of intellectuals—the *philosophes*—who brought to eighteenth-century France a spirit of critical inquiry based on reason and experiment. Like his fellow *philosophes* Voltaire, Condorcet, Helvétius, and others, Diderot applied scientific methods and empirical observation derived largely from the observations and thoughts of Bacon, Newton, and Locke to the study of politics, society, human behavior, and religion. Thus, the *philosophes* led a kind of intellectual insurrection against what they called the superstition of the Church and the ignorance of political processes that supported the despotism of absolute monarchy. As Diderot himself put it, these intellectuals were leading "a revolution in the minds of men to free them from prejudice," and they took up their work by applying criticism to Diderot's three classes of facts: "the acts of divinity, the phenomena of nature, and the actions of men."

Diderot and the *philosophes* believed that an increase of knowledge and understanding could bring about human progress, but they doubted that the unexamined processes of "civilization" would guarantee such positive change. As in the *Supplement to the Voyage of Bougainville*, Diderot could go so far as to suggest that European civilization had actually corrupted human nature by creating artificial tastes and desires. Nonetheless, because he believed that human nature and human institutions were subject to the same laws that governed the operations of natural phenomena, Diderot believed that it was not too late for Europeans to break out of their customary social habits and change themselves for the better. In this belief that institutions could, and should, be changed, these Enlightenment thinkers differed from the humanist thinkers of the Renaissance, who used classical thought primarily to legitimate the authority of the Church and monarchy. Diderot was certainly not moderate in his support for individual and intellectual freedom, having written that "men will never be free till the last king is strangled with the entrails of the last priest." While this statement sounds incendiary, Diderot did not advocate violent revolution, for he thought that gradual reform in the structure of society and its laws could finally succeed in nurturing the basic goodness and virtue in all human beings whose original propensity for virtue had been corrupted by social practices and civil institutions.

With his colleague Jean d'Alembert, and a few others known as the Encyclopedists, Diderot embarked on an ambitious project to tabulate and catalog all that was known to philosophy, science, the arts, and the trades in the eighteenth century. Diderot completed the massive eleven volumes of *The Encyclopedia, or Classified Dictionary of the Sciences, Arts, and Occupations* between 1751 and 1772, announcing in the Prospectus (1750) its purpose not only of collecting facts about what could be known, but to discover the underlying principles of any connection or links among the various sciences and arts: "[We want] to make use of the links to reveal the [underlying] principles more forcefully and the results more clearly; to indicate the close or distant connections between the beings which form nature, and which have concerned men; . . . to form a general map of the efforts of the human mind in all activities, over all the centuries." Clearly, the *Encyclopédie* embodied Diderot's injunction that "All things must be examined without sparing anyone's sensibilities." Despite early attempts to censor and ban the *Encyclopédie*—Diderot had already in 1749 spent 100 days in the Bastille for his iconoclastic writing—Diderot persisted in his spirited task to see the first edition through to its 4,000 subscribers, and its further distribution in a number of cheaper, popular editions. While d'Alembert took charge of the essays on mathematics and science, Diderot was responsible for the overall project in general and for the essays on industrial arts and technology in particular. His articles for the vast compendium fill three volumes of his twenty-volume collected works, and these articles range from technology to aesthetics.

Diderot published few other works as he labored on the *Encyclopédie*, but once it was finished he tried his hand again at fiction and critical essays. In about 1770, he began the *Supplement to the Voyage of Bougainville*, which, like his *Rameau's Nephew* and *The Dream of d'Alembert*, remained in manuscript during Diderot's lifetime. Ironically, an Abbé Bourlet de Vauxcelles ordered the publication of the *Supplement* in 1796; the Abbé hoped to discredit the revolutionary Jacobins in France by mocking Diderot's work and holding it up as an example of the "pernicious doctrines" of the *philosophes*, whose work was thought to have inspired the French Revolution.

Diderot began the *Supplement* as a review of the travel accounts of Louis Antoine de Bougainville, the first Frenchman to sail around the world and the man who gave the name *bougainvillea* to the flowering vine. Bougainville's accounts, first published between 1766 and 1769, were collected in one volume as *Voyage Around the World* in 1771. Bougainville had described the expulsion of the Jesuits from Paraguay in 1768, at which he had been present, and had refuted the popular view (stemming from accounts of Magellan's visit to Patagonia) that the natives of Tierra del Fuego were giants. Moreover, Bougainville, like other European travelers to the South Seas, described Tahiti as a kind of Blessed Isles. In the European imagination, the people of the South Seas were thought to live an idyllic life of ease and sexual freedom, released from the necessity of labor by a bountiful nature whose laws the islanders happily followed in their own social practices.

We can see Diderot's interest in natural law in the *Supplement*, where he contrasts the apparent sexual freedom of the Tahitians with the cultural and religious taboos governing sexual practices in Europe. He observes that civil and religious laws—in this case, especially the law and custom of monogamy—lead primarily to hypocrisy, because European men and women still secretly follow the compelling sexual urges of that greater force, natural law. Although Diderot rejected the primitivist idea that the people of the New World were "noble savages" living in a state of natural innocence, health, and happiness, he nonetheless conceives of the Tahitians as an ideal society against which to criticize, even to parody, the hypocrisy, tyranny, and self-righteousness of Europeans. Distinguishing between "natural" and "artificial" desires, Diderot points out that the restrictions of European religion and culture have created a kind of internal civil war within the European mind. His depiction of the European as a person tormented by the struggle between powerful natural desires and artificial moral impositions and constraints in some ways anticipates Nietzsche's analysis of morality and Freud's conception of the conflict between the unconscious and conscious. For Diderot, as habits and fears replace human beings' natural impulse to do good, people become divided both within and among themselves.

SUGGESTED READINGS

For Diderot's biography, see A. M. Wilson's *Diderot* (1972). Among the numerous studies of Diderot's thought, including the *Supplement,* see Geoffrey Bremner's *Order and Chance: The Pattern of Diderot's Thought* (1983), L. G. Crocker's *Diderot's Chaotic Order* (1974), and O. Fellows's *Diderot* (1977).

Supplement to the Voyage of Bougainville

OR DIALOGUE BETWEEN A AND B
ON THE DISADVANTAGE OF ATTACHING MORAL IDEAS TO
CERTAIN PHYSICAL ACTIONS INCOMPATIBLE THEREWITH

Translated by Jean Stewart and Jonathan Kemp

At quanto meliora monet, pregnantiaque istis.
Dives opis Natura suæ, tu si modo recte
Dispensare velis, ac non fugienda petendis.
Immiscere! Tuo vitio rerumne labores,
Nil referre putas?[1]
—(HORAT. *Sat. lib I, Sat II line 73 et seq.*)

1. JUDGMENT ON BOUGAINVILLE'S *VOYAGE*

A: That superb starry sky, under which we came back yesterday and which seemed to promise us glorious weather for to-day, hasn't kept its word.
B: Why do you say that?
A: The fog is so thick that we can't see the nearby trees.
B: That is true; but suppose the fog, which only stays in the lower part of the atmosphere because it is sufficiently charged with moisture, should fall to earth?
A: But suppose, on the contrary, it rises and gains the upper regions of the atmosphere, where the density is less, and it cannot become saturated, as the chemists say?

---

[1] How much better, and how conflicting with all that, is the advice of Nature, beautiful giver of her wealth, if only you are ready to manage properly and not to confound things desirable with those undesirable! Do you think that it does not matter, whether your troubles are due to your fault or to circumstances? [Translators' note]

B: Well then, we must wait.

A: And while waiting, what are you doing?

B: I'm reading.

A: Still this *Voyage* of Bougainville's?

B: Yes, still.

A: I don't understand that man at all. The study of mathematics, which presupposes a sedentary life, occupied his youth; then suddenly he changed from this retired and contemplative life to the active, hard, roving and unsettled life of an explorer.

B: Not at all. The vessel is only a floating house, and if you regard the navigator, who crosses immense distances, as enclosed and motionless within his narrow surroundings, you will visualize him going round the world on a plank just as you and I explore the universe on your floor.

A: Another apparently curious thing is the contradiction between the character of the man and of his enterprise. Bougainville has a taste for the amusements of society: he loves women, plays and good food; he accepts the whirl of fashion with as good grace as he did the inconstancy of the element on which he has been tossed. He is amiable and gay: a true well-balanced Frenchman; on the one hand, a treatise on the differential and integral calculus, on the other, a voyage round the world.

B: He is like everybody else: he enjoys himself after toil, and applies himself to work after relaxation.

A: What do you think of his *Voyage?*

B: So far as I can judge from a fairly superficial reading, I should relate its value to three principal points: a better knowledge of our old earth and its inhabitants, greater security on the seas which he sailed, sounding with the lead, and greater accuracy in our maps and charts. Bougainville started with the necessary understanding and qualities for these ends: philosophy, courage and truthfulness; a keen vision which seized everything and shortened the times of observation; circumspection and patience; the desire to see, to be enlightened and to learn; a knowledge of the calculus, mechanics, geometry, astronomy, and a sufficient smattering of natural history.

A: And his style?

B: Without affection; its tone is practical, simple and clear, particularly if you understand the language of seamen.

A: Was it a long voyage?

B: I have traced it on this globe. You see the line of red dots?

A: Which starts from Nantes?

B: And runs to the Straits of Magellan, enters the Pacific Ocean, winds between these islands forming the immense archipelago which stretches from the Philippines to New Holland, skirts Madagascar, the Cape of Good Hope, continues into the Atlantic, follows the African coast and rejoins itself where the navigators embarked.

A: They had a hard time?

B: Every navigator exposes himself, and consents to expose himself, to the perils of air, fire, land and water. But, after having wandered whole months between sea and sky, between life and death, after having been lashed by storms, menaced with death from shipwreck, disease, lack of food and water, that one of these unfortunates should come, with his ship wrecked, to fall dying with exhaustion and wretchedness at the feet of a brazen monster who refuses assistance or who pitilessly makes him wait for the most urgent help, that is dreadful. . . .

A: A crime worthy of heavy punishment.

B: One of those calamities on which the explorer has not counted.

A: And should not have to count. I believed that the European powers sent to govern their overseas possessions only honest souls, good men, people full of humanity and capable of compassion. . . .

B: That is the last thing they care about!

A: There are some queer things in that *Voyage* of Bougainville's.

B: Many.

A: Didn't he assert that wild animals approached men, and that birds came and perched on them, before they knew the danger of that familiarity?

B: Others had said it before him.

A: How does he explain the existence of certain animals on islands separated from all the continents by enormous expanses of sea? Who took the wolf, the fox, the dog, stag and snake there?

B: He explains nothing; he only attests the fact.

A: But how do you explain it?

B: Who knows the primitive history of our globe? How many wide areas of land, now isolated, were once continuous? The only phenomenon on which we could form some conjectures is the direction of the body of waters which separated them.

A: How so?

B: By the general form of the erosion. Some day we will amuse ourselves with this research, if you agree. For the moment, do you see this island called the Lancers? Anybody would ask, from the inspection of its position on the globe, who has put people on it; what means of communication joined them to the rest of their species; what happens about multiplication on an area no more than a league in diameter?

A: They kill and eat themselves, and perhaps therefrom arises a very old and very natural primary epoch of cannibalism, of island origin.

B: Or multiplication is limited by some superstitious law; the child is crushed in its mother's womb, trodden under the feet of a priestess.

A: Or men are sacrificed under the knife of a priest; or they have recourse to the castration of males. . . .

B: Or to the infibulation of females. From all that, there result different cruel customs, both necessary and bizarre, whose cause is lost in the mists of antiquity, and which put philosophers to the torture to explain them. It is a fairly constant observation that supernatural and divine institutions strengthen and preserve themselves by being transformed, ultimately, into civil and national laws; and that civil and national institutions become consecrated, and degenerate into supernatural and divine precepts.

A: That is one of the most disastrous of vicious circles.

B: One more link added to the chains which bind us.

A: Wasn't he in Paraguay at the time of the expulsion of the Jesuits?

B: Yes.

A: What did he say about it?

B: Less than he could have said; but enough to teach us that these cruel Spartans in the black habit used their Indian slaves like the Lacedemonians[2] did their helots. They condemned them to hard labour, sweated them, and left them no rights of property; kept them under the opium of superstition; exacted from them profound veneration; strode among them, lash in hand, striking every one,

---

[2]The Spartans, or Lacedemonians, were ancient Greeks known for austerity, self-discipline, and severity of manner.

irrespective of sex or age. Another hundred years and their expulsion would have become impossible, or the motive of a war between these monks and the sovereign whose authority they would have undermined little by little.

A: And these Patagonians about whom Doctor Maty and La Condamine of the Academy[3] have made so much fuss?

B: They are fine people, who come and embrace you, crying "Chaoua"; strong, vigorous, hardly ever exceeding five feet six inches in height, with nothing enormous about them except their girth, the largeness of their heads and the thickness of their limbs. Born with a taste for the marvellous, which exaggerates everything around him, how could the man leave a just proportion to objects, when he has, so to speak, to justify the journey he has made and the difficulties he had in going so far to see them?

A: And what does he think of the savage?

B: It seems that the cruel character which is sometimes found in him comes from his having to defend himself against wild beasts. He is innocent and gentle wherever nothing troubles his repose and security. Every war is born from the common claim to the same property. One civilized man has a common claim with another civilized man to the possession of a field of which each occupies one end; and this field becomes the subject of dispute between them.

A: And the tiger has a common claim, with the savage, to the possession of a forest; that is the first of all claims and the oldest cause of wars.... Have you seen the Tahitian whom Bougainville took on board and brought to this country?

B: I've seen him; he is named Aotourou. The first land he saw he took for the native land of the explorers. Either they had deceived him about the length of the voyage, or, naturally misled by the apparent short distance from the shore of the sea where he lived to where the sky seemed to limit it at the horizon, he was ignorant of the real extent of the earth. The idea of the communal enjoyment of women was so well established in his mind that he threw himself upon the first European woman he met and prepared very seriously to treat her with true Tahitian courtesy. He was bored among us. The Tahitian alphabet having no b, c, d, f, g, q, x, y, nor z, he could never learn to speak our language, which presented too many foreign articulations and new sounds for his inflexible organs of speech. He never ceased to sigh for his own country, and I am not surprised. Bougainville's *Voyage* is the only one which has given me a taste for any other country than my own. Until reading this I had thought that nowhere was there anything so good as at home, with the result that I believed the same for every inhabitant of the earth: a natural effect of the attraction of the soil, an attraction which holds for good things which one enjoys at home and which one has not the same certainty of finding elsewhere.

A: What! Don't you think that the Parisian is convinced that he might grow corn in the Roman Campagna as in the fields of the Beauce?[4]

B: Indeed, no. Bougainville sent Aotourou back, after having provided for his expenses and ensured his return.

A: Oh, Aotourou! How glad you will be to see your father and mother again, and your brothers, sisters, lovers and fellow-countrymen! What will you tell them about us?

---

[3]Matthew Maty (1718–1776), Dutch physician and writer, moved to England in 1741 to become librarian of the British Museum and a member of the Royal Society; Charles Mary la Condamine (1701–1774), French writer and traveler, author of *A Journal of a Voyage to the Equator*. One item of the debate was whether giants existed in Patagonia.

[4]A marshy and a fertile corn-growing district, respectively, in France.

B: Only a little, and that they won't believe.

A: Why only a little?

B: Because he has understood only a few things, and because he will not find in his language any terms corresponding to those things which he has understood.

A: And why won't they believe him?

B: Because after comparing their ways with ours, they would much rather take Aotourou for a liar, than believe us to be so mad.

A: Really?

B: I don't doubt it. The life of a savage is simple, and our societies are such complex mechanisms. The Tahitian is at a primary stage in the development of the world, the European is at its old age. The interval separating us is greater than that between the new-born child and the decrepit old man. He understands nothing of our customs, our laws, or he sees in them only fetters disguised in a hundred ways; fetters which can only excite indignation and hatred in a being for whom liberty is one of the most profound of feelings.

A: Are you wanting to make a fable about Tahiti?

B: It is not a fable; and you would have no doubt of the sincerity of Bougainville, if you knew the *Supplement* to his *Voyage*.

A: Where is this *Supplement* to be found?

B: There on the table.

A: Won't you entrust it to me?

B: No; but we could run through it together if you agree.

A: Certainly, I should like to do so. See, the fog is going now, and the blue sky is beginning to appear. It seems to be my lot always to be wrong with you, even in the smallest things; I must be very good to forgive you such continual superiority!

B: Hold on! read. Let's skip this preamble which doesn't matter and go straight to the farewell of one of the island chiefs to our explorers. This will give you some idea of the eloquence of these people.

A: How did Bougainville understand these farewells spoken in a language of which he was ignorant?

B: You will see. It is an old man speaking.

2. THE OLD MAN'S FAREWELL

He was the father of a large family. At the arrival of the Europeans, he looked disdainfully at them, showing neither astonishment, fear nor curiosity. They accosted him. He turned his back on them, and withdrew into his hut. His silence and his anxiety revealed his thoughts only too well: he lamented within himself for the great days of his country, now eclipsed. At the departure of Bougainville, when the inhabitants ran in a crowd to the shore, clinging to his garments, embracing his companions and weeping, the old man came forward with a stern air and said:

"Weep, poor folk of Tahiti, weep! Would that this were the arrival and not the departure of these ambitious and wicked men. One day you will know them better. One day they will return, in one hand the piece of wood you now see attached to the belt of this one, and the other grasping the blade you now see hanging from the belt of another. And with these they will enslave you, murder you or subject you to their extravagances and vices. One day you will serve under them, as corrupted, as vile, as loathsome as themselves.

"But I console myself; I am reaching the end of my journey; I shall not live to see the calamity I foretell. Oh people of Tahiti! Oh my friends! You have a means to escape this tragic future; but I would rather die than counsel it. Let them go their ways, let them live."

Then, addressing himself to Bougainville, he continued:

"And you, chief of these brigands who obey you, quickly take your vessel from our shores. We are innocent, we are happy; and you can only spoil our happiness. We follow the pure instincts of nature; and you have tried to wipe its impress from our souls. Here everything belongs to everybody. You have preached to us I know not what distinctions between 'mine' and 'thine.' Our daughters and our wives are common to us all. You have shared this privilege with us; and you have lighted passions in them before unknown. They have become maddened in your arms; you have become ferocious in theirs. They have begun to hate each other; you have slain each other for them, and they have returned to us stained with your blood.

"We are a free people; and now you have planted in our country the title deeds of our future slavery. You are neither god nor demon; who are you, then, to make slaves? Orou! You understand the language of these men, tell us all, as you have told me, what they have written on this sheet of metal: 'This country is ours.' This country yours? And why? Because you have walked thereon? If a Tahitian landed one day on your shores, and scratched on one of your rocks or on the bark of your trees: 'This country belongs to the people of Tahiti'— what would you think?

"You are the strongest! And what of that? When someone took one of the contemptible trifles with which your vessel is filled, you cried out and you were revenged. Yet at the same time in the depths of your heart you plotted the theft of a whole country! You are not a slave; you would suffer death rather than be one; yet you want to enslave us. Do you think the Tahitian does not know how to defend his liberty and to die? The Tahitian you want to seize like a wild animal is your brother. You are both children of nature; what right have you over him that he has not over you? When you came, did we rush upon you, did we pillage your ship? Did we seize you and expose you to the arrows of our enemies? Did we yoke you with the animals for toil in our fields? No. We respected our own likeness in you. Leave us to our ways; they are wiser and more honest than yours. We do not want to barter what you call our ignorance for your useless civilization. Everything that is necessary and good for us we possess. Do we deserve contempt, because we have not known how to develop superfluous wants? When we hunger, we have enough to eat; when we are cold we have wherewith to clothe us. You have been in our huts; what is lacking there, in your opinion? You may pursue as far as you like what you call the comforts of life; but allow sensible people to stop, when they would only have obtained imaginary good from the continuation of their painful efforts. If you persuade us to exceed the narrow limits of our wants, when shall we ever finish toiling? When shall we enjoy ourselves? We have reduced the sum of our annual and daily labours to the least possible, because nothing seems to us preferable to repose. Go to your own country to agitate and torment yourself as much as you like; leave us in peace. Do not worry us with your artificial needs nor with your imaginary virtues. Look on these men; see how upright, healthy and robust they are. Look on these women; see how upright, healthy, fresh and beautiful they are. Take this bow; it is my own. Call one, two, three or four of your friends to help you and try to bend it. I can bend it myself, alone. I till the soil. I climb mountains. I pierce the forest. I can run a league on the plains in less than an hour. Your young companions would be hard put to follow me, yet I am more than ninety years old.

"Woe unto this island! Woe to these people of Tahiti and to all who will come after them, woe from the day you first visited us! We should know only one disease; that to which all men, animals and plants are subject—old age; but you have brought us another; you have infected our blood.

"It will perhaps be necessary to exterminate our daughters, wives, children, with our own hands; all those who have approached your women; those who have approached your men.

"Our fields shall be soaked with the foul blood which has passed from your veins into ours; or else our children, condemned to nourish and perpetuate the evil which you have given to the fathers and mothers, will transmit it for ever to their descendants. Villains! You will be the guilty ones; guilty either of the ravages of disease that will follow the fatal embraces of your people, or of the murders which we shall commit to stop the spread of the poison.

"You speak of crimes! Do you know any more enormous than your own? What is your punishment for him who kills his neighbour?—death by the sword; what is your punishment for the coward who poisons?—death by fire. Compare your crime to his; tell us then, poisoner of whole peoples, what should be the torment you deserve? But a short while ago, the young Tahitian girl yielded herself to the transports and embraces of the Tahitian youth; waited impatiently until her mother, authorized by her having reached the age of marriage, should remove her veil and make naked her breast. She was proud to excite the desire and to attract the amorous glances of unknown men, of relatives, of her brother. Without dread and without shame, in our presence, in the midst of a circle of innocent Tahitians, to the sound of flutes, between the dances, she accepted the caresses of the one to whom her young heart and the secret voice of her senses urged her. The idea of crime and the peril of disease came with you. Our enjoyments, once so sweet, are now accompanied by remorse and terror. That man in black who stands near you listening to me, has spoken to our lads. I do not know what he has said to our girls. But our lads are hesitant; our girls blush. Plunge if you will into the dark depths of the forest with the perverse companion of your pleasure; but let the good and simple Tahitians reproduce themselves without shame, under the open sky, in the full light of day. What finer and more noble feeling could you put in place of that with which we have inspired them, and which animates them now? They think that the moment to enrich the nation and the family with a new citizen is come, and they glory in it. They eat to live and to grow; they grow in order to multiply and they find in it nothing vicious nor shameful.

"Listen to the continuation of your crimes. You had hardly come among our people than they became thieves. You had scarcely landed on our soil, than it reeked with blood. That Tahitian who ran to meet you, to receive you crying 'Taio! friend, friend,' you slew. And why did you slay him? . . . because he had been taken by the glitter of your little serpents' eggs. He gave you of his fruits; he offered you his wife and daughter, he ceded you his hut; yet you killed him for a handful of beads which he had taken without having asked. And the people? At the noise of your murderous shot, terror seized them, and they fled to the mountains. But be assured that they would not have waited long to descend again. Then you would all have perished, but for me. Ah! why did I pacify them, why did I hold them back, why do I still restrain them, even now? I do not know; for you deserve no pity; for you have a ferocious soul which will never feel it. You have wandered, you and yours, everywhere in our island. You have been respected; you have enjoyed all things; you have found neither barrier nor refusal in your ways; you have been invited within, you have sat, and all the abundance of our country has been spread before you. When you desired young girls, only excepting those who had not yet the privilege of unveiling their faces and breasts, their mothers have presented to you all the others, quite naked. You have possessed the tender victim of the duties of hospitality; flowers and leaves were heaped up for you and her; musicians sounded their instruments; nothing has spoiled the sweetness, nor hindered the freedom of your caresses nor of hers. They have sung the anthem exhorting you to be a man, and our child to be a woman, yielding and voluptuous. They danced around your couch. And it was when you came from the arms of this woman, after experiencing on her breast the sweetest of all intoxications, that you slew her brother, friend or father.

"You have done still worse. Look over there, see that enclosure bristling with weapons. These arms which have menaced only your enemies are now turned against our own children. See these unhappy companions of our pleasures. See their sadness, the grief of their fathers and the despair of their mothers. They are those condemned to die, either by our hands or by the diseases you have given them.

"Away now, unless your cruel eyes revel in the spectacle of death. Go now, go; and may the guilty seas which spared you on your voyage hither, absolve themselves and avenge us, by engulfing you before you return.

"And you, oh people of Tahiti! Go into your huts, go, all of you; and let these strangers as they leave hear only the roar of the tide and see only the foam of its fury whitening a deserted shore."

He had scarcely finished before the crowd of people had disappeared. A vast silence reigned over the whole island, and only the keen whistling of the wind and the dull sound of the breakers along the shore could be heard. One might have said that the air and the sea, conscious of the voice of the aged man, were moved to obey him.

B: Ah! . . . well, what do you think of it?

A: This speech seems vehement to me; but in spite of something abrupt and wild about it I seem to detect European ideas and turns of phrase.

B: Remember that it's a translation from Tahitian into Spanish, then from Spanish into French. The old man had come, at night, to that Orou, whom he had called upon in his speech, and in whose home the use of the Spanish language had been preserved from time immemorial. Orou had written out the old man's harangue in Spanish; and Bougainville had a copy of it in his hand while the old man was speaking.

A: I see only too well why Bougainville has suppressed this fragment. But that's not all there is; and my curiosity about the rest is not tepid.

B: What follows will perhaps interest you less.

A: That doesn't matter.

B: It is a conversation between the almoner[5] of the expedition and an inhabitant of the island.

A: With Orou?

B: Yes, Orou. When Bougainville's vessel neared Tahiti, a great number of dug-out canoes were launched on the water. In an instant his ship was surrounded by natives; wherever he turned his eyes he saw demonstrations of surprise and goodwill. They threw provisions on board, held out their arms to him, tied on to the vessel and climbed its sides. They filled his launch. They shouted to the land, from which came answering cries, and the inhabitants of the island ran out. They all land; they take possession of the members of the crew, whom they allot among themselves. Each takes his guest to his hut, the men with their arms round their waists, the women stroking their cheeks. Imagine yourself there; be a witness in thought, of this spectacle of hospitality, and tell me your opinion of the human species.

---

[5] A priest.

A: Very beautiful.

B: But I should perhaps forget to tell you of a very strange event. This scene of goodwill and humanity was suddenly stirred by the cries of a man shouting for help; it was the servant of one of Bougainville's officers. Some young Tahitians had thrown themselves on him, laid him on the ground, undressed him and were preparing to do him the civility of Tahitian custom.

A: What! these simple souls, these primitive people, so good, so honest...?

B: You misunderstand. This servant was a woman disguised as a man. Undiscovered by any of the crew, during the whole of a long voyage, the Tahitians had divined her sex at the first glance. Her name was Barré. She was born in Burgundy, was neither ugly nor pretty and was twenty-six years old. She had never before left her village, and her first idea for travelling was to make a journey round the world. She showed wisdom and courage at all times.

A: These frail creatures often contain heroic spirits.

3. Discussion between the Almoner and Orou

B: In the sharing of Bougainville's crew among the Tahitians, the almoner was allotted to Orou; they were about the same age, thirty-five to thirty-six. Orou had then only his wife and three daughters, called Asto, Palli and Thia. They undressed the almoner, bathed his face, hands and feet, and served him a wholesome and frugal meal. When he was about to go to bed, Orou, who had been absent with his family, reappeared, and presenting to him his wife and three daughters, all naked, said: "You have eaten, you are young and in good health; if you sleep alone you will sleep badly, for man needs a companion beside him at night. There is my wife, there are my daughters; choose the one who pleases you best. But if you wish to oblige me you will give preference to the youngest of my daughters, who has not yet had any children." The mother added: "Alas! But it's no good complaining about it; poor Thia! it is not her fault."

The almoner answered that his religion, his office, good morals and decency would not allow him to accept these offers.

Orou replied: "I do not know what this thing is that you call 'religion'; but I can only think ill of it, since it prevents you from tasting an innocent pleasure to which nature, the sovereign mistress, invites us all; prevents you from giving existence to one of your own kind, from doing a service which a father, mother and children all ask of you, from doing something for a host who has received you well, and from enriching a nation, by giving it one more citizen. I do not know what this thing is which you call your 'office' but your first duty is to be a man and to be grateful. I do not suggest that you should introduce into your country the ways of Orou, but Orou, your host and friend, begs you to lend yourself to the ways of Tahiti. Whether the ways of Tahiti are better or worse than yours is an easy question to decide. Has the land of your birth more people than it can feed? If so your ways are neither worse nor better than ours. But can it feed more than it has? Our ways are better than yours. As to the sense of decency which you offer as objection, I understand you; I agree that I was wrong, and I ask your pardon. I do not want you to injure your health; if you are tired, you must have rest; but I hope that you will not continue to sadden us. See the care you have made appear on all these faces; they fear lest you should have found blemishes on them which merit your disdain. But when it is only the pleasure of doing honour to one of my daughters, amidst her companions and sisters, and of doing a good action, won't that suffice you? Be generous!"

THE ALMONER: It's not that: they are all equally beautiful; but my religion! my office!

OROU: They are mine and I offer them to you; they are their own and they give themselves to you. Whatever may be the purity of conscience which the thing "religion" and the thing "office" prescribe, you can accept them without scruple. I am not abusing my authority at all; be sure that I know and respect the rights of the individual."

Here the truthful almoner agrees that Providence had never exposed him to such violent temptation. He was young, he became agitated and tormented; he turned his eyes away from the lovely suppliants, and then regarded them again; he raised his hands and eyes to the sky. Thia, the youngest, clasped his knees and said: "Stranger, do not distress my father and mother, do not afflict me. Honour me in the hut, among my own people; raise me to the rank of my sisters, who mock me. Asto, the eldest, already had three children; the second, Palli, has two; but Thia has none at all. Stranger, honest stranger, do not repulse me; make me a mother, make me a child that I can one day lead by the hand, by my side, here in Tahiti; who may be seen held at my breast in nine months' time; one of whom I shall be so proud and who will be part of my dowry when I go from my parents' hut to another's. I shall perhaps be more lucky with you than with our young Tahitians. If you will grant me this favour I shall never forget you; I shall bless you all my life. I shall write your name on my arm and on your son's; we shall pronounce it always with joy. And when you leave these shores, my good wishes will go with you on the seas till you reach your own land."

The candid almoner said that she clasped his knees, and gazed into his eyes so expressively and so touchingly; that she wept; that her father, mother and sisters withdrew; that he remained alone with her, and that, still saying "my religion, my office," he found himself the next morning lying beside the young girl, who overwhelmed him with caresses, and who invited her parents and sisters, when they came to their bed in the morning, to join their gratitude to hers. Asto and Palli, who had withdrawn, returned bringing food, fruits and drink. They kissed their sister and made vows over her. They all ate together.

Then Orou, left alone with the almoner, said to him:

"I see that my daughter is well satisfied with you and I thank you. But would you teach me what is meant by this word 'religion' which you have repeated so many times and so sorrowfully?"

The almoner, after having mused a moment answered: "Who made your hut and the things which furnish it?"

OROU: I did.

THE ALMONER: Well then, we believe that this world and all that it contains is the work of a maker.

OROU: Has he feet, hands and a head then?

THE ALMONER: No.

OROU: Where is his dwelling-place?

THE ALMONER: Everywhere.

OROU: Here too?

THE ALMONER: Here.

OROU: We have never seen him.

THE ALMONER: One doesn't see him.

OROU: That's an indifferent father, then! He must be old, for he will at least be as old as his work.

THE ALMONER: He does not age. He spoke to our ancestors, gave them laws, prescribed the manner in which he wished to be honoured; he ordered a certain behaviour as being good, and he forbade them certain other actions as being wicked.

OROU: I follow you; and one of the actions he forbade them, as wicked, was to lie with a woman or a girl? Why, then, did he make two sexes?

THE ALMONER: That they might unite; but with certain requisite conditions, after certain preliminary ceremonies in consequence of which the man belongs to the woman and only to her; and the woman belongs to the man, and only to him.

OROU: For their whole lives?

THE ALMONER: For the whole of their lives.

OROU: So that if it happened that a woman should lie with a man other than her husband, or a husband with another woman . . . but that couldn't happen. Since the maker is there and this displeases him, he will know how to prevent them doing it.

THE ALMONER: No; he lets them do it, and they sin against the law of God (for it is thus we call the great maker) against the law of the country; and they commit a crime.

OROU: I should be sorry to offend you by what I say, but if you would permit me, I would give you my opinion.

THE ALMONER: Speak.

OROU: I find these singular precepts opposed to nature and contrary to reason, made to multiply crimes and to plague at every moment this old maker, who has made everything, without help of hands, or head, or tools, who is everywhere and is not seen anywhere, who exists to-day and to-morrow and yet is not a day older, who commands and is not obeyed, who can prevent and yet does not do so. Contrary to nature because these precepts suppose that a free, thinking and sentient being can be the property of a being like himself. On what is this law founded? Don't you see that in your country they have confused the thing which has neither consciousness nor thought, nor desire, nor will; which one picks up, puts down, keeps or exchanges, without injury to it, or without its complaining, have confused this with the thing which cannot be exchanged or acquired, which has liberty, will, desire, which can give or refuse itself for a moment or for ever, which laments and suffers, and which cannot become an article of commerce, without its character being forgotten and violence done to its nature; contrary to the general law of existence? In fact, nothing could appear to you more senseless than a precept which refuses to admit that change which is a part of us, which commands a constancy which cannot be found there and which violates the liberty of the male and female by chaining them for ever to each other; more senseless than a fidelity which limits the most capricious of enjoyments to one individual; than an oath of the immutability of two beings made of flesh; and all that in the face of a sky which never for a moment remains the same, in caverns which threaten destruction, below a rock which falls to powder, at the foot of a tree which cracks, on a stone which rocks? Believe me, you have made the condition of man worse than that of animals. I do not know what your great maker may be; but I rejoice that he has never spoken to our forefathers, and I wish that he may never speak to our children; for he might tell them the same foolishness, and they commit the folly of believing it. Yesterday, at supper, you mentioned "magistrates" and "priests," whose authority regulates your conduct; but, tell me, are they the masters of good and evil? Can they make what is just to be unjust, and unjust, just? Does it rest with them to attribute good to harmful actions, and evil to innocent or useful actions? You could not think it, for, at that rate, there would be neither true nor false, good nor bad, beautiful nor ugly; or at any rate only what pleased your great maker, your magistrates and your priests to pronounce so. And from one moment to another you would be obliged to change your ideas and your conduct. One day someone would tell you, on behalf of one of your three masters, to kill, and you would be obliged by your conscience to kill; another day, "steal," and you would have to steal; or "do not eat this fruit" and you would not dare to eat it; "I forbid you this vegetable or animal" and you would take care not to touch them. There is no good thing that could not be forbidden you, and no wickedness that you could not be ordered to do. And what would you be reduced to, if your three masters, disagreeing among themselves, should at once permit, enjoin and forbid you the same thing, as I believe must often happen. Then, to please the priest you must become embroiled with the magistrate; to satisfy the magistrate you must displease the great maker; and to make yourself agreeable to the great maker you must renounce nature. And do you know what will happen then? You will neglect all of them, and you will be neither man, nor citizen nor pious; you will be nothing; you will be out of favour with all the kinds of authorities, at odds even with yourself, tormented by your heart, persecuted by your enraged masters; and wretched as I saw you yesterday evening when I offered my wife and daughters to you, and you cried out, "But my religion, my office!"

Do you want to know what is good and what is bad in all times and in all places? Hold fast to the nature of things and of actions; to your relations with your fellows; to the influence of your conduct on your individual usefulness and the general good. You are mad if you believe that there is anything, high or low in the universe, which can add to or subtract from the laws of nature. Her eternal will is that good should be preferred to evil, and the general good to the individual good. You may ordain the opposite but you will not be obeyed. You will multiply the number of malefactors and the wretched by fear, punishment and remorse. You will deprave consciences; you will corrupt minds. They will not know what to do or what to avoid. Disturbed in their state of innocence, at ease with crime, they will have lost their guiding star. Answer me sincerely; in spite of the express orders of your three lawgivers, does a young man, in your country, never lie with a young girl without their permission?

THE ALMONER: I should deceive you if I asserted it.

OROU: Does a woman who has sworn to belong only to her husband never give herself to another man?

THE ALMONER: Nothing is more common.

OROU: Your lawgivers either punish or do not punish; if they punish they are ferocious beasts who fight against nature; if they do not punish, they are imbeciles who have exposed their authority to contempt by an empty prohibition.

THE ALMONER: The culprits who escape the severity of the law are punished by popular condemnation.

OROU: That is to say, justice is exercised through the lack of common sense of the whole nation, and the foolishness of opinion does duty for laws.

THE ALMONER: A girl who has been dishonoured will not find a husband.

OROU: Dishonoured! Why?

THE ALMONER: An unfaithful wife is more or less despised.

OROU: Despised! But why?

THE ALMONER: The young man is called a cowardly seducer.

OROU: A coward, a seducer! But why?

THE ALMONER: The father and mother and child are desolated. The unfaithful husband is a libertine; the betrayed husband shares his wife's shame.

OROU: What a monstrous tissue of extravagances you've just revealed to me! And yet you don't say everything; for as soon as one allows oneself to dispose at pleasure of the ideas of justice and ownership, to take away or to give an arbitrary character to things, to attribute or deny good or evil to certain actions, capriciously, then one can be censorious, vindictive, suspicious, tyrannical, envious, jealous, deceitful. There is spying, quarrelling, cheating and lying; daughters deceive their parents, wives their husbands. Girls, yes, I don't doubt it, will strangle their infants, suspicious fathers will hate and neglect theirs, mothers will leave them and abandon them to their fates. And crime and debauchery will show themselves in all their forms. I know all that as if I had lived among you. It is so, because it must be so; and your society, of which your leader boasts because of its good regulations, will only be a swarm of hypocrites who secretly trample all laws under foot; or of unfortunates who are themselves the instruments of their own suffering in submitting; or of imbeciles in whom prejudices have quite stifled the voice of nature; or of abnormal monsters in whom nature does not protest her rights.

THE ALMONER: So it would seem. But don't you marry, then?

OROU: Yes, we marry.

THE ALMONER: But what does it consist in?

OROU: A mutual consent to live in the same hut and to lie in the same bed for as long as we find it good to do so.

THE ALMONER: And when you find it no longer good?

OROU: We separate.

THE ALMONER: What becomes of the children?

OROU: Oh stranger! Your last question finally reveals to me the profound misery of your country. You must understand, my friend, that here the birth of a child is always a good fortune, and its death a subject for regret and tears. A child is precious because he ought to become a man; therefore we have a care for it, quite other than for our animals and plants. A child born causes both domestic and public joy. It is an increase of fortune for the hut and of strength for the nation. It means more hands and arms in Tahiti. We see in him a farmer, fisher, hunter, soldier, husband and father. When she returns from her husband's cabin to that of her parents, a woman takes with her the children which she had taken as dowry; those born during their companionship are shared; and as nearly as can be, males and females are divided, so that each one retains an equal number of boys and girls.

THE ALMONER: But the children are a charge for a long time before they give any service.

OROU: We allot for their maintenance and for that of old people, one-sixth part of all the produce of the country; this allowance goes with them. Thus you see that the more numerous a Tahitian family is, the richer it is.

THE ALMONER: A sixth part!

OROU: Yes; it is a certain means for increasing the population, for securing respect for the aged and for preserving the children.

THE ALMONER: Your married couples take each other back again sometimes?

OROU: Very often; however, the shortest duration of a marriage is from one moon to another.

THE ALMONER: Unless the woman is pregnant; must they then live together for at least nine months?

OROU: You are mistaken; the paternity, like the allowance, goes with the child everywhere.

THE ALMONER: You spoke of the children which a woman brought as dowry to her husband.

OROU: Certainly. There's my eldest daughter who has three children; they are progressing, they are healthy and beautiful, they promise to be strong. If it takes her fancy to marry, she will take them with her, they are hers. Her husband will receive them joyfully, and his wife would only be dearer to him if she were pregnant with a fourth.

THE ALMONER: By him?

OROU: By him, or someone else. The more children our girls have, the more they are sought after; the stronger and more vigorous our lads are, the richer are they. Also, just as much as we are careful to preserve the ones from the approach of men, and the others from commerce with women, before the age of fecundity, after that age we equally exhort them to reproduce, when they are fit to do so. You could not believe the importance of the service you will have done my daughter Thia, if you have given her a child. Her mother will no longer say to her at each moon, "But, Thia, what are you thinking of? You never get pregnant; you are nineteen and ought already to have two children, and yet have none at all. Who will look after you? If you lose all your youth like this, what will you do in your old age? Thia, you must have some defect which keeps men away from you. Cure yourself of it, my child; at your age I had been three times a mother."

THE ALMONER: What precautions do you take to protect your adolescent boys and girls?

OROU: That is the principal object of education at home and the most important point of public morality. Our boys, until the age of twenty-two, two or three years after puberty, remain covered with a long tunic, their loins girded with a little chain. Before the age of marriage, our girls would not dare to go out without a white veil. Taking off the chain, or lifting the veil are faults which are seldom committed, because we early teach them the unpleasant consequences. But as soon as the male has reached his full growth, when the symptoms of virility are regularly present, and the frequent effusion of the seminal fluid and its quality confirm it; when the young girl is languid, bored, and is mature enough to feel desires, to inspire them and to satisfy them usefully, then the father takes off his son's chain, and cuts the nail of the middle finger of his right hand. The mother takes off her daughter's veil. The one can then ask of women, and be asked: the other can walk in public with her face uncovered and her breast bare, and accept or refuse the caresses of a man. One merely indicates in advance to the boy which girls, and to the girl which boys, they should prefer. The day of freedom is a great occasion for the boy or girl.

If it is a girl, in the evening the young boys assemble round the hut and the air resounds the whole night through with their songs and the sounds of instruments. On the day, she is led by her father and mother to an enclosure, where there is dancing and exercises of jumping, running and fighting. The man is displayed naked before her, from all aspects and in all attitudes. If it is a boy, it is the young girls who, in his presence, do the ceremonies and honours of the feast, and show him the woman naked, without reserve and without secrecy. The rest of the ceremony is fulfilled on a bed of leaves, as you saw when you first came among us. At the fall of day, the girl goes back to her parents' hut, or to that of the man she has chosen, and stays there so long as it pleases her.

THE ALMONER: This feast, then, is not at all a wedding-day?

OROU: Just so. . . .

• • •

A: What's that I see in the margin?

B: It's a note, where the good almoner says that the teachings of the parents concerning the girls' and boys' choices were full of good sense, and very fine and useful observations. But he has suppressed this catechism, which would have appeared to people as corrupt and superficial as ourselves, as unpardonably licentious; adding, however, that it was not without regret that he had deleted these details, which would have shown, firstly, how far a nation which occupied itself ceaselessly with an important object could be led in its researches without the aid of physics and anatomy; secondly, the difference between the ideas of beauty in a country where the forms are related to a momentary pleasure, and among a people where they are appreciated for a more constant utility. There, to be beautiful, a striking complexion, wide forehead, large eyes, fine and delicate features, a slender waist, a small mouth, small hands and feet are required. . . . Here almost every one of these elements does not enter into the calculation. The woman whom everyone regards and whom desire pursues is she who bears promise of many children (the woman of Cardinal d'Ossat) who will be active, intelligent, courageous, healthy and robust. There is almost nothing in common between the Venus of Athens[6] and the Tahitian one; the former is a wanton Venus, the latter a fertile Venus. A Tahitian woman said scornfully one day to another woman of the country: "You are beautiful, but you make ugly children; I am ugly, but I produce beautiful children, and it is me that men prefer."

After this note by the almoner, Orou continues:

OROU: What a happy moment it is for a young girl and for her parents when it is verified that she is pregnant! She gets up, runs, throws her arms round the necks of her father and mother. With transports of mutual joyfulness she tells, and they learn, of this event. "Mother, father, kiss me; I am pregnant!—Is it really true?—Absolutely true.—And whose is it?—It was done with so and so" . . .

THE ALMONER: How can she name the father of her child?

OROU: Why do you want her not to know it? It is the same with the duration of our loves as with that of our marriages; it is at least from one moon to the following one.

THE ALMONER: And this rule is really scrupulously observed?

OROU: You shall judge. In the first place the interval between two moons is not long; but where two fathers have a well-founded claim to the formation of a child, it no longer belongs to its mother.

THE ALMONER: Who does it belong to then?

OROU: To the one to whom it pleases her to give it; that's her sole privilege. And a child being for its own sake a source of interest and riches, you can imagine that among us, libertines are rare. And that the youths keep away from them.

THE ALMONER: You have your libertines then? I am much comforted.

OROU: We have even more than one sort; but you make me stray from my subject. When one of our girls is pregnant, if the father of the child is a fine young man well built, brave, intelligent, and hard working, the hope that the child will inherit the qualities of the father intensifies the joy. Our child has only the shame of bad choice. You can imagine what value we attach to health, beauty, strength, industriousness and courage; you can imagine how, without any interference, the prerogatives of blood are bound to be perpetuated among us. You have been in many countries, now tell me if you have seen in any of them as many fine men and beautiful women as in Tahiti! Look at me; what do you think of me? Well, there are ten thousand men here, who are taller and more robust; but not one braver than I; therefore the mothers often nominate me to their daughters.

THE ALMONER: But of all these children that you can have produced outside your own hut, how many come back to you?

OROU: One fourth, male or female. There is established among us a circulation of men, women and children or of hands of all ages and functions, which is of quite other importance than the circulation of your commodities, which are only the products of them.

---

[6]The Greek goddess of love.

THE ALMONER: So I conceive. What are these black veils that I've noticed from time to time?

OROU: The sign of sterility, either a defect of birth or a consequence of advanced age. She who discards the veil and mingles with men, is a libertine; he who lifts this veil and approaches a sterile woman, is a libertine.

THE ALMONER: And these grey veils?

OROU: The sign of the periodic indisposition. She who discards this veil, and mingles with men, is a libertine; he who lifts it and approaches the indisposed woman, is a libertine.

THE ALMONER: Have you punishments for such licentiousness?

OROU: Nothing except the blame!

THE ALMONER: Can a father lie with his daughter, a mother with her son, a brother with his sister, a husband with another's wife?

OROU: Why not?

THE ALMONER: We'll let fornication pass; but adultery, incest! . . .

OROU: What do you mean by your words: "fornication," "adultery," "incest"?

THE ALMONER: Crimes, horrible crimes, for any one of which people are burnt in my country.

OROU: Whether you burn or don't burn in your country doesn't matter to me. But you will not judge the morals of Europe by those of Tahiti, nor, consequently, the morals of Tahiti by those of Europe. We must have a more certain rule than that; and what shall that be? Do you know any other than the general good and personal utility? Now tell me what there is in your crime of "incest" which is contrary to these two objectives of our actions. You are mistaken, my friend, if you believe that once a law is published, a dishonourable word invented, a punishment decreed, all is said. Answer me now, what do you understand by "incest"?

THE ALMONER: But an incest . . .

OROU: An "incest"? Was it long ago that your great maker, without head, hands or tools made the world?

THE ALMONER: No.

OROU: Did he make the whole human race at once?

THE ALMONER: No. He created only one man and one woman.

OROU: Had they any children?

THE ALMONER: Assuredly.

OROU: Suppose that the first two parents had had only girls, and that their mother dies first, or that they had had only boys and that the wife had lost her husband.

THE ALMONER: You embarrass me; but whatever you say, incest is a horrible crime; let us speak of something else.

OROU: It pleases you to say so. I am not going to speak as long as you will not tell me what this abominable crime of "incest" is.

THE ALMONER: Well, I grant you that perhaps incest injures nothing in nature; but doesn't it suffice that it menaces the political constitution? What would become of the security of a leader and the tranquillity of a state, if the whole of a nation composed of several million people, should find itself centred about fifty fathers of families?

OROU: At the worst it would be that where there is only one great society, there would be fifty smaller ones, more happiness and one crime the less.

THE ALMONER: But I fancy, however, that even here, a son rarely lies with his mother.

OROU: Unless he has much respect for her, and a tenderness which makes him forget the disparity in age and prefer a woman of forty to a girl of nineteen.

THE ALMONER: And the commerce of fathers with their daughters?

OROU: Hardly more frequent, unless the girl is ugly and little sought after. If her father loves her, he helps her to prepare her dowry of children.

THE ALMONER: I imagine from this that the lot of women whom nature has not endowed cannot be a happy one in Tahiti.

OROU: That proves to me that you haven't a high opinion of the generosity of our young people.

THE ALMONER: As for the union of brother and sister, I do not doubt but that is very common.

OROU: And greatly approved.

THE ALMONER: To hear you, this passion, which produces so many crimes and evils in our country, must be quite innocent here.

OROU: Stranger! You are lacking in both judgment and memory; in judgment, because whenever anything is forbidden one is tempted to do the forbidden thing and one does it; in memory, because you don't remember what I've told you. We have dissolute old women who go out at night without their black veils, and receive men, when nothing can result from their connection; if they are recognized or surprised, exile to the north of the island or slavery is their punishment. We have precocious girls who lift their veils in spite of their parents (and we have a closed place for them in the hut); youths who remove their chain before the time prescribed by nature and by the law (and we reprove their parents for it); women for whom the period of pregnancy seems too long; women and girls who are not too careful about wearing their grey veils. But, in fact, we do not attach great importance to any of these faults, and you would hardly believe how the idea of personal and public wealth, joined in our minds with the idea of population, purifies our manners in this respect.

THE ALMONER: The passion of two men for the same woman, or the desire of two women or two girls for the same man, doesn't that ever cause trouble?

OROU: I have yet seen only four cases of that; the choice of the man or of the woman settles everything. Violence by a man would be a grave fault; but a public complaint is necessary and it is almost unheard of that a girl or woman complains. The only thing that I have noticed, is that our women have less compassion for ugly men than our youths have for the women poorly endowed by nature; and that doesn't worry us.

THE ALMONER: You hardly know jealousy, from what I can see; but marital tenderness and maternal love, those powerful and sweet feelings, if they are not strangers here, must be very feeble.

OROU: We have replaced them by another, which in another fashion is quite general, powerful and lasting, namely interest. Now be sincere, leave all that prating about virtues, which is incessantly on your comrades' lips but which is not at all in the depths of their hearts. Tell me, if in any country whatever there is a father who, without shame which checks him, would not rather lose his child, a husband who would not rather lose his wife, than his fortune and ease for the rest of his life. Be sure that wherever a man shall be as attached to the preservation of his fellow man as to his bed, his health, his repose, his hut, his produce, and his fields, he will do for him all that it is possible for him to do. It is here that tears moisten the pillow of a sick child; it is here that we prize a fertile woman, a daughter ripe for marriage, an adolescent boy. Here it is that we are occupied with their establishment, because their preservation is always a gain, and their loss always a diminution of fortune.

THE ALMONER: I fear too well that this savage is right. The miserable peasant in our country who wears out his wife to spare his horse, lets his child perish without succour and calls in a doctor for his cattle.

OROU: I don't quite understand what you've just said; but when you return to your very civilized country try to introduce this motive there; and it is then that the worth of every child that's born, and the importance of population will be felt. Shall I tell you a secret? But take care that you do not give it away. You arrive here; we give our women and girls to you; you are astonished; you show a gratitude which makes us laugh; you thank us when we lay on you and on your companions the heaviest of all impositions. We have not asked for money, we have not thrown ourselves on your merchandise, we have scorned the goods: but our women and our girls have just drawn the very blood from your veins. When you shall be gone, you will have left us children; do you not think this tribute levied on your person, on your own flesh, is well worth any other? And if you want to appreciate the value of it, imagine that you had two hundred leagues of coast to sail by, and that at every twenty miles a similar tribute was exacted. We have immense areas of fallow land; we lack hands to cultivate it; and we have asked them of you. We have to make up for calamitous epidemics; and we have used you to fill the void which they have made. We have to fight neighbouring enemies and need soldiers; and we have begged you to make them for us. Our women and girls outnumber the men, and we have associated you in our task. Amongst these women and girls are some from whom we have not been able to get children, and it is these we have exposed to your first embraces. We have to pay dues in men to a neighbouring oppressor; it is you and your comrades who will defray this for us; and in five or six years we shall send him your sons, if they are worth less than the others. Healthier and more robust than you are, we saw at once that you surpassed us in intelligence; and at once we destined some of our most beautiful women and girls to collect the seed of a race better than our own. It's an experiment that we have made, and one which may prove successful. We have drawn from you and yours the only part of you that we could; and know that, savages as we are, we know how to scheme. Go where you will; and you will always find a man as subtle as yourself. He will always give you only what is no good to himself, and will always ask of you something that is useful to him. If he gives you a piece of gold for a piece of iron, it is because the gold is of no value to him and he prizes the iron. But tell me though, why you are not dressed like the others? What does this long robe that covers you from head to feet signify, and this pointed sack which falls over your shoulders, or which you pull over your ears?

THE ALMONER: It is because, as you see me, I belong to a society of men, called monks in my country. The most sacred of their vows is to approach no woman and to beget no children.

OROU: What do you do then?

THE ALMONER: Nothing.

OROU: And your magistrate allows that kind of laziness, the worst of all?

THE ALMONER: He does more; he respects it and sees that it is respected.

OROU: My first idea was that nature, some accident, or a cruel art had deprived you of the power of reproducing your like; and that out of pity they would rather let you live than kill you. But, monk, my daughter tells me that you are a man, and one as robust as any Tahitian, and that she has hopes that your repeated embraces will not be unfruitful. Now that I understand why you cried out yesterday evening "But my religion! my office!," could you tell me the motive of the favour and respect which the magistrates accord to you?

THE ALMONER: I do not know.

OROU: You at least know for what reason, being a man, you have freely condemned yourself not to be one?

THE ALMONER: That would be too long and too difficult to explain to you.

OROU: And this vow of sterility, is the monk very faithful to it?

THE ALMONER: No.

OROU: I was sure of it. Do you also have female monks?

THE ALMONER: Yes.

OROU: As wise as the male monks?

THE ALMONER: More closely confined, they wither from sadness and perish from boredom.

OROU: And the injury done to nature is revenged. Oh! What a villanous country! If everything is arranged there as you tell me, you are more barbarous than we are.

. . .

The good almoner then recounts that he passed the rest of the day going about the island, visiting the huts, and that in the evening, after supper, the father and mother having begged him to sleep with the second of their daughters, Palli was presented to him in the same undress as Thia, and that he cried out several times during the night: "My religion! my office!"; that the third night he had been moved by the same remorse with Asto, the eldest; and that he granted the fourth night, out of politeness, to the wife of his host.

4. CONTINUATION OF THE DIALOGUE

A: I like that polite almoner.

B: I like much more the manners of Tahiti and Orou's discourse.

A: Although a little on the European model.

B: I don't doubt it. You see, here the good almoner complains of the briefness of his stay in Tahiti, and of the difficulty of knowing better the customs of a people wise enough to have stopped themselves of their own accord at a median level of development, or happy enough to live in a climate where the fertility assures them a long torpid existence, active enough to provide the necessities of life, and sufficiently indolent for their innocence, repose and happiness to have nothing to fear from a too-rapid progress of enlightenment. Nothing was evil there by law or opinion, there was only what was evil in itself. Labour and the harvests were done collectively. The accepted meaning of the word property was very narrow. The passion of love, reduced there to a simple physical appetite, produced none of our disturbances. The whole island seemed like one large family, where each hut represented the different apartments of one large mansion. He ends by declaring that these Tahitians will always be in his thoughts, that he was tempted to fling his vestments into the ship and pass the rest of his days among them, and that he feared very much that he would rue more than once not having done so.

A: But in spite of all this praise, what useful conclusions are to be drawn from the strange manners and customs of an uncivilized people?

B: I see that as soon as some physical causes, for example, the necessity for conquering the barrenness of the soil, have stimulated man's sagacity, this impetus carries him much beyond his immediate objective, and that when the period of need has passed, he is carried off into the limitless realm of fantasy, from which there is no coming back. May the happy people of Tahiti stay where they are! I see that except in this remote corner of our globe, there has never been morality and perhaps never will be anywhere.

A: Then what do you understand by morality?

B: I understand a general submission, and a conduct consequent on good or bad laws. If the laws are good, morals are good; if the laws are bad, morals are bad; if laws, good or bad, are not observed at all, that worst condition of a society, then there is no morality at all. Now, how can laws be observed if they contradict one another? Examine the history of various epochs and nations, both ancient and modern, and you will find men subjected to three codes of law, the laws of nature, civil law and the law of religion, and constrained to infringe alternately all these codes, which have never been in agreement. From this it follows that there has never been in any country, as Orou guessed of ours, either man, or citizen or truly pious person.

A: From which you conclude, no doubt, that in basing morality on the eternal relations which exist between men, the law of religion may become superfluous, and that civil law ought only to be the enunciation of the laws of nature.

B: And that, under pain of multiplying the wicked instead of making the good.

A: Or that, if it be judged necessary to keep all three codes, the last two should only be exact copies of the first, which we carry always graven in our hearts and which will always be the most powerful.

B: That's not very exact. We have at birth only a similarity of organization with other beings, the same needs, an attraction towards the same pleasures, a common aversion for the same pains; that is what makes man as he is, and which ought to be the basis of the morality suitable for him.

A: That's not easy.

B: It is so difficult that I would willingly believe the most primitive people on earth, a Tahitian, who has held scrupulously to the laws of nature, nearer to a good code of laws than any civilized people.

A: Because it is easier for him to get rid of his too-great primitiveness, than it is for us to retrace our steps and remedy our abuses.

B: Above all, those which have to do with the relations between men and women.

A: That may be. But let's begin at the beginning. Let us sincerely question nature and see what answer she gives us about this.

B: I agree.

A: Does marriage exist in nature?

B: If by marriage you understand the preference which one female gives to one male above all other males, or which a male gives to one female above all other females, a mutual preference, in consequence of which they form a more or less lasting association which perpetuates the species by the reproduction of individuals, then marriage does exist in nature.

A: I think as you do; for this preference is observed not only in the human species, but also in other species of animals, as witness the host of males who pursue one female in our countryside in spring, of whom only one obtains the title of husband. What about love-making?

B: If by this you understand those means, forcible or delicate, which passion inspires, both in the male and in the female, in order to obtain that preference which leads to the sweetest, most important and most general of pleasures, then love-making does exist in nature.

A: I think so too. Witness the variety of pretty tricks done by the male to please the female; and by the female to excite and secure the desire of the male. And coquetry?...

B: ...Is a lie, which consists in feigning a passion that is not felt and in promising a preference that will not be granted. The male flirt plays with the female; the female flirt plays with the male; a contemptible game which sometimes leads to terrible catastrophes; a ridiculous performance for which the deceiver and deceived are equally punished by the loss of some of the most precious moments of their lives.

A: According to you, then, coquetry is unnatural.

B: I don't say that.

A: And constancy?

B: I can tell you nothing better about it than what Orou said to the almoner: the poor vanity of two children who don't understand themselves, whose momentary intoxication blinds them to the mutability of everything which surrounds them!

A: And faithfulness, that rare phenomenon?

B: In our country, almost always the infatuation and torture of the honest man or honest woman; a chimera in Tahiti.

A: Jealousy?

B: The passion of a destitute and avaricious animal which fears a lack; in man an unjust feeling, a consequence of our false morals and of a property-right extended to a feeling, thinking, desiring and free object.

A: Jealousy, then, you think, does not exist in nature?

B: I don't say that. Vices and virtues equally exist in nature.

A: The jealous man is melancholy.

B: Like a tyrant, because he is conscious of it.

A: What about modesty?

B: Ah! Now you involve me in a course on the morality of love-making. A man wants to be neither disturbed nor distracted in his pleasures; those of love are followed by a weakness which would leave him at the mercy of his enemy. That is all there can be natural in modesty; all the rest is custom.—The almoner remarks in a third piece which I have not read to you, that the Tahitian does not blush for the involuntary movements which are excited in him when near his wife, surrounded by his daughters; that the latter see this, are moved, but never embarrassed. As soon as women became the property of men and the furtive enjoyment of a girl was regarded as a theft, then the words "modesty," "reserve," "propriety" were born, and imaginary virtues and vices. In a word, it was wished to raise between the two sexes barriers which should prevent them from a mutual invitation to violate these laws which had been imposed on them, and which often produced the opposite effect, by heating the imagination and exciting desires. When I see trees planted round our palaces, and clothes arranged so as both to show and to hide part of a woman's breast, I seem to recognize a secret return to the forest and an appeal for the liberty of our primeval dwelling. The Tahitian would say to us: "Why do you hide yourself? What are you ashamed of? Are you doing evil when you bow to the most powerful impulse in nature? Man, offer yourself frankly if it pleases you. Woman, if this man is agreeable to you, receive him with the same freedom."

A: Don't worry yourself. Even if we begin like civilized men, it is rare if we don't finish like the Tahitian.

B: Yes. These conventional preliminaries consume half the life of a man of character.

A: Yes, I agree; but what does it matter, if this pernicious urge of the human mind against which you were inveighing just now, is the more moderated because of it? A philosopher, in our days, when asked why men courted women, and not women, men, answered that it was natural to ask from the one who could always give.

B: That reason has always appeared to me more ingenious than sound. Nature, indecently if you like, drives one sex indiscriminately towards the other; and in some conceivable condition of animal and primitive mankind, perhaps not existing anywhere....

A: Not even in Tahiti?

B: No...the gap which should separate man from woman would be crossed by the most amorous. If they wait and flee, pursue and escape, attack and defend, it is because the passion, unequal in its progress, does not operate in them with equal force. From which it follows that sensual pleasure develops, is consummated and is extinguished on the one side, while it has hardly begun to arise on the other, and both remain miserable because of this. That is a faithful picture of what would happen with two free and perfectly innocent young people. But when the woman has learnt, either by experience or education, the more or less cruel consequences of a delicious moment, her heart chills at the approach of the man. The man's heart does not shiver; his senses command him and he obeys. The woman's senses make themselves understood, but she fears to heed them. It is the man's role to make her forget her fears, to intoxicate her and to seduce her. The man keeps whole his natural urge towards the woman; the natural urge of the woman towards the man, a geometrician would say, was directly proportional to the intensity of her passion and inversely proportional to the magnitude of her fears; a ratio which is complicated by a myriad different elements in our society, which practically all conspire to increase the faint-heartedness of the one sex and the duration of the pursuit by the other. It is a kind of tactics in which the resources of the defence and the means of attack are about on a level. The resistance of the woman has been consecrated; the violence of the man is considered contemptible. Violence which would be only a trifling injury in Tahiti, becomes a crime in our cities.

A: But how has it happened that an act whose end is so solemn, and to which nature invites us by the most powerful attraction, that the noblest, most delicious and most innocent of pleasures should have become the most fruitful source of our depravities and our evils?

B: Orou explained it at least ten times to the almoner; now listen again and try to remember it. It is by the tyranny of man, who has converted the possession of a woman into the possession of a chattel;[7] by the manners and customs which have overloaded with stipulations the union of marriage; by civil laws which have subjected marriage to an infinity of formalities; by the very nature of our society, where the diversity of fortune and rank has instituted privileges and rules of what is and is not done; by a peculiar contradiction common to all existing societies, whereby the birth of a child, always regarded as an increase of wealth for the nation, more often and more certainly means an increase of poverty to the family; by the political opinions of sovereigns who relate everything to their own interest and security; by religious institutions which have applied the names vices and virtues to actions which were not susceptible to any morality.

How far we are from naturalness and happiness! The empire of nature cannot be destroyed; you may try to thwart it with obstacles, but it will prevail. Write as much as you please on the tablets of bronze—to use an expression of wise Marcus Aurelius—that the voluptuous movement of two bellies together is a crime, but the heart of man will only be torn between the menace of your proscription and the violence of his feelings. But the unruly heart will not cease to demand; and your terrifying inscription will disappear from our eyes a hundred times during the course of a lifetime. Chisel it in marble: Thou shalt not eat of ixion or of griffon; thou shalt know only thy wife; thou shalt not be a husband to thy sister. But you will not fail to increase the punishment in proportion to the oddity of your prohibitions; you will become ferocious, but you will never succeed in making me contrary to nature.

A: How short the law of nations would be, if it conformed exactly to the law of nature! How many errors and vices would man be spared!

B: Would you like to know the condensed history of almost all our miseries? Here it is. There existed a natural man; an artificial man was introduced within this

---

[7] I.e., to turn women into property.

man; and within this cavern a civil war breaks out, which lasts for life. Sometimes the natural man is stronger; sometimes he is felled by the artificial, moral man; and in both cases the miserable monster is plagued, tortured, tormented, stretched on the rack; ceaselessly lamenting, always wretched, whether a false enthusiasm of glory transports him and intoxicates him, or a false shame bows him and casts him down. Nevertheless there are extreme circumstances which bring man back to his original simplicity.

A: Want and sickness, two great exorcists.

B: You have named them. In reality, what becomes of all these conventional virtues then? In want, a man is remorseless; and in sickness a woman is without shame.

A: So I have observed.

B: But another phenomenon which will not have escaped you either, is that the return of the artificial and moral man follows step by step the progress from illness to convalescence, and from convalescence to a state of health. The moment when the bodily infirmity ceases is the one when the internal civil war begins again, and almost always to the disadvantage of the invader.

A: That's true. I have myself experienced in convalescence, that the natural man had deadly strength against the artificial and moral man. But now tell me, must we civilize man or abandon him to his instincts?

B: Must you have a precise answer?

A: Undoubtedly.

B: If you propose to be his tyrant, then civilize him, persecute him all you are able with a morality contrary to nature; fetter him in all ways; impede his actions with a thousand obstacles; frighten him with phantoms, make eternal the war in the cavern, and let the natural man be always shackled at the feet of the moral man. But do you want him to be happy and free? Then don't meddle with his affairs; plenty of unforeseen events will lead him towards understanding and to corruptness. And always remain convinced, that it is not for your sake but for theirs that these cunning law-givers have moulded you and made you unnatural like you are. I appeal to all political, civil, and religious institutions; examine them deeply; and I shall be greatly deceived, if you don't find the human race bowed century after century under the yoke which a handful of scoundrels resolved to put upon it. Beware of anyone who wants to order things. To regulate, is always to make oneself master of the others by hampering them; and the Calabrians[8] are almost the only ones on whom the flattery of legislators has not yet imposed.

A: Does this anarchy of the Calabrians please you?

B: I appeal to experience; and I wager that their barbarism is less vicious than our courtesy. How many trifling rascalities here counterbalance the atrociousness of a few great crimes about which so much is made. I look upon uncivilized men as a multitude of scattered and isolated springs. Doubtless if it happened that some of these springs collided, one or other of them would break. To obviate this difficulty, an individual of profound wisdom and sublime genius assembled these springs and made a mechanism of them. And in this mechanism called society, all the springs were set acting and reacting against one another, endlessly fatigued; and he broke more of them in a day under this state of control, than he would have broken in a year under the anarchy of nature. But what a smash! What devastation! What enormous destruction of the little springs when two, three, or four of these enormous machines clashed violently!

A: So you prefer the condition of brute and primitive nature?

---

[8]Inhabitants of the mountainous region in southeastern Italy.

B: I should not dare pronounce on it; but I know that many times the townsman has been known to leave all and go back to the forest; and that one has never seen the man of the forest clothe himself and establish himself in the town.

A: I have often thought that the sum of good and evil varied for each individual; but that the joy and pain of any species of animal had its limit which it could not exceed, and that perhaps our efforts gave us, in the last analysis, as many inconveniences as advantages; so that we have only tormented ourselves in increasing the two sides of an equation between which there existed an eternal and necessary equality. Nevertheless I do not doubt that the average life of the civilized man is not longer than the average life of a savage.

B: And if the time a machine lasts is not a true measure of its degree of wear, what would you conclude?

A: I see that on the whole, you would incline to believe men the more wicked and unhappy the more they are civilized.

B: I shall not review all the countries of the earth; but I will warn you that you will only find the condition of man a happy one in Tahiti, and supportable in one corner of Europe. There suspicious masters, jealous of their security, are occupied in keeping him in what you call brutishness.

A: In Venice, perhaps?

B: Why not? You will not deny, at least, that nowhere is there less acquired understanding, less artificial morality, and fewer chimerical vices and virtues.

A: I wasn't expecting such praise of that government.

B: And I'm not giving it. I am showing you a kind of compensation for slavery, that every traveller has felt and commended.

A: A poor compensation!

B: Perhaps. The Greeks proscribed the man who added a string to the lyre of Mercury.[9]

A: And that prohibition is a bloody satire on their first law-givers. It is the first string that must be cut.

B: You understand me. Wherever there is a lyre there are strings. So long as the natural appetites are adulterated, count on evil women.

A: Like La Reymer.

B: Or horrible men.

A: Like Gardeil.

B: And on people ill-fated for no reason at all.

A: Like Tanié, Mademoiselle de la Chaux, the Chevalier Desroches and Madame de la Carlière.[10] It's certain one would seek in vain in Tahiti for examples of depravity like the first two, and of misery like the last three. What shall we do then? Shall we return to nature, or submit to the laws?

B: We must speak against insane laws until they are reformed; while waiting, we must submit to them. Anyone who infringes a bad law by his own private authority authorizes all others to infringe the good ones. There is less inconvenience in being mad among madmen, than in being wise alone. Let us tell ourselves, let us cry out unceasingly, that shame, punishment and dishonour have been attached to actions innocent in themselves; but let us not commit these actions, because shame, punishment and dishonour are the greatest of all evils. Let us copy the good almoner, a monk in France, a primitive man in Tahiti.

---

[9]Roman god of merchants, associated with Hermes, the Greek messenger god who invented the lyre from a tortoise shell, using sheep gut for strings.

[10]These are characters from two of Diderot's shorter works, *This Is Not a Story* and *On the Inconsistency of Public Judgment on Private Behavior*.

A: Take the dress of the country one's going to, and keep that of the country where one is.

B: And above all be scrupulously honest and sincere with those fragile beings who cannot delight us without renouncing the most precious advantages of our society.... And now, what's become of that thick fog?

A: It has disappeared.

B: And shall we be free again, after dinner, to go out or remain here?

A: That will depend, I think, rather more on the ladies than on us.

B: Always these women! One can't take a step without meeting them somewhere.

A: What if we should read the discussion between the almoner and Orou to them?

B: What do you think they would say about it?

A: I know nothing about that.

B: And what would they think about it?

A: Perhaps the opposite of what they would say.

GOTTHOLD EPHRAIM LESSING
[1729–1781]

Each of the great ages of Western civilization can be associated with a city, a place where the ideals and impulses of the age are most fully articulated. We associate the classical ideal, for example, with Athens, the medieval world with Rome, the Renaissance, perhaps, with Florence. The Enlightenment was centered in Paris, for that city, with its rational city planning, its wide boulevards and classical buildings, became the site where Diderot and his fellow *philosophes* planned their comprehensive *Encyclopedia*, where political philosophers dreamed of rational utopias, and where André le Notre designed the geometry of the Versailles gardens.

France in the seventeenth and eighteenth centuries was centered, but Germany was scattered. The Holy Roman Empire had left Germany fragmented into 300 separate states, governed by competing petty rulers. Some attempted to rise above the general mediocrity and made pretensions to enlightenment. Frederick the Great of Prussia, for example, invited Voltaire and other intellectuals to his court, and Voltaire told Frederick that Berlin, the capital of Prussia, would be "the Athens of Germany, perhaps of Europe." But privately Voltaire said that Berlin was more like Sparta than Athens.

The political fragmentation that left Germany "unenlightened" was compounded by a zealous and oppressive Lutheranism. Although Luther had sought to free Christians from the power of the Catholic hierarchy, his insistence on the authority of scripture and commitment to salvation by faith (not reason) alone became articles of oppressive dogmatism. Many German Lutherans, absolutely convinced of the rightness of their doctrines, were intolerant toward divergent religious opinions and were particularly hostile to the rational Deism of the *philosophes*. Facing such formidable political and religious obstacles, the German Enlightenment, or *Aufklärung*, was slow in arriving. It was almost a century after Bacon and Descartes that Gottfried Wilhelm Leibniz, the father of the German Enlightenment, and Gotthold Ephraim Lessing, its central literary figure, sought distinctively German models for enlightenment. In his criticism, his philosophical and theological writings, and, especially, in his plays, Lessing challenged the French influence in German literature and culture. In doing so, he prepared the way for the Golden Age of German literature in the generation that followed.

LIFE

He was born in 1729, the son of a Lutheran minister in Saxony. Lessing's career as a critic, journalist, theater manager, and playwright broke his local ties with Saxony and took him to Leipzig, Berlin, Wittenberg, Hamburg, and Vienna as he developed an ideal of German drama and culture that transcended the petty differences between the separate states. Similarly, his religious progress from orthodox Lutheranism, to Deism, and, finally, to his own religious philosophy, embodied the German Enlightenment's ideal of broad religious tolerance.

A bookish youth, Lessing entered Leipzig University in 1746, ostensibly to study theology. But he soon became more interested in drama and wrote a series of comedies for theaters in the town, a course of action disapproved of by his father, who pulled him out of the university and brought him home for a period of reflection and reformation. When Lessing returned to Leipzig, this time to study medicine, he once again became entangled in the theater. He went on to Berlin where he became a successful journalist, literary critic, translator, and playwright. One of his plays from this period, *The Jews* (1749), a defense of Jews against the religious bigotry of the time, looked forward in some of its themes and characters to *Nathan the Wise*.

Although he returned to the study of medicine in 1751 at the University of Wittenberg, receiving a degree in 1752, literature, not medicine, remained his abiding professional interest. Back in Berlin in 1755, he issued a six-volume collection of his works, including epigrams, comedies, and, most significantly, the first German domestic tragedy, *Miss Sara Sampson,* a work that begins the history of modern German drama. In the play, Lessing chose not to model his work on the French tragedians Corneille and Racine, thereby liberating the German drama from its slavish dependency on France. He chose instead the inspiration of the British theater, especially a work by George Lillo, *The London Merchant.* In 1758, he went a step further, going to German folklore for his sources in a dramatic sketch, *Dr. Faust,* a manuscript that has since been lost. The German drama, Lessing thought, could not find appropriate models in the refined formalism of the French theater. Shakespeare, with his truth to nature and reality, was a much more appropriate mentor. In the great plays from his later years, *Minna from Barnhelm* (1767), *Emilia Galotti* (1772), and *Nathan the Wise* (1779), Lessing established a modern German theater freed from imitation of the French and expressing the world view of the German Enlightenment.

WORK

In *Minna from Barnhelm,* Lessing spoke for a broader German identity by turning the petty political divisions and the deference to French culture into the stuff of comedy. A romance between a Prussian officer and a woman from Saxony is thwarted by political suspicion and intrigue. At a crucial moment in the play, the misunderstandings between the divided Germans are overshadowed by the foppish fawning of a French officer. As they counter the transparent scheming of the Frenchman, the Saxons and the Prussians resolve their differences so that the marriage can take place. On the stage at least, the unity of the comic resolution could transform political pettiness and cultural sycophancy.

In his religious views, Lessing also sought to reconcile differences. While Voltaire and the French *philosophes* adopted an anticlerical stance and attacked oppressive and hypocritical religious institutions, especially the Roman Catholic Church, Lessing, writing in the context of dogmatic German Lutheranism, criticized the intolerance of sects that considered themselves the only true religion. He saw Christianity as an expression of a stage in humankind's evolving spiritual quest. Belief in a dogmatic revealed religion, Lessing thought, would be replaced by a rational spirituality that saw all religions as simply different manifestations of a spiritual impulse common to all people. He considered the Bible a historical document, the Old and New Testaments revealing developing stages in humankind's religious growth. With enlightenment, humankind would no longer be dependent on revelation or on scripture, for the rational person who understood the spirit of religion would know that religion finally is not a matter of outward forms, of institutional ceremonies, or of conformity to scriptural injunctions. In the final analysis, religion is an expression of the inner experience of each individual; it is a matter of the heart.

After he had been forbidden to publish theological essays in which he argued his position, Lessing set out in *Nathan the Wise* to explain his religious views in drama. The first German play in blank verse—another of Lessing's attempts to link the German drama to Shakespeare and the English drama rather than to French sources—the play centers in a parable, the story of the three rings borrowed from Boccaccio's *Decameron*. Lessing modified the story to fit his purposes, but its crucial issue remains the same: Which of three indistinguishable rings representing the three major religions—Judaism, Christianity, and Islam—is the true one? In the play, the parable is told by Nathan, a Jewish merchant in Jerusalem at the time of the Third Crusade in 1192. Saladin, the enlightened Moslem ruler of the city, asks Nathan which of the three religions is the true one, hoping to trap the rich merchant in an answer that will justify confiscating his money to support the government. But Nathan proves his wisdom by responding with the parable, and Saladin is so impressed with Nathan's answer that he gives up his scheme to trick him. The play that surrounds the parable tells the story of a Christian Templar and the Jewish stepdaughter of Nathan who, though drawn to each other, are put off by their religious differences. By the end of the play, they learn that they are really brother and sister, the children of Saladin's brother, a Christian convert. So they are Christian, Moslem, and Jew, but more than that, they are all members of one family; their religious differences pale in significance to their family ties.

Although earlier versions of the parable show the Christian ring to be the true one or suggest that a test will distinguish one ring as authentic, Lessing alters the story and provides no such tests to prove one ring more authentic than the others. Indeed, his point is that there is no one true ring. Each of the rings is true to one who believes in it. Lessing goes a step further to suggest that the truth of any one of the rings will not be established by proving the other rings false, but rather by the faithfulness, goodness, and tolerance of the person who believes in it.

In its message that narrow religious bigotry must be overcome and that all religions are expressions of a common human spirituality, *Nathan the Wise* is a document of the Enlightenment. In reconciling differences and stressing unifying factors, it is particularly German in its enlightenment. In seeing religion as an expression of the individual's inner spirituality and defining it as a matter of the heart, however, the play looks forward to romanticism and to the age of Goethe and Schiller that was soon to follow.

SUGGESTED READINGS

F. Andrew Brown in *Gotthold Ephraim Lessing* (1971) provides a useful introduction to Lessing and his career. Edmund Fuller's *The Pageant of the Theatre* (1965) discusses Lessing's dramas. Two interesting commentaries on the ring parable appear in Henry E. Allison's *Lessing and the Enlightenment* (1966) and F. W. Kaufman's "Nathan's Crisis," *Monatshafte* 48 (1956): 277–80.

FROM *NATHAN THE WISE*

The Parable of the Rings

Translated by Bayard Quincy Morgan

SALADIN:
  Come nearer, Jew!—Still nearer!—Close to me!—
  And have no fear!
NATHAN:
                        That's for your foe to feel!
SALADIN:
  You say you're Nathan?
NATHAN:
                                    Yes.
SALADIN:
                                    Wise Nathan?
NATHAN:
                                    No.
SALADIN:
  If you don't say it, yet the people do.
NATHAN:
  May be; the people!
SALADIN:
                        Yet you don't suppose
  That I am scornful of the people's voice?—
  I long have had a wish to know the man
  Whom they call wise.
NATHAN:
                        And if it were in scorn
  They called him so? If to the people "wise"
  Were nothing more than "shrewd"? and shrewd were he   10
  Who knew his interest well?
SALADIN:
                        Of course you mean
  His genuine interest?
NATHAN:
                        Why then indeed
  Most selfish were most shrewd. And shrewd and wise
  Were one.
SALADIN:
                        I hear you prove what you'd deny.—
  Mankind's true interests, to the folk unknown,
  Are known to you; at least you've tried to know them;
  You've pondered them; and that alone produces
  The wise man.
NATHAN:
                        As each thinker thinks he is.
SALADIN:
  Enough of modesty! For when one longs
  To hear dry reason, constant modesty   20

Is sickening. [*He jumps up.*] Let's come to business, Jew.
But with sincerity!
NATHAN:
                              Your Highness, I
Will surely serve you so that I shall seem
Well worth your custom.
SALADIN:
                              Serve me? what?
NATHAN:
                                        You shall
Obtain the best in all things; have it, too,
At lowest rates.
SALADIN:
                    What do you mean? I hope
It's not your wares?—I'll let my sister haggle
And bargain with you. [*Aside.*] That's for listening ears!
[*Aloud.*] With you as merchant I have no concern.
NATHAN:
Then doubtless you will wish to know what I   30
Have met or noted on my way about
The foe, who is indeed astir again? If I
May plainly speak . . .
SALADIN:
                    That too is not the goal
I'm steering for with you. Of that I know
All that I need.—In short . . .
NATHAN:
                              Command me, Sultan.
SALADIN:
I seek instruction from you now in quite
A different field.—Since you're accounted wise:
Then tell me, pray—what faith, or moral law,
Has most appeal for you?
NATHAN:
                              Your Highness knows
I am a Jew.   40
SALADIN:
          And I a Mussulman.
The Christian stands between us.—Of these three
Religions only one can be the true one.—
A man like you does not remain where chance
Of birth has cast him: if he so remains,
It's out of insight, reasons, better choice.
Well, then! such insight I would share with you.
Let me the reasons know, which I have had
No time to ponder out. Reveal to me
The choice determined by these reasons plain—
Of course in confidence—that I as well   50
May make your choice my own.—This startles you?
You weigh me with your eye?—It may well be
No other Sultan has had such caprice;

Although I think it not unworthy quite
Of any Sultan.—Am I right?—Then speak!—
Speak out!—Or would you have a moment's time
To think it over? Good; I'll grant you that.—
[*Aside.*] Has she been listening? I will go and see;
I'll ask if she approves of me. [*Aloud.*] Reflect!
Reflect, make haste! For I shall soon return.   60
     [*He goes into the ante-room into which* SITTAH *withdrew.*]

· · ·

NATHAN:

   H'm! h'm!—how strange!—I'm all confused.—What would
The Sultan have of me?—I thought of money;
And he wants—truth. Yes, truth! And wants it so—
So bare and blank—as if the truth were coin!—
And were it coin, which anciently was weighed!—
That might be done! But coin from modern mints,
Which but the stamp creates, which you but count
Upon the counter—truth is not like that!
As one puts money in his purse, just so
One puts truth in his head? Which here is Jew?   10
Which, I or he?—But stay!—Suppose in truth
He did not ask for truth!—I must admit,
Suspicion that he used the truth as trap
Would be too small by far.—Too small?—What is
Too small for one so great?—That's right, that's right:
He rushed into the house incontinent!
One knocks, one listens, surely, when one comes
As friend.—I must tread warily!—But how?—
To be a Jew outright won't do at all.—
But not to be a Jew will do still less.   20
For if no Jew, he might well ask, then why
Not Mussulman?—That's it! And that can save me!
Not only children can be quieted
With fables.—See, he comes. Well, let him come!

· · ·

SALADIN [*returning, aside*]:

   There, now the coast is clear!—[*Aloud.*] I hope I come
Not prematurely?—You are at an end
With your deliberations.—Well then, speak!
No soul will hear us.

NATHAN:

               Let the whole world listen.

SALADIN:

   So sure is Nathan of his case? Now there
Is wisdom! Not to hide the truth! To stake
One's all upon it! Life and limb! One's goods
And blood!

NATHAN:
> Yes, when it's needful and of use.

SALADIN:
> Henceforth I may expect to hold by rights
> One of my names, Reformer of the world
> And of the law.

NATHAN:
> Indeed, a handsome title!
> But, Sultan, ere I draw the final veil,
> Allow me, please, to tell an ancient story.

SALADIN:
> Why not? I always was a friend of tales
> Well told.

NATHAN:
> To tell them *well* is not, I fear,
> My forte.

SALADIN:
> Proud modesty again?—Tell on!

NATHAN:
> In days of yore, there dwelt in eastern lands
> A man who had a ring of priceless worth
> Received from hands beloved. The stone it held,
> An opal, shed a hundred colors fair,
> And had the magic power that he who wore it,
> Trusting its strength, was loved of God and men.
> No wonder therefore that this eastern man
> Would never cease to wear it; and took pains
> To keep it in his household for all time.
> He left the ring to that one of his sons
> He loved the best; providing that in turn
> That son bequeath to his most favorite son
> The ring; and thus, regardless of his birth,
> The dearest son, by virtue of the ring,
> Should be the head, the prince of all his house.—
> You follow, Sultan.

SALADIN:
> Perfectly. Continue!

NATHAN:
> At last this ring, passed on from son to son,
> Descended to a father of three sons;
> All three of whom were duly dutiful,
> All three of whom in consequence he needs
> Must love alike. But yet from time to time,
> Now this, now that one, now the third—as each
> Might be with him alone, the other two
> Not sharing then his overflowing heart—
> Seemed worthiest of the ring; and so to each
> He promised it, in pious frailty.
> This lasted while it might.—Then came the time
> For dying, and the loving father finds
> Himself embarrassed. It's a grief to him
> To wound two of his sons, who have relied

10

20

30

40

Upon his word.—What's to be done?—He sends
In secret to a jeweler, of whom
He orders two more rings, in pattern like
His own, and bids him spare nor cost nor toil   50
To make them in all points identical.
The jeweler succeeds. And when he brings
The rings to him, the sire himself cannot
Distinguish them from the original.
In glee and joy he calls his sons to him,
Each by himself, confers on him his blessing—
His ring as well—and dies.—You hear me, Sultan?

SALADIN [*who, taken aback, has turned away*]:
I hear, I hear you!—Finish now your fable
Without delay.—I'm waiting!

NATHAN:

I am done.
For what ensues is wholly obvious.—   60
Scarce is the father dead when all three sons
Appear, each with his ring, and each would be
The reigning prince. They seek the facts, they quarrel,
Accuse. In vain; the genuine ring was not
Demonstrable; [*he pauses for a reply*] almost as little as
Today the genuine faith.

SALADIN:

You mean this as
The answer to my question?...

NATHAN:

What I mean
Is merely an excuse, if I decline
Precisely to distinguish those three rings
Which with intent the father ordered made   70
That sharpest eyes might not distinguish them.

SALADIN:
The rings!—Don't trifle with me!—I should think
That those religions which I named to you
Might be distinguished readily enough.
Down to their clothing; down to food and drink!

NATHAN:
In all respects except their basic grounds.—
Are they not grounded all in history,
Or writ or handed down?—But history
Must be accepted wholly upon faith—
Not so?—Well then, whose faith are we least like   80
To doubt? Our people's, surely? Those whose blood
We share? the ones who from our childhood gave
Us proofs of love? who never duped us, but
When it was for our good to be deceived?—
How can I trust my fathers less than you
Trust yours? Or turn about.—Can I demand
That to your forebears you should give the lie
That mine be not gainsaid? Or turn about.

The same holds true of Christians. Am I right?—

SALADIN [*aside*]:

    By Allah, yes! The man is right. I must

    Be still.

NATHAN:

          Let's come back to our rings once more.

    As we have said: the sons preferred complaint;

    And each swore to the judge, he had received

    The ring directly from his father's hand.—

    As was the truth!—And long before had had

    His father's promise, one day to enjoy

    The privilege of the ring.—No less than truth!—

    His father, each asserted, could not have

    Been false to him; and sooner than suspect

    This thing of him, of such a loving father:

    He must accuse his brothers—howsoever

    Inclined in other things to think the best

    Of them—of some false play; and he the traitors

    Would promptly ferret out; would take revenge.

SALADIN:

    And then, the judge?—I am all ears to hear

    What you will have the judge decide. Speak on!

NATHAN:

    Thus said the judge: unless you swiftly bring

    Your father here to me, I'll bid you leave

    My judgment seat. Think you that I am here

    For solving riddles? Would you wait, perhaps,

    Until the genuine ring should rise and speak?—

    But stop! I hear the genuine ring enjoys

    The magic power to make its wearer loved,

    Beloved of God and men. That must decide!

    For spurious rings can surely not do that!—

    Whom then do two of you love most? Quick, speak!

    You're mute? The rings' effect is only backward,

    Not outward? Each one loves himself the most?—

    O then you are, all three, deceived deceivers!

    Your rings are false, all three. The genuine ring

    No doubt got lost. To hide the grievous loss,

    To make it good, the father caused three rings

    To serve for one.

SALADIN:

          O splendid, splendid!

NATHAN:

                So,

    The judge went on, if you'll not have my counsel,

    Instead of verdict, go! My counsel is:

    Accept the matter wholly as it stands.

    If each one from his father has his ring,

    Then let each one believe his ring to be

    The true one.—Possibly the father wished

    To tolerate no longer in his house

The tyranny of just one ring!—And know:
That you, all three, he loved; and loved alike;
Since two of you he'd not humiliate
To favor one.—Well then! Let each aspire
To emulate his father's unbeguiled,
Unprejudiced affection! Let each strive
To match the rest in bringing to the fore
The magic of the opal in his ring!
Assist that power with all humility,
With benefaction, hearty peacefulness,   140
And with profound submission to God's will!
And when the magic powers of the stones
Reveal themselves in children's children's children:
I bid you, in a thousand thousand years,
To stand again before this seat. For then
A wiser man than I will sit as judge
Upon this bench, and speak. Depart!—So said
The modest judge.

SALADIN:
                    God! God!

NATHAN:
                              Now, Saladin,
If you would claim to be that wiser man,
The promised one...   150

SALADIN [*rushing to him and seizing his hand, which he retains*]:
I, dust? I, nothing? God!

NATHAN:
What is the matter, Saladin?

SALADIN:
                    Dear Nathan!—
The thousand thousand years your judge assigned
Are not yet up.—His judgment seat is not
For me.—Go!—Go!—But be my friend.

THE WORLD CONTEXT

MATSUO BASHŌ
[1644–1694]

In the last months of his life, Matsuo Bashō handed a poem to one of his numerous students:

> Do not copy me—
> do not be like a cantaloupe
> cut into halves.

This advice was not easy to follow. Although Bashō did not invent the short poetic form known today as the haiku, his poems had mastered the form by broadening its emotional and thematic possibilities; in effect, Bashō became the standard by which all later haiku were measured. Among students and adults, haiku are very popular around the world; dozens of magazines and contests are devoted each year to its practitioners. To serious admirers, however, Bashō is much more than an expert poet; long after his death, he remains a sage or religious teacher.

Published eight years after his death, Bashō's most famous work, *Oku no Hosomichu* (*Narrow Road through the Provinces*) could be classified as travel literature, but it is totally different from the travels of Candide, Lemuel Gulliver, or Benjamin Franklin. Bashō's journey is best characterized as a pilgrimage to natural and artificial shrines, where he experiences the connections or relationships between places, their histories, previous visitors, friends, and himself. Bashō uses brief poems and carefully written prose to capture intimate, intense moments of coalescence, the times when his life and the place being visited come together. These passages are like a series of photographs in which the camera is pointed both outward and inward, bringing the two dimensions together—the poet in the place.

These moments are not peculiar to Japanese writers or to Asia in general; today we use the metaphor of "mountaintop" or "peak" experiences to describe them because they often literally occur on mountaintops, for westerners as well as for Bashō. This kind of experience, however, was not the standard material of the Enlightenment writers included in this anthology, although writers concerned with these experiences existed in the West, using different poetic forms, especially during the romantic period of the nineteenth century. Whereas Voltaire, Swift, and Franklin were public figures using their ideas and writings to effect social and political changes, Bashō led a simple, almost monastic life. Often withdrawn from society and available only to a few disciples and other poets, he earned the title "saint of haiku."

In *Narrow Road through the Provinces*, Bashō shows his mastery of two literary traditions, the poetic diary and *haikai*. Dating from the eighth or ninth century in Japan was a tradition of using the diary or journal not only for recording events, but as an artistic form, shaped by an aesthetic purpose, and regularly containing poetry as well as prose. The tradition of *haikai* or "linked verse" involved alternating short, pithy three-line poems with two-line poems to form an extended sequence of poems. A review of these terms might be helpful.

Strictly speaking, *haikai* is the name given to the sequence of alternating poems mentioned above and usually written by two or more poets. Imagine three poets sitting cross-legged together. The poet Boncho begins with a three-line poem, formally called a *hokku* in Bashō's day:

> in town
> the smells of things
> summer moon

Bashō responds:

> it's hot it's hot
> at each portal the sigh

Kyorai responds:

> not twice weeded
> and already the rice
> is earing
> —Translated by Maeda Cana

Thirty-three stanzas later, the *haikai* anthology was ended and was called "Summer Moon." The skill of each poet is shown in the way in which his stanza responds or is "linked" to the previous stanza. The stanzas are linked together not by a common plot or theme running throughout the collection, but by word play, innuendo, emotion, atmosphere, and contrast.

Haikai had its source in a similar form called *renga*, which was developed in the thirteenth century and was characterized by seriousness and elegance, with one hundred or more stanzas. *Haikai*—with *hai* meaning "play" and *kai* meaning "friendly exchange of words"—was developed in the sixteenth century and represented a liberated *renga* using popular, even vulgar, topics, and often containing fewer than one hundred stanzas. Under Bashō's influence, *haikai* found a middle ground between elegance and vulgarity, a truthful and beautiful reconciliation of the poet with the reality of the moment.

LIFE

Born in the province of Iga in 1644 with the name Matsuo Munefusa, Bashō was the son of a minor samurai serving the Todo family. Bashō studied linked verse with Yoshitada, the heir of the Todo dynasty, who wrote under the pen name of Sengin. When Yoshitada died, Bashō turned from the life of a samurai to poetry. He moved to Kyoto, where he studied poetry and apparently had a mistress named Juteini. His first volume of poetry, *Kai Oi (The Seashell Game)*, was completed in his hometown of Ueno City and published in 1671. In 1672, he moved to Edo (Tokyo), which was a young, thriving city. Changing his pen name from Sobo to Tosei, Bashō became associated with Soin, a master poet, who taught him the importance of writing about ordinary life.

Bashō's work began to appear in numerous anthologies, and disciples gathered around him. In 1680 they built him a house and presented him with a young Japanese banana tree, *bashō*, which provided a name for his house, and eventually a new pen name. According to tradition, Bashō gained recognition with this haiku written shortly after settling in his new home:

> *kare eda ni*
> *karasu no tomarikeri*
> *aki no kure*

> On a withered branch
> a crow has settled—
> autumn nightfall.
> –TRANSLATED BY HAROLD G. HENDERSON

Before Bashō's work, this poetic form had become stiff and formalized, encumbered with rules. He opened up new possibilities with his homely images and the easy movement from object to season. Bashō advised his followers: "Do not seek to follow in the footsteps of the men of old; seek what they sought."

With the priest Buccho, Bashō studied Zen Buddhism, which has its roots in Taoism as well as traditional Buddhism, and his perception of the world began to change. Nobuyuki Yuasa, a fine translator, calls attention to Bashō's description of his new awareness: "What is important is to keep our mind high in the world of true understanding, and returning to the world of our daily experience to seek therein the truth of beauty. No matter what we may be doing at a given moment, we must not forget that it has a bearing upon our everlasting self which is poetry."

In 1684, Bashō went on his first major journey to a region southwest of Edo; the account of it, which combined both prose and poetry, was published as *The Record of a Weather-Exposed Skeleton*. After his return to Edo, his work appeared in several important anthologies, including *Frog Contest,* which contains Bashō's most famous poem.

> *Furu ike ya*
> *Kawazu tobikomu*
> *Mizu no oto*

> The ancient pond
> A frog jumps in—
> Sound of water.

Although a technical definition of haiku stipulates a three-line stanza with alternating 5,7,5 syllables in the lines, it is not always possible to translate Japanese into English and retain the syllable count. Donald Keene's translation above has fewer syllables in English, but Nobuyuki Yuasa's version below contains several more:

> Breaking the silence
> Of an ancient pond,
> A frog jumped into water—
> A deep resonance.

The latter version is more explanatory, making accommodations for a Western reader who is perhaps unfamiliar with the lean flashes of reality in haiku. The original poem itself is a model haiku; the first line sets the scene in nature, and the last two lines suggest an instant insight or new perspective. On a first reading, the poet seems to be describing an objective scene with a simple literal meaning: One can imagine sitting by a pond in absolute quiet and then hearing the sound of a frog plopping into the water as it dives, and perhaps seeing the ripples resonate outward in broad, ever-widening circles. But without stretching the situation at all, one can also easily make the connection between the image of a pond and the poet's consciousness, and a moment when the sound of the frog hitting the water resonates within the psyche, bringing a rich and total focus to the poet's attention, connecting the internal reality with the external scene. No philosophy, no psychology, just a brief window into a connecting moment.

Bashō's second major journey, in 1688, which followed the same route as his first journey, resulted in two works, *The Records of a Travel-Worn Satchel* and *A Visit to Sarashina Village*. Through experience, Bashō was learning how to balance prose with poetry; his message was becoming clearer, as witnessed by a passage in *The Records of a Travel-Worn Satchel:* "All who have achieved real excellence in any art, possess one thing in common, that is, a mind to obey nature, to be one with nature, throughout the four seasons of the year. Whatever such a mind sees is a flower, and whatever such a mind dreams of is the moon."

In *The Narrow Road through the Provinces*, Bashō records his third major journey, which was begun in the spring of 1689 and lasted more than two years. Before leaving Edo at the age of forty-five, he sold his house, suggesting that he did not expect to return. More than the previous two journeys, this one represented a culminating pilgrimage and his mature vision of the meaning of life. Back once again in Edo, he spent four years writing and revising the work. At the age of fifty he began his final journey in the spring of 1694, setting out for the south of Japan. En route, he got sick and died that same year. *The Narrow Road through the Provinces* was first published in 1702.

WORK

In a mixture of biography and fiction, prose and poetry, *The Narrow Road through the Provinces* describes visits to temples, historical shrines, poet friends, and intensely beautiful vistas. Bashō passes through gates, climbs mountains, and looks at the moon. But he is not simply a tourist on a sightseeing trip with his pen as a camera. He is on a religious pilgrimage that is best described in Zen Buddhist terms. He is not looking for Christian salvation, but a series of moments in consciousness where he perfectly blends with the scene at hand in what might almost be called a "mystical identification" with the outside world, the flow of reality.

At the outset of the pilgrimage, Bashō is nervous, filled with anxiety. Careful preparations have to be made. Travel was difficult at that time, even dangerous, and his goal was a relatively unexplored portion of Japan—a fine symbol of those deep areas of consciousness that he expects to open up and engage. Each passage through a barrier gate represents another stage in Bashō's quest. The experience of the first, the Shirakawa Barrier, is captured by Bashō's travel companion, Sora, who describes the change of clothes that was part of the rite of passage through the gate.

Bashō does not simply wish to record his visits to shrines in his writings, but to use his writing as a means of making a deep connection with a place and a moment. Many of the famous shrines on his itinerary, like the Islands of Matsushima, have been celebrated in other literary works, but it is characteristic of Bashō's poems that in such sacred sites he often makes a direct connection with ordinary reality using ordinary, everyday subjects.

> Autumn is cool now—
> Let us peel a feast with both hands,
> Melon and eggplant.
> —TRANSLATED BY EARL MINER

Our English language seems to fail us when we speak of these matters, especially when we use words such as "mystical identification" or "mystical union" to describe Bashō's connection with the places he visits. The shrines themselves are typically places of extraordinary beauty or where some important historical event took place; they are places visited by other poets and recreated in poems. The shrines therefore are layered with meanings, in the same way that, for Roman Catholics, Lourdes in France is the sacred site of a Marian vision, a pilgrimage site, a tourist spot, and a place of healing. There is a difference, however; with Lourdes there is an underlying reference to a transcendent reality, to Mary or God. But with Bashō's shrines, the radiance is immanent rather than transcendent. It is a question of being open to the particular beauty of a place and connecting with or participating in it.

It is typical of Bashō that a simple or seemingly insignificant thing becomes the lightning rod for a Zen experience. At the Tada Shrine, a samurai's helmet evokes several meanings of loss associated with past dynasties and wars. But the ultimate and final loss—death itself—is accentuated by the chirp of a cricket inside the helmet, suggesting the living person who once wore the helmet but now is dead.

> What a loss is here:
> Beneath the warrior's splendid helmet
> A chirping cricket.

If Bashō can capture this moment of connection in a brief poem, then it is possible that his reader may have a similar experience reading the poem. The poem then does not appeal to the intellect; it does not explain in logical terms how the world is connected. Rather the poem speaks to the intuition or the imagination, which can immediately grasp the moment of connection. An appropriate response then to this kind of poem is an "Ahhhhh" or a sigh or "I see!" or "I get it!"

Bashō is particularly famous for invoking a quality called *sabi* to link his verses; *sabi* is an atmosphere of sadness and loneliness from the past that colors the present, as in the following poem:

> I heard the unblown flute
> In the deep summer shadows
> Of the Temple of Suma.
> —TRANSLATED BY R. H. BLYTH

Often for pilgrims it was not simply a question of visiting a shrine, but visiting it at the right time of year or during a full moon. Toward the end of his journey, Bashō passes through the Uguisu Barrier, crosses a mountain pass, and arrives at an inn whose host advises him to take advantage of the moonlight at the Myōjin shrine at Kei. Bashō prepares the reader for the shrine in prose: "The shrine had an aura of divinity, and down upon it poured the moonlight between the trees onto the white sand, making it look as if a thick frost had spread over all." In the past, an abbot started a tradition of carrying sand into the shrine area for the comfort of worshipers; Bashō's haiku makes this connection.

> Divinely pure,
> The moonlight sparkles on the sand
> Borne by the Archabbot.

The light of the moon reflecting on the sand is analogous to the poet's imagination or consciousness fully participating in the sacredness of that shrine, a kind of climax for Bashō's journey.

Bashō has had a continuing influence in Japan. Early in the twentieth century, when Japanese writers admired Western romantic poets such as Wordsworth, Byron, Goethe, and Hoffmann, they considered Bashō to be a Japanese romantic. When French symbolist poets such as Baudelaire, Mallarmé, and Verlaine became the vogue in Japan, Bashō also was made a symbolist, with his deep appreciation for the connection of all things. Bashō and the haiku were largely discovered at the turn of the century by westerners. The short, lean poem particularly appealed to British and American imagist poets such as Ezra Pound, Amy Lowell, Richard Aldington, H.D., and William Carlos Williams. Today the haiku is well-known throughout the United States and Europe.

SUGGESTED READINGS

Full-length studies, including biographies, are provided by Kenkichi Yamamoto's *Bashō* (1957) and Makoto Ueda's *Matsuo Bashō* (1970). Historical context is provided by Donald Keene's *Anthology of Japanese Literature* (1955), Earl Miner's *Japanese Linked Poetry: An Account with Translations of Renga and Haikai Sequences* (1979), D. T. Suzuki's *Zen and Japanese Culture* (especially ch. 7, "Zen and Haiku"), and Harold G. Henderson's *An Introduction to Haiku* (1958). A succinct introduction to *haikai* is included in Maeda Cana's translation of Bashō's *Monkey's Raincoat* (1973). Nobuyuki Yuasa has a good translation and helpful introduction in *The Narrow Road to the Deep North and Other Travel Sketches* (1966). A comparison between Eastern and Western literature can be found in R. H. Blyth's *Zen in English Literature and Oriental Classics* (1960).

The Narrow Road
through the Provinces

Translated by Earl Miner

The months and days are the wayfarers of the centuries,[1] and as yet another year comes round, it, too, turns traveler. Sailors whose lives float away as they labor on boats, horsemen who encounter old age as they draw the horse around once more by the bit, they also spend their days in travel and make their home in wayfaring.

---

[1]Echoing the Preface of *Ch'un yeh yen t'ao li tu*, by Li Po (701–762). [All notes for this selection are translator's notes.]

Over the centuries many famous men have met death on the way; and I, too, though I do not know what year it began, have long yielded to the wind like a loosened cloud and, unable to give up my wandering desires, have taken my way along the coast. Last autumn,[2] as I cleaned the old cobwebs from my dilapidated house by the riverside,[3] I found that the year had suddenly drawn to its close. As the sky of the new year filled with the haze of spring, I thought of going beyond the Shirakawa Barrier,[4] and so possessed was I by some peripatetic urge that I thought I had an invitation from the god of travelers himself and so became unable to settle down to anything. I mended my underpants, re-corded my rain hat, and took three bits of moxa cautery. I could not put from my mind how lovely the moon must be at Matsushima. I disposed of my property and moved to Sampū's villa.[5]

> My old grasshut,
> Lived in now by another generation,
> Is decked out with dolls.

This and the rest of the first eight stanzas of a *haikai*[6] I left posted on a pillar of my cottage.

The twenty-seventh of the Third Month, the sky at dawn was hazed over, and observing the pale soft light of the moon as it faded from the sky,[7] I looked beyond to where the peak of Mount Fuji rose dimly in the sky, and then nearer at hand from Ueno to Yanaka, wondering when I would again see these cherry blossoms. I felt a heaviness of heart. Everyone with whom I was on close terms assembled the night before I was to leave and saw me off on the boat. As I was landing at a place called Senju, my heart was burdened by the thought of the many miles stretching ahead, and my tears fell over such a parting on the illusory path of this world.

> With spring leaving,
> The birds cry out regret, the fish
> Have tears in their eyes.

That poem marked the beginning of the pilgrimage, but it was difficult to set forth. There were all my friends gathered to see me off and apparently prepared to stand there till they saw the last of my back vanish down the road.

This year, that is to say 1689, the thought suddenly entered my head to go on an aimless wandering through distant provinces. I knew that the sufferings of travel are said to bring a fall of frost to one's head, like snow from a Chinese sky; still, there were places I had heard of but had not yet seen. To live long enough to arrive back home was a happiness I could not rely upon. With thoughts of such kinds occupying my mind, I found that at last I had made my way to the post station of Sōka. The pack of things on my bony, thin shoulders was giving me pain. Setting out with nothing but what I could bear myself, I carried a stout paper raincoat to keep out the chill at night, a cotton kimono, raingear, something in the way of ink and brush—and various things given me as farewell presents and therefore difficult to dispose of. It was the traveler's dilemma, knowing them a hindrance and unable to throw them away.

---

[2]Early autumn of 1688, after returning from travel to Suma and Sarashina.
[3]Referring to a residence of some months at his house along the Sumida River in Edo, now Tokyo.
[4]Alluding to a poem by Priest Nōin (998–1050), *GSIS*, IX: 518, and possibly also to a verse by Li Po.
[5]Sampū (1648–1733), proper surname Sugiyama, was a follower of Bashō in poetry.
[6]It was common to think of the first eight stanzas of a *haikai* (as also in the earlier linked verse, *renga*) as comprising the opening unit. They were commonly written on one fold of a sheet of paper.
[7]Echoing a passage from the chapter, "Hahakigi" in *The Tale of Genji* (trans. Waley, I, ii).

We paid homage at the shrine of the god of Muro no Yashima. Sora,[8] who accompanied me on the journey, explained: "The god enshrined here is called the Flower Blooming Princess and is the same as the deity of Sengen Shrine on Mount Fuji. She was called Muro no Yashima after giving birth to Lord Hohodemi when she had entered into a house without doors and set herself on fire to prove his divinity.[9] It is because of such a background that poets associate smoke with this place." It is also forbidden here to eat the *konoshiro* fish, which smells when overheated, but almost everybody knows the outlines of such stories.

The thirtieth, we are stopping at a place in the foothills of Mount Nikkō. The owner of the inn approached us. "People call me Buddha Gozaemon," he said. "I am honest in all my dealings—people will tell you as much—so spend a night of your travels at ease in my little inn." Had the Buddha appeared, then, in temporary form in this corrupt world of ours, perhaps to save one like myself, a mendicant or pilgrim in the habit of an itinerant priest? If one examined the innkeeper's conduct closely, one would discover no calculation or worldliness, only a thoroughly honest man. He was a kind such as the Confucian *Analects* speak of, with a strength of will and rugged honesty close to the ideal virtue—an admirable purity of disposition.

The first of the Fourth Month, we worshiped at the shrine on this mountain. Long ago the characters used for Mount Nikkō were the "Nikō" meaning "Double Rough," but when the Great Teacher Kūkai set up a temple here, he changed the name to "Nikkō" or "Sun's Radiance." It is not clear whether or not he had foreseen what would be a thousand years later, but now the light of this radiant place reaches everywhere, extending the benefit of the temple to the last corner of the country, assisting all four classes[10] in the peaceable and prosperous conduct of their affairs. More might be said, but feeling hesitant at such a place, I put aside my brush.

> As all begins afresh,
> On the green leaves, on the young leaves
> The brightness of the sun.

It is strange to see the late spring haze draping Blackhair Mountain, and patches of white snow lingering whitely, also belying its name. As Sora put it:

> Shaving off the old,
> Here beneath Blackhair Mountain,
> We don summer clothes.[11]

Sora belongs to the Kawai clan, and his given name is Sōgorō. His house was so close to mine that its eaves touched the fronds of my Banana Plant Hut,[12] and he

---

[8]Sora (1650–1711), surname Iwanami (later Kawai), was a disciple of Bashō, accompanied him on at least one other journey, and kept a record of the present journey, *The Diary of Sora*. The differences between Sora's detailed factual account and Bashō's reveal how substantially Bashō altered actual events in the interests of art.

[9]A story in the *Kojiki* says that the princess announced her pregnancy after but one night with her husband. To prove it his, she gave birth safely in a closed, burning room; hence the child's name, Hohodemi, "Visible by Firelight." See *Kojiki*, ed. Kurano Kenji (Tokyo, 1958), *Nihon Koten Bungaku Taikei*, pp. 133–135. For another version, see *Nihongi*, trans. W. G. Aston (London, 1956), pp. 70–73.

[10]The four classes are those of feudal Japan: soldiers, farmers, artisans, and merchants. Bashō obliquely praises the shogunate.

[11]The verses play on "shaving" and the name of the mountain. They also refer to the change from winter to summer clothes on the 1st of the Fourth Month, the actual date of the visit to Nikkō. In addition, Sora alludes to his change to religious garb that Bashō mentions later on.

[12]The description is of course heightened. Bashō took his poetic name from his Banana Plant Hut (Bashō-an).

helps me with my kitchen work. Now he is with me on this trip, taking pleasure in being able to look on Matsushima and Kisa Bay, willing to endure the hardships of travel. On the morning we set out, he took the tonsure, put on a priest's black robes and changed the characters for his given name, Sōgo, from those with a worldly meaning to others with a religious significance. It was in connection with these matters that he wrote his poem on Blackhair Mountain. Since there is the deeper religious significance to the changing of clothes, that last line has special significance.

Climbing the mountainside for half a mile or so up from the shrine, we came upon a waterfall. It flew down a hundred feet or more from cavernous boulders at the peak to hundreds of rocks below, gathering at last into a fresh, clear pool. Because one can enter a hollow in the rocks and see the cascade from behind, it is called Rearview Falls.

> For a little while,
> Hidden in the hermitage of the falls,
> Starting summer seclusion.[13]

Having an acquaintance at a place called Kurobane in the Nasu area, I cut across the plain from Nikkō, seeking to get straight over. As we walked on, we could just make out a village ahead in the distance, when rain began to fall and the day grew dark. We hired lodging for the night at a farmhouse, and at dawn the next day we once again set off across the plain. We came upon an untethered horse grazing. A man was cutting hay nearby, and when we asked for help, we discovered that he was not a person without human feeling, even though he had been coarsened by his work in the fields.

"What can I do?" he asked, implying that he could not leave his work. "On the other hand, the paths on this plain are a network of routes, and a traveler who does not know his way is sure to get lost. You can't let that happen. Take the horse as far as he will carry you and then send him back."

His two young children came running along as guides, though following the horse. One was a girl who told us her name was Kasane. Thinking it an elegant name he had not heard before, Sora wrote:

> Pretty Kasane,
> Or the eightfold maidenflower,
> Is what it must mean.[14]

Coming at last to a village, we wedged some money for the use of a horse into an opening in the saddle and sent it back.

In Kurobane we visited the place of a man called, I think, Jōbōji, who was officer in charge of the fief in the lord's absence. Although he had no expectation of our visit, he seemed to take great pleasure in seeing us and talked with us for days and nights together. His younger brother, with the pen name Tōsui, came to keep us constant company. He also took us to his own house and got us invitations to the houses of relatives. A number of days passed by in this fashion, and on one of them

---

[13] Bashō alludes to the practice priests sometimes followed of secluding themselves in a room for thirty days of summer hermit life.

[14] The maidenflower is a kind of wild pink and a traditional symbol for Japanese girls or women (see *The Diary of Izumi Shikibu*, p. 146). Sora treats "Kasane" to mean something like "multifoliate."

we made an excursion to the outskirts of Kurobane. We took a look at the former dog-shooting grounds and made our way through the well-known bamboo thicket of Nasu to the tomb of Lady Tamamo.[15] From there we paid a visit to the Hachiman Shrine. When we were told that the time Nasu no Yoichi transfixed the fan with an arrow at the Battle of Yashima he had prayed for success to this Hachiman of his clan, we were impressed all the more. We returned to Tōsui's house as darkness fell.

Kōmyōji, a temple for Shugen ascetics, is not far from his house. We paid a visit to it, worshiping in the Founder's Hall.

> I pray I may fill
> Clogs as worthy as the Founder's:
> Crossing far summer hills.

Beyond Ungan Temple in this province are the remains of the hermitage of my religious instructor, Bucchō Oshō.[16] He once sent me a poem:

> The grass thatched hut
> Does not measure even five feet
> In height and width;
> I might knock it into bundles
> If it did not save me from the rains.

"I wrote these two stanzas on a rock near the hut, using a piece of pine charcoal," he added.

A crowd of people decided on their own to come with me when I spoke of going back for a look at the remains, walking off with my staff to Ungan Temple. There was a large number of young people among them who led us a merry time until, without realizing it, we had arrived at the foothill below the temple. The mountains appeared to extend a great distance beyond, and the paths through the valleys grew ever fainter in the distance. The pines and cedars clustered darkly together, the mosses beneath them dripping with water. Even the summer sky, which ought to have been sunny clear through, was cold to look upon. At a place outside the gate to the temple grounds, there is a spot from which one can see all ten famous views. We stood there for a time by a bridge, and then crossed it, entering into the main gate.

Now we wondered where we might find traces of Bucchō's hermitage and so scaled the mountain behind the temple, discovering the tiny hut built on stones and backing upon a cave. Its appearance brought to mind the deathly isolation of Priest Yuan Miao and the hut on the rocks of Priest Fa Yun.[17]

> The noisy woodpecker, too,
> Spares the hut still standing in silence
> In summer-clustered trees

I left that patchwork of verses on a beam.

---

[15] It will be observed how military matters, and archery in particular, unify the Kurobane episode. On Lady Tamamo, see n. 18. Hachiman is the god of war. The famous story of Yoichi's remarkable archery can be found in *The Tale of the Heike* and many other versions. A member of the Minamoto forces, he pierced with an arrow from great range the rising sun emblem on a fan attached by the Taira enemy to the mast of a ship in the Inland Sea. The Battle of Yashima was a climax in the Gempei Wars of the twelfth century.

[16] Bucchō (1644–1716) was a Zen priest.

[17] The Sung priest Yuan Miao immured himself for fifteen years, and the Liang bishop Fa Yun was associated with the isolated temple he had built on rocks.

From Kurobane we go to Sesshōseki. Jōbōji had lent me a horse, and the man leading it said to me, "Please write down a poem for me." He seemed to me to have surprisingly refined tastes for a groom, so I wrote:

> Cutting across the moor,
> Draw still the horse you lead along—
> Hear the wood thrush again.

Sesshōseki turned out to be slightly off toward the loom of the mountains from the Hot Springs of Nasu.[18] The stone itself retains its poisonous properties, and such insects as bees and butterflies lay dead around it so thickly that we could scarcely see the sand underneath. The willow that Priest Saigyō wrote of, "Rippling in the pure spring water,"[19] is at the village of Ashino, where it still grows on the ridge between two paddyfields. The magistrate of this area had sometimes said to me, "I wish that I could show you that willow of Saigyō's," and I had wondered just where it might be. And today I have actually come and stood in its shade.

> Planted, the single field—
> All too soon I must leave the shade
> Of Saigyō's willow.

As the restless days of travel were piling up, we came at last to the Shirakawa Barrier, and my unsettled feelings gave way to calm. It surpasses what Taira Kanemori implied when he wrote from here, "If I could but convey / To those at home some hint of this."[20] One of the three barriers in the northeastern provinces, Shirakawa has always had special appeal to poets and other men of letters. The richly leaved branches were the more precious because the autumn wind heard by Priest Nōin still lingers in the ears, and an image remains of its famous scarlet autumn leaves. The white hydrangeas are pale as linen and the wild rose blossoms vie with them for whiteness, the whole giving the feeling of snow in its coloring. Fujiwara Kiyosuke[21] has set down how a man came to this barrier and tidied his headgear before he would cross it.

> The white hydrangeas
> Enough to deck the head with fancy dress
> For crossing the barrier.

> —SORA

In such fashion we passed through, proceeding till we forded the Abukuma River. On the left, Mount Aizu towered, and on the right lay the villages Iwaki, Sōma, and Miharu, which were divided by hills from Hitachi and Shimotsuke

---

[18]The name Sesshōseki means "life-quelling stone," taken from the stone described. Poisonous gases no doubt related to the geological formations producing the hot springs made the stone seem mortal. The stone was said to be a metamorphosis of Lady Tamamo (see n. 15), a fox in human guise who successfully ensnared the attentions of Emperor Konoe (r. 1141–1155) till exposed by a diviner. She then fled to the north and ended as this poisonous stone.

[19]Alluding to a poem by Priest Saigyō (1118–1190), SKKS, III: 262, made famous by reference to it in a nō play. Saigyō is the poet most often mentioned or alluded to in The Narrow Road, the next, Priest Nōin. Both were itinerant poets like Bashō.

[20]Quoting from a poem by Kanemori (d. 990), SIS, VI: 339.

[21]The passage is a tissue of allusion. Bashō echoes in succession poems by Priest Nōin, GSIS, IX: 518; by Minamoto Yorimasa (1104–1180) on the leaves, SZS, VI: 364; by Oe no Sadashige (dates unknown) on the appearance of snow, SGSIS, VI: 492; and by Fujiwara Kiyosuke (1104–1177), who set down the story in his Fukuro Sōshi about one Taketa Kuniyuki.

Provinces. We passed Kagenuma, but since the sky was clouded, we missed the chance to see the reflections in its waters. At the posting town of Sukagawa we visited Tōkyū,[22] and we lingered on there for four or five days. When we met him, he asked, "How was it crossing the Shirakawa Barrier?"

"The hardships of our long journey," I answered, "had left us exhausted and feeling oppressed. Added to that there was the almost overwhelming beauty of the area, the associations with men of former times, and what had been written about it long ago. There was so much to take in that I was able to write but little verse."

> Here they begin,
> The celebrated places of the provinces,
> With a song of the fields.

"I only wrote that, thinking that it would be a pity to cross the Shirakawa Barrier without writing something."

Tōkyū responded by adding a second unit to my verses, Sora the third. After a time we had written three sets of *haikai*.

In a nook near this post station there is a great chestnut tree. A priest who has turned his back upon the world lives in its shade. Was not that the kind of life Saigyō described in remote mountains, where one just picked up horse chestnuts from the ground? The thought brought a tranquility of spirit with it, and I jotted down the things that follow:

> The character for "chestnut" is made up of "west" written above "tree." It therefore suggests the Western Paradise and recalls that during his lifetime the Bodhisattva Gyōgi made up his staffs or pillars entirely from this wood.

To which I added,

> It is a common flower
> That the worldly think not worth their note,
> Chestnut at the hermit's eaves.[23]

Just twelve miles from Tōkyū's house, and removed some distance from the Hiwada post station, is Asaka Hill. It is not far from the road in a largely marshy countryside. The time was at hand for cutting that kind of iris I had heard called "blue flag," and accordingly I asked the people of the area, "Which plant is it that they call 'blue flag'?" I asked a number of people, but none of them could say. As I went about the marshes, inquiring everywhere, with "blue flags, blue flags" on my lips, the sun had started to glide down toward the mountain rim before I was aware. Turning right at Nihonmatsu, we had a quick look at the cave of Kurozuka and walked on to spend the night at Fukushima.

The next morning we inquired after the clothes-printing stone of Shinobu. We found the hamlet to be a small village lying beneath the rise of the hills. The stone itself is half buried in the ground. The village children came to us to tell the story of the stone.

"Long ago," they said, "it was at the top of the hill. But the farmers were so upset by the way visitors to it trampled their grain, that they had the stone brought down here into the valley. It lies on its side with the printing surface down." It is possible that the story deserves some credit.

---

[22]Tōkyū, or Sagara Izaemon (1638–1715), probably met Bashō during residence in Edo.

[23]The poem is typical in a number of ways. It refers to a humble flower, and displays a characteristic mingling of description and symbolism. Also, like many in *The Narrow Road*, it was used as an initial stanza or *hokku* for successive linkings with stanzas by Sora and others.

> Planting the rice sprouts,
> Busy hands recall the ancient dyeing
> On the Shinobu print-stone.

We crossed the river at Tsukinowa Ford and emerged in a post town called Se no Ue. Three and a half miles farther on, just to the left of the hills, there is a site recalling Vice-Governor Satō.[24] Having heard that the hamlet of Iizuka was in the vicinity of Sabano, we walked on inquiring everywhere. For all our questions, we came at last to a hill called Maruyama, the site of the vice governor's palace. When people told us of the grand gate that had stood at the foot of the hill, the image of the past led me to tears. At an old temple nearby there remain the graves of the whole Satō household, and standing between those of the two brave young wives, I wiped my eyes. They may have been women, but they had left a name for bravery to the world. There is a famous Chinese monument that made all visitors weep, but we need not seek so far for such a stone. Upon entering the temple to ask for tea, we were told that the sword of Yoshitsune and the pannier of Benkei were kept there as treasures.[25]

> The pannier and sword:
> Use them to decorate the Boys' Festival
> Along with carp streamers.[26]

That happened on the first of the Fifth Month.

From there we went on to Iizuka for lodging. It is a place with hot springs, and so we took accommodation at a place offering such bathing. What we discovered was a dirt-floored room with rice mats spread out. Such a hovel had little appeal. Since there was no lamp, either, we had to rely upon the faint light of the sunken hearth to prepare our bedclothes and get to bed. As night came on, thunder rumbled and rain came down in a torrent, leaking from the roof above our beds. To add to it, we were attacked by fleas and mosquitoes. I was unable to sleep and had an attack of colic. I thought that I was about to go under. The short night of the season was at last over, and once again we set out on our travels. The distress of the night still weighed upon me, however, and I felt very low. We engaged a horse and with it we got to the post station of Kōri.

It is not a very reassuring state of affairs to have this illness while the road we must take lies vague and far ahead. Our tour is a pilgrimage through remote back country. I thought of the lack of stability in human affairs and of resigning myself to leaving my body behind in a forsaken area. The thought that I would die halfway on my journey seemed to me the will of heaven, and my spirits revived. In my new mood I stepped along jauntily, and one might say that—as we came to Ōkido in Date—I was dotty.

We passed through the castle towns of Abumizuri and Shiroishi. We had come to the Kasajima Territory and therefore inquired of people where we might find

---

[24]Satō Motoharu died fighting in the area in 1189 on behalf of the doomed cause of Yoshitsune (see next footnote).

[25]The story of Minamoto Yoshitsune and his strong faithful companion, Priest Benkei, is one of the most romantic narratives of Japanese chivalry. After achieving great things in battle, Yoshitsune was said to have been hounded down by troops of his jealous brother, the shogun Yoritomo, and to have died by his own hand in 1189 at the age of thirty. Since Sora's *Diary* says explicitly that they did not enter the temple, Bashō's artistic heightening can easily be glimpsed.

[26]Bashō characteristically deflates some of the air of romance by relating the heroic symbols to the cloth or paper carp flown on poles, one for each son of the house, on the 5th of the Fifth Month.

the grave of Fujiwara Sanekata.[27] "The hamlet you can see dimly off to the right," we were told, "is called Minowa, and beyond that lies Kasajima. There you can still find the Kasajima Shrine of the god of travelers and the pampas grass that was a keepsake to Priest Saigyō."[28] The rains of the Fifth Month had set in, however, leaving the side roads all but impassable, and in my weakened condition it was best just to pass through the country, only looking from a distance upon Minowa and Kasajima. The suggestion of raincoats and rainhats[29] was altogether appropriate to this rainy season, and so I wrote:

> Yes, Kasajima—
> Over what foul roads does it lie
> Beneath summer rains?

We stopped overnight at Iwanuma.

The following morning we went to see the pine of Takekuma—and, truly, it wakes you up, as the legend says. The roots of a single tree divide near the top of the soil into trunks, so retaining the shape that men wrote of long ago. One cannot help recalling Priest Nōin and his poem.[30] Perhaps it was because, so long ago, the man newly arrived as governor of Mutsu Province had had the pines cut down for piling under the Natori River bridge that when Priest Nōin came here on his second visit he should write, "No trace remains, / Not this time, of the famous pine . . ." They told us there that the pines have often been cut down and replanted, but now they look as if their age has been guarded a millennium, and they are truly a splendid stand. There are the verses by Kyōhaku.[31]

> You late cherry blossoms,
> Do not forget to show Bashō the pine
> Of far Takekuma.

To answer such a parting present given as we left Edo:

> The cherry blossoms
> Have yielded after three moons' passage
> To these two pines.[32]

We crossed Natori River and entered Sendai. It was the fourth of the Fifth Month, the day for decking houses with iris leaves. We located an inn and stayed

---

[27]Sanekata, a poet and provincial governor, died in 998 while living in exile from the capital. Bashō feels sympathy and kinship.

[28]Alluding to Saigyō's poem on Sanekata, *SKKS*, VII: 793, regretting that Sanekata remains only a name in the world, with only withered pampas grass a reminder of him.

[29]The *mino-* of Minowa means a straw raincoat, and the *kasa-* of Kasajima suggests in this context a sedge rainhat.

[30]Nōin's poem (*GSIS*, XVIII: 1,043), echoed later by Bashō, runs:

> No trace remains,
> Not this time, of the famous pine
> That grew at Takekuma—
> Have ten centuries slipped away
> Before I came to look again?

[31]Kyōhaku (d. 1696) was a disciple of Bashō.

[32]Both the months and Bashō have passed along. The play on two and three recalls a poem, *GSIS*, XVIII: 1,042, saying that if you ask the people in the capital about the two pines of Takekuma, they will turn you off with talk of three moons.

over for four or five days. There is a painter named Kaemon[33] living here. I had heard that he was a person of great sensibility and so sought him out. "The famous old places," he told me, "are grown quite obscure. For some time I have been trying to ferret them out." He undertook to be our guide for a day. Miyagi Moor was overgrown with bush clover and so gave rich promise of autumn scenery. At other places with poetic associations—Tamada, Yokono, and Tsutsujigaoka—the pony grass was in full flower. We went into a pinewoods so thick that the rays of the sun could not filter through, and learned that its name was "Under the Trees." Even long ago, the extraordinarily heavy dews of the place led a poet to exclaim, "Companions of your lord, / Tell His Highness, 'Wear your rainhat!' "[34] The day at last grew dark as we paid our homage at Yakushi Temple, Tenjin Shrine, and such places. Kaemon had given me maps he had sketched of Matsushima, Shiogama, and other famous places in the area, and he revealed himself to be the discriminating person he is by presenting me, as a parting gift, two pairs of walking sandals corded with iris-blue thongs.

> The purple irises
> Are bound henceforth to my feet—
> Thongs of straw sandals.

Following the route marked on the maps Kaemon had given us, we found along the narrow road to the north that the sedge of the ten-stranded mat did indeed exist.[35] They say that even now ten-stranded sedge mats are presented annually to the lord of the Sendai fief.

The stone monument of Tsubo is at Taga Castle in Ichikawa Village.

The monument is over six feet high and just about three feet wide. Its surface is so covered with moss that one can only make out its inscription by the depressions. It tells of distances to the four corners of the country. There is also: "This castle was built in 724 by Lord Ōno Azumabito,[36] provincial state secretary and military commander, and restored in 762 by Lord Emi Asakari,[37] who was similarly a commander entrusted with pacifying the area, and also counselor and governor of the Eastern Provinces. The first day of the Twelfth Month." That would be in the reign of Emperor Shōmu.

From long ago the monument has been an adornment of verse and the subject of numerous stories. Ours is a world in which even mountains crumble with time, rivers change their courses, and roads go in altered routes. Stones disappear beneath the surface of the earth, great trees wither away, and saplings take their place. There are seldom any certain vestiges of what has been. Yet in this place there are wholly trustworthy memorials of events a millennium ago and, as I stand here looking upon them with my own eyes, I have the feeling of having actually seen what motivated men in ancient times. Such an experience is a benefit of wayfaring, and rejoicing over the gift of life, I forgot about the rigors of travel and was overcome even to tears.

---

[33]Kitano Kaemon (d. 1746) was also a *haikai* poet. The irises with which the paragraph begins and ends were associated with the Boys' Festival of the 5th of the Fifth Month and with the Sendai area.

[34]From an Eastern Song, *KKS*, XX: 1,091. Some Eastern Songs were from this area.

[35]The full phrase is a poetic expression for sedge. The sentence also refers to the road from which Bashō fashioned his title.

[36]Lord Ōno went to the province with Fujiwara Umakai (d. 737).

[37]Asakari was executed with his father after rebelling in 762.

We inquired afterwards about the Tama River in Noda and the Stone of Oki. At the famous Sue no Matsuyama,[38] a temple has been built with the same name rendered in Chinese fashion—Matsushōzan. Graves dot the intervals between the pines of the woods. The most intimate promises of lovers, made never to change,[39] have their outcome in these graves, and the thought made time seem yet crueler, just as the vesper bell sounded from Shiogama. The sky from which the summer rain had been falling cleared somewhat, and in the faint glowing of the moon over the water in the early dark, the form of Magaki Isle seemed near at hand. The little boats of the fishermen row in together, and from the babble of voices as they divide their catch, one can well understand the meaning of the old poet who wrote, "How sad the hands upon the net lines," and feel the touching sorrow of the scene.[40] That night I heard blind minstrels strumming their *biwa* lutes and chanting their north-country ballads. The instruments are not those used to accompany the military ballads, nor yet those used for the military ballad drama.[41] They make an artless, back-country rhythm above which the reciters raise their voices, and though recitation at one's pillow side is not very restful, it was still a triumph that such an accomplishment should have survived in the provinces.

Early the next morning we paid homage to Myōjin Shrine in Shiogama. This shrine was restored by the lord of the province[42] and now has a main building with magnificent sturdy pillars and a splendid painted ceiling. Its stone steps rise high aloft, and from above the brightness of the morning sun sparkles on the vermilion lacquer of its fence. In this unparadisiacal back country, the virtues of the gods have led to the building of such splendid shrines. It is a very precious feature of our national traditions. In front of the main shrine building there are votive lanterns, and on the front lid of one of them is written, "Presented in 1187 by Izumi Saburō."[43] It was remarkable how vividly an image from five centuries ago took shape before me there. He was a brave man, a soldier loyal and filial, whose fame is alive to this day and earns him the admiration of everyone. It was written long ago: "We should bend our efforts to stay on the Way and hold to the grand principles of loyalty. So doing, we shall be accompanied by honor."[44]

The day was close to noon. Hiring a boat, we set out for Matsushima.[45] The distance is about five miles, but we soon landed at Ojima Beach.

What one can say about the place is sure to have little novelty, but Matsushima is the finest beauty spot of Japan and for it there is no need to feel ashamed of a comparison with Lake Tung-t'ing or the West Lake at Hangchow, the best that

---

[38] The Stone of Oki and Sue no Matsuyama are celebrated in numerous poems; see, for example, *The Diary of Izumi Shikibu*, p. 110.

[39] An allusion to a passage in *The Song of Everlasting Remorse (Ch'ang hên ko)* by Po Chü-i (772–846), long one of the most popular Chinese poems in Japan as well as China.

[40] Echoing an Eastern Song, *KKS*, XX: 1,088. The original meant, "What charm in hands upon the net lines," but as Bashō's context makes clear, the meaning of *kanashi* had changed in some six or seven centuries.

[41] That is, a style different from those for reciting the *Heike Monogatari* and the *kōwakamai*.

[42] The lord was the powerful Date Masamune (1565–1636), who patronized a number of arts and who founded the shrine in 1607.

[43] Izumi Saburō, i.e., Fujiwara Tadahira (d. 1189) was the only one of the three sons of Hidehira (see n. 52) who followed their promise to him to remain faithful to the ill-starred Yoshitsune.

[44] This echoes a Chinese classic, but which one is a matter much disputed.

[45] Matsushima is one of the great beauty spots of Japan, an island off the coast from Sendai. Bashō's account is no doubt the best known of writings of visits to the island.

China can offer. The sea comes in from the southeast and over the years has beaten out an inlet over six miles around, and within the arc the tide comes in an eagre as it does at Che-chiang. There were islands beyond counting, some tall ones pointing each its finger toward heaven, and other low ones crawling on their bellies across the sea. Some islands are piled up in two layers, others in three; some on the left stand aloof from each other, others join hands on the right. Some look as if they were children being carried on the back, yet others as if they were being hugged—in the manner in which parents or grandparents fondle their young ones. The needles of the pines are a rich green; the sprays of the trees are blown in a whirl by the sea winds, and yet their lovely twisted forms seem to have been assumed of their own accord. The deep attraction of the place is that of the loveliest face made lovelier.[46] It must have been the special care of the god of hills, Ōyamatsumi, in the remote past of the mighty gods. And who is there that could paint or describe the handiwork of Zōka, the demiurge of heaven and earth?

The island coastline of Ojima juts from the main body of land, an island looking like a peninsula. One can still see the site of the detached temple of the Zen Priest Ungo, along with such other things as the stone he sat upon for meditation.[47] In the shade of the pines there were also one or two priests who had renounced the world, leading the lives of hermits in their grass-thatched huts, above which rose the thin smoke of fires built of pine cones or fallen needles. Of course I do not know them, but their life is appealing. As I approached them, the moon rose, sparkling upon the sea, creating a loveliness different from that in daylight. We went back to the inlet and looked for lodging. Our room was in the upper of two storeys, and we opened our window, enjoying our traveler's sleep in the freshest of breezes, borne upon us with the strangest feeling of delicacy. Sora wrote a poem.

> Here at Matsushima,
> O wood thrush, the plumage of cranes
> Would add to your song.

I decided to be silent as a poet in such a place, but though I intended to go to sleep, I could not. When I left my old hut to set out on this trip, Sodō gave me a Chinese poem on Matsushima and Hara Anteki gave me his *waka* on Matsugaura.[48] Opening my pilgrim's knapsack, I took out these poems for my companions that night. I also had the opening verses by Sampū and those by Dakushi.[49]

The eleventh we worshiped at Zuigan Temple. Long ago the first of its thirty-two abbots, Makabe Heishirō, went to T'ang China after taking orders and on his return founded this temple.[50] When the Zen Priest Ungo later came here, his great virtue enabled him to attain comprehensive understanding of Buddhist teaching, and he set about to refurbish the chief Zen temples, to put gold leaf on their walls and to decorate their altars till they shone with dazzling brightness. The temple is become

---

[46]Echoing Su Tung-p'o (1036–1101), *Yin hu-shang ch'u ch'ing hou yü.*

[47]Priest Ungo (1582–1658) had gone from the capital (now Kyoto) to a temple supported by the rich Date daimiate. The site must have been abandoned not long before Bashō's visit.

[48]Yamaguchi Sodō (1642–1716) was a *haikai* poet and Hara Anteki (dates unknown) a physician and *tanka* poet.

[49]For Sampū, see n. 5; the dates of Nakagawa Dakushi are unknown.

[50]Makabe Heishirō was a prominent priest during the Kamakura period (i.e., *ca.* 1185–1382). Bashō has him going to T'ang rather than Sung China and has changed the date of this paragraph from the 9th, and the next from the 10th. He mistakes the founder and gets thirty-two generations of abbots from no source known today. The Kenbutsu Bashō wonders about later in the paragraph flourished *ca.* 1107–1123.

a great center of piety and learning—a temple which makes people think that the Buddha's Paradise was achieved here. I wondered where the temple of Kenbutsu might be.

On the twelfth we took Hiraizumi as our aim. With memories of places like the Pine of Anewa or the Bridge of Odae celebrated in many poems, we walked over roads where there were but few tracks, roads used only by hunters and grass-cutters, and so became unable to say which direction lay where, losing our way completely but at last coming out in the harbor town of Ishinomaki. I looked across the waters at Mount Kinka, which Yakamochi had written about for Emperor Shōmu as the blossoming of gold flowers,[51] and I saw in the harbor hundreds of the little boats that ply along the coast, while in the village the houses lay so close as to struggle with each other for room, and above them the smoke from cooking fires spiraled up over an area as far as the eye could see. We had come here with no intention of visiting at all, and now when we sought to rent lodgings we found that there was no one who let them. At last we found a pitiful little place to spend the night, and the next morning we set out once again on random travel over unknown roads. We walked along the embankment of the Kitakami River, getting glimpses from afar of places celebrated in verse—the Sode Ford, the Pasture of Obachi, and the Reed Plain of Mano. Trudging on a road along a lengthy expanse of marshy ground, we found that the countryside weighed heavily upon our feelings. We came to a place called Toima and there spent the night. At last, the next day, we arrived in Hiraizumi. The distance we had covered was more than forty-five miles.

The splendors of the three generations of Hiraizumi[52] now comprise the briefest of dreams, and of the grand façade there are only faint remains stretching out for two and a half miles. Hidehira's castle is now leveled to overgrown fields, and of all the splendors of his past, only Mount Kinkei retains its form. Climbing up to the high ramparts of what had been Yoshitsune's stronghold, one can see below the Kitakami River flowing in a wide stream from the south. The Koromo River pours past the site of loyal Izumi Saburō's castle, then beneath these ramparts, and at last into the Kitakami. The old relics of others like Yasuhira are to be found separated to the west at Koromo Barrier, which controlled the southern approach and probably was meant to protect the area against incursions by the northern tribesmen. Yoshitsune and his brave adherents took refuge in this citadel, but the most famous names claim the world only a little while, and now the level grass covers their traces. What Tu Fu wrote[53] came to my mind—

> The country crumbles, but mountains and rivers endure;
> A late spring visits the castle, replacing it with green grasses . . .

and sitting down on my pilgrim's hat I wept over the ruins of time.

> The summer grasses:
> The high bravery of men-at-arms,
> The vestiges of dream.

---

[51] Alluding to a poem by Ōtomo Yakamochi (718–785), *MYS*, XVIII: 4,097.

[52] The rebellious but splendid court at Hiraizumi was established by Fujiwara Kiyohira (d. 1126) in 1094. Its next two generations were those of his descendants: Motohira (d. 1157) and Hidehira (d. 1187). Hidehira's eldest son, Yasuhira (d. 1189), disregarded his father's charge to support Yoshitsune. His betrayal led the ruthless Yoritomo in turn to destroy him and Hiraizumi in 1189. See n. 43.

[53] Bashō adapts lines from "A Spring View" (*Ch'un wang*) by the T'ang poet, Tu Fu (712–770).

And by Sora:

> The white hydrangeas—
> One can see in them Kanefusa,
> Brave when white-haired.[54]

I saw at last with astonishment the wonders of Chūson Temple, of which I had heard before. In one hall there are statues of the three great generations of Hiraizumi, in the other their coffins and three statues of the Buddha. But the seven sacred treasures had been scattered, the jeweled door was broken by the wind, and the gilt pillars were moldered by frost and snow. Yet a place that ought long since to have been utterly reduced and left level under the turf has been enclosed not long ago, and with the roof retiled it withstands the wind and the rain. It is preserved for a time as a remembrance of the past.

> The brightness lasts
> Undimmed by ages of summer rain:
> The Temple of Light.

We looked for a moment upon the road to the north, where it ran obscurely off toward Nambu, and went our way, stopping that night at Iwade. We had decided to pass by Ogurozaki and Mizunoojima, following a route past Narugo Hot Springs to the Barrier of Shitomae, then crossing the mountains to Dewa Province. Because there are so few travelers on this route, the barrier guards treated us with great suspicion, and we were let through only after much delay. We struggled up a steep mountain trail and, finding that the day had grown dark, stumbled into the house of a provincial border guard and asked to be let lodging for the night. A fierce rainstorm howled for three days, keeping us in those worthless lodgings in the mountains.

> Fleas and lice,
> And the sound of horses pissing
> Disturb my pillow.

Our host told us that high mountains separated this area from Dewa and that since the roads were not at all clearly defined we would do best to make the crossing with a guide. "By all means," I told him, and the person he found for us turned out to be a most reliable-looking young man with a short curved sword at his waist and a live-oak staff. I thought to myself, "We will surely run into trouble today," and followed close after him, overcome with fright. As our host had warned us, we had to struggle over high, heavily forested mountains, where not a single birdsong was to be heard. It was so dark beneath the trees and so thick with leafy growth that we might have been journeying by night. And as Tu Fu wrote, "Whirlwinds of dust blow down from the clouds, bringing darkness."[55] We struggled to make our way through dense patches of bamboo grass. We forded streams, and we stumbled over stones. Dripping with a cold sweat, we came out at last on the Mogami plain. The young man who had guided us said, "I have never made this crossing without something happening. We have really done something wonderful to get here without trouble." We parted amid rejoicing on both sides and later heard confirmation of what the guide had said. It made us tremble to think of what we had gone through.

---

[54] One of the heroes of the Yoshitsune saga, Kanefusa showed great bravery when Yoshitsune and his family met destruction at Hiraizumi. See *Gikeiki*, vii and viii.

[55] From *Chêng fu ma ch'en huo t'o yen tung chung*.

At Obanazawa we inquired after a man called Seifū who, though a rich merchant, had no vulgarity in him.[56] He had often been to and from the capital and so knew what wayfaring was like. He pressed us to stay with him for a few days—to refresh ourselves after the rigors of so long a journey—and took all manner of good care of us. I wrote some verses while staying with him.

> I sit for a spell,[57]
> Taking the coolness as my house,
> Idling in comfort.

> Come, jump out, there—
> Under the silkworm nursery,
> The croak of a toad.

> Taking its image
> From a little cosmetic brush,
> Flowering rouge-thistle.

Sora added:

> Minding their silkworms,
> People keep the simple appearance
> Of ages long past.

In the fief of Yamagata there is a mountain temple called Ryushaku. Established by the Great Teacher Jikaku,[58] it is situated in an area of great quiet and evident purity. Having been urged to visit it, we set out off our main course from Obanazawa, the distance being some fifteen miles. It was still afternoon when we arrived. Arranging with the priests for temple lodgings at the foot of the mountain, we ascended the slope to the temple proper. The mountain seemed to be built up of rocks upon boulders. The pines and oaks were manifestly old, and the very stones and earth, lying under their smooth shroud of moss, gave off an atmosphere of great age. The doors of the temple pavilion up there on the rocks were all barred. There was not so much as a sound. Coasting around the brink of the grounds, as if we were creeping over the stones, we paid a manner of worship at the temple, but it was the scenery that struck a stillness in our hearts, purifying them from worldly defilement.

> In seclusion, silence.
> Shrilling into the mountain boulder,
> The cicada's rasp.

Deciding to board a boat down the Mogami River, we went to a place called Ōishida and awaited fair weather. During the delay, someone from the area told us "the seeds of *haikai* sown in this place long ago continue to grow, but we cannot forget how the art flowered here in former times and long for such success again.

---

[56]Suzuki Seifū (1651–1721) of the Shimadaya. The first two sentences reflect feudal prejudice against merchants, as well as the way merchants rose above it, commonly by following the cultivated pursuits of the military aristocracy, from which Bashō himself came.

[57]"I sit for a spell," etc. The poem uses some dialect. "Come, jump out, there," etc. That the toads are intended to be poetic can be understood by the fact that two love poems lie behind this: *MYS*, X: 2,265 and XVI: 3,818. "Taking its image," etc. Rouge-thistle is an aster resembling a thistle; its flowers are used for make-up, and this lies behind Bashō's association. Seifū was a merchant dealing with these flowers (which had other commercial value as well), a product of the area. "Minding their silkworms," etc. The appearance is probably that of bent peasant forms in clothing traditional for the work.

[58]Jikaku (794–865) is said to have founded the temple in 860 on the commission of Emperor Seiwa (r. 858–876).

Minds as simple as ours could use instruction in an art more elegant than our piping on reed flutes. As far as understanding the central principles of this art are concerned, we grope along with our feet, losing our way between new ways and old. We are guideless and perplexed. We certainly do not wish to let pass the opportunity given by your visit." They would not take no for an answer. We composed a sheaf of poems with them, leaving it behind. In such fashion my journey has allowed the style I practice to become known even in so remote an area as this.

The Mogami River begins in Michinoku Province, and its upper reaches mark the boundary of Yamagata. In the middle of its course there are such hazardous places as Goten and Hayabusa. Thereafter it flows along the northern side of Mount Itajiki and empties into the sea at Sakata. Along both its banks the mountains rose upon us as if to close over the river, and the vegetation was wildly luxuriant. Yet through such passage boats drop downstream towards the sea. Was it not because they carried rice that they were called riceboats in our older poetry? We passed Shiraito Falls cascading among a cluster of freshly leaved trees, and the Pavilion of the Immortals standing hard by the river. The swollen current rages along, a certain danger to our boat plying on.

> The summer rains
> Collected in a surging current:
> The Mogami River.

The third of the Sixth Month, we climbed Mount Haguro. We inquired after a man called Zushi Sakichi and, with his good offices, met the auxiliary bishop, Egaku,[59] a man of unusual warmth. He put us up in an outlying temple, the Minamidani, and treated us to a banquet.

The fourth there was a gathering for composing *haikai* at the main seat of the temple. My opening verses ran:

> How gratifying it is—
> Snow patches fragrant in the summer wind
> At Minamidani.[60]

The fifth we worshiped at Haguro Gongen. It is not at all clear when its founder, the Great Teacher Nōjo, lived.[61] It appears in the *Engi Rites* as "The Shrine of Ushū Satoyama." But that must be the result of some copyist's mistaking the similar characters, *sato* and *kuro*. Moreover, Ushū Kuroyama must have arisen from the omission of the *-shu* and changing the pronunciation of *u* to *ha:* Haguroyama. The reason the province is called Dewa, or Producing of Feathers, is, according to the *Fudoki*,[62] that the plumage of birds was sent from here to the court. With Gassan and Yudono, Mount Haguro is one of the three principal temples of the area and an affiliate of Kan'ei Temple back in Edo. It is a place where the discipline of concentration and insight practiced in Tendai Buddhism has brightened the world like the moon and where, in addition, the doctrine of Enlightenment Through Tranquility in the Law has been like an accompanying lamp in the night. The

---

[59]Sakichi (d. 1693) was a *haikai* poet; Egaku (d. 1707) an acting bishop. The 3rd of the Sixth Month is July 19 by our calendar.

[60]Sora's *Diary* makes clear that the poem as composed on the journey (like some others) originally ran differently. The first version may be rendered, "... The snow patches given a fragrance / By the sound of the wind." There is an echo of a Chinese poem in a popular collection of the time.

[61]Nōjo is said to be the third son of Emperor Sushun (r. 587–592).

[62]In Bashō's time, reference books falsely attributed the explanation to the *Fudoki*. Dewa is the Japanese name for the province, and Ushū the Sinified.

priests' quarters consist of a row of buildings where the ascetics diligently practice various forms of discipline. People value the efficacy of this holy mountain and restrain their fears. Its success deserves to continue and to keep the area a center for such admirable good work.

The eighth we climbed Mount Gassan. It entailed wrapping of scarves about our bodies, putting on headdresses of bound cotton strips, calling on all our strength to guide us as we climbed up the almost twenty miles. We walked in snow and ice in a cold mountain atmosphere among the clouds and mists, as if in the high heavens beside the paths of the sun and moon. It was an agony to breathe, and our bodies seemed to mutter against us. But at last we reached the summit, finding that the sun had set and the moon was risen. Arranging for a place to sleep, we spread out bamboo grass, with fine bamboos for a pillow. It was on such beds that we waited out the night. When the sun rose and melted away the clouds, we descended to Yudono.

Here Gassan the swordsmith chose the waters of the area for their miraculous tempering power.[63] Purifying himself in them, his mind and body made right, he would hammer out a sword. When he put "Gassan" to a masterwork, it was something the world would treasure. In China they used to temper swords in the waters of Lung-chüan Spring, and the waters chosen here by Gassan are of that order of excellence. He was a person who admired such figures as Kan Chiang and his wife Mo-yeh of the Wu dynasty, they who made the famous swords to which they gave their own names, and he well understood how little common was the dedication necessary to make outstanding things.

While sitting down on a stone to rest, I noticed a cherry tree only three feet high and about half blossomed out. Although it is buried by the snow that piles up so deeply here, this late blossomer does not forget the spring, and I found its spirit touching. It is as though the plum blossoms in dead summer that one reads of in Chinese verse were giving off their fragrance here, or as if the touching cherry tree that Bishop Gyōson wrote of had blossomed again, and such recollections make this tree seem yet more precious.[64]

The customary discipline of pilgrims does not allow me to give a detailed description of the area around Mount Yudono, and more than that, we are not even to write of it. Returning from Gassan to our lodging at Minamidani, at the urging of Egaku we wrote out on poem cards some of the verses we had composed in our walking tour of the three mountains of Dewa.

> How cool it is—
> The crescent moon seen faintly
> On Mount Haguro.[65]

> The peak of clouds
> Forms and crumbles, forms and crumbles—
> But Gassan in moonlight!

---

[63] Gassan flourished in the late eleventh century.

[64] Gyōson (1057–1135) was a Tendai ecclesiastic; the poem Bashō alludes to speaks of a mountain cherry like this, far from the sight of men: KYS, IX: 556.

[65] "The peak of clouds," etc. Contrasting day and night scenes, cloud peaks and actual mountain, the original plays on *Tsuki no yama*, both meaning the mountain in moonlight and giving the Japanese reading for "Gassan" (Moon-mountain). "No one may relate," etc. Referring to the rules about not describing the area. For his part, Bashō can also not explain, only show that he was moved. "My tears fall," etc. Sora's *Diary* records that there were so many offerings that they blew about on the paths, apparently ignored by the ascetics.

> No one may relate
> The mysteries of Mount Yudono;
> Yet tears wet my sleeves.

And Sora:

> My tears fall on the path
> As I tread the unregarded offerings
> Of Mount Yudono temples.

We left Mount Haguro and went to the castle town of Tsurugaoka, where we were taken to the house of Nagayama Shigeyuki,[66] a samurai, and there composed a set of *haikai*. Sakichi was also there to see us off as we boarded the boat for Sakata Harbor. We took lodging at the house of a physician who had taken En'an Fugyoku[67] as his poetic name.

> Southwards Mount Atsumi,
> Then looking north to breezy Fuku Bay,
> And the cool of the evening.

> The River Mogami,
> Thrusts the sun and ends the day's heat
> In the cooling sea.

Whether rivers or hills, sea or land, the scenery we had already looked upon had been magnificent. Now my heart urged me to look at Kisa Bay.[68] We walked northeast from the port of Sakata, crossing mountains, limping along rocky shores, swishing across sandy beaches, and covering well over twenty miles, and that just as at last the sun was sinking brightly to the west, as the strong onshore breeze stirred up the sand, and as the rain threw into a dim haze the islands, the sea, and Mount Chōkai. The rain cast a darkness over the scenery, and I felt as though I were groping in shadows. But it is "a landscape also of special beauty when veiled by the rain," and we could hope for another surpassing view when the veil of rain had lifted. With such thoughts we barely squeezed into "a fisherman's reed hut / On Kisa Bay."[69]

The next morning the sky was very clear and, just as the sun was shining its brightest, we set our boat upon the bay. We headed for Nōin Isle, where we inquired after some sign of the place where Priest Nōin had lived so peacefully for three years. Then we crossed back to the shore of the mainland to the place famous for the cherry tree of Priest Saigyō's poem, and saw an aged tree, a keepsake of Saigyō.[70] By the coast there is an imperial mausoleum, which is said to be that of

---

[66] Shigeyuki (dates unknown) was a poet of Bashō's school. It is believed that Sakichi (see n. 59), mentioned in the next sentence, was somehow connected with Shigeyuki and had accompanied Bashō as far as Tsurugaoka.

[67] Fugyoku (d. 1697) had joined Bashō's poetic school after practicing other styles.

[68] Kisa Bay is a large inlet about twenty-five miles northeast of Sakata; a famous beauty spot, it has about a hundred islands within it and there were then about thirty towns along its coast.

[69] The beauty of scenery veiled or unveiled by rain recalls a poem by Su Tung-p'o, *Yin hu-shang ch'u ch'ing hou yü,* in which he also compares the scene to the beauty of Lady Hsi-shih, who was voluptuous with either little or heavy cosmetics, as Bashō suggests in his next poem. See also n. 72. The sublimity of the prose in the paragraph characteristically concludes with a humble reed hut, echoing a poem of Priest Nōin, *GSIS,* IX: 519.

[70] The poem was then thought to be by Saigyō:

> At the Bay of Kisa
> The cherry tree is buried under
> The lapping ocean waves,
> And the little boats of fisherfolk
> Row along above the blossoms.

Empress Jingū.[71] The temple of the area is Kanmanju. I had never heard before that Empress Jingū had visited the area. What is one to make of the story? Seated in the banquet room of this temple, with the reed lattice rolled up, we could see a wide panorama lying before us. To the south, islands, the sea, and Mount Chōkai looming up to support the heavens and reflected below in the waters of Kisa Bay. To the west, the Muyamuya Barrier cuts across the road, and to the east there runs an embankment and far beyond it, dim in the distance, the road to Akita. Again, off to the north, where the surf seems to draw the sea back and forth, is a place called Shiogoshi. Kisa Bay extends more than two miles each way. It reminds me of Matsushima, but with this difference: Matsushima carried an air of people smiling; Kisa Bay suggests rather the gloom of a frown. It is not just that it is melancholy—more than that, there is an impression of pain, and the effect is that of a beautiful woman whose heart is sorely troubled.

> Pink flowering silk-trees,
> Dimmed in the rain like the beauty of Hsi Shih,
> The Bay of Kisa.[72]

> At Shiogoshi Inlet:
> Cranes wetting spindly legs in the shallows,
> The sea breathing coolness.

Sora wrote some verses at the time of the summer festival there.

> The Bay of Kisa—
> What special food can be eaten
> On festival day?

Teiji, a merchant from Mino Province, wrote:

> The fisher huts—
> Their rain shutters taken off for benches
> In the cool of the evening.

And Sora wrote upon seeing two ospreys nesting on a rock,

> Waves will not wash it:
> There is the fond bond of husband and wife
> In the nest of the osprey.

A number of days passed in our taking leave of the people of Sakata, but at last we turned our attention to the cloud-covered road to the south along this far side of the country. The thought of the distance to be covered makes one's heart ache—I hear that it is more than 280 miles to the capital of Kaga Province. But we set out, crossing the Nezu Barrier, set foot in the province of Echigo for the first time, and at last reached the Ichiburi Barrier into Etchū Province. During the nine days of that stage, my spirits were greatly afflicted by the heat and the wet weather, and since my illness broke out again, that part of my travel record must be left vacant.

---

[71] Empress Jingū was queen of Emperor Chūai and regent from 201 to 269. But dates that early are very suspect and her association with the area was wholly legendary, as Bashō's skepticism suggests. Cf. n. 102.

[72] "Pink flowering silk-trees," etc. The beauty of the scene is compared to the beauty of Hsi Shih, lovely even in frowns; she was sent as a present to Kou-chien of the Yüeh by Fu-chai of the Wu dynasty. "The Bay of Kisa," etc. The place was famous for its shellfish. Sora wonders what more festive food the village could turn to. Little is known of Teiji, though he was a merchant with the surname Miyabe and is thought to have been from Gifu (near modern Nagoya), where Bashō may have met him and taken him into his school. "Waves will not wash it," etc. Washing waves represent betrayal in love in court poetry, and Sora alludes to an anonymous Eastern Song, *KKS*, XX: 1,093. See *The Diary of Izumi Shikibu*, nn. 17 and 18.

First month of autumn—
This eve of the Seventh-Night Festival
Is unlike other nights.[73]

The wild dark ocean:
Streaming over it to Sado Island,
The river of stars.

Today we passed the most trying part of our north-country journey, going through dangerous places with such horrible names as Deserting-Parents–Abandoned-Children, Excluded Dog, and Rejected Horse. I was so tired that I searched out a pillow and lay down as soon as I could. Two young women were talking, however, in the next room but one, toward the front of the building. Mingled with their voices was that of an old man, and from what was said I understood that the women were from Niigata in Echigo Province, and that they were prostitutes. They were on their way to worship at the Ise Shrine, and the man had come to see them as far as this barrier at Ichiburi. He would go back to Niigata tomorrow, while they were writing letters and giving him various broken messages to carry back.

The conversation floated to me. "We are as they say waves falling upon the beach, coming to ruin on the shore, expecting no better end than 'fisherwomen' like us ever have. People treat us with disgust, and we fall lower and lower. Each night we are pledged to love a different man. To have to endure such a shameful life, what terrible things must we have done in a previous existence?"

I fell to sleep with their words in my ears, and just as we were setting out the next morning, the two women came up to us weeping.

"We don't know what route to take," they said, "and so we are terribly worried about our trip. Our anxiety has made us miserable about what lies ahead, and we wonder, may we follow you—at a distance far enough so we would not embarrass you? Your clothes show that you are priests, and that means you will have pity. The boundless grace of the Buddha can be bestowed even on such as we, so please help our souls to enter his Way." They continued in tears as they spoke.

"I regret it very much," I told them, "but we are not so much traveling anywhere as stopping here and there for periods of time. It would really be better for you if you accompanied ordinary travelers. The favor of the gods should enable you to get to Ise without trouble." With that we set out on our way, but the great pity of their situation troubled me for some time.

Prostitutes and priest
Slept under a roof lent a beauty
By bush clover and moon.[74]

I spoke out the verses to Sora, who set them down in his *Diary*.

They say that the Kurobe has forty-eight rapids, and although I do not know how many rivers we crossed, we came at last to a bay called Nago. We were told that while it was not the proper spring season for seeing the famous wisteria at

---

[73]"First month of autumn," etc. It is the Seventh Month of the lunar calendar; on the Tanabata Festival of the 7th, see *The Diary of Izumi Shikibu*, n. 26. "The wild dark ocean," etc. Sado lies off the coast of Niigata city. "The river of stars" is the Milky Way. The vast panorama and the force of nature suggest the insignificance of man.

[74]The flowering bush clover symbolizes the women as the moon does the poet-priest. The poem is esteemed for the kinship, beauty, and pathos it implies Bashō found in the encounter. It is not in Sora's *Diary* and therefore was written later, probably to have a love episode after the manner of a "love-verse" in linked poetry.

nearby Tako, the place was still worth a look in early autumn. When we as
where it was, we were told, "Well, you would have to go about twelve miles along
the coast and so into that area hidden by the mountains. There are only a few
miserable huts of fishermen, and you probably would not be able to obtain lodging
for the night." Intimidated by that, we walked on to Kaga Province.

> The ripening grain,
> Walking in the fragrance while on the right
> The rocky shore of the sea.

   Crossing Mount Unohana and the Pass of Kurikara, we arrived in Kanazawa on
the fifteenth of the Seventh Month. We encountered a merchant with the *haikai*
name of Kasho,[75] traveling here from Osaka, and we shared lodgings with him.
There was a man of these parts, Isshō,[76] who was, I had heard, devoted to the
art of poetry. His name as a writer was increasingly heard, and many who were
not themselves poets had come to know of him. I discovered that he had died last
winter, and now his elder brother proposed a memorial service at which we would
compose elegiac verse.

> Shake, little grave mound!
> The voice with which I cry is at one
> With the autumn wind.

And on being invited to a thatched hermitage:

> Autumn is cool now—
> Let us peel a feast with both hands,
> Melon and eggplant.

There were others composed on the road.

> Crimson on red,
> The sun sets with yet remaining heat,
> But autumn is in the wind.

At a place called Komatsu,

> How nice it sounds,
> This name, Komatsu, where wind ruffles over
> The bush clover and pampas.

   We paid a visit to the Tada Shrine here in Komatsu. The helmet and part of
the fabric of the armor of Sanemori are preserved in the shrine.[77] I was told that
these things were presented to Sanemori long ago, while he still adhered to the
Minamoto cause, by Lord Yoshitomo.[78] Certainly they were not the possessions of
any ordinary samurai. The visor and the earflaps were laterally engraved and inlaid
with gold arabesque of a chrysanthemum pattern. A goldwork dragon ornamented
the crown, and at the front of the crown were the hoe-shaped crests on either side.
The records describe with great vividness the events of those times, telling how
Kiso no Yoshinaka had grieved over Sanemori and sent these two possessions to the

---

[75] Kasho (d. 1731) was a follower of Bashō's school.

[76] Although a provincial poet, Kosugi Isshō (1653–1688) was very talented and was one of the first to
practice Bashō's mature style successfully. The two poets must have been eager for the meeting they were
denied, as Bashō's passionate elegy shows.

[77] Saitō Sanemori (1111–1183), killed at the battle of Shinohara in the area Bashō was visiting, had dyed
his white hair so as not to be dissuaded from, or derided in, battle. He had changed allegiance from the
Minamoto to the losing Taira in the Gempei Wars, and his is a story of loss in many ways.

[78] Minamoto Yoshitomo (1147–1199) was father of Yoritomo, who founded Minamoto rule of the
country, and of the legendary tragic Yoshitsune.

shrine along with a letter of supplication.[79] Higuchi Jirō was said to be the bearer of these relics. I wrote some verses reflecting on the story.

> What a loss is here:
> Beneath the warrior's splendid helmet
> A chirping cricket.

On our way to Yamanaka Hot Springs, the peak of Shirane regarded us from behind as we walked along.[80] At the bottom of a mountain on our left we came upon a temple of Kannon. After Cloistered Emperor Kazan had visited the Kannons of thirty-three places in succession, he had this statue of the great Bodhisattva of Mercy installed, and it is said that it was he who gave the temple its name, Nata, made up from parts of "Nachi" and "Tanigumi."[81] The rocks on the slopes of the temple are varied in shape. Pines now grown old were planted along them, and little reed-thatched temples have been perched on the rocky outcroppings. Altogether it is a fine place.

> These stones excel
> The stones of Ishiyama in whiteness:
> The autumn wind.[82]

We took the waters of the spa. Their efficacy is said to rival the waters of Ariake.[83]

> At Yamanaka—
> Asters cannot match the fragrance
> Of the life-giving waters.[84]

The master of the hot springs lodge is called Kumenosuke, and he is still a youngster.[85] His father[86] had a taste for *haikai,* and years ago when Teishitsu of the capital visited here while still a fledgling poet, he was so put to shame by the performance of this lad's father that he returned to the capital, became a pupil of Teitoku, and so gradually became known to the world. They say that after he grew famous he took for his poetic teaching no fees from people of this one remote village. Of course all this is a tale of events long ago.

---

[79] Minamoto Yoshinaka (1154–1184), brought up in Kiso, was a skillful but inflammatory general on the Minamoto side during the Gempei Wars. He was killed by Yoritomo's troops when he rebelled. Higuchi Jirō, or Kanemitsu, mentioned a bit later, was one of Yoshinaka's four famous lieutenants and died with him in battle.

[80] Shirane, or Shirayama, is one of the three most famous mountains of Japan and separated three of the ancient provinces in what is now the area of Ishikawa Prefecture.

[81] Emperor Kazan (r. 984–986) abdicated to religious life at the age of eighteen. Nachi and Tanigumi are places in present Wakayama and Gifu Prefectures, the former the first, the latter the last, of the thirty-three temples visited by Kazan and so appropriate as the basis for the name of his temple.

[82] "The stones of Ishiyama," etc. These verses have aroused a great deal of discussion. The most widely accepted version of their meaning is that though the famous Ishiyama Temple near Lake Biwa has famous white stones, those are not as white as those of this hill of stones (*ishiyama*). Bashō's grammar is slightly ambiguous, suggesting a whiteness to the autumn wind, as in such a court poem as that by Fujiwara Teika (1162–1241), *SKKS,* XV: 1,336.

[83] Ariake is thought to be a mistake for Arima, near what is now Kobe City.

[84] The poem refers to a Chinese legend about a large aster or chrysanthemum bedewed with drops of sweet water conducive to long life.

[85] Kumenosuke, or Izumiya Matabē (1676–1751), about thirteen years old when Bashō made his visit.

[86] The father (d. 1679) also had the business name of Izumiya Matabē. The Teishitsu whom he embarrassed was Yasuhara Masahira (1610–1673), a distinguished *haikai* poet of the school of Matsunaga Teitoku (1570–1653).

Sora has fallen ill with abdominal trouble. Because he has relatives at N_ _
in Ise, he is going ahead alone.

> Walking, walking on,
> Though I collapse I shall be buried
> On a bush-clover plain.[87]

He wrote down the verses and left them with me. There are the sufferings of the
one who goes, and the unhappiness of him left behind, each like one of two wild
ducks lost from each other.[88] I responded with verses.

> From today the dew
> Will erase the inscription on my hat,
> "I travel with a friend."[89]

I have stopped at a temple called Zenshō on the outskirts of the castle town of
Daishōji. This is still Kaga Province. Sora had stopped here the night before and
left a poem behind.

> Throughout the night,
> Sleeplessly listening to the autumn wind—
> Parted and in hills remote.

"Parted for a night, parted for a thousand leagues."[90] I too heard that autumn wind
as I lay in the same temple dormitory, and when dawn began to brighten the sky,
the voices of priests at their morning recitations came distinct to my ear. After a
time the assembly bell rang for breakfast, and I joined the priests in their dining hall.
Thinking that I had to get into Echizen Province today, I felt rather in a hurry, but
as I started down the steps from the dining hall, young priests crowded about me,
holding out paper and an inkstone. It happened to be the time when the willows
of the temple garden were dropping their leaves, so I wrote:

> The willow leaves fall—
> After sweeping the temple garden
> I hope I can leave.[91]

Anxious to get on, I just scribbled it down, as if my sandals were already in motion.

At Yoshizaki on the border of Echizen Province I took to a boat and was rowed
across the inlet to look at the pines of Shiogoshi.[92]

> All through the night
> The waves have been borne ashore
> By the furious wind,
> And the moonlight sparkled in the water
> Dripping from the Shiogoshi pines.
>
> —SAIGYŌ[93]

---

[87] Some editors see an allusion in this poem to Saigyō's poem from his personal collection, *Sankashū,*
Zoku Kokka Taikan, 7,837.

[88] Faithful wild ducks were emblems of close friends or married pairs.

[89] Bashō and Sora had evidently followed the traveler's custom, when making up a pair, of writing on
their bamboo hats, "I am one of two journeying together."

[90] The expression was proverbial in Chinese poems.

[91] The poem alludes to the custom of one's performing some menial task like cleaning a room or garden
before leaving a Zen temple where one had spent the night. Bashō seems the more human for his irritation
with the young priests.

[92] Shiogoshi, on the Japan Sea side of the island, was famous for its stand of fifty or so pines; from there
Bashō heads south.

[93] The poem is not really by Saigyō.

The poem has been posted on behalf of numerous views in this area. Adding a line or even a word to its five lines would be as superfluous as adding a sixth finger to one's hand.[94]

The head priest of Tenryū Temple in Maruoka was a man with whom I had had connections for a very long time, and so it was that I visited him. There was also a man named Hokushi from Kanazawa, who had promised to see me off from his city, but he gradually lengthened his time with me until now we were here at this temple together.[95] All along the way he was reluctant to pass by any place of special beauty without composing verse, and from time to time he recited for me several excellent poems. Now that we were parting at last, I wrote a poem for him.

> Scribbled all over,
> The summer fan might be rejected now,
> But for its memories.[96]

About fifty blocks, as it were, from the town, I turned into the hills and went to worship at Eihei Temple. It was founded by the Zen Priest Dōgen.[97] Wishing, as a devout priest might well do, to avoid the attractions of the capital, he came off to this forsaken place in the hills, leaving worldly affairs behind.

Because Fukui lies only about six and a half miles away, I set out after finishing the evening meal. In the twilight the road was uncertain underfoot. There is a cultivated samurai named Tōsai living here.[98] Many years ago now he came to Edo and called on me—it must be above ten years past. I thought that he must be very aged by this time, or even dead, but when I asked people about him they said that, no, he was still quite alive and told me where I might find him. It turned out to be a place secluded in the center of town, a shabby little structure but delightfully overgrown with moonflowers and gourd vines, its entrance all but hidden by a profusion of cockscomb and broom tree. I said to myself, "This *has* to be the place." I knocked at the entrance and there appeared a woman of the most ragged appearance. "Where do you come from, Your Reverence?" she asked. "The man of the house has gone to the place of Mr. What-ever-it-was nearby. If you want to speak with him, you had best inquire there." Her manner suggested that she was Tōsai's wife.

Thinking that such beauty in an unpromising place was like some tale of old,[99] I at last inquired after Tōsai and stayed with him two nights. I told him that I thought the harbor of Tsuruga would be a good place to see the autumn moon and started to take my leave. At that Tōsai said he would accompany me and, tucking up the hem of his kimono into his sash, he started off with a jaunty air to guide me.

As we walked on, I found that the imposing peak of Shirane was at last screened from sight, and the top of Mount Hina stood out clearly. We crossed Asamuzu Bridge, and upon arriving at Tamae found that its famous reeds were headed out.[100]

---

[94] Bashō echoes *Chuang Tzu,* Chap. VIII.

[95] Tachibana Hokushi (d. 1718) was a poet of Bashō's school. The temple mentioned is in Matsuoka, not Maruoka, which is nearby.

[96] A fan is no longer needed in the cooler weather of autumn, yet in spite of being scribbled on, it is precious for its associations. It is a metaphor for Hokushi, and for Bashō's reluctance to part.

[97] Priest Dōgen (1200–1253) was founder of Sōtō Zen Buddhism.

[98] Kambe or Sugiura Tōsai (d. 1700) was an important *haikai* poet of the Teitoku school.

[99] Talk of "some tale of old" brings to the surface the recollection of the Yūgao chapter of *The Tale of Genji,* which underlies the whole Fukui episode and in which there is the remark, "You hear of such things in tales of old."

[100] The reeds of Tamae were famous enough, but the whole passage is built into a *michiyuki,* or travel passage with beautiful names (e.g., Uguisu Barrier, the Barrier of the Warbler) and associations, a technique common in a number of Japanese literary forms.

We passed Uguisu Barrier by the side, crossed over Yunō Pass, and on Mount Kaeru near the ruins of Hiuchi Castle I heard the first geese coming south. At dusk on the evening of the autumn full moon, I took lodgings at the harbor of Tsuruga.

The moon was splendid that night. When I asked, "Can we hope to see the moon like this tomorrow night?" my host told me, "Given the changeable nature of the weather in this area, it is difficult to predict a fair or cloudy night."[101] He poured me sake and, at his suggestion, we paid a night visit to the Myōjin shrine at Kei, which honors Emperor Chūai.[102] The shrine had an aura of divinity, and down upon it poured the moonlight between the trees onto the white sand, making it look as if a thick frost had spread over all.

My host told me, "Long ago, the second Archabbot observed the ordeal faced by worshipers at this shrine, and he himself cut away plants, carried earth and sand, gathered the marshy waters into a pool, and so tidied the area that worshipers needed fear no discomfort.[103] This ancient example has lasted on as an unbroken tradition, and still today you will see sand carried into the shrine. It is called 'The Archabbot's Sand-bearing.'" I wrote some verses.

> Divinely pure,
> The moonlight sparkles on the sand
> Borne by the Archabbot.

Just as my host had foretold, it rained the next night.

> In the north country
> The night of the full autumn moon,
> Untrustworthy weather.

The next day, the sixteenth, the sky had cleared, and thinking that I would like to look for the famous little colored clams, I took a boat to the Beach of Iro.[104] It is a passage of about fifteen miles. A man called Tenya Something-or-other went with me, his servants taking an ample provision of lunchboxes and sake flasks.[105] We settled in the boat and set off with a smart wind, arriving in no time at all. On the beach, where there were but few huts of fishermen, there was a pitiable little Nichiren temple. It was there that we sat, and as we drank tea, heating and drinking sake, I felt the particular melancholy of an autumn evening.

> The lonely sadness,
> Exceeding even that of Suma Beach,
> These shores of autumn.

> In intervals of surf,
> The little colored shells are jumbled
> With bush-clover rubbish.[106]

At my request, Tōsai wrote an outline of the events of the day and left it at the temple.

---

[101] The implication, sanctioned by proverbs from the Chinese and Japanese past, is to enjoy the moon on the clear night before, even though it is not wholly full.

[102] Emperor Chūai is said to be the fourteenth emperor of Japan and to have ruled 192–200. Cf. n. 71.

[103] Bashō varies from other accounts; editors say that the event took place in 1301, and that the second archabbot died in 1319.

[104] The clams are those made famous by Saigyō's poem, *Sankashū, Zoku Kokka Taikan,* 8,189.

[105] Tenya Gorōzaemon (dates unknown) was a *haikai* poet. The passage is actually about four miles.

[106] The two poems vary greatly, the first being subjective and allusive to the sadness of Suma Beach (from *The Tale of Genji* and other stories), the second, objective with its image of bits of broken bush-clover mingling with the famous shells.

Rotsū met me as I was going back to Tsuruga Harbor, and from there accompanied me to Mino Province.[107] Our pace quickened by going on horseback, it was not long before we entered the town of Ōgaki, where Sora had arrived from Ise and where Etsujin had also hurried in by horse. We all gathered at Jokō's house. Master Zensen, Keikō and his sons, and many others among my close friends came, by day and by night. They looked upon me as if I had come back from the dead, sympathized with me for the hardships of travel, and rejoiced with me that I had come through. The strain of travel still weighed upon me. But because it was already the sixth of the Ninth Month, I resolved to get on to observe the rare ceremonies at the Great Shrines of Ise.[108] And so, boarding a boat yet again—

> Parting for Futami Bay
> Is like tearing the body from the clam-shell:
> Autumn goes to its end.[109]

CHIKAMATSU MONZAEMON
[1653–1724]

Often considered to be Japan's greatest playwright, Chikamatsu Monzaemon is sometimes compared to Shakespeare because of his breadth of vision and his extensive influence on later Japanese theater. The comparison can often mislead readers, however, for Japanese theater, especially the *jōruri* puppet theater, now called *bunraku*, for which Chikamatsu wrote his plays, differs fundamentally in its theatrical effects, music, stage, and performance from traditional Western theater. Relying upon the combined effects of spectacle, the rhythmic pacing of the *samisen* (a stringed instrument), and the varied intonation and voicing of the master chanter, the puppet plays may be compared to the earliest Greek dramas, in which a single speaker retold an incident from the Homeric tales or from familiar myths. In *jōruri* plays, similarly, a single master chanter serves as the voices for all the puppets, which are manipulated by three other puppet masters who are veiled in black costumes and who remain utterly expressionless to focus attention on the nearly life-sized puppets, which seem to come alive during the performance. Like the Nō dramas from which they evolved, *jōruri* plays often are based on great stories from classic tales, like the *Tale of Genji* or *Tale of Heike*. Although his drama contains numerous allusions to these works, in many of his plays Chikamatsu turned to historical characters and to contemporary incidents involving ordinary people. These in turn have now been retold through the later *Kabuki* theater and in some novels. Junichuro Tanizaki's *Some Prefer Nettles* (1929) details with fine sensitivity the importance of the puppet theater to Japanese culture and turns especially upon the play we select here, *The Love Suicides at Amijima.*

Before studying Chikamatsu himself, it is important to understand a little about the early Tokugawa period during which he wrote. In 1614, Tokugawa Ieyasu emerged

---

[107] The names of a number of Bashō's friends and pupils follow. Yasomura or Inbe Rotsū (1648–1738) was in Bashō's school. Ochi Etsujin (d. *ca.* 1739) was a prominent member of it. Kondō Jokō entered it in 1687. Tsuda Zensen (dates unknown) belonged, as did also Miyazaki Keikō (d. 1693) and his three sons. As in *haikai* or *renga* linked verse, the passage of time speeds up just before the last verse, a great distance and many people being covered here.

[108] The rare ceremonies, which were held every twenty-one years, took place on the 10th and 13th of the Ninth Month of 1689.

[109] Futami Bay is near the Ise Shrines, but *Futami* may also be taken as shell-body.

as victor at the end of a long series of wars among feudal rivals, and set himself up as the first shogun of Japan. Maintaining the divine-right emperor as a mere spectacle of power in Kyoto, the Tokugawa shogunate at Edo (now Tokyo) had become the functional center of power. Under Tokugawa, the process of national unification, or *bakuhan*, began, resulting in Japan's relative isolation from the rest of the world until 1868, when the Meiji Restoration opened the doors to visitors again. To preserve the national identity, the Tokugawa shoguns allowed only the Dutch to trade with Japanese merchants. Rather like the people of Bacon's Bensalem in *The New Atlantis*, the Japanese kept in touch with some Western practices by means of this highly regulated Dutch trade, while at the same time preserving their native tradition and religion from outside influences.

During the Tokugawa period, education and social practices were based on neo-Confucianism, although religious life in Japan still was based on the mixed Buddhism and Shintoism it had inherited from earlier periods. The Confucianist doctrines promoted an ordered society divided into distinct groups—the warriors, or *samurai*, the farmers, the artisans, and the merchants. Like their Western counterparts, the merchant classes rose in wealth and influence during this period, although they were still subject to the authority of the samurai. As Donald Keene points out in his introduction to the plays of Chikamatsu, it was for (and about) the merchant class that some of the greatest writers of this era wrote, including the novelist Ihara Saikaku, author of the comic *Five Women Who Loved Love;* Matsuo Bashō, whose haiku were popular among the merchants; and Chikamatsu, whose plays often concern life in what was known as the "gay quarters," licensed pleasure quarters where the merchants and samurai could spend their surplus wealth on the entertainments of beautiful courtesans. Indeed, Chikamatsu was one of the first dramatists in world literature to take up the lives of ordinary men and women as material worthy of the tragedy. Sanctioned in Japanese culture during this era, the pleasure quarters observed rather formal standards of etiquette, and the courtesans occupied a strict hierarchy with titles of their ranks based on names from poems and plays: Pines, Plum-blossoms, and Maple-leaves and Tides, Reflections, and Moons, for example, name the two highest-ranking categories. When, as in *The Love Suicides at Amijima,* a man fell in love with a courtesan, he could offer to buy out her contract and set her free, but often at a price that exceeded his means. In Chikamatsu's plays, only through *shinjū*, or love suicide, could the ruined and tormented lover or couple escape. Like Goethe's *Sorrows of Young Werther*, which set off a series of imitation suicides in late eighteenth-century Germany, Chikamatsu's love suicide plays, beginning with his first play *The Love Suicides at Sonezaki* (1703), were so popular and influential that the government had to intervene in 1722 to ban such *shinjū* plays in order to stem the growing number of actual suicides in Japan in the early eighteenth century.

LIFE

Chikamatsu Monzaemon was born into a samurai family in the province of Echizen, and moved to Kyoto as a teenager, where he served as a personal attendant to a noble family. As early as 1661, he published some haiku in a family collection, but it was not until 1683, when he wrote *The Soga Successors,* that he published his first *jōruri*, or puppet play, although there is some disagreement as to whether he wrote some earlier plays. With the publication of *Kagekiyo Victorious,* as Donald Keene notes in his introduction to Chikamatsu's plays, Chikamatsu produced what many consider the first "new" puppet play, abandoning the conventional language of the *jōruri*. For the next twenty years, Chikamatsu wrote primarily for the Kabuki theater, working closely with the greatest actor of the period, Sakata Tojuro. With the production of *The Love Suicides at Sonezaki* (1703), a puppet play that received high acclaim and wide popularity, Chikamatsu, in the last years of his life, turned exclusively to writing the *jōruri*. Of these he wrote three kinds: the *jidaimono*, or history play, such as *The Battles of Coxinga* (1715); the *sewamono*, or play of contemporary domestic life, such as *The Uprooted Pine* (1718); and finally the *shinjū*, or suicide play, such as Chikamatsu's masterpiece, *The Love Suicides at Amijima* (1721), which we print here.

WORK

The hero of *The Love Suicides at Amijima* is Kamiya Jihei, a paper merchant who struggles between his love for Koharu, a young courtesan whom he has met at the "gay district," and love for his wife, Osan. Thus, like Madame de Clèves, who must choose between the Duc de Nemours and her husband, Jihei finds himself facing that classic dilemma of tragedy and the novel both in the East and the West: the conflicting demands of duty and personal desire. The Japanese define this opposition as one between *giri* (duty and social responsibility) and *ninjō* (human feelings or passion). Koharu too is bound by *giri*, which would demand that she give up Jihei to his wife. Torn between their obligations to family and friends, the impossibility of leading a fulfilling life together on Earth because of shame and possible reprisals, the two lovers decide that *shinjū* or a ritual love suicide offers the only escape from the impossible demands of the material and transitory world. They believe they will be reunited in the paradise that awaits them after death. As Koharu says in Act III, "What have we to grieve about? Though in this world we could not stay together, in the next and through each successive world to come until the end of time we shall be husband and wife." Yet even in their preparations for death, they must consider their mutual *giri* to Osan, and so determine to die apart to minimize their offense to her.

The play is steeped in literary allusions and Buddhist symbolism that many Western readers will miss, even with heavy annotations. In Act III, as the lovers make their *michiyuki*, or farewell journey, they pass over six bridges, each symbolizing the threshold into a new world. The journey involves a symbolic passage into the Buddhist underworld, a descent that must take place before the lovers can cross the Onari bridge (a bridge whose name suggests "to become Buddha") onto the "other shore" (nirvana) of Amijima, where they will die. *Ami* ("net") in the play's title alludes to two doctrines: the karmic "Heaven's net" of Chapter 73 of the *Tao te Ching* ("Heaven's net is wide; coarse are the meshes, yet nothing slips through"), and the net of redemption offered by Amida Nyorai—the Amida buddha. Thus, Jihei and Koharu inevitably fall into the net of suffering that leads from their actions, yet that fall also involves the possibility of their eventual fulfillment in the next world.

SUGGESTED READINGS

For an interesting account of the Japanese puppet theater, see Barbara Adachi's *The Voices and Hands of Bunraku* (1978). Critical works that offer an introduction to the drama of Chikamatsu include C. Andrew Gerstle's *Circles of Fantasy: Convention in the Plays of Chikamatsu* (1986), Donald Keene's *Japanese Literature: An Introduction for Westerners* (1955), and the introduction to Donald Keene's superb collection, *Major Plays of Chikamatsu* (1961). Donald H. Shively focuses especially upon our play in *The Love Suicide at Amijima: A Study of a Japanese Domestic Tragedy* (1953).

The Love Suicides at Amijima

Translated by Donald Keene

CAST OF CHARACTERS

KAMIYA JIHEI, *aged 28, a paper merchant*
KONAYA MAGOEMON, *his brother, a flour merchant*
GOZAEMON, *Jihei's father-in-law*
TAHEI, *a rival for Koharu*
DEMBEI, *proprietor of the Yamato House*
SANGORŌ, *Jihei's servant*
KANTARŌ, *aged 6, Jihei's son*
A MINSTREL PRIEST
PORTERS, FISHERMEN, PERSONS OF THE QUARTER

KOHARU, *aged 19, a courtesan at the Kinokuni House in Sonezaki*
OSAN, *Jihei's wife*
OSAN'S MOTHER *(who is also Jihei's aunt), aged 56*
OSUE, *aged 4, Jihei's daughter*
PROPRIETRESS *at Kawachi House*
KIYO, *a receptionist*
TAMA, *Osan's servant*
SUGI, *Koharu's maid*
MAIDS, PROSTITUTES, SERVANTS

ACT I

Scene 1

*A street in Sonezaki New Quarter, Osaka.
Time: November 4, 1720.*

NARRATOR:
> *Sanjō bakkara fungoro nokkoro*
> *Chokkoro fungoro de*
> *Mate tokkoro wakkara yukkuru*
> *Wakkara yukkuru ta ga*
> *Kasa wo wanga ranga ra su*
> *Sora ga kunguru kunguru mo*
> *Renge rengere bakkara fungoro.*[1]

The love of a prostitute is deep beyond measure; it's a bottomless sea of affection that cannot be emptied or dried. By Shell River,[2] love songs in every mood fill the air, and hearts stop short at the barrier of doorway lanterns. Men roam the streets in high spirits, humming snatches of puppet plays, mimicking the actors, or singing bawdy ballads as they pass; others are drawn into the houses by samisens played in upstairs rooms. But here is a visitor who hides his face, avoiding the gift day.[3] See how he creeps along, afraid to be forced into spending too much!

Kiyo, the receptionist, notices him.

KIYO: Who's this trying to avoid me?

NARRATOR: She snatches again and again at his hood-flap; he dodges her twice or thrice, but this is a valuable customer, and she refuses to let him escape. At last she pounces on him with the cry:

KIYO: No more of your nonsense! Come along!

NARRATOR: And the customer, caught flap and cap, is trapped into folly by this female Kagekiyo.

---

[1]Scholars have been unable to discover the meaning of these rhythmic lines.
[2]The Shijimi River bordering Sonezaki Quarter.
[3]Days when customers in the Gay Quarters gave presents to proprietors of the teahouses.

Among the flowers on display—even the bridges are called Plum and Cherry Blossom[4]—here is Koharu of the Kinokuni House, now graduated from the smock of a bath attendant in the South to the garments of love in the New Quarter.[5] Is her name "Second Spring" a sign that she is fated to leave behind a fleeting name in November?

"Who has sent for me tonight?" she wonders, uncertain as a dove in the uncertain light of a standing lantern. A prostitute passes her, then turns back.

PROSTITUTE: Is that you, Koharu? Where have you been keeping yourself? We don't get invited to the same parties any more, and I never see you or hear a word from you. Have you been sick? Your face looks thinner. Somebody was telling me that the master at your place now gives all your customers a thorough examination and hardly lets you out of the house, all on account of your Kamiji.[6] But I've also heard that you're to be ransomed by Tahei and go live with him in the country—in Itami, was it? Is it true?

KOHARU: I'd be much obliged if you'd please stop talking about Itami! The relations between Jihei and myself, I'm sorry to say, are not as close as people suppose. It's that loud-mouthed Tahei who's started the rumors and spread them everywhere, until every last customer has deserted me. The master blames Kamiya Jihei, and he's done everything to keep us from meeting. Why, I'm not even allowed to receive letters from Jihei. Tonight, strangely enough, I've been sent to Kawashō. My customer's a samurai, I'm told. But I keep worrying that I might meet that dreadful Tahei on the way. I feel exactly as if I had some mortal enemy. Do you suppose he might be over there?

PROSTITUTE: If you feel that way about Tahei, you'd better hide quickly. Look— coming out of the first block—there's one of those street minstrels, singing his nonsense hymns. I can see in the crowd round him a dissolute-looking fellow with his hair tricked up in some funny style—the stuck-up swell! I'm sure it's Tahei. Oh—they're heading this way!

NARRATOR: A moment later the defrocked priest, in a flat cap and ink-black robes with the sleeves tucked back, comes bumbling along, surrounded by a crowd of idlers. He bangs at random on his bell, mixing his nonsense with the burden of a hymn.

MINSTREL:
"Fan Kuai's[7] style was no great shakes—
See how Asahina of Japan used to break down gates!"
He rips through the gate bars and tangle of felled trees,
Slays Uryōko and Saryōko and passes the barrier, As time passes by.
Namamida Namaida Namamida Namaida.
Ei Ei Ei Ei Ei.
"Though I wander all over,
The sad world holds no one
Who looks like my dear Matsuyama!"
—He weeps, he howls, only to burst into laughs.
"How wretched that I must end my life in madness!"
He falls prostrate, the grass for his pallet,

---

[4]Umeda and Sakura Bridges over the Shijimi.

[5]The Shimanouchi and Sonezaki Quarters, respectively.

[6]That is, Kamiya Jihei.

[7]The characters the minstrel refers to in his song are historical and fictional figures who play important roles in Chikamatsu's earlier plays.

A sight too sad for the eyes to behold.
Namamida Namaida Namamida Namaida.
Ei Ei Ei Ei Ei.
Tokubei of the dyer's shop,
Since he first fell in love with Fusa,
Has yielded to passion that absorbs his fortune,
A love stained so deep lye itself cannot cleanse it.
Namamida Namaida Namamida Namaida
Namamida Namaida.

SUGI: Excuse me, priest.

MINSTREL: What is it?

SUGI: It's bad luck to sing those songs, just when stories about love suicides in the Quarter have at last quieted down. Why don't you give us instead a *nembutsu* song on the journey from *The Battles of Coxinga?*[8]

NARRATOR: Sugi offers him some coins from her sleeve.

MINSTREL:
For a mere one or two coppers
You can't expect to travel all the way,
Three thousand leagues to the Land of Great Ming!
It doesn't pay, it doesn't pray Amida Buddha.[9]

NARRATOR: Grumbling in this strain, he moves on.

Scene 2

The Kawachi House, a Sonezaki teahouse.

NARRATOR: Koharu slips away, under cover of the crowd, and hurries into the Kawachi House.

PROPRIETRESS: Well, well, I hadn't expected you so soon.—It's been ages even since I've heard your name mentioned. What a rare visitor you are, Koharu! And what a long time it's been!

NARRATOR: The proprietress greets Koharu cheerfully.

KOHARU: Oh—you can be heard as far as the gate. Please don't call me Koharu in such a loud voice. That horrible Ri Tōten[10] is out there. I beg you, keep your voice down.

NARRATOR: Were her words overheard? In bursts a party of three men.

TAHEI: I must thank you first of all, dear Koharu, for bestowing a new name on me, Ri Tōten. I never was called *that* before. Well, friends, this is the Koharu I've confided to you about—the good-hearted, good-natured, good-in-bed Koharu. Step up and meet the whore who's started all the rivalry! Will I soon be the lucky man and get Koharu for my wife? Or will Kamiya Jihei ransom her?

NARRATOR: He swaggers up.

KOHARU: I don't want to hear another word. If you think it's such an achievement to start unfounded rumors about someone you don't even know, throw yourself into it, say what you please. But I don't want to hear.

---

[8]Chikamatsu's most popular play, a history play first performed in 1715.
[9]The Land of Great Ming refers to China. Amida Buddha, the Buddha of Infinite Life and Light, is the central deity of Pure Land or Jōdo Buddhism, which maintains that invoking the name of Buddha leads to rebirth in the Western Paradise.
[10]The antagonist in *The Battles of Coxinga.*

NARRATOR: She steps away suddenly, but he sidles up again.

TAHEI: You may not want to hear me, but the clink of my gold coins will make you listen! What a lucky girl you are! Just think—of all the many men in Temma and the rest of Osaka, you chose Jihei the paper dealer, the father of two children, with his cousin for his wife and his uncle for his father-in-law! A man whose business is so tight he's at his wits' ends every sixty days merely to pay the wholesalers' bills! Do you think he'll be able to fork over nearly ten *kamme*[11] to ransom you? That reminds me of the mantis who picked a fight with an oncoming vehicle! But look at me—I haven't a wife, a father-in-law, a father, or even an uncle, for that matter. Tahei the Lone Wolf—that's the name I'm known by. I admit that I'm no match for Jihei when it comes to bragging about myself in the Quarter, but when it comes to money, I'm an easy winner. If I pushed with all the strength of my money, who knows what I might conquer?—How about it, men?—Your customer tonight, I'm sure, is none other than Jihei, but I'm taking over. The Lone Wolf's taking over. Hostess! Bring on the saké! On with the saké!

PROPRIETRESS: What are you saying? Her customer tonight is a samurai, and he'll be here any moment. Please amuse yourself elsewhere.

NARRATOR: But Tahei's look is playful.

TAHEI: A customer's a customer, whether he's a samurai or a townsman. The only difference is that one wears swords and the other doesn't. But even if this samurai wears his swords he won't have five or six—there'll only be two, the broadsword and dirk. I'll take care of the samurai and borrow Koharu afterwards. [*To* KOHARU.] You may try to avoid me all you please, but some special connection from a former life must have brought us together. I owe everything to that ballad-singing priest—what a wonderful thing the power of prayer is! I think I'll recite a prayer of my own. Here, this ashtray will be my bell, and my pipe the hammer. This is fun.
Chan Chan Cha Chan Chan.
Ei Ei Ei Ei Ei.
Jihei the paper dealer—
Too much love for Koharu
Has made him a foolscap,
He wastepapers sheets of gold
Till his fortune's shredded to confetti
And Jihei himself is like scrap paper
You can't even blow your nose on!
Hail, Hail Amida Buddha!
Namaida Namaida Namaida.

NARRATOR: As he prances wildly, roaring his song, a man appears at the gate, so anxious not to be recognized that he wears, even at night, a wicker hat.

TAHEI: Well, Toilet paper's showed up! That's quite a disguise! Why don't you come in, Toilet paper? If my prayer's frightened you, say a Hail Amida! Here, I'll take off your hat!

NARRATOR: He drags the man in and examines him: it is the genuine article, a two-sworded samurai, somber in dress and expression, who glares at Tahei through his woven hat, his eyeballs round as gongs. Tahei, unable to utter either a Hail or an Amida, gasps "Haaa!" in dismay, but his face is unflinching.

---

[11] A *kamme* is worth 1,000 *momme* of silver; one *momme* was worth 3.75 grams of silver. As the play indicates, ten *kamme* was considered to be a lot of money.

TAHEI: Koharu, I'm a townsman. I've never worn a sword, but I've lots of New Silver[12] at my place, and I think that the glint could twist a mere couple of swords out of joint. Imagine that wretch from the toilet paper shop, with a capital as thin as tissue, trying to compete with the Lone Wolf! That's the height of impertinence! I'll wander down now from Sakura Bridge to Middle Street, and if I meet that Wastepaper along the way, I'll trample him under foot. Come on, men.

NARRATOR: Their gestures, at least, have a cavalier assurance as they swagger off, taking up the whole street.

    The samurai customer patiently endures the fool, indifferent to his remarks because of the surroundings, but every word of gossip about Jihei, whether for good or ill, affects Koharu. She is so depressed that she stands there blankly, unable even to greet her guest. Sugi, the maid from the Kinokuni House, runs up from home, looking annoyed.

SUGI: When I left you here a while ago, Miss Koharu, your guest hadn't appeared yet, and they gave me a terrible scolding when I got back for not having checked on him. I'm very sorry, sir, but please excuse me a minute.

NARRATOR: She lifts the woven hat and examines the face.

SUGI: Oh—it's not him! There's nothing to worry about, Koharu. Ask your guest to keep you for the whole night, and show him how sweet you can be. Give him a barrelful of nectar! Good-by, madam, I'll see you later, honey.

NARRATOR: She takes her leave with a cloying stream of puns. The extremely hard-baked samurai is furious.

SAMURAI: What's the meaning of this? You'd think from the way she appraised my face that I was a tea canister or a porcelain cup! I didn't come here to be trifled with. It's difficult enough for me to leave the Residence even by day, and in order to spend the night away I had to ask the senior officer's permission and sign the register. You can see how complicated the regulations make things. But I'm in love, miss, just from hearing about you, and I wanted very badly to spend a night with you. I came here a while ago without an escort and made the arrangements with the teahouse. I had been looking forward to your kind reception, a memory to last me a lifetime, but you haven't so much as smiled at me or said a word of greeting. You keep your head down, as if you were counting money in your lap. Aren't you afraid of getting a stiff neck? Madam—I've never heard the like. Here I come to a teahouse, and I must play the part of night nurse in a maternity room!

PROPRIETRESS: You're quite right, sir. Your surprise is entirely justified, considering that you don't know the reasons. This girl is deeply in love with a customer named Kamiji. It's been Kamiji today and Kamiji tomorrow, with nobody else allowed a chance at her. Her other customers have scattered in every direction, like leaves in a storm. When two people get so carried away with each other, it often leads to trouble, for both the customer and the girl. In the first place, it interferes with business, and the owner, whoever he may be, is bound to prevent it. That's why all her guests are examined. Koharu is naturally depressed—it's only to be expected. You are annoyed, which is equally to be expected. But, speaking as the proprietress here, it seems to me that the essential thing is for you to meet each other halfway and cheer up. Come, have a drink.—Act a little more lively, Koharu.

NARRATOR: Koharu, without answering, lifts her tear-stained face.

---

[12]Coins of high value.

KOHARU: Tell me, samurai, they say that, if you're going to kill yourself anyway, people who die during the Ten Nights[13] are sure to become Buddhas. Is that really true?

SAMURAI: How should I know? Ask the priest at your family temple.

KOHARU: Yes, that's right. But there's something I'd like to ask a samurai. If you're committing suicide, it'd be a lot more painful, wouldn't it, to cut your throat rather than hang yourself?

SAMURAI: I've never tried cutting my throat to see whether or not it hurt. Please ask more sensible questions.—What an unpleasant girl!

NARRATOR: Samurai though he is, he looks nonplussed.

PROPRIETRESS: Koharu, that's a shocking way to treat a guest the first time you meet him. I'll go and get my husband. We'll have some saké together. That ought to liven things a bit.

NARRATOR: The gate she leaves is illumined by the evening moon low in the sky; the clouds and the passers in the street have thinned.

For long years there has lived in Temma, the seat of the mighty god,[14] though not a god himself, Kamiji, a name often bruited by the gongs of worldly gossip, so deeply, hopelessly, is he tied to Koharu by the ropes of an ill-starred love. Now is the tenth moon, the month when no gods will unite them;[15] they are thwarted in their love, unable to meet. They swore in the last letters they exchanged that if only they could meet, that day would be their last. Night after night Jihei, ready for death, trudges to the Quarter, distractedly, as though his soul had left a body consumed by the fires of love.

At a roadside eating stand he hears people gossiping about Koharu. "She's at Kawashō with a samurai customer," someone says, and immediately Jihei decides, "It will be tonight!"

He peers through the latticework window and sees a guest in the inside room, his face obscured by a hood. Only the moving chin is visible, and Jihei cannot hear what is said.

JIHEI: Poor Koharu! How thin her face is! She keeps it averted from the lamp. In her heart she's thinking only of me. I'll signal her that I'm here, and we'll run off together. Then which will it be—Umeda or Kitano?[16] Oh—I want to tell her I'm here. I want to call her.

NARRATOR: He beckons with his heart, his spirit flies to her, but his body, like a cicada's cast-off shell, clings to the latticework. He weeps with impatience.

The guest in the inside room gives a great yawn.

SAMURAI: What a bore, playing nursemaid to a prostitute with worries on her mind!—The street seems quiet now. Let's go to the end room. We can at least distract ourselves by looking at the lanterns. Come with me.

NARRATOR: They go together to the outer room. Jihei, alarmed, squeezes into the patch of shadow under the lattice window. Inside they do not realize that anyone eavesdrops.

SAMURAI: I've been noticing your behavior and the little things you've said this evening. It's plain to me that you intend a love suicide with Kamiji, or whatever his name is—the man the hostess mentioned. I'm sure I'm right. I realize that

---

[13] A period from the sixth to the fifteenth of the tenth month during which Pure Land ceremonies were held; a popular saying suggested that those who died during this time would attain immediate salvation.

[14] Tenjin Shrine was located in Temma, one of the three major districts of Osaka; Temma Tenjin was one of the guardian deities of Osaka.

[15] In the tenth month all the gods assembled at Izumo, leaving the god of marriage absent from Osaka.

[16] Places north and east of Sonezaki with well-known cemeteries; both names are associated with the god Temma Tenjin.

no amount of advice or reasoning is likely to penetrate the ears of somebody bewitched by the god of death, but I must say that you're exceedingly foolish. The boy's family won't blame him for his recklessness, but they will blame and hate you. You'll be shamed by the public exposure of your body. Your parents may be dead, for all I know, but if they're alive, you'll be punished in hell as a wicked daughter. Do you suppose that you'll become a Buddha? You and your lover won't even be able to fall smoothly into hell together! What a pity—and what a tragedy! This is only our first meeting but, as a samurai, I can't let you die without trying to save you. No doubt money's the problem. I'd like to help, if five or ten *ryō*[17] would be of service. I swear by the god Hachiman[18] and by my good fortune as a samurai that I will never reveal to anyone what you tell me. Open your heart without fear.

NARRATOR: He whispers these words. She joins her hands and bows.

KOHARU: I'm extremely grateful. Thank you for your kind words and for swearing an oath to me, someone you've never had for a lover or even a friend. I'm so grateful that I'm crying.—Yes, it's as they say, when you've something on your mind it shows on your face. You were right. I have promised Kamiji to die with him. But we've been completely prevented from meeting by my master, and Jihei, for various reasons, can't ransom me at once. My contracts with my former master and my present one still have five years to run. If somebody else claimed me during that time, it would be a blow to me, of course, but a worse disgrace to Jihei's honor. He suggested that it would be better if we killed ourselves, and I agreed. I was caught by obligations from which I could not withdraw, and I promised him before I knew what I was doing. I said, "We'll watch for a chance, and I'll slip out when you give the signal." "Yes," he said, "slip out somehow." Ever since then I've been leading a life of uncertainty, never knowing from one day to the next when my last hour will come.

I have a mother living in a back alley south of here. She has no one but me to depend on, and she does piecework to eke out a living. I keep thinking that after I'm dead she'll become a beggar or an outcast, and maybe she'll die of starvation. That's the only sad part about dying. I have just this one life. I'm ashamed that you may think me a coldhearted woman, but I must endure the shame. The most important thing is that I don't want to die. I beg you, please help me to stay alive.

NARRATOR: As she speaks the samurai nods thoughtfully. Jihei, crouching outside, hears her words with astonishment; they are so unexpected to his manly heart that he feels like a monkey who has tumbled from a tree. He is frantic with agitation.

JIHEI [*to himself*]: Then was everything a lie? Ahhh—I'm furious! For two whole years I've been bewitched by that rotten she-fox! Shall I break in and kill her with one blow of my sword? Or shall I satisfy my anger by shaming her to her face?

NARRATOR: He gnashes his teeth and weeps in chagrin. Inside the house Koharu speaks through her tears.

KOHARU: It's a curious thing to ask, but would you please show the kindness of a samurai and become my customer for the rest of this year and into next spring? Whenever Jihei comes, intent on death, please interfere and force him to postpone and postpone his plan. In this way our relations can be broken quite

---

[17]Gold pieces.
[18]A god of war and protector of warriors.

naturally. He won't have to kill himself, and my life will also be saved.—What evil connection from a former existence made us promise to die? How I regret it now!

NARRATOR: She weeps, leaning on the samurai's knee.

SAMURAI: Very well, I'll do as you ask. I think I can help you.—But there's a draft blowing. Somebody may be watching.

NARRATOR: He slams shut the latticework *shōji*.[19] Jihei, listening outside, is in a frenzy.

JIHEI: Exactly what you'd expect from a whore, a cheap whore! I misjudged her foul nature. She robbed the soul from my body, the thieving harlot! Shall I slash her down or run her through? What am I to do?

NARRATOR: The shadows of two profiles fall on the *shōji*.

JIHEI: I'd like to give her a taste of my fist and trample her.—What are they chattering about? See how they nod to each other! Now she's bowing to him, whispering and sniveling. I've tried to control myself—I've pressed my chest, I've stroked it—but I can't stand any more. This is too much to endure!

NARRATOR: His heart pounds wildly as he unsheathes his dirk, a Magoroku of Seki. "Koharu's side must be here," he judges, and stabs through an opening in the latticework. But Koharu is too far away for his thrust, and though she cries out in terror, she remains unharmed. Her guest instantly leaps at Jihei, grabs his hands, and jerks them through the latticework. With his sword knot he quickly and securely fastens Jihei's hands to the window upright.

SAMURAI: Don't make any outcry, Koharu. You are not to look at him.

NARRATOR: At this moment the proprietor and his wife return. They exclaim in alarm.

SAMURAI: This needn't concern you. Some ruffian ran his sword through the *shōji*, and I've tied his arms to the latticework. I have my own way of dealing with him. Don't untie the cord. If you attract a crowd, the place is sure to be thrown in an uproar. Let's all go inside. Come with me, Koharu. We'll go to bed.

NARRATOR: Koharu answers, "Yes," but she recognizes the handle of the dirk, and the memory—if not the blade—transfixes her breast.

KOHARU: There're always people doing crazy things in the Quarter when they've had too much to drink. Why don't you let him go without making any trouble? I think that's best, don't you, Kawashō?

SAMURAI: Out of the question. Do as I say—inside, all of you. Koharu, come along.

NARRATOR: Jihei can still see their shadows even after they enter the inner room, but he is bound to the spot, his hands held in fetters which grip him the tighter as he struggles, his body beset by suffering as he tastes a living shame worse than a dog's. More determined than ever to die, he sheds tears of blood, a pitiful sight.

Tahei the Lone Wolf returns from his carousing.

TAHEI: That's Jihei standing by Kawashō's window. I'll give him a tossing.

NARRATOR: He catches Jihei by the collar and starts to lift him over his back.

JIHEI: Owww!

TAHEI: Owww? What kind of weakling are you? Oh, I see—you're tied here. You must've been pulling off a robbery. You dirty pickpocket! You rotten pickpocket!

---

[19] A window or door sash covered with thin paper.

NARRATOR: He drubs Jihei mercilessly.

TAHEI: You burglar! You convict!

NARRATOR: He kicks him wildly.

TAHEI: Kamiya Jihei's been caught burgling, and they've tied him up!

NARRATOR: Passersby and people of the neighborhood, attracted by his shouts, quickly gather. The samurai rushes from the house.

SAMURAI: Who's calling him a burglar? You? Tell what Jihei's stolen! Out with it!

NARRATOR: He seizes Tahei and forces him into the dirt. Tahei rises to his feet only for the samurai to kick him down again and again. He grips Tahei.

SAMURAI: Jihei! Trample him to your heart's content!

NARRATOR: He pushes Tahei under Jihei's feet. Bound though he is, Jihei stamps furiously over Tahei's face. Tahei, thoroughly trampled and covered with mire, gets to his feet and glares around him.

TAHEI [*to bystander*]: How could you fools stand there calmly and let him step on me? I've memorized every one of your faces, and I intend to pay you back. Remember that!

NARRATOR: He makes his escape, still determined to have the last word. The spectators burst out laughing.

VOICES: Listen to him brag, even after he's been trampled on! Let's throw him from the bridge and give him a drink of water! Don't let him get away!

NARRATOR: They chase after him. When the crowd has dispersed, the samurai approaches Jihei and unfastens the knots. He shows his face with his hood removed.

JIHEI: Magoemon! My brother! How shaming!

NARRATOR: He sinks to the ground and weeps, prostrating himself in the dirt.

KOHARU: Are you his brother, sir?

NARRATOR: Koharu runs to them. Jihei, catching her by the front of the kimono, forces her to the ground.

JIHEI: Beast! She-fox! I'd sooner trample on you than on Tahei!

NARRATOR: He raises his foot, but Magoemon calls out.

MAGOEMON: That's the kind of foolishness responsible for all your trouble. A prostitute's business is to deceive men. Have you just now waked up to that? I've seen to the bottom of her heart the very first time I met her, but you're so scatter-brained that in over two years of intimacy with the woman you never discovered what she was thinking. Instead of stamping on Koharu, why don't you use your feet on your own misguided disposition?—It's deplorable. You're my younger brother, but you're almost thirty, and you've got a six-year-old boy and a four-year-old girl, Kantarō and Osue. You run a shop with a thirty-six-foot frontage, but you don't seem to realize that your whole fortune's collapsing. You shouldn't have to be lectured to by your brother. Your father-in-law is your aunt's husband, and your mother-in-law is your aunt. They've always been like real parents to you. Your wife Osan is my cousin too. The ties of marriage are multiplied by those of blood. But when the family has a reunion the only subject of discussion is our mortification over your incessant visits to Sonezaki. I feel sorry for our poor aunt. You know what a stiff-necked gentleman of the old school her husband Gozaemon is. He's forever flying into a rage and saying, "We've been tricked by your nephew. He's deserted our daughter. I'll take Osan back and ruin Jihei's reputation throughout Temma." Our aunt, with all the heartache to bear herself, sometimes sides with him and sometimes with you. She's worried herself sick. What an ingrate, not to appreciate how she's defended you in your shame! This one offense is enough to make you the target for Heaven's future punishment!

I realized that your marriage couldn't last much longer at this rate. I decided, in the hopes of relieving our aunt's worries, that I'd see with my own eyes what kind of woman Koharu was, and work out some sort of solution afterwards. I consulted the proprietor here, then came myself to investigate the cause of your sickness. I see now how natural it was that you should desert your wife and children. What a faithful prostitute you discovered! I congratulate you!

And here I am, Magoemon the Miller, known far and wide for my paragon of a brother, dressed up like a masquerader at a festival or maybe a lunatic! I put on swords for the first time in my life, and announced myself, like a bit player in a costume piece, as an officer at a residence. I feel like an absolute idiot with these swords, but there's nowhere I can dispose of them now.—It's so infuriating—and ridiculous—that it's given me a pain in the chest.

NARRATOR: He gnashes his teeth and grimaces, attempting to hide his tears. Koharu, choking the while with emotion, can only say:

KOHARU: Yes, you're entirely right.

NARRATOR: The rest is lost in tears. Jihei pounds the earth with his fist.

JIHEI: I was wrong. Forgive me, Magoemon. For three years I've been possessed by that witch. I've neglected my parents, relatives—even my wife and children—and wrecked my fortune, all because I was deceived by Koharu, that sneak thief! I'm utterly mortified. But I'm through with her now, and I'll never set foot here again. Weasel! Vixen! Sneak thief! Here's proof that I've broken with her!

NARRATOR: He pulls out the amulet bag which has rested next to his skin.

JIHEI: Here are the written oaths we've exchanged, one at the beginning of each month, twenty-nine in all. I return them. This means our love and affection are over. Take them.

NARRATOR: He flings the notes at her.

JIHEI: Magoemon, collect from her my pledges. Please make sure you get them all. Then burn them with your own hands. [To KOHARU.] Hand them to my brother.

KOHARU: As you wish.

NARRATOR: In tears, she surrenders the amulet bag. Magoemon opens it.

MAGOEMON: One, two, three, four . . . ten . . . twenty-nine. They're all here. There's also a letter from a woman. What's this?

NARRATOR: He starts to unfold it.

KOHARU: That's an important letter. I can't let you see it.

NARRATOR: She clings to Magoemon's arm, but he pushes her away. He holds the letter to the lamplight and examines the address, "To Miss Koharu from Kamiya Osan." As soon as he reads the words, he casually thrusts the letter into his kimono.

MAGOEMON: Koharu. A while ago I swore by my good fortune as a samurai, but now Magoemon the Miller swears by his good fortune as a businessman that he will show this letter to no one, not even his wife. I alone will read it, then burn it with the oaths. You can trust me. I will not break this oath.

KOHARU: Thank you. You save my honor.

NARRATOR: She bursts into tears again.

JIHEI [laughs contemptuously]: Save your honor! You talk like a human being! [To MAGOEMON.] I don't want to see her cursed face another minute. Let's go. No—I can't hold so much resentment and bitterness! I'll kick her one in the face, a memory to treasure for the rest of my life. Excuse me, please.

NARRATOR: He strides up to Koharu and stamps on the ground.

JIHEI: For three years I've loved you, delighted in you, longed for you, adored you, but today my foot will say my only farewells.

NARRATOR: He kicks her sharply on the forehead and bursts into tears. The brothers leave, forlorn figures. Koharu, unhappy woman, raises her voice in lament as she watches them go. Is she faithful or unfaithful? Her true feelings are hidden in the words penned by Jihei's wife, a letter no one has seen. Jihei goes his separate way without learning the truth.

ACT II

Scene: The house and shop of Kamiya Jihei.
Time: Ten days later.

NARRATOR: The busy street that runs straight to Tenjin Bridge named for the god of Temma, bringer of good fortune, is known as the Street Before the Kami,[20] and here a paper shop does business under the name Kamiya Jihei. The paper is honestly sold, the shop well situated; it is a long-established firm, and customers come thick as raindrops.

    Outside crowds pass in the street, on their way to the Ten Nights service, while inside the husband dozes in the *kotatsu*,[21] shielded from draughts by a screen at his pillow. His wife Osan keeps solitary, anxious watch over shop and house.

OSAN: The days are so short—it's dinnertime already, but Tama still hasn't returned from her errand to Ichinokawa.[22] I wonder what can be keeping her. That scamp Sangorō isn't back either. The wind is freezing. I'm sure the children will both be cold. He doesn't even realize that it's time for Osue to be nursed. Heaven preserve me from ever becoming such a fool! What an infuriating creature!

NARRATOR: She speaks to herself.

KANTARŌ: Mama, I've come back all by myself.

NARRATOR: Her son, the older child, runs up to the house.

OSAN: Kantarō—is that you? What happened to Osue and Sangorō?

KANTARŌ: They're playing by the shrine. Osue wanted her milk and she was bawling her head off.

OSAN: I was sure she would. Oh—your hands and feet are frozen stiff as nails! Go and warm yourself at the *kotatsu*. Your father's sleeping there.—What am I to do with that idiot?

NARRATOR: She runs out impatiently to the shop just as Sangorō shuffles back, alone.

OSAN: Come here, you fool! Where have you left Osue?

SANGORŌ: You know, I must've lost her somewhere. Maybe somebody's picked her up. Should I go back for her?

OSAN: How could you? If any harm has come to my precious child, I'll beat you to death!

NARRATOR: But even as she screams at him, the maid Tama returns with Osue on her back.

TAMA: The poor child—I found her in tears at the corner. Sangorō, when you're supposed to look after the child, do it properly.

---

[20] *Kami* means both "god" and "paper."
[21] A coal-burning fireplace or brazier constructed of a wooden frame covered by a quilt and usually located in the center of a room.
[22] A vegetable market at the north end of Tenjin Bridge in the Temma district.

OSAN: You poor dear. You must want your milk.

NARRATOR: She joins the others by the *kotatsu* and suckles the child.

OSAN: Tama—give that fool a taste of something that he'll remember!

NARRATOR: Sangorō shakes his head.

SANGORŌ: No, thanks. I gave each of the children two tangerines just a while ago at the shrine, and I tasted five myself.

NARRATOR: Fool though he is, bad puns come from him nimbly enough, and the others can only smile despite themselves.

TAMA: Oh—I've become so involved with this half-wit that I almost forgot to tell you, ma'am, that Mr. Magoemon and his aunt are on their way here from the west.

OSAN: Oh dear! I'll have to wake Jihei in that case. [*To* JIHEI.] Please get up. Mother and Magoemon are coming. They'll be upset again if you let them see you, a businessman, sleeping in the afternoon, with the day so short as it is.

JIHEI: All right.

NARRATOR: He struggles to a sitting position and, with his abacus in one hand, pulls his account book to him with the other.

JIHEI: Two into ten goes five, three into nine goes three, three into six goes two, seven times eight is fifty-six.

NARRATOR: His fifty-six-year-old aunt enters with Magoemon.

JIHEI: Magoemon, aunt. How good of you. Please come in. I was in the midst of some urgent calculations. Four nines makes thirty-six *momme*. Three sixes make eighteen *fun*. That's two *momme* less two *fun*.[23] Kantarō! Osue! Granny and Uncle have come! Bring the tobacco tray! One times three makes three. Osan, serve the tea!

NARRATOR: He jabbers away.

AUNT: We haven't come for tea or tobacco. Osan, you're young I know, but you're the mother of two children, and your excessive forbearance does you no credit. A man's dissipation can always be traced to his wife's carelessness. Remember, it's not only the man who's disgraced when he goes bankrupt and his marriage breaks up. You'd do well to take notice of what's going on and assert yourself a bit more.

MAGOEMON: It's foolish to hope for any results, aunt. The scoundrel even deceives me, his elder brother. Why should he take to heart criticism from his wife? Jihei—you played me for a fool. After showing me how you returned Koharu's pledges, here you are, not ten days later, redeeming her! What does this mean? I suppose your urgent calculations are of Koharu's debts! I've had enough!

NARRATOR: He snatches away the abacus and flings it clattering into the hallway.

JIHEI: You're making an enormous fuss without any cause. I haven't crossed the threshold since the last time I saw you except to go twice to the wholesalers in Imabashi and once to the Tenjin Shrine. I haven't even thought of Koharu, much less redeemed her.

AUNT: None of your evasions! Last evening at the Ten Nights service I heard the people in the congregation gossiping. Everybody was talking about the great patron from Temma who'd fallen in love with a prostitute named Koharu from the Kinokuni House in Sonezaki. They said he'd driven away her other guests and was going to ransom her in the next couple of days. There was all kinds of gossip about the abundance of money and fools even in these days of high prices.

---

[23] Twenty *fun* made two *momme*; see note 11.

My husband Gozaemon has been hearing about Koharu constantly, and he's sure that her great patron from Temma must be you, Jihei. He told me, "He's your nephew, but for me he's a stranger, and my daughter's happiness is my chief concern. Once he ransoms the prostitute he'll no doubt sell his wife to a brothel. I intend to take her back before he starts selling her clothes."

He was halfway out of the house before I could restrain him. "Don't get so excited. We can settle this calmly. First we must make sure whether or not the rumors are true."

That's why Magoemon and I are here now. He was telling me a while ago that the Jihei of today was not the Jihei of yesterday—that you'd broken all connections with Sonezaki and completely reformed. But now I hear that you've had a relapse. What disease can this be?

Your father was my brother. When the poor man was on his deathbed, he lifted his head from the pillow and begged me to look after you, as my son-in-law and nephew. I've never forgotten those last words, but your perversity has made a mockery of his request!

NARRATOR: She collapses in tears of resentment. Jihei claps his hands in sudden recognition.

JIHEI: I have it! The Koharu everybody's gossiping about is the same Koharu, but the great patron who's to redeem her is a different man. The other day, as my brother can tell you, Tahei—they call him the Lone Wolf because he hasn't any family or relations—started a fight and was trampled on. He gets all the money he needs from his home town, and he's been trying for a long time to redeem Koharu. I've always prevented him, but I'm sure he's decided that now is his chance. I have nothing to do with it.

NARRATOR: Osan brightens at his words.

OSAN: No matter how forbearing I might be—even if I were an angel—you don't suppose I'd encourage my husband to redeem a prostitute! In this instance at any rate there's not a word of untruth in what my husband has said. I'll be a witness to that, Mother.

NARRATOR: Husband's and wife's words tally perfectly.

AUNT: Then it's true?

NARRATOR: The aunt and nephew clap their hands with relief.

MAGOEMON: Well, I'm happy it's over, anyway. To make us feel doubly reassured, will you write an affidavit which will dispel any doubts your stubborn uncle may have?

JIHEI: Certainly. I'll write a thousand if you like.

MAGOEMON: Splendid! I happen to have bought this on the way here.

NARRATOR: Magoemon takes from the fold of his kimono a sheet of oath-paper from Kumano, the sacred characters formed by flocks of crows.[24] Instead of vows of eternal love, Jihei now signs under penalty of Heaven's wrath an oath that he will sever all ties and affections with Koharu. "If I should die, may Bonten and Taishaku above, and the Four Great Kings below afflict me!"[25] So the text runs, and to it is appended the names of many Buddhas and gods. He signs his name, Kamiya Jihei, in bold characters, imprints the oath with a seal of blood, and proffers it.

---

[24] The Shinto shrine at Kumano issued such paper with crow-shaped characters on the face and the obverse side blank for writing oaths.

[25] Bonten and Taishaku are the Japanese version of the Hindu gods Brahma, ruler of the world, and Sakra (Indra), god of battle; the four kings are the Deva kings who served Sakra.

OSAN: It's a great relief to me, too. Mother, I have you and Magoemon to thank. Jihei and I have had two children, but this is his firmest pledge of affection. I hope you share my joy.

AUNT: Indeed we do. I'm sure that Jihei will settle down and his business will improve, now that he's in this frame of mind. It's been entirely for his sake and for love of the grandchildren that we've intervened. Come, Magoemon, let's be on our way. I'm anxious to set my husband's mind at ease.—It's become chilly here. See that the children don't catch cold.—This too we owe to the Buddha of the Ten Nights. I'll say a prayer of thanks before I go. Hail, Amida Buddha!

NARRATOR: She leaves, her heart innocent as Buddha's. Jihei is perfunctory even about seeing them to the door. Hardly have they crossed the threshold than he slumps down again at the *kotatsu*. He pulls the checked quilting over his head.

OSAN: You still haven't forgotten Sonezaki, have you?

NARRATOR: She goes up to him in disgust and tears away the quilting. He is weeping; a waterfall of tears streams along the pillow, deep enough to bear him afloat. She tugs him upright and props his body against the *kotatsu* frame. She stares into his face.

OSAN: You're acting outrageously, Jihei. You shouldn't have signed that oath if you felt so reluctant to leave her. The year before last, on the middle day of the Boar of the tenth moon, we lit the first fire in the *kotatsu* and celebrated by sleeping here together, pillow to pillow. Ever since then—did some demon or snake creep into my bosom that night?—for two whole years I've been condemned to keep watch over an empty nest. I thought that tonight at least, thanks to Mother and Magoemon, we'd share sweet words in bed as husbands and wives do, but my pleasure didn't last long. How cruel of you, how utterly heartless! Go ahead, cry your eyes out, if you're so attached to her. Your tears will flow into Shijimi River and Koharu, no doubt, will ladle them out and drink them! You're ignoble, inhuman.

NARRATOR: She embraces his knees and throws herself over him, moaning in supplication. Jihei wipes his eyes.

JIHEI: If tears of grief flowed from the eyes and tears of anger from the ears, I could show my heart without saying a word. But my tears all pour in the same way from my eyes, and there's no difference in their color. It's not surprising that you can't tell what's in my heart. I have not a shred of attachment left for that vampire in human skin, but I bear a grudge against Tahei. He has all the money he wants, no wife or children. He's schemed again and again to redeem her, but Koharu refused to give in, at least until I broke with her. She told me time and again, "You have nothing to worry about. I'll never let myself be redeemed by Tahei, not even if my ties with you are ended and I can no longer stay by your side. If my master is induced by Tahei's money to deliver me to him, I'll kill myself in a way that'll do you credit!" But think—not ten days have passed since I broke with her, and she's to be redeemed by Tahei! That rotten whore! That animal! No, I haven't a trace of affection left for her, but I can just hear how Tahei will be boasting. He'll spread the word around Osaka that my business has come to a standstill and I'm hard pressed for money. I'll meet with contemptuous stares from the wholesalers. I'll be dishonored. My heart is broken and my body burns with shame. What a disgrace! How maddening! I've passed the stage of shedding hot tears, tears of blood, sticky tears—my tears now are of molten iron!

NARRATOR: He collapses with weeping. Osan pales with alarm.

OSAN: If that's the situation, poor Koharu will surely kill herself.

JIHEI: You're too well bred, despite your intelligence, to understand her likes! What makes you suppose that faithless creature would kill herself? Far from it—she's probably taking moxa treatments and medicine to prolong her life!

OSAN: No, that's not true. I was determined never to tell you so long as I lived, but I'm afraid of the crime I'd be committing if I concealed the facts and let her die with my knowledge. I will reveal my great secret. There is not a grain of deceit in Koharu. It was I who schemed to end the relations between you. I could see signs that you were drifting towards suicide. I felt so unhappy that I wrote a letter, begging her as one woman to another to break with you, though I knew how painful it would be. I asked her to save your life. The letter must have moved her. She answered that she would give you up, though you were more precious than life itself, because she could not shirk her duty to me. I've kept her letter with me ever since—it's been like a protective charm. Could such a noble-hearted woman violate her promise and brazenly marry Tahei? When a woman—I no less than another—has given herself completely to a man, she does not change. I'm sure she'll kill herself. I'm sure of it. Ahhh—what a dreadful thing to have happened! Save her, please.

NARRATOR: Her voice rises in agitation. Her husband is thrown into a turmoil.

JIHEI: There was a letter in an unknown woman's hand among the written oaths she surrendered to my brother. It must have been from you. If that's the case, Koharu will surely commit suicide.

OSAN: Alas! I'd be failing in the obligations I owe her as another woman if I allowed her to die. Please go to her at once. Don't let her kill herself.

NARRATOR: Clinging to her husband, she melts in tears.

JIHEI: But what can I possibly do? It'd take half the amount of her ransom in earnest money merely to keep her out of Tahei's clutches. I can't save Koharu's life without administering a dose of 750 *momme* in New Silver. How could I raise that much money in my present financial straits? Even if I crush my body to powder, where will the money come from?

OSAN: Don't exaggerate the difficulties. If that's all you need, it's simple enough.

NARRATOR: She goes to the wardrobe, and opening a small drawer takes out a bag fastened with cords of twisted silk. She unhesitantly tears it open and throws down a packet which Jihei retrieves.

JIHEI: What's this? Money? Four hundred *momme* in New Silver? How in the world—

NARRATOR: He stares astonished at this money he never put there.

OSAN: I'll tell you later where this money came from. I've scraped it together to pay the bill for Iwakuni paper that falls due the day after tomorrow. We'll have to ask Magoemon to help us keep the business from betraying its insolvency. But Koharu comes first. The packet contains 400 *momme*. That leaves 350 *momme* to raise.

NARRATOR: She unlocks a large drawer. From the wardrobe lightly fly kite-colored Hachijō silks; a Kyoto crepe kimono lined in pale brown, insubstantial as her husband's life which flickers today and may vanish tomorrow; a padded kimono of Osue's, a flaming scarlet inside and out—Osan flushes with pain to part with it; Kantarō's sleeveless, unlined jacket—if she pawns this, he'll be cold this winter. Next comes a garment of striped Gunnai silk lined in pale blue and never worn, and then her best formal costume—heavy black silk dyed with her family crest, an ivy leaf in a ring. They say that those joined by marriage ties can even go naked at home, though outside the house clothes make the man: she snatches up even her husband's finery, a silken cloak, making fifteen articles in all.

OSAN: The very least the pawnshop can offer is 30 *momme* in New Silver.

NARRATOR: Her face glows as though she already held the money she needs; she hides in the one bundle her husband's shame and her own obligation, and puts her love in besides.

OSAN: It doesn't matter if the children and I have nothing to wear. My husband's reputation concerns me more. Ransom Koharu. Save her. Assert your honor before Tahei.

NARRATOR: But Jihei's eyes remain downcast all the while, and he is silently weeping.

JIHEI: Yes, I can pay the earnest money and keep her out of Tahei's hands. But once I've redeemed her, I'll either have to maintain her in a separate establishment or bring her here. Then what will become of you?

NARRATOR: Osan is at a loss to answer.

OSAN: Yes, what shall I do? Shall I become your children's nurse or the cook? Or perhaps the retired mistress of the house?

NARRATOR: She falls to the floor with a cry of woe.

JIHEI: That would be too selfish. I'd be afraid to accept such generosity. Even if the punishment for my crimes against my parents, against Heaven, against the gods and the Buddhas fails to strike me, the punishment for my crimes against my wife alone will be sufficient to destroy all hope for the future life. Forgive me, I beg you.

NARRATOR: He joins his hands in tearful entreaty.

OSAN: Why should you bow before me? I don't deserve it. I'd be glad to rip the nails from my fingers and toes, to do anything which might serve my husband. I've been pawning my clothes for some time in order to scrape together the money for the paper wholesalers' bills. My wardrobe is empty, but I don't regret it in the least. But it's too late now to talk of such things. Hurry, change your cloak and go to her with a smile.

NARRATOR: He puts on an under kimono of Gunnai silk, a robe of heavy black silk, and a striped cloak. His sash of figured damask holds a dirk of middle length worked in gold: Buddha surely knows that tonight it will be stained with Koharu's blood.

JIHEI: Sangorō! Come here!

NARRATOR: Jihei loads the bundle on the servant's back, intending to take him along. Then he firmly thrusts the wallet next to his skin and starts towards the gate.

VOICE: Is Jihei at home?

NARRATOR: A man enters, removing his fur cap. They see—good heavens!—that it is Gozaemon.

OSAN AND JIHEI: Ahhh—how fortunate that you should come at this moment!

NARRATOR: Husband and wife are upset and confused. Gozaemon snatches away Sangorō's bundle and sits heavily. His voice is sharp.

GOZAEMON: Stay where you are, harlot!—My esteemed son-in-law, what a rare pleasure to see you dressed in your finest attire, with a dirk and a silken cloak! Ahhh—that's how a gentleman of means spends his money! No one would take you for a paper dealer. Are you perchance on your way to the New Quarter? What commendable perseverance! You have no need for your wife, I take it. —Give her a divorce. I've come to take her home with me.

NARRATOR: He speaks needles and his voice is bitter. Jihei has not a word to reply.

OSAN: How kind of you, Father, to walk here on such a cold day. Do have a cup of tea.

NARRATOR: Offering the teacup serves as an excuse for edging closer.

OSAN: Mother and Magoemon came here a while ago, and they told my husband how much they disapproved of his visits to the New Quarter. Jihei was in tears and he wrote out an oath swearing he had reformed. He gave it to Mother. Haven't you seen it yet?

GOZAEMON: His written oath? Do you mean this?

NARRATOR: He takes the paper from his kimono.

GOZAEMON: Libertines scatter vows and oaths wherever they go, as if they were monthly statements of accounts. I thought there was something peculiar about this oath, and now that I am here I can see I was right. Do you still swear to Bonten and Taishaku? Instead of such nonsense, write out a bill of divorcement!

NARRATOR: He rips the oath to shreds and throws down the pieces. Husband and wife exchange looks of alarm, stunned into silence. Jihei touches his hands to the floor and bows his head.

JIHEI: Your anger is justified. If I were still my former self, I would try to offer explanations, but today I appeal entirely to your generosity. Please let me stay with Osan. I promise that even if I become a beggar or an outcast and must sustain life with the scraps that fall from other people's chopsticks, I will hold Osan in high honor and protect her from every harsh and bitter experience. I feel so deeply indebted to Osan that I cannot divorce her. You will understand that this is true as time passes and I show you how I apply myself to my work and restore my fortune. Until then please shut your eyes and allow us to remain together.

NARRATOR: Tears of blood stream from his eyes and his face is pressed to the matting in contrition.

GOZAEMON: The wife of an outcast! That's all the worse. Write the bill of divorcement at once! I will verify and seal the furniture and clothes Osan brought in her dowry.

NARRATOR: He goes to the wardrobe. Osan is alarmed.

OSAN: My clothes are all here. There's no need to examine them.

NARRATOR: She runs up to forestall him, but Gozaemon pushes her aside and jerks open a drawer.

GOZAEMON: What does this mean?

NARRATOR: He opens another drawer: it too is empty. He pulls out every last drawer, but not so much as a foot of patchwork cloth is to be seen. He tears open the wicker hampers, long boxes, and clothes chests.

GOZAEMON: Stripped bare, are they?

NARRATOR: His eyes set in fury. Jihei and Osan huddle under the striped *kotatsu* quilts, ready to sink into the fire with humiliation.

GOZAEMON: This bundle looks suspicious.

NARRATOR: He unties the knots and dumps out the contents.

GOZAEMON: As I thought! You were sending these to the pawnshop, I take it. Jihei—you'd strip the skin from your wife's and your children's bodies to squander the money on your whore! Dirty thief! You're my wife's nephew, but an utter stranger to me, and I'm under no obligation to suffer for your sake. I'll explain to Magoemon what has happened and ask him to make good whatever inroads you've already made on Osan's belongings. But first, the bill of divorcement!

NARRATOR: Even if Jihei could escape through seven padlocked doors, eight thicknesses of chains, and a hundred girdling walls, he could not evade so stringent a demand.

JIHEI: I won't use a brush to write the bill of divorcement. Here's what I'll do instead! Good-by, Osan.

NARRATOR: He lays his hand on his dirk, but Osan clings to him.

OSAN: Father—Jihei admits that he's done wrong and he's apologized in every way. You press your advantage too hard. Jihei may be a stranger, but his children are your grandchildren. Have you no affection for them? I will not accept a bill of divorcement.

NARRATOR: She embraces her husband and raises her voice in tears.

GOZAEMON: Very well. I won't insist on it. Come with me, woman.

NARRATOR: He pulls her to her feet.

OSAN: No, I won't go. What bitterness makes you expose to such shame a man and wife who still love each other? I will not suffer it.

NARRATOR: She pleads with him, weeping, but he pays her no heed.

GOZAEMON: Is there some greater shame? I'll shout it through the town!

NARRATOR: He pulls her up, but she shakes free. Caught by the wrist she totters forward when—alas!—her toes brush against her sleeping children. They open their eyes.

CHILDREN: Mother dear, why is Grandfather, the bad man, taking you away? Whom will we sleep beside now?

NARRATOR: They call out after her.

OSAN: My poor dears! You've never spent a night away from Mother's side since you were born. Sleep tonight beside your father. [To JIHEI.] Please don't forget to give the children their tonic before breakfast.—Oh, my heart is broken!

NARRATOR: These are her parting words. She leaves her children behind, abandoned as in the woods; the twin-trunked bamboo of conjugal love is sundered forever.

ACT III

Scene 1

Sonezaki New Quarter, in front of the Yamato House.
Time: That night.

NARRATOR: This is Shijimi River, the haunt of love and affection. Its flowing water and the feet of passersby are stilled now at two in the morning, and the full moon shines clear in the sky. Here in the street a dim doorway lantern is marked "Yamatoya Dembei" in a single scrawl. The night watchman's clappers take on a sleepy cadence as he totters by on uncertain legs. The very thickness of his voice crying, "Beware of fire! Beware of fire!" tells how far advanced the night is. A serving woman from the upper town comes along, followed by a palanquin. "It's terribly late," she remarks to the bearers as she clatters open the side door of the Yamato House and steps inside.

SERVANT: I've come to take back Koharu of the Kinokuni House.

NARRATOR: Her voice is faintly heard outside. A few moments later, after hardly time enough to exchange three or four words of greeting, she emerges.

SERVANT: Koharu is spending the night. Bearers, you may leave now and get some rest. [To proprietress, inside the doorway.] Oh, I forgot to tell you, madam. Please keep an eye on Koharu. Now that the ransom to Tahei has been arranged and the money's been accepted, we're merely her custodians. Please don't let her drink too much saké.

NARRATOR: She leaves, having scattered at the doorway the seeds that before morning will turn Jihei and Koharu to dust.

At night between two and four even the teahouse kettle rests; the flame flickering in the low candle stand narrows; and the frost spreads in the cold river-wind of the deepening night. The master's voice breaks the stillness.

DEMBEI [*to* JIHEI]: It's still the middle of the night. I'll send somebody with you. [*To servants.*] Mr. Jihei is leaving. Wake Koharu. Call her here.

NARRATOR: Jihei slides open the side door.

JIHEI: No, Dembei, not a word to Koharu. I'll be trapped here till dawn if she hears I'm leaving. That's why I'm letting her sleep and slipping off this way. Wake her up after sunrise and send her back then. I'm returning home now and will leave for Kyoto immediately on business. I have so many engagements that I may not be able to return in time for the interim payment. Please use the money I gave you earlier this evening to clear my account. I'd like you also to send 150 *me* of Old Silver to Kawashō for the moon-viewing party last month. Please get a receipt. Give Saietsubō from Fukushima[26] one piece of silver as a contribution to the Buddhist altar he's bought, and tell him to use it for a memorial service. Wasn't there something else? Oh yes—give Isoichi a tip of four silver coins. That's the lot. Now you can close up and get to bed. Good-by. I'll see you when I return from Kyoto.

NARRATOR: Hardly has he taken two or three steps than he turns back.

JIHEI: I forgot my dirk. Fetch it for me, won't you?—Yes, Dembei, this is one respect in which it's easier being a townsman. If I were a samurai and forgot my sword, I'd probably commit suicide on the spot!

DEMBEI: I completely forgot that I was keeping it for you. Yes, here's the knife with it.

NARRATOR: He gives the dirk to Jihei, who fastens it firmly into his sash.

JIHEI: I feel secure as long as I have this. Good night!

NARRATOR: He goes off.

DEMBEI: Please come back to Osaka soon! Thank you for your patronage!

NARRATOR: With this hasty farewell Dembei rattles the door bolt shut; then not another sound is heard as the silence deepens. Jihei pretends to leave, only to creep back again with stealthy steps. He clings to the door of the Yamato House. As he peeps within he is startled by shadows moving towards him. He takes cover at the house across the way until the figures pass.

Magoemon the Miller, his heart pulverized with anxiety over his younger brother, comes first, followed by the apprentice Sangorō with Jihei's son Kantarō on his back. They hurry along until they spy the lantern of the Yamato House. Magoemon pounds on the door.

MAGOEMON: Excuse me. Kamiya Jihei's here, isn't he? I'd like to see him a moment.

NARRATOR: Jihei thinks, "It's my brother!" but dares not stir from his place of concealment. From inside a man's sleep-laden voice is heard.

DEMBEI: Jihei left a while ago saying he was going up to Kyoto. He's not here.

NARRATOR: Not another sound is heard. Magoemon's tears fall unchecked.

MAGOEMON [*to himself*]: I ought to have met him on the way if he'd been going home. I can't understand what takes him to Kyoto. Ahhh—I'm trembling all over with worry. I wonder if he didn't take Koharu with him.

NARRATOR: The thought pierces his heart; unable to bear the pain, he pounds again on the door.

DEMBEI: Who is it, so late at night? We've gone to bed.

MAGOEMON: I'm sorry to disturb you, but I'd like to ask one more thing. Has Koharu of the Kinokuni House left? I was wondering if she mightn't have gone with Jihei.

---

[26]Perhaps a priest who presided over entertainment in the Gay Quarters, or a male entertainer; Fukushima bordered Sonezaki to the west.

DEMBEI: What's that? Koharu's upstairs, fast asleep.

MAGOEMON: That's a relief, anyway. There's no fear of a lovers' suicide. But where is he hiding himself causing me all this anxiety? He can't imagine the agony of suspense that the whole family is going through on his account. I'm afraid that bitterness towards his father-in-law may make him forget himself and do something rash. I brought Kantarō along, hoping he would help to dissuade Jihei, but the gesture was in vain. I wonder why I failed to meet him?

NARRATOR: He murmurs to himself, his eyes moist with tears. Jihei's hiding place is close enough for him to hear every word. He chokes with emotion, but can only swallow his tears.

MAGOEMON: Sangorō! Where does the fool go night after night? Don't you know anywhere else?

NARRATOR: Sangorō imagines that he himself is the fool referred to.

SANGORŌ: I know a couple of places, but I'm too embarrassed to mention them.

MAGOEMON: You know them? Where are they? Tell me.

SANGORŌ: Please don't scold me when you've heard. Every night I wander down below the warehouses by the market.

MAGOEMON: Imbecile! Who's asking about that? Come on, let's search the back streets. Don't let Kantarō catch a chill. The poor kid's having a cold time of it, thanks to that useless father of his. Still, if the worst the boy experiences is the cold I won't complain. I'm afraid that Jihei may cause him much greater pain. The scoundrel!

NARRATOR: But beneath the rancor in his heart of hearts is profound pity.

MAGOEMON: Let's look at the back street!

NARRATOR: They pass on. As soon as their figures have gone off a distance Jihei runs from his hiding place. Standing on tiptoes he gazes with yearning after them and cries out in his heart.

JIHEI: He cannot leave me to my death, though I am the worst of sinners! I remain to the last a burden to him! I'm unworthy of such kindness!

NARRATOR: He joins his hands and kneels in prayer.

JIHEI: If I may make one further request of your mercy, look after my children!

NARRATOR: These are his only words; for a while he chokes with tears.

JIHEI: At any rate, our decision's been made. Koharu must be waiting.

NARRATOR: He peers through a crack in the side door of the Yamato House and glimpses a figure.

JIHEI: That's Koharu, isn't it? I'll let her know I'm here.

NARRATOR: He clears his throat, their signal. "Ahem, ahem"—the sound blends with the clack of wooden clappers as the watchman comes from the upper street, coughing in the night wind. He hurries on his round of fire warning, "Take care! Beware!" Even this cry has a dismal sound to one in hiding. Jihei, concealing himself like the god of Katsuragi,[27] lets the watchman pass. He sees his chance and rushes to the side door, which softly opens from within.

JIHEI: Koharu?

KOHARU: Were you waiting? Jihei—I want to leave quickly.

NARRATOR: She is all impatience, but the more hastily they open the door, the more likely people will be to hear the casters turning. They lift the door; it gives a moaning that thunders in their ears and in their hearts. Jihei lends a hand from

---

[27] A god associated with Mount Katsuragi; he was so ugly that he only came out at night to work on a bridge he was building between Mount Katsuragi and Mount Kimpu.

the outside, but his fingertips tremble with the trembling of his heart. The door opens a quarter of an inch, a half, an inch—an inch ahead are the tortures of hell, but more than hell itself they fear the guardian-demon's eyes. At last the door opens, and with the joy of New Year's morn Koharu slips out. They catch each other's hands. Shall they go north or south, west or east? Their pounding hearts urge them on, though they know not to what destination: turning their backs on the moon reflected in Shijimi River, they hurry eastward as fast as their legs will carry them.

Scene 2

The farewell journey of many bridges.

NARRATOR:
    The running hand in texts of Nō is always Konoe style;[28]
    An actor in a woman's part is sure to wear a purple hat.
    Does some teaching of the Buddha as rigidly decree
    That men who spend their days in evil haunts must end like this?
    Poor creatures, though they would discover today their destiny in the Sutra of Cause and Effect,[29] tomorrow the gossip of the world will scatter like blossoms the scandal of Kamiya Jihei's love suicide, and, carved in cherry wood, his story to the last detail will be printed in illustrated sheets.

    Jihei, led on by the spirit of death—if such there be among the gods—is resigned to this punishment for neglect of his trade. But at times—who could blame him?—his heart is drawn to those he has left behind, and it is hard to keep walking on. Even in the full moon's light, this fifteenth night of the tenth moon, he cannot see his way ahead—a sign perhaps of the darkness in his heart? The frost now falling will melt by dawn but, even more quickly than this symbol of human frailty, the lovers themselves will melt away. What will become of the fragrance that lingered when he held her tenderly at night in their bedchamber?

    This bridge, Tenjin Bridge, he has crossed every day, morning and night, gazing at Shijimi River to the west. Long ago, when Tenjin, then called Michizane, was exiled to Tsukushi, his plum tree, following its master, flew in one bound to Dazaifu, and here is Plum-field Bridge. Green Bridge recalls the aged pine that followed later, and Cherry Bridge the tree that withered away in grief over parting. Such are the tales still told, bespeaking the power of a single poem.[30]

JIHEI: Though born the parishioner of so holy and mighty a god, I shall kill you and then myself. If you ask the cause, it was that I lacked even the wisdom that might fill a tiny Shell Bridge. Our stay in this world has been short as an autumn day. This evening will be the last of your nineteen, of my twenty-eight years. The time has come to cast away our lives. We promised we'd remain together faithfully, till you were an old woman and I an old man, but before we knew each other three full years, we have met this disaster. Look, there is Ōe Bridge. We follow the river from Little Naniwa Bridge to Funairi Bridge. The farther we journey, the closer we approach the road to death.

---

[28]A style of calligraphy dating from the sixteenth century, used for printing texts of Nō plays.
[29]The Karma Sutra, a sacred Buddhist scripture, that relates action in a chain of cause and effect.
[30]The bridges named here are those the lovers cross on their journey east from Sonezaki to Amijima.

NARRATOR: He laments. She clings to him.

KOHARU: Is this already the road to death?

NARRATOR: Falling tears obscure from each the other's face and threaten to immerse even the Horikawa bridges.

JIHEI: A few steps north and I could glimpse my house, but I will not turn back. I will bury in my breast all thoughts of my children's future, all pity for my wife. We cross southward over the river. Why did they call a place with as many buildings as a bridge has piers "Eight Houses"? Hurry, we want to arrive before the down-river boat from Fushimi comes—with what happy couples sleeping aboard!

Next is Temma Bridge, a frightening name for us about to depart this world. Here the two streams Yodo and Yamato join in one great river, as fish with water, and as Koharu and I, dying on one blade will cross together the River of Three Fords.[31] I would like this water for our tomb offering!

KOHARU: What have we to grieve about? Though in this world we could not stay together, in the next and through each successive world to come until the end of time we shall be husband and wife. Every summer for my devotions I have copied the All Compassionate and All Merciful Chapter of the Lotus Sutra,[32] in the hope that we may be reborn on one lotus.

NARRATOR: They cross over Kyō Bridge and reach the opposite shore.

KOHARU: If I can save living creatures at will when once I mount a lotus calyx in Paradise and become a Buddha, I want to protect women of my profession, so that never again will there be love suicides.

NARRATOR: This unattainable prayer stems from worldly attachment, but it touchingly reveals her heart.

They cross Onari Bridge. The waters of Noda Creek[33] are shrouded with morning haze; the mountain tips show faintly white.

JIHEI: Listen—the voices of the temple bells begin to boom. How much farther can we go on this way? We are not fated to live any longer—let us make an end quickly. Come this way.

NARRATOR: Tears are strung with the 108 beads of the rosaries in their hands. They have come now to Amijima, to the Daichō Temple;[34] the overflowing sluice gate of a little stream beside a bamboo thicket will be their place of death.

Scene 3

Amijima.

JIHEI: No matter how far we walk, there'll never be a spot marked "For Suicides." Let us kill ourselves here.

NARRATOR: He takes her hand and sits on the ground.

KOHARU: Yes, that's true. One place is as good as another to die. But I've been thinking on the way that if they find our dead bodies together people will say that Koharu and Jihei committed a lovers' suicide. Osan will think then that I

---

[31] *Mitsuse-gawa*, the river in the Buddhist underworld that one must cross to reach the land of the dead; Jihei hopes that people will use water from the Yodo and Yamato as offerings to the gods in their prayers to himself and Koharu.

[32] This section of the Buddhist scripture tells the story of the Goddess of Mercy.

[33] A small river northwest of Amijima.

[34] The 108 beads represent the 108 passions or ties to the world that the teller of the beads attempts to subdue; Daichō temple is a Jōdo or Pure Land temple in the Amijima section of Osaka.

treated as mere scrap paper the letter I sent promising her, when she asked me not to kill you, that I would not, and vowing to break all relations. She will be sure that I lured her precious husband into a lovers' suicide. She will despise me as a one-night prostitute, a false woman with no sense of decency. I fear her contempt more than the slander of a thousand or ten thousand strangers. I can imagine how she will resent and envy me. That is the greatest obstacle to my salvation. Kill me here, then choose another spot, far away, for yourself.

NARRATOR: She leans against him. Jihei joins in her tears of pleading.

JIHEI: What foolish worries! Osan has been taken back by my father-in-law. I've divorced her. She and I are strangers now. Why should you feel obliged to a divorced woman? You were saying on the way that you and I will be husband and wife through each successive world until the end of time. Who can criticize us, who can be jealous if we die side by side?

KOHARU: But who is responsible for your divorce? You're even less reasonable than I. Do you suppose that our bodies will accompany us to the afterworld? We may die in different places, our bodies may be pecked by kites and crows, but what does it matter as long as our souls are twined together? Take me with you to heaven or to hell!

NARRATOR: She sinks again in tears.

JIHEI: You're right. Our bodies are made of earth, water, fire, and wind, and when we die they revert to emptiness. But our souls will not decay, no matter how often reborn. And here's a guarantee that our souls will be married and never part!

NARRATOR: He whips out his dirk and slashes off his black locks at the base of the top knot.

JIHEI: Look, Koharu. As long as I had this hair I was Kamiya Jihei, Osan's husband, but cutting it has made me a monk. I have fled the burning house of the three worlds of delusion; I am a priest, unencumbered by wife, children, or worldly possessions. Now that I no longer have a wife named Osan, you owe her no obligations either.

NARRATOR: In tears he flings away the hair.

KOHARU: I am happy.

NARRATOR: Koharu takes up the dirk and ruthlessly, unhesitantly, slices through her flowing Shimada coiffure. She casts aside the tresses she has so often washed and combed and stroked. How heartbreaking to see their locks tangled with the weeds and midnight frost of this desolate field!

JIHEI: We have escaped the inconstant world, a nun and a priest. Our duties as husband and wife belong to our profane past. It would be best to choose quite separate places for our deaths, a mountain for one, the river for the other. We will pretend that the ground above this sluice gate is a mountain. You will die there. I shall hang myself by this stream. The time of our deaths will be the same, but the method and place will differ. In this way we can honor to the end our duty to Osan. Give me your under sash.

NARRATOR: Its fresh violet color and fragrance will be lost in the winds of impermanence; the crinkled silk long enough to wind twice round her body will bind two worlds, this and the next. He firmly fastens one end to the crosspiece of the sluice, then twists the other into a noose for his neck. He will hang for love of his wife like the "pheasant in the hunting grounds."[35]

---

[35] An allusion to a poem by Otomo no Yakamochi (718–785); the pheasant calling to its mate attracts the attention of the hunters.

Koharu watches Jihei prepare for his death. Her eyes swim with tears, her mind is distraught.

KOHARU: Is that how you're going to kill yourself?—If we are to die apart, I have only a little while longer by your side. Come near me.

NARRATOR: They take each other's hands.

KOHARU: It's over in a moment with a sword, but I'm sure you'll suffer. My poor darling!

NARRATOR: She cannot stop the silent tears.

JIHEI: Can suicide ever be pleasant, whether by hanging or cutting the throat? You mustn't let worries over trifles disturb the prayers of your last moments. Keep your eyes on the westward-moving moon, and worship it as Amida himself.[36] Concentrate your thoughts on the Western Paradise. If you have any regrets about leaving the world, tell me now, then die.

KOHARU: I have none at all, none at all. But I'm sure you must be worried about your children.

JIHEI: You make me cry all over again by mentioning them. I can almost see their faces, sleeping peacefully, unaware, poor dears, that their father is about to kill himself. They're the one thing I can't forget.

NARRATOR: He droops to the ground with weeping. The voices of the crows leaving their nests at dawn rival his sobs. Are the crows mourning his fate? The thought brings more tears.

JIHEI: Listen to them. The crows have come to guide us to the world of the dead. There's an old saying that every time somebody writes an oath on the back of a Kumano charm, three crows of Kumano die on the holy mountain. The first words we've written each New Year have been vows of love, and how often we've inscribed oaths at the beginning of the month! If each oath has killed three crows, what a multitude must have perished! Their cries have always sounded like "beloved, beloved," but hatred for our crime of taking life makes their voices ring tonight "revenge, revenge!" Whose fault is it they demand revenge? Because of me you will die a painful death. Forgive me!

NARRATOR: He takes her in his arms.

KOHARU: No, it's my fault!

NARRATOR: They cling to each other, face pressed to face; their sidelocks, drenched with tears, freeze in the winds blowing over the fields. Behind them echoes the voice of the Daichō Temple.

JIHEI: Even the long winter night seems short as our lives.

NARRATOR: Dawn is already breaking, and matins can be heard. He draws her to him.

JIHEI: The moment has come for our glorious end. Let there be no tears on your face when they find you later.

KOHARU: There won't be any.

NARRATOR: She smiles. His hands, numbed by the frost, tremble before the pale vision of her face, and his eyes are first to cloud. He is weeping so profusely that he cannot control the blade.

KOHARU: Compose yourself—but be quick!

NARRATOR: Her encouragement lends him strength; the invocations to Amida carried by the wind urge a final prayer. *Namu Amida Butsu.*[37] He thrusts in the

---

[36] Amida Buddha's paradise, the Pure Land, was in the west.

[37] The traditional prayer or invocation of Amida's name; it roughly means "Adoration for the Buddha of Infinite Light and Life."

saving sword. Stabbed, she falls backwards, despite his staying hand, and struggles in terrible pain. The point of the blade has missed her windpipe, and these are the final tortures before she can die. He writhes with her in agony, then painfully summons his strength again. He draws her to him, and plunges his dirk to the hilt. He twists the blade in the wound, and her life fades away like an unfinished dream at dawning.

He arranges her corpse head to the north, face to the west, lying on her right side,[38] and throws his cloak over her. He turns away at last, unable to exhaust with tears his grief over parting. He pulls the sash to him and fastens the noose around his neck. The service in the temple has reached the closing section, the prayers for the dead. "Believers and unbelievers will equally share in the divine grace,"[39] the voices proclaim, and at the final words Jihei jumps from the sluice gate.

JIHEI: May we be reborn on one lotus! Hail Amida Buddha!

NARRATOR: For a few moments he writhes like a gourd swinging in the wind, but gradually the passage of his breath is blocked as the stream is dammed by the sluice gate, where his ties with this life are snapped.

Fishermen out for the morning catch find the body in their net.

FISHERMEN: A dead man! Look, a dead man! Come here, everybody!

NARRATOR: The tale is spread from mouth to mouth. People say that they who were caught in the net of Buddha's vow[40] immediately gained salvation and deliverance, and all who hear the tale of the Love Suicides at Amijima are moved to tears.

OLAUDAH EQUIANO
[1745–1797]

About two years before the publication of the misadventures of Voltaire's ill-fated hero Candide, an eleven-year-old African was kidnapped from his home in Essaka, in what is now Nigeria. An innocent, like Candide, this young man was taken into slavery and was eventually sold to traders on the coast, from which he would embark on a very real journey into misfortune, oppression, and despair. The book that tells his eloquent tale of betrayal, enslavement, misadventure, and finally emancipation, *The Interesting Narrative of the Life of Olaudah Equiano, or Gustavus Vassa the African,* was published in London in 1789. Although a few slaves had told their stories in print before—most notably Ignatius Sancho and Ottobah Cugoano—*Equiano's Travels,* as it is often called, marks a crucial moment in the development of a significant new literary genre, the slave narrative. Reflecting its author's spiritual and intellectual resolution and framing the incidents of his life as a slave within a deeply felt humanitarian perspective, this book would inspire over the next century such works as Frederick Douglass's *Narrative of the Life of Frederick Douglass, an American Slave* (1845) and Harriet Jacobs's *Incidents in the Life of a Slave Girl* (1861), which we include in our nineteenth-century selections.

---

[38] Imitating the position of the dying Sakyamuni Buddha.
[39] The final refrain of a Pure Land memorial prayer.
[40] In contrast to the fishermen who find only the body in their net, the souls of Koharu and Jihei have been caught in the net (*ami*) of Buddha and so will be freed from the cycle of rebirth.

LIFE

Equiano's "round unvarnished tale," as it was called in an early review, begins with a brief description of his birth in 1745 in Essaka, a village in Eboe, an area that is today part of eastern Nigeria. His father, as he tells us, was one of the chief elders, the Embrenche, of his community, and as a child Equiano was blessed with good omens. In the first chapter of his book, Equiano describes the society, religious beliefs, and customs of the Ibo people with whom he spent his childhood. Unlike the Yoruba, who occupied territory near the Ibo culture in what is now Nigeria, the Ibo had a village culture. Within each village, a council of elders settled matters that affected the community and mediated disputes between parties. Nonetheless, a village assembly, which was open to all except the *osu* or slaves, ensured that members of the village had a voice in the decision-making process. As becomes evident in Chinua Achebe's *Things Fall Apart,* which describes the Ibo traditions in place more than a century after Equiano's death, the Ibo also were organized along a complex system of age group, kinship, and ritual ties. In the eighteenth century, the Ibo engaged in an intricate network of trade with other interdependent Ibo villages and with their neighbors to the south who inhabited the city-states in the Niger delta region. Among the commodities traded were slaves, and when he was about eleven, Equiano was kidnapped by a raiding party and eventually taken to the coast to be sold into slavery.

Equiano's story up to this point would be fairly typical of the thousands of slaves who were kidnapped by rival tribes or parties of raiders, who would exchange their victims for rifles, textiles, tobacco, iron, brass, and other items. Sometimes, as in Equiano's case, the slaves would pass hands on their journey to the coastal towns along the Gold Coast or in the Niger delta, where they were held in forts until sold to the European slave traders, packed into the infamous "slavers," the crowded ships that would take them to the West Indies or the United States. In his narrative, Equiano describes the horrible conditions aboard the slave ship, the anxieties and sorrows he suffered upon being traded from place to place and being separated from his sister. After being kidnapped, Equiano was taken to Barbados, then to Virginia, where he was sold to a plantation owner. Within a few months he was sold again to Michael Henry Pascal, a British naval captain, with whom Equiano sailed to England, Holland, and North America, where his ship engaged in battles during the Seven Years' War. Through Pascal, Equiano learned to read and write, and he was treated with kindness and with some measure of respect by Pascal's relatives the Guerins, in London. Nonetheless, in 1763 Pascal sold Equiano to Captain James Doran, who took him to the West Indies, where he finally ended up the property of Robert King, a Quaker merchant.

Equiano notes early that his name Olaudah means "fortunate one," and although his life would suggest the opposite, he reminds readers who haven't seen the horrors of the slave trade that, by comparison with most African slaves, he can only consider himself "as a particular favourite of Heaven." Indeed, King finally enabled Equiano to buy his freedom in 1767, after which Equiano returned to London, where he launched a life of adventure. Attracted by the life he'd come to know as a seafarer and small trader, Equiano traveled to the Mediterranean, America, the West Indies, and even to the Arctic, with the Phipps Expedition of 1772. In 1786, he was appointed Commissary of Provisions and Stores to help oversee the resettling of freed slaves in Sierra Leone, although a disagreement with the authorities caused him to resign this post. Nonetheless, Equiano stayed in England to become one of the leading black proponents of abolition and a key figure in the antislavery movement. In 1792, Equiano married Susanna Cullen, with whom he spent the next five years in England. He died in 1797, shortly after the death of one of his two daughters, leaving behind a substantial estate for his wife and surviving daughter.

WORK

After its publication in 1789, *The Life of Olaudah Equiano* met with enormous popularity in England and the United States (eight English editions and one American edition by 1794), and it contributed to the growing antislavery movement in England that eventually led to the freeing of all slaves in the British colonies in 1834. Whereas Voltaire's *Candide* invents the hapless travels of an innocent hero to criticize European society in general, *The Life of Olaudah Equiano* recounts its author's experiences in order, as Equiano says, to promote "the interests of humanity." Given the wide travels and the numerous accounts of voyages to new lands, battles at sea, and captivity, *The Life of Olaudah Equiano* shares some of the features of works such as *Candide* and even Swift's *Gulliver's Travels*. As Paul Edwards, editor and commentator on Equiano's works, has noted, "the situation has a touch of both Robinson Crusoe and Gulliver: from one point of view, his is a story of economic and moral survival on the bleak rock of slavery, a study in initiative and adaptability not entirely unlike Robinson Crusoe's; and from another, it is a tale, like Gulliver's, of new perspectives gained by physical alienation, in this case of the black man in a white world." Yet, we are constantly reminded in Equiano's story that the hardships he endures and the oppression he suffers are not fiction but reality.

SUGGESTED READINGS

A complete text of *The Life of Olaudah Equiano* is available in Henry Louis Gates, Jr., ed., *The Classic Slave Narratives* (1987); Paul Edwards has edited an abridged edition, *Equiano's Travels* (1967), and has introduced the standard facsimile edition, *The Life of Olaudah Equiano, or Gustavus Vassa the African* (1969). Angela Costanzo's *Surprizing Narrative: Olaudah Equiano and the Beginning of Black Autobiography* (1987) and Catherine Obianuju Acholonu's *The Igbo Roots of Olaudah Equiano* (1989) are two book-length studies of Equiano's life and work. Paul Edwards's *Black Writers in England, 1760–1890* (1991) and Keith Sandiford's *Measuring the Moment: Strategies of Protest in Eighteenth-Century Afro-English Writing* (1988) contain discussions of Equiano's narrative, as do two collections of essays on the slave narrative in general, John Sekora and Darwin T. Turner, eds., *The Art of the Slave Narrative: Original Essays in Criticism and Theory* (1982), and Charles T. Davis and Henry Louis Gates, Jr., eds., *The Slave's Narrative* (1985).

The Interesting Narrative of the Life of Olaudah Equiano, or Gustavus Vassa the African

FROM
CHAPTER 1

I. I believe it is difficult for those who publish their own memoirs to escape the imputation of vanity. Nor is this the only disadvantage under which they labour: it is also their misfortune, that whatever is uncommon is rarely, if ever, believed, and from what is obvious we are apt to turn with disgust, and to charge the writer of it with impertinence. People generally think those memoirs only worthy to be read or remembered which abound in great or striking events; those in short, which, in a high degree, excite either admiration or pity: all others they consign to contempt and oblivion. It is therefore, I confess, not a little hazardous in a private and obscure individual, and a stranger too, thus to solicit the indulgent attention of the public;

especially when I own I offer here the history of neither a saint, a hero, nor a tyrant. I believe there are a few events in my life which have not happened to many. It is true the incidents of it are numerous; and did I consider myself an European, I might say my sufferings were great: but when I compare my lot with that of most of my countrymen, I regard myself as a *particular favourite of Heaven,* and acknowledge the mercies of Providence in every occurrence of my life. If, then, the following narrative does not appear sufficiently interesting to engage general attention, let my motive be some excuse for its publication. I am not so foolishly vain as to expect from it either immortality or literary reputation. If it affords any satisfaction to my numerous friends, at whose request it has been written, or in the smallest degree promotes the interests of humanity, the ends for which it was undertaken will be fully attained, and every wish of my heart gratified. Let it therefore be remembered that, in wishing to avoid censure, I do not aspire to praise.

II. That part of Africa, known by the name of Guinea, to which the trade of slaves is carried on, extends along the coast above 3,400 miles, from Senegal to Angola, and includes a variety of kingdoms. Of these the most considerable is the kingdom of Benin, both as to extent and wealth, the richness and culture of the soil, the power of its king, and the number and warlike disposition of its inhabitants. It is situated nearly under the line, and extends along the coast about 170 miles, but runs back into the interior of Africa to a distance hitherto, I believe, unexplored by any traveller; and seems only terminated at length by the empire of Abyssinia, near 1,500 miles from its beginning. This kingdom is divided into many provinces or districts; in one of the most remote and fertile of which, named Essaka, situated in a charming fruitful vale, I was born, in the year 1745. The distance of this province from the capital of Benin and the sea coast must be very considerable: for I had never heard of white men or Europeans, nor of the sea; and our subjection to the king of Benin was little more than nominal. Every transaction of the government, as far as my slender observation extended, was conducted by the chiefs or elders of the place. The manners and government of a people who have little commerce with other countries, are generally very simple; and the history of what passes in one family or village, may serve as a specimen of the whole nation. My father was one of those elders or chiefs of whom I have spoken, and was stiled Embrenche; a term, as I remember, importing the highest distinction, and signifying in our language "a mark of grandeur." ...

FROM
CHAPTER 2

...I have already acquainted the reader with the time and place of my birth. My father, besides many slaves, had a numerous family, of which seven lived to grow up, including myself and a sister, who was the only daughter. As I was the youngest of the sons, I became, of course, the greatest favourite with my mother, and was always with her, and she used to take particular pains to form my mind. I was trained up from my earliest years in the art of war: my daily exercise was shooting and throwing javelins; and my mother adorned me with emblems, after the manner of our greatest warriors. In this way I grew up till I was turned the age of eleven, when an end was put to my happiness in the following manner:—When the grown people in the neighbourhood were gone far in the fields to labour, the children generally assembled together in some of the neighbours' premises to play; and some of us often used to get up into a tree to look out for any assailant, or kidnapper, that might come upon us. For they sometimes took those opportunities of our parents' absence, to attack and carry off as many as they could seize. One day, as I was watching at the top of a tree in our yard, I saw one of those people come into the yard of our next neighbour but one, to kidnap, there being many stout young people in it. Immediately on this I gave the alarm of the rogue, and he was surrounded by the stoutest of them, who entangled him with cords, so that he could not escape till some of the grown people came and secured him.

II. But alas! ere long it was my fate to be thus attacked, and to be carried off, when none of the grown people were nigh. One day, when all our people were gone out to their work as usual, and only I and my sister were left to mind the house, two men and a woman got over our walls, and in a moment seized us both; and without giving us time to cry out, or to make any resistance, they stopped our mouths and ran off with us into the nearest wood. Here they tied our hands, and continued to carry us as far as they could, till night came on, when we reached a small house, where the robbers halted for refreshment and spent the night. We were then unbound, but were unable to take any food; and being quite overpowered by fatigue and grief, our only relief was some sleep, which allayed our misfortune for a short time. The next morning we left the house, and continued travelling all the day. For a long time we had kept the woods, but at last we came into a road which I believed I knew. I had now some hopes of being delivered; for we had advanced but a little way before I discovered some people at a distance, on which I began to cry out for their assistance; but my cries had no other effect than to make them tie me faster and stop my mouth; they then put me into a large sack. They also stopped my sister's mouth, and tied her hands; and in this manner we proceeded till we were out of sight of these people.

When we went to rest the following night, they offered us some victuals; but we refused it; and the only comfort we had was in being in one another's arms all that night, and bathing each other with tears. But alas! we were soon deprived of even the small comfort of weeping together. The next day proved one of greater sorrow than I had yet experienced; for my sister and I were then separated, while we lay clasped in each other's arms. It was in vain that we besought them not to part us; she was torn from me, and immediately carried away, while I was left in a state of distraction not to be described. I cried and grieved continually; and for several days did not eat any thing but what they forced into my mouth. At length, after many days' travelling, during which I had often changed masters, I got into the hands of a chieftain, in a pleasant country. This man had two wives and some children, and they all used me extremely well, and did all they could to comfort me; particularly the first wife, who was something like my mother. Although I was a great many days' journey from my father's house, yet these people spoke exactly the same language with us. This first master of mine, as I may call him, was a smith, and my principal employment was working his bellows, which were the same kind as I had seen in my vicinity. They were in some respects not unlike the stoves here in gentlemen's kitchens; and were covered over with leather, and in the middle of that leather a stick was fixed, and a person stood up and worked it, in the same manner as is done to pump water out of a cask with a hand pump. I believe it was gold he worked, for it was of a lovely bright yellow colour, and was worn by the women on their wrists and ankles.

I was there, I suppose, about a month, and they at length used to trust me some little distance from the house. I employed this liberty in embracing every opportunity to inquire the way to my own home: and I also sometimes, for the same purpose, went with the maidens, in the cool of the evenings, to bring pitchers of water from the springs for the use of the house. I had also remarked where the sun rose in the morning, and set in the evening, as I had travelled along: and had observed that my father's house was towards the rising of the sun. I therefore determined to seize the first opportunity of making my escape, and to shape my course for that quarter; for I was quite oppressed and weighed down by grief after my mother and friends; and my love of liberty, ever great, was strengthened by the mortifying circumstance of not daring to eat with the free-born children, although I was mostly their companion.

III. While I was projecting my escape, one day an unlucky event happened, which quite disconcerted my plan, and put an end to my hopes. I used to be sometimes employed in assisting an elderly woman slave to cook and take care of the poultry: and one morning, while I was feeding some chickens, I happened to toss a small pebble at one of them, which hit it on the middle, and directly killed it. The old slave having soon after missed the chicken, inquired after it; and on my relating the accident (for I told her the truth, because my mother would never suffer me to tell a lie) she flew into a violent passion, threatened that I should suffer for it; and, my master being out, she immediately went and told her mistress what I had done. This alarmed me very much, and I expected an instant flogging, which to me was uncommonly dreadful; for I had seldom been beaten at home. I therefore resolved to fly; and accordingly I ran into a thicket that was hard by, and hid myself in the bushes. Soon afterwards my mistress and the slave returned, and, not seeing me, they searched all the house, but not finding me, and I not making answer when they called me, they thought I had run away, and the whole neighbourhood was raised in the pursuit of me.

In that part of the country, as well as in ours, the houses and villages were skirted with woods, or shrubberies, and the bushes were so thick that a man could readily conceal himself in them, so as to elude the strictest search. The neighbours continued the whole day looking for me, and several times many of them came within a few yards of the place where I lay hid. I expected every moment, when I heard a rustling among the trees, to be found out, and punished by my master. But they never discovered me, though they often were so near that I even heard their conjectures, as they were looking about for me; and I now learned from them, that any attempt to return home would be hopeless. Most of them supposed I had fled towards home; but the distance was so great, and the way so intricate, that they thought I could never reach it, and that I should be lost in the woods. When I heard this I was seized with a violent panic, and abandoned myself to despair. Night too began to approach, and aggravated all my fears. I had before entertained hopes of getting home and had determined when it should be dark to make the attempt; but I was now convinced it was fruitless, and began to consider that, if possibly I could escape all other animals, I could not those of the human kind; and that, not knowing the way, I must perish in the woods. Thus was I like the hunted deer:

> Ev'ry leaf, and ev'ry whisp'ring breath
> Convey'd a foe, and ev'ry foe a death.

I heard frequent rustlings among the leaves, and being pretty sure they were snakes, I expected every instant to be stung by them. This increased my anguish, and the horror of my situation became now quite insupportable. I at length quitted the thicket, very faint and hungry, for I had not eaten nor drunk any thing all the day. I crept to my master's kitchen, from whence I set out at first, which was an open shed, and laid myself down in the ashes with an anxious wish for death to relieve me from all my pains. I was scarcely awake in the morning, when the old woman slave, who was the first up, came to light the fire, and saw me in the fire place. She was very much surprised to see me, and could scarcely believe her own eyes. She now promised to intercede for me, and went for her master, who soon after came, and, having slightly reprimanded me, ordered me to be taken care of, and not ill treated.

IV. Soon after this my master's only daughter and child by his first wife, sickened and died, which affected him so much that for some time he was almost frantic, and really would have killed himself, had he not been watched and prevented. However, in a small time afterwards he recovered, and I was again sold. I was now carried to the left of the sun's rising, through many dreary wastes and dismal woods, amidst the hideous roaring of wild beasts. The people I was sold to used to carry me very often, when I was tired, either on their shoulders or on their backs. I saw many convenient well-built sheds along the road, at proper distances, to accommodate the merchants and travellers. They lie in those buildings along with their wives, who often accompany them: and they always go well armed.

From the time I left my own nation I always found somebody that understood me till I came to the sea coast. The languages of different nations did not totally differ, nor were they so copious as those of the Europeans, particularly the English. They were therefore easily learned; and, while I was journeying thus through Africa, I acquired two or three different tongues. In this manner I had been travelling for a considerable time, when one evening, to my great surprise, whom should I see brought to the house where I was, but my dear sister? As soon as she saw me she gave a loud shriek, and ran into my arms. I was quite overpowered: neither of us could speak; but for a considerable time, clung to each other in mutual embraces, unable to do any thing but weep. Our meeting affected all who saw us; and indeed I must acknowledge, in honour of those sable destroyers of human rights, that I never met with any ill treatment, or saw any offered to their slaves, except tying them, when necessary, to keep them from running away.

When these people knew we were brother and sister, they indulged us to be together; and the man, to whom I supposed we belonged, lay with us, he in the middle, while she and I held one another by the hands across his breast all night; and thus for a while we forgot our misfortunes in the joy of being together. But even this small comfort was soon to have an end, for scarcely had the fatal morning appeared, when she was again torn from me for ever! I was now more miserable, if possible, than before. The small relief which her presence gave me from pain was gone, and the wretchedness of my situation was redoubled by my anxiety after her fate, and my apprehensions lest her sufferings should be greater than mine, when I could not be with her to alleviate them.

Yes, dear partner of all my childish sports! Sharer of my joys and sorrows; happy should I have ever esteemed myself to encounter every misery for you, and to procure your freedom by the sacrifice of my own! Though you were early forced from my arms, your image has been always rivetted in my heart, from which neither time nor fortune has been able to remove it: so that, while the thoughts of your sufferings have damped my prosperity, they have mingled with adversity and increased its bitterness. To that Heaven, which protects the weak from the strong, I commit the care of your innocence and virtues, if they have not already received their full reward, and if your youth and delicacy have not long since fallen victims to the violence of the African trader, the pestilential stench of a Guinea ship, the seasoning in the European colonies, or the lash and lust of a brutal and unrelenting overseer.

I did not long remain after my sister. I was again sold, and carried through a number of places, till, after travelling a considerable time, I came to a town called Tinmah, in the most beautiful country I had yet seen in Africa. It was extremely rich, and there were many rivulets which flowed through it, and supplied a large pond in the centre of the town, where the people washed. Here I first saw and tasted cocoa nuts, which I thought superior to any nuts I had ever tasted before; and the trees which were loaded, were also interspersed among the houses, which had commodious shades adjoining, and were in the same manner as ours, the insides being neatly plastered and whitewashed. Here I also saw and tasted, for the first time, sugar-cane. Their money consisted of little white shells, the size of the fingernail. I was sold for one hundred and seventy-two of these, by a merchant who lived at this place. I had been about two or three days at his house, when a wealthy widow, a neighbour of his came there one evening, and brought with her an only son, a young gentleman about my own age and size. Here they saw me; and, having taken a fancy to me, I was bought of the merchant, and went home with them. Her house and premises were situated close to one of those rivulets I have mentioned, and were the finest I ever saw in Africa: they were very extensive, and she had a number of slaves to attend her. The next day I was washed and perfumed, and when meal-time came, I was led into the presence of my mistress, and ate and drank before her with her son. This filled me with astonishment; and I could scarcely avoid expressing my surprise that the young gentleman should suffer me, who was bound, to eat with him who was free; and not only so, but that he would not at any time either eat or drink till I had taken first, because I was the eldest, which was agreeable to our custom. Indeed every thing here, and their treatment of me, made me forget that I was a slave. The language of these people resembled ours so nearly, that we understood each other perfectly. They had also the very same customs as we. There were likewise slaves daily to attend us, while my young master and I, with other boys, sported with our darts, and bows and arrows, as I had been used to do at home. In this resemblance to my former happy state, I passed about two months; and now I began to think I was to be adopted into the family, and was beginning to be reconciled to my situation, and to forget by degrees my misfortunes, when all at once the delusion vanished; for, without the least previous knowledge, one morning, early, while my dear master and companion was still asleep, I was awakened out of my reverie to fresh sorrow, and hurried away even amongst the uncircumcised.

Thus, at the very moment I dreamed of the greatest happiness, I found myself most miserable; and it seemed as if fortune wished to give me this taste of joy, only to render the reverse more poignant. The change I now experienced was as painful as it was sudden and unexpected. It was a change indeed from a state of bliss to a scene which is inexpressible by me, as it discovered to me an element I had never before beheld, and of which till then had no idea; and wherein such instances of hardship and cruelty continually occurred, as I can never reflect on but with horror.

V. All the nations and people I had hitherto passed through resembled our own in their manners, customs, and language: but I came at length to a country, the inhabitants of which differed from us in all these particulars. I was very much struck with this difference, especially when I came among a people who did not circumcise, and who ate without washing their hands. They cooked their provisions also in iron pots, and had European cutlasses and cross bows, which were unknown to us; and fought with their fists among themselves. Their women were not so modest as ours, for they ate, drank, and slept with their men. But, above all, I was amazed to see no sacrifices or offerings among them. In some of those places the people ornamented themselves with scars, and likewise filed their teeth very sharp. They sometimes wanted to ornament me in the same manner, but I would not suffer them; hoping that I might sometime be among a people who did not thus disfigure themselves, as I thought they did. At last I came to the banks of a large river, covered with canoes, in which the people appeared to live, with their household utensils, and provisions of all kinds. I was beyond measure astonished at this, as I had never before seen any water larger than a pond or a rivulet: and my surprise was mingled with no small fear when I was put into one of these canoes, and we began to paddle and move along the river. We continued going on thus till night; and when we came to land, and made fires on the banks, each family by themselves, some dragged their canoes on shore, others cooked in theirs, and laid in them all night. Those on the land had mats, of which they made tents, some in the shape of little houses: in these we slept: and after the morning meal, we embarked again, and proceeded as before. I was often very much astonished to see some of the women as well as the men, jump into the water, dive to the bottom, come up again, and swim about. Thus I continued to travel, both by land and by water, through different countries and various nations, till at the end of six or seven months after I had been kidnapped, I arrived at the sea coast.

It would be tedious and uninteresting to relate all the incidents which befell me during this journey, and which I have not yet forgotten, or to mention the various lands I passed through, and the manners and customs of the different people among whom I lived: I shall therefore only observe, that in all the places where I was, the soil was exceedingly rich; the pomkins, aedas, plantains, yams, &c. &c. were in great abundance, and of incredible size. There were also large quantities of different gums, though not used for any purpose; and every where a great deal of tobacco. The cotton even grew quite wild; and there was plenty of red wood. I saw no mechanics whatever in all the way, except such as I have mentioned. The chief employment in all these countries was agriculture, and both the males and females, as with us, were brought up to it, and trained in the arts of war.

The first object that saluted my eyes when I arrived on the coast was the sea, and a slave ship, which was then riding at anchor, and waiting for its cargo. These filled me with astonishment, that was soon converted into terror, which I am yet at a loss to describe, and much more the then feelings of my mind when I was carried on board. I was immediately handled and tossed up to see if I was sound, by some of the crew; and I was now persuaded that I had got into a world of bad spirits, and that they were going to kill me. Their complexions too, differing so much from ours, their long hair, and the language they spoke, which was very different from any I had ever heard, united to confirm me in this belief. Indeed such were the horrors of my views and fears at the moment, that if ten thousand worlds had been my own, I would have freely parted with them all to have exchanged my condition with the meanest slave in my own country. When I looked round the ship too, and saw a large furnace or copper boiling and a multitude of black people, of every description, chained together, every one of their countenances expressing dejection and sorrow, I no longer doubted of my fate; and, quite overpowered with horror and anguish, I fell motionless on the deck, and fainted. When I recovered a little, I found some black people about me, who I believed were some of those who brought me on board, and had been receiving their pay: they talked to me in order to cheer me, but all in vain. I asked them if we were not to be eaten by those white men with horrible looks, red faces, and long hair. They told me I was not: and one of the crew brought me a small portion of spirituous liquor in a wine glass; but, being afraid of him, I would not take it out of his hand. One of the blacks therefore took it from him and gave it to me, and I took a little down my palate, which, instead of reviving me, as they thought it would, threw me into the greatest consternation at the strange feeling it produced, having never tasted any such liquor before.

Soon after this the blacks who brought me on board went off, and left me abandoned to despair. I now saw myself deprived of all chance of return-ing to my native country, or even the least glimpse of gaining the shore, which I now considered as friendly; and I even wished for my former slavery, in preference to my present situation, which was filled with horrors of every kind, still heightened by my ignorance of what I was to undergo. I was not long suffered to indulge my grief. I was soon put down under the decks, and there I received such a salutation in my nostrils as I had never experienced in my life: so that, with the loathsomeness of the stench, and with my crying together, I became so sick and low that I was not able to eat, nor had I the least desire to taste any thing. I now wished for the last friend, death, to relieve me; but soon, to my grief, two of the white men offered me eatables; and, on my refusing to eat, one of them held me fast by the hands, and laid me across, I think, the windlass, and tied my feet, while the other flogged me severely. I had never experienced any thing of this kind before, and although, not being used to the water, I naturally feared that element the first time I saw it, yet nevertheless, could I have got over the nettings, I would have jumped over the side, but I could not; and besides the crew used to watch us very closely, who were not chained down to the decks, lest we should leap into the water. I have seen some of these poor African prisoners most severely cut for attempting to do so, and hourly whipped for not eating. This indeed was often the case with myself. In a little time after, amongst the poor chained men, I found some of my own nation, which in a small degree gave ease to my mind. I inquired of these what was to be done with us. They gave me to understand we were to be carried to these white people's country to work for them. I was then a little revived, and thought if it were no worse than working, my situation was not so desperate. But still I feared I should be put to death, the white people looked and acted, as I thought, in so savage a manner; for I had never seen among any people such instances of brutal cruelty: and this is not only shewn towards us blacks, but also to some of the whites themselves. One white man in particular I saw, when we were permitted to be on deck, flogged so unmercifully with a large rope near the foremast, that he died in consequence of it; and they tossed him over the side as they would have done a brute. This made me fear these people the more; and I expected nothing less than to be treated in the same manner. I could not help expressing my fearful apprehensions to some of my countrymen; I asked them if these people had no country, but lived in this hollow place, the ship. They told me they did not, but came from a distant one. "Then," said I, "how comes it, that in all our country we never heard of them?" They told me, because they lived so very far off. I then asked, where their women were: had they any like themselves. I was told they had. "And why," said I, "do we not see them?" They answered, because they were left behind. I asked how the vessel could go. They told me they could not tell; but that there was cloth put upon the masts by the help of the ropes I saw, and then the vessel went on; and the white men had some spell or magic they put in the water, when they liked, in order to stop the vessel. I was exceedingly amazed at this account, and really thought they were spirits. I therefore wished much to be from amongst them, for I expected they would sacrifice me; but my wishes were in vain, for we were so quartered that it was impossible for any of us to make our escape.

VI. While we stayed on the coast I was mostly on deck; and one day, to my great astonishment, I saw one of these vessels coming in with the sails up. As soon as the whites saw it, they gave a great shout, at which we were amazed; and the more so as the vessel appeared larger by approaching nearer. At last she came to an anchor in my sight, and when the anchor was let go, I and my countrymen who saw it, were lost in astonishment to observe the vessel stop, and were now convinced it was done by magic. Soon after this the other ship got her boats out, and they came on board of us, and the people of both ships seemed very glad to see each other. Several of the strangers also shook hands with us black people, and made motions with their hands, signifying, I suppose, we were to go to their country; but we did not understand them. At last, when the ship, in which we were, had got in all her cargo, they made ready with many fearful noises, and we were all put under deck, so that we could not see how they managed the vessel.

But this disappointment was the least of my grief. The stench of the hold, while we were on the coast, was so intolerably loathsome, that it was dangerous to remain there for any time, and some of us had been permitted to stay on the deck for the fresh air; but now that the whole ship's cargo were confined together, it became absolutely pestilential. The closeness of the place, and the heat of the climate, added to the number in the ship, being so crowded that each had scarcely room to turn himself, almost suffocated us. This produced copious perspirations, so that the air soon became unfit for respiration, from a variety of loathsome smells, and brought on a sickness among the slaves, of which many died, thus falling victims to the improvident avarice, as I may call it, of their purchasers. This deplorable situation was again aggravated by the galling of the chains, now become insupportable; and the filth of necessary tubs, into which the children often fell, and were almost suffocated. The shrieks of the women, and the groans of the dying, rendered it a scene of horror almost inconceivable. Happily, perhaps, for myself, I was soon reduced so low here that it was thought necessary to keep me almost continually on deck; and from my extreme youth, I was not put in fetters. In this situation I expected every hour to share the fate of my companions, some of whom were almost daily brought upon deck at the point of death, and I began to hope that death would soon put an end to my miseries. Often did I think many of the inhabitants of the deep much more happy than myself; I envied them the freedom they enjoyed, and as often wished I could change my condition for theirs. Every circumstance I met with served only to render my state more painful, and heighten my apprehensions and my opinion of the cruelty of the whites. One day they had taken a number of fishes; and when they had killed and satisfied themselves with as many as they thought fit, to our astonishment who were on the deck, rather than give any of them to us to eat, as we expected, they tossed the remaining fish into the sea again, although we begged and prayed for some as well as we could, but in vain; and some of my countrymen, being pressed by hunger, took an opportunity, when they thought no one saw them, of trying to get a little privately; but were discovered, and the attempt procured for them some very severe floggings.

One day, when we had a smooth sea and moderate wind, two of my wearied countrymen, who were chained together, (I was near them at the time) preferring death to such a life of misery, somehow made through the nettings and jumped into the sea: immediately another quite dejected fellow, who on account of his illness was suffered to be out of irons also followed their example; and I believe many more would very soon have done the same, if they had not been prevented by the ship's crew, who were instantly alarmed. Those of us who were the most active were in a moment put down under the deck; and there was such a noise and confusion amongst the people of the ship as I never heard before, to stop her and get the boat out to go after the slaves. However, two of the wretches were drowned; but they got the other, and afterward flogged him unmercifully, for thus attempting to prefer death to slavery. In this manner we continued to undergo more hardships than I can now relate, hardships which are inseparable from this accursed trade. Many a time we were near suffocation from the want of fresh air, being deprived thereof for days together. This, and the stench of the necessary tubs, carried off many.

II. During our passage I first saw flying fishes, which surprised me very much: they used frequently to fly across the ship, and many of them fell on the deck. I also now first saw the use of the quadrant. I had often with astonishment seen the mariners make observations with it, and I could not think what it meant. They at last took notice of my surprise: and one of them, willing to increase it, as well as to gratify my curiosity, made me one day look through it. The clouds appeared to me to be land, which disappeared as they passed along. This heightened my wonder; and I was now more persuaded than ever that I was in another world, and that every thing about me was magic. At last we came in sight of the island of Barbadoes, at which the whites on board gave a great shout, and made many signs of joy to us. We did not know what to think of this, but as the vessel drew nearer we plainly saw the harbour, and other ships of different kinds and sizes; and we soon anchored amongst them off Bridge Town. Many merchants and planters now came on board, though it was in the evening. They put us in separate parcels, and examined us attentively. They also made us jump, and pointed to the land, signifying we were to go there. We thought by this we should be beaten by these ugly men, as they appeared to us; and, when soon after we were all put down under the deck again, there was much dread and trembling among us, and nothing but bitter cries to be heard all the night from these apprehensions, insomuch that at last the white people got some old slaves from the land to pacify us. They told us we were not to be eaten, but to work, and were soon to go on land, where we should see many of our country people. This report eased us much; and, sure enough, soon after we landed, there came to us Africans of all languages.

We were conducted immediately to the merchant's yard, where we were all pent up together like so many sheep in a fold, without regard to sex or age. As every object was new to me, every thing I saw filled me with surprise. What struck me first was that the houses were built with bricks in stories, and were in every other respect different from those I had seen in Africa; but I was still more astonished at seeing people on horseback. I did not know what this could mean; and indeed I thought these people full of nothing but magical arts. While I was in this astonishment one of my fellow prisoners spoke to a countryman of his about the horses, who said they were the same kind they had in their country. I understood them, though they were from a distant part of Africa, and I thought it odd I had not seen any horses there; but afterwards, when I came to converse with different Africans, I found they had many horses amongst them, and much larger than those I then saw.

We were not many days in the merchant's custody before we were sold after the usual manner, which is this:—On a signal given, such as the beat of a drum, the buyers rush at once into the yard where the slaves are confined, and make choice of that parcel they like best. The noise and clamour with which this is attended, and the eagerness visible in the countenances of the buyers, serve not a little to increase the apprehensions of the terrified Africans, who may well be supposed to consider them the ministers of that destruction to which they think themselves devoted. In this manner, without scruple, are relations and friends separated, most of them never to see each other again. I remember in the vessel in which I was brought over in, in the man's apartment, there were several brothers, who, in the sale, were sold in different lots; and it was very moving on this occasion to see their distress and hear their cries at parting. O, ye nominal Christians! might not an African ask you, "learned you this from your God, who says unto you, Do unto all men as you would men should do unto you? Is it not enough that we are torn from our country and friends, to toil for your luxury and lust of gain? Must every tender feeling be likewise sacrificed to your avarice? Are the dearest friends and relations now rendered more dear by their separation from the rest of their kindred, still to be parted from each other, and thus prevented from cheering the gloom of slavery, with the small comfort of being together, and mingling their sufferings and sorrows? Why are parents to lose their children, brothers their sisters, or husbands their wives? Surely this is a new refinement in cruelty, which, while it has no advantage to atone for it, thus aggravates distress, and adds fresh horrors even to the wretchedness of slavery." . . .

FROM
CHAPTER 5

. . . I have sometimes heard it asserted that a negro cannot earn his master the first cost; but nothing can be further from the truth. I suppose nine tenths of the mechanics throughout the West-Indies are negro slaves; and I well know the coopers among them earn two dollars a-day; the carpenters the same, and oftentimes more; also the masons, smiths, and fishermen, &c. and I have known many slaves whose masters would not take a thousand pounds current for them. But surely this assertion refutes itself: for, if it be true, why do the planters and merchants pay such a price for slaves? And, above all, why do those, who make this assertion, exclaim the most loudly against the abolition of the slave trade? So much are men blinded, and to such inconsistent arguments are they driven by mistaken interest! I grant, indeed, that slaves are sometimes, by half-feeding, half-clothing, over-working, and stripes, reduced so low, that they are turned out as unfit for service, and left to perish in the woods, or to expire on a dunghill.

My master[1] was several times offered by different gentlemen one hundred guineas for me; but he always told them he would not sell me, to my great joy: and I used to double my diligence and care for fear of getting into the hands of these men, who did not allow a valuable slave the common support of life. Many of them used to find fault with my master for feeding his slaves so well as he did; although I often went hungry, and an Englishman might think my fare very indifferent: but he used to tell them he always would do it, because the slaves thereby looked better and did more work.

While I was thus employed by my master, I was often a witness to cruelties of every kind, which were exercised on my unhappy fellowslaves. I used frequently to have different cargoes of new negroes in my care for sale; and it was almost a constant practice with our clerks, and other whites, to commit violent depredations on the chastity of the female slaves; and to these atrocities I was, though with reluctance, obliged to submit at all times, being unable to help them. When we have had some of these slaves on board my master's vessels to carry them to other islands, or to America, I have known our mates commit these acts most shamefully, to the disgrace not of christians only, but of men. I have even known them gratify their brutal passion with females not ten years old; and these abominations some of them practised to such a scandalous excess, that one of our captains discharged the mate and others on that account. And yet in Montserrat I have seen a negro-man staked to the ground, and cut most shockingly, and then his ears cut off, bit by bit, because he had been connected with a white woman, who was a common prostitute! As if it were no crime in the whites to rob an innocent African girl of her virtue; but most heinous in a black man only to gratify a passion of nature, where the temptation was offered by one of a different colour, though the most abandoned woman of her species.

VII. One Mr. D——, told me he had sold 41,000 negroes, and he once cut off a negro-man's leg for running away. I asked him if the man had died in the operation,

---

[1]Robert King

how he, as a christian, could answer, for the horrid act, before God. And he told me, answering was a thing of another world; what he thought and did were policy. I told him that the christian doctrine taught us "to do unto others as we would that others should do unto us." He then said that his scheme had the desired effect—it cured that man and some others of running away.

Another negro-man was half hanged, and then burnt, for attempting to poison a cruel overseer. Thus, by repeated cruelties, are the wretched first urged to despair, and then murdered, because they still retain so much of human nature about them as to wish to put an end to their misery, and to retaliate on their tyrants! These overseers are, indeed, for the most part, persons of the worst character of any denomination of men in the West-Indies. Unfortunately, many humane gentlemen, by not residing on their estates, are obliged to leave the management of them in the hands of these human butchers, who cut and mangle the slaves in a shocking manner, on the most trivial occasions, and altogether treat them, in every respect, like brutes. They pay no regard to the situation of pregnant women, nor the least attention to the lodging of the field negroes. Their huts, which ought to be well covered, and the place dry where they take their short repose, are often open sheds, built in damp places; so that, when the poor creatures return tired from the toils of the field, they contract many disorders, from being exposed to the damp air in this uncomfortable state, while they are heated, and their pores are open.

The neglect certainly conspires with many others to cause a decrease in the births, as well as in the lives of the grown negroes. I can quote many instances of gentlemen who reside on their own estates in the West-Indies, and then the scene is quite changed; the negroes are treated with lenity and proper care, by which their lives are prolonged, and their masters profited. To the honour of humanity, I know several gentlemen who managed their estates in this manner, and found that benevolence was their true interest. And, among many I could mention in Montserrat,[2] whose slaves looked remarkably well, and never needed any fresh supplies of negroes, (and there are many other estates, especially in Barbadoes, which, from such judicious treatment, need no fresh stock of negroes at any time) I have the honour of knowing a most worthy and humane gentleman, who is a native of Barbadoes, and has estates there.[3] This gentleman has written a treatise on the usage of his own slaves. He allows them two hours for refreshment at mid-day, and many other indulgences and comforts, particularly in their lying; and, besides this, he raises more provisions on his estate than they can destroy; so that by these attentions he saves the lives of his negroes, and keeps them healthy, and as happy as the condition of slavery can admit. I myself, as shall appear in the sequel, managed an estate, where, by such attentions, the negroes were uncommonly cheerful and healthy, and did more work by half than by the common mode of treatment they usually do. For want, therefore, of such care and attention to the poor negroes, and otherwise oppressed as they are, it is no wonder that the decrease should require 20,000 new negroes annually to fill up the vacant places of the dead.

Even in Barbadoes, notwithstanding those humane exceptions which I have mentioned and others with which I am acquainted that justly make it quoted as a place where slaves meet with the best treatment, and need fewest recruits of any in the West-Indies; yet this island requires 1,000 negroes annually to keep up the original stock, which is only 80,000. So that the whole term of a negro's life may be said to be there, but sixteen years![4] And yet the climate here is in every respect

---

[2]Mr. Dubury, and many others, in Montserrat.
[3]Sir Philip Gibbes, Bart. Barbadoes.
[4]Benezet's "Account of Guinea," p. 16.

the same as that from which they are taken, except in being more wholesome. Do the British colonies decrease in this manner? And yet what a prodigious difference is there between an English and West-India climate?

VIII. While I was in Montserrat I knew a negro-man, one Emanuel Sankey, who endeavoured to escape from his miserable bondage, by concealing himself on board of a London ship. But fate did not favour the poor oppressed man; for, being discovered when the vessel was under sail, he was delivered up again to his master. This christian master immediately pinned the wretch to the ground, at each wrist and ankle, and then took some sticks of sealing wax, lighted them, and dropped it all over his back. There was another master noted for cruelty:—I believe he had not a slave but had been cut, and pieces fairly taken out of the flesh: and after they had been punished thus, he used to make them get into a long wooden box, or case, he had for that purpose, and shut them up during pleasure. It was just about the height and breadth of man; and the poor wretches had no room when in the case to move.

It was very common in several of the islands, particularly in St. Kitt's, for the slaves to be branded with the initial letters of their master's name, and a load of heavy iron hooks hung about their necks. Indeed on the most trivial occasions they were loaded with chains, and often instruments of torture were added. The iron muzzle, thumb-screws, &c. are so well known as not to need a description, and were sometimes applied for the slightest faults. I have seen a negro beaten till some of his bones were broken, for only letting a pot boil over. It is not uncommon, after a flogging, to make slaves go on their knees and thank their owners, and pray, or rather say, "God bless you." I have often asked many of the men slaves (who used to go several miles to their wives, and late in the night, after having been wearied with a hard day's labour) why they went so far for wives, and did not take them of their own master's negro-women, and particularly those who lived together as household slaves. Their answers have ever been—"Because when the master or mistress choose to punish the women, they make the husbands flog their own wives, and that we could not bear to do." Is it surprising such usage should drive the poor creatures to despair, and make them seek a refuge in death, from those evils which render their lives intolerable—while

> With shudd'ring horror pale, and eyes aghast,
> They view their lamentable lot, and find
> No rest?

This they frequently do. A negro-man, on board a vessel of my master's, while I belonged to her, having been put in irons for some trifling misdemeanour, and kept in that state some days, being weary of life, took an opportunity of jumping overboard into the sea; however he was picked up without being drowned. Another, whose life was also a burden to him, resolved to starve himself to death, and refused to eat any victuals: this procured him a severe flogging; and he also on the first occasion that offered, jumped overboard at Charles Town, but was saved.

Nor is there any greater reward shewn to the little property than there is to the persons and lives of the negroes. I have already related an instance or two of particular oppression, out of many which I have witnessed; but the following is frequent in all the islands:—The wretched field-slaves, after toiling all the day for an unfeeling owner, who gives them but little victuals, steal sometimes a few moments from rest or refreshment to gather some small portion of grass, according as their time will admit. This they commonly tie up in a parcel; either a bits worth (sixpence) or half a bit's worth, and bring it to town, or to the market to

sell. Nothing is more common than for the white people, on this occasion, to take
the grass from them without paying for it; and not only so, but too often also, to
my knowledge, our clerks and many others, at the same time have committed acts
of violence on the poor, wretched, and helpless females; whom I have seen for
hours stand crying to no purpose, and get no redress or pay of any kind. Is not this
one common and crying sin enough to bring down God's judgment on the islands?
He tells us the oppressor and the oppressed are both in his hands; and if these are
not the poor, the broken-hearted, the blind, the captive, the bruised, of which our
Saviour speaks, who are they? . . .

FROM
CHAPTER 7

III. We set sail once more for Montserrat, and arrived there safe; but much
out of humour with our friend, the silversmith. When we had unladen the vessel,
and I had sold my venture, finding myself master of about forty-seven pounds, I
consulted my true friend, the Captain, how I should proceed in offering my master
the money for my freedom. He told me to come on a certain morning, when
he and my master would be at breakfast together. Accordingly, on that morning
I went, and met the Captain there, as he had appointed. When I went in I made
my obeisance to my master, and with my money in my hand, and many fears in
my heart, I prayed him to be as good as his offer to me, when he was pleased
to promise me my freedom as soon as I could purchase it. This speech seemed
to confound him; he began to recoil; and my heart that instant sunk within me.
"What," said he, "give you your freedom? Why, where did you get the money?
Have you got forty pounds sterling?" "Yes, sir," I answered. "How did you get
it?" replied he. I told him, "very honestly." The Captain then said he knew I
got the money very honestly and with much industry, and that I was particularly
careful. On which my master replied, I got money much faster than he did; and
said he would not have made me the promise which he did, had he thought I
should have got the money so soon. "Come, come," said my worthy Captain,
clapping my master on the back, "Come, Robert, (which was his name) I think
you must let him have his freedom. You have laid your money out very well; you
have received good interest for it all this time, and here is now the principal at
last. I know Gustavus has earned you more than a hundred a year, and he will still
save you money, as he will not leave you. Come, Robert, take the money." My
master then said, he would not be worse than his promise; and, taking the money,
told me to go to the Secretary at the Register Office, and get my manumission
drawn up.

These words of my master were like a voice from heaven to me: in an instant
all my trepidation was turned into unutterable bliss, and I most reverently bowed
myself with gratitude, unable to express my feelings, but by the overflowing of my
eyes, and a heart replete with thanks to God; while my true and worthy friend,
the Captain, congratulated us both with a peculiar degree of heartfelt pleasure. As
soon as the first transports of my joy were over, and that I had expressed my thanks
to these my worthy friends in the best manner I was able, I rose with a heart full
of affection and reverence, and left the room, in order to obey my master's joyful
mandate of going to the Register Office. As I was leaving the house I called to
mind the words of the Psalmist, in the 126th Psalm, and like him, "I glorified God
in my heart, in whom I trusted." These words had been impressed on my mind
from the very day I was forced from Deptford to the present hour, and I now saw
them, as I thought, fulfilled and verified.

My imagination was all rapture as I flew to the Register Office; and in this respect, like the apostle Peter[5] (whose deliverance from prison was so sudden and extraordinary, that he thought he was in a vision) I could scarcely believe I was awake. Heavens! who could do justice to my feelings at this moment? Not conquering heroes themselves, in the midst of a triumph—Not the tender mother who has just regained her long-lost infant, and presses it to her heart—Not the weary, hungry mariner, at the sight of the desired friendly port—Not the lover, when he once more embraces his beloved mistress, after she has been ravished from his arms!—All within my breast was tumult, wildness, and delirium! My feet scarcely touched the ground; for they were winged with joy, and, like Elijah, as he rose to Heaven, they "were with lightning sped as I went on." Every one I met I told of my happiness, and blazed about the virtue of my amiable master and Captain.

When I got to the office and acquainted the Register with my errand, he congratulated me on the occasion, and told me he would draw up my manumission for half-price, which was a guinea. I thanked him for his kindness; and, having received it and paid him, I hastened to my master to get him to sign it, that I might be fully released. Accordingly he signed the manumission that day; so that, before night, I, who had been a slave in the morning, trembling at the will of another, was become my own master, and completely free. I thought this was the happiest day I had ever experienced; and my joy was still heightened by the blessings and prayers of many of the sable race, particularly the aged, to whom my heart had ever been attached with reverence.

As the form of my manumission has something peculiar in it, and expresses the absolute power and dominion one man claims over his fellow, I shall beg leave to present it before my readers at full length.[6]

IV. In short, the fair as well as black people immediately styled me by a new appellation,—to me the most desirable in the world,—which was "Freeman," and, at the dances I gave, my Georgia superfine blue clothes made no indifferent appearance, as I thought. Some of the sable females, who formerly stood aloof, now began to relax and appear less coy; but my heart was still fixed on London, where I hoped to be ere long. So that my worthy Captain, and his owner, my late master, finding that the bent of my mind was towards London, said to me, "We hope you won't leave us, but that you will still be with the vessels." Here gratitude bowed me down; and none but the generous mind can judge of my feelings, struggling between inclination and duty. However, notwithstanding my wish to be in London, I obediently answered my benefactors that I would go in the vessel, and not leave them; and from that day I was entered on board as an able-bodied seaman, at thirty-six shillings per month, besides what perquisites I could make. My intention was to make a voyage or two, entirely to please these my honoured patrons; but I determined that the year following, if it pleased God, I would see Old England once more, and surprise my old master, Captain Pascal, who was hourly in my mind; for I still loved him, notwithstanding his usage to me, and I pleased myself with thinking of what he would say when he saw what the Lord had done for me in so short a time, instead of being, as he might perhaps suppose, under the cruel yoke of some planter.

With such reveries I used often to entertain myself, and shorten the time till my return; and now, being as in my original free African style, I embarked on board the Nancy, after having got all things ready for our voyage. In this state of serenity we sailed for St. Eustatia; and having smooth seas and calm weather,

---

[5]Acts xii. 9.
[6]In the original, the manumission appears in an index not included here [Editor's note].

we soon arrived there; after taking our cargo on board, we proceeded to Savannah in Georgia, in August, 1766. While we were there, as usual, I used to go for the cargo up the rivers in boats; and, when on this business, I have been frequently beset by Alligators, which were very numerous on that coast and river. I have shot many of them when they have been near getting into our boats; which we have with great difficulty sometimes prevented, and have been very much frightened at them. I have seen a young one sold in Georgia alive for sixpence.

During our stay at this place, one evening a slave belonging to Mr. Read, a merchant of Savannah, came near our vessel, and began to use me very ill. I entreated him, with all the patience of which I was master, to desist, as I knew there was little or no law for a free negro here. But the fellow, instead of taking my advice, persevered in his insults, and even struck me. At this I lost all temper, and fell on him, and beat him soundly. The next morning his master came to our vessel, as we lay alongside the wharf, and desired me to come ashore that he might have me flogged all round the town, for beating his negro slave! I told him he had insulted me, and had given the provocation by first striking me. I had also told my Captain the whole affair that morning, and desired him to go along with me to Mr. Read, to prevent bad consequences; but he said that it did not signify . . .

FROM
CHAPTER 12

Tortures, murder, and every other imaginable barbarity and iniquity, are practised upon the poor slaves with impunity. I hope the slave trade will be abolished. I pray it may be an event at hand. The great body of manufacturers, uniting in the cause, will considerably facilitate and expedite it; and as I have already stated, it is most substantially their interest and advantage, and as such the nation's at large, except those persons concerned in manufacturing neck-yokes, collars, chains, hand-cuffs, leg-bolts, drags, thumb-screws, iron muzzles, and coffins; cats, scourges, and other instruments of torture used in the slave-trade. In a short time one sentiment will alone prevail, from motives of interest as well as justice and humanity. Europe contains one hundred and twenty millions of inhabitants. Query—How many millions doth Africa contain? Supposing the Africans, collectively and individually, to expend £5. a head in raiment and furniture yearly, when civilized, &c. an immensity beyond the reach of imagination!

This I conceive to be a theory founded upon facts, and therefore an infallible one. If the blacks were permitted to remain in their own country, they would double themselves every fifteen years. In proportion to such increase will be the demand for manufactures. Cotton and indigo grow spontaneously in most parts of Africa; a consideration this of no small consequence to the manufacturing towns of Great Britain. It opens a most immense, glorious, and happy prospect; the clothing, &c. of a continent ten thousand miles in circumference, and immensely rich in productions of every denomination in return for manufactures.

VII. Since the first publication of my narrative, I have been in a great variety of scenes[7] in many parts of Great-Britain, Ireland, and Scotland, an account of which might well be added here; but as this would swell the volume too much, I shall only observe in general, that in May 1791, I sailed from Liverpool to Dublin, where I

---

[7]Viz. Some curious adventures beneath the earth, in a river in Manchester,—and a most astonishing one under the Peak of Derbyshire—and in September 1792, I went 90 fathoms down St. Anthony's Colliery, at Newcastle, under the river Tyne, some hundreds of yards on the Durham side.

was very kindly received, and from thence to Cork, and then travelled over many counties in Ireland. I was every where exceedingly well treated, by persons of all ranks. I found the people extremely hospitable, particularly in Belfast, where I took my passage on board of a vessel for Clyde, on the 29th of January, and arrived at Greenock on the 30th.—Soon after I returned to London, where I found persons of note from Holland and Germany, who requested me to go there; and I was glad to hear that an edition of my Narrative had been printed in both places, also in New York. I remained in London till I heard the debate in the house of Commons on the slave-trade, April the 2d and 3d. I then went to Soham in Cambridgeshire, and was married on the 7th of April to Miss Cullen, daughter of James and Ann Cullen, late of Ely.[8]

I have only therefore to request the reader's indulgence, and conclude. I am far from the vanity of thinking there is any merit in this narrative: I hope censure will be suspended, when it is considered that it was written by one who was as unwilling as unable to adorn the plainness of truth by the colouring of imagination. My life and fortune have been extremely chequered, and my adventures various. Even those I have related are considerably abridged. If any incident in this little work should appear uninteresting and trifling to most readers, I can only say, as my excuse for mentioning it, that almost every event of my life made an impression on my mind, and influenced my conduct. I early accustomed myself to look at the hand of God in the minutest occurrence, and to learn from it a lesson of morality and religion; and in this light every circumstance I have related was, to me, of importance. After all, what makes any event important, unless by its observation we become better and wiser, and learn *to do justly, to love mercy, and to walk humbly before God?* To those who are possessed of this spirit, there is scarcely any book or incident so trifling that does not afford some profit, while to others the experience of ages seems of no use; and even to pour out to them the treasures of wisdom is throwing the jewels of instruction away.

BACKGROUND TEXTS

MARIE LE JARS DE GOURNAY
[C. 1565–1645]

In 1585, when Marie Le Jars de Gournay was nineteen, she came upon a copy of Montaigne's essays, and his words excited her so deeply that she required a sedative. In 1588, when her mother took her to Paris to be presented at court, de Gournay seized the chance to turn her debut into an escape from her family, who believed women should not be educated. From her hotel, she sent Montaigne a letter so eloquent that he immediately came to call and asked her mother for permission to adopt her. De Gournay did not go to live with the Montaignes, but Montaigne made long visits to her home in Picardy, and during daily walks the two discussed the expansion and revision of his *Essays*. De Gournay soon published a collection of her poetry, prose, and Latin translations titled

---

[8]See *Gentleman's Magazine* for April 1792, *Literary and Biographical Magazine and British Review* for May 1792, and the *Edinburgh Historical Register or Monthly Intelligencer* for April 1792.

M. de Montaigne's Promenade, by his Adopted Daughter (1594). Upon Montaigne's death in 1592, at the request of his wife, de Gournay prepared the text of the 1595 edition of his essays, for which she wrote an impassioned prefatory defense of the author. In 1598, she brought out an even more definitive edition of the *Essays*.

At the age of thirty-four, de Gournay settled permanently in Paris, determined to support herself as a writer and scholar. She wrote treatises on education, philology, and politics, translations from Latin, and a wide range of poems, dialogues, and autobiographical pieces on the condition of a woman writer. Margarite de Valois gave her a small pension and invited her to the brilliant salon she kept, where de Gournay mingled with poets, writers, prelates, and politicians. In hopes of augmenting a precarious income, she and her companion–housekeeper Nicole Jamin conducted home experiments with alchemy.

Throughout her career, de Gournay made many devoted friends, but she continually drew fire as a woman who took outspoken political and social positions and who refused to be silenced; she was mocked for her appearance, for her alchemical experiments, even for keeping three pet cats. She was frequently caricatured in plays taking aim at the French Academy, which she had helped to found. She died while working on a collected edition of her writings.

In her essay *On the Equality of Men and Women,* published in 1622, de Gournay appeals to many authorities, including Gnostic and Apocryphal Christian texts excluded from the Bible, and to French folklore as well. She places particular emphasis on the noncanonical tradition surrounding Mary Magdalene, including stories that say she was actually the most favored of Jesus' followers, an "apostle to the Apostles" who ministered after the crucifixion for some thirty years in the south of France. De Gournay claims that she is forgoing the opportunity to mention the many individual instances of women's bravery, loyalty, and intelligence, for fear that they will be considered mere idiosyncratic acts; instead, she promises to cite only evidence of accepted authorities attesting to the natural endowments given all womankind. Yet, in this seemingly scattered essay (which in fact cites many particular examples of women's courage and capabilities), de Gournay looks hard at the origins of sexism, meets head-on some traditional arguments about women's inferiority, and points relentlessly to equal education as the key to equal power for women.

Highly praised during her lifetime, her work, like that of many women writers, was allowed to lapse into obscurity soon after her death. Feminist critics are turning to her once again as an early defender of the rights of women and as one of the first women in the field of literary theory.

On the Equality of Men and Women

Translated by Patricia Clark Smith

Most people who defend women against men's boasts of superiority turn right around and claim that women are really the superior sex. I, who want to avoid all such extremes, am content to assert that men and women are equals; in the matter of the sexes, claims of either superiority or inferiority go against nature.

Of course, I know that for some men it's not enough to declare they are the superior sex. They want to confine women to domesticity, and to that sphere only. But women can always console themselves with the knowledge that the men who hold such opinions are exactly those whom they themselves would least wish to emulate. If those misogynists had themselves been born women, they would justify all the spleen vomited upon our sex. They cherish the conviction that their own worth depends simply upon their maleness, because they have heard trumpeted through the streets the myth that women have neither worth nor ability, being deficient both in their minds and in the organs of their bodies. Such men wax eloquent as they preach these maxims; they can do so because for them *dignity, ability, mind, body, organs* are only empty words. These men have yet to learn that the main characteristic of an oaf is that he puts his trust in slogans, superstition, and hearsay.

You can easily see what happens when savants like these compare the two sexes: they say that at her best woman can only aspire to equal a very ordinary man. They simply cannot conceive of a great woman, were her sex to be changed, as the match of a great man, any more than they can imagine a mere mortal man elevating himself to the status of a god.

Hercules only bested twelve monsters in twelve combats, but these misogynists are more powerful than he, for with a single word they lay low half the world. And yet, how can anybody believe that people like these men, who promote themselves on the basis of others' weaknesses, are truly powerful in their own beings? Above all, these men seem to think they can absolve themselves of their shameless insulting of women simply by slathering praise on their own sex, as if their loose talk, no matter whether true or false, became more believable the more outrageous it grew. God knows, I am all too well acquainted with this race of men whose idle banter gets instantly transmuted into proverbs. They are among the men who most fiercely despise women. But there, now; if they can simply go about issuing decrees proclaiming themselves to be fine fellows, why shouldn't they turn around and degrade women by a similar fiat?

As someone who considers herself a fair judge of the worth and capability of women, I am not going to try to prove my contentions here by setting out my own reasons for valuing women, for reasons are open to debate. Nor will I cite examples of great women, even though they abound. I shall rely instead upon the authority of God himself, upon the authority of the pillars of the Church, and upon the authority of the great thinkers who have illumined the universe. But let us first turn to these last-named glorious witnesses, reserving God and the Holy Fathers, like hoarded treasure, for later.

[Socrates and Plato], to whom everyone grants divinity . . . both assign women the same rights, faculties, and functions as men, in their *Republic* and everywhere else. Moreover, they maintain that women have often surpassed the men of their country, since women actually invented some of their fine arts, and some have excelled at and taught better and more authoritatively than any man all sorts of perfections and virtues throughout the most famous cities of antiquity, including Alexandria, [which became] the greatest city of the Roman Empire after Rome herself. These two philosophers, themselves miracles of nature, believed that the most important speeches in their books took on a finer luster when spoken by Diotima and Aspasia. Socrates is not afraid to name Diotima as his teacher and preceptor in the highest realms of knowledge, and he himself became the teacher and preceptor of all mankind. . . .

Given all Socrates' words about women's accomplishments, it is easy to see how, when he lets slip some remarks during Xenophon's *Symposium* about women having less judgment than men, he is attributing that lack to the ignorance and inexperience in which women are brought up, or else to a general falling-off in society; besides, he also allows a wide margin for exceptions. But the men who make up the misogynist proverbs don't understand subtleties like that.

Perhaps women do attain excellence less often than men. But isn't it a wonder that the lack of good teaching —or, rather, the overabundance of wretched teaching—has not kept women from attaining anything at all? Is there a greater difference between a man and a woman than there is between one woman and another, taking into account each person's education and the circumstances of his or her upbringing, whether in city or hamlet, in one or another nation? And wouldn't the gap people often notice between men's and women's accomplishments be bridged if women were educated and given experience equal to men in business affairs and in arts and letters? Education is so very crucial; when even one aspect of it, such as being taught how to play a part in social affairs, is denied to Italian women, but is made easily available to their French and English sisters, the Italians are almost always outshone by the French and English. (I say *almost* always because particular Italian women have succeeded brilliantly, and we have had two Italian queens to whose prudence France owes a great deal.) Surely education could equalize the faculties of men and women. We can see from the previous example how simply through being schooled in one area—that is, in the social arts of being a hostess—the lesser have triumphed over the greater, for Italian women by nature have a more delicate air than French or English women, and they are naturally more capable of refining the spirits of those around them, as is evident when their Italian men are compared to Frenchmen and Englishmen.

In his treatise on the virtuous deeds of women, Plutarch contends that virtue is identical in men and in women. Seneca similarly proclaims in the *Consolations* that we must believe that nature has in no way slighted women, nor has she limited their virtues or their minds more than men's; rather, she has given women an equal measure of energy and ability to perform honest laudable deeds.

Leaving [Seneca and Plutarch], let us see what the third member of the triumvirate of human wisdom and morality has to say in his essays. [Montaigne] remarks that, though he isn't sure why it should be so, he has rarely seen a woman worthy to be a leader of men. But is he not thus comparing women in particular with mankind in general? And is this not in itself a confession that he is afraid of falling into error if he goes beyond generalizing about women? (Though, to be sure, he could easily enough have made excuses for his reservations on the grounds of women's scant and shameful education.) Moreover, in another part of his *Essays,* he forgets to mention that Plato gives authority to women in the *Republic,* and also omits to note that Antistines denied there was any difference between the talents and virtues of the two sexes....

Is it really necessary to cite one by one the infinite number of other illustrious authors, ancient and modern, among them Erasmus, Poliziano, and Agrippa, as well as that honest and capable instructor of courtiers [Castiglione], in addition to the many poets who are opposed to misogynists and who attest to women's advantages, aptitudes, and abilities to discharge all offices and perform all worthy acts? Indeed, women can console themselves with the knowledge that their detractors do not come off well in arguments against any able opponent. A shrewd man, even if he actually believed women to be inferior, would not contend that women's worth falls short of man's, nor would he assert that women are undeservedly praised. In order to invalidate the testimony of all these eminent authors who praise women, he would have to call them a rampaging herd of wild buffalo. Indeed, he would have to proclaim entire great civilizations like Smyrna to be nations of wild buffalo. For, according to Tacitus, in the olden times the people of Smyrna, in order to appear more noble than their neighbors, would go about claiming descent from either Tantalus, Jupiter's son, or from Theseus, Neptune's grandson, or else from an Amazon; in their eyes, descent from the Amazon weighed equally with descent from the gods.

Salic law, which denies women the right to wear the crown, prevails only in France.[1] It was invented at the time of Pharamond, when our forefathers were

---

[1]Salic law is the rule of succession in a number of European royal families that bars male or female descendants in the female line from succeeding to titles.

thinking of nothing but the war against the Empire whose yoke they longed to throw off, and the female body seemed to them then less fit for bearing arms, given the need to bear children and to nurse them. Nevertheless it must be noted that among the Peers of France, who were originally created to be personal companions to the King, as their name suggests, there are women Peeresses who in their own right are entitled to the same privileges and suffrage as male Peers. The Lacedemonians, that brave and generous people, consulted their wives on all matters both public and private. And we French have been well-served by the invention of the office of Regent as the equivalent of King; without it, how many times would the State have vanished from the earth? We can speak first-hand from the time of our own trials about the need for this device of Regency during the minorities of male rulers.

Tacitus says that those bellicose people the Germans, who were at last overcome after more than two hundred years of war, bestowed a dowry upon their prospective wives, instead of vice-versa, and some of the German territories were governed solely by women. Moreover, when Aeneas gives Dido the sceptre of Ilium, scholars tell us the act derives from the fact that at one time eldest daughters like Dido ruled the royal houses.[2] Could there be two more beautiful arguments against Salic law than these? Also, plainly, neither our ancient Gauls nor the Carthaginians despised women, for when the two peoples were united in the army of Hannibal to cross the Alps, they designated the Gallic women to be the arbiters of their differences.

When men strip women of their right to the greatest advantages, it may be that the theft and the consequent suffering are due to the inequality of physical strength rather than to any moral lacking on the part of women, and physical strength is such a low virtue that the beasts surpass man in that regard, just as men surpass women. It is again Tacitus who tells us that where might reigns, all justice, honesty, and even modesty are attributed to the victor. What wonder, then, that ability and worth in general are accorded to men, to the exclusion of women?

Moreover, the human animal is really neither man nor woman, the sexes having been created not simply, but rather *secundum quid,* as the theologians tell us; that is to say, only for the purpose of propagation. The only unique thing about this human animal is the human soul, and the old joke—*What is most like a tomcat on a windowsill?—A female cat on a windowsill!*—is fitting here, if we may allow ourselves a moment for laughter. Men and women are so much one creature that if a man is more than a woman, then a woman is more than a man. Man was created male and female, say the scriptures, counting the two as one. Hence, Jesus Christ is called the Son of Man, even though he is really only the son of a woman. The great Saint Basil says the virtue of a man and a woman are the same, since God bestowed on both the same creation and the same honor: *masculum et feminam fecit eos.* Now, those whose natures are the same must behave in the same way, and similar deeds must be accorded equal value and equal praise. Such is the testimony of Basil, that mighty pillar and venerable witness of the Church.

It is well to remember that certain ancient quibblers were so arrogant they would deny that the female sex was created in God's image; they'd have us believe that man's resemblance to God depends chiefly on his beard. Logically, it would then follow that women could not resemble men, since they don't resemble He after whom men are shaped.

God himself has given women the gift of prophesy in equal measure with man, and He has set women to be judges, teachers, and leaders of his faithful people in peace and in war. Moreover, he has caused them to triumph with him in the greatest of victories, which they have then spread to other parts of the world. . . .

---

[2]De Gournay mistakenly believes that Aeneas makes Dido the Queen of Troy.

To continue with my list of holy witnesses, though Saint Paul bans women from the ministry and bids them be silent in church, it is evident that he does so not out of contempt, but because he fears they will present a temptation by showing themselves so brilliantly in public, as they must if they are to minister and preach, and being so much more well-endowed with beauty and grace than men. I maintain that the lack of contempt for women in the New Testament is evident, even without taking into consideration Saint Peter's great respect for Saint Petronilla, and without mentioning Mary Magdalene, who is named in the Church as the equal of the Apostles, *par Apostolis*. And indeed, as everyone in Provence is aware, the Church and the Apostles themselves made an exception to the rule of silence for that very woman, who preached for thirty years after Christ's death at the church of Sainte Baume near Marseille.[3] If anyone further questions the evidence that women have preached, one may well ask what the Sibyls were doing, if not preaching across the Universe by divine inspiration the future advent of Jesus Christ?[4] Among the ancient nations, all have agreed that women as well as men could be priests. And Christians must at least concede that women are able to administer the sacrament of baptism—but is it then fair that women are forbidden to administer the other sacraments? People say that the need to save the souls of dying infants forced the Church Fathers, however reluctantly, to permit women to baptise. But surely those men didn't think of themselves as agreeing to violate and defame a sacrament out of mere need when they consented to let women perform baptisms! It is clear they banned women from administering the other sacraments only in order to maintain more completely male authority, either because they themselves were male, or because, perversely or not, they wished to ensure peace between the two sexes by weakening and devaluing one of them. Surely Saint Jerome writes wisely on this point when he says that in the matter of service to God, the spirit and the doctrine must always be considered, but not the sex, a verdict which should be extended to allow women . . . to perform all honest acts and pursue all worthwhile knowledge. Allowing women to do so would carry out the intentions of this Saint who honors and stoutly defends women. Saint John the Eagle, most beloved of the Evangelists, did not despise women, nor did Saint Peter, Saint Paul, or the two Church Fathers Basil and Jerome; Jerome addresses his epistles specifically to women. I needn't go into the infinite number of saints and Church Fathers who concur with them in their writings.

As for Judith, I should not even bother to mention what she did if hers had been an act that depended solely upon the will of the doer; I won't list here deeds of that sort, even if they are legion, and as heroic as the acts that crown the most illustrious men.[5] Here, I am trying not to record individual acts of courage by women, for fear that they will appear to be mere idiosyncratic outbursts of personal strength, rather than brave deeds that are illustrative of gifts common to all womankind.

---

[3]A great deal of folklore surrounds Mary Magdalene, who was at one time venerated nearly equally with the Virgin Mary. De Gournay is drawing on the tradition that Magdalene and her sister Martha made their way to Provence, where Mary preached and Martha slew a dragon by pouring holy water on its head. At Ste. Baume ("Holy Tree"), the site of an old pagan shrine, Mary is said to have lived and preached for thirty years without touching food or drink, and her presence there reputedly ensured a good vintage for the local winemakers.

[4]The Sibyl was originally an oracular spirit represented by a succession of priestesses at Cumae in Italy. By the first century B.C.E., there were said to be ten Sibyls at different locations around Europe. In the Middle Ages, the *Sibylline Books,* collections of their oracles, were doctored by Christians to make it seem as though the Sibyls foretold the coming of Christ.

[5]The Book of Judith, one of the Apocryphal books of the Old Testament, tells the story of how a young Jewish widow saves the besieged town of Bethulia by cutting off the head of the enemy war chief Holofernes when he falls into a drunken sleep.

But Judith's deed does deserve to be mentioned here. Her plan grew in the heart of a young woman surrounded by many weak and fainthearted men, and, faced with the dire and difficult task of saving a city, a whole population of the faithful, Judith's act, rather than being totally voluntary, seems to me to have been divinely inspired, and divine inspiration seems a privilege especially accorded to women. The Maid of Orleans' deeds seem similar, growing out of similar desperate circumstances, although Joan of Arc acted for an even larger cause, the salvation of a great kingdom and its monarch:

> This noble maid, skilled in the arts of Mars,
> Mows squadrons down, and braves the heat of wars,
> With fabric stiff she binds her maiden chest:
> One rosy nipple gleams on each round breast.
> To gain laurel and glory for her crown,
> She'll face the most illustrious warriors down!

Let us add that Mary Magdalene is the only soul to whom the Redeemer spoke these words and promised this great grace: *Wherever the Gospel shall be preached, there they shall refer to you.*[6] And Jesus Christ announced his glad and glorious resurrection first to women, in order that they, according to one of the Church Fathers, might become Apostles to the Apostles themselves, with this express mission: *Go,* He said to this same Mary Magdalene, *and tell Peter and the Apostles what you have seen.* And earlier He announced His incarnation equally to women as well as to men in the person of Anna, who recognized Him at the same instant as good Saint Simon. That miraculous birth, furthermore, was predicted by the Sibyls alone among the Gentiles, a great honor for the female sex. And what an honor for women as well was the dream of Pilate's wife, a dream which was sent to a woman, bypassing all men on such an exalted occasion!

If men boast that Jesus Christ was born a member of their sex, we women may retort that He had to be incarnated as a man, for had He been born a woman He could not as a young person have mingled without scandal with the multitudes at all hours of the day and night, in the way He needed to in order to convert, succor, and save humankind; this is especially true, considering the hostility He faced from the Jewish people. And yet, if a person is so feeble-minded as to need to imagine a Male or a Female God (granted that in the French language His name does have a masculine ring) and consequently needs to elevate one sex over the other in order to honor the Incarnation of God's son, that person exposes himself as someone who is as poor a philosopher as he is a theologian. At any rate, the advantages men derive from claiming Jesus as a member of their sex . . . are compensated for by His most precious conception within the body of a woman, and by that woman's utterly perfect claim to bear the name of perfection, alone of all created beings since our first parents fell from grace, this woman set apart from others also by her Assumption into heaven.

Finally, if Scripture has declared the husband to be the head of the wife, it would be the greatest foolishness for men to take this as a seal of their nobility. The examples, authorities, and arguments chronicled in this essay prove that the favors and graces bestowed upon men and women are equal, even identical. And God Himself has spoken: *the two shall be as one;* and, further, *the man shall leave his mother and father, and cleave unto his wife.* Undoubtedly, man was designated the head

---

[6]Jesus does not speak these words to Mary Magdalene in the canonical four gospels, nor does he call her "Apostle to the Apostles." De Gournay's source is uncertain, but Mary Magdalene is accorded a high degree of respect in the Gnostic tradition and in the folklore of southern France (cf. note 3).

of the family only because of the explicit need to promote peace within marriage. Obviously, that need required that one of the pair yield to the other, and the greater physical strength of the man meant that he would not be the one who would submit. . . .

Even if it were true, as some contend, that submission was first imposed upon women because of the sin of the apple, that leaves us still a long way from concluding that man is more noble than woman. If you should happen to believe that the Scriptures command woman to yield to man, if you believe that women are utterly unfit to stand up to men in an argument, see what absurdity follows: Woman has been found worthy of being created in God's image; worthy to take part in the most holy Eucharist; worthy of seeing visions of God, and even of being possessed by the Holy Spirit. And yet, woman is deemed unfit to receive the benefits and privileges of the human male.

Is this not the same as saying that human men are more valuable than God Himself? And do such views not elevate the human male above all Mysteries, and thus commit the greatest of blasphemies?

RENÉ DESCARTES
[1596–1650]

French philosopher, mathematician, and scientist René Descartes is, along with Francis Bacon, one of the founders of modern thought. If Bacon is the father of empiricism and experimental science, Descartes is the father of rationalism and theoretical science. He set out to create a single, mathematically based method for all the sciences and in doing so developed the systematic practice of "methodical doubt" or "Cartesian skepticism." He describes this process in his two most important philosophic treatises, *Discourse on Method* (1637) and *Meditations* (1642). The passage from the *Discourse on Method* that follows is an account of the revelatory moment when he discovered this method and its fundamental truth. Descartes was in the Bavarian army during the winter of 1619–1620, and, on one particularly cold day, he crawled into a stove to keep warm. He stayed there all day meditating, and when he emerged several hours later, he claims, his philosophy was half finished. In his meditations Descartes began by doubting the existence of all things and all convictions about the world, seeking any conviction that resisted such skepticism. He discovered that he could doubt everything except that he was doubting. By this method he arrived at his fundamental truth, *cogito ergo sum* ("I think, therefore I am").

By relocating the source of truth in the mind or the self, rather than in the external world or a divine being, Descartes changed the direction of Western thought. Instead of looking to past learning as a repository of truth, as his Renaissance predecessors had done, he regarded works of the past as compilations of error. He sought truth in the mind alone. Intuition, "clear and distinct" ideas that could not be doubted such as his *cogito ergo sum,* became the starting points from which he deduced other truths. He summarized this position in one of his twenty-one *Rules for the Direction of the Mind:* "In the subjects we propose to investigate, our inquiries should be directed, not to what others have thought, nor to what we ourselves conjecture, but to what we can clearly and perspicuously behold and with certainty deduce; for knowledge is not won in any other way." Although he began by retreating into the self and relying on his own powers of reasoning, Descartes did not end in isolation or solipsism. From the certainty of his individualistic starting point, he deduced the existence of God and of a material reality, and he believed that others would arrive at the same conclusions; for "the power of forming a good judgment and of properly distinguishing the true from the false, which is properly speaking what is called Good sense or Reason, is by nature equal in all men." Uniting individualism with Reason, Descartes thus articulated two of the major premises of the Enlightenment that earned it the epithet the Age of Reason.

Discourse on Method

Translated by Elizabeth S. Haldane and G. R. T. Ross

I was then in Germany, to which country I had been attracted by the wars which are not yet at an end. And as I was returning from the coronation of the Emperor to join the army, the setting in of winter detained me in a quarter where, since I found no society to divert me, while fortunately I had also no cares or passions to trouble me, I remained the whole day shut up alone in a stove-heated room, where I had complete leisure to occupy myself with my own thoughts. One of the first of the considerations that occurred to me was that there is very often less perfection in works composed of several portions, and carried out by the hands of various masters, than in those on which one individual alone has worked. Thus we see that buildings planned and carried out by one architect alone are usually more beautiful and better proportioned than those which many have tried to put in order and improve, making use of old walls which were built with other ends in view. In the same way also, those ancient cities which, originally mere villages, have become in the process of time great towns, are usually badly constructed in comparison with those which are regularly laid out on a plain by a surveyor who is free to follow his own ideas. Even though, considering their buildings each one apart, there is often as much or more display of skill in the one case than in the other, the former have large buildings and small buildings indiscriminately placed together, thus rendering the streets crooked and irregular, so that it might be said that it was chance rather than the will of men guided by reason that led to such an arrangement. And if we consider that this happens despite the fact that from all time there have been certain officials who have had the special duty of looking after the buildings of private individuals in order that they may be public ornaments, we shall understand how difficult it is to bring about much that is satisfactory in operating only upon the works of others. Thus I imagined that those people who were once half-savage, and who have become civilized only by slow degrees, merely forming their laws as the disagreeable necessities of their crimes and quarrels constrained them, could not succeed in establishing so good a system of government as those who, from the time they first came together as communities, carried into effect the constitution laid down by some prudent legislator. Thus it is quite certain that the constitution of the true Religion whose ordinances are of God alone is incomparably better regulated than any other. And, to come down to human affairs, I believe that if Sparta was very flourishing in former times, this was not because of the excellence of each and every one of its laws, seeing that many were very strange and even contrary to good morals, but because, being drawn up by one individual, they all tended towards the same end. And similarly I thought that the sciences found in books—in those at least whose reasonings are only probable and which have no demonstrations, composed as they are of the gradually accumulated opinions of many different individuals— do not approach so near to the truth as the simple reasoning which a man of common sense can quite naturally carry out respecting the things which come immediately before him. Again I thought that since we have all been children before being men, and since it has for long fallen to us to be governed by our appetites and by our teachers (who often enough contradicted one another, and none of whom perhaps counselled us always for the best), it is almost impossible that our judgments should be so excellent or solid as they should have been had we had complete use of our reason since our birth, and had we been guided by its means alone.

It is true that we do not find that all the houses in a town are rased to the ground for the sole reason that the town is to be rebuilt in another fashion, with streets made more beautiful; but at the same time we see that many people cause their own houses to be knocked down in order to rebuild them, and that sometimes they are forced so to do where there is danger of the houses falling of themselves, and when the foundations are not secure. From such examples I argued to myself that there was no plausibility in the claim of any private individual to reform a state by altering everything, and by overturning it throughout, in order to set it right again. Nor is it likewise probable that the whole body of the Sciences, or the order of teaching established by the Schools, should be reformed. But as regards all the opinions which up to this time I had embraced, I thought I could not do better than endeavour once for all to sweep them completely away, so that they might later on be replaced, either by others which were better, or by the same, when I had made them conform to the uniformity of a rational scheme. And I firmly believed that by this means I should succeed in directing my life much better than if I had only built on old foundations, and relied on principles of which I allowed myself to be in youth persuaded without having inquired into their truth. For although in so doing I recognised various difficulties, these were at the same time not unsurmountable, nor comparable to those which are found in reformation of the most insignificant kind in matters which concern the public. In the case of great bodies it is too difficult a task to raise them again when they are once thrown down, or even to keep them in their places when once thoroughly shaken; and their fall cannot be otherwise than very violent. Then as to any imperfections that they may possess (and the very diversity that is found between them is sufficient to tell us that these in many cases exist) custom has doubtless greatly mitigated them, while it has also helped us to avoid, or insensibly corrected a number against which mere foresight would have found it difficult to guard. And finally the imperfections are almost always more supportable than would be the process of removing them, just as the great roads which wind about amongst the mountains become, because of being frequented, little by little so well-beaten and easy that it is much better to follow them than to try to go more directly by climbing over rocks and descending to the foot of precipices.

This is the reason why I cannot in any way approve of those turbulent and unrestful spirits who, being called neither by birth nor fortune to the management of public affairs, never fail to have always in their minds some new reforms. And if I thought that in this treatise there was contained the smallest justification for this folly, I should be very sorry to allow it to be published. My design has never extended beyond trying to reform my own opinion and to build on a foundation which is entirely my own. If my work has given me a certain satisfaction, so that I here present to you a draft of it, I do not do so because I wish to advise anybody

to imitate it. Those to whom God has been most beneficent in the bestowal of
His graces will perhaps form designs which are more elevated; but I fear much
that this particular one will seem too venturesome for many. The simple resolve to
strip oneself of all opinions and beliefs formerly received is not to be regarded as
an example that each man should follow, and the world may be said to be mainly
composed of two classes of minds neither of which could prudently adopt it. There
are those who, believing themselves to be cleverer than they are, cannot restrain
themselves from being precipitate in judgment and have not sufficient patience to
arrange their thoughts in proper order; hence, once a man of this description had
taken the liberty of doubting the principles he formerly accepted, and had deviated
from the beaten track, he would never be able to maintain the path which must
be followed to reach the appointed end more quickly, and he would hence remain
wandering astray all through his life. Secondly, there are those who having reason
or modesty enough to judge that they are less capable of distinguishing truth from
falsehood than some others from whom instruction might be obtained, are right in
contenting themselves with following the opinions of these others rather than in
searching better ones for themselves.

For myself I should doubtless have been of these last if I had never had more
than a single master, or had I never known the diversities which have from all time
existed between the opinions of men of the greatest learning. But I had been taught,
even in my College days, that there is nothing imaginable so strange or so little
credible that it has not been maintained by one philosopher or other, and I further
recognised in the course of my travels that all those whose sentiments are very
contrary to ours are yet not necessarily barbarians or savages, but may be possessed
of reason in as great or even a greater degree than ourselves. I also considered
how very different the self-same man, identical in mind and spirit, may become,
according as he is brought up from childhood amongst the French or Germans,
or has passed his whole life amongst Chinese or cannibals. I likewise noticed how
even in the fashions of one's clothing the same thing that pleased us ten years ago,
and which will perhaps please us once again before ten years are passed, seems at
the present time extravagant and ridiculous. I thus concluded that it is much more
custom and example that persuade us than any certain knowledge, and yet in spite
of this the voice of the majority does not afford a proof of any value in truths a
little difficult to discover, because such truths are much more likely to have been
discovered by one man than by a nation. I could not, however, put my finger on a
single person whose opinions seemed preferable to those of others, and I found that
I was, so to speak, constrained myself to undertake the direction of my procedure.

But like one who walks alone and in the twilight I resolved to go so slowly,
and to use so much circumspection in all things, that if my advance was but very
small, at least I guarded myself well from falling. I did not wish to set about the final
rejection of any single opinion which might formerly have crept into my beliefs
without having been introduced there by means of Reason, until I had first of all
employed sufficient time in planning out the task which I had undertaken, and in
seeking the true Method of arriving at a knowledge of all the things of which my
mind was capable.

Among the different branches of Philosophy, I had in my younger days to a
certain extent studied Logic; and in those of Mathematics, Geometrical Analysis and
Algebra—three arts or sciences which seemed as though they ought to contribute
something to the design I had in view. But in examining them I observed in respect
to Logic that the syllogisms and the greater part of the other teaching served better
in explaining to others those things that one knows (or like the art of Lully, in

enabling one to speak without judgment of those things of which one is ignorant) than in learning what is new. And although in reality Logic contains many precepts which are very true and very good, there are at the same time mingled with them so many others which are hurtful or superfluous, that it is almost as difficult to separate the two as to draw a Diana or a Minerva out of a block of marble which is not yet roughly hewn. And as to the Analysis of the ancients and the Algebra of the moderns, besides the fact that they embrace only matters the most abstract, such as appear to have no actual use, the former is always so restricted to the consideration of symbols that it cannot exercise the Understanding without greatly fatiguing the Imagination; and in the latter one is so subjected to certain rules and formulas that the result is the construction of an art which is confused and obscure, and which embarrasses the mind, instead of a science which contributes to its cultivation. This made me feel that some other Method must be found, which, comprising the advantages of the three, is yet exempt from their faults. And as a multiplicity of laws often furnishes excuses for evil-doing, and as a State is hence much better ruled when, having but very few laws, these are most strictly observed; so, instead of the great number of precepts of which Logic is composed, I believed that I should find the four which I shall state quite sufficient, provided that I adhered to a firm and constant resolve never on any single occasion to fail in their observance.

The first of these was to accept nothing as true which I did not clearly recognise to be so: that is to say, carefully to avoid precipitation and prejudice in judgments, and to accept in them nothing more than what was presented to my mind so clearly and distinctly that I could have no occasion to doubt it.

The second was to divide up each of the difficulties which I examined into as many parts as possible, and as seemed requisite in order that it might be resolved in the best manner possible.

The third was to carry on my reflections in due order, commencing with objects that were the most simple and easy to understand, in order to rise little by little, or by degrees, to knowledge of the most complex, assuming an order, even if a fictitious one, among those which do not follow a natural sequence relatively to one another.

The last was in all cases to make enumerations so complete and reviews so general that I should be certain of having omitted nothing.

Those long chains of reasoning, simple and easy as they are, of which geometricians make use in order to arrive at the most difficult demonstrations, had caused me to imagine that all those things which fall under the cognizance of man might very likely be mutually related in the same fashion; and that, provided only that we abstain from receiving anything as true which is not so, and always retain the order which is necessary in order to deduce the one conclusion from the other, there can be nothing so remote that we cannot reach to it, nor so recondite that we cannot discover it. And I had not much trouble in discovering which objects it was necessary to begin with, for I already knew that it was with the most simple and those most easy to apprehend. Considering also that of all those who have hitherto sought for the truth in the Sciences, it has been the mathematicians alone who have been able to succeed in making any demonstrations, that is to say producing reasons which are evident and certain, I did not doubt that it had been by means of a similar kind that they carried on their investigations. I did not at the same time hope for any practical result in so doing, except that my mind would become accustomed to the nourishment of truth and would not content itself with false reasoning. But for all that I had no intention of trying to master all those particular sciences that receive in common the name of Mathematics; but observing that, although their objects are different, they do not fail to agree in this, that they take nothing under consideration but the various relationships or proportions which are present in these objects, I thought that it would be better if I only examined these proportions in their general aspect, and without viewing them otherwise than in the objects which would serve most to facilitate a knowledge of them. Not that I should in any way restrict them to these objects, for I might later on all the more easily apply them to all other objects to which they were applicable. Then, having carefully noted that in order to comprehend the proportions I should sometimes require to consider each one in particular, and sometimes merely keep them in mind, or take them in groups, I thought that, in order the better to consider them in detail, I should picture them in the form of lines, because I could find no method more simple nor more capable of being distinctly represented to my imagination and senses. I considered, however, that in order to keep them in my memory or to embrace several at once, it would be essential that I should explain them by means of certain formulas, the shorter the better. And for this purpose it was requisite that I should borrow all that is best in Geometrical Analysis and Algebra, and correct the errors of the one by the other.

As a matter of fact, I can venture to say that the exact observation of the few precepts which I had chosen gave me so much facility in sifting out all the questions embraced in these two sciences, that in the two or three months which I employed in examining them—commencing with the most simple and general, and making each truth that I discovered a rule for helping me to find others—not only did I arrive at the solution of many questions which I had hitherto regarded as most difficult, but, towards the end, it seemed to me that I was able to determine in the case of those of which I was still ignorant, by what means, and in how far, it was possible to solve them. In this I might perhaps appear to you to be very vain if you did not remember that having but one truth to discover in respect to each matter, whoever succeeds in finding it knows in its regard as much as can be known. It is the same as with a child, for instance, who has been instructed in Arithmetic and has made an addition according to the rule prescribed; he may be sure of having found as regards the sum of figures given to him all that the human mind can know. For, in conclusion, the Method which teaches us to follow the true order and enumerate exactly every term in the matter under investigation contains everything which gives certainty to the rules of Arithmetic.

But what pleased me most in this Method was that I was certain by its means of exercising my reason in all things, if not perfectly, at least as well as was in my power. And besides this, I felt in making use of it that my mind gradually accustomed itself to conceive of its objects more accurately and distinctly; and not having restricted this Method to any particular matter, I promised myself to apply it as usefully to the difficulties of other sciences as I had done to those of Algebra. Not that on this account I dared undertake to examine just at once all those that might present themselves; for that would itself have been contrary to the order which the Method prescribes. But having noticed that the knowledge of these difficulties must be dependent on principles derived from Philosophy in which I yet found nothing to be certain, I thought that it was requisite above all to try to establish certainty in it. I considered also that since this endeavour is the most important in all the world, and that in which precipitation and prejudice were most to be feared, I should not try to grapple with it till I had attained to a much riper age than that of three and twenty, which was the age I had reached. I thought, too, that I should first of all employ much time in preparing myself for the work by eradicating from my mind all the wrong opinions which I had up to this time accepted, and accumulating a variety of experiences fitted later on to afford matter for my reasonings, and by ever exercising myself in the Method which I had prescribed, in order more and more to fortify myself in the power of using it. . . .

FROM

PART 4

I do not know that I ought to tell you of the first meditations there made by me, for they are so metaphysical and so unusual that they may perhaps not be acceptable to everyone. And yet at the same time, in order that one may judge whether the foundations which I have laid are sufficiently secure, I find myself constrained in some measure to refer to them. For a long time I had remarked that it is sometimes requisite in common life to follow opinions which one knows to be most uncertain, exactly as though they were indisputable, as has been said above. But because in this case I wished to give myself entirely to the search after Truth, I thought that it was necessary for me to take an apparently opposite course, and to reject as absolutely false everything as to which I could imagine the least ground of doubt, in order to see if afterwards there remained anything in my belief that was entirely certain. Thus, because our senses sometimes deceive us, I wished to suppose that nothing is just as they cause us to imagine it to be; and because there are men who deceive themselves in their reasoning and fall into paralogisms, even concerning the simplest matters of geometry, and judging that I was as subject to error as was any other, I rejected as false all the reasons formerly accepted by me as demonstrations. And since all the same thoughts and conceptions which we have while awake may also come to us in sleep, without any of them being at that time true, I resolved to assume that everything that ever entered into my mind was no more true than the illusions of my dreams. But immediately afterwards I noticed that whilst I thus wished to think all things false, it was absolutely essential that the "I" who thought this should be some[thing], and remarking that this truth *"I think, therefore I am"* was so certain and so assured that all the most extravagant suppositions brought forward by the sceptics were incapable of shaking it, I came to the conclusion that I could receive it without scruple as the first principle of the Philosophy for which I was seeking.

And then, examining attentively that which I was, I saw that I could conceive that I had no body, and that there was no world nor place where I might be; but yet that I could not for all that conceive that I was not. On the contrary, I saw from the very fact that I thought of doubting the truth of other things, it very evidently and certainly followed that I was; on the other hand if I had only ceased from thinking, even if all the rest of what I had ever imagined had really existed, I should have no reason for thinking that I had existed. From that I knew that I was a substance the whole essence or nature of which is to think, and that for its existence there is no need of any place, nor does it depend on any material thing; so that this "me," that is to say, the soul by which I am what I am, is entirely distinct from body, and is even more easy to know than is the latter; and even if body were not, the soul would not cease to be what it is.

After this I considered generally what in a proposition is requisite in order to be true and certain; for since I had just discovered one which I knew to be such, I thought that I ought also to know in what this certainty consisted. And having remarked that there was nothing at all in the statement *"I think, therefore I am"* which assures me of having thereby made a true assertion, excepting that I see very clearly that to think it is necessary to be, I came to the conclusion that I might assume, as a general rule, that the things which we conceive very clearly and distinctly are all true—remembering, however, that there is some difficulty in ascertaining which are those that we distinctly conceive.

FATHER CHRESTIEN LE CLERCQ
[C. 1641–1698]

AND

A MICMAC ELDER
[C. 1640–1695]

This account of cultural confrontation was recorded by Father Chrestien Le Clercq, a member of the Recollect order who worked as a missionary, linguist, and interpreter among the Micmacs. The Micmac are woodlands people who speak an Algonquin language; they have lived in the vicinity of the present-day Canadian Maritime Provinces, Quebec, and northern New England for more than two thousand years. French missionaries first arrived among them in the early 1500s. Le Clercq served in Canada between 1675 and 1687, but his *Nouvelle Relation de Gaspesia*, the story of his experiences in Canada written for his superiors back in France, was not printed until 1791. The encounter he describes here took place in about 1676 in present-day New Brunswick; as the selection begins, Le Clercq has just been speaking of the hardships Europeans endure when they travel with American Indians, and is reminded of what he once heard a Micmac elder say about the comparative merits of European and Algonquin ways of life. Le Clercq's response to the Micmac elder's speech may be somewhat colored by the already potent myth of the Noble Savage, but Le Clercq lived for a long time among the Micmac, and he seems to have been one of the few white men, especially one of the few clerics, whom the native people of the Gaspesian Peninsula held in some regard.

The speech of the Micmac elder is one of many similar ones recorded by missionaries, colonists, and travelers in New France and elsewhere throughout the Americas during the sixteenth and seventeenth centuries. Like Diderot's fictional Orou in the *Supplement to the Voyage of Bougainville*, the elder speaking here offers a trenchant criticism of European customs, and he poses the most significant question native populations everywhere repeatedly asked European colonists: If European culture is so wonderful, why are so many Europeans leaving it behind and moving to other lands?

One important difference between the speeches of Diderot's fictional South Seas islander and this historical Micmac speaker is that the deadpan wit, the ironic edge, and the rhetorical power of actual American Indian oratory can be heard coming through even in Le Clercq's French transcription; contemporary American Indian scholars believe that Le Clercq has probably given us a fair approximation of the words of a seventeenth-century American Indian.

[You Tell Us That France Is an Earthly Paradise]
Translated by Patricia Clark Smith

I pass over other styles of camping practiced by our Micmac Indians because all I can say is that it is always very uncomfortable for French people who travel with them; every one of their camps is meager and miserable. Nonetheless, they value their portable dwellings more highly than the finest houses we build.

A party of Micmacs testified to this one day when some gentlemen from Isle Percée [a French trading center] asked me to interpret while they tried to persuade the Indians of the advantages of living like French people. The Frenchmen were quite surprised when the Micmac leader, who had been listening very patiently to all the French speeches I had been translating for him and his people, turned to me and spoke these words:

"I'm surprised the French are as stupid as they seem to be, judging from what you have just been telling us about how they want us to abandon our poles and bark for those stone and wooden houses they are always talking about, the ones they claim tower as high as the trees. Perhaps their houses at home *are* that big, but why would people who stand five or six feet tall need to live in a place sixty to eighty feet high? You've seen for yourself, Father, how our wigwams give us every convenience your homes do; you know how in our houses we can relax, drink, sleep, eat, and have a good time with our friends when we feel like it. But that's not all I have to say," he added, eyeing one of our captains.

"Brother, I know you think your people are better off and wiser than we are. But we camp where we like, and we don't depend on any lord of the manor for our lodging. Maybe you're just not as strong as we are; when you travel, you can't carry your halls and houses on your backs! You have to arrange ahead of time for places to stay at every stop along your route, or else you have to rent rooms from strangers. We can truly say our home is everywhere because we just set up our camp wherever we are without having to ask anybody's permission.

"As long as we're talking frankly like this, I want to tell you it's insulting, the way you always lecture us about how our country is a little hell compared to France. You keep on telling us we're the poorest and most unhappy people on earth, living here without religion, without manners, without honor, without government, without any rules, living just like the forest animals. And you're always pointing out how we lack bread, wine, and a thousand other comforts that abound in Europe, that earthly paradise where your every need is satisfied.

"Well, Brother, if you don't yet know what our people really think about you and your whole nation, then it's time somebody told you the truth. Believe me, as miserable as we seem in your eyes, we're happier than you in this one crucial thing: we are content with what little we have. And you are simply fooling yourselves if you think you can convince us your country is better than ours. If France is such an earthly paradise, then why would any sane man want to leave it? Why abandon your wives, children, relatives, and friends? Why risk your life and your property year after year, through all seasons on stormy seas, just to sail to a strange and barbarous country you call the most wretched in the world? You notice how our people don't even try to get passage to France; we have good reason to think we'd hate it, given that year after year we see more of you French leave France to come over here and enrich yourselves in our country. Anyway, we strongly suspect that even though you men all look like masters and captains over here, you must really be only simple workmen and servants and slaves back at home in your own country. We can see how you value our old rags and our poorest beaverskin clothes, even things we consider past wearing, and we see the way you eagerly fish for cod in our waters to make up for your own misery and oppressive poverty.

"As for us Micmac, we find all the richness and comfort we need right here in our ancestral land, without having to risk our lives on long voyages. And while we feel sorry for you as we sit back and watch you work, we have to marvel at your fussiness and your anxiety as you toil day and night to load up your ships with our codfish. We can see for ourselves that your people must live almost exclusively on the cod you catch here. It is everlastingly nothing but cod—cod for breakfast, cod at noon, cod for supper, cod and more cod, until finally you crave something else more tasty, and then you are forced to turn to us, whom you so despise, and beg us to go hunting game for you so you can feast.

"I ask you just this one question: which person is wisest and happiest, he who labors without stopping and just barely makes enough to get by? Or he who enjoys his life and finds all he needs through the pleasures of hunting and fishing?

"It is true," he said, "that we haven't always had the bread and the wine your France produces. But haven't you heard the stories about how before the French arrived here the Micmac people used to live much longer than we do now? Today we no longer have among us elders who reach one hundred and thirty or forty years, and that is so because we are gradually adopting your way of life. The most long-lived of us now are the ones who scorn your bread and wine and brandy and who keep to our native diet of beaver and moose and waterfowl and fish, in accord with the ways of our ancestors and all Micmac people. Hear me now, Brother, because I tell you this with an open heart: there is no Micmac who doesn't consider himself infinitely more happy and more powerful than any of you French."

* * *

Whatever you may think of this reasoning, I must say that I myself would consider these Indians more fortunate than ourselves, and would even concede that the lives of these barbarians could arouse envy, if only they had the teachings, the understanding, and the means to salvation a merciful God has given us. Their lives aren't vexed like ours by a thousand annoyances. They have nothing like the ranks or offices in the military and in the judicial system that we so ambitiously pursue. They have no private possessions, so they are free from trickery and lawsuits over inheritances. The very titles of sergeant, attorney, clerk, judge, and president are unknown to them. They direct all their ambition toward ambushing and killing numbers of beaver, moose, fur seal, and other animals to get their meat for food and skins for clothing.

These people live in great harmony, never quarreling and never beating one another except when they are drunk. Instead, they mutually aid one another when someone is in need, and they do so with great kindness and without expecting any praise for their charity. There is continual joy in their wigwams. Their large families do not embarrass them, for instead of being annoyed by their children, they look upon them as riches, and the more children there are, the more fortunate the family. Since they never expect that children will rise to a higher station in life than their parents, they are free from worry about accumulating wealth to advance their children in society. As a result, the natural way of making love prevails among them, and the conjugal relations between husband and wife are never repressed as they are in Europe by the selfish fear of having too many children. This duty of fathering and raising children, considered so onerous in Europe, is seen by the Indians as honorable, advantageous, and practical, and he who has the most children is the most honored among his people. Children will support their parents in old age, and contribute to the joy of those who gave birth to them. In truth, these people dwell together, father and children, like the first kings of the earth, who lived when the world was new by hunting and fishing, and upon vegetables and sagamite,[1] for their stew, I think, must be very like the pottage Jacob begged of Esau before ceding to him his blessing . . .

---

[1] Sagamite is a stew of pounded dried corn, something like cornmeal mush; Le Clercq here compares it to the mess of pottage of *Genesis* 27, the savory dish of lentils for which Jacob traded his birthright. This dish was more usually called *samp* by the Micmac, but French and English colonists throughout the northeastern settlements of America settled on *sagamite*, borrowed from the Algonquin-speaking Anishnabe (Chippewa) people living farther inland. *Succotash*, a cognate word, has passed into common American English to mean a stew of corn and lima beans.

GOTTFRIED WILHELM LEIBNIZ
[1646–1716]

Although Gottfried Wilhelm Leibniz was one of the great systematic thinkers and mathematicians of his own time, he is probably best remembered in our time as the model for Voltaire's Pangloss in *Candide*. Voltaire's satiric simplification of Leibniz's reconciliation of scientific empiricism and traditional theism reduces Leibniz's unified world view to the absurd soundbite: "This is the best of all possible worlds." But Leibniz was a many-talented man who made original contributions in many fields—in mathematics, logic, philosophy, law, history, linguistics, and the sciences. His creation of the infinitesimal calculus at the same time as Newton led to some bitter arguments over which man deserved credit for the invention. Leibniz presented considerably more complex analyses and arguments for his optimistic rationalism than the facile proofs offered by Pangloss. The son of a philosopher at the University of Leipzig and father himself to the German Enlightenment, or *Aufklärung*, Leibniz spent his working life as a government agent and diplomat. His philosophy, in its attempts to reconcile and unify opposing positions, sometimes takes on the virtues of diplomacy, and in doing so earns Bertrand Russell's description as "optimistic, orthodox, fantastic, and shallow." Even so, as a rationalist, Leibniz sometimes went to extremes. He believed, for example, that arguments could be resolved if "words of vague and uncertain meanings" were replaced with mathematical "fixed symbols." Then differences in metaphysics or ethics could be settled in the same way that mathematical issues are resolved: "If controversies were to arise, there would be no need of disputation between two philosophers than between two accountants. For it would suffice to take their pencils in their hands, to sit down to their slates, and to say to each other (with a friend as witness, if they liked): Let us calculate."

The passage we include below, from a supplement to Leibniz's *Theodicy* (1710), treats theological issues, stating them as logical syllogisms and then methodically addressing the premises. This systematic method might be seen as a step toward reducing such complex matters to calculations. Leibniz's Panglossian conclusion is stated in his final sentence, "that the kingdom of God is the most perfect of all possible states or governments, and that consequently the little evil there is, is required for the consummation of the immense good which is found there." His arguments in arriving at this conclusion are examples of the facile reasoning that Voltaire satirized in Pangloss's unremitting optimism.

FROM

Supplement *to* Theodicy

Translated by George M. Duncan with revisions by Philip P. Wiener

[A VINDICATION OF GOD'S JUSTICE]

Some intelligent persons have desired that this supplement be made [to *Theodicy*], and I have the more readily yielded to their wishes as in this way I have an opportunity again to remove certain difficulties and to make some observations which were not sufficiently emphasized in the work itself.

I. *Objection.* Whoever does not choose the best is lacking in power, or in knowledge, or in goodness.

God did not choose the best in creating this world.

Therefore, God has been lacking in power, or in knowledge, or in goodness.

Answer. I deny the minor, that is, the second premise of this syllogism; and our opponent proves it by this:

Prosyllogism. Whoever makes things in which there is evil, which could have been made without any evil, or the making of which could have been omitted, does not choose the best.

God has made a world in which there is evil; a world, I say, which could have been made without any evil, or the making of which could have been omitted altogether.

Therefore, God has not chosen the best.

Answer. I grant the minor of this prosyllogism; for it must be confessed that there is evil in this world which God has made, and that it was possible to make a world without evil, or even not to create a world at all, for its creation has depended on the free will of God; but I deny the major, that is, the first of the two premises of the prosyllogism, and I might content myself with simply demanding its proof; but in order to make the matter clearer, I have wished to justify this denial by showing that the best plan is not always that which seeks to avoid evil, since it may happen that the *evil is accompanied by a greater good.* For example, a general of an army will prefer a great victory with a slight wound to a condition without wound and without victory. We have proved this more fully in the large work by making it clear, by instances taken from mathematics and elsewhere, that an imperfection in the part may be required for a greater perfection in the whole. In this I have followed the opinion of St. Augustine, who has said a hundred times, that God has permitted evil in order to bring about good, that is, a greater good; and that of Thomas Aquinas (in libr. II. sent. dist. 32, qu. I, art. 1), that the permitting of evil tends to the good of the universe. I have shown that the ancients called Adam's fall *felix culpa,* a happy sin, because it had been retrieved with immense advantage by the incarnation of the Son of God, who has given to the universe something nobler than anything that ever would have been among creatures except for it. For the sake of a clearer understanding, I have added, following many good authors, that it was in accordance with order and the general good that God allowed to certain creatures the opportunity of exercising their liberty, even when he foresaw that they would turn to evil, but which he could so well rectify; because it was not fitting that, in order to hinder sin, God should always act in an extraordinary manner. To overthrow this objection, therefore, it is sufficient to show that a world with evil might be better than a world without evil; but I have gone even farther, in the work, and have even proved that this universe must be in reality better than every other possible universe.

II. *Objection.* If there is more evil than good in intelligent creatures, then there is more evil than good in the whole work of God.

Now, there is more evil than good in intelligent creatures.

Therefore, there is more evil than good in the whole work of God.

Answer. I deny the major and the minor of this conditional syllogism. As to the major, I do not admit it at all, because this pretended deduction from a part to the whole, from intelligent creatures to all creatures, supposes tacitly and without proof that creatures destitute of reason cannot enter into comparison nor into account with those which possess it. But why may it not be that the surplus of good in the non-intelligent creatures which fill the world, compensates for, and even incomparably surpasses, the surplus of evil in the rational creatures? It is true that the value of the latter is greater; but, in compensation, the others are beyond comparison the more numerous, and it may be that the proportion of number and quantity surpasses that of value and of quality.

As to the minor, that is no more to be admitted; that is, it is not at all to be admitted that there is more evil than good in the intelligent creatures. There is no need even of granting that there is more evil than good in the human race, because it is possible, and in fact very probable, that the glory and the perfection of the blessed are incomparably greater than the misery and the imperfection of the damned, and that here the excellence of the total good in the smaller number exceeds the total evil in the greater number. The blessed approach the Divinity, by means of a Divine Mediator, as near as may suit these creatures, and make such progress in good as is impossible for the damned to make the evil, approach as nearly as they may to the nature of demons. God is infinite, and the devil is limited; the good may and does go to infinity, while evil has its bounds. It is therefore possible, and is credible, that in the comparison of the blessed and the damned, the contrary of that which I have said might happen in the comparison of intelligent and non-intelligent creatures, takes place; namely, it is possible that in the comparison of the happy and the unhappy, the proportion of degree exceeds that of number, and that in the comparison of intelligent and non-intelligent creatures, the proportion of number is greater than that of value. I have the right to suppose that a thing is possible so long as its impossibility is not proved; and indeed that which I have here advanced is more than a supposition.

But in the second place, if I should admit that there is more evil than good in the human race, I still have good grounds for not admitting that there is more evil than good in all intelligent creatures. For there is an inconceivable number of genii, and perhaps of other rational creatures. And an opponent could not prove that in all the City of God, composed as well of genii as of rational animals without number and of an infinity of kinds, evil exceeds good. And although in order to answer an objection, there is no need of proving that a thing is, when its mere possibility suffices; yet, in this work, I have not omitted to show that it is a consequence of the supreme perfection of the Sovereign of the universe, that the kingdom of God is the most perfect of all possible states or governments, and that consequently the little evil there is, is required for the consummation of the immense good which is found there.

MARY ASTELL
[1666–1731]

"Such a paradise as your mother Eve forfeited," but with "no serpents to deceive you, whilst you entertain yourselves in those delicious gardens": With this vivid imagery of redemption, Mary Astell envisioned in *A Serious Proposal to the Ladies* (1692) her utopia, a monastery where Englishwomen could worship God, educate themselves, and rejoice in one another's friendship. Astell anticipated that the proposal would not be welcomed by men because it would permit women access to the learning they had monopolized, and she feared people of both sexes might be made uncomfortable by the resemblance of her proposed women's academy to nunneries, which Protestant propaganda luridly depicted as brothels. Astell's fears were justified. *A Serious Proposal* did attract some favorable attention, but the birth of academic institutions for women did not come until the nineteenth century.

Mary Astell was born to a middle-class family in Newcastle, England, where an uncle who was a clergyman taught her philosophy and the elements of logic she was to wield so skillfully in her own writing. In 1688 she moved to London, where she made friends among the clergy and the minor nobility, counting on their patronage for her upkeep.

Lady Mary Wortley Montagu, twenty-three years younger, the powerful "she-meteor" among British intellectuals, became Astell's lifelong friend, despite the differences in their ages and their temperaments.

Unlike Montagu, Mary Astell was a conservative on all matters except the issue of education for women. A number of her writings defend the positions of the Church of England. Although she had platonic friendships with men, she chose to remain single. She argued for women's equality and catalogued all the injustices and the woes married women endured in *Some Reflections Upon Marriage* (1700), but she nonetheless believed that, by the laws of God, marriage required the subordination of women to men. Only a single woman could hope to enjoy the intellectual and spiritual refreshment of Astell's "delicious gardens."

FROM

A Serious Proposal to the Ladies

Now as to the proposal, it is to erect a *Monastery*, or if you will (to avoid giving offense to the scrupulous and injudicious, by names which though innocent in themselves, have been abused by superstitious practices), we will call it a *Religious Retirement*, and such as shall have a double aspect, being not only a retreat from the world for those who desire that advantage, but likewise, an institution and previous discipline, to fit us to do the greatest good in it; such an institution as this (if I do not mightily deceive myself) would be the most probable method to amend the present and improve the future age. For here those who are convinced of the emptiness of earthly enjoyments, who are sick of the vanity of the world and its impertinencies, may find more substantial and satisfying entertainments, and need not be confined to what they justly loathe. Those who are desirous to know and fortify their weak side, first do good to themselves, that hereafter they may be capable of doing more good to others; or for their greater security are willing to avoid *temptation*, may get out of that danger which a continual stay in view of the enemy, and the familiarity and unwearied application of the temptation may expose them to; and gain an opportunity to look into themselves, to be acquainted at home and no longer the greatest strangers to their own hearts. Such as are willing in a more peculiar and undisturbed manner, to attend the great business they came into the world about, the service of GOD and improvement of their own minds, may find a convenient and blissful recess from the noise and hurry of the world. A world so cumbersome, so infectious, that although through the grace of GOD and their own strict watchfulness, they are kept from sinking down into its corruptions, 'twill however damp their flight to Heaven, hinder them from attaining any eminent pitch of virtue.

You are therefore, ladies, invited into a place where you shall suffer no other confinement, but to be kept out of the road of sin: You shall not be deprived of your grandeur but only exchange the vain pomps and pageantry of the world, empty titles and forms of state, for the true and solid greatness of being able to despise them. You will not only quit the chat of insignificant people for an ingenious conversation; the froth of flashy wit for real wisdom; idle tales for instructive discourses. The deceitful flatteries of those who, under pretense of loving and admiring you, really served their *own* base ends, for the seasonable reproofs and wholesome counsels of your hearty well-wishers and affectionate friends, which will procure you those perfections your feigned lovers pretended you had, and kept you from obtaining. No uneasy task will be enjoined you, all your labor being only to prepare for the highest degrees of that glory, the very lowest of which is more than at present you are able to conceive, and the prospect of it sufficient to outweigh all the pains of religion, were there any in it, as really there are none. All that is required of you, is only to be as happy as possibly you can, and to make sure of a felicity that will fill all the capacities of your souls!

. . .

But because we were not made for ourselves, nor can by any means so effectually glorify GOD, and do good to our own souls, as by doing offices of charity and beneficence to others; and to the intent that every virtue, and the highest degrees of every virtue, may be exercised and promoted the most that may be; your retreat shall be so managed as not to exclude the good works of an *active* from the pleasure and serenity of a *contemplative* life, but by a due mixture of both retain all the advantages and avoid the inconveniences that attend either. It shall not so cut you off from the world as to hinder you from bettering and improving it, but rather qualify you to do it the greatest good, and be a seminary to stock the kingdom with pious and prudent ladies, whose good example, it is to be hoped, will so influence the rest of their sex that women may no longer pass for those little useless and impertinent animals, which the ill conduct of too many has caused 'em to be mistaken for.

We have hitherto considered our retirement only in relation to religion, which is indeed its *main*, I may say its *only* design; nor can this be thought too contracting a word, since religion is the adequate business of our lives and, largely considered, takes in all we have to do, nothing being a fit employment for a rational creature which has not either a *direct* or *remote* tendency to this great and *only* end. But because, as we have all along observed, religion never appears in its true beauty but when it is accompanied with wisdom and discretion; and that without a good understanding, we can scarce be *truly*, but never *eminently* good; being liable to a thousand seductions and mistakes (for even the men themselves, if they have not a competent degree of knowledge, are carried about with every wind of doctrine). Therefore, one great end of this institution shall be, to expel that cloud of ignorance which custom has involved us in, to furnish our minds with a stock of solid and useful knowledge, that the souls of women may no longer be the only unadorned and neglected things. It is not intended that our *religious* should waste their time and trouble their heads about such unconcerning matters as the vogue of the world has turned up for learning, the impertinency of which has been excellently exposed by an ingenious pen, but busy themselves in a serious enquiry after *necessary* and *perfective* truths, something which it *concerns* them to know, and which tends to their real interest and perfection, and what that is the excellent author just now mentioned will sufficiently inform them.[1] Such a course of study will neither be too troublesome nor out of the reach of a female *virtuoso*,[2] for it is not intended she should spend her hours in learning *words* but *things*, and therefore no more languages than are necessary to acquaint her with useful authors. Nor need she trouble herself in turning over a great number of books, but take care to understand and digest a few well chosen and good ones. Let her but obtain right ideas, and be truly acquainted with the nature of those objects that present themselves to her mind, and then no matter whether or no she be able to tell what fanciful people have said about them: And thoroughly to understand Christianity as professed by the Church of England will be sufficient to confirm her in the truth, though she have not a catalogue of those particular errors which oppose it. Indeed a learned education

---

[1] Astell refers to her friend the Reverend John Norris and his 1690 treatise *Reflections upon the Conduct of Human Life*.
[2] A scholar.

of the women will appear so unfashionable that I began to startle at the singularity of the proposition, but was extremely pleased when I found a late ingenious author (whose book I met with since the writing of this) agree with me in my opinion. For speaking of the repute that learning was in about 150 years ago, *It was so very modish* (says he) *that the fair sex seemed to believe that Greek and Latin added to their charms: and Plato and Aristotle untranslated, were frequent ornaments of their closets. One would think by the effects, that it was a proper way of educating them, since there are no accounts in history of so many great women in any one age, as are to be found between the years 15 and 1600.*[3]

For since GOD has given women as well as men intelligent souls, why should they be forbidden to improve them? Since he has not denied us the faculty of thinking, why should we not (at least in gratitude to him) employ our thoughts on himself, their noblest object, and not unworthily bestow them on trifles and gaieties and secular affairs? Being the soul was created for the contemplation of truth as well as for the fruition of good, is it not as cruel and unjust to exclude women from the knowledge of the one as from the enjoyment of the other? Especially since the will is blind, and cannot choose but by the direction of the understanding; or to speak more properly, since the soul always *wills* according as she *understands*, so that if she understands amiss, she wills amiss. And as exercise enlarges and exalts any faculty, so through want of using it becomes cramped and lessened; if therefore we make little or no use of our understandings, we shall shortly have none to use; and the more contracted and unemployed the deliberating and directive power is, the more liable is the elective to unworthy and mischievous choices. What is it but the want of an ingenious education that renders the generality of feminine conversations so insipid and foolish and their solitude so insupportable? Learning is therefore necessary to render them more agreeable and useful in company, and to furnish them with becoming entertainments when alone, that so they may not be driven to those miserable shifts, which too many make use of to put off their time, that precious talent that never lies on the hands of a judicious person.

. . .

There is a sort of learning indeed which is worse than the greatest ignorance: a woman may study plays and romances all her days, and be a great deal more knowing but never a jot the wiser. Such a knowledge as this serves only to instruct and put her forward in the practice of the greatest follies, yet how can they justly blame her who forbid, or at least won't afford opportunity of better? A rational mind *will* be employed, it will never be satisfied in doing nothing, and if you neglect to furnish it with good materials, 'tis like to take up with such as come to hand.

We pretend not that women should teach in the Church, or usurp authority where it is not allowed them; permit us only to understand our *own* duty, and not be forced to take it upon trust from others; to be at least so far learned, as to be able to form in our minds a true idea of Christianity, it being so very necessary to fence us against the danger of these *last* and *perilous days*, in which deceivers, a part of whose character is to *lead captive silly women*, need not *creep into houses*, since they have authority to proclaim their errors on the *house top*. And let us also acquire a true practical knowledge, such as will convince us of the absolute necessity of *holy living* as well as of *right believing*, and that no heresy is more dangerous than that of an ungodly and wicked life. And since the French tongue is understood by most ladies, methinks they may much better improve it by the study of philosophy (as I hear the

---

[3] Astell quotes from William Wottons's *Reflections upon Ancient and Modern Learning* (1694).

French Ladies do), Descartes, Malebranche[4] and others, than by reading idle *novels* and *romances*. 'Tis strange we should be so forward to imitate their fashions and fopperies, and have no regard to what really deserves our imitation. And why shall it not be thought as genteel to understand *French philosophy*, as to be accoutered in a *French mode?* Let therefore the famous Madam Dacier, Scudéry, &c, and our own incomparable Orinda,[5] excite the emulation of the English ladies.

The ladies, I'm sure, have no reason to dislike this proposal, but I know not how the men will resent it to have their enclosure broke down, and women invited to taste of that tree of knowledge they have so long unjustly *monopolized*. But they must excuse me if I be as partial to my own sex as they are to theirs, and think women as capable of learning as men are, and that it becomes them as well. For I cannot imagine wherein the hurt lies, if instead of doing mischief to one another, by an uncharitable and vain conversation, women be enabled to inform and instruct those of their own sex at least; the Holy Ghost having left it on record, that Priscilla as well as her husband, catechized the eloquent Apollos and the great Apostle found no fault with her.[6] It will therefore be very proper for our ladies to spend part of their time in this retirement in adorning their minds with useful knowledge.

LADY MARY WORTLEY MONTAGU
[1689–1762]

The eighteenth century in England has been characterized as an age of prose because the literary marketplace gave rise to the novel, histories, biographies, travel and exploration narratives, and diaries. Another popular literary form was the collection of "familiar" letters by persons of public importance, including politicians, actors, writers, well-to-do travelers taking the "Grand Tour" of continental Europe, or explorers and diplomats journeying to lands beyond the familiar boundaries of Europe. European readers were fascinated with what they considered to be exotic cultures. Whetted early in the century by the Galland translation of *Thousand and One Nights* from Arabic into French and the opening of increased trade and European presence in the Levant, curiosity about the Orient virtually guaranteed the popularity of published accounts—genuine and invented—of travels to China, India, the Middle East, and Palestine. Europeans also liked to see their own customs and manners through the eyes of non-European travelers, giving rise to satire and social criticism in the form of letters from imaginary visitors. Two of the most important of these invented travels are Montesquieu's *Persian Letters* (1754), which purports to be a series of letters recording the observations of three Persians—Rica, Usbek, and Rhedi; and Oliver Goldsmith's *The Citizen of the World* (1762), which similarly masquerades as a series of letters from a Chinese philosopher, Lien Chi Altangi, temporarily visiting England.

Among the genuine travelers in the eighteenth century was Lady Mary Wortley Montagu, whose husband, Edward Wortley Montagu, was made ambassador to Con-

---

[4]René Descartes (1596–1650) and Nicholas de Malebranche (1638–1715) were both seventeenth-century French philosophers.

[5]Anne Dacier (1654–1720) translated Homer into French. Madeleine de Scudéry (1607–1701) wrote romances infused with her considerable learning. "Orinda" was the literary nickname of Katherine Philips (1631–1664), a reclusive poet whose work was circulated only in manuscript and widely praised by many famous contemporary British writers.

[6]Priscilla was an early Roman Christian of humble background; she spoke up in public and corrected a learned male convert on points of Jesus' teachings, and so has figured as a hero to Christian feminists. See *Acts* 18: 24–26.

stantinople in 1716. Born Mary Pierrepont, daughter of Evelyn Pierrepont, a Whig peer who eventually became Lord of Dorchester, Lady Mary early demonstrated a keen critical intelligence and a desire to learn, which led her to teach herself Latin and to read avidly in the classics and the popular novels of her time. Her wit and conversation, for which she was well known in London circles, was sharpened in her father's home where she attracted the attention of his friends, including the writers Joseph Addison, Richard Steele, and William Congreve. In 1712, at age twenty-four, against her father's will she eloped with Wortley and began to extend her reputation for cultivation and learning, contributing poems and essays within an elite literary circle that included Alexander Pope, against whom she later wrote some pointed satirical poems.

In 1716, Wortley was appointed Ambassador to the Porte, and he and Lady Mary departed for Turkey in January 1717, staying until May 1718. While in Turkey, Lady Mary learned the native language and acquired some knowledge of Turkish literature. In addition, she sought out information about smallpox inoculation, which she introduced into England upon her return and for which she met with stubborn resistance and skepticism from prominent English physicians. During this stay, Lady Mary kept notes and wrote letters (some of which appear never to have been intended for the addressee) that she later compiled into what is known as her brilliant *Turkish Letters,* not published until 1763, a year after her death in London at the age of seventy-four. Lady Mary spent most of her last years in Italy and France, having freed herself from what turned out to be an unhappy marriage and being disappointed in her love for a young Italian writer, Francesco Algarotti. After leaving England in 1739, she lived alone for almost twenty-one years, rather like Voltaire's Candide, on a small farm where she literally tended her garden and wrote in her journal. In addition to her letters, for which she was highly praised, Lady Mary wrote the satirical *Town Eclogues* and *Court Poems* (1716), and a periodical, *The Nonsense of Common-Sense* (1737-1738), which she took up to defend her friend Robert Walpole against attacks by Tory writers, including Pope.

Unlike the fictional constructs of Montesquieu and Goldsmith, Lady Mary's letters attempt, as nearly as possible for a European observer, to account for the manners and customs she witnessed directly in her travels to Turkey. The letters give us a rare opportunity to witness Turkish society from a European woman's point of view, in this case relatively untainted by most of the prejudices common in travel narratives about the East. Remarkably, Lady Mary records in the letters below her view of a Turkish harem and a mosque, spaces usually forbidden to Western travelers, into which Lady Mary was admitted. Lady Mary avoids romanticizing or demeaning Turkey, as other European writers were wont to do when writing about the Orient, but the letters do show some of those strategies of domesticating the Other that Edward Said describes in his *Orientalism,* an important study of European representations of the East.

FROM

The Turkish Letters

... I was invited to dine with the Grand Vizier's lady,[1] and it was with a great deal of pleasure I prepared myself for an entertainment which was never given before to any Christian. I thought I should very little satisfy her curiosity (which I did not doubt was a considerable motive to the invitation) by going in a dress she was used to see, and therefore dressed myself in the court habit of Vienna,

---

[1] Sultana Hafitén, widow of Sultan Mustafa II, who ruled from 1695 to 1703; the Grand Vizier was the chief authority in the Ottoman Empire, second only to the Sultan.

which is much more magnificent than ours. However, I chose to go *incognita,* to avoid any disputes about ceremony, and went in a Turkish coach, only attended by my woman that held up my train, and the Greek lady who was my interpretress. I was met at the court door by her black eunuch, who helped me out of the coach with great respect, and conducted me through several rooms, where her she-slaves, finely dressed, were ranged on each side. In the innermost I found the lady sitting on her sofa, in a sable vest. She advanced to meet me, and presented me half a dozen of her friends with great civility. She seemed a very good-[looking] woman, near fifty years old. I was surprised to observe so little magnificence in her house, the furniture being all very moderate; and, except the habits and number of her slaves, nothing about her that appeared expensive. She guessed at my thoughts, and told me that she was no longer of an age to spend either her time or money in superfluities; that her whole expense was in charity, and her whole employment praying to God. There was no affectation in this speech; both she and her husband are entirely given up to devotion. He never looks upon any other woman; and, what is much more extraordinary, touches no bribes, notwithstanding the example of all his predecessors. He is so scrupulous in this point, that he would not accept Mr. W————'s present, till he had been assured over and over that it was a settled perquisite of his place at the entrance of every ambassador.

She entertained me with all kind of civility till dinner came in, which was served, one dish at a time, to a vast number, all finely dressed after their manner, which I do not think so bad as you have perhaps heard it represented. I am a very good judge of their eating, having lived three weeks in the house of an *effendi*[2] at Belgrade, who gave us very magnificent dinners, dressed by his own cooks, which the first week pleased me extremely; but I own I then began to grow weary of it, and desired our own cook might add a dish or two after our manner. But I attribute this to custom. I am very much inclined to believe an Indian, that had never tasted of either, would prefer their cookery to ours. Their sauces are very high, all the roast very much done. They use a great deal of rich spice. The soup is served for the last dish; and they have at least as great variety of ragouts as we have. I was very sorry I could not eat of as many as the good lady would have had me, who was very earnest in serving me of every thing. The treat concluded with coffee and perfumes, which is a high mark of respect; two slaves kneeling *censed* my hair, clothes, and handkerchief. After this ceremony, she commanded her slaves to play and dance, which they did with their guitars in their hands; and she excused to me their want of skill, saying she took no care to accomplish them in that art.

I returned her thanks, and soon after took my leave. I was conducted back in the same manner I entered; and would have gone straight to my own house; but the Greek lady with me earnestly solicited me to visit the *kiyàya's* lady,[3] saying, he was the second officer in the empire, and ought indeed to be looked upon as the first, the Grand Vizier having only the name, while he exercised the authority. I had found so little diversion in this *harém,* that I had no mind to go into another. But her importunity prevailed with me, and I am extreme glad that I was so complaisant.

All things here were with quite another air than at the Grand Vizier's; and the very house confessed the difference between an old devote and a young beauty. It was nicely clean and magnificent. I was met at the door by two black eunuchs, who led me through a long gallery between two ranks of beautiful young girls, with their hair finely plaited, almost hanging to their feet, all dressed in fine light damasks, brocaded with silver. I was sorry that decency did not permit me to stop to consider

---

[2]Literally "sir" or "master," but used in general to indicate a member of the upper ranks of society; an aristocrat.

[3]The Lieutenant's wife; i.e., the wife of the Grand Vizier's deputy.

them nearer. But that thought was lost upon my entrance into a large room, or rather pavilion, built round with gilded sashes, which were most of them thrown up, and the trees planted near them gave an agreeable shade, which hindered the sun from being troublesome. The jessamines and honeysuckles that twisted round their trunks, shedding a soft perfume, increased by a white marble fountain playing sweet water in the lower part of the room, which fell into three or four basins with a pleasing sound. The roof was painted with all sort of flowers, falling out of gilded baskets, that seemed tumbling down. On a sofa, raised three steps, and covered with fine Persian carpets, sat the *kiyàya's* lady, leaning on cushions of white satin, embroidered; and at her feet sat two young girls, the eldest about twelve years old, lovely as angels, dressed perfectly rich, and almost covered with jewels. But they were hardly seen near the fair *Fatima* (for that is her name), so much her beauty effaced every thing I have seen, all that has been called lovely either in England or Germany, and [I] must own that I never saw any thing so gloriously beautiful, nor can I recollect a face that would have been taken notice of near hers. She stood up to receive me, saluting me after their fashion, putting her hand upon her heart with a sweetness full of majesty, that no court breeding could ever give. She ordered cushions to be given to me, and took care to place me in the corner, which is the place of honour. I confess, though the Greek lady had before given me a great opinion of her beauty, I was so struck with admiration, that I could not for some time speak to her, being wholly taken up in gazing. That surprising harmony of features! that charming result of the whole! that exact proportion of body! that lovely bloom of complexion unsullied by art! the unutterable enchantment of her smile!—But her eyes!—large and black, with all the soft languishment of the blue! every turn of her face discovering some new charm.

After my first surprise was over, I endeavoured, by nicely examining her face, to find out some imperfection, without any fruit of my search, but being clearly convinced of the error of that vulgar notion, that a face perfectly regular would not be agreeable; nature having done for her with more success, what Apelles[4] is said to have essayed, by a collection of the most exact features, to form, a perfect face, and to that, a behaviour so full of grace and sweetness, such easy motions, with an air so majestic, yet free from stiffness or affectation, that I am persuaded, could she be suddenly transported upon the most polite throne of Europe, nobody would think her other than born and bred to be a queen, though educated in a country we call barbarous. To say all in a word, our most celebrated English beauties would vanish near her.

She was dressed in a *caftán* of gold brocade, flowered with silver, very well fitted to her shape, and shewing to advantage the beauty of her bosom, only shaded by the thin gauze of her shift. Her drawers were pale pink, green and silver, her slippers white, finely embroidered: her lovely arms adorned with bracelets of diamonds, and her broad girdle set round with diamonds; upon her head a rich Turkish handkerchief of pink and silver, her own fine black hair hanging a great length in various tresses, and on one side of her head some bodkins of jewels. I am afraid you will accuse me of extravagance in this description. I think I have read somewhere that women always speak in rapture when they speak of beauty, but I cannot imagine why they should not be allowed to do so. I rather think it [a] virtue to be able to admire without any mixture of desire or envy. The gravest writers have spoken with great warmth of some celebrated pictures and statues. The workmanship of Heaven certainly excels all our weak imitations, and, I think,

---

[4]The most famous Greek painter of antiquity (c. fourth century B.C.E.).

has a much better claim to our praise. For me, I am not ashamed to own I took more pleasure in looking on the beauteous Fatima, than the finest piece of sculpture could have given me.

She told me the two girls at her feet were her daughters, though she appeared too young to be their mother. Her fair maids were ranged below the sofa, to the number of twenty, and put me in mind of the pictures of the ancient nymphs. I did not think all nature could have furnished such a scene of beauty. She made them a sign to play and dance. Four of them immediately began to play some soft airs on instruments between a lute and a guitar, which they accompanied with their voices, while the others danced by turns. This dance was very different from what I had seen before. Nothing could be more artful, or more proper to raise certain ideas. The tunes so soft!—the motions so languishing!—accompanied with pauses and dying eyes! half-falling back, and then recovering themselves in so artful a manner, that I am very positive the coldest and most rigid prude upon earth could not have looked upon them without thinking of something not to be spoken of. I suppose you may have read that the Turks have no music but what is shocking to the ears; but this account is from those who never heard any but what is played in the streets, and is just as reasonable as if a foreigner should take his ideas of the English music from the bladder and string, and marrow-bones and cleavers. I can assure you that the music is extremely pathetic; 'tis true I am inclined to prefer the Italian, but perhaps I am partial. I am acquainted with a Greek lady who sings better than Mrs. Robinson,[5] and is very well skilled in both, who gives the preference to the Turkish. 'Tis certain they have very fine natural voices; these were very agreeable. When the dance was over, four fair slaves came into the room with silver censers in their hands, and perfumed the air with amber, aloes-wood, and other rich scents. After this they served me coffee upon their knees in the finest japan china, with *soucoupes*[6] of silver, gilt. The lovely Fatima entertained me all this time in the most polite agreeable manner, calling me often *Guzél sultanum*, or the beautiful sultana, and desiring my friendship with the best grace in the world, lamenting that she could not entertain me in my own language.

When I took my leave, two maids brought in a fine silver basket of embroidered handkerchiefs; she begged I would wear the richest for her sake, and gave the others to my woman and interpretress. I retired through the same ceremonies as before, and could not help fancying I had been some time in Mahomet's paradise, so much I was charmed with what I had seen. I know not how the relation of it appears to you. I wish it may give you part of my pleasure; for I would have my dear sister share in all the diversions of, &c.

To the Abbot———[the Abbé Conti]

Adrianople, May 17, O.S. [1717]

...I went...to see the mosque of Sultan Selim I,[7] which is a building very well worth the curiosity of a traveller. I was dressed in my Turkish habit, and admitted without scruple: though I believe they guessed who I was, by the extreme officiousness of the doorkeeper to shew me every part of it. It is situated very advantageously in the midst of the city, and in the highest part, making a very

---

[5] Anastasia Robinson, an opera singer and contemporary of Lady Mary.
[6] Saucers.
[7] Ruler of Ottoman Empire (1512–1520).

noble show. The first court has four gates, and the innermost three. They are both of them surrounded with cloisters, with marble pillars of the Ionic order, finely polished and of very lively colours; the whole pavement being white marble, the roof of the cloisters being divided into several cupolas or domes, leaded, with gilt balls on the top. In the midst of each court [are] fine fountains of white marble; before the great gate of the mosque, a portico, with green marble pillars. It has five gates, the body of the mosque being one prodigious dome.

I understand so little of architecture, I dare not pretend to speak of the proportions. It seemed to me very regular; this I am sure of, it is vastly high, and I thought it the noblest building I ever saw. It had two rows of marble galleries on pillars, with marble balusters; the pavement marble, covered with Persian carpets, and, in my opinion, it is a great addition to its beauty, that it is not divided into pews, and incumbered with forms and benches like our churches; nor the pillars (which are most of them red and white marble) disfigured by the little tawdry images and pictures that give the Roman Catholic churches the air of toy-shops. The walls seemed to me inlaid with such very lively colours, in small flowers, I could not imagine what stones had been made use of. But going nearer, I saw they were crusted with japan china, which has a very beautiful effect. In the midst hung a vast lamp of silver, gilt; besides which, I do verily believe, there were at least two thousand of a lesser size. This must look very glorious when they are all lighted; but that being at night, no women are suffered to enter. Under the large lamp is a great pulpit of carved wood, gilt; and just by it, a fountain to wash, which you know is an essential part of their devotion. In one corner is a little gallery, inclosed with gilded lattices, for the Grand Signior. At the upper end, a large niche, very like an altar, raised two steps, covered with gold brocade, and, standing before it, two silver gilt candlesticks, the height of a man, and in them white wax candles, as thick as a man's waist. The outside of the mosque is adorned with four towers, vastly high, gilt on the top, from whence the *imaums* call the people to prayers. I had the curiosity to go up one of them, which is contrived so artfully, as to give surprise to all that see it. There is but one door, which leads to three different staircases, going to the three different stories of the tower, in such a manner, that three priests may ascend, rounding, without ever meeting each other; a contrivance very much admired.

Behind the mosque is an exchange full of shops, where poor artificers are lodged *gratis*. I saw several dervises at their prayers here. They are dressed in a plain piece of woollen, with their arms bare, and a woollen cap on their heads, like a high-crowned hat without brims. I went to see some other mosques, built much after the same manner, but not comparable in point of magnificence to this I have described, which is infinitely beyond any church in Germany or England; I won't talk of other countries I have not seen. The seraglio does not seem a very magnificent palace. But the gardens [are] very large, plentifully supplied with water, and full of trees: which is all I know of them, having never been in them. . . .

TO THE COUNTESS OF———[MAR]

Pera of Constantinople, March 10, O.S. [1718]

. . . I went to see the Sultana Hafitén, favourite of the late Emperor Mustapha, who, you know, (or perhaps you don't know) was deposed by his brother, the reigning Sultan Achmet, and died a few weeks after, being poisoned, as it was generally believed. This lady was, immediately after his death, saluted with an absolute order to leave the seraglio, and choose herself a husband from the great men at the Porte.[8] I suppose you may imagine her overjoyed at this proposal. Quite contrary: these women, who are called, and esteem themselves, queens, look upon this liberty as the greatest disgrace and affront that can happen to them. She threw herself at the Sultan's feet, and begged him to poignard her, rather than use his brother's widow with that contempt. She represented to him, in agonies of sorrow, that she was privileged from this misfortune, by having brought five princes into the Ottoman family; but all the boys being dead, and only one girl surviving, this excuse was not received, and she [was] compelled to make her choice. She chose Bekir Effendi, then secretary of state, and above fourscore years old, to convince the world that she firmly intended to keep the vow she had made, of never suffering a second husband to approach her bed; and since she must honour some subject so far as to be called his wife, she would choose him as a mark of her gratitude, since it was he that had presented her at the age of ten years old, to her last lord. But she has never permitted him to pay her one visit; though it is now fifteen years she has been in his house, where she passes her time in uninterrupted mourning, with a constancy very little known in Christendom, especially in a widow of twenty-one, for she is now but thirty-six. She has no black eunuchs for her guard, her husband being obliged to respect her as a queen, and not inquire at all into what is done in her apartment, where I was led into a large room, with a sofa the whole length of it, adorned with white marble pillars like a *ruelle,*[9] covered with pale blue figured velvet on a silver ground, with cushions of the same, where I was desired to repose till the Sultana appeared, who had contrived this manner of reception to avoid rising up at my entrance, though she made me an inclination of her head when I rose up to her. I was very glad to observe a lady that had been distinguished by the favour of an emperor, to whom beauties were every day presented from all parts of the world. But she did not seem to me to have ever been half so beautiful as the fair Fatima I saw at Adrianople; though she had the remains of a fine face, more decayed by sorrow than time. But her dress was something so surprisingly rich, I cannot forbear describing it to you. She wore a vest called *donalma,* and which differs from a *caftán* by longer sleeves, and folding over at the bottom. It was of purple cloth, strait to her shape, and thick set, on each side, down to her feet, and round the sleeves, with pearls of the best water, of the same size as their buttons commonly are. You must not suppose I mean as large as those of my Lord ———, but about the bigness of a pea; and to these buttons large loops of diamonds, in the form of those gold loops so common upon birthday coats. This habit was tied, at the waist, with two large tassels of smaller pearl, and round the arms embroidered with large diamonds: her shift fastened at the bottom with a great diamond, shaped like a lozenge; her girdle as broad as the broadest English ribbon, entirely covered with diamonds. Round her neck she wore three chains, which reached to her knees: one of large pearl, at the bottom of which hung a fine coloured emerald, as big as a turkey-egg; another, consisting of two hundred emeralds, close joined together, of the most lively green, perfectly matched, every one as large as a half-crown piece, and as thick as three crown pieces; and another of small emeralds, perfectly round. But her earrings eclipsed all the rest. They were two diamonds, shaped exactly like pears, as large as a big hazel-nut. Round her *talpoche*[10] she had four strings of pearl, the whitest and most perfect in the world, at least enough to make four necklaces,

---

[8]The official name of the Turkish government, taken from the high gate at the entrance to the building housing the Grand Vizier's administrative offices.

[9]A passageway or lane.

[10]A kind of bonnet with elongated sides.

every one as large as the Duchess of Marlborough's, and of the same size, fastened with two roses, consisting of a large ruby for the middle stone, and round them twenty drops of clean diamonds to each. Beside this, her head-dress was covered with bodkins of emeralds and diamonds. She wore large diamond bracelets, and had five rings on her fingers, all single diamonds, (except Mr. Pitt's[11]) the largest I ever saw in my life. It is for jewellers to compute the value of these things; but, according to the common estimation of jewels in our part of the world, her whole dress must be worth above a hundred thousand pounds sterling. This I am very sure of, that no European queen has half the quantity; and the empress's jewels, though very fine, would look very mean near hers.

She gave me a dinner of fifty dishes of meat, which (after their fashion) were placed on the table but one at a time, and was extremely tedious. But the magnificence of her table answered very well to that of her dress. The knives were of gold, the hafts set with diamonds. But the piece of luxury that grieved my eyes was the tablecloth and napkins, which were all tiffany, embroidered with silks and gold, in the finest manner, in natural flowers. It was with the utmost regret that I made use of these costly napkins, as finely wrought as the finest handkerchiefs that ever came out of this country. You may be sure, that they were entirely spoiled before dinner was over. The sherbet (which is the liquor they drink at meals) was served in china bowls; but the covers and salvers massy gold. After dinner, water was brought in a gold basin, and towels of the same kind of the napkins, which I very unwillingly wiped my hands upon; and coffee was served in china, with gold *soucoupes*.

The Sultana seemed in very good humour, and talked to me with the utmost civility. I did not omit this opportunity of learning all that I possibly could of the seraglio, which is so entirely unknown among us. She assured me, that the story of the Sultan's throwing a handkerchief is altogether fabulous; and the manner upon that occasion, no other but that he sends the *kyslár agá,* to signify to the lady the honour he intends her. She is immediately complimented upon it by the others, and led to the bath, where she is perfumed and dressed in the most magnificent and becoming manner. The Emperor precedes his visit by a royal present, and then comes into her apartment: neither is there any such thing as her creeping in at the bed's foot. She said, that the first he made choice of was always after the first in rank, and not the mother of the eldest son, as other writers would make us believe. Sometimes the Sultan diverts himself in the company of all his ladies, who stand in a circle round him. And she confessed that they were ready to die with jealousy and envy of the happy she that he distinguished by any appearance of preference. But this seemed to me neither better nor worse than the circles in most courts, where the glance of the monarch is watched, and every smile waited for with impatience, and envied by those who cannot obtain it.

She never mentioned the Sultan[12] without tears in her eyes, yet she seemed very fond of the discourse. "My past happiness," said she, "appears a dream to me. Yet I cannot forget that I was beloved by the greatest and most lovely of mankind. I was chosen from all the rest, to make all his campaigns with him; I would not survive him, if I was not passionately fond of the princess my daughter. Yet all my tenderness for her was hardly enough to make me preserve my life. When I lost him, I passed a whole twelvemonth without seeing the light. Time has softened my despair; yet I now pass some days every week in tears, devoted to the memory of my Sultan."

---

[11] William Pitt, Earl of Chatham (1708–1778), a powerful English statesman.
[12] Sultan Mustafa II, who died in 1703.

There was no affectation in these words. It was easy to see she was in a deep melancholy, though her good humour made her willing to divert me.

She asked me to walk in her garden, and one of her slaves immediately brought her a *pellice*[13] of rich brocade lined with sables. I waited on her into the garden, which had nothing in it remarkable but the fountains; and from thence she shewed me all her apartments. In her bed-chamber her toilet was displayed, consisting of two looking-glasses, the frames covered with pearls, and her night *talpoche* set with bodkins of jewels, and near it three vests of fine sables, every one of which is, at least, worth a thousand dollars (two hundred pounds English money). I don't doubt these rich habits were purposely placed in sight, but they seemed negligently thrown on the sofa. When I took my leave of her, I was complimented with perfumes, as at the Grand Vizier's, and presented with a very fine embroidered handkerchief. Her slaves were to the number of thirty, besides ten little ones, the eldest not above seven years old. These were the most beautiful girls I ever saw, all richly dressed; and I observed that the Sultana took a great deal of pleasure in these lovely children, which is a vast expense; for there is not a handsome girl of that age to be bought under a hundred pounds sterling. They wore little garlands of flowers, and their own hair, braided, which was all their head-dress; but their habits all of gold stuffs. These served her coffee, kneeling; brought water when she washed, &c. It is a great part of the business of the older slaves to take care of these girls, to learn them to embroider, and serve them as carefully as if they were children of the family.

Now, do I fancy that you imagine I have entertained you, all this while, with a relation that has, at least, received many embellishments from my hand? This is but too like (say you) the Arabian Tales: these embroidered napkins! and a jewel as large as a turkey's egg!—You forget, dear sister, those very tales were written by an author of this country, and (excepting the enchantments) are a real representation of the manners here. We travellers are in very hard circumstances: If we say nothing but what has been said before us, we are dull, and we have observed nothing. If we tell any thing new, we are laughed at as fabulous and romantic, not allowing for the difference of ranks, which afford difference of company, more curiosity, or the changes of customs, that happen every twenty years in every country. But people judge of travellers exactly with the same candour, good nature, and impartiality, they judge of their neighbours upon all occasions. For my part, if I live to return amongst you, I am so well acquainted with the morals of all my dear friends and acquaintance, that I am resolved to tell them nothing at all, to avoid the imputation (which their charity would certainly incline them to) of my telling too much. But I depend upon your knowing me enough to believe whatever I seriously assert for truth; though I give you leave to be surprised at an account so new to you.

But what would you say if I told you, that I have been in a harém, where the winter apartment was wainscoted with inlaid work of mother-of-pearl, ivory of different colours, and olive wood, exactly like the little boxes you have seen brought out of this country; and those rooms designed for summer, the walls all crusted with japan china, the roofs gilt, and the floors spread with the finest Persian carpets? Yet there is nothing more true; such is the palace of my lovely friend, the fair Fatima, whom I was acquainted with at Adrianople. I went to visit her yesterday; and, if possible, she appeared to me handsomer than before. She met me at the door of her chamber, and, giving me her hand with the best grace in the world—"You Christian ladies," said she, with a smile that made her as handsome as an angel, "have the reputation of inconstancy, and I did not expect, whatever goodness you expressed

---

[13] A long cloak lined with fur.

for me at Adrianople, that I should ever see you again. But I am now convinced that I have really the happiness of pleasing you; and, if you knew how I speak of you amongst our ladies, you would be assured that you do me justice if you think me your friend." She placed me in the corner of the sofa, and I spent the afternoon in her conversation, with the greatest pleasure in the world.

The Sultana Hafitén is, what one would naturally expect to find a Turkish lady, willing to oblige, but not knowing how to go about it; and it is easy to see in her manner, that she has lived secluded from the world. But Fatima has all the politeness and good breeding of a court; with an air that inspires, at once, respect and tenderness; and now I understand her language, I find her wit as engaging as her beauty. She is very curious after the manners of other countries, and has not that partiality for her own, so common to little minds. A Greek that I carried with me, who had never seen her before, (nor could have been admitted now, if she had not been in my train,) shewed that surprise at her beauty and manner which is unavoidable at the first sight, and said to me in Italian, "This is no Turkish lady, she is certainly some Christian." Fatima guessed she spoke of her, and asked what she said. I would not have told, thinking she would have been no better pleased with the compliment than one of our court beauties to be told she had the air of a Turk; but the Greek lady told it her; and she smiled, saying, "It is not the first time I have heard so: my mother was a Poloneze, taken at the siege of Caminiec;[14] and my father used to rally me, saying, He believed his Christian wife had found some Christian gallant; for I had not the air of a Turkish girl." I assured her, that, if all the Turkish ladies were like her, it was absolutely necessary to confine them from public view, for the repose of mankind; and proceeded to tell her what a noise such a face as hers would make in London or Paris. "I can't believe you," replied she agreeably; "if beauty was so much valued in your country as you say, they would never have suffered you to leave it." Perhaps, dear sister, you laugh at my vanity in repeating this compliment; but I only do it as I think it very well turned, and give it you as an instance of the spirit of her conversation.

Her house was magnificently furnished, and very well fancied; her winter rooms being furnished with figured velvet on gold grounds, and those for summer with fine Indian quilting embroidered with gold. The houses of the great Turkish ladies are kept clean with as much nicety as those in Holland. This was situated in a high part of the town; and from the windows of her summer apartment we had the prospect of the sea, the islands, and the Asian mountains. . . .

THOMAS JEFFERSON
[1743–1826]

As much as any American politician of his time, Thomas Jefferson embodied the spirit of the Enlightenment: he believed that a people who had access to free education and had the support of democratic institutions could best govern themselves.

Jefferson himself had tremendous breadth as a human being: he was a scientist, an architect, a philosopher, a statesman, a farmer, and a politician. Born into the Virginia aristocracy, Jefferson grew up quickly; his father died when young Thomas was fourteen,

---

[14]Camieniec, a chief town in the Russian district of Podolio, a part of the Ottoman Empire since 1672, had long been a site of fighting between Poles and Turks; Turkey lost Camieniec to Russia in 1795.

leaving him 2,700 acres and a large number of slaves. After an education at the College of William and Mary, he practiced law and began his political career at the age of twenty-six, when he was elected to the Virginia House of Burgesses. His marriage brought him more land, and inevitably he was thrust into colonial issues and an anti-British faction. Before his political career was finished, he served as a minister to France, the U.S. secretary of state, vice president, and president of the United States. He was in his early thirties, however, when he became recognized throughout the colonies for his intellectual and literary brilliance.

In the spring of 1776, as the war with England began to warm up, and as Thomas Paine's pamphlet *Common Sense* preached the politics of independence, the Continental Congress appointed a committee of five to draft a formal declaration of independence. Thomas Jefferson was largely responsible for the first version of this declaration.

It is important to emphasize that this document is not simply a "declaration of independence," but a succinct philosophical statement justifying the principles by which such an act of separation might take place. The document has a neat three-part structure: a statement of the rational basis for having and supporting government, a detailed description of the abuses of the current English government, and a logical, inevitable conclusion that independence is right and necessary. Jefferson's acquaintance with "natural rights" philosophers such as Locke and Rousseau put him into contention with Alexander Hamilton and the Federalist party, who believed that government exists to restrain humanity's evil, animal side and to protect private property and the rights of a growing merchant class. In Jefferson's view, the philosophical foundations for independence are self-evident truths about human equality and the human rights to life, liberty, and the pursuit of happiness. Obviously, these principles were not self-evident to monarchs and other despots, or to anyone—then or now—who takes a pessimistic or cynical view about human nature. If equality and unalienable rights belong to individuals—especially in a "state of nature"—then governments are created to protect and support these rights. If a government does not adequately conform to this "social contract," then a people have a right and duty to sever relations with it. Similar ideas were later expressed in the French Declaration of the Rights of Man and Citizen (1789), a guiding document for the French Revolution.

The Declaration of Independence is a splendid example of how a philosophical manifesto could be put into practice and serve as a basis for a constitution and a new form of government, a democratic form of government.

The Declaration of Independence

THE UNANIMOUS DECLARATION OF THE
THIRTEEN UNITED STATES OF AMERICA

When in the Course of human events, it becomes necessary for one people to dissolve the political bands which have connected them with another, and to assume among the powers of the earth, the separate and equal station to which the Laws of Nature and of Nature's God entitle them, a decent respect to the opinions of mankind requires that they should declare the causes which impel them to the separation. We hold these truths to be self-evident, that all men are created equal, that they are endowed by their Creator with certain unalienable Rights, that among these are Life, Liberty and the pursuit of Happiness. That to secure these rights, Governments are instituted among Men, deriving their just powers from the consent of the governed, That whenever any Form of Government becomes destructive of these ends, it is the Right of the People to alter or to abolish it, and to institute new Government, laying its foundation on such principles and organizing its powers in such form, as to them shall seem most likely to effect their Safety and Happiness. Prudence, indeed, will dictate that Governments long established should not be changed for light and transient causes; and accordingly all experience hath shewn, that mankind are more disposed to suffer, while evils are sufferable, than to right themselves by abolishing the forms to which they are accustomed. But when a long train of abuses and usurpations, pursuing invariably the same Object evinces a design to reduce them under absolute Despotism, it is their right, it is their duty, to throw off such Government, and to provide new Guards for their future security. Such has been the patient sufferance of these Colonies; and such is now the necessity which constrains them to alter their former Systems of Government. The history of the present King of Great Britain is a history of repeated injuries and usurpations, all having in direct object the establishment of an absolute Tyranny over these States. To prove this, let Facts be submitted to a candid world. He has refused his Assent to Laws, the most wholesome and necessary for the public good. He has forbidden his Governors to pass Laws of immediate and pressing importance, unless suspended in their operation till his Assent should be obtained; and when so suspended, he has utterly neglected to attend to them. He has refused to pass other Laws for the accommodation of large districts of people, unless those people would relinquish the right of Representation in the Legislature, a right inestimable to them and formidable to tyrants only. He has called together legislative bodies at places unusual, uncomfortable, and distant from the depository of their public Records, for the sole purpose of fatiguing them into compliance with his measures. He has dissolved Representative Houses repeatedly, for opposing with manly firmness his invasions on the rights of the people. He has refused for a long time, after such dissolutions, to cause others to be elected; whereby the Legislative powers, incapable of Annihilation, have returned to the People at large for their exercise; the State remaining in the mean time exposed to all the dangers of invasion from without, and convulsions within. He has endeavoured to prevent the population of these States; for that purpose obstructing the Laws for Naturalization of Foreigners; refusing to pass others to encourage their migrations hither, and raising the conditions of new Appropriations of Lands. He has obstructed the Administration of Justice, by refusing his Assent to Laws for establishing Judiciary powers. He has made Judges dependent on his Will alone, for the tenure of their offices, and the amount and payment of their salaries. He has erected a multitude of New Offices, and sent hither swarms of Officers to harrass our people, and eat out their substance. He has kept among us, in times of peace, standing Armies without the Consent of our legislatures. He has affected to render the Military independent of and superior to the Civil power. He has combined with others to subject us to a jurisdiction foreign to our constitution, and unacknowledged by our laws; giving his Assent to their Acts of pretended Legislation: For Quartering large bodies of armed troops among us: For protecting them, by a mock Trial, from punishment for any Murders which they should commit on the Inhabitants of these States: For cutting off our Trade with all parts of the world: For imposing Taxes on us without our Consent: For depriving us in many cases of the benefits of Trial by Jury: For transporting us beyond Seas to be tried for pretended offences: For abolishing the free System of English Laws in a neighbouring Province, establishing therein an Arbitrary government, and enlarging its Boundaries so as to render it at once an example and fit instrument for introducing the same absolute rule into these Colonies: For taking away our Charters, abolishing our most valuable Laws, and altering fundamentally the Forms of our Governments: For suspending our own Legislatures, and declaring themselves invested with power to legislate for us in all cases whatsoever. He has abdicated Government here, by declaring us out of his Protection and waging War against us. He has plundered our seas, ravaged our Coasts, burnt our towns, and destroyed the Lives of our people. He is at this time transporting large Armies of foreign Mercenaries to compleat the works of death, desolation and tyranny, already begun with circumstances of Cruelty & perfidy scarcely paralleled in the most barbarous ages, and totally unworthy the Head of a civilized nation. He has constrained our fellow Citizens taken Captive on the high Seas to bear Arms against their Country, to become the executioners of their friends and Brethren, or to fall themselves by their Hands. He has excited domestic insurrections amongst us, and has endeavoured to bring on the inhabitants of our frontiers, the merciless Indian Savages, whose known rule of warfare, is an undistinguished destruction of all ages, sexes and conditions. In every stage of these Oppressions We have Petitioned for Redress in the most humble terms: Our repeated Petitions have been answered only by repeated injury. A Prince, whose character is thus marked by every act which may define a Tyrant, is unfit to be the ruler of a free people. Nor have We been wanting in attentions to our British brethren. We have warned them from time to time of attempts by their legislature to extend an unwarrantable jurisdiction over us. We have reminded them of the circumstances of our emigration and settlement here. We have appealed to their native justice and magnanimity, and we have conjured them by the ties of our common kindred to disavow these usurpations, which, would inevitably interrupt our connections and correspondence. They too have been deaf to the voice of justice and of consanguinity. We must, therefore, acquiesce in the necessity, which denounces our Separation, and hold them, as we hold the rest of mankind, Enemies in War, in Peace Friends.

We, therefore, the Representatives of the united States of America, in General Congress, Assembled, appealing to the Supreme Judge of the world for the rectitude of our intentions, do, in the Name, and by Authority of the good People of these Colonies, solemnly publish and declare, That these United Colonies are, and of Right ought to be Free and Independent States; that they are Absolved from all Allegiance to the British Crown, and that all political connection between them and the State of Great Britain, is and ought to be totally dissolved; and that as Free and Independent States, they have full Power to levy War, conclude Peace, contract Alliances, establish Commerce, and to do all other Acts and Things which Independent States may of right do. And for the support of this Declaration, with a firm reliance on the protection of divine Providence, we mutually pledge to each other our Lives, our Fortunes and our sacred Honor.

MARY WOLLSTONECRAFT
[1759–1797]

In the early 1790s, Thomas Paine's *Rights of Man* reached enormous popularity among the working people in England. In that book Paine attacked the aristocracy for abusing the false privileges of hereditary wealth, arguing that all men have the right to elect their governors and to take part in shaping the laws to which they are subject. While Paine advocated the rights of men, Mary Wollstonecraft argued for the rights of both men and women, the latter of whom Paine had largely overlooked. In her first important political treatise, *A Vindication of the Rights of Men* (1790), Wollstonecraft defended her friend Richard Price against Edmund Burke's famous *Reflections on the Revolution in France* (1790), which attacked Price's principles of egalitarianism and support for the beginning revolution in France. Two years later, in *A Vindication of the Rights of Woman* (1792), she anatomized the condition of women in England and called for an end to the abuses in domestic, social, and political life that women had to endure. In the celebrated Age of Reason, with its emphasis upon liberty and independence, she argued, women had been left out of the picture. In the Enlightenment spirit that informs its arguments, *A Vindication* embraces wide-reaching injustices in society. Wollstonecraft criticizes the moral turpitude and idleness of the aristocracy; exposes the institution of hereditary property as an instrument that perpetuates unmerited social and economic distinctions; and advocates that friendship based on reason, understanding, and affection replace mere passion that dies on the wing as the basis for relationships between men and women.

Although the way toward defending women's rights had been partially prepared in England by Mary Astell's *Some Reflections upon Marriage* (1700) and Catherine Macaulay's *Letters on Education* (1790), which argued that if women received an education equal to that of men they would equal men in intellectual achievement, Wollstonecraft's *A Vindication of the Rights of Woman* pointed more directly to the blatant injustice of the present "false system of education" that left women with few job opportunities and that reduced their powers of reason to mere cunning. Wollstonecraft argues that women's education prepares them only for superficial conversation, shallow thinking, and ornamental accomplishments, designed to enable them only to become "alluring objects for the moment," to amuse and titillate men. Thus, women not only become subordinate to and dependent upon men for their economic and social standing, but they cannot become capable and contributing citizens because such education stifles their natural powers of reason. Robbed of their ability to exercise independent judgment, women under the present system become victims of custom, unable to exercise their virtue and thus unable to prepare their souls for that glorious world beyond death "where there is neither marriage, nor giving in marriage." As Wollstonecraft writes, "I shall only insist that men have increased that inferiority [of women] till women are almost sunk below the standard of rational creatures," and she calls upon women to "let the practice of every duty be subordinate to the grand one of improving our minds, and preparing our affections for a more exalted state."

A Vindication of the Rights of Woman elicited a strong reaction from many conservative writers, who responded with virulent attacks upon her character as much as upon her free thinking. After her untimely death in September 1797, her husband William Godwin added fuel to this fire by publishing, rather naïvely, a completely candid biography of her life, *Memoirs of the Author of "A Vindication of the Rights of Woman."* Despite the attacks of many contemporaries, Wollstonecraft found sympathetic readers among the budding feminist writers of her age, including the English writers Mary Hays and Mary Ann Evans (George Eliot), and the American feminists Lucretia Mott and Elizabeth Cady Stanton, who organized the first women's rights convention in Seneca Falls, New York, in 1848; moreover, *A Vindication* was available in American, French, and German editions throughout the nineteenth century. The fortune of her work has taken a positive turn in our century, and her work finally receives the respect it deserves. Emma Goldman eloquently sums up Wollstonecraft's life and work in a brief tribute to her: "The treasure of her soul, the wisdom of her life's philosophy, the depth of her World of thought, the intensity of her battle for human emancipation and especially her indomitable struggle for the liberation of her own sex, are even today so far ahead of the average grasp that we may indeed claim for her the rare exception which nature has created once in a century."

A Vindication of the Rights of Woman

INTRODUCTION TO THE FIRST EDITION

After considering the historic page, and viewing the living world with anxious solicitude, the most melancholy emotions of sorrowful indignation have depressed my spirits, and I have sighed when obliged to confess, that either nature has made a great difference between man and man, or that the civilization which has hitherto taken place in the world has been very partial. I have turned over various books written on the subject of education, and patiently observed the conduct of parents and the management of schools; but what has been the result?—a profound conviction that the neglected education of my fellow-creatures is the grand source of the misery I deplore; and that women, in particular, are rendered weak and wretched by a variety of concurring causes, originating from one hasty conclusion. The conduct and manners of women, in fact, evidently prove that their minds are not in a healthy state; for, like the flowers which are planted in too rich a soil, strength and usefulness are sacrificed to beauty; and the flaunting leaves, after having pleased a fastidious eye, fade, disregarded on the stalk, long before the season when they ought to have arrived at maturity. One cause of this barren blooming I attribute to a false system of education, gathered from the books written on this subject by men who, considering females rather as women than human creatures, have been more anxious to make them alluring mistresses than affectionate wives and rational mothers; and the understanding of the sex has been so bubbled by this specious homage, that the civilized women of the present century, with a few exceptions, are only anxious to inspire love, when they ought to cherish a nobler ambition, and by their abilities and virtues exact respect.

In a treatise, therefore, on female rights and manners, the works which have been particularly written for their improvement must not be overlooked; especially when it is asserted, in direct terms, that the minds of women are enfeebled by false refinement; that the books of instruction, written by men of genius, have had the same tendency as more frivolous productions; and that, in the true style of Mahometanism, they are treated as a kind of subordinate beings, and not as a part of the human species, when improveable reason is allowed to be the dignified distinction which raises men above the brute creation, and puts a natural sceptre in a feeble hand.

Yet, because I am a woman, I would not lead my readers to suppose that I mean violently to agitate the contested question respecting the quality or inferiority of the sex; but as the subject lies in my way, and I cannot pass it over without subjecting the main tendency of my reasoning to misconstruction, I shall stop a moment to deliver, in a few words, my opinion. In the government of the physical world it is observable that the female in point of strength is, in general, inferior to the male. This is the law of nature; and it does not appear to be suspended or abrogated in favour of woman. A degree of physical superiority cannot, therefore, be denied—and it is a noble prerogative! But not content with this natural pre-eminence, men endeavour to sink us still lower, merely to render us alluring objects for a moment; and women, intoxicated by the adoration which men, under the influence of their senses, pay them, do not seek to obtain a durable interest in their hearts, or to become the friends of the fellow creatures who find amusement in their society.

I am aware of an obvious inference:—from every quarter have I heard exclamations against masculine women; but where are they to be found? If by this appellation men mean to inveigh against their ardour in hunting, shooting, and gaming, I shall most cordially join in the cry; but if it be against the imitation of manly virtues, or, more properly speaking, the attainment of those talents and virtues, the exercise of which ennobles the human character, and which raise females in the scale of animal being, when they are comprehensively termed mankind;—all those who view them with a philosophic eye must, I should think, wish with me, that they may every day grow more and more masculine.

This discussion naturally divides the subject. I shall first consider women in the grand light of human creatures, who, in common with men, are placed on this earth to unfold their faculties; and afterwards I shall more particularly point out their peculiar designation.

I wish also to steer clear of an error which many respectable writers have fallen into; for the instruction which has hitherto been addressed to women, has rather been applicable to *ladies,* if the little indirect advice, that is scattered through Sandford and Merton,[1] be excepted; but, addressing my sex in a firmer tone, I pay particular attention to those in the middle class, because they appear to be in the most natural state. Perhaps the seeds of false-refinement, immorality, and vanity, have ever been shed by the great. Weak, artificial beings, raised above the common wants and affections of their race, in a premature unnatural manner, undermine the very foundation of virtue, and spread corruption through the whole mass of society! As a class of mankind they have the strongest claim to pity; the education of the rich tends to render them vain and helpless, and the unfolding mind is not strengthened by the practice of those duties which dignify the human character. They only live to amuse themselves, and by the same law which in nature invariably produces certain effects, they soon only afford barren amusement.

But as I purpose taking a separate view of the different ranks of society, and of the moral character of women, in each, this hint is, for the present, sufficient; and I have only alluded to the subject, because it appears to me to be the very essence of an introduction to give a cursory account of the contents of the work it introduces.

My own sex, I hope, will excuse me, if I treat them like rational creatures, instead of flattering their *fascinating* graces, and viewing them as if they were in a state of perpetual childhood, unable to stand alone. I earnestly wish to point out in what true dignity and human happiness consists—I wish to persuade women to endeavour to acquire strength, both of mind and body, and to convince them that the soft phrases, susceptibility of heart, delicacy of sentiment, and refinement of taste, are almost synonymous with epithets of weakness, and that those beings who are only the objects of pity and that kind of love, which has been termed its sister, will soon become objects of contempt.

Dismissing, then, those pretty feminine phrases, which the men condescendingly use to soften our slavish dependence, and despising that weak elegancy of mind, exquisite sensibility, and sweet docility of manners, supposed to be the sexual characteristics of the weaker vessel, I wish to shew that elegance is inferior to virtue, that the first object of laudable ambition is to obtain a character as a human being, regardless of the distinction of sex; and that secondary views should be brought to this simple touchstone.

This is a rough sketch of my plan; and should I express my conviction with the energetic emotions that I feel whenever I think of the subject, the dictates of experience and reflection will be felt by some of my readers. Animated by this important object, I shall disdain to cull my phrases or polish my style;—I aim at being useful, and sincerity will render me unaffected; for, wishing rather to persuade

---

[1] *The History of Sandford and Merton* (1783–1789), a popular children's book by Thomas Day.

by the force of my arguments, than dazzle by the elegance of my language, I shall not waste my time in rounding periods, or in fabricating the turgid bombast of artificial feelings, which, coming from the head, never reach the heart. I shall be employed about things, not words! and, anxious to render my sex more respectable members of society, I shall try to avoid that flowery diction which has slided from essays into novels, and from novels into familiar letters and conversation.

These pretty superlatives, dropping glibly from the tongue, vitiate the taste, and create a kind of sickly delicacy that turns away from simple unadorned truth; and a deluge of false sentiments and overstretched feelings, stifling the natural emotions of the heart, render the domestic pleasures insipid, that ought to sweeten the exercise of those severe duties, which educate a rational and immortal being for a nobler field of action.

The education of women has, of late, been more attended to than formerly; yet they are still reckoned a frivolous sex, and ridiculed or pitied by the writers who endeavour by satire or instruction to improve them. It is acknowledged that they spend many of the first years of their lives in acquiring a smattering of accomplishments; meanwhile strength of body and mind are sacrificed to libertine notions of beauty, to the desire of establishing themselves,—the only way women can rise in the world,—by marriage. And this desire making mere animals of them, when they marry they act as such children may be expected to act:—they dress; they paint, and nickname God's creatures. Surely these weak beings are only fit for a seraglio!—Can they be expected to govern a family with judgment, or take care of the poor babes whom they bring into the world?

If then it can be fairly deduced from the present conduct of the sex, from the prevalent fondness for pleasure which takes place of ambition and those nobler passions that open and enlarge the soul; that the instruction which women have hitherto received has only tended, with the constitution of civil society, to render them insignificant objects of desire—mere propagators of fools!—if it can be proved that in aiming to accomplish them, without cultivating their understandings, they are taken out of their sphere of duties, and made ridiculous and useless when the short-lived bloom of beauty is over,[2] I presume that *rational* men will excuse me for endeavouring to persuade them to become more masculine and respectable.

Indeed the word masculine is only a bugbear: there is little reason to fear that women will acquire too much courage or fortitude; for their apparent inferiority with respect to bodily strength, must render them, in some degree, dependent on men in the various relations of life; but why should it be increased by prejudices that give a sex to virtue, and confound simple truths with sensual reveries?

Women are, in fact, so much degraded by mistaken notions of female excellence, that I do not mean to add a paradox when I assert, that this artificial weakness produces a propensity to tyrannize, and gives birth to cunning, the natural opponent of strength, which leads them to play off those contemptible infantine airs that undermine esteem even whilst they excite desire. Let men become more chaste and modest, and if women do not grow wiser in the same ratio, it will be clear that they have weaker understandings. It seems scarcely necessary to say, that I now speak of the sex in general. Many individuals have more sense than their male relatives; and, as nothing preponderates where there is a constant struggle for an equilibrium, without it has naturally more gravity, some women govern their husbands without degrading themselves, because intellect will always govern.

---

[2]A lively writer, I cannot recollect his name, asks what business women turned of forty have to do in the world? [Wollstonecraft's note]

THE NINETEENTH CENTURY

❦

The Romantic Self
and Social Reality

TIME LINE FOR THE NINETEENTH CENTURY

Date	History and Politics
1770–1790	1789 French Revolution.
1790–1800	1791 U.S. Bill of Rights ratified.
	1793 Reign of Terror begins; Louis XVI beheaded.
	1794 Slavery abolished in French colonies.
	1796 Edict of Peking forbids the importation of opium into China.
1800–1810	1802 Slave rebellion in French Santo Domingo led by Toussaint L'Ouverture.
	1808 U.S. prohibits importation of slaves from Africa.
	1809 Ecuador gains independence from Spain.
1810–1820	1810 Height of Napoleon's power.
	1811 Luddites destroy factory machines in northern England.
	1813 Simón Bolívar becomes dictator in Venezuela.
	1814 Lord Hastings, Governor of India, declares war on Gurkhas in Nepal.
	1815 Battle of Waterloo.
	1819 Peterloo Massacre in Manchester.
1820–1830	1822 Brazil becomes independent of Portugal.
	1823 Mexico becomes a republic; Monroe Doctrine.
	1829 Slavery abolished in Mexico.
1830–1840	1830 Revolution in Paris; Louis Phillipe becomes King of France.
	1832 Britain: First Reform Bill.
	1833 Abolition of slavery in British colonies.
	1836 The Alamo.
	1837 Victoria becomes Queen of Great Britain.
	1839 Outbreak of first Opium War between Britain and China; Independent Republic of Natal founded by Boers.

Science, Culture, and Technology

Literature

1774 Goethe, *The Sorrows of Young Werther.*

1791 Paine, *Rights of Man.*

1792 Wollstonecraft, *A Vindication of the Rights of Woman.*

1793 David, *The Murder of Marat.*

1793 Blake, *The Marriage of Heaven and Hell.*

1795 Haydn completes the twelve London Symphonies.

1794 Blake, *Songs of Innocence and Experience.*

1798 Malthus, *Essay on the Principle of Population.*

1798 Wordsworth and Coleridge, *Lyrical Ballads.*

1799 Rosetta Stone found near Rosetta, Egypt.

1800 Schlegel, "Talk on Mythology."

1807 Fulton's *Clermont* navigates in the Hudson River.

1808 Beethoven, *Symphony No. 5.*

1808 Goethe, *Faust*, Part I.

1809 Lamarck, *Principles of Zoology.*

1810 Goya, *The Disasters of War.*

1811 Stephenson, first locomotive.

1812 The Brothers Grimm, *Fairy Tales.*

1813 Austen, *Pride and Prejudice.*

1814 Scott, *Waverley.*

1816 Rossini, *The Barber of Seville.*

1818 Mary Shelley, *Frankenstein*; de Staël, *French Revolution.*

1819 Géricault, *The Raft of the Medusa.*

1819 Keats, *Odes*; Hoffmann, "The Mines of Falun."

1820 Ampère discovers electrical current.

1824 Erie Canal finished.

1830 Delacroix, *Liberty Guiding the People.*

1830 Balzac begins *The Human Comedy*; Stendhal, *The Red and the Black.*

1832 Hiroshige, *Fifty-Three Stages of the Tokaido.*

1832 Goethe, *Faust*, Part II.

1833 Lyell, *Principles of Geology.*

1834 Babbage invents principle of the computer.

1837 Pushkin, *The Bronze Horseman.*

1839 Goodyear vulcanizes rubber; Daguerre develops the daguerreotype photographic process.

1839 Poe, "The Fall of the House of Usher."

(Continued on next page)

TIME LINE FOR THE NINETEENTH CENTURY (Continued)

Date	*History and Politics*
1840–1850	1841 Britain proclaims sovereignty over Hong Kong.
	1842 Orange Free State established by Boers.
	1844 Daniel O'Connell found guilty of conspiracy against British rule in Ireland.
	1846 First Sikh War ends; Treaty of Lahore; Polish revolt.
	1848 Revolt in Paris; Louis Napoleon elected President; revolution in Vienna; Metternich resigns; revolutions in Venice, Berlin, Milan, Parma, Rome; Czech revolt in Prague; Treaty of Guadalupe Hildago ends Mexican–U.S. War.
	1849 Mazzini proclaims Rome a republic; revolts in Dresden and Baden; British defeat Sikhs at Chillianwalla; Britain annexes the Punjab.
1850–1860	1850 Outbreak of Anglo–Kaffir War; Taiping Rebellion in China.
	1852 South African Republic (Transvaal) established.
	1854 Commodore Perry negotiates first Japanese– American treaty; Republican Party formed in U.S.
	1855 Crimean War.
	1856 Britain annexes Oudh, India, and Natal.
	1857 Peace of Paris ends Anglo–Persian War; Indian mutiny against British rule; Irish Republican Brotherhood (Fenians) founded; Czar Alexander II begins emancipation of Russian serfs.
	1858 Treaty of Tientsin ends Anglo–Chinese War; British proclaim peace in India.
	1859 Franco–Austrian War.
1860–1870	1860 Garibaldi proclaims Victor Emmanuel II King of Italy; Abraham Lincoln elected president.
	1861 Beginning of U.S. Civil War.
	1862 Bismarck becomes Prussian Prime Minister.
	1863 Emancipation Proclamation; French capture Mexico City; Maximilian of Austria named emperor of Mexico.
	1865 End of Civil War; Lincoln assassinated; abolition of slavery in the U.S.
	1866 Austro–Italian War.

Science, Culture, and Technology

Literature

1840 Tocqueville, *Democracy in America*.

1843 Prescott, *History of the Conquest of Mexico*.

1844 Turner, *Rain, Steam, and Speed*.

1846 Smithsonian Institution founded; Howe invents sewing machine; Berlioz, *Damnation of Faust*.

1847 California Gold Rush.

1847 Charlotte Brontë, *Jane Eyre*; Emily Brontë, *Wuthering Heights*; Thackeray, *Vanity Fair*.

1848 Marx and Engels, *The Communist Manifesto*.

1849 Dickens, *David Copperfield*.

1850 Hawthorne, *The Scarlet Letter*.

1851 Melville, *Moby Dick*.

1852 Stowe, *Uncle Tom's Cabin*.

1855 Whitman, "Song of Myself."

1857 Liszt, *Eine Faust Symphonie*.

1857 Baudelaire, *Les Fleurs du Mal*.

1859 Gounod, *Faust*; first oil well drilled at Titusville, Pa.

1859 Darwin, *Origin of Species*.

1861 Pasteurization introduced following Pasteur's work on microorganisms.

1861 Jacobs, *Incidents in the Life of a Slave Girl*.

1862 Turgenev, *Fathers and Sons*.

1863 Manet, *Olympia*.

1864 Thoreau, *The Maine Woods*.

1865 Mendel discovers laws of genetic inheritance; Schubert, *Unfinished Symphony*.

1867 Nobel manufactures dynamite.

(Continued on next page)

TIME LINE FOR THE NINETEENTH CENTURY (Continued)

Date	*History and Politics*
	1868 Russia sells Alaska to U.S.; revolution in Spain; Shogun Kekei of Japan abdicates; Meiji Dynasty restored.
	1869 Opening of Suez Canal.
1870–1880	1870 Franco–Prussian War; revolt in Paris; Third Republic established in France.
	1871 Paris Commune.
	1873 Republic proclaimed in Spain; famine in Bengal.
	1874 End of Ashanti War.
	1877 Queen Victoria proclaimed empress of India; Satsuma revolt in Japan suppressed.
	1879 British–Zulu War.
1880–1890	1880 Boer Republic under Kruger.
	1881 Political parties founded in Japan.
	1885 Congo becomes personal possession of Leopold II of Belgium.
	1886 First Indian National Congress.
1890–1900	1890 First general election in Japan.
	1891 Famine in Russia.
	1895 End of China–Japan War; Rhodesia founded.
	1899 Boer War; Dreyfus pardoned.
1900–1910	1901 Death of Queen Victoria; Boxer Rebellion in China.
	1902 Anglo–Japanese Treaty recognizes independence of Korea and China; end of Boer War.
	1903 British complete conquest of Nigeria.

Science, Culture, and Technology   *Literature*

1868 Brahms, *German Requiem.*

1869 Rimbaud, *Poems.*

1871 Stanley meets Livingstone.   1871 Eliot, *Middlemarch.*

1872 Whistler, *The Artist's Mother.*
1873 Japan adopts European calendar.

1874 First impressionist exhibition, Paris.   1876 Mallarmé, "L'Après-midi d'un faune."
1875 Bizet, *Carmen*; Schliemann, *Troy and*   1877 Flaubert, "A Simple Heart."
          Its Remains.
1876 Bell invents telephone.   1878 Hardy, *The Return of the Native.*

1879 Edison develops incandescent lamp.   1879 Ibsen, *A Doll's House.*
1880 Rodin, *The Thinker.*   1880 Dostoevsky, *The Brothers*
          Karamazov.
1885 Benz develops prototype of auto-   1883 Nietzsche, *Thus Spake Zarathustra*;
          mobile; van Gogh, *The Potato Eaters.*   Hopkins, *Life among the Piutes.*
1886 Statue of Liberty dedicated.   1884 Twain, *Huckleberry Finn.*

1888 Eastman develops hand camera;   1885 Zola, *Germinal.*
          Jack the Ripper.
1889 Eiffel Tower.   1886 Tolstoy, *The Death of Ivan Ilyitch.*
1890 Frazer, *The Golden Bough*; W. James,   1890 Ōgai, "The Dancing Girl."
          The Principles of Psychology.
1892 Diesel patents heavy oil engine;   1891 Doyle, *The Adventures of Sherlock*
          Monet paints Rouen Cathedral.   *Holmes.*
1893 Dvořák, *New World Symphony.*   1892 Gilman, *The Yellow Wallpaper.*
1894 Debussy, *L'Après-midi d'un faune.*   1894 Chopin, "The Story of an Hour."
1895 Röntgen discovers X rays; first   1895 Tagore, "The Hungry Stones"; Freud
          motion picture.   and Breuer, *Studies in Hysteria.*
1896 Nobel endows Nobel Prizes.
1900 Planck develops quantum theory;
          Freud, *Interpretation of Dreams.*
1902 Gauguin, *Riders to the Sea.*   1902 Conrad, *Heart of Darkness*; Gorky,
          Lower Depths.
1903 Wright Brothers' first flight.   1903 Shaw, *Man and Superman.*

(Continued on next page)

TIME LINE FOR THE NINETEENTH CENTURY (Continued)

Date	History and Politics
	1905 Sinn Fein Party founded in Dublin; Sun Yat-sen organizes a union to expel Manchus from China.
	1908 Union of South Africa established.
1910–1920	1910 Japan annexes Korea; revolution in Portugal; China abolishes slavery.
	1911 Mexican civil war.
	1912 Sun Yat-sen founds Kuomintang (Chinese National Party).
	1913 Balkan War.
	1914 World War I.

INTRODUCTION

IN THE LAST QUARTER of the eighteenth century, the American and French revolutions brought changes in political and social life that influenced all corners of the world. During the century that followed, the political map of nearly every continent was redrawn, the processes of manufacture and economic relationships were transformed, and the assumptions and ideals of the scientific revolution and the Enlightenment were profoundly revised.

The romantic movement in literature and the arts expressed a revolutionary change in consciousness, one that turned away from the rational public discourse of the Enlightenment to adopt the private voice of poetic subjectivism. Romantic scholar Morse Peckham has described romanticism as the most radical shift in the Western mind since the movement into cities in Greece in the fifth century B.C.E. Unlike their eighteenth-century predecessors, who often envisioned society as a systematic and harmonious order, an artificial contract between rational individuals seeking their enlightened self-interest, the romantics saw society as organic and dynamic, an expression of elemental oppositions and primal forces that surfaced in the revolutions. From the romantic perspective, the individual was also defined by conflict; alienated from society and at war within, the romantic protagonist often revealed this inner conflict by impulsive and self-destructive behavior.

The beginning of the romantic period can be dated from the publication of Goethe's *The Sorrows of Young Werther*, published in 1774, or from the time of the American and French revolutions. In many ways the age was one of oppositions and contradictions. The romantics celebrated spiritual enlightenment as the life around them became in-

Science, Culture, and Technology	Literature
1904 Weber, *The Protestant Ethic and the Spirit of Capitalism*; Puccini, *Madame Butterfly*.	1904 Chekhov, *The Cherry Orchard*.
1905 Einstein, special theory of relativity; Les Fauves artist group founded.	
1909 Peary reaches North Pole.	
1910 Stravinsky, *The Firebird*; Evans completes excavation of Cnossus, Crete.	
1911 Mahler, *Das Lied von der Erde*; Matisse, *Red Studio*.	
1912 *Titanic* disaster.	
1913 Russell and Whitehead, *Principia Mathematica*; Bohr develops theory of atomic structure; Armory Show introduces cubism and post-impressionism in U.S.	
1914 Ford pioneers the assembly line.	

creasingly secular and materialistic. They idealized dynamic individualism and the spirit of humanity as industrialism turned the great masses of working people into time-serving machines. The impetus for social change spurred continuing revolutionary movements throughout the century, while growing governmental bureaucracies made change difficult and unlikely. The individual and social realities spurred the romantics to idealistic visions of a better world, but they also prompted realistic disillusionment. Romantic idealism seems inevitably to have been accompanied by a constraining realism: despair undermined energy, determinism limited the impulse for freedom, the past restricted the possibilities of the present. This countering realism grew stronger as the century progressed. The period is usually broken into two parts, divided around the middle of the century into the romantic and realistic periods. However, the tension between romantic idealism and constraining realism is characteristic of the period from the beginning.

Whether expressing an idealistic vision or describing the complexities of the real world, the artists of the nineteenth century worked on a grand scale. The symphonies of Beethoven and Brahms, the operas of Verdi and Wagner, and the novels of Dickens and Tolstoy are all monuments of artistic ambition. Goethe's romantic reconstruction of the Faust legend into a cosmic drama and Emily Brontë's unique tale of generational struggle on the Yorkshire moors typify the romantic consciousness as it awakened from the rationalism that William Blake called "Newton's sleep." The romantics sought to free themselves from the mechanistic materialism of the scientific world view, to explore the deeper dimensions of the self, and to establish a human community based on organic rather than mechanistic principles. Their explorations into subjectivity made them aware of the gap between the romantic vision and the realities of their time.

The Romantic and Realistic Periods

Symbolically at least, the nineteenth century began on July 14, 1789, the decisive day when the French revolutionaries took over the Bastille. In the Declaration of Independence, Jefferson had summed up the political ideals of the Enlightenment; the French Jacobins turned them into the revolutionary slogan "*liberté, fraternité, égalité*" and took to the streets. Even though they espoused the democratic, antimonarchical ideals of the Enlightenment, the Jacobins broke with their predecessors' commitment to reasoned and evolutionary change. The superstition and oppression of the past, they believed, could be overthrown only by arms, not by argument. Their violent successes became examples emulated around the world by those who similarly wanted to throw off feudal oppression, monarchy, or colonial exploitation.

In the century that followed the storming of the Bastille, revolutionary movements arose throughout Europe. The year 1848 became the "year of revolution," when virtually simultaneous armed insurrections began in Paris and spread to nearly every European country. Appropriately, it was also the year in which Marx and Engels published *The Communist Manifesto*, which described history as an ongoing series of class struggles. Revolutionary gains were often countered by reactionary movements, but the struggle continued throughout the century. In some cases, in Britain for example, democratic gains were achieved with relatively little bloodshed. But in other places, the struggle to overthrow the old regimes of aristocrats and kings left the streets flowing with blood. We remember the French Revolution most vividly in the images of the guillotine and the Reign of Terror.

Many of the revolutionary movements were more nationalistic than democratic. In Germany and Italy, nationalism weakened loyalties to local princes and prompted movements to unify smaller states into larger nations. Throughout Europe, loyalty to national identities aroused more passionate allegiance than the Enlightenment's ideal of rational universalism.

No figure better represents the contradictory impulses of the century than Napoleon. Son of a Corsican attorney, Napoleon was a commoner who rose to power as a military strategist in the aftermath of the French Revolution. He began as an officer in the revolutionary army of the people, but he became the emperor of most of Europe, a dictator who replaced the ruling monarchs with members of his own family. If he embodied on the one hand the ideals of the Revolution, on the other he represented their betrayal. As the charismatic "unifier" of Europe, he abolished the power of hereditary princes only to become the tyrant that Nietzsche would later describe as "the synthesis of brute and Superman."

The revolutionary and Napoleonic models for social change were imitated around the world, especially in Latin America. On the island of Haiti, Toussaint L'Ouverture led an unsuccessful slave revolt in 1791, and in 1810 Miguel Hidalgo launched the movement that would eventually free Mexico from Spanish rule. In the first two decades of the nineteenth century, Simón Bolívar fought to liberate much of South America from Spain and to establish democratic governments. Although he was successful in ousting Spain, Bolívar's Napoleonic dream of uniting the Latin American nations was frustrated by ambitious tyrants who fought among themselves. Like their French model, the Latin American revolutions began with liberal democratic ideals but ended in dictatorships.

After Napoleon's defeat, the victorious European powers were more concerned with seeking their own economic advantage in other parts of the world than with promoting democracy. Gradually, they set themselves up as the colonial owners or managers of much of the rest of the globe. The competition to establish colonial spheres of influence in Africa, Asia, and other less-developed regions was known as "the Great Game"; by 1900 the European nations controlled over four-fifths of the land surface of the globe. The maps of

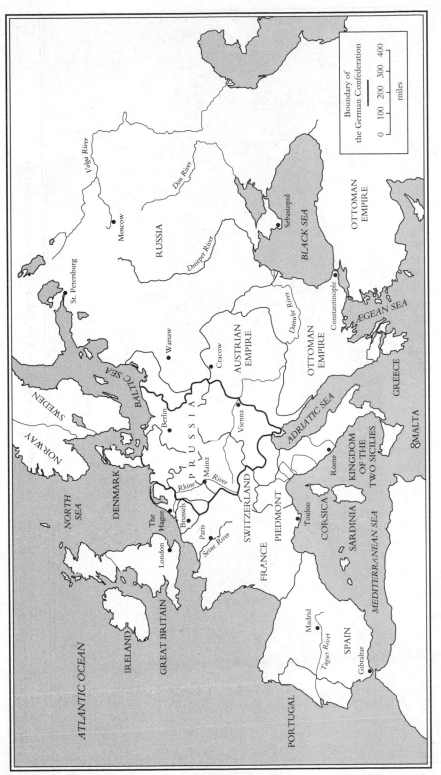

EUROPE IN 1848

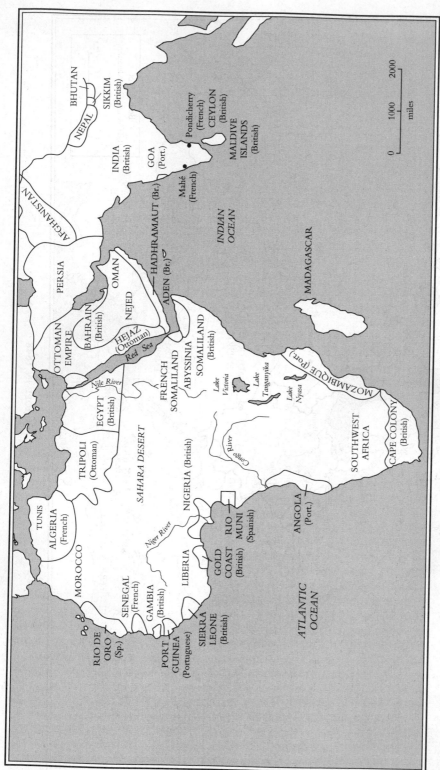

EUROPEAN COLONIES IN AFRICA AND WESTERN ASIA, MID-NINETEENTH CENTURY

Asia and Africa were colored to identify their absentee owners. Britain, most successful of the gamesters, circled the globe in British red with an empire on which the sun never set.

While the political maps of Europe and the world were being redrawn, the Industrial Revolution was transforming the processes of manufacture, the demography of Europe, and the social lives of millions. The Industrial Revolution encompasses a series of inventions beginning in the mid-eighteenth century that transformed manufacturing, transportation, and agriculture. The new machines enabled the creation of factories and, with the use of steam power to run the machines, the factories could be clustered into new industrial towns. Although some of the machines were developed in the eighteenth century, the new demographics of the industrial cities were largely a nineteenth-century phenomenon with Britain leading the rest of Europe in industrialization and urbanization. Of the major European nations, only Russia remained relatively untouched.

The Industrial Revolution increased the general level of prosperity, especially for the bourgeoisie, the growing class of capitalists who owned and developed the new factories and their professional colleagues who managed and maintained the new social order. As this urban middle class grew during the century, they sought political power to match their increasing economic importance. With political influence, they broadened the electorate to consolidate their power, removed restrictions in the marketplace, promoted free trade, and increased educational opportunity. As literacy expanded, a new audience and a new literary marketplace were created. In the industrialized nations, the arts, literature among them, were produced by a growing commercial establishment. The old feudal patronage system, where the writer or painter was supported by the benevolence of an aristocratic sponsor, was gone, displaced by a marketplace where novelists or portrait painters or sculptors supported themselves by selling their work. Popular magazines addressed to readers from different social classes also multiplied during the century. More and more, commercial success defined artistic achievement.

The new readers wanted literary works that described their experiences and expressed their values. This new middle-class audience is in large part responsible for making the nineteenth century the great age of the novel. Because a majority of novel readers were women, the marketplace also encouraged female writers such as Jane Austen, George Sand, and the Brontë sisters to write about women's lives. Male novelists also often wrote about female characters in such great works of the period as Tolstoy's *Anna Karenina* and Flaubert's *Madame Bovary*. Many of Henrik Ibsen's social dramas, including plays such as *A Doll's House* that depicted bourgeois life for a bourgeois audience, addressed women's concerns. Although we often associate rigidly patriarchal attitudes with the bourgeois culture of the time, it is important to note that the cultural marketplace of the nineteenth century enabled some women and minorities to question the established order and describe the world from more marginal perspectives.

The Industrial Revolution increased material prosperity and broadened cultural opportunity; it also created massive social problems. Workers were lured from the countryside into the industrial cities to join the growing urban proletariat. The new cities were jerry-built boomtowns with few public services, poor sanitation, and crowded housing. Industrial workers, whose wages were set by the forces of competition, had no protection against unemployment or brutal working conditions. Even the existing welfare system did not provide services for many of them. Realistic novelists such as Charles Dickens, Elizabeth Gaskell, and Émile Zola exposed the social problems created by industrialization. Other writers and artists were so daunted by the materialism of the period that they idealized the preindustrial Middle Ages. In that more organic society, they believed, human beings had not been reduced to cogs in a grim industrial machine.

The Industrial Revolution physically embodied the scientific materialism of the Renaissance and Enlightenment. Based on an analysis of the processes of production into their component parts, the factory system rationalized manufacture by dividing labor among many different workers. This specialization of labor was the central feature in Adam Smith's mid-eighteenth-century treatise on the *Wealth of Nations*. Smith believed that a rational economy would be accompanied by a harmonious society brought into being by the guiding "invisible hand" of the competitive marketplace. His economic theory did not predict the visible horrors of the industrial cities and the hostilities of the class struggle that became increasingly apparent as the nineteenth century progressed.

ROMANTIC AND REALISTIC LITERATURE

Like the revolutionaries who rejected gradual reform and took their cause into the streets, the romantic writers and artists revolted against the ideals of their neoclassical predecessors. They thought empiricism superficial, for it was limited to the visible world and to objective reality, and it could not reveal more important subjective and invisible truths. Art that merely tried to imitate the visible world, the stated aim of the neoclassicists, was for the romantics mechanical and empty. As writers and artists, they rejected the artistic rules that guided their predecessors. Instead of using the carefully balanced couplets and elevated language of Alexander Pope and his followers, the romantic poets wrote in freer lyric forms that emulated the language of common people. Goethe's *Faust*, for example, does not employ a single verse form such as Shakespearean iambic pentameter. It is written in a variety of lyric forms, shifting its tone, meter, and formal structure from one scene to the next, and its language ranges from an elevated discourse in heaven to the slang of the barroom. Many romantic works are characterized by a hybridization of forms. Wordsworth and Coleridge's *Lyrical Ballads*, for example, combines the lyric, a high cultural form, and the ballad, a low cultural form. Blake's *Marriage of Heaven and Hell* mixes lyric, prose, biblical aphorism, and narrative.

The romantics modified the progressive optimism of the Enlightenment. Simply knowing that the Church promoted superstition and that governments served the interests of the few had proved insufficient to end fear and oppression. Neither knowledge—the preoccupation of the eighteenth-century thinkers—nor active revolution had been able to change the world. The material gains brought about by science, industry, and material progress paled in comparison to the losses. The poet William Blake lamented England's "green and pleasant land," now blighted and blackened by the factories, and Wordsworth deplored the spiritual loss brought on by the preoccupation with "getting and spending."

The romantics also rebelled against conventions. In social intercourse, they thought the manners and decorum that had seemed so important to the eighteenth century masked the true person and discouraged the communion that romantic friends craved. Determined to express themselves more honestly and deeply, the romantics retreated into introspection and withdrew from society. Sometimes they became boorish rebels whose bluntness made them unwelcome in polite society. In a more heroic mode, the romantic assumed the role of liberator, a Prometheus rebelling against the established order to free humankind from oppression.

Goethe's novel *The Sorrows of Young Werther* became a manifesto of the romantic rebellion against the Age of Reason. Published in 1774 during the Sturm und Drang (storm and stress) movement in Germany, the novel is one of the earliest works of European romanticism. Its hero, an educated young man, abandons a post in the diplomatic service to go off by himself into the country and brood on his alienation. He is saved from his despair when he falls in love with a simple and natural country girl, but she is engaged to an unimaginative businessman. Even after she marries her fiancé, Werther continues to love her, a romantic obsession that finally leads to suicide, the tragic triumph of emotion over reason. Werther's sincerity, his refusal to compromise his inner truth, his absolute consistency even to death, presented a revolutionary alternative to the pale heroes of the Age of Reason. Goethe's readers imitated Werther's excessive emotion, adopted his canary yellow waistcoat and blue jacket as a mode of dress, and a few even committed suicide. These reactions were extreme, but, as William Blake put it in stating one of the credos of romanticism, "The road to excess leads to the palace of wisdom."

The romantics' revolution was not just a reaction against their predecessors in the Age of Reason. They were also rebelling against the dominant culture of their own time. While their contemporaries affirmed material progress, moderation, objective truth, and science, the artists and poets celebrated spiritual insight, intensity, subjectivity, and the primitive. Indeed, the image of the artist as an outsider, an alien or exile, emerges during this period, when the artists so often felt themselves counter to the dominant values of their time. Their ideals were not new. We have seen them as an undercurrent in many works of the Enlightenment. In the late eighteenth century, however, what had been an undercurrent became the artistic mainstream.

Challenging the rationalism and materialism of the dominant culture, the romantic writers and artists affirmed contrary and oppositional values. Most of all, they celebrated nature. The world of the *philosophes* was primarily an urban one, a well-ordered city or an artificial, formal garden. The romantics, on the other hand, preferred country to city and untamed nature to cultivated gardens. Several of the English romantic poets moved to the Lake District in northeastern England, and American romantics such as Thoreau went off to live by themselves in the woods.

Nature was a much broader concept for the romantics than simply rocks and trees. It referred to the human as well as the physical world. In human terms, "natural" described the spontaneous, unaffected, emotional person. "The child is father to the man," Wordsworth wrote, because the child had not yet been cut off from nature and taught to suppress natural impulses. Thus the child could teach the adult forgotten spiritual truths. Similarly, peasants untutored in the artificial affectations of the city possessed a natural understanding and lived a truer and fuller life than their urban cousins. This romantic attraction to the childlike and the primitive prompted an interest in folk literature. In the early nineteenth century, Sir Walter Scott collected Scottish and English ballads and the brothers Grimm in Germany collected and retold folk and fairy tales.

Emotion was "natural"; reason was learned. In their celebration of feeling, the romantics redefined the meaning of doubt. For Descartes, writing at the beginning of the Age of Reason, skepticism was an intellectual method: Doubting everything except that he was doubting became the starting point for his rational construction of knowledge. But when Alfred, Lord Tennyson, writing two centuries later, was driven to doubt and despair by the death of his closest friend, he regained belief not by rationally appreciating his own thought processes, but rather by remembering the love that he had felt for his friend. That feeling confirmed an ultimate meaning in the universe and gave him an argument for living.

For the romantics, thought began in feeling. Their test for truth was an inner test. They did not look for objective evidence, for confirmation outside themselves. Rather they looked within, to the truths of emotion and, especially, of imagination. Poets became the new philosopher kings or, as Percy Shelley described them, "legislators" of humankind, because they could lift the veil between the material and immaterial, see the spiritual truths beyond, and communicate them to the rest of humanity. While the classical artists of the Enlightenment sought to represent the outer world and developed rules for successful imitation, the romantics sought inner truths of the imagination and their works celebrated the unfettered expression of that inner vision. As Wordsworth put it, poetry resulted from "emotion recollected in tranquility."

As a result, romantic art is much more personal than the art of the eighteenth century. The lyric poets of the period write in the first person, singing, like Walt Whitman, songs of themselves. Wordsworth's romantic epic is a long autobiographical poem, *The Prelude*, describing the growth of the poet's mind. This journey into the self is often confusing and may even be dangerous. Leaving behind the objective world of everyday reality and freed from the constraints of society, the romantic enters an unfamiliar world of dreams and nightmares. The quest sometimes takes the form of a night journey into an anarchic and threatening underworld, like Faust's Walpurgisnacht. Its strangeness, for male authors, is often connected with its femininity: For Faust, the journey to the underworld becomes a journey to the realm of the Mothers, and Elis Froebom's journey into E.T.A. Hoffmann's "The Mines of Falun" is linked to the search for the Metal Queen, an earth goddess. This journey into the dark side of the self, its repressed, violent, and irrational aspects, may yield greater self-understanding, but it can also bring destruction. Elis Froebom does not return from his descent into the mine, and Keats knows that melancholy "dwells with Beauty" and that Beauty must die. For the male poets of the romantic period the feminine, the primitive, and the irrational are linked and they represent forces that both empower and threaten them.

Attracted by the promise of empowerment, the romantics could be cut off from the rest of humanity and destroyed by the divisions and contradictions within. If they survived this inner journey, the romantics believed, they would be rewarded with greater self-understanding and also with a deeper connection to their fellow human beings. The romantic route to community was through self-exploration, for in learning about oneself, we make the paradoxical discovery that uniqueness is something all human beings have in common. The journey into the self was not to be in the end an isolating one, for it led to empathy and the recovery of a common humanity. But this discovery had a melancholy side, for the common human condition was suffering and death. This realistic counter-awareness always tempers the romantic consciousness.

Later in the period, realism overcame idealism. At the beginning of the century, the poets believed that common country folk, because they were closer to nature, could embody the spiritual truths that the poets were seeking. As the century went on and cities grew, it was not so easy to retreat into the country or to celebrate folk wisdom. In realistic novels, the dominant literary form during the second half of the nineteenth century, realists such as Flaubert detailed the material banality of the bourgeoisie and the spiritual vacuity of the common human condition. Even though Emily Brontë is telling a romantic story in *Wuthering Heights*, her realistic picture of domestic life on the Yorkshire moors is not an attractive one. In the view of Dostoevsky's cynically realistic Grand Inquisitor, the great mass of humanity desired bread rather than freedom. Science seemed to have material explanations for everything, and when Darwin's evolutionary theory, published in 1859, reduced humans to animals and explained the creation as a random process, many were ready to accept Nietzsche's assertion that "God is dead." The realists simply tried to describe ordinary people and everyday things objectively, without any suggestion that they were part of a larger design or had deep spiritual understanding. Flaubert, in "A Simple Heart," seems to be mocking the search for such significance when he makes Félicité's holy spirit a bedraggled parrot. The naturalists, writers such as Émile Zola in France and Theodore Dreiser in the United States, went a Darwinian step further than the realists. Life is not simply ordinary and trivial, they suggested, it is physically determined, and human beings, like the rest of the animal creation, are driven by biological needs and instinctual desires.

In spite of their cynicism and apparent objectivity, the realists often affirmed the power of imagination to create community. For all his shallowness and petty materialism, Tolstoy's Ivan Ilyitch becomes fully human as he faces death, and his story elicits our romantic empathy with him. Even though the realistic side of Flaubert may have looked upon such provincial characters as Félicité and Madame Bovary with ironic disdain, his romantic side was so drawn to identify with them that he exclaimed, "I am Madame Bovary!"

This division in the consciousness of the nineteenth century between the romantic and realistic is particularly important to the growing body of literature that treated the situation of women. In Ibsen's *A Doll's House* and the stories by Charlotte Perkins Gilman and Kate Chopin, the female protagonists seek to alleviate patriarchal oppression by drawing on inner resources of the self. Their success in doing so is at best problematic; Nora Helmer's life after she shuts the door on her marriage is a matter for speculation. The most complete triumph over such oppression is probably that of Linda Brent in a slave narrative that describes its heroine's escape from the doubly oppressive patriarchy of slavery. In this autobiographical account, Harriet Jacobs combines the romantic journey to freedom with the historical realities of her life.

Even though the nineteenth century was an age of intensive colonial enterprise, there is surprisingly little direct treatment of the colonies and their peoples in the European literature of the period. In novels, fortunes are inherited from colonial relatives and characters occasionally disappear to China, India, Africa, or Australia. But colonialism was peripheral to the experience of most Europeans, and the colonies largely remained exotic settings for "oriental" tales and adventure stories. To the colonized, however, the presence of Europeans was a daily fact of life. The works we have chosen to represent the world context for this period are all concerned with the effects of Western culture on nonwesterners. Describing her first contact with Europeans, Sarah Winnemucca Hopkins, a Piute Indian in Nevada, recounts the Indians' surprising conclusions about the strangers. Mori Ōgai from Japan, a society that had been very reluctant to engage with the West, symbolizes the attraction of the West to a Japanese student in the figure of his German dancer-lover. Rabindranath Tagore writes of India's divided consciousness. Schooled in the literature of European romanticism, Tagore translates romantic themes and motifs to fit the colonial context. In *Broken Ties*, for example, the narrator Srivlas tries to reconcile the Western empiricism and rationalism of his university education with traditional Indian spiritual values. His attempt to do so, like the quests undertaken by the romantic heroes of the West, proves dangerous and brings suffering and loss. But it also unites him with Damini, the woman who both represents spiritual consciousness and rejects the confining roles traditionally assigned to women in India.

FAUST AND WUTHERING HEIGHTS

Two works define our romantic themes, Goethe's *Faust* (published in two parts in 1808 and 1832) and Emily Brontë's *Wuthering Heights* (1847). Goethe's dramatic poem, a romantic re-creation of the Renaissance Faust story, has long been considered the work that epitomizes European romanticism. Brontë's novel, a haunting and violent love story, treats romantic themes from a feminine point of view.

At the beginning of *Faust* we meet a scholar who has mastered all the established branches of learning—law, medicine, theology, natural science—and is dissatisfied with all of them, for mere accomplishments of the mind do not satisfy the longings of his heart. They do not relieve his inner emptiness. For the man of reason, this emotional crisis is beyond rational comprehension or control. So, at the moment of his greatest achievement, he experiences disillusion, dejection, and frustration and is driven to suicidal despair. If he survives this crisis, his life will take a new direction. When Faust calls up his repressed Mephistopheles, he abandons rationality to explore the irrational: He gives up controlled experimentation to immerse himself in experience; he turns from the achievements of the mind to try the pleasures of the body; he gives up the ideal of perfection to celebrate imperfection. Probing the divisions within himself, Faust also explores the conventional dichotomies of Western culture. His journey takes him from external and empirical reality into internal and mysterious truths, from the objective realm, conventionally construed as masculine, into the subjective underworld of the feminine. Faust's journey resembles that of the classical epic hero, but he does not go to the underworld to meet the shade of his father, as Achilles and Aeneas do. His underworld journey through manic Walpurgisnacht and the tragic affair with Gretchen lead in Part II to the realm of the Mothers.

Faust's Walpurgisnacht releases him from the constraints of rationality. He is no longer in control of himself or his world. Acting spontaneously, he stabs Valentine, and he is helpless to prevent the destruction of Gretchen and her family. By linking his destiny to inner knowledge rather than outward achievement, Faust learns that his creative power is inextricably entangled with the dark and destructive dimensions of the self. In Part II, Faust attempts to overcome guilt and solipsism and to act for the betterment of others. We include the first scene of Act I, where Faust seeks solace in nature after the death of Gretchen, and Act V, in which he undertakes a redeeming social project just before his death. This final effort, draining marshes for a housing development, is an imperfect achievement. His egotism leads to the sacrifice of Baucis and Philemon, but the project also embodies altruism and social concern, and this concern turns *Faust* from the tragedy of Gretchen that ends Part I to the divine comedy that ends Part II. Faust's crude attempt at altruism redeems him as an imperfect yet striving human being. And the closing acceptance of imperfection affirms the underlying principle of realism, that limitations of time and place and flaws in human character inevitably constrain the idealistic romantic impulse.

Emily Brontë's *Wuthering Heights* makes the romantic motifs found in *Faust* unfamiliar by giving them a feminine treatment. So strange has this novel seemed to many of its readers that it has often been characterized as an eccentric story unlike anything else written at the time. Brontë's passionate and violent characters and the setting in the remote Yorkshire moors of northern England, an area so uncivilized that it is characterized at one point in the novel as "a misanthropist's heaven," seem unlike the characters and situations in other novels of the period. The two framing narrators, Lockwood and Nelly Dean, mediate this strange story for more conventional readers.

Like Faust, Brontë's protagonist is a divided figure. Torn between her natural impulses and her desire for civilized restraint, between the two halves of herself symbolized by Heathcliff and Edgar Linton, Catherine Earnshaw makes a fatal mistake when she chooses to marry Edgar. By rejecting Heathcliff, she denies her inner self, for, as she tells Nelly, "I *am* Heathcliff . . . so don't talk of our separation again—it is impracticable." But the marriage does separate them: It leads to Heathcliff's disappearance and to his vengeful return when he seeks to take control of Wuthering Heights and destroy it. Catherine's own decline begins with her marriage and ultimately leads to her death.

Heathcliff's commanding presence has made him seem to many readers the central figure, but he is really an outsider, a disrupting force who incites the violent conflicts of the story. His background is mysterious. He has been identified as a gypsy, or as one of the thousands of Irish workers who migrated to England in the 1840s to escape the famine in Ireland, or even as a black from the colonies. Whatever his origins, he is clearly an alien in Yorkshire, not part of the established patriarchal households represented by Wuthering Heights and Thrushcross Grange. Oppressed by Hindley and scorned by Linton, Heathcliff is allied with Catherine and embodies her unrestrained, natural, feminine side. If she is Heathcliff, he is Catherine. Their identity is part of nature; their place, Penistone Crags, a natural rock formation out on the moors turned into a castle of the imagination. When Catherine chooses Edgar, she denies at least half of herself. Thrushcross Grange, a cultivated park walled off from the wild moors, is an orderly household. Although Edgar Linton is weak and ineffectual, he nonetheless represents patriarchal order in this outpost of civilization.

Wuthering Heights is sometimes viewed as the love tragedy of Catherine and Heathcliff, but their story, like that of Faust and Gretchen, takes up only part of the novel. There has been great suffering and loss in the course of the story, but Heathcliff and Catherine are romantic spirits, primordial forces in an elemental realm of the imagination. They may live on as spirits of the moors, as the shepherd boy at the end suggests, but their deaths do not resolve the conflicts between the worlds of Wuthering Heights and Thrushcross Grange.

That process is left for the generation of Catherine Linton and Hareton Earnshaw to carry out. At the end of the novel, as Cathy teaches Hareton his letters, we see the beginnings of a new order that may unite the two houses. Hareton and Cathy articulate a more realistic world view as they seek to survive and achieve a modicum of civilization. If Heathcliff and the first Catherine are siblings to the romantic rebels and Byronic heroes of the first part of the century, Hareton and the second Catherine are related to realistic figures such as Flaubert's Félicité. Although *Wuthering Heights* at first seems to be an iconoclastic and eccentric work, Brontë's melding of romantic and realistic themes is like that in many other works of the time.

SUGGESTED READINGS

Some histories of the nineteenth century helpful to students of literature include E. J. Hobsbaum's three volumes, *The Age of Revolution, 1789–1848* (1962), *The Age of Capital, 1848–1875* (1975), and *The Age of Empire, 1875–1914* (1987); and Roland N. Stromberg's *European Intellectual History Since 1789* (1966). Among the useful works on romanticism are Mario Praz's *The Romantic Agony* (1956) and Lilian Furst's *The Contours of European Romanticism* (1979), which treat European romanticism broadly. R. F. Gleckner and G. E. Enscoe have collected essays by several writers in *Romanticism: Points of View* (1962). R. W. Harris's *Romanticism and the Social Order, 1780–1830* puts romanticism into its social and historical context. Meyer Abrams's classic *The Mirror and the Lamp* (1953) and W. J. Bate's *From Classic to Romantic* (1946) discuss romantic literary theory. Marilyn Butler revises some established ideas about British romanticism in *Romantics, Rebels and Reactionaries* (1981), and R. W. B. Lewis includes the American romantics in his classic study of nineteenth-century American literature, *The American Adam* (1955). Among the useful works on realism are George Becker's collection of *Documents of Literary Realism* (1963); Erich Auerbach's essays 19 and 20 in *Mimesis* (1946); Harry Levin's *The Gates of Horn* (1963), which discusses the work of five French realists, and his essay "What Is Realism?" in *Contexts of Criticism* (1957); Jacques Barzun's *Darwin, Marx, Wagner* (1941), which treats the work of three dominant figures of the century and their influence on our time; and C. P. Snow's *The Realists* (1978), discussing the work of eight realistic novelists of the nineteenth century.

REPRESENTATIVE TEXTS

JOHANN WOLFGANG VON GOETHE
[1749–1832]

Goethe's lifetime, from 1749 to 1832, may encompass the greatest shift in consciousness of any period in Western thought. It bridges the Enlightenment, with its belief in reason, objectivity, and rational control, and the romantic age, which celebrates feeling, subjectivity, and imagination. At the heart of the period and at just about the midpoint of Goethe's life was the French Revolution, the event that, more than any other, came to symbolize the violent transition from rational order to passionate subjectivity that was taking place.

More than any other single figure of the time, Goethe was the man of his age. Poet, playwright, autobiographer, novelist, critic, and journalist, Goethe seemed to try his hand at nearly every literary form. He was a painter, theater manager, statesman, bureaucrat, educational theorist, and scientist as well. He was a "Renaissance man." After meeting Goethe, Napoleon is said to have remarked, "*Voilà un homme!*" (This is a man!). Goethe's masterwork, the long dramatic poem *Faust,* the story of another Renaissance man, is in many ways the defining work of European romanticism.

LIFE

Born in Frankfurt into an affluent bourgeois family, Goethe had a happy childhood before going off to the University of Leipzig when he was sixteen. There he published his first volumes of poetry, but he left for health reasons before completing his degree. In 1770 he went to the University of Strasbourg to study law, and there met J. G. Herder, the critic and philosopher who was the formative influence on the Sturm und Drang (storm and stress) movement, a German literary movement of the 1770s that sought to overthrow the cult of rationalism by emphasizing feeling, imagination, and natural simplicity. The Sturm und Drang, led by Herder, Friedrich Schiller, and Goethe, was the first onslaught of German romanticism. Influenced by Herder, Goethe wrote *Götz von Berlichingen* (1773), the first major literary work of the movement, and *The Sorrows of Young Werther* (1774), the movement's major work. The story of a sensitive young man driven to suicide by his alienation from the conventional world, his emotional absolutism, and his frustrated passion for a country girl, *Werther* took Europe by storm. Werther's blue coat and yellow waistcoat became the fashion and a rash of suicides occurred in the wake of the novel's popularity, similar to those that followed Chikamatsu's *shinju* plays in Japan. Thomas Carlyle said that the book caught the spirit of the age and gave expression to "the nameless unrest and longing discontent which was then agitating every bosom."

In 1775 Goethe moved to Weimar, where he spent most of the rest of his life working as a government official and diplomat for the reigning duke, Charles Augustus, while continuing to write and carry out scientific investigations. The poems of his early years in Weimar modify the extreme emotionalism of his sturm und drang works to reveal a growing objectivity. Nature becomes less a projection of the author's moods than something existing in its own right. A more classical bent in Goethe's work was encouraged by his visit to Italy in 1786–1787. The works from this Italian period, especially *Iphigenie in Tauris* (1787) and the *Roman Elegies* (1788–1789), celebrate classical ideals and humanity's power to free itself from the delusions of its own consciousness.

In the 1790s Goethe, like nearly all Europeans of the time, was caught up in the French Revolution and its aftermath. He accompanied Charles Augustus on a disastrous military campaign in France in 1792. Out of these experiences, Goethe wrote several books: the war dramas *Hermann and Dorothea* (1797) and *The Natural Daughter* (1804), and his most important work during this period, *Wilhelm Meister's Apprenticeship* (1796), a bildungsroman—a novel devoted to describing the learning process, the "apprenticeship," of a young person learning about life. Goethe had worked on the novel for several years, and it might be said to describe his learning process during his first two decades in Weimar.

Among Goethe's most productive years were those at the turn of the century when he collaborated with Friedrich Schiller. From 1794 until Schiller's death in 1805, the two writers formed a friendship and literary collaboration similar to that of Wordsworth and Coleridge in England. Schiller's classicism reinforced the classical direction in Goethe's work, as the two men collaborated on several literary magazines and other writing projects. Schiller especially encouraged Goethe's work on *Faust*.

After Schiller's death, Goethe's writing took a more romantic direction in the psychological novel *Elective Affinities* (1809), which explores the night side of human relationships. Goethe also continued his scientific work, publishing in 1805–1810 his most important scientific papers on the *Theory of Color*. In the later years of his life, Goethe became interested in non-Western literature, developing an ideal of a *Weltliteratur* (world literature) that transcended national differences to advance a universal civilization. His own poems in the *Divan of West and East* (1819) were inspired by Persian poetry, and attempt to marry East and West. By the last decade of his life, Goethe had become a reigning sage, and Weimar a place of pilgrimage for writers, artists, and intellectuals from all over Europe.

Goethe worked on *Faust* throughout his life. The *Urfaust*, an early version of the poem that was not published during Goethe's lifetime, was probably written in the early 1870s. The first published version, *Faust, a Fragment*, appeared in 1790 and the completed *Faust, Part I* in 1808. *Faust, Part II*, which Goethe worked on in the last years of his life, was published after his death in 1832. Goethe said of this life's work that it would always be unfinished: "The whole will always remain a fragment." And in a suppressed valediction for the play, he challenged his readers to make sense of it: "Our play is rather like the whole life of man / We make a start, we make an end— / But make a whole of it? Well, do so if you can."

WORK

Goethe's challenge defines one of the central critical issues presented by *Faust*: whether or not it can be read as a unified and coherent work of art. Because it was written at different periods throughout Goethe's life, many commentators have read it as an autobiographical poem telling of Goethe's intellectual and creative growth. Like Goethe, Faust is a Renaissance man. Restless and dissatisfied with the limitations of his human situation, he seeks greater knowledge and experience. The two warring souls within him may characterize two competing aspects of Goethe's character, his Enlightenment, scientific side, and his intuitive, poetic side. The two aspects of human nature represented by Mephistopheles and Faust, worldly cynicism and optimistic striving, may also reveal crucial contradictions in Goethe's own character.

But Faust is also representative of his time, a kind of modern Everyman, going through the dialectical transition from the Enlightenment into the romantic age and embodying in his own mind and experience the contradictions of the time. The original folk stories of the Faust legend emerged in the late Middle Ages as a way of articulating the change from the Church-dominated hierarchical consciousness of the Middle Ages to the humanism of the Renaissance. The struggle between these competing points of view can be seen in Marlowe's version of the story, *The Tragical History of Doctor Faustus* (c. 1592). Goethe's *Faust* reflects a similar period of transition, one caught between the Enlightenment's ideal of objective utopianism and the subjectivity of the romantic age. At the core of Goethe's poem is a contradiction: God challenges Satan to make Faust discontented; Faust bets Mephistopheles that he cannot make him contented. Many of the play's ambiguities and the questions that it leaves open at the end derive from this contradiction: Is Faust saved or damned? Is he ever satisfied with his lot? Is the work tragic or comic? These issues are caught up in the dialectical oppositions of the drama.

By beginning with a folk story as the basis for his poem, Goethe exemplifies the romantic interest in the primitive, for in the simple stories of the people, the romantics thought they could get beneath the veneer of civilization and get in touch with nature. But Goethe significantly transformed the original folk story. *Faust* is no longer a contest between good and evil, or between the power of the Church and the individual. Goethe's *Faust* explores instead alternative world views, different aspects of Faust's consciousness. When he rejects "word" and "mind" as adequate translations for the beginning of the Gospel of St. John and substitutes instead, "In the beginning was the Deed," Faust bespeaks the division within himself and the choice that Mephistopheles will offer him. Rejecting "mind," Faust turns his back on his past, on his role as an Enlightenment scholar. Affirming the "Deed," he chooses experience and action, to become a man of the world, of the body rather than the mind, of the parts of himself that he has previously ignored. From this perspective, Mephistopheles is not so much a separate character or a representation of evil as he is a projection of Faust's consciousness, a representative of one of the "two souls" that reside within Faust's breast. The poem pits Mephistopheles' cynicism and despair against Faust's optimism; it explores the interplay between the physical and spiritual, the human and divine.

Mephistopheles does not offer Faust a chance to break rules or to challenge authority but rather a chance to explore another reality. Rather than mind, he offers body; rather than idea, he offers experience. But the immersion in experience is dangerous; acting in the moment, from emotional spontaneity rather than rational consideration, can have tragic consequences. Valentine's death, for example, is an unforeseen result of Faust's affair with Margaret. Unthinking action inevitably leads to errors. And Faust's search for the fullest expression of his nature leads to tragic errors that result in the destruction of Margaret, her family, and Baucis and Philemon. If Mephistopheles is not a representative of evil in Goethe's poem, Faust is not an unqualified representative of good. In both aspects of his character, the divided Faust is caught in ambiguities and paradoxes.

In its full version, *Faust* is over 12,000 lines long. Many anthologies reprint only the first part of the play, Faust's wager with Mephistopheles and the Margaret story. This truncated version misrepresents the movement of the whole drama and makes *Faust* even more of a fragment than it is. We have added here some sections of Part II that suggest the structure of the whole: the opening scene in which Faust seeks solace in nature and all of the final act, which describes Faust's project to reclaim a marsh for a housing development. But we have not been able to include many other sections that present Faust's quest in highly symbolic form and foreshadow the end of the drama. His marriage to Helen of Troy and his journey to the realm of the Mothers are especially important preparation for Faust's final ascension with the "Woman soul." His visit to the realm of the Mothers transforms the usual journey of epic heroes like Achilles and Aeneas, who go to the underworld to learn their destiny from the shades of their fathers. Faust must visit the realm of the Mothers, for his quest, like that in many works of romantic literature, seeks the place and identity of the Eternal-Feminine.

Nineteenth-century readers tended to see *Faust* as a drama of a man redeemed by striving, for in spite of his mistakes, Faust never ceases searching for the good. He is never satisfied with the limitations of the experiences that Mephistopheles offers him. These early critics often pointed to the last act in Part II, where Faust drains a marsh to develop a housing project, as an indication that Faust has transcended his selfishness and redeemed his earlier errors by engaging in altruistic service to humankind. Modern readers, less enamored of development and less willing to affirm action for its own sake, have not been so easily convinced that Faust has changed or grown. After all, they point out, Baucis and Philemon are sacrificed so that Faust's development scheme can proceed. The ending of the play, then, becomes problematic. Is it tragic or comic? Is Faust redeemed? Or is the end a cosmic mockery? Stuart Atkins suggests these paradoxical ambiguities when he describes *Faust* as "the drama of a man destroyed by the larger force than himself which is life and yet enjoying triumph in inevitable defeat."

SUGGESTED READINGS

Any writer as prolific and various as Goethe is bound to prompt a considerable critical and biographical interest. Among the useful introductory books on Goethe and his work are Barker Fairley's *A Study of Goethe* (1947), Henry Hatfield's *Goethe: A Critical Introduction* (1963), and Terence J. Reed's *Goethe* (1984). The Norton Critical Edition of *Faust* (1976), edited by Cyrus Hamlin, includes a selection of critical essays on the play. Among the many critical books on *Faust,* students may find Stuart Atkins's *Goethe's Faust: A Literary Analysis* (1964) and Jane K. Brown's *Goethe's Faust: The German Tragedy* (1986) particularly helpful. Goethe's poem has prompted many literary retellings of the Faust story in the last two centuries. Some are included in this anthology, but of particular interest is Thomas Mann's *Doktor Faustus* (1947), in which Mann uses the Faust story to satirize Hitler's Third Reich.

FROM

Faust

Translated by Charles E. Passage

CHARACTERS IN THE PROLOGUE IN HEAVEN

THE LORD	MICHAEL
RAPHAEL	MEPHISTOPHELES
GABRIEL	

CHARACTERS IN THE TRAGEDY

FAUST	A STUDENT
MEPHISTOPHELES	ELIZABETH, *an acquaintance of* MARGARET
WAGNER, *a student*	WITCHES, *old and young;*
LIESCHEN	WIZARDS; WILL-O'-THE-WISP;
MARGARET *(also* GRETCHEN*)*	PROKTOPHANTASMIST; THE BEAUTY;
MARTHA, MARGARET*'s neighbor*	SERVIBILIS; MONKEYS; SPIRITS; ANIMALS;
VALENTINE, MARGARET*'s brother*	APPRENTICES; COUNTRY-FOLK; CITIZENS;
OLD PEASANT	BEGGAR; STUDENTS; *etc.*

CHARACTERS IN PART II

FAUST	LEMURS
MEPHISTOPHELES *in various guises*	*The* FOUR GRAY WOMEN: WANT, GUILT,
ARIEL	CARE, DISTRESS
BAUCIS	A PENITENT
PHILEMON	DOCTOR MARIANUS
A TRAVELER	CHORUS OF ANGELS *and* PENITENTS *and*
THE THREE MIGHTY MEN	*various Heavenly characters*
LYNCEUS	

PROLOGUE IN HEAVEN

RAPHAEL:

> The sun sings as it sang of old
> With brother spheres in rival sound,
> In thundrous motion onward rolled
> Completing its appointed round.
> The angels draw strength from the sight,

Though fathom it no angel may;
The great works of surpassing might
Are grand as on Creation day.[1]   250

GABRIEL:
And swift beyond conception flies
The turning earth, now dark, now bright,
With clarity of paradise
Succeeding deep and dreadful night;
The sea in foam from its broad source
Against the base of cliffs is hurled,
And down the sphere's eternal course
Both cliff and sea are onward whirled.

MICHAEL:
And storms a roaring battle wage
From sea to land, from land to sea,   260
And forge a chain amid their rage,
A chain of utmost potency.
There blazing lightning-flashes sear
The path for bursting thunder's way—
And yet thy heralds, Lord, revere
The mild procession of thy day.

ALL THREE:
The angels draw strength from the sight,
Though fathom it no angel may;
The great works of surpassing might
Are grand as on Creation day.   270

MEPHISTOPHELES:
Since you, O Lord, approach again and see
These people here and ask us how we do,
And since you used to like my company,
Behold me also here among this crew.
Excuse me, I can not be eloquent,
Not even if I'm scorned by all your staff;
My grand style would provoke your merriment
If you had not forgotten how to laugh.
Of suns and worlds there's nothing I can say;
How men torment themselves is what I see.   280
The little earth-god stays the same perpetually
And still is just as odd as on Creation day.
He would be better off at least
If you had not endowed him with the heavens' light;
He terms it Reason and exerts the right
To be more brute than any beast.
He seems like—craving pardon of Your Grace—
One of the spindle-shank grasshopper race
That flit around and as they hop
Sing out their ancient ditty where they stop.   290
He should stay in the grass where he has sung!
He sticks his nose in every pile of dung.

---

[1] The line numbers are those of the original poem. We have omitted the "Dedication" and the "Prologue in the Theater" that precede this section.

THE LORD:

    Is there no more that you could add?

    Is finding fault all you can do?

    Is nothing on earth ever right with you?

MEPHISTOPHELES:

    No, Lord! I find things there, as always, downright bad.

    The human race in all its woes I so deplore

    I hate to plague the poor things any more.

THE LORD:

    Do you know Faust?

MEPHISTOPHELES:

                The Doctor?

THE LORD:

                            And my servant.

MEPHISTOPHELES:

    He serves you in a curious way, I think.   300

    Not earthly is the poor fool's food and drink.

    An inner ferment drives him far

    And he is half aware that he is mad;

    From heaven he demands the fairest star,

    From earth all peaks of pleasure to be had,

    And nothing near and nothing far

    Will calm his troubled heart or make it glad.

THE LORD:

    Though now he serves me but confusedly,

    I soon shall guide him on toward what is clear.

    The gardener knows, when green comes to the tree,   310

    That flowers and fruit will deck the coming year.

MEPHISTOPHELES:

    What will you bet you lose him if you give

    Me your permission now to steer

    Him gently down my path instead?

THE LORD:

    As long as he on earth may live,

    To you such shall not be gainsaid.

    Man errs as long as he can strive.

MEPHISTOPHELES:

    Thank you for that; for with the dead

    I never hankered much to be.

    It is the plump, fresh cheeks that mean the most to me.   320

    I'm out to corpses calling at my house;

    I play the way the cat does with the mouse.

THE LORD:

    Good, then! The matter is agreed!

    Divert this spirit from his primal source,

    And if you can ensnare him, lead

    Him with you on your downward course;

    And stand abashed when you have to confess:

    A good man harried in his dark distraction

    Can still perceive the ways of righteousness.

MEPHISTOPHELES:

    All right! It won't be any long transaction.   330

    I have no fears at all for my bet's sake.

And once I've won, let it be understood
You will admit my triumph as you should.
Dust shall he eat, and call it good,
Just like my aunt, the celebrated snake.

THE LORD:

There too feel wholly free to try;
Toward your kind I have borne no hate.
Of all the spirits that deny,
The scoffer burdens me with slightest weight.
Man's activeness can all too easily go slack,   340
He loves to be in ease unqualified;
Hence I set a companion at his side
To goad him like a devil from the back.
   But you, true sons of gods, may you
Rejoice in beauty that is full and true!
May that which is evolving and alive
Encompass you in bonds that Love has wrought;
And what exists in wavering semblance, strive
To' fix in final permanence of thought.

       [*The heavens close, the* ARCHANGELS *disperse.*]

MEPHISTOPHELES:

From time to time I like to see the Boss,   350
And with him like to keep things on the level.
It's really nice in one of such high class
To be so decent with the very Devil.

THE FIRST PART OF THE TRAGEDY

Night

FAUST *restless in his chair at his desk in a narrow and high-vaulted Gothic room.*

FAUST:

I've read, alas! through philosophy,
Medicine and jurisprudence too,
And, to my grief, theology
With ardent labor studied through.
And here I stand with all my lore,
Poor fool, no wiser than before!
I'm Master, I'm Doctor, and with my reading   360
These ten years now I have been leading
My scholars on wild-goose hunts, out
And in, cross-lots, and round about—
To find that nothing can be known!
This burns my very marrow and bone.
I'm shrewder, it's true, than all the tribes
Of Doctors and Masters and priests and scribes;
Neither doubts nor scruples now can daunt me,
Neither hell nor devils now can haunt me—
But by the same token I lose all delight.   370
I don't pretend to know anything aright,
I don't pretend to have in mind

Things I could teach to improve mankind.
Nor have I lands nor treasure hoards,
Nor honors and splendors the world affords;
No dog would want to live this way!
And so I've yielded to magic's sway,
To see if spirits' force and speech
Might not bring many a mystery in reach;
So I no longer need to go   380
On saying things that I don't know;
So I may learn the things that hold
The world together at its core,
So I may potencies and seeds behold,
And trade in empty words no more.

   O if, full moon, you did but shine
Your last upon this pain of mine,
Whom I have watched ascending bright
Here at my desk in mid of night;
Then over books and papers here,   390
Sad friend, you would come into view.
Ah, could I on some mountain height
Rove beneath your mellow light,
Drift on with spirits round mountain caves,
Waft over meadows your dim light laves,
And, clear of learning's fumes, renew
Myself in baths of healing dew!

   Am I still in this prison stall?
Accursed, musty hole-in-the-wall,
Where the very light of heaven strains   400
But dully through the painted panes!

   By these enormous book-piles bounded
Which dust bedecks and worms devour,
Which are by sooty charts surrounded
Up to the vaultings where they tower;
With jars shelved round me, and retorts,
With instruments packed in and jammed,
Ancestral junk together crammed—
Such is your world! A world of sorts!

   Do you still wonder why your heart   410
Is choked with fear within your breast?
Why nameless pain checks every start
Toward life and leaves you so oppressed?
Instead of Nature's living sphere
Wherein God placed mankind of old,
Brute skeletons surround you here
And dead men's bones and smoke and mold.

   Flee! Up! And out into the land!
Does not this mystic book indeed,
From Nostradamus'[2] very hand,   420
Give all the guidance that you need?
Then you will recognize the courses

---

[2] French astrologer and physician Michel de Notredame (1503–1566).

Of stars; within you will unfold,
At Nature's prompting, your soul's forces
As spirits speech with spirits hold.
In vain this arid brooding here
The sacred signs to clarify—
You spirits who are hovering near,
If you can hear me, give reply!

        [He opens the book and glimpses the sign of the macrocosm.]

Ha! Suddenly what rapture at this view   430
Goes rushing through my senses once again!
I feel a youthful joy of life course new
And ardent through my every nerve and vein.
Was it a god who wrote these signs whereby
My inward tempest-rage is stilled
And my poor heart with joy is filled
And with a mystic impulse high
The powers of Nature all around me are revealed?
Am I a god? I feel so light!
In these pure signs I see the whole   440
Of operative Nature spread before my soul.
Now what the wise man says I understand aright:
"The spirit world is not locked off from thee;
Thy heart is dead, thy mind's bolt drawn!
Up, scholar, and bathe cheerfully
Thy earthly breast in rosy dawn!"

                      [He contemplates the sign.]

How all things interweave to form the Whole,
Each in another finds its life and goal!
How each of heaven's powers soars and descends
And each to each the golden buckets lends;   450
On fragrant-blessed wings
From heaven piercing to earth's core
Till all the cosmos sweetly rings!
   O what a sight!—A sight, but nothing more!
Where can I grasp you, Nature without end?
You breasts, where? Source of all our lives,[3]
On which both heaven and earth depend,
Toward you my withered heart so strives—
You flow, you swell, and must I thirst in vain?

    [Impatiently he turns pages of the book and glimpses the sign of the Earth Spirit.]

How differently I am affected by this sign!   460
You, Spirit of the Earth, are nearer me,
I feel more potent energy,
I feel aglow as with new wine.
I feel the strength to brave the world, to go
And shoulder earthly weal and earthly woe,
To wrestle with the tempests there,
In shipwreck's grinding crash not to despair.

---

[3]The image is that of a mother-earth goddess, perhaps like the ancient Diana of Ephesus, who was
represented with innumerable breasts that gave suck to all creatures.

Clouds gather over me—
The moon conceals its light—
The lamp has vanished!   470
Mists rise!—Red lightnings dart and flash
About my head—Down from
The vaulted roof cold horror blows
And seizes me!
Spirit implored, I feel you hovering near.
Reveal yourself!
O how my heart is rent with fear!
With new emotion
My senses riot in wild commotion!
My heart surrenders to you utterly!   480
You must! You must! though it cost life to me!
> [*He seizes the book and mystically pronounces the sign of the
> Spirit. A reddish flame flashes. The* SPIRIT *appears in the flame.*]

SPIRIT:
    Who calls me?

FAUST [*cowering*]:
                    Ghastly shape!

SPIRIT:
                                    With might
    You have compelled me to appear,
    You have long sucked about my sphere,
    Now—

FAUST:
            No! I cannot bear the sight!

SPIRIT:
    You begged so breathlessly to bring me near
    To hear my voice and see my face as well;
    I bow before your strong compulsive spell,
    And here I am!—What childish fear
    Besets you, superman! Where is the soul that cried?   490
    Where is the heart that made and bore a world inside
    Itself and sought amid its gleeful pride
    To be with spirits equal and allied?
    Where are you, Faust, whose voice called out to me,
    Who forced yourself on me so urgently?
    Are you the one who, having felt my breath,
    Now tremble to your being's depth,
    A terrified and cringing worm?

FAUST:
    Shall I give way before you, thing of flame?
    I am your equal. Faust is my name!   500

SPIRIT:
    In tides of life, in action's storm
    I surge as a wave,
    Swaying ceaselessly;
    Birth and the grave,
    An endless sea,
    A changeful flowing,
    A life all glowing:

I work in the hum of the loom of time
Weaving the living raiment of godhead sublime.
FAUST:
    O you who roam the world from end to end,   510
    Restless Spirit, I feel so close to you!
SPIRIT:
    You are like the spirit you comprehend,
    Not me!

                        [Disappears.]

FAUST [*overwhelmed*]:
    Not you?
    Whom then?
    I, image of the godhead!
    Not even rank with you!

                        [A knock.]

    God's death! I know who's there—my famulus[4]—
    This puts an end to my great joy!
    To think that dry-bones should destroy   520
    The fullness of these visions thus!
          [Enter WAGNER *in a dressing gown and nightcap, a*
          lamp in his hand. FAUST *turns around impatiently.]*

WAGNER:
    Excuse me! I heard you declaiming;
    It surely was a Grecian tragedy?
    There I would like some more proficiency,
    Today it gets so much acclaiming.
    I've sometimes heard it said a preacher
    Could profit with an actor for a teacher.
FAUST:
    Yes, if the preacher is an actor too,
    As may on some occasions be the case.
WAGNER:
    Oh, cooped up in one's museum all year through   530
    And hardly seeing folks except on holidays,
    Hardly by telescope, how can one find
    Persuasive skills wherewith to guide mankind?
FAUST:
    Unless you feel it you will not succeed;
    Unless up from your soul it wells
    And all your listeners' hearts compels
    By utmost satisfaction of a need,
    You'll always fail. With paste and glue,
    By grinding others' feasts for hash,
    By blowing your small flame up too   540
    Above your paltry pile of ash,
    High praise you'll get in apes' and children's sight,
    If that's what suits your hankering—
    But heart with heart you never will unite
    If from your heart it does not spring.

---

[4]A graduate assistant to a professor.

WAGNER:
> Delivery makes the speaker's real success,
> And that's just where I feel my backwardness.

FAUST:
> Try for an honest win! Why rail
> Like any bell-loud fool there is?
> Good sense and reason will prevail   550
> Without a lot of artifice.
> If you have serious things to say,
> Why hunt for words out of your way?
> Your flashy speeches on which you have pinned
> The frilly cutouts of men's artistry
> Are unrefreshing as the misty wind
> That sighs through withered leaves autumnally!

WAGNER:
> Oh Lord! How long is art,
> How short our life! And ever
> Amid my work and critical endeavor   560
> Despair besets my head and heart.
> How difficult the means are to come by
> That get one back up to the source,
> And then before one finishes mid-course,
> Poor devil, one must up and die.

FAUST:
> Is that the sacred font, a parchment roll,
> From which a drink will sate your thirst forever?
> Refreshment will delight you never
> Unless it surges up from your own soul.

WAGNER:
> But what delight there is in pages   570
> That lead us to the spirit of the ages!
> In seeing how before us wise men thought
> And how far glorious progress has been brought.

FAUST:
> O yes, up to the furthest star!
> My friend, the eras and past ages are
> For us a book with seven seals.[5]
> What you the spirit of the ages call
> Is only those men's spirits after all
> Held as a mirror that reveals
> The times. They're often just a source of gloom!   580
> You take one look at them and run away.
> A trash can and a littered storage room,
> At best a plot for some heroic play
> With excellent pragmatic saws
> That come resoundingly from puppets' jaws.

WAGNER:
> But then the world! The mind and heart of man!
> To learn about those things is our whole aim.

---

[5]See Revelation 5:1.

FAUST:

Yes, call it learning if you can!
But who dares call a child by its right name?
The few who such things ever learned,
Who foolishly their brimming hearts unsealed   590
And to the mob their feelings and their thoughts revealed,
Were in all ages crucified or burned.
But it is late into the night, my friend,
We must break off now for the present.

WAGNER:

I would have liked to stay awake and spend
The time in talk so learned and so pleasant.
But since tomorrow will be Easter Day,
I'll ask some further questions if I may.
I have industriously pursued my studying;   600
I know a lot, but would like to know everything.

[*Exit.*]

FAUST [*alone*]:

Why hope does not abandon all such brains
That cling forever to such shallow stuff!
They dig for treasure and are glad enough
To turn up angleworms for all their pains!
   May such a human voice presume to speak
Where spirits closed around me in full ranks?
And yet for this one time I give you thanks,
Of all earth's sons the poorest and most weak.
You pulled me back from the despair and panic   610
That threatened to destroy my very mind.
That vision loomed so vast and so titanic
That I felt dwarfed and of the dwarfish kind.
   I, image of the godhead, who supposed
Myself so near eternal verity,
Who reveled in celestial clarity,
My earthly substance quite deposed,
I, more than cherub, whose free strength presumed
To flow through Nature's veins, myself creating,
Thereby in godlike life participating,   620
How I must pay for my expostulating!
There by a word of thunder I was consumed!
   Your equal I dare not pretend to be;
If I had power to make you come to me,
I did not have the power to make you stay.
In that brief moment's ecstasy
I felt so small and yet so great;
You thrust me backwards cruelly
To my uncertain human fate.
Who will instruct me? What must I not do?   630
Should I give every impulse play?
Alas, our very actions, like our sorrows too,
Build obstacles in our life's way.
   On the most glorious things mind can conceive
Things strange and ever stranger force intrusion;

Once we the good things of this world achieve,
We term the better things cheat and delusion.
The noble feelings that conferred our life
Are paralyzed amid our earthly strife.
    If Fantasy once soared through endless space   640
And hopefully aspired to the sublime,
She is content now with a little place
When joys have foundered in the gulf of time.
Deep down within the heart Care builds her nest
And causing hidden pain she broods,
And brooding restlessly she troubles joy and rest;
Assuming ever different masks and moods,
She may appear as house and home, as child, as wife,
As poison, dagger, flood, or fire;
You dread what never does transpire,   650
And what you never lose you grieve for all your life.
    I am not like the gods! Too sharp I feel that thrust!
I am more like the worm that burrows in the dust,
That living there and finding sustenance
Is crushed beneath a passing foot by chance.
    Is all of this not dust that these walls hold
Upon their hundred shelves oppressing me?
The rubbish which with nonsense thousandfold
Confines me in this world of moths distressfully?
Should I find *here* the things I need?   660
When in perhaps a thousand books I read
That men have been tormented everywhere,
Though one may have been happy here and there?—
What is your grinning message, hollow skull,
But that your brain, like mine, once sought the day
In all its lightness, but amid the twilight dull,
Lusting for truth, went miserably astray?
And all you instruments make fun of me
With wheel and cog and drum and block:
I stood before the door, you should have been the key;   670
Your wards are intricate but do not turn the lock.
Mysterious in broad daylight,
Nature's veil can not be filched by you,
And what she keeps back from your prying spirit's sight
You will not wrest from her by lever or by screw.
You old contrivances unused by me,
You served my father's needs, hence here you stay.
You, ancient scroll, have blackened steadily
As long as dull lamps on this desk have smoked away.
Better if I had squandered my small estate   680
Than sweat and by that little be oppressed!
Whatever you inherit from your late
Forebears, see that it is possessed.
Things unused are a burden of great weight;
The hour can use what it alone creates, at best.
    But why does my gaze fix on that spot over there?
Is that small bottle then a magnet to my eyes?

Why is all suddenly so bright and fair
As when in a dark wood clear moonlight round us lies?
    Rare phial, I salute you as I draw   690
You down with reverence and with awe.
In you I honor human skill and art.
You essence of all lovely slumber-flowers,
You extract of all subtle deadly powers,
Unto your master now your grace impart!
I see you, and my suffering is eased,
I clasp you, and my strugglings have ceased,
The flood tide of my spirit ebbs away.
To open seas I am shown forth by signs,
Before my feet the mirror-water shines,   700
And I am lured to new shores by new day.
    A fiery chariot comes on airy pinions
Down toward me! I feel ready now and free
To rise by new paths unto aether's wide dominions,
To newer spheres of pure activity.
This higher life! This godlike ecstasy!
And you, but now a worm, have you acquired such worth?
Yes, only turn your back decisively
Upon the lovely sun of earth!
By your presumptuous will, fling wide the portals   710
Past which each man would rather slink away.
Now is the time to prove by deeds that mortals
Yield not to gods in dignity's array:
To shrink not back from that dark cavern where
Imagination sees itself to torment damned,
To press on toward that thoroughfare
Around whose narrow mouth all hell is spanned:
To take that step with cheer, to force egress—
Though at the risk of passing into nothingness.
    Come down, you glass of crystal purity,   720
Come forth out of your ancient case to me
Who have not thought of you these many years.
You used to gleam amid my father's feasts
And used to gladden earnest guests
As you were passed from hand to hand with cheers.
Your gorgeous braid of pictures deftly twined,
The drinker's pledge to tell of them in rhyme
And drain your hollow rondure at one time,
These bring back many youthful nights to mind;
I shall not this time pass you to a neighbor,   730
To prove my wit upon your art I shall not labor;
Here is a juice that makes one drunk with no delay.
Its brownish liquid streams and fills your hollow.
This final drink which now shall follow,
Which I prepared and which I choose to swallow,
Be it a festive high salute to coming day!
                 [*He lifts the glass to his lips.*]
               [*A peal of bells and choral song.*]

CHORUS OF ANGELS:
> Christ is arisen!
> Joy to the mortal
> Whom the pernicious
> Lingering, inherited   740
> Dearths encompassed.

FAUST:
> What bright clear tone, what whirring drone profound
> Makes me put this glass from my lips away?
> Do you deep bells already sound
> The solemn first hour of the Easter Day?
> Do you choirs sing the song that once such comfort gave
> When angels sang it by the darkness of a grave
> Assuring a new covenant that day?

CHORUS OF WOMEN:
> With spices enbalmed
> Here we had carried Him,   750
> We, His devoted,
> Here we had buried Him;
> With winding cloths
> Cleanly we wrapped Him;
> But, alas, we find
> Christ is not here.

CHORUS OF ANGELS:
> Christ is arisen!
> Blessed the loving
> Who stood the troubling,
> Stood the healing,   760
> Chastening test.

FAUST:
> Why seek here in the dust for me,
> You heavenly tones so mighty and so mild?
> Ring out around where gentle souls may be.
> I hear your tidings but I lack for faith,
> And Miracle is Faith's most favored child.
> As high as to those spheres I dare not soar
> Whence sound these tidings of great joy;
> Yet by these sounds, familiar since I was a boy,
> I now am summoned back to life once more.   770
> Once there would downward rush to me the kiss
> Of heavenly love in solemn Sabbath hour;
> Then plenitude of bell tones rang with mystic power
> And prayer had the intensity of bliss;
> Past comprehension sweet, a yearning
> Drove me to wander field and forest where
> Amid a thousand hot tears burning
> I felt a world arise which was most fair.
> The merry games of youth are summoned by that song,
> And free delight of springtime festival;   780
> And by that memory with childlike feeling strong
> I am kept from this final step of all.

Sing on, sweet songs, in that celestial strain!
A teardrop falls, the earth has me again!
CHORUS OF DISCIPLES:
  If from the dead
  He has ascended,
  Living, sublime,
  Glorious on high,
  If He in His growth
  Nears creative joy,   790
  We, alas, are still here
  On the bosom of earth.
  He has left His own
  Behind here to languish;
  Master, we mourn
  Thy happiness.
CHORUS OF ANGELS:
  Christ is arisen
  From the womb of decay;
  Bonds that imprison
  You, rend gladsome away!   800
  For you as you praise Him,
  Proving your love,
  Fraternally sharing,
  Preaching and faring,
  Rapture proclaiming,
  For you the Master is near,
  For you He is here.

Outside the City Gate

All sorts of people coming out for a walk.

SEVERAL APPRENTICES:
  But why go up the hill?
OTHERS:
  We're going to the Hunting Lodge up there.
THE FIRST ONES:
  We'd rather walk out to the Mill.   810
ONE APPRENTICE:
  I'd suggest you go to the Reservoir.
THE SECOND:
  It's not a pleasant walk, you know.
OTHERS:
  How about you?
A THIRD:
           I'll go where the others go.
A FOURTH:
  Come on to Burgdorf! There you're sure to find good cheer,
  The prettiest girls and also first-rate beer,
  And the best fights you'll ever face.

A FIFTH:
>You glutton, do you itch to go
>For your third drubbing in a row?
>I have a horror of that place.

SERVING GIRL:
>No, no! I'm going back now, if you please.   820

ANOTHER:
>We'll surely find him standing by those poplar trees.

THE FIRST GIRL:
>For me that's no great lucky chance;
>He'll walk at your side and he'll dance
>With none but you upon the lea.
>What good will your fun be to me?

THE OTHER GIRL:
>He won't be there alone today; he said
>He'd bring along the curlyhead.

SCHOLAR:
>Damn! How those lusty wenches hit their stride!
>Brother, come on! We'll walk it at their side.
>Strong beer, tobacco with a bite,   830
>A girl decked in her best, just suit my appetite.

GIRL OF THE MIDDLE CLASS:
>Just see those handsome boys! It certainly
>Is just a shame and a disgrace;
>They could enjoy the very best society,
>And after serving girls they chase.

SECOND SCHOLAR [*to the* FIRST]:
>Don't go so fast! Behind us are two more,
>Both very nicely dressed;
>One is my neighbor from next door
>In whom I take an interest.
>They walk demurely, but you'll see   840
>How they will overtake us finally.

THE FIRST:
>No, Brother, I don't like things in my way.
>Quick! Let's not lose these wildfowl on our chase.
>The hand that wields the broom on Saturday
>On Sunday will provide the best embrace.

CITIZEN:
>No, this new burgomaster, I don't care for him,
>And now he's in, he daily gets more grim.
>And for the city, what's he done?
>Don't things get worse from day to day?
>More rules than ever to obey,   850
>And taxes worse than any yet, bar none.

BEGGAR [*sings*]:
>Kind gentlemen and ladies fair,
>So rosy-cheeked and gay of dress,
>Be good enough to hear my prayer,
>Relieve my want and my distress.
>Let me not vainly tune my lay.

Glad is the giver and only he.
Now that all men keep holiday,
Be there a harvest day for me.

ANOTHER CITIZEN:

There's nothing better for Sunday or a holiday   860
Than talk about war and war's alarms,
When off in Turkey people up in arms
Are battling in a far-off fray.
You sip your glass, stand by the window side,
And down the river watch the painted vessels glide,
Then come home in the evening all at ease,
Blessing peace and the times of peace.

THIRD CITIZEN:

Yes, neighbor, that's the way I like it too:
Let them beat out each other's brains,
Turn everything up wrong-end-to,   870
So long as here at home our good old way remains.

OLD WOMAN [to the MIDDLE-CLASS GIRLS]:

Heyday! How smart! My young and pretty crew!
Now who could help but fall for you?—
But don't act quite so proud. You'll do!
And what you're after, I could help you to.

MIDDLE-CLASS GIRL:

Come, Agatha! I don't want to be seen
In public with such witches. It's quite true
My future lover last Saint Andrew's E'en
In flesh and blood she let me view[6]—

THE OTHER GIRL:

She showed me mine too in her crystal glass,   880
A soldier type, with dashing friends behind him;
I look for him in every one I pass
And yet I just don't seem to find him.

SOLDIERS:

Castles and towers,
Ramparts so high,
Girls of disdainful
Scorn-casting eye,
I'd like to win!
Keen is the contest,
Grand is the pay!   890
    We'll let the trumpets
Sound out the call,
Whether to joy
Or to downfall.
There's an assault!
That is the life!
Maidens and castles
Surrender in strife.

---

[6]On November 30 Saint Andrew, the patron saint of the unmarried, offers visions of future lovers and spouses.

Keen is the contest,
Grand is the pay!   900
And then the soldiers
Go marching away.

[Enter FAUST and WAGNER.]

FAUST:
From ice are released the streams and brooks
At springtime's lovely, life-giving gaze;
Now hope smiles green down valley ways;
Old Winter feebly flees to nooks
Of rugged hills, and as he hies
Casts backward from him in his flight
Impotent showers of gritty ice
In streaks over meadows newly green.   910
But the sun permits of nothing white,
Everything is growth and striving,
All things are in colors reviving,
And lack of flowers in the countryside
By gay-clad humans is supplied.
Turn and from these heights look down
And backwards yonder toward the town.
From the hollow, gloomy gate
Streams a throng in motley array.
All want to sun themselves today.   920
The Lord's resurrection they celebrate
For they are themselves new risen from tombs:
From squalid houses' dingy rooms,
From tradesman's and apprentice' chains,
From crushing streets and choking lanes,
From roof's and gable's oppressive mass,
From their churches' everlasting night,
They are all brought forth into the light.
See now, just see how swiftly they pass
And scatter to fields' and gardens' grass   930
And how so many merry boats
The river's length and breadth there floats,
How almost sinking with its load
That last barque pushes from the quay.
From even the hillside's distant road
Bright costumes glimmer colorfully.
Sounds of village mirth arise,
Here is the people's true paradise.
Both great and small send up a cheer:
"Here I am human, I can *be* human here!"   940

WAGNER:
Doctor, to take a walk with you
Is an honor and a gain, of course,
But come here alone, that I'd never do,
Because I am a foe of all things coarse.
This fiddling, shouting, bowling, I detest
And all that with it goes along;
They rage as if by fiends possessed

And call it pleasure, call it song!
        [Peasants under the linden tree. Dance and song.]
The shepherd for the dance got dressed
In wreath and bows and fancy vest,
And bravely did he show.   950
Beneath the linden lass and lad
Were dancing round and round like mad.
Juchhe! Juchhe!
Juchheisa! Heisa! He!
So went the fiddlebow.
    In through the crowd he pushed in haste
And jostled one girl in the waist
All with his sharp elbow.
The buxom lass, she turned her head,   960
"Well, that was stupid, now!" she said.
Juchhe! Juchhe!
Juchheisa! Heisa! He!
"Don't be so rude, fine fellow!"
    The ring spun round with all its might,
They danced to left, they danced to right,
And see the coattails go!
And they got red, and they got warm,
And breathless waited arm in arm,
Juchhe! Juchhe!
Juchheisa! Heisa! He!   970
A hip against an elbow.
    "Don't be so free! How many a maid
Has been betrothed and been betrayed
By carrying on just so!"
And yet he coaxed her to one side,
And from the linden far and wide
Juchhe! Juchhe!
Juchheisa! Heisa! He!
Rang shout and fiddlebow.   980
OLD PEASANT:
    Doctor, it's really nice of you
Not to shun our mirth today,
And such a learnèd master too,
To mingle with the folk this way.
Therefore accept our finest stein
Filled with cool drink and let me first
Present it with this wish of mine:
May it not only quench your thirst—
May all its count of drops be added to
The sum of days that are allotted you.   990
FAUST:
    I take the cooling drink you offer me
And wish you thanks and all prosperity.
          [The people gather around in a circle.]
OLD PEASANT:
    Indeed it was most kind of you

On this glad day to come here thus,
For in the evil days gone by
You proved a friend to all of us.
Many a man is here alive
Because your father in the past
Saved him from raging fever's fury
When he had stemmed the plague at last.   1000
And as a young man you went too
Among the houses of the pest;
Many a corpse they carried out
But you came healthy from the test.
You bore up under trials severe;
The Helper yonder helped the helper here.

ALL:
Good health attend the proven man,
Long may he help, as help he can!

FAUST:
Bow to Him yonder who provides
His help and teaches help besides.   1010
[*He walks on with* WAGNER.]

WAGNER:
What feelings must be yours, O noble man,
Before the veneration of this crowd!
O fortunate indeed is one who can
So profit from the gifts with which he is endowed!
The fathers show you to their sons,
Each asks and pushes in and runs,
The fiddle stops, the dancer waits,
They stand in rows where you pass by,
And all their caps go flying high:
A little more and they would bend the knee   1020
As if there passed the Venerabile.

FAUST:
Only a few steps more now up to yonder stone
And we shall rest from our long walk. Up there
I often used to sit and brood alone
And rack myself with fasting and with prayer.
Then rich in hope, in faith secure,
By wringing of hands, by tears and sighs,
I sought the plague's end to assure
By forcing the Lord of the skies.
Praise sounds like mockery on the people's part.   1030
If you could only read within my heart
How little father and son
Were worthy of the fame they won!
My father was a man of honor but obscure
Who over Nature and her holy spheres would brood
In his own way and with capricious mood,
Though wholly upright, to be sure.
With other adepts of the art he locked
Himself in his black kitchen and from lists

Of endless recipes sought to concoct   1040
A blend of the antagonists.[7]
There a Red Lion—a wooer to aspire—
Was in a warm bath with the Lily wed,
And both were then tormented over open fire
From one into the other bridal bed.
If the Young Queen was then espied
In rainbow hues within the flask,
There was our medicine; the patients died,
And "Who got well?" none thought to ask.
Thus we with hellish tonics wrought more ills   1050
Among these valleys and these hills,
And raged more fiercely, than the pest.
I gave the poison out to thousands with my hand;
They withered, and I have to stand
And hear the ruthless killers blessed.

WAGNER:
How can such things make you downcast?
Has not a good man done sufficient
In being conscientious and proficient
At skills transmitted from the past?
If you respect your father in your youth,   1060
You will receive his fund of knowledge whole;
If as a man you swell the store of truth,
Your son can then achieve a higher goal.

FAUST:
O happy he who still can hope
To rise out of the sea of errors here!
What one most needs to know exceeds his scope,
And what one knows is useless and unclear.
But let us not spoil hours that are so fair
With these dark melancholy thoughts of mine!
See how beneath the sunset air   1070
The green-girt cottages all shine.
The sun moves on, the day has spent its force,
Yonder it speeds, new day eliciting.
O that I am swept upward on no wing
To follow it forever in its course!
Then I would see by deathless evening rays
The silent world beneath my feet,
All valleys calmed, all mountaintops ablaze,
And silver brooks with golden rivers meet.
No mountains then would block my godlike flight   1080
For all the chasms gashed across their ways;
And soon the sea with its warmed bays
Would open to my wondering sight.
But now the goddess seems to sink down finally;
But a new impulse wakes in me,

---

[7]Using actual sixteenth-century terms, Goethe describes the manufacture of "the Philosopher's Stone" in an alchemist's laboratory ("black kitchen").

I hasten forth to drink her everlasting light,
With day in front of me and at my back the night,
With waves down under me and over me the sky.
A glorious dream, dreamed while the day declined.
Alas, that to the pinions of the mind   1090
No wing corporeal is joined as their ally.
And yet inborn in all our race
Is impulse upward, forward, and along,
When overhead and lost in azure space
The lark pours forth its trilling song,
When over jagged pine tree heights
The full-spread eagle wheels its flights,
And when across the seas and plains
Onward press the homing cranes.

WAGNER:
I have had moody hours of my own,   1100
But such an impulse I have never known.
The spectacle of woods and fields soon cloys,
I'll never envy birds their pinionage;
But how we *are* borne on by mental joys
From book to book, from page to page!
How sweet and fair the winter nights become,
A blessed life glows warm in every limb,
And oh! if one unrolls a noble parchment tome,
The whole of heaven then comes down to him.

FAUST:
By one impulse alone are you possessed,   1110
O may you never know the other!
Two souls abide, alas, within my breast,
And each one seeks for riddance from the other.
The one clings with a dogged love and lust
With clutching parts unto this present world,
The other surges fiercely from the dust
Unto sublime ancestral fields.
If there are spirits in the air
Between the earth and heaven holding sway,
Descend out of your golden fragrance there   1120
And to new life of many hues sweep me away!
Yes, if a magic mantle were but mine,
And if to far-off lands it bore me,
Not for all costly raiment placed before me
Would I exchange it; kings' cloaks I would decline!

WAGNER:
Do not invoke that well-known troop
That stream above us in the murky air,
Who from all quarters down on mankind swoop
And bring the thousand perils they prepare.
With whetted spirit fangs down from the north   1130
They pitch upon you with their arrowy tongues;
Out of the morning's east they issue forth
To prey with parching breath upon your lungs;
And if the south up from the desert drives

Those which heap fire on fire upon your brain,
The west brings on the swarm that first revives
Then drowns you as it drowns the field and plain.
They listen eagerly, on mischief bent,
And to deceive us, willingly comply,
They often pose as being heaven sent   1140
And lisp like angels when they lie.
But let us go. The world has all turned grey,
The air is chill, mist closes out the day.
With nightfall one enjoys a room.—
Why do you stand and stare with wondering gaze?
What so arrests you out there in the gloom?

FAUST:
Do you see that black dog that through the stubble strays?

WAGNER:
He looks quite unremarkable to me.

FAUST:
Look close! What do you take the beast to be?

WAGNER:
A poodle, searching with his natural bent   1150
And snuffing for his master's scent.

FAUST:
Do you see how he spirals round us, snail-
shell-wise, and ever closer on our trail?
And if I'm not mistaken, he lays welts
Of fire behind him in his wake.

WAGNER:
I see a plain black poodle, nothing else;
Your eyes must be the cause of some mistake.

FAUST:
I seem to see deft snares of magic laid
For future bondage round our feet somehow.

WAGNER:
I see him run about uncertain and afraid   1160
Because he sees two strangers, not his master now.

FAUST:
The circle narrows, he is near!

WAGNER:
You see! It's just a dog, no phantom here.
He growls, he doubts, lies belly-flat and all,
And wags his tail. All doggish protocol.

FAUST:
Come here! Come join our company!

WAGNER:
He's just a foolish pup. You see?
You stop, and he will wait for you,
You speak to him, and he'll jump up on you,
Lose something, and he'll fetch it quick,   1170
Or go in water for a stick.

FAUST:
You must be right, I see there's not a trace
Of spirits. It's his training he displays.

WAGNER:
> A sage himself will often find
> He likes a dog that's trained to mind.
> Yes, he deserves your favor totally,
> A model scholar of the students, he.
>> [*They go in through the city gate.*]

Study Room

FAUST *entering with the poodle.*

FAUST:
> From field and meadow I withdraw
> Which deepest darkness now bedecks,
> With holy and foreboding awe
> The better soul within us wakes.   1180
> Asleep now are my wild desires,
> My vehement activity;
> The love of mankind now aspires,
> The love of God aspires in me.
>> Be quiet, poodle! Why should you romp and rove?
> What are you snuffing there at the sill?
> Go and lie down behind the stove,
> I'll give you my best pillow if you're still.
> Out there on the hill-road back to town   1190
> You amused us by running and frisking your best;
> Now accept your keep from me; lie down
> And be a welcome and quiet guest.
>> Ah, when in our close cell by night
> The lamp burns with a friendly cheer,
> Then deep within us all grows bright
> And hearts that know themselves grow clear.
> Reason begins once more to speak
> And hope begins to bloom again,
> The brooks of life we yearn to seek   1200
> And to life's source, ah! to attain.
>> Stop growling, poodle! With the sacred tones that rise
> And now my total soul embrace,
> Your animal noise is out of place.
> We are accustomed to having men despise
> What they do not understand;
> The good and the beautiful they misprize,
> Finding it cumbersome, they scowl and growl;
> Must a dog, like men, set up a howl?
>> But alas! with the best of will I feel no more   1210
> Contentment welling up from my heart's core.
> Why must the stream so soon run dry
> And we again here thirsting lie?
> These things experiences familiarize.
> But this lack can find compensation,
> The supernatural we learn to prize,
> And then we long for revelation,

Which nowhere burns more nobly or more bright
Than here in the New Testament. Tonight
An impulse urges me to reach   1220
Out for this basic text and with sincere
Emotion make its holy meaning clear
Within my own beloved German speech.

[*He opens a volume and sets about it.*]

It says: "In the beginning was the *Word*."[8]
Already I am stuck! And who will help afford?
Mere word I cannot possibly so prize,
I must translate it otherwise.
Now if the Spirit lends me proper light,
"In the beginning was the *Mind*" would be more nearly right.
Consider that first line with care,   1230
The pen must not be overhasty there!
Can it be mind that makes and shapes all things?
It should read: "In the beginning was the *Power*."
But even as I write down this word too,
Something warns me that it will not do.
Now suddenly the Spirit prompts me in my need,
I confidently write: "In the beginning was the *Deed!*"
    If I'm to share this room with you,
Poodle, that howling must be curbed.
And stop that barking too!   1240
I cannot be disturbed
By one who raises such a din.
One of us must give in
And leave this cell we're in.
I hate to drive you out of here,
But the door is open, the way is clear.
But what is this I see?
Can such things happen naturally?
Is this reality or fraud?
My poodle grows both long and broad!   1250
He rises up with might;
No dog's shape this! This can't be right!
What phantom have I harbored thus?
He's like a hippopotamus
With fiery eyes and ghastly teeth.
O, I see what's beneath!
For such a mongrel of hell
The Key of Solomon works well.[9]

SPIRITS [*in the corridor*]:

Captive inside there is one of us,
Stay out here, follow him none of us.   1260
Like a fox in an iron snare
A lynx of hell is cornered in there.
But take heed!

---

[8]John 1:1.

[9]*Solomon's Key*, or the *Clavicula Salomonis*, was a standard book used by magicians in the Middle Ages.
It gave the rules for controlling spirits.

Hover to, hover fro,
Above, below,
And pretty soon he'll be freed.
If you can help him in aught
Don't leave him caught.
Many a turn he has done
Helping us every one.   1270

FAUST:

To deal with the beast before
Me, I'll use the spell of the four:[10]
  Salamander shall kindle,
Undine shall coil,
Sylph shall dwindle,
Kobold shall toil.
  Lacking the lore
Of the elements four,
Not knowing aright
Their use and might,   1280
None shall be lord
Of the spirit horde.
  Vanish in flame,
Salamander!
Together rush and stream,
Undine!
In meteor glory gleam,
Sylph!
Bring help to the house,
Incubus! Incubus!   1290
Step forth and make an ending! Thus!
  None of the four
Lurks in the beast.
He lies and grins at me as before,
I have not harmed him in the least.
You'll hear me tell
A stronger spell.
  Do you, fellow, live
As hell's fugitive?
See this sign now[11]   1300
To which they bow,
The black hordes of hell!
  With hair abristle he starts to swell.
  Forfeiter of bliss,
Can you read this?
The never-created
Of name unstated,
Diffused through all heavens' expanse,
Transpierced by the infamous lance?

---

[10] The spirits of the four elements: Fire, Water, Air, and Earth.

[11] The sign INRI or JNRJ, abbreviation for "Jesus the Nazarene, King of the Jews" (*Jesus Nazarenus Rex Judaeorum*), which Pilate had inscribed on the cross that held the body of Jesus at the crucifixion (John 19:19). Faust apparently holds a crucifix over the shape-shifting spirit-beast.

Back of the stove he flees from my spells,   1310
There like an elephant he swells,
He fills the room entire,
He melts like a mist of sleet.
Rise ceilingwards no higher!
Fall down at your master's feet.
You see that mine is no idle threat.
With sacred flame I will scorch you yet.
Await not the might
Of the triply burning light!¹²
Await not the sight   1320
Of my arts in their fullest measure!

      [As the mist falls away, MEPHISTOPHELES *steps forth*
      from behind the stove, dressed as a traveling scholar.]

MEPHISTOPHELES:
Why all the fuss? What is the gentleman's pleasure?
FAUST:
So this was what was in the cur!
A traveling scholar? That's the best joke I've heard yet.
MEPHISTOPHELES:
I salute you, learned Sir.
You had me in a mighty sweat.
FAUST:
What is your name?
MEPHISTOPHELES:
          For one so disesteeming
The word, the question seems so small to me,
And for a man disdainful of all seeming,
Who searches only for reality.   1330
FAUST:
With gentlemen like you, their nature is deduced
Quite often from the name that's used,
As all too patently applies
When you are named Corrupter, Liar, God of Flies.¹³
All right, who are you then?
MEPHISTOPHELES:
          Part of that Force which would
Do evil ever yet forever works the good.
FAUST:
What sense is there beneath that riddling guise?
MEPHISTOPHELES:
I am the Spirit that constantly denies!
And rightly so; for everything that's ever brought
To life deserves to come to naught.   1340
Better if nothing ever came to be.
Thus all that you call sin, you see,
And havoc—evil, in short—is meant
To be my proper element.

---

¹²The "sign" of the Trinity.
¹³The "Baal-Zebub the god of Ekron" of II Kings 1:2, usually etymologized as "the god of flies" or
"the fly-god."

FAUST:
> You call yourself a part, yet stand quite whole before me there?

MEPHISTOPHELES:
> It is the modest truth that I declare.
> Now folly's little microcosm, man,
> Boasts *himself* whole as often as he can. . . .
> I am part of the part which once was absolute,
> Part of the Darkness which gave birth to Light,   1350
> The haughty Light, which now seeks to dispute
> The ancient rank and range of Mother Night,
> But unsuccessfully, because, try as it will,
> It is stuck fast to bodies still.
> It streams from bodies, bodies it makes fair,
> A body hinders its progression; thus I hope
> It won't be long before its scope
> Will in the bodies' ruination share.

FAUST:
> I see your fine objectives now!
> Wholesale annihilation fails somehow,   1360
> So you go at it one by one.

MEPHISTOPHELES:
> I don't get far, when all is said and done.
> The thing opposed to Nothingness,
> This stupid earth, this Somethingness,
> For all that I have undertaken
> Against it, still remains unshaken;
> In spite of tempest, earthquake, flood, and flame
> The earth and ocean calmly stay the same.
> And as for that damned stuff, the brood of beasts and man,
> With them there's nothing I can do.   1370
> To think how many I have buried too!
> Fresh blood runs in their veins just as it always ran.
> And so it goes. Sometimes I could despair!
> In earth, in water, and in air
> A thousand growing things unfold,
> In dryness, wetness, warmth, and cold!
> Had I not specially reserved the flame,
> I wouldn't have a thing in my own name.

FAUST:
> So you shake your cold devil's fist
> Clenched in futile rage malign,   1380
> So you the endless Power resist,
> The creative, living, and benign!
> Some other goal had best be sought,
> Chaos' own fantastic son!

MEPHISTOPHELES:
> We really shall give this some thought
> And talk about it more anon.
> Right now, however, might I go?

FAUST:
> Why you should ask, I don't quite see.
> Now that we've made acquaintance, though,
> Come any time to visit me.   1390

Here is the window, there the doors,
The chimney too is practical.

MEPHISTOPHELES:

Must I confess? To leave this room of yours
There is a trifling obstacle.
The witch's foot[14] there on the sill—

FAUST:

The pentagram distresses you?
But tell me now, O son of hell,
If that prevents you, how did you get through?
Could such a spirit be so blind?

MEPHISTOPHELES:

Observe it carefully. It's ill designed.   1400
One point there, facing outward as it were,
Is just a bit disjoined, you see.

FAUST:

Now what a lucky chance for me!
And so you are my prisoner?
And all by merest accident!

MEPHISTOPHELES:

The poodle did not notice when in he went.
Things now take on a different shape:
The Devil's caught and can't escape.

FAUST:

But why not use the window to withdraw?

MEPHISTOPHELES:

With devils and with spirits it's a law: 1410
Where they slipped in, they must go out.
The first is up to us, the second leaves no doubt:
There we are slaves.

FAUST:

                              So hell has its own law?
I find that good, because a pact could then
Perhaps be worked out with you gentlemen?

MEPHISTOPHELES:

What once is promised, you will revel in,
No skimping and no spreading thin.
But such things can't be done so fast,
We'll speak of that when next we meet.
And now I beg you first and last   1420
To let me make my fair retreat.

FAUST:

Just for a single moment yet remain
And tell me of some pleasant news.

MEPHISTOPHELES:

No, let me go now! I'll come back again,
Then you can ask me all you choose.

FAUST:

I never had a plan so bold

---

[14]Another term for the pentagram, a symbol made up of interlocking triangles to form a five-pointed star used to ward off evil spirits.

As capturing you. You walked into the snare.
Whoever holds the Devil, let him hold!
A second time he will not have him there.

MEPHISTOPHELES:
I am quite ready, if you choose,   1430
To keep you company and stay,
But on condition that I use
My worthy skills to while the time away.

FAUST:
I'd like to see them, so feel free,
Just so the skills work pleasantly.

MEPHISTOPHELES:
Your senses will, my friend, gain more
In this hour than you've known before
In one whole year's monotony.
And what my dainty spirits sing you,
The lovely images they bring you   1440
Will be no empty magic play.
Your sense of smell shall be delighted,
Your sense of taste shall be excited,
And feelings will sweep you away.
No preparation shall we need;
We are assembled, so proceed!

SPIRITS:
Vanish, you gloomy
Vaultings above!
Lovelier hue
Of aether's blue   1450
Be shed in here!
O might the darkling
Clouds melt for once!
Stars begin sparkling;
Mellower suns
Shine now in here.
Sons of the air,
Of beauty rare,
Hover thronging,
Wafting in light.   1460
Ardent longing
Follows their flight.
Raiment in strands
Shed as streamer bands
Cover the lands,
Cover the groves
Where lovers vow,
Lost in reverie,
Lifelong loves.
Arbors on arbors!   1470
Lush greenery!
Masses of grapes
Tumble from vines
Into presses and vats,
Gush now as brooks

Of foaming wines,
Trickle as rills
Through gorges that wind,
Leaving the hills
Far behind,   1480
Widening to lakes
Around the abundance
Of verdant heights.
And then the birds
Drink delight,
Fly to the sun,
Fly to the bright
Islands that gleam
Drifting and glittering
Upon the stream;   1490
There we hear choirs
Of jubilant throngs,
See them on meadows,
At dances and songs,
Disporting free
In festivity;
Climbing, some,
Over the peaks,
Skimming, some,
Over the lakes,
Still others fly;   1500
All toward the high
Joy of existence,
All toward the distance
Of loving stars.

MEPHISTOPHELES:
He is asleep. Well done, my dainty, airy youngsters!
You lulled him loyally, my songsters!
I am much in your debt for such a concert.
You are not yet the man to hold the Devil fast!
Around him your sweet dream illusions cast   1510
And steep him in a sea of fancy;
But now I need a rat's tooth to divest
This threshold of its necromancy.
No lengthy incantation will be needed,
Here comes one rustling up, and my word will be heeded.
The Master of the rats and mice,
Of bedbugs, flies, and frogs and lice,
Commands you boldly to appear
And gnaw this carven threshold clear
Where he has daubed a jot of oil—   1520
Ah, there you scamper up to toil!
Get right to work! I'm hemmed in by the wedge
That's right there on the outer edge.
Just one more bite and then it's done.—
Now, till we meet again, Faustus, dream on!

FAUST [*waking*]:
Have I been once again betrayed?

The spirit throng has fled so utterly
That I but dreamed the Devil came and stayed
And that a poodle got away from me?

Study Room (II)

FAUST:
A knock? Come in! Who now comes bothering me?   1530
MEPHISTOPHELES:
It's I.
FAUST:
Come in!
MEPHISTOPHELES:
A third call there must be.
FAUST:
Come in, then!
MEPHISTOPHELES:
That's the way I like to hear you.
We shall, I trust, get on quite well,
For I have come here to dispel
Your moods, and as a noble squire be near you,
Clad all in scarlet and gold braid,
With my short cape of stiff silk made,
A rooster feather on my hat,
A long sharp rapier at my side,
And I advise you to provide   1540
Yourself a costume just like that,
So you, untrammeled and set free,
Can find out just what life can be.
FAUST:
No matter what might be my own attire,
I would feel life cramped anyway.
I am too old merely to play,
Too young to be without desire.
What can the world give me? Renounce,
Renounce shalt thou, thou shalt renounce!
That is the everlasting song   1550
Dinned in our ears throughout the course
Of all our lives, which all life long
Each hour sings until it's hoarse.
Mornings I wake with horror and could weep
Hot tears at seeing the new sun
Which will not grant me in its sweep
Fulfillment of a single wish, not one,
Which mars anticipated joys
Themselves with willful captiousness
And with a thousand petty frets destroys   1560
My eager heart's creativeness.
At nightfall I must lie down ill at ease
Upon my couch of misery where
There will be neither rest nor peace,
Wild dreams will terrify me even there.
The god that in my heart abides

Can stir my soul's profoundest springs;
He over all my energies presides
But cannot alter outward things.
Existence is a weight by which I am oppressed,
With death desired, life something to detest.

MEPHISTOPHELES:
And yet Death never is a wholly welcome guest.

FAUST:
O happy he around whose brow Death winds
The blood-stained wreath in victory's radiance,
Or he whom in a girl's embrace Death finds
After the hectic whirling of the dance!
O, had I in my exultation sunk
Down dead before the lofty Spirit's power!

MEPHISTOPHELES:
And yet a brownish potion was not drunk
By someone on a certain midnight hour.

FAUST:
Spying, it seems, amuses you.

MEPHISTOPHELES:
                              I dare
Not claim omniscience, but of much I am aware.

FAUST:
If from that harrowing confusion
A sweet familiar tone drew me away,
Belied me with a child's profusion
Of memories from a former day,
I now curse everything that holds the soul
Enchanted by the lures of sorcery
And charms it in this dreary hole
By sweet illusion and duplicity!
Cursed be the lofty self-opinion
With which the mind itself deludes!
Cursed be phenomena's dominion
Which on our senses so intrudes!
Cursed be the cheating dream obsessions
With name and fame that have us so beguiled!
Cursed be what we have deemed possessions:
Servant and plow, and wife and child!
Cursed be old Mammon when with treasure
He lures to deeds adventurous
Or when for idleness and pleasure
He spreads the pillows soft for us!
Cursed be the nectar of the grape!
Cursed be love at its happiest!
And cursed be hope! And cursed be faith!
And cursed be patience more than all the rest!

CHORUS OF SPIRITS [invisible]:
Woe! Woe!
You have destroyed
The beauteous world
With mighty fist;

1570

1580

1590

1600

1610

It crumbles, it collapses!
A demigod has shattered it!
We carry
The fragments to the void,
We grieve
For beauty so destroyed.
More mightily,
Son of earth,
More splendidly
Bring it to birth,   1620
Rebuild it in the heart of you!
Begin a new
Life course
With senses clear,
And may new songs
Hail it with cheer!

MEPHISTOPHELES:
These are the minions
From my dominions.
Precociously wise,
Deeds and desires they now advise.   1630
Out of solitude
Where senses and saps are glued,
To the wide world's view
They lure and summon you.
Cease toying with your sorrow then,
Which tears your life as vulture-talons tear;
The worst of company makes you aware
You are a man with other men.
This does not indicate
That you're to run with the pack;   1640
I am not one of the great,
But if you want a track
Through life together with me,
I'll adapt myself quite willingly
To be yours right here and now.
I am your fellow,
If it suits you, to the grave,
I am your servant and your slave.

FAUST:
And what am I supposed to do for you?

MEPHISTOPHELES:
There's lots of time before that's due.   1650

FAUST:
No, no! The Devil is an egoist
And does not willingly assist
Another just for God's sake. I insist
You make all your conditions clear;
Such a slave is one to fear.

MEPHISTOPHELES:
I'll bind myself to be your servant *here*
And at your beck and call wait tirelessly,

If when there in the *yonder* we appear
You will perform the same for me.
FAUST:
 The yonder is of small concern.   1660
 Once you have smashed this world to pieces,
 The other one may come to be in turn.
 It is out of this earth that my joy springs
 And this sun shines upon my sufferings;
 Once free of them, this trouble ceases;
 Then come what may and as time brings.
 About all that I do not wish to hear,
 Whether in future there is hate and love
 And whether in that yonder sphere
 There is a new beneath and new above.   1670
MEPHISTOPHELES:
 In this mood you dare venture it. Just make
 The compact, and I then will undertake
 To turn my skills to joy. I'll give you more
 Than any man has ever seen before.
FAUST:
 Poor, sorry Devil, what could you deliver?
 Was human mind in lofty aspiration ever
 Comprehended by the likes of you?
 Do you have food that does not satisfy? Or do
 You have red gold that will run through
 The hand like quicksilver and away?   1680
 A game that none may win who play?
 A girl who in my very arms
 Will pledge love to my neighbor with her eyes?
 Or honor with its godlike charms
 Which like a shooting star flashes and dies?
 Show me the fruit that rots right on the tree,
 And trees that every day leaf out anew!
MEPHISTOPHELES:
 Such a demand does not daunt me,
 Such treasures I can furnish you.
 But still the time will come around, good friend, 1690
 When we shall want to relish things in peace.
FAUST:
 If ever I lie down upon a bed of ease,
 Then let that be my final end!
 If you can cozen me with lies
 Into a self-complacency,
 Or can beguile with pleasures you devise,
 Let that day be the last for me!
 This bet I offer!
MEPHISTOPHELES:
     Done!
FAUST:
     And I agree:
 If I to any moment say:
 Linger on! You are so fair!   1700

Put me in fetters straightaway,
Then I can die for all I care!
Then toll bells for my funeral,
Then of your service you are free,
The clock may stop, the clock hand fall,
And time be past and done for me!

MEPHISTOPHELES:

Consider well, we shall remember this.

FAUST:

And that would be quite right of you.
I have committed no presumptuousness.
I am a slave no matter what I do,   1710
Yours or another's, we may dismiss.

MEPHISTOPHELES:

I will begin right with your doctoral feast
And be your slave this very day.
For life and death's sake, though, just one thing, if I may:
Just write a line or two at least.

FAUST:

You ask for written forms, you pedant? Can
You never have known man, or known the word of man?
Is it not enough that by the word I gave
The die of all my days is finally cast?
Does not the world down all its rivers rave,   1720
And should a promise hold me fast?
But this illusion in our hearts is set
And who has ever wanted to uproot it yet?
Happy the man whose heart is true and pure,
No sacrifice he makes will he regret!
A parchment, though, with seal and signature,
That is a ghost at which all people shy.
The word is dead before the ink is dry
And wax and leather hold the mastery.
What, evil spirit, do you want from me?   1730
Bronze, marble, parchment, paper? And then
Am I to write with stylus, chisel, or a pen?
The choice is yours and wholly free.

MEPHISTOPHELES:

Why carry on so heatedly
And force your eloquence so high?
Just any little scrap will do;
You sign it with a drop of blood.

FAUST:

If that is satisfactory to you,
We'll let it stand at that absurdity.

MEPHISTOPHELES:

Blood is a juice of very special kind.   1740

FAUST:

I'll honor this pact, you need not be afraid!
The aim of all my strength and mind
Will be to keep this promise I have made.
I puffed myself up far too grand;

In your class I deserve to be.
The mighty Spirit spurned me and
Nature locks herself from me.
The thread of thought is snapped off short,
Knowledge I loathe of every sort.
Let us now sate our ardent passion   1750
In depths of sensuality!
Let miracles of every fashion
Be brought in veils of mystery!
Let us plunge in the flood of time and chance,
Into the tide of circumstance!
Let grief and gratification,
Success and frustration
Spell one another as they can;
Restless doing is the only way for man.
MEPHISTOPHELES:
There is no goal or limit set.   1760
Snatch tidbits as impulse prompts you to,
Take on the wing whatever you can get!
And may you digest what pleases you.
Just help yourself and don't be coy.
FAUST:
But I tell you there is no talk of joy.
I vow myself to frenzy, agonies of gratification,
Enamored hatred, quickening frustration.
Cured of the will to knowledge now, my mind
And heart shall be closed to no sorrow any more
And all that is the lot of human kind   1770
I want to feel down to my senses' core,
Grasp with my mind their worst things and their best,
Heap all their joys and troubles on my breast,
And thus my self to their selves' limits to extend,
And like them perish foundering at the end.
MEPHISTOPHELES:
Believe me, many a thousand year
I've chewed this rugged food, and I well know
That from the cradle to the bier
No man digests this ancient sourdough.
This whole, believe the likes of us,   1780
For deity alone was made.
He dwells in timeless radiance glorious,
Us he has relegated to the shade,
You, day and night alone can aid.
FAUST:
But I am set on it.
MEPHISTOPHELES:
                    Easy said!
There's just one thing that could go wrong:
Time is short and art is long;
You could, I think, be taught and led.
Choose a poet for your associate,
Let the gentleman's thoughts have their free bent   1790

To heap upon your reverend pate
All noble qualities he can invent:
The lion's nobility,
The fleetness of the hind,
The fiery blood of Italy,
The Northman's steadfast mind.
Have him for you the secret find
Of magnanimity and guile combined,
Then make you fall in love by plan
While youthful passions are in flame.   1800
I'd like myself to meet just such a man,
I'd give him "Sir Microcosm" for a name.

FAUST:
What am I then, if seeking to attain
That toward which all my senses strain,
The crown of mankind, is in vain?

MEPHISTOPHELES:
You're after all—just what you are.
Wear wigs of a million ringlets as you will,
Put ell-thick soles beneath your feet, and still
You will remain just what you are.

FAUST:
I feel that I have fruitlessly amassed   1810
All treasures of the human mind,
And now when I sit down at last
No fresh strength wells within my heart, I find;
I'm not one hair's breadth taller nor one whit
Closer to the infinite.

MEPHISTOPHELES:
These matters, my good Sir, you see
Much in the ordinary light;
We must proceed more cleverly
Before life's joys have taken flight.
What the Devil! You've got hands and feet,   1820
You've got a head, you've got a prat;
Are all the things that I find sweet
Less mine for all of that?
If I can buy six stallions, can
I not call their strength also mine?
I race along and am a proper man
As if their four-and-twenty legs were mine.
Come on, then! Let this brooding be!
And off into the world with me!
I tell you, any speculative fellow   1830
Is like a beast led round and round
By demons on a heath all dry and yellow
When on all sides lies good green pasture ground.

FAUST:
But how do we begin?

MEPHISTOPHELES:
First we will get away.
What kind of dungeon is this anyway?

What kind of life do you lead if
You bore yourself and bore the youngsters stiff?
Leave that to Neighbor Sleek-and-Slow.
Why go on threshing straw? There is no doubt
The best things that you know   1840
You dare not tell the boys about.
I hear one now out in the hall.

FAUST:

I simply cannot see him now.

MEPHISTOPHELES:

The poor lad has been waiting, after all,
And must not go uncomforted somehow.
Come, lend your cap and gown to me;
The mask will suit me admirably.
                                    [*He changes clothes.*]
Just trust my wits and I'll succeed.
A quarter of an hour is all I need.
Meanwhile get ready for your travels with all speed.   1850
                                                   [*Exit* FAUST.]

MEPHISTOPHELES [*in* FAUST's *long gown*]:

Scorn reason and the lore of mind,
Supremest powers of mankind,
Just let the Prince of Lies endow
Your strength with his illusions now,
And I will have you unconditionally—
Fate has conferred on him a mind
That urges ever onward with incontinency,
Whose eager striving is of such a kind
That early joys are overleaped and left behind.
I'll drag him through wild life at last,   1860
Through shallow insipidity,
I'll make him wriggle, stultify, stick fast,
And in his insatiety
His greedy lips will find that food and drink float past.
He will vainly beg refreshment on the way.
Had his lot not been with the Devil cast,
He would go to the Devil anyway.
                                    [*Enter a* STUDENT.]

STUDENT:

I've been here just a short time, Sir,
And come to you with deference
To meet a man, and see and hear,   1870
Of whom all speak with reverence.

MEPHISTOPHELES:

I must approve your courtesy.
A man like other men you see.
Have you inquired around elsewhere?

STUDENT:

Take me, I entreat you, in your care.
I come with fresh blood, spirits high,
And money in tolerable supply.
My mother was loath to have me go,

But I would like to learn and know.

MEPHISTOPHELES:
Then this is just the place to come. 1880

STUDENT:
Frankly, I'd rather be back home.
I feel confined within these walls,
I'm ill at ease amid these halls,
The space is cramped, you never see
Green country or a single tree,
And in these rooms with benches lined
I lose my hearing, sight, and mind.

MEPHISTOPHELES:
It all depends on habit. Right at first
The infant will not take its mother's breast,
But then it finds relief from thirst 1890
And soon it feeds away with zest.
So you to Wisdom's breast will turn
And every day more strongly yearn.

STUDENT:
I'll hang upon her neck with all affection
If you will set me in the right direction.

MEPHISTOPHELES:
First tell me, before we go on,
What course have you decided on?

STUDENT:
I want to be quite erudite;
I'd like to comprehend aright
What all there is on earth, in heaven as well, 1900
In science and in nature too.

MEPHISTOPHELES:
You're on the right track, I can tell;
Just see that nothing distracts you.

STUDENT:
With body and soul it shall be done.
But to be frank, I would like in some ways
A little freedom and some fun
On pleasant summer holidays.

MEPHISTOPHELES:
Make good use of your time, so fast it flies.
You'll gain time if you just will organize.
And so, dear friend, I would advise 1910
First off *collegium logicum*.[15]
There you will get your mind well braced
In Spanish boots[16] so tightly laced
That it will henceforth toe the taut
And cautiously marked line of thought
And not go will-o'-the-wisping out
And in, across, and round about.

---

[15] A course in logic.
[16] An instrument of torture consisting of metal boots that were screwed tighter and tighter.

They will spend days on teaching you
About how things you used to do—
Like eating, drinking—just like that,
Need One! Two! Three! for getting at.
For with thought-manufactures
It's like a weaver's masterpiece:
A thousand threads one treadle plies,
The shuttles dart back to and fro,
Unseen the threads together flow,
A thousand knots one movement ties;
Then comes the philosopher to have his say
And proves things have to be this way:
The first being so, the second so,
The third and fourth are so-and-so;
If first and second were absent, neither
Would third and fourth be present either.
All scholars find this very clever,
None have turned weavers yet, however.
Whoever wants to know and write about
A living thing, first drives the spirit out;
He has the parts then in his grasp,
But gone is the spirit's holding-clasp.
Encheiresin naturae[17] chemists call it now,
Mocking themselves, they know not how.

STUDENT:

I don't just get all you imply.

MEPHISTOPHELES:

It will go better by and by,
Once you have all these things principified
And properly classified.

STUDENT:

I feel as dazed by all you've said
As if a mill wheel spun inside my head.

MEPHISTOPHELES:

Above all else you next must turn
To metaphysics. See that you learn
Profoundly and with might and main
What does not fit the human brain.
For what fits in—or misfits—grand
Resounding phrases are on hand.
But this semester most of all
Keep schedule, be punctual.
You'll have five classes every day;
Be in there on the stroke of the bell.
See that you are prepared as well,
With paragraphs worked up in such a way
That you can see with just a look

1920

1930

1940

1950

1960

---

[17]"Nature's hand-hold," the term of J. R. Spielmann, an eighteenth-century chemist, for the power
that holds biological components together in a living organism.

There's nothing said but what is in the book;
And take your notes with dedication
As if the Holy Ghost gave the dictation!

STUDENT:

No second time need I be told,
I see its usefulness all right;
What one gets down in black and white
One can take home and feel consoled.

MEPHISTOPHELES:

But name your field of concentration!

STUDENT:

I don't feel law is just the thing for me.

MEPHISTOPHELES:

I cannot blame you there especially,   1970
Well do I know the law school situation.
Laws are perpetrated like disease
Hereditary in some families;
From generation to generation they are bred
And furtively from place to place they spread.
Sense turns to nonsense, wise works to a mire.
Woe that you are a grandson and born late!
About the legal right that is innate
In man, they do not so much as inquire.

STUDENT:

You make my own aversion still more great.   1980
He whom you teach is fortunate.
I'd almost take theology, in a way.

MEPHISTOPHELES:

I wouldn't want to lead you astray.
That branch of learning, once you do begin it,
It's so hard to avoid the path of sin,
There's so much hidden poison lurking in it
And you can hardly tell this from the medicine.
Again it's best to follow only one man there
And by that master's statements swear.
Cling hard and fast to words, in sum;   1990
Then through sure portals you will come
To Certainty's own templed home.

STUDENT:

But words must have ideas too behind them.

MEPHISTOPHELES:

Quite so! But just don't fret too much to no avail,
Because just when ideas fail
Words will crop up, and timely you will find them.
With words you can most excellently dispute,
Words can a system constitute,
In words you can put faith and not be shaken,
And from a word not one iota can be taken.   2000

STUDENT:

Forgive me for so importuning you,
But I must trouble you again.
Would you say just a telling word or two

About the course in medicine?
Three years is a short time, and O my God!
The field itself is far too broad.
With just a little hint alone
One feels it would not seem so great.
MEPHISTOPHELES [*aside*]:
I've had enough of this dry tone,
I've got to play the Devil straight.   2010
                    [*aloud*]
The gist of medicine is grasped with ease;
You study through the great world and the small
To let it go on after all
As God may please.
In vain you'll go a-roving scientifically,
There each learns only what he can;
But one who grasps the moment, he
Is truly the right man.
You've got a good build on the whole,
And you won't lack for impudence;   2020
If you just have self-confidence
You'll have the trust of many a soul.
And learn to manage women, of that make sure;
For all their endless Ah!'s and Oh!'s
And thousand woes
Depend on one point only for their cure,
And if you're halfway decent about that,
You'll have them all under your hat.
First, by a title win their confidence
That your skills many skills transcend,   2030
Then you can finger every little thing and be
Welcome where others wait for years on end.
Know how to take her little pulse, and grasp her
With slyly passionate glances while you clasp her
Around her trim and slender waist
To see how tightly she is laced.
STUDENT:
Now that's more like it! The where and how I see!
MEPHISTOPHELES:
Grey, my dear friend, is all of theory,
And verdant is life's golden tree.
STUDENT:
I swear it's all just like a dream to me.   2040
Might I come back another time to sound
Your wisdom to its depths profound?
MEPHISTOPHELES:
I'll gladly do anything I may.
STUDENT:
It's just impossible to go away
Unless you take my album here and sign.
Would you do me the honor of a line?
MEPHISTOPHELES:
With pleasure.
                    [*He writes and gives the album back.*]

STUDENT [*reads*]:
> Eritis sicut Deus, scientes bonum et malum.[18]
> > [*He respectfully closes the book and takes his leave.*]

MEPHISTOPHELES:
> Just follow that old saying and my cousin, the snake,
> And you will surely tremble for your God's-likeness' sake!   2050
> > [*Reenter* FAUST.]

FAUST:
> And where do we go now?

MEPHISTOPHELES:
> > The choice is up to you.
> We'll see the small world first, and then the great one too.
> What joy, what profit will be yours
> As you sail glibly through this course!

FAUST:
> But with this long beard on my face
> I lack for easy social grace.
> This bold attempt will never work with me,
> I never could get on in company,
> In front of others I feel small and harassed,
> I'll be continually embarrassed.   2060

MEPHISTOPHELES:
> Good friend, all that is needed, time will give.
> Once you have confidence, you will know how to live.

FAUST:
> How do we travel, though, and get about?
> Do you have servants, coach and pair?

MEPHISTOPHELES:
> All we need do is spread this mantle out
> And it will take us through the air.
> But see that on this daring flight
> Beginning now you travel light.
> A little fire gas I will now prepare
> Will lift us to the upper air,   2070
> And if we're light, we'll go up fast from here.
> Congratulations on your new career!

. . .

Witch's Kitchen[19]

A large cauldron stands over the fire on a low hearth. Amid the steam rising from it various forms are seen. A MONKEY *sits by the kettle skimming it and watching that it does not boil over. The* HE-MONKEY *sits nearby with the young ones, warming himself. Walls and ceiling are hung with the most bizarre paraphernalia of witchcraft.*

FAUST:
> I am revolted by this crazy witchery;
> I shall be cured, you guarantee,

---

[18]"Ye shall be as gods, knowing good and evil" (Genesis 3:5), Satan's temptation to Eve in the Garden of Eden.

[19]Scene V, "Auerbach's Cellar in Leipzig," in which Mephistopheles astounds some drunken students by drawing wine from a table, has been omitted.

In this stark raving rookery?
Must I seek counsel from an aged crone?   2340
And will her filthy cookery
Take thirty years off from my flesh and bone?
Alas for me if you can nothing better find!
Already hope has vanished, I despair.
Has neither Nature nor a wholesome mind
Devised a balm to cure me anywhere?

MEPHISTOPHELES:
Ah, now, my friend, you're talking sense once more.
There is a natural way to make you young again,
But that is in another book, and on that score
It forms a curious chapter even then.   2350

FAUST:
I want to hear it.

MEPHISTOPHELES:
        Good! A way without recourse
To money, medicine, or sorcery:
Straight to the fields direct your course
And start to dig immediately;
There keep yourself and keep your mind
Within a circle close confined,
Eat only unadulterated food,
Live with the beasts as beast, and count it good
To strew the harvest field with your own dung;
There is no better way, believe me,   2360
Up to age eighty to stay young.

FAUST:
I am not used to that, nor could I ever stand
To take a shovel in my hand.
For me that narrow life would never do.

MEPHISTOPHELES:
Well, then it's to the witch for you.

FAUST:
But why just this old hag? What makes
You say that *you* can't brew the cup?

MEPHISTOPHELES:
A pretty pastime that! I could put up
A thousand bridges in the time it takes.
This work needs skill and knowledge, it is true,   2370
But it requires some patience too.
A quiet mind may work for years on end
But time alone achieves the potent blend.
And as for what there may be to it,
There's many an odd ingredient.
The Devil taught her how to brew it,
But by himself the Devil cannot do it.
        [*catching sight of the* ANIMALS]
Ah, see the cute breed by the fire!
That is the maid, that is the squire.
        [*to the* ANIMALS]
Where is the lady of the house?   2380

THE ANIMALS:
> Out of the house
> On a carouse
> Up chimney and away.

MEPHISTOPHELES:
> How long does she rampage today?

THE ANIMALS:
> Until we get our paws warm, anyway.

MEPHISTOPHELES [*to* FAUST]:
> How do you like these cunning creatures?

FAUST:
> Repulsive to the nth degree.

MEPHISTOPHELES:
> No, discourse such as this one features
> Is just the kind that most entrances me.
>
> > [*to the* ANIMALS]
>
> Now, you accursed puppets you,   2390
> Why are you paddling in that broth, pray tell?

THE ANIMALS:
> We're cooking up some beggars' stew.

MEPHISTOPHELES:
> You'll have a good big clientele.

THE HE-MONKEY [*coming over and fawning on* MEPHISTOPHELES]:
> O roll the dice
> And make me nice
> And rich with gains!
> My lot is bad,
> But if I had
> Some money, I'd have brains.

MEPHISTOPHELES:
> How happy would this monkey be   2400
> If he could play the lottery!

> [*Meanwhile the young monkeys have been playing
> with a large globe and now roll it forward.*]

THE HE-MONKEY:
> That is the world;
> Spun and twirled,
> It never ceases;
> It rings like glass,
> But hollow, alas,
> It breaks to pieces.
> Here it gleams bright,
> And here more bright,
> Alive am I.   2410
> Dear son, I say
> Keep far away,
> For you must die.
> It's made of clay,
> And splinters fly.

MEPHISTOPHELES:
> And why the sieve?

THE HE-MONKEY [*takes it down*]:
  I'd know you if
  You were a thief.[20]
        [*He runs to the* SHE-MONKEY *and has her look through it.*]
  Look through the sieve:
  You see the thief   2420
  And name him not?
MEPHISTOPHELES [*going over to the fire*]:
  And why the pot?
THE HE-MONKEY AND THE SHE-MONKEY:
  The silly sot!
  Not know the pot,
  Not know the kettle?
MEPHISTOPHELES:
  Uncivil beast!
THE HE-MONKEY:
  Here, take the whisk
  And sit on the settle.
        [*He has* MEPHISTOPHELES *sit down.*]
FAUST [*has all this time been standing in front of a mirror, now going up to it, now step-*
        ping back away from it]:
  What do I see with form divine
  Upon this magic mirror shine?   2430
  O Love, lend me the swiftest of your pinions
  And take me off to her dominions!
  Unless I stand right here in this one place
  And do not venture to go near,
  I see her misted only and unclear.—
  A woman of the utmost grace!
  Can any woman be so fair?
  In this recumbent body do I face
  The essence of all heavens here?
  Is there on earth the like of it?   2440
MEPHISTOPHELES:
  It's natural, if a god will six whole days expend
  And then himself shout bravo! in the end,
  That something smart must come of it.
  Go right ahead and gaze your fill;
  Just such a sweetheart I can well provide,
  And lucky is the man who will
  Then take her with him as his bride.
        [FAUST *keeps right on looking into the mirror.* MEPHISTOPHELES
        sprawls on the settle and toys with the whisk as he goes on speaking.]
  I sit here like a king upon his throne,
  I hold a scepter, and I lack a crown alone.
        [*The* ANIMALS, *who have been going through all kinds of odd motions*
        helter-skelter, bring MEPHISTOPHELES *a crown amid loud cries.*]
THE ANIMALS:
  O just be so good
  As with sweat and blood   2450

---

[20]Thieves were supposed to be recognizable as such when viewed through a sieve.

To glue this crown and lime it.
> [*They handle the crown clumsily and break it
> in two pieces, then hop around with the pieces.*]
Now it is done!
We talk, look, and run,
We listen and rhyme it—
FAUST [*toward the mirror*]:
  I'm going crazy here, I feel!
MEPHISTOPHELES [*pointing to the* ANIMALS]:
  My own head now almost begins to reel.
THE ANIMALS:
  If we have luck
  And don't get stuck
  We'll make sense yet!
FAUST [*as before*]:
  My heart is catching fire within!
  Let's get away from here, and fast!
MEPHISTOPHELES [*in his previous posture*]:
  This much you'll have to grant at least:
  As poets they are genuine.
[*The kettle, which the* SHE-MONKEY *has left unwatched, begins to boil over. A great flame
flashes up the chimney. Down through the flame comes the* WITCH *with hideous screams.*]
THE WITCH:
  Ow! Ow! Ow! Ow!
  Damnable brute! Accursed sow!
  Neglect the kettle, scorch your mate!
  Accursed beast!
> [*catching sight of* FAUST *and* MEPHISTOPHELES]
  What have we here?
  Who are you here?
  What do you want?
  Who has sneaked in?
  Flames and groans
  Consume your bones!
> [*She dips the skimmer into the kettle and scoops flames at* FAUST,
> MEPHISTOPHELES, *and the* ANIMALS. *The* ANIMALS *whimper.*]
MEPHISTOPHELES [*reverses the whisk he is holding and goes smashing the glasses and
  pots*]:
  Crash! And smash!
  There goes your trash!
  Your glassware's done!
  It's all in fun,
  I'm only beating time,
  Carrion, to your rhyme.
> [*as the* WITCH *falls back in fury and horror*]
  You recognize me, Bone-bag? Skeleton?
  You know your master and your lord?
  What keeps me now from going on
  To pulverize you and your monkey horde!
  For my red coat you have such small respect?
  My rooster feather you don't recognize?
  Is my face hidden? Or do you expect
  I'll state my name and enterprise?

2460

2470

2480

THE WITCH:

    O Sir, forgive this rude salute from me!

    And yet no horse hoof do I see;   2490

    And then where is your raven pair?

MEPHISTOPHELES:

    This time I'll let you get away with it.

    It has been quite some while, I will admit,

    Since last we met. And to be fair,

    The culture that has licked the world up slick

    Has even with the Devil turned the trick.

    The northern phantom is no longer to be found;

    Where will you see horns, tail, or claws around?

    As for the foot, which I can't do without,

    It would work me much social harm, I fear;   2500

    And so, like many a young man, I've gone about

    With padded calves this many a long year.

THE WITCH [dancing]:

    I'll lose my mind for jubilation

    To see Squire Satan back in circulation!

MEPHISTOPHELES:

    Woman, I forbid that appellation!

THE WITCH:

    Why? What harm has it ever done?

MEPHISTOPHELES:

    It's long since passed to fable books and vanished.

    Yet people are no better off. The Evil One

    They're rid of, but their evils are not banished.

    Just call me Baron, that will do.   2510

    I am a cavalier like any cavalier.

    You do not doubt my noble blood, and you

    Can see the coat of arms that I wear here.

                     [He makes an indecent gesture.]

THE WITCH [laughing immoderately]:

    Ha! Ha! Just like you, that I'll swear!

    Oh you're a rogue, just as you always were!

MEPHISTOPHELES [to FAUST]:

    Learn this, my friend! This is the way

    To handle witches any day.

THE WITCH:

    Now, gentlemen, how can I be of use?

MEPHISTOPHELES:

    A good glass of the well-known juice,

    But of your oldest, is what I'm after;   2520

    It's years that put the powers in those brews.

THE WITCH:

    Why, sure! Here is a bottle on my shelf

    From which I sometimes take a nip myself

    And which no longer has a trace of stink.

    I'll gladly pour you out a little glass.

                     [softly]

    But if this man here unprepared should drink,

    You know he'll die before two hours pass.

MEPHISTOPHELES:

    He's a good friend, and I mean things to thrive with him;

    Give him the best your kitchen offers, serve him well.

    So draw your circle, speak your spell,   2530

    And fill his cup right to the brim.

[*With bizarre gestures the* WITCH *describes a circle and places strange things inside it. Meanwhile the glasses begin to ring and the kettle to boom and make music. Finally she fetches a great book and disposes the monkeys within the circle to serve her as a lectern and to hold torches. She beckons* FAUST *to come to her.*]

FAUST [*to* MEPHISTOPHELES]:

    Now tell me, what is all this leading to?

    These frantic motions and this wild ado

    And all of this disgusting stuff

    I've known and hated long enough.

MEPHISTOPHELES:

    On, nonsense! It's just for the fun of it!

    And don't be such a prig! As a physician,

    She needs to hocus-pocus just a bit

    So that the juice can work on your condition.

                 [*He gets* FAUST *into the circle.*]

THE WITCH [*begins to declaim with great bombast out of a book*]:

    This must ye ken!   2540

    From one take ten;

    Skip two; and then

    Even up three,

    And rich you'll be.

    Leave out the four.

    From five and six,

    Thus says the witch,

    Make seven and eight,

    And all is straight.

    And nine is one,   2550

    And ten is none.

    This is the witch's one-times-one!

FAUST:

    I think the hag's in fever and delirium.

MEPHISTOPHELES:

    Oh, there is lots more still to come.

    As I well know, the whole book's in that vein.

    I've wasted much time going through its pages,

    For total paradox will still remain

    A mystery alike to fools and sages.

    My friend, the art is old and new.

    For ages it has been the thing to do,   2560

    By Three and One, and One and Three,

    To broadcast error in guise of verity.

    And so they teach and jabber unperturbed;

    With fools, though, who is going to bother?

    Man has a way of thinking, when he hears a word,

    That certainly behind it lies some thought or other.

THE WITCH [*continues*]:

    The lofty force

Of wisdom's source
Is from the whole world hidden.
Once give up thinking,   2570
And in a twinkling
It's granted you unbidden.

FAUST:
What nonsense is she spouting now before us?
My head is going to split before too long.
I feel as if I'm listening to a chorus
Of fools a hundred thousand strong.

MEPHISTOPHELES:
Enough, O worthy Sibyl! Pray, no more!
Bring on your potion now, and pour
A goblet quickly to the brim;
My friend is safe, your drink won't injure him.   2580
He is a man of many titles,
And many a dram has warmed his vitals.
         [*With many ceremonies the* WITCH *pours out the drink in a*
              goblet. As FAUST *raises it to his mouth a little flame arises.*]
Just drink it down. Go on! You'll love
The way it makes your heart soar higher.
What! With the Devil hand-in-glove
And boggle at a little fire?
              [*The* WITCH *dissolves the circle.* FAUST *steps forth.*]
Come right on out! You must not rest.

THE WITCH:
And may the dram do you much good!

MEPHISTOPHELES [*to the* WITCH]:
If you have any favor to request,
Just tell me on Walpurgis,[21] if you would.   2590

THE WITCH:
Here is a spell; say it occasionally
And you'll see strange results without a doubt.

MEPHISTOPHELES [*to* FAUST]:
Just come along, entrust yourself to me.
You must perspire now necessarily
To get the force to penetrate both in and out.
I'll teach you later all the joys of indolence,
And soon to your heart's pleasure you'll commence
To feel how Cupid rises up and hops about.

FAUST:
Just one more quick look in the mirror there!
That womanly form was O! So fair!   2600

MEPHISTOPHELES:
No, no! For soon, alive before you here
The paragon of women shall appear.

---

[21] The Bloksberg, highest peak of the Harz Mountains, was the traditional scene of devils' orgies on St.
Walpurga's Night, April 30.

[*aside*]

With that drink in you, you will find
All women Helens to your mind.

A Street

FAUST:

Fair lady, may I be so free
As to offer my arm and company?

MARGARET:

I'm neither a lady nor fair, and may
Go unescorted on my way.

[*She disengages herself and goes on.*]

FAUST:

By heaven, but that child is sweet!
Like none I ever chanced to meet.   2610
So virtuous and modest, yes,
But with a touch of spunkiness.
Her lips so red, her cheek so bright,
I never shall forget the sight.
The shy way she cast down her eye
Has pressed itself deep in my heart;
And then the quick and short reply,
That was the most delightful part!

[*Enter* MEPHISTOPHELES.]

You must get me that girl, you hear?

MEPHISTOPHELES:

Which one?

FAUST:

She just went by me here.   2620

MEPHISTOPHELES:

That one? She just came from the priest,
He absolved her from her sins and all;
I stole up near the confessional.
She's just a simple little thing,
Went to confession just for nothing.
On such as she I have no hold.

FAUST:

And yet she's past fourteen years old.

MEPHISTOPHELES:

Why, you talk just like Jack the Rake
Who wants all flowers to bloom for his sake
And fancies that no honor is,   2630
Or favor, but the picking's his.
It doesn't always work that way.

FAUST:

Dear Master Laudable, I say
Don't bother me with your legality!
And I am telling you outright,
Unless that creature of delight
Lies in my arms this very night,
At midnight we part company.

MEPHISTOPHELES:
    Remember there are limits! I
    Need fourteen days at least to try   2640
    And find an opportunity.
FAUST:
    Had I but seven hours clear,
    I wouldn't need the Devil near
    To lead that girl astray for me.
MEPHISTOPHELES:
    You're talking like a Frenchman. Wait!
    And don't be put out or annoyed:
    What good's a thing too soon enjoyed?
    The pleasure is not half so great
    As when you first parade the doll
    Through every sort of folderol   2650
    And knead and pat and shape her well,
    The way that all French novels tell.
FAUST:
    I've appetite enough without it.
MEPHISTOPHELES:
    With no more joking now about it:
    I'm telling you that pretty child
    Will not be hurriedly beguiled.
    There's nothing to be gained by force;
    To cunning we must have recourse.
FAUST:
    Get me some of that angel's attire!
    Lead me to her place of rest!
    Get me the kerchief from her breast,   2660
    A garter for my love's desire!
MEPHISTOPHELES:
    Just so you see that I do heed
    Your pain and serve your every need,
    We shall not waste a single minute.
    I'll take you to her room and put you in it.
FAUST:
    And shall I see her? have her?
MEPHISTOPHELES:
                            No!
    She'll be at a neighbor's when we go.
    And all alone there you can dwell
    Upon the fragrance of her cell   2670
    And hope for future joys as well.
FAUST:
    Can we go now?
MEPHISTOPHELES:
                    It's too soon yet.
FAUST:
    Get me a gift for her, and don't forget.

                                                                [Exit.]

MEPHISTOPHELES:
    What! Gifts so soon! That's fine! He'll be right in his glory!

I know a lot of pretty places
Where there are buried treasure cases;
I must go through my inventory!

[*Exit.*]

Evening

A small, neat room. MARGARET *braiding her hair and doing it up.*

MARGARET:
    I'd give a good deal if I knew
    Who was that gentleman today!
    He had a very gallant way   2680
    And comes of noble lineage too.
    That much I could read from his face—
    Or he'd not be so bold in the first place.

[*Exit.*]

[*Enter* FAUST *and* MEPHISTOPHELES.]

MEPHISTOPHELES:
    Come on! But softly. In you go!
FAUST [*after a silence*]:
    I beg you, leave me here alone.
MEPHISTOPHELES [*peering about*]:
    Not every girl's this neat, you know?

[*Exit.*]

FAUST [*looking all around*]:
    Welcome, lovely twilight gloom
    That hovers in this sacred room!
    Seize on my heart, sweet love pangs who
    Both live and languish on hope's own dew.   2690
    How everything here is imbued
    With stillness, order, and content!
    Here in this poverty, what plenitude!
    Here in this prison, what ravishment!
        [*He throws himself into the leather armchair beside the bed.*]
    O you who have both joy and sorrow known
    From times gone by, clasp me too in your arms!
    How often at this patriarchal throne
    Children have gathered round about in swarms!
    Perhaps my sweetheart, plump-cheeked, used to stand
    Here grateful for a Christmas present and   2700
    Devoutly kiss her grandsire's withered hand.
    I feel your spirit, maiden, playing
    About me, breathing order, plenitude,
    And every day in mother-fashion saying
    The cloth upon the table must be fresh renewed
    And underfoot clean sand be strewed.
    Dear hand! so godlike! In it lies
    What turns a cottage to a paradise.
    And here!
            [*He lifts the bed curtains.*]
    What chill of rapture seizes me!

Here I could linger on for hours.   2710
Here, Nature, you with your creative powers
From light dreams brought the angel forth to be;
Here lay the child, her bosom warm
With life; here tenderly there grew
With pure and sacred help from you
The godlike image of her form.
　　And you? What purpose brought you here?
How I am touched with shame sincere!
What do you want? Why is your heart so sore?
O sorry Faust! I know you now no more.   2720
　　Does magic haze surround me everywhere?
I pressed for pleasure with no least delay,
And in a love dream here I melt away!
Are we the toys of every breath of air?
　　If she this moment now were to come by,
What punishment your impudence would meet!
The loud-mouth lummox—O how small!—would lie
Dissolved in shame before her feet.

　　　　　　　　　[*Enter* MEPHISTOPHELES.]

MEPHISTOPHELES:
　　Quick now! I see her at the gate.
FAUST:
　　Away! And never to come back!   2730
MEPHISTOPHELES:
　　Here is a casket of some weight,
　　I took it elsewhere from a rack.
　　Just put it in her clothespress there,
　　It'll make her head swim, that I'll swear.
　　I put some little baubles in it
　　To bait another bauble and win it.
　　A girl's a girl and play is play.
FAUST:
　　I wonder . . . should I?
MEPHISTOPHELES:
　　　　　　　　　　　　You delay?
　　You wouldn't maybe want to keep the baubles?
　　In that case I advise Your Lust   2740
　　To save my pretty daytime, just
　　Don't bother me with further troubles.
　　You are not miserly, I trust!
　　I scratch my head, I rub my hands—
　　　　　[*He puts the casket in the clothespress and pushes the lock shut again.*]
　　Off and away now!
　　To get that lovely child to play now
　　Into your heart's desires and plans.
　　And you stand all
　　Poised to proceed to lecture hall,
　　And as if in the flesh, and grey,   2750
　　Physics and Metaphysics led the way.
　　Come on!

　　　　　　　　　　　　　　　　　　　　　　　　　　　　　　[*Exeunt.*]

　　　　　　　[*Enter* MARGARET *with a lamp.*]

MARGARET:
   It's close in here, there is no air.
                    [*She opens the window.*]
   And yet it's not so warm out there.
   I feel so odd, I can't say how—
   I do wish Mother would come home now.
   I'm chilled all over, and shivering!
   I'm such a foolish, timid thing!
             [*She begins to sing as she undresses.*]

    There was a king of Thule
   True even to the grave,   2760
   To whom a golden goblet
   His dying mistress gave.
    Naught did he hold more dear,
   He drained it every feast;
   And from his eye a tear
   Welled each time as he ceased.
    When life was nearly done,
   His towns he totaled up,
   Begrudged his heir not one,
   But did not give the cup.   2770
    There with his vassals all
   At royal board sat he
   In high ancestral hall
   Of his castle by the sea.
    The old toper then stood up,
   Quaffed off his last life-glow,
   And flung the sacred cup
   Down to the flood below.
    He saw it fall, and drink,
   And sink deep in the sea;   2780
   Then did his eyelids sink,
   And no drop more drank he.
[*She opens the clothespress to put her clothes away and catches sight of the jewel casket.*]
   How did this pretty casket get in here?
   I locked the press, I'm sure. How queer!
   What can it have inside it? Can it be
   That someone left it as security
   For money Mother has provided?
   Here on a ribbon hangs a little key—
   I think I'll have a look inside it!
   What's this? O Lord in heaven! See!   2790
   I've never seen the like in all my days!
   A noble lady with such jewelry
   Could walk with pride on holidays.
   I wonder how this chain would look on me?
   Such glorious things! Whose could they be?
            [*She puts it on and steps up to the mirror.*]
   If just these earrings could be mine!
   One looks so different in them right away.
   What good does beauty do, young thing? It may
   Be very well to wonder at,
   But people let it go at that;   2800

They praise you half in pity.
Gold serves all ends,
On gold depends
Everything. Ah, we poor!

Promenade

FAUST *pacing up and down in thought.* MEPHISTOPHELES *comes to him.*

MEPHISTOPHELES:
Now by the element of hell! By love refused!
I wish I knew a stronger oath that could be used!
FAUST:
What's this? What's griping you so badly?
I've never seen a face the like of this!
MEPHISTOPHELES:
Why, I'd surrender to the Devil gladly
If I were not the Devil as it is!   2810
FAUST:
Have you gone off your head? I grant
It suits you, though, to rave and rant.
MEPHISTOPHELES:
Just think, those jewels for Gretchen that I got,
Some priest has made off with the lot!—
Her mother got to see the things,
Off went her dire imaginings;
That woman's got some sense of smell,
She has prayerbook-sniffing on the brain,
A whiff of any item, and she can tell
Whether the thing is sacred or profane.   2820
That jewelry she spotted in a minute
As having no great blessing in it.
"My child," she cried, "ill-gotten good
Ensnares the soul, consumes the blood.
Before Our Lady we will lay it,
With heaven's manna she'll repay it."[22]
Margretlein pulled a pouty face,
Called it a gift horse, and in any case
She thought he wasn't godless, he
Who sneaked it in so cleverly.   2830
The mother had a priest drop by;
No sooner did he the trick espy
Than his eyes lit up with what he saw.
"This shows an upright mind," quoth he,
"Self-conquest gains us victory.
The church has a good healthy maw,
She's swallowed up whole countries, still
She never yet has eaten her fill.
The church, dear ladies, alone has health
For digestion of ill-gotten wealth."   2840

---

[22]Revelation 2:17: "To him that overcometh will I give to eat of the hidden manna."

FAUST:
> That's nothing but the usual game,
> A king and a Jew can do the same.

MEPHISTOPHELES:
> Then up he scooped brooch, chain, and rings
> As if they were just trivial things
> With no more thanks, if's, and's, or but's
> Than if they were a bag of nuts,
> Promised them celestial reward—
> All edified, they thanked him for it.

FAUST:
> And Gretchen?

MEPHISTOPHELES:
>   Sits lost now in concern,
> Not knowing yet which way to turn;   2850
> Thinks day and night about the gems,
> But more of him from whom the present stems.

FAUST:
> I hate to see the dear girl worry.
> Get her a new set in a hurry.
> The first one wasn't too much anyway.

MEPHISTOPHELES:
> My gentleman finds this mere child's play.

FAUST:
> And here's the way I want it. Go
> Make friends there with that neighbor. Show
> You're not a devil made of sugar water,
> Get those new gems and have them brought her.   2860

MEPHISTOPHELES:
> Sir, I obey with all my heart.

>   [*Exit* FAUST.]

> This fool in love will huff and puff
> The sun and moon and stars apart
> To get his sweetheart pastime stuff.

>   [*Exit.*]

The Neighbor's House

MARTHA *alone.*

MARTHA:
> Now God forgive my husband, he
> Has not done the right thing by me.
> Way off into the world he's gone,
> And leaves me on the straw alone.
> Yet he surely had no cause on my part,
> God knows I loved him with all my heart.   2870
>   [*She weeps.*]
> He could be dead!—If I just knew for sure!
> Or had a statement with a signature!
>   [*Enter* MARGARET.]

MARGARET:
> Dame Martha!

MARTHA:

What is it, Gretelchen?

MARGARET:

My knees are sinking under me.
I've found one in my press again,
Another casket, of ebony,
And this time it's a gorgeous set
Far richer than the first one yet.

MARTHA:

This time you mustn't tell your mother,
Off it would go to church just like the other.   2880

MARGARET:

O look at them! Just see! Just see!

MARTHA [putting them on her]:

You *are* a lucky creature!

MARGARET:

Unfortunately
In church or on the street I do not dare
Be seen in them, or anywhere.

MARTHA:

You just come over frequently,
Put on the jewels in secret here,
Walk by the mirror an hour or so in privacy,
And we'll enjoy them, never fear.
There'll come a chance, a holiday, before we're done,
Where you can show them to the people one by one,   2890
A necklace first, pearl ear-drops next; your mother
Won't notice it, or we'll make up some thing or other.

MARGARET:

But who could bring both caskets here?
There's something not quite right...

[A knock.]

Oh, dear!

Could that be Mother coming here?

MARTHA [looking through the blinds]:

It's a strange gentleman—Come in!

[MEPHISTOPHELES steps in.]

MEPHISTOPHELES:

I'm so free as to step right in,
The ladies must excuse my liberty.

[Steps back respectfully before MARGARET.]

I wish to see Dame Martha Schwerdtlein, if I may.

MARTHA:

Right here! What might the gentleman have to say?   2900

MEPHISTOPHELES [aside to her]:

I know you now, that is enough for me.
You have distinguished company.
Forgive my freedom, I shall then
Return this afternoon again.

MARTHA [aloud]:

Child, think of it! The gentleman takes
You for some lady! For mercy's sakes!

MARGARET:
> I'm just a poor young girl; I find
> The gentleman is far too kind.
> These gems do not belong to me.

MEPHISTOPHELES:
> Oh, it's not just the jewelry.   2910
> She has a quick glance, and a way!
> I am delighted I may stay.

MARTHA:
> What is your errand then? I'm very—

MEPHISTOPHELES:
> I wish my tidings were more merry.
> I trust you will not make me rue this meeting:
> Your husband is dead and sends you greeting.

MARTHA:
> He's dead! That faithful heart! Oh, my!
> My husband's dead! Oh! I shall die!

MARGARET:
> Dear lady, Oh! Do not despair!

MEPHISTOPHELES:
> Now listen to the sad affair.   2920

MARGARET:
> I hope I never, never love.
> Such loss as this I would die of.

MEPHISTOPHELES:
> Glad must have sad, sad must have glad, as always.

MARTHA:
> O tell me all about his dying!

MEPHISTOPHELES:
> At Padua, by Saint Anthony's
> They buried him, and he is lying
> In ground well sanctified and blest
> At cool and everlasting rest.

MARTHA:
> And there is nothing else you bring?

MEPHISTOPHELES:
> Yes, one request and solemn enterprise: 2930
> Three hundred Masses for him you should have them sing.
> My pockets are quite empty otherwise.

MARTHA:
> What, not a luck-piece, or a trinket such
> As any journeyman deep in his pack would hoard
> As a remembrance token stored
> And sooner starve or beg than use it!

MEPHISTOPHELES:
> Madam, it grieves me very much;
> Indeed he did not waste his money or lose it.
> And much did he his failings then deplore,
> Yes, and complained of his hard luck still more.   2940

MARGARET:
> To think that human fortunes so miscarry!
> Many's the Requiem I'll pray for him, I'm sure.

MEPHISTOPHELES:
    Ah, you deserve now very soon to marry,
    A child of such a kindly nature.
MARGARET:
    It's not yet time for that. Oh, no!
MEPHISTOPHELES:
    If not a husband, then meanwhile a beau.
    It's one of heaven's greatest graces
    To hold so dear a thing in one's embraces.
MARGARET:
    It's not the custom here for one.
MEPHISTOPHELES:
    Custom or not, it still is done.   2950
MARTHA:
    But tell me more!
MEPHISTOPHELES:
                    I stood at his bedside—
    Half-rotten straw it was and little more
    Than horse manure; but in good Christian style he died,
    Yet found he had still further items on his score.
    "How I detest myself!" he cried with dying breath,
    "For having left my business and my wife!
    Ah, that remembrance is my death.
    If she would just forgive me in this life!"—
MARTHA [*weeping*]:
    The good man! I long since forgave.
MEPHISTOPHELES:
    "God knows, though, she was more to blame than I."   2960
MARTHA:
    It's a lie! And he with one foot in the grave!
MEPHISTOPHELES:
    Oh, he was talking through his hat
    There at the end, if I am half a judge.
    "I had no time to sit and yawn," he said,
    "First children and then earning children's bread,
    Bread in the widest sense, at that,
    And could not even eat my share in peace."
MARTHA:
    Did he forget my love, how I would drudge
    Both day and night and never cease?
MEPHISTOPHELES:
    No, he remembered that all right.   2970
    "As I put out from Malta," he went on,
    "I prayed for wife and children fervently;
    Then heaven too disposed things favorably
    So our ship took a Turkish galleon
    With treasure for the great Sultan aboard.
    Then bravery came in for reward
    And I got, as was only fair,
    My own well calculated share."
MARTHA:
    What! Where? Do you suppose he buried it?

MEPHISTOPHELES:
Who knows where the four winds have carried it?   2980
A pretty girl took him in tow when he
Was roaming Naples there without a friend;
She showed him so much love and loyalty
He bore the marks right to his blessed end.
MARTHA:
The rogue! He robbed his children like a thief!
And all that misery and grief
Could not prevent the shameful life he led.
MEPHISTOPHELES:
But that, you see, is why he's dead.
Were I in your place now, you know,
I'd mourn him for a decent year and then   2990
Be casting round meanwhile to find another beau.
MARTHA:
Oh Lord, the kind my first man was,
I'll never in this world find such again.
There never was a fonder fool than mine.
Only, he liked the roving life too much,
And foreign women, and foreign wine,
And then, of course, those devilish dice.
MEPHISTOPHELES:
Well, well, it could have worked out fine
If he had only taken such
Good care on his part to be nice.   3000
I swear on those terms it is true
I would myself exchange rings with you.
MARTHA:
Oh, the gentleman has such joking ways!
MEPHISTOPHELES [*aside*]:
It's time for me to be pushing onward!
She'd hold the very Devil to his word.
                    [*to* GRETCHEN]
How are things with your heart these days?
MARGARET:
What do you mean, Sir?
MEPHISTOPHELES [*aside*]:
                    O you innocents!
Ladies, farewell!
MARGARET:
                    Farewell.
MARTHA:
                    One word yet! What I crave is
Some little piece of evidence
Of when and how my sweetheart died and where his grave is.   3010
I've always been a friend of orderliness,
I'd like to read his death note in the weekly press.
MEPHISTOPHELES:
Good woman, what two witnesses report
Will stand as truth in any court.
I have a friend, quite serious,

I'll bring him to the judge with us.
I'll go and get him.

MARTHA:

Do that! Do!

MEPHISTOPHELES:

This lady will be with you too?
A splendid lad, much traveled. He
Shows ladies every courtesy.   3020

MARGARET:

The gentleman would make me blush for shame.

MEPHISTOPHELES:

Before no earthly king that one could name.

MARTHA:

Out in the garden to the rear
This afternoon we'll expect both of you here.

A Street

FAUST:

How is it? Will it work? Will it succeed?

MEPHISTOPHELES:

Ah, bravo! I find you aflame indeed.
Gretchen is yours now pretty soon.
You meet at neighbor Martha's house this afternoon.
The woman is expressly made
To work the pimp and gypsy trade!   3030

FAUST:

Good!

MEPHISTOPHELES:

Ah, but something is required of us.

FAUST:

One good turn deserves another.

MEPHISTOPHELES:

We will depose some testimony or other
To say her husband's bones are to be found
In Padua in consecrated ground.

FAUST:

Fine! First we'll need to do some journey-going.

MEPHISTOPHELES:

Sancta simplicitas! For that we need not fuss.
Just testify, and never mind the knowing.

FAUST:

Think of a better plan, or nothing doing.

MEPHISTOPHELES:

O saintly man! and sanctimonious!   3040
False witness then you never bore
In all your length of life before?
Have you not with great power given definition
Of God, the world, and all the world's condition,
Of man, man's heart, man's mind, and what is more,
With brazen brow and with no lack of breath?
And when you come right down to it,

You knew as much about them, you'll admit,
As you know of this Mister Schwerdtlein's death!
FAUST:
    You are a liar and a sophist too.   3050
MEPHISTOPHELES:
    Or would be, if I didn't know a thing or two.
    Tomorrow will you not deceive
    Poor Gretchen and then make her believe
    The vows of soul-felt love you swear?
FAUST:
    And from my heart.
MEPHISTOPHELES:
                All good and fair!
    Then comes eternal faith, and love still higher,
    Then comes the super-almighty desire—
    Will that be heartfelt too, I inquire?
FAUST:
    Stop there! It will!—If I have feeling,
    And for this feeling, for this reeling   3060
    Seek a name, and finding none,
    With all my senses through the wide world run,
    And clutch at words supreme, and claim
    That boundless, boundless is the flame
    That burns me, infinite and never done,
    Is that a devilish, lying game?
MEPHISTOPHELES:
    I still am right!
FAUST:
               Mark this and heed it,
    And spare me further waste of throat and lung:
    To win an argument takes no more than a tongue,
    That's all that's needed.   3070
    But come, this chatter fills me with disgust,
    For you are right, primarily because I must.

A Garden

MARGARET *on* FAUST*'s arm,* MARTHA *with* MEPHISTOPHELES, *strolling up and down.*

MARGARET:
    I feel, Sir, you are only sparing me
    And shaming me by condescending so.
    A traveler, from charity,
    Will often take things as they go.
    I realize my conversation can
    Not possibly amuse such an experienced man.
FAUST:
    One glance of yours, one word delights me more
    Than all of this world's wisdom-store.   3080
                  [*He kisses her hand.*]
MARGARET:
    How can you kiss it? It must seem to you

So coarse, so rough a hand to kiss.
What kinds of tasks have I not had to do!
You do not know how strict my mother is.

[*They pass on.*]

MARTHA:

And so, Sir, you are traveling constantly?

MEPHISTOPHELES:

Business and duty keep us on our way.
Many a place one leaves regretfully,
But then one simply cannot stay.

MARTHA:

It may well do while in one's prime
To rove about the world as a rolling stone,   3090
But then comes the unhappy time,
And dragging to the grave, a bachelor, alone,
Was never good for anyone.

MEPHISTOPHELES:

Ah, such with horror I anticipate.

MARTHA:

Then act, dear Sir, before it is too late.

[*They pass on.*]

MARGARET:

But out of sight is out of mind!
Your courtesy comes naturally;
But you have friends in quantity
Who are more clever than my kind.

FAUST:

Dear girl, believe me, clever in that sense   3100
Means usually a close self-interest.

MARGARET:

Really?

FAUST:

       To think simplicity and innocence
Are unaware their sacred way is best,
That lowliness and sweet humility
Are bounteous Nature's highest gifts—

MARGARET:

Think only for a moment's time of me,
I shall have time enough to think of you.

FAUST:

Then you are much alone?

MARGARET:

Yes, our house is a little one,
And yet it must be tended to.   3110
We have no maid, hence I must cook and sweep and knit
And sew, and do the errands early and late;
And then my mother is a bit
Too strict and strait.
And yet she has no need to scrimp and save this way;
We could live better far than others, you might say;
My father left a sizeable estate,

A house and garden past the city gate.
But I have rather quiet days of late.
My brother is a soldier, 3120
My little sister died;
The child did sometimes leave me with my patience tried,
And yet I'd gladly have the trouble back again,
She was so dear to me.
FAUST:
An angel, if like you.
MARGARET:
I brought her up; she dearly loved me too.
She was born following my father's death.
Mother we thought at her last breath,
She was so miserable, but then
She slowly, slowly got her strength again.
It was impossible for her to nurse 3130
The little mite herself, of course,
And so I raised her all alone
On milk and water; she became my own.
In my arms, in my lap she smiled,
Wriggled, and grew up to be a child.
FAUST:
You must have known the purest happiness.
MARGARET:
But many trying hours nonetheless.
At night her little cradle used to stand
Beside my bed, and she had but to stir
And I was there at hand, 3140
Sometimes to feed her, sometimes to comfort her,
Sometimes when she would not be still, to rise
And pace the floor with her to soothe her cries,
And yet be at the washtub early, do
The marketing and tend the hearth fire too,
And every morrow like today.
One's spirits are not always cheerful, Sir, that way;
Yet food is relished better, as is rest.
[*They pass on.*]
MARTHA:
Poor women! They are badly off indeed,
A bachelor is hard to change, they say. 3150
MEPHISTOPHELES:
Someone like you is all that I would need
To set me on a better way.
MARTHA:
But is there no one, Sir, that you have found?
Speak frankly, is your heart in no wise bound?
MEPHISTOPHELES:
The proverb says: A wife and one's own household
Are worth their weight in pearls and gold.
MARTHA:
But I mean, have you felt no inclination?

MEPHISTOPHELES:
I have met everywhere with much consideration.
MARTHA:
But has your heart in no case been impressed?
MEPHISTOPHELES:
With ladies one must not presume to jest.   3160
MARTHA:
Oh, you misunderstand me!
MEPHISTOPHELES:
                    What a shame! I find
I understand—that you are very kind.
                    [*They pass on.*]
FAUST:
And so you did, my angel, recognize
Me in the garden here at the first look?
MARGARET:
Did you not see how I cast down my eyes?
FAUST:
And you forgive the liberty I took
And all my impudence before
When you had just left the cathedral door?
MARGARET:
I was confused, the experience was all new.
No one could say bad things of me.   3170
Ah, thought I, could he possibly
Have noted something brazen or bold in you?
He seemed to think here was a girl he could
Treat in just any way he would.
I must confess that then I hardly knew
What soon began to argue in your favor;
But I was angry with myself, however,
For not becoming angrier with you.
FAUST:
My darling!
MARGARET:
           Wait!
    [*She picks a star flower and plucks the petals off it one by one.*]
FAUST:
                    What is it? A bouquet?
MARGARET:
No, just a game.
FAUST:
           What?
MARGARET:
                    You'd laugh at me if I should say.   3180
    [*She murmurs something as she goes on plucking.*]
FAUST:
What are you murmuring?
MARGARET [*half aloud*]:
                    He loves me—loves me not.
FAUST:
You lovely creature of the skies!

MARGARET [*continuing*]:
   Loves me—not—loves me—not—
               [*with delight as she reaches the last petal*]
   He loves me!
FAUST:
             Yes, my child! And let this language of
   The flowers be your oracle. He loves you!
   Do you know what that means? He loves you!
               [*He takes both her hands.*]
MARGARET:
   I'm trembling!
FAUST:
   O do not tremble! Let this glance
   And let this pressure of my hands
   Say what is inexpressible: 3190
   To yield oneself entirely and to feel
   A rapture that must be everlasting!
   Eternal!—Its end would be despair.
   No! Without end! Without end!
      [MARGARET *presses his hands, disengages herself, and runs*
       off. He stands in thought for a moment, then follows her.]
MARTHA [*coming along*]:
   It's getting dark.
MEPHISTOPHELES:
           We must be on our way.
MARTHA:
   I'd ask you gentlemen to stay,
   But this is such a wicked neighborhood.
   It seems that no one has a thing to do
   Or put his mind to
   But watch his neighbor's every move and stir.   3200
   No matter what one does, there's always talk.
   What of our couple?
MEPHISTOPHELES:
          They've flown up the arbor walk.
   The wanton butterflies!
MARTHA:
         He seems to take to her.
MEPHISTOPHELES:
   And she to him. Such is the world's old way.

A Summer House

MARGARET *comes running in, hides behind the door, puts her finger to her lips, and peeps through the crack.*

MARGARET:
   He's coming!
              [FAUST *comes along.*]
FAUST:
       Little rogue, to tease me so!

I'll catch you!
                    [*He kisses her.*]
MARGARET [*embracing him and returning his kiss*]:
        From my heart I love you so!
                    [MEPHISTOPHELES *knocks.*]
FAUST [*stamping his foot*]:
    Who's there?
MEPHISTOPHELES:
                A friend!
FAUST:
                A beast!
MEPHISTOPHELES:
                        It's time for us to go.
                    [MARTHA *comes along.*]
MARTHA:
    Yes, it is late, Sir.
FAUST:
                May I not escort you, though?
MARGARET:
    My mother would—farewell!
FAUST:
                        Ah, must I leave you then?
    Farewell!
MARTHA:
            Adieu!
MARGARET:
        But soon to meet again!   3210
                    [*Exeunt* FAUST *and* MEPHISTOPHELES.]
    Dear Lord! What things and things there can
    Come to the mind of such a man!
    I stand abashed, and for the life of me
    Cannot do other than agree.
    A simple child, I cannot see
    Whatever it is he finds in me.

                                                    [*Exit.*]

                        Forest and Cavern
FAUST:
    Spirit sublime, thou gavest me, gavest me all
    For which I asked. Thou didst not turn in vain
    Thy countenance upon me in the fire.
    Thou gavest me glorious Nature for my kingdom,   3220
    And power to feel it and enjoy it. No
    Cold, marveling observation didst thou grant me,
    Deep vision to her very heart thou hast
    Vouchsafed, as into the heart of a friend.
    Thou dost conduct the ranks of living creatures
    Before me and teachest me to know my brethren
    In quiet bush, in air, and in the water.
    And when the storm in forest roars and snarls,
    And the giant fir comes crashing down, and, falling,

Crushes its neighbor boughs and neighbor stems,   3230
And hills make hollow thunder of its fall,
Then dost thou guide me to safe caverns, showest
Me then unto myself, and my own bosom's
Profound and secret wonders are revealed.
And when before my sight the pure moon rises
And casts its mellow comfort, then from crags
And rain-sprent bushes there come drifting toward me
The silvery forms from ages now gone by,
Allaying meditation's austere pleasure.
    That no perfection is to man allotted,   3240
I now perceive. Along with this delight
That brings me near and nearer to the gods,
Thou gavest me this companion whom I can
No longer do without, however he
Degrades me to myself or insolently
Turns thy gifts by a breath to nothingness.
Officiously he fans a frantic fire
Within my bosom for that lovely girl.
Thus from desire I stagger to enjoyment
And in enjoyment languish for desire.   3250
                    [*Enter* MEPHISTOPHELES.]

MEPHISTOPHELES:
  Won't you have had enough of this life presently?
  How can it in the long run do for you?
  All well and good to try it out and see,
  But then go on to something new!

FAUST:
  I do wish you had more to do
  Than pester me on a good day.

MEPHISTOPHELES:
  All right, then, I won't bother you.
  You dare not mean that anyway.
  In you, friend, gruff, uncivil, and annoyed,
  There's nothing much to lose, indeed.   3260
  The whole day long you keep my time employed!
  But from my master's nose it's hard to read
  What pleases him and what one should avoid.

FAUST:
  Now there is just the proper tone!
  He wants my thanks for having been annoying.

MEPHISTOPHELES:
  What kind of life would you now be enjoying,
  Poor son of earth, without the help I've shown?
  But I have long since cured you anyhow
  From gibberish your imagination talked,
  And if it weren't for me you would have walked   3270
  Right off this earthly globe by now.
  Why should you mope around and stare
  Owl-like at cave and rocky lair?
  Why suck up food from soggy moss and trickling stone
  Just like a toad all, all alone?

A fine sweet pastime! That stick-in-the-mud
Professor still is in your blood.

FAUST:
Can you conceive the fresh vitality
This wilderness existence gives to me?
But if you could conceive it, yes,   3280
You would be devil enough to block my happiness.

MEPHISTOPHELES:
A superterrestrial delight!
To lie around on dewy hills at night,
Clasp earth and heaven to you in a rapture,
Inflate yourself to deity's great size,
Delve to earth's core by impulse of surmise,
All six days' creation in your own heart capture,
In pride of power enjoy I know not what,
In ecstasy blend with the All there on the spot,
The son of earth dissolved in vision,   3290
And then the lofty intuition—

[with a gesture]

To end—just how, I must not mention.

FAUST:
O vile!

MEPHISTOPHELES:
That does not please you much; meanwhile
You have the right to speak your moral "Vile!"
Before chaste ears one must not talk about
What chaste hearts cannot do without.
All right: occasional pleasure of a lie
To yourself, is something I will not deny;
But you won't last long in that vein.
Soon you will be elsewhere attracted,   3300
Or if it goes too long, distracted
To madness or to anguished pain.
Enough of this! Your sweetheart sits there in her room,
Around her everything is gloom.
You never leave her thoughts, and she
Loves you just overwhelmingly.
Passion came to flood first on your part,
As melting snow will send a brooklet running high;
You poured all that into her heart,
And now your brook is running dry.   3310
It seems to me, instead of playing king
In woodland wilds, so great a lord
Might help the childish little thing
And give her loving some reward.
Time hangs upon her like a pall,
She stands by the window, watches the clouds along
And past the ancient city wall.
"If I were a little bird!" so goes her song
Half the night and all day long.
Sometimes cheerful, mostly sad and of   3320
No further power of tears,

Then calm again, so it appears,
And always in love.

FAUST:
Serpent! Serpent!

MEPHISTOPHELES [*aside*]:
Admit I've got you there!

FAUST:
Infamous being! Begone! And do not dare
So much as speak that lovely creature's name!
Do not arouse desire in me to where
Half-maddened senses burst in open flame!

MEPHISTOPHELES:
What, then? She thinks you fled from her,   3330
And more or less that's just what did occur.

FAUST:
I am near her, and even if I were
Afar, I could not lose her or forget;
The very body of the Lord, when her
Lips touch it, rouses envy and regret.

MEPHISTOPHELES:
My friend, I've often envied you indeed
The twin roes that among the lilies feed.

FAUST:
Pander, begone!

MEPHISTOPHELES:
                    Fine! I laugh while you rail.
The God that created girls and boys
Saw that the noblest power He enjoys   3340
Was seeing that occasion should not fail.
Come on, then! What a shame this is!
You're going to your sweetheart's room
And not off to your doom.

FAUST:
What if I do find heaven in her arms?
What if in her embrace my spirit warms?
Do I not still feel her distress?
Am I not still the fugitive, the homeless,
The monster without rest or purpose sweeping
Like a cataract from crag to crag and leaping   3350
In frenzy of desire to the abyss?
While at one side, she, with her childlike mind,
Dwells in a cottage on the Alpine slope
With all her quiet life confined
Within her small world's narrow scope.
And I, the God-detested,
Had not enough, but wrested
The crag away and scattered
Its ruins as they shattered
To undermine her and her peace as well!   3360
The victim you demanded, fiend of hell!
Help, Devil, make this time of anguish brief!
Let it be soon if it must be!

Let her fate crash in ruins over me,
Together let us come to grief.
MEPHISTOPHELES:
Ah, now it seethes again and glows!
Go in and comfort her, you lout!
A head like yours beholds the close
Of doom as soon as he sees no way out.
Hurrah for men that bravely dare!   3370
You're half bedeviled anyway;
There's nothing sillier in the world, I say,
Than being a devil in despair.

Gretchen's Room

GRETCHEN *at her spinning wheel, alone.*

GRETCHEN:
My peace is gone,
My heart is sore,
I'll find it never
And nevermore.
    When he does not come
I live in a tomb,
The world is all   3380
Bitter as gall.
    O, my poor head
Is quite distraught,
And my poor mind
Is overwrought.
    My peace is gone,
My heart is sore,
I'll find it never
And nevermore.
    I look from my window
Only to greet him,   3390
I leave the house
Only to meet him.
    His noble gait
And form and guise,
The smile of his mouth,
The spell of his eyes,
    The magic in
Those words of his,
The clasp of his hand,
And oh!—his kiss.   3400
    My peace is gone,
My heart is sore,
I'll find it never
And nevermore.
    My bosom aches
To feel him near,
Oh, could I clasp

And hold him here
    And kiss and kiss him   3410
Whom I so cherish,
Beneath his kisses
I would perish!

Martha's Garden

MARGARET:
  Promise me, Henry!
FAUST:
             If I can!
MARGARET:
  About religion, what do you feel now, say?
  You are a good, warmhearted man,
  And yet I fear you're not inclined that way.
FAUST:
  Leave that, my child! That I love you, you feel;
  For those I love, my flesh and blood I'd give,
  And no one's church or feelings would I steal.   3420
MARGARET:
  But that is not enough! One must believe!
FAUST:
  Must one?
MARGARET:
         O, if I had some influence!
  You do not even revere the sacraments.
FAUST:
  I do revere them.
MARGARET:
         But without desire.
  It's long since you have gone to Mass or to confession.
  Do you believe in God?
FAUST:
         My darling, who can say:
  I believe in God?
  Ask priest or sage you may,
  And their replies seem odd
  Mockings of the asker.
MARGARET:
         Then you do not believe?   3430
FAUST:
  My answer, dear one, do not misconceive!
  Who can name
  Him, or proclaim:
  I believe in Him?
  Who is so cold
  As to make bold
  To say: I do not believe in Him?
  The all-embracing,
  The all-sustaining,
  Does He not hold and sustain   3440

You, me, Himself?
Does heaven not arch high above us?
Does earth not lie firm here below?
And do not everlasting stars
Rise with a kindly glance?
Do I not gaze into your eyes,
And do not all things crowd
Into your head and heart,
Working in eternal mystery
Invisibly visible at your side?   3450
Let these things fill your heart, vast as they are,
And when you are entirely happy in that feeling,
Then call it what you will:
Heart, Fortune, Love, or God!
I have no name for it.
Feeling is everything,
Names are sound and smoke
Obscuring heaven's glow.

MARGARET:
That is all very good and fair;
The priest says much the same, although   3460
He used a different wording as he spoke.

FAUST:
It is said everywhere
By all hearts underneath the sky of day,
Each heart in its own way;
So why not I in mine?

MARGARET:
It sounds all right when you express it so;
There's something not quite right about it, though;
You have no Christianity.

FAUST:
Dear child!

MARGARET:
                    It has this long time troubled me
To find you keep the company you do.   3470

FAUST:
How so?

MARGARET:
                The person whom you have with you,
In my profoundest being I abhor,
And nothing in my life before
So cut me to the heart
As this man's face when he came near.

FAUST:
My darling, have no fear.

MARGARET:
His presence roils my blood, yet for my part,
People otherwise win my heart;
Much as I yearn to have you near,
This person inspires in me a secret fear,   3480

And if I take him for a scoundrel too,
God forgive me for the wrong I do!

FAUST:

Such queer fish also have to be.

MARGARET:

To live with him would never do for me!
Let him but so much as appear,
He looks about with such a sneer
And half enraged;
Nothing can keep his sympathy engaged;
Upon his brow it's written clear
That he can hold no person dear.   3490
In your embrace I feel so free,
So warm, so yielded utterly;
His presence chokes me, chills me through and through.

FAUST:

O you intuitive angel, you!

MARGARET:

This so overwhelms me, that when
He joins us, be it where it may,
It seems that I no longer love you then.
With him there, I could never pray.
This eats my very heart; and you,
Henry, must feel the same thing too.   3500

FAUST:

This is a matter of antipathy.

MARGARET:

I must be going.

FAUST:

O, when will it be
That I may for a little hour rest
In your embrace in quiet, breast to breast?

MARGARET:

If I but slept alone, this very night
I'd leave the door unbolted, you realize,
But Mother's sleep is always light,
And if she took us by surprise,
I would die on the spot, I think.

FAUST:

There is no need for that, my dear!   3510
Here is a little phial. A mere
Three drops into her drink
Will shroud up Nature in deep sleep.

MARGARET:

What will I not do for your sake?
It will not harm her, though, to take?

FAUST:

Would I propose it, Love, if that were so?

MARGARET:

I look at you, dear man, and do not know
What so compels me to your will;

Already I have done so much for you
That there is little left for me to do.   3520

                                                                    [*Exit.*]

[*Enter* MEPHISTOPHELES.]

MEPHISTOPHELES:
The little monkey's gone?
FAUST:

You spied again?

MEPHISTOPHELES:

I could

Not help but hear it word for word:
Professor had his catechism heard;
I hope it does you lots of good.
Girls have a way of wanting to find out
Whether a man's conventionally devout.
They think: he gave in there, he'll truckle to us, no doubt.
FAUST:
You, monster, do not realize
How this good loyal soul can be
So full of faith and trust—
Which things alone suffice
To make her bliss—and worry holily
For fear she must look on her best beloved as lost.
MEPHISTOPHELES:
You supersensual sensual wooer,
A girl has got you on a puppet wire.
FAUST:
You misbegotten thing of filth and fire!
MEPHISTOPHELES:
She's mighty clever too at physiognomy:
When I am present, she feels—how, she's not just sure,
My mask bodes meaning at a hidden level;
She thinks beyond a doubt I'm a "Genie,"   3540
And possibly the very Devil.
Tonight, then—?
FAUST:

What is that to you?

MEPHISTOPHELES:
I have my pleasure in it too!

At the Well

GRETCHEN *and* LIESCHEN *with pitchers.*

LIESCHEN:
About Barbie, I suppose you've heard?
GRETCHEN:
I get out very little. Not a word.
LIESCHEN:
Why, Sibyl was telling me today.
She's finally gone down Fools' Way.
That's what grand airs will do!

GRETCHEN:

How so?

LIESCHEN:

It stinks!
She's feeding two now when she eats and drinks.

GRETCHEN:

Ah!

LIESCHEN:

Serves her right! And long enough   3550
She hung around that fellow. All that stuff!
It was walk and jaunt
Out to the village and dancing haunt,
And everywhere she had to shine,
Always treating her to pastry and wine;
She got to think her good looks were so fine
She lost her self-respect and nothing would do
But she accepted presents from him too.
It was kiss and cuddle, and pretty soon
The flower that she had was gone.   3560

GRETCHEN:

O the poor thing!

LIESCHEN:

Is it pity that you feel!
When our kind sat at the spinning wheel
And our mothers wouldn't let us out at night,
There she was with her lover at sweet delight
Down on the bench in the dark entryway
With never an hour too long for such play.
So let her go now with head bowed down
And do church penance in a sinner's gown!

GRETCHEN:

But surely he'll take her as his wife!

LIESCHEN:

He'd be a fool! A chipper lad   3570
Finds fun is elsewhere to be had.
Besides, he's gone.

GRETCHEN:

O, that's not fair!

LIESCHEN:

If she gets him, she'll find it bad.
The boys will rip her wreath, and what's more,
They'll strew chopped straw around her door![23]

[*Exit.*]

GRETCHEN [*walking home*]:

How firmly I could once inveigh
When any young girl went astray!
For others' sins I could not find
Words enough to speak my mind!
Black as it was, blacker it had to be,   3580

---

[23] A traditional way of punishing unfaithful wives.

And still it wasn't black enough for me.
I thanked my stars and was so game,
And now I stand exposed to shame!
Yet all that led me to this pass
Was so good, and so dear, alas!

Zwinger[24]

In a niche of the wall a statue of the Mater dolorosa *with jugs of flowers in front of it.*

GRETCHEN [*puts fresh flowers in the jugs*]:
 O deign
Amid your pain
To look in mercy on my grief.
 With sword thrust through
The heart of you,
You gaze up to your Son in death.   3590
 To Him on high
You breathe your sigh
For His and your distressful grief.
 Who knows
What throes
Wrack me, flesh and bone?
What makes my poor heart sick with fear
And what it is I plead for here,
Only you know, you alone!   3600
 No matter where I go,
I know such woe, such woe
Here within my breast!
I am not quite alone,
Alas! I weep, I moan,
My heart is so distressed.
 The flowerpots at my window
Had only tears for dew
When early in the morning
I picked these flowers for you.
 When bright into my room
The early sun had come,   3610
Upon my bed in gloom
I sat, with sorrow numb.
 Help! Rescue me from shame and death!
O deign
Amid your pain
To look in mercy on my grief!

---

[24] *Zwinger* is an untranslatable term for the open space between the last houses of a town and the inside of the city walls, sometimes the open space between two parallel city walls. Gretchen has sought the most out-of-the-way spot in the city for her private devotions. The *Mater dolorosa* is a statue of Mary, the mother of Jesus, in an attitude of grief as she beholds the crucifixion; in accordance with Luke 2:35 her visible heart is pierced with a sword. The text freely adapts the famous thirteenth-century hymn *Stabat mater dolorosa.*

Night

The street in front of GRETCHEN's *door.* VALENTINE, *a soldier, Gretchen's brother.*

VALENTINE:
 When I used to be in a merry crowd
 Where many a fellow liked to boast,   3620
 And lads in praise of girls grew loud
 And to their fairest raised a toast
 And drowned praise in glasses' overflow,
 Then, braced on my elbows, I
 Would sit with calm assurance by
 And listen to their braggadocio;
 Then I would stroke my beard and smile
 And take my brimming glass in hand
 And say: "To each his own! Meanwhile
 Where is there one in all the land   3630
 To hold a candle or compare
 With my sister Gretel anywhere?"
 Clink! Clank! the round of glasses went;
 "He's right!" some shouted in assent,
 "The glory of her sex!" cried some,
 And all the braggarts sat there dumb.
 But now!—I could tear my hair and crawl
 Right up the side of the smooth wall!—
 Now every rascal that comes near
 Can twit me with a jibe or sneer!   3640
 With every chance word dropped I sweat
 Like one who has not paid a debt.
 I'd knock the whole lot down if I
 Could only tell them that they lie.
  What have we here? Who's sneaking along?
 There are two of them, if I'm not wrong.
 If he's the one, I'll grab his hide,
 He won't get out of here alive!
       [*Enter* FAUST *and* MEPHISTOPHELES.]

FAUST:
 How from the window of that sacristy
 The vigil lamp casts forth its flickering light   3650
 Sidewise faint and fainter down the night,
 And darkness closes around totally.
 So in my heart the darkness reigns.

MEPHISTOPHELES:
 And I feel like a cat with loving-pains
 That sneaks up fire escapes and crawls
 And slinks along the sides of walls;
 I feel so cozy at it, and so right,
 With a bit of thievery, a bit of rutting to it.
 Through all my limbs I feel an ache for
 The glorious Walpurgis Night.   3660
 Day after tomorrow brings us to it;
 Then one knows what he stays awake for.

FAUST:
    Will it come to the top, that treasure
    I see glimmering over there?
MEPHISTOPHELES:
    You very soon will have the pleasure
    Of lifting the pot to upper air.
    Just recently I took a squint:
    It's full of ducats shiny from the mint.
FAUST:
    Not a jewel, not a ring
    To add to others of my girl's?   3670
MEPHISTOPHELES:
    I do believe I saw a string
    Of something that looked much like pearls.
FAUST:
    That's good. I really hate to go
    Without a gift to take with me.
MEPHISTOPHELES:
    You needn't fuss and trouble so
    About enjoying something free.
    But now that all the stars are in the sky,
    You'll hear a real art work from me:
    I'll sing her a moral lullaby
    To befool her the more certainly.   3680
                        [He sings to the zither.]
    What dost thou here
    With dawn so near,
    O Katie dear,
    Outside your sweetheart's door?
    Maiden, beware
    Of entering there
    Lest forth you fare
    A maiden nevermore.
        Maidens, take heed!
    Once do the deed,
    And all you need
    Is: Good night, you poor things!   3690
    If you're in love,
    To no thief give
    The thing you have
    Except with wedding rings.
VALENTINE [*steps forward*]:
    Who is it you're luring? By the Element!
    You accursed rat-catcher, you!
    To the Devil first with the instrument!
    Then to the Devil with the singer too!   3700
MEPHISTOPHELES:
    The zither's smashed, there's nothing left of it.
VALENTINE:
    And next there is a skull to split!
MEPHISTOPHELES [*to* FAUST]:
    Don't flinch, Professor, and don't fluster!
    Come close in by me, and don't tarry.

Quick! Whip out your feather duster!
Just thrust away and I will parry.

VALENTINE:
Then parry this!

MEPHISTOPHELES:
Why not?

VALENTINE:
This too!

MEPHISTOPHELES:
Of course!

VALENTINE:
I think the Devil fights in you!
What's this? My hand is going lame.

MEPHISTOPHELES [*to* FAUST]:
Thrust home!

VALENTINE [*falls*]:
O!

MEPHISTOPHELES:
There, the lummox is quite tame.   3710
Come on! It's time for us to disappear.
Soon they will raise a murderous hue and cry.
With the police I always can get by,
But of the court of blood I stand in fear.

MARTHA [*at the window*]:
Come out! Come out!

GRETCHEN [*at the window*]:
Bring out a light!

MARTHA [*as before*]:
They swear and scuffle, shout and fight.

PEOPLE:
Here's one already dead!

MARTHA [*coming out*]:
Where are the murderers? Have they fled?

GRETCHEN [*coming out*]:
Who's lying here?

PEOPLE:
Your mother's son.

GRETCHEN:
Almighty God! I am undone!   3720

VALENTINE:
I'm dying! That's a tale
Soon told and sooner done.
Why do you women stand and wail?
Come close and hear me, everyone!
[*They all gather around him.*]
My Gretchen, see! too young you are
And not yet wise enough by far,
You do not manage right.
In confidence I'll tell you more:
You have turned out to be a whore,
And being one, be one outright.   3730

GRETCHEN:
My brother! God! What do you mean?

VALENTINE:
Leave our Lord God out of this farce. What's done
Is done, alas! and cannot be undone.
And what comes next will soon be seen.
You started secretly with one,
It won't be long till others come,
And when a dozen more have had you,
The whole town will have had you too.
   When shame is born, she first appears
Stealthily amid the world
And with the veil of darkness furled 3740
About her head and ears.
First one would gladly slay her outright.
But as she grows and waxes bold,
She walks quite naked in the daylight,
But is no fairer to behold.
The uglier her visage grows,
The more by open day she goes.
   The time already I foresee
When all the decent citizenry
Will from you, harlot, turn away 3750
As from a plague corpse in their way.
Your heart will sink within you when
They look you in the eye! No more
Golden chains will you wear then![25]
Or stand by the altar in church as before!
No more in collars of fine lace
Will you come proudly to the dancing place!
Off to a dismal corner you will slouch
Where the beggars and the cripples crouch.
And even though God may forgive, 3760
Accursed here on earth you still will live.
MARTHA:
Commend your soul to God! Will you
Take blasphemy upon you too?
VALENTINE:
If I could reach your withered skin and bone,
You shameless, pandering, old crone,
I do believe that I could win
Full pardon for my every sin!
GRETCHEN:
My brother! What pain of hell for me!
VALENTINE:
I tell you, let your weeping be!
When you gave up your honor, you gave 3770
The fiercest heart-stab I could know.

---

[25]As Goethe had observingly read, a Frankfurt police ordinance of the fifteenth century forbade promiscuous women to wear jewelry, silk, satin, or damask, and denied them the use of a pew in church. This latter requirement would force them to remain at the rear with the "beggars and the cripples."

Now through the sleep of death I go
To God, a soldier true and brave.

[*Dies.*]

Cathedral

Service, organ, and choir. GRETCHEN *among many people. An* EVIL SPIRIT *behind Gretchen.*

EVIL SPIRIT:
How different, Gretchen, it was
When still full of innocence
You approached this altar,
From your little dog-eared prayer book
Murmuring prayers,   3780
Half childish play,
Half God in heart!
Gretchen!
Where are your thoughts?
Within your heart
What deed of crime?
Do you pray for your mother's soul that slept
Away unto the long, long pain because of you?
Whose blood is on your doorstep?
—And underneath your heart
Does not a new life quicken,   3790
Tormenting itself and you
With its premonitory presence?

GRETCHEN:
Alas! Alas!
If I could be rid of the thoughts
That rush this way and that way
Despite my will!

CHOIR:
Dies irae, dies illa
solvet saeclum in favilla.[26]

[*The organ sounds.*]

EVIL SPIRIT:
Wrath seizes you!
The trumpet sounds!   3800
The graves shudder!
And your heart
From ashen rest,
For flames of torment
Once more reconstituted,
Quakes forth.

GRETCHEN:
If I were out of here!

---

[26]The opening of the greatest of medieval hymns, the *Dies irae*, composed before 1250, probably by Thomas of Celano, and used in masses of the dead: "The day of wrath, that day / Shall dissolve the world in fire." Through nineteen three-line stanzas the hymn describes the end of the world and the Last Judgment.

I feel as if the organ were
Stifling my breath,
As if the choir dissolved
My inmost heart.   3810

CHOIR:

Judex ergo cum sedebit,
quidquid latet adparebit,
nil inultum remanebit.[27]

GRETCHEN:

I cannot breathe!
The pillars of the wall
Imprison me!
The vaulted roof
Crushes me!—Air!

EVIL SPIRIT:

Concealment! Sin and shame
Are not concealed.   3820
Air? Light?
Woe to you!

CHOIR:

Quid sum miser tunc dicturus?
Quem patronum rogaturus?
Cum vix justus sit securus.[28]

EVIL SPIRIT:

The clarified avert
Their countenances from you.
The pure shudder to reach
Out hands to you.   3830
Woe!

CHOIR:

Quid sum miser tunc dicturus?

GRETCHEN:

Neighbor! Your smelling-bottle!

[She falls in a faint.]

Walpurgis Night

The Harz Mountains. Vicinity of Schierke and Elend.[29]

MEPHISTOPHELES:

Now don't you long for broomstick-transportation?
I'd like the toughest he-goat there can be.
We're far yet, by this route, from destination.

---

[27]"Therefore when the Judge shall sit, / Whatever is hidden shall appear, / Nothing shall remain unavenged."

[28]"What shall I, wretched, say? / What patron shall I call upon? / When scarcely the just man is safe."

[29]Saint Walpurgis (Walpurga, Walburga, Valburg, d. 780) was a niece of Saint Boniface and herself a missionary to Germany. By coincidence, her church calendar day, April 30, fell together with the pagan festivals on the eve of May Day, the end of winter and the beginning of summer. Under the Christian dispensation, those festivals, like the Hallowe'en festivals (Oct. 31) at the end of summer and the beginning of winter, passed into folklore as devils' orgies. Folklore further localized those orgies on the Brocken, highest peak of the Harz Mountains in central Germany. From the village of Elend a two- or three-hour walk leads past the village of Schierke to a desolate plateau and finally to the top of the Brocken.

FAUST:

Since my legs still are holding out so sturdily,
This knotty stick will do for me.
Why take a short cut anyway?
Slinking through this labyrinth of alleys, 3840
Then climbing cliffs above these valleys
Where streams plunge down in everlasting spray,
Such is the spice of pleasure on this way!
Springtime over birches weaves its spell,
It's sensed already by the very pine;
Why should it not affect our limbs as well?

MEPHISTOPHELES:

There's no such feeling in these limbs of mine!
Within me all is winter's chill;
On my path I'd prefer the frost and snow.
How drearily the reddish moon's disc, still 3850
Not full, is rising with belated glow
And giving such bad light that any step now
Will have us bumping into rock or tree!
I'll call a will-o'-the-wisp,[30] if you'll allow.
I see one burning merrily.
Hey, there, my friend! May I request your flare?
Why flash for nothing over there?
Just be so good and light our way up here.

WILL-O'-THE-WISP:

I hope sheer awe will give me mastery
Over my natural instability; 3860
Most commonly we go a zigzag career.

MEPHISTOPHELES:

Ho, ho! It's man you want to imitate!
Now in the Devil's name, go straight!
Or else I'll blow your flicker-life right out.

WILL-O'-THE-WISP:

You are the master here beyond a doubt,
And so I'll do my best to serve you nicely.
Remember, though! The mountain is magic-mad tonight,
And if you want a will-o'-the-wisp to lend you light
You mustn't take these matters too precisely.

    [FAUST, MEPHISTOPHELES, WILL-O'-THE-WISP *in alternating song.*] 3870

Having entered, as it seems,
Realms of magic and of dreams,
Guide us well so that we may
Get along our upward way
Through the vast and empty waste.

    Tree after tree, with what mad haste
They rush past us as we go,
See the boulders bending low,
And the rocks of long-nosed sort,
How they snore and how they snort.

---

[30]A will-o'-the-wisp (*ignis fatuus,* Jack-o'-Lantern) is a conglomeration of phosphorescent gas from decayed vegetation in swamps. By night it resembles an eerily swaying lantern.

Athwart the turf, the stones athwart,   3880
Brook and brooklet speeds along.
Is it rustling? Is it song?
Do I hear love's sweet lament
Singing of days from heaven sent?
What we hope and what we love!
And the echo is retold
Like a tale from times of old.
    To-whit! To-whoo! it sounds away,
Screech owl, plover, and the jay;
Have all these stayed wide awake?   3890
Are those efts amid the brake?
Long of haunch and thick of paunch!
And the roots that wind and coil
Snakelike out of stone and soil
Knot the bonds of wondrous snares,
Scare us, take us unawares;
Out of tough and living gnarls
Polyp arms reach out in snarls
For the traveler's foot. Mice scurry
Thousand-colored by drove and flurry   3900
Through the moss and through the heather!
And the fireflies in ascent
Densely swarm and swirl together,
Escort to bewilderment.
    Have we stopped or are we trying
To continue onward flying?
Everything is whirling by,
Rocks and trees are making faces,
Wandering lights in many places
Bloat and bulge and multiply.   3910

MEPHISTOPHELES:
Grab my cloak-end and hold tight.
Here's a sort of medium height
Which for our amazement shows
How Mammon in the mountain glows.

FAUST:
How oddly in the valley bottoms gleams
A dull glow like the break of day,
And even in the chasm's deepest seams
It probes and gropes its searching way.
There steam puffs forth, there vapor twines,
Here through the mist the splendor shines,   3920
Now dwindling to a slender thread,
Now gushing like a fountainhead.
It fans out in a hundred veins
A long stretch of the valley run,
Then where the narrow pass constrains
Its course, it merges into one.
There sparks are gusting high and higher
Like golden sand strewn on the night.
Look! There along its entire height
The cliff-face kindles into fire.   3930

MEPHISTOPHELES:
> Has not Sir Mammon done some fine contriving
> To illuminate his palace hall?
> You're lucky to have seen it all.
> But now I scent the boisterous guests arriving.

FAUST:
> How the wind's bride rides the air!
> How she beats my back with cuff and blow!

MEPHISTOPHELES:
> Grab on to this cliff's ancient ribs with care
> Or she will hurl you to the chasm far below.
> A mist has thickened the night.
> Hark! Through the forests, what a crashing!   3940
> The startled owls fly up in fright.
> Hark! The splitting and the smashing
> Of pillars in the greenwood hall!
> Boughs strain and snap and fall.
> The tree trunks' mighty moaning!
> The tree roots' creaking and groaning!
> In fearful entanglement they all
> Go tumbling to their crushing fall,
> And through the wreckage-littered hollows
> The hissing wind howls and wallows.   3950
> Do you hear voices there on high?
> In the distance, or nearby?
> Yes, the mountain all along
> Is bathed in frenzied magic song.

WITCHES [*in chorus*]:
> The witches to the Brocken ride,
> The stubble is yellow, the corn is green.
> There with great crowds up every side,
> Seated on high, Lord Urian[31] is seen.
> And on they go over stock and stone,
> The he-goat st——s from the f——ts of the crone.[32]
>   3960

A VOICE:
> Old Baubo[33] by herself comes now,
> Riding on a farrow sow.

CHORUS:
> Pay honor where honor is due!
> Dame Baubo, up and on with you!
> A mother astride a husky sow,
> The whole witch crew can follow now.

A VOICE:
> Which way did *you* come?

A VOICE:
>   By Ilsenstein crest.
> And I took a peep in an owlet's nest:

---

[31] The Devil.
[32] "The he-goat stinks from the farts of the crone."
[33] In Greek mythology, an obscene and bestial nurse of Demeter.

What eyes she made at me!

A VOICE:

O go to hell!

Why must you drive so hard!   3970

A VOICE:

She skinned me alive,
I'll never survive!

WITCHES [*chorus*]:

The way is broad, the way is long,
O what a mad and crazy throng!
The broomstick scratches, the pitchfork pokes,
The mother bursts open, the infant chokes.

WITCHMASTERS [*semi-chorus*]:

We creep along like a snail in his house,
The women are always up ahead.
For traveling to the Devil's house,
Women are a thousand steps ahead.

THE OTHER HALF:

Why, that's no cause for sorry faces!   3980
Women need the thousand paces;
But let them hurry all they can,
One jump is all it takes a man.

A VOICE [*above*]:

Come on along from Felsensee there, you!

VOICES [*from below*]:

We'd like to make the top there too.
We wash and are as clean as clean can be,
And still the same sterility.

BOTH CHORUSES:

The wind has died, the star has fled,
The dull moon hides, and in its stead   3990
The whizzings of our magic choir
Strike forth a thousand sparks of fire.

A VOICE [*from below*]:

Wait! Wait! Or I'll get left!

A VOICE [*from above*]:

Who's calling from that rocky cleft?

A VOICE [*from below*]:

Take me with you! Take me with you!
Three hundred years I have been climbing
And still can't make the top, I find.
I'd like to be with my own kind.

BOTH CHORUSES:

A broom or stick will carry you,
A pitchfork or a he-goat too;   4000
Whoever cannot fly today
Is lost forever, you might say.

HALF-WITCH [*below*]:

Here all these years I've minced along;
How did the others get so far ahead?
I have no peace at home, and yet
Can't get in here where I belong.

CHORUS OF WITCHES:
>The salve puts courage in a hag,
>A sail is made from any rag,
>For a ship any trough will do;
>None flies unless today he flew. 4010

BOTH CHORUSES:
>And when the topmost peak we round
>Just coast along and graze the ground,
>So far and wide the heath will be
>Hid by your swarm of witchery.

>*[They alight.]*

MEPHISTOPHELES:
>They push and shove, they bustle and gab,
>They hiss and swirl, they hustle and blab!
>They glow, shed sparks, and stink and burn!
>The very witches' element!
>Hold tight to me, or we'll be swept apart in turn.
>Where are you?

FAUST:
>   Here!

MEPHISTOPHELES:
>   What? Swept so far so soon? 4020
>I must invoke my house-right and call the tune.
>Squire Voland[34] comes! Give ground, sweet rabble, ground!
>Grab on to me, Professor! In one bound
>We'll give this mob the slip quite easily;
>It's too mad even for the likes of me.
>There's something shining with a very special flare
>Down in those bushes. Curiosity
>Impels me. Come! We'll drop in there.

FAUST:
>You Spirit of Contradiction! Be my guiding light!
>I think it was a move that made good sense: 4030
>We travel to the Brocken on Walpurgis Night
>To isolate ourselves up here by preference.

MEPHISTOPHELES:
>Just see the jolly fires! Why here
>A club has gathered for good cheer.
>In little circles one is not alone.

FAUST:
>I'd rather be up there, I own.
>I see the glow and twisting smoke.
>The crowd streams toward the Evil One;
>There many a riddle must be undone.

MEPHISTOPHELES:
>And many a riddle also spun. 4040
>But let the great world revel away,
>Here where it's quiet we shall stay.
>It is a usage long since instituted

---

[34] Another name for the Devil.

That in the great world little worlds are constituted.
I see young witches naked and bare,
And old ones clothed more prudently;
For my sake, show them courtesy,
The effort is small, the jest is rare.
I hear some tuning up of instruments.
Damned whine and drone! One must get used to it.   4050
Come on! Come on! Now there's no help for it,
I'll go in first and prepare your entrance,
And you will owe me for another work of mine.
This is no little space, you must admit, my friend.
Look, and your eye can hardly see the end.
A hundred bonfires burn there in a line;
There's dancing, chatting, cooking, drinking, making love;
What better things than these can you think of?

FAUST:

In which of your roles will you now appear,
Magician or Devil, to introduce me here?   4060

MEPHISTOPHELES:

Most commonly I go incognito,
But on such gala days one lets one's Orders show.
I have no Garter to distinguish me,
But here the cloven hoof is held in dignity.
You see that snail that's creeping toward us there
Its feelers have already spied
My presence somehow in the air;
I couldn't hide here even if I tried.
Come on! We'll stroll along from fire to fire,
I'll be the wooer and you can be the squire.   4070

[*to some people who are sitting around some dying embers*]

Old gentlemen, what are you doing here?
I'd praise you if I found you in the midst of cheer
Surrounded by the noise and youthful riot;
Alone at home we get our fill of quiet.

GENERAL:

Who can put any faith in nations,
Do for them all you may have done?
With women and with populations
Youth is always number one.

PRIME MINISTER:

They're too far off the right course now today,
I still stick with the men of old;   4080
For frankly, when we had our way,
That was the actual Age of Gold.

PARVENU:

We weren't so stupid either, you'll allow,
And often did what we should not;
But everything is topsy-turvy now
Just when we'd like to keep the things we've got.

AUTHOR:

Where can you read a publication
With even a modicum of sense?

As for the younger generation,
They are the height of impudence.   4090
MEPHISTOPHELES [*who suddenly looks very old*]:
I feel men ripe for doomsday, now my legs
Are climbing Witches' Hill in their last climb;
And since my cask is running dregs,
The world is also running out of time.
HUCKSTER WITCH:
O Sirs, don't pass me by this way!
Don't miss this opportunity!
Just give my wares some scrutiny,
All sorts of things are on display.
Across the earth you will not find
A booth like this; no item here, not one   4100
But what has good sound mischief done
At some time to the world and human kind.
No dagger here but what has dripped with gore,
No cup but what has served to pour
Consuming poison in some healthy frame,
No jewel but what has misled to her shame
Some lovely girl, no sword but of the kind
That stabbed an adversary from behind.
MEPHISTOPHELES:
Cousin, you're out of date in times like these.
What's done is past, what's past is done.   4110
Get in a stock of novelties!
With us it's novelties or none.
FAUST:
If I don't lose my mind! But I declare
This really is what I would call a fair!
MEPHISTOPHELES:
The whole mad rout is pushing on above;
You're being shoved, though you may think you shove.
FAUST:
Now who is that?
MEPHISTOPHELES:
                        Observe her with some care,
For that is Lilith.
FAUST:
                    Who?
MEPHISTOPHELES:
                        Adam's first wife.
Beware of her resplendent hair,
The one adornment that she glories in,   4120
Once she entraps a young man in that snare,
She won't so quickly let him out again.
FAUST:
That old witch with the young one sitting there,
They've kicked their heels around, that pair!
MEPHISTOPHELES:
No rest for them today. Ah! They're beginning
Another dance. Come on! Let's get into the swing.

FAUST [*dancing with the* YOUNG WITCH]:
    A lovely dream once came to me;
    In it I saw an apple tree,
    Two lovely apples shone upon it,
    They charmed me so, I climbed up on it.   4130
THE BEAUTY:
    Apples always were your craze
    From Paradise to present days.
    I feel joy fill me through and through
    To think my garden bears them too.
MEPHISTOPHELES [*with the* OLD WITCH]:
    A dismal dream once came to me;
    In it I saw a cloven tree,
    It had a ―― ―― ――;
    Yet ―― as it was, it charmed my soul.
THE OLD WITCH:
    I proffer now my best salute
    To the Knight with the Horse's Hoof!
    So if your ―― ―― ――, go to it,   4140
    Unless ―― ―― won't let you do it.
PROKTOPHANTASMIST:
    Accursed mob! This is presumptuous!
    Was it not long since proved to you
    Ghosts do not have the same feet humans do?
    And here you dance just like the rest of us!
THE BEAUTY [*dancing*]:
    And what does *he* want at our ball?
FAUST [*dancing*]:
    Oh, he turns up just anywhere at all.
    What others dance, he must evaluate.
    If there's a step about which he can't prate,   4150
    It's just as if the step had not occurred.
    It bothers him the most when we go forward.
    If you would run in circles round about
    The way he does in his old mill,
    He'd call it good and sing its praises still,
    Especially if his opinion were sought out.
PROKTOPHANTASMIST:
    But you're still here! Oh! This is insolent!
    Begone! Why, we brought in Enlightenment!
    This Devil's pack, with them all rules are flouted.
    We are so clever, yet there is no doubt about it: 4160
    There's still a ghost at Tegel. How long have I swept
    Illusions out, and still I find they're kept.
THE BEAUTY:
    Then go away and let us have the field.
PROKTOPHANTASMIST:
    I tell you spirits to your faces
    I will not stand for any traces
    Of spirit despotism I can't wield.
                    [*The dancing goes on.*]
    I just can't win today, no matter what I do.
    But I can always take a trip;

And I still hope, before I'm done, to slip
One over on the devils and the writers too.   4170
MEPHISTOPHELES:
Down in the nearest puddle he will plump,
That is the best assuagement he can find;
If leeches feast upon his rump,
He will be cured of ghosts and his own mind.

[*to* FAUST, *who has left the dance*]

Why do you leave that pretty girl
Who in the dance so sweetly sang?
FAUST:
Because a little red mouse sprang
Out of her mouth while she was singing.
MEPHISTOPHELES:
What's wrong with that? The mouse was still not grey.
Why raise such questions and be bringing   4180
Them to a trysting hour anyway?
FAUST:
Then I saw—
MEPHISTOPHELES:
                    What?
FAUST:
                          Mephisto, do you see
A pale girl standing over there alone?
She drags herself but slowly from the place
And seems to move with shackled feet.
I must confess she has the sweet
Look of my kindly Gretchen's face.
MEPHISTOPHELES:
Let that be! That bodes well for no one.
It is a magic image, lifeless, an eidolon.
Encounters with such are not good;   4190
The fixed stare freezes human blood
And one is turned almost to stone—
You've heard of the Medusa,[35] I suppose.
FAUST:
Indeed, a corpse's eyes are those,
Unshut by loving hand. That is the breast
That Gretchen offered for my rest,
That is the dear, sweet body I have known.
MEPHISTOPHELES:
You easily misguided fool, that's magic art.
She looks to every man like his own sweetheart.
FAUST:
What suffering! And what delight!   4200
My eyes can not shift from that sight.
How oddly round that lovely throat there lies
A single band of scarlet thread
No broader than a knife has bled.

---

[35]The Medusa, her hair made of serpents, turned men into stone by looking at them. She was slain by Perseus, who cut off her head.

MEPHISTOPHELES:
Quite right! And I can see it likewise.
Beneath her arm she also carries that same head
Since Perseus cut it off for her.
And you crave for illusion still!
Come, let us climb that little hill,
The Prater is no merrier,[36]   4210
And if I haven't been misled,
I actually see a theater.
What's being given?
SERVIBILIS:
                    A minute yet before it starts.
A new play, last of seven in a row;
That is the number given in these parts.
A dilettant made up the show,
And dilettanti take the parts.
Forgive me, Sirs, if I now disappear;
I just delight in running up the curtain.
MEPHISTOPHELES:
I'm glad to find you on the Blocksberg here,   4220
It's just where you belong, that's certain.
ARIEL:
If mind or Nature gave you wings
    And any wing discloses,
Follow where my leading brings
    You to the Hill of Roses.
ORCHESTRA [*pianissimo*]:
Gauze of mist and cloud-bank's edge
    Are touched with streaks of dawn.
Breeze in branch and wind in sedge,
    And everything is gone.

Gloomy Day[37]

A field.

FAUST: In misery! Desperate! Long wandering pitifully upon the earth and now
    in prison! Locked up as a wrongdoer for ghastly torments in a jail, that lovely,
    unfortunate creature! To come to this! To this!—Perfidious, worthless Spirit, and
    this you kept from me!—Stand there, yes, stand there! Roll those devilish eyes
    furiously in your head! Stand and defy me with your unbearable presence! In
    prison! In irrevocable misery! Delivered over to evil spirits and to judging, heart-
    less humanity! And meanwhile you lull me with insipid dissipations, conceal her
    increasing misery from me, and let her go helpless to destruction!
MEPHISTOPHELES: She is not the first.
FAUST: Cur! Monster of abomination!—Turn him, Infinite Spirit, turn the worm
    back into his canine form, the way he used to like to trot along in front of me

---

[36] The Prater is a famous park in Vienna.
[37] Scene 22, "Walpurgis-Night's Dream," a puzzling scene seldom included in dramatic productions of
Faust, has been omitted.

often in time of night, and roll at the feet of the harmless traveler, and cling to the shoulders of one who fell. Turn him back into his favorite shape, so he can crawl on his belly in the sand up to me and I can kick him, the reprobate!—Not the first!—Grief! Grief beyond the grasp of any human soul, that more than one creature has sunk to the depths of such misery, that the first did not atone for the guilt of all the others in her writhing and deathly agony before the eyes of Eternal Forgiveness! It grinds through my marrow and my life, the misery of this one alone; you grin complacently over the fate of thousands!

MEPHISTOPHELES: Now we are once again at the limit of our wits, where the minds of you mortals go overboard. Why do you make common cause with us if you can't go through with it? You want to fly and are not proof to dizziness? Did we force ourselves on you, or you on us?

FAUST: Do not bare your ravening fangs at me that way! I loathe it!—Great and glorious Spirit who didst deign to appear to me, who knowest my heart and my soul, why dost thou forge me together with this infamous associate who gloats on harm and revels in destruction?

MEPHISTOPHELES: Are you through?

FAUST: Save her! Or woe to you! The ghastliest of curses upon you unto millennia!

MEPHISTOPHELES: I cannot loose the avenger's bonds, nor open his locks.—Save her!—Who was it plunged her into ruin? I or you? [FAUST *gazes wildly about.*] So you reach for thunderbolts? Lucky they were not given to you miserable mortals! To pulverize an innocent person in his path is the way of the tyrant, in order to relieve his feelings.

FAUST: Take me there! She shall be free!

MEPHISTOPHELES: And the risk you run? Remember: blood-guilt from your hand still lies upon the city. Over the place where the slain man fell hover avenging spirits in wait for the returning murderer.

FAUST: This yet from you? A world of murder and death upon you, monster! Take me there, I say, and set her free!

MEPHISTOPHELES: I will take you, and what I *can* do: hear! Do I have all power in heaven and on earth? The jailer's senses I will becloud, *you* get possession of his keys and lead her out yourself with your human hand. I will stand watch! The magic horses are ready, I will carry you away. This much I can do.

FAUST: Up and away!

Night, Open Country

FAUST, MEPHISTOPHELES, *rushing on black horses.*

FAUST:
 What are they doing yonder on Gallows Rock?
MEPHISTOPHELES:
 I don't know what they're brewing or doing.   4400
FAUST:
 They soar and swoop, bending and stooping.
MEPHISTOPHELES:
 A crew of witches.
FAUST:
 They strew and bless.
MEPHISTOPHELES:
 On past! On past!

Dungeon

FAUST *in front of a little iron door, with a bunch of keys and a lamp.*

FAUST:
A horror long unfamiliar over me crawls,
Grief seizes me, grief common to human kind.
She is imprisoned in these clammy walls,
Her crime a fond illusion of the mind.
You shrink back from her door
Afraid to see her once more!
On! Delay brings Death up from behind.

[*He seizes the lock.*]
[*Singing is heard from inside.*]

My mother, the whore,
She murdered me!
My father, the rogue,
He has eaten me!
Little sister has laid
My bones away
In a place of cool, cool shade.
And I am turned into a woodland bird;
Fly away! Fly away!

FAUST [*unlocking the door*]:
She does not dream her lover can thus hear
Her clanking chains, her rustling straw so near.

[*He enters.*]

MARGARET [*cowering on her pallet*]:
They're coming. O how bitter it is to die!

FAUST [*softly*]:
Be still! Be still! I come to set you free.

MARGARET [*throwing herself at his feet*]:
If you are human, feel my misery.

FAUST:
You'll wake the jailer with your cry!

[*He takes hold of the chains to unlock them.*]

MARGARET [*on her knees*]:
Who was it, headsman, who could give
You so much power!
You take me at the midnight hour.
Have pity on me, let me live!
Is tomorrow morning not time enough?

[*She stands up.*]

Am I not still so young, so young!
To die so soon!
And I was beautiful, and that was my undoing.
My friend was near, now he is near no more.
My wreath lies torn, the flowers scattered that I wore.
O do not seize me so violently!
What have I done to you? O pity me!
Let me not in vain implore,

4410

4420

4430

I never saw you in my life before!   4440
FAUST:
    Will I survive such misery!
MARGARET:
    I am now wholly in your might.
    First let me nurse my child again.
    I fondled it all through the night;
    They took it from me just to cause me pain,
    And now they say that I have slain
    My child. Now I shall never more be glad.
    And they sing songs about me! How can they be
    So wicked! So runs an ancient story, but who bade
    Them make that tale fit me!   4450
FAUST [*falling on his knees*]:
    A lover at your feet implores
    You to come forth out of these woeful doors.
MARGARET [*kneels with him*]:
    O let us kneel and call upon the saints in prayer!
    Look! Underneath that stair,
    Beneath that threshold there,
    Hell seethes! Beneath the floor
    The Evil One
    Makes ghastly noise
    Of tumult and uproar!
FAUST [*loudly*]:
    Gretchen! Gretchen!   4460
MARGARET [*attentively*]:
    That was my beloved's voice!
                        [*She jumps up. Her chains fall off.*]
    Where is he? I heard him calling me.
    No one can stop me. I am free!
    To his arms I will fly,
    And at his heart I'll lie!
    Gretchen, he called! He stood there at that door.
    And through the howling din of hell's uproar,
    Through the wrath of devils' mocking noise
    I recognized that sweet, that loving voice.
FAUST:
    I *am* here!
MARGARET:
                You! O say that once again!   4470
                    [*embracing him*]
    It *is* he! Where is anguish now, or pain?
    Where is my prison's agony?
    You come to set me free!
    And I am saved!—
    There is the street once more where I
    That first time saw you passing by.
    There is the cheerful garden too
    With Martha and me waiting for you.
FAUST [*trying to lead her away*]:
    Come with me! Come with me!

MARGARET:

O tarry!

I gladly tarry where you tarry.

[caressing him]

FAUST:

Hurry!
Unless you hurry,
It will cost us a bitter price.

MARGARET:

What! Can you no longer kiss?
So briefly gone, so soon returned,
My friend, and kissing all unlearned?
Why am I frightened with such strange alarms,
When from your words, your glances, overwhelmingly
I once felt all of heaven in your arms,
When you would kiss as though to stifle me?
Kiss me now, or
I will kiss you!

[She embraces him.]

Alas! your lips are cold,
And dumb.
What has become
Of your loving?
Who has robbed me of it?

[She turns away from him.]

FAUST:

Come! Follow me! My darling, be bold!
I'll love you with a passion thousandfold,
Only come with me! That's all I'd have you do!

MARGARET [turning toward him]:

But is it you? But is it really you?

FAUST:

It is! But come with me!

MARGARET:

You loose my chain,

And take me back into your arms again.
How is it that you do not shrink from me?—
Do you know who it is, my friend, you're setting free?

FAUST:

Come! Come! Deep night will soon be done.

MARGARET:

I sent my mother to her death,
I drowned my child—the one
Born to both you and me—yes, to you too.
It is you! I can not believe it yet.
Give me your hand! It is no dream!
Your dear hand!—O! But it is wet!
Wipe it off. But still I seem
To see blood on it.
My God! What have you done!
Put up your sword,
That much I ask!

4480

4490

4500

4510

FAUST:
> O let the past be past and done
> Or you will be my death.

MARGARET:
> No, you must stay alive!   4520
> The graves I will describe for you,
> And you must see to them
> This coming morning;
> The best spot give to my mother,
> And next to her my brother;
> Bury me off a little way,
> But not too far away;
> And the babe at my right breast.
> No one else will lie by me!—
> To nestle at your side so lovingly,   4530
> That was a rapture sweet and blest!
> But for me that will never come again.
> It seems as if I had to force my way to you,
> As if you spurned me away from you;
> Yet it is you, and your look is so winsome.

FAUST:
> If you feel it is I, then come!

MARGARET:
> Out there?

FAUST:
> To freedom.

MARGARET:
> If the grave is there,
> If Death is waiting, come!
> From there to my eternal bed   4540
> But not one step beyond—
> You go? O Henry, if I could go too!

FAUST:
> You can! If you but will! There is the door.

MARGARET:
> I cannot go! For me hope is no more.
> What good is flight? They only hunt me down.
> It is so wretched to have to beg,
> And with an evil conscience too!
> It is so wretched to wander far from home,
> And they would catch me anyway!

FAUST:
> I will stay with you.   4550

MARGARET:
> O quick! O quick!
> Save your poor child.
> Go up the path
> That skirts the brook
> And across the bridge
> To the woods beyond,
> Left, where the plank is
> In the pond.

Catch it quick!
It tries to rise,   4560
It struggles still!
Save it! Save it!

FAUST:

Control yourself!
One step, and you are free!

MARGARET:

If only we were past the hill!
There sits my mother on a stone,
And I am cold with dread!
There sits my mother on a stone
And shakes her head.
She does not beckon, does not nod, her head sinks lower,   4570
She slept so long, she wakes no more.
She slept so we might love.
O those were happy times!

FAUST:

If all things fail that I can say,
Then I must carry you away.

MARGARET:

No, let me go! I will not suffer violence!
Let go the hand that murderously holds me so fast!
I did all things to please you in the past.

FAUST:

The day shows grey. My love! My love!

MARGARET:

Yes, daylight penetrates. The final day.   4580
It was to be my wedding day.
Tell no one you have been with Gretchen.
Alas! rough hands
Have ripped the wreath I wore.
And we shall meet once more,
But not at the dance.
The crowd wells forth, it swells and grows
And overflows
The streets, the square;
The staff is broken, the death knell fills the air.[38]   4590
How I am seized and bound!
I am already at the block.
The neck of every living soul around
Foresenses the ax blade and its shock.
The crowd is silent as a tomb.

FAUST:

Would I were never born!

[MEPHISTOPHELES *appears outside.*]

MEPHISTOPHELES:

Up! Or it is your doom.
Useless dallying! Shilly-shallying!

---

[38]The judge broke a wand as a way to symbolize a death sentence.

My horses shudder outside the door,[39]
It is the break of day.   4600
MARGARET:
   What rises out of the floor?
   He! He! Send him away!
   What does he want in this sacred place?[40]
   He comes for me!
FAUST:
                   You shall live!
MARGARET:
   Judgment of God! Myself to Thee I give!
MEPHISTOPHELES [*to* FAUST]:
   Come on! Come on! Or I'll leave you here with her.
MARGARET:
   Father, I am Thine! Deliver me!
   You angels! Sacred hosts, descend!
   Guard me about, protect me and defend!
   Henry! I shudder to behold you.   4610
MEPHISTOPHELES:
   She is condemned!
A VOICE [*from above*]:
                     Is saved!
MEPHISTOPHELES [*to* FAUST]:
                             Hither to me!
   [*Disappears with* FAUST.]
A VOICE [*from within, dying away*]:
   Henry! Henry!

THE SECOND PART OF THE TRAGEDY

Act One

Pleasant Region

FAUST *reclining on flowery greensward, restless, trying to sleep. Twilight. A ring of spirits hovering and flitting, graceful tiny forms.*

ARIEL[41] [*song accompanied by Aeolian harps*]:
   When the blossoms of the spring
   Float as rain down to the earth,
   When green fields are shimmering
   For all who are of this world's birth,
   Elfins of high spirit race
   Haste to help where help they can;
   Be he holy, be he base,
   They grieve for the grieving man.   4620

---

[39] They are magic horses of the night and cannot bear the light of day.

[40] A condemned person's place of confinement was inaccessible to evil spirits; that Mephistopheles dares intrude is a sign of his desperation lest he lose Faust.

[41] Ariel and the Elves symbolize the curative powers of Nature.

You airy hoverers where this head now lies,
Reveal yourselves in noble elfin guise,
Assuage the frantic turmoil of his soul,
Withdraw the fiery bitter arrows of remorse,
From horror lived through, purge and make him whole.
    Four are the watches of night's course,
Be prompt to keep them gladly and in full.
First, on cool pillows let his head be laid,
Then bathe him in the Lethe of the dew;
Lithe shall his strained and stiffened limbs be made   4630
And rest deliver him to day, all new.
Perform the fairest elfin rite,
Restore him to the holy light.

CHORUS [*singly, by twos, and in combination, alternately and together*]:
    When the air lies warm and calm
Over green-hemmed field and dale,
Twilight wafts a fragrant balm,
Wafts sweet mists in veil on veil,
Whispers softly of sweet peace,
Rocks the heart to childlike rest,
Grants this weary man's eyes ease,   4640
Shuts the portals of the west.
    Night has come with total dark,
Holily star moves to star,
Sovereign fire and feeble spark
Glitters near and glows afar,
Glitters here lake-mirrored, glows
High up in the clear of night;
Sealing joy in deep repose,
Reigns the moon in fullest light.
    Now these hours are snuffed out,   4650
Pain and joy have died away;
Health is certain; banish doubt,
Put your trust in coming day.
Green dawn valleys, hills are pillows
Fluffed for shadowed rest and sweet,
Harvestwards in silver billows
Sway and surge the tides of wheat.
    Wish on wishes to obtain,
Look to skies all bright aloft.
Lightest fetters still restrain,   4660
Sleep is seed coat: sluff it off!
Though the many shrink and waver,
Do not tarry to make bold;
All things tend in that man's favor
Who perceives and takes swift hold.
    [*Tremendous tumult proclaims the approach of the sun.*]

ARIEL:
Hark! the horal tempest nears!
Sounding but to spirit ears
Where the newborn day appears.

Cliff gates, rasping, open; under
Phoebus' chariot wheels rolls thunder;   4670
What mighty din the daylight brings!
Drumrolls pounding, trumpets sounding,
Eyesight-dazzling, ear-astounding,
Unheard be such unheard things.[42]
Into headed flowers dart!
Lie there still in deepest part,
Under leaves, in clefts of rock:
Deafness comes of such a shock!

FAUST:

Life's pulse, renewed in vigor, throbs to greet
Aethereal dawning of the gentle light.   4680
New-quickened, Earth, thou breathest at my feet,
Thou who wert also constant through the night;
Already thou conferrest joy once more
And rousest resolution of great might
To strive for highest being evermore.
  In shimmering dawn revealed the world now lies,
The thousand voices of the forest soar,
A radiance streams in glory from the skies
Though mists in valleys still are drifted deep,
And branches fresh with life emerge and rise   4690
From fragrant glens where they were drowned in sleep;
By dull depths yielded up, hue clears on hue
Where pearls from glistening bloom and petal weep,
And paradise emerges to my view.
  Lift up your eyes!—Each giant mountain height
Proclaims the solemnest of hours anew.
They soonest catch the everlasting light
Which will thereafter unto us descend.
Now down the Alpine lawns steep-sloping, bright
New radiance and clarity extend   4700
And step by step their last objectives gain.
The sun comes forth! But when I that way tend,
I am struck blind, I turn aside in pain.
  So is it with our yearning hopes that tried
And finally their utmost wish attain
When portals of fulfillment open wide.
And now as those eternal depths upraise
Flame so tremendous, we stand terrified;
We sought to set the torch of life ablaze
And find ourselves engulfed in seas of fire!   4710
Is it great love, or hate, whose burning gaze
Strikes now a mighty grief, now vast desire,
Till we turn backwards to the earth and run
And veil ourselves in youth's soft cloud attire?

---

[42]Because such sounds ("sounding but to spirit ears") would, if received by physical ears, drive the
hearer to madness, if not annihilate him.

Behind me only be the shining sun!
The cataract that through the cleft rock roars
To ever mounting rapture has me won;
From plunge to plunge it overflows and pours
Itself in thousands and uncounted streams
While high in air mist-veil on mist-veil soars.   4720
But O how glorious through the storm there gleams
The changeless, ever changeful rainbow bent,
Sometimes distinct, sometimes with shattered beams,
Dispensing showers of cool and fragrant scent.
Man's effort is there mirrored in that strife.
Reflect and by reflection comprehend:
There in that rainbow's radiance *is* our life.[43]

Act Five[44]

Open Country

A TRAVELER:

Those dark lindens, well I know them,
Standing in their strength of age;
Once again I pass below them
After such long pilgrimage.
Here, then, is the place at last;
That same cottage sheltered me,
On those dunes I once was cast
By the tempest-ridden sea.
I should like to bless my hosts,   11050
Such a kindly, sturdy pair,
Who were old then on these coasts,
All too old still to be there.
What good folk they used to be!
Shall I knock? Call out?—Good greeting!
If your hospitality
Still brings good to strangers meeting.

BAUCIS [*a little old woman, very ancient*]:

Welcome, comer, softly speak,
Do not break my husband's rest;
From his sleep the old man, weak,   11060
Draws brief waking's rapid zest.

TRAVELER:

Tell me, Mother, is it you
Who once saved the young man's life?
To whom now fresh thanks are due,

---

[43] The complex thought may be paraphrased: Humankind is no match for the sun; its vital force is more appropriately symbolized by the cataract that rushes onward because its nature is to rush onward; human achievement is a by-product like the rainbow, sometimes realized in full, more often realized only in segments of its shattered arch.

[44] After a series of symbolic adventures, including a marriage to Helen of Troy, a visit to the underworld realm of the Mothers, and the experience of a new classical golden age, Faust, now an old man of 100 years, has reached the final days of his life. Yet he is still an active man, as the development project he undertakes in this act indicates.

Both to husband and to wife?
Are you Baucis, who to my
Half-dead lips new life once gave?
     [*The husband appears.*]
You Philemon, who saved my
Drowning treasure from the wave?   11070
By the flames of your quick fire,
By your bell's sweet silver sound,
That adventure grim and dire
Safe conclusion from you found.
 Let me step down here a way,
Gazing on the boundless sea;
Let me kneel and let me pray,
For my heart oppresses me.
     [*He walks forward on the dune.*]
PHILEMON [*to* BAUCIS]:
 Hurry now to set the table
 Underneath the garden trees.   11080
 Let him go, he is not able
 To believe what his eye sees.
     [*standing next to the* TRAVELER]
 That by which you were mistreated,
 Wave on wild wave foaming, lies—
 See you!—as a garden treated,
 As a scene from Paradise.
 Aging, I was not on hand
 To be helpful as before;
 While my strength waned, waves were banned
 Far out from the former shore.   11090
 Clever lords set daring wights
 Dredging ditches, damming, diking,
 Curbing ocean's sovereign rights,
 Ruling it to their own liking.
 Field on field, see! green and sweet,
 Meadow, garden, forest, town.—
 Come, however, come and eat,
 For the sun will soon be down.—
 Sails loom there against the west
 Seeking port and safe repair;   11100
 Like the birds, they know their nest,
 For the harbor now is there.
 Thus at furthest range of sight
 Lies the blue fringe of the main,
 All the rest to left and right
 Is a thickly peopled plain.
     [*In the garden. The three at table.*]
BAUCIS:
 You are silent? do not eat
 Though your lips are starved for food?
PHILEMON:
 He is marveling at the feat;
 Tell him how those matters stood.   11110

BAUCIS:
    As for marvels, this was one!
    Even now it troubles me;
    For the whole affair was done
    Not as rightful things should be.
PHILEMON:
    Should the Emperor be to blame
    If he let him have this shore?
    Did a herald not proclaim
    That with trumpets at our door?
    Near our dunes they first were seen;
    Swiftly tents and shacks appeared.   11120
    But amid the verdant green
    Soon a palace was upreared.
BAUCIS:
    Daytimes, noisy varlets might
    Vainly hack and delve away;
    Where the flamelets swarmed by night
    Stood a dike the following day.
    Human sacrifices bled,
    Nighttime heard them shriek and wail,
    Seawards rolled the tides of red,
    Morning saw a new canal.   11130
    Godless is he, and he still
    Wants our cottage, wants our trees,
    As a swaggering neighbor, will
    Have us as dependencies.
PHILEMON:
    Yet he offered us a fine
    Homestead on the new-made land.
BAUCIS:
    Trust no bottom dredged from brine,
    On your headland make your stand!
PHILEMON:
    To our chapel come away
    Final sunlight to behold,
    Let us sound the bells and pray   11140
    Kneeling to the God of old.

Palace

Spacious ornamental garden; a large, straight canal. FAUST *in extreme old age, walking and meditating.*

LYNCEUS THE TOWER WARDEN [*through a speaking-trumpet*]:
    The sun sinks down, the final ships
    Are moving briskly into port.
    One mighty barque makes for the slips
    On the canal close by your court.
    The colored ensigns flutter faster,
    The sturdy masts stand tall and straight,
    The boatman hails you as his master,

And Fortune hails you as most great.   11150
                      [*The little bell rings out on the dune.*]
FAUST [*starting up*]:
    Accursed bell! In profanation,
    Like spiteful shot it wounds my ear;
    Before me lies my vast creation,
    Vexation dogs me at the rear;
    The envious sound reminds me still
    Complete possession is not mine,
    The brown hut on the linden hill,
    The moldering church is still not mine.
    If I desired its coolness, I
    Would seek its alien shade with fear,   11160
    A thorn to my foot, a thorn to my eye.
    Would I were far away from here!
TOWER WARDEN [*as above*]:
    How gaily comes the boat with sails
    Before the gentle evening gales.
    How swift its course looms up with hoard
    Of boxes, bales, and chests aboard.
              [*A splendid ship richly and colorfully laden with produce of
              foreign climes.* MEPHISTOPHELES. *The* THREE MIGHTY MEN.]
CHORUS:
    And so we land,
    And so we meet.
    Our master and
    Our lord we greet.   11170
              [*They disembark; the wares are brought ashore.*]
MEPHISTOPHELES:
    So we have proved ourselves, content
    If we our master's praises earn.
    We had but two ships when we went
    But now have twenty on return.
    The mighty things that we have wrought
    Show by the cargo we have brought.
    Free ocean is mind's liberation:
    Who there cares for deliberation!
    What counts is sudden grasp and grip
    To catch a fish or catch a ship,   11180
    And once you have control of three,
    A fourth is hooked quite easily;
    The fifth is in a sorry plight
    For you have might and therefore right.
    "What" is the question, never "How."
    If I don't mix up stern and bow,
    Then business, war, and piracy
    Are an unsevered trinity.
THE THREE MIGHTY MEN:
    No thanks we get!
    We get no thanks!   11190
    Our master thinks
    Our cargo stinks.

He makes a face,
He takes no pleasure
For all we bring
Him royal treasure.

MEPHISTOPHELES:
Expect no more.
What do you care?
After all,
You got your share.

THE MEN:
That was only
In sport. Now we
Demand to share
Equally.

MEPHISTOPHELES:
First arrange
In hall on hall
These costly items
One and all.
Once he sees
The precious sight,
Once he reckons
Costs aright,
He won't skimp
You in the least,
He'll give the fleet
Feast on feast.
The gay birds come with morning's tide
And for them I can best provide.

[*The cargo is removed.*]

MEPHISTOPHELES [*to* FAUST]:
With solemn brow, with somber glance
You take these noble gifts of Chance;
Your wisdom has been glorified,
The shore and ocean are allied,
In swift career from shore the sea
Accepts your vessels willingly;
Admit that now your arm extends
From here to earth's extremest ends.
Here it began, on this spot stood
The very first poor shack of wood;
A little ditch was scraped in loam
Where now the oar leaps swift with foam.
Your own high thought, your servers' toil
Have won the prize from sea and soil.
From here ...

FAUST:
                O be that "here" accursed!
It's just the thing I mind the worst.
I must tell you as my ally
I cannot bear it, I am maimed
In heart, blow after blow, thereby,

11200

11210

11220

11230

And telling you, I am ashamed.
Those old folks up there ought to move,
I'd like those lindens for my seat;   11240
Those few trees not my own disprove
My worldwide claims and spell defeat.
There for the prospect I would now
Build scaffolding from bough to bough
And open vistas looking on
All the things that I have done,
And have in one view all combined
This masterpiece of human mind,
With shrewd sense spurring active feats
Throughout far nations' dwelling seats.   11250
   This is the torment of the rack,
In wealth perceiving what we lack.
The sound of bells, the lindens' bloom
Give me the sense of church and tomb;
The will that nothing could withstand
Is broken here upon this sand.
What can I do about it? Tell
Me! I am frantic from that bell.

MEPHISTOPHELES:
   Such nuisance cannot help but gall
   You, that is only natural.   11260
   Who would deny it? Far and near
   That jangling grates on every ear.
   And that damned ding-dong-diddle, why!
   It shrouds the cheerful evening sky,
   It butts in on your every turn
   From baby-bath to funeral urn,
   As if between the ding and dong
   Life were a mere dream all along.

FAUST.
   Resistance, stubborn selfishness
   Can spoil the lordliest success,   11270
   Until in angry pain one must
   Grow tired at last of being just.

MEPHISTOPHELES:
   Why should you fuss about things here
   When colonizing's your career?

FAUST:
   Then go and get them off my path!—
   You know the pretty homestead where
   I mean to move the aged pair.

MEPHISTOPHELES:
   We'll move them out to their new ground
   Before there's time to look around.
   For any violence that's done   11280
   A pretty place will soon atone.
                    [*He gives a shrill whistle.*]
                [*Enter the* THREE MIGHTY MEN.]
   Come! Do as your lord bids you do.

Tomorrow he will feast the crew.
THE THREE:
  The old man met us with a slight.
  A nice feast is no more than right.

                                                      [*Exeunt.*]

MEPHISTOPHELES [*ad spectatores*]:
  What happed of old now haps anew:
  For there was Naboth's vineyard too. (I Kings 21)[45]

                    Deep Night

LYNCEUS THE TOWER WARDEN [*on the watchtower, singing*]:
  For sight I was born,
  For viewing was set;
  To watchtower sworn,
  I love the world yet.
  I gaze out afar,
  I see what is near,   11290
  The moon and the star,
  The forest and deer.
  Thus splendors of ages
  On all sides I view;
  As I found them all good,
  So I find myself too.
  You fortunate eyes,
  For all you have seen,   11300
  Whatever it was,
  It still was so fine!

                    [*A pause.*]

    Not alone for my delight
  Am I stationed here so high;
  In the darkness of the night
  Monstrous horror strikes my eye!
  I see sparks that dart and blow
  Through the linden trees' twin night,
  Strong and stronger twists the glow   11310
  As the wind's draft fans it bright.
  Hah! the cottage is on fire!
  Walls that moist and mossy stand;
  Speedy rescue they require
  And no rescue is at hand.
  Oh! those kindly aged folk,
  Always careful with their fire,
  Now are victims of the smoke
  In disaster dread and dire!
  Flames flame up, red stands the shape   11320
  Of that black and mossy shell;
  If those good folk could escape
  From that wildly burning hell!

---

[45] See 1 Kings 21. When Naboth refused to sell his vineyard to King Ahab, Queen Jezebel had Naboth arrested and killed.

Tongues of lightning lightly leap,
Through the leaves and branches sweep;
Withered boughs, they flare and burn,
Falling with a sudden blaze.
Must my eyes so much discern?
Alas for my far-sighted gaze!
Now the chapel goes down crashing, 11330
Crushed by weight of limb and bough,
Pointed flames go writhing, flashing
To the highest treetops now.
Scarlet burns each hollow tree
To the very roots at last.

            [*A long pause. Song.*]

What was once a joy to see
After centuries has passed.

FAUST [*on the balcony, toward the dunes*]:
Above me what a whimpering dirge.
The word is here, the sound is late;
My warder wails; my deep thoughts urge 11340
That this deed was precipitate.
But if the lindens have been wrecked
And left as charred stumps hideously,
A lookout I shall soon erect
To face out toward infinity.
I also see the new house where
In peace the aged couple stays,
Who, sensing my kind wish and care,
Will now enjoy their latter days.

MEPHISTOPHELES AND THE THREE [*below*]:
We come at a good rapid trot, 11350
But go off well, the thing did not.
We rapped, we knocked, we rapped again,
And still they would not let us in.
We battered and we knocked away,
The rotten door fell in and lay;
We shouted out in threat and call
But found they heard us not at all.
As happens in such cases, they
Just would not hear, would not obey;
We had no time to waste or spare 11360
And soon we cleared them out of there.
The couple's sufferings were slight,
And all they did was die of fright.
A stranger there put up a show
Of force and had to be laid low.
Amid the brief course of the match
Some scattered coals got in the thatch,
And now the fire is blazing free
To the cremation of all three.

FAUST:
To all my words then you were deaf! 11370
I wanted an exchange, not theft.

Upon this ruthless action be
My curse! Share in it equally!

CHORUS:
The ancient saying still makes sense:
Bow willingly to violence;
But if you bravely make resistance,
Risk house and home—and your existence.

[*Exeunt.*]

FAUST [*on the balcony*]:
The stars conceal their gaze and shining,
The fire sinks smoldering and declining;
A faint gust fans it fitfully
And wafts its smoke and scent to me.   11380
Too rashly bidden, too rashly done!—
What glides so spectrally toward me?

Midnight

Enter FOUR GREY WOMEN.

THE FIRST:
My name is Want.
THE SECOND:
                    My name is Guilt.
THE THIRD:
My name is Care.
THE FOURTH:
                    My name is Distress.
THREE [*together*]:
The door is fast-bolted, we cannot get in,
The owner is wealthy, we'll never get in.
WANT:
Here I turn to shadow.
GUILT:
                    Here I have no place.
DISTRESS:
From me is averted the much-pampered face.
CARE:
You sisters, you can not and may not get in,   11390
But Care through the keyhole will make her way in.
                    [CARE *disappears.*]
WANT:
O sisters, grey sisters, away let us glide.
GUILT:
I'll be your ally and walk close at your side.
DISTRESS:
And close on your footsteps will follow Distress.
THE THREE:
Hard rides now the cloud, disappears now the star,
From behind, from behind, from afar, from afar
There comes now our brother, and his name is—Death.

                    [*Exeunt.*]

FAUST [*in the palace*]:
    Four I saw come, but only three go hence,
    And of their speech I could not catch the sense.
    "Distress" I heard, and like caught breath   11400
    A gloomy rhyme-word followed—"Death."
    It sounded hollow, hushed with ghostly fear.
    I've still not fought my way into the clear.
    If I could sweep my path from magic free
    And quite unlearn the spells of sorcery,
    If I could face you, Nature, as a man,
    It then would be worth while to be a man.
        Such was I once, before I cursed to doom
    Both myself and the world in that dark room.
    The air so teems with monsters ghostly shaped   11410
    That no one knows how they can be escaped.
    If *one* day laughs amid sweet reason's light,
    Dreams weave us round with cobwebs that same night.
    If vernal fields make our glad hearts beat faster,
    A bird croaks; and what does he croak? Disaster.
    Ensnared by superstition soon and late,
    It works and shows itself and hints our fate,
    And daunted we stand helpless in the gloom.
        The door creaks, yet no one comes in the room.
                  [*shaken*]
    Is someone here?
CARE:
                Well may you ask. I am.   11420
FAUST:
    And you, who are you then?
CARE:
                But here I am.
FAUST:
    Go back, then!
CARE:
              I am in my proper station.
FAUST [*angered at first, then appeased; to himself*]:
    Then watch yourself and speak no incantation.
CARE:
    If no ear for me were found,
    In the heart I still would sound.
    In my ever changeful guise
    Fearful force I exercise,
    On the highroad, on the sea
    Bearing you dread company,
    Ever found though sought for never,   11430
    Cursed and yet cajoled forever.
        But have you never yet known Care?
FAUST:
    I have but raced on through the world;
    I seized on every pleasure by the hair;
    What did not satisfy, I let go by,
    And what eluded me, I let it be.
    I have but craved, accomplished my delight,

Then wished anew, and so with main and might
Stormed through my life; first grandly and with passion,
But now more wisely, in more prudent fashion.   11440
I know enough about the world of men,
The prospect yonder is beyond our ken;
A fool is he who that way blinks his eyes
And fancies kindred beings in the skies.
Let him stand firm here and here look around:
This world is not mute if the man is sound.
Why need he stray off to eternity!
What he knows here is certainty.
So let him walk along his earthly day:
If spirits haunt him, let him go his way,   11450
Find joy and torment in his forward stride,
And at each moment be unsatisfied.

CARE:
One whom I can once possess
Finds the whole world profitless;
Eternal gloom descends and lies,
For him suns neither set nor rise;
With external senses whole,
Darkness dwells within his soul,
On the earth there is no treasure
He can grasp or own with pleasure,   11460
He starves in plenty, and for him
Weal and woe become mere whim;
Be it bliss or be it sorrow,
He postpones it till the morrow;
Living in the future ever,
He succeeds in no endeavor.

FAUST:
Stop! You will not succeed with me!
I will not hear such folly. Hence!
Hearing this evil litany
Could addle wisest men's good sense.   11470

CARE:
Whether he should go or stay,
His decision seeps away;
At broad highways' midmost he
Gropes by half-steps hesitantly.
He gets deep and deeper lost,
Sees all things as purpose-crossed,
Burdening himself and others,
Breathing deeply as he smothers,
Neither dead nor yet alive,
Succumb he can't, nor yet survive.   11480
Galling "O, I should!" combined
With his painful "Never mind...,"
Liberated and suppressed,
Semi-sleeping with no rest,
He is fixed in place and groomed
For the hell to which he's doomed.

FAUST:
Unholy specters! Thus you have betrayed
The race of humans time and time again,
And out of days of mere indifference made
A filthy snarl and tangled net of pain.   11490
From demons one can scarcely be quite free,
Not to be broken are the spirit ties,
And yet your power, great as it may be,
O Care, I will not recognize.

CARE:
Then feel it now, as I behind
Me leave my curse and turn from you.
Since human beings all their lives are blind,
Now, Faustus, be you just so too!

[*She breathes upon him. Exit.*]

FAUST [*blinded*]:
The night seems deep and deeper to be sinking,
Bright light still shines within myself alone.   11500
I hasten to enact what I am thinking;
No will imposes save the master's own.
Up, servers, from your couches, every man,
And gladly see the boldness of my plan!
Take up your tools, swing shovel now and spade!
Bring instantly to flower the lands surveyed.
Strict ordering and swift diligence
Will yield the fairest recompense.
In this great task one mind commands
Sufficiently a thousand hands.   11510

Great Forecourt of the Palace

Torches.

MEPHISTOPHELES [*as Foreman leading the way*]:
This way! This way! Come on! Come on!
You shambling lemur batches,[46]
You semi-natures made of bone
And frazzled sinew patches.

LEMURS [*in chorus*]:
We come at call, we are on hand,
And as we heard by half,
There is, they say, a spacious land
That we're supposed to have.
    Sharp-pointed stakes, here's your supply,
Here is the measuring chain;   11520
The summons was for us, but why,
Quite slips our minds again.

---

[46]Roman spirits of the unrighteous dead, represented as skeletons held together by their funeral wrappings.

MEPHISTOPHELES:

No fussing now for elegance,
Just go by your own measurements;
The tallest should lie down upon the ground,
The rest can lift the sod up all around.
Just sink the longish trench four-sided
With which our forebears were provided.
Out of the palace to the narrow home,
That is the sorry end to which we come.   11530

LEMURS [*digging and making droll gestures*]:

When I was young and lived and loved,
Methought that was full sweet,
When frolic rang and mirth was loud
There I would stir my feet.
    Now spiteful Age has struck at me
And hit me with his crutch;
I stumbled on a yawning grave—
Why must they open such!

FAUST [*coming from the palace and groping his way by the doorposts*]:

O how this clang of spades delights my soul!
These are the many who perform my toil   11540
And reconcile the earth with its own soil
And for the waves set up a goal
And gird tight limits round the sea.

MEPHISTOPHELES [*aside*]:

And yet all your activity
Serves us, with dam and dike creation;
For Neptune the great water devil
You are preparing one big revel.
You all are lost in every wise—
The elements are our allies,
And things head for annihilation.   11550

FAUST:

Foreman!

MEPHISTOPHELES:

        Here!

FAUST:

            By any means you may,
Get workmen here by throngs and hordes,
Incite with strictness and rewards,
Entice them, urge them, give them pay!
I want to have reports each day of how
The trench proceeds that we are starting now.

MEPHISTOPHELES [*half-aloud*]:

They talked no trench when last they gave
Reports to me, but of a grave.

FAUST:

A swamp there by the mountain lies,
Infecting everything attained;   11560
If that foul pool could once be drained,
The feat would outstrip every prize.

For many millions I shall open spaces
Where they, not safe but active-free, have dwelling places.
Verdant the fields and fruitful; man and beast
Alike upon that newest earth well pleased,
Shall settle soon the mighty strength of hill
Raised by a bold and busy people's will,
And here inside, a land like Paradise.
Then let the outer flood to dike's rim rise, 11570
And as it eats and seeks to crush by force,
The common will will rush to stem its course.
To this opinion I am given wholly
And this is wisdom's final say:
Freedom and life belong to that man solely
Who must reconquer them each day.
Thus child and man and old man will live here
Beset by peril year on busy year.
Such in their multitudes I hope to see
On free soil standing with a people free. 11580
Then to that moment I could say:
Linger on, you are so fair!
Nor can the traces of my earthly day
In many aeons pass away.—
Foresensing all the rapture of that dream,
This present moment gives me joy supreme.

[FAUST *sinks back; the* LEMURS *take hold
of him and lay him down on the ground.*]

MEPHISTOPHELES:
No joy could sate him, no bliss could satisfy,
He chased his changeful vision to the last;
This final moment, paltry, void, and dry,
The poor wretch wants to hold it fast. 11590
Time masters him who could withstand
My power, the old man lies here on the sand.
The clock has stopped—

CHORUS:
Has stopped. As death-still as the midnight.
The clock hand falls.

MEPHISTOPHELES:
It falls. And "it is finished."

CHORUS:
And all is over.

MEPHISTOPHELES:
Over! Stupid word!
Does it make sense?
Over, and sheerest naught, total indifference!
All this creating comes to what?
To make things as if they were not.
"A thing is over now!" What does that mean? 11600
The same as if the thing had never been,
Yet circles round and round as if it *were*.
Eternal Emptiness I still prefer.

Burial

LEMUR [*solo*]:
　　O, who so badly built this house
　　With shovel and with spade?
LEMURS [*chorus*]:
　　For you, mute guest in hempen shroud,
　　It's far too finely made.
LEMUR [*solo*]:
　　And who so badly decked the hall?
　　Of tables, chairs, not any?
LEMURS [*chorus*]
　　The lease was short-termed. After all,　　　　　　　　　　11610
　　Believers are so many.
MEPHISTOPHELES:
　　Here lies the body; if the spirit strays,
　　I'll soon confront it with that blood-signed scroll—
　　They have so many methods nowadays
　　To cheat the Devil of a soul.
　　Our old way seems to give offense,
　　Our new way they do not condone;
　　Once I'd have done it all alone,
　　Where now I have to have assistants.
　　　　We're badly off on every score.
　　Old rights, time-honored ways of yore—　　　　　　　　11620
　　There's nothing left that you can trust.
　　Time was, a soul rode up the final gasp;
　　Then as with quickest mouse I'd make a thrust
　　And whoops! there she would be tight in my grasp.
　　Now they hang back, won't leave the dismal place,
　　Inside the filthy corpse they tarry late;
　　The elements in mutual hate
　　Expel them finally by sheer disgrace.
　　And if I fret for days and hours now,　　　　　　　　　11630
　　There still are questions of When? Where? and How?
　　Old Death has lost his rapid strength; about
　　The very Whether? there has long been doubt.
　　On dead-stiff limbs I've doted often, then
　　A false alarm and off they walked again.
　　　　[*Fantastic and imperious conjuring gestures.*]
　　Come on, then! On the double! All of you
　　Lords of the straight, lords of the crooked horn,
　　Chips off the ancient block, you devils born,
　　And bring the jaws of hell up with you too.
　　For hell has many, many sets of jaws,　　　　　　　　　11640
　　By different ranks and standings it devours,
　　But we won't haggle over rules and laws
　　From now on in this final game of ours.
　　　　[*The hideous jaws of hell open on the left.*]
　　The eyeteeth gape; up from the vaulted pit
　　There seethes a tide of flame in raging flow,
　　And through the steam-clouds in the back of it

I see the fiery city all aglow.
The red tide breaks in surges to the very teeth,
The damned swim, hoping rescue, up the bath;
But the hyena champs them back beneath   11650
And they retrace in pain their burning path.
There's much more off in nooks you may perceive,
The scariest things jammed in the tightest space!
It's good to scare the sinners: they believe
It's only an imaginary place.
                    [*to the* FAT DEVILS *with short, straight horns*]
You paunchy rascals with the cheeks that burn,
All fattened up on brimstone, how you glow!
Short dumpy things with necks that cannot turn,
Watch for a gleam of phosphor here below:
That will be Soul, or Psyche with the wings;[47]   11660
Once they're pulled off, she's just a nasty worm;
I'll set my seal on her, then off she slings
Down to the whirlwind and the fiery storm!
    Those nether regions watch with care,
You lard-guts! Duty bids you so.
For if she deigns to dwell down there
We do not just exactly know.
The navel's where she likes to hide—
Watch there, she might whisk past you to one side.
                    [*to the* LEAN DEVILS *with long, crooked horns*]
You fancy bucks, you giant fuglemen,   11670
Keep sawing air, don't stop from first to last.
With arms and sharp claws spread, be ready when
The fluttering thing on fleeing wing comes past.
She surely must find her old house a bore;
Then too, the "genius"[48] also wants to soar.
                    [*Glory from above, on the right.*]

THE HEAVENLY HOST:
    Follow, you envoys
    Of celestial joys
    In unhurried flight:
    Sinners forgiving,
    Dust to make living;   11680
    Down from above
    Tokens of love
    To all creatures giving
    In hovering flight.

MEPHISTOPHELES:
    Discords I hear and mawkish whimpering
    Coming from topside with unwelcome light.
    It's that half-boy-half-maiden simpering
    In which a canting taste takes such delight.
    In our depravity, you know, we meant

---

[47]*Psyche*, the Greek word for *soul*, represented as a butterfly.
[48]The spirit that inhabits the human body.

And planned destruction for the human race;   11690
The most disgraceful thing we could invent
Would, in *their* worship, be in place.
   Just see the minions mince and charm!
They've snitched a lot of souls in just this wise
By turning our own weapons to our harm;
They're devils too, though in disguise.
To lose out now would mean eternal shame;
Up to that grave, then, and cling fast to same!

CHORUS OF ANGELS [*strewing roses*]:
  Refulgence of roses
  Fragrance expending!   11700
  Tremulous, swaying,
  Life-force conveying,
  Branchlet-bewisped
  Buds now unclasped,
  Bloom fullest and best.
    Springtime arise,
  Crimson and green;
  Bring Paradise
  To him at his rest.

MEPHISTOPHELES [*to the* SATANS]:
  Why do you duck and wince? Is that hell's play?   11710
  Stand firm and let them strew away.
  Back to your stations, gawks, and stay!
  They fancy they are going to snow
  Hot devils under with their posy show.
  Your breath will melt and shrivel that away.
  Now blow, you puff-cheeks! There! Enough! Enough!
  You've bleached and blanched them with your huff and puff.—
  Don't blow so lustily, shut snout and nose!
  O, now you've overblown your blows.
  You must learn when to stop! When will you learn!   11720
  They're shriveled, but they're going to scorch and burn!
  As bright and poisonous flames they're drifting near!
  Stand firm against them, crowd together here!
  All courage vanishes, strength ebbs away.
  The devils scent strange fires' caressing play.

ANGELS [*chorus*]:
  Blossoms of joy,
  Flames of high gladness,
  Love they expend,
  Bliss they portend,
  Heart as it may:
  Truth in their words,   11730
  Clear aetherwards
  Eternal hordes,
  Limitless day!

MEPHISTOPHELES:
  O curses on this ninny band!
  Upon their heads the Satans stand.
  The louts turn cartwheels down the path

And plop ass-backwards into hell.
Take comfort from your well deserved hot bath!
I'm staying on here for a spell.—   11740
                    [*knocking aside the drifting roses*]
Will-o'-the-wisps, begone! Shine as you will,
Once caught, you're little turds of jelly still.
Why flutter so? Just go away! And quick!
Like pitch and sulphur to my neck they stick!

ANGELS [*chorus*]:
  What you may not possess
  You must abjure;
  What gives your heart distress
  You must not endure.
  If it crowds in by force,
  We must take valiant course.   11750
  Love only lovers
  Brings to the door.

MEPHISTOPHELES:
  My head and liver burn, my heart is rent.
  A super-devilish element!
  Worse stinging far than hell's own fire.—
  That's why you lift laments so dire,
  Unhappy lovers, who forever crane
  Your necks to look at loved ones who disdain.
      Me too! But what makes my head that way tend?
  Am I not sworn to fight them to the end?   11760
  I used to find them such a hateful sight.
  Has something alien pierced me through and through?
  I love to have these darling boys in view.
  What keeps me now from cursing them tonight?
  If *I* am gulled at this late date,
  Who will then as "the Fool" be styled?
  These handsome rascals that I hate
  Seem just too lovely, and I am beguiled.—
      Now pretty lads, come tell me true:
  Are you too not of Lucifer's family?   11770
  You're just so nice, I'd like a kiss from you,
  I feel you're just the thing for me.
  It comes so cozily, so naturally,
  As if we'd met a thousand times before,
  So kitten-sly and raffishly;
  With every glance you charm me more and more.
  Come closer, grant me just one glance!

ANGELS:
  But why do you fall back when we advance?
  We move up closer; meet us if you can.
          [*The* ANGELS, *moving about, come to occupy the entire space.*]

MEPHISTOPHELES [*who is forced into the proscenium*]:
  You call *us* spirits damned, but you   11780
  Are the real witch-masters tried and true,
  For you seduce both maid and man.—
  O cursed adventure! Do you claim

This is the element of love?
My entire body is aflame,
I hardly feel the burning from above.—
You hover to and fro; come down and stir
Your lovely limbs in ways a trifle worldlier.
Your seriousness is most becoming for a while,
But just for once I'd like to see you smile;   11790
That would give me a pleasure unsurpassed.
I mean the kind of looks that lovers cast.
A flicker of the lips, and there we'll have it.
I like you best, there, lad so slim and tall,
But clergy-looks don't go with you at all.
Give me a glance that's just the least bit avid.
Then, too, you could more decent-nakedly appear;
Those flowing robes are all too morals-emphasizing—
They turn their backs—a glimpse now from the rear!—
The little monkeys are so appetizing!   11800
CHORUS OF ANGELS:
     Turn, flames of love,
     Toward clarity;
     Be the self-damned saved
     By verity;
     Self-redeemed be they
     From evil's sway,
     Blessed to be
     In the totality.
MEPHISTOPHELES [getting control of himself]:
     What is this!—I am raw with sores all round,
     A very Job, shocked at the state he's in   11810
     And yet triumphant as he looks within
     Himself and trusts himself and his own kin;
     My noble devil parts are safe and sound,
     The love infection breaks out through the skin.
     Now that the cursed flames are out, I call
     Down curses, as you well deserve, on one and all!
CHORUS OF ANGELS:
     Sacred ardors!
     Whom you surround
     Has full life found
     With the good, in bliss.   11820
     Ascend up allied
     And praises wreathe,
     In air purified
     The spirit may breathe!
           [They ascend, bearing with them FAUST's immortal part.]
MEPHISTOPHELES [looking about]:
     What's this?—Now where can they have gone?
     You juveniles have caught me by surprise
     And off to heaven with the booty flown.
     So that's why they were nibbling at this grave!
     They've made off with my great and unique prize,
     The soul which he to me once pledged and gave,   11830
     They've smuggled it away, that's what they've done.

To whom can I go for redress?
Who will get me my well-earned right?
You have been fooled in your old days. Confess,
However, you deserve your sorry plight.
I have outrageously mismanaged,
A mighty outlay—shamefully!—is lost,
Absurd amour and common lust have managed
To catch the canny Devil to his cost.
But if the one of wise experience got   11840
Himself involved in that mad, childish game,
Still, slight the folly was most surely not
Which caught him at the last and overcame.

Mountain Gorges

Forest, cliff, wilderness. Holy anchorites,[49] *disposed up the mountainside, stationed in the ravines.*

CHORUS AND ECHO:
   Woodlands, they falter toward it,
   Cliffsides, they weigh against it,
   Root-snarls, they clutch into it,
   Tree dense to tree up along it.
   Waves in a foaming welter,
   Nethermost cave yields shelter.
   Lions in silence rove   11850
   Friendly and tame around,
   Reverencing holy ground,
   Love's holy treasure-trove.
PATER ECSTATICUS[50] [*floating up and down*]:
   Ecstasy's ceaseless fire,
   Love's bond of hot desire,
   Seething heart of pain,
   Foaming joy divine.
   Arrows, transfix me!
   Lances, enforce me!
   Cudgels, batter me!   11860
   Lightning bolts, shatter me!
   So the All may utterly
   Abolish the Nullity,
   Gleam the fixed star above,
   Essence of endless love.
PATER PROFUNDUS[51] [*lower region*]:
   As rocky chasms here beneath
   On deeper chasms base their thrusts,
   As countless brooklets, shining, seethe
   In downward leaps and foaming gusts,

---

[49] The holy anchorites are hermits of the early Christian centuries who withdrew into the wilderness to devote their entire existences to the adoration of God. Goethe here makes them symbols of intense aspiration utterly possessed by love.

[50] The title given to Saint Anthony; this spirit is mystical with a longing for the infinite.

[51] The title of St. Bernard of Clairvaux; a spirit of the lower region (profundus), this spirit is earthy and sense-bound.

As upward to the air above   11870
The tall tree in its power strains,
Just so, it is almighty Love
That forms all things and all sustains.
    There is a roaring all around
As if woods were billows under gales,
And yet there falls with gracious sound
The wealth of waters to the vales,
As if bound to bring moisture there;
The lightning flash of flaming dart
That struck to purify the air   11880
And purge infection from its heart—
    All are Love's messengers proclaiming
Creation's ceaseless workings multifold.
May my soul also know such flaming,
Where spirit, now perplexed and cold,
In gross net of the senses caught,
Is riveted in chains that smart.
O God! Assuage and calm my thought,
Illuminate my needy heart!
PATER SERAPHICUS[52] [*middle region*]:
    What cloud of dawning at this minute   11890
Parts the pine trees' floating hair?
Do I guess what lives within it?
Here is a youthful spirit choir.
CHORUS OF BLESSED BOYS:[53]
    Tell us, Father, where we wander,
Tell us, kind man, who we are.
Happy are we, and so tender
Is the life that we all bear.
PATER SERAPHICUS:
    Children, you were midnight-born,[54]
Sense and spirit half attained;
From your parents you were torn,   11900
For the angels you were gained.
One who loves, before your faces
You feel present; draw, then, near;
Rugged earthways left no traces
On you as you now appear.
Come you down, and with the loan
Of my earthly-bounded eyes,
Using them as if your own,
View the land that round you lies.
                     [*He takes them into himself.*]
These are trees; these, cliffsides jutting;   11910
That, a waterfall that plunges,
By its awesome down-course cutting
Short the steep path as it lunges.

---

[52]The title of St. Francis of Assisi; this spirit is self-denying and concerned for others.
[53]The souls of the infant dead.
[54]Children born at midnight were thought to have little chance of living.

BLESSED BOYS [*from within*]:
Х This is mighty to behold,
Х But a place in which to grieve,
Х Chills us with a terror cold.
Х Good man, kind man, let us leave.
PATER SERAPHICUS:
Х Rise to higher spheres; mature
Х Unobserved by any eyes,
Х As, in ways forever pure,   11920
Х God's own presence fortifies.
Х For throughout free air above
Х Spirits taste no other food
Х Than revelation of eternal Love
Х Which nurtures to beatitude.
CHORUS OF BLESSED BOYS [*circling about the highest peaks*]:
Х Gladly entwine
Х Hands in a ring,
Х With feelings divine
Х Dance and sing.
Х Trust in the lore   11930
Х Divinely told,
Х Him you adore
Х You shall behold.
ANGELS [*soaring in the higher atmosphere, bearing the immortal part of* FAUST]:
Х Delivered is he now from ill,
Х Whom we a spirit deemed:
Х "Who strives forever with a will,
Х By us can be redeemed."
Х And if in him the higher Love
Х Has had a share, to meet him
Х Will come the blessed host above   11940
Х And warmly greet him
THE YOUNGER ANGELS:
Х Loving-holy penitents,
Х By the roses that they rained,
Х Helped us to the triumph gained
Х In this task of eminence,
Х Helped to win this treasured soul.
Х Demons yielded from their goal,
Х Devils at our onslaught fled.
Х Spirits felt Love's pain instead
Х Of their usual hellish anguish;   11950
Х Bitter pangs could even vanquish
Х The arch-Satan's self. Exult!
Х Joyous is the high result!
THE MORE PERFECTED ANGELS:
Х Earth remnants still arrest us,
Х Hard to endure;
Х Were he made of asbestos,[55]
Х He is not pure.

---

[55]Although asbestos is an unburnable material, it is nonetheless material and thus not spiritual.

When once strong spirit force
Subsumes man's elements,
No angels can divorce
The quintessence
Of dual self made one;
The two parts allied
Eternal Love alone
Can then divide.

THE YOUNGER ANGELS:
Misted at rocky height
Spirits appear
Moving closer in sight
As they haste along.
The cloudlets grow more clear,
I see a lively throng
Of blessed boys,
From earth's oppression free,
Joined in a ring,
Glad with the joys
Of spheres so beauteously
Decked with new spring.
With these let him begin,
And, rising with them, win
Perfection gradually.

THE BLESSED BOYS:
With joy we receive
Him in pupa stage;
In him we achieve
Angelic pledge.
Unravel the cocoon strands
Around him rife.
Great he already stands
With holy life.

DOCTOR MARIANUS[56] [*in the highest, purest cell*]:
The prospect here is free,
The mind uplifting.
There ladies move past me
Upward drifting.
The Glorious One beneath
Her starry wreath
In splendor there is seen,
All Heaven's Queen.

                              [*enraptured*]
    Highest mistress of the world,
Admit me, in this blue
Tent of heaven here unfurled,
To thy mystery's view.
What earnestly and tenderly
Stirs men's hearts, approve,

11960

11970

11980

11990

12000

---

[56] A teacher of the cult of the Virgin Mary.

And all things they bring to thee
In holy joy of love.
    Courage fights invincibly
Till thou bidd'st it cease,
Ardor mellows suddenly
As thou givest peace.
Virgin pure in fairest sense,
Mother, of all honor worth,   12010
Queen in eminence,
Of gods the peer by birth.
    Around her dense-
ly gather clouds,
Penitents
In gentle crowds
About her knees,
Bright aether breathing,
Mercy beseeching.
    To thee, inviolate,   12020
It is not denied
That the easily misled
Should in thee confide.
    In their weakness swept away,
Hard they are to save;
Who of his own power may
Wrest chains from lust's slave?
Whose foot will not fail him fast
On the slippery path?
Who is not deceived at last   12030
By a cozening breath?

        [*The* MATER GLORIOSA *soars forth.*]

CHORUS OF FEMALE PENITENTS:
Thou soarest on high
To eternal realms.
O hear our cry!
Peerless art thou,
Merciful art thou!

MAGNA PECCATRIX (St. Luke 7:36):[57]
By the love which at the feet
Of thy transfigured Son God-born
Shed tears as though of balsam sweet
Despite the Pharisee's high scorn;   12040
By the alabaster ointment box
Shedding fragrance down on Him,
By the hair and flowing locks
Which then dried each sacred limb—

MULIER SAMARITANA (St. John 4):[58]
By the well whereto were driven
Abram's herds, and by the well-dips

---

[57] The "greatly sinful woman" who washed Jesus' feet at the house of the Pharisee.
[58] The "woman of Samaria" who drew water for Jesus to drink.

Whence a cooling drink was given
To the Saviour's thirsting lips;
By the spring of purity
Which from thence outpours and flows   12050
Ever clear and copiously
As through all the worlds it goes—

MARIA AEGYPTIACA [*Acta Sanctorum*]:[59]
By the consecrated tomb
Where the Lord was laid of yore,
By the arm that beckoned doom,
Thrusting me back from the door;
By the forty-year repentance
That I lived in desert waste,
By the blessed farewell sentence
That upon the sand I traced—   12060

ALL THREE:
Thou who never dost deny
Help to those whose sins are great,
And eternally on high
Dost repentance elevate,
Grant to this good soul as well,
Who did only once transgress,
Hardly knowing that she fell—
Grant remission limitless.

UNA POENITENTIUM, ONCE NAMED GRETCHEN [*nestling close*]:
Deign, O deign,
Amid thy reign   12070
In radiance,
To look in mercy on my joy.
My once beloved,
No more troubled,
Joins me in joy.

BLESSED BOYS [*drawing near in a circling movement*]:
So soon he has outgrown us
In might of limb;
Reward will soon be shown us
For care of him.
Too little time we sojourned   12080
For life to reach us,
But those things he has learned,
And he will teach us.

A PENITENT, ONCE NAMED GRETCHEN:
Amid the noble choir of Heaven
He hardly knows that self of his,
He guesses not the new life given,
Yet of the holy host he is.
See how he wrests himself out free
Of his integument of earth,

---

[59]Mary of Egypt was forbidden to enter the Church of the Holy Sepulchre in Jerusalem and did penance in the desert for forty-eight years.

How in ethereal raiment he 12090
Shows youthful vigor in new birth.
Vouchsafe to me to be his guide,
His eyes still dazzle with new day.
MATER GLORIOSA:
Rise, and in higher spheres abide;
He will sense you and find the way.
DOCTOR MARIANUS [*prostrate on his face, in adoration*]:
Gaze upward to that saving glance;
Toward beatitude,
Gentle penitents, advance,
Be changed with gratitude.
Let every better sense be keen 12100
To do thee service duly;
Virgin, Mother, and our Queen,
Goddess, help us truly.
CHORUS MYSTICUS:
All transitory
Things represent;
Inadequates here
Become event,
Ineffables here,
Accomplishment;
The Eternal-Feminine 12110
Draws us onward.[60]

EMILY BRONTË
[1818–1848]

The realistic side of nineteenth-century literature is most fully articulated in the novel, the dominant literary form of the era. The novelists document the everyday life of average people and through their detailed narratives enable their readers to observe and share the lives of others. We feel the frustrations of Austen's Elizabeth Bennett and identify with the aspirations of Dickens's David Copperfield. We are drawn to exclaim with Flaubert, "I am Madame Bovary!" as we read his day-by-day account of her life. We can even empathize with Hawthorne's adulteress or Dostoevsky's ax-murderer as they are individualized in the details of their novels.

Realism is essential to Emily Brontë's *Wuthering Heights* (1847), a unique and haunting story of love and revenge that may be, as one critic has described it, "the twentieth century's

---

[60]These lines can be interpreted as follows. All transitory things are—as in Plato's doctrine—imperfect reflections of divine realities. Humankind's utmost striving while on earth is necessary, but it requires the complement of heavenly assistance. Transition from earthly form into eternal form is accomplished, but no words are adequate to describe it. The Eternal-Feminine is the unfailing inspiration, the moving force giving impetus in earthly life as in the life hereafter to strive from lesser stages upward toward infinite perfection. That perfection is Love; in Dante's final line of the *Paradiso*, "the Love that moves the sun and the other stars."

favorite nineteenth-century novel." Brontë details her natural setting, the remote moors of Yorkshire, a rural county in northeastern England. She describes the passing seasons on the moors, the unsettled weather that changes suddenly from calm to storm, as she traces the equally stormy lives of the rugged people who live in this harsh and exposed environment. Her characters are rooted in their place and time; some of her peasant characters speak in a Yorkshire accent so thick that it requires translation. We must believe in the reality of these characters and their setting to accept the extraordinary story Brontë has to tell of unrestrained emotions, violent passions, and the dark side of life. Like *Faust*, this romantic story explores the limits of nature, feeling, and subjectivity. A saga covering three generations, the novel presents a confrontation between conflicting forces: nature and civilization, wild and tame, passion and reason, female and male. By the end of the novel, as in *Faust*, the romantic extremes have been restrained, but the toll that this process takes is great.

LIFE

One of six extraordinary children, Emily Brontë, born in 1818, was the fourth daughter of an Evangelical clergyman of the Church of England. Her mother died when she was three and her two oldest sisters, Maria and Elizabeth, died of tuberculosis in 1825 when they were still children. The four remaining Brontë children, Charlotte (1816–1855), Branwell (1817–1848), Emily, and Anne (1820–1849), were raised by their pious aunt and their father in the parsonage at Haworth, a remote mill village on the Yorkshire moors. Isolated by geography and by social class, the Brontë children were thrown into their own company. They entertained themselves by reading the books in their father's library—especially the poems of Byron, the novels of Sir Walter Scott, and the works of Milton—and they entertained each other by writing and illustrating long romantic fantasies. Working in pairs, Charlotte and Branwell created the legends of the fantasy kingdom of Angria while Emily and Anne wrote of Gondal. In these juvenile romances can be found the beginnings of the characters and situations of their later novels.

All four of the children had difficulty breaking away from the family and from Yorkshire. Although they all went away to school and took positions as governesses or tutors away from Haworth, all eventually returned. Of the four surviving children, Emily seems to have been the most incapable of living away from home. When Emily was away at Roe Head School, Charlotte said that she thought Emily "would die, if she did not go home." She lasted only one year at the school in Brussels where she and Charlotte went to study and her term as a governess near Halifax in 1839 took her away for an even shorter period of time. She was drawn back by her attachment to the family and the legends of Gondal and by her love of the moors. Her poetry, as well as *Wuthering Heights*, reveals the depth of her attachment to the natural setting of her childhood home.

All four of the children had artistic talent. Branwell, a painter, never established himself as an artist, but his talent can be seen in some of his paintings, which are on display in the parsonage in Haworth, now a Brontë museum and library. The three sisters all became published writers. Using male pseudonyms, Charlotte, Emily, and Anne published a volume of *Poems by Currer, Ellis, and Acton Bell* in 1846. The book was virtually unnoticed at the time: Only two copies were sold in the first year. Several of their novels, on the other hand, were best-sellers and have become classics. Charlotte wrote four novels; the best-known are *Jane Eyre* (1847) and *Villette* (1853). Anne's two novels, *Agnes Grey* (1847) and *The Tenant of Wildfell Hall* (1848), less successful than the works of her sisters, are still worth reading. Emily's one novel, *Wuthering Heights*, is the most unusual and perhaps the most puzzling of all the Brontë novels.

The early deaths of all the Brontë children have contributed to the romantic legends that have grown up about them. Branwell, a victim of alcoholism and drug addiction, died in

1848 at 31. Emily, at age 30, died a few months later. Anne was only 29 when she died in 1849. Charlotte, who lived the longest and was the only one to marry, died in 1855 at 38.

Charlotte described Emily as "not a person of a demonstrative character"; indeed, most contemporary accounts make her out to be a withdrawn and secretive person. Ellen Nussey, a family friend, described her as "a tall, lithe creature, with a grace half-queenly, half-untamed in her sudden and supple movements, wearing with picturesque negligence her ample purple-splashed skirts; her face clear and pale; her very dark and plenteous brown hair fastened up behind with a Spanish comb; her large grey-hazel eyes, now full of indolent indulgent humour, now glimmering with hidden meanings, now quickened into flame by a flash of indignation." If she was secretive in the parsonage, she became more expressive on the moors where she liked to roam with her dogs. Ellen Nussey described her at a spring on the moors, playing "like a young child with the tadpoles in the water, making them swim about and then... moralizing on the strong and the weak, the brave and the cowardly, as she chased them with her hand." Her love of nature is apparent in *Wuthering Heights*; out on the moors or at Penistone Crags, Heathcliff and Catherine become fully themselves, become part of nature. In this celebration of nature Emily Brontë is the most romantic of the Victorian novelists.

WORK

To its detailed observation of the natural world, *Wuthering Heights* adds many other romantic elements. The opening chapters, when Lockwood first visits Wuthering Heights and is unsettled by the dream of the waif outside the window of his paneled bedroom, seem to come from the Gothic novels of the time, which featured remote houses, cruel and brutal relationships, horrific and supernatural occurrences. Brontë also evokes the Byronic hero, especially in the character of Heathcliff. Brooding, melancholy, solitary, and self-destructive, these outlaw-rebels earned their name from the notorious heroes of some of Lord Byron's poems, figures such as Manfred and Cain. It is Catherine who speaks with the voice of the Byronic hero, however, when she describes a dream about going to heaven: "I was only going to say that heaven did not seem to be my home; and I broke my heart with weeping to come back to earth; and the angels were so angry that they flung me out, into the middle of the heath on the top of Wuthering Heights; where I woke sobbing for joy." Catherine has been suckled on a pagan creed; her world is animated by the forces of nature and charged with unrestrained energy and violent passion. Her natural supernaturalism is of a renegade kind.

Like Faust, Catherine is divided, torn between warring halves of herself. In the most famous passage in the novel, Catherine tells Nelly of the differences between her relationships with Edgar Linton and Heathcliff. Using nature imagery, she says that her love for Edgar "is like the foliage in the woods. Time will change it... as winter changes the trees. My love for Heathcliff resembles the eternal rocks beneath—a source of little visible delight, but necessary. Nelly, I *am* Heathcliff." Nevertheless, Catherine marries Linton, choosing the superficial and the temporary over the deep impulses of her being. This decision separates her from Heathcliff, from Wuthering Heights, and from the moors and it begins Heathcliff's vengeance and her slow decline to death. If she ever brings the two halves of herself together again, it is only after both she and Heathcliff have died.

Heathcliff represents the deepest levels of Catherine's being, but he is also a disruptive figure in the novel. When Mr. Earnshaw surprises his family by bringing home the dark waif from Liverpool, he introduces the catalyst that will divide Catherine and Hindley, Earnshaws and Lintons, nature and civilization, male and female. On the realistic level of the story, he is a mysterious figure. Some have suggested that he is Earnshaw's illegitimate son who will challenge the legitimate children for rights to his father's property. Others have seen him as a gypsy, or as one of the many Irish migrants who roamed northern

England in the hungry 1840s, or even as a black from one of the colonies who has found his way to Liverpool. In any case, he is outside of the established lines of inheritance, forced into dependency or outlawry to secure a place for himself. As a woman, Catherine shares his role as an outsider. They are natural soulmates.

Brontë mitigates the strangeness of her tale by telling it through two narrators. The first narrator is Lockwood, a southerner who thinks of himself as a misanthrope and identifies with Heathcliff when he first meets him. He soon learns that his misanthropy does not compare with Heathcliff's. Most of what he tells us, however, is told to him in turn by Nelly Dean, a garrulous, gossipy servant woman who has been present at most of the events she describes and who tells them in a matter-of-fact way that belies their strangeness. This double narration has the effect of making the story believable and ambiguous. One wonders just how much of the story Lockwood is capable of understanding and how much Nelly is covering up in her narration.

Even though the story is one of emotional extremes and violent oppositions, the details of setting, chronology, and plot are very carefully worked out. The places in the novel and the distances between them are based on the topography of the moors around Haworth. Many of the places in the novel are thinly disguised versions of actual places. Similarly, the chronology, which spans three generations of the Earnshaw and Linton families and is told in a series of flashbacks, carefully unfolds the events of the novel in relation to each other. The details of wills and property settlements are also carefully worked out. Thus, for all its romantic excess, *Wuthering Heights* is very thoroughly grounded in realistic detail.

The end of the novel confirms this realistic side of the story. Counterpointed to the account of Heathcliff's death and funeral are the realistic scenes showing the next generation of Hareton Earnshaw and the younger Catherine as they begin life anew. They are diminished versions of Heathcliff and the first Catherine, but their marriage may be the beginning of a new community unriven by the forces that destroyed the generation preceding them.

SUGGESTED READINGS

Winifred Gérin's *Emily Brontë: A Biography* (1971) is the standard account of Emily Brontë's life. Linda H. Peterson includes several essays on the novel from different critical perspectives in her Case Study volume published in 1992. Two essays of particular interest are Dorothy Van Ghent's chapter on *Wuthering Heights* in *The English Novel: Form and Function* (1953) and the feminist discussion of the novel by Sandra M. Gilbert and Susan Gubar in *The Madwoman in the Attic* (1979).

Wuthering Heights

CHAPTER 1

1801——I have just returned from a visit to my landlord—the solitary neighbour that I shall be troubled with. This is certainly a beautiful country! In all England, I do not believe that I could have fixed on a situation so completely removed from the stir of society. A perfect misanthropist's heaven—and Mr. Heathcliff and I are such a suitable pair to divide the desolation between us. A capital fellow! He little imagined how my heart warmed towards him when I beheld his black eyes withdraw so suspiciously under their brows, as I rode up, and when his fingers sheltered themselves, with a jealous resolution, still further in his waistcoat, as I announced my name.

"Mr. Heathcliff?" I said.

A nod was the answer.

"Mr. Lockwood, your new tenant, sir. I do myself the honour of calling as soon as possible after my arrival, to express the hope that I have not inconvenienced you by my perseverance in soliciting the occupation of Thrushcross Grange: I heard, yesterday, you had had some thoughts—"

"Thrushcross Grange is my own, sir," he interrupted, wincing, "I should not allow any one to inconvenience me, if I could hinder it—walk in!"

The "walk in," was uttered with closed teeth and expressed the sentiment, "Go to the Deuce!" Even the gate over which he leant manifested no sympathizing movement to the words, and I think that circumstance determined me to accept the invitation: I felt interested in a man who seemed more exaggeratedly reserved than myself.

When he saw my horse's breast fairly pushing the barrier, he did pull out his hand to unchain it, and then sullenly preceded me up the causeway, calling, as we entered the court—

"Joseph, take Mr. Lockwood's horse; and bring up some wine."

"Here we have the whole establishment of domestics, I suppose," was the reflection, suggested by this compound order. "No wonder the grass grows up between the flags, and cattle are the only hedge-cutters."

Joseph was an elderly, nay, an old man, very old, perhaps, though hale and sinewy.

"The Lord help us!" he soliloquized in an undertone of peevish displeasure, while relieving me of my horse: looking, meantime, in my face so sourly that I charitably conjectured he must have need of divine aid to digest his dinner, and his pious ejaculation had no reference to my unexpected advent.

Wuthering Heights is the name of Mr. Heathcliff's dwelling. "Wuthering" being a significant provincial adjective, descriptive of the atmospheric tumult to which its station is exposed in stormy weather. Pure, bracing ventilation they must have up there, at all times, indeed: one may guess the power of the north wind, blowing over the edge, by the excessive slant of a few stunted firs at the end of the house; and by a range of gaunt thorns all stretching their limbs one way, as if craving alms of the sun. Happily, the architect had foresight to build it strong: the narrow windows are deeply set in the wall, and the corners defended with large jutting stones.

Before passing the threshold, I paused to admire a quantity of grotesque carving lavished over the front, and especially about the principal door, above which, among a wilderness of crumbling griffins and shameless little boys, I detected the date "1500," and the name "Hareton Earnshaw." I would have made a few comments, and requested a short history of the place from the surly owner, but his attitude at the door appeared to demand my speedy entrance, or complete departure, and I had no desire to aggravate his impatience, previous to inspecting the penetralium.

One step brought us into the family sitting-room, without any introductory lobby or passage: they call it here "the house" preeminently. It includes kitchen and parlour, generally, but I believe at Wuthering Heights the kitchen is forced to retreat altogether into another quarter; at least I distinguished a chatter of tongues, and a clatter of culinary utensils deep within; and I observed no signs of roasting, boiling, or baking about the huge fire-place; nor any glitter of copper saucepans and tin cullenders on the walls. One end, indeed, reflected splendidly both light and heat from ranks of immense pewter dishes, interspersed with silver jugs and tankards, towering row after row, in a vast oak dresser, to the very roof. The latter had never been underdrawn: its entire anatomy lay bare to an inquiring eye, except where a frame of wood laden with oat-cakes, and clusters of legs of beef, mutton, and ham, concealed it. Above the chimney were sundry villanous old guns, and a couple of horse-pistols, and, by way of ornament, three gaudily-painted canisters disposed along its ledge. The floor was of smooth, white stone; the chairs, high-backed, primitive structures, painted green, one or two heavy black ones lurking in the shade. In an arch under the dresser, reposed a huge, liver-coloured bitch pointer surrounded by a swarm of squealing puppies, and other dogs haunted other recesses.

The apartment and furniture would have been nothing extraordinary as belonging to a homely, northern farmer, with a stubborn countenance, and stalwart limbs set out to advantage in knee-breeches and gaiters. Such an individual, seated in his arm-chair, his mug of ale frothing on the round table before him, is to be seen in any circuit of five or six miles among these hills, if you go at the right time, after dinner. But Mr. Heathcliff forms a singular contrast to his abode and style of living. He is a dark-skinned gypsy in aspect, in dress and manners a gentleman, that is, as much a gentleman as many a country squire: rather slovenly, perhaps, yet not looking amiss with his negligence, because he has an erect and handsome figure—and rather morose. Possibly, some people might suspect him of a degree of under-bred pride; I have a sympathetic chord within that tells me it is nothing of the sort: I know, by instinct, his reserve springs from an aversion to showy displays of feeling—to manifestations of mutual kindliness. He'll love and hate, equally under cover, and esteem it a species of impertinence to be loved or hated again—No, I'm running on too fast—I bestow my own attributes over-liberally on him. Mr. Heathcliff may have entirely dissimilar reasons for keeping his hand out of the way when he meets a would-be acquaintance, to those which actuate me. Let me hope my constitution is almost peculiar: my dear mother used to say I should never have a comfortable home, and only last summer I proved myself perfectly unworthy of one.

While enjoying a month of fine weather at the sea-coast, I was thrown into the company of a most fascinating creature, a real goddess in my eyes, as long as she took no notice of me. I "never told my love" vocally; still, if looks have language, the merest idiot might have guessed I was over head and ears: she understood me at last, and looked a return—the sweetest of all imaginable looks. And what did I do? I confess it with shame—shrunk icily into myself, like a snail; at every glance retired colder and farther; till, finally, the poor innocent was led to doubt her own senses, and, overwhelmed with confusion at her supposed mistake, persuaded her mamma to decamp.

By this curious turn of disposition I have gained the reputation of deliberate heartlessness, how undeserved, I alone can appreciate.

I took a seat at the end of the hearthstone opposite that towards which my landlord advanced, and filled up an interval of silence by attempting to caress the canine mother, who had left her nursery and was sneaking wolfishly to the back of my legs, her lip curled up, and her white teeth watering for a snatch.

My caress provoked a long, guttural gnarl.

"You'd better let the dog alone," growled Mr. Heathcliff in unison, checking fiercer demonstrations with a punch of his foot. "She's not accustomed to be spoiled—not kept for a pet."

Then, striding to a side-door, he shouted again—

"Joseph!"

Joseph mumbled indistinctly in the depths of the cellar, but gave no intimation of ascending; so his master dived down to him, leaving me *vis-à-vis* the ruffianly bitch and a pair of grim, shaggy sheep dogs, who shared with her a jealous guardianship over all my movements.

Not anxious to come in contact with their fangs, I sat still; but, imagining they would scarcely understand tacit insults, I unfortunately indulged in winking and making faces at the trio, and some turn of my physiognomy so irritated madam, that she suddenly broke into a fury and leapt on my knees. I flung her back, and hastened to interpose the table between us. This proceeding roused the whole hive. Half-a-dozen four-footed fiends, of various sizes and ages, issued from hidden dens to the common centre. I felt my heels and coat-laps peculiar subjects of assault; and, parrying off the larger combatants as effectually as I could with the poker, I was constrained to demand, aloud, assistance from some of the household in re-establishing peace.

Mr. Heathcliff and his man climbed the cellar steps with vexatious phlegm. I don't think they moved one second faster than usual, though the hearth was an absolute tempest of worrying and yelping.

Happily, an inhabitant of the kitchen made more dispatch; a lusty dame, with tucked-up gown, bare arms, and fire-flushed cheeks, rushed into the midst of us flourishing a frying-pan; and used that weapon, and her tongue, to such purpose, that the storm subsided magically, and she only remained, heaving like a sea after a high wind, when her master entered on the scene.

"What the devil is the matter?" he asked, eyeing me in a manner that I could ill endure after this inhospitable treatment.

"What the devil, indeed!" I muttered. "The herd of possessed swine could have had no worse spirits in them than those animals of yours, sir. You might as well leave a stranger with a brood of tigers!"

"They won't meddle with persons who touch nothing," he remarked, putting the bottle before me, and restoring the displaced table. "The dogs do right to be vigilant. Take a glass of wine?"

"No, thank you."

"Not bitten, are you?"

"If I had been, I would have set my signet on the biter."

Heathcliff's countenance relaxed into a grin.

"Come, come," he said, "you are flurried, Mr. Lockwood. Here, take a little wine. Guests are so exceedingly rare in this house that I and my dogs, I am willing to own, hardly know how to receive them. Your health, sir!"

I bowed and returned the pledge, beginning to perceive that it would be foolish to sit sulking for the misbehaviour of a pack of curs: besides, I felt loath to yield the fellow further amusement, at my expense, since his humour took that turn.

He—probably swayed by prudential considerations of the folly of offending a good tenant—relaxed a little, in the laconic style of chipping off his pronouns and auxiliary verbs, and introduced what he supposed would be a subject of interest to me, a discourse on the advantages and disadvantages of my present place of retirement.

I found him very intelligent on the topics we touched; and, before I went home, I was encouraged so far as to volunteer another visit to-morrow.

He evidently wished no repetition of my intrusion. I shall go, notwithstanding. It is astonishing how sociable I feel myself compared with him.

CHAPTER 2

Yesterday afternoon set in misty and cold. I had half a mind to spend it by my study fire, instead of wading through heath and mud to Wuthering Heights.

On coming up from dinner, however (N. B. I dine between twelve and one o'clock; the housekeeper, a matronly lady taken as a fixture along with the house, could not, or would not comprehend my request that I might be served at five.)—on mounting the stairs with this lazy intention, and stepping into the room, I saw a servant-girl on her knees, surrounded by brushes and coal-scuttles, and raising an infernal dust as she extinguished the flames with heaps of cinders. This spectacle drove me back immediately; I took my hat, and, after a four miles' walk, arrived at Heathcliff's garden gate just in time to escape the first feathery flakes of a snow shower.

On that bleak hill-top the earth was hard with a black frost, and the air made me shiver through every limb. Being unable to remove the chain, I jumped over, and, running up the flagged causeway bordered with straggling gooseberry bushes, knocked vainly for admittance, till my knuckles tingled and the dogs howled.

"Wretched inmates!" I ejaculated, mentally, "you deserve perpetual isolation from your species for your churlish inhospitality. At least, I would not keep my doors barred in the day time. I don't care—I will get in!"

So resolved, I grasped the latch and shook it vehemently. Vinegar-faced Joseph projected his head from a round window of the barn.

"Whet are ye for?" he shouted. "T' maister's dahn i' t'fowld. Goa rahnd by th' end ut' laith, if yah went tuh spake tull him."[1]

"Is there nobody inside to open the door?" I hallooed, responsively.

"They's nobbut t' missis; and shoo'll nut oppen't an ye mak yer flaysome dins till neeght."[2]

"Why? cannot you tell her who I am, eh, Joseph?"

"Nor-ne me! Aw'll hae noa hend wi't," muttered the head vanishing.

The snow began to drive thickly. I seized the handle to essay another trial, when a young man, without coat, and shouldering a pitchfork, appeared in the yard behind. He hailed me to follow him, and, after marching through a washhouse and a paved area containing a coal-shed, pump, and pigeon cote, we at length arrived in the large, warm, cheerful apartment where I was formerly received.

It glowed delightfully in the radiance of an immense fire, compounded of coal, peat, and wood; and near the table, laid for a plentiful evening meal, I was pleased to observe the "missis," an individual whose existence I had never previously suspected.

I bowed and waited, thinking she would bid me take a seat. She looked at me, leaning back in her chair, and remained motionless and mute.

"Rough weather!" I remarked. "I'm afraid, Mrs. Heathcliff, the door must bear the consequence of your servants' leisure attendance: I had hard work to make them hear me!"

She never opened her mouth. I stared—she stared also. At any rate, she kept her eyes on me, in a cool, regardless manner, exceedingly embarrassing and disagreeable.

"Sit down," said the young man, gruffly. "He'll be in soon."

I obeyed; and hemmed, and called the villain Juno, who deigned, at this second interview, to move the extreme tip of her tail, in token of owning my acquaintance.

"A beautiful animal!" I commenced again. "Do you intend parting with the little ones, madam?"

"They are not mine," said the amiable hostess more repellingly than Heathcliff himself could have replied.

"Ah, your favourites are among these!" I continued, turning to an obscure cushion full of something like cats.

"A strange choice of favourites," she observed scornfully.

Unluckily, it was a heap of dead rabbits. I hemmed once more, and drew closer to the hearth, repeating my comment on the wildness of the evening.

---

[1] *T'fowld:* the fold; *ut' laith:* of the barn.
[2] *Nobbut:* only; *flaysome:* frightening.

"You should not have come out," she said, rising and reaching from the chimney-piece two of the painted canisters.

Her position before was sheltered from the light; now, I had a distinct view of her whole figure and countenance. She was slender, and apparently scarcely past girlhood: an admirable form, and the most exquisite little face that I have ever had the pleasure of beholding: small features, very fair; flaxen ringlets, or rather golden, hanging loose on her delicate neck; and eyes—had they been agreeable in expression, they would have been irresistible. Fortunately for my susceptible heart, the only sentiment they evinced hovered between scorn and a kind of desperation, singularly unnatural to be detected there.

The canisters were almost out of her reach; I made a motion to aid her; she turned upon me as a miser might turn if any one attempted to assist him in counting his gold.

"I don't want your help," she snapped, "I can get them for myself."

"I beg your pardon," I hastened to reply.

"Were you asked to tea?" she demanded, tying an apron over her neat black frock, and standing with a spoonful of the leaf poised over the pot.

"I shall be glad to have a cup," I answered.

"Were you asked?" she repeated.

"No," I said, half smiling. "You are the proper person to ask me."

She flung the tea back, spoon and all, and resumed her chair in a pet, her forehead corrugated, and her red under-lip pushed out, like a child's, ready to cry.

Meanwhile, the young man had slung onto his person a decidedly shabby upper garment, and, erecting himself before the blaze, looked down on me from the corner of his eyes, for all the world as if there were some mortal feud unavenged between us. I began to doubt whether he were a servant or not; his dress and speech were both rude, entirely devoid of the superiority observable in Mr. and Mrs. Heathcliff; his thick, brown curls were rough and uncultivated, his whiskers encroached bearishly over his cheeks, and his hands were embrowned like those of a common labourer. Still his bearing was free, almost haughty, and he showed none of a domestic's assiduity in attending on the lady of the house.

In the absence of clear proofs of his condition, I deemed it best to abstain from noticing his curious conduct, and, five minutes afterwards, the entrance of Heathcliff relieved me, in some measure, from my uncomfortable state.

"You see, sir, I am come according to promise!" I exclaimed, assuming the cheerful; "and I fear I shall be weather-bound for half an hour, if you can afford me shelter during that space."

"Half an hour?" he said, shaking the white flakes from his clothes; "I wonder you should select the thick of a snow-storm to ramble about in. Do you know that you run a risk of being lost in the marshes? People familiar with these moors often miss their road on such evenings, and, I can tell you, there is no chance of a change at present."

"Perhaps I can get a guide among your lads, and he might stay at the Grange till morning—could you spare me one?"

"No, I could not."

"Oh, indeed! Well, then, I must trust to my own sagacity."

"Umph."

"Are you going to mak th' tea?" demanded he of the shabby coat, shifting his ferocious gaze from me to the young lady.

"Is *he* to have any?" she asked, appealing to Heathcliff.

"Get it ready, will you?" was the answer, uttered so savagely that I started. The tone in which the words were said revealed a genuine bad nature. I no longer felt inclined to call Heathcliff a capital fellow.

When the preparations were finished, he invited me with—

"Now, sir, bring forward your chair." And we all, including the rustic youth, drew round the table, an austere silence prevailing while we discussed our meal.

I thought, if I had caused the cloud, it was my duty to make an effort to dispel it. They could not every day sit so grim and taciturn, and it was impossible, however ill-tempered they might be, that the universal scowl they wore was their every day countenance.

"It is strange," I began in the interval of swallowing one cup of tea and receiving another, "it is strange how custom can mould our tastes and ideas; many could not imagine the existence of happiness in a life of such complete exile from the world as you spend, Mr. Heathcliff; yet, I'll venture to say, that, surrounded by your family, and with your amiable lady as the presiding genius over your home and heart—"

"My amiable lady!" he interrupted, with an almost diabolical sneer on his face. "Where is she—my amiable lady?"

"Mrs. Heathcliff, your wife, I mean."

"Well, yes—Oh! you would intimate that her spirit has taken the post of ministering angel, and guards the fortunes of Wuthering Heights, even when her body is gone. Is that it?"

Perceiving myself in a blunder, I attempted to correct it. I might have seen there was too great a disparity between the ages of the parties to make it likely that they were man and wife. One was about forty, a period of mental vigour at which men seldom cherish the delusion of being married for love, by girls: that dream is reserved for the solace of our declining years. The other did not look seventeen.

Then it flashed upon me—"The clown at my elbow, who is drinking his tea out of a basin and eating his bread with unwashed hands, may be her husband. Heathcliff, junior, of course. Here is the consequence of being buried alive: she has thrown herself away upon that boor, from sheer ignorance that better individuals existed! A sad pity—I must beware how I cause her to regret her choice."

The last reflection may seem conceited; it was not. My neighbour struck me as bordering on repulsive. I knew, through experience, that I was tolerably attractive.

"Mrs. Heathcliff is my daughter-in-law," said Heathcliff, corroborating my surmise. He turned, as he spoke, a peculiar look in her direction, a look of hatred, unless he has a most perverse set of facial muscles that will not, like those of other people, interpret the language of his soul.

"Ah, certainly—I see now; you are the favoured possessor of the beneficent fairy," I remarked, turning to my neighbour.

This was worse than before: the youth grew crimson, and clenched his fist with every appearance of a meditated assault. But he seemed to recollect himself, presently, and smothered the storm in a brutal curse, muttered on my behalf, which, however, I took care not to notice.

"Unhappy in your conjectures, sir!" observed my host; "we neither of us have the privilege of owning your good fairy; her mate is dead. I said she was my daughter-in-law, therefore, she must have married my son."

"And this young man is—"

"Not my son, assuredly!"

Heathcliff smiled again, as if it were rather too bold a jest to attribute the paternity of that bear to him.

"My name is Hareton Earnshaw," growled the other; "and I'd counsel you to respect it!"

"I have shown no disrespect," was my reply, laughing internally at the dignity with which he announced himself.

He fixed his eye on me longer than I cared to return the stare, for fear I might be tempted either to box his ears, or render my hilarity audible. I began to feel unmistakably out of place in that pleasant family circle. The dismal spiritual atmosphere overcame, and more than neutralized the glowing physical comforts round me; and I resolved to be cautious how I ventured under those rafters a third time.

The business of eating being concluded, and no one uttering a word of sociable conversation, I approached a window to examine the weather.

A sorrowful sight I saw: dark night coming down prematurely, and sky and hills mingled in one bitter whirl of wind and suffocating snow.

"I don't think it possible for me to get home now, without a guide," I could not help exclaiming. "The roads will be buried already; and, if they were bare, I could scarcely distinguish a foot in advance."

"Hareton, drive those dozen sheep into the barn porch. They'll be covered if left in the fold all night; and put a plank before them," said Heathcliff.

"How must I do?" I continued, with rising irritation.

There was no reply to my question; and, on looking round, I saw only Joseph bringing in a pail of porridge for the dogs, and Mrs. Heathcliff, leaning over the fire, diverting herself with burning a bundle of matches which had fallen from the chimney-piece as she restored the tea-canister to its place.

The former, when he had deposited his burden, took a critical survey of the room, and, in cracked tones, grated out—

"Aw woonder hagh yah can faishion tuh stand thear i' idleness un war, when all on 'em's goan aght! Bud yah're a nowt, and it's noa use talking—yah'll niver mend uh yer ill ways; bud goa raight tuh t' divil, like yer mother afore ye!"[3]

I imagined, for a moment, that this piece of eloquence was addressed to me; and, sufficiently enraged, stepped towards the aged rascal with an intention of kicking him out of the door.

Mrs. Heathcliff, however, checked me by her answer.

"You scandalous old hypocrite!" she replied. "Are you not afraid of being carried away bodily, whenever you mention the devil's name? I warn you to refrain from provoking me, or I'll ask your abduction as a special favour. Stop, look here, Joseph," she continued, taking a long, dark book from a shelf. "I'll show you how far I've progressed in the Black Art—I shall soon be competent to make a clear house of it. The red cow didn't die by chance; and your rheumatism can hardly be reckoned among providential visitations!"

"Oh, wicked, wicked!" gasped the elder, "may the Lord deliver us from evil!"

"No, reprobate! you are a castaway—be off, or I'll hurt you seriously! I'll have you all modelled in wax and clay; and the first who passes the limits I fix, shall—I'll not say what he shall be done to—but, you'll see! Go, I'm looking at you!"

The little witch put a mock malignity into her beautiful eyes, and Joseph, trembling with sincere horror, hurried out praying and ejaculating "wicked" as he went.

I thought her conduct must be prompted by a species of dreary fun; and, now that we were alone, I endeavoured to interest her in my distress.

"Mrs. Heathcliff," I said, earnestly, "you must excuse me for troubling you—I presume, because, with that face, I'm sure you cannot help being good-hearted. Do point out some landmarks by which I may know my way home. I have no more idea how to get there than you would have how to get to London!"

---

[3] *Un war:* and worse.

"Take the road you came," she answered, ensconcing herself in a chair, with a candle, and the long book open before her. "It is brief advice, but as sound as I can give."

"Then, if you hear of me being discovered dead in a bog, or a pit full of snow, your conscience won't whisper that it is partly your fault?"

"How so? I cannot escort you. They wouldn't let me go to the end of the garden-wall."

"*You!* I should be sorry to ask you to cross the threshold, for my convenience, on such a night," I cried. "I want you to *tell* me my way, not to *show* it; or else to persuade Mr. Heathcliff to give me a guide."

"Who? There is himself, Earnshaw, Zillah, Joseph, and I. Which would you have?"

"Are there no boys at the farm?"

"No, those are all."

"Then it follows that I am compelled to stay."

"That you may settle with your host. I have nothing to do with it."

"I hope it will be a lesson to you, to make no more rash journeys on these hills," cried Heathcliff's stern voice from the kitchen entrance. "As to staying here, I don't keep accommodations for visitors; you must share a bed with Hareton, or Joseph, if you do."

"I can sleep on a chair in this room," I replied.

"No, no! A stranger is a stranger, be he rich or poor—it will not suit me to permit any one the range of the place while I am off guard!" said the unmannerly wretch.

With this insult my patience was at an end. I uttered an expression of disgust, and pushed past him into the yard, running against Earnshaw in my haste. It was so dark that I could not see the means of exit, and, as I wandered round, I heard another specimen of their civil behaviour amongst each other.

At first, the young man appeared about to befriend me.

"I'll go with him as far as the park," he said.

"You'll go with him to hell!" exclaimed his master, or whatever relation he bore. "And who is to look after the horses, eh?"

"A man's life is of more consequence than one evening's neglect of the horses; somebody must go," murmured Mrs. Heathcliff, more kindly than I expected.

"Not at your command!" retorted Hareton. "If you set store on him, you'd better be quiet."

"Then I hope his ghost will haunt you; and I hope Mr. Heathcliff will never get another tenant, till the Grange is a ruin!" she answered sharply.

"Hearken, hearken, shoo's cursing on em!" muttered Joseph, towards whom I had been steering.

He sat within earshot, milking the cows by the aid of a lantern which I seized unceremoniously, and, calling out that I would send it back on the morrow, rushed to the nearest postern.

"Maister, maister, he's staling t' lantern!" shouted the ancient, pursuing my retreat. "Hey, Gnasher! Hey, dog! Hey, Wolf, holld him, holld him!"

On opening the little door, two hairy monsters flew at my throat, bearing me down and extinguishing the light, while a mingled guffaw, from Heathcliff and Hareton, put the copestone on my rage and humiliation.

Fortunately, the beasts seemed more bent on stretching their paws, and yawning and flourishing their tails, than devouring me alive; but they would suffer no resurrection, and I was forced to lie till their malignant masters pleased to deliver me: then hatless, and trembling with wrath, I ordered the miscreants to let me out—on their peril to keep me one minute longer—with several incoherent threats of retaliation that, in their indefinite depth of virulency, smacked of King Lear.

The vehemence of my agitation brought on a copious bleeding at the nose, and still Heathcliff laughed, and still I scolded. I don't know what would have concluded the scene had there not been one person at hand rather more rational than myself, and more benevolent than my entertainer. This was Zillah, the stout housewife, who at length issued forth to inquire into the nature of the uproar. She thought that some of them had been laying violent hands on me, and, not daring to attack her master, she turned her vocal artillery against the younger scoundrel.

"Well, Mr. Earnshaw," she cried, "I wonder what you'll have agait[4] next! Are we going to murder folk on our very door-stones? I see this house will never do for me—look at t' poor lad, he's fair choking! Wisht, wisht! you mun'n't go on so—come in, and I'll cure that. There now, hold ye still."

With these words she suddenly splashed a pint of icy water down my neck, and pulled me into the kitchen. Mr. Heathcliff followed, his accidental merriment expiring quickly in his habitual moroseness.

I was sick exceedingly, and dizzy and faint; and thus compelled, perforce, to accept lodgings under his roof. He told Zillah to give me a glass of brandy, and then passed on to the inner room, while she condoled with me on my sorry predicament, and having obeyed his orders, whereby I was somewhat revived, ushered me to bed.

Chapter 3

While leading the way upstairs, she recommended that I should hide the candle, and not make a noise, for her master had an odd notion about the chamber she would put me in, and never let anybody lodge there willingly.

I asked the reason.

She did not know, she answered; she had only lived there a year or two; and they had so many queer goings on, she could not begin to be curious.

Too stupified to be curious myself, I fastened my door and glanced round for the bed. The whole furniture consisted of a chair, a clothes-press, and a large oak case, with squares cut out near the top, resembling coach windows.

Having approached this structure, I looked inside, and perceived it to be a singular sort of old-fashioned couch, very conveniently designed to obviate the necessity for every member of the family having a room to himself. In fact, it formed a little closet, and the ledge of a window, which it enclosed, served as a table.

I slid back the panelled sides, got in with my light, pulled them together again, and felt secure against the vigilance of Heathcliff, and every one else.

The ledge, where I placed my candle, had a few mildewed books piled up in one corner; and it was covered with writing scratched on the paint. This writing, however, was nothing but a name repeated in all kinds of characters, large and small—*Catherine Earnshaw,* here and there varied to *Catherine Heathcliff,* and then again to *Catherine Linton.*

In vapid listlessness I leant my head against the window, and continued spelling over Catherine Earnshaw—Heathcliff—Linton, till my eyes closed; but they had not rested five minutes when a glare of white letters started from the dark, as vivid as spectres—the air swarmed with Catherines; and rousing myself to dispel

---

[4]*Agait:* going on.

the obtrusive name, I discovered my candle wick reclining on one of the antique volumes, and perfuming the place with an odour of roasted calf-skin.

I snuffed it off, and, very ill at ease under the influence of cold and lingering nausea, sat up, and spread open the injured tome on my knee. It was a Testament, in lean type, and smelling dreadfully musty: a fly-leaf bore the inscription—"Catherine Earnshaw, her book," and a date some quarter of a century back.

I shut it, and took up another, and another, till I had examined all. Catherine's library was select, and its state of dilapidation proved it to have been well used, though not altogether for a legitimate purpose; scarcely one chapter had escaped a pen and ink commentary—at least, the appearance of one—covering every morsel of blank that the printer had left.

Some were detached sentences; other parts took the form of a regular diary, scrawled in an unformed, childish hand. At the top of an extra page, quite a treasure probably when first lighted on, I was greatly amused to behold an excellent caricature of my friend Joseph, rudely yet powerfully sketched.

An immediate interest kindled within me for the unknown Catherine, and I began, forthwith, to decypher her faded hieroglyphics.

"An awful Sunday!" commenced the paragraph beneath. "I wish my father were back again. Hindley is a detestable substitute—his conduct to Heathcliff is atrocious—H. and I are going to rebel—we took our initiatory step this evening.

"All day had been flooding with rain; we could not go to church, so Joseph must needs get up a congregation in the garret; and, while Hindley and his wife basked downstairs before a comfortable fire—doing anything but reading their Bibles, I'll answer for it—Heathcliff, myself, and the unhappy plough-boy were commanded to take our Prayer-books, and mount. We were ranged in a row, on a sack of corn, groaning and shivering, and hoping that Joseph would shiver too, so that he might give us a short homily for his own sake. A vain idea! The service lasted precisely three hours; and yet my brother had the face to exclaim, when he saw us descending—

"'What, done already?'

"On Sunday evenings we used to be permitted to play, if we did not make much noise; now a mere titter is sufficient to send us into corners!

"'You forget you have a master here,' says the tyrant. 'I'll demolish the first who puts me out of temper! I insist on perfect sobriety and silence. Oh, boy! was that you? Frances, darling, pull his hair as you go by; I heard him snap his fingers.'

"Frances pulled his hair heartily; and then went and seated herself on her husband's knee, and there they were, like two babies, kissing and talking nonsense by the hour—foolish palaver that we should be ashamed of.

"We made ourselves as snug as our means allowed in the arch of the dresser. I had just fastened our pinafores together, and hung them up for a curtain, when in comes Joseph, on an errand from the stables. He tears down my handywork, boxes my ears, and croaks—

"'T' maister nobbut just buried, and Sabbath nut oe'red, und t'sahnd uh't gospel still i' yer lugs, and yah darr be laiking! shame on ye! sit ye dahn, ill childer! they's good books eneugh if ye'll read 'em; sit ye dahn, and think uh yer sowls!'[5]

"Saying this, he compelled us so to square our positions that we might receive, from the far-off fire, a dull ray to show us the text of the lumber he thrust upon us.

"I could not bear the employment. I took my dingy volume by the scroop,[6] and hurled it into the dog-kennel, vowing I hated a good book.

---

[5] Oe'red: over; t'sahnd: the sound; lugs: ears; darr be laiking: dare be playing.
[6] The back of the cover of a book.

"Heathcliff kicked his to the same place.

"Then there was a hubbub!

"'Maister Hindley!' shouted our chaplain. 'Maister, coom hither! Miss Cathy's riven th' back off "Th' Helmet uh Salvation," un' Heathcliff's pawsed his fit[7] intuh t' first part uh "T' Brooad Way to Destruction"! It's fair flaysome ut yah let 'em goa on this gait. Ech! th' owd man ud uh laced 'em properly—bud he's goan!'

"Hindley hurried up from his paradise on the hearth, and seizing one of us by the collar, and the other by the arm, hurled both into the back-kitchen, where, Joseph asseverated, 'owd Nick' would fetch us as sure as we were living; and, so comforted, we each sought a separate nook to await his advent.

"I reached this book, and a pot of ink from a shelf, and pushed the house-door ajar to give me light, and I have got the time on with writing for twenty minutes; but my companion is impatient and proposes that we should appropriate the dairy woman's cloak, and have a scamper on the moors, under its shelter. A pleasant suggestion—and then, if the surly old man come in, he may believe his prophesy verified—we cannot be damper, or colder, in the rain than we are here."

I suppose Catherine fulfilled her project, for the next sentence took up another subject; she waxed lachrymose.

"How little did I dream that Hindley would ever make me cry so!" she wrote. "My head aches, till I cannot keep it on the pillow; and still I can't give over. Poor Heathcliff! Hindley calls him a vagabond, and won't let him sit with us, nor eat with us any more; and, he says, he and I must not play together, and threatens to turn him out of the house if we break his orders.

"He has been blaming our father (how dared he?) for treating H. too liberally; and swears he will reduce him to his right place—"

I began to nod drowsily over the dim page; my eye wandered from manuscript to print. I saw a red ornamented title—"Seventy Times Seven, and the First of the Seventy-First. A Pious Discourse delivered by the Reverend Jabes Branderham, in the Chapel of Gimmerden Sough." And while I was, half consciously, worrying my brain to guess what Jabes Branderham would make of his subject, I sank back in bed, and fell asleep.

Alas, for the effects of bad tea and bad temper! what else could it be that made me pass such a terrible night? I don't remember another that I can at all compare with it since I was capable of suffering.

I began to dream, almost before I ceased to be sensible of my locality. I thought it was morning, and I had set out on my way home, with Joseph for a guide. The snow lay yards deep in our road; and, as we floundered on, my companion wearied me with constant reproaches that I had not brought a pilgrim's staff, telling me I could never get into the house without one, and boastfully flourishing a heavy-headed cudgel, which I understood to be so denominated.

For a moment I considered it absurd that I should need such a weapon to gain admittance into my own residence. Then, a new idea flashed across me. I was not going there; we were journeying to hear the famous Jabes Branderham preach from the text—"Seventy Times Seven"; and either Joseph, the preacher, or I had committed the "First of the Seventy-First," and were to be publicly exposed and excommunicated.

We came to the chapel. I have passed it really in my walks, twice or thrice; it lies in a hollow, between two hills—an elevated hollow, near a swamp, whose

---

[7] *Pawsed his fit:* made a hole with his foot.

peaty moisture is said to answer all the purposes of embalming on the few corpses deposited there. The roof has been kept whole hitherto, but, as the clergyman's stipend is only twenty pounds per annum, and a house with two rooms, threatening speedily to determine into one, no clergyman will undertake the duties of pastor, especially as it is currently reported that his flock would rather let him starve than increase the living by one penny from their own pockets. However, in my dream, Jabes had a full and attentive congregation: and he preached—good God—what a sermon! Divided into *four hundred and ninety* parts, each fully equal to an ordinary address from the pulpit, and each discussing a separate sin! Where he searched for them, I cannot tell; he had his private manner of interpreting the phrase, and it seemed necessary the brother should sin different sins on every occasion.

They were of the most curious character—odd transgressions that I never imagined previously.

Oh, how weary I grew. How I writhed, and yawned, and nodded, and revived! How I pinched and pricked myself, and rubbed my eyes, and stood up, and sat down again, and nudged Joseph to inform me if he would *ever* have done!

I was condemned to hear all out; finally, he reached the "*First of the Seventy-First.*" At that crisis, a sudden inspiration descended on me; I was moved to rise and denounce Jabes Branderham as the sinner of the sin that no Christian need pardon.

"Sir," I exclaimed, "sitting here, within these four walls, at one stretch, I have endured and forgiven the four hundred and ninety heads of your discourse. Seventy times seven times have I plucked up my hat and been about to depart— Seventy times seven times have you preposterously forced me to resume my seat. The four hundred and ninety-first is too much. Fellow martyrs, have at him! Drag him down, and crush him to atoms, that the place which knows him may know him no more!"

"*Thou art the Man!*" cried Jabes, after a solemn pause, leaning over his cushion. "Seventy times seven times didst thou gapingly contort thy visage—seventy times seven did I take counsel with my soul—Lo, this is human weakness; this also may be absolved! The First of the Seventy-First is come. Brethren, execute upon him the judgment written! such honour have all His saints!"

With that concluding word, the whole assembly, exalting their pilgrim's staves, rushed round me in a body, and I, having no weapon to raise in self-defence, commenced grappling with Joseph, my nearest and most ferocious assailant, for his. In the confluence of the multitude, several clubs crossed; blows, aimed at me, fell on other sconces. Presently the whole chapel resounded with rappings and counter-rappings. Every man's hand was against his neighbour; and Branderham, unwilling to remain idle, poured forth his zeal in a shower of loud taps on the boards of the pulpit, which resounded so smartly that, at last, to my unspeakable relief, they woke me.

And what was it that had suggested the tremendous tumult, what had played Jabes's part in the row? Merely the branch of a fir tree that touched my lattice, as the blast wailed by, and rattled its dry cones against the panes!

I listened doubtingly an instant; detected the disturber, then turned and dozed, and dreamt again; if possible, still more disagreeably than before.

This time, I remembered I was lying in the oak closet, and I heard distinctly the gusty wind, and the driving of the snow; I heard, also, the fir-bough repeat its teasing sound, and ascribed it to the right cause; but it annoyed me so much, that I resolved to silence it, if possible; and, I thought, I rose and endeavoured to unhasp the casement. The hook was soldered into the staple, a circumstance observed by me when awake, but forgotten.

"I must stop it, nevertheless!" I muttered, knocking my knuckles through the glass, and stretching an arm out to seize the importunate branch: instead of which, my fingers closed on the fingers of a little, ice-cold hand!

The intense horror of nightmare came over me; I tried to draw back my arm, but the hand clung to it, and a most melancholy voice sobbed—

"Let me in—let me in!"

"Who are you?" I asked, struggling, meanwhile, to disengage myself.

"Catherine Linton," it replied, shiveringly (why did I think of *Linton?* I had read *Earnshaw* twenty times for Linton). "I'm come home, I'd lost my way on the moor!"

As it spoke, I discerned, obscurely, a child's face looking through the window. Terror made me cruel; and, finding it useless to attempt shaking the creature off, I pulled its wrist on to the broken pane, and rubbed it to and fro till the blood ran down and soaked the bed-clothes: still it wailed, "Let me in!" and maintained its tenacious gripe, almost maddening me with fear.

"How can I?" I said at length. "Let *me* go, if you want me to let you in!"

The fingers relaxed, I snatched mine through the hole, hurriedly piled the books up in a pyramid against it, and stopped my ears to exclude the lamentable prayer.

I seemed to keep them closed above a quarter of an hour, yet, the instant I listened again, there was the doleful cry moaning on!

"Begone!" I shouted, "I'll never let you in, not if you beg for twenty years!"

"It's twenty years," mourned the voice, "twenty years, I've been a waif for twenty years!"

Thereat began a feeble scratching outside, and the pile of books moved as if thrust forward.

I tried to jump up, but could not stir a limb; and so yelled aloud, in a frenzy of fright.

To my confusion, I discovered the yell was not ideal. Hasty footsteps approached my chamber door; somebody pushed it open, with a vigorous hand, and a light glimmered through the squares at the top of the bed. I sat shuddering yet, and wiping the perspiration from my forehead: the intruder appeared to hesitate, and muttered to himself.

At last, he said in a half-whisper, plainly not expecting an answer—

"Is any one here?"

I considered it best to confess my presence, for I knew Heathcliff's accents, and feared he might search further, if I kept quiet.

With this intention, I turned and opened the panels. I shall not soon forget the effect my action produced.

Heathcliff stood near the entrance, in his shirt and trousers, with a candle dripping over his fingers, and his face as white as the wall behind him. The first creak of the oak startled him like an electric shock: the light leaped from his hold to a distance of some feet, and his agitation was so extreme that he could hardly pick it up.

"It is only your guest, sir," I called out, desirous to spare him the humiliation of exposing his cowardice further. "I had the misfortune to scream in my sleep, owing to a frightful nightmare. I'm sorry I disturbed you."

"Oh, God confound you, Mr. Lockwood! I wish you were at the—" commenced my host, setting the candle on a chair, because he found it impossible to hold it steady.

"And who showed you up to this room?" he continued, crushing his nails into his palms, and grinding his teeth to subdue the maxillary convulsions. "Who was it? I've a good mind to turn them out of the house this moment!"

"It was your servant, Zillah," I replied, flinging myself on to the floor, and rapidly resuming my garments. "I should not care if you did, Mr. Heathcliff; she richly deserves it. I suppose that she wanted to get another proof that the place was haunted, at my expense. Well, it is—swarming with ghosts and goblins! You have reason in shutting it up, I assure you. No one will thank you for a doze in such a den!"

"What do you mean?" asked Heathcliff, "and what are you doing? Lie down and finish out the night, since you *are* here; but, for heaven's sake! don't repeat that horrid noise. Nothing could excuse it, unless you were having your throat cut!"

"If the little fiend had got in at the window, she probably would have strangled me!" I returned. "I'm not going to endure the persecutions of your hospitable ancestors again. Was not the Reverend Jabes Branderham akin to you on the mother's side? And that minx, Catherine Linton, or Earnshaw, or however she was called—she must have been a changeling—wicked little soul! She told me she had been walking the earth these twenty years: a just punishment for her mortal transgressions, I've no doubt!"

Scarcely were these words uttered, when I recollected the association of Heathcliff's with Catherine's name in the book, which had completely slipped from my memory till thus awakened. I blushed at my inconsideration; but, without showing further consciousness of the offence, I hastened to add—

"The truth is, sir, I passed the first part of the night in—" here, I stopped afresh—I was about to say "perusing those old volumes"; then it would have revealed my knowledge of their written, as well as their printed contents; so, correcting myself, I went on—"in spelling over the name scratched on that window-ledge. A monotonous occupation, calculated to set me asleep, like counting, or—"

"What *can* you mean by talking in this way to *me!*" thundered Heathcliff with savage vehemence. "How—how *dare* you, under my roof—God! he's mad to speak so!" And he struck his forehead with rage.

I did not know whether to resent this language, or pursue my explanation; but he seemed so powerfully affected that I took pity and proceeded with my dreams, affirming I had never heard the appellation of "Catherine Linton" before, but reading it often over produced an impression which personified itself when I had no longer my imagination under control.

Heathcliff gradually fell back into the shelter of the bed as I spoke, finally sitting down almost concealed behind it. I guessed, however, by his irregular and intercepted breathing, that he struggled to vanquish an access of violent emotion.

Not liking to show him that I heard the conflict, I continued my toilette rather noisily, looked at my watch, and soliloquized on the length of the night—

"Not three o'clock yet! I could have taken oath it had been six. Time stagnates here—we must surely have retired to rest at eight!"

"Always at nine in winter, and always rise at four," said my host, suppressing a groan, and, as I fancied, by the motion of his shadow's arm, dashing a tear from his eyes.

"Mr. Lockwood," he added, "you may go into my room; you'll only be in the way, coming downstairs so early; and your childish outcry has sent sleep to the devil for me."

"And for me, too," I replied. "I'll walk in the yard till daylight, and then I'll be off; and you need not dread a repetition of my intrusion. I am now quite cured of seeking pleasure in society, be it country or town. A sensible man ought to find sufficient company in himself."

"Delightful company!" muttered Heathcliff. "Take the candle, and go where you please. I shall join you directly. Keep out of the yard, though; the dogs are unchained, and the house—Juno mounts sentinel there, and—nay, you can only ramble about the steps and passages. But, away with you! I'll come in two minutes."

I obeyed, so far as to quit the chamber; when, ignorant where the narrow lobbies led, I stood still, and was witness, involuntarily, to a piece of superstition on the part of my landlord, which belied, oddly, his apparent sense.

He got on to the bed and wrenched open the lattice, bursting, as he pulled at it, into an uncontrollable passion of tears.

"Come in! come in!" he sobbed. "Cathy, do come. Oh, do—*once* more! Oh! my heart's darling, hear me *this* time—Catherine, at last!"

The spectre showed a spectre's ordinary caprice; it gave no sign of being; but the snow and wind whirled wildly through, even reaching my station, and blowing out the light.

There was such anguish in the gush of grief that accompanied this raving, that my compassion made me overlook its folly, and I drew off, half angry to have listened at all, and vexed at having related my ridiculous nightmare, since it produced that agony, though *why*, was beyond my comprehension.

I descended cautiously to the lower regions and landed in the back-kitchen, where a gleam of fire, raked compactly together, enabled me to rekindle my candle.

Nothing was stirring except a brindled, grey cat, which crept from the ashes and saluted me with a querulous mew.

Two benches, shaped in sections of a circle, nearly enclosed the hearth; on one of these I stretched myself, and Grimalkin mounted the other. We were both of us nodding, ere any one invaded our retreat; and then it was Joseph shuffling down a wooden ladder that vanished in the roof, through a trap: the ascent to his garret, I suppose.

He cast a sinister look at the little flame which I had enticed to play between the ribs, swept the cat from its elevation, and bestowing himself in the vacancy, commenced the operation of stuffing a three-inch pipe with tobacco; my presence in his sanctum was evidently esteemed a piece of impudence too shameful for remark. He silently applied the tube to his lips, folded his arms, and puffed away.

I let him enjoy the luxury, unannoyed; and after sucking out the last wreath, and heaving a profound sigh, he got up, and departed as solemnly as he came.

A more elastic footstep entered next, and now I opened my mouth for a "good morning," but closed it again, the salutation unachieved; for Hareton Earnshaw was performing his orisons, *sotto voce*, in a series of curses directed against every object he touched, while he rummaged a corner for a spade or shovel to dig through the drifts. He glanced over the back of the bench, dilating his nostrils, and thought as little of exchanging civilities with me as with my companion, the cat.

I guessed by his preparations that egress was allowed, and leaving my hard couch, made a movement to follow him. He noticed this, and thrust at an inner door with the end of his spade, intimating by an inarticulate sound, that there was the place where I must go, if I changed my locality.

It opened into the house, where the females were already astir, Zillah, urging flakes of flame up the chimney with a colossal bellows, and Mrs. Heathcliff, kneeling on the hearth, reading a book by the aid of the blaze.

She held her hand interposed between the furnace-heat and her eyes, and seemed absorbed in her occupation; desisting from it only to chide the servant for covering her with sparks, or to push away a dog, now and then, that snoozled its nose over-forwardly into her face.

I was surprised to see Heathcliff there also. He stood by the fire, his back towards me, just finishing a stormy scene to poor Zillah, who ever and anon interrupted her labour to pluck up the corner of her apron, and heave an indignant groan.

"And you, you worthless—" he broke out as I entered, turning to his daughter-in-law, and employing an epithet as harmless as duck, or sheep, but generally represented by a dash—"there you are at your idle tricks again! The rest of them do earn their bread—you live on my charity! Put your trash away, and find something to do. You shall pay me for the plague of having you eternally in my sight—do you hear, damnable jade?"

"I'll put my trash away, because you can make me, if I refuse," answered the young lady, closing her book, and throwing it on a chair. "But I'll not do anything, though you should swear your tongue out, except what I please!"

Heathcliff lifted his hand, and the speaker sprang to a safer distance, obviously acquainted with its weight.

Having no desire to be entertained by a cat and dog combat, I stepped forward briskly, as if eager to partake the warmth of the hearth, and innocent of any knowledge of the interrupted dispute. Each had enough decorum to suspend further hostilities: Heathcliff placed his fists, out of temptation, in his pockets; Mrs. Heathcliff curled her lip and walked to a seat far off, where she kept her word by playing the part of a statue during the remainder of my stay.

That was not long. I declined joining their breakfast, and, at the first gleam of dawn, took an opportunity of escaping into the free air, now clear and still, and cold as impalpable ice.

My landlord hallooed for me to stop, ere I reached the bottom of the garden, and offered to accompany me across the moor. It was well he did, for the whole hill-back was one billowy, white ocean, the swells and falls not indicating corresponding rises and depressions in the ground: many pits, at least, were filled to a level; and entire ranges of mounds, the refuse of the quarries, blotted from the chart which my yesterday's walk left pictured in my mind.

I had remarked on one side of the road, at intervals of six or seven yards, a line of upright stones, continued through the whole length of the barren: these were erected, and daubed with lime, on purpose to serve as guides in the dark, and also, when a fall, like the present, confounded the deep swamps on either hand with the firmer path: but, excepting a dirty dot pointing up here and there, all traces of their existence had vanished; and my companion found it necessary to warn me frequently to steer to the right or left, when I imagined I was following, correctly, the windings of the road.

We exchanged little conversation, and he halted at the entrance of Thrushcross park, saying, I could make no error there. Our adieux were limited to a hasty bow, and then I pushed forward, trusting to my own resources, for the porter's lodge is untenanted as yet.

The distance from the gate to the Grange is two miles: I believe I managed to make it four, what with losing myself among the trees, and sinking up to the neck in snow, a predicament which only those who have experienced it can appreciate. At any rate, whatever were my wanderings, the clock chimed twelve as I entered the house; and that gave exactly an hour for every mile of the usual way from Wuthering Heights.

My human fixture and her satellites rushed to welcome me; exclaiming, tumultuously, they had completely given me up: everybody conjectured that I perished last night; and they were wondering how they must set about the search for my remains.

I bid them be quiet, now that they saw me returned, and, benumbed to my very heart, I dragged upstairs, whence, after putting on dry clothes, and pacing to and fro thirty or forty minutes, to restore the animal heat, I am adjourned to my study, feeble as a kitten, almost too much so to enjoy the cheerful fire and smoking coffee which the servant has prepared for my refreshment.

CHAPTER 4

What vain weather-cocks we are! I, who had determined to hold myself independent of all social intercourse, and thanked my stars that, at length, I had lighted on a spot where it was next to impracticable—I, weak wretch, after maintaining till dusk a struggle with low spirits and solitude, was finally compelled to strike my colours; and, under pretence of gaining information concerning the necessities of my establishment, I desired Mrs. Dean, when she brought in supper, to sit down while I ate it, hoping sincerely she would prove a regular gossip, and either rouse me to animation, or lull me to sleep by her talk.

"You have lived here a considerable time," I commenced; "did you not say sixteen years?"

"Eighteen, sir; I came, when the mistress was married, to wait on her; after she died, the master retained me for his house-keeper."

"Indeed."

There ensued a pause. She was not a gossip, I feared, unless about her own affairs, and those could hardly interest me.

However, having studied for an interval, with a fist on either knee, and a cloud of meditation over her ruddy countenance, she ejaculated—

"Ah, times are greatly changed since then!"

"Yes," I remarked, "you've seen a good many alterations, I suppose?"

"I have: and troubles too," she said.

"Oh, I'll turn the talk on my landlord's family!" I thought to myself. "A good subject to start—and that pretty girl-widow, I should like to know her history: whether she be a native of the country, or, as is more probable, an exotic that the surly *indigenae* will not recognise for kin."

With this intention I asked Mrs. Dean why Heathcliff let Thrushcross Grange, and preferred living in a situation and residence so much inferior.

"Is he not rich enough to keep the estate in good order?" I enquired.

"Rich, sir!" she returned. "He has, nobody knows what money, and every year it increases. Yes, yes, he's rich enough to live in a finer house than this, but he's very near—close-handed; and, if he had meant to flit to Thrushcross Grange, as soon as he heard of a good tenant he could not have borne to miss the chance of getting a few hundreds more. It is strange people should be so greedy, when they are alone in the world!"

"He had a son, it seems?"

"Yes, he had one—he is dead."

"And that young lady, Mrs. Heathcliff, is his widow?"

"Yes."

"Where did she come from originally?"

"Why, sir, she is my late master's daughter; Catherine Linton was her maiden name. I nursed her, poor thing! I did wish Mr. Heathcliff would remove here, and then we might have been together again."

"What, Catherine Linton!" I exclaimed, astonished. But a minute's reflection convinced me it was not my ghostly Catherine. "Then," I continued, "my predecessor's name was Linton?"

"It was."

"And who is that Earnshaw, Hareton Earnshaw, who lives with Mr. Heathcliff? are they relations?"

"No; he is the late Mrs. Linton's nephew."

"The young lady's cousin, then?"

"Yes; and her husband was her cousin also—one, on the mother's—the other, on the father's side. Heathcliff married Mr. Linton's sister."

"I see the house at Wuthering Heights has 'Earnshaw' carved over the front door. Are they an old family?"

"Very old, sir; and Hareton is the last of them, as our Miss Cathy is of us—I mean, of the Lintons. Have you been to Wuthering Heights? I beg your pardon for asking; but I should like to hear how she is!"

"Mrs. Heathcliff? She looked very well, and very handsome; yet, I think, not very happy."

"Oh dear, I don't wonder! And how did you like the master?"

"A rough fellow, rather, Mrs. Dean. Is not that his character?"

"Rough as a saw-edge, and hard as whinstone! The less you meddle with him the better."

"He must have had some ups and downs in life to make him such a churl. Do you know anything of his history?"

"It's a cuckoo's, sir—I know all about it, except where he was born, and who were his parents, and how he got his money, at first. And Hareton has been cast out like an unfledged dunnock! The unfortunate lad is the only one, in all this parish, that does not guess how he has been cheated!"

"Well, Mrs. Dean, it will be a charitable deed to tell me something of my neighbours—I feel I shall not rest, if I go to bed; so, be good enough to sit and chat an hour."

"Oh, certainly, sir! I'll just fetch a little sewing, and then I'll sit as long as you please. But you've caught cold; I saw you shivering, and you must have some gruel to drive it out."

The worthy woman bustled off; and I crouched nearer the fire; my head felt hot, and the rest of me chill: moreover, I was excited, almost to a pitch of foolishness, through my nerves and brain. This caused me to feel, not uncomfortable, but rather fearful, as I am still, of serious effects from the incidents of today and yesterday.

She returned presently, bringing a smoking basin, and a basket of work; and, having placed the former on the hob, drew in her seat, evidently pleased to find me so companionable.

Before I came to live here, she commenced, waiting no further invitation to her story, I was almost always at Wuthering Heights, because my mother had nursed Mr. Hindley Earnshaw, that was Hareton's father, and I got used to playing with the children. I ran errands too, and helped to make hay, and hung about the farm ready for anything that anybody would set me to.

One fine summer morning—it was the beginning of harvest, I remember—Mr. Earnshaw, the old master, came downstairs, dressed for a journey; and, after he had told Joseph what was to be done during the day, he turned to Hindley, and Cathy, and me—for I sat eating my porridge with them—and he said, speaking to his son—

"Now, my bonny man, I'm going to Liverpool, to-day. What shall I bring you? You may choose what you like; only let it be little, for I shall walk there and back; sixty miles each way, that is a long spell!"

Hindley named a fiddle, and then he asked Miss Cathy; she was hardly six years old, but she could ride any horse in the stable, and she chose a whip.

He did not forget me, for he had a kind heart, though he was rather severe, sometimes. He promised to bring me a pocketful of apples and pears, and then he kissed his children good-bye, and set off.

It seemed a long while to us all—the three days of his absence—and often did little Cathy ask when he would be home. Mrs. Earnshaw expected him by supper-time, on the third evening; and she put the meal off hour after hour; there were no signs of his coming, however, and at last the children got tired of running down to the gate to look. Then it grew dark; she would have had them to bed, but they begged sadly to be allowed to stay up; and, just about eleven o'clock, the door-latch was raised quietly and in stept the master. He threw himself into a chair, laughing and groaning, and bid them all stand off, for he was nearly killed—he would not have such another walk for the three kingdoms.

"And at the end of it, to be flighted[8] to death!" he said, opening his great coat, which he held bundled up in his arms, "See here, wife; I was never so beaten with anything in my life; but you must e'en take it as a gift of God, though it's as dark almost as if it came from the devil."

We crowded round, and, over Miss Cathy's head, I had a peep at a dirty, ragged, black-haired child; big enough both to walk and talk—indeed, its face looked older than Catherine's—yet, when it was set on its feet, it only stared round, and repeated over and over again some gibberish that nobody could understand. I was frightened, and Mrs. Earnshaw was ready to fling it out of doors: she did fly up—asking how he could fashion to bring that gipsy brat into the house, when they had their own bairns to feed and fend for? What he meant to do with it, and whether he were mad?

The master tried to explain the matter; but he was really half dead with fatigue, and all that I could make out, amongst her scolding, was a tale of his seeing it starving, and houseless, and as good as dumb in the streets of Liverpool, where he picked it up and inquired for its owner. Not a soul knew to whom it belonged, he said, and his money and time being both limited, he thought it better to take it home with him at once, than run into vain expenses there; because he was determined he would not leave it as he found it.

Well, the conclusion was that my mistress grumbled herself calm; and Mr. Earnshaw told me to wash it, and give it clean things, and let it sleep with the children.

Hindley and Cathy contented themselves with looking and listening till peace was restored; then, both began searching their father's pockets for the presents he had promised them. The former was a boy of fourteen, but when he drew out what had been a fiddle, crushed to morsels in the great coat, he blubbered aloud, and Cathy, when she learnt the master had lost her whip in attending on the stranger, showed her humour by grinning and spitting at the stupid little thing, earning for her pains a sound blow from her father to teach her cleaner manners.

They entirely refused to have it in bed with them, or even in their room, and I had no more sense, so I put it on the landing of the stairs, hoping it might be gone on the morrow. By chance, or else attracted by hearing his voice, it crept to Mr. Earnshaw's door and there he found it on quitting his chamber. Inquiries were made as to how it got there; I was obliged to confess, and in recompense for my cowardice and inhumanity was sent out of the house.

This was Heathcliff's first introduction to the family. On coming back a few days afterwards, for I did not consider my banishment perpetual, I found they had christened him "Heathcliff"; it was the name of a son who died in childhood, and it has served him ever since, both for Christian and surname.

Miss Cathy and he were now very thick; but Hindley hated him, and to say the truth I did the same; and we plagued and went on with him shamefully, for I wasn't reasonable enough to feel my injustice, and the mistress never put in a word on his behalf when she saw him wronged.

---

[8] *Flighted:* frightened.

He seemed a sullen, patient child, hardened, perhaps, to ill-treatment: he would stand Hindley's blows without winking or shedding a tear, and my pinches moved him only to draw in a breath, and open his eyes as if he had hurt himself by accident, and nobody was to blame.

This endurance made old Earnshaw furious when he discovered his son persecuting the poor, fatherless child, as he called him. He took to Heathcliff strangely, believing all he said (for that matter, he said precious little, and generally the truth) and petting him up far above Cathy, who was too mischievous and wayward for a favourite.

So, from the very beginning, he bred bad feeling in the house; and at Mrs. Earnshaw's death, which happened in less than two years after, the young master had learnt to regard his father as an oppressor rather than a friend, and Heathcliff as a usurper of his parent's affections and his privileges, and he grew bitter with brooding over these injuries.

I sympathised a while, but, when the children fell ill of the measles and I had to tend them, and take on me the cares of a woman at once, I changed my ideas. Heathcliff was dangerously sick, and while he lay at the worst he would have me constantly by his pillow; I suppose he felt I did a good deal for him, and he hadn't wit to guess that I was compelled to do it. However, I will say this, he was the quietest child that ever nurse watched over. The difference between him and the others forced me to be less partial. Cathy and her brother harassed me terribly; *he* was as uncomplaining as a lamb, though hardness, not gentleness, made him give little trouble.

He got through, and the doctor affirmed it was in a great measure owing to me, and praised me for my care. I was vain of his commendations, and softened towards the being by whose means I earned them, and thus Hindley lost his last ally; still I couldn't dote on Heathcliff, and I wondered often what my master saw to admire so much in the sullen boy who never, to my recollection, repaid his indulgence by any sign of gratitude. He was not insolent to his benefactor; he was simply insensible, though knowing perfectly the hold he had on his heart, and conscious he had only to speak and all the house would be obliged to bend to his wishes.

As an instance, I remember Mr. Earnshaw once bought a couple of colts at the parish fair, and gave the lads each one. Heathcliff took the handsomest, but it soon fell lame, and when he discovered it, he said to Hindley—

"You must exchange horses with me; I don't like mine, and if you won't I shall tell your father of the three thrashings you've given me this week, and show him my arm, which is black to the shoulder."

Hindley put out his tongue, and cuffed him over the ears.

"You'd better do it at once," he persisted, escaping to the porch (they were in the stable); "you will have to, and if I speak of these blows, you'll get them again with interest."

"Off, dog!" cried Hindley, threatening him with an iron weight, used for weighing potatoes and hay.

"Throw it," he replied, standing still, "and then I'll tell how you boasted that you would turn me out of doors as soon as he died, and see whether he will not turn you out directly."

Hindley threw it, hitting him on the breast, and down he fell, but staggered up immediately, breathless and white, and had not I prevented it, he would have gone just so to the master, and got full revenge by letting his condition plead for him, intimating who had caused it.

"Take my colt, gipsy, then!" said young Earnshaw. "And I pray that he may break your neck; take him, and be damned, you beggarly interloper! and wheedle

my father out of all he has, only afterwards show him what you are, imp of Satan
—And take that, I hope he'll kick out your brains!"

Heathcliff had gone to loose the beast, and shift it to his own stall. He was passing
behind it, when Hindley finished his speech by knocking him under its feet, and
without stopping to examine whether his hopes were fulfilled, ran away as fast as
he could.

I was surprised to witness how coolly the child gathered himself up, and went on
with his intention, exchanging saddles and all, and then sitting down on a bundle of
hay to overcome the qualm which the violent blow occasioned, before he entered
the house.

I persuaded him easily to let me lay the blame of his bruises on the horse; he
minded little what tale was told since he had what he wanted. He complained so
seldom, indeed, of such stirs as these, that I really thought him not vindictive—I
was deceived completely, as you will hear.

CHAPTER 5

In the course of time, Mr. Earnshaw began to fail. He had been active and
healthy, yet his strength left him suddenly; and when he was confined to the
chimney-corner he grew grievously irritable. A nothing vexed him, and suspected
slights of his authority nearly threw him into fits.

This was especially to be remarked if any one attempted to impose upon, or
domineer over, his favourite: he was painfully jealous lest a word should be spoken
amiss to him, seeming to have got into his head the notion that, because he liked
Heathcliff, all hated, and longed to do him an ill-turn.

It was a disadvantage to the lad, for the kinder among us did not wish to fret the
master, so we humoured his partiality; and that humouring was rich nourishment
to the child's pride and black tempers. Still it became in a manner necessary; twice,
or thrice, Hindley's manifestations of scorn, while his father was near, roused the
old man to a fury. He seized his stick to strike him, and shook with rage that he
could not do it.

At last, our curate (we had a curate then who made the living answer by teaching
the little Lintons and Earnshaws, and farming his bit of land himself) he advised
that the young man should be sent to college, and Mr. Earnshaw agreed, though
with a heavy spirit, for he said—

"Hindley was naught, and would never thrive as where he wandered."

I hoped heartily we should have peace now. It hurt me to think the master
should be made uncomfortable by his own good deed. I fancied the discontent of
age and disease arose from his family disagreements, as he would have it that it did;
really, you know, sir, it was in his sinking frame.

We might have got on tolerably, notwithstanding, but for two people, Miss
Cathy and Joseph, the servant; you saw him, I dare say, up yonder. He was, and is
yet, most likely, the wearisomest, self-righteous pharisee that ever ransacked a Bible
to rake the promises to himself, and fling the curses on his neighbours. By his knack
of sermonizing and pious discoursing, he contrived to make a great impression
on Mr. Earnshaw, and the more feeble the master became, the more influence he
gained.

He was relentless in worrying him about his soul's concerns, and about ruling his
children rigidly. He encouraged him to regard Hindley as a reprobate; and, night
after night, he regularly grumbled out a long string of tales against Heathcliff and

Catherine; always minding to flatter Earnshaw's weakness by heaping the heaviest blame on the last.

Certainly, she had ways with her such as I never saw a child take up before; and she put all of us past our patience fifty times and oftener in a day: from the hour she came downstairs, till the hour she went to bed, we had not a minute's security that she wouldn't be in mischief. Her spirits were always at high-water mark, her tongue always going—singing, laughing, and plaguing everybody who would not do the same. A wild, wicked slip she was—but she had the bonniest eye, and sweetest smile, and lightest foot in the parish; and, after all, I believe she meant no harm; for when once she made you cry in good earnest, it seldom happened that she would not keep you company, and oblige you to be quiet that you might comfort her.

She was much too fond of Heathcliff. The greatest punishment we could invent for her was to keep her separate from him: yet she got chided more than any of us on his account.

In play, she liked, exceedingly, to act the little mistress; using her hands freely, and commanding her companions: she did so to me, but I would not bear slapping and ordering; and so I let her know.

Now, Mr. Earnshaw did not understand jokes from his children: he had always been strict and grave with them; and Catherine, on her part, had no idea why her father should be crosser and less patient in his ailing condition, than he was in his prime.

His peevish reproofs wakened in her a naughty delight to provoke him; she was never so happy as when we were all scolding her at once, and she defying us with her bold, saucy look, and her ready words; turning Joseph's religious curses into ridicule, baiting me, and doing just what her father hated most, showing how her pretended insolence, which he thought real, had more power over Heathcliff than his kindness; how the boy would do *her* bidding in anything, and *his* only when it suited his own inclination.

After behaving as badly as possible all day, she sometimes came fondling to make it up at night. "Nay, Cathy," the old man would say, "I cannot love thee; thou'rt worse than thy brother. Go, say thy prayers, child, and ask God's pardon. I doubt thy mother and I must rue that we ever reared thee!"

That made her cry, at first; and then, being repulsed continually hardened her, and she laughed if I told her to say she was sorry for her faults, and beg to be forgiven.

But the hour came, at last, that ended Mr. Earnshaw's troubles on earth. He died quietly in his chair one October evening, seated by the fire-side.

A high wind blustered round the house, and roared in the chimney: it sounded wild and stormy, yet it was not cold, and we were all together—I, a little removed from the hearth, busy at my knitting, and Joseph reading his Bible near the table (for the servants generally sat in the house then, after their work was done). Miss Cathy had been sick, and that made her still; she leant against her father's knee, and Heathcliff was lying on the floor with his head in her lap.

I remember the master, before he fell into a doze, stroking her bonny hair—it pleased him rarely to see her gentle—and saying—

"Why canst thou not always be a good lass, Cathy?"

And she turned her face up to his, and laughed, and answered—

"Why cannot you always be a good man, father?"

But as soon as she saw him vexed again, she kissed his hand, and said she would sing him to sleep. She began singing very low, till his fingers dropped from hers, and his head sank on his breast. Then I told her to hush, and not stir, for fear she should wake him. We all kept as mute as mice a full half-hour, and should have done so longer, only Joseph, having finished his chapter, got up and said that he must rouse the master for prayers and bed. He stepped forward, and called him by name, and touched his shoulder, but he would not move—so he took the candle and looked at him.

I thought there was something wrong as he set down the light; and seizing the children each by an arm, whispered them to "frame[9] upstairs, and make little din—they might pray alone that evening—he had summut to do."

"I shall bid father good-night first," said Catherine, putting her arms round his neck, before we could hinder her.

The poor thing discovered her loss directly—she screamed out—

"Oh, he's dead, Heathcliff! he's dead!"

And they both set up a heart-breaking cry.

I joined my wail to theirs, loud and bitter; but Joseph asked what we could be thinking of to roar in that way over a saint in heaven.

He told me to put on my cloak and run to Gimmerton for the doctor and the parson. I could not guess the use that either would be of, then. However, I went, through wind and rain, and brought one, the doctor, back with me; the other said he would come in the morning.

Leaving Joseph to explain matters, I ran to the children's room; their door was ajar, I saw they had never laid down, though it was past midnight; but they were calmer, and did not need me to console them. The little souls were comforting each other with better thoughts than I could have hit on; no parson in the world ever pictured heaven so beautifully as they did, in their innocent talk; and, while I sobbed and listened, I could not help wishing we were all there safe together.

Chapter 6

Mr. Hindley came home to the funeral; and—a thing that amazed us, and set the neighbours gossiping right and left—he brought a wife with him.

What she was, and where she was born he never informed us; probably, she had neither money nor name to recommend her, or he would scarcely have kept the union from his father.

She was not one that would have disturbed the house much on her own account. Every object she saw, the moment she crossed the threshold, appeared to delight her; and every circumstance that took place about her, except the preparing for the burial, and the presence of the mourners.

I thought she was half silly, from her behaviour while that went on; she ran into her chamber, and made me come with her, though I should have been dressing the children; and there she sat shivering and clasping her hands, and asking repeatedly—

"Are they gone yet?"

Then she began describing with hysterical emotion the effect it produced on her to see black; and started, and trembled, and, at last, fell a weeping—and when I asked what was the matter? answered, she didn't know; but she felt so afraid of dying!

I imagined her as little likely to die as myself. She was rather thin, but young, and fresh complexioned, and her eyes sparkled as bright as diamonds. I did remark, to be sure, that mounting the stairs made her breathe very quick, that the least

---

[9] *Frame:* go.

sudden noise set her all in a quiver, and that she coughed troublesomely sometimes: but I knew nothing of what these symptoms portended, and had no impulse to sympathize with her. We don't in general take to foreigners here, Mr. Lockwood, unless they take to us first.

Young Earnshaw was altered considerably in the three years of his absence. He had grown sparer, and lost his colour, and spoke and dressed quite differently; and, on the very day of his return, he told Joseph and me we must thenceforth quarter ourselves in the back-kitchen, and leave the house for him. Indeed, he would have carpeted and papered a small spare room for a parlour; but his wife expressed such pleasure at the white floor, and huge glowing fire-place, at the pewter dishes, and delf-case, and dog-kennel, and the wide space there was to move about in, where they usually sat, that he thought it unnecessary to her comfort, and so dropped the intention.

She expressed pleasure, too, at finding a sister among her new acquaintance, and she prattled to Catherine, and kissed her, and ran about with her, and gave her quantities of presents, at the beginning. Her affection tired very soon, however, and when she grew peevish, Hindley became tyrannical. A few words from her, evincing a dislike to Heathcliff, were enough to rouse in him all his old hatred of the boy. He drove him from their company to the servants, deprived him of the instructions of the curate, and insisted that he should labour out of doors instead, compelling him to do so, as hard as any other lad on the farm.

Heathcliff bore his degradation pretty well at first, because Cathy taught him what she learnt, and worked or played with him in the fields. They both promised fair to grow up as rude as savages, the young master being entirely negligent how they behaved, and what they did, so they kept clear of him. He would not even have seen after their going to church on Sundays, only Joseph and the curate reprimanded his carelessness when they absented themselves, and that reminded him to order Heathcliff a flogging, and Catherine a fast from dinner or supper.

But it was one of their chief amusements to run away to the moors in the morning and remain there all day, and the after-punishment grew a mere thing to laugh at. The curate might set as many chapters as he pleased for Catherine to get by heart, and Joseph might thrash Heathcliff till his arm ached; they forgot everything the minute they were together again, at least the minute they had contrived some naughty plan of revenge; and many a time I've cried to myself to watch them growing more reckless daily, and I not daring to speak a syllable for fear of losing the small power I still retained over the unfriended creatures.

One Sunday evening, it chanced that they were banished from the sitting-room, for making a noise, or a light offence of the kind, and when I went to call them to supper, I could discover them nowhere.

We searched the house, above and below, and the yard and stables; they were invisible; and, at last, Hindley in a passion told us to bolt the doors, and swore nobody should let them in that night.

The household went to bed; and I, too anxious to lie down, opened my lattice and put my head out to hearken, though it rained, determined to admit them in spite of the prohibition, should they return.

In a while, I distinguished steps coming up the road, and the light of a lantern glimmered through the gate.

I threw a shawl over my head and ran to prevent them from waking Mr. Earnshaw by knocking. There was Heathcliff, by himself; it gave me a start to see him alone.

"Where is Miss Catherine?" I cried hurriedly. "No accident, I hope?"

"At Thrushcross Grange," he answered, "and I would have been there too, but they had not the manners to ask me to stay."

"Well, you will catch it!" I said, "you'll never be content till you're sent about your business. What in the world led you wandering to Thrushcross Grange?"

"Let me get off my wet clothes, and I'll tell you all about it, Nelly," he replied.

I bid him beware of rousing the master, and while he undressed, and I waited to put out the candle, he continued—

"Cathy and I escaped from the wash-house to have a ramble at liberty, and getting a glimpse of the Grange lights, we thought we would just go and see whether the Lintons passed their Sunday evenings standing shivering in corners, while their father and mother sat eating and drinking, and singing and laughing, and burning their eyes out before the fire. Do you think they do? Or reading sermons, and being catechised by their man-servant, and set to learn a column of Scripture names, if they don't answer properly?"

"Probably not," I responded. "They are good children, no doubt, and don't deserve the treatment you receive, for your bad conduct."

"Don't you cant, Nelly," he said. "Nonsense! We ran from the top of the Heights to the park, without stopping—Catherine completely beaten in the race, because she was barefoot. You'll have to seek for her shoes in the bog to-morrow. We crept through a broken hedge, groped our way up the path, and planted ourselves on a flower-plot under the drawing-room window. The light came from thence; they had not put up the shutters, and the curtains were only half closed. Both of us were able to look in by standing on the basement, and clinging to the ledge, and we saw—ah! it was beautiful—a splendid place carpeted with crimson, and crimson-covered chairs and tables, and a pure white ceiling bordered by gold, a shower of glass-drops hanging in silver chains from the centre, and shimmering with little soft tapers. Old Mr. and Mrs. Linton were not there. Edgar and his sister had it entirely to themselves; shouldn't they have been happy? We should have thought ourselves in heaven! And now, guess what your good children were doing? Isabella—I believe she is eleven, a year younger than Cathy—lay screaming at the farther end of the room, shrieking as if witches were running red hot needles into her. Edgar stood on the hearth weeping silently, and in the middle of the table sat a little dog shaking its paw and yelping, which, from their mutual accusations, we understood they had nearly pulled in two between them. The idiots! That was their pleasure! to quarrel who should hold a heap of warm hair, and each begin to cry because both, after struggling to get it, refused to take it. We laughed outright at the petted things, we did despise them! When would you catch me wishing to have what Catherine wanted? or find us by ourselves, seeking entertainment in yelling, and sobbing, and rolling on the ground, divided by the whole room? I'd not exchange, for a thousand lives, my condition here, for Edgar Linton's at Thrushcross Grange—not if I might have the privilege of flinging Joseph off the highest gable, and painting the house-front with Hindley's blood!"

"Hush, hush!" I interrupted. "Still you have not told me, Heathcliff, how Catherine is left behind?"

"I told you we laughed," he answered. "The Lintons heard us, and with one accord, they shot like arrows to the door; there was silence, and then a cry, 'Oh, mamma, mamma! Oh, papa! Oh, mamma, come here. Oh, papa, oh!' They really did howl out, something in that way. We made frightful noises to terrify them still more, and then we dropped off the ledge, because somebody was drawing the bars, and we felt we had better flee. I had Cathy by the hand, and was urging her on, when all at once she fell down.

" 'Run, Heathcliff, run!' she whispered. 'They have let the bull-dog loose, and he holds me!'

"The devil had seized her ankle, Nelly; I heard his abominable snorting. She did not yell out—no! She would have scorned to do it, if she had been spitted on the horns of a mad cow. I did, though; I vociferated curses enough to annihilate any fiend in Christendom, and I got a stone and thrust it between his jaws, and tried with all my might to cram it down his throat. A beast of a servant came up with a lantern, at last, shouting—

" 'Keep fast, Skulker, keep fast!'

"He changed his note, however, when he saw Skulker's game. The dog was throttled off, his huge, purple tongue hanging half a foot out of his mouth, and his pendant lips streaming with bloody slaver.

"The man took Cathy up; she was sick, not from fear, I'm certain, but from pain. He carried her in; I followed, grumbling execrations and vengeance.

" 'What prey, Robert?' hallooed Linton from the entrance.

" 'Skulker has caught a little girl, sir,' he replied, 'and there's a lad here,' he added, making a clutch at me, 'who looks an out-and-outer! Very like, the robbers were for putting them through the window, to open the doors to the gang after all were asleep, that they might murder us at their ease. Hold your tongue, you foul-mouthed thief, you! you shall go to the gallows for this. Mr. Linton, sir, don't lay by your gun!'

" 'No, no, Robert!' said the old fool. 'The rascals knew that yesterday was my rent-day; they thought to have me cleverly. Come in; I'll furnish them a reception. There, John, fasten the chain. Give Skulker some water, Jenny. To beard a magistrate in his strong-hold, and on the Sabbath, too! Where will their insolence stop? Oh, my dear Mary, look here! Don't be afraid, it is but a boy—yet the villain scowls so plainly in his face, would it not be a kindness to the country to hang him at once, before he shows his nature in acts, as well as features?'

"He pulled me under the chandelier, and Mrs. Linton placed her spectacles on her nose and raised her hands in horror. The cowardly children crept nearer also, Isabella lisping—

" 'Frightful thing! Put him in the cellar, papa. He's exactly like the son of the fortune-teller that stole my tame pheasant. Isn't he, Edgar?'

"While they examined me, Cathy came round; she heard the last speech, and laughed. Edgar Linton, after an inquisitive stare, collected sufficient wit to recognise her. They see us at church, you know, though we seldom meet them elsewhere.

" 'That's Miss Earnshaw!' he whispered to his mother, 'and look how Skulker has bitten her—how her foot bleeds!'

" 'Miss Earnshaw? Nonsense!' cried the dame, 'Miss Earnshaw scouring the country with a gipsy! And yet, my dear, the child is in mourning—surely it is—and she may be lamed for life!'

" 'What culpable carelessness in her brother!' exclaimed Mr. Linton, turning from me to Catherine. 'I've understood from Shielders' (that was the curate, sir) 'that he lets her grow up in absolute heathenism. But who is this? Where did she pick up this companion? Oho! I declare he is that strange acquisition my late neighbour made in his journey to Liverpool—a little Lascar, or an American or Spanish castaway.'

" 'A wicked boy, at all events,' remarked the old lady, 'and quite unfit for a decent house! Did you notice his language, Linton? I'm shocked that my children should have heard it.'

"I recommended cursing—don't be angry, Nelly—and so Robert was ordered to take me off. I refused to go without Cathy; he dragged me into the garden, pushed the lantern into my hand, assured me that Mr. Earnshaw should be informed of my behaviour, and bidding me march directly, secured the door again.

"The curtains were still looped up at one corner; and I resumed my station as spy, because, if Catherine had wished to return, I intended shattering their great glass panes to a million fragments, unless they let her out.

"She sat on the sofa quietly. Mrs. Linton took off the grey cloak of the dairy maid which we had borrowed for our excursion, shaking her head, and expostulating with her, I suppose; she was a young lady and they made a distinction between her treatment and mine. Then the woman servant brought a basin of warm water, and washed her feet; and Mr. Linton mixed a tumbler of negus, and Isabella emptied a plateful of cakes into her lap, and Edgar stood gaping at a distance. Afterwards, they dried and combed her beautiful hair, and gave her a pair of enormous slippers, and wheeled her to the fire, and I left her, as merry as she could be, dividing her food between the little dog and Skulker whose nose she pinched as he ate; and kindling a spark of spirit in the vacant blue eyes of the Lintons—a dim reflection from her own enchanting face. I saw they were full of stupid admiration; she is so immeasurably superior to them—to everybody on earth, is she not, Nelly?"

"There will more come of this business than you reckon on," I answered, covering him up and extinguishing the light. "You are incurable, Heathcliff, and Mr. Hindley will have to proceed to extremities, see if he won't."

My words came truer than I desired. The luckless adventure made Earnshaw furious. And then Mr. Linton, to mend matters, paid us a visit himself on the morrow; and read the young master such a lecture on the road he guided his family, that he was stirred to look about him, in earnest.

Heathcliff received no flogging, but he was told that the first word he spoke to Miss Catherine should ensure a dismissal; and Mrs. Earnshaw undertook to keep her sister-in-law in due restraint, when she returned home; employing art, not force—with force she would have found it impossible.

CHAPTER 7

Cathy stayed at Thrushcross Grange five weeks, till Christmas. By that time her ankle was thoroughly cured, and her manners much improved. The mistress visited her often, in the interval, and commenced her plan of reform by trying to raise her self-respect with fine clothes and flattery, which she took readily: so that, instead of a wild, hatless little savage jumping into the house, and rushing to squeeze us all breathless, there alighted from a handsome black pony a very dignified person with brown ringlets falling from the cover of a feathered beaver, and a long cloth habit which she was obliged to hold up with both hands that she might sail in.

Hindley lifted her from her horse, exclaiming delightedly—

"Why, Cathy, you are quite a beauty! I should scarcely have known you—you look like a lady now. Isabella Linton is not to be compared with her, is she, Frances?"

"Isabella has not her natural advantages," replied his wife, "but she must mind and not grow wild again here. Ellen, help Miss Catherine off with her things. Stay, dear, you will disarrange your curls—let me untie your hat."

I removed the habit, and there shone forth beneath, a grand plaid silk frock, white trousers, and burnished shoes; and, while her eyes sparkled joyfully when the dogs came bounding up to welcome her, she dare hardly touch them lest they should fawn upon her splendid garments.

She kissed me gently—I was all flour making the Christmas cake, and it would not have done to give me a hug—and then she looked round for Heathcliff. Mr. and Mrs. Earnshaw watched anxiously their meeting, thinking it would enable them to judge, in some measure, what grounds they had for hoping to succeed in separating the two friends.

Heathcliff was hard to discover, at first. If he were careless and uncared for, before Catherine's absence, he had been ten times more so, since.

Nobody but I even did him the kindness to call him a dirty boy, and bid him wash himself, once a week; and children of his age seldom have a natural pleasure in soap and water. Therefore, not to mention his clothes, which had seen three months' service in mire and dust, and his thick uncombed hair, the surface of his face and hands was dismally beclouded. He might well skulk behind the settle, on beholding such a bright, graceful damsel enter the house, instead of a rough-headed counterpart of himself, as he expected.

"Is Heathcliff not here?" she demanded, pulling off her gloves, and displaying fingers wonderfully whitened with doing nothing, and staying indoors.

"Heathcliff, you may come forward," cried Mr. Hindley, enjoying his discomfiture and gratified to see what a forbidding young blackguard he would be compelled to present himself. "You may come and wish Miss Catherine welcome, like the other servants."

Cathy, catching a glimpse of her friend in his concealment, flew to embrace him; she bestowed seven or eight kisses on his cheek within the second, and then stopped, and drawing back, burst into a laugh, exclaiming—

"Why, how very black and cross you look! and how—how funny and grim! But that's because I'm used to Edgar and Isabella Linton. Well, Heathcliff, have you forgotten me?"

She had some reason to put the question, for shame and pride threw double gloom over his countenance, and kept him immovable.

"Shake hands, Heathcliff," said Mr. Earnshaw, condescendingly; "once in a way, that is permitted."

"I shall not!" replied the boy, finding his tongue at last, "I shall not stand to be laughed at, I shall not bear it!"

And he would have broken from the circle, but Miss Cathy seized him again.

"I did not mean to laugh at you," she said, "I could not hinder myself. Heathcliff, shake hands, at least! What are you sulky for? It was only that you looked odd. If you wash your face and brush your hair, it will be all right. But you are so dirty!"

She gazed concernedly at the dusky fingers she held in her own, and also at her dress, which she feared had gained no embellishment from its contact with his.

"You needn't have touched me!" he answered, following her eye and snatching away his hand. "I shall be as dirty as I please, and I like to be dirty, and I will be dirty."

With that he dashed head foremost out of the room, amid the merriment of the master and mistress, and to the serious disturbance of Catherine, who could not comprehend how her remarks should have produced such an exhibition of bad temper.

After playing lady's maid to the new-comer, and putting my cakes in the oven, and making the house and kitchen cheerful with great fires befitting Christmas eve, I prepared to sit down and amuse myself by singing carols, all alone, regardless of Joseph's affirmations that he considered the merry tunes I chose as next door to songs.

He had retired to private prayer in his chamber, and Mr. and Mrs. Earnshaw were engaging Missy's attention by sundry gay trifles bought for her to present to the little Lintons, as an acknowledgment of their kindness.

They had invited them to spend the morrow at Wuthering Heights, and the invitation had been accepted, on one condition: Mrs. Linton begged that her darlings might be kept carefully apart from that "naughty, swearing boy."

Under these circumstances I remained solitary. I smelt the rich scent of the heating spices; and admired the shining kitchen utensils, the polished clock, decked in holly, the silver mugs ranged on a tray ready to be filled with mulled ale for supper; and, above all, the speckless purity of my particular care—the scoured and well-swept floor.

I gave due inward applause to every object, and then I remembered how old Earnshaw used to come in when all was tidied, and call me a cant lass,[10] and slip a shilling into my hand, as a Christmas box; and from that I went on to think of his fondness for Heathcliff, and his dread lest he should suffer neglect after death had removed him; and that naturally led me to consider the poor lad's situation now, and from singing I changed my mind to crying. It struck me soon, however, there would be more sense in endeavouring to repair some of his wrongs than shedding tears over them. I got up and walked into the court to seek him.

He was not far; I found him smoothing the glossy coat of the new pony in the stable, and feeding the other beasts, according to custom.

"Make haste, Heathcliff!" I said, "the kitchen is so comfortable—and Joseph is upstairs; make haste, and let me dress you smart before Miss Cathy comes out, and then you can sit together, with the whole hearth to yourselves, and have a long chatter till bedtime."

He proceeded with his task and never turned his head towards me.

"Come—are you coming?" I continued. "There's a little cake for each of you, nearly enough; and you'll need half an hour's donning."

I waited five minutes, but getting no answer left him. Catherine supped with her brother and sister-in-law: Joseph and I joined at an unsociable meal seasoned with reproofs on one side and sauciness on the other. His cake and cheese remained on the table all night for the fairies. He managed to continue work till nine o'clock, and then marched dumb and dour to his chamber.

Cathy sat up late, having a world of things to order for the reception of her new friends: she came into the kitchen, once, to speak to her old one, but he was gone, and she only stayed to ask what was the matter with him, and then went back.

In the morning, he rose early; and, as it was a holiday, carried his ill-humour onto the moors, not re-appearing till the family were departed for church. Fasting and reflection seemed to have brought him to a better spirit. He hung about me for a while, and having screwed up his courage, exclaimed abruptly—

"Nelly, make me decent, I'm going to be good."

"High time, Heathcliff," I said, "you *have* grieved Catherine; she's sorry she ever came home, I dare say! It looks as if you envied her, because she is more thought of than you."

The notion of *envying* Catherine was incomprehensible to him, but the notion of grieving her he understood clearly enough.

"Did she say she was grieved?" he inquired, looking very serious.

"She cried when I told her you were off again this morning."

"Well, *I* cried last night," he returned, "and I had more reason to cry than she."

"Yes, you had the reason of going to bed with a proud heart and an empty stomach," said I. "Proud people breed sad sorrows for themselves. But, if you be ashamed of your touchiness, you must ask pardon, mind, when she comes in.

---

[10] *Cant:* lively.

You must go up and offer to kiss her, and say—you know best what to say, only do it heartily, and not as if you thought her converted into a stranger by her grand dress. And now, though I have dinner to get ready, I'll steal time to arrange you so that Edgar Linton shall look quite a doll beside you: and that he does. You are younger, and yet, I'll be bound, you are taller and twice as broad across the shoulders—you could knock him down in a twinkling. Don't you feel that you could?"

Heathcliff's face brightened a moment; then it was overcast afresh, and he sighed.

"But, Nelly, if I knocked him down twenty times, that wouldn't make him less handsome, or me more so. I wish I had light hair and a fair skin, and was dressed and behaved as well, and had a chance of being as rich as he will be!"

"And cried for mamma, at every turn," I added, "and trembled if a country lad heaved his fist against you, and sat at home all day for a shower of rain. O, Heathcliff, you are showing a poor spirit! Come to the glass, and I'll let you see what you should wish. Do you mark those two lines between your eyes; and those thick brows, that instead of rising arched, sink in the middle; and that couple of black fiends, so deeply buried, who never open their windows boldly, but lurk glinting under them, like devil's spies? Wish and learn to smooth away the surly wrinkles, to raise your lids frankly, and change the fiends to confident, innocent angels, suspecting and doubting nothing, and always seeing friends where they are not sure of foes. Don't get the expression of a vicious cur that appears to know the kicks it gets are its desert, and yet hates all the world, as well as the kicker, for what it suffers."

"In other words, I must wish for Edgar Linton's great blue eyes, and even forehead," he replied. "I do—and that won't help me to them."

"A good heart will help you to a bonny face, my lad," I continued, "if you were a regular black; and a bad one will turn the bonniest into something worse than ugly. And now that we've done washing, and combing, and sulking—tell me whether you don't think yourself rather handsome? I'll tell you, I do. You're fit for a prince in disguise. Who knows but your father was Emperor of China, and your mother an Indian queen, each of them able to buy up, with one week's income, Wuthering Heights and Thrushcross Grange together? And you were kidnapped by wicked sailors, and brought to England. Were I in your place, I would frame high notions of my birth; and the thoughts of what I was should give me courage and dignity to support the oppressions of a little farmer!"

So I chattered on; and Heathcliff gradually lost his frown, and began to look quite pleasant, when, all at once, our conversation was interrupted by a rumbling sound moving up the road and entering the court. He ran to the window, and I to the door, just in time to behold the two Lintons descend from the family carriage, smothered in cloaks and furs, and the Earnshaws dismount from their horses—they often rode to church in winter. Catherine took a hand of each of the children, and brought them into the house, and set them before the fire, which quickly put colour into their white faces.

I urged my companion to hasten now, and show his amiable humour, and he willingly obeyed; but ill luck would have it that, as he opened the door leading from the kitchen on one side, Hindley opened it on the other. They met, and the master, irritated at seeing him clean and cheerful, or, perhaps, eager to keep his promise to Mrs. Linton, shoved him back with a sudden thrust, and angrily bade Joseph "keep the fellow out of the room—send him into the garret till dinner is over. He'll be cramming his fingers in the tarts, and stealing the fruit, if left alone with them a minute."

"Nay, sir," I could not avoid answering, "he'll touch nothing, not he—and, I suppose, he must have his share of the dainties as well as we."

"He shall have his share of my hand, if I catch him downstairs again till dark," cried Hindley. "Begone, you vagabond! What! you are attempting the coxcomb, are you? Wait till I get hold of those elegant locks—see if I won't pull them a bit longer!"

"They are long enough already," observed Master Linton, peeping from the door-way; "I wonder they don't make his head ache. It's like a colt's mane over his eyes!"

He ventured this remark without any intention to insult; but Heathcliff's violent nature was not prepared to endure the appearance of impertinence from one whom he seemed to hate, even then, as a rival. He seized a tureen of hot apple-sauce, the first thing that came under his gripe, and dashed it full against the speaker's face and neck—who instantly commenced a lament that brought Isabella and Catherine hurrying to the place.

Mr. Earnshaw snatched up the culprit directly and conveyed him to his chamber, where, doubtless, he administered a rough remedy to cool the fit of passion, for he reappeared red and breathless. I got the dishcloth, and, rather spitefully, scrubbed Edgar's nose and mouth, affirming it served him right for meddling. His sister began weeping to go home, and Cathy stood by, confounded, blushing for all.

"You should not have spoken to him!" she expostulated with Master Linton. "He was in a bad temper, and now you've spoilt your visit, and he'll be flogged—I hate him to be flogged! I can't eat my dinner. Why did you speak to him, Edgar?"

"I didn't," sobbed the youth, escaping from my hands, and finishing the remainder of the purification with his cambric pocket-handkerchief. "I promised mamma that I wouldn't say one word to him, and I didn't!"

"Well, don't cry!" replied Catherine, contemptuously. "You're not killed. Don't make more mischief—my brother is coming—be quiet! Give over, Isabella! Has anybody hurt *you?*"

"There, there, children—to your seats!" cried Hindley, bustling in. "That brute of a lad has warmed me nicely. Next time, Master Edgar, take the law into your own fists—it will give you an appetite!"

The little party recovered its equanimity at sight of the fragrant feast. They were hungry after their ride, and easily consoled, since no real harm had befallen them.

Mr. Earnshaw carved bountiful platefuls; and the mistress made them merry with lively talk. I waited behind her chair, and was pained to behold Catherine, with dry eyes and an indifferent air, commence cutting up the wing of a goose before her.

"An unfeeling child," I thought to myself, "how lightly she dismisses her old playmate's troubles. I could not have imagined her to be so selfish."

She lifted a mouthful to her lips; then she set it down again: her cheeks flushed, and the tears gushed over them. She slipped her fork to the floor, and hastily dived under the cloth to conceal her emotion. I did not call her unfeeling long, for I perceived she was in purgatory throughout the day, and wearying to find an opportunity of getting by herself, or paying a visit to Heathcliff, who had been locked up by the master, as I discovered on endeavouring to introduce to him a private mess of victuals.

In the evening we had a dance. Cathy begged that he might be liberated then, as Isabella Linton had no partner; her entreaties were vain, and I was appointed to supply the deficiency.

We got rid of all gloom in the excitement of the exercise, and our pleasure was increased by the arrival of the Gimmerton band, mustering fifteen strong: a trumpet, a trombone, clarionets, bassoons, French horns, and a bass viol, besides singers. They go the rounds of all the respectable houses, and receive contributions every Christmas, and we esteemed it a first-rate treat to hear them.

After the usual carols had been sung, we set them to songs and glees. Mrs. Earnshaw loved the music, and so they gave us plenty.

Catherine loved it too; but she said it sounded sweetest at the top of the steps, and she went up in the dark; I followed. They shut the house door below, never noting our absence, the place was so full of people. She made no stay at the stairs' head, but mounted farther, to the garret where Heathcliff was confined, and called him. He stubbornly declined answering for a while; she persevered, and finally persuaded him to hold communion with her through the boards.

I let the poor things converse unmolested, till I supposed the songs were going to cease, and the singers to get some refreshment: then, I clambered up the ladder to warn her.

Instead of finding her outside, I heard her voice within. The little monkey had crept by the skylight of one garret, along the roof, into the skylight of the other, and it was with the utmost difficulty I could coax her out again.

When she did come, Heathcliff came with her; and she insisted that I should take him into the kitchen, as my fellow-servant had gone to a neighbour's to be removed from the sound of our "devil's psalmody," as it pleased him to call it.

I told them I intended, by no means, to encourage their tricks; but as the prisoner had never broken his fast since yesterday's dinner, I would wink at his cheating Mr. Hindley that once.

He went down; I set him a stool by the fire, and offered him a quantity of good things; but he was sick and could eat little, and my attempts to entertain him were thrown away. He leant his two elbows on his knees, and his chin on his hands, and remained wrapt in dumb meditation. On my inquiring the subject of his thoughts, he answered gravely—

"I'm trying to settle how I shall pay Hindley back. I don't care how long I wait, if I can only do it, at last. I hope he will not die before I do!"

"For shame, Heathcliff!" said I. "It is for God to punish wicked people; we should learn to forgive."

"No, God won't have the satisfaction that I shall," he returned. "I only wish I knew the best way! Let me alone, and I'll plan it out: while I'm thinking of that, I don't feel pain."

But, Mr. Lockwood, I forget these tales cannot divert you. I'm annoyed how I should dream of chattering on at such a rate; and your gruel cold, and you nodding for bed! I could have told Heathcliff's history, all that you need hear, in half-a-dozen words.

Thus interrupting herself, the housekeeper rose, and proceeded to lay aside her sewing; but I felt incapable of moving from the hearth, and I was very far from nodding.

"Sit still, Mrs. Dean," I cried, "do sit still, another half hour! You've done just right to tell the story leisurely. That is the method I like; and you must finish in the same style. I am interested in every character you have mentioned, more or less."

"The clock is on the stroke of eleven, sir."

"No matter—I'm not accustomed to go to bed in the long hours. One or two is early enough for a person who lies till ten."

"You shouldn't lie till ten. There's the very prime of the morning gone long before that time. A person who has not done one half his day's work by ten o'clock runs a chance of leaving the other half undone."

"Nevertheless, Mrs. Dean, resume your chair; because to-morrow I intend lengthening the night till afternoon. I prognosticate for myself an obstinate cold, at least."

"I hope not, sir. Well, you must allow me to leap over some three years; during that space Mrs. Earnshaw—"

"No, no, I'll allow nothing of the sort! Are you acquainted with the mood of mind in which, if you were seated alone, and the cat licking its kitten on the rug before you, you would watch the operation so intently that puss's neglect of one ear would put you seriously out of temper?"

"A terribly lazy mood, I should say."

"On the contrary, a tiresomely active one. It is mine, at present, and, therefore, continue minutely. I perceive that people in these regions acquire over people in towns the value that a spider in a dungeon does over a spider in a cottage, to their various occupants; and yet the deepened attraction is not entirely owing to the situation of the looker-on. They *do* live more in earnest, more in themselves, and less in surface change, and frivolous external things. I could fancy a love for life here almost possible; and I was a fixed unbeliever in any love of a year's standing. One state resembles setting a hungry man down to a single dish on which he may concentrate his entire appetite, and do it justice; the other, introducing him to a table laid out by French cooks. He can perhaps extract as much enjoyment from the whole, but each part is a mere atom in his regard and remembrance."

"Oh! here we are the same as anywhere else, when you get to know us," observed Mrs. Dean, somewhat puzzled at my speech.

"Excuse me," I responded; "you, my good friend, are a striking evidence against that assertion. Excepting a few provincialisms of slight consequence, you have no marks of the manners that I am habituated to consider as peculiar to your class. I am sure you have thought a great deal more than the generality of servants think. You have been compelled to cultivate your reflective faculties, for want of occasions for frittering your life away in silly trifles."

Mrs. Dean laughed.

"I certainly esteem myself a steady, reasonable kind of body," she said, "not exactly from living among the hills and seeing one set of faces, and one series of actions, from year's end to year's end; but I have undergone sharp discipline which has taught me wisdom; and then, I have read more than you would fancy, Mr. Lockwood. You could not open a book in this library that I have not looked into, and got something out of also, unless it be that range of Greek and Latin, and that of French—and those I know one from another: it is as much as you can expect of a poor man's daughter.

"However, if I am to follow my story in true gossip's fashion, I had better go on; and instead of leaping three years, I will be content to pass to the next summer—the summer of 1778, that is, nearly twenty-three years ago."

Chapter 8

On the morning of a fine June day, my first bonny little nursling, and the last of the ancient Earnshaw stock, was born.

We were busy with the hay in a far-away field, when the girl that usually brought our breakfasts came running, an hour too soon, across the meadow and up the lane, calling me as she ran.

"Oh, such a grand bairn!" she panted out. "The finest lad that ever breathed! But the doctor says missis must go; he says she's been in a consumption these many months. I heard him tell Mr. Hindley: and now she has nothing to keep her, and she'll be dead before winter. You must come home directly. You're to nurse it,

Nelly—to feed it with sugar and milk, and take care of it, day and night. I wish I were you, because it will be all yours when there is no missis!"

"But is she very ill?" I asked, flinging down my rake, and tying my bonnet.

"I guess she is; yet she looks bravely," replied the girl, "and she talks as if she thought of living to see it grow a man. She's out of her head for joy, it's such a beauty! If I were her, I'm certain I should not die. I should get better at the bare sight of it, in spite of Kenneth. I was fairly mad at him. Dame Archer brought the cherub down to master, in the house, and his face just began to light up, when the old croaker steps forward, and, says he—'Earnshaw, it's a blessing your wife has been spared to leave you this son. When she came, I felt convinced we shouldn't keep her long; and now, I must tell you, the winter will probably finish her. Don't take on, and fret about it too much, it can't be helped. And besides, you should have known better than to choose such a rush of a lass!' "

"And what did the master answer?" I enquired.

"I think he swore—but I didn't mind him, I was straining to see the bairn," and she began again to describe it rapturously. I, as zealous as herself, hurried eagerly home to admire, on my part, though I was very sad for Hindley's sake; he had room in his heart only for two idols—his wife and himself: he doted on both, and adored one, and I couldn't conceive how he would bear the loss.

When we got to Wuthering Heights, there he stood at the front door; and, as I passed in, I asked, how was the baby?

"Nearly ready to run about, Nell!" he replied, putting on a cheerful smile.

"And the mistress?" I ventured to inquire, "the doctor says she's—"

"Damn the doctor!" he interrupted, reddening. "Frances is quite right—she'll be perfectly well by this time next week. Are you going upstairs? will you tell her that I'll come, if she'll promise not to talk? I left her because she would not hold her tongue; and she must—tell her Mr. Kenneth says she must be quiet."

I delivered this message to Mrs. Earnshaw; she seemed in flighty spirits, and replied merrily—

"I hardly spoke a word, Ellen, and there he has gone out twice, crying. Well, say I promise I won't speak; but that does not bind me not to laugh at him!"

Poor soul! Till within a week of her death that gay heart never failed her; and her husband persisted doggedly, nay, furiously, in affirming her health improved every day. When Kenneth warned him that his medicines were useless at that stage of the malady, and he needn't put him to further expense by attending her, he retorted—

"I know you need not—she's well—she does not want any more attendance from you! She never was in a consumption. It was a fever; and it is gone—her pulse is as slow as mine now, and her cheek as cool."

He told his wife the same story, and she seemed to believe him; but one night, while leaning on his shoulder, in the act of saying she thought she should be able to get up to-morrow, a fit of coughing took her—a very slight one. He raised her in his arms; she put her two hands about his neck, her face changed, and she was dead.

As the girl had anticipated, the child Hareton fell wholly into my hands. Mr. Earnshaw, provided he saw him healthy, and never heard him cry, was contented, as far as regarded him. For himself, he grew desperate; his sorrow was of that kind that will not lament. He neither wept nor prayed—he cursed and defied—execrated God and man, and gave himself up to reckless dissipation.

The servants could not bear his tyrannical and evil conduct long: Joseph and I were the only two that would stay. I had not the heart to leave my charge; and besides, you know, I had been his foster sister, and excused his behaviour more readily than a stranger would.

Joseph remained to hector over tenants and labourers, and because it was his vocation to be where there was plenty of wickedness to reprove.

The master's bad ways and bad companions formed a pretty example for Catherine and Heathcliff. His treatment of the latter was enough to make a fiend of a saint. And, truly, it appeared as if the lad *were* possessed of something diabolical at that period. He delighted to witness Hindley degrading himself past redemption; and became daily more notable for savage sullenness and ferocity.

I could not half tell what an infernal house we had. The curate dropped calling, and nobody decent came near us, at last, unless Edgar Linton's visits to Miss Cathy might be an exception. At fifteen she was the queen of the country-side; she had no peer, and she did turn out a haughty, headstrong creature! I own I did not like her after her infancy was past; and I vexed her frequently by trying to bring down her arrogance; she never took an aversion to me, though. She had a wondrous constancy to old attachments; even Heathcliff kept his hold on her affections unalterably, and young Linton, with all his superiority, found it difficult to make an equally deep impression.

He was my late master; that is his portrait over the fireplace. It used to hang on one side, and his wife's on the other; but hers has been removed, or else you might see something of what she was. Can you make that out?

Mrs. Dean raised the candle, and I discerned a soft-featured face, exceedingly resembling the young lady at the Heights, but more pensive and amiable in expression. It formed a sweet picture. The long light hair curled slightly on the temple; the eyes were large and serious; the figure almost too graceful. I did not marvel how Catherine Earnshaw could forget her first friend for such an individual. I marvelled much how he, with a mind to correspond with his person, could fancy my idea of Catherine Earnshaw.

"A very agreeable portrait," I observed to the housekeeper. "Is it like?"

"Yes," she answered; "but he looked better when he was animated; that is his every day countenance; he wanted spirit in general."

Catherine had kept up her acquaintance with the Lintons since her five weeks' residence among them; and as she had no temptation to show her rough side in their company, and had the sense to be ashamed of being rude where she experienced such invariable courtesy, she imposed unwittingly on the old lady and gentleman, by her ingenious cordiality; gained the admiration of Isabella, and the heart and soul of her brother—acquisitions that flattered her from the first, for she was full of ambition, and led her to adopt a double character without exactly intending to deceive anyone.

In the place where she heard Heathcliff termed a "vulgar young ruffian," and "worse than a brute," she took care not to act like him; but at home she had small inclination to practise politeness that would only be laughed at, and restrain an unruly nature when it would bring her neither credit nor praise.

Mr. Edgar seldom mustered courage to visit Wuthering Heights openly. He had a terror of Earnshaw's reputation, and shrunk from encountering him, and yet he was always received with our best attempts at civility: the master himself avoided offending him, knowing why he came, and if he could not be gracious, kept out of the way. I rather think his appearance there was distasteful to Catherine; she was not artful, never played the coquette, and had evidently an objection to her two friends meeting at all; for when Heathcliff expressed contempt of Linton, in his presence, she could not half coincide, as she did in his absence; and when Linton evinced disgust and antipathy to Heathcliff, she dare not treat his sentiments with indifference, as if depreciation of her playmate were of scarcely any consequence to her.

I've had many a laugh at her perplexities and untold troubles, which she vainly strove to hide from my mockery. That sounds ill-natured—but she was so proud, it became really impossible to pity her distresses, till she should be chastened into more humility.

She did bring herself, finally, to confess, and confide in me. There was not a soul else that she might fashion into an adviser.

Mr. Hindley had gone from home, one afternoon, and Heathcliff presumed to give himself a holiday on the strength of it. He had reached the age of sixteen then, I think, and without having bad features or being deficient in intellect, he contrived to convey an impression of inward and outward repulsiveness that his present aspect retains no traces of.

In the first place, he had, by that time, lost the benefit of his early education: continual hard work, begun soon and concluded late, had extinguished any curiosity he once possessed in pursuit of knowledge, and any love for books or learning. His childhood's sense of superiority, instilled into him by the favours of old Mr. Earnshaw, was faded away. He struggled long to keep up an equality with Catherine in her studies and yielded with poignant though silent regret: but he yielded completely; and there was no prevailing on him to take a step in the way of moving upward, when he found he must, necessarily, sink beneath his former level. Then personal appearance sympathised with mental deterioration; he acquired a slouching gait, and ignoble look; his naturally reserved disposition was exaggerated into an almost idiotic excess of unsociable moroseness; and he took a grim pleasure, apparently, in exciting the aversion rather than the esteem of his few acquaintance.

Catherine and he were constant companions still, at his seasons of respite from labour; but he had ceased to express his fondness for her in words, and recoiled with angry suspicion from her girlish caresses, as if conscious there could be no gratification in lavishing such marks of affection on him. On the before-named occasion he came into the house to announce his intention of doing nothing, while I was assisting Miss Cathy to arrange her dress: she had not reckoned on his taking it into his head to be idle, and imagining she would have the whole place to herself, she managed, by some means, to inform Mr. Edgar of her brother's absence, and was then preparing to receive him.

"Cathy, are you busy, this afternoon?" asked Heathcliff. "Are you going any-where?"

"No, it is raining," she answered.

"Why have you that silk frock on, then?" he said. "Nobody coming here, I hope?"

"Not that I know of," stammered Miss, "but you should be in the field now, Heathcliff. It is an hour past dinner time; I thought you were gone."

"Hindley does not often free us from his accursed presence," observed the boy. "I'll not work any more to-day, I'll stay with you."

"O, but Joseph will tell," she suggested. "You'd better go!"

"Joseph is loading lime on the farther side of Pennistow Crag; it will take him till dark, and he'll never know."

So saying he lounged to the fire, and sat down. Catherine reflected an instant, with knitted brows—she found it needful to smooth the way for an intrusion.

"Isabella and Edgar Linton talked of calling this afternoon," she said, at the conclusion of a minute's silence. "As it rains, I hardly expect them; but they may come, and if they do, you run the risk of being scolded for no good."

"Order Ellen to say you are engaged, Cathy," he persisted. "Don't turn me out for those pitiful, silly friends of yours! I'm on the point, sometimes, of complaining that they—but I'll not—"

"That they what?" cried Catherine, gazing at him with a troubled countenance. "Oh, Nelly!" she added petulantly, jerking her head away from my hands, "you've combed my hair quite out of curl! That's enough, let me alone. What are you on the point of complaining about, Heathcliff?"

"Nothing—only look at the almanack on that wall." He pointed to a framed sheet hanging near the window, and continued—

"The crosses are for the evenings you have spent with the Lintons, the dots for those spent with me. Do you see? I've marked every day."

"Yes—very foolish; as if I took notice!" replied Catherine in a peevish tone. "And where is the sense of that?"

"To show that I *do* take notice," said Heathcliff.

"And should I always be sitting with you?" she demanded, growing more irritated. "What good do I get? What do you talk about? You might be dumb or a baby for anything you say to amuse me, or for anything you do, either!"

"You never told me before that I talked too little, or that you disliked my company, Cathy!" exclaimed Heathcliff in much agitation.

"It is no company at all, when people know nothing and say nothing," she muttered.

Her companion rose up, but he hadn't time to express his feelings further, for a horse's feet were heard on the flags, and, having knocked gently, young Linton entered, his face brilliant with delight at the unexpected summons he had received.

Doubtless Catherine marked the difference between her friends as one came in, and the other went out. The contrast resembled what you see in exchanging a bleak, hilly, coal country, for a beautiful fertile valley; and his voice and greeting were as opposite as his aspect. He had a sweet, low manner of speaking, and pronounced his words as you do: that's less gruff than we talk here, and softer.

"I'm not come too soon, am I?" he said, casting a look at me. I had begun to wipe the plate, and tidy some drawers at the far end in the dresser.

"No," answered Catherine. "What are you doing there, Nelly?"

"My work, Miss," I replied. (Mr. Hindley had given me directions to make a third party in any private visits Linton chose to pay.)

She stepped behind me and whispered crossly, "Take yourself and your dusters off; when company are in the house, servants don't commence scouring and cleaning in the room where they are!"

"It's a good opportunity, now that master is away," I answered aloud: "he hates me to be fidgetting over these things in his presence. I'm sure Mr. Edgar will excuse me."

"I hate you to be fidgetting in *my* presence," exclaimed the young lady imperiously, not allowing her guest time to speak. She had failed to recover her equanimity since the little dispute with Heathcliff.

"I'm sorry for it, Miss Catherine!" was my response; and I proceeded assiduously with my occupation.

She, supposing Edgar could not see her, snatched the cloth from my hand, and pinched me, with a prolonged wrench, very spitefully on the arm.

I've said I did not love her, and rather relished mortifying her vanity, now and then; besides, she hurt me extremely, so I started up from my knees, and screamed out—

"O, Miss, that's a nasty trick! you have no right to nip me, and I'm not going to bear it!"

"I didn't touch you, you lying creature!" cried she, her fingers tingling to repeat the act, and her ears red with rage. She never had power to conceal her passion, it always set her whole complexion in a blaze.

"What's that, then?" I retorted, showing a decided purple witness to refute her.

She stamped her foot, wavered a moment, and then, irresistibly impelled by the naughty spirit within her, slapped me on the cheek a stinging blow that filled both eyes with water.

"Catherine, love! Catherine!" interposed Linton, greatly shocked at the double fault of falsehood and violence which his idol had committed.

"Leave the room, Ellen!" she repeated, trembling all over.

Little Hareton, who followed me everywhere, and was sitting near me on the floor, at seeing my tears commenced crying himself, and sobbed out complaints against "wicked Aunt Cathy," which drew her fury on to his unlucky head: she seized his shoulders, and shook him till the poor child waxed livid, and Edgar thoughtlessly laid hold of her hands to deliver him. In an instant one was wrung free, and the astonished young man felt it applied over his own ear in a way that could not be mistaken for jest.

He drew back in consternation. I lifted Hareton in my arms, and walked off to the kitchen with him, leaving the door of communication open, for I was curious to watch how they would settle their disagreement.

The insulted visitor moved to the spot where he had laid his hat, pale and with a quivering lip.

"That's right!" I said to myself. "Take warning and begone! It's a kindness to let you have a glimpse of her genuine disposition."

"Where are you going?" demanded Catherine, advancing to the door.

He swerved aside and attempted to pass.

"You must not go!" she exclaimed energetically.

"I must and shall!" he replied in a subdued voice.

"No," she persisted, grasping the handle; "not yet, Edgar Linton—sit down; you shall not leave me in that temper. I should be miserable all night, and I won't be miserable for you!"

"Can I stay after you have struck me?" asked Linton.

Catherine was mute.

"You've made me afraid, and ashamed of you," he continued; "I'll not come here again!"

Her eyes began to glisten and her lids to twinkle.

"And you told a deliberate untruth!" he said.

"I didn't!" she cried, recovering her speech. "I did nothing deliberately—Well, go, if you please—get away! And now I'll cry—I'll cry myself sick!"

She dropped down on her knees by a chair and set to weeping in serious earnest.

Edgar persevered in his resolution as far as the court; there he lingered. I resolved to encourage him.

"Miss is dreadfully wayward, sir!" I called out. "As bad as any marred child[11]—you'd better be riding home, or else she will be sick, only to grieve us."

The soft thing looked askance through the window: he possessed the power to depart, as much as a cat possesses the power to leave a mouse half killed, or a bird half eaten.

Ah, I thought, there will be no saving him—He's doomed, and flies to his fate!

And so it was; he turned abruptly, hastened into the house again, shut the door behind him; and, when I went in a while after to inform them that Earnshaw had

---

[11]*Marred child:* spoiled child.

come home rabid drunk, ready to pull the old place about our ears (his ordinary frame of mind in that condition), I saw the quarrel had merely effected a closer intimacy—had broken the outworks of youthful timidity, and enabled them to forsake the disguise of friendship, and confess themselves lovers.

Intelligence of Mr. Hindley's arrival drove Linton speedily to his horse, and Catherine to her chamber. I went to hide little Hareton, and to take the shot out of the master's fowling piece, which he was fond of playing with in his insane excitement, to the hazard of the lives of any who provoked, or even attracted his notice too much; and I had hit upon the plan of removing it, that he might do less mischief, if he did go the length of firing the gun.

CHAPTER 9

He entered, vociferating oaths dreadful to hear; and caught me in the act of stowing his son away in the kitchen cupboard. Hareton was impressed with a wholesome terror of encountering either his wild beast's fondness or his madman's rage; for in one he ran a chance of being squeezed and kissed to death, and in the other of being flung into the fire, or dashed against the wall; and the poor thing remained perfectly quiet wherever I chose to put him.

"There, I've found it out at last!" cried Hindley, pulling me back by the skin of the neck, like a dog. "By heaven and hell, you've sworn between you to murder that child! I know how it is, now, that he is always out of my way. But, with the help of Satan, I shall make you swallow the carving knife, Nelly! You needn't laugh; for I've just crammed Kenneth, head-downmost, in the Blackhorse marsh; and two is the same as one—and I want to kill some of you, I shall have no rest till I do!"

"But I don't like the carving knife, Mr. Hindley," I answered; "it has been cutting red herrings. I'd rather be shot, if you please."

"You'd rather be damned!" he said, "and so you shall. No law in England can hinder a man from keeping his house decent, and mine's abominable! open your mouth."

He held the knife in his hand, and pushed its point between my teeth: but, for my part, I was never much afraid of his vagaries. I spat out, and affirmed it tasted detestably—I would not take it on any account.

"Oh!" said he, releasing me, "I see that hideous little villain is not Hareton: I beg your pardon, Nell. If it be, he deserves flaying alive for not running to welcome me, and for screaming as if I were a goblin. Unnatural cub, come hither! I'll teach thee to impose on a good-hearted, deluded father. Now, don't you think the lad would be handsomer cropped? It makes a dog fiercer, and I love something fierce—get me a scissors—something fierce and trim! Besides, it's infernal affectation—devilish conceit it is—to cherish our ears: we're asses enough without them. Hush, child, hush! well, then, it is my darling! wisht, dry thy eyes—there's a joy; kiss me; what! it won't? kiss me, Hareton! Damn thee, kiss me! By God, as if I would rear such a monster! As sure as I'm living, I'll break the brat's neck."

Poor Hareton was squalling and kicking in his father's arms with all his might, and redoubled his yells when he carried him upstairs and lifted him over the banister. I cried out that he would frighten the child into fits, and ran to rescue him.

As I reached them, Hindley leant forward on the rails to listen to a noise below, almost forgetting what he had in his hands.

"Who is that?" he asked, hearing some one approaching the stair's foot.

I leant forward also, for the purpose of signing to Heathcliff, whose step I recognized, not to come further; and, at the instant when my eye quitted Hareton, he gave a sudden spring, delivered himself from the careless grasp that held him, and fell.

There was scarcely time to experience a thrill of horror before we saw that the little wretch was safe. Heathcliff arrived underneath just at the critical moment; by a natural impulse, he arrested his descent, and setting him on his feet, looked up to discover the author of the accident.

A miser who has parted with a lucky lottery ticket for five shillings, and finds next day he has lost in the bargain five thousand pounds, could not show a blanker countenance than he did on beholding the figure of Mr. Earnshaw above. It expressed, plainer than words could do, the intensest anguish at having made himself the instrument of thwarting his own revenge. Had it been dark, I dare say, he would have tried to remedy the mistake by smashing Hareton's skull on the steps; but we witnessed his salvation; and I was presently below with my precious charge pressed to my heart.

Hindley descended more leisurely, sobered and abashed.

"It is your fault, Ellen," he said, "you should have kept him out of sight; you should have taken him from me! Is he injured anywhere?"

"Injured!" I cried angrily, "If he's not killed, he'll be an idiot! Oh! I wonder his mother does not rise from her grave to see how you use him. You're worse than a heathen—treating your own flesh and blood in that manner!"

He attempted to touch the child, who, on finding himself with me, sobbed off his terror directly. At the first finger his father laid on him, however, he shrieked again louder than before, and struggled as if he would go into convulsions.

"You shall not meddle with him!" I continued, "He hates you—they all hate you—that's the truth! A happy family you have; and a pretty state you're come to!"

"I shall come to a prettier, yet, Nelly!" laughed the misguided man, recovering his hardness. "At present, convey yourself and him away. And, hark you, Heathcliff! clear you too, quite from my reach and hearing. I wouldn't murder you to-night, unless, perhaps, I set the house on fire; but that's as my fancy goes—"

While saying this he took a pint bottle of brandy from the dresser, and poured some into a tumbler.

"Nay, don't!" I entreated, "Mr. Hindley, do take warning. Have mercy on this unfortunate boy, if you care nothing for yourself!"

"Any one will do better for him than I shall," he answered.

"Have mercy on your own soul!" I said, endeavouring to snatch the glass from his hand.

"Not I! on the contrary, I shall have great pleasure in sending it to perdition, to punish its Maker," exclaimed the blasphemer. "Here's to its hearty damnation!"

He drank the spirits, and impatiently bade us go; terminating his command with a sequel of horrid imprecations, too bad to repeat or remember.

"It's a pity he cannot kill himself with drink," observed Heathcliff, muttering an echo of curses back when the door was shut. "He's doing his very utmost; but his constitution defies him. Mr. Kenneth says he would wager his mare, that he'll outlive any man on this side Gimmerton, and go to the grave a hoary sinner; unless some happy chance out of the common course befall him."

I went into the kitchen and sat down to lull my little lamb to sleep. Heathcliff, as I thought, walked through to the barn. It turned out, afterwards, that he only got as far as the other side the settle, when he flung himself on a bench by the wall, removed from the fire, and remained silent.

I was rocking Hareton on my knee, and humming a song that began—

"It was far in the night, and the bairnies grat,
The mither beneath the mools heard that,"[12]

when Miss Cathy, who had listened to the hubbub from her room, put her head in, and whispered—

"Are you alone, Nelly?"

"Yes, Miss," I replied.

She entered and approached the hearth. I, supposing she was going to say something, looked up. The expression of her face seemed disturbed and anxious. Her lips were half asunder as if she meant to speak; and she drew a breath, but it escaped in a sigh, instead of a sentence.

I resumed my song, not having forgotten her recent behaviour.

"Where's Heathcliff?" she said, interrupting me.

"About his work in the stable," was my answer.

He did not contradict me; perhaps he had fallen into a doze.

There followed another long pause, during which I perceived a drop or two trickle from Catherine's cheek to the flags.

Is she sorry for her shameful conduct? I asked myself. That will be a novelty, but she may come to the point as she will—I shan't help her!

No, she felt small trouble regarding any subject, save her own concerns.

"Oh, dear!" she cried at last. "I'm very unhappy!"

"A pity," observed I. "You're hard to please—so many friends and so few cares, and can't make yourself content!"

"Nelly, will you keep a secret for me?" she pursued, kneeling down by me, and lifting her winsome eyes to my face with that sort of look which turns off bad temper, even when one has all the right in the world to indulge it.

"Is it worth keeping?" I inquired, less sulkily.

"Yes, and it worries me, and I must let it out! I want to know what I should do. To-day, Edgar Linton has asked me to marry him, and I've given him an answer. Now, before I tell you whether it was a consent, or denial, you tell me which it ought to have been."

"Really, Miss Catherine, how can I know?" I replied. "To be sure, considering the exhibition you performed in his presence this afternoon, I might say it would be wise to refuse him: since he asked you after that, he must either be hopelessly stupid or a venturesome fool."

"If you talk so, I won't tell you any more," she returned, peevishly, rising to her feet, "I accepted him, Nelly. Be quick, and say whether I was wrong!"

"You accepted him? then, what good is it discussing the matter? You have pledged your word, and cannot retract."

"But, say whether I should have done so—do!" she exclaimed in an irritated tone, chafing her hands together, and frowning.

"There are many things to be considered before that question can be answered properly," I said sententiously. "First and foremost, do you love Mr. Edgar?"

"Who can help it? Of course I do," she answered.

Then I put her through the following catechism: for a girl of twenty-two, it was not injudicious.

"Why do you love him, Miss Cathy?"

---

[12] *Bairnies grat:* babies cried; *mools:* earth.

"Nonsense, I do—that's sufficient."

"By no means; you must say why."

"Well, because he is handsome, and pleasant to be with."

"Bad," was my commentary.

"And because he is young and cheerful."

"Bad, still."

"And because he loves me."

"Indifferent, coming there."

"And he will be rich, and I shall like to be the greatest woman of the neighbourhood, and I shall be proud of having such a husband."

"Worst of all! And now, say how you love him."

"As everybody loves—You're silly, Nelly."

"Not at all—Answer."

"I love the ground under his feet, and the air over his head, and everything he touches, and every word he says—I love all his looks, and all his actions, and him entirely, and altogether. There now!"

"And why?"

"Nay—you are making a jest of it; it is exceedingly ill-natured! It's no jest to me!" said the young lady, scowling, and turning her face to the fire.

"I'm very far from jesting, Miss Catherine," I replied. "You love Mr. Edgar, because he is handsome, and young, and cheerful, and rich, and loves you. The last, however, goes for nothing. You would love him without that, probably; and with it, you wouldn't, unless he possessed the four former attractions."

"No, to be sure not: I should only pity him—hate him, perhaps, if he were ugly, and a clown."

"But there are several other handsome, rich young men in the world; handsomer, possibly, and richer than he is. What should hinder you from loving them?"

"If there be any, they are out of my way. I've seen none like Edgar."

"You may see some; and he won't always be handsome, and young, and may not always be rich."

"He is now; and I have only to do with the present. I wish you would speak rationally."

"Well, that settles it—if you have only to do with the present, marry Mr. Linton."

"I don't want your permission for that—I *shall* marry him; and yet you have not told me whether I'm right."

"Perfectly right; if people be right to marry only for the present. And now, let us hear what you are unhappy about. Your brother will be pleased; the old lady and gentleman will not object, I think; you will escape from a disorderly, comfortless home into a wealthy, respectable one; and you love Edgar, and Edgar loves you. All seems smooth and easy—where is the obstacle?"

"*Here!* and *here!*" replied Catherine, striking one hand on her forehead, and the other on her breast. "In whichever place the soul lives—in my soul, and in my heart, I'm convinced I'm wrong!"

"That's very strange! I cannot make it out."

"It's my secret; but if you will not mock at me, I'll explain it; I can't do it distinctly, but I'll give you a feeling of how I feel."

She seated herself by me again: her countenance grew sadder and graver, and her clasped hands trembled.

"Nelly, do you never dream queer dreams?" she said, suddenly, after some minutes' reflection.

"Yes, now and then," I answered.

"And so do I. I've dreamt in my life dreams that have stayed with me ever after, and changed my ideas; they've gone through and through me, like wine through water, and altered the colour of my mind. And this is one—I'm going to tell it—but take care not to smile at any part of it."

"Oh! don't, Miss Catherine!" I cried. "We're dismal enough without conjuring up ghosts and visions to perplex us. Come, come, be merry, and like yourself! Look at little Hareton—*he's* dreaming nothing dreary. How sweetly he smiles in his sleep!"

"Yes; and how sweetly his father curses in his solitude! You remember him, I dare say, when he was just such another as that chubby thing—nearly as young and innocent. However, Nelly, I shall oblige you to listen—it's not long; and I've no power to be merry to-night."

"I won't hear it, I won't hear it!" I repeated, hastily.

I was superstitious about dreams then, and am still; and Catherine had an unusual gloom in her aspect, that made me dread something from which I might shape a prophecy, and foresee a fearful catastrophe.

She was vexed, but she did not proceed. Apparently taking up another subject, she recommenced in a short time.

"If I were in heaven, Nelly, I should be extremely miserable."

"Because you are not fit to go there," I answered. "All sinners would be miserable in heaven."

"But it is not for that. I dreamt, once, that I was there."

"I tell you I won't harken to your dreams, Miss Catherine! I'll go to bed," I interrupted again.

She laughed, and held me down, for I made a motion to leave my chair.

"This is nothing," cried she; "I was only going to say that heaven did not seem to be my home; and I broke my heart with weeping to come back to earth; and the angels were so angry that they flung me out, into the middle of the heath on the top of Wuthering Heights; where I woke sobbing for joy. That will do to explain my secret, as well as the other. I've no more business to marry Edgar Linton than I have to be in heaven; and if the wicked man in there had not brought Heathcliff so low, I shouldn't have thought of it. It would degrade me to marry Heathcliff now; so he shall never know how I love him; and that, not because he's handsome, Nelly, but because he's more myself than I am. Whatever our souls are made of, his and mine are the same, and Linton's is as different as a moonbeam from lightning, or frost from fire."

Ere this speech ended, I became sensible of Heathcliff's presence. Having noticed a slight movement, I turned my head, and saw him rise from the bench, and steal out, noiselessly. He had listened till he heard Catherine say it would degrade her to marry him, and then he stayed to hear no farther.

My companion, sitting on the ground, was prevented by the back of the settle from remarking his presence or departure; but I started, and bade her hush!

"Why?" she asked, gazing nervously round.

"Joseph is here," I answered, catching opportunely, the roll of his cartwheels up the road; "and Heathcliff will come in with him. I'm not sure whether he were not at the door this moment."

"Oh, he couldn't overhear me at the door!" said she. "Give me Hareton, while you get the supper, and when it is ready ask me to sup with you. I want to cheat my uncomfortable conscience, and be convinced that Heathcliff has no notion of these things. He has not, has he? He does not know what being in love is?"

"I see no reason that he should not know, as well as you," I returned; "and if *you* are his choice, he'll be the most unfortunate creature that ever was born! As soon as you become Mrs. Linton, he loses friend, and love, and all! Have you considered how you'll bear the separation, and how he'll bear to be quite deserted in the world? Because, Miss Catherine—"

"He quite deserted! we separated!" she exclaimed, with an accent of indignation. "Who is to separate us, pray? They'll meet the fate of Milo![13] Not as long as I live, Ellen—for no mortal creature. Every Linton on the face of the earth might melt into nothing, before I could consent to forsake Heathcliff. Oh, that's not what I intend—that's not what I mean! I shouldn't be Mrs. Linton were such a price demanded! He'll be as much to me as he has been all his lifetime. Edgar must shake off his antipathy, and tolerate him, at least. He will when he learns my true feelings towards him. Nelly, I see now, you think me a selfish wretch, but, did it never strike you that if Heathcliff and I married, we should be beggars? whereas, if I marry Linton, I can aid Heathcliff to rise, and place him out of my brother's power."

"With your husband's money, Miss Catherine?" I asked. "You'll find him not so pliable as you calculate upon: and, though I'm hardly a judge, I think that's the worst motive you've given yet for being the wife of young Linton."

"It is not," retorted she, "it is the best! The others were the satisfaction of my whims; and for Edgar's sake, too, to satisfy him. This is for the sake of one who comprehends in his person my feelings to Edgar and myself. I cannot express it; but surely you and everybody have a notion that there is, or should be, an existence of yours beyond you. What were the use of my creation if I were entirely contained here? My great miseries in this world have been Heathcliff's miseries, and I watched and felt each from the beginning; my great thought in living is himself. If all else perished, and *he* remained, I should still continue to be; and, if all else remained, and he were annihilated, the Universe would turn to a mighty stranger. I should not seem a part of it. My love for Linton is like the foliage in the woods. Time will change it, I'm well aware, as winter changes the trees. My love for Heathcliff resembles the eternal rocks beneath—a source of little visible delight, but necessary. Nelly, I *am* Heathcliff—he's always, always in my mind—not as a pleasure, any more than I am always a pleasure to myself—but as my own being—so, don't talk of our separation again—it is impracticable; and—"

She paused, and hid her face in the folds of my gown; but I jerked it forcibly away. I was out of patience with her folly!

"If I can make any sense of your nonsense, Miss," I said, "it only goes to convince me that you are ignorant of the duties you undertake in marrying; or else that you are a wicked, unprincipled girl. But trouble me with no more secrets. I'll not promise to keep them."

"You'll keep that?" she asked, eagerly.

"No, I'll not promise," I repeated.

She was about to insist, when the entrance of Joseph finished our conversation; and Catherine removed her seat to a corner, and nursed Hareton, while I made the supper.

After it was cooked, my fellow servant and I began to quarrel who should carry some to Mr. Hindley; and we didn't settle it till all was nearly cold. Then we came to the agreement that we would let him ask, if he wanted any, for we feared particularly to go into his presence when he had been some time alone.

"Und hah isn't that nowt comed in frough th' field, be this time? What is he abaht? girt eedle seeght!"[14] demanded the old man, looking round for Heathcliff.

"I'll call him," I replied. "He's in the barn, I've no doubt."

---

[13] A Greek athlete who was caught in the tree he was trying to split and was eaten by wolves.
[14] *Girt eedle seeght:* great idle sight.

I went and called, but got no answer. On returning, I whispered to Catherine that he had heard a good part of what she said, I was sure; and told how I saw him quit the kitchen just as she complained of her brother's conduct regarding him.

She jumped up in a fine fright, flung Hareton onto the settle, and ran to seek for her friend herself, not taking leisure to consider why she was so flurried, or how her talk would have affected him.

She was absent such a while that Joseph proposed we should wait no longer. He cunningly conjectured they were staying away in order to avoid hearing his protracted blessing. They were "ill eneugh for ony fahl manners," he affirmed. And, on their behalf, he added that night a special prayer to the usual quarter of an hour's supplication before meat, and would have tacked another to the end of the grace, had not his young mistress broken in upon him with a hurried command that he must run down the road, and, wherever Heathcliff had rambled, find and make him re-enter directly!

"I want to speak with him, and I *must*, before I go upstairs," she said. "And the gate is open, he is somewhere out of hearing; for he would not reply, though I shouted at the top of the fold as loud as I could."

Joseph objected at first; she was too much in earnest, however, to suffer contradiction; and at last he placed his hat on his head, and walked grumbling forth.

Meantime, Catherine paced up and down the floor, exclaiming—

"I wonder where he is—I wonder where he *can* be! What did I say, Nelly? I've forgotten. Was he vexed at my bad humour this afternoon? Dear! tell me what I've said to grieve him. I do wish he'd come. I do wish he would!"

"What a noise for nothing!" I cried, though rather uneasy myself. "What a trifle scares you! It's surely no great cause of alarm that Heathcliff should take a moonlight saunter on the moors, or even lie too sulky to speak to us, in the hay-loft. I'll engage he's lurking there. See if I don't ferret him out!"

I departed to renew my search; its result was disappointment, and Joseph's quest ended in the same.

"Yon lad gets war un war!" observed he on re-entering. "He's left th' yate ut t' full swing, and Miss's pony has trodden dahn two rigs uh corn, un plottered through, raight o'er intuh t' meadow! Hahsomdiver, t' maister 'ull play t' divil to-morn, and he'll do weel. He's patience itsseln wi' sich careless, offald craters—patience itsseln, he is! Bud he'll nut be soa allus—yah's see, all on ye! Yah mumn't drive him aht uf his heead fur nowt!"[15]

"Have you found Heathcliff, you ass?" interrupted Catherine. "Have you been looking for him, as I ordered?"

"Aw sud more likker look for th' horse," he replied. "It 'ud be tuh more sense. Bud Aw can look for norther[16] horse, nur man uf a neeght loike this—as black as t' chimbley! und Hathecliff's noan t' chap tuh coom ut *maw* whistle——happen he'll be less hard uh hearing wi' *ye!*"

It *was* a very dark evening for summer: the clouds appeared inclined to thunder, and I said we had better all sit down; the approaching rain would be certain to bring him home without further trouble.

However, Catherine would not be persuaded into tranquillity. She kept wandering to and fro, from the gate to the door, in a state of agitation which permitted

---

[15] *War un war:* worse and worse; *yate:* gate; *plottered:* scrambled; *offald:* worthless.
[16] *Norther:* neither.

no repose; and at length took up a permanent situation on one side of the wall, near the road, where, heedless of my expostulations, and the growling thunder, and the great drops that began to plash around her, she remained, calling at intervals, and then listening, and then crying outright. She beat Hareton, or any child, at a good, passionate fit of crying.

About midnight, while we still sat up, the storm came rattling over the Heights in full fury. There was a violent wind, as well as thunder, and either one or the other split a tree off at the corner of the building; a huge bough fell across the roof, and knocked down a portion of the east chimney-stack, sending a clatter of stones and soot into the kitchen fire.

We thought a bolt had fallen in the middle of us, and Joseph swung onto his knees, beseeching the Lord to remember the Patriarchs Noah and Lot; and, as in former times, spare the righteous, though he smote the ungodly. I felt some sentiment that it must be a judgment on us also. The Jonah, in my mind, was Mr. Earnshaw, and I shook the handle of his den that I might ascertain if he were yet living. He replied audibly enough, in a fashion which made my companion vociferate more clamorously than before that a wide distinction might be drawn between saints like himself, and sinners like his master. But the uproar passed away in twenty minutes, leaving us all unharmed, excepting Cathy, who got thoroughly drenched for her obstinacy in refusing to take shelter, and standing bonnetless and shawlless to catch as much water as she could with her hair and clothes.

She came in and lay down on the settle, all soaked as she was, turning her face to the back, and putting her hands before it.

"Well, Miss!" I exclaimed, touching her shoulder; "you are not bent on getting your death, are you? Do you know what o'clock it is? Half-past twelve. Come! come to bed; there's no use waiting longer on that foolish boy—he'll be gone to Gimmerton, and he'll stay there now. He guesses we shouldn't wake for him till this late hour; at least, he guesses that only Mr. Hindley would be up; and he'd rather avoid having the door opened by the master."

"Nay, nay, he's noan at Gimmerton!" said Joseph. "Aw's niver wonder, bud he's at t' bothom uf a bog-hoile. This visitation worn't for nowt, und Aw wod hev ye tuh look aht, Miss—yah muh be t' next. Thank Hivin for all! All warks togither for gooid tuh them as is chozzen and piked aht froo' th' rubbidge![17] Yah knaw whet t' Scripture ses—"

And he began quoting several texts; referring us to the chapters and verses where we might find them.

I, having vainly begged the wilful girl to rise and remove her wet things, left him preaching and her shivering, and betook myself to bed with little Hareton, who slept as fast as if every one had been sleeping round him.

I heard Joseph read on a while afterwards; then I distinguished his slow step on the ladder, and then I dropt asleep.

Coming down somewhat later than usual, I saw, by the sun-beams piercing the chinks of the shutters, Miss Catherine still seated near the fire-place. The house door was ajar, too; light entered from its unclosed windows; Hindley had come out, and stood on the kitchen hearth, haggard and drowsy.

"What ails you, Cathy?" he was saying when I entered; "you look as dismal as a drowned whelp. Why are you so damp and pale, child?"

"I've been wet," she answered reluctantly, "and I'm cold, that's all."

---

[17] *Rubbidge:* rubbish.

"Oh, she is naughty!" I cried, perceiving the master to be tolerably sober. "She got steeped in the shower of yesterday evening, and there she has sat the night through, and I couldn't prevail on her to stir."

Mr. Earnshaw stared at us in surprise. "The night through," he repeated. "What kept her up, not fear of the thunder, surely? That was over, hours since."

Neither of us wished to mention Heathcliff's absence, as long as we could conceal it; so I replied, I didn't know how she took it into her head to sit up; and she said nothing.

The morning was fresh and cool; I threw back the lattice, and presently the room filled with sweet scents from the garden; but Catherine called peevishly to me—

"Ellen, shut the window. I'm starving!" And her teeth chattered as she shrunk closer to the almost extinguished embers.

"She's ill," said Hindley, taking her wrist, "I suppose that's the reason she would not go to bed. Damn it! I don't want to be troubled with more sickness here. What took you into the rain?"

"Running after t'lads, as usuald!" croaked Joseph, catching an opportunity, from our hesitation, to thrust in his evil tongue.

"If Aw wur yah, maister, Aw'd just slam t'boards i' their faces all on 'em, gentle and simple! Never a day ut yah're off, but yon cat uh Linton comes sneaking hither; and Miss Nelly shoo's a fine lass! shoo sits watching for ye i' t'kitchen; and as yah're in at one door, he's aht at t'other; und, then, wer grand lady goes a coorting uf hor side! It's bonny behaviour, lurking amang t'flields, after twelve ut' night, wi that fahl, flaysome divil uf a gipsy, Heathcliff! They think *Aw'm* blind; but Aw'm noan, nowt ut t'soart! Aw seed young Linton, boath coming and going, and Aw seed *yah*" (directing his discourse on me), "yah gooid fur nowt, slattenly witch! nip up und bolt intuh th' hahs, t' minute yah heard t'maister's horse fit clatter up t' road."[18]

"Silence, eavesdropper!" cried Catherine. "None of your insolence before me! Edgar Linton came yesterday, by chance, Hindley; and it was *I* who told him to be off, because I knew you would not like to have met him as you were."

"You lie, Cathy, no doubt," answered her brother, "and you are a confounded simpleton! But never mind Linton, at present. Tell me, were you not with Heathcliff last night? Speak the truth, now. You need not be afraid of harming him: though I hate him as much as ever, he did me a good turn a short time since, that will make my conscience tender of breaking his neck. To prevent it, I shall send him about his business this very morning; and after he's gone, I'd advise you all to look sharp, I shall only have the more humour for you!"

"I never saw Heathcliff last night," answered Catherine, beginning to sob bitterly: "and if you do turn him out of doors, I'll go with him. But, perhaps, you'll never have an opportunity—perhaps, he's gone." Here she burst into uncontrollable grief, and the remainder of her words were inarticulate.

Hindley lavished on her a torrent of scornful abuse, and bid her get to her room immediately, or she shouldn't cry for nothing! I obliged her to obey; and I shall never forget what a scene she acted, when we reached her chamber. It terrified me. I thought she was going mad, and I begged Joseph to run for the doctor.

It proved the commencement of delirium; Mr. Kenneth, as soon as he saw her, pronounced her dangerously ill; she had a fever.

He bled her, and he told me to let her live on whey and water-gruel, and take care she did not throw herself downstairs, or out of the window; and then he left,

---

[18] *Hahs:* house; *horse fit:* horse feet.

for he had enough to do in the parish where two or three miles was the ordinary distance between cottage and cottage.

Though I cannot say I made a gentle nurse, and Joseph and the master were no better; and though our patient was as wearisome and headstrong as a patient could be, she weathered it through.

Old Mrs. Linton paid us several visits, to be sure, and set things to rights, and scolded and ordered us all; and when Catherine was convalescent, she insisted on conveying her to Thrushcross Grange: for which deliverance we were very grateful. But the poor dame had reason to repent of her kindness; she and her husband both took the fever, and died within a few days of each other.

Our young lady returned to us, saucier and more passionate, and haughtier than ever. Heathcliff had never been heard of since the evening of the thunder-storm, and, one day, I had the misfortune, when she had provoked me exceedingly, to lay the blame of his disappearance on her (where indeed it belonged, as she well knew). From that period, for several months, she ceased to hold any communication with me, save in the relation of a mere servant. Joseph fell under a ban also; he *would* speak his mind, and lecture her all the same as if she were a little girl; and she esteemed herself a woman, and our mistress, and thought that her recent illness gave her a claim to be treated with consideration. Then the doctor had said that she would not bear crossing much, she ought to have her own way; and it was nothing less than murder, in her eyes, for any one to presume to stand up and contradict her.

From Mr. Earnshaw and his companions she kept aloof; and tutored by Kenneth, and serious threats of a fit that often attended her rages, her brother allowed her whatever she pleased to demand, and generally avoided aggravating her fiery temper. He was rather *too* indulgent in humouring her caprices; not from affection, but from pride, he wished earnestly to see her bring honour to the family by an alliance with the Lintons, and, as long as she let him alone, she might trample us like slaves for ought he cared!

Edgar Linton, as multitudes have been before and will be after him, was infatuated; and believed himself the happiest man alive on the day he led her to Gimmerton chapel, three years subsequent to his father's death.

Much against my inclination, I was persuaded to leave Wuthering Heights and accompany her here. Little Hareton was nearly five years old, and I had just begun to teach him his letters. We made a sad parting, but Catherine's tears were more powerful than ours. When I refused to go, and when she found her entreaties did not move me, she went lamenting to her husband and brother. The former offered me munificent wages; the latter ordered me to pack up. He wanted no women in the house, he said, now that there was no mistress; and as to Hareton, the curate should take him in hand, by and by. And so I had but one choice left, to do as I was ordered. I told the master he got rid of all decent people only to run to ruin a little faster; I kissed Hareton good-bye; and, since then, he has been a stranger, and it's very queer to think it, but I've no doubt he has completely forgotten all about Ellen Dean and that he was ever more than all the world to her, and she to him!

At this point of the housekeeper's story, she chanced to glance towards the time-piece over the chimney; and was in amazement on seeing the minute-hand measure half-past one. She would not hear of staying a second longer. In truth, I felt rather disposed to defer the sequel of her narrative myself: and now that she is vanished to her rest, and I have meditated for another hour or two, I shall summon courage to go, also, in spite of aching laziness of head and limbs.

CHAPTER 10

A charming introduction to a hermit's life! Four weeks' torture, tossing and sickness! Oh, these bleak winds, and bitter, northern skies, and impassable roads, and dilatory country surgeons! And, oh, this dearth of the human physiognomy, and, worse than all, the terrible intimation of Kenneth that I need not expect to be out of doors till spring!

Mr. Heathcliff has just honoured me with a call. About seven days ago he sent me a brace of grouse—the last of the season. Scoundrel! He is not altogether guiltless in this illness of mine; and that I had a great mind to tell him. But, alas! how could I offend a man who was charitable enough to sit at my bedside a good hour, and talk on some other subject than pills and draughts, blisters and leeches?

This is quite an easy interval. I am too weak to read, yet I feel as if I could enjoy something interesting. Why not have up Mrs. Dean to finish her tale? I can recollect its chief incidents, as far as she had gone. Yes, I remember her hero had run off, and never been heard of for three years; and the heroine was married. I'll ring; she'll be delighted to find me capable of talking cheerfully.

Mrs. Dean came.

"It wants twenty minutes, sir, to taking the medicine," she commenced.

"Away, away with it!" I replied; "I desire to have—"

"The doctor says you must drop the powders."

"With all my heart! Don't interrupt me. Come and take your seat here. Keep your fingers from that bitter phalanx of vials. Draw your knitting out of your pocket—that will do—now continue the history of Mr. Heathcliff, from where you left off, to the present day. Did he finish his education on the Continent, and come back a gentleman? or did he get a sizer's place at college? or escape to America, and earn honours by drawing blood from his foster country? or make a fortune more promptly, on the English highways?"

"He may have done a little in all these vocations, Mr. Lockwood; but I couldn't give my word for any. I stated before that I didn't know how he gained his money; neither am I aware of the means he took to raise his mind from the savage ignorance into which it was sunk; but, with your leave, I'll proceed in my own fashion, if you think it will amuse and not weary you. Are you feeling much better this morning?"

"Much."

"That's good news."

I got Miss Catherine and myself to Thrushcross Grange; and to my agreeable disappointment, she behaved infinitely better than I dared to expect. She seemed almost over-fond of Mr. Linton; and even to his sister, she showed plenty of affection. They were both very attentive to her comfort, certainly. It was not the thorn bending to the honeysuckles, but the honeysuckles embracing the thorn. There were no mutual concessions; one stood erect, and the others yielded; and who *can* be ill-natured and bad-tempered, when they encounter neither opposition nor indifference?

I observed that Mr. Edgar had a deep-rooted fear of ruffling her humour. He concealed it from her; but if ever he heard me answer sharply, or saw any other servant grow cloudy at some imperious order of hers, he would show his trouble by a frown of displeasure that never darkened on his own account. He, many a time, spoke sternly to me about my pertness; and averred that the stab of a knife could not inflict a worse pang than he suffered at seeing his lady vexed.

Not to grieve a kind master, I learnt to be less touchy; and, for the space of half a year, the gunpowder lay as harmless as sand, because no fire came near to explode it. Catherine had seasons of gloom and silence, now and then: they were respected with sympathizing silence by her husband, who ascribed them to an alteration in her constitution, produced by her perilous illness, as she was never subject to depression of spirits before. The return of sunshine was welcomed by answering sunshine from him. I believe I may assert that they were really in possession of deep and growing happiness.

It ended. Well, we *must* be for ourselves in the long run; the mild and generous are only more justly selfish than the domineering; and it ended when circumstances caused each to feel that the one's interest was not the chief consideration in the other's thoughts.

On a mellow evening in September, I was coming from the garden with a heavy basket of apples which I had been gathering. It had got dusk, and the moon looked over the high wall of the court, causing undefined shadows to lurk in the corners of the numerous projecting portions of the building. I set my burden on the house steps by the kitchen door, and lingered to rest and draw in a few more breaths of the soft, sweet air; my eyes were on the moon, and my back to the entrance, when I heard a voice behind me say—

"Nelly, is that you?"

It was a deep voice, and foreign in tone; yet there was something in the manner of pronouncing my name which made it sound familiar. I turned about to discover who spoke, fearfully, for the doors were shut, and I had seen nobody on approaching the steps.

Something stirred in the porch; and moving nearer, I distinguished a tall man dressed in dark clothes, with dark face and hair. He leant against the side, and held his fingers on the latch, as if intending to open for himself.

"Who can it be?" I thought. "Mr. Earnshaw? Oh, no! The voice has no resemblance to his."

"I have waited here an hour," he resumed, while I continued staring; "and the whole of that time all round has been as still as death. I dared not enter. You do not know me? Look, I'm not a stranger!"

A ray fell on his features; the cheeks were sallow, and half covered with black whiskers; the brows lowering, the eyes deep set and singular. I remembered the eyes.

"What!" I cried, uncertain whether to regard him as a worldly visitor, and I raised my hands in amazement. "What! you come back? Is it really you? Is it?"

"Yes, Heathcliff," he replied, glancing from me up to the windows, which reflected a score of glittering moons, but showed no lights from within. "Are they at home—where is she? Nelly, you are not glad—you needn't be so disturbed. Is she here? Speak! I want to have one word with her—your mistress. Go, and say some person from Gimmerton desires to see her."

"How will she take it?" I exclaimed. "What will she do? The surprise bewilders me—it will put her out of her head! And you *are* Heathcliff? But altered! Nay, there's no comprehending it. Have you been for a soldier?"

"Go, and carry my message," he interrupted impatiently; "I'm in hell till you do!"

He lifted the latch, and I entered; but when I got to the parlour where Mr. and Mrs. Linton were, I could not persuade myself to proceed.

At length, I resolved on making an excuse to ask if they would have the candles lighted, and I opened the door.

They sat together in a window whose lattice lay back against the wall, and displayed, beyond the garden trees and the wild green park, the valley of Gimmerton, with a long line of mist winding nearly to its top (for very soon after you pass the chapel, as you may have noticed, the sough that runs from the marshes joins a beck which follows the bend of the glen). Wuthering Heights rose above this silvery vapour; but our old house was invisible—it rather dips down on the other side.

Both the room and its occupants, and the scene they gazed on, looked wondrously peaceful. I shrank reluctantly from performing my errand, and was actually going away, leaving it unsaid, after having put my question about the candles, when a sense of my folly compelled me to return, and mutter—

"A person from Gimmerton wishes to see you, ma'am."

"What does he want?" asked Mrs. Linton.

"I did not question him," I answered.

"Well, close the curtains, Nelly," she said; "and bring up tea. I'll be back again directly."

She quitted the apartment; Mr. Edgar inquired carelessly, who it was?

"Some one the mistress does not expect," I replied. "That Heathcliff, you recollect him, sir, who used to live at Mr. Earnshaw's."

"What, the gipsy—the plough-boy?" he cried. "Why did you not say so to Catherine?"

"Hush! you must not call him by those names, master," I said. "She'd be sadly grieved to hear you. She was nearly heart-broken when he ran off; I guess his return will make a jubilee to her."

Mr. Linton walked to a window on the other side of the room that overlooked the court. He unfastened it, and leant out. I suppose they were below, for he exclaimed, quickly—

"Don't stand there, love! Bring the person in, if it be any one particular."

Ere long, I heard the click of the latch, and Catherine flew upstairs, breathless and wild, too excited to show gladness; indeed, by her face, you would rather have surmised an awful calamity.

"Oh, Edgar, Edgar!" she panted, flinging her arms round his neck. "Oh, Edgar, darling! Heathcliff's come back—he is!" And she tightened her embrace to a squeeze.

"Well, well," cried her husband, crossly, "don't strangle me for that! He never struck me as such a marvellous treasure. There is no need to be frantic!"

"I know you didn't like him," she answered, repressing a little the intensity of her delight. "Yet, for my sake, you must be friends now. Shall I tell him to come up?"

"Here?" he said, "into the parlour?"

"Where else?" she asked.

He looked vexed, and suggested the kitchen as a more suitable place for him.

Mrs. Linton eyed him with a droll expression—half angry, half laughing at his fastidiousness.

"No," she added, after a while; "I cannot sit in the kitchen. Set two tables here, Ellen; one for your master and Miss Isabella, being gentry; the other for Heathcliff and myself, being of the lower orders. Will that please you, dear? Or must I have a fire lighted elsewhere? If so, give directions. I'll run down and secure my guest. I'm afraid the joy is too great to be real!"

She was about to dart off again; but Edgar arrested her.

"*You* bid him step up," he said, addressing me; "and, Catherine, try to be glad, without being absurd! The whole household need not witness the sight of your welcoming a runaway servant as a brother."

I descended and found Heathcliff waiting under the porch, evidently anticipating an invitation to enter. He followed my guidance without waste of words, and I ushered him into the presence of the master and mistress, whose flushed cheeks betrayed signs of warm talking. But the lady's glowed with another feeling when her friend appeared at the door; she sprang forward, took both his hands, and led him to Linton; and then she seized Linton's reluctant fingers and crushed them into his.

Now fully revealed by the fire and candlelight, I was amazed, more than ever, to behold the transformation of Heathcliff. He had grown a tall, athletic, well-formed man, beside whom my master seemed quite slender and youth-like. His upright carriage suggested the idea of his having been in the army. His countenance was much older in expression and decision of feature than Mr. Linton's; it looked intelligent, and retained no marks of former degradation. A half-civilized ferocity lurked yet in the depressed brows and eyes full of black fire, but it was subdued; and his manner was even dignified, quite divested of roughness, though too stern for grace.

My master's surprise equalled or exceeded mine: he remained for a minute at a loss how to address the ploughboy, as he had called him. Heathcliff dropped his slight hand, and stood looking at him coolly till he chose to speak.

"Sit down, sir," he said, at length. "Mrs. Linton, recalling old times, would have me give you a cordial reception, and, of course, I am gratified when anything occurs to please her."

"And I also," answered Heathcliff, "especially if it be anything in which I have a part. I shall stay an hour or two willingly."

He took a seat opposite Catherine, who kept her gaze fixed on him as if she feared he would vanish were she to remove it. He did not raise his to her often; a quick glance now and then sufficed; but it flashed back, each time more confidently, the undisguised delight he drank from hers.

They were too much absorbed in their mutual joy to suffer embarrassment. Not so Mr. Edgar; he grew pale with pure annoyance, a feeling that reached its climax when his lady rose, and stepping across the rug, seized Heathcliff's hands again, and laughed like one beside herself.

"I shall think it a dream to-morrow!" she cried. "I shall not be able to believe that I have seen, and touched, and spoken to you once more—and yet, cruel Heathcliff! you don't deserve this welcome. To be absent and silent for three years, and never to think of me!"

"A little more than you have thought of me!" he murmured. "I heard of your marriage, Cathy, not long since; and, while waiting in the yard below, I meditated this plan: just to have one glimpse of your face, a stare of surprise, perhaps, and pretended pleasure; afterwards settle my score with Hindley; and then prevent the law by doing execution on myself. Your welcome has put these ideas out of my mind; but beware of meeting me with another aspect next time! Nay, you'll not drive me off again. You were really sorry for me, were you? Well, there was cause. I've fought through a bitter life since I last heard your voice, and you must forgive me, for I struggled only for you."

"Catherine, unless we are to have cold tea, please to come to the table," interrupted Linton, striving to preserve his ordinary tone, and a due measure of politeness. "Mr. Heathcliff will have a long walk, wherever he may lodge to-night; and I'm thirsty."

She took her post before the urn; and Miss Isabella came, summoned by the bell; then, having handed their chairs forward, I left the room.

The meal hardly endured ten minutes. Catherine's cup was never filled, she could neither eat nor drink. Edgar had made a slop in his saucer, and scarcely swallowed a mouthful.

Their guest did not protract his stay that evening above an hour longer. I asked, as he departed, if he went to Gimmerton?

"No, to Wuthering Heights," he answered, "Mr. Earnshaw invited me when I called this morning."

Mr. Earnshaw invited *him!* and *he* called on Mr. Earnshaw! I pondered this sentence painfully after he was gone. Is he turning out a bit of a hypocrite, and coming into the country to work mischief under a cloak? I mused—I had a presentiment, in the bottom of my heart, that he had better have remained away.

About the middle of the night, I was wakened from my first nap by Mrs. Linton gliding into my chamber, taking a seat on my bed-side, and pulling me by the hair to rouse me.

"I cannot rest, Ellen," she said by way of apology. "And I want some living creature to keep me company in my happiness! Edgar is sulky, because I'm glad of a thing that does not interest him. He refuses to open his mouth, except to utter pettish, silly speeches; and he affirmed I was cruel and selfish for wishing to talk when he was so sick and sleepy. He always contrives to be sick at the least cross! I gave a few sentences of commendation to Heathcliff, and he, either for a headache or a pang of envy, began to cry: so I got up and left him."

"What use is it praising Heathcliff to him?" I answered. "As lads they had an aversion to each other, and Heathcliff would hate just as much to hear him praised—it's human nature. Let Mr. Linton alone about him, unless you would like an open quarrel between them."

"But does it not show great weakness?" pursued she. "I'm not envious: I never feel hurt at the brightness of Isabella's yellow hair, and the whiteness of her skin; at her dainty elegance, and the fondness all the family exhibit for her. Even you, Nelly, if we have a dispute sometimes, you back Isabella, at once; and I yield like a foolish mother—I call her a darling, and flatter her into a good temper. It pleases her brother to see us cordial, and that pleases me. But they are very much alike; they are spoiled children, and fancy the world was made for their accommodation; and, though I humour both, I think a smart chastisement might improve them, all the same."

"You're mistaken, Mrs. Linton," said I. "They humour you: I know what there would be to do if they did not! You can well afford to indulge their passing whims, as long as their business is to anticipate all your desires. You may, however, fall out, at last, over something of equal consequence to both sides; and then those you term weak are very capable of being as obstinate as you!"

"And then we shall fight to the death, shan't we, Nelly?" she returned laughing. "No! I tell you, I have such faith in Linton's love that I believe I might kill him, and he wouldn't wish to retaliate."

I advised her to value him the more for his affection.

"I do," she answered, "but he needn't resort to whining for trifles. It is childish; and, instead of melting into tears because I said that Heathcliff was now worthy of any one's regard, and it would honour the first gentleman in the country to be his friend, he ought to have said it for me, and been delighted from sympathy. He must get accustomed to him, and he may as well like him. Considering how Heathcliff has reason to object to him, I'm sure he behaved excellently!"

"What do you think of his going to Wuthering Heights?" I inquired. "He is reformed in every respect, apparently—quite a Christian—offering the right hand of fellowship to his enemies all round!"

"He explained it," she replied. "I wondered as much as you. He said he called to gather information concerning me, from you, supposing you resided there still; and Joseph told Hindley, who came out and fell to questioning him of what he had been doing, and how he had been living; and finally, desired him to walk in. There were some persons sitting at cards; Heathcliff joined them; my brother lost some money to him; and, finding him plentifully supplied, he requested that he would come again in the evening, to which he consented. Hindley is too reckless to select his acquaintance prudently; he doesn't trouble himself to reflect on the causes he might have for mistrusting one whom he has basely injured. But Heathcliff affirms his principal reason for resuming a connection with his ancient persecutor is a wish to install himself in quarters at walking distance from the Grange, and an attachment to the house where we lived together, and likewise a hope that I shall have more opportunities of seeing him there than I could have if he settled in Gimmerton. He means to offer liberal payment for permission to lodge at the Heights; and doubtless my brother's covetousness will prompt him to accept the terms; he was always greedy, though what he grasps with one hand, he flings away with the other."

"It's a nice place for a young man to fix his dwelling in!" said I. "Have you no fear of the consequences, Mrs. Linton?"

"None for my friend," she replied. "His strong head will keep him from danger; a little for Hindley, but he can't be made morally worse than he is; and I stand between him and bodily harm. The event of this evening has reconciled me to God and humanity! I had risen in angry rebellion against providence. Oh, I've endured very, very bitter misery, Nelly! If that creature knew how bitter, he'd be ashamed to cloud its removal with idle petulance. It was kindness for him which induced me to bear it alone: had I expressed the agony I frequently felt, he would have been taught to long for its alleviation as ardently as I. However, it's over, and I'll take no revenge on his folly; I can afford to suffer anything, hereafter! Should the meanest thing alive slap me on the cheek, I'd not only turn the other, but I'd ask pardon for provoking it; and, as a proof, I'll go make my peace with Edgar instantly. Good-night—I'm an angel!"

In this self-complacent conviction she departed; and the success of her fulfilled resolution was obvious on the morrow: Mr. Linton had not only abjured his peevishness (though his spirits seemed still subdued by Catherine's exuberance of vivacity), but he ventured no objection to her taking Isabella with her to Wuthering Heights in the afternoon; and she rewarded him with such a summer of sweetness and affection in return, as made the house a paradise for several days; both master and servants profiting from the perpetual sunshine.

Heathcliff—Mr. Heathcliff I should say in future—used the liberty of visiting at Thrushcross Grange cautiously, at first: he seemed estimating how far its owner would bear his intrusion. Catherine, also, deemed it judicious to moderate her expressions of pleasure in receiving him; and he gradually established his right to be expected.

He retained a great deal of the reserve for which his boyhood was remarkable, and that served to repress all startling demonstrations of feeling. My master's uneasiness experienced a lull, and further circumstances diverted it into another channel for a space.

His new source of trouble sprang from the not anticipated misfortune of Isabella Linton evincing a sudden and irresistible attraction towards the tolerated guest. She was at that time a charming young lady of eighteen; infantile in manners, though possessed of keen wit, keen feelings, and a keen temper, too, if irritated. Her brother, who loved her tenderly, was appalled at this fantastic preference. Leaving aside the degradation of an alliance with a nameless man, and the possible fact that his property, in default of heirs male, might pass into such a one's power, he had sense to comprehend Heathcliff's disposition—to know that, though his exterior was altered, his mind was unchangeable, and unchanged. And he dreaded that mind; it revolted him; he shrank forebodingly from the idea of committing Isabella to its keeping.

He would have recoiled still more had he been aware that her attachment rose unsolicited, and was bestowed where it awakened no reciprocation of sentiment; for the minute he discovered its existence, he laid the blame on Heathcliff's deliberate designing.

We had all remarked, during some time, that Miss Linton fretted and pined over something. She grew cross and wearisome, snapping at and teasing Catherine continually, at the imminent risk of exhausting her limited patience. We excused her to a certain extent, on the plea of ill health—she was dwindling and fading before our eyes. But one day, when she had been peculiarly wayward, rejecting her breakfast, complaining that the servants did not do what she told them; that the mistress would allow her to be nothing in the house, and Edgar neglected her; that she had caught a cold with the doors being left open, and we let the parlour fire go out on purpose to vex her; with a hundred yet more frivolous accusations, Mrs. Linton peremptorily insisted that she should get to bed; and, having scolded her heartily, threatened to send for the doctor.

Mention of Kenneth caused her to exclaim, instantly, that her health was perfect, and it was only Catherine's harshness which made her unhappy.

"How can you say I am harsh, you naughty fondling?" cried the mistress, amazed at the unreasonable assertion. "You are surely losing your reason. When have I been harsh, tell me?"

"Yesterday," sobbed Isabella, "and now!"

"Yesterday!" said her sister-in-law. "On what occasion?"

"In our walk along the moor; you told me to ramble where I pleased, while you sauntered on with Mr. Heathcliff!"

"And that's your notion of harshness?" said Catherine, laughing. "It was no hint that your company was superfluous; we didn't care whether you kept with us or not; I merely thought Heathcliff's talk would have nothing entertaining for your ears."

"Oh, no," wept the young lady; "you wished me away, because you knew I liked to be there!"

"Is she sane?" asked Mrs. Linton, appealing to me. "I'll repeat our conversation, word for word, Isabella; and you point out any charm it could have had for you."

"I don't mind the conversation," she answered. "I wanted to be with—"

"Well!" said Catherine, perceiving her hesitate to complete the sentence.

"With him; and I won't be always sent off!" she continued, kindling up. "You are a dog in the manger, Cathy, and desire no one to be loved but yourself!"

"You are an impertinent little monkey!" exclaimed Mrs. Linton, in surprise. "But I'll not believe this idiocy! It is impossible that you can covet the admiration of Heathcliff—that you can consider him an agreeable person! I hope I have misunderstood you, Isabella?"

"No, you have not," said the infatuated girl. "I love him more than ever you loved Edgar; and he might love me if you would let him!"

"I wouldn't be you for a kingdom, then!" Catherine declared, emphatically—and she seemed to speak sincerely. "Nelly, help me to convince her of her madness. Tell her what Heathcliff is—an unreclaimed creature, without refinement, without cultivation; an arid wilderness of furze and whinstone. I'd as soon put that little canary into the park on a winter's day as recommend you to bestow your heart on him! It is deplorable ignorance of his character, child, and nothing else, which makes that dream enter your head. Pray don't imagine that he conceals depths of benevolence and affection beneath a stern exterior! He's not a rough diamond—a pearl-containing oyster of a rustic; he's a fierce, pitiless, wolfish man. I never say to him, 'Let this or that enemy alone, because it would be ungenerous or cruel to harm them'; I say, 'Let them alone, because *I* should hate them to be wronged': and he'd crush you, like a sparrow's egg, Isabella, if he found you a troublesome charge. I know he couldn't love a Linton; and yet he'd be quite capable of marrying your fortune and expectations. Avarice is growing with him a besetting sin. There's my picture; and I'm his friend—so much so, that had he thought seriously to catch you, I should, perhaps, have held my tongue, and let you fall into his trap."

Miss Linton regarded her sister-in-law with indignation.

"For shame! for shame!" she repeated, angrily. "You are worse than twenty foes, you poisonous friend!"

"Ah! you won't believe me, then?" said Catherine. "You think I speak from wicked selfishness?"

"I'm certain you do," retorted Isabella; "and I shudder at you!"

"Good!" cried the other. "Try for yourself, if that be your spirit; I have done, and yield the argument to your saucy insolence."

"And I must suffer for her egotism!" she sobbed, as Mrs. Linton left the room. "All, all is against me; she has blighted my single consolation. But she uttered falsehoods, didn't she? Mr. Heathcliff is not a fiend; he has an honourable soul, and a true one, or how could he remember her?"

"Banish him from your thoughts, Miss," I said. "He's a bird of bad omen; no mate for you. Mrs. Linton spoke strongly, and yet I can't contradict her. She is better acquainted with his heart than I, or any one besides; and she never would represent him as worse than he is. Honest people don't hide their deeds. How has he been living? how has he got rich? why is he staying at Wuthering Heights, the house of a man whom he abhors? They say Mr. Earnshaw is worse and worse since he came. They sit up all night together continually; and Hindley has been borrowing money on his land, and does nothing but play and drink: I heard only a week ago—it was Joseph who told me—I met him at Gimmerton."

"'Nelly,' he said, 'we's hae a Crahnr's 'quest enah, at ahr folks.[19] One on 'em's a'most getten his finger cut off wi' hauding t'other froo' sticking hisseln loike a cawlf. That's maister, yah knaw, ut's soa up uh going tuh t'grand 'sizes.[20] He's noan feard uh t' Bench uh judges, norther Paul, nur Peter, nur John, nor Mathew, nor noan on 'em, nut he! He fair like's—he langs tuh set his brazened face agean 'em! And yon bonny lad Heathcliff, yah mind, he's a rare un! He cau girn a laugh,[21] as weel's onybody at a raight divil's jest. Does he niver say nowt of his fine living amang us, when he goas tuh t' Grange? This is t' way on't—up at sun-dahn; dice, brandy, cloised shutters, und can'le lught till next day, at nooin—then, t'fooil gangs banning un raving tuh his cham'er, makking dacent fowks dig thur fingers i' thur lugs fur varry shaume; un' the' knave, wah, he carn cahnt his brass, un ate, un' sleep, un' off tuh his neighbour's tuh gossip wi' t' wife. I' course, he tells Dame Catherine hah hor father's goold runs intuh his pocket, and her fathur's son gallops dahn t' broad road, while he flees afore tuh oppen t' pikes.'[22] Now, Miss Linton, Joseph is an old rascal, but no liar; and, if his account of Heathcliff's conduct be true, you would never think of desiring such a husband, would you?"

"You are leagued with the rest, Ellen!" she replied. "I'll not listen to your slanders. What malevolence you must have to wish to convince me that there is no happiness in the world!"

Whether she would have got over this fancy if left to herself, or persevered in nursing it perpetually, I cannot say; she had little time to reflect. The day after, there was a justice-meeting at the next town; my master was obliged to attend; and Mr. Heathcliff, aware of his absence, called rather earlier than usual.

---

[19] *Crahnr's 'quest:* coroner's inquest; *enah:* soon.
[20] *T'grand 'sizes:* the grand assizes or court sessions.
[21] *Girn a laugh:* show the teeth while laughing.
[22] *Gangs banning:* goes cursing; *wah, he carn cahnt his brass.* why, he can count his money.

Catherine and Isabella were sitting in the library, on hostile terms, but silent. The latter, alarmed at her recent indiscretion, and the disclosure she had made of her secret feelings in a transient fit of passion; the former, on mature consideration, really offended with her companion; and, if she laughed again at her pertness, inclined to make it no laughing matter to *her*.

She did laugh as she saw Heathcliff pass the window. I was sweeping the hearth, and I noticed a mischievous smile on her lips. Isabella, absorbed in her meditations, or a book, remained till the door opened, and it was too late to attempt an escape, which she would gladly have done had it been practicable.

"Come in, that's right!" exclaimed the mistress, gaily, pulling a chair to the fire. "Here are two people sadly in need of a third to thaw the ice between them, and you are the very one we should both of us choose. Heathcliff, I'm proud to show you, at last, somebody that dotes on you more than myself. I expect you to feel flattered. Nay, it's not Nelly; don't look at her! My poor little sister-in-law is breaking her heart by mere contemplation of your physical and moral beauty. It lies in your own power to be Edgar's brother! No, no, Isabella, you shan't run off," she continued, arresting, with feigned playfulness, the confounded girl who had risen indignantly. "We were quarrelling like cats about you, Heathcliff; and I was fairly beaten in protestations of devotion and admiration; and, moreover, I was informed that if I would but have the manners to stand aside, my rival, as she will have herself to be, would shoot a shaft into your soul that would fix you for ever, and send my image into eternal oblivion!"

"Catherine," said Isabella, calling up her dignity, and disdaining to struggle from the tight grasp that held her, "I'd thank you to adhere to the truth and not slander me, even in joke! Mr. Heathcliff, be kind enough to bid this friend of yours release me: she forgets that you and I are not intimate acquaintants, and what amuses her is painful to me beyond expression."

As the guest answered nothing, but took his seat, and looked thoroughly indifferent what sentiments she cherished concerning him, she turned, and whispered an earnest appeal for liberty to her tormentor.

"By no means!" cried Mrs. Linton in answer. "I won't be named a dog in the manger again. You *shall* stay: now then, Heathcliff, why don't you evince satisfaction at my pleasant news? Isabella swears that the love Edgar has for me is nothing to that she entertains for you. I'm sure she made some speech of the kind, did she not, Ellen? And she has fasted ever since the day before yesterday's walk, from sorrow and rage that I despatched her out of your society, under the idea of its being unacceptable."

"I think you belie her," said Heathcliff, twisting his chair to face them. "She wishes to be out of my society now, at any rate!"

And he stared hard at the object of discourse, as one might do at a strange repulsive animal, a centipede from the Indies, for instance, which curiosity leads one to examine in spite of the aversion it raises.

The poor thing couldn't bear that; she grew white and red in rapid succession, and, while tears beaded her lashes, bent the strength of her small fingers to loosen the firm clutch of Catherine, and perceiving that as fast as she raised one finger off her arm, another closed down, and she could not remove the whole together, she began to make use of her nails, and their sharpness presently ornamented the detainer's with crescents of red.

"There's a tigress!" exclaimed Mrs. Linton, setting her free, and shaking her hand with pain. "Begone, for God's sake, and hide your vixen face! How foolish to reveal those talons to *him*. Can't you fancy the conclusions he'll draw? Look, Heathcliff! they are instruments that will do execution—you must beware of your eyes."

"I'd wrench them off her fingers, if they ever menaced me," he answered brutally, when the door had closed after her. "But what did you mean by teasing the creature in that manner, Cathy? You were not speaking the truth, were you?"

"I assure you I was," she returned. "She has been pining for your sake several weeks; and raving about you this morning, and pouring forth a deluge of abuse, because I represented your failings in a plain light for the purpose of mitigating her adoration. But don't notice it further. I wished to punish her sauciness, that's all. I like her too well, my dear Heathcliff, to let you absolutely seize and devour her up."

"And I like her too ill to attempt it," said he, "except in a very ghoulish fashion. You'd hear of odd things, if I lived alone with that mawkish, waxen face; the most ordinary would be painting on its white the colours of the rainbow, and turning the blue eyes black, every day or two; they detestably resemble Linton's."

"Delectably," observed Catherine. "They are dove's eyes—angel's!"

"She's her brother's heir, is she not?" he asked, after a brief silence.

"I should be sorry to think so," returned his companion. "Half-a-dozen nephews shall erase her title, please Heaven! Abstract your mind from the subject, at present. You are too prone to covet your neighbour's goods: remember *this* neighbour's goods are mine."

"If they were *mine*, they would be none the less that," said Heathcliff, "but though Isabella Linton may be silly, she is scarcely mad; and, in short, we'll dismiss the matter, as you advise."

From their tongues, they did dismiss it; and Catherine, probably, from her thoughts. The other, I felt certain, recalled it often in the course of the evening; I saw him smile to himself—grin rather—and lapse into ominous musing whenever Mrs. Linton had occasion to be absent from the apartment.

I determined to watch his movements. My heart invariably cleaved to the master's, in preference to Catherine's side; with reason, I imagined, for he was kind, and trustful, and honourable: and she—she could not be called the *opposite*, yet she seemed to allow herself such wide latitude that I had little faith in her principles, and still less sympathy for her feelings. I wanted something to happen which might have the effect of freeing both Wuthering Heights and the Grange of Mr. Heathcliff, quietly, leaving us as we had been prior to his advent. His visits were a continual nightmare to me; and, I suspected, to my master also. His abode at the Heights was an oppression past explaining. I felt that God had forsaken the stray sheep there to its own wicked wanderings, and an evil beast prowled between it and the fold, waiting his time to spring and destroy.

CHAPTER 11

Sometimes, while meditating on these things in solitude, I've got up in a sudden terror, and put on my bonnet to go see how all was at the farm; I've persuaded my conscience that it was a duty to warn him how people talked regarding his ways; and then I've recollected his confirmed bad habits, and, hopeless of benefiting him, have flinched from re-entering the dismal house, doubting if I could bear to be taken at my word.

One time I passed the old gate, going out of my way, on a journey to Gimmerton. It was about the period that my narrative has reached—a bright, frosty afternoon, the ground bare, and the road hard and dry.

I came to a stone where the highway branches off on to the moor at your left hand; a rough sand-pillar, with the letters W. H. cut on its north side, on the east,

G., and on the south-west, T. G. It serves as guide-post to the Grange, and Heights, and village.

The sun shone yellow on its grey head, reminding me of summer; and I cannot say why, but all at once, a gush of child's sensations flowed into my heart. Hindley and I held it a favourite spot twenty years before.

I gazed long at the weather-worn block; and, stooping down, perceived a hole near the bottom still full of snail-shells and pebbles, which we were fond of storing there with more perishable things; and, as fresh as reality, it appeared that I beheld my early playmate seated on the withered turf, his dark, square head bent forward, and his little hand scooping out the earth with a piece of slate.

"Poor Hindley!" I exclaimed, involuntarily.

I started—my bodily eye was cheated into a momentary belief that the child lifted its face and stared straight into mine! It vanished in a twinkling; but, immediately, I felt an irresistible yearning to be at the Heights. Superstition urged me to comply with this impulse. Supposing he should be dead! I thought—or should die soon! —supposing it were a sign of death!

The nearer I got to the house the more agitated I grew; and on catching sight of it, I trembled every limb. The apparition had outstripped me; it stood looking through the gate. That was my first idea on observing an elf-locked, brown-eyed boy setting his ruddy countenance against the bars. Further reflection suggested this must be Hareton, *my* Hareton, not altered greatly since I left him, ten months since.

"God bless thee, darling!" I cried, forgetting instantaneously my foolish fears. "Hareton, it's Nelly—Nelly, thy nurse."

He retreated out of arm's length, and picked up a large flint.

"I am come to see thy father, Hareton," I added, guessing from the action that Nelly, if she lived in his memory at all, was not recognised as one with me.

He raised his missile to hurl it; I commenced a soothing speech, but could not stay his hand. The stone struck my bonnet; and then ensued, from the stammering lips of the little fellow, a string of curses, which, whether he comprehended them or not, were delivered with practised emphasis, and distorted his baby features into a shocking expression of malignity.

You may be certain this grieved more than angered me. Fit to cry, I took an orange from my pocket, and offered it to propitiate him.

He hesitated, and then snatched it from my hold, as if he fancied I only intended to tempt and disappoint him.

I showed another, keeping it out of his reach.

"Who has taught you those fine words, my barn,"[23] I inquired. "The curate?"

"Damn the curate, and thee! Gie me that," he replied.

"Tell us where you got your lessons, and you shall have it," said I. "Who's your master?"

"Devil daddy," was his answer.

"And what do you learn from Daddy?" I continued.

He jumped at the fruit; I raised it higher. "What does he teach you?" I asked.

"Naught," said he, "but to keep out of his gait. Daddy cannot bide me, because I swear at him."

"Ah! and the devil teaches you to swear at Daddy?" I observed.

"Aye—nay," he drawled.

"Who then?"

---

[23] *Barn:* bairn, child.

"Heathcliff."

I asked if he liked Mr. Heathcliff?

"Aye!" he answered again.

Desiring to have his reasons for liking him, I could only gather the sentences—"I known't—he pays Dad back what he gies to me—he curses Daddy for cursing me—he says I mun do as I will."

"And the curate does not teach you to read and write, then?" I pursued.

"No, I was told the curate should have his —— teeth dashed down his —— throat, if he stepped over the threshold. Heathcliff had promised that!"

I put the orange in his hand, and bade him tell his father that a woman called Nelly Dean was waiting to speak with him, by the garden gate.

He went up the walk, and entered the house; but, instead of Hindley, Heathcliff appeared on the door stones, and I turned directly and ran down the road as hard as ever I could race, making no halt till I gained the guide post, and feeling as scared as if I had raised a goblin.

This is not much connected with Miss Isabella's affair; except that it urged me to resolve further on mounting vigilant guard, and doing my utmost to check the spread of such bad influence at the Grange, even though I should wake a domestic storm by thwarting Mrs. Linton's pleasure.

The next time Heathcliff came, my young lady chanced to be feeding some pigeons in the court. She had never spoken a word to her sister-in-law for three days; but she had likewise dropped her fretful complaining, and we found it a great comfort.

Heathcliff had not the habit of bestowing a single unnecessary civility on Miss Linton, I knew. Now, as soon as he beheld her, his first precaution was to take a sweeping survey of the house-front. I was standing by the kitchen window, but I drew out of sight. He then stept across the pavement to her, and said something: she seemed embarrassed, and desirous of getting away; to prevent it, he laid his hand on her arm. She averted her face; he apparently put some question which she had no mind to answer. There was another rapid glance at the house, and supposing himself unseen, the scoundrel had the impudence to embrace her.

"Judas! Traitor!" I ejaculated. "You are a hypocrite too, are you? A deliberate deceiver."

"Who is, Nelly?" said Catherine's voice at my elbow. I had been over-intent on watching the pair outside to mark her entrance.

"Your worthless friend!" I answered warmly; "the sneaking rascal yonder. Ah, he has caught a glimpse of us—he is coming in! I wonder will he have the art to find a plausible excuse for making love to Miss, when he told you he hated her?"

Mrs. Linton saw Isabella tear herself free, and run into the garden; and a minute after, Heathcliff opened the door.

I couldn't withhold giving some loose to my indignation; but Catherine angrily insisted on silence, and threatened to order me out of the kitchen, if I dared be so presumptuous as to put in my insolent tongue.

"To hear you, people might think *you* were the mistress!" she cried. "You want setting down in your right place! Heathcliff, what are you about, raising this stir? I said you must let Isabella alone!—I beg you will, unless you are tired of being received here, and wish Linton to draw the bolts against you!"

"God forbid that he should try!" answered the black villain. I detested him just then. "God keep him meek and patient! Every day I grow madder after sending him to heaven!"

"Hush!" said Catherine, shutting the inner door. "Don't vex me. Why have you disregarded my request? Did she come across you on purpose?"

"What is it to you?" he growled. "I have a right to kiss her, if she chooses, and you have no right to object. I'm not *your* husband: *you* needn't be jealous of me!"

"I'm not jealous *of* you," replied the mistress, "I'm jealous *for* you. Clear your face, you shan't scowl at me! If you like Isabella, you shall marry her. But do you like her? Tell the truth, Heathcliff! There, you won't answer. I'm certain you don't!"

"And would Mr. Linton approve of his sister marrying that man?" I inquired.

"Mr. Linton should approve," returned my lady decisively.

"He might spare himself the trouble," said Heathcliff; "I could do as well without his approbation. And as to you, Catherine, I have a mind to speak a few words now, while we are at it. I want you to be aware that I *know* you have treated me infernally—infernally! Do you hear? And if you flatter yourself that I don't perceive it, you are a fool; and if you think I can be consoled by sweet words you are an idiot; and if you fancy I'll suffer unrevenged, I'll convince you of the contrary, in a very little while! Meantime, thank you for telling me your sister-in-law's secret. I swear I'll make the most of it. And stand you aside!"

"What new phase of his character is this?" exclaimed Mrs. Linton, in amazement. "I've treated you infernally—and you'll take revenge! How will you take it, ungrateful brute? How have I treated you infernally?"

"I seek no revenge on you," replied Heathcliff less vehemently. "That's not the plan. The tyrant grinds down his slaves and they don't turn against him, they crush those beneath them. You are welcome to torture me to death for your amusement, only allow me to amuse myself a little in the same style, and refrain from insult, as much as you are able. Having levelled my palace, don't erect a hovel and complacently admire your own charity in giving me that for a home. If I imagined you really wished me to marry Isabella, I'd cut my throat!"

"Oh, the evil is that I am *not* jealous, is it?" cried Catherine. "Well, I won't repeat my offer of a wife: it is as bad as offering Satan a lost soul. Your bliss lies, like his, in inflicting misery. You prove it. Edgar is restored from the ill-temper he gave way to at your coming; I begin to be secure and tranquil; and you, restless to know us at peace, appear resolved on exciting a quarrel. Quarrel with Edgar, if you please, Heathcliff, and deceive his sister; you'll hit on exactly the most efficient method of revenging yourself on me."

This conversation ceased. Mrs. Linton sat down by the fire, flushed and gloomy. The spirit which served her was growing intractable: she could neither lay nor control it. He stood on the hearth, with folded arms, brooding on his evil thoughts; and in this position I left them to seek the master, who was wondering what kept Catherine below so long.

"Ellen," said he, when I entered, "have you seen your mistress?"

"Yes, she's in the kitchen, sir," I answered. "She's sadly put out by Mr. Heathcliff's behaviour: and, indeed, I do think it's time to arrange his visits on another footing. There's harm in being too soft, and now it's come to this—" And I related the scene in the court, and, as near as I dared, the whole subsequent dispute. I fancied it could not be very prejudicial to Mrs. Linton, unless she made it so afterwards, by assuming the defensive for her guest.

Edgar Linton had difficulty in hearing me to the close. His first words revealed that he did not clear his wife of blame.

"This is insufferable!" he exclaimed. "It is disgraceful that she should own him for a friend, and force his company on me! Call me two men out of the hall, Ellen. Catherine shall linger no longer to argue with the low ruffian—I have humoured her enough."

He descended, and bidding the servants wait in the passage, went, followed by me, to the kitchen. Its occupants had recommenced their angry discussion; Mrs.

Linton, at least, was scolding with renewed vigour; Heathcliff had moved to the window, and hung his head, somewhat cowed by her violent rating apparently.

He saw the master first, and made a hasty motion that she should be silent; which she obeyed, abruptly, on discovering the reason of his intimation.

"How is this?" said Linton, addressing her; "what notion of propriety must you have to remain here, after the language which has been held to you by that blackguard? I suppose, because it is his ordinary talk, you think nothing of it—you are habituated to his baseness, and, perhaps, imagine I can get used to it too!"

"Have you been listening at the door, Edgar?" asked the mistress, in a tone particularly calculated to provoke her husband, implying both carelessness and contempt of his irritation.

Heathcliff, who had raised his eyes at the former speech, gave a sneering laugh at the latter, on purpose, it seemed, to draw Mr. Linton's attention to him.

He succeeded; but Edgar did not mean to entertain him with any high flights of passion.

"I have been so far forbearing with you, sir," he said, quietly; "not that I was ignorant of your miserable, degraded character, but I felt you were only partly responsible for that; and Catherine wishing to keep up your acquaintance, I acquiesced—foolishly. Your presence is a moral poison that would contaminate the most virtuous: for that cause, and to prevent worse consequences, I shall deny you, hereafter, admission into this house, and give notice, now, that I require your instant departure. Three minutes' delay will render it involuntary and ignominious."

Heathcliff measured the height and breadth of the speaker with an eye full of derision.

"Cathy, this lamb of yours threatens like a bull!" he said. "It is in danger of splitting its skull against my knuckles. By God, Mr. Linton, I'm mortally sorry that you are not worth knocking down!"

My master glanced towards the passage, and signed me to fetch the men: he had no intention of hazarding a personal encounter.

I obeyed the hint; but Mrs. Linton, suspecting something, followed, and when I attempted to call them, she pulled me back, slammed the door to, and locked it.

"Fair means!" she said, in answer to her husband's look of angry surprise. "If you have not the courage to attack him, make an apology, or allow yourself to be beaten. It will correct you of feigning more valour than you possess. No, I'll swallow the key before you shall get it! I'm delightfully rewarded for my kindness to each! After constant indulgence of one's weak nature, and the other's bad one, I earn, for thanks, two samples of blind ingratitude, stupid to absurdity! Edgar, I was defending you and yours; and I wish Heathcliff may flog you sick, daring to think an evil thought of me!"

It did not need the medium of a flogging to produce that effect on the master. He tried to wrest the key from Catherine's grasp; and for safety she flung it into the hottest part of the fire; whereupon Mr. Edgar was taken with a nervous trembling, and his countenance grew deadly pale. For his life he could not avert that access of emotion: mingled anguish and humiliation overcame him completely. He leant on the back of a chair, and covered his face.

"Oh, heavens! In old days this would win you knighthood!" exclaimed Mrs. Linton. "We are vanquished! we are vanquished! Heathcliff would as soon lift a finger at you as the king would march his army against a colony of mice. Cheer up, you shan't be hurt! Your type is not a lamb, it's a sucking leveret."

"I wish you joy of the milk-blooded coward, Cathy!" said her friend. "I compliment you on your taste: and that is the slavering, shivering thing you preferred to me! I would not strike him with my fist, but I'd kick him with my foot, and experience considerable satisfaction. Is he weeping, or is he going to faint for fear?"

The fellow approached and gave the chair on which Linton rested a push. He'd better have kept his distance: my master quickly sprang erect, and struck him full on the throat a blow that would have levelled a slighter man.

It took his breath for a minute; and, while he choked, Mr. Linton walked out by the back door into the yard, and from thence, to the front entrance.

"There! you've done with coming here," cried Catherine. "Get away, now; he'll return with a brace of pistols, and half a dozen assistants. If he did overhear us, of course, he'd never forgive you. You've played me an ill turn, Heathcliff! But go—make haste! I'd rather see Edgar at bay than you."

"Do you suppose I'm going with that blow burning in my gullet?" he thundered. "By hell, no! I'll crush his ribs in like a rotten hazel-nut, before I cross the threshold! If I don't floor him now, I shall murder him sometime, so, as you value his existence, let me get at him!"

"He is not coming," I interposed, framing a bit of a lie. "There's the coachman, and the two gardeners; you'll surely not wait to be thrust into the road by them! Each has a bludgeon, and master will, very likely, be watching from the parlour windows to see that they fulfil his orders."

The gardeners and coachman *were* there; but Linton was with them. They had already entered the court. Heathcliff, on second thoughts, resolved to avoid a struggle against three underlings; he seized the poker, smashed the lock from the inner door, and made his escape as they tramped in.

Mrs. Linton, who was very much excited, bid me accompany her upstairs. She did not know my share in contributing to the disturbance, and I was anxious to keep her in ignorance.

"I'm nearly distracted, Nelly!" she exclaimed, throwing herself on the sofa. "A thousand smiths' hammers are beating in my head! Tell Isabella to shun me—this uproar is owing to her; and should she or any one else aggravate my anger at present, I shall get wild. And, Nelly, say to Edgar, if you see him again to-night, that I'm in danger of being seriously ill. I wish it may prove true. He has startled and distressed me shockingly! I want to frighten him. Besides, he might come and begin a string of abuse, or complainings; I'm certain I should recriminate, and God knows where we should end! Will you do so, my good Nelly? You are aware that I am no way blameable in this matter. What possessed him to turn listener? Heathcliff's talk was outrageous, after you left us; but I could soon have diverted him from Isabella, and the rest meant nothing. Now, all is dashed wrong by the fool's-craving to hear evil of self that haunts some people like a demon! Had Edgar never gathered our conversation, he would never have been the worse for it. Really, when he opened on me in that unreasonable tone of displeasure, after I had scolded Heathcliff till I was hoarse for *him*, I did not care, hardly, what they did to each other, especially as I felt that, however the scene closed, we should all be driven asunder for nobody knows how long! Well, if I cannot keep Heathcliff for my friend, if Edgar will be mean and jealous, I'll try to break their hearts by breaking my own. That will be a prompt way of finishing all, when I am pushed to extremity! But it's a deed to be reserved for a forlorn hope; I'd not take Linton by surprise with it. To this point he has been discreet in dreading to provoke me; you must represent the peril of quitting that policy, and remind him of my passionate temper, verging, when kindled, on frenzy. I wish you could dismiss that apathy out of your countenance, and look rather more anxious about me!"

The stolidity with which I received these instructions was, no doubt, rather exasperating, for they were delivered in perfect sincerity; but I believed a person who could plan the turning of her fits of passion to account, beforehand, might, by exerting her will, manage to control herself tolerably even while under their influence; and I did not wish to "frighten" her husband, as she said, and multiply his annoyances for the purpose of serving her selfishness.

Therefore I said nothing when I met the master coming towards the parlour; but I took the liberty of turning back to listen whether they would resume their quarrel together.

He began to speak first.

"Remain where you are, Catherine," he said, without any anger in his voice, but with much sorrowful despondency. "I shall not stay. I am neither come to wrangle, nor be reconciled; but I wish just to learn whether, after this evening's events, you intend to continue your intimacy with—"

"Oh, for mercy's sake," interrupted the mistress, stamping her foot, "for mercy's sake, let us hear no more of it now! Your cold blood cannot be worked into a fever; your veins are full of ice-water, but mine are boiling, and the sight of such chillness makes them dance."

"To get rid of me, answer my question," persevered Mr. Linton. "You *must* answer it; and that violence does not alarm me. I have found that you can be as stoical as any one, when you please. Will you give up Heathcliff hereafter, or will you give up me? It is impossible for you to be *my* friend and *his* at the same time; and I absolutely *require* to know which you choose."

"I require to be let alone!" exclaimed Catherine furiously. "I demand it! Don't you see I can scarcely stand? Edgar, you—you leave me!"

She rung the bell till it broke with a twang: I entered leisurely. It was enough to try the temper of a saint, such senseless, wicked rages! There she lay dashing her head against the arm of the sofa, and grinding her teeth, so that you might fancy she would crash them to splinters!

Mr. Linton stood looking at her in sudden compunction and fear. He told me to fetch some water. She had no breath for speaking.

I brought a glass full; and, as she would not drink, I sprinkled it on her face. In a few seconds she stretched herself out stiff, and turned up her eyes, while her cheeks, at once blanched and livid, assumed the aspect of death.

Linton looked terrified.

"There is nothing in the world the matter," I whispered. I did not want him to yield, though I could not help being afraid in my heart.

"She has blood on her lips!" he said, shuddering.

"Never mind!" I answered, tartly. And I told him how she had resolved, previous to his coming, on exhibiting a fit of frenzy.

I incautiously gave the account aloud, and she heard me, for she started up—her hair flying over her shoulders, her eyes flashing, the muscles of her neck and arms standing out preternaturally. I made up my mind for broken bones, at least; but she only glared about her for an instant, and then rushed from the room.

The master directed me to follow; I did, to her chamber door; she hindered me from going farther by securing it against me.

As she never offered to descend to breakfast next morning, I went to ask whether she would have some carried up.

"No!" she replied, peremptorily.

The same question was repeated at dinner and tea; and again on the morrow after, and received the same answer.

Mr. Linton, on his part, spent his time in the library, and did not inquire concerning his wife's occupations. Isabella and he had had an hour's interview, during which he tried to elicit from her some sentiment of proper horror for Heathcliff's advances; but he could make nothing of her evasive replies, and was obliged to close the examination unsatisfactorily; adding, however, a solemn warning, that if she were so insane as to encourage that worthless suitor, it would dissolve all bonds of relationship between herself and him.

CHAPTER 12

While Miss Linton moped about the park and garden, always silent, and almost always in tears; and her brother shut himself up among books that he never opened—wearying, I guessed, with a continual vague expectation that Catherine, repenting her conduct, would come of her own accord to ask pardon, and seek a reconciliation—and while *she* fasted pertinaciously, under the idea, probably, that at every meal, Edgar was ready to choke for her absence, and pride alone held him from running to cast himself at her feet, I went about my household duties, convinced that the Grange had but one sensible soul in its walls, and that lodged in my body.

I wasted no condolences on Miss, nor any expostulations on my mistress, nor did I pay attention to the sighs of my master, who yearned to hear his lady's name, since he might not hear her voice.

I determined they should come about as they pleased for me; and though it was a tiresomely slow process, I began to rejoice at length in a faint dawn of its progress, as I thought at first.

Mrs. Linton, on the third day, unbarred her door; and having finished the water in her pitcher and decanter, desired a renewed supply, and a basin of gruel, for she believed she was dying. That I set down as a speech meant for Edgar's ears; I believed no such thing, so I kept it to myself, and brought her some tea and dry toast.

She ate and drank eagerly; and sank back on her pillow again, clenching her hands and groaning.

"Oh, I will die," she exclaimed, "since no one cares anything about me. I wish I had not taken that."

Then a good while after I heard her murmur—

"No, I'll not die—he'd be glad—he does not love me at all—he would never miss me!"

"Did you want anything, ma'am?" I enquired, still preserving my external composure, in spite of her ghastly countenance and strange exaggerated manner.

"What is that apathetic being doing?" she demanded, pushing the thick entangled locks from her wasted face. "Has he fallen into a lethargy, or is he dead?"

"Neither," replied I; "if you mean Mr. Linton. He's tolerably well, I think, though his studies occupy him rather more than they ought; he is continually among his books, since he has no other society."

I should not have spoken so, if I had known her true condition, but I could not get rid of the notion that she acted a part of her disorder.

"Among his books!" she cried, confounded. "And I dying! I on the brink of the grave! My God! does he know how I'm altered?" continued she, staring at her reflection in a mirror, hanging against the opposite wall. "Is that Catherine Linton? He imagines me in a pet—in play, perhaps. Cannot you inform him that it is frightful earnest? Nelly, if it be not too late, as soon as I learn how he feels, I'll choose between these two: either to starve at once—that would be no punishment unless he had a heart—or to recover and leave the country. Are you speaking the truth about him now? Take care. Is he actually so utterly indifferent for my life?"

"Why, ma'am," I answered, "the master has no idea of your being deranged; and, of course, he does not fear that you will let yourself die of hunger."

"You think not? Cannot you tell him I will?" she returned. "Persuade him—speak of your own mind—say you are certain I will!"

"No, you forget, Mrs. Linton," I suggested, "that you have eaten some food with a relish this evening, and to-morrow you will perceive its good effects."

"If I were only sure it would kill him," she interrupted, "I'd kill myself directly! These three awful nights, I've never closed my lids—and oh, I've been tormented! I've been haunted, Nelly! But I begin to fancy you don't like me. How strange! I thought, though everybody hated and despised each other, they could not avoid loving me—and they have all turned to enemies in a few hours. *They* have, I'm positive; the people *here*. How dreary to meet death, surrounded by their cold faces! Isabella, terrified and repelled, afraid to enter the room, it would be so dreadful to watch Catherine go. And Edgar standing solemnly by to see it over; then offering prayers of thanks to God for restoring peace to his house, and going back to his *books!* What, in the name of all that feels, has he to do with *books*, when I am dying?"

She could not bear the notion which I had put into her head of Mr. Linton's philosophical resignation. Tossing about, she increased her feverish bewilderment to madness, and tore the pillow with her teeth; then raising herself up all burning, desired that I would open the window. We were in the middle of winter, the wind blew strong from the northeast, and I objected.

Both the expressions flitting over her face, and the changes of her moods, began to alarm me terribly; and brought to my recollection her former illness, and the doctor's injunction that she should not be crossed.

A minute previously she was violent; now, supported on one arm, and not noticing my refusal to obey her, she seemed to find childish diversion in pulling the feathers from the rents she had just made, and ranging them on the sheet according to their different species: her mind had strayed to other associations.

"That's a turkey's," she murmured to herself; "and this is a wild-duck's; and this is a pigeon's. Ah, they put pigeons' feathers in the pillows—no wonder I couldn't die! Let me take care to throw it on the floor when I lie down. And here is a moor-cock's; and this—I should know it among a thousand—it's a lapwing's. Bonny bird; wheeling over our heads in the middle of the moor. It wanted to get to its nest, for the clouds touched the swells, and it felt rain coming. This feather was picked up from the heath, the bird was not shot; we saw its nest in the winter, full of little skeletons. Heathcliff set a trap over it, and the old ones dare not come. I made him promise he'd never shoot a lapwing after that, and he didn't. Yes, here are more! Did he shoot my lapwings, Nelly? Are they red, any of them? Let me look."

"Give over with that baby-work!" I interrupted, dragging the pillow away, and turning the holes towards the mattress, for she was removing its contents by handfuls. "Lie down and shut your eyes, you're wandering. There's a mess! The down is flying about like snow!"

I went here and there collecting it.

"I see in you, Nelly," she continued, dreamily, "an aged woman—you have grey hair, and bent shoulders. This bed is the fairy cave under Penistone Crag, and you are gathering elf-bolts[24] to hurt our heifers; pretending, while I am near, that they

---

[24] Arrowheads.

are only locks of wool. That's what you'll come to fifty years hence; I know you are not so now. I'm not wandering: you're mistaken, or else I should believe you really *were* that withered hag, and I should think I *was* under Penistone Crag, and I'm conscious it's night, and there are two candles on the table making the black press shine like jet."

"The black press? where is that?" I asked. "You are talking in your sleep!"

"It's against the wall, as it always is," she replied. "It *does* appear odd—I see a face in it!"

"There is no press in the room, and never was," said I, resuming my seat, and looping up the curtain that I might watch her.

"Don't *you* see that face?" she enquired, gazing earnestly at the mirror.

And say what I could, I was incapable of making her comprehend it to be her own; so I rose and covered it with a shawl.

"It's behind there still!" she pursued, anxiously. "And it stirred. Who is it? I hope it will not come out when you are gone! Oh! Nelly, the room is haunted! I'm afraid of being alone!"

I took her hand in mine, and bid her be composed, for a succession of shudders convulsed her frame, and she *would* keep straining her gaze towards the glass.

"There's nobody here!" I insisted. "It was *yourself*, Mrs. Linton; you knew it a while since."

"Myself," she gasped, "and the clock is striking twelve! It's true, then; that's dreadful!"

Her fingers clutched the clothes, and gathered them over her eyes. I attempted to steal to the door with an intention of calling her husband; but I was summoned back by a piercing shriek. The shawl had dropped from the frame.

"Why, what *is* the matter?" cried I. "Who is coward now? Wake up! That is the glass—the mirror, Mrs. Linton; and you see yourself in it, and there am I too, by your side."

Trembling and bewildered, she held me fast, but the horror gradually passed from her countenance; its paleness gave place to a glow of shame.

"Oh, dear! I thought I was at home," she sighed. "I thought I was lying in my chamber at Wuthering Heights. Because I'm weak, my brain got confused, and I screamed unconsciously. Don't say anything; but stay with me. I dread sleeping, my dreams appal me."

"A sound sleep would do you good, ma'am," I answered; "and I hope this suffering will prevent your trying starving again."

"Oh, if I were but in my own bed in the old house!" she went on bitterly, wringing her hands. "And that wind sounding in the firs by the lattice. Do let me feel it—it comes straight down the moor—do let me have one breath!"

To pacify her, I held the casement ajar, a few seconds. A cold blast rushed through; I closed it, and returned to my post.

She lay still now, her face bathed in tears. Exhaustion of body had entirely subdued her spirit; our fiery Catherine was no better than a wailing child!

"How long is it since I shut myself in here?" she asked, suddenly reviving.

"It was Monday evening," I replied, "and this is Thursday night, or rather Friday morning, at present."

"What! of the same week?" she exclaimed. "Only that brief time?"

"Long enough to live on nothing but cold water and ill-temper," observed I.

"Well, it seems a weary number of hours," she muttered doubtfully; "it must be more. I remember being in the parlour after they had quarrelled; and Edgar being cruelly provoking, and me running into this room desperate. As soon as ever I had barred the door, utter blackness overwhelmed me, and I fell on the floor. I couldn't explain to Edgar how certain I felt of having a fit, or going raging mad, if he persisted in teasing me! I had no command of tongue, or brain, and he did not guess my agony, perhaps; it barely left me sense to try to escape from him and his voice. Before I recovered sufficiently to see and hear, it began to be dawn; and, Nelly, I'll tell you what I thought, and what has kept recurring and recurring till I feared for my reason. I thought as I lay there with my head against that table leg, and my eyes dimly discerning the grey square of the window, that I was enclosed in the oak-panelled bed at home; and my heart ached with some great grief which, just waking, I could not recollect. I pondered, and worried myself to discover what it could be; and, most strangely, the whole last seven years of my life grew a blank! I did not recall that they had been at all. I was a child; my father was just buried, and my misery arose from the separation that Hindley had ordered between me and Heathcliff. I was laid alone, for the first time, and, rousing from a dismal doze after a night of weeping, I lifted my hand to push the panels aside: it struck the table-top! I swept it along the carpet, and then memory burst in—my late anguish was swallowed in a paroxysm of despair. I cannot say why I felt so wildly wretched—it must have been temporary derangement, for there is scarcely cause. But, supposing at twelve years old, I had been wrenched from the Heights, and every early association, and my all in all, as Heathcliff was at that time, and been converted at a stroke into Mrs. Linton, the lady of Thrushcross Grange, and the wife of a stranger; an exile, and outcast, thenceforth, from what had been my world. You may fancy a glimpse of the abyss where I grovelled! Shake your head as you will, Nelly, *you* have helped to unsettle me! You should have spoken to Edgar, indeed you should, and compelled him to leave me quiet! Oh, I'm burning! I wish I were out of doors—I wish I were a girl again, half savage, and hardy, and free; and laughing at injuries, not maddening under them! Why am I so changed? why does my blood rush into a hell of tumult at a few words? I'm sure I should be myself were I once among the heather on those hills. Open the window again wide, fasten it open! Quick, why don't you move?"

"Because I won't give you your death of cold," I answered.

"You won't give me a chance of life, you mean," she said sullenly. "However, I'm not helpless yet, I'll open it myself."

And sliding from the bed before I could hinder her, she crossed the room, walking very uncertainly, threw it back, and bent out, careless of the frosty air that cut about her shoulders as keen as a knife.

I entreated, and finally attempted to force her to retire. But I soon found her delirious strength much surpassed mine (she *was* delirious, I became convinced by her subsequent actions, and ravings).

There was no moon, and everything beneath lay in misty darkness; not a light gleamed from any house, far or near; all had been extinguished long ago; and those at Wuthering Heights were never visible—still she asserted she caught their shining.

"Look!" she cried eagerly, "that's my room, with the candle in it, and the trees swaying before it; and the other candle is in Joseph's garret. Joseph sits up late, doesn't he? He's waiting till I come home that he may lock the gate. Well, he'll wait a while yet. It's a rough journey, and a sad heart to travel it; and we must pass by Gimmerton Kirk, to go that journey! We've braved its ghosts often together, and dared each other to stand among the graves and ask them to come. But Heathcliff, if I dare you now, will you venture? If you do, I'll keep you. I'll not lie there by myself; they may bury me twelve feet deep, and throw the church down over me, but I won't rest till you are with me. I never will!"

She paused, and resumed with a strange smile, "He's considering—he'd rather I'd come to him! Find a way, then! not through that Kirkyard. You are slow! Be content, you always followed me!"

Perceiving it vain to argue against her insanity, I was planning how I could reach something to wrap about her, without quitting my hold of herself, for I could not trust her alone by the gaping lattice, when, to my consternation, I heard the rattle of the door-handle, and Mr. Linton entered. He had only then come from the library; and, in passing through the lobby, had noticed our talking and been attracted by curiosity, or fear, to examine what it signified at that late hour.

"Oh, sir!" I cried, checking the exclamation risen to his lips at the sight which met him, and the bleak atmosphere of the chamber. "My poor mistress is ill, and she quite masters me; I cannot manage her at all; pray, come and persuade her to go to bed. Forget your anger, for she's hard to guide any way but her own."

"Catherine ill?" he said, hastening to us. "Shut the window, Ellen! Catherine! why—"

He was silent; the haggardness of Mrs. Linton's appearance smote him speechless, and he could only glance from her to me in horrified astonishment.

"She's been fretting here," I continued, "and eating scarcely anything, and never complaining; she would admit none of us till this evening, and so we couldn't inform you of her state, as we were not aware of it ourselves, but it is nothing."

I felt I uttered my explanations awkwardly; the master frowned. "It is nothing, is it, Ellen Dean?" he said sternly. "You shall account more clearly for keeping me ignorant of this!" And he took his wife in his arms, and looked at her with anguish.

At first she gave him no glance of recognition—he was invisible to her abstracted gaze. The delirium was not fixed, however; having weaned her eyes from contemplating the outer darkness, by degrees she centred her attention on him, and discovered who it was that held her.

"Ah! you are come, are you, Edgar Linton?" she said, with angry animation. "You are one of those things that are ever found when least wanted, and when you are wanted, never! I suppose we shall have plenty of lamentations, now—I see we shall—but they can't keep me from my narrow home out yonder, my resting place where I'm bound before spring is over! There it is, not among the Lintons, mind, under the chapel-roof; but in the open air with a head-stone, and you may please yourself, whether you go to them, or come to me!"

"Catherine, what have you done?" commenced the master. "Am I nothing to you, any more? Do you love that wretch, Heath—"

"Hush!" cried Mrs. Linton. "Hush, this moment! You mention that name and I end the matter instantly, by a spring from the window! What you touch at present, you may have; but my soul will be on that hilltop before you lay hands on me again. I don't want you, Edgar; I'm past wanting you. Return to your books. I'm glad you possess a consolation, for all you had in me is gone."

"Her mind wanders, sir," I interposed. "She has been talking nonsense the whole evening; but, let her have quiet and proper attendance, and she'll rally. Hereafter, we must be cautious how we vex her."

"I desire no further advice from you," answered Mr. Linton. "You knew your mistress's nature, and you encouraged me to harass her. And not to give me one hint of how she has been these three days! It was heartless! Months of sickness could not cause such a change!"

I began to defend myself, thinking it too bad to be blamed for another's wicked waywardness!

"I knew Mrs. Linton's nature to be headstrong and domineering," cried I; "but I didn't know that you wished to foster her fierce temper! I didn't know that, to humour her, I should wink at Mr. Heathcliff. I performed the duty of a faithful servant in telling you, and I have got a faithful servant's wages! Well, it will teach me to be careful next time. Next time you may gather intelligence for yourself!"

"The next time you bring a tale to me, you shall quit my service, Ellen Dean," he replied.

"You'd rather hear nothing about it, I suppose, then, Mr. Linton?" said I. "Heathcliff has your permission to come a–courting to Miss, and to drop in at every opportunity your absence offers, on purpose to poison the mistress against you?"

Confused as Catherine was, her wits were alert at applying our conversation.

"Ah! Nelly has played traitor," she exclaimed, passionately. "Nelly is my hidden enemy. You witch! So you do seek elf-bolts to hurt us! Let me go, and I'll make her rue! I'll make her howl a recantation!"

A maniac's fury kindled under her brows; she struggled desperately to disengage herself from Linton's arms. I felt no inclination to tarry the event; and, resolving to seek medical aid on my own responsibility, I quitted the chamber.

In passing the garden to reach the road, at a place where a bridle hook is driven into the wall, I saw something white moved irregularly, evidently by another agent than the wind. Notwithstanding my hurry, I stayed to examine it, lest ever after I should have the conviction impressed on my imagination that it was a creature of the other world.

My surprise and perplexity were great to discover, by touch more than vision, Miss Isabella's springer, Fanny, suspended by a handkerchief, and nearly at its last gasp.

I quickly released the animal, and lifted it into the garden. I had seen it follow its mistress upstairs, when she went to bed, and wondered much how it could have got out there, and what mischievous person had treated it so.

While untying the knot round the hook, it seemed to me that I repeatedly caught the beat of horses' feet galloping at some distance; but there were such a number of things to occupy my reflections that I hardly gave the circumstance a thought, though it was a strange sound, in that place, at two o'clock in the morning.

Mr. Kenneth was fortunately just issuing from his house to see a patient in the village as I came up the street; and my account of Catherine Linton's malady induced him to accompany me back immediately.

He was a plain, rough man; and he made no scruple to speak his doubts of her surviving this second attack, unless she were more submissive to his directions than she had shown herself before.

"Nelly Dean," said he, "I can't help fancying there's an extra cause for this. What has there been to do at the Grange? We've odd reports up here. A stout, hearty lass like Catherine does not fall ill for a trifle; and that sort of people should not either. It's hard work bringing them through fevers, and such things. How did it begin?"

"The master will inform you," I answered; "but you are acquainted with the Earnshaws' violent dispositions, and Mrs. Linton caps them all. I may say this; it commenced in a quarrel. She was struck during a tempest of passion with a kind of fit. That's her account, at least; for she flew off in the height of it, and locked herself up. Afterwards, she refused to eat, and now she alternately raves and remains in a half dream, knowing those about her, but having her mind filled with all sorts of strange ideas and illusions."

"Mr. Linton will be sorry?" observed Kenneth, interrogatively.

"Sorry? He'll break his heart should anything happen!" I replied. "Don't alarm him more than necessary."

"Well, I told him to beware," said my companion, "and he must bide the consequences of neglecting my warning! Hasn't he been thick with Mr. Heathcliff lately?"

"Heathcliff frequently visits at the Grange," answered I, "though more on the strength of the mistress having known him when a boy, than because the master likes his company. At present, he's discharged from the trouble of calling; owing to some presumptuous aspirations after Miss Linton which he manifested. I hardly think he'll be taken in again."

"And does Miss Linton turn a cold shoulder on him?" was the doctor's next question.

"I'm not in her confidence," returned I, reluctant to continue the subject.

"No, she's a sly one," he remarked, shaking his head. "She keeps her own counsel! But she's a real little fool. I have it from good authority that last night (and a pretty night it was!) she and Heathcliff were walking in the plantation at the back of your house, above two hours; and he pressed her not to go in again, but just mount his horse and away with him! My informant said she could only put him off by pledging her word of honour to be prepared on their first meeting after that: when it was to be, he didn't hear, but you urge Mr. Linton to look sharp!"

This news filled me with fresh fears; I outstripped Kenneth, and ran most of the way back. The little dog was yelping in the garden yet. I spared a minute to open the gate for it, but instead of going to the house door, it coursed up and down snuffing the grass, and would have escaped to the road, had I not seized and conveyed it in with me.

On ascending to Isabella's room, my suspicions were confirmed: it was empty. Had I been a few hours sooner, Mrs. Linton's illness might have arrested her rash step. But what could be done now? There was a bare possibility of overtaking them if pursued instantly. *I* could not pursue them, however; and I dare not rouse the family, and fill the place with confusion; still less unfold the business to my master, absorbed as he was in his present calamity, and having no heart to spare for a second grief!

I saw nothing for it but to hold my tongue, and suffer matters to take their course; and Kenneth being arrived, I went with a badly composed countenance to announce him.

Catherine lay in a troubled sleep; her husband had succeeded in soothing the access of frenzy; he now hung over her pillow, watching every shade, and every change of her painfully expressive features.

The doctor, on examining the case for himself, spoke hopefully to him of its having a favourable termination, if we could only preserve around her perfect and constant tranquillity. To me, he signified the threatening danger was not so much death, as permanent alienation of intellect.

I did not close my eyes that night, nor did Mr. Linton; indeed, we never went to bed; and the servants were all up long before the usual hour, moving through the house with stealthy tread, and exchanging whispers as they encountered each other in their vocations. Every one was active but Miss Isabella; and they began to remark how sound she slept. Her brother too asked if she had risen, and seemed impatient for her presence, and hurt that she showed so little anxiety for her sister-in-law.

I trembled lest he should send me to call her; but I was spared the pain of being the first proclaimant of her flight. One of the maids, a thoughtless girl, who had been on an early errand to Gimmerton, came panting upstairs, open-mouthed, and dashed into the chamber, crying—

"Oh, dear, dear! What mun we have next? Master, master, our young lady—"

"Hold your noise!" cried I hastily, enraged at her clamorous manner.

"Speak lower, Mary—What is the matter?" said Mr. Linton. "What ails your young lady?"

"She's gone, she's gone! Yon' Heathcliff's run off wi' her!" gasped the girl.

"That is not true!" exclaimed Linton, rising in agitation. "It cannot be—how has the idea entered your head? Ellen Dean, go and seek her—it is incredible—it cannot be."

As he spoke he took the servant to the door, and then repeated his demand to know her reasons for such an assertion.

"Why, I met on the road a lad that fetches milk here," she stammered, "and he asked whether we wern't in trouble at the Grange. I thought he meant for Missis's sickness, so I answered, yes. Then, says he, 'They's somebody gone after 'em, I guess?' I stared. He saw I knew naught about it, and he told how a gentleman and lady had stopped to have a horse's shoe fastened at a blacksmith's shop, two miles out of Gimmerton, not very long after midnight! and how the blacksmith's lass had got up to spy who they were: she knew them both directly. And she noticed the man—Heathcliff it was, she felt certain, nob'dy could mistake him, besides—put a sovereign in her father's hand for payment. The lady had a cloak about her face; but having desired a sup of water, while she drank, it fell back, and she saw her very plain. Heathcliff held both bridles as they rode on, and they set their faces from the village, and went as fast as the rough roads would let them. The lass said nothing to her father, but she told it all over Gimmerton this morning."

I ran and peeped, for form's sake, into Isabella's room: confirming, when I returned, the servant's statement. Mr. Linton had resumed his seat by the bed; on my re-entrance, he raised his eyes, read the meaning of my blank aspect, and dropped them without giving an order, or uttering a word.

"Are we to try any measures for overtaking and bringing her back?" I inquired. "How should we do?"

"She went of her own accord," answered the master; "she had a right to go if she pleased. Trouble me no more about her. Hereafter she is only my sister in name, not because I disown her, but because she has disowned me."

And that was all he said on the subject; he did not make a single inquiry further, or mention her in any way, except directing me to send what property she had in the house to her fresh home, wherever it was, when I knew it.

CHAPTER 13

For two months the fugitives remained absent; in those two months, Mrs. Linton encountered and conquered the worst shock of what was denominated a brain fever. No mother could have nursed an only child more devotedly than Edgar tended her. Day and night, he was watching, and patiently enduring all the annoyances that irritable nerves and a shaken reason could inflict; and, though Kenneth remarked that what he saved from the grave would only recompense his care by forming the source of constant future anxiety—in fact, that his health and strength were being sacrificed to preserve a mere ruin of humanity—he knew no limits in gratitude and joy when Catherine's life was declared out of danger; and hour after hour he would sit beside her, tracing the gradual return to bodily health, and flattering his too sanguine hopes with the illusion that her mind would settle back to its right balance also, and she would soon be entirely her former self.

The first time she left her chamber was at the commencement of the following March. Mr. Linton had put on her pillow, in the morning, a handful of golden crocuses; her eye, long stranger to any gleam of pleasure, caught them in waking, and shone delighted as she gathered them eagerly together.

"These are the earliest flowers at the Heights!" she exclaimed. "They remind me of soft thaw winds, and warm sunshine, and nearly melted snow. Edgar, is there not a south wind, and is not the snow almost gone?"

"The snow is quite gone down here, darling," replied her husband, "and I only see two white spots on the whole range of moors. The sky is blue, and the larks are singing, and the becks and brooks are all brim full. Catherine, last spring at this time, I was longing to have you under this roof; now, I wish you were a mile or two up those hills; the air blows so sweetly, I feel that it would cure you."

"I shall never be there, but once more!" said the invalid, "and then you'll leave me, and I shall remain for ever. Next spring you'll long again to have me under this roof, and you'll look back and think you were happy to-day."

Linton lavished on her the kindest caresses, and tried to cheer her by the fondest words; but, vaguely regarding the flowers, she let the tears collect on her lashes and stream down her cheeks unheeding.

We knew she was really better, and, therefore, decided that long confinement to a single place produced much of this despondency, and it might be partially removed by a change of scene.

The master told me to light a fire in the many-weeks-deserted parlour, and to set an easy-chair in the sunshine by the window; and then he brought her down, and she sat a long while enjoying the genial heat, and, as we expected, revived by the objects round her, which, though familiar, were free from the dreary associations investing her hated sickchamber. By evening, she seemed greatly exhausted; yet no arguments could persuade her to return to that apartment, and I had to arrange the parlour sofa for her bed, till another room could be prepared.

To obviate the fatigue of mounting and descending the stairs, we fitted up this, where you lie at present, on the same floor with the parlour; and she was soon strong enough to move from one to the other, leaning on Edgar's arm.

Ah, I thought myself, she might recover, so waited on as she was. And there was double cause to desire it, for on her existence depended that of another; we cherished the hope that in a little while Mr. Linton's heart would be gladdened, and his lands secured from a stranger's gripe, by the birth of an heir.

I should mention that Isabella sent to her brother, some six weeks from her departure, a short note, announcing her marriage with Heathcliff. It appeared dry and cold; but at the bottom was dotted in with pencil an obscure apology, and an entreaty for kind remembrance and reconciliation, if her proceeding had offended him; asserting that she could not help it then, and being done, she had now no power to repeal it.

Linton did not reply to this, I believe; and, in a fortnight more, I got a long letter, which I considered odd coming from the pen of a bride just out of the honeymoon. I'll read it, for I keep it yet. Any relic of the dead is precious, if they were valued living.

Dear Ellen, it begins.

I came last night to Wuthering Heights, and heard, for the first time, that Catherine has been, and is yet, very ill. I must not write to her, I suppose, and my brother is either too angry or too distressed to answer what I send him. Still, I must write to somebody, and the only choice left me is you.

Inform Edgar that I'd give the world to see his face again—-that my heart returned to Thrushcross Grange in twenty-four hours after I left it, and is there at this moment, full of warm feelings for him, and Catherine! *I can't follow it, though* –(those words are underlined)—they need not expect me, and they may draw what conclusions they please; taking care, however, to lay nothing at the door of my weak will or deficient affection.

The remainder of the letter is for yourself alone. I want to ask you two questions: the first is—

How did you contrive to preserve the common sympathies of human nature when you resided here? I cannot recognise any sentiment which those around share with me.

The second question, I have great interest in; it is this—

Is Mr. Heathcliff a man? If so, is he mad? And if not, is he a devil? I shan't tell my reasons for making this inquiry; but I beseech you to explain, if you can, what I have married—that is, when you call to see me; and you must call, Ellen, very soon. Don't write, but come, and bring me something from Edgar.

Now, you shall hear how I have been received in my new home, as I am led to imagine the Heights will be. It is to amuse myself that I dwell on such subjects as the lack of external comforts; they never occupy my thoughts, except at the moment when I miss them. I should laugh and dance for joy, if I found their absence was the total of my miseries, and the rest was an unnatural dream!

The sun set behind the Grange, as we turned on to the moors; by that, I judged it to be six o'clock; and my companion halted half-an-hour, to inspect the park, and the gardens, and, probably, the place itself, as well as he could; so it was dark when we dismounted in the paved yard of the farmhouse, and your old fellow-servant, Joseph, issued out to receive us by the light of a dip candle. He did it with a courtesy that redounded to his credit. His first act was to elevate his torch to a level with my face, squint malignantly, project his under-lip, and turn away.

Then he took the two horses, and led them into the stables; reappearing for the purpose of locking the outer gate, as if we lived in an ancient castle.

Heathcliff stayed to speak to him, and I entered the kitchen—a dingy, untidy hole; I dare say you would not know it, it is so changed since it was in your charge.

By the fire stood a ruffianly child, strong in limb and dirty in garb, with a look of Catherine in his eyes and about his mouth.

"This is Edgar's legal nephew," I reflected—"mine in a manner; I must shake hands, and—yes—I must kiss him. It is right to establish a good understanding at the beginning."

I approached, and, attempting to take his chubby fist, said—

"How do you do, my dear?"

He replied in a jargon I did not comprehend.

"Shall you and I be friends, Hareton?" was my next essay at conversation.

An oath, and a threat to set Throttler on me if I did not "frame off," rewarded my perseverance.

"Hey, Throttler, lad!" whispered the little wretch, rousing a half-bred bull-dog from its lair in a corner. "Now, wilt tuh be ganging?" he asked authoritatively.

Love for my life urged a compliance; I stepped over the threshold to wait till the others should enter. Mr. Heathcliff was nowhere visible; and Joseph, whom I followed to the stables and requested to accompany me in, after staring and muttering to himself, screwed up his nose and replied—

"Mim! mim! mim! Did iver Christian body hear owt like it? Minching un' munching! Hah can Aw tell whet ye say?"[25]

"I say, I wish you to come with me into the house!" I cried, thinking him deaf, yet highly disgusted at his rudeness.

"Nor nuh me![26] Aw getten summut else to do," he answered, and continued his work, moving his lantern jaws meanwhile, and surveying my dress and countenance (the former a great deal too fine, but the latter, I'm sure, as sad as he could desire) with sovereign contempt.

I walked round the yard, and through a wicket, to another door, at which I took the liberty of knocking, in hopes some more civil servant might shew himself.

After a short suspense, it was opened by a tall, gaunt man, without neckerchief, and otherwise extremely slovenly; his features were lost in masses of shaggy hair that

---

[25] *Minching un' munching:* mincing and mouthing.
[26] *Nor nuh me:* not me.

hung on his shoulders; and *his* eyes, too, were like a ghostly Catherine's, with all their beauty annihilated.

"What's your business here?" he demanded, grimly. "Who are you?"

"My name *was* Isabella Linton," I replied. "You've seen me before, sir. I'm lately married to Mr. Heathcliff; and he has brought me here—I suppose by your permission."

"Is he come back, then?" asked the hermit, glaring like a hungry wolf.

"Yes—we came just now," I said; "but he left me by the kitchen door; and when I would have gone in, your little boy played sentinel over the place, and frightened me off by the help of a bull-dog."

"It's well the hellish villain has kept his word!" growled my future host, searching the darkness beyond me in expectation of discovering Heathcliff; and then he indulged in a soliloquy of execrations, and threats of what he would have done had the "fiend" deceived him.

I repented having tried this second entrance, and was almost inclined to slip way before he finished cursing, but ere I could execute that intention, he ordered me in, and shut and re-fastened the door.

There was a great fire, and that was all the light in the huge apartment, whose floor had grown a uniform grey; and the once brilliant pewter dishes, which used to attract my gaze when I was a girl, partook of a similar obscurity, created by tarnish and dust.

I inquired whether I might call the maid, and be conducted to a bed-room? Mr. Earnshaw vouchsafed no answer. He walked up and down, with his hands in his pockets, apparently quite forgetting my presence; and his abstraction was evidently so deep, and his whole aspect so misanthropical, that I shrank from disturbing him again.

You'll not be surprised, Ellen, at my feeling particularly cheerless, seated in worse than solitude on that inhospitable hearth, and remembering that four miles distant lay my delightful home, containing the only people I loved on earth; and there might as well be the Atlantic to part us, instead of those four miles: I could not overpass them!

I questioned with myself—where must I turn for comfort? and—mind you don't tell Edgar, or Catherine—above every sorrow beside, this rose pre-eminent—despair at finding nobody who could or would be my ally against Heathcliff!

I had sought shelter at Wuthering Heights, almost gladly, because I was secured by that arrangement from living alone with him; but he knew the people we were coming amongst, and he did not fear their intermeddling.

I sat and thought a doleful time; the clock struck eight, and nine, and still my companion paced to and fro, his head bent on his breast, and perfectly silent, unless a groan or a bitter ejaculation forced itself out at intervals.

I listened to detect a woman's voice in the house, and filled the interim with wild regrets and dismal anticipations, which, at last, spoke audibly in irrepressible sighing and weeping.

I was not aware how openly I grieved, till Earnshaw halted opposite, in his measured walk, and gave me a stare of newly awakened surprise. Taking advantage of his recovered attention, I exclaimed—

"I'm tired with my journey, and I want to go to bed! Where is the maid-servant? Direct me to her, as she won't come to me!"

"We have none," he answered; "you must wait on yourself!"

"Where must I sleep, then?" I sobbed—I was beyond regarding self-respect, weighed down by fatigue and wretchedness.

"Joseph will show you Heathcliff's chamber," said he; "open that door—he's in there."

I was going to obey, but he suddenly arrested me, and added in the strangest tone—

"Be so good as to turn your lock, and draw your bolt—don't omit it!"

"Well!" I said. "But why, Mr. Earnshaw?" I did not relish the notion of deliberately fastening myself in with Heathcliff.

"Look here!" he replied, pulling from his waistcoat a curiously constructed pistol, having a double-edged spring knife attached to the barrel. "That's a great tempter to a desperate man, is it not? I cannot resist going up with this, every night, and trying his door. If once I find it open, he's done for! I do it invariably, even though the minute before I have been recalling a hundred reasons that should make me refrain: it is some devil that urges me to thwart my own schemes by killing him. You fight against that devil, for love, as long as you may; when the time comes, not all the angels in heaven shall save him!"

I surveyed the weapon inquisitively; a hideous notion struck me. How powerful I should be possessing such an instrument! I took it from his hand, and touched the blade. He looked astonished at the expression my face assumed during a brief second. It was not horror, it was covetousness. He snatched the pistol back, jealously; shut the knife, and returned it to its concealment.

"I don't care if you tell him," said he. "Put him on his guard, and watch for him. You know the terms we are on, I see; his danger does not shock you."

"What has Heathcliff done to you?" I asked. "In what has he wronged you to warrant this appalling hatred? Wouldn't it be wiser to bid him quit the house?"

"No," thundered Earnshaw; "should he offer to leave me, he's a dead man: persuade him to attempt it, and you are a murderess! Am I to lose *all*, without a chance of retrieval? Is Hareton to be a beggar? Oh, damnation! I *will* have it back; and I'll have *his* gold too; and then his blood; and hell shall have his soul! It will be ten times blacker with that guest than ever it was before!"

You've acquainted me, Ellen, with your old master's habits. He is clearly on the verge of madness—he was so last night, at least. I shuddered to be near him, and thought on the servant's ill-bred moroseness as comparatively agreeable.

He now recommenced his moody walk, and I raised the latch, and escaped into the kitchen.

Joseph was bending over the fire, peering into a large pan that swung above it; and a wooden bowl of oatmeal stood on the settle close by. The contents of the pan began to boil, and he turned to plunge his hand into the bowl; I conjectured that this preparation was probably for our supper, and, being hungry, I resolved it should be eatable; so, crying out sharply, "*I'll* make the porridge!" I removed the vessel out of his reach, and proceeded to take off my hat and riding habit. "Mr. Earnshaw," I continued, "directs me to wait on myself: I will. I'm not going to act the lady among you, for fear I should starve."

"Gooid Lord!" he muttered, sitting down, and stroking his ribbed stockings from the knee to the ankle. "If they's tuh be fresh ortherings—just when Aw getten used tuh two maisters, if Aw mun hev a *mistress* set o'er my heead, it's loike time tuh be flitting. Aw niver *did* think tuh say t' day ut Aw mud lave th' owld place—but Aw daht it's nigh at hend!"[27]

This lamentation drew no notice from me; I went briskly to work, sighing to remember a period when it would have been all merry fun, but compelled speedily to drive off the remembrance. It racked me to recall past happiness, and the greater

---

[27] *Aw daht:* I don't doubt; *at hend:* at hand.

peril there was of conjuring up its apparition, the quicker the thible[28] ran round, and the faster the handfuls of meal fell into the water.

Joseph beheld my style of cookery with growing indignation.

"Thear!" he ejaculated. "Hareton, thah willut sup thy porridge tuh neeght; they'll be nowt bud lumps as big as maw nave. Thear, agean! Aw'd fling in bowl un all, if Aw wer yah! Thear, pale t' guilp off, un' then yah'll hae done wi't. Bang, bang. It's a marcy t' bothom isn't deaved aht!"[29]

It *was* rather a rough mess, I own, when poured into the basins; four had been provided, and a gallon pitcher of new milk was brought from the dairy, which Hareton seized and commenced drinking and spilling from the expansive lip.

I expostulated, and desired that he should have his in a mug; affirming that I could not taste the liquid treated so dirtily. The old cynic chose to be vastly offended at this nicety; assuring me, repeatedly, that "the barn was every bit as gooid" as I, "and every bit as wollsome," and wondering how I could fashion to be so conceited; meanwhile, the infant ruffian continued sucking; and glowered up at me defyingly, as he slavered into the jug.

"I shall have my supper in another room," I said. "Have you no place you call a parlour?"

"*Parlour!*" he echoed, sneeringly, "*parlour!* Nay, we've noa *parlours.* If yah dunnut loike wer company, they's maister's; un' if yah dunnut loike maister, they's us."

"Then I shall go upstairs," I answered; "shew me a chamber!"

I put my basin on a tray, and went myself to fetch some more milk.

With great grumblings, the fellow rose and preceded me in my ascent: we mounted to the garrets, he opening a door, now and then, to look into the apartments we passed.

"Here's a rahm," he said, at last, flinging back a cranky board on hinges. "It's weel eneugh tuh ate a few porridge in. They's a pack uh corn i' t' corner, thear, meeterly clane; if yah're feared uh muckying yer grand silk cloes, spread yer hankerchir ut t' top on't."[30]

The "rahm" was a kind of lumber-hole smelling strong of malt and grain; various sacks of which articles were piled around, leaving a wide, bare space in the middle.

"Why, man!" I exclaimed, facing him angrily, "this is not a place to sleep in. I wish to see my bed-room."

"*Bed-rume!*" he repeated, in a tone of mockery. "Yah's see all t' *bed-rumes* thear is—yon's mine."

He pointed into the second garret, only differing from the first in being more naked about the walls, and having a large, low, curtainless bed, with an indigo-coloured quilt, at one end.

"What do I want with yours?" I retorted. "I suppose Mr. Heathcliff does not lodge at the top of the house, does he?"

"Oh! it's Maister *Hathecliff's* yah're wenting?" cried he, as if making a new discovery. "Couldn't ye uh said soa, at onst? un then, Aw mud uh telled ye, 'baht all this wark,[31] ut that's just one yah cannut sea—he allas keeps it locked, un' nob'dy iver mells[32] on't but hisseln."

---

[28] A smooth stick for stirring broth or porridge.
[29] *Nave:* fist; *pale t' guilp off:* cool off the iron pot by taking out a ladleful and then dropping it in again; *deaved:* broken, stunned.
[30] *Meeterly clane:* fairly clean; *muckying:* dirtying.
[31] *'Baht all this wark:* without all this work.
[32] *Mells:* meddles.

"You've a nice house, Joseph," I could not refrain from observing, "and pleasant inmates; and I think the concentrated essence of all the madness in the world took up its abode in my brain the day I linked my fate with theirs! However, that is not to the present purpose—there are other rooms. For heaven's sake, be quick, and let me settle somewhere!"

He made no reply to this adjuration; only plodding doggedly down the wooden steps, and halting before an apartment which, from that halt and the superior quality of its furniture, I conjectured to be the best one.

There was a carpet, a good one; but the pattern was obliterated by dust; a fire-place hung with cut paper, dropping to pieces; a handsome oak-bedstead with ample crimson curtains of rather expensive material and modern make. But they had evidently experienced rough usage; the valances hung in festoons, wrenched from their rings, and the iron rod supporting them was bent in an arc on one side, causing the drapery to trail upon the floor. The chairs were also damaged, many of them severely; and deep indentations deformed the panels of the walls.

I was endeavouring to gather resolution for entering, and taking possession, when my fool of a guide announced—

"This here is t' maister's."

My supper by this time was cold, my appetite gone, and my patience exhausted. I insisted on being provided instantly with a place of refuge, and means of repose.

"Whear the divil—" began the religious elder. "The Lord bless us! The Lord forgie us! Whear the *hell* wold ye gang? ye marred, wearisome nowt![33] Yah seen all bud Hareton's bit uf a cham'er. They's nut another hoile tuh lig dahn in i' th' hahse!"

I was so vexed, I flung my tray and its contents on the ground; and then seated myself at the stairs-head, hid my face in my hands, and cried.

"Ech! ech!" exclaimed Joseph. "Weel done, Miss Cathy! weel done, Miss Cathy! Hahsiver, t' maister sall just tum'le o'er them brocken pots, un' then we's hear summut; we's hear hah it's tuh be. Gooid-fur-nowt madling! yah desarve pining froo this tuh Churstmas, flinging t' precious gifts uh God under fooit i' yer flaysome rages! Bud Aw'm mista'em if yah shew yer sperrit lang. Will Hathecliff bide sich bonny ways, think ye? Aw nobbut wish he muh cotch ye i' that plisky. Aw nobbut wish he may."[34]

And so he went scolding to his den beneath, taking the candle with him, and I remained in the dark.

The period of reflection succeeding this silly action compelled me to admit the necessity of smothering my pride, and choking my wrath, and bestirring myself to remove its effects.

An unexpected aid presently appeared in the shape of Throttler, whom I now recognised as a son of our old Skulker; it had spent its whelphood at the Grange, and was given by my father to Mr. Hindley. I fancy it knew me: it pushed its nose against mine by way of salute, and then hastened to devour the porridge, while I groped from step to step, collecting the shattered earthenware, and drying the spatters of milk from the banister with my pocket-handkerchief.

Our labours were scarcely over when I heard Earnshaw's tread in the passage; my assistant tucked in his tail, and pressed to the wall; I stole into the nearest doorway. The dog's endeavour to avoid him was unsuccessful, as I guessed by a

---

[33] *Marred, wearisome nowt:* spoiled, worrisome naught.
[34] *Pining:* starving; *plisky:* rage.

scutter downstairs, and a prolonged, piteous yelping. I had better luck. He passed on, entered his chamber, and shut the door.

Directly after, Joseph came up with Hareton, to put him to bed. I had found shelter in Hareton's room, and the old man, on seeing me, said—

"They's rahm fur boath yah un yer pride, nah, Aw sud think i' th' hahse. It's empty; yah muh hev it all tuh yerseln, un Him as allas maks a third, i' sich ill company!"

Gladly did I take advantage of this intimation; and the minute I flung myself into a chair, by the fire, I nodded, and slept.

My slumber was deep and sweet, though over far too soon. Mr. Heathcliff awoke me; he had just come in, and demanded, in his loving manner, what I was doing there?

I told him the cause of my staying up so late—that he had the key of our room in his pocket.

The adjective *our* gave mortal offence. He swore it was not, nor ever should be mine; and he'd—but I'll not repeat his language, nor describe his habitual conduct; he is ingenious and unresting in seeking to gain my abhorrence! I sometimes wonder at him with an intensity that deadens my fear: yet, I assure you, a tiger or a venomous serpent could not rouse terror in me equal to that which he wakens. He told me of Catherine's illness, and accused my brother of causing it; promising that I should be Edgar's proxy in suffering, till he could get a hold of him.

I do hate him—I am wretched—I have been a fool! Beware of uttering one breath of this to any one at the Grange. I shall expect you every day—don't disappoint me!

Isabella.

Chapter 14

As soon as I had perused this epistle, I went to the master, and informed him that his sister had arrived at the Heights, and sent me a letter expressing her sorrow for Mrs. Linton's situation, and her ardent desire to see him; with a wish that he would transmit to her, as early as possible, some token of forgiveness by me.

"Forgiveness!" said Linton. "I have nothing to forgive her, Ellen. You may call at Wuthering Heights this afternoon, if you like, and say that I am not *angry*, but I'm *sorry* to have lost her: especially as I can never think she'll be happy. It is out of the question my going to see her, however; we are eternally divided; and should she really wish to oblige me, let her persuade the villain she has married to leave the country."

"And you won't write her a little note, sir?" I asked, imploringly.

"No," he answered. "It is needless. My communication with Heathcliff's family shall be as sparing as his with mine. It shall not exist!"

Mr. Edgar's coldness depressed me exceedingly; and all the way from the Grange I puzzled my brains how to put more heart into what he said, when I repeated it; and how to soften his refusal of even a few lines to console Isabella.

I dare say she had been on the watch for me since morning. I saw her looking through the lattice, as I came up the garden causeway, and I nodded to her; but she drew back, as if afraid of being observed.

I entered without knocking. There never was such a dreary, dismal scene as the formerly cheerful house presented! I must confess that, if I had been in the young lady's place, I would, at least, have swept the hearth and wiped the tables with a duster. But she already partook of the pervading spirit of neglect which encompassed her. Her pretty face was wan and listless; her hair uncurled, some locks hanging lankly down, and some carelessly twisted round her head. Probably she had not touched her dress since yester evening.

Hindley was not there. Mr. Heathcliff sat at a table, turning over some papers in his pocket-book; but he rose when I appeared, asked me how I did, quite friendly, and offered me a chair.

He was the only thing there that seemed decent, and I thought he never looked better. So much had circumstances altered their positions, that he would certainly have struck a stranger as a born and bred gentleman, and his wife as a thorough little slattern!

She came forward eagerly to greet me; and held out one hand to take the expected letter.

I shook my head. She wouldn't understand the hint, but followed me to a sideboard, where I went to lay my bonnet, and importuned me in a whisper to give her directly what I had brought.

Heathcliff guessed the meaning of her manœuvres, and said—

"If you have got anything for Isabella, as no doubt you have, Nelly, give it to her. You needn't make a secret of it; we have no secrets between us."

"Oh, I have nothing," I replied, thinking it best to speak the truth at once. "My master bid me tell his sister that she must not expect either a letter or a visit from him at present. He sends his love, ma'am, and his wishes for your happiness, and his pardon for the grief you have occasioned; but he thinks that after this time, his household, and the household here, should drop intercommunication, as nothing good could come of keeping it up."

Mrs. Heathcliff's lip quivered slightly, and she returned to her seat in the window. Her husband took his stand on the hearthstone, near me, and began to put questions concerning Catherine.

I told him as much as I thought proper of her illness, and he extorted from me, by cross-examination, most of the facts connected with its origin.

I blamed her, as she deserved, for bringing it all on herself; and ended by hoping that he would follow Mr. Linton's example, and avoid future interference with his family, for good or evil.

"Mrs. Linton is now just recovering," I said; "she'll never be like she was, but her life is spared, and if you really have a regard for her, you'll shun crossing her way again. Nay, you'll move out of this country entirely; and that you may not regret it, I'll inform you Catherine Linton is as different now from your old friend Catherine Earnshaw, as that young lady is different from me! Her appearance is changed greatly, her character much more so; and the person who is compelled, of necessity, to be her companion, will only sustain his affection hereafter by the remembrance of what she once was, by common humanity, and a sense of duty!"

"That is quite possible," remarked Heathcliff, forcing himself to seem calm, "quite possible that your master should have nothing but common humanity, and a sense of duty to fall back upon. But do you imagine that I shall leave Catherine to his *duty* and *humanity?* and can you compare my feelings respecting Catherine, to his? Before you leave this house, I must exact a promise from you, that you'll get me an interview with her: consent, or refuse, I *will* see her! What do you say?"

"I say, Mr. Heathcliff," I replied, "you must not—you never shall, through my means. Another encounter between you and the master would kill her altogether!"

"With your aid that may be avoided," he continued, "and should there be danger of such an event—should he be the cause of adding a single trouble more to her existence—why, I think, I shall be justified in going to extremes! I wish you had sincerity enough to tell me whether Catherine would suffer greatly from his loss. The fear that she would restrains me: and there you see the distinction between our feelings. Had he been in my place, and I in his, though I hated him with a hatred that turned my life to gall, I never would have raised a hand against him. You may look incredulous, if you please! I never would have banished him from her society, as long as she desired his. The moment her regard ceased, I would have torn his heart out, and drank his blood! But, till then—if you don't believe me, you don't know me—till then, I would have died by inches before I touched a single hair of his head!"

"And yet," I interrupted, "you have no scruples in completely ruining all hopes of her perfect restoration, by thrusting yourself into her remembrance, now, when she has nearly forgotten you, and involving her in a new tumult of discord and distress."

"You suppose she has nearly forgotten me?" he said. "Oh, Nelly! you know she has not! You know as well as I do, that for every thought she spends on Linton, she spends a thousand on me! At a most miserable period of my life, I had a notion of the kind; it haunted me on my return to the neighbourhood last summer, but only her own assurance could make me admit the horrible idea again. And then, Linton would be nothing, nor Hindley, nor all the dreams that ever I dreamt. Two words would comprehend my future—*death* and *hell*; existence, after losing her, would be hell.

"Yet I was a fool to fancy for a moment that she valued Edgar Linton's attachment more than mine. If he loved with all the powers of his puny being, he couldn't love as much in eighty years as I could in a day. And Catherine has a heart as deep as I have; the sea could be as readily contained in that horse-trough, as her whole affection be monopolized by him. Tush! He is scarcely a degree dearer to her than her dog, or her horse. It is not in him to be loved like me: how can she love in him what he has not?"

"Catherine and Edgar are as fond of each other as any two people can be!" cried Isabella, with sudden vivacity. "No one has a right to talk in that manner, and I won't hear my brother depreciated in silence!"

"Your brother is wondrous fond of you too, isn't he?" observed Heathcliff scornfully. "He turns you adrift on the world with surprising alacrity."

"He is not aware of what I suffer," she replied. "I didn't tell him that."

"You have been telling him something, then—you have written, have you?"

"To say that I was married, I did write—you saw the note."

"And nothing since?"

"No."

"My young lady is looking sadly the worse for her change of condition," I remarked. "Somebody's love comes short in her case, obviously—whose I may guess; but, perhaps, I shouldn't say."

"I should guess it was her own," said Heathcliff. "She degenerates into a mere slut! She is tired of trying to please me, uncommonly early. You'd hardly credit it, but the very morrow of our wedding, she was weeping to go home. However, she'll suit this house so much the better for not being over nice, and I'll take care she does not disgrace me by rambling abroad."

"Well, sir," returned I, "I hope you'll consider that Mrs. Heathcliff is accustomed to be looked after and waited on; and that she has been brought up like an only daughter, whom every one was ready to serve. You must let her have a maid to keep things tidy about her, and you must treat her kindly. Whatever be your notion of Mr. Edgar, you cannot doubt that she has a capacity for strong attachments, or she wouldn't have abandoned the elegancies, and comforts, and friends of her former home, to fix contentedly, in such a wilderness as this, with you."

"She abandoned them under a delusion," he answered, "picturing in me a hero of romance, and expecting unlimited indulgences from my chivalrous devotion. I can hardly regard her in the light of a rational creature, so obstinately has she persisted in forming a fabulous notion of my character, and acting on the false impressions she cherished. But, at last, I think she begins to know me. I don't perceive the silly smiles and grimaces that provoked me at first; and the senseless incapability of discerning that I was in earnest when I gave her my opinion of her infatuation, and herself. It was a marvellous effort of perspicacity to discover that I did not love her. I believed, at one time, no lessons could teach her that! And yet it is poorly learnt; for this morning she announced, as a piece of appalling intelligence, that I had actually succeeded in making her hate me! A positive labour of Hercules, I assure you! If it be achieved, I have cause to return thanks. Can I trust your assertion, Isabella? Are you sure you hate me? If I let you alone for half-a-day, won't you come sighing and wheedling to me again? I dare say she would rather I had seemed all tenderness before you; it wounds her vanity, to have the truth exposed. But I don't care who knows that the passion was wholly on one side, and I never told her a lie about it. She cannot accuse me of showing one bit of deceitful softness. The first thing she saw me do, on coming out of the Grange, was to hang up her little dog; and when she pleaded for it the first words I uttered were a wish that I had the hanging of every being belonging to her, except one: possibly she took that exception for herself. But no brutality disgusted her. I suppose she has an innate admiration of it, if only her precious person were secure from injury! Now, was it not the depth of absurdity—of genuine idiocy—for that pitiful, slavish, mean-minded brach[35] to dream that I could love her? Tell your master, Nelly, that I never, in all my life, met with such an abject thing as she is. She even disgraces the name of Linton; and I've sometimes relented, from pure lack of invention, in my experiments on what she could endure, and still creep shamefully cringing back! But tell him, also, to set his fraternal and magisterial heart at ease, that I keep strictly within the limits of the law. I have avoided, up to this period, giving her the slightest right to claim a separation; and, what's more, she'd thank nobody for dividing us. If she desired to go she might: the nuisance of her presence outweighs the gratification to be derived from tormenting her!"

"Mr. Heathcliff," said I, "this is the talk of a madman, and your wife, most likely, is convinced you are mad; and, for that reason, she has borne with you hitherto: but now that you say she may go, she'll doubtless avail herself of the permission. You are not so bewitched, ma'am, are you, as to remain with him of your own accord?"

"Take care, Ellen!" answered Isabella, her eyes sparkling irefully; there was no misdoubting by their expression, the full success of her partner's endeavours to make himself detested. "Don't put faith in a single word he speaks. He's a lying fiend, a monster, and not a human being! I've been told I might leave him before; and I've made the attempt, but I dare not repeat it! Only, Ellen, promise you'll not mention a syllable of his infamous conversation to my brother or Catherine. Whatever he may pretend, he wishes to provoke Edgar to desperation: he says he has married me on purpose to obtain power over him; and he shan't obtain it—I'll die first! I just hope, I pray, that he may forget his diabolical prudence, and kill me! The single pleasure I can imagine is to die, or to see him dead!"

"There—that will do for the present!" said Heathcliff. "If you are called upon in a court of law, you'll remember her language, Nelly! And take a good look at that countenance—she's near the point which would suit me. No, you're not fit to

---

[35] *Brach:* bitch-hound.

be your own guardian, Isabella, now; and I, being your legal protector, must retain you in my custody, however distasteful the obligation may be. Go upstairs; I have something to say to Ellen Dean in private. That's not the way—upstairs, I tell you! Why, this is the road upstairs, child!"

He seized, and thrust her from the room; and returned muttering—

"I have no pity! I have no pity! The more the worms writhe, the more I yearn to crush out their entrails! It is a moral teething, and I grind with greater energy, in proportion to the increase of pain."

"Do you understand what the word pity means?" I said, hastening to resume my bonnet. "Did you ever feel a touch of it in your life?"

"Put that down!" he interrupted, perceiving my intention to depart. "You are not going yet. Come here now, Nelly: I must either persuade or compel you to aid me in fulfilling my determination to see Catherine, and that without delay. I swear that I meditate no harm; I don't desire to cause any disturbance, or to exasperate or insult Mr. Linton; I only wish to hear from herself how she is, and why she has been ill; and to ask if anything that I could do would be of use to her. Last night, I was in the Grange garden six hours, and I'll return there to-night; and every night I'll haunt the place, and every day, till I find an opportunity of entering. If Edgar Linton meets me, I shall not hesitate to knock him down, and give him enough to ensure his quiescence while I stay. If his servants oppose me, I shall threaten them off with these pistols. But wouldn't it be better to prevent my coming in contact with them, or their master? And you could do it so easily! I'd warn you when I came, and then you might let me in unobserved, as soon as she was alone, and watch till I departed, your conscience quite calm: you would be hindering mischief."

I protested against playing that treacherous part in my employer's house; and besides, I urged the cruelty and selfishness of his destroying Mrs. Linton's tranquillity, for his satisfaction.

"The commonest occurrence startles her painfully," I said. "She's all nerves, and she couldn't bear the surprise, I'm positive. Don't persist, sir! or else, I shall be obliged to inform my master of your designs, and he'll take measures to secure his house and its inmates from any such unwarrantable intrusions!"

"In that case, I'll take measures to secure you, woman!" exclaimed Heathcliff; "you shall not leave Wuthering Heights till to-morrow morning. It is a foolish story to assert that Catherine could not bear to see me; and as to surprising her, I don't desire it: you must prepare her—ask her if I may come. You say she never mentions my name, and that I am never mentioned to her. To whom should she mention me if I am a forbidden topic in the house? She thinks you are all spies for her husband. Oh, I've no doubt she's in hell among you! I guess by her silence, as much as any thing, what she feels. You say she is often restless, and anxious-looking—is that a proof of tranquillity? You talk of her mind being unsettled. How the devil could it be otherwise, in her frightful isolation. And that insipid, paltry creature attending her from *duty* and *humanity*! From *pity* and *charity*! He might as well plant an oak in a flowerpot, and expect it to thrive, as imagine he can restore her to vigour in the soil of his shallow cares! Let us settle it at once; will you stay here, and am I to fight my way to Catherine over Linton and his footmen? Or will you be my friend, as you have been hitherto, and do what I request? Decide! because there is no reason for my lingering another minute, if you persist in your stubborn ill-nature!"

Well, Mr. Lockwood, I argued and complained, and flatly refused him fifty times; but in the long run he forced me to an agreement. I engaged to carry a letter from him to my mistress; and should she consent, I promised to let him have intelligence of Linton's next absence from home, when he might come, and get in as he was able. I wouldn't be there, and my fellow servants should be equally out of the way.

Was it right or wrong? I fear it was wrong, though expedient. I thought I prevented another explosion by my compliance; and I thought, too, it might create a favourable crisis in Catherine's mental illness: and then I remembered Mr. Edgar's stern rebuke of my carrying tales; and I tried to smooth away all disquietude on the subject, by affirming, with frequent iteration, that that betrayal of trust, if it merited so harsh an appellation, should be the last.

Notwithstanding, my journey homeward was sadder than my journey thither; and many misgivings I had, ere I could prevail on myself to put the missive into Mrs. Linton's hand.

But here is Kenneth; I'll go down, and tell him how much better you are. My history is *dree*[36] as we say, and will serve to wile away another morning.

Dree, and dreary! I reflected as the good woman descended to receive the doctor; and not exactly of the kind which I should have chosen to amuse me. But never mind! I'll extract wholesome medicines from Mrs. Dean's bitter herbs; and firstly, let me beware of the fascination that lurks in Catherine Heathcliff's brilliant eyes. I should be in a curious taking if I surrendered my heart to that young person, and the daughter turned out a second edition of the mother!

CHAPTER 15

Another week over—and I am so many days nearer health, and spring! I have now heard all my neighbour's history, at different sittings, as the housekeeper could spare time from more important occupations. I'll continue it in her own words, only a little condensed. She is, on the whole, a very fair narrator and I don't think I could improve her style.

In the evening, she said, the evening of my visit to the Heights, I knew, as well as if I saw him, that Mr. Heathcliff was about the place; and I shunned going out, because I still carried his letter in my pocket, and didn't want to be threatened, or teased any more.

I had made up my mind not to give it till my master went somewhere, as I could not guess how its receipt would affect Catherine. The consequence was, that it did not reach her before the lapse of three days. The fourth was Sunday, and I brought it into her room after the family were gone to church.

There was a man-servant left to keep the house with me, and we generally made a practice of locking the doors during the hours of service; but on that occasion the weather was so warm and pleasant that I set them wide open, and, to fulfil my engagement, as I knew who would be coming, I told my companion that the mistress wished very much for some oranges, and he must run over to the village and get a few, to be paid for on the morrow. He departed, and I went upstairs.

Mrs. Linton sat in a loose, white dress, with a light shawl over her shoulders, in the recess of the open window, as usual. Her thick, long hair had been partly removed at the beginning of her illness, and now she wore it simply combed in its natural tresses over her temples and neck. Her appearance was altered, as I had told Heathcliff, but when she was calm, there seemed unearthly beauty in the change.

The flash of her eyes had been succeeded by a dreamy and melancholy softness; they no longer gave the impression of looking at the objects around her; they appeared always to gaze beyond, and far beyond—you would have said out of

---

[36] *Dree:* sad.

this world. Then, the paleness of her face—its haggard aspect having vanished as she recovered flesh—and the peculiar expression arising from her mental state, though painfully suggestive of their causes, added to the touching interest which she wakened, and—invariably to me, I know, and to any person who saw her, I should think—refuted more tangible proofs of convalescence and stamped her as one doomed to decay.

A book lay spread on the sill before her, and the scarcely perceptible wind fluttered its leaves at intervals. I believe Linton had laid it there, for she never endeavoured to divert herself with reading, or occupation of any kind, and he would spend many an hour in trying to entice her attention to some subject which had formerly been her amusement.

She was conscious of his aim, and in her better moods endured his efforts placidly, only showing their uselessness by now and then suppressing a wearied sigh, and checking him at last with the saddest of smiles and kisses. At other times, she would turn petulantly away, and hide her face in her hands, or even push him off angrily; and then he took care to let her alone, for he was certain of doing no good.

Gimmerton chapel bells were still ringing; and the full, mellow flow of the beck in the valley came soothingly on the ear. It was a sweet substitute for the yet absent murmur of the summer foliage, which drowned that music about the Grange when the trees were in leaf. At Wuthering Heights it always sounded on quiet days, following a great thaw or a season of steady rain; and of Wuthering Heights, Catherine was thinking as she listened—that is, if she thought, or listened, at all—but she had the vague, distant look I mentioned before, which expressed no recognition of material things either by ear or eye.

"There's a letter for you, Mrs. Linton," I said, gently inserting it in one hand that rested on her knee. "You must read it immediately, because it wants an answer. Shall I break the seal?"

"Yes," she answered, without altering the direction of her eyes.

I opened it—it was very short.

"Now," I continued, "read it."

She drew away her hand, and let it fall. I replaced it in her lap, and stood waiting till it should please her to glance down; but that movement was so long delayed that at last I resumed—

"Must I read it, ma'am? It is from Mr. Heathcliff."

There was a start, and a troubled gleam of recollection, and a struggle to arrange her ideas. She lifted the letter, and seemed to peruse it; and when she came to the signature she sighed; yet still I found she had not gathered its import, for, upon my desiring to hear her reply, she merely pointed to the name, and gazed at me with mournful and questioning eagerness.

"Well, he wishes to see you," said I, guessing her need of an interpreter. "He's in the garden by this time, and impatient to know what answer I shall bring."

As I spoke, I observed a large dog, lying on the sunny grass beneath, raise its ears, as if about to bark, and then smoothing them back, announce by a wag of the tail that some one approached whom it did not consider a stranger.

Mrs. Linton bent forward, and listened breathlessly. The minute after, a step traversed the hall; the open house was too tempting for Heathcliff to resist walking in: most likely he supposed that I was inclined to shirk my promise, and so resolved to trust to his own audacity.

With straining eagerness Catherine gazed towards the entrance of her chamber. He did not hit the right room directly; she motioned me to admit him; but he found it out, ere I could reach the door, and in a stride or two was at her side, and had her grasped in his arms.

He neither spoke, nor loosed his hold, for some five minutes, during which period he bestowed more kisses than ever he gave in his life before, I dare say; but then my mistress had kissed him first, and I plainly saw that he could hardly bear, for downright agony, to look into her face! The same conviction had stricken him as me, from the instant he beheld her, that there was no prospect of ultimate recovery there—she was fated, sure to die.

"Oh, Cathy! Oh, my life! how can I bear it?" was the first sentence he uttered, in a tone that did not seek to disguise his despair.

And now he stared at her so earnestly that I thought the very intensity of his gaze would bring tears into his eyes; but they burned with anguish, they did not melt.

"What now?" said Catherine, leaning back, and returning his look with a suddenly clouded brow: her humour was a mere vane for constantly varying caprices. "You and Edgar have broken my heart, Heathcliff! And you both come to bewail the deed to me, as if you were the people to be pitied! I shall not pity you, not I. You have killed me—and thriven on it, I think. How strong you are! How many years do you mean to live after I am gone?"

Heathcliff had knelt on one knee to embrace her; he attempted to rise, but she seized his hair, and kept him down.

"I wish I could hold you," she continued, bitterly, "till we were both dead! I shouldn't care what you suffered. I care nothing for your sufferings. Why shouldn't you suffer? I do! Will you forget me—will you be happy when I am in the earth? Will you say twenty years hence, 'That's the grave of Catherine Earnshaw. I loved her long ago, and was wretched to lose her; but it is past. I've loved many others since—my children are dearer to me than she was, and, at death, I shall not rejoice that I am going to her, I shall be sorry that I must leave them!' Will you say so, Heathcliff?"

"Don't torture me till I'm as mad as yourself," cried he, wrenching his head free, and grinding his teeth.

The two, to a cool spectator, made a strange and fearful picture. Well might Catherine deem that heaven would be a land of exile to her, unless, with her mortal body, she cast away her mortal character also. Her present countenance had a wild vindictiveness in its white cheek, and a bloodless lip and scintillating eye; and she retained in her closed fingers a portion of the locks she had been grasping. As to her companion, while raising himself with one hand, he had taken her arm with the other; and so inadequate was his stock of gentleness to the requirements of her condition, that on his letting go, I saw four distinct impressions left blue in the colourless skin.

"Are you possessed with a devil," he pursued, savagely, "to talk in that manner to me, when you are dying? Do you reflect that all those words will be branded in my memory, and eating deeper eternally, after you have left me? You know you lie to say I have killed you; and, Catherine, you know that I could as soon forget you as my existence! Is it not sufficient for your infernal selfishness, that while you are at peace I shall writhe in the torments of hell?"

"I shall not be at peace," moaned Catherine, recalled to a sense of physical weakness by the violent, unequal throbbing of her heart, which beat visibly and audibly under this excess of agitation.

She said nothing further till the paroxysm was over; then she continued, more kindly—

"I'm not wishing you greater torment than I have, Heathcliff! I only wish us never to be parted—and should a word of mine distress you hereafter, think I feel the same distress underground, and for my own sake, forgive me! Come here and kneel down again! You never harmed me in your life. Nay, if you nurse anger, that will be worse to remember than my harsh words! Won't you come here again? Do!"

Heathcliff went to the back of her chair, and leant over, but not so far as to let her see his face, which was livid with emotion. She bent round to look at him; he would not permit it; turning abruptly, he walked to the fire-place, where he stood, silent, with his back towards us.

Mrs. Linton's glance followed him suspiciously: every movement woke a new sentiment in her. After a pause, and a prolonged gaze, she resumed, addressing me in accents of indignant disappointment—

"Oh, you see, Nelly! he would not relent a moment, to keep me out of the grave! *That* is how I'm loved! Well, never mind! That is not *my* Heathcliff. I shall love mine yet; and take him with me—he's in my soul. And," added she, musingly, "the thing that irks me most is this shattered prison, after all. I'm tired, tired of being enclosed here. I'm wearying to escape into that glorious world, and to be always there; not seeing it dimly through tears, and yearning for it through the walls of an aching heart; but really with it, and in it. Nelly, you think you are better and more fortunate than I; in full health and strength. You are sorry for me—very soon that will be altered. I shall be sorry for *you.* I shall be incomparably beyond and above you all. I *wonder* he won't be near me!" She went on to herself. "I thought he wished it. Heathcliff, dear! you should not be sullen now. Do come to me, Heathcliff."

In her eagerness she rose and supported herself on the arm of the chair. At that earnest appeal, he turned to her, looking absolutely desperate. His eyes wide, and wet at last, flashed fiercely on her; his breast heaved convulsively. An instant they held asunder; and then how they met I hardly saw, but Catherine made a spring, and he caught her, and they were locked in an embrace from which I thought my mistress would never be released alive. In fact, to my eyes, she seemed directly insensible. He flung himself into the nearest seat, and on my approaching hurriedly to ascertain if she had fainted, he gnashed at me, and foamed like a mad dog, and gathered her to him with greedy jealousy. I did not feel as if I were in the company of a creature of my own species; it appeared that he would not understand, though I spoke to him; so I stood off, and held my tongue, in great perplexity.

A movement of Catherine's relieved me a little presently: she put up her hand to clasp his neck, and bring her cheek to his, as he held her; while he, in return, covering her with frantic caresses, said wildly—

"You teach me now how cruel you've been—cruel and false. *Why* did you despise me? *Why* did you betray your own heart, Cathy? I have not one word of comfort. You deserve this. You have killed yourself. Yes, you may kiss me, and cry; and wring out my kisses and tears. They'll blight you—they'll damn you. You loved me—then what *right* had you to leave me? What right—answer me—for the poor fancy you felt for Linton? Because misery, and degradation, and death, and nothing that God or Satan could inflict would have parted us, *you*, of your own will, did it. I have not broken your heart—*you* have broken it—and in breaking it, you have broken mine. So much the worse for me, that I am strong. Do I want to live? What kind of living will it be when you—oh, God! would *you* like to live with your soul in the grave?"

"Let me alone. Let me alone," sobbed Catherine. "If I've done wrong, I'm dying for it. It is enough! You left me too; but I won't upbraid you! I forgive you. Forgive me!"

"It is hard to forgive, and to look at those eyes, and feel those wasted hands," he answered. "Kiss me again; and don't let me see your eyes! I forgive what you have done to me. I love *my* murderer—but *yours!* How can I?"

They were silent—their faces hid against each other, and washed by each other's tears. At least, I suppose the weeping was on both sides; as it seemed Heathcliff *could* weep on a great occasion like this.

I grew very uncomfortable, meanwhile; for the afternoon wore fast away, the man whom I had sent off returned from his errand, and I could distinguish, by the shine of the westering sun up the valley, a concourse thickening outside Gimmerton chapel porch.

"Service is over," I announced. "My master will be here in half-an-hour."

Heathcliff groaned a curse, and strained Catherine closer—she never moved.

Ere long I perceived a group of the servants passing up the road towards the kitchen wing. Mr. Linton was not far behind; he opened the gate himself, and sauntered slowly up, probably enjoying the lovely afternoon that breathed as soft as summer.

"Now he is here," I exclaimed. "For heaven's sake, hurry down! You'll not meet any one on the front stairs. Do be quick; and stay among the trees till he is fairly in."

"I must go, Cathy," said Heathcliff, seeking to extricate himself from his companion's arms. "But, if I live, I'll see you again before you are asleep. I won't stray five yards from your window."

"You must not go!" she answered, holding him as firmly as her strength allowed. "You shall not, I tell you."

"For one hour," he pleaded, earnestly.

"Not for one minute," she replied.

"I *must*—Linton will be up immediately," persisted the alarmed intruder.

He would have risen, and unfixed her fingers by the act—she clung fast, gasping; there was mad resolution in her face.

"No!" she shrieked. "Oh, don't, don't go. It is the last time! Edgar will not hurt us. Heathcliff, I shall die! I shall die!"

"Damn the fool. There he is," cried Heathcliff, sinking back into his seat. "Hush, my darling! Hush, hush, Catherine! I'll stay. If he shot me so, I'd expire with a blessing on my lips."

And there they were fast again. I heard my master mounting the stairs—the cold sweat ran from my forehead; I was horrified.

"Are you going to listen to her ravings?" I said, passionately. "She does not know what she says. Will you ruin her, because she has not wit to help herself? Get up! You could be free instantly. That is the most diabolical deed that ever you did. We are all done for—master, mistress, and servant."

I wrung my hands, and cried out; and Mr. Linton hastened his step at the noise. In the midst of my agitation, I was sincerely glad to observe that Catherine's arms had fallen relaxed, and her head hung down.

"She's fainted or dead," I thought, "so much the better. Far better that she should be dead, than lingering a burden and a misery-maker to all about her."

Edgar sprang to his unbidden guest, blanched with astonishment and rage. What he meant to do, I cannot tell; however, the other stopped all demonstrations, at once, by placing the lifeless-looking form in his arms.

"Look there," he said. "Unless you be a fiend, help her first—then you shall speak to me!"

He walked into the parlour, and sat down. Mr. Linton summoned me, and with great difficulty, and after resorting to many means, we managed to restore her to sensation; but she was all bewildered; she sighed, and moaned, and knew nobody. Edgar, in his anxiety for her, forgot her hated friend. I did not. I went at the earliest opportunity, and besought him to depart, affirming that Catherine was better, and he should hear from me in the morning, how she passed the night.

"I shall not refuse to go out of doors," he answered; "but I shall stay in the garden; and, Nelly, mind you keep your word to-morrow. I shall be under those larch trees. Mind! or I pay another visit, whether Linton be in or not."

He sent a rapid glance through the half-open door of the chamber, and ascertaining that what I stated was apparently true, delivered the house of his luckless presence.

CHAPTER 16

About twelve o'clock that night was born the Catherine you saw at Wuthering Heights, a puny, seven months' child; and two hours after, the mother died, having never recovered sufficient consciousness to miss Heathcliff, or know Edgar.

The latter's distraction at his bereavement is a subject too painful to be dwelt on; its after effects showed how deep the sorrow sunk.

A great addition, in my eyes, was his being left without an heir. I bemoaned that, as I gazed on the feeble orphan; and I mentally abused old Linton for—what was only natural partiality—the securing his estate to his own daughter, instead of his son's.

An unwelcomed infant it was, poor thing! It might have wailed out of life, and nobody cared a morsel, during those first hours of existence. We redeemed the neglect afterwards; but its beginning was as friendless as its end is likely to be.

Next morning—bright and cheerful out of doors—stole softened in through the blinds of the silent room, and suffused the couch and its occupant with a mellow, tender glow.

Edgar Linton had his head laid on the pillow, and his eyes shut. His young and fair features were almost as death-like as those of the form beside him, and almost as fixed; but *his* was the hush of exhausted anguish, and *hers* of perfect peace. Her brow smooth, her lids closed, her lips wearing the expression of a smile. No angel in heaven could be more beautiful than she appeared; and I partook of the infinite calm in which she lay. My mind was never in a holier frame than while I gazed on that untroubled image of Divine rest. I instinctively echoed the words she had uttered, a few hours before. "Incomparably beyond, and above us all! Whether still on earth or now in heaven, her spirit is at home with God!"

I don't know if it be a peculiarity in me, but I am seldom otherwise than happy while watching in the chamber of death, should no frenzied or despairing mourner share the duty with me. I see a repose that neither earth nor hell can break; and I feel an assurance of the endless and shadowless hereafter—the Eternity they have entered—where life is boundless in its duration, and love in its sympathy, and joy in its fulness. I noticed on that occasion how much selfishness there is even in a love like Mr. Linton's, when he so regretted Catherine's blessed release!

To be sure, one might have doubted, after the wayward and impatient existence she had led, whether she merited a haven of peace at last. One might doubt in seasons of cold reflection, but not then, in the presence of her corpse. It asserted its own tranquillity, which seemed a pledge of equal quiet to its former inhabitant.

"Do you believe such people *are* happy in the other world, sir? I'd give a great deal to know."

I declined answering Mrs. Dean's question, which struck me as something heterodox. She proceeded—

"Retracing the course of Catherine Linton, I fear we have no right to think she is: but we'll leave her with her Maker."

The master looked asleep, and I ventured soon after sunrise to quit the room and steal out to the pure, refreshing air. The servants thought me gone to shake off the drowsiness of my protracted watch; in reality, my chief motive was seeing Mr. Heathcliff. If he had remained among the larches all night, he would have heard nothing of the stir at the Grange, unless, perhaps, he might catch the gallop of the messenger going to Gimmerton. If he had come nearer, he would probably be aware, from the lights flitting to and fro, and the opening and shutting of the outer doors, that all was not right within.

I wished, yet feared, to find him. I felt the terrible news must be told, and I longed to get it over, but *how* to do it I did not know.

He was there—at least a few yards further in the park; leant against an old ash tree, his hat off, and his hair soaked with the dew that had gathered on the budded branches, and fell pattering round him. He had been standing a long time in that position, for I saw a pair of ousels passing and repassing scarcely three feet from him, busy in building their nest, and regarding his proximity no more than that of a piece of timber. They flew off at my approach, and he raised his eyes and spoke—

"She's dead!" he said; "I've not waited for you to learn that. Put your handkerchief away—don't snivel before me. Damn you all! she wants none of *your* tears!"

I was weeping as much for him as her: we do sometimes pity creatures that have none of the feeling either for themselves or others; and when I first looked into his face, I perceived that he had got intelligence of the catastrophe; and a foolish notion struck me that his heart was quelled and he prayed, because his lips moved and his gaze was bent on the ground.

"Yes, she's dead!" I answered, checking my sobs and drying my cheeks. "Gone to heaven, I hope, where we may, everyone, join her, if we take due warning, and leave our evil ways to follow good!"

"Did *she* take due warning, then?" asked Heathcliff, attempting a sneer. "Did she die like a saint? Come, give me a true history of the event. How did—"

He endeavoured to pronounce the name, but could not manage it; and compressing his mouth, he held a silent combat with his inward agony, defying, meanwhile, my sympathy with an unflinching, ferocious stare.

"How did she die?" he resumed, at last—fain, notwithstanding his hardihood, to have a support behind him, for, after the struggle, he trembled, in spite of himself, to his very finger-ends.

"Poor wretch!" I thought; "you have a heart and nerves the same as your brother men! Why should you be so anxious to conceal them? Your pride cannot blind God! You tempt Him to wring them, till He forces a cry of humiliation!"

"Quietly as a lamb!" I answered, aloud. "She drew a sigh, and stretched herself, like a child reviving, and sinking again to sleep; and five minutes after I felt one little pulse at her heart, and nothing more!"

"And—and did she ever mention me?" he asked, hesitating, as if he dreaded the answer to his question would introduce details that he could not bear to hear.

"Her senses never returned—she recognised nobody from the time you left her," I said. "She lies with a sweet smile on her face; and her latest ideas wandered back to pleasant early days. Her life closed in a gentle dream—may she wake as kindly in the other world!"

"May she wake in torment!" he cried, with frightful vehemence, stamping his foot, and groaning in a sudden paroxysm of ungovernable passion. "Why, she's a liar to the end! Where is she? Not *there*—not in heaven—not perished—where? Oh! you said you cared nothing for my sufferings! And I pray one prayer—I repeat it till my tongue stiffens—Catherine Earnshaw, may you not rest, as long as I am living! You said I killed you—haunt me, then! The murdered *do* haunt their murderers, I believe. I know that ghosts *have* wandered on earth. Be with me always—take any form—drive me mad! only *do* not leave me in this abyss, where I cannot find you! Oh, God! it is unutterable! I *cannot* live without my life! I *cannot* live without my soul!"

He dashed his head against the knotted trunk; and, lifting up his eyes, howled, not like a man, but like a savage beast getting goaded to death with knives and spears.

I observed several splashes of blood about the bark of the tree, and his hand and forehead were both stained; probably the scene I witnessed was a repetition of others acted during the night. It hardly moved my compassion—it appalled me; still I felt reluctant to quit him so. But the moment he recollected himself enough to notice me watching, he thundered a command for me to go, and I obeyed. He was beyond my skill to quiet or console!

Mrs. Linton's funeral was appointed to take place on the Friday following her decease; and till then her coffin remained uncovered, and strewn with flowers and scented leaves, in the great drawing-room. Linton spent his days and nights there, a sleepless guardian; and—a circumstance concealed from all but me—Heathcliff spent his nights, at least, outside, equally a stranger to repose.

I held no communication with him; still I was conscious of his design to enter, if he could; and on the Tuesday, a little after dark, when my master, from sheer fatigue, had been compelled to retire a couple of hours, I went and opened one of the windows, moved by his perseverance to give him a chance of bestowing on the fading image of his idol one final adieu.

He did not omit to avail himself of the opportunity, cautiously and briefly—too cautiously to betray his presence by the slightest noise; indeed, I shouldn't¹ have discovered that he had been there, except for the disarrangement of the drapery about the corpse's face, and for observing on the floor a curl of light hair, fastened with a silver thread, which, on examination, I ascertained to have been taken from a locket hung round Catherine's neck. Heathcliff had opened the trinket and cast out its contents, replacing them by a black lock of his own. I twisted the two, and enclosed them together.

Mr. Earnshaw was, of course, invited to attend the remains of his sister to the grave; he sent no excuse, but he never came; so that besides her husband, the mourners were wholly composed of tenants and servants. Isabella was not asked.

The place of Catherine's interment, to the surprise of the villagers, was neither in the chapel, under the carved monument of the Lintons, nor yet by the tombs of her own relations, outside. It was dug on a green slope, in a corner of the kirkyard, where the wall is so low that heath and bilberry plants have climbed over it from the moor; and peat mould almost buries it. Her husband lies in the same spot, now; and they have each a simple headstone above, and a plain grey block at their feet, to mark the graves.

CHAPTER 17

That Friday made the last of our fine days, for a month. In the evening, the weather broke; the wind shifted from south to northeast, and brought rain first, and then sleet and snow.

On the morrow one could hardly imagine that there had been three weeks of summer: the primroses and crocuses were hidden under wintry drifts; the larks were silent, the young leaves of the early trees smitten and blackened. And dreary, and chill, and dismal that morrow did creep over! My master kept his room. I took possession of the lonely parlour, converting it into a nursery; and there I was sitting, with the moaning doll of a child laid on my knee, rocking it to and fro, and watching, meanwhile, the still driving flakes build up the uncurtained window, when the door opened, and some person entered, out of breath and laughing!

My anger was greater than my astonishment for a minute; I supposed it one of the maids, and I cried—

"Have done! How dare you show your giddiness here? What would Mr. Linton say if he heard you?"

"Excuse me!" answered a familiar voice, "but I know Edgar is in bed, and I cannot stop myself."

With that, the speaker came forward to the fire, panting and holding her hand to her side.

"I have run the whole way from Wuthering Heights!" she continued, after a pause. "Except where I've flown. I couldn't count the number of falls I've had. Oh, I'm aching all over! Don't be alarmed. There shall be an explanation as soon as I can give it—only just have the goodness to step out and order the carriage to take me on to Gimmerton, and tell a servant to seek up a few clothes in my wardrobe."

The intruder was Mrs. Heathcliff. She certainly seemed in no laughing predicament: her hair streamed on her shoulders, dripping with snow and water; she was dressed in the girlish dress she commonly wore, befitting her age more than her position—a low frock, with short sleeves, and nothing on either head or neck. The frock was of light silk, and clung to her with wet; and her feet were protected merely by thin slippers; add to this a deep cut under one ear, which only the cold prevented from bleeding profusely, a white face scratched and bruised, and a frame hardly able to support itself through fatigue, and you may fancy my first fright was not much allayed when I had leisure to examine her.

"My dear young lady," I exclaimed, "I'll stir nowhere, and hear nothing, till you have removed every article of your clothes, and put on dry things; and certainly you shall not go to Gimmerton to-night; so it is needless to order the carriage."

"Certainly, I shall," she said; "walking or riding; yet I've no objection to dress myself decently; and—ah, see how it flows down my neck now! The fire does make it smart."

She insisted on my fulfilling her directions, before she would let me touch her; and not till after the coachman had been instructed to get ready, and a maid set to pack up some necessary attire, did I obtain her consent for binding the wound and helping to change her garments.

"Now, Ellen," she said, when my task was finished, and she was seated in an easy chair on the hearth, with a cup of tea before her, "you sit down opposite me, and put poor Catherine's baby away—I don't like to see it! You mustn't think I care little for Catherine, because I behaved so foolishly on entering. I've cried too, bitterly—yes, more than any one else has reason to cry. We parted unreconciled, you remember, and I shan't forgive myself. But for all that, I was not going to sympathise with him—the brute beast! O, give me the poker! This is the last thing of his I have about me." She slipped the gold ring from her third finger, and threw it on the floor. "I'll smash it!" she continued, striking with childish spite. "And then I'll burn it!" and she took and dropped the misused article among the coals. "There! he shall buy another, if he gets me back again. He'd be capable of coming to seek me, to tease Edgar—I dare not stay, lest that notion should possess his wicked head! And besides, Edgar has not been kind, has he? And I won't come suing for his assistance; nor will I bring him into more trouble. Necessity compelled me to seek shelter here; though, if I had not learnt he was out of the way, I'd have halted at the kitchen, washed my face, warmed myself, got you to bring what I wanted, and departed again to anywhere out of the reach of my accursed—of that incarnate goblin! Ah, he was in such a fury! If he had caught me! It's a pity Earnshaw is not his match in strength—I wouldn't have run till I'd seen him all but demolished, had Hindley been able to do it!"

"Well, don't talk so fast, Miss!" I interrupted, "you'll disorder the handkerchief I have tied round your face, and make the cut bleed again. Drink your tea, and take breath and give over laughing. Laughter is sadly out of place under this roof, and in your condition!"

"An undeniable truth," she replied. "Listen to that child! It maintains a constant wail—send it out of my hearing, for an hour; I shan't stay any longer."

I rang the bell, and committed it to a servant's care; and then I inquired what had urged her to escape from Wuthering Heights in such an unlikely plight, and where she meant to go, as she refused remaining with us.

"I ought, and I wish to remain," answered she, "to cheer Edgar and take care of the baby, for two things, and because the Grange is my right home. But I tell you, he wouldn't let me! Do you think he could bear to see me grow fat and merry; and could bear to think that we were tranquil, and not resolve on poisoning our comfort? Now, I have the satisfaction of being sure that he detests me to the point of its annoying him seriously to have me within ear-shot, or eye-sight. I notice, when I enter his presence, the muscles of his countenance are involuntarily distorted into an expression of hatred; partly arising from his knowledge of the good causes I have to feel that sentiment for him, and partly from original aversion. It is strong enough to make me feel pretty certain that he would not chase me over England, supposing I contrived a clear escape; and therefore I must get quite away. I've recovered from my first desire to be killed by him. I'd rather he'd kill himself! He has extinguished my love effectually, and so I'm at my ease. I can recollect yet how I loved him; and can dimly imagine that I could still be loving him, if—no, no! Even if he had doted on me, the devilish nature would have revealed its existence somehow. Catherine had an awfully perverted taste to esteem him so dearly, knowing him so well. Monster! would that he could be blotted out of creation, and out of my memory!"

"Hush, hush! He's a human being," I said. "Be more charitable; there are worse men than he is yet!"

"He's not a human being," she retorted; "and he has no claim on my charity. I gave him my heart, and he took and pinched it to death; and flung it back to me. People feel with their hearts, Ellen, and since he has destroyed mine, I have not power to feel for him, and I would not, though he groaned from this to his dying day, and wept tears of blood for Catherine! No, indeed, indeed, I wouldn't!" And here Isabella began to cry; but, immediately dashing the water from her lashes, she recommenced.

"You asked, what has driven me to flight at last? I was compelled to attempt it, because I had succeeded in rousing his rage a pitch above his malignity. Pulling out the nerves with red hot pincers requires more coolness than knocking on the head. He was worked up to forget the fiendish prudence he boasted of, and proceeded to murderous violence. I experienced pleasure in being able to exasperate him: the sense of pleasure woke my instinct of self-preservation, so I fairly broke free, and if ever I come into his hands again he is welcome to a signal revenge.

"Yesterday, you know, Mr. Earnshaw should have been at the funeral. He kept himself sober for the purpose—tolerably sober; not going to bed mad at six o'clock and getting up drunk at twelve. Consequently, he rose, in suicidal low spirits, as fit for the church as for a dance; and instead, he sat down by the fire and swallowed gin or brandy by tumblerfuls.

"Heathcliff—I shudder to name him!—has been a stranger in the house from last Sunday till to-day. Whether the angels have fed him, or his kin beneath, I cannot tell; but he has not eaten a meal with us for nearly a week. He has just come home at dawn, and gone upstairs to his chamber; locking himself in—as if anybody dreamt of coveting his company! There he has continued, praying like a Methodist; only the deity he implored is senseless dust and ashes; and God, when addressed, was curiously confounded with his own black father! After concluding these precious orisons—and they lasted generally till he grew hoarse, and his voice was strangled in his throat—he would be off again; always straight down to the Grange! I wonder Edgar did not send for a constable, and give him into custody! For me, grieved as I was about Catherine, it was impossible to avoid regarding this season of deliverance from degrading oppression as a holiday.

"I recovered spirits sufficient to hear Joseph's eternal lectures without weeping; and to move up and down the house, less with the foot of a frightened thief than formerly. You wouldn't think that I should cry at anything Joseph could say, but he and Hareton are detestable companions. I'd rather sit with Hindley, and hear his awful talk, than with 't' little maister,' and his staunch supporter, that odious old man!

"When Heathcliff is in, I'm often obliged to seek the kitchen and their society, or starve among the damp, uninhabited chambers; when he is not, as was the case this week, I establish a table and chair at one corner of the house fire, and never mind how Mr. Earnshaw may occupy himself; and he does not interfere with my arrangements. He is quieter now than he used to be, if no one provokes him; more sullen and depressed, and less furious. Joseph affirms he's sure he's an altered man; that the Lord has touched his heart, and he is saved 'so as by fire.' I'm puzzled to detect signs of the favourable change, but it is not my business.

"Yester-evening, I sat in my nook reading some old books till late on towards twelve. It seemed so dismal to go upstairs, with the wild snow blowing outside, and my thoughts continually reverting to the kirkyard and the new made grave! I dared hardly lift my eyes from the page before me, that melancholy scene so instantly usurped its place.

"Hindley sat opposite, his head leant on his hand, perhaps meditating on the same subject. He had ceased drinking at a point below irrationality, and had neither stirred nor spoken during two or three hours. There was no sound through the house but the moaning wind which shook the windows every now and then, the faint crackling of the coals, and the click of my snuffers as I removed at intervals the long wick of the candle. Hareton and Joseph were probably fast asleep in bed. It was very, very sad, and while I read, I sighed, for it seemed as if all joy had vanished from the world, never to be restored.

"The doleful silence was broken at length by the sound of the kitchen latch. Heathcliff had returned from his watch earlier than usual, owing, I suppose, to the sudden storm.

"That entrance was fastened, and we heard him coming round to get in by the other. I rose with an irrepressible expression of what I felt on my lips, which induced my companion, who had been staring towards the door, to turn and look at me.

"'I'll keep him out five minutes,' he exclaimed. 'You won't object?'

"'No, you may keep him out the whole night, for me,' I answered. 'Do! put the key in the lock, and draw the bolts.'

"Earnshaw accomplished this ere his guest reached the front; he then came and brought his chair to the other side of my table, leaning over it, and searching in my eyes for a sympathy with the burning hate that gleamed from his: as he both looked and felt like an assassin, he couldn't exactly find that; but he discovered enough to encourage him to speak.

" 'You and I,' he said, 'have each a great debt to settle with the man out yonder! If we were neither of us cowards, we might combine to discharge it. Are you as soft as your brother? Are you willing to endure to the last, and not once attempt a repayment?'

" 'I'm weary of enduring now,' I replied, 'and I'd be glad of a retaliation that wouldn't recoil on myself; but treachery and violence are spears pointed at both ends—they wound those who resort to them, worse than their enemies.'

" 'Treachery and violence are a just return for treachery and violence!' cried Hindley. 'Mrs. Heathcliff, I'll ask you to do nothing but sit still and be dumb. Tell me now, can you? I'm sure you would have as much pleasure as I in witnessing the conclusion of the fiend's existence; he'll be *your* death unless you overreach him—and he'll be *my* ruin. Damn the hellish villain! He knocks at the door as if he were master here already! Promise to hold your tongue, and before that clock strikes—it wants three minutes of one—you're a free woman!'

"He took the implements which I described to you in my letter from his breast, and would have turned down the candle. I snatched it away, however, and seized his arm.

" 'I'll not hold my tongue!' I said; 'you mustn't touch him. Let the door remain shut and be quiet!'

" 'No! I've formed my resolution, and by God, I'll execute it!' cried the desperate being. 'I'll do you a kindness in spite of yourself, and Hareton justice! And you needn't trouble your head to screen me; Catherine is gone. Nobody alive would regret me, or be ashamed, though I cut my throat this minute—and it's time to make an end!'

"I might as well have struggled with a bear, or reasoned with a lunatic. The only resource left me was to run to a lattice, and warn his intended victim of the fate which awaited him.

" 'You'd better seek shelter somewhere else to-night!' I exclaimed in a rather triumphant tone. 'Mr. Earnshaw has a mind to shoot you, if you persist in endeavouring to enter.'

" 'You'd better open the door, you—' he answered, addressing me by some elegant term that I don't care to repeat.

" 'I shall not meddle in the matter,' I retorted again. 'Come in, and get shot, if you please! I've done my duty.'

"With that I shut the window, and returned to my place by the fire, having too small a stock of hypocrisy at my command to pretend any anxiety for the danger that menaced him.

"Earnshaw swore passionately at me, affirming that I loved the villain yet, and calling me all sorts of names for the base spirit I evinced. And I, in my secret heart (and conscience never reproached me) thought what a blessing it would be for *him*, should Heathcliff put him out of misery; and what a blessing for *me*, should he send Heathcliff to his right abode! As I sat nursing these reflections, the casement behind me was banged on to the floor by a blow from the latter individual, and his black countenance looked blightingly through. The stanchions stood too close to suffer his shoulders to follow, and I smiled, exulting in my fancied security. His hair and clothes were whitened with snow, and his sharp cannibal teeth, revealed by cold and wrath, gleamed through the dark.

" 'Isabella, let me in, or I'll make you repent!' he 'girned,'[37] as Joseph calls it.

" 'I cannot commit murder,' I replied. 'Mr. Hindley stands sentinel with a knife and loaded pistol.'

" 'Let me in by the kitchen door!' he said.

" 'Hindley will be there before me,' I answered. 'And that's a poor love of yours that cannot bear a shower of snow! We were left at peace in our beds as long as the summer moon shone, but the moment a blast of winter returns, you must run for shelter! Heathcliff, if I were you, I'd go stretch myself over her grave and die like a faithful dog. The world is surely not worth living in now, is it? You had distinctly impressed on me the idea that Catherine was the whole joy of your life. I can't imagine how you think of surviving her loss.'

" 'He's there, is he?' exclaimed my companion, rushing to the gap. 'If I can get my arm out I can hit him!'

"I'm afraid, Ellen, you'll set me down as really wicked; but you don't know all, so don't judge! I wouldn't have aided or abetted an attempt on even *his* life, for anything. Wish that he were dead, I must; and therefore I was fearfully disappointed, and unnerved by terror for the consequences of my taunting speech, when he flung himself on Earnshaw's weapon and wrenched it from his grasp.

"The charge exploded, and the knife, in springing back, closed into its owner's wrist. Heathcliff pulled it away by main force, slitting up the flesh as it passed on, and thrust it dripping into his pocket. He then took a stone, struck down the division between two windows, and sprung in. His adversary had fallen senseless with excessive pain and the flow of blood that gushed from an artery, or a large vein.

"The ruffian kicked and trampled on him, and dashed his head repeatedly against the flags, holding me with one hand, meantime, to prevent me summoning Joseph.

"He exerted preter-human self-denial in abstaining from finishing him completely; but getting out of breath, he finally desisted, and dragged the apparently inanimate body onto the settle.

"There he tore off the sleeve of Earnshaw's coat, and bound up the wound with brutal roughness, spitting and cursing during the operation, as energetically as he had kicked before.

"Being at liberty, I lost no time in seeking the old servant, who, having gathered by degrees the purport of my hasty tale, hurried below, gasping, as he descended the steps two at once.

" 'Whet is thur tuh do, nah? whet is thur tuh do, nah?'

" 'There's this to do,' thundered Heathcliff, 'that your master's mad; and should he last another month, I'll have him to an asylum. And how the devil did you come to fasten me out, you toothless hound? Don't stand muttering and mumbling there. Come, I'm not going to nurse him. Wash that stuff away; and mind the sparks of your candle—it is more than half brandy!'

" 'Und soa, yah been murthering on him!' exclaimed Joseph, lifting his hands and eyes in horror. 'If iver Aw seed a seeght loike this! May the Lord—'

"Heathcliff gave him a push onto his knees in the middle of the blood, and flung a towel to him; but instead of proceeding to dry it up, he joined his hands, and began a prayer which excited my laughter from its odd phraseology. I was in the condition of mind to be shocked at nothing; in fact, I was as reckless as some malefactors show themselves at the foot of the gallows.

---

[37] '*Girned:* snarled.

"'Oh, I forgot you,' said the tyrant. 'You shall do that. Down with you. And you conspire with him against me, do you, viper? There, that is work fit for you!'

"He shook me till my teeth rattled, and pitched me beside Joseph, who steadily concluded his supplications and then rose, vowing he would set off for the Grange directly. Mr. Linton was a magistrate, and though he had fifty wives dead, he should inquire into this.

"He was so obstinate in his resolution that Heathcliff deemed it expedient to compel from my lips a recapitulation of what had taken place; standing over me, heaving with malevolence, as I reluctantly delivered the account in answer to his questions.

"It required a great deal of labour to satisfy the old man that Heathcliff was not the aggressor; especially with my hardly wrung replies. However, Mr. Earnshaw soon convinced him that he was alive still; he hastened to administer a dose of spirits, and by their succour his master presently regained motion and consciousness.

"Heathcliff, aware that his opponent was ignorant of the treatment received while insensible, called him deliriously intoxicated; and said he should not notice his atrocious conduct further, but advised him to get to bed. To my joy, he left us after giving this judicious counsel, and Hindley stretched himself on the hearth-stone. I departed to my own room, marvelling that I had escaped so easily.

"This morning, when I came down, about half-an-hour before noon, Mr. Earnshaw was sitting by the fire, deadly sick; his evil genius, almost as gaunt and ghastly, leant against the chimney. Neither appeared inclined to dine, and having waited till all was cold on the table, I commenced alone.

"Nothing hindered me from eating heartily; and I experienced a certain sense of satisfaction and superiority, as, at intervals, I cast a look towards my silent companions, and felt the comfort of a quiet conscience within me.

"After I had done, I ventured on the unusual liberty of drawing near the fire, going round Earnshaw's seat, and kneeling in the corner beside him.

"Heathcliff did not glance my way, and I gazed up and contemplated his features almost as confidently as if they had been turned to stone. His forehead, that I once thought so manly, and that I now think so diabolical, was shaded with a heavy cloud; his basilisk eyes were nearly quenched by sleeplessness, and weeping, perhaps, for the lashes were wet then; his lips devoid of their ferocious sneer, and sealed in an expression of unspeakable sadness. Had it been another, I would have covered my face in the presence of such grief. In *his* case, I was gratified; and ignoble as it seems to insult a fallen enemy, I couldn't miss this chance of sticking in a dart; his weakness was the only time when I could taste the delight of paying wrong for wrong."

"Fie, fie, Miss!" I interrupted. "One might suppose you had never opened a Bible in your life. If God afflict your enemies, surely that ought to suffice you. It is both mean and presumptuous to add your torture to his!"

"In general, I'll allow that it would be, Ellen," she continued. "But what misery laid on Heathcliff could content me, unless I have a hand in it? I'd rather he suffered *less*, if I might cause his sufferings and he might *know* that I was the cause. Oh, I owe him so much. On only one condition can I hope to forgive him. It is, if I may take an eye for an eye, a tooth for a tooth; for every wrench of agony, return a wrench, reduce him to my level. As he was the first to injure, make him the first to implore pardon; and then—why then, Ellen, I might show you some generosity. But it is utterly impossible I can ever be revenged, and therefore I cannot forgive him. Hindley wanted some water, and I handed him a glass, and asked him how he was.

" 'Not as ill as I wish,' he replied. 'But leaving out my arm, every inch of me is as sore as if I had been fighting with a legion of imps!'

" 'Yes, no wonder,' was my next remark. 'Catherine used to boast that she stood between you and bodily harm: she meant that certain persons would not hurt you, for fear of offending her. It's well people don't *really* rise from their grave, or, last night, she might have witnessed a repulsive scene! Are not you bruised, and cut over your chest and shoulders?'

" 'I can't say,' he answered; 'but what do you mean? Did he dare to strike me when I was down?'

" 'He trampled on, and kicked you, and dashed you on the ground,' I whispered. 'And his mouth watered to tear you with his teeth; because he's only half a man—not so much.'

"Mr. Earnshaw looked up, like me, to the countenance of our mutual foe, who, absorbed in his anguish, seemed insensible to anything around him; the longer he stood, the plainer his reflections revealed their blackness through his features.

" 'Oh, if God would but give me strength to strangle him in my last agony, I'd go to hell with joy,' groaned the impatient man, writhing to rise, and sinking back in despair, convinced of his inadequacy for the struggle.

" 'Nay, it's enough that he has murdered one of you,' I observed aloud. 'At the Grange, every one knows your sister would have been living now, had it not been for Mr. Heathcliff. After all, it is preferable to be hated than loved by him. When I recollect how happy we were—how happy Catherine was before he came—I'm fit to curse the day.'

"Most likely, Heathcliff noticed more the truth of what was said, than the spirit of the person who said it. His attention was roused, I saw, for his eyes rained down tears among the ashes, and he drew his breath in suffocating sighs.

"I stared full at him, and laughed scornfully. The clouded windows of hell flashed a moment towards me; the fiend which usually looked out, however, was so dimmed and drowned that I did not fear to hazard another sound of derision.

" 'Get up, and begone out of my sight,' said the mourner.

"I guessed he uttered those words, at least, though his voice was hardly intelligible.

" 'I beg your pardon,' I replied. 'But I loved Catherine too; and her brother requires attendance which, for her sake, I shall supply. Now that she's dead, I see her in Hindley; Hindley has exactly her eyes, if you had not tried to gouge them out and made them black and red, and her—'

" 'Get up, wretched idiot, before I stamp you to death!' he cried, making a movement that caused me to make one also.

" 'But then,' I continued, holding myself ready to flee, 'if poor Catherine had trusted you, and assumed the ridiculous, contemptible, degrading title of Mrs. Heathcliff, she would soon have presented a similar picture! *She* wouldn't have borne your abominable behaviour quietly; her detestation and disgust must have found voice.'

"The back of the settle and Earnshaw's person interposed between me and him; so instead of endeavouring to reach me, he snatched a dinner knife from the table and flung it at my head. It struck beneath my ear, and stopped the sentence I was uttering; but, pulling it out, I sprang to the door and delivered another which I hope went a little deeper than his missile.

"The last glimpse I caught of him was a furious rush on his part, checked by the embrace of his host; and both fell locked together on the hearth.

"In my flight through the kitchen I bid Joseph speed to his master; I knocked over Hareton, who was hanging a litter of puppies from a chair-back in the doorway;

and, blest as a soul escaped from purgatory, I bounded, leaped, and flew down the steep road; then, quitting its windings, shot direct across the moor, rolling over banks, and wading through marshes; precipitating myself, in fact, towards the beacon light of the Grange. And far rather would I be condemned to a perpetual dwelling in the infernal regions, than even for one night abide beneath the roof of Wuthering Heights again."

Isabella ceased speaking, and took a drink of tea; then she rose, and bidding me put on her bonnet and a great shawl I had brought, and turning a deaf ear to my entreaties for her to remain another hour, she stepped onto a chair, kissed Edgar's and Catherine's portraits, bestowed a similar salute on me, and descended to the carriage accompanied by Fanny, who yelped wild with joy at recovering her mistress. She was driven away, never to revisit this neighbourhood; but a regular correspondence was established between her and my master when things were more settled.

I believe her new abode was in the south, near London; there she had a son born, a few months subsequent to her escape. He was christened Linton, and, from the first, she reported him to be an ailing, peevish creature.

Mr. Heathcliff, meeting me one day in the village, inquired where she lived. I refused to tell. He remarked that it was not of any moment, only she must beware of coming to her brother; she should not be with him, if he had to keep her himself.

Though I would give no information, he discovered, through some of the other servants, both her place of residence and the existence of the child. Still he didn't molest her; for which forbearance she might thank his aversion, I suppose.

He often asked about the infant, when he saw me; and on hearing its name, smiled grimly, and observed—

"They wish me to hate it too, do they?"

"I don't think they wish you to know any thing about it," I answered.

"But I'll have it," he said, "when I want it. They may reckon on that!"

Fortunately, its mother died before the time arrived, some thirteen years after the decease of Catherine, when Linton was twelve, or a little more.

On the day succeeding Isabella's unexpected visit, I had no opportunity of speaking to my master: he shunned conversation, and was fit for discussing nothing. When I could get him to listen, I saw it pleased him that his sister had left her husband, whom he abhorred with an intensity which the mildness of his nature would scarcely seem to allow. So deep and sensitive was his aversion, that he refrained from going anywhere where he was likely to see or hear of Heathcliff. Grief, and that together, transformed him into a complete hermit: he threw up his office of magistrate, ceased even to attend church, avoided the village on all occasions, and spent a life of entire seclusion within the limits of his park and grounds, only varied by solitary rambles on the moors, and visits to the grave of his wife, mostly at evening, or early morning before other wanderers were abroad.

But he was too good to be thoroughly unhappy long. *He* didn't pray for Catherine's soul to haunt him. Time brought resignation, and a melancholy sweeter than common joy. He recalled her memory with ardent, tender love, and hopeful aspiring to the better world, where, he doubted not, she was gone.

And he had earthly consolation and affections, also. For a few days, I said, he seemed regardless of the puny successor to the departed: that coldness melted as fast as snow in April, and ere the tiny thing could stammer a word or totter a step, it wielded a despot's sceptre in his heart.

It was named Catherine, but he never called it the name in full, as he had never called the first Catherine short, probably because Heathcliff had a habit of doing so.

The little one was always Cathy; it formed to him a distinction from the mother, and yet, a connection with her; and his attachment sprang from its relation to her, far more than from its being his own.

I used to draw a comparison between him and Hindley Earnshaw, and perplex myself to explain satisfactorily why their conduct was so opposite in similar circumstances. They had both been fond husbands, and were both attached to their children; and I could not see how they shouldn't both have taken the same road, for good or evil. But, I thought in my mind, Hindley, with apparently the stronger head, has shown himself sadly the worse and the weaker man. When his ship struck, the captain abandoned his post; and the crew, instead of trying to save her, rushed into riot and confusion, leaving no hope for their luckless vessel. Linton, on the contrary, displayed the true courage of a loyal and faithful soul: he trusted God; and God comforted him. One hoped, and the other despaired: they chose their own lots, and were righteously doomed to endure them.

But you'll not want to hear my moralizing, Mr. Lockwood: you'll judge as well as I can, all these things; at least, you'll think you will, and that's the same.

The end of Earnshaw was what might have been expected; it followed fast on his sister's: there were scarcely six months between them. We, at the Grange, never got a very succinct account of his state preceding it; all that I did learn was on occasion of going to aid in the preparations for the funeral. Mr. Kenneth came to announce the event to my master.

"Well, Nelly," said he, riding into the yard one morning, too early not to alarm me with an instant presentiment of bad news. "It's yours and my turn to go into mourning at present. Who's given us the slip now, do you think?"

"Who?" I asked in a flurry.

"Why, guess!" he returned, dismounting, and slinging his bridle on a hook by the door. "And nip up the corner of your apron; I'm certain you'll need it."

"Not Mr. Heathcliff, surely?" I exclaimed.

"What! would you have tears for him?" said the doctor. "No, Heathcliff's a tough young fellow; he looks blooming to-day—I've just seen him. He's rapidly regaining flesh since he lost his better half."

"Who is it, then, Mr. Kenneth?" I repeated impatiently.

"Hindley Earnshaw! Your old friend Hindley," he replied, "and my wicked gossip; though he's been too wild for me this long while. There! I said we should draw water. But cheer up! He died true to his character, drunk as a lord. Poor lad; I'm sorry, too. One can't help missing an old companion, though he had the worst tricks with him that ever man imagined, and has done me many a rascally turn. He's barely twenty-seven, it seems; that's your own age; who would have thought you were born in one year!"

I confess this blow was greater to me than the shock of Mrs. Linton's death: ancient associations lingered round my heart; I sat down in the porch and wept as for a blood relation, desiring Kenneth to get another servant to introduce him to the master.

I could not hinder myself from pondering on the question—"Had he had fair play?" Whatever I did, that idea would bother me: it was so tiresomely pertinacious that I resolved on requesting leave to go to Wuthering Heights, and assist in the last duties to the dead. Mr. Linton was extremely reluctant to consent, but I pleaded eloquently for the friendless condition in which he lay; and I said my old master and foster brother had a claim on my services as strong as his own. Besides, I reminded him that the child, Hareton, was his wife's nephew, and, in the absence of nearer kin, he ought to act as its guardian; and he ought to and must inquire how the property was left, and look over the concerns of his brother-in-law.

He was unfit for attending to such matters then, but he bid me speak to his lawyer; and at length permitted me to go. His lawyer had been Earnshaw's also: I called at the village, and asked him to accompany me. He shook his head, and advised that Heathcliff should be let alone, affirming, if the truth were known, Hareton would be found little else than a beggar.

"His father died in debt," he said; "the whole property is mortgaged, and the sole chance for the natural heir is to allow him an opportunity of creating some interest in the creditor's heart, that he may be inclined to deal leniently towards him."

When I reached the Heights, I explained that I had come to see everything carried on decently, and Joseph, who appeared in sufficient distress, expressed satisfaction at my presence. Mr. Heathcliff said he did not perceive that I was wanted, but I might stay and order the arrangements for the funeral, if I chose.

"Correctly," he remarked, "that fool's body should be buried at the cross-roads, without ceremony of any kind. I happened to leave him ten minutes, yesterday afternoon; and, in that interval, he fastened the two doors of the house against me, and he has spent the night in drinking himself to death deliberately! We broke in this morning, for we heard him snorting like a horse; and there he was, laid over the settle: flaying and scalping would not have wakened him. I sent for Kenneth, and he came; but not till the beast had changed into carrion: he was both dead and cold and stark; and so you'll allow, it was useless making more stir about him!"

The old servant confirmed this statement, but muttered—

"Aw'd rayther he'd goan hisseln fur t'doctor! Aw sud uh taen tent[38] un t'maister better nur him—un he warn't deead when Aw left, nowt uh t'soart!"

I insisted on the funeral being respectable. Mr. Heathcliff said I might have my own way there too; only, he desired me to remember that the money for the whole affair came out of his pocket.

He maintained a hard, careless deportment, indicative of neither joy nor sorrow; if anything, it expressed a flinty gratification at a piece of difficult work successfully executed. I observed once, indeed, something like exultation in his aspect: it was just when the people were bearing the coffin from the house. He had the hypocrisy to represent a mourner; and previous to following with Hareton, he lifted the unfortunate child on to the table and muttered, with peculiar gusto—

"Now, my bonny lad, you are *mine*! And we'll see if one tree won't grow as crooked as another, with the same wind to twist it!"

The unsuspecting thing was pleased at this speech; he played with Heathcliff's whiskers, and stroked his cheek, but I divined its meaning and observed tartly—

"That boy must go back with me to Thrushcross Grange, sir. There is nothing in the world less yours than he is!"

"Does Linton say so?" he demanded.

"Of course—he has ordered me to take him," I replied.

"Well," said the scoundrel, "we'll not argue the subject now; but I have a fancy to try my hand at rearing a young one, so intimate to your master that I must supply the place of this with my own, if he attempt to remove it. I don't engage to let Hareton go, undisputed; but I'll be pretty sure to make the other come! Remember to tell him."

This hint was enough to bind our hands. I repeated its substance on my return, and Edgar Linton, little interested at the commencement, spoke no more of

---

[38] *Sud uh taen tent:* should have taken care.

interfering. I'm not aware that he could have done it to any purpose, had he been ever so willing.

The guest was now the master of Wuthering Heights: he held firm possession, and proved to the attorney, who, in his turn, proved it to Mr. Linton, that Earnshaw had mortgaged every yard of land he owned for cash to supply his mania for gaming; and he, Heathcliff, was the mortgagee.

In that manner, Hareton, who should now be the first gentleman in the neighbourhood, was reduced to a state of complete dependence on his father's inveterate enemy; and lives in his own house as a servant deprived of the advantage of wages, and quite unable to right himself, because of his friendlessness, and his ignorance that he has been wronged.

CHAPTER 18

The twelve years, continued Mrs. Dean, following that dismal period, were the happiest of my life: my greatest troubles, in their passage, rose from our little lady's trifling illnesses, which she had to experience in common with all children, rich and poor.

For the rest, after the first six months, she grew like a larch, and could walk and talk too, in her own way, before the heath blossomed a second time over Mrs. Linton's dust.

She was the most winning thing that ever brought sunshine into a desolate house—a real beauty in face, with the Earnshaws' handsome dark eyes, but the Lintons' fair skin, and small features, and yellow curling hair. Her spirit was high, though not rough, and qualified by a heart sensitive and lively to excess in its affections. That capacity for intense attachments reminded me of her mother; still she did not resemble her, for she could be soft and mild as a dove, and she had a gentle voice, and pensive expression: her anger was never furious; her love never fierce; it was deep and tender.

However, it must be acknowledged, she had faults to foil her gifts. A propensity to be saucy was one; and a perverse will that indulged children invariably acquire, whether they be good tempered or cross. If a servant chanced to vex her, it was always: "I shall tell papa!" And if he reproved her, even by a look, you would have thought it a heartbreaking business: I don't believe he ever did speak a harsh word to her.

He took her education entirely on himself, and made it an amusement. Fortunately, curiosity and a quick intellect urged her into an apt scholar; she learnt rapidly and eagerly, and did honour to his teaching.

Till she reached the age of thirteen, she had not once been beyond the range of the park by herself. Mr. Linton would take her with him a mile or so outside, on rare occasions; but he trusted her to no one else. Gimmerton was an unsubstantial name in her ears; the chapel, the only building she had approached or entered, except her own home. Wuthering Heights and Mr. Heathcliff did not exist for her; she was a perfect recluse, and, apparently, perfectly contented. Sometimes, indeed, while surveying the country from her nursery window, she would observe—

"Ellen, how long will it be before I can walk to the top of those hills? I wonder what lies on the other side—is it the sea?"

"No, Miss Cathy," I would answer, "it is hills again just like these."

"And what are those golden rocks like, when you stand under them?" she once asked.

The abrupt descent of Penistone Crags particularly attracted her notice, especially when the setting sun shone on it and the topmost heights, and the whole extent of landscape besides lay in shadow.

I explained that they were bare masses of stone, with hardly enough earth in their clefts to nourish a stunted tree.

"And why are they bright so long after it is evening here?" she pursued.

"Because they are a great deal higher up than we are," replied I; "you could not climb them, they are too high and steep. In winter the frost is always there before it comes to us; and, deep into summer, I have found snow under that black hollow on the north-east side!"

"Oh, you have been on them!" she cried, gleefully. "Then I can go, too, when I am a woman. Has papa been, Ellen?"

"Papa would tell you, Miss," I answered, hastily, "that they are not worth the trouble of visiting. The moors, where you ramble with him, are much nicer; and Thrushcross park is the finest place in the world."

"But I know the park, and I don't know those," she murmured to herself. "And I should delight to look round me from the brow of that tallest point—my little pony, Minny, shall take me some time."

One of the maids mentioning the Fairy cave quite turned her head with a desire to fulfil this project; she teased Mr. Linton about it; and he promised she should have the journey when she got older. But Miss Catherine measured her age by months, and—

"Now, am I old enough to go to Penistone Crags?" was the constant question in her mouth.

The road thither wound close by Wuthering Heights. Edgar had not the heart to pass it; so she received as constantly the answer—

"Not yet, love, not yet."

I said Mrs. Heathcliff lived above a dozen years after quitting her husband. Her family were of a delicate constitution: she and Edgar both lacked the ruddy health that you will generally meet in these parts. What her last illness was, I am not certain; I conjecture they died of the same thing, a kind of fever, slow at its commencement, but incurable, and rapidly consuming life towards the close.

She wrote to inform her brother of the probable conclusion of a four months' indisposition under which she had suffered; and entreated him to come to her, if possible, for she had much to settle, and she wished to bid him adieu, and deliver Linton safely into his hands. Her hope was, that Linton might be left with him, as he had been with her; his father, she would fain convince herself, had no desire to assume the burden of his maintenance or education.

My master hesitated not a moment in complying with her request; reluctant as he was to leave home at ordinary calls, he flew to answer this; commending Catherine to my peculiar vigilance in his absence, with reiterated orders that she must not wander out of the park, even under my escort: he did not calculate on her going unaccompanied.

He was away three weeks: the first day or two, my charge sat in a corner of the library, too sad for either reading or playing: in that quiet state she caused me little trouble; but it was succeeded by an interval of impatient, fretful weariness; and being too busy, and too old then, to run up and down amusing her, I hit on a method by which she might entertain herself.

I used to send her on her travels round the grounds—now on foot, and now on a pony; indulging her with a patient audience of all her real and imaginary adventures, when she returned.

The summer shone in full prime; and she took such a taste for this solitary rambling that she often contrived to remain out from breakfast till tea; and then the evenings were spent in recounting her fanciful tales. I did not fear her breaking bounds, because the gates were generally locked, and I thought she would scarcely venture forth alone, if they had stood wide open.

Unluckily, my confidence proved misplaced. Catherine came to me, one morning, at eight o'clock, and said she was that day an Arabian merchant, going to cross the Desert with his caravan; and I must give her plenty of provision for herself and beasts, a horse and three camels, personated by a large hound and a couple of pointers.

I got together good store of dainties, and slung them in a basket on one side of the saddle; and she sprang up as gay as a fairy, sheltered by her wide-brimmed hat and gauze veil from the July sun, and trotted off with a merry laugh, mocking my cautious counsel to avoid galloping, and come back early.

The naughty thing never made her appearance at tea. One traveller, the hound, being an old dog and fond of its ease, returned; but neither Cathy, nor the pony, nor the two pointers were visible in any direction; and I despatched emissaries down this path, and that path, and, at last, went wandering in search of her myself.

There was a labourer working at a fence round a plantation, on the borders of the grounds. I enquired of him if he had seen our young lady.

"I saw her at morn," he replied; "she would have me to cut her a hazel switch, and then she leapt her galloway over the hedge yonder, where it is lowest, and galloped out of sight."

You may guess how I felt at hearing this news. It struck me directly she must have started for Penistone Crags.

"What will become of her?" I ejaculated, pushing through a gap which the man was repairing, and making straight to the high road.

I walked as if for a wager, mile after mile, till a turn brought me in view of the Heights, but no Catherine could I detect, far or near.

The Crags lie about a mile and a half beyond Mr. Heathcliff's place, and that is four from the Grange, so I began to fear night would fall ere I could reach them.

"And what if she should have slipped in, clambering among them," I reflected, "and been killed, or broken some of her bones?"

My suspense was truly painful; and, at first, it gave me delightful relief to observe, in hurrying by the farm-house, Charlie, the fiercest of the pointers, lying under a window, with swelled head and bleeding ear.

I opened the wicket and ran to the door, knocking vehemently for admittance. A woman whom I knew, and who formerly lived at Gimmerton, answered: she had been servant there since the death of Mr. Earnshaw.

"Ah," said she, "you are come a seeking your little mistress! don't be frightened. She's here safe—but I'm glad it isn't the master."

"He is not at home then, is he?" I panted, quite breathless with quick walking and alarm.

"No, no," she replied, "both he and Joseph are off, and I think they won't return this hour or more. Step in and rest you a bit."

I entered, and beheld my stray lamb seated on the hearth, rocking herself in a little chair that had been her mother's, when a child. Her hat was hung against the wall, and she seemed perfectly at home, laughing and chattering, in the best spirits imaginable, to Hareton, now a great, strong lad of eighteen, who stared at her with considerable curiosity and astonishment; comprehending precious little of the fluent succession of remarks and questions which her tongue never ceased pouring forth.

"Very well, Miss," I exclaimed, concealing my joy under an angry countenance. "This is your last ride, till papa comes back. I'll not trust you over the threshold again, you naughty, naughty girl."

"Aha, Ellen!" she cried gaily, jumping up, and running to my side. "I shall have a pretty story to tell to-night—and so you've found me out. Have you ever been here in your life before?"

"Put that hat on, and home at once," said I. "I'm dreadfully grieved at you, Miss Cathy, you've done extremely wrong! It's no use pouting and crying; that won't repay the trouble I've had, scouring the country after you. To think how Mr. Linton charged me to keep you in; and you stealing off so; it shows you are a cunning little fox, and nobody will put faith in you any more."

"What have I done?" sobbed she, instantly checked. "Papa charged me nothing: he'll not scold me, Ellen—he's never cross, like you!"

"Come, come!" I repeated. "I'll tie the riband. Now, let us have no petulance. Oh, for shame. You thirteen years old, and such a baby!"

This exclamation was caused by her pushing the hat from her head, and retreating to the chimney out of my reach.

"Nay," said the servant, "don't be hard on the bonny lass, Mrs. Dean. We made her stop—she'd fain have ridden forwards, afeard you should be uneasy. Hareton offered to go with her, and I thought he should. It's a wild road over the hills."

Hareton, during the discussion, stood with his hands in his pockets, too awkward to speak, though he looked as if he did not relish my intrusion.

"How long am I to wait?" I continued, disregarding the woman's interference. "It will be dark in ten minutes. Where is the pony, Miss Cathy? And where is Phœnix? I shall leave you, unless you be quick, so please yourself."

"The pony is in the yard," she replied, "and Phœnix is shut in there. He's bitten—and so is Charlie. I was going to tell you all about it; but you are in a bad temper, and don't deserve to hear."

I picked up her hat, and approached to reinstate it; but perceiving that the people of the house took her part, she commenced capering round the room; and, on my giving chase, ran like a mouse, over and under and behind the furniture, rendering it ridiculous for me to pursue.

Hareton and the woman laughed, and she joined them, and waxed more impertinent still; till I cried, in great irritation—

"Well, Miss Cathy, if you were aware whose house this is, you'd be glad enough to get out."

"It's *your* father's, isn't it?" said she, turning to Hareton.

"Nay," he replied, looking down, and blushing bashfully.

He could not stand a steady gaze from her eyes, though they were just his own.

"Whose, then—your master's?" she asked.

He coloured deeper, with a different feeling, muttered an oath, and turned away.

"Who is his master?" continued the tiresome girl, appealing to me. "He talked about 'our house,' and 'our folk.' I thought he had been the owner's son. And he never said, Miss; he should have done, shouldn't he, if he's a servant?"

Hareton grew black as a thunder-cloud, at this childish speech. I silently shook my questioner, and, at last, succeeded in equipping her for departure.

"Now, get my horse," she said, addressing her unknown kinsman as she would one of the stable-boys at the Grange. "And you may come with me. I want to see where the goblin hunter rises in the marsh, and to hear about the *fairishes,* as you call them—but make haste! What's the matter? Get my horse, I say."

"I'll see thee damned, before I be *thy* servant!" growled the lad.

"You'll see me *what?*" asked Catherine in surprise.

"Damned—thou saucy witch!" he replied.

"There, Miss Cathy! you see you have got into pretty company," I interposed. "Nice words to be used to a young lady! Pray don't begin to dispute with him. Come, let us seek for Minny ourselves, and begone."

"But, Ellen," cried she, staring, fixed in astonishment. "How dare he speak so to me? Mustn't he be made to do as I ask him? You wicked creature, I shall tell papa what you said—Now then!"

Hareton did not appear to feel this threat; so the tears sprung into her eyes with indignation. "You bring the pony," she exclaimed, turning to the woman, "and let my dog free this moment!"

"Softly, Miss," answered the addressed. "You'll lose nothing by being civil. Though Mr. Hareton, there, be not the master's son, he's your cousin; and I was never hired to serve you."

"*He* my cousin!" cried Cathy with a scornful laugh.

"Yes, indeed," responded her reprover.

"Oh, Ellen! don't let them say such things," she pursued in great trouble. "Papa is gone to fetch my cousin from London—my cousin is a gentleman's son. That my—" she stopped, and wept outright; upset at the bare notion of relationship with such a clown.

"Hush, hush!" I whispered, "people can have many cousins and of all sorts, Miss Cathy, without being any the worse for it; only they needn't keep their company, if they be disagreeable and bad."

"He's not, he's not my cousin, Ellen!" she went on, gathering fresh grief from reflection, and flinging herself into my arms for refuge from the idea.

I was much vexed at her and the servant for their mutual revelations; having no doubt of Linton's approaching arrival, communicated by the former, being reported to Mr. Heathcliff; and feeling as confident that Catherine's first thought on her father's return would be to seek an explanation of the latter's assertion concerning her rude-bred kindred.

Hareton, recovering from his disgust at being taken for a servant, seemed moved by her distress; and, having fetched the pony round to the door, he took, to propitiate her, a fine crooked-legged terrier whelp from the kennel, and putting it into her hand, bid her wisht, for he meant naught.

Pausing in her lamentations, she surveyed him with a glance of awe and horror, then burst forth anew.

I could scarcely refrain from smiling at this antipathy to the poor fellow, who was a well-made, athletic youth, good-looking in features, and stout and healthy, but attired in garments befitting his daily occupations of working on the farm, and lounging among the moors after rabbits and game. Still, I thought I could detect in his physiognomy a mind owning better qualities than his father ever possessed. Good things lost amid a wilderness of weeds, to be sure, whose rankness far over-topped their neglected growth; yet, notwithstanding, evidence of a wealthy soil that might yield luxuriant crops under other and favourable circumstances. Mr. Heathcliff, I believe, had not treated him physically ill; thanks to his fearless nature, which offered no temptation to that course of oppression; it had none of the timid susceptibility that would have given zest to ill-treatment, in Heathcliff's judgment. He appeared to have bent his malevolence on making him a brute: he was never taught to read or write; never rebuked for any bad habit which did not annoy his keeper; never led a single step towards virtue, or guarded by a single precept against vice. And from what I heard, Joseph contributed much to his deterioration by a narrow-minded partiality which prompted him to flatter and pet him, as a boy, because he was the head of the old family. And as he had been in the habit of accusing Catherine Earnshaw and Heathcliff, when children, of putting the master past his patience, and compelling him to seek solace in drink, by what he termed their "offald[39] ways," so at present he laid the whole burden of Hareton's faults on the shoulders of the usurper of his property.

If the lad swore, he wouldn't correct him; nor however culpably he behaved. It gave Joseph satisfaction, apparently, to watch him go the worst lengths. He allowed that he was ruined; that his soul was abandoned to perdition; but then, he reflected that Heathcliff must answer for it. Hareton's blood would be required at his hands; and there lay immense consolation in that thought.

Joseph had instilled into him a pride of name, and of his lineage; he would, had he dared, have fostered hate between him and the present owner of the Heights, but his dread of that owner amounted to superstition; and he confined his feelings regarding him to muttered innuendoes and private comminations.

I don't pretend to be intimately acquainted with the mode of living customary in those days at Wuthering Heights. I only speak from hearsay; for I saw little. The villagers affirmed Mr. Heathcliff was *near,* and a cruel hard landlord to his tenants; but the house, inside, had regained its ancient aspect of comfort under female management; and the scenes of riot common in Hindley's time were not now enacted within its walls. The master was too gloomy to seek companionship with any people, good or bad, and he is yet.

This, however, is not making progress with my story. Miss Cathy rejected the peace-offering of the terrier, and demanded her own dogs, Charlie and Phœnix. They came limping, and hanging their heads; and we set out for home, sadly out of sorts, every one of us.

I could not wring from my little lady how she had spent the day; except that, as I supposed, the goal of her pilgrimage was Penistone Crags; and she arrived without adventure to the gate of the farm-house, when Hareton happened to issue forth, attended by some canine followers who attacked her train.

They had a smart battle, before their owners could separate them: that formed an introduction. Catherine told Hareton who she was, and where she was going; and asked him to show her the way, finally beguiling him to accompany her.

He opened the mysteries of the Fairy cave, and twenty other queer places; but, being in disgrace, I was not favoured with a description of the interesting objects she saw.

I could gather, however, that her guide had been a favourite till she hurt his feelings by addressing him as a servant; and Heathcliff's housekeeper hurt hers by calling him her cousin.

Then the language he had held to her rankled in her heart; she who was always "love," and "darling," and "queen," and "angel," with everybody at the Grange, to be insulted so shockingly by a stranger! She did not comprehend it; and hard work I had to obtain a promise that she would not lay the grievance before her father.

I explained how he objected to the whole household at the Heights, and how sorry he would be to find she had been there; but I insisted most on the fact, that if she revealed my negligence of his orders, he would perhaps be so angry that I should have to leave; and Cathy couldn't bear that prospect: she pledged her word, and kept it, for my sake—after all, she was a sweet little girl.

---

[39] *Offald:* disreputable.

A letter, edged with black, announced the day of my master's return. Isabella was dead; and he wrote to bid me get mourning for his daughter, and arrange a room and other accommodations for his youthful nephew.

Catherine ran wild with joy at the idea of welcoming her father back, and indulged most sanguine anticipations of the innumerable excellencies of her "real" cousin.

The evening of their expected arrival came. Since early morning, she had been busy, ordering her own small affairs; and now, attired in her new black frock—poor thing! her aunt's death impressed her with no definite sorrow—she obliged me, by constant worrying, to walk with her down through the grounds to meet them.

"Linton is just six months younger than I am," she chattered, as we strolled leisurely over the swells and hollows of mossy turf, under shadow of the trees. "How delightful it will be to have him for a playfellow! Aunt Isabella sent papa a beautiful lock of his hair; it was lighter than mine—more flaxen, and quite as fine. I have it carefully preserved in a little glass box; and I've often thought what pleasure it would be to see its owner. Oh! I am happy—and papa, dear, dear papa! Come, Ellen, let us run! come run!"

She ran, and returned and ran again, many times before my sober footsteps reached the gate, and then she seated herself on the grassy bank beside the path, and tried to wait patiently, but that was impossible; she couldn't be still a minute.

"How long they are!" she exclaimed. "Ah, I see some dust on the road—they are coming! No! When will they be here? May we not go a little way—half a mile, Ellen, only just half a mile? Do say yes, to that clump of birches at the turn!"

I refused staunchly; and, at length, her suspense was ended: the travelling carriage rolled in sight.

Miss Cathy shrieked, and stretched out her arms, as soon as she caught her father's face, looking from the window. He descended, nearly as eager as herself; and a considerable interval elapsed ere they had a thought to spare for any but themselves.

While they exchanged caresses, I took a peep in to see after Linton. He was asleep in a corner, wrapped in a warm, fur-lined cloak, as if it had been winter. A pale, delicate, effeminate boy, who might have been taken for my master's younger brother, so strong was the resemblance; but there was a sickly peevishness in his aspect that Edgar Linton never had.

The latter saw me looking; and having shaken hands, advised me to close the door, and leave him undisturbed; for the journey had fatigued him.

Cathy would fain have taken one glance; but her father told her to come on, and they walked together up the park, while I hastened before to prepare the servants.

"Now, darling," said Mr. Linton, addressing his daughter, as they halted at the bottom of the front steps, "your cousin is not so strong or so merry as you are, and he has lost his mother, remember, a very short time since; therefore, don't expect him to play and run about with you directly. And don't harass him much by talking—let him be quiet this evening, at least, will you?"

"Yes, yes, papa," answered Catherine; "but I do want to see him; and he hasn't once looked out."

The carriage stopped; and the sleeper, being roused, was lifted to the ground by his uncle.

"This is your cousin Cathy, Linton," he said, putting their little hands together. "She's fond of you already; and mind you don't grieve her by crying to-night. Try to be cheerful now; the travelling is at an end, and you have nothing to do but rest and amuse yourself as you please."

"Let me go to bed, then," answered the boy, shrinking from Catherine's salute; and he put his fingers to his eyes to remove incipient tears.

"Come, come, there's a good child," I whispered, leading him in. "You'll make her weep too—see how sorry she is for you!"

I do not know whether it were sorrow for him, but his cousin put on as sad a countenance as himself, and returned to her father. All three entered, and mounted to the library, where tea was laid ready.

I proceeded to remove Linton's cap and mantle, and placed him on a chair by the table; but he was no sooner seated than he began to cry afresh. My master inquired what was the matter.

"I can't sit on a chair," sobbed the boy.

"Go to the sofa, then, and Ellen shall bring you some tea," answered his uncle, patiently.

He had been greatly tried during the journey, I felt convinced, by his fretful, ailing charge.

Linton slowly trailed himself off, and lay down. Cathy carried a foot-stool and her cup to his side.

At first she sat silent; but that could not last; she had resolved to make a pet of her little cousin, as she would have him to be; and she commenced stroking his curls, and kissing his cheek, and offering him tea in her saucer, like a baby. This pleased him, for he was not much better; he dried his eyes, and lightened into a faint smile.

"Oh, he'll do very well," said the master to me, after watching them a minute. "Very well, if we can keep him, Ellen. The company of a child of his own age will instil new spirit into him soon, and by wishing for strength he'll gain it."

"Aye, if we can keep him!" I mused to myself; and sore misgivings came over me that there was slight hope of that. And then, I thought, however will that weakling live at Wuthering Heights, between his father and Hareton? What playmates and instructors they'll be.

Our doubts were presently decided—even earlier than I expected. I had just taken the children upstairs, after tea was finished, and seen Linton asleep—he would not suffer me to leave him till that was the case. I had come down, and was standing by the table in the hall, lighting a bed-room candle for Mr. Edgar, when a maid stepped out of the kitchen and informed me that Mr. Heathcliff's servant, Joseph, was at the door, and wished to speak with the master.

"I shall ask him what he wants first," I said, in considerable trepidation. "A very unlikely hour to be troubling people, and the instant they have returned from a long journey. I don't think the master can see him."

Joseph had advanced through the kitchen, as I uttered these words, and now presented himself in the hall. He was donned in his Sunday garments, with his most sanctimonious and sourest face; and holding his hat in one hand and his stick in the other, he proceeded to clean his shoes on the mat.

"Good evening, Joseph," I said, coldly. "What business brings you here to-night?"

"It's Maister Linton Aw mun spake tull," he answered, waving me disdainfully aside.

"Mr. Linton is going to bed; unless you have something particular to say, I'm sure he won't hear it now," I continued. "You had better sit down in there, and entrust your message to me."

"Which is his rahm?" pursued the fellow, surveying the range of closed doors.

I perceived he was bent on refusing my mediation; so very reluctantly I went up to the library, and announced the unseasonable visitor, advising that he should be dismissed till next day.

Mr. Linton had no time to empower me to do so, for he mounted close at my heels, and, pushing into the apartment, planted himself at the far side of the table, with his two fists clapped on the head of his stick, and began in an elevated tone, as if anticipating opposition—

"Hathecliff has send me for his lad, un Aw 'munn't goa back 'baht him."[40]

Edgar Linton was silent a minute; an expression of exceeding sorrow overcast his features; he would have pitied the child on his own account; but, recalling Isabella's hopes and fears, and anxious wishes for her son, and her commendations of him to his care, he grieved bitterly at the prospect of yielding him up, and searched in his heart how it might be avoided. No plan offered itself: the very exhibition of any desire to keep him would have rendered the claimant more peremptory: there was nothing left but to resign him. However, he was not going to rouse him from his sleep.

"Tell Mr. Heathcliff," he answered, calmly, "that his son shall come to Wuthering Heights to-morrow. He is in bed, and too tired to go the distance now. You may also tell him that the mother of Linton desired him to remain under my guardianship; and, at present, his health is very precarious."

"Noa!" said Joseph, giving a thud with his prop on the floor, and assuming an authoritative air. "Noa! that manes nowt—Hathecliff maks noa 'cahnt uh t' mother, nur yah norther—bud he'll hev his lad; und Aw mun tak him—soa nah yah knaw!"

"You shall not to-night!" answered Linton, decisively. "Walk down stairs at once, and repeat to your master what I have said. Ellen, show him down. Go—"

And, aiding the indignant elder with a lift by the arm, he rid the room of him, and closed the door.

"Varrah weel!" shouted Joseph, as he slowly drew off. "Tuh morn, he's come hisseln, un' thrust *him* aht, if yah darr!"

CHAPTER 20

To obviate the danger of this threat being fulfilled, Mr. Linton commissioned me to take the boy home early, on Catherine's pony, and, said he—

"As we shall now have no influence over his destiny, good or bad, you must say nothing of where he is gone to my daughter; she cannot associate with him hereafter, and it is better for her to remain in ignorance of his proximity, lest she should be restless, and anxious to visit the Heights. Merely tell her, his father sent for him suddenly, and he has been obliged to leave us."

Linton was very reluctant to be roused from his bed at five o'clock, and astonished to be informed that he must prepare for further travelling; but I softened off the matter by stating that he was going to spend some time with his father, Mr. Heathcliff, who wished to see him so much, he did not like to defer the pleasure till he should recover from his late journey.

"My father?" he cried, in strange perplexity. "Mamma never told me I had a father. Where does he live? I'd rather stay with uncle."

"He lives a little distance from the Grange," I replied, "just beyond those hills— not so far but you may walk over here, when you get hearty. And you should be

---

[40] *Baht him:* without him.

glad to go home, and to see him. You must try to love him, as you did your mother, and then he will love you."

"But why have I not heard of him before?" asked Linton; "why didn't mamma and he live together, as other people do?"

"He had business to keep him in the north," I answered; "and your mother's health required her to reside in the south."

"And why didn't mamma speak to me about him?" persevered the child. "She often talked of uncle, and I learnt to love him long ago. How am I to love papa? I don't know him."

"Oh, all children love their parents," I said. "Your mother, perhaps, thought you would want to be with him, if she mentioned him often to you. Let us make haste. An early ride on such a beautiful morning is much preferable to an hour's more sleep."

"Is *she* to go with us?" he demanded. "The little girl I saw yesterday?"

"Not now," replied I.

"Is uncle?" he continued.

"No, I shall be your companion there," I said.

Linton sank back on his pillow, and fell into a brown study.

"I won't go without uncle," he cried at length; "I can't tell where you mean to take me."

I attempted to persuade him of the naughtiness of showing reluctance to meet his father; still he obstinately resisted any progress towards dressing, and I had to call for my master's assistance in coaxing him out of bed.

The poor thing was finally got off with several delusive assurances that his absence should be short; that Mr. Edgar and Cathy would visit him; and other promises, equally ill-founded, which I invented and reiterated at intervals throughout the way.

The pure heather-scented air, and the bright sunshine, and the gentle canter of Minny relieved his despondency, after a while. He began to put questions concerning his new home, and its inhabitants, with greater interest and liveliness.

"Is Wuthering Heights as pleasant a place as Thrushcross Grange?" he inquired, turning to take a last glance into the valley, whence a light mist mounted and formed a fleecy cloud on the skirts of the blue.

"It is not so buried in trees," I replied, "and it is not quite so large, but you can see the country beautifully, all round; and the air is healthier for you—fresher and dryer. You will, perhaps, think the building old and dark at first—though it is a respectable house, the next best in the neighbourhood. And you will have such nice rambles on the moors! Hareton Earnshaw—that is Miss Cathy's other cousin, and so yours in a manner—will show you all the sweetest spots; and you can bring a book in fine weather, and make a green hollow your study; and, now and then, your uncle may join you in a walk: he does, frequently, walk out on the hills."

"And what is my father like?" he asked. "Is he as young and handsome as uncle?"

"He's as young," said I, "but he has black hair and eyes, and looks sterner, and he is taller and bigger altogether. He'll not seem to you so gentle and kind at first, perhaps, because it is not his way—still, mind you be frank and cordial with him; and naturally he'll be fonder of you than any uncle, for you are his own."

"Black hair and eyes!" mused Linton. "I can't fancy him. Then I am not like him, am I?"

"Not much," I answered. Not a morsel, I thought, surveying with regret the white complexion and slim frame of my companion, and his large languid eyes—his mother's eyes, save that, unless a morbid touchiness kindled them a moment, they had not a vestige of her sparkling spirit.

"How strange that he should never come to see mamma and me," he murmured. "Has he ever seen me? If he have, I must have been a baby—I remember not a single thing about him!"

"Why, Master Linton," said I, "three hundred miles is a great distance; and ten years seem very different in length to a grown up person, compared with what they do to you. It is probable Mr. Heathcliff proposed going, from summer to summer, but never found a convenient opportunity; and now it is too late. Don't trouble him with questions on the subject: it will disturb him for no good."

The boy was fully occupied with his own cogitations for the remainder of the ride, till we halted before the farm-house garden gate. I watched to catch his impressions in his countenance. He surveyed the carved front and low-browed lattices, the straggling gooseberry bushes and crooked firs, with solemn intentness, and then shook his head: his private feelings entirely disapproved of the exterior of his new abode; but he had sense to postpone complaining—there might be compensation within.

Before he dismounted, I went and opened the door. It was half-past six; the family had just finished breakfast; the servant was clearing and wiping down the table. Joseph stood by his master's chair telling some tale concerning a lame horse; and Hareton was preparing for the hay-field.

"Hallo, Nelly!" cried Mr. Heathcliff, when he saw me. "I feared I should have to come down and fetch my property myself. You've brought it, have you? Let us see what we can make of it."

He got up and strode to the door: Hareton and Joseph followed in gaping curiosity. Poor Linton ran a frightened eye over the faces of the three.

"Sure-ly," said Joseph after a grave inspection, "he's swopped wi' ye, maister, an' yon's his lass!"

Heathcliff, having stared his son into an ague of confusion, uttered a scornful laugh.

"God! what a beauty! what a lovely, charming thing!" he exclaimed. "Haven't they reared it on snails and sour milk, Nelly? Oh, damn my soul! but that's worse than I expected—and the devil knows I was not sanguine!"

I bid the trembling and bewildered child get down, and enter. He did not thoroughly comprehend the meaning of his father's speech, or whether it were intended for him: indeed, he was not yet certain that the grim, sneering stranger was his father; but he clung to me with growing trepidation, and on Mr. Heathcliff's taking a seat, and bidding him "come hither," he hid his face on my shoulder, and wept.

"Tut, tut!" said Heathcliff, stretching out a hand and dragging him roughly between his knees, and then holding up his head by the chin. "None of that nonsense! We're not going to hurt thee, Linton—isn't that thy name? Thou art thy mother's child, entirely! Where is *my* share in thee, puling chicken?"

He took off the boy's cap and pushed back his thick flaxen curls, felt his slender arms, and his small fingers; during which examination, Linton ceased crying, and lifted his great blue eyes to inspect the inspector.

"Do you know me?" asked Heathcliff, having satisfied himself that the limbs were all equally frail and feeble.

"No!" said Linton, with a gaze of vacant fear.

"You've heard of me, I dare say?"

"No," he replied again.

"No? What a shame of your mother, never to waken your filial regard for me! You are my son, then, I'll tell you; and your mother was a wicked slut to leave you in ignorance of the sort of father you possessed. Now, don't wince, and colour up! Though it *is* something to see you have not white blood. Be a good lad; and I'll do for you. Nelly, if you be tired you may sit down; if not get home again. I guess you'll report what you hear and see, to the cipher at the Grange; and this thing won't be settled while you linger about it."

"Well," replied I, "I hope you'll be kind to the boy, Mr. Heathcliff, or you'll not keep him long, and he's all you have akin in the wide world that you will ever know—remember."

"I'll be *very* kind to him, you needn't fear!" he said, laughing. "Only nobody else must be kind to him—I'm jealous of monopolizing his affection. And, to begin my kindness, Joseph! bring the lad some breakfast. Hareton, you infernal calf, begone to your work. Yes, Nell," he added when they were departed, "my son is prospective owner of your place, and I should not wish him to die till I was certain of being his successor. Besides, he's *mine,* and I want the triumph of seeing *my* descendent fairly lord of their estates; my child hiring their children to till their fathers' lands for wages. That is the sole consideration which can make me endure the whelp—I despise him for himself, and hate him for the memories he revives! But that consideration is sufficient; he's as safe with me, and shall be tended as carefully as your master tends his own. I have a room upstairs, furnished for him in handsome style; I've engaged a tutor, also, to come three times a week, from twenty miles distance, to teach him what he pleases to learn. I've ordered Hareton to obey him; and in fact I've arranged everything with a view to preserve the superior and the gentleman in him, above his associates. I do regret, however, that he so little deserves the trouble. If I wished any blessing in the world, it was to find him a worthy object of pride, and I'm bitterly disappointed with the whey-faced whining wretch!"

While he was speaking, Joseph returned, bearing a basin of milk-porridge, and placed it before Linton. He stirred round the homely mess with a look of aversion, and affirmed he could not eat it.

I saw the old man-servant shared largely in his master's scorn of the child, though he was compelled to retain the sentiment in his heart, because Heathcliff plainly meant his underlings to hold him in honour.

"Cannot ate it?" repeated he, peering in Linton's face, and subduing his voice to a whisper, for fear of being overheard. "But Maister Hareton nivir ate nowt else, when he wer a little un: und what wer gooid eneugh fur him's gooid eneugh fur yah, Aw's rayther think!"

"I *shan't* eat it!" answered Linton, snappishly. "Take it away."

Joseph snatched up the food indignantly, and brought it to us.

"Is there owt ails th' victuals?" he asked, thrusting the tray under Heathcliff's nose.

"What should ail them?" he said.

"Wah!" answered Joseph, "yon dainty chap says he cannut ate 'em. Bud Aw guess it's raight! His mother wer just soa—we wer a'most too mucky tuh sow t' corn fur makking her breead."

"Don't mention his mother to me," said the master, angrily. "Get him something that he can eat, that's all. What is his usual food, Nelly?"

I suggested boiled milk or tea; and the housekeeper received instructions to prepare some.

Come, I reflected, his father's selfishness may contribute to his comfort. He perceives his delicate constitution, and the necessity of treating him tolerably. I'll console Mr. Edgar by acquainting him with the turn Heathcliff's humour has taken.

Having no excuse for lingering longer, I slipped out, while Linton was engaged in timidly rebuffing the advances of a friendly sheep-dog. But he was too much on the alert to be cheated: as I closed the door, I heard a cry, and a frantic repetition of the words—

"Don't leave me! I'll not stay here! I'll not stay here!'

Then the latch was raised and fell: they did not suffer him to come forth. I mounted Minny, and urged her to a trot; and so my brief guardianship ended.

CHAPTER 21

We had sad work with little Cathy that day: she rose in high glee, eager to join her cousin; and such passionate tears and lamentations followed the news of his departure, that Edgar himself was obliged to sooth her, by affirming he should come back soon; he added, however, "if I can get him"; and there were no hopes of that.

This promise poorly pacified her, but time was more potent; and though still, at intervals, she inquired of her father when Linton would return, before she did see him again, his features had waxed so dim in her memory that she did not recognise him.

When I chanced to encounter the housekeeper of Wuthering Heights, in paying business-visits to Gimmerton, I used to ask how the young master got on; for he lived almost as secluded as Catherine herself, and was never to be seen. I could gather from her that he continued in weak health, and was a tiresome inmate. She said Mr. Heathcliff seemed to dislike him ever longer and worse, though he took some trouble to conceal it. He had an antipathy to the sound of his voice, and could not do at all with his sitting in the same room with him many minutes together.

There seldom passed much talk between them; Linton learnt his lessons, and spent his evenings in a small apartment they called the parlour; or else lay in bed all day, for he was constantly getting coughs, and colds, and aches, and pains of some sort.

"And I never knew such a faint-hearted creature," added the woman; "nor one so careful of hisseln. He *will* go on, if I leave the window open, a bit late in the evening. Oh! it's killing, a breath of night air! And he must have a fire in the middle of summer; and Joseph's 'bacca pipe is poison; and he must always have sweets and dainties, and always milk, milk for ever—heeding naught how the rest of us are pinched in winter; and there he'll sit, wrapped in his furred cloak in his chair by the fire, and some toast and water, or other slop on the hob to sip at; and if Hareton, for pity, comes to amuse him—Hareton is not bad-natured, though he's rough—they're sure to part, one swearing and the other crying. I believe the master would relish Earnshaw's thrashing him to a mummy, if he were not his son; and I'm certain he would be fit to turn him out of doors, if he knew half the nursing he gives hisseln. But then, he won't go into danger of temptation; he never enters the parlour, and should Linton show those ways in the house where he is, he sends him upstairs directly."

I divined, from this account, that utter lack of sympathy had rendered young Heathcliff selfish and disagreeable, if he were not so originally; and my interest in him, consequently, decayed, though still I was moved with a sense of grief at his lot, and a wish that he had been left with us.

Mr. Edgar encouraged me to gain information; he thought a great deal about him, I fancy, and would have run some risk to see him; and he told me once to ask the housekeeper whether he ever came into the village?

She said he had only been twice, on horseback, accompanying his father; and both times he pretended to be quite knocked up for three or four days afterwards.

That housekeeper left, if I recollect rightly, two years after he came; and another, whom I did not know, was her successor: she lives there still.

Time wore on at the Grange in its former pleasant way, till Miss Cathy reached sixteen. On the anniversary of her birth we never manifested any signs of rejoicing, because it was also the anniversary of my late mistress's death. Her father invariably spent that day alone in the library; and walked, at dusk, as far as Gimmerton kirkyard, where he would frequently prolong his stay beyond midnight. Therefore Catherine was thrown on her own resources for amusement.

This twentieth of March was a beautiful spring day, and when her father had retired, my young lady came down dressed for going out, and said she had asked to have a ramble on the edge of the moors with me; and Mr. Linton had given her leave, if we went only a short distance and were back within the hour.

"So make haste, Ellen!" she cried. "I know where I wish to go; where a colony of moor game are settled. I want to see whether they have made their nests yet."

"That must be a good distance up," I answered; "they don't breed on the edge of the moor."

"No, it's not," she said. "I've gone very near with papa."

I put on my bonnet and sallied out, thinking nothing more of the matter. She bounded before me, and returned to my side, and was off again like a young greyhound; and, at first, I found plenty of entertainment in listening to the larks singing far and near, and enjoying the sweet, warm sunshine, and watching her, my pet and my delight, with her golden ringlets flying loose behind, and her bright cheek, as soft and pure in its bloom as a wild rose, and her eyes radiant with cloudless pleasure. She was a happy creature, and an angel, in those days. It's a pity she could not be content.

"Well," said I, "where are your moor game, Miss Cathy? We should be at them—the Grange park-fence is a great way off now."

"Oh, a little further—only a little further, Ellen," was her answer, continually. "Climb to that hillock, pass that bank, and by the time you reach the other side, I shall have raised the birds."

But there were so many hillocks and banks to climb and pass, that, at length, I began to be weary, and told her we must halt, and retrace our steps.

I shouted to her, as she had outstripped me, a long way; she either did not hear or did not regard, for she still sprang on, and I was compelled to follow. Finally, she dived into a hollow; and before I came in sight of her again, she was two miles nearer Wuthering Heights than her own home; and I beheld a couple of persons arrest her, one of whom I felt convinced was Mr. Heathcliff himself.

Cathy had been caught in the fact of plundering, or, at least, hunting out the nests of the grouse.

The Heights were Heathcliff's land, and he was reproving the poacher.

"I've neither taken any nor found any," she said, as I toiled to them, expanding her hands in corroboration of the statement. "I didn't mean to take them; but papa told me there were quantities up here, and I wished to see the eggs."

Heathcliff glanced at me with an ill-meaning smile, expressing his acquaintance with the party, and, consequently, his malevolence towards it, and demanded who "papa" was?

"Mr. Linton of Thrushcross Grange," she replied. "I thought you did not know me, or you wouldn't have spoken in that way."

"You suppose papa is highly esteemed and respected then?" he said, sarcastically.

"And what are you?" inquired Catherine, gazing curiously on the speaker. "That man I've seen before. Is he your son?"

She pointed to Hareton, the other individual, who had gained nothing but increased bulk and strength by the addition of two years to his age: he seemed as awkward and rough as ever.

"Miss Cathy," I interrupted, "it will be three hours instead of one that we are out, presently. We really must go back."

"No, that man is not my son," answered Heathcliff, pushing me aside. "But I have one, and you have seen him before, too; and, though your nurse is in a hurry, I think both you and she would be the better for a little rest. Will you just turn this nab of heath,[41] and walk into my house? You'll get home earlier for the ease; and you shall receive a kind welcome."

I whispered Catherine that she mustn't, on any account, accede to the proposal; it was entirely out of the question.

"Why?" she asked, aloud. "I'm tired of running, and the ground is dewy—I can't sit here. Let us go, Ellen! Besides, he says I have seen his son. He's mistaken, I think; but I guess where he lives—at the farm-house I visited in coming from Penistone Crags. Don't you?"

"I do. Come, Nelly, hold your tongue—it will be a treat for her to look in on us. Hareton, get forwards with the lass. You shall walk with me, Nelly."

"No, she's not going to any such place," I cried, struggling to release my arm which he had seized; but she was almost at the doorstones already, scampering round the brow at full speed. Her appointed companion did not pretend to escort her; he shyed off by the road-side, and vanished.

"Mr. Heathcliff, it's very wrong," I continued; "you know you mean no good. And there she'll see Linton, and all will be told, as soon as ever we return; and I shall have the blame."

"I want her to see Linton," he answered; "he's looking better these few days; it's not often he's fit to be seen. And we'll soon persuade her to keep the visit secret—where is the harm of it?"

"The harm of it is, that her father would hate me if he found I suffered her to enter your house; and I am convinced you have a bad design in encouraging her to do so," I replied.

"My design is as honest as possible. I'll inform you of its whole scope," he said. "That the two cousins may fall in love, and get married. I'm acting generously to your master; his young chit has no expectations, and should she second my wishes, she'll be provided for, at once, as joint successor with Linton."

"If Linton died," I answered, "and his life is quite uncertain, Catherine would be the heir."

"No, she would not," he said. "There is no clause in the will to secure it so; his property would go to me; but, to prevent disputes, I desire their union, and am resolved to bring it about."

"And I'm resolved she shall never approach your house with me again," I returned, as we reached the gate, where Miss Cathy waited our coming.

Heathcliff bid me be quiet; and, preceding us up the path, hastened to open the door. My young lady gave him several looks, as if she could not exactly make up her mind what to think of him; but now he smiled when he met her eye, and softened his voice in addressing her, and I was foolish enough to imagine the memory of her mother might disarm him from desiring her injury.

---

[41]A knob or projecting escarpment on a hill.

Linton stood on the hearth. He had been out walking in the fields, for his cap was on, and he was calling to Joseph to bring him dry shoes.

He had grown tall of his age, still wanting some months of sixteen. His features were pretty yet, and his eye and complexion brighter than I remembered them, though with merely temporary lustre borrowed from the salubrious air and genial sun.

"Now, who is that?" asked Mr. Heathcliff, turning to Cathy. "Can you tell?"

"Your son?" she said, having doubtfully surveyed first one and then the other.

"Yes, yes," answered he; "but is this the only time you have beheld him? Think! Ah! you have a short memory. Linton, don't you recall your cousin, that you used to tease us so with wishing to see?"

"What, Linton!" cried Cathy, kindling into joyful surprise at the name. "Is that little Linton? He's taller than I am! Are you Linton?"

The youth stepped forward, and acknowledged himself: she kissed him fervently, and they gazed with wonder at the change time had wrought in the appearance of each.

Catherine had reached her full height; her figure was both plump and slender, elastic as steel, and her whole aspect sparkling with health and spirits. Linton's looks and movements were very languid, and his form extremely slight; but there was a grace in his manner that mitigated these defects, and rendered him not unpleasing.

After exchanging numerous marks of fondness with him, his cousin went to Mr. Heathcliff, who lingered by the door, dividing his attention between the objects inside and those that lay without, pretending, that is, to observe the latter, and really noting the former alone.

"And you are my uncle, then!" she cried, reaching up to salute him. "I thought I liked you, though you were cross, at first. Why don't you visit at the Grange with Linton? To live all these years such close neighbours, and never see us, is odd; what have you done so for?"

"I visited it once or twice too often before you were born," he answered. "There—damn it! If you have any kisses to spare, give them to Linton—they are thrown away on me."

"Naughty Ellen!" exclaimed Catherine, flying to attack me next with her lavish caresses. "Wicked Ellen! to try to hinder me from entering. But I'll take this walk every morning in future. May I, uncle—and sometimes bring papa? Won't you be glad to see us?"

"Of course!" replied the uncle, with a hardly suppressed grimace, resulting from his deep aversion to both the proposed visitors. "But stay," he continued, turning towards the young lady. "Now I think of it, I'd better tell you. Mr. Linton has a prejudice against me; we quarrelled at one time of our lives, with unchristian ferocity; and, if you mention coming here to him, he'll put a veto on your visits altogether. Therefore, you must not mention it, unless you be careless of seeing your cousin hereafter. You may come, if you will, but you must not mention it."

"Why did you quarrel?" asked Catherine, considerably crestfallen.

"He thought me too poor to wed his sister," answered Heathcliff, "and was grieved that I got her. His pride was hurt, and he'll never forgive it."

"That's wrong!" said the young lady: "some time, I'll tell him so. But Linton and I have no share in your quarrel. I'll not come here, then; he shall come to the Grange."

"It will be too far for me," murmured her cousin; "to walk four miles would kill me. No, come here, Miss Catherine, now and then, not every morning, but once or twice a week."

The father launched towards his son a glance of bitter contempt.

"I am afraid, Nelly, I shall lose my labour," he muttered to me. "Miss Catherine, as the ninny calls her, will discover his value, and send him to the devil. Now, if it had been Hareton—do you know that, twenty times a day, I covet Hareton, with all his degradation? I'd have loved the lad had he been some one else. But I think he's safe from *her* love. I'll pit him against that paltry creature, unless it bestir itself briskly. We calculate it will scarcely last till it is eighteen. Oh, confound the vapid thing. He's absorbed in drying his feet, and never looks at her—Linton!"

"Yes, father," answered the boy.

"Have you nothing to show your cousin, anywhere about; not even a rabbit, or a weasel's nest? Take her into the garden, before you change your shoes; and into the stable to see your horse."

"Wouldn't you rather sit here?" asked Linton, addressing Cathy in a tone which expressed reluctance to move again.

"I don't know," she replied, casting a longing look to the door, and evidently eager to be active.

He kept his seat, and shrank closer to the fire.

Heathcliff rose, and went into the kitchen, and from thence to the yard, calling out for Hareton.

Hareton responded, and presently the two re-entered. The young man had been washing himself, as was visible by the glow on his cheeks, and his wetted hair.

"Oh, I'll ask *you,* uncle," cried Miss Cathy, recollecting the housekeeper's assertion. "That's not my cousin, is he?"

"Yes," he replied, "Your mother's nephew. Don't you like him?"

Catherine looked queer.

"Is he not a handsome lad?" he continued.

The uncivil little thing stood on tiptoe, and whispered a sentence in Heathcliff's ear.

He laughed; Hareton darkened; I perceived he was very sensitive to suspected slights, and had obviously a dim notion of his inferiority. But his master or guardian chased the frown by exclaiming—

"You'll be the favourite among us, Hareton! She says you are a—what was it? Well, something very flattering. Here! you go with her round the farm. And behave like a gentleman, mind! Don't use any bad words; and don't stare, when the young lady is not looking at you, and be ready to hide your face when she is; and, when you speak, say your words slowly, and keep your hands out of your pockets. Be off, and entertain her as nicely as you can."

He watched the couple walking past the window. Earnshaw had his countenance completely averted from his companion. He seemed studying the familiar landscape with a stranger's and an artist's interest.

Catherine took a sly look at him, expressing small admiration. She then turned her attention to seeking out objects of amusement for herself, and tripped merrily on, lilting a tune to supply the lack of conversation.

"I've tied his tongue," observed Heathcliff. "He'll not venture a single syllable, all the time! Nelly, you recollect me at his age—nay, some years younger. Did I ever look so stupid, so 'gaumless,'[42] as Joseph calls it?"

"Worse," I replied, "because more sullen with it."

"I've a pleasure in him," he continued reflecting aloud. "He has satisfied my expectations. If he were a born fool I should not enjoy it half so much. But he's no fool; and I can sympathise with all his feelings, having felt them myself. I know

---

[42] *Gaumless:* witless, befuddled.

what he suffers now, for instance, exactly—it is merely a beginning of what he shall suffer, though. And he'll never be able to emerge from his bathos of coarseness and ignorance. I've got him faster than his scoundrel of a father secured me, and lower; for he takes a pride in his brutishness. I've taught him to scorn everything extra-animal as silly and weak. Don't you think Hindley would be proud of his son, if he could see him? almost as proud as I am of mine. But there's this difference; one is gold put to the use of paving stones, and the other is tin polished to ape a service of silver. *Mine* has nothing valuable about it; yet I shall have the merit of making it go as far as such poor stuff can go. *His* had first-rate qualities, and they are lost—rendered worse than unavailing. I have nothing to regret; he would have more than any but I are aware of. And the best of it is, Hareton is damnably fond of me! You'll own that I've outmatched Hindley there. If the dead villain could rise from his grave to abuse me for his offspring's wrongs, I should have the fun of seeing the said offspring fight him back again, indignant that he should dare to rail at the one friend he has in the world!"

Heathcliff chuckled a fiendish laugh at the idea; I made no reply, because I saw that he expected none.

Meantime, our young companion, who sat too removed from us to hear what was said, began to evince symptoms of uneasiness, probably repenting that he had denied himself the treat of Catherine's society for fear of a little fatigue.

His father remarked the restless glances wandering to the window, and the hand irresolutely extended towards his cap.

"Get up, you idle boy!" he exclaimed with assumed heartiness. "Away after them! they are just at the corner, by the stand of hives."

Linton gathered his energies, and left the hearth. The lattice was open, and, as he stepped out, I heard Cathy inquiring of her unsociable attendant, what was that inscription over the door?

Hareton stared up, and scratched his head like a true clown.

"It's some damnable writing," he answered. "I cannot read it."

"Can't read it?" cried Catherine; "I can read it: it's English. But I want to know why it is there."

Linton giggled—the first appearance of mirth he had exhibited.

"He does not know his letters," he said to his cousin. "Could you believe in the existence of such a colossal dunce?"

"Is he all as he should be?" asked Miss Cathy seriously, "or is he simple—not right? I've questioned him twice now, and each time he looked so stupid I think he does not understand me; I can hardly understand *him*, I'm sure!"

Linton repeated his laugh, and glanced at Hareton tauntingly, who certainly did not seem quite clear of comprehension at that moment.

"There's nothing the matter but laziness, is there, Earnshaw?" he said. "My cousin fancies you are an idiot. There you experience the consequence of scorning 'book-larning,' as you would say. Have you noticed, Catherine, his frightful Yorkshire pronunciation?"

"Why, where the devil is the use on't?" growled Hareton, more ready in answering his daily companion. He was about to enlarge further, but the two youngsters broke into a noisy fit of merriment; my giddy Miss being delighted to discover that she might turn his strange talk to matter of amusement.

"Where is the use of the devil in that sentence?" tittered Linton. "Papa told you not to say any bad words, and you can't open your mouth without one. Do try to behave like a gentleman, now do!"

"If thou weren't more a lass than a lad, I'd fell thee this minute, I would; pitiful lath of a crater!" retorted the angry boor, retreating, while his face burnt with mingled rage and mortification; for he was conscious of being insulted, and embarrassed how to resent it.

Mr. Heathcliff, having overheard the conversation as well as I, smiled when he saw him go, but immediately afterwards cast a look of singular aversion on the flippant pair, who remained chattering in the door-way: the boy finding animation enough while discussing Hareton's faults and deficiencies, and relating anecdotes of his goings on; and the girl relishing his pert and spiteful sayings, without considering the ill-nature they evinced. But I began to dislike, more than to compassionate, Linton, and to excuse his father, in some measure, for holding him cheap.

We stayed till afternoon: I could not tear Miss Cathy away, before: but happily my master had not quitted his apartment, and remained ignorant of our prolonged absence.

As we walked home, I would fain have enlightened my charge on the characters of the people we had quitted; but she got it into her head that I was prejudiced against them.

"Aha!" she cried, "you take papa's side, Ellen—you are partial, I know, or else you wouldn't have cheated me so many years into the notion that Linton lived a long way from here. I'm really extremely angry, only I'm so pleased, I can't show it! But you must hold your tongue about my uncle: he's *my* uncle, remember, and I'll scold papa for quarrelling with him."

And so she ran on, till I dropped endeavouring to convince her of her mistake. She did not mention the visit that night, because she did not see Mr. Linton. Next day it all came out, sadly to my chagrin; and still I was not altogether sorry: I thought the burden of directing and warning would be more efficiently borne by him than me, but he was too timid in giving satisfactory reasons for his wish that she would shun connection with the household of the Heights, and Catherine liked good reasons for every restraint that harassed her petted will.

"Papa!" she exclaimed, after the morning's salutations, "guess whom I saw yesterday, in my walk on the moors. Ah, papa, you started! you've not done right, have you, now? I saw—But listen, and you shall hear how I found you out, and Ellen, who is in league with you, and yet pretended to pity me so, when I kept hoping, and was always disappointed about Linton's coming back!"

She gave a faithful account of her excursion and its consequences; and my master, though he cast more than one reproachful look at me, said nothing till she had concluded. The he drew her to him, and asked if she knew why he had concealed Linton's near neighbourhood from her? Could she think it was to deny her a pleasure that she might harmlessly enjoy?

"It was because you disliked Mr. Heathcliff," she answered.

"Then you believe I care more for my own feelings than yours, Cathy?" he said. "No, it was not because I disliked Mr. Heathcliff, but because Mr. Heathcliff dislikes me; and is a most diabolical man, delighting to wrong and ruin those he hates, if they give him the slightest opportunity. I knew that you could not keep up an acquaintance with your cousin, without being brought into contact with him; and I knew he would detest you, on my account; so, for your own good, and nothing else, I took precautions that you should not see Linton again. I meant to explain this some time as you grew older, and I'm sorry I delayed it!"

"But Mr. Heathcliff was quite cordial, papa," observed Catherine, not at all convinced; "and *he* didn't object to our seeing each other: he said I might come to his house when I pleased, only I must not tell you, because you had quarrelled with him, and would not forgive him for marrying Aunt Isabella. And you won't—*you* are the one to be blamed. He is willing to let *us* be friends—at least Linton and I—and you are not."

My master, perceiving that she would not take his word for her uncle-in-law's evil disposition, gave a hasty sketch of his conduct to Isabella, and the manner in which Wuthering Heights became his property. He could not bear to discourse long upon the topic, for though he spoke little of it, he still felt the same horror and detestation of his ancient enemy that had occupied his heart ever since Mrs. Linton's death. "She might have been living yet, if it had not been for him!" was his constant bitter reflection; and, in his eyes, Heathcliff seemed a murderer.

Miss Cathy, conversant with no bad deeds except her own slight acts of disobedience, in justice and passion, rising from hot temper and thoughtlessness, and repented of on the day they were committed, was amazed at the blackness of spirit that could brood on and cover revenge for years, and deliberately prosecute its plans, without a visitation of remorse. She appeared so deeply impressed and shocked at this new view of human nature—excluded from all her studies and all her ideas till now—that Mr. Edgar deemed it unnecessary to pursue the subject. He merely added—

"You will know hereafter, darling, why I wish you to avoid his house and family; now, return to your old employments and amusements, and think no more about them!"

Catherine kissed her father, and sat down quietly to her lessons for a couple of hours, according to custom; then she accompanied him into the grounds, and the whole day passed as usual: but in the evening, when she had retired to her room, and I went to help her to undress, I found her crying, on her knees by the bedside.

"Oh, fie, silly child!" I exclaimed. "If you had any real griefs, you'd be ashamed to waste a tear on this little contrariety. You never had one shadow of substantial sorrow, Miss Catherine. Suppose, for a minute, that master and I were dead, and you were by yourself in the world—how would you feel, then? Compare the present occasion with such an affliction as that, and be thankful for the friend you have, instead of coveting more."

"I'm not crying for myself, Ellen," she answered, "it's for him. He expected to see me again to-morrow, and there, he'll be so disappointed—and he'll wait for me, and I shan't come!"

"Nonsense!" said I, "do you imagine he has thought as much of you as you have of him? Hasn't he Hareton for a companion? Not one in a hundred would weep at losing a relation they had just seen twice, for two afternoons. Linton will conjecture how it is, and trouble himself no further about you."

"But may I not write a note to tell him why I cannot come?" she asked, rising to her feet. "And just send those books I promised to lend him? His books are not as nice as mine, and he wanted to have them extremely, when I told him how interesting they were. May I not, Ellen?"

"No, indeed, no, indeed!" replied I with decision. "Then he would write to you, and there'd never be an end of it. No, Miss Catherine, the acquaintance must be dropped entirely—so papa expects, and I shall see that it is done!"

"But how can one little note—" she recommenced, putting on an imploring countenance.

"Silence!" I interrupted. "We'll not begin with your little notes. Get into bed!"

She threw at me a very naughty look, so naughty that I would not kiss her good-night at first: I covered her up, and shut her door, in great displeasure; but, repenting half-way, I returned softly, and lo! there was Miss, standing at the table with a bit of blank paper before her and a pencil in her hand, which she guiltily slipped out of sight, on my re-entrance.

"You'll get nobody to take that, Catherine," I said, "if you write it; and at present I shall put out your candle."

I set the extinguisher on the flame, receiving as I did so a slap on my hand, and a petulant "cross thing!" I then quitted her again, and she drew the bolt in one of her worst, most peevish humours.

The letter was finished and forwarded to its destination by a milk-fetcher who came from the village, but that I didn't learn till some time afterwards. Weeks passed on, and Cathy recovered her temper, though she grew wondrous fond of stealing off to corners by herself, and often, if I came near her suddenly while reading, she would start, and bend over the book, evidently desirous to hide it; and I detected edges of loose paper sticking out beyond the leaves.

She also got a trick of coming down early in the morning, and lingering about the kitchen, as if she were expecting the arrival of something; and she had a small drawer in a cabinet in the library, which she would trifle over for hours, and whose key she took special care to remove when she left it.

One day, as she inspected this drawer, I observed that the playthings and trinkets, which recently formed its contents, were transmuted into bits of folded paper.

My curiosity and suspicions were roused; I determined to take a peep at her mysterious treasures; so, at night, as soon as she and my master were safe upstairs, I searched and readily found among my house keys, one that would fit the lock. Having opened, I emptied the whole contents into my apron, and took them with me to examine at leisure in my own chamber.

Though I could not but suspect, I was still surprised to discover that they were a mass of correspondence—daily almost, it must have been—from Linton Heathcliff, answers to documents forwarded by her. The earlier dated were embarrassed and short; gradually, however, they expanded into copious love letters, foolish as the age of the writer rendered natural, yet with touches, here and there, which I thought were borrowed from a more experienced source.

Some of them struck me as singularly odd compounds of ardour and flatness; commencing in strong feeling, and concluding in the affected, wordy way that a schoolboy might use to a fancied, incorporeal sweetheart.

Whether they satisfied Cathy, I don't know, but they appeared very worthless trash to me.

After turning over as many as I thought proper, I tied them in a handkerchief and set them aside, re-locking the vacant drawer.

Following her habit, my young lady descended early, and visited the kitchen: I watched her go to the door, on the arrival of a certain little boy; and, while the dairy maid filled his can, she tucked something into his jacket pocket, and plucked something out.

I went round by the garden, and laid wait for the messenger, who fought valorously to defend his trust, and we spilt the milk between us; but I succeeded in abstracting the epistle, and, threatening serious consequences if he did not look sharp home, I remained under the wall, and perused Miss Cathy's affectionate composition. It was more simple and more eloquent than her cousin's—very pretty and very silly. I shook my head, and went meditating into the house.

The day being wet, she could not divert herself with rambling about the park; so, at the conclusion of her morning studies, she resorted to the solace of the drawer. Her father sat reading at the table; and I, on purpose, had sought a bit of work in some unripped fringes of the window curtain, keeping my eye steadily fixed on her proceedings.

Never did any bird flying back to a plundered nest which it had left brim-ful of chirping young ones, express more complete despair in its anguished cries and flutterings, than she by her single "Oh!" and the change that transfigured her late happy countenance. Mr. Linton looked up.

"What is the matter, love? Have you hurt yourself?" he said.

His tone and look assured her *he* had not been the discoverer of the hoard.

"No, papa—" she gasped. "Ellen! Ellen! come upstairs—I'm sick!"

I obeyed her summons, and accompanied her out.

"Oh, Ellen! you have got them," she commenced immediately, dropping on her knees, when we were enclosed alone. "O, give them to me, and I'll never never do so again! Don't tell papa. You have not told papa, Ellen, say you have not! I've been exceedingly naughty, but I won't do it any more!"

With a grave severity in my manner, I bid her stand up.

"So," I exclaimed, "Miss Catherine, you are tolerably far on, it seems—you may well be ashamed of them! A fine bundle of trash you study in your leisure hours, to be sure: why, it's good enough to be printed! And what do you suppose the master will think, when I display it before him? I haven't shown it yet, but you needn't imagine I shall keep your ridiculous secrets. For shame! And you must have led the way in writing such absurdities; he would not have thought of beginning, I'm certain."

"I didn't! I didn't!" sobbed Cathy, fit to break her heart. "I didn't once think of loving him till—"

"*Loving!*" cried I, as scornfully as I could utter the word. "*Loving!* Did anybody ever hear the like! I might just as well talk of loving the miller who comes once a year to buy our corn. Pretty loving, indeed, and both times together you have seen Linton hardly four hours in your life! Now here is the babyish trash. I'm going with it to the library; and we'll see what your father says to such *loving.*"

She sprang at her precious epistles, but I held them above my head; and then she poured out further frantic entreaties that I would burn them—do anything rather than show them. And being really fully as inclined to laugh as scold, for I esteemed it all girlish vanity, I at length relented in a measure, and asked—

"If I consent to burn them, will you promise faithfully, neither to send nor receive a letter again, nor a book—for I perceive you have sent him books—nor locks of hair, nor rings, nor playthings?"

"We don't send playthings!" cried Catherine, her pride overcoming her shame.

"Nor anything at all, then, my lady!" I said. "Unless you will, here I go."

"I promise, Ellen!" she cried, catching my dress. "Oh, put them in the fire, do, do!"

But when I proceeded to open a place with the poker, the sacrifice was too painful to be borne. She earnestly supplicated that I would spare her one or two.

"One or two, Ellen, to keep for Linton's sake!"

I unknotted the handkerchief, and commenced dropping them in from an angle, and the flame curled up the chimney.

"I will have one, you cruel wretch!" she screamed, darting her hand into the fire, and drawing forth some half consumed fragments, at the expense of her fingers.

"Very well—and I will have some to exhibit to papa!" I answered, shaking back the rest into the bundle, and turning anew to the door.

She emptied her blackened pieces into the flames, and motioned me to finish the immolation. It was done; I stirred up the ashes, and interred them under a shovel-full of coals; and she mutely, and with a sense of intense injury, retired to her private apartment. I descended to tell my master that the young lady's qualm of sickness was almost gone, but I judged it best for her to lie down a while.

She wouldn't dine; but she re-appeared at tea, pale and red about the eyes, and marvellously subdued in outward aspect.

Next morning, I answered the letter by a slip of paper inscribed, "Master Heathcliff is requested to send no more notes to Miss Linton, as she will not receive them." And, thenceforth, the little boy came with vacant pockets.

CHAPTER 22

Summer drew to an end, and early Autumn: it was past Michaelmas, but the harvest was late that year, and a few of our fields were still uncleared.

Mr. Linton and his daughter would frequently walk out among the reapers; at the carrying of the last sheaves, they stayed till dusk, and the evening happening to be chill and damp, my master caught a bad cold, that, settling obstinately on his lungs, confined him indoors throughout the whole of the winter, nearly without intermission.

Poor Cathy, frightened from her little romance, had been considerably sadder and duller since its abandonment; and her father insisted on her reading less, and taking more exercise. She had his companionship no longer; I esteemed it a duty to supply its lack, as much as possible, with mine: an inefficient substitute, for I could only spare two or three hours, from my numerous diurnal occupations, to follow her footsteps, and then my society was obviously less desirable than his.

On an afternoon in October, or the beginning of November—a fresh watery afternoon, when the turf and paths were rustling with moist, withered leaves, and the cold, blue sky was half hidden by clouds, dark grey streamers, rapidly mounting from the west, and boding abundant rain—I requested my young lady to forego her ramble because I was certain of showers. She refused; and I unwillingly donned a cloak, and took my umbrella to accompany her on a stroll to the bottom of the park: a formal walk which she generally affected if low-spirited—and that she invariably was when Mr. Edgar had been worse than ordinary; a thing never known from his confession, but guessed both by her and me from his increased silence, and the melancholy of his countenance.

She went sadly on: there was no running or bounding now, though the chill wind might well have tempted her to a race. And often, from the side of my eye, I could detect her raising a hand, and brushing something off her cheek.

I gazed round for a means of diverting her thoughts. On one side of the road rose a high, rough bank, where hazels and stunted oaks, with their roots half exposed, held uncertain tenure: the soil was too loose for the latter; and strong winds had blown some nearly horizontal. In summer, Miss Catherine delighted to climb along these trunks, and sit in the branches, swinging twenty feet above the ground; and I, pleased with her agility, and her light, childish heart, still considered it proper to scold every time I caught her at such an elevation, but so that she knew there was no necessity for descending. From dinner to tea she would lie in her breeze-rocked cradle, doing nothing except singing old songs—my nursery lore—to herself, or watching the birds, joint tenants, feed and entice their young ones to fly, or nestling with closed lids, half thinking, half dreaming, happier than words can express.

"Look, Miss!" I exclaimed, pointing to a nook under the roots of one twisted tree. "Winter is not here yet. There's a little flower, up yonder, the last bud from the multitude of blue-bells that clouded those turf steps in July with a lilac mist. Will you clamber up, and pluck it to show to papa?"

Cathy stared a long time at the lonely blossom trembling in its earthy shelter, and replied, at length—

"No, I'll not touch it—but it looks melancholy, does it not, Ellen?"

"Yes," I observed, "about as starved and sackless[43] as you—your cheeks are bloodless; let us take hold of hands and run. You're so low, I dare say I shall keep up with you."

---

[43] *Sackless:* feeble.

"No," she repeated, and continued sauntering on, pausing, at intervals, to muse over a bit of moss, or a tuft of blanched grass, or a fungus spreading its bright orange among the heaps of brown foliage; and, ever and anon, her hand was lifted to her averted face.

"Catherine, why are you crying, love?" I asked, approaching and putting my arm over her shoulder. "You mustn't cry because papa has a cold; be thankful it is nothing worse."

She now put no further restraint on her tears; her breath was stifled by sobs.

"Oh, it *will* be something worse," she said. "And what shall I do when papa and you leave me, and I am by myself? I can't forget your words, Ellen, they are always in my ear. How life will be changed, how dreary the world will be, when papa and you are dead."

"None can tell, whether you won't die before us," I replied. "It's wrong to anticipate evil. We'll hope there are years and years to come before any of us go: master is young, and I am strong, and hardly forty-five. My mother lived till eighty, a canty dame to the last. And suppose Mr. Linton were spared till he saw sixty, that would be more years than you have counted, Miss. And would it not be foolish to mourn a calamity above twenty years beforehand?"

"But Aunt Isabella was younger than papa," she remarked, gazing up with timid hope to seek further consolation.

"Aunt Isabella had not you and me to nurse her," I replied. "She wasn't as happy as master; she hadn't as much to live for. All you need do, is to wait well on your father, and cheer him by letting him see you cheerful; and avoid giving him anxiety on any subject—mind that, Cathy! I'll not disguise but you might kill him, if you were wild and reckless, and cherished a foolish, fanciful affection for the son of a person who would be glad to have him in his grave; and allowed him to discover that you fretted over the separation he has judged it expedient to make."

"I fret about nothing on earth except papa's illness," answered my companion. "I care for nothing in comparison with papa. And I'll never—never—oh, never, while I have my senses, do an act, or say a word to vex him. I love him better than myself, Ellen; and I know it by this: I pray every night that I may live after him, because I would rather be miserable than that he should be—that proves I love him better than myself."

"Good words," I replied. "But deeds must prove it also; and after he is well, remember you don't forget resolutions formed in the hour of fear."

As we talked, we neared a door that opened on the road; and my young lady, lightening into sunshine again, climbed up, and seated herself on the top of the wall, reaching over to gather some hips that bloomed scarlet on the summit branches of the wild rose trees, shadowing the highway side; the lower fruit had disappeared, but only birds could touch the upper, except from Cathy's present station.

In stretching to pull them, her hat fell off; and as the door was locked, she proposed scrambling down to recover it. I bid her be cautious lest she got a fall, and she nimbly disappeared.

But the return was no such easy matter; the stones were smooth and neatly cemented, and the rosebushes and blackberry stragglers could yield no assistance in re-ascending. I, like a fool, didn't recollect that till I heard her laughing, and exclaiming—

"Ellen! you'll have to fetch the key, or else I must run round to the porter's lodge. I can't scale the ramparts on this side!"

"Stay where you are," I answered, "I have my bundle of keys in my pocket; perhaps I may manage to open it; if not, I'll go."

Catherine amused herself with dancing to and fro before the door, while I tried all the large keys in succession. I had applied the last, and found that none would do; so, repeating my desire that she would remain there, I was about to hurry home as fast as I could when an approaching sound arrested me. It was the trot of a horse; Cathy's dance stopped, and in a minute the horse stopped also.

"Who is that?" I whispered.

"Ellen, I wish you could open the door," whispered back my companion, anxiously.

"Ho, Miss Linton!" cried a deep voice (the rider's). "I'm glad to meet you. Don't be in haste to enter, for I have an explanation to ask and obtain."

"I shan't speak to you, Mr. Heathcliff!" answered Catherine. "Papa says you are a wicked man, and you hate both him and me; and Ellen says the same."

"That is nothing to the purpose," said Heathcliff. (He it was.) "I don't hate my son, I suppose, and it is concerning him that I demand your attention. Yes! you have cause to blush. Two or three months since, were you not in the habit of writing to Linton? making love in play, eh? You deserved, both of you, flogging for that! You especially, the elder, and less sensitive, as it turns out. I've got your letters, and if you give me any pertness, I'll send them to your father. I presume you grew weary of the amusement, and dropped it, didn't you? Well, you dropped Linton with it, into a Slough of Despond. He was in earnest—in love—really. As true as I live, he's dying for you—breaking his heart at your fickleness, not figuratively, but actually. Though Hareton has made him a standing jest for six weeks, and I have used more serious measures, and attempted to frighten him out of his idiocy, he gets worse daily, and he'll be under the sod before summer, unless you restore him!"

"How can you lie so glaringly to the poor child!" I called from the inside. "Pray ride on! How can you deliberately get up such paltry falsehoods? Miss Cathy, I'll knock the lock off with a stone. You won't believe that vile nonsense. You can feel in yourself, it is impossible that a person should die for love of a stranger."

"I was not aware there were eaves-droppers," muttered the detected villain. "Worthy Mrs. Dean, I like you, but I don't like your double dealing," he added, aloud. "How could *you* lie so glaringly, as to affirm I hated the 'poor child'? And invent bugbear stories to terrify her from my door-stones? Catherine Linton (the very name warms me), my bonny lass, I shall be from home all this week; go and see if I have not spoken truth; do, there's a darling! Just imagine your father in my place, and Linton in yours; then think how you would value your careless lover, if he refused to stir a step to comfort you, when your father, himself, entreated him; and don't, from pure stupidity, fall into the same error. I swear, on my salvation, he's going to his grave, and none but you can save him!"

The lock gave way, and I issued out.

"I swear Linton is dying," repeated Heathcliff, looking hard at me. "And grief and disappointment are hastening his death. Nelly, if you won't let her go, you can walk over yourself. But I shall not return till this time next week; and I think your master himself would scarcely object to her visiting her cousin!"

"Come in," said I, taking Cathy by the arm and half forcing her to re-enter, for she lingered, viewing with troubled eyes, the features of the speaker, too stern to express his inward deceit.

He pushed his horse close, and, bending down, observed—

"Miss Catherine, I'll own to you that I have little patience with Linton—and Hareton and Joseph have less. I'll own that he's with a harsh set. He pines for kindness, as well as love; and a kind word from you would be his best medicine. Don't mind Mrs. Dean's cruel cautions, but be generous, and contrive to see him. He dreams of you day and night, and cannot be persuaded that you don't hate him, since you neither write nor call."

I closed the door, and rolled a stone to assist the loosened lock in holding it; and spreading my umbrella, I drew my charge underneath, for the rain began to drive through the moaning branches of the trees, and warned us to avoid delay.

Our hurry prevented any comment on the encounter with Heathcliff, as we stretched towards home; but I divined instinctively that Catherine's heart was clouded now in double darkness. Her features were so sad, they did not seem hers: she evidently regarded what she had heard as every syllable true.

The master had retired to rest before we came in. Cathy stole to his room to inquire how he was; he had fallen asleep. She returned, and asked me to sit with her in the library. We took our tea together; and afterwards she lay down on the rug, and told me not to talk, for she was weary.

I got a book, and pretended to read. As soon as she supposed me absorbed in my occupation, she recommenced her silent weeping: it appeared, at present, her favourite diversion. I suffered her to enjoy it a while; then I expostulated, deriding and ridiculing all Mr. Heathcliff's assertions about his son, as if I were certain she would coincide. Alas! I hadn't the skill to counteract the effect his account had produced; it was just what he intended.

"You may be right, Ellen," she answered; "but I shall never feel at ease till I know. And I must tell Linton it is not my fault that I don't write; and convince him that I shall not change."

What use were anger and protestations against her silly credulity? We parted that night hostile; but next day beheld me on the road to Wuthering Heights, by the side of my wilful young mistress's pony. I couldn't bear to witness her sorrow, to see her pale, dejected countenance, and heavy eyes; and I yielded in the faint hope that Linton himself might prove, by his reception of us, how little of the tale was founded on fact.

CHAPTER 23

The rainy night had ushered in a misty morning—half frost, half drizzle—and temporary brooks crossed our path, gurgling from the uplands. My feet were thoroughly wetted; I was cross and low, exactly the humour suited for making the most of these disagreeable things.

We entered the farm-house by the kitchen way to ascertain whether Mr. Heathcliff were really absent, because I put slight faith in his own affirmation.

Joseph seemed sitting in a sort of elysium alone, beside a roaring fire; a quart of ale on the table near him, bristling with large pieces of toasted oat cake, and his black, short pipe in his mouth.

Catherine ran to the hearth to warm herself. I asked if the master were in?

My question remained so long unanswered, that I thought the old man had grown deaf, and repeated it louder.

"Na—ay!" he snarled, or rather screamed through his nose. "Na—ay! yah muh goa back whear yah coom frough."

"Joseph!" cried a peevish voice, simultaneously with me, from the inner room. "How often am I to call you? There are only a few red ashes now. Joseph! come this moment."

Vigorous puffs, and a resolute stare into the grate, declared he had no ear for this appeal. The housekeeper and Hareton were invisible; one gone on an errand, and the other at his work, probably. We knew Linton's tones and entered.

"Oh, I hope you'll die in a garret! starved to death," said the boy, mistaking our approach for that of his negligent attendant.

He stopped, on observing his error; his cousin flew to him.

"Is that you, Miss Linton?" he said, raising his head from the arm of the great chair in which he reclined. "No—don't kiss me. It takes my breath—dear me! Papa said you would call," continued he, after recovering a little from Catherine's embrace, while she stood by looking very contrite. "Will you shut the door, if you please? you left it open, and those—those *detestable* creatures won't bring coals to the fire. It's so cold!"

I stirred up the cinders, and fetched a scuttle-full myself. The invalid complained of being covered with ashes; but he had a tiresome cough, and looked feverish and ill, so I did not rebuke his temper.

"Well, Linton," murmured Catherine, when his corrugated brow relaxed. "Are you glad to see me? Can I do you any good?"

"Why didn't you come before?" he said. "You should have come, instead of writing. It tired me dreadfully, writing those long letters. I'd far rather have talked to you. Now, I can neither bear to talk, nor anything else. I wonder where Zillah is! Will you (looking at me) step into the kitchen and see?"

I had received no thanks for my other service; and being unwilling to run to and fro at his behest, I replied—

"Nobody is out there but Joseph."

"I want to drink," he exclaimed, fretfully, turning away. "Zillah is constantly gadding off to Gimmerton since papa went. It's miserable! And I'm obliged to come down here—they resolved never to hear me upstairs."

"Is your father attentive to you, Master Heathcliff?" I asked, perceiving Catherine to be checked in her friendly advances.

"Attentive? He makes *them* a little more attentive, at least," he cried. "The wretches! Do you know, Miss Linton, that brute Hareton laughs at me. I hate him—indeed, I hate them all—they are odious beings."

Cathy began searching for some water; she lighted on a pitcher in the dresser, filled a tumbler, and brought it. He bid her add a spoonful of wine from a bottle on the table; and, having swallowed a small portion, appeared more tranquil, and said she was very kind.

"And are you glad to see me?" asked she, reiterating her former question, and pleased to detect the faint dawn of a smile.

"Yes, I am. It's something new to hear a voice like yours!" he replied, "but I *have* been vexed, because you wouldn't come. And papa swore it was owing to me; he called me a pitiful, shuffling, worthless thing; and said you despised me; and if he had been in my place, he would be more the master of the Grange than your father, by this time. But you don't despise me, do you, Miss—"

"I wish you would say Catherine, or Cathy!" interrupted my young lady. "Despise you? No! Next to papa, and Ellen, I love you better than anybody living. I don't love Mr. Heathcliff, though; and I dare not come when he returns; will he stay away many days?"

"Not many," answered Linton, "but he goes onto the moors frequently, since the shooting season commenced, and you might spend an hour or two with me, in his absence. Do! say you will! I think I should not be peevish with you; you'd not provoke me, and you'd always be ready to help me, wouldn't you?"

"Yes," said Catherine, stroking his long soft hair; "if I could only get papa's consent, I'd spend half my time with you. Pretty Linton! I wish you were my brother!"

"And then you would like me as well as your father?" observed he, more cheerfully. "But papa says you would love me better than him and all the world, if you were my wife—so I'd rather you were that!"

"No! I should never love anybody better than papa," she returned gravely. "And people hate their wives, sometimes; but not their sisters and brothers, and if you were the latter, you would live with us, and papa would be as fond of you as he is of me."

Linton denied that people ever hated their wives; but Cathy affirmed they did, and in her wisdom, instanced his own father's aversion to her aunt.

I endeavoured to stop her thoughtless tongue. I couldn't succeed till everything she knew was out. Master Heathcliff, much irritated, asserted her relation was false.

"Papa told me; and papa does not tell falsehoods!" she answered pertly.

"*My* papa scorns yours!" cried Linton. "He calls him a sneaking fool!"

"Yours is a wicked man," retorted Catherine, "and you are very naughty to dare to repeat what he says. He must be wicked, to have made Aunt Isabella leave him as she did!"

"She didn't leave him," said the boy; "you shan't contradict me!"

"She did!" cried my young lady.

"Well, I'll tell *you* something!" said Linton. "Your mother hated your father, now then."

"Oh!" exclaimed Catherine, too enraged to continue.

"And she loved mine!" added he.

"You little liar! I hate you now," she panted, and her face grew red with passion.

"She did! she did!" sang Linton, sinking into the recess of his chair, and leaning back his head to enjoy the agitation of the other disputant, who stood behind.

"Hush, Master Heathcliff!" I said; "that's your father's tale too, I suppose."

"It isn't—you hold your tongue!" he answered. "She did, she did, Catherine, she did, she did!"

Cathy, beside herself, gave the chair a violent push, and caused him to fall against one arm. He was immediately seized by a suffocating cough that soon ended his triumph.

It lasted so long that it frightened even me. As to his cousin, she wept with all her might, aghast at the mischief she had done, though she said nothing.

I held him till the fit exhausted itself. Then he thrust me away, and leant his head down, silently. Catherine quelled her lamentations also, took a seat opposite, and looked solemnly into the fire.

"How do you feel now, Master Heathcliff?" I inquired, after waiting ten minutes.

"I wish *she* felt as I do," he replied, "spiteful, cruel thing! Hareton never touches me, he never struck me in his life. And I was better to-day—and there—" his voice died in a whimper.

"*I* didn't strike you!" muttered Cathy, chewing her lip to prevent another burst of emotion.

He sighed and moaned like one under great suffering, and kept it up for a quarter of an hour, on purpose to distress his cousin, apparently, for whenever he caught a stifled sob from her, he put renewed pain and pathos into the inflexions of his voice.

"I'm sorry I hurt you, Linton!" she said at length, racked beyond endurance. "But *I* couldn't have been hurt by that little push; and I had no idea that you could, either—you're not much, are you, Linton? Don't let me go home thinking I've done you harm! Answer, speak to me."

"I can't speak to you," he murmured, "you've hurt me so, that I shall lie awake all night, choking with this cough! If you had it you'd know what it was; but *you'll* be comfortably asleep, while I'm in agony—and nobody near me! I wonder how you would like to pass those fearful nights!" And he began to wail aloud for very pity of himself.

"Since you are in the habit of passing dreadful nights," I said, "it won't be Miss who spoils your ease; you'd be the same, had she never come. However, she shall not disturb you again—and perhaps you'll get quieter when we leave you."

"Must I go?" asked Catherine dolefully, bending over him. "Do you want me to go, Linton?"

"You can't alter what you've done," he replied pettishly, shrinking from her, "unless you alter it for the worse, by teasing me into a fever."

"Well, then I must go?" she repeated.

"Let me alone, at least," said he; "I can't bear your talking!"

She lingered, and resisted my persuasions to departure, a tiresome while, but as he neither looked up nor spoke, she finally made a movement to the door and I followed.

We were recalled by a scream. Linton had slid from his seat on to the hearthstone, and lay writhing in the mere perverseness of an indulged plague of a child, determined to be as grievous and harassing as it can.

I thoroughly gauged his disposition from his behaviour, and saw at once it would be folly to attempt humouring him. Not so my companion: she ran back in terror, knelt down, and cried, and soothed, and entreated, till he grew quiet from lack of breath, by no means from compunction at distressing her.

"I shall lift him on to the settle," I said, "and he may roll about as he pleases; we can't stop to watch him. I hope you are satisfied, Miss Cathy, that *you* are not the person to benefit him, and that his condition of health is not occasioned by attachment to you. Now then, there he is! Come away; as soon as he knows there is nobody by to care for his nonsense, he'll be glad to lie still!"

She placed a cushion under his head, and offered him some water; he rejected the latter, and tossed uneasily on the former, as if it were a stone, or a block of wood.

She tried to put it more comfortably.

"I can't do with that," he said, "it's not high enough!"

Catherine brought another to lay above it.

"That's *too* high!" murmured the provoking thing.

"How must I arrange it, then?" she asked despairingly.

He twined himself up to her, as she half knelt by the settle, and converted her shoulder into a support.

"No, that won't do!" I said. "You'll be content with the cushion, Master Heathcliff! Miss has wasted too much time on you already; we cannot remain five minutes longer."

"Yes, yes, we can!" replied Cathy. "He's good and patient, now. He's beginning to think I shall have far greater misery than he will to-night, if I believe he is the worse for my visit; and then, I dare not come again. Tell the truth about it, Linton, for I mustn't come, if I have hurt you."

"You must come, to cure me," he answered. "You ought to come because you have hurt me. You know you have, extremely! I was not as ill when you entered, as I am at present—was I?"

"But you've made yourself ill by crying, and being in a passion."

"I didn't do it all," said his cousin. "However, we'll be friends now. And you want me—you would wish to see me sometimes, really?"

"I told you I did!" he replied impatiently. "Sit on the settle and let me lean on your knee. That's as mamma used to do, whole afternoons together. Sit quite still, and don't talk, but you may sing a song if you can sing, or you may say a nice, long interesting ballad—one of those you promised to teach me—or a story. I'd rather have a ballad, though: begin."

Catherine repeated the longest she could remember. The employment pleased both mightily. Linton would have another, and after that another, notwithstanding my strenuous objections; and so they went on until the clock struck twelve, and we heard Hareton in the court, returning for his dinner.

"And to-morrow, Catherine, will you be here to-morrow?" asked young Heathcliff, holding her frock, as she rose reluctantly.

"No!" I answered, "nor next day neither." She, however, gave a different response, evidently, for his forehead cleared as she stooped and whispered in his ear.

"You won't go to-morrow, recollect, Miss!" I commenced, when we were out of the house. "You are not dreaming of it, are you?"

She smiled.

"Oh, I'll take good care!" I continued; "I'll have that lock mended, and you can escape by no way else."

"I can get over the wall," she said, laughing. "The Grange is not a prison, Ellen, and you are not my jailer. And besides, I'm almost seventeen. I'm a woman—and I'm certain Linton would recover quickly if he had me to look after him. I'm older than he is, you know, and wiser, less childish, am I not? And he'll soon do as I direct him with some slight coaxing. He's a pretty little darling when he's good. I'd make such a pet of him, if he were mine. We should never quarrel, should we, after we were used to each other? Don't you like him, Ellen?"

"Like him?" I exclaimed. "The worst-tempered bit of a sickly slip that ever struggled into its teens! Happily, as Mr. Heathcliff conjectured, he'll not win twenty! I doubt whether he'll see spring, indeed—and small loss to his family, whenever he drops off; and lucky it is for us that his father took him. The kinder he was treated, the more tedious and selfish he'd be! I'm glad you have no chance of having him for a husband, Miss Catherine!"

My companion waxed serious at hearing this speech. To speak of his death so regardlessly wounded her feelings.

"He's younger than I," she answered, after a protracted pause of meditation, "and he ought to live the longest; he will—he must live as long as I do. He's as strong now as when he first came into the North, I'm positive of that! It's only a cold that ails him, the same as papa has. You say papa will get better, and why shouldn't he?"

"Well, well," I cried, "after all, we needn't trouble ourselves; for listen, Miss—and mind, I'll keep my word—if you attempt going to Wuthering Heights again, with or without me, I shall inform Mr. Linton, and, unless he allows it, the intimacy with your cousin must not be revived."

"It has been revived!" muttered Cathy sulkily.

"Must not be continued, then!" I said.

"We'll see!" was her reply, and she set off at a gallop, leaving me to toil in the rear.

We both reached home before our dinnertime; my master supposed we had been wandering through the park, and therefore he demanded no explanation of our absence. As soon as I entered, I hastened to change my soaked shoes and stockings; but sitting such a while at the Heights had done the mischief. On the succeeding morning, I was laid up; and during three weeks I remained incapacitated for attending to my duties—a calamity never experienced prior to that period, and never, I am thankful to say, since.

My little mistress behaved like an angel in coming to wait on me, and cheer my solitude: the confinement brought me exceedingly low. It is wearisome, to a stirring active body, but few have slighter reasons for complaint than I had. The moment Catherine left Mr. Linton's room, she appeared at my bed-side. Her day was divided between us; no amusement usurped a minute: she neglected her meals, her studies, and her play; and she was the fondest nurse that ever watched. She must have had a warm heart, when she loved her father so, to give so much to me!

I said her days were divided between us; but the master retired early, and I generally needed nothing after six o'clock, thus the evening was her own.

Poor thing, I never considered what she did with herself after tea. And though frequently, when she looked in to bid me good-night, I remarked a fresh colour in her cheeks, and a pinkness over her slender fingers; instead of fancying the hue borrowed from a cold ride across the moors, I laid it to the charge of a hot fire in the library.

CHAPTER 24

At the close of three weeks, I was able to quit my chamber, and move about the house. And on the first occasion of my sitting up in the evening, I asked Catherine to read to me, because my eyes were weak. We were in the library, the master having gone to bed: she consented, rather unwillingly, I fancied; and imagining my sort of books did not suit her, I bid her please herself in the choice of what she perused.

She selected one of her own favourites, and got forward steadily about an hour; then came frequent questions.

"Ellen, are not you tired? Hadn't you better lie down now? You'll be sick, keeping up so long, Ellen."

"No, no, dear, I'm not tired," I returned, continually.

Perceiving me immovable, she essayed another method of showing her dis-relish for her occupation. It changed to yawning, and stretching, and—

"Ellen, I'm tired."

"Give over then and talk," I answered.

That was worse: she fretted and sighed, and looked at her watch till eight; and finally went to her room, completely overdone with sleep, judging by her peevish, heavy look, and the constant rubbing she inflicted on her eyes.

The following night she seemed more impatient still; and on the third from recovering my company, she complained of a head-ache, and left me.

I thought her conduct odd; and having remained alone a long while, I resolved on going, and inquiring whether she were better, and asking her to come and lie on the sofa, instead of upstairs, in the dark.

No Catherine could I discover upstairs, and none below. The servants affirmed they had not seen her. I listened at Mr. Edgar's door—all was silence. I returned to her apartment, extinguished my candle, and seated myself in the window.

The moon shone bright; a sprinkling of snow covered the ground, and I reflected that she might, possibly, have taken it into her head to walk about the garden, for refreshment. I did detect a figure creeping along the inner fence of the park, but it was not my young mistress; on its emerging into the light, I recognised one of the grooms.

He stood a considerable period, viewing the carriage-road through the grounds; then started off at a brisk pace, as if he had detected something, and reappeared presently, leading Miss's pony; and there she was, just dismounted, and walking by its side.

The man took his charge stealthily across the grass towards the stable. Cathy entered by the casement-window of the drawing-room, and glided noiselessly up to where I awaited her.

She put the door gently to, slipped off her snowy shoes, untied her hat, and was proceeding, unconscious of my espionage, to lay aside her mantle, when I suddenly rose and revealed myself. The surprise petrified her an instant: she uttered an inarticulate exclamation, and stood fixed.

"My dear Miss Catherine," I began, too vividly impressed by her recent kindness to break into a scold, "where have you been riding out at this hour? And why should you try to deceive me, by telling a tale? Where have you been? Speak!"

"To the bottom of the park," she stammered. "I didn't tell a tale."

"And nowhere else?" I demanded.

"No," was the muttered reply.

"Oh, Catherine," I cried, sorrowfully. "You know you have been doing wrong, or you wouldn't be driven to uttering an untruth to me. That does grieve me. I'd rather be three months ill, than hear you frame a deliberate lie."

She sprang forward, and bursting into tears, threw her arms round my neck.

"Well, Ellen, I'm so afraid of you being angry," she said. "Promise not to be angry, and you shall know the very truth. I hate to hide it."

We sat down in the window-seat; I assured her I would not scold, whatever her secret might be, and I guessed it, of course; so she commenced—

"I've been to Wuthering Heights, Ellen, and I've never missed going a day since you fell ill; except thrice before, and twice after you left your room. I gave Michael books and pictures to prepare Minny every evening, and to put her back in the stable; you mustn't scold *him* either, mind. I was at the Heights by half-past six, and generally stayed till half-past eight, and then galloped home. It was not to amuse myself that I went; I was often wretched all the time. Now and then, I was happy, once in a week perhaps. At first, I expected there would be sad work persuading you to let me keep my word to Linton, for I had engaged to call again next day, when we quitted him; but, as you stayed upstairs on the morrow, I escaped that trouble; and while Michael was refastening the lock of the park door in the afternoon, I got possession of the key, and told him how my cousin wished me to visit him, because he was sick, and couldn't come to the Grange; and how papa would object to my going. And then I negotiated with him about the pony. He is fond of reading, and he thinks of leaving soon to get married, so he offered, if I would lend him books out of the library, to do what I wished; but I preferred giving him my own, and that satisfied him better.

"On my second visit, Linton seemed in lively spirits; and Zillah—that is their housekeeper—made us a clean room and a good fire, and told us that, as Joseph was out at a prayer-meeting and Hareton Earnshaw was off with his dogs—robbing our woods of pheasants, as I heard afterwards—we might do what we liked.

"She brought me some warm wine and gingerbread, and appeared exceedingly good-natured; and Linton sat in the arm-chair, and I in the little rocking chair on the hearthstone, and we laughed and talked so merrily, and found so much to say; we planned where we would go, and what we would do in summer. I needn't repeat that, because you would call it silly.

"One time, however, we were near quarrelling. He said the pleasantest manner of spending a hot July day was lying from morning till evening on a bank of heath in the middle of the moors, with the bees humming dreamily about among the bloom, and the larks singing high up over head, and the blue sky and bright sun shining steadily and cloudlessly. That was his most perfect idea of heaven's happiness. Mine was rocking in a rustling green tree, with a west wind blowing, and bright, white clouds flitting rapidly above; and not only larks, but throstles, and blackbirds, and linnets, and cuckoos pouring out music on every side, and the moors seen at a distance, broken into cool dusky dells; but close by, great swells of long grass undulating in waves to the breeze; and woods and sounding water, and the whole world awake and wild with joy. He wanted all to lie in an ecstacy of peace; I wanted all to sparkle, and dance in a glorious jubilee.

"I said his heaven would be only half alive, and he said mine would be drunk; I said I should fall asleep in his, and he said he could not breathe in mine, and began to grow very snappish. At last, we agreed to try both as soon as the right weather came; and then we kissed each other and were friends. After sitting still an hour, I looked at the great room with its smooth, uncarpeted floor, and thought how nice it would be to play in, if we removed the table; and I asked Linton to call Zillah in to help us, and we'd have a game at blind-man's buff—she should try to catch us; you used to, you know, Ellen. He wouldn't; there was no pleasure in it, he said, but he consented to play at ball with me. We found two in a cupboard, among a heap of old toys: tops, and hoops, and battledores, and shuttlecocks. One was marked C., and the other H.; I wished to have the C., because that stood for Catherine, and the H. might be for Heathcliff, his name; but the bran came out of H., and Linton didn't like it.

"I beat him constantly; and he got cross again, and coughed, and returned to his chair. That night, though, he easily recovered his good humour; he was charmed with two or three pretty songs—*your* songs, Ellen; and when I was obliged to go, he begged and entreated me to come the following evening, and I promised.

"Minny and I went flying home as light as air: and I dreamt of Wuthering Heights, and my sweet, darling cousin, till morning.

"On the morrow, I was sad; partly because you were poorly, and partly that I wished my father knew, and approved of my excursions: but it was beautiful moonlight after tea; and, as I rode on, the gloom cleared.

"I shall have another happy evening, I thought to myself, and what delights me more, my pretty Linton will.

"I trotted up their garden, and was turning round to the back, when that fellow Earnshaw met me, took my bridle, and bid me go in by the front entrance. He patted Minny's neck, and said she was a bonny beast, and appeared as if he wanted me to speak to him. I only told him to leave my horse alone, or else it would kick him.

"He answered in his vulgar accent.

"'It wouldn't do mitch hurt if it did'; and surveyed its legs with a smile.

"I was half inclined to make it try; however, he moved off to open the door, and, as he raised the latch, he looked up to the inscription above, and said, with a stupid mixture of awkwardness and elation—

"'Miss Catherine! I can read yon, nah.'

"'Wonderful,' I exclaimed. 'Pray let us hear you—you *are* grown clever!'

"He spelt, and drawled over by syllables, the name—

"'Hareton Earnshaw.'

"'And the figures?' I cried, encouragingly, perceiving that he came to a dead halt.

"'I cannot tell them yet,' he answered.

"'Oh, you dunce!' I said, laughing heartily at his failure.

"The fool stared, with a grin hovering about his lips, and a scowl gathering over his eyes, as if uncertain whether he might not join in my mirth; whether it were not pleasant familiarity, or what it really was, contempt.

"I settled his doubts by suddenly retrieving my gravity, and desiring him to walk away, for I came to see Linton, not him.

"He reddened—I saw that by the moonlight—dropped his hand from the latch, and skulked off, a picture of mortified vanity. He imagined himself to be as accomplished as Linton, I suppose, because he could spell his own name; and was marvellously discomfited that I didn't think the same."

"Stop, Miss Catherine, dear!" I interrupted. "I shall not scold, but I don't like your conduct there. If you had remembered that Hareton was your cousin as much as Master Heathcliff, you would have felt how improper it was to behave in that way. At least, it was praiseworthy ambition for him to desire to be as accomplished as Linton; and probably he did not learn merely to show off; you had made him ashamed of his ignorance before, I have no doubt; and he wished to remedy it and please you. To sneer at his imperfect attempt was very bad breeding. Had *you* been brought up in his circumstances, would you be less rude? He was as quick and as intelligent a child as ever you were, and I'm hurt that he should be despised now, because that base Heathcliff has treated him so unjustly."

"Well, Ellen, you won't cry about it, will you?" she exclaimed, surprised at my earnestness. "But wait, and you shall hear if he conned his A B C to please me; and if it were worth while being civil to the brute. I entered; Linton was lying on the settle, and half got up to welcome me.

" 'I'm ill to-night, Catherine, love,' he said, 'and you must have all the talk, and let me listen. Come, and sit by me. I was sure you wouldn't break your word, and I'll make you promise again, before you go.'

"I knew now that I mustn't tease him, as he was ill; and I spoke softly and put no questions, and avoided irritating him in any way. I had brought some of my nicest books for him; he asked me to read a little of one, and I was about to comply, when Earnshaw burst the door open, having gathered venom with reflection. He advanced direct to us, seized Linton by the arm, and swung him off the seat.

" 'Get to thy own room!' he said in a voice almost inarticulate with passion; and his face looked swelled and furious. 'Take her there if she comes to see thee—thou shalln't keep me out of this. Begone, wi' ye both!'

"He swore at us, and left Linton no time to answer, nearly throwing him into the kitchen; and he clenched his fist, as I followed, seemingly longing to knock me down. I was afraid, for a moment, and I let one volume fall; he kicked it after me, and shut us out.

"I heard a malignant, crackly laugh by the fire, and turning, beheld that odious Joseph, standing rubbing his bony hands, and quivering.

" 'Aw wer sure he'd sarve ye eht! He's a grand lad! He's gotten t'raight sperrit in him! He knaws—Aye, he knaws, as weel as Aw do, who sud be t'maister yonder. Ech, ech, ech! He mad ye skift[44] properly! Ech, ech, ech!'

" 'Where must we go?' I said to my cousin, disregarding the old wretch's mockery.

"Linton was white and trembling. He was not pretty then, Ellen. Oh, no! he looked frightful! for his thin face and large eyes were wrought into an expression of frantic, powerless fury. He grasped the handle of the door, and shook it—it was fastened inside.

" 'If you don't let me in, I'll kill you! If you don't let me in, I'll kill you!' he rather shrieked than said. 'Devil! devil! I'll kill you, I'll kill you!'

"Joseph uttered his croaking laugh again.

" 'Thear, that's t'father!' he cried. 'That's father! We've allas summut uh orther side in us. Niver heed Hareton, lad—dunnut be 'feard—he cannot get at thee!'

"I took hold of Linton's hands, and tried to pull him away; but he shrieked so shockingly that I dared not proceed. At last, his cries were choked by a dreadful fit of coughing; blood gushed from his mouth, and he fell on the ground.

"I ran into the yard, sick with terror; and called for Zillah, as loud as I could. She soon heard me; she was milking the cows in a shed behind the barn, and hurrying from her work, she inquired what there was to do?

---

[44] *Skift:* move away quickly.

"I hadn't breath to explain; dragging her in, I looked about for Linton. Earnshaw had come out to examine the mischief he had caused, and he was then conveying the poor thing upstairs. Zillah and I ascended after him; but he stopped me at the top of the steps, and said I shouldn't go in, I must go home.

"I exclaimed that he had killed Linton and I *would* enter.

"Joseph locked the door, and declared I should do 'no sich stuff,' and asked me whether I were 'bahn to be as mad as him.'

"I stood crying, till the housekeeper re-appeared; she affirmed he would be better in a bit, but he couldn't do with that shrieking and din, and she took me, and nearly carried me into the house.

"Ellen, I was ready to tear my hair off my head! I sobbed and wept so that my eyes were almost blind; and the ruffian you have such sympathy with stood opposite, presuming every now and then to bid me 'wisht,' and denying that it was his fault; and finally, frightened by my assertions that I would tell papa, and that he should be put in prison and hanged, he commenced blubbering himself, and hurried out to hide his cowardly agitation.

"Still, I was not rid of him: when at length they compelled me to depart, and I had got some hundred yards off the premises, he suddenly issued from the shadow of the road-side, and checked Minny and took hold of me.

"'Miss Catherine, I'm ill grieved,' he began, 'but it's rayther too bad—'

"I gave him a cut with my whip, thinking perhaps he would murder me. He let go, thundering one of his horrid curses, and I galloped home more than half out of my senses.

"I didn't bid you good-night, that evening; and I didn't go to Wuthering Heights, the next. I wished to, exceedingly; but I was strangely excited, and dreaded to hear that Linton was dead, sometimes; and sometimes shuddered at the thoughts of encountering Hareton.

"On the third day I took courage; at least, I couldn't bear longer suspense and stole off once more. I went at five o'clock, and walked, fancying I might manage to creep into the house, and up to Linton's room, unobserved. However, the dogs gave notice of my approach: Zillah received me, and saying 'the lad was mending nicely,' showed me into a small, tidy, carpeted apartment, where, to my inexpressible joy, I beheld Linton laid on a little sofa, reading one of my books. But he would neither speak to me nor look at me, through a whole hour, Ellen. He has such an unhappy temper—and what quite confounded me, when he did open his mouth it was to utter the falsehood that I had occasioned the uproar, and Hareton was not to blame!

"Unable to reply, except passionately, I got up and walked from the room. He sent after me a faint 'Catherine!' He did not reckon on being answered so, but I wouldn't turn back; and the morrow was the second day on which I stayed at home, nearly determined to visit him no more.

"But it was so miserable going to bed, and getting up, and never hearing anything about him, that my resolution melted into air before it was properly formed. It *had* appeared wrong to take the journey once; now it seemed wrong to refrain. Michael came to ask if he must saddle Minny; I said 'Yes,' and considered myself doing a duty as she bore me over the hills.

"I was forced to pass the front windows to get to the court; it was no use trying to conceal my presence.

"'Young master is in the house,' said Zillah, as she saw me making for the parlour.

"I went in; Earnshaw was there also, but he quitted the room directly. Linton sat in the great arm-chair half asleep; walking up to the fire, I began in a serious tone, partly meaning it to be true—

" 'As you don't like me, Linton, and as you think I come on purpose to hurt you, and pretend that I do so every time, this is our last meeting—let us say good-bye; and tell Mr. Heathcliff that you have no wish to see me, and that he mustn't invent any more falsehoods on the subject.'

" 'Sit down and take your hat off, Catherine,' he answered. 'You are so much happier than I am, you ought to be better. Papa talks enough of my defects, and shows enough scorn of me, to make it natural I should doubt myself. I doubt whether I am not altogether as worthless as he calls me, frequently; and then I feel so cross and bitter, I hate everybody! I *am* worthless, and bad in temper, and bad in spirit, almost always—and if you choose, you *may* say good-bye. You'll get rid of an annoyance. Only, Catherine, do me this justice; believe that if I might be as sweet, and as kind, and as good as you are, I would be, as willingly and more so, than as happy and as healthy. And believe that your kindness has made me love you deeper than if I deserved your love, and though I couldn't, and cannot help showing my nature to you, I regret it and repent it, and shall regret and repent it, till I die!'

"I felt he spoke the truth; and I felt I must forgive him; and, though he should quarrel the next moment, I must forgive him again. We were reconciled, but we cried, both of us, the whole time I stayed. Not entirely for sorrow, yet I *was* sorry Linton had that distorted nature. He'll never let his friends be at ease, and he'll never be at ease himself!

"I have always gone to his little parlour, since that night; because his father returned the day after. About three times, I think, we have been merry and hopeful, as we were the first evening; the rest of my visits were dreary and troubled—now, with his selfishness and spite; and now, with his sufferings: but I've learnt to endure the former with nearly as little resentment as the latter.

"Mr. Heathcliff purposely avoids me. I have hardly seen him at all. Last Sunday, indeed, coming earlier than usual, I heard him abusing poor Linton, cruelly, for his conduct of the night before. I can't tell how he knew of it, unless he listened. Linton had certainly behaved provokingly; however, it was the business of nobody but me; and I interrupted Mr. Heathcliff's lecture by entering and telling him so. He burst into a laugh, and went away, saying he was glad I took that view of the matter. Since then, I've told Linton he must whisper his bitter things.

"Now, Ellen, you have heard all; and I can't be prevented from going to Wuthering Heights, except by inflicting misery on two people; whereas, if you'll only not tell papa, my going need disturb the tranquillity of none. You'll not tell, will you? It will be very heartless if you do."

"I'll make up my mind on that point by to-morrow, Miss Catherine," I replied. "It requires some study; and so I'll leave you to your rest, and go think it over."

I thought it over aloud, in my master's presence; walking straight from her room to his, and relating the whole story, with the exception of her conversations with her cousin, and any mention of Hareton.

Mr. Linton was alarmed and distressed more than he would acknowledge to me. In the morning, Catherine learnt my betrayal of her confidence, and she learnt also that her secret visits were to end.

In vain she wept and writhed against the interdict, and implored her father to have pity on Linton: all she got to comfort her was a promise that he would write, and give him leave to come to the Grange when he pleased; but explaining that he must no longer expect to see Catherine at Wuthering Heights. Perhaps, had he been aware of his nephew's disposition and state of health, he would have seen fit to withhold even that slight consolation.

CHAPTER 25

"These things happened last winter, sir," said Mrs. Dean; "hardly more than a year ago. Last winter, I did not think, at another twelve months' end, I should be amusing a stranger to the family with relating them! Yet, who knows how long you'll be a stranger? You're too young to rest always contented, living by yourself; and I some way fancy no one could see Catherine Linton, and not love her. You smile; but why do you look so lively and interested, when I talk about her? and why have you asked me to hang her picture over your fireplace? and why—"

"Stop, my good friend!" I cried. "It may be very possible that I should love her; but would she love me? I doubt it too much to venture my tranquillity by running into temptation; and then my home is not here. I'm of the busy world, and to its arms I must return. Go on. Was Catherine obedient to her father's commands?"

"She was," continued the housekeeper. "Her affection for him was still the chief sentiment in her heart; and he spoke without anger. He spoke in the deep tenderness of one about to leave his treasures amid perils and foes, where his remembered words would be the only aid that he could bequeath to guide her.

He said to me, a few days afterwards—

"I wish my nephew would write, Ellen, or call. Tell me, sincerely, what you think of him—is he changed for the better, or is there a prospect of improvement, as he grows a man?"

"He's very delicate, sir," I replied; "and scarcely likely to reach manhood; but this I can say, he does not resemble his father; and if Miss Catherine had the misfortune to marry him, he would not be beyond her control, unless she were extremely and foolishly indulgent. However, master, you'll have plenty of time to get acquainted with him, and see whether he would suit her: it wants four years and more to his being of age."

Edgar sighed; and, walking to the window, looked out towards Gimmerton Kirk. It was a misty afternoon, but the February sun shone dimly, and we could just distinguish the two fir trees in the yard, and the sparely scattered gravestones.

"I've prayed often," he half soliloquized, "for the approach of what is coming; and now I begin to shrink, and fear it. I thought the memory of the hour I came down that glen a bridegroom would be less sweet than the anticipation that I was soon, in a few months, or, possibly, weeks, to be carried up, and laid in its lonely hollow! Ellen, I've been very happy with my little Cathy. Through winter nights and summer days she was a living hope at my side. But I've been as happy musing by myself among those stones, under that old church—lying, through the long June evenings, on the green mound of her mother's grave, and wishing, yearning for the time when I might lie beneath it. What can I do for Cathy? How must I quit her? I'd not care one moment for Linton being Heathcliff's son; nor for his taking her from me, if he could console her for my loss. I'd not care that Heathcliff gained his ends, and triumphed in robbing me of my last blessing! But should Linton be unworthy—only a feeble tool to his father—I cannot abandon her to him! And, hard though it be to crush her buoyant spirit, I must persevere in making her sad while I live, and leaving her solitary when I die. Darling! I'd rather resign her to God, and lay her in the earth before me."

"Resign her to God, as it is, sir," I answered, "and if we should lose you—which may He forbid—under His providence, I'll stand her friend and counsellor to the last. Miss Catherine is a good girl; I don't fear that she will go wilfully wrong; and people who do their duty are always finally rewarded."

Spring advanced; yet my master gathered no real strength, though he resumed his walks in the grounds with his daughter. To her inexperienced notions, this itself was a sign of convalescence; and then his cheek was often flushed, and his eyes were bright: she felt sure of his recovering.

On her seventeenth birthday, he did not visit the churchyard; it was raining, and I observed—

"You'll surely not go out to-night, sir?"

He answered—

"No, I'll defer it this year, a little longer."

He wrote again to Linton, expressing his great desire to see him; and, had the invalid been presentable, I've no doubt his father would have permitted him to come. As it was, being instructed, he returned an answer, intimating that Mr. Heathcliff objected to his calling at the Grange; but his uncle's kind remembrance delighted him, and he hoped to meet him, sometimes, in his rambles, and personally to petition that his cousin and he might not remain long so utterly divided.

That part of his letter was simple, and probably his own. Heathcliff knew he could plead eloquently enough for Catherine's company, then—

"I do not ask," he said, "that she may visit here; but am I never to see her, because my father forbids me to go to her home, and you forbid her to come to mine? Do, now and then, ride with her towards the Heights; and let us exchange a few words, in your presence! We have done nothing to deserve this separation; and you are not angry with me—you have no reason to dislike me, you allow, yourself. Dear uncle! send me a kind note to-morrow; and leave to join you anywhere you please, except at Thrushcross Grange. I believe an interview would convince you that my father's character is not mine; he affirms I am more your nephew than his son; and though I have faults which render me unworthy of Catherine, she has excused them, and, for her sake, you should also. You inquire after my health—it is better; but while I remain cut off from all hope, and doomed to solitude, or the society of those who never did, and never will like me, how can I be cheerful and well?"

Edgar, though he felt for the boy, could not consent to grant his request; because he could not accompany Catherine.

He said, in summer, perhaps, they might meet: meantime, he wished him to continue writing at intervals, and engaged to give him what advice and comfort he was able by letter; being well aware of his hard position in his family.

Linton complied; and had he been unrestrained, would probably have spoiled all by filling his epistles with complaints and lamentations; but his father kept a sharp watch over him; and, of course, insisted on every line that my master sent being shown; so, instead of penning his peculiar personal sufferings and distresses, the themes constantly uppermost in his thoughts, he harped on the cruel obligation of being held asunder from his friend and love; and gently intimated that Mr. Linton must allow an interview soon, or he should fear he was purposely deceiving him with empty promises.

Cathy was a powerful ally at home; and, between them, they at length persuaded my master to acquiesce in their having a ride or a walk together, about once a week, under my guardianship, and on the moors nearest the Grange, for June found him still declining; and, though he had set aside, yearly, a portion of his income for my young lady's fortune, he had a natural desire that she might retain—or, at least, return in a short time to—the house of her ancestors; and he considered her only prospect of doing that was by a union with his heir; he had no idea that the latter was failing almost as fast as himself; nor had any one, I believe: no doctor visited the Heights, and no one saw Master Heathcliff to make report of his condition, among us.

I, for my part, began to fancy my forebodings were false, and that he must be actually rallying, when he mentioned riding and walking on the moors, and seemed so earnest in pursuing his object.

I could not picture a father treating a dying child as tyrannically and wickedly as I afterwards learnt Heathcliff had treated him, to compel this apparent eagerness; his efforts redoubling the more imminently his avaricious and unfeeling plans were threatened with defeat by death.

CHAPTER 26

Summer was already past its prime, when Edgar reluctantly yielded his assent to their entreaties, and Catherine and I set out on our first ride to join her cousin.

It was a close, sultry day, devoid of sunshine, but with a sky too dappled and hazy to threaten rain; and our place of meeting had been fixed at the guide-stone, by the crossroads. On arriving there, however, a little herd-boy, despatched as a messenger, told us that—

"Maister Linton wer just ut this side th' Heights: and he'd be mitch obleeged to us to gang on a bit further."

"Then Master Linton has forgot the first injunction of his uncle," I observed: "he bid us keep on the Grange land, and here we are, off at once."

"Well, we'll turn our horses' heads round, when we reach him," answered my companion; "our excursion shall lie towards home."

But when we reached him, and that was scarcely a quarter of a mile from his own door, we found he had no horse, and we were forced to dismount, and leave ours to graze.

He lay on the heath, awaiting our approach, and did not rise till we came within a few yards. Then he walked so feebly, and looked so pale, that I immediately exclaimed—

"Why, Master Heathcliff, you are not fit for enjoying a ramble this morning. How ill you do look!"

Catherine surveyed him with grief and astonishment; she changed the ejaculation of joy on her lips, to one of alarm, and the congratulation on their long postponed meeting, to an anxious inquiry, whether he were worse than usual?

"No—better—better!" he panted, trembling, and retaining her hand as if he needed its support, while his large blue eyes wandered timidly over her; the hollowness round them, transforming to haggard wildness the languid expression they once possessed.

"But you have been worse," persisted his cousin, "worse than when I saw you last—you are thinner, and—"

"I'm tired," he interrupted, hurriedly. "It is too hot for walking, let us rest here. And, in the morning, I often feel sick—papa says I grow so fast."

Badly satisfied, Cathy sat down, and he reclined beside her.

"This is something like your paradise," said she, making an effort at cheerfulness. "You recollect the two days we agreed to spend in the place and way each thought pleasantest? This is nearly yours, only there are clouds; but then, they are so soft and mellow, it is nicer than sunshine. Next week, if you can, we'll ride down to the Grange Park, and try mine."

Linton did not appear to remember what she talked of; and he had evidently great difficulty in sustaining any kind of conversation. His lack of interest in the subjects she started, and his equal incapacity to contribute to her entertainment, were so obvious that she could not conceal her disappointment. An indefinite alteration had come over his whole person and manner. The pettishness that might be caressed into fondness, had yielded to a listless apathy; there was less of the peevish temper of a child which frets and teases on purpose to be soothed, and more of the self-absorbed moroseness of a confirmed invalid, repelling consolation, and ready to regard the good-humoured mirth of others as an insult.

Catherine perceived, as well as I did, that he held it rather a punishment, than a gratification, to endure our company; and she made no scruple of proposing, presently, to depart.

That proposal, unexpectedly, roused Linton from his lethargy, and threw him into a strange state of agitation. He glanced fearfully towards the Heights, begging she would remain another half-hour, at least.

"But, I think," said Cathy, "you'd be more comfortable at home than sitting here; and I cannot amuse you to-day, I see, by my tales, and songs, and chatter; you have grown wiser than I, in these six months; you have little taste for my diversions now; or else, if I could amuse you, I'd willingly stay."

"Stay to rest yourself," he replied. "And, Catherine, don't think, or say that I'm *very* unwell—it is the heavy weather and heat that make me dull; and I walked about, before you came, a great deal, for me. Tell uncle, I'm in tolerable health, will you?"

"I'll tell him that *you* say so, Linton. I couldn't affirm that you are," observed my young lady, wondering at his pertinacious assertion of what was evidently an untruth.

"And be here again next Thursday," continued he, shunning her puzzled gaze. "And give him my thanks for permitting you to come—my best thanks, Catherine. And—and if you *did* meet my father, and he asked you about me, don't lead him to suppose that I've been extremely silent and stupid; don't look sad and downcast, as you *are* doing—he'll be angry."

"I care nothing for his anger," exclaimed Cathy, imagining she would be its object.

"But I do," said her cousin, shuddering. "*Don't* provoke him against me, Catherine, for he is very hard."

"Is he severe to you, Master Heathcliff?" I inquired. "Has he grown weary of indulgence, and passed from passive, to active hatred?"

Linton looked at me, but did not answer; and, after keeping her seat by his side another ten minutes, during which his head fell drowsily on his breast, and he uttered nothing except suppressed moans of exhaustion or pain, Cathy began to seek solace in looking for bilberries, and sharing the produce of her researches with me: she did not offer them to him, for she saw further notice would only weary and annoy.

"Is it half an hour now, Ellen?" she whispered in my ear, at last. "I can't tell why we should stay. He's asleep, and papa will be wanting us back."

"Well, we must not leave him asleep," I answered; "wait till he wakes and be patient. You were mighty eager to set off, but your longing to see poor Linton has soon evaporated!"

"Why did *he* wish to see me?" returned Catherine. "In his crossest humours, formerly, I liked him better than I do in his present curious mood. It's just as if it were a task he was compelled to perform—this interview—for fear his father should scold him. But I'm hardly going to come to give Mr. Heathcliff pleasure, whatever reason he may have for ordering Linton to undergo this penance. And, though I'm glad he's better in health, I'm sorry he's so much less pleasant, and so much less affectionate to me."

"You think *he is* better in health, then?" I said.

"Yes," she answered; "because he always made such a great deal of his sufferings, you know. He is not tolerably well, as he told me to tell papa, but he's better, very likely."

"Then you differ with me, Miss Cathy," I remarked; "I should conjecture him to be far worse."

Linton here started from his slumber in bewildered terror, and asked if any one had called his name.

"No," said Catherine; "unless in dreams. I cannot conceive how you manage to doze, out of doors, in the morning."

"I thought I heard my father," he gasped, glancing up to the frowning nab above us. "You are sure nobody spoke?"

"Quite sure," replied his cousin. "Only Ellen and I were disputing concerning your health. Are you truly stronger, Linton, than when we separated in winter? If you be, I'm certain one thing is not stronger—your regard for me—speak, are you?"

The tears gushed from Linton's eyes as he answered—

"Yes, yes, I am!"

And, still under the spell of the imaginary voice, his gaze wandered up and down to detect its owner.

Cathy rose.

"For to-day we must part," she said. "And I won't conceal that I have been sadly disappointed with our meeting, though I'll mention it to nobody but you—not that I stand in awe of Mr. Heathcliff!"

"Hush," murmured Linton; "for God's sake, hush! He's coming." And he clung to Catherine's arm, striving to detain her; but, at that announcement, she hastily disengaged herself, and whistled to Minny, who obeyed her like a dog.

"I'll be here next Thursday," she cried, springing to the saddle. "Good-bye. Quick, Ellen!"

And so we left him, scarcely conscious of our departure, so absorbed was he in anticipating his father's approach.

Before we reached home, Catherine's displeasure softened into a perplexed sensation of pity and regret largely blended with vague, uneasy doubts about Linton's actual circumstances, physical and social; in which I partook, though I counselled her not to say much, for a second journey would make us better judges.

My master requested an account of our ongoings: his nephew's offering of thanks was duly delivered, Miss Cathy gently touching on the rest: I also threw little light on his inquiries, for I hardly knew what to hide, and what to reveal.

CHAPTER 27

Seven days glided away, every one marking its course by the henceforth rapid alteration of Edgar Linton's state. The havoc that months had previously wrought was now emulated by the inroads of hours.

Catherine, we would fain have deluded yet, but her own quick spirit refused to delude her. It divined, in secret, and brooded on the dreadful probability, gradually ripening into certainty.

She had not the heart to mention her ride, when Thursday came round; I mentioned it for her, and obtained permission to order her out of doors; for the library, where her father stopped a short time daily—the brief period he could bear to sit up—and his chamber had become her whole world. She grudged each moment that did not find her bending over his pillow, or seated by his side. Her countenance grew wan with watching and sorrow, and my master gladly dismissed her to what he flattered himself would be a happy change of scene and society, drawing comfort from the hope that she would not now be left entirely alone after his death.

He had a fixed idea, I guessed by several observations he let fall, that as his nephew resembled him in person, he would resemble him in mind; for Linton's letters bore few or no indications of his defective character. And I, through pardonable weakness, refrained from correcting the error; asking myself what good there would be in disturbing his last moments with information that he had neither power nor opportunity to turn to account.

We deferred our excursion till the afternoon; a golden afternoon of August— every breath from the hills so full of life, that it seemed whoever respired it, though dying, might revive.

Catherine's face was just like the landscape—shadows and sunshine flitting over it, in rapid succession; but the shadows rested longer and the sunshine was more transient, and her poor little heart reproached itself for even that passing forgetfulness of its cares.

We discerned Linton watching at the same spot he had selected before. My young mistress alighted, and told me that as she was resolved to stay a very little while, I had better hold the pony and remain on horseback; but I dissented; I wouldn't risk losing sight of the charge committed to me a minute; so we climbed the slope of heath together.

Master Heathcliff received us with greater animation on this occasion; not the animation of high spirits though, nor yet of joy; it looked more like fear.

"It is late!" he said, speaking short, and with difficulty. "Is not your father very ill? I thought you wouldn't come."

"*Why* won't you be candid?" cried Catherine, swallowing her greeting. "Why cannot you say at once, you don't want me? It is strange, Linton, that for the second time, you have brought me here on purpose, apparently, to distress us both, and for no reason besides!"

Linton shivered, and glanced at her, half supplicating, half ashamed; but his cousin's patience was not sufficient to endure this enigmatical behaviour.

"My father *is* very ill," she said, "and why am I called from his bedside—why didn't you send to absolve me from my promise, when you wished I wouldn't keep it? Come! I desire an explanation; playing and trifling are completely banished out of my mind, and I can't dance attendance on your affections, now!"

"My affections!" he murmured; "what are they? For heaven's sake, Catherine, don't look so angry! Despise me as much as you please; I am a worthless, cowardly wretch—I can't be scorned enough! but I'm too mean for your anger—hate my father, and spare me, for contempt!"

"Nonsense!" cried Catherine in a passion. "Foolish, silly boy! And there! he trembles, as if I were really going to touch him! You needn't bespeak contempt, Linton; anybody will have it spontaneously, at your service. Get off! I shall return home; it is folly dragging you from the hearth-stone, and pretending—what do we pretend? Let go my frock! If I pitied you for crying and looking so very frightened, you should spurn such pity. Ellen, tell him how disgraceful this conduct is. Rise, and don't degrade yourself into an abject reptile—*don't*."

With streaming face and an expression of agony, Linton had thrown his nerveless frame along the ground; he seemed convulsed with exquisite terror.

"Oh!" he sobbed, "I cannot bear it! Catherine, Catherine, I'm a traitor too, and I dare not tell you! But leave me and I shall be killed! *Dear* Catherine, my life is in your hands; and you have said you loved me—and if you did, it wouldn't harm you. You'll not go, then? kind, sweet, good Catherine! And perhaps you *will* consent—and he'll let me die with you!"

My young lady, on witnessing his intense anguish, stooped to raise him. The old feeling of indulgent tenderness overcame her vexation, and she grew thoroughly moved and alarmed.

"Consent to what?" she asked. "To stay? Tell me the meaning of this strange talk, and I will. You contradict your own words, and distract me! Be calm and frank, and confess at once all that weighs on your heart. You wouldn't injure me, Linton, would you? You wouldn't let any enemy hurt me, if you could prevent it? I'll believe you are a coward, for yourself, but not a cowardly betrayer of your best friend."

"But my father threatened me," gasped the boy, clasping his attenuated fingers, "and I dread him—I dread him! I *dare* not tell!"

"Oh well!" said Catherine, with scornful compassion, "keep your secret, *I'm* no coward—save yourself, I'm not afraid!"

Her magnanimity provoked his tears; he wept wildly, kissing her supporting hands, and yet could not summon courage to speak out.

I was cogitating what the mystery might be, and determined Catherine should never suffer to benefit him or any one else, by my good will; when hearing a rustle among the ling,[45] I looked up, and saw Mr. Heathcliff almost close upon us, descending the Heights. He didn't cast a glance towards my companions, though they were sufficiently near for Linton's sobs to be audible; but hailing me in the almost hearty tone he assumed to none besides, and the sincerity of which I couldn't avoid doubting, he said—

"It is something to see you so near to my house, Nelly! How are you at the Grange? Let us hear! The rumour goes," he added in a lower tone, "that Edgar Linton is on his death-bed—perhaps they exaggerate his illness?"

"No; my master is dying," I replied; "it is true enough. A sad thing it will be for us all, but a blessing for him!"

"How long will he last, do you think?" he asked.

"I don't know," I said.

"Because," he continued, looking at the two young people, who were fixed under his eye—Linton appeared as if he could not venture to stir, or raise his head, and Catherine could not move, on his account—"Because that lad yonder seems determined to beat me—and I'd thank his uncle to be quick, and go before him. Hallo! Has the whelp been playing that game long? I *did* give him some lessons about snivelling. Is he pretty lively with Miss Linton generally?"

"Lively? no—he has shown the greatest distress," I answered. "To see him, I should say, that instead of rambling with his sweetheart on the hills, he ought to be in bed, under the hands of a doctor."

"He shall be, in a day or two," muttered Heathcliff. "But first—get up, Linton! Get up!" he shouted. "Don't grovel on the ground, there—up this moment!"

Linton had sunk prostrate again in another paroxysm of helpless fear, caused by his father's glance towards him, I suppose: there was nothing else to produce such humiliation. He made several efforts to obey, but his little strength was annihilated for the time, and he fell back again with a moan.

Mr. Heathcliff advanced, and lifted him to lean against a ridge of turf.

"Now," said he with curbed ferocity, "I'm getting angry—and if you don't command that paltry spirit of yours—Damn you! Get up, directly!"

---

[45] *Ling:* heather.

"I will, father!" he panted. "Only, let me alone, or I shall faint! I've done as you wished, I'm sure. Catherine will tell you that—that I—have been cheerful. Ah! keep by me, Catherine; give me your hand."

"Take mine," said his father; "stand on your feet! There now—she'll lend you her arm. That's right, look at *her*. You would imagine I was the devil himself, Miss Linton, to excite such horror. Be so kind as to walk home with him, will you? He shudders, if I touch him."

"Linton, dear!" whispered Catherine, "I can't go to Wuthering Heights—papa has forbidden me. He'll not harm you, why are you so afraid?"

"I can never re-enter that house," he answered. "I am *not* to re-enter it without you!"

"Stop!" cried his father. "We'll respect Catherine's filial scruples. Nelly, take him in, and I'll follow your advice concerning the doctor, without delay."

"You'll do well," replied I, "but I must remain with my mistress. To mind your son is not my business."

"You are very stiff!" said Heathcliff; "I know that—but you'll force me to pinch the baby, and make it scream, before it moves your charity. Come then, my hero. Are you willing to return, escorted by me?"

He approached once more, and made as if he would seize the fragile being; but shrinking back, Linton clung to his cousin, and implored her to accompany him, with a frantic importunity that admitted no denial.

However I disapproved, I couldn't hinder her; indeed, how could she have refused him herself? What was filling him with dread, we had no means of discerning, but there he was, powerless under its gripe, and any addition seemed capable of shocking him into idiocy.

We reached the threshold; Catherine walked in; and I stood waiting till she had conducted the invalid to a chair, expecting her out immediately; when Mr. Heathcliff, pushing me forward, exclaimed—

"My house is not stricken with the plague, Nelly; and I have a mind to be hospitable to-day; sit down, and allow me to shut the door."

He shut and locked it also. I started.

"You shall have tea, before you go home," he added. "I am by myself. Hareton is gone with some cattle to the Lees—and Zillah and Joseph are off on a journey of pleasure. And, though I'm used to being alone, I'd rather have some interesting company, if I can get it. Miss Linton, take your seat by *him*. I give you what I have; the present is hardly worth accepting; but I have nothing else to offer. It is Linton, I mean. How she does stare! It's odd what a savage feeling I have to anything that seems afraid of me! Had I been born where laws are less strict, and tastes less dainty, I should treat myself to a slow vivisection of those two, as an evening's amusement."

He drew in his breath, struck the table, and swore to himself—

"By hell! I hate them."

"I'm not afraid of you!" exclaimed Catherine, who could not hear the latter part of his speech.

She stepped close up, her black eyes flashing with passion and resolution.

"Give me that key—I will have it!" she said. "I wouldn't eat or drink here, if I were starving."

Heathcliff had the key in his hand that remained on the table. He looked up, seized with a sort of surprise at her boldness, or, possibly, reminded by her voice and glance, of the person from whom she inherited it.

She snatched at the instrument, and half succeeded in getting it out of his loosened fingers; but her action recalled him to the present; he recovered it speedily.

"Now, Catherine Linton," he said, "stand off, or I shall knock you down; and that will make Mrs. Dean mad."

Regardless of this warning, she captured his closed hand and its contents again.

"We *will* go!" she repeated, exerting her utmost efforts to cause the iron muscles to relax; and finding that her nails made no impression, she applied her teeth pretty sharply.

Heathcliff glanced at me a glance that kept me from interfering a moment. Catherine was too intent on his fingers to notice his face. He opened them suddenly, and resigned the object of dispute; but, ere she had well secured it, he seized her with the liberated hand, and, pulling her on his knee, administered with the other a shower of terrific slaps on both sides of the head, each sufficient to have fulfilled his threat, had she been able to fall.

At this diabolical violence, I rushed on him furiously.

"You villain!" I began to cry, "you villain!"

A touch on the chest silenced me; I am stout, and soon put out of breath; and, what with that and the rage, I staggered dizzily back, and felt ready to suffocate, or to burst a blood-vessel.

The scene was over in two minutes; Catherine, released, put her two hands to her temples, and looked just as if she were not sure whether her ears were off or on. She trembled like a reed, poor thing, and leant against the table perfectly bewildered.

"I know how to chastise children, you see," said the scoundrel, grimly, as he stooped to repossess himself of the key, which had dropped to the floor. "Go to Linton now, as I told you; and cry at your ease! I shall be your father to-morrow—all the father you'll have in a few days—and you shall have plenty of that—you can bear plenty—you're no weakling—you shall have a daily taste, if I catch such a devil of a temper in your eyes again!"

Cathy ran to me instead of Linton, and knelt down, and put her burning cheek on my lap, weeping aloud. Her cousin had shrunk into a corner of the settle, as quiet as a mouse, congratulating himself, I dare say, that the correction had lighted on another than him.

Mr. Heathcliff, perceiving us all confounded, rose, and expeditiously made the tea himself. The cups and saucers were laid ready. He poured it out, and handed me a cup.

"Wash away your spleen," he said. "And help your own naughty pet and mine. It is not poisoned, though I prepared it. I'm going out to seek your horses."

Our first thought, on his departure, was to force an exit somewhere. We tried the kitchen door, but that was fastened outside; we looked at the windows—they were too narrow for even Cathy's little figure.

"Master Linton," I cried, seeing we were regularly imprisoned, "you know what your diabolical father is after, and you shall tell us, or I'll box your ears, as he has done your cousin's."

"Yes, Linton; you must tell," said Catherine. "It was for your sake I came; and it will be wickedly ungrateful if you refuse."

"Give me some tea, I'm thirsty, and then I'll tell you," he answered. "Mrs. Dean, go away. I don't like you standing over me. Now, Catherine, you are letting your tears fall into my cup! I won't drink that. Give me another."

Catherine pushed another to him, and wiped her face. I felt disgusted at the little wretch's composure, since he was no longer in terror for himself. The anguish he had exhibited on the moor subsided as soon as ever he entered Wuthering Heights; so I guessed he had been menaced with an awful visitation of wrath if he failed in decoying us there; and, that accomplished, he had no further immediate fears.

"Papa wants us to be married," he continued, after sipping some of the liquid. "And he knows your papa wouldn't let us marry now; and he's afraid of my dying, if we wait; so we are to be married in the morning, and you are to stay here all night; and, if you do as he wishes, you shall return home next day, and take me with you."

"Take you with her, pitiful changeling?" I exclaimed. "*You* marry? Why, the man is mad, or he thinks us fools, every one. And do you imagine that beautiful young lady, that healthy, hearty girl, will tie herself to a little perishing monkey like you? Are you cherishing the notion that *anybody*, let alone Miss Catherine Linton, would have you for a husband? You want whipping for bringing us in here at all, with your dastardly, puling tricks; and—don't look so silly now! I've a very good mind to shake you severely, for your contemptible treachery, and your imbecile conceit."

I did give him a slight shaking, but it brought on the cough, and he took to his ordinary resource of moaning and weeping, and Catherine rebuked me.

"Stay all night? No!" she said, looking slowly round. "Ellen, I'll burn that door down, but I'll get out."

And she would have commenced the execution of her threat directly, but Linton was up in alarm, for his dear self, again. He clasped her in his two feeble arms, sobbing—

"Won't you have me, and save me? Not let me come to the Grange? Oh! darling Catherine! you mustn't go, and leave me, after all. You *must* obey my father, you *must!*"

"I must obey my own," she replied, "and relieve him from this cruel suspense. The whole night! What would he think? he'll be distressed already. I'll either break or burn a way out of the house. Be quiet! You're in no danger—but, if you hinder me—Linton, I love papa better than you!"

The mortal terror he felt of Mr. Heathcliff's anger restored to the boy his coward's eloquence. Catherine was near distraught; still, she persisted that she must go home, and tried entreaty, in her turn, persuading him to subdue his selfish agony.

While they were thus occupied, our jailer re-entered.

"Your beasts have trotted off," he said, "and—Now, Linton! snivelling again? What has she been doing to you? Come, come—have done, and get to bed. In a month or two, my lad, you'll be able to pay her back her present tyrannies, with a vigorous hand. You're pining for pure love, are you not? nothing else in the world—and she shall have you! There, to bed! Zillah won't be here to-night; you must undress yourself. Hush! hold your noise! Once in your own room, I'll not come near you, you needn't fear. By chance, you've managed tolerably. I'll look to the rest."

He spoke these words, holding the door open for his son to pass; and the latter achieved his exit exactly as a spaniel might, which suspected the person who attended on it of designing a spiteful squeeze.

The lock was re-secured. Heathcliff approached the fire, where my mistress and I stood silent. Catherine looked up, and instinctively raised her hand to her cheek: his neighbourhood revived a painful sensation. Anybody else would have been incapable of regarding the childish act with sternness, but he scowled on her, and muttered—

"Oh, you are not afraid of me? Your courage is well disguised—you *seem* damnably afraid!"

"I *am* afraid now," she replied; "because if I stay, papa will be miserable; and how can I endure making him miserable—when he—when he—Mr. Heathcliff, *let* me go home! I promise to marry Linton—papa would like me to, and I love him—and why should you wish to force me to do what I'll willingly do of myself?"

"Let him dare to force you!" I cried. "There's law in the land, thank God, there is! though we *be* in an out-of-the-way place. I'd inform, if he were my own son, and it's felony without benefit of clergy!"

"Silence!" said the ruffian. "To the devil with your clamour! I don't want *you* to speak. Miss Linton, I shall enjoy myself remarkably in thinking your father will be miserable; I shall not sleep for satisfaction. You could have hit on no surer way of fixing your residence under my roof, for the next twenty-four hours, than informing me that such an event would follow. As to your promise to marry Linton, I'll take care you shall keep it, for you shall not quit the place till it is fulfilled."

"Send Ellen then, to let papa know I'm safe!" exclaimed Catherine, weeping bitterly. "Or marry me now. Poor papa! Ellen, he'll think we're lost. What shall we do?"

"Not he! He'll think you are tired of waiting on him, and run off, for a little amusement," answered Heathcliff. "You cannot deny that you entered my house of your own accord, in contempt of his injunctions to the contrary. And it is quite natural that you should desire amusement at your age; and that you should weary of nursing a sick man, and that man *only* your father. Catherine, his happiest days were over when your days began. He cursed you, I dare say, for coming into the world (I did, at least). And it would just do if he cursed you as *he* went out of it. I'd join him. I don't love you! How should I? Weep away. As far as I can see, it will be your chief diversion hereafter, unless Linton make amends for other losses; and your provident parent appears to fancy he may. His letters of advice and consolation entertained me vastly. In his last, he recommended my jewel to be careful of his; and kind to her when he got her. Careful and kind—that's paternal! But Linton requires his whole stock of care and kindness for himself. Linton can play the little tyrant well. He'll undertake to torture any number of cats if their teeth be drawn, and their claws pared. You'll be able to tell his uncle fine tales of his *kindness,* when you get home again, I assure you."

"You're right there!" I said; "explain your son's character. Show his resemblance to yourself; and then, I hope, Miss Cathy will think twice before she takes the cockatrice!"

"I don't much mind speaking of his amiable qualities now," he answered, "because she must either accept him, or remain a prisoner, and you along with her, till your master dies. I can detain you both, quite concealed, here. If you doubt, encourage her to retract her word, and you'll have an opportunity of judging!"

"I'll not retract my word," said Catherine. "I'll marry him, within this hour, if I may go to Thrushcross Grange afterwards. Mr. Heathcliff, you're a cruel man, but you're not a fiend; and you won't, from *mere* malice, destroy, irrevocably, all my happiness. If papa thought I had left him on purpose, and if he died before I returned, could I bear to live? I've given over crying; but I'm going to kneel here, at your knee; and I'll not get up, and I'll not take my eyes from your face, till you look back at me! No, don't turn away! *do* look! You'll see nothing to provoke you. I don't hate you. I'm not angry that you struck me. Have you never loved *anybody,* in all your life, uncle? *never?* Ah! you must look once—I'm so wretched—you can't help being sorry and pitying me."

"Keep your eft's fingers off; and move, or I'll kick you!" cried Heathcliff, brutally repulsing her. "I'd rather be hugged by a snake. How the devil can you dream of fawning on me? I *detest* you!"

He shrugged his shoulders—shook himself, indeed, as if his flesh crept with aversion, and thrust back his chair, while I got up, and opened my mouth, to commence a downright torrent of abuse; but I was rendered dumb in the middle of the first sentence, by a threat that I should be shown into a room by myself, the very next syllable I uttered.

It was growing dark—we heard a sound of voices at the garden gate. Our host hurried out, instantly; *he* had his wits about him; *we* had not. There was a talk of two or three minutes, and he returned alone.

"I thought it had been your cousin Hareton," I observed to Catherine. "I wish he would arrive! Who knows but he might take our part?"

"It was three servants sent to seek you from the Grange," said Heathcliff, overhearing me. "You should have opened a lattice and called out; but I could swear that chit is glad you didn't. She's glad to be obliged to stay, I'm certain."

At learning the chance we had missed, we both gave vent to our grief without control, and he allowed us to wail on till nine o'clock; then he bid us go upstairs, through the kitchen, to Zillah's chamber, and I whispered my companion to obey; perhaps we might contrive to get through the window there, or into a garret, and out by its skylight.

The window, however, was narrow like those below, and the garret trap was safe from our attempts; for we were fastened in as before.

We neither of us lay down: Catherine took her station by the lattice, and watched anxiously for morning—a deep sigh being the only answer I could obtain to my frequent entreaties that she would try to rest.

I seated myself in a chair, and rocked, to and fro, passing harsh judgment on my many derelictions of duty; from which, it struck me then, all the misfortunes of all my employers sprang. It was not the case, in reality, I am aware; but it was, in my imagination, that dismal night, and I thought Heathcliff himself less guilty than I.

At seven o'clock he came, and inquired if Miss Linton had risen.

She ran to the door immediately, and answered—

"Yes."

"Here, then," he said, opening it, and pulling her out.

I rose to follow, but he turned the lock again. I demanded my release.

"Be patient," he replied; "I'll send up your breakfast in a while."

I thumped on the panels, and rattled the latch angrily; and Catherine asked why I was still shut up? He answered, I must try to endure it another hour, and they went away.

I endured it two or three hours; at length, I heard a footstep, not Heathcliff's.

"I've brought you something to eat," said a voice; "oppen t' door!"

Complying eagerly, I beheld Hareton, laden with food enough to last me all day.

"Tak it," he added, thrusting the tray into my hand.

"Stay one minute," I began.

"Nay!" cried he, and retired, regardless of any prayers I could pour forth to detain him.

And there I remained enclosed, the whole day, and the whole of the next night; and another, and another. Five nights and four days I remained, altogether, seeing nobody but Hareton, once every morning, and he was a model of a jailer—surly, and dumb, and deaf to every attempt at moving his sense of justice or compassion.

CHAPTER 28

On the fifth morning, or rather afternoon, a different step approached—lighter and shorter—and, this time, the person entered the room. It was Zillah, donned in her scarlet shawl, with a black silk bonnet on her head, and a willow basket swung to her arm.

"Eh, dear! Mrs. Dean," she exclaimed. "Well! there is a talk about you at Gimmerton. I never thought but you were sunk in the Blackhorse marsh, and Missy with you, till master told me you'd been found, and he'd lodged you here! What, and you must have got on an island, sure? And how long were you in the hole? Did master save you, Mrs. Dean? But you're not so thin—you've not been so poorly, have you?"

"Your master is a true scoundrel!" I replied. "But he shall answer for it. He needn't have raised that tale—it shall all be laid bare!"

"What do you mean?" asked Zillah. "It's not his tale: they tell that in the village—about your being lost in the marsh; and I calls to Earnshaw, when I come in—"

" 'Eh, they's queer things, Mr. Hareton, happened since I went off. It's a sad pity of that likely young lass, and cant Nelly Dean.'

"He stared. I thought he had not heard aught, so I told him the rumour.

"The master listened, and he just smiled to himself, and said—

" 'If they have been in the marsh, they are out now, Zillah. Nelly Dean is lodged, at this minute, in your room. You can tell her to flit, when you go up; here is the key. The bog-water got into her head, and she would have run home, quite flighty, but I fixed her, till she came round to her senses. You can bid her go to the Grange, at once, if she be able, and carry a message from me, that her young lady will follow in time to attend the Squire's funeral.' "

"Mr. Edgar is not dead?" I gasped. "Oh! Zillah, Zillah!"

"No, no—sit you down, my good mistress," she replied; "you're right sickly yet. He's not dead: Doctor Kenneth thinks he may last another day. I met him on the road and asked."

Instead of sitting down, I snatched my outdoor things, and hastened below, for the way was free.

On entering the house, I looked about for some one to give information of Catherine.

The place was filled with sunshine, and the door stood wide open, but nobody seemed at hand.

As I hesitated whether to go off at once, or return and seek my mistress, a slight cough drew my attention to the hearth.

Linton lay on the settle, sole tenant, sucking a stick of sugar-candy, and pursuing my movements with apathetic eyes.

"Where is Miss Catherine?" I demanded, sternly, supposing I could frighten him into giving intelligence, by catching him thus, alone.

He sucked on like an innocent.

"Is she gone?" I said.

"No," he replied; "she's upstairs—she's not to go; we won't let her."

"You won't let her, little idiot!" I exclaimed. "Direct me to her room immediately, or I'll make you sing out sharply."

"Papa would make you sing out, if you attempted to get there," he answered. "He says I'm not to be soft with Catherine; she's my wife, and it's shameful that she should wish to leave me! He says, she hates me, and wants me to die, that she may have my money, but she shan't have it; and she shan't go home! She never shall! she may cry, and be sick as much as she pleases!"

He resumed his former occupation, closing his lids, as if he meant to drop asleep.

"Master Heathcliff," I resumed, "have you forgotten all Catherine's kindness to you, last winter, when you affirmed you loved her, and when she brought you books, and sung you songs, and came many a time through wind and snow to see you? She wept to miss one evening, because you would be disappointed; and you felt then, that she was a hundred times too good to you; and now you believe the lies your father tells, though you know he detests you both! And you join him against her. That's fine gratitude, is it not?"

The corner of Linton's mouth fell, and he took the sugar-candy from his lips.

"Did she come to Wuthering Heights, because she hated you?" I continued. "Think for yourself! As to your money, she does not even know that you will have any. And you say she's sick; and yet, you leave her alone, up there in a strange house! *You*, who have felt what it is to be so neglected! You could pity your own sufferings, and she pitied them, too, but you won't pity hers! I shed tears, Master Heathcliff, you see—an elderly woman, and a servant merely—and you, after pretending such affection, and having reason to worship her almost, store every tear you have for yourself, and lie there quite at ease. Ah! you're a heartless, selfish boy!"

"I can't stay with her," he answered crossly. "I'll not stay, by myself. She cries so I can't bear it. And she won't give over, though I say I'll call my father. I did call him once; and he threatened to strangle her, if she was not quiet, but she began again, the instant he left the room; moaning and grieving, all night long, though I screamed for vexation that I couldn't sleep."

"Is Mr. Heathcliff out?" I inquired, perceiving that the wretched creature had no power to sympathise with his cousin's mental tortures.

"He's in the court," he replied, "talking to Doctor Kenneth, who says uncle is dying, truly, at last. I'm glad, for I shall be master of the Grange after him— and Catherine always spoke of it as *her* house. It isn't hers! It's mine—papa says everything she has is mine. All her nice books are mine; she offered to give me them, and her pretty birds, and her pony Minny, if I would get the key of our room, and let her out; but I told her she had nothing to give, they were all, all mine. And then she cried, and took a little picture from her neck, and said I should have that—two pictures in a gold case, on one side her mother, and on the other, uncle, when they were young. That was yesterday—I said *they* were mine, too; and tried to get them from her. The spiteful thing wouldn't let me; she pushed me off, and hurt me. I shrieked out—that frightens her—she heard papa coming, and she broke the hinges, and divided the case and gave me her mother's portrait; the other she attempted to hide; but papa asked what was the matter and I explained it. He took the one I had away; and ordered her to resign hers to me; she refused, and he—he struck her down, and wrenched it off the chain, and crushed it with his foot."

"And were you pleased to see her struck?" I asked, having my designs in encouraging his talk.

"I winked," he answered. "I wink to see my father strike a dog, or a horse, he does it so hard. Yet I was glad at first—she deserved punishing for pushing me: but when papa was gone, she made me come to the window and showed me her cheek cut on the inside, against her teeth, and her mouth filling with blood; and then she gathered up the bits of the picture, and went and sat down with her face to the wall, and she has never spoken to me since, and I sometimes think she can't speak for pain. I don't like to think so! but she's a naughty thing for crying continually; and she looks so pale and wild, I'm afraid of her!"

"And you can get the key if you choose?" I said.

"Yes, when I am upstairs," he answered; "but I can't walk upstairs now."

"In what apartment is it?" I asked.

"Oh," he cried, "I shan't tell *you* where it is! It is our secret. Nobody, neither Hareton, nor Zillah are to know. There! you've tired me—go away, go away!" And he turned his face onto his arm, and shut his eyes, again.

I considered it best to depart without seeing Mr. Heathcliff; and bring a rescue for my young lady, from the Grange.

On reaching it, the astonishment of my fellow servants to see me, and their joy also, was intense; and when they heard that their little mistress was safe, two or three were about to hurry up, and shout the news at Mr. Edgar's door: but I bespoke the announcement of it, myself.

How changed I found him, even in those few days! He lay an image of sadness, and resignation, waiting his death. Very young he looked: though his actual age was thirty-nine, one would have called him ten years younger, at least. He thought of Catherine, for he murmured her name. I touched his hand, and spoke.

"Catherine is coming, dear master!" I whispered; "she is alive, and well; and will be here I hope to-night."

I trembled at the first effects of this intelligence: he half rose up, looked eagerly round the apartment, and then sunk back in a swoon.

As soon as he recovered, I related our compulsory visit, and detention at the Heights. I said Heathcliff forced me to go in, which was not quite true; I uttered as little as possible against Linton; nor did I describe all his father's brutal conduct, my intentions being to add no bitterness, if I could help it, to his already overflowing cup.

He divined that one of his enemy's purposes was to secure the personal property, as well as the estate, to his son, or rather himself; yet why he did not wait till his decease, was a puzzle to my master, because ignorant how nearly he and his nephew would quit the world together.

However, he felt his will had better be altered. Instead of leaving Catherine's fortune at her own disposal, he determined to put it in the hands of trustees, for her use during life, and for her children, if she had any, after her. By that means, it could not fall to Mr. Heathcliff should Linton die.

Having received his orders, I despatched a man to fetch the attorney, and four more, provided with serviceable weapons, to demand my young lady of her jailer. Both parties were delayed very late. The single servant returned first.

He said Mr. Green, the lawyer, was out when he arrived at his house, and he had to wait two hours for his re-entrance: and then Mr. Green told him he had a little business in the village that must be done, but he would be at Thrushcross Grange before morning.

The four men came back unaccompanied, also. They brought word that Catherine was ill, too ill to quit her room, and Heathcliff would not suffer them to see her.

I scolded the stupid fellows well, for listening to that tale, which I would not carry to my master; resolving to take a whole bevy up to the Heights, at daylight, and storm it, literally, unless the prisoner were quietly surrendered to us.

Her father *shall* see her, I vowed, and vowed again, if that devil be killed on his own doorstones in trying to prevent it!

Happily, I was spared the journey, and the trouble.

I had gone downstairs at three o'clock to fetch a jug of water; and was passing through the hall with it in my hand, when a sharp knock at the front door made me jump.

"Oh! it is Green," I said, recollecting myself, "—only Green," and I went on, intending to send somebody else to open it; but the knock was repeated, not loud, and still importunately.

I put the jug on the banister, and hastened to admit him myself.

The harvest moon shone clear outside. It was not the attorney. My own sweet little mistress sprung on my neck sobbing—

"Ellen! Ellen! Is papa alive?"

"Yes!" I cried, "yes, my angel, he is! God be thanked, you are safe with us again!"

She wanted to run, breathless as she was, upstairs to Mr. Linton's room; but I compelled her to sit down on a chair, and made her drink, and washed her pale face, chafing it into a faint colour with my apron. Then I said I must go first, and tell of her arrival; imploring her to say, she should be happy with young Heathcliff.

She stared, but soon comprehending why I counselled her to utter the falsehood, she assured me she would not complain.

I couldn't abide to be present at their meeting. I stood outside the chamber-door a quarter of an hour, and hardly ventured near the bed, then.

All was composed, however; Catherine's despair was as silent as her father's joy. She supported him calmly, in appearance; and he fixed on her features his raised eyes, that seemed dilating with ecstasy.

He died blissfully, Mr. Lockwood; he died so. Kissing her cheek, he murmured—

"I am going to her, and you, darling child, shall come to us"; and never stirred or spoke again, but continued that rapt, radiant gaze, till his pulse imperceptibly stopped, and his soul departed. None could have noticed the exact minute of his death, it was so entirely without a struggle.

Whether Catherine had spent her tears, or whether the grief were too weighty to let them flow, she sat there dry-eyed till the sun rose; she sat till noon, and would still have remained, brooding over that death-bed, but I insisted on her coming away, and taking some repose.

It was well I succeeded in removing her, for at dinner-time appeared the lawyer, having called at Wuthering Heights to get his instructions how to behave. He had sold himself to Mr. Heathcliff, and that was the cause of his delay in obeying my master's summons. Fortunately, no thought of worldly affairs crossed the latter's mind, to disturb him, after his daughter's arrival.

Mr. Green took upon himself to order everything and everybody about the place. He gave all the servants but me, notice to quit. He would have carried his delegated authority to the point of insisting that Edgar Linton should not be buried beside his wife, but in the chapel, with his family. There was the will, however, to hinder that, and my loud protestations against any infringement of its directions.

The funeral was hurried over; Catherine, Mrs. Linton Heathcliff now, was suffered to stay at the Grange, till her father's corpse had quitted it.

She told me that her anguish had at last spurred Linton to incur the risk of liberating her. She heard the men I sent, disputing at the door, and she gathered the sense of Heathcliff's answer. It drove her desperate. Linton, who had been conveyed up to the little parlour soon after I left, was terrified into fetching the key before his father re-ascended.

He had the cunning to unlock, and re-lock the door, without shutting it; and when he should have gone to bed, he begged to sleep with Hareton, and his petition was granted, for once.

Catherine stole out before break of day. She dare not try the doors, lest the dogs should raise an alarm; she visited the empty chambers, and examined their windows; and, luckily, lighting on her mother's, she got easily out of its lattice, and onto the ground, by means of the fir tree, close by. Her accomplice suffered for his share in the escape, notwithstanding his timid contrivances.

CHAPTER 29

The evening after the funeral, my young lady and I were seated in the library; now musing mournfully, one of us despairingly, on our loss, now venturing conjectures as to the gloomy future.

We had just agreed the best destiny which could await Catherine, would be a permission to continue resident at the Grange, at least during Linton's life: he being allowed to join her there, and I to remain as housekeeper. That seemed rather too favourable an arrangement to be hoped for, and yet I did hope, and began to cheer up under the prospect of retaining my home, and my employment, and, above all, my beloved young mistress, when a servant—one of the discarded ones, not yet departed—rushed hastily in, and said, "that devil Heathcliff" was coming through the court: should he fasten the door in his face?

If we had been mad enough to order that proceeding, we had not time. He made no ceremony of knocking, or announcing his name; he was master, and availed himself of the master's privilege to walk straight in, without saying a word.

The sound of our informant's voice directed him to the library; he entered, and motioning him out, shut the door.

It was the same room into which he had been ushered, as a guest, eighteen years before: the same moon shone through the window; and the same autumn landscape lay outside. We had not yet lighted a candle, but all the apartment was visible, even to the portraits on the wall—the splendid head of Mrs. Linton, and the graceful one of her husband.

Heathcliff advanced to the hearth. Time had little altered his person either. There was the same man, his dark face rather sallower, and more composed, his frame a stone or two heavier, perhaps, and no other difference.

Catherine had risen with an impulse to dash out, when she saw him.

"Stop!" he said, arresting her by the arm. "No more runnings away! Where would you go? I'm come to fetch you home; and I hope you'll be a dutiful daughter, and not encourage my son to further disobedience. I was embarrassed how to punish him, when I discovered his part in the business—he's such a cobweb, a pinch would annihilate him—but you'll see by his look that he has received his due! I brought him down one evening, the day before yesterday, and just set him in a chair, and never touched him afterwards. I sent Hareton out, and we had the room to ourselves. In two hours, I called Joseph to carry him up again; and, since then, my presence is as potent on his nerves as a ghost; and I fancy he sees me often, though I am not near. Hareton says he wakes and shrieks in the night by the hour together; and calls you to protect him from me; and, whether you like your precious mate or not, you must come—he's your concern now; I yield all my interest in him to you."

"Why not let Catherine continue here?" I pleaded, "and send Master Linton to her. As you hate them both, you'd not miss them; they *can* only be a daily plague to your unnatural heart."

"I'm seeking a tenant for the Grange," he answered; "and I want my children about me, to be sure—besides, that lass owes me her services for her bread; I'm not going to nurture her in luxury and idleness after Linton is gone. Make haste and get ready now. And don't oblige me to compel you."

"I shall," said Catherine. "Linton is all I have to love in the world, and, though you have done what you could to make him hateful to me, and me to him, you *cannot* make us hate each other! and I defy you to hurt him when I am by, and I defy you to frighten me."

"You are a boastful champion!" replied Heathcliff; "but I don't like you well enough to hurt him: you shall get the full benefit of the torment, as long as it lasts. It is not I who will make him hateful to you—it is his own sweet spirit. He's as bitter as gall at your desertion, and its consequences; don't expect thanks for this noble devotion. I heard him draw a pleasant picture to Zillah of what he would do, if he were as strong as I. The inclination is there, and his very weakness will sharpen his wits to find a substitute for strength."

"I know he has a bad nature," said Catherine; "he's your son. But I'm glad I've a better, to forgive it; and I know he loves me and for that reason I love him. Mr. Heathcliff, *you* have *nobody* to love you; and, however miserable you make us, we shall still have the revenge of thinking that your cruelty rises from your greater misery! You *are* miserable, are you not? Lonely, like the devil, and envious like him? *Nobody* loves you—*nobody* will cry for you, when you die! I wouldn't be you!"

Catherine spoke with a kind of dreary triumph: she seemed to have made up her mind to enter into the spirit of her future family, and draw pleasure from the griefs of her enemies.

"You shall be sorry to be yourself presently," said her father-in-law, "if you stand there another minute. Begone, witch, and get your things."

She scornfully withdrew.

In her absence, I began to beg for Zillah's place at the Heights, offering to resign her mine; but he would suffer it on no account. He bid me be silent, and then, for the first time, allowed himself a glance round the room, and a look at the pictures. Having studied Mrs. Linton, he said—

"I shall have that at home. Not because I need it, but—"

He turned abruptly to the fire, and continued, with what, for lack of a better word, I must call a smile—

"I'll tell you what I did yesterday! I got the sexton, who was digging Linton's grave, to remove the earth off her coffin lid, and I opened it. I thought, once, I would have stayed there, when I saw her face again—it is hers yet—he had hard work to stir me; but he said it would change, if the air blew on it, and so I struck one side of the coffin loose, and covered it up—not Linton's side, damn him! I wish he'd been soldered in lead—and I bribed the sexton to pull it away, when I'm laid there, and slide mine out too. I'll have it made so, and then, by the time Linton gets to us, he'll not know which is which!"

"You were very wicked, Mr. Heathcliff!" I exclaimed; "were you not ashamed to disturb the dead?"

"I disturbed nobody, Nelly," he replied; "and I gave some ease to myself. I shall be a great deal more comfortable now; and you'll have a better chance of keeping me underground, when I get there. Disturbed her? No! she has disturbed me, night and day, through eighteen years—incessantly—remorselessly—till yesternight; and yesternight, I was tranquil. I dreamt I was sleeping the last sleep, by that sleeper, with my heart stopped, and my cheek frozen against hers."

"And if she had been dissolved into earth, or worse, what would you have dreamt of then?" I said.

"Of dissolving with her, and being more happy still!" he answered. "Do you suppose I dread any change of that sort? I expected such a transformation on raising the lid, but I'm better pleased that it should not commence till I share it. Besides, unless I had received a distinct impression of her passionless features, that strange feeling would hardly have been removed. It began oddly. You know, I was wild after she died, and eternally, from dawn to dawn, praying her to return to me—her spirit. I have a strong faith in ghosts; I have a conviction that they can, and do exist, among us!

"The day she was buried there came a fall of snow. In the evening I went to the churchyard. It blew bleak as winter—all round was solitary: I didn't fear that her fool of a husband would wander up the den so late; and no one else had business to bring them there.

"Being alone, and conscious two yards of loose earth was the sole barrier between us, I said to myself—

" 'I'll have her in my arms again! If she be cold, I'll think it is this north wind that chills *me*; and if she be motionless, it is sleep.'

"I got a spade from the toolhouse, and began to delve with all my might—it scraped the coffin; I fell to work with my hands; the wood commenced cracking about the screws, I was on the point of attaining my object, when it seemed that I heard a sigh from some one above, close at the edge of the grave, and bending down. 'If I can only get this off,' I muttered, 'I wish they may shovel in the earth over us both!' and I wrenched at it more desperately still. There was another sigh, close at my ear. I appeared to feel the warm breath of it displacing the sleet-laden wind. I knew no living thing in flesh and blood was by; but as certainly as you perceive the approach to some substantial body in the dark, though it cannot be discerned, so certainly I felt that Cathy was there, not under me, but on the earth.

"A sudden sense of relief flowed from my heart through every limb. I relinquished my labour of agony, and turned consoled at once, unspeakably consoled. Her presence was with me; it remained while I re-filled the grave, and led me home. You may laugh, if you will, but I was sure I should see her there. I was sure she was with me, and I could not help talking to her.

"Having reached the Heights, I rushed eagerly to the door. It was fastened; and, I remember, that accursed Earnshaw and my wife opposed my entrance. I remember stopping to kick the breath out of him, and then hurrying upstairs, to my room, and hers. I looked round impatiently—I felt her by me—I could *almost* see her, and yet I *could not!* I ought to have sweat blood then, from the anguish of my yearning, from the fervour of my supplications to have but one glimpse! I had not one. She showed herself, as she often was in life, a devil to me! And, since then, sometimes more, and sometimes less, I've been the sport of that intolerable torture! Infernal—keeping my nerves at such a stretch, that, if they had not resembled catgut, they would, long ago, have relaxed to the feebleness of Linton's.

"When I sat in the house with Hareton, it seemed that on going out, I should meet her; when I walked on the moors I should meet her coming in. When I went from home, I hastened to return; she *must* be somewhere at the Heights, I was certain! And when I slept in her chamber—I was beaten out of that—I couldn't lie there; for the moment I closed my eyes, she was either outside the window, or sliding back the panels, or entering the room, or even resting her darling head on the same pillow as she did when a child. And I must open my lids to see. And so I opened and closed them a hundred times a night—to be always disappointed! It racked me! I've often groaned aloud, till that old rascal Joseph no doubt believed that my conscience was playing the fiend inside of me.

"Now since I've seen her, I'm pacified—a little. It was a strange way of killing, not by inches, but by fractions of hair-breadths, to beguile me with the spectre of a hope, through eighteen years!"

Mr. Heathcliff paused and wiped his forehead. His hair clung to it, wet with perspiration; his eyes were fixed on the red embers of the fire; the brows not contracted, but raised next the temples, diminishing the grim aspect of his countenance, but imparting a peculiar look of trouble, and a painful appearance of mental tension towards one absorbing subject. He only half addressed me, and I maintained silence—I didn't like to hear him talk!

After a short period, he resumed his meditation on the picture, took it down, and leant it against the sofa to contemplate it at better advantage; and while so occupied Catherine entered, announcing that she was ready, when her pony should be saddled.

"Send that over to-morrow," said Heathcliff to me, then turning to her he added, "You may do without your pony; it is a fine evening, and you'll need no ponies at Wuthering Heights, for what journeys you take, your own feet will serve you—Come along."

"Good-bye, Ellen!" whispered my dear little mistress. As she kissed me, her lips felt like ice. "Come and see me, Ellen, don't forget."

"Take care you do no such thing, Mrs. Dean!" said her new father. "When I wish to speak to you I'll come here. I want none of your prying at my house!"

He signed her to precede him; and casting back a look that cut my heart, she obeyed.

I watched them from the window walk down the garden. Heathcliff fixed Catherine's arm under his, though she disputed the act, at first, evidently, and with rapid strides, he hurried her into the alley, whose trees concealed them.

CHAPTER 30

I have paid a visit to the Heights, but I have not seen her since she left; Joseph held the door in his hand, when I called to ask after her, and wouldn't let me pass. He said Mrs. Linton was "thrang,"[46] and the master was not in. Zillah has told me something of the way they go on, otherwise I should hardly know who was dead, and who living.

She thinks Catherine haughty, and does not like her, I can guess by her talk. My young lady asked some aid of her, when she first came, but Mr. Heathcliff told her to follow her own business, and let his daughter-in-law look after herself, and Zillah willingly acquiesced, being a narrow-minded, selfish woman. Catherine evinced a child's annoyance at this neglect; repaid it with contempt, and thus enlisted my informant among her enemies, as securely as if she had done her some great wrong.

I had a long talk with Zillah, about six weeks ago, a little before you came, one day when we foregathered on the moor; and this is what she told me.

"The first thing Mrs. Linton did," she said, "on her arrival at the Heights, was to run upstairs without even wishing good-evening to me and Joseph; she shut herself into Linton's room, and remained till morning. Then, while the master and Earnshaw were at breakfast, she entered the house and asked all in a quiver if the doctor might be sent for? her cousin was very ill."

" 'We know that!' answered Heathcliff, 'but his life is not worth a farthing, and I won't spend a farthing on him.'

" 'But I cannot tell how to do,' she said, 'and if nobody will help me, he'll die!'

" 'Walk out of the room!' cried the master, 'and let me never hear a word more about him! None here care what becomes of him; if you do, act the nurse; if you do not, lock him up and leave him.'

"Then she began to bother me, and I said I'd had enough plague with the tiresome thing; we each had our tasks, and hers was to wait on Linton; Mr. Heathcliff bid me leave that labour to her.

"How they managed together, I can't tell. I fancy he fretted a great deal, and moaned hisseln, night and day; and she had precious little rest, one could guess by her white face, and heavy eyes. She sometimes came into the kitchen all wildered like, and looked as if she would fain beg assistance: but I was not going to disobey the master. I never dare disobey him, Mrs. Dean, and though I thought it wrong that Kenneth should not be sent for, it was no concern of mine, either to advise or complain; and I always refused to meddle.

"Once or twice, after we had gone to bed, I've happened to open my door again, and seen her sitting crying, on the stairs' top; and then I've shut myself in, quick, for fear of being moved to interfere. I did pity her then, I'm sure; still, I didn't wish to lose my place, you know!

---

[46] *Thrang:* busy.

"At last, one night she came boldly into my chamber, and frightened me out of my wits, by saying—

" 'Tell Mr. Heathcliff that his son is dying—I'm sure he is, this time. Get up, instantly, and tell him!'

"Having uttered this speech, she vanished again. I lay a quarter of an hour listening and trembling. Nothing stirred—the house was quiet.

" 'She's mistaken,' I said to myself. 'He's got over it. I needn't disturb them.' And I began to doze. But my sleep was marred a second time, by a sharp ringing of the bell—the only bell we have, put up on purpose for Linton; and the master called to me, to see what was the matter, and inform them that he wouldn't have that noise repeated.

"I delivered Catherine's message. He cursed to himself, and in a few minutes, came out with a lighted candle, and proceeded to their room. I followed. Mrs. Heathcliff was seated by the bedside, with her hands folded on her knees. Her father-in-law went up, held the light to Linton's face, looked at him, and touched him; afterwards he turned to her.

" 'Now—Catherine,' he said, 'how do you feel?'

"She was dumb.

" 'How do you feel, Catherine?' he repeated.

" 'He's safe, and I'm free,' she answered, 'I should feel well—but,' she continued with a bitterness she couldn't conceal, 'you have left me so long to struggle against death, alone, that I feel and see only death! I feel like death!'

"And she looked like it, too! I gave her a little wine. Hareton and Joseph, who had been wakened by the ringing and the sound of feet, and heard our talk from outside, now entered. Joseph was fain, I believe, of the lad's removal: Hareton seemed a thought bothered, though he was more taken up with staring at Catherine than thinking of Linton. But the master bid him get off to bed again—we didn't want his help. He afterwards made Joseph remove the body to his chamber, and told me to return to mine, and Mrs. Heathcliff remained by herself.

"In the morning, he sent me to tell her she must come down to breakfast. She had undressed, and appeared going to sleep, and said she was ill; at which I hardly wondered. I informed Mr. Heathcliff, and he replied—

" 'Well, let her be till after the funeral; and go up now and then to get her what is needful; and as soon as she seems better, tell me.'

"Cathy stayed upstairs a fortnight, according to Zillah, who visited her twice a day, and would have been rather more friendly, but her attempts at increasing kindness were proudly and promptly repelled.

"Heathcliff went up once, to show her Linton's will. He had bequeathed the whole of his, and what had been her, moveable property to his father. The poor creature was threatened, or coaxed, into that act during her week's absence, when his uncle died. The lands, being a minor, he could not meddle with. However, Mr. Heathcliff has claimed and kept them in his wife's right, and his also, I suppose legally. At any rate Catherine, destitute of cash and friends, cannot disturb his possession.

"Nobody," said Zillah, "ever approached her door, except that once, but I; and nobody asked anything about her. The first occasion of her coming down into the house, was on a Sunday afternoon.

"She had cried out, when I carried up her dinner, that she couldn't bear any longer being in the cold; and I told her the master was going to Thrushcross Grange; and Earnshaw and I needn't hinder her from descending; so, as soon as she heard Heathcliff's horse trot off, she made her appearance, donned in black, and her yellow curls combed back behind her ears, as plain as a Quaker; she couldn't comb them out.

"Joseph and I generally go to chapel on Sundays," (the Kirk, you know, has no minister now, explained Mrs. Dean, and they call the Methodists' or Baptists' place, I can't say which it is, at Gimmerton, a chapel). "Joseph had gone," she continued, "but I thought proper to bide at home. Young folks are always the better for an elder's over-looking, and Hareton, with all his bashfulness, isn't a model of nice behaviour. I let him know that his cousin would very likely sit with us, and she had been always used to see the Sabbath respected, so he had as good leave his guns and bits of in-door work alone, while she stayed.

"He coloured up at the news, and cast his eyes over his hands and clothes. The train-oil and gunpowder were shoved out of sight in a minute. I saw he meant to give her his company; and I guessed, by his way, he wanted to be presentable; so, laughing, as I durst not laugh when the master is by, I offered to help him, if he would, and joked at his confusion. He grew sullen, and began to swear.

"Now, Mrs. Dean," she went on, seeing me not pleased by her manner, "you happen think your young lady too fine for Mr. Hareton, and happen you're right; but, I own, I should love well to bring her pride a peg lower. And what will all her learning and her daintiness do for her, now? She's as poor as you or I—poorer, I'll be bound; you're saving, and I'm doing my little all, that road."[47]

Hareton allowed Zillah to give him her aid; and she flattered him into a good humour; so, when Catherine came, half forgetting her former insults, he tried to make himself agreeable, by the housekeeper's account.

"Missis walked in," she said, "as chill as an icicle, and as high as a princess. I got up and offered her my seat in the arm-chair. No, she turned up her nose at my civility. Earnshaw rose too, and bid her come to the settle, and sit close by the fire; he was sure she was starved.

" 'I've been starved a month and more,' she answered, resting on the word, as scornful as she could.

"And she got a chair for herself, and placed it at a distance from both of us.

"Having sat till she was warm, she began to look round, and discovered a number of books in the dresser; she was instantly upon her feet again, stretching to reach them, but they were too high up.

"Her cousin, after watching her endeavours a while, at last summoned courage to help her; she held her frock, and he filled it with the first that came to hand.

"That was a great advance for the lad. She didn't thank him; still, he felt gratified that she had accepted his assistance, and ventured to stand behind as she examined them, and even to stoop and point out what struck his fancy in certain old pictures which they contained; nor was he daunted by the saucy style in which she jerked the page from his finger; he contented himself with going a bit farther back, and looking at her instead of the book.

"She continued reading, or seeking for something to read. His attention became, by degrees, quite centred in the study of her thick, silky curls; her face he couldn't see, and she couldn't see him. And, perhaps, not quite awake to what he did, but attracted like a child to a candle, at last he proceeded from staring to touching; he put out his hand and stroked one curl, as gently as if it were a bird. He might have stuck a knife into her neck, she started round in such a taking.

" 'Get away, this moment! How dare you touch me? Why are you stopping there?' she cried, in a tone of disgust. 'I can't endure you! I'll go up stairs again, if you come near me.'

---

[47] *That road:* that way.

"Mr. Hareton recoiled, looking as foolish as he could do; he sat down in the settle, very quiet, and she continued turning over her volumes, another half hour; finally, Earnshaw crossed over, and whispered to me—

" 'Will you ask her to read to us, Zillah? I'm stalled of doing naught; and I do like—I could like to hear her! Dunnot say I wanted it, but ask of yourseln.'

" 'Mr. Hareton wishes you would read to us, ma'am,' I said, immediately. 'He'd take it very kind—he'd be much obliged.'

"She frowned; and, looking up, answered—

" 'Mr. Hareton, and the whole set of you, will be good enough to understand that I reject any pretence at kindness you have the hypocrisy to offer! I despise you, and will have nothing to say to any of you! When I would have given my life for one kind word, even to see one of your faces, you all kept off. But I won't complain to you! I'm driven down here by the cold, not either to amuse you, or enjoy your society.'

" 'What could I ha' done?' began Earnshaw. 'How was I to blame?'

" 'Oh! you are an exception,' answered Mrs. Heathcliff. 'I never missed such a concern as you.'

" 'But I offered more than once, and asked,' he said, kindling up at her pertness, 'I asked Mr. Heathcliff to let me wake for you—'

" 'Be silent! I'll go out of doors, or anywhere, rather than have your disagreeable voice in my ear!' said my lady.

"Hareton muttered, she might go to hell, for him! and unslinging his gun, restrained himself from his Sunday occupations no longer.

"He talked now, freely enough; and she presently saw fit to retreat to her solitude: but the frost had set in, and, in spite of her pride, she was forced to condescend to our company, more and more. However, I took care there should be no further scorning at my good nature. Ever since, I've been as stiff as herself; and she has no lover, or liker among us—and she does not deserve one—for, let them say the least word to her, and she'll curl back without respect of any one! She'll snap at the master himself, and as good as dares him to thrash her; and the more hurt she gets, the more venomous she grows."

At first, on hearing this account from Zillah, I determined to leave my situation, take a cottage, and get Catherine to come and live with me; but Mr. Heathcliff would as soon permit that, as he would set up Hareton in an independent house; and I can see no remedy, at present, unless she could marry again; and that scheme, it does not come within my province to arrange.

Thus ended Mrs. Dean's story. Notwithstanding the doctor's prophecy, I am rapidly recovering strength, and, though it be only the second week in January, I propose getting out on horseback, in a day or two, and riding over to Wuthering Heights, to inform my landlord that I shall spend the next six months in London; and, if he likes, he may look out for another tenant to take the place, after October—I would not pass another winter here, for much.

CHAPTER 31

Yesterday was bright, calm, and frosty. I went to the Heights as I proposed; my housekeeper entreated me to bear a little note from her to her young lady, and I did not refuse, for the worthy woman was not conscious of anything odd in her request.

The front door stood open, but the jealous gate was fastened, as at my last visit; I knocked and invoked Earnshaw from among the garden beds; he unchained it, and I entered. The fellow is as handsome a rustic as need be seen. I took particular notice of him this time; but then he does his best, apparently, to make the least of his advantages.

I asked if Mr. Heathcliff were at home? He answered, no; but he would be in at dinner-time. It was eleven o'clock, and I announced my intention of going in, and waiting for him, at which he immediately flung down his tools and accompanied me, in the office of watchdog, not as a substitute for the host.

We entered together; Catherine was there, making herself useful in preparing some vegetables for the approaching meal; she looked more sulky, and less spirited than when I had seen her first. She hardly raised her eyes to notice me, and continued her employment with the same disregard to common forms of politeness, as before; never returning my bow and good morning by the slightest acknowledgment.

"She does not seem so amiable," I thought, "as Mrs. Dean would persuade me to believe. She's a beauty, it is true; but not an angel."

Earnshaw surlily bid her remove her things to the kitchen.

"Remove them yourself," she said, pushing them from her, as soon as she had done, and retiring to a stool by the window, where she began to carve figures of birds and beasts, out of the turnip parings in her lap.

I approached her, pretending to desire a view of the garden; and, as I fancied, adroitly dropped Mrs. Dean's note onto her knee, unnoticed by Hareton—but she asked aloud—

"What is that?" And chucked it off.

"A letter from your old acquaintance, the housekeeper at the Grange," I answered, annoyed at her exposing my kind deed, and fearful lest it should be imagined a missive of my own.

She would gladly have gathered it up at this information, but Hareton beat her; he seized, and put it in his waistcoat, saying Mr. Heathcliff should look at it first.

Thereat, Catherine silently turned her face from us, and, very stealthily, drew out her pocket-handkerchief and applied it to her eyes; and her cousin, after struggling a while to keep down his softer feelings, pulled out the letter and flung it on the floor beside her as ungraciously as he could.

Catherine caught and perused it eagerly; then she put a few questions to me concerning the inmates, rational and irrational, of her former home; and gazing towards the hills, murmured in soliloquy—

"I should like to be riding Minny down there! I should like to be climbing up there—Oh! I'm tired—I'm *stalled*, Hareton!"

And she leant her pretty head back against the sill, with half a yawn and half a sigh, and lapsed into an aspect of abstracted sadness, neither caring nor knowing whether we remarked her.

"Mrs. Heathcliff," I said, after sitting some time mute, "you are not aware that I am an acquaintance of yours? so intimate, that I think it strange you won't come and speak to me. My housekeeper never wearies of talking about and praising you; and she'll be greatly disappointed if I return with no news of, or from you, except that you received her letter, and said nothing!"

She appeared to wonder at this speech and asked—

"Does Ellen like you?"

"Yes, very well," I replied unhesitatingly.

"You must tell her," she continued, "that I would answer her letter, but I have no materials for writing, not even a book from which I might tear a leaf."

"No books!" I exclaimed. "How do you contrive to live here without them, if I may take the liberty to inquire? Though provided with a large library, I'm frequently very dull at the Grange; take my books away, and I should be desperate!"

"I was always reading, when I had them," said Catherine, "and Mr. Heathcliff never reads; so he took it into his head to destroy my books. I have not had a glimpse of one, for weeks. Only once, I searched through Joseph's store of theology, to his great irritation; and once, Hareton, I came upon a secret stock in your room—some Latin and Greek, and some tales and poetry; all old friends. I brought the last here—and you gathered them, as a magpie gathers silver spoons, for the mere love of stealing! They are of no use to you; or else you concealed them in the bad spirit, that as you cannot enjoy them, nobody else shall. Perhaps *your* envy counselled Mr. Heathcliff to rob me of my treasures? But I've most of them written on my brain and printed in my heart, and you cannot deprive me of those!"

Earnshaw blushed crimson, when his cousin made this revelation of his private literary accumulations, and stammered an indignant denial of her accusations.

"Mr. Hareton is desirous of increasing his amount of knowledge," I said, coming to his rescue. "He is not *envious* but *emulous* of your attainments. He'll be a clever scholar in a few years!"

"And he wants *me* to sink into a dunce, meantime," answered Catherine. "Yes, I hear him trying to spell and read to himself, and pretty blunders he makes! I wish you would repeat Chevy Chase, as you did yesterday; it was extremely funny! I heard you—and I heard you turning over the dictionary, to seek out the hard words, and then cursing, because you couldn't read their explanations!"

The young man evidently thought it too bad that he should be laughed at for his ignorance, and then laughed at for trying to remove it. I had a similar notion, and, remembering Mrs. Dean's anecdote of his first attempt at enlightening the darkness in which he had been reared, I observed—

"But, Mrs. Heathcliff, we have each had a commencement, and each stumbled and tottered on the threshold, and had our teachers scorned, instead of aiding us, we should stumble and totter yet."

"Oh!" she replied, "I don't wish to limit his acquirements. Still, he has no right to appropriate what is mine, and make it ridiculous to me with his vile mistakes and mis-pronunciations! Those books, both prose and verse, were consecrated to me by other associations, and I hate to have them debased and profaned in his mouth! Besides, of all, he has selected my favourite pieces that I love the most to repeat, as if out of deliberate malice!"

Hareton's chest heaved in silence a minute; he laboured under a severe sense of mortification and wrath, which it was no easy task to suppress.

I rose, and, from a gentlemanly idea of relieving his embarrassment, took up my station in the door-way, surveying the external prospect, as I stood.

He followed my example, and left the room, but presently re-appeared, bearing half-a-dozen volumes in his hands, which he threw into Catherine's lap, exclaiming—

"Take them! I never want to hear, or read, or think of them again!"

"I won't have them, now!" she answered. "I shall connect them with you, and hate them."

She opened one that had obviously been often turned over, and read a portion in the drawling tone of a beginner; then laughed, and threw it from her.

"And listen!" she continued provokingly, commencing a verse of an old ballad in the same fashion.

But his self-love would endure no further torment. I heard, and not altogether disapprovingly, a manual check given to her saucy tongue. The little wretch had done her utmost to hurt her cousin's sensitive though uncultivated feelings, and a physical argument was the only mode he had of balancing the account and repaying its effects on the inflicter.

He afterwards gathered the books and hurled them on the fire. I read in his countenance what anguish it was to offer that sacrifice to spleen. I fancied that as they consumed, he recalled the pleasure they had already imparted, and the triumph and ever increasing pleasure he had anticipated from them; and, I fancied, I guessed the incitement to his secret studies, also. He had been content with daily labour and rough animal enjoyments, till Catherine crossed his path. Shame at her scorn, and hope of her approval were his first prompters to higher pursuits; and instead of guarding him from one, and winning him the other, his endeavours to raise himself had produced just the contrary result.

"Yes, that's all the good that such a brute as you can get from them!" cried Catherine, sucking her damaged lip, and watching the conflagration with indignant eyes.

"You'd *better* hold your tongue, now!" he answered fiercely.

And his agitation precluding further speech, he advanced hastily to the entrance, where I made way for him to pass. But, ere he had crossed the door-stones, Mr. Heathcliff, coming up the causeway, encountered him and laying hold of his shoulder, asked—

"What's to do now, my lad?"

"Naught, naught!" he said, and broke away, to enjoy his grief and anger in solitude.

Heathcliff gazed after him, and sighed.

"It will be odd, if I thwart myself!" he muttered, unconscious that I was behind him. "But, when I look for his father in his face, I find *her* every day more! How the devil is he so like? I can hardly bear to see him."

He bent his eyes to the ground, and walked moodily in. There was a restless, anxious expression in his countenance I had never remarked there before, and he looked sparer in person.

His daughter-in-law, on perceiving him through the window, immediately escaped to the kitchen, so that I remained alone.

"I'm glad to see you out of doors again, Mr. Lockwood," he said in reply to my greeting, "from selfish motives partly; I don't think I could readily supply your loss in this desolation. I've wondered, more than once, what brought you here."

"An idle whim, I fear, sir," was my answer, "or else an idle whim is going to spirit me away. I shall set out for London next week; and I must give you warning, that I feel no disposition to retain Thrushcross Grange, beyond the twelvemonths I agreed to rent it. I believe I shall not live there any more."

"Oh, indeed! you're tired of being banished from the world, are you?" he said. "But, if you be coming to plead off paying for a place you won't occupy, your journey is useless. I never relent in exacting my due, from any one."

"I'm coming to plead off nothing about it!" I exclaimed, considerably irritated. "Should you wish it, I'll settle with you now," and I drew my notebook from my pocket.

"No, no," he replied coolly; "you'll leave sufficient behind, to cover your debts, if you fail to return. I'm not in such a hurry—sit down and take your dinner with us; a guest that is safe from repeating his visit, can generally be made welcome. Catherine! bring the things in—where are you?"

Catherine re-appeared, bearing a tray of knives and forks.

"You may get your dinner with Joseph," muttered Heathcliff aside, "and remain in the kitchen till he is gone."

She obeyed his directions very punctually; perhaps she had no temptation to transgress. Living among clowns and misanthropists, she probably cannot appreciate a better class of people, when she meets them.

With Mr. Heathcliff, grim and saturnine, on one hand, and Hareton, absolutely dumb, on the other, I made a somewhat cheerless meal, and bid adieu early. I would have departed by the back way to get a last glimpse of Catherine, and annoy old Joseph; but Hareton received orders to lead up my horse, and my host himself escorted me to the door, so I could not fulfil my wish.

"How dreary life gets over in that house!" I reflected, while riding down the road. "What a realization of something more romantic than a fairy tale it would have been for Mrs. Linton Heathcliff, had she and I struck up an attachment, as her good nurse desired, and migrated together into the stirring atmosphere of the town!"

CHAPTER 32

1802.—This September, I was invited to devastate the moors of a friend, in the North; and, on my journey to his abode, I unexpectedly came within fifteen miles of Gimmerton. The hostler at a roadside public-house was holding a pail of water to refresh my horses, when a cart of very green oats, newly reaped, passed by, and he remarked—

"Yon's frough Gimmerton, nah! They're allas three wick' after other folk wi' ther harvest."

"Gimmerton?" I repeated—my residence in that locality had already grown dim and dreamy. "Ah! I know! How far is it from this?"

"Happen fourteen mile' o'er th' hills, and a rough road," he answered.

A sudden impulse seized me to visit Thrushcross Grange. It was scarcely noon, and I conceived that I might as well pass the night under my own roof, as in an inn. Besides, I could spare a day easily, to arrange matters with my landlord, and thus save myself the trouble of invading the neighbourhood again.

Having rested a while, I directed my servant to inquire the way to the village; and, with great fatigue to our beasts, we managed the distance in some three hours.

I left him there, and proceeded down the valley alone. The grey church looked greyer, and the lonely churchyard lonelier. I distinguished a moor sheep cropping the short turf on the graves. It was sweet, warm weather—too warm for travelling; but the heat did not hinder me from enjoying the delightful scenery above and below; had I seen it nearer August, I'm sure it would have tempted me to waste a month among its solitudes. In winter, nothing more dreary, in summer, nothing more divine, than those glens shut in by hills, and those bluff, bold swells of heath.

I reached the Grange before sunset, and knocked for admittance; but the family had retreated into the back premises, I judged by one thin, blue wreath curling from the kitchen chimney, and they did not hear.

I rode into the court. Under the porch, a girl of nine or ten sat knitting, and an old woman reclined on the horse-steps, smoking a meditative pipe.

"Is Mrs. Dean within?" I demanded of the dame.

"Mistress Dean? Nay!" she answered, "shoo doesn't bide here; shoo's up at th' Heights."

"Are you the housekeeper, then?" I continued.

"Eea, Aw keep th' hause," she replied.

"Well, I'm Mr. Lockwood, the master. Are there any rooms to lodge me in, I wonder? I wish to stay here all night."

"T' maister!" she cried in astonishment. "Whet, whoiver knew yah wur coming? Yah sud ha' send word! They's nowt norther dry, nor mensful[48] abaht t' place—nowt there isn't!"

She threw down her pipe and bustled in, the girl followed, and I entered too; soon perceiving that her report was true, and, moreover, that I had almost upset her wits by my unwelcome apparition.

I bid her be composed—I would go out for a walk; and, meantime, she must try to prepare a corner of a sitting-room for me to sup in, and a bed-room to sleep in. No sweeping and dusting, only good fires and dry sheets were necessary.

She seemed willing to do her best; though she thrust the hearth-brush into the grates in mistake for the poker, and mal-appropriated several other articles of her craft; but I retired, confiding in her energy for a resting-place against my return.

Wuthering Heights was the goal of my proposed excursion. An after-thought brought me back, when I had quitted the court.

"All well at the Heights?" I enquired of the woman.

"Eea, f'r owt Ee knaw!" she answered, skurrying away with a pan of hot cinders.

I would have asked why Mrs. Dean had deserted the Grange; but it was impossible to delay her at such a crisis, so I turned away and made my exit, rambling leisurely along with the glow of a sinking sun behind, and the mild glory of a rising moon in front—one fading, and the other brightening, as I quitted the park, and climbed the stony by-road branching off to Mr. Heathcliff's dwelling.

Before I arrived in sight of it, all that remained of day was a beamless, amber light along the west; but I could see every pebble on the path, and every blade of grass by that splendid moon.

I had neither to climb the gate, nor to knock—it yielded to my hand.

That is an improvement! I thought. And I noticed another, by the aid of my nostrils, a fragrance of stocks and wall flowers, wafted on the air, from amongst the homely fruit trees.

Both doors and lattices were open; and yet, as is usually the case in a coal district, a fine, red fire illumined the chimney; the comfort which the eye derives from it, renders the extra heat endurable. But the house of Wuthering Heights is so large, that the inmates have plenty of space for withdrawing out of its influence; and, accordingly, what inmates there were had stationed themselves not far from one of the windows. I could both see them and hear them talk before I entered, and looked and listened in consequence, being moved thereto by a mingled sense of curiosity and envy that grew as I lingered.

"Con-*trary!*" said a voice, as sweet as a silver bell—"That for the third time, you dunce! I'm not going to tell you, again—Recollect, or I pull your hair!"

"Contrary, then," answered another, in deep, but softened tones. "And now, kiss me, for minding so well."

"No, read it over first correctly, without a single mistake."

The male speaker began to read. He was a young man, respectably dressed, and seated at a table, having a book before him. His handsome features glowed with pleasure, and his eyes kept impatiently wandering from the page to a small white hand over his shoulder, which recalled him by a smart slap on the cheek, whenever its owner detected such signs of inattention.

Its owner stood behind; her light shining ringlets blending, at intervals, with his brown locks, as she bent to superintend his studies; and her face—it was lucky he

---

[48] *Norther dry, nor mensful:* neither dry nor proper.

could not see her face, or he would never have been so steady. I could, and I bit my lip, in spite, at having thrown away the chance I might have had of doing something besides staring at its smiting beauty.

The task was done, not free from further blunders, but the pupil claimed a reward, and received at least five kisses, which, however, he generously returned. Then, they came to the door, and from their conversation, I judged they were about to issue out and have a walk on the moors. I supposed I should be condemned in Hareton Earnshaw's heart, if not by his mouth, to the lowest pit in the infernal regions if I showed my unfortunate person in his neighbourhood then, and feeling very mean and malignant, I skulked round to seek refuge in the kitchen.

There was unobstructed admittance on that side also; and, at the door, sat my old friend, Nelly Dean, sewing and singing a song, which was often interrupted from within, by harsh words of scorn and intolerance, uttered in far from musical accents.

"Aw'd rayther, by th' haulf, hev 'em swearing i' my lugs frough morn tuh neeght, nur hearken yah, hahsiver!" said the tenant of the kitchen, in answer to an unheard speech of Nelly's. "It's a blazing shaime, ut Aw cannut oppen t' Blessed Book, bud yah set up them glories tuh Sattan, un' all t' flaysome wickednesses ut iver wer born intuh t' warld! Oh! yah're a raight nowt, un' shoo's another; un' that poor lad 'ull be lost, atween ye. Poor lad!" he added, with a groan; "he's witched, Aw'm sartin on't! O, Lord, judge 'em, for they's norther law nur justice amang wer rullers!"

"No! or we should be sitting in flaming fagots, I suppose," retorted the singer. "But wisht, old man, and read your Bible, like a Christian, and never mind me. This is 'Fairy Annie's Wedding'—a bonny tune—it goes to a dance."

Mrs. Dean was about to recommence, when I advanced, and recognising me directly, she jumped to her feet, crying—

"Why, bless you, Mr. Lockwood! How could you think of returning in this way? All's shut up at Thrushcross Grange. You should have given us notice!"

"I've arranged to be accommodated there, for as long as I shall stay," I answered. "I depart again to-morrow. And how are you transplanted here, Mrs. Dean? tell me that."

"Zillah left, and Mr. Heathcliff wished me to come, soon after you went to London, and stay till you returned. But, step in, pray! Have you walked from Gimmerton this evening?"

"From the Grange," I replied; "and, while they make me lodging room there, I want to finish my business with your master, because I don't think of having another opportunity in a hurry."

"What business, sir?" said Nelly, conducting me into the house. "He's gone out, at present, and won't return soon."

"About the rent," I answered.

"Oh! then it is with Mrs. Heathcliff you must settle," she observed, "or rather with me. She has not learnt to manage her affairs yet, and I act for her; there's nobody else."

I looked surprised.

"Ah! you have not heard of Heathcliff's death, I see!" she continued.

"Heathcliff dead?" I exclaimed, astonished. "How long ago?"

"Three months since—but, sit down, and let me take your hat, and I'll tell you all about it. Stop, you have had nothing to eat, have you?"

"I want nothing. I have ordered supper at home. You sit down too. I never dreamt of his dying! Let me hear how it came to pass. You say you don't expect them back for some time—the young people?"

"No—I have to scold them every evening, for their late rambles, but they don't care for me. At least, have a drink of our old ale; it will do you good—you seem weary."

She hastened to fetch it, before I could refuse, and I heard Joseph asking whether "it warn't a crying scandal that she should have fellies at her time of life? And then, to get them jocks[49] out uh t' Maister's cellar! He fair shaamed to 'bide still and see it."

She did not stay to retaliate, but re-entered, in a minute, bearing a reaming, silver pint, whose contents I lauded with becoming earnestness. And afterwards she furnished me with the sequel of Heathcliff's history. He had a "queer" end, as she expressed it.

I was summoned to Wuthering Heights, within a fortnight of your leaving us, she said; and I obeyed joyfully, for Catherine's sake.

My first interview with her grieved and shocked me! she had altered so much since our separation. Mr. Heathcliff did not explain his reasons for taking a new mind about my coming here; he only told me he wanted me, and he was tired of seeing Catherine; I must make the little parlour my sitting room, and keep her with me. It was enough if he were obliged to see her once or twice a day.

She seemed pleased at this arrangement; and, by degrees, I smuggled over a great number of books and other articles, that had formed her amusement at the Grange; and flattered myself we should get on in tolerable comfort.

The delusion did not last long. Catherine, contented at first, in a brief space grew irritable and restless. For one thing, she was forbidden to move out of the garden, and it fretted her sadly to be confined to its narrow bounds, as Spring drew on; for another, in following the house, I was forced to quit her frequently, and she complained of loneliness; she preferred quarrelling with Joseph in the kitchen, to sitting at peace in her solitude.

I did not mind their skirmishes; but Hareton was often obliged to seek the kitchen also, when the master wanted to have the house to himself; and, though, in the beginning, she either left it at his approach, or quietly joined in my occupations, and shunned remarking, or addressing him—and though he was always as sullen and silent as possible—after a while, she changed her behaviour, and became incapable of letting him alone: talking at him; commenting on his stupidity and idleness; expressing her wonder how he could endure the life he lived—how he could sit a whole evening staring into the fire, and dozing.

"He's just like a dog, is he not, Ellen?" she once observed, "or a cart-horse? He does his work, eats his food, and sleeps, eternally! What a blank, dreary mind he must have! Do you ever dream, Hareton? And, if you do, what is it about? But you can't speak to me!"

Then she looked at him; but he would neither open his mouth, nor look again.

"He's perhaps dreaming now," she continued. "He twitched his shoulder as Juno twitches hers. Ask him, Ellen."

"Mr. Hareton will ask the master to send you upstairs, if you don't behave!" I said. He had not only twitched his shoulder, but clenched his fist, as if tempted to use it.

"I know why Hareton never speaks, when I am in the kitchen," she exclaimed, on another occasion. "He is afraid I shall laugh at him. Ellen, what do you think?

---

[49] *Fellies:* fellows; *jocks:* jugs.

He began to teach himself to read once; and, because I laughed, he burned his books, and dropped it—was he not a fool?"

"Were not you naughty?" I said; "answer me that."

"Perhaps I was," she went on, "but I did not expect him to be so silly. Hareton, if I gave you a book, would you take it now? I'll try!"

She placed one she had been perusing on his hand; he flung it off, and muttered, if she did not give over, he would break her neck.

"Well, I shall put it here," she said, "in the table drawer, and I'm going to bed."

Then she whispered me to watch whether he touched it, and departed. But he would not come near it, and so I informed her in the morning, to her great disappointment. I saw she was sorry for his persevering sulkiness and indolence. Her conscience reproved her for frightening him off improving himself; she had done it effectually.

But her ingenuity was at work to remedy the injury; while I ironed, or pursued other stationary employments I could not well do in the parlour, she would bring some pleasant volume, and read it aloud to me. When Hareton was there, she generally paused in an interesting part, and left the book lying about—that she did repeatedly; but he was as obstinate as a mule, and, instead of snatching at her bait, in wet weather he took to smoking with Joseph, and they sat like automatons, one on each side of the fire, the elder happily too deaf to understand her wicked nonsense, as he would have called it, the younger doing his best to seem to disregard it. On fine evenings the latter followed his shooting expeditions, and Catherine yawned and sighed, and teased me to talk to her, and ran off into the court or garden, the moment I began; and, as a last resource, cried and said she was tired of living, her life was useless.

Mr. Heathcliff, who grew more and more disinclined to society, had almost banished Earnshaw out of his apartment. Owing to an accident, at the commencement of March, he became for some days a fixture in the kitchen. His gun burst while out on the hills by himself; a splinter cut his arm, and he lost a good deal of blood before he could reach home. The consequence was, that, perforce, he was condemned to the fire-side and tranquillity, till he made it up again.

It suited Catherine to have him there: at any rate, it made her hate her room upstairs more than ever; and she would compel me to find out business below, that she might accompany me.

On Easter Monday, Joseph went to Gimmerton fair with some cattle; and, in the afternoon, I was busy getting up linen in the kitchen. Earnshaw sat, morose as usual, at the chimney corner, and my little mistress was beguiling an idle hour with drawing pictures on the window panes, varying her amusement by smothered bursts of songs, and whispered ejaculations, and quick glances of annoyance and impatience in the direction of her cousin, who steadfastly smoked, and looked into the grate.

At a notice that I could do with her no longer intercepting my light, she removed to the hearthstone. I bestowed little attention on her proceedings, but, presently, I heard her begin—

"I've found out, Hareton, that I want—that I'm glad—that I should like you to be my cousin, now, if you had not grown so cross to me, and so rough."

Hareton returned no answer.

"Hareton, Hareton, Hareton! do you hear?" she continued.

"Get off wi' ye!" he growled, with uncompromising gruffness.

"Let me take that pipe," she said, cautiously advancing her hand, and abstracting it from his mouth.

Before he could attempt to recover it, it was broken, and behind the fire. He swore at her and seized another.

"Stop," she cried, "you must listen to me, first; and I can't speak while those clouds are floating in my face."

"Will you go to the devil!" he exclaimed, ferociously, "and let me be!"

"No," she persisted, "I won't—I can't tell what to do to make you talk to me, and you are determined not to understand. When I call you stupid, I don't mean anything—I don't mean that I despise you. Come, you shall take notice of me, Hareton—you are my cousin, and you shall own me."

"I shall have naught to do wi' you, and your mucky pride, and your damned, mocking tricks!" he answered. "I'll go to hell, body and soul, before I look sideways after you again! Side out of t' gait,[50] now; this minute!"

Catherine frowned, and retreated to the window-seat, chewing her lip, and endeavouring, by humming an eccentric tune, to conceal a growing tendency to sob.

"You should be friends with your cousin, Mr. Hareton," I interrupted, "since she repents of her sauciness! It would do you a great deal of good—it would make you another man, to have her for a companion."

"A companion!" he cried; "when she hates me, and does not think me fit to wipe her shoon! Nay, if it made me a king, I'd not be scorned for seeking her good will any more."

"It is not I who hate you, it is you who hate me!" wept Cathy, no longer disguising her trouble. "You hate me as much as Mr. Heathcliff does, and more."

"You're a damned liar," began Earnshaw; "why have I made him angry, by taking your part then, a hundred times? and that, when you sneered at, and despised me, and—Go on plaguing me, and I'll step in yonder, and say you worried me out of the kitchen!"

"I didn't know you took my part," she answered, drying her eyes; "and I was miserable and bitter at everybody; but, now I thank you and beg you to forgive me, what can I do besides?"

She returned to the hearth, and frankly extended her hand.

He blackened, and scowled like a thunder cloud, and kept his fists resolutely clenched, and his gaze fixed on the ground.

Catherine, by instinct, must have divined it was obdurate perversity, and not dislike, that prompted this dogged conduct; for, after remaining an instant undecided, she stooped, and impressed on his cheek a gentle kiss.

The little rogue thought I had not seen her, and, drawing back, she took her former station by the window, quite demurely.

I shook my head reprovingly; and then she blushed, and whispered—

"Well! what should I have done, Ellen? He wouldn't shake hands, and he wouldn't look. I must show him some way that I like him, that I want to be friends."

Whether the kiss convinced Hareton, I cannot tell; he was very careful, for some minutes, that his face should not be seen; and when he did raise it, he was sadly puzzled where to turn his eyes.

Catherine employed herself in wrapping a handsome book neatly in white paper; and having tied it with a bit of riband, and addressed it to "Mr. Hareton Earnshaw,"

---

[50] *Side out of t' gait:* get out of the way.

she desired me to be her ambassadress, and convey the present to its destined recipient.

"And tell him, if he'll take it, I'll come and teach him to read it right," she said, "and, if he refuse it, I'll go upstairs, and never tease him again."

I carried it, and repeated the message, anxiously watched by my employer. Hareton would not open his fingers, so I laid it on his knee. He did not strike it off either. I returned to my work. Catherine leaned her head and arms on the table, till she heard the slight rustle of the covering being removed; then she stole away, and quietly seated herself beside her cousin. He trembled, and his face glowed. All his rudeness and all his surly harshness had deserted him—he could not summon courage, at first, to utter a syllable, in reply to her questioning look, and her murmured petition.

"Say you forgive me, Hareton, do! You can make me so happy, by speaking that little word."

He muttered something inaudible.

"And you'll be my friend?" added Catherine, interrogatively.

"Nay! you'll be ashamed of me every day of your life," he answered. "And the more, the more you know me, and I cannot bide it."

"So, you won't be my friend?" she said, smiling as sweet as honey, and creeping close up.

I overheard no further distinguishable talk; but, on looking round again, I perceived two such radiant countenances bent over the page of the accepted book, that I did not doubt the treaty had been ratified on both sides, and the enemies were, thenceforth, sworn allies.

The work they studied was full of costly pictures; and those, and their position, had charm enough to keep them unmoved, till Joseph came home. He, poor man, was perfectly aghast at the spectacle of Catherine seated on the same bench with Hareton Earnshaw, leaning her hand on his shoulder; and confounded at his favourite's endurance of her proximity. It affected him too deeply to allow an observation on the subject that night. His emotion was only revealed by the immense sighs he drew, as he solemnly spread his large Bible on the table, and overlaid it with dirty bank-notes from his pocket-book, the produce of the day's transactions. At length, he summoned Hareton from his seat.

"Tak' these in tuh t' maister, lad," he said, "un' bide theare; Aw's gang up tuh my awn rahm. This hoile's norther mensful, nor seemly fur us—we mun side aht, and search another!"[51]

"Come, Catherine," I said, "we must 'side out,' too—I've done my ironing, are you ready to go?"

"It is not eight o'clock!" she answered, rising unwillingly, "Hareton, I'll leave this book upon the chimney-piece, and I'll bring some more to-morrow."

"Ony books ut yah leave, Aw suall tak' intuh th' hahse," said Joseph, "un' it 'ull be mitch if yah find 'em agean; soa, yah muh plase yourseln!"

Cathy threatened that his library should pay for hers; and, smiling as she passed Hareton, went singing upstairs, lighter of heart, I venture to say, than ever she had been under that roof before, except, perhaps, during her earliest visits to Linton.

The intimacy, thus commenced, grew rapidly, though it encountered temporary interruptions. Earnshaw was not to be civilized with a wish; and my young lady was no philosopher, and no paragon of patience; but both their minds tending

---

[51]*Hoile:* house; *side aht:* get out.

to the same point—one loving and desiring to esteem, and the other loving and desiring to be esteemed—they contrived in the end to reach it.

You see, Mr. Lockwood, it was easy enough to win Mrs. Heathcliff's heart; but now, I'm glad you did not try. The crown of all my wishes will be the union of those two; I shall envy no one on their wedding-day—there won't be a happier woman than myself in England!

CHAPTER 33

On the morrow of that Monday, Earnshaw being still unable to follow his ordinary employments, and, therefore, remaining about the house, I speedily found it would be impracticable to retain my charge beside me, as heretofore.

She got downstairs before me, and out into the garden, where she had seen her cousin performing some easy work; and when I went to bid them come to breakfast, I saw she had persuaded him to clear a large space of ground from currant and gooseberry bushes, and they were busy planning together an importation of plants from the Grange.

I was terrified at the devastation which had been accomplished in a brief half hour; the black currant trees were the apple of Joseph's eye, and she had just fixed her choice of a flower bed in the midst of them!

"There! That will be all shewn to the master," I exclaimed, "the minute it is discovered. And what excuse have you to offer for taking such liberties with the garden? We shall have a fine explosion on the head of it: see if we don't! Mr. Hareton, I wonder you should have no more wit, than to go and make that mess at her bidding!"

"I'd forgotten they were Joseph's," answered Earnshaw, rather puzzled, "but I'll tell him I did it."

We always ate our meals with Mr. Heathcliff. I held the mistress's post in making tea and carving; so I was indispensable at table. Catherine usually sat by me; but to-day, she stole nearer to Hareton, and I presently saw she would have no more discretion in her friendship, than she had in her hostility.

"Now, mind you don't talk with and notice your cousin too much," were my whispered instructions as we entered the room. "It will certainly annoy Mr. Heathcliff, and he'll be mad at you both."

"I'm not going to," she answered.

The minute after, she had sidled to him, and was sticking primroses in his plate of porridge.

He dared not speak to her, there; he dared hardly look, and yet she went on teasing, till he was twice on the point of being provoked to laugh; and I frowned, and then she glanced towards the master, whose mind was occupied on other subjects than his company, as his countenance evinced, and she grew serious for an instant, scrutinizing him with deep gravity. Afterwards she turned, and re-commenced her nonsense; at last, Hareton uttered a smothered laugh.

Mr. Heathcliff started; his eye rapidly surveyed our faces. Catherine met it with her accustomed look of nervousness, and yet defiance, which he abhorred.

"It is well you are out of my reach," he exclaimed. "What fiend possesses you to stare back at me, continually, with those infernal eyes? Down with them! and don't remind me of your existence again. I thought I had cured you of laughing!"

"It was me," muttered Hareton.

"What do you say?" demanded the master.

Hareton looked at his plate, and did not repeat the confession.

Mr. Heathcliff looked at him a bit, and then silently resumed his breakfast, and his interrupted musing.

We had nearly finished, and the two young people prudently shifted wider asunder, so I anticipated no further disturbance during that sitting, when Joseph appeared at the door, revealing by his quivering lip and furious eyes, that the outrage committed on his precious shrubs was detected.

He must have seen Cathy and her cousin about the spot before he examined it, for while his jaws worked like those of a cow chewing its cud, and rendered his speech difficult to understand, he began—

"Aw mun hev my wage, and Aw mun goa! Aw *hed* aimed tuh dee, wheare Aw'd sarved fur sixty year; un' Aw thowt Aw'd lug my books up intuh t' garret, un' all my bits uh stuff, un' they sud hev t' kitchen tuh theirseln; fur t' sake uh quietness. It wur hard tuh gie up my awn hearthstun, bud Aw thowt Aw *could* do that! Bud nah, shoo's taan my garden frough me, un' by th' heart, Maister, Aw cannot stand it! Yah muh bend tuh th' yoak, an ye will—*Aw'* noan used to't and an ow'd man doesn't sooin get used tuh new barthens.[52] Aw'd rayther arn my bite an' my sup, wi' a hammer in th' road!"

"Now, now, idiot!" interrupted Heathcliff, "cut it short! What's your grievance? I'll interfere in no quarrels between you and Nelly. She may thrust you into the coal-hole for anything I care."

"It's noan Nelly!" answered Joseph. "Aw sudn't shift fur Nelly[53]—nasty, ill nowt as shoo is. Thank God! *shoo* cannot stale t'sowl uh nob'dy! Shoo wer niver soa handsome, bud whet a body mud look at her 'baht winking. It's yon flaysome, graceless quean, ut's witched ahr lad, wi' her bold een, un' her forrard ways till—Nay! It fair brusts my heart! He's forgetten all E done for him, un made on him, un' goan un' riven up a whole row ut t' grandest currant trees i' t' garden!" And here he lamented outright, unmanned by a sense of his bitter injuries, and Earnshaw's ingratitude and dangerous condition.

"Is the fool drunk?" asked Mr. Heathcliff. "Hareton, is it you he's finding fault with?"

"I've pulled up two or three bushes," replied the young man, "but I'm going to set 'em again."

"And why have you pulled them up?" said the master.

Catherine wisely put in her tongue.

"We wanted to plant some flowers there," she cried. "I'm the only person to blame, for I wished him to do it."

"And who the devil gave *you* leave to touch a stick about the place?" demanded her father-in-law, much surprised. "And who ordered *you* to obey her?" he added, turning to Hareton.

The latter was speechless; his cousin replied—

"You shouldn't grudge a few yards of earth for me to ornament, when you have taken all my land!"

"Your land, insolent slut? you never had any!" said Heathcliff.

"And my money," she continued, returning his angry glare, and, meantime, biting a piece of crust, the remnant of her breakfast.

"Silence!" he exclaimed. "Get done, and begone!"

---

[52] *Barthens:* literally, places or berths for cattle.
[53] *Sudn't shift fur Nelly:* shouldn't leave because of Nelly.

"And Hareton's land, and his money," pursued the reckless thing. "Hareton and I are friends now; and I shall tell him all about you!"

The master seemed confounded a moment; he grew pale, and rose up, eyeing her all the while, with an expression of mortal hate.

"If you strike me, Hareton will strike you!" she said; "so you may as well sit down."

"If Hareton does not turn you out of the room, I'll strike him to hell," thundered Heathcliff. "Damnable witch! dare you pretend to rouse him against me? Off with her! Do you hear? Fling her into the kitchen! I'll kill her, Ellen Dean, if you let her come into my sight again!"

Hareton tried under his breath to persuade her to go.

"Drag her away!" he cried savagely. "Are you staying to talk?" And he approached to execute his own command.

"He'll not obey you, wicked man, any more!" said Catherine, "and he'll soon detest you, as much as I do!"

"Wisht! wisht!" muttered the young man reproachfully. "I will not hear you speak so to him. Have done!"

"But you won't let him strike me?" she cried.

"Come then!" he whispered earnestly.

It was too late—Heathcliff had caught hold of her.

"Now *you* go!" he said to Earnshaw. "Accursed witch! this time she has provoked me, when I could not bear it; and I'll make her repent it for ever!"

He had his hand in her hair; Hareton attempted to release the locks, entreating him not to hurt her that once. His black eyes flashed; he seemed ready to tear Catherine in pieces, and I was just worked up to risk coming to the rescue, when of a sudden, his fingers relaxed, he shifted his grasp from her head to her arm, and gazed intently in her face. Then, he drew his hand over his eyes, stood a moment to collect himself apparently, and turning anew to Catherine, said with assumed calmness—

"You must learn to avoid putting me in a passion, or I shall really murder you, some time! Go with Mrs. Dean, and keep with her, and confine your insolence to her ears. As to Hareton Earnshaw, if I see him listen to you, I'll send him seeking his bread where he can get it! Your love will make him an outcast, and a beggar. Nelly, take her, and leave me, all of you! Leave me!"

I led my young lady out; she was too glad of her escape, to resist; the other followed, and Mr. Heathcliff had the room to himself, till dinner.

I had counselled Catherine to get her upstairs; but, as soon as he perceived her vacant seat, he sent me to call her. He spoke to none of us, ate very little, and went out directly afterwards, intimating that he should not return before evening.

The two new friends established themselves in the house, during his absence, where I heard Hareton sternly check his cousin, on her offering a revelation of her father-in-law's conduct to his father.

He said he wouldn't suffer a word to be uttered to him, in his disparagement; if he were the devil, it didn't signify; he would stand by him; and he'd rather she would abuse himself, as she used to, than begin on Mr. Heathcliff.

Catherine was waxing cross at this; but he found means to make her hold her tongue, by asking, how she would like *him* to speak ill of her father? and then she comprehended that Earnshaw took the master's reputation home to himself, and was attached by ties stronger than reason could break—chains, forged by habit, which it would be cruel to attempt to loosen.

She showed a good heart, thenceforth, in avoiding both complaints and expressions of antipathy concerning Heathcliff, and confessed to me her sorrow that she had endeavoured to raise a bad spirit between him and Hareton; indeed, I don't believe she has ever breathed a syllable, in the latter's hearing, against her oppressor, since.

When this slight disagreement was over, they were thick again, and as busy as possible, in their several occupations, of pupil and teacher. I came in to sit with them, after I had done my work, and I felt so soothed and comforted to watch them, that I did not notice how time got on. You know, they both appeared, in a measure, my children: I had long been proud of one, and now, I was sure, the other would be a source of equal satisfaction. His honest, warm, and intelligent nature shook off rapidly the clouds of ignorance and degradation in which it had been bred; and Catherine's sincere commendations acted as a spur to his industry. His brightening mind brightened his features, and added spirit and nobility to their aspect. I could hardly fancy it the same individual I had beheld on the day I discovered my little lady at Wuthering Heights, after her expedition to the Crags.

While I admired, and they laboured, dusk drew on, and with it returned the master. He came upon us quite unexpectedly, entering by the front way, and had a full view of the whole three, ere we could raise our heads to glance at him.

Well, I reflected, there was never a pleasanter, or more harmless sight; and it will be a burning shame to scold them. The red fire-light glowed on their two bonny heads, and revealed their faces, animated with the eager interest of children; for, though he was twenty-three, and she eighteen, each had so much of novelty to feel and learn, that neither experienced nor evinced the sentiments of sober disenchanted maturity.

They lifted their eyes together, to encounter Mr. Heathcliff. Perhaps you have never remarked that their eyes are precisely similar, and they are those of Catherine Earnshaw. The present Catherine has no other likeness to her, except a breadth of forehead, and a certain arch of the nostril that makes her appear rather haughty, whether she will or not. With Hareton the resemblance is carried farther; it is singular, at all times—then, it was particularly striking, because his senses were alert, and his mental faculties wakened to unwonted activity.

I suppose this resemblance disarmed Mr. Heathcliff: he walked to the hearth in evident agitation, but it quickly subsided, as he looked at the young man; or, I should say, altered its character, for it was there yet.

He took the book from his hand, and glanced at the open page, then returned it without any observation, merely signing Catherine away. Her companion lingered very little behind her, and I was about to depart also, but he bid me sit still.

"It is a poor conclusion, is it not," he observed, having brooded a while on the scene he had just witnessed. "An absurd termination to my violent exertions? I get levers and mattocks to demolish the two houses, and train myself to be capable of working like Hercules, and when everything is ready, and in my power, I find the will to lift a slate off either roof has vanished! My old enemies have not beaten me; now would be the precise time to revenge myself on their representatives: I could do it; and none could hinder me. But where is the use? I don't care for striking, I can't take the trouble to raise my hand! That sounds as if I had been labouring the whole time, only to exhibit a fine trait of magnanimity. It is far from being the case—I have lost the faculty of enjoying their destruction, and I am too idle to destroy for nothing.

"Nelly, there is a strange change approaching—I'm in its shadow at present. I take so little interest in my daily life, that I hardly remember to eat, and drink. Those two, who have left the room, are the only objects which retain a distinct material appearance to me; and that appearance causes me pain, amounting to agony. About *her* I won't speak; and I don't desire to think; but I earnestly wish she were invisible—her presence invokes only maddening sensations. *He* moves me differently; and yet if I could do it without seeming insane, I'd never see him again! You'll perhaps think me rather inclined to become so," he added, making an effort to smile, "if I try to describe the thousand forms of past associations and ideas he awakens, or embodies—But you'll not talk of what I tell you, and my mind is so eternally secluded in itself, it is tempting, at last, to turn it out to another.

"Five minutes ago, Hareton seemed a personification of my youth, not a human being. I felt to him in such a variety of ways, that it would have been impossible to have accosted him rationally.

"In the first place, his startling likeness to Catherine connected him fearfully with her. That, however, which you may suppose the most potent to arrest my imagination, is actually the least, for what is not connected with her to me? and what does not recall her? I cannot look down to this floor, but her features are shaped on the flags! In every cloud, in every tree—filling the air at night, and caught by glimpses in every object by day, I am surrounded with her image! The most ordinary faces of men and women—my own features—mock me with a resemblance. The entire world is a dreadful collection of memoranda that she did exist, and that I have lost her!

"Well, Hareton's aspect was the ghost of my immortal love, of my wild endeavours to hold my right, my degradation, my pride, my happiness, and my anguish—

"But it is frenzy to repeat these thoughts to you; only it will let you know why, with a reluctance to be always alone, his society is no benefit, rather an aggravation of the constant torment I suffer; and it partly contributes to render me regardless how he and his cousin go on together. I can give them no attention, any more."

"But what do you mean by a *change*, Mr. Heathcliff?" I said, alarmed at his manner, though he was neither in danger of losing his senses, nor dying; according to my judgment he was quite strong and healthy; and, as to his reason, from childhood he had a delight in dwelling on dark things, and entertaining odd fancies. He might have had a monomania on the subject of his departed idol; but on every other point his wits were as sound as mine.

"I shall not know that, till it comes," he said, "I'm only half conscious of it now."

"You have no feeling of illness, have you?" I asked.

"No, Nelly, I have not," he answered.

"Then, you are not afraid of death?" I pursued.

"Afraid? No!" he replied. "I have neither a fear, nor a presentiment, nor a hope of death. Why should I? With my hard constitution, and temperate mode of living, and unperilous occupations, I ought to, and probably *shall* remain above ground, till there is scarcely a black hair on my head. And yet I cannot continue in this condition! I have to remind myself to breathe—almost to remind my heart to beat! And it is like bending back a stiff spring; it is by compulsion that I do the slightest act not prompted by one thought, and by compulsion, that I notice anything alive, or dead, which is not associated with one universal idea. I have a single wish, and my whole being and faculties are yearning to attain it. They have yearned towards it so long, and so unwaveringly, that I'm convinced it *will* be reached—and *soon*—because it has devoured my existence. I am swallowed in the anticipation of its fulfilment.

"My confessions have not relieved me, but they may account for some otherwise unaccountable phases of humour, which I show. O, God! It is a long fight, I wish it were over!"

He began to pace the room, muttering terrible things to himself, till I was inclined to believe, as he said Joseph did, that conscience had turned his heart to an earthly hell. I wondered greatly how it would end.

Though he seldom before had revealed this state of mind, even by looks, it was his habitual mood, I had no doubt: he asserted it himself; but not a soul, from his general bearing, would have conjectured the fact. You did not, when you saw him, Mr. Lockwood; and at the period of which I speak, he was just the same as then, only fonder of continued solitude, and perhaps still more laconic in company.

CHAPTER 34

For some days after that evening, Mr. Heathcliff shunned meeting us at meals; yet he would not consent, formally, to exclude Hareton and Cathy. He had an aversion to yielding so completely to his feelings, choosing rather to absent himself; and eating once in twenty-four hours seemed sufficient sustenance for him.

One night, after the family were in bed, I heard him go downstairs, and out at the front door: I did not hear him re-enter and, in the morning, I found he was still away.

We were in April then: the weather was sweet and warm, the grass as green as showers and sun could make it, and the two dwarf apple trees, near the southern wall, in full bloom.

After breakfast, Catherine insisted on my bringing a chair, and sitting with my work under the fir trees at the end of the house; and she beguiled Hareton, who had perfectly recovered from his accident, to dig and arrange her little garden, which was shifted to that corner by the influence of Joseph's complaints.

I was comfortably revelling in the spring fragrance around, and the beautiful soft blue overhead, when my young lady, who had run down near the gate to procure some primrose roots for a border, returned only half laden, and informed us that Mr. Heathcliff was coming in.

"And he spoke to me," she added with a perplexed countenance.

"What did he say?" asked Hareton.

"He told me to begone as fast as I could," she answered. "But he looked so different from his usual look that I stopped a moment to stare at him."

"How?" he enquired.

"Why, almost bright and cheerful—No, almost nothing—*very much* excited, and wild and glad!" she replied.

"Night-walking amuses him, then," I remarked, affecting a careless manner. In reality, as surprised as she was, and, anxious to ascertain the truth of her statement, for to see the master looking glad would not be an every day spectacle, I framed an excuse to go in.

Heathcliff stood at the open door; he was pale, and he trembled; yet, certainly, he had a strange joyful glitter in his eyes that altered the aspect of his whole face.

"Will you have some breakfast?" I said, "You must be hungry rambling about all night!"

I wanted to discover where he had been; but I did not like to ask directly.

"No, I'm not hungry," he answered, averting his head, and speaking rather contemptuously, as if he guessed I was trying to divine the occasion of his good humour.

I felt perplexed: I didn't know whether it were not a proper opportunity to offer a bit of admonition.

"I don't think it right to wander out of doors," I observed, "instead of being in bed: it is not wise, at any rate, this moist season. I dare say you'll catch a bad cold, or a fever—you have something the matter with you now!"

"Nothing but what I can bear," he replied, "and with the greatest pleasure, provided you'll leave me alone. Get in, and don't annoy me."

I obeyed; and, in passing, I noticed he breathed as fast as a cat.

"Yes!" I reflected to myself, "we shall have a fit of illness. I cannot conceive what he has been doing!"

That noon, he sat down to dinner with us, and received a heaped-up plate from my hands, as if he intended to make amends for previous fasting.

"I've neither cold, nor fever, Nelly," he remarked, in allusion to my morning's speech. "And I'm ready to do justice to the food you give me."

He took his knife and fork, and was going to commence eating, when the inclination appeared to become suddenly extinct. He laid them on the table, looked eagerly towards the window, then rose and went out.

We saw him walking, to and fro, in the garden, while we concluded our meal; and Earnshaw said he'd go and ask why he would not dine; he thought we had grieved him some way.

"Well, is he coming?" cried Catherine, when her cousin returned.

"Nay," he answered, "but he's not angry; he seemed rare and pleased indeed; only, I made him impatient by speaking to him twice; and then he bid me be off to you; he wondered how I could want the company of any body else."

I set his plate, to keep warm, on the fender: and after an hour or two, he re-entered, when the room was clear, in no degree calmer: the same unnatural—it was unnatural—appearance of joy under his black brows; the same bloodless hue, and his teeth visible, now and then, in a kind of smile; his frame shivering, not as one shivers with chill or weakness, but as a tight-stretched cord vibrates—a strong thrilling, rather than trembling.

I will ask what is the matter, I thought, or who should? And I exclaimed—

"Have you heard any good news, Mr. Heathcliff? You look uncommonly animated."

"Where should good news come from, to me?" he said. "I'm animated with hunger; and, seemingly, I must not eat."

"Your dinner is here," I returned; "why won't you get it?"

"I don't want it now," he muttered, hastily. "I'll wait till supper. And, Nelly, once for all, let me beg you to warn Hareton and the other away from me. I wish to be troubled by nobody—I wish to have this place to myself."

"Is there some new reason for this banishment?" I inquired. "Tell me why you are so queer, Mr. Heathcliff? Where were you last night? I'm not putting the question through idle curiosity, but—"

"You are putting the question through very idle curiosity," he interrupted, with a laugh. "Yet, I'll answer it. Last night, I was on the threshold of hell. To-day, I am within sight of my heaven. I have my eyes on it—hardly three feet to sever me! And now you'd better go. You'll neither see nor hear anything to frighten you, if you refrain from prying."

Having swept the hearth and wiped the table, I departed more perplexed than ever.

He did not quit the house again that afternoon, and no one intruded on his solitude, till, at eight o'clock, I deemed it proper, though unsummoned, to carry a candle and his supper to him.

He was leaning against the ledge of an open lattice, but not looking out; his face was turned to the interior gloom. The fire had smouldered to ashes; the room was filled with the damp, mild air of the cloudy evening, and so still, that not only the murmur of the beck down Gimmerton was distinguishable, but its ripples and its gurgling over the pebbles, or through the large stones which it could not cover.

I uttered an ejaculation of discontent at seeing the dismal grate, and commenced shutting the casements, one after another, till I came to his.

"Must I close this?" I asked, in order to rouse him, for he would not stir.

The light flashed on his features, as I spoke. Oh, Mr. Lockwood, I cannot express what a terrible start I got, by the momentary view! Those deep black eyes! That smile, and ghastly paleness! It appeared to me, not Mr. Heathcliff, but a goblin; and, in my terror, I let the candle bend towards the wall, and it left me in darkness.

"Yes, close it," he replied, in his familiar voice. "There, that is pure awkwardness! Why did you hold the candle horizontally? Be quick, and bring another."

I hurried out in a foolish state of dread, and said to Joseph—

"The master wishes you to take him a light, and rekindle the fire." For I dared not go in myself again just then.

Joseph rattled some fire into the shovel, and went; but he brought it back, immediately, with the supper tray in his other hand, explaining that Mr. Heathcliff was going to bed, and he wanted nothing to eat till morning.

We heard him mount the stairs directly; he did not proceed to his ordinary chamber, but turned into that with the panelled bed. Its window, as I mentioned before, is wide enough for anybody to get through, and it struck me that he plotted another midnight excursion, which he had rather we had no suspicion of.

"Is he a ghoul, or a vampire?" I mused. I had read of such hideous, incarnate demons. And then I set myself to reflect how I had tended him in infancy; and watched him grow to youth; and followed him almost through his whole course; and what absurd nonsense it was to yield to that sense of horror.

"But where did he come from, the little dark thing, harboured by a good man to his bane?" muttered superstition, as I dozed into unconsciousness. And I began, half dreaming, to weary myself with imaging some fit parentage for him; and repeating my waking meditations, I tracked his existence over again, with grim variations; at last, picturing his death and funeral; of which, all I can remember is, being exceedingly vexed at having the task of dictating an inscription for his monument, and consulting the sexton about it; and, as he had no surname, and we could not tell his age, we were obliged to content ourselves with the single word, "Heathcliff." That came true; we were. If you enter the kirkyard, you'll read on his headstone only that, and the date of his death.

Dawn restored me to common sense. I rose, and went into the garden, as soon as I could see, to ascertain if there were any foot-marks under his window. There were none.

"He has stayed at home," I thought, "and he'll be all right, to-day!"

I prepared breakfast for the household, as was my usual custom, but told Hareton and Catherine to get theirs ere the master came down, for he lay late. They preferred taking it out of doors, under the trees, and I set a little table to accommodate them.

On my re-entrance, I found Mr. Heathcliff below. He and Joseph were conversing about some farming business; he gave clear, minute directions concerning the matter discussed, but he spoke rapidly, and turned his head continually aside, and had the same excited expression, even more exaggerated.

When Joseph quitted the room, he took his seat in the place he generally chose, and I put a basin of coffee before him. He drew it nearer, and then rested in his arms on the table, and looked at the opposite wall, as I supposed, surveying one particular portion, up and down, with glittering, restless eyes, and with such eager interest, that he stopped breathing, during half a minute together.

"Come now," I exclaimed, pushing some bread against his hand. "Eat and drink that, while it is hot. It has been waiting near an hour."

He didn't notice me, and yet he smiled. I'd rather have seen him gnash his teeth than smile so.

"Mr. Heathcliff! master!" I cried. "Don't, for God's sake, stare as if you saw an unearthly vision."

"Don't, for God's sake, shout so loud," he replied. "Turn round, and tell me, are we by ourselves?"

"Of course," was my answer, "of course, we are!"

Still, I involuntarily obeyed him, as if I were not quite sure.

With a sweep of his hand, he cleared a vacant space in front among the breakfast things, and leant forward to gaze more at his ease.

Now, I perceived he was not looking at the wall, for when I regarded him alone, it seemed exactly that he gazed at something within two yards distance. And, whatever it was, it communicated, apparently, both pleasure and pain, in exquisite extremes; at least, the anguished, yet raptured expression of his countenance suggested that idea.

The fancied object was not fixed, either; his eyes pursued it with unwearied vigilance, and, even in speaking to me, were never weaned away.

I vainly reminded him of his protracted abstinence from food; if he stirred to touch anything in compliance with my entreaties, if he stretched his hand out to get a piece of bread, his fingers clenched, before they reached it, and remained on the table, forgetful of their aim.

I sat, a model of patience, trying to attract his absorbed attention from its engrossing speculation, till he grew irritable, and got up, asking why I would not allow him to have his own time in taking his meals? and saying that, on the next occasion, I needn't wait; I might set the things down, and go.

Having uttered these words, he left the house, slowly sauntered down the garden path, and disappeared through the gate.

The hours crept anxiously by: another evening came. I did not retire to rest till late, and when I did, I could not sleep. He returned after midnight, and, instead of going to bed, shut himself into the room beneath. I listened, and tossed about; and, finally, dressed and descended. It was too irksome to lie up there, harassing my brain with a hundred idle misgivings.

I distinguished Mr. Heathcliff's step, restlessly measuring the floor; and he frequently broke the silence by a deep inspiration, resembling a groan. He muttered detached words also; the only one I could catch was the name of Catherine, coupled with some wild term of endearment or suffering, and spoken as one would speak to a person present—low and earnest, and wrung from the depth of his soul.

I had not courage to walk straight into the apartment; but I desired to divert him from his reverie, and, therefore fell foul of the kitchen fire, stirred it, and began to scrape the cinders. It drew him forth sooner than I expected. He opened the door immediately, and said—

"Nelly, come here—is it morning? Come in with your light."

"It is striking four," I answered; "you want a candle to take upstairs—you might have lit one at this fire."

"No, I don't wish to go upstairs," he said. "Come in, and kindle *me* a fire, and do anything there is to do about the room."

"I must blow the coals red first, before I can carry any," I replied, getting a chair and the bellows.

He roamed to and fro, meantime, in a state approaching distraction; his heavy sighs succeeding each other so thick as to leave no space for common breathing between.

"When day breaks, I'll send for Green," he said; "I wish to make some legal inquiries of him while I can bestow a thought on those matters, and while I can act calmly. I have not written my will yet, and how to leave my property, I cannot determine! I wish I could annihilate it from the face of the earth."

"I would not talk so, Mr. Heathcliff," I interposed. "Let your will be, a while— you'll be spared to repent of your many injustices, yet! I never expected that your nerves would be disordered: they are, at present, marvellously so, however; and, almost entirely, through your own fault. The way you've passed these three last days might knock up a Titan. Do take some food, and some repose. You need only look at yourself in a glass to see how you require both. Your cheeks are hollow, and your eyes blood-shot, like a person starving with hunger, and going blind with loss of sleep."

"It is not my fault, that I cannot eat or rest," he replied. "I assure you it is through no settled designs. I'll do both, as soon as I possibly can. But you might as well bid a man struggling in the water, rest within arms-length of the shore! I must reach it first, and then I'll rest. Well, never mind Mr. Green; as to repenting of my injustices, I've done no injustice, and I repent of nothing—I'm too happy, and yet I'm not happy enough. My soul's bliss kills my body, but does not satisfy itself."

"Happy, master?" I cried. "Strange happiness! If you would hear me without being angry, I might offer some advice that would make you happier."

"What is that?" he asked. "Give it."

"You are aware, Mr. Heathcliff," I said, "that from the time you were thirteen years old, you have lived a selfish, unchristian life; and probably hardly had a Bible in your hands during all that period. You must have forgotten the contents of the book, and you may not have space to search it now. Could it be hurtful to send for some one—some minister of any denomination, it does not matter which, to explain it, and show you how very far you have erred from its precepts, and how unfit you will be for its heaven, unless a change takes place before you die?"

"I'm rather obliged than angry, Nelly," he said, "for you remind me of the manner that I desire to be buried in. It is to be carried to the churchyard, in the evening. You and Hareton may, if you please accompany me—and mind, particularly, to notice that the sexton obeys my directions concerning the two coffins! No minister need come; nor need anything be said over me. I tell you, I have nearly attained *my* heaven; and that of others is altogether unvalued and uncoveted by me!"

"And supposing you persevered in your obstinate fast, and died by that means, and they refused to bury you in the precincts of the Kirk?" I said, shocked at his godless indifference. "How would you like it?"

"They won't do that," he replied; "if they did, you must have me removed secretly; and if you neglect it, you shall prove, practically, that the dead are not annihilated!"

As soon as he heard the other members of the family stirring he retired to his den, and I breathed freer. But in the afternoon, while Joseph and Hareton were at their work, he came into the kitchen again, and with a wild look, bid me come, and sit in the house—he wanted somebody with him.

I declined, telling him plainly that his strange talk and manner frightened me, and I had neither the nerve nor the will to be his companion, alone.

"I believe you think me a fiend!" he said, with his dismal laugh, "something too horrible to live under a decent roof!"

Then turning to Catherine, who was there, and who drew behind me at his approach, he added, half sneeringly—

"Will *you* come, chuck? I'll not hurt you. No! to you, I've made myself worse than the devil. Well, there is *one* who won't shrink from my company! By God!

she's relentless. Oh, damn it! It's unutterably too much for flesh and blood to bear, even mine."

He solicited the society of no one more. At dusk, he went into his chamber. Through the whole night, and far into the morning, we heard him groaning, and murmuring to himself. Hareton was anxious to enter, but I bid him fetch Mr. Kenneth, and he should go in and see him.

When he came, and I requested admittance and tried to open the door, I found it locked; and Heathcliff bid us be damned. He was better, and would be left alone; so the doctor went away.

The following evening was very wet; indeed it poured down, till day-dawn; and, as I took my morning walk round the house, I observed the master's window swinging open, and the rain driving straight in.

He cannot be in bed, I thought; those showers would drench him through! He must either be up, or out. But I'll make no more ado, I'll go boldly and look!

Having succeeded in obtaining entrance with another key, I ran to unclose the panels, for the chamber was vacant; quickly pushing them aside, I peeped in. Mr. Heathcliff was there—laid on his back. His eyes met mine so keen and fierce, I started; and then he seemed to smile.

I could not think him dead, but his face and throat were washed with rain; the bedclothes dripped, and he was perfectly still. The lattice, flapping to and fro, had grazed one hand that rested on the sill; no blood trickled from the broken skin, and when I put my fingers to it, I could doubt no more—he was dead and stark!

I hasped the window; I combed his black long hair from his forehead; I tried to close his eyes—to extinguish, if possible, that frightful, life-like gaze of exultation, before any one else beheld it. They would not shut; they seemed to sneer at my attempts, and his parted lips and sharp, white teeth sneered too! Taken with another fit of cowardice, I cried out for Joseph. Joseph shuffled up and made a noise, but resolutely refused to meddle with him.

"Th' divil's harried off his soul," he cried, "and he muh hev his carcass intuh t' bargin, for ow't Aw care! Ech! what a wicked un he looks girnning[54] at death!" and the old sinner grinned in mockery.

I thought he intended to cut a caper round the bed; but suddenly composing himself, he fell on his knees, and raised his hands, and returned thanks that the lawful master and the ancient stock were restored to their rights.

I felt stunned by the awful event; and my memory unavoidably recurred to former times with a sort of oppressive sadness. But poor Hareton, the most wronged, was the only one that really suffered much. He sat by the corpse all night, weeping in bitter earnest. He pressed its hand, and kissed the sarcastic, savage face that every one else shrank from contemplating; and bemoaned him with that strong grief which springs naturally from a generous heart, though it be tough as tempered steel.

Kenneth was perplexed to pronounce of what disorder the master died. I concealed the fact of his having swallowed nothing for four days, fearing it might lead to trouble, and then, I am persuaded he did not abstain on purpose; it was the consequence of his strange illness, not the cause.

We buried him, to the scandal of the whole neighbourhood, as he had wished. Earnshaw, and I, the sexton and six men to carry the coffin, comprehended the whole attendance.

The six men departed when they had let it down into the grave: we stayed to see it covered. Hareton, with a streaming face, dug green sods, and laid them over

---

[54]*Girnning:* grinning.

the brown mould himself. At present it is as smooth and verdant as its companion mounds—and I hope its tenant sleeps as soundly. But the country folks, if you asked them, would swear on their Bible that he *walks*. There are those who speak to having met him near the church, and on the moor, and even within this house. Idle tales, you'll say, and so say I. Yet that old man by the kitchen fire affirms he has seen two on 'em looking out of his chamber window, on every rainy night, since his death—and an odd thing happened to me about a month ago.

I was going to the Grange one evening—a dark evening threatening thunder—and, just at the turn of the Heights, I encountered a little boy with a sheep and two lambs before him; he was crying terribly, and I supposed the lambs were skittish, and would not be guided.

"What is the matter, my little man?" I asked.

"They's Heathcliff and a woman, yonder, under t' Nab," he blubbered, "un' Aw darnut pass 'em."

I saw nothing; but neither the sheep nor he would go on, so I bid him take the road lower down.

He probably raised the phantoms from thinking, as he traversed the moors alone, on the nonsense he had heard his parents and companions repeat—yet still, I don't like being out in the dark, now; and I don't like being left by myself in this grim house. I cannot help it, I shall be glad when they leave it, and shift to the Grange!

"They are going to the Grange, then?" I said.

"Yes," answered Mrs. Dean, "as soon as they are married; and that will be on New Year's day."

"And who will live here then?"

"Why, Joseph will take care of the house, and, perhaps, a lad to keep him company. They will live in the kitchen, and the rest will be shut up."

"For the use of such ghosts as choose to inhabit it," I observed.

"No, Mr. Lockwood," said Nelly, shaking her head. "I believe the dead are at peace, but it is not right to speak of them with levity."

At that moment the garden gate swung to; the ramblers were returning.

"*They* are afraid of nothing," I grumbled, watching their approach through the window. "Together they would brave Satan and all his legions."

As they stepped onto the door-stones, and halted to take a last look at the moon, or, more correctly, at each other, by her light, I felt irresistibly impelled to escape them again; and, pressing a remembrance into the hand of Mrs. Dean, and disregarding her expostulations at my rudeness, I vanished through the kitchen, as they opened the house-door, and so should have confirmed Joseph in his opinion of his fellow-servant's gay indiscretions, had he not, fortunately, recognised me for a respectable character by the sweet ring of a sovereign at his feet.

My walk home was lengthened by a diversion in the direction of the Kirk. When beneath its walls, I perceived decay had made progress, even in seven months: many a window showed black gaps deprived of glass; and slates jutted off, here and there, beyond the right line of the roof, to be gradually worked off in coming autumn storms.

I sought, and soon discovered, the three head-stones on the slope next the moor—the middle one, grey, and half buried in heath—Edgar Linton's only harmonized by the turf, and moss creeping up its foot—Heathcliff's still bare.

I lingered round them, under that benign sky; watched the moths fluttering among the heath and hare-bells; listened to the soft wind breathing through the grass; and wondered how any one could ever imagine unquiet slumbers for the sleepers in that quiet earth.

❧

WESTERN TEXTS

WILLIAM BLAKE

[1757–1827]

Perhaps no writer of the early nineteenth century represents the revolt against the empirical philosophy of the Enlightenment more than the English poet, printmaker, and visionary William Blake. Imbued with the spirit of the age of revolution and romanticism, Blake strenuously condemns what he deems the slavish following of religious, social, and aesthetic conventions that stifled individual freedom and creativity in his day, and defiantly declares his personal independence from them: "I must create my own system or be enslav'd by another man's." Blake believed that God resides within each human being, and it was his goal to use his imaginative works to free other people and enable them to see the divine spirit within themselves and so to build up a world of beauty, joy, peace, and freedom. He stated this goal poetically in the preface to *Milton,* one of his longer visionary works:

> I will not cease from Mental Flight,
> Nor shall my sword sleep in my hand
> Till we have built Jerusalem,
> In England's green and pleasant land.

Although his contemporaries largely neglected Blake's work, his fiery celebration of the imagination, his revolt against neoclassical standards, and his exuberant energy and spirit of reform have earned him in the twentieth century a reputation as one of the most important romantic poets.

LIFE

William Blake was born in London on November 28, 1757, the son of a hosier. He grew up in London, where he very early displayed a talent for drawing and a proclivity for visionary encounters with a world beyond the senses. When he was eight years old, for example, his father reprimanded Blake for telling him about seeing bright winged angels in a tree, and throughout his life Blake reported conversing with angels and other visitors from the spirit world who often guided his work. Never receiving a formal education, Blake received instruction in drawing from Henry Parr's school and at age fourteen was apprenticed as an engraver with James Basire, engraver for the Society of Antiquaries. Here he exercised his talents on drawing likenesses from relics of ancient kings and queens and of biblical figures, such as Joseph of Arimathea, while reading extensively and trying his hand at poetry. One project in particular, the engravings for Jacob Bryant's *New System or Analysis of Ancient Mythology* (1774–1776), introduced Blake to ancient myths from around the world. Bryant's comparative approach to mythology and his attempt to show that myths as varied as those from Egypt, Greece, and Rome might all derive from the same origin may have influenced Blake as he went on in later years to develop his own mythology. Certainly, as we learn from *A Descriptive Catalogue,* Blake followed Bryant in believing that "[t]he antiquities of every Nation under Heaven are the same thing, as Jacob Bryant and all antiquaries have proved."

After his seven-year apprenticeship to Basire and a brief stint studying at the Royal Academy of Art, for whose conventions he developed a strong distaste, Blake set up as an engraver in London, where he associated with Henry Fuseli and John Flaxman, fellow artists who both encouraged and influenced Blake's highly idiosyncratic work. In 1782, Blake married Catherine Boucher, who assisted him in his various activities, which now included, in addition to writing and engraving his own works, giving lessons in drawing and doing commercial engraving. After the death of Blake's younger brother, Robert, in 1787, Blake reported having conversations with his spirit, who was said to have inspired Blake in his visionary works. In 1800 Blake accepted the generosity of William Hayley, a conventional poet and patron of the arts, who encouraged the Blakes to move to a cottage at Felpham, on the Sussex seacoast. Here Hayley provided Blake with the means to pursue his own work, but he tried to tether Blake's imagination and direct him toward more publicly acceptable, conventional tastes. As a result of his quarreling with Hayley, whom he called the "Enemy of my Spiritual Life while he pretends to be the Friend of my Corporeal," Blake returned to 17 South Molton Street, London, in 1803, having narrowly escaped from being prosecuted for sedition.

To the end of his life, Blake managed to eke out a living with commercial engraving and printing projects, but he continued to apply his fullest energies to his longer prophetic works, including *Jerusalem* and *The Four Zoas,* even after the dismal failure of an exhibition of his work in 1809. The visionary poet and artist was somewhat vindicated in his later years, having attracted the devotion and critical praise of younger artists such as John Varley, John Linnel, and Samuel Palmer, who helped support the impoverished poet. Turning in his old age primarily to painting and drawing, Blake completed superb illustrations for the works of Virgil and Dante and for the Book of Job. He died on August 12, 1827, reportedly singing with joy.

WORK

Blake's first publication was a collection of lyrical poems written just before and during his apprenticeship to Basire. The only work of Blake's printed by conventional means, *Poetical Sketches* (1783) contains lyrics on traditional topics, such as the seasons, love, and poetry. Nonetheless, in these lyrics we see the beginnings of that sublime tone, subtle irony, and deviation from convention that characterize his mature work. Moreover, as in "How sweet I roam'd from field to field," some of the lyrics anticipate Blake's concern with the distinction between innocence and experience that informs his first major work, the *Songs of Innocence and Experience* (1794). Blake produced the twenty-eight copies of the combined *Songs of Innocence and Experience* using the innovative method of relief etching that he developed, which he used for all of his subsequent publications. In these works, Blake combines engraving, watercolor, and poetry to create what some critics call his "composite art," a multimedia presentation of his poetry that aims to achieve a profound impression on the reader and gives the works a sense of fluidity and process.

In 1789, Blake completed *Songs of Innocence,* which appears to present from the resilient and hopeful view of a child the social and moral problems that plagued London. By 1794, Blake had added the companion poems comprising the *Songs of Experience* that treat the same topics of the earlier poems but from the more critical (some would say cynical) and sinister perspective of the adult. Although some critics equate innocence with childhood and experience with adulthood, these two categories more accurately represent, in Blake's terms, "two contrary states of the human soul," for either perspective is available to the human consciousness regardless of age. Indeed, Blake's masterful irony disturbs even the pleasant and joyful surfaces of the *Songs of Innocence* with the potential for a more sinister account of what takes place in each poem. In "The Chimney Sweeper," for example, little Tom Dacre's dream may be enough to keep him "happy & warm," but the moral slogan of the last line—"So if all do their duty, they need not fear harm"—reminds us of the innumerable tracts, tales, and poems written in Blake's day to enjoin working people to submit cheerfully to a life of labor. Thus, the poem anticipates the radical protest of its companion poem in *Songs of Experience,* in which the young chimney sweeper is aware of the hypocrisy of his parents, who would sell him into slavery and then congratulate themselves on having done their duty to "God & his Priest & King." While Blake disdained the Enlightenment rationalism of Voltaire and Rousseau, as is evident in "Mock on Mock on Voltaire Rousseau," Blake's satire, directed at the hypocrisy and moral turpitude of those who uncritically follow the crowd, shows some similarities with that of his Enlightenment adversaries.

If *Songs of Innocence and Experience* presents a society parasitic upon genius, innocence, and those whose spirit and energy are as yet unfettered by religious, social, political, and moral convention, it also celebrates the vitality, imagination, and independence of those who challenge the institutions that create the "mind-forg'd manacles." Because Blake saw his work as "an endeavor to restore what the ancients call the golden age," what he hoped to do through his unique combination of poetic and visual art was to awaken the vital poetic genius within all human beings. Thus, from the *Songs of Innocence and Experience* to *The Four Zoas,* Blake challenges the reader to become an active participant in the construction of meaning. Moreover, writing in the age of the French Revolution, the age of political radicals such as Mary Wollstonecraft, William Godwin, and Thomas Paine, Blake's call for imaginative freedom is also a call for political and social freedom, including the freedom of women from subordination to men and the freedom of slaves, as articulated in one of his early myths, *Visions of the Daughters of Albion* (1791–1792). Throughout his increasingly arcane "Lambeth prophecies" such as *America* (1793), *Europe* (1794), *The Book of Urizen* (1794), and *The Book of Los* (1795), Blake attacked the moral authoritarianism, religious falsehood, and materialism of his time. In the longer prophecies, such as *Milton* (1804), *Jerusalem* (1804), and *The Four Zoas* (c. 1796–1807), which remained incomplete at his death, Blake further elaborated his complex myth and envisioned a world set free from its political, social, and religious fetters by the power of the imagination. The biblical rhetoric and diction, the formal experimentalism, and the private myth-making that Blake undertook in these later works appear in *The Marriage of Heaven and Hell* (1793), one of Blake's earliest, most important, and most accessible prophetic works.

The Marriage of Heaven and Hell might be described as a compendium of Blake's ideas, displayed in a literary-aesthetic form that defies categorization. In addition to the colored plates and the "illuminated printing" of this work, *The Marriage of Heaven and Hell* involves a hybridization of many literary forms including biblical prophecy, satire, autobiography, aphorism, lyric, and prose. The poem is a direct satire of Emanuel Swedenborg's *Heaven and Hell,* in which Swedenborg anticipates in "memorable relations" the eventual reconciliation of good and evil. Indeed, Blake's poem challenges the very system of binary oppositions upon which Swedenborg's doctrine is based. Nothing, in Blake's view, is either good or bad except as the beholder makes it so. As in "The Tyger," from *Songs of Experience,* Blake shows here that the hand that framed the tiger also framed the lamb, and he subjects the binary system underlying the Western valuation of good and evil to a devastating critique. Indeed, the prophetic bard in this poem positions himself squarely opposite the empiricist and rationalist intellectual tradition of the Enlightenment, attacks the system-builders who have relied upon reason alone to construct their vision of the world, and denounces those who have perverted the dynamic, imaginative vision of prophecy by changing it into fixed forms of religious doctrine. Here Blake shows his utter disdain, even contempt, for anything that is static or frozen into convention and custom, a point poignantly expressed in his claim that "without contraries there is no progression." Thus, the "marriage" of the title is ironic, for Blake's poem ultimately advocates not reconciliation but ongoing dialectic; "opposition," as he puts it, "is true friendship."

Although Blake's philosophy admits of few generalizations, *The Marriage of Heaven and Hell* shows that Blake sees the material world as the product of the Fall. He recognizes that only through acknowledging the Fall and embracing the body, rather than denying it as orthodox Christianity would, can human beings be redeemed. Like the utopian socialist Fourier, Blake believes that the repression of desire poisons both the body and the mind or spirit: "He who desires but acts not breeds pestilence." Blake recognizes the interdependence of mind and body, and condemns that form of religion that outlaws the body and in so doing cuts off the spirit from the primary source of its energy.

The major agency of repression is reason, represented in Blake's later prophecies by Urizen, a figure who represents the withering of faculties that occurs when one accepts the limits of the five senses. As Blake puts it in Plate 14, "man has closed himself up, till he sees all things thro' narrow chinks of his cavern." Here we encounter the major paradox of Blake's thought. Although the five senses impose limits upon reason, which in turn becomes the "outward circumference of energy," it is only through the full and active engagement of the senses that we may be redeemed from the body and recognize our true spiritual existence. In *Europe,* for example, Blake writes that "Five windows light the cavern'd Man." These windows are the five senses that are "the chief inlets of Soul in this age." That is, the senses in this life are remnants of the "enlarg'd and numerous senses" of our spiritual life. Thus, we must learn to use them to their fullest, for they bring a clarity of vision that finally frees us from the limits of empiricism. It is Blake's hope, in *The Marriage of Heaven and Hell* and in his later works, to engage our faculties to their fullest and so cleanse our perceptions so that we, too, will see "the infinite in every thing."

SUGGESTED READINGS

A new critical biography of William Blake, E. P. Thompson's *Witness Against the Best: William Blake and the Moral Law* (1993), places Blake's work in its historical and intellectual context, as does David V. Erdman's *Blake: Prophet Against Empire* (1954; revised 1964). Many general studies of Blake's work are available, including Northrop Frye's classic study *Fearful Symmetry* (1947); Ann Mellor's *Blake's Human Form Divine* (1974); Mark Schorer's *William Blake: The Politics of Vision* (1946); and E. D. Hirsch's *Innocence and Experience* (1969). Three excellent books on Blake's printmaking and art are David Bindman's *Blake as an Artist* (1977), Morris Eaves's *William Blake's Theory of Art* (1982), and Robert N. Essick's *William Blake, Printmaker* (1980). Michael Ferber's *The Social Vision of William Blake* (1985) combines a sociohistorical analysis of the poems with a discussion of Blake's significance for our own time.

"How sweet I roam'd from field to field"

How sweet I roam'd from field to field,
    And tasted all the summer's pride,
'Till I the prince of love[1] beheld,
    Who in the sunny beams did glide!

He shew'd me lilies for my hair,
    And blushing roses for my brow;
He led me through his gardens fair,
    Where all his golden pleasures grow.

---

[1]In Greek mythology, Eros or Cupid.

With sweet May dews my wings were wet,
    And Phoebus[2] fir'd my vocal rage;
He caught me in his silken net,
    And shut me in his golden cage.

He loves to sit and hear me sing,
    Then, laughing, sports and plays with me;
Then stretches out my golden wing,
    And mocks my loss of liberty.

TO THE MUSES

Whether on Ida's[1] shady brow,
    Or in the chambers of the East,
The chambers of the sun, that now
    From antient melody have ceas'd;

Whether in Heav'n ye wander fair,
    Or the green corners of the earth,
Or the blue regions of the air,
    Where the melodious winds have birth;

Whether on chrystal[2] rocks ye rove,
    Beneath the bosom of the sea
Wand'ring in many a coral grove,
    Fair Nine,[3] forsaking Poetry!

How have you left the antient love
    That bards of old enjoy'd in you!
The languid strings do scarcely move!
    The sound is forc'd, the notes are few!

FROM

SONGS of INNOCENCE

INTRODUCTION

Piping down the valleys wild
Piping songs of pleasant glee
On a cloud I saw a child.
And he laughing said to me.

10

10

---

[2]Phoebus Apollo, "the bright one"; the Greek god of music, prophecy, and poetry.
TO THE MUSES
    [1]A mountain in Phrygia, associated with many events in classical mythology and the Trojan War.
    [2]Blake's nonstandard spellings and inconsistent spelling will be retained throughout; obvious slips have been silently corrected.
    [3]The nine Muses, daughters of Zeus and Mnemosyne (memory), who inspired writers, poets, musicians, and other creative artists.

Pipe a song about a Lamb;
So I piped with merry chear,
Piper pipe that song again—
So I piped, he wept to hear.

Drop thy pipe thy happy pipe
Sing thy songs of happy chear,
So I sung the same again   10
While he wept with joy to hear

Piper sit thee down and write
In a book that all may read—
So he vanish'd from my sight.
And I pluck'd a hollow reed.

And I made a rural pen,
And I stain'd the water clear,
And I wrote my happy songs
Every child may joy to hear   20

THE LAMB

Little Lamb who made thee
　Dost thou know who made thee
Gave thee life & bid thee feed.
By the stream & o'er the mead;
Gave thee clothing of delight,
Softest clothing wooly bright;
Gave thee such a tender voice,
Making all the vales rejoice!
　Little Lamb who made thee
　Dost thou know who made thee   10

　Little Lamb I'll tell thee,
　Little Lamb I'll tell thee!
He is called by thy name,
For he calls himself a Lamb:
He is meek & he is mild,
He became a little child:
I a child & thou a lamb,
We are called by his name.
　Little Lamb God bless thee.
　Little Lamb God bless thee.   20

THE LITTLE BLACK BOY.

My mother bore me in the southern wild,
And I am black, but O! my soul is white;
White as an angel is the English child:
But I am black as if bereav'd of light.

My mother taught me underneath a tree
And sitting down before the heat of day,
She took me on her lap and kissed me,
And pointing to the east began to say.

Look on the rising sun: there God does live
And gives his light, and gives his heat away.   10
And flowers and trees and beasts and men recieve
Comfort in morning joy in the noon day.

And we are put on earth a little space,
That we may learn to bear the beams of love,
And these black bodies and this sun-burnt face
Is but a cloud, and like a shady grove.

For when our souls have learn'd the heat to bear
The cloud will vanish we shall hear his voice.
Saying: come out from the grove my love & care,
And round my golden tent like lambs rejoice.   20

Thus did my mother say and kissed me,
And thus I say to little English boy.
When I from black and he from white cloud free,
And round the tent of God like lambs we joy:

I'll shade him from the heat till he can bear,
To lean in joy upon our fathers knee.
And then I'll stand and stroke his silver hair,
And be like him and he will then love me.

THE CHIMNEY SWEEPER

When my mother died I was very young,
And my father sold me while yet my tongue,
Could scarcely cry weep weep weep weep.
So your chimneys I sweep & in soot I sleep.

Theres little Tom Dacre, who cried when his head
That curl'd like a lambs back, was shav'd, so I said.
Hush Tom never mind it, for when your head's bare,
You know that the soot cannot spoil your white hair.

And so he was quiet, & that very night,
As Tom was a sleeping he had such a sight,   10
That thousands of sweepers Dick, Joe Ned & Jack
Were all of them lock'd up in coffins of black

And by came an Angel who had a bright key,
And he open'd the coffins & set them all free.
Then down a green plain leaping laughing they run
And wash in a river and shine in the Sun.

Then naked & white, all their bags left behind,
They rise upon clouds, and sport in the wind.
And the Angel told Tom if he'd be a good boy,
He'd have God for his father & never want joy.   20

And so Tom awoke and we rose in the dark
And got with our bags & our brushes to work.
Tho' the morning was cold, Tom was happy & warm,
So if all do their duty, they need not fear harm.

HOLY THURSDAY

Twas on a Holy Thursday[1] their innocent faces clean
The children walking two & two in red & blue & green
Grey headed beadles walkd before with wands as white as snow
Till into the high dome of Pauls[2] they like Thames[3] waters flow

O what a multitude they seemd these flowers of London town
Seated in companies they sit with radiance all their own
The hum of multitudes was there but multitudes of lambs
Thousands of little boys & girls raising their innocent hands

Now like a mighty wind they raise to heaven the voice of song
Or like harmonious thunderings the seats of heaven among   10
Beneath them sit the aged men wise guardians[4] of the poor
Then cherish pity, lest you drive an angel from your door

FROM

SONGS of EXPERIENCE

INTRODUCTION.

Hear the voice of the Bard!
Who Present, Past, & Future sees
Whose ears have heard,
The Holy Word,
That walk'd among the ancient trees.

Calling the lapsed Soul
And weeping in the evening dew;
That might controll,
The starry pole;
And fallen fallen light renew!   10

---

[1] Normally designates Ascension Day, the fortieth day after Easter. The annual charity-school services, to which this poem refers, were held on the first Thursday in May, unless that day fell on Ascension Day. Thus, Blake is being ironic here.
[2] St. Paul's Cathedral in London.
[3] River that runs through London.
[4] The overseers or governors of the charity schools.

O Earth O Earth return!
Arise from out the dewy grass;
Night is worn,
And the morn
Rises from the slumberous mass.

Turn away no more:
Why wilt thou turn away
The starry floor
The watry shore
Is giv'n thee till the break of day.   20

EARTH'S ANSWER

Earth rais'd up her head,
From the darkness dread & drear.
Her light fled:
Stony dread!
And her locks cover'd with grey despair.

Prison'd on watry shore
Starry Jealousy does keep my den
Cold and hoar
Weeping o'er
I hear the Father of the ancient men   10

Selfish father of men
Cruel jealous selfish fear
Can delight
Chain'd in night
The virgins of youth and morning bear.

Does spring hide its joy
When buds and blossoms grow?
Does the sower?
Sow by night?
Or the plowman in darkness plow?   20

Break this heavy chain,
That does freeze my bones around
Selfish! vain,
Eternal bane!
That free Love with bondage bound.

HOLY THURSDAY

Is this a holy thing to see,
In a rich and fruitful land,
Babes reducd to misery,
Fed with cold and usurous hand?

Is that trembling cry a song?
Can it be a song of joy?
And so many children poor?
It is a land of poverty!

And their sun does never shine.
And their fields are bleak & bare.   10
And their ways are fill'd with thorns.
It is eternal winter there.

For where-e'er the sun does shine,
And where-e'er the rain does fall:
Babe can never hunger there,
Nor poverty the mind appall.

THE CHIMNEY SWEEPER

A little black thing among the snow:
Crying weep, weep, in notes of woe!
Where are thy father & mother? say?
They are both gone up to the church to pray.

Because I was happy upon the heath,
And smil'd among the winters snow:
They clothed me in the clothes of death,
And taught me to sing the notes of woe.

And because I am happy, & dance & sing,
They think they have done me no injury: 10
And are gone to praise God & his Priest & King
Who make up a heaven of our misery.

THE SICK ROSE

O Rose thou art sick.
The invisible worm,
That flies in the night
In the howling storm:

Has found out thy bed
Of crimson joy:
And his dark secret love
Does thy life destroy.

THE TYGER

Tyger Tyger, burning bright,
In the forests of the night;
What immortal hand or eye,
Could frame thy fearful symmetry?

In what distant deeps or skies
Burnt the fire of thine eyes!
On what wings dare he aspire?
What the hand, dare sieze the fire?

And what shoulder, & what art,   10
Could twist the sinews of thy heart?
And when thy heart began to beat,
What dread hand? & what dread feet?

What the hammer? what the chain,
In what furnace was thy brain?
What the anvil? what dread grasp,
Dare its deadly terrors clasp?

When the stars threw down their spears
And water'd heaven with their tears:
Did he smile his work to see?
Did he who made the Lamb make thee?   20

Tyger, Tyger burning bright,
In the forests of the night:
What immortal hand or eye,
Dare frame thy fearful symmetry?

LONDON

I wander thro' each charter'd⁵ street,
Near where the charter'd Thames does flow.
And mark in every face I meet
Marks of weakness, marks of woe.

In every cry of every Man,
In every Infants cry of fear,
In every voice: in every ban,
The mind-forg'd manacles I hear

How the Chimney-sweepers cry
Every blackning Church appalls,   10
And the hapless Soldiers sigh,
Runs in blood down Palace walls

But most thro' midnight streets I hear
How the youthful Harlots curse
Blasts the new-born Infants tear
And blights with plagues the Marriage hearse

---

⁵London's charters granted certain liberties and privileges to its citizens, and also demarcated the rights of property.

THE *MARRIAGE* of HEAVEN and HELL

PLATE 2[1]

THE ARGUMENT.

Rintrah[2] roars & shakes his fires in the burdend air;
Hungry clouds swag on the deep

Once meek, and in a perilous path,
The just man kept his course along
The vale of death.
Roses are planted where thorns grow.
And on the barren heath
Sing the honey bees.

Then the perilous path was planted:
And a river, and a spring   10
On every cliff and tomb;
And on the bleached bones
Red clay brought forth.

Till the villain left the paths of ease,
To walk in perilous paths, and drive
The just man into barren climes.

Now the sneaking serpent walks
In mild humility.
And the just man rages in the wilds
Where lions roam.   20

Rintrah roars & shakes his fires in the burdend air;
Hungry clouds swag on the deep.

PLATE 3

As a new heaven is begun, and it is now thirty-three years[3] since its advent:
the Eternal Hell revives. And lo! Swedenborg is the Angel sitting at the tomb; his
writings are the linen clothes folded up.[4] Now is the dominion of Edom, & the
return of Adam into Paradise; see Isaiah XXXIV & XXXV Chap:[5]

---

[1]The plate numbers refer to Blake's artwork, not reproduced in this edition, on which the text appears.

[2]A mythic figure in Blake's works who represents the angry prophet, like Isaiah. The imagery of this section draws in part upon Isaiah 34 and 35, which Blake mentions in the following section.

[3]Emanuel Swedenborg (1688–1772), whose works Blake parodies here, predicted that the Last Judgment would occur in 1757, the year of Blake's birth. Writing in 1790, Blake thus refers to his own birth and sets up Swedenborg as a kind of John the Baptist and himself as a kind of Christ, who was crucified and resurrected at age 33.

[4]Blake alludes here to the resurrection of Christ as described in Matthew 28:1–7 and John 20:1–10.

[5]In Genesis 27–28 and 36, Edom refers to Esau, the son of Isaac, at the time he will triumph over his deceitful brother Jacob, who had tricked their father into giving him Esau's rightful blessing. Isaiah 34 and 35 describe God's judgment upon the wicked descendants of Edom and the redemption of the just. The symbolic density here is typical of *The Marriage of Heaven and Hell*, where Blake condenses biblical allusions into a myth that resonates politically to the moment and promise of the French Revolution, and psychologically to the possibility for the imaginative and spiritual redemption of the individual.

Without Contraries is no progression. Attraction and Repulsion, Reason and Energy, Love and Hate, are necessary to Human existence.

From these contraries spring what the religious call Good & Evil. Good is the passive that obeys Reason[.] Evil is the active springing from Energy.

Good is Heaven. Evil is Hell.

PLATE 4
THE VOICE OF THE DEVIL

All Bibles or sacred codes. have been the causes of the following Errors.

1. That Man has two real existing principles Viz: a Body & a Soul.

2. That Energy. calld Evil. is alone from the Body. & that Reason. calld Good. is alone from the Soul.

3. That God will torment Man in Eternity for following his Energies. But the following Contraries to these are True

1 Man has no Body distinct from his Soul for that calld Body is a portion of Soul discernd by the five Senses, the chief inlets of Soul in this age

2 Energy is the only life and is from the Body and Reason is the bound or outward circumference of Energy.

3 Energy is Eternal Delight

PLATE 5

Those who restrain desire, do so because theirs is weak enough to be restrained; and the restrainer or reason usurps its place & governs the unwilling.

And being restraind it by degrees becomes passive till it is only the shadow of desire.

The history of this is written in Paradise Lost. & the Governor or Reason is call'd Messiah.

And the original Archangel or possessor of the command of the heavenly host, is calld the Devil or Satan and his children are call'd Sin & Death[6]

But in the Book of Job Miltons Messiah is call'd Satan.[7]

For this history has been adopted by both parties

It indeed appear'd to Reason as if Desire was cast out, but the Devils account is, that the Messi[PL 6]ah fell. & formed a heaven of what he stole from the Abyss

This is shewn in the Gospel, where he prays to the Father to send the comforter or Desire that Reason may have Ideas to build on, the Jehovah of the Bible being no other than he, who dwells in flaming fire. Know that after Christs death, he became Jehovah.

But in Milton; the Father is Destiny, the Son, a Ratio[8] of the five senses. & the Holy-ghost, Vacuum!

Note. The reason Milton wrote in fetters when he wrote of Angels & God, and at liberty when of Devils & Hell, is because he was a true Poet and of the Devils party without knowing it

---

[6]See *Paradise Lost* 2.758–69.

[7]Because God allows Satan to punish the just man Job, as Milton's Messiah punishes Satan in Book 6 of *Paradise Lost*.

[8]i.e., reduced from the senses; an example of Blake's impatience with the empiricism of John Locke and his followers.

A Memorable Fancy.

As I was walking among the fires of hell, delighted with the enjoyments of Genius; which to Angels look like torment and insanity. I collected some of their Proverbs: thinking that as the sayings used in a nation, mark its character, so the Proverbs of Hell, shew the nature of Infernal wisdom better than any description of buildings or garments.

When I came home; on the abyss of the five senses, where a flat sided steep frowns over the present world. I saw a mighty Devil folded in black clouds, hovering on the sides of the rock, with cor[PL 7]roding fires he wrote the following sentence now percieved by the minds of men, & read by them on earth.

How do you know but ev'ry Bird that cuts the airy way,
Is an immense world of delight, clos'd by your senses five?

Proverbs of Hell.

In seed time learn, in harvest teach, in winter enjoy.
Drive your cart and your plow over the bones of the dead.
The road of excess leads to the palace of wisdom.
Prudence is a rich ugly old maid courted by Incapacity.
He who desires but acts not, breeds pestilence.
The cut worm forgives the plow.
Dip him in the river who loves water.
A fool sees not the same tree that a wise man sees.
He whose face gives no light, shall never become a star.
Eternity is in love with the productions of time.   10
The busy bee has no time for sorrow.
The hours of folly are measur'd by the clock, but of wisdom: no clock
      can measure.
All wholsom food is caught without a net or a trap.
Bring out number weight & measure in a year of dearth.
No bird soars too high. if he soars with his own wings.
A dead body. revenges not injuries.
The most sublime act is to set another before you.
If the fool would persist in his folly he would become wise
Folly is the cloke of knavery.
Shame is Prides cloke.   20

PLATE 8

Prisons are built with stones of Law, Brothels with bricks of Religion.
The pride of the peacock is the glory of God.
The lust of the goat is the bounty of God.
The wrath of the lion is the wisdom of God.
The nakedness of woman is the work of God.
Excess of sorrow laughs. Excess of joy weeps.
The roaring of lions, the howling of wolves, the raging of the stormy
      sea, and the destructive sword. are portions of eternity too great for
      the eye of man.
The fox condemns the trap, not himself.
Joys impregnate. Sorrows bring forth.

Let man wear the fell of the lion. woman the fleece of the sheep.   30
The bird a nest, the spider a web, man friendship.
The selfish smiling fool. & the sullen frowning fool. shall be both
 thought wise. that they may be a rod.
What is now proved was once, only imagin'd.
The rat, the mouse, the fox, the rabbet; watch the roots, the lion, the
 tyger, the horse, the elephant, watch the fruits.
The cistern contains: the fountain overflows
One thought. fills immensity.
Always be ready to speak your mind, and a base man will avoid you.
Every thing possible to be believ'd is an image of truth.
The eagle never lost so much time. as when he submitted to learn of
 the crow.

PLATE 9

The fox provides for himself. but God provides for the lion.   40
Think in the morning, Act in the noon, Eat in the evening, Sleep in the
 night.
He who has sufferd you to impose on him knows you.
As the plow follows words, so God rewards prayers.
The tygers of wrath are wiser than the horses of instruction
Expect poison from the standing water.
You never know what is enough unless you know what is more than
 enough.
Listen to the fools reproach! it is a kingly title!
The eyes of fire, the nostrils of air, the mouth of water, the beard of
 earth.
The weak in courage is strong in cunning.
The apple tree never asks the beech how he shall grow, nor the lion. the   50
 horse, how he shall take his prey.
The thankful reciever bears a plentiful harvest.
If others had not been foolish, we should be so.
The soul of sweet delight, can never be defil'd,
When thou seest an Eagle, thou seest a portion of Genius. lift up thy
 head!
As the catterpiller chooses the fairest leaves to lay her eggs on, so the
 priest lays his curse on the fairest joys.
To create a little flower is the labour of ages.
Damn. braces: Bless relaxes.
The best wine is the oldest. the best water the newest.
Prayers plow not! Praises reap not!
Joys laugh not! Sorrows weep not!   60

PLATE 10

The head Sublime, the heart Pathos, the genitals Beauty, the hands &
 feet Proportion.
As the air to a bird or the sea to a fish, so is contempt to the contempt-
 ible.
The crow wish'd every thing was black, the owl, that every thing was
 white.
Exuberance is Beauty.
If the lion was advise'd by the fox. he would be cunning.

Improve[me]nt makes strait roads, but the crooked roads without
    Improvement, are roads of Genius.
Sooner murder an infant in its cradle than nurse unacted desires
Where man is not nature is barren.
Truth can never be told so as to be understood, and not be believ'd.
Enough! or Too Much 70

PLATE 11

    The ancient Poets animated all sensible objects with Gods or Geniuses, calling them by the names and adorning them with the properties of woods, rivers, mountains, lakes, cities, nations, and whatever their enlarged & numerous senses could percieve.

And particularly they studied the genius of each city & country. placing it under its mental deity.

Till a system was formed, which some took advantage of & enslav'd the vulgar by attempting to realize or abstract the mental deities from their objects; thus began Priesthood.

Choosing forms of worship from poetic tales.

And at length they pronouncd that the Gods had orderd such things.

Thus men forgot that All deities reside in the human breast.

PLATE 12

A MEMORABLE FANCY.

The Prophets Isaiah and Ezekiel dined with me, and I asked them how they dared so roundly to assert. that God spake to them; and whether they did not think at the time, that they would be misunderstood, & so be the cause of imposition.

Isaiah answer'd. I saw no God, nor heard any, in a finite organical perception; but my senses discover'd the infinite in every thing, and as I was then perswaded, & remain confirm'd; that the voice of honest indignation is the voice of God, I cared not for consequences but wrote.

Then I asked: does a firm perswasion that a thing is so, make it so?

He replied. All poets believe that it does, & in ages of imagination this firm perswasion removed mountains; but many are not capable of a firm perswasion of any thing.

Then Ezekiel said. The philosophy of the east taught the first principles of human perception   some nations held one principle for the origin & some another, we of Israel taught that the Poetic Genius (as you now call it) was the first principle and all the others merely derivative, which was the cause of our despising the Priests & Philosophers of other countries, and prophecying that all Gods [PL 13] would at last be proved to originate in ours & to be the tributaries of the Poetic Genius, it was this. that our great poet King David desired so fervently & invokes so patheticly, saying by this he conquers enemies & governs kingdoms; and we so loved our God. that we cursed in his name all the deities of surrounding nations, and asserted that they had rebelled; from these opinions the vulgar came to think that all nations would at last be subject to the jews.

This said he, like all firm perswasions, is come to pass, for all nations believe the jews code and worship the jews god, and what greater subjection can be

I heard this with some wonder, & must confess my own conviction. After dinner I ask'd Isaiah to favour the world with his lost works, he said none of equal value was lost. Ezekiel said the same of his.

I also asked Isaiah what made him go naked and barefoot three years? he answerd, the same that made our friend Diogenes the Grecian.[9]

I then asked Ezekiel. why he eat dung, & lay so long on his right & left side?[10] he answerd. the desire of raising other men into a perception of the infinite   this the North American tribes practise. & is he honest who resists his genius or conscience. only for the sake of present ease or gratification?

PLATE 14

The ancient tradition that the world will be consumed in fire at the end of six thousand years is true. as I have heard from Hell.

For the cherub with his flaming sword is hereby commanded to leave his guard at tree of life, and when he does, the whole creation will be consumed, and appear infinite. and holy whereas it now appears finite & corrupt.

This will come to pass by an improvement of sensual enjoyment.

But first the notion that man has a body distinct from his soul, is to be expunged; this I shall do, by printing in the infernal method, by corrosives, which in Hell are salutary and medicinal, melting apparent surfaces away, and displaying the infinite which was hid.[11]

If the doors of perception were cleansed every thing would appear to man as it is, infinite.

For man has closed himself up, till he sees all things thro' narrow chinks of his cavern.

PLATE 15

A MEMORABLE FANCY

I was in a Printing house in Hell & saw the method in which knowledge is transmitted from generation to generation.

In the first chamber was a Dragon-Man, clearing away the rubbish from a caves mouth; within, a number of Dragons were hollowing the cave,

In the second chamber was a Viper folding round the rock & the cave, and others adorning it with gold silver and precious stones.

In the third chamber was an Eagle with wings and feathers of air, he caused the inside of the cave to be infinite, around were numbers of Eagle like men, who built palaces in the immense cliffs.

In the fourth chamber were Lions of flaming fire raging around & melting the metals into living fluids.

In the fifth chamber were Unnam'd forms, which cast the metals into the expanse.

There they were reciev'd by Men who occupied the sixth chamber, and took the forms of books & were arranged in libraries.

---

[9]Isaiah had walked naked as a portent and warning to Egypt and Ethiopia (Isaiah 20:3), Diogenes (c. 400–325 B.C.E) was a Greek philosopher of the Cynic school, which denounced the artificial comforts of civilization in favor of an austere simplicity.

[10]See Ezekiel 4:4–6 and 12.

[11]Here and in the section that follows Blake describes the process of "illuminated printing," the method of relief etching that he developed for producing his prophetic works.

PLATE 16

The Giants who formed this world into its sensual existence and now seem to live in it in chains, are in truth. the causes of its life & the sources of all activity, but the chains are, the cunning of weak and tame minds. which have power to resist energy, according to the proverb, the weak in courage is strong in cunning.

Thus one portion of being, is the Prolific. the other, the Devouring: to the devourer it seems as if the producer was in his chains, but it is not so, he only takes portions of existence and fancies that the whole.

But the Prolific would cease to be Prolific unless the Devourer as a sea recieved the excess of his delights.

Some will say, Is not God alone the Prolific? I answer, God only Acts & Is, in existing beings or Men.

These two classes of men are always upon earth, & they should be enemies; whoever tries [PL 17] to reconcile them seeks to destroy existence.

Religion is an endeavour to reconcile the two.

Note. Jesus Christ did not wish to unite but to seperate them, as in the Parable of sheep and goats! & he says I came not to send Peace but a Sword.[12]

Messiah or Satan or Tempter was formerly thought to be one of the Antediluvians[13] who are our Energies.

A MEMORABLE FANCY[14]

An Angel came to me and said   O pitiable foolish young man! O horrible! O dreadful state! consider the hot burning dungeon thou art preparing for thyself to all eternity, to which thou art going in such career.

I said, perhaps you will be willing to shew me my eternal lot & we will contemplate together upon it and see whether your lot or mine is most desirable

So he took me thro' a stable & thro' a church & down into the church vault at the end of which was a mill: thro' the mill we went, and came to a cave. down the winding cavern we groped our tedious way till a void boundless as a nether sky appeard beneath us. & we held by the roots of trees and hung over this immensity, but I said, if you please we will commit ourselves to this void, and see whether providence is here also, if you will not I will? but he answerd, do not presume O youngman but as we here remain behold thy lot which will soon appear when the darkness passes away

So I remaind with him sitting in the twisted [PL 18] root of an oak. he was suspended in a fungus which hung with the head downward into the deep;

By degrees we beheld the infinite Abyss, fiery as the smoke of a burning city; beneath us at an immense distance was the sun, black but shining[;] round it were fiery tracks on which revolv'd vast spiders, crawling after their prey; which flew or rather swum in the infinite deep, in the most terrific shapes of animals sprung from corruption. & the air was full of them, & seemd composed of them; these are Devils. and are called Powers of the air, I now asked my companion which was my eternal lot? he said, between the black & white spiders

But now, from between the black & white spiders a cloud and fire burst and rolled thro the deep   blackning all beneath, so that the nether deep grew black as

---

[12]See Matthew 10:34 for the parable of sheep and goats; Matthew 25:33 for Christ bearing the sword.
[13]Those who lived before the great flood.
[14]This section is a Swiftean parody of the abstract and rationalistic theology that Blake believes perverts the perception of divinity or spiritual reality in his time.

a sea & rolled with a terrible noise: beneath us was nothing now to be seen but a black tempest, till looking east between the clouds & the waves, we saw a cataract of blood mixed with fire and not many stones throw from us appeard and sunk again the scaly fold of a monstrous serpent[.] at last to the east, distant about three degrees appeard a fiery crest above the waves[.] slowly it reared like a ridge of golden rocks till we discoverd two globes of crimson fire, from which the sea fled away in clouds of smoke, and now we saw, it was the head of Leviathan, his forehead was divided into streaks of green & purple like those on a tygers forehead: soon we saw his mouth & red gills hang just above the raging foam tinging the black deep with beams of blood, advancing toward [PL 19] us with all the fury of a spiritual existence.

My friend the Angel climb'd up from his station into the mill; I remain'd alone, & then this appearance was no more, but I found myself sitting on a pleasant bank beside a river by moon light hearing a harper who sung to the harp, & his theme was, The man who never alters his opinion is like standing water, & breeds reptiles of the mind.

But I arose, and sought for the mill, & there I found my Angel, who surprised asked me, how I escaped?

I answerd. All that we saw was owing to your metaphysics: for when you ran away, I found myself on a bank by moonlight hearing a harper, But now we have seen my eternal lot, shall I shew you yours? he laughd at my proposal; but I by force suddenly caught him in my arms, & flew westerly thro' the night, till we were elevated above the earths shadow: then I flung myself with him directly into the body of the sun, here I clothed myself in white, & taking in my hand Swedenborgs volumes sunk from the glorious clime, and passed all the planets till we came to saturn, here I staid to rest & then leap'd into the void, between saturn & the fixed stars.[15]

Here said I! is your lot, in this space, if space it may be calld, Soon we saw the stable and the church, & I took him to the altar and open'd the Bible, and lo! it was a deep pit, into which I descended driving the Angel before me, soon we saw seven houses of brick,[16] one we enterd; in it were a [PL 20] number of monkeys, baboons, & all of that species chaind by the middle, grinning and snatching at one another, but witheld by the shortness of their chains: however I saw that they sometimes grew numerous, and then the weak were caught by the strong and with a grinning aspect, first coupled with & then devourd, by plucking off first one limb and then another till the body was left a helpless trunk. this after grinning & kissing it with seeming fondness they devourd too; and here & there I saw one savourily picking the flesh off of his own tail; as the stench terribly annoyd us both we went into the mill, & I in my hand brought the skeleton of a body, which in the mill was Aristotles Analytics.[17]

So the Angel said: thy phantasy has imposed upon me & thou oughtest to be ashamed.

I answerd: we impose on one another, & it is but lost time to converse with you whose works are only Analytics

Opposition is true Friendship.

---

[15]In the Ptolemaic cosmos, Saturn was the most distant planet, beyond which was a band of fixed stars. Swedenborg believed that the stars were inhabited by spirits and angels.

[16]Perhaps the seven churches in Asia to which John addresses the prophecy of Revelation (Revelations 1:4).

[17]Treatises on logic and science.

PLATE 21

I have always found that Angels have the vanity to speak of themselves as the only wise; this they do with a confident insolence sprouting from systematic reasoning;

Thus Swedenborg boasts that what he writes is new; tho' it is only the Contents or Index of already publish'd books

A man carried a monkey about for a shew, & because he was a little wiser than the monkey, grew vain, and conciev'd himself as much wiser than seven men. It is so with Swedenborg; he shews the folly of churches & exposes hypocrites, till he imagines that all are religious. & himself the single [PL 22] one on earth that ever broke a net.

Now hear a plain fact: Swedenborg has not written one new truth: Now hear another: he has written all the old falshoods.

And now hear the reason. He conversed with Angels who are all religious, & conversed not with Devils who all hate religion, for he was incapable thro' his conceited notions.

Thus Swedenborgs writings are a recapitulation of all superficial opinions, and an analysis of the more sublime, but no further.

Have now another plain fact: Any man of mechanical talents may from the writings of Paracelsus or Jacob Behmen,[18] produce ten thousand volumes of equal value with Swedenborg's. and from those of Dante or Shakespear, an infinite number.

But when he has done this, let him not say that he knows better than his master, for he only holds a candle in sunshine.

A Memorable Fancy

Once I saw a Devil in a flame of fire. who arose before an Angel that sat on a cloud. and the Devil utterd these words.

The worship of God is. Honouring his gifts in other men each according to his genius. and loving the [PL 23] greatest men best, those who envy or calumniate great men hate God, for there is no other God.

The Angel hearing this became almost blue but mastering himself he grew yellow, & at last white pink & smiling, and then replied,

Thou Idolater, is not God One? & is not he visible in Jesus Christ? and has not Jesus Christ given his sanction to the law of ten commandments and are not all other men fools, sinners, & nothings?

The Devil answer'd; bray a fool in a morter with wheat. yet shall not his folly be beaten out of him: if Jesus Christ is the greatest man, you ought to love him in the greatest degree; now hear how he has given his sanction to the law of ten commandments: did he not mock at the sabbath, and so mock the sabbaths God? murder those who were murderd because of him? turn away the law from the woman taken in adultery? steal the labor of others to support him? bear false witness when he omitted making a defence before Pilate? covet when he pray'd for his disciples, and when he bid them shake off the dust of their feet against such as refused to lodge them? I tell you, no virtue can exist without breaking these

---

[18]Paracelsus (c. 1490–1541), a Swiss physician and alchemist, associated with the occult sciences and the pursuit of the elixir of life; Behmen is Jakob Böhme (1575–1624), a German mystic and theosophist whose work influenced Blake.

ten commandments. Jesus was all virtue, and acted from im[PL 24]pulse. not from rules.

When he had so spoken: I beheld the Angel who stretched out his arms embracing the flame of fire & he was consumed and arose as Elijah.[19]

Note. This Angel, who is now become a Devil, is my particular friend: we often read the Bible together in its infernal or diabolical sense which the world shall have if they behave well

I have also: The Bible of Hell: which the world shall have whether they will or no.

One Law for the Lion & Ox is Oppression

PLATE 25

A SONG OF LIBERTY[20]

1. The Eternal Female groand! it was heard over all the Earth:
2. Albions[21] coast is sick silent; the American meadows faint!
3. Shadows of Prophecy shiver along by the lakes and the rivers and mutter across the ocean? France rend down thy dungeon;[22]
4. Golden Spain burst the barriers of old Rome;
5. Cast thy keys O Rome[23] into the deep down falling, even to eternity down falling,
6. And weep
7. In her trembling hands she took the new born terror howling:
8. On those infinite mountains of light now barr'd out by the atlantic sea,[24] the new born fire stood before the starry king!
9. Flag'd with grey brow'd snows and thunderous visages the jealous wings wav'd over the deep.
10. The speary hand burned aloft, unbuckled was the shield, forth went the hand of jealousy among the flaming hair, and [PL 26] hurl'd the new born wonder thro' the starry night.
11. The fire, the fire, is falling!
12. Look up! look up! O citizen of London. enlarge thy countenance; O Jew, leave counting gold! return to thy oil and wine; O African! black African! (go. winged thought widen his forehead.)
13. The fiery limbs, the flaming hair, shot like the sinking sun into the western sea.
14. Wak'd from his eternal sleep, the hoary element roaring fled away:
15. Down rushd beating his wings in vain the jealous king; his grey brow'd councellors, thunderous warriors, curl'd veterans, among helms, and shields, and chariots[,] horses, elephants: banners, castles, slings and rocks,

---

[19]See 2 Kings 2:11 where Elijah, riding on a fiery chariot, rises on a whirlwind of flame.

[20]Blake bound this poem, etched in 1792, to some of the versions of *The Marriage of Heaven and Hell*. Capturing the revolutionary spirit of the time, this symbolic narrative describes the birth of the spirit of revolution, later called Orc in Blake's mythology, and his struggle with the forces of tyranny, later embodied more fully in Blake's myth as Urizen.

[21]England.

[22]An allusion to the storming of the Bastille on July 14, 1789, which marked the beginning of the French Revolution.

[23]The power and authority of the Roman Catholic Pope.

[24]Atlantis; here as a prelapsarian utopia of freedom.

16. Falling, rushing, ruining! buried in the ruins, on Urthona's[25] dens.

17. All night beneath the ruins, then their sullen flames faded emerge round the gloomy king,

18. With thunder and fire: leading his starry hosts thro' the waste wilderness [PL 27] he promulgates his ten commands,[26] glancing his beamy eyelids over the deep in dark dismay,

19. Where the son of fire in his eastern cloud, while the morning plumes her golden breast,

20. Spurning the clouds written with curses, stamps the stony law to dust, loosing the eternal horses from the dens of night, crying

Empire is no more! and now the lion & wolf shall cease.[27]

CHORUS

Let the Priests of the Raven of dawn, no longer in deadly black. with hoarse note curse the sons of joy. Nor his accepted brethren whom, tyrant, he calls free: lay the bound or build the roof. Nor pale religious letchery call that virginity, that wishes but acts not!

For every thing that lives is Holy

"Mock on Mock on Voltaire Rousseau"

Mock on Mock on Voltaire Rousseau
Mock on Mock on tis all in vain
You throw the sand against the wind
And the wind blows it back again

And every sand becomes a Gem
Reflected in the beams divine
Blown back they blind the mocking Eye
But still in Israels paths they shine

The Atoms of Democritus
And Newtons Particles of light   10
Are sands upon the Red sea shore
Where Israels tents do shine so bright

---

[25] "Earth Owner"; in later works Urthona is a spirit of imagination and creativity. His confinement here symbolizes the collapse of creative power and liberty under the "mind forg'd manacles" of political and religious dogma.

[26] The Ten Commandments of Moses, associated here with the demise of true religious inspiration and the formation of religious institutions and reductive forms of sectarianism.

[27] See Isaiah 65:17–25; the creation of the New Jerusalem will bring in a time when "the wolf and the lamb shall feed together, / the lion shall eat straw like the ox; / and dust shall be the serpent's food." Compare also Blake's concluding apothegm to Plate 24: "One Law for the Lion & Ox is Oppression."

WILLIAM WORDSWORTH
[1770–1850]

Few poets embody what William Hazlitt, referring to the early nineteenth century, called the "spirit of the age" so much as William Wordsworth. A self-conscious reformer in his youth, Wordsworth supported the early stages of the French Revolution, hoping that it would inspire England to take steps toward political reform. That spirit of reform carried over into his early poetry, not only in his intensive focus upon the lives of poor rustics and the loss of "domestic feeling" within a community assailed by industrial change and the accumulation of people in cities, but in his very poetic style. Declaring the poetic diction of eighteenth-century poetry stale and uninspiring, Wordsworth announced a new poetic diction that would eschew the proprieties of neoclassicism and incorporate the language of common people into the hallowed demesnes of the poem. So much did Wordsworth convince his readers of his revolutionary status that 1798, the year in which he and Samuel Taylor Coleridge published *Lyrical Ballads,* stands for many literary critics as a threshold date marking the advent of romantic poetry in England. Although Wordsworth completed most of his great poetry between 1793 and 1807, he continued writing until his death in 1850. Spanning the period from the French Revolution until well into the Victorian era, Wordsworth's poetic output offers a unique record of the transformations in political and poetic sentiment in the nineteenth century. In Wordsworth's middle and later years, this movement involves a falling off from a fervent desire for revolutionary change to a more temperate acceptance of the status quo, for which many younger poets, notably Byron and Browning, berated him. Nonetheless, this "lost leader," as Browning dubbed him, had ardent supporters throughout the nineteenth and twentieth centuries, and undoubtedly remains one of the most influential poets of the nineteenth century.

LIFE

William Wordsworth was born April 7, 1770, in the small Cumberland village of Cockermouth near the English Lake District. The son of a lawyer who managed the vast estates of the Earl of Lonsdale, Wordsworth at first enjoyed a pleasant childhood in the family along the banks of River Derwent. When he was seven years old, however, his mother died and the family, including his three brothers and his sister, Dorothy, went to live among different relatives. William went with his brother Richard to Hawkshead, Lancashire, to live with Anne Tyson while they attended grammar school. During these formative days, which he remembers fondly in his great work *The Prelude* (1805 and 1850), Wordsworth spent much of his free time roaming the surrounding countryside and hills.

Wordsworth's father died in 1783, and although he had left an estate of nearly 5,000 pounds claimed against the Earl of Lonsdale, the Earl withheld payment, leaving the Wordsworth children dependent upon their uncles. In 1787, Wordsworth entered St. John's College, Cambridge, taking a minimal interest in his courses while pursuing a prodigious and broad range of independent reading in the classics, Italian, and contemporary English literature. Leaving Cambridge in January 1791, Wordsworth took a degree without distinction, and disappointed his uncles' hopes that he would take a position in the Church. The summer before taking his degree, Wordsworth traveled to France and toured on foot through the Swiss and Italian Alps with his friend Robert Jones. France in the summer of 1790 was in a ferment of revolutionary hope and fear; as Wordsworth writes in *The Prelude,* Book 9, "The land all swarmed with passion" and the people were "risen up / Fresh as the morning star." The Revolution had begun a year before with the storming of the Bastille on July 14, 1789, and sympathizers with the revolutionary principles saw in France the possibility for the overthrow of absolutism. A new age and spirit was being born; Book 10 of *The Prelude* expresses Wordsworth's sense of hope in those early years of the Revolution: "Bliss was it in that dawn to be alive."

Wordsworth would return to France in 1791 when a more somber mood hung on the Revolution. With Louis XVI under house arrest and division within the National Assembly, Paris was in confusion. Although Wordsworth was not in France during the execution of Louis and Marie Antoinette in January and October 1793, respectively, Wordsworth felt from England the shock that jarred all of Europe at the Reign of Terror that followed shortly thereafter. During the Reign of Terror—a series of trials and summary executions aimed at quelling anti-republican sentiment and eliminating traitors—more than 2,600 people were executed in fifteen months. In the words of Wordsworth's *Prelude*, Book 10, it was "A woeful time for them whose hopes did still / Outlast the shock." Although some intellectuals throughout Europe continued to support the Revolution even through the shadow of the guillotine, seeing violence as an unfortunate but necessary stage of radical transformation, the Reign of Terror tempered or extinguished altogether the hopes that before had been so profound. In the *Ode: Intimations of Immortality*, Wordsworth's struggle to find "abundant recompense" from the loss of innocence and glory serves as a metaphor for the struggle of many Europeans whose vision of an egalitarian society gave way to disenchantment in the violent wake of the Revolution.

During the turbulent years of the Revolution, Wordsworth was in England, taking walking tours, drifting in and out of London's radical circles (which included William Godwin and Mary Wollstonecraft), visiting his friends and family, and finally setting up home with his sister Dorothy Wordsworth, first at Racedown in 1795, later at Alfoxden in 1798, and finally at Grasmere in the heart of the English Lake District in 1799 after a brief trip to Germany. In 1797, while at Racedown, Wordsworth began his famous friendship and collaboration with Samuel Taylor Coleridge. In 1798, Wordsworth and Coleridge published *Lyrical Ballads*, seen by many critics as the founding text of English romanticism. "Lines Composed a Few Miles above Tintern Abbey," the first poem in our selection, was published as the final poem in *Lyrical Ballads*.

Wordsworth and Coleridge conceived of *Lyrical Ballads* as an experiment to see how far poetry could use the "real language of men in a state of vivid sensation" to convey the importance of ordinary actions and incidents. Hence, Wordsworth's poems in *Lyrical Ballads* describe "incidents and situations from common life" and attempt to invoke the noble simplicity of the rustics and common people who inhabit his poems. Rejecting the stilted poetic diction of neoclassical poets such as Alexander Pope, Wordsworth attempted to capture—in a "purified" form—the natural rhythms and inflections of rustic life, for there, it was thought, people had more direct access to the permanent truths and noble feelings of nature itself. As he wrote in one of the poems in the collection, "One impulse from a vernal wood / May teach you more of man, / Of moral evil and of good, / Than all the sages can." *Lyrical Ballads* was praised by a few discriminating readers, such as William Hazlitt, as the sign of a new spirit of poetry, but many critics trained in the neoclassical principles of the eighteenth century delivered mixed reviews of the book. Nonetheless, even those critics who objected to the lowly subject matter of the collaboration and its outright dismissal of poetic decorum had to acknowledge that the poems contained a depth of feeling that was admirable and new.

"Tintern Abbey" and the later *Ode: Intimations of Immortality* (composed between 1802 and 1804) are more highly stylized than most of the poems in *Lyrical Ballads*, but both poems do demonstrate Wordsworth's intense interest in exploring the relationships between feeling and consciousness, mind and nature, and the past and present. In their philosophical musing and their displaced grappling with the great concerns of the Revolution, "Tintern Abbey" and the *Ode* mark the beginning and end of one of Wordsworth's most productive phases, between 1798 and 1802. He did, nonetheless, continue to write poetry—including what some think to be his greatest work, the fourteen-book *Prelude*—for almost another forty years. Having established a home at Grasmere with his wife, Mary Hutchinson, and his sister, Wordsworth set up a thriving poetic "cottage industry." Between 1798 and 1850, Wordsworth published many other poems, including *Poems in Two Volumes* in 1807, *The Excursion* in 1814, and *Yarrow Revisited, and Other Poems* in 1835. *The Prelude,* Wordsworth's heavily revised autobiographical poem of epic proportions, remained unpublished until shortly after his death on April 23, 1850.

WORK

Often erroneously called a "nature poet" (in the sense of a poet who merely describes the natural world and the landscape), Wordsworth primarily describes the relationship between mind and nature, what he sees as the reciprocal interaction between nature and human consciousness. Looking forward to a long philosophical poem that he and Coleridge had projected as his life's goal, Wordsworth delineated what turned out to be the subject matter for almost all of his poems, and especially *The Prelude*. In the "Prospectus to *The Recluse,*" Wordsworth dismisses the typical mythological subject matter of epic, and turns his attention instead to "the Mind of Man— / My haunt, and the main region of my song." What he hopes to show in the course of this work is

> How exquisitely the individual Mind
> (And the progressive powers perhaps no less
> Of the whole species) to the external World
> Is fitted:—and how exquisitely, too—
> Theme this but little heard of among men
> The external World is fitted to the Mind.

The primary experience of nature, in both its beautiful and terrifying aspects, Wordsworth believes, is vitally important for sustaining and invigorating the spiritual strength and creative power of human beings through later times of trial, loss, and confinement in places that offer less inspiration. The sustenance that these initial moments of contact with nature offer, however, depends upon a reciprocating power—rendered variously as a "wise passiveness" and an "auxiliar light"—from the heart and mind of the person encountering the natural object. These moments of intensive and reflexive experience become for Wordsworth "spots of time" with a "fructifying virtue." That is, this moment of mutual dialogue generates in the subject the power to restore the old and to awaken new feelings at a later time.

Critics often describe the Wordsworthian encounter with nature as a dialectical process, an interaction between two apparently discordant and separate entities that produces a kind of unity between them. This dialectic, a process that runs throughout European romanticism, drives the experience of the narrator of "Tintern Abbey" as the discontinuity between the present and past experience of the landscape at first opens a disturbing gap between the past and present self. But that gap allows him to find a new strength. Thus, "Tintern Abbey" begins with returning to a scene that the narrator had previously visited. Looking out over the landscape, the narrator superimposes the remembered landscape upon the present landscape. The composite landscape that results points to certain losses, but also to certain gains, that the poet has experienced over time. In *The Prelude,* Wordsworth describes the experience this way:

> so wide appears
> The vacancy between me and those days
> Which yet have such self-presence in my mind

> That sometimes when I think of them I seem
> Two consciousnesses—conscious of myself,
> And of some other being.

That other being, as we see in "Tintern Abbey" and in the *Ode,* may be variously the natural child, the naïve "roe" bounding among the hills, as Wordsworth did at Hawkshead; or the political child, an equally naïve tourist or spectator of the Revolution who remains innocent of the blood of kings and commoners he witnesses in France. Thus, in these two poems—in their celebration of childhood, their failure to recuperate a lost innocence, and their attempt to find compensation in an understanding of that loss—Wordsworth captures what William Hazlitt calls the "spirit of the age" of post-Revolutionary romanticism.

SUGGESTED READINGS

Of the biographies of Wordsworth, Stephen Gill's recent *William Wordsworth: A Life* (1990) offers a very readable and comprehensive approach to the life and the poetry. Among the general critical works, Geoffrey Hartman's classic *Wordsworth's Poetry 1787–1814* (1964) still offers the best overall introduction, and a new collection of essays edited by Kenneth R. Johnston and Gene W. Ruoff, *The Age of William Wordsworth: Critical Essays on the Romantic Tradition* (1987), provides a good selection of recent criticism. Two books that have generated important discussion about Wordsworth's poetry recently are Marjorie Levinson's *Wordsworth's Great Period Poems* (1986) and Alan Liu's *Wordsworth: The Sense of History* (1989). For books specifically addressing *Lyrical Ballads* and *The Prelude,* see Stephen Maxfield Parrish's *The Art of the Lyrical Ballads* (1973), Mary Jacobus's *Tradition and Experiment in the "Lyrical Ballads" 1798* (1976), Herbert Lindenberger's *On Wordsworth's "Prelude"* (1963), and Richard J. Onorato's *The Character of the Poet: Wordsworth in "The Prelude"* (1971).

Lines Composed a Few Miles above Tintern Abbey[1]

Five years have past; five summers, with the length
Of five long winters! and again I hear
These waters,[2] rolling from their mountain-springs
With a soft inland murmur.—Once again
Do I behold these steep and lofty cliffs,
That on a wild secluded scene impress
Thoughts of more deep seclusion; and connect
The landscape with the quiet of the sky.
The day is come when I again repose
Here, under this dark sycamore, and view   10
These plots of cottage-ground, these orchard-tufts,
Which at this season, with their unripe fruits,
Are clad in one green hue, and lose themselves

---

[1]Tintern Abbey was then, as it is now, a ruined monastery in Monmouthshire.
[2]The Wye, a river that runs through Wales and western England.

'Mid groves and copses. Once again I see
These hedge-rows, hardly hedge-rows, little lines
Of sportive wood run wild: these pastoral farms,
Green to the very door; and wreaths of smoke
Sent up, in silence, from among the trees!
With some uncertain notice, as might seem
Of vagrant dwellers in the houseless woods,   20
Or of some Hermit's cave, where by his fire
The Hermit sits alone.
                These beauteous forms,
Through a long absence, have not been to me
As is a landscape to a blind man's eye:
But oft, in lonely rooms, and 'mid the din
Of towns and cities, I have owed to them
In hours of weariness, sensations sweet,
Felt in the blood, and felt along the heart;
And passing even into my purer mind,
With tranquil restoration:—feelings too   30
Of unremembered pleasure: such, perhaps,
As have no slight or trivial influence
On that best portion of a good man's life,
His little, nameless, unremembered, acts
Of kindness and of love. Nor less, I trust,
To them I may have owed another gift,
Of aspect more sublime; that blessed mood,
In which the burden of the mystery,
In which the heavy and the weary weight
Of all this unintelligible world,   40
Is lightened:—that serene and blessed mood,
In which the affections gently lead us on,—
Until, the breath of this corporeal frame
And even the motion of our human blood
Almost suspended, we are laid asleep
In body, and become a living soul:
While with an eye made quiet by the power
Of harmony, and the deep power of joy,
We see into the life of things.
                    If this
Be but a vain belief, yet, oh! how oft—   50
In darkness and amid the many shapes
Of joyless daylight; when the fretful stir
Unprofitable, and the fever of the world,
Have hung upon the beatings of my heart—
How oft, in spirit, have I turned to thee,
O sylvan Wye! thou wanderer through the woods,
How often has my spirit turned to thee!

    And now, with gleams of half-extinguished thought,
With many recognitions dim and faint,
And somewhat of a sad perplexity,   60
The picture of the mind revives again:

While here I stand, not only with the sense
Of present pleasure, but with pleasing thoughts
That in this moment there is life and food
For future years. And so I dare to hope,
Though changed, no doubt, from what I was when first
I came among these hills; when like a roe
I bounded o'er the mountains, by the sides
Of the deep rivers, and the lonely streams,
Wherever nature led: more like a man   70
Flying from something that he dreads, than one
Who sought the thing he loved. For nature then
(The coarser pleasures of my boyish days,
And their glad animal movements all gone by)
To me was all in all.—I cannot paint
What then I was. The sounding cataract
Haunted me like a passion: the tall rock,
The mountain, and the deep and gloomy wood,
Their colours and their forms, were then to me
An appetite; a feeling and a love,   80
That had no need of a remoter charm,
By thought supplied, nor any interest
Unborrowed from the eye.—That time is past,
And all its aching joys are now no more,
And all its dizzy raptures. Not for this
Faint I, nor mourn nor murmur; other gifts
Have followed; for such loss, I would believe,
Abundant recompense. For I have learned
To look on nature, not as in the hour
Of thoughtless youth; but hearing oftentimes   90
The still, sad music of humanity,
Nor harsh nor grating, though of ample power
To chasten and subdue. And I have felt
A presence that disturbs me with the joy
Of elevated thoughts; a sense sublime
Of something far more deeply interfused,
Whose dwelling is the light of setting suns,
And the round ocean and the living air,
And the blue sky, and in the mind of man:
A motion and a spirit, that impels   100
All thinking things, all objects of all thought,
And rolls through all things. Therefore am I still
A lover of the meadows and the woods,
And mountains; and of all that we behold
From this green earth; of all the mighty world
Of eye, and ear,—both what they half create,
And what perceive; well pleased to recognize
In nature and the language of the sense,
The anchor of my purest thoughts, the nurse,
The guide, the guardian of my heart, and soul   110
Of all my moral being.
                        Nor perchance,
If I were not thus taught, should I the more

Suffer my genial[3] spirits to decay:
For thou art with me here upon the banks
Of this fair river; thou my dearest Friend,[4]
My dear, dear Friend; and in thy voice I catch
The language of my former heart, and read
My former pleasures in the shooting lights
Of thy wild eyes. Oh! yet a little while
May I behold in thee what I was once,   120
My dear, dear Sister! and this prayer I make,
Knowing that Nature never did betray
The heart that loved her; 'tis her privilege,
Through all the years of this our life, to lead
From joy to joy: for she can so inform
The mind that is within us, so impress
With quietness and beauty, and so feed
With lofty thoughts, that neither evil tongues,
Rash judgements, nor the sneers of selfish men,
Nor greetings where no kindness is, nor all   130
The dreary intercourse of daily life,
Shall e'er prevail against us, or disturb
Our cheerful faith, that all which we behold
Is full of blessings. Therefore let the moon
Shine on thee in thy solitary walk;
And let the misty mountain-winds be free
To blow against thee: and, in after years,
When these wild ecstasies shall be matured
Into a sober pleasure; when thy mind
Shall be a mansion for all lovely forms,   140
Thy memory be as a dwelling-place
For all sweet sounds and harmonies; oh! then,
If solitude, or fear, or pain, or grief,
Should be thy portion, with what healing thoughts
Of tender joy wilt thou remember me,
And these my exhortations! Nor, perchance—
If I should be where I no more can hear
Thy voice, nor catch from thy wild eyes these gleams
Of past existence—wilt thou then forget
That on the banks of this delightful stream   150
We stood together; and that I, so long
A worshipper of Nature, hither came
Unwearied in that service: rather say
With warmer love—oh! with far deeper zeal
Of holier love. Nor wilt thou then forget,
That after many wanderings, many years
Of absence, these steep woods and lofty cliffs,
And this green pastoral landscape, were to me
More dear, both for themselves and for thy sake!

---

[3] Creative and generative of both imaginative works and social feeling.
[4] Dorothy Wordsworth, the poet's sister.

Ode: Intimations of Immortality

The Child is Father of the Man;
And I could wish my days to be
Bound each to each by natural piety.[1]

1

There was a time when meadow, grove, and stream,
The earth, and every common sight,
    To me did seem
    Apparelled in celestial light,
The glory and the freshness of a dream.
It is not now as it hath been of yore;—
    Turn wheresoe'er I may,
      By night or day,
The things which I have seen I now can see no more.

2

    The Rainbow comes and goes,   10
    And lovely is the Rose;
    The Moon doth with delight
Look round her when the heavens are bare;
    Waters on a starry night
    Are beautiful and fair;
  The sunshine is a glorious birth;
  But yet I know, where'er I go,
That there hath past away a glory from the earth.

3

Now, while the birds thus sing a joyous song,
    And while the young lambs bound   20
    As to the tabor's sound,
To me alone there came a thought of grief:
A timely utterance gave that thought relief,
    And I again am strong:
The cataracts blow their trumpets from the steep;
No more shall grief of mine the season wrong;
I hear the Echoes through the mountains throng,
The Winds come to me from the fields of sleep,
    And all the earth is gay;
      Land and sea   30

---

[1] These are the final lines from an earlier poem, "My Heart Leaps Up."

Give themselves up to jollity,
　　And with the heart of May
Doth every Beast keep holiday;—
　　Thou Child of Joy,
Shout round me, let me hear thy shouts, thou happy Shepherd-boy!

4

Ye blessèd Creatures, I have heard the call
　　Ye to each other make; I see
The heavens laugh with you in your jubilee;
　　My heart is at your festival,
　　My head hath its coronal,   40
The fulness of your bliss, I feel—I feel it all.
　　Oh evil day! if I were sullen
　　While Earth herself is adorning,
　　　This sweet May-morning,
　　And the Children are culling
　　　On every side,
　　In a thousand valleys far and wide,
　　Fresh flowers; while the sun shines warm,
And the Babe leaps up on his Mother's arm:—
　　I hear, I hear, with joy I hear!   50
　　—But there's a Tree, of many, one,
A single Field which I have looked upon,
Both of them speak of something that is gone:
　　The Pansy at my feet
　　Doth the same tale repeat:
Whither is fled the visionary gleam?
Where is it now, the glory and the dream?

5

Our birth is but a sleep and a forgetting:
The Soul that rises with us, our life's Star,
　　Hath had elsewhere its setting,   60
　　And cometh from afar:
　　Not in entire forgetfulness,
　　And not in utter nakedness,
But trailing clouds of glory do we come
　　From God, who is our home:
Heaven lies about us in our infancy!
Shades of the prison-house begin to close
　　Upon the growing Boy,
　　　But He
Beholds the light, and whence it flows,   70
　　He sees it in his joy;
The Youth, who daily farther from the east
　　Must travel, still is Nature's Priest,
　　And by the vision splendid

Is on his way attended;
At length the Man perceives it die away,
And fade into the light of common day.

6

Earth fills her lap with pleasures of her own;
Yearnings she hath in her own natural kind,
And, even with something of a Mother's mind,   80
    And no unworthy aim,
    The homely Nurse doth all she can
To make her Foster-child, her Inmate Man,
    Forget the glories he hath known,
And that imperial palace whence he came.

7

Behold the Child among his new-born blisses,
A six years' Darling of a pigmy size!
See, where 'mid work of his own hand he lies,
Fretted by sallies of his mother's kisses,
With light upon him from his father's eyes!   90
See, at his feet, some little plan or chart,
Some fragment from his dream of human life,
Shaped by himself with newly-learnèd art;
    A wedding or a festival,
    A mourning or a funeral;
        And this hath now his heart,
    And unto this he frames his song:
        Then will he fit his tongue
To dialogues of business, love, or strife;
    But it will not be long   100
    Ere this be thrown aside,
    And with new joy and pride
The little Actor cons another part;
Filling from time to time his 'humorous stage'[2]
With all the Persons, down to palsied Age,
That Life brings with her in her equipage;
    As if his whole vocation
    Were endless imitation.

8

Thou, whose exterior semblance doth belie
    Thy Soul's immensity;
Thou best Philosopher, who yet dost keep   110
Thy heritage, thou Eye among the blind,

─────────────
[2]From a sonnet dedicated to Fulke Greville in Elizabethan poet Samuel Daniel's *Musophilus* (1599).

That, deaf and silent, read'st the eternal deep,
Haunted for ever by the eternal mind,—
    Mighty Prophet! Seer blest!
    On whom those truths do rest,
Which we are toiling all our lives to find,
In darkness lost, the darkness of the grave;
Thou, over whom thy Immortality
Broods like the Day, a Master o'er a Slave,   120
A Presence which is not to be put by;
Thou little Child, yet glorious in the might
Of heaven-born freedom on thy being's height,
Why with such earnest pains dost thou provoke
The years to bring the inevitable yoke,
Thus blindly with thy blessedness at strife?
Full soon thy Soul shall have her earthly freight,
And custom lie upon thee with a weight,
Heavy as frost, and deep almost as life!

9

    O joy! that in our embers   130
    Is something that doth live,
    That nature yet remembers
    What was so fugitive!
The thought of our past years in me doth breed
Perpetual benediction: not indeed
For that which is most worthy to be blest;
Delight and liberty, the simple creed
Of Childhood, whether busy or at rest,
With new-fledged hope still fluttering in his breast:—
    Not for these I raise   140
    The song of thanks and praise;
  But for those obstinate questionings
  Of sense and outward things,
  Fallings from us, vanishings;
  Blank misgivings of a Creature
Moving about in worlds not realized,
High instincts before which our mortal Nature
Did tremble like a guilty Thing surprised:
    But for those first affections,
    Those shadowy recollections,   150
  Which, be they what they may,
Are yet the fountain light of all our day,
Are yet a master light of all our seeing;
  Uphold us, cherish, and have power to make
Our noisy years seem moments in the being
Of the eternal Silence: truths that wake,
    To perish never;
Which neither listlessness, nor mad endeavour,
    Nor Man nor Boy,
Nor all that is at enmity with joy,   160
Can utterly abolish or destroy!

Hence in a season of calm weather
    Though inland far we be,
Our Souls have sight of that immortal sea
    Which brought us hither,
    Can in a moment travel thither,
And see the Children sport upon the shore,
And hear the mighty waters rolling evermore.

10

Then sing, ye Birds, sing, sing a joyous song!
    And let the young Lambs bound
    As to the tabor's sound!   170
We in thought will join your throng,
    Ye that pipe and ye that play,
    Ye that through your hearts today
    Feel the gladness of the May!
What though the radiance which was once so bright
Be now for ever taken from my sight,
    Though nothing can bring back the hour
Of splendour in the grass, of glory in the flower;
    We will grieve not, rather find   180
    Strength in what remains behind;
    In the primal sympathy
    Which having been must ever be;
    In the soothing thoughts that spring
    Out of human suffering;
    In the faith that looks through death,
In years that bring the philosophic mind.

11

And O, ye Fountains, Meadows, Hills, and Groves,
Forebode not any severing of our loves!
Yet in my heart of hearts I feel your might;   190
I only have relinquished one delight
To live beneath your more habitual sway.
I love the Brooks which down their channels fret,
Even more than when I tripped lightly as they;
The innocent brightness of a new-born Day
        Is lovely yet;
The Clouds that gather round the setting sun
Do take a sober colouring from an eye
That hath kept watch o'er man's mortality;
Another race hath been, and other palms are won.   200
Thanks to the human heart by which we live,
Thanks to its tenderness, its joys, and fears,
To me the meanest flower that blows can give
Thoughts that do often lie too deep for tears.

The Prelude (1805)

FROM

Book First

Fair seed-time had my soul, and I grew up
Fostered alike by beauty and by fear,
Much favored in my birthplace, and no less
In that beloved vale to which erelong
I was transplanted. Well I call to mind—
'Twas at an early age, ere I had seen   310
Nine summers—when upon the mountain slope
The frost and breath of frosty wind had snapped
The last autumnal crocus, 'twas my joy
To wander half the night among the cliffs
And the smooth hollows where the woodcocks ran
Along the open turf. In thought and wish
That time, my shoulder all with springes[1] hung,
I was a fell destroyer. On the heights
Scudding away from snare to snare, I plied
My anxious visitation, hurrying on,   320
Still hurrying, hurrying onward. Moon and stars
Were shining o'er my head; I was alone,
And seemed to be a trouble to the peace
That was among them. Sometimes it befel
In these night-wanderings, that a strong desire
O'erpowered my better reason, and the bird
Which was the captive of another's toils
Became my prey; and when the deed was done
I heard among the solitary hills
Low breathings coming after me, and sounds   330
Of undistinguishable motion, steps
Almost as silent as the turf they trod.

Nor less in springtime, when on southern banks
The shining sun had from her knot of leaves
Decoyed the primrose flower, and when the vales
And woods were warm, was I a plunderer then
In the high places, on the lonesome peaks,
Where'er among the mountains and the winds
The mother-bird had built her lodge. Though mean
My object and inglorious, yet the end   340
Was not ignoble. Oh, when I have hung
Above the raven's nest, by knots of grass
And half-inch fissures in the slippery rock
But ill sustained, and almost, as it seemed,
Suspended by the blast which blew amain,
Shouldering the naked crag, oh, at that time

---

[1] Traps.

While on the perilous ridge I hung alone,
With what strange utterance did the loud dry wind
Blow through my ears; the sky seemed not a sky
Of earth, and with what motion moved the clouds!   350

The mind of man is framed even like the breath
And harmony of music. There is a dark
Invisible workmanship that reconciles
Discordant elements, and makes them move
In one society. Ah me, that all
The terrors, all the early miseries,
Regrets, vexations, lassitudes, that all
The thoughts and feelings which have been infused
Into my mind, should ever have made up
The calm existence that is mine when I   360
Am worthy of myself. Praise to the end,
Thanks likewise for the means! But I believe
That Nature, oftentimes, when she would frame
A favored being, from his earliest dawn
Of infancy doth open out the clouds
As at the touch of lightning, seeking him
With gentlest visitation; not the less,
Though haply aiming at the self-same end,
Does it delight her sometimes to employ
Severer interventions, ministry   370
More palpable—and so she dealt with me.

One evening—surely I was led by her—
I went alone into a shepherd's boat,
A skiff that to a willow-tree was tied
Within a rocky cave, its usual home.
'Twas by the shores of Patterdale, a vale
Wherein I was a stranger, thither come
A schoolboy traveller at the holidays.
Forth rambled from the village inn alone,
No sooner had I sight of this small skiff,   380
Discovered thus by unexpected chance,
Than I unloosed her tether and embarked.
The moon was up, the lake was shining clear
Among the hoary mountains; from the shore
I pushed, and struck the oars, and struck again
In cadence, and my little boat moved on
Even like a man who moves with stately step
Though bent on speed. It was an act of stealth
And troubled pleasure. Nor without the voice
Of mountain-echoes did my boat move on,   390
Leaving behind her still on either side
Small circles glittering idly in the moon,
Until they melted all into one track
Of sparkling light. A rocky steep uprose
Above the cavern of the willow-tree,

And now, as suited one who proudly rowed
With his best skill, I fixed a steady view
Upon the top of that same craggy ridge,
The bound of the horizon—for behind
Was nothing but the stars and the grey sky.   400
She was an elfin pinnace;[2] lustily
I dipped my oars into the silent lake,
And as I rose upon the stroke my boat
Went heaving through the water like a swan—
When from behind that craggy steep, till then
The bound of the horizon, a huge cliff,
As if with voluntary power instinct,
Upreared its head. I struck, and struck again,
And, growing still in stature, the huge cliff
Rose up between me and the stars, and still   410
With measured motion, like a living thing
Strode after me. With trembling hands I turned
And through the silent water stole my way
Back to the cavern of the willow-tree.
There, in her mooring-place, I left my bark
And through the meadows homeward went with grave
And serious thoughts; and after I had seen
That spectacle, for many days my brain
Worked with a dim and undetermined sense
Of unknown modes of being. In my thoughts   420
There was a darkness—call it solitude
Or blank desertion—no familiar shapes
Of hourly objects, images of trees,
Of sea or sky, no colours of green fields,
But huge and mighty forms that do not live
Like living men moved slowly through my mind
By day, and were the trouble of my dreams.

    Wisdom and spirit of the universe,
Thou soul that art the eternity of thought,
That giv'st to forms and images a breath   430
And everlasting motion—not in vain,
By day or star-light, thus from my first dawn
Of childhood didst thou intertwine for me
The passions that build up our human soul,
Not with the mean and vulgar works of man,
But with high objects, with enduring things,
With life and Nature, purifying thus
The elements of feeling and of thought,
And sanctifying by such discipline
Both pain and fear, until we recognise   440
A grandeur in the beatings of the heart. . . .

---

[2] A small boat.

SAMUEL TAYLOR COLERIDGE
[1772–1834]

Coleridge was one of the most lively and fecund minds of his generation. Like Goethe and Goethe's Faust, he took all of human knowledge for his inquiry, including the classics, history, philosophy, music, art, theology, and literary criticism. Providing the intellectual bridge between German romanticism and the England of his day, Coleridge incorporated key ideas concerning the godlike role of the artist, the centrality of the creative imagination, the organic structure of reality, and the mythic connection between consciousness and nature. His search for a comprehensive system that would unite the individual with nature began with a cognitive principle: He wanted to establish that the mind does not simply "collect" sensations and reflect upon them (the mechanism of "associationism"), but also actively, creatively, shapes perception. Although we do not entirely create our realities ("idealism"), Coleridge believed, we certainly qualify and formulate our sensations. This kind of mental activity was integral to Coleridge's conviction that art, in its broadest function, "is the mediatress between, and reconciler of, nature and man."

LIFE

Born October 21, 1772, Samuel Taylor Coleridge was the son of a clergyman and schoolmaster who died when Coleridge was nine. Shortly thereafter he was sent to Christ's Hospital in London, where he received a classical education and dabbled in metaphysics, theology, and social satire. After a year at Jesus College, Cambridge, he enlisted in the Light Dragoons under the name of Silas Tompkin Comberbach, but he was ill-suited for military life and returned to Cambridge. In 1794 he met Robert Southey, and together they made plans for a utopian society in America, which they called a pantisocracy. Coleridge agreed to marry Sarah Fricker as part of his scheme with Southey. When the pantisocracy plans fell apart, Coleridge nevertheless married Sarah in 1795, after having left Cambridge without a degree. Following the birth of their first son, David Hartley—named after Coleridge's favorite philosopher at the time—they moved to a cottage at Nether Stowey.

In 1797 a close friendship arose between Coleridge and William Wordsworth that significantly changed both their personal and professional lives. Coleridge's admiration for Wordsworth was initially unqualified: "Wordsworth is a very great man, the only man to whom *at all times* and *in all modes of excellence* I feel myself inferior." Their long conversations and periods of creativity led to the publication of *Lyrical Ballads* (1798), a book that changed the course of English literature and ushered in an era of imaginative genius that would later be called *romanticism*. In that same year, an annuity of 150 pounds from Josiah and Tom Wedgwood—the family famous for pottery—allowed Coleridge to concentrate on his writing. In September 1798, Wordsworth and his sister Dorothy journeyed with Coleridge to Germany, where his study of German philosophy, especially of Kant, profoundly influenced his ideas about nature and the imagination.

Laudanum, a tincture of opium, was prescribed for Coleridge's poor health, for painful attacks of rheumatism in particular. During the winter of 1800–1801 heavy doses of opium persuaded Coleridge of his debilitating addiction. This recognition contributed to periods of depression and Coleridge's own uncertainty about his worth as a person, writer, and thinker. A journey to Malta and other parts of Europe in 1804, designed as a rest cure for mind and body, ended up a disaster. He returned to England even more addicted to opium, estranged from his wife, and plagued by financial problems.

In retrospect, Coleridge's friends seemed to think he did not live up to his potential as a poet or critic; Coleridge's own doubts and regrets supported this conclusion. Undoubtedly his poor mental and physical health furthered his tendency to leave written works unfinished. Nevertheless, the quantity and variety of his writing, including notebooks and marginalia, is very impressive.

Because of financial need, in 1808 he began a series of public lectures on poetry and drama, which he would continue over the next few years. His lectures on Shakespeare are particularly important for their insight into Shakespeare's characters. Coleridge also wrote for newspapers. His periodical *The Friend* continued in publication for over a year. A play, *Remorse,* was successfully produced in 1813. Finally in 1816, relief came to Coleridge's life in the person of James Gillman, a Highgate doctor, who took Coleridge into his home and looked after his health. There he spent the last eighteen years of his life, actively writing plays and essays devoted to religious and social subjects. His most important piece of prose, *Biographia Literaria,* a mixture of autobiography, criticism, and philosophy, was published in 1817. Even his conversations, which were known for their brilliance and charm, were recorded and published.

WORK

Coleridge wrote his best poems, and in fact, most of his poems—nearly four-fifths of his total poetic output—during the period 1798–1802. Coleridge is most famous for three poems of the supernatural: "The Rime of the Ancient Mariner," "Kubla Khan," and "Christabel," the last two of which are unfinished. These poems reveal an interest in the mysterious, supernatural world of the Gothic. His love for exotic travelogues shows up in both "The Ancient Mariner" and "Kubla Khan." The original edition of *Lyrical Ballads* began with Coleridge's "The Rime of the Ancient Mariner" and concluded with Wordsworth's "Tintern Abbey." The idea of linking "lyrical" with "ballad" indicates the two poets' interest in capturing elemental experience in a poem that combined popular story with polite poetic forms. "The Rime of the Ancient Mariner" is the only imitation of a genuine folk ballad in the collection. In *Biographia Literaria,* Coleridge describes their plan for the anthology: Wordsworth was to write poems that would "give the charm of novelty to things of every day," and direct the mind "to the loveliness and the wonders of the world before us." Coleridge would choose "persons and characters supernatural" for poems that would contain "a semblance of truth sufficient to procure for these shadows of imagination that willing suspension of disbelief for the moment, which constitutes poetic faith."

Some of the details in "The Ancient Mariner" were gleaned from accounts of voyages around Cape Horn and into the Pacific, so that Coleridge's striking descriptions of phosphorescence at night and other travel details ring true. The poem hinges on a transformation of consciousness through the agency of a spirit world. The mariner, without attention or deliberate thought, kills an albatross, one of God's creatures. He then must learn the consequences of this act while developing a different way of perceiving the natural world. The mariner draws upon the tradition of wanderer: Ahasuerus the Wandering Jew and the Flying Dutchman—the man who, after committing a sin, must live out his penance by wandering the earth and telling his story to others, presumably to save them from a similar fate.

It is not far-fetched to see in Coleridge's propensity for wandering and solitude something of the ancient mariner's solitary life-style. In fact, the major images of the poem—sea, calm, wind, murder, bird, sailing, snakes—have equivalents to inner states of mind or psyche, so that the poem can be read as both a literal voyage and an allegory of the mind or soul.

When Mrs. Anna Barbauld, a writer and critic, accused the poem of having no moral, Coleridge replied that he thought the poem had too much of a moral and concluded: "It ought to have had no more moral than the Arabian Nights' tale of the merchant's sitting down to eat dates by the side of a well, and throwing the shells aside, and lo! a genie starts up, and says he *must* kill the aforesaid merchant, *because* one of the date shells had, it seems, put out the eye of the genie's son" (*Table Talk*).

Coleridge claimed that "Kubla Khan," named after the grandson of Genghis Khan, was composed in an opium reverie that was interrupted by a visitor, an explanation that has caused a great deal of controversy among commentators. The first two-thirds of the poem has elements that suggest stream-of-consciousness writing: an exotic location, dreamlike imagery with sexual overtones, an elusive situation, and lush sound patterns. The symbolism of the "deep romantic chasm" is not only mysterious and erotic, but connotes danger with the "Ancestral voices prophesying war!" On one level, the poem is about the unconscious, sacred origin of the creative process, which erupts like a fountain and returns to the earth, and about the precocious, dangerous poet with "flashing eyes" and "floating hair." Undoubtedly, there are numerous other meanings as well.

A concern with nature is evident in many of Coleridge's poems, but a higher priority is given to the inner life, the nature of introspection, the formative importance of the imagination, and the sinuous motion of moods and dreams—much of which we would now call psychology. Like other romantics, such as E.T.A. Hoffmann and Novalis, Coleridge explored the shadowy valleys of faith and despair, lofty creation, and cataclysmic destruction.

SUGGESTED READINGS

E. K. Chambers's *Samuel Taylor Coleridge* (1938) is the standard biography; Nicholas Roe's *Wordsworth and Coleridge: The Radical Years* (1988) provides a more specialized biography. Walter Jackson Bate's *Coleridge* (1968) has a broad commentary on Coleridge and his work. I. A. Richards's *Coleridge on Imagination* (1934) focuses on Coleridge's critical distinctions involving imagination and myth. J. Beer's *Coleridge's Poetic Intelligence* (1975) and Humphrey House's *Coleridge* (1953) explore individual poems. For the sources of "Kubla Khan" and "The Rime of the Ancient Mariner," see John Livingston Lowes, *The Road to Xanadu* (1927).

Kubla Khan

In Xanadu did Kubla Khan[1]
A stately pleasure-dome decree:
Where Alph,[2] the sacred river, ran
Through caverns measureless to man
    Down to a sunless sea.

---

[1]Mongol emperor (1215?–1294).
[2]Perhaps the Alpheus River, but certainly a primordial river.

So twice five miles of fertile ground
With walls and towers were girdled round:
And here were gardens bright with sinuous rills,
Where blossomed many an incense-bearing tree;
And here were forests ancient as the hills,   10
Enfolding sunny spots of greenery.

But oh! that deep romantic chasm which slanted
Down the green hill athwart a cedarn cover!
A savage place! as holy and enchanted
As e'er beneath a waning moon was haunted
By woman wailing for her demon-lover!
And from this chasm, with ceaseless turmoil seething,
As if this earth in fast thick pants were breathing,
A mighty fountain momently was forced;
Amid whose swift half-intermitted burst   20
Huge fragments vaulted like rebounding hail,
Or chaffy grain beneath the thresher's flail:
And 'mid these dancing rocks at once and ever
It flung up momently the sacred river.
Five miles meandering with a mazy motion
Through wood and dale the sacred river ran,
Then reached the caverns measureless to man,
And sank in tumult to a lifeless ocean:
And 'mid this tumult Kubla heard from far
Ancestral voices prophesying war!   30
    The shadow of the dome of pleasure
    Floated midway on the waves;
    Where was heard the mingled measure
    From the fountain and the caves.
It was a miracle of rare device,
A sunny pleasure-dome with caves of ice!
    A damsel with a dulcimer
    In a vision once I saw:
    It was an Abyssinian maid,
    And on her dulcimer she played,
    Singing of Mount Abora.   40
    Could I revive within me,
    Her symphony and song,
    To such a deep delight 'twould win me,
That with music loud and long,
I would build that dome in air,
That sunny dome! those caves of ice!
And all who heard should see them there,
And all should cry, Beware! Beware!
His flashing eyes, his floating hair!   50
Weave a circle round him thrice,
And close your eyes with holy dread,
For he on honey-dew hath fed,
And drunk the milk of Paradise.

The Rime of the Ancient Mariner

IN SEVEN PARTS

Facile credo, plures esse Naturas invisibiles quam visibiles in rerum universitate. Sed horum omnium familiam quis nobis enarrabit? et gradus et cognationes et discrimina et singulorum munera? Quid agunt? quae loca habitant? Harum rerum notitiam semper ambivit ingenium humanum, nunquam attigit. Juvat, interea, non diffiteor, quandoque in animo, tanquam in tabulâ, majoris et melioris mundi imaginem contemplari: ne mens assuefacta hodiernae vitae minutiis se contrahat nimis, et tota subsidat in pusillas cogitationes. Sed veritati interea invigilandum est, modusque servandus, ut certa ab incertis, diem a nocte, distinguamus. —T. BURNET, *Archaeol. Phil.* p. 68.[1]

ARGUMENT

How a Ship having passed the Line was driven by storms to the cold Country towards the South Pole; and how from thence she made her course to the tropical Latitude of the Great Pacific Ocean; and of the strange things that befell; and in what manner the Ancyent Marinere came back to his own Country.

PART 1

It is an ancient Mariner,
And he stoppeth one of three.
"By thy long gray beard and glittering eye,
Now wherefore stopp'st thou me?

An ancient Mariner meeteth three Gallants bidden to a wedding-feast, and detaineth one.

"The Bridegroom's doors are opened wide,
And I am next of kin,
The guests are met, the feast is set:
May'st hear the merry din."

He holds him with his skinny hand;
"There was a ship," quoth he.
"Hold off! unhand me, gray-beard loon!"
Eftsoons[2] his hand dropt he.   10

He holds him with his glittering eye—
The Wedding-Guest stood still,
And listens like a three years' child.
The Mariner hath his will.

The Wedding-Guest is spellbound by the eye of the old seafaring man and constrained to hear his tale.

---

[1]Latin epigraph: "I readily believe that there are more invisible than visible Natures in the universe. But who will explain for us the family of all these beings, and the ranks and relations and distinguishing features and functions of each? What do they do? What places do they inhabit? The human mind has always sought the knowledge of these things, but never attained it. Meanwhile I do not deny that it is helpful sometimes to contemplate in the mind, as on a tablet, the image of a greater and better world, lest the intellect, habituated to the petty things of daily life, narrow itself and sink wholly into trivial thoughts. But at the same time we must be watchful for the truth and keep a sense of proportion, so that we may distinguish the certain from the uncertain, day from night." [Thomas Burnet, 1692]

[2]At once.

The Wedding-Guest sat on a stone:
He cannot choose but hear;
And thus spake on that ancient man,
The bright-eyed Mariner.   20

"The ship was cheered, the harbor cleared,
Merrily did we drop
Below the kirk,[3] below the hill,
Below the light-house top.

"The sun came up upon the left,   *The Mariner tells how the ship*
Out of the sea came he!   *sailed southward with a good*
And he shone bright, and on the right   *wind and fair weather, till it*
Went down into the sea.   *reached the Line.*

"Higher and higher every day,
Till over the mast at noon[4]—"   30
The Wedding-Guest here beat his breast,
For he heard the loud bassoon.

The bride hath paced into the hall,   *The Wedding-Guest heareth*
Red as a rose is she;   *the bridal music; but the*
Nodding their heads before her goes   *Mariner continueth his tale.*
The merry minstrelsy.

The Wedding-Guest he beat his breast,
Yet he cannot choose but hear;
And thus spake on that ancient man,
The bright-eyed Mariner.   40

"And now the Storm-blast came, and he   *The ship driven by a storm*
Was tyrannous and strong: *toward the south pole.*
He struck with his o'ertaking wings,
And chased us south along.

"With sloping masts and dipping prow,
As who pursued with yell and blow
Still treads the shadow of his foe,
And forward bends his head,
The ship drove fast, loud roared the blast,
And southward aye we fled.   50

"And now there came both mist and snow,
And it grew wondrous cold:
And ice, mast-high, came floating by,
As green as emerald.

---

[3]Church.
[4]The sun is straight up at noon at the equator.

"And through the drifts the snowy clifts
Did send a dismal sheen:
Nor shapes of men nor beasts we ken—
The ice was all between.

*The land of ice, and of fearful
sounds where no living thing
was to be seen.*

"The ice was here, the ice was there,
The ice was all around:
It cracked and growled, and roared and howled,
Like noises in a swound!⁵   60

"At length did cross an Albatross,
Through the fog it came;
As if it had been a Christian soul,
We hailed it in God's name.

*Till a great sea-bird called the
Albatross, came through the
snow-fog, and was received
with great joy and hospitality.*

"It ate the food it ne'er had eat,
And round and round it flew.
The ice did split with a thunder-fit;
The helmsman steered us through!   70

"And a good south wind sprung up behind;
The Albatross did follow,
And every day, for food or play,
Came to the mariners' hollo!

*And lo! the Albatross proveth
a bird of good omen, and
followeth the ship as it
returned northward through fog
and floating ice.*

"In mist or cloud, on mast or shroud,
It perched for vespers nine;
Whiles all the night, through fog-smoke white,
Glimmered the white moon-shine."

"God save thee, ancient Mariner!
From the fiends, that plague thee thus!—
Why look'st thou so?"—"With my cross-bow
I shot the Albatross!"

*The ancient Mariner
inhospitably killeth the pious
bird of good omen.*   80

PART 2

"The Sun now rose upon the right:⁶
Out of the sea came he,
Still hid in mist, and on the left
Went down into the sea.

"And the good south wind still blew behind,
But no sweet bird did follow,
Nor any day for food or play
Came to the mariners' hollo!   90

---

⁵Swoon.
⁶Having rounded Cape Horn, the ship heads north with the sunrise on the right side.

"And I had done a hellish thing,
And it would work 'em woe:
For all averred, I had killed the bird
That made the breeze to blow.
Ah, wretch! said they, the bird to slay,
That made the breeze to blow!

"Nor dim nor red, like God's own head,
The glorious Sun uprist:
Then all averred, I had killed the bird
That brought the fog and mist.
Twas right, said they, such birds to slay,
That bring the fog and mist.

"The fair breeze blew, the white foam flew,
The furrow followed free;
We were the first that ever burst
Into that silent sea.

"Down dropt the breeze, the sails dropt down,
Twas sad as sad could be;
And we did speak only to break
The silence of the sea!

"All in a hot and copper sky,
The bloody Sun, at noon,
Right up above the mast did stand,
No bigger than the Moon.

"Day after day, day after day,
We stuck, nor breath nor motion;
As idle as a painted ship
Upon a painted ocean.

"Water, water, everywhere,
And all the boards did shrink;
Water, water, everywhere,
Nor any drop to drink.

"The very deep did rot: O Christ!
That ever this should be!
Yea, slimy things did crawl with legs
Upon the slimy sea.

"About, about, in reel and rout
The death-fires[7] danced at night;
The water, like a witch's oils,
Burnt green, and blue and white.

*His shipmates cry out against
the ancient Mariner, for killing
the bird of good luck.*

*But when the fog cleared off
they justify the same, and thus
make themselves accomplices in
the crime.* 100

*The fair breeze continues; the
ship enters the Pacific Ocean,
and sails northward, even till it
reaches the Line.*

*The ship hath been suddenly
becalmed.* 110

*And the Albatross begins to be
avenged.* 120

*A Spirit had followed them;
one of the invisible inhabitants
of this planet, neither departed
souls nor angels; concerning
whom the learned Jew,
Josephus, and the Platonic
Constantinopolitan, Michael
Psellus, may be consulted.* 130

---

[7]The corposant, or St. Elmo's fire, on the ship's rigging.

"And some in dreams assured were
Of the Spirit that plagued us so;
Nine fathom deep he had followed us
From the land of mist and snow.

They are very numerous, and
there is no climate or element
without one or more.

"And every tongue, through utter drought,
Was withered at the root;
We could not speak, no more than if
We had been choked with soot.

"Ah! well-a-day! what evil looks
Had I from old and young!
Instead of the cross, the Albatross
About my neck was hung.

The shipmates, in their sore
distress, would fain throw   140
the whole guilt on the ancient
Mariner: in sign whereof they
hang the dead sea-bird round
his neck.

PART 3

"There passed a weary time. Each throat
Was parched, and glazed each eye.
A weary time! a weary time!
How glazed each weary eye,
When looking westward, I beheld
A something in the sky.

The ancient Mariner beholdeth
a sign in the element afar off.

"At first it seemed a little speck,
And then it seemed a mist;
It moved and moved, and took at last
A certain shape, I wist.[8]

150

"A speck, a mist, a shape, I wist!
And still it neared and neared:
As if it dodged a water-sprite,
It plunged and tacked and veered.

"With throats unslaked, with black lips baked,
We could nor laugh nor wail;
Through utter drought all dumb we stood!
I bit my arm, I sucked the blood,
And cried, A sail! a sail!

At its nearer approach, it
seemeth him to be a ship; and
at a dear ransom he freeth his
speech from the bonds of thirst.   160

"With throats unslaked, with black lips baked,
Agape they heard me call:
Gramercy![9] they for joy did grin,
And all at once their breath drew in,
As they were drinking all.

A flash of joy;

"See! see! (I cried) she tacks no more!
Hither to work us weal[10]

And horror follows. For can it
be a ship that comes onward

---

[8]Knew.
[9]French *grand-merci,* "great thanks."
[10]Benefit.

Without a breeze, without a tide,
She steadies with upright keel!

without wind or tide?   170

"The western wave was all aflame,
The day was well nigh done!
Almost upon the western wave
Rested the broad bright Sun;
When that strange shape drove suddenly
Betwixt us and the Sun.

"And straight the Sun was flecked with bars,
(Heaven's Mother send us grace!)
As if through a dungeon-grate he peered
With broad and burning face.

*It seemeth him but the
skeleton of a ship.*

                    180

"Alas! (thought I, and my heart beat loud)
How fast she nears and nears!
Are those her sails that glance in the Sun,
Like restless gossameres?[11]

"Are those her ribs through which the Sun
Did peer, as through a grate?
And is that Woman all her crew?
Is that a Death? and are there two?
Is Death that woman's mate?

*And its ribs are seen as bars
on the face of the setting Sun.
The Specter-Woman and her
Deathmate, and no other on
board the skeleton-ship.*

                    190

"Her lips were red, her looks were free,
Her locks were yellow as gold:
Her skin was as white as leprosy,
The Night-mare Life-in-Death was she,
Who thicks man's blood with cold.

Like vessel, like crew!

"The naked hulk alongside came,
And the twain were casting dice;
'The game is done! I've won! I've won!'
Quoth she, and whistles thrice.

*Death and Life-in-Death have
diced for the ship's crew, and
she (the latter) winneth the
ancient Mariner.*

"The Sun's rim dips; the stars rush out:
At one stride comes the dark;
With far-heard whisper, o'er the sea,
Off shot the specter-bark.

*No twilight within the courts
of the Sun.*   200

"We listened and looked sideways up!
Fear at my heart, as at a cup,
My life-blood seemed to sip!
The stars were dim, and thick the night,
The steersman's face by his lamp gleamed white;
From the sails the dew did drip—
Till clomb above the eastern bar

At the rising of the Moon,

---

[11]A film of cobwebs.

The hornéd Moon, with one bright star
Within the nether tip.   210

"One after one, by the star-dogged Moon,   *One after another,*
Too quick for groan or sigh,
Each turned his face with a ghastly pang,
And cursed me with his eye.

"Four times fifty living men,   *His shipmates drop down*
(And I heard nor sigh nor groan)   *dead.*
With heavy thump, a lifeless lump
They dropt down one by one.

"The souls did from their bodies fly—   *But Life-in-Death begins her*   220
They fled to bliss or woe!   *work on the ancient Mariner.*
And every soul, it passed me by
Like the whizz of my cross-bow!"

PART 4

"I fear thee, ancient Mariner!   *The Wedding-Guest feareth*
I fear thy skinny hand!   *that a Spirit is talking to him;*
And thou art long, and lank, and brown,
As is the ribbed sea-sand.

"I fear thee and thy glittering eye,
And thy skinny hand, so brown."—
"Fear not, fear not, thou Wedding-Guest!   *But the ancient Mariner*   230
This body dropt not down.   *assureth him of his bodily life,*
                                                  and proceedeth to relate his
                                                  horrible penance.
"Alone, alone, all, all alone,
Alone on a wide, wide sea!
And never a saint took pity on
My soul in agony.

"The many men, so beautiful!   *He despiseth the creatures of*
And they all dead did lie: *the calm.*
And a thousand thousand slimy things
Lived on; and so did I.

"I looked upon the rotting sea,   *And envieth that they should*   240
And drew my eyes away;   *live, and so many lie dead.*
I looked upon the rotting deck,
And there the dead men lay.

"I looked to heaven, and tried to pray;
But or ever a prayer had gusht,
A wicked whisper came, and made
My heart as dry as dust.

"I closed my lids, and kept them close,
And the balls like pulses beat;
For the sky and the sea, and the sea and the sky   250
Lay like a load on my weary eye,
And the dead were at my feet.

"The cold sweat melted from their limbs,
Nor rot nor reek did they:
The look with which they looked on me
Had never passed away.

"An orphan's curse would drag to hell
A spirit from on high;
But oh! more horrible than that
Is a curse in a dead man's eye!   260
Seven days, seven nights, I saw that curse,
And yet I could not die.

"The moving Moon went up the sky,
And nowhere did abide:
Softly she was going up,
And a star or two beside—

"Her beams bemocked the sultry main,
Like April hoar-frost spread;
But where the ship's huge shadow lay,
The charmèd water burnt alway
A still and awful red.

"Beyond the shadow of the ship,
I watched the water-snakes:
They moved in tracks of shining white,
And when they reared, the elfish light
Fell off in hoary flakes.

"Within the shadow of the ship
I watched their rich attire:
Blue, glossy green, and velvet black,
They coiled and swam; and every track   280
Was a flash of golden fire.

"O happy living things! no tongue
Their beauty might declare:
A spring of love gushed from my heart,
And I blessed them unaware;
Sure my kind saint took pity on me,
And I blessed them unaware.

"The selfsame moment I could pray;
And from my neck so free
The Albatross fell off, and sank   290
Like lead into the sea."

*But the curse liveth for him in
the eye of the dead men.*

*In his loneliness and fixedness
he yearneth towards the
journeying Moon, and the
stars that still sojourn, yet still
move onward; and everywhere
the blue sky belongs to them,
and is their appointed rest, and
their native country and their
own natural homes, which they
enter unannounced, as lords
that are certainly expected, and
yet there is a silent joy at their
arrival.*   270

*By the light of the Moon he
beholdeth God's creatures of
the great calm.*

*Their beauty and their
happiness.*

He blesseth them in his heart.

The spell begins to break.

PART 5

"Oh sleep! it is a gentle thing,
Beloved from pole to pole!
To Mary Queen the praise be given!
She sent the gentle sleep from Heaven,
That slid into my soul.

"The silly[12] buckets on the deck,
That had so long remained,
I dreamt that they were filled with dew;
And when I awoke, it rained.

*By grace of the holy Mother,
the ancient Mariner is refreshed
with rain.*

300

"My lips were wet, my throat was cold,
My garments all were dank;
Sure I had drunken in my dreams,
And still my body drank.

"I moved, and could not feel my limbs:
I was so light—almost
I thought that I had died in sleep,
And was a blessed ghost.

"And soon I heard a roaring wind:
It did not come anear;
But with its sound it shook the sails,
That were so thin and sere.

*He heareth sounds and seeth
strange sights and commotions
in the sky and the elements.*

310

"The upper air burst into life!
And a hundred fire-flags sheen,[13]
To and fro they were hurried about!
And to and fro, and in and out,
The wan stars danced between.

"And the coming wind did roar more loud,
And the sails did sigh like sedge;
And the rain poured down from one black cloud;
The Moon was at its edge.

320

"The thick black cloud was cleft, and still
The Moon was at its side:
Like waters shot from some high crag,
The lightning fell with never a jag,
A river steep and wide.

"The loud wind never reached the ship,
Yet now the ship moved on!

*The bodies of the ship's crew
are inspired, and the ship
moves on;*

---

[12]Unused.
[13]Shone; these are the Southern Lights.

Beneath the lightning and the Moon
The dead men gave a groan.
330

"They groaned, they stirred, they all uprose,
Nor spake, nor moved their eyes;
It had been strange, even in a dream,
To have seen those dead men rise.

"The helmsman steered, the ship moved on;
Yet never a breeze up blew;
The mariners all 'gan work the ropes,
Where they were wont do do;
They raised their limbs like lifeless tools—
We were a ghastly crew.
340

"The body of my brother's son
Stood by me, knee to knee:
The body and I pulled at one rope,
But he said nought to me."

"I fear thee, ancient Mariner!"
"Be calm, thou Wedding-Guest!
'Twas not those souls that fled in pain,
Which to their corses[14] came again,
But a troop of spirits blest:

*But not by the souls of the
men, nor by demons of earth
or middle air, but by a blessed
troop of angelic spirits, sent
down by the invocation of the
guardian saint.*
350

"For when it dawned—they dropped their arms,
And clustered round the mast;
Sweet sounds rose slowly through their mouths,
And from their bodies passed.

"Around, around, flew each sweet sound,
Then darted to the Sun;
Slowly the sounds came back again,
Now mixed, now one by one.

"Sometimes a-dropping from the sky
I heard the skylark sing;
Sometimes all little birds that are,
How they seemed to fill the sea and air
With their sweet jargoning![15]
360

"And now 'twas like all instruments,
Now like a lonely flute;
And now it is an angel's song,
That makes the heavens be mute.

"It ceased; yet still the sails made on
A pleasant noise till noon,

---

[14] Corpses.   [15] Warbling.

A noise like of a hidden brook
In the leafy month of June,
That to the sleeping woods all night
Singeth a quiet tune.

"Till noon we quietly sailed on,
Yet never a breeze did breathe:
Slowly and smoothly went the ship,
Moved onward from beneath.

"Under the keel nine fathom deep,
From the land of mist and snow,
The Spirit slid: and it was he
That made the ship to go.
The sails at noon left off their tune,
And the ship stood still also.

The lonesome Spirit from the south pole carries on the ship as far as the Line, in obedience to the angelic troop, but still requireth vengeance.

"The Sun, right up above the mast,
Had fixed her to the ocean:
But in a minute she 'gan stir,
With a short uneasy motion—
Backwards and forwards half her length
With a short uneasy motion.

"Then like a pawing horse let go,
She made a sudden bound:
It flung the blood into my head,
And I fell down in a swound.

"How long in that same fit I lay,
I have not[16] to declare;
But ere my living life returned,
I heard, and in my soul discerned,
Two voices in the air.

The Polar Spirit's fellow demons, the invisible inhabitants of the element, take part in his wrong; and two of them relate, one to the other that penance long and heavy for the ancient Mariner hath been accorded to the Polar Spirit, who returneth southward.

"'Is it he?' quoth one, 'Is this the man?
By Him who died on cross,
With his cruel bow he laid full low
The harmless Albatross.

"'The Spirit who bideth by himself
In the land of mist and snow,
He loved the bird that loved the man
Who shot him with his bow.'

"The other was a softer voice,
As soft as honey-dew:
Quoth he, 'The man hath penance done,
And penance more will do.'"

370

380

390

400

---

[16]That is, "I do not know."

PART 6

FIRST VOICE

" 'But tell me, tell me! speak again,
Thy soft response renewing—
What makes that ship drive on so fast?
What is the ocean doing?'

410

SECOND VOICE

" 'Still as a slave before his lord,
The ocean hath no blast;
His great bright eye most silently
Up to the Moon is cast—

" 'If he may know which way to go;
For she guides him smooth or grim.
See, brother, see! how graciously
She looketh down on him.'

420

FIRST VOICE

" 'But why drives on that ship so fast,
Without or wave or wind?'

*The Mariner hath been cast
into a trance; for the angelic
power causeth the vessel to
drive northward faster than
human life could endure.*

SECOND VOICE

" 'The air is cut away before,
And closes from behind.'
" 'Fly, brother, fly! more high, more high!
Or we shall be belated:
For slow and slow that ship will go,
When the Mariner's trance is abated.'

"I woke, and we were sailing on
As in a gentle weather:
'Twas night, calm night, the moon was high;
The dead men stood together.

*The supernatural motion is
retarded; the Mariner awakes,
and his penance begins anew.*

430

"All stood together on the deck,
For a charnel-dungeon fitter:
All fixed on me their stony eyes,
That in the Moon did glitter.

"The pang, the curse, with which they died,
Had never passed away:
I could not draw my eyes from theirs,
Nor turn them up to pray.

440

"And now this spell was snapt: once more
I viewed the ocean green,
And looked far forth, yet little saw
Of what had else been seen—

The curse is finally expiated.

"Like one, that on a lonesome road
Doth walk in fear and dread,
And having once turned round, walks on,
And turns no more his head;
Because he knows, a frightful fiend   450
Doth close behind him tread.

"But soon there breathed a wind on me,
Nor sound nor motion made:
Its path was not upon the sea,
In ripple or in shade.

"It raised my hair, it fanned my cheek
Like a meadow-gale of spring—
It mingled strangely with my fears,
Yet it felt like a welcoming.

"Swiftly, swiftly flew the ship,
Yet she sailed softly too: 460
Sweetly, sweetly blew the breeze—
On me alone it blew.

"Oh! dream of joy! is this indeed   *And the ancient Mariner*
The light-house top I see?   *beholdeth his native country.*
Is this the hill? is this the kirk?
Is this mine own countree?

"We drifted o'er the harbor-bar,
And I with sobs did pray—
O let me be awake, my God!   470
Or let me sleep alway.

"The harbor-bay was clear as glass,
So smoothly it was strewn!
And on the bay the moonlight lay,
And the shadow of the Moon.

"The rock shone bright, the kirk no less,
That stands above the rock:
The moonlight steeped in silentness
The steady weathercock.

"And the bay was white with silent light   480
Till, rising from the same,
Full many shapes, that shadows were,   *The angelic spirits leave the*
In crimson colors came.   *dead bodies,*

"A little distance from the prow
Those crimson shadows were:
I turned my eyes upon the deck—
Oh, Christ! what saw I there!

"Each corse lay flat, lifeless and flat,
And, by the holy rood![17]
A man all light, a seraph-man,[18]
On every corse there stood.

And appear in their own forms 490
of light.

"This seraph-band, each waved his hand,
It was a heavenly sight!
They stood as signals to the land,
Each one a lovely light;

"This seraph-band, each waved his hand,
No voice did they impart—
No voice; but oh! the silence sank
Like music on my heart.

"But soon I heard the dash of oars,   500
I heard the Pilot's cheer;
My head was turned perforce away,
And I saw a boat appear.

"The Pilot and the Pilot's boy,
I heard them coming fast:
Dear Lord in Heaven! it was a joy
The dead men could not blast.

"I saw a third—I heard his voice:
It is the Hermit good!
He singeth loud his godly hymns   510
That he makes in the wood.
He'll shrieve my soul, he'll wash away
The Albatross's blood."

PART 7

"This Hermit good lives in that wood
Which slopes down to the sea.
How loudly his sweet voice he rears!
He loves to talk with marineres
That come from a far countree.

The Hermit of the wood,

"He kneels at morn, and noon, and eve—
He hath a cushion plump: 520
It is the moss that wholly hides
The rotted old oak-stump.

---

[17] Cross.
[18] The highest rank of angels.

"The skiff-boat neared: I heard them talk,
'Why, this is strange, I trow!
Where are those lights so many and fair,
That signal made but now?'

" 'Strange, by my faith!' the Hermit said—   *Approacheth the ship with*
'And they answered not our cheer!   *wonder.*
The planks looked warped! and see those sails,
How thin they are and sere!   530
I never saw aught like to them,
Unless perchance it were

" 'Brown skeletons of leaves that lag
My forest-brook along;
When the ivy-tod[19] is heavy with snow,
And the owlet whoops to the wolf below,
That eats the she-wolf's young.'

" 'Dear Lord! it hath a fiendish look—
(The Pilot made reply)
I am a-feared'—'Push on, push on!'   540
Said the Hermit cheerily.

"The boat came closer to the ship,
But I nor spake nor stirred;
The boat came close beneath the ship,
And straight a sound was heard.

"Under the water it rumbled on,   *The ship suddenly sinketh.*
Still louder and more dread:
It reached the ship, it split the bay;
The ship went down like lead.

"Stunned by that loud and dreadful sound,   *The ancient Mariner is saved*   550
Which sky and ocean smote,   *in the Pilot's boat.*
Like one that hath been seven days drowned
My body lay afloat;
But swift as dreams, myself I found
Within the Pilot's boat.

"Upon the whirl, where sank the ship,
The boat spun round and round;
And all was still, save that the hill
Was telling of the sound.

"I moved my lips—the Pilot shrieked   560
And fell down in a fit;
The holy Hermit raised his eyes,
And prayed where he did sit.

_____
[19]Clump.

"I took the oars: the Pilot's boy,
Who now doth crazy go,
Laughed loud and long, and all the while
His eyes went to and fro.
'Ha! ha!' quoth he, 'full plain I see,
The Devil knows how to row.'

"And now, all in my own countree,   570
I stood on the firm land!
The Hermit stepped forth from the boat,
And scarcely he could stand.

" 'O shrieve me, shrieve me, holy man!'   *The ancient Mariner earnestly*
The Hermit crossed his brow.   *entreateth the Hermit to*
'Say quick,' quoth he, 'I bid thee say—   *shrieve him; and the penance*
What manner of man art thou?'   *of life falls on him.*

"Forthwith this frame of mine was wrenched
With a woful agony,
Which forced me to begin my tale;   580
And then it left me free.

"Since then, at an uncertain hour,   *And ever and anon throughout*
That agony returns;   *his future life an agony*
And till my ghastly tale is told,   *constraineth him to travel from*
This heart within me burns.   *land to land,*

"I pass, like night, from land to land;
I have strange power of speech;
That moment that his face I see,
I know the man that must hear me:
To him my tale I teach.   590

"What loud uproar bursts from that door!
The wedding-guests are there:
But in the garden-bower the bride
And bride-maids singing are:
And hark the little vesper bell,
Which biddeth me to prayer!

"O Wedding-Guest! this soul hath been
Alone on a wide, wide sea:
So lonely 'twas, that God himself
Scarce seeméd there to be.   600

"Oh sweeter than the marriage-feast,
'Tis sweeter far to me,
To walk together to the kirk
With a goodly company!—

"To walk together to the kirk,
And all together pray,

While each to his great Father bends,
Old men, and babes, and loving friends,
And youths and maidens gay!

"Farewell, farewell! but this I tell
To thee, thou Wedding-Guest!
He prayeth well, who loveth well
Both man and bird and beast.

And to teach by his own   610
example love and reverence
to all things that God made
and loveth.

"He prayeth best, who loveth best
All things both great and small;
For the dear God who loveth us,
He made and loveth all."

The Mariner, whose eye is bright,
Whose beard with age is hoar,
Is gone: and now the Wedding-Guest
Turned from the bridegroom's door.

620

He went like one that hath been stunned,
And is of sense forlorn:
A sadder and a wiser man,
He rose the morrow morn.

E. T. A. HOFFMANN
[1776–1822]

Without knowing the name of E. T. A. Hoffmann, many of us first glimpse the eerie beauty of his work through some childhood Christmas encounter with Tchaikovsky's *Nutcracker Suite*. Hoffmann tales such as "The Nutcracker and the King of the Mice" and "The Mines of Falun" exemplify two important aspects of romanticism. First, Hoffmann draws upon his own native northern and central European folk traditions, such as the sinister sand-man who visits fretful children and the earth-spirits who haunt mines, recognizing in them an imaginative source as rich as Greek and Roman myth. Second, in his tales Hoffmann explores the uncanny and the grotesque, valuing the supernatural as an important aspect of nature. Hoffmann's ghosts, apparitions, and dreams are always more worthy of attention than the pronouncements of respectable burghers; the supernatural calls out to his heroes and heroines so powerfully because it is a manifestation of some repressed guilt or longing hidden within their own hearts.

LIFE

It is not surprising that Hoffmann's works should often center on a lonely young person such as Elis Froebom of "The Mines of Falun." Hoffmann's parents separated soon after his birth in 1776 in Königsberg in East Prussia, and he grew up with a fragile mother unable to cope with her circumstances, an ailing grandmother, and a stern uncle. Hoffmann spoke of these years as "an arid heath, without blossom or flower." Happily, one cheerful unmarried aunt loved him, and his playmate Theodor von Hippel would prove a staunch friend for all their days. Hoffmann also discovered an emotional outlet and solace in music. Although gifted in many arts—acting, painting, stage design, and literature—music was Hoffmann's first and enduring love. In homage to Mozart he changed his baptismal name from Wilhelm to Amadeus.

Despite his artistic bent, the young Hoffmann chose the profession of law. He did well at the university, and seemed destined for a comfortable government career, but in 1796 after a scandalous love affair with a married cousin, he fled to Glogau in what is now Poland. This episode was the first of many disruptions in Hoffmann's life. Like Edgar Allan Poe, his spiritual heir, and like many of his fictional characters, Hoffmann was one of those people who naturally seek the edge of chaos, who subconsciously invite upheaval as soon as they find themselves in a settled situation.

Hoffmann was transferred in 1800 to the pleasant Polish city of Posen, where he pursued the arts while serving the Prussian Polish High Court. When he married Michalina Roher Trzynska, the proper daughter of a civil official, he seemed to have at last entered respectable adulthood, but in 1802 Hoffmann drew a widely circulated cartoon of the imperious local commanding general as a drummer-boy beating a fierce tattoo upon a teapot with a kitchen spoon. He was punished with a transfer to the tiny village of Plock, deep in central Poland. In April 1804, Theodor von Hippel, by now titled and wealthy, reappeared in Hoffmann's life. As he would on many successive occasions, von Hippel pulled strings and got him transferred to Warsaw, a vibrant center of art and culture where Hoffmann thrived; he established an orchestra in his spare time and began composing innovative music. Although seldom performed today, his pieces suggest bold aural images and emotions; Wagner learned much from him.

When Napoleon defeated the Prussians, Hoffmann's idyll shattered. In 1807, he was deported to Berlin for refusing to take a French oath of allegiance. While his wife remained stranded in Warsaw, their child died in an epidemic. The trauma of separation and grief seems to have killed their love, but they remained together. The couple eked out a grim living in Berlin until 1808, when Hoffmann was made director of a musical theater in Bamberg, where he began writing short stories.

Hoffmann once wrote that Beethoven's greatness came from "the endless longing that is the very essence of romanticism"; now in midlife he tasted that "essence" for himself by falling wildly in love with a sixteen-year-old music student. When she married in 1812, Hoffmann fled the city. From then on he turned more and more to fiction, with hopeless love one of his recurring themes.

For the next two years, through the dreary confusion of the Napoleonic Wars, Hoffmann and his long-suffering wife drifted back and forth between Dresden and Leipzig. He took such a keen interest in closely observing battles that he once got shot; his *Battle Symphony* sought to depict musically the Battle of Dresden. Even in his composing, Hoffmann was growing more and more attracted to storytelling. His first book, *Fantasiestucke in Callots Manier (Fantasy-pieces in the Style of Callot)* was published in 1814. In that same year, with von Hippel's help, Hoffmann found work at the Supreme Court in Berlin, where he lived until his death in 1822.

Always conscientious about his legal duties, Hoffmann managed at the same time to lead a bon vivant's life and write prolifically. His novel *Die Elixiere des Teufels (The Devil's Elixir)* appeared in 1816, and more stories, including "The Mines of Falun," came out under the general title of *Die Serapionsbruder (The Serapion Brotherhood)* in separate volumes between 1819 and 1821. At the end of his life, Hoffmann got into another face-off with authority when the King of Prussia appointed him head of a commission to sniff out traitors. Hoffmann, who championed free speech, kept declaring suspects innocent even when he himself personally disliked them. His last years were spent in ill health made worse by alcoholism and near-bankruptcy.

WORK

In "The Mines of Falun," the uncanny impinges subtly upon a quite solid nineteenth-century Europe of commerce and pleasure, with the East India Company, sailors' carouses, actual Swedish mines, and explanations of profit-sharing. Like many romantic protagonists, Elis is alone in a crowd, emotionally unfulfilled; like Faust who thirsts for "the breasts of life," he cannot quench his desire with liquor or a woman's love. Like Faust's, his dissatisfaction with his present calling seems darkly linked with family history and old guilts; he miraculously survives the storm in which his father drowned, and his mother dies during his last voyage. In time, Elis encounters a series of other father and mother figures, some of whom exact revenge for Elis's acts of omission and his attempts to lead a normal life.

In his first conversation with the mysterious Torbern, Elis dwells upon his longing for the nurturing mother he has lost, and perhaps that nostalgia gives Torbern the clue that Elis is a potential votary of that sternest of mothers, the Metal Queen. Hoffmann is playing on very old beliefs about mines; myths from widely separated cultures view miners and metalsmiths as people who have made pacts with the goddess. While ordinary people content themselves pottering about on the surface of the female earth, She reserves her real secrets for those who dare a descent into Her darkness. Like Faust, Elis learns that quests cannot be abandoned simply because one decides it might be nice to lead a normal life. Nature, the rich mother/mistress who "lays bare her most secret treasures," demands absolute loyalty; she is both nurturer and devourer, and her rules are not human rules.

As in Keats's "Lamia," "Hyperion," and "La Belle Dame sans Merci"; Coleridge's "Christabel"; many of Poe's tales; and a number of other romantic texts written by men, fear of women permeates this story. The memory of Elis's beloved mother evokes in him racking guilt. Ulla, the "bright angel," first arouses his desires, then her father plays a trick on him that drives him in despair toward the mine and his second vision of the Metal Queen; finally, she snares him in a marriage promise that will mean his death. As for the Queen herself, merely to look upon her is to be bound to her, and to look away from her means the reluctant beholder will be turned to stone. Hoffmann's suggestions about sexuality in this no-exit tale are grim indeed.

SUGGESTED READINGS

E. F. Bleiler's biographical sketch of Hoffmann in the introduction to his edition of *The Best Tales of Hoffmann* (1963) is dry but serviceable. James McGlathery's *Mysticism and Sexuality: E. T. A. Hoffmann* (1981) traces the origins of Hoffmann's beliefs and sensibilities. Wolfgang Kayser's *The Grotesque in Art and Literature* (1981) is a classic text on the Gothic genre.

The Mines of Falun

Translated by E. F. Bleiler

One bright, sunny day in July the whole population of Goethaborg was assembled at the harbour. A fine East Indiaman, happily returned from her long voyage, was lying at anchor, with her long, homeward-bound pennant and the Swedish flag fluttering gaily in the azure sky. Hundreds of boats, skiffs and other small craft, thronged with rejoicing seafolk, were going to and fro on the mirroring waters of the Goethaelf, and the cannon of Masthuggetorg thundered their far-echoing greeting out to sea. The gentlemen of the East India Company were walking up and down on the quay, reckoning up, with smiling faces, the plentiful profits they had netted, and rejoicing at the yearly increasing success of their hazardous enterprise and at the growing commercial importance of their good town of Goethaborg. For the same reasons everybody looked at these brave adventurers with pleasure and pride, and shared their rejoicing; for their success brought sap and vigour into the whole life of the place.

The crew of the East Indiaman, about a hundred strong, landed in a number of boats (gaily dressed with flags for the occasion) and prepared to hold their Hoensning. That is the name of the feast which the sailors hold on such occasions; it often goes on for several days. Musicians went before them in strange, gay dresses; some played lustily on violins, oboes, fifes and drums, while others sang merry songs. After them came the crew, walking two and two; some, with gay ribbons on their hats and jackets, waved fluttering streamers; others danced and skipped; and all of them shouted and cheered at the tops of their voices, till the sounds of merriment rang far and wide.

Thus the gay procession passed through the streets, and on to the suburb of Haga, where a feast was ready for them in a tavern.

Here the best of "Oel" flowed in rivers and bumper after bumper was quaffed. Women joined them, as is always the case when sailors come home from a long voyage; dancing began, and wilder and wilder grew the revel, and louder and louder the din.

One sailor only—a slender, handsome lad of about twenty or a little less—had slipped away and was sitting alone outside, on the bench at the door of the tavern.

Two or three of his shipmates came out to him, and one of them cried, laughing loudly:

"Now then, Elis Froebom! are you going to be a donkey, as usual, and sit out here sulking instead of joining the sport like a man? Why, you might as well part company from the old ship altogether, and set sail on your own hook as fight shy of the Hoensning. One would think you were a regular long-shore landlubber, and had never been afloat on blue water. All the same, you've got as good pluck as any sailor that walks a deck—ay, and as cool and steady a head in a gale of wind as ever I came athwart; but you see, you can't take your liquor! You'd sooner keep the ducats in your pocket than serve them out to the land-sharks ashore here. Here, lad! take a drink of that; or Naecken, the sea-devil, and all the Troll will be foul of your hawse[1] before you know where you are!"

Elis Froebom jumped up quickly from the bench, glared angrily at his shipmates, took the tumbler—which was filled to the brim with brandy—and emptied it at a draught; then he said:

"You see I can take my glass with any man of you, Ivens; and you can ask the captain if I'm a good sailor or not; so stow away that long tongue of yours and sheer off! I don't care about all this drink and row here; and what I'm doing out here by myself's no business of yours; you have nothing to do with it."

"All right, my hearty!" answered Ivens. "I know all about it. You're one of these Nerica men—and a moony lot the whole cargo of them are too. They're the sort that would rather sit and pipe their eye about nothing particular than take a good glass and see what the women at home are made of, after a twelve-month's cruise! But just you belay there a bit. Steer full and bye, and stand off and on, and I'll send somebody out to you that'll cut you adrift in a pig's whisper from that old bench where you've cast your anchor."

---

[1] The part of a ship's bow where anchor-cables are fastened.

They went, and presently a very pretty girl came out of the tavern and sat down bedside the melancholy Elis, who was still sitting, silent and thoughtful, on the bench. From her dress and general appearance there could be no doubt as to her calling. But the life she was leading had not yet quite marred the delicacy of the wonderfully tender features of her beautiful face; there was no trace of repulsive boldness about the expression of her dark eyes—rather a quiet, melancholy longing.

"Aren't you coming to join your shipmates, Elis?" she said. "Now that you're back safe and sound, after all you've gone through on your long voyage, aren't you glad to be home in the old country again?"

The girl spoke in a soft, gentle voice, putting her arms about him. Elis Froebom looked into her eyes as if roused from a dream. He took her hand; he pressed her to his breast. It was evident that what she had said had made its way to his heart.

"Ah!" he said, as if collecting his thoughts, "it's no use talking about enjoying myself. I can't join in all that riot and uproar; there's no pleasure in it, for me. You go back. Sing and shout like the rest of them, if you can, and let gloomy, melancholy Elis stay out here by himself; he would only spoil your pleasure. Wait a minute, though! I like you, and I want you to think of me sometimes, when I'm away on the sea again."

With that he took two shining ducats out of his pocket and a beautiful Indian handkerchief from his breast, and gave them to the girl. Her eyes streamed with tears; she rose, laid the money on the bench, and said:

"Oh, keep your ducats; they only make me miserable; but I'll wear the hand-kerchief in remembrance of you. You're not likely to find me next year when you hold your Hoensning in the Haga."

And she crept slowly away down the street, with her hands pressed to her face.

Elis fell back into his gloomy reveries. At length, as the uproar in the tavern grew loud and wild, he cried:

"Oh, I wish I were deep, deep beneath the sea! for there's nobody left in the wide, wide world that I can be happy with now!"

A deep, harsh voice spoke, close behind him: "You must have been most unfortunate, youngster, to wish to die, just when life should be opening before you."

Elis looked round, and saw an old miner leaning with folded arms against the boarded wall of the tavern, looking down at him with a grave, penetrating stare.

As Elis looked at him, a feeling came to him as if some familiar figure had suddenly come into the deep, wild solitude in which he had thought himself lost. He pulled himself together, and told the old miner that his father had been a stout sailor, but had perished in the storm from which he himself had been saved as if by a miracle; that his two soldier brothers had died in battle, and he had supported his mother with the liberal pay he drew for sailing to the East Indies. He said he had been obliged to follow the life of a sailor, having been brought up to it from childhood, and it had been a great piece of good fortune that he got into the service of the East India Company. This voyage, the profits had been greater than usual, and each of the crew had been given a sum of money over and above his pay; so that he had hastened, in the highest spirits, with his pockets full of ducats, to the little cottage where his mother lived. But strange faces looked at him from the windows, and a young woman who opened the door to him at last told him in a cold, harsh tone that his mother had died three months earlier, and that he would find the few bits of things that were left, after paying the funeral expenses, waiting for him at the Town Hall.

The death of his mother broke his heart. He felt alone in the world—as much so as if he had been wrecked on some lonely reef, helpless and miserable. All his life at sea seemed to him to have been a mistaken, purposeless driving. And when he thought of his mother, perhaps badly looked after by strangers, he thought it a wrong and horrible thing that he should have gone to sea at all, instead of staying at home and taking proper care of her. His comrades had dragged him to the Hoensning in spite of himself, and he had thought too that the uproar and even the drink might deaden his pain; but instead of that, all the veins in his breast seemed to be bursting, and he felt as if he would bleed to death.

"Well," said the old miner, "you'll soon be off to sea again, Elis, and then your sorrow will soon be over. Old folks must die; there's no help for that. She has only gone from this miserable world to a better."

"Ah!" said Elis, "it is just because nobody believes in my sorrow, and that they all think me a fool to feel it—I say it's that which is driving me out of the world! I won't go to sea any more; I'm sick of living altogether. When the ship used to go flying along through the water, with all sails set, spreading like wings, the waves playing and dashing in exquisite music, and the wind singing in the rigging, my heart used to bound. Then I could hurrah and shout on deck like the best of them. And when I was on lookout duty of dark, quiet nights, I used to think about getting home, and how glad my dear old mother would be to have me back. I could enjoy a Hoensning like the rest of them then. And when I had shaken the ducats into mother's lap and given her the handkerchiefs and all the other pretty things I had brought home, her eyes would sparkle with pleasure, and she would clap her hands for joy, and run out and in, and fetch me ale which she had kept for my homecoming. And when I sat with her evenings, I would tell her of all the strange folks I had seen, and their ways and customs, and about the wonderful things I had come across in my long voyages. This delighted her; and she would tell me of my father's wonderful cruises in the far North, and lots of strange sailor's yarns which I had heard a hundred times but never could hear too often. Ah! who will give me that happiness back again? What should I do among my shipmates? They would only laugh at me. Where should I find any heart for my work? There would be no purpose to it."

"It gives me real satisfaction to listen to you, youngster," said the old miner. "I have been observing you, without your knowledge, for the last hour or two, and have had my own enjoyment in doing so. All that you have said and done has shown me that you have a very thoughtful mind, and a character and nature pious, simple, and sincere. Heaven could have given you no more precious gifts; but you were never in all your born days in the least cut out for a sailor. How could the wild, unsettled sailor's life suit a meditative, melancholy Neriker like you?—for I can see that you come from Nerica by your features and whole appearance. You are right to say goodbye to that life forever. But you're not going to walk about idle, with your hands in your pockets? Take my advice, Elis Froebom. Go to Falun, and be a miner. You are young and strong. You'll soon be a first-class pick-hand; then a hewer; presently a surveyor, and so get higher and higher. You have a lot of ducats in your pocket. Take care of them; invest them; add more to them. Very likely you'll soon get a 'Hemmans' of your own, and then a share in the works. Take my advice, Elis Froebom; be a miner."

The old man's words caused him a sort of fear.

"What?" he cried. "Would you have me leave the bright, sunny sky that revives and refreshes me, and go down into that hell-like abyss, and dig and tunnel like a mole for metals and ores, merely to gain a few wretched ducats? Oh, never!"

"The usual thing," said the old man. "People despise what they have had no chance of knowing anything about! As if all the constant wearing, petty anxieties inseparable from business up here on the surface, were nobler than the miner's work. To his skill, knowledge, and untiring industry Nature lays bare her most secret treasures. You speak of gain with contempt, Elis Froebom. Well, there's something infinitely higher in question here, perhaps: the mole tunnels the ground from blind instinct; but it may be, in the deepest depths, by the pale glimmer of the mine candle, men's eyes get to see clearer, and at length, growing stronger and stronger, acquire the power of reading in the stones, the gems, and the minerals, the mirroring of secrets which are hidden above the clouds. You know nothing about mining, Elis. Let me tell you a little."

He sat down on the bench beside Elis, and began to describe the various processes minutely, placing all the details before him in the clearest and brightest colours. He talked of the mines of Falun, in which he said he had worked since he was a boy; he described the great main-shaft, with its dark brown sides; he told how incalculably rich the mine was in gems of the finest water. More and more vivid grew his words, more and more glowing his face. He went, in his description, through the different shafts as if they had been the alleys of some enchanted garden. The jewels came to life, the fossils began to move; the wondrous pyrosmalite and the almandine[2] flashed in the light of the miner's candles; the rock crystals glittered, and darted their rays.

Elis listened intently. The old man's strange way of speaking of all these subterranean marvels as if he were standing in the midst of them impressed him deeply. His breast felt stifled; it seemed to him as if he were already down in these depths with the old man, and would never look upon the friendly light of day again. And yet it seemed as though the old man were opening to him a new and unknown world, to which he really properly belonged, and that he had somehow felt all the magic of that world in mystic forebodings since his boyhood.

"Elis Froebom," said the old man at last, "I have laid before you all the glories of a calling for which Nature really destined you. Think the subject over well, and then act as your better judgment counsels you."

He rose quickly from the bench and strode away without any goodbye to Elis, without looking at him even. Soon he disappeared from his sight.

Meanwhile quietness had set in in the tavern. The strong ale and brandy had got the upper hand. Many of the sailors had gone away with the girls; others were lying snoring in corners. Elis—who could go no more to his old home—asked for, and was given, a little room to sleep in.

Scarcely had he thrown himself, worn and weary as he was, upon his bed, when dreams began to wave their pinions over him. He thought he was sailing in a beautiful vessel on a sea calm and clear as a mirror, with a dark, cloudy sky vaulted overhead. But when he looked down into the sea he presently saw that what he had thought was water was a firm, transparent, sparkling substance, in the shimmer of which the ship, in a wonderful manner, melted away, so that he found himself standing upon this floor of crystal, with a vault of black rock above him, for that was rock which he had taken at first for clouds. Impelled by some power unknown to him he stepped onward, but at that moment everything around him began to move, and wonderful plants and flowers, of glittering metal, came shooting up out of the crystal mass he was standing on, and entwined their leaves and blossoms in the loveliest manner. The crystal floor was so transparent that Elis could distinctly see the roots of these plants. But soon, as his glance penetrated deeper and deeper, he saw, far, far down in the depths, innumerable beautiful maidens, embracing each other with white, gleaming arms; and it was from their hearts that the roots, plants, and flowers were growing. And when these maidens smiled, a sweet sound rang all

---

[2]Pyrosmalite and almandine are varieties of brightly colored crystals.

through the vault above, and the wonderful metal-flowers shot up higher and waved their leaves and branches in joy. An indescribable sense of rapture came upon the lad; a world of love and passionate longing awoke in his heart.

"Down, down to you!" he cried, and threw himself with outstretched arms down upon the crystal ground. But it gave way under him, and he seemed to be floating in shimmering ether.

"Ha! Elis Froebom; what do you think of this world of glory?" a strong voice cried. It was the old miner. But as Elis looked at him, he seemed to expand into gigantic size, and to be made of glowing metal. Elis was beginning to be terrified; but a brilliant light came darting like a sudden lightning flash out of the depths of the abyss, and the earnest face of a grand, majestic woman appeared. Elis felt the rapture of his heart swelling and swelling into destroying pain. The old man had hold of him, and cried:

"Take care, Elis Froebom! That is the queen. You may look up now."

He turned his head involuntarily, and saw the stars of the night sky shining through a cleft in the vault overhead. A gentle voice called his name as if in inconsolable sorrow. It was his mother's. He thought he saw her form up at the cleft. But it was a young and beautiful woman who was calling him, and stretching her hands down into the vault.

"Take me up!" he cried to the old man. "I tell you I belong to the upper world, and its familiar, friendly sky."

"Take care, Froebom," said the old man solemnly; "be faithful to the queen, whom you have devoted yourself to."

But now, when he looked down again into the immobile face of the majestic woman, he felt that his personality dissolved away into glowing molten stone. He screamed aloud in nameless fear and awoke from this dream of wonder, whose rapture and terror echoed deep within his being.

"I suppose I could scarcely help dreaming all this extraordinary stuff," he said to himself, as he collected his senses with difficulty; "the old miner told me so much about the glories of the subterranean world that of course my head's quite full of it. But I never in my life felt as I do now. Perhaps I'm still dreaming. No, no; I suppose I must be a little out of sorts. Let's get into the open air. The fresh sea breeze'll soon set me all right."

He pulled himself together, and ran to the Klippa Haven, where the uproar of the Hoensning was breaking out again. But he soon found that all enjoyment passed him by, that he couldn't hold any thought fast in his mind, that presages and wishes to which he could give no name went crossing each other in his mind. He thought of his dead mother with the bitterest sorrow; but then, again, it seemed to him that what he most longed for was to see that girl again—the one whom he gave the handkerchief to—who had spoken so nicely to him the evening before. And yet he was afraid that if she were to come to meet him out of some street, she would turn out in the end to be the old miner. And he was afraid of *him*; though, at the same time, he would have liked to hear more from him of the wonders of the mine.

Driven hither and thither by all these fancies, he looked down into the water, and then he thought he saw the silver ripples hardening into the sparkling glimmer in which the grand ships melted away, while the dark clouds, which were beginning to gather and obscure the blue sky, seemed to sink down and thicken into a vault of rock. He was in his dream again, gazing into the immobile face of the majestic woman, and the devouring pain of passionate longing took possession of him as before.

His shipmates roused him from his reverie to go and join one of their processions, but an unknown voice seemed to whisper in his ear:

"What are you doing here? Away, away! Your home is in the mines of Falun. There all the glories which you saw in your dream are waiting for you. Away, away to Falun!"

For three days Elis hung and loitered about the streets of Goethaborg, constantly haunted by the wonderful images of his dream, continually urged by the unknown voice. On the fourth day he was standing at the gate through which the road to Gefle goes, when a tall man walked through it, passing him. Elis fancied he recognized in this man the old miner, and he hastened on after him, but could not overtake him.

He followed him on and on, without stopping.

He knew he was on the road to Falun, and this circumstance quieted him in a curious way; for he felt certain that the voice of destiny had spoken to him through the old miner, and that it was he who was now leading him on to his appointed place and fate.

And in fact, many times—particularly if there was any uncertainty about the road—he saw the old man suddenly appear out of some ravine, or from thick bushes, or gloomy rocks, stalk away before him, without looking round, and then disappear again.

At last, after journeying for many weary days, Elis saw in the distance two great lakes with a thick vapour rising between them. As he mounted the hill to westward, he saw some towers and black roofs rising through the smoke. The old man appeared before him, grown to gigantic size, pointed with outstretched hand towards the vapour, and disappeared again among the rocks.

"There lies Falun," said Elis, "the end of my journey."

He was right; for people, coming up from behind him, said the town of Falun lay between the lakes Runn and Warpann, and that the hill he was ascending was the Guffrisberg, where the main shaft of the mine was.

He went bravely on. But when he came to the enormous gulf, like the jaws of hell itself, the blood curdled in his veins, and he stood as if turned to stone at the sight of this colossal work of destruction.

The main shaft of the Falun mines is some twelve hundred feet long, six hundred feet broad, and a hundred and eighty feet deep. Its dark brown sides go, at first for the most part, perpendicularly down, till about halfway they are sloped inwards towards the center by enormous accumulations of stones and refuse. In these, and on the sides, there peeped out here and there timberings of old shafts, formed of strong shores set close together and strongly rabbeted at the ends, in the way that log houses are built. Not a tree, not a blade of grass to be seen in all the bare, blank, crumbling congeries of stony chasms; the pointed, jagged, indented masses of rock tower aloft all round in wonderful forms, often like monstrous animals turned to stone, often like colossal human beings. In the abyss itself lie in wild confusion— pell-mell—stones, slag, and scoria, and an eternal, stupefying sulphurous vapour rises from the depths, as if the hell-broth, whose reek poisons and kills all the green gladsomeness of nature, were being brewed down below. One would think this was where Dante went down and saw the Inferno, with all its horror and immitigable pain.

As Elis looked down into this monstrous abyss, he remembered what an old sailor, one of his shipmates, had told him once. This shipmate of his, at a time when he was down with fever, thought the sea had suddenly all gone dry, and the boundless depths of the abyss had opened under him, so that he saw all the horrible creatures of the deep twining and writhing about in dreadful contortions among thousands of extraordinary shells and groves of coral, till they died, and lay dead, with their mouths all gaping. The old sailor said that to see such a vision meant death, ere long, in the waves; and in fact very soon he did fall overboard, no one knew exactly how, and was drowned without possibility of rescue. Elis thought of that: for indeed the abyss seemed to him to be a good deal like the bottom of the sea run dry; and the black rocks, and the blue and red slag and scoria, were like horrible monsters shooting out polyp-arms at him. Two or three miners happened just then to be coming up from work in the mine, and in their dark mining clothes, with their black, grimy faces, they were much like ugly, diabolical creatures of some sort, slowly and painfully crawling and forcing their way up to the surface.

Elis felt a shudder of dread go through him, and—what he had never experienced in all his career as a sailor—he became giddy. Unseen hands seemed to be dragging him down into the abyss.

He closed his eyes and ran a few steps away from it, and it was not till he began climbing up the Guffrisberg again, far from the shaft, and could look up at the bright, sunny sky, that he quite lost the feeling of terror which had taken possession of him. He breathed freely once more, and cried, from the depths of his heart:

"Lord of my Life! what are the dangers of the sea compared with the horror which dwells in that awful abyss of rock? The storm may rage, the black clouds may come whirling down upon the breaking billows, but the beautiful, glorious sun soon gets the mastery again and the storm is past. But never does the sun penetrate into these black, gloomy caverns; never a freshening breeze of spring can revive the heart down there. No! I shall not join you, black earthworms! Never could I bring myself to lead that terrible life."

He resolved to spend that night in Falun, and set off back to Goethaborg the first thing in the morning.

When he got to the market place, he found a crowd of people there. A train of miners with their mine candles in their hands, and musicians before them, was halted before a handsome house. A tall, slightly built middle-aged man came out, looking around him with kindly smiles. It was easy to see by his frank manner, his open brow, and his bright, dark-blue eyes that he was a genuine Dalkarl. The miners formed a circle around him, and he shook them each cordially by the hand, saying kindly words to them all.

Elis learned that this was Pehrson Dahlsjoe, Alderman, and owner of a fine "Fraelse" at Stora-Kopparberg. "Fraelse" is the name given in Sweden to landed property leased out for the working of the lodes of copper and silver contained in it. The owners of these lands have shares in the mines and are responsible for their management.

Elis was told, further, that the Assizes were just over that day, and that then the miners went round in procession to the houses of the aldermen, the chief engineers and the minemasters, and were hospitably entertained.

When he looked at these fine, handsome fellows, with their kindly, frank faces, he forgot all about the earthworms he had seen coming up the shaft. The healthy gladsomeness which broke out afresh in the whole circle, as if new-fanned by a spring breeze, when Pehrson Dahlsjoe came out, was of a different sort from the senseless noise and uproar of the sailors' Hoensning. The manner in which these miners enjoyed themselves went straight to the serious Elis's heart. He felt indescribably happy; but he could scarce restrain his tears when some of the young pickmen sang an ancient ditty in praise of the miner's calling, and of the happiness of his lot, to a simple melody which touched his heart and soul.

When this song was ended, Pehrson Dahlsjoe opened his door, and the miners all went into his house one after another. Elis followed involuntarily and stood at the threshold, so that he could see the whole spacious room where the miners took their places on benches. Then the doors at the side opposite to him opened, and a beautiful young lady in evening dress came in. She was in the full glory of the freshest bloom of youth, tall and slender with dark hair in many curls, and a bodice fastened with rich clasps. The miners all stood up, and a low murmur of pleasure ran through their ranks. "Ulla Dahlsjoe!" they said. "What a blessing Heaven has bestowed on our hearty alderman in her!" Even the oldest miners' eyes sparkled when she gave them her hand in kindly greeting, as she did to them all. Then she brought beautiful silver tankards, filled them with splendid ale (such as Falun is famous for), and handed them to the guests with a face beaming with kindness and hospitality.

When Elis saw her a lightning flash seemed to go through his heart, kindling all the heavenly bliss, the love-longings, the passionate ardour lying hidden and imprisoned there. For it was Ulla Dahlsjoe who had held out the hand of rescue to him in his mysterious dream. He thought he understood now the deep significance of that dream, and, forgetting the old miner, praised the stroke of fortune which had brought him to Falun.

Alas! he felt he was but an unknown, unnoticed stranger, standing there on the doorstep miserable, comfortless, alone—and he wished he had died before he saw Ulla, as he now must perish for love and longing. He could not move his eyes from the beautiful creature, and as she passed close to him, he pronounced her name in a low, trembling voice. She turned and saw him standing there with a face as red as fire, unable to utter a syllable. So she went up to him and said, with a sweet smile:

"I suppose you are a stranger, friend, since you are dressed as a sailor. Well! why are you standing at the door? Come in and join us."

Elis felt as if in the blissful paradise of some happy dream, from which he would presently waken to inexpressible wretchedness. He emptied the tankard which she had given him; and Pehrson Dahlsjoe came up, and after kindly shaking hands with him, asked him where he came from and what had brought him to Falun.

Elis felt the warming power of the noble liquor in his veins, and looking Dahlsjoe in the eye, he felt happy and courageous. He told him he was a sailor's son and had been at sea since his childhood, had just come home from the East Indies and found his mother dead; that he was now alone in the world; that the wild sea life had become altogether distasteful to him; that his keenest inclination led him to a miner's calling, and that he wished to get employment as a miner here in Falun. The latter statement, quite the reverse of his recent determination, escaped him involuntarily; it was as if he could not have said anything else to the alderman, as if it were the most ardent desire of his soul, although he had not known it himself till now.

Pehrson Dahlsjoe looked at him long and carefully, as if he would read his heart; then he said:

"I cannot suppose, Elis Froebom, that it is mere thoughtless fickleness and the love of change that lead you to give up the calling you have followed hitherto, nor that you have omitted to weigh maturely and consider all the difficulties and hardships of the miner's life before making up your mind to take to it. It is an old belief with us that the mighty elements with which the miner has to deal, and which he controls so bravely, destroy him unless he strains all his being to keep command of them—if he gives place to other thoughts which weaken that vigour which he has to reserve wholly for his constant conflict with Earth and Fire. But if you have properly tested the sincerity of your inward call and it has withstood the trial, you are come in a good hour. Workmen are wanted in my part of the mine. If you like, you can stay here with me, and tomorrow the Captain will take you down with him, and show you what to do."

Elis's heart swelled with gladness at this. He thought no more of the terror of the awful, hell-like abyss into which he had looked. The thought that he was going to see Ulla every day and live under the same roof with her filled him with rapture and delight. He gave way to the sweetest hopes.

Pehrson Dahlsjoe told the miners that a young hand had applied for employment, and presented him to them then and there. They all looked approvingly at the well-knit lad, and thought he was quite cut out for a miner, what with his light, powerful figure, his industry and straightforwardness.

One of the men, well advanced in years, came and shook hands with him cordially, saying he was Head Captain in Pehrson Dahlsjoe's part of the mine, and would be very glad to give him any help and instruction in his power. Elis had to sit down beside this man, who at once began, over his tankard of ale, to describe with much minuteness the sort of work which Elis would have to commence with.

Elis remembered the old miner whom he had seen at Goethaborg, and strangely enough found he was able to repeat nearly all that he had told him.

"Ay," cried the Head Captain. "Where can you have learned all that? It's most surprising! There can't be a doubt that you will be the finest pickman in the mine in a very short time."

Ulla—going back and forth among the guests and attending to them—often nodded kindly to Elis, and told him to be sure and enjoy himself. "You're not a stranger now, you know," she said, "but one of the household. You have nothing more to do with the treacherous sea—the rich mines of Falun are your home."

A heaven of bliss and rapture dawned upon Elis at these words of Ulla's. It was evident that she liked to be near him; and Pehrson Dahlsjoe watched his quiet earnestness of character with manifest approval.

But Elis's heart beat violently when he stood again by the reeking hell-mouth, and went down the mine with the Captain, in his miner's clothes, with the heavy, iron-shod Dalkarl shoes on his feet. Hot vapours soon threatened to suffocate him, and then presently the candles flickered in the cutting draughts of cold air that blew in the lower levels. They went down deeper and deeper, on iron ladders at last scarcely a foot wide; and Elis found that his sailor's adroitness at climbing was not of the slightest service to him there.

They got to the lowest depths of the mine at last, and the Captain showed him what work he was to do.

Elis thought of Ulla. Like some bright angel he saw her hovering over him, and he forgot all the terror of the abyss, and the hardness of the labour.

It was clear in all his thoughts that it was only if he devoted himself with all the power of his mind, and with all the exertion which his body would endure, to mining work here with Pehrson Dahlsjoe, that there was any possibility of his fondest hopes being some day realized. Wherefore it came about that he was as good at his work as the most practiced hand in an incredibly short space of time.

Staunch Pehrson Dahlsjoe got to like this good, industrious lad better and better every day, and often told him plainly that he had found in him one whom he regarded as a dear son as well as a first-class mine-hand. Also Ulla's regard for him became more and more unmistakable. Often, when he was going to his work and there was any prospect of danger, she would enjoin him with tears in her eyes to be sure to take care of himself. And she would come running to meet him when he came back, and always had the finest of ale or some other refreshment ready for him. His heart danced for joy one day when Pehrson said to him that as he had brought a good sum of money with him, there could be no doubt that—with his habits of economy and industry—he would soon have a Hemmans, or perhaps even a Fraelse; and then not a mineowner in all Falun would refuse if he asked for his daughter. Elis would have liked to tell him at once how unspeakably he loved Ulla, and how all his hopes of happiness were based upon her. But unconquerable shyness and the doubt whether Ulla really liked him—though he often thought she did—sealed his lips.

One day it chanced that Elis was at work in the lowest depths of the mine, shrouded in thick, sulphurous vapour, so that his candle only shed a feeble glimmer and he could scarcely distinguish the run of the lode. Suddenly he heard—as if coming from some still deeper cutting—a knocking as if somebody was at work with a pick-hammer. As that sort of work was scarcely possible at such a depth, and as he knew nobody was down there that day but himself—because the Captain had all the men employed in another part of the mine—this knocking and hammering struck him as strange and uncanny. He stopped working and listened to the hollow sounds, which seemed to come nearer and nearer. All at once he saw, close by him, a black shadow and—as a keen draught of air blew away the sulphur vapour—the old miner whom he had seen in Goethaborg.

"Good luck," he cried, "good luck to Elis Froebom, down here among the stones! What do you think of the life, comrade?"

Elis would have liked to ask in what wonderful way the old man had got into the mine; but he kept striking his hammer on the rocks with such force that the sparks went whirling all round, and the mine rang as if with distant thunder. Then he cried, in a terrible voice:

"There's a grand run of trap[3] just here; but a scurvy, ignorant scoundrel like you sees nothing in it but a narrow streak of 'trumm' not worth a beanstalk. Down here you're a sightless mole, and you'll always be a mere abomination to the Metal Prince. You're of no use up above either—trying to get hold of the pure Regulus; which you never will—hey! You want to marry Pehrson Dahlsjoe's daughter; that's what you've taken to mine work for, not from any love of it. Mind what you're after, doubleface; take care that the Metal Prince, whom you are trying to deceive, doesn't take you and dash you down so that the sharp rocks tear you limb from limb. And Ulla will never be your wife; that much I tell you."

Elis's anger was kindled at the old man's insulting words.

"What are you doing," he cried, "here in my master, Herr Pehrson Dahlsjoe's shaft, where I am doing my duty and working as hard at it as I can? Be off out of this the way you came, or we'll see which of us two will dash the other's brains out down here."

With which he placed himself in a threatening attitude and swung his hammer about the old man's ears; he only gave a sneering laugh, and Elis saw with terror how he swarmed up the narrow ladder rungs like a squirrel, and disappeared amongst the black labyrinths of the chasms.

The young man felt paralyzed in all his limbs; he could not go on with his work, but went up. When the old Head Captain—who had been busy in another part of the mine—saw him, he cried:

"For God's sake, Elis, what has happened to you? You're as pale as death. I suppose it's the sulphur gas; you're not accustomed to it yet. Here, take a drink, my lad; that'll do you good."

Elis took a good mouthful of brandy out of the flask which the Head Captain handed to him; and then, feeling better, told him what had happened down in

---

[3] Trap is a kind of igneous rock that is crushed and used to make roadbeds.

the mine, as also how he had made the uncanny old miner's acquaintance in Goethaborg.

The Head Captain listened silently; then dubiously shook his head and said:

"That must have been old Torbern that you met, Elis; and I see now that there really is something in the tales that people tell about him. More than one hundred years ago, there was a miner here of the name of Torbern. He seems to have been one of the first to bring mining into a flourishing condition at Falun here, and in his time profits far exceeded anything that we know of now. Nobody at that time knew so much about mining as Torbern, who had great scientific skill and thoroughly understood all the ins and outs of the business. The richest lodes seemed to disclose themselves to him, as if he was endowed with higher powers peculiar to himself; and as he was a gloomy, meditative man, without wife or child—with no regular home, indeed—and very seldom came up to the surface, it couldn't fail that a story soon went about that he was in compact with the mysterious power which dwells in the bowels of the earth and creates metals. Disregarding Torbern's solemn warnings—for he always prophesied that some calamity would happen as soon as the miners' impulse to work ceased to be sincere love for the marvellous metals and ores—people went on enlarging the excavations more and more for the sake of mere profit, till on St. John's Day[4] of the year 1678, came the terrible landslip and subsidence which formed our present enormous main shaft, laying waste the whole of the works, as they were then, in the process. It was only after many months' labour that several of the shafts were with much difficulty put into workable order again. Nothing was seen or heard of Torbern. There seemed to be no doubt that he had been at work down below at the time of the catastrophe, so that there could be no question what his fate had been. But not long after, particularly when the work was beginning to go better again, the miners said they had seen old Torbern in the mine, and that he had given them valuable advice and pointed out rich lodes to them. Others had come across him at the top of the main shaft, walking round it, sometimes lamenting, sometimes shouting in wild anger. Other young fellows have come here in the way you yourself did, saying that an old miner had advised them to take to mining and shown them the way to Falun. This always happened when there was a scarcity of hands; very likely it was Torbern's way of helping on the cause. But if it really was he whom you had those words with in the mine, and if he spoke of a fine run of trap there isn't a doubt that there must be a grand vein of ore thereabouts, and we must see tomorrow if we can come across it. Of course you remember that we call rich veins of the kind 'trap-runs,' and that a 'trumm' is a vein which goes subdividing into several smaller ones, and probably gets lost altogether."

When Elis, tossed hither and thither by various thoughts went into Pehrson Dahlsjoe's, Ulla did not come to meet him as usual. She was sitting with downcast looks and—as he thought—eyes which had been weeping; and beside her was a handsome young fellow, holding her hand and trying to say all sorts of kind and amusing things to which she seemed to pay little attention. Pehrson Dahlsjoe took Elis—who, seized by gloomy presentiments, was keeping a dark glance riveted on the pair—into another room, and said:

"Well, Elis, you will soon have it in your power to give me a proof of your regard and sincerity. I have always looked upon you as a son, but you will soon

---

[4]Saint John's Day falls on June 24, near the summer solstice; in old European folklore, it was thought to be a good day for discovering buried treasure.

take the place of one altogether. The man whom you see in there is a well-to-do merchant, Eric Olavsen by name, from Goethaborg. I am giving him my daughter for his wife, at his desire. He will take her to Goethaborg, and then you will be left alone with me, my only support in my declining years. Well, you say nothing? You turn pale? I trust this step doesn't displease you, and that now that I'm going to lose my daughter you are not going to leave me too? But I hear Olavsen mentioning my name; I must go in."

With which he went back to the room.

Elis felt a thousand red-hot irons tearing at his heart. He could find no words, no tears. In wild despair he ran out, out of the house, away to the great mine shaft.

That monstrous chasm had a terrible appearance by day; but now, when night had fallen and the moon was just peeping down into it, the desolate crags looked like a numberless horde of horrible monsters, the dire brood of hell, rolling and writhing in wildest confusion all about its reeking sides and clefts, and flashing up fiery eyes and shooting forth glowing claws to clutch the race of mortals.

"Torbern, Torbern," Elis cried in a terrible voice which made the rocks re-echo. "Torbern, I am here; you were not wrong—I was a wretched fool to fix my hopes on any earthly love, up on the surface here. My treasure, my life, everything for me, is down below. Torbern! take me down with you! Show me the richest veins, the lodes of ore, the glowing metal! I will dig and bore, and toil and labour. Never, never more will I come back to see the light of day. Torbern! Torbern! take me down to you!"

He took his flint and steel from his pocket, lighted his candle, and went quickly down the shaft, into the deep cutting where he had been on the previous day, but he saw nothing of the old man. But what was his amazement when, at the deepest point, he saw the vein of metal with the utmost clearness and distinctness, so that he could trace every one of its ramifications and its risings and fallings. But as he kept his gaze fixed more and more firmly on this wonderful vein, a dazzling light seemed to come shining through the shaft, and the walls of rock grew transparent as crystal. That mysterious dream which he had had in Goethaborg came back upon him. He was looking upon those Elysian Fields of glorious metallic trees and plants on which, by way of fruits, buds, and blossoms, hung jewels streaming with fire. He saw the maidens and he looked on the face of the mighty queen. She put out her arms, drew him to her, and pressed him to her breast. Then a burning ray darted through his heart, and all his consciousness was merged in a feeling of floating in waves of some blue, transparent, glittering mist.

"Elis Froebom! Elis Froebom!" a powerful voice from above cried out, and the reflection of torches began shining in the shaft. It was Pehrson Dahlsjoe who had come down with the Captain to search for the lad, who had been seen running in the direction of the main shaft like a mad creature.

They found him standing as if turned to stone, with his face pressed against the cold, hard rock.

"What are you doing down here in the nighttime, you foolish fellow?" cried Pehrson. "Pull yourself together, and come up with us. Who knows what good news you may hear."

Elis went up in profound silence after Dahlsjoe, who did not cease to rate him soundly for exposing himself to such danger. It was broad daylight when they got to the house.

Ulla threw herself into Elis's arms with a great cry and called him the fondest names, and Pehrson said to him:

"You foolish fellow! How could I help seeing, long ago, that you were in love with Ulla, and that it was on her account, in all probability, that you were working so hard in the mine? Neither could I help seeing that she was just as fond of you. Could I wish for a better son-in-law than a fine, hearty, hard-working, honest miner—than just yourself, Elis? What vexed me was that you never would speak."

"We scarcely knew ourselves," said Ulla, "how fond we were of each other."

"However that may be," said Pehrson, "I was annoyed that Elis didn't tell me openly and candidly of his love for you, and that was why I made up the story about Eric Olavsen, which was so nearly being the death of you, you silly fellow. Not but what I wished to try you, Ulla, into the bargain. Eric Olavsen has been married for many a day, and I give my daughter to you, Elis Froebom, for, I say again, I couldn't wish for a better son-in-law."

Tears of joy and happiness ran down Elis's cheeks. The highest bliss which his imagination had pictured had come to pass so suddenly and unexpectedly that he could scarcely believe it was anything but another blissful dream. The work people came to dinner, at Dahlsjoe's invitation, in honour of the event. Ulla had dressed in her prettiest attire, and looked more charming than ever, so that they all cried, over and over again, "Eh! what a sweet and charming creature Elis has for his wife! May God bless them and make them happy!"

Yet the terror of the previous night still lay upon Elis's pale face, and he often stared about him as if he were far away from all that was going on round him. "Elis, darling, what is the matter?" Ulla asked anxiously. He pressed her to his heart and said, "Yes, yes, you are my own, and all is well." But in the midst of all his happiness he often felt as though an icy hand clutched at his heart, and a dismal voice asked him:

"Is it your highest aim to be engaged to Ulla? Wretched fool! Have you not looked upon the face of the queen?"

He felt himself overpowered by an indescribable feeling of anxiety. He was haunted and tortured by the thought that one of the workmen would suddenly assume gigantic proportions, and to his horror he would recognize in him Torbern, come to remind him, in a terrible manner, of the subterranean realm of gems and metals to which he had devoted himself.

And yet he could see no reason why the spectral old man should be hostile to him, or what connection there was between his mining work and his love.

Pehrson, seeing Elis's disordered condition, attributed it to the trouble he had gone through and his nocturnal visit to the mine. Not so Ulla, who, seized by a secret presentiment, implored her lover to tell her what terrible thing had happened to him to tear him away from her so entirely. This almost broke his heart. It was in vain that he tried to tell her of the wonderful face which had revealed itself to him in the depths of the mine. Some unknown power seemed to seal his lips forcibly; he felt as though the terrible face of the queen were looking out from his heart, so that if he mentioned her, everything about him would turn to stone, to dark, black rock, as at the sight of the Medusa's frightful head. All the glory and magnificence which had filled him with rapture in the abyss appeared to him now as a pandemonium of immitigable torture, deceptively decked out to allure him to his ruin.

Dahlsjoe told him he must stay at home for a few days to shake off the sickness which he seemed to have fallen into. And during this time Ulla's affection, which now streamed bright and clear from her candid, childlike heart, drove away the memory of his fateful adventure in the mine depths. Joy and happiness brought him back to life and to belief in his good fortune, and in the impossibility of its being ever interfered with by any evil power.

When he went down the pit again, everything appeared quite different to what it used to be. The most glorious veins lay clear and distinct before his eyes. He worked twice as zealously as before; he forgot everything else. When he got to the surface again, it cost him an effort to remember Pehrson Dahlsjoe, even his Ulla. He felt as if divided into two halves, as if his better self, his real personality, went down to the central point of the earth, and there rested in bliss in the queen's arms, whilst *he* went to his dark dwelling in Falun. When Ulla spoke of their love, and the happiness of their future life together, he would begin to talk of the splendours of the depths, and the inestimably precious treasures that lay hidden there, and in so doing would get entangled in such wonderful, incomprehensible sayings that alarm and terrible anxiety took possession of the poor child, who could not divine why Elis should be so completely altered from his former self. He kept telling the Captain and Dahlsjoe himself with the greatest delight, that he had discovered the richest veins and the most magnificent trap-runs, and when these turned out to be nothing but unproductive rock, he would laugh contemptuously and say that none but he understood the secret signs, the significant writing, fraught with hidden meaning, which the queen's own hand had inscribed on the rocks, and that it was sufficient to understand those signs without bringing to light what they indicated.

The old Captain looked sorrowfully at Elis, who spoke, with wild gleaming eyes of the glorious paradise which glowed down in the depths of the earth. "That terrible old Torbern has been at him," he whispered in Dahlsjoe's ear.

"Pshaw! don't believe these miners' yarns," cried Dahlsjoe. "He's a deep-thinking serious fellow, and love has turned his head, that's all. Wait till the marriage is over, then we'll hear no more of the trap-runs, the treasures, and the subterranean paradise."

The wedding day fixed by Dahlsjoe came at last. For a few days previously Elis had been more tranquil, more serious, more sunk in deep reflection than ever. But, on the other hand, never had he shown such affection for Ulla as at this time. He could not leave her for a moment, and never went down the mine at all. He seemed to have forgotten his restless excitement about mining work, and never a word of the subterranean kingdom crossed his lips. Ulla was all rapture. Her fear lest the dangerous powers of the subterranean world, of which she had heard old miners speak, had been luring him to his destruction, had left her; and Dahlsjoe too said, laughing to the Captain, "You see, Elis was only a little light-headed for love of my Ulla."

Early on the morning of the wedding day, which was St. John's Day as it chanced, Elis knocked at the door of Ulla's room. She opened it, and started back terrified at the sight of Elis, dressed in his wedding clothes, deadly pale, with dark gloomy fire sparkling in his eyes.

"I only want to tell you, my beloved Ulla," he said, in a faint, trembling voice, "that we are just arrived at the summit of the highest good fortune which it is possible for mortals to attain. Everything has been revealed to me in the night which is just over. Down in the depths below, hidden in chlorite and mica, lies the cherry-coloured sparkling almandine, on which the tablet of our lives is graven. I have to give it to you as a wedding present. It is more splendid than the most glorious blood-red carbuncle,[5] and when, united in truest affection, we look into its streaming splendour together, we shall see and understand the peculiar manner in which our hearts and souls have grown together into the wonderful branch which shoots from the queen's heart, at the central point of the globe. All

---

[5] Any of several kinds of red gemstones.

that is necessary is that I go and bring this stone to the surface, and that I will do now, as fast as I can. Take care of yourself meanwhile, darling. I will be back in a little while."

Ulla implored him with bitter tears to give up all idea of such a dreamlike undertaking, for she felt a strong presentiment of disaster; but Elis declared that without this stone he should never know a moment's peace or happiness, and that there was not the slightest danger of any kind. He pressed her fondly to his heart, and was gone.

The guests were all assembled to accompany the bridal pair to the church of Copparberg, where they were to be married, and a crowd of girls, who were to be the bridesmaids and walk in procession before the bride (as is the custom of the place), were laughing and playing round Ulla. The musicians were tuning their instruments to begin a wedding march. It was almost noon, but Elis had not made his appearance. Suddenly some miners came running up, horror in their pale faces, with the news that there had been a terrible catastrophe, a subsidence of the earth, which had destroyed the whole of Pehrson Dahlsjoe's part of the mine.

"Elis! oh, Elis! you are gone!" screamed Ulla, wildly, and fell as if dead. Then for the first time Dahlsjoe learned from the Captain that Elis had gone down the main shaft in the morning. Nobody else had been in the mine, the rest of the men having been invited to the wedding. Dahlsjoe and all the others hurried off to search, at the imminent danger of their own lives. In vain! Elis Froebom was not to be found. There could be no question but that the earth-fall had buried him in the rock. And thus came desolation and mourning upon the house of brave Pehrson Dahlsjoe, at the moment when he thought he was assured of peace and happiness for the remainder of his days.

Long had stout Pehrson Dahlsjoe been dead, his daughter Ulla long lost sight of and forgotten. Nobody in Falun remembered them. More than fifty years had gone by since Froebom's luckless wedding day, when it chanced that some miners who were making a connection passage between two shafts found, at a depth of three hundred yards, buried in vitriolated water, the body of a young miner, which seemed when they brought it to the daylight to be turned to stone.

The young man looked as if he were lying in a deep sleep, so perfectly preserved were the features of his face, so wholly without trace of decay his new suit of miner's clothes, and even the flowers in his breast. The people of the neighbourhood all collected round the young man, but no one recognized him or could say who he had been, and none of the workmen missed any comrade.

The body was going to be taken to Falun, when out of the distance an old, old woman came creeping slowly and painfully up on crutches.

"Here's the old St. John's Day grandmother!" the miners said. They had given her this name because they had noticed that every year she came up to the main shaft on Saint John's Day, and looked down into its depths, weeping, lamenting, and wringing her hands as she crept round it, then went away again.

The moment she saw the body she threw away her crutches, lifted her arms to Heaven, and cried, in the most heart-rending way.

"Oh! Elis Froebom! Oh, my sweet, sweet bridegroom!"

And she huddled down beside the body, took the stone hands and pressed them to her heart, chilled with age, but throbbing still with the fondest love, like some naphtha flame under the surface ice.

"Ah!" she said, looking round at the spectators, "nobody, nobody among you remembers poor Ulla Dahlsjoe, this poor boy's happy bride fifty long years ago. When I went away, in my terrible sorrow and despair, to Ornaes, old Torbern comforted me, and told me I should see my poor Elis, who was buried in the rock upon our wedding day, once more here upon earth. And I have come every year and looked for him. And now this blessed meeting has been granted me this day. Oh, Elis! Elis! my beloved husband!"

She wound her arms about him as if she would never part from him more, and the people all stood around in the deepest emotion.

Fainter and fainter grew her sobs and sighs, till they ceased to be audible.

The miners closed around. They would have raised poor Ulla, but she had breathed out her life upon her bridegroom's body. The spectators noticed now that it was beginning to crumble into dust. The appearance of petrifaction had been deceptive.

In the church of Copparberg, where they were to have been married fifty years earlier, the miners laid in the earth the ashes of Elis Froebom, and with them the body of her who had been thus "Faithful unto death."

JOHN KEATS
[1795–1821]

During his brief life, John Keats wrote a handful of poems that put him in the front rank of English romantic poets. His particular contribution to romantic poetics consists of his brilliant use of imagery to portray the life of sensuous experience. His poems explore the pain and suffering that result from the fleeting nature of beauty and the impermanence of youth. As in Goethe's portrait of Young Werther, Keats depicts the sensitive poet with a heightened awareness of life's brevity and pain. In reaction to these thorns, the poet in several poems yearns to flee temporal existence and live forever in the realms of imagination or art.

LIFE

Keats's early education was at a school in Enfield, where the headmaster's son, Charles Cowden Clarke, took a particular interest in him and greatly encouraged his literary interests. Keats was eight when his father, the manager of a stable, was killed in a riding accident. When Keats was fourteen his mother died from tuberculosis, a disease that ran through the family, eventually killing Keats's brother and the poet himself. Keats was pulled out of school when his grandmother appointed an unimaginative tea merchant named Richard Abbey to be his guardian. Abbey guided Keats into medical studies. Although he spent four years as an apprentice and continued in medicine at Guy's Hospital in London in 1815, he soon abandoned medicine for poetry, having met Leigh Hunt, a political radical, critic, and poet.

Keats was twenty-two when Hunt sponsored his first book of poems in 1817. This volume included "On First Looking into Chapman's Homer" and "Sleep and Poetry," poems that reflected his talent and his seriousness about poetry as a vocation. Hunt also opened the door to a literary world where Keats met other prominent writers and artists, including Shelley, Hazlitt, and Haydon.

Following Milton's example of using classical themes for long poems, Keats undertook an overly ambitious project, *Endymion,* which was published in 1818. *Endymion* contains some 4,000 lines of rich, almost luxuriant images of a mortal, Endymion, who searches for and eventually finds a goddess symbolizing beauty. The year 1818 also saw family problems for Keats. His brother George and his wife emigrated to Kentucky, where they lost their money in a bad investment. Keats was left to care for his younger brother, Tom, who had contracted tuberculosis and was slowly wasting away, dying in December of that year. Keats himself went on a walking tour of northern England and returned with a severe sore throat, a warning sign of tuberculosis, the family malady.

During the same winter, 1818, Keats fell madly in love with Fanny Brawne. In the latter part of 1819 they became engaged, but were never married. Within the context of family problems, his own economic poverty, and his devotion to Fanny Brawne, Keats, within a nine-month period—January to September 1819—wrote the great poems of his career: "The Eve of St. Agnes," "La Belle Dame sans Merci: A Ballad," six magnificent odes, "Lamia," and a number of fine sonnets.

In an early poem, "Sleep and Poetry," Keats set up a program for his own development as a poet, which was modeled after the careers of epic poets such as Virgil and Milton. He was to begin with pastoral poems: "First the realm I'll pass / Of Flora, and old Pan: sleep in the grass, / Feed upon apples red, and strawberries, / And choose each pleasure that my fancy sees." Eventually he would grow beyond these poems: "Yes, I must pass them for a nobler life, / Where I may find the agonies, the strife / Of human hearts." Keats mastered the first stage, that of creating pictures and delighting in the sensuous surface of reality. Although he was rapidly maturing as a writer, he did not live long enough to fulfill completely his goal of dealing with the dark or painful complexities of human experience.

In February of 1820, Keats coughed up blood. The tuberculosis that had claimed both his mother and brother threatened his life. Advised to go to a warmer climate for the winter, Keats suffered through his last months in Italy. He died in Rome on February 23, 1821.

WORK

Keats's letters provide us with a broad picture of his interests, both personal and intellectual. In them he talks about people, the cultural scene in London, the nature and role of the poet, his family, his love for Fanny Brawne, his ideas about life and death. One of his ideals he termed *negative capability:* "that is when man is capable of being in uncertainties, Mysteries, doubts, without any irritable reaching after fact & reason" (To G. & T. Keats, 1817). Keats questions whether logic or a philosophical system can finally satisfy or explain the intricacies of the human spirit. An individual can appreciate the flux of life only by remaining content with half-knowledge, contradictory knowledge, without grasping after answers, the comfort of rational certainties. Only then does it become possible to imaginatively sympathize with the changing variety of life. Shakespeare, for example, was willing to submerge his own character in order to enter into the diverse characters of his plays. Following this idea, Keats maintained that a poet should have no character, no identity: "it is not itself—it has no self—it is every thing and nothing—It has no character—it enjoys light and shade; it lives in gusto, be it foul or fair, high or low, rich or poor, mean or elevated—It has as much delight in conceiving an Iago as an Imogen" (To R. Woodhouse, 1818).

In his letters, Keats develops romantic notions about the importance of beauty and intensity in poetry: "the excellence of every Art is its intensity, capable of making all disagreeables evaporate, from their being in close relationship with Beauty & Truth" (To G. & T. Keats, 1817). There is a kind of truth in art that is different from logical truth or scientific truth: "The Imagination may be compared to Adam's dream—he awoke and found it truth . . . I have never yet been able to perceive how any thing can be known for truth by consecutive reasoning. . . . However it may be, O for a Life of Sensations rather than of Thoughts!" (To B. Bailey, 1817). The poetic key that brings access to the truth of the imagination is the image, and Keats's own poems illustrate this.

"La Belle Dame sans Merci: A Ballad" picks up the motif of the *femme fatale*, who exacts a stern price for her sexual favors. Rich details are used to create the otherworldly reality of the seduction scenes; the connection between sex and death is a lingering byproduct of the experience. One of Keats's constant themes is the suffering that an awareness of mortality brings to the sensitive young poet. In "Ode to Autumn," the season itself is experienced in all of its ripeness and "mellow fruitfulness," with the underlying recognition that winter death is just moments away. Keats captures a kind of timelessness in the second stanza with a personification of Autumn lost in the reveries of harvest. A variation on this theme is developed in his "Ode to a Nightingale," where sensuous image is piled on sensuous image. The poet requests a drink that will release him from wordly cares, "where but to think is to be full of sorrow." Again tempted by death, the poet vows to use poetry, not drunkenness, to join the nightingale, which becomes a symbolic "immortal Bird" whose song resounds through the centuries and in faraway lands.

The scenes of lovers on the urn in the "Ode on a Grecian Urn" provide another occasion to lament the transience of youth and to celebrate timeless art that creates the illusion of holding on to life's sweetness. In the final stanza, the poet is able to admit the limitations of art with the words "Cold pastoral!" The last two lines of the poem involving beauty and truth have spawned innumerable explanations of their meaning or meanings. In a letter to Bailey (November 22, 1817), Keats wrote: "I am certain of nothing but of the holiness of the Heart's affections and the truth of Imagination—What the imagination seizes as Beauty must be truth." Keats expresses a sentiment that has become almost a truism since the romantic age: Besides the "truth of reason," which measures and evaluates the objective world, there is also an "intuitive or imaginative truth," which arises from and reveals the heart-felt relations with person and nature that make life both possible and worthwhile.

SUGGESTED READINGS

Two excellent biographies are W. J. Bate's *John Keats* (1963) and A. Ward's *John Keats: The Making of a Poet* (1963). Commentary on individual poems can be found in Douglas Bush's *Selected Poems and Letters* (1959) and C. L. Finney's *The Evolution of Keats' Poetry*, 2 vols. (1936). C. T. Watts's *A Preface to Keats* (1985) is useful. For Keats's letters, see Lionel Trilling, *The Selected Letters of John Keats* (1951).

La Belle Dame sans Merci:[1] A Ballad

1

O what can ail thee, knight-at-arms,
    Alone and palely loitering?
The sedge has withered from the lake,
    And no birds sing.

---

[1] "The Beautiful Lady without Pity," the title of a medieval poem by Alain Chartier.

2

O what can ail thee, knight-at-arms,
    So haggard and so woe-begone?
The squirrel's granary is full,
    And the harvest's done.

3

I see a lily on thy brow,
    With anguish moist and fever dew,   10
And on thy cheek a fading rose
    Fast withereth too.

4

"I met a lady in the meads[2]
    Full beautiful—a faery's child,
Her hair was long, her foot was light,
    And her eyes were wild.

5

"I made a garland for her head,
    And bracelets too, and fragrant zone;[3]
She looked at me as she did love,
    And made sweet moan.   20

6

"I set her on my pacing steed,
    And nothing else saw all day long,
For sidelong would she bend and sing
    A faery's song.

7

"She found me roots of relish sweet,
    And honey wild, and manna dew,
And sure in language strange she said
    'I love thee true.'

---

[2]Meadows.   [3]Girdle.

8

"She took me to her elfin grot,[4]
  And there she wept and sighed full sore,
And there I shut her wild wild eyes   30
  With kisses four.

9

"And there she lullèd me asleep,
  And there I dreamed—Ah! woe betide!
The latest dream I ever dreamt
  On the cold hill side.

10

"I saw pale kings and princes too,
  Pale warriors, death-pale were they all;
They cried, 'La Belle Dame sans Merci
  Hath thee in thrall!'   40

11

"I saw their starved lips in the gloam[5]
  With horrid warning gapèd wide,
And I awoke, and found me here,
  On the cold hill's side.

12

"And this is why I sojourn here,
  Alone and palely loitering,
Though the sedge is withered from the lake,
  And no birds sing."

Ode to a Nightingale

1

My heart aches, and a drowsy numbness pains
  My sense, as though of hemlock I had drunk,
Or emptied some dull opiate to the drains
  One minute past, and Lethe-wards[1] had sunk:

---

[4]Grotto.   [5]Twilight.
ODE TO A NIGHTINGALE
[1]Lethe is the river of forgetfulness in Greek mythology.

'Tis not through envy of thy happy lot,
  But being too happy in thine happiness,—
    That thou, light-wingéd Dryad[2] of the trees,
      In some melodious plot
  Of beechen green, and shadows numberless,
    Singest of summer in full-throated ease.   10

2

O, for a draught of vintage! that hath been
  Cool'd a long age in the deep-delvéd earth,
Tasting of Flora and the country green,
  Dance, and Provençal song, and sunburnt mirth!
O for a beaker full of the warm South,
  Full of the true, the blushful Hippocrene,[3]
    With beaded bubbles winking at the brim,
      And purple-stainéd mouth;
  That I might drink, and leave the world unseen,
    And with thee fade away into the forest dim: 20

3

Fade far away, dissolve, and quite forget
  What thou among the leaves hast never known,
The weariness, the fever, and the fret
  Here, where men sit and hear each other groan;
Where palsy shakes a few, sad, last gray hairs,
  Where youth grows pale, and spectre-thin, and dies;
    Where but to think is to be full of sorrow
      And leaden-eyed despairs,
  Where Beauty cannot keep her lustrous eyes,
    Or new Love pine at them beyond to-morrow.   30

4

Away! away! for I will fly to thee,
  Not charioted by Bacchus and his pards,[4]
But on the viewless wings of Poesy,
  Though the dull brain perplexes and retards:
Already with thee! tender is the night,
  And haply[5] the Queen-Moon is on her throne,
    Cluster'd around by all her starry Fays;[6]
      But here there is no light,
Save what from heaven is with the breezes blown
    Through verdurous glooms and winding mossy ways.   40

---

[2] Wood nymph.
[3] Fountain of the Muses on Mt. Helicon in Greece.
[4] Leopards.
[5] Perhaps.
[6] Fairies.

5

I cannot see what flowers are at my feet,
  Nor what soft incense hangs upon the boughs,
But, in embalmèd darkness, guess each sweet
  Wherewith the seasonable month endows
The grass, the thicket, and the fruit-tree wild;
  White hawthorn, and the pastoral eglantine;
    Fast fading violets cover'd up in leaves;
      And mid-May's eldest child,
  The coming musk-rose, full of dewy wine,
    The murmurous haunt of flies on summer eves.   50

6

Darkling[7] I listen; and, for many a time
  I have been half in love with easeful Death,
Call'd him soft names in many a musèd rhyme,
  To take into the air my quiet breath;
Now more than ever seems it rich to die,
  To cease upon the midnight with no pain,
    While thou art pouring forth thy soul abroad
      In such an ecstasy!
  Still wouldst thou sing, and I have ears in vain—
    To thy high requiem become a sod.   60

7

Thou wast not born for death, immortal Bird!
  No hungry generations tread thee down;
The voice I hear this passing night was heard
  In ancient days by emperor and clown:
Perhaps the self-same song that found a path
  Through the sad heart of Ruth,[8] when, sick for home,
  She stood in tears amid the alien corn;
    The same that oft-times hath
Charm'd magic casements, opening on the foam
    Of perilous seas, in faery lands forlorn.   70

8

Forlorn! the very word is like a bell
  To toll me back from thee to my sole self!
Adieu! the fancy cannot cheat so well
  As she is fam'd to do, deceiving elf.

---

[7] In the dark.
[8] Ruth from the Book of Ruth in the Bible.

Adieu! adieu! thy plaintive anthem fades
  Past the near meadows, over the still stream,
     Up the hill-side; and now 'tis buried deep
     In the next valley-glades:
     Was it a vision, or a waking dream?
     Fled is that music:—Do I wake or sleep?   80

Ode on a Grecian Urn

1

Thou still unravish'd bride of quietness,
  Thou foster-child of silence and slow time,
Sylvan historian, who canst thus express
  A flowery tale more sweetly than our rhyme:
What leaf-fring'd legend haunts about thy shape
  Of deities or mortals, or of both,
     In Tempe or the dales of Arcady?[1]
  What men or gods are these? What maidens loth?
What mad pursuit? What struggle to escape?
     What pipes and timbrels? What wild ecstasy?   10

2

Heard melodies are sweet, but those unheard
  Are sweeter; therefore, ye soft pipes, play on;
Not to the sensual ear, but, more endear'd,
  Pipe to the spirit ditties of no tone:
Fair youth, beneath the trees, thou canst not leave
  Thy song, nor ever can those trees be bare;
     Bold lover, never, never canst thou kiss,
Though winning near the goal—yet, do not grieve;
     She cannot fade, though thou hast not thy bliss,
For ever wilt thou love, and she be fair!   20

3

Ah, happy, happy boughs! that cannot shed
  Your leaves, nor ever bid the spring adieu;
And, happy melodist, unweariéd,
  For ever piping songs for ever new:
More happy love! more happy, happy love!
  For ever warm and still to be enjoy'd,

---

[1]Tempe is a lovely valley in Greece near Mount Olympus; Arcady, a region in the Peloponnese, symbolizes rural beauty.

For ever panting, and for ever young;
All breathing human passion far above,
   That leaves a heart high-sorrowful and cloy'd,
     A burning forehead, and a parching tongue.   30

4

Who are these coming to the sacrifice?
   To what green altar, O mysterious priest,
Lead'st thou that heifer lowing at the skies,
   And all her silken flanks with garlands drest?
What little town by river or sea shore,
   Or mountain-built with peaceful citadel,
     Is emptied of this folk, this pious morn?
And, little town, thy streets for evermore
   Will silent be; and not a soul to tell
     Why thou art desolate, can e'er return.   40

5

O Attic[2] shape! Fair attitude! with brede[3]
   Of marble men and maidens overwrought,
With forest branches and the trodden weed;
   Thou, silent form, dost tease us out of thought
As doth eternity: Cold pastoral!
   When old age shall this generation waste,
     Thou shalt remain, in midst of other woe
Than ours, a friend to man, to whom thou say'st,
   "Beauty is truth, truth beauty,"—that is all
     Ye know on earth, and all ye need to know.   50

Ode to Autumn

1

Season of mists and mellow fruitfulness,
   Close bosom-friend of the maturing sun;
Conspiring with him how to load and bless
   With fruit the vines that round the thatch-eves run;
To bend with apples the moss'd cottage-trees,
   And fill all fruit with ripeness to the core;
     To swell the gourd, and plump the hazel shells
     With a sweet kernel; to set budding more,

---

[2]Attica is the region in Greece where Athens is located.
[3]Pattern.

And still more, later flower for the bees,
Until they think warm days will never cease,
For Summer has o'er-brimm'd their clammy cells.

10

2

Who hath not seen thee oft amid thy store?
Sometimes whoever seeks abroad may find
Thee sitting careless on a granary floor,
Thy hair soft-lifted by the winnowing wind;
Or on a half-reap'd furrow sound asleep,
Drows'd with the fume of poppies, while thy hook
Spares the next swath and all its twinéd flowers:
And sometimes like a gleaner thou dost keep
Steady thy laden head across a brook;
Or by a cyder-press, with patient look,
Thou watchest the last oozings hours by hours.

20

3

Where are the songs of Spring? Ay, where are they?
Think not of them, thou hast thy music too,—
While barréd clouds bloom the soft-dying day,
And touch the stubble-plains with rosy hue;
Then in a wailful choir the small gnats mourn
Among the river sallows,[1] borne aloft
Or sinking as the light wind lives or dies;
And full-grown lambs loud bleat from hilly bourn;
Hedge-crickets sing; and now with treble soft
The red-breast whistles from a garden-croft;[2]
And gathering swallows twitter in the skies.

30

ALEXANDER PUSHKIN
[1799–1837]

The three great romantic writers in Russia during the early nineteenth century were Nikolai Gogol, Mikhail Lermontov, and Alexander Pushkin. Pushkin holds the place for Russian literature that Shakespeare does for English, or Goethe for German literature. Because of its formal and stylistic diversity, range, and innovation, like Shakespeare's and Goethe's, Pushkin's work does not easily fall into a single category. Indeed, his greatest work, *Eugene Onegin,* a novel written in verse and modeled on Byron's *Don Juan,* combines

---

[1]Willows.
[2]Enclosed farmland.

features of the romantic lyric but looks forward to the shift toward realism in its depiction of character and its straightforward plot. *Onegin,* like Pushkin's other works, celebrates in true romantic form the genius and independence of the "natural man" who does not hesitate to challenge conventional authority and power.

LIFE

Alexander Pushkin was born in Moscow in 1799; his father was a minor writer and his mother the granddaughter of an Ethiopian slave in the court of Peter the Great who eventually became a landowner and general. Pushkin was proud of both his boyar ancestry on his father's side and his African ancestry on his mother's, and he came to honor the latter in *The Negro of Peter the Great,* a novel that remained incomplete at his death in 1837. Trained at home to read and speak French, as were most aristocratic children in early nineteenth-century Russia, Pushkin in his youth wrote poetry in French rather than his native Russian. Eventually he attended the lycée at Tsarskoe Selo, a highly selective and elite school that specialized in turning the sons of aristocrats into soldiers and civil servants. While at school, Pushkin wrote poetry, a comic play, a novel, and a short story—in Russian now—exercising early his talent to explore to mastery, and even parody, the dominant forms of literature.

Steeped in the Enlightenment tradition of political and social thought that was standard fare at the lycée, Pushkin graduated in 1817 and took a position with the Foreign Office in St. Petersburg. Two poems that he wrote during this early period, "Freedom" (1817) and "The Village" (1819), show Pushkin's flirtation with revolutionary ideas—especially sympathy for the plight of the serfs, a qualified attack on Tsar Alexander's despotism, and a more general (and less threatening) love of freedom. This flirtation, however, along with his membership in a revolutionary group called The Green Lamp, ultimately led to his exile in the south under charges of circulating seditious literature. In Ekaterinoslav, his place of exile, Pushkin was taken in by the Raevsky family, who introduced him to the work of Byron. During the early 1820s, Pushkin, who was now with General Raevsky in Kishinev and eventually Odessa, on the Black Sea, found himself in a rich cultural ferment of Romanian, Greek, Jewish, Armenian, and even Gypsy traditions. In Odessa there were many Greek refugees in exile from their country, now under the domination of Turkey. Like Byron and Shelley in England, Pushkin grew sympathetic to the revolt of the Greeks against the occupying Turks. Indeed, Byron's work grew increasingly important to Pushkin as he finished some of the most important poems of his southern cycle—*The Prisoner of the Caucasus* (1822), *The Fountain of Bakhchisarai* (1823), and *The Gipsies* (1824)—and began writing *Eugene Onegin.* With the publication of these Byronic narrative poems, Pushkin's genius was immediately recognized. The free form and rebel heroes of the poems, their interest in "natural man," and the disenchantment with authoritarian rule clearly set Pushkin among the great romantics of his age.

In 1824, after a disagreement with the governor, Pushkin was again exiled to his mother's estate at Mikhailovskoye, where he continued to work on *Eugene Onegin* and completed a second masterpiece, *Boris Godunov* (1825), a tragedy written in verse. Consistent with Pushkin's opposition to French classicism and his quest for freer form, *Boris Godunov* rejects the strict "unities" of French classical tragedy in favor of a Shakespearean openness. Because of the unconventional form, the play, like Byron's *Manfred,* remained popular as a closet drama, but was not produced until 1870. In 1825, following Tsar Alexander's death and the Decembrist revolt, Pushkin met with the new tsar, Nicholas, who extended both a pardon and patronage to Pushkin. Pushkin thought his work would now be free from censorship, but Nicholas proved him wrong when he objected to portions of

Boris Godunov. In 1831, Pushkin married Natalia Goncharov, whose love of court society and flirtatiousness led six years later to Pushkin's death in a duel with one of her suitors, a French émigré named Baron d'Anthes.

WORK

Begun in 1823 and published in chapter form through 1830, *Eugene Onegin*, like Byron's *Don Juan*, grew by accretion. It is the story of the love between a young man who has left St. Petersburg to live on the estate of his uncle and the young Tatanya, the daughter of a nearby family. The episodes of *Onegin* often leave the two main characters aside to pursue other, what some might consider digressive themes and scenes, which include stories about minor characters, descriptions of places, and observations on literature. Through the digressive stanzas, the verse novel offers a detailed panorama of Russian culture in the early nineteenth century, including the politics of the Decembrist revolt and the influence of European literature on early Russian romanticism.

During the 1830s, Pushkin began publishing a series of "little plays," dramatic narrative poems that treat important cultural moments or ideas. *The Stone Guest* retells the story of Don Juan, and *Mozart and Salieri* depicts Salieri's fabled jealousy of Mozart, a theme revived in our time by Peter Shaffer's *Amadeus*. Pushkin identifies Mozart's work with spontaneity and genius, in contrast to the studied craftsmanship of Salieri's work, which cannot reach the same creative heights and so frustrates the otherwise competent musician. In addition, Pushkin wrote during the 1830s a number of short stories and novellas, including *The Queen of Spades* (1834) and *The Captain's Daughter* (1836), the latter of which returns to a historical event, the Pugachev rebellion, for a story that objectively depicts the land-owning classes in the nineteenth century.

The Bronze Horseman (completed in 1833 and published in 1837), which we include here, is one of Pushkin's literary treatments of Tsar Peter the Great, the horseman of the bronze statue. The story takes place during the great flood of St. Petersburg in 1824, and poignantly sets up a contrast between Peter's greatness and the incidents in the life of the petty clerk Yevgeni. Pushkin praises the building of St. Petersburg, the work and vision of Tsar Peter, in response to those who questioned the wisdom of building on such a desolate site, constantly threatened by the sea. In the poem, the destructive potential of the sea suggests a severe historical necessity that threatens to desolate the works of human creativity and craft. Once for Pushkin an image of freedom, as it is in Byron's poetry, the sea here becomes a predatory beast that feeds upon the city.

In *The Bronze Horseman,* Yevgeni, a prototype of the ubiquitous clerks that one finds in Gogol and Dostoevsky, loses all that he loves in the flood. In his bitter disappointment, he castigates Peter, the city's founder, by scorning the statue of the Bronze Horseman, which seems to come to life and chase him through the city. Yevgeni's vision of ruin contrasts with Peter's vision for the city as he studies the bleak Baltic coastland upon which he, Faust-like, wants to found a city to mark both his own greatness and the greatness of his nation. Peter's reclamation of the barren land stands as a heroic act of imagination and power. But the triumph of human creativity over natural forces ultimately fails, and Yevgeni and others like him must bear the burden of Peter's lack of total mastery. The opposition between Yevgeni and Peter also has a political dimension, for it roused early critics to see the poem as an opposition between the state and the individual—hence the original censorship imposed by Tsar Nicholas. Critics disagree over which character represents the hero: Peter or Yevgeni. Is Peter a creative genius who defies natural desolation and realizes his vision in the building of the city, or is he a despot whose overreaching ambition leads to the desolation of the small people like Yevgeni? Is Yevgeni simply the common person who falls in the sway of greater human, political, and natural powers, or is he a hero who despite his weakness challenges these powers, a spokesperson for the oppressed masses whose helpless defiance nonetheless foreshadows a revolution?

SUGGESTED READINGS

Students interested in Pushkin's life should consult the biographies by Henri Troyat (1936; trans. 1950) and David Magarshack (1967). Among works of general criticism, see Walter N. Vickery's *Alexander Pushkin* (1970), John Bayley's *Pushkin: A Comparative Commentary* (1971), and William M. Todd's "Pushkin" in *Handbook of Russian Literature*, ed. Victor Terras (1985). On *The Bronze Horseman*, Edmund Wilson's "In Honor of Pushkin" in *The Triple Thinkers* (1952) offers a good introduction. See also Waclaw Lednicki's *Pushkin's Bronze Horseman: The Story of a Masterpiece* (1955), the chapter on history and heroic poetry in John Bayley's *Pushkin: A Comparative Commentary*, and the chapter devoted to the poem in A. D. P. Briggs's *Alexander Pushkin: A Critical Study* (1983).

The Bronze Horseman

Translated by D. M. Thomas

A TALE OF ST. PETERSBURG

Introduction

On a shore washed by desolate waves, *he*[1] stood,
Full of high thoughts, and gazed into the distance.
The broad river rushed before him; a wretched skiff
Sped on it in solitude. Here and there,
Like black specks on the mossy, marshy banks,
Were huts, the shelter of the hapless Finn;
And forest, never visited by rays
Of the mist-shrouded sun, rustled all round.

And he thought: From here we will outface the Swede;
To spite our haughty neighbour I shall found   10
A city here.[2] By nature we are fated
To cut a window through to Europe,
To stand with a firm foothold on the sea.
Ships of every flag, on waves unknown
To them, will come to visit us, and we
Shall revel in the open sea.

A hundred years have passed, and the young city,
The grace and wonder of the northern lands,

---

[1] Peter I, the Great (1672–1725), tsar of Russia from 1682 to 1725, who led the westernization of Russia, often by stern measures.

[2] With the aid of Italian and French architects, in 1703 Peter began to construct St. Petersburg, or Petrograd; the new city was a monument to Peter's plans for westernizing Russia and a symbol of strength against longtime foes, including Sweden, just across the Baltic.

Out of the gloom of forests and the mud
Of marshes splendidly has risen; where once   20
The Finnish fisherman, the sad stepson
Of nature, standing alone on the low banks,
Cast into unknown waters his worn net,
Now huge harmonious palaces and towers
Crowd on the bustling banks; ships in their throngs
Speed from all ends of the earth to the rich quays;
The Neva³ is clad in granite; bridges hang
Poised over her waters; her islands are covered
With dark-green gardens, and before the younger
Capital, ancient Moscow has grown pale,   30
Like a widow in purple before a new empress.

I love you, Peter's creation, I love your stern
Harmonious look, the Neva's majestic flow,
Her granite banks, the iron tracery
Of your railings, the transparent twilight and
The moonless glitter of your pensive nights,
When in my room I write or read without
A lamp, and slumbering masses of deserted
Streets shine clearly, and the Admiralty spire
Is luminous, and, without letting in   40
The dark of night to golden skies, one dawn
Hastens to relieve another, granting
A mere half-hour to night. I love
The motionless air and frost of your harsh winter,
The sledges coursing along the solid Neva,
Girls' faces brighter than roses, and the sparkle
And noise and sound of voices at the balls,
And, at the hour of the bachelor's feast, the hiss
Of foaming goblets and the pale-blue flame
Of punch. I love the warlike energy   50
Of Mars' Field,⁴ the uniform beauty of the troops
Of infantry and of the horses, tattered
Remnants of those victorious banners in array
Harmoniously swaying, the gleam of those
Bronze helmets, shot through in battle. O martial
Capital,⁵ I love the smoke and thunder
Of your fortress, when the empress of the north
Presents a son to the royal house, or when
Russia celebrates another victory
Over the foe, or when the Neva, breaking   60
Her blue ice, bears it to the seas, exulting,
Scenting spring days.

        Flaunt your beauty, Peter's
City, and stand unshakeable like Russia,

---

³The river that runs through St. Petersburg into the Baltic; the poem is based on the devastating flood of 1824 when the Neva overflowed its banks.
⁴The parade grounds in St. Petersburg.
⁵St. Petersburg was capital of Russia from 1712 to 1914, when the capital moved to Moscow.

So that even the conquered elements may make
Their peace with you; let the Finnish waves
Forget their enmity and ancient bondage,
And let them not disturb with empty spite
Peter's eternal sleep!

There was a dreadful time—the memory of it
Is still fresh ... I will begin my narrative   70
Of it for you, my friends. My tale will be sad.

                                        1

November over darkened Petrograd.
With a roar of waves splashing against the edges
Of her shapely bounds, the Neva tossed
Like a sick man in his restless bed.
It was already late and dark; against
The window angrily the rain was beating,
And the wind blew, howling sadly. At that time
Came young Yevgeni home, from friends ... We'll call
Our hero by this name. It's pleasant, and   80
Has long been congenial to my pen.
We do not need his surname, though perhaps
In times gone by it shone, under the pen
Of Karamzin,[6] rang forth in our native legends;
But now it is forgotten by the world
And fame. Our hero lives in Kolomna,[7] works
Somewhere, avoids the paths of the famous, mourns
Neither dead relatives nor the forgotten past.

And so, having come home, Yevgeni tossed
His cloak aside, undressed, lay down. But for   90
A long time could not fall asleep, disturbed
By divers thoughts. What did he think about?
About the fact that he was poor, by toil
Would have to earn honour and independence;
That God might have granted him more brains and money;
That there are lazy devils, after all,
For whom life is so easy! That he had been
A clerk for two years; he also thought the weather
Was not becoming any calmer; that
The river was still rising; as like as not,   100
The bridges on the Neva had been raised,
And for two or three days he would be cut off
From Parasha. At that point Yevgeni sighed
From his heart, and fell to dreaming like a poet.

---

[6]Nikolai Mikhailovich Karamzin (1766–1825), Russian writer and historian, author of the *History of the Russian State* (1818–1824).
[7]At the time, an outlying suburb of Petersburg.

'Get married? Me? Why not! It would be hard,
Of course; but then, I'm young and healthy, ready
To toil day and night; somehow or other
I'll fix myself a humble, simple shelter
Where Parasha and I can live in quiet.
After a year or two I'll get a job,   110
And Parasha will bring up our children . . . Then
We shall begin to live, and thus we'll go
Hand in hand to the grave, and our grandchildren
Will bury us . . .'

Thus he dreamed. And he felt sad that night,
And wished the wind would not howl gloomily,
The rain not beat so angrily at the window . . .

At last he closed his sleepy eyes. And now
The foul night thins, and the pale day draws on . . .
The dreadful day!

         All night the Neva rushed   120
Towards the sea against the storm, unable
To overcome the madness of the winds . . .
She could no longer carry on the struggle . . .
By morning, throngs of people on her banks
Admired the spray, the mountains and the foam
Of maddened waters. But harried by the gale
Out of the gulf, the Neva turned back, angry,
Turbulent, and swamped the islands. The weather
Raged more fiercely, Neva swelled up and roared,
Bubbling like a cauldron; suddenly   130
Hurled herself on the city like a beast.
Everything ran before her, everything
Suddenly became deserted—suddenly
The waters flowed into the cellars underground,
The canals surged up to the railings,
And Petropolis floated up, like Triton,[8]
Plunged to the waist in water.

    Siege! Assault! The sly waves climb like thieves
Through the windows. Scudding boats smash the panes
With their sterns. Hawkers' trays, fragments of huts,   140
Beams, roofs, the wares of thrifty trading,
The chattels of pale poverty, bridges swept
Away by the storm, coffins from the buried
Cemetery—all float along the streets!

    The people gaze upon the wrath of God
And await their doom. Alas! All's swept away:
Shelter and food—where shall they find them?

---

[8] A sea god, son of the chief god of the sea, Poseidon, and Amphitrite, a sea goddess; Triton calmed the waters by sounding a conch shell.

In that dread year the late Tsar in his glory
Still ruled Russia. He came out on to the balcony,
Sad, troubled, and said: 'Tsars cannot master   150
The divine elements.' He sat down and with thoughtful
Sorrowful eyes gazed on the dire disaster:
The squares like lakes; broad rivers of streets
Pouring into them. The palace a sad island.
The Tsar spoke—from end to end of the city,
Along streets near and far, a dangerous journey
Through the storm waters, generals set off
To save the people, drowning in their homes.

There, in Peter's square, where in the corner
A new house towers, where over the lofty porch   160
Two guardian lions stand like living creatures
With upraised paw—there sat, astride the marble
Beast, hatless, his arms crossed tightly,
Motionless and fearfully pale, Yevgeni.
He was afraid, poor fellow, not for himself.
He did not hear the greedy billow rise,
Lapping his soles; he did not feel the rain
Lashing his face, nor the wind, wildly howling,
Tear his hat from his head. His desperate gaze
Was fixed on one distant point. Like mountains,   170
There the waves rose up from the seething depths,
And raged, there the storm howled, there wreckage
Rushed to and fro . . . God, God! There—
Alas!—so close to the waves, almost by the gulf
Itself, is an unpainted fence and a willow
And a small ramshackle house: there they live,
A widow and her daughter, Parasha, his dream . . .
Or is all this a dream? Is all our life
Nothing but an empty dream, heaven's jest?

And he, as though bewitched, as if riveted   180
To the marble, cannot get down! Around him
Is water and nothing else! And, his back turned
To him, in unshakeable eminence, over
The angry river, the turbulent Neva, stands
The Image, with outstretched arm, on his bronze horse.

2

But now, satiated with destruction, wearied
By her insolent violence, the Neva drew back,
Revelling in the chaos she had caused,
And carelessly abandoning her booty.
Thus a marauder, bursting into a village with   190
His savage band, smashes, slashes, shatters,
And robs; shrieks, gnashing of teeth, violence,
Oaths, panic, howls! And weighed down by their plunder,

Fearing pursuit, exhausted, the robbers leave
For home, dropping their plunder on the way.

The water fell, the roadway was visible,
And my Yevgeni, in hope and fear and grief,
Hastened with sinking heart to the scarcely abated
River. But full of their victory the waves
Still seethed angrily, as though beneath them   200
Fires were smouldering; foam still covered them,
And heavily the Neva breathed, like a horse
Galloping home from battle. Yevgeni looks:
He sees a boat; he runs towards his find;
Shouts to the ferryman—and for ten kopecks
The carefree ferryman rows him across the billows.

And long the experienced oarsman struggled with
The stormy waves, and all the time the skiff
Was on the point of plunging with its rash crew
To the depths, between the ranges of the waves   210
—And at last he reached the bank.
                              The wretched man
Runs down a familiar street to familiar places.
He gazes, and can recognize nothing.
A dreadful vision! All is piled up before him:
This has been hurled down, that has been torn away;
The little houses have become twisted, others
Have completely collapsed, others have been shifted
By the waves; all around, as on a battlefield,
Corpses are strewn. Yevgeni rushes headlong,
Remembering nothing, exhausted by torments,   220
To the place where fate awaits him with unknown tidings,
As with a sealed letter. And now he is
Already rushing through the suburb, and here
Is the bay, and close by is the house . . .
What is this? . . .
                  He stopped. Went back and turned.
Looked . . . walked forward . . . looked again.
Here is the place where their house stood;
Here is the willow. There were gates here—swept
Away, evidently. But where is the house?
And, full of gloomy anxiety, he walks, he walks   230
Around, talks loudly to himself—and then,
Striking his forehead with his hand, he laughed.

Darkness fell upon the city, shaking
With terror; long its people did not sleep,
But talked among themselves of the past day.

Dawn's light shone over the pale capital
And found no trace of the disaster; loss
Was covered by a purple cloak. And life
Resumed its customary order. People
Walked coldly, impassively, along cleared streets.   240

Government officials, leaving their night's shelter,
Went to their jobs. The indomitable tradesman
Opened his cellar looted by the Neva,
Hoping to make good his loss at his neighbour's expense.
Boats were being hauled away from courtyards.

    Already Count Khvostov,[9] beloved of heaven,
Was singing the disaster of Neva's banks
In his immortal verses.

                           But my poor, poor
Yevgeni! . . . Alas! his confused mind could not endure
The shocks he had suffered. His ears still heard   250
The boom of Neva and the winds. Silently
He wandered round, filled with dreadful thoughts.
Some sort of dream tormented him. A week,
A month, went by—still he did not go home.
When the time ran out, his landlord leased
His abandoned nook to a poor poet. Yevgeni
Did not come to collect his belongings. He grew
A stranger to the world. All day he wandered
On foot, and slept at night on the embankment;
He fed on scraps handed to him through windows.   260
Tattered and mouldy grew his shabby clothes.
Children threw stones at him. Often the whips
Of coachmen lashed him, for he could not find his way;
It seemed he noticed nothing, deafened by
An inner turmoil. And so he dragged out his life,
Neither beast nor man, neither this nor that,
Not of the living world nor of the dead . . .

    Once he was sleeping on the Neva banks.
The days of summer were declining towards autumn.
A sickly wind was breathing. The sullen wave
Splashed against the embankment, reproachfully   270
Grumbling and beating against the smooth steps,
Like a petitioner at the door of judges
Who keep turning him away. The poor wretch woke.
It was dark: rain dripped, the wind howled gloomily;
A distant watchman traded cries with it.
Yevgeni started up; recalled his nightmare;
Hastily he set off wandering, until
He suddenly stopped—and slowly began to cast
His eyes around, with wild fear on his face.   280
He found himself at the foot of the pillars of
The great house. Over the porch the lions stood
On guard, like living creatures, with their paws
Upraised; and eminently dark and high
Above the railed-in rock, with arm outstretched,
The Image, mounted on his horse of bronze.

---

[9]A minor poet and contemporary of Pushkin.

Yevgeni shuddered. Terribly his thoughts
Grew clear in him. He recognized the place
Where the flood played, where greedy waves had pressed,
Rioting round him angrily, and the lions,   290
And the square, and him who motionlessly
Held aloft his bronze head in the darkness,
Him by whose fateful will the city had
Been founded on the sea . . . How terrible
He was in the surrounding murk! What thought
Was on his brow, what strength was hidden in him!
And in that steed what fire! Where do you gallop,
Proud steed, and where will you plant your hoofs?
O mighty master of fate! was it not thus,
Towering on the precipice's brink,   300
You reared up Russia with your iron curb?

    The poor madman walked around the pedestal
Of the Image, and brought wild looks to bear
On the countenance of the lord of half the world.
His breast contracted, his brow was pressed against
The cold railings, his eyes were sealed by mist,
Flames ran through his heart, his blood boiled.
Sombrely he stood before the statue;
His teeth clenched, his hands tightened, trembling
With wrath, possessed by a dark power, he whispered: 310
'All right then, wonder-worker, just you wait!'
And suddenly set off running at breakneck speed.
It seemed to him that the face of the dead Tsar,
Momentarily flaring up with rage,
Was slowly turning . . . Across the empty square
He runs, and hears behind him—like the rumble
Of thunder—the clash and clangor of hoofs
Heavily galloping over the shaking square.
And lit by the pale moonlight, stretching out
His hand aloft, the Bronze Horseman rushes   320
After him on his ponderously galloping mount;
And all night long, wherever the madman ran,
The Bronze Horseman followed with a ringing clatter.

    And from that time, whenever his wanderings took him
Into that square, confusion appeared on his face.
Hastily he would press his hand to his heart,
As though to ease its torment, he would doff
His tattered cap, he would not raise his troubled
Eyes, and would go on by some roundabout way.

    A small island can be seen off-shore. Sometimes   330
A fisherman out late will moor there with
His net and cook his meagre supper. Or
Some civil servant, boating on a Sunday,
Will pay a visit to the barren island.
No grass grows, not a blade. The flood, in sport,

Had driven a ramshackle little house there.
Above the water it had taken root
Like a black bush. Last spring a wooden barge
Carried away the wreckage. By the threshold
They found my madman, and on that very spot
For the love of God they buried his cold corpse.   340

HARRIET A. JACOBS (LINDA BRENT)
[C. 1813–1897]

In the eighteenth and nineteenth centuries, among white residents of the United States and Canada, the romantic impulse often took the form of dreams about starting life anew amid the great western territories, places for the most part not yet inscribed by European ideas and codes of behavior. The North American West was for many the symbolic direction of promise and potential self-fulfillment, and the early history of the United States is still often popularly imagined as the story of pioneers of European origin "winning" the West as they travel across it and redeem it from native peoples and from its own wildness.

This perspective was not shared by all living in North America. For the enslaved African-American people of the southern United States, the direction of hope, the crucial journey, lay not to the west but to the north, toward the free states, and more particularly toward Canada, after the Fugitive Slave Law of 1850 subjected runaway slaves within U.S. borders to deportation. In words that appear to be about patient endurance and the sufferings of biblical peoples, spirituals and work songs encode or "signify" enslaved singers' longing for the journey north, and even actual information about how to get there; for example, the "sweet chariot" that swings low to carry us home and the "drinking gourd" we are urged to follow are both secret references to the Big Dipper, an easily recognizable constellation whose lines point to the North Star, that indispensable guide to those fleeing northward under cover of night. Harriet Jacobs was one of the many slaves who made that journey and wrote about it. To protect those who had helped her to escape, she used the pseudonym "Linda Brent," and changed the names of almost all the people and places figuring in her life in the South.

LIFE

Jacobs was born into slavery in about 1813 in Edenton, North Carolina. She was orphaned early; her maternal grandmother, Molly Horniblow ("Aunt Martha"), was a freedwoman who made her living as a baker. When Jacobs was eleven, her first mistress died, and she was bequeathed to the three-year-old daughter of Dr. James Norcom ("Dr. Flint"). Norcom soon began a dogged campaign of sexual harassment against Jacobs. When he forbade her to marry the African-American freedman whom she loved, she exercised the only option of resistance open to her and took for her lover another influential white man, the young lawyer Samuel Treadwell Sawyer ("Mr. Sands"), by whom she bore two children, Joseph and Louisa Matilda.

In 1835, Dr. Norcom punished Jacobs for continuing to refuse him by exiling her to his plantation, where slaves were treated more brutally than in town; next, he threatened to bring her children to the plantation and make them suffer particularly hard enslavement. Jacobs reasoned that if she were to disappear, Norcom would find her motherless children a mere burden and might sell them to an agent secretly representing their white father, whom she hoped would then free them.

For nearly seven years, while most people believed her dead or fled to the North, she hid in a cramped crawl space in the attic of her grandmother's house, afraid to reveal her presence even to her own children. Sawyer was indeed able to purchase Joseph and Louisa Matilda, but he never got around to the crucial legal matter of setting them free.

Jacobs at last escaped by boat in 1842 to New York City, where she worked as a nursemaid for the family of the editor Nathaniel Parker Willis. There, she met Frederick Douglass, the most prominent writer and orator who had escaped slavery, and Amy Post and Lydia Maria Child, writers active in the causes of abolition and women's rights. There, too, she was at last reunited with her children. Her son Joseph became a sailor, a livelihood that kept him out of slavery's reach, but Jacobs and Louisa Matilda were traced to New York by the vengeful Norcom and his now-adult daughter. The Norcoms threatened to reclaim Jacobs and her daughter until Willis's wife purchased Jacobs and set her free.

Jacobs's friends urged her to tell her story, but for some time she held back because of the pain and shame of revealing the sexual history so central to that telling. (It is worthwhile to remember that more than 130 years later, it is still hard for women and men of our time to speak about histories of rape and childhood sexual abuse.) Above all, Jacobs feared her daughter Louisa Matilda's reaction to her story, especially because Jacobs's grandmother, who was supportive in all else, had condemned Jacobs for becoming Sawyer's lover and getting pregnant by him. Finally Jacobs agreed to write her autobiography, hoping that she might galvanize women to oppose the evils of slavery. With some help from editor Lydia Maria Child—whose work on the text was demonstrably that of an editor, not a ghostwriter—Jacobs brought out *Incidents in the Life of a Slave Girl* in 1861. Once Louisa Matilda knew the story, she embraced her mother along with her history, rejoicing in Jacobs's courage.

After the Civil War, Jacobs did relief work for freed slaves in the South and raised money for that cause in England. Toward the latter part of her life, she ran a boardinghouse in Cambridge, Massachusetts; she died in 1897. Louisa Matilda Jacobs continued her mother's work in relief and civil rights.

WORK

Although slavery was practiced in many parts of the world, only in the United States did the slave narrative come to be a true genre of literature, one that emerges out of a rich blend of African, American, and European sources: the argument-by-storytelling and the rhythmic power of African tribal oratory; the verisimilitude of realism; the melodramatic formulations and personal pleas to "Dear Reader" of the sentimental novel; the hairbreadth escapes of the picaresque tradition. This is not to say that the narrow escapes, hideous suffering, and heartfelt pleas did not actually occur, but the narrators learn the means of their telling from oral and written expression they have previously encountered.

Finally, the real people of these narratives share with the fictional personae of contemporary European-American romantic literature the determination of the individual to speak one's own name, to insist on one's own identity, through acts of open rebellion or carefully masked defiance against a larger society. A number of prominent white abolitionists in the United States and in England were themselves writers of romantic fiction and poetry, and felt able to sympathize with the African-American writers on the ground of shared struggles against a dominant society that discouraged freedom. Many, such as Harriet Beecher Stowe, John Greenleaf Whittier, and Lydia Maria Child, helped to sponsor the lectures and publications of slaves who had escaped to the North. But as Frederick Douglass, the author of the best known of all slave narratives, would remark in 1855, the free person, however sympathetic, "cannot see things in the same light with the slave, because he does not, and cannot, look from the same point from which the slave does."

After the Civil War, many scholars came to regard the narratives as merely political propaganda, ephemeral literature of little value except as curiosities. In the last decades of the twentieth century, the recovery and rereading of slave narratives has been an important project of historians, anthropologists, folklorists, musicologists, and people in quest of the African-American vision of the antebellum South. Literary critics have come to appreciate the narratives for their own literary worth, and to realize how deeply they have influenced African-American writing. As Rosa Bontemps remarked in 1966, "From the narrative came the spirit and vitality and the angle of vision responsible for the most effective prose writing by black American writers from William Wells Brown to Charles W. Chesnutt, from W.E.B. DuBois to Richard Wright, Ralph Ellison, and James Baldwin." Bontemps's observation has been corroborated by African-American writing of recent decades; many readers have found their way back to the slave narratives through Alex Haley's *Roots,* Toni Morrison's *Beloved,* or similar works.

The slave narratives produced in the United States—more than 6,000 existing book-length narratives, Works Progress Administration interviews, and occasional essays, it has been estimated—vary greatly in many ways. But as James Olney and other scholars have pointed out, these texts share certain features of form and structure. For example, the authors often give accounts of how they learned to read and write and of the crucial role literacy plays in resisting slavery; they often include descriptions of slave auctions, and feature an account of one spectacularly brutal master or overseer. Most have a story to tell about one particularly strong and resolute slave who resists white authority, and most remark upon how avowedly Christian slaveholders are worse than ones who aren't especially religious. All these tropes can be found in Jacobs, as can two other features whose significance may easily escape contemporary readers. First, slave narratives were always printed with testimonials and portraits and other prefatory material attesting to the author's existence and truthfulness; second, with astonishing consistency, the narratives' opening sentences begin, "I was born . . ." Such features in the published narratives served to combat charges that these books and stories were mere abolitionist propaganda, heavily doctored or created by white zealots. But the testimonials, the portraits, and especially the ability to put into writing the words *I was born* were also a way for the freed author to insist upon his or her very existence as a human being, a man or a woman capable of thought, feeling, and speech.

As Charles T. Davis and Henry Louis Gates, Jr., note in *The Slave's Narrative,* twentieth-century historians have continued to be more likely to detect "bias" in the slaves' accounts and "authenticity" in the masters'. Jacobs's story, especially her startling account of her seven years of life spent in the crawl space, was read skeptically by many until 1985, when Jean Fagin Yellin brought to light letters, house blueprints, and other documents that proved Jacobs's authorship and her reliability.

Jacobs's narrative differs significantly from slave narratives by men in several important ways. First, she makes a specific appeal to a *female* audience, the Northern white sisterhood who might be aroused to outrage by her story. Women could not yet vote in the United States, but Jacobs hoped for action they might take outside of suffrage to persuade men to vote against slavery. Second, she speaks with great frankness of the sexual persecution she endured, of the sexual choices she made within the constraints of slavery, and of how the sexual subjugation of black women by white men poisons black and white families alike. Finally, while many male slave narratives center upon an unattached heroic young man who contrives mainly by his own strength and wits to win his way to freedom, Jacobs tells us about a resourceful and mutually supportive network of courageous women, in and out of slavery, who are working to liberate one another, and to free one another's children.

SUGGESTED READINGS

Jean Fagin Yellin's edition of *Incidents in the Life of a Slave Girl* (1987) contains etchings, photographs, maps, and descriptions of key people and places in Jacobs's narrative, together with Yellin's brilliant and moving reconstruction of Jacobs's life and the making of her book. Charles T. Davis and Henry Louis Gates, Jr.'s *The Slave's Narrative* (1991) brings together essays on many aspects of the genre. See especially their introduction, and James Olney's essay "'I Was Born': Slave Narratives, Their Status as Autobiography and as Literature," pp. 148–74. Houston A. Baker, Jr., in *Blues, Ideology, and Afro-American Literature* (1987), suggests many connections between slave narratives and other expressions of African-American culture.

FROM

Incidents in the Life of a Slave Girl

CHAPTER 1. CHILDHOOD

I was born a slave; but I never knew it till six years of happy childhood had passed away. My father was a carpenter, and considered so intelligent and skilful in his trade, that, when buildings out of the common line were to be erected, he was sent for from long distances, to be head workman. On condition of paying his mistress two hundred dollars a year, and supporting himself, he was allowed to work at his trade, and manage his own affairs. His strongest wish was to purchase his children; but, though he several times offered his hard earnings for that purpose, he never succeeded. In complexion my parents were a light shade of brownish yellow, and were termed mulattoes. They lived together in a comfortable home; and, though we were all slaves, I was so fondly shielded that I never dreamed I was a piece of merchandise, trusted to them for safe keeping, and liable to be demanded of them at any moment. I had one brother, William, who was two years younger than myself—a bright, affectionate child. I had also a great treasure in my maternal grandmother, who was a remarkable woman in many respects. She was the daughter of a planter in South Carolina, who, at his death, left her mother and his three children free, with money to go to St. Augustine, where they had relatives. It was during the Revolutionary War; and they were captured on their passage, carried back, and sold to different purchasers. Such was the story my grandmother used to tell me; but I do not remember all the particulars. She was a little girl when she was captured and sold to the keeper of a large hotel. I have often heard her tell how hard she fared during childhood. But as she grew older she evinced so much intelligence, and was so faithful, that her master and mistress could not help seeing it was for their interest to take care of such a valuable piece of property. She became an indispensable personage in the household, officiating in all capacities, from cook and wet nurse to seamstress. She was much praised for her cooking; and her nice crackers became so famous in the neighborhood that many people were desirous of obtaining them. In consequence of numerous requests of this kind, she asked permission of her mistress to bake crackers at night, after all the household work was done; and she obtained leave to do it, provided she would clothe herself and her children from the profits. Upon these terms, after working hard all day for her mistress, she began her midnight bakings, assisted by her two oldest children. The business proved profitable; and each year she laid by a little, which was saved for a fund to purchase her children. Her master died, and the property was divided among his heirs. The widow had her dower in the hotel, which she continued to keep open. My grandmother remained in her service as a slave; but her children were divided among her master's children. As she had five, Benjamin, the youngest one, was sold, in order that each heir might have an equal portion of dollars and cents. There was so little difference in our ages that he seemed more like my brother than my uncle. He was a bright, handsome lad, nearly white; for he inherited the complexion my grandmother had derived from Anglo-Saxon ancestors. Though only ten years old, seven hundred and twenty dollars were paid for him. His sale was a terrible blow to my grandmother; but she was naturally hopeful, and she went to work with renewed energy, trusting in time to be able to purchase some of her children. She had laid up three hundred dollars, which her mistress one day begged as a loan, promising to pay her soon. The reader probably knows that no promise or writing given to a slave is legally binding; for, according to Southern laws, a slave, *being* property, can *hold* no property. When my grandmother lent her hard earnings to her mistress, she trusted solely to her honor. The honor of a slaveholder to a slave!

To this good grandmother I was indebted for many comforts. My brother Willie and I often received portions of the crackers, cakes, and preserves, she made to sell; and after we ceased to be children we were indebted to her for many more important services.

Such were the unusually fortunate circumstances of my early childhood. When I was six years old, my mother died; and then, for the first time, I learned, by the talk around me, that I was a slave. My mother's mistress was the daughter of my grandmother's mistress. She was the foster sister of my mother; they were both nourished at my grandmother's breast. In fact, my mother had been weaned at three months old, that the babe of the mistress might obtain sufficient food. They played together as children; and, when they became women, my mother was a most faithful servant to her whiter foster sister. On her death-bed her mistress promised that her children should never suffer for any thing; and during her lifetime she kept her word. They all spoke kindly of my dead mother, who had been a slave merely in name, but in nature was noble and womanly. I grieved for her, and my young mind was troubled with the thought who would now take care of me and my little brother. I was told that my home was now to be with her mistress; and I found it a happy one. No toilsome or disagreeable duties were imposed upon me. My mistress was so kind to me that I was always glad to do her bidding, and proud to labor for her as much as my young years would permit. I would sit by her side for hours, sewing diligently, with a heart as free from care as that of any free-born white child. When she thought I was tired, she would send me out to run and jump; and away I bounded, to gather berries or flowers to decorate her room. Those were happy days—too happy to last. The slave child had no thought for the morrow; but there came that blight, which too surely waits on every human being born to be a chattel.

When I was nearly twelve years old, my kind mistress sickened and died. As I saw the cheek grow paler, and the eye more glassy, how earnestly I prayed in my heart that she might live! I loved her; for she had been almost like a mother to me. My prayers were not answered. She died, and they buried her in the little churchyard, where, day after day, my tears fell upon her grave.

I was sent to spend a week with my grandmother. I was now old enough to begin to think of the future; and again and again I asked myself what they would do with me. I felt sure I should never find another mistress so kind as the one who was gone. She had promised my dying mother that her children should never suffer for any thing; and when I remembered that, and recalled her many proofs of attachment to me, I could not help having some hopes that she had left me free. My friends were almost certain it would be so. They thought she would be sure to do it, on account of my mother's love and faithful service. But, alas! we all know that the memory of a faithful slave does not avail much to save her children from the auction block.

After a brief period of suspense, the will of my mistress was read, and we learned that she had bequeathed me to her sister's daughter, a child of five years old. So vanished our hopes. My mistress had taught me the precepts of God's Word: "Thou shalt love thy neighbor as thyself." "Whatsoever ye would that men should do unto you, do ye even so unto them." But I was her slave, and I suppose she did not recognize me as her neighbor. I would give much to blot out from my memory that one great wrong. As a child, I loved my mistress; and, looking back on the happy days I spent with her, I try to think with less bitterness of this act of injustice. While I was with her, she taught me to read and spell; and for this privilege, which so rarely falls to the lot of a slave, I bless her memory.

She possessed but few slaves; and at her death those were all distributed among her relatives. Five of them were my grandmother's children, and had shared the same milk that nourished her mother's children. Notwithstanding my grandmother's long and faithful service to her owners, not one of her children escaped the auction block. These God-breathing machines are no more, in the sight of their masters, than the cotton they plant, or the horses they tend.

Chapter 2. The New Master and Mistress

Dr. Flint, a physician in the neighborhood, had married the sister of my mistress, and I was now the property of their little daughter. It was not without murmuring that I prepared for my new home; and what added to my unhappiness, was the fact that my brother William was purchased by the same family. My father, by his nature, as well as by the habit of transacting business as a skilful mechanic, had more of the feelings of a freeman than is common among slaves. My brother was a spirited boy; and being brought up under such influences, he early detested the name of master and mistress. One day, when his father and his mistress had happened to call him at the same time, he hesitated between the two; being perplexed to know which had the strongest claim upon his obedience. He finally concluded to go to his mistress. When my father reproved him for it, he said, "You both called me, and I didn't know which I ought to go to first."

"You are *my* child," replied our father, "and when I call you, you should come immediately, if you have to pass through fire and water."

Poor Willie! He was now to learn his first lesson of obedience to a master. Grandmother tried to cheer us with hopeful words, and they found an echo in the credulous hearts of youth.

When we entered our new home we encountered cold looks, cold words, and cold treatment. We were glad when the night came. On my narrow bed I moaned and wept, I felt so desolate and alone.

I had been there nearly a year, when a dear little friend of mine was buried. I heard her mother sob, as the clods fell on the coffin of her only child, and I turned away from the grave, feeling thankful that I still had something left to love. I met my grandmother, who said, "Come with me, Linda;" and from her tone I knew that something sad had happened. She led me apart from the people, and then said, "My child, your father is dead." Dead! How could I believe it? He had died so suddenly I had not even heard that he was sick. I went home with my grandmother. My heart rebelled against God, who had taken from me mother, father, mistress, and friend. The good grandmother tried to comfort me. "Who knows the ways of God?" said she. "Perhaps they have been kindly taken from the evil days to come." Years afterwards I often thought of this. She promised to be a mother to her grandchildren, so far as she might be permitted to do so; and strengthened by her love, I returned to my master's. I thought I should be allowed to go to my father's house the next morning; but I was ordered to go for flowers, that my mistress's house might be decorated for an evening party. I spent the day gathering flowers and weaving them into festoons, while the dead body of my father was lying within a mile of me. What cared my owners for that? he was merely a piece of property. Moreover, they thought he had spoiled his children, by teaching them to feel that they were human beings. This was blasphemous doctrine for a slave to teach; presumptuous in him, and dangerous to the masters.

The next day I followed his remains to a humble grave beside that of my dear mother. There were those who knew my father's worth, and respected his memory.

My home now seemed more dreary than ever. The laugh of the little slave-children sounded harsh and cruel. It was selfish to feel so about the joy of others. My brother moved about with a very grave face. I tried to comfort him, by saying, "Take courage, Willie; brighter days will come by and by."

"You don't know any thing about it, Linda," he replied. "We shall have to stay here all our days; we shall never be free."

I argued that we were growing older and stronger, and that perhaps we might, before long, be allowed to hire our own time, and then we could earn money to buy our freedom. William declared this was much easier to say than to do; moreover, he did not intend to *buy* his freedom. We held daily controversies upon this subject.

Little attention was paid to the slaves' meals in Dr. Flint's house. If they could catch a bit of food while it was going, well and good. I gave myself no trouble on that score, for on my various errands I passed my grandmother's house, where there was always something to spare for me. I was frequently threatened with punishment if I stopped there; and my grandmother, to avoid detaining me, often stood at the gate with something for my breakfast or dinner. I was indebted to *her* for all my comforts, spiritual or temporal. It was *her* labor that supplied my scanty wardrobe. I have a vivid recollection of the linsey-woolsey dress given me every winter by Mrs. Flint. How I hated it! It was one of the badges of slavery.

While my grandmother was thus helping to support me from her hard earnings, the three hundred dollars she had lent her mistress were never repaid. When her mistress died, her son-in-law, Dr. Flint, was appointed executor. When grandmother applied to him for payment, he said the estate was insolvent, and the law prohibited payment. It did not, however, prohibit him from retaining the silver candelabra, which had been purchased with that money. I presume they will be handed down in the family, from generation to generation.

My grandmother's mistress had always promised her that, at her death, she should be free; and it was said that in her will she made good the promise. But when the estate was settled, Dr. Flint told the faithful old servant that, under existing circumstances, it was necessary she should be sold.

On the appointed day, the customary advertisement was posted up, proclaiming that there would be a "public sale of negroes, horses, &c." Dr. Flint called to tell my grandmother that he was unwilling to wound her feelings by putting her up at auction, and that he would prefer to dispose of her at private sale. My grandmother saw through his hypocrisy; she understood very well that he was ashamed of the job. She was a very spirited woman, and if he was base enough to sell her, when her mistress intended she should be free, she was determined the public should know it. She had for a long time supplied many families with crackers and preserves; consequently, "Aunt Marthy," as she was called, was generally known, and every body who knew her respected her intelligence and good character. Her long and faithful service in the family was also well known, and the intention of her mistress to leave her free. When the day of sale came, she took her place among the chattels, and at the first call she sprang upon the auction-block. Many voices called out, "Shame! Shame! Who is going to sell *you*, aunt Marthy? Don't stand there! That is no place for *you*." Without saying a word, she quietly awaited her fate. No one bid for her. At last, a feeble voice said, "Fifty dollars." It came from a maiden lady, seventy years old, the sister of my grandmother's deceased mistress. She had lived forty years under the same roof with my grandmother; she knew how faithfully she had served her owners, and how cruelly she had been defrauded of her rights; and she resolved to protect her. The auctioneer waited for a higher bid; but her wishes were respected; no one bid above her. She could neither read nor write; and when the bill of sale was made out, she signed it with a cross. But what consequence was that, when she had a big heart overflowing with human kindness? She gave the old servant her freedom.

At that time, my grandmother was just fifty years old. Laborious years had passed since then; and now my brother and I were slaves to the man who had defrauded her of her money, and tried to defraud her of her freedom. One of my mother's sisters, called Aunt Nancy, was also a slave in his family. She was a kind, good aunt to me; and supplied the place of both housekeeper and waiting maid to her mistress. She was, in fact, at the beginning and end of every thing.

Mrs. Flint, like many southern women, was totally deficient in energy. She had not strength to superintend her household affairs; but her nerves were so strong, that she could sit in her easy chair and see a woman whipped, till the blood trickled from every stroke of the lash. She was a member of the church; but partaking of the Lord's supper did not seem to put her in a Christian frame of mind. If dinner was not served at the exact time on that particular Sunday, she would station herself in the kitchen, and wait till it was dished, and then spit in all the kettles and pans that had been used for cooking. She did this to prevent the cook and her children from eking out their meagre fare with the remains of the gravy and other scrapings. The slaves could get nothing to eat except what she chose to give them. Provisions were weighed out by the pound and ounce, three times a day. I can assure you she gave them no chance to eat wheat bread from her flour barrel. She knew how many biscuits a quart of flour would make, and exactly what size they ought to be.

Dr. Flint was an epicure. The cook never sent a dinner to his table without fear and trembling; for if there happened to be a dish not to his liking, he would either order her to be whipped, or compel her to eat every mouthful of it in his presence. The poor, hungry creature might not have objected to eating it; but she did object to having her master cram it down her throat till she choked.

They had a pet dog, that was a nuisance in the house. The cook was ordered to make some Indian mush for him. He refused to eat, and when his head was held over it, the froth flowed from his mouth into the basin. He died a few minutes after. When Dr. Flint came in, he said the mush had not been well cooked, and that was the reason the animal would not eat it. He sent for the cook, and compelled her to eat it. He thought that the woman's stomach was stronger than the dog's; but her sufferings afterwards proved that he was mistaken. This poor woman endured many cruelties from her master and mistress; sometimes she was locked up, away from her nursing baby, for a whole day and night.

When I had been in the family a few weeks, one of the plantation slaves was brought to town, by order of his master. It was near night when he arrived, and Dr. Flint ordered him to be taken to the work house, and tied up to the joist, so that his feet would just escape the ground. In that situation he was to wait till the doctor had taken his tea. I shall never forget that night. Never before, in my life, had I heard hundreds of blows fall, in succession, on a human being. His piteous groans, and his "O, pray don't, massa," rang in my ear for months afterwards. There were many conjectures as to the cause of this terrible punishment. Some said master accused him of stealing corn; others said the slave had quarrelled with his wife, in presence of the overseer, and had accused his master of being the father of her child. They were both black, and the child was very fair.

I went into the work house next morning, and saw the cowhide still wet with blood, and the boards all covered with gore. The poor man lived, and continued to quarrel with his wife. A few months afterwards Dr. Flint handed them both over to a slavetrader. The guilty man put their value into his pocket, and had the satisfaction of knowing that they were out of sight and hearing. When the mother was delivered into the trader's hands, she said, "You *promised* to treat me well." To which he replied, "You have let your tongue run too far; damn you!" She had forgotten that it was a crime for a slave to tell who was the father of her child.

From others than the master persecution also comes in such cases. I once saw a young slave girl dying soon after the birth of a child nearly white. In her agony she cried out, "O Lord, come and take me!" Her mistress stood by, and mocked at her like an incarnate fiend. "You suffer, do you?" she exclaimed. "I am glad of it. You deserve it all, and more too."

The girl's mother said, "The baby is dead, thank God; and I hope my poor child will soon be in heaven, too."

"Heaven!" retorted the mistress. "There is no such place for the like of her and her bastard."

The poor mother turned away, sobbing. Her dying daughter called her, feebly, and as she bent over her, I heard her say, "Don't grieve so, mother; God knows all about it; and HE will have mercy upon me."

Her sufferings, afterwards, became so intense, that her mistress felt unable to stay; but when she left the room, the scornful smile was still on her lips. Seven children called her mother. The poor black woman had but the one child, whose eyes she saw closing in death, while she thanked God for taking her away from the greater bitterness of life.

· · ·

CHAPTER 5. THE TRIALS OF GIRLHOOD

During the first years of my service in Dr. Flint's family, I was accustomed to share some indulgences with the children of my mistress. Though this seemed to me no more than right, I was grateful for it, and tried to merit the kindness by the faithful discharge of my duties. But I now entered on my fifteenth year—a sad epoch in the life of a slave girl. My master began to whisper foul words in my ear. Young as I was, I could not remain ignorant of their import. I tried to treat them with indifference or contempt. The master's age, my extreme youth, and the fear that his conduct would be reported to my grandmother, made him bear this treatment for many months. He was a crafty man, and resorted to many means to accomplish his purposes. Sometimes he had stormy, terrific ways, that made his victims tremble; sometimes he assumed a gentleness that he thought must surely subdue. Of the two, I preferred his stormy moods, although they left me trembling. He tried his utmost to corrupt the pure principles my grandmother had instilled. He peopled my young mind with unclean images, such as only a vile monster could think of. I turned from him with disgust and hatred. But he was my master. I was compelled to live under the same roof with him—where I saw a man forty years my senior daily violating the most sacred commandments of nature. He told me I was his property; that I must be subject to his will in all things. My soul revolted against the mean tyranny. But where could I turn for protection? No matter whether the slave girl be as black as ebony or as fair as her mistress. In either case, there is no shadow of law to protect her from insult, from violence, or even from death; all these are inflicted by fiends who bear the shape of men. The mistress, who ought to protect the helpless victim, has no other feelings towards her but those of jealousy and rage. The degradation, the wrongs, the vices, that grow out of slavery, are more than I can describe. They are greater than you would willingly believe. Surely, if you credited one half the truths that are told you concerning the helpless millions suffering in this cruel bondage, you at the north would not help to tighten the yoke. You surely would refuse to do for the master, on your own soil, the mean and cruel work which trained bloodhounds and the lowest class of whites do for him at the south.

Every where the years bring to all enough of sin and sorrow; but in slavery the very dawn of life is darkened by these shadows. Even the little child, who is accustomed to wait on her mistress and her children, will learn, before she is twelve years old, why it is that her mistress hates such and such a one among the slaves. Perhaps the child's own mother is among those hated ones. She listens to violent outbreaks of jealous passion, and cannot help understanding what is the cause. She will become prematurely knowing in evil things. Soon she will learn to tremble when she hears her master's footfall. She will be compelled to realize that she is no longer a child. If God has bestowed beauty upon her, it will prove her greatest curse. That which commands admiration in the white woman only hastens the degradation of the female slave. I know that some are too much brutalized by slavery to feel the humiliation of their position; but many slaves feel it most acutely, and shrink from the memory of it. I cannot tell how much I suffered in the presence of these wrongs, nor how I am still pained by the retrospect. My master met me at every turn, reminding me that I belonged to him, and swearing by heaven and earth that he would compel me to submit to him. If I went out for a breath of fresh air, after a day of unwearied toil, his footsteps dogged me. If I knelt by my mother's grave, his dark shadow fell on me even there. The light heart which nature had given me became heavy with sad forebodings. The other slaves in my master's house noticed the change. Many of them pitied me; but none dared to ask the cause. They had no need to inquire. They knew too well the guilty practices under that roof; and they were aware that to speak of them was an offence that never went unpunished.

I longed for some one to confide in. I would have given the world to have laid my head on my grandmother's faithful bosom, and told her all my troubles. But Dr. Flint swore he would kill me, if I was not as silent as the grave. Then, although my grandmother was all in all to me, I feared her as well as loved her. I had been accustomed to look up to her with a respect bordering upon awe. I was very young, and felt shamefaced about telling her such impure things, especially as I knew her to be very strict on such subjects. Moreover, she was a woman of a high spirit. She was usually very quiet in her demeanor; but if her indignation was once roused, it was not very easily quelled. I had been told that she once chased a white gentleman with a loaded pistol, because he insulted one of her daughters. I dreaded the consequences of a violent outbreak; and both pride and fear kept me silent. But though I did not confide in my grandmother, and even evaded her vigilant watchfulness and inquiry, her presence in the neighborhood was some protection to me. Though she had been a slave, Dr. Flint was afraid of her. He dreaded her scorching rebukes. Moreover, she was known and patronized by many people; and he did not wish to have his villainy made public. It was lucky for me that I did not live on a distant plantation, but in a town not so large that the inhabitants were ignorant of each other's affairs. Bad as are the laws and customs in a slaveholding community, the doctor, as a professional man, deemed it prudent to keep up some outward show of decency.

O, what days and nights of fear and sorrow that man caused me! Reader, it is not to awaken sympathy for myself that I am telling you truthfully what I suffered in slavery. I do it to kindle a flame of compassion in your hearts for my sisters who are still in bondage, suffering as I once suffered.

I once saw two beautiful children playing together. One was a fair white child; the other was her slave, and also her sister. When I saw them embracing each other, and heard their joyous laughter, I turned sadly away from the lovely sight. I foresaw the inevitable blight that would fall on the little slave's heart. I knew how soon her laughter would be changed to sighs. The fair child grew up to be a still fairer woman. From childhood to womanhood her pathway was blooming with flowers, and overarched by a sunny sky. Scarcely one day of her life had been clouded when the sun rose on her happy bridal morning.

How had those years dealt with her slave sister, the little playmate of her childhood? She, also, was very beautiful; but the flowers and sunshine of love were not for her. She drank the cup of sin, and shame, and misery, whereof her persecuted race are compelled to drink.

In view of these things, why are ye silent, ye free men and women of the north? Why do your tongues falter in maintenance of the right? Would that I had more ability! But my heart is so full, and my pen is so weak! There are noble men and women who plead for us, striving to help those who cannot help themselves. God bless them! God give them strength and courage to go on! God bless those, every where, who are laboring to advance the cause of humanity!

CHAPTER 6. THE JEALOUS MISTRESS

I would ten thousand times rather that my children should be the half-starved paupers of Ireland than to be the most pampered among the slaves of America. I would rather drudge out my life on a cotton plantation, till the grave opened to give me rest, than to live with an unprincipled master and a jealous mistress. The felon's home in a penitentiary is preferable. He may repent, and turn from the error of his ways, and so find peace; but it is not so with a favorite slave. She is not allowed to have any pride of character. It is deemed a crime in her to wish to be virtuous.

Mrs. Flint possessed the key to her husband's character before I was born. She might have used this knowledge to counsel and to screen the young and the innocent among her slaves; but for them she had no sympathy. They were the objects of her constant suspicion and malevolence. She watched her husband with unceasing vigilance; but he was well practised in means to evade it. What he could not find opportunity to say in words he manifested in signs. He invented more than were ever thought of in a deaf and dumb asylum. I let them pass, as if I did not understand what he meant; and many were the curses and threats bestowed on me for my stupidity. One day he caught me teaching myself to write. He frowned, as if he was not well pleased; but I suppose he came to the conclusion that such an accomplishment might help to advance his favorite scheme. Before long, notes were often slipped into my hand. I would return them, saying, "I can't read them, sir." "Can't you?" he replied; "then I must read them to you." He always finished the reading by asking, "Do you understand?" Sometimes he would complain of the heat of the tea room, and order his supper to be placed on a small table in the piazza. He would seat himself there with a well-satisfied smile, and tell me to stand by and brush away the flies. He would eat very slowly, pausing between the mouthfuls. These intervals were employed in describing the happiness I was so foolishly throwing away, and in threatening me with the penalty that finally awaited my stubborn disobedience. He boasted much of the forbearance he had exercised towards me, and reminded me that there was a limit to his patience. When I succeeded in avoiding opportunities for him to talk to me at home, I was ordered to come to his office, to do some errand. When there, I was obliged to stand and listen to such language as he saw fit to address to me. Sometimes I so openly expressed my contempt for him that he would become violently enraged, and I wondered why he did not strike me. Circumstanced as he was, he probably thought it was better policy to be forbearing. But the state of things grew worse and worse daily. In desperation I told him that I must and would apply to my grandmother for protection. He threatened me with death, and worse than death, if I made any complaint to her. Strange to say, I did not despair. I was naturally of a buoyant disposition, and always I had a hope of somehow getting out of his clutches. Like many a poor, simple slave before me, I trusted that some threads of joy would yet be woven into my dark destiny.

I had entered my sixteenth year, and every day it became more apparent that my presence was intolerable to Mrs. Flint. Angry words frequently passed between her and her husband. He had never punished me himself, and he would not allow any body else to punish me. In that respect, she was never satisfied; but, in her angry moods, no terms were too vile for her to bestow upon me. Yet I, whom she detested so bitterly, had far more pity for her than he had, whose duty it was to make her life happy. I never wronged her, or wished to wrong her; and one word of kindness from her would have brought me to her feet.

After repeated quarrels between the doctor and his wife, he announced his intention to take his youngest daughter, then four years old, to sleep in his apartment. It was necessary that a servant should sleep in the same room, to be on hand if the child stirred. I was selected for that office, and informed for what purpose that arrangement had been made. By managing to keep within sight of people, as much as possible, during the day time, I had hitherto succeeded in eluding my master, though a razor was often held to my throat to force me to change this line of policy. At night I slept by the side of my great aunt, where I felt safe. He was too prudent to come into her room. She was an old woman, and had been in the family many years. Moreover, as a married man, and a professional man, he deemed it necessary to save appearances in some degree. But he resolved to remove the obstacle in the way of his scheme; and he thought he had planned it so that he should evade suspicion. He was well aware how much I prized my refuge by the side of my old aunt, and he determined to dispossess me of it. The first night the doctor had the little child in his room alone. The next morning, I was ordered to take my station as nurse the following night. A kind Providence interposed in my favor. During the day Mrs. Flint heard of this new arrangement, and a storm followed. I rejoiced to hear it rage.

After a while my mistress sent for me to come to her room. Her first question was, "Did you know you were to sleep in the doctor's room?"

"Yes, ma'am."

"Who told you?"

"My master."

"Will you answer truly all the questions I ask?"

"Yes, ma'am."

"Tell me, then, as you hope to be forgiven, are you innocent of what I have accused you?"

"I am."

She handed me a Bible, and said, "Lay your hand on your heart, kiss this holy book, and swear before God that you tell me the truth."

I took the oath she required, and I did it with a clear conscience.

"You have taken God's holy word to testify your innocence," said she. "If you have deceived me, beware! Now take this stool, sit down, look me directly in the face, and tell me all that has passed between your master and you."

I did as she ordered. As I went on with my account her color changed frequently, she wept, and sometimes groaned. She spoke in tones so sad, that I was touched by her grief. The tears came to my eyes; but I was soon convinced that her emotions arose from anger and wounded pride. She felt that her marriage vows were desecrated, her dignity insulted; but she had no compassion for the poor victim of her husband's perfidy. She pitied herself as a martyr; but she was incapable of feeling for the condition of shame and misery in which her unfortunate, helpless slave was placed.

Yet perhaps she had some touch of feeling for me; for when the conference was ended, she spoke kindly, and promised to protect me. I should have been much comforted by this assurance if I could have had confidence in it; but my experiences in slavery had filled me with distrust. She was not a very refined woman, and had not much control over her passions. I was an object of her jealousy, and, consequently, of her hatred; and I knew I could not expect kindness or confidence from her under the circumstances in which I was placed. I could not blame her. Slaveholders' wives feel as other women would under similar circumstances. The fire of her temper kindled from small sparks, and now the flame became so intense that the doctor was obliged to give up his intended arrangement.

I knew I had ignited the torch, and I expected to suffer for it afterwards; but I felt too thankful to my mistress for the timely aid she rendered me to care much about that. She now took me to sleep in a room adjoining her own. There I was an object of her especial care, though not of her especial comfort, for she spent many a sleepless night to watch over me. Sometimes I woke up, and found her bending over me. At other times she whispered in my ear, as though it was her husband who was speaking to me, and listened to hear what I would answer. If she startled me, on such occasions, she would glide stealthily away; and the next morning she would tell me I had been talking in my sleep, and ask who I was talking to. At last, I began to be fearful for my life. It had been often threatened; and you can imagine, better than I can describe, what an unpleasant sensation it must produce to wake up in the dead of night and find a jealous woman bending over you. Terrible as this experience was, I had fears that it would give place to one more terrible.

My mistress grew weary of her vigils; they did not prove satisfactory. She changed her tactics. She now tried the trick of accusing my master of crime, in my presence, and gave my name as the author of the accusation. To my utter astonishment, he replied, "I don't believe it: but if she did acknowledge it, you tortured her into exposing me." Tortured into exposing him! Truly, Satan had no difficulty in distinguishing the color of his soul! I understood his object in making this false representation. It was to show me that I gained nothing by seeking the protection of my mistress; that the power was still all in his own hands. I pitied Mrs. Flint. She was a second wife, many years the junior of her husband; and the hoary-headed miscreant was enough to try the patience of a wiser and better woman. She was completely foiled, and knew not how to proceed. She would gladly have had me flogged for my supposed false oath; but, as I have already stated, the doctor never allowed any one to whip me. The old sinner was politic. The application of the lash might have led to remarks that would have exposed him in the eyes of his children and grandchildren. How often did I rejoice that I lived in a town where all the inhabitants knew each other! If I had been on a remote plantation, or lost among the multitude of a crowded city, I should not be a living woman at this day.

The secrets of slavery are concealed like those of the Inquisition. My master was, to my knowledge, the father of eleven slaves. But did the mothers dare to tell who was the father of their children? Did the other slaves dare to allude to it, except in whispers among themselves? No, indeed! They knew too well the terrible consequences.

My grandmother could not avoid seeing things which excited her suspicions. She was uneasy about me, and tried various ways to buy me; but the neverchanging answer was always repeated: "Linda does not belong to *me*. She is my daughter's property, and I have no legal right to sell her." The conscientious man! He was too scrupulous to *sell* me; but he had no scruples whatever about committing a much greater wrong against the helpless young girl placed under his guardianship, as his daughter's property. Sometimes my persecutor would ask me whether I would like to be sold. I told him I would rather be sold to any body than to lead such a life as I did. On such occasions he would assume the air of a very injured individual, and reproach me for my ingratitude. "Did I not take you into the house, and make you the companion of my own children?" he would say. "Have I ever treated you like a negro? I have never allowed you to be punished, not even to please your mistress. And this is the recompense I get, you ungrateful girl!" I answered that he had reasons of his own for screening me from punishment, and that the course he pursued made my mistress hate me and persecute me. If I wept, he would say, "Poor child! Don't cry! don't cry! I will make peace for you with your mistress. Only let me arrange matters in my own way. Poor, foolish girl! you don't know what is for your own good. I would cherish you. I would make a lady of you. Now go, and think of all I have promised you."

I did think of it.

Reader, I draw no imaginary pictures of southern homes. I am telling you the plain truth. Yet when victims make their escape from this wild beast of Slavery, northerners consent to act the part of bloodhounds, and hunt the poor fugitive back into his den, "full of dead men's bones, and all uncleanness." Nay, more, they are not only willing, but proud, to give their daughters in marriage to slaveholders. The poor girls have romantic notions of a sunny clime, and of the flowering vines that all the year round shade a happy home. To what disappointments are they destined! The young wife soon learns that the husband in whose hands she has placed her happiness pays no regard to his marriage vows. Children of every shade of complexion play with her own fair babies, and too well she knows that they are born unto him of his own household. Jealousy and hatred enter the flowery home, and it is ravaged of its loveliness.

Southern women often marry a man knowing that he is the father of many little slaves. They do not trouble themselves about it. They regard such children as property, as marketable as the pigs on the plantation; and it is seldom that they do not make them aware of this by passing them into the slavetrader's hands as soon as possible, and thus getting them out of their sight. I am glad to say there are some honorable exceptions.

I have myself known two southern wives who exhorted their husbands to free those slaves towards whom they stood in a "parental relation;" and their request was granted. These husbands blushed before the superior nobleness of their wives' natures. Though they had only counselled them to do that which it was their duty to do, it commanded their respect, and rendered their conduct more exemplary. Concealment was at an end, and confidence took the place of distrust.

Though this bad institution deadens the moral sense, even in white women, to a fearful extent, it is not altogether extinct. I have heard southern ladies say of Mr. Such a one, "He not only thinks it no disgrace to be the father of those little niggers, but he is not ashamed to call himself their master. I declare, such things ought not to be tolerated in any decent society!"

Chapter 7. The Lover

Why does the slave ever love? Why allow the tendrils of the heart to twine around objects which may at any moment be wrenched away by the hand of violence? When separations come by the hand of death, the pious soul can bow in resignation, and say, "Not my will, but thine be done, O Lord!" But when the ruthless hand of man strikes the blow, regardless of the misery he causes, it is hard to be submissive. I did not reason thus when I was a young girl. Youth will be youth. I loved, and I indulged the hope that the dark clouds around me would turn out a bright lining. I forgot that in the land of my birth the shadows are too dense for light to penetrate. A land

> "Where laughter is not mirth; nor thought the mind;
> Nor words a language; nor e'en men mankind.
> Where cries reply to curses, shrieks to blows,
> And each is tortured in his separate hell."[1]

There was in the neighborhood a young colored carpenter; a free born man. We had been well acquainted in childhood, and frequently met together afterwards. We became mutually attached, and he proposed to marry me. I loved him with all the ardor of a young girl's first love. But when I reflected that I was a slave, and that the laws gave no sanction to the marriage of such, my heart sank within me. My lover wanted to buy me; but I knew that Dr. Flint was too wilful and arbitrary a man to consent to that arrangement. From him, I was sure of experiencing all sorts of opposition, and I had nothing to hope from my mistress. She would have been delighted to have got rid of me, but not in that way. It would have relieved her mind of a burden if she could have seen me sold to some distant state, but if I was married near home I should be just as much in her husband's power as I had previously been,—for the husband of a slave has no power to protect her. Moreover, my mistress, like many others, seemed to think that slaves had no right to any family ties of their own; that they were created merely to wait upon the

---

[1] George Gordon, Lord Byron, "The Lament of Tasso," iv, 7–10.

family of the mistress. I once heard her abuse a young slave girl, who told her that a colored man wanted to make her his wife. "I will have you peeled and pickled,[2] my lady," said she, "if I even hear you mention that subject again. Do you suppose that I will have you tending *my* children with the children of that nigger?" The girl to whom she said this had a mulatto child, of course not acknowledged by its father. The poor black man who loved her would have been proud to acknowledge his helpless offspring.

Many and anxious were the thoughts I revolved in my mind. I was at a loss what to do. Above all things, I was desirous to spare my lover the insults that had cut so deeply into my own soul. I talked with my grandmother about it, and partly told her my fears. I did not dare to tell her the worst. She had long suspected all was not right, and if I confirmed her suspicions I knew a storm would rise that would prove the overthrow of all my hopes.

This love-dream had been my support through many trials; and I could not bear to run the risk of having it suddenly dissipated. There was a lady in the neighborhood, a particular friend of Dr. Flint's, who often visited the house. I had a great respect for her, and she had always manifested a friendly interest in me. Grandmother thought she would have great influence with the doctor. I went to this lady, and told her my story. I told her I was aware that my lover's being a free-born man would prove a great objection; but he wanted to buy me; and if Dr. Flint would consent to that arrangement, I felt sure he would be willing to pay any reasonable price. She knew that Mrs. Flint disliked me; therefore, I ventured to suggest that perhaps my mistress would approve of my being sold, as that would rid her of me. The lady listened with kindly sympathy, and promised to do her utmost to promote my wishes. She had an interview with the doctor, and I believe she pleaded my cause earnestly; but it was all to no purpose.

How I dreaded my master now! Every minute I expected to be summoned to his presence; but the day passed, and I heard nothing from him. The next morning, a message was brought to me: "Master wants you in his study." I found the door ajar, and I stood a moment gazing at the hateful man who claimed a right to rule me, body and soul. I entered, and tried to appear calm. I did not want him to know how my heart was bleeding. He looked fixedly at me, with an expression which seemed to say, "I have half a mind to kill you on the spot." At last he broke the silence, and that was a relief to both of us.

"So you want to be married, do you?" said he, "and to a free nigger."

"Yes, sir."

"Well, I'll soon convince you whether I am your master, or the nigger fellow you honor so highly. If you *must* have a husband, you may take up with one of my slaves."

What a situation I should be in, as the wife of one of *his* slaves, even if my heart had been interested!

I replied, "Don't you suppose, sir, that a slave can have some preference about marrying? Do you suppose that all men are alike to her?"

"Do you love this nigger?" said he, abruptly.

"Yes, sir."

"How dare you tell me so!" he exclaimed, in great wrath. After a slight pause, he added, "I supposed you thought more of yourself; that you felt above the insults of such puppies."

---

[2]"Peeled and pickled" refers to the practice of whipping a slave and then rinsing the wounds with salt water.

I replied, "If he is a puppy I am a puppy, for we are both of the negro race. It is right and honorable for us to love each other. The man you call a puppy never insulted me, sir; and he would not love me if he did not believe me to be a virtuous woman."

He sprang upon me like a tiger, and gave me a stunning blow. It was the first time he had ever struck me; and fear did not enable me to control my anger. When I had recovered a little from the effects, I exclaimed, "You have struck me for answering you honestly. How I despise you!"

There was silence for some minutes. Perhaps he was deciding what should be my punishment; or, perhaps, he wanted to give me time to reflect on what I had said, and to whom I had said it. Finally, he asked, "Do you know what you have said?"

"Yes, sir; but your treatment drove me to it."

"Do you know that I have a right to do as I like with you,—that I can kill you, if I please?"

"You have tried to kill me, and I wish you had; but you have no right to do as you like with me."

"Silence!" he exclaimed, in a thundering voice. "By heavens, girl, you forget yourself too far! Are you mad? If you are, I will soon bring you to your senses. Do you think any other master would bear what I have borne from you this morning? Many masters would have killed you on the spot. How would you like to be sent to jail for your insolence?"

"I know I have been disrespectful, sir," I replied; "but you drove me to it; I couldn't help it. As for the jail, there would be more peace for me there than there is here."

"You deserve to go there," said he, "and to be under such treatment, that you would forget the meaning of the word *peace*. It would do you good. It would take some of your high notions out of you. But I am not ready to send you there yet, notwithstanding your ingratitude for all my kindness and forbearance. You have been the plague of my life. I have wanted to make you happy, and I have been repaid with the basest ingratitude; but though you have proved yourself incapable of appreciating my kindness, I will be lenient towards you, Linda. I will give you one more chance to redeem your character. If you behave yourself and do as I require, I will forgive you and treat you as I always have done; but if you disobey me, I will punish you as I would the meanest slave on my plantation. Never let me hear that fellow's name mentioned again. If I ever know of your speaking to him, I will cowhide you both; and if I catch him lurking about my premises, I will shoot him as soon as I would a dog. Do you hear what I say? I'll teach you a lesson about marriage and free niggers! Now go, and let this be the last time I have occasion to speak to you on this subject."

Reader, did you ever hate? I hope not. I never did but once; and I trust I never shall again. Somebody has called it "the atmosphere of hell;" and I believe it is so.

For a fortnight the doctor did not speak to me. He thought to mortify me; to make me feel that I had disgraced myself by receiving the honorable addresses of a respectable colored man, in preference to the base proposals of a white man. But though his lips disdained to address me, his eyes were very loquacious. No animal ever watched its prey more narrowly than he watched me. He knew that I could write, though he had failed to make me read his letters; and he was now troubled lest I should exchange letters with another man. After a while he became weary of silence; and I was sorry for it. One morning, as he passed through the hall, to leave the house, he contrived to thrust a note into my hand. I thought I had better read it, and spare myself the vexation of having him read it to me. It expressed regret for the blow he had given me, and reminded me that I myself was wholly to blame for it. He hoped I had become convinced of the injury I was doing myself by incurring his displeasure. He wrote that he had made up his mind to go to Louisiana; that he should take several slaves with him, and intended I should be one of the number. My mistress would remain where she was; therefore I should have nothing to fear from that quarter. If I merited kindness from him, he assured me that it would be lavishly bestowed. He begged me to think over the matter, and answer the following day.

The next morning I was called to carry a pair of scissors to his room. I laid them on the table, with the letter beside them. He thought it was my answer, and did not call me back. I went as usual to attend my young mistress to and from school. He met me in the street, and ordered me to stop at his office on my way back. When I entered, he showed me his letter, and asked me why I had not answered it. I replied, "I am your daughter's property, and it is in your power to send me, or take me, wherever you please." He said he was very glad to find me so willing to go, and that we should start early in the autumn. He had a large practice in the town, and I rather thought he had made up the story merely to frighten me. However that might be, I was determined that I would never go to Louisiana with him.

Summer passed away, and early in the autumn Dr. Flint's eldest son was sent to Louisiana to examine the country, with a view to emigrating. That news did not disturb me. I knew very well that I should not be sent with *him*. That I had not been taken to the plantation before this time, was owing to the fact that his son was there. He was jealous of his son; and jealousy of the overseer had kept him from punishing me by sending me into the fields to work. Is it strange that I was not proud of these protectors? As for the overseer, he was a man for whom I had less respect than I had for a bloodhound.

Young Mr. Flint did not bring back a favorable report of Louisiana, and I heard no more of that scheme. Soon after this, my lover met me at the corner of the street, and I stopped to speak to him. Looking up, I saw my master watching us from his window. I hurried home, trembling with fear. I was sent for, immediately, to go to his room. He met me with a blow. "When is mistress to be married?" said he, in a sneering tone. A shower of oaths and imprecations followed. How thankful I was that my lover was a free man, that my tyrant had no power to flog him for speaking to me in the street!

Again and again I revolved in my mind how all this would end. There was no hope that the doctor would consent to sell me on any terms. He had an iron will, and was determined to keep me, and to conquer me. My lover was an intelligent and religious man. Even if he could have obtained permission to marry me while I was a slave, the marriage would give him no power to protect me from my master. It would have made him miserable to witness the insults I should have been subjected to. And then, if we had children, I knew they must "follow the condition of the mother." What a terrible blight that would be on the heart of a free, intelligent father! For *his* sake, I felt that I ought not to link his fate with my own unhappy destiny. He was going to Savannah to see about a little property left him by an uncle; and hard as it was to bring my feelings to it, I earnestly entreated him not to come back. I advised him to go to the Free States, where his tongue would not be tied, and where his intelligence would be of more avail to him. He left me, still hoping the day would come when I could be bought. With me the lamp of hope had gone out. The dream of my girlhood was over. I felt lonely and desolate.

Still I was not stripped of all. I still had my good grandmother, and my affectionate brother. When he put his arms round my neck, and looked into my eyes, as if to read there the troubles I dared not tell, I felt that I still had something to love. But even that pleasant emotion was chilled by the reflection that he might be torn from me at any moment, by some sudden freak of my master. If he had known how we love each other, I think he would have exulted in separating us. We often planned together how we could get to the north. But, as William remarked, such things are easier said than done. My movements were very closely watched, and we had no means of getting any money to defray our expenses. As for grandmother, she was strongly opposed to her children's undertaking any such project. She had not forgotten poor Benjamin's sufferings, and she was afraid that if another child tried to escape, he would have a similar or a worse fate. To me, nothing seemed more dreadful than my present life. I said to myself, "William *must* be free. He shall go to the north, and I will follow him." Many a slave sister has formed the same plans.

. . .

CHAPTER 10. A PERILOUS PASSAGE IN THE SLAVE GIRL'S LIFE

After my lover went away, Dr. Flint contrived a new plan. He seemed to have an idea that my fear of my mistress was his greatest obstacle. In the blandest tones, he told me that he was going to build a small house for me, in a secluded place, four miles away from the town. I shuddered; but I was constrained to listen, while he talked of his intention to give me a home of my own, and to make a lady of me. Hitherto, I had escaped my dreaded fate, by being in the midst of people. My grandmother had already had high words with my master about me. She had told him pretty plainly what she thought of his character, and there was considerable gossip in the neighborhood about our affairs, to which the open-mouthed jealousy of Mrs. Flint contributed not a little. When my master said he was going to build a house for me, and that he could do it with little trouble and expense, I was in hopes something would happen to frustrate his scheme; but I soon heard that the house was actually begun. I vowed before my Maker that I would never enter it. I had rather toil on the plantation from dawn till dark; I had rather live and die in jail, than drag on, from day to day, through such a living death. I was determined that the master, whom I so hated and loathed, who had blighted the prospects of my youth, and made my life a desert, should not, after my long struggle with him, succeed at last in trampling his victim under his feet. I would do any thing, every thing, for the sake of defeating him. What *could* I do? I thought and thought, till I became desperate, and made a plunge into the abyss.

And now, reader, I come to a period in my unhappy life, which I would gladly forget if I could. The remembrance fills me with sorrow and shame. It pains me to tell you of it; but I have promised to tell you the truth, and I will do it honestly, let it cost me what it may. I will not try to screen myself behind the plea of compulsion from a master; for it was not so. Neither can I plead ignorance or thoughtlessness. For years, my master had done his utmost to pollute my mind with foul images, and to destroy the pure principles inculcated by my grandmother, and the good mistress of my childhood. The influences of slavery had had the same effect on me that they had on other young girls; they had made me prematurely knowing, concerning the evil ways of the world. I knew what I did, and I did it with deliberate calculation.

But, O, ye happy women, whose purity has been sheltered from childhood, who have been free to choose the objects of your affection, whose homes are protected by law, do not judge the poor desolate slave girl too severely! If slavery had been abolished, I, also, could have married the man of my choice; I could have had a home shielded by the laws; and I should have been spared the painful task of confessing what I am now about to relate; but all my prospects had been blighted by slavery. I wanted to keep myself pure; and, under the most adverse circumstances, I tried hard to preserve my self-respect; but I was struggling alone in the powerful grasp of the demon Slavery; and the monster proved too strong for me. I felt as if I was forsaken by God and man; as if all my efforts must be frustrated; and I became reckless in my despair.

I have told you that Dr. Flint's persecutions and his wife's jealousy had given rise to some gossip in the neighborhood. Among others, it chanced that a white unmarried gentleman had obtained some knowledge of the circumstances in which I was placed. He knew my grandmother, and often spoke to me in the street. He became interested for me, and asked questions about my master, which I answered in part. He expressed a great deal of sympathy, and a wish to aid me. He constantly sought opportunities to see me, and wrote to me frequently. I was a poor slave girl, only fifteen years old.

So much attention from a superior person was, of course, flattering; for human nature is the same in all. I also felt grateful for his sympathy, and encouraged by his kind words. It seemed to me a great thing to have such a friend. By degrees, a more tender feeling crept into my heart. He was an educated and eloquent gentleman; too eloquent, alas, for the poor slave girl who trusted in him. Of course I saw whither all this was tending. I knew the impassable gulf between us; but to be an object of interest to a man who is not married, and who is not her master, is agreeable to the pride and feelings of a slave, if her miserable situation has left her any pride or sentiment. It seems less degrading to give one's self, than to submit to compulsion. There is something akin to freedom in having a lover who has no control over you, except that which he gains by kindness and attachment. A master may treat you as rudely as he pleases, and you dare not speak; moreover, the wrong does not seem so great with an unmarried man, as with one who has a wife to be made unhappy. There may be sophistry in all this; but the condition of a slave confuses all principles of morality, and, in fact, renders the practice of them impossible.

When I found that my master had actually begun to build the lonely cottage, other feelings mixed with those I have described. Revenge, and calculations of interest, were added to flattered vanity and sincere gratitude for kindness. I knew nothing would enrage Dr. Flint so much as to know that I favored another; and it was something to triumph over my tyrant even in that small way. I thought he would revenge himself by selling me, and I was sure my friend, Mr. Sands, would buy me. He was a man of more generosity and feeling than my master, and I thought my freedom could be easily obtained from him. The crisis of my fate now came so near that I was desperate. I shuddered to think of being the mother of children that should be owned by my old tyrant. I knew that as soon as a new fancy took him, his victims were sold far off to get rid of them; especially if they had children. I had seen several women sold, with his babies at the breast. He never allowed his offspring by slaves to remain long in sight of himself and his wife. Of a man who was not my master I could ask to have my children well supported; and in this case, I felt confident I should obtain the boon. I also felt quite sure that they would be made free. With all these thoughts revolving in my mind, and seeing no other way of escaping the doom I so much dreaded, I made a headlong plunge. Pity me, and pardon me, O virtuous reader! You never knew what it is to be a slave; to be entirely unprotected by law or custom; to have the laws reduce you to the condition of a chattel, entirely subject to the will of another. You never exhausted your ingenuity in avoiding the snares, and eluding the power of a hated tyrant; you never shuddered at the sound of his footsteps, and trembled within hearing of his voice. I know I did wrong. No one can feel it more sensibly than I do. The painful and humiliating memory will haunt me to my dying day. Still, in looking back, calmly, on the events of my life, I feel that the slave woman ought not to be judged by the same standard as others.

The months passed on. I had many unhappy hours. I secretly mourned over the sorrow I was bringing on my grandmother, who had so tried to shield me from harm. I knew that I was the greatest comfort of her old age, and that it was a source of pride to her that I had not degraded myself, like most of the slaves. I wanted to confess to her that I was no longer worthy of her love; but I could not utter the dreaded words.

As for Dr. Flint, I had a feeling of satisfaction and triumph in the thought of telling *him*. From time to time he told me of his intended arrangements, and I was silent. At last, he came and told me the cottage was completed, and ordered me to go to it. I told him I would never enter it. He said, "I have heard enough of such talk as that. You shall go, if you are carried by force; and you shall remain there."

I replied, "I will never go there. In a few months I shall be a mother."

He stood and looked at me in dumb amazement, and left the house without a word. I thought I should be happy in my triumph over him. But now that the truth was out, and my relatives would hear of it, I felt wretched. Humble as were their circumstances, they had pride in my good character. Now, how could I look them in the face? My self-respect was gone! I had resolved that I would be virtuous, though I was a slave. I had said, "Let the storm beat! I will brave it till I die." And now, how humiliated I felt!

I went to my grandmother. My lips moved to make confession, but the words stuck in my throat. I sat down in the shade of a tree at her door and began to sew. I think she saw something unusual was the matter with me. The mother of slaves is very watchful. She knows there is no security for her children. After they have entered their teens she lives in daily expectation of trouble. This leads to many questions. If the girl is of a sensitive nature, timidity keeps her from answering truthfully, and this well-meant course has a tendency to drive her from maternal counsels. Presently, in came my mistress, like a mad woman, and accused me concerning her husband. My grandmother, whose suspicions had been previously awakened, believed what she said. She exclaimed, "O Linda! has it come to this? I had rather see you dead than to see you as you now are. You are a disgrace to your dead mother." She tore from my fingers my mother's wedding ring and her silver thimble. "Go away!" she exclaimed, "and never come to my house, again." Her reproaches fell so hot and heavy, that they left me no chance to answer. Bitter tears, such as the eyes never shed but once, were my only answer. I rose from my seat, but fell back again, sobbing. She did not speak to me; but the tears were running down her furrowed cheeks, and they scorched me like fire. She had always been so kind to me! *So* kind! How I longed to throw myself at her feet, and tell her all the truth! But she had ordered me to go, and never to come there again. After a few minutes, I mustered strength, and started to obey her. With what feelings did I now close that little gate, which I used to open with such an eager hand in my childhood! It closed upon me with a sound I never heard before.

Where could I go? I was afraid to return to my master's. I walked on recklessly, not caring where I went, or what would become of me. When I had gone four or five miles, fatigue compelled me to stop. I sat down on the stump of an old tree. The stars were shining through the boughs above me. How they mocked me, with their bright, calm light! The hours passed by, and as I sat there alone a chilliness and deadly sickness came over me. I sank on the ground. My mind was full of horrid thoughts. I prayed to die; but the prayer was not answered. At last, with great effort I roused myself, and walked some distance further, to the house of a woman who had been a friend of my mother. When I told her why I was there, she spoke soothingly to me; but I could not be comforted. I thought I could bear my shame if I could only be reconciled to my grandmother. I longed to open my heart to her. I thought if she could know the real state of the case, and all I had been bearing for years, she would perhaps judge me less harshly. My friend advised me to send for her. I did so; but days of agonizing suspense passed before she came. Had she utterly forsaken me? No. She came at last. I knelt before her, and told her the things that had poisoned my life; how long I had been persecuted; that I saw no way of escape; and in an hour of extremity I had become desperate. She listened in silence. I told her I would bear any thing and do any thing, if in time I had hopes of obtaining her forgiveness. I begged of her to pity me, for my dead mother's sake. And she did pity me. She did not say, "I forgive you;" but she looked at me lovingly, with her eyes full of tears. She laid her old hand gently on my head, and murmured, "Poor child! Poor child!"

. . .

Chapter 12. Fear of Insurrection

Not far from this time Nat Turner's insurrection broke out; and the news threw our town into great commotion.[3] Strange that they should be alarmed, when their slaves were so "contented and happy"! But so it was.

It was always the custom to have a muster every year. On that occasion every white man shouldered his musket. The citizens and the so-called country gentlemen wore military uniforms. The poor whites took their places in the ranks in every-day dress, some without shoes, some without hats. This grand occasion had already passed; and when the slaves were told there was to be another muster, they were surprised and rejoiced. Poor creatures! They thought it was going to be a holiday. I was informed of the true state of affairs, and imparted it to the few I could trust. Most gladly would I have proclaimed it to every slave; but I dared not. All could not be relied on. Mighty is the power of the torturing lash.

By sunrise, people were pouring in from every quarter within twenty miles of the town. I knew the houses were to be searched; and I expected it would be done by country bullies and the poor whites. I knew nothing annoyed them so much as to see colored people living in comfort and respectability; so I made arrangements for them with especial care. I arranged every thing in my grandmother's house as neatly as possible. I put white quilts on the beds, and decorated some of the rooms with flowers. When all was arranged, I sat down at the window to watch. Far as my eye could reach, it rested on a motley crowd of soldiers. Drums and fifes were discoursing martial music. The men were divided into companies of sixteen, each headed by a captain. Orders were given, and the wild scouts rushed in every direction, wherever a colored face was to be found.

It was a grand opportunity for the low whites, who had no negroes of their own to scourge. They exulted in such a chance to exercise a little brief authority, and show their subserviency to the slaveholders; not reflecting that the power which trampled on the colored people also kept themselves in poverty, ignorance, and moral degradation. Those who never witnessed such scenes can hardly believe what I know was inflicted at this time on innocent men, women, and children, against

[3]Nat Turner led a slave insurrection on August 21 and 22, 1831, in Southhampton County, Virginia, near Jacobs's home in Edenton, North Carolina, in which fifty-five white people were killed. Months of brutal terrorist attacks on both slave and freed African Americans followed in the wake of the rebellion.

whom there was not the slightest ground for suspicion. Colored people and slaves who lived in remote parts of the town suffered in an especial manner. In some cases the searchers scattered powder and shot among their clothes, and then sent other parties to find them, and bring them forward as proof that they were plotting insurrection. Every where men, women, and children were whipped till the blood stood in puddles at their feet. Some received five hundred lashes; others were tied hands and feet, and tortured with a bucking paddle, which blisters the skin terribly. The dwellings of the colored people, unless they happened to be protected by some influential white person, who was nigh at hand, were robbed of clothing and every thing else the marauders thought worth carrying away. All day long these unfeeling wretches went round, like a troop of demons, terrifying and tormenting the helpless. At night, they formed themselves into patrol bands, and went wherever they chose among the colored people, acting out their brutal will. Many women hid themselves in woods and swamps, to keep out of their way. If any of the husbands or fathers told of these outrages, they were tied up to the public whipping post, and cruelly scourged for telling lies about white men. The consternation was universal. No two people that had the slightest tinge of color in their faces dared to be seen talking together.

I entertained no positive fears about our household, because we were in the midst of white families who would protect us. We were ready to receive the soldiers whenever they came. It was not long before we heard the tramp of feet and the sound of voices. The door was rudely pushed open; and in they tumbled, like a pack of hungry wolves. They snatched at every thing within their reach. Every box, trunk, closet, and corner underwent a thorough examination. A box in one of the drawers containing some silver change was eagerly pounced upon. When I stepped forward to take it from them, one of the soldiers turned and said angrily, "What d'ye foller us fur? D'ye s'pose white folks is come to steal?"

I replied, "You have come to search; but you have searched that box, and I will take it, if you please."

At that moment I saw a white gentleman who was friendly to us; and I called to him, and asked him to have the goodness to come in and stay till the search was over. He readily complied. His entrance into the house brought in the captain of the company, whose business it was to guard the outside of the house, and see that none of the inmates left it. This officer was Mr. Litch, the wealthy slaveholder whom I mentioned, in the account of neighboring planters, as being notorious for his cruelty. He felt above soiling his hands with the search. He merely gave orders; and, if a bit of writing was discovered, it was carried to him by his ignorant followers, who were unable to read.

My grandmother had a large trunk of bedding and table cloths. When that was opened, there was a great shout of surprise; and one exclaimed, "Where'd the damned niggers git all dis sheet an' table clarf?"

My grandmother, emboldened by the presence of our white protector, said, "You may be sure we didn't pilfer 'em from *your* houses."

"Look here, mammy," said a grim-looking fellow without any coat, "you seem to feel mighty gran' 'cause you got all them 'ere fixens. White folks oughter have 'em all."

His remarks were interrupted by a chorus of voices shouting, "We's got 'em! We's got 'em! Dis 'ere yaller gal's got letters!"

There was a general rush for the supposed letter, which, upon examination, proved to be some verses written to me by a friend. In packing away my things, I had overlooked them. When their captain informed them of their contents, they seemed much disappointed. He inquired of me who wrote them. I told him it was one of my friends. "Can you read them?" he asked. When I told him I could, he swore, and raved, and tore the paper into bits. "Bring me all your letters!" said he, in a commanding tone. I told him I had none. "Don't be afraid," he continued, in an insinuating way. "Bring them all to me. Nobody shall do you any harm." Seeing I did not move to obey him, his pleasant tone changed to oaths and threats. "Who writes to you? half free niggers?" inquired he. I replied, "O, no; most of my letters are from white people. Some request me to burn them after they are read, and some I destroy without reading."

An exclamation of surprise from some of the company put a stop to our conversation. Some silver spoons which ornamented an old-fashioned buffet had just been discovered. My grandmother was in the habit of preserving fruit for many ladies in the town, and of preparing suppers for parties; consequently she had many jars of preserves. The closet that contained these was next invaded, and the contents tasted. One of them, who was helping himself freely, tapped his neighbor on the shoulder, and said, "Wal done! Don't wonder de niggers want to kill all de white folks, when dey live on 'sarves" [meaning preserves]. I stretched out my hand to take the jar, saying, "You were not sent here to search for sweetmeats."

"And what *were* we sent for?" said the captain, bristling up to me. I evaded the question.

The search of the house was completed, and nothing found to condemn us. They next proceeded to the garden, and knocked about every bush and vine, with no better success. The captain called his men together, and, after a short consultation, the order to march was given. As they passed out of the gate, the captain turned back, and pronounced a malediction on the house. He said it ought to be burned to the ground, and each of its inmates receive thirty-nine lashes. We came out of this affair very fortunately; not losing any thing except some wearing apparel.

Towards evening the turbulence increased. The soldiers, stimulated by drink, committed still greater cruelties. Shrieks and shouts continually rent the air. Not daring to go to the door, I peeped under the window curtain. I saw a mob dragging along a number of colored people, each white man, with his musket upraised, threatening instant death if they did not stop their shrieks. Among the prisoners was a respectable old colored minister. They had found a few parcels of shot in his house, which his wife had for years used to balance her scales. For this they were going to shoot him on Court House Green. What a spectacle was that for a civilized country! A rabble, staggering under intoxication, assuming to be the administrators of justice!

The better class of the community exerted their influence to save the innocent, persecuted people; and in several instances they succeeded, by keeping them shut up in jail till the excitement abated. At last the white citizens found that their own property was not safe from the lawless rabble they had summoned to protect them. They rallied the drunken swarm, drove them back into the country, and set a guard over the town.

The next day, the town patrols were commissioned to search colored people that lived out of the city; and the most shocking outrages were committed with perfect impunity. Every day for a fortnight, if I looked out, I saw horsemen with some poor panting negro tied to their saddles, and compelled by the lash to keep up with their speed, till they arrived at the jail yard. Those who had been whipped too unmercifully to walk were washed with brine, tossed into a cart, and carried to jail. One black man, who had not fortitude to endure scourging, promised to give information about the conspiracy. But it turned out that he knew nothing at all. He had not even heard the name of Nat Turner. The poor fellow had, however, made up a story, which augmented his own sufferings and those of the colored people.

The day patrol continued for some weeks, and at sundown a night guard was substituted. Nothing at all was proved against the colored people, bond or free. The wrath of the slaveholders was somewhat appeased by the capture of Nat Turner. The imprisoned were released. The slaves were sent to their masters, and the free were permitted to return to their ravaged homes. Visiting was strictly forbidden on the plantations. The slaves begged the privilege of again meeting at their little church in the woods, with their burying ground around it. It was built by the colored people, and they had no higher happiness than to meet there and sing hymns together, and pour out their hearts in spontaneous prayer. Their request was denied, and the church was demolished. They were permitted to attend the white churches, a certain portion of the galleries being appropriated to their use. There, when every body else had partaken of the communion, and the benediction had been pronounced, the minister said, "Come down, now, my colored friends." They obeyed the summons, and partook of the bread and wine, in commemoration of the meek and lowly Jesus, who said, "God is your Father, and all ye are brethren."

CHAPTER 13. THE CHURCH AND SLAVERY

After the alarm caused by Nat Turner's insurrection had subsided, the slaveholders came to the conclusion that it would be well to give the slaves enough of religious instruction to keep them from murdering their masters. The Episcopal clergyman offered to hold a separate service on Sundays for their benefit. His colored members were very few, and also very respectable—a fact which I presume had some weight with him. The difficulty was to decide on a suitable place for them to worship. The Methodist and Baptist churches admitted them in the afternoon; but their carpets and cushions were not so costly as those at the Episcopal church. It was at last decided that they should meet at the house of a free colored man, who was a member.

I was invited to attend, because I could read. Sunday evening came, and, trusting to the cover of night, I ventured out. I rarely ventured out by daylight, for I always went with fear, expecting at every turn to encounter Dr. Flint, who was sure to turn me back, or order me to his office to inquire where I got my bonnet, or some other article of dress. When the Rev. Mr. Pike came, there were some twenty persons present. The reverend gentleman knelt in prayer, then seated himself, and requested all present, who could read, to open their books, while he gave out the portions he wished them to repeat or respond to.

His text was, "Servants, be obedient to them that are your masters according to the flesh, with fear and trembling, in singleness of your heart, as unto Christ."

Pious Mr. Pike brushed up his hair till it stood upright, and, in deep, solemn tones, began: "Hearken, ye servants! Give strict heed unto my words. You are rebellious sinners. Your hearts are filled with all manner of evil. 'Tis the devil who tempts you. God is angry with you, and will surely punish you, if you don't forsake your wicked ways. You that live in town are eye-servants behind your master's back. Instead of serving your masters faithfully, which is pleasing in the sight of your heavenly Master, you are idle, and shirk your work. God sees you. You tell lies. God hears you. Instead of being engaged in worshipping him, you are hidden away somewhere, feasting on your master's substance; tossing coffee-grounds with some wicked fortuneteller, or cutting cards with another old hag. Your masters may not find you out, but God sees you, and will punish you. O, the depravity of your hearts! When your master's work is done, are you quietly together, thinking of the goodness of God to such sinful creatures? No; you are quarrelling, and tying up little bags of roots to bury under the door-steps to poison each other with. God sees you. You men steal away to every grog shop to sell your master's corn, that you may buy rum to drink. God sees you. You sneak into the back streets, or among the bushes, to pitch coppers. Although your masters may not find you out, God sees you; and he will punish you. You must forsake your sinful ways, and be faithful servants. Obey your old master and your young master—your old mistress and your young mistress. If you disobey your earthly master, you offend your heavenly Master. You must obey God's commandments. When you go from here, don't stop at the corners of the streets to talk, but go directly home, and let your master and mistress see that you have come."

The benediction was pronounced. We went home, highly amused at brother Pike's gospel teaching, and we determined to hear him again. I went the next Sabbath evening, and heard pretty much a repetition of the last discourse. At the close of the meeting, Mr. Pike informed us that he found it very inconvenient to meet at the friend's house, and he should be glad to see us, every Sunday evening, at his own kitchen.

I went home with the feeling that I had heard the Reverend Mr. Pike for the last time. Some of his members repaired to his house, and found that the kitchen sported two tallow candles; the first time, I am sure, since its present occupant owned it, for the servants never had any thing but pine knots. It was so long before the reverend gentleman descended from his comfortable parlor that the slaves left, and went to enjoy a Methodist shout. They never seem so happy as when shouting and singing at religious meetings. Many of them are sincere, and nearer to the gate of heaven than sanctimonious Mr. Pike, and other longfaced Christians, who see wounded Samaritans, and pass by on the other side.

The slaves generally compose their own songs and hymns; and they do not trouble their heads much about the measure. They often sing the following verses:

"Old Satan is one busy ole man;
 He rolls dem blocks all in my way;
But Jesus is my bosom friend;
 He rolls dem blocks away.

"If I had died when I was young,
 Den how my stam'ring tongue would have sung;
But I am ole, and now I stand
 A narrow chance for to tread dat heavenly land."

I well remember one occasion when I attended a Methodist class meeting. I went with a burdened spirit, and happened to sit next a poor, bereaved mother, whose heart was still heavier than mine. The class leader was the town constable—a man who bought and sold slaves, who whipped his brethren and sisters of the church at the public whipping post, in jail or out of jail. He was ready to perform that Christian office any where for fifty cents. This white-faced, black-hearted brother came near us, and said to the stricken woman, "Sister, can't you tell us how the Lord deals with your soul? Do you love him as you did formerly?"

She rose to her feet, and said, in piteous tones, "My Lord and Master, help me! My load is more than I can bear. God has hid himself from me, and I am left in darkness and misery." Then, striking her breast, she continued, "I can't tell you what is in here! They've got all my children. Last week they took the last one. God only knows where they've sold her. They let me have her sixteen years, and then—O! O! Pray for her brothers and sisters! I've got nothing to live for now. God make my time short!"

She sat down, quivering in every limb. I saw that constable class leader become crimson in the face with suppressed laughter, while he held up his handkerchief, that those who were weeping for the poor woman's calamity might not see his merriment. Then, with assumed gravity, he said to the bereaved mother, "Sister, pray to the Lord that every dispensation of his divine will may be sanctified to the good of your poor needy soul!"

The congregation struck up a hymn, and sung as though they were as free as the birds that warbled round us,—

> "Ole Satan thought he had a mighty aim;
> He missed my soul, and caught my sins.
> Cry Amen, cry Amen, cry Amen to God!
>
> "He took my sins upon his back;
> Went muttering and grumbling down to hell.
> Cry Amen, cry Amen, cry Amen to God!
>
> "Ole Satan's church is here below.
> Up to God's free church I hope to go.
> Cry Amen, cry Amen, cry Amen to God!"

Precious are such moments to the poor slaves. If you were to hear them at such times, you might think they were happy. But can that hour of singing and shouting sustain them through the dreary week, toiling without wages, under constant dread of the lash?

The Episcopal clergyman, who, ever since my earliest recollection, had been a sort of god among the slaveholders, concluded, as his family was large, that he must go where money was more abundant. A very different clergyman took his place. The change was very agreeable to the colored people, who said, "God has sent us a good man this time." They loved him, and their children followed him for a smile or a kind word. Even the slaveholders felt his influence. He brought to the rectory five slaves. His wife taught them to read and write, and to be useful to her and themselves. As soon as he was settled, he turned his attention to the needy slaves around him. He urged upon his parishioners the duty of having a meeting expressly for them every Sunday, with a sermon adapted to their comprehension. After much argument and importunity, it was finally agreed that they might occupy the gallery of the church on Sunday evenings. Many colored people, hitherto unaccustomed to attend church, now gladly went to hear the gospel preached. The sermons were simple, and they understood them. Moreover, it was the first time they had ever been addressed as human beings. It was not long before his white parishioners began to be dissatisfied. He was accused of preaching better sermons to the negroes than he did to them. He honestly confessed that he bestowed more pains upon those sermons than upon any others; for the slaves were reared in such ignorance that it was a difficult task to adapt himself to their comprehension. Dissensions arose in the parish. Some wanted he should preach to them in the evening, and to the slaves in the afternoon. In the midst of these disputings his wife died, after a very short illness. Her slaves gathered round her dying bed in great sorrow. She said, "I have tried to do you good and promote your happiness; and if I have failed, it has not been for want of interest in your welfare. Do not weep for me; but prepare for the new duties that lie before you. I leave you all free. May we meet in a better world." Her liberated slaves were sent away, with funds to establish them comfortably. The colored people will long bless the memory of that truly Christian woman. Soon after her death her husband preached his farewell sermon, and many tears were shed at his departure.

Several years after, he passed through our town and preached to his former congregation. In his afternoon sermon he addressed the colored people. "My friends," said he, "it affords me great happiness to have an opportunity of speaking to you again. For two years I have been striving to do something for the colored people of my own parish; but nothing is yet accomplished. I have not even preached a sermon to them. Try to live according to the word of God, my friends. Your skin is darker than mine; but God judges men by their hearts, not by the color of their skins." This was strange doctrine from a southern pulpit. It was very offensive to slaveholders. They said he and his wife had made fools of their slaves, and that he preached like a fool to the negroes.

I knew an old black man, whose piety and childlike trust in God were beautiful to witness. At fifty-three years old he joined the Baptist church. He had a most earnest desire to learn to read. He thought he should know how to serve God better if he could only read the Bible. He came to me, and begged me to teach him. He said he could not pay me, for he had no money; but he would bring me nice fruit when the season for it came. I asked him if he didn't know it was contrary to law; and that slaves were whipped and imprisoned for teaching each other to read. This brought the tears into his eyes. "Don't be troubled, uncle Fred," said I. "I have no thoughts of refusing to teach you. I only told you of the law, that you might know the danger, and be on your guard." He thought he could plan to come three times a week without its being suspected. I selected a quiet nook, where no intruder was likely to penetrate, and there I taught him his A, B, C. Considering his age, his progress was astonishing. As soon as he could spell in two syllables he wanted to spell out words in the Bible. The happy smile that illuminated his face put joy into my heart. After spelling out a few words, he paused, and said, "Honey, it 'pears when I can read dis good book I shall be nearer to God. White man is got all de sense. He can larn easy. It ain't easy for ole black man like me. I only wants to read dis book, dat I may know how to live; den I hab no fear 'bout dying."

I tried to encourage him by speaking of the rapid progress he had made. "Hab patience, child," he replied. "I larns slow."

I had no need of patience. His gratitude, and the happiness I imparted, were more than a recompense for all my trouble.

At the end of six months he had read through the New Testament, and could find any text in it. One day, when he had recited unusually well, I said, "Uncle Fred, how do you manage to get your lessons so well?"

"Lord bress you, chile," he replied. "You nebber gibs me a lesson dat I don't pray to God to help me to understan' what I spells and what I reads. And he *does* help me, chile. Bress his holy name!"

There are thousands, who, like good uncle Fred, are thirsting for the water of life; but the law forbids it, and the churches withhold it. They send the Bible to heathen abroad, and neglect the heathen at home. I am glad that missionaries go out to the dark corners of the earth; but I ask them not to overlook the dark corners at home. Talk to American slaveholders as you talk to savages in Africa. Tell *them* it is wrong to traffic in men. Tell them it is sinful to sell their own children, and atrocious to violate their own daughters. Tell them that all men are brethren, and that man has no right to shut out the light of knowledge from his brother. Tell them they are answerable to God for sealing up the Fountain of Life from souls that are thirsting for it.

There are men who would gladly undertake such missionary work as this; but, alas! their number is small. They are hated by the south, and would be driven from its soil, or dragged to prison to die, as others have been before them. The field is ripe for the harvest, and awaits the reapers. Perhaps the great grandchildren of uncle

Fred may have freely imparted to them the divine treasures, which he sought by stealth, at the risk of the prison and the scourge.

Are doctors of divinity blind, or are they hypocrites? I suppose some are the one, and some the other; but I think if they felt the interest in the poor and the lowly, that they ought to feel, they would not be so *easily* blinded. A clergyman who goes to the south, for the first time, has usually some feeling, however vague, that slavery is wrong. The slaveholder suspects this, and plays his game accordingly. He makes himself as agreeable as possible; talks on theology, and other kindred topics. The reverend gentleman is asked to invoke a blessing on a table loaded with luxuries. After dinner he walks round the premises, and sees the beautiful groves and flowering vines, and the comfortable huts of favored household slaves. The southerner invites him to talk with these slaves. He asks them if they want to be free, and they say, "O, no, massa." This is sufficient to satisfy him. He comes home to publish a "South-Side View of Slavery," and to complain of the exaggerations of abolitionists. He assures people that he has been to the south, and seen slavery for himself; that it is a beautiful "patriarchal institution;" that the slaves don't want their freedom; that they have hallelujah meetings, and other religious privileges.

What does *he* know of the half-starved wretches toiling from dawn till dark on the plantations? of mothers shrieking for their children, torn from their arms by slave traders? of young girls dragged down into moral filth? of pools of blood around the whipping post? of hounds trained to tear human flesh? of men screwed into cotton gins to die? The slaveholder showed him none of these things, and the slaves dared not tell of them if he had asked them.

There is a great difference between Christianity and religion at the south. If a man goes to the communion table, and pays money into the treasury of the church, no matter if it be the price of blood, he is called religious. If a pastor has offspring by a woman not his wife, the church dismiss him, if she is a white woman; but if she is colored, it does not hinder his continuing to be their good shepherd.

When I was told that Dr. Flint had joined the Episcopal church, I was much surprised. I supposed that religion had a purifying effect on the character of men; but the worst persecutions I endured from him were after he was a communicant. The conversation of the doctor, the day after he had been confirmed, certainly gave *me* no indication that he had "renounced the devil and all his works." In answer to some of his usual talk, I reminded him that he had just joined the church. "Yes, Linda," said he. "It was proper for me to do so. I am getting on in years, and my position in society requires it, and it puts an end to all the damned slang. You would do well to join the church, too, Linda."

"There are sinners enough in it already," rejoined I. "If I could be allowed to live like a Christian, I should be glad."

"You can do what I require; and if you are faithful to me, you will be as virtuous as my wife," he replied.

I answered that the Bible didn't say so.

His voice became hoarse with rage. "How dare you preach to me about your infernal Bible!" he exclaimed. "What right have you, who are my negro, to talk to me about what you would like, and what you wouldn't like? I am your master, and you shall obey me."

No wonder the slaves sing,—

> "Ole Satan's church is here below;
> Up to God's free church I hope to go."
>
> • • •

CHAPTER 21. THE LOOPHOLE OF RETREAT

A small shed had been added to my grandmother's house years ago. Some boards were laid across the joists at the top, and between these boards and the roof was a very small garret, never occupied by any thing but rats and mice. It was a pent roof, covered with nothing but shingles, according to the southern custom for such buildings. The garret was only nine feet long and seven wide. The highest part was three feet high, and sloped down abruptly to the loose board floor. There was no admission for either light or air. My uncle Phillip, who was a carpenter, had very skilfully made a concealed trap-door, which communicated with the storeroom. He had been doing this while I was waiting in the swamp. The storeroom opened upon a piazza. To this hole I was conveyed as soon as I entered the house. The air was stifling; the darkness total. A bed had been spread on the floor. I could sleep quite comfortably on one side; but the slope was so sudden that I could not turn on the other without hitting the roof. The rats and mice ran over my bed; but I was weary, and I slept such sleep as the wretched may, when a tempest has passed over them. Morning came. I knew it only by the noises I heard; for in my small den day and night were all the same. I suffered for air even more than for light. But I was not comfortless. I heard the voices of my children. There was joy and there was sadness in the sound. It made my tears flow. How I longed to speak to them! I was eager to look on their faces; but there was no hole, no crack, through which I could peep. This continued darkness was oppressive. It seemed horrible to sit or lie in a cramped position day after day, without one gleam of light. Yet I would have chosen this, rather than my lot as a slave, though white people considered it an easy one; and it was so compared with the fate of others. I was never cruelly over-worked; I was never lacerated with the whip from head to foot; I was never so beaten and bruised that I could not turn from one side to the other; I never had my heel-strings cut to prevent my running away; I was never chained to a log and forced to drag it about, while I toiled in the fields from morning till night; I was never branded with hot iron, or torn by bloodhounds. On the contrary, I had always been kindly treated, and tenderly cared for, until I came into the hands of Dr. Flint. I had never wished for freedom till then. But though my life in slavery was comparatively devoid of hardships, God pity the woman who is compelled to lead such a life!

My food was passed up to me through the trap-door my uncle had contrived; and my grandmother, my uncle Phillip, and aunt Nancy would seize such opportunities as they could, to mount up there and chat with me at the opening. But of course this was not safe in the daytime. It must all be done in darkness. It was impossible for me to move in an erect position, but I crawled about my den for exercise. One day I hit my head against something, and found it was a gimlet. My uncle had left it sticking there when he made the trap-door. I was as rejoiced as Robinson Crusoe could have been at finding such a treasure. It put a lucky thought into my head. I said to myself, "Now I will have some light. Now I will see my children." I did not dare to begin my work during the daytime, for fear of attracting attention. But I groped round; and having found the side next the street, where I could frequently see my children, I stuck the gimlet in and waited for evening. I bored three rows of holes, one above another; then I bored out the interstices between. I thus succeeded in making one hole about an inch long and an inch broad. I sat by it till late into the night, to enjoy the little whiff of air that floated in. In the morning I watched for my children. The first person I saw in the street was Dr. Flint. I had a shuddering, superstitious feeling that it was a bad omen. Several familiar faces passed by. At last I heard the merry laugh of children, and presently two sweet little faces were looking up at me, as though they knew I was there, and were conscious of the joy they imparted. How I longed to *tell* them I was there!

My condition was now a little improved. But for weeks I was tormented by hundreds of little red insects, fine as a needle's point, that pierced through my skin, and produced an intolerable burning. The good grandmother gave me herb teas and cooling medicines, and finally I got rid of them. The heat of my den was intense, for nothing but thin shingles protected me from the scorching summer's sun. But I had my consolations. Through my peeping-hole I could watch the children, and when they were near enough, I could hear their talk. Aunt Nancy brought me all the news she could hear at Dr. Flint's. From her I learned that the doctor had written to New York to a colored woman, who had been born and raised in our neighborhood, and had breathed his contaminating atmosphere. He offered her a reward if she could find out any thing about me. I know not what was the nature of her reply; but he soon after started for New York in haste, saying to his family that he had business of importance to transact. I peeped at him as he passed on his way to the steamboat. It was a satisfaction to have miles of land and water between us, even for a little while; and it was a still greater satisfaction to know that he believed me to be in the Free States. My little den seemed less dreary than it had done. He returned, as he did from his former journey to New York, without obtaining any satisfactory information. When he passed our house next morning, Benny was standing at the gate. He had heard them say that he had gone to find me, and he called out, "Dr. Flint, did you bring my mother home? I want to see her." The doctor stamped his foot at him in a rage, and exclaimed, "Get out of the way, you little damned rascal! If you don't, I'll cut off your head."

Benny ran terrified into the house, saying, "You can't put me in jail again. I don't belong to you now." It was well that the wind carried the words away from the doctor's ear. I told my grandmother of it, when we had our next conference at the trap-door; and begged of her not to allow the children to be impertinent to the irascible old man.

Autumn came, with a pleasant abatement of heat. My eyes had become accustomed to the dim light, and by holding my book or work in a certain position near the aperture I contrived to read and sew. That was a great relief to the tedious monotony of my life. But when winter came, the cold penetrated through the thin shingle roof, and I was dreadfully chilled. The winters there are not so long, or so severe, as in northern latitudes; but the houses are not built to shelter from cold, and my little den was peculiarly comfortless. The kind grandmother brought me bed-clothes and warm drinks. Often I was obliged to lie in bed all day to keep comfortable; but with all my precautions, my shoulders and feet were frostbitten. O, those long, gloomy days, with no object for my eye to rest upon, and no thoughts to occupy my mind, except the dreary past and the uncertain future! I was thankful when there came a day sufficiently mild for me to wrap myself up and sit at the loophole to watch the passers by. Southerners have the habit of stopping and talking in the streets, and I heard many conversations not intended to meet my ears. I heard slave-hunters planning how to catch some poor fugitive. Several times I heard allusions to Dr. Flint, myself, and the history of my children, who, perhaps, were playing near the gate. One would say, "I wouldn't move my little finger to catch her, as old Flint's property." Another would say, "I'll catch *any* nigger for the reward. A man ought to have what belongs to him, if he *is* a damned brute." The opinion was often expressed that I was in the Free States. Very rarely did any one suggest that I might be in the vicinity. Had the least suspicion rested on my grandmother's house, it would have been burned to the ground. But it was the last place they thought of. Yet there was no place, where slavery existed, that could have afforded me so good a place of concealment.

Dr. Flint and his family repeatedly tried to coax and bribe my children to tell something they had heard said about me. One day the doctor took them into a shop, and offered them some bright little silver pieces and gay handkerchiefs if they would tell where their mother was. Ellen shrank away from him, and would not speak; but Benny spoke up, and said, "Dr. Flint, I don't know where my mother is. I guess she's in New York; and when you go there again, I wish you'd ask her to come home, for I want to see her; but if you put her in jail, or tell her you'll cut her head off, I'll tell her to go right back."

• • •

CHAPTER 23. STILL IN PRISON

When spring returned, and I took in the little patch of green the aperture commanded, I asked myself how many more summers and winters I must be condemned to spend thus. I longed to draw in a plentiful draught of fresh air, to stretch my cramped limbs, to have room to stand erect, to feel the earth under my feet again. My relatives were constantly on the lookout for a chance of escape; but none offered that seemed practicable, and even tolerably safe. The hot summer came again, and made the turpentine drop from the thin roof over my head.

During the long nights I was restless for want of air, and I had no room to toss and turn. There was but one compensation; the atmosphere was so stifled that even mosquitos would not condescend to buzz in it. With all my detestation of Dr. Flint, I could hardly wish him a worse punishment, either in this world or that which is to come, than to suffer what I suffered in one single summer. Yet the laws allowed *him* to be out in the free air, while I, guiltless of crime, was pent up here, as the only means of avoiding the cruelties the laws allowed him to inflict upon me! I don't know what kept life within me. Again and again, I thought I should die before long; but I saw the leaves of another autumn whirl through the air, and felt the touch of another winter. In summer the most terrible thunder storms were acceptable, for the rain came through the roof, and I rolled up my bed that it might cool the hot boards under it. Later in the season, storms sometimes wet my clothes through and through, and that was not comfortable when the air grew chilly. Moderate storms I could keep out by filling the chinks with oakum.

But uncomfortable as my situation was, I had glimpses of things out of doors, which made me thankful for my wretched hiding-place. One day I saw a slave pass our gate, muttering, "It's his own, and he can kill it if he will." My grandmother told me that woman's history. Her mistress had that day seen her baby for the first time, and in the lineaments of its fair face she saw a likeness to her husband. She turned the bondwoman and her child out of doors, and forbade her ever to return. The slave went to her master, and told him what had happened. He promised to talk with her mistress, and make it all right. The next day she and her baby were sold to a Georgia trader.

Another time I saw a woman rush wildly by, pursued by two men. She was a slave, the wet nurse of her mistress's children. For some trifling offence her mistress ordered her to be stripped and whipped. To escape the degradation and the torture, she rushed to the river, jumped in, and ended her wrongs in death.

Senator Brown, of Mississippi, could not be ignorant of many such facts as these, for they are of frequent occurrence in every Southern State. Yet he stood up in the

Congress of the United States, and declared that slavery was "a great moral, social, and political blessing; a blessing to the master, and a blessing to the slave!"[4]

I suffered much more during the second winter than I did during the first. My limbs were benumbed by inaction, and the cold filled them with cramp. I had a very painful sensation of coldness in my head; even my face and tongue stiffened, and I lost the power of speech. Of course it was impossible, under the circumstances, to summon any physician. My brother William came and did all he could for me. Uncle Phillip also watched tenderly over me; and poor grandmother crept up and down to inquire whether there were any signs of returning life. I was restored to consciousness by the dashing of cold water in my face, and found myself leaning against my brother's arm, while he bent over me with streaming eyes. He afterwards told me he thought I was dying, for I had been in an unconscious state sixteen hours. I next became delirious, and was in great danger of betraying myself and my friends. To prevent this, they stupefied me with drugs. I remained in bed six weeks, weary in body and sick at heart. How to get medical advice was the question. William finally went to a Thompsonian doctor, and described himself as having all my pains and aches.[5] He returned with herbs, roots, and ointment. He was especially charged to rub on the ointment by a fire; but how could a fire be made in my little den? Charcoal in a furnace was tried, but there was no outlet for the gas, and it nearly cost me my life. Afterwards coals, already kindled, were brought up in an iron pan, and placed on bricks. I was so weak, and it was so long since I had enjoyed the warmth of a fire, that those few coals actually made me weep. I think the medicines did me some good; but my recovery was very slow. Dark thoughts passed through my mind as I lay there day after day. I tried to be thankful for my little cell, dismal as it was, and even to love it, as part of the price I had paid for the redemption of my children. Sometimes I thought God was a compassionate Father, who would forgive my sins for the sake of my sufferings. At other times, it seemed to me there was no justice or mercy in the divine government. I asked why the curse of slavery was permitted to exist, and why I had been so persecuted and wronged from youth upward. These things took the shape of mystery, which is to this day not so clear to my soul as I trust it will be hereafter.

In the midst of my illness, grandmother broke down under the weight of anxiety and toil. The idea of losing her, who had always been my best friend and a mother to my children, was the sorest trial I had yet had. O, how earnestly I prayed that she might recover! How hard it seemed, that I could not tend upon her, who had so long and so tenderly watched over me!

One day the screams of a child nerved me with strength to crawl to my peeping-hole, and I saw my son covered with blood. A fierce dog, usually kept chained, had seized and bitten him. A doctor was sent for, and I heard the groans and screams of my child while the wounds were being sewed up. O, what torture to a mother's heart, to listen to this and be unable to go to him!

But childhood is like a day in spring, alternately shower and sunshine. Before night Benny was bright and lively, threatening the destruction of the dog; and great was his delight when the doctor told him the next day that the dog had bitten another boy and been shot. Benny recovered from his wounds; but it was long before he could walk.

---

[4]Jacobs refers to a speech made by Albert G. Brown (1813–1880) on February 24, 1854, during congressional debate on the Kansas–Nebraska Bill.

[5]Thompsonians, named after Samuel Thomson (1763–1843), attempted to cure disease by raising the internal body temperature.

When my grandmother's illness became known, many ladies, who were her customers, called to bring her some little comforts, and to inquire whether she had every thing she wanted. Aunt Nancy one night asked permission to watch with her sick mother, and Mrs. Flint replied, "I don't see any need of your going. I can't spare you." But when she found other ladies in the neighborhood were so attentive, not wishing to be outdone in Christian charity, she also sallied forth, in magnificent condescension, and stood by the bedside of her who had loved her in her infancy, and who had been repaid by such grievous wrongs. She seemed surprised to find her so ill, and scolded uncle Phillip for not sending for Dr. Flint. She herself sent for him immediately, and he came. Secure as I was in my retreat, I should have been terrified if I had known he was so near me. He pronounced my grandmother in a very critical situation, and said if her attending physician wished it, he would visit her. Nobody wished to have him coming to the house at all hours, and we were not disposed to give him a chance to make out a long bill.

As Mrs. Flint went out, Sally told her the reason Benny was lame was, that a dog had bitten him. "I'm glad of it," replied she. "I wish he had killed him. It would be good news to send to his mother. *Her* day will come. The dogs will grab *her* yet." With these Christian words she and her husband departed, and, to my great satisfaction, returned no more.

I heard from uncle Phillip, with feelings of unspeakable joy and gratitude, that the crisis was passed and grandmother would live. I could now say from my heart, "God is merciful. He has spared me the anguish of feeling that I caused her death."

• • •

CHAPTER 29. PREPARATIONS FOR ESCAPE

I hardly expect that the reader will credit me, when I affirm that I lived in that little dismal hole, almost deprived of light and air, and with no space to move my limbs, for nearly seven years.[6] But it is a fact; and to me a sad one, even now; for my body still suffers from the effects of that long imprisonment, to say nothing of my soul. Members of my family, now living in New York and Boston, can testify to the truth of what I say.

Countless were the nights that I sat late at the little loophole scarcely large enough to give me a glimpse of one twinkling star. There, I heard the patrols and slave-hunters conferring together about the capture of runaways, well knowing how rejoiced they would be to catch me.

Season after season, year after year, I peeped at my children's faces, and heard their sweet voices, with a heart yearning all the while to say, "Your mother is here." Sometimes it appeared to me as if ages had rolled away since I entered upon that gloomy, monotonous existence. At times, I was stupefied and listless; at other times I became very impatient to know when these dark years would end, and I should again be allowed to feel the sunshine, and breathe the pure air.

After Ellen left us, this feeling increased. Mr. Sands had agreed that Benny might go to the north whenever his uncle Phillip could go with him; and I was anxious to be there also, to watch over my children, and protect them so far as I was able. Moreover, I was likely to be drowned out of my den, if I remained much longer; for the slight roof was getting badly out of repair, and uncle Phillip was

---

[6]Jacobs lived in her grandmother's attic crawl space from August 1835 to June 1842.

afraid to remove the shingles, lest some one should get a glimpse of me. When storms occurred in the night, they spread mats and bits of carpet, which in the morning appeared to have been laid out to dry; but to cover the roof in the daytime might have attracted attention. Consequently, my clothes and bedding were often drenched; a process by which the pains and aches in my cramped and stiffened limbs were greatly increased. I revolved various plans of escape in my mind, which I sometimes imparted to my grandmother, when she came to whisper with me at the trap-door. The kind-hearted old woman had an intense sympathy for runaways. She had known too much of the cruelties inflicted on those who were captured. Her memory always flew back at once to the sufferings of her bright and handsome son, Benjamin, the youngest and dearest of her flock. So, whenever I alluded to the subject, she would groan out, "O, don't think of it, child. You'll break my heart." I had no good old aunt Nancy now to encourage me; but my brother William and my children were continually beckoning me to the north.

And now I must go back a few months in my story. I have stated that the first of January was the time for selling slaves, or leasing them out to new masters. If time were counted by heart-throbs, the poor slaves might reckon years of suffering during that festival so joyous to the free. On the New Year's day preceding my aunt's death, one of my friends, named Fanny, was to be sold at auction, to pay her master's debts. My thoughts were with her during all the day, and at night I anxiously inquired what had been her fate. I was told that she had been sold to one master, and her four little girls to another master, far distant; that she had escaped from her purchaser, and was not to be found. Her mother was the old Aggie I have spoken of. She lived in a small tenement belonging to my grandmother, and built on the same lot with her own house. Her dwelling was searched and watched, and that brought the patrols so near me that I was obliged to keep very close in my den. The hunters were somehow eluded; and not long afterwards Benny accidentally caught sight of Fanny in her mother's hut. He told his grandmother, who charged him never to speak of it, explaining to him the frightful consequences; and he never betrayed the trust. Aggie little dreamed that my grandmother knew where her daughter was concealed, and that the stooping form of her old neighbor was bending under a similar burden of anxiety and fear; but these dangerous secrets deepened the sympathy between the two old persecuted mothers.

My friend Fanny and I remained many weeks hidden within call of each other; but she was unconscious of the fact. I longed to have her share my den, which seemed a more secure retreat than her own; but I had brought so much trouble on my grandmother, that it seemed wrong to ask her to incur greater risks. My restlessness increased. I had lived too long in bodily pain and anguish of spirit. Always I was in dread that by some accident, or some contrivance, slavery would succeed in snatching my children from me. This thought drove me nearly frantic, and I determined to steer for the North Star at all hazards.[7] At this crisis, Providence opened an unexpected way for me to escape. My friend Peter came one evening, and asked to speak with me. "Your day has come, Linda," said he. "I have found a chance for you to go to the Free States. You have a fortnight to decide." The news seemed too good to be true; but Peter explained his arrangements, and told me all that was necessary was for me to say I would go. I was going to answer him with a joyful yes, when the thought of Benny came to my mind. I told him the temptation was exceedingly strong, but I was terribly afraid of Dr. Flint's alleged power over my child, and that I could not go and leave him behind. Peter remonstrated earnestly.

---

[7]Runaway slaves, who often traveled by night, were guided by the North Star.

He said such a good chance might never occur again; that Benny was free, and could be sent to me; and that for the sake of my children's welfare I ought not to hesitate a moment. I told him I would consult with uncle Phillip. My uncle rejoiced in the plan, and bade me go by all means. He promised, if his life was spared, that he would either bring or send my son to me as soon as I reached a place of safety. I resolved to go, but thought nothing had better be said to my grandmother till very near the time of departure. But my uncle thought she would feel it more keenly if I left her so suddenly. "I will reason with her," said he, "and convince her how necessary it is, not only for your sake, but for hers also. You cannot be blind to the fact that she is sinking under her burdens." I was not blind to it. I knew that my concealment was an ever-present source of anxiety, and that the older she grew the more nervously fearful she was of discovery. My uncle talked with her, and finally succeeded in persuading her that it was absolutely necessary for me to seize the chance so unexpectedly offered.

The anticipation of being a free woman proved almost too much for my weak frame. The excitement stimulated me, and at the same time bewildered me. I made busy preparations for my journey, and for my son to follow me. I resolved to have an interview with him before I went, that I might give him cautions and advice, and tell him how anxiously I should be waiting for him at the north. Grandmother stole up to me as often as possible to whisper words of counsel. She insisted upon my writing to Dr. Flint, as soon as I arrived in the Free States, and asking him to sell me to her. She said she would sacrifice her house, and all she had in the world, for the sake of having me safe with my children in any part of the world. If she could only live to know *that* she could die in peace. I promised the dear old faithful friend that I would write to her as soon as I arrived, and put the letter in a safe way to reach her; but in my own mind I resolved that not another cent of her hard earnings should be spent to pay rapacious slaveholders for what they called their property. And even if I had not been unwilling to buy what I had already a right to possess, common humanity would have prevented me from accepting the generous offer, at the expense of turning my aged relative out of house and home, when she was trembling on the brink of the grave.

I was to escape in a vessel; but I forbear to mention any further particulars. I was in readiness, but the vessel was unexpectedly detained several days. Meantime, news came to town of a most horrible murder committed on a fugitive slave, named James. Charity, the mother of this unfortunate young man, had been an old acquaintance of ours. I have told the shocking particulars of his death, in my description of some of the neighboring slaveholders. My grandmother, always nervously sensitive about runaways, was terribly frightened. She felt sure that a similar fate awaited me, if I did not desist from my enterprise. She sobbed, and groaned, and entreated me not to go. Her excessive fear was somewhat contagious, and my heart was not proof against her extreme agony. I was grievously disappointed, but I promised to relinquish my project.

When my friend Peter was apprised of this, he was both disappointed and vexed. He said, that judging from our past experience, it would be a long time before I had such another chance to throw away. I told him it need not be thrown away; that I had a friend concealed near by, who would be glad enough to take the place that had been provided for me. I told him about poor Fanny, and the kind-hearted, noble fellow, who never turned his back upon any body in distress, white or black, expressed his readiness to help her. Aggie was much surprised when she found that we knew her secret. She was rejoiced to hear of such a chance for Fanny, and arrangements were made for her to go on board the vessel the next night. They both supposed that I had long been at the north, therefore my name was not mentioned in the transaction. Fanny was carried on board at the appointed time, and stowed away in a very small cabin. This accommodation had been purchased at a price that would pay for a voyage to England. But when one proposes to go to fine old England, they stop to calculate whether they can afford the cost of the pleasure; while in making a bargain to escape from slavery, the trembling victim is ready to say, "Take all I have, only don't betray me!"

The next morning I peeped through my loophole, and saw that it was dark and cloudy. At night I received news that the wind was ahead, and the vessel had not sailed. I was exceedingly anxious about Fanny, and Peter too, who was running a tremendous risk at my instigation. Next day the wind and weather remained the same. Poor Fanny had been half dead with fright when they carried her on board, and I could readily imagine how she must be suffering now. Grandmother came often to my den, to say how thankful she was I did not go. On the third morning she rapped for me to come down to the storeroom. The poor old sufferer was breaking down under her weight of trouble. She was easily flurried now. I found her in a nervous, excited state, but I was not aware that she had forgotten to lock the door behind her, as usual. She was exceedingly worried about the detention of the vessel. She was afraid all would be discovered, and then Fanny, and Peter, and I, would all be tortured to death, and Phillip would be utterly ruined, and her house would be torn down. Poor Peter! If he should die such a horrible death as the poor slave James had lately done, and all for his kindness in trying to help me, how dreadful it would be for us all! Alas, the thought was familiar to me, and had sent many a sharp pang through my heart. I tried to suppress my own anxiety, and speak soothingly to her. She brought in some allusion to aunt Nancy, the dear daughter she had recently buried, and then she lost all control of herself. As she stood there, trembling and sobbing, a voice from the piazza called out, "Whar is you, aunt Marthy?" Grandmother was startled, and in her agitation opened the door, without thinking of me. In stepped Jenny, the mischievous housemaid, who had tried to enter my room, when I was concealed in the house of my white benefactress. "I's bin huntin ebery whar for you, aunt Marthy," said she. "My missis wants you to send her some crackers." I had slunk down behind a barrel, which entirely screened me, but I imagined that Jenny was looking directly at the spot, and my heart beat violently. My grandmother immediately thought what she had done, and went out quickly with Jenny to count the crackers locking the door after her. She returned to me, in a few minutes, the perfect picture of despair. "Poor child!" she exclaimed, "my carelessness has ruined you. The boat ain't gone yet. Get ready immediately, and go with Fanny. I ain't got another word to say against it now; for there's no telling what may happen this day."

Uncle Phillip was sent for, and he agreed with his mother in thinking that Jenny would inform Dr. Flint in less than twenty-four hours. He advised getting me on board the boat, if possible; if not, I had better keep very still in my den, where they could not find me without tearing the house down. He said it would not do for him to move in the matter, because suspicion would be immediately excited; but he promised to communicate with Peter. I felt reluctant to apply to him again, having implicated him too much already; but there seemed to be no alternative. Vexed as Peter had been by my indecision, he was true to his generous nature, and said at once that he would do his best to help me, trusting I should show myself a stronger woman this time.

He immediately proceeded to the wharf, and found that the wind had shifted, and the vessel was slowly beating down stream. On some pretext of urgent necessity, he offered two boatmen a dollar apiece to catch up with her. He was of lighter complexion than the boatmen he hired, and when the captain saw them coming so rapidly, he thought officers were pursuing his vessel in search of the runaway slave he had on board. They hoisted sails, but the boat gained upon them, and the indefatigable Peter sprang on board.

The captain at once recognized him. Peter asked him to go below, to speak about a bad bill he had given him. When he told his errand, the captain replied, "Why, the woman's here already; and I've put her where you or the devil would have a tough job to find her."

"But it is another woman I want to bring," said Peter. "*She* is in great distress, too, and you shall be paid any thing within reason, if you'll stop and take her."

"What's her name?" inquired the captain.

"Linda," he replied.

"That's the name of the woman already here," rejoined the captain. "By George! I believe you mean to betray me."

"O!" exclaimed Peter, "God knows I wouldn't harm a hair of your head. I am too grateful to you. But there really *is* another woman in great danger. Do have the humanity to stop and take her!"

After a while they came to an understanding. Fanny, not dreaming I was any where about in that region, had assumed my name, though she had called herself Johnson. "Linda is a common name," said Peter, "and the woman I want to bring is Linda Brent."

The captain agreed to wait at a certain place till evening, being handsomely paid for his detention.

Of course, the day was an anxious one for us all. But we concluded that if Jenny had seen me, she would be too wise to let her mistress know of it; and that she probably would not get a chance to see Dr. Flint's family till evening, for I knew very well what were the rules in that household. I afterwards believed that she did not see me; for nothing ever came of it, and she was one of those base characters that would have jumped to betray a suffering fellow being for the sake of thirty pieces of silver.

I made all my arrangements to go on board as soon as it was dusk. The intervening time I resolved to spend with my son. I had not spoken to him for seven years, though I had been under the same roof, and seen him every day, when I was well enough to sit at the loophole. I did not dare to venture beyond the storeroom; so they brought him there, and locked us up together, in a place concealed from the piazza door. It was an agitating interview for both of us. After we had talked and wept together for a little while, he said, "Mother, I'm glad you're going away. I wish I could go with you. I knew you was here; and I have been *so* afraid they would come and catch you!"

I was greatly surprised, and asked him how he had found it out.

He replied, "I was standing under the eaves, one day, before Ellen went away, and I heard somebody cough up over the wood shed. I don't know what made me think it was you, but I did think so. I missed Ellen, the night before she went away; and grandmother brought her back into the room in the night; and I thought maybe she'd been to see *you,* before she went, for I heard grandmother whisper to her, 'Now go to sleep; and remember never to tell.'"

I asked him if he ever mentioned his suspicions to his sister. He said he never did; but after he heard the cough, if he saw her playing with other children on that side of the house, he always tried to coax her round to the other side, for fear they would hear me cough, too. He said he had kept a close lookout for Dr. Flint, and if he saw him speak to a constable, or a patrol, he always told grandmother. I now recollected that I had seen him manifest uneasiness, when people were on that side of the house, and I had at the time been puzzled to conjecture a motive for his actions. Such prudence may seem extraordinary in a boy of twelve years, but slaves, being surrounded by mysteries, deceptions, and dangers, early learn to be suspicious and watchful, and prematurely cautious and cunning. He had never asked a question of grandmother, or uncle Phillip, and I had often heard him chime in with other children, when they spoke of my being at the north.

I told him I was now really going to the Free States, and if he was a good, honest boy, and a loving child to his dear old grandmother, the Lord would bless him, and bring him to me, and we and Ellen would live together. He began to tell me that grandmother had not eaten any thing all day. While he was speaking, the door was unlocked, and she came in with a small bag of money, which she wanted me to take. I begged her to keep a part of it, at least, to pay for Benny's being sent to the north; but she insisted, while her tears were falling fast, that I should take the whole. "You may be sick among strangers," she said, "and they would send you to the poorhouse to die." Ah, that good grandmother!

For the last time I went up to my nook. Its desolate appearance no longer chilled me, for the light of hope had risen in my soul. Yet, even with the blessed prospect of freedom before me, I felt very sad at leaving forever that old homestead, where I had been sheltered so long by the dear old grandmother; where I had dreamed my first young dream of love; and where, after that had faded away, my children came to twine themselves so closely round my desolate heart. As the hour approached for me to leave, I again descended to the storeroom. My grandmother and Benny were there. She took me by the hand, and said, "Linda, let us pray." We knelt down together, with my child pressed to my heart, and my other arm round the faithful, loving old friend I was about to leave forever. On no other occasion has it ever been my lot to listen to so fervent a supplication for mercy and protection. It thrilled through my heart, and inspired me with trust in God.

Peter was waiting for me in the street. I was soon by his side, faint in body, but strong of purpose. I did not look back upon the old place, though I felt that I should never see it again.

CHAPTER 30. NORTHWARD BOUND

I never could tell how we reached the wharf. My brain was all of a whirl, and my limbs tottered under me. At an appointed place we met my uncle Phillip, who had started before us on a different route, that he might reach the wharf first, and give us timely warning if there was any danger. A row-boat was in readiness. As I was about to step in, I felt something pull me gently, and turning round I saw Benny, looking pale and anxious. He whispered in my ear, "I've been peeping into the doctor's window, and he's at home. Good by, mother. Don't cry; I'll come." He hastened away. I clasped the hand of my good uncle, to whom I owed so much, and of Peter, the brave, generous friend who had volunteered to run such terrible risks to secure my safety. To this day I remember how his bright face beamed with joy, when he told me he had discovered a safe method for me to escape. Yet that intelligent, enterprising, noble-hearted man was a chattel! liable, by the laws of a country that calls itself civilized, to be sold with horses and pigs! We parted in silence. Our hearts were all too full for words!

Swiftly the boat glided over the water. After a while, one of the sailors said, "Don't be down-hearted, madam. We will take you safely to your husband, in ———." At first I could not imagine what he meant; but I had presence of mind to think that it probably referred to something the captain had told him; so I thanked him, and said I hoped we should have pleasant weather.

When I entered the vessel the captain came forward to meet me. He was an elderly man, with a pleasant countenance. He showed me to a little box of a cabin, where sat my friend Fanny. She started as if she had seen a spectre. She gazed on me in utter astonishment, and exclaimed, "Linda, can this be *you?* or is it your ghost?" When we were locked in each other's arms, my overwrought feelings could no longer be restrained. My sobs reached the ears of the captain, who came and very kindly reminded us, that for his safety, as well as our own, it would be prudent for us not to attract any attention. He said that when there was a sail in sight he wished us to keep below; but at other times, he had no objection to our being on deck. He assured us that he would keep a good lookout, and if we acted prudently, he thought we should be in no danger. He had represented us as women going to meet our husbands in ———. We thanked him, and promised to observe carefully all the directions he gave us.

Fanny and I now talked by ourselves, low and quietly, in our little cabin. She told me of the sufferings she had gone through in making her escape, and of her terrors while she was concealed in her mother's house. Above all, she dwelt on the agony of separation from all her children on that dreadful auction day. She could scarcely credit me, when I told her of the place where I had passed nearly seven years. "We have the same sorrows," said I. "No," replied she, "you are going to see your children soon, and there is no hope that I shall ever even hear from mine."

The vessel was soon under way, but we made slow progress. The wind was against us. I should not have cared for this, if we had been out of sight of the town; but until there were miles of water between us and our enemies, we were filled with constant apprehensions that the constables would come on board. Neither could I feel quite at ease with the captain and his men. I was an entire stranger to that class of people, and I had heard that sailors were rough, and sometimes cruel. We were so completely in their power, that if they were bad men, our situation would be dreadful. Now that the captain was paid for our passage, might he not be tempted to make more money by giving us up to those who claimed us as property? I was naturally of a confiding disposition, but slavery had made me suspicious of every body. Fanny did not share my distrust of the captain or his men. She said she was afraid at first, but she had been on board three days while the vessel lay in the dock, and nobody had betrayed her, or treated her otherwise than kindly.

The captain soon came to advise us to go on deck for fresh air. His friendly and respectful manner, combined with Fanny's testimony, reassured me, and we went with him. He placed us in a comfortable seat, and occasionally entered into conversation. He told us he was a Southerner by birth, and had spent the greater part of his life in the Slave States, and that he had recently lost a brother who traded in slaves. "But," said he, "it is a pitiable and degrading business, and I always felt ashamed to acknowledge my brother in connection with it." As we passed Snaky Swamp, he pointed to it, and said, "There is a slave territory that defies all the laws." I thought of the terrible days I had spent there, and though it was not called Dismal Swamp, it made me feel very dismal as I looked at it.

I shall never forget that night. The balmy air of spring was so refreshing! And how shall I describe my sensations when we were fairly sailing on Chesapeake Bay? O, the beautiful sunshine! the exhilarating breeze! and I could enjoy them without fear or restraint. I had never realized what grand things air and sunlight are till I had been deprived of them.

Ten days after we left land we were approaching Philadelphia. The captain said we should arrive there in the night, but he thought we had better wait till morning, and go on shore in broad daylight, as the best way to avoid suspicion.

I replied, "You know best. But will you stay on board and protect us?"

He saw that I was suspicious, and he said he was sorry, now that he had brought us to the end of our voyage, to find I had so little confidence in him. Ah, if he had ever been a slave he would have known how difficult it was to trust a white man. He assured us that we might sleep through the night without fear; that he would take care we were not left unprotected. Be it said to the honor of this captain, Southerner as he was, that if Fanny and I had been white ladies, and our passage lawfully engaged, he could not have treated us more respectfully. My intelligent friend, Peter, had rightly estimated the character of the man to whose honor he had intrusted us.

The next morning I was on deck as soon as the day dawned. I called Fanny to see the sun rise, for the first time in our lives, on free soil; for such I *then* believed it to be. We watched the reddening sky, and saw the great orb come up slowly out of the water, as it seemed. Soon the waves began to sparkle, and every thing caught the beautiful glow. Before us lay the city of strangers. We looked at each other, and the eyes of both were moistened with tears. We had escaped from slavery, and we supposed ourselves to be safe from the hunters. But we were alone in the world, and we had left dear ties behind us; ties cruelly sundered by the demon Slavery.

WALT WHITMAN
[1819–1892]

One measure of Walt Whitman is the praise of writers, past and present, for how Whitman has revealed to them their own creativity and self-worth. With his free rhythms and open structure, his sexual directness, his colloquial vocabulary, his democratic inclusion of all peoples in his writing, he has empowered generations of readers. Ezra Pound, who at first took a fastidious dislike to Whitman, conceded "He *is* America. His crudity is an exceeding great stench, but it *is* America." For Allen Ginsberg, Whitman was a "lonely old courage teacher" who dared to honor homosexual lovers. Pablo Neruda could not remember when he first read Whitman, but thanked him because "you gathered / for me / everything; / everything that came forth / was harvested by you / galloping in the alfalfa, / picking poppies for me, / visiting the rivers, / coming into the kitchens / in the afternoon." African-American feminist June Jordan celebrates "this great American poet of democracy as cosmos, this poet of a continent as consciousness, the poet of the many people as one people, this poet of a diction comprehensible to all."

Walt Whitman worked at projecting a hearty and very public persona; by the end of his life, his face was emblazoned on cigar boxes, and a Whitman fan club in England venerated a lock of his hair and a stuffed canary that had once been his pet. But the man who boasted "I sound my barbaric yawp over the roofs of the world" was secretive about his inner life, and there are nearly as many mysteries about the private Whitman as there are about his greatest American contemporary, Emily Dickinson.

LIFE

Whitman was born at West Hills on Long Island on May 31, 1819, the second of eight children of a loving mother and the father for whom he was named. The elder Walt, according to his son, was "mean, angered, unjust," an alcoholic who had trouble making ends meet. Whitman's best legacy from his father was political; Thomas Paine was a family friend, and the Whitmans supported liberal and feminist causes. When Whitman was four his father abandoned farming and turned to buying or building houses and quickly mortgaging them, so the family moved almost yearly. Whitman deeply loved his mother and his baby brother Jeff, but household life on the whole was cramped and harsh, and he left school at twelve for a string of jobs as printer's devil, teacher, job-printer, house builder, and newspaper editor.

Whitman's early writings, such as his mawkish temperance novel *Franklin Evans: Or, The Inebriate,* showed little promise. But the imaginative soil from which *Leaves of Grass* sprang in 1855 was, as he said, "plowed and manured" well before he began to write that astonishing book. During his years editing, carpentering, and writing formula fiction, Whitman was also tirelessly reading—Shakespeare, the Bible, Greek and Roman literature, the English romantics, the *Bhagavad Gita,* and other Asian texts. From his contemporaries he mainly gauged how he did *not* want to write: He would avoid "rippling" cadences, elaborate "poetical images," a "tedious and affected" voice. Music—folk songs and spirituals, grand opera and oratorios—enraptured him. From opera especially he was learning the techniques of antiphony, of long flexible narrative lines, of setting off powerful lyric sections in the manner of arias. Above all, like other great naturalists and poets, the young Whitman was a born voyeur and loafer and eavesdropper, a friendly spy taking note of nesting birds and seasonal weeds and molting snakes, a hanger-out registering all the sights and sounds and smells of working people's lives.

The 1855 *Leaves of Grass,* published at Whitman's own expense, contained twelve poems and a preface that made plain Whitman knew he was doing something big and daring. He was casting aside conventional versification, trying instead to catch the rhythms of "the grand American expression," "brawny enough and limber and full enough" to match any poetry. For the frontispiece Whitman chose an engraving of himself lounging in an open-necked work shirt like "one of the roughs," the plain working men he loved and to whom he sought to give voice.

Leaves of Grass got almost no critical notice except for anonymous reviews by its author. But Ralph Waldo Emerson wrote, "I greet you at the beginning of a great career, which must yet have had a long foreground somewhere, for such a start." Without asking permission, Whitman used Emerson's letter to promote his book; Emerson didn't seem to mind, but the literary establishment thought this self-promotion confirmed Whitman's vulgarity.

Through the rest of Whitman's life, *Leaves of Grass* would be his chief work, continually enlarged, revised, rearranged, lovingly tended, growing like the graveyard grass in section 6 of "Song of Myself" out of all he experienced. In the third edition in 1860, he added two sections now titled "Children of Adam" and "Calamus." The poems of the former deal in a frank and grimly dutiful way with heterosexual love: "It is I, you women, I make my way, / I am stern, acrid, large, undissuadable, but I love you, / I do not hurt you any more than is necessary for you, / I pour the stuff to start sons and daughters fit for these States." In the "Calamus" poems, where Whitman celebrates male relationships, "the dear love of comrades," the language is less explicit, and far more tender: These poems and the gay male love they celebrate are like phallic calamus or wild iris, flourishing in secret on the "margins of pond waters," remote from the paths most men will admit to walking.

Whitman's actual sexual history was one of his most guarded secrets. His hints about past mistresses and illegitimate children, hints perhaps intended to discourage importunate gay admirers, have never been substantiated. No sexual relationship of Whitman's, heterosexual or gay, has ever been documented, but clearly his strongest attractions were to young working-class men. It may be that the celebratory poet of "the body electric" experienced little genital sex over his lifetime, finding himself less threatened in the role of a "loving and hugging" comrade. Perhaps, as he suggests in section 27 of

"Song of Myself," his responses were so strong that a little went a long way: "To touch my person to someone else's is about as much as I can stand." In any case, the 1860 *Leaves of Grass,* with "Children of Adam" and "Calamus" included against the advice of Emerson and others, lost Whitman many advocates.

The Civil War affected Whitman profoundly. In 1862, when his brother George suffered a mild wound at Fredericksburg, Whitman traveled to Washington to nurse him, and there found a second true vocation as an unpaid "wound dresser," tending the injured and soothing the dying; eventually, Whitman found a clerkship in a federal office to support himself. He fetched patients treats of candy and pickles and tobacco, played Twenty Questions with them, or just listened to them talk of war and home. During these war years in Washington, Whitman agonized over his unrequited passion for Peter Doyle, a young streetcar conductor, but in the Union hospital wards, Whitman's nurturing tenderness toward younger men was welcomed, and his experiences found their way into *Leaves of Grass.* Sightings of President Lincoln in the streets of the capital also moved him profoundly. Although the two never met, tradition has it that Lincoln admired *Leaves of Grass,* and on seeing Whitman in a crowd remarked, "He looks like a man." At Lincoln's death Whitman wrote "When Lilacs Last in the Dooryard Bloomed," one of the great elegiac poems of Western literature.

After the war, Whitman was forced out of his job when his boss came across a copy of *Leaves of Grass* and charged him with obscenity; friends rallied, and he was given a clerkship in the attorney general's office. In 1871, he published the fifth edition of *Leaves of Grass* and *Democratic Vistas,* a plea for Americans to beware materialism and seek instead to evolve into a visionary spiritual and cultural democracy, a theme echoed in "Passage to India." But Whitman was no pure democrat; he fiercely opposed universal suffrage, especially for freed slaves.

In 1873, Whitman had a stroke and returned north to New Jersey to recuperate at his brother George's house; his mother died soon after. He was never again fully well, but he continued to revise and rearrange *Leaves* while his fame grew to a cult in the United States and Europe. In 1879, this poet who had imaginatively cataloged the North American continent at last saw for himself the American West, as far as the Rockies: "wonders, revelations I wouldn't have missed for my life . . . the Prairie States, *the real America,*" he reported. He died in Camden on March 26, 1892.

WORK

"Song of Myself" is Whitman's epic. The epic hero is not a warrior like Odysseus nor a pilgrim soul like Dante's nor even an idealistic developing poet like the "I" of Wordsworth's *Prelude.* Whitman's "Me Myself" is both spirit and body, "hankering, gross, mystical, nude," a self who contains all creation, who has intimate connections to dinosaurs and runaway slaves, to Bowery prostitutes and opera singers and longshoremen, to alligators snoozing on riverbanks and the remotest of stars; his is a uniquely American, democratic self, one that "mutter[s] the word En Masse." His heroic act is to apprehend and pass on this revelation of the democracy of creation, a vision available to all. And yet he is not special, he is no miracle, except in the way each of us, even the ants and the "heap'd stones, elder, mullein, and pokeweed," are miracles. And Whitman assures us in the haunting last lines of the poem that he is hanging out, loafing somewhere, encouraging the reader's own journey to discover universal democracy:

> Failing to fetch me at first keep encouraged,
> Missing me one place search another,
> I stop somewhere waiting for you.

SUGGESTED READINGS

The definitive biography of Whitman remains Gay Wilson Allen's *The Solitary Singer: A Critical Biography of Walt Whitman* (1955); Justin Kaplan's *Walt Whitman* (1980) is highly readable. David S. Reynolds's *Beneath the American Renaissance: The Subversive Imagination in the Age of Emerson and Melville* (1988) is an excellent overview of Whitman's era, and contains fine chapters on Whitman's humor, his sensuality, and his connection to popular reform movements. E. H. Miller's *"Song of Myself": A Mosaic of Interpretations* (1989) provides extensive close readings of Whitman's central work.

FROM

Song of Myself

1

I Celebrate myself, and sing myself,
And what I assume you shall assume,
For every atom belonging to me as good belongs to you.

I loafe and invite my soul,
I lean and loafe at my ease observing a spear of summer grass.

My tongue, every atom of my blood, form'd from this soil, this air,
Born here of parents born here from parents the same, and their parents the
    same,
I, now thirty-seven years old in perfect health begin,
Hoping to cease not till death.

Creeds and schools in abeyance,   10
Retiring back a while sufficed at what they are, but never forgotten,
I harbor for good or bad, I permit to speak at every hazard,
Nature without check with original energy.

2

Houses and rooms are full of perfumes, the shelves are crowded with perfumes,
I breathe the fragrance myself and know it and like it,
The distillation would intoxicate me also, but I shall not let it.

The atmosphere is not a perfume, it has no taste of the distillation, it is odorless,
It is for my mouth forever, I am in love with it,
I will go to the bank by the wood and become undisguised and naked,
I am mad for it to be in contact with me.   20

The smoke of my own breath,
Echoes, ripples, buzz'd whispers, love-root, silk-thread, crotch and vine,
My respiration and inspiration, the beating of my heart, the passing of blood and
    air through my lungs,
The sniff of green leaves and dry leaves, and of the shore and dark-color'd sea-
    rocks, and of hay in the barn,

The sound of the belch'd words of my voice loos'd to the eddies of the wind,
A few light kisses, a few embraces, a reaching around of arms,
The play of shine and shade on the trees as the supple boughs wag,
The delight alone or in the rush of the streets, or along the fields and hill-sides,
The feeling of health, the full-noon trill, the song of me rising from bed and
    meeting the sun.

Have you reckon'd a thousand acres much? have you reckon'd the earth much?   30
Have you practis'd so long to learn to read?
Have you felt so proud to get at the meaning of poems?

Stop this day and night with me and you shall possess the origin of all poems,
You shall possess the good of the earth and sun, (there are millions of suns left,)
You shall no longer take things at second or third hand, nor look through the
    eyes of the dead, nor feed on the spectres in books,
You shall not look through my eyes either, nor take things from me,
You shall listen to all sides and filter them from your self.

. . .

5

I believe in you my soul, the other I am must not abase itself to you,
And you must not be abased to the other.

Loafe with me on the grass, loose the stop from your throat,   40
Not words, not music or rhyme I want, not custom or lecture, not even the
    best,
Only the lull I like, the hum of your valvèd voice.

I mind how once we lay such a transparent summer morning,
How you settled your head athwart my hips and gently turn'd over upon me,
And parted the shirt from my bosom-bone, and plunged your tongue to my
    bare-script heart,
And reach'd till you felt my beard, and reach'd till you held my feet.

Swiftly arose and spread around me the peace and knowledge that pass all the
    argument of the earth,
And I know that the hand of God is the promise of my own,
And I know that the spirit of God is the brother of my own,
And that all the men ever born are also my brothers, and the women my sisters
    and lovers,   50
And that a kelson[1] of the creation is love,
And limitless are leaves stiff or drooping in the fields,
And brown ants in the little wells beneath them,
And mossy scabs of the worm fence, heap'd stones, elder, mullein and poke-
    weed.

---

[1]A kelson is the superstructure of a ship's keel.

6

A child said *What is the grass?* fetching it to me with full hands;
How could I answer the child? I do not know what it is any more than he.
I guess it must be the flag of my disposition, out of hopeful green stuff woven.

Or I guess it is the handkerchief of the Lord,
A scented gift and remembrancer designedly dropt,
Bearing the owner's name someway in the corners, that we may see and remark,
  and say *Whose?*

Or I guess the grass is itself a child, the produced babe of the vegetation.

Or I guess it is a uniform hieroglyphic,
And it means, Sprouting alike in broad zones and narrow zones,
Growing among black folks as among white,
Kanuck,² Tuckahoe,³ Congressman, Cuff,⁴ I give them the same, I receive them
  the same.

And now it seems to me the beautiful uncut hair of graves.

Tenderly will I use you curling grass,
It may be you transpire from the breasts of young men,
It may be if I had known them I would have loved them,
It may be you are from old people, or from offspring taken soon out of their
  mothers' laps,
And here you are the mothers' laps.

This grass is very dark to be from the white heads of old mothers,
Darker than the colorless beards of old men,
Dark to come from under the faint red roofs of mouths.

O I perceive after all so many uttering tongues,
And I perceive they do not come from the roofs of mouths for nothing.

I wish I could translate the hints about the dead young men and women,
And the hints about old men and mothers, and the offspring taken soon out of
  their laps.

What do you think has become of the young and old men?
And what do you think has become of the women and children?

They are alive and well somewhere,
The smallest sprout shows there is really no death,
And if ever there was it led forward life, and does not wait at the end to arrest it,
And ceas'd the moment life appear'd.

---

²French Canadian.
³Resident of tidewater Virginia.
⁴African American

All goes onward and outward, nothing collapses,
And to die is different from what any one supposed, and luckier.

. . .

16

I am of old and young, of the foolish as much as the wise,
Regardless of others, ever regardful of others,
Maternal as well as paternal, a child as well as a man,
Stuff'd with the stuff that is coarse and stuff'd with the stuff that is fine,   90
One of the Nation of many nations, the smallest the same and the largest the
    same,
A Southerner soon as a Northerner, a planter nonchalant and hospitable down
    by the Oconee I live,
A Yankee bound my own way ready for trade, my joints the limberest joints on
    earth and the sternest joints on earth,
A Kentuckian walking the vale of the Elkhorn in my deer-skin leggings, a
    Louisianian or Georgian,
A boatman over lakes or bays or along coasts, a Hoosier, Badger, Buckeye;[5]

At home on Kanadian snow-shoes or up in the bush, or with fishermen off
    Newfoundland,
At home in the fleet of ice-boats, sailing with the rest and tacking,
At home on the hills of Vermont or in the woods of Maine, or the Texan ranch,
Comrade of Californians, comrade of free North-Westerners, (loving their big
    proportions,)
Comrade of raftsmen and coalmen, comrade of all who shake hands and
    welcome to drink and meat,
A learner with the simplest, a teacher of the thoughtfullest,   100
A novice beginning yet experient of myriads of seasons,
Of every hue and caste am I, of every rank and religion,
A farmer, mechanic, artist, gentleman, sailor, quaker,
Prisoner, fancy-man, rowdy, lawyer, physician, priest,
I resist any thing better than my own diversity,
Breathe the air but leave plenty after me,
And am not stuck up, and am in my place.

(The moth and the fish-eggs are in their place,
The bright suns I see and the dark suns I cannot see are in their place,   110
The palpable is in its place and the impalpable is in its place.)

17

These are really the thoughts of all men in all ages and lands, they are not
    original with me,
If they are not yours as much as mine they are nothing, or next to nothing,

---

[5]Nicknames, respectively, for natives of Indiana, Wisconsin, and Ohio.

If they are not the riddle and the untying of the riddle they are nothing,
If they are not just as close as they are distant they are nothing.

This is the grass that grows wherever the land is and the water is,
This the common air that bathes the globe.

· · ·

20

Who goes there? hankering, gross, mystical, nude;
How is it I extract strength from the beef I eat?

What is a man anyhow? what am I? what are you?   120

All I mark as my own you shall offset it with your own,
Else it were time lost listening to me.

I do not snivel that snivel the world over,
That months are vacuums and the ground but wallow and filth.

Whimpering and truckling fold with powders for invalids, conformity goes to
    the fourth-remov'd,
I wear my hat as I please indoors or out.

Why should I pray? why should I venerate and be ceremonious?

Having pried through the strata, analyzed to a hair, counsel'd with doctors and
    calculated close,
I find no sweeter fat than sticks to my own bones.

In all people I see myself, none more and not one a barleycorn less,   130
And the good or bad I say of myself I say of them.

I know I am solid and sound,
To me the converging objects of the universe perpetually flow,
All are written to me, and I must get what the writing means.

I know I am deathless,
I know this orbit of mine cannot be swept by a carpenter's compass,
I know I shall not pass like a child's carlacue[6] cut with a burnt stick at night.

I know I am august,
I do not trouble my spirit to vindicate itself or be understood,
I see that the elementary laws never apologize,   140
(I reckon I behave no prouder than the level I plant my house by, after all.)

---

[6] A curlicue.

I exist as I am, that is enough,
If no other in the world be aware I sit content,
And if each and all be aware I sit content.

One world is aware and by far the largest to me, and that is myself,
And whether I come to my own to-day or in ten thousand or ten million years,
I can cheerfully take it now, or with equal cheerfulness I can wait.

My foothold is tenon'd and mortis'd in granite,
I laugh at what you call dissolution,
And I know the amplitude of time.   150

21

I am the poet of the Body and I am the poet of the Soul,
The pleasures of heaven are with me and the pains of hell are with me,
The first I graft and increase upon myself, the latter I translate into a new
    tongue.

I am the poet of the woman the same as the man,
And I say it is as great to be a woman as to be a man,
And I say there is nothing greater than the mother of men.

I chant the chant of dilation or pride,
We have had ducking and deprecating about enough,
I show that size is only development.

Have you outstript the rest? are you the President?   160
It is a trifle, they will more than arrive there every one, and still pass on.

I am he that walks with the tender and growing night,
I call to the earth and sea half-held by the night.

Press close bare-bosom'd night—press close magnetic nourishing night!
Night of south winds—night of the large few stars!
Still nodding night—mad naked summer night.

Smile O voluptuous cool-breath'd earth!
Earth of the slumbering and liquid trees!
Earth of departed sunset—earth of the mountains misty-topt!
Earth of the vitreous pour of the full moon just tinged with blue!   170
Earth of shine and dark mottling the tide of the river!
Earth of the limpid gray of clouds brighter and clearer for my sake!
Far-swooping elbow'd earth—rich apple-blossom'd earth!
Smile, for your lover comes.

Prodigal, you have given me love—therefore I to you give love!
O unspeakable passionate love.

. . .

24

Walt Whitman, a kosmos, of Manhattan the son,
Turbulent, fleshy, sensual, eating, drinking and breeding,
No sentimentalist, no stander above men and women or apart from them,
No more modest than immodest.   180

Unscrew the locks from the doors!
Unscrew the doors themselves from their jambs!

Whoever degrades another degrades me,
And whatever is done or said returns at last to me.

Through me the afflatus surging and surging, through me the current and index.

I speak the pass-word primeval, I give the sign of democracy,
By God! I will accept nothing which all cannot have their counterpart of on the
    same terms.

Through me many long dumb voices,
Voices of the interminable generations of prisoners and slaves,
Voices of the diseas'd and despairing and of thieves and dwarfs,   190
Voices of cycles of preparation and accretion,
And of the threads that connect the stars, and of wombs and of the father-stuff,
And of the rights of them the others are down upon,
Of the deform'd, trivial, flat, foolish, despised,
Fog in the air, beetles rolling balls of dung.

Through me forbidden voices,
Voices of sexes and lusts, voices veil'd and I remove the veil,
Voices indecent by me clarified and transfigur'd.

I do not press my fingers across my mouth,
I keep as delicate around the bowels as around the head and heart,   200
Copulation is no more rank to me than death is.

I believe in the flesh and the appetites,
Seeing, hearing, feeling, are miracles, and each part and tag of me is a miracle.

Divine am I inside and out, and I make holy whatever I touch or am touch'd
    from,
The scent of these arm-pits aroma finer than prayer,
This head more than churches, bibles, and all the creeds.

If I worship one thing more than another it shall be the spread of my own body,
    or any part of it,
Translucent mould of me it shall be you!
Shaded ledges and rests it shall be you!
Firm masculine colter[7] it shall be you!   210

---

[7]The cutting edge of a plow; metaphorically, the penis.

Whatever goes to the tilth of me it shall be you!
You my rich blood! your milky stream pale strippings of my life!
Breast that presses against other breasts it shall be you!
My brain it shall be your occult convolutions!
Root of wash'd sweet-flag! timorous pond-snipe! nest of guarded duplicate eggs!
    it shall be you!
Mix'd tussled hay of head, beard, brawn, it shall be you!
Trickling sap of maple, fibre of manly wheat, it shall be you!
Sun so generous it shall be you!
Vapors lighting and shading my face it shall be you!   220
You sweaty brooks and dews it shall be you!
Winds whose soft-tickling genitals rub against me it shall be you!
Broad muscular fields, branches of live oak, loving lounger in my winding paths,
    it shall be you!
Hands I have taken, face I have kiss'd, mortal I have ever touch'd, it shall be
    you.

I dote on myself, there is that lot of me and all so luscious,
Each moment and whatever happens thrills me with joy,
I cannot tell how my ankles bend, nor whence the cause of my faintest wish,
Nor the cause of the friendship I emit, nor the cause of the friendship I take
    again.

That I walk up my stoop, I pause to consider if it really be,
A morning-glory at my window satisfies me more than the metaphysics of
    books.

To behold the day-break!   230
The little light fades the immense and diaphanous shadows,
The air tastes good to my palate.

Hefts of the moving world at innocent gambols silently rising freshly exuding,
Scooting obliquely high and low.

Something I cannot see puts upward libidinous prongs,
Seas of bright juice suffuse heaven.

The earth by the sky staid with, the daily close of their junction,
The heav'd challenge from the east that moment over my head,
The mocking taunt. See then whether you shall be master!

                                    . . .

                                    28

Is this then a touch? quivering me to a new identity,   240
Flames and ether making a rush for my veins,
Treacherous tip of me reaching and crowding to help them,
My flesh and blood playing out lightning to strike what is hardly different from
    myself,

On all sides prurient provokers stiffening my limbs,
Straining the udder of my heart for its withheld drip,
Behaving licentious toward me, taking no denial,
Depriving me of my best as for a purpose,
Unbuttoning my clothes, holding me by the bare waist,
Deluding my confusion with the calm of the sunlight and pasture-fields,
Immodestly sliding the fellow-senses away,   250
They bribed to swap off with touch and go and graze at the edges of me,
No consideration, no regard for my draining strength or my anger,
Fetching the rest of the herd around to enjoy them a while,
Then all uniting to stand on a headland and worry me.

The sentries desert every other part of me,
They have left me helpless to a red marauder,
They all come to the headland to witness and assist against me.

I am given up by traitors,
I talk wildly, I have lost my wits, I and nobody else am the greatest traitor,
I went myself first to the headland, my own hands carried me there.   260

You villain touch! what are you doing? my breath is tight in its throat,
Unclench your floodgates, you are too much for me.

29

Blind loving wrestling touch, sheath'd hooded sharp-tooth'd touch!
Did it make you ache so, leaving me?

Parting track'd by arriving, perpetual payment of perpetual loan,
Rich showering rain, and recompense richer afterward.

Sprouts take and accumulate, stand by the curb prolific and vital,
Landscapes projected masculine, full-sized and golden.

. . .

31

I believe a leaf of grass is no less than the journey-work of the stars,
And the pismire is equally perfect, and a grain of sand, and the egg of the
    wren,   270
And the tree-toad is a chef-d'œuvre for the highest,
And the running blackberry would adorn the parlors of heaven,
And the narrowest hinge in my hand puts to scorn all machinery,
And the cow crunching with depress'd head surpasses any statue,
And a mouse is miracle enough to stagger sextillions of infidels.

I find I incorporate gneiss, coal, long-threaded moss, fruits, grains, esculent
    roots,

And am stucco'd with quadrupeds and birds all over,
And have distanced what is behind me for good reasons,
But call any thing back again when I desire it.

In vain the speeding or shyness,   280
In vain the plutonic rocks send their old heat against my approach,
In vain the mastodon retreats beneath its own powder'd bones,
In vain objects stand leagues off and assume manifold shapes,
In vain the ocean settling in hollows and the great monsters lying low,
In vain the buzzard houses herself with the sky,
In vain the snake slides through the creepers and logs,
In vain the elk takes to the inner passes of the woods,
In vain the razor-bill'd auk sails far north to Labrador,
I follow quickly, I ascend to the nest in the fissure of the cliff.

32

I think I could turn and live with animals, they are so placid and self-contain'd,   290
I stand and look at them long and long.

They do not sweat and whine about their condition,
They do not lie awake in the dark and weep for their sins,
They do not make me sick discussing their duty to God,
Not one is dissatisfied, not one is demented with the mania of owning things,
Not one kneels to another, nor to his kind that lived thousands of years ago,
Not one is respectable or unhappy over the whole earth.

So they show their relations to me and I accept them,
They bring me tokens of myself, they evince them plainly in their possession.

I wonder where they get those tokens,   300
Did I pass that way huge times ago and negligently drop them?

Myself moving forward then and now and forever,
Gathering and showing more always and with velocity,
Infinite and omnigenous, and the like of these among them,
Not too exclusive toward the reachers of my remembrancers,

Picking out here one that I love, and now go with him on brotherly terms.

A gigantic beauty of a stallion, fresh and responsive to my caresses,
Head high in the forehead, wide between the ears,
Limbs glossy and supple, tail dusting the ground,
Eyes full of sparkling wickedness, ears finely cut, flexibly moving.   310

His nostrils dilate as my heels embrace him,
His well-built limbs tremble with pleasure as we race around and return.

I but use you a minute, then I resign you, stallion,
Why do I need your paces when I myself out-gallop them?
Even as I stand or sit passing faster than you.

33

Space and Time! now I see it is true, what I guess'd at,
What I guess'd when I loaf'd on the grass,
What I guess'd while I lay alone in my bed,
And again as I walk'd the beach under the paling stars of the morning.

My ties and ballasts leave me, my elbows rest in sea-gaps,   320
I skirt sierras, my palms cover continents,
I am afoot with my vision.

By the city's quadrangular houses—in log huts, camping with lumbermen,
Along the ruts of the turnpike, along the dry gulch and rivulet bed,
Weeding my onion-patch or hoeing rows of carrots and parsnips, crossing
    savannas, trailing in forests,
Prospecting, gold-digging, girdling the trees of a new purchase,
Scorch'd ankle-deep by the hot sand, hauling my boat down the shallow river,
Where the panther walks to and fro on a limb overhead, where the buck turns
    furiously at the hunter,
Where the rattlesnake suns his flabby length on a rock, where the otter is
    feeding on fish,
Where the alligator in his tough pimples sleeps by the bayou,   330
Where the black bear is searching for roots or honey, where the beaver pats the
    mud with his paddle-shaped tail;
Over the growing sugar, over the yellow-flower'd cotton plant, over the rice in
    its low moist field,
Over the sharp-peak'd farm house, with its scallop'd scum and slender shoots
    from the gutters,
Over the western persimmon, over the long-leav'd corn, over the delicate
    blue-flower flax,
Over the white and brown buckwheat, a hummer and buzzer there with the
    rest,
Over the dusky green of the rye as it ripples and shades in the breeze;
Scaling mountains, pulling myself cautiously up, holding on by low scragged
    limbs,
Walking the path worn in the grass and beat through the leaves of the brush,
Where the quail is whistling betwixt the woods and the wheat-lot,
Where the bat flies in the Seventh-month eve, where the great goldbug drops
    through the dark,   340
Where the brook puts out of the roots of the old tree and flows to the meadow,
Where cattle stand and shake away flies with the tremulous shuddering of their
    hides,
Where the cheese-cloth hangs in the kitchen, where andirons straddle the
    hearth-slab, where cobwebs fall in festoons from the rafters;
Where trip-hammers crash, where the press is whirling its cylinders,
Wherever the human heart beats with terrible throes under its ribs,
Where the pear-shaped balloon is floating aloft, (floating in it myself and looking
    composedly down,)

. . .

Looking in at the shop-windows of Broadway the whole forenoon, flatting the
    flesh of my nose on the thick plate glass,

Wandering the same afternoon with my face turn'd up to the clouds, or down a
    lane or along the beach,
My right and left arms round the sides of two friends, and I in the middle;
Coming home with the silent and dark-cheek'd bush-boy, (behind me he rides
    at the drape of the day,)   350
Far from the settlements studying the print of animals' feet, or the moccasin
    print,
By the cot in the hospital reaching lemonade to a feverish patient,
Nigh the coffin'd corpse when all is still, examining with a candle;
Voyaging to every port to dicker and adventure,
Hurrying with the modern crowd as eager and fickle as any,
Hot toward one I hate, ready in my madness to knife him,
Solitary at midnight in my back yard, my thoughts gone from me a long while,
Walking the old hills of Judæa with the beautiful gentle God by my side,
Speeding through space, speeding through heaven and the stars,
Speeding amid the seven satellites and the broad ring, and the diameter of eighty
    thousand miles,   360
Speeding with tail'd meteors, throwing fire-balls like the rest,
Carrying the crescent child that carries its own full mother in its belly,
Storming, enjoying, planning, loving, cautioning,
Backing and filling, appearing and disappearing,
I tread day and night such roads.

. . .

48

I have said that the soul is not more than the body,
And I have said that the body is not more than the soul,
And nothing, not God, is greater to one than one's self is,
And whoever walks a furlong without sympathy walks to his own funeral drest
    in his shroud,
And I or you pocketless of a dime may purchase the pick of the earth,   370
And to glance with an eye or show a bean in its pod confounds the learning of
    all times,
And there is no trade or employment but the young man following it may
    become a hero,
And there is no object so soft but it makes a hub for the wheel'd universe,
And I say to any man or woman, Let your soul stand cool and composed before
    a million universes.

And I say to mankind, Be not curious about God,
For I who am curious about each am not curious about God,
(No array of terms can say how much I am at peace about God and about
    death.)

I hear and behold God in every object, yet understand God not in the least,
Nor do I understand who there can be more wonderful than myself.

Why should I wish to see God better than this day?   380
I see something of God each hour of the twenty-four, and each moment then,
In the faces of men and women I see God, and in my own face in the glass,

I find letters from God dropt in the street, and every one is sign'd by God's
    name,
And I leave them where they are, for I know that wheresoe'er I go,
Others will punctually come for ever and ever.

49

And as to you Death, and you bitter hug of mortality, it is idle to try to alarm
    me.

To his work without flinching the accoucheur[8] comes,
I see the elder-hand pressing receiving supporting,
I recline by the sills of the exquisite flexible doors,
And mark the outlet, and mark the relief and escape.   390

And as to you Corpse I think you are good manure, but that does not offend
    me,
I smell the white roses sweet-scented and growing,
I reach to the leafy lips, I reach to the polish'd breasts of melons.

And as to you Life I reckon you are the leavings of many deaths,
(No doubt I have died myself ten thousand times before.)

I hear you whispering there O stars of heaven,
O suns—O grass of graves—O perpetual transfers and promotions,
If you do not say any thing how can I say any thing?

Of the turbid pool that lies in the autumn forest,
Of the moon that descends the steeps of the soughing twilight,   400
Toss, sparkles of day and dusk—toss on the black stems that decay in the muck,
Toss to the moaning gibberish of the dry limbs.

I ascend from the moon, I ascend from the night,
I perceive that the ghastly glimmer is noonday sunbeams reflected,
And debouch to the steady and central from the offspring great or small.

50

There is that in me—I do not know what it is—but I know it is in me.

Wrench'd and sweaty—calm and cool then my body becomes,
I sleep—I sleep long.

I do not know it—it is without name—it is a word unsaid,
It is not in any dictionary, utterance, symbol.   410

Something it swings on more than the earth I swing on,
To it the creation is the friend whose embracing awakes me.

---

[8] A midwife or obstetrician.

Perhaps I might tell more. Outlines! I plead for my brothers and sisters.
Do you see O my brothers and sisters?
It is not chaos or death—it is form, union, plan—it is eternal life—it is Happiness.

51

The past and present wilt—I have fill'd them, emptied them,
And proceed to fill my next fold of the future.

Listener up there! what have you to confide to me?
Look in my face while I snuff the sidle of evening,
(Talk honestly, no one else hears you, and I stay only a minute longer.)   420

Do I contradict myself?
Very well then I contradict myself,
(I am large, I contain multitudes.)

I concentrate toward them that are nigh, I wait on the door-slab.

Who has done his day's work? who will soonest be through with his supper?
Who wishes to walk with me?

Will you speak before I am gone? will you prove already too late?

52

The spotted hawk swoops by and accuses me, he complains of my gab and my
    loitering.

I too am not a bit tamed, I too am untranslatable,
I sound my barbaric yawp over the roofs of the world.   430

The last scud of day holds back for me,
It flings my likeness after the rest and true as any on the shadow'd wilds,
It coaxes me to the vapor and the dusk.

I depart as air, I shake my white locks at the runaway sun,
I effuse my flesh in eddies, and drift it in lacy jags.

I bequeath myself to the dirt to grow from the grass I love,
If you want me again look for me under your boot-soles.

You will hardly know who I am or what I mean,
But I shall be good health to you nevertheless,
And filter and fibre your blood.   440

Failing to fetch me at first keep encouraged,
Missing me one place search another,
I stop somewhere waiting for you.

GUSTAVE FLAUBERT
[1821–1880]

More than any other writer of the century, perhaps, Gustave Flaubert can be described as the exemplar of realism. *Madame Bovary* (1856), his masterwork, models the objective narrative technique and commonplace subject matter of the realists, and Flaubert's statements about writing articulate the basic concepts of their literary theory. Flaubert's achievements were not gained without struggle, for his romantic impulses were strong. Unlike Dickens, Balzac, or Dostoevsky, who infused their depictions of urban life with a personal mythology, Flaubert satisfied his conflicting inclinations in separate works, alternating between excessive and indulgent romances and carefully controlled realistic novels.

LIFE

Born into a medical family in Rouen in 1821, Flaubert claimed that his detailed and clinical powers of observation were the result of having "a doctor's eye." The provincial life he saw in his native Normandy often seemed diseased, affected by stultifying conventionality. As a schoolboy, he compiled lists of *idées reçues* (received ideas) to mock the banality of bourgeois life. For relief from provincial tedium, he began writing exotic romantic stories, including *The Memoirs of a Fool,* written at age sixteen, recounting his secret love for an older married woman. He escaped Normandy by going to Paris to study law, but, after failing his examinations and suffering a nervous breakdown, he withdrew from the university and returned to his home in 1846. Although he took occasional trips to Paris and traveled to Greece, North Africa, and the Middle East, Flaubert spent the rest of his life living uneventfully and writing in Normandy.

WORK

When some friends advised him to burn the manuscript of his extravagant narrative *The Temptation of St. Anthony* and suggested that he try instead to write a more "down to earth" novel based on an actual case of a local doctor's wife who had deceived her husband, Flaubert began *Madame Bovary*. Writing the novel took five years and forced him into very disciplined habits of composition. "The author, in his work," he wrote, "must be like God in the Universe, present everywhere and visible nowhere." Although he was contemptuous of the bourgeois provincialism of his characters and of Emma Bovary's romantic delusions, Flaubert attempted to enter sympathetically into her world and to record the sordid story with absolute objectivity. He measured his success as an artist by his capacity to enter "at every moment into skins which are antipathetic to me." He claimed victory in this struggle between his art and his temperament when he asserted, "I am Madame Bovary." As his heroine, he could be everywhere in his novel, yet visible nowhere.

The discipline required of the novelist was formal and verbal as well as psychological. Besides the detached and objective point of view, Flaubert sought absolute economy of expression and precise concreteness, with each detail contributing to unity of tone. He wanted his style to be "as rhythmical as verse and as precise as the language of science." The subject matter of the story, he believed, was not important. The important thing was to choose *le seul mot juste,* the one right word. But many of Flaubert's readers were unimpressed by the artistic merits of the novel and believed that the subject matter did in fact matter. They were outraged by Flaubert's account of Emma's adulteries. After the novel appeared in 1856, the French government brought charges against Flaubert for "outraging public morals and religion." At the trial he narrowly escaped conviction, and in the process he gained public notoriety.

Flaubert's next novel, *Salammbô* (1863), returned to romantic excesses. A historical novel that takes place in ancient Carthage, it indulges in lush orientalism, describing the unrestrained indulgences of its Eastern setting in extravagant language. *A Sentimental Education* (1869) returned to the realistic style of *Madame Bovary*. An account of the passion of its young hero, Frederic Moreau, for an older woman, the novel is set against a very detailed historical context of the period preceding the coup d'état of 1851. Flaubert had reworked this novel several times, beginning it many years earlier in *The Memoirs of a Fool*. Similarly, his next book, *The Temptation of St. Anthony* (1874), was one that he had rewritten at different stages of his life. His changing religious views can be traced in the various versions, from his early antireligious nihilism to his later respect for religion in the final published version.

Flaubert's last published work, *Three Tales* (1877), reveals both sides of his character in the sharply contrasting stories: "A Simple Heart," "The Legend of St. Julian Hospitaller," and "Herodias." As different as these three stories are from each other, they are all, like *The Temptation of St. Anthony,* saint's lives. "A Simple Heart," closest to *Madame Bovary* in its subject matter and technique, shows Flaubert's ability to sympathize with his provincial characters and to understand their lives from the inside. Félicité's life, unlike Emma Bovary's, is not sordid; rather, it is a triumph of the commonplace, a simple life that achieves saintly dignity.

"A Simple Heart" follows many of the conventions of the traditional saint's tale. The course of Félicité's life structures the story, which begins with her childhood and ends with her beatific death. Her life, like those of the saints, is a series of trials. She is orphaned as a child and mistreated by the family that takes her in. Her lover betrays her, and those she loves most—Virginie, her nephew, her mistress, and even her parrot—die and leave her alone. She performs heroic acts, such as fending off the bull, and suffers persecution when she is beaten on the road. Her death, on a saint's day, is marked by a beatific vision.

It is also a very realistic story. Writing of Normandy where he lived nearly all his life, Flaubert describes in precise detail the small provincial town of Pont-l'Évêque and the surrounding countryside. "A Simple Heart," like *Madame Bovary*, is a story of disillusionment, as, one by one, everything that Félicité holds dear is lost or taken away. Her life seems to belie her name, for it is a recitation of suffering and loss. Her vision at the end, which conflates the bedraggled parrot with the Holy Spirit, climaxes this catalog with the absurd and pathetic illusion of an illiterate peasant. Viewed from the outside, Félicité's life appears only as an ironic contrast to the saints' lives which her life seems to imitate.

But Flaubert's sympathetic understanding of Félicité and her world gives the story power, for in getting inside her innocence, he is able to reveal the spirituality of this most common life. We may recognize Madame Aubain's selfishness and contempt for her servant, but Félicité is innocent of such awareness, and when she loses her mistress, she loses much of the meaning of her life. Flaubert's objectivity makes us aware both of Madame Aubain's coldness and of her importance to Félicité. Likewise, from an exterior view, Félicité's love for Loulou, her parrot, appears comic and grotesque, but viewed from the sympathetic interior understanding that Flaubert achieves, her power to love the bird defines her saintliness. In the drab, gray world of the sculleries and the Norman countryside in which she lives, the parrot brings an exotic touch of color and becomes the central point in the spiritual vision that ultimately focuses her life.

The model of the saint's life that plays in the background of the story acts as a romantic paradigm against which we view the triviality and absurdity of Félicité's life. But the sympathetic understanding of Félicité that Flaubert's realistic technique makes possible closes the gap between the saintly ideal and the absurd reality, just as the creature's story in *Frankenstein* qualifies and counters Victor's horror over his creation. The awareness of the gap between ideal perfection and imperfect reality informs both the idealism of the early romantics and the realism of their successors.

SUGGESTED READINGS

Two useful introductions to Flaubert and his work are Victor Brombert's *The Novels of Flaubert* (1966), which includes a chapter on "A Simple Heart," and Peter Cortland's *A Reader's Guide to Flaubert* (1968). Raymond Giraud provides a variety of modern critical essays by various writers in *Flaubert: A Collection of Critical Essays* (1964). Julian Barnes's novel *Flaubert's Parrot* (1984) tells a contemporary story based on Flaubert's life and on themes from "A Simple Heart."

A Simple Heart

Translated by Arthur McDowall

1

Madame Aubain's servant Félicité was the envy of the ladies of Pont-l'Évêque[1] for half a century.

She received a hundred francs a year. For that she was cook and general servant, and did the sewing, washing, and ironing; she could bridle a horse, fatten poultry, and churn butter—and she remained faithful to her mistress, unamiable as the latter was.

Mme. Aubain had married a gay bachelor without money who died at the beginning of 1809, leaving her with two small children and a quantity of debts. She then sold all her property except the farms of Toucques and Geffosses, which brought in five thousand francs a year at most, and left her house in Saint-Melaine for a less expensive one that had belonged to her family and was situated behind the market.

This house had a slate roof and stood between an alley and a lane that went down to the river. There was an unevenness in the levels of the rooms which made you stumble. A narrow hall divided the kitchen from the "parlour" where Mme. Aubain spent her day, sitting in a wicker easy chair by the window. Against the panels, which were painted white, was a row of eight mahogany chairs. On an old piano under the barometer a heap of wooden and cardboard boxes rose like a pyramid. A stuffed armchair stood on either side of the Louis-Quinze chimney-piece, which was in yellow marble with a clock in the middle of it modelled like a temple of Vesta.[2] The whole room was a little musty, as the floor was lower than the garden.

The first floor began with "Madame's" room: very large, with a pale-flowered wall-paper and a portrait of "Monsieur" as a dandy of the period. It led to a smaller room, where there were two children's cots without mattresses. Next came the drawing-room, which was always shut up and full of furniture covered with sheets. Then there was a corridor leading to a study. The shelves of a large bookcase were

---

[1] A village in Normandy.
[2] The Roman goddess of the hearth.

respectably lined with books and papers, and its three wings surrounded a broad writing-table in darkwood. The two panels at the end of the room were covered with pen-drawings, water-colour landscapes, and engravings by Audran,[3] all relics of better days and vanished splendour. Félicité's room on the top floor got its light from a dormer-window, which looked over the meadows.

She rose at daybreak to be in time for Mass, and worked till evening without stopping. Then, when dinner was over, the plates and dishes in order, and the door shut fast, she thrust the log under the ashes and went to sleep in front of the hearth with her rosary in her hand. Félicité was the stubbornest of all bargainers; and as for cleanness, the polish on her saucepans was the despair of other servants. Thrifty in all things, she ate slowly, gathering off the table in her fingers the crumbs of her loaf—a twelve-pound loaf expressly baked for her, which lasted for three weeks.

At all times of year she wore a print handkerchief fastened with a pin behind, a bonnet that covered her hair, grey stockings, a red skirt, and a bibbed apron—such as hospital nurses wear—over her jacket.

Her face was thin and her voice sharp. At twenty-five she looked like forty. From fifty onwards she seemed of no particular age; and with her silence, straight figure, and precise movements she was like a woman made of wood, and going by clockwork.

2

She had had her love-story like another.

Her father, a mason, had been killed by falling off some scaffolding. Then her mother died, her sisters scattered, and a farmer took her in and employed her, while she was still quite little, to herd the cows at pasture. She shivered in rags and would lie flat on the ground to drink water from the ponds; she was beaten for nothing, and finally turned out for the theft of thirty sous which she did not steal. She went to another farm, where she became dairy-maid; and as she was liked by her employers her companions were jealous of her.

One evening in August (she was then eighteen) they took her to the assembly at Colleville. She was dazed and stupefied in an instant by the noise of the fiddlers, the lights in the trees, the gay medley of dresses, the lace, the gold crosses, and the throng of people jigging all together. While she kept shyly apart a young man with a well-to-do air, who was leaning on the shaft of a cart and smoking his pipe, came up to ask her to dance. He treated her to cider, coffee, and cake, and bought her a silk handkerchief; and then, imagining she had guessed his meaning, offered to see her home. At the edge of a field of oats he pushed her roughly down. She was frightened and began to cry out; and he went off.

One evening later she was on the Beaumont road. A big hay-wagon was moving slowly along; she wanted to get in front of it, and as she brushed past the wheels she recognized Theodore. He greeted her quite calmly, saying she must excuse it all because it was "the fault of the drink." She could not think of any answer and wanted to run away.

He began at once to talk about the harvest and the worthies of the commune, for his father had left Colleville for the farm at Les Écots, so that now he and she were neighbours. "Ah!" she said. He added that they thought of settling him in life. Well, he was in no hurry; he was waiting for a wife to his fancy. She dropped her

---

[3]Gérard Audran (1640–1703) made engravings of famous paintings for use in home decoration.

head; and then he asked her if she thought of marrying. She answered with a smile that it was mean to make fun of her.

"But I am not, I swear!"—and he passed his left hand round her waist. She walked in the support of his embrace; their steps grew slower. The wind was soft, the stars glittered, the huge wagon-load of hay swayed in front of them, and dust rose from the dragging steps of the four horses. Then, without a word of command, they turned to the right. He clasped her once more in his arms, and she disappeared into the shadow.

The week after Theodore secured some assignations with her.

They met at the end of farmyards, behind a wall, or under a solitary tree. She was not innocent as young ladies are—she had learned knowledge from the animals—but her reason and the instinct of her honour would not let her fall. Her resistance exasperated Theodore's passion; so much so that to satisfy it—or perhaps quite artlessly—he made her an offer of marriage. She was in doubt whether to trust him, but he swore great oaths of fidelity.

Soon he confessed to something troublesome; the year before his parents had bought him a substitute for the army, but any day he might be taken again, and the idea of serving was a terror to him. Félicité took this cowardice of his as a sign of affection, and it redoubled hers. She stole away at night to see him, and when she reached their meeting-place Theodore racked her with his anxieties and urgings.

At last he declared that he would go himself to the prefecture for information, and would tell her the result on the following Sunday, between eleven and midnight.

When the moment came she sped towards her lover. Instead of him she found one of his friends.

He told her that she would not see Theodore any more. To ensure himself against conscription he had married an old woman, Madame Lehoussais, of Toucques, who was very rich.

There was an uncontrollable burst of grief. She threw herself on the ground, screamed, called to the God of mercy, and moaned by herself in the fields till daylight came. Then she came back to the farm and announced that she was going to leave; and at the end of the month she received her wages, tied all her small belongings with a handkerchief, and went to Pont-l'Évêque.

In front of the inn there she made inquiries of a woman in a widow's cap, who, as it happened, was just looking for a cook. The girl did not know much, but her willingness seemed so great and her demands so small that Mme. Aubain ended by saying:

"Very well, then, I will take you."

A quarter of an hour afterwards Félicité was installed in her house.

She lived there at first in a tremble, as it were, at "the style of the house" and the memory of "Monsieur" floating over it all. Paul and Virginie, the first aged seven and the other hardly four, seemed to her beings of a precious substance; she carried them on her back like a horse; it was a sorrow to her that Mme. Aubain would not let her kiss them every minute. And yet she was happy there. Her grief had melted in the pleasantness of things all round.

Every Thursday regular visitors came in for a game of boston, and Félicité got the cards and foot-warmers ready beforehand. They arrived punctually at eight and left before the stroke of eleven.

On Monday mornings the dealer who lodged in the covered passage spread out all his old iron on the ground. Then a hum of voices began to fill the town, mingled with the neighing of horses, bleating of lambs, grunting of pigs, and the sharp rattle of carts along the street. About noon, when the market was at its height, you might see a tall, hook-nosed old countryman with his cap pushed back making his appearance at the door. It was Robelin, the farmer of Geffosses. A little later came Liébard, the farmer from Toucques—short, red, and corpulent—in a grey jacket and gaiters shod with spurs.

Both had poultry or cheese to offer their landlord. Félicité was invariably a match for their cunning, and they went away filled with respect for her.

At vague intervals Mme. Aubain had a visit from the Marquis de Gremanville, one of her uncles, who had ruined himself by debauchery and now lived at Falaise on his last remaining morsel of land. He invariably came at the luncheon hour, with a dreadful poodle whose paws left all the furniture in a mess. In spite of efforts to show his breeding, which he carried to the point of raising his hat every time he mentioned "my late father," habit was too strong for him; he poured himself out glass after glass and fired off improper remarks. Félicité edged him politely out of the house—"You have had enough, Monsieur de Gremanville! Another time!"—and she shut the door on him.

She opened it with pleasure to M. Bourais, who had been a lawyer. His baldness, his white stock, frilled shirt, and roomy brown coat, his way of rounding the arm as he took snuff—his whole person, in fact, created that disturbance of mind which overtakes us at the sight of extraordinary men.

As he looked after the property of "Madame" he remained shut up with her for hours in "Monsieur's" study, though all the time he was afraid of compromising himself. He respected the magistracy immensely, and had some pretensions to Latin.

To combine instruction and amusement he gave the children a geography book made up of a series of prints. They represented scenes in different parts of the world: cannibals with feathers on their heads, a monkey carrying off a young lady, Bedouins in the desert, the harpooning of a whale, and so on. Paul explained these engravings to Félicité; and that, in fact, was the whole of her literary education. The children's education was undertaken by Guyot, a poor creature employed at the town hall, who was famous for his beautiful hand and sharpened his penknife on his boots.

When the weather was bright the household set off early for a day at Geffosses Farm.

Its courtyard is on a slope, with the farmhouse in the middle, and the sea looks like a grey streak in the distance.

Félicité brought slices of cold meat out of her basket, and they breakfasted in a room adjoining the dairy. It was the only surviving fragment of a country house which was now no more. The wallpaper hung in tatters, and quivered in the draughts. Mme. Aubain sat with bowed head, overcome by her memories; the children became afraid to speak. "Why don't you play, then?" she would say, and off they went.

Paul climbed into the barn, caught birds, played at ducks and drakes over the pond, or hammered with his stick on the big casks which boomed like drums. Virginie fed the rabbits or dashed off to pick cornflowers, her quick legs showing their embroidered little drawers.

One autumn evening they went home by the fields. The moon was in its first quarter, lighting part of the sky; and mist floated like a scarf over the windings of the Toucques. Cattle, lying out in the middle of the grass, looked quietly at the four people as they passed. In the third meadow some of them got up and made a half-circle in front of the walkers. "There's nothing to be afraid of," said Félicité, as she stroked the nearest on the back with a kind of crooning song; he wheeled round and the others did the same. But when they crossed the next pasture there was a formidable bellow. It was a bull, hidden by the mist. Mme. Aubain was about to run. "No! no! don't go so fast!" They mended their pace, however, and heard a loud breathing behind them which came nearer. His hoofs thudded on the meadow grass like hammers; why, he was galloping now! Félicité turned round, and tore up clods of earth with both hands and threw them in his eyes. He lowered his muzzle, waved his horns, and quivered with fury, bellowing terribly. Mme. Aubain, now at the end of the pasture with her two little ones, was looking wildly for a place to get over the high bank. Félicité was retreating, still with her face to the bull, keeping up a shower of clods which blinded him, and crying all the time, "Be quick! be quick!"

Mme. Aubain went down into the ditch, pushed Virginie first and then Paul, fell several times as she tried to climb the bank, and managed it at last by dint of courage.

The bull had driven Félicité to bay against a rail-fence; his slaver was streaming into her face; another second, and he would have gored her. She had just time to slip between two of the rails, and the big animal stopped short in amazement.

This adventure was talked of at Pont-l'Évêque for many a year. Félicité did not pride herself on it in the least, not having the barest suspicion that she had done anything heroic.

Virginie was the sole object of her thoughts, for the child developed a nervous complaint as a result of her fright, and M. Poupart, the doctor, advised sea-bathing at Trouville. It was not a frequented place then. Mme. Aubain collected information, consulted Bourais, and made preparations as though for a long journey.

Her luggage started a day in advance, in Liébard's cart. The next day he brought round two horses, one of which had a lady's saddle with a velvet back to it, while a cloak was rolled up to make a kind of seat on the crupper of the other. Mme. Aubain rode on that, behind the farmer. Félicité took charge of Virginie, and Paul mounted M. Lechaptois' donkey, lent on condition that great care was taken of it.

The road was so bad that its five miles took two hours. The horses sank in the mud up to their pasterns, and their haunches jerked abruptly in the effort to get out; or else they stumbled in the ruts, and at other moments had to jump. In some places Liébard's mare came suddenly to a halt. He waited patiently until she went on again, talking about the people who had properties along the road, and adding moral reflections to their history. So it was that as they were in the middle of Toucques, and passed under some windows bowered with nasturtiums, he shrugged his shoulders and said: "There's a Mme. Lehoussais lives there; instead of taking a young man she . . ." Félicité did not hear the rest; the horses were trotting and the donkey galloping. They all turned down a bypath; a gate swung open and two boys appeared; and the party dismounted in front of a manure-heap at the very threshold of the farmhouse door.

When Mme. Liébard saw her mistress she gave lavish signs of joy. She served her a luncheon with a sirloin of beef, tripe, black-pudding, a fricassee of chicken, sparkling cider, a fruit tart, and brandied plums; seasoning it all with compliments to Madame, who seemed in better health; Mademoiselle, who was "splendid" now; and Monsieur Paul, who had "filled out" wonderfully. Nor did she forget their deceased grandparents, whom the Liébards had known, as they had been in the service of the family for several generations. The farm, like them, had the stamp of antiquity. The beams on the ceiling were worm-eaten, the walls blackened with smoke, and the window-panes grey with dust. There was an oak dresser laden with every sort of useful article—jugs, plates, pewter bowls, wolf-traps, and sheep-shears; and a huge syringe made the children laugh. There was not a tree in the three courtyards without mushrooms growing at the bottom of it or a tuft of mistletoe on its boughs. Several of them had been thrown down by the wind. They had taken root again at the middle; and all were bending under their wealth of apples.

The thatched roofs, like brown velvet and of varying thickness, withstood the heaviest squalls. The cart-shed, however, was falling into ruin. Mme. Aubain said she would see about it, and ordered the animals to be saddled again.

It was another half-hour before they reached Trouville. The little caravan dismounted to pass Écores—it was an overhanging cliff with boats below it—and three minutes later they were at the end of the quay and entered the courtyard of the Golden Lamb, kept by good Mme. David.

From the first days of their stay Virginie began to feel less weak, thanks to the change of air and the effect of the sea-baths. These, for want of a bathing-dress, she took in her chemise; and her nurse dressed her afterwards in a coastguard's cabin which was used by the bathers.

In the afternoons they took the donkey and went off beyond the Black Rocks, in the direction of Hennequeville. The path climbed at first through ground with dells in it like the green sward of a park, and then reached a plateau where grass fields and arable lay side by side. Hollies rose stiffly out of the briary tangle at the edge of the road; and here and there a great withered tree made zigzags in the blue air with its branches.

They nearly always rested in a meadow, with Deauville on their left, Havre on their right, and the open sea in front. It glittered in the sunshine, smooth as a mirror and so quiet that its murmur was scarcely to be heard; sparrows chirped in hiding and the immense sky arched over it all. Mme. Aubain sat doing her needlework; Virginie plaited rushes by her side; Félicité pulled up lavender, and Paul was bored and anxious to start home.

Other days they crossed the Toucques in a boat and looked for shells. When the tide went out sea-urchins, starfish, and jelly-fish were left exposed; and the children ran in pursuit of the foam-flakes which scudded in the wind. The sleepy waves broke on the sand and unrolled all along the beach; it stretched away out of sight, bounded on the land-side by the dunes which parted it from the Marsh, a wide meadow shaped like an arena. As they came home that way, Trouville, on the hill-slope in the background, grew bigger at every step, and its miscellaneous throng of houses seemed to break into a gay disorder.

On days when it was too hot they did not leave their room. From the dazzling brilliance outside light fell in streaks between the laths of the blinds. There were no sounds in the village; and on the pavement below not a soul. This silence round them deepened the quietness of things. In the distance, where men were caulking, there was a tap of hammers as they plugged the hulls, and a sluggish breeze wafted up the smell of tar.

The chief amusement was the return of the fishing-boats. They began to tack as soon as they had passed the buoys. The sails came down on two of the three masts; and they drew on with the foresail swelling like a balloon, glided through the splash of the waves, and when they had reached the middle of the harbour suddenly dropped anchor. Then the boats drew up against the quay. The sailors threw quivering fish over the side; a row of carts was waiting, and women in cotton bonnets darted out to take the baskets and give their men a kiss.

One of them came up to Félicité one day, and she entered the lodgings a little later in a state of delight. She had found a sister again—and then Nastasie Barette, "wife of Leroux," appeared, holding an infant at her breast and another child with her right hand, while on her left was a little cabin boy with his hands on his hips and a cap over his ear.

After a quarter of an hour Mme. Aubain sent them off; but they were always to be found hanging about the kitchen, or encountered in the course of a walk. The husband never appeared.

Félicité was seized with affection for them. She bought them a blanket, some shirts, and a stove; it was clear that they were making a good thing out of her. Mme. Aubain was annoyed by this weakness of hers, and she did not like the liberties taken by the nephew, who said "thee" and "thou" to Paul. So as Virginie was coughing and the fine weather gone, she returned to Pont-l'Évêque.

There M. Bourais enlightened her on the choice of a boys' school. The one at Caen was reputed to be the best, and Paul was sent to it. He said his good-byes bravely, content enough at going to live in a house where he would have companions.

Mme. Aubain resigned herself to her son's absence as a thing that had to be. Virginie thought about it less and less. Félicité missed the noise he made. But she found an occupation to distract her; from Christmas onward she took the little girl to catechism every day.

3

After making a genuflexion at the door she walked up between the double rows of chairs under the lofty nave, opened Mme. Aubain's pew, sat down, and began to look about her. The choir stalls were filled with the boys on the right and the girls on the left, and the curé stood by the lectern. On a painted window in the apse the Holy Ghost looked down upon the Virgin. Another window showed her on her knees before the child Jesus, and a group carved in wood behind the altar-shrine represented St. Michael overthrowing the dragon.

The priest began with a sketch of sacred history. The Garden, the Flood, the Tower of Babel, cities in flames, dying nations, and overturned idols passed like a dream before her eyes; and the dizzying vision left her with reverence for the Most High and fear of his wrath. Then she wept at the story of the Passion. Why had they crucified Him, when He loved the children, fed the multitudes, healed the blind, and had willed, in His meekness, to be born among the poor, on the dung-heap of a stable? The sowings, harvests, wine-presses, all the familiar things that the Gospel speaks of, were a part of her life. They had been made holy by God's passing; and she loved the lambs more tenderly for her love of the Lamb, and the doves because of the Holy Ghost.

She found it hard to imagine Him in person, for He was not merely a bird, but a flame as well, and a breath at other times. It may be His light, she thought, which flits at night about the edge of the marshes, His breathing which drives on the clouds, His voice which gives harmony to the bells; and she would sit rapt in adoration, enjoying the cool walls and the quiet of the church.

Of doctrines she understood nothing—did not even try to understand. The curé discoursed, the children repeated their lesson, and finally she went to sleep, waking up with a start when their wooden shoes clattered on the flagstones as they went away.

It was thus that Félicité, whose religious education had been neglected in her youth, learned the catechism by dint of hearing it; and from that time she copied all Virginie's observances, fasting as she did and confessing with her. On Corpus Christi Day they made a festal altar together.

The first communion loomed distractingly ahead. She fussed over the shoes, the rosary, the book and gloves; and how she trembled as she helped Virginie's mother to dress her!

All through the mass she was racked with anxiety. She could not see one side of the choir because of M. Bourais but straight in front of her was the flock of maidens, with white crowns above their hanging veils, making the impression of a field of snow; and she knew her dear child at a distance by her dainty neck and thoughtful air. The bell tinkled. The heads bowed, and there was silence. As the organ pealed, singers and congregation took up the "Agnus Dei";[4] then the procession of the boys began, and after them the girls rose. Step by step, with their hands joined in prayer, they went towards the lighted altar, knelt on the first step, received the sacrament in turn, and came back in the same order to their places. When Virginie's turn came Félicité leaned forward to see her; and with the imaginativeness of deep and tender feeling it seemed to her that she actually was the child; Virginie's face became hers, she was dressed in her clothes, it was her heart beating in her breast. As the moment came to open her mouth she closed her eyes and nearly fainted.

She appeared early in the sacristy next morning for Monsieur the curé to give her the communion. She took it with devotion, but it did not give her the same exquisite delight.

Mme. Aubain wanted to make her daughter into an accomplished person; and as Guyot could not teach her music or English she decided to place her in the Ursuline Convent at Honfleur as a boarder. The child made no objection. Félicité sighed and thought that Madame lacked feeling. Then she reflected that her mistress might be right; matters of this kind were beyond her.

So one day an old spring-van drew up at the door, and out of it stepped a nun to fetch the young lady. Félicité hoisted the luggage on to the top, admonished the driver, and put six pots of preserves, a dozen pears, and a bunch of violets under the seat.

At the last moment Virginie broke into a fit of sobbing; she threw her arms round her mother, who kissed her on the forehead, saying over and over "Come, be brave! be brave!" The step was raised, and the carriage drove off.

Then Mme. Aubain's strength gave way; and in the evening all her friends—the Lormeau family, Mme. Lechaptois, the Rochefeuille ladies, M. de Houppeville, and Bourais—came in to console her.

To be without her daughter was very painful for her at first. But she heard from Virginie three times a week, wrote to her on the other days, walked in the garden, and so filled up the empty hours.

From sheer habit Félicité went into Virginie's room in the mornings and gazed at the walls. It was boredom to her not to have to comb the child's hair now, lace up her boots, tuck her into bed—and not to see her charming face perpetually and hold her hand when they went out together. In this idle condition she tried making lace. But her fingers were too heavy and broke the threads; she could not attend to anything, she had lost her sleep, and was, in her own words, "destroyed."

To "divert herself" she asked leave to have visits from her nephew Victor.

He arrived on Sundays after mass, rosy-cheeked, bare-chested, with the scent of the country he had walked through still about him. She laid her table promptly and they had lunch, sitting opposite each other. She ate as little as possible herself to save expense, but stuffed him with food so generous that at last he went to sleep. At the first stroke of vespers she woke him up, brushed his trousers, fastened his tie, and went to church, leaning on his arm with maternal pride.

Victor was always instructed by his parents to get something out of her—a packet of moist sugar, it might be, a cake of soap, spirits, or even money at times. He brought his things for her to mend and she took over the task, only too glad to have a reason for making him come back.

---

[4]A prayer to Christ, addressed to the "Lamb of God."

In August his father took him off on a coasting voyage. It was holiday time, and she was consoled by the arrival of the children. Paul, however, was getting selfish, and Virginie was too old to be called "thou" any longer; this put a constraint and barrier between them.

Victor went to Morlaix, Dunkirk, and Brighton in succession and made Félicité a present on his return from each voyage. It was a box made of shells the first time, a coffee cup the next, and on the third occasion a large gingerbread man. Victor was growing handsome. He was well made, had a hint of a moustache, good honest eyes, and a small leather hat pushed backwards like a pilot's. He entertained her by telling stories embroidered with nautical terms.

On a Monday, July 14, 1819 (she never forgot the date), he told her that he had signed on for the big voyage and next night but one he would take the Honfleur boat and join his schooner, which was to weigh anchor from Havre before long. Perhaps he would be gone two years.

The prospect of this long absence threw Félicité into deep distress; one more good-bye she must have, and on the Wednesday evening, when Madame's dinner was finished, she put on her clogs and made short work of the twelve miles between Pont-l'Évêque and Honfleur.

When she arrived in front of the Calvary she took the turn to the right instead of the left, got lost in the timber-yards, and retraced her steps; some people to whom she spoke advised her to be quick. She went all round the harbour basin, full of ships, and knocked against hawsers; then the ground fell away, lights flashed across each other, and she thought her wits had left her, for she saw horses up in the sky.

Others were neighing by the quay-side, frightened at the sea. They were lifted by a tackle and deposited in a boat, where passengers jostled each other among cider casks, cheese baskets, and sacks of grain; fowls could be heard clucking, the captain swore; and a cabin-boy stood leaning over the bows, indifferent to it all. Félicité, who had not recognized him, called "Victor!" and he raised his head; all at once, as she was darting forwards, the gangway was drawn back.

The Honfleur packet, women singing as they hauled it, passed out of harbour. Its framework creaked and the heavy waves whipped its bows. The canvas had swung round, no one could be seen on board now; and on the moon-silvered sea the boat made a black speck which paled gradually, dipped, and vanished.

As Félicité passed by the Calvary she had a wish to commend to God what she cherished most, and she stood there praying a long time with her face bathed in tears and her eyes towards the clouds. The town was asleep, coastguards were walking to and fro; and water poured without cessation through the holes in the sluice, with the noise of a torrent. The clocks struck two.

The convent parlour would not be open before day. If Félicité were late Madame would most certainly be annoyed; and in spite of her desire to kiss the other child she turned home. The maids at the inn were waking up as she came in to Pont-l'Évêque.

So the poor slip of a boy was going to toss for months and months at sea! She had not been frightened by his previous voyages. From England or Brittany you came back safe enough; but America, the colonies, the islands—these were lost in a dim region at the other end of the world.

Félicité's thoughts from that moment ran entirely on her nephew. On sunny days she was harassed by the idea of thirst; when there was a storm she was afraid of the lightning on his account. As she listened to the wind growling in the chimney or carrying off the slates she pictured him lashed by that same tempest, at the top of a shattered mast, with his body thrown backwards under a sheet of foam; or else (with a reminiscence of the illustrated geography) he was being eaten by savages, captured in a wood by monkeys, or dying on a desert shore. And never did she mention her anxieties.

Mme. Aubain had anxieties of her own, about her daughter. The good sisters found her an affectionate but delicate child. The slightest emotion unnerved her. She had to give up the piano.

Her mother stipulated for regular letters from the convent. She lost patience one morning when the postman did not come, and walked to and fro in the parlour from her armchair to the window. It was really amazing; not a word for four days!

To console Mme. Aubain by her own example Félicité remarked:

"As for me, Madame, it's six months since I heard . . ."

"From whom, pray?"

"Why . . . from my nephew," the servant answered gently.

"Oh! your nephew!" And Mme. Aubain resumed her walk with a shrug of the shoulders, as much as to say: "I was not thinking of him! And what is more, it's absurd! A scamp of a cabin-boy—what does he matter? . . . whereas my daughter . . . why, just think!"

Félicité, though she had been brought up on harshness, felt indignant with Madame—and then forgot. It seemed the simplest thing in the world to her to lose one's head over the little girl. For her the two children were equally important; a bond in her heart made them one, and their destinies must be the same.

She heard from the chemist that Victor's ship had arrived at Havana. He had read this piece of news in a gazette.

Cigars—they made her imagine Havana as a place where no one does anything but smoke, and there was Victor moving among the negroes in a cloud of tobacco. Could you, she wondered, "in case you needed," return by land? What was the distance from Pont-l'Évêque? She questioned M. Bourais to find out.

He reached for his atlas and began explaining the longitudes; Félicité's consternation provoked a fine pedantic smile. Finally he marked with his pencil a black, imperceptible point in the indentations of an oval spot, and said as he did so, "Here it is." She bent over the map; the maze of coloured lines wearied her eyes without conveying anything; and on an invitation from Bourais to tell him her difficulty she begged him to show her the house where Victor was living. Bourais threw up his arms, sneezed, and laughed immensely: a simplicity like hers was a positive joy. And Félicité did not understand the reason; how could she when she expected, very likely, to see the actual image of her nephew—so stunted was her mind!

A fortnight afterwards Liébard came into the kitchen at market-time as usual and handed her a letter from her brother-in-law. As neither of them could read she took it to her mistress.

Mme. Aubain, who was counting the stitches in her knitting, put the work down by her side, broke the seal of the letter, started, and said in a low voice, with a look of meaning:

"It is bad news . . . that they have to tell you. Your nephew . . ."

He was dead. The letter said no more.

Félicité fell on to a chair, leaning her head against the wainscot; and she closed her eyelids, which suddenly flushed pink. Then with bent forehead, hands hanging, and fixed eyes, she said at intervals:

"Poor little lad! poor little lad!"

Liébard watched her and heaved sighs. Mme. Aubain trembled a little.

She suggested that Félicité should go to see her sister at Trouville. Félicité answered by a gesture that she had no need.

There was a silence. The worthy Liébard thought it was time for them to withdraw.

Then Félicité said:

"They don't care, not they!"

Her head dropped again; and she took up mechanically, from time to time, the long needles on her work-table.

Women passed in the yard with a barrow of dripping linen.

As she saw them through the window-panes she remembered her washing; she had put it to soak the day before, to-day she must wring it out; and she left the room.

Her plank and tub were at the edge of the Toucques. She threw a pile of linen on the bank, rolled up her sleeves, and taking her wooden beater dealt lusty blows whose sound carried to the neighbouring gardens. The meadows were empty, the river stirred in the wind; and down below long grasses wavered, like the hair of corpses floating in the water. She kept her grief down and was very brave until the evening; but once in her room she surrendered to it utterly, lying stretched on the mattress with her face in the pillow and her hands clenched against her temples.

Much later she heard, from the captain himself, the circumstances of Victor's end. They had bled him too much at the hospital for yellow fever. Four doctors held him at once. He had died instantly, and the chief had said:

"Bah! there goes another!"

His parents had always been brutal to him. She preferred not to see them again; and they made no advances, either because they forgot her or from the callousness of the wretchedly poor.

Virginie began to grow weaker.

Tightness in her chest, coughing, continual fever, and veinings on her cheek-bones betrayed some deep-seated complaint. M. Poupart had advised a stay in Provence. Mme. Aubain determined on it, would have brought her daughter home at once but for the climate of Pont-l'Évêque.

She made an arrangement with a job-master, and he drove her to the convent every Tuesday. There is a terrace in the garden, with a view over the Seine. Virginie took walks there over the fallen vine-leaves, on her mother's arm. A shaft of sunlight through the clouds made her blink sometimes, as she gazed at the sails in the distance and the whole horizon from the castle of Tancarville to the light-houses at Havre. Afterwards they rested in the arbour. Her mother had secured a little cask of excellent Malaga; and Virginie, laughing at the idea of getting tipsy, drank a thimble-full of it, no more.

Her strength came back visibly. The autumn glided gently away. Félicité reassured Mme. Aubain. But one evening, when she had been out on a commission in the neighbourhood, she found M. Poupart's gig at the door. He was in the hall, and Mme. Aubain was tying her bonnet.

"Give me my foot-warmer, purse, gloves! Quicker, come!"

Virginie had inflammation of the lungs; perhaps it was hopeless.

"Not yet!" said the doctor, and they both got into the carriage under whirling flakes of snow. Night was coming on and it was very cold.

Félicité rushed into the church to light a taper. Then she ran after the gig, came up with it in an hour, and jumped lightly in behind. As she hung on by the fringes a thought came into her mind: "The courtyard has not been shut up; supposing burglars got in!" And she jumped down.

At dawn next day she presented herself at the doctor's. He had come in and started for the country again. Then she waited in the inn, thinking that a letter would come by some hand or other. Finally, when it was twilight, she took the Lisieux coach.

The convent was at the end of a steep lane. When she was about half-way up it she heard strange sounds—a death-bell tolling. "It is for someone else," thought Félicité, and she pulled the knocker violently.

After some minutes there was a sound of trailing slippers, the door opened ajar, and a nun appeared.

The good sister, with an air of compunction, said that "she had just passed away." On the instant the bell of St. Leonard's tolled twice as fast.

Félicité went up to the second floor.

From the doorway she saw Virginie stretched on her back, with her hands joined, her mouth open, and head thrown back under a black crucifix that leaned towards her, between curtains that hung stiffly, less pale than was her face. Mme. Aubain, at the foot of the bed which she clasped with her arms, was choking with sobs of agony. The mother superior stood on the right. Three candlesticks on the chest of drawers made spots of red, and the mist came whitely through the windows. Nuns came and took Mme. Aubain away.

For two nights Félicité never left the dead child. She repeated the same prayers, sprinkled holy water over the sheets, came and sat down again, and watched her. At the end of the first vigil she noticed that the face had grown yellow, the lips turned blue, the nose was sharper, and the eyes sunk in. She kissed them several times, and would not have been immensely surprised if Virginie had opened them again; to minds like hers the supernatural is quite simple. She made the girl's toilette, wrapped her in her shroud, lifted her down into her bier, put a garland on her head, and spread out her hair. It was fair, and extraordinarily long for her age. Félicité cut off a big lock and slipped half of it into her bosom, determined that she should never part with it.

The body was brought back to Pont-l'Évêque, as Mme. Aubain intended; she followed the hearse in a closed carriage.

It took another three-quarters of an hour after the mass to reach the cemetery. Paul walked in front, sobbing. M. Bourais was behind, and then came the chief residents, the women shrouded in black mantles, and Félicité. She thought of her nephew; and because she had not been able to pay these honours to him her grief was doubled, as though the one were being buried with the other.

Mme. Aubain's despair was boundless. It was against God that she first rebelled, thinking it unjust of Him to have taken her daughter from her—she had never done evil and her conscience was so clear! Ah, no!—she ought to have taken Virginie off to the south. Other doctors would have saved her. She accused herself now, wanted to join her child, and broke into cries of distress in the middle of her dreams. One dream haunted her above all. Her husband, dressed as a sailor, was returning from a long voyage, and shedding tears he told her that he had been ordered to take Virginie away. Then they consulted how to hide her somewhere.

She came in once from the garden quite upset. A moment ago—and she pointed out the place—the father and daughter had appeared to her, standing side by side, and they did nothing, but they looked at her.

For several months after this she stayed inertly in her room. Félicité lectured her gently; she must live for her son's sake, and for the other, in remembrance of "her."

"Her?" answered Mme. Aubain, as though she were just waking up. "Ah, yes! . . . yes! . . . You do not forget her!" This was an allusion to the cemetery, where she was strictly forbidden to go.

Félicité went there every day.

Precisely at four she skirted the houses, climbed the hill, opened the gate, and came to Virginie's grave. It was a little column of pink marble with a stone underneath and a garden plot enclosed by chains. The beds were hidden under a coverlet of flowers. She watered their leaves, freshened the gravel, and knelt down to break up the earth better. When Mme. Aubain was able to come there she felt a relief and a sort of consolation.

Then years slipped away, one like another, and their only episodes were the great festivals as they recurred—Easter, the Assumption, All Saints' Day. Household occurrences marked dates that were referred to afterwards. In 1825, for instance, two glaziers white-washed the hall; in 1827 a piece of the roof fell into the courtyard and nearly killed a man. In the summer of 1828 it was Madame's turn to offer the consecrated bread; Bourais, about this time, mysteriously absented himself; and one by one the old acquaintances passed away: Guyot, Liébard, Mme. Lechaptois, Robelin, and Uncle Gremanville, who had been paralysed for a long time.

One night the driver of the mail-coach announced the Revolution of July[5] in Pont-l'Évêque. A new sub-prefect was appointed a few days later—Baron de Larsonnière, who had been consul in America, and brought with him, besides his wife, a sister-in-law and three young ladies, already growing up. They were to be seen about on their lawn, in loose blouses, and they had a negro and a parrot. They paid a call on Mme. Aubain which she did not fail to return. The moment they were seen in the distance Félicité ran to let her mistress know. But only one thing could really move her feelings—the letters from her son.

He was swallowed up in a tavern life and could follow no career. She paid his debts, he made new ones; and the sighs that Mme. Aubain uttered as she sat knitting by the window reached Félicité at her spinning-wheel in the kitchen.

They took walks together along the espaliered wall, always talking of Virginie and wondering if such and such a thing would have pleased her and what, on some occasion, she would have been likely to say.

All her small belongings filled a cupboard in the two-bedded room. Mme. Aubain inspected them as seldom as she could. One summer day she made up her mind to it—and some moths flew out of the wardrobe.

Virginie's dresses were in a row underneath a shelf, on which there were three dolls, some hoops, a set of toy pots and pans, and the basin that she used. They took out her petticoats as well, and the stockings and handkerchiefs, and laid them out on the two beds before folding them up again. The sunshine lit up these poor things, bringing out their stains and the creases made by the body's movements. The air was warm and blue, a blackbird warbled, life seemed bathed in a deep sweetness. They found a little plush hat with thick, chestnut-coloured pile; but it was eaten all over by moths. Félicité begged it for her own. Their eyes met fixedly and filled with tears; at last the mistress opened her arms, the servant threw herself into them, and they embraced each other, satisfying their grief in a kiss that made them equal.

It was the first time in their lives, Mme. Aubain's nature not being expansive. Félicité was as grateful as though she had received a favour, and cherished her mistress from that moment with the devotion of an animal and a religious worship.

The kindness of her heart unfolded.

When she heard the drums of a marching regiment in the street she posted herself at the door with a pitcher of cider and asked the soldiers to drink. She nursed cholera patients and protected the Polish refugees;[6] one of these even declared that he wished to marry her. They quarrelled, however; for when she came back from the Angelus one morning she found that he had got into her kitchen and made himself a vinegar salad which he was quietly eating.

After the Poles came father Colmiche, an old man who was supposed to have committed atrocities in '93.[7] He lived by the side of the river in the ruins of a pigsty.

---

[5] In 1830 the Bourbons were expelled and Louis-Philippe became king of France.
[6] After Russia suppressed the Polish uprisings in 1831, many Polish refugees came to France.
[7] The Reign of Terror during the French Revolution began in 1793.

The little boys watched him through the cracks in the wall, and threw pebbles at him which fell on the pallet where he lay constantly shaken by a catarrh; his hair was very long, his eyes inflamed, and there was a tumour on his arm bigger than his head. She got him some linen and tried to clean up his miserable hole; her dream was to establish him in the bake-house, without letting him annoy Madame. When the tumour burst she dressed it every day; sometimes she brought him cake, and would put him in the sunshine on a truss of straw. The poor old man, slobbering and trembling, thanked her in his worn-out voice, was terrified that he might lose her, and stretched out his hands when he saw her go away. He died; and she had a mass said for the repose of his soul.

That very day a great happiness befell her; just at dinner-time appeared Mme. de Larsonnière's negro, carrying the parrot in its cage, with perch, chain, and padlock. A note from the baroness informed Mme. Aubain that her husband had been raised to a prefecture and they were starting that evening; she begged her to accept the bird as a memento and mark of her regard.

For a long time he had absorbed Félicité's imagination, because he came from America; and that name reminded her of Victor, so much so that she made inquiries of the negro. She had once gone so far as to say "How Madame would enjoy having him!"

The negro repeated the remark to his mistress; and as she could not take the bird away with her she chose this way of getting rid of him.

4

His name was Loulou. His body was green and the tips of his wings rose-pink; his forehead was blue and his throat golden.

But he had the tiresome habits of biting his perch, tearing out his feathers, sprinkling his dirt about, and spattering the water of his tub. He annoyed Mme. Aubain, and she gave him to Félicité for good.

She endeavoured to train him; soon he could repeat "Nice boy! Your servant, sir! Good morning, Marie!" He was placed by the side of the door, and astonished several people by not answering to the name Jacquot, for all parrots are called Jacquot. People compared him to a turkey and a log of wood, and stabbed Félicité to the heart each time. Strange obstinacy on Loulou's part!—directly you looked at him he refused to speak.

None the less he was eager for society; for on Sundays, while the Rochefeuille ladies, M. de Houppeville, and new familiars—Onfroy the apothecary, Monsieur Varin, and Captain Mathieu—were playing their game of cards, he beat the windows with his wings and threw himself about so frantically that they could not hear each other speak.

Bourais' face, undoubtedly, struck him as extremely droll. Directly he saw it he began to laugh—and laugh with all his might. His peals rang through the courtyard and were repeated by the echo; the neighbours came to their windows and laughed too; while M. Bourais, gliding along under the wall to escape the parrot's eye, and hiding his profile with his hat, got to the river and then entered by the garden gate. There was a lack of tenderness in the looks which he darted at the bird.

Loulou had been slapped by the butcher-boy for making so free as to plunge his head into his basket; and since then he was always trying to nip him through his shirt. Fabu threatened to wring his neck, although he was not cruel, for all his tattooed arms and large whiskers. Far from it; he really rather liked the parrot, and in a jovial humour even wanted to teach him to swear. Félicité, who was alarmed by such proceedings, put the bird in the kitchen. His little chain was taken off and he roamed about the house.

His way of going downstairs was to lean on each step with the curve of his beak, raise the right foot, and then the left; and Félicité was afraid that these gymnastics brought on fits of giddiness. He fell ill and could not talk or eat any longer. There was a growth under his tongue, such as fowls have sometimes. She cured him by tearing the pellicle off with her finger-nails. Mr. Paul was thoughtless enough one day to blow some cigar smoke into his nostrils, and another time when Mme. Lormeau was teasing him with the end of her umbrella he snapped at the ferrule. Finally he got lost.

Félicité had put him on the grass to refresh him, and gone away for a minute, and when she came back—no sign of the parrot! She began by looking for him in the shrubs, by the waterside, and over the roofs, without listening to her mistress's cries of "Take care, do! You are out of your wits!" Then she investigated all the gardens in Pont-l'Évêque, and stopped the passers-by. "You don't ever happen to have seen my parrot, by any chance, do you?" And she gave a description of the parrot to those who did not know him. Suddenly, behind the mills at the foot of the hill she thought she could make out something green that fluttered. But on the top of the hill there was nothing. A hawker assured her that he had come across the parrot just before, at Saint-Melaine, in Mère Simon's shop. She rushed there; they had no idea of what she meant. At last she came home exhausted, with her slippers in shreds and despair in her soul; and as she was sitting in the middle of the garden-seat at Madame's side, telling the whole story of her efforts, a light weight dropped on to her shoulder—it was Loulou! What on earth had he been doing? Taking a walk in the neighbourhood, perhaps!

She had some trouble in recovering from this, or rather never did recover. As the result of a chill she had an attack of quinsy,[8] and soon afterwards an earache. Three years later she was deaf; and she spoke very loud, even in church. Though Félicité's sins might have been published in every corner of the diocese without dishonour to her or scandal to anybody, his Reverence the priest thought it right now to hear her confession in the sacristy only.

Imaginary noises in the head completed her upset. Her mistress often said to her, "Heavens! how stupid you are!" "Yes, Madame," she replied, and looked about for something.

Her little circle of ideas grew still narrower; the peal of church-bells and the lowing of cattle ceased to exist for her. All living beings moved as silently as ghosts. One sound only reached her ears now—the parrot's voice.

Loulou, as though to amuse her, reproduced the click-clack of the turn-spit, the shrill call of a man selling fish, and the noise of the saw in the joiner's house opposite; when the bell rang he imitated Mme. Aubain's "Félicité! the door! the door!"

They carried on conversations, he endlessly reciting the three phrases in his repertory, to which she replied with words that were just as disconnected but uttered what was in her heart. Loulou was almost a son and a lover to her in her

---

[8] Tonsillitis.

isolated state. He climbed up her fingers, nibbled at her lips, and clung to her kerchief; and when she bent her forehead and shook her head gently to and fro, as nurses do, the great wings of her bonnet and the bird's wings quivered together.

When the clouds massed and the thunder rumbled Loulou broke into cries, perhaps remembering the downpours in his native forests. The streaming rain made him absolutely mad; he fluttered wildly about, dashing up to the ceiling, upset everything, and went out through the window to dabble in the garden; but he was back quickly to perch on one of the fire-dogs and hopped about to dry himself, exhibiting his tail and his beak in turn.

One morning in the terrible winter of 1837 she had put him in front of the fireplace because of the cold. She found him dead, in the middle of his cage: head downwards, with his claws in the wires. He had died from congestion, no doubt. But Félicité thought he had been poisoned with parsley, and though there was no proof of any kind her suspicions inclined to Fabu.

She wept so piteously that her mistress said to her, "Well, then, have him stuffed!"

She asked advice from the chemist, who had always been kind to the parrot. He wrote to Havre, and a person called Fellacher undertook the business. But as parcels sometimes got lost in the coach she decided to take the parrot as far as Honfleur herself.

Along the sides of the road were leafless apple-trees, one after the other. Ice covered the ditches. Dogs barked about the farms; and Félicité, with her hands under her cloak, her little black sabots[9] and her basket, walked briskly in the middle of the road.

She crossed the forest, passed High Oak, and reached St. Gatien.

A cloud of dust rose behind her, and in it a mail-coach, carried away by the steep hill, rushed down at full gallop like a hurricane. Seeing this woman who would not get out of the way, the driver stood up in front and the postilion shouted too. He could not hold in his four horses, which increased their pace, and the two leaders were grazing her when he threw them to one side with a jerk of the reins. But he was wild with rage, and lifting his arm as he passed at full speed, gave her such a lash from waist to neck with his big whip that she fell on her back.

Her first act, when she recovered consciousness, was to open her basket. Loulou was happily none the worse. She felt a burn in her right cheek, and when she put her hands against it they were red; the blood was flowing.

She sat down on a heap of stones and bound up her face with her handkerchief. Then she ate a crust of bread which she had put in the basket as a precaution, and found a consolation for her wound in gazing at the bird.

When she reached the crest of Ecquemauville she saw the Honfleur lights sparkling in the night sky like a company of stars; beyond, the sea stretched dimly. Then a faintness overtook her and she stopped; her wretched childhood, the disillusion of her first love, her nephew's going away, and Virginie's death all came back to her at once like the waves of an oncoming tide, rose to her throat, and choked her.

Afterwards, at the boat, she made a point of speaking to the captain, begging him to take care of the parcel, though she did not tell him what was in it.

Fellacher kept the parrot a long time. He was always promising it for the following week. After six months he announced that a packing-case had started, and then

---

[9]Wooden shoes.

nothing more was heard of it. It really seemed as though Loulou was never coming back. "Ah, they have stolen him!" she thought.

He arrived at last, and looked superb. There he was, erect upon a branch which screwed into a mahogany socket, with a foot in the air and his head on one side, biting a nut which the bird-stuffer—with a taste for impressiveness—had gilded.

Félicité shut him up in her room. It was a place to which few people were admitted, and held so many religious objects and miscellaneous things that it looked like a chapel and bazaar in one.

A big cupboard impeded you as you opened the door. Opposite the window commanding the garden a little round one looked into the court; there was a table by the folding-bed with a water-jug, two combs, and a cube of blue soap in a chipped plate. On the walls hung rosaries, medals, several benign Virgins, and a holy water vessel made out of cocoa-nut; on the chest of drawers, which was covered with a cloth like an altar, was the shell box that Victor had given her, and after that a watering-can, a toy-balloon, exercise-books, the illustrated geography, and a pair of young lady's boots; and, fastened by its ribbons to the nail of the looking-glass, hung the little plush hat! Félicité carried observances of this kind so far as to keep one of Monsieur's frock-coats. All the old rubbish which Mme. Aubain did not want any longer she laid hands on for her room. That was why there were artificial flowers along the edge of the chest of drawers and a portrait of the Comte d'Artois[10] in the little window recess.

With the aid of a bracket Loulou was established over the chimney, which jutted into the room. Every morning when she woke up she saw him there in the dawning light, and recalled old days and the smallest details of insignificant acts in a deep quietness which knew no pain.

Holding, as she did, no communication with anyone, Félicité lived as insensibly as if she were walking in her sleep. The Corpus Christi processions roused her to life again. Then she went round begging mats and candlesticks from the neighbours to decorate the altar they put up in the street.

In church she was always gazing at the Holy Ghost in the window, and observed that there was something of the parrot in him. The likeness was still clearer, she thought, on a crude colour-print representing the baptism of Our Lord. With his purple wings and emerald body he was the very image of Loulou.

She bought him, and hung him up instead of the Comte d'Artois, so that she could see them both together in one glance. They were linked in her thoughts; and the parrot was consecrated by his association with the Holy Ghost, which became more vivid to her eye and more intelligible. The Father could not have chosen to express Himself through a dove, for such creatures cannot speak; it must have been one of Loulou's ancestors, surely. And though Félicité looked at the picture while she said her prayers she swerved a little from time to time towards the parrot.

She wanted to join the Ladies of the Virgin, but Mme. Aubain dissuaded her.

And then a great event loomed up before them—Paul's marriage.

He had been a solicitor's clerk to begin with, and then tried business, the Customs, the Inland Revenue, and made efforts, even, to get into the Rivers and Forests. By an inspiration from heaven he had suddenly, at thirty-six, discovered his real line—the Registrar's Office. And there he showed such marked capacity

---

[10] Title of Charles X, the last of the Bourbon kings. He ruled between 1824 and 1830 and died in 1836 in exile.

that an inspector had offered him his daughter's hand and promised him his influence.

So Paul, grown serious, brought the lady to see his mother.

She sniffed at the ways of Pont-l'Évêque, gave herself great airs, and wounded Félicité's feelings. Mme. Aubain was relieved at her departure.

The week after came news of M. Bourais' death in an inn in Lower Brittany. The rumour of suicide was confirmed, and doubts arose as to his honesty. Mme. Aubain studied his accounts, and soon found out the whole tale of his misdoings—embezzled arrears, secret sales of wood, forged receipts, etc. Besides that he had an illegitimate child, and "relations with a person at Dozulé."

These shameful facts distressed her greatly. In March 1853 she was seized with a pain in the chest; her tongue seemed to be covered with film, and leeches did not ease the difficult breathing. On the ninth evening of her illness she died, just at seventy-two.

She passed as being younger, owing to the bands of brown hair which framed her pale, pock-marked face. There were few friends to regret her, for she had a stiffness of manner which kept people at a distance.

But Félicité mourned for her as one seldom mourns for a master. It upset her ideas and seemed contrary to the order of things, impossible and monstrous, that Madame should die before her.

Ten days afterwards, which was the time it took to hurry there from Besançon, the heirs arrived. The daughter-in-law ransacked the drawers, chose some furniture, and sold the rest; and then they went back to their registering.

Madame's armchair, her small round table, her foot-warmer, and the eight chairs were gone! Yellow patches in the middle of the panels showed where the engravings had hung. They had carried off the two little beds and the mattresses, and all Virginie's belongings had disappeared from the cupboard. Félicité went from floor to floor dazed with sorrow.

The next day there was a notice on the door, and the apothecary shouted in her ear that the house was for sale.

She tottered, and was obliged to sit down. What distressed her most of all was to give up her room, so suitable as it was for poor Loulou. She enveloped him with a look of anguish when she was imploring the Holy Ghost, and formed the idolatrous habit of kneeling in front of the parrot to say her prayers. Sometimes the sun shone in at the attic window and caught his glass eye, and a great luminous ray shot out of it and put her in an ecstasy.

She had a pension of three hundred and eighty francs a year which her mistress had left her. The garden gave her a supply of vegetables. As for clothes, she had enough to last her to the end of her days, and she economized in candles by going to bed at dusk.

She hardly ever went out, as she did not like passing the dealer's shop, where some of the old furniture was exposed for sale. Since her fit of giddiness she dragged one leg; and as her strength was failing Mère Simon, whose grocery business had collapsed, came every morning to split the wood and pump water for her.

Her eyes grew feeble. The shutters ceased to be thrown open. Years and years passed, and the house was neither let nor sold.

Félicité never asked for repairs because she was afraid of being sent away. The boards on the roof rotted; her bolster was wet for a whole winter. After Easter she spat blood.

Then Mère Simon called in a doctor. Félicité wanted to know what was the matter with her. But she was too deaf to hear, and the only word which reached her was "pneumonia." It was a word she knew, and she answered softly "Ah! like Madame," thinking it natural that she should follow her mistress.

The time for the festal shrines was coming near. The first one was always at the bottom of the hill, the second in front of the post-office, and the third towards the middle of the street. There was some rivalry in the matter of this one, and the women of the parish ended by choosing Mme. Aubain's courtyard.

The hard breathing and fever increased. Félicité was vexed at doing nothing for the altar. If only she could at least have put something there! Then she thought of the parrot. The neighbours objected that it would not be decent. But the priest gave her permission, which so intensely delighted her that she begged him to accept Loulou, her sole possession, when she died.

From Tuesday to Saturday, the eve of the festival, she coughed more often. By the evening her face had shrivelled, her lips stuck to her gums, and she had vomitings; and at twilight next morning, feeling herself very low, she sent for a priest.

Three kindly women were round her during the extreme unction. Then she announced that she must speak to Fabu. He arrived in his Sunday clothes, by no means at his ease in the funereal atmosphere.

"Forgive me," she said, with an effort to stretch out her arm; "I thought it was you who had killed him."

What did she mean by such stories? She suspected him of murder—a man like him! He waxed indignant, and was on the point of making a row.

"There," said the women, "she is no longer in her senses, you can see it well enough!"

Félicité spoke to shadows of her own from time to time. The women went away, and Mère Simon had breakfast. A little later she took Loulou and brought him close to Félicité with the words:

"Come, now, say good-bye to him!"

Loulou was not a corpse, but the worms devoured him; one of his wings was broken, and the tow was coming out of his stomach. But she was blind now; she kissed him on the forehead and kept him close against her cheek. Mère Simon took him back from her to put him on the altar.

5

Summer scents came up from the meadows; flies buzzed; the sun made the river glitter and heated the slates. Mère Simon came back into the room and fell softly asleep.

She woke at the noise of bells; the people were coming out from vespers. Félicité's delirium subsided. She thought of the procession and saw it as if she had been there.

All the school children, the church-singers, and the firemen walked on the pavement, while in the middle of the road the verger armed with his hallebard and the beadle with a large cross advanced in front. Then came the schoolmaster, with an eye on the boys, and the sister, anxious about her little girls; three of the daintiest, with angelic curls, scattered rose-petals in the air; the deacon controlled the band with outstretched arms; and two censer-bearers turned back at every step towards the Holy Sacrament, which was borne by Monsieur the curé, wearing his beautiful chasuble, under a canopy of dark-red velvet held up by four churchwardens. A crowd of people pressed behind, between the white cloths covering the house walls, and they reached the bottom of the hill.

A cold sweat moistened Félicité's temples. Mère Simon sponged her with a piece of linen, saying to herself that one day she would have to go that way.

The hum of the crowd increased, was very loud for an instant and then went further away.

A fusillade shook the window-panes. It was the postilions saluting the monstrance.[11] Félicité rolled her eyes and said as audibly as she could: "Does he look well?" The parrot was weighing on her mind.

Her agony began. A death-rattle that grew more and more convulsed made her sides heave. Bubbles of froth came at the corners of her mouth and her whole body trembled.

Soon the booming of the ophicleides,[12] the high voices of the children, and the deep voices of the men were distinguishable. At intervals all was silent, and the tread of feet, deadened by the flowers they walked on, sounded like a flock pattering on grass.

The clergy appeared in the courtyard. Mère Simon clambered on to a chair to reach the attic window, and so looked down straight upon the shrine. Green garlands hung over the altar, which was decked with a flounce of English lace. In the middle was a small frame with relics in it; there were two orange-trees at the corners, and all along stood silver candlesticks and china vases, with sunflowers, lilies, peonies, foxgloves, and tufts of hortensia. This heap of blazing colour slanted from the level of the altar to the carpet which went on over the pavement; and some rare objects caught the eye. There was a silver-gilt sugar-basin with a crown of violets; pendants of Alençon stone glittered on the moss, and two Chinese screens displayed their landscapes. Loulou was hidden under roses, and showed nothing but his blue forehead, like a plaque of lapis lazuli.

The churchwardens, singers, and children took their places round the three sides of the court. The priest went slowly up the steps, and placed his great, radiant golden sun[13] upon the lace. Everyone knelt down. There was a deep silence; and the censers glided to and fro on the full swing of their chains.

An azure vapour rose up into Félicité's room. Her nostrils met it; she inhaled it sensuously, mystically; and then closed her eyes. Her lips smiled. The beats of her heart lessened one by one, vaguer each time and softer, as a fountain sinks, an echo disappears; and when she sighed her last breath she thought she saw an opening in the heavens, and a gigantic parrot hovering above her head.

FYODOR DOSTOEVSKY
[1821–1881]

Dostoevsky's novels are like a laboratory in which all the major ideas floating around in the heads of Europeans in the second half of the nineteenth century are dissected. The ideas are not examined abstractly as in a philosophy text, but as the mental tools of flesh-and-blood individuals—that is, as lived ideas. Nicholas Berdyaev writes that ideas for Dostoevsky "are fiery billows, never frozen categories . . . they are the destiny of living

---

[11] The container for the consecrated host.
[12] A deep-toned brass wind instrument.
[13] The monstrance.

being, its burning motive-power." What sort of ideas? Romantic ideas about freedom and art, about the boundaries of reason and the shadow side of human consciousness; socialist ideas about atheism, revolution, and social progress; orthodox ideas about sin, penance, and forgiveness; totalitarian ideas about law and order, prisons, and social privilege; populist ideas about peasants, nationalism, Christianity, and Russia's destiny in the world. It would be a mistake to read Dostoevsky's novels solely as a pale mask for his autobiography; nevertheless, his own inner conflicts and spiritual odyssey become the basis for his fictional heroes.

LIFE

Fyodor Mikhailovich Dostoevsky was born October 30, 1821, in Moscow. His father, an impoverished nobleman, was a doctor at a public hospital for the poor, where the family lived. The setting provided an early introduction to pain and suffering. His mother was sickly and died when he was sixteen. In 1837, he was enrolled at the Military Engineering School in St. Petersburg. En route to school, he saw a government courier beat his coachman with his fists: "This revolting scene remained in my memory for the rest of my life," he wrote in 1876. During his five years at this school his primary interest was in literature.

While Fyodor was away at school, his retired father, who had a reputation for brutality, was murdered by his peasants on a small estate. Dostoevsky resigned his army commission in 1844, and with some inherited money from his father devoted himself to writing. The result was the publication of *Poor Folk* in 1846, which portrayed the lives of the lower classes. It was a big success, especially with Vissarion Belinsky, the most important critic of the time. Dostoevsky immediately became involved with a young literary set and with the secret activities of Petrashevsky's socialist circle.

In reaction to the Revolution of 1848 in France and a fear that the winds of reform might blow through Russia, the Tsar had socialists, including Dostoevsky, rounded up and arrested in Moscow. They were tried and sentenced to death. At the very last moment, as they were led blindfolded before the firing squad—in a prearranged sadistic plot to scare the young intellectuals—a reprieve was granted. Not surprisingly, Dostoevsky never forgot that moment. He spent the next four years in penal servitude in Siberia.

While in prison, he underwent a profound conversion. He questioned the progressive, even revolutionary, ideas of his youth and replaced them with a more orthodox belief in the evil potential of human nature, the cleansing benefits of suffering, the redemptive power of love, and a faith in the prophetic mission of the Russian peasant. He also experienced his first epileptic seizure, a condition that would haunt him the rest of his life. A disastrous marriage to a consumptive widow lasted until her death in 1864.

After nearly ten years of exile in Siberia, Dostoevsky was finally permitted to return to European Russia, and eventually to St. Petersburg. After a tempestuous affair, he married his stenographer, Anna Gregorievna Snitkin, who brought some semblance of order and stability to his life. For a time he was plagued by money problems, his brother's debts, and his own debilitating bouts with gambling; nevertheless, he was writing some of the finest novels of the Western world, while periodically fleeing to Europe to avoid creditors.

In 1864 he used a scurrilous persona to chastise Russian intellectuals in the first of his major novels, *Notes from Underground*. Others followed: *Crime and Punishment* (1866), *The Idiot* (1868), and *The Possessed* (1871). During the last ten years of his life, he enjoyed comparatively easy circumstances, along with popularity and respect. *A Raw Youth* was published in 1875, and from 1876 to 1880, he wrote a monthly journal, *The Diary of a Writer.* The climax of his writing career was a book he had planned for years, *The Brothers Karamazov* (1880), which was a huge success. Less than a year after its publication, he died on January 28, 1881.

WORK

The Brothers Karamazov, from which "The Grand Inquisitor" is taken, is the story of a parricide. Typically, the characters in Dostoevsky's major novels are situated in crisis, usually a crime. Rarely are his characters seen in ordinary, everyday situations—the humdrum of work or play, complacency or habit—such as we might find in Chekhov's short stories. Dostoevsky tends to place them on the margins between freedom and captivity, love and hate, crime and forgiveness, sin and salvation, life and death. Dostoevsky uses the intensity of conflict in his characters to bypass mundane concerns in order to explore the ultimate questions of existence.

In a strangely modern family configuration, father Karamazov has one son by his first wife, two sons by his second wife, and one illegitimate son by a simple-minded peasant. The wives die and the sons are raised by relatives so that the father can pursue his crude, hedonistic ways. The sons grow up to be very different in personality and interests, but nevertheless representative of the diverse, conflicting parts of Dostoevsky himself. Dmitri is passionate and tempestuous like his father. Alyosha is innocent and saintly. The illegitimate Smerdyakov is a degenerate and an epileptic who eventually kills his father. Ivan is the intellectual, torn between doubt and faith, hope and nihilism, reflecting most directly Dostoevsky's own inner division. Ivan struggles with the idea of a loving God who could permit so much suffering on earth, especially by innocent children. All of the brothers live life passionately.

In what Ivan calls a poem in prose, he reads "The Grand Inquisitor" to Alyosha. The setting for his prose poem is Seville, Spain, during the height of the Inquisition in the sixteenth century. After fifteen centuries, Jesus has finally returned to earth to heal and comfort his people. He is immediately arrested and isolated by the inquisitor. In a very persuasive and moving monologue, the inquisitor explains to Jesus why the Church as an institution had to betray Jesus' original mission by enslaving the people with miracle, mystery, and authority. According to the inquisitor, the masses of people were incapable of handling the freedom intended by Jesus and were willing to exchange it for the illusion of freedom and bread.

Ivan's piece is a strong indictment of religious institutions as the inquisitor fluctuates between being a powerful apologist for institutional cynicism and a lonely, disillusioned atheist. In a perfect response to the inquisitor's degradation, Jesus kisses him on the lips and departs.

In the part of the novel that follows "The Grand Inquisitor," there is a discussion with Father Zossima, a true holy man who is offered by Dostoevsky as an alternative to the inquisitor. Father Zossima preaches unconditional love for our fallen world: "Love all God's creation, the whole and every grain of sand in it. Love every leaf, every ray of God's light. Love the animals, love the plants, love everything. If you love everything, you will perceive the divine mystery in things. Once you perceive it, you will begin to comprehend it better every day. And you will come at last to love the whole world with an all-embracing love."

Dostoevsky did not intend Ivan's prose poem to be a pamphlet setting out a series of answers and prescribing a course of action. As a literary gem, it was meant to raise questions and stimulate multiple interpretations. It was part of Dostoevsky's genius that he could wrestle free from the ordinary boundaries of nineteenth-century consciousness and call into question the institutions and programs of Western culture, thereby exposing a spiritual wasteland that would plague the sensibilities of modern writers.

SUGGESTED READINGS

Excellent biographical studies are found in David Magarshack's *Dostoevsky* (1963) and F. M. Terras's *Dostoevsky: Life, Work, and Criticism* (1984). Ernest J. Simmons's *Dostoevsky: The Making of a Novelist* (1950) describes the influences that shaped Dostoevsky's maturation as a writer. Nicholas Berdyaev's *Dostoevsky: An Interpretation* (1957) is particularly interested in Dostoevsky's version of Christianity. Vyacheslav Ivanov's *Freedom and the Tragic Life: A Study in Dostoevsky* (1952) focuses on philosophical issues. Malcolm Jones and Garth M. Terry, editors, *New Essays on Dostoevsky* (1983), and René Wellek, editor, *Dostoevsky: A Collection of Critical Essays* (1962), provide a wide spectrum of views on Dostoevsky's life and writing. Dmitri Mirsky's *History of Russian Literature* (1963) contains a broad overview of Russian literature and a literary context for Dostoevsky.

The Brothers Karamazov

Translated by Constance Garnett

THE GRAND INQUISITOR

"... *Do you know, Alyosha—don't laugh! I made a poem about a year ago. If you can waste another ten minutes on me, I'll tell it to you.*"

"*You wrote a poem?*"

"*Oh, no, I didn't write it,*" laughed Ivan, "*and I've never written two lines of poetry in my life. But I made up this poem in prose and I remembered it. I was carried away when I made it up. You will be my first reader—that is, listener. Why should an author forego even one listener?*" smiled Ivan. "*Shall I tell it to you?*"

"*I am all attention,*" said Alyosha.

"*My poem is called 'The Grand Inquisitor'; it's a ridiculous thing, but I want to tell it to you.*"

"Even this must have a preface—that is, a literary preface," laughed Ivan, "and I am a poor hand at making one. You see, my action takes place in the sixteenth century, and at that time, as you probably learnt at school, it was customary in poetry to bring down heavenly powers on earth. Not to speak of Dante, in France clerks, as well as the monks in the monasteries, used to give regular performances in which the Madonna, the saints, the angels, Christ, and God Himself were brought on the stage. In those days it was done in all simplicity. In Victor Hugo's 'Notre Dame de Paris' an edifying and gratuitous spectacle was provided for the people in the Hotel de Ville of Paris in the reign of Louis XI in honor of the birth of the dauphin. It was called *Le bon jugement de la très sainte et gracieuse Vierge Marie*,[1] and she appears herself on the stage and pronounces her *bon jugement*. Similar plays, chiefly from the Old Testament, were occasionally performed in Moscow, too, up to the times of Peter the Great. But besides plays there were all sorts of legends and ballads scattered about the world, in which the saints and angels and all the powers of Heaven took

---

[1] The good judgment of the saintly and gracious Virgin Mary.

part when required. In our monasteries the monks busied themselves in translating, copying, and even composing such poems—and even under the Tatars. There is, for instance, one such poem (of course, from the Greek), 'The Wanderings of Our Lady Through Hell,' with descriptions as bold as Dante's. Our Lady visits Hell, and the Archangel Michael leads her through the torments. She sees the sinners and their punishment. There she sees among others one noteworthy set of sinners in a burning lake; some of them sink to the bottom of the lake so that they can't swim out, and 'these God forgets'—an expression of extraordinary depth and force. And so Our Lady, shocked and weeping, falls before the throne of God and begs for mercy for all in Hell—for all she has seen there, and indiscriminately. Her conversation with God is immensely interesting. She beseeches Him, she will not desist, and when God points to the hands and feet of her Son, nailed to the Cross, and asks, 'How can I forgive His tormentors?' she bids all the saints, all the martyrs, all the angels and archangels to fall down with her and pray for mercy on all without distinction. It ends by her winning from God a respite of suffering every year from Good Friday till Trinity day, and the sinners at once raise a cry of thankfulness from Hell, chanting, 'Thou art just, O Lord, in this judgment.' Well, my poem would have been of that kind if it had appeared at that time. He comes on the scene in my poem, but He says nothing, only appears and passes on. Fifteen centuries have passed since He promised to come in His glory, fifteen centuries since His prophet wrote, 'Behold, I come quickly';[2] 'Of that day and that hour knoweth no man, neither the Son, but the Father,'[3] as He Himself predicted on earth. But humanity awaits him with the same faith and with the same love. Oh, with greater faith, for it is fifteen centuries since man has ceased to see signs from Heaven.

> No signs from Heaven come today
> To add to what the heart doth say.

There was nothing left but faith in what the heart doth say. It is true there were many miracles in those days. There were saints who performed miraculous cures; some holy people, according to their biographies, were visited by the Queen of Heaven herself. But the devil did not slumber, and doubts were already arising among men of the truth of these miracles. And just then there appeared in the north of Germany a terrible new heresy. 'A huge star like to a torch' (that is, to a church) 'fell on the sources of the waters and they became bitter.' These heretics began blasphemously denying miracles. But those who remained faithful were all the more ardent in their faith. The tears of humanity rose up to Him as before, awaiting His coming, loved Him, hoped for Him, yearned to suffer and die for Him as before. And so many ages mankind had prayed with faith and fervor, 'O Lord our God, hasten Thy coming,' so many ages called upon Him, that in His infinite mercy He deigned to come down to His servants. Before that day He had come down, He had visited some holy men, martyrs, and hermits, as is written in their 'Lives.' Among us, Tyutchev,[4] with absolute faith in the truth of his words, bore witness that

> Bearing the Cross, in slavish dress,
> Weary and worn, the Heavenly King
> Our mother, Russia, came to bless,
> And through our land went wandering.

And that certainly was so, I assure you.

---

[2] Revelations 22:7.
[3] Mark 13:32.
[4] A Russian poet (1803–1873).

"And behold, He deigned to appear for a moment to the people, to the tortured, suffering people, sunk in iniquity, but loving Him like children. My story is laid in Spain, in Seville, in the most terrible time of the Inquisition, when fires were lighted every day to the glory of God, and 'in the splendid *auto da fé*[5] the wicked heretics were burnt.' Oh, of course, this was not the coming in which He will appear according to His promise at the end of time in all His heavenly glory, and which will be sudden 'as lightning flashing from east to west.'[6] No, He visited His children only for a moment, and there where the flames were crackling round the heretics. In His infinite mercy He came once more among men in that human shape in which He walked among men for three years fifteen centuries ago. He came down to the 'hot pavement' of the southern town in which on the day before almost a hundred heretics had, *ad majorem gloriam Dei,*[7] been burnt by the cardinal, the Grand Inquisitor, in a magnificent *auto da fé,* in the presence of the king, the court, the knights, the cardinals, the most charming ladies of the court, and the whole population of Seville.

"He came softly, unobserved, and yet, strange to say, every one recognized Him. That might be one of the best passages in the poem. I mean, why they recognized Him. The people are irresistibly drawn to Him, they surround Him, they flock about Him, follow Him. He moves silently in their midst with a gentle smile of infinite compassion. The sun of love burns in His heart, light and power shine from His eyes, and their radiance, shed on the people, stirs their hearts with responsive love. He holds out His hands to them, blesses them, and a healing virtue comes from contact with Him, even with His garments. An old man in the crowd, blind from childhood, cries out, 'O Lord, heal me and I shall see Thee!' and, as it were, scales fall from his eyes and the blind man sees Him. The crowd weeps and kisses the earth under His feet. Children throw flowers before Him, sing, and cry hosannah. 'It is He—it is He!' all repeat. 'It must be He, it can be no one but Him!' He stops at the steps of the Seville cathedral at the moment when the weeping mourners are bringing in a little open white coffin. In it lies a child of seven, the only daughter of a prominent citizen. The dead child lies hidden in flowers. 'He will raise your child,' the crowd shouts to the weeping mother. The priest, coming to meet the coffin, looks perplexed and frowns, but the mother of the dead child throws herself at His feet with a wail. 'If it is Thou, raise my child!' she cries, holding out her hands to Him. The procession halts, the coffin is laid on the steps at His feet. He looks with compassion, and His lips once more softly pronounce, 'Maiden, arise!'[8] and the maiden arises. The little girl sits up in the coffin and looks round, smiling with wide-open wondering eyes, holding a bunch of white roses they had put in her hand.

"There are cries, sobs, confusion among the people, and at that moment the cardinal himself, the Grand Inquisitor, passes by the cathedral. He is an old man, almost ninety, tall and erect, with a withered face and sunken eyes, in which there is still a gleam of light. He is not dressed in his gorgeous cardinal's robes, as he was the day before, when he was burning the enemies of the Roman Church—at that moment he was wearing his coarse, old, monk's cassock. At a distance behind him come his gloomy assistants and slaves and the 'holy guard.' He stops at the sight of the crowd and watches it from a distance. He sees everything; he sees them set the

---

[5] Literally, "act of faith"; indicates the burning of a heretic.
[6] Matthew 24:27.
[7] "For the greater glory of God," the Jesuits' motto.
[8] Mark 5:41.

coffin down at His feet, sees the child rise up, and his face darkens. He knits his thick grey brows and his eyes gleam with a sinister fire. He holds out his finger and bids the guards take Him. And such is his power, so completely are the people cowed into submission and trembling obedience to him, that the crowd immediately makes way for the guards, and in the midst of deathlike silence they lay hands on Him and lead Him away. The crowd instantly bows down to the earth, like one man, before the old inquisitor. He blesses the people in silence and passes on. The guards lead their prisoner to the close, gloomy, vaulted prison in the ancient palace of the Holy Inquisition and shut Him in it. The day passes and is followed by the dark, burning 'breathless' night of Seville. The air is 'fragrant with laurel and lemon.' In the pitch darkness the iron door of the prison is suddenly opened and the Grand Inquisitor himself comes in with a light in his hand. He is alone; the door is closed at once behind him. He stands in the doorway and for a minute or two gazes into His face. At last he goes up slowly, sets the light on the table and speaks.

"'Is it Thou? Thou?' but receiving no answer, he adds at once, 'Don't answer, be silent. What canst Thou say, indeed? I know too well what Thou wouldst say. And Thou hast no right to add anything to what Thou hadst said of old. Why, then, art Thou come to hinder us? For Thou hast come to hinder us, and Thou knowest that. But dost Thou know what will be tomorrow? I know not who Thou art and care not to know whether it is Thou or only a semblance of Him, but tomorrow I shall condemn Thee and burn Thee at the stake as the worst of heretics. And the very people who have today kissed Thy feet, tomorrow at the faintest sign from me will rush to heap up the embers of Thy fire. Knowest Thou that? Yes, maybe Thou knowest it,' he added with thoughtful penetration, never for a moment taking his eyes off the Prisoner."

"I don't quite understand, Ivan. What does it mean?" Alyosha, who had been listening in silence, said with a smile. "Is it simply a wild fantasy, or a mistake on the part of the old man—some impossible *qui pro quo?*"[9]

"Take it as the last," said Ivan, laughing, "if you are so corrupted by modern realism and can't stand anything fantastic. If you like it to be a case of mistaken identity, let it be so. It is true," he went on, laughing, "the old man was ninety, and he might well be crazy over his set idea. He might have been struck by the appearance of the Prisoner. It might, in fact, be simply his ravings, the delusion of an old man of ninety, overexcited by the *auto da fé* of a hundred heretics the day before. But does it matter to us after all whether it was a mistake of identity or a wild fantasy? All that matters is that the old man should speak out, should speak openly of what he has thought in silence for ninety years."

"And the Prisoner too is silent? Does He look at him and not say a word?"

"That's inevitable in any case," Ivan laughed again. "The old man has told Him He hasn't the right to add anything to what He has said of old. One may say it is the most fundamental feature of Roman Catholicism, in my opinion at least. 'All has been given by Thee to the Pope,' they say, 'and all, therefore, is still in the Pope's hands, and there is no need for Thee to come now at all. Thou must not meddle for the time, at least.' That's how they speak and write, too—the Jesuits, at any rate. I have read it myself in the works of their theologians. 'Hast Thou the right to reveal to us one of the mysteries of that world from which Thou hast come?' my old man asks Him, and answers the question for Him. 'No, Thou has not; that Thou mayest not add to what has been said of old, and mayest not take from men the freedom which Thou didst exalt when Thou wast on earth. Whatsoever Thou

---

[9]Misunderstanding.

revealest anew will encroach on men's freedom of faith; for it will be manifest as a miracle, and the freedom of their faith was dearer to Thee than anything in those days fifteen hundred years ago. Didst Thou not often say then, "I will make you free"?[10] But now Thou hast seen these "free" men,' the old man adds suddenly, with a pensive smile. 'Yes, we've paid dearly for it,' he goes on, looking sternly at Him, 'but at last we have completed that work in Thy name. For fifteen centuries we have been wrestling with Thy freedom, but now it is ended and over for good. Dost Thou not believe that it's over for good? Thou lookest meekly at me and deignest not even to be wroth with me. But let me tell Thee that now, today, people are more persuaded than ever that they have perfect freedom, yet they have brought their freedom to us and laid it humbly at our feet. But that has been our doing. Was this what Thou didst? Was this Thy freedom?' "

"I don't understand again," Alyosha broke in. "Is he ironical, is he jesting?"

"Not a bit of it! He claims it as a merit for himself and his Church that at last they have vanquished freedom and have done so to make men happy. 'For now' (he is speaking of the Inquisition, of course) 'for the first time it has become possible to think of the happiness of men. Man was created a rebel; and how can rebels be happy? Thou wast warned,' he says to Him. 'Thou hast had no lack of admonitions, and warnings, but Thou didst not listen to those warnings; Thou didst reject the only way by which men might be made happy. But, fortunately, departing Thou didst hand on the work to us. Thou hast promised, Thou hast established by Thy word, Thou hast given to us the right to bind and to unbind, and now, of course, Thou canst not think of taking it away. Why, then, hast Thou come to hinder us?' "

"And what's the meaning of 'no lack of admonitions and warnings'?" asked Alyosha.

"Why, that's the chief part of what the old man must say.

" 'The wise and dread Spirit, the spirit of self-destruction and nonexistence,' the old man goes on, 'the great spirit talked with Thee in the wilderness, and we are told in the books that he "tempted" Thee.[11] Is that so? And could anything truer be said than what he revealed to Thee in three questions and what Thou didst reject, and what in the books is called "the temptation"? And yet if there has ever been on earth a real stupendous miracle, it took place on that day, on the day of the three temptations. The statement of those three questions was itself the miracle. If it were possible to imagine simply for the sake of argument that those three questions of the dread spirit had perished utterly from the books, and that we had to restore them and to invent them anew, and to do so had gathered together all the wise men of the earth—rulers, chief priests, learned men, philosophers, poets—and had set them the task to invent three questions, such as would not only fit the occasion, but express in three words, three human phrases, the whole future history of the world and of humanity—dost Thou believe that all the wisdom of the earth united could have invented anything in depth and force equal to the three questions which were actually put to Thee then by the wise and mighty spirit in the wilderness? From those questions alone, from the miracle of their statement, we can see that we have here to do not with the fleeting human intelligence, but with the absolute and eternal. For in those three questions the whole subsequent history of mankind is, as it were, brought together into one whole, and foretold, and in them are united all the unsolved historical contradictions of human nature. At the time it could

---

[10]For example, John 8:36.
[11]The story of Satan's temptation of Jesus is told in Matthew 4:1–11 and in Luke 4:1–13.

not be so clear, since the future was unknown; but now that fifteen hundred years have passed, we see that everything in those three questions was so justly divined and foretold, and has been so truly fulfilled, that nothing can be added to them or taken from them.

"'Judge Thyself who was right—Thou or he who questioned Thee then? Remember the first question; its meaning, in other words, was this: "Thou wouldst go into the world, and art going with empty hands, with some promise of freedom which men in their simplicity and their natural unruliness cannot even understand, which they fear and dread—for nothing has ever been more insupportable for a man and a human society than freedom. But seest Thou these stones in this parched and barren wilderness? Turn them into bread, and mankind will run after Thee like a flock of sheep, grateful and obedient, though forever trembling, lest Thou withdraw Thy hand and deny them Thy bread." But Thou wouldst not deprive man of freedom and didst reject the offer, thinking, what is that freedom worth, if obedience is bought with bread? Thou didst reply that man lives not by bread alone. But dost Thou know that for the sake of that earthly bread the spirit of the earth will rise up against Thee and will strive with Thee and overcome Thee, and all will follow him, crying, "Who can compare with this beast? He has given us fire from heaven!"[12] Dost Thou know that the ages will pass, and humanity will proclaim by the lips of their sages that there is no crime, and therefore no sin; there is only hunger? "Feed men, and then ask of them virtue!" that's what they'll write on the banner which they will raise against Thee, and with which they will destroy Thy temple. Where Thy temple stood will rise a new building; the terrible tower of Babel[13] will be built again, and though, like the one of old, it will not be finished, yet Thou mightest have prevented that new tower and have cut short the sufferings of men for a thousand years; for they will come back to us after a thousand years of agony with their tower. They will seek us again, hidden underground in the catacombs, for we shall be again persecuted and tortured. They will find us and cry to us, "Feed us, for those who have promised us fire from heaven haven't given it!" And then we shall finish building their tower, for he finishes the building who feeds them. And we alone shall feed them in Thy name, declaring falsely that it is in Thy name. Oh, never, never can they feed themselves without us! No science will give them bread so long as they remain free. In the end they will lay their freedom at our feet, and say to us, "Make us your slaves, but feed us." They will understand themselves, at last, that freedom and bread enough for all are inconceivable together, for never, never will they be able to share between them! They will be convinced, too, that they can never be free, for they are weak, vicious, worthless and rebellious. Thou didst promise them the bread of Heaven, but, I repeat again, can it compare with earthly bread in the eyes of the weak, ever-sinful and ignoble race of man? And if for the sake of the bread of Heaven thousands and tens of thousands shall follow Thee, what is to become of the millions and tens of thousands of millions of creatures who will not have the strength to forego the earthly bread for the sake of the heavenly? Or dost Thou care only for the tens of thousands of the great and strong, while the millions, numerous as the sands of the sea, who are weak but love Thee, must exist only for the sake of the great and strong? No, we care for the weak, too. They are sinful and rebellious, but in the end they too will become obedient. They will marvel at us and look on us as gods, because we are ready to endure the

---

[12]Revelations, 13:4, 13.
[13]Genesis 11.

freedom which they have found so dreadful and to rule over them—so awful it will seem to them to be free. But we shall tell them that we are Thy servants and rule them in Thy name. We shall deceive them again, for we will not let Thee come to us again. That deception will be our suffering, for we shall be forced to lie.

" 'This is the significance of the first question in the wilderness, and this is what Thou hast rejected for the sake of that freedom which Thou hast exalted above everything. Yet in this question lies hidden the great secret of this world. Choosing "bread," Thou wouldst have satisfied the universal and everlasting craving of humanity—to find someone to worship. So long as man remains free he strives for nothing so incessantly and so painfully as to find someone to worship. But man seeks to worship what is established beyond dispute, so that all men would agree at once to worship it. For these pitiful creatures are concerned not only to find what one or the other can worship, but to find something that all would believe in and worship; what is essential is that all may be *together* in it. This craving for *community* of worship is the chief misery of every man individually and of all humanity from the beginning of time. For the sake of common worship they've slain each other with the sword. They have set up gods and challenged one another, "Put away your gods and come and worship ours, or we will kill you and your gods!" And so it will be to the end of the world, even when gods disappear from the earth; they will fall down before idols just the same. Thou didst know, Thou couldst not but have known, this fundamental secret of human nature, but Thou didst reject the one infallible banner which was offered Thee to make all men bow down to Thee alone—the banner of earthly bread; and Thou hast rejected it for the sake of freedom and the bread of Heaven. Behold what Thou didst further. And all again in the name of freedom! I tell Thee that man is tormented by no greater anxiety than to find someone quickly to whom he can hand over the gift of freedom with which the ill-fated creature is born. But only one who can appease their conscience can take over their freedom. In bread there was offered Thee an invincible banner; give bread, and man will worship Thee, for nothing is more certain than bread. But if someone else gains possession of his conscience—oh! then he will cast away Thy bread and follow after him who has ensnared his conscience. In that Thou wast right. For the secret of man's being is not only to live but to have something to live for. Without a stable conception of the object of life, man would not consent to go on living, and would rather destroy himself than remain on earth, though he had bread in abundance. That is true. But what happened? Instead of taking men's freedom from them, Thou didst make it greater than ever! Didst Thou forget that man prefers peace, and even death, to freedom of choice in the knowledge of good and evil? Nothing is more seductive for man than his freedom of conscience, but nothing is a greater cause of suffering. And behold, instead of giving a firm foundation for setting the conscience of man at rest forever, Thou didst choose all that is exceptional, vague and enigmatic; Thou didst choose what was utterly beyond the strength of men, acting as though Thou didst not love them at all—Thou who didst come to give Thy life for them! Instead of taking possession of man's freedom, Thou didst increase it, and burdened the spiritual kingdom of mankind with its sufferings forever. Thou didst desire man's free love, that he should follow Thee freely, enticed and taken captive by Thee. In place of the rigid, ancient law, man must hereafter with free heart decide for himself what is good and what is evil, having only Thy image before him as his guide. But didst Thou not know he would at last reject even Thy image and Thy truth, if he is weighed down with the fearful burden of free choice? They will cry aloud at last that the truth is not in Thee, for they could not have been left in greater confusion and suffering than Thou hast caused, laying upon them so many cares and unanswerable problems.

" 'So that, in truth, Thou didst Thyself lay the foundation for the destruction of Thy kingdom, and no one is more to blame for it. Yet what was offered Thee? There are three powers, three powers alone, able to conquer and to hold captive forever the conscience of these impotent rebels for their happiness—those forces are miracle, mystery and authority. Thou hast rejected all three and hast set the example for doing so. When the wise and dread spirit set Thee on the pinnacle of the temple and said to Thee, "If Thou wouldst know whether Thou art the Son of God then cast Thyself down, for it is written: the angels shall hold him up lest he fall and bruise himself, and Thou shalt know then whether Thou art the Son of God and shalt prove then how great is Thy faith in Thy Father." But Thou didst refuse and wouldst not cast Thyself down. Oh! of course, Thou didst proudly and well like God; but the weak, unruly race of men, are they gods? Oh, Thou didst know then that in taking one step, in making one movement to cast Thyself down, Thou wouldst be tempting God and have lost all Thy faith in Him, and wouldst have been dashed to pieces against that earth which Thou didst come to save. And the wise spirit that tempted Thee would have rejoiced. But I ask again, are there many like Thee? And couldst Thou believe for one moment that men, too, could face such a temptation? Is the nature of men such that they can reject miracle, and at the great moments of their life, the moments of their deepest, most agonizing spiritual difficulties, cling only to the free verdict of the heart? Oh, Thou didst know that Thy deed would be recorded in books, would be handed down to remote times and the utmost ends of the earth, and Thou didst hope that man, following Thee, would cling to God and not ask for a miracle. But Thou didst not know that when man rejects miracle he rejects God too; for man seeks not so much God as the miraculous. And as man cannot bear to be without the miraculous, he will create new miracles of his own for himself, and will worship deeds of sorcery and witchcraft, though he might be a hundred times over a rebel, heretic and infidel. Thou didst not come down from the Cross when they shouted to Thee, mocking and reviling Thee, "Come down from the Cross and we will believe that Thou art He."[14] Thou didst not come down, for again Thou wouldst not enslave man by a miracle, and didst crave faith given freely, not based on miracle. Thou didst crave for free love and not the base raptures of the slave before the might that has overawed him forever. But Thou didst think too highly of men therein, for they are slaves, of course, though rebellious by nature. Look round and judge; fifteen centuries have passed; look upon them. Whom hast Thou raised up to Thyself? I swear, man is weaker and baser by nature than Thou hast believed him! Can he, can he do what Thou didst? By showing him so much respect, Thou didst, as it were, cease to feel for him, for Thou didst ask far too much from him—Thou who hast loved him more than Thyself! Respecting him less, Thou wouldst have asked less of him. That would have been more like love, for his burden would have been lighter. He is weak and vile. What though he is everywhere now rebelling against our power, and proud of his rebellion? It is the pride of a child and a schoolboy. They are little children rioting and barring out the teacher at school. But their childish delight will end; it will cost them dear. They will cast down temples and drench the earth with blood. But they will see at last, the foolish children, that, though they are rebels, they are impotent rebels, unable to keep up their own rebellion. Bathed in their foolish tears, they will recognize at last that He who created them rebels must have meant to mock at them. They will say this in despair, and their utterance will be a blasphemy which will make them

---

[14]Mark 15:32.

more unhappy still, for man's nature cannot bear blasphemy, and in the end always avenges it on itself. And so unrest, confusion and unhappiness—that is the present lot of man after Thou didst bear so much for their freedom! Thy great prophet tells in vision and in image that he saw all those who took part in the first resurrection and that there were of each tribe twelve thousand. But if there were so many of them, they must have been not men but gods. They had borne Thy cross, they had endured scores of years in the barren, hungry wilderness, living upon locusts and roots—and Thou mayest indeed point with pride at those children of freedom, of free love, of free and splendid sacrifice for Thy name. But remember that they were only some thousands; and what of the rest? And how are the other weak ones to blame, because they could not endure what the strong have endured? How is the weak soul to blame that it is unable to receive such terrible gifts? Canst Thou have simply come to the elect and for the elect? But if so, it is a mystery and we cannot understand it. And if it is a mystery, we too have a right to preach a mystery, and to teach them that it's not the free judgment of their hearts, not love, that matters, but a mystery which they must follow blindly, even against their conscience. So we have done. We have corrected Thy work and have founded it upon *miracle, mystery* and *authority*. And men rejoiced that they were again led like sheep, and that the terrible gift that had brought them such suffering was, at last, lifted from their hearts. Were we right teaching them this? Speak! Did we not love mankind, so meekly acknowledging their feebleness, lovingly lightening their burden, and permitting their weak nature even sin with our sanction? Why hast Thou come now to hinder us? And why dost Thou look silently and searchingly at me with Thy mild eyes? Be angry. I don't want Thy love, for I love Thee not. And what use is it for me to hide anything from Thee? Don't I know to Whom I am speaking? All that I can say is known to Thee already. And is it for me to conceal from Thee our mystery? Perhaps it is Thy will to hear it from my lips. Listen, then. We are not working with Thee, but with *him*—that is our mystery. It's long—eight centuries—since we have been on *his* side and not on Thine. Just eight centuries ago, we took from him what Thou didst reject with scorn, that last gift he offered Thee, showing Thee all the kingdoms of the earth.[15] We took from him Rome and the sword of Cæsar, and proclaimed ourselves sole rulers of the earth, though hitherto we have not been able to complete our work. But whose fault is that? Oh, the work is only beginning, but it has begun. It has long to await completion and the earth has yet much to suffer, but we shall triumph and shall be Cæsars, and then we shall plan the universal happiness of man. But Thou mightest have taken even the sword of Cæsar. Why didst Thou reject that last gift? Hadst Thou accepted that last counsel of the mighty spirit, Thou wouldst have accomplished all that man seeks on earth—that is, someone to worship, someone to keep his conscience, and some means of uniting all in one unanimous and harmonious ant heap, for the craving for universal unity is the third and last anguish of men. Mankind as a whole has always striven to organize a universal state. There have been many great nations with great histories, but the more highly they were developed the more unhappy they were, for they felt more acutely than other people the craving for world-wide union. The great conquerors, Timours and Genghis Khans,[16] whirled like hurricanes over the face of the earth, striving to subdue its people, and they too were but the unconscious expression of the same craving for universal unity. Hadst Thou taken the world and Cæsar's

---

[15]In 401, Pope Innocent I claimed authority over the Roman Church, establishing an institution competitive with the Roman Empire.

[16]Timour, or Timur (c. 1336–1405), and Genghis Khan (c. 1167–1227) were Mongol conquerors.

purple, Thou wouldst have founded the universal state and have given universal peace. For who can rule men if not he who holds their conscience and their bread in his hands? We have taken the sword of Cæsar, and in taking it, of course, have rejected Thee and followed *him*. Oh, ages are yet to come of the confusion of free thought, of their science and cannibalism. For having begun to build their tower of Babel without us, they will end, of course, with cannibalism. But then the beast will crawl to us and lick our feet and spatter them with tears of blood. And we shall sit upon the beast and raise the cup, and on it will be written, "Mystery." But then, and only then, the reign of peace and happiness will come for men. Thou art proud of Thine elect, but Thou hast only the elect, while we give rest to all. And besides, how many of those elect, those mighty ones who could become elect, have grown weary waiting for Thee, and have transferred and will transfer the powers of their spirit and the warmth of their heart to the other camp, and end by raising their *free* banner against Thee. Thou didst Thyself lift up that banner. But with us all will be happy and will no more rebel, nor destroy one another as under Thy freedom. Oh, we shall persuade them that they will only become free when they renounce their freedom to us and submit to us. And shall we be right or shall we be lying? They will be convinced that we are right, for they will remember the horrors of slavery and confusion to which Thy freedom brought them. Freedom, free thought and science, will lead them into such straits and will bring them face to face with such marvels and insoluble mysteries that some of them, the fierce and rebellious, will destroy themselves; others, rebellious but weak, will destroy one another, while the rest, weak and the unhappy, will crawl fawning to our feet and whine to us: "Yes, you were right, you alone possess His mystery, and we come back to you, save us from ourselves!"

"'Receiving bread from us, they will see clearly that we take the bread made by their hands from them, to give it to them, without any miracle. They will see that we do not change the stones to bread, but in truth they will be more thankful for taking it from our hands than for the bread itself! For they will remember only too well that in old days, without our help, even the bread they made turned to stones in their hands, while since they have come back to us, the very stones have turned to bread in their hands. Too, too well they know the value of complete submission! And until men know that, they will be unhappy. Who is most to blame for their not knowing it, speak? Who scattered the flock and sent it astray on unknown paths? But the flock will come together again and will submit once more, and then it will be once for all. Then we shall give them the quiet humble happiness of weak creatures such as they are by nature. Oh, we shall persuade them at last not to be proud, for Thou didst lift them up and thereby taught them to be proud. We shall show them that they are weak, that they are only pitiful children, but that childlike happiness is the sweetest of all. They will become timid and will look to us and huddle close to us in fear, as chicks to the hen. They will marvel at us and will be awe-stricken before us, and will be proud at our being so powerful and clever, that we have been able to subdue such a turbulent flock of thousands of millions. They will tremble impotently before our wrath, their minds will grow fearful, they will be quick to shed tears like women and children, but they will be just as ready at a sign from us to pass to laughter and rejoicing, to happy mirth and childish song. Yes, we shall set them to work, but in their leisure hours we shall make their life like a child's game, with children's songs and innocent dance. Oh, we shall allow them even sin; they are weak and helpless, and they will love us like children because we allow them to sin. We shall tell them that every sin will be expiated, if it is done with our permission, that we allow them to sin because we love them, and the punishment for these sins we take upon ourselves. And we shall take it upon ourselves, and they will adore us as their saviors who have taken on themselves their sins before God. And they will have no secrets from us. We shall allow or forbid them to live with their wives and mistresses, to have or not to have children—according to whether they have been obedient or disobedient—and they will submit to us gladly and cheerfully. The most painful secrets of their conscience, all, all they will bring to us, and we shall have an answer for all. And they will be glad to believe our answer, for it will save them from the great anxiety and terrible agony they endure at present in making a free decision for themselves. And all will be happy, all the millions of creatures, except the hundred thousand who rule over them. For only we, we who guard the mystery, shall be unhappy. There will be thousands of millions of happy babes, and a hundred thousand sufferers who have taken upon themselves the curse of the knowledge of good and evil. Peacefully they will die, peacefully they will expire in Thy name, and beyond the grave they will find nothing but death. But we shall keep the secret, and for their happiness we shall allure them with the reward of heaven and eternity. Though if there were anything in the other world, it certainly would not be for such as they. It is prophesied that Thou wilt come again in victory, Thou wilt come with Thy chosen, the proud and strong, but we will say that they have only saved themselves, but we have saved all. We are told that the harlot who sits upon the beast, and holds in her hands the *mystery*, shall be put to shame, that the weak will rise up again, and will rend her royal purple and will strip naked her loathsome body.[17] But then I will stand up and point out to Thee the thousand millions of happy children who have known no sin. And we who have taken their sins upon us for their happiness will stand up before Thee and say: "Judge us if Thou canst and darest." Know that I fear Thee not. Know that I too have been in the wilderness, I too have lived on roots and locusts, I too prized the freedom with which Thou hast blessed men, and I too was striving to stand among Thy elect, among the strong and powerful, thirsting "to make up the number." But I awakened and would not serve madness. I turned back and joined the ranks of those *who have corrected Thy work.* I left the proud and went back to the humble, for the happiness of the humble. What I say to Thee will come to pass, and our dominion will be built up. I repeat, tomorrow Thou shalt see that obedient flock who at a sign from me will hasten to heap up the hot cinders about the pile on which I shall burn Thee for coming to hinder us. For if anyone has ever deserved our fires, it is Thou. Tomorrow I shall burn Thee. *Dixi.*'"[18]

Ivan stopped. He was carried away as he talked and spoke with excitement; when he had finished, he suddenly smiled.

Alyosha had listened in silence; toward the end he was greatly moved and seemed several times on the point of interrupting, but restrained himself. Now his words came with a rush.

"But . . . that's absurd!" he cried, flushing. "Your poem is in praise of Jesus, not in blame of Him—as you meant it to be. And who will believe you about freedom? Is that the way to understand it? That's not the idea of it in the Orthodox Church . . . That's Rome, and not even the whole of Rome, it's false—those are the worst of the Catholics, the Inquisitors, the Jesuits! . . . And there could not be such a fantastic creature as your Inquisitor. What are these sins of mankind they take on themselves? Who are these keepers of the mystery who have taken some curse upon themselves for the happiness of mankind? When have they been seen? We know the Jesuits,

---

[17] The Whore of Babylon in Revelations 17.
[18] The closing word for a religious pronouncement, meaning "I have spoken."

they are spoken ill of, but surely they are not what you describe? They are not that at all, not at all.... They are simply the Romish army for the earthly sovereignty of the world in the future, with the Pontiff of Rome for Emperor... that's their ideal, but there's no sort of mystery or lofty melancholy about it.... It's simple lust of power, of filthy earthly gain, of domination—something like a universal serfdom with them as masters—that's all they stand for. They don't even believe in God, perhaps. Your suffering inquisitor is a mere fantasy."

"Stay, stay," laughed Ivan, "how hot you are! A fantasy you say, let it be so! Of course it's a fantasy. But allow me to say: do you really think that the Roman Catholic movement of the last centuries is actually nothing but the lust of power, of filthy earthly gain? Is that Father Païssy's teaching?"

"No, no, on the contrary, Father Païssy did once say something the same as you... but of course it's not the same, not a bit the same," Alyosha hastily corrected himself.

"A precious admission, in spite of your 'not a bit the same.' I ask you why your Jesuits and inquisitors have united simply for vile material gain? Why can there not be among them one martyr oppressed by great sorrow and loving humanity? You see, only suppose that there was one such man among all those who desire nothing but filthy material gain—if there's only one like my old inquisitor, who had himself eaten roots in the desert and made frenzied efforts to subdue his flesh to make himself free and perfect. But yet all his life he loved humanity, and suddenly his eyes were opened, and he saw that it is no great moral blessedness to attain perfection and freedom, if at the same time one gains the conviction that billions of God's creatures have been created as a mockery, that they will never be capable of using their freedom, that these poor rebels can never turn into giants to complete the tower, that it was not for such geese that the great idealist dreamt his dream of harmony. Seeing all that, he turned back and joined—the clever people. Surely that could have happened?"

"Joined whom, what clever people?" cried Alyosha, completely carried away. "They have no such great cleverness and no mysteries and secrets.... Perhaps nothing but atheism, that's all their secret. Your inquisitor does not believe in God, that's his secret!"

"What if it is so! At last you have guessed it. It's perfectly true that that's the whole secret, but isn't that suffering, at least for a man like that, who has wasted his whole life in the desert and yet could not shake off his incurable love of humanity? In his old age he reached the clear conviction that nothing but the advice of the great dread spirit could build up any tolerable sort of life for the feeble, unruly, 'incomplete, empirical creatures created in jest.' And so, convinced of this, he sees that he must follow the counsel of the wise spirit, the dread spirit of death and destruction, and therefore accept lying and deception, and lead men consciously to death and destruction, and yet deceive them all the way so that they may not notice where they are being led, that the poor, blind creatures may at least on the way think themselves happy. And note, the deception is in the name of Him in Whose ideal the old man had so fervently believed all his life long. Is not that tragic? And if only one such stood at the head of the whole army 'filled with the lust of power only for the sake of filthy gain'—would not one such be enough to make a tragedy? More than that, one such standing at the head is enough to create the actual leading idea of the Roman Church with all its armies and Jesuits, its highest idea. I tell you frankly that I firmly believe that there has always been such a man among those who stood at the head of the movement. Who knows, there may have been some such even among the Roman Popes. Who knows, perhaps the spirit of that accursed old man who loves mankind so obstinately in his own way is to be found even now in a whole multitude of such old men, existing not by chance but by agreement, as a secret league formed long ago for the guarding of the mystery, to guard it from the weak and the unhappy, so as to make them happy. No doubt it is so, and so it must be indeed. I fancy that even among the Masons there's something of the same mystery at the bottom, and that that's why the Catholics so detest the Masons as their rivals breaking up the unity of the idea, while it is so essential that there should be one flock and one shepherd.... But from the way I defend my idea I might be an author impatient of your criticism. Enough of it."

"You are perhaps a Mason yourself!" broke suddenly from Alyosha. "You don't believe in God," he added, speaking this time very sorrowfully. He fancied besides that his brother was looking at him ironically. "How does your poem end?" he asked, suddenly looking down. "Or was it the end?"

"I meant it to end like this: When the Inquisitor ceased speaking, he waited some time for his Prisoner to answer him. His silence weighed down upon him. He saw the Prisoner had listened intently all the time, looking gently in his face and evidently not wishing to reply. The old man longed for Him to say something, however bitter and terrible. But He suddenly approached the old man in silence and softly kissed him on his bloodless, aged lips. That was all his answer. The old man shuddered. His lips moved. He went to the door, opened it, and said to him: 'Go, and come no more.... Come not at all, never, never!' And he let him out into the dark alleys of the town. The Prisoner went away."

"And the old man?"

"The kiss glows in his heart, but the old man adheres to his idea."

"And you with him, you too?" cried Alyosha, mournfully.

Ivan laughed.

"Why, it's all nonsense, Alyosha. It's only a senseless poem of a senseless student, who could never write two lines of verse. Why do you take it so seriously? Surely you don't suppose I am going straight off to the Jesuits, to join the men who are correcting His work? Good Lord, it's no business of mine. I told you, all I want is to live on to thirty, and then... dash the cup to the ground!"

"But the little sticky leaves, and the precious tombs, and the blue sky, and the woman you love! How will you live, how will you love them?" Alyosha cried sorrowfully. "With such a hell in your heart and your head, how can you? No, that's just what you are going away for, to join them... if not, you will kill yourself, you can't endure it!"

"There is a strength to endure everything," Ivan said with a cold smile.

"What strength?"

"The strength of the Karamazovs—the strength of the Karamazov baseness."

"To sink into debauchery, to stifle your soul with corruption, yes?"

"Possibly even that... only perhaps till I am thirty I shall escape it, and then—"

"How will you escape it? By what will you escape it? That's impossible with your ideas."

"In the Karamazov way, again."

" 'Everything is lawful,' you mean? Everything is lawful, is that it?"

Ivan scowled, and all at once turned strangely pale.

"Ah, you've caught up yesterday's phrase, which so offended Miüsov—and which Dmitri pounced upon so naïvely and paraphrased!" he smiled queerly. "Yes, if you like, 'everything is lawful' since the word has been said. I won't deny it. And Mitya's version isn't bad."

Alyosha looked at him in silence.

"I thought that going away from here I have you at least," Ivan said suddenly, with unexpected feeling; "but now I see that there is no place for me even in your heart, my dear hermit. The formula, 'all is lawful,' I won't renounce—will you renounce me for that, yes?"

Alyosha got up, went to him and softly kissed him on the lips.

"That's plagiarism," cried Ivan, highly delighted. "You stole that from my poem. Thank you, though. Get up, Alyosha, it's time we were going, both of us."

They went out, but stopped when they reached the entrance of the restaurant.

"Listen, Alyosha," Ivan began in a resolute voice, "if I am really able to care for the sticky little leaves, I shall only love them remembering you. It's enough for me that you are somewhere here, and I shan't lose my desire for life yet. Is that enough for you? Take it as a declaration of love if you like. And now you go to the right and I to the left. And it's enough, do you hear—enough! I mean even if I don't go away tomorrow (I think I certainly shall go) and we meet again, don't say a word more on these subjects. I beg that particularly. And about Dmitri, too, I ask you especially never speak to me again," he added, with sudden irritation; "it's all exhausted, it has all been said over and over again, hasn't it? And I'll make you one promise in return for it. When, at thirty, I want to 'dash the cup to the ground,' wherever I may be I'll come to have one more talk with you, even though it were from America—you may be sure of that. I'll come on purpose. It will be very interesting to have a look at you, to see what you'll be by that time. It's rather a solemn promise, you see. And we really may be parting for seven years or ten. Come, go now to your Pater Seraphicus, he is dying. If he dies without you, you will be angry with me for having kept you. Good-bye, kiss me once more; that's right, now go."

HENRIK IBSEN
[1828–1906]

Recalling his childhood in Skien, a village in rural Norway, Henrik Ibsen described the view from the window of his room as "only buildings, nothing green." And the buildings that he particularly remembered—the church, the jail, the pillory, and the madhouse—may have been the models from his childhood for the institutions that constrain and oppress the characters in his great social dramas.

Often called the "father of the modern drama," Ibsen is best known for realistic plays such as *A Doll's House* (1879), *An Enemy of the People* (1882), and *Hedda Gabler* (1890), written in the last quarter of the century. These plays explore the ways in which bourgeois values and social conventions deny individuals opportunities for growth and fulfillment. Very different from the romantic comedies and melodramas that were the standard theatrical fare at the time, Ibsen's plays often shocked nineteenth-century audiences who went to the theater to be amused. But they moved other playwrights and changed the course of drama, influencing especially such modern dramatists as George Bernard Shaw in England and Eugene O'Neill and Arthur Miller in the United States—heirs to a dramatic tradition Shaw called "Ibsenism."

LIFE

Born the son of a prosperous businessman in Skien in 1828, Ibsen learned early the precariousness of bourgeois respectability. When he was nine, his father's business failed and the family was forced to move ignominiously out of town. At fifteen, he left home to become a druggist's apprentice at Grimstad, where he spent six years and fathered an illegitimate child—a buried secret in Ibsen's life like the secrets in many of his plays. He moved to Christiania (now Oslo) in 1850 with hopes of entering the university, but he failed part of the entrance examinations and went to work in the theater instead. For the next fourteen years as producer, director, and writer, Ibsen learned the craft of the theater. But he did not begin writing his great plays until he left Norway in 1864 for Italy and Germany, where he lived for twenty-seven years at the height of his writing career. There he completed *Brand* and *Peer Gynt*, poems in which he related the legendary and mythological subject matter of his early work to contemporary Norway.

In Europe he also wrote his great social dramas, beginning in 1877 with *The Pillars of Society* and followed by the scandalous *A Doll's House* (1879) and *Ghosts* (1881). All three plays presented pillars of village life—marriage, the family, and the Church—as oppressive and hypocritical institutions, forcing buried secrets that threaten to destroy the lives of the protagonists. In *The Wild Duck* (1884), *An Enemy of the People* (1882), and *Rosmersholm* (1882), the secrets become lies, and the plays study characters who are afraid to tell the truth. The psychological dimension becomes increasingly important, especially in later plays such as *The Lady from the Sea* (1888), *Hedda Gabler* (1890), and *The Master Builder* (1892), which study the psychological effects on women of their subordinate role in society and the effects on men of their aggressive dominance.

Although he is best known for his realistic social dramas, Ibsen was also a symbolic and mythological writer. Much of his early work was devoted to historical and mythological subjects, culminating in *Brand* (1865) and *Peer Gynt* (1867), two dramatic poems that use traditional materials to comment indirectly on contemporary Norway. In the last plays of the 1890s, in works such as *John Gabriel Borkman* (1896) and *When We Dead Awaken* (1899), Ibsen turned to a more symbolic and visionary style. In this less realistic mode, Ibsen could be considered father to such symbolic dramatists as William Butler Yeats and Tennessee Williams.

Ibsen returned to Norway in 1891 and spent the last fifteen years of his life in Christiania, where he died in 1906. Appropriately, his dying word was "*tvertimod*," meaning "on the contrary."

WORK

Nearly all of Ibsen's social plays present a hero or heroine constrained by social institutions—the Church, marriage, and middle-class respectability. These characters are not simply victims of social forces; through bad choices, mistakes, and weaknesses of character they suppress guilty secrets or tell lies and collude in creating their own difficulties. The plays nearly always center on a moment of crisis when the secret or lie is revealed and the hero or heroine must choose how to meet the revelation.

Many of Ibsen's most interesting characters are women whose marriages deny them opportunities for personal growth. For many of these women, their subordination has tragic consequences, as in the destruction of Mrs. Alving and her son in *Ghosts* and the suicide of Hedda Gabler. Honored by a Norwegian feminist society at the end of his life for his treatment of women's issues, Ibsen commented, with a touch of his characteristic contrariness, "I am not quite clear as to just what this women's rights movement really is. To me it has seemed a problem of mankind in general." Even though Ibsen may not have written with a feminist agenda, he took his female characters seriously. The moral issues they faced were just as significant as those confronted by his male characters.

One of Ibsen's earliest social dramas, *A Doll's House* does not end tragically as some of his later plays do, but its critique of bourgeois marriage is just as telling as in the darker plays. Ibsen worked within the conventions of the "well-made play." The action is focused in time and place, occurring over three days and taking place within the confines of the Helmers' living room. The plot turns melodramatically on the letter that reveals Nora's secret, but the issues raised by the play are far more serious than the inconsequential misunderstandings in popular comedies; and the ending, instead of restoring the Helmers' marriage and affirming accepted domestic virtues, shocked its nineteenth-century audience by reversing their conventional expectations.

Ibsen underscores the irony in his reversal of convention by setting the play at Christmas, the domestic holiday when families gather and family histories come to light. Nora and Torvald must confront their past, but unlike Scrooge in Dickens's story, who is changed by doing so, the Helmers remain unchanged and unable to resolve the contradictions in their incompatible marriage. Torvald cannot compromise his desire to advance at the bank and Nora admits that she cannot remain in so confining a marriage.

Critics have sometimes been bothered by the apparent inconsistency in the character of Nora, wondering whether the domestic butterfly of the first act could turn into the courageous rebel of the last. But Nora is not really a different person at the end of the play; she simply hid her independence and courage earlier. Her "transformation" is more of a revelation, which Ibsen develops in rich detail. The differences between Nora and Mrs. Linde, the facts of her personal history, and the contrast between her courage and Torvald's conventionality show us that she is not changed in a single night like Scrooge, but is, at the end, simply acting consistently with the person she has always been. Ibsen's dramatic skill in using the characters Mrs. Linde and Krogstad as foils to draw out the hidden sides of Nora and Torvald prepares us for the inevitability of the ending.

SUGGESTED READINGS

The standard biography is Michael Meyer's *Ibsen: A Biography* (1971). Some good introductions to Ibsen's work include David Thomas's *Henrik Ibsen* (1983) and Brian Downs's two books *Ibsen: The Intellectual Background* (1948) and *A Study of Six Plays by Ibsen* (1950). J. W. McFarlane has edited a useful collection of critical essays, *Henrik Ibsen: A Critical Anthology* (1970). George Bernard Shaw's classic *The Quintessence of Ibsenism* (1891) provides a discussion of Ibsen's work and ideas by his most important disciple. Elizabeth Hardwick's "Ibsen's Women" in *Seduction and Betrayal* (1974) includes a chapter on Nora Helmer.

A Doll's House

Translated by Eva Le Gallienne

CHARACTERS

TORVALD HELMER, *a lawyer*
NORA, *his wife*
DOCTOR RANK
MRS. KRISTINE LINDE
NILS KROGSTAD, *an attorney*

THE HELMERS' THREE SMALL CHILDREN
ANNE-MARIE, *nurse at the Helmers'*
HELENE, *maid at the Helmers'*
A PORTER

The action takes place in the Helmer residence.

ACT 1

A comfortable room furnished with taste, but not expensively. In the back wall a door on the right leads to the hall, another door on the left leads to HELMER's *study. Between the two doors a piano. In the left wall, center, a door; farther downstage a window. Near the window a round table with an armchair and a small sofa. In the right wall upstage a door, and further downstage a porcelain stove round which are grouped a couple of armchairs and a rocking chair. Between the stove and the door stands a small table. Engravings on the walls. A whatnot with china objects and various bric-a-brac. A small bookcase with books in fancy bindings. The floor is carpeted; a fire burns in the stove. A winter day.*

NORA: Be sure and hide the Christmas tree carefully, Helene, the children mustn't see it till this evening, when it's all decorated. [*To the* PORTER, *taking out her purse*] How much?

PORTER: Fifty, Ma'am.

NORA: Here you are. No—keep the change.

[*The* PORTER *thanks her and goes.* NORA *closes the door. She laughs gaily to herself as she takes off her outdoor things. Takes a bag of macaroons out of her pocket and eats a couple, then she goes cautiously to the door of her husband's study and listens*] Yes—he's home. [*She goes over to the table right, humming to herself again.*]

HELMER [*From his study*]: Is that my little lark twittering out there?

NORA [*Busily undoing the packages*]: Yes, it is.

HELMER: Is that my little squirrel bustling about?

NORA: Yes.

HELMER: When did my squirrel get home?

NORA: Just this minute. [*She puts the bag of macaroons back in her pocket and wipes her mouth*] Oh, Torvald, do come in here! You must see what I have bought.

HELMER: Now, don't disturb me! [*A moment afterwards he opens the door and looks in—pen in hand*] Did you say "bought"? That—all *that*? Has my little spendthrift been flinging money about again?

NORA: But, Torvald, surely this year we ought to let ourselves go a bit! After all, it's the first Christmas we haven't had to be careful.

HELMER: Yes, but that doesn't mean we can afford to *squander* money.

NORA: Oh, Torvald, we can squander a bit, can't we? Just a little tiny bit? You're going to get a big salary and you'll be making lots and lots of money.

HELMER: After the first of the year, yes. But remember there'll be three whole months before my salary falls due.

NORA: We can always borrow in the meantime.

HELMER: Nora! [*Goes to her and pulls her ear playfully*] There goes my little featherbrain! Let's suppose I borrowed a thousand crowns today, you'd probably squander it all during Christmas week; and then let's suppose that on New Year's Eve a tile blew off the roof and knocked my brains out—

NORA [*Puts her hand over his mouth*]: Don't say such frightful things!

HELMER: But let's suppose it happened—then what?

NORA: If anything as terrible as *that* happened, I shouldn't care whether I owed money or not.

HELMER: But what about the people I'd borrowed from?

NORA: Who cares about them? After all they're just strangers.

HELMER: Oh, Nora, Nora! What a little woman you are! But seriously, Nora, you know my feelings about such things. I'll have no borrowing—I'll have no debts! There can be no freedom—no, nor beauty either—in a home based upon loans and credit. We've held out bravely up to now, and we shall continue to do so for the short time that remains.

NORA [*Goes toward the stove*]: Just as you like, Torvald.

HELMER [*Following her*]: Come, come; the little lark mustn't droop her wings. Don't tell me my little squirrel is sulking! [*He opens his purse*] Nora! Guess what I have here!

NORA [*Turns quickly*]: Money!

HELMER: There you are! [*He hands her some notes*] Don't you suppose I know that money is needed at Christmas time?

NORA [*Counts the notes*]: Ten, twenty, thirty, forty. Oh thank you, thank you, Torvald—this'll last me a long time!

HELMER: Better see that it does!

NORA: Oh, it will—I know. But do come here. I want to show you everything I've bought, and all so cheap too! Here are some new clothes for Ivar, and a little sword—and this horse and trumpet are for Bob, and here's a doll for Emmy—and a doll's bed. They're not worth much, but she's sure to tear them to pieces in a minute anyway. This is some dress material and handkerchiefs for the maids. Old Anne-Marie really should have had something better.

HELMER: And what's in that other parcel?

NORA [*With a shriek*]: No, Torvald! You can't see that until this evening!

HELMER: I can't, eh? But what about you—you little squanderer? Have you thought of anything for yourself?

NORA: Oh, there's nothing I want, Torvald.

HELMER: Of course there is!—now tell me something sensible you'd really like to have.

NORA: But there's nothing—really! Except of course—

HELMER: Well?

NORA [*She fingers the buttons on his coat; without looking at him*]: Well—If you really want to give me something—you might—you might—

HELMER: Well, well, out with it!

NORA [*Rapidly*]: You might give me some money, Torvald—just anything you feel you could spare; and then one of these days I'll buy myself something with it.

HELMER: But Nora—

NORA: Oh, please do, dear Torvald—I beg you to! I'll wrap it up in beautiful gold paper and hang it on the Christmas tree. Wouldn't that be fun?

HELMER: What's the name of the bird that eats up money?

NORA: The Spendthrift bird—I know! But do let's do as I say, Torvald!—it will give me a chance to choose something I really need. Don't you think that's a sensible idea? Don't you?

HELMER [*Smiling*]: Sensible enough—providing you really *do* buy something for yourself with it. But I expect you'll fritter it away on a lot of unnecessary household expenses, and before I know it you'll be coming to me for more.

NORA: But, Torvald—

HELMER: You can't deny it, Nora dear. [*Puts his arm round her waist*] The Spendthrift is a sweet little bird—but it costs a man an awful lot of money to support one!

NORA: How can you say such nasty things—I save all I can!

HELMER: Yes, I dare say—but that doesn't amount to much!

NORA [*Hums softly and smiles happily*]: You don't know, Torvald, what expenses we larks and squirrels have!

HELMER: You're a strange little creature; exactly like your father. You'll go to any lengths to get a sum of money—but as soon as you have it, it just slips through your fingers. You don't know yourself what's become of it. Well, I suppose

one must just take you as you are. It's in your blood. Oh, yes! such things are
hereditary, Nora.

NORA: I only wish I had inherited a lot of Father's qualities.

HELMER: And I wouldn't wish you any different than you are, my own sweet little
lark. But Nora, it's just occurred to me—isn't there something a little—what
shall I call it—a little guilty about you this morning?

NORA: About me?

HELMER: Yes. Look me straight in the eye.

NORA [*Looking at him*]: Well?

HELMER [*Wags a threatening finger at her*]: Has my little sweet-tooth been breaking
rules today?

NORA: No! What makes you think that?

HELMER: Are you sure the sweet-tooth didn't drop in at the confectioner's?

NORA: No, I assure you, Torvald—

HELMER: She didn't nibble a little candy?

NORA: No, really not.

HELMER: Not even a macaroon or two?

NORA: No, Torvald, I assure you—really—

HELMER: There, there! Of course I'm only joking.

NORA [*Going to the table right*]: It would never occur to me to go against your
wishes.

HELMER: Of course I know that—and anyhow—you've given me your word—
[*Goes to her*] Well, my darling, I won't pry into your little Christmas secrets.
They'll be unveiled tonight under the Christmas tree.

NORA: Did you remember to ask Dr. Rank?

HELMER: No, it really isn't necessary. He'll take it for granted he's to dine with
us. However, I'll ask him, when he stops by this morning. I've ordered some
specially good wine. I am so looking forward to this evening, Nora, dear!

NORA: So am I—And the children will have such fun!

HELMER: Ah! How nice it is to feel secure; to look forward to a good position with
an ample income. It's a wonderful prospect—isn't it, Nora?

NORA: It's simply marvelous!

HELMER: Do you remember last Christmas? For three whole weeks—you locked
yourself up every evening until past midnight—making paper flowers for the
Christmas tree—and a lot of other wonderful things you wanted to surprise us
with. I was never so bored in my life!

NORA: I wasn't a bit bored.

HELMER [*Smiling*]: But it all came to rather a sad end, didn't it, Nora?

NORA: Oh, do you have to tease me about that again! How could I help the cat
coming in and tearing it all to pieces.

HELMER: Of course you couldn't help it, you poor darling! You meant to give us
a good time—that's the main thing. But it's nice to know those lean times are
over.

NORA: It's wonderful!

HELMER: Now I don't have to sit here alone, boring myself to death; and you don't
have to strain your dear little eyes, and prick your sweet little fingers—

NORA [*Claps her hands*]: No, I don't—do I, Torvald! Oh! How lovely it all is. [*Takes
his arm*] I want to tell you how I thought we'd arrange things after Christmas.
[*The doorbell rings*] Oh there's the bell. [*Tidies up the room a bit*] It must be a
visitor—how tiresome!

HELMER: I don't care to see any visitors, Nora—remember that.

HELENE [*In the doorway*]: There's a lady to see you, Ma'am.

NORA: Well, show her in.

HELENE [*To* HELMER]: And the Doctor's here too, Sir.

HELMER: Did he go straight to my study?

HELENE: Yes, he did, Sir.

[HELMER *goes into his study.* HELENE *ushers in* MRS. LINDE
who is dressed in traveling clothes, and closes the door behind her.]

MRS. LINDE [*In subdued and hesitant tone*]: How do you do, Nora?

NORA [*Doubtfully*]: How do you do?

MRS. LINDE: You don't recognize me, do you?

NORA: No, I don't think—and yet—I seem to— [*With a sudden outburst*] Kristine!
Is it really you?

MRS. LINDE: Yes; it's really I!

NORA: Kristine! And to think of my not knowing you! But how could I when—
[*More softly*] You've changed so, Kristine!

MRS. LINDE: Yes I suppose I have. After all—it's nine or ten years—

NORA: Is it *that* long since we met? Yes, so it is. Oh, these last eight years have been
such happy ones! Fancy your being in town! And imagine taking that long trip
in midwinter! How brave you are!

MRS. LINDE: I arrived by the morning boat.

NORA: You've come for the Christmas holidays, I suppose—what fun! Oh, what a
good time we'll have! Do take off your things. You're not cold, are you? [*Helping
her*] There; now we'll sit here by the stove. No, you take the arm-chair; I'll sit
here in the rocker. [*Seizes her hands*] Now you look more like yourself again. It
was just at first—you're a bit paler, Kristine—and perhaps a little thinner.

MRS. LINDE: And much, much older, Nora.

NORA: Well, perhaps a *little* older—a tiny, tiny bit—not much, though. [*She
suddenly checks herself; seriously*] Oh, but, Kristine! What a thoughtless wretch I
am, chattering away like that—Dear, darling Kristine, do forgive me!

MRS. LINDE: What for, Nora, dear?

NORA [*Softly*]: You lost your husband, didn't you, Kristine! You're a widow.

MRS. LINDE: Yes; my husband died three years ago.

NORA: Yes, I remember; I saw it in the paper. Oh, I *did* mean to write to you,
Kristine! But I kept on putting it off, and all sorts of things kept coming in the
way.

MRS. LINDE: I understand, dear Nora.

NORA: No, it was beastly of me, Kristine! Oh, you poor darling! What you must
have gone through!—And he died without leaving you anything, didn't he?

MRS. LINDE: Yes.

NORA: And you have no children?

MRS. LINDE: No.

NORA: Nothing then?

MRS. LINDE: Nothing— Not even grief, not even regret.

NORA [*Looking at her incredulously*]: But how is that possible, Kristine?

MRS. LINDE [*Smiling sadly and stroking her hair*]: It sometimes happens, Nora.

NORA: Imagine being so utterly alone! It must be dreadful for you, Kristine! I have
three of the loveliest children! I can't show them to you just now, they're out
with their nurse. But I want you to tell me all about yourself—

MRS. LINDE: No, no; I'd rather hear about you, Nora—

NORA: No, I want you to begin. I'm not going to be selfish today. I'm going to
think only of you. Oh! but one thing I *must* tell you. You haven't heard about
the wonderful thing that's just happened to us, have you?

MRS. LINDE: No. What is it?

NORA: My husband's been elected president of the Joint Stock Bank!

MRS. LINDE: Oh, Nora— How splendid!

NORA: Yes; isn't it? You see, a lawyer's position is so uncertain, especially if he refuses to handle any cases that are in the least bit—shady; Torvald is very particular about such things—and I agree with him, of course! You can imagine how glad we are. He's to start at the Bank right after the New Year; he'll make a big salary and all sorts of percentages. We'll be able to live quite differently from then on—we'll have everything we want. Oh, Kristine! I'm so happy and excited! Won't it be wonderful to have lots and lots of money, and nothing to worry about!

MRS. LINDE: It certainly would be wonderful to have enough for one's needs.

NORA: Oh, not just for one's *needs*, Kristine! But heaps and heaps of money!

MRS. LINDE [*With a smile*]: Nora, Nora, I see you haven't grown up yet! I remember at school you were a frightful spendthrift.

NORA [*Quietly; smiling*]: Yes; that's what Torvald always says. [*Holding up her forefinger*] But I haven't had much chance to be a spendthrift. We have had to work hard—both of us.

MRS. LINDE: You too?

NORA: Oh yes! I did all sorts of little jobs: needlework, embroidery, crochet—that sort of thing. [*Casually*] And other things as well. I suppose you know that Torvald left the Government service right after we were married. There wasn't much chance of promotion in his department, and of course he had to earn more money when he had me to support. But that first year he overworked himself terribly. He had to undertake all sorts of odd jobs, worked from morning till night. He couldn't stand it; his health gave way and he became deathly ill. The doctors said he absolutely *must* spend some time in the South.

MRS. LINDE: Yes, I heard you spent a whole year in Italy.

NORA: Yes, we did. It wasn't easy to arrange, I can tell you. It was just after Ivar's birth. But of course we had to go. It was a wonderful trip, and it saved Torvald's life. But it cost a fearful lot of money, Kristine.

MRS. LINDE: Yes, it must have.

NORA: Twelve hundred dollars! Four thousand eight hundred crowns! That's an awful lot of money, you know.

MRS. LINDE: You were lucky to have it.

NORA: Well, you see, we got it from Father.

MRS. LINDE: Oh, I see. Wasn't it just about that time that your father died?

NORA: Yes, it was, Kristine. Just think! I wasn't able to go to him—I couldn't be there to nurse him! I was expecting Ivar at the time and then I had my poor sick Torvald to look after. Dear, darling Papa! I never saw him again, Kristine. It's the hardest thing I have had to go through since my marriage.

MRS. LINDE: I know you were awfully fond of him. And after that you went to Italy?

NORA: Yes; then we had the money, you see; and the doctors said we must lose no time; so we started a month later.

MRS. LINDE: And your husband came back completely cured?

NORA: Strong as an ox!

MRS. LINDE: But—what about the doctor then?

NORA: How do you mean?

MRS. LINDE: Didn't the maid say something about a doctor, just as I arrived?

NORA: Oh, yes; Dr. Rank. He's our best friend—it's not a professional call; he stops in to see us every day. No, Torvald hasn't had a moment's illness since; and the children are strong and well, and so am I. [*Jumps up and claps her hands*] Oh

Kristine, Kristine! How lovely it is to be alive and happy! But how disgraceful of me! Here I am talking about nothing but myself! [*Seats herself upon a footstool close to* KRISTINE *and lays her arms on her lap*] Please don't be cross with me— Is it really true, Kristine, that you didn't love your husband? Why did you marry him, then?

MRS. LINDE: Well, you see—Mother was still alive; she was bedridden; completely helpless; and I had my two younger brothers to take care of. I didn't think it would be right to refuse him.

NORA: No, I suppose not. I suppose he had money then?

MRS. LINDE: Yes, I believe he was quite well off. But his business was precarious, Nora. When he died it all went to pieces, and there was nothing left.

NORA: And then—?

MRS. LINDE: Then I had to struggle along as best I could. I had a small shop for a while, and then I started a little school. These last three years have been one long battle—but it is over now, Nora. My dear mother is at rest— She doesn't need me any more. And my brothers are old enough to work, and can look after themselves.

NORA: You must have such a free feeling!

MRS. LINDE: No—only one of complete emptiness. I haven't a soul to live for! [*Stands up restlessly*] I suppose that's why I felt I had to get away. I should think here it would be easier to find something to do—something to occupy one's thoughts. I might be lucky enough to get a steady job here—some office work, perhaps—

NORA: But that's so terribly tiring, Kristine; and you look so tired already. What you need is a rest. Couldn't you go to some nice watering-place?

MRS. LINDE [*Going to the window*]: I have no father to give me the money, Nora.

NORA [*Rising*]: Oh, please don't be cross with me!

MRS. LINDE [*Goes to her*]: My dear Nora, you mustn't be cross with me! In my sort of position it's hard not to become bitter. One has no one to work for, and yet one can't give up the struggle. One must go on living, and it makes one selfish. I'm ashamed to admit it—but, just now, when you told me the good news about your husband's new position—I was glad—not so much for your sake as for mine.

NORA: How do you mean? Oh of course—I see! You think Torvald might perhaps help you.

MRS. LINDE: That's what I thought, yes.

NORA: And so he shall, Kristine. Just you leave it to me. I'll get him in a really good mood—and then bring it up quite casually. Oh, it would be such fun to help you!

MRS. LINDE: How good of you, Nora dear, to bother on my account! It's especially good of you—after all, you've never had to go through any hardship.

NORA: I? Not go through any—?

MRS. LINDE [*Smiling*]: Well— Good Heavens—a little needlework, and so forth— You're just a child, Nora.

NORA [*Tosses her head and paces the room*]: You needn't be so patronizing!

MRS. LINDE: No?

NORA: You're just like all the rest. You all think I'm incapable of being serious—

MRS. LINDE: Oh, come now—

NORA: You seem to think I've had no troubles—that I've been through nothing in my life!

MRS. LINDE: But you've just told me all your troubles, Nora dear.

NORA: I've only told you trifles! [*Softly*] I haven't mentioned the important thing.

MRS. LINDE: Important thing? What do you mean?

NORA: I know you look down on me, Kristine; but you really shouldn't. You take pride in having worked so hard and so long for your mother.

MRS. LINDE: I don't look down on anyone, Nora; I can't help feeling proud and happy too, to have been able to make Mother's last days a little easier—

NORA: And you're proud of what you did for your brothers, too.

MRS. LINDE: I think I have a right to be.

NORA: Yes, so do I. But I want you to know, Kristine—that I, too, have something to be proud of.

MRS. LINDE: I don't doubt that. But what are you referring to?

NORA: Hush! We must talk quietly. It would be dreadful if Torvald overheard us! He must never know about it! No one must know about it, except you.

MRS. LINDE: And what is it, Nora?

NORA: Come over here. [*Draws her down beside her on sofa*] Yes, I have something to be proud and happy about too. I saved Torvald's life, you see.

MRS. LINDE: Saved his life? But how?

NORA: I told you about our trip to Italy. Torvald would never have recovered if it hadn't been for that.

MRS. LINDE: Yes, I know—and your father gave you the necessary money.

NORA [*Smiling*]: That's what everyone thinks—Torvald too; but—

MRS. LINDE: Well—?

NORA: Papa never gave us a penny. I raised the money myself.

MRS. LINDE: All that money! You?

NORA: Twelve hundred dollars. Four thousand eight hundred crowns. What do you think of that?

MRS. LINDE: But, Nora, how on earth did you do it? Did you win it in the lottery?

NORA [*Contemptuously*]: The lottery! Of course not! Any fool could have done that!

MRS. LINDE: Where did you get it then?

NORA [*Hums and smiles mysteriously*]: H'm; tra-la-la-la.

MRS. LINDE: You certainly couldn't have borrowed it.

NORA: Why not?

MRS. LINDE: A wife can't borrow without her husband's consent.

NORA [*Tossing her head*]: Oh I don't know! If a wife has a good head on her shoulders—and has a little sense of business—

MRS. LINDE: I don't in the least understand, Nora—

NORA: Well, you needn't. I never said I borrowed the money. I may have got it in some other way. [*Throws herself back on the sofa*] Perhaps I got it from some admirer. After all when one is as attractive as I am—!

MRS. LINDE: What a mad little creature you are!

NORA: I'm sure you're dying of curiosity, Kristine—

MRS. LINDE: Nora, are you sure you haven't been a little rash?

NORA [*Sitting upright again*]: Is it rash to save one's husband's life?

MRS. LINDE: But mightn't it be rash to do such a thing behind his back?

NORA: But I couldn't tell him—don't you understand that! He wasn't even supposed to know how ill he was. The doctors didn't tell him—they came to me privately, told me his life was in danger and that he could only be saved by living in the South for a while. At first I tried persuasion; I cried, I begged, I cajoled—I said how much I longed to take a trip abroad like other young wives; I reminded him of my condition and told him he ought to humor me—and finally, I came right out and suggested that we borrow the money. But then, Kristine, he was almost angry; he said I was being frivolous and that it was his duty as my husband not to indulge my whims and fancies—I think that's what he called them. Then

I made up my mind he must be saved in spite of himself—and I thought of a way.

MRS. LINDE: But didn't he ever find out from your father that the money was not from him?

NORA: No; never. You see, Papa died just about that time. I was going to tell him all about it and beg him not to give me away. But he was so very ill—and then, it was no longer necessary—unfortunately.

MRS. LINDE: And you have never confided all this to your husband?

NORA: Good heavens, no! That's out of the question! He's much too strict in matters of that sort. And besides—Torvald could never bear to think of owing anything to me! It would hurt his self-respect—wound his pride. It would ruin everything between us. Our whole marriage would be wrecked by it!

MRS. LINDE: Don't you think you'll ever tell him?

NORA [*Thoughtfully; half-smiling*]: Perhaps some day—a long time from now when I'm no longer so pretty and attractive. No! Don't laugh! Some day when Torvald is no longer as much in love with me as he is now; when it no longer amuses him to see me dance and dress-up and act for him—then it might be useful to have something in reserve. [*Breaking off*] Oh, what nonsense! That time will never come! Well—what do you think of my great secret, Kristine? Haven't I something to be proud of too? It's caused me endless worry, though. It hasn't been easy to fulfill my obligations. You know, in business there are things called installments, and quarterly interest—and they're dreadfully hard to meet on time. I've had to save a little here and there, wherever I could. I couldn't save much out of the housekeeping, for of course Torvald had to live well. And I couldn't let the children go about badly dressed; any money I got for them, I spent on them, the darlings!

MRS. LINDE: Poor Nora! I suppose it had to come out of your own allowance.

NORA: Yes, of course. But after all, the whole thing was my doing. Whenever Torvald gave me money to buy some new clothes, or other things I needed, I never spent more than half of it; I always picked out the simplest cheapest dresses. It's a blessing that almost anything looks well on me—so Torvald never knew the difference. But it's been hard sometimes, Kristine. It's so nice to have pretty clothes—isn't it?

MRS. LINDE: I suppose it is.

NORA: And I made money in other ways too. Last winter I was lucky enough to get a lot of copying to do. I shut myself up in my room every evening and wrote far into the night. Sometimes I was absolutely exhausted—but it was fun all the same—working like that and earning money. It made me feel almost like a man!

MRS. LINDE: How much have you managed to pay off?

NORA: Well, I really don't know exactly. It's hard to keep track of things like that. All I know is—I've paid every penny I could scrape together. There were times when I didn't know which way to turn! [*Smiles*] Then I used to sit here and pretend that some rich old gentleman had fallen madly in love with me—

MRS. LINDE: What are you talking about? *What* old gentleman?

NORA: I'm just joking! And then he was to die and when they opened his will, there in large letters were to be the words: "I leave all my fortune to that charming Nora Helmer to be handed over to her immediately."

MRS. LINDE: But who *is* this old gentleman?

NORA: Good heavens, can't you understand? There never *was* any such old gentleman; I just used to make him up, when I was at the end of my rope and didn't know where to turn for money. But it doesn't matter now—the tiresome old fellow can stay where he is as far as I am concerned. I no longer need him nor his money; for now my troubles are over. [*Springing up*] Oh, isn't it wonderful to think of, Kristine. No more troubles! No more worry! I'll be able to play and romp about with the children; I'll be able to make a charming lovely home for Torvald—have everything just as he likes it. And soon spring will be here, with its great blue sky. Perhaps we might take a little trip—I might see the ocean again. Oh, it's so marvelous to be alive and to be happy!

[*The hall doorbell rings.*]

MRS. LINDE [*Rising*]: There's the bell. Perhaps I had better go.

NORA: No, no; do stay! It's probably just someone for Torvald.

HELENE [*In the doorway*]: Excuse me, Ma'am; there's a gentleman asking for Mr. Helmer—but the doctor's in there—and I didn't know if I should disturb him—

NORA: Who is it?

KROGSTAD [*In the doorway*]: It is I, Mrs. Helmer.

[MRS. LINDE *starts and turns away to the window.*]

NORA [*Goes a step toward him, anxiously; in a low voice*]: You? What is it? Why do you want to see my husband?

KROGSTAD: It's to do with Bank business—more or less. I have a small position in the Joint Stock Bank, and I hear your husband is to be the new president.

NORA: Then it's just—?

KROGSTAD: Just routine business, Mrs. Helmer; nothing else.

NORA: Then, please be good enough to go into his study.

[KROGSTAD *goes. She bows indifferently while she closes the door into the hall. Then she goes to the stove and tends the fire.*]

MRS. LINDE: Who was that man, Nora?

NORA: A Mr. Krogstad—he's a lawyer.

MRS. LINDE: I was right then.

NORA: Do you know him?

MRS. LINDE: I used to know him—many years ago. He worked in a law office in our town.

NORA: Yes, so he did.

MRS. LINDE: How he has changed!

NORA: He was unhappily married, they say.

MRS. LINDE: Is he a widower now?

NORA: Yes—with lots of children. There! That's better! [*She closes the door of the stove and moves the rocking chair a little to one side.*]

MRS. LINDE: I'm told he's mixed up in a lot of rather questionable business.

NORA: He may be; I really don't know. But don't let's talk about business—it's so tiresome.

[DR. RANK *comes out of* HELMER'*s room.*]

RANK [*Still in the doorway*]: No, no, I won't disturb you. I'll go in and see your wife for a moment. [*Sees* MRS. LINDE] Oh, I beg your pardon. I seem to be in the way here, too.

NORA: Of course not! [*Introduces them*] Dr. Rank—Mrs. Linde.

RANK: Well, well, I've often heard that name mentioned in this house; didn't I pass you on the stairs when I came in?

MRS. LINDE: Yes; I'm afraid I climb them very slowly. They wear me out!

RANK: A little on the delicate side—eh?

MRS. LINDE: No; just a bit overtired.

RANK: I see. So I suppose you've come to town for a good rest—on a round of dissipation!

MRS. LINDE: I have come to look for work.

RANK: Is that the best remedy for tiredness?

MRS. LINDE: One has to live, Doctor.

RANK: Yes, I'm told that's necessary.

NORA: Oh, come now, Dr. Rank! You're not above wanting to live yourself!

RANK: That's true enough. No matter how wretched I may be, I still want to hang on as long as possible. All my patients have that feeling too. Even the *morally* sick seem to share it. There's a wreck of a man in there with Helmer now—

MRS. LINDE [*Softly*]: Ah!

NORA: Whom do you mean?

RANK: A fellow named Krogstad, he's a lawyer—you wouldn't know anything about him. He's thoroughly depraved—rotten to the core— Yet even he declared, as though it were a matter of paramount importance, that he must live.

NORA: Really? What did he want with Torvald?

RANK: I've no idea; I gathered it was some Bank business.

NORA: I didn't know that Krog—that this man Krogstad had anything to do with the Bank?

RANK: He seems to have some sort of position there. [*To* MRS. LINDE] I don't know if this is true in your part of the country—but there are men who make it a practice of prying about in other people's business, searching for individuals of doubtful character—and having discovered their secret, place them in positions of trust, where they can keep an eye on them, and make use of them at will. Honest men—men of strong moral fiber—they leave out in the cold.

MRS. LINDE: Perhaps the weaklings need more help.

RANK [*Shrugs his shoulders*]: That point-of-view is fast turning society into a clinic.

[NORA, *deep in her own thoughts, breaks into half-stifled laughter and claps her hands.*]

RANK: Why should that make you laugh? I wonder if you've any idea what "society" is?

NORA: Why should I care about your tiresome old "society"? I was laughing at something quite different—something frightfully amusing. Tell me, Dr. Rank— will all the employees at the Bank be dependent on Torvald now?

RANK: Is *that* what strikes you as so amusing?

NORA [*Smiles and hums*]: Never you mind! Never you mind! [*Walks about the room*] What fun to think that we—that Torvald—has such power over so many people. [*Takes the bag from her pocket*] Dr. Rank, how about a macaroon?

RANK: Well, well!— Macaroons, eh? I thought they were forbidden here.

NORA: These are some Kristine brought—

MRS. LINDE: What! I—

NORA: Now, you needn't be so frightened. How could you possibly know that Torvald had forbidden them? He's afraid they'll spoil my teeth. Oh, well—just for once! Don't you agree, Dr. Rank? There you are! [*Puts a macaroon into his mouth*] You must have one too, Kristine. And I'll have just one—just a tiny one, or at most two. [*Walks about again*] Oh dear, I am so happy! There's just one thing in all the world that would give me the greatest pleasure.

RANK: What's that?

NORA: It's something I long to say in front of Torvald.

RANK: What's to prevent you?

NORA: Oh, I don't dare; it isn't nice.

MRS. LINDE: Not nice?

RANK: It might be unwise, then; but you can certainly say it to us. What is it you so long to say in front of Torvald?

NORA: I'd so love to say "Damn!—damn!—damn it all!"

RANK: Have you gone crazy?

MRS. LINDE: Good gracious, Nora—

RANK: Go ahead and say it—here he comes!

NORA [*Hides the macaroons*]: Hush—sh—sh.

[HELMER *comes out of his room; he carries his hat and overcoat.*]

NORA [*Going to him*]: Well, Torvald, dear, did you get rid of him?

HELMER: He has just gone.

NORA: Let me introduce you—this is Kristine, who has just arrived in town—-

HELMER: Kristine? I'm sorry—but I really don't—

NORA: Mrs. Linde, Torvald, dear—Kristine Linde.

HELMER: Oh yes! I suppose you're one of my wife's school friends?

MRS. LINDE: Yes; we knew each other as children.

NORA: Imagine, Torvald! She came all that long way just to talk to you.

HELMER: How do you mean?

MRS. LINDE: Well, it wasn't exactly—

NORA: Kristine is tremendously good at office-work, and her great dream is to get a position with a really clever man—so she can improve still more, you see—

HELMER: Very sensible, Mrs. Linde.

NORA: And when she heard that you had become president of the Bank—it was in the paper, you know—she started off at once; you *will* try and do something for Kristine, won't you, Torvald? For my sake?

HELMER: It's by no means impossible. You're a widow, I presume?

MRS. LINDE: Yes.

HELMER: And you've already had business experience?

MRS. LINDE: A good deal.

HELMER: Then, I think it's quite likely I may be able to find a place for you.

NORA [*Clapping her hands*]: There, you see! You see!

HELMER: You have come at a good moment, Mrs. Linde.

MRS. LINDE: How can I ever thank you—?

HELMER [*Smiling*]: Don't mention it. [*Puts on his overcoat*] But just now, I'm afraid you must excuse me—

RANK: I'll go with you. [*Fetches his fur coat from the hall and warms it at the stove.*]

NORA: Don't be long, Torvald, dear.

HELMER: I shan't be more than an hour.

NORA: Are you going too, Kristine?

MRS. LINDE [*Putting on her outdoor things*]: Yes; I must go and find a place to live.

HELMER: We can all go out together.

NORA [*Helping her*]: How tiresome that we're so cramped for room, Kristine; otherwise—

MRS. LINDE: Oh, you mustn't think of that! Good bye, dear Nora, and thanks for everything.

NORA: Good bye for the present. Of course you'll come back this evening. And you too, Dr. Rank—eh? If you're well enough? But of course you'll be well enough! Wrap up warmly now! [*They go out talking, into the hall; children's voices are heard on the stairs*] Here they come! Here they come! [*She runs to the outer door and opens it. The nurse,* ANNE-MARIE, *enters the hall with the children*] Come in, come in—you darlings! Just look at them, Kristine. Aren't they sweet?

RANK: No chattering in this awful draught!

HELMER: Come along, Mrs. Linde; you have to be a mother to put up with this!

[DR. RANK, HELMER, *and* MRS. LINDE *go down the stairs;* ANNE-MARIE *enters the room with the children;* NORA *comes in too, shutting the door behind her.*]

NORA: How fresh and bright you look! And what red cheeks! Like apples and roses. [*The children chatter to her during what follows*] Did you have a good time? Splendid!

You gave Emmy and Bob a ride on your sled? Both at once? You *are* a clever boy, Ivar! Let me hold her for a bit, Anne-Marie. My darling little doll-baby. [*Takes the smallest from the nurse and dances with her*] All right, Bobbie! Mama will dance with you too. You threw snowballs, did you? I should have been in on that! Never mind, Anne; I'll undress them myself—oh, do let me—it's such fun. Go on into the nursery, you look half-frozen. There's some hot coffee in there on the stove. [*The nurse goes into the room on the left.* NORA *takes off the children's things and throws them down anywhere, while the children all talk together*] Not really! You were chased by a big dog? But he didn't bite you? No; dogs don't bite tiny little doll-babies! Don't touch the packages, Ivar. What's in them? Wouldn't you like to know! No. No! Careful! It might bite! Come on, let's play. What will we play? Hide-and-seek? Let's play hide-and-seek. Bob, you hide first! Do you want me to? All right! I'll hide first then.

[*She and the children play, laughing and shouting, all over the room and in the adjacent room to the left. Finally* NORA *hides under the table; the children come rushing in, look for her, but cannot find her, hear her half-suppressed laughter, rush to the table, lift up the cover and see her. Loud shouts of delight. She creeps out, as though to frighten them. More shouts. Meanwhile there has been a knock at the door leading into the hall. No one has heard it. Now the door is half-opened and* KROGSTAD *appears. He waits a little—the game continues.*]

KROGSTAD: I beg your pardon, Mrs. Helmer—

NORA [*With a stifled scream, turns round and half jumps up*]: Oh! What do you want?

KROGSTAD: Excuse me; the outer door was ajar—someone must have forgotten to close it—

NORA [*Standing up*]: My husband is not at home, Mr. Krogstad.

KROGSTAD: I know that.

NORA: Then, what do you want here?

KROGSTAD: I want a few words with you.

NORA: With——? [*To the children, softly*] Go in to Anne-Marie. What? No—the strange man won't do Mama any harm; when he's gone we'll go on playing. [*She leads the children into the right hand room, and shuts the door behind them; uneasy, in suspense*] You want to speak to me?

KROGSTAD: Yes, I do.

NORA: Today? But it's not the first of the month yet—

KROGSTAD: No, it is Christmas Eve. It's up to you whether your Christmas is a merry one.

NORA: What is it you want? Today I can't possibly—

KROGSTAD: That doesn't concern me for the moment. This is about something else. You have a few minutes, haven't you?

NORA: I suppose so; although—

KROGSTAD: Good. I was sitting in the restaurant opposite, and I saw your husband go down the street—

NORA: Well?

KROGSTAD: —with a lady.

NORA: What of it?

KROGSTAD: May I ask if that lady was a Mrs. Linde?

NORA: Yes.

KROGSTAD: She's just come to town, hasn't she?

NORA: Yes. Today.

KROGSTAD: Is she a good friend of yours?

NORA: Yes, she is. But I can't imagine—

KROGSTAD: I used to know her too.

NORA: Yes, I know you did.

KROGSTAD: Then you know all about it. I thought as much. Now, tell me: is Mrs. Linde to have a place in the Bank?

NORA: How dare you question me like this, Mr. Krogstad—you, one of my husband's employees! But since you ask—you might as well know. Yes, Mrs. Linde is to have a position at the Bank, and it is I who recommended her. Does that satisfy you, Mr. Krogstad?

KROGSTAD: I was right, then.

NORA [*Walks up and down*]: After all, one has a little influence, now and then. Even if one is only a woman it doesn't always follow that—people in subordinate positions, Mr. Krogstad, ought really to be careful how they offend anyone who—h'm—

KROGSTAD: —has influence?

NORA: Precisely.

KROGSTAD [*Taking another tone*]: Then perhaps you'll be so kind, Mrs. Helmer, as to use your influence on *my* behalf?

NORA: What? How do you mean?

KROGSTAD: Perhaps you'll be good enough to see that I *retain* my subordinate position?

NORA: But, I don't understand. Who wants to take it from you?

KROGSTAD: Oh, don't try and play the innocent! I can well understand that it would be unpleasant for your friend to associate with me; and I understand too, whom I have to thank for my dismissal.

NORA: But I assure you—

KROGSTAD: Never mind all that—there is still time. But I advise you to use your influence to prevent this.

NORA: But, Mr. Krogstad, I *have* no influence—absolutely none!

KROGSTAD: Indeed! I thought you just told me yourself—

NORA: You misunderstood me—*really* you did! You must know my husband would never be influenced by me!

KROGSTAD: Your husband and I were at the University together—I know him well. I don't suppose he's any more inflexible than other married men.

NORA: Don't you dare talk disrespectfully about my husband, or I'll show you the door!

KROGSTAD: The little lady's plucky.

NORA: I'm no longer afraid of you. I'll soon be free of all this—after the first of the year.

KROGSTAD [*In a more controlled manner*]: Listen to me, Mrs. Helmer. This is a matter of life and death to me. I warn you I shall fight with all my might to keep my position in the Bank.

NORA: So it seems.

KROGSTAD: It's not just the salary; that is the least important part of it— It's something else— Well, I might as well be frank with you. I suppose you know, like everyone else, that once—a long time ago—I got into quite a bit of trouble.

NORA: I have heard something about it, I believe.

KROGSTAD: The matter never came to court; but from that time on, all doors were closed to me. I then went into the business with which you are familiar. I had to do something; and I don't think I've been among the worst. But now I must get away from all that. My sons are growing up, you see; for their sake I'm determined to recapture my good name. This position in the Bank was to be the first step; and now your husband wants to kick me back into the mud again.

NORA: But I tell you, Mr. Krogstad, it's not in my power to help you.

KROGSTAD: Only because you don't really want to; but I can compel you to do it, if I choose.

NORA: You wouldn't tell my husband that I owe you money?

KROGSTAD: And suppose I were to?

NORA: But that would be an outrageous thing to do! [*With tears in her voice*] My secret—that I've guarded with such pride—such joy! I couldn't bear to have him find it out in such an ugly, hateful way—to have him find it out from you! I couldn't bear it! It would be too horribly unpleasant!

KROGSTAD: Only unpleasant, Mrs. Helmer?

NORA [*Vehemently*]: But just you do it! You'll be the one to suffer; for then my husband will *really* know the kind of man you are—there'll be no chance of keeping your job then!

KROGSTAD: Didn't you hear my question? I asked if it were only unpleasantness you feared?

NORA: If my husband got to know about it, he'd naturally pay you off at once, and then we'd have nothing more to do with you.

KROGSTAD [*Takes a step towards her*]: Listen, Mrs. Helmer: Either you have a very bad memory, or you know nothing about business. I think I'd better make the position clear to you.

NORA: What do you mean?

KROGSTAD: When your husband fell ill, you came to me to borrow twelve hundred dollars.

NORA: I didn't know what else to do.

KROGSTAD: I promised to find you the money—

NORA: And you did find it.

KROGSTAD: I promised to find you the money, on certain conditions. At that time you were so taken up with your husband's illness and so anxious to procure the money for your journey, that you probably did not give much thought to details. Perhaps I'd better remind you of them. I promised to find you the amount in exchange for a note, which I drew up.

NORA: Yes, and I signed it.

KROGSTAD: Very good. But then I added a clause, stating that your father would stand sponsor for the debt. This clause your father was to have signed.

NORA: Was to—? He did sign it.

KROGSTAD: I left the date blank, so that your father himself should date his signature. You recall that?

NORA: Yes, I believe—

KROGSTAD: Then I gave you the paper, and you were to mail it to your father. Isn't that so?

NORA: Yes.

KROGSTAD: And you must have mailed it at once; for five or six days later you brought me back the document with your father's signature; and then I handed you the money.

NORA: Well? Haven't I made my payments punctually?

KROGSTAD: Fairly—yes. But to return to the point: That was a sad time for you, wasn't it, Mrs. Helmer?

NORA: It was indeed!

KROGSTAD: Your father was very ill, I believe?

NORA: Yes—he was dying.

KROGSTAD: And he did die soon after, didn't he?

NORA: Yes.

KROGSTAD: Now tell me, Mrs. Helmer: Do you happen to recollect the date of your father's death: the day of the month, I mean?

NORA: Father died on the 29th of September.

KROGSTAD: Quite correct. I have made inquiries. Now here is a strange thing, Mrs. Helmer— [*Produces a paper*] something rather hard to explain.

NORA: What do you mean? What strange thing?

KROGSTAD: The strange thing about it is, that your father seems to have signed this paper three days after his death!

NORA: I don't understand—

KROGSTAD: Your father died on the 29th of September. But look at this: his signature is dated October 2nd! Isn't that rather strange, Mrs. Helmer? [NORA *is silent*] Can you explain that to me? [NORA *continues silent*] It is curious, too, that the words "October 2nd" and the year are not in your father's handwriting, but in a handwriting I seem to know. This could easily be explained, however; your father might have forgotten to date his signature, and someone might have added the date at random, before the fact of your father's death was known. There is nothing wrong in that. It all depends on the signature itself. It is of course genuine, Mrs. Helmer? It was your father himself who wrote his name here?

NORA [*After a short silence, throws her head back and looks defiantly at him*]: No, it wasn't. I wrote Father's name.

KROGSTAD: I suppose you realize, Mrs. Helmer, what a dangerous confession that is?

NORA: Why should it be dangerous? You will get your money soon enough!

KROGSTAD: I'd like to ask you a question: Why didn't you send the paper to your father?

NORA: It was impossible. Father was too ill. If I had asked him for his signature, he'd have wanted to know what the money was for. In his condition I simply could not tell him that my husband's life was in danger. That's why it was impossible.

KROGSTAD: Then wouldn't it have been wiser to give up the journey?

NORA: How could I? That journey was to save my husband's life. I simply couldn't give it up.

KROGSTAD: And it never occurred to you that you weren't being honest with me?

NORA: I really couldn't concern myself with that. You meant nothing to me— In fact I couldn't help disliking you for making it all so difficult—with your cold, business-like clauses and conditions—when you knew my husband's life was at stake.

KROGSTAD: You evidently haven't the faintest idea, Mrs. Helmer, what you have been guilty of. Yet let me tell you that it was nothing more and nothing worse that made me an outcast from society.

NORA: You don't expect me to believe that you ever did a brave thing to save your wife's life?

KROGSTAD: The law takes no account of motives.

NORA: It must be a very bad law, then!

KROGSTAD: Bad or not, if I produce this document in court, you will be condemned according to the law.

NORA: I don't believe that for a minute. Do you mean to tell me that a daughter has no right to spare her dying father worry and anxiety? Or that a wife has no right to save her husband's life? I may not know much about it—but I'm sure there must be something or other in the law that permits such things. You as a lawyer should be aware of that. You don't seem to know very much about the law, Mr. Krogstad.

KROGSTAD: Possibly not. But business—the kind of business we are concerned with—I *do* know something about. Don't you agree? Very well, then; do as you please. But I warn you: if I am made to suffer a second time, you shall keep me company. [*Bows and goes out through the hall.*]

NORA [*Stands a while thinking, then tosses her head*]: What nonsense! He's just trying to frighten me. I'm not such a fool as all that! [*Begins folding the children's clothes. Pauses*] And yet—? No, it's impossible! After all—I only did it for love's sake.

CHILDREN [*At the door, left*]: Mamma, the strange man has gone now.

NORA: Yes, yes, I know. But don't tell anyone about the strange man. Do you hear? Not even Papa!

CHILDREN: No, Mamma; now will you play with us again?

NORA: No, not just now.

CHILDREN: But Mamma! You promised!

NORA: But I can't just now. Run back to the nursery; I have so much to do. Run along now! Run along, my darlings! [*She pushes them gently into the inner room, and closes the door behind them. Sits on the sofa, embroiders a few stitches, but soon pauses*] No! [*Throws down the work, rises, goes to the hall door and calls out*] Helene, bring the tree in to me, will you? [*Goes to table, right, and opens the drawer; again pauses*] No, it's utterly impossible!

HELENE [*Carries in the Christmas tree*]: Where shall I put it, Ma'am?

NORA: Right there; in the middle of the room.

HELENE: Is there anything else you need?

NORA: No, thanks; I have everything.

[HELENE, *having put down the tree, goes out.*]

NORA [*Busy dressing the tree*]: We'll put a candle here—and some flowers here—that dreadful man! But it's just nonsense! There's nothing to worry about. The tree will be lovely. I'll do everything to please you, Torvald; I'll sing for you, I'll dance for you—

[*Enter* HELMER *by the hall door, with a bundle of documents.*]

NORA: Oh! You're back already?

HELMER: Yes. Has somebody been here?

NORA: No. Nobody.

HELMER: That's odd. I just saw Krogstad leave the house.

NORA: Really? Well—as a matter of fact—Krogstad was here for a moment.

HELMER: Nora—I can tell by your manner—he came here to ask you to put in a good word for him, didn't he?

NORA: Yes, Torvald.

HELMER: And you weren't supposed to tell me he'd been here—You were to do it as if of your own accord—isn't that it?

NORA: Yes, Torvald; but—

HELMER: Nora, Nora! How could you consent to such a thing! To have dealings with a man like that—make him promises! And then to lie about it too!

NORA: Lie!

HELMER: Didn't you tell me that nobody had been here? [*Threatens with his finger*] My little bird must never do that again! A song-bird must sing clear and true! No false notes! [*Puts arm around her*] Isn't that the way it should be? Of course it is! [*Lets her go*] And now we'll say no more about it. [*Sits down before the fire*] It's so cozy and peaceful here! [*Glances through the documents.*]

NORA [*Busy with the tree, after a short silence*]: Torvald!

HELMER: Yes.

NORA: I'm so looking forward to the Stenborgs' fancy dress party, day after tomorrow.

HELMER: And I can't wait to see what surprise you have in store for me.

NORA: Oh, it's so awful, Torvald!

HELMER: *What* is?

NORA: I can't think of anything amusing. Everything seems so silly, so pointless.

HELMER: Has my little Nora come to *that* conclusion?

NORA [*Behind his chair, with her arms on the back*]: Are you very busy, Torvald?

HELMER: Well—

NORA: What are all those papers?

HELMER: Just Bank business.

NORA: Already!

HELMER: The board of directors has given me full authority to do some re-organizing—to make a few necessary changes in the staff. I'll have to work on it during Christmas week. I want it all settled by the New Year.

NORA: I see. So that was why that poor Krogstad—

HELMER: H'm.

NORA [*Still leaning over the chair-back and slowly stroking his hair*]: If you weren't so very busy, I'd ask you to do me a great, great favor, Torvald.

HELMER: Well, let's hear it! Out with it!

NORA: You have such perfect taste, Torvald; and I do so want to look well at the fancy dress ball. Couldn't you take me in hand, and decide what I'm to be, and arrange my costume for me?

HELMER: Well, well! So we're not so self-sufficient after all! We need a helping hand, do we?

NORA: Oh, please, Torvald! I know I shall *never* manage without your help!

HELMER: I'll think about it; we'll hit on something.

NORA: Oh, how sweet of you! [*Goes to the tree again; pauses*] Those red flowers show up beautifully! Tell me, Torvald; did that Krogstad do something very wrong?

HELMER: He committed forgery. Have you any idea of what that means?

NORA: Perhaps he did it out of necessity?

HELMER: Or perhaps he was just fool-hardy, like so many others. I am not so harsh as to condemn a man irrevocably for one mistake.

NORA: No, of course not!

HELMER: A man has a chance to rehabilitate himself, if he honestly admits his guilt and takes his punishment.

NORA: Punishment—

HELMER: But that wasn't Krogstad's way. He resorted to tricks and evasions; became thoroughly demoralized.

NORA: You really think it would—?

HELMER: When a man has that sort of thing on his conscience his life becomes a tissue of lies and deception. He's forced to wear a mask—even with those nearest to him—his own wife and children even. And the children—that's the worst part of it, Nora.

NORA: Why?

HELMER: Because the whole atmosphere of the home would be contaminated. The very air the children breathed would be filled with evil.

NORA [*Closer behind him*]: Are you sure of that?

HELMER: As a lawyer, I know it from experience. Almost all cases of early delinquency can be traced to dishonest mothers.

NORA: Why—only mothers?

HELMER: It usually stems from the mother's side; but of course it can come from the father too. We lawyers know a lot about such things. And this Krogstad has been deliberately poisoning his own children for years, by surrounding them with lies and hypocrisy—that is why I call him demoralized. [*Holds out both hands to her*] So my sweet little Nora must promise not to plead his cause. Shake hands on it. Well? What's the matter? Give me your hand. There! That's all settled. I assure you it would have been impossible for me to work with him. It literally gives me a feeling of physical discomfort to come in contact with such people. [NORA *draws her hand away, and moves to the other side of the Christmas tree.*]

NORA: It's so warm here. And I have such a lot to do.

HELMER [*Rises and gathers up his papers*]: I must try and look through some of these papers before dinner. I'll give some thought to your costume too. Perhaps I may even find something to hang in gilt paper on the Christmas tree! [*Lays his hand on her head*] My own precious little song-bird! [*He goes into his study and closes the door after him.*]

NORA [*Softly, after a pause*]: It can't be—! It's impossible. Of course it's impossible!

ANNE-MARIE [*At the door, left*]: The babies keep begging to come in and see Mamma.

NORA: No, no! Don't let them come to me! Keep them with you, Anne-Marie.

ANNE-MARIE: Very well, Ma'am. [*Shuts the door.*]

NORA [*Pale with terror*]: Harm my children!—Corrupt my home! [*Short pause. She throws back her head*] It's not true! I know it's not! It could never, never be true!

[*Curtain*]

ACT 2

The same room. In the corner, beside the piano, stands the Christmas tree, stripped and with the candles burnt out. NORA's *outdoor things lie on the sofa.* NORA, *alone, is walking about restlessly. At last she stops by the sofa, and picks up her cloak.*

NORA [*Puts the cloak down again*]: Did someone come in? [*Goes to the hall and listens*] No; no one; of course no one will come today, Christmas Day; nor tomorrow either. But perhaps— [*Opens the door and looks out*] No, there's nothing in the mail-box; it's quite empty. [*Comes forward*] Oh nonsense! He only meant to frighten me. There won't be any trouble. It's all impossible! Why, I— I have three little children!

[ANNE-MARIE *enters from the left, with a large cardboard box.*]

ANNE-MARIE: Well—I found the box with the fancy dress clothes at last, Miss Nora.

NORA: Thanks; put it on the table.

ANNE-MARIE [*Does so*]: I'm afraid they're rather shabby.

NORA: If I had my way I'd tear them into a thousand pieces!

ANNE-MARIE: Good gracious! They can be repaired—just have a little patience.

NORA: I'll go and get Mrs. Linde to help me.

ANNE-MARIE: I wouldn't go out again in this awful weather! You might catch cold, Miss Nora, and get sick.

NORA: Worse things might happen— How are the children?

ANNE-MARIE: The poor little things are playing with their Christmas presents; but—

NORA: Have they asked for me?

ANNE-MARIE: They're so used to having Mamma with them.

NORA: I know, but, you see, Anne-Marie, I won't be able to be with them as much as I used to.

ANNE-MARIE: Well, little children soon get used to anything.

NORA: You really think so? Would they forget me if I went away for good?

ANNE-MARIE: Good gracious!—for good!

NORA: Tell me something, Anne-Marie—I've so often wondered about it—how could you bear to part with your child—give it up to strangers?

ANNE-MARIE: Well, you see, I had to—when I came to nurse my little Nora.

NORA: Yes—but how could you *bear* to do it?

ANNE-MARIE: I couldn't afford to say "no" to such a good position. A poor girl who's been in trouble must take what comes. Of course *he* never offered to help me—the wicked sinner!

NORA: Then I suppose your daughter has forgotten all about you.

ANNE-MARIE: No—indeed she hasn't! She even wrote to me—once when she was confirmed and again when she was married.

NORA [*Embracing her*]: Dear old Anne-Marie—you were a good mother to me when I was little.

ANNE-MARIE: But then my poor little Nora *had* no mother of her own!

NORA: And if ever my little ones were left without—you'd look after them, wouldn't you?—Oh, that's just nonsense! [*Opens the box*] Go back to them. Now I must— Just you wait and see how lovely I'll look tomorrow!

ANNE-MARIE: My Miss Nora will be the prettiest person there! [*She goes into the room on the left.*]

NORA [*Takes the costume out of the box, but soon throws it down again*]: I wish I dared go out—I'm afraid someone might come. I'm afraid something might happen while I'm gone. That's just silly! No one will come. I must try not to think— This muff needs cleaning. What pretty gloves—they're lovely! I must put it out of my head! One, two, three, four, five, six— [*With a scream*] Ah! They're here!

[*Goes toward the door, then stands irresolute.* MRS. LINDE *enters from the hall, where she has taken off her things.*]

NORA: Oh, it's you, Kristine! There's no one else out there, is there? I'm so glad you have come!

MRS. LINDE: I got a message you'd been asking for me.

NORA: Yes, I just happened to be passing by. There's something I want you to help me with. Sit down here on the sofa. Now, listen: There's to be a fancy dress ball at the Stenborgs' tomorrow evening—they live just overhead—and Torvald wants me to go as a Neapolitan peasant girl, and dance the tarantella;[1] I learned it while we were in Capri.

MRS. LINDE: So you're going to give a real performance, are you?

NORA: Torvald wants me to. Look, here's the costume; Torvald had it made for me down there. But it's all torn, Kristine, and I don't know whether—

MRS. LINDE: Oh, we'll soon fix that. It's only the trimming that has come loose here and there. Have you a needle and thread? Oh, yes. Here's everything I need.

NORA: It's awfully good of you!

MRS. LINDE [*Sewing*]: So you're going to be all dressed up, Nora—what fun! You know—I think I'll run in for a moment—just to see you in your costume— I haven't really thanked you for last night. I had such a happy time!

NORA [*Rises and walks across the room*]: Somehow it didn't seem as nice to me as usual. I wish you'd come to town a little earlier, Kristine. Yes—Torvald has a way of making things so gay and cozy.

MRS. LINDE: Well—so have you. That's your father coming out in you! But tell me—is Doctor Rank always so depressed?

---

[1] A whirling dance from southern Italy, once thought to be a remedy for the bite of the tarantula.

NORA: No; last night it was worse than usual. He's terribly ill, you see—tuberculosis of the spine, or something. His father was a frightful man, who kept mistresses and all that sort of thing—that's why his son has been an invalid from birth—

MRS. LINDE [*Lets her sewing fall into her lap*]: Why, Nora! what do you know about such things?

NORA [*Moving about the room*]: After all—I've had three children; and those women who look after one at childbirth know almost as much as doctors; and they love to gossip.

MRS. LINDE [*Goes on sewing, a short pause*]: Does Doctor Rank come here every day?

NORA: Every single day. He's Torvald's best friend, you know—always has been; and he's *my* friend too. He's almost like one of the family.

MRS. LINDE: Do you think he's quite sincere, Nora? I mean—isn't he inclined to flatter people?

NORA: Quite the contrary. What gave you that impression?

MRS. LINDE: When you introduced us yesterday he said he had often heard my name mentioned here; but I noticed afterwards that your husband hadn't the faintest notion who I was. How could Doctor Rank—?

NORA: He was quite right, Kristine. You see Torvald loves me so tremendously that he won't share me with anyone; he wants me all to himself, as he says. At first he used to get terribly jealous if I even mentioned any of my old friends back home; so naturally I gave up doing it. But I often talk to Doctor Rank about such things—he likes to hear about them.

MRS. LINDE: Listen to me, Nora! In many ways you are still a child. I'm somewhat older than you, and besides, I've had much more experience. I think you ought to put a stop to all this with Dr. Rank.

NORA: Put a stop to what?

MRS. LINDE: To the whole business. You said something yesterday about a rich admirer who was to give you money—

NORA: One who never existed, unfortunately. Go on.

MRS. LINDE: Has Doctor Rank money?

NORA: Why yes, he has.

MRS. LINDE: And he has no one dependent on him?

NORA: No, no one. But—

MRS. LINDE: And he comes here every single day?

NORA: Yes—I've just told you so.

MRS. LINDE: It's surprising that a sensitive man like that should be so importunate.

NORA: I don't understand you—

MRS. LINDE: Don't try to deceive me, Nora. Don't you suppose I can guess who lent you the twelve hundred dollars?

NORA: You must be out of your mind! How could you ever think such a thing? Why, he's a friend of ours; he comes to see us every day! The situation would have been impossible!

MRS. LINDE: So it wasn't he, then?

NORA: No, I assure you. Such a thing never even occurred to me. Anyway, he didn't have any money at that time; he came into it later.

MRS. LINDE: Perhaps that was just as well, Nora, dear.

NORA: No—it would never have entered my head to ask Dr. Rank— Still—I'm sure that if I did ask him—

MRS. LINDE: But you won't, of course.

NORA: No, of course not. Anyway—I don't see why it should be necessary. But I'm sure that if I talked to Doctor Rank—

MRS. LINDE: Behind your husband's back?

NORA: I want to get that thing cleared up; after all, that's behind his back too. I must get clear of it.

MRS. LINDE: That's just what I said yesterday; but—

NORA [*Walking up and down*]: It's so much easier for a man to manage things like that—

MRS. LINDE: One's own husband, yes.

NORA: Nonsense. [*Stands still*] Surely if you pay back everything you owe—the paper is returned to you?

MRS. LINDE: Naturally.

NORA: Then you can tear it into a thousand pieces, and burn it up—the nasty, filthy thing!

MRS. LINDE [*Looks at her fixedly, lays down her work, and rises slowly*]: Nora, you are hiding something from me.

NORA: You can see it in my face, can't you?

MRS. LINDE: Something's happened to you since yesterday morning, Nora, what is it?

NORA [*Going towards her*]: Kristine—! [*Listens*] Hush! Here comes Torvald! Go into the nursery for a little while. Torvald hates anything to do with sewing. Get Anne-Marie to help you.

MRS. LINDE [*Gathers the things together*]: Very well; but I shan't leave until you have told me all about it. [*She goes out to the left, as* HELMER *enters from the hall.*]

NORA [*Runs to meet him*]: Oh, I've missed you so, Torvald, dear!

HELMER: Was that the dressmaker—?

NORA: No, it was Kristine. She's helping me fix my costume. It's going to look so nice.

HELMER: Wasn't that a good idea of mine?

NORA: Splendid! But don't you think it was good of me to let you have your way?

HELMER: Good of you! To let your own husband have his way! There, there, you crazy little thing; I'm only teasing. Now I won't disturb you. You'll have to try the dress on, I suppose.

NORA: Yes—and I expect you've work to do.

HELMER: I have. [*Shows her a bundle of papers*] Look. I've just come from the Bank— [*Goes towards his room.*]

NORA: Torvald.

HELMER [*Stopping*]: Yes?

NORA: If your little squirrel were to beg you—with all her heart—

HELMER: Well?

NORA: Would you do something for her?

HELMER: That depends on what it is.

NORA: Be a darling and say "Yes," Torvald! Your squirrel would skip about and play all sorts of pretty tricks—

HELMER: Well—out with it!

NORA: Your little lark would twitter all day long—

HELMER: She does that anyway!

NORA: I'll pretend to be an elf and dance for you in the moonlight, Torvald.

HELMER: Nora—you're surely not getting back to what we talked about this morning?

NORA [*Coming nearer*]: Oh, Torvald, dear, I do most humbly beg you—!

HELMER: You have the temerity to bring that up again?

NORA: You must give in to me about this, Torvald! You *must* let Krogstad keep his place!

HELMER: I'm giving his place to Mrs. Linde.

NORA: That's awfully sweet of you. But instead of Krogstad—couldn't you dismiss some other clerk?

HELMER: This is the most incredible obstinacy! Because you were thoughtless enough to promise to put in a good word for him, am I supposed to—?

NORA: That's not the reason, Torvald. It's for your own sake. Didn't you tell me yourself he writes for the most horrible newspapers? He can do you no end of harm. Oh! I'm so afraid of him—

HELMER: I think I understand; you have some unpleasant memories—that's why you're frightened.

NORA: What do you mean?

HELMER: Aren't you thinking of your father?

NORA: Oh, yes—of course! You remember how those awful people slandered poor Father in the newspapers? If you hadn't been sent to investigate the matter, and been so kind and helpful—he might have been dismissed.

HELMER: My dear Nora, there is a distinct difference between your father and me. Your father's conduct was not entirely unimpeachable. But mine is; and I trust it will remain so.

NORA: You never know what evil-minded people can think up. We could be so happy now, Torvald, in our lovely, peaceful home—you and I and the children! Oh! I implore you, Torvald—!

HELMER: The more you plead his cause the less likely I am to keep him on. It's already known at the Bank that I intend to dismiss Krogstad. If I were to change my mind, people might say I'd done it at the insistence of my wife—

NORA: Well—what of that?

HELMER: Oh, nothing, of course! As long as the obstinate little woman gets her way! I'd simply be the laughing-stock of the whole staff; they'd think I was weak and easily influenced—I should soon be made to feel the consequences. Besides—there is one factor that makes it quite impossible for Krogstad to work at the Bank as long as I'm head there.

NORA: What could that be?

HELMER: His past record I might be able to overlook—

NORA: Yes, you might, mightn't you, Torvald—?

HELMER: And I'm told he's an excellent worker. But unfortunately we were friendly during our college days. It was one of those impetuous friendships that subsequently often prove embarrassing. He's tactless enough to call me by my first name—regardless of the circumstances—and feels quite justified in taking a familiar tone with me. At any moment he comes out with "Torvald" this, and "Torvald" that! It's acutely irritating. It would make my position at the Bank intolerable.

NORA: You're surely not serious about this, Torvald?

HELMER: Why not?

NORA: But—it's all so petty.

HELMER: Petty! So you think I'm petty!

NORA: Of course not, Torvald—just the opposite; that's why—

HELMER: Never mind; you call my motives petty; so I must be petty too! Petty! Very well!—We'll put an end to this now—once and for all. [HELMER *goes to the door into the hall and calls* HELENE.]

NORA: What do you want?

HELMER [*Searching among his papers*]: I want this thing settled. [HELENE *enters*] Take this letter, will you? Get a messenger and have him deliver it at once! It's urgent. Here's some money.

HELENE: Very good, Sir. [*Goes with the letter.*]

HELMER [*Putting his papers together*]: There, little Miss Obstinacy.

NORA [*Breathless*]: Torvald—what was in that letter?

HELMER: Krogstad's dismissal.

NORA: Call her back, Torvald! There's still time. Call her back! For my sake, for your own sake, for the sake of the children, don't send that letter! Torvald, do you hear? You don't realize what may come of this!

HELMER: It's too late.

NORA: Too late, yes.

HELMER: Nora, dear; I forgive your fears—though it's not exactly flattering to me to think I could ever be afraid of any spiteful nonsense Krogstad might choose to write about me! But I forgive you all the same—it shows how much you love me. [*Takes her in his arms*] And that's the way it should be, Nora darling. No matter what happens, you'll see—I have strength and courage for us both. My shoulders are broad—I'll bear the burden.

NORA [*Terror-struck*]: How do you mean?

HELMER: The whole burden, my darling. Don't you worry any more.

NORA [*With decision*]: No! You mustn't—I won't let you!

HELMER: Then we'll share it, Nora, as man and wife. That is as it should be. [*Petting her*] Are you happy now? There! Don't look at me like a frightened little dove! You're just imagining things, you know— Now don't you think you ought to play the tarantella through—and practice your tambourine? I'll go into my study and close both doors, then you won't disturb me. You can make all the noise you like! [*Turns round in doorway*] And when Rank comes, just tell him where I am. [*He nods to her, and goes with his papers to his room, closing the door.*]

NORA [*Bewildered with terror, stands as though rooted to the ground, and whispers*]: He'd do it too! He'd do it—in spite of anything! But he mustn't—never, never! Anything but that! There must be some way out! What shall I do? [*The hall bell rings*] Dr. Rank—! Anything but that—anything, *anything* but that!

[NORA *draws her hands over her face, pulls herself together, goes to the door and opens it.* RANK *stands outside hanging up his fur coat. During the following scene, darkness begins to fall.*]

NORA: How are you, Doctor Rank? I recognized your ring. You'd better not go in to Torvald just now; I think he's busy.

RANK: How about you? [*Enters and closes the door.*]

NORA: You know I always have an hour to spare for you.

RANK: Many thanks. I'll make use of that privilege as long as possible.

NORA: What do you mean—as long as possible?

RANK: Does that frighten you?

NORA: No—but it's such a queer expression. Has anything happened?

RANK: I've been expecting it for a long time, but I never thought it would come quite so soon.

NORA: What is it you have found out? Doctor Rank, please tell me!

RANK [*Sitting down by the stove*]: I haven't much time left. There's nothing to do about it.

NORA [*With a sigh of relief*]: Oh! Then—it's about you—?

RANK: Of course. What did you think? It's no use lying to one's self. I am the most miserable of all my patients, Mrs. Helmer. These past few days I've been taking stock of my position—and I find myself completely bankrupt. Within a month, I shall be rotting in the church-yard.

NORA: What a ghastly way to talk!

RANK: The whole business is pretty ghastly, you see. And the worst of it is, there are so many ghastly things to be gone through before it's over. I've just one last examination to make, then I shall know approximately when the final dissolution will begin. There's something I want to say to you: Helmer's sensitive nature is repelled by anything ugly. I couldn't bear to have him near me when—

NORA: But Doctor Rank—

RANK: No, I couldn't bear it! I won't have him there—I shall bar my door against him— As soon as I am absolutely certain of the worst, I'll send you my visiting-card marked with a black cross; that will mean the final horror has begun.

NORA: Doctor Rank—you're absolutely impossible today! And I did so want you to be in a good humor.

RANK: With death staring me in the face? And why should I have to expiate another's sins! What justice is there in that? Well—I suppose in almost every family there are some such debts that have to be paid.

NORA [*Stopping her ears*]: Don't talk such nonsense! Come along! Cheer up!

RANK: One might as well laugh. It's really very funny when you come to think of it—that my poor innocent spine should be made to suffer for my father's exploits!

NORA [*At table, left*]: He was much addicted to asparagus-tips and paté de foie gras, wasn't he?

RANK: Yes; and truffles.

NORA: Oh, of course—truffles, yes. And I suppose oysters too?

RANK: Oh, yes! Masses of oysters, certainly!

NORA: And all the wine and champagne that went with them! It does seem a shame that all these pleasant things should be so damaging to the spine, doesn't it?

RANK: Especially when it's a poor miserable spine that never had any of the fun!

NORA: Yes, that's the biggest shame of all!

RANK [*Gives her a searching look*]: H'm—

NORA [*A moment later*]: Why did you smile?

RANK: No; you were the one that laughed.

NORA: No; you were the one that smiled, Doctor Rank!

RANK [*Gets up*]: You're more of a rogue than I thought you were.

NORA: I'm full of mischief today.

RANK: So it seems.

NORA [*With her hands on his shoulders*]: Dear, dear Doctor Rank, don't go and die and leave Torvald and me.

RANK: Oh, you won't miss me long! Those who go away—are soon forgotten.

NORA [*Looks at him anxiously*]: You really believe that?

RANK: People develop new interests, and soon—

NORA: What do you mean—new interests?

RANK: That'll happen to you and Helmer when I am gone. You seem to have made a good start already. What was that Mrs. Linde doing here last evening?

NORA: You're surely not jealous of poor old Kristine!

RANK: Yes, I am. She will be my successor in this house. When I'm gone she'll probably—

NORA: Sh—hh! She's in there.

RANK: She's here again today? You see!

NORA: She's just helping me with my costume. Good heavens, you *are* in an unreasonable mood! [*Sits on sofa*] Now do try to be good, Doctor Rank. Tomorrow you'll see how beautifully I'll dance; and then you can pretend I'm doing it all to please you—and Torvald too, of course—that's understood.

RANK [*After a short silence*]: You know—sitting here talking to you so informally—I simply can't imagine what would have become of me, if I had never had this house to come to.

NORA [*Smiling*]: You really *do* feel at home with us, don't you?

RANK [*In a low voice—looking straight before him*]: And to be obliged to leave it all—

NORA: Nonsense! You're not going to leave anything.

RANK [*In the same tone*]: And not to be able to leave behind one even the smallest proof of gratitude; at most a fleeting regret—an empty place to be filled by the first person who comes along.

NORA: And supposing I were to ask you for—? No—

RANK: For what?

NORA: For a great proof of your friendship.

RANK: Yes?—Yes?

NORA: No, I mean—if I were to ask you to do me a really tremendous favor—

RANK: You'd really, for once, give me that great happiness?

NORA: Oh, but you don't know what it is.

RANK: Then tell me.

NORA: I don't think I can, Doctor Rank. It's much too much to ask—it's not just a favor—I need your help and advice as well—

RANK: So much the better. I've no conception of what you mean. But tell me about it. You trust me, don't you?

NORA: More than anyone. I know you are my best and truest friend—that's why I can tell you. Well then, Doctor Rank, there is something you must help me prevent. You know how deeply, how intensely Torvald loves me; he wouldn't hesitate for a moment to give up his life for my sake.

RANK [*Bending towards her*]: Nora—do you think he is the only one who—?

NORA [*With a slight start*]: Who—what?

RANK: Who would gladly give his life for you?

NORA [*Sadly*]: I see.

RANK: I was determined that you should know this before I—went away. There'll never be a better chance to tell you. Well, Nora, now you know, and you must know too that you can trust me as you can no one else.

NORA [*Standing up; simply and calmly*]: Let me get by—

RANK [*Makes way for her, but remains sitting*]: Nora—

NORA [*In the doorway*]: Bring in the lamp, Helene. [*Crosses to the stove*] Oh, dear Doctor Rank, that was really horrid of you.

RANK [*Rising*]: To love you just as deeply as—as someone else does; is that horrid?

NORA: No—but the fact of your telling me. There was no need to do that.

RANK: What do you mean? Did you know—?

[HELENE *enters with the lamp; sets it on the table and goes out again.*]

RANK: Nora—Mrs. Helmer—tell me, did you know?

NORA: Oh, how do I know what I knew or didn't know. I really can't say— How could you be so clumsy, Doctor Rank? It was all so nice.

RANK: Well, at any rate, you know now that I stand ready to serve you body and soul. So—tell me.

NORA [*Looking at him*]: After this?

RANK: I beg you to tell me what it is.

NORA: I can't tell you anything now.

RANK: But you must! Don't punish me like that! Let me be of use to you; I'll do anything for you—anything within human power.

NORA: You can do nothing for me now. Anyway—I don't really need help. I was just imagining things, you see. Really! That's all it was! [*Sits in the rocking chair, looks at him and smiles*] Well—you're a nice one, Doctor Rank! Aren't you a bit ashamed, now that the lamp's been lit?

RANK: No; really not. But I suppose I'd better go now—for good?

NORA: You'll do no such thing! You must come here just as you always have. Torvald could never get on without you!

RANK: But how about *you?*

NORA: You know I always love to have you here.

RANK: Yes—I suppose that's what misled me. I can't quite make you out. I've often felt you liked being with me almost as much as being with Helmer.

NORA: Well—you see— There are the people one loves best—and yet there are others one would almost rather *be* with.

RANK: Yes—there's something in that.

NORA: When I was still at home, it was of course Papa whom I loved best. And yet whenever I could, I used to slip down to the servants' quarters. I loved being with them. To begin with, they never lectured me a bit, and it was such fun to hear them talk.

RANK: I see; and now you have me instead!

NORA [*Jumps up and hurries toward him*]: Oh, dear, darling Doctor Rank. I didn't mean it like that! It's just that now, Torvald comes first—the way Papa did. *You* understand—!

[*HELENE enters from the hall.*]

HELENE: I beg your pardon, Ma'am— [*Whispers to NORA, and gives her a card.*]

NORA [*Glancing at card*]: Ah! [*Puts it in her pocket.*]

RANK: Anything wrong?

NORA: No, nothing! It's just—it's my new costume—

RANK: Isn't that your costume—there?

NORA: Oh, that one, yes. But this is a different one. It's one I've ordered—Torvald mustn't know—

RANK: So *that's* the great secret!

NORA: Yes, of course it is! Go in and see him, will you? He's in his study. Be sure and keep him there as long as—

RANK: Don't worry; he shan't escape me. [*Goes into HELMER's room.*]

NORA [*To HELENE*]: He's waiting in the kitchen?

HELENE: Yes, he came up the back stairs—

NORA: Why didn't you tell him I was busy?

HELENE: I did, but he insisted.

NORA: He won't go away?

HELENE: Not until he has spoken to you, Ma'am.

NORA: Very well, then; show him in; but quietly, Helene—and don't say a word to anyone; it's about a surprise for my husband.

HELENE: I understand, Ma'am. [*She goes out.*]

NORA: It's coming! It's going to happen after all! No, no! It can't happen. It *can't!* [*She goes to HELMER's door and locks it. HELENE opens the hall door for KROGSTAD, and shuts it after him. He wears a traveling-coat, boots, and a fur cap.*]

NORA [*Goes towards him*]: Talk quietly; my husband is at home.

KROGSTAD: What's that to me?

NORA: What is it you want?

KROGSTAD: I want to make sure of something.

NORA: Well—what is it? Quickly!

KROGSTAD: I suppose you know I've been dismissed.

NORA: I couldn't prevent it, Mr. Krogstad. I did everything in my power, but it was useless.

KROGSTAD: So that's all your husband cares about you! He must realize what I can put you through, and yet, in spite of that, he dares to—

NORA: You don't imagine my husband knows about it?

KROGSTAD: No—I didn't really suppose he did. I can't imagine my friend Torvald Helmer showing that much courage.

NORA: I insist that you show respect when speaking of my husband, Mr. Krogstad!

KROGSTAD: With all due respect, I assure you! But am I right in thinking—since you are so anxious to keep the matter secret—that you have a clearer idea today than you had yesterday, of what you really did?

NORA: Clearer than *you* could ever give me!

KROGSTAD: Of course! I who know so little about the law—!

NORA: What do you want of me?

KROGSTAD: I just wanted to see how you were getting on, Mrs. Helmer. I've been thinking about you all day. You see—even a mere money-lender, a cheap journalist—in short, someone like me—is not entirely without feeling.

NORA: Then prove it; think of my little children.

KROGSTAD: Did you or your husband think of mine? But that's not the point. I only wanted to tell you not to take this matter too seriously. I shan't take any action—for the present, at least.

NORA: You won't, will you? I was sure you wouldn't!

KROGSTAD: It can all be settled quite amicably. It needn't be made public. It needn't go beyond us three.

NORA: But, my husband must never know.

KROGSTAD: How can you prevent it? Can you pay off the balance?

NORA: No, not immediately.

KROGSTAD: Have you any way of raising the money within the next few days?

NORA: None—that I will make use of.

KROGSTAD: And if you had, it would have made no difference. Even if you were to offer me the entire sum in cash—I still wouldn't give you back your note.

NORA: What are you going to do with it?

KROGSTAD: I shall simply keep it—I shall guard it carefully. No one, outside the three of us, shall know a thing about it. So, if you have any thought of doing something desperate—

NORA: I shall.

KROGSTAD: —of running away from home, for instance—

NORA: I shall!

KROGSTAD: —or perhaps even something worse—

NORA: How could you guess that?

KROGSTAD: —then put all such thoughts out of your head.

NORA: How did you know that I had thought of *that?*

KROGSTAD: Most of us think of *that*, at first. I thought of it, too; but I didn't have the courage—

NORA [*Tonelessly*]: I haven't either.

KROGSTAD [*Relieved*]: No; you haven't the courage for it either, have you?

NORA: No! I haven't, I haven't!

KROGSTAD: Besides, it would be a very foolish thing to do. You'll just have to get through one domestic storm—and then it'll all be over. I have a letter for your husband, here in my pocket—

NORA: Telling him all about it?

KROGSTAD: Sparing you as much as possible.

NORA [*Quickly*]: He must never read that letter. Tear it up, Mr. Krogstad! I will manage to get the money somehow—

KROGSTAD: Excuse me, Mrs. Helmer, but I thought I just told you—

NORA: Oh, I'm not talking about the money I owe you. Just tell me how much money you want from my husband—I will get it somehow!

KROGSTAD: I want no money from your husband.

NORA: What *do* you want then?

KROGSTAD: Just this: I want a new start; I want to make something of myself; and your husband shall help me do it. For the past eighteen months my conduct has been irreproachable. It's been a hard struggle—I've lived in abject poverty; still, I was content to work my way up gradually, step by step. But now I've been kicked out, and now I shall not be satisfied to be merely reinstated—taken back on sufferance. I'm determined to make something of myself, I tell you. I intend to continue working in the Bank—but I expect to be promoted. Your husband shall create a new position for me—

NORA: He'll never do it!

KROGSTAD: Oh, yes he will; I know him—he'll do it without a murmur; he wouldn't dare do otherwise. And then—you'll see! Within a year I'll be his right hand man. It'll be Nils Krogstad, not Torvald Helmer, who'll run the Joint Stock Bank.

NORA: That will never happen.

KROGSTAD: No? Would you, perhaps—?

NORA: Yes! I have the courage for it now.

KROGSTAD: You don't frighten me! A dainty, pampered little lady such as you—

NORA: You'll see, you'll see!

KROGSTAD: Yes, I dare say! How would you like to lie there under the ice—in that freezing, pitch-black water? And in the spring your body would be found floating on the surface—hideous, hairless, unrecognizable—

NORA: You can't frighten me!

KROGSTAD: You can't frighten me either. People don't do that sort of thing, Mrs. Helmer. And, anyway, what would be the use? I'd still have your husband in my power.

NORA: You mean—afterwards? Even if I were no longer—?

KROGSTAD: Remember—I'd still have your reputation in my hands! [NORA *stands speechless and looks at him*] Well, I've given you fair warning. I wouldn't do anything foolish, if I were you. As soon as Helmer receives my letter, I shall expect to hear from him. And just remember this: I've been forced back into my former way of life—and your husband is responsible. I shall never forgive him for it. Good-bye, Mrs. Helmer.

[*Goes out through the hall.* NORA *hurries to the door, opens it a little, and listens.*]

NORA: He's gone. He didn't leave the letter. Of course he didn't—that would be impossible! [*Opens the door further and further*] What's he doing? He's stopped outside the door. He's not going down the stairs. Has he changed his mind? Is he—? [*A letter falls into the box.* KROGSTAD'*s footsteps are heard gradually receding down the stairs.* NORA *utters a suppressed shriek, and rushes forward towards the sofa table; pause*] It's in the letter-box! [*Slips shrinkingly up to the hall door*] It's there!— Torvald, Torvald—now we are lost!

[MRS. LINDE *enters from the left with the costume.*]

MRS. LINDE: There, I think it's all right now. If you'll just try it on—?

NORA [*Hoarsely and softly*]: Come here, Kristine.

MRS. LINDE [*Throws down the dress on the sofa*]: What's the matter with you? You look upset.

NORA: Come here. Do you see that letter? Do you see it—in the letter-box?

MRS. LINDE: Yes, yes, I see it.

NORA: It's from Krogstad—

MRS. LINDE: Nora—you don't mean Krogstad lent you the money!

NORA: Yes; and now Torvald will know everything.

MRS. LINDE: It'll be much the best thing for you both, Nora.

NORA: But you don't know everything. I committed forgery—

MRS. LINDE: Good heavens!

NORA: Now, listen to me, Kristine; I want you to be my witness—

MRS. LINDE: How do you mean "witness"? What am I to—?

NORA: If I should go out of my mind—that might easily happen—

MRS. LINDE: Nora!

NORA: Or if something should happen to me—something that would prevent my being here—!

MRS. LINDE: Nora, Nora, you're quite beside yourself!

NORA: In case anyone else should insist on taking all the blame upon himself—the whole blame—you understand—

MRS. LINDE: Yes, but what makes you think—?

NORA: Then you must bear witness to the fact that that isn't true. I'm in my right mind now; I know exactly what I'm saying; and I tell you nobody else knew anything about it; I did the whole thing on my own. Just remember that.

MRS. LINDE: Very well—I will. But I don't understand at all.

NORA: No—of course—you couldn't. It's the wonderful thing—It's about to happen, don't you see?

MRS. LINDE: What "wonderful thing"?

NORA: The wonderful—wonderful thing! But it must never be allowed to happen—never. It would be too terrible.

MRS. LINDE: I'll go and talk to Krogstad at once.

NORA: No, don't go to him! He might do you some harm.

MRS. LINDE: There was a time—he would have done anything in the world for me.

NORA: He?

MRS. LINDE: Where does he live?

NORA: How do I know—? Yes— [*Feels in her pocket*] Here's his card. But the letter, the letter—!

HELMER [*From his study; knocking on the door*]: Nora!

NORA [*Shrieks in terror*]: Oh! What is it? What do you want?

HELMER: Don't be frightened! We're not coming in; anyway, you've locked the door. Are you trying on?

NORA: Yes, yes, I'm trying on. I'm going to look so pretty, Torvald.

MRS. LINDE [*Who has read the card*]: He lives just round the corner.

NORA: But it won't do any good. It's too late now. The letter is in the box.

MRS. LINDE: I suppose your husband has the key?

NORA: Of course.

MRS. LINDE: Krogstad must ask for his letter back, unread. He must make up some excuse—

NORA: But this is the time that Torvald usually—

MRS. LINDE: Prevent him. Keep him occupied. I'll come back as quickly as I can. [*She goes out hastily by the hall door.*]

NORA [*Opens* HELMER's *door and peeps in*]: Torvald!

HELMER [*In the study*]: Well? May one venture to come back into one's own living-room? Come along, Rank—now we shall see— [*In the doorway*] Why—what's this?

NORA: What, Torvald dear?

HELMER: Rank led me to expect some wonderful disguise.

RANK [*In the doorway*]: That's what I understood. I must have been mistaken.

NORA: Not till tomorrow evening! Then I shall appear in all my splendor!

HELMER: But you look quite tired, Nora, dear. I'm afraid you've been practicing too hard.

NORA: Oh, I haven't practiced at all yet.

HELMER: You ought to, though—

NORA: Yes—I really should, Torvald! But I can't seem to manage without your help. I'm afraid I've forgotten all about it.

HELMER: Well—we'll see what we can do. It'll soon come back to you.

NORA: You will help me, won't you, Torvald? Promise! I feel so nervous—all those people! You must concentrate on me this evening—forget all about business. *Please*, Torvald, dear—promise me you will!

HELMER: I promise. This evening I'll be your slave—you sweet, helpless little thing—! Just one moment, though—I want to see— [*Going to hall door.*]

NORA: What do you want out there?

HELMER: I just want to see if there are any letters.

NORA: Oh, don't, Torvald! Don't bother about that now!

HELMER: Why not?

NORA: *Please* don't, Torvald! There aren't any.

HELMER: Just let me take a look— [*Starts to go.*]

[NORA, *at the piano, plays the first bars of the tarantella.*]

HELMER [*Stops in the doorway*]: Aha!

NORA: I shan't be able to dance tomorrow if I don't rehearse with you!

HELMER [*Going to her*]: Are you really so nervous, Nora, dear?

NORA: Yes, I'm terrified! Let's rehearse right away. We've plenty of time before dinner. Sit down and play for me, Torvald, dear; direct me—guide me; you know how you do!

HELMER: With pleasure, my darling, if you wish me to. [*Sits at piano.*]

[NORA *snatches the tambourine out of the box, and hurriedly drapes herself in a long parti-colored shawl; then, with a bound, stands in the middle of the floor and cries out.*]

NORA: Now play for me! Now I'll dance!

[HELMER *plays and* NORA *dances.* RANK *stands at the piano behind* HELMER *and looks on.*]

HELMER [*Playing*]: Too fast! Too fast!

NORA: I can't help it!

HELMER: Don't be so violent, Nora!

NORA: That's the way it *should* be!

HELMER [*Stops*]: No, no; this won't do at all!

NORA [*Laughs and swings her tambourine*]: You see? What did I tell you?

RANK: I'll play for her.

HELMER [*Rising*]: Yes, do—then I'll be able to direct her.

[RANK *sits down at the piano and plays;* NORA *dances more and more wildly.* HELMER *stands by the stove and addresses frequent corrections to her; she seems not to hear. Her hair breaks loose, and falls over her shoulders. She does not notice it, but goes on dancing.* MRS. LINDE *enters and stands spellbound in the doorway.*]

MRS. LINDE: Ah—!

NORA [*Dancing*]: We're having such fun, Kristine!

HELMER: Why, Nora, dear, you're dancing as if your life were at stake!

NORA: It is! It is!

HELMER: Rank, stop! This is absolute madness. Stop, I say!

[RANK *stops playing, and* NORA *comes to a sudden standstill.*]

HELMER [*Going toward her*]: I never would have believed it. You've forgotten everything I ever taught you.

NORA [*Throws the tambourine away*]: I told you I had!

HELMER: This needs an immense amount of work.

NORA: That's what I said; you see how important it is! You must work with me up to the very last minute. Will you promise me, Torvald?

HELMER: I most certainly will!

NORA: This evening and all day tomorrow you must think of nothing but me. You mustn't open a single letter—mustn't even *look* at the mail-box.

HELMER: Nora! I believe you're still worried about that wretched man—

NORA: Yes—yes, I am!

HELMER: Nora— Look at me—there's a letter from him in the box, isn't there?

NORA: Maybe—I don't know; I believe there is. But you're not to read anything of that sort now; nothing must come between us until the party's over.

RANK [*Softly, to* HELMER]: Don't go against her.

HELMER [*Putting his arm around her*]: Very well! The child shall have her way. But tomorrow night, when your dance is over—

NORA: Then you'll be free.

[HELENE *appears in the doorway, right.*]

HELENE: Dinner is served, Ma'am.

NORA: We'll have champagne, Helene.

HELENE: Very good, Ma'am. [*Goes out.*]

HELMER: Quite a feast, I see!

NORA: Yes—a real feast! We'll stay up till dawn drinking champagne! [*Calling out*] Oh, and we'll have macaroons, Helene—lots of them! Why not—for once!

HELMER [*Seizing her hand*]: Come, come! Not so violent! Be my own little lark again.

NORA: I will, Torvald. But now—both of you go in—while Kristine helps me with my hair.

RANK [*Softly, as they go*]: Is anything special the matter? I mean—anything—?

HELMER: No, no; nothing at all. It's just this childish fear I was telling you about. [*They go out to the right.*]

NORA: Well?

MRS. LINDE: He's gone out of town.

NORA: I saw it in your face.

MRS. LINDE: He'll be back tomorrow evening. I left a note for him.

NORA: You shouldn't have bothered. You couldn't prevent it anyway. After all, there's a kind of joy in waiting for the wonderful thing to happen.

MRS. LINDE: I don't understand. What *is* this thing you're waiting for?

NORA: I can't explain. Go in and join them. I'll be there in a moment.

[MRS. LINDE *goes into the dining room.* NORA *stands for a moment as though pulling herself together; then looks at her watch.*]

NORA: Five o'clock. Seven hours till midnight. Twenty-four hours till the next midnight and then the tarantella will be over. Twenty-four and seven? I've thirty-one hours left to live.

[HELMER *appears at the door, right.*]

HELMER: Well! What has become of the little lark?

NORA [*Runs to him with open arms*]: Here she is!

[*Curtain*]

ACT 3

The same room. The table, with the chairs around it, has been moved to stage-center. A lighted lamp on the table. The hall door is open. Dance music is heard from the floor above. MRS. LINDE *sits by the table absent-mindedly turning the pages of a book. She tries to read, but seems unable to keep her mind on it. Now and then she listens intently and glances towards the hall door.*

MRS. LINDE [*Looks at her watch*]: Where can he be? The time is nearly up. I hope he hasn't— [*Listens again*] Here he is now. [*She goes into the hall and cautiously opens the outer door; cautious footsteps are heard on the stairs; she whispers*] Come in; there is no one here.

KROGSTAD [*In the doorway*]: I found a note from you at home. What does it mean?

MRS. LINDE: I simply *must* speak to you.

KROGSTAD: Indeed? But why here? Why in this house?

MRS. LINDE: I couldn't see you at my place. My room has no separate entrance. Come in; we're quite alone. The servants are asleep, and the Helmers are upstairs at a party.

KROGSTAD [*Coming into the room*]: Well, well! So the Helmers are dancing tonight, are they?

MRS. LINDE: Why shouldn't they?

KROGSTAD: Well—why not!

MRS. LINDE: Let's have a talk, Krogstad.

KROGSTAD: Have we two anything to talk about?

MRS. LINDE: Yes. A great deal.

KROGSTAD: I shouldn't have thought so.

MRS. LINDE: But then, you see—you have never really understood me.

KROGSTAD: There wasn't much to understand, was there? A woman is heartless enough to break off with a man, when a better match is offered; it's quite an ordinary occurrence.

MRS. LINDE: You really think me heartless? Did you think it was so easy for me?

KROGSTAD: Wasn't it?

MRS. LINDE: You really believed that, Krogstad?

KROGSTAD: If not, why should you have written to me as you did?

MRS. LINDE: What else could I do? Since I was forced to break with you, I felt it was only right to try and kill your love for me.

KROGSTAD [*Clenching his hands together*]: So that was it! And you did this for money!

MRS. LINDE: Don't forget I had my mother and two little brothers to think of. We couldn't wait for you, Krogstad; things were so unsettled for you then.

KROGSTAD: That may be; but, even so, you had no right to throw me over—not even for their sake.

MRS. LINDE: Who knows? I've often wondered whether I did right or not.

KROGSTAD [*More softly*]: When I had lost you, I felt the ground crumble beneath my feet. Look at me. I'm like a shipwrecked man clinging to a raft.

MRS. LINDE: Help may be nearer than you think.

KROGSTAD: Help was here! Then you came and stood in the way.

MRS. LINDE: I knew nothing about it, Krogstad. I didn't know until today that I was to replace *you* at the Bank.

KROGSTAD: Very well—I believe you. But now that you do know, will you withdraw?

MRS. LINDE: No; I'd do you no good by doing that.

KROGSTAD: "Good" or not—I'd withdraw all the same.

MRS. LINDE: I have learnt to be prudent, Krogstad—I've had to. The bitter necessities of life have taught me that.

KROGSTAD: And life has taught me not to believe in phrases.

MRS. LINDE: Then life has taught you a very wise lesson. But what about deeds? Surely you must still believe in them?

KROGSTAD: How do you mean?

MRS. LINDE: You just said you were like a shipwrecked man, clinging to a raft.

KROGSTAD: I have good reason to say so.

MRS. LINDE: Well—I'm like a shipwrecked *woman* clinging to a raft. I have no one to mourn for, no one to care for.

KROGSTAD: You made your choice.

MRS. LINDE: I *had* no choice, I tell you!

KROGSTAD: What then?

MRS. LINDE: Since we're both of us shipwrecked, couldn't we join forces, Krogstad?
KROGSTAD: You don't mean—?
MRS. LINDE: Two people on a raft have a better chance than one.
KROGSTAD: Kristine!
MRS. LINDE: Why do you suppose I came here to the city?
KROGSTAD: You mean—you thought of me?
MRS. LINDE: I can't live without work; all my life I've worked, as far back as I can
   remember; it's always been my one great joy. Now I'm quite alone in the world;
   my life is empty—aimless. There's not much joy in working for one's self. You
   could help me, Nils; you could give me something and someone to work for.
KROGSTAD: I can't believe all this. It's an hysterical impulse—a woman's exaggerated
   craving for self-sacrifice.
MRS. LINDE: When have you ever found me hysterical?
KROGSTAD: You'd really be willing to do this? Tell me honestly—do you quite
   realize what my past has been?
MRS. LINDE: Yes.
KROGSTAD: And you know what people think of me?
MRS. LINDE: Didn't you just say you'd have been a different person if you'd been
   with me?
KROGSTAD: I'm sure of it.
MRS. LINDE: Mightn't that still be true?
KROGSTAD: You really mean this, Kristine, don't you? I can see it in your face. Are
   you sure you have the courage—?
MRS. LINDE: I need someone to care for, and your children need a mother. We two
   need each other, Nils. I have faith in your fundamental goodness. I'm not afraid.
KROGSTAD [*Seizing her hands*]: Thank you—thank you, Kristine. I'll make others
   believe in me too—I won't fail you! But—I'd almost forgotten—
MRS. LINDE [*Listening*]: Hush! The tarantella! You must go!
KROGSTAD: Why? What is it?
MRS. LINDE: Listen! She's begun her dance; as soon as she's finished dancing, they'll
   be down.
KROGSTAD: Yes—I'd better go. There'd have been no need for all that—but, of
   course, you don't know what I've done about the Helmers.
MRS. LINDE: Yes, I do, Nils.
KROGSTAD: And yet you have the courage to—?
MRS. LINDE: I know you were desperate—I understand.
KROGSTAD: I'd give anything to undo it!
MRS. LINDE: You can. Your letter's still in the mail-box.
KROGSTAD: Are you sure?
MRS. LINDE: Quite, but—
KROGSTAD [*Giving her a searching look*]: Could that be it? You're doing all this to save
   your friend? You might as well be honest with me! Is that it?
MRS. LINDE: I sold myself once for the sake of others, Nils; I'm not likely to do it
   again.
KROGSTAD: I'll ask for my letter back unopened.
MRS. LINDE: No, no.
KROGSTAD: Yes, of course. I'll wait till Helmer comes; I'll tell him to give me back
   the letter—I'll say it refers to my dismissal—and ask him not to read it—
MRS. LINDE: No, Nils; don't ask for it back.
KROGSTAD: But wasn't that actually your reason for getting me to come here?
MRS. LINDE: Yes, in my first moment of fear. But that was twenty-four hours
   ago, and since then I've seen incredible things happening here. Helmer must

know the truth; this wretched business must no longer be kept secret; it's time those two came to a thorough understanding; there's been enough deceit and subterfuge.

KROGSTAD: Very well, if you like to risk it. But there's one thing I can do, and at once—

MRS. LINDE [*Listening*]: You must go now. Make haste! The dance is over; we're not safe here another moment.

KROGSTAD: I'll wait for you downstairs.

MRS. LINDE: Yes, do; then you can see me home.

KROGSTAD: Kristine! I've never been so happy! [KROGSTAD *goes out by the outer door. The door between the room and the hall remains open.*]

MRS. LINDE [*Arranging the room and getting her outdoor things together*]: How different things will be! Someone to work for, to live for; a home to make happy! How wonderful it will be to try!—I wish they'd come— [*Listens*] Here they are! I'll get my coat— [*Takes bonnet and cloak.* HELMER's *and* NORA's *voices are heard outside, a key is turned in the lock, and* HELMER *drags* NORA *almost by force into the hall. She wears the Italian costume with a large black shawl over it. He is in evening dress and wears a black domino,*[2] *open.*]

NORA [*Struggling with him in the doorway*]: No, no! I don't want to come home; I want to go upstairs again; I don't want to leave so early!

HELMER: Come—Nora dearest!

NORA: I beg you, Torvald! Please, *please*—just one hour more!

HELMER: Not one single minute more, Nora darling; don't you remember our agreement? Come along in, now; you'll catch cold.

[*He leads her gently into the room in spite of her resistance.*]

MRS. LINDE: Good evening.

NORA: Kristine!

HELMER: Why, Mrs. Linde! What are you doing here so late?

MRS. LINDE: Do forgive me. I did so want to see Nora in her costume.

NORA: Have you been waiting for me all this time?

MRS. LINDE: Yes; I came too late to catch you before you went upstairs, and I didn't want to go away without seeing you.

HELMER [*Taking* NORA's *shawl off*]: And you *shall* see her, Mrs. Linde! She's worth looking at I can tell you! Isn't she lovely?

MRS. LINDE: Oh, Nora! How perfectly—!

HELMER: Absolutely exquisite, isn't she? That's what everybody said. But she's obstinate as a mule, is my sweet little thing! I don't know what to do with her. Will you believe it, Mrs. Linde, I had to drag her away by force?

NORA: You'll see—you'll be sorry, Torvald, you didn't let me stay, if only for another half-hour.

HELMER: Do you hear that, Mrs. Linde? Now, listen to this: She danced her tarantella to wild applause, and she deserved it, too, I must say—though, perhaps, from an artistic point of view, her interpretation was a bit too realistic. But never mind—the point is, she made a great success, a phenomenal success. Now— should I have allowed her to stay on and spoil the whole effect? Certainly not! I took my sweet little Capri girl—my capricious little Capri girl, I might say—in my arms; a rapid whirl round the room, a low curtsey to all sides, and—as they say in novels—the lovely apparition vanished! An exit should always be effective,

---

[2]A long cloak worn with a mask to a masquerade.

Mrs. Linde; but I can't get Nora to see that. Phew! It's warm here. [*Throws his domino on a chair and opens the door to his room*] Why—there's no light on in here! Oh no, of course— Excuse me— [*Goes in and lights candles.*]

NORA [*Whispers breathlessly*]: Well?

MRS. LINDE [*Softly*]: I've spoken to him.

NORA: And—?

MRS. LINDE: Nora—you must tell your husband everything—

NORA [*Tonelessly*]: I knew it!

MRS. LINDE: You have nothing to fear from Krogstad; but you must speak out.

NORA: I shan't.

MRS. LINDE: Then the letter will.

NORA: Thank you, Kristine. Now I know what I must do. Hush—!

HELMER [*Coming back*]: Well, have you finished admiring her, Mrs. Linde?

MRS. LINDE: Yes, and now I must say good-night.

HELMER: Oh—must you be going already? Does this knitting belong to you?

MRS. LINDE [*Takes it*]: Oh, thank you; I almost forgot it.

HELMER: So you knit, do you?

MRS. LINDE: Yes.

HELMER: Why don't you do embroidery instead?

MRS. LINDE: Why?

HELMER: Because it's so much prettier. Now watch! You hold the embroidery in the left hand—so—and then, in the right hand, you hold the needle, and guide it—so—in a long graceful curve—isn't that right?

MRS. LINDE: Yes, I suppose so—

HELMER: Whereas, knitting can never be anything but ugly. Now, watch! Arms close to your sides, needles going up and down—there's something Chinese about it!— That really was splendid champagne they gave us.

MRS. LINDE: Well, good-night, Nora; don't be obstinate any more.

HELMER: Well said, Mrs. Linde!

MRS. LINDE: Good-night, Mr. Helmer.

HELMER [*Accompanying her to the door*]: Good-night, good-night; I hope you get home safely. I'd be only too glad to—but you've such a short way to go. Good-night, good-night. [*She goes;* HELMER *shuts the door after her and comes forward again*] Well—thank God we've got rid of her; she's a dreadful bore, that woman.

NORA: You must be tired, Torvald.

HELMER: I? Not in the least.

NORA: But, aren't you sleepy?

HELMER: Not a bit. On the contrary, I feel exceedingly lively. But what about you? You seem to be very tired and sleepy.

NORA: Yes, I am very tired. But I'll soon sleep now.

HELMER: You see! I was right not to let you stay there any longer.

NORA: Everything you do is always right, Torvald.

HELMER [*Kissing her forehead*]: There's my sweet, sensible little lark! By the way, did you notice how gay Rank was this evening?

NORA: Was he? I didn't get a chance to speak to him.

HELMER: I didn't either, really; but it's a long time since I've seen him in such a jolly mood. [*Gazes at* NORA *for a while, then comes nearer her*] It's so lovely to be home again—to be here alone with you. You glorious, fascinating creature!

NORA: Don't look at me like that, Torvald.

HELMER: Why shouldn't I look at my own dearest treasure?—at all this loveliness that is mine, wholly and utterly mine—mine alone!

NORA [*Goes to the other side of the table*]: You mustn't talk to me like that tonight.

HELMER [*Following*]: You're still under the spell of the tarantella—and it makes you even more desirable. Listen! The other guests are leaving now. [*More softly*] Soon the whole house will be still, Nora.

NORA: I hope so.

HELMER: Yes, you do, don't you, my beloved. Do you know something—when I'm out with you among a lot of people—do you know why it is I hardly speak to you, why I keep away from you, and only occasionally steal a quick glance at you; do you know why that is? It's because I pretend that we love each other in secret, that we're secretly engaged, and that no one suspects there is anything between us.

NORA: Yes, yes; I know your thoughts are always round me.

HELMER: Then, when it's time to leave, and I put your shawl round your smooth, soft, young shoulders—round that beautiful neck of yours—I pretend that you are my young bride, that we've just come from the wedding, and that I'm taking you home for the first time—that for the first time I shall be alone with you—quite alone with you, in all your tremulous beauty. All evening I have been filled with longing for you. As I watched you swaying and whirling in the tarantella—my pulses began to throb until I thought I should go mad; that's why I carried you off—made you leave so early—

NORA: Please go, Torvald! Please leave me. I don't want you like this.

HELMER: What do you mean? You're teasing me, aren't you, little Nora? Not want me—! Aren't I your husband—?

[*A knock at the outer door.*]

NORA [*Starts*]: Listen—!

HELMER [*Going toward the hall*]: Who is it?

RANK [*Outside*]: It is I; may I come in a moment?

HELMER [*In a low tone, annoyed*]: Why does he have to bother us now! [*Aloud*] Just a second! [*Opens door*] Well! How nice of you to look in.

RANK: I heard your voice, and I thought I'd like to stop in a minute. [*Looks round*] These dear old rooms! You must be so cozy and happy here, you two!

HELMER: I was just saying how gay and happy you seemed to be, upstairs.

RANK: Why not? Why shouldn't I be? One should get all one can out of life; all one can, for as long as one can. That wine was excellent—

HELMER: Especially the champagne.

RANK: You noticed that, did you? It's incredible how much I managed to get down.

NORA: Torvald drank plenty of it too.

RANK: Oh?

NORA: It always puts him in such a jolly mood.

RANK: Well, why shouldn't one have a jolly evening after a well-spent day?

HELMER: Well-spent! I'm afraid mine wasn't much to boast of!

RANK [*Slapping him on the shoulder*]: But mine was, you see?

NORA: Did you by any chance make a scientific investigation, Doctor Rank?

RANK: Precisely.

HELMER: Listen to little Nora, talking about scientific investigations!

NORA: Am I to congratulate you on the result?

RANK: By all means.

NORA: It was good then?

RANK: The best possible, both for the doctor and the patient—certainty.

NORA [*Quickly and searchingly*]: Certainty?

RANK: Absolute certainty. Wasn't I right to spend a jolly evening after that?

NORA: You were quite right, Doctor Rank.

HELMER: I quite agree! Provided you don't have to pay for it, tomorrow.

RANK: You don't get anything for nothing in this life.

NORA: You like masquerade parties, don't you, Dr. Rank?

RANK: Very much—when there are plenty of amusing disguises—

NORA: What shall we two be at our next masquerade?

HELMER: Listen to her! Thinking of the next party already!

RANK: We two? I'll tell you. You must go as a precious talisman.

HELMER: How on earth would you dress that!

RANK: That's easy. She'd only have to be herself.

HELMER: Charmingly put. But what about you? Have you decided what you'd be?

RANK: Oh, definitely.

HELMER: Well?

RANK: At the next masquerade party I shall be invisible.

HELMER: That's a funny notion!

RANK: There's a large black cloak—you've heard of the invisible cloak, haven't you? You've only to put it around you and no one can see you any more.

HELMER [*With a suppressed smile*]: Quite true!

RANK: But I almost forgot what I came for. Give me a cigar, will you, Helmer? One of the dark Havanas.

HELMER: Of course—with pleasure. [*Hands cigar case.*]

RANK [*Takes one and cuts the end off*]: Thanks.

NORA [*Striking a wax match*]: Let me give you a light.

RANK: I thank you. [*She holds the match. He lights his cigar at it*] And now, I'll say good-bye!

HELMER: Good-bye, good-bye, my dear fellow.

NORA: Sleep well, Doctor Rank.

RANK: Thanks for the wish.

NORA: Wish me the same.

RANK: You? Very well, since you ask me— Sleep well. And thanks for the light. [*He nods to them both and goes out.*]

HELMER [*In an undertone*]: He's had a lot to drink.

NORA [*Absently*]: I dare say. [HELMER *takes his bunch of keys from his pocket and goes into the hall*] Torvald! What do you want out there?

HELMER: I'd better empty the mail-box; it's so full there won't be room for the papers in the morning.

NORA: Are you going to work tonight?

HELMER: No—you know I'm not.—Why, what's this? Someone has been at the lock.

NORA: The lock—?

HELMER: Yes—that's funny! I shouldn't have thought that the maids would— Here's a broken hair-pin. Why—it's one of yours, Nora.

NORA [*Quickly*]: It must have been the children—

HELMER: You'll have to stop them doing that— There! I got it open at last. [*Takes contents out and calls out towards the kitchen*] Helene?—Oh, Helene; put out the lamp in the hall, will you? [*He returns with letters in his hand, and shuts the door to the hall*] Just look how they've stacked up. [*Looks through them*] Why, what's this?

NORA [*At the window*]: The letter! Oh, Torvald! No!

HELMER: Two visiting cards—from Rank.

NORA: From Doctor Rank?

HELMER [*Looking at them*]: Doctor Rank, physician. They were right on top. He must have stuck them in just now, as he left.

NORA: Is there anything on them?

HELMER: There's a black cross over his name. Look! What a gruesome thought. Just as if he were announcing his own death.

NORA: And so he is.

HELMER: What do you mean? What do you know about it? Did he tell you anything?

NORA: Yes. These cards mean that he has said good-bye to us for good. Now he'll lock himself up to die.

HELMER: Oh, my poor friend! I always knew he hadn't long to live, but I never dreamed it would be quite so soon—! And to hide away like a wounded animal—

NORA: When the time comes, it's best to go in silence. Don't you think so, Torvald?

HELMER [*Walking up and down*]: He'd become such a part of us. I can't imagine his having gone for good. With his suffering and loneliness he was like a dark, cloudy background to our lives—it made the sunshine of our happiness seem even brighter— Well, I suppose it's for the best—for him at any rate. [*Stands still*] And perhaps for us too, Nora. Now we are more than ever dependent on each other. [*Takes her in his arms*] Oh, my beloved wife! I can't seem to hold you close enough. Do you know something, Nora. I often wish you were in some great danger—so I could risk body and soul—my whole life—everything, everything, for your sake.

NORA [*Tears herself from him and says firmly*]: Now you must read your letters, Torvald.

HELMER: No, no; not tonight. I want to be with you, my beloved wife.

NORA: With the thought of your dying friend—?

HELMER: Of course— You are right. It's been a shock to both of us. A hideous shadow has come between us—thoughts of death and decay. We must try and throw them off. Until then—we'll stay apart.

NORA [*Her arms round his neck*]: Torvald! Good-night! Good-night!

HELMER [*Kissing her forehead*]: Good-night, my little song-bird. Sleep well! Now I'll go and read my letters. [*He goes with the letters in his hand into his room and shuts the door.*]

NORA [*With wild eyes, gropes about her, seizes* HELMER*'s domino, throws it round her, and whispers quickly, hoarsely, and brokenly*]: I'll never see him again. Never, never, never. [*Throws her shawl over her head*] I'll never see the children again. I'll never see them either—Oh the thought of that black, icy water! That fathomless—! If it were only over! He has it now; he's reading it. Oh, not yet—please! Not yet! Torvald, good-bye—! Good-bye to you and the children!

> [*She is rushing out by the hall; at the same moment* HELMER *flings his door open, and stands there with an open letter in his hand.*]

HELMER: Nora!

NORA [*Shrieks*]: Ah—!

HELMER: What does this mean? Do you know what is in this letter?

NORA: Yes, yes, I know. Let me go! Let me out!

HELMER [*Holds her back*]: Where are you going?

NORA [*Tries to break away from him*]: Don't try to save me, Torvald!

HELMER [*Falling back*]: So it's true! It's true what he writes? It's too horrible! It's impossible—it can't be true.

NORA: It *is* true. I've loved you more than all the world.

HELMER: Oh, come now! Let's have no silly nonsense!

NORA [*A step nearer him*]: Torvald—!

HELMER: Do you realize what you've done?

NORA: Let me go—I won't have you suffer for it! I won't have you take the blame!

HELMER: Will you stop this play-acting! [*Locks the outer door*] You'll stay here and give an account of yourself. Do you understand what you have done? Answer me! Do you understand it?

NORA [*Looks at him fixedly, and says with a stiffening expression*]: I think I'm beginning to understand for the first time.

HELMER [*Walking up and down*]: God! What an awakening! After eight years to discover that you who have been my pride and joy—are no better than a hypocrite, a liar—worse than that—a criminal! It's too horrible to think of! [*NORA says nothing, and continues to look fixedly at him*] I might have known what to expect. I should have foreseen it. You've inherited all your father's lack of principle—be silent!—all of your father's lack of principle, I say!—no religion, no moral code, no sense of duty. This is my punishment for shielding him! I did it for your sake; and this is my reward!

NORA: I see.

HELMER: You've destroyed my happiness. You've ruined my whole future. It's ghastly to think of! I'm completely in the power of this scoundrel; he can force me to do whatever he likes, demand whatever he chooses; order me about at will; and I shan't dare open my mouth! My entire career is to be wrecked and all because of a lawless, unprincipled woman!

NORA: If I were no longer alive, then you'd be free.

HELMER: Oh yes! You're full of histrionics! Your father was just the same. Even if you "weren't alive," as you put it, what good would that do me? None whatever! He could publish the story all the same; I might even be suspected of collusion. People might say I was behind it all—that I had prompted you to do it. And to think I have you to thank for all this—you whom I've done nothing but pamper and spoil since the day of our marriage. Now do you realize what you've done to me?

NORA [*With cold calmness*]: Yes.

HELMER: It's all so incredible, I can't grasp it. But we must try and come to some agreement. Take off that shawl. Take it off, I say! Of course, we must find some way to appease him—the matter must be hushed up at any cost. As far as we two are concerned, there must be no change in our way of life—in the eyes of the world, I mean. You'll naturally continue to live here. But you won't be allowed to bring up the children—I'd never dare trust them to you—God! to have to say this to the woman I've loved so tenderly— There can be no further thought of happiness between us. We must save what we can from the ruins—we can save appearances, at least— [*A ring; HELMER starts*] What can that be? At this hour! You don't suppose he—! Could he—? Hide yourself, Nora; say you are ill.

[*NORA stands motionless. HELMER goes to the door and opens it.*]

HELENE [*Half dressed, in the hall*]: It's a letter for Mrs. Helmer.

HELMER: Give it to me. [*Seizes the letter and shuts the door*] It's from him. I shan't give it to you. I'll read it myself.

NORA: Very well.

HELMER [*By the lamp*]: I don't dare open it; this may be the end—for both of us. Still—I must know. [*Hastily tears the letter open; reads a few lines, looks at an enclosure; with a cry of joy*] Nora! [*NORA looks inquiringly at him*] Nora!—I can't believe it—I must read it again. But it's true—it's really true! Nora, I am saved! I'm saved!

NORA: What about me?

HELMER: You too, of course; we are both of us saved, both of us. Look!—he's sent you back your note—he says he's sorry for what he did and apologizes for it—that due to a happy turn of events he— Oh, what does it matter what he says! We are saved, Nora! No one can harm you now. Oh, Nora, Nora—;

but let's get rid of this hateful thing. I'll just see— [*Glances at the I.O.U.*] No, no—I won't even look at it; I'll pretend it was all a horrible dream. [*Tears the I.O.U. and both letters in pieces. Throws them into the fire and watches them burn*] There! Now it's all over— He said in his letter you've known about this since Christmas Eve— you must have had three dreadful days, Nora!

NORA: Yes. It's been very hard.

HELMER: How you must have suffered! And you saw no way out but—No! We'll forget the whole ghastly business. We'll just thank God and repeat again and again: It's over; all over! Don't you understand, Nora? You don't seem to grasp it: It's over. What's the matter with you? Why do you look so grim? My poor darling little Nora, I understand; but you mustn't worry—because I've forgiven you, Nora; I swear I have; I've forgiven everything. You did what you did because you loved me—I see that now.

NORA: Yes—that's true.

HELMER: You loved me as a wife should love her husband. You didn't realize what you were doing—you weren't able to judge how wrong it was. Don't think this makes you any less dear to me. Just you lean on me; let me guide you and advise you; I'm not a man for nothing! There's something very endearing about a woman's helplessness. And try and forget those harsh things I said just now. I was frantic; my whole world seemed to be tumbling about my ears. Believe me, I've forgiven you, Nora—I swear it—I've forgiven everything.

NORA: Thank you for your forgiveness, Torvald. [*Goes out, to the right.*]

HELMER: No! Don't go. [*Looking through the doorway*] Why do you have to go in there?

NORA [*Inside*]: I want to get out of these fancy-dress clothes.

HELMER [*In the doorway*]: Yes, do, my darling. Try to calm down now, and get back to normal, my poor frightened little song-bird. Don't you worry—you'll be safe under my wings—they'll protect you. [*Walking up and down near the door*] How lovely our home is, Nora! You'll be sheltered here; I'll cherish you as if you were a little dove I'd rescued from the claws of some dreadful hawk. You'll see—your poor fluttering little heart will soon grow calm again. Tomorrow all this will appear in quite a different light—things will be just as they were. I won't have to keep on saying I've forgiven you—you'll be able to sense it. You don't really think I could ever drive you away, do you? That I could even so much as reproach you for anything? You'd understand if you could see into my heart. When a man forgives his wife whole-heartedly—as I have you—it fills him with such tenderness, such peace. She seems to belong to him in a double sense; it's as though he'd brought her to life again; she's become more than his wife—she's become his child as well. That's how it will be with us, Nora—my own bewildered, helpless little darling. From now on you mustn't worry about anything; just open your heart to me; just let me be both will and conscience to you. [NORA *enters in everyday dress*] What's all this? I thought you were going to bed. You've changed your dress?

NORA: Yes, Torvald; I've changed my dress.

HELMER: But what for? At this hour?

NORA: I shan't sleep tonight.

HELMER: But, Nora dear—

NORA [*Looking at her watch*]: It's not so very late— Sit down, Torvald; we have a lot to talk about. [*She sits at one side of the table.*]

HELMER: Nora—what does this mean? Why that stern expression?

NORA: Sit down. It'll take some time. I have a lot to say to you.

[HELMER *sits at the other side of the table.*]

HELMER: You frighten me, Nora. I don't understand you.

NORA: No, that's just it. You don't understand me; and I have never understood you either—until tonight. No, don't interrupt me. Just listen to what I have to say. This is to be a final settlement, Torvald.

HELMER: How do you mean?

NORA [*After a short silence*]: Doesn't anything special strike you as we sit here like this?

HELMER: I don't think so—why?

NORA: It doesn't occur to you, does it, that though we've been married for eight years, this is the first time that we two—man and wife—have sat down for a serious talk?

HELMER: What do you mean by serious?

NORA: During eight whole years, no—more than that—ever since the first day we met—we have never exchanged so much as one serious word about serious things.

HELMER: Why should I perpetually burden you with all my cares and problems? How could you possibly help me to solve them?

NORA: I'm not talking about cares and problems. I'm simply saying we've never once sat down seriously and tried to get to the bottom of anything.

HELMER: But, Nora, darling—why should you be concerned with serious thoughts?

NORA: That's the whole point! You've never understood me—A great injustice has been done me, Torvald; first by Father, and then by you.

HELMER: What a thing to say! No two people on earth could ever have loved you more than we have!

NORA [*Shaking her head*]: You never loved me. You just thought it was fun to be in love with me.

HELMER: This is fantastic!

NORA: Perhaps. But it's true all the same. While I was still at home I used to hear Father airing his opinions and they became my opinions; or if I didn't happen to agree, I kept it to myself—he would have been displeased otherwise. He used to call me his doll-baby, and played with me as I played with my dolls. Then I came to live in your house—

HELMER: What an expression to use about our marriage!

NORA [*Undisturbed*]: I mean—from Father's hands I passed into yours. You arranged everything according to your tastes, and I acquired the same tastes, or I pretended to—I'm not sure which—a little of both, perhaps. Looking back on it all, it seems to me I've lived here like a beggar, from hand to mouth. I've lived by performing tricks for you, Torvald. But that's the way you wanted it. You and Father have done me a great wrong. You've prevented me from becoming a real person.

HELMER: Nora, how can you be so ungrateful and unreasonable! Haven't you been happy here?

NORA: No, never. I thought I was; but I wasn't really.

HELMER: Not—not happy!

NORA: No; only merry. You've always been so kind to me. But our home has never been anything but a play-room. I've been your doll-wife, just as at home I was Papa's doll-child. And the children in turn, have been my dolls. I thought it fun when you played games with me, just as they thought it fun when I played games with them. And that's been our marriage, Torvald.

HELMER: There may be a grain of truth in what you say, even though it is distorted and exaggerated. From now on things will be different. Play-time is over now; tomorrow lessons begin!

NORA: Whose lessons? Mine, or the children's?

HELMER: Both, if you wish it, Nora, dear.

NORA: Torvald, I'm afraid you're not the man to teach me to be a real wife to you.

HELMER: How can you say that?

NORA: And I'm certainly not fit to teach the children.

HELMER: Nora!

NORA: Didn't you just say, a moment ago, you didn't dare trust them to me?

HELMER: That was in the excitement of the moment! You mustn't take it so seriously!

NORA: But you were quite right, Torvald. That job is beyond me; there's another job I must do first: I must try and educate myself. You could never help me to do that; I must do it quite alone. So, you see—that's why I'm going to leave you.

HELMER [Jumping up]: What did you say—?

NORA: I shall never get to know myself—I shall never learn to face reality—unless I stand alone. So I can't stay with you any longer.

HELMER: Nora! Nora!

NORA: I am going at once. I'm sure Kristine will let me stay with her tonight—

HELMER: But, Nora—this is madness! I shan't allow you to do this. I shall forbid it!

NORA: You no longer have the power to forbid me anything. I'll only take a few things with me—those that belong to me. I shall never again accept anything from you.

HELMER: Have you lost your senses?

NORA: Tomorrow I'll go home—to what *was* my home, I mean. It might be easier for me there, to find something to do.

HELMER: You talk like an ignorant child, Nora—!

NORA: Yes. That's just why I must educate myself.

HELMER: To leave your home—to leave your husband, and your children! What do you suppose people would say to that?

NORA: It makes no difference. This is something I *must* do.

HELMER: It's inconceivable! Don't you realize you'd be betraying your most sacred duty?

NORA: What do you consider that to be?

HELMER: Your duty towards your husband and your children— I surely don't have to tell you that!

NORA: I've another duty just as sacred.

HELMER: Nonsense! What duty do you mean?

NORA: My duty towards myself.

HELMER: Remember—before all else you are a wife and mother.

NORA: I don't believe that anymore. I believe that before all else I am a human being, just as you are—or at least that I should try and become one. I know that most people would agree with you, Torvald—and that's what they say in books. But I can no longer be satisfied with what most people say—or what they write in books. I must think things out for myself—get clear about them.

HELMER: Surely your position in your home is clear enough? Have you no sense of religion? Isn't that an infallible guide to you?

NORA: But don't you see, Torvald—I don't really know what religion is.

HELMER: Nora! How *can* you!

NORA: All I know about it is what Pastor Hansen told me when I was confirmed. He taught me what he thought religion was—said it was *this* and *that*. As soon as I get away by myself, I shall have to look into that matter too, try and decide whether what he taught me was right—or whether it's right for *me*, at least.

HELMER: A nice way for a young woman to talk! It's unheard of! If religion means nothing to you, I'll appeal to your conscience; you must have some sense of ethics, I suppose? Answer me! Or have you none?

NORA: It's hard for me to answer you, Torvald. I don't think I know—all these things bewilder me. But I *do* know that I think quite differently from you about them. I've discovered that the law, for instance, is quite different from what I had imagined; but I find it hard to believe it can be right. It seems it's criminal for a woman to try and spare her old, sick, father, or save her husband's life! I can't agree with that.

HELMER: You talk like a child. You have no understanding of the society we live in.

NORA: No, I haven't. But I'm going to try and learn. I want to find out which of us is right—society or I.

HELMER: You are ill, Nora; you have a touch of fever; you're quite beside yourself.

NORA: I've never felt so sure—so clear-headed—as I do tonight.

HELMER: "Sure and clear-headed" enough to leave your husband and your children?

NORA: Yes.

HELMER: Then there is only one explanation possible.

NORA: What?

HELMER: You don't love me any more.

NORA: No; that is just it.

HELMER: Nora!— What are you saying!

NORA: It makes me so unhappy, Torvald; for you've always been so kind to me. But I can't help it. I don't love you any more.

HELMER [*Mastering himself with difficulty*]: You feel "sure and clear-headed" about this too?

NORA: Yes, utterly sure. That's why I can't stay here any longer.

HELMER: And can you tell me how I lost your love?

NORA: Yes, I can tell you. It was tonight—when the wonderful thing didn't happen; I knew then you weren't the man I always thought you were.

HELMER: I don't understand.

NORA: For eight years I've been waiting patiently; I knew, of course, that such things don't happen every day. Then, when this trouble came to me—I thought to myself: Now! Now the wonderful thing will happen! All the time Krogstad's letter was out there in the box, it never occurred to me for a single moment that you'd think of submitting to his conditions. I was absolutely convinced that you'd defy him—that you'd tell him to publish the thing to all the world; and that then—

HELMER: You mean you thought I'd let my wife be publicly dishonored and disgraced?

NORA: No. What I thought you'd do, was to take the blame upon yourself.

HELMER: Nora—!

NORA: I know! You think I never would have accepted such a sacrifice. Of course I wouldn't! But my word would have meant nothing against yours. That was the wonderful thing I hoped for, Torvald, hoped for with such terror. And it was to prevent that, that I chose to kill myself.

HELMER: I'd gladly work for you day and night, Nora—go through suffering and want, if need be—but one doesn't sacrifice one's honor for love's sake.

NORA: Millions of women have done so.

HELMER: You think and talk like a silly child.

NORA: Perhaps. But you neither think nor talk like the man I want to share my life with. When you'd recovered from your fright—and you never thought of me, only of yourself—when you had nothing more to fear—you behaved as though none of this had happened. I was your little lark again, your little doll—whom you would have to guard more carefully than ever, because she was so weak and frail. [*Stands up*] At that moment it suddenly dawned on me that I have been living here for eight years with a stranger and that I'd borne him three children. I can't bear to think about it! I could tear myself to pieces!

HELMER [*Sadly*]: I see, Nora—I understand; there's suddenly a great void between us— Is there no way to bridge it?

NORA: Feeling as I do now, Torvald—I could never be a wife to you.

HELMER: But, if I were to change? Don't you think I'm capable of that?

NORA: Perhaps—when you no longer have your doll to play with.

HELMER: It's inconceivable! I *can't* part with you, Nora. I can't endure the thought.

NORA [*Going into room on the right*]: All the more reason it should happen. [*She comes back with outdoor things and a small traveling-bag, which she places on a chair.*]

HELMER: But not at once, Nora—not now! At least wait till tomorrow.

NORA [*Putting on cloak*]: I can't spend the night in a strange man's house.

HELMER: Couldn't we go on living here together? As brother and sister, if you like—as friends.

NORA [*Fastening her hat*]: You know very well that wouldn't last, Torvald. [*Puts on the shawl*] Good-bye. I won't go in and see the children. I know they're in better hands than mine. Being what I am—how can I be of any use to them?

HELMER: But surely, some day, Nora—?

NORA: How can I tell? How do I know what sort of person I'll become?

HELMER: You are my wife, Nora, now and always!

NORA: Listen to me, Torvald—I've always heard that when a wife deliberately leaves her husband as I am leaving you, he is legally freed from all responsibility towards her. At any rate, I release you now from all responsibility. You mustn't feel yourself bound, any more than I shall. There must be complete freedom on both sides. Here is your ring. Now give me mine.

HELMER: That too?

NORA: That too.

HELMER: Here it is.

NORA: So—it's all over now. Here are the keys. The servants know how to run the house—better than I do. I'll ask Kristine to come by tomorrow, after I've left town; there are a few things I brought with me from home; she'll pack them up and send them on to me.

HELMER: You really mean it's over, Nora? *Really* over? You'll never think of me again?

NORA: I expect I shall often think of you; of you—and the children, and this house.

HELMER: May I write to you?

NORA: No—never. You mustn't! Please!

HELMER: At least, let me send you—

NORA: Nothing!

HELMER: But, you'll let me help you, Nora—

NORA: No, I say! I can't accept anything from strangers.

HELMER: Must I always be a stranger to you, Nora?

NORA [*Taking her traveling-bag*]: Yes. Unless it were to happen—the most wonderful thing of all—

HELMER: What?

NORA: Unless we both could change so that— Oh, Torvald! I no longer *believe* in miracles, you see!

HELMER: Tell me! Let *me* believe! Unless we both could change so that—?

NORA: —So that our life together might truly be a marriage. Good-bye. [*She goes out by the hall door.*]

HELMER [*sinks into a chair by the door with his face in his hands*]: Nora! Nora! [*He looks around the room and rises*] She is gone! How empty it all seems! [*A hope springs up in him*] The most wonderful thing of all—?

[*From below is heard the reverberation of a heavy door closing.*]

[*Curtain*]

LEO TOLSTOY

[1828–1910]

Leo Tolstoy was the most famous Russian of his time. Two giant novels, *War and Peace* and *Anna Karenina,* elevated him in literary circles, but his fame became worldwide when he turned his attention to the political and spiritual issues of his day, writing books and pamphlets that criticized governments and charted a new spirituality for his followers. During the last years of his life people came from all over the world to visit him at his country estate. Actually, it is deceptive to suggest that Tolstoy was first a great novelist who then turned into a moralist; his whole life was a continuous struggle between the body and the spirit, between reason and faith. In a romantic vein he celebrated the life of the peasant, the simple values of people who live close to the earth and close to their hearts. In contrast, his aristocratic background seemed hollow and hypocritical. Nevertheless, he was attracted to the benefits of the city, to books and literate conversation, as well as to the decadent pleasures provided by city life. As Tolstoy tried to reconcile his life with his art, he reflected a larger conflict in the nineteenth century between the rational ideals of the Enlightenment and the fresh vision of romanticism.

LIFE

Tolstoy was born on August 28, 1828, to Count Nikolaj Tolstoy and his wife, the former Princess Volkonsky, on the large country estate of Yasnaya Polyana, some 120 miles south of Moscow. The deaths of his mother when he was two, his father when he was nine, and a guardian aunt when he was thirteen forced him to be on his own. With his primary attention on wine, women, and gambling, Tolstoy failed several courses at the University of Kazan, where he studied oriental languages and law. He left the university in 1847 without a degree and returned to Yasnaya Polyana, where he tried to improve the living conditions of his serfs. Frustrated by the suspicion of the peasants, Leo journeyed with his brother Nikolaj to the Caucasus, where he joined the army and fought a war against Muslims, and a bit later against the French and English in the Crimean War. From these experiences came *Sevastopol Sketches* (1855), which along with an earlier work, *Childhood* (1852), brought him recognition.

Uneasy with literary society, he visited Europe and continued his writing at Yasnaya Polyana, where he established a progressive school for the children of his illiterate workers. At age thirty-four he married Sofia, the high-strung eighteen-year-old daughter of a court doctor. They had thirteen children. During the years 1863–1869 he wrote his monumental novel *War and Peace.* Although this novel focuses on the invasion of Russia by Napoleon, it is the panoramic, epic-like sweep of the novel and the vibrant world of characters and settings that establish it as one of the greatest novels ever written. There are battle scenes and military heroes, but in the end love, marriage, and family are the lasting victors. Scholars have criticized Tolstoy's portrait of Napoleon and his theory of fatalistic history, but the real heart of the novel is the detailed evocation of Russian life, episode after episode building into a coherent nineteenth-century literary world.

When Sofia insisted that they winter in Moscow, Leo became a census taker and for the first time confronted the appalling poverty and degradation of the poor working classes in Moscow's slums—men, women, and children being ground down by a kind of slave labor in the factories. In contrast, Tolstoy's own luxurious life-style deeply troubled his conscience, and he was determined to simplify his life. He cut wood, swept floors, and plowed fields. He went barefoot in the summer, made his own leather boots, and wore a peasant blouse and trousers. He drank a brew of barley and acorns rather than coffee, and wrote his second great novel, *Anna Karenina* (1875–1877), a story of contemporary manners. In this novel, Anna and Vronsky's illicit love is successful initially in defying the conventional codes of marriage, but the power of social mores eventually descends on them. The once-radiant Anna becomes wretchedly unhappy and tragically ends her life in suicide.

After completing *Anna Karenina*, Tolstoy was exhausted and suffered a profound psychological and moral crisis over the futility of material success and the relentless movement of time toward death. He was rich and famous, but he questioned the value of his greatest novels. His autobiography, *A Confession* (1879), which is in the tradition of both St. Augustine's and Rousseau's *Confessions,* describes this crisis of faith and includes a poignant fable about a traveler in the steppes who is attacked by a furious wild beast: "To save himself the traveler gets into a waterless well; but at the bottom of it he sees a dragon with jaws wide open to devour him. The unhappy man dares not get out for fear of the wild beast, and dares not descend for fear of the dragon, so he catches hold of the branch of a wild plant growing in a crevice of the well. His arms grow tired, and he feels that he must soon perish...he sees two mice, one black and one white, gradually making their way round the stem of the wild plant on which he is hanging, nibbling it through. The plant will soon give way and break off, and he will fall into the jaws of the dragon...still hanging, he looks around him, and, finding some drops of honey on the leaves of the wild plant, he stretches out his tongue and licks them."

Knowing that the dragon of death awaited him, Tolstoy found that the honey was no longer sweet. Death, after all, had claimed his brother; his son Petya died in 1873 and a beloved Aunt Toinette died in 1874. He was no longer interested in literature as art, but in literature as message. He turned to religion; he studied the scriptures and the history of Christianity. He wrestled with the concept of God. He tried to emulate the piety of Russian peasants and he took to visiting monasteries, the most famous of which is the Optina Monastery, made famous by Dostoevsky in *The Brothers Karamazov.*

It was the Sermon on the Mount, especially Matthew 5:39 ("Do not resist evil"), that became his program for moral and spiritual reform. He was attracted by the beatitudes, the idea of dispossession of goods, pacifism, and strict self-control. Tolstoy's daring, courageous experiment was to take Jesus' Sermon on the Mount seriously and to actually try to live accordingly. By stripping Christianity of institutions, priesthood, and ritual, Tolstoy attempted to recreate a basic, moral Christianity that would liberate Russians from the bondage of what he perceived as a corrupt religion controlled by the Church.

From then on, writing fiction was less important than producing a series of books and pamphlets explaining his own version of Jesus' teachings. *What I Believe* (1883) describes Jesus' pacifism, "Turn your cheek, love your enemies." In *What Then Must We Do* (1884), he described the plight of the impoverished classes in Moscow, deplored the evils of money, and prescribed a return to the land. In 1888, he gave up meat, alcohol, and tobacco. He attempted to embody his fundamental beliefs in several short stories and one rather propagandistic novel, *Resurrection* (1900), in which Prince Nekhludov comes to terms with the consequences of his promiscuity and the burdens of wealth through a spiritual resurrection. In *The Kingdom of God Is Within You* (1894), he expressed his opposition to the religious ritual and the abuses of Church power. His particular form of Christian anarchy is summed up in five commandments: 1) Do not be angry at anyone; 2) Do not commit adultery; 3) Do not swear any oaths; 4) Do not repay evil with evil; 5) Love your enemies and be good to both enemies and friends.

His war on orthodoxy eventually led to his excommunication in 1901. But outside Russia his reputation grew, as did his support for persecuted groups. Christians, Jews, Muslims, and Buddhists from all over the world came to Yasnaya Polyana to sit at his feet. Mahatma Gandhi first came to know Tolstoy through *The Kingdom of God Is Within You* and they corresponded. Although his doctrine of nonviolence did not appeal to Russian Marxists, Tolstoy's ideas shaped the twentieth-century practices of not only Gandhi but Martin Luther King, Jr., and Dorothy Day, the founder of the Catholic Worker movement. Gandhi founded farms in South Africa and India based on Tolstoyan principles. Tolstoy himself admired the writings of Emerson, Thoreau, and Whitman in the United States. He also looked to Goethe, Dickens, and Montaigne for inspiration. He was familiar with Buddhist writings, the Koran, and Lao-tzu.

With world popularity and regular visits from his followers, life at home was not tranquil. Sofia became increasingly jealous, and when Tolstoy threatened to give up his holdings and distribute them to the poor, she protested. He was troubled by his failure to live up to his own ideals, and on November 8, 1910, he wrote Sofia a farewell letter and secretly departed Yasnaya Polyana. Falling ill on a train, he spent his final days in a stationmaster's house at Astapovo. Sofia was prevented from seeing him, her husband of forty-eight years, until he slipped into a coma. He died on November 20.

WORK

The moving story *The Death of Ivan Ilyitch* (1886) belongs to the second major period of Tolstoy's life when, after his spiritual crisis, he focused on reconciling life, literature, and morality. The plot of this work is simple and straightforward; as indicated by the title, there is no suspense about the outcome. Ivan Ilyitch is a judge, a public official, who is making his way up the social and institutional ladder, when one day he has a minor accident while fixing a curtain and his life is radically turned around. As he grows weaker, slowly dying, he experiences all the loneliness and isolation that had been his own normal, bureaucratic style of handling his clientele and family. The veil of officialdom that had formerly separated him from all his personal and public associations now prevents him from receiving any real communications from doctors, friends, wife, and children. It is as if members of the middle class have mysteriously lost their ability to speak honestly with each other, to sincerely express their feelings. Instead they are caught up in the language of manners, in hedging and obfuscation, in the jargon of professions, hiding or denying the language of the heart.

Unfortunately, Ivan Ilyitch has created his bed and is condemned to lie in it during the remainder of his life, a time when he most desires and needs human contact in order to face the awesome reality of death. Two characters are able to pierce Ivan's isolation: his frightened, shy son, Volodya, and the servant Gerasim. The implications are clear: The son is not yet old enough to be corrupted by social affectations and can therefore act on his genuine feelings. Gerasim's saving grace is his social class: As a peasant and servant he is used to dealing with sickness and death; being close to nature, close to the earth, he handles both of them honestly and directly, while treating Ivan with compassion and truthfulness. Implicit in the unfolding of Ivan's painful dilemma is Tolstoy's criticism of society and the Church, which fail individuals when they most need aid and comfort.

As in his other writings, Tolstoy used physical details to evoke the sights and smells of a dying man. The self-serving responses to the announcement of Ivan Ilyitch's death in the first paragraphs of the story set the tone for relationships in the rest of the story. Ivan's own painful self-centeredness is finally alleviated at the end of the story, during the final moments of his life, when he faces the truth about his essentially empty life and thereby achieves a kind of release from his fear of death. As he plunges toward the light at the bottom of a psychological hole, he murmurs to himself, "Death is over" and "It's no more."

Critic Vladimir Lakshin summed up Tolstoy's place among Russia's literary masters: "We like Chekhov, admire Dostoevsky, love Pushkin, but Tolstoy? As a combination artist, philosopher, public figure and human being he is *neobychny* [unparalleled, incomparable]."

SUGGESTED READINGS

Ernest J. Simmons's *Leo Tolstoy* (1946) and Henri Troyat's *Tolstoy* (1967) provide good biographies. R. F. Christian's *Tolstoy: A Critical Introduction* (1969) is a broad overview of Tolstoy's writing. E. B. Greenwood's *Tolstoy: The Comprehensive Vision* (1975) and Philip Rahv's *Image and Idea* (1949) have individual chapters on *The Death of Ivan Ilyitch*. Ralph Matlaw's *Tolstoy: A Collection of Critical Essays* (1967) includes a spectrum of critical opinions.

The Death of Ivan Ilyitch

Translated by Constance Garnett

1

Inside the great building of the Law Courts, during the interval in the hearing of the Melvinsky case, the members of the judicial council and the public prosecutor were gathered together in the private room of Ivan Yegorovitch Shebek, and the conversation turned upon the celebrated Krasovsky case. Fyodor Vassilievitch hotly maintained that the case was not in the jurisdiction of the court. Yegor Ivanovitch stood up for his own view; but from the first Pyotr Ivanovitch, who had not entered into the discussion, took no interest in it, but was looking through the newspapers which had just been brought in.

"Gentlemen!" he said, "Ivan Ilyitch is dead!"

"You don't say so!"

"Here, read it," he said to Fyodor Vassilievitch, handing him the fresh still damp-smelling paper.

Within a black margin was printed: "Praskovya Fyodorovna Golovin with heartfelt affliction informs friends and relatives of the decease of her beloved husband, member of the Court of Justice, Ivan Ilyitch Golovin, who passed away on the 4th of February. The funeral will take place on Thursday at one o'clock."

Ivan Ilyitch was a colleague of the gentlemen present, and all liked him. It was some weeks now since he had been taken ill; his illness had been said to be incurable. His post had been kept open for him, but it had been thought that in case of his death Alexyeev might receive his appointment, and either Vinnikov or Shtabel would succeed to Alexyeev's. So that on hearing of Ivan Ilyitch's death, the first thought of each of the gentlemen in the room was of the effect this death might have on the transfer or promotion of themselves or their friends.

"Now I am sure of getting Shtabel's place or Vinnikov's," thought Fyodor Vassilievitch. "It was promised me long ago, and the promotion means eight hundred rubles additional income, besides the grants for office expenses."

"Now I shall have to petition for my brother-in-law to be transferred from Kaluga," thought Pyotr Ivanovitch. "My wife will be very glad. She won't be able to say now that I've never done anything for her family."

"I thought somehow that he'd never get up from his bed again," Pyotr Ivanovitch said aloud. "I'm sorry!"

"But what was it exactly was wrong with him?"

"The doctors could not decide. That's to say, they did decide, but differently. When I saw him last, I thought he would get over it."

"Well, I positively haven't called there ever since the holidays. I've kept meaning to go."

"Had he any property?"

"I think there's something, very small, of his wife's. But something quite trifling."

"Yes, one will have to go and call. They live such a terribly long way off."

"A long way from you, you mean. Everything's a long way from your place."

"There, he can never forgive me for living the other side of the river," said Pyotr Ivanovitch, smiling at Shebek. And they began to talk of the great distances between different parts of the town, and went back into the court.

Besides the reflections upon the changes and promotions in the service likely to ensue from this death, the very fact of the death of an intimate acquaintance excited in every one who heard of it, as such a fact always does, a feeling of relief that "it is he that is dead, and not I."

"Only think! he is dead, but here am I all right," each one thought or felt. The more intimate acquaintances, the so-called friends of Ivan Ilyitch, could not help thinking too that now they had the exceedingly tiresome social duties to perform of going to the funeral service and paying the widow a visit of condolence.

The most intimately acquainted with their late colleague were Fyodor Vassilievitch and Pyotr Ivanovitch.

Pyotr Ivanovitch had been a comrade of his at the school of jurisprudence, and considered himself under obligations to Ivan Ilyitch.

Telling his wife at dinner of the news of Ivan Ilyitch's death and his reflections as to the possibility of getting her brother transferred into their circuit, Pyotr Ivanovitch, without lying down for his usual nap, put on his frockcoat and drove to Ivan Ilyitch's.

At the entrance before Ivan Ilyitch's flat stood a carriage and two hired flies.[1] Downstairs in the entry near the hat-stand there was leaning against the wall a coffin-lid with tassels and braiding freshly rubbed up with pipeclay. Two ladies were taking off their cloaks. One of them he knew, the sister of Ivan Ilyitch; the other was a lady he did not know. Pyotr Ivanovitch's colleague, Shvarts, was coming down; and from the top stair, seeing who it was coming in, he stopped and winked at him, as though to say: "Ivan Ilyitch has made a mess of it; it's a very different matter with you and me."

Shvarts's face, with his English whiskers[2] and all his thin figure in his frockcoat, had, as it always had, an air of elegant solemnity; and this solemnity, always such a contrast to Shvarts's playful character, had a special piquancy here. So thought Pyotr Ivanovitch.

---

[1] Horse-drawn cabs.
[2] Side whiskers.

Pyotr Ivanovitch let the ladies pass on in front of him, and walked slowly up the stairs after them. Shvarts had not come down, but was waiting at the top. Pyotr Ivanovitch knew what for; he wanted obviously to settle with him where their game of *vint*[3] was to be that evening. The ladies went up to the widow's room; while Shvarts, with his lips tightly and gravely shut and amusement in his eyes, with a twitch of his eyebrows motioned Pyotr Ivanovitch to the right, to the room where the dead man was.

Pyotr Ivanovitch went in, as people always do on such occasions, in uncertainty as to what he would have to do there. One thing he felt sure of—that crossing oneself never comes amiss on such occasions. As to whether it was necessary to bow down while doing so, he did not feel quite sure, and so chose a middle course. On entering the room he began crossing himself, and made a slight sort of bow. So far as the movements of his hands and head permitted him, he glanced while doing so about the room. Two young men, one a high school boy, nephews probably, were going out of the room, crossing themselves. An old lady was standing motionless; and a lady, with her eyebrows queerly lifted, was saying something to her in a whisper. A deacon in a frockcoat, resolute and hearty, was reading something aloud with an expression that precluded all possibility of contradiction. A young peasant who used to wait at table, Gerasim, walking with light footsteps in front of Pyotr Ivanovitch, was sprinkling something on the floor. Seeing this, Pyotr Ivanovitch was at once aware of the faint odor of the decomposing corpse. On his last visit to Ivan Ilyitch Pyotr Ivanovitch had seen this peasant in his room; he was performing the duties of a sicknurse, and Ivan Ilyitch liked him particularly. Pyotr Ivanovitch continued crossing himself and bowing in a direction intermediate between the coffin, the deacon, and the holy pictures on the table in the corner. Then when this action of making the sign of the cross with his hand seemed to him to have been unduly prolonged, he stood still and began to scrutinize the dead man.

The dead man lay, as dead men always do lie, in a peculiarly heavy dead way, his stiffened limbs sunk in the cushions of the coffin, and his head bent back forever on the pillow, and thrust up, as dead men always do, his yellow waxen forehead with bald spots on the sunken temples, and his nose that stood out sharply and, as it were, squeezed on the upper lip. He was much changed, even thinner since Pyotr Ivanovitch had seen him, but his face—as always with the dead—was more handsome, and, above all, more impressive than it had been when he was alive. On the face was an expression of what had to be done having been done, and rightly done. Besides this, there was too in that expression a reproach or a reminder for the living. This reminder seemed to Pyotr Ivanovitch uncalled for, or, at least, to have nothing to do with him. He felt something unpleasant; and so Pyotr Ivanovitch once more crossed himself hurriedly, and, as it struck him, too hurriedly, not quite in accordance with the proprieties, turned and went to the door. Shvarts was waiting for him in the adjoining room, standing with his legs apart and both hands behind his back playing with his top hat. A single glance at the playful, sleek, and elegant figure of Shvarts revived Pyotr Ivanovitch. He felt that he, Shvarts, was above it, and would not give way to depressing impressions. The mere sight of him said plainly: the incident of the service over the body of Ivan Ilyitch cannot possibly constitute a sufficient ground for recognizing the business of the session suspended,—in other words, in no way can it hinder us from shuffling and cutting a pack of cards this evening, while the footman sets four unsanctified candles on the table for us; in fact, there is no ground for supposing that this incident could prevent us from spending

---

[3]Bridge.

the evening agreeably. He said as much indeed to Pyotr Ivanovitch as he came out, proposing that the party should meet at Fyodor Vassilievitch's. But apparently it was Pyotr Ivanovitch's destiny not to play *vint* that evening. Praskovya Fyodorovna, a short, fat woman who, in spite of all efforts in a contrary direction, was steadily broader from her shoulders downwards, all in black, with lace on her head and her eyebrows as queerly arched as those of the lady standing beside the coffin, came out of her own apartments with some other ladies, and conducting them to the dead man's room, said: "The service will take place immediately; come in."

Shvarts, making an indefinite bow, stood still, obviously neither accepting nor declining this invitation. Praskovya Fyodorovna, recognizing Pyotr Ivanovitch, sighed, went right up to him, took his hand, and said, "I know that you were a true friend of Ivan Ilyitch's . . . " and looked at him, expecting from him the suitable action in response to these words. Pyotr Ivanovitch knew that, just as before he had to cross himself, now what he had to do was to press her hand, to sigh and to say, "Ah, I was indeed!" And he did so. And as he did so, he felt that the desired result had been attained; that he was touched, and she was touched.

"Come, since it's not begun yet, I have something I want to say to you," said the widow. "Give me your arm."

Pyotr Ivanovitch gave her his arm, and they moved towards the inner rooms, passing Shvarts, who winked gloomily at Pyotr Ivanovitch.

"So much for our *vint*! Don't complain if we find another partner. You can make a fifth when you do get away," said his humorous glance.

Pyotr Ivanovitch sighed still more deeply and despondently, and Praskovya Fyodorovna pressed his hand gratefully. Going into her drawing-room, which was upholstered with pink cretonne and lighted by a dismal-looking lamp, they sat down at the table, she on a sofa and Pyotr Ivanovitch on a low ottoman with deranged springs which yielded spasmodically under his weight. Praskovya Fyodorovna was about to warn him to sit on another seat, but felt such a recommendation out of keeping with her position, and changed her mind. Sitting down on the ottoman, Pyotr Ivanovitch remembered how Ivan Ilyitch had arranged this drawing-room, and had consulted him about this very pink cretonne with green leaves. Seating herself on the sofa, and pushing by the table (the whole drawing-room was crowded with furniture and things), the widow caught the lace of her black fichu[4] in the carving of the table. Pyotr Ivanovitch got up to disentangle it for her; and the ottoman, freed from his weight, began bobbing up spasmodically under him. The widow began unhooking her lace herself, and Pyotr Ivanovitch again sat down, suppressing the mutinous ottoman springs under him. But the widow could not quite free herself, and Pyotr Ivanovitch rose again, and again the ottoman became mutinous and popped up with a positive snap. When this was all over, she took out a clean cambric handkerchief and began weeping. Pyotr Ivanovitch had been chilled off by the incident with the lace and the struggle with the ottoman springs, and he sat looking sullen. This awkward position was cut short by the entrance of Sokolov, Ivan Ilyitch's butler, who came in to announce that the place in the cemetery fixed on by Praskovya Fyodorovna would cost two hundred rubles. She left off weeping, and with the air of a victim glancing at Pyotr Ivanovitch, said in French that it was very terrible for her. Pyotr Ivanovitch made a silent gesture signifying his unhesitating conviction that it must indeed be so.

"Please, smoke," she said in a magnanimous, and at the same time, crushed voice, and she began discussing with Sokolov the question of the price of the site for the grave.

---

[4] Shawl.

Pyotr Ivanovitch, lighting a cigarette, listened to her very circumstantial inquiries as to the various prices of sites and her decision as to the one to be selected. Having settled on the site for the grave, she made arrangements also about the choristers. Sokolov went away.

"I see to everything myself," she said to Pyotr Ivanovitch, moving on one side the albums that lay on the table; and noticing that the table was in danger from the cigarette-ash, she promptly passed an ash-tray to Pyotr Ivanovitch, and said: "I consider it affectation to pretend that my grief prevents me from looking after practical matters. On the contrary, if anything could—not console me . . . but distract me, it is seeing after everything for him." She took out her handkerchief again, as though preparing to weep again; and suddenly, as though struggling with herself, she shook herself, and began speaking calmly: "But I've business to talk about with you."

Pyotr Ivanovitch bowed, carefully keeping in check the springs of the ottoman, which had at once begun quivering under him.

"The last few days his sufferings were awful."

"Did he suffer very much?" asked Pyotr Ivanovitch.

"Oh, awfully! For the last moments, hours indeed, he never left off screaming. For three days and nights in succession he screamed incessantly. It was insufferable. I can't understand how I bore it; one could hear it through three closed doors. Ah, what I suffered!"

"And was he really conscious?" asked Pyotr Ivanovitch.

"Yes," she whispered, "up to the last minute. He said good-bye to us a quarter of an hour before his death, and asked Volodya to be taken away too."

The thought of the sufferings of a man he had known so intimately, at first as a light-hearted boy, a schoolboy, then grown up as a partner at whist, in spite of the unpleasant consciousness of his own and this woman's hypocrisy, suddenly horrified Pyotr Ivanovitch. He saw again that forehead, the nose that seemed squeezing the lip, and he felt frightened for himself. "Three days and nights of awful suffering and death. Why, that may at once, any minute, come upon me too," he thought, and he felt for an instant terrified. But immediately, he could not himself have said how, there came to his support the customary reflection that this had happened to Ivan Ilyitch and not to him, and that to him this must not and could not happen; that in thinking thus he was giving way to depression, which was not the right thing to do, as was evident from Shvarts's expression of face. And making these reflections, Pyotr Ivanovitch felt reassured, and began with interest inquiring details about Ivan Ilyitch's end, as though death were a mischance peculiar to Ivan Ilyitch, but not at all incidental to himself.

After various observations about the details of the truly awful physical sufferings endured by Ivan Ilyitch (these details Pyotr Ivanovitch learned only through the effect Ivan Ilyitch's agonies had had on the nerves of Praskovya Fyodorovna), the widow apparently thought it time to get to business.

"Ah, Pyotr Ivanovitch, how hard it is, how awfully, awfully hard!" and she began to cry again.

Pyotr Ivanovitch sighed, and waited for her to blow her nose. When she had done so, he said, "Indeed it is," and again she began to talk, and brought out what was evidently the business she wished to discuss with him; that business consisted in the inquiry as to how on the occasion of her husband's death she was to obtain a grant from the government. She made a show of asking Pyotr Ivanovitch's advice about a pension. But he perceived that she knew already to the minutest details, what he did not know himself indeed, everything that could be got out of the government on the ground of this death; but that what she wanted to find out was, whether there were not any means of obtaining a little more? Pyotr Ivanovitch tried to imagine such means; but after pondering a little, and out of politeness abusing the government for its stinginess, he said that he believed that it was impossible to obtain more. Then she sighed and began unmistakably looking about for an excuse for getting rid of her visitor. He perceived this, put out his cigarette, got up, pressed her hand, and went out into the passage.

In the dining-room, where was the bric-à-brac clock that Ivan Ilyitch had been so delighted at buying, Pyotr Ivanovitch met the priest and several people he knew who had come to the service for the dead, and saw too Ivan Ilyitch's daughter, a handsome young lady. She was all in black. Her very slender figure looked even slenderer than usual. She had a gloomy, determined, almost wrathful expression. She bowed to Pyotr Ivanovitch as though he were to blame in some way. Behind the daughter, with the same offended air on his face, stood a rich young man, whom Pyotr Ivanovitch knew, too, an examining magistrate, the young lady's *fiancé*, as he had heard. He bowed dejectedly to him, and would have gone on into the dead man's room, when from the staircase there appeared the figure of the son, the high school boy, extraordinarily like Ivan Ilyitch. He was the little Ivan Ilyitch over again as Pyotr Ivanovitch remembered him at school. His eyes were red with crying, and had that look often seen in unclean boys of thirteen or fourteen.[5] The boy, seeing Pyotr Ivanovitch, scowled morosely and bashfully. Pyotr Ivanovitch nodded to him and went into the dead man's room. The service for the dead began—candles, groans, incense, tears, sobs. Pyotr Ivanovitch stood frowning, staring at his feet in front of him. He did not once glance at the dead man, and right through to the end did not once give way to depressing influences, and was one of the first to walk out. In the hall there was no one. Gerasim, the young peasant, darted out of the dead man's room, tossed over with his strong hand all the fur cloaks to find Pyotr Ivanovitch's, and gave it him.

"Well, Gerasim, my boy?" said Pyotr Ivanovitch, so as to say something. "A sad business, isn't it?"

"It's God's will. We shall come to the same," said Gerasim, showing his white, even, peasant teeth in a smile, and, like a man in a rush of extra work, he briskly opened the door, called up the coachman, saw Pyotr Ivanovitch into the carriage, and darted back to the steps as though bethinking himself of what he had to do next.

Pyotr Ivanovitch had a special pleasure in the fresh air after the smell of incense, of the corpse, and of carbolic acid.

"Where to?" asked the coachman.

"It's not too late, I'll still go round to Fyodor Vassilievitch's."

And Pyotr Ivanovitch drove there. And he did, in fact, find them just finishing the first rubber, so that he came just at the right time to take a hand.

2

The previous history of Ivan Ilyitch was the simplest, the most ordinary, and the most awful.

Ivan Ilyitch died at the age of forty-five, a member of the Judicial Council. He was the son of an official, whose career in Petersburg through various ministries and departments had been such as leads people into that position in which, though it is distinctly obvious that they are unfit to perform any kind of real duty, they yet cannot, owing to their long past service and their official rank, be dismissed; and

---

[5]A look that suggests impure, sexual thoughts or acts.

they therefore receive a specially created fictitious post, and by no means fictitious thousands—from six to ten—on which they go on living till extreme old age. Such was the privy councilor, the superfluous member of various superfluous institutions, Ilya Efimovitch Golovin.

He had three sons. Ivan Ilyitch was the second son. The eldest son's career was exactly like his father's, only in a different department, and he was by now close upon that stage in the service in which the same sinecure would be reached. The third son was the unsuccessful one. He had in various positions always made a mess of things, and was now employed in the railway department. And his father and his brothers, and still more their wives, did not merely dislike meeting him, but avoided, except in extreme necessity, recollecting his existence. His sister had married Baron Greff, a Petersburg official of the same stamp as his father-in-law. Ivan Ilyitch was *le phénix de la famille*,[6] as people said. He was not so frigid and precise as the eldest son, nor so wild as the youngest. He was the happy mean between them—a shrewd, lively, pleasant, and well-bred man. He had been educated with his younger brother at the school of jurisprudence. The younger brother had not finished the school course, but was expelled when in the fifth class. Ivan Ilyitch completed the course successfully. At school he was just the same as he was later on all his life—an intelligent fellow, highly good-humored and sociable, but strict in doing what he considered to be his duty. His duty he considered whatever was so considered by those persons who were set in authority over him. He was not a toady as a boy, nor later on as a grown-up person; but from his earliest years he was attracted, as a fly to the light, to persons of good standing in the world, assimilated their manners and their views of life, and established friendly relations with them. All the enthusiasms of childhood and youth passed, leaving no great traces in him; he gave way to sensuality and to vanity, and latterly when in the higher classes at school to liberalism, but always keeping within certain limits which were unfailingly marked out for him by his instincts.

At school he had committed actions which had struck him beforehand as great vileness, and gave him a feeling of loathing for himself at the very time he was committing them. But later on, perceiving that such actions were committed also by men of good position, and were not regarded by them as base, he was able, not to regard them as good, but to forget about them completely, and was never mortified by recollections of them.

Leaving the school of jurisprudence in the tenth class, and receiving from his father a sum of money for his outfit, Ivan Ilyitch ordered his clothes at Sharmer's, hung on his watchchain a medallion inscribed *respice finem*,[7] said good-bye to the prince who was the principal of his school, had a farewell dinner with his comrades at Donon's, and with all his new fashionable belongings—traveling trunk, linen, suits of clothes, shaving and toilet appurtenances, and traveling rug, all ordered and purchased at the very best shops—set off to take the post of secretary on special commissions for the governor of a province, a post which had been obtained for him by his father.

In the province Ivan Ilyitch without loss of time made himself a position as easy and agreeable as his position had been in the school of jurisprudence. He did his work, made his career, and at the same time led a life of well-bred social gaiety. Occasionally he visited various districts on official duty, behaved with dignity both with his superiors and his inferiors; and with exactitude and an incorruptible honesty

---

[6]"The phoenix of the family"; that is, a prodigy.
[7]"Regard the end." (Latin)

of which he could not help feeling proud, performed the duties with which he was entrusted, principally having to do with the dissenters.[8] When engaged in official work he was, in spite of his youth and taste for frivolous amusement, exceedingly reserved, official, and even severe. But in social life he was often amusing and witty, and always good-natured, well-bred, and *bon enfant*,[9] as was said of him by his chief and his chief's wife, with whom he was like one of the family.

In the province there was, too, a connection with one of the ladies who obtruded their charms on the stylish young lawyer. There was a dressmaker, too, and there were drinking bouts with smart officers visiting the neighborhood, and visits to a certain outlying street after supper; there was a rather cringing obsequiousness in his behavior, too, with his chief, and even his chief's wife. But all this was accompanied with such a tone of the highest breeding, that it could not be called by harsh names; it all came under the rubric of the French saying, *Il faut que la jeunesse se passe.*[10] Everything was done with clean hands, in clean shirts, with French phrases, and, what was of most importance, in the highest society, and consequently with the approval of people of rank.

Such was Ivan Ilyitch's career for five years, and then came a change in his official life. New methods of judicial procedure were established; new men were wanted to carry them out. And Ivan Ilyitch became such a new man. Ivan Ilyitch was offered the post of examining magistrate, and he accepted it in spite of the fact that this post was in another province, and he would have to break off all the ties he had formed and form new ones. Ivan Ilyitch's friends met together to see him off, had their photographs taken in a group, presented him with a silver cigarette-case, and he set off to his new post.

As an examining magistrate, Ivan Ilyitch was as *comme il faut*,[11] as well-bred, as adroit in keeping official duties apart from private life, and as successful in gaining universal respect, as he had been as secretary of private commissions. The duties of his new office were in themselves of far greater interest and attractiveness for Ivan Ilyitch. In his former post it had been pleasant to pass in his smart uniform from Sharmer's through the crowd of petitioners and officials waiting timorously and envying him, and to march with his easy swagger straight into the governor's private room, there to sit down with him to tea and cigarettes. But the persons directly subject to his authority were few. The only such persons were the district police superintendents and the dissenters, when he was serving on special commissions. And he liked treating such persons affably, almost like comrades; liked to make them feel that he, able to annihilate them, was behaving in this simple, friendly way with them. But such people were then few in number. Now as an examining magistrate Ivan Ilyitch felt that every one—every one without exception—the most dignified, the most self-satisfied people, all were in his hands, and that he had but to write certain words on a sheet of paper with a printed heading, and this dignified self-satisfied person would be brought before him in the capacity of a defendant or a witness; and if he did not care to make him sit down, he would have to stand up before him and answer his questions. Ivan Ilyitch never abused this authority of his; on the contrary, he tried to soften the expression of it. But the consciousness of this power and the possibility of softening its effect constituted for him the chief interest and attractiveness of his new position. In the work itself, in the preliminary

---

[8]The Old Believers, a sect that broke away from the Russian Orthodox Church in the seventeenth century; members were subject to numerous legal restrictions.

[9]"Good child." (French)

[10]"Youth must have its way." (French)

[11]"As it should be." (French)

inquiries, that is, Ivan Ilyitch very rapidly acquired the art of setting aside every consideration irrelevant to the official aspect of the case, and of reducing every case, however complex, to that form in which it could in a purely external fashion be put on paper, completely excluding his personal view of the matter, and what was of paramount importance, observing all the necessary formalities. All this work was new. And he was one of the first men who put into practical working the reforms in judicial procedure enacted in 1864.[12]

On settling in a new town in his position as examining magistrate, Ivan Ilyitch made new acquaintances, formed new ties, took up a new line, and adopted a rather different attitude. He took up an attitude of somewhat dignified aloofness towards the provincial authorities, while he picked out the best circle among the legal gentlemen and wealthy gentry living in the town, and adopted a tone of slight dissatisfaction with the government, moderate liberalism, and lofty civic virtue. With this, while making no change in the elegance of his get-up, Ivan Ilyitch in his new office gave up shaving, and left his beard free to grow as it liked. Ivan Ilyitch's existence in the new town proved to be very agreeable; the society which took the line of opposition to the governor was friendly and good; his income was larger, and he found a source of increased enjoyment in whist, at which he began to play at this time; and having a faculty for playing cards good-humoredly, and being rapid and exact in his calculations, he was as a rule on the winning side.

After living two years in the new town, Ivan Ilyitch met his future wife. Praskovya Fyodorovna Mihel was the most attractive, clever, and brilliant girl in the set in which Ivan Ilyitch moved. Among other amusements and recreations after his labors as a magistrate, Ivan Ilyitch started a light, playful flirtation with Praskovya Fyodorovna.

Ivan Ilyitch when he was an assistant secretary had danced as a rule; as an examining magistrate he danced only as an exception. He danced now as it were under protest, as though to show "that though I am serving on the new reformed legal code, and am of the fifth class in official rank, still if it comes to a question of dancing, in that line, too, I can do better than others." In this spirit he danced now and then towards the end of the evening with Praskovya Fyodorovna, and it was principally during these dances that he won the heart of Praskovya Fyodorovna. She fell in love with him. Ivan Ilyitch had no clearly defined intention of marrying; but when the girl fell in love with him, he put the question to himself: "After all, why not get married?"

The young lady, Praskovya Fyodorovna, was of good family, nice-looking. There was a little bit of property. Ivan Ilyitch might have reckoned on a more brilliant match, but this was a good match. Ivan Ilyitch had his salary; she, he hoped, would have as much of her own. It was a good family; she was a sweet, pretty, and perfectly *comme il faut* young woman. To say that Ivan Ilyitch got married because he fell in love with his wife and found in her sympathy with his views of life, would be as untrue as to say that he got married because the people of his world approved of the match. Ivan Ilyitch was influenced by both considerations; he was doing what was agreeable to himself in securing such a wife, and at the same time doing what persons of higher standing looked upon as the correct thing.

And Ivan Ilyitch got married.

The process itself of getting married and the early period of married life, with the conjugal caresses, the new furniture, the new crockery, the new house linen, all up to the time of his wife's pregnancy, went off very well; so that Ivan Ilyitch had

---

[12]After the emancipation of the serfs in 1861, the entire legal system was reformed in 1864.

already begun to think that so far from marriage breaking up that kind of frivolous, agreeable, lighthearted life, always decorous and always approved by society, which he regarded as the normal life, it would even increase its agreeableness. But at that point, in the early months of his wife's pregnancy, there came in a new element, unexpected, unpleasant, tiresome and unseemly, which could never have been anticipated, and from which there was no escape.

His wife, without any kind of reason, it seemed to Ivan Ilyitch, *de gaieté de coeur,*[13] as he expressed it, began to disturb the agreeableness and decorum of their life. She began without any sort of justification to be jealous, exacting in her demands on his attention, squabbled over everything, and treated him to the coarsest and most unpleasant scenes.

At first Ivan Ilyitch hoped to escape from the unpleasantness of this position by taking up the same frivolous and well-bred line that had served him well on other occasions of difficulty. He endeavored to ignore his wife's ill-humor, went on living lightheartedly and agreeably as before, invited friends to play cards, tried to get away himself to the club or to his friends. But his wife began on one occasion with such energy, abusing him in such coarse language, and so obstinately persisted in her abuse of him every time he failed in carrying out her demands, obviously having made up her mind firmly to persist until he gave way, that is, stayed at home and was as dull as she was, that Ivan Ilyitch took alarm. He perceived that matrimony, at least with his wife, was not invariably conducive to the pleasures and proprieties of life; but, on the contrary, often destructive of them, and that it was therefore essential to erect some barrier to protect himself from these disturbances. And Ivan Ilyitch began to look about for such means of protecting himself. His official duties were the only thing that impressed Praskovya Fyodorovna, and Ivan Ilyitch began to use his official position and the duties arising from it in his struggle with his wife to fence off his own independent world apart.

With the birth of the baby, the attempts at nursing it, and the various unsuccessful experiments with foods, with the illnesses, real and imaginary, of the infant and its mother, in which Ivan Ilyitch was expected to sympathize, though he never had the slightest idea about them, the need for him to fence off a world apart for himself outside his family life became still more imperative. As his wife grew more irritable and exacting, so did Ivan Ilyitch more and more transfer the center of gravity of his life to his official work. He became fonder and fonder of official life, and more ambitious than he had been.

Very quickly, not more than a year after his wedding, Ivan Ilyitch had become aware that conjugal life, though providing certain comforts, was in reality a very intricate and difficult business towards which one must, if one is to do one's duty, that is, lead the decorous life approved by society, work out for oneself a definite line, just as in the government service.

And such a line Ivan Ilyitch did work out for himself in his married life. He expected from his home life only those comforts—of dinner at home, of housekeeper and bed—which it could give him, and, above all, that perfect propriety in external observances required by public opinion. For the rest, he looked for good-humored pleasantness, and if he found it he was very thankful. If he met with antagonism and querulousness, he promptly retreated into the separate world he had shut off for himself in his official life, and there he found solace.

Ivan Ilyitch was prized as a good official, and three years later he was made assistant public prosecutor. The new duties of this position, their dignity, the

---

[13]Literally, "out of gaiety of heart" (French); arbitrarily.

possibility of bringing any one to trial and putting any one in prison, the publicity of the speeches and the success Ivan Ilyitch had in that part of his work,—all this made his official work still more attractive to him.

Children were born to him. His wife became steadily more querulous and ill-tempered, but the line Ivan Ilyitch had taken up for himself in home life put him almost out of reach of her grumbling.

After seven years of service in the same town, Ivan Ilyitch was transferred to another province with the post of public prosecutor. They moved, money was short, and his wife did not like the place they had moved to. The salary was indeed a little higher than before, but their expenses were larger. Besides, a couple of children died, and home life consequently became even less agreeable for Ivan Ilyitch.

For every mischance that occurred in their new place of residence, Praskovya Fyodorovna blamed her husband. The greater number of subjects of conversation between husband and wife, especially the education of the children, led to questions which were associated with previous quarrels, and quarrels were ready to break out at every instant. There remained only those rare periods of being in love which did indeed come upon them, but never lasted long. These were the islands at which they put in for a time, but they soon set off again upon the ocean of concealed hostility, that was made manifest in their aloofness from one another. This aloofness might have distressed Ivan Ilyitch if he had believed that this ought not to be so, but by now he regarded this position as perfectly normal, and it was indeed the goal towards which he worked in his home life. His aim was to make himself more and more free from the unpleasant aspects of domestic life and to render them harmless and decorous. And he attained this aim by spending less and less time with his family; and when he was forced to be at home, he endeavored to secure his tranquillity by the presence of outsiders. The great thing for Ivan Ilyitch was having his office. In the official world all the interest of life was concentrated for him. And this interest absorbed him. The sense of his own power, the consciousness of being able to ruin any one he wanted to ruin, even the external dignity of his office, when he made his entry into the court or met subordinate officials, his success in the eyes of his superiors and his subordinates, and, above all, his masterly handling of cases, of which he was conscious,—all this delighted him and, together with chats with his colleagues, dining out, and whist, filled his life. So that, on the whole, Ivan's life still went on in the way he thought it should go—agreeably, decorously.

So he lived for another seven years. His eldest daughter was already sixteen, another child had died, and there was left only one other, a boy at the high school, a subject of dissension. Ivan Ilyitch wanted to send him to the school of jurisprudence, while Praskovya Fyodorovna to spite him sent him to the high school. The daughter had been educated at home, and had turned out well; the boy too did fairly well at his lessons.

3

Such was Ivan Ilyitch's life for seventeen years after his marriage. He had been prosecutor a long while by now, and had refused several appointments offered him, looking out for a more desirable post, when there occurred an unexpected incident which utterly destroyed his peace of mind. Ivan Ilyitch had been expecting to be appointed presiding judge in a university town, but a certain Goppe somehow stole a march on him and secured the appointment. Ivan Ilyitch took offense, began upbraiding him, and quarrelled with him and with his own superiors. A coolness was felt towards him, and on the next appointment that was made he was again passed over.

This was in the year 1880. That year was the most painful one in Ivan Ilyitch's life. During that year it became evident on the one hand that his pay was insufficient for his expenses; on the other hand, that he had been forgotten by every one, and that what seemed to him the most monstrous, the cruelest injustice, appeared to other people as a quite commonplace fact. Even his father felt no obligation to assist him. He felt that every one had deserted him, and that every one regarded his position with an income of three thousand five hundred rubles as a quite normal and even fortunate one. He alone, with a sense of the injustice done him, and the everlasting nagging of his wife and the debts he had begun to accumulate, living beyond his means, knew that his position was far from being normal.

The summer of that year, to cut down his expenses, he took a holiday and went with his wife to spend the summer in the country at her brother's.

In the country, with no official duties to occupy him, Ivan Ilyitch was for the first time a prey not to simple boredom, but to intolerable depression; and he made up his mind that things could not go on like that, and that it was absolutely necessary to take some decisive steps.

After a sleepless night spent by Ivan Ilyitch walking up and down the terrace, he determined to go to Petersburg to take active steps and to get transferred to some other department, so as to revenge himself on *them,* the people, that is, who had not known how to appreciate him.

Next day, in spite of all the efforts of his wife and his mother-in-law to dissuade him, he set off to Petersburg.

He went with a single object before him—to obtain a post with an income of five thousand. He was ready now to be satisfied with a post in any department, of any tendency, with any kind of work. He must only have a post—a post with five thousand, in the executive department, the banks, the railways, the Empress Marya's institutions,[14] even in the customs duties—what was essential was five thousand, and essential it was, too, to get out of the department in which they had failed to appreciate his value.

And, behold, this quest of Ivan Ilyitch's was crowned with wonderful, unexpected success. At Kursk there got into the same first-class carriage F. S. Ilyin, an acquaintance, who told him of a telegram just received by the governor of Kursk, announcing a change about to take place in the ministry—Pyotr Ivanovitch was to be superseded by Ivan Semyonovitch.

The proposed change, apart from its significance for Russia, had special significance for Ivan Ilyitch from the fact that by bringing to the front a new person, Pyotr Petrovitch, and obviously, therefore, his friend Zahar Ivanovitch, it was in the highest degree propitious to Ivan Ilyitch's own plans. Zahar Ivanovitch was a friend and school-fellow of Ivan Ilyitch's.

At Moscow the news was confirmed. On arriving at Petersburg, Ivan Ilyitch looked up Zahar Ivanovitch, and received a positive promise of an appointment in his former department—that of justice.

A week later he telegraphed to his wife: *"Zahar Miller's place. At first report I receive appointment."*

Thanks to these changes, Ivan Ilyitch unexpectedly obtained, in the same department as before, an appointment which placed him two stages higher than his former colleagues, and gave him an income of five thousand, together with the

---

[14]Charitable institutions founded by the Empress Marya, wife of Paul I.

official allowance of three thousand five hundred for traveling expenses. All his ill-humor with his former enemies and the whole department was forgotten, and Ivan Ilyitch was completely happy.

Ivan Ilyitch went back to the country more lighthearted and good-tempered than he had been for a very long while. Praskovya Fyodorovna was in better spirits, too, and peace was patched up between them. Ivan Ilyitch described what respect every one had shown him in Petersburg; how all those who had been his enemies had been put to shame, and were cringing now before him; how envious they were of his appointment, and still more of the high favor in which he stood at Petersburg.

Praskovya Fyodorovna listened to this, and pretended to believe it, and did not contradict him in anything, but confined herself to making plans for her new arrangements in the town to which they would be moving. And Ivan Ilyitch saw with delight that these plans were his plans; that they were agreed; and that his life after this disturbing hitch in its progress was about to regain its true, normal character of lighthearted agreeableness and propriety.

Ivan Ilyitch had come back to the country for a short stay only. He had to enter upon the duties of his new office on the 10th of September; and besides, he needed some time to settle in a new place, to move all his belongings from the other province, to purchase and order many things in addition; in short, to arrange things as settled in his own mind, and almost exactly as settled in the heart too of Praskovya Fyodorovna.

And now when everything was so successfully arranged, and when he and his wife were agreed in their aim, and were, besides, so little together, they got on with one another as they had not got on together since the early years of their married life. Ivan Ilyitch had thought of taking his family away with him at once; but his sister and his brother-in-law, who had suddenly become extremely cordial and intimate with him and his family, were so pressing in urging them to stay that he set off alone.

Ivan Ilyitch started off; and the lighthearted temper produced by his success, and his good understanding with his wife, one thing backing up another, did not desert him all the time. He found a charming set of apartments, the very thing both husband and wife had dreamed of. Spacious, lofty reception-rooms in the old style, a comfortable, dignified-looking study for him, rooms for his wife and daughter, a schoolroom for his son, everything as though planned on purpose for them. Ivan Ilyitch himself looked after the furnishing of them, chose the wallpapers, bought furniture, by preference antique furniture, which had a peculiar *comme-il-faut* style to his mind, and it all grew up and grew up, and really attained the ideal he had set before himself. When he had half finished arranging the house, his arrangement surpassed his own expectations. He saw the *comme-il-faut* character, elegant and free from vulgarity, that the whole would have when it was all ready. As he fell asleep he pictured to himself the reception-room as it would be. Looking at the drawing-room, not yet finished, he could see the hearth, the screen, the *étagère*,[15] and the little chairs dotted here and there, the plates and dishes on the wall, and the bronzes as they would be when they were all put in their places. He was delighted with the thought of how he would impress Praskovya and Lizanka, who had taste too in this line. They would never expect anything like it. He was particularly successful in coming across and buying cheap old pieces of furniture, which gave a peculiarly aristocratic air to the whole. In his letters he purposely disparaged everything so as to surprise them. All this so absorbed him that the duties of his new

---

[15]Bookcase.

office, though he was so fond of his official work, interested him less than he had expected. During sittings of the court he had moments of inattention; he pondered the question which sort of cornices to have on the window-blinds, straight or fluted. He was so interested in this business that he often set to work with his own hands, moved a piece of furniture, or hung up curtains himself. One day he went up a ladder to show a workman, who did not understand, how he wanted some hangings draped, made a false step and slipped; but, like a strong and nimble person, he clung on, and only knocked his side against the corner of a frame. The bruised place ached, but it soon passed off. Ivan Ilyitch felt all this time particularly good-humored and well. He wrote: "I feel fifteen years younger." He thought his house-furnishing would be finished in September, but it dragged on to the middle of October. But then the effect was charming; not he only said so, but every one who saw it told him so too.

In reality, it was all just what is commonly seen in the houses of people who are not exactly wealthy but want to look like wealthy people, and so succeed only in being like one another—hangings, dark wood, flowers, rugs and bronzes, everything dark and highly polished, everything that all people of a certain class have so as to be like all people of a certain class. And in his case it was all so like that it made no impression at all; but it all seemed to him somehow special. When he met his family at the railway station and brought them to his newly furnished rooms, all lighted up in readiness, and a footman in a white tie opened the door into an entry decorated with flowers, and then they walked into the drawing-room and the study, uttering cries of delight, he was very happy, conducted them everywhere, eagerly drinking in their praises, and beaming with satisfaction. The same evening, while they talked about various things at tea, Praskovya Fyodorovna inquired about his fall, and he laughed and showed them how he had gone flying, and how he had frightened the upholsterer.

"It's as well I'm something of an athlete. Another man might have been killed, and I got nothing worse than a blow here; when it's touched it hurts, but it's going off already; just a bruise."

And they began to live in their new abode, which, as is always the case, when they had got thoroughly settled in they found to be short of just one room, and with their new income, which, as always, was only a little—some five hundred rubles—too little, and everything went very well. Things went particularly well at first, before everything was quite finally arranged, and there was still something to do to the place—something to buy, something to order, something to move, something to make to fit. Though there were indeed several disputes between husband and wife, both were so well satisfied, and there was so much to do, that it all went off without serious quarrels. When there was nothing left to arrange, it became a little dull, and something seemed to be lacking, but by then they were making acquaintances and forming habits, and life was filled up again.

Ivan Ilyitch, after spending the morning in the court, returned home to dinner, and at first he was generally in a good humor, although this was apt to be upset a little, and precisely on account of the new abode. Every spot on the table-cloth, on the hangings, the string of a window blind broken, irritated him. He had devoted so much trouble to the arrangement of the rooms that any disturbance of their order distressed him. But, on the whole, the life of Ivan Ilyitch ran its course as, according to his conviction, life ought to do—easily, agreeably, and decorously. He got up at nine, drank his coffee, read the newspaper, then put on his official uniform, and went to the court. There the routine of the daily work was ready mapped out for him, and he stepped into it at once. People with petitions, inquiries in the office, the office itself, the sittings—public and preliminary. In all this the great thing necessary was to exclude everything with the sap of life in it, which always disturbs the regular course of official business, not to admit any sort of relations with people except the official relations; the motive of all intercourse had to be simply the official motive, and the intercourse itself to be only official. A man would come, for instance, anxious for certain information. Ivan Ilyitch, not being the functionary on duty, would have nothing whatever to do with such a man. But if this man's relation to him as a member of the court is such as can be formulated on official stamped paper—within the limits of such a relation Ivan Ilyitch would do everything, positively everything he could, and in doing so would observe the semblance of human friendly relations, that is, the courtesies of social life. But where the official relation ended, there everything else stopped too. This art of keeping the official aspect of things apart from his real life, Ivan Ilyitch possessed in the highest degree; and through long practice and natural aptitude, he had brought it to such a pitch of perfection that he even permitted himself at times, like a skilled specialist as it were in jest, to let the human and official relations mingle. He allowed himself this liberty just because he felt he had the power at any moment if he wished it to take up the purely official line again and to drop the human relation. This thing was not simply easy, agreeable, and decorous; in Ivan Ilyitch's hands it attained a positively artistic character. In the intervals of business he smoked, drank tea, chatted a little about politics, a little about public affairs, a little about cards, but most of all about appointments in the service. And tired, but feeling like some artist who has skillfully played his part in the performance, one of the first violins in the orchestra, he returned home. At home his daughter and her mother had been paying calls somewhere, or else some one had been calling on them; the son had been at school, had been preparing his lessons with his teachers, and duly learning correctly what was taught at the high school. Everything was as it should be. After dinner, if there were no visitors, Ivan Ilyitch sometimes read some book of which people were talking, and in the evening sat down to work, that is, read official papers, compared them with the laws, sorted depositions, and put them under the laws. This he found neither tiresome nor entertaining. It was tiresome when he might have been playing *vint;* but if there were no *vint* going on, it was better anyway than sitting alone or with his wife. Ivan Ilyitch's pleasures were little dinners, to which he invited ladies and gentlemen of good social position, and such methods of passing the time with them as were usual with such persons, so that his drawing-room might be like all other drawing-rooms.

Once they even gave a party—a dance. And Ivan Ilyitch enjoyed it, and everything was very successful, except that it led to a violent quarrel with his wife over the tarts and sweetmeats. Praskovya Fyodorovna had her own plan; while Ivan Ilyitch insisted on getting everything from an expensive pastry-cook, and ordered a great many tarts, and the quarrel was because these tarts were left over and the pastry-cook's bill came to forty-five rubles. The quarrel was a violent and unpleasant one, so much so that Praskovya Fyodorovna called him "Fool, imbecile." And he clutched at his head, and in his anger made some allusion to a divorce. But the party itself was enjoyable. There were all the best people, and Ivan Ilyitch danced with Princess Trufanov, the sister of the one so well known in connection with the charitable association called "Bear my Burden." His official pleasures lay in the gratification of his pride; his social pleasures lay in the gratification of his vanity. But Ivan Ilyitch's most real pleasure was the pleasure of playing *vint.* He admitted to himself that, after all, after whatever unpleasant incidents there had been in his life, the pleasure which burned like a candle before all others was sitting with good players, and not noisy partners, at *vint;* and, of course, a four-hand game (playing with five was never a success, though one pretends to like it particularly), and with good cards, to play a shrewd, serious game, then supper and a glass of wine. And after *vint,* especially after winning some small stakes (winning large sums was unpleasant), Ivan Ilyitch went to bed in a particularly happy frame of mind.

So they lived. They moved in the very best circle, and were visited by people of consequence and young people.

In their views of their circle of acquaintances, the husband, the wife, and the daughter were in complete accord; and without any expressed agreement on the subject, they all acted alike in dropping and shaking off various friends and relations, shabby persons who swooped down upon them in their drawing-room with Japanese plates on the walls, and pressed their civilities on them. Soon these shabby persons ceased fluttering about them, and none but the very best society was seen at the Golovins. Young men began to pay attention to Lizanka; and Petrishtchev, the son of Dmitry Ivanovitch Petrishtchev, and the sole heir of his fortune, an examining magistrate, began to be so attentive to Lizanka, that Ivan Ilyitch had raised the question with his wife whether it would not be as well to arrange a sledge drive for them, or to get up some theatricals. So they lived. And everything went on in this way without change, and everything was very nice.

4

All were in good health. One could not use the word ill-health in connection with the symptoms Ivan Ilyitch sometimes complained of, namely, a queer taste in his mouth and a sort of uncomfortable feeling on the left side of the stomach.

But it came to pass that this uncomfortable feeling kept increasing, and became not exactly a pain, but a continual sense of weight in his side and the cause of an irritable temper. This irritable temper, continually growing, began at last to mar the agreeable easiness and decorum that had reigned in the Golovin household. Quarrels between the husband and wife became more and more frequent, and soon all the easiness and amenity of life had fallen away, and mere propriety was maintained with difficulty. Scenes became again more frequent. Again there were only islands in the sea of contention—and but few of these—at which the husband and wife could meet without an outbreak. And Praskovya Fyodorovna said now, not without grounds, that her husband had a trying temper. With her characteristic exaggeration, she said he had always had this awful temper, and she had needed all her sweetness to put up with it for twenty years. It was true that it was he now who began the quarrels. His gusts of temper always broke out just before dinner, and often just as he was beginning to eat, at the soup. He would notice that some piece of the crockery had been chipped, or that the food was not nice, or that his son put his elbow on the table, or his daughter's hair was not arranged as he liked it. And whatever it was, he laid the blame of it on Praskovya Fyodorovna. Praskovya Fyodorovna had at first retorted in the same strain, and said all sorts of horrid things to him; but on two occasions, just at the beginning of dinner, he had flown into such a frenzy that she perceived it was due to physical derangement, and was brought on by taking food, and she controlled herself; she did not reply, but simply made haste to get dinner over. Praskovya Fyodorovna took great credit to herself for this exercise of self-control. Making up her mind that her husband had a fearful temper, and made her life miserable, she began to feel sorry for herself. And the more she felt for herself, the more she hated her husband. She began to wish he were dead; yet could not wish it, because then there would be no income. And this exasperated her against him even more. She considered herself dreadfully unfortunate, precisely because even his death could not save her, and she felt irritated and concealed it, and this hidden irritation on her side increased his irritability.

After one violent scene, in which Ivan Ilyitch had been particularly unjust, and after which he had said in explanation that he certainly was irritable, but that it was due to illness, she said that if he were ill he ought to take steps, and insisted on his going to see a celebrated doctor.

He went. Everything was as he had expected; everything was as it always is. The waiting and the assumption of dignity, that professional dignity he knew so well, exactly as he assumed it himself in court, and the sounding and listening and questions that called for answers that were foregone conclusions and obviously superfluous, and the significant air that seemed to insinuate—you only leave it all to us, and we will arrange everything, for us it is certain and incontestable how to arrange everything, everything in one way for every man of every sort. It was all exactly as in his court of justice. Exactly the same air as he put on in dealing with a man brought up for judgment, the doctor put on for him.

The doctor said: This and that proves that you have such-and-such a thing wrong inside you; but if that is not confirmed by analysis of this and that, then we must assume this and that. If we assume this and that, then—and so on. To Ivan Ilyitch there was only one question of consequence, Was his condition dangerous or not? But the doctor ignored that irrelevant inquiry. From the doctor's point of view this was a side issue, not the subject under consideration; the only real question was the balance of probabilities between a loose kidney, chronic catarrh, and appendicitis. It was not a question of the life of Ivan Ilyitch, but the question between the loose kidney and the intestinal appendix. And this question, as it seemed to Ivan Ilyitch, the doctor solved in a brilliant manner in favor of the appendix, with the reservation that analysis of the water[16] might give a fresh clue, and that then the aspect of the case would be altered. All this was point for point identical with what Ivan Ilyitch had himself done in brilliant fashion a thousand times over in dealing with some man on his trial. Just as brilliantly the doctor made his summing-up, and triumphantly, gaily even, glanced over his spectacles at the prisoner in the dock. From the doctor's summing-up Ivan Ilyitch deduced the conclusion—that things looked bad, and that he, the doctor, and most likely every one else, did not care, but that things looked bad for him. And this conclusion impressed Ivan Ilyitch morbidly, arousing in him a great feeling of pity for himself, of great anger against this doctor who could be unconcerned about a matter of such importance.

But he said nothing of that. He got up, and, laying the fee on the table, he said, with a sigh, "We sick people probably often ask inconvenient questions. Tell me, is this generally a dangerous illness or not?"

The doctor glanced severely at him with one eye through his spectacles, as though to say: "Prisoner at the bar, if you will not keep within the limits of the questions allowed you, I shall be compelled to take measures for your removal from the precincts of the court." "I have told you what I thought necessary and suitable already," said the doctor; "the analysis will show anything further." And the doctor bowed him out.

Ivan Ilyitch went out slowly and dejectedly, got into his sledge, and drove home. All the way home he was incessantly going over all the doctor had said, trying to translate all these complicated, obscure, scientific phrases into simple language, and to read in them an answer to the question, Is it bad—is it very bad, or nothing much as yet? And it seemed to him that the upshot of all the doctor had said was that it was

---

[16]Urine.

very bad. Everything seemed dismal to Ivan Ilyitch in the streets. The sledge-drivers were dismal, the houses were dismal, the people passing, and the shops were dismal. This ache, this dull gnawing ache, that never ceased for a second, seemed, when connected with the doctor's obscure utterances, to have gained a new, more serious significance. With a new sense of misery Ivan Ilyitch kept watch on it now.

He reached home and began to tell his wife about it. His wife listened; but in the middle of his account his daughter came in with her hat on, ready to go out with her mother. Reluctantly she half sat down to listen to these tedious details, but she could not stand it for long, and her mother did not hear his story to the end.

"Well, I'm very glad," said his wife; "now you must be sure and take the medicine regularly. Give me the prescription; I'll send Gerasim to the chemist's!" And she went to get ready to go out.

He had not taken a breath while she was in the room, and he heaved a deep sigh when she was gone.

"Well," he said, "may be it really is nothing as yet."

He began to take the medicine, to carry out the doctor's directions, which were changed after the analysis of the water. But it was just at this point that some confusion arose, either in the analysis or in what ought to have followed from it. The doctor himself, of course, could not be blamed for it, but it turned out that things had not gone as the doctor had told him. Either he had forgotten or told a lie, or was hiding something from him.

But Ivan Ilyitch still went on just as exactly carrying out the doctor's direction, and in doing so he found comfort at first.

From the time of his visit to the doctor Ivan Ilyitch's principal occupation became the exact observance of the doctor's prescriptions as regards hygiene and medicine and the careful observation of his ailment in all the functions of his organism. Ivan Ilyitch's principal interest came to be people's ailments and people's health. When anything was said in his presence about sick people, about deaths and recoveries, especially in the case of an illness resembling his own, he listened, trying to conceal his excitement, asked questions, and applied what he heard to his own trouble.

The ache did not grow less; but Ivan Ilyitch made great efforts to force himself to believe that he was better. And he succeeded in deceiving himself so long as nothing happened to disturb him. But as soon as he had a mischance, some unpleasant words with his wife, a failure in his official work, an unlucky hand at *vint,* he was at once acutely sensible of his illness. In former days he had borne with such mishaps, hoping soon to retrieve the mistake, to make a struggle, to reach success later, to have a lucky hand. But now he was cast down by every mischance and reduced to despair. He would say to himself: "Here I'm only just beginning to get better, and the medicine has begun to take effect, and now this mischance or disappointment." And he was furious against the mischance or the people who were causing him the disappointment and killing him, and he felt that this fury was killing him, but could not check it. One would have thought that it should have been clear to him that this exasperation against circumstances and people was aggravating his disease, and that therefore he ought not to pay attention to the unpleasant incidents. But his reasoning took quite the opposite direction. He said that he needed peace, and was on the watch for everything that disturbed his peace, and at the slightest disturbance of it he flew into a rage. What made his position worse was that he read medical books and consulted doctors. He got worse so gradually that he might have deceived himself, comparing one day with another, the difference was so slight. But when he consulted the doctors, then it seemed to him that he was getting worse, and very rapidly so indeed. And in spite of this, he was continually consulting the doctors.

That month he called on another celebrated doctor. The second celebrity said almost the same as the first, but put his questions differently; and the interview with this celebrity only redoubled the doubts and terrors of Ivan Ilyitch. A friend of a friend of his, a very good doctor, diagnosed the disease quite differently; and in spite of the fact that he guaranteed recovery, by his questions and his suppositions he confused Ivan Ilyitch even more and strengthened his suspicions. A homeopath gave yet another diagnosis of the complaint, and prescribed medicine, which Ivan Ilyitch took secretly for a week; but after a week of the homeopathic medicine he felt no relief, and losing faith both in the other doctor's treatment and in this, he fell into even deeper depression. One day a lady of his acquaintance talked to him of the healing wrought by the holy pictures. Ivan Ilyitch caught himself listening attentively and believing in the reality of the facts alleged. This incident alarmed him. "Can I have degenerated to such a point of intellectual feebleness?" he said to himself. "Nonsense! it's all rubbish. I must not give way to nervous fears, but fixing on one doctor, adhere strictly to his treatment. That's what I will do. Now it's settled. I won't think about it, but till next summer I will stick to the treatment, and then I shall see. Now I'll put a stop to this wavering!" It was easy to say this, but impossible to carry it out. The pain in his side was always dragging at him, seeming to grow more acute and ever more incessant; it seemed to him that the taste in his mouth was queerer, and there was a loathsome smell even from his breath, and his appetite and strength kept dwindling. There was no deceiving himself; something terrible, new, and so important that nothing more important had ever been in Ivan Ilyitch's life, was taking place in him, and he alone knew of it. All about him did not or would not understand, and believed that everything in the world was going on as before. This was what tortured Ivan Ilyitch more than anything. Those of his own household, most of all his wife and daughter, who were absorbed in a perfect whirl of visits, did not, he saw, comprehend it at all, and were annoyed that he was so depressed and exacting, as though he were to blame for it. Though they tried indeed to disguise it, he saw he was a nuisance to them; but that his wife had taken up a definite line of her own in regard to his illness, and stuck to it regardless of what he might say and do. This line was expressed thus: "You know," she would say to acquaintances, "Ivan Ilyitch cannot, like all other simple-hearted folks, keep to the treatment prescribed him. One day he'll take his drops and eat what he's ordered, and go to bed in good time; the next day, if I don't see to it, he'll suddenly forget to take his medicine, eat sturgeon (which is forbidden by the doctors), yes, and sit up at *vint* till past midnight."

"Why, when did I do that?" Ivan Ilyitch asked in vexation one day at Pyotr Ivanovitch's.

"Why, yesterday, with Shebek."

"It makes no difference. I couldn't sleep for pain."

"Well, it doesn't matter what you do it for, only you'll never get well like that, and you make us wretched."

Praskovya Fyodorovna's external attitude to her husband's illness, openly expressed to others and to himself, was that Ivan Ilyitch was to blame in the matter of his illness, and that the whole illness was another injury he was doing to his wife. Ivan Ilyitch felt that the expression of this dropped from her unconsciously, but that made it no easier for him.

In his official life, too, Ivan Ilyitch noticed, or fancied he noticed, a strange attitude to him. At one time it seemed to him that people were looking inquisitively at him, as a man who would shortly have to vacate his position; at another time his friends would suddenly begin chaffing him in a friendly way over his nervous fears, as though that awful and horrible, unheard-of thing that was going on within him, incessantly gnawing at him, and irresistibly dragging him away somewhere, were the most agreeable subject for joking. Shvarts especially, with his jocoseness, his liveliness, and his *comme-il-faut* tone, exasperated Ivan Ilyitch by reminding him of himself ten years ago.

Friends came sometimes to play cards. They sat down to the card-table; they shuffled and dealt the new cards. Diamonds were led and followed by diamonds, the seven. His partner said, "Can't trump," and played the two of diamonds. What then? Why, delightful, capital, it should have been—he had a trump hand. And suddenly Ivan Ilyitch feels that gnawing ache, that taste in his mouth, and it strikes him as something grotesque that with that he could be glad of a trump hand.

He looks at Mihail Mihailovitch, his partner, how he taps on the table with his red hand, and affably and indulgently abstains from snatching up the trick, and pushes the cards towards Ivan Ilyitch so as to give him the pleasure of taking them up, without any trouble, without even stretching out his hand. "What, does he suppose that I'm so weak that I can't stretch out my hand?" thinks Ivan Ilyitch, and he forgets the trumps, and trumps his partner's cards, and plays his trump hand without making three tricks; and what's the most awful thing of all is that he sees how upset Mihail Mihailovitch is about it, while he doesn't care a bit, and it's awful for him to think why he doesn't care.

They all see that he's in pain, and say to him, "We can stop if you're tired. You go and lie down." Lie down? No, he's not in the least tired; they will play the rubber. All are gloomy and silent. Ivan Ilyitch feels that it is he who has brought this gloom upon them, and he cannot disperse it. They have supper, and the party breaks up, and Ivan Ilyitch is left alone with the consciousness that his life is poisoned for him and poisons the life of others, and that this poison is not losing its force, but is continually penetrating more and more deeply into his whole existence.

And with the consciousness of this, and with the physical pain in addition, and the terror in addition to that, he must lie in his bed, often not able to sleep for pain the greater part of the night; and in the morning he must get up again, dress, go to the law-court, speak, write, or, if he does not go out, stay at home for all the four-and-twenty hours of the day and night, of which each one is a torture. And he had to live thus on the edge of the precipice alone, without one man who would understand and feel for him.

5

In this way one month, then a second, passed by. Just before the New Year his brother-in-law arrived in the town on a visit to them. Ivan Ilyitch was at the court when he arrived. Praskovya Fyodorovna had gone out shopping. Coming home and going into his study, he found there his brother-in-law, a healthy, florid man, engaged in unpacking his trunk. He raised his head, hearing Ivan Ilyitch's step, and for a second stared at him without a word. That stare told Ivan Ilyitch everything. His brother-in-law opened his mouth to utter an "Oh!" of surprise, but checked himself. That confirmed it all.

"What! have I changed?"

"Yes, there is a change."

And all Ivan Ilyitch's efforts to draw him into talking of his appearance his brother-in-law met with obstinate silence. Praskovya Fyodorovna came in; the brother-in-law went to see her. Ivan Ilyitch locked his door and began gazing at himself in the looking-glass, first full face, then in profile. He took up his photograph, taken with his wife, and compared the portrait with what he saw in the looking-glass. The change was immense. Then he bared his arm to the elbow, looked at it, pulled the sleeve down again, sat down on an ottoman and felt blacker than night.

"I mustn't, I mustn't," he said to himself, jumped up, went to the table, opened some official paper, tried to read it, but could not. He opened the door, went into the drawing-room. The door into the drawing-room was closed. He went up to it on tiptoe and listened.

"No, you're exaggerating," Praskovya Fyodorovna was saying.

"Exaggerating? You can't see it. Why, he's a dead man. Look at his eyes—there's no light in them. But what's wrong with him?"

"No one can tell. Nikolaev" (that was another doctor) "said something, but I don't know, Leshtchetitsky" (this was the celebrated doctor) "said the opposite."

Ivan Ilyitch walked away, went to his own room, lay down, and fell to musing. "A kidney—a loose kidney." He remembered all the doctors had told him, how it had been detached, and how it was loose; and by an effort of imagination he tried to catch that kidney and to stop it, to strengthen it. So little was needed, he fancied. "No, I'll go again to Pyotr Ivanovitch" (this was the friend who had a friend a doctor). He rang, ordered the horse to be put in, and got ready to go out.

"Where are you off to, Jean?"[17] asked his wife with a peculiarly melancholy and exceptionally kind expression.

This exceptionally kind expression exasperated him. He looked darkly at her.

"I want to see Pyotr Ivanovitch."

He went to the friend, who had a friend a doctor. And with him to the doctor's. He found him in, and had a long conversation with him.

Reviewing the anatomical and physiological details of what, according to the doctor's view, was taking place within him, he understood it all. It was just one thing—a little thing wrong with the intestinal appendix. It might all come right. Only strengthen one sluggish organ, and decrease the undue activity of another, and absorption would take place, and all would be set right. He was a little late for dinner. He ate his dinner, talked cheerfully, but it was a long while before he could go to his own room to work. At last he went to his study, and at once sat down to work. He read his legal documents and did his work, but the consciousness never left him of having a matter of importance very near to his heart which he had put off, but would look into later. When he had finished his work, he remembered that the matter near his heart was thinking about the intestinal appendix. But he did not give himself up to it; he went into the drawing-room to tea. There were visitors; and there was talking, playing on the piano, and singing; there was the young examining magistrate, the desirable match for the daughter. Ivan Ilyitch spent the evening, as Praskovya Fyodorovna observed, in better spirits than any of them; but he never forgot for an instant that he had the important matter of the intestinal appendix put off for consideration later. At eleven o'clock he said good night and went to his own room. He had slept alone since his illness in a little room adjoining his study. He went in, undressed, and took up a novel of Zola,[18] but did not read it; he fell to thinking. And in his imagination the desired recovery of the intestinal appendix had taken place. There had been absorption, rejection, re-establishment of the regular action.

"Why, it's all simply that," he said to himself. "One only wants to assist nature." He remembered the medicine, got up, took it, lay down on his back, watching for the medicine to act beneficially and overcome the pain. "It's only to take it regularly and avoid injurious influences; why, already I feel rather better, much better." He

---

[17]French version of Ivan.

[18]Émile Zola (1840–1902), a French novelist criticized by Tolstoy for his crude, naturalistic writing.

began to feel his side; it was not painful to the touch. "Yes, I don't feel it—really, much better already." He put out the candle and lay on his side. "The appendix is getting better, absorption." Suddenly he felt the familiar, old, dull, gnawing ache, persistent, quiet, in earnest. In his mouth the same familiar loathsome taste. His heart sank, and his brain felt dim, misty. "My God, my God!" he said, "again, again, and it will never cease." And suddenly the whole thing rose before him in quite a different aspect. "Intestinal appendix! kidney!" he said to himself. "It's not a question of the appendix, not a question of the kidney, but of life and . . . death. Yes, life has been and now it's going, going away, and I cannot stop it. Yes. Why deceive myself? Isn't it obvious to every one, except me, that I'm dying, and it's only a question of weeks, of days—at once perhaps. There was light, and now there is darkness. I was here, and now I am going! Where?" A cold chill ran over him, his breath stopped. He heard nothing but the throbbing of his heart.

"I shall be no more, then what will there be? There'll be nothing. Where then shall I be when I'm no more? Can this be dying? No; I don't want to!" He jumped up, tried to light the candle; and fumbling with trembling hands, he dropped the candle and the candlestick on the floor and fell back again on the pillow. "Why trouble? it doesn't matter," he said to himself, staring with open eyes into the darkness. "Death. Yes, death. And they—all of them—don't understand, and don't want to understand, and feel no pity. They are playing." (He caught through the closed doors the far-away cadence of a voice and the accompaniment.) "They don't care, but they will die too. Fools! Me sooner and them later; but it will be the same for them. And they are merry. The beasts!" Anger stifled him. And he was agonizingly, insufferably miserable. "It cannot be that all men always have been doomed to this awful horror!" He raised himself.

"There is something wrong in it; I must be calm. I must think it all over from the beginning." And then he began to consider. "Yes, the beginning of my illness. I knocked my side, and I was just the same, that day and the days after; it ached a little, then more, then doctors, then depression, misery, and again doctors; and I've gone on getting closer and closer to the abyss. Strength growing less. Nearer and nearer. And here I am, wasting away, no light in my eyes. I think of how to cure the appendix, but this is death. Can it be death?" Again a horror came over him; gasping for breath, he bent over, began feeling for the matches, and knocked his elbow against the bedside table. It was in his way and hurt him; he felt furious with it, in his anger knocked against it more violently, and upset it. And in despair, breathless, he fell back on his spine waiting for death to come that instant.

The visitors were leaving at that time. Praskovya Fyodorovna was seeing them out. She heard something fall, and came in.

"What is it?"

"Nothing. I dropped something by accident."

She went out, brought a candle. He was lying, breathing hard and fast, like a man who has run a mile, and staring with fixed eyes at her.

"What is it, Jean?"

"No—othing, I say. I dropped something."—"Why speak? She won't understand," he thought.

She certainly did not understand. She picked up the candle, lighted it for him, and went out hastily. She had to say good-bye to a departing guest. When she came back, he was lying in the same position on his back, looking upwards.

"How are you—worse?"

"Yes."

She shook her head, sat down.

"Do you know what, Jean? I wonder if we hadn't better send for Leshtchetitsky to see you here?"

This meant calling in the celebrated doctor, regardless of expense. He smiled malignantly, and said no. She sat a moment longer, went up to him, and kissed him on the forehead.

He hated her with all the force of his soul when she was kissing him, and had to make an effort not to push her away.

"Good night. Please God, you'll sleep."

"Yes."

6

Ivan Ilyitch saw that he was dying, and was in continual despair.

At the bottom of his heart Ivan Ilyitch knew that he was dying; but so far from growing used to this idea, he simply did not grasp it—he was utterly unable to grasp it.

The example of the syllogism that he had learned in Kiseveter's logic[19]—Caius is a man, men are mortal, therefore Caius is mortal—had seemed to him all his life correct only as regards Caius, but not at all as regards himself. In that case it was a question of Caius, a man, an abstract man, and it was perfectly true, but he was not Caius, and was not an abstract man; he had always been a creature quite, quite different from all others; he had been little Vanya with a mamma and papa, and Mitya and Volodya, with playthings and a coachman and a nurse; afterwards with Katenka, with all the joys and griefs and ecstasies of childhood, boyhood, and youth. What did Caius know of the smell of the leathern ball Vanya had been so fond of? Had Caius kissed his mother's hand like that? Caius had not heard the silk rustle of his mother's skirts. He had not made a riot at school over the pudding. Had Caius been in love like that? Could Caius preside over the sittings of the court?

And Caius certainly was mortal, and it was right for him to die; but for me, little Vanya, Ivan Ilyitch, with all my feelings and ideas—for me it's a different matter. And it cannot be that I ought to die. That would be too awful.

That was his feeling.

"If I had to die like Caius, I should have known it was so, some inner voice would have told me so. But there was nothing of the sort in me. And I and all my friends, we felt that it was not at all the same as with Caius. And now here it is!" he said to himself. "It can't be! It can't be, but it is! How is it? How's one to understand it?" And he could not conceive it, and tried to drive away this idea as false, incorrect, and morbid, and to supplant it by other, correct, healthy ideas. But this idea, not as an idea merely, but as it were an actual fact, came back again and stood confronting him.

And to replace this thought he called up other thoughts, one after another, in the hope of finding support in them. He tried to get back into former trains of thought, which in old days had screened off the thought of death. But, strange to say, all that had in old days covered up, obliterated the sense of death, could not now produce the same effect. Latterly, Ivan Ilyitch spent the greater part of his time in these efforts to restore his old trains of thought which had shut off death. At one time he would say to himself, "I'll put myself into my official work; why, I used to live in it." And he would go to the law-courts, banishing every doubt. He would enter into conversation with his colleagues, and would sit carelessly, as his old habit was, scanning the crowd below dreamily, and with both his wasted hands he would lean on the arms of the oak arm-chair just as he always did; and bending over to a

---

[19]Karl Kiesewetter (1766–1819) wrote a popular textbook, *Outline of Logic* (1796).

colleague, pass the papers to him and whisper to him, then suddenly dropping his eyes and sitting up straight, he would pronounce the familiar words that opened the proceedings. But suddenly in the middle, the pain in his side, utterly regardless of the stage he had reached in his conduct of the case, began its work. It riveted Ivan Ilyitch's attention. He drove away the thought of it, but it still did its work, and then *It* came and stood confronting him and looked at him, and he felt turned to stone, and the light died away in his eyes, and he began to ask himself again, "Can it be that It is the only truth?" And his colleagues and his subordinates saw with surprise and distress that he, the brilliant, subtle judge, was losing the thread of his speech, was making blunders. He shook himself, tried to regain his self-control, and got somehow to the end of the sitting, and went home with the painful sense that his judicial labors could not as of old hide from him what he wanted to hide; that he could not by means of his official work escape from *It*. And the worst of it was that It drew him to itself not for him to do anything in particular, but simply for him to look at It straight in the face, to look at It and, doing nothing, suffer unspeakably.

And to save himself from this, Ivan Ilyitch sought amusements, other screens, and these screens he found, and for a little while they did seem to save him; but soon again they were not so much broken down as let the light through, as though It pierced through everything, and there was nothing that could shut It off.

Sometimes during those days he would go into the drawing-room he had furnished, that drawing-room where he had fallen, for which—how bitterly ludicrous it was for him to think of it!—for the decoration of which he had sacrificed his life, for he knew that it was that bruise that had started his illness. He went in and saw that the polished table had been scratched by something. He looked for the cause, and found it in the bronze clasps of the album, which had been twisted on one side. He took up the album, a costly one, which he had himself arranged with loving care, and was vexed at the carelessness of his daughter and her friends. Here a page was torn, here the photographs had been shifted out of their places. He carefully put it to rights again and bent the clasp back.

Then the idea occurred to him to move all this setting up of the albums to another corner where the flowers stood. He called the footman; or his daughter or his wife came to help him. They did not agree with him, contradicted him; he argued, got angry. But all that was very well, since he did not think of It; It was not in sight.

But then his wife would say, as he moved something himself, "Do let the servants do it, you'll hurt yourself again," and all at once It peeped through the screen; he caught a glimpse of It. He caught a glimpse of It, but still he hoped It would hide itself. Involuntarily, though, he kept watch on his side; there it is just the same still, aching still, and now he cannot forget it, and *It* is staring openly at him from behind the flowers. What's the use of it all?

"And it's the fact that here, at that curtain, as if it had been storming a fort, I lost my life. Is it possible? How awful and how silly! It cannot be! It cannot be, and it is."

He went into his own room, lay down, and was again alone with It. Face to face with It, and nothing to be done with It. Nothing but to look at It and shiver.

7

How it came to pass during the third month of Ivan Ilyitch's illness, it would be impossible to say, for it happened little by little, imperceptibly, but it had come to pass that his wife and his daughter and his son and their servants and their acquaintances, and the doctors, and, most of all, he himself—all were aware that all interest in him for other people consisted now in the question how soon he would leave his place empty, free the living from the constraint of his presence, and be set free himself from his sufferings.

He slept less and less; they gave him opium, and began to inject morphine. But this did not relieve him. The dull pain he experienced in the half-asleep condition at first only relieved him as a change, but then it became as bad, or even more agonizing, than the open pain. He had special things to eat prepared for him according to the doctors' prescriptions; but these dishes became more and more distasteful, more and more revolting to him.

Special arrangements, too, had to be made for his other physical needs, and this was a continual misery to him. Misery from the uncleanliness, the unseemliness, and the stench, from the feeling of another person having to assist in it.

But just from this most unpleasant side of his illness there came comfort to Ivan Ilyitch. There always came into his room on these occasions to clear up for him the peasant who waited on table, Gerasim.

Gerasim was a clean, fresh, young peasant, who had grown stout and hearty on the good fare in town. Always cheerful and bright. At first the sight of this lad, always cleanly dressed in the Russian style, engaged in this revolting task, embarrassed Ivan Ilyitch.

One day, getting up from the night-stool,[20] too weak to replace his clothes, he dropped on to a soft low chair and looked with horror at his bare, powerless thighs, with the muscles so sharply standing out on them.

Then there came in with light, strong steps Gerasim, in his thick boots, diffusing a pleasant smell of tar from his boots, and bringing in the freshness of the winter air. Wearing a clean hempen apron, and a clean cotton shirt, with his sleeves tucked up on his strong, bare young arms, without looking at Ivan Ilyitch, obviously trying to check the radiant happiness in his face so as not to hurt the sick man, he went up to the night-stool.

"Gerasim," said Ivan Ilyitch faintly.

Gerasim started, clearly afraid that he had done something amiss, and with a rapid movement turned towards the sick man his fresh, good-natured, simple young face, just beginning to be downy with the first growth of beard.

"Yes, your honor."

"I'm afraid this is very disagreeable for you. You must excuse me. I can't help it."

"Why, upon my word, sir!" And Gerasim's eyes beamed, and he showed his white young teeth in a smile. "What's a little trouble? It's a case of illness with you, sir."

And with his deft, strong arms he performed his habitual task, and went out, stepping lightly. And five minutes later, treading just as lightly, he came back.

Ivan Ilyitch was still sitting in the same way in the arm-chair.

"Gerasim," he said, when the latter had replaced the night-stool all sweet and clean, "please help me; come here." Gerasim went up to him. "Lift me up. It's difficult for me alone, and I've sent Dmitry away."

Gerasim went up to him; as lightly as he stepped he put his strong arms round him, deftly and gently lifted and supported him, with the other hand pulled up his trousers, and would have set him down again. But Ivan Ilyitch asked him to carry him to the sofa. Gerasim, without effort, carefully not squeezing him, led him, almost carrying him, to the sofa, and settled him there.

---

[20]Commode.

"Thank you; how neatly and well . . . you do everything."

Gerasim smiled again, and would have gone away. But Ivan Ilyitch felt his presence such a comfort that he was reluctant to let him go.

"Oh, move that chair near me, please. No, that one, under my legs. I feel easier when my legs are higher."

Gerasim picked up the chair, and without letting it knock, set it gently down on the ground just at the right place, and lifted Ivan Ilyitch's legs on to it. It seemed to Ivan Ilyitch that he was easier just at the moment when Gerasim lifted his legs higher.

"I'm better when my legs are higher," said Ivan Ilyitch. "Put that cushion under me."

Gerasim did so. Again he lifted his legs to put the cushion under them. Again it seemed to Ivan Ilyitch that he was easier at that moment when Gerasim held his legs raised. When he laid them down again, he felt worse.

"Gerasim," he said to him, "are you busy just now?"

"Not at all, sir," said Gerasim, who had learned among the town-bred servants how to speak to gentlefolks.

"What have you left to do?"

"Why, what have I to do? I've done everything, there's only the wood to chop for to-morrow."

"Then hold my legs up like that—can you?"

"To be sure, I can." Gerasim lifted the legs up. And it seemed to Ivan Ilyitch that in that position he did not feel the pain at all.

"But how about the wood?"

"Don't you trouble about that, sir. We shall have time enough."

Ivan Ilyitch made Gerasim sit and hold his legs, and began to talk to him. And, strange to say, he fancied he felt better while Gerasim had hold of his legs.

From that time forward Ivan Ilyitch would sometimes call Gerasim, and get him to hold his legs on his shoulders, and he liked talking with him. Gerasim did this easily, readily, simply, and with a good-nature that touched Ivan Ilyitch. Health, strength, and heartiness in all other people were offensive to Ivan Ilyitch; but the strength and heartiness of Gerasim did not mortify him, but soothed him.

Ivan Ilyitch's great misery was due to the deception that for some reason or other every one kept up with him—that he was simply ill, and not dying, and that he need only keep quiet and follow the doctor's orders, and then some great change for the better would be the result. He knew that whatever they might do, there would be no result except more agonizing sufferings and death. And he was made miserable by this lie, made miserable at their refusing to acknowledge what they all knew and he knew, by their persisting in lying to him about his awful position, and in forcing him too to take part in this lie. Lying, lying, this lying carried on over him on the eve of his death, and destined to bring that terrible, solemn act of his death down to the level of all their visits, curtains, sturgeons for dinner . . . was a horrible agony for Ivan Ilyitch. And, strange to say, many times when they had been going through the regular performance over him, he had been within a hair's-breadth of screaming at them: "Cease your lying! You know, and I know, that I'm dying; so do, at least, give over lying!" But he had never had the spirit to do this. The terrible, awful act of his dying was, he saw, by all those about him, brought down to the level of a casual, unpleasant, and to some extent indecorous, incident (somewhat as they would behave with a person who should enter a drawing-room smelling unpleasant). It was brought down to this level by that very decorum to which he had been enslaved all his life. He saw that no one felt for him, because no one would even grasp his position. Gerasim was the only person who recognized the position, and felt sorry for him. And that was why Ivan Ilyitch was only at ease with Gerasim. He felt comforted when Gerasim sometimes supported his legs for whole nights at a stretch, and would not go away to bed, saying, "Don't you worry yourself, Ivan Ilyitch, I'll get sleep enough yet," or when suddenly dropping into the familiar peasant forms of speech, he added: "If thou weren't sick, but as 'tis, 'twould be strange if I didn't wait on thee." Gerasim alone did not lie; everything showed clearly that he alone understood what it meant, and saw no necessity to disguise it, and simply felt sorry for his sick, wasting master. He even said this once straight out, when Ivan Ilyitch was sending him away.

"We shall all die. So what's a little trouble?" he said, meaning by this to express that he did not complain of the trouble just because he was taking this trouble for a dying man, and he hoped that for him too some one would be willing to take the same trouble when his time came.

Apart from this deception, or in consequence of it, what made the greatest misery for Ivan Ilyitch was that no one felt for him as he would have liked them to feel for him. At certain moments, after prolonged suffering, Ivan Ilyitch, ashamed as he would have been to own it, longed more than anything for some one to feel sorry for him, as for a sick child. He longed to be petted, kissed, and wept over, as children are petted and comforted. He knew that he was an important member of the law-courts, that he had a beard turning grey, and that therefore it was impossible. But still he longed for it. And in his relations with Gerasim there was something approaching to that. And that was why being with Gerasim was a comfort to him. Ivan Ilyitch longs to weep, longs to be petted and wept over, and then there comes in a colleague, Shebek; and instead of weeping and being petted, Ivan Ilyitch puts on his serious, severe, earnest face, and from mere inertia gives his views on the effect of the last decision in the Court of Appeal, and obstinately insists upon them. This falsity around him and within him did more than anything to poison Ivan Ilyitch's last days.

8

It was morning. All that made it morning for Ivan Ilyitch was that Gerasim had gone away, and Pyotr the footman had come in; he had put out the candles, opened one of the curtains, and begun surreptitiously setting the room to rights. Whether it were morning or evening, Friday or Sunday, it all made no difference; it was always just the same thing. Gnawing, agonizing pain never ceasing for an instant; the hopeless sense of life always ebbing away, but still not yet gone; always swooping down on him that fearful, hated death, which was the only reality, and always the same falsity. What were days, or weeks, or hours of the day to him?

"Will you have tea, sir?"

"He wants things done in their regular order. In the morning the family should have tea," he thought, and only said—

"No."

"Would you care to move on to the sofa?"

"He wants to make the room tidy, and I'm in his way. I'm uncleanness, disorder," he thought, and only said—

"No, leave me alone."

The servant still moved busily about his work. Ivan Ilyitch stretched out his hand. Pyotr went up to offer his services.

"What can I get you?"

"My watch."

Pyotr got out the watch, which lay just under his hand, and gave it to him.

"Half-past eight. Are they up?"

"Not yet, sir. Vladimir Ivanovitch" (that was his son) "has gone to the high school, and Praskovya Fyodorovna gave orders that she was to be waked if you asked for her. Shall I send word?"

"No, no need." Should I try some tea? he thought.

"Yes, tea . . . bring it."

Pyotr was on his way out. Ivan Ilyitch felt frightened of being left alone. "How keep him? Oh, the medicine. Pyotr, give me my medicine. Oh well, may be, medicine may still be some good." He took the spoon, drank it. "No, it does no good. It's all rubbish, deception," he decided, as soon as he tasted the familiar, mawkish, hopeless taste. "No, I can't believe it now. But the pain, why this pain? If it would only cease for a minute." And he groaned. Pyotr turned round. "No, go on. Bring the tea."

Pyotr went away. Ivan Ilyitch, left alone, moaned, not so much from the pain, awful as it was, as from misery. Always the same thing again and again, all these endless days and nights. If it would only be quicker. Quicker to what? Death, darkness. No, no. Anything better than death!

When Pyotr came in with the tea on a tray, Ivan Ilyitch stared for some time absent-mindedly at him, not grasping who he was and what he wanted. Pyotr was disconcerted by this stare. And when he showed he was disconcerted, Ivan Ilyitch came to himself.

"Oh yes," he said, "tea, good, set it down. Only help me to wash and put on a clean shirt."

And Ivan Ilyitch began his washing. He washed his hands slowly, and then his face, cleaned his teeth, combed his hair, and looked in the looking-glass. He felt frightened at what he saw, especially at the way his hair clung limply to his pale forehead. When his shirt was being changed, he knew he would be still more terrified if he glanced at his body, and he avoided looking at himself. But at last it was all over. He put on his dressing-gown, covered himself with a rug, and sat in the armchair to drink his tea. For one moment he felt refreshed; but as soon as he began to drink the tea, again there was the same taste, the same pain. He forced himself to finish it, and lay down, stretched out his legs. He lay down and dismissed Pyotr.

Always the same. A gleam of hope flashes for a moment, then again the sea of despair roars about him again, and always pain, always pain, always heartache, and always the same thing. Alone it is awfully dreary; he longs to call some one, but he knows beforehand that with others present it will be worse. "Morphine again—only to forget again. I'll tell him, the doctor, that he must think of something else. It can't go on, it can't go on like this."

One hour, two hours pass like this. Then there is a ring at the front door. The doctor, perhaps. Yes, it is the doctor, fresh, hearty, fat, and cheerful, wearing that expression that seems to say, "You there are in a panic about something, but we'll soon set things right for you." The doctor is aware that this expression is hardly fitting here, but he has put it on once and for all, and can't take it off, like a man who has put on a frockcoat to pay a round of calls.

In a hearty, reassuring manner the doctor rubs his hands.

"I'm cold. It's a sharp frost. Just let me warm myself," he says with an expression, as though it's only a matter of waiting a little till he's warm, and as soon as he's warm he'll set everything to rights.

"Well, now, how are you?"

Ivan Ilyitch feels that the doctor would like to say, "How's the little trouble?" but that he feels that he can't talk like that, and says, "How did you pass the night?"

Ivan Ilyitch looks at the doctor with an expression that asks—

"Is it possible you're never ashamed of lying?"

But the doctor does not care to understand this look.

And Ivan Ilyitch says—

"It's always just as awful. The pain never leaves me, never ceases. If only there were something!"

"Ah, you're all like that, all sick people say that. Come, now, I do believe I'm thawed; even Praskovya Fyodorovna, who's so particular, could find no fault with my temperature. Well, now I can say good morning." And the doctor shakes hands.

And dropping his former levity, the doctor, with a serious face, proceeds to examine the patient, feeling his pulse, to take his temperature, and then the tappings and soundings begin.

Ivan Ilyitch knows positively and indubitably that it's all nonsense and empty deception; but when the doctor, kneeling down, stretches over him, putting his ear first higher, then lower, and goes through various gymnastic evolutions over him with a serious face, Ivan Ilyitch is affected by this, as he used sometimes to be affected by the speeches of the lawyers in court, though he was perfectly well aware that they were telling lies all the while and why they were telling lies.

The doctor, kneeling on the sofa, was still sounding him, when there was the rustle of Praskovya Fyodorovna's silk dress in the doorway, and she was heard scolding Pyotr for not having let her know that the doctor had come.

She comes in, kisses her husband, and at once begins to explain that she has been up a long while, and that it was only through a misunderstanding that she was not there when the doctor came.

Ivan Ilyitch looks at her, scans her all over, and sets down against her her whiteness and plumpness, and the cleanness of her hands and neck, and the glossiness of her hair, and the gleam full of life in her eyes. With all the force of his soul he hates her. And when she touches him it makes him suffer from the thrill of hatred he feels for her.

Her attitude to him and his illness is still the same. Just as the doctor had taken up a certain line with the patient which he was not now able to drop, so she too had taken up a line with him—that he was not doing something he ought to do, and was himself to blame, and she was lovingly reproaching him for his neglect, and she could not now get out of this attitude.

"Why, you know, he won't listen to me; he doesn't take his medicine at the right times. And what's worse still, he insists on lying in a position that surely must be bad for him—with his legs in the air."

She described how he made Gerasim hold his legs up.

The doctor smiled with kindly condescension that said, "Oh well, it can't be helped, these sick people do take up such foolish fancies; but we must forgive them."

When the examination was over, the doctor looked at his watch, and then Praskovya Fyodorovna informed Ivan Ilyitch that it must, of course, be as he liked, but she had sent to-day for a celebrated doctor, and that he would examine him, and have a consultation with Mihail Danilovitch (that was the name of their regular doctor).

"Don't oppose it now, please. This I'm doing entirely for my own sake," she said ironically, meaning it to be understood that she was doing it all for his sake, and was only saying this to give him no right to refuse her request. He lay silent, knitting his brows. He felt that he was hemmed in by such a tangle of falsity that it was hard to disentangle anything from it.

Everything she did for him was entirely for her own sake, and she told him she was doing for her own sake what she actually was doing for her own sake as something so incredible that he would take it as meaning the opposite.

At half-past eleven the celebrated doctor came. Again came the sounding, and then grave conversation in his presence and in the other room about the kidney and the appendix, and questions and answers, with such an air of significance, that again, instead of the real question of life and death, which was now the only one that confronted him, the question that came uppermost was of the kidney and the appendix, which were doing something not as they ought to do, and were for that reason being attacked by Mihail Danilovitch and the celebrated doctor, and forced to mend their ways.

The celebrated doctor took leave of him with a serious, but not a hopeless face. And to the timid question that Ivan Ilyitch addressed to him while he lifted his eyes, shining with terror and hope, up towards him, Was there a chance of recovery? he answered that he could not answer for it, but that there was a chance. The look of hope with which Ivan Ilyitch watched the doctor out was so piteous that, seeing it, Praskovya Fyodorovna positively burst into tears, as she went out of the door to hand the celebrated doctor his fee in the next room.

The gleam of hope kindled by the doctor's assurance did not last long. Again the same room, the same pictures, the curtains, the wallpaper, the medicine-bottles, and ever the same, his aching suffering body. And Ivan Ilyitch began to moan; they gave him injections, and he sank into oblivion. When he waked up it was getting dark; they brought him his dinner. He forced himself to eat some broth; and again everything the same, and again the coming night.

After dinner at seven o'clock, Praskovya Fyodorovna came into his room, dressed as though to go to a *soirée*,[21] with her full bosom laced in tight, and traces of powder on her face. She had in the morning mentioned to him that they were going to the theatre. Sarah Bernhardt[22] was visiting the town, and they had a box, which he had insisted on their taking. By now he had forgotten about it, and her smart attire was an offense to him. But he concealed this feeling when he recollected that he had himself insisted on their taking a box and going, because it was an aesthetic pleasure, beneficial and instructive for the children.

Praskovya Fyodorovna came in satisfied with herself, but yet with something of a guilty air. She sat down, asked how he was, as he saw, simply for the sake of asking, and not for the sake of learning anything, knowing indeed that there was nothing to learn, and began telling him how absolutely necessary it was; how she would not have gone for anything, but the box had been taken, and Liza, their daughter, and Petrishtchev (the examining lawyer, the daughter's suitor) were going, and that it was out of the question to let them go alone. But that she would have liked much better to stay with him. If only he would be sure to follow the doctor's prescription while she was away.

"Oh, and Fyodor Dmitryevitch" (the suitor) "would like to come in. May he? And Liza?"

"Yes, let them come in."

The daughter came in, in evening clothes, her fresh young body showing, while his body made him suffer so. But she made a show of it; she was strong, healthy, obviously in love, and impatient of the illness, suffering, and death that hindered her happiness.

Fyodor Dmitryevitch came in too in evening dress, his hair curled *à la Capoul*,[23] with his long sinewy neck tightly fenced round by a white collar, with his vast

---

[21] Evening event.
[22] A popular French actress (1844–1923).
[23] "According to Capoul," a French style.

expanse of white chest and strong thighs displayed in narrow black trousers, with one white glove in his hand and a crush opera hat.

Behind him crept in unnoticed the little high school boy in his new uniform, poor fellow, in gloves, and with those awful blue rings under his eyes that Ivan Ilyitch knew the meaning of.

He always felt sorry for his son. And pitiable indeed was his scared face of sympathetic suffering. Except Gerasim, Ivan Ilyitch fancied that Volodya was the only one that understood and was sorry.

They all sat down; again they asked how he was. A silence followed. Liza asked her mother about the opera-glass. An altercation ensued between the mother and daughter as to who had taken it, and where it had been put. It turned into an unpleasant squabble.

Fyodor Dmitryevitch asked Ivan Ilyitch whether he had seen Sarah Bernhardt? Ivan Ilyitch could not at first catch the question that was asked him, but then he said, "No, have you seen her before?"

"Yes, in *Adrienne Lecouvreur*."[24]

Praskovya Fyodorovna observed that she was particularly good in that part. The daughter made some reply. A conversation sprang up about the art and naturalness of her acting, that conversation that is continually repeated and always the same.

In the middle of the conversation Fyodor Dmitryevitch glanced at Ivan Ilyitch and relapsed into silence. The others looked at him and became mute, too. Ivan Ilyitch was staring with glittering eyes straight before him, obviously furious with them. This had to be set right, but it could not anyhow be set right. This silence had somehow to be broken. No one would venture on breaking it, and all began to feel alarmed that the decorous deception was somehow breaking down, and the facts would be exposed to all. Liza was the first to pluck up courage. She broke the silence. She tried to cover up what they were all feeling, but inadvertently she gave it utterance.

"*If we are going*, though, it's time to start," she said, glancing at her watch, a gift from her father; and with a scarcely perceptible meaning smile to the young man, referring to something only known to themselves, she got up with a rustle of her skirts.

They all got up, said good-bye, and went away. When they were gone, Ivan Ilyitch fancied he was easier; there was no falsity—that had gone away with them, but the pain remained. That continual pain, that continual terror, made nothing harder, nothing easier. It was always worse.

Again came minute after minute, hour after hour, still the same and still no end, and ever more terrible the inevitable end.

"Yes, send Gerasim," he said in answer to Pyotr's question.

9

Late at night his wife came back. She came in on tiptoe, but he heard her, opened his eyes, and made haste to close them again. She wanted to send away Gerasim and sit up with him herself instead. He opened his eyes and said, "No, go away."

"Are you in great pain?"

---

[24]A play by Eugène Scribe (1791–1861), a commercial playwright disliked by Tolstoy.

"Always the same."

"Take some opium."

He agreed, and drank it. She went away.

Till three o'clock he slept a miserable sleep. It seemed to him that he and his pain were being thrust somewhere into a narrow, deep, black sack, and they kept pushing him further and further in, and still could not thrust him to the bottom. And this operation was awful to him, and was accompanied with agony. And he was afraid, and yet wanted to fall into it, and struggled and yet tried to get into it. And all of a sudden he slipped and fell and woke up. Gerasim, still the same, is sitting at the foot of the bed half-dozing peacefully, patient. And he is lying with his wasted legs clad in stockings, raised on Gerasim's shoulders, the same candle burning in the alcove, and the same interminable pain.

"Go away, Gerasim," he whispered.

"It's all right, sir. I'll stay a bit longer."

"No, go away."

He took his legs down, lay sideways on his arm, and he felt very sorry for himself. He only waited till Gerasim had gone away into the next room; he could restrain himself no longer, and cried like a child. He cried at his own helplessness, at his awful loneliness, at the cruelty of people, at the cruelty of God, at the absence of God.

"Why hast Thou done all this? What brought me to this? Why, why torture me so horribly?"

He did not expect an answer, and wept indeed that there was and could be no answer. The pain grew more acute again, but he did not stir, did not call. He said to himself, "Come, more then; come, strike me! But what for? What have I done to Thee? what for?"

Then he was still, ceased weeping, held his breath, and was all attention; he listened, as it were, not to a voice uttering sounds, but to the voice of his soul, to the current of thoughts that rose up within him.

"What is it you want?" was the first clear idea capable of putting into words that he grasped.

"What? Not to suffer, to live," he answered.

And again he was utterly plunged into attention so intense that even the pain did not distract him.

"To live? Live how?" the voice of his soul was asking.

"Why, live as I used to live before—happily and pleasantly."

"As you used to live before—happily and pleasantly?" queried the voice. And he began going over in his imagination the best moments of his pleasant life. But strange to say, all these best moments of his pleasant life seemed now not at all what they had seemed then. All—except the first memories of childhood—there, in his childhood there had been something really pleasant in which one could have lived if it had come back. But the creature who had this pleasant experience was no more; it was like a memory of some one else.

As soon as he reached the beginning of what had resulted in him as he was now, Ivan Ilyitch, all that had seemed joys to him then now melted away before his eyes and were transformed into something trivial, and often disgusting.

And the further he went from childhood, the nearer to the actual present, the more worthless and uncertain were the joys. It began with life at the school of jurisprudence. Then there had still been something genuinely good; then there had been gaiety; then there had been friendship; then there had been hopes. But in the higher classes these good moments were already becoming rarer. Later on, during the first period of his official life, at the governor's, good moments appeared; but it was all mixed, and less and less of it was good. And further on even less was good, and the further he went the less good there was.

His marriage . . . as gratuitous as the disillusion of it and the smell of his wife's breath and the sensuality, the hypocrisy! And that deadly official life, and anxiety about money, and so for one year, and two, and ten, and twenty, and always the same thing. And the further he went, the more deadly it became. "As though I had been going steadily downhill, imagining that I was going uphill. So it was in fact. In public opinion I was going uphill, and steadily as I got up it, life was ebbing away from me. . . . And now the work's done, there's nothing left but to die.

"But what is this? What for? It cannot be! It cannot be that life has been so senseless, so loathsome? And if it really was so loathsome and senseless, then why die, and die in agony? There's something wrong.

"Can it be I have not lived as one ought?" suddenly came into his head. "But how not so, when I've done everything as it should be done?" he said, and at once dismissed this only solution of all the enigma of life and death at something utterly out of the question.

"What do you want now? To live? Live how? Live as you live at the courts when the usher booms out: 'The Judge is coming!' . . . The judge is coming, the judge is coming," he repeated to himself. "Here he is, the judge! But I'm not to blame!" he shrieked in fury. "What's it for?" And he left off crying, and turning with his face to the wall, fell to pondering always on the same question, "What for, why all this horror?"

But however much he pondered, he could not find an answer. And whenever the idea struck him, as it often did, that it all came of his never having lived as he ought, he thought of all the correctness of his life and dismissed the strange idea.

10

Another fortnight had passed. Ivan Ilyitch could not now get up from the sofa. He did not like lying in bed, and lay on the sofa. And lying almost all the time facing the wall, in loneliness he suffered all the inexplicable agonies, and in loneliness pondered always that inexplicable question, "What is it? Can it be true that it's death?" And an inner voice answered, "Yes, it is true." "Why these agonies?" and a voice answered, "For no reason." Beyond and besides this there was nothing.

From the very beginning of his illness, ever since Ivan Ilyitch first went to the doctor's, his life had been split up into two contradictory moods, which were continually alternating—one was despair and the anticipation of an uncomprehended and awful death; the other was hope and an absorbed watching over the actual condition of his body. First there was nothing confronting him but a kidney or intestine which had temporarily declined to perform its duties, then there was nothing but unknown awful death, which there was no escaping.

These two moods had alternated from the very beginning of the illness; but the further the illness progressed, the more doubtful and fantastic became the conception of the kidney, and the more real the sense of approaching death.

He had but to reflect on what he had been three months before and what he was now, to reflect how steadily he had been going downhill, for every possibility of hope to be shattered.

Of late, in the loneliness in which he found himself, lying with his face to the back of the sofa, a loneliness in the middle of a populous town and of his numerous acquaintances and his family, a loneliness than which none more complete could be found anywhere—not at the bottom of the sea, not deep down in the earth;—of late in this fearful loneliness Ivan Ilyitch had lived only in imagination in the past. One by one the pictures of his past rose up before him. It always began from what was nearest in time and went back to the most remote, to childhood, and rested there. If Ivan Ilyitch thought of the stewed prunes that had been offered him for dinner that day, his mind went back to the damp, wrinkled French plum of his childhood, of its peculiar taste and the flow of saliva when the stone was sucked; and along with this memory of a taste there rose up a whole series of memories of that period—his nurse, his brother, his playthings. "I mustn't . . . it's too painful," Ivan Ilyitch said to himself, and he brought himself back to the present. The button on the back of the sofa and the creases in the morocco. "Morocco's dear, and doesn't wear well; there was a quarrel over it. But the morocco was different, and different too the quarrel when we tore father's portfolio and were punished, and mamma bought us the tarts." And again his mind rested on his childhood, and again it was painful, and he tried to drive it away and think of something else.

And again at that point, together with that chain of associations, quite another chain of memories came into his heart, of how his illness had grown up and become more acute. It was the same there, the further back the more life there had been. There had been both more that was good in life and more of life itself. And the two began to melt into one. "Just as the pain goes on getting worse and worse, so has my whole life gone on getting worse and worse," he thought. One light spot was there at the back, at the beginning of life, and then it kept getting blacker and blacker, and going faster and faster. "In inverse ratio to the square of the distance from death," thought Ivan Ilyitch. And the image of a stone falling downwards with increasing velocity sank into his soul. Life, a series of increasing sufferings, falls more and more swiftly to the end, the most fearful sufferings. "I am falling." He shuddered, shifted himself, would have resisted, but he knew beforehand that he could not resist; and again, with eyes weary with gazing at it, but unable not to gaze at what was before him, he stared at the back of the sofa and waited, waited expecting that fearful fall and shock and dissolution. "Resistance is impossible," he said to himself. "But if one could at least comprehend what it's for? Even that's impossible. It could be explained if one were to say that I hadn't lived as I ought. But that can't be alleged," he said to himself, thinking of all the regularity, correctness, and propriety of his life. "That really can't be admitted," he said to himself, his lips smiling ironically as though some one could see his smile and be deceived by it. "No explanation! Agony, death. . . . What for?"

11

So passed a fortnight. During that fortnight an event occurred that had been desired by Ivan Ilyitch and his wife. Petrishtchev made a formal proposal. This took place in the evening. Next day Praskovya Fyodorovna went in to her husband, resolving in her mind how to inform him of Fyodor Dmitryevitch's proposal, but that night there had been a change for the worse in Ivan Ilyitch. Praskovya Fyodorovna found him on the same sofa, but in a different position. He was lying on his face, groaning, and staring straight before him with a fixed gaze.

She began talking of remedies. He turned his stare on her. She did not finish what she had begun saying; such hatred of her in particular was expressed in that stare.

"For Christ's sake, let me die in peace," he said.

She would have gone away, but at that moment the daughter came in and went up to say good morning to him. He looked at his daughter just as at his wife, and to her inquiries how he was, he told her drily that they would soon all be rid of him. Both were silent, sat a little while, and went out.

"How are we to blame?" said Liza to her mother. "As though we had done it! I'm sorry for papa, but why punish us?"

At the usual hour the doctor came. Ivan Ilyitch answered, "Yes, no," never taking his exasperated stare from him, and towards the end he said, "Why, you know that you can do nothing, so let me be."

"We can relieve your suffering," said the doctor.

"Even that you can't do; let me be."

The doctor went into the drawing-room and told Praskovya Fyodorovna that it was very serious, and that the only resource left them was opium to relieve his sufferings, which must be terrible. The doctor said his physical sufferings were terrible, and that was true; but even more terrible than his physical sufferings were his mental sufferings, and in that lay his chief misery.

His moral sufferings were due to the fact that during that night, as he looked at the sleepy, good-natured, broad-cheeked face of Gerasim, the thought had suddenly come into his head, "What if in reality all my life, my conscious life, has been not the right thing?" The thought struck him that what he had regarded before as an utter impossibility, that he had spent his life not as he ought, might be the truth. It struck him that those scarcely detected impulses of struggle within him against what was considered good by persons of higher position, scarcely detected impulses which he had dismissed, that they might be the real thing, and everything else might be not the right thing. And his official work, and his ordering of his daily life and of his family, and these social and official interests,—all that might be not the right thing. He tried to defend it all to himself. And suddenly he felt all the weakness of what he was defending. And it was useless to defend it.

"But if it's so," he said to himself, "and I am leaving life with the consciousness that I have lost all that was given me, and there's no correcting it, then what?" He lay on his back and began going over his whole life entirely anew. When he saw the footman in the morning, then his wife, then his daughter, then the doctor, every movement they made, every word they uttered, confirmed for him the terrible truth that had been revealed to him in the night. In them he saw himself, saw all in which he had lived, and saw distinctly that it was all not the right thing; it was a horrible, vast deception that concealed both life and death. This consciousness intensified his physical agonies, multiplied them tenfold. He groaned and tossed from side to side and pulled at the covering over him. It seemed to him that it was stifling him and weighing him down. And for that he hated them.

They gave him a big dose of opium; he sank into unconsciousness; but at dinner-time the same thing began again. He drove them all away, and tossed from side to side.

His wife came to him and said, "Jean, darling, do this for my sake" (for my sake?). "It can't do harm, and it often does good. Why, it's nothing. And often in health people——"

He opened his eyes wide.

"What? Take the sacrament? What for? No. Besides . . ."

She began to cry.

"Yes, my dear. I'll send for our priest, he's so nice."

"All right, very well," he said.

When the priest came and confessed him he was softened, felt as it were a relief from his doubts, and consequently from his sufferings, and there came a moment of hope. He began once more thinking of the intestinal appendix and the possibility of curing it. He took the sacrament with tears in his eyes.

When they laid him down again after the sacrament for a minute, he felt comfortable, and again the hope of life sprang up. He began to think about the operation which had been suggested to him. "To live, I want to live," he said to himself. His wife came in to congratulate him; she uttered the customary words and added—

"It's quite true, isn't it, that you're better?"

Without looking at her, he said, "Yes."

Her dress, her figure, the expression of her face, the tone of her voice,—all told him the same: "Not the right thing. All that in which you lived and are living is lying, deceit, hiding life and death away from you." And as soon as he had formed that thought, hatred sprang up in him, and with that hatred agonizing physical sufferings, and with these sufferings the sense of inevitable, approaching ruin. Something new was happening; there were screwing and shooting pains, and a tightness in his breathing.

The expression of his face as he uttered that "Yes" was terrible. After uttering that "Yes," looking her straight in the face, he turned on to his face, with a rapidity extraordinary in his weakness, and shrieked—

"Go away, go away, let me be!"

12

From that moment there began the scream that never ceased for three days, and was so awful that through two closed doors one could not hear it without horror. At the moment when he answered his wife he grasped that he had fallen, that there was no return, that the end had come, quite the end, while doubt was still as unsolved, still remained doubt.

"Oo! Oo—o! Oo!" he screamed in varying intonations. He had begun screaming, "I don't want to!" and so had gone on screaming on the same vowel sound—oo!

All those three days, during which time did not exist for him, he was struggling in that black sack into which he was being thrust by an unseen resistless force. He struggled as the man condemned to death struggles in the hands of the executioner, knowing that he cannot save himself. And every moment he felt that in spite of all his efforts to struggle against it, he was getting nearer and nearer to what terrified him. He felt that his agony was due both to his being thrust into this black hole and still more to his not being able to get right into it. What hindered him from getting into it was the claim that his life had been good. That justification of his life held him fast and would not let him get forward, and it caused him more agony than all.

All at once some force struck him in the chest, in the side, and stifled his breathing more than ever; he rolled forward into the hole, and there at the end there was some sort of light. It had happened with him, as it had sometimes happened to him in a railway carriage, when he had thought he was going forward while he was going back, and all of a sudden recognized his real direction.

"Yes, it has all been not the right thing," he said to himself, "but that's no matter." He could, he could do the right thing. "What is the right thing?" he asked himself, and suddenly he became quiet.

This was at the end of the third day, two hours before his death. At the very moment the schoolboy had stealthily crept into his father's room and gone up to his bedside. The dying man was screaming and waving his arms. His hand fell on the schoolboy's head. The boy snatched it, pressed it to his lips, and burst into tears.

At that very moment Ivan Ilyitch had rolled into the hole, and caught sight of the light, and it was revealed to him that his life had not been what it ought to have been, but that that could still be set right. He asked himself, "What is the right thing?"—and became quiet, listening. Then he felt some one was kissing his hand. He opened his eyes and glanced at his son. He felt sorry for him. His wife went up to him. He glanced at her. She was gazing at him with open mouth, the tears unwiped streaming over her nose and cheeks, a look of despair on her face. He felt sorry for her.

"Yes, I'm making them miserable," he thought. "They're sorry, but it will be better for them when I die." He would have said this, but had not the strength to utter it. "Besides, why speak, I must act," he thought. With a glance to his wife he pointed to his son and said—

"Take away . . . sorry for him. . . . And you too . . ." He tried to say "forgive," but said "forgo" . . . and too weak to correct himself, shook his hand, knowing that He would understand Whose understanding mattered.

And all at once it became clear to him that what had tortured him and would not leave him was suddenly dropping away all at once on both sides and on ten sides and on all sides. He was sorry for them, must act so that they might not suffer. Set them free and be free himself of those agonies. "How right and how simple!" he thought. "And the pain?" he asked himself. "Where's it gone? Eh, where are you, pain?"

He began to watch for it.

"Yes, here it is. Well, what of it, let the pain be.

"And death. Where is it?"

He looked for his old accustomed terror of death, and did not find it. "Where is it? What death?" There was no terror, because death was not either.

In the place of death there was light.

"So this is it!" he suddenly exclaimed aloud.

"What joy!"

To him all this passed in a single instant, and the meaning of that instant suffered no change after. For those present his agony lasted another two hours. There was a rattle in his throat, a twitching in his wasted body. Then the rattle and the gasping came at longer and longer intervals.

"It is over!" some one said over him.

He caught those words and repeated them in his soul.

"Death is over," he said to himself. "It's no more."

He drew in a breath, stopped midway in the breath, stretched and died.

EMILY DICKINSON
[1830–1886]

Emily Dickinson's poems, in one sense, have not had very much influence on succeeding generations of writers; it is hard to name a single poet whose poems look or sound like Dickinson's crafted miniatures. But in another way her influence has been vast, especially (but not only) for women, in that she, like Whitman, teaches writers audacity. The female voices that speak Emily Dickinson's poems are daring, subversive, uncompromising. They belong in the company of Goethe's Faust, of Brontë's Cathy and Heathcliff, for they weigh old assumptions and find them wanting, speak about desires deemed improper by society, defy convention and invite cataclysm. Dickinson's work reminds us that the romantic hero, the person who tests the limits of God's and society's tolerance, who always thirsts for something beyond, who experiences suicidal despair and shattering joy, can be a woman writing in an upstairs bedroom.

LIFE

In some ways, we know a fair amount about Emily Dickinson. The outward circumstances of her life were so few and mild that a visit to an ophthalmologist or the first prize awarded her bread at the local fair count as significant events in the chronology. We know that her recipe for Black Cake called for nineteen eggs; we know that she loved to kiss her baby nephew on the fat crease of his neck. We know, in short, many of the sorts of details often absent from male biography. But we know little of her inner life except that it was intense. We do not know the name or even the sex of the person to whom in the early 1860s she wrote a series of anguished and openly erotic love letters, nor do we know whether those letters were ever sent. We do not know why she chose to refrain from publishing all but eight of her more than 1,700 poems, although at her death she left some 700 of them carefully copied out and hand-sewn into packets. Nor do we know why, after a rather lively childhood and adolescence, she sought a more and more secluded life.

Dickinson was born on December 10, 1830, in Amherst, Massachusetts, a beautiful village in the Berkshire hills whose vigorous intellectual life centered around Amherst College, for which her father and later her brother Austin served as treasurer. The Dickinson children were in awe all their lives of their stern but affectionate father, and Dickinson was exceptionally close to her brother Austin and her sister Lavinia. Dickinson herself had an excellent education at Amherst Academy, and later during a single year at Mount Holyoke Female Seminary. Dickinson's was not the typical watered-down "female curriculum" of her day; her basic knowledge of botany, astronomy, physics, theology, and other subjects is evident throughout the poems. At Mount Holyoke, Dickinson revealed her independent turn of mind. When Mary Lyon, the revered founder, asked the assembled students to rise if they hoped to become Christians, only Dickinson remained seated. As is abundantly manifested in her poems, Dickinson balked at conventional pieties and at easy answers to the large theological questions.

The beginning of Dickinson's gradual withdrawal from society can probably be dated from her leaving Mount Holyoke. As many have pointed out, her isolation may have been strategic. The amount of housework, child-care, and social obligation visited upon even an unmarried daughter in a large family allowed little time for poetry. Perhaps the mystery grows less mysterious in the light of nineteenth-century works by other women: In Mary Shelley's *Frankenstein*, the monster's lonely time in the hut adjacent to the DeLacy cottage, where he is the free unseen observer and interpreter of all their doings, actually proves the most pleasurable and creative time he will know; in Charlotte Perkins Gilman's "The Yellow Wallpaper," the heroine converts her enforced isolation into a private self-assertion and flowering of imagination, even if it is a morbid one. Later in her life, in the upstairs bedroom where she did most of her writing, Dickinson once pantomimed for her niece Martha the act of locking herself in, saying "It's just a turn—and freedom, Mattie!"

After Dickinson's departure from Mount Holyoke, she made a few trips with her family. In 1855, she visited Washington and Philadelphia with her father, then serving a term in Congress. In Philadelphia she met the married minister Charles Wadsworth, perhaps the person to whom, in the late 1850s and early 1860s, she addressed the "Master letters," painful expressions of hopeless longing that may never have been mailed. On the other hand, there is ample evidence that Dickinson's deepest erotic and emotional attachments were to women.

Dickinson had written poems from adolescence on, but in the early 1860s—the time of the emotional crises hinted at in the Master letters—her creativity burgeoned. In 1862, in response to an essay by Thomas Wentworth Higginson in *The Atlantic Monthly* giving advice to young would-be writers, Dickinson sent him four poems, asking him in an unsigned letter to tell her whether he thought they "breathed"; she penciled her name lightly on a card, which she enclosed in a separate envelope. Higginson was too conventional to appreciate fully Dickinson's work—he often objected to the unorthodoxy of her grammar and vocabulary—but he was a generous lifelong mentor. Her childhood friend Helen Hunt Jackson, author of the popular romance *Ramona,* also respected Dickinson's work and kept urging her to publish, but her pleas were largely in vain. Dickinson cringed at the way her few published poems were altered and regularized by editors, and her reluctance to have her work tampered with may partially explain her reluctance to let it go out into the world. Certainly, even those closest to her did not guess how prolifically she wrote. At times during the 1860s, Dickinson seems to have written one or more poems a day.

Besides the mysterious private anguish of rejection or loss that occasioned the Master letters, other griefs and complicated situations befell Dickinson in her adult life. Her eyesight was threatened in some way in the 1860s, a problem serious enough to compel her to leave home and seek months of treatment in Boston in 1864. Whether her ailment was psychosomatic or not, the threat of loss of vision must have terrified this most visual of writers.

Death was never far from any nineteenth-century household, but particular deaths were especially painful for Dickinson—several young men she had known died during the Civil War; her father, in 1874; her favorite nephew, Gilbert, in 1883; her beloved friend Judge Otis Lord in the following year. Not only death, but the slow process of dying, was a very present reality for Dickinson. Her mother, no brilliant intellectual but a pleasant and nurturing woman when she was well, became essentially an invalid in 1855, and until her death in 1882 the responsibility of nursing her fell mostly to Emily and Lavinia, her unmarried daughters.

In 1882, Dickinson's adored elder brother Austin embarked upon a passionate, adulterous affair with Mabel Loomis Todd, the artistic young wife of an Amherst professor, a relationship that would endure until Austin's death in 1895. The lovers did not seek to divorce their partners, although everyone in both families knew what was going on, and the affair seems to have been an open secret throughout the scandalized community. Emily and Lavinia, at whose house the lovers often trysted, were apparently caught in the crossfire of family loyalties, but neither sister recorded a word about the situation.

In her last years, Dickinson saw no one face-to-face except certain family members and household servants, allowing her rare guests to sit in an adjacent room and speak to her through a door left slightly ajar. She died on May 15, 1886, of Bright's disease. Shortly afterward, Lavinia discovered more than a thousand poems in various drawers and initially gave them to Austin's wife, Susan, with the thought that Susan might oversee their publication. In two years, when Susan had made no effort to do so, Lavinia took the poems back and gave them to Dickinson's old mentor, Higginson, and Mabel Loomis Todd, Austin's lover, herself something of a poet. The two jointly oversaw two small editions of selected poems in 1890 and 1891; in 1896, Todd brought out a third selection. These editions did exactly what Dickinson had feared in their smoothing-out and normalizing of her distinctive voice. Thomas Johnson's edition of 1955, nearly seventy years after Dickinson's death, was the first to attempt to reproduce the poems as Dickinson had recorded them.

WORK

Dickinson once disingenuously claimed to Higginson that her major influences were Keats, the Brownings, and the Bible; elsewhere, she would name Shakespeare and her lexicon as the books she depended upon. She disavowed knowing her greatest poetic contemporary, Walt Whitman, whose work she had been told was "disgraceful." We know she had a particular affinity for the work of other women such as the Brontës and George Eliot. But the form of her poetry was shaped by very homely influences indeed

—principally, the "common meter" of hymn books. Her poems are also influenced by valentines and memorial verses for the dead, both avidly written and collected by genteel Amherst residents.

Out of this conventional background, Emily Dickinson forged her extraordinary poems, the more extraordinary because the revolutionary things they say occur within such everyday structures. In hymn meter, she wonders whether God is not playing a game of hide-and-seek with his children, one that might end, horribly, with the major player having gone away, leaving people staring at their deaths into a nothingness (338); she takes the supposedly comforting phrase "the Lord giveth, and the Lord taketh away" and pushes it to its logical extreme, envisioning a God who is at once a stingy banker, a sneaky burglar, and overall a father to whose capricious principles of spiritual economy we are subjected as he gives us people to love and then snatches them away (49). Elsewhere, she envisions ecstatic erotic unions with a figure who may be a mortal lover, a version of Christ, or both (249); in either case, these are poems that defy and demand more and harder answers than churches or preachers may provide. She prefers painful truth, however discouraging, to any smoothing over (241). Dickinson's eye for natural subjects is matchless; like Whitman and Thoreau, she is able to see beyond the usual pretty subject. Her poems deal with rats, frogs, snakes, and bats as well as bluebirds, and she looks steadily at nature's darker side.

Perhaps most compelling of all is Dickinson's exploration of female power and powerlessness. She unflinchingly records a dream in which a flaccid worm she'd thoughtlessly permitted in her bedroom turns into a menacing male snake "ringed with power" (1670); she pictures a spirited girl child who inwardly thwarts all adult efforts to repress her (613); she envisions standing in relation to some master, whether God or a human lover, as a gun to its owner, with its explosive power to kill directed at fellow female creatures (754). In a poem that for many modern readers seems to evoke experience of repeated sexual abuse, Dickinson asserts that a woman's life amounts to brief moments of feverish freedom bracketed by long periods of helpless oppression (512).

Dickinson's heroic voices defy the whole weight of nineteenth-century theology, patriarchy, and the ideal of the woman as "the angel in the house"; coming from a woman in small-town New England in the nineteenth century, that is heroism indeed.

Suggested Readings

Richard Sewall's *The Life of Emily Dickinson* (1974) is a rich, full biography. Susan Howe's *My Emily Dickinson* (1985) is a contemporary poet and scholar's exposition of various feminist issues in Dickinson's poetry. Suzanne Juhasz, ed., *Feminist Critics Read Emily Dickinson* (1983) contains many good essays. J. Dobson's *Dickinson and the Strategies of Reticence: The Woman Writer in Nineteenth-Century America* (1989) explores issues of gender and creative survival.

338: "I know that He exists"

I know that He exists.
Somewhere—in Silence—
He has hid his rare life
From our gross eyes.

'Tis an instant's play.
'Tis a fond Ambush—

Just to make Bliss
Earn her own surprise!

But—should the play
Prove piercing earnest—
Should the glee—glaze—   10
In Death's—stiff—stare—

Would not the fun
Look too expensive!
Would not the jest—
Have crawled too far!

49: "I never lost as much but twice"

I never lost as much but twice,
And that was in the sod.
Twice have I stood a beggar
Before the door of God!

Angels—twice descending
Reimbursed my store—
Burglar! Banker—Father!
I am poor once more!

376: "Of Course—I prayed—"

Of Course—I prayed—
And did God Care?
He cared as much as on the Air
A Bird—had stamped her foot—
And cried "Give Me"—
My Reason—Life—
I had not had—but for Yourself—

'Twere better Charity
To leave me in the Atom's Tomb—
Merry, and Nought, and gay, and numb—   10
Than this smart Misery.

986: "A narrow Fellow in the Grass"

A narrow Fellow in the Grass
Occasionally rides—
You may have met Him—did you not
His notice sudden is—

The Grass divides as with a Comb—
A spotted shaft is seen—
And then it closes at your feet
And opens further on—

He likes a Boggy Acre
A Floor too cool for Corn—   10
Yet when a Boy, and Barefoot—
I more than once at Noon
Have passed, I thought, a Whip lash
Unbraiding in the Sun
When stooping to secure it
It wrinkled, and was gone—

Several of Nature's People
I know, and they know me—
I feel for them a transport
Of cordiality—   20

But never met this Fellow
Attended, or alone
Without a tighter breathing
And Zero at the Bone—

861: "Split the Lark—and you'll find the Music—"

Split the Lark—and you'll find the Music—
Bulb after Bulb, in Silver rolled—
Scantily dealt to the Summer Morning
Saved for your Ear when Lutes be old.

Loose the Flood—you shall find it patent—
Gush after Gush, reserved for you—
Scarlet Experiment! Sceptic Thomas![1]
Now, do you doubt that your Bird was true?

1670: "In Winter in my Room"

In Winter in my Room
I came upon a Worm—
Pink, lank and warm—
But as he was a worm
And worms presume
Not quite with him at home—

---

[1]"Doubting Thomas," the disciple who declared he would not believe Jesus had risen unless he could place his fingers in Jesus' wounds; see John 20:24–29.

Secured him by a string
To something neighboring
And went along.

A Trifle afterward   10
A thing occurred
I'd not believe it if I heard
But state with creeping blood—
A snake with mottles rare
Surveyed my chamber floor
In feature as the worm before
But ringed with power—

The very string with which
I tied him—too
When he was mean and new   20
That string was there—

I shrank—"How fair you are"!
Propitiation's claw—
"Afraid," he hissed
"Of me"?
"No cordiality"—
He fathomed me—
Then to a Rhythm *Slim*
Secreted in his Form
As Patterns swim   30
Projected him.

That time I flew
Both eyes his way
Lest he pursue
Nor ever ceased to run
Till in a distant Town
Towns on from mine
I set me down
This was a dream.

613: "They shut me up in Prose—"

They shut me up in Prose—
As when a little Girl
They put me in the Closet—
Because they liked me "still"—

Still! Could themself have peeped—
And seen my Brain—go round—
They might as wise have lodged a Bird
For Treason—in the Pound—

Himself has but to will
And easy as a Star   10
Abolish his Captivity—
And laugh—No more have I—

435: "Much Madness is divinest Sense—"

Much Madness is divinest Sense—
To a discerning Eye—
Much Sense—the starkest Madness—   *Enlightenment*
'Tis the Majority   *thought*
In this, as All, prevail—
Assent—and you are sane—
Demur—you're straightway dangerous—
And handled with a Chain—

241: "I like a look of Agony"

I like a look of Agony,
Because I know it's true—
Men do not sham Convulsion,
Nor simulate, a Throe—

The Eyes glaze once—and that is Death—
Impossible to feign
The Beads upon the Forehead
By homely Anguish strung.

249: "Wild Nights—Wild Nights!"

Wild Nights—Wild Nights!
Were I with thee   *Spiritual*
Wild Nights should be   *ecstasy*
Our luxury!   *sexual encounter*
                                                     or
Futile—the Winds—   *spiritual encounter*
To a Heart in port—
Done with the Compass—
Done with the Chart!

Rowing in Eden—
Ah, the Sea!   10
Might I but moor—Tonight—
In Thee!

612: "It would have starved a Gnat—"

It would have starved a Gnat—
To live so small as I—
And yet I was a living Child—
With Food's necessity

Upon me—like a Claw—
I could no more remove
Than I could coax a Leech away—
Or make a Dragon—move—

Nor like the Gnat—had I—
The privilege to fly   10
And seek a Dinner for myself—
How mightier He—than I—

Nor like Himself—the Art
Upon the Window Pane
To gad my little Being out—
And not begin—again—

754: "My Life had stood—a Loaded Gun—"

My Life had stood—a Loaded Gun—
In Corners—till a Day
The Owner passed—identified—
And carried Me away—

And now We roam in Sovereign Woods—
And now We hunt the Doe—
And every time I speak for Him—
The Mountains straight reply—

And do I smile, such cordial light
Upon the Valley glow—   10
It is as a Vesuvian face
Had let its pleasure through—

And when at Night—Our good Day done—
I guard My Master's Head—
'Tis better than the Eider-Duck's
Deep Pillow—to have shared—

To foe of His—I'm deadly foe—
None stir the second time—
On whom I lay a Yellow Eye—
Or an emphatic Thumb—   20

Though I than He—may longer live
He longer must—than I—
For I have but the power to kill,
Without—the power to die—

512: "The Soul has Bandaged moments—"

The Soul has Bandaged moments—
When too appalled to stir—
She feels some ghastly Fright come up
And stop to look at her—

Salute her—with long fingers—
Caress her freezing hair—
Sip, Goblin, from the very lips
The Lover—hovered—o'er—
Unworthy, that a thought so mean
Accost a Theme—so—fair—   10

The soul has moments of Escape—
When bursting all the doors—
She dances like a Bomb, abroad,
And swings upon the Hours,

As do the Bee—delirious borne—
Long Dungeoned from his Rose—
Touch Liberty—then know no more,
But Noon, and Paradise—

The Soul's retaken moments—
When, Felon led along,   20
With shackles on the plumed feet,
And staples, in the Song,

The Horror welcomes her, again,
These, are not brayed of Tongue—

443: "I tie my Hat—I crease my Shawl—"

I tie my Hat—I crease my Shawl—
Life's little duties do—precisely—
As the very least
Were infinite—to me—

I put new Blossoms in the Glass—
And throw the old—away—
I push a petal from my Gown
That anchored there—I weigh
The time 'twill be till six o'clock
I have so much to do—   10
And yet—Existence—some way back—
Stopped—struck—my ticking—through—
We cannot put Ourself away
As a completed Man
Or Woman—When the Errand's done
We came to Flesh—upon—
There may be—Miles on Miles of Nought—
Of Action—sicker far—
To simulate—is stinging work—
To cover what we are   20
From Science—and from Surgery—
Too Telescopic Eyes
To bear on us unshaded—
For their—sake—not for Ours—

'Twould start them—
We—could tremble—
But since we got a Bomb—
And held it in our Bosom—
Nay—Hold it—it is calm—

Therefore—we do life's labor—   30
Though life's Reward—be done—
With scrupulous exactness—
To hold our Senses—on—

67: "Success is counted sweetest"

Success is counted sweetest
By those who ne'er succeed.
To comprehend a nectar
Requires sorest need.

Not one of all the purple Host
Who took the Flag today
Can tell the definition
So clear of Victory

As he defeated—dying—
On whose forbidden ear   10
The distant strains of triumph
Burst agonized and clear!

KATE CHOPIN
[1851–1904]

During the first half of the twentieth century, Kate Chopin was thought of either as a minor writer whose stories of Creole life in Louisiana were part of the local color movement of the late nineteenth century, or as the author of a scandalous novel. Otherwise, her work was largely ignored until the 1960s, when a new generation of readers discovered the unrelenting realism and provocative themes beneath the local color in her stories. Her most important work, the novel *The Awakening* (1899), is now recognized as one of the classics of American feminism.

LIFE

As the daughter of a mother descended from the French Creole aristocracy and an Irish immigrant father who had become a successful merchant in St. Louis, Katherine O'Flaherty, born in 1851, had a privileged childhood. Even though her father died in a railway accident when she was four, she attended Catholic convent schools in St. Louis and made her debut in St. Louis society when she was eighteen. In 1870 she married Oscar Chopin, a Creole cotton trader. After a wedding trip to Europe, the Chopins settled in Louisiana, first in New Orleans and then in Coutierville in Natchitoches Parish in central Louisiana. They had six children before Oscar died in 1883 of swamp fever. After her husband's death, Katherine, financially independent, moved back to St. Louis with her children, where she began her writing career in earnest, publishing her first poems and stories in 1889.

WORK

The most important intellectual influence in her life was probably Frederick Kohlben-heyer, her physician in St. Louis, who became her confidant in the mid-1880s. An agnostic, he encouraged her to read Darwin and Thomas Huxley and to give up Catholicism. She also read the work of such American regional writers as Sarah Orne Jewett and Mary E. Wilkins Freeman and, especially, the French realists Flaubert, Zola, and de Maupassant. This reading encouraged the realistic directions in her own writing as she explored the ways in which her characters were influenced by their environment, as women caught in the social mores of nineteenth-century America, or as members of one of the ethnic and racial groups in Louisiana: Creoles, descendants of the French and Spanish colonists; Cajuns, descendants of eighteenth-century French-Canadian immigrants to Louisiana; blacks; and Indians. De Maupassant was a particularly important influence. She translated several of his stories into English, and many of her stories, including "The Story of an Hour," use the same kind of irony, the tight construction, and the surprise turn at the end that typified de Maupassant's work.

Nearly all of Kate Chopin's literary work was published in the 1890s. She wrote several poems, nearly a hundred stories, and three novels during the decade. Her first novel, *At Fault* (1890), set in the Louisiana backcountry, tells the story of a troubled relationship between a widow and a married man. Her stories about the same region began to appear in national magazines. She published two collections of stories, *Bayou Folk* (1894) and *A Night in Acadie* (1897). She wrote a second novel, *Young Dr. Gosse,* early in the decade, but later destroyed the manuscript after she could not find a publisher for it. Her reputation, both in her own time and since, has rested largely on her third novel, *The Awakening* (1899). It is the story of Edna Pontellier, a young wife and mother, who is awakened to her own desires and feelings through relationships with Robert Lebrun, a romantic man she meets while on vacation, and Mademoiselle Reisz, an artist. She neglects her social duties and angers her husband, has an affair, leaves her marriage, and finally ends her life by drowning. The novel shocked readers in the 1890s. Reviewers called it a "vulgar story," one that "should be labeled a poison." Even Willa Cather dismissed it as only "a Creole Bovary," an imitation of Flaubert's novel *Madame Bovary*, that had similarly scandalized the French. *The Awakening* was banned from libraries and Chopin was shunned in St. Louis society. Only in the last three decades has Chopin's novel been recognized as much more than a shocking piece of conventional fiction or mock French realism. In the novel, she adopted the conventions of French realism to study an American woman coming to an awareness of the confining social conventions that denied her full humanity. Although it is set in Louisiana, as many of her short stories are, it is much more than a work of regional interest.

"The Story of an Hour" could also have been titled "The Awakening," for it, too, describes a moment of awareness when Mrs. Mallard realizes how she really feels about her life and situation. The news of her husband's death shocks her into an awareness that seems to overtake her against her will. The tight focus of the story and the double surprise in the ending show that Chopin had learned her craft well from de Maupassant. Mrs. Mallard's awakening allies her with Nora Helmer, the heroine of Ibsen's *A Doll's House*, and the woman in Charlotte Perkins Gilman's "The Yellow Wallpaper," as one of many "new women" in the literature of the period—women who sought to control their own lives rather than be defined by marriage and their relationships to men.

SUGGESTED READINGS

Emily Toth's *Kate Chopin: A Solitary Soul* (1989) adds a good deal of new biographical information about the author to that in Per Seyersted's *Kate Chopin: A Critical Biography* (1969), the standard work on Chopin's life. Barbara C. Ewell's *Kate Chopin* (1986) is a good critical introduction to all of Chopin's work. Discussion of her short stories can also be found in B. Bender, "Kate Chopin's Lyrical Short Stories," *Studies in Short Fiction II* (1974), 257–66.

The Story of an Hour

Knowing that Mrs. Mallard was afflicted with heart trouble, great care was taken to break to her as gently as possible the news of her husband's death.

It was her sister Josephine who told her, in broken sentences; veiled hints that revealed in half concealing. Her husband's friend Richards was there, too, near her. It was he who had been in the newspaper office when intelligence of the railroad disaster was received, with Brently Mallard's name leading the list of "killed." He had only taken the time to assure himself of its truth by a second telegram, and had hastened to forestall any less careful, less tender friend in bearing the sad message.

She did not hear the story as many women have heard the same, with a paralyzed inability to accept its significance. She wept at once, with sudden, wild abandonment, in her sister's arms. When the storm of grief had spent itself she went away to her room alone. She would have no one follow her.

There stood, facing the open window, a comfortable, roomy armchair. Into this she sank, pressed down by a physical exhaustion that haunted her body and seemed to reach into her soul.

She could see in the open square before her house the tops of trees that were all aquiver with the new spring life. The delicious breath of rain was in the air. In the street below a peddler was crying his wares. The notes of a distant song which some one was singing reached her faintly, and countless sparrows were twittering in the eaves.

There were patches of blue sky showing here and there through the clouds that had met and piled one above the other in the west facing her window.

She sat with her head thrown back upon the cushion of the chair, quite motionless, except when a sob came up into her throat and shook her, as a child who has cried itself to sleep continues to sob in its dreams.

She was young, with a fair, calm face, whose lines bespoke repression and even a certain strength. But now there was a dull stare in her eyes, whose gaze was fixed away off yonder on one of those patches of blue sky. It was not a glance of reflection, but rather indicated a suspension of intelligent thought.

There was something coming to her and she was waiting for it, fearfully. What was it? She did not know; it was too subtle and elusive to name. But she felt it, creeping out of the sky, reaching toward her through the sounds, the scents, the color that filled the air.

Now her bosom rose and fell tumultuously. She was beginning to recognize this thing that was approaching to possess her, and she was striving to beat it back with her will—as powerless as her two white slender hands would have been.

When she abandoned herself a little whispered word escaped her slightly parted lips. She said it over and over under her breath: "free, free, free!" The vacant stare and the look of terror that had followed it went from her eyes. They stayed keen and bright. Her pulses beat fast, and the coursing blood warmed and relaxed every inch of her body.

She did not stop to ask if it were or were not a monstrous joy that held her. A clear and exalted perception enabled her to dismiss the suggestion as trivial.

She knew that she would weep again when she saw the kind, tender hands folded in death; the face that had never looked save with love upon her, fixed and gray and dead. But she saw beyond that bitter moment a long procession of years to come that would belong to her absolutely. And she opened and spread her arms out to them in welcome.

There would be no one to live for her during those coming years; she would live for herself. There would be no powerful will bending hers in that blind persistence with which men and women believe they have a right to impose a private will upon a fellow-creature. A kind intention or a cruel intention made the act seem no less a crime as she looked upon it in that brief moment of illumination.

And yet she had loved him—sometimes. Often she had not. What did it matter! What could love, the unsolved mystery, count for in face of this possession of self-assertion which she suddenly recognized as the strongest impulse of her being!

"Free! Body and soul free!" she kept whispering.

Josephine was kneeling before the closed door with her lips to the keyhole, imploring for admission. "Louise, open the door! I beg; open the door—you will make yourself ill. What are you doing, Louise? For heaven's sake open the door."

"Go away. I am not making myself ill." No; she was drinking in a very elixir of life through that open window.

Her fancy was running riot along those days ahead of her. Spring days, and summer days, and all sorts of days that would be her own. She breathed a quick prayer that life might be long. It was only yesterday she had thought with a shudder that life might be long.

She arose at length and opened the door to her sister's importunities. There was a feverish triumph in her eyes, and she carried herself unwittingly like a goddess of Victory. She clasped her sister's waist, and together they descended the stairs. Richards stood waiting for them at the bottom.

Some one was opening the front door with a latchkey. It was Brently Mallard who entered, a little travel-stained, composedly carrying his gripsack and umbrella. He had been far from the scene of accident, and did not even know there had been one. He stood amazed at Josephine's piercing cry; at Richards' quick motion to screen him from the view of his wife.

But Richards was too late.

When the doctors came they said she had died of heart disease—of joy that kills.

SYMBOLIST POETRY
[c. 1857–c. 1898]

Challenging the Enlightenment view that close observation of the objective world would lead to the discovery of laws that governed nature and mind, the romantics turned inward to plumb the depths of subjectivity—the unconscious mind and emotion—in search of truth and beauty. For the romantics, the poet or artist inspired by genius fulfilled the role of prophet for an age that seemed to have lost its soul in the selfish pursuit of material gain in a world where human relations seemed to turn on the "cash nexus." For Percy Shelley, writing in *A Defence of Poetry* (1821; published 1840), "Poetry, and the principle of Self, of which money is the visible incarnation, are the God and Mammon of the world"; poetry, a shadowy visitation of what is divine in human beings, in Shelley's words, could "defeat the curse" of materialism, and so had a social as well as an aesthetic function. Nonetheless, in the work of Shelley and other romantic writers such as Pushkin, Keats, and Novalis, we can hear a romanticism played in a minor key, a poetry of uncertainty and hesitation. Keats's "Ode on Melancholy," for example, reminds us that Melancholy "dwells with Beauty—Beauty that must die" and that the hand of Joy "is ever at his lips / Bidding adieu." As the nineteenth century progressed and writers more fully began to perceive the pettiness, hypocrisy, and drudgery of human life, this more sinister side of romanticism influenced the movements known as aestheticism, decadence, and symbolism, the most important of these. While realist and naturalist writers such as Balzac, Chekhov, and Flaubert attempted to capture life as it really was, to record the world in all of its dreary and sordid detail, the symbolists turned against the real, hoping to evoke in their highly allusive and metaphorically dense poetry a purer, transcendent reality in the work of art itself.

The three poets we include in this section represent the symbolist movement in its broadest sense. Despite differences in tone, style, and content, Charles Baudelaire (1821–1867), Arthur Rimbaud (1854–1891), and Stéphane Mallarmé (1842–1898) share an aesthetic sensibility that involves an effort to evoke a pure state of feeling, a mysterious sense of the ineffable, even though they might be doomed to fail in that attempt. Critics sometimes see Baudelaire and Rimbaud as precursors to symbolism, transitional poets between French romanticism and symbolism, but they agree that Mallarmé epitomizes the movement. All three poets in varying degrees sought to free poetry from the conventional structure and versification respected by the Parnassian poets; to create a verse that would imitate the tones and elusiveness of music; and to evoke, rather than describe, a sense of pure feeling and transcendent beauty. Moreover, all three poets exerted a profound influence upon late nineteenth-century and modernist poetry, including that of William Butler Yeats, T. S. Eliot, and Rainer Maria Rilke.

LIVES OF CHARLES BAUDELAIRE, ARTHUR RIMBAUD, AND STÉPHANE MALLARMÉ

Charles Baudelaire was born in Paris in 1821 into a family of respectable means. His father, François Baudelaire, died in 1825, after which Charles was raised by his mother, Caroline Defayis, and stepfather, Jacques Aupick, whom the boy deeply resented. Baudelaire attended school at the Collège de Lyon, where Aupick had moved the family in 1830, and later at the Lycée Louis-le-Grand, after returning to Paris in 1836. Here Baudelaire began to develop the deep sense of boredom, or *ennui*, that became a major theme in his poetry. Against his stepfather's wishes, the young Baudelaire plunged into a life of literature and libertinism, cultivating in his writing and life a bohemian dandyism. Shortly after foiling his parents' attempt to ship him off to Calcutta in 1841, Baudelaire began his relationship with Jeanne Duval, a Creole woman who is the "black Venus" in many of his poems. After 1844, Baudelaire lived on a tightly restricted inheritance and immersed himself in the cafés of the Latin Quarter, where he began writing some of the poems that would appear in his most important work, *The Flowers of Evil* (1857), which appeared the same year as Flaubert's *Madame Bovary* and caused a similar public outrage. In the 1840s, Baudelaire also spent much time in galleries and museums, and his *Salons* (1845, 1846, and 1859) and essays on the painting of Eugène Delacroix and Constantin Guys, among others, represent a formidable body of art criticism. In the midst of the "drunkenness" of the Revolution of 1848, Baudelaire discovered (and later translated) the works of Edgar Allan Poe, with whom he strongly identified as an outcast, and whose formalist poetic principles he found strikingly similar to his own. In 1862, Baudelaire published a collection of prose poems, now called *Paris Spleen*, and in the same year he had a stroke that he interpreted as a portent of his death. Living in poverty, his genius largely unrecognized, Baudelaire died in Paris on August 31, 1867.

Just three years before Baudelaire published *The Flowers of Evil*, Arthur Rimbaud was born in Charleville, in the north of France. Having been abandoned at age six by his father, an army captain, Rimbaud was raised under the rigid moral regime of his mother, Vitalie (Cuif) Rimbaud. A prodigy at school, Rimbaud in his early teens began to write verses in Greek and Latin, as well as in French. At the Collège de Charleville, Georges Izambard, the youngest tutor in the college, recognized Rimbaud's genius and encouraged him in his work. When in 1870 the young poet was arrested for vagrancy, after having fled on foot from his home to Paris for a taste of freedom, Izambard bailed him out and tried to reconcile him to his mother. Of the potent independence he felt at that moment, Rimbaud writes in "Ma Bohème": "I followed you, Muse! Beneath your spell, / Oh, la, la, what glorious loves I dreamed." Soon after his return home, Rimbaud escaped again to Paris, but he was back in Charleville at the outset of the Paris Commune of March 1871, an uprising of radical and moderate republicans led by the national guard in Paris against the interim government of Adolphe Thiers. In Charleville, Rimbaud cultivated a vagrant look, and although he abandoned his formal studies he read Paul Verlaine, Baudelaire, and Baudelaire's translations of Poe. He began to develop his theory that the poet was a *voyant*, a seer whose words were to give a presentiment of the ineffable. Rimbaud sent a packet of his poems to Verlaine, who invited this "adolescent satan," as the older poet called him, to Paris. The *voyant*, in Rimbaud's view, had to degrade himself completely, to descend into a state of total abandon and disorientation of the senses in order to become a poet. In a famous statement from his "Lettre du voyant" (1871), Rimbaud claimed "Je est un autre," that is, "I is an other," to express the self-alienation, suffering, and madness from which poetry rises. For this philosophy, Rimbaud earned himself a place among *les poètes maudits*, the damned poets, so named by Verlaine in a critical and biographical study by that title published in 1884. Included among the damned were Mallarmé and Verlaine himself. In the summer of 1871, Rimbaud began to write *The Drunken Boat,* his autobiographical masterpiece, in which the wayward path of the boat becomes a symbol for the poetic vocation. After two years of a reckless companionship with Verlaine that ended in a violent argument, Rimbaud published *A Season in Hell* (1873), and by 1875 he had completed the poems in *Illuminations* (published 1886). After failing to renew his friendship with Verlaine, Rimbaud found himself once more a vagabond, traveling to Germany, serving briefly as a Dutch soldier (he deserted shortly after arriving in Batavia), and wandering around Europe, working for a while as an interpreter for a circus and taking various odd jobs. In the 1880s, Rimbaud abandoned poetry for business; hoping to gain financial independence he worked variously as a soldier, a coffee trader, and even a gun-runner, traveling from Cyprus to Aden, into Abyssinia, and back to France. Rimbaud's dazzling career ended in Marseilles in November 1891 when, attended by his sister, he died of complications arising from a tumor on his leg.

Although he was born before Rimbaud, Stéphane Mallarmé comes last in our discussion, for he completed his major works later than Rimbaud and, more than any other poet, he strove to articulate and to practice the principles of symbolism, both in his literary criticism and in his poetry. Mallarmé was born in Paris in 1842, the son of Numa-Florence-Joseph Mallarmé, a government official, and Elisabeth-Félicie Desmolins. His mother died when he was five years old, and Mallarmé was sent to boarding school and was separated from his younger sister, with whom he maintained a close friendship until her death in 1857. After attending various boarding schools, the young poet graduated from the lycée at Sens in 1860, after failing his first exam. Taking a job as an accountant, Mallarmé became an enthusiastic reader of Baudelaire and Poe, and with the encouragement of Emmanuel des Essarts, a teacher and poet, Mallarmé published his first poems in 1862. With the death of his father in April 1863, Mallarmé married Marie Gebhard and began his long, improbable career as an English teacher, first at Tournon and eventually, from 1871 to 1885, in Paris. Since the 1860s, Mallarmé had been writing poetry in earnest, at first imitating Baudelaire, but always attempting to go beyond Baudelaire by divorcing the poem's symbols from any connection to the world outside the poem, creating a dense symbolic network within the poem, which he perceived—following Poe—as a hermetically sealed world of its own. Although no major collection of his poetry appeared until 1887 (*Les Poésies*), his influence in literary circles and the poems and essays that appeared intermittently under their own covers or in periodicals earned him the attention of Verlaine, who included an essay on Mallarmé in *Les Poètes maudits,* published in 1884. One year later, the poet of nothingness, as Jean-Paul Sartre called him, took a post at the Collège Rollin in Paris, where he taught until 1894, the year Claude Debussy's *Prélude à l'Après-Midi d'un Faune,* based on Mallarmé's poem, premiered in Paris. Having become a patron of young writers and a friend of many leading artists, musicians, and writers such as Édouard Manet, Huysmans, and the young Paul Valéry, Mallarmé died at Valvins in 1898.

WORK

As Valéry noted in *The Existence of Symbolism* (1939), symbolism "was not a school. On the contrary, it included many schools of the most divergent types," although, as he went on to say, "Aesthetics divided them; Ethics united them." Keeping in mind the distinctions among the brute scenes of Baudelaire's *Flowers of Evil*, the reeling discontinuities of Rimbaud's *The Drunken Boat*, and the hermetically sealed polish of

Mallarmé's "The Afternoon of a Faun," readers can recognize a shared attempt in these works to transcend the monotonies of the everyday and to repudiate the getting and spending of the marketplace that realist and naturalist writers made into the stock of their literary trade. If romantic and symbolist poets share a common goal to refashion a consciousness eroded by what Valéry called the "reign of universal haste," they are distinguished in part by the contrast between the romantic poets' attempt to convey philosophical ideas and transform the world and the symbolist poets' attempt to cultivate a pure poetry that rejects philosophy altogether and transcends the world. From Baudelaire and Rimbaud to Mallarmé, there is an increasing emphasis upon the symbol as a means to evoke the mystery of language itself, rather than to refer to some subjective consciousness or some objective, material world.

For Baudelaire, Rimbaud, and Mallarmé, the symbol serves as a point of convergence for many things and so remains deliberately ambiguous and resonant. In striving for the evocativeness of music in their works, later symbolists such as Verlaine, Laforgue, and Valéry sought to capture tones, fragrances, sensations, and intuitions rather than concrete images or rational ideas. They aimed to record the negation of a thing rather than the thing itself, the space of an impression after it dissolves before the eye or ear of the reader. To quote from Mallarmé's "Crisis in Poetry," a key essay in his important collection *Divagations* (1897): "I say: a flower! and, out of the forgetfulness where my voice banishes any contour, inasmuch as it arises, an idea itself and fragrant, the one absent from all bouquets." We can see this move to link all things through their afterpresence as early as Baudelaire's "Correspondences," which evokes the "pervasiveness of everlasting things" as colors, scents, and sounds commingle and correspond "Like long-drawn echoes afar converging / In harmonies darksome and profound." Or, in Verlaine's phrase from "The Art of Poetry" (1884), "Never the Color, always the Shade, / always the nuance is supreme!"

Edgar Allan Poe's rejection of the role of inspiration in poetic composition and his focus upon deliberate craftsmanship appealed to Baudelaire, who spoke of his writing as a "travail," a labor. Although Baudelaire shared the Parnassian and romantic poet's quest for beauty, he believed that it would be found not in airy flights of the imagination but rather in the very midst of the most revolting realities. Hence, as its title suggests, *The Flowers of Evil* explores the sordid and the grotesque, partly in order to shock its readers out of their complacency and to move them to find beauty in the ugliness, wretchedness, and viciousness of their everyday lives. For Baudelaire, *ennui*—the profound boredom and habitual superficiality of the everyday—allows human beings to ignore their more sinister, more disgusting and petty selves. In "To the Reader" he declares himself the poet of evil who promises to hold up a mirror to reflect the horrible beauty that his hypocritical readers refuse to confront. Baudelaire's poetry places the ideal and what he calls *Spleen*—a profound and restless malaise—into a tense imbalance, and rather than reconcile them in a romantic idyll or declaration of hope, he throws the responsibility for closure over to his readers. In poems such as "The Swan" and "The Voyage," Baudelaire touches upon the infinite, the purity of *azure*, the deep blue, further celebrated in Mallarmé's "The Azure," that suggests transcendence and hints at absolute beauty. In poems like these, Baudelaire's work most anticipates the symbolism of the later poets.

Like Baudelaire, Rimbaud was a self-conscious craftsman who experimented with nearly all of the traditional forms of nineteenth-century French poetry and who went further than Baudelaire to break with conventions, both poetic and social. Rimbaud tried to realize in his life and work a Baudelairean, even Nietzschean, vision beyond good and evil, and so he cultivated an exacting excess and disorder. As he wrote to Izambard in May 1871, "Now, I am degrading myself as much as possible. Why? I want to be a poet, and I am working to make myself a seer:...It is a question of reaching the unknown by the derangement of all the senses. The sufferings are enormous, but one has to be strong, one has to be born a poet, and I know I am a poet." The poet's indulgence in degradation does not stem from a hedonistic passion for the forbidden, but rather out of a deep, perhaps metaphysical, contempt for the world. His contempt for the petty vulgarity of materialism and his passion for life is evident in *The Drunken Boat,* which vacillates erratically beneath its apparently smooth surface, between a dream of escape and a desire to find some secure moorings. In this great autobiographical poem, Rimbaud's antagonistic experience is stretched tightly across metaphoric oppositions and contrasting images, and the voice that says at once that it cares and does not care seems to be that of the poet, poised at the moment of embarking on his short-lived but intoxicating poetic career, which he brought to an abrupt end. If the logical consequence of the distrust of language and the confrontation with a hopelessly distracted audience is silence, if silence is the only pure medium, then Rimbaud's adieu to writing may be the ultimate expression of symbolism.

With roots in the poetry of Baudelaire and Rimbaud, whose respective "Correspondences" and "Vowels" suggest that poetry should move toward some absolute purity, symbolism was perfected in the hands of Stéphane Mallarmé and Paul Verlaine in the 1880s and 1890s. Although a poem such as "Windows" shows an affinity in setting and tone to the short stories of Flaubert or de Maupassant, Mallarmé's poetry repudiates realism and naturalism in general and Parnassian poetry, which emphasized objective description, in particular. In so doing, he emphasized the evocative powers of language to approximate the infinite, as in "The Azure." His "Crisis in Poetry" repudiated description and called for a language not of the thing but of approximation: "It is not *description* which can unveil the efficacy and beauty of monuments, seas, or the human face in all their maturity and native state, but rather evocation, *allusion, suggestion.*" Thus, Mallarmé rejected the idea of a one-to-one correspondence between word and thing, preferring instead to use words to tease out resonances that would defy any attempt to come up with a fixed meaning. As Mallarmé put it in "The Evolution of Literature," an interview published in *Echo de Paris* in 1891: "To *name* an object is largely to destroy poetic enjoyment, which comes from gradual divination. The ideal is to *suggest* the object." Rather than mirror the mundane realities and petty materialism of his world, Mallarmé strove to create in his poetry a purely aesthetic space, a second-order reality, by eliminating the traces of the world present in language itself. "The Afternoon of a Faun" displays the result of the poet's task to dissolve the residues of the real in order to make a new, synthetic world within the poem. Here Mallarmé attempts to maximize pure consciousness as a negation of the material world that otherwise constrains his or her potential. As Paul Valéry said, "Never did the ivory tower seem so high," but, perhaps, never did it look so beautiful.

SUGGESTED READINGS

For biographies of these three writers, see Enid Starkie's *Baudelaire* (1953), Starkie's *Arthur Rimbaud* (1968), and Austin Gill's *The Early Mallarmé*, 2 vols. (1979, 1986). Among the many works on symbolism, Arthur Symons's *The Symbolist Movement in Literature* (1899) and Edmund Wilson's discussion of the symbolists in *Axel's Castle* (1931) remain classics, although students should supplement those works with more recent studies such as Carol de Dobay Rifelj's *Word and Figure: The Language of Nineteenth-Century French Poetry* (1986) and David Michael Hertz's *The Turning of the Word: The Musico-Literary Poetics of the Symbolist Movement* (1987). Laurence M. Porter's *The Crisis of French Symbolism* (1990) contains an illuminating discussion of the problems of defining symbolism and its relation to other poetic movements in the nineteenth century. Volumes 4 and 5 of P. E. Charvet's *A Literary History of France* (1967) offer useful introductions to the writers included here, as does Wallace Fowlie's *Climate of Violence: The French Literary Tradition from Baudelaire to the Present* (1967).

CHARLES BAUDELAIRE
[1821–1867]

To the Reader

Translated by Stanley Kunitz

Ignorance, error, cupidity, and sin
Possess our souls and exercise our flesh;
Habitually we cultivate remorse
As beggars entertain and nurse their lice.

Our sins are stubborn. Cowards when contrite
We overpay confession with our pains,
And when we're back again in human mire
Vile tears, we think, will wash away our stains.

Thrice-potent Satan in our cursèd bed
Lulls us to sleep, our spirit overkissed,   10
Until the precious metal of our will
Is vaporized—that cunning alchemist!

Who but the Devil pulls our waking-strings!
Abominations lure us to their side;
Each day we take another step to hell,
Descending through the stench, unhorrified.

Like an exhausted rake who mouths and chews
The martyrized breast of an old withered whore
We steal, in passing, whatever joys we can,
Squeezing the driest orange all the more.   20

Packed in our brains incestuous as worms
Our demons celebrate in drunken gangs,
And when we breathe, that hollow rasp is Death
Sliding invisibly down into our lungs.

If the dull canvas of our wretched life
Is unembellished with such pretty ware
As knives or poison, pyromania, rape,
It is because our soul's too weak to dare!

But in this den of jackals, monkeys, curs,
Scorpions, buzzards, snakes—this paradise   30
Of filthy beasts that screech, howl, grovel, grunt—
In this menagerie of mankind's vice

There's one supremely hideous and impure!
Soft-spoken, not the type to cause a scene,
He'd willingly make rubble of the earth
And swallow up creation in a yawn.

I mean *Ennui!* who in his hookah-dreams
Produces hangmen and real tears together.
How well you know this fastidious monster, reader,
—Hypocrite reader, you—my double! my brother!   40

The Albatross

Translated by Kate Flores

Ofttimes, for diversion, seafaring men
Capture albatross, those vast birds of the seas
That accompany, at languorous pace,
Boats plying their way through bitter straits.

Having scarce been taken aboard
These kings of the blue, awkward and shy,
Piteously their great white wings
Let droop like oars at their sides.

This wingèd voyager, how clumsy he is and weak!
He just now so lovely, how comic and ugly!   10
One with a stubby pipe teases his beak,
Another mimics, limping, the cripple who could fly!

The Poet resembles this prince of the clouds,
Who laughs at hunters and haunts the storms;
Exiled to the ground amid the jeering pack,
His giant wings will not let him walk.

Correspondences

Translated by Kate Flores

Nature is a temple from whose living columns
Commingling voices emerge at times;
Here man wanders through forests of symbols
Which seem to observe him with familiar eyes.

Like long-drawn echoes afar converging
In harmonies darksome and profound,
Vast as the night and vast as light,
Colors, scents and sounds correspond.

There are fragrances fresh as the flesh of children,
Sweet as the oboe, green as the prairie,   10
—And others overpowering, rich and corrupt,

Possessing the pervasiveness of everlasting things,
Like benjamin, frankincense, amber, myrrh,
Which the raptures of the senses and the spirit sing.

Spleen

Translated by Barbara Gibbs

When the oppressive sky weighs like a cover
On the sick spirit, in the toils of ennui,
And embracing the horizon's curve
Pours on us, sadder than nights, a dark day;

When earth becomes a humid dungeon
Where Hope like a bat strikes her timid
Wing against the walls and beats on
The decaying ceiling with her head;

When the rain spreading its immense trails
Imitates a vast prison of bars,   10
And a mute crowd of infamous spiders
Comes to hang its threads at the back of our brains,

Bells suddenly leap furiously,
Launching a dreadful clamor to heaven,
Like wandering spirits without a country
Who start to complain stubbornly.

—And long hearses without drums or music drag
In slow file through my soul; Hope vanquished
Weeps, and atrocious, despotic Anguish
Plants on my bowed head her black flag.   20

The Swan

Translated by Kate Flores

To Victor Hugo

1

Andromache,[1] I think of you! —This little stream,
Poor wretched mirror resplendent once
With all the grandeur of your widow's grief,
This deceptive Simoïs,[2] heightened with your tears,

Has suddenly, as I wandered through the new Carrousel,
Restored a fertile memory of mine.
—Old Paris is no more (the contours of a city
Change, alas! more quickly than a mortal heart);

---

[1] Wife of the Trojan hero Hector and mother of Astyanax, both of whom were killed by the Greeks; after the fall of Troy, Andromache was taken as a slave by Pyrrhus (Neoptolomus), the son of her husband's killer, Achilles; Pyrrhus eventually gave Andromache to Helenus, Hector's brother, who had also been taken by the Greeks.

[2] A river in the vicinity of Troy.

Only in spirit do I see that regiment of booths,
That array of makeshift capitals and posts,   10
The turf, the rough stones greened by the puddle waters,
And, gleaming in the cases, the jumbled bric-a-brac.

There at one time a menagerie stood;
There I saw one morning, at the hour when, under cold clear skies,
The working world awakes, and the cleaners of the streets
Hurl into the quiet air a dismal hurricane,

A swan who had escaped his cage,
And, padding the dry pavement with his webbed feet,
Trailed his snowy plumage along the scraggly ground.
Beside a waterless gutter the creature opened his beak   20

And tremulously bathing his wings in the dust, cried,
His heart full of the lovely lake of his birth:
"Water, when the deluge? Tempests, when do you thunder?"
I can see that hapless one, strange and fatal myth,

Toward the heavens, sometimes, like Ovid's man,
Toward the heavens ironical and cruelly blue,
Bend his thirsting head upon his convulsive neck,
As though addressing reproaches unto God!

2

Paris changes! but my melancholy alters not a whit!
New palaces, scaffoldings, stocks,   30
Old neighborhoods to me are all allegory now,
And now my cherished remembrances are heavier than rocks!

Thus before this Louvre an image dejects me:
I think of my glorious swan, with his mad gestures,
Like the exiled, ridiculous and sublime,
And wrung by a truceless yearning! and then of you,

Andromache, fallen from a mighty husband's arms,
A lowly creature, beneath the hand of supernal Pyrrhus,
Bending down distraught beside an empty tomb;
Widow of Hector, alas! and wife to Helenus!   40

I think upon the Negress, tubercular and wasted,
Groveling in the mud, and seeking, with haggard eye,
Beyond the massive wall of mist,
Magnificent Africa's absent coconut palms;

Of all who have lost what cannot ever be regained,
Not ever! of those who drink their fill of tears
And suckle of Sorrow like a good she-wolf!
Of scrawny orphans desiccating like flowers!

Thus in the forest of my spirit's exile
An old Remembrance echoes full blast like a horn!   50

I think upon sailors forgotten on isles,
Of the captured, the defeated! . . . and of so many more!

The Voyage

Translated by Barbara Gibbs

To Maxime du Camp

1

To the child, in love with maps and pictures,
The universe is vast as his appetite.
Ah how immense the world is by lamplight!
How small the world is in recollection!

One morning we set out, our brains full of fire,
Our hearts swollen with rancor and harsh longing,
And we go, following the wave's rhythm,
Cradling our infinite on the seas' finite:

Some are glad to leave a squalid birthplace,
Or their abhorred cradles; some, astrologers   10
Drowned in a woman's eyes, their tyrannical
Circe[1] of the dangerous perfumes.

Not to be turned to beasts, they make themselves
Drunk on space and light and the flaming skies;
The frost that bites them, the suns that tan them,
Slowly wear away the marks of kisses.

But the true travelers are those who leave
For leaving's sake; light hearts like balloons,
They never swerve from their fatality,
And say, without knowing why: "Let us go on!"   20

Those whose desires have the shape of clouds,
Who dream, like a recruit of the cannon,
Of boundless, changing, unknown pleasures
Whose name the human mind has never known!

2

We imitate—horror!—the top and ball,
Waltzing and skipping; even in our sleep
Curiosity torments and rolls us
Like a merciless Angel whipping suns.

Strange lot, in which the goal displaces itself,
And being nowhere may be anywhere!   30

---

[1] The island sorceress in *The Odyssey* who changed men and women into beasts.

In which Man, whose hope never flags, goes always
Running like a madman in search of rest!

Our soul's a ship seeking its Icaria;[2]
A voice shouts from the bridge: "Open your eyes!"
From the top, ardent and mad, another cries:
"Love...glory...happiness!" Hell is a sandbar!

Each island signaled by the man on watch
Is an Eldorado[3] promised by Fate;
Imagination, preparing her feast,
Sees only a reef in the dawning light.   40

Poor lover of chimerical countries!
Must we toss him in chains, or in the sea, this
Inventor of Americas, this drunken
Sailor whose vision poisons the abyss?

Such is the old vagrant who paws the mud
And dreams, nose in air, of dazzling Edens;
His bewitched eye beholds a Capua[4]
All around, where the candle lights a hovel.

                                  3

Marvelous travelers! What noble tales
We read in your eyes profound as oceans!
Show us your chests of splendid memories,   50
Astounding jewels, made of wind and stars.

We will sail without steam or canvas!
Enliven the boredom of our prisons;
Pass across our spirits, stretched like canvases,
Your memories in their frames of horizons.

Tell us, what have you seen?

                                  4

                                  "We have seen stars
And billows; and we have also seen sands;
And, despite shocks and unforeseen disasters,
We were often bored, as you were here.   60

The sun's splendor above violet seas,
The splendor of cities in the setting sun,
Made our hearts burn with restless ardor
To plunge into a sky of seductive light.

---

[2]An island in the Aegean named after Icarus, the boy who fell to the sea having flown too close to the sun when he and his father, Daedalus, escaped prison on waxen wings. In French literature, Icaria is associated with utopian quests, as in Étienne Cabet's *Voyage to Icaria* (1840).

[3]Legendary city of gold that enflamed the colonial quests of Spanish conquistadors in the sixteenth century.

[4]A city in southern Italy notorious for its luxury and libertinism.

The richest cities, the noblest landscapes,
Never possess the mysterious
Attraction of those chance makes out of clouds.
And desire kept us forever anxious.

—Enjoyment augments the strength of desire.
Desire, ancient tree that thrives on pleasure,   70
All the while your bark thickens and hardens,
Your branches would look more closely on the sun!

When will you stop growing, great tree, longer
Lived than the cypress? —Yet we were careful
To cull a few sketches for your album,
Brothers who think all that's exotic fair!

We bowed before idols with trunks, and
Thrones constellated with shining jewels,
And carven palaces whose fairy pomp
Would make your bankers ruinous dreams.   80

Costumes like a drunkenness for the eyes
We say; women with painted teeth and nails,
And skilled fakirs whom the snake caresses."

5

And then, after that what?

6

"O childish brains!

Lest we forget the most important thing,
Everywhere, without wishing to, we viewed,
From top to bottom of the fatal ladder,
The dull pageant of everlasting sin:

Woman, conceited slave, neither amused
Nor disgusted by her self-worship;   90
Man, hot, gluttonous tyrant, hard and grasping,
Slave of a slave, gutter in the sewer;

The hangman enjoying, the martyr sobbing,
The fete that spices and perfumes the blood;
The despot unnerved by power's poison,
The mob in love with the brutalizing whip;

A great many religions like our own,
All scaling heaven; Holiness seeking
Its pleasure in nails and haircloth, as a
Delicate wallows in a feather bed;   100

Babbling Mankind, drunk with its own genius,
And mad as it ever was, crying out

To God, in its furious agony:
'O my fellow, my master, I curse thee!'

And the less stupid, bold lovers of Madness,
Fleeing the herd fenced in by Destiny,
To take refuge in a vast opium!
—Thus the everlasting news of the whole globe."

7

A bitter knowledge we gain by traveling!
The world, monotonous and small, today,   110
Yesterday, tomorrow, reflects our image:
Dreadful oasis in a waste of boredom!

Shall we depart or stay? Stay if you can;
Depart if you must. Some run, others crouch
To deceive the watchful, deadly foe, Time!
There are those, alas! who run without rest,

Like the wandering Jew[5] and the apostles,
Whom nothing suffices, carriage or ship,
To flee that base retiary; others
Wear him out without leaving their cradles.   120

When at last he has his foot on our backs,
Then we'll be able to hope and cry: on!
Just as we used to set out for China,
Eyes fixed on the horizon and hair streaming,

We will embark on the sea of Darkness
With the joyous hearts of young passengers;
Listen to those charming, mournful voices
Singing: "Come this way, who desire to eat

The perfumed Lotus![6] Here are gathered the
Miraculous fruits your hearts hunger for;   130
Come and grow drunk on the strange mildness
Of this afternoon without an ending."

We know the ghost by its familiar speech;
Our Pylades stretch out their arms to us.
"To renew your heart, swim towards your Electra!"[7]
Cries she whose knees we kissed in former days.

---

[5]A legendary Jew, condemned to roam the world until Judgment Day for mocking Christ on his way
to the Crucifixion.

[6]The fabled plant that induces a state of blissful indolence and forgetfulness; an allusion to the land of
the Lotus-eaters in Book 9 of *The Odyssey*, in which voices of the dead lured the sailors to this land of
happy stupor.

[7]Pylades was the loyal friend of Orestes, son of King Agamemnom and his faithless wife Clytemnestra;
Electra, Orestes' sister, saved her brother from being murdered by Aegisthus, their mother's lover, who
helped her kill Agamemnon when he returned to Mycenae after the Trojan War. Electra eventually married
Pylades; both symbolize the faithful companion.

[handwritten: beauty to be found in midst of reality]

Death, old captain, it's time to weigh anchor!
This country bores us, O Death! Let us set sail!
If the sea and sky are as black as ink,
Our hearts, you know well, are bursting with rays!   140

Pour your poison on us; let it comfort
Us! We long, so does this fire burn our brains,
To dive into the gulf, Hell or Heaven,
What matter? Into the Unknown in search of the *new!*

[handwritten: The sea — absolute beauty imagination ennui — boredom, complacency — images to shock us out of it]

STÉPHANE MALLARMÉ
[1842–1898]

Windows

Translated by Daisy Aldan

Disgusted with the dreary hospital, and the rank fumes
Rising with the banal whiteness of the curtains
Toward the great crucifix tired of the bare wall,
The man destined for death slyly straightens his old spine,

Shuffles, less to warm his rotting body
Than to watch the sun on the stones, to press
His ashen gaunt and skeletal face
To the panes which a clear beautiful ray attempts to tinge,

And his mouth, feverish and greedy for the azure,
As when young, he breathed his prize,   10
A virginal cheek! soils
With a long bitter kiss the warm golden panes.

Drunk, forgetting the horror of the holy oil,
The herb teas, the clock and the inflicted bed,
The cough, he lives again; and when twilight bleeds on the tiles,
His eye on the horizon gorged with light,

Sees golden ships, fine as swans,
On a scented river of purple, sleepily
Rocking the rich faun flash of their lines
In a great calm charged with memory!   20

In this way, disgusted with the blunt-souled man
Who wallows in contentment, where only his appetites
Devour him, and who insists on fetching this filth
To present to his wife nursing her children,

I flee and I cling to all those windows
From where one turns one's back on life, and hallowed,
In their glass, washed by eternal dews,
Gilded by the chaste morning of the Infinite

I see myself and I brag I am an angel! and I die, and I long
—Let the glass be art, let it be mysticism—   30
To be reborn, wearing my dream as a crown,
In a past heaven where Beauty flourished!

But, alas! Here—below is master; its curse
Sickens me at times even in this safe shelter,
And the foul vomit of Stupidity
Makes me stop up my nose in face of the azure.

Is there a way for Me who knows bitterness,
To shatter the crystal insulted by the monster
And to escape with my two featherless wings
—Even at the risk of falling in eternity?   40

The Azure

Translated by Kate Flores

In serene irony the infinite azure,
Languidly lovely as the flowers, smites
The impotent poet cursing his genius
Across a barren wilderness of Sorrows.

Fleeing with eyes closed, I feel it probe
Deep as a racking remorse
My empty soul. Where escape? And what eerie night
To hurl, O remains, against this heart-mangling scorn?

O fogs, come forth! Pour your monotonous ashes
In long shreds of haze across the skies,   10
Drowning the livid quagmire of the autumns
And rearing a vast ceiling of silence!

And you, from the lethal morasses emerge and gather
As you come the slime and the vapid reeds,
Dear Ennui, to stuff with untiring hands
The great blue holes the birds maliciously make.

More! Let the sad chimneys unceasingly
Smoke, and a wandering prison of soot
Blot out in the horror of their murky trails
The sun dying yellowish on the horizon!   20

—The Sky is dead. —Toward you I run! O matter, give
Oblivion of the cruel Ideal and of Sin

To this martyr who comes to share the straw
Where men's contented cattle lie,

For here I wish, since at the last my brain, empty
As the pot of paint lying at the foot of a wall,
The art to adorn the woeful Idea possesses no more,
To yawn disconsolately to a desolate death . . .

In vain! The Azure triumphs, and in the bells
I hear it sing. My soul, it becomes a voice   30
Instilling us with fear anew of its awful victory,
And from the living metal comes in bluenesses the Angelus![1]

It whirls through the mist as of old and cleaves
Like a resolute sword your intrinsic agony;
In the helpless and hopeless revolt what escape?
I am obsessed. The Azure! The Azure! The Azure! The Azure!

The Afternoon of a Faun

Translated by Frederick Morgan

ECLOGUE

The Faun

These nymphs, I would make them endure.

Their delicate flesh-tint so clear,
it hovers yet upon the air
heavy with foliage of sleep.

Was it a dream I loved? My doubt,
hoarded of old night, culminates
in many a subtle branch, that stayed
the very forest's self and proves
alas! that I alone proposed
the ideal failing of the rose   10
as triumph of my own. Think now . . .
and if the women whom you gloze
picture a wish of your fabled senses!
Faun, the illusion takes escape
from blue cold eyes, like a spring in tears,
of the purer one: and would you say
of her, the other, made of sighs,
that she contrasts, like the day breeze

---

[1]A prayer said three times a day to commemorate the Incarnation of Christ and to honor the Virgin Mary.

warmly astir now in your fleece!
No! through the moveless, half-alive   20
languor that suffocates in heat
freshness of morning, if it strive,
no water sounds save what is poured
upon the grove sparged with accords
by this my flute; and the sole wind
prompt from twin pipes to be exhaled
before dispersal of the sound
in arid shower without rain
is—on the unwrinkled, unstirred
horizon—calm and clear to the eye,   30
the artificial breath of in-
spiration, which regains the sky.

Sicilian shores of a calm marsh,
despoilèd by my vanity
that vies with suns, tacit beneath
the flower-sparkle, now RELATE
how here I cut the hollow reeds
that talent tames; when, on pale gold
of distant greens that dedicate
their vine to fountains, undulates   40
an animal whiteness in repose:
and how at sound of slow prelude
with which the pipes first come to life
this flight of swans, no! naiads flees
or plunges . . .

        Limp in the tawny hour
all is afire but shows no trace
by what art those too many brides
longed-for by him who seeks the *A*
all at once decamped; then shall I wake
to the primal fire, alone and straight,   50
beneath an ancient surge of light,
even as one of you, lilies!
by strength of my simplicity.

Other than the soft nothingness
their lips made rumor of, the kiss,
which gives assurance in low tones
of the two perfidious ones,
my breast, immaculate of proof,
attests an enigmatic bite,
imputed to some august tooth;   60
leave it! such mystery made choice
of confidant: the vast twinned reed—
beneath blue sky we give it voice:
diverting to itself the cheek's
turmoil, it dreams, in a long solo,
that we amused the beauty here-

about by false bewilderments
between it and our naïve song;
dreams too that from the usual dream
of back or flawless flank traced by   70
my shuttered glances, it makes fade,
tempered to love's own pitch, a vain,
monotonous, sonorous line.

Oh instrument of flights, try then,
cunning Syrinx,[1] to bloom again
by lakes where you await me! I,
proud of my murmur, shall discourse
at length of goddesses; and by
idolatries warmly portrayed
remove more cinctures from their shades: 80
thus, when from grapes their clarity
I suck, to banish a regret
deflected by my strategy,
laughing, I raise the cluster high
and empty to the summer sky,
and breathing into its bright skins,
craving the grace of drunkenness,
I gaze them through till night begins.

Oh nymphs, let us once more expand
various MEMORIES. *My eye,*   90
piercing the reeds, darted at each
immortal neck-and-shoulders, which
submerged its burning in the wave
with a cry of rage to the forest sky;
and the splendid shower of their hair
in shimmering limpidities,
oh jewels, vanishes! I run;
when, at my feet, all interlaced
(bruised by the languor which they taste
of this sickness of being two),   100
I come upon them where they sleep
amid their own chance arms alone;
and seizing them, together still
entwined, I fly to this massed bloom—
detested by the frivolous shade—
of roses draining all perfume
in the sun's heat; where our frisk play
may mirror the consumèd day.
I worship you, oh wrath of virgins,
savage joy of the sacred burden   110
sliding its nakedness to flee

---

[1] An Arcadian nymph, transformed into a clump of reeds in order to escape Pan, who used the reeds to make the first shepherd's pipe (panpipe).

my lips that drink, all fiery—
like tremor of a lightning-flash!—
the secret terror of the flesh:
from feet of the inhuman one
to her shy sister's heart, who is
forsaken at the instant by
an innocence, moist with wild tears
or humors of a brighter cheer.
My crime is, that in gaiety   120
of vanquishing these traitor fears
I parted the disheveled tuft
of kisses which the gods had kept
so closely mingled; for I scarce
moved to conceal a burning laugh
beneath glad sinuosities
of one alone (holding the child,
naïve and never blushing, by
a single finger, that her white-
swan candor might take tinge of shame   130
from kindling of her sister's flame):
when from my arms, that are undone
by obscure passings, this my prey
forever thankless slips away
unpitying the sob which still
intoxicated me.

                                    Ah well!
Others will draw me towards joy,
their tresses knotted to my brow's
twin horns: you know, my passion, how
each pomegranate, purple now   140
and fully ripened, bursts—and hums
with bees; and our blood, taking fire
from her who will possess it, flows
for the timeless swarm of all desire.
At the hour when this wood is tinged
with ash and gold, a festival
flares up in the extinguished leaves:
Etna!² it's on your slopes, visited
by Venus³ setting down her heels
artless upon your lava, when   150
a solemn slumber thunders, or
the flame expires.   I hold the queen!

Oh certain punishment...

                                    But no,
the spirit empty of words, and
this weighed-down body late succumb

---

²Volcano on the eastern coast of Sicily.
³The Roman goddess of love.

to the proud silence of midday;
no more—lying on the parched sand,
forgetful of the blasphemy,
I must sleep, in my chosen way,
wide-mouthed to the wine-fostering sun! 160

Couple, farewell; I soon shall see
the shade wherein you merged as one.

ARTHUR RIMBAUD
[1854–1891]

The Drunken Boat
Translated by Louise Varèse

As I came down the impassable Rivers,
I felt no more the bargemen's guiding hands,
Targets for yelling red-skins they were nailed
Naked to painted poles.

What did I care for any crews,
Carriers of English cotton or of Flemish grain!
Bargemen and all that hubbub left behind,
The waters let me go my own free way.

In the furious lashings of the tides,
Emptier than children's minds, I through that winter 10
Ran! And great peninsulas unmoored
Never knew more triumphant uproar than I knew.

The tempest blessed my wakings on the sea.
Light as a cork I danced upon the waves,
Eternal rollers of the deep sunk dead,
Nor missed at night the lanterns' idiot eyes!

Sweeter than sour apples to a child,
Green waters seeped through all my seams,
Washing the stains of vomit and blue wine,
And swept away my anchor and my helm. 20

And since then I've been bathing in the Poem
Of star-infused and milky Sea,
Devouring the azure greens, where, flotsam pale,
A brooding corpse at times drifts by;

Where, dyeing suddenly the blue,
Rhythms delirious and slow in the blaze of day,
Stronger than alcohol, vaster than your lyres,
Ferment the bitter reds of love!

I know the lightning-opened skies, waterspouts,
Eddies and surfs; I know the night,   30
And dawn arisen like a colony of doves,
And sometimes I have seen what men have thought they saw!

I've seen the low sun, fearful with mystic signs,
Lighting with far flung violet arms,
Like actors in an ancient tragedy,
The fluted waters shivering far away.

I've dreamed green nights of dazzling snows,
Slow kisses on the eyelids of the sea,
The terrible flow of unforgettable saps,
And singing phosphors waking yellow and blue.   40

Months through I've followed the assaulting tides
Like maddened cattle leaping up the reefs,
Nor ever thought the Marys'[1] luminous feet
Could curb the muzzle of the panting Deep.

I've touched, you know, fantastic Floridas
Mingling the eyes of panthers, human-skinned, with flowers!
And rainbows stretched like endless reins
To glaucous flocks beneath the seas.

I've seen fermenting marshes like enormous nets
Where in the reeds a whole Leviathan[2] decays!   50
Crashings of waters in the midst of calms!
Horizons toward far chasms cataracting!

Glaciers and silver suns, fiery skies and pearly seas,
Hideous wrecks at the bottom of brown gulfs
Where giant serpents vermin ridden   \
Drop with black perfumes from the twisted trees!

I would show children those dorados,
And golden singing fishes in blue seas.
Foam flowers have blest my aimless wanderings,
Ineffable winds have given me wings.   60

Tired of poles and zones, sometimes the martyred sea,
Rolling me gently on her sobbing breast,
Lifted her shadow flowers with yellow cups toward me
And I stayed there like a woman on her knees.

---

[1]The three Marys of the New Testament: Mary, mother of Jesus; Mary Magdalen; and Mary of Bethany.
[2]A sea monster, symbolizing evil in the Bible.

Island, I sailed, and on my gunnels tossed
Quarrels and droppings of the pale-eyed birds,
While floating slowly past my fragile bands,
Backward the drowned went dreaming by.

But I, lost boat in the cove's trailing tresses,
Tossed by the tempest into birdless space,   70
Whose water-drunken carcass never would have salvaged
Old Monitor or Galleon of the Hanseatic League;[3]

Who, ridden by violet mists, steaming and free,
Pierced the sky reddening like a wall,
Covered with lichens of the sun and azure's phlegm,
Preserves that all good poets love,

Who, spotted with electric crescents ran,
Mad plank with escort of black hypocamps,
While Augusts with their hammer blows tore down
The sea-blue, spiral-flaming skies;   80

Who trembling felt Behemoth's[4] rut
And Maelstroms[5] groaning fifty leagues away,
Eternal scudder through the quiescent blue,
I long for Europe's parapets!

I've seen sidereal archipelagos! Islands
Whose delirious skies open for wanderers:
"Is it in such bottomless nights you sleep, exiled,
O countless golden birds, O Force to come?"

True I have wept too much! Dawns are heartbreaking;
Cruel all moons and bitter the suns.   90
Drunk with love's acrid torpors,
O let my keel burst! Let me go to the sea!

If I desire any European water, it's the black pond
And cold, where toward perfumed evening
A sad child on his knees sets sail
A boat as frail as a May butterfly.

I can no longer, bathed in your languors, O waves,
Obliterate the cotton carriers' wake,
Nor cross the pride of pennants and of flags,
Nor swim past prison hulks' hateful eyes!   100

---

[3] A confederation of towns in northern Germany organized in the Middle Ages to protect commercial and trade interests.
[4] A huge beast.
[5] A large whirlpool, named after a two-mile-wide whirlpool off the northwest coast of Norway.

Vowels

Translated by Louise Varèse

A black, E white, I red, U green, O blue;
Someday I'll tell your latent birth O vowels:
A, a black corset hairy with gaudy flies
That bumble round all stinking putrefactions,

Gulfs of darkness; E, candors of steam and tents,
Icicles' proud spears, white kings, and flutter of para-
    sols;
I, purple blood coughed up, laughter of lovely lips
In anger or ecstatic penitence;

U, cycles, divine vibrations of virescent seas,
Peace of the pastures sown with animals, peace   10
Of the wrinkles that alchemy stamps on studious brows;

O, Clarion supreme, full of strange stridences,
Silences crossed by Angels and Worlds:
—Omega, the violet ray of His Eyes!

ANTON CHEKHOV
[1860–1904]

In both his plays and his short stories, Anton Chekhov wrote about ordinary people in ordinary situations, but the simplicity of his style is deceptive. In the small details, in the nuances of attitude and gesture, lie his genius for invoking, in all their beauty and pathos, the profound ambiguities and complexities of human life. As a stylist, Chekhov redefined both drama and short fiction, preparing them for the twentieth century. He was able to capture a uniquely "modern" consciousness: Self-knowledge is uncertain and communication between individuals is always problematic and ambiguous. Missed communication is frequent in a rapidly changing society. His writings reflect the uncertainty about ordinary life and the loss of faith in traditional beliefs at the turn of the century.

In 1886, when Chekhov was twenty-six years old, he described his writing technique: "I do not remember working more than a day on *any single* story of mine . . . I wrote my stories as reporters write their news about fires: mechanically, half-consciously, without worrying about either the reader or themselves." While studying medicine, Chekhov was supporting his family in Moscow by writing. He had already published almost 300 stories in the popular magazines of St. Petersburg and Moscow. He would write 300 more in the next year. This was an apprenticeship for the young writer; he wrote and wrote and wrote, learning a style of writing that would be a trademark in many of his stories. In a letter to his brother, he talks about the use of suggestive detail to evoke a whole scene: "You have to choose small details in describing nature, grouping them in such a way that if you close your eyes after reading it you can picture the whole thing. For example, you'll get a picture of a moonlight night if you write that on the dam of the mill a piece of broken bottle flashed like a bright star and the black shadow of a dog or a wolf rolled by like a ball."

In a letter to A. S. Suvorin, it is clear that Chekhov is charting a totally different path from the tempestuous psychological treatments of Dostoevsky's novels, one that would be traveled by generations of modern writers; the letter contains a concise definition of realism: "I think that it is not for writers to solve such questions as the existence of God, pessimism, etc. The writer's function is only to describe by whom, how, and under what conditions the questions of God and pessimism were discussed. The artist must be only an impartial witness of his characters and what they said, not their judge."

LIFE

Anton Chekhov was born at Taganrog on January 17, 1860. He attended a Greek preparatory school and later the Taganrog secondary school. In 1879, three years after his father went bankrupt and the family fled to Moscow, Anton started medical school and began to sell humorous stories to help support his family. When Chekhov was twenty-three, he contracted tuberculosis, which eventually took his life. With a visit to St. Petersburg in 1885, a year after receiving his medical degree, Chekhov discovered that he was already famous and had attracted the attention of an important novelist of the 1840s, Dmitri Grigorovich. Grigorovich in turn introduced him to Aleksei Suvorin, who would publish many of his most famous stories in his newspaper, *Novoe Vremya* (*New Times*). Suvorin even created a special literary supplement for Chekhov's work. In 1887, Chekhov's first play, *Ivanov,* was produced in Moscow, thereby launching his literary career in the drama. Already known as a fine writer of short stories, Chekhov would break ground in two major literary forms and set standards of excellence for numerous writers in the twentieth century.

After the production of *Ivanov,* Chekhov's life was rather ordinary for a Russian doctor of the late nineteenth century, with the exception of a strenuous visit in 1890 through Siberia to the penal colony on the island of Sakhalin. Under Tolstoy's humanitarian influence, Chekhov made the trip and later described the inhumane conditions of the prisoners in a book, *The Island of Sakhalin* (1893–1894). In 1892, he purchased the Melikhova estate, fifty miles south of Moscow in the village of Melikhova, where he lived with his parents and spent his time writing, caring for patients, and contributing to local service projects. In 1897, Chekhov's health began to fail and he was forced to sell the Melikhova estate and move to the warmer climate of Yalta, where he spent the last part of his life writing some of his best plays and cultivating strong friendships with Tolstoy and Maxim Gorky.

His most famous plays were written in the 1890s and early 1900s for the Moscow Art Theatre, which was directed by Konstantin Stanislavsky, one of the geniuses of modern theater. In addition to *The Cherry Orchard* (1904), his plays of this period include *The Seagull* (1896), *Uncle Vanya* (1900), and *The Three Sisters* (1901). In 1901, Chekhov married an actress from the Moscow Art Theatre, Olga Leonardovna Knipper, and during the happy years of this marriage he wrote his masterpiece about the passing of the old order and the rise of the middle class, *The Cherry Orchard.* This final play was produced on January 17, 1904, Chekhov's birthday. As it was also the twenty-fifth anniversary of Chekhov's literary career, a grand celebration was planned for opening night. Nemirovich-Danchenko, the co-director of the theater, paid the final tribute of the evening by saying to Chekhov: "Our theater is so much indebted to your talent, to your tender heart and pure soul, that you have every right to say 'This is my theater.'" Chekhov died six months later on July 2, 1904, at the Badenweiler spa in the Black Forest.

WORK

Chekhov is a master stylist, a poet really, able to use a few poignant details to evoke a whole scene or character. With great skill, he creates atmosphere and mood as he ranges over both urban and rural life. Quick to deflate the arrogant and pretentious, he is equally harsh with the crudities of life lived close to the soil. Characteristic of his later work is the focus on people's isolation, their inability to communicate with one another, and the oppressive boredom that grinds away at a person's vitality. Maxim Gorky, a famous Russian dramatist and fiction writer of the early twentieth century, summarizes Chekhov's attitudes toward his subjects: "Detesting all that was vulgar and unclean, he described the seamy side of life in the lofty language of the poet, with the gentle smile of the humorist, and the bitter inner reproach beneath the polished surface of his stories is scarcely noticeable... No one ever understood the tragic nature of life's trifles so clearly and intuitively as Chekhov did, never before has a writer been able to hold up to human beings such a ruthlessly truthful picture of all that was shameful and pitiable in the dingy chaos of middle-class life."

It is often said that Chekhov's plays do not have a plot, and that this absence defines his approach to realism. Chekhov himself said that he wanted to show life as it is lived by ordinary people: "A play should be written in which people arrive, go away, have dinner, talk about the weather, and play cards. Life must be exactly as it is, and people as they are—not on stilts....Let everything on the stage be just as complicated, and at the same time just as simple as it is in life." The arrival and departure of people frame the action of *The Cherry Orchard,* but within the play's boundaries Chekhov reveals the intricacy and subtlety of human behavior. If Chekhov's major contribution to theater was showing how drama was as much embedded in the internal struggles of characters as in plot action, he uses the disposition of a bankrupt estate in *The Cherry Orchard* to depict people trapped within their personalities and circumstances, incapable of decisive action on the one hand or of expressing their true feelings on the other. For Lyubov, Gaev, and the landowning elite, the cherry orchard symbolizes the privilege of money and tradition and an ignorance of the price the serf class had to pay for such unproductive, foolish luxury. The student Trofimov recognizes the burden of economic oppression represented by the orchard, and with youthful bombast, champions work as the pathway to a new Russian Eden—a nineteenth-century "myth of progress." In between the positions of the old and young is Lopahin, who embodies the crass materialism of a new, pragmatic middle class.

Chekhov's answer to the limited, often shallow perspectives of his characters is not a particular political philosophy that might address the turmoil of a changing Russia. A few of his short stories, such as "The Beggar" and "The Bet," seem to bear the imprint of Tolstoy's nonviolent philosophy, but Chekhov's stories and plays are rarely ideological in the sense that a story can be neatly packaged by a moral or easily reduced to a philosophical statement. Always there seems to be a restrained drama that seldom reaches the scale of tragedy, and more often than not touches on pathos and comedy. People make mistakes and suffer, but in the background is Chekhov's abiding faith in the quiet dignity of love and work, the life of simplicity and diligence. Maxim Gorky observes, "I have never met anyone who felt the importance of work as the basis of culture so profoundly and diversely as A.P. [Anton Pavlovich]... He loved building, planting gardens, adorning the earth, he felt the poetry of work."

In a letter of September 15, 1903, Chekhov chooses to describe *The Cherry Orchard* not as a tragedy of the old Russian aristocracy, "but as comedy, in places even a farce." Certainly the play is filled with comic moments. With cultural pretensions, servants mimic the aristocrats, who in turn betray their own limitations with inappropriate gestures and remarks. Gaev, for example, dilutes his opinions with exclamations from playing billiards. Semyonov-Pishtchik, a neighboring landowner, snatches Lyubov's medicines and swallows all the pills. Instead of a match between Varya and Lopahin, a relationship that would reconcile social classes, the conversation drifts to the weather and a broken thermometer. There is nothing comic, however, about the play's final scene, which overflows with pathos. A sense of the inevitable is played out when the old butler Firs finds that he has been locked out of the house and forgotten. In a final repudiation of the old regime in which he was born a serf, he exclaims, "Ech! I'm good for nothing." As he lies down to die, the sound of the ax felling the cherry orchard can be heard in the background.

SUGGESTED READINGS

Ernest J. Simmons's *Chekhov: A Biography* (1962) is a substantial biography. Beverly Hahn's *Chekhov: A Study of Major Stories and Plays* (1977) and R. L. Jackson's *Chekhov: A Collection of Critical Essays* (1967) contain various perspectives on Chekhov's life and work. Ralph E. Matlaw (editor), *Anton Chekhov's Short Stories: Texts of the Stories, Backgrounds, Criticism* (Norton Critical Edition, 1975), provides excellent translations of major short stories and helpful background. René Wellek and N. D. Wellek's *Chekhov: New Perspectives* (1984) is a collection of contemporary criticism.

The Cherry Orchard

Translated by Constance Garnett

CHARACTERS

MADAME RANEVSKY (LYUBOV ANDREYEVNA), *the owner of the cherry orchard*
ANYA, *her daughter, aged seventeen*
VARYA, *her adopted daughter, aged twenty-four*
GAEV, LEONID ANDREYEVITCH, *brother of Madame Ranevsky*
LOPAHIN, YERMOLAY ALEXEYEVITCH, *a merchant*
TROFIMOV, PYOTR SERGEYEVITCH, *a student*
SEMYONOV-PISHTCHIK, *a landowner*
CHARLOTTA IVANOVNA, *a governess*

EPIHODOV, SEMYON PANTALEYEVITCH, *a clerk*
DUNYASHA, *a maid*
FIRS, *an old valet, aged eighty-seven*
YASHA, *a young valet*
A VAGRANT
THE STATIONMASTER
A POST-OFFICE CLERK
VISITORS
SERVANTS

The action takes place on the estate of MADAME RANEVSKY

ACT 1

A room, which has always been called the nursery. One of the doors leads into ANYA's *room. Dawn, sun rises during the scene. May, the cherry trees in flower, but it is cold in the garden with the frost of early morning. Windows closed.*

[*Enter* DUNYASHA *with a candle and* LOPAHIN *with a book in his hand.*]
LOPAHIN: The train's in, thank God. What time is it?
DUNYASHA: Nearly two o'clock. [*Puts out the candle.*] It's daylight already.
LOPAHIN: The train's late! Two hours, at least. [*Yawns and stretches.*] I'm a pretty one; what a fool I've been. Came here on purpose to meet them at the station and dropped asleep.... Dozed off as I sat in the chair. It's annoying.... You might have waked me.
DUNYASHA: I thought you had gone. [*Listens.*] There, I do believe they're coming!

LOPAHIN: [*Listens.*] No, what with the luggage and one thing and another. [*A pause.*] Lyubov Andreyevna has been abroad five years; I don't know what she is like now. . . . She's a splendid woman. A good-natured, kind-hearted woman. I remember when I was a lad of fifteen, my poor father—he used to keep a little shop here in the village in those days—gave me a punch in the face with his fist and made my nose bleed. We were in the yard here, I forget what we'd come about—he had had a drop. Lyubov Andreyevna—I can see her now—she was a slim young girl then—took me to wash my face, and then brought me into this very room, into the nursery. "Don't cry, little peasant," says she, "it will be well in time for your wedding day." . . . [*A pause.*] Little peasant. . . . My father was a peasant, it's true, but here am I in a white waistcoat and brown shoes, like a pig in a bun shop. Yes, I'm a rich man, but for all my money, come to think, a peasant I was, and a peasant I am. [*Turns over the pages of the book.*] I've been reading this book and I can't make head or tail of it. I fell asleep over it. [*A pause.*]

DUNYASHA: The dogs have been awake all night, they feel that the mistress is coming.

LOPAHIN: Why, what's the matter with you, Dunyasha?

DUNYASHA: My hands are all of a tremble. I feel as though I should faint.

LOPAHIN: You're a spoilt soft creature, Dunyasha. And dressed like a lady too, and your hair done up. That's not the thing. One must know one's place.

> [*Enter* EPIHODOV *with a nosegay; he wears a pea jacket and highly polished creaking topboots; he drops the nosegay as he comes in.*]

EPIHODOV [*picking up the nosegay*]: Here! the gardener's sent this, says you're to put it in the dining room. [*Gives* DUNYASHA *the nosegay.*]

LOPAHIN: And bring me some kvass.[1]

DUNYASHA: I will. [*Goes out.*]

EPIHODOV: It's chilly this morning, three degrees of frost, though the cherries are all in flower. I can't say much for our climate. [*Sighs.*] I can't. Our climate is not often propitious to the occasion. Yermolay Alexeyevitch, permit me to call your attention to the fact that I purchased myself a pair of boots the day before yesterday, and they creak, I venture to assure you, so that there's no tolerating them. What ought I to grease them with?

LOPAHIN: Oh, shut up! Don't bother me.

EPIHODOV: Every day some misfortune befalls me. I don't complain. I'm used to it, and I wear a smiling face. [DUNYASHA *comes in, hands* LOPAHIN *the kvass.*] I am going. [*Stumbles against a chair, which falls over.*] There! [*As though triumphant*] There you see now, excuse the expression, an accident like that among others. . . . It's positively remarkable. [*Goes out.*]

DUNYASHA: Do you know, Yermolay Alexeyevitch, I must confess, Epihodov has made me a proposal.

LOPAHIN: Ah!

DUNYASHA: I'm sure I don't know. . . . He's a harmless fellow, but sometimes when he begins talking, there's no making anything of it. It's all very fine and expressive, only there's no understanding it. I've a sort of liking for him too. He loves me to distraction. He's an unfortunate man; every day there's something. They tease him about it—two and twenty misfortunes they call him.

LOPAHIN [*listening*]: There! I do believe they're coming.

DUNYASHA: They are coming! What's the matter with me? . . . I'm cold all over.

---

[1]Russian beer.

LOPAHIN: They really are coming. Let's go and meet them. Will she know me? It's five years since I saw her.

DUNYASHA [*in a flutter*]: I shall drop this very minute.... Ah, I shall drop.

[*There is a sound of two carriages driving up to the house.* LOPAHIN *and* DUNYASHA *go out quickly. The stage is left empty. A noise is heard in the adjoining rooms.* FIRS, *who has driven to meet* MADAME RANEVSKY, *crosses the stage hurriedly leaning on a stick. He is wearing old-fashioned livery and a high hat. He says something to himself, but not a word can be distinguished. The noise behind the scenes goes on increasing. A voice: "Come, let's go in here." Enter* LYUBOV ANDREYEVNA, ANYA, *and* CHARLOTTA IVANOVNA *with a pet dog on a chain, all in travelling dresses.* VARYA *in an outdoor coat with a kerchief over her head,* GAEV, SEMYONOV-PISHTCHIK, LOPAHIN, DUNYASHA *with bag and parasol, servants with other articles. All walk across the room.*]

ANYA: Let's come in here. Do you remember what room this is, mamma?

LYUBOV [*joyfully, through her tears*]: The nursery!

VARYA: How cold it is, my hands are numb. [*To* LYUBOV ANDREYEVNA] Your rooms, the white room and the lavender one, are just the same as ever, mamma.

LYUBOV: My nursery, dear delightful room.... I used to sleep here when I was little.... [*Cries.*] And here I am, like a little child.... [*Kisses her brother and* VARYA, *and then her brother again.*] Varya's just the same as ever, like a nun. And I knew Dunyasha. [*Kisses* DUNYASHA.]

GAEV: The train was two hours late. What do you think of that? Is that the way to do things?

CHARLOTTA [*to* PISHTCHIK]: My dog eats nuts, too.

PISHTCHIK [*wonderingly*]: Fancy that!

[*They all go out except* ANYA *and* DUNYASHA.]

DUNYASHA: We've been expecting you so long. [*Takes* ANYA's *hat and coat.*]

ANYA: I haven't slept for four nights on the journey. I feel dreadfully cold.

DUNYASHA: You set out in Lent, there was snow and frost, and now? My darling! [*Laughs and kisses her.*] I *have* missed you, my precious, my joy. I must tell you ... I can't put it off a minute....

ANYA [*wearily*]: What now?

DUNYASHA: Epihodov, the clerk, made me a proposal just after Easter.

ANYA: It's always the same thing with you.... [*Straightening her hair*] I've lost all my hairpins.... [*She is staggering from exhaustion.*]

DUNYASHA: I don't know what to think, really. He does love me, he does love me so!

ANYA [*looking towards her door, tenderly*]: My own room, my windows just as though I had never gone away. I'm home! Tomorrow morning I shall get up and run into the garden.... Oh, if I could get to sleep! I haven't slept all the journey, I was so anxious and worried.

DUNYASHA: Pyotr Sergeyevitch came the day before yesterday.

ANYA [*joyfully*]: Petya!

DUNYASHA: He's asleep in the bathhouse, he has settled in there. I'm afraid of being in their way, says he. [*Glancing at her watch*] I was to have waked him, but Varvara Mihalovna told me not to. Don't you wake him, says she.

[*Enter* VARYA *with a bunch of keys at her waist.*]

VARYA: Dunyasha, coffee and make haste.... Mamma's asking for coffee.

DUNYASHA: This very minute. [*Goes out.*]

VARYA: Well, thank God, you've come. You're home again [*petting her*]. My little darling has come back! My precious beauty has come back again!

ANYA: I have had a time of it!

VARYA: I can fancy.

ANYA: We set off in Holy Week—it was so cold then, and all the way Charlotta would talk and show off her tricks. What did you want to burden me with Charlotta for?

VARYA: You couldn't have travelled all alone, darling. At seventeen!

ANYA: We got to Paris at last, it was cold there—snow. I speak French shockingly. Mamma lives on the fifth floor, I went up to her and there were a lot of French people, ladies, an old priest with a book. The place smelt of tobacco and so comfortless. I felt sorry, oh! so sorry for mamma all at once, I put my arms round her neck, and hugged her and wouldn't let her go. Mamma was as kind as she could be, and she cried....

VARYA [*through her tears*]: Don't speak of it, don't speak of it!

ANYA: She had sold her villa at Mentone, she had nothing left, nothing. I hadn't a farthing left either, we only just had enough to get here. And mamma doesn't understand! When we had dinner at the stations, she always ordered the most expensive things and gave the waiters a whole rouble. Charlotta's just the same. Yasha too must have the same as we do; it's simply awful. You know Yasha is mamma's valet now, we brought him here with us.

VARYA: Yes, I've seen the young rascal.

ANYA: Well, tell me—have you paid the arrears on the mortgage?

VARYA: How could we get the money?

ANYA: Oh, dear! Oh, dear!

VARYA: In August the place will be sold.

ANYA: My goodness!

LOPAHIN: [*Peeps in at the door and moos like a cow.*] Moo! [*Disappears.*]

VARYA [*weeping*]: There, that's what I could do to him [*shakes her fist*].

ANYA [*embracing* VARYA, *softly*]: Varya, has he made you an offer? [VARYA *shakes her head.*] Why, but he loves you. Why is it you don't come to an understanding? What are you waiting for?

VARYA: I believe that there never will be anything between us. He has a lot to do, he has no time for me... and takes no notice of me. Bless the man, it makes me miserable to see him.... Everyone's talking of our being married, everyone's congratulating me, and all the while there's really nothing in it; it's all like a dream. [*In another tone*] You have a new brooch like a bee.

ANYA [*mournfully*]: Mamma bought it. [*Goes into her own room and in a lighthearted childish tone*] And you know, in Paris I went up in a balloon!

VARYA: My darling's home again! My pretty is home again!

[DUNYASHA *returns with the coffee pot and is making the coffee.*]

VARYA [*standing at the door*]: All day long, darling, as I go about looking after the house, I keep dreaming all the time. If only we could marry you to a rich man, then I should feel more at rest. Then I would go off by myself on a pilgrimage to Kiev, to Moscow... and so I would spend my life going from one holy place to another.... I would go on and on.... What bliss!

ANYA: The birds are singing in the garden. What time is it?

VARYA: It must be nearly three. It's time you were asleep, darling. [*Going into* ANYA's *room*] What bliss!

[YASHA *enters with a rug and a travelling bag.*]

YASHA: [*Crosses the stage, mincingly.*] May one come in here, pray?

DUNYASHA: I shouldn't have known you, Yasha. How you have changed abroad.

YASHA: H'm!... And who are you?

DUNYASHA: When you went away, I was that high. [*Shows distance from floor.*] Dunyasha, Fyodor's daughter.... You don't remember me!

YASHA: H'm!... You're a peach! [*Looks round and embraces her: she shrieks and drops a saucer.* YASHA *goes out hastily.*]

VARYA [*in the doorway, in a tone of vexation*]: What now?

DUNYASHA [*through her tears*]: I have broken a saucer.

VARYA: Well, that brings good luck.

ANYA [*coming out of her room*]: We ought to prepare mamma: Petya is here.

VARYA: I told them not to wake him.

ANYA [*dreamily*]: It's six years since father died. Then only a month later little brother Grisha was drowned in the river, such a pretty boy he was, only seven. It was more than mamma could bear, so she went away, went away without looking back [*shuddering*]. . . . How well I understand her, if only she knew! [*A pause.*] And Petya Trofimov was Grisha's tutor, he may remind her.

[*Enter* FIRS: *he is wearing a pea jacket and a white waistcoat.*]

FIRS: [*Goes up to the coffee pot, anxiously.*] The mistress will be served here. [*Puts on white gloves.*] Is the coffee ready? [*Sternly to* DUNYASHA] Girl! Where's the cream?

DUNYASHA: Ah, mercy on us! [*Goes out quickly.*]

FIRS [*fussing round the coffee pot*]: Ech! you good-for-nothing! [*Muttering to himself*] Come back from Paris. And the old master used to go to Paris too . . . horses all the way. [*Laughs.*]

VARYA: What is it, Firs?

FIRS: What is your pleasure? [*Gleefully*] My lady has come home! I have lived to see her again! Now I can die. [*Weeps with joy.*]

[*Enter* LYUBOV ANDREYEVNA, GAEV *and* SEMYONOV-PISHTCHIK; *the latter is in a short-waisted full coat of fine cloth, and full trousers.* GAEV, *as he comes in, makes a gesture with his arms and his whole body, as though he were playing billiards.*]

LYUBOV: How does it go? Let me remember. Cannon off the red!

GAEV: That's it—in off the white! Why, once, sister, we used to sleep together in this very room, and now I'm fifty-one, strange as it seems.

LOPAHIN: Yes, time flies.

GAEV: What do you say?

LOPAHIN: Time, I say, flies.

GAEV: What a smell of patchouli![2]

ANYA: I'm going to bed. Good night, mamma. [*Kisses her mother.*]

LYUBOV: My precious darling. [*Kisses her hands.*] Are you glad to be home? I can't believe it.

ANYA: Good night, uncle.

GAEV [*kissing her face and hands*]: God bless you! How like you are to your mother! [*To his sister*] At her age you were just the same, Lyuba.

[ANYA *shakes hands with* LOPAHIN *and* PISHTCHIK, *then goes out, shutting the door after her.*]

LYUBOV: She's quite worn out.

PISHTCHIK: Aye, it's a long journey, to be sure.

VARYA [*to* LOPAHIN *and* PISHTCHIK]: Well, gentlemen? It's three o'clock and time to say good-by.

LYUBOV: [*Laughs.*] You're just the same as ever, Varya. [*Draws her to her and kisses her.*] I'll just drink my coffee and then we will all go and rest. [FIRS *puts a cushion under her feet.*] Thanks, friend. I am so fond of coffee, I drink it day and night. Thanks, dear old man. [*Kisses* FIRS.]

VARYA: I'll just see whether all the things have been brought in. [*Goes out.*]

LYUBOV: Can it really be me sitting here? [*Laughs.*] I want to dance about and clap my hands. [*Covers her face with her hands.*] And I could drop asleep in a moment! God knows I love my country, I love it tenderly; I couldn't look out of the

---

[2] East Indian perfume.

window in the train, I kept crying so. [*Through her tears*] But I must drink my coffee, though. Thank you, Firs, thanks, dear old man. I'm so glad to find you still alive.

FIRS: The day before yesterday.

GAEV: He's rather deaf.

LOPAHIN: I have to set off for Harkov directly, at five o'clock.... It is annoying! I wanted to have a look at you, and a little talk.... You are just as splendid as ever.

PISHTCHIK [*breathing heavily*]: Handsomer, indeed.... Dressed in Parisian style... completely bowled me over.

LOPAHIN: Your brother, Leonid Andreyevitch here, is always saying that I'm a low-born knave, that I'm a money grubber, but I don't care one straw for that. Let him talk. Only I do want you to believe in me as you used to. I do want your wonderful tender eyes to look at me as they used to in the old days. Merciful God! My father was a serf of your father and of your grandfather, but you—you—did so much for me once, that I've forgotten all that; I love you as though you were my kin... more than my kin.

LYUBOV: I can't sit still, I simply can't.... [*Jumps up and walks about in violent agitation.*] This happiness is too much for me.... You may laugh at me, I know I'm silly.... My own bookcase. [*Kisses the bookcase.*] My little table.

GAEV: Nurse died while you were away.

LYUBOV: [*Sits down and drinks coffee.*] Yes, the Kingdom of Heaven be hers! You wrote me of her death.

GAEV: And Anastasy is dead. Squinting Petruchka has left me and is in service now with the police captain in the town. [*Takes a box of caramels out of his pocket and sucks one.*]

PISHTCHIK: My daughter, Dashenka, wishes to be remembered to you.

LOPAHIN: I want to tell you something very pleasant and cheering [*glancing at his watch*]. I'm going directly... there's no time to say much... well, I can say it in a couple of words. I needn't tell you your cherry orchard is to be sold to pay your debts; the 22nd of August is the date fixed for the sale; but don't you worry, dearest lady, you may sleep in peace, there is a way of saving it.... This is what I propose. I beg your attention! Your estate is not twenty miles from the town, the railway runs close by it, and if the cherry orchard and the land along the river bank were cut up into building plots and then let on lease for summer villas, you would make an income of at least 25,000 roubles a year out of it.

GAEV: That's all rot, if you'll excuse me.

LYUBOV: I don't quite understand you, Yermolay Alexeyevitch.

LOPAHIN: You will get a rent of at least 25 roubles a year for a three-acre plot from summer visitors, and if you say the word now, I'll bet you what you like there won't be one square foot of ground vacant by the autumn, all the plots will be taken up. I congratulate you; in fact, you are saved. It's a perfect situation with that deep river. Only, of course, it must be cleared—all the old buildings, for example, must be removed, this house too, which is really good for nothing and the old cherry orchard must be cut down.

LYUBOV: Cut down? My dear fellow, forgive me, but you don't know what you are talking about. If there is one thing interesting—remarkable indeed—in the whole province, it's just our cherry orchard.

LOPAHIN: The only thing remarkable about the orchard is that it's a very large one. There's a crop of cherries every alternate year, and then there's nothing to be done with them, no one buys them.

GAEV: This orchard is mentioned in the "Encyclopaedia."

LOPAHIN [*glancing at his watch*]: If we don't decide on something and don't take some steps, on the 22nd of August the cherry orchard and the whole estate too will be sold by auction. Make up your minds! There is no other way of saving it, I'll take my oath on that. No, no!

FIRS: In old days, forty or fifty years ago, they used to dry the cherries, soak them, pickle them, make jam too, and they used—

GAEV: Be quiet, Firs.

FIRS: And they used to send the preserved cherries to Moscow and to Harkov by the wagon-load. That brought the money in! And the preserved cherries in those days were soft and juicy, sweet and fragrant. . . . They knew the way to do them then. . . .

LYUBOV: And where is the recipe now?

FIRS: It's forgotten. Nobody remembers it.

PISHTCHIK [*to* LYUBOV ANDREYEVNA]: What's it like in Paris? Did you eat frogs there?

LYUBOV: Oh, I ate crocodiles.

PISHTCHIK: Fancy that now!

LOPAHIN: There used to be only the gentlefolks and the peasants in the country, but now there are these summer visitors. All the towns, even the small ones, are surrounded nowadays by these summer villas. And one may say for sure, that in another twenty years there'll be many more of these people and that they'll be everywhere. At present the summer visitor only drinks tea in his verandah, but maybe he'll take to working his bit of land too, and then your cherry orchard would become happy, rich and prosperous. . . .

GAEV [*indignant*]: What rot!

[*Enter* VARYA *and* YASHA.]

VARYA: There are two telegrams for you, mamma. [*Takes out keys and opens an old-fashioned bookcase with a loud crack.*] Here they are.

LYUBOV: From Paris. [*Tears the telegrams, without reading them.*] I have done with Paris.

GAEV: Do you know, Lyuba, how old that bookcase is? Last week I pulled out the bottom drawer and there I found the date branded on it. The bookcase was made just a hundred years ago. What do you say to that? We might have celebrated its jubilee. Though it's an inanimate object, still it is a *book* case.

PISHTCHIK [*amazed*]: A hundred years! Fancy that now.

GAEV: Yes. . . . It is a thing . . . [*feeling the bookcase*]. Dear, honored, bookcase! Hail to thee who for more than a hundred years hast served the pure ideals of good and justice; thy silent call to fruitful labor has never flagged in those hundred years, maintaining [*in tears*] in the generations of man, courage and faith in a brighter future and fostering in us ideals of good and social consciousness. [*A pause.*]

LOPAHIN: Yes. . . .

LYUBOV: You are just the same as ever, Leonid.

GAEV [*a little embarrassed*]: Cannon off the right into the pocket!

LOPAHIN [*looking at his watch*]: Well, it's time I was off.

YASHA [*handing* LYUBOV ANDREYEVNA *medicine*]: Perhaps you will take your pills now.

PISHTCHIK: You shouldn't take medicines, my dear madam . . . they do no harm and no good. Give them here . . . honored lady. [*Takes the pillbox, pours the pills into the hollow of his hand, blows on them, puts them in his mouth and drinks off some kvass.*] There!

LYUBOV [*in alarm*]: Why, you must be out of your mind!

PISHTCHIK: I have taken all the pills.

LOPAHIN: What a glutton! [*All laugh.*]

FIRS: His honor stayed with us in Easter week, ate a gallon and a half of cucumbers. . . . [*Mutters.*]

LYUBOV: What is he saying?

VARYA: He has taken to muttering like that for the last three years. We are used to it.

YASHA: His declining years!

[CHARLOTTA IVANOVNA, *a very thin, lanky figure in a white dress with a lorgnette in her belt, walks across the stage.*]

LOPAHIN: I beg your pardon, Charlotta Ivanovna, I have not had time to greet you. [*Tries to kiss her hand.*]

CHARLOTTA [*pulling away her hand*]: If I let you kiss my hand, you'll be wanting to kiss my elbow, and then my shoulder.

LOPAHIN: I've no luck today! [*All laugh.*] Charlotta Ivanovna, show us some tricks!

LYUBOV: Charlotta, do show us some tricks!

CHARLOTTA: I don't want to. I'm sleepy. [*Goes out.*]

LOPAHIN: In three weeks' time we shall meet again. [*Kisses* LYUBOV ANDREYEVNA's *hand.*] Good-by till then—I must go. [*To* GAEV] Good-by. [*Kisses* PISHTCHIK.] Good-by. [*Gives his hand to* VARYA, *then to* FIRS *and* YASHA.] I don't want to go. [*To* LYUBOV ANDREYEVNA] If you think over my plan for the villas and make up your mind, then let me know; I will lend you 50,000 roubles. Think of it seriously.

VARYA [*angrily*]: Well, do go, for goodness sake.

LOPAHIN: I'm going, I'm going. [*Goes out.*]

GAEV: Low-born knave! I beg pardon, though . . . Varya is going to marry him, he's Varya's fiancé.

VARYA: Don't talk nonsense, uncle.

LYUBOV: Well, Varya, I shall be delighted. He's a good man.

PISHTCHIK: He is, one must acknowledge, a most worthy man. And my Dashenka . . . says too that . . . she says . . . various things. [*Snores, but at once wakes up.*] But all the same, honored lady, could you oblige me . . . with a loan of 240 roubles . . . to pay the interest on my mortgage tomorrow?

VARYA [*dismayed*]: No, no.

LYUBOV: I really haven't any money.

PISHTCHIK: It will turn up. [*Laughs.*] I never lose hope. I thought everything was over, I was a ruined man, and lo and behold—the railway passed through my land and . . . they paid me for it. And something else will turn up again, if not today, then tomorrow . . . Dashenka'll win two hundred thousand . . . she's got a lottery ticket.

LYUBOV: Well, we've finished our coffee, we can go to bed.

FIRS: [*Brushes* GAEV, *reprovingly.*] You have got on the wrong trousers again! What am I to do with you?

VARYA [*softly*]: Anya's asleep. [*Softly opens the window.*] Now the sun's risen, it's not a bit cold. Look, mamma, what exquisite trees! My goodness! And the air! The starlings are singing!

GAEV: [*Opens another window.*] The orchard is all white. You've not forgotten it, Lyuba? That long avenue that runs straight, straight as an arrow, how it shines on a moonlight night. You remember? You've not forgotten?

LYUBOV [*looking out of the window into the garden*]: Oh, my childhood, my innocence! It was in this nursery I used to sleep, from here I looked out into the orchard, happiness waked with me every morning and in those days the orchard was just the same, nothing has changed. [*Laughs with delight.*] All, all white! Oh, my orchard! After the dark gloomy autumn, and the cold winter; you are young again, and full of happiness, the heavenly angels have never left you. . . . If I could cast off the burden that weighs on my heart, if I could forget the past!

GAEV: H'm! and the orchard will be sold to pay our debts; it seems strange. . . .

LYUBOV: See, our mother walking . . . all in white, down the avenue! [*Laughs with delight.*] It is she!

GAEV: Where?

VARYA: Oh, don't, mamma!

LYUBOV: There is no one. It was my fancy. On the right there, by the path to the arbor, there is a white tree bending like a woman....

[*Enter* TROFIMOV *wearing a shabby student's uniform and spectacles.*]

LYUBOV: What a ravishing orchard! White masses of blossom, blue sky....

TROFIMOV: Lyubov Andreyevna! [*She looks round at him.*] I will just pay my respects to you and then leave you at once. [*Kisses her hand warmly.*] I was told to wait until morning, but I hadn't the patience to wait any longer....

[LYUBOV ANDREYEVNA *looks at him in perplexity.*]

VARYA [*through her tears*]: This is Petya Trofimov.

TROFIMOV: Petya Trofimov, who was your Grisha's tutor.... Can I have changed so much?

[LYUBOV ANDREYEVNA *embraces him and weeps quietly.*]

GAEV [*in confusion*]: There, there, Lyuba.

VARYA [*crying*]: I told you, Petya, to wait till tomorrow.

LYUBOV: My Grisha... my boy... Grisha... my son!

VARYA: We can't help it, mamma, it is God's will.

TROFIMOV [*softly through his tears*]: There... there.

LYUBOV [*weeping quietly*]: My boy was lost... drowned. Why? Oh, why, dear Petya? [*More quietly*] Anya is asleep in there, and I'm talking loudly... making this noise.... But, Petya? Why have you grown so ugly? Why do you look so old?

TROFIMOV: A peasant woman in the train called me a mangy-looking gentleman.

LYUBOV: You were quite a boy then, a pretty little student, and now your hair's thin—and spectacles. Are you really a student still?

[*Goes towards the door.*]

TROFIMOV: I seem likely to be a perpetual student.

LYUBOV: [*Kisses her brother, then* VARYA.] Well, go to bed.... You are older too, Leonid.

PISHTCHIK: [*Follows her.*] I suppose it's time we were asleep.... Ugh! my gout. I'm staying the night! Lyubov Andreyevna, my dear soul, if you could... tomorrow morning... 240 roubles.

GAEV: That's always his story.

PISHTCHIK: 240 roubles... to pay the interest on my mortgage.

LYUBOV: My dear man, I have no money.

PISHTCHIK: I'll pay it back, my dear... a trifling sum.

LYUBOV: Oh, well. Leonid will give it you... You give him the money, Leonid.

GAEV: Me give it him! Let him wait till he gets it!

LYUBOV: It can't be helped, give it him. He needs it. He'll pay it back.

[LYUBOV ANDREYEVNA, TROFIMOV, PISHTCHIK *and* FIRS *go out.* GAEV, VARYA *and* YASHA *remain.*]

GAEV: Sister hasn't got out of the habit of flinging away her money. [*To* YASHA] Get away, my good fellow, you smell of the hen house.

YASHA [*with a grin*]: And you, Leonid Andreyevitch, are just the same as ever.

GAEV: What's that? [*To* VARYA] What did he say?

VARYA [*to* YASHA]: Your mother has come from the village; she has been sitting in the servants' room since yesterday, waiting to see you.

YASHA: Oh, bother her!

VARYA: For shame!

YASHA: What's the hurry? She might just as well have come tomorrow.

[*Goes out.*]

VARYA: Mamma's just the same as ever, she hasn't changed a bit. If she had her own way, she'd give away everything.

GAEV: Yes. [*A pause.*] If a great many remedies are suggested for some disease, it means that the disease is incurable. I keep thinking and racking my brains; I have many schemes, a great many, and that really means none. If we could only come in for a legacy from somebody, or marry our Anya to a very rich man, or we might go to Yaroslavl and try our luck with our old aunt, the Countess. She's very, very rich, you know.

VARYA: [*Weeps.*] If God would help us.

GAEV: Don't blubber. Aunt's very rich, but she doesn't like us. First, sister married a lawyer instead of a nobleman.... [ANYA *appears in the doorway.*] And then her conduct, one can't call it virtuous. She is good, and kind, and nice, and I love her, but, however one allows for extenuating circumstances, there's no denying that she's an immoral woman. One feels it in her slightest gesture.

VARYA [*in a whisper*]: Anya's in the doorway.

GAEV: What do you say? [*A pause.*] It's queer, there seems to be something wrong with my right eye. I don't see as well as I did. And on Thursday when I was in the district Court...

[*Enter* ANYA.]

VARYA: Why aren't you asleep, Anya?

ANYA: I can't get to sleep.

GAEV: My pet. [*Kisses* ANYA*'s face and hands.*] My child. [*Weeps.*] You are not my niece, you are my angel, you are everything to me. Believe me, believe...

ANYA: I believe you, uncle. Everyone loves you and respects you... but, uncle dear, you must be silent... simply be silent. What were you saying just now about my mother, about your own sister? What made you say that?

GAEV: Yes, yes... [*Puts his hand over his face.*] Really, that was awful! My God, save me! And today I made a speech to the bookcase... so stupid! And only when I had finished, I saw how stupid it was.

VARYA: It's true, uncle, you ought to keep quiet. Don't talk, that's all.

ANYA: If you could keep from talking, it would make things easier for you, too.

GAEV: I won't speak. [*Kisses* ANYA *and* VARYA*'s hands.*] I'll be silent. Only this is about business. On Thursday I was in the district Court; well, there was a large party of us there and we began talking of one thing and another, and this and that, and do you know, I believe that it will be possible to raise a loan on an I.O.U. to pay the arrears on the mortgage.

VARYA: If the Lord would help us!

GAEV: I'm going on Tuesday; I'll talk of it again. [*To* VARYA] Don't blubber. [*To* ANYA] Your mamma will talk to Lopahin; of course, he won't refuse her. And as soon as you're rested you shall go to Yaroslavl to the Countess, your great-aunt. So we shall all set to work in three directions at once, and the business is done. We shall pay off arrears, I'm convinced of it. [*Puts a caramel in his mouth.*] I swear on my honor, I swear by anything you like, the estate shan't be sold [*excitedly*]. By my own happiness, I swear it! Here's my hand on it, call me the basest, vilest of men, if I let it come to an auction! Upon my soul I swear it!

ANYA: [*Her equanimity has returned, she is quite happy.*]   How good you are, uncle, and how clever! [*Embraces her uncle.*] I'm at peace now! Quite at peace! I'm happy!

[*Enter* FIRS.]

FIRS [*reproachfully*]: Leonid Andreyevitch, have you no fear of God? when are you going to bed?

GAEV: Directly, directly. You can go, Firs. I'll... yes, I will undress myself. Come, children, by-by. We'll go into details tomorrow, but now go to bed. [*Kisses* ANYA *and* VARYA] I'm a man of the eighties. They run down that period, but still I can say I have had to suffer not a little for my convictions in my life. It's not for nothing that the peasant loves me. One must know the peasant! One must know how...

ANYA: At it again, uncle!

VARYA: Uncle dear, you'd better be quiet!

FIRS [*angrily*]: Leonid Andreyevitch!

GAEV: I'm coming. I'm coming. Go to bed. Potted the shot—there's a shot for you! A beauty! [*Goes out*, FIRS *hobbling after him.*]

ANYA: My mind's at rest now. I don't want to go to Yaroslavl, I don't like my great-aunt, but still my mind's at rest. Thanks to uncle.

[*Sits down.*]

VARYA: We must go to bed. I'm going. Something unpleasant happened while you were away. In the old servants' quarters there are only the old servants, as you know—Efimyushka, Polya and Yevstigney—and Karp too. They began letting stray people in to spend the night—I said nothing. But all at once I heard they had been spreading a report that I gave them nothing but pease pudding to eat. Out of stinginess, you know.... And it was all Yevstigney's doing.... Very well, I said to myself.... If that's how it is, I thought, wait a bit. I sent for Yevstigney. ... [*Yawns.*] He comes.... "How's this, Yevstigney," I said, "you could be such a fool as to?..." [*Looking at* ANYA] Anitchka! [*A pause.*] She's asleep. [*Puts her arm round* ANYA.] Come to bed...come along! [*Leads her.*] My darling has fallen asleep! Come... [*They go.*]

[*Far away beyond the orchard a shepherd plays on a pipe.* TROFIMOV *crosses the stage and, seeing* VARYA *and* ANYA, *stands still.*]

VARYA: 'Sh! asleep, asleep. Come, my own.

ANYA [*softly, half asleep*]: I'm so tired. Still those bells. Uncle...dear...mamma and uncle....

VARYA: Come, my own, come along.

[*They go into* ANYA's *room.*]

TROFIMOV [*tenderly*]: My sunshine! My spring.

ACT 2

The open country. An old shrine, long abandoned and fallen out of the perpendicular; near it a well, large stones that have apparently once been tombstones, and an old garden seat. The road to GAEV's *house is seen. On one side rise dark poplars; and there the cherry orchard begins. In the distance a row of telegraph poles and far, far away on the horizon there is faintly outlined a great town, only visible in very fine clear weather. It is near sunset.* CHARLOTTA, YASHA *and* DUNYASHA *are sitting on the seat.* EPIHODOV *is standing near, playing something mournful on a guitar. All sit plunged in thought.* CHARLOTTA *wears an old forage cap; she has taken a gun from her shoulder and is tightening the buckle on the strap.*

CHARLOTTA [*musingly*]: I haven't a real passport of my own, and I don't know how old I am, and I always feel that I'm a young thing. When I was a little girl, my father and mother used to travel about to fairs and give performances—very good ones. And I used to dance *salto mortale*[3] and all sorts of things. And when papa and mamma died, a German lady took me and had me educated. And so I grew up and became a governess. But where I came from, and who I am, I

---

[3]"Leap of death" (Italian); that is, a standing somersault.

don't know.... Who my parents were, very likely they weren't married... I
don't know. [*Takes a cucumber out of her pocket and eats.*] I know nothing at all. [*A
pause.*] One wants to talk and has no one to talk to... I have nobody.

EPIHODOV: [*Plays on the guitar and sings.*] "What care I for the noisy world! What
care I for friends or foes!" How agreeable it is to play on the mandolin!

DUNYASHA: That's a guitar, not a mandolin. [*Looks in a hand mirror and powders
herself.*]

EPIHODOV: To a man mad with love, it's a mandolin. [*Sings.*] "Were her heart but
aglow with love's mutual flame." [YASHA *joins in.*]

CHARLOTTA: How shockingly these people sing! Foo! Like jackals!

DUNYASHA [*to* YASHA]: What happiness, though, to visit foreign lands.

YASHA: Ah, yes! I rather agree with you there. [*Yawns, then lights a cigar.*]

EPIHODOV: That's comprehensible. In foreign lands everything has long since
reached full complexion.

YASHA: That's so, of course.

EPIHODOV: I'm a cultivated man, I read remarkable books of all sorts, but I can
never make out the tendency I am myself precisely inclined for, whether to live
or to shoot myself, speaking precisely, but nevertheless I always carry a revolver.
Here it is... [*Shows revolver.*]

CHARLOTTA: I've had enough, and now I'm going. [*Puts on the gun.*] Epihodov,
you're a very clever fellow, and a very terrible one too, all the women must
be wild about you. Br-r-r! [*Goes.*] These clever fellows are all so stupid; there's
not a creature for me to speak to.... Always alone, alone, nobody belonging to
me... and who I am, and why I'm on earth, I don't know. [*Walks away slowly.*]

EPIHODOV: Speaking precisely, not touching upon other subjects, I'm bound to
admit about myself, that destiny behaves mercilessly to me, as a storm to a little
boat. If, let us suppose, I am mistaken, then why did I wake up this morning, to
quote an example, and look round, and there on my chest was a spider of fearful
magnitude... like this. [*Shows with both hands.*] And then I take up a jug of kvass,
to quench my thirst, and in it there is something in the highest degree unseemly
of the nature of a cockroach. [*A pause.*] Have you read Buckle?[4] [*A pause.*] I am
desirous of troubling you, Dunyasha, with a couple of words.

DUNYASHA: Well, speak.

EPIHODOV: I should be desirous to speak with you alone. [*Sighs.*]

DUNYASHA [*embarrassed*]: Well—only bring me my mantle first. It's by the cupboard.
It's rather damp here.

EPIHODOV: Certainly. I will fetch it. Now I know what I must do with my revolver.
[*Takes the guitar and goes off playing on it.*]

YASHA: Two and twenty misfortunes! Between ourselves, he's a fool. [*Yawns.*]

DUNYASHA: God grant he doesn't shoot himself! [*A pause.*] I am so nervous, I'm
always in a flutter. I was a little girl when I was taken into our lady's house, and
now I have quite grown out of peasant ways, and my hands are white, as white
as a lady's. I'm such a delicate, sensitive creature, I'm afraid of everything. I'm
so frightened. And if you deceive me, Yasha, I don't know what will become of
my nerves.

YASHA: [*Kisses her.*] You're a peach! Of course a girl must never forget herself; what
I dislike more than anything is a girl being flighty in her behavior.

---

[4]Henry Thomas Buckle's *History of Civilization in England* (1857–1861) was considered to be very
enlightened and progressive during Chekhov's time.

DUNYASHA: I'm passionately in love with you, Yasha; you are a man of culture—you can give your opinion about anything. [*A pause.*]

YASHA: [*Yawns.*] Yes, that's so. My opinion is this: if a girl loves anyone, that means that she has no principles. [*A pause.*] It's pleasant smoking a cigar in the open air. [*Listens.*] Someone's coming this way . . . it's the gentlefolk. [DUNYASHA *embraces him impulsively.*] Go home, as though you had been to the river to bathe; go by that path, or else they'll meet you and suppose I have made an appointment with you here. That I can't endure.

DUNYASHA [*coughing softly*]: The cigar has made my head ache. . . .

[*Goes off.* YASHA *remains sitting near the shrine.*
Enter LYUBOV ANDREYEVNA, GAEV *and* LOPAHIN.]

LOPAHIN: You must make up your mind once for all—there's no time to lose. It's quite a simple question, you know. Will you consent to letting the land for building or not? One word in answer: Yes or no? Only one word!

LYUBOV: Who is smoking such horrible cigars here? [*Sits down.*]

GAEV: Now the railway line has been brought near, it's made things very convenient. [*Sits down.*] Here we have been over and lunched in town. Cannon off the white! I should like to go home and have a game.

LYUBOV: You have plenty of time.

LOPAHIN: Only one word! [*Beseechingly*] Give me an answer!

GAEV [*yawning*]: What do you say?

LYUBOV: [*Looks in her purse.*] I had quite a lot of money here yesterday, and there's scarcely any left today. My poor Varya feeds us all on milk soup for the sake of economy; the old folks in the kitchen get nothing but pease pudding, while I waste my money in a senseless way. [*Drops purse, scattering gold pieces.*] There, they have all fallen out [*annoyed*]!

YASHA: Allow me, I'll soon pick them up. [*Collects the coins.*]

LYUBOV: Pray do, Yasha. And what did I go off to the town to lunch for? Your restaurant's a wretched place with its music and the tablecloth smelling of soap. . . . Why drink so much, Leonid? And eat so much? And talk so much? Today you talked a great deal again in the restaurant, and all so inappropriately. About the era of the 'seventies, about the decadents.[5] And to whom? Talking to waiters about decadents!

LOPAHIN: Yes.

GAEV [*waving his hand*]: I'm incorrigible; that's evident. [*Irritably to* YASHA] Why is it you keep fidgeting about in front of us!

YASHA: [*Laughs.*] I can't help laughing when I hear your voice.

GAEV [*to his sister*]: Either I or he . . .

LYUBOV: Get along! Go away, Yasha.

YASHA: [*Gives* LYUBOV ANDREYEVNA *her purse.*] Directly [*hardly able to suppress his laughter*]. This minute. . . . [*Goes off.*]

LOPAHIN: Deriganov, the millionaire, means to buy your estate. They say he is coming to the sale himself.

LYUBOV: Where did you hear that?

LOPAHIN: That's what they say in town.

GAEV: Our aunt in Yaroslavl has promised to send help; but when, and how much she will send, we don't know.

---

[5]A name applied to late-nineteenth-century artists who explored the dark and macabre sides of human experience.

LOPAHIN: How much will she send? A hundred thousand? Two hundred?

LYUBOV: Oh, well! . . . Ten or fifteen thousand, and we must be thankful to get that.

LOPAHIN: Forgive me, but such reckless people as you are—such queer, unbusi-
nesslike people—I never met in my life. One tells you in plain Russian your
estate is going to be sold, and you seem not to understand it.

LYUBOV: What are we to do? Tell us what to do.

LOPAHIN: I do tell you every day. Every day I say the same thing. You absolutely
must let the cherry orchard and the land on building leases; and do it at once, as
quick as may be—the auction's close upon us! Do understand! Once make up
your mind to build villas, and you can raise as much money as you like, and then
you are saved.

LYUBOV: Villas and summer visitors—forgive me saying so—it's so vulgar.

GAEV: There I perfectly agree with you.

LOPAHIN: I shall sob, or scream, or fall into a fit. I can't stand it! You drive me mad!
[*To* GAEV] You're an old woman!

GAEV: What do you say?

LOPAHIN: An old woman! [*Gets up to go.*]

LYUBOV [*in dismay*]: No, don't go! Do stay, my dear friend! Perhaps we shall think
of something.

LOPAHIN: What is there to think of?

LYUBOV: Don't go, I entreat you! With you here it's more cheerful, anyway. [*A
pause.*] I keep expecting something, as though the house were going to fall about
our ears.

GAEV [*in profound dejection*]: Potted the white! It fails—a kiss.

LYUBOV: We have been great sinners. . . .

LOPAHIN: You have no sins to repent of.

GAEV: [*Puts a caramel in his mouth.*] They say I've eaten up my property in caramels.
[*Laughs.*]

LYUBOV: Oh, my sins! I've always thrown my money away recklessly like a lunatic. I
married a man who made nothing but debts. My husband died of champagne—
he drank dreadfully. To my misery I loved another man, and immediately—it was
my first punishment—the blow fell upon me, here, in the river . . . my boy was
drowned and I went abroad—went away for ever, never to return, not to see that
river again . . . I shut my eyes, and fled, distracted, and *he* after me . . . pitilessly,
brutally. I bought a villa at Mentone, for *he* fell ill there, and for three years I
had no rest day or night. His illness wore me out, my soul was dried up. And last
year, when my villa was sold to pay my debts, I went to Paris and there he robbed
me of everything and abandoned me for another woman; and I tried to poison
myself. . . . So stupid, so shameful! . . . And suddenly I felt a yearning for Russia,
for my country, for my little girl. . . . [*Dries her tears.*] Lord, Lord, be merciful!
Forgive my sins! Do not chastise me more! [*Takes a telegram out of her pocket.*] I got
this today from Paris. He implores forgiveness, entreats me to return. [*Tears up
the telegram.*] I fancy there is music somewhere. [*Listens.*]

GAEV: That's our famous Jewish orchestra. You remember, four violins, a flute and
a double bass.

LYUBOV: That still in existence? We ought to send for them one evening, and give
a dance.

LOPAHIN: [*Listens.*] I can't hear. . . . [*Hums softly.*] "For money the Germans will
turn a Russian into a Frenchman." [*Laughs.*] I did see such a piece at the theater
yesterday! It was funny!

LYUBOV: And most likely there was nothing funny in it. You shouldn't look at
plays, you should look at yourself a little oftener. How gray your lives are! How
much nonsense you talk.

LOPAHIN: That's true. One may say honestly, we live a fool's life. [*Pause.*] My father was a peasant, an idiot; he knew nothing and taught me nothing, only beat me when he was drunk, and always with his stick. In reality I am just such another blockhead and idiot. I've learnt nothing properly. I write a wretched hand. I write so that I feel ashamed before folks, like a pig.

LYUBOV: You ought to get married, my dear fellow.

LOPAHIN: Yes . . . that's true.

LYUBOV: You should marry our Varya, she's a good girl.

LOPAHIN: Yes.

LYUBOV: She's a good-natured girl, she's busy all day long, and what's more, she loves you. And you have liked her for ever so long.

LOPAHIN: Well? I'm not against it. . . . She's a good girl. [*Pause.*]

GAEV: I've been offered a place in the bank: 6,000 roubles a year. Did you know?

LYUBOV: You would never do for that! You must stay as you are.

[*Enter* FIRS *with overcoat.*]

FIRS: Put it on, sir, it's damp.

GAEV [*putting it on*]: You bother me, old fellow.

FIRS: You can't go on like this. You went away in the morning without leaving word. [*Looks him over.*]

LYUBOV: You look older, Firs!

FIRS: What is your pleasure?

LOPAHIN: You look older, she said.

FIRS: I've had a long life. They were arranging my wedding before your papa was born. . . . [*Laughs.*] I was the head footman before the emancipation came.[6] I wouldn't consent to be set free then; I stayed on with the old master. . . . [*A pause.*] I remember what rejoicings they made and didn't know themselves what they were rejoicing over.

LOPAHIN: Those were fine old times. There was flogging anyway.

FIRS [*not hearing*]: To be sure! The peasants knew their place, and the masters knew theirs; but now they're all at sixes and sevens, there's no making it out.

GAEV: Hold your tongue, Firs. I must go to town tomorrow. I have been promised an introduction to a general, who might let us have a loan.

LOPAHIN: You won't bring that off. And you won't pay your arrears, you may rest assured of that.

LYUBOV: That's all his nonsense. There is no such general.

[*Enter* TROFIMOV, ANYA, *and* VARYA.]

GAEV: Here come our girls.

ANYA: There's mamma on the seat.

LYUBOV [*tenderly*]: Come here, come along. My darlings! [*Embraces* ANYA *and* VARYA.] If you only knew how I love you both. Sit beside me, there, like that.

[*All sit down.*]

LOPAHIN: Our perpetual student is always with the young ladies.

TROFIMOV: That's not your business.

LOPAHIN: He'll soon be fifty, and he's still a student.

TROFIMOV: Drop your idiotic jokes.

LOPAHIN: Why are you so cross, you queer fish?

TROFIMOV: Oh, don't persist!

LOPAHIN: [*Laughs.*] Allow me to ask you what's your idea of me?

TROFIMOV: I'll tell you my idea of you, Yermolay Alexeyevitch: you are a rich man, you'll soon be a millionaire. Well, just as in the economy of nature a wild beast

---

[6]Tsar Alexander II emancipated the serfs in 1861.

is of use, who devours everything that comes in his way, so you too have your use.

[*All laugh.*]

VARYA: Better tell us something about the planets, Petya.

LYUBOV: No, let us go on with the conversation we had yesterday.

TROFIMOV: What was it about?

GAEV: About pride.

TROFIMOV: We had a long conversation yesterday, but we came to no conclusion. In pride, in your sense of it, there is something mystical. Perhaps you are right from your point of view; but if one looks at it simply, without subtlety, what sort of pride can there be, what sense is there in it, if a man in his physiological formation is very imperfect, if in the immense majority of cases he is coarse, dull-witted, profoundly unhappy? One must give up glorification of self. One should work, and nothing else.

GAEV: One must die in any case.

TROFIMOV: Who knows? And what does it mean—dying? Perhaps man has a hundred senses, and only the five we know are lost at death, while the other ninety-five remain alive.

LYUBOV: How clever you are, Petya!

LOPAHIN [*ironically*]: Fearfully clever!

TROFIMOV: Humanity progresses, perfecting its powers. Everything that is beyond its ken now will one day become familiar and comprehensible; only we must work, we must with all our powers aid the seeker after truth. Here among us in Russia the workers are few in number as yet. The vast majority of the intellectual people I know, seek nothing, do nothing, are not fit as yet for work of any kind. They call themselves intellectual, but they treat their servants as inferiors, behave to the peasants as though they were animals, learn little, read nothing seriously, do practically nothing, only talk about science and know very little about art. They are all serious people, they all have severe faces, they all talk of weighty matters and air their theories, and yet the vast majority of us—ninety-nine per cent—live like savages, at the least thing fly to blows and abuse, eat piggishly, sleep in filth and stuffiness, bugs everywhere, stench and damp and moral impurity. And it's clear all our fine talk is only to divert our attention and other people's. Show me where to find the crèches[7] there's so much talk about, and the reading rooms? They only exist in novels: in real life there are none of them. There is nothing but filth and vulgarity and Asiatic apathy. I fear and dislike very serious faces. I'm afraid of serious conversations. We should do better to be silent.

LOPAHIN: You know, I get up at five o'clock in the morning, and I work from morning to night; and I've money, my own and other people's, always passing through my hands, and I see what people are made of all round me. One has only to begin to do anything to see how few honest, decent people there are. Sometimes when I lie awake at night, I think: "Oh! Lord, thou hast given us immense forests, boundless plains, the widest horizons, and living here we ourselves ought really to be giants."

LYUBOV: You ask for giants! They are no good except in storybooks; in real life they frighten us.

[EPIHODOV *advances in the background, playing on the guitar.*]

LYUBOV [*dreamily*]: There goes Epihodov.

ANYA [*dreamily*]: There goes Epihodov.

---

[7]Day nurseries.

GAEV: The sun has set, my friends.

TROFIMOV: Yes.

GAEV [*not loudly, but, as it were, declaiming*]: O nature, divine nature, thou art bright with eternal luster, beautiful and indifferent! Thou, whom we call mother, thou dost unite within thee life and death! Thou dost give life and dost destroy!

VARYA [*in a tone of supplication*]: Uncle!

ANYA: Uncle, you are at it again!

TROFIMOV: You'd much better be cannoning off the red!

GAEV: I'll hold my tongue, I will.

[*All sit plunged in thought. Perfect stillness. The only thing audible is the muttering of* FIRS. *Suddenly there is a sound in the distance, as it were from the sky—the sound of a breaking harp string, mournfully dying away.*]

LYUBOV: What is that?

LOPAHIN: I don't know. Somewhere far away a bucket fallen and broken in the pits. But somewhere very far away.

GAEV: It might be a bird of some sort—such as a heron.

TROFIMOV: Or an owl.

LYUBOV: [*Shudders.*] I don't know why, but it's horrid. [*A pause.*]

FIRS: It was the same before the calamity—the owl hooted and the samovar hissed all the time.

GAEV: Before what calamity?

FIRS: Before the emancipation. [*A pause.*]

LYUBOV: Come, my friends, let us be going; evening is falling. [*To* ANYA] There are tears in your eyes. What is it, darling? [*Embraces her.*]

ANYA: Nothing, mamma; it's nothing.

TROFIMOV: There is somebody coming.

[*The* WAYFARER *appears in a shabby white forage cap and an overcoat; he is slightly drunk.*]

WAYFARER: Allow me to inquire, can I get to the station this way?

GAEV: Yes. Go along that road.

WAYFARER: I thank you most feelingly [*coughing*]. The weather is superb. [*Declaims*] My brother, my suffering brother!... Come out to the Volga! Whose groan do you hear?... [*To* VARYA] Mademoiselle, vouchsafe a hungry Russian thirty kopeks.

[VARYA *utters a shriek of alarm.*]

LOPAHIN [*angrily*]: There's a right and a wrong way of doing everything!

LYUBOV [*hurriedly*]: Here, take this. [*Looks in her purse.*] I've no silver. No matter— here's gold for you.

WAYFARER: I thank you most feelingly! [*Goes off.*]

[*Laughter.*]

VARYA [*frightened*]: I'm going home—I'm going... Oh, mamma, the servants have nothing to eat, and you gave him gold!

LYUBOV: There's no doing anything with me. I'm so silly! When we get home, I'll give you all I possess. Yermolay Alexeyevitch, you will lend me some more...!

LOPAHIN: I will.

LYUBOV: Come, friends, it's time to be going. And Varya, we have made a match of it for you. I congratulate you.

VARYA [*through her tears*]: Mamma, that's not a joking matter.

LOPAHIN: "Ophelia, get thee to a nunnery!"[8]

---

[8]Lopahin is quoting lines from a scene in Shakespeare's *Hamlet* (III, i, 139–42) where Hamlet taunts Ophelia.

GAEV: My hands are trembling; it's a long while since I had a game of billiards.

LOPAHIN: "Ophelia! Nymph, in thy orisons be all my sins remember'd."

LYUBOV: Come, it will soon be suppertime.

VARYA: How he frightened me! My heart's simply throbbing.

LOPAHIN: Let me remind you, ladies and gentlemen: on the 22nd of August the cherry orchard will be sold. Think about that! Think about it!

[*All go off, except* TROFIMOV *and* ANYA.]

ANYA [*laughing*]: I'm grateful to the wayfarer! He frightened Varya and we are left alone.

TROFIMOV: Varya's afraid we shall fall in love with each other, and for days together she won't leave us. With her narrow brain she can't grasp that we are above love. To eliminate the petty and transitory which hinders us from being free and happy—that is the aim and meaning of our life. Forward! We go forward irresistibly towards the bright star that shines yonder in the distance. Forward! Do not lag behind, friends.

ANYA: [*Claps her hands.*] How well you speak! [*A pause.*] It is divine here today.

TROFIMOV: Yes, it's glorious weather.

ANYA: Somehow, Petya, you've made me so that I don't love the cherry orchard as I used to. I used to love it so dearly. I used to think that there was no spot on earth like our garden.

TROFIMOV: All Russia is our garden. The earth is great and beautiful—there are many beautiful places in it. [*A pause.*] Think only, Anya, your grandfather, and great-grandfather, and all your ancestors were slave owners—the owners of living souls—and from every cherry in the orchard, from every leaf, from every trunk there are human creatures looking at you. Cannot you hear their voices? Oh, it is awful! Your orchard is a fearful thing, and when in the evening or at night one walks about the orchard, the old bark on the trees glimmers dimly in the dusk, and the old cherry trees seem to be dreaming of centuries gone by and tortured by fearful visions. Yes! We are at least two hundred years behind, we have really gained nothing yet, we have no definite attitude to the past, we do nothing but theorize or complain of depression or drink vodka. It is clear that to begin to live in the present we must first expiate our past, we must break with it; and we can expiate it only by suffering, by extraordinary unceasing labor. Understand that, Anya.

ANYA: The house we live in has long ceased to be our own, and I shall leave it, I give you my word.

TROFIMOV: If you have the house keys, fling them into the well and go away. Be free as the wind.

ANYA [*in ecstasy*]: How beautifully you said that!

TROFIMOV: Believe me, Anya, believe me! I am not thirty yet, I am young, I am still a student, but I have gone through so much already! As soon as winter comes I am hungry, sick, careworn, poor as a beggar, and what ups and downs of fortune have I not known! And my soul was always, every minute, day and night, full of inexplicable forebodings. I have a foreboding of happiness, Anya. I see glimpses of it already.

ANYA [*pensively*]: The moon is rising.

[EPIHODOV *is heard playing still the same mournful song on the guitar. The moon rises. Somewhere near the poplars* VARYA *is looking for* ANYA *and calling "Anya! where are you?"*]

TROFIMOV: Yes, the moon is rising. [*A pause.*] Here is happiness—here it comes! It is coming nearer and nearer; already I can hear its footsteps. And if we never see it—if we may never know it—what does it matter? Others will see it after us.

VARYA'S VOICE: Anya! Where are you?

TROFIMOV: That Varya again! [*Angrily*] It's revolting!

ANYA: Well, let's go down to the river. It's lovely there.

TROFIMOV: Yes, let's go.

[*They go.*]

VARYA'S VOICE: Anya! Anya!

ACT 3

A drawing room divided by an arch from a larger drawing room. A chandelier burning. The Jewish orchestra, the same that was mentioned in Act 2, is heard playing in the anteroom. It is evening. In the larger drawing room they are dancing the grand chain. The voice of SEMYONOV-PISHTCHIK: *"Promenade à une paire!" Then enter the drawing room in couples first* PISHTCHIK *and* CHARLOTTA IVANOVNA, *then* TROFIMOV *and* LYUBOV ANDREYEVNA, *thirdly* ANYA *with the* POST OFFICE CLERK, *fourthly* VARYA *with the* STATION MASTER, *and other guests.* VARYA *is quietly weeping and wiping away her tears as she dances. In the last couple is* DUNYASHA. *They move across the drawing room.* PISHTCHIK *shouts:* "Grand rond, balancez!" *and* "Les Cavaliers à genou et remerciez vos dames."[9]

[FIRS *in a swallow-tail coat brings in seltzer water on a tray.* PISHTCHIK *and* TROFIMOV *enter the drawing room.*]

PISHTCHIK: I am a full-blooded man; I have already had two strokes. Dancing's hard work for me, but as they say, if you're in the pack, you must bark with the rest. I'm as strong, I may say, as a horse. My parent, who would have his joke—may the Kingdom of Heaven be his!—used to say about our origin that the ancient stock of the Semyonov-Pishtchiks was derived from the very horse that Caligula made a member of the senate. [*Sits down.*] But I've no money, that's where the mischief is. A hungry dog believes in nothing but meat. . . . [*Snores, but at once wakes up.*] That's like me . . . I can think of nothing but money.

TROFIMOV: There really is something horsy about your appearance.

PISHTCHIK: Well . . . a horse is a fine beast . . . a horse can be sold.

[*There is the sound of billiards being played in an adjoining room.* VARYA *appears in the arch leading to the larger drawing room.*]

TROFIMOV [*teasing*]: Madame Lopahin! Madame Lopahin!

VARYA [*angrily*]: Mangy-looking gentleman!

TROFIMOV: Yes, I am a mangy-looking gentleman, and I'm proud of it!

VARYA [*pondering bitterly*]: Here we have hired musicians and nothing to pay them! [*Goes out.*]

TROFIMOV [*to* PISHTCHIK]: If the energy you have wasted during your lifetime in trying to find the money to pay your interest had gone to something else, you might in the end have turned the world upside down.

PISHTCHIK: Nietzsche,[10] the philosopher, a very great and celebrated man . . . of enormous intellect . . . says in his works, that one can make forged bank notes.

TROFIMOV: Why, have you read Nietzsche?

PISHTCHIK: What next . . . Dashenka told me. . . . And now I am in such a position, I might just as well forge bank notes. The day after tomorrow I must pay 310 roubles—130 I have procured. [*Feels in his pockets, in alarm.*] The money's gone!

---

[9] The instructions for the French dance are: "Promenade à une paire," promenade by couples; "Grand rond, balancez," grand round and swing; "Les Cavaliers à genou et remerciez vos dames," gentlemen, kneel and thank your ladies.

[10] Friedrich Nietzsche (1844–1900), a German philosopher.

I have lost my money! [*Through his tears*] Where's the money? [*Gleefully*] Why, here it is behind the lining. . . . It has made me hot all over.

[*Enter* LYUBOV ANDREYEVNA *and* CHARLOTTA IVANOVNA.]

LYUBOV: [*Hums the Lezginka.*[11]] Why is Leonid so long? What can he be doing in town? [*To* DUNYASHA] Offer the musicians some tea.

TROFIMOV: The sale hasn't taken place, most likely.

LYUBOV: It's the wrong time to have the orchestra, and the wrong time to give a dance. Well, never mind. [*Sits down and hums softly.*]

CHARLOTTA: [*Gives* PISHTCHIK *a pack of cards.*] Here's a pack of cards. Think of any card you like.

PISHTCHIK: I've thought of one.

CHARLOTTA: Shuffle the pack now. That's right. Give it here, my dear Mr. Pishtchik. *Eins, zwei, drei*[12]—now look, it's in your breast pocket.

PISHTCHIK [*taking a card out of his breast pocket*]: The eight of spades! Perfectly right! [*Wonderingly*] Fancy that now!

CHARLOTTA [*holding pack of cards in her hands, to* TROFIMOV]: Tell me quickly which is the top card.

TROFIMOV: Well, the queen of spades.

CHARLOTTA: It is! [*To* PISHTCHIK] Well, which card is uppermost?

PISHTCHIK: The ace of hearts.

CHARLOTTA: It is! [*Claps her hands, pack of cards disappears.*] Ah! what lovely weather it is today!

[*A mysterious feminine voice which seems coming out of the floor answers her.* "Oh, yes, it's magnificent weather, madam."]

CHARLOTTA: You are my perfect ideal.

VOICE: And I greatly admire you too, madam.

STATION MASTER [*applauding*]: The lady ventriloquist—bravo!

PISHTCHIK [*wonderingly*]: Fancy that now! Most enchanting Charlotta Ivanovna. I'm simply in love with you.

CHARLOTTA: In love? [*Shrugging shoulders*] What do you know of love, *guter Mensch, aber schlechter Musikant.*[13]

TROFIMOV: [*Pats* PISHTCHIK *on the shoulder.*] You dear old horse. . . .

CHARLOTTA: Attention, please! Another trick! [*Takes a travelling rug from a chair.*] Here's a very good rug; I want to sell it [*shaking it out*]. Doesn't anyone want to buy it?

PISHTCHIK [*wonderingly*]: Fancy that!

CHARLOTTA: *Eins, zwei, drei!* [*Quickly picks up rug she has dropped; behind the rug stands* ANYA; *she makes a curtsey, runs to her mother, embraces her and runs back into the larger drawing room amidst general enthusiasm.*]

LYUBOV: [*Applauds.*] Bravo! Bravo!

CHARLOTTA: Now again! *Eins, zwei, drei!* [*Lifts up the rug; behind the rug stands* VARYA, *bowing.*]

PISHTCHIK [*wonderingly*]: Fancy that now!

CHARLOTTA: That's the end. [*Throws the rug at* PISHTCHIK, *makes a curtsey, runs into the larger drawing room.*]

PISHTCHIK: [*Hurries after her.*] Mischievous creature! Fancy! [*Goes out.*]

---

[11]The music for a courtship dance from the Caucasus mountains.
[12]"One, two, three" (German).
[13]"Good man but bad musician" (German).

LYUBOV: And still Leonid doesn't come. I can't understand what he's doing in the town so long! Why, everything must be over by now. The estate is sold, or the sale has not taken place. Why keep us so long in suspense?

VARYA [*trying to console her*]: Uncle's bought it. I feel sure of that.

TROFIMOV [*ironically*]: Oh, yes!

VARYA: Great-aunt sent him an authorization to buy it in her name, and transfer the debt. She's doing it for Anya's sake, and I'm sure God will be merciful. Uncle will buy it.

LYUBOV: My aunt in Yaroslavl sent fifteen thousand to buy the estate in her name, she doesn't trust us—but that's not enough even to pay the arrears. [*Hides her face in her hands.*] My fate is being sealed today, my fate . . .

TROFIMOV [*teasing* VARYA]: Madame Lopahin.

VARYA [*angrily*]: Perpetual student! Twice already you've been sent down from the University.

LYUBOV: Why are you angry, Varya? He's teasing you about Lopahin. Well, what of that? Marry Lopahin if you like, he's a good man, and interesting; if you don't want to, don't! Nobody compels you, darling.

VARYA: I must tell you plainly, mamma, I look at the matter seriously; he's a good man, I like him.

LYUBOV: Well, marry him. I can't see what you're waiting for.

VARYA: Mamma. I can't make him an offer myself. For the last two years, everyone's been talking to me about him. Everyone talks; but he says nothing or else makes a joke. I see what it means. He's growing rich, he's absorbed in business, he has no thoughts for me. If I had money, were it ever so little, if I had only a hundred roubles, I'd throw everything up and go far away. I would go into a nunnery.

TROFIMOV: What bliss!

VARYA [*to* TROFIMOV]: A student ought to have sense! [*In a soft tone with tears*] How ugly you've grown, Petya! How old you look! [*To* LYUBOV ANDREYEVNA, *no longer crying*] But I can't do without work, mamma; I must have something to do every minute.

[*Enter* YASHA.]

YASHA [*hardly restraining his laughter*]: Epihodov has broken a billiard cue! [*Goes out.*]

VARYA: What is Epihodov doing here? Who gave him leave to play billiards? I can't make these people out. [*Goes out.*]

LYUBOV: Don't tease her, Petya. You see she has grief enough without that.

TROFIMOV: She is so very officious, meddling in what's not her business. All the summer she's given Anya and me no peace. She's afraid of a love affair between us. What's it to do with her? Besides, I have given no grounds for it. Such triviality is not in my line. We are above love!

LYUBOV: And I suppose I am beneath love. [*Very uneasily*] Why is it Leonid's not here? If only I could know whether the estate is sold or not! It seems such an incredible calamity that I really don't know what to think. I am distracted . . . I shall scream in a minute . . . I shall do something stupid. Save me, Petya, tell me something, talk to me!

TROFIMOV: What does it matter whether the estate is sold today or not? That's all done with long ago. There's no turning back, the path is overgrown. Don't worry yourself, dear Lyubov Andreyevna. You mustn't deceive yourself; for once in your life you must face the truth!

LYUBOV: What truth? You see where the truth lies, but I seem to have lost my sight, I see nothing. You settle every great problem so boldly, but tell me, my dear boy, isn't it because you're young—because you haven't yet understood one of your problems through suffering? You look forward boldly, and isn't it that you don't see and don't expect anything dreadful because life is still hidden from your young eyes? You're bolder, more honest, deeper than we are, but think, be just a little magnanimous, have pity on me. I was born here, you know, my father and mother lived here, my grandfather lived here, I love this house. I can't conceive of life without the cherry orchard, and if it really must be sold, then sell me with the orchard. [*Embraces* TROFIMOV, *kisses him on the forehead.*] My boy was drowned here. [*Weeps.*] Pity me, my dear kind fellow.

TROFIMOV: You know I feel for you with all my heart.

LYUBOV: But that should have been said differently, so differently. [*Takes out her handkerchief, telegram falls on the floor.*] My heart is so heavy today. It's so noisy here my soul is quivering at every sound, I'm shuddering all over, but I can't go away; I'm afraid to be quiet and alone. Don't be hard on me, Petya . . . I love you as though you were one of ourselves. I would gladly let you marry Anya—I swear I would—only, my dear boy, you must take your degree, you do nothing—you're simply tossed by fate from place to place. That's so strange. It is, isn't it? And you must do something with your beard to make it grow somehow. [*Laughs.*] You look so funny!

TROFIMOV: [*Picks up the telegram.*] I've no wish to be a beauty.

LYUBOV: That's a telegram from Paris. I get one every day. One yesterday and one today. That savage creature is ill again, he's in trouble again. He begs forgiveness, beseeches me to go, and really I ought to go to Paris to see him. You look shocked, Petya. What am I to do, my dear boy, what am I to do? He is ill, he is alone and unhappy, and who'll look after him, who'll keep him from doing the wrong thing, who'll give him his medicine at the right time? And why hide it or be silent? I love him, that's clear. I love him! I love him! He's a millstone about my neck, I'm going to the bottom with him, but I love that stone and can't live without it. [*Presses* TROFIMOV's *hand.*] Don't think ill of me, Petya, don't tell me anything, don't tell me . . .

TROFIMOV [*through his tears*]: For God's sake forgive my frankness: why, he robbed you!

LYUBOV: No! No! No! You mustn't speak like that. [*Covers her ears.*]

TROFIMOV: He is a wretch! You're the only person that doesn't know it! He's a worthless creature! A despicable wretch!

LYUBOV [*getting angry, but speaking with restraint*]: You're twenty-six or twenty-seven years old, but you're still a schoolboy.

TROFIMOV: Possibly.

LYUBOV: You should be a man at your age! You should understand what love means! And you ought to be in love yourself. You ought to fall in love! [*Angrily*] Yes, yes, and it's not purity in you, you're simply a prude, a comic fool, a freak.

TROFIMOV [*in horror*]: The things she's saying!

LYUBOV: I am above love! You're not above love, but simply as our Firs here says, "You are a good-for-nothing." At your age not to have a mistress!

TROFIMOV [*in horror*]: This is awful! The things she is saying! [*Goes rapidly into the larger drawing room clutching his head.*] This is awful! I can't stand it! I'm going. [*Goes off, but at once returns.*] All is over between us! [*Goes off into the anteroom.*]

LYUBOV: [*Shouts after him.*] Petya! Wait a minute! You funny creature! I was joking! Petya!

[*There is a sound of somebody running quickly downstairs and suddenly falling with a crash.* ANYA *and* VARYA *scream, but there is a sound of laughter at once.*]

LYUBOV: What has happened?

[ANYA *runs in.*]

ANYA [*laughing*]: Petya's fallen downstairs! [*Runs out.*]

LYUBOV: What a queer fellow that Petya is!

[*The* STATION MASTER *stands in the middle of the larger room and reads "The Magdalene," by Alexey Tolstoy.[14] They listen to him, but before he has recited many lines strains of a waltz are heard from the anteroom and the reading is broken off. All dance.* TROFIMOV, ANYA, VARYA *and* LYUBOV ANDREYEVNA *come in from the anteroom.*]

LYUBOV: Come, Petya—come, pure heart! I beg your pardon. Let's have a dance! [*Dances with* PETYA.]

    [ANYA *and* VARYA *dance.* FIRS *comes in, puts his stick down near the side door.* YASHA *also comes into the drawing room and looks on at the dancing.*]

YASHA: What is it, old man?

FIRS: I don't feel well. In the old days we used to have generals, barons and admirals dancing at our balls, and now we send for the post office clerk and the station master and even they're not overanxious to come. I am getting feeble. The old master, the grandfather, used to give sealing wax for all complaints. I have been taking sealing wax for twenty years or more. Perhaps that's what's kept me alive.

YASHA: You bore me, old man! [*Yawns.*] It's time you were done with.

FIRS: Ach, you're a good-for-nothing! [*Mutters.*]

    [TROFIMOV *and* LYUBOV ANDREYEVNA *dance in the larger room and then on to the stage.*]

LYUBOV: *Merci.* I'll sit down a little. [*Sits down.*] I'm tired.

    [*Enter* ANYA.]

ANYA [*excitedly*]: There's a man in the kitchen has been saying that the cherry orchard's been sold today.

LYUBOV: Sold to whom?

ANYA: He didn't say to whom. He's gone away.

    [*She dances with* TROFIMOV, *and they go off into the larger room.*]

YASHA: There was an old man gossiping there, a stranger.

FIRS: Leonid Andreyevitch isn't here yet, he hasn't come back. He has his light overcoat on, *demi-saison,*[15] he'll catch cold for sure. Ach! Foolish young things!

LYUBOV: I feel as though I should die. Go, Yasha, find out to whom it has been sold.

YASHA: But he went away long ago, the old chap. [*Laughs.*]

LYUBOV [*with slight vexation*]: What are you laughing at? What are you pleased at?

YASHA: Epihodov is so funny. He's a silly fellow, two and twenty misfortunes.

LYUBOV: Firs, if the estate is sold, where will you go?

FIRS: Where you bid me, there I'll go.

LYUBOV: Why do you look like that? Are you ill? You ought to be in bed.

FIRS: Yes [*ironically*]. Me go to bed and who's to wait here? Who's to see to things without me? I'm the only one in all the house.

YASHA: [*To* LYUBOV ANDREYEVNA.] Lyubov Andreyevna, permit me to make a request of you; if you go back to Paris again, be so kind as to take me with you. It's positively impossible for me to stay here [*looking about him; in an undertone*]. There's no need to say it, you see for yourself—an uncivilized country, the people have no morals, and then the dullness! The food in the kitchen's abominable, and then Firs runs after one muttering all sorts of unsuitable words. Take me with you, please do!

---

[14]A sentimental poem by a distant relative of Leo Tolstoy.

[15]"Between seasons"; a light, all-weather coat (French).

[*Enter* PISHTCHIK.]

PISHTCHIK: Allow me to ask you for a waltz, my dear lady. [LYUBOV ANDREYEVNA *goes with him.*] Enchanting lady, I really must borrow of you just 180 roubles [*dances*], only 180 roubles. [*They pass into the larger room.*]

YASHA: [*Hums softly.*] "Knowest thou my soul's emotion."

[*In the larger drawing room, a figure in a gray top hat and in check trousers is gesticulating and jumping about. Shouts of "Bravo, Charlotta Ivanovna."*]

DUNYASHA: [*She has stopped to powder herself.*] My young lady tells me to dance. There are plenty of gentlemen, and too few ladies, but dancing makes me giddy and makes my heart beat. Firs, the post office clerk said something to me just now that quite took my breath away.

[*Music becomes more subdued.*]

FIRS: What did he say to you?

DUNYASHA: He said I was like a flower.

YASHA: [*Yawns.*] What ignorance! [*Goes out.*]

DUNYASHA: Like a flower. I am a girl of such delicate feelings, I am awfully fond of soft speeches.

FIRS: Your head's being turned.

[*Enter* EPIHODOV.]

EPIHODOV: You have no desire to see me, Dunyasha. I might be an insect. [*Sighs.*] Ah! life!

DUNYASHA: What is it you want?

EPIHODOV: Undoubtedly you may be right. [*Sighs.*] But of course, if one looks at it from that point of view, if I may so express myself, you have, excuse my plain speaking, reduced me to a complete state of mind. I know my destiny. Every day some misfortune befalls me and I have long ago grown accustomed to it, so that I look upon my fate with a smile. You gave me your word, and though I—

DUNYASHA: Let us have a talk later, I entreat you, but now leave me in peace, for I am lost in reverie. [*Plays with her fan.*]

EPIHODOV: I have a misfortune every day, and if I may venture to express myself, I merely smile at it, I even laugh.

[VARYA *enters from the larger drawing room.*]

VARYA: You still have not gone, Epihodov. What a disrespectful creature you are, really! [*To* DUNYASHA] Go along, Dunyasha! [*To* EPIHODOV] First you play billiards and break the cue, then you go wandering about the drawing room like a visitor!

EPIHODOV: You really cannot, if I may so express myself, call me to account like this.

VARYA: I'm not calling you to account, I'm speaking to you. You do nothing but wander from place to place and don't do your work. We keep you as a counting-house clerk, but what use you are I can't say.

EPIHODOV [*offended*]: Whether I work or whether I walk, whether I eat or whether I play billiards, is a matter to be judged by persons of understanding and my elders.

VARYA: You dare to tell me that! [*Firing up*] You dare! You mean to say I've no understanding. Begone from here! This minute!

EPIHODOV [*intimidated*]: I beg you to express yourself with delicacy.

VARYA [*beside herself with anger*]: This moment! get out! away! [*He goes towards the door, she following him.*] Two and twenty misfortunes! Take yourself off! Don't let me set eyes on you! [EPIHODOV *has gone out, behind the door his voice,* "I shall lodge a complaint against you."] What! You're coming back? [*Snatches up the stick* FIRS *has put down near the door.*] Come! Come! Come! I'll show you! What! You're coming? Then take that! [*She swings the stick, at the very moment that* LOPAHIN *comes in.*]

LOPAHIN: Very much obliged to you!

VARYA [*angrily and ironically*]: I beg your pardon!

LOPAHIN: Not at all! I humbly thank you for your kind reception!

VARYA: No need of thanks for it. [*Moves away, then looks round and asks softly*] I haven't hurt you?

LOPAHIN: Oh, no! Not at all! There's an immense bump coming up, though!

VOICES FROM LARGER ROOM: Lopahin has come! Yermolay Alexeyevitch!

PISHTCHIK: What do I see and hear? [*Kisses* LOPAHIN.] There's a whiff of cognac about you, my dear soul, and we're making merry here too!

[*Enter* LYUBOV ANDREYEVNA.]

LYUBOV: Is it you, Yermolay Alexeyevitch? Why have you been so long? Where's Leonid?

LOPAHIN: Leonid Andreyevitch arrived with me. He is coming.

LYUBOV [*in agitation*]: Well! Well! Was there a sale? Speak!

LOPAHIN [*embarrassed, afraid of betraying his joy*]: The sale was over at four o'clock. We missed our train—had to wait till half-past nine. [*Sighing heavily*] Ugh! I feel a little giddy.

[*Enter* GAEV. *In his right hand he has purchases, with his left hand is wiping away his tears.*]

LYUBOV: Well, Leonid? What news? [*Impatiently, with tears*] Make haste, for God's sake!

GAEV: [*Makes her no answer, simply waves his hand. To* FIRS, *weeping.*] Here, take them; there's anchovies, Kertch herrings. I have eaten nothing all day. What I have been through! [*Door into the billiard room is open. There is heard a knocking of balls and the voice of* YASHA *saying "Eighty-seven."* GAEV's *expression changes, he leaves off weeping.*] I am fearfully tired. Firs, come and help me change my things. [*Goes to his own room across the larger drawing room.*]

PISHTCHIK: How about the sale? Tell us, do!

LYUBOV: Is the cherry orchard sold?

LOPAHIN: It is sold.

LYUBOV: Who has bought it?

LOPAHIN: I have bought it.

[*A pause.* LYUBOV *is crushed; she would fall down if she were not standing near a chair and table.* VARYA *takes keys from her waistband, flings them on the floor in middle of drawing room and goes out.*]

LOPAHIN: I have bought it! Wait a bit, ladies and gentlemen, pray. My head's a bit muddled, I can't speak. [*Laughs.*] We came to the auction. Deriganov was there already. Leonid Andreyevitch only had 15,000 and Deriganov bid 30,000, besides the arrears, straight off. I saw how the land lay. I bid against him. I bid 40,000, he bid 45,000, I said 55, and so he went on, adding 5 thousands and I adding 10. Well...So it ended. I bid 90, and it was knocked down to me. Now the cherry orchard's mine! Mine! [*Chuckles.*] My God, the cherry orchard's mine! Tell me that I'm drunk, that I'm out of my mind, that it's all a dream. [*Stamps with his feet.*] Don't laugh at me! If my father and my grandfather could rise from their graves and see all that has happened! How their Yermolay, ignorant, beaten Yermolay, who used to run about barefoot in winter, how that very Yermolay has bought the finest estate in the world! I have bought the estate where my father and grandfather were slaves, where they weren't even admitted into the kitchen. I am asleep, I am dreaming! It is all fancy, it is the work of your imagination plunged in the darkness of ignorance. [*Picks up keys, smiling fondly.*] She threw away the keys; she means to show she's not the housewife now. [*Jingles the keys.*] Well, no matter. [*The orchestra is heard tuning up.*] Hey, musicians!

Play! I want to hear you. Come, all of you, and look how Yermolay Lopahin will take the axe to the cherry orchard, how the trees will fall to the ground! We will build houses on it and our grandsons and great-grandsons will see a new life springing up there. Music! Play up!

[Music begins to play. LYUBOV ANDREYEVNA *has sunk into a chair and is weeping bitterly.]*

LOPAHIN [*reproachfully*]: Why, why didn't you listen to me? My poor friend! Dear lady, there's no turning back now. [*With tears*] Oh, if all this could be over, oh, if our miserable disjointed life could somehow soon be changed!

PISHTCHIK: [*Takes him by the arm, in an undertone.*] She's weeping, let us go and leave her alone. Come. [*Takes him by the arm and leads him into the larger drawing room.*]

LOPAHIN: What's that? Musicians, play up! All must be as I wish it. [*With irony*] Here comes the new master, the owner of the cherry orchard! [*Accidentally tips over a little table, almost upsetting the candelabra.*] I can pay for everything!

[Goes out with PISHTCHIK. *No one remains on the stage or in the larger drawing room except* LYUBOV, *who sits huddled up, weeping bitterly. The music plays softly.* ANYA *and* TROFIMOV *come in quickly.* ANYA *goes up to her mother and falls on her knees before her.* TROFIMOV *stands at the entrance to the larger drawing room.]*

ANYA: Mamma! Mamma, you're crying, dear, kind, good mamma! My precious! I love you! I bless you! The cherry orchard is sold, it is gone, that's true, that's true! But don't weep, mamma! Life is still before you, you have still your good, pure heart! Let us go, let us go, darling, away from here! We will make a new garden, more splendid than this one; you will see it, you will understand. And joy, quiet, deep joy, will sink into your soul like the sun at evening! And you will smile, mamma! Come, darling, let us go!

ACT 4

Same as in First Act. There are neither curtains on the windows nor pictures on the walls: only a little furniture remains piled up in a corner as if for sale. There is a sense of desolation; near the outer door and in the background of the scene are packed trunks, travelling bags, etc. On the left the door is open, and from here the voices of VARYA *and* ANYA *are audible.* LOPAHIN *is standing waiting.* YASHA *is holding a tray with glasses full of champagne. In front of the stage* EPIHODOV *is tying up a box. In the background behind the scene a hum of talk from the peasants who have come to say good-by. The voice of* GAEV: *"Thanks, brothers, thanks!"*

YASHA: The peasants have come to say good-by. In my opinion, Yermolay Alex-eyevitch, the peasants are good-natured, but they don't know much about things.

[The hum of talk dies away. Enter across front of stage LYUBOV ANDREYEVNA *and* GAEV. *She is not weeping, but is pale; her face is quivering—she cannot speak.]*

GAEV: You gave them your purse, Lyuba. That won't do—that won't do!

LYUBOV: I couldn't help it! I couldn't help it!

[Both go out.]

LOPAHIN [*in the doorway, calls after them*]: You will take a glass at parting? Please do. I didn't think to bring any from the town, and at the station I could only get one bottle. Please take a glass. [*A pause.*] What? You don't care for any? [*Comes away from the door.*] If I'd known, I wouldn't have bought it. Well, and I'm not going to drink it. [YASHA *carefully sets the tray down on a chair.*] You have a glass, Yasha, anyway.

YASHA: Good luck to the travellers, and luck to those that stay behind! [*Drinks.*] This champagne isn't the real thing, I can assure you.

LOPAHIN: It cost eight roubles the bottle. [*A pause.*] It's devilish cold here.

YASHA: They haven't heated the stove today—it's all the same since we're going. [*Laughs.*]

LOPAHIN: What are you laughing for?

YASHA: For pleasure.

LOPAHIN: Though it's October, it's as still and sunny as though it were summer. It's just right for building! [*Looks at his watch; says in doorway*] Take note, ladies and gentlemen, the train goes in forty-seven minutes; so you ought to start for the station in twenty minutes. You must hurry up!

[TROFIMOV *comes in from out of doors wearing a greatcoat.*]

TROFIMOV: I think it must be time to start, the horses are ready. The devil only knows what's become of my galoshes; they're lost. [*In the doorway.*] Anya! My galoshes aren't here. I can't find them.

LOPAHIN: And I'm getting off to Harkov. I am going in the same train with you. I'm spending all the winter at Harkov. I've been wasting all my time gossiping with you and fretting with no work to do. I can't get on without work. I don't know what to do with my hands, they flap about so queerly, as if they didn't belong to me.

TROFIMOV: Well, we're just going away, and you will take up your profitable labors again.

LOPAHIN: Do take a glass.

TROFIMOV: No, thanks.

LOPAHIN: Then you're going to Moscow now?

TROFIMOV: Yes. I shall see them as far as the town, and tomorrow I shall go on to Moscow.

LOPAHIN: Yes, I daresay, the professors aren't giving any lectures, they're waiting for your arrival.

TROFIMOV: That's not your business.

LOPAHIN: How many years have you been at the University?

TROFIMOV: Do think of something newer than that—that's stale and flat. [*Hunts for galoshes.*] You know we shall most likely never see each other again, so let me give you one piece of advice at parting: don't wave your arms about—get out of the habit. And another thing, building villas, reckoning up that the summer visitors will in time become independent farmers—reckoning like that, that's not the thing to do either. After all, I am fond of you: you have fine delicate fingers like an artist, you've a fine delicate soul.

LOPAHIN: [*Embraces him.*] Good-by, my dear fellow. Thanks for everything. Let me give you money for the journey, if you need it.

TROFIMOV: What for? I don't need it.

LOPAHIN: Why, you haven't got a halfpenny.

TROFIMOV: Yes, I have, thank you. I got some money for a translation. Here it is in my pocket, [*anxiously*] but where can my galoshes be!

VARYA [*from the next room*]: Take the nasty things! [*Flings a pair of galoshes onto the stage.*]

TROFIMOV: Why are you so cross, Varya? h'm!...but those aren't my galoshes.

LOPAHIN: I sowed three thousand acres with poppies in the spring, and now I have cleared forty thousand profit. And when my poppies were in flower, wasn't it a picture! So here, as I say, I made forty thousand, and I'm offering you a loan because I can afford to. Why turn up your nose? I am a peasant—I speak bluntly.

TROFIMOV: Your father was a peasant, mine was a chemist—and that proves absolutely nothing whatever. [LOPAHIN *takes out his pocketbook.*] Stop that—stop that. If you were to offer me two hundred thousand I wouldn't take it. I am an independent man, and everything that all of you, rich and poor alike, prize so highly and hold so dear, hasn't the slightest power over me—it's like so much fluff fluttering in the air. I can get on without you. I can pass by you. I am strong and proud. Humanity is advancing towards the highest truth, the highest happiness, which is possible on earth, and I am in the front ranks.

LOPAHIN: Will you get there?

TROFIMOV: I shall get there. [*A pause.*] I shall get there, or I shall show others the way to get there.

[*In the distance is heard the stroke of an axe on a tree.*]

LOPAHIN: Good-by, my dear fellow; it's time to be off. We turn up our noses at one another, but life is passing all the while. When I am working hard without resting, then my mind is more at ease, and it seems to me as though I too know what I exist for; but how many people there are in Russia, my dear boy, who exist, one doesn't know what for. Well, it doesn't matter. That's not what keeps things spinning. They tell me Leonid Andreyevitch has taken a situation. He is going to be a clerk at the bank—6,000 roubles a year. Only, of course, he won't stick to it—he's too lazy.

ANYA [*in the doorway*]: Mamma begs you not to let them chop down the orchard until she's gone.

TROFIMOV: Yes, really, you might have the tact. [*Walks out across the front of the stage.*]

LOPAHIN: I'll see to it! I'll see to it! Stupid fellows! [*Goes out after him.*]

ANYA: Has Firs been taken to the hospital?

YASHA: I told them this morning. No doubt they have taken him.

ANYA [*to* EPIHODOV, *who passes across the drawing room*]: Semyon Pantaleyevitch, inquire, please, if Firs has been taken to the hospital.

YASHA [*in a tone of offense*]: I told Yegor this morning—why ask a dozen times?

EPIHODOV: Firs is advanced in years. It's my conclusive opinion no treatment would do him good; it's time he was gathered to his fathers. And I can only envy him. [*Puts a trunk down on a cardboard hatbox and crushes it.*] There, now, of course—I knew it would be so.

YASHA [*jeeringly*]: Two and twenty misfortunes!

VARYA [*through the door*]: Has Firs been taken to the hospital?

ANYA: Yes.

VARYA: Why wasn't the note for the doctor taken too?

ANYA [*from the adjoining room*]: Where's Yasha? Tell him his mother's come to say good-by to him.

YASHA: [*Waves his hand.*] They put me out of all patience! [DUNYASHA *has all this time been busy about the luggage. Now, when* YASHA *is left alone, she goes up to him.*]

DUNYASHA: You might just give me one look, Yasha. You're going away. You're leaving me. [*Weeps and throws herself on his neck.*]

YASHA: What are you crying for? [*Drinks the champagne.*] In six days I shall be in Paris again. Tomorrow we shall get into the express train and roll away in a flash. I can scarcely believe it! *Vive la France!* It doesn't suit me here—it's not the life for me; there's no doing anything. I have seen enough of the ignorance here. I have had enough of it. [*Drinks champagne.*] What are you crying for? Behave yourself properly, and then you won't cry.

DUNYASHA: [*Powders her face, looking in a pocket mirror.*] Do send me a letter from Paris. You know how I loved you, Yasha—how I loved you! I am a tender creature, Yasha.

YASHA: Here they are coming!

[*Busies himself about the trunks, humming softly. Enter* LYUBOV ANDREYEVNA, GAEV, ANYA *and* CHARLOTTA IVANOVNA.]

GAEV: We ought to be off. There's not much time now [*looking at* YASHA]. What a smell of herrings!

LYUBOV: In ten minutes we must get into the carriage. [*Casts a look about the room.*] Farewell, dear house, dear old home of our fathers! Winter will pass and spring will come, and then you will be no more; they will tear you down! How much those walls have seen! [*Kisses her daughter passionately.*] My treasure, how bright you look! Your eyes are sparkling like diamonds! Are you glad? Very glad?

ANYA: Very glad! A new life is beginning, mamma.

GAEV: Yes, really, everything is all right now. Before the cherry orchard was sold, we were all worried and wretched, but afterwards, when once the question was settled conclusively, irrevocably, we all felt calm and even cheerful. I am a bank clerk now—I am a financier—cannon off the red. And you, Lyuba, after all, you are looking better; there's no question of that.

LYUBOV: Yes. My nerves are better, that's true. [*Her hat and coat are handed to her.*] I'm sleeping well. Carry out my things, Yasha. It's time. [*To* ANYA] My darling, we shall soon see each other again. I am going to Paris. I can live there on the money your Yaroslavl auntie sent us to buy the estate with—hurrah for auntie!—but that money won't last long.

ANYA: You'll come back soon, mamma, won't you? I'll be working up for my examination in the high school, and when I have passed that, I shall set to work and be a help to you. We will read all sorts of things together, mamma, won't we? [*Kisses her mother's hands.*] We will read in the autumn evenings. We'll read lots of books, and a new wonderful world will open out before us [*dreamily*]. Mamma, come soon.

LYUBOV: I shall come, my precious treasure. [*Embraces her.*]

[*Enter* LOPAHIN. CHARLOTTA *softly hums a song.*]

GAEV: Charlotta's happy; she's singing!

CHARLOTTA: [*Picks up a bundle like a swaddled baby.*] By, by, my baby. [*A baby is heard crying: "Ooah! ooah!"*] Hush, hush, my pretty boy! [*Ooah! ooah!*] Poor little thing! [*Throws the bundle back.*] You must please find me a situation. I can't go on like this.

LOPAHIN: We'll find you one, Charlotta Ivanovna. Don't you worry yourself.

GAEV: Everyone's leaving us. Varya's going away. We have become of no use all at once.

CHARLOTTA: There's nowhere for me to be in the town. I must go away. [*Hums.*] What care I . . .

[*Enter* PISHTCHIK.]

LOPAHIN: The freak of nature!

PISHTCHIK [*gasping.*]: Oh! . . . let me get my breath. . . . I'm worn out . . . my most honored . . . Give me some water.

GAEV: Want some money, I suppose? Your humble servant! I'll go out of the way of temptation. [*Goes out.*]

PISHTCHIK: It's a long while since I have been to see you . . . dearest lady. [*To* LOPAHIN] You are here . . . glad to see you . . . a man of immense intellect . . . take . . . here [*gives* LOPAHIN] . . . 400 roubles. That leaves me owing 840.

LOPAHIN [*shrugging his shoulders in amazement*]: It's like a dream. Where did you get it?

PISHTCHIK: Wait a bit . . . I'm hot . . . a most extraordinary occurrence! Some Englishmen came along and found in my land some sort of white clay. [*To* LYUBOV ANDREYEVNA] And 400 for you . . . most lovely . . . wonderful. [*Gives money.*] The rest later. [*Sips water.*] A young man in the train was telling me just now that a great philosopher advises jumping off a housetop. "Jump!" says he; "the whole gist of the problem lies in that." [*Wonderingly*] Fancy that, now! Water, please!

LOPAHIN: What Englishmen?

PISHTCHIK: I have made over to them the rights to dig the clay for twenty-four years... and now, excuse me... I can't stay... I must be trotting on. I'm going to Znoikovo... to Kardamanovo.... I'm in debt all round. [*Sips.*] ... To your very good health!... I'll come in on Thursday.

LYUBOV: We are just off to the town, and tomorrow I start for abroad.

PISHTCHIK: What! [*In agitation*] Why to the town? Oh, I see the furniture... the boxes. No matter... [*through his tears*] ... no matter... men of enormous intellect... these Englishmen.... Never mind... be happy. God will succor you ... no matter... everything in this world must have an end. [*Kisses* LYUBOV ANDREYEVNA's *hand.*] If the rumor reaches you that my end has come, think of this... old horse, and say: "There once was such a man in the world... Semyonov Pishtchik... the Kingdom of Heaven be his!"... most extraordinary weather... yes. [*Goes out in violent agitation, but at once returns and says in the doorway*] Dashenka wishes to be remembered to you. [*Goes out.*]

LYUBOV: Now we can start. I leave with two cares in my heart. The first is leaving Firs ill. [*Looking at her watch*] We have still five minutes.

ANYA: Mamma, Firs has been taken to the hospital. Yasha sent him off this morning.

LYUBOV: My other anxiety is Varya. She is used to getting up early and working; and now, without work, she's like a fish out of water. She is thin and pale, and she's crying, poor dear! [*A pause.*] You are well aware, Yermolay Alexeyevitch, I dream of marrying her to you, and everything seemed to show that you would get married. [*Whispers to* ANYA *and motions to* CHARLOTTA *and both go out.*] She loves you—she suits you. And I don't know—I don't know why it is you seem, as it were, to avoid each other. I can't understand it!

LOPAHIN: I don't understand it myself, I confess. It's queer somehow, altogether. If there's still time, I'm ready now at once. Let's settle it straight off, and go ahead; but without you, I feel I shan't make her an offer.

LYUBOV: That's excellent. Why, a single moment's all that's necessary. I'll call her at once.

LOPAHIN: And there's champagne all ready too [*looking into the glasses*]. Empty! Someone's emptied them already. [YASHA *coughs.*] I call that greedy.

LYUBOV [*eagerly*]: Capital! We will go out. Yasha, *allez!*[16] I'll call her in. [*At the door*] Varya, leave all that; come here. Come along! [*Goes out with* YASHA.]

LOPAHIN [*looking at his watch*]: Yes.

[*A pause. Behind the door, smothered laughter and whispering, and, at last, enter* VARYA.]

VARYA [*looking a long while over the things*]: It is strange, I can't find it anywhere.

LOPAHIN: What are you looking for?

VARYA: I packed it myself, and I can't remember. [*A pause.*]

LOPAHIN: Where are you going now, Varvara Mihailova?

VARYA: I? To the Ragulins. I have arranged to go to them to look after the house—as a housekeeper.

LOPAHIN: That's in Yashnovo? It'll be seventy miles away. [*A pause.*] So this is the end of life in this house!

VARYA [*looking among the things*]: Where is it? Perhaps I put it in the trunk. Yes, life in this house is over—there will be no more of it.

LOPAHIN: And I'm just off to Harkov—by this next train. I've a lot of business there. I'm leaving Epihodov here, and I've taken him on.

VARYA: Really!

---

[16]"Go" (French).

LOPAHIN: This time last year we had snow already, if you remember; but now it's so fine and sunny. Though it's cold, to be sure—three degrees of frost.

VARYA: I haven't looked. [*A pause.*] And besides, our thermometer's broken.

[*A pause. Voice at the door from the yard:* "Yermolay Alexeyevitch!"]

LOPAHIN [*as though he had long been expecting this summons*]: This minute!

[LOPAHIN *goes out quickly.* VARYA *sitting on the floor and laying her head on a bag full of clothes, sobs quietly. The door opens.* LYUBOV ANDREYEVNA *comes in cautiously.*]

LYUBOV: Well? [*A pause.*] We must be going.

VARYA [*Has wiped her eyes and is no longer crying*]: Yes, mamma, it's time to start. I shall have time to get to the Ragulins today, if only you're not late for the train.

LYUBOV [*in the doorway*]: Anya, put your things on.

[*Enter* ANYA, *then* GAEV *and* CHARLOTTA IVANOVNA. GAEV *has on a warm coat with a hood. Servants and cabmen come in.* EPIHODOV *bustles about the luggage.*]

LYUBOV: Now we can start on our travels.

ANYA [*joyfully*]: On our travels!

GAEV: My friends—my dear, my precious friends! Leaving this house forever, can I be silent? Can I refrain from giving utterance at leave-taking to those emotions which now flood all my being?

ANYA [*supplicatingly*]: Uncle!

VARYA: Uncle, you mustn't!

GAEV [*dejectedly*]: Cannon and into the pocket . . . I'll be quiet. . . .

[*Enter* TROFIMOV *and afterwards* LOPAHIN.]

TROFIMOV: Well, ladies and gentlemen, we must start.

LOPAHIN: Epihodov, my coat!

LYUBOV: I'll stay just one minute. It seems as though I have never seen before what the walls, what the ceilings in this house were like, and now I look at them with greediness, with such tender love.

GAEV: I remember when I was six years old sitting in that window on Trinity Day watching my father going to church.

LYUBOV: Have all the things been taken?

LOPAHIN: I think all. [*Putting on overcoat, to* EPIHODOV] You, Epihodov, mind you see everything is right.

EPIHODOV [*in a husky voice*]: Don't you trouble, Yermolay Alexeyevitch.

LOPAHIN: Why, what's wrong with your voice?

EPIHODOV: I've just had a drink of water, and I choked over something.

YASHA [*contemptuously*]: The ignorance!

LYUBOV: We are going—and not a soul will be left here.

LOPAHIN: Not till the spring.

VARYA: [*Pulls a parasol out of a bundle, as though about to hit someone with it.* LOPAHIN *makes a gesture as though alarmed.*] What is it? I didn't mean anything.

TROFIMOV: Ladies and gentlemen, let us get into the carriage. It's time. The train will be in directly.

VARYA: Petya, here they are, your galoshes, by that box. [*With tears*] And what dirty old things they are!

TROFIMOV [*putting on his galoshes*]: Let us go, friends!

GAEV [*greatly agitated, afraid of weeping*]: The train—the station! Double balk, ah!

LYUBOV: Let us go!

LOPAHIN: Are we all here? [*Locks the side door on left.*] The things are all here. We must lock up. Let us go!

ANYA: Good-by, home! Good-by to the old life!

TROFIMOV: Welcome to the new life!

[TROFIMOV *goes out with* ANYA. VARYA *looks round the room and goes out slowly.* YASHA *and* CHARLOTTA IVANOVNA, *with her dog, go out.*]

LOPAHIN: Till the spring, then! Come, friends, till we meet!

[*Goes out.* LYUBOV ANDREYEVNA *and* GAEV *remain alone. As though they had been waiting for this, they throw themselves on each other's necks, and break into subdued smothered sobbing, afraid of being overheard.*]

GAEV [*in despair*]: Sister, my sister!

LYUBOV: Oh, my orchard!—my sweet, beautiful orchard! My life, my youth, my happiness, good-by! good-by!

VOICE OF ANYA [*calling gaily*]: Mamma!

VOICE OF TROFIMOV [*gaily, excitedly*]: Aa—oo!

LYUBOV: One last look at the walls, at the windows. My dear mother loved to walk about this room.

GAEV: Sister, sister!

VOICE OF ANYA: Mamma!

VOICE OF TROFIMOV: Aa—oo!

LYUBOV: We are coming.

[*They go out. The stage is empty. There is the sound of the doors being locked up, then of the carriages driving away. There is silence. In the stillness there is the dull stroke of an axe on a tree, clanging with a mournful lonely sound. Footsteps are heard.* FIRS *appears in the doorway on the right. He is dressed as always—in a pea jacket and white waistcoat with slippers on his feet. He is ill.*]

FIRS: [*Goes up to the doors, and tries the handles.*] Locked! They have gone.... [*Sits down on sofa.*] They have forgotten me.... Never mind...I'll sit here a bit.... I'll be bound Leonid Andreyevitch hasn't put his fur coat on and has gone off in his thin overcoat. [*Sighs anxiously.*] I didn't see after him.... These young people... [*Mutters something that can't be distinguished.*] Life has slipped by as though I hadn't lived. [*Lies down.*] I'll lie down a bit.... There's no strength in you, nothing left you—all gone! Ech! I'm good for nothing.

[*Lies motionless. A sound is heard that seems to come from the sky, like a breaking harp string, dying away mournfully. All is still again, and there is heard nothing but the strokes of the axe far away in the orchard.*]

CHARLOTTE PERKINS GILMAN
[1860–1935]

One common motif in romantic literature is the fatal woman who haunts the hero's life. She may be human or supernatural. She may deliberately pursue the hero, or she may actually try to discourage him from following her. She may with evil intent seduce the hero away from his mission or his intended destiny, or she may actually help him to realize that destiny more fully by encouraging him to explore the subconscious, forbidden, "feminine" sides of his own psyche. More often than not, an encounter with such a figure, like the Metal Queen in Hoffmann's "The Mines at Falun," ends in the hero's death. In all her lethal attractiveness, she is the romantic era's version of Eve.

Texts by women may incorporate romantic heroes and fatal women, but in the nineteenth century many women also created the obverse of that duo, the *female* hero and the fatal *man*. Like the fatal woman, the fatal man takes many forms. Emily Brontë's dashing Heathcliff in *Wuthering Heights* encourages Cathy to explore her sexuality and assert her own strength, but the constraints of Cathy's society simply cannot tolerate that much unbridled natural energy and impulse in women. Cathy must give up Heathcliff, and having once experienced him, she must die for lack of him and all he stands for.

The physician–husband of Charlotte Perkins Gilman's "The Yellow Wallpaper" is a different sort of fatal man. Unlike Heathcliff, John presses his nameless wife more and more to conform with the patriarchal society's impossible notions of what women should be—that is, depleted, spiritless, pleasant, and obedient. He is her smiling, well-intentioned jailer and tormentor.

LIFE

Charlotte Perkins Gilman wrote in part out of her own experience. This writer, artist, editor, and social reformer born in 1860 was descended from a number of famous nineteenth-century advocates of human rights. Her great-aunt Harriet Beecher Stowe, author of *Uncle Tom's Cabin,* was her childhood idol. Gilman's father deserted his wife and three children early in Gilman's life, perhaps because doctors had forbidden the couple to have more children. Gilman grew up with plenty of reason to question the nineteenth century's ideal of marriage, which featured a kindly, authoritarian father-provider and a mother who was the flawless "angel in the house," content to accede to the father's wise judgments and finding her fulfillment in comforting, nourishing, and gladdening her family circle.

Despite Gilman's extreme doubts about marriage, at twenty-four she wed Charles Walter Stetson, a pleasant, conventional artist, and immediately grew depressed as household duties infringed upon her writing. When her depression deepened with the birth of her daughter ten months after the marriage, Gilman sought the help of the famous "nerve specialist" S. Weir Mitchell, whose popular "rest cure" for troubled women was a month's regimen of bed rest, heavy meals, baths, and massage, followed by a return to home and full immersion in household duties. He ordered Gilman to keep her baby beside her at all times, to allow herself only two hours of "intellectual life" a day, and above all "never to touch pen, brush, or pencil" for the rest of her life. Gilman followed the prescription, but she grew rapidly worse, bursting into tears at the sight of her child, cuddling a doll she secretly made from rags, hiding deep in closets to try to escape the fear and despair that stalked her. Both she and Stetson recognized that the treatment and their marriage were failing, and he agreed to a divorce and to take primary responsibility for their daughter. Release from marriage and motherhood proved her cure; Gilman went on to a full life as a writer, editor, and lecturer. Her published writings include *Herland* (1915), a spirited feminist utopian fantasy; *Women and Economics: A Study of the Economic Relation between Men and Women as a Factor in Social Evolution* (1898), which argues that our society imprisons women in their homes with the "sexuo-economic" relationship and then defines the work that is done in homes as women's natural lot; and *The Living of Charlotte Perkins Gilman* (1935), her autobiography. Eventually, she made a happy second marriage, and she and her daughter were able to enjoy a close and loving relationship. Far ahead of her time, she advocated child care shared by both parents, communal households with shared duties, birth control, premarital agreements, and economic and legal rights for women. She also believed in the right to take one's own life, and when she learned in 1935 that she had terminal breast cancer, she chose a quiet and dignified suicide.

WORK

"The Yellow Wallpaper" is not strictly autobiographical; Walter Stetson, far from being an overbearing patriarch, helped Gilman as best he could and even praised this story, written six years after Gilman's crisis. Not everyone liked the story; William Dean Howells, who had retired from the editorship of *The Atlantic Monthly*, tried to help her place the story with his successor, but that editor declared that he could not possibly publish it, saying, "I could not forgive myself if I made others as miserable as I have made myself." It eventually was printed in *The New England Magazine* in 1901. Gilman sent a copy to Dr. Mitchell, who did not reply, but who was said to have later acknowledged to friends that he had altered his methods after reading it. In her autobiography Gilman says that if that rumor was true, she would feel her life had not been in vain.

"The Yellow Wallpaper" is more than an indictment of one particular insensitive doctor or foolish medical treatment, and it is more than just a good psychological horror story; in its brief scope, it takes a devastating look at the oppressive relationships between middle-class husband and wife, doctor and patient, society and the artist, the patriarchy and women in bondage within it. It invokes the Gothic conventions of the spooky isolated mansion, the mysterious chamber of barred windows, the sense of some alien presence in the house, partly to say that the true horror story concerns not monsters but nineteenth-century men and women in ordinary marriages and professional relationships. This woman, even to herself, is nameless; she is so demoralized she can only whisper the truth of her oppression in the tiniest voice, can only write it in the most secret of places, and must then continue to blame her oppression upon her own failure to conform cheerfully to it. Ironically, John—"I am a doctor, dear, and I know"—bases all his "knowledge" upon a fantasy of what women are and what they need; the quieter she is, the more at peace he believes her to be. The wife's "fancies," on the other hand—that she is growing worse, that John is wrong, that she is in a prison—are real. When she is driven further and further back upon herself, she undertakes her great heroic action against the men and the society who are killing her—not by directly attacking them, but by seeing an image of herself in the Rorschach-like wallpaper and endeavoring to free that woman. In a way, as frightening as the ending is, it might be said that the wife has gained some power over her situation; she has found a task in which she can take pride and pleasure, and she can even, by the final lines, express what she truly feels about John. In madness, she has found her way to a terrible freedom. The painful power of this story probably accounts for the fact that it remained out of print for nearly fifty years, until a Feminist Press reprint in 1973 awakened a keen interest in Gilman's work.

SUGGESTED READINGS

Gary Scharnhorst's *Charlotte Perkins Gilman* (1985) is a sound critical biography. Mary A. Hill's *Charlotte Perkins Gilman: The Making of a Radical Feminist 1860–1896* (1980) describes the shaping of Gilman's feminist politics. Ann J. Lane's biography *To Herland and Beyond: The Life and Works of Charlotte Perkins Gilman* (1990) is a highly readable account of the complex ways in which Gilman's feminist theory found expression in her life.

The Yellow Wallpaper

It is very seldom that mere ordinary people like John and myself secure ancestral halls for the summer.

A colonial mansion, a hereditary estate, I would say a haunted house and reach the height of romantic felicity—but that would be asking too much of fate!

Still I will proudly declare that there is something queer about it.

Else, why should it be let so cheaply? And why have stood so long untenanted?

John laughs at me, of course, but one expects that.

John is practical in the extreme. He has no patience with faith, an intense horror of superstition, and he scoffs openly at any talk of things not to be felt and seen and put down in figures.

John is a physician, and *perhaps*—(I would not say it to a living soul, of course, but this is dead paper and a great relief to my mind)—*perhaps* that is one reason I do not get well faster.

You see, he does not believe I am sick! And what can one do?

If a physician of high standing, and one's own husband, assures friends and relatives that there is really nothing the matter with one but temporary nervous depression—a slight hysterical tendency—what is one to do?

My brother is also a physician, and also of high standing, and he says the same thing.

So I take phosphates or phosphites—whichever it is—and tonics, and air and exercise, and journeys, and am absolutely forbidden to "work" until I am well again.

Personally, I disagree with their ideas.

Personally, I believe that congenial work, with excitement and change, would do me good.

But what is one to do?

I did write for a while in spite of them; but it *does* exhaust me a good deal—having to be so sly about it, or else meet with heavy opposition.

I sometimes fancy that in my condition, if I had less opposition and more society and stimulus—but John says the very worst thing I can do is to think about my condition, and I confess it always makes me feel bad.

So I will let it alone and talk about the house.

The most beautiful place! It is quite alone, standing well back from the road, quite three miles from the village. It makes me think of English places that you read about, for there are hedges and walls and gates that lock, and lots of separate little houses for the gardeners and people.

There is a *delicious* garden! I never saw such a garden—large and shady, full of box-bordered paths, and lined with long grape-covered arbors with seats under them.

There were greenhouses, but they are all broken now.

There was some legal trouble, I believe, something about the heirs and co-heirs; anyhow, the place has been empty for years.

That spoils my ghostliness, I am afraid, but I don't care—there is something strange about the house—I can feel it.

I even said so to John one moonlight evening, but he said what I felt was a draught, and shut the window.

I get unreasonably angry with John sometimes. I'm sure I never used to be so sensitive. I think it is due to this nervous condition.

But John says if I feel so I shall neglect proper self-control; so I take pains to control myself—before him, at least, and that makes me very tired.

I don't like our room a bit. I wanted one downstairs that opened onto the piazza and had roses all over the window, and such pretty old-fashioned chintz hangings! But John would not hear of it.

He said there was only one window and not room for two beds, and no near room for him if he took another.

He is very careful and loving, and hardly lets me stir without special direction.

I have a schedule prescription for each hour in the day; he takes all care from me, and so I feel basely ungrateful not to value it more.

He said he came here solely on my account, that I was to have perfect rest and all the air I could get. "Your exercise depends on your strength, my dear," said he, "and your food somewhat on your appetite; but air you can absorb all the time." So we took the nursery at the top of the house.

It is a big, airy room, the whole floor nearly, with windows that look all ways, and air and sunshine galore. It was a nursery first, and then playroom and gymnasium, I should judge, for the windows are barred for little children, and there are rings and things in the walls.

The paint and paper look as if a boys' school had used it. It is stripped off—the paper—in great patches all around the head of my bed, about as far as I can reach, and in a great place on the other side of the room low down. I never saw a worse paper in my life. One of those sprawling, flamboyant patterns committing every artistic sin.

It is dull enough to confuse the eye in following, pronounced enough constantly to irritate and provoke study, and when you follow the lame uncertain curves for a little distance they suddenly commit suicide—plunge off at outrageous angles, destroy themselves in unheard-of contradictions.

The color is repellent, almost revolting: a smouldering unclean yellow, strangely faded by the slow-turning sunlight. It is a dull yet lurid orange in some places, a sickly sulphur tint in others.

No wonder the children hated it! I should hate it myself if I had to live in this room long.

There comes John, and I must put this away—he hates to have me write a word.

We have been here two weeks, and I haven't felt like writing before, since that first day.

I am sitting by the window now, up in this atrocious nursery, and there is nothing to hinder my writing as much as I please, save lack of strength.

John is away all day, and even some nights when his cases are serious.

I am glad my case is not serious!

But these nervous troubles are dreadfully depressing.

John does not know how much I really suffer. He knows there is no reason to suffer, and that satisfies him.

Of course it is only nervousness. It does weigh on me so not to do my duty in any way!

I meant to be such a help to John, such a real rest and comfort, and here I am a comparative burden already!

Nobody would believe what an effort it is to do what little I am able—to dress and entertain, and order things.

It is fortunate Mary is so good with the baby. Such a dear baby!

And yet I *cannot* be with him, it makes me so nervous.

I suppose John never was nervous in his life. He laughs at me so about this wallpaper!

At first he meant to repaper the room, but afterward he said that I was letting it get the better of me, and that nothing was worse for a nervous patient than to give way to such fancies.

He said that after the wallpaper was changed it would be the heavy bedstead, and then the barred windows, and then that gate at the head of the stairs, and so on.

"You know the place is doing you good," he said, "and really, dear, I don't care to renovate the house just for a three months' rental."

"Then do let us go downstairs," I said. "There are such pretty rooms there."

Then he took me in his arms and called me a blessed little goose, and said he would go down cellar, if I wished, and have it whitewashed into the bargain.

But he is right enough about the beds and windows and things.

It is as airy and comfortable a room as anyone need wish, and, of course, I would not be so silly as to make him uncomfortable just for a whim.

I'm really getting quite fond of the big room, all but that horrid paper.

Out of one window I can see the garden—those mysterious deep-shaded arbors, the riotous old-fashioned flowers, and bushes and gnarly trees.

Out of another I get a lovely view of the bay and a little private wharf belonging to the estate. There is a beautiful shaded lane that runs down there from the house. I always fancy I see people walking in these numerous paths and arbors, but John has cautioned me not to give way to fancy in the least. He says that with my imaginative power and habit of story-making, a nervous weakness like mine is sure to lead to all manner of excited fancies, and that I ought to use my will and good sense to check the tendency. So I try.

I think sometimes that if I were only well enough to write a little it would relieve the press of ideas and rest me.

But I find I get pretty tired when I try.

It is so discouraging not to have any advice and companionship about my work. When I get really well, John says we will ask Cousin Henry and Julia down for a long visit; but he says he would as soon put fireworks in my pillow-case as to let me have those stimulating people about now.

I wish I could get well faster.

But I must not think about that. This paper looks to me as if it *knew* what a vicious influence it had!

There is a recurrent spot where the pattern lolls like a broken neck and two bulbous eyes stare at you upside down.

I get positively angry with the impertinence of it and the everlastingness. Up and down and sideways they crawl, and those absurd unblinking eyes are everywhere. There is one place where two breadths didn't match, and the eyes go all up and down the line, one a little higher than the other.

I never saw so much expression in an inanimate thing before, and we all know how much expression they have! I used to lie awake as a child and get more entertainment and terror out of blank walls and plain furniture than most children could find in a toy-store.

I remember what a kindly wink the knobs of our big old bureau used to have, and there was one chair that always seemed like a strong friend.

I used to feel that if any of the other things looked too fierce I could always hop into that chair and be safe.

The furniture in this room is no worse than inharmonious, however, for we had to bring it all from downstairs. I suppose when this was used as a playroom they had to take the nursery things out, and no wonder! I never saw such ravages as the children have made here.

The wallpaper, as I said before, is torn off in spots, and it sticketh closer than a brother—they must have had perseverance as well as hatred.

Then the floor is scratched and gouged and splintered, the plaster itself is dug out here and there, and this great heavy bed, which is all we found in the room, looks as if it had been through the wars.

But I don't mind it a bit—only the paper.

There comes John's sister. Such a dear girl as she is, and so careful of me! I must not let her find me writing.

She is a perfect and enthusiastic housekeeper, and hopes for no better profession. I verily believe she thinks it is the writing which made me sick!

But I can write when she is out, and see her a long way off from these windows.

There is one that commands the road, a lovely shaded winding road, and one that just looks off over the country. A lovely country, too, full of great elms and velvet meadows.

This wallpaper has a kind of sub-pattern in a different shade, a particularly irritating one, for you can only see it in certain lights, and not clearly then.

But in the places where it isn't faded and where the sun is just so—I can see a strange, provoking, formless sort of figure that seems to skulk about behind that silly and conspicuous front design.

There's sister on the stairs!

Well, the Fourth of July is over! The people are all gone, and I am tired out. John thought it might do me good to see a little company, so we just had Mother and Nellie and the children down for a week.

Of course I didn't do a thing. Jennie sees to everything now.

But it tired me all the same.

John says if I don't pick up faster he shall send me to Weir Mitchell[1] in the fall.

But I don't want to go there at all. I had a friend who was in his hands once, and she says he is just like John and my brother, only more so!

Besides, it is such an undertaking to go so far.

I don't feel as if it was worthwhile to turn my hand over for anything, and I'm getting dreadfully fretful and querulous.

I cry at nothing, and cry most of the time.

Of course I don't when John is here, or anybody else, but when I am alone.

And I am alone a good deal just now. John is kept in town very often by serious cases, and Jennie is good and lets me alone when I want her to.

So I walk a little in the garden or down that lovely lane, sit on the porch under the roses, and lie down up here a good deal.

I'm getting really fond of the room in spite of the wallpaper. Perhaps *because of* the wallpaper.

It dwells in my mind so!

I lie here on this great immovable bed—it is nailed down, I believe—and follow that pattern about by the hour. It is as good as gymnastics, I assure you. I start, we'll say, at the bottom, down in the corner over there where it has not been touched, and I determine for the thousandth time that I *will* follow that pointless pattern to some sort of a conclusion.

I know a little of the principle of design, and I know this thing was not arranged on any laws of radiation, or alternation, or repetition, or symmetry, or anything else that I ever heard of.

It is repeated, of course, by the breadths, but not otherwise.

Looked at in one way, each breadth stands alone; the bloated curves and flourishes—a kind of "debased Romanesque" with delirium tremens—go waddling up and down in isolated columns of fatuity.

But, on the other hand, they connect diagonally, and the sprawling outlines run off in great slanting waves of optic horror, like a lot of wallowing sea-weeds in full chase.

---

[1]S. Weir Mitchell was the actual name of the doctor who prescribed the "rest cure" for Gilman; see headnote.

The whole thing goes horizontally, too, at least it seems so, and I exhaust myself trying to distinguish the order of its going in that direction.

They have used a horizontal breadth for a frieze, and that adds wonderfully to the confusion.

There is one end of the room where it is almost intact, and there, when the crosslights fade and the low sun shines directly upon it, I can almost fancy radiation after all—the interminable grotesque seems to form around a common center and rush off in headlong plunges of equal distraction.

It makes me tired to follow it. I will take a nap, I guess.

I don't know why I should write this.

I don't want to.

I don't feel able.

And I know John would think it absurd. But I *must* say what I feel and think in some way—it is such a relief!

But the effort is getting to be greater than the relief.

Half the time now I am awfully lazy, and lie down ever so much. John says I mustn't lose my strength, and has me take cod liver oil and lots of tonics and things, to say nothing of ale and wine and rare meat.

Dear John! He loves me very dearly, and hates to have me sick. I tried to have a real earnest reasonable talk with him the other day, and tell him how I wish he would let me go and make a visit to Cousin Henry and Julia.

But he said I wasn't able to go, nor able to stand it after I got there; and I did not make out a very good case for myself, for I was crying before I had finished.

It is getting to be a great effort for me to think straight. Just this nervous weakness, I suppose.

And dear John gathered me up in his arms, and just carried me upstairs and laid me on the bed, and sat by me and read to me till it tired my head.

He said I was his darling and his comfort and all he had, and that I must take care of myself for his sake, and keep well.

He says no one but myself can help me out of it, that I must use my will and self-control and not let any silly fancies run away with me.

There's one comfort—the baby is well and happy, and does not have to occupy this nursery with the horrid wallpaper.

If we had not used it, that blessed child would have! What a fortunate escape! Why, I wouldn't have a child of mine, an impressionable little thing, live in such a room for worlds.

I never thought of it before, but it is lucky that John kept me here after all; I can stand it so much easier than a baby, you see.

Of course I never mention it to them any more—I am too wise—but I keep watch for it all the same.

There are things in that wallpaper that nobody knows about but me, or ever will.

Behind that outside pattern the dim shapes get clearer every day.

It is always the same shape, only very numerous.

And it is like a woman stooping down and creeping about behind that pattern. I don't like it a bit. I wonder—I begin to think—I wish John would take me away from here!

It is so hard to talk with John about my case, because he is so wise, and because he loves me so.

But I tried it last night.

It was moonlight. The moon shines in all around just as the sun does.

I hate to see it sometimes, it creeps so slowly, and always comes in by one window or another.

John was asleep and I hated to waken him, so I kept still and watched the moonlight on that undulating wallpaper till I felt creepy.

The faint figure behind seemed to shake the pattern, just as if she wanted to get out.

I got up softly and went to feel and see if the paper *did* move, and when I came back John was awake.

"What is it, little girl?" he said. "Don't go walking about like that—you'll get cold."

I thought it was a good time to talk, so I told him that I really was not gaining here, and that I wished he would take me away.

"Why, darling!" said he. "Our lease will be up in three weeks, and I can't see how to leave before.

"The repairs are not done at home, and I cannot possibly leave town just now. Of course, if you were in any danger, I could and would, but you really are better, dear, whether you can see it or not. I am a doctor, dear, and I know. You are gaining flesh and color, your appetite is better, I feel really much easier about you."

"I don't weigh a bit more," said I, "nor as much; and my appetite may be better in the evening when you are here but it is worse in the morning when you are away!"

"Bless her little heart!" said he with a big hug. "She shall be as sick as she pleases! But now let's improve the shining hours by going to sleep, and talk about it in the morning!"

"And you won't go away?" I asked gloomily.

"Why, how can I, dear? It is only three weeks more and then we will take a nice little trip of a few days while Jennie is getting the house ready. Really, dear, you are better!"

"Better in body perhaps—" I began, and stopped short, for he sat up straight and looked at me with such a stern, reproachful look that I could not say another word.

"My darling," said he, "I beg of you, for my sake and for our child's sake, as well as for your own, that you will never for one instant let that idea enter your mind! There is nothing so dangerous, so fascinating, to a temperament like yours. It is a false and foolish fancy. Can you not trust me as a physician when I tell you so?"

So of course I said no more on that score, and we went to sleep before long. He thought I was asleep first, but I wasn't and lay there for hours trying to decide whether that front pattern and the back pattern really did move together or separately.

On a pattern like this, by daylight, there is a lack of sequence, a defiance of law, that is a constant irritant to a normal mind.

The color is hideous enough, and unreliable enough, and infuriating enough, but the pattern is torturing.

You think you have mastered it, but just as you get well under way in following, it turns a back-somersault and there you are. It slaps you in the face, knocks you down, and tramples upon you. It is like a bad dream.

The outside pattern is a florid arabesque, reminding one of a fungus. If you can imagine a toadstool in joints, an interminable string of toadstools, budding and sprouting in endless convolutions—why, that is something like it.

That is, sometimes!

There is one marked peculiarity about this paper, a thing nobody seems to notice but myself, and that is that it changes as the light changes.

When the sun shoots in through the east window—I always watch for that first long, straight ray—it changes so quickly that I never can quite believe it.

That is why I watch it always.

By moonlight—the moon shines in all night when there is a moon—I wouldn't know it was the same paper.

At night in any kind of light, in twilight, candlelight, lamplight, and worst of all by moonlight, it becomes bars! The outside pattern, I mean, and the woman behind it is as plain as can be.

I didn't realize for a long time what the thing was that showed behind, that dim sub-pattern, but now I am quite sure it is a woman.

By daylight she is subdued, quiet. I fancy it is the pattern that keeps her so still. It is so puzzling. It keeps me quiet by the hour.

I lie down ever so much now. John says it is good for me, and to sleep all I can.

Indeed he started the habit by making me lie down for an hour after each meal.

It is a very bad habit, I am convinced, for you see, I don't sleep.

And that cultivates deceit, for I don't tell them I'm awake—oh, no!

The fact is I am getting a little afraid of John.

He seems very queer sometimes, and even Jennie has an inexplicable look.

It strikes me occasionally, just as a scientific hypothesis, that perhaps it is the paper!

I have watched John when he did not know I was looking, and come into the room suddenly on the most innocent excuses, and I've caught him several times *looking at the paper!* And Jennie too. I caught Jennie with her hand on it once.

She didn't know I was in the room, and when I asked her in a quiet, a very quiet voice, with the most restrained manner possible, what she was doing with the paper, she turned around as if she had been caught stealing, and looked quite angry—asked me why I should frighten her so!

Then she said that the paper stained everything it touched, that she had found yellow smooches on all my clothes and John's and she wished we would be more careful!

Did not that sound innocent? But I know she was studying that pattern, and I am determined that nobody shall find it out but myself!

Life is very much more exciting now than it used to be. You see, I have something more to expect, to look forward to, to watch. I really do eat better, and am more quiet than I was.

John is so pleased to see me improve! He laughed a little the other day, and said I seemed to be flourishing in spite of my wallpaper.

I turned it off with a laugh. I had no intention of telling him it was *because* of the wallpaper—he would make fun of me. He might even want to take me away.

I don't want to leave now until I have found it out. There is a week more, and I think that will be enough.

I'm feeling so much better!

I don't sleep much at night, for it is so interesting to watch developments; but I sleep a good deal during the daytime.

In the daytime it is tiresome and perplexing.

There are always new shoots on the fungus, and new shades of yellow all over it. I cannot keep count of them, though I have tried conscientiously.

It is the strangest yellow, that wallpaper! It makes me think of all the yellow things I ever saw—not beautiful ones like buttercups, but old, foul, bad yellow things.

But there is something else about that paper—the smell! I noticed it the moment we came into the room, but with so much air and sun it was not bad. Now we have had a week of fog and rain, and whether the windows are open or not, the smell is here.

It creeps all over the house.

I find it hovering in the dining-room, skulking in the parlor, hiding in the hall, lying in wait for me on the stairs.

It gets into my hair.

Even when I go to ride, if I turn my head suddenly and surprise it—there is that smell!

Such a peculiar odor, too! I have spent hours in trying to analyze it, to find what it smelled like.

It is not bad—at first—and very gentle, but quite the subtlest, most enduring odor I ever met.

In this damp weather it is awful. I wake up in the night and find it hanging over me.

It used to disturb me at first. I thought seriously of burning the house—to reach the smell.

But now I am used to it. The only thing I can think of that it is like is the *color* of the paper! A yellow smell.

There is a very funny mark on this wall, low down, near the mopboard. A streak that runs round the room. It goes behind every piece of furniture, except the bed, a long, straight, even *smooch,* as if it had been rubbed over and over.

I wonder how it was done and who did it, and what they did it for. Round and round and round—round and round and round—it makes me dizzy!

I really have discovered something at last.

Through watching so much at night, when it changes so, I have finally found out.

The front pattern *does* move—and no wonder! The woman behind shakes it!

Sometimes I think there are a great many women behind, and sometimes only one, and she crawls around fast, and her crawling shakes it all over.

Then in the very bright spots she keeps still, and in the very shady spots she just takes hold of the bars and shakes them hard.

And she is all the time trying to climb through. But nobody could climb through that pattern—it strangles so; I think that is why it has so many heads.

They get through, and then the pattern strangles them off and turns them upside down, and makes their eyes white!

If those heads were covered or taken off it would not be half so bad.

I think that woman gets out in the daytime!

And I'll tell you why—privately—I've seen her!

I can see her out of every one of my windows!

It is the same woman, I know, for she is always creeping, and most women do not creep by daylight.

I see her in that long shaded lane, creeping up and down. I see her in those dark grape arbors, creeping all around the garden.

I see her on that long road under the trees, creeping along, and when a carriage comes she hides under the blackberry vines.

I don't blame her a bit. It must be very humiliating to be caught creeping by daylight!

I always lock the door when I creep by daylight. I can't do it at night, for I know John would suspect something at once.

And John is so queer now that I don't want to irritate him. I wish he would take another room! Besides, I don't want anybody to get that woman out at night but myself.

I often wonder if I could see her out of all the windows at once.

But, turn as fast as I can, I can only see out of one at one time.

And though I always see her, she *may* be able to creep faster than I can turn! I have watched her sometimes away off in the open country, creeping as fast as a cloud shadow in a wind.

If only that top pattern could be gotten off from the under one! I mean to try it, little by little.

I have found out another funny thing, but I shan't tell it this time! It does not do to trust people too much.

There are only two more days to get this paper off, and I believe John is beginning to notice. I don't like the look in his eyes.

And I heard him ask Jennie a lot of professional questions about me. She had a very good report to give.

She said I slept a good deal in the daytime.

John knows I don't sleep very well at night, for all I'm so quiet!

He asked me all sorts of questions, too, and pretended to be very loving and kind.

As if I couldn't see through him!

Still, I don't wonder he acts so, sleeping under this paper for three months.

It only interests me, but I feel sure John and Jennie are affected by it.

Hurrah! This is the last day, but it is enough. John is to stay in town over night, and won't be out until this evening.

Jennie wanted to sleep with me—the sly thing; but I told her I should undoubtedly rest better for a night all alone.

That was clever, for really I wasn't alone a bit! As soon as it was moonlight and that poor thing began to crawl and shake the pattern, I got up and ran to help her.

I pulled and she shook. I shook and she pulled, and before morning we had peeled off yards of that paper.

A strip about as high as my head and half around the room.

And then when the sun came and that awful pattern began to laugh at me, I declared I would finish it today!

We go away tomorrow, and they are moving all my furniture down again to leave things as they were before.

Jennie looked at the wall in amazement, but I told her merrily that I did it out of pure spite at the vicious thing.

She laughed and said she wouldn't mind doing it herself, but I must not get tired.

How she betrayed herself that time!

But I am here, and no person touches this paper but Me—not *alive!*

She tried to get me out of the room—it was too patent! But I said it was so quiet and empty and clean now that I believed I would lie down again and sleep all I could, and not to wake me even for dinner—I would call when I woke.

So now she is gone, and the servants are gone, and the things are gone, and there is nothing left but that great bedstead nailed down, with the canvas mattress we found on it.

We shall sleep downstairs tonight, and take the boat home tomorrow.

I quite enjoy the room, now it is bare again.

How those children did tear about here!

This bedstead is fairly gnawed!

But I must get to work.

I have locked the door and thrown the key down into the front path.

I don't want to go out, and I don't want to have anybody come in, till John comes.

I want to astonish him.

I've got a rope up here that even Jennie did not find. If that woman does get out, and tries to get away, I can tie her!

But I forgot I could not reach far without anything to stand on!

This bed will *not* move!

I tried to lift and push it until I was lame, and then I got so angry I bit off a little piece at one corner—but it hurt my teeth.

Then I peeled off all the paper I could reach standing on the floor. It sticks horribly and the pattern just enjoys it! All those strangled heads and bulbous eyes and waddling fungus growths just shriek with derision!

I am getting angry enough to do something desperate. To jump out of the window would be admirable exercise, but the bars are too strong even to try.

Besides I wouldn't do it. Of course not. I know well enough that a step like that is improper and might be misconstrued.

I don't like to *look* out of the windows even—there are so many of those creeping women, and they creep so fast.

I wonder if they all come out of that wallpaper as I did?

But I am securely fastened now by my well-hidden rope—you don't get *me* out in the road there!

I suppose I shall have to get back behind the pattern when it comes night, and that is hard!

It is so pleasant to be out in this great room and creep around as I please!

I don't want to go outside. I won't, even if Jennie asks me to.

For outside you have to creep on the ground, and everything is green instead of yellow.

But here I can creep smoothly on the floor, and my shoulder just fits in that long smooch around the wall, so I cannot lose my way.

Why, there's John at the door!

It is no use, young man, you can't open it!

How he does call and pound!

Now he's crying to Jennie for an axe.

It would be a shame to break down that beautiful door!

"John, dear!" said I in the gentlest voice. "The key is down by the front steps, under a plantain leaf!"

That silenced him for a few moments.

Then he said, very quietly indeed, "Open the door, my darling!"

"I can't," said I. "The key is down by the front door under a plantain leaf!" And then I said it again, several times, very gently and slowly, and said it so often that he had to go and see, and he got it of course, and came in. He stopped short by the door.

"What is the matter?" he cried. "For God's sake, what are you doing!"

I kept on creeping just the same, but I looked at him over my shoulder.

"I've got out at last," said I, "in spite of you and Jane. And I've pulled off most of the paper, so you can't put me back!"

Now why should that man have fainted? But he did, and right across my path by the wall, so that I had to creep over him every time!

🌿

THE WORLD CONTEXT

SARAH WINNEMUCCA HOPKINS
[C. 1844–1891]

Sarah Winnemucca Hopkins was an interpreter and educator among her own Paiute people; her 1883 *Life among the Piutes: Their Wrongs and Claims* is an autobiography, a genre highly developed in the oral tradition of American Indians. Hers is one of the earliest American Indian autobiographies to be set down in writing; it is also distinguished by the fact that Hopkins herself, not some anthropologist, determined the shape of her story. When she submitted her manuscript, written in phonetic English, to her editor, Mary Mann, both she and Mann agreed that the editing should consist only in the correction of spelling and grammar. Mann noted in her brief preface to the work, "At this moment, when the United States seem waking up to their duty to the original possessors of our immense territory, it is of the first importance to hear what only an Indian and an Indian woman can tell." Hopkins gives an invaluable account of first contacts between Euro-Americans and American Indians in the Great Basin area, bringing to that account her powerful skills as a storyteller.

In the last half of the twentieth century, the American Indian population of the United States has grown swiftly, and was nearing three million at the 1990 census. That figure represents a triumph of hard-won survival and continuance, for the story of American Indian–white relations in the previous four centuries was largely one of attempted genocide on the part of the Euro-Americans by both violent and subtle means, practiced sometimes deliberately, sometimes unwittingly. Contrary to popular images derived from Western novels and movies, actual wars waged with guns, cavalry, and bugles make up the least significant part of that story; many other factors besides warfare reduced the American Indian population of North America from an estimated five million before 1492 to a nadir of about 250,000 in 1890.

The single most devastating cause of American Indian death was disease. Until the coming of the Europeans, smallpox, measles, the bubonic plague, cholera, typhoid, pleurisy, scarlet fever, diphtheria, mumps, whooping cough, gonorrhea, pneumonia, malaria, and yellow fever were unknown in the Western Hemisphere, and the native peoples had no built-up resistance from previous exposure to these pathogens. Besides the normal spread of epidemics, there are abundant records of communicable diseases such as smallpox and addictive substances such as alcohol being deliberately introduced into tribal communities; in 1763, for example, Lord Jeffrey Amherst wrote to his lieutenant approving a plan to spread smallpox, noting, "You will do well to try to innoculate the Indians by means of blankets as well as to try every other method that can serve to extirpate this exorable [sic] race."

Cultural repression and the willful destruction of American Indian ways of life were nearly as effective as disease in undermining American Indian populations. Government and missionary boarding schools worked hard to assimilate the children who were compelled to attend them. Although many American Indian parents tried to keep their children at home, often students were kidnapped or forcibly taken by agents for the schools. Once the children were ensconced in such institutions, contact with their families was discouraged or forbidden; students were shamed and punished if they tried to speak their birth language or observe native religious and cultural practices. Church and Bureau of

Indian Affairs records and inscriptions in boarding school cemeteries are testaments to the fact that although many of these children died of disease, a great number simply wasted away from loneliness and despair.

Even within the American Indian communities themselves, native religious practices were outlawed and otherwise interfered with. Missionaries, soldiers, anthropologists, and curio collectors stole or confiscated sacred objects such as medicine pouches, ritual masks, fetishes, and sun-dance poles. White settlers often built directly on top of sites sacred to the native people. The natural environment itself was altered; plants and animals upon which tribal life depended grew more sparse when whites encroached upon their habitats. Sometimes indigenous harvests or animal populations were deliberately destroyed; the great buffalo herds of the Western plains were systematically slaughtered by hired killers such as Buffalo Bill Cody, not only for their hides or because they interfered with the passage of wagon trains and the railroad, but because their presence sustained the way of life of most American Indian nations on the Great Plains.

Above all, American Indian lands were routinely confiscated through force, trickery, and broken treaties, and people were forcibly herded by the United States military and local government officials into smaller and smaller confines inadequate to support a concentrated human population. Some of those historic forced marches into cramped and alien territory—the Cherokee Trail of Tears in the late 1830s, or the Navajos' Long Walk of the 1860s—are relatively familiar to modern-day people, but in fact no Indian nation in the Americas escaped encroachment and the steady loss of its land base. Each nation's story of interaction with whites and the consequences of those encounters is at once unique and wearily familiar.

Such acts of removal were spiritually devastating for American Indian peoples, all of whom identified their very essence with the particular terrain they had learned to live within so harmoniously. The land for them was not potential farmland or acreage containing natural resources meant to be extracted, nor yet a backdrop for their own actions, as the English term "landscape" implies. Rather, for tribal peoples no natural form is without spiritual essence: Land is a complexly interrelated community of spiritual and conscious beings, only a small part of whom are human, and human beings must learn to interact properly with this community. As twentieth-century Laguna Pueblo writer Leslie Silko has phrased it in describing her people's idea of land,

> Rocks and clay are part of the Mother. They emerge in various forms, but at some time before, they were smaller particles or great boulders. At a later time they may again become what they once were. Dust.
> A rock has being or spirit, although we may not understand it. The spirit may differ from the spirit we know in animals or plants or in ourselves. In the end we may all originate from the depths of the earth. Perhaps this is how all beings share in the spirit of the earth. We do not know.

The world view Silko describes is fundamentally different from that of the conquistador, the sod-buster, the forty-niner, the wildcatter, the present-day developer. Our world text from nineteenth-century American Indians deals with the suffering that occurs when land is jointly occupied by American Indians and Euro-Americans, people with different world views and unequal technological power.

LIFE

Sarah Winnemucca Hopkins was born about 1844, probably near the present-day Carson City, Nevada. She was a member of the Paiute nation, or Piute, as she preferred to spell it. In the Great Basin region of what is now Utah, Nevada, and eastern Oregon and California, her Uto-Aztecan–speaking people lived peacefully within a simple economy based on roots, berries, piñon nuts, and the jackrabbits they hunted with clubs, managing to avoid all but incidental contact with the European invaders until the silver strikes of the mid-nineteenth century brought white people flooding into the Reno–Carson City vicinity. In this excerpt from Hopkins's autobiography, which we will look at in more detail shortly, she vividly recalls the traumatic initial meetings with white people experienced by her and her family.

After the events here chronicled, Hopkins's world became thoroughly intertwined with white culture. Although she was strongly resistant and fearful as a young girl first encountering parties of whites, she eventually went along with her grandfather's and her father's choice to try to cooperate with white people in an effort to save what they could of their lands and way of life. She became an expressive and fluent speaker of English, and a gifted interpreter; although the degree of her literacy is a matter of some debate, she did at least learn to write phonetic English. She interpreted for her father before military and local white assemblages, and she acted in sentimental pantomimes depicting Paiute life and history for white audiences, posing in *tableaux vivantes* entitled "The Indian Camp," "The War Council," and the like, in Virginia City and elsewhere, even at the Metropolitan Theater in San Francisco in 1864.

As she came to experience the colonizers more extensively, numerous encounters with corrupt government-appointed Indian agents and private citizens eroded her tentative trust. One especially bitter personal memory for her was the time she returned to her home area to introduce her new husband to her people; by this time, Hopkins was in her twenties and already well respected in the Great Basin region for her skills as an interpreter and negotiator. The young couple was greeted by a drunken party of prominent white male citizens who staged a perverted version of a *shivaree*, a hazing to which newlywed white couples were subjected in western frontier towns. The white men in this case imitated Paiute mourning songs and attempted without success to force the newlyweds to drink whiskey.

Hopkins decided that she preferred the military rather than any other white authority to be in charge of her people, for in her experience they were more apt to be fair and had some familiarity with Paiute ways; "There were no Custers," she writes, "among the officers in Nevada." Accordingly she became a scout, an interpreter, and a spokesperson for the army, trying to persuade Paiutes and members of other Great Basin nations to accept removal to reservations. Although Hopkins has been criticized in her time and in ours for being a sellout, clearly she was simply seeking the course that would be the best among many sorry choices. She continued to protest the actions of government agents and to urge that her people not be split up but quartered all together at the Malheur reservation.

In 1870, when Hopkins wrote a letter to *Harper's Weekly* protesting the government's treatment of the Paiutes, she attracted the attention of the Eastern intellectual establishment. In 1881 she made a lecture tour in Massachusetts, where she spoke at the homes of elite members of the transcendental movement such as Ralph Waldo Emerson and John Greenleaf Whittier. Mary Mann, the wife of the eminent educator Horace Mann, encouraged Hopkins to write her story and helped her to get it published; Mann's insistence that she had done little to Hopkins's manuscript save to normalize spelling and punctuation seems to be truthful. Later in her life, Hopkins helped to found an Indian school near Lovelock, Nevada. She died in Monida, Montana, on October 16, 1891.

WORK

In writing *Life among the Piutes*, Hopkins may conceivably have been influenced by white autobiographies and slave narratives, but some scholars doubt this on the grounds that she seems not to have been so much a reader as a fluent and powerful speaker who managed to set down her story in phonetic English orthography. A number of ways of recounting people's lives were practiced in American Indian cultures. Many nations kept pictorial or verbal "counts," calendar histories recording important events that sometimes included adventures that had befallen one person among them. The reciting of "coup tales" was also a custom in many American Indian nations; in the presence of witnesses who might vouch for the story or contradict it, a person would tell and sometimes pantomime a feat of bravery that brought honor to the tribe, often a tale about striking an enemy at close range. Sarah Winnemucca Hopkins's autobiography resembles these traditions and differs from white autobiographical traditions in a crucial way; she sees her story throughout as taking place in the context of her people and their collective history. Even when she recounts courageous acts, they are told as events that affect a whole tribe and are performed for the sake of that tribe. The governing narrative structure is not, as it would be in a white autobiography, the growth and advancement of self, marked off by turning points in her life; she does not even bother to record such seemingly significant moments as her conversion to Christianity or her courtship and marriage. Instead, the narrative of events in her life is structured around Paiute history.

In the excerpt we present here, the first chapter of the autobiography, Hopkins is anything but childlike in her skill at re-creating the perceptions and reactions of her child-self during her tribe's initial encounters with whites. She renders vividly the frightening otherness of the white settlers as seen by the Paiute people; Euro-American men, with their large pale eyes and fluffy beards, look like giant owls, and an African-American man wearing a red shirt, glimpsed at a distance, seems to be a man lit ablaze and horribly charred. Moreover, an accident of history confirms the Paiutes' worst fears about whites when the Donner party passes through Nevada; this poorly led and mismanaged band of settlers for whom the present-day Donner Pass is named started too late in the season to cross the Sierra Nevada, and resorted to cannibalism during the snowbound winter. This same Donner party, as Hopkins reveals, wantonly set fire to a cache of Paiute supplies stored against the winter as they passed near Carson City on their doomed journey into the high country. Understandably, the Paiutes do not try to warn these people that the snows are about to close in. When the Paiutes learn of the Donner party's fate, they know for certain that these "owls" are not only wanton destroyers of others' supplies, but cannibals as well.

Later, when a group of white people first approaches their camp, Hopkins's mother buries her and her cousin in sand up to their necks and heaps sagebrush over them to save the children from being eaten. The terrified little girls remain buried for a whole day. The text makes clear that Hopkins regards her experience of the coming of the whites and this resulting entombment as a sort of first death; she believes that her second and final death will be less terrifying. As the chapter progresses, many of the settlers prove to be kind, and some proffer beguiling gifts. But Hopkins makes it clear that the coming of the white people and the native people's varying reactions toward them begins very quickly to fragment her family and her tribe.

SUGGESTED READINGS

In *Great Documents in American Indian History* (1973), Wayne Moquin and Charles Van Doren provide a good sampler of American Indian oral tales, histories, speeches, constitutions, manifestos, and legal briefs. H. David Brumble's *American Indian Autobiography* (1988), Gretchen Bataille and Kay Sands's *American Indian Women: Telling Their Lives* (1984), Arnold Krupat's *For Those Who Come After* (1985), and Hertha Dawn Wong's *Sending My Heart Back Across the Years* (1990) are all good studies of the autobiographical genre in Native American writing. Gae Whitney Canfield's *Sarah Winnemucca of the Northern Paiutes* (1983) is a full biography of Hopkins.

Life among the Piutes: Their Wrongs and Claims

CHAPTER 1

First Meeting of Piutes and Whites.

I was born somewhere near 1844, but am not sure of the precise time. I was a very small child when the first white people came into our country. They came like a lion, yes, like a roaring lion, and have continued so ever since, and I have never forgotten their first coming. My people were scattered at that time over nearly all the territory now known as Nevada. My grandfather was chief of the entire Piute nation, and was camped near Humboldt Lake, with a small portion of his tribe, when a party travelling eastward from California was seen coming. When the news was brought to my grandfather, he asked what they looked like? When told that they had hair on their faces, and were white, he jumped up and clasped his hands together, and cried aloud,—

"My white brothers,—my long-looked for white brothers have come at last!"

He immediately gathered some of his leading men, and went to the place where the party had gone into camp. Arriving near them, he was commanded to halt in a manner that was readily understood without an interpreter. Grandpa at once made signs of friendship by throwing down his robe and throwing up his arms to show them he had no weapons; but in vain,—they kept him at a distance. He knew not what to do. He had expected so much pleasure in welcoming his white brothers to the best in the land, that after looking at them sorrowfully for a little while, he came away quite unhappy. But he would not give them up so easily. He took some of his most trustworthy men and followed them day after day, camping near them at night, and travelling in sight of them by day, hoping in this way to gain their confidence. But he was disappointed, poor dear old soul!

I can imagine his feelings, for I have drank deeply from the same cup. When I think of my past life, and the bitter trials I have endured, I can scarcely believe I live, and yet I do; and, with the help of Him who notes the sparrow's fall, I mean to fight for my down-trodden race while life lasts.

Seeing they would not trust him, my grandfather left them, saying, "Perhaps they will come again next year." Then he summoned his whole people, and told them this tradition:—

"In the beginning of the world there were only four, two girls and two boys. Our forefather and mother were only two, and we are their children. You all know that a great while ago there was a happy family in this world. One girl and one boy were dark and the others were white. For a time they got along together without quarrelling, but soon they disagreed, and there was trouble. They were cross to one another and fought, and our parents were very much grieved. They prayed that their children might learn better, but it did not do any good; and afterwards the whole household was made so unhappy that the father and mother saw that they must separate their children; and then our father took the dark boy and girl, and the white boy and girl, and asked them, 'Why are you so cruel to each other?' They hung down their heads, and would not speak. They were ashamed. He said to them, 'Have I not been kind to you all, and given you everything your hearts wished for? You do not have to hunt and kill your own game to live upon. You see, my dear children, I have power to call whatsoever kind of game we want to eat; and I also have the power to separate my dear children, if they are not good to each other.' So he separated his children by a word. He said, 'Depart from each other, you cruel children;—go across the mighty ocean and do not seek each other's lives.'

"So the light girl and boy disappeared by that one word, and their parents saw them no more, and they were grieved, although they knew their children were happy. And by-and-by the dark children grew into a large nation; and we believe it is the one we belong to, and that the nation that sprung from the white children will some time send some one to meet us and heal all the old trouble. Now, the white people we saw a few days ago must certainly be our white brothers, and I want to welcome them. I want to love them as I love all of you. But they would not let me; they were afraid. But they will come again, and I want you one and all to promise that, should I not live to welcome them myself, you will not hurt a hair on their heads, but welcome them as I tried to do."

How good of him to try and heal the wound, and how vain were his efforts! My people had never seen a white man, and yet they existed, and were a strong race. The people promised as he wished, and they all went back to their work.

The next year came a great emigration, and camped near Humboldt Lake. The name of the man in charge of the trains was Captain Johnson, and they stayed three days to rest their horses, as they had a long journey before them without water. During their stay my grandfather and some of his people called upon them, and they all shook hands, and when our white brothers were going away they gave my grandfather a white tin plate. Oh, what a time they had over that beautiful gift,—it was so bright! They say that after they left, my grandfather called for all his people to come together, and he then showed them the beautiful gift which he had received from his white brothers. Everybody was so pleased; nothing like it was ever seen in our country before. My grandfather thought so much of it that he bored holes in it and fastened it on his head, and wore it as his hat. He held it in as much admiration as my white sisters hold their diamond rings or a sealskin jacket. So that winter they talked of nothing but their white brothers. The following spring there came great news down the Humboldt River, saying that there were some more of the white brothers coming, and there was something among them that was burning all in a blaze. My grandfather asked them what it was like. They told him it looked like a man; it had legs and hands and a head, but the head had quit burning, and it was left quite black. There was the greatest excitement among my people everywhere about the men in a blazing fire. They were excited because they did not know there were any people in the world but the two,—that is, the Indians and the whites; they thought that was all of us in the beginning of the world, and, of course, we did not know where the others had come from, and we don't know yet. Ha! ha! oh, what a laughable thing that was! It was two negroes wearing red shirts!

The third year more emigrants came, and that summer Captain Fremont, who is now General Fremont.

My grandfather met him, and they were soon friends. They met just where the railroad crosses Truckee River, now called Wadsworth, Nevada. Captain Fremont gave my grandfather the name of Captain Truckee, and he also called the river after him. Truckee is an Indian word, it means *all right*, or *very well*. A party of twelve of my people went to California with Captain Fremont. I do not know just how long they were gone.

• • •

When my grandfather went to California he helped Captain Fremont fight the Mexicans. When he came back he told the people what a beautiful country California was. Only eleven returned home, one having died on the way back.

They spoke to their people in the English language, which was very strange to them all.

Captain Truckee, my grandfather, was very proud of it, indeed. They all brought guns with them. My grandfather would sit down with us for hours, and would say over and over again, "Goodee gun, goodee, goodee gun, heap shoot." They also brought some of the soldiers' clothes with all their brass buttons, and my people were very much astonished to see the clothes, and all that time they were peaceable toward their white brothers. They had learned to love them, and they hoped more of them would come. Then my people were less barbarous than they are nowadays.

That same fall, after my grandfather came home, he told my father to take charge of his people and hold the tribe, as he was going back to California with as many of his people as he could get to go with him. So my father took his place as Chief of the Piutes, and had it as long as he lived. Then my grandfather started back to California again with about thirty families. That same fall, very late, the emigrants kept coming. It was this time that our white brothers first came amongst us. They could not get over the mountains, so they had to live with us. It was on Carson River, where the great Carson City stands now. You call my people bloodseeking. My people did not seek to kill them, nor did they steal their horses,—no, no, far from it. During the winter my people helped them. They gave them such as they had to eat. They did not hold out their hands and say:—

"You can't have anything to eat unless you pay me." No,—no such word was used by us savages at that time; and the persons I am speaking of are living yet; they could speak for us if they choose to do so.

The following spring, before my grandfather returned home, there was a great excitement among my people on account of fearful news coming from different tribes, that the people whom they called their white brothers were killing everybody that came in their way, and all the Indian tribes had gone into the mountains to save their lives. So my father told all his people to go into the mountains and hunt and lay up food for the coming winter. Then we all went into the mountains. There was a fearful story they told us children. Our mothers told us that the whites were killing everybody and eating them. So we were all afraid of them. Every dust that we could see blowing in the valleys we would say it was the white people. In the late fall my father told his people to go to the rivers and fish, and we all went to Humboldt River, and the women went to work gathering wild seed, which they grind between the rocks. The stones are round, big enough to hold in the hands. The women did this when they got back, and when they had gathered all they could they put it in one place and covered it with grass, and then over the grass mud. After it is covered it looks like an Indian wigwam.

Oh, what a fright we all got one morning to hear some white people were coming. Every one ran as best they could. My poor mother was left with my little sister and me. Oh, I never can forget it. My poor mother was carrying my little sister on her back, and trying to make me run; but I was so frightened I could not move my feet, and while my poor mother was trying to get me along my aunt overtook us, and she said to my mother: "Let us bury our girls, or we shall all be killed and eaten up." So they went to work and buried us, and told us if we heard any noise not to cry out, for if we did they would surely kill us and eat us. So our mothers buried me and my cousin, planted sage bushes over our faces to keep the sun from burning them, and there we were left all day.

Oh, can any one imagine my feelings *buried alive*, thinking every minute that I was to be unburied and eaten up by the people that my grandfather loved so much? With my heart throbbing, and not daring to breathe, we lay there all day. It seemed that the night would never come. Thanks be to God! the night came at last. Oh, how I cried and said: "Oh, father, have you forgotten me? Are you never coming for me?" I cried so I thought my very heartstrings would break.

At last we heard some whispering. We did not dare to whisper to each other, so we lay still. I could hear their footsteps coming nearer and nearer. I thought my heart was coming right out of my mouth. Then I heard my mother say, " 'T is right here!" Oh, can any one in this world ever imagine what were my feelings when I was dug up by my poor mother and father? My cousin and I were once more happy in our mothers' and fathers' care, and we were taken to where all the rest were.

I was once buried alive; but my second burial shall be for ever, where no father or mother will come and dig me up. It shall not be with throbbing heart that I shall listen for coming footsteps. I shall be in the sweet rest of peace,—I, the chieftain's weary daughter.

Well, while we were in the mountains hiding, the people that my grandfather called our white brothers came along to where our winter supplies were.[1] They set everything we had left on fire. It was a fearful sight. It was all we had for the winter, and it was all burnt during that night. My father took some of his men during the night to try and save some of it, but they could not; it had burnt down before they got there.

These were the last white men that came along that fall. My people talked fearfully that winter about those they called our white brothers. My people said they had something like awful thunder and lightning, and with that they killed everything that came in their way.

This whole band of white people perished in the mountains, for it was too late to cross them. We could have saved them, only my people were afraid of them. We never knew who they were, or where they came from. So, poor things, they must have suffered fearfully, for they all starved there. The snow was too deep.

Early in the following spring, my father told all his people to go to the mountains, for there would be a great emigration that summer. He told them he had had a wonderful dream, and wanted to tell them all about it.

He said, "Within ten days come together at the sink of Carson, and I will tell you my dream."

The sub-chiefs went everywhere to tell their people what my father had told them to say; and when the time came we all went to the sink of Carson.

Just about noon, while we were on the way, a great many of our men came to meet us, all on their horses. Oh, what a beautiful song they sang for my father as they came near us! We passed them, and they followed us, and as we came near to the encampment, every man, woman, and child were out looking for us. They had a place all ready for us. Oh, how happy everybody was! One could hear laughter everywhere, and songs were sung by happy women and children.

My father stood up and told his people to be merry and happy for five days. It is a rule among our people always to have five days to settle anything. My father told them to dance at night, and that the men should hunt rabbits and fish, and some were to have games of football, or any kind of sport or playthings they wished, and the women could do the same, as they had nothing else to do. My people were so happy during the five days,—the women ran races, and the men ran races on foot and on horses.

My father got up very early one morning, and told his people the time had come,—that we could no longer be happy as of old, as the white people we called our brothers had brought a great trouble and sorrow among us already. He went on and said,—

"These white people must be a great nation, as they have houses that move. It is wonderful to see them move along. I fear we will suffer greatly by their coming to our country; they come for no good to us, although my father said they were our brothers, but they do not seem to think we are like them. What do you all think about it? Maybe I am wrong. My dear children, there is something telling me that I

---

[1] Apparently the infamous Donner party; see headnote.

am not wrong, because I am sure they have minds like us, and think as we do; and I know that they were doing wrong when they set fire to our winter supplies. They surely knew it was our food."

And this was the first wrong done to us by our white brothers.

Now comes the end of our merrymaking.

Then my father told his people his fearful dream, as he called it. He said,—

"I dreamt this same thing three nights,—the very same. I saw the greatest emigration that has yet been through our country. I looked North and South and East and West, and saw nothing but dust, and I heard a great weeping. I saw women crying, and I also saw my men shot down by the white people. They were killing my people with something that made a great noise like thunder and lightning, and I saw the blood streaming from the mouths of my men that lay all around me. I saw it as if it was real. Oh, my dear children! You may all think it is only a dream,—nevertheless, I feel that it will come to pass. And to avoid bloodshed, we must all go to the mountains during the summer, or till my father comes back from California. He will then tell us what to do. Let us keep away from the emigrant roads and stay in the mountains all summer. There are to be a great many pine-nuts this summer, and we can lay up great supplies for the coming winter, and if the emigrants don't come too early, we can take a run down and fish for a month, and lay up dried fish. I know we can dry a great many in a month, and young men can go into the valleys on hunting excursions, and kill as many rabbits as they can. In that way we can live in the mountains all summer and all winter too."

So ended my father's dream. During that day one could see old women getting together talking over what they had heard my father say. They said,—

"It is true what our great chief has said, for it was shown to him by a higher power. It is not a dream. Oh, it surely will come to pass. We shall no longer be a happy people, as we now are; we shall no longer go here and there as of old; we shall no longer build our big fires as a signal to our friends, for we shall always be afraid of being seen by those bad people."

"Surely they don't eat people?"

"Yes, they do eat people, because they ate each other up in the mountains last winter."

This was the talk among the old women during the day.

"Oh, how grieved we are! Oh, where will it end?"

That evening one of our doctors called for a council, and all the men gathered together in the council-tent to hear what their medicine man had to say, for we all believe our doctor is greater than any human being living. We do not call him a medicine man because he gives medicine to the sick, as your doctors do. Our medicine man cures the sick by the laying on of hands, and we have doctresses as well as doctors. We believe that our doctors can communicate with holy spirits from heaven. We call heaven the Spirit Land.

Well, when all the men get together, of course there must be smoking the first thing. After the pipe has passed round five times to the right, it stops, and then he tells them to sing five songs. He is the leader in the song-singing. He sings heavenly songs, and he says he is singing with the angels. It is hard to describe these songs. They are all different, and he says the angels sing them to him.

Our doctors never sing war-songs, except at a war-dance, as they never go themselves on the war-path. While they were singing the last song, he said,—

"Now I am going into a trance. While I am in the trance you must smoke just as you did before; not a word must be spoken while I am in the trance."

About fifteen minutes after the smoking was over, he began to make a noise as if he was crying a great way off. The noise came nearer and nearer, until he breathed, and after he came to, he kept on crying. And then he prophesied, and told the people that my father's dream was true in one sense of the word,—that is, "Our people will not all die at the hands of our white brothers. They will kill a great many with their guns, but they will bring among us a fearful disease that will cause us to die by hundreds."

We all wept, for we believed this word came from heaven.

So ended our feast, and every family went to its own home in the pine-nut mountains, and remained there till the pine-nuts were ripe. They ripen about the last of June.

Late in that fall, there came news that my grandfather was on his way home. Then my father took a great many of his men and went to meet his father, and there came back a runner, saying, that all our people must come together. It was said that my grandfather was bringing bad news. All our people came to receive their chieftain; all the old and young men and their wives went to meet him. One evening there came a man, saying that all the women who had little children should go to a high mountain. They wanted them to go because they brought white men's guns, and they made such a fearful noise, it might even kill some of the little children. My grandfather had lost one of his men while he was away.

So all the women that had little children went. My mother was among the rest; and every time the guns were heard by us, the children would scream. I thought, for one that my heart would surely break. So some of the women went down from the mountain and told them not to shoot any more, or their children would die with fright. When our mothers brought us down to our homes the nearer we came to the camp, the more I cried,—

"Oh, mother, mother, don't take us there!" I fought my mother,—I bit her. Then my father came, and took me in his arms and carried me to the camp. I put my head in his bosom, and would not look up for a long time. I heard my grandfather say,—

"So the young lady is ashamed because her sweetheart has come to see her. Come, dearest, that won't do after I have had such a hard time to come to see my sweetheart, that she should be ashamed to look at me."

Then he called my two brothers to him, and said to them, "Are you glad to see me?" And my brothers both told him that they were glad to see him. Then my grandfather said to them,—

"See that young lady; she does not love her sweetheart any more, does she? Well, I shall not live if she does not come and tell me she loves me. I shall take that gun, and I shall kill myself."

That made me worse than ever, and I screamed and cried so hard that my mother had to take me away. So they kept weeping for the little one three or four days. I did not make up with my grandfather for a long time. He sat day after day, and night after night, telling his people about his white brothers. He told them that the whites were really their brothers, that they were very kind to everybody, especially to children; that they were always ready to give something to children. He told them what beautiful things their white brothers had,—what beautiful clothes they wore, and about the big houses that go on the mighty ocean, and travel faster than any horse in the world. His people asked him how big they were. "Well, as big as that hill you see there, and as high as the mountain over us."

"Oh, that is not possible,—it would sink, surely."

"It is every word truth, and that is nothing to what I am going to tell you. Our white brothers are a mighty nation, and have more wonderful things than that. They have a gun that can shoot a ball bigger than my head, that can go as far off as that mountain you see over there."

The mountain he spoke of at that time was about twenty miles across from where we were. People opened their eyes when my grandfather told of the many battles they had with the Mexicans, and about their killing so many of the Mexicans, and taking their big city away from them, and how mighty they were. These wonderful things were talked about all winter long. The funniest thing was that he would sing some of the soldier's roll-calls, and the air to the Star-spangled Banner, which everybody learned during the winter.

He then showed us a more wonderful thing than all the others that he had brought. It was a paper, which he said could talk to him. He took it out and he would talk to it, and talk with it. He said, "This can talk to all our white brothers, and our white sisters, and their children. Our white brothers are beautiful, and our white sisters are beautiful, and their children are beautiful!" He also said the paper can travel like the wind, and it can go and talk with their fathers and brothers and sisters, and come back to tell what they are doing, and whether they are well or sick.

After my grandfather told us this, our doctors and doctresses said,—

"If they can do this wonderful thing, they are not truly human, but pure spirits. None but heavenly spirits can do such wonderful things. We can communicate with the spirits, yet we cannot do wonderful things like them. Oh, our great chieftain, we are afraid your white brothers will yet make your people's hearts bleed. You see if they don't; for we can see it. Their blood is all around us, and the dead are lying all about us, and we cannot escape it. It will come. Then you will say our doctors and doctresses did know. Dance, sing, play, it will do no good; we cannot drive it away. They have already done the mischief, while you were away."

But this did not go far with my grandfather. He kept talking to his people about the good white people, and told them all to get ready to go with him to California the following spring.

Very late that fall, my grandfather and my father and a great many more went down to the Humboldt River to fish. They brought back a great many fish, which we were very glad to get; for none of our people had been down to fish the whole summer.

When they came back, they brought us more news. They said there were some white people living at the Humboldt sink. They were the first ones my father had seen face to face. He said they were not like "humans." They were more like owls than any thing else. They had hair on their faces, and had white eyes, and looked beautiful.

I tell you we children had to be very good, indeed, during the winter; for we were told that if we were not good they would come and eat us up. We remained there all winter; the next spring the emigrants came as usual, and my father and grandfather and uncles, and many more went down on the Humboldt River on fishing excursions. While they were thus fishing, their white brothers came upon them and fired on them, and killed one of my uncles, and wounded another. Nine more were wounded, and five died afterwards. My other uncle got well again, and is living yet. Oh, that was a fearful thing, indeed!

After all these things had happened, my grandfather still stood up for his white brothers.

Our people had council after council, to get my grandfather to give his consent that they should go and kill those white men who were at the sink of Humboldt. No; they could do nothing of the kind while he lived. He told his people that his word was more to him than his son's life, or any one else's life either.

"Dear children," he said, "think of your own words to me;—you promised. You want me to say to you, Go and kill those that are at the sink of Humboldt. After your promise, how dare you to ask me to let your hearts be stained with the blood of those who are innocent of the deed that has been done to us by others? Is not my dear beloved son laid alongside of your dead, and you say I stand up for their lives. Yes, it is very hard, indeed; but, nevertheless, I know and you know that those men who live at the sink are not the ones that killed our men."

While my grandfather was talking, he wept, and men, women, and children, were all weeping. One could hardly hear him talking.

After he was through talking, came the saddest part. The widow of my uncle who was killed, and my mother and father all had long hair. They cut off their hair, and also cut long gashes in their arms and legs, and they were all bleeding as if they would die with the loss of blood. This continued for several days, for this is the way we mourn for our dead. When the woman's husband dies, she is first to cut off her hair, and then she braids it and puts it across his breast; then his mother and sisters, his father and brothers and all his kinsfolk cut their hair. The widow is to remain unmarried until her hair is the same length as before, and her face is not to be washed all that time, and she is to use no kind of paint, nor to make any merriment with other women until the day is set for her to do so by her father-in-law, or if she has no father-in-law, by her mother-in-law, and then she is at liberty to go where she pleases. The widower is at liberty when his wife dies; but he mourns for her in the same way, by cutting his hair off.

It was late that fall when my grandfather prevailed with his people to go with him to California. It was this time that my mother accompanied him. Everything had been got ready to start on our journey. My dear father was to be left behind. How my poor mother begged to stay with her husband! But my grandfather told her that she could come back in the spring to see her husband; so we started for California, leaving my poor papa behind. All my kinsfolk went with us but one aunt and her children.

The first night found us camped at the sink of Carson, and the second night we camped on Carson River. The third day, as we were travelling along the river, some of our men who were ahead, came back and said there were some of our white brothers' houses ahead of us. So my grandfather told us all to stop where we were while he went to see them. He was not gone long, and when he came back he brought some hard bread which they gave him. He told us that was their food, and he gave us all some to taste. That was the first I ever tasted.

Then my grandfather once more told his people that his paper talked for him, and he said,—

"Just as long as I live and have that paper which my white brothers' great chieftain has given me, I shall stand by them, come what will." He held the paper up towards heaven and kissed it, as if it was really a person. "Oh, if I should lose this," he said, "we shall all be lost. So, children, get your horses ready, and we will go on, and we will camp with them to-night, or by them, for I have a sweetheart along who is dying for fear of my white brothers." He meant me; for I was always crying and hiding under somebody's robes, for we had no blankets then.

Well, we went on; but we did not camp with them, because my poor mother and brothers and sisters told my grandfather that I was sick with crying for fright, and for him not to camp too close to them. The women were speaking two words for themselves and one for me, for they were just as afraid as I was. I had seen my brother Natchez crying when the men came back, and said there were white men ahead of us. So my grandfather did as my mother wished him to do, and we went on by them; but I did not know it, as I had my head covered while we were passing their camp. I was riding behind my older brother, and we went on and camped quite a long way from them that night.

So we travelled on to California, but did not see any more of our white brothers till we got to the head of Carson River, about fifteen miles above where great Carson City now stands.

"Now give me the baby." It was my baby-sister that grandpa took from my mother, and I peeped from under my mother's fur, and I saw some one take my little sister. Then I cried out,—

"Oh, my sister! Don't let them take her away."

And once more my poor grandfather told his people that his white brothers and sisters were very kind to children. I stopped crying, and looked at them again. Then I saw them give my brother and sister something white. My mother asked her father what it was, and he said it was *Pe-har-be*, which means sugar. Just then one of the women came to my mother with some in her hand, and grandpa said:—

"Take it, my child."

Then I held out my hand without looking. That was the first gift I ever got from a white person, which made my heart very glad.

When they went away, my grandfather called me to him, and said I must not be afraid of the white people, for they are very good. I told him that they looked so very bad I could not help it.

We travelled with them at that time two days, and the third day we all camped together where some white people were living in large white houses. My grandpa went to one of the houses, and when he came back he said his white brothers wanted him to come and get some beef and hard bread. So he took four men with him to get it, and they gave him four boxes of hard bread and a whole side of beef, and the next morning we got our horses ready to go on again. There was some kind of a fight,—that is, the captain of the train was whipping negroes who were driving his team. That made my poor grandfather feel very badly. He went to the captain, and told him he would not travel with him. He came back and said to his people that he would not travel with his white brothers any farther. We travelled two days without seeing any more of my grandfather's white brothers. At last we came to a very large encampment of white people, and they ran out of their wagons, or wood-houses, as we called them, and gathered round us. I was riding behind my brother. I was so afraid, I told him to put his robe over me, but he did not do so. I scratched him and bit him on his back, and then my poor grandfather rode up to the tents where they were, and he was asked to stay there all night with them. After grandpa had talked awhile, he said to his people that he would camp with his brothers. So he did. Oh, what nice things we all got from my grandpa's white brothers! Our men got red shirts, and our women got calico for dresses. Oh, what a pretty dress my sister got! I did not get anything, because I hid all the time. I was hiding under some robes. No one knew where I was. After all the white people were gone, I heard my poor mother cry out:—

"Oh, where is my little girl? Oh, father, can it be that the white people have carried her away? Oh, father, go and find her,—go, go, and find her!" And I also heard my brothers and sister cry. Yet I said nothing, because they had not called me to get some of the pretty things. When they began to cry, I began crawling out, and then my grandfather scolded me, and told me that his brothers loved good children, but not bad ones like me. How I did cry, and wished that I had staid at home with my father! I went to sleep crying.

I did not forget what had happened. There was a house near where we camped. My grandfather went down to the house with some of his men, and pretty soon we saw them coming back. They were carrying large boxes, and we were all looking at them. My mother said there were two white men coming with them.

"Oh, mother, what shall I do? Hide me!"

I just danced round like a wild one, which I was. I was behind my mother. When they were coming nearer, I heard my grandpa say,—

"Make a place for them to sit down."

Just then, I peeped round my mother to see them. I gave one scream, and said,—

"Oh, mother, the owls!"

I only saw their big white eyes, and I thought their faces were all hair. My mother said,—

"I wish you would send your brothers away, for my child will die."

I imagined I could see their big white eyes all night long. They were the first ones I had ever seen in my life.

We went on the next day, and passed some more of our white brothers' houses, as we called their wagons at that time. We camped on the Sanvada mountains and spent the night. My grandfather said everything that was good about the white people to me. At last we were camped upon the summit, and it snowed very hard all night, and in the morning my grandfather told his people to hurry and get their horses, and travel on, for fear we might get snowed into the mountains. That night we overtook some emigrants who were camped there to rest their oxen. This time I watched my grandfather to see what he would do. He said, "I am going to show them my rag friend again." As he rode up to one of their tents, three white men came out to him; then they took him to a large tent. Quite a number of white men came out to him. I saw him take out the paper he called his rag friend and give it to one of the men who stood looking at it; then he looked up and came toward him and held out his hand to my grandfather, and then the rest of the white men did the same all round. Then the little children and the women did the same, and I saw the little ones running to their tents and back again with something in their hands, and they were giving it to each man. The next morning I could not eat, and said to my mother,—

"Let us go back to father—let us not go with grandpa, for he is bad." My poor mother said, "We can't go alone; we would all be killed if we go, for we have no rag friend as father has. And dear, you must be good, and grandpa will love you just as well as ever. You must do what he tells you to do."

Oh, how badly I did feel! I held my two hands over my face, and was crying as if my heart would break.

"My dear, don't cry; here comes grandpa."

I heard him say,—

"Well, well, is my sweetheart never going to stop crying? Come, dear, I have something for my baby; come and see what it is."

So I went to him with my head down, not because I was afraid he would whip me,—no—no, for Indians do not whip their children. Oh, how happy I was when he told me he would give me something very beautiful. It was a little cup, and it made me very glad, indeed; and he told me it was to drink water out of, not to wear. He said,—

"I am going to tell you what I did with a beautiful gift I received from my white brothers. It was of the same kind, only it was flat and round, and it was as bright as your cup is now."

He said to his wife, "Give me my bright hat"; and she did so.

"You see I used to wear it on my head, because my white brother did not tell me what it was for." Then he began to laugh, and he laughed so long! then he stopped and said, "it was not to wear, but to eat out of, and I have made myself a fool by wearing it as a hat. Oh, how my brothers did laugh at me because I wore it at our first fight with Mexicans in Mexico. Now, dearest children, I do not want you to think my brothers laughed at me to make fun of me; no—no—it was because I wore the tin plate for a hat, that's all."

He also said they had much prettier things than this to eat out of. He went on and told us never to take anything belonging to them or lying outside of his white brothers' houses. "They hang their clothes out of doors after washing them; but they are not thrown away, and for fear some of you might think so and take them, I tell you about it. Therefore, never take anything unless they give it to you; then they will love you."

So I kept thinking over what he said to me about the good white people, and saying to myself, "I will make friends with them when we come into California."

When we came to Sacramento valley (it is a very beautiful valley), my grandfather said to his people that a great many of his white brothers were there, and he knew a great many of them; but we would not go there,—we would go on to Stockton. There he had a very good brother, who had a very big house, made of red stone; it was so high that it would tire any one to go up to some of the rooms. My uncle, my mother's brother, asked him how many rooms were up there? My grandpa said,—

"We have to climb up three times to get to the top." They all laughed, as much as to say my grandpa lied. He said, "You will not laugh when I show you what wonderful things my white brothers can do. I will tell you something more wonderful than that. My brother has a big house that runs on the river, and it whistles and makes a beautiful noise, and it has a bell on it which makes a beautiful noise also." My uncle asked again how big it was.

"Oh, you will see for yourself; we will get there to-morrow night. We will stop there ten days, and you can see for yourselves, and then you will know, my brothers, that what I have told you is true."

After travelling all day we went into camp for the night. We had been there but a little while, and there came a great many men on horseback, and camped near us. I ran to my mother and said I was sleepy, and wanted to go to bed. I did so because I did not want to see them, and I knew grandpa would have them come to see us. I heard him say he was going to see them. I lay down quietly for a little while, and then got up and looked round to see if my brother was going too. There was no one but my mother and little sister. They had all gone to see them.

"Lie down, dear," my mother said.

I did so, but I did not sleep for a long time, for I was thinking about the house that runs on the water. I wondered what it was like. I kept saying to myself, "Oh, I wish it was to-morrow now." I heard mother say,—

"They are coming." Pretty soon I heard grandpa say, "They are not my brothers." Mother said, "Who are they?"

"They are what my brothers call Mexicans. They are the people we fought; if they knew who I was they would kill me, but they shall not know. I am not going to show them my rag friend, for fear my rag friend will tell of me."

Oh my! oh my! That made me worse than ever. I cried, so that one could have heard my poor heart beat. Oh, how I wished I was back with my father again! All the children were not afraid of the white people—only me. My brothers would go everywhere with grandpa. I would not have been so afraid of them if I had not been told by my own father and grandmamma that the white people would kill little children and eat them.

Everything was all right, and the next day we went on our journey, and after a whole day's journey we came within a mile of the town. The sun was almost down when grandpa stopped and said,—

"Now, one and all, listen as you go on. You will hear the water-house bell ring."

So we did, and pretty soon we heard the prettiest noise we had ever heard in all our life-time. It became dark before we got to the town, but we could see something like stars away ahead of us. Oh, how I wished I had staid with my father in our own country. I cried out, saying,—

"Oh, mother, I am so afraid. I cannot go to the white people. They are so much like the owls with their big white eyes. I cannot make friends with them."

I kept crying until we came nearer the town, and camped for the night. My grandpa said to his men,—

"Unsaddle your horses while I go and see my friend."

He came back in a few moments, and said:—

"Turn your horses into the corral, and now we will go to bed without making any fire."

So we did, and I for one was glad. But although very tired I could not sleep, for grandpa kept telling us that at daybreak we would hear the water-house's whistle. The next morning my mother waked me, and I got up and looked round me. I found no one but mother.

"Oh, where is sister, mother?"

"Oh, she has gone with the rest to see the water-house."

"Mother, did you hear it whistle?"

"Yes, we all heard it, and it made such a fearful noise! The one that whistled has gone on. But another came in just like it, and made just such a noise. Your brother was here awhile ago. He said the water-house had many looking-glasses all round it, and when it came in it was so tired, it breathed so hard, it made us almost deaf."

"Say, mother, let us go and see."

But mother said,—

"No, your brother said there were so many white people that one can hardly get along. We will wait until your grandpa comes, and hear what they all say. A'n't you hungry, my child?"

I said, "Yes."

"Your brother brought something that tastes like sugar."

It was cake, and I ate so much it made me sick.

I was sick all day and night, and the next day I had the chills. Oh, I was very, very sick; my poor mother thought I would die. I heard her say to grandpa one day,—

"The sugar-bread was poisoned which your white brother gave us to eat, and it has made my poor little girl so sick that I am afraid she will die." My poor mother and brothers and sisters were crying; mother had me in her arms. My grandpa came and took me in his arms and said to me,—

"Open your eyes, dear, and see your grandpa!" I did as he told me, because I had not forgotten what mother had said to me, to do whatever he told me to do, and then he would love me. The reason I had not opened my eyes was because my head ached so badly that it hurt me so I shut them again. My poor mother cried the more, and all our people gathered around us and began to cry. My mother said to grandpa,—

"Can there be anything done for her?"

"Dear daughter," he said, "I am sorry you have such bad hearts against my white brothers. I have eaten some sugar-bread, and so have you, and all the rest of us, and we did not get sick. Dear daughter, you should have blessed the strange food before you gave it to your child to eat; maybe that is why she is sick."

It is a law among us that all strange food is blessed before eaten, and also clothing of any kind that is given to us by any one, Indians or white people, must be blessed before worn. So all my people came together and prayed over me, but it was all in vain. I do not know how long I was sick, but very long. I was indeed poisoned, not by the bread I had eaten, but by poison oak. My face swelled so that I could not see for a long time, but I could hear everything. At last some one came that had a voice like an angel. I really thought it must be an angel, for I had been taught by my father that an angel comes to watch the sick one and take the soul to the spirit land. I kept thinking it must be so, and I learned words from the angel (as I thought it). I could not see, for my eyes were swollen shut. These were the words, "Poor little girl, it is too bad!" It was said so often by the pretty sweet voice, I would say it over and over when I was suffering so badly, and would cry out, "Poor little girl, it is too bad!" At last I began to get well, and I could hear my grandpa say the same words.

Then I began to see a little, and the first thing I asked my mother, was, "What was the angel saying to me?" Oh, how frightened my poor mother was! She cried out,—

"Oh, father, come here! My little girl is talking to the angels,—she is dying."

My sister and brothers ran to her, crying, and for the first time since I was sick I cried out, "Oh, don't, don't cry! I am getting well,—indeed I am. Stop crying, and give me something to eat. I was only asking you what the angel meant by saying 'Poor little girl, it is too bad!'"

"Oh," says grandpa, "it is the good white woman; I mean my white sister, who comes here to see you. She has made you well. She put some medicine on your face, and has made you see. Ain't you glad to see?"

I said, "Can I see her now?"

"Yes, she will come pretty soon; she comes every day to see you."

Then my mother came with something for me to eat, but I said, "Wait, grandpa, tell me more about the good woman."

He said, "My dear child, she is truly an angel, and she has come every day to see you. You will love her, I know."

"Dear grandpa, will she come pretty soon? I want to see her."

Grandpa said, "I will go and get her. You won't be afraid, will you?"

So my grandpa went. I tried my best to eat, but I could not, it was so hard.

My sister said, "They are coming."

I said, "Mother, fix my eyes so I can see the angel. Has it wings, mother?"

Mother said, "You will see for yourself."

Just then they came, and grandpa said, "Here she is." The first thing she did she put her beautiful white hand on my forehead. I looked at her; she was, indeed, a beautiful angel. She said the same words as before. I asked my grandpa what she was saying. Then he told me what she meant by it. I began to get well very fast, and this sweet angel came every day and brought me something nice to eat; and oh, what pretty dresses she brought me. When she brought the dresses she talked to my grandpa a long time, and she cried, and after she went away he said to my mother,—

"The dresses which my white sister gave my child were her dead child's clothes, so they should be burned." I began to cry, because I did not want them burned. He said to me,—

"Don't cry, my child; you will get nicer ones than these if you learn to love my white sister."

Of course the clothes were burned, and after I got well my grandpa took great delight in taking us all to see his white brothers and sisters, and I knew what he meant when he said "my little girls;" I knew he meant me and sister, and he also would say "my little boys," when he was talking about my brothers.

He would say, pointing to my brother, "my Natchez"; he always said this. So the white people called one of my brothers Natchez, and he has had that name to this day.

So I came to love the white people. We left Stockton and went on farther to a place called San Joaquin River. It took us only one day to go there. We only crossed that river at that time.

One of my grandpa's friends was named Scott, and the other Bonsal. After we got there, his friend killed beef for him and his people. We stayed there some time. Then grandpa told us that he had taken charge of Mr. Scott's cattle and horses, and he was going to take them all up to the mountains to take care of them for his brothers. He wanted my uncles and their families and my mother and her two sons and three daughters to stay where they were; that is, he told his dear daughter that he wanted her two sons to take care of a few horses and cows that would be left. My mother began to cry, and said,—

"Oh, father, don't leave us here! My children might get sick, and there would be no one to speak for us; or something else might happen." He again said, "I don't think my brothers will do anything that is wrong to you and your children." Then my mother asked my grandfather if he would take my sister with him. My poor mother felt that her daughter was unsafe, for she was young and very good-looking.

"I would like to take her along," he said, "but I want her to learn how to work and cook. Scott and Bonsal say they will take the very best care of you and the children. It is not as if I was going to leave you here really alone; your brothers will be with you." So we staid. Two men owned the ferry, and they had a great deal of money. So my brothers took care of their horses and cows all winter, and they paid them well for their work. But, oh, what trouble we had for a while! The men whom my grandpa called his brothers would come into our camp and ask my mother to give our sister to them. They would come in at night, and we would all scream and cry; but that would not stop them. My sister, and mother, and my uncles all cried and said, "Oh, why did we come? Oh, we shall surely all be killed some night." My uncles and brothers would not dare to say a word, for fear they would be shot down. So we used to go away every night after dark and hide, and come back to our camp every morning. One night we were getting ready to go, and there came five men. The fire was out; we could see two men come into the tent and shut off the postles outside. My uncles and my brothers made such a noise! I don't know what happened; when I woke I asked my mother if they had killed my sister. She said, "We are all safe here. Don't cry."

"Where are we, mother?"

"We are in a boarding-house."

"Are my uncles killed?"

"No, dear, they are all near here too."

I said, "Sister, where are you? I want to come to you."

She said, "Come on."

I laid down, but I could not sleep. I could hear my poor sister's heart beat. Early the next morning we got up and went down stairs, for it was upstairs where we slept. There were a great many in the room. When we came down, my mother said, "We will go outside."

My sister said, "There is no outlet to the house. We can't get out."

Mother looked round and said, "No, we cannot get out." I as usual began to cry. My poor sister! I ran to her, I saw tears in her eyes. I heard some one speak close to my mother. I looked round and saw Mr. Scott holding the door open. Mother said, "Children, come."

He went out with us and pointed to our camp, and shook his head, and motioned to mother to go into a little house where they were cooking. He took my hand in his, and said the same words that I had learned, "Poor little girl." I could see by his looks that he pitied me, so I was not afraid of him. We went in and sat down on the floor. Oh, what pretty things met my eyes. I was looking all round the room, and I saw beautiful white cups, and every beautiful thing on something high and long, and around it some things that were red.

I said to my sister, "Do you know what those are?" for she had been to the house before with my brothers. She said, "That high thing is what they use when eating, and the white cups are what they drink hot water from, and the red things you see is what they sit upon when they are eating." There was one now near us, and I thought if I could sit upon it I should be so happy! I said to my mother, "Can I sit on that one?" She said, "No, they would whip you." I did not say any more, but sat looking at the beautiful red chair. By-and-by the white woman went out, and I wished in my heart I could go and sit upon it while she was gone. Then she came in with her little child in her arms. As she came in she went right to the very chair I wanted to sit in so badly, and set her child in it. I looked up to my mother, and said, "Will she get a whipping?"

"No, dear, it belongs to her father."

So I said no more. Pretty soon a man came in. She said something to him, and he went out, and in a little while they all came in and sat round that high thing, as I called it. That was the table. It was all very strange to me, and they were drinking the hot water as they ate. I thought it was indeed hot water. After they got through, they all went out again, but Mr. Scott staid and talked to the woman and the man a long time. Then the woman fixed five places and the men went out and brought in my brothers, and kept talking to them. My brother said, "Come and sit here, and you, sister, sit there." But as soon as I sat down in the beautiful chair I began to look at the pretty picture on the back of the chair. "Dear, sit nice and eat, or the white woman will whip you," my mother said. I was quiet, but did not eat much. I tasted the black hot water; I did not like it. It was coffee that we called hot water. After we had done, brother said, "Mother, come outside; I want to talk to you." So we all went out. Brother said, "Mother, Mr. Scott wants us all to stay here. He says you and sister are to wash dishes, and learn all kinds of work. We are to stay here all the time and sleep upstairs, and the white woman is going to teach my sister how to sew. I think, dear mother, we had better stay, because grandpa said so, and our father Scott will take good care of us. He is going up into the mountains to see how grandpa is getting along, and he says he will take my uncles with him." All the time brother was talking, my mother and sister were crying. I did not cry, for I wanted to stay so that I could sit in the beautiful red chairs. Mother said,—

"Dear son, you know if we stay here sister will be taken from us by the bad white man. I would rather see her die than see her heart full of fear every night."

"Yes, dear mother, we love our dear sister, and if you say so we will go to papa."

"Yes, dear son, let us go and tell him what his white brothers are doing to us."

"Then I will go and tell Mr. Scott we want to go to our papa." He was gone some time, and at last came back.

"Mother," he says, "we can't go,—that is, brother and I must stay;—but you and sister can go if you wish to."

"Oh no, my dear children, how can I go and leave you here? Oh, how can that bad man keep you from going? You are not his children. How dare he say you cannot go with your mother? He is not your father; he is nothing but a bad white man, and he dares to say you cannot go. Your own father did not say you should not come with me. Oh, had my dear husband said those words I would not have been here to-day, and see my dear children suffer from day to day. Oh, if your father only knew how his children were suffering, I know he would kill that white man who tried to take your sister. I cannot see for my life why my father calls them his white brothers. They are not people; they have no thought, no mind, no love. They are beasts, or they would know I, a lone woman, am here with them. They tried to take my girl from me and abuse her before my eyes and yours too, and oh, you must go too."

"Oh, mother, here he comes!"

My mother got up. She held out her two hands to him, and cried out,—

"Oh, good father, don't keep my children from me. If you have a heart in you, give them back to me. Let me take them to their good father, where they can be cared for."

We all cried to see our poor mother pleading for us. Mother held on to him until he gave some signs of letting her sons go with her; then he nodded his head,—they might go. My poor mother's crying was turned into joy, and we were all glad. The wagon was got ready,—we were to ride in it. Oh, how I jumped about because I was going to ride in it! I ran up to sister, and said,—

"Ain't you glad we are going to ride in that beautiful red house?" I called it house. My sister said,—

"Not I, dear sister, for I hate everything that belongs to the white dogs. I would rather walk all the way; oh, I hate them so badly!"

When everything was got ready, we got into the red house, as we called the wagon. I soon got tired of riding in the red house and went to sleep. Nothing happened during the day, and after awhile mother told us not to say a word about why we left, for grandpa might get mad with us. So we got to our people, and grandpa ran out to meet us. We were all glad to see him. The white man staid all night, and went home the next day. After he left us my grandpa called my brothers to him.

"Now, my dear little boys, I have something to tell you that will make you happy. Our good father (he did not say my white brother, but he said our good father) has left something with me to give you, and he also told me that he had given you some money for your work. He says you are all good boys, and he likes you very much; and he told me to give you three horses apiece, which makes six in all, and he wants you and your brother to go back and to go on with the same work, and he will pay you well for it. He is to come back in three days; then if you want to go with him you can."

Brother said, "Will mother and sisters go too?"

"No, they will stay with me." My brothers were so happy over their horses.

Now, my dear reader, there is no word so endearing as the word father, and that is why we call all good people father or mother; no matter who it is,—negro, white man, or Indian, and the same with the women. Grandpa talked to my mother a long time, but I did not hear what he said to her, as I went off to play with the other children. But the first thing I knew the white man came and staid four days. Then all the horses were got up, and he saw them all, and the cattle also. I could see my poor mother and sister crying now and then, but I did not know what for. So one morning the man was going away, and I saw mother getting my brothers' horses ready too. I ran to my mother, and said, "Mother, what makes you cry so?" Grandpa was talking to her. He said, "They will not be hurt; they will have quite a number of horses by the time we are ready to go back to our home again."

I knew then that my brothers were going back with this man. Oh, then I began to cry, and said everything that was bad to them. I threw myself down upon the ground.

"Oh, brothers, I will never see them any more. They will kill them, I know. Oh, you naughty, naughty grandpa, you want my poor brothers to be killed by the bad men. You don't know what they do to us. Oh, mother, run,—bring them back again!"

Oh, how we missed our brothers for a long time. We did not see them for a long time, but the men came now and then. They never brought my brothers with them. After they went away, grandpa would come in with his rag friend in hand and say to mother, "My friend here says my boys are all right, not sick."

My mother said, "Father, why can you not have them come and see us sometimes?"

"Dear daughter, we will get ready to go home. It is time now that the snow is off the mountains. In ten days more we will go, and we will get the children as we go by."

Oh, how happy everybody was! Everybody was singing here and there, getting beautiful dresses made, and before we started we had a thanksgiving dance. The day we were to start we partook of the first gathering of food for that summer. So that morning everybody prayed, and sang songs, and danced, and ate before starting. It was all so nice, and everybody was so happy because they were going to see their dear country and the dear ones at home. Grandpa took all the horses belonging to the white men. After we got home the horses were put into the corral for all night, and the two white men counted their horses the next morning. They gave my grandpa eight horses for his work, and two or three horses each to some of the people. To my two brothers they gave sixteen horses and some money, and after we all got our horses, grandpa said to his people,—

"Now, my children, you see that what I have told you about my white brothers is true. You see we have not worked very much, and they have given us all horses. Don't you see they are good people?"

All that time, neither my uncles nor my mother had told what the white men did while we were left all alone.

So the day was set for starting. It was to be in five days. We had been there three days when we saw the very men who were so bad to us. Yes, they were talking to grandpa. Mother said to sister,—

"They are talking about us. You see they are looking this way."

Sister said, "Oh, mother, I hope grandpa will not do such a wicked thing as to give me to those bad men."

Oh, how my heart beat! I saw grandpa shake his head, and he looked mad with them. He came away and left them standing there. From that day my grandma took my sister under her care, and we got along nicely.

Then we started for our home, and after travelling some time we arrived at the head of Carson River. There we met some of our people, and they told us some very bad news, indeed, which made us all cry. They said almost all the tribe had died off, and if one of a family got sick it was a sure thing that the whole family would die. He said the white men had poisoned the Humboldt River, and our people had drank the water and died off. Grandpa said,—

"Is my son dead?"

"No, he has been in the mountains all the time, and all who have been there are all right."

The men said a great many of our relations had died off.

We staid there all night, and the next day our hair was all cut off. My sister and my mother had such beautiful hair!

So grandpa said to the man,—

"Go and tell our people we are coming. Send them to each other, and tell my son to come to meet us."

So we went on our journey, and after travelling three days more we came to a place called Genoa, on the west side of Carson River, at the very place where I had first seen a white man. A saw-mill and a grist-mill were there, and five more houses.

We camped in the very same place where we did before. We staid there a long time waiting for my father to come to meet us. At last my cousin rode into our camp one evening, and said my father was coming with many of his people. We heard them as they came nearer and nearer; they were all crying, and then we cried too, and as they got off their horses they fell into each other's arms, like so many little children, and cried as if their hearts would break, and told what they had suffered since we went away, and how our people had died off. As soon as one would get sick he would drink water and die right off. Every one of them was in mourning also, and they talked over the sad things which had happened to them during the time we were away. One and all said that the river must have been poisoned by the white people, because that they had prayed, and our spirit-doctors had tried to cure the sick; they too died while they were trying to cure them. After they had told grandpa all, he got angry and said,—

"My dear children, I am heartily sorry to hear your sad story; but I cannot and will not believe my white brothers would do such a thing. Oh, my dear children, do not think so badly of our white fathers, for if they had poisoned the river, why, my dear children, they too would have died when they drank of the water. It is this, my dear children, it must be some fearful disease or sickness unknown to us, and therefore, my dear children, don't blame our brothers. The whole tribe have called me their father, and I have loved you all as my dear children, and those who have died are happy in the Spirit-land, though we mourn their loss here on earth. I know my grandchildren and daughters and brothers are in that happy bright Spirit-land, and I shall soon see them there. Some of you may live a long time yet, and don't let your hearts work against your white fathers; if you do, you will not get along. You see they are already here in our land; here they are all along the river, and we must let our brothers live with us. We cannot tell them to go away. I know your good hearts. I know you won't say *kill them*. Surely you all know that they are human. Their lives are just as dear to them as ours to us. It is a very sad thing indeed to have to lose so many of our dear ones; but maybe it was to be. We can do nothing but mourn for their loss." He went on to say,—

"My dear children, you all know the tradition says: 'Weep not for your dead; but sing and be joyful, for the soul is happy in the Spirit-land.' But it is natural for man or woman to weep, because it relieves our hearts to weep together, and we all feel better afterwards."

Every one hung their heads while grandpa talked on. Now and then one could hear some of them cry out, just as the Methodists cry out at their meetings; and grandpa said a great many beautiful things to his people. He talked so long, I for one wished he would stop, so I could go and throw myself into my father's arms, and tell him what the white people were. At last he stopped, and we all ran to our father and threw our arms around his neck, and cried for joy; and then mother came with little sister. Papa took her in his arms, and mother put her hand in his bosom, and we all wept together, because mother had lost two sisters, and their husbands, and all their children but one girl; and thus passed away the day. Grandpa had gone off during our meeting with father, and prayer was offered, and every one washed their face, and were waiting for something else. Pretty soon grandpa came, and said: "This is my friend," holding up his paper in his hand. "Does it look as if it could talk and ask for anything? Yet it does. It can ask for something to eat for me and my people. Yet, it is nothing but a rag. Oh, wonderful things my white brothers can do. I have taken it down to them, and it has asked for sacks of flour for us to eat. Come, we will go and get them." So the men went down and got the flour. Grandpa took his son down to see the white men, and by-and-by we saw them coming back. They had given my father a red blanket and a red shirt.

RABINDRANATH TAGORE
[1861–1941]

Rabindranath Tagore, the leading figure of the Bengali renaissance during the late nineteenth and early twentieth century, was truly a Renaissance man. A poet, novelist, dramatist, essayist, philosopher, journalist, editor, teacher, painter, and musician, Tagore has, more than any figure during the last century other than Gandhi, come to represent India. William Rothenstein praised him to George Bernard Shaw as the model of Eastern wisdom: "He represents all that is religious, literary, scholarly and aristocratic in Bengal, and if there were no other representative we should look upon India as the most perfect country in the world."

LIFE

Born in 1861 into a prominent Brahman family of writers and thinkers, Tagore inherited the divided consciousness of colonial India. He described "Western imperialism" as "the greatest trial in [India's] history." The British had instituted an "impersonal empire, where the rulers were over us but not among us," Tagore wrote, and the colonial experience had "so disintegrated and demoralized... our people that many wondered if India could ever rise again by the genius of her own people." Nevertheless, Tagore did not reject all things British. He compared himself to "a migratory bird having two homes," Bengal and Britain. His education, partly in Calcutta and partly in England, introduced him to literatures in Sanskrit, Bengali, and English, and all three became part of his personal cultural heritage. So his project to regenerate his people and bring them back to "such a thing as our own mind" was based on a program of synthesizing the best from East and West into a new global culture that he called "the Universal human spirit."

At the time of Tagore's birth, India was "the jewel in the crown" of British imperialism—the largest and most important of all the British colonies. But by the 1880s the movement for Indian nationalism and independence, the Congress Movement, had begun to challenge British hegemony on the subcontinent. The Bengali literary renaissance was part of this emerging nationalistic consciousness, for it sought to establish a literature and culture that would represent "our reaction against the culture of Europe and its ideals, [and] a newborn sense of self-respect." The new Bengali literature was written in Bengali, the everyday language of the people of northeast India. It did not use Sanskrit, the traditional "literary" language of Bengal, and it rejected English as the language of the oppressor. It also departed from the traditional poetic forms and mythological subject matter. Instead, in such modern literary forms as the novel and short story, it realistically described the lives of common people, often drawing on folktales and songs for its models and inspiration.

Tagore's literary career was ignited by his contact with rural India after he returned from school in England. His father sent him to oversee some family estates in the Ganges River valley, and there Tagore rediscovered his native land. He heard the language of the peasants, learned their songs, and absorbed the unchanging life of rural India. The stories and poems that he wrote in the 1890s and in the first decade of the twentieth century reveal the influence of this experience in the country. Their language is realistic and vernacular, and their literary models are not traditional Sanskrit poems but rather the songs and stories of the peasants. In the country the cosmopolitan Tagore found the enduring themes of India.

WORK

His short stories, many of them written during the 1890s, often describe the confrontation between city and country as one of the defining divisions of colonial India. Typically in these stories, a city dweller, anglicized by his Western education and contact with the British, is reminded of his Indian roots by an unsettling experience in the countryside. Such is the experience, for example, of the government clerk in "The Hungry Stones." Tagore's poems, many of them songs based on traditional Indian folk songs, caught the attention of Western poets and writers with the publication of the English translation of *Gitanjali* (*Song Offerings*) in 1912. William Butler Yeats, who was similarly exploring his heritage through Irish folktale and myth, found a soul-brother in Tagore: "A whole people, a whole civilisation, immeasurably strange to us," Yeats wrote, "seems to have been taken up into this imagination; and yet we are not moved because of its strangeness, but because we have met our own image, . . . or heard, perhaps for the first time in literature, our voice as in a dream." Largely on the basis of the English *Gitanjali*, Tagore was awarded the Nobel Prize for literature in 1913.

Tagore's novels—the best known are *Gora* (1910) and *Ghare-baire* (*The Home and the World*, 1916)—are more political than his stories and poems. They present India as desiring independence but saddled with the mentality of a subject nation. Tagore never viewed independence as an end in itself, but rather as part of a process of regaining national self-respect. He saw in Mahatma Gandhi, the leader of the Indian independence movement, a figure who had synthesized East and West as Tagore himself was trying to do. Gandhi, Tagore wrote, had taken the message of Christianity—the doctrine "that God became man in order to save humanity by taking the burden of its sin and suffering on himself"—and turned it into a principle of nonviolent struggle. In doing this, Gandhi became an expression of "the genius of India [which] has taken from her aggressors the most spiritually significant principle of their culture and fashioned of it a new message of hope for mankind."

Besides his writing, Tagore devoted himself to social causes, to the restoration of rural village life in India, and to the school he founded in 1901, which he turned into an international university in 1921, an institution "for the study of the different cultures and religions of the world and to create that mutual sympathy, understanding and tolerance on which alone can the unity of mankind rest." His international fame made him a world traveler, and in his later years he often lectured at universities in Europe and America. He died in Calcutta in 1941.

The two stories that we have included present the divided Indian consciousness in different ways. The psychological divisions in the narrator of the tale in "The Hungry Stones"—between his daytime and nighttime selves, his rational and emotional sides—enlarge into the divisions within Indian society between the town and the country, the English governmental bureaucracy and the traditional rural culture, the present and the past. The comic plot shows the mysterious castle in the countryside scaring the city boy back to the city while the tale itself imitates in its form the framed tales of the *Arabian Nights* tradition.

The short bildungsroman, *Broken Ties*, links the self-realization of its narrator, Srivilas, with his growing awareness of his cultural identity. He and Satish, his idolized alter ego, enact the extremes in divided India in the first two parts of the novella as they convert from atheists into followers of a mystical guru. As atheists, inhabiting half of a partitioned house in Calcutta, a house suggestive of their divided country, they celebrate the Western values of empiricism, rationality, and materialism, values derived from the works of the British utilitarians: Malthus, Bentham, Mill, and Herbert Spencer. Going to the opposite extreme to become disciples of the guru Lilananda Swami, they travel about rural India chanting prayers, beating drums, and seeking ecstatic fulfillment and emotional release. But neither of these opposite ways of life is finally fulfilling. It is Damini, the rebellious follower of the swami, who teaches Srivilas how to be spiritual and physical at the same time. When they return together to Calcutta they are part of a new, independent generation that offends both pious traditionalists and liberated urbanites. But Srivilas's learning is not complete until he learns the final truth of suffering—final at least for the story—when he must deal with Damini's death. By the end of the story, the conflict between Eastern mysticism and Western empiricism has been transcended and Srivilas has managed to reconcile within himself the cultural oppositions he has lived through. Tagore borrowed the forms of the short story and the novella from the West, but the substance of his stories is profoundly Indian.

SUGGESTED READINGS

The best biography of Tagore in English is Krishna Kripalani's *Rabindranath Tagore: A Biography* (1980). Mary Lago's *Rabindranath Tagore* (1976) is a useful introduction to Tagore's life and work, and her article "Modes of Questioning in Tagore's Short Stories," *Studies in Short Fiction* 5 (Fall 1967, 24–36), discusses several of the stories in terms of a process of moral questioning, an approach that can also be used with the stories in this book.

The Hungry Stones

Translated by Panna Lal Basu

My kinsman and myself were returning to Calcutta from our Puja[1] trip when we met the man in a train. From his dress and bearing we took him at first for an up-country Mahomedan, but we were puzzled as we heard him talk. He discoursed upon all subjects so confidently that you might think the Disposer of All Things consulted him at all times in all that He did. Hitherto we had been perfectly happy, as we did not know that secret and unheard-of forces were at work, that the Russians had advanced close to us, that the English had deep and secret policies, that confusion among the native chiefs had come to a head. But our newly-acquired friend said with a sly smile: "There happen more things in heaven and earth, Horatio, than are reported in your newspapers."[2] As we had never stirred out of our homes before, the demeanour of the man struck us dumb with wonder. Be the topic ever so trivial, he would quote science, or comment on the *Vedas*,[3] or repeat quatrains from some Persian poet; and as we had no pretence to a knowledge of science or the *Vedas* or Persian, our admiration for him went on increasing, and my kinsman, a theosophist, was firmly convinced that our fellow-passenger must have been supernaturally inspired by some strange "magnetism" or "occult power," by an "astral body" or something of that kind. He listened to the tritest saying that fell from the lips of our extraordinary companion with devotional rapture, and secretly took down notes of his conversation. I fancy that the extraordinary man saw this, and was a little pleased with it.

---

[1] A Hindu religious holiday.

[2] An allusion to Hamlet's remark to Horatio, "There are more things in heaven and earth, Horatio, / Than are dreamt of in your philosophy" (*Hamlet* I, v).

[3] The primary scriptures of Hinduism.

When the train reached the junction, we assembled in the waiting-room for the connection. It was then 10 P.M., and as the train, we heard, was likely to be very late, owing to something wrong in the lines, I spread my bed on the table and was about to lie down for a comfortable doze, when the extraordinary person deliberately set about spinning the following yarn. Of course, I could get no sleep that night.

When, owing to a disagreement about some questions of administrative policy, I threw up my post at Junagarh, and entered the service of the Nizam of Hyderabad, they appointed me at once, as a strong young man, collector of cotton duties at Barich.

Barich is a lovely place. The *Susta* "chatters over stony ways and babbles on the pebbles," tripping, like a skilful dancing girl, in through the woods below the lonely hills. A flight of 150 steps rises from the river, and above that flight, on the river's brim and at the foot of the hills, there stands a solitary marble palace. Around it there is no habitation of man—the village and the cotton mart of Barich being far off.

About 250 years ago the Emperor Mahmud Shah II. had built this lonely palace for his pleasure and luxury. In his days jets of rose-water spurted from its fountains, and on the cold marble floors of its spray-cooled rooms young Persian damsels would sit, their hair dishevelled before bathing, and, splashing their soft naked feet in the clear water of the reservoirs, would sing, to the tune of the guitar, the *ghazals*[4] of their vineyards.

The fountains play no longer; the songs have ceased; no longer do snow-white feet step gracefully on the snowy marble. It is but the vast and solitary quarters of cess-collectors like us, men oppressed with solitude and deprived of the society of women. Now, Karim Khan, the old clerk of my office, warned me repeatedly not to take up my abode there. "Pass the day there, if you like," said he, "but never stay the night." I passed it off with a light laugh. The servants said that they would work till dark, and go away at night. I gave my ready assent. The house had such a bad name that even thieves would not venture near it after dark.

At first the solitude of the deserted palace weighed upon me like a nightmare. I would stay out, and work hard as long as possible, then return home at night jaded and tired, go to bed and fall asleep.

Before a week had passed, the place began to exert a weird fascination upon me. It is difficult to describe or to induce people to believe; but I felt as if the whole house was like a living organism slowly and imperceptibly digesting me by the action of some stupefying gastric juice.

Perhaps the process had begun as soon as I set my foot in the house, but I distinctly remember the day on which I first was conscious of it.

It was the beginning of summer, and the market being dull I had no work to do. A little before sunset I was sitting in an arm-chair near the water's edge below the steps. The *Susta* had shrunk and sunk low; a broad patch of sand on the other side glowed with the hues of evening; on this side the pebbles at the bottom of the clear shallow waters were glistening. There was not a breath of wind anywhere, and the still air was laden with an oppressive scent from the spicy shrubs growing on the hills close by.

As the sun sank behind the hill-tops a long dark curtain fell upon the stage of day, and the intervening hills cut short the time in which light and shade mingle at

---

[4]A popular love poem or song.

sunset. I thought of going out for a ride, and was about to get up when I heard a footfall on the steps behind. I looked back, but there was no one.

As I sat down again, thinking it to be an illusion, I heard many footfalls, as if a large number of persons were rushing down the steps. A strange thrill of delight, slightly tinged with fear, passed through my frame, and though there was not a figure before my eyes, methought I saw a bevy of joyous maidens coming down the steps to bathe in the *Susta* in that summer evening. Not a sound was in the valley, in the river, or in the palace, to break the silence, but I distinctly heard the maidens' gay and mirthful laugh, like the gurgle of a spring gushing forth in a hundred cascades, as they ran past me, in quick playful pursuit of each other, towards the river, without noticing me at all. As they were invisible to me, so I was, as it were, invisible to them. The river was perfectly calm, but I felt that its still, shallow, and clear waters were stirred suddenly by the splash of many an arm jingling with bracelets, that the girls laughed and dashed and spattered water at one another, that the feet of the fair swimmers tossed the tiny waves up in showers of pearl.

I felt a thrill at my heart—I cannot say whether the excitement was due to fear or delight or curiosity. I had a strong desire to see them more clearly, but naught was visible before me; I thought I could catch all that they said if I only strained my ears; but however hard I strained them, I heard nothing but the chirping of the cicadas in the woods. It seemed as if a dark curtain of 250 years was hanging before me, and I would fain lift a corner of it tremblingly and peer through, though the assembly on the other side was completely enveloped in darkness.

The oppressive closeness of the evening was broken by a sudden gust of wind, and the still surface of the *Susta* rippled and curled like the hair of a nymph, and from the woods wrapt in the evening gloom there came forth a simultaneous murmur, as though they were awakening from a black dream. Call it reality or dream, the momentary glimpse of that invisible mirage reflected from a far-off world, 250 years old, vanished in a flash. The mystic forms that brushed past me with their quick unbodied steps, and loud, voiceless laughter, and threw themselves into the river, did not go back wringing their dripping robes as they went. Like fragrance wafted away by the wind they were dispersed by a single breath of the spring.

Then I was filled with a lively fear that it was the Muse that had taken advantage of my solitude and possessed me—the witch had evidently come to ruin a poor devil like myself making a living by collecting cotton duties. I decided to have a good dinner—it is the empty stomach that all sorts of incurable diseases find an easy prey. I sent for my cook and gave orders for a rich, sumptuous *moghlai*[5] dinner, redolent of spices and *ghi*.

Next morning the whole affair appeared a queer fantasy. With a light heart I put on a *sola*[6] hat like the *sahebs*,[7] and drove out to my work. I was to have written my quarterly report that day, and expected to return late; but before it was dark I was strangely drawn to my house—by what I could not say—I felt they were all waiting, and that I should delay no longer. Leaving my report unfinished I rose, put on my *sola* hat, and startling the dark, shady, desolate path with the rattle of my carriage, I reached the vast silent palace standing on the gloomy skirts of the hills.

On the first floor the stairs led to a very spacious hall, its roof stretching wide over ornamental arches resting on three rows of massive pillars, and groaning day and night under the weight of its own intense solitude. The day had just closed,

---

[5] Spicy food; ghi is butter.
[6] Pith helmet.
[7] A term meaning "sir," often applied derisively to the British.

and the lamps had not yet been lighted. As I pushed the door open a great bustle seemed to follow within, as if a throng of people had broken up in confusion, and rushed out through the doors and windows and corridors and verandas and rooms, to make its hurried escape.

As I saw no one I stood bewildered, my hair on end in a kind of ecstatic delight, and a faint scent of *attar*[8] and unguents almost effaced by age lingered in my nostrils. Standing in the darkness of that vast desolate hall between the rows of those ancient pillars, I could hear the gurgle of fountains plashing on the marble floor, a strange tune on the guitar, the jingle of ornaments and the tinkle of anklets, the clang of bells tolling the hours, the distant note of *nahabat*,[9] the din of the crystal pendants of chandeliers shaken by the breeze, the song of *bulbuls*[10] from the cages in the corridors, the cackle of storks in the gardens, all creating round me a strange unearthly music.

Then I came under such a spell that this intangible, inaccessible, unearthly vision appeared to be the only reality in the world—and all else a mere dream. That I, that is to say, Srijut So-and-so, the eldest son of So-and-so of blessed memory, should be drawing a monthly salary of Rs. 450 by the discharge of my duties as collector of cotton duties, and driving in my dog-cart to my office every day in a short coat and *sola* hat, appeared to me to be such an astonishingly ludicrous illusion that I burst into a horse-laugh, as I stood in the gloom of that vast silent hall.

At that moment my servant entered with a lighted kerosene lamp in his hand. I do not know whether he thought me mad, but it came back to me at once that I was in very deed Srijut So-and-so, son of So-and-so of blessed memory, and that, while our poets, great and small, alone could say whether inside or outside the earth there was a region where unseen fountains perpetually played and fairy guitars, struck by invisible fingers, sent forth an eternal harmony, this at any rate was certain, that I collected duties at the cotton market at Barich, and earned thereby Rs. 450 per mensem as my salary. I laughed in great glee at my curious illusion, as I sat over the newspaper at my camp-table, lighted by the kerosene lamp.

After I had finished my paper and eaten my *moghlai* dinner, I put out the lamp, and lay down on my bed in a small side-room. Through the open window a radiant star, high above the Avalli hills skirted by the darkness of their woods, was gazing intently from millions and millions of miles away in the sky at Mr. Collector lying on a humble camp-bedstead. I wondered and felt amused at the idea, and do not know when I fell asleep or how long I slept; but I suddenly awoke with a start, though I heard no sound and saw no intruder—only the steady bright star on the hilltop had set, and the dim light of the new moon was stealthily entering the room through the open window, as if ashamed of its intrusion.

I saw nobody, but felt as if some one was gently pushing me. As I awoke she said not a word, but beckoned me with her five fingers bedecked with rings to follow her cautiously. I got up noiselessly, and, though not a soul save myself was there in the countless apartments of that deserted palace with its slumbering sounds and waking echoes, I feared at every step lest any one should wake up. Most of the rooms of the palace were always kept closed, and I had never entered them.

I followed breathless and with silent steps my invisible guide—I cannot now say where. What endless dark and narrow passages, what long corridors, what silent and solemn audience-chambers and close secret cells I crossed!

Though I could not see my fair guide, her form was not invisible to my mind's eye,—an Arab girl, her arms, hard and smooth as marble, visible through

---

[8]A jasmine-scented perfume.

[9]A musical instrument.

[10]Songbirds like nightingales, often mentioned in Persian poetry.

her loose sleeves, a thin veil falling on her face from the fringe of her cap, and a curved dagger at her waist! Methought that one of the thousand and one Arabian Nights had been wafted to me from the world of romance, and that at the dead of night I was wending my way through the dark narrow alleys of slumbering Bagdad to a trysting-place fraught with peril.

At last my fair guide stopped abruptly before a deep blue screen, and seemed to point to something below. There was nothing there, but a sudden dread froze the blood in my heart—methought I saw there on the floor at the foot of the screen a terrible negro eunuch dressed in rich brocade, sitting and dozing with outstretched legs, with a naked sword on his lap. My fair guide lightly tripped over his legs and held up a fringe of the screen. I could catch a glimpse of a part of the room spread with a Persian carpet—some one was sitting inside on a bed—I could not see her, but only caught a glimpse of two exquisite feet in gold-embroidered slippers, hanging out from loose saffron-coloured *paijamas* and placed idly on the orange-coloured velvet carpet. On one side there was a bluish crystal tray on which a few apples, pears, oranges, and bunches of grapes in plenty, two small cups and a gold-tinted decanter were evidently awaiting the guest. A fragrant intoxicating vapour, issuing from a strange sort of incense that burned within, almost overpowered my senses.

As with trembling heart I made an attempt to step across the outstretched legs of the eunuch, he woke up suddenly with a start, and the sword fell from his lap with a sharp clang on the marble floor.

A terrific scream made me jump, and I saw I was sitting on that camp-bedstead of mine sweating heavily; and the crescent moon looked pale in the morning light like a weary sleepless patient at dawn; and our crazy Meher Ali was crying out, as is his daily custom, "Stand back! Stand back!!" while he went along the lonely road.

Such was the abrupt close of one of my Arabian Nights; but there were yet a thousand nights left.

Then followed a great discord between my days and nights. During the day I would go to my work worn and tired, cursing the bewitching night and her empty dreams, but as night came my daily life with its bonds and shackles of work would appear a petty, false, ludicrous vanity.

After nightfall I was caught and overwhelmed in the snare of a strange intoxication. I would then be transformed into some unknown personage of a bygone age, playing my part in unwritten history; and my short English coat and tight breeches did not suit me in the least. With a red velvet cap on my head, loose *paijamas,* an embroidered vest, a long flowing silk gown, and coloured handkerchiefs scented with *attar,* I would complete my elaborate toilet, sit on a high-cushioned chair, and replace my cigarette with a many-coiled *narghileh*[11] filled with rose-water, as if in eager expectation of a strange meeting with the beloved one.

I have no power to describe the marvellous incidents that unfolded themselves, as the gloom of the night deepened. I felt as if in the curious apartments of that vast edifice the fragments of a beautiful story, which I could follow for some distance, but of which I could never see the end, flew about in a sudden gust of the vernal breeze. And all the same I would wander from room to room in pursuit of them the whole night long.

Amid the eddy of these dream-fragments, amid the smell of *henna* and the twanging of the guitar, amid the waves of air charged with fragrant spray, I would catch like a flash of lightning the momentary glimpse of a fair damsel. She it was who had saffron-coloured *paijamas,* white ruddy soft feet in gold-embroidered

---

[11] A water pipe.

slippers with curved toes, a close-fitting bodice wrought with gold, a red cap, from which a golden frill fell on her snowy brow and cheeks.

She had maddened me. In pursuit of her I wandered from room to room, from path to path among the bewildering maze of alleys in the enchanted dreamland of the nether world of sleep.

Sometimes in the evening, while arraying myself carefully as a prince of the blood-royal before a large mirror, with a candle burning on either side, I would see a sudden reflection of the Persian beauty by the side of my own. A swift turn of her neck, a quick eager glance of intense passion and pain glowing in her large dark eyes, just a suspicion of speech on her dainty red lips, her figure, fair and slim, crowned with youth like a blossoming creeper, quickly uplifted in her graceful tilting gait, a dazzling flash of pain and craving and ecstasy, a smile and a glance and a blaze of jewels and silk, and she melted away. A wild gust of wind, laden with all the fragrance of hills and woods, would put out my light, and I would fling aside my dress and lie down on my bed, my eyes closed and my body thrilling with delight, and there around me in the breeze, amid all the perfume of the woods and hills, floated through the silent gloom many a caress and many a kiss and many a tender touch of hands, and gentle murmurs in my ears, and fragrant breaths on my brow; or a sweetly-perfumed kerchief was wafted again and again on my cheeks. Then slowly a mysterious serpent would twist her stupefying coils about me; and heaving a heavy sigh, I would lapse into insensibility, and then into a profound slumber.

One evening I decided to go out on my horse—I do not know who implored me to stay—but I would listen to no entreaties that day. My English hat and coat were resting on a rack, and I was about to take them down when a sudden whirlwind, crested with the sands of the *Susta* and the dead leaves of the Avalli hills, caught them up, and whirled them round and round, while a loud peal of merry laughter rose higher and higher, striking all the chords of mirth till it died away in the land of sunset.

I could not go out for my ride, and the next day I gave up my queer English coat and hat for good.

That day again at dead of night I heard the stifled heart-breaking sobs of some one—as if below the bed, below the floor, below the stony foundation of that gigantic palace, from the depths of a dark damp grave, a voice piteously cried and implored me: "Oh, rescue me! Break through these doors of hard illusion, deathlike slumber and fruitless dreams, place me by your side on the saddle, press me to your heart, and, riding through hills and woods and across the river, take me to the warm radiance of your sunny rooms above!"

Who am I? Oh, how can I rescue thee? What drowning beauty, what incarnate passion shall I drag to the shore from this wild eddy of dreams? O lovely ethereal apparition! Where didst thou flourish and when? By what cool spring, under the shade of what date-groves, wast thou born—in the lap of what homeless wanderer in the desert? What Bedouin snatched thee from thy mother's arms, an opening bud plucked from a wild creeper, placed thee on a horse swift as lightning, crossed the burning sands, and took thee to the slave-market of what royal city? And there, what officer of the Badshah,[12] seeing the glory of thy bashful blossoming youth, paid for thee in gold, placed thee in a golden palanquin, and offered thee as a present for the seraglio of his master? And O, the history of that place! The music of the *sareng*,[13] the jingle of anklets, the occasional flash of daggers and the glowing

---

[12]The emperor.
[13]A sort of violin.

wine of Shiraz poison, and the piercing flashing glance! What infinite grandeur, what endless servitude! The slave-girls to thy right and left waved the *chamar*,[14] as diamonds flashed from their bracelets; the Badshah, the king of kings, fell on his knees at thy snowy feet in bejewelled shoes, and outside the terrible Abyssinian eunuch, looking like a messenger of death, but clothed like an angel, stood with a naked sword in his hand! Then, O, thou flower of the desert, swept away by the blood-stained dazzling ocean of grandeur, with its foam of jealousy, its rocks and shoals of intrigue, on what shore of cruel death wast thou cast, or in what other land more splendid and more cruel?

Suddenly at this moment that crazy Meher Ali screamed out: "Stand back! Stand back!! All is false! All is false!!" I opened my eyes and saw that it was already light. My *chaprasi*[15] came and handed me my letters, and the cook waited with a *salam*[16] for my orders.

I said: "No, I can stay here no longer." That very day I packed up, and moved to my office. Old Karim Khan smiled a little as he saw me. I felt nettled, but said nothing, and fell to my work.

As evening approached I grew absent-minded; I felt as if I had an appointment to keep; and the work of examining the cotton accounts seemed wholly useless; even the *Nizamat*[17] of the Nizam did not appear to be of much worth. Whatever belonged to the present, whatever was moving and acting and working for bread seemed trivial, meaningless, and contemptible.

I threw my pen down, closed my ledgers, got into my dog-cart, and drove away. I noticed that it stopped of itself at the gate of the marble palace just at the hour of twilight. With quick steps I climbed the stairs, and entered the room.

A heavy silence was reigning within. The dark rooms were looking sullen as if they had taken offence. My heart was full of contrition, but there was no one to whom I could lay it bare, or of whom I could ask forgiveness. I wandered about the dark rooms with a vacant mind. I wished I had a guitar to which I could sing to the unknown: "O fire, the poor moth that made a vain effort to fly away has come back to thee! Forgive it but this once, burn its wings and consume it in thy flame!"

Suddenly two tear-drops fell from overhead on my brow. Dark masses of clouds overcast the top of the Avalli hills that day. The gloomy woods and the sooty waters of the *Susta* were waiting in terrible suspense and in an ominous calm. Suddenly land, water, and sky shivered, and a wild tempest-blast rushed howling through the distant pathless woods, showing its lightning-teeth like a raving maniac who had broken his chains. The desolate halls of the palace banged their doors, and moaned in the bitterness of anguish.

The servants were all in the office, and there was no one to light the lamps. The night was cloudy and moonless. In the dense gloom within I could distinctly feel that a woman was lying on her face on the carpet below the bed—clasping and tearing her long dishevelled hair with desperate fingers. Blood was trickling down her fair brow, and she was now laughing a hard, harsh, mirthless laugh, now bursting into violent wringing sobs, now rending her bodice and striking at her bare bosom, as the wind roared in through the open window, and the rain poured in torrents and soaked her through and through.

All night there was no cessation of the storm or of the passionate cry. I wandered from room to room in the dark, with unavailing sorrow. Whom could I console

---

[14] Fly whisks.

[15] Clerk.

[16] A Muslim greeting, accompanied by bowing the head and touching the brow with the right hand.

[17] Royalty.

when no one was by? Whose was this intense agony of sorrow? Whence arose this inconsolable grief?

And the mad man cried out: "Stand back! Stand back!! All is false! All is false!!"

I saw that the day had dawned, and Meher Ali was going round and round the palace with his usual cry in that dreadful weather. Suddenly it came to me that perhaps he also had once lived in that house, and that, though he had gone mad, he came there every day, and went round and round, fascinated by the weird spell cast by the marble demon.

Despite the storm and rain I ran to him and asked: "Ho, Meher Ali, what is false?"

The man answered nothing, but pushing me aside went round and round with his frantic cry, like a bird flying fascinated about the jaws of a snake, and made a desperate effort to warn himself by repeating: "Stand back! Stand back!! All is false! All is false!!"

I ran like a mad man through the pelting rain to my office, and asked Karim Khan: "Tell me the meaning of all this!"

What I gathered from that old man was this: That at one time countless unrequited passions and unsatisfied longings and lurid flames of wild blazing pleasure raged within that palace, and that the curse of all the heart-aches and blasted hopes had made its every stone thirsty and hungry, eager to swallow up like a famished ogress any living man who might chance to approach. Not one of those who lived there for three consecutive nights could escape these cruel jaws, save Meher Ali, who had escaped at the cost of his reason.

I asked: "Is there no means whatever of my release?" The old man said: "There is only one means, and that is very difficult. I will tell you what it is, but first you must hear the history of a young Persian girl who once lived in that pleasure-dome. A stranger or a more bitterly heart-rending tragedy was never enacted on this earth."

Just at this moment the coolies announced that the train was coming. So soon? We hurriedly packed up our luggage, as the train steamed in. An English gentleman, apparently just aroused from slumber, was looking out of a first-class carriage endeavouring to read the name of the station. As soon as he caught sight of our fellow-passenger, he cried, "Hallo," and took him into his own compartment. As we got into a second-class carriage, we had no chance of finding out who the man was nor what was the end of his story.

I said: "The man evidently took us for fools and imposed upon us out of fun. The story is pure fabrication from start to finish." The discussion that followed ended in a lifelong rupture between my theosophist kinsman and myself.

Broken Ties

Translated by Panna Lal Basu

CHAPTER I
UNCLE

1

When I first met Satish he appeared to me like a constellation of stars, his eyes shining, his tapering fingers like flames of fire, his face glowing with a youthful radiance. I was surprised to find that most of his fellow-students hated him, for no other fault than that he resembled himself more than he resembled others. Because with men, as well as with some insects, taking the colour of the surroundings is often the best means of self-protection.

The students in the hostel where I lived could easily guess my reverence for Satish. This caused them discomfort, and they never missed an opportunity of reviling him in my hearing. If you have a speck of grit in your eye it is best not to rub it. And when words smart it is best to leave them unanswered.

But one day the calumny against Satish was so gross that I could not remain silent.

Yet the trouble was that I hardly knew anything about Satish. We never had even a word between us, while some of the other students were his close neighbours, and some his distant relatives. These affirmed, with assurance, that what they said was true; and I affirmed, with even greater assurance, that it was incredible. Then all the residents of the hostel bared their arms, and cried: 'What impertinence!'

That night I was vexed to tears. Next day, in an interval between lectures, when Satish was reading a book lying at full length on the grass in College Square, I went up to him without any introduction, and spoke to him in a confused manner, scarcely knowing what I said. Satish shut his book, and looked in my face. Those who have not seen his eyes will not know what that look was like.

Satish said to me: 'Those who libel me do so, not because they love to know the truth, but because they love to believe evil of me. Therefore it is useless to try to prove to them that the calumny is untrue.'

'But,' I said, 'the liars must be——'

'They are not liars,' interrupted Satish.

'I have a neighbour,' he went on, 'who has epileptic fits. Last winter I gave him a blanket. My servant came to me in a furious temper, and told me that the boy only feigned the disease. These students who malign me are like that servant of mine. They believe what they say. Possibly my fate has awarded me an extra blanket which they think would have suited them better.'

I asked him a question: 'Is it true what they say, that you are an atheist?'

He said: 'Yes.'

I bent my head to the ground. I had been arguing with my fellow-students that Satish could not possibly be an atheist.

I had received two severe blows at the outset of my short acquaintance with Satish. I had imagined that he was a Brahman, but I had come to know that Satish belonged to a Bania[1] family, and I in whose veins flowed a bluer blood was bound duly to despise all Banias. Secondly, I had a rooted belief that atheists were worse than murderers, nay, worse even than beef-eaters.

Nobody could have imagined, even in a dream, that I would ever sit down and take my meals with a Bania student, or that my fanatical zeal in the creed of atheism would surpass even that of my instructor. Yet both these things came to pass.

Wilkins was our professor in the College. His learning was on a level with his contempt for his pupils. He felt that it was a menial occupation to teach literature to Bengali students. Therefore, in our Shakespeare class, he would give us the synonym for 'cat' as 'a quadruped of the feline species.' But Satish was excused from taking notes. The Professor told him: 'I will make good to you the hours wasted in this class when you come to my room.'

The other less favoured students used to ascribe this indulgent treatment of Satish to his fair complexion and to his profession of atheism. Some of the more worldly-wise among them went to Wilkins's study with a great show of enthusiasm

---

[1] The Hindu caste of tradesmen.

to borrow from him some book on Positivism. But he refused, saying that it would be too hard for them. That they should be held unfit even to cultivate atheism made their minds all the more bitter against Satish.

2

Jagamohan was Satish's uncle. He was a notorious atheist of that time. It would be inadequate to say that he did not believe in God. One ought rather to say that he vehemently believed in no God. As the business of a captain in the navy is rather to sink ships than to steer, so it was Jagamohan's business to sink the creed of theism, wherever it put its head above the water.

The order of his arguments ran like this:

(1) If there be a God, then we must owe our intelligence to Him.

(2) But our intelligence clearly tells us that there is no God.

(3) Therefore God Himself tells us that there is no God.

'Yet you Hindus,' he would continue, 'have the effrontery to say that God exists. For this sin thirty-three million gods and goddesses exact penalties from you people, pulling your ears hard for your disobedience.'

Jagamohan was married when he was a mere boy. Before his wife died he had read Malthus.[2] He never married again.

His younger brother, Harimohan, was the father of Satish. Harimohan's nature was so exactly the opposite of his elder brother's that people might suspect me of fabricating it for the purpose of writing a story. But only stories have to be always on their guard to sustain their reader's confidence. Facts have no such responsibility, and laugh at our incredulity. So, in this world, there are abundant instances of two brothers, the exact opposites of one another, like morning and evening.

Harimohan, in his infancy, had been a weakly child. His parents had tried to keep him safe from the attacks of all maladies by barricading him behind amulets and charms, dust taken from holy shrines, and blessings bought from innumerable Brahmans at enormous expense. When Harimohan grew up, he was physically quite robust, yet the tradition of his poor health lingered on in the family. So nobody claimed from him anything more arduous than that he should continue to live. He fulfilled his part, and did hold on to his life. Yet he never allowed his family to forget for a moment that life in his case was more fragile than in most other mortals. Thus he managed to divert towards himself the undivided attention of all his aunts and his mother, and had specially prepared meals served to him. He had less work and more rest than other members of the family. He was never allowed to forget that he was under the special protection, not only of his aforesaid mother and aunts, but also of the countless gods and goddesses presiding in the three regions of earth, heaven, and air. He thus acquired an attitude of prayerful dependence towards all the powers of the world, both seen and unseen,—sub-inspectors, wealthy neighbours, highly placed officials, let alone sacred cows and Brahmans.

Jagamohan's anxieties went altogether in an opposite direction. He would give a wide berth to men of power, lest the slightest suspicion of snobbishness should cling to him. It was this same sentiment which had greatly to do with his defiance of the gods. His knees were too stiff to bend before those from whom favour could be expected.

Harimohan got himself married at the proper time, that is to say, long before the time. After three sisters and three brothers, Satish was born. Everybody was struck

---

[2]Thomas Malthus (1766–1834), English economist whose *Essay on Population* (1798) argued that population growth would inevitably outpace the growth of the food supply.

by his resemblance to his uncle, and Jagamohan took possession of him, as if he were his own son.

At first Harimohan was glad of this, having regard to the educational advantage of the arrangement; for Jagamohan had the reputation of being the most eminent scholar of that period.

He seemed to live within the shell of his English books. It was easy to find the rooms he occupied in the house by the rows of books about the walls, just as it is easy to find out the bed of a stream by its lines of pebbles.

Harimohan petted and spoilt his eldest son, Purandar, to his heart's content. He had an impression that Purandar was too delicate to survive the shock of being denied anything he wanted. His education was neglected. No time was lost in getting him married, and yet nobody could keep him within the connubial limits. If Harimohan's daughter-in-law expressed any disapprobation of his vagaries in that direction, Harimohan would get angry with her and ascribe his son's conduct to her want of tact and charm.

Jagamohan entirely took charge of Satish to save him from similar paternal solicitude. Satish acquired a mastery of the English language while he was still a child, and the inflammatory doctrines of Mill and Bentham[3] set his brain on fire, till he began to burn like a living torch of atheism.

Jagamohan treated Satish, not as his junior, but as his boon companion. He held the opinion that veneration in human nature was a superstition, specially designed to make men into slaves. Some son-in-law of the family wrote to him a letter, with the usual formal beginning:

'To the gracious feet of——'

Jagamohan wrote an answer, arguing with him as follows:

MY DEAR NOREN—Neither you nor I know what special significance it gives to the feet to call them 'gracious.' Therefore the epithet is worse than useless, and had better be dropped. And then it is apt to give one a nervous shock when you address your letter only to the feet, completely ignoring their owner. But you should understand, that so long as my feet are attached to my body, you should never dissociate them from their context.

Next, you should bear in mind that human feet have not the advantage of prehensibility, and it is sheer madness to offer anything to them, confounding their natural function.

Lastly, your use of the plural inflection to the word 'feet,' instead of the dual, may denote special reverence on your part (because there are animals with four feet which have your particular veneration) but I consider it my duty to disabuse your mind of all errors concerning my own zoological identity.—Yours,   JAGAMOHAN.

Jagamohan used to discuss with Satish subjects which are usually kept out of sight in conversation. If people objected to this plainness of speech with one so young, he would say that you can only drive away hornets by breaking in their nest. So you can only drive away the shamefulness of certain subjects by piercing through the shame itself.

When Satish had completed his College course, Harimohan tried his best to extricate him from his uncle's sphere of influence. But when once the noose is fixed round the neck, it only grows tighter by pulling at it. Harimohan became more and more annoyed at his brother, the more Satish proved recalcitrant. If this

---

[3]James Mill (1773–1836) and Jeremy Bentham (1748–1832), English utilitarian philosophers, economic theorists, and political scientists. The utilitarians argued that the purpose of government was to create the greatest happiness for the greatest number.

atheism of his son and elder brother had been merely a matter of private opinion, Harimohan could have tolerated it. He was quite ready to pass off dishes of fowl as 'kid curry.'[4] But matters had now become so desperate that even lies became powerless to whitewash the culprits. What brought things to a head was this:

The positive side of Jagamohan's atheistic creed consisted in doing good to others. He felt a special pride in it, because doing good, for an atheist, was a matter of unmitigated loss. It had no allurements of merit and no deterrents of punishment in the hereafter. If he was asked what concern he had in bringing about 'the greatest happiness of the greatest number,' he used to answer that his best incentive was that he could expect nothing in return. He would say to Satish:

'Baba,[5] we are atheists. And therefore the very pride of it should keep us absolutely stainless. Because we have no respect for any being higher than ourselves, therefore we must respect ourselves.'

There were some leather shops in the neighbourhood kept by Muhammadans. The uncle and nephew bestirred themselves with great zeal in doing good to these Muhammadans and their untouchable leather workers.[6] This made Harimohan beside himself with indignation. Since he knew that any appeal to Scriptures, or to tradition, would have no effect upon these two renegades, he complained to his brother concerning the wasting of his patrimony.

'When my expenditure,' his brother answered, 'comes up to the amount you have spent upon your full-fed Brahman priests, we shall be quits.'

One day Harimohan's people were surprised to find that a preparation was going on in Jagamohan's quarters for a grand feast. The cooks and waiters were all Mussulmans. Harimohan called for his son, and said to him angrily:

'I hear that you are going to give a feast to all your reverend friends, the leather workers.'

Satish replied that he was far too poor to think of it. His uncle had invited them.

Purandar, Satish's elder brother, was equally indignant. He threatened to drive all the unclean guests away. When Harimohan expressed his protest to his brother, he answered:

'I never make any objection to your offering food to your idols. You should make no objection to my offering food to my gods.'

'Your gods!' exclaimed Harimohan.

'Yes, my gods,' his brother answered.

'Have you become a theist all of a sudden?' sneered Harimohan.

'No!' his brother replied. 'Theists worship the God who is invisible. You idolaters worship gods who are visible, but dumb and deaf. The gods I worship are both visible and audible, and it is impossible not to believe in them.'

'Do you really mean to say,' cried Harimohan, 'that these leather workers and Mussulmans are your gods?'

'Indeed, they are,' said Jagamohan; 'you shall see their miraculous power when I put food before them. They will actually swallow it, which I defy your gods to do. It delights my heart to see my gods perform such divine wonders. If you are not morally blind, it will delight your heart also.'

Purandar came to his uncle, and told him in a high-pitched voice that he was prepared to take desperate measures to stop the proceedings. Jagamohan laughed at him, and said:

---

[4] In Bengal kid curry is often eaten without blame. But fowl curry would come within the prohibitions. [Translator's note]

[5] A term of endearment, literally "father." [Translator's note]

[6] As leather is made from the hides of dead animals, those who work in leather are regarded as unclean by orthodox Hindus. Only the very lowest castes are tanners. [Translator's note]

'You monkey! If you ever try to lay hands on my gods, you will instantly discover how powerful they are, and I shall not have to do anything to defend them.'

Purandar was even a greater coward than his father. He was a tyrant only where he was sure of receiving submission. In this case he did not dare to pick a quarrel with his Muhammadan neighbours. So he came to Satish, and reviled him. Satish gazed at him with those wonderful eyes of his, and remained silent.

The feast was a great success.

3

Harimohan could not take this insult passively. He declared war. The property on whose income the whole family subsisted was a temple endowment. Harimohan brought a suit in the law court against his brother, accusing him of such grave breaches of propriety as made him unworthy of remaining the trustee of a religious endowment. Harimohan had as many witnesses as ever he wished. The whole Hindu neighbourhood was ready to support him.

Jagamohan professed in open court that he had no faith in gods or idols of any description whatever; that all eatable food was for him food to be eaten; that he never bothered his head to find out the particular limb of Brahma from which the Muhammadans had issued, and therefore he had not the smallest hesitation in taking food in their company.

The judge ruled Jagamohan to be unfit to hold the temple property. Jagamohan's lawyers assured him that the decision could be upset by an appeal to the higher Court. But Jagamohan refused to appeal. He said he could not cheat even the gods whom he did not believe in. Only those who had the intelligence to believe such things had the conscience to cheat them.

His friends asked him: 'How are you going to maintain yourself?'

He answered: 'If I have nothing else to eat, I shall be content to gulp down my last breath.'

After this, a partition was made of the family house. A wall was raised from the ground floor to the upper storey, dividing the house into two parts.

Harimohan had great faith in the selfish sanity of prudence in human nature. He was certain that the savour of good living would tempt Satish into his golden trap, away from the empty nest of Jagamohan. But Satish gave another proof that he had neither inherited his father's conscience nor his sanity. He remained with his uncle.

Jagamohan was so accustomed to look upon Satish as his own that he was not surprised to find him remaining on his side after the partition.

But Harimohan knew his brother's temperament very well. He went about talking to people, explaining that the reason why Jagamohan did not let go his hold on Satish was that he expected to make a good thing out of Satish's presence, keeping him as a kind of hostage.

Harimohan almost shed tears while he said to his neighbour: 'Could my brother ever imagine that I was going to starve him? Since he is cunning enough to concoct this diabolical plot against me, I shall wait and see whether he is cleverer than I am.'

Harimohan's talk about Satish reached Jagamohan's ears. Jagamohan was surprised at his own stupidity in not anticipating such a turn of events.

He said: 'Good-bye, Satish.'

Satish was absolutely certain that nothing could make Jagamohan change his mind, so he had to take his leave, after having spent his eighteen years of life in his uncle's company.

When Satish had put his books and bedding on the top of the carriage, and driven away, Jagamohan shut the door of his room, and flung himself on the floor. When evening came, and the old servant knocked at the door with the lighted lamp, he got no answer.

Alas for the greatest happiness of the greatest number! The estimate in number is not the only measure of human affairs. The man who counts 'one' may go beyond all arithmetic when the heart does the sum. When Satish took his departure, he at once became infinite to Jagamohan.

Satish went into a students' lodging to share a room with one of his friends. Harimohan shed tears while meditating on the neglect of filial duties in this god-forsaken age. Harimohan had a very tender heart.

After the partition, Purandar dedicated a room in their portion of the house to the family god. It gave him a peculiar pleasure to know that his uncle must be execrating him for the noise raised every morning and every evening by the sacred conches and prayer gongs.

In order to maintain himself, Satish secured a post as a private tutor. Jagamohan obtained an appointment as head master of a high school. And it became a religious duty with Harimohan and Purandar to persuade parents and guardians to take away their boys from the malign influence of the atheist Jagamohan.

4

One day, after a very long interval of absence, Satish came to Jagamohan. These two had given up the usual form of greeting[7] which passes between elder and younger.

Jagamohan embraced Satish, led him to a chair, and asked him for the news.

There was news indeed!

A girl named Nonibala had taken shelter with her widowed mother in the house of the mother's brother. So long as her mother lived, there was no trouble. But a short time ago her mother had died. Her cousins were rascals. One of their friends had taken away this girl. Then, suspecting her of infidelity, after a while he made her life a constant torture. This had happened in the house next to the one where Satish had his tutorship. Satish wanted to save her from this misery, but he had no money or shelter of his own. Therefore he had come to his uncle. The girl was about to give birth to a child.

Jagamohan, when he heard the story, was filled with indignation. He was not the man to calculate coldly the consequence of his deeds, and he at once said to his nephew: 'I have the room in which I keep my books. I can put the girl there.'

'But what about your books?' Satish asked in surprise. Very few books, however, were now remaining. During the time when he had been unable to secure an appointment, he had been obliged to eke out a living by selling his books.

Jagamohan said: 'Bring the girl at once.'

'She is waiting downstairs,' said Satish. 'I have brought her here.' Jagamohan ran downstairs, and found the girl crouching in the corner, wrapped in her *sari,* looking like a bundle of clothes.

Jagamohan, in his deep bass voice, said at once: 'Come, little Mother, why do you sit in the dust?'

The girl covered her face, and burst into tears. Jagamohan was not a man to give way to emotion, but his eyes were wet as he turned to Satish and said: 'The burden that this girl is bearing is ours.'

Then he said to the girl: 'Mother, don't be shy on my account. My schoolfellows used to call me "Mad Jagai," and I am the same madcap even now.'

---

[7]This greeting in Bengal is for the younger to touch the feet of the elder. [Translator's note]

Then, without hesitation, he took the girl by both her hands, and raised her. The veil dropped from off her face.

The girl's face was fresh and young, and there was no line of hardness or vice in it. The inner purity of her heart had not been stained, just as a speck of dust does not soil a flower. Jagamohan took Nonibala to his upper room, and said to her: 'Mother, look what a state my room is in! The floor is all unswept. Everything is upside down; and as for myself, I have no fixed hour for my bath or my meals. Now that you have come to my house, everything will be put right, and even this mad Jagai will be made respectable.'

Nonibala had never felt before, even when her mother lived, how much one person could be to another; because her mother had looked upon her, not so much as a daughter, but as a young girl who had to be watched.

Jagamohan employed an elderly woman servant to help Nonibala. At first Noni was afraid lest Jagamohan should refuse to take food from her hand because of her impurity. But it turned out that Jagamohan refused to take his meals unless they were cooked and served by Noni.

Jagamohan was aware that a great wave of calumny was about to break over his head. Noni also felt that it was inevitable, and she had no peace of mind. Within a day or two it began.

The servant who waited on her had at first supposed that Noni was Jagamohan's daughter. But she came one day, saying hard things to Noni, and resigned her service in contempt. Noni became pale with fear, thinking of Jagamohan.

Jagamohan said to her: 'My little Mother, the full moon is up in the horizon of my life, so the time is ripe for the flood-tide of revilement. But, however muddy the water may become, it will never stain my moonlight.'

An aunt of Jagamohan's came to Harimohan's quarters, and said to him: 'Jagai, what a disgrace, what a disgrace! Wipe off this stain of sin from your house.'

Jagamohan answered: 'You are pious people, and this advice is worthy of you. But if I try to drive away all relics of sin, what will become of the sinner?'

Some old grandmother of a woman came to him, and said: 'Send this wench away to the hospital. Harimohan is ready to bear all the cost.'

Jagamohan said: 'But she is my mother. Because some one is ready to pay expenses, should I send my mother to the hospital?'

The grandmother opened her eyes wide with surprise and said: 'Who is this you call your mother?'

Jagamohan replied: 'She who nourished life within her womb, and risks her life to give birth to children. I cannot call that scoundrel-father of the child "Father." He can only cause trouble, keeping himself safely out of it.'

Harimohan's whole body shrank with the utter infamy of the thing. That a fallen woman should be sheltered only on the other side of the wall, and in the midst of a household sacred to the memory of generations of mothers and grandmothers! The disgrace was intolerable.

Harimohan at once surmised that Satish was mixed up in this affair, and that his uncle was encouraging him in his shameful conduct. He was so sure of his facts that he went about spreading the news. Jagamohan did not say a single word to contradict him.

'For us atheists,' he said, 'the only heaven waiting for good deeds is calumny.'

The more the rumour of Jagamohan's doings became distorted, the more he seemed to enjoy it, and his laughter rang loud in the sky. Harimohan and respectable people of his class could never imagine that the uncle could go so far as to jest openly on such a subject, and indulge in loud unseemly buffoonery about it with his own nephew.

Though Purandar had been carefully avoiding that part of the house where his uncle lived, he vowed that he would never rest till he had driven the girl away from her shelter.

At the time when Jagamohan had to go to his school he would shut up all access to his quarters, and he would come back the moment he had any leisure to see how Noni was faring.

One day at noon Purandar, with the help of a bamboo ladder, crossed the boundary wall and jumped down into Jagamohan's part of the house. Nonibala had been resting after the morning meal. The door of her room was open. Purandar, when he saw the sleeping figure of Noni, gave a great start, and shouted out in anger: 'So *you* are here, are you?'

Noni woke up and saw Purandar before her. She became pale as death, and her limbs shrank under her. She felt powerless to run away or to utter a single word.

Purandar, trembling with rage, shouted out: 'Noni!'

Just then Jagamohan entered the room from behind, and cried: 'Get out of this room.'

Purandar's whole body began to swell up like an angry cat.

Jagamohan said: 'If you don't get out at once, I will call in the police.'

Purandar darted a terrible glance at Noni, and went out. Noni fainted.

Jagamohan now understood the whole situation. By questioning, he found out that Satish had been aware that Purandar had seduced Noni; but, fearing an angry brawl, he had not informed Jagamohan of the fact.

For days after this incident Noni trembled like a bamboo leaf. Then she gave birth to a dead child.

One midnight Purandar had driven Noni away from her room, kicking her in anger. Since then he had sought her in vain. When he suddenly found her in his uncle's house, he was seized with an uncontrollable passion of jealousy. He was sure that Satish had enticed her away from him, to keep her for his own pleasure, and had then put her in the very next house to his own in order to insult him. This was more than any mortal man could bear.

Harimohan heard all about it. Indeed, Purandar never took any pains to hide these doings from his father, for his father looked upon his son's moral aberrations with a kindly indulgence. But Harimohan thought it contrary to all notions of decency for Satish to snatch away this girl whom his elder brother, Purandar, had looked upon with favour. He devoutly hoped that Purandar would be successful in recovering his spoil.

It was the time of the Christmas holidays. Jagamohan attended Noni night and day. One evening he was translating a novel of Sir Walter Scott's to her, when Purandar burst into the room with another young man.

When Jagamohan was about to call for the police, the young man said: 'I am Noni's cousin. I have come to take her away.'

Jagamohan caught hold of Purandar by his neck, and shoved him out of the room and down the stairs. He then turned to the other young man and said: 'You are a villain and a scoundrel! You assert this cousin's right of yours to wreck her life, not to protect her.'

The young man hurried away. But when he had got to a safe distance, he threatened Jagamohan with legal steps in order to rescue his ward.

Noni said within herself: 'O Earth, open and swallow me up!'[8]

---

[8]The reference is to Sita in the Ramayana, who uttered this cry when in extreme trouble. [Translator's note]

Jagamohan called Satish, and said to him: 'Let me leave this place and go to some up-country town with Noni. It will kill her if this is repeated.'

Satish urged that his brother was certain to follow her when once he had got the clue.

'Then what do you propose?' said Jagamohan.

'Let me marry Noni,' was the answer.

'Marry Noni!'

'Yes, according to the civil marriage rites.'

Jagamohan stood up and went to Satish, and pressed him to his heart.

5

Since the partition of the house, Harimohan had not once entered the house to see his elder brother. But that day he came in, dishevelled, and said:

'Dada,[9] what disaster is this you are planning?'

'I am saving everybody from disaster,' said Jagamohan.

'Satish is just like a son to you,' said Harimohan, 'and yet you can have the heart to see him married to that woman of the street!'

'Yes,' he replied, 'I have brought him up almost as my own son, and I consider that my pains have borne fruit at last.'

'Dada,' said Harimohan, 'I humbly acknowledge my defeat at your hands. I am willing to write away half my property to you, if only you will not take revenge on me like this.'

Jagamohan started up from his chair and bellowed out:

'You want to throw me your dirty leavings, as you throw a dog a bone! I am an atheist— remember that! I am not a pious man like you! I neither take revenge, nor beg for favours.'

Harimohan hastened round to Satish's lodgings. He cried out to him:

'Satish! What in the world are you going to do? Can you think of no other way of ruining yourself? Are you determined to plunge the whole family into this hideous shame?'

Satish answered: 'I have no particular desire to marry. I only do it in order to save my family from hideous shame.'

Harimohan shouted: 'Have you not got the least spark of conscience left in you? That girl, who is almost like a wife to your brother————'

Satish caught him up sharply: 'What? Like a wife. Not that word, sir, if you please!'

After that, Harimohan became wildly abusive in his language, and Satish remained silent.

What troubled Harimohan most was that Purandar openly advertised his intention to commit suicide if Satish married Noni. Purandar's wife told him that this would solve a difficult problem—if only he would have the courage to do it.

Satish sedulously avoided Noni all these days, but, when the proposed marriage was settled, Jagamohan asked Satish that Noni and he should try to know each other better before they were united in wedlock. Satish consented.

Jagamohan fixed a date for their first talk together. He said to Noni:

'My little Mother, you must dress yourself up for this occasion.'

Noni bent her eyes to the ground.

'No, no,' said he, 'don't be shy, Noni. I have a great longing to see you nicely dressed, and you must satisfy my desire.'

---

[9] Elder brother. [Translator's note]

He had specially selected some Benares silk and a bodice and veil for Noni. He gave these things to her.

Noni prostrated herself at his feet. This made Jagamohan get up hurriedly. He snatched away his feet from her embrace, and said:

'I see, Noni, I have miserably failed in clearing your mind of all this superstitious reverence. I may be your elder in age, but don't you know you are greater than I am, for you are my mother?'

He kissed her on her forehead and said:

'I have had an invitation to go out, and I shall be late back this evening.'

Noni clasped his hand and said:

'Baba, I want your blessing to-night.'

Jagamohan replied:

'Mother, I see that you are determined to turn me into a theist in my old age. I wouldn't give a brass farthing for a blessing, myself. Yet I cannot help blessing you when I see your face.'

Jagamohan put his hand under her chin, and raised her face, and looked into it silently, while tears ran down her cheeks.

6

In the evening a man ran up to the place where Jagamohan was having his dinner, and brought him back to his house.

He found the dead body of Noni, stretched on the bed, dressed in the things he had given her. In her hand was a letter. Satish was standing by her head. Jagamohan opened the letter, and read:

> Baba, forgive me. I could not do what you wanted. I tried my best, but I could never forget him. My thousand salutations to your gracious feet.   —NONIBALA, the Sinner.

CHAPTER II
SATISH

1

The last words of Jagamohan, the atheist, to his nephew, Satish, were: 'If you have a fancy for funeral ceremony, don't waste it on your uncle,—reserve it for your father.'

This is how he came by his death.

When the plague first broke out in Calcutta, the poor citizens were less afraid of the epidemic than of the preventive staff who wore its badge. Satish's father, Harimohan, was sure that their Mussulman neighbours, the untouchable leather-dealers, would be the first to catch it, and thereupon defile him and his kith and kin by dragging them along into a common end. Before he fled from his house, Harimohan went over to offer refuge to his elder brother, saying: 'I have taken a house on the river at Kalna, if you——'

'Nonsense!' interrupted Jagamohan. 'How can I desert these people?'

'Which people?'

'These leather-dealers of ours.'

Harimohan made a grimace and left his brother without further parley. He next proceeded to his son's lodgings, and to him simply said: 'Come along.'

Satish's refusal was equally laconic. 'I have work to do here,' he replied.

'As pall-bearer to the leather-dealers, I suppose?'

'Yes, sir; that is, if my services be needed.'

'Yes, sir, indeed! You scamp, you scoundrel, you atheist! If need be you're quite ready to consign fourteen generations of your ancestors to perdition, I have no doubt!'

Convinced that the Kali Yuga[10] had touched its lowest depth, Harimohan returned home, despairing of the salvation of his next of kin. In order to protect himself against contamination he covered sheets of foolscap with the name of Kali, the protecting goddess, in his neatest handwriting.

Harimohan left Calcutta. The plague and the preventive officials duly made their appearance in the locality; and for dread of being dragged off to the plague hospital, the wretched victims dared not call in medical aid. After a visit to one of these hospitals, Jagamohan shook his head and remarked: 'What if these people are falling ill,—that does not make them criminals.'

Jagamohan schemed and contrived till he obtained permission to use his own house as a private plague hospital. Some of us students offered to assist Satish in nursing: there was a qualified doctor among our number.

The first patient in our hospital was a Mussulman. He died. The next was Jagamohan himself. He did not survive either. He said to Satish: 'The religion I have all along followed has given me its last reward. There is nothing to complain of.'

Satish had never taken the dust[11] of his uncle's feet while living. After Jagamohan's death he made that obeisance for the first and last time.

'Fit death for an atheist!' scoffed Harimohan when he first came across Satish after the cremation.

'That is so, sir!' agreed Satish, proudly.

2

Just as, when the flame is blown out, the light suddenly and completely disappears, so did Satish after his uncle's death. He went out of our ken altogether.

We had never been able to fathom how deeply Satish loved his uncle. Jagamohan was alike father and friend to him,—and, it may be said, son as well; for the old man had been so regardless of himself, so unmindful of worldly concerns, that it used to be one of the chief cares of Satish to look after him and keep him safe from disaster. Thus had Satish received from and given to his uncle his all.

What the bleakness of his bereavement meant for Satish, it was impossible for us to conceive. He struggled against the agony of negation, refusing to believe that such absolute blankness could be true: that there could be emptiness so desolate as to be void even of Truth. If that which seemed one vast 'No' had not also its aspect of 'Yes,' would not the whole universe leak away through its yawning gap into nothingness?

For two years Satish wandered from place to place,—we had no contact with him. We threw ourselves with all the greater zeal into our self-appointed tasks. We made it a special point to shock those who professed belief in any kind of religion, and the fields of good work we selected were such that not a good soul had a good word left for us. Satish had been our flower; when he dropped off, we, the thorns, cast off our sheaths and gloried in our sharpness.

---

[10] According to the Hindu Shastras the present age, the Kali Yuga, is the Dark Age when Dharma (civilization) will be at its lowest ebb. [Translator's note]

[11] Touching the feet of a revered elder, and then one's own head, is called taking the dust of the feet. It is the formal way of doing reverence. [Translator's note]

3

Two years had passed since we lost sight of Satish. My mind revolted against harbouring the least thing evil against him, nevertheless I could not help suspecting that the high pitch at which he used to be kept strung must have been flattened down by this shock.

Uncle Jagamohan had once said of a *Sannyasin:*[12] 'As the money-changer tests the ring of each coin, so does the world test each man by the response he gives to shocks of loss and pain, and the resistance he offers to the craze for cheap salvation. Those who fail to ring true are cast aside as worthless. These wandering ascetics have been so rejected, as being unfit to take part in the world's commerce,—yet the vagabonds swagger about, boasting that it is they who have renounced the world! The worthy are permitted no loophole of escape from duty,—only withered leaves are allowed to fall off the tree.'

Had it come to this, that Satish, of all people, had joined the ranks of the withered and the worthless? Was he, then, fated to leave on the black touchstone of bereavement his mark of spuriousness?

While assailed with these misgivings, news suddenly reached us that Satish (our Satish, if you please!) was making the heavens resound with his cymbals in some out-of-the-way village, singing frenzied *kirtans*[13] as a follower of Lilananda Swami, the Vaishnava revivalist!

It had passed my comprehension, when I first began to know Satish, how he could ever have come to be an atheist. I was now equally at a loss to understand how Lilananda Swami could have managed to lead him in such a dance with his *kirtans.*

And how on earth were we to show our faces? What laughter there would be in the camp of the enemy,—whose number, thanks to our folly, was legion! Our band waxed mightily wroth with Satish. Many of them said they had known from the very first that there was no rational substance in him,—he was all frothy idealism. And I now discovered how much I really loved Satish. He had dealt his ardent sect of atheists their death-blow, yet I could not be angry with him.

Off I started to hunt up Lilananda Swami. River after river I crossed, and trudged over endless fields. The nights I spent in grocers' shops. At last in one of the villages I came up against Satish's party.

It was then two o'clock in the afternoon. I had been hoping to catch Satish alone. Impossible! The cottage which was honoured with the Swami's presence was packed all round with crowds of his disciples. There had been *kirtans* all the morning; those who had come from a distance were now waiting to have their meal served.

As soon as Satish caught sight of me, he dashed up and embraced me fervidly. I was staggered. Satish had always been extremely reserved. His outward calm had been the only measure of his depth of feeling. He now appeared as though intoxicated.

The Swami was resting in the front room, with the door ajar. He could see us. At once came the call, in a deep voice: 'Satish!'

Satish was back inside, all in a flurry.

'Who is that?' inquired the Swami.

---

[12] A Brahman ascetic.

[13] The *kirtan* is a kind of devotional oratorio sung to the accompaniment of drums and cymbals, the libretto ranging over the whole gamut of human emotions, which are made the vehicle for communion with the Divine Lover. As their feelings get worked up, the singers begin to sway their bodies with, and finally dance to, the rhythm. [Translator's note]

'Srivilas, a great friend of mine,' Satish reported.

During these years I had managed to make a name for myself in our little world. A learned Englishman had remarked, on hearing one of my English speeches: 'The man has a wonderful——.' But let that be. Why add to the number of my enemies? Suffice it to say that, from the students up to the students' grandparents, the reputation had travelled round that I was a rampaging atheist who could bestride the English language and race her over the hurdles at breakneck speed in the most marvellous manner.

I somehow felt that the Swami was pleased to have me here. He sent for me. I merely hinted at the usual salutation as I entered his room,—that is to say, my joined hands were uplifted, but my head was not lowered.

This did not escape the Swami. 'Here, Satish!' he ordered. 'Fill me that pipe of mine.'

Satish set to work. But as he lit the tinder, it was I who was set ablaze within. Moreover, I was getting fidgety, not knowing where to sit. The only seat in the room was a wooden bedstead on which was spread the Swami's carpet. Not that I confessed to any qualms about occupying a corner of the same carpet on which the great man was installed, but somehow my sitting down did not come off. I remained standing near the door.

It appeared that the Swami was aware of my having won the Premchand-Roychand[14] scholarship. 'My son,' he said to me, 'it is good for the pearl diver if he succeeds in reaching the bottom, but he would die if he had to stay there. He must come up for the free breath of life. If you would live, you must now come up to the light, out of the depths of your learning. You have enjoyed the fruits of your scholarship, now try a taste of the joys of its renunciation.'

Satish handed his Master the lighted pipe and sat down on the bare floor near his feet. The Swami leant back and stretched his legs out towards Satish, who began gently to massage them. This was more than I could stand. I left the room. I could, of course, see that this ordering about of Satish and making him fetch and carry was deliberately directed at me.

The Swami went on resting. All the guests were duly served by the householder with a meal of kedgeree. From five o'clock the *kirtans* started again and went on till ten in the night.

When I got Satish alone at last, I said to him: 'Look here, Satish! You have been brought up in the atmosphere of freedom from infancy. How have you managed to get yourself entangled in this kind of bondage today? Is Uncle Jagamohan, then, so utterly dead?'

Partly because the playfulness of affection prompted it, partly, perhaps, because precision of description required it, Satish used to reverse the first two syllables of my name and call me Visri.[15]

'Visri,' he replied, 'while Uncle was alive he gave me freedom in life's field of work,—the freedom which the child gets in the playground. After his death it is he, again, who has given me freedom on the high seas of emotion,—the freedom which the child gains when it comes back to its mother's arms. I have enjoyed to the full the freedom of life's day-time; why should I now deprive myself of the freedom of its evening? Be sure that both these are the gift of that same uncle of ours.'

'Whatever you may say,' I persisted, 'Uncle could have nothing to do with this kind of pipe-filling, leg-massaging business. Surely this is no picture of freedom.'

---

[14]The highest prize at the Calcutta University. [Translator's note]
[15]Ungainly, ugly. [Translator's note]

'That,' argued Satish, 'was the freedom on shore. There Uncle gave full liberty of action to our limbs. This is freedom on the ocean. Here the confinement of the ship is necessary for our progress. That is why my Master keeps me bound to his service. This massaging is helping me to cross over.'

'It does not sound so bad,' I admitted, 'the way you put it. But, all the same, I have no patience with a man who can thrust out his legs at you like that.'

'He can do it,' explained Satish, 'because he has no need of such service. Had it been for himself, he might have felt ashamed to ask it. The need is mine.'

I realised that the world into which Satish had been transported had no place for me, his particular friend. The person, whom Satish has so effusively embraced, was not Srivilas, but a representative of all humanity,—just an idea. Such ideas are like wine. When they get into the head any one can be embraced and wept over—I, only as much as anybody else. But whatever joys may be the portion of the ecstatic one, what can such embrace signify to me, the other party? What satisfaction am I to get, merely to be accounted one of the ripples on a grand, difference-obliterating flood,—I, the individual I?

However, further argument was clearly useless. Nor could I make up my mind to desert Satish. So, as his satellite, I also danced from village to village, carried along the current of *kirtan* singing.

The intoxication of it gradually took hold of me. I also embraced all and sundry, wept without provocation, and tended the feet of the Master. And one day, in a moment of curious exaltation, Satish was revealed to me in a light for which there can be no other name than divine.

4

With the capture of two such egregious, college-educated atheists as we were, the fame of Lilananda Swami spread far and wide. His Calcutta disciples now pressed him to take up his headquarters at the metropolis.

So Swami Lilananda came on to Calcutta.

Shivatosh had been a devoted follower of Lilananda. Whenever the Swami visited Calcutta he had stayed with Shivatosh. And it was the one delight of Shivatosh's life to serve the Master, together with all his disciples, when they thus honoured his house. When he died he bequeathed all his property to the Swami, leaving only a life-interest in the income to his young childless widow. It was his hope that this house of his would become a pilgrim-centre for the sect.

This was the house where we now went into residence.

During our ecstatic progress through the villages I had been in an elated mood, which I now found it difficult to keep up in Calcutta. In the wonderland of emotion, where we had been revelling, the mystic drama of the courting of the Bride within us and the Bridegroom who is everywhere was being played. And a fitting accompaniment to it had been the symphony of the broad grazing greens, the shaded ferry landing-places, the enraptured expanse of the noonday leisure, the deep evening silences vibrant with the tremolo of cicadas. Ours had been a dream progress to which the open skies of the countryside offered no obstacle. But with our arrival at Calcutta we knocked our heads against its hardness, we got jostled by its crowds, and our dream was at an end.

Yet, was not this the same Calcutta where, within the confines of our students' lodgings, we had once put our whole soul into our studies, by day and by night; where we had pondered over and discussed the problems of our country with our fellow-students in the College Square; where we had served as volunteers at the holding of our National Assemblies; where we had responded to the call of Uncle Jagamohan, and taken the vow to free our minds from all slavery imposed by Society or State? Yes, it was in this self-same Calcutta that, in the flood-tide of our youth, we had pursued our course, regardless of the revilement of stranger and kindred alike, proudly breasting all contrary currents like a boat in full sail. Why, then, should we now fail, in this whirlpool of suffering humanity, ridden with pleasure and pain, driven by hunger and thirst, to keep up the exaltation proper to our tear-drenched cult of emotional Communion?

As I manfully made the attempt, I was beset with doubts at every step. Was I then a mere weakling: unfaithful to my ideal: unworthy of strenuous endeavour? When I turned to Satish, to see how he fared, I found on his countenance no sign to show that Calcutta, for him, represented any geographical reality whatsoever. In the mystic world where he dwelt, all this city life meant no more than a mirage.

5

We two friends took up our quarters, with the Master, in Shivatosh's house. We had come to be his chief disciples, and he would have us constantly near his person.

With our Master and our fellow-disciples we were absorbed day and night in discussing emotions in general and the philosophy of spiritual emotion in particular. Into the very thick of the abstruse complexities which thus engaged our attention, the ripple of a woman's laughter would now and again find its way from the inner apartments.[16] Sometimes there would be heard, in a clear, high-toned voice, the call 'Bami!'—evidently a maid-servant of that name.

These were doubtless but trivial interruptions for minds soaring, almost to vanishing point, into the empyrean of idea. But to me they came as a grateful shower of rain upon a parched and thirsty soil. When little touches of life, like shed flower petals, were blown across from the unknown world behind the wall, then all in a moment I could understand that the wonderland of our quest was just there,—where the keys jingled, tied to the corner of Bami's sari; where the sound of the broom rose from the swept floor, and the smell of the cooking from the kitchen,—all trifles, but all true. That world, with its mingling of fine and coarse, bitter and sweet,—that itself was the heaven where Emotion truly held sway.

The name of the widow was Damini. We could catch momentary glimpses of her through opening doors and flapping curtains. But the two of us grew to be so much part and parcel of the Master as to share his privilege,[17] and very soon these doors and curtains were no longer barriers in our case.

Damini[18] was the lightning which gleams within the massed clouds of July. Without, the curves of youth enveloped her in their fulness, within flashed fitful fires. Thus runs an entry in Satish's diary:

> In Nonibala I have seen the Universal Woman in one of her aspects,—the woman who takes on herself the whole burden of sin, who gives up life itself for the sinner's sake, and in dying leaves for the world the balm of immortality. In Damini I see another aspect of Universal Woman. This one has nothing to do with death,—she is the Artist of the Art of Life. She blossoms out, in limitless profusion, in form and scent and movement. She is not for rejection; refuses to entertain the ascetic; and is vowed to resist the least farthing of payment to the tax-gathering Winter Wind.

It is necessary to relate Damini's previous history.

At the time when the coffers of her father, Annada, were overflowing with proceeds of his jute business, Damini was married to Shivatosh. So long, Shivatosh's fortune had consisted only in his pedigree: it could now count a more substantial

---

[16]The women's part of the house. [Translator's note]
[17]Women do not observe *purdah* with religious ascetics. [Translator's note]
[18]Damini means Lightning. [Translator's note]

addition. Annada bestowed on his son-in-law a house in Calcutta and sufficient money to keep him for life. There were also lavish gifts of furniture and ornaments made to his daughter.

Annada, further, made a futile attempt to take Shivatosh into his own business. But the latter had no interest in worldly concerns. An astrologer had once predicted to Shivatosh that, on the happening of a special conjunction of the stars, his soul would gain its emancipation whilst still in the flesh. From that day he lived in this hope alone, and ceased to find charm in riches, or even in objects still more charming. It was while in this frame of mind that he had become a disciple of Lilananda Swami.

In the meantime, with the subsidence of the jute boom, the full force of the adverse wind caught the heavy-laden bark of Annada's fortune and toppled it over. All his property was sold up and he had hardly enough left to make a bare living.

One evening Shivatosh came into the inner apartments and said to his wife: 'The Master is here. He has some words of advice for you and bids you attend.'

'I cannot go to him now,' answered Damini. 'I haven't the time.'

What? No time! Shivatosh went up nearer and found his wife seated in the gathering dusk, in front of the open safe, with her ornaments spread out before her. 'What in the world is keeping you?' inquired he.

'I am arranging my jewels,' was the reply.

So that was the reason for her lack of time. Indeed!

The next day, when Damini opened the safe, she found her jewel-box missing. 'My jewels?' she exclaimed, turning inquiringly to her husband.

'But you offered them to the Master. Did not his call reach you at the very moment?—for he sees into the minds of men. He has deigned, in his mercy, to save you from the lure of pelf.'

Damini's indignation rose to white heat.

'Give me back my ornaments!' she commanded.

'Why, what will you do with them?'

'They were my father's gift to me. I would return them to him.'

'They have gone to a better place,' said Shivatosh. 'Instead of pandering to worldly needs they are dedicated to the service of devotees.'

That is how the tyrannical imposition of faith began. And the pious ritual of exorcism, in all its cruelty, continued to be practised in order to rid Damini's mind of its mundane affections and desires.

So, while her father and her little brother were starving by inches, Damini had to prepare daily, with her own hands, meals for the sixty or seventy disciples who thronged the house with the Master. She would sometimes rebelliously leave out the salt, or contrive to get the viands scorched, but that did not avail to gain her any respite from her penance.

At this juncture Shivatosh died: and in departing he awarded his wife the supreme penalty for her want of faith,—he committed his widow, with all her belongings, to the guardianship of the Master.

6

The house was in a constant tumult with rising waves of fervour. Devotees kept streaming in from all quarters to sit at the feet of the Master. And yet Damini, who had gained the Presence without effort of her own, thrust aside her good fortune with contumely.

Did the Master call her for some special mark of his favour she would keep aloof, pleading a headache. If he had occasion to complain of some special omission of personal attention on her part, she would confess to have been away at the theatre. The excuse was lacking in truth, but not in rudeness.

The other women disciples were aghast at Damini's ways. First, her attire was not such as widows[19] should affect. Secondly, she showed no eagerness to drink in the Master's words of wisdom. Lastly, her demeanour had none of the reverential restraint which the Master's presence demanded. 'What a shame,' exclaimed they. 'We have seen many awful women, but not one so outrageous.'

The Swami used to smile. 'The Lord,' said he, 'takes a special delight in wrestling with a valiant opponent. When Damini has to own defeat, her surrender will be absolute.'

He began to display an exaggerated tolerance for her contumacy. That vexed Damini still more, for she looked on it as a more cunning form of punishment. And one day the Master caught her in a fit of laughter, mimicking to one of her companions the excessive suavity of his manner towards herself. Still he had not a word of rebuke, and repeated simply that the final *dénouement* would be all the more extraordinary, to which end the poor thing was but the instrument of Providence, and so herself not to blame.

This was how we found her when we first came. The *dénouement* was indeed extraordinary. I can hardly bring myself to write on further. Moreover, what happened is so difficult to tell. The network of suffering, which is woven behind the scenes, is not of any pattern set by the Scriptures, nor of our own devising. Hence the frequent discords between the inner and the outer life—discords that hurt, and wail forth in tears.

There came, at length, the dawn when the harsh crust of rebelliousness cracked and fell to pieces, and the flower of self-surrender came through and held up its dew-washed face. Damini's service became so beautiful in its truth that it descended on the devotees like the blessing of the very Divinity of their devotions.

And when Damini's lightning flashes had matured into a steady radiance, Satish looked on her and saw that she was beautiful; but I say this, that Satish gazed only on her beauty, failing to see Damini herself.

In Satish's room there hung a portrait of the Swami sitting in meditation, done on a porcelain medallion. One day he found it on the floor,—in fragments. He put it down to his pet cat. But other little mischiefs began to follow, which were clearly beyond the powers of the cat. There was some kind of disturbance in the air, which now and again broke out in unseen electric shocks.

How others felt, I know not, but a growing pain gnawed at my heart. Sometimes I thought that this constant ecstasy of emotion was proving too much for me. I wanted to give it all up and run away. The old work of teaching the leather-dealers' children seemed, in its unalloyed prose, to be now calling me back.

One afternoon when the Master was taking his siesta, and the weary disciples were at rest, Satish for some reason went off into his own room at this unusual hour. His progress was suddenly arrested at the threshold. There was Damini, her thick tresses dishevelled, lying prone on the floor, beating her head on it as she moaned: 'Oh, you stone, you stone, have mercy on me, have mercy and kill me outright!'

Satish, trembling from head to foot with a nameless fear, fled from the room.

7

It was a rule with Swami Lilananda to go off once a year to some remote, out-of-the-way place, away from the crowd. With the month of Magh[20] came round the time for his journey. Satish was to attend on him.

---

[19] Hindu widows in Bengal are supposed to dress in simple white (sometimes plain brown silk), without border, or ornamentation. [Translator's note]

[20] January–February. [Translator's note]

I asked to go too. I was worn to the very bone with the incessant emotional excitement of our cult, and felt greatly in need of physical movement as well as of mental quiet.

The Master sent for Damini. 'My little mother,' he told her, 'I am about to leave you for the duration of my travels. Let me arrange for your stay meanwhile with your aunt, as usual.'

'I would accompany you,' said Damini.

'You could hardly bear it, I am afraid. Our journeying will be troublesome.'

'Of course I can bear it,' she answered. 'Pray have no concern about any trouble of mine.'

Lilananda was pleased at this proof of Damini's devotion. In former years, this opportunity had been Damini's holiday time,—the one thing to which she had looked forward through the preceding months. 'Miraculous!' thought the Swami. 'How wondrously does even stone become as wax in the Lord's melting-pot of emotion.'

So Damini had her way, and came along with us.

8

The spot we reached, after hours of tramping in the sun, was a little promontory on the sea-coast, shaded by cocoa-nut palms. Profound was the solitude and the tranquillity which reigned there, as the gentle rustle of the palm tassels merged into the idle plash of the girdling sea. The place looked like a tired hand of the sleepy shore, limply fallen upon the surface of the waters. On this open hand stood a bluish-green hill, and inside the hill was a sculptured cave-temple of bygone days, which, for all its serene beauty, was the cause of much disquiet amongst antiquarians as to the origin, style, and subject-matter of its sculptures.

Our intention had been to return to the village where we had made our halt, after paying a visit to this temple. That was now seen to be impossible. The day was fast declining, and the moon was long past its full. Lilananda Swami at length decided that we should pass the night in the cave.

All four of us sat down to rest on the sandy soil beneath the cocoa-nut groves fringing the sea. The sunset glow bent lower and lower over the western horizon, as though Day was making its parting obeisance to approaching Night.

The Master's voice broke forth in song—one of his own composition:

> The day has waned, when at last we meet at the turning;
> And as I try to see thy face, the last ray of evening fades into the night.

We had heard the song before, but never with such complete *rapport* between singer, audience, and surroundings. Damini was affected to tears. The Swami went on to the second verse:

> I shall not grieve that the darkness comes between thee and my sight,—
> Only, for a moment, stand before me, that I may kiss thy feet and wipe them with my hair.

When he had come to the end, the placid even-tide, enveloping sky and waters, was filled, like some ripe, golden fruit, with the bursting sweetness of melody.

Damini rose and went up to the Master. As she prostrated herself at his feet, her loose hair slipped off her shoulders and was scattered over the ground on either side. She remained long thus before she raised her head.

9 *(From Satish's Diary)*

There were several chambers within the temple. In one of these I spread my blanket and laid myself down. The darkness pent up inside the cave seemed alive, like some great black monster, its damp breath bedewing my body. I began to be haunted by the idea that this was the first of all created animals, born in the beginning of time, with no eyes or ears, but just one enormous appetite. Confined within this cavern for endless ages it knew nothing, having no mind; but having sensibility it felt; and wept and wept in silence.

Fatigue overpowered my limbs like a dead weight, but sleep came not. Some bird, or perhaps bat, flitted in from the outside, or out from the inside,—its wings beating the air as it flew from darkness to darkness; when the draught reached my body it sent a shiver through me, making my flesh creep.

I thought I would go and get some sleep outside. But I could not recollect the direction in which the entrance was. As I crawled on my hands and knees along the way which appeared the right one, I knocked against the cave wall. When I tried a different side, I nearly tumbled into a hollow in which the water dripping through the cracks had collected.

I crawled back to my blanket and stretched myself on it again. Again was I possessed with the fancy that I had been taken right into the creature's maw and could not extricate myself; that I was the victim of a blind hunger which was licking me with its slimy saliva, through which I would be sucked and digested noiselessly, little by little.

I felt that only sleep could save me. My living, waking consciousness was evidently unable to bear such close embrace of this horrible, suffocating obscurity—fit only for the dead to suffer. I cannot say how long after it came upon me,—or whether it was really sleep at all,—but a thin veil of oblivion fell at last over my senses. And while in such half-conscious state I actually felt a deep breathing somewhere near my bare feet. Surely it was not that primeval creature of my imagining!

Then something seemed to cling about my feet. Some real wild animal this time,—was my first thought. But there was nothing furry in its touch. What if it was some species of serpent or reptile, of features and body unknown to me, of whose method of absorbing its prey I could form no idea? All the more loathsome seemed the softness of it,—of this terrible, unknown mass of hunger.

What between dread and disgust, I could not even utter a cry. I tried to push it away with ineffectual thrusts with my legs. Its face seemed to be touching my feet, on which its panting breath fell thickly. What kind of a face had it, I wondered. I launched a more vigorous kick as the stupor left me. I had at first supposed there was no fur, but what felt like a mane now brushed across my legs. I struggled up into a sitting posture.

Something stole away in the darkness. There was also a curious kind of sound. Could it have been sobbing?

CHAPTER III
DAMINI

1

We are back in our quarters in the village, near a temple, in a two-storeyed house belonging to one of the Swami's disciples, which had been placed at our disposal. Since our return we see but little of Damini, though she is still in charge of our household affairs. She has made friends with the neighbouring women, and spends most of her spare time in going about with them from one house to another.

The Swami is not particularly pleased. Damini's heart, thinks he, does not yet respond to the call of the ethereal heights. All its fondness is still for earthen walls. In her daily work of looking after the devotees,—formerly like an act of worship with her,—a trace of weariness has become noticeable. She makes mistakes. Her service has lost its radiance.

The Master, at heart, begins to be afraid of her again. Between her brows there darkens a gathering frown; her temple is ruffled with fitful breezes; the loosening knot of her hair lowers over her neck; the pressure of her lips, the gleams from the corner of her eye, her sudden wayward gestures presage a rebellious storm.

The Swami turned to his *kirtans* with renewed attention. The wandering bee, he hoped, would be brought to drink deep of the honey, once enticed in by its fragrance. And so the short cool days were filled to the brim with the foaming wine of ecstatic song.

But no, Damini refused to be caught. The exasperated Swami laughed out one day: 'The Lord is out hunting: the resolute flight of the deer adds zest to the chase: but succumb she must, in the end.'

When we had first come to know Damini, she was not to be found among the band of devotees clustering round the Master. That, however, did not attract our notice then. But now, her empty place had become conspicuous. Her frequent absences smote us tempestuously.

The Swami put this down to her pride, and that hurt his own pride. As for me,—but what does it matter what I thought?

One day the Master mustered up courage to say in his most dulcet tones: 'Damini, my little mother, do you think you will have a little time to spare this afternoon? If so——'

'No,' said Damini.

'Would you mind telling me why?'

'I have to assist in making sweetmeats at the Nandi's.'

'Sweetmeats? What for?'

'They have a wedding on.'

'Is your assistance so indispensably——?'

'I promised to be there.'

Damini whisked out of the room without waiting for further questioning.

Satish, who was there with us, was dumbfounded. So many men of learning, wealth, and fame had surrendered at the feet of the Master, and this slip of a girl,—what gave her such hardihood of assurance?

Another evening Damini happened to be at home. The Master had addressed himself to some specially important topic. After his discourse had progressed awhile, something in our faces gave him pause. He found our attention wandering. On looking round he discovered that Damini, who had been seated in the room, sewing in hand, was not to be seen. He understood the reason of our distraction. She was not there, not there, not there,—the refrain now kept worrying him too. He began to lose the thread of his discourse, and at last gave it up altogether.

The Swami left the room and went off to Damini's door. 'Damini,' he called. 'Why are you all alone here? Will you not come and join us?'

'I am engaged,' said Damini.

The baffled Swami could see, as he passed by the half-open door, a captive kite in a cage. It had somehow struck against the telegraph wires, and had been lying wounded when Damini rescued it from the pestering crows, and she had been tending it since.

The kite was not the only object which engaged Damini's solicitude. There was a mongrel pup, whose looks were on a par with its breeding. It was discord personified. Whenever it heard our cymbals, it would look up to heaven and voice forth a prolonged complaint. The gods, being fortunate, did not feel bound to give it a hearing. The poor mortals whose ears happened to be within reach were woefully agonised.

One afternoon, when Damini was engaged in practising horticulture in sundry cracked pots on the roof-terrace, Satish came up and asked her point-blank: 'Why is it you have given up coming over there altogether?'

'Over where?'

'To the Master.'

'Why, what need have you people of me?'

'We have no need,—but surely the need is yours.'

'No, no!' flung out Damini. 'Not at all, not at all!'

Taken aback by her heat, Satish gazed at her in silence. Then he mused aloud: 'Your mind lacks peace. If you would gain peace——'

'Peace from you,—you who are consumed day and night with your excitement,— where have *you* the peace to give? Leave me alone, I beg and pray you. I was at peace. I would be at peace.'

'You see but the waves on the surface. If you have the patience to dive deep, you will find all calm there.'

Damini wrung her hands as she cried: 'I beseech you, for the Lord's sake, don't insist on my diving downwards. If only you will give up all hope of my conversion, I may yet live.'

2

My experience has never been large enough to enable me to penetrate the mysteries of woman's mind. Judging from what little I have seen of the surface from the outside, I have come to the belief that women are ever ready to bestow their heart where sorrow cannot but be their lot. They will either string their garland of acceptance[21] for some brute of a man who will trample it under foot and defile it in the mire of his passions, or dedicate it to some idealist, on whose neck it will get no hold, attenuated as he is, like the dream-stuff of his imaginings.

When left to do their own choosing, women invariably reject ordinary men like me, made up of gross and fine, who know woman to be just woman,—that is to say, neither a doll of clay made to serve for our pastime, nor a transcendental melody to be evoked at our master touch. They reject us, because we have neither the forceful delusions of the flesh, nor the roseate illusions of fancy: we can neither break them on the wheel of our desire, nor melt them in the glow of our fervour to be cast in the mould of our ideal.

Because we know them only for what they are, they may be friendly, but cannot love us. We are their true refuge, for they can rely on our devotion; but our self-dedication comes so easy that they forget it has a price. So the only reward we get is to be used for their purposes; perchance to win their respect. But I am afraid my excursions into the region of psychology are merely due to personal grievances, which have my own experience behind them. The fact probably is, what we thus lose is really our gain,—anyway, that is how we may console ourselves.

Damini avoids the Master because she cannot bear him. She fights shy of Satish because for him her feelings are of the opposite description. I am the only person, near at hand, with whom there is no question either of love or hate. So whenever I am with her, Damini talks away to me of unimportant matters concerning the old days, the present times, or the daily happenings at the neighbours' houses. These talks usually take place on the shaded part of the roof-terrace, which serves as a passage between our several rooms on the second storey, where Damini sits slicing betel-nuts.

---

[21] In the old days, when a girl had to choose between several suitors, she signified her choice by putting a garland round the neck of the accepted one. [Translator's note]

What I could not understand was, how these trifling talks should have attracted the notice of Satish's emotion-clouded vision. Even suppose the circumstance was not so trifling, had I not often been told that, in the world where Satish dwelt, there were no such disturbing things as circumstances at all? The Mystic Union, in which personified cosmic forces were assisting, was an eternal drama, not an historical episode. Those who are rapt with the undying flute strains, borne along by the ceaseless zephyrs which play on the banks of the ever-flowing Jamuna[22] of that mystic paradise, have no eyes or ears left for the ephemeral doings immediately around them. This much at least is certain, that before our return from the cave, Satish used to be much denser in his perception of worldly events.

For this difference I may have been partly responsible. I also had begun to absent myself from our *kirtans* and discourses, perhaps with a frequency which could not elude even Satish. One day he came round on inquiry, and found me running after Damini's mongoose,—a recent acquisition,—trying to lure it into bondage with a pot of milk, which I had procured from the local milkman. This occupation, viewed as an excuse, was simply hopeless. It could easily have waited till the end of our sitting. For the matter of that, the best thing clearly would have been to leave the mongoose to its own devices, thus at one stroke demonstrating my adherence to the two principal tenets of our cult,—Compassion for all creatures, and Passion for the Lord.

That is why, when Satish came up, I had to feel ashamed. I put down the pot, then and there, and tried to edge away along the path which led back to self-respect.

But Damini's behaviour took me by surprise. She was not in the least abashed as she asked: 'Where are you off to, Srivilas Babu?'

I scratched my head, as I mumbled: 'I was thinking of joining the——'

'They must have finished by this time. Do sit down.'

This coming from Damini, in the presence of Satish, made my ears burn.

Damini turned to Satish. 'I am in awful trouble with the mongoose,' she said. 'Last night it stole a chicken from the Mussulman quarters over there. I dare not leave it loose any longer. Srivilas Babu has promised to look out for a nice big hamper to keep it in.'

It seemed to me that it was my devotion to her which Damini was using the mongoose to show off. I was reminded how the Swami had given orders to Satish so as to impress me. The two were the same thing.

Satish made no reply, and his departure was somewhat abrupt. I gazed on Damini and could see her eyes flash out as they followed his disappearing figure; while on her lips there set a hard, enigmatic smile.

What conclusion Damini had come to she herself knew best; the only result apparent to me was that she began to send for me on all kinds of flimsy pretexts. Sometimes she would make sweetmeats, which she pressed on me. One day I could not help suggesting: 'Let's offer some to Satish as well.'

'That would only annoy him,' said Damini.

And it happened that Satish, passing that way, caught me in the act of being thus regaled.

In the drama which was being played, the hero and the heroine spoke their parts 'aside.' I was the one character who, being of no consequence, had to speak out. This sometimes made me curse my lot; none the less, I could not withstand the temptation of the petty cash with which I was paid off, from day to day, for taking up the rôle of middleman.

---

[22] A major river in Bengal that flows into the Ganges.

3

For some days Satish clanged his cymbals and danced his *kirtans* with added vigour. Then one day he came to me and said: 'We cannot keep Damini with us any longer.'

'Why?' I asked.

'We must free ourselves altogether from the influence of women.'

'If that be a necessity,' said I, 'there must be something radically wrong with our system.'

Satish stared at me in amazement.

'Woman is a natural phenomenon,' I continued, undaunted, 'who will have her place in the world, however much we may try to get rid of her. If your spiritual welfare depends on ignoring her existence, then its pursuit will be like the chasing of a phantom, and will so put you to shame, when the illusion is gone, that you will not know where to hide yourself.'

'Oh, stop your philosophising!' exclaimed Satish. 'I was talking practical politics. It is only too evident that women are emissaries of Maya,[23] and at Maya's behest ply on us their blandishments,—for they cannot fulfil the design of their Mistress unless they overpower our reason. So we must steer clear of them if we would keep our intellect free.'

I was about to make my reply, when Satish stopped me with a gesture, and went on: 'Visri, old fellow! let me tell you plainly: if the hand of Maya is not visible to you, that is because you have allowed yourself to be caught in her net. The vision of beauty with which she has ensnared you to-day will vanish, and with the beauty will disappear the spectacles of desire, through which you now see it as greater than all the world. Where the noose of Maya is so glaringly obvious, why be foolhardy enough to take risks?'

'I admit all that,' I rejoined. 'But, my dear fellow, the all-pervading net of Maya was not cast by my hands, nor do I know the way to escape through it. Since we have not the power to evade Maya, our spiritual striving should help us, while acknowledging her, to rise above her. Because it does not take such a course, we have to flounder about in vain attempts to cut away the half of Truth.'

'Well, well, let's have your idea a little more clearly,' said Satish.

'We must sail the boat of our life,' I proceeded, 'along the current of nature, in order to reach beyond it. Our problem is, not how to get rid of this current, but how to keep the boat afloat in its channel until it is through. For that, a rudder is necessary.'

'You people who have ceased to be loyal to the Master,—how can I make you understand that in *him* we have just this rudder? You would regulate your spiritual life according to your own whims. That way death lies!' Satish went to the Master's chamber, and fell to tending his feet with fervour.

The same evening, when Satish lit the Master's pipe, he also put forward his plaint against Maya and her emissaries. The smoking of one pipe, however, did not suffice for its adjudication. Evening after evening, pipe after pipe was exhausted, yet the Master was unable to make up his mind.

From the very beginning Damini had given the Swami no end of trouble. Now the girl had managed to set up this eddy in the midst of the smooth course of the devotees' progress. But Shivatosh had thrown her and her belongings so absolutely

---

[23] Or Mahamaya, the Hindu goddess who produces illusions of sensory experience.

on the Master's hands that he knew not how or where to cast her off. What made it more difficult still was that he harboured a secret fear of his ward.

And Satish, in spite of all the doubled and quadrupled enthusiasm which he put into his *kirtans,* in spite of all the pipe-filling and massaging in which he tried to rest his heart, was not allowed to forget for a moment that Maya had taken up her position right across the line of his spiritual advance.

One day some *kirtan* singers of repute had arrived, and were to sing in the evening at the temple next door. The *kirtan* would last far into the night. I managed to slip away after the preliminary overture, having no doubt that, in so thick a crowd, no one would notice my absence.

Damini that evening had completely thrown off her reserve. Things which are difficult to speak of, which refuse to leave one's choking throat, flowed from her lips so simply, so sweetly. It was as if she had suddenly come upon some secret recess in her heart, so long hidden away in darkness,—as if, by some strange chance, she had gained the opportunity to stand before her own self, face to face.

Just at this time Satish came up from behind and stood there hesitating, without our being aware of it at the moment. Not that Damini was saying anything very particular, but there were tears in her eyes,—all her words, in fact, were then welling up from some tear-flooded depth. When Satish arrived, the *kirtan* could not have been anywhere near its end. I divined that he must have been goaded with repeated inward urgings to have left the temple then.

As Satish came round into our view, Damini rose with a start, wiped her eyes, and made off towards her room. Satish, with a tremor in his voice, said: 'Damini, will you listen to me? I would have a word with you.'

Damini slowly retraced her steps, and came and sat down again. I made as though to take myself off, but an imploring glance from her restrained me from stirring. Satish, who seemed to have made some kind of effort meanwhile, came straight to the point.

'The need,' said he to Damini, 'which brought the rest of us to the Master, was not yours when you came to him.'

'No,' avowed Damini expectantly.

'Why, then, do you stay amongst his devotees?'

Damini's eyes flamed up as she cried: 'Why do I stay? Because I did not come of my own accord! I was a helpless creature, and everyone knew my lack of faith. Yet I was bound hand and foot by your devotees in this dungeon of devotion. What avenue of escape have you left me?'

'We have now decided,' stated Satish, 'that if you would go to stay with some relative all your expenses will be found.'

'You have decided, have you?'

'Yes.'

'Well, then,—I have not!'

'Why, how will that inconvenience you?'

'Am I a pawn in your game, that you devotees should play me, now this way, now the other?'

Satish was struck dumb.

'I did not come,' continued Damini, 'wanting to please your devotees. And I am not going away at the bidding of the lot of you, merely because I don't happen to please you!'

Damini covered her face with her hands and burst out sobbing as she ran into her room and slammed the door.

Satish did not return to the *kirtan* singing. He sank down in a corner of the adjoining roof-terrace and brooded there in silence.

The sound of the breakers on the distant seashore came, wafted along the south breeze, like despairing sighs, rising up to the watching star clusters, from the very heart of the Earth.

I spent the night wandering round and round along the dark, deserted village lanes.

4

The World of Reality has made a determined onslaught on the Mystic Paradise, within the confines of which the Master sought to keep Satish and myself content by repeatedly filling for us the cup of symbolism with the nectar of idea. Now the clash of the actual with the symbolic bids fair to overturn the latter and spill its emotional contents in the dust. The Master is not blind to this danger.

Satish is no longer himself. Like a paper kite, with its regulating knot gone, he is still high in the skies, but may at any moment begin to gyrate groundwards. There is no falling off as yet in the outward rigour of his devotional and disciplinary exercises, but a closer scrutiny reveals the totter of weakening.

As for my condition, Damini has left nothing so vague in it as to require any guess-work. The more she notices the fear in the Master's face, and the pain in Satish's, the oftener she makes me dance attendance on her.

At last it came to this, that when we were engaged in talk with the Master, Damini would sometimes appear in the doorway and interrupt us with: 'Srivilas Babu, would you mind coming over this way?' without even condescending to add what I was wanted for.

The Swami would glance up at me; Satish would glance up at me; I would hesitate for a moment between them and her; then I would glance up at the door,—and in a trice I was off the fence and out of the room. An effort would be made, after my exit, to go on with the talk, but the effort would soon get the better of the talk, whereupon the latter would stop.

Everything seemed to be falling to pieces around us. The old compactness was gone.

We two had come to be the pillars of the sect. The Master could not give up either of us without a struggle. So he ventured once more to make an overture to Damini. 'My little mother,' said he, 'the time is coming for us to proceed to the more arduous part of our journey. You had better return from here.'

'Return where?'

'Home, to your aunt.'

'That cannot be.'

'Why?' asked the Swami.

'First of all,' said Damini, 'she is not my own aunt at all. Why should she bear my burden?'

'All your expenses shall be borne by us.'

'Expenses are not the only burden. It is no part of her duty to be saddled with looking after me.'

'But, Damini,' urged the Swami in his desperation, 'can I keep you with me for ever?'

'Is that a question for me to answer?'

'But where will you go when I am dead?'

'I was never allowed,' returned Damini icily, 'to have the responsibility of thinking that out. I have been made to realise too well that in this world I have neither home nor property; nothing at all to call my own. That is what makes my burden so heavy to bear. It pleased you to take it up. You shall not now cast it on another!'

Damini went off.

'Lord, have mercy!' sighed the Swami.

Damini had laid on me the command to procure for her some good Bengali books. I need hardly say that by 'good' Damini did not mean spiritual, of the quality affected by our sect. Nor need I pause to make it clear that Damini had no compunction in asking anything from me. It has not taken her long to find out that making demands on me was the easiest way of making me amends. Some kinds of trees are all the better for being pruned: that was the kind of person I seemed to be where Damini was concerned.

Well, the books I ordered were unmitigatedly modern. The author was distinctly less influenced by Manu[24] than by Man himself. The packet was delivered by the postman to the Swami. He raised his eyebrows, as he opened it, and asked: 'Hullo, Srivilas, what are these for?'

I remained silent.

The Master gingerly turned over some of the pages, as he remarked for my benefit that he had never thought much of the author, having failed to find in his writings the correct spiritual flavour.

'If you read them carefully, sir,' I suddenly blurted out, 'you will find his writings not to be lacking in the flavour of Truth.' The fact is, rebellion had been long brewing within me. I was feeling done to death with mystic emotion. I was nauseated with shedding tears over abstract human feelings, to the neglect of living human creatures.

The Master blinked at me curiously before he replied: 'Very well, my son, carefully read them I will.' He tucked the books away under the bolster on which he reclined. I could perceive that his idea was not to surrender them to me.

Damini, from behind the door, must have got wind of this, for at once she stepped in and asked: 'Haven't the books you ordered for me arrived yet?'

I remained silent.

'My little mother!' said the Swami. 'These books are not fit for you to read.'

'How should you know that?'

The Master frowned. 'How, at least, could you know better?'

'I have read the author: you, perhaps, have not.'

'Why, then, need you read him over again?'

'When *you* have any need,' Damini flared up, 'nothing is allowed to stand in *your* way. It is only *I* who am to have no needs!'

'You forget yourself, Damini. I am a *sannyasin*. I have no worldly desires.'

'You forget that I am not a *sannyasin*. I have a desire to read these books. Will you kindly let me have them?'

The Swami drew out the books from under his bolster and tossed them across to me. I handed them over to Damini.

In the end, the books that Damini would have read alone by herself, she now began to send for me to read out to her. It was in that same shaded veranda along our rooms that these readings took place. Satish passed and repassed, longing to join in, but could not, unasked.

One day we had come upon a humorous passage, and Damini was rocking with laughter. There was a festival on at the temple and we had supposed that Satish would be there. But we heard a door open behind, through which Satish unexpectedly appeared and came and sat down beside us.

Damini's laughter was at once cut short. I also felt awkward. I wanted badly to say something to Satish, but no words would come, and I went on silently turning

---

[24]The Hindu law-giver. [Translator's note]

over page after page of my book. He rose, and left as abruptly as he had come. Our reading made no further progress that day.

Satish may very likely have understood that while he envied the absence of reserve between Damini and me, its presence was just what I envied in his case. That same day he petitioned the Master to be allowed to go off on a solitary excursion along the sea-coast, promising to be back within a week. 'The very thing, my son!' acquiesced the Swami, with enthusiasm.

Satish departed. Damini did not send for me to read to her any more, nor had she anything else to ask of me. Neither did I see her going to her friends, the women of the neighbourhood. She kept her room, with closed doors.

Some days passed thus. One afternoon, when the Master was deep in his siesta, and I was writing a letter seated out on our veranda, Satish suddenly turned up. Without so much as a glance at me, he walked straight up to Damini's door, knocking as he called: 'Damini, Damini.'

Damini came out at once. A strangely altered Satish met her inquiring gaze. Like a storm-battered ship, with torn rigging and tattered sails, was his condition,—eyes wild, hair dishevelled, features drawn, garments dusty.

'Damini,' said Satish, 'I asked you to leave us. That was wrong of me. I beg your forgiveness.'

'Oh, don't say that,' cried the distressed Damini, clasping her hands.

'You must forgive me,' he repeated. 'I will never again allow that pride to overcome me, which led me to think I could take you or leave you, according to my own spiritual requirements. Such sin will never cross my mind again, I promise you. Do you also promise me one thing?'

'Command me!' said Damini, making humble obeisance.

'You must join us, and not keep aloof like this.'

'I will join you,' said Damini. 'I will sin no more.' Then, as she bowed low again to take the dust of his feet, she repeated, 'I will sin no more.'

5

The stone was melted again. Damini's bewildering radiance remained undimmed, but it lost its heat. In worship and ritual and service her beauty blossomed out anew. She was never absent from the *kirtan* singing, nor when the Master gave his readings and discourses. There was a change in her raiment also. She reverted to the golden brown of plain tussore,[25] and whenever we saw her she seemed fresh from her toilet.

The severest test came in her intercourse with the Master. When she made her salutation to him, I could catch the glint of severely repressed temper through her half-closed eyelids. I knew very well that she could not bear to take orders from the Master; nevertheless, so complete was her self-suppression, that the Swami was able to screw up the courage to repeat his condemnation of the obnoxious tone of that outrageously modern Bengali writer. The next day there was a heap of flowers near his seat, and under them were the torn pages of the books of the objectionable author.

I had always noticed that the attendance on the Master by Satish was specially intolerable to Damini. Even now, when the Master asked him for some personal service, Damini would try to hustle past Satish and forestall him. This, however, was not possible in every case; and while Satish kept blowing on the tinder to get it

---

[25] The tussore silk-worm is a wild variety, and its cocoon has to be used after the moth has cut its way out and flown away, thus not being killed in the process of unwinding the silk. Hence tussore silk is deemed specially suitable for wear on occasions of divine worship. [Translator's note]

into a blaze for the Master's pipe, Damini would have much ado to keep herself in hand by grimly repeating under her breath, 'I will sin no more. I will sin no more.'

But what Satish had tried for did not come off. On the last occasion of Damini's self-surrender, he had seen the beauty of the surrender only, not of the self behind it. This time Damini herself had become so true for him that she eclipsed all strains of music, and all thoughts of philosophy. Her reality had become so dominant that Satish could no longer lose himself in his visions, nor think of her merely as an aspect of Universal Woman. It was not she who, as before, set off for him the melodies which filled his mind; rather, these melodies had now become part of the halo which encircled her person.

I should not, perhaps, leave out the minor detail that Damini had no longer any use for me. Her demands on me had suddenly ceased altogether. Of my colleagues, who used to assist in beguiling her leisure, the kite was dead, the mongoose had escaped, and as for the mongrel puppy, its manners having offended the Master's susceptibilities, it had been given away. Thus, bereft both of occupation and companionship, I returned to my old place in the assembly surrounding the Master, though the talking and singing and doing that went on there had all alike become horribly distasteful to me.

6

The laboratory of Satish's mind was not amenable to any outside laws. One day, as he was compounding therein, for my special benefit, a weird mixture of ancient philosophy and modern science, with reason as well as emotion promiscuously thrown in, Damini burst in upon us, panting:

'Oh, do come, both of you, come quick!'

'Whatever is the matter?' I cried, as I leapt up.

'Nabin's wife has taken poison, I think,' she said.

Nabin was a neighbour, one of our regular *kirtan* singers—an ardent disciple. We hurried after Damini, but when we arrived his wife was dead.

We pieced together her story. Nabin's wife had brought her motherless younger sister to live with them. She was a very pretty girl, and when Nabin's brother had last been home, he was so taken with her that their marriage was speedily arranged. This greatly relieved her elder sister, for, high caste as they were, a suitable bridegroom was not easy to find. The wedding-day had been fixed some months later, when Nabin's brother would have completed his college course. Meanwhile Nabin's wife lit upon the discovery that her husband had seduced her sister. She forthwith insisted on his marrying the unfortunate girl,—for which, as it happened, he did not require much persuasion. The wedding ceremony had just been put through, whereupon the elder sister had made away with herself by taking poison.

There was nothing to be done. The three of us slowly wended our way back, to find the usual throng round the Master. They sang a *kirtan* to him, and he waxed ecstatic in his usual manner, and began to dance with them.

That evening the moon was near its full. One corner of our terrace was overhung by the branch of a *chalta* tree. At the edge of the shadow, under its thick foliage, sat Damini lost in silent thought. Satish was softly pacing up and down our veranda behind her. I had a hobby for diary-writing, in which I was indulging, alone in my room, with the door wide open.

That evening the *koil*[26] could not sleep; stirred by the south breeze the leaves too were speaking out, and the moonlight, shimmering on them, smiled in response.

---

[26] A bird with a hooting call.

Something must also have stirred within Satish, for he suddenly turned his steps towards the terrace and went and stood near Damini.

Damini looked round with a start, adjusted her *sari*[27] over the back of her head, and rose as if to leave. Satish called, 'Damini!'

She stopped at once, and turning to him appealingly with folded hands she said, 'My Master, may I ask you a question?'

Satish looked at her inquiringly, but made no reply.

Damini went on: 'Tell me truly, of what use to the world is this thing with which your sect is occupied day and night? Whom have you been able to save?'

I came out from my room and stood on the veranda.

Damini continued: 'This passion, passion, passion on which you harp,—did you not see it in its true colours to-day? It has neither religion nor duty; it regards neither wife nor brother, nor the sanctuary of home; it knows neither pity nor trust, nor modesty, nor shame. What way have you discovered to save men from the hell of this cruel, shameless, soul-killing passion?'

I could not contain myself, but cried out: 'Oh yes, we have hit upon the wonderful device of banishing Woman right away from our territory, so as to make our pursuit of passion quite safe!'

Without paying any heed to my words, Damini spoke on to Satish: 'I have learnt nothing at all from your Master. He has never given me one moment's peace of mind. Fire cannot quench fire. The road along which he is taking his devotees leads neither to courage, nor restraint, nor peace. That poor woman who is dead,—her heart's blood was sucked dry by this Fury, Passion, who killed her. Did you not see the hideous countenance of the murderess? For God's sake, my Master, I implore you, do not sacrifice me to that Fury. Oh, save me, for if anybody can save me, it is you!'

For a space all three of us kept silent. So poignant became the silence all around, it seemed to me that the vibrating drone of the *cicadas* was but a swoon-thrill of the pallid sky.

Satish was the first to speak. 'Tell me,' said he to Damini, 'what is it you would have me do for you?'

'Be my *guru!* I would follow none else. Give me some creed—higher than all this—which can save me. Do not let me be destroyed, together with the Divinity which is in me.'

Satish drew himself up straight, as he responded: 'So be it.'

Damini prostrated herself at his feet, her forehead touching the ground, and remained long thus, in reverential adoration, murmuring: 'Oh, my Master, my Master, save me, save me, save me from all sin.'

7

Once more there was a mighty sensation in our world, and a storm of vituperation in the newspapers—for Satish had again turned renegade.

At first he had defiantly proclaimed active disbelief in all religion and social convention. Next, with equal vehemence, he had displayed active belief in gods and goddesses, rites and ceremonies, not excluding the least of them. Now, lastly, he had thrown to the winds all the rubbish-heaps both of religious and irreligious cults, and had retired into such simple peacefulness that no one could even guess what he believed, or what he did not. True, he took up good works as of old; but there was nothing aggressive about it this time.

---

[27] A formal recognition of the presence of an elder. [Translator's note]

There was another event over which the newspapers exhausted all their resources of sarcasm and virulence. That was the announcement of Damini's marriage with me. The mystery of this marriage none will perhaps fathom,—but why need they?

CHAPTER IV

SRIVILAS

1

There was once an indigo factory on this spot. All that now remains of it are some tumble-down rooms belonging to the old house, the rest having crumbled into dust. When returning homewards, after performing Damini's last rites, the place, as we passed by it, somehow appealed to me, and I stayed on alone.

The road leading from the river-side to the factory gate is flanked by an avenue of *sissoo* trees. Two broken pillars still mark the site of the gateway, and portions of the garden wall are standing here and there. The only other memento of the past is the brick-built mound over the grave of some Mussulman servant of the factory. Through its cracks, wild flowering shrubs have sprung up. Covered with blossoms they sway to the breeze and mock at death, like merry maidens shaking with laughter while they chaff the bridegroom on his wedding-day. The banks of the garden pool have caved in and let the water trickle away, leaving the bottom to serve as a bed for a coriander patch. As I sit out on the roadside, under the shade of the avenue, the scent of the coriander, in flower, goes through and through my brain.

I sit and muse. The factory, of which these remnants are left, like the skeleton of some dead animal by the wayside, was once alive. From it flowed waves of pleasure and pain in a stormy succession, which then seemed to be endless. Its terribly efficient English proprietor, who made the very blood of his sweating cultivators run indigo-blue,—how tremendous was he compared to puny me! Nevertheless, Mother Earth girded up her green mantle, undismayed, and set to work so thoroughly to plaster over the disfigurement wrought by him and his activities, that the few remaining traces require but a touch or two more to vanish for ever.

This scarcely novel reflection, however, was not what my mind ruminated over. 'No, no!' it protested. 'One dawn does not succeed another merely to smear fresh plaster[28] over the floor. True, the Englishman of the factory, together with the rest of its abominations, are all swept away into oblivion like a handful of dust,—but my Damini!'

Many will not agree with me, I know. Shankaracharya's[29] philosophy spares no one. All the world is *maya,* a trembling dewdrop on the lotus leaf. But Shankaracharya was a *sannyasin.* 'Who is your wife, who your son?' were questions he asked, without understanding their meaning. Not being a *sannyasin* myself, I know full well that Damini is not a vanishing dewdrop on the lotus leaf.

But, I am told, there are householders also, who say the same thing. That may be. They are mere householders, who have lost only the mistress of their house.

---

[28] The wattle-and-daub cottages of a Bengal village are cleaned and renovated every morning by a moist clay mixture being smeared by the housewife over the plinth and floors. [Translator's note]

[29] Or Shankara, an eighth-century Hindu theologian, sometimes said to be the founder of the principal sects of Hinduism.

Their home is doubtless *maya,* and so likewise is its mistress. These are their own handiwork, and when done with any broom is good enough for sweeping their fragments clean away.

I did not keep house long enough to settle down as a householder, nor is mine the temperament of a *sannyasin,*—that saved me. So the Damini whom I gained became neither housewife nor *maya.* She ever remained true to herself,—my Damini. Who dares to call her a shadow?

Had I known Damini only as mistress of my house, much of this would never have been written. It is because I knew her in a greater, truer relation, that I have no hesitation in putting down the whole truth, recking nothing of what others may say.

Had it been my lot to live with Damini, as others do in the everyday world, the household routine of toilet and food and repose would have sufficed for me as for them. And after Damini's death, I could have heaved a sigh and exclaimed with Shankaracharya: 'Variegated is the world of *maya!*' before hastening to honour the suggestion of some aunt, or other well-meaning elder, by another attempt to sample its variety by marrying again. But I had not adjusted myself to the domestic world, like a foot in a comfortable old shoe. From the very outset I had given up hope of happiness,—no, no, that is saying too much; I was not so non-human as that. Happiness I certainly hoped for, but I did not arrogate to myself the right to claim it.

Why? Because it was I who persuaded Damini to give her consent to our marriage. Not for us was the first auspicious vision[30] in the rosy glow of festive lamps, to the rapturous strains of wedding pipes. We married in the broad light of day, with eyes wide open.

2

When we went away from Lilananda Swami, the time came to think of ways and means, as well as of a sheltering roof. We had all along been more in danger of surfeit than of starvation, with the hospitality which the devotees of the Master pressed on us, wherever we went with him. We had almost come to forget that to be a householder involves the acquiring, or building, or at least the renting of a house, so accustomed had we become to cast the burden of its supply upon another, and to look on a house as demanding from us only the duty of making ourselves thoroughly comfortable in it.

At length we recollected that Uncle Jagamohan had bequeathed his share of the house to Satish. Had the will been left in Satish's custody, it would by this time have been wrecked, like a paper boat, on the waves of his emotion. It happened, however, to be with me; for I was the executor. There were three conditions attached to the bequest which I was responsible for carrying out. No religious worship was to be performed in the house. The ground floor was to be used as a school for the leather-dealers' children. And after Satish's death, the whole property was to be applied for the benefit of that community. Piety was the one thing Uncle Jagamohan could not tolerate. He looked on it as more defiling even than worldliness; and probably these provisions, which he facetiously referred to in English as 'sanitary precautions,' were intended as a safeguard against the excessive piety which prevailed in the adjoining half of the house.

'Come along,' I said to Satish. 'Let's go to your Calcutta house.'

---

[30] At one stage of the wedding ceremony a red screen is placed round the Bride and Bridegroom, and they are asked to look at each other. This is the Auspicious Vision. [Translator's note]

'I am not quite ready for that yet,' Satish replied.

I did not understand him.

'There was a day,' he explained, 'when I relied wholly on reason, only to find at last that reason could not support the whole of life's burden. There was another day, when I placed my reliance on emotion, only to discover it to be a bottomless abyss. The reason and the emotion, you see, were alike mine. Man cannot rely on himself alone. I dare not return to town until I have found my support.'

'What then do you suggest?' I asked.

'You two go on to the Calcutta house. I would wander alone for a time. I seem to see glimpses of the shore. If I allow it out of my sight now, I may lose it for ever.'

As soon as we were by ourselves, Damini said to me: 'That will never do! If he wanders about alone, who is to look after him? Don't you remember in what plight he came back when he last went wandering? The very idea of it fills me with fear.'

Shall I tell the truth? This anxiety of Damini's stung me like a hornet, leaving behind the smart of anger. Had not Satish wandered about for two whole years after Uncle Jagamohan's death,—had that killed him? My question did not remain unuttered. Rather, some of the smart of the sting got expressed with it.

'I know, Srivilas Babu,' Damini replied. 'It takes a great deal to kill a man. But why should he be allowed to suffer at all, so long as the two of us are here to prevent it?'

The two of us! Half of that meant this wretched creature, Srivilas! It is of course a law of the world, that in order to save some people from suffering others shall suffer. All the inhabitants of the earth may be divided into two such classes. Damini had found out to which I belonged. It was compensation, indeed, that she included herself in the same class.

I went and said to Satish: 'All right, then, let us postpone our departure to town. We can stay for a time in that dilapidated house on the river-side. They say it is subject to ghostly visitations. This will serve to keep off human visitors.'

'And you two?' inquired Satish.

'Like the ghosts, we shall keep in hiding as far as possible.'

Satish threw a nervous glance at Damini,—there may have been a suggestion of dread in it.

Damini clasped her hands as she said imploringly: 'I have accepted you as my *guru*. Whatever my sins may have been, let them not deprive me of the right to serve you.'

3

I must confess that this frenzied pertinacity of Satish's quest is beyond my understanding. There was a time when I would have laughed to scorn the very idea. Now I had ceased to laugh. What Satish was pursuing was fire indeed, no will-o'-the-wisp. When I realised how its heat was consuming him, the old arguments of Uncle Jagamohan's school refused to pass my lips. Of what avail would it be to find, with Herbert Spencer, that the mystic sense might have originated in some ghostly superstition, or that its message could be reduced to some logical absurdity? Did we not see how Satish was burning,—his whole being aglow?

Satish was perhaps better off when his days were passing in one round of excitement,—singing, dancing, serving the Master,—the whole of his spiritual effort exhausting itself in the output of the moment. Since he has lapsed into outward quiet, his spirit refuses to be controlled any longer. There is now no question of seeking emotional satisfaction. The inward struggle for realisation is so tremendous within him, that we are afraid to look on his face.

I could remain silent no longer. 'Satish,' I suggested, 'don't you think it would be better to go to some *guru* who could show you the way and make your spiritual progress easier?'

This only served to annoy him. 'Oh, do be quiet, Visri,' he broke out irritably. 'For goodness' sake keep quiet! What does one want to make it easier for? Delusion alone is easy. Truth is always difficult.'

'But would it not be better,' I tried again, 'if some *guru* were to guide you along the path of Truth?'

Satish was almost beside himself. 'Will you never understand,' he groaned, 'that I am not running after any geographical truth? The Dweller within can only come to me along my own true path. The path of the *guru* can only lead to the *guru's* door.'

What a number of opposite principles have I heard enunciated by this same mouth of Satish! I, Srivilas, once the favourite disciple of Uncle Jagamohan,—who would have threatened me with a big stick if I had called him Master,—had actually been made by Satish to massage the legs of Lilananda Swami. And now not even a week has passed but he needs must preach to me in this strain! However, as I dared not smile, I maintained a solemn silence.

'I have now understood,' Satish went on, 'why our Scriptures say that it is better to die in one's own *dharma*[31] rather than court the terrible fate of taking the *dharma* of another. All else may be accepted as gifts, but if one's *dharma* is not one's own, it does not save, but kills. I cannot gain my God as alms from anybody else. If I get Him at all, it shall be I who win Him. If I do not, even death is better.'

I am argumentative by nature, and could not give in so easily. 'A poet,' said I, 'may get a poem from within himself. But he who is not a poet needs must take it from another.'

'I am a poet,' said Satish, without blenching.

That finished the matter. I came away.

Satish had no regular hours for meals or sleep. There was no knowing where he was to be found next. His body began to take on the unsubstantial keenness of an over-sharpened knife. One felt this could not go on much longer. Yet I could not muster up courage to interfere. Damini, however, was utterly unable to bear it. She was grievously incensed at God's ways. With those who ignored Him, God was powerless,—was it fair thus to take it out of one who was helplessly prostrate at His feet? When Damini used to wax wroth with Lilananda Swami, she knew how to bring it home to him. Alas, she knew not how to bring her feelings home to God!

Anyhow, she spared no pains in trying to get Satish to be regular in satisfying his physical needs. Numberless and ingenious were her contrivances to get this misfit creature to conform to domestic regulations. For a considerable space Satish made no overt objection to her endeavours. But one morning he waded across the shallow river to the broad sand-bed along the opposite bank, and there disappeared from sight.

The sun rose to the meridian; it gradually bent over to the west; but there was no sign of Satish. Damini waited for him, fasting, till she could contain herself no longer. She put some food on a salver, and with it toiled through the knee-deep water, and at last found herself on the sand-bank.

It was a vast expanse on which not a living creature of any kind was to be seen. The sun was cruel. Still more so were the glowing billows of sand, one succeeding the other, like ranks of crouching sentinels guarding the emptiness. As she stood on

---

[31] A key concept in Hinduism with many meanings. In this passage, it refers to the essential quality of one's nature.

the edge of this spreading pallor, where all limits seemed to have been lost, where no call could meet with any response, no question with any answer, Damini's heart sank within her. It was as if her world had been wiped away and reduced to the dull blank of original colourlessness. One vast 'No' seemed to be stretched at her feet. No sound, no movement, no red of blood, no green of vegetation, no blue of sky,—but only the drab of sand. It looked like the lipless grin of some giant skull, the tongueless cavern of its jaws gaping with an eternal petition of thirst to the unrelenting fiery skies above.

While she was wondering in what direction to proceed, the faint track of footsteps caught Damini's eye. These she pursued, and went on and on, over the undulating surface, till they stopped at a pool on the farther side of a sand-drift. Along the moist edge of the water could be seen the delicate tracery of the claw-marks of innumerable water-fowl. Under the shade of the sand-drift sat Satish.

The water was the deepest of deep blue. The fussy snipe were poking about on its margin, bobbing their tails and fluttering their black-and-white wings. At some distance were a flock of wild duck quacking vigorously, and seeming never to get the preening of their feathers done to their own satisfaction. When Damini reached the top of the mound, which formed one bank of the pool, the ducks took themselves off in a body, with a great clamour and beating of wings.

Satish looked round and saw Damini. 'Why are you here?' he cried.

'I have brought you something to eat,' said Damini.

'I want nothing,' said Satish.

'It is very late——' ventured Damini.

'Nothing at all,' repeated Satish.

'Let me then wait a little,' suggested Damini. 'Perhaps later on——?'

'Oh, why will you——' burst out Satish, but as his glance fell on Damini's face he stopped short.

Damini said nothing further. Tray in hand she retraced her steps through the sand, which glared round her like the eye of a tiger in the dark.

Tears had always been rarer in Damini's eyes than lightning flashes. But when I saw her that evening,—seated on the floor, her feet stretched out before her,—she was weeping. When she saw me her tears seemed to burst through some obstruction and showered forth in torrents. I cannot tell what it felt like within my breast. I came near and sat down on one side.

When she had calmed herself a little I inquired: 'Why does Satish's health make you so anxious?'

'What else have I to be anxious about?' she asked simply. 'All the rest he has to think out for himself. There I can neither understand nor help.'

'But consider, Damini,' I said. 'When man's mind puts forth all its energy into one particular channel, his bodily needs become reduced correspondingly. That is why, in the presence of great joy or great sorrow, man does not hunger or thirst. Satish's state of mind is now such that it will do him no harm even if you do not look after his body.'

'I am a woman,' replied Damini. 'The building up of the body with our own body, with our life itself, is our *dharma*. It is woman's own creation. So when we women see the body suffer, our spirit refuses to be comforted.'

'That is why,' I retorted, 'those who are busy with things of the spirit seem to have no eyes for you, the guardians of mere bodies!'

'Haven't they!' Damini flared up. 'So wonderful, rather, is the vision of their eyes, it turns everything topsy-turvy.'

'Ah, woman,' said I to myself. 'That is what fascinates you. Srivilas, my boy, next time you take birth, take good care to be born in the world of topsy-turvydom.'

4

The wound which Satish inflicted on Damini that day on the sands had this result, that he could not remove from his mind the agony he had seen in her eyes. During the succeeding days he had to go through the purgatory of showing her special consideration. It was long since he had freely conversed with us. Now he would send for Damini and talk to her. The experiences and struggles through which he was passing were the subject of these talks.

Damini had never been so exercised by his indifference as she now was by his solicitude. She felt sure this could not last, because the cost was too much to pay. Some day or other Satish's attention would be drawn to the state of the account, and he would discover how high the price was; then would come the crash. The more regular Satish became in his meals and rest, as a good householder should, the more anxious became Damini, the more she felt ashamed of herself. It was almost as if she would be relieved to find Satish becoming rebellious. She seemed to be saying: 'You were quite right to hold aloof. Your concern for me is only punishing yourself. That I cannot bear!—I must,' she appeared to conclude, 'make friends with the neighbours again, and see if I cannot contrive to keep away from the house.'

One night we were roused by a sudden shout: 'Srivilas! Damini!' It must have been past midnight, but Satish could not have taken count of the hour. How he passed his nights we knew not, but the way he went on seemed to have cowed the very ghosts into flight.

We shook off our slumbers, and came out of our respective rooms to find Satish on the flagged pavement in front of the house, standing alone in the darkness. 'I have understood!' he exclaimed as he saw us. 'I have no more doubts.'

Damini softly went up and sat down on the pavement. Satish absently followed her example and sat down too. I also followed suit.

'If I keep going,' said Satish, 'in the same direction along which He comes to me, then I shall only be going further and further away from Him. If I proceed in the opposite direction, then only can we meet.'

I silently gazed at his flaming eyes. As a geometrical truth what he said was right enough. But what in the world was it all about?

'He loves form,' Satish went on, 'so He is continually descending towards form. We cannot live by form alone, so we must ascend towards His formlessness. He is free, so His play is within bonds. We are bound, so we find our joy in freedom. All our sorrow is because we cannot understand this.'

We kept as silent as the stars.

'Do you not understand, Damini?' pursued Satish. 'He who sings proceeds from his joy to the tune; he who hears, from the tune to joy. One comes from freedom into bondage, the other goes from bondage into freedom; only thus can they have their communion. He sings and we hear. He ties the bonds as He sings to us, we untie them as we hear Him.'

I cannot say whether Damini understood Satish's words, but she understood Satish. With her hands folded on her lap she kept quite still.

'I was hearing His song through the night,' Satish went on, 'till in a flash the whole thing became clear to me. Then I could not keep it to myself, and called out to you. All this time I had been trying to fashion Him to suit myself, and so was deprived.—O Desolator! Breaker of ties! Let me be shattered to pieces within you, again and again, for ever and ever. Bonds are not for me, that is why I cannot hold on to bonds for long. Bonds are yours, and so are you kept eternally bound to creation. Play on, then, with our forms and let me take my flight into your formlessness.—O Eternal, you are mine, mine, mine!'—Satish departed into the night towards the river.

After that night, Satish lapsed back into his old ways, forgetful of all claims of rest or nourishment. As to when his mind would rise into the light of ecstasy, or lapse into the depths of gloom, we could make no guess. May God help her who has taken on herself the burden of keeping such a creature within the wholesomeness of worldly habit....

5

It had been stiflingly oppressive the whole day. In the night a great storm burst on us. We had our several rooms along a veranda, in which a light used to be kept burning all night. That was now blown out. The river was lashed into foaming waves, and a flood of rain burst forth from the clouds. The splashing of the waves down below, and the dashing of the torrents from above, played the cymbals in this chaotic revel of the gods. Nothing could be seen of the deafening movements which resounded within the depths of the darkness, and made the sky, like a blind child, break into shivers of fright. Out of the bamboo thickets pierced a scream as of some bereaved giantess. From the mango groves burst the cracking and crashing of breaking timber. The river-side echoed with the deep thuds of falling masses from the crumbling banks. Through the bare ribs of our dilapidated house the keen blasts howled and howled like infuriated beasts.

On such a night the fastenings of the human mind are shaken loose. The storm gains entry and plays havoc within, scattering into disorder its well-arranged furniture of convention, tossing about its curtains of decorous restraint in disturbing revealment. I could not sleep. But what can I write of the thoughts which assailed my sleepless brain? They do not concern this story.

'Who is that?' I heard Satish cry out all of a sudden in the darkness.

'It is I,—Damini,' came the reply. 'Your windows are open, and the rain is streaming in. I have come to close them.'

As she was doing this, she found Satish had got out of his bed. He seemed to stand and hesitate, just for a moment, and then he went out of the room.

Damini went back to her own room and sat long on the threshold. No one returned. The fury of the wind went on increasing in violence.

Damini could sit quiet no longer. She also left the house. It was hardly possible to keep on one's feet in the storm. The sentinels of the revelling gods seemed to be scolding Damini and repeatedly thrusting her back. The rain made desperate attempts to pervade every nook and cranny of the sky.

A flash rent the sky from end to end with terrific tearing thunder. It revealed Satish standing on the river brink. With a supreme effort Damini reached him in one tempestuous rush, outvying the wind. She fell prone at his feet. The shriek of the storm was overcome by her cry: 'At your feet, I swear I had no thought of sin against your God! Why punish me thus?'

Satish stood silent.

'Thrust me into the river with your feet, if you would be rid of me. But return you must!'

Satish came back. As he re-entered the house he said: 'My need for Him whom I seek is immense,—so absolutely, that I have no need for anything else at all. Damini, have pity on me and leave me to Him.'

After a space of silence Damini said: 'I will.'

6

I knew nothing of this at the time, but heard it all from Damini afterwards. So when I saw through my open door the two returning figures pass along the veranda to their rooms, the desolation of my lot fell heavy on my heart and took me by the throat. I struggled up from my bed. Further sleep was impossible that night.

Next morning, what a changed Damini met my eyes! The demon dance of last night's storm seemed to have left all its ravages on this one forlorn girl. Though I knew nothing of what had happened, I felt bitterly angry with Satish.

'Srivilas Babu,' said Damini, 'will you take me on to Calcutta?'

I could guess all that these words meant for her; so I asked no question. But, in the midst of the torture within me, I felt the balm of consolation. It was well that Damini should take herself away from here. Repeated buffeting against the rock could only end in the vessel being broken up.

At parting, Damini made her obeisance to Satish, saying: 'I have grievously sinned at your feet. May I hope for pardon?'

Satish, with his eyes fixed on the ground, replied: 'I also have sinned. Let me first purge my sin away, and then will I claim forgiveness.'

It became clear to me, on our way to Calcutta, what a devastating fire had all along been raging within Damini. I was so scorched by its heat that I could not restrain myself from breaking out in revilement of Satish.

Damini stopped me frenziedly. 'Don't you dare talk so in my presence!' she exclaimed. 'Little do you know what he saved me from! You can only see my sorrow. Had you no eyes for the sorrow he has been through, in order to save me? The hideous tried once to destroy the beautiful, and got well kicked for its pains.—Serve it right!—Serve it right!'—Damini began to beat her breast violently with her clenched hands. I had to hold them back by main force.

When we arrived in the evening, I left Damini at her aunt's and went over to a lodging-house, where I used to be well known. My old acquaintances started at sight of me. 'Have you been ill?' they cried.

By next morning's post I got a letter from Damini. 'Take me away,' she wrote. 'There is no room for me here.'

It appeared that her aunt would not have her. Scandal about us was all over the town. The Pooja numbers of the weekly newspapers had come out shortly after we had given up Lilananda Swami. All the instruments for our execution had been kept sharpened. The carnage turned out to be worthy of the occasion. In our *shastras*[32] the sacrifice of she-animals is prohibited. But, in the case of modern human sacrifice, a woman victim seems to add to the zest of the performers. The mention of Damini's name was skilfully avoided. But no less was the skill which did away with all doubt as to the intention. Anyhow, it had resulted in this shrinkage of room in the house of Damini's distant aunt.

Damini had lost her parents. But I had an idea that her brother was living. I asked Damini for his address, but she shook her head, saying they were too poor. The fact was, Damini did not care to place her brother in an awkward position. What if he also came to say there was no room?

'Where will you stay, then?' I had to inquire.

'I will go back to Lilananda Swami.'

I could not trust myself to speak for a time,—I was so overcome. Was this, then, the last cruel trick which Fate had held in reserve?

'Will the Swami take you back?' I asked at length.

'Gladly!'

Damini understood men. Sect mongers rejoice more in capturing adherents than in comprehending truths. Damini was quite right. There would be no dearth of room for her at Lilananda's, but——

---

[32] Hindu scriptures.

'Damini,' I said, just at this juncture. 'There is another way. If you promise not to be angry, I will mention it.'

'Tell me,' said Damini.

'If it is at all possible for you to think of marrying a creature, such as I am——'

'What are you saying, Srivilas Babu?' interrupted Damini. 'Are you mad?'

'Suppose I am,' said I. 'One can sometimes solve insoluble problems by becoming mad. Madness is like the wishing carpet of the *Arabian Nights*. It can waft one over the thousand petty considerations which obstruct the everyday world.'

'What do you call petty considerations?'

'Such as: What will people think?—What will happen in the future?—and so on, and so forth.'

'And what about the vital considerations?'

'What do you call vital?' I asked in my turn.

'Such as, for instance: What will be your fate if you marry a creature like me?' said Damini.

'If that be a vital consideration, I am reassured. For I cannot possibly be in a worse plight than now. Any movement of my prostrate fortune, even though it be a turning over to the other side, cannot but be a sign of improvement.'

Of course I could not believe that some telepathic news of my state of mind had never reached Damini. Such news, however, had not, so far, come under the head of 'Important'—at least it had not called for any notice to be taken. Now action was definitely demanded of her.

Damini was lost in silent thought.

'Damini,' I said, 'I am only one of the very ordinary sort of men,—even less, for I am of no account in the world. To marry me, or not to marry me, cannot make enough difference to be worth all this thought.'

Tears glistened in Damini's eyes. 'Had you been an ordinary man, it would not have cost me a moment's hesitation,' she said.

After another long silence, Damini murmured: 'You know what I am.'

'You also know what I am,' I rejoined.

Thus was the proposal mooted, relying more on things unspoken than on what was said.

7

Those who, in the old days, had been under the spell of my English speeches had mostly shaken off their fascination during my absence; except only Naren, who still looked on me as one of the rarest products of the age. A house belonging to him was temporarily vacant. In this we took shelter.

It seemed at first that my proposal would never be rescued from the ditch of silence, into which it had lumbered at the very start; or at all events that it would require any amount of discussion and repair work before it could be hauled back on the high road of 'yes' or 'no.'

But man's mind was evidently created to raise a laugh against mental science, with its sudden practical jokes. In the spring, which now came upon us, the Creator's joyous laughter rang through and through this hired dwelling of ours.

All this while Damini never had the time to notice that I was anybody at all; or it may be that the dazzling light from a different quarter had kept her blinded. Now that her world had shrunk around her, it was reduced to me alone. So she had no help but to look on me with seeing eyes. Perhaps it was the kindness of my fate which contrived that this should be her first sight of me.

By river and hill and seashore have I wandered along with Damini, as one of Lilananda's *kirtan* party, setting the atmosphere on fire with passionate song, to the beat of drum and cymbal. Great sparks of emotion were set free as we rang the changes on the text of the Vaishanava poet: *The noose of love hath bound my heart to thy feet.* Yet the curtain which hid me from Damini was not burnt away.

But what was it that happened in this Calcutta lane? The dingy houses, crowding upon one another, blossomed out like flowers of paradise. Verily God vouchsafed to us a miracle. Out of this brick and mortar He fashioned a harp-string to voice forth His melody. And with His wand He touched me, the least of men, and made me, all in a moment, wonderful.

When the curtain is there, the separation is infinite; when it is lifted, the distance can be crossed in the twinkling of an eye. So it took no time at all. 'I was in a dream,' said Damini. 'It wanted this shock to wake me. Between that "you" of mine and this "you" of mine, there was a veil of stupor. I salute my Master again and again, for it is he who dispelled it.'

'Damini,' I said, 'do not keep your gaze on me like that. Before, when you made the discovery that this creation of God is not beautiful, I was able to bear it; but it will be difficult to do so now.'

'I am making the discovery,' she replied, 'that this creation of God has its beauty.'

'Your name will go down in history!' I exclaimed. 'The planting of the explorer's flag on the South Pole heights was child's play to this discovery of yours. "Difficult" is not the word for it. You will have achieved the impossible!'

I had never realised before how short our spring month of Phalgun[33] is. It has only thirty days, and each of the days is not a minute more than twenty-four hours. With the infinite time which God has at His disposal, such parsimony I failed to understand!

'This mad freak that you are bent on,' said Damini; 'what will your people have to say to it?'

'My people are my best friends. So they are sure to turn me out of their house.'

'What next?'

'Next it will be for you and me to build up a home, fresh from the very foundations, that will be our own special creation.'

'You must also fashion afresh the mistress of your house, from the very beginning. May she also be your creation, with no trace left of her old battered condition!'

We fixed a day in the following month for the wedding. Damini insisted that Satish should be brought over.

'What for?' I asked.

'He must give me away.'

Where the madcap was wandering I was not sure. I had written several letters, but with no reply. He could hardly have given up that old haunted house, otherwise my letters would have been returned as undelivered. The chances were that he had not the time to be opening and reading letters.

'Damini,' said I, 'you must come with me and invite him personally. This is not a case for sending a formal invitation letter. I could have gone by myself, but my courage is not equal to it. For all we know, he may be on the other side of the river, superintending the preening of ducks' feathers. To follow him there is a desperate venture of which you alone are capable!'

Damini smiled. 'Did I not swear I would never pursue him there again?'

'You swore you would not go to him with food any more. That does not cover your going over to invite him to a repast!'

---

[33] Spring.

8

This time everything passed off smoothly. We each took Satish by one hand and brought him along with us back to Calcutta. He was as pleased as a child receiving a pair of new dolls!

Our idea had been to have a quiet wedding. But Satish would have none of that. Moreover, there were the Mussulman friends of Uncle Jagamohan. When they heard the news, they were so extravagantly jubilant that the neighbours must have thought it was for the Amir of Kabul or the Nizam of Hyderabad, at the very least. But the height of revelry was reached by the newspapers in a very orgy of calumny. Our hearts, however, were too full to harbour any resentment. We were quite willing to allow the blood-thirstiness of the readers to be satisfied, and the pockets of the proprietors to be filled,—along with our blessings to boot.

'Come and occupy my house, Visri, old fellow,' said Satish.

'Come with us, too,' I added. 'Let us set to work together over again.'

'No, thank you,' said Satish. 'My work is elsewhere.'

'You won't be allowed to go till you have assisted at our house-warming,' insisted Damini.

This function was not going to be a crowded affair, Satish being the only guest. But it was all very well for him to say: 'Come and occupy my house.' That had already been done by his father, Harimohan,—not directly, but through a tenant. Harimohan would have entered into possession himself, but his worldly and other-worldly advisers warned him that it was best not to risk it,—a Mussulman having died there of the plague. Of course the tenant to whom it was offered ran the same spiritual and physical risks, but then why need he be told?

How we got the house out of Harimohan's clutches is a long story. The Mussulman leather-dealers were our chief allies. When they got to know the contents of the will, we found further legal steps to be superfluous.

The allowance which I had all along been getting from home was now stopped. It was all the more of a joy to us to undertake together the toil of setting up house without outside assistance. With the seal of Premchand-Roychand it was not difficult for me to secure a professorship. I was able to supplement my income by publishing notes on the prescribed text-books, which were eagerly availed of as patent nostrums for passing examinations. I need not have done so much, for our own wants were few. But Damini insisted that Satish should not have to worry about his own living while we were here to prevent it.

There was another thing about which Damini did not say a word. I had to attend to it secretly. That was the education of her brother's son and the marriage of his daughter. Both of these matters were beyond the means of her brother himself. His house was barred to us, but pecuniary assistance has no caste to stand in the way of its acceptance. Moreover, acceptance did not necessarily involve acknowledgment. So I had to add the sub-editorship of a newspaper to my other occupations.

Without consulting Damini, I engaged a cook and two servants. Without consulting me, Damini sent them packing the very next day. When I objected, she made me conscious how ill-judged was my attempted consideration for her. 'If I am not allowed,' she said, 'to do my share of work while you are slaving away, where am I to hide my shame?'

My work outside and Damini's work at home flowed on together like the confluent Ganges and Jumna. Damini also began to teach sewing to the leather-dealers' little girls. She was determined not to take defeat at my hands. I am not enough of a poet to sing how this Calcutta house of ours became Brindaban[34] itself,

---

[34]A center for Hindu pilgrimage in north central India.

our labours the flute strains which kept it enraptured. All I can say is that our days did not drag, neither did they merely pass by,—they positively danced along.

One more springtime came and went; but never another.

Ever since her return from the cave-temple Damini had suffered from a pain in her breast, of which, however, she then told no one. This suddenly took a turn for the worse, and when I asked her about it she said: 'This is my secret wealth, my touchstone. With it, as dower, I was able to come to you. Otherwise I would not have been worthy.'

The doctors, each of them, had a different name for the malady. Neither did they agree in their prescriptions. When my little hoard of gold was blown away between the cross-fire of the doctors' fees and the chemist's bills, the chapter of medicament came to an end, and change of air was advised. As a matter of fact, hardly anything of changeable value was left to us except air.

'Take me to the place from which I brought the pain,' said Damini. 'It has no dearth of air.'

When the month of Magh ended with its full moon and Phalgun began, while the sea heaved and sobbed with the wail of its lonely eternity, Damini, taking the dust of my feet, bade farewell to me with the words:

'I have not had enough of you. May you be mine again in our next birth.'

MORI ŌGAI
[1862–1922]

The last few decades of the Tokugawa period (1603–1868), a time of rigidly enforced isolationism for Japan, correspond roughly with the wave of romanticism sweeping through Europe. Like their European contemporaries, Japanese writers of the nineteenth century witnessed rapid social and economic changes: the decline of neo-Confucianism and the rigid social hierarchy it helped to legitimate, an acceleration of demand for a reform of government to better accommodate a rising middle class, the gradual opening of Japan to trade with the West, growing dependence upon money as a means of exchange, and the commercialization of art and literature. In 1854, the Tokugawa shogunate that had ruled for over 200 years was threatened when Commodore Perry and the Japanese signed the Treaty of Kanagawa, which opened Japanese ports to American ships; four years later the Commercial Treaty of 1858 between the United States and Japan opened more ports and brought Japan into the world of international trade. Strongly opposed by clans who exploited the antiforeign sentiment welling up in Japan against the Emperor and the Tokugawa Shogun, whom many saw as selling out their national identity, a number of clan leaders called the Satcho Hito group took control of the government and led the Japanese into the modern world through the so-called Meiji Restoration.

The Meiji leadership encouraged a careful exchange of ideas and technology with the West, announcing in its charter of 1868 that "knowledge shall be sought from all the world and thus shall the foundation of the Imperial polity be strengthened." Entering the world marketplace of ideas and commodities involved major changes in the way the Japanese conducted their educational system, legal system, military, and industry; one area that remained inviolate, however, was religion. The traditional Shintoism was promoted under the Meiji leadership both as a spiritual practice and as a means to maintain a sense of national identity under the emperor, said to be a descendant of the Sun Goddess. Even when a parliamentary government was established under the constitution of 1889 that protected the civil rights of Japanese citizens, the emperor's place remained secure; article three of the constitution, for example, stated that the emperor was "sacred and inviolable." Loyalty to the emperor and the modernization of the military led Japan to defeat first China in 1894 and then Russia, which was trying to gain territory in Manchuria and Korea, in 1905. Apparently the decision to send young intellectuals abroad to bring back ideas for rebuilding the Japanese system had succeeded, and with these victories Western leaders recognized Japan as a major world power.

One of the young intellectuals sent to Europe was Mori Ōgai, one of the greatest writers of the Meiji period, an army doctor with connections to the highest ranking bureaucracy. Steeped in the tradition of the *samurai,* Japanese and Chinese literature, and European science and literature, Ōgai was one of the first great Japanese writers whose birth, education, and career combined to span the newly made bridge between East and West. Although loyal to the values of the oligarchy and the traditional rule of *giri,* or obligation to one's public responsibilities, Ōgai also appreciated some of the values of the West, including its emphasis upon individual talent and freedom. Obviously, *giri* does not reconcile well with individualism, and in Ōgai's work we see the struggle to bring the two into some kind of meaningful balance between a disciplined deference to authority and a reasoned self-enlightenment. Along with his contemporary Natsume Sōseki, Ōgai founded a school of fiction writing opposed to the prevailing literary naturalism of Meiji literature.

LIFE

Mori Ōgai was born Mori Rinatro in 1862 in the small town of Tsuwano in western Japan. Keeping up a tradition that went back several generations, Ōgai's father Shizuo was a doctor in the service of the *daimyō,* or feudal lord, and Ōgai received the education to follow in his father's footsteps. By age five, Ōgai began the study of Confucius and Mencius, and at age seven he entered the fief school, where he excelled at his study of these Chinese philosophers, mathematics, medicine, and Dutch. Here he won annual prizes for his scholarship. Shortly after the dissolution of the fiefdoms, Ōgai left Tsuwano for Tokyo, where he took up the study of German—the language of choice for medical professionals—and lived with Nishi Amane, a prominent scholar and bureaucrat in the Department of Military Affairs, whose special interest was Western civilization. By 1874 Ōgai, two years underage, enrolled in the preparatory course for medical school and began his medical training under the direction of German professors in 1877 at the University of Tokyo, from which he graduated in 1881. In that same year he entered the Medical Corps, hoping to travel to Europe. Within three years, Ōgai received orders to go to Berlin to study hygiene and the administration of medicine in the German army. In Germany, Ōgai pursued his medical studies, read widely in German literature and philosophy, including the works of Goethe, Schiller, and Heine, and fell in love with a German woman. He left a diary, *Doitsu nikki,* of these years, and we can get some sense of his impressions from Ōgai's earliest short stories, written shortly after his return to Japan. "Maihime" ("The Dancing Girl"), Ōgai's first short story, describes the disappointed love affair of Ōta Toyotarō, who, like Ōgai, had been sent to Berlin to study German culture. Other stories that treat the German experience are "Utakata no ki" ("A Record of Froth on the Water") and "Fumizukai" ("The Courier"), written a few years after his return to Japan.

When he returned to Japan in the fall of 1888, after visiting London and Paris, Ōgai started a literary magazine called *Shiragami zōshi,* in which he published his own and other works of fiction, translations of European and American writers, and literary criticism. Ōgai also published a collection of translations called *Omokage* (*Vestiges*), in which he developed a new style of form and diction. In addition, he became involved in public health and in urban planning projects, taking up the cause of the working classes who needed housing and health care. After a year-long, unsuccessful marriage that ended in 1890 and a one-year tour of Korea during the Sino–Japanese War in 1894, Ōgai founded an avant-garde journal called *Mezamashigusa* (*Remarkable Notes*), which ended in 1900 when he entered what he called his "years of exile" in the remote town of Kokura, banished for his zealous attempt to move Japanese science and art into the modern era too quickly. At forty, Ōgai returned to Tokyo in 1902 and began another journal, *Mannensō* (*Eternal Grasses*), only to have another war—the Russo–Japanese war of 1904–1905—interrupt his work as writer, critic, scholar, and translator. With the end of the war, Ōgai returned to Tokyo and focused his energies on an incredible array of literary tasks. He wrote and produced plays actively seeking to modernize Japanese drama, translated works of European literature and philosophy, and wrote poetry and fiction. Among the works of this later period are his famous translation of Goethe's *Faust* (1913); *Shizuka*, a historical drama based on a traditional character from the Nō and Kabuki theater; *Kamen* (*Mask*), a play that speaks out against naturalism and argues that in the interest of social harmony one should cloak emotions that would disturb others; and the autobiographical quartet of novels *Vita sekusuarisu* (*Vita Sexualis*, 1909, which was banned), *Seinen* (*Youth*, 1911), *Gan* (*Wild Geese*, 1913), and *Kaijin* (*Destruction*), which remained unfinished.

In the last years of his life, Ōgai turned more attention to philosophy and history, writing many stories dealing with the Tokugawa period, including "The Last Will and Testament of Okitsu Yagoemon" (1912), a historically displaced meditation on the ritual suicide of General Nogi following the death of Emperor Meiji in 1912. He also wrote a story set in the Middle Ages, "Sanshō dayū" ("Sansho the Bailiff"), and some dealing with China, including "Kanzan Jitoku" concerning the celebrated Han Shan, the author of the Cold Mountain poems. Ōgai's interest in historical themes, incidents, and people also led him to write three historical works centering around the life of Shibue Chūsai, whose education and career as a doctor in the late Tokugawa period were close enough to Ōgai's to allow him to create a kind of spiritual and intellectual double of himself in the life of Chūsai. As he fought a kidney ailment and possibly a long-term tuberculosis in the last years of his life, Mori Ōgai tenaciously clung to what he called his "will to write," and he continued working and writing almost to the very end of his life on July 9, 1922.

Work

During the nineteenth century, Japanese literature turned from imitation of the Chinese and Japanese classics toward a literature more vitally engaged with the immediate present and the inner life of the individual writer. Poets Kagawa Kageki (1768–1843) and Uchiyama Mayumi (1784–1852), and *haikai* master Kobayashi Issa, like Wordsworth in England, rejected the use of conventional poetic devices and diction. They argued that the poet should disregard *giri*, duty or obligation imposed by tradition, in favor of a more personal style that would set the writer free to explore his or her own creative powers. Writers such as Takizawa Bakin (1767–1848) introduced a new kind of novel, the *yomihon*, or reading books. These books drew upon Buddhist stories, Japanese theater, and Japanese feudal history to set up elaborate plots with romantic heroes and mystical events. With the beginning of the Meiji period, as Japanese writers came into contact with European romanticism, realism, and naturalism, the *gesaku* notion of literature as a mere pastime or diversion gave way to the idea that literature should portray an accurate copy of human behavior, a picture of the fine detail of everyday life in its drudgery as well as its splendor. Under the influence of Turgenev, whose work he translated, Futabatei Shimei (1864–1909) published *Ukigumo* (*Floating Cloud*, 1887–1889), whose tormented character Utsumi Bunzo resembles those forlorn souls who adorn the pages of Flaubert and Chekhov. Against the dominant force of the realists and naturalists, who in Japan tended to focus on sexual more than social depravity, Ōgai adopted the idealist aesthetics of Karl Robert von Hartmann, the author of a two-volume work on the history of German aesthetics and the philosophy of the beautiful. Revealing a certain affinity for romanticism, Ōgai criticized writers such as Zola for their stark description of unpalatable emotion. Ōgai preferred to remove his reader beyond the drudgery of the everyday; as he noted in "Shōsetsuron" ("On the Novel," 1889), the "desire to seek real facts has never hindered dreams of visiting the Infinite."

"Maihime" ("The Dancing Girl"), which appeared in 1890 and deals with Ōgai's experience in Germany, pulls in the direction of realism in its account of the disappointments of its protagonist, Ōta Toyotarō, yet it also conveys a sense of the promise that love ignites in the young couple. Ōta Toyotarō, like Ōgai, arrives in Berlin on an official mission to study. Dismissed because of unfavorable reports about his seriousness, he meets Elise, a young German dancer with whom he falls in love. Eventually, Ōta learns that he can return to Japan and restore his name, but only if he leaves Elise, now pregnant. Much of the story revolves around his anguished attempt to reach a decision, torn between a compelling sense of tradition-laden obligation to his homeland and a profound pull toward the new sense of self-responsibility, symbolized in part by Elise—a kind of European doppelgänger who represents the attraction of the West. Ōta Toyotarō thus becomes a symbol of the Japanese mind as it cautiously opens up to non-Japanese influences and cultures.

SUGGESTED READINGS

For general criticism combined with biographical information on Ōgai, see Richard John Bowring's *Mori Ōgai and the Modernization of Japanese Culture* (1979), J. Thomas Rimer's *Mori Ōgai* (1975), and Eric W. Johnson's "The Historical Fiction and Biography of Mori Ōgai," in *The Journal of the Association of Teachers of Japanese* (November 1972). J. Thomas Rimer's *Youth and Other Stories* (1994) presents a selection of Ōgai's short stories translated into English.

The Dancing Girl

Translated by Richard Bowring

They have finished loading the coal, and the tables here in the second-class saloon stand in silence. Even the bright glare from the electric lights seems wasted, for tonight the group of card players who usually gather here of an evening are staying in a hotel and I am left alone on board.

It is now five years since the hopes I cherished for so long were fulfilled and I received orders to go to Europe. When I arrived here in the port of Saigon, I was struck by the strangeness of everything I saw and heard. I wonder how many thousands of words I wrote every day as I jotted down random thoughts in my travel diary. It was published in a newspaper at the time and was highly praised, but now I shudder to think how any sensitive person must have reacted to my childish ideas and my presumptuous rhetoric. I even recorded details of the common flora and fauna, the geology, and the local customs as if they were rarities. Now, on my way home, the notebooks that I bought intending to use for a diary remain untouched. Could it be that while studying in Germany I developed a kind of *nil admirari* attitude? No, there is another reason.

Returning to Japan, I feel a very different person from when I set out. Not only do I still feel dissatisfied with my studies, but I have also learned how sad this transient life can be. I am now aware of the fallibility of human emotions, but in particular I realize what a fickle heart I have myself. To whom could I possibly show a record of fleeting impressions that might well be right one day and wrong the next? Perhaps this is why my diary was never written. No, there is another reason.

Twenty days or more have passed since we left Brindisi.[1] Usually it is the custom at sea to while away the cares of travel even in the company of utter strangers, but I have shut myself up in my cabin under the pretext of feeling somewhat indisposed. I seldom speak to my fellow travelers, for I am tormented by a hidden remorse.

At first this pain was a mere wisp of cloud that brushed against my heart, hiding the mountain scenery of Switzerland and dulling my interest in Italy's ancient ruins. Then gradually I grew weary of life and weary of myself, and suffered the most heart-rending anguish. Now, remorse has settled in the depths of my heart, the merest shadow. And yet, with everything I read and see it causes me renewed pain, evoking feelings of extreme nostalgia, like a form reflected in a mirror or the echo of a voice.

How can I ever rid myself of such remorse? If it were of a different nature I could perhaps soothe my feelings by expressing them in poetry. But it is so deeply engraved upon my heart that I fear this is impossible. And yet, as there is no one here this evening, and it will be some while before the cabin boy comes to turn off the light, I think I will try to record the outline of my story here.

Thanks to a very strict education at home since childhood, my studies lacked nothing, despite the fact that I had lost my father at an early age. When I studied at the school in my former fief, and in the preparatory course for the university in Tokyo, and later in the Faculty of Law, the name Ōta Toyotarō was always at the top of the list. Thus, no doubt, I brought some comfort to my mother who had found in me, her only child, the strength to go through life. At nineteen I received my degree and was praised for having achieved greater honor than had any other student since the founding of the university. I joined a government department and spent three pleasant years in Tokyo with my mother, whom I had called up from the country. Being especially high in the estimation of the head of my department, I was then given orders to travel to Europe and study matters connected with my particular section. Stirred by the thought that now I had the opportunity to make my name and raise my family fortunes, I was not too sorry to leave even my mother, although she was over fifty. So it was that I left home far behind and arrived in Berlin.

I had the vague hope of accomplishing great feats and was used to working hard under pressure. But suddenly here I was, standing in the middle of this most modern of European capitals. My eyes were dazzled by its brilliance, my mind was dazed by the riot of color. To translate Unter den Linden as 'under the Bodhi tree'[2] would suggest a quiet secluded spot. But just come and see the groups of men and women sauntering along the pavements that line each side of that great thoroughfare as it runs, straight as a die, through the city. It was still in the days

---

[1] A port town in southeastern Italy.

[2] A street lined with lime trees in Berlin. Ōgai may also allude to the classic poem by Walter von der Vogelweide (c. 1170–1230), a medieval German lyric poet. The linden is a lime tree; the Bodhi tree is the sacred fig tree, associated with Gautama Buddha, who attained enlightenment meditating beneath this "tree of wisdom."

when Wilhelm I would come to his window and gaze down upon his capital. The tall, broad-shouldered officers in their colorful dress uniform, and the attractive girls, their hair made up in the Parisian style, were everywhere a delight to the eye. Carriages ran silently on asphalt roads. Just visible in the clear sky between the towering buildings were fountains cascading with the sound of heavy rain. Looking into the distance, one could see the statue of the goddess on the victory column. She seemed to be floating halfway to heaven from the midst of the green trees on the other side of the Brandenburg Gate.[3] All these myriad sights were gathered so close at hand that it was quite bewildering for the newcomer. But I had promised myself that I would not be impressed by such captivating scenes of beauty and I continually closed my mind to these external objects that bore in on me.

The Prussian officials were all happy to welcome me when I pulled on the bell rope, asked for an interview, and handed over my open letter of introduction, explaining to them why I had come. They promised to tell me whatever I wished to know once formal application had been received from the Legation. I was fortunate enough to have learned both French and German at home, and no sooner was I introduced than they asked where and when I had learned to speak so well.

I had already obtained official permission to enter Berlin University and so I enrolled to study politics whenever my duties might permit. After one or two months, when the official preliminaries had been carried out and my investigations were making good progress, I sent off a report on the most urgent matters, and the rest I wrote down in a number of notebooks. As far as the university was concerned, there was no chance of providing special courses for would-be politicians, as I had naively hoped. I was irresolute for a while, but then, deciding to attend two or three law lectures, I paid the fee and went to listen.

Some three years passed in this way like a dream. But there is always a time when, come what may, one's true nature reveals itself. I had obeyed my father's dying words and had done what my mother had taught me. From the beginning I had studied willingly, proud to hear myself praised as an infant prodigy, and later I had labored unremittingly in the happy knowledge that my department head was pleased with my excellent work. But all that time I had been a mere passive, mechanical being with no real awareness of myself. Now, however, at the age of twenty-five, perhaps because I had been exposed to the liberal ways of the university for some time, there grew within me a kind of uneasiness; it seemed as if my real self, which had been lying dormant deep down, was gradually appearing on the surface and threatening my former assumed self. I realized that I would be happy neither as a high-flying politician nor as a lawyer learning statutes off by heart and pronouncing sentence.

My mother, I thought to myself, had tried to make me into a walking dictionary, and my department head had tried to turn me into an incarnation of the law. The former I might just be able to stand, but the latter was out of the question. Up to then I had answered him with scrupulous care even in quite trifling matters, but from that time on, I often argued in my reports that one should not be bothered with petty legal details. Once a person grasped the spirit of the law, I grandly said, everything would solve itself. In the university I abandoned the law lectures, and became more interested in history and literature; eventually I moved into the world of the arts.

My department head had obviously tried to turn me into a machine that could be manipulated as he desired. He could hardly have been very pleased with someone

---

[3]A magnificent gate in Berlin, designed in the Doric style by Karl Langhaus and completed in 1791.

who entertained such independent ideas and held such unusual views. I was in a precarious situation. If that were all, however, it would not have been enough to undermine my position. But among the students studying at Berlin at the time was an influential group with whom I did not see eye to eye. They were only suspicious of me at first, but then they began to slander me. They may have had good reason.

Attributing the fact that I neither drank nor played billiards with them to apparent stubbornness and self-restraint on my part, they ridiculed and envied me. But this was because they did not know me. How could anyone else know the reason for my behavior when I did not know it myself? I felt like the leaves of the silk-tree which shrink and shy away when they are touched. I felt as unsure of myself as a young girl. Ever since my youth I had followed the advice of my elders and kept to the path of learning and obedience. If I had succeeded, it was not through being courageous. I might have seemed capable of arduous study, but I had deceived not only myself but others too. I had simply followed a path that I was made to follow. The fact that external matters did not disturb me was not because I had the courage to reject them or ignore them, but rather because I was afraid and tied myself hand and foot. Before I left home I was convinced I was a man of talent. I believed deeply in my own powers of endurance. Yes, but even that was short-lived. I felt quite the hero until the ship left Yokohama, but then I found myself weeping uncontrollably. I thought it strange at the time, but it was my true nature showing through. Perhaps it had been with me from my birth; or perhaps it came about because my father died and I was brought up by my mother.

The ridicule of the students was only to be expected, but it was stupid of them to be jealous of such a weak and pitiful mind.

I used to see women sitting in the cafés soliciting for custom; their faces were heavily made up and their clothes were gaudy. But I never had the courage to go and approach them. Nor did I have the nerve to join in with those men about town, with their tall hats, their pince-nez, and that aristocratic nasal accent so peculiar to Prussians. Not having the heart for such things, I found I could not mix with my more lively fellow countrymen, and because of this barrier between us, they bore a grudge against me. Then they started telling tales, and thus I was accused of crimes I had not committed and had to put up with so much hardship in so short a time.

One evening I sauntered through the Tiergarten and then walked down Unter den Linden. On the way back to my lodgings in Monbijoustrasse, I came in front of the old church in Klosterstrasse. How many times, I wonder, had I passed through that sea of lights, entered this gloomy passage, and stood enraptured, gazing at the three-hundred-year-old church that lay set back from the road. Opposite it stood some houses with the washing hanging out to dry on poles on the roofs, and a bar where an old Jew with long whiskers was standing idly by the door; there was also a tenement house with one flight of steps running directly to the upper rooms and another leading down to the home of a blacksmith who lived in the cellar.

Just as I was walking past I noticed a young girl sobbing against the closed door of the church. She must have been about sixteen or seventeen. Her light golden hair flowed down from under the scarf around her head, and her dress was spotlessly clean. Surprised by my footsteps, she turned around. Only a poet could really do her justice. Her eyes were blue and clear, but filled with a wistful sadness. They were shaded by long eyelashes which half hid her tears. Why was it that in one glance over her shoulder she pierced the defenses of my heart?

Perhaps it was because of some profound grief that she was standing there in tears oblivious of all else. The coward in me was overcome by compassion and sympathy, and without thinking I went to her side.

'Why are you crying?' I asked. 'Perhaps because I am a stranger here I may be able to help you all the more.' I was astounded by my audacity.

Startled, she stared into my sallow face, but she must have seen my sincerity from my expression.

'You look a kind sort of person,' she sobbed. 'Not cruel like him or my mother!'

Her tears had stopped for a moment, but now they overflowed again and ran down her lovely cheeks.

'Help me! You must help me from having to lose all sense of shame. My mother beat me because I did not agree to his proposal. My father has just died and we have to bury him tomorrow. But we don't have a penny in the house.'

She dissolved into tears again. I gazed at her as she hung her head and trembled.

'If I am to take you home, you must calm down,' I said. 'Don't let everyone hear you. We're out in the street.'

She had inadvertently lain her head on my shoulder while I was speaking. Suddenly she looked up and, giving me the same startled glance as before, she fled from me in shame.

She walked quickly, as if unwilling for people to see her, and I followed. Through a large door across the road from the church was a flight of old worn stone steps. Up these steps on the third floor was a door so small that one needed to bend down to enter. The girl pulled on the twisted end of a rusty piece of wire.

'Who's there?' came a hoarse voice from inside.

'It's Elise. I'm back.'

She had hardly finished speaking when the door was roughly pulled open by an old woman. Although her hair was graying and her brow clearly showed the traces of poverty and suffering, it was not an evil face. She was wearing an old dress of some wool and cotton material and had on some dirty slippers. When Elise pointed to me and went inside, the old woman slammed the door in my face as if she had been waiting impatiently.

I stood there vacantly for a while. Then, by the light of an oil lamp, I noticed a name painted on the door in lacquer: 'Ernst Weigert', and below, 'Tailor'. I presumed it was the name of the girl's dead father. Inside I heard voices raised as if in argument, then all was quiet again. The door was reopened, and the old woman, apologizing profusely for such impolite behavior, invited me in.

The door opened into the kitchen. On the right was a low window with spotlessly clean linen curtains. On the left was a roughly-built brick stove. The door of the room facing me was half open and I saw inside a bed covered with a white sheet. The dead man must have been lying there. She opened a door next to the stove and led me to an attic; it faced onto the street and had no real ceiling. The beams sloping down from the corners of the roof to the window were covered with paper, and below that, where there was only room enough to stoop, was a bed. On the table in the middle of the room was spread a beautiful woollen cloth on which were arranged two books, a photograph album, and a vase with a bunch of flowers. They seemed somehow too expensive for the place. Standing shyly beside the table was the girl.

She was exceedingly attractive. In the lamplight her pallid face had a faint blush, and the slender beauty of her hands and feet seemed hardly to belong to the daughter of a poor family. She waited until the old woman had left the room and then spoke. She had a slight accent.

'It was thoughtless of me to lead you here. Please forgive me. But you looked so very kind. You won't despise me, will you. I suppose you don't know Schaumberg, the man we were relying on for my father's funeral tomorrow. He's the manager at the Viktoria Theater. I have been working for him for two years so I thought he was bound to help us; but he took advantage of our misfortune and tried to force me to do what he wished. You must help. I promise to pay you back from the little I earn, even if I have to go hungry. If not, then my mother says. . . .'

She burst into tears and stood there trembling. There was an irresistible appeal in her eyes as she gazed up at me. Did she know the effect her eyes had on me, or was it unintentional?

I had two or three silver marks in my pocket, but that would probably not have been enough. So I took off my watch and laid it on the table.

'This will help you for the time being,' I said. 'Tell the pawnbroker's man if he calls on Ōta at 3 Monbijoustrasse, I'll redeem it.'

The girl looked startled but grateful. As I put out my hand to say goodbye, she raised it to her lips and covered it with tears.

Alas, what evil fate brought her to my lodgings to thank me? She looked so beautiful there standing by the window where I used to sit reading all day long surrounded by the works of Schopenhauer and Schiller.[4] From that time on our relationship gradually deepened. When my countrymen got to know, they immediately assumed that I was seeking my pleasures in the company of dancing girls. But it was as yet nothing more than a foolish trifling affair.

One of my fellow countrymen—I will not give his name, but he was known as a mischief-maker—reported to my department head that I was frequenting theaters and seeking the company of actresses. My superior was in any case resentful that I was neglecting my proper studies, and so he eventually told the Legation to abolish my post and terminate my employment. The Minister at the Legation passed this order on, advising me that they would pay the fare if I returned home immediately, but that I could expect no official help if I decided to stay on. I asked for one week's grace, and it was while I was thus worrying what to do that I received two letters which brought me the most intense pain I think I have ever suffered. They had both been sent at almost the same time, but one was written by my mother and the other by a friend telling me of her death, the death of the mother who was so dear to me. I cannot bear to repeat here what she wrote. Tears prevent my pen from writing more.

The relationship between Elise and myself had in fact been more innocent than had appeared to others. Her father had been poor and her education had been meager. At the age of fifteen she had answered an advertisement by a dancing master and had learned that disreputable trade. When she had finished the course, she went to the Viktoria Theater and was now the second dancer of the group. But the life of a dancer is precarious. As the writer Hackländer[5] has said, they are today's slaves, tied by a poor wage and driven hard with rehearsals in the daytime and performances at night. In the theater dressing room they can make up and dress themselves in beautiful clothes; but outside they often do not have enough clothes or food for themselves and life is very hard for those who have to support their parents or families. It was said that, as a result, it was rare for them not to fall into the lowest of all professions.

Elise had escaped this fate, partly owing to her modest nature and partly because of her father's careful protection. Ever since a child, she had in fact liked reading,

---

[4]Arthur Schopenhauer (1788–1860), German philosopher influenced by Hindu thought; Friedrich von Schiller (1759–1805), German writer of literary, critical, and historical works.

[5]Friedrich Wilhelm von Hackländer (1807–1877), a minor German novelist and playwright.

but all she could lay her hands on were poor novels of the type lent by the circulating libraries, known by their cry of '*Colportage*'. After meeting me, she began to read the books I lent her, and gradually her tastes improved and she lost her accent. Soon the mistakes in her letters to me became fewer. And so there had grown up between us a kind of teacher–pupil relationship. When she heard of my untimely dismissal, she went pale. I concealed the fact that it was connected with her, but she asked me not to tell her mother. She was afraid that if her mother knew I had lost financial support for my studies she would want nothing more to do with me.

There is no need to describe it in detail here, but it was about this time that my feeling for her suddenly changed to one of love and the bond between us deepened. The most important decision of my life lay before me. It was a time of real crisis. Some perhaps may wonder and criticize my behavior, but my affection for Elise had been strong ever since our first meeting, and now I could read in her expression sympathy for my misfortune and sadness at the prospect of parting. The way she stood there, a picture of loveliness, her hair hanging loose—I was distraught by so much suffering and powerless in the face of such enchantment.

The day I had arranged to meet the Minister approached. Fate was pressing. If I returned home like this, I should have failed in my studies and bear a disgraced name. I would never be able to re-establish myself. But on the other hand, if I stayed, I could not see any way of obtaining funds to support my studies.

At this point, my friend Aizawa Kenkichi, with whom I am now travelling home, came to my aid. He was private secretary to Count Amakata in Tokyo, and he saw the report of my dismissal in the Official Gazette. He persuaded the editor of a certain newspaper to make me their foreign correspondent, so I could stay in Berlin and send back reports on various topics such as politics and the arts.

The salary they offered was a pittance, but by changing my lodgings and eating lunch at a cheaper restaurant, I would just be able to make ends meet. While I was trying to decide, Elise showed her love by throwing me a life line. I don't know how she did it, but she managed to win over her mother, and I was accepted as a lodger in their rooms. It was not long before Elise and I found ourselves pooling our meager resources, and managed, even in the midst of all our troubles, to enjoy life.

After breakfast, Elise either went to rehearsals, or, when she was free, would stay at home. I would go to the coffee shop on Königsstrasse with its narrow frontage and its long deep interior. There, in a room lit by an open skylight, I used to read all the newspapers and jot down the odd note or two in pencil. Here would come young men with no regular job, old men who lived quite happily by lending out the little money that they had, and jobbers stealing time off from their work at the Exchange to put their feet up for a while. I wonder what they made of the strange Japanese who sat among them writing busily on the cold stone table, quite oblivious that the cup of coffee the waitress had brought was getting cold, and who was always going back and forth to the wall where the newspapers were hanging open in long wooden frames. When Elise had rehearsals, she would call in about one o'clock on her way home. Some of the people there must have looked askance when we left together, myself and this girl who seemed as if she could dance in the palm of your hand.

I neglected my studies. When she came home from the theater, Elise would sit in a chair and sew, and I would write my articles on the table by her side, using the faint light of the lamp hanging from the ceiling. These articles were quite unlike my earlier reports when I had raked up onto paper the dead leaves of laws and statutes. Now I wrote about the lively political scene and criticized the latest trends in literature and the arts, carefully composing the articles to the best of my ability, more in the style of Heine than Börne.[6] During this time Wilhelm I and Friedrich III died in quick succession. Writing particularly detailed reports on subjects such as the accession of the new emperor and the fall of Bismarck, I found myself from then on much busier than I had expected, and it was difficult to read the few books I had or return to my studies. I had not cancelled my registration at the university, but I could not afford to pay the fees and so seldom went to any lectures.

Yes, I neglected my studies. But I did become expert in a different sphere—popular education, for this was more advanced in Germany than in any other European country. No sooner had I become a correspondent than I was constantly reading and writing about the variety of excellent discussions appearing in the newspapers and journals, and I brought to this work the perception gained from my studies as a university student. My knowledge of the world, which up to then had been rather limited, thus became much broader, and I reached a stage undreamed of by most of my compatriots studying there. They could barely read the editorials in the German newspapers.

Then came the winter of 1888. They spread grit on the pavements of the main streets and shoveled the snow into piles. Although the ground in the Klosterstrasse area was bumpy and uneven, the surface became smooth with ice. It was sad to see the starved sparrows frozen to death on the ground when you opened the door in the mornings. We lit a fire in the stove to warm the room, but it was still unbearably cold. The north European winter penetrated the stone walls and pierced our cotton clothes. A few evenings before, Elise had fainted on stage and had been helped home by some friends. She felt ill from then on and rested. But she brought up whatever she tried to eat and it was her mother who first suggested that it might be morning sickness. Even without this my future was uncertain. What could I possibly do if it were true?

It was Sunday morning. I was at home, but felt somewhat uneasy. Elise did not feel bad enough to go to bed; she sat on a chair drawn up close to the small fireplace but said little. There was the sound of someone at the door and her mother, who had been in the kitchen, hurried in with a letter for me. I recognized Aizawa's handwriting immediately, but the stamp was Prussian and it was postmarked Berlin. Feeling puzzled, I opened the letter. The news was totally unexpected: 'Arrived yesterday evening as part of Count Amakata's suite. The Count says he wants to see you immediately. If your fortunes are ever to be restored, now is the time. Excuse brevity but sent in great haste.'

I stared at the letter.

'Is it from home?' asked Elise. 'It's not bad news, is it?'

She was probably thinking it was connected with my salary from the newspaper.

'No,' I replied. 'There's no need to worry. You've heard me mention Aizawa. Well, he's just arrived in Berlin with his Minister. He wants to see me. He says it's urgent, so I'd better go along without delay.'

Not even a mother seeing off her beloved only child could have been more solicitous. Thinking I was to have an interview with the Count, Elise fought back her illness. She chose a clean white shirt and got out my *Gehrock*, a coat with two rows of buttons, which she had carefully stored away. She helped me into it, and even tied my cravat for me.

---

[6]Heinrich Heine (1797–1856), a leading liberal German writer and poet, who worked in Paris as a foreign correspondent for German newspapers; Karl Ludwig Börne (1786–1837), German republican writer and satirist. Heine, whose style is more subtle and ironic than Börne's, which is overtly satirical and polemical, looked up to Börne as a young man and wrote a tribute to him.

'Now no one will be able to say you look a disgrace. Look in my mirror,' she said. 'Why so miserable? I wish I could come too!'

She straightened my suit a little.

'But when I see you dressed up like this, you somehow don't look like my Toyotarō.'

She thought for a moment.

'If you do become rich and famous, you'll never leave me, will you. Even if my illness does not turn out to be what Mother says it is.'

'What! Rich and famous?' I smiled. 'I lost the desire to enter politics years ago. I don't even want to see the Count. I'm just going to meet an old friend whom I have not seen for a very long time.'

The first-class *Droschke*[7] that her mother had ordered drew up under the window, the wheels creaking in the snow. I put on my gloves, slung my slightly soiled overcoat about my shoulders without putting my arms through the sleeves, and picked up my hat. I kissed Elise goodbye and went downstairs. She opened the ice-covered window to see me off, her hair blowing in the north wind.

I got out at the entrance to the Kaiserhof. Inquiring the room number of Private Secretary Aizawa from the doorman, I climbed the marble staircase. It had been a long time since I had last been there. I came to an antechamber where there was a plush sofa by the central pillar and directly ahead a mirror. Here I took off my coat and, passing along a corridor, arrived at Aizawa's door. I hesitated a little. How would he greet me? When we were at university together, he had been so impressed by my correct behavior. I entered the room and we met face to face. He seemed stouter and sturdier than of old, but he had the same naturally cheerful disposition and did not appear to be concerned about my misconduct. But we were given no time to discuss in detail what had happened since we had last met, for I was called in and interviewed by the Count. He entrusted me with the translation of some urgent documents written in German. I accepted them and took my leave. Aizawa followed me out and invited me to lunch.

During the meal it was he who asked all the questions and I who gave the answers, because his career had been in the main uneventful, whereas the story of my life was full of troubles and adversity.

He listened as I told him about my unhappy experiences with complete frankness. He was often surprised, but never tried to blame me. On the contrary he ridiculed my boorish countrymen. But when I had finished my tale he became serious and remonstrated with me. Things had reached this pass because I was basically weak-willed, but there was no point in laboring the fact now, he said. Nevertheless, how long could a man of talent and learning like myself remain emotionally involved with a mere chit of a girl and lead such an aimless life? At this stage Count Amakata merely needed me for my German. Since he knew the reason for my dismissal, Aizawa would make no attempt to make him change his preconception of me—it would do neither of us any good if the Count were to think that we were trying to deceive him. But there was no better way to recommend people than by displaying their talents. I should show the Count how good I was and so try to win his confidence. As for the girl, she might be sincerely in love with me and our passions deeply involved, but there was certainly no meeting of minds—I had merely allowed myself to slip into what was an accepted practice. I must decide to give her up, he urged.

---

[7] A carriage for hire.

When he mapped out my future like this, I felt like a man adrift who spies a mountain in the distance. But the mountain was still covered in cloud. I was not sure whether I would reach it, or even if I did, whether it would bring satisfaction. Life was pleasant even in the midst of poverty and Elise's love was hard to reject. Being so weak-willed I could make no decision there and then, so I merely promised to follow my friend's advice for a while, and try and break off the affair. When it came to losing something close to me, I could resist my enemies, but never could refuse my friends.

We parted about four o'clock. As I came out of the hotel restaurant the wind hit me in the face. A fire had been burning in a big tiled stove inside, so when the double glass doors closed behind me and I stood outside in the open, the cold of the afternoon pierced my thin overcoat and seemed all the more intense. I shivered, and there was a strange chill in my heart too.

I finished the translation in one night. Thereafter I found myself going to the Kaiserhof quite often. At first the Count spoke only of business, but after a while he brought up various things that had happened at home recently and asked my opinion. When the occasion arose, he would tell me about the mistakes people had made on the voyage out, and would burst out laughing.

A month went by. Then one day he suddenly turned to me.

'I'm leaving for Russia tomorrow. Will you come with me?' he asked.

I had not seen Aizawa for several days as he was busy with official business, and the request took me totally by surprise.

'How could I refuse?' I replied.

I must confess that I did not answer as the result of a quick decision. When I am suddenly asked a question by someone whom I trust, I instantly agree without weighing up the consequences. Not only do I agree, but, despite knowing how difficult the matter will be, I often hide my initial thoughtlessness by persevering and carrying it out.

That day I was given not only the translation fee but also my travel money. When I got home I gave the fee to Elise. With this she would be able to support herself and her mother until such time as I returned from Russia. She said she had been to see a doctor, who confirmed that she was pregnant. Being anaemic she hadn't realized her condition for some months. She had also received a message from the theater telling her that she had been dismissed as she had been away for so long. She had only been off work for a month, so there was probably some other reason for such severity. Believing implicitly in my sincerity, she did not seem unduly worried about the impending journey.

The journey was not long by train and so there was little to prepare. I just packed into a small suitcase a hired black suit, a copy of the *Almanach de Gotha,* and two or three dictionaries. In view of recent depressing events, I felt it would be miserable for Elise after my departure. I was also anxious lest she should cry at the station, so I took the step of sending her and her mother out early the next morning to visit friends. I collected up my things and locked the door on my way out, leaving the key with the cobbler who lived at the entrance.

What is there to tell of my travels in Russia? My duties as an interpreter suddenly lifted me from the mundane and dropped me above the clouds into the Russian court. Accompanying the Count's party, I went to St Petersburg, where I was overwhelmed by the ornate architecture of the palace, which represented for me the greatest splendors of Paris transported into the midst of ice and snow. Above all I remember the countless flickering yellow candles, the light reflected by the multitude of decorations and epaulets, and the fluttering fans of the court ladies, who forgot the cold outside as they sat in the warmth from the exquisitely carved and inlaid fireplaces. As I was the most fluent French speaker in the party, I had to circulate between host and guest and interpret for them.

But I had not forgotten Elise. How could I? She sent me letters every day. On the day I left, she had wanted to avoid the unaccustomed sadness of sitting alone by lamplight, and so had talked late into the night at a friend's house. Then, feeling tired, she returned home and immediately went to bed. Next morning, she wondered if she had not just dreamed she was alone. But when she got up, her depression and sense of loneliness were worse than the time when she had been scratching a living and had not known where the next meal was coming from. This was what she told me in her first letter.

Later letters seemed to be written in great distress, and each of them began in the same way.

'Ah! Only now do I realize the depth of my love for you. As you say you have no close relatives at home, you will stay here if you find you can make a good living, won't you? My love must tie you here to me. Even if that proves impossible and you have to return home, I could easily come with my mother. But where would we get the money for the fare? I had always intended to stay here and wait for the day you became famous, whatever I had to do. But the pain of separation grows stronger every day, even though you are only on a short trip and have only been away about twenty days. It was a mistake to have thought that parting was just a passing sorrow. My pregnancy is at last beginning to be obvious, so you cannot reject me now, whatever happens. I quarrel a lot with Mother. But she has given in, now she sees how much more determined I am than I used to be. When I travel home with you, she's talking of going to stay with some distant relatives who live on a farm near Stettin. If, as you say in your last letter, you are doing important work for the Minister, we can somehow manage the fare. How I long for the day you return to Berlin.'

It was only after reading this letter that I really understood my predicament. How could I have been so insensitive! I had been proud to have made a decision about my own course of action and that of others unrelated to me. But it had been made in entirely favorable rather than adverse conditions. When I tried to clarify my relationship with others, the emotions that I had formerly trusted became confused.

I was already on very good terms with the Count. But in my shortsightedness I only took into consideration the duties that I was then undertaking. The gods might have known how this was connected to my hopes for the future, but I never gave it a thought. Was my passion cooling? When Aizawa had first recommended me, I had felt that the Count's confidence would be hard to gain, but now I had to some extent won his trust. When Aizawa had said things like, 'If we continue to work together after you return to Japan,' I wondered whether he had really been hinting that this was what the Count was saying. It was true that Aizawa was my friend, but he would not have been able to tell me openly since it was an official matter. Now that I thought about it, I wondered whether he had perhaps told the Count what I had rashly promised him—that I was going to sever my connections with Elise.

When I first came to Germany, I thought that I had discovered my true nature, and I swore never to become used as a machine again. But perhaps it was merely the pride of a bird that had been given momentary freedom to flap its wings and yet still had its legs bound. There was no way I could loose the bonds. The rope had first been in the hands of my department head, and now, alas, it was in the hands of the Count.

It happened to be New Year's Day when I returned to Berlin with the Count's party. I left them at the station and took a cab home. In Berlin no one sleeps on New Year's Eve and it is the custom to lie in late the next morning. Every single house was quiet. The snow on the road had frozen hard into ruts in the bitter cold and shone brightly in the sunlight. The cab turned into Klosterstrasse and pulled up at the entrance to the house. I heard a window open but saw nothing from inside the cab. I got the driver to take my bag and was just about to climb the steps when Elise came flying down to meet me. She cried out and flung her arms around my neck. At this the driver was a little startled and mumbled something in his beard that I could not hear.

'Oh! Welcome home! I would have died if you had not returned!' she cried.

Up to now I had prevaricated. At times the thought of Japan and the desire to seek fame seemed to overcome my love, but at this precise moment all my hesitation left me and I hugged her. She laid her head on my shoulder and wept tears of happiness.

'Which floor do I take it to?' growled the driver as he hurried up the stairs with the luggage.

I gave a few silver coins to her mother, who had come to the door to meet me, and asked her to pay the driver. Elise held me by the hand and hurried into the room. I was surprised to see a pile of white cotton and lace lying on the table. She laughed and pointed to the pile.

'What do you think of all the preparations?' she said.

She picked up a piece of material and I saw it was a baby's nappy.

'You cannot imagine how happy I am!' she said. 'I wonder if our child will have your dark eyes. Ah, your eyes that I have only been able to dream about. When it's born, you will do the right thing, won't you? You'll give it your name and no one else's, won't you?'

She hung her head.

'You may laugh at me for being silly, but I will be so happy the day we go to church.'

Her uplifted eyes were full of tears.

I did not call on the Count for two or three days because I thought he might be tired from the journey, and so I stayed at home. Then, one evening, a messenger came bearing an invitation. When I arrived, the Count greeted me warmly and thanked me for my work in Russia. He then asked me whether I felt like returning to Japan with him. I knew so much and my knowledge of languages alone was of great value, he said. He had thought that, seeing I had been so long in Germany, I might have some ties here, but he had asked Aizawa and had been relieved to hear that this was not the case.

I could not possibly deny what appeared to be the situation. I was shaken, but of course found it impossible to contradict what Aizawa had told him. If I did not take this chance, I might lose not only my homeland but also the very means by which I might retrieve my good name. I was suddenly struck by the thought that I might die in this sea of humanity, in this vast European capital. I showed my lack of moral fiber and agreed to go.

It was shameless. What could I say to Elise when I returned? As I left the hotel my mind was in indescribable turmoil. I wandered, deep in thought, not caring where I was going. Time and time again I was cursed at by the drivers of carriages that I bumped into and I jumped back startled. After a while I looked around and found I was in the Tiergarten. I half collapsed onto a bench by the side of the path. My head was on fire and felt as if someone were pounding it with a hammer as I leaned back. How long did I lie there like a corpse? The terrible cold creeping into the marrow of my bones woke me up. It was nighttime and the thickly falling snow had piled up an inch high on my shoulders and the peak of my cap.

It must have been past eleven. Even the tracks of the horse-drawn trams along Mohabit and Karlstrasse were buried under the snow and the gas lamps around the

Brandenburg Gate gave out a bleak light. My feet were frozen stiff when I tried to get up, and I had to rub them with my hands before I could move.

I walked slowly and it must have been past midnight when I got to Klosterstrasse. I don't know how I got there. It was early January and the bars and tea shops on Unter den Linden must have been full, but I remember nothing of that. I was completely obsessed by the thought that I had committed an unforgivable crime.

In the fourth-floor attic Elise was evidently not yet asleep, for a bright gleam of light shone out into the night sky. The falling snowflakes were like a flock of small white birds, and the light kept on disappearing and reappearing as if the plaything of the wind. As I went in through the door I realized how weary I was. The pain in my joints was so unbearable that I half crawled up the stairs. I went through the kitchen, opened the door of the room, and stumbled inside. Elise was sewing nappies by the table and turned round.

'What have you been doing?' she gasped. 'Just look at you!'

She had good reason to be shocked. My face was as pale as a corpse. I had lost my cap somewhere on the way and my hair was in a frightful mess. My clothes were torn and dirty from the muddy snow as I had stumbled many times along the road.

I remember trying to reply, but I could say nothing. Unable to stand because my knees were shaking so violently, I tried to grab a chair, but then I fell to the floor.

It was some weeks later that I regained consciousness. I had just babbled in a high fever while Elise tended me. Then one day Aizawa had come to visit me, saw for himself what I had hidden from him, and arranged matters by only telling the Count that I was ill. When I first set eyes on Elise again, tending me at the bedside, I was shocked at her altered appearance. She had become terribly thin and her blood-shot eyes were sunk into her gray cheeks. With Aizawa's help she had not wanted for daily necessities, it was true, but this same benefactor had spiritually killed her.

As he told me later, she had heard from Aizawa about the promise I had given him and how I had agreed to the Count's proposal that evening. She had jumped up from her chair, her face ashen pale, and crying out, 'Toyotarō! How could you deceive me!', she had suddenly collapsed. Aizawa had called her mother and together they had put her to bed. When she awoke some time later, her eyes were fixed in a stare and she could not recognize those around her. She cried out my name, abused me, tore her hair, and bit the coverlet. Then she suddenly seemed to remember something and started to look for it. Everything her mother gave her she threw away, except the nappies that were on the table. These she stared at for a moment, then pressed them to her face and burst into tears.

From that time on, she was never violent, but her mind was almost completely unhinged and she became as simple-minded as a child. The doctor said there was no hope of recovery, for it was an illness called paranoia that had been brought on by sudden excessive emotion. They tried to remove her to the Dalldorf Asylum, but she cried out and refused to go. She would continually clasp a nappy to her breast and bring it out to look at, and this seemed to make her content. Although she did not leave my sickbed, she did not seem to be really aware of what was going on. Just occasionally she would repeat the word 'medicine', as if remembering it.

I recovered from my illness completely. How often did I hold her living corpse in my arms and shed bitter tears? When I left with the Count for the journey back to Japan, I discussed the matter with Aizawa and gave her mother enough to eke out a bare existence; I also left some money to pay for the birth of the child that I had left in the womb of the poor mad girl.

Friends like Aizawa Kenkichi are rare indeed, and yet to this very day there remains a part of me that curses him.

❧

BACKGROUND TEXTS

=================

MADAME DE STAËL (GERMAINE NECKER)
[1766–1817]

Germaine Necker, better known as Madame de Staël, witnessed, commented upon, and made herself a part of the French Revolution, the rise of Napoleon, the restoration of the monarchy in 1814, and the influx of German thought into France, an undertaking speeded by her friendship with Friedrich Schlegel and Goethe, among others, and the publication of her *On Germany* in 1813. Adding to the praises of writers such as Stendhal and Benjamin Constant, Lord Byron, who met de Staël during the summer of 1816 at Lake Geneva, called her "the first female writer of this, perhaps any age."

Germaine Necker was the daughter of Jacques Necker, the Director of Finance under Louis XVI at the time of the French Revolution, and Suzanne Curchod, through whose salon in Paris passed many of the great intellectuals of the day, including Buffon, Diderot, and Talleyrand. Introduced early to the ideas of the *philosophes* and to Montesquieu and Rousseau, the inquisitive young woman developed a keen love for free inquiry, independent thinking, and a belief in the powers of reason, which later led her to support movements for independence and reform throughout Europe, despite her father's close contact with the court of Louis XVI. After she married the baron de Staël-Holstein, the Swedish ambassador to Paris, in 1785, Madame de Staël's own salon in Paris became a major center for intellectual activity and the exchange of ideas. Her marriage did not last, but her salon continued to be a vital center of French intellectual life, except for intermittent interruptions during the Revolution and during her repeated periods of exile ordered by Napoleon. In these years, she traveled widely and set up a salon in exile at the château Coppet on Lake Geneva, which drew writers, artists, and politicians from all over Europe.

The salon in France at the end of the eighteenth century was a formal institution for promoting discussion about art, literature, philosophy, and politics. Dynamic and highly respected, leaders of salons, such as Madame de Staël, were renowned for their extensive learning, ready wit, and social savoir faire, and wielded considerable influence among intellectuals and people of high social standing. De Staël's influence, unlike that of other salon figures, spread through her critical work and creative writing as well, including *Letters on Rousseau* (1788), *On Literature Considered in its Relationship to Social Institutions* (1800), the novels *Delphine* (1802) and *Corinne* (1807), and her *On Germany* (1813), which for the first time set out the distinction between "classic" and "romantic" as the opposition between an art that has already attained perfection and a more dynamic art that is perfectible. Her distinction between classic and romantic may have influenced Ruskin's conception of the Gothic in *The Stones of Venice*. The selection from Madame de Staël's work presented here demonstrates her pivotal position between the eighteenth and nineteenth centuries and her familiarity with the central figures of European romanticism, in this case Napoleon Bonaparte. The sketch of Napoleon comes from *Considerations on the Principal Events of the French Revolution* (1818), and it shows her talent to construct perceptive critical generalizations and to evoke character by means of description. For some writers, especially Lord Byron, Napoleon represented the heroic but flawed principles of high romanticism embodied in the theater of politics and international power. De Staël's portrait gives us some sense of the dangers of such a character, when principle gives way to the arbitrary wielding of power.

Considerations on the Principal Events of the French Revolution

Translated by Morroe Berger

[NAPOLEON]

Part III, Chapter 26. Treaty of Campo Formio, 1797[1]
General Bonaparte's Arrival in Paris

The Directory[2] was not inclined to peace, not because it wished to extend French rule beyond the Rhine and the Alps but because it believed war useful for the propagation of the republican system. Its plan was to surround France with a belt of republics. One of the great faults of the French—a consequence of their social customs—is to imitate each other and to want to be imitated. They take the natural differences in men's or even nations' ways of thinking as a hostile feeling against themselves.

General Bonaparte was certainly less serious and less sincere than the Directory in the love of republican ideas, but he was much more shrewd in estimating a situation. He sensed that peace would become popular in France because passions were subsiding and people were weary of sacrifices; so he signed the Treaty of Campo Formio with Austria.

General Bonaparte distinguished himself as much by his character and mind as by his victories, and the imagination of the French was beginning to attach itself to him strongly. A tone of moderation and nobility prevailed in his style, which contrasted with the revolutionary gruffness of the civil leaders of France. The warrior spoke like a magistrate, while the magistrates expressed themselves with martial violence.

It was with this feeling, at least, that I saw him for the first time in Paris. I could find no words of reply when he came to me to tell me that he had sought my father at Coppet and that he regretted having passed through Switzerland without having seen him. But when I was somewhat recovered from the confusion of admiration, a very strong sense of fear followed. Bonaparte at that time had no power; he was even believed to be somewhat threatened by the jealous suspicions of the Directory. So the fear he inspired was caused only by the extraordinary effect of his person upon nearly all who approached him. I had seen men worthy of respect, and I had seen fierce men: there was nothing in the impression Bonaparte produced upon me that recalled either the former or the latter. I very quickly saw, in the various occasions I had to meet him during his stay in Paris, that his character could not be defined by the words we ordinarily use; he was neither good, nor fierce, nor gentle, nor cruel, like others we know. Such a being, having no equals, could neither feel nor arouse any sympathy: he was more than a human being or less than one. His appearance, his mind, and his speech were foreign in nature—an added advantage for subjugating the French.

Far from being reassured by seeing Bonaparte more often, I was made increasingly apprehensive. I had a vague feeling that no emotion of the heart could influence him. He considers a human being a fact or a thing, not a fellow man. He does not hate nor does he love. For him, there is nothing but himself; all others are ciphers.

Every time I heard him speak I was struck by his superiority: yet it had no resemblance to that of men educated and cultivated by study or by social intercourse,

---

[1] The Treaty of Campo Formio in 1797, following the defeat of Prussia two years before, sealed Napoleon's popularity in France.

[2] The ruling body in France from 1795 to 1799, when Napoleon seized power and made himself First Consul in the coup d'état of 18 Brumaire (November 9, 1799).

such as may be found in England or France. But his speech showed a feeling for the situation, like the hunter's for his prey. Sometimes he related the political and military events of his life in a very interesting way; he even had a touch of Italian imagination in the stories that permitted some humor. Nothing, however, could overcome my unconquerable aversion for what I saw in him. I sensed in his soul a cold and sharp sword that froze as it wounded. I sensed in his mind a deep irony that nothing could escape—neither greatness, nor beauty, nor even his own glory. For he despised the nation whose support he wanted, and no spark of enthusiasm could be found in his need to awe the human race.

It was in the interval between Bonaparte's return and his departure for Egypt— that is, toward the end of 1797—that I saw him several times in Paris; and never could I rid myself of the difficulty in breathing that I felt in his presence. One day I was at table between him and the Abbé Siéyès[3]—an extraordinary spot, had I been able to foresee the future! I studied his face carefully, but whenever he noticed my searching glances he seemed to erase all expression from his eyes, as if they had turned to marble. His face became blank, except for the faint smile into which he shaped his lips, as a precaution, to confound anyone who might wish to observe the external signs of his thoughts.

His face, at that time lean and pale, was rather pleasant. Since then he has become fat, which ill suits him; we need to believe that such a man is tormented by his own nature, in order to tolerate the fact that this nature makes others suffer so. As he is short, though his body is long, he looks much better on horseback than on foot. In everything, it is war and only war that suits him. His conduct in company is awkward without being shy. He appears somewhat scornful when he controls himself and somewhat common when relaxed. Scorn suits him better, so he readily adopts it.

The Directory gave General Bonaparte an official reception which, in several respects, should be regarded as an important moment in the history of the Revolution. The courtyard of the Luxembourg Palace was chosen for the ceremony. No room would have been large enough to hold the crowd it attracted; there were spectators at all the windows and on all the roofs. The five Directors,[4] in Roman dress, were seated upon a platform at the end of the courtyard.

Bonaparte came dressed very simply, followed by his *aides-de-camp*, all taller than he but almost stooped by the respect they showed him. The *élite* of France present there covered the victorious general with applause. He was the hope of everyone: republicans, royalists, all saw the present and the future resting in his powerful hand.

Alas! What has happened to those days of glory and peace France anticipated twenty years ago! All these good things were in the hand of one man. What has he done with them?

· · ·

FROM
Part IV, Chapter XX. On Exile

... During the twelve years of exile to which Napoleon condemned me, I often reflected that he could not feel the misfortune of being barred from France. He did not have a single memory of France in his heart. Only the rocks of Corsica[5] recalled

---

[3] Emmanuel-Joseph Siéyès (1748–1836), a political theorist of the French Revolution, who became a member of the Directory and helped set up the coup d'état of 18 Brumaire.

[4] The executive branch of the Directory; the five were Paul François Barras, Sieyès, Roger Ducos, Louis Jérôme Gohier, and Jean François Moulin.

[5] The Mediterranean island off the western coast of Italy where Napoleon was born.

to him the days of his childhood, but the daughter of M. Necker was more French than he.

I sensed more quickly than others—and I pride myself on it—Bonaparte's tyrannical character and intentions. The true friends of liberty are in this respect guided by an instinct that does not deceive them. But my position, at the outset of the Consulate,[6] was made more painful by the fact that respectable society in France thought it saw in Bonaparte the man who had saved them from anarchy or Jacobinism. They therefore vigorously condemned the spirit of opposition I displayed toward him.

I still remember one of the drawing-room tortures, if I may put it this way, that French aristocrats can, when it suits them, so expertly inflict upon those who do not share their opinions. A large part of the old nobility came around to supporting Bonaparte—some, as has since been seen, in order to return to their practices as courtiers, and others hoping that the First Consul would restore the former dynasty. People knew that I strongly opposed the form of government Napoleon was following and preparing, and the advocates of arbitrary power, according to their custom, described as anti-social those opinions that tended to raise the dignity of people. If some *emigrés* who returned under Bonaparte's rule were reminded of the fury with which they then blamed the friends of liberty, who consistently supported but one system, they might learn tolerance in looking back upon their errors.

I was the first woman Bonaparte exiled, but he soon banished many others of various opinions. Since women, on the one hand, could in no way further his political schemes, and since, on the other hand, they were less susceptible than men to the fears and hopes that power dispensed, they irritated him like so many rebels, and he took pleasure in saying offensive and vulgar things to them. He hated the spirit of chivalry as much as he sought pomp—a bad choice among the old customs. He retained, also, from his early ways during the Revolution, a certain Jacobin antipathy for the brilliant society of Paris, over which women exerted much influence. He feared their wit, which, it must be admitted, is particularly characteristic of Frenchwomen.

Bonaparte wanted me to praise him in my writings, not, certainly, that an additional eulogy would have been noticed in the fumes of incense surrounding him, but it annoyed him that I was the only writer the French knew who had published under his rule without making any mention of his majestic existence. And he ended by suppressing my book on Germany with incredible fury. Until then my misfortune had consisted only in my removal from Paris, but after that I was forbidden all travel, and I was threatened with prison for the rest of my days. The contagious nature of exile, an invention worthy of the Roman emperors, was the most bitter aggravation of this penalty. Those who came to see the exiles exposed themselves to exile in turn. Most of the Frenchmen I knew avoided me like the plague. This seemed comic to me when I did not suffer too much from it. . . .

Part V, Chapter 14. Bonaparte's Conduct upon His Return

If it was criminal to recall Bonaparte, it was silly to try to disguise such a man as a constitutional monarch. As he was taken back, a military dictatorship should have been handed to him, conscription re-established, and the nation called to arms—in short, no one should have bothered about liberty when independence

---

[6]The name of the French government between 18 Brumaire, 1799, and Napoleon's proclamation of Empire in 1804; after naming himself First Consul, Napoleon was elected Consul for life.

was in danger. In being made to adopt language quite contrary to what had been his own for fifteen years, Bonaparte's reputation necessarily suffered. Clearly, it was only because he was forced by circumstances that he could proclaim principles so different from those he had followed when he was all-powerful.

Now what is such a man when he allows himself to be coerced? The terror he used to inspire, the power that came from that terror, no longer existed; he was a muzzled bear who could still be heard to grumble but whose masters made dance as they pleased. A man who detested abstract ideas and legal restraints, instead of being made to talk about constitutions for hours on end, should have been on the field of battle four days after his arrival in Paris, before the preparations of the Allies were completed and especially while the shock caused by his return still stunned the imagination. He should have aroused the passions of the Italians and the Poles, promised the Spaniards to expiate his errors by giving them back their parliament—in short, liberty should have been regarded as a weapon and not an obstacle.

Indeed, how could Bonaparte have put up with the constitution he was made to proclaim? When the responsible ministers resisted his will, what would he have done with them?

Military Jacobinism, one of the world's greatest scourges, was, if still possible, Bonaparte's only resort. When he uttered the words law and liberty, Europe was reassured: it sensed that this was no longer its old and terrible adversary.

FRIEDRICH SCHLEGEL
[1772–1829]

Like Coleridge in England, the German Friedrich von Schlegel has come to be recognized as one of the most important romantic theorists and critics of the nineteenth century. Novalis, the inspired poet of *Hymns to the Night,* said about Schlegel in 1800: "If anyone was born to be the apostle for our time, it is you... the St. Paul of the new religion... with this religion begins a new world history. You understand the secrets of the age."

Born in Hanover on March 10, 1772, the son of a Protestant minister, Schlegel studied the classics at Göttingen in 1790. As for other German philosophers, the study of Greek language, philosophy, and culture was, for Schlegel, the model of a whole and harmonious education. With his brother August Wilhelm Schlegel, Friedrich began to publish the quarterly *Athenaeum* in 1798. It was in this journal that his famous definition of romantic poetry appeared, the first lines of which are: "Romantic poetry is a progressive universal poetry. Its mission is not merely to reunite all separate genres of poetry and to put poetry in touch with philosophy and rhetoric. It will, and should... amalgamate poetry and prose, genius and criticism, the poetry of art and the poetry of nature, render poetry living and social, and life and society poetic, poeticize wit, fill and saturate the forms of art with solid cultural material of every kind, and inspire them with vibrations of humor."

In 1802, Schlegel went to Paris where he studied Sanskrit. He was one of the first German scholars to exalt the study of ancient India, to claim that Indian mythology could be favorably compared with Greek myth and was useful to romantic poets. In 1808 he published *On the Wisdom and Language of the Indians.*

Schlegel's optimistic hope for the healing and synthesizing future of poetry was based to a large extent on his belief in the unity of art, myth, and religion during the early stages of human existence. In other words, all of human culture had once fit together harmoniously and people were whole and healthy; then it all became fragmented, divided, and unhealthy. The new poetry was to act as a synthesizing agent that would restore an ultimate spiritual vision of harmony. In this program, "myth" came to replace poetry or literature as the umbrella under which art, philosophy, and religion might be united, even as Greek myth served as such a synthesizing agent for the ancient Greeks. Schlegel redirects the role of criticism by elevating it into a synthesizing, holistic enterprise, one that would unite all fields of learning.

Schlegel then redefines the role of poet as myth-maker. Goethe and others believed that myth could not be consciously created by individuals; Schlegel calls upon poets to create new myths for the modern world, myths that will create a unified vision. The importance placed on myth by German writers and thinkers of the early nineteenth century has a commanding influence on Western thought into the twentieth century.

FROM

Talk on Mythology

Translated by Ernst Behler and Roman Struc

Considering your serious reverence for art, I wish to challenge you, my friends, to ask yourselves this question: should the force of inspiration also in poetry continue to split up and, when it has exhausted itself by struggling against the hostile element, end up in lonely silence? Are the most sacred things always to remain nameless and formless, and be left in darkness to chance? Is love indeed invincible, and is there an art worthy of the name if it does not have the power to bind the spirit of love with its magic word, to make the spirit of love follow and obey it, and to inspire its beautiful creations in accordance with its necessary freedom?

You above all others must know what I mean. You yourselves have written poetry, and while doing so you must often have felt the absence of a firm basis for your activity, a matrix, a sky, a living atmosphere.

The modern poet must create all these things from within himself, and many have done it splendidly; up to now, however, each poet separately and each work from its very beginning, like a new creation out of nothing.

I will go right to the point. Our poetry, I maintain, lacks a focal point, such as mythology was for the ancients; and one could summarize all the essentials in which modern poetry is inferior to the ancient in these words: We have no mythology. But, I add, we are close to obtaining one or, rather, it is time that we earnestly work together to create one.

For it will come to us by an entirely opposite way from that of previous ages, which was everywhere the first flower of youthful imagination, directly joining and imitating what was most immediate and vital in the sensuous world. The new mythology, in contrast, must be forged from the deepest depths of the spirit; it must be the most artful of all works of art, for it must encompass all the others; a new bed and vessel for the ancient, eternal fountainhead of poetry, and even the infinite poem concealing the seeds of all other poems.

You may well smile at this mystical poem and the disorder that might originate from the abundance of poetic creations. But the highest beauty, indeed the highest order is yet only that of chaos, namely of such a one that waits only for the touch of love to unfold as a harmonious world, of such a chaos as the ancient mythology and poetry were. For mythology and poetry are one and inseparable. All poems of antiquity join one to the other, till from ever increasing masses and members the whole is formed. Everything interpenetrates everything else, and everywhere there is one and the same spirit, only expressed differently. And thus it is truly no empty image to say: Ancient poetry is a single, indivisible, and perfect poem. Why should what has once been not come alive again? In a different way, to be sure. And why not in a more beautiful, a greater way?

. . . .

. . . It is not a sensitivity to this or that nor a passion that smolders and dies again, but a clear fragrance that hovers invisibly visible over the whole; everywhere eternal longing finds an accord from the depths of the simple work which in calm greatness breathes the spirit of original love.

And is not this soft reflection of the godhead in man the actual soul, the kindling spark of all poetry? Mere representation of man, passions, and actions does not truly amount to anything, as little as using artificial forms does, even if you shuffle and turn over the old stuff together millions of times. That is only the visible, the external body, for when the soul has been extinguished what is left is only the lifeless corpse of poetry. When that spark of inspiration breaks out in works, however, a new phenomenon stands before us, alive and in the beautiful glory of light and love.

And what else is any wonderful mythology but hieroglyphic expression of surrounding nature in this transfigured form of imagination and love?

Mythology has one great advantage. What usually escapes our consciousness can here be perceived and held fast through the senses and spirit like the soul in the body surrounding it, through which it shines into our eyes and speaks to our ear.

. . .

. . . For this is the beginning of all poetry, to cancel the progression and laws of rationally thinking reason, and to transplant us once again into the beautiful confusion of imagination, into the original chaos of human nature, for which I know as yet no more beautiful symbol than the motley throng of the ancient gods.

Why won't you arise and revive those splendid forms of great antiquity? Try for once to see the old mythology, steeped in Spinoza and in those views which present-day physics must excite in every thinking person, and everything will appear to you in new splendor and vitality.

But to accelerate the genesis of the new mythology, the other mythologies must also be reawakened according to the measure of their profundity, their beauty, and their form. If only the treasures of the Orient were as accessible to us as those of Antiquity. What new source of poetry could then flow from India if a few German artists with their catholicity and profundity of mind, with the genius for translation which is their own, had the opportunity which a nation growing ever more dull and brutal barely knows how to use. In the Orient we must look for the most sublime form of the Romantic, and only when we can draw from the source, perhaps will the semblance of southern passion which we find so charming in Spanish poetry appear to us occidental and sparse.

In general, one must be able to press toward the goal by more than one way. Let each pursue his own in joyful confidence, in the most individual manner; for nowhere has the right of individuality more validity—provided individuality is what this word defines: indivisible unity and an inner and vital coherence—than here where the sublime is at issue. From this standpoint I would not hesitate to say that the true value, indeed the virtue of man is his originality.

. . .

And thus let us, by light and life, hesitate no longer, but accelerate, each according to his own mind, that great development to which we were called. Be worthy of the greatness of the age and the fog will vanish from your eyes; and there will be light before you. All thinking is a divining, but man is only now beginning to realize his divining power. What immense expansion will this power experience, and especially now! It seems to me that he who could understand the age—that is, those great principles of general rejuvenation and of eternal revolution—would be able to succeed in grasping the poles of mankind, to recognize and to know the activity of the first men as well as the nature of the Golden Age which is to come. Then the empty chatter would stop and man would become conscious of what he is: he would understand the earth and the sun.

This is what I mean by the new mythology.

CHARLES DARWIN
[1809–1882]

The naturalist who established the theory of biological evolution, Charles Darwin remains nearly as controversial a figure in our time as he was in his own day. Educated at Cambridge for the clergy, Darwin was changed by his voyage on the HMS *Beagle* from 1831 to 1836, where he served as the ship's naturalist. Impressed by the differences between the species on offshore islands such as the Galápagos Islands off the coast of Ecuador and the species on the continent, Darwin set out to explain how such differences occurred. Influenced by other scientists who were working on related problems, especially geologist Sir Charles Lyell and biologist Alfred Russel Wallace, and by the work of T. R. Malthus, the economist whose *Essay on the Principle of Population* had described the human world as a struggle for survival, Darwin published his comprehensive theory in *On the Origin of Species by Means of Natural Selection, or the Preservation of Favoured Races in the Struggle for Life* (1859).

Although many of Darwin's ideas had been circulating in scientific circles for many years before 1859, *Origin of Species* brought the ideas together and presented them to a much wider audience. It provoked immediate and intense controversy, especially over the implications of Darwin's ideas to the generally accepted religious doctrine that the creation was the result of a special and immutable act of God. Instead of a universe designed by God, Darwin seemed to propose one governed by chance. The idea of natural selection, or the "struggle for existence," was in itself unsettling, for it made violence and struggle the fundamental truths of the cosmos, and turned nature from the benign and peaceable kingdom envisioned in the past into a realm, as Tennyson described it, "red in tooth and claw." The passages we have chosen from *Origin of Species* and *The Descent of Man* (1871) present Darwin's idea of natural selection and his application of it to the human realm.

Origin of Species

[THE STRUGGLE FOR EXISTENCE]

The Term, Struggle for Existence, Used in a Large Sense

I should premise that I use this term in a large and metaphorical sense including dependence of one being on another, and including (which is more important) not only the life of the individual, but success in leaving progeny. Two canine animals, in a time of dearth, may be truly said to struggle with each other which shall get food and live. But a plant on the edge of a desert is said to struggle for life against the

drought, though more properly it should be said to be dependent on ﹍
A plant which annually produces a thousand seeds, of which only one of an ave﹍
comes to maturity, may be more truly said to struggle with the plants of the same
and other kinds which already clothe the ground. The mistletoe is dependent on
the apple and a few other trees, but can only in a far-fetched sense be said to
struggle with these trees, for, if too many of these parasites grow on the same tree,
it languishes and dies. But several seedling mistletoes, growing close together on the
same branch, may more truly be said to struggle with each other. As the mistletoe
is disseminated by birds, its existence depends on them; and it may methodically be
said to struggle with other fruit-bearing plants, in tempting the birds to devour and
thus disseminate its seeds. In these several senses, which pass into each other, I use
for convenience' sake the general term of Struggle for Existence.

Geometrical Ratio of Increase

A struggle for existence inevitably follows from the high rate at which all organic
beings tend to increase. Every being, which during its natural lifetime produces
several eggs or seeds, must suffer destruction during some period of its life, and
during some season or occasional year, otherwise, on the principle of geometrical
increase, its numbers would quickly become so inordinately great that no country
could support the product. Hence, as more individuals are produced than can
possibly survive, there must in every case be a struggle for existence, either one
individual with another of the same species, or with the individuals of distinct
species, or with the physical conditions of life. It is the doctrine of Malthus[1] applied
with manifold force to the whole animal and vegetable kingdoms; for in this case
there can be no artificial increase of food, and no prudential restraint from marriage.
Although some species may be now increasing, more or less rapidly, in numbers, all
cannot do so, for the world would not hold them.

There is no exception to the rule that every organic being naturally increases at
so high a rate, that, if not destroyed, the earth would soon be covered by the progeny
of a single pair. Even slow-breeding man has doubled in twenty-five years, and at
this rate, in less than a thousand years, there would literally not be standing-room
for his progeny. Linnaeus[2] has calculated that if an annual plant produced only two
seeds—and there is no plant so unproductive as this—and their seedlings next year
produced two, and so on, then in twenty years there should be a million plants.
The elephant is reckoned the slowest breeder of all known animals, and I have taken
some pains to estimate its probable minimum rate of natural increase; it will be
safest to assume that it begins breeding when thirty years old, and goes on breeding
till ninety years old, bringing forth six young in the interval, and surviving till one
hundred years old; if this be so, after a period of from 740 to 750 years there would
be nearly nineteen million elephants alive, descended from the first pair.

But we have better evidence on this subject than mere theoretical calculations,
namely, the numerous recorded cases of the astonishingly rapid increase of various
animals in a state of nature, when circumstances have been favourable to them
during two or three following seasons. Still more striking is the evidence from
our domestic animals of many kinds which have run wild in several parts of the
world; if the statements of the rate of increase of slow-breeding cattle and horses in
South America, and latterly in Australia, had not been well authenticated, they would

---

[1] Thomas Malthus (1766–1834), the English essayist who argued that population growth would inevitably outstrip the growth in the food supply.

[2] Carolus Linnaeus (1707–1778), a Swedish botanist and the originator of the system of taxonomic classification.

have been incredible. So it is with plants; cases could be given of introduced plants which have become common throughout whole islands in a period of less than ten years. Several of the plants, such as the cardoon and a tall thistle, which are now the commonest over the whole plains of La Plata, clothing square leagues of surface almost to the exclusion of every other plant, have been introduced from Europe; and there are plants which now range in India, as I hear from Dr. Falconer, from Cape Comorin to the Himalaya, which have been imported from America since its discovery. In such cases, and endless others could be given, no one supposes, that the fertility of the animals or plants has been suddenly and temporarily increased in any sensible degree. The obvious explanation is that the conditions of life have been highly favourable, and that there has consequently been less destruction of the old and young, and that nearly all the young have been enabled to breed. Their geometrical ratio of increase, the result of which never fails to be surprising, simply explains their extraordinarily rapid increase and wide diffusion in their new homes.

In a state of nature almost every full-grown plant annually produces seed, and amongst animals there are very few which do not annually pair. Hence we may confidently assert, that all plants and animals are tending to increase at a geometrical ratio,—that all would rapidly stock every station in which they could anyhow exist,—and that this geometrical tendency to increase must be checked by destruction at some period of life. Our familiarity with the larger domestic animals tends, I think, to mislead us: we see no great destruction falling on them, but we do not keep in mind that thousands are annually slaughtered for food, and that in a state of nature an equal number would have somehow to be disposed of.

The only difference between organisms which annually produce eggs or seeds by the thousand, and those which produce extremely few, is, that the slow-breeders would require a few more years to people, under favourable conditions, a whole district, let it be ever so large. The condor lays a couple of eggs and the ostrich a score, and yet in the same country the condor may be the more numerous of the two; the Fulmar petrel lays but one egg, yet it is believed to be the most numerous bird in the world. One fly deposits hundreds of eggs, and another, like the hippobosca, a single one; but this difference does not determine how many individuals of the two species can be supported in a district. A large number of eggs is of some importance to those species which depend on a fluctuating amount of food, for it allows them rapidly to increase in number. But the real importance of a large number of eggs or seeds is to make up for much destruction at some period of life; and this period in the great majority of cases is an early one. If an animal can in any way protect its own eggs or young, a small number may be produced, and yet the average stock be fully kept up; but if many eggs or young are destroyed, many must be produced, or the species will become extinct. It would suffice to keep up the full number of a tree, which lived on an average for a thousand years, if a single seed were produced once in a thousand years, supposing that this seed were never destroyed, and could be ensured to germinate in a fitting place. So that, in all cases, the average number of any animal or plant depends only indirectly on the number of its eggs or seeds.

In looking at Nature, it is most necessary to keep the foregoing considerations always in mind—never to forget that every single organic being may be said to be striving to the utmost to increase in numbers; that each lives by a struggle at some period of its life; that heavy destruction inevitably falls either on the young or old, during each generation or at recurrent intervals. Lighten any check, mitigate the destruction ever so little, and the number of the species will almost instantaneously increase to any amount.

· · ·

Why, it may be asked, until recently did nearly all the most eminent living naturalists and geologists disbelieve in the mutability of species? It cannot be asserted that organic beings in a state of nature are subject to no variation; it cannot be proved that the amount of variation in the course of long ages is a limited quality; no clear distinction has been, or can be, drawn between species and well-marked varieties. It cannot be maintained that species when intercrossed are invariably sterile, and varieties invariably fertile; or that sterility is a special endowment and sign of creation. The belief that species were immutable productions was almost unavoidable as long as the history of the world was thought to be of short duration; and now that we have acquired some idea of the lapse of time, we are too apt to assume, without proof, that the geological record is so perfect that it would have afforded us plain evidence of the mutation of species, if they had undergone mutation.

But the chief cause of our natural unwillingness to admit that one species has given birth to clear and distinct species, is that we are always slow in admitting great changes of which we do not see the steps. The difficulty is the same as that felt by so many geologists, when Lyell[3] first insisted that long lines of inland cliffs had been formed, the great valleys excavated, by the agencies which we see still at work. The mind cannot possibly grasp the full meaning of the term of even a million years; it cannot add up and perceive the full effects of many slight variations, accumulated during an almost infinite number of generations.

Although I am fully convinced of the truth of the views given in this volume under the form of an abstract, I by no means expect to convince experienced naturalists whose minds are stocked with a multitude of facts all viewed, during a long course of years, from a point of view directly opposite to mine. It is so easy to hide our ignorance under such expressions as the "plan of creation," "unity of design," &c., and to think that we give an explanation when we only re-state a fact. Any one whose disposition leads him to attach more weight to unexplained difficulties than to the explanation of a certain number of facts will certainly reject the theory. A few naturalists, endowed with much flexibility of mind, and who have already begun to doubt the immutability of species, may be influenced by this volume; but I look with confidence to the future,—to young and rising naturalists, who will be able to view both sides of the question with impartiality. Whoever is led to believe that species are mutable will do good service by conscientiously expressing his conviction; for thus only can the load of prejudice by which this subject is overwhelmed be removed. . . .

. . .

It is interesting to contemplate a tangled bank, clothed with many plants of many kinds, with birds singing on the bushes, with various insects flitting about, and with worms crawling through the damp earth, and to reflect that these elaborately constructed forms, so different from each other, and dependent upon each other in so complex a manner, have all been produced by laws acting around us. These laws, taken in the largest sense, being Growth with Reproduction; Inheritance which is almost implied by reproduction; Variability from the indirect and direct action of the conditions of life, and from use and disuse: a Ratio of Increase so high as to lead

---

[3] Sir Charles Lyell (1797–1875), a British geologist.

to a Struggle for Life, and as a consequence to Natural Selection, entailing Divergence of Character and the Extinction of less-improved forms. Thus, from the war of nature, from famine and death, the most exalted object which we are capable of conceiving, namely, the production of the higher animals, directly follows. There is grandeur in this view of life, with its several powers, having been originally breathed by the Creator into a few forms or into one; and that, whilst this planet has gone cycling on according to the fixed law of gravity, from so simple a beginning endless forms most beautiful and most wonderful have been, and are being evolved.

FROM

The Descent of Man

. . . The main conclusion arrived at in this work, namely, that man is descended from some lowly organised form, will, I regret to think, be highly distasteful to many. But there can hardly be a doubt that we are descended from barbarians. The astonishment which I felt on first seeing a party of Fuegians[1] on a wild and broken shore will never be forgotten by me, for the reflection at once rushed into my mind—such were our ancestors. These men were absolutely naked and bedaubed with paint, their long hair was tangled, their mouths, frothed with excitement, and their expression was wild, startled, and distrustful. They possessed hardly any arts, and like wild animals lived on what they could catch; they had no government, and were merciless to every one not of their own small tribe. He who has seen a savage in his native land will not feel much shame, if forced to acknowledge that the blood of some more humble creature flows in his veins. For my own part I would as soon be descended from that heroic little monkey, who braved his dreaded enemy in order to save the life of his keeper, or from that old baboon, who descending from the mountains, carried away in triumph his young comrade from a crowd of astonished dogs—as from a savage who delights to torture his enemies, offers up bloody sacrifices, practises infanticide without remorse, treats his wives like slaves, knows no decency, and is haunted by the grossest superstitions.

Man may be excused for feeling some pride at having risen, though not through his own exertions, to the very summit of the organic scale; and the fact of his having thus risen, instead of having been aboriginally placed there, may give him hope for a still higher destiny in the distant future. But we are not here concerned with hopes or fears, only with the truth as far as our reason permits us to discover it; and I have given the evidence to the best of my ability. We must, however, acknowledge, as it seems to me, that man with all his noble qualities, with sympathy which feels for the most debased, with benevolence which extends not only to other men but to the humblest living creature, with his god-like intellect which has penetrated into the movements and constitution of the solar system—with all these exalted powers—Man still bears in his bodily frame the indelible stamp of his lowly origin.

---

[1]Natives of Tierra del Fuego at the southern tip of South America.

HENRY DAVID THOREAU
[1817–1862]

Henry David Thoreau, natural historian, philosopher, and essayist, is best known for *Walden* (1854), his complex meditation upon living simply in the cabin he built for himself on the outskirts of Concord, Massachusetts, and for *Civil Disobedience* (1849), his essay defining the lines between a government's prerogatives and an individual's rights. But many readers find their favorite Thoreau among his journals and lesser-known books such as *The Maine Woods*. In 1846, while Thoreau still was living intermittently on the shores of Walden Pond, he experienced deep wilderness for the first time on an expedition to northern Maine, where he climbed Mount Ktaadn. In a dialect of Algonquin, *Ktaadn* means "Big Mountain"; the usual spelling today is "Katahdin." The mountain now lies within Baxter State Park, and Thoreau's route closely parallels the present Abol Trail, where a spring bears his name.

Only a handful of white people had preceded Thoreau's party in scaling Ktaadn, the first place in the continental United States to catch the rays of the rising sun. Thoreau, raised amid the gentler woods and rolling mountains of Massachusetts, tells us that he finds on Ktaadn a natural world that seems utterly indifferent to human beings. Here, he gropes for titanic images to suggest the rawest and most elemental edge of a creation still awesomely in progress, and he compares himself, a person who has dared to set foot on these wild slopes, to Satan, Milton's fallen angel scrabbling through the realms of Chaos and Old Night. The forbidding being Thoreau hears speaking through this welter of rock and cloud is female; here is the innermost voice of the Mother when she is being most utterly herself, and on this height she feels no obligation to whisper comforting assurances that we human beings are her beloved children.

Our text is taken from the posthumously published *The Maine Woods,* but Thoreau's account of climbing Ktaadn first appeared in *The Union Magazine* in 1848.

The Maine Woods

KTAADN

...While my companions were seeking a suitable spot for this purpose,[1] I improved the little daylight that was left in climbing the mountain alone. We were in a deep and narrow ravine, sloping up to the clouds, at an angle of nearly forty-five degrees, and hemmed in by walls of rock, which were at first covered with low trees, then with impenetrable thickets of scraggy birches and spruce-trees, and with moss, but at last bare of all vegetation but lichens, and almost continually draped in clouds. Following up the course of the torrent which occupied this—and I mean to lay some emphasis on this word *up*—pulling myself up by the side of perpendicular falls of twenty or thirty feet, by the roots of firs and birches, and then, perhaps, walking a level rod or two in the thin stream, for it took up the whole road, ascending by huge steps, as it were, a giant's stairway, down which a river flowed, I had soon cleared the trees, and paused on the successive shelves, to look back over the country. The

---

[1] A campsite.

torrent was from fifteen to thirty feet wide, without a tributary, and seemingly not diminishing in breadth as I advanced; but still it came rushing and roaring down, with a copious tide, over and amidst masses of bare rock, from the very clouds, as though a water-spout had just burst over the mountain. Leaving this at last, I began to work my way, scarcely less arduous than Satan's anciently through Chaos, up the nearest, though not the highest peak.[2] At first scrambling on all fours over the tops of ancient black spruce-trees, (*Abies nigra,*) old as the flood, from two to ten or twelve feet in height, their tops flat and spreading, and their foliage blue and nipt with cold, as if for centuries they had ceased growing upward against the bleak sky, the solid cold. I walked some good rods erect upon the tops of these trees, which were overgrown with moss and mountain-cranberries. It seemed that in the course of time they had filled up the intervals between the huge rocks, and the cold wind had uniformly levelled all over. Here the principle of vegetation was hard put to it. There was apparently a belt of this kind running quite round the mountain, though, perhaps, nowhere so remarkable as here. Once, slumping through, I looked down ten feet, into a dark and cavernous region, and saw the stem of a spruce, on whose top I stood, as on a mass of coarse basket-work, fully nine inches in diameter at the ground. These holes were bears' dens, and the bears were even then at home. This was the sort of garden I made my way *over,* for an eighth of a mile, at the risk, it is true, of treading on some of the plants, not seeing any path *through* it—certainly the most treacherous and porous country I ever travelled.

> "———nigh founder'd, on he fares,
> Treading the crude consistence, half on foot,
> Half flying."[3]

But nothing could exceed the toughness of the twigs,—not one snapped under my weight, for they had slowly grown. Having slumped, scrambled, rolled, bounced, and walked, by turns, over this scraggy country, I arrived upon a side-hill, or rather side-mountain, where rocks, gray, silent rocks, were the flocks and herds that pastured, chewing a rocky cud at sunset. They looked at me with hard gray eyes, without a bleat or a low. This brought me to the skirt of a cloud, and bounded my walk that night. But I had already seen that Maine country when I turned about, waving, flowing, rippling, down below.

When I returned to my companions, they had selected a camping-ground on the torrent's edge, and were resting on the ground; one was on the sick list, rolled in a blanket, on a damp shelf of rock. It was a savage and dreary scenery enough; so wildly rough, that they looked long to find a level and open space for the tent. We could not well camp higher, for want of fuel; and the trees here seemed so evergreen and sappy, that we almost doubted if they would acknowledge the influence of fire; but fire prevailed at last, and blazed here, too, like a good citizen of the world. Even at this height we met with frequent traces of moose, as well as of bears. As here was no cedar, we made our bed of coarser feathered spruce; but at any rate the feathers were plucked from the live tree. It was, perhaps, even a more grand and desolate place for a night's lodging than the summit would have been, being in the neighborhood of those wild trees, and of the torrent. Some more aerial and finer-spirited winds rushed and roared through the ravine all night, from time to time arousing our fire, and dispersing the embers about. It was as if we lay in the

---

[2]Here, and in the two verse passages quoted below, Thoreau alludes to Book II of Milton's *Paradise Lost,* where Satan on his reconnaissance mission to spy on the newly created earth must travel through the realm of Chaos.

[3]Milton, *Paradise Lost* II, 940–42.

very nest of a young whirlwind. At midnight, one of my bedfellows, being startled in his dreams by the sudden blazing up to its top of a fir-tree, whose green boughs were dried by the heat, sprang up, with a cry, from his bed, thinking the world on fire, and drew the whole camp after him.

In the morning, after whetting our appetite on some raw pork, a wafer of hard bread, and a dipper of condensed cloud or water-spout, we all together began to make our way up the falls, which I have described; this time choosing the right hand, or highest peak, which was not the one I had approached before. But soon my companions were lost to my sight behind the mountain ridge in my rear, which still seemed ever retreating before me, and I climbed alone over huge rocks, loosely poised, a mile or more, still edging toward the clouds—for though the day was clear elsewhere, the summit was concealed by mist. The mountain seemed a vast aggregation of loose rocks, as if sometime it had rained rocks, and they lay as they fell on the mountain sides, nowhere fairly at rest, but leaning on each other, all rocking-stones, with cavities between, but scarcely any soil or smoother shelf. They were the raw materials of a planet dropped from an unseen quarry, which the vast chemistry of nature would anon work up, or work down, into the smiling and verdant plains and valleys of earth. This was an undone extremity of the globe; as in lignite we see coal in the process of formation.

At length I entered within the skirts of the cloud which seemed forever drifting over the summit, and yet would never be gone, but was generated out of that pure air as fast as it flowed away; and when, a quarter of a mile further, I reached the summit of the ridge, which those who have seen in clearer weather say is about five miles long, and contains a thousand acres of table-land, I was deep within the hostile ranks of clouds, and all objects were obscured by them. Now the wind would blow me out a yard of clear sunlight, wherein I stood; then a gray, dawning light was all it could accomplish, the cloud line ever rising and falling with the wind's intensity. Sometimes it seemed as if the summit would be cleared in a few moments and smile in sunshine: but what was gained on one side was lost on another. It was like sitting in a chimney and waiting for the smoke to blow away. It was, in fact, a cloud-factory,—these were the cloud-works, and the wind turned them off done from the cool, bare rocks. Occasionally, when the windy columns broke in to me, I caught sight of a dark, damp crag to the right or left; the mist driving ceaselessly between it and me. It reminded me of the creations of the old epic and dramatic poets, of Atlas, Vulcan, the Cyclops, and Prometheus.[4] Such was Caucasus and the rock where Prometheus was bound. Æschylus[5] had no doubt visited such scenery as this. It was vast, Titanic, and such as man never inhabits. Some part of the beholder, even some vital part, seems to escape through the loose grating of his ribs as he ascends. He is more lone than you can imagine. There is less of substantial thought and fair understanding in him, than in the plains where men inhabit. His reason is dispersed and shadowy, more thin and subtile like the air. Vast, Titanic, inhuman Nature has got him at disadvantage, caught him alone, and pilfers him of some of his divine faculty. She does not smile on him as in the plains. She

---

[4] In Greek mythology, Atlas ("he who dares") and Prometheus ("forethought") were both descended from the Titans, the giant children of the primordial couple Uranus and Gaea. For rebelling against Zeus, Atlas was condemned to stand in a remote corner of the world supporting the sky on his shoulders; Prometheus, as punishment for creating human beings and stealing the gods' fire for them, was chained to a rock in the Caucasus where an eagle fed each day upon his liver, which regenerated every night. Vulcan is the crippled Roman god of fire, forges, and smithies; the Cyclopes, in Greek mythology, were a race of one-eyed giants.

[5] Aeschylus (525–456 B.C.E.) is the Greek playwright who wrote of Prometheus' mountain ordeal.

seems to say sternly, why came ye here before your time? This ground is not prepared for you. Is it not enough that I smile in the valleys? I have never made this soil for thy feet, this air for thy breathing, these rocks for thy neighbors. I cannot pity nor fondle thee here, but forever relentlessly drive thee hence to where I *am* kind. Why seek me where I have not called thee, and then complain because you find me but a stepmother? Shouldst thou freeze or starve, or shudder thy life away, here is no shrine, nor altar, nor any access to my ear.

> "Chaos and ancient Night, I come no spy
> With purpose to explore or to disturb
> The secrets of your realm, but * * *
> * * * * * * * as my way
> Lies through your spacious empire up to light."[6]

The tops of mountains are among the unfinished parts of the globe, whither it is a slight insult to the gods to climb and pry into their secrets, and try their effect on our humanity. Only daring and insolent men, perchance, go there. Simple races, as savages, do not climb mountains—their tops are sacred and mysterious tracts never visited by them. Pomola[7] is always angry with those who climb to the summit of Ktaadn.

. . .

I found my companions where I had left them, on the side of the peak, gathering the mountain cranberries, which filled every crevice between the rocks, together with blue berries, which had a spicier flavor the higher up they grew, but were not the less agreeable to our palates. When the country is settled and roads are made, these cranberries will perhaps become an article of commerce. From this elevation, just on the skirts of the clouds, we could overlook the country west and south for a hundred miles. There it was, the State of Maine, which we had seen on the map, but not much like that. Immeasurable forest for the sun to shine on, that eastern *stuff* we hear of in Massachusetts. No clearing, no house. It did not look as if a solitary traveller had cut so much as a walking-stick there. Countless lakes,—Moosehead in the southwest, forty miles long by ten wide, like a gleaming silver platter at the end of the table; Chesuncook eighteen long by three wide, without an island; Millinocket, on the south, with its hundred islands; and a hundred others without a name; and mountains also, whose names, for the most part, are known only to the Indians. The forest looked like a firm grass sward, and the effect of these lakes in its midst has been well compared by one who has since visited this same spot, to that of a "mirror broken into a thousand fragments, and wildly scattered over the grass, reflecting the full blaze of the sun." It was a large farm for somebody, when cleared. According to the Gazetteer, which was printed before the boundary question was settled, this single Penobscot county in which we were, was larger than the whole State of Vermont, with its fourteen counties; and this was only a part of the wild lands of Maine. We are concerned now, however, about natural, not political limits. We were about eighty miles as the bird flies from Bangor, or one hundred and fifteen as we had ridden, and walked, and paddled. We had to console ourselves with the reflection that this view was probably as good as that from the peak, as far as it went, and what were a mountain without its attendant clouds and mists? Like ourselves, neither Bailey nor Jackson had obtained a clear view from the summit.[8]

---

[6]Milton, *Paradise Lost* II, 970–74.
[7]Thoreau probably refers to Pomona, the Roman goddess of domestic orchards.
[8]Earlier white explorers of Ktaadn.

Setting out on our return to the river, still at an early hour in the day, we decided to follow the course of the torrent, which we supposed to be Murch Brook, as long as it would not lead us too far out of our way. We thus travelled about four miles in the very torrent itself, continually crossing and recrossing it, leaping from rock to rock, and jumping with the stream down falls of seven or eight feet, or sometimes sliding down on our backs in a thin sheet of water. This ravine had been the scene of an extraordinary freshet in the spring, apparently accompanied by a slide from the mountain. It must have been filled with a stream of stones and water, at least twenty feet above the present level of the torrent. For a rod or two on either side of its channel, the trees were barked and splintered up to their tops, the birches bent over, twisted, and sometimes finely split like a stable-broom; some a foot in diameter snapped off, and whole clumps of trees bent over with the weight of rocks piled on them. In one place we noticed a rock two or three feet in diameter, lodged nearly twenty feet high in the crotch of a tree. For the whole four miles, we saw but one rill emptying in, and the volume of water did not seem to be increased from the first. We travelled thus very rapidly with a downward impetus, and grew remarkably expert at leaping from rock to rock, for leap we must, and leap we did, whether there was any rock at the right distance or not. It was a pleasant picture when the foremost turned about and looked up the winding ravine, walled in with rocks and the green forest, to see at intervals of a rod or two, a red-shirted or green-jacketed mountaineer against the white torrent, leaping down the channel with his pack on his back, or pausing upon a convenient rock in the midst of the torrent to mend a rent in his clothes, or unstrap the dipper at his belt to take a draught of the water. At one place we were startled by seeing, on a little sandy shelf by the side of the stream, the fresh print of a man's foot, and for a moment realized how Robinson Crusoe felt in a similar case; but at last we remembered that we had struck this stream on our way up, though we could not have told where, and one had descended into the ravine for a drink. The cool air above, and the continual bathing of our bodies in mountain water, alternate foot, sitz, douche, and plunge baths, made this walk exceedingly refreshing, and we had travelled only a mile or two after leaving the torrent, before every thread of our clothes was as dry as usual, owing perhaps to a peculiar quality in the atmosphere.

After leaving the torrent, being in doubt about our course, Tom threw down his pack at the foot of the loftiest spruce tree at hand, and shinned up the bare trunk some twenty feet, and then climbed through the green tower, lost to our sight, until he held the topmost spray in his hand.[9] McCauslin,[10] in his younger days, had marched through the wilderness with a body of troops, under General Somebody, and with one other man did all the scouting and spying service. The General's word was: "Throw down the top of that tree," and there was no tree in the Maine woods so high that it did not lose its top in such a case. I have heard a story of two men being lost once in these woods, nearer to the settlements than this, who climbed the loftiest pine they could find, some six feet in diameter at the ground, from whose top they discovered a solitary clearing and its smoke. When at this height, some two hundred feet from the ground, one of them became dizzy, and fainted

---

[9]"The spruce-tree," says Springer in '51, "is generally selected, principally for the superior facilities which its numerous limbs afford the climber. To gain the first limbs of this tree, which are from twenty to forty feet from the ground, a smaller tree is undercut and lodged against it, clambering up which the top of the spruce is reached. In some cases, when a very elevated position is desired, the spruce-tree is lodged against the trunk of some lofty pine, up which we ascend to a height twice that of the surrounding forest."

To indicate the direction of pines, he throws down a branch, and a man at the ground takes the bearing. [Thoreau's note]

[10]A member of Thoreau's party.

in his companion's arms, and the latter had to accomplish the descent with him, alternately fainting and reviving, as best he could. To Tom we cried, where away does the summit bear? where the burnt lands? The last he could only conjecture; he descried, however, a little meadow and pond, lying probably in our course, which we concluded to steer for. On reaching this secluded meadow, we found fresh tracks of moose on the shore of the pond, and the water was still unsettled as if they had fled before us. A little further, in a dense thicket, we seemed to be still on their trail. It was a small meadow, of a few acres, on the mountain side, concealed by the forest, and perhaps never seen by a white man before, where one would think that the moose might browse and bathe, and rest in peace. Pursuing this course, we soon reached the open land, which went sloping down some miles toward the Penobscot.

Perhaps I most fully realized that this was primeval, untamed, and forever untameable *Nature,* or whatever else men call it, while coming down this part of the mountain. We were passing over "Burnt Lands," burnt by lightning, perchance, though they showed no recent marks of fire hardly so much as a charred stump, but looked rather like a natural pasture for the moose and deer, exceedingly wild and desolate, with occasional strips of timber crossing them, and low poplars springing up, and patches of blueberries here and there. I found myself traversing them familiarly, like some pasture run to waste, or partially reclaimed by man; but when I reflected what man, what brother or sister or kinsman of our race made it and claimed it, I expected the proprietor to rise up and dispute my passage. It is difficult to conceive of a region uninhabited by man. We habitually presume his presence and influence everywhere. And yet we have not seen pure Nature, unless we have seen her thus vast, and drear, and inhuman, though in the midst of cities. Nature was here something savage and awful, though beautiful. I looked with awe at the ground I trod on, to see what the Powers had made there, the form and fashion and material of their work. This was that Earth of which we have heard, made out of Chaos and old Night. Here was no man's garden, but the unhandselled[11] globe. It was not lawn, nor pasture, nor mead, nor woodland, nor lea, nor arable, nor waste-land. It was the fresh and natural surface of the planet Earth, as it was made forever and ever,—to be the dwelling of man, we say,—so Nature made it, and man may use it if he can. Man was not to be associated with it. It was Matter, vast, terrific,—not his Mother Earth that we have heard of, not for him to tread on, or be buried in,—no, it were being too familiar even to let his bones lie there—the home this of Necessity and Fate. There was there felt the presence of a force not bound to be kind to man. It was a place for heathenism and superstitious rites,—to be inhabited by men nearer of kin to the rocks and to wild animals than we. We walked over it with a certain awe, stopping from time to time to pick the blueberries which grew there, and had a smart and spicy taste. Perchance where *our* wild pines stand, and leaves lie on their forest floor in Concord, there were once reapers, and husbandmen planted grain; but here not even the surface had been scarred by man, but it was a specimen of what God saw fit to make this world. What is it to be admitted to a museum, to see a myriad of particular things, compared with being shown some star's surface, some hard matter in its home! I stand in awe of my body, this matter to which I am bound has become so strange to me. I fear not spirits, ghosts, of which I am one,—*that* my body might,—but I fear bodies, I tremble to meet them. What is this Titan that has possession of me? Talk of mysteries!—think of our life in nature,—daily to be shown matter, to come in contact with it,—rocks, trees, wind on our cheeks! the *solid* earth! the *actual* world! the *common sense! Contact! Contact! Who* are we? *where* are we?

---

[11] Something not yet put into use.

KARL MARX
[1818-1883]

AND

FRIEDRICH ENGELS
[1820-1895]

"The philosophers have only *interpreted* the world; the point is to *change* it." Karl Marx, a doctor of philosophy from the University of Berlin, spent his lifetime studying the causes of human oppression and designing a social system called communism to put an end to it.

Marx was born in Prussia in 1818. After receiving his doctorate in 1841, he became editor of the *Rheinische Zeitung*, a radical newspaper in Cologne. He met Friedrich Engels there, and married Jenny von Westphalen; both remained Marx's lifelong companions. With Engels he collaborated on *The German Ideology* in 1845–1846 and *The Communist Manifesto* in 1848. Over the next twenty years, supported in part by Engels, Marx wrote his great work, *Capital*. He published the first volume in 1867, and Engels published the remaining two after Marx's death, in 1885 and 1894, respectively.

The *Communist Manifesto*, commissioned by the Communist League in London in 1847, is noteworthy for its tone. Part I, which we include here, announces the arrival of the world revolutionary movement. It portrays humankind as divided throughout history into opposing social classes, which narrow down to two in the modern era: the bourgeoisie (the owners of the means of production) and the proletariat (those who must sell their labor in order to survive). It explains the dynamic of the Industrial Revolution. It claims that the bourgeois revolution has gone out of control, until "what the bourgeoisie . . . produces, above all, is its own grave-diggers."

Part II, which we do not include, responds to concerns people had that the communists would abolish private property, the family, education, marriage, national boundaries, and other "eternal truths" such as morality and religion. One by one, Engels demonstrates that these seemingly universal phenomena have a bourgeois character. Then he lists the measures the proletariat will take to bring about social justice once it comes to power. These include the abolition of private property, a graduated income tax, the centralization of credit, and equality of labor.

Communist Manifesto

I. BOURGEOIS AND PROLETARIANS[1]

The history of all hitherto existing society is the history of class struggles.

Freeman and slave, patrician and plebeian, lord and serf, guild-master and journeyman, in a word, oppressor and oppressed, stood in constant opposition to one another, carried on an uninterrupted, now hidden, now open fight, a fight that each time ended, either in a revolutionary re-constitution of society at large, or in the common ruin of the contending classes.

---

[1] "By bourgeoisie is meant the class of modern Capitalists, owners of the means of social production and employers of wage-labour. By proletariat, the class of modern wage-labourers who, having no means of production of their own, are reduced to selling their labour-power in order to live" (Engels, 1888).

In the earlier epochs of history, we find almost everywhere a complicated arrangement of society into various orders, a manifold gradation of social rank. In ancient Rome we have patricians, knights, plebeians, slaves; in the Middle Ages, feudal lords, vassals, guild-masters, journeymen, apprentices, serfs; in almost all of these classes, again, subordinate gradations.

The modern bourgeois society that has sprouted from the ruins of feudal society has not done away with class antagonisms. It has but established new classes, new conditions of oppression, new forms of struggle in place of the old ones.

Our epoch, the epoch of the bourgeoisie, possesses, however, this distinctive feature: it has simplified the class antagonisms: Society as a whole is more and more splitting up into two great hostile camps, into two great classes directly facing each other: Bourgeoisie and Proletariat.

From the serfs of the Middle Ages sprang the chartered burghers of the earliest towns. From these burgesses the first elements of the bourgeoisie were developed.

The discovery of America, the rounding of the Cape, opened up fresh ground for the rising bourgeoisie. The East-Indian and Chinese markets, the colonisation of America, trade with the colonies, the increase in the means of exchange and in commodities generally, gave to commerce, to navigation, to industry, an impulse never before known, and thereby, to the revolutionary element in the tottering feudal society, a rapid development.

The feudal system of industry, under which industrial production was monopolised by closed guilds, now no longer sufficed for the growing wants of the new markets. The manufacturing system took its place. The guild-masters were pushed on one side by the manufacturing middle class; division of labour between the different corporate guilds vanished in the face of division of labour in each single workshop.

Meantime the markets kept ever growing, the demand ever rising. Even manufacture no longer sufficed. Thereupon, steam and machinery revolutionised industrial production. The place of manufacture was taken by the giant, Modern Industry, the place of the industrial middle class, by industrial millionaires, the leaders of whole industrial armies, the modern bourgeois.

Modern industry has established the world-market, for which the discovery of America paved the way. This market has given an immense development to commerce, to navigation, to communication by land. This development has, in its turn, reacted on the extension of industry; and in proportion as industry, commerce, navigation, railways extended, in the same proportion the bourgeoisie developed, increased its capital, and pushed into the background every class handed down from the Middle Ages.

We see, therefore, how the modern bourgeoisie is itself the product of a long course of development, of a series of revolutions in the modes of production and of exchange.

Each step in the development of the bourgeoisie was accompanied by a corresponding political advance of that class. An oppressed class under the sway of the feudal nobility, an armed and self-governing association in the mediaeval commune; here independent urban republic (as in Italy and Germany), there taxable "third estate" of the monarchy (as in France), afterwards, in the period of manufacture proper, serving either the semi-feudal or the absolute monarchy as a counterpoise against the nobility, and, in fact, corner-stone of the great monarchies in general, the bourgeoisie has at last, since the establishment of Modern Industry and of the world-market, conquered for itself, in the modern representative State, exclusive political sway. The executive of the modern State is but a committee for managing the common affairs of the whole bourgeoisie.

The bourgeoisie, historically, has played a most revolutionary part.

The bourgeoisie, wherever it has got the upper hand, has put an end to all feudal, patriarchal, idyllic relations. It has pitilessly torn asunder the motley feudal ties that bound man to his "natural superiors," and has left remaining no other nexus between man and man than naked self-interest, than callous "cash payment." It has drowned the most heavenly ecstasies of religious fervour, of chivalrous enthusiasm, of philistine sentimentalism, in the icy water of egotistical calculation. It has resolved personal worth into exchange value, and in place of the numberless indefeasible chartered freedoms, has set up that single, unconscionable freedom—Free Trade. In one word, for exploitation, veiled by religious and political illusions, it has substituted naked, shameless, direct, brutal exploitation.

The bourgeoisie has stripped of its halo every occupation hitherto honoured and looked up to with reverent awe. It has converted the physician, the lawyer, the priest, the poet, the man of science, into its paid wage-labourers.

The bourgeoisie has torn away from the family its sentimental veil, and has reduced the family relation to a mere money relation.

The bourgeoisie has disclosed how it came to pass that the brutal display of vigour in the Middle Ages, which Reactionists so much admire, found its fitting complement in the most slothful indolence. It has been the first to show what man's activity can bring about. It has accomplished wonders far surpassing Egyptian pyramids, Roman aqueducts, and Gothic cathedrals; it has conducted expeditions that put in the shade all former Exoduses of nations and crusades.

The bourgeoisie cannot exist without constantly revolutionising the instruments of production, and thereby the relations of production, and with them the whole relations of society. Conservation of the old modes of production in unaltered form, was, on the contrary, the first condition of existence for all earlier industrial classes. Constant revolutionising of production, uninterrupted disturbance of all social conditions, everlasting uncertainty and agitation distinguish the bourgeois epoch from all earlier ones. All fixed, fast-frozen relations, with their train of ancient and venerable prejudices and opinions, are swept away, all new-formed ones become antiquated before they can ossify. All that is solid melts into air, all that is holy is profaned, and man is at last compelled to face with sober senses, his real conditions of life, and his relations with his kind.

The need of a constantly expanding market for its product chases the bourgeoisie over the whole surface of the globe. It must nestle everywhere, settle everywhere, establish connexions everywhere.

The bourgeoisie has through its exploitation of the world-market given a cosmopolitan character to production and consumption in every country. To the great chagrin of Reactionists, it has drawn from under the feet of industry the national ground on which it stood. All old-established national industries have been destroyed or are daily being destroyed. They are dislodged by new industries, whose introduction becomes a life and death question for all civilised nations, by industries that no longer work up indigenous raw material, but raw material drawn from the remotest zones; industries whose products are consumed, not only at home, but in every quarter of the globe. In place of the old wants, satisfied by the productions of the country, we find new wants, requiring for their satisfaction the products of distant lands and climes. In place of the old local and national seclusion and self-sufficiency, we have intercourse in every direction, universal inter-dependence of nations. And as in material, so also in intellectual production. The intellectual creations of individual nations become common property. National one-sidedness and narrow-mindedness become more and more impossible, and from the numerous national and local literatures, there arises a world literature.

The bourgeoisie, by the rapid improvement of all instruments of production, by the immensely facilitated means of communication, draws all, even the most barbarian, nations into civilisation. The cheap prices of its commodities are the heavy artillery with which it batters down all Chinese walls, with which it forces the barbarians' intensely obstinate hatred of foreigners to capitulate. It compels all nations, on pain of extinction, to adopt the bourgeois mode of production; it compels them to introduce what it calls civilisation into their midst, *i.e.*, to become bourgeois themselves. In one word, it creates a world after its own image.

The bourgeoisie has subjected the country to the rule of the towns. It has created enormous cities, has greatly increased the urban population as compared with the rural, and has thus rescued a considerable part of the population from the idiocy of rural life. Just as it has made the country dependent on the towns, so it has made barbarian and semi-barbarian countries dependent on the civilised ones, nations of peasants on nations of bourgeois, the East on the West.

The bourgeoisie keeps more and more doing away with the scattered state of the population, of the means of production, and of property. It has agglomerated population, centralised means of production, and has concentrated property in a few hands. The necessary consequence of this was political centralisation. Independent, or but loosely connected provinces, with separate interests, laws, governments and systems of taxation, became lumped together into one nation, with one government, one code of laws, one national class-interest, one frontier and one customs-tariff.

The bourgeoisie, during its rule of scarce one hundred years, has created more massive and more colossal productive forces than have all preceding generations together. Subjection of Nature's forces to man, machinery, application of chemistry to industry and agriculture, steam-navigation, railways, electric telegraphs, clearing of whole continents for cultivation, canalisation of rivers, whole populations conjured out of the ground—what earlier century had even a presentiment that such productive forces slumbered in the lap of social labour?

We see then: the means of production and of exchange, on whose foundation the bourgeoisie built itself up, were generated in feudal society. At a certain stage in the development of these means of production and of exchange, the conditions under which feudal society produced and exchanged, the feudal organisation of agriculture and manufacturing industry, in one word, the feudal relations of property became no longer compatible with the already developed productive forces; they became so many fetters. They had to be burst asunder; they were burst asunder.

Into their place stepped free competition, accompanied by a social and political constitution adapted to it, and by the economical and political sway of the bourgeois class.

A similar movement is going on before our own eyes. Modern bourgeois society with its relations of production, of exchange and of property, a society that has conjured up such gigantic means of production and of exchange, is like the sorcerer, who is no longer able to control the powers of the nether world whom he has called up by his spells. For many a decade past the history of industry and commerce is but the history of the revolt of modern productive forces against modern conditions of production, against the property relations that are the conditions for the existence of the bourgeoisie and of its rule. It is enough to mention the commercial crises that by their periodical return put on its trial, each time more threateningly, the existence of the entire bourgeois society. In these crises a great part not only of the existing products, but also of the previously created productive forces, are periodically destroyed. In these crises there breaks out an epidemic that, in all earlier epochs, would have seemed an absurdity—the epidemic of over-production. Society suddenly finds itself put back into a state of momentary barbarism; it appears as if a famine, a universal war of devastation had cut off the supply of every means of subsistence; industry and commerce seem to be destroyed; and why? Because there is too much civilisation, too much means of subsistence, too much industry, too much commerce. The productive forces at the disposal of society no longer tend to further the development of the conditions of bourgeois property; on the contrary, they have become too powerful for these conditions, by which they are fettered, and so soon as they overcome these fetters, they bring disorder into the whole of bourgeois society, endanger the existence of bourgeois property. The conditions of bourgeois society are too narrow to comprise the wealth created by them. And how does the bourgeoisie get over these crises? On the one hand by enforced destruction of a mass of productive forces; on the other, by the conquest of new markets, and by the more thorough exploitation of the old ones. That is to say, by paving the way for more extensive and more destructive crises, and by diminishing the means whereby crises are prevented.

The weapons with which the bourgeoisie felled feudalism to the ground are now turned against the bourgeoisie itself.

But not only has the bourgeoisie forged the weapons that bring death to itself; it has also called into existence the men who are to wield those weapons—the modern working class—the proletarians.

In proportion as the bourgeoisie, *i.e.*, capital, is developed, in the same proportion is the proletariat, the modern working class, developed—a class of labourers, who live only so long as they find work, and who find work only so long as their labour increases capital. These labourers, who must sell themselves piece-meal, are a commodity, like every other article of commerce, and are consequently exposed to all the vicissitudes of competition, to all the fluctuations of the market.

Owing to the extensive use of machinery and to division of labour, the work of the proletarians has lost all individual character, and consequently, all charm for the workman. He becomes an appendage of the machine, and it is only the most simple, most monotonous, and most easily acquired knack, that is required of him. Hence, the cost of production of a workman is restricted, almost entirely, to the means of subsistence that he requires for his maintenance, and for the propagation of his race. But the price of a commodity, and therefore also of labour, is equal to its cost of production. In proportion, therefore, as the repulsiveness of the work increases, the wage decreases. Nay more, in proportion as the use of machinery and division of labour increases, in the same proportion the burden of toil also increases, whether by prolongation of the working hours, by increase of the work exacted in a given time or by increased speed of the machinery, etc.

Modern industry has converted the little workshop of the patriarchal master into the great factory of the industrial capitalist. Masses of labourers, crowded into the factory, are organised like soldiers. As privates of the industrial army they are placed under the command of a perfect hierarchy of officers and sergeants. Not only are they slaves of the bourgeois class, and of the bourgeois State; they are daily and hourly enslaved by the machine, by the over-looker, and, above all, by the individual bourgeois manufacturer himself. The more openly this despotism proclaims gain to be its end and aim, the more petty, the more hateful and the more embittering it is.

The less the skill and exertion of strength implied in manual labour, in other words, the more modern industry becomes developed, the more is the labour of men superseded by that of women. Differences of age and sex have no longer any distinctive social validity for the working class. All are instruments of labour, more or less expensive to use, according to their age and sex.

No sooner is the exploitation of the labourer by the manufacturer, so far, at an end, that he receives his wages in cash, than he is set upon by the other portions of the bourgeoisie, the landlord, the shopkeeper, the pawnbroker, etc.

The lower strata of the middle class—the small tradespeople, shopkeepers, and retired tradesmen generally, the handicraftsmen and peasants—all these sink gradually into the proletariat, partly because their diminutive capital does not suffice for the scale on which Modern Industry is carried on, and is swamped in the competition with the large capitalists, partly because their specialised skill is rendered worthless by new methods of production. Thus the proletariat is recruited from all classes of the population.

The proletariat goes through various stages of development. With its birth begins its struggle with the bourgeoisie. At first the contest is carried on by individual labourers, then by the workpeople of a factory, then by the operatives of one trade, in one locality, against the individual bourgeois who directly exploits them. They direct their attacks not against the bourgeois conditions of production, but against the instruments of production themselves; they destroy imported wares that compete with their labour, they smash to pieces machinery, they set factories ablaze, they seek to restore by force the vanished status of the workman of the Middle Ages.

At this stage the labourers still form an incoherent mass scattered over the whole country, and broken up by their mutual competition. If anywhere they unite to form more compact bodies, this is not yet the consequence of their own active union, but of the union of the bourgeoisie, which class, in order to attain its own political ends, is compelled to set the whole proletariat in motion, and is moreover yet, for a time, able to do so. At this stage, therefore, the proletarians do not fight their enemies, but the enemies of their enemies, the remnants of absolute monarchy, the landowners, the non-industrial bourgeois, the petty bourgeoisie. Thus the whole historical movement is concentrated in the hands of the bourgeoisie; every victory so obtained is a victory for the bourgeoisie.

But with the development of industry the proletariat not only increases in number; it becomes concentrated in greater masses, its strength grows, and it feels that strength more. The various interests and conditions of life within the ranks of the proletariat are more and more equalised, in proportion as machinery obliterates all distinctions of labour, and nearly everywhere reduces wages to the same low level. The growing competition among the bourgeois, and the resulting commercial crises, make the wages of the workers ever more fluctuating. The unceasing improvement of machinery, ever more rapidly developing, makes their livelihood more and more precarious; the collisions between individual workmen and individual bourgeois take more and more the character of collisions between two classes. Thereupon the workers begin to form combinations (Trades Unions) against the bourgeois; they club together in order to keep up the rate of wages; they found permanent associations in order to make provision beforehand for these occasional revolts. Here and there the contest breaks out into riots.

Now and then the workers are victorious, but only for a time. The real fruit of their battles lies, not in the immediate result, but in the ever-expanding union of the workers. This union is helped on by the improved means of communication that are created by modern industry and that place the workers of different localities in contact with one another. It was just this contact that was needed to centralise the numerous local struggles, all of the same character, into one national struggle between classes. But every class struggle is a political struggle. And that union, to attain which the burghers of the Middle Ages, with their miserable highways, required centuries, the modern proletarians, thanks to railways, achieve in a few years.

This organisation of the proletarians into a class, and consequently into a political party, is continually being upset again by the competition between the workers themselves. But it ever rises up again, stronger, firmer, mightier. It compels legislative recognition of particular interests of the workers, by taking advantage of the divisions among the bourgeoisie itself. Thus the ten-hours' bill in England was carried.

Altogether collisions between the classes of the old society further, in many ways, the course of development of the proletariat. The bourgeoisie finds itself involved in a constant battle. At first with the aristocracy; later on, with those portions of the bourgeoisie itself, whose interests have become antagonistic to the progress of industry; at all times, with the bourgeoisie of foreign countries. In all these battles it sees itself compelled to appeal to the proletariat, to ask for its help, and thus, to drag it into the political arena. The bourgeoisie itself, therefore, supplies the proletariat with its own elements of political and general education, in other words, it furnishes the proletariat with weapons for fighting the bourgeoisie.

Further, as we have already seen, entire sections of the ruling classes are, by the advance of industry, precipitated into the proletariat, or are at least threatened in their conditions of existence. These also supply the proletariat with fresh elements of enlightenment and progress.

Finally, in times when the class struggle nears the decisive hour, the process of dissolution going on within the ruling class, in fact within the whole range of society, assumes such a violent, glaring character, that a small section of the ruling class cuts itself adrift, and joins the revolutionary class, the class that holds the future in its hands. Just as, therefore, at an earlier period, a section of the nobility went over to the bourgeoisie, so now a portion of the bourgeoisie goes over to the proletariat, and in particular, a portion of the bourgeois ideologists, who have raised themselves to the level of comprehending theoretically the historical movement as a whole.

Of all the classes that stand face to face with the bourgeoisie today, the proletariat alone is a really revolutionary class. The other classes decay and finally disappear in the face of Modern Industry; the proletariat is its special and essential product.

The lower middle class, the small manufacturer, the shopkeeper, the artisan, the peasant, all these fight against the bourgeoisie, to save from extinction their existence as fractions of the middle class. They are therefore not revolutionary, but conservative. Nay more, they are reactionary, for they try to roll back the wheel of history. If by chance they are revolutionary, they are so only in view of their impending transfer into the proletariat, they thus defend not their present, but their future interests, they desert their own standpoint to place themselves at that of the proletariat.

The "dangerous class,"[2] the social scum, that passively rotting mass thrown off by the lowest layers of old society, may, here and there, be swept into the movement by a proletarian revolution; its conditions of life, however, prepare it far more for the part of a bribed tool of reactionary intrigue.

---

[2] The German name for this underclass is the *Lumpenproletariat*.

In the conditions of the proletariat, those of old society at large are already virtually swamped. The proletarian is without property; his relation to his wife and children has no longer anything in common with the bourgeois family-relations; modern industrial labour, modern subjection to capital, the same in England as in France, in America as in Germany, has stripped him of every trace of national character. Law, morality, religion, are to him so many bourgeois prejudices, behind which lurk in ambush just as many bourgeois interests.

All the preceding classes that got the upper hand, sought to fortify their already acquired status by subjecting society at large to their conditions of appropriation. The proletarians cannot become masters of the productive forces of society, except by abolishing their own previous mode of appropriation, and thereby also every other previous mode of appropriation. They have nothing of their own to secure and to fortify; their mission is to destroy all previous securities for, and insurances of, individual property.

All previous historical movements were movements of minorities, or in the interests of minorities. The proletarian movement is the self-conscious, independent movement of the immense majority, in the interests of the immense majority. The proletariat, the lowest stratum of our present society, cannot stir, cannot raise itself up, without the whole superincumbent strata of official society being sprung into the air.

Though not in substance, yet in form, the struggle of the proletariat with the bourgeoisie is at first a national struggle. The proletariat of each country must, of course, first of all settle matters with its own bourgeoisie.

In depicting the most general phases of the development of the proletariat, we traced the more or less veiled civil war, raging within existing society, up to the point where that war breaks out into open revolution, and where the violent overthrow of the bourgeoisie lays the foundation for the sway of the proletariat.

Hitherto, every form of society has been based, as we have already seen, on the antagonism of oppressing and oppressed classes. But in order to oppress a class, certain conditions must be assured to it under which it can, at least, continue its slavish existence. The serf, in the period of serfdom, raised himself to membership in the commune, just as the petty bourgeois, under the yoke of feudal absolutism, managed to develop into a bourgeois. The modern labourer, on the contrary, instead of rising with the progress of industry, sinks deeper and deeper below the conditions of existence of his own class. He becomes a pauper, and pauperism develops more rapidly than population and wealth. And here it becomes evident, that the bourgeoisie is unfit any longer to be the ruling class in society, and to impose its conditions of existence upon society as an over-riding law. It is unfit to rule because it is incompetent to assure an existence to its slave within his slavery, because it cannot help letting him sink into such a state, that it has to feed him, instead of being fed by him. Society can no longer live under this bourgeoisie, in other words, its existence is no longer compatible with society.

The essential condition for the existence, and for the sway of the bourgeois class, is the formation and augmentation of capital; the condition for capital is wage-labour. Wage-labour rests exclusively on competition between the labourers. The advance of industry, whose involuntary promoter is the bourgeoisie, replaces the isolation of the labourers, due to competition, by their revolutionary combination, due to association. The development of Modern Industry, therefore, cuts from under its feet the very foundation on which the bourgeoisie produces and appropriates products. What the bourgeoisie, therefore, produces, above all, is its own grave-diggers. Its fall and the victory of the proletariat are equally inevitable.

FRIEDRICH NIETZSCHE
[1844–1900]

Friedrich Nietzsche, one of the most controversial nineteenth-century philosophers, was also one of the most influential. Born in Prussia, the son of a Lutheran minister, Nietzsche went to the Universities of Bonn and Leipzig before becoming, in 1869, a professor of classical philology at the University of Basel in Switzerland, a post he held for ten years. In his early works, *The Birth of Tragedy from the Spirit of Music* (1872) and *Untimely Meditations* (1873–1876), Nietzsche wrote, in part, as an apostle of the composer Richard Wagner. But he broke with Wagner at the end of the decade and, after resigning from the university, went on in the 1880s to write the works on which his reputation is based: *Thus Spake Zarathustra* (1883–1884), *Beyond Good and Evil* (1886), and *The Genealogy of Morals* (1887). In 1889 he suffered a mental breakdown and was largely incapacitated during the last decade of his life.

A Darwinian who saw life as struggle, Nietzsche thought that human behavior could be accounted for by a single basic drive, the will to power. His ideal was the superman (*Übermensch*), a superior man who creatively employs both his passion and his reason to become a higher type. Such fulfillment, Nietzsche thought, was thwarted by both Enlightenment rationalism, which encouraged disembodied conformism, and by Christianity, which celebrated weakness and failure. The superman, by contrast, was Dionysian, celebrating the passions and the body as well as the mind, affirming this world and the present moment rather than seeking otherworldly consolation, and taking responsibility for his own freedom and destiny. The passages we include below, from *Thus Spake Zarathustra*, describe the superman and illustrate Nietzsche's style, a literary way of writing philosophy that has been adopted by such later philosophers as Sartre and Camus, who develop their philosophical ideas in novels and plays. The influence of Nietzsche's ideas on twentieth-century writers, especially the existentialists, has been profound.

Thus Spake Zarathustra
Translated by Thomas Common

[THE SUPERMAN]

FROM
PART ONE

3

When Zarathustra arrived at the nearest town which adjoineth the forest, he found many people assembled in the market-place; for it had been announced that a rope-dancer would give a performance. And Zarathustra spake thus unto the people:

I teach you the Superman. Man is something that is to be surpassed. What have ye done to surpass man?

All beings hitherto have created something beyond themselves: and ye want to be the ebb of that great tide, and would rather go back to the beast than surpass man?

What is the ape to man? A laughing-stock, a thing of shame. And just the same shall man be to the Superman: a laughing-stock, a thing of shame.

Ye have made your way from the worm to man, and much within you is still worm. Once were ye apes, and even yet man is more of an ape than any of the apes.

Even the wisest among you is only a disharmony and hybrid of plant and phantom. But do I bid you become phantoms or plants?

Lo, I teach you the Superman!

The Superman is the meaning of the earth. Let your will say: The Superman *shall be* the meaning of the earth!

I conjure you, my brethren, *remain true to the earth,* and believe not those who speak unto you of superearthly hopes! Poisoners are they, whether they know it or not.

Despisers of life are they, decaying ones and poisoned ones themselves, of whom the earth is weary: so away with them!

Once blasphemy against God was the greatest blasphemy; but God died, and therewith also those blasphemers. To blaspheme the earth is now the dreadfulest sin, and to rate the heart of the unknowable higher than the meaning of the earth!

Once the soul looked contemptuously on the body, and then that contempt was the supreme thing:—the soul wished the body meagre, ghastly, and famished. Thus it thought to escape from the body and the earth.

Oh, that soul was itself meagre, ghastly, and famished; and cruelty was the delight of that soul!

But ye, also, my brethren, tell me: What doth your body say about your soul? Is your soul not poverty and pollution and wretched self-complacency?

Verily, a polluted stream is man. One must be a sea, to receive a polluted stream without becoming impure.

Lo, I teach you the Superman: he is that sea; in him can your great contempt be submerged.

What is the greatest thing ye can experience? It is the hour of great contempt. The hour in which even your happiness becometh loathsome unto you, and so also your reason and virtue.

The hour when ye say: "What good is my happiness! It is poverty and pollution and wretched self-complacency. But my happiness should justify existence itself!"

The hour when ye say: "What good is my reason! Doth it long for knowledge as the lion for his food? It is poverty and pollution and wretched self-complacency!"

The hour when ye say: "What good is my virtue! As yet it hath not made me passionate. How weary I am of my good and my bad! It is all poverty and pollution and wretched self-complacency!"

The hour when ye say: "What good is my justice! I do not see that I am fervour and fuel. The just, however, are fervour and fuel!"

The hour when ye say: "What good is my pity! Is not pity the cross on which he is nailed who loveth man? But my pity is not a crucifixion."

Have ye ever spoken thus? Have ye ever cried thus? Ah! would that I had heard you crying thus!

It is not your sin—it is your self-satisfaction that crieth unto heaven; your very sparingness in sin crieth unto heaven!

Where is the lightning to lick you with its tongue? Where is the frenzy with which ye should be inoculated?

Lo, I teach you the Superman: he is that lightning, he is that frenzy!—

When Zarathustra had thus spoken, one of the people called out: "We have now heard enough of the rope-dancer; it is time now for us to see him!" And all the people laughed at Zarathustra. But the rope-dancer, who thought the words applied to him, began his performance.

PART FOUR

1

When I came unto men for the first time, then did I commit the anchorite folly, the great folly: I appeared on the market-place.

And when I spake unto all, I spake unto none. In the evening, however, rope-dancers were my companions, and corpses; and I myself almost a corpse.

With the new morning, however, there came unto me a new truth: then did I learn to say: "Of what account to me are market-place and populace and populace-noise and long populace-ears!"

Ye higher men, learn *this* from me: On the market-place no one believeth in higher men. But if ye will speak there, very well! The populace, however, blinketh: "We are all equal."

"Ye higher men,"—so blinketh the populace—"there are no higher men, we are all equal; man is man, before God—we are all equal!"

Before God!—Now, however, this God hath died. Before the populace, however, we will not be equal. Ye higher men, away from the market-place!

2

Before God!—Now however this God hath died! Ye higher men, this God was your greatest danger.

Only since he lay in the grave have ye again arisen. Now only cometh the great noontide, now only doth the higher man become—master!

Have ye understood this word, O my brethren? Ye are frightened: do your hearts turn giddy? Doth the abyss here yawn for you? Doth the hell-hound here yelp at you?

Well! Take heart! ye higher men! Now only travaileth the mountain of the human future. God hath died: now do *we* desire—the Superman to live.

3

The most careful ask to-day: "How is man to be maintained?" Zarathustra however asketh, as the first and only one: "How is man to be *surpassed?*"

The Superman, I have at heart; *that* is the first and only thing to me—and *not* man: not the neighbour, not the poorest, not the sorriest, not the best.—

O my brethren, what I can love in man is that he is a going over and a going under. And also in you there is much that maketh me love and hope.

In that ye have despised, ye higher men, that maketh me hope. For the great despisers are the great reverers.

In that ye have despaired, there is much to honour. For ye have not learned to submit yourselves, ye have not learned petty policy.

For to-day have the petty people become master: they all preach submission and humility and policy and diligence and consideration and the long *et cetera* of petty virtues.

Whatever is of the effeminate type, whatever originateth from the servile type, and especially the populace-mishmash:—*that* wisheth now to be master of all human destiny—O disgust! Disgust! Disgust!

That asketh and asketh and never tireth: "How is man to maintain himself best, longest, most pleasantly?" Thereby—are they the masters of today.

These masters of today—surpass them, O my brethren—these petty people: *they* are the Superman's greatest danger!

Surpass, ye higher men, the petty virtues, the petty policy, the sand-grain considerateness, the ant-hill trumpery, the pitiable comfortableness, the "happiness of the greatest number"—!

And rather despair than submit yourselves. And verily, I love you, because ye know not today how to live, ye higher men! For thus do *ye* live—best!

4

Have ye courage, O my brethren? Are ye stout-hearted? *Not* the courage before witnesses, but anchorite and eagle courage, which not even a God any longer beholdeth?

Cold souls, mules, the blind and the drunken, I do not call stout-hearted. He hath heart who knoweth fear, but *vanquisheth* it; who seeth the abyss, but with *pride*.

He who seeth the abyss, but with eagle's eyes,—he who with eagle's talons *graspeth* the abyss: he hath courage.— —

5

"Man is evil"—so said to me for consolation, all the wisest ones. Ah, if only it be still true today! For the evil is man's best force.

"Man must become better and eviler"—so do *I* teach. The evilest is necessary for the Superman's best.

It may have been well for the preacher of the petty people to suffer and be burdened by men's sin. I, however, rejoice in great sin as my great *consolation.*—

Such things, however, are not said for long ears. Every word, also, is not suited for every mouth. These are fine far-away things: at them sheep's claws shall not grasp!

6

Ye higher men, think ye that I am here to put right what ye have put wrong?

Or that I wished henceforth to make snugger couches for you sufferers? Or show you restless, miswandering, misclimbing ones, new and easier footpaths?

Nay! Nay! Three times Nay! Always more, always better ones of your type shall succumb,—for ye shall always have it worse and harder. Thus only—

—Thus only groweth man aloft to the height where the lightning striketh and shattereth him: high enough for the lightning!

Towards the few, the long, the remote go forth my soul and my seeking: of what account to me are your many little, short miseries!

Ye do not yet suffer enough for me! For ye suffer from yourselves, ye have not yet suffered *from man.* Ye would lie if ye spake otherwise! None of you suffereth from what *I* have suffered.— —

7

It is not enough for me that the lightning no longer doeth harm. I do not wish to conduct it away: it shall learn—to work for *me.*—

My wisdom hath accumulated long like a cloud, it becometh stiller and darker. So doeth all wisdom which shall one day bear *lightnings.*—

Unto these men of today will I not be *light,* nor be called light. *Them*—will I blind: lightning of my wisdom! put out their eyes!

8

Do not will anything beyond your power: there is a bad falseness in those who will beyond their power.

Especially when they will great things! For they awaken distrust in great things, these subtle false-coiners and stage-players:—

—Until at last they are false towards themselves, squint-eyed, whited cankers, glossed over with strong words, parade virtues and brilliant false deeds.

Take good care there, ye higher men! For nothing is more precious to me, and rarer, than honesty.

Is this today not that of the populace? The populace however knoweth not what is great and what is small, what is straight and what is honest: it is innocently crooked, it ever lieth.

9

Have a good distrust today, ye higher men, ye enheartened ones! Ye open-hearted ones! And keep your reasons secret! For this today is that of the populace.

What the populace once learned to believe without reasons, who could—refute it to them by means of reasons?

And on the market-place one convinceth with gestures. But reasons make the populace distrustful.

And when truth hath once triumphed there, then ask yourselves with good distrust: "What strong error hath fought for it?"

Be on your guard also against the learned! They hate you, because they are unproductive! They have cold, withered eyes before which every bird is unplumed.

Such persons vaunt about not lying: but inability to lie is still far from being love of truth. Be on your guard!

Freedom from fever is still far from being knowledge! Refrigerated spirits I do not believe in. He who cannot lie, doth not know what truth is.

10

If ye would go up high, then use your own legs! Do not get yourselves *carried* aloft; do not seat yourselves on other people's backs and heads!

Thou hast mounted, however, on horseback? Thou now ridest briskly up to thy goal? Well, my friend! But thy lame foot is also with thee on horseback!

When thou reachest thy goal, when thou alightest from thy horse: precisely on thy *height,* thou higher man,—then wilt thou stumble!

11

Ye creating ones, ye higher men! One is only pregnant with one's own child.

Do not let yourselves be imposed upon or put upon! Who then is *your* neighbour? Even if ye act "for your neighbour"—ye still do not create for him!

Unlearn, I pray you, this "for," ye creating ones: your very virtue wisheth you to have naught to do with "for" and "on account of" and "because." Against these false little words shall ye stop your ears.

"For one's neighbour," is the virtue only of the petty people: there it is said "like and like," and "hand washeth hand":—they have neither the right nor the power for *your* self-seeking!

In your self-seeking, ye creating ones, there is the foresight and foreseeing of the pregnant! What no one's eye hath yet seen, namely, the fruit—this, sheltereth and saveth and nourisheth your entire love.

Where your entire love is, namely, with your child, there is also your entire virtue! Your work, your will is *your* "neighbour": let no false values impose upon you!

12

Ye creating ones, ye higher men! Whoever hath to give birth is sick; whoever hath given birth, however, is unclean.

Ask women: one giveth birth, not because it giveth pleasure. The pain maketh hens and poets cackle.

Ye creating ones, in you there is much uncleanness. That is because ye have had to be mothers.

A new child: oh, how much new filth hath also come into the world! Go apart! He who hath given birth shall wash his soul!

13

Be not virtuous beyond your powers! And seek nothing from yourselves opposed to probability!

Walk in the footsteps in which your fathers' virtue hath already walked! How would ye rise high, if your fathers' will should not rise with you?

He, however, who would be a firstling, let him take care lest he also become a lastling! And where the vices of your fathers are, there should ye not set up as saints!

He whose fathers were inclined for women, and for strong wine and flesh of wildboar swine; what would it be if he demanded chastity of himself?

A folly would it be! Much, verily, doth it seem to me for such a one, if he should be the husband of one or of two or of three women.

And if he founded monasteries, and inscribed over their portals: "The way to holiness,"—I should still say: What good is it! it is a new folly!

He hath founded for himself a penance-house and refuge-house: much good may it do! But I do not believe in it.

In solitude there groweth what any one bringeth into it—also the brute in one's nature. Thus is solitude inadvisable unto many.

Hath there ever been anything filthier on earth than the saints of the wilderness? *Around them* was not only the devil loose—but also the swine.

14

Shy, ashamed, awkward, like the tiger whose spring hath failed—thus, ye higher men, have I often seen you slink aside. A *cast* which ye made had failed.

But what doth it matter, ye dice-players! Ye had not learned to play and mock, as one must play and mock! Do we not ever sit at a great table of mocking and playing?

And if great things have been a failure with you, have ye yourselves therefore—been a failure? And if ye yourselves have been a failure, hath man therefore—been a failure? If man, however, hath been a failure: well then! never mind!

15

The higher its type, always the seldomer doth a thing succeed. Ye higher men here, have ye not all—been failures?

Be of good cheer; what doth it matter? How much is still possible! Learn to laugh at yourselves, as ye ought to laugh!

What wonder even that ye have failed and only half-succeeded, ye half-shattered ones! Doth not—man's *future* strive and struggle in you?

Man's furthest, profoundest, star-highest issues, his prodigious powers—do not all these foam through one another in your vessel?

What wonder that many a vessel shattereth! Learn to laugh at yourselves, as ye ought to laugh! Ye higher men, Oh, how much is still possible!

And verily, how much hath already succeeded! How rich is this earth in small, good, perfect things, in well-constituted things!

Set around you small, good, perfect things, ye higher men. Their golden maturity healeth the heart. The perfect teacheth one to hope.

16

What hath hitherto been the greatest sin here on earth? Was it not the word of him who said: "Woe unto them that laugh now!"

Did he himself find no cause for laughter on the earth? Then he sought badly. A child even findeth cause for it.

He—did not love sufficiently: otherwise would he also have loved us, the laughing ones! But he hated and hooted us; wailing and teeth-gnashing did he promise us.

Must one then curse immediately, when one doth not love? That—seemeth to me bad taste. Thus did he, however, this absolute one. He sprang from the populace.

And he himself just did not love sufficiently; otherwise would he have raged less because people did not love him. All great love doth not *seek* love:—it seeketh more.

Go out of the way of all such absolute ones! They are a poor sickly type, a populace-type: they look at this life with ill-will, they have an evil eye for this earth.

Go out of the way of all such absolute ones! They have heavy feet and sultry hearts:—they do not know how to dance. How could the earth be light to such ones!

17

Tortuously do all good things come nigh to their goal. Like cats they curve their backs, they purr inwardly with their approaching happiness,—all good things laugh.

His step betrayeth whether a person already walketh on *his own* path: just see me walk! He, however, who cometh nigh to his goal, danceth.

And verily, a statue have I not become, not yet do I stand there stiff, stupid and stony, like a pillar; I love fast racing.

And though there be on earth fens and dense afflictions, he who hath light feet runneth even across the mud, and danceth, as upon well-swept ice.

Lift up your hearts, my brethren, high, higher! And do not forget your legs! Lift up also your legs, ye good dancers, and better still, if ye stand upon your heads!

18

This crown of the laughter, this rose-garland crown: I myself have put on this crown, I myself have consecrated my laughter. No one else have I found to-day potent enough for this.

Zarathustra the dancer, Zarathustra the light one, who beckoneth with his pinions, one ready for flight, beckoning unto all birds, ready and prepared, a blissfully light-spirited one:—

Zarathustra the soothsayer, Zarathustra the sooth-laugher, no impatient one, no absolute one, one who loveth leaps and side-leaps; I myself have put on this crown!

19

Lift up your hearts, my brethren, high, higher! And do not forget your legs! Lift up also your legs, ye good dancers, and better still if ye stand upon your heads!

There are also heavy animals in a state of happiness, there are club-footed ones from the beginning. Curiously do they exert themselves, like an elephant which endeavoureth to stand upon its head.

Better, however, to be foolish with happiness than foolish with misfortune, better to dance awkwardly than walk lamely. So learn, I pray you, my wisdom, ye higher men: even the worst thing hath two good reverse sides,—

—Even the worst thing hath good dancing-legs: so learn, I pray you, ye higher men, to put yourselves on your proper legs!

So unlearn, I pray you, the sorrow-sighing, and all the populace-sadness! Oh, how sad the buffoons of the populace seem to me today! This today, however, is that of the populace.

20

Do like unto the wind when it rusheth forth from its mountain-caves: unto its own piping will it dance; the seas tremble and leap under its footsteps.

That which giveth wings to asses, that which milketh the lionesses:—praised be that good, unruly spirit, which cometh like a hurricane unto all the present and unto all the populace,—

—Which is hostile to thistle-heads and puzzle-heads, and to all withered leaves and weeds:—praised be this wild, good, free spirit of the storm, which danceth upon fens and afflictions, as upon meadows!

Which hateth the consumptive populace-dogs, and all the ill-constituted, sullen brood:—praised be this spirit of all free spirits, the laughing storm, which bloweth dust into the eyes of all the melanopic and melancholic!

Ye higher men, the worst thing in you is that ye have none of you learned to dance as ye ought to dance—to dance beyond yourselves! What doth it matter that ye have failed!

How many things are still possible! So *learn* to laugh beyond yourselves! Lift up your hearts, ye good dancers, high! higher! And do not forget the good laughter!

This crown of the laughter, this rose-garland crown: to you, my brethren, do I cast this crown! Laughing have I consecrated; ye higher men, *learn*, I pray you—to laugh!

THE
TWENTIETH
CENTURY

❧

The Modern Age and
the Emerging World Culture

TIME LINE FOR THE TWENTIETH CENTURY

Date	*History and Politics*
1890–1900	
1900–1910	
1910–1920	1914 World War I begins.
	1916 T. E. Lawrence in Arabia.
	1917 United States enters war.
	1918 World War I armistice signed; Bolshevik Revolution in Russia.
	1919 Prohibition amendment ratified; First League of Nations meeting.
1920–1930	1920 Women's suffrage passed in United States; Irish independence; Gandhi emerges as leader of Indian independence movement; Sacco and Vanzetti arrested.
	1922 Formation of the Soviet Union.
	1925 Hindenburg elected president of Germany; Hitler, *Mein Kampf*, vol. 1.
	1927 "Black Friday"; German economy collapses.
	1928 Chiang Kai-shek, President of China.
	1929 Stock market crash.
1930–1940	
	1932 Roosevelt elected president; New Deal begins.

Science, Culture, and Technology   *Literature*

1895 Freud and Breuer, *Studies in Hysteria.*

1902 Conrad, *Heart of Darkness.*

1907 Picasso, *Les Demoiselles d'Avignon.*   1903 Du Bois, *The Souls of Black Folk.*

1913 Armory Show introduces cubism and   1912 Synge, *Playboy of the Western World.*
     postimpressionism in United States;
     Stravinsky, *The Rite of Spring.*

1914 Henry Ford pioneers the assembly   1913 Lawrence, *Sons and Lovers;* Proust,
     line.   *Swann's Way.*

                                              1914 Joyce, "The Dead."

1915 Einstein, general theory of relativity;   1915 Kafka, *The Metamorphosis.*
     Duchamp, beginnings of Dada
     movement; Margaret Sanger jailed
     for *Family Limitation;* Film: *Birth of a
     Nation,* Griffith.

1918 Spengler, *Decline of the West.*   1918 Hopkins, *Poems.*

1919 Bauhaus founded by Gropius.

1921 Wittgenstein, *Tractatus Logico-   1920 Colette, *Chéri.*
     philosophicus.*

1922 Lord Carnarvon discovers the tomb of   1922 Eliot, *The Waste Land;* Akhmatova,
     Tutankhamen.   *Anno Domini MCMXXI.*

1923 Le Corbusier, *Towards a New   1923 Rilke, *Sonnets to Orpheus.*
     Architecture.*

                                              1924 Lu Xun, "The New Year's Sacrifice";
                                                   O'Casey, *Juno and the Paycock.*

1925 Scopes trial; Film: *Potemkin,* Eisenstein. 1925 Fitzgerald, *The Great Gatsby.*

1926 Television demonstrated.   1926 Hemingway, *The Sun Also Rises;*
                                                   O'Neill, *The Great God Brown.*

1927 Lindbergh's flight across the Atlantic;   1927 Hesse, *Steppenwolf.*
     Film: *The Jazz Singer,* first full-length
     talking picture.

1928 Gershwin, *An American in Paris;* Ravel, 1928 Sholokhov, *And Quiet Flows the Don;*
     Bolero; Fleming discovers penicillin.   Yeats, *The Tower.*

1929 St. Valentine's Day massacre; O'Keeffe,   1929 Faulkner, *The Sound and the Fury;*
     Black Flower and Blue Larkspur.   Woolf, *A Room of One's Own;*
                                                   Remarque, *All Quiet on the Western
                                                   Front.*

1931 Dali, *Persistence of Memory;* Empire   1930 Musil, *The Man without Qualities.*
     State Building.

(Continued on next page)

TIME LINE FOR THE TWENTIETH CENTURY (Continued)

Date	*History and Politics*
	1933 American bank holiday; repeal of Prohibition; Hitler granted dictatorial powers.
	1936 Italy annexes Abyssinia; Mussolini and Hitler proclaim Rome–Berlin Axis; Edward VIII abdicates; Spanish Civil War; Chiang Kai-shek declares war on Japan.
	1938 Germany occupies Sudetenland; Munich Conference.
	1939 World War II.
1940–1950	1940 Trotsky assassinated in Mexico.
	1941 Pearl Harbor; United States enters war.
	1944 D-Day, June 6.
	1945 VE Day, May 8; United States drops atomic bomb on Hiroshima and Nagasaki; Japan surrenders; Arab League founded; United Nations founded.
	1946 Nuremberg Tribunal.
	1947 Indian independence.
	1948 Gandhi assassinated; Israel founded.
	1949 People's Republic of China proclaimed by Mao Zedong; End of Greek civil war.
1950–1960	1950 Korean War.
	1951 End of Allied occupation in Japan; Rosenbergs sentenced to death.
	1952 First hydrogen bomb exploded; Mau Mau rebellion in Kenya.
	1953 Tito elected president of Yugoslavia; Stalin succeeded by Malenkov in U.S.S.R.; Reza Shah Pahlavi monarchy established in Iran.
	1954 Senator McCarthy censured by Senate; *Brown vs. Board of Education* desegregation decision.
	1955 West Germany joins NATO.
	1956 Suez crisis; Soviet invasion of Hungary.

Science, Culture, and Technology	*Literature*
1932 Lindbergh kidnapping; Calder, mobiles; Amelia Earhart's solo flight across the Atlantic.	1932 Huxley, *Brave New World*.
1936 Keynes, *General Theory of Employment, Interest, and Money;* Carlson develops xerography.	1933 Stein, *The Autobiography of Alice B. Toklas*.
1937 Picasso, *Guernica*.	1935 Neruda, *Residence on Earth;* Lorca, *Lament for Ignacio Mejías*.
	1939 Steinbeck, *The Grapes of Wrath*.
1940 Lascaux caves discovered.	1940 Wright, *Native Son;* Koestler, *Darkness at Noon*.
	1941 Brecht, *Mother Courage and Her Children;* Borges, "The Garden of Forking Paths."
1942 Fermi splits the atom.	1943 Sartre, *The Flies;* Ellison, "Flying Home."
1947 Wright, Johnson Research Building; Dead Sea Scrolls discovered.	1947 *The Diary of Anne Frank*.
1948 Bell Labs develop transistor; Pollock, *Composition No. 1*.	1948 Pound, *The Pisan Cantos*.
	1951 Salinger, *Catcher in the Rye*.
	1952 Beckett, *Waiting for Godot;* Lessing, "The Old Chief Mshlanga."
1953 Crick and Watson model structure of DNA; Skinner, *Science and Human Behavior;* de Beauvoir, *The Second Sex*.	1953 Kawabata, "The Moon on the Water."
	1954 Amis, *Lucky Jim*.
1955 Montgomery, Alabama, bus boycott.	
	1956 Ginsberg, *Howl;* Osborne, *Look Back in Anger*.

(Continued on next page)

TIME LINE FOR THE TWENTIETH CENTURY (Continued)

Date	*History and Politics*
	1957 European Economic Community established; Ghana wins independence.
	1959 Cuban revolution; homelands established in South Africa.
1960–1970	1960 Bay of Pigs invasion; Eichmann found guilty; 69 demonstrators killed in Sharpeville, South Africa.
	1961 Berlin Wall; American combat troops sent to Vietnam.
	1962 Algerian independence.
	1963 President Kennedy assassinated.
	1965 Vietnam War escalated.
	1966 Cultural Revolution in China.
	1967 Arab–Israeli 6-Day War.
	1968 Martin Luther King, Jr., and Robert Kennedy assassinated; Prague Spring; student uprisings in Paris and U.S.
1970–1980	1970 Four Kent State students killed.
	1972 Nixon goes to China.
	1973 OPEC cartel triples oil prices.
	1974 Nixon resigns over Watergate.
	1975 End of Vietnam War.
	1976 Soweto protests in South Africa.
	1977 Sadat of Egypt visits Jerusalem.
	1979 Khomeini establishes Islamic Republic in Iran.
1980–1990	1980 Walesa leads Solidarity strike in Gdansk; Iraq–Iran War.
	1981 Sadat assassinated.
	1985 Gorbachev named leader of U.S.S.R.
	1988 End of Iraq–Iran War.
	1989 End of Communist regimes in Eastern Europe; Berlin Wall torn down; Tiananmen Square demonstrators shot.
1990–	1990 Mandela released from prison; Mexico City becomes world's most populous city.
	1994 First multiracial elections in South Africa; self-rule granted to Palestinians in Israeli-occupied territory.

Science, Culture, and Technology

1957 Launching of *Sputnik,* first space satellite; Bernstein, *West Side Story.*

1958 Beatnik movement; Presley, "Heartbreak Hotel."

1961 Yury Gagarin, first man in space.

1963 Pop art.

1965 Malcolm X assassinated; op art.

1967 Beatles, *Sgt. Pepper's Lonely Hearts Club Band.*

1968 Woodstock.

1969 Armstrong and Aldrin first men on the moon.

1976 Haley, *Roots.*

1978 Wozniak and Jobs develop the personal computer.

1981 AIDS virus identified.

Literature

1957 Baldwin, "Sonny's Blues"; Pasternak, *Doctor Zhivago;* Camus, "The Guest."

1958 Achebe, *Things Fall Apart.*

1959 Grass, *The Tin Drum.*

1960 Duras, *Hiroshima Mon Amour.*

1963 Takenishi, "The Rite."

1964 Lessing, *African Stories.*

1968 Arendt, *Men in Dark Times.*

1969 Momaday, *The Way to Rainy Mountain;* Kundera, "The Hitchhiking Game."

1970 Narayan, "A Horse and Two Goats"; Solzhenitsyn, Nobel Acceptance Speech.

1972 Marquez, "A Very Old Man with Enormous Wings."

1973 Rich, *Diving into the Wreck.*

1978 Desai, "The Farewell Party."

1979 Dyson, *Disturbing the Universe.*

1982 Wiesel, *Legends of Our Time.*

1984 Rifaat, "My World of the Unknown."

1988 Rushdie, *The Satanic Verses.*

1990 Fuentes, "The Prisoner of Las Lomas."

INTRODUCTION

NEARLY EVERY AGE SINCE THE RENAISSANCE has thought of itself as modern, in the sense of being up-to-date or current. Historians often use the term "modern" to characterize the last four centuries or so. Our century shares many aspects of its modernity with the three centuries that preceded it. We have in common a belief in progress, an orientation toward the future, and an assumption that human beings have the power to direct and define their lives. We usually place more credence in invention than in tradition, more faith in reason than in emotion or intuition.

Many writers and artists of the early twentieth century, however, were conscious of radical changes that were taking place in their time that made it different from the past. These changes were reflected in science, religion, philosophy, and politics, and made their time distinctively "modern." After the destruction of World War I, people, especially in cities, began to question meaning and value, experiencing what some writers described as alienation and a loss of faith in traditional institutions. Artists modified old forms or created new ones to reflect this reorientation and its focus on consciousness. Cultural historians now distinguish between "modern," which describes the disruption of life between World War I and World War II, and "contemporary," which represents a wide variety of responses to living in a world of nuclear energy, high technology, and changing national boundaries. The modern period was marked by disillusionment with Western institutions and values. In the contemporary period, the wide dissemination of minority and national voices throughout the world has contributed to an exploration of new sources of value and meaning.

MODERNISM

The modernist period, dating roughly from the 1890s to World War II, was a time of intellectual, cultural, social, and political crisis—a time when old beliefs, customary ways of living, and traditional forms of governance were challenged and often replaced. These lines from "The Second Coming," written in 1920 by William Butler Yeats (1865–1939), one of Europe's most visionary poets, capture the spirit of the age that witnessed the cataclysmic change of the Bolshevik Revolution, the horror of World War I, and the collapse of accepted truths in science, religion, and politics:

> Things fall apart; the center cannot hold;
> Mere anarchy is loosed upon the world,
> The blood-dimmed tide is loosed, and everywhere
> The ceremony of innocence is drowned;
> The best lack all conviction, while the worst
> Are full of passionate intensity.

The anarchy Yeats describes stemmed from many cultural and political sources. Nietzsche threatened organized religion with his pronouncement about the death of God, and Sir James Frazer's *The Golden Bough* (1890) demonstrated with compelling evidence drawn from anthropological studies of primitive societies that the doctrines and rituals of Christianity bore unsettling resemblances to totemistic and magical religions. The scientific community, which in the nineteenth century had progressed to a belief that science could explain nearly all material phenomena, was transformed by the advent of quantum physics and the theory of relativity. The Newtonian universe in which motion, force, gravity, and the like were believed to be governed by immutable laws gave way to the complex theories of scientists such as Max Planck (1858–1947), Albert Einstein

(1879–1955), Niels Bohr (1885–1962), and Werner Heisenberg (1901–1976). In 1905, Einstein proposed that space and time are not absolute entities as they appear from our commonsense perspective, but are relative to each other in what he called a "space–time continuum." Einstein's theory of relativity replaced the customary three-dimensional view of things, adding time as a necessary fourth dimension in any physical description of an object. In 1927, Werner Heisenberg's experiments with electrons led to his famous "uncertainty principle," which implied that scientists could not accurately describe reality because electrons could be measured either as waves or as particles. The work of these scientists paved the way for the discovery of a fascinating subatomic world which, to paraphrase Yeats's "The Second Coming," would eventually "vex the world to nightmare" with the nuclear bomb.

If fundamental concepts such as God, time, space, and matter were merely convenient and expedient "fictions," as the philosopher Hans Vaihinger concluded in 1911, what then of human values, language, literature, art, culture, the state, or the self? Such philosophers as Ludwig Wittgenstein (1889–1951), Bertrand Russell (1872–1970), and later A. J. Ayer (1910–1989) sought in the spirit of science to limit the philosopher's realm to demonstrable "facts" about the physical universe. As "logical positivists," they relegated questions of human ideals and metaphysics to the realm of emotions or the irrational. The Viennese philosopher Wittgenstein focused a great deal of attention on language, demanding that abstract and imprecise terms such as "God," "beauty," and "truth" be exorcised from the lexicon, leaving behind a precise, scientific language that would correspond directly to experience. Wittgenstein and the Swiss linguist Ferdinand de Saussure (1857–1913) believed that language systems were subject to certain identifiable (but not natural or inevitable) laws that could be discovered and mapped. Language was a game and all we could ever really know were the rules of the game.

Later thinkers such as anthropologist Claude Lévi-Strauss (born 1908) expanded the concept of linguistic laws to culture, arguing that human beings act according to certain social codes, deep structures within each culture that govern religious, social, and cultural practices. Carl Gustav Jung (1875–1961) believed that these codes were not relative to particular cultures or historical periods, but were universal and timeless. In myth, literature, art, and religious symbols, Jung found what he called "archetypes," or age-old symbols, such as the Quest, the Great Mother, and the Wise Man, that suggested that human beings in diverse times and cultures shared a common spiritual and psychic heritage. Moreover, Jung believed that the outward or physical forms of religion might change or evolve, but the deep spiritual needs remain relatively constant and must be addressed by each generation. Jung's explorations of world religions and his investigations of dreams, in stark contrast to the positivist philosophy that had turned its back on the soul, offered a path for a spiritual rebirth.

While Jung offered to lead "modern man in search of a soul," to borrow the title from one of his books, others railed against the losses that people in the modern era had already racked up in the name of progress. Oswald Spengler in *Decline of the West* (1918) predicted that the West had lived out its allotted cycle of glory, citing World War I as a point of no return in the spiral downward to final desolation. The massive trench warfare of World War I (1914–1917) was more horrible than anyone could have anticipated. Soldiers died more hideous deaths—by gassing, shelling, and aerial bombardment—and more troops of more nationalities were slaughtered under grimmer conditions than in any previous war. Even the memories of earlier conflicts were distant ones, for Europe had not suffered a widespread war for nearly a century. The young men who fought in the trenches had been nursed on comfortable pieties about God, country, and bravery, and had not even grown up before they became the "lost generation," wiped out on the battlefields or disillusioned by the destruction of the Great War.

Novelists such as Franz Kafka (1883–1924), André Gide (1869–1951), and Thomas Mann (1875–1955) depicted in their works images of Europeans filled with anxiety, thrown into a valueless world of hedonism and senseless competition, and sinking into powerlessness and decadence. This picture was accentuated by certain European aristocrats who believed that democracy was a threat to social order; José Ortega y Gasset's *The Revolt of the Masses* (1930) predicted that government by the many would topple Western civilization.

T. S. Eliot's *The Waste Land* (1922), probably the classic description of this modernist malaise, presented modern urban society as a sterile, materialistic wasteland, where even the search for meaning was filled with detours and dead ends. The poem pieced together a series of realistic vignettes of banal urban life with a patchwork of fragments from the great literary works of the past, shards of a broken and forgotten tradition. Communication between individuals was faulty or nonexistent, and sexual relations were mechanical and alienating. Although there were suggestions at the end of the poem about potential sources of healing, like much modernist writing from the first half of the twentieth century *The Waste Land* was less concerned with a cure than with a description of the cultural sickness.

This condition of alienation and fragmentation nonetheless produced feverish cultural activity. Avant-garde movements in art, music, and literature abounded, giving some credence to Octavio Paz's insight that "Modernity is a sort of creative self-destruction." Artists, musicians, and writers almost seemed to be trying to outpace the dizzying technological changes. In 1909 the Italian writer Filippo Marinetti (1876–1944) launched futurism, which strove to capture in the arts the aggressive and iconoclastic spirit of the new science and the quick pace of industrial and technological change. Other avant-garde movements such as fauvism, expressionism, cubism, vorticism, and surrealism turned against what they saw as the monotonous dominion of the bourgeoisie in social and cultural life.

Everywhere, writers and artists sought to disrupt the complacency of the middle classes whose materialism, tepid conservatism, and timid conformity seemed to suffocate the arts. Taking to heart the scientists' claims that we cannot know reality and that we may not share a common reality, painters such as French postimpressionist Paul Cézanne (1839–1906); the Russian Wassily Kandinsky (1866–1944), founder of *Der Blaue Reiter;* and Pablo Picasso (1881–1973), the leading cubist, turned painting toward a complex, geometrical play of surfaces. In their creations, which defied the earlier works of academic realists, objects and figures were fragmented and distorted through multiple planes transversing the canvas. In music, Viennese composer Arnold Schönberg (1874–1951) and Russian composer Igor Stravinsky (1882–1971) similarly toppled the harmonic and melodic conventions of music by introducing atonality and polytonality. Atonality completely dismissed the concept of key; polytonality allowed the composer to intermix keys at will. In both cases, the result was dissonance and discord. When Stravinsky's ballet *The Rite of Spring* opened in Paris in 1913, shocked patrons rioted. The distortion and disruption of these works captured the centrifugal force of early twentieth-century Europe, which seemed to be splitting apart as events spun out of control.

MODERNIST LITERATURE

Literary artists were also caught up in the effort to criticize, shock, and so revitalize the sensibilities of the bourgeoisie. In "September 1913," Yeats lashed out at the Dublin middle classes whose obtuseness prevented a collection of impressionist paintings from being acquired by the city:

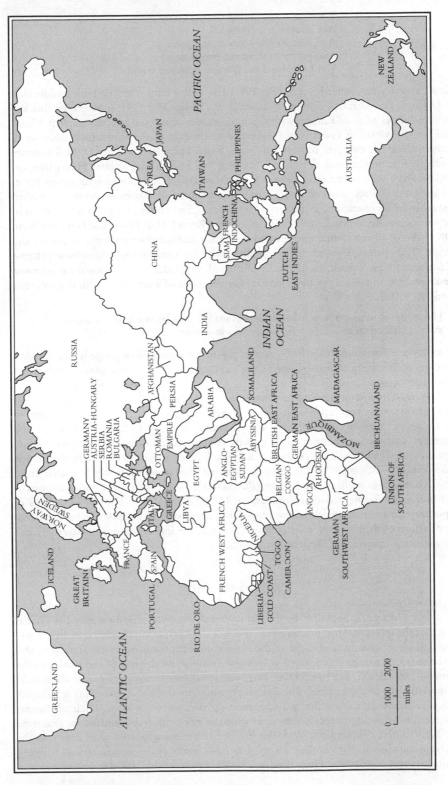

EUROPE, AFRICA, ASIA, AND AUSTRALIA, 1914

> What need you, being come to sense,
> But fumble in a greasy till
> And add the halfpence to the pence
> And prayer to shivering prayer, until
> You have dried the marrow from the bone?

Yeats's countryman James Joyce (1882–1941) also found fault with the Irish middle class in *Dubliners* (1914) and *A Portrait of the Artist as a Young Man* (1916), before he shocked the sensibilities of all of Europe with the more experimental and sexually explicit *Ulysses* (1922). The works of Franz Kafka awakened his readers to the frightening isolation of individuals in the modern, bureaucratic state. English novelist and poet D. H. Lawrence (1885–1930), putting into fiction the "vitalism" of French philosopher Henri Bergson (1859–1941), who celebrated an *élan vital* (vital spirit) against the deadening rationality of the logical positivists, shocked readers with his sexually explicit themes and the unabashed sensuality of his characters. Futurism, expressionism, and cubism found kindred spirits in writers such as Ezra Pound (1885–1972), Gottfried Benn (1886–1956), and Gertrude Stein (1874–1946), all of whom experimented with form and narrative structure in poetry and fiction. The challenge was to match the changes in consciousness with nonlinear patterns of language. Stein's work, in particular, disrupted the reader's conventional expectations for a narrative to tell a story by exploding the very idea of a sentence, as in this example from "As a Wife Has a Cow":

> Has made, as it has made as it has made, has made has to be as a wife has a cow, a love story. Has made as to be as a wife has a cow a love story.

James Joyce's *Finnegans Wake* (1939) carried the new theories of language to their logical conclusion, inventing words by assembling familiar sounds into strange and ambiguous new letter combinations.

The most important developments in fiction were those of Joyce and Virginia Woolf (1882–1941), who developed a new type of psychological novel as they experimented with ways to represent the "stream of consciousness" in prose. In flowing, unpunctuated sentences that merged memory and present awareness, following an associative logic, they presented the mental life of their characters. Albert Camus (1913–1960), the French existentialist philosopher of the absurd, captured the sense of being alienated from social conventions such as family, funerals, marriage, and courtrooms with his portrait of Meursault's fragmented consciousness in *The Stranger* (1942). The various forms of experimentation in the work of the modernists were ways to unsettle the conventional expectations of their readers, to make them aware of the incoherence of modern life and the alienating influence of modern institutions.

WORLD WAR II

World War I was supposed to be the war to end all wars, but very soon after 1917 it was clear that the forces that had produced the first war were preparing another one. Economic conflicts, ultranationalism, the rise of dictators, competition among colonial powers, and the stresses of a worldwide depression brought Europe, and the rest of the world, to the point of explosion in the late 1930s. Two contradictory versions of Western civilization formed the base of the conflict. The Fascists presented themselves as preservers or restorers of a pure European culture that would reverse the decline of the West. Their opponents saw them as achieving order only by destroying the free democratic institutions that were the West's finest achievement. With the rise of fascism, many people were drawn to the Marxian conclusion that conflict was the inevitable result of the contradictions between capitalism and democracy. Thus, dismayed by the failure of the capitalist governments to put a stop to Hitler, Mussolini, and Franco, people were drawn into the Communist Party and other leftist movements to form a diverse and committed Popular Front opposed to fascism. Their opposition was dramatically and tragically expressed during the Spanish Civil War (1936–1939), when International Brigades of idealistic leftists volunteered to fight beside the Spanish Republicans in an effort to preserve the democratic second Spanish Republic against a coalition of conservative and fascist forces under Francisco Franco.

In other ways, however, the world was not prepared for World War II. The scale of the conflict was unprecedented, for it reached beyond Europe to involve China, Japan, and the colonial possessions of the European powers in Africa and Asia. It was the last grand gesture of colonialism and would be a major cause of its destruction. Second, people were not prepared for the extent of the devastation, the leveling of whole cities with aerial bombardment, or for the civilian genocide of the Holocaust. There was no way to comprehend the massive suffering, torture, and deaths of millions of Jews, Gypsies, homosexuals, and others whom the Nazis deemed unfit to live. These atrocities were carried out with deliberate, scientific efficiency as the principles of industrial organization and technological productivity were applied to the business of mass murder. Finally, the end of the war, with the dropping of the atomic bombs on Hiroshima and Nagasaki, raised unsettling ethical and technological questions. Would atomic energy restore our belief in progress and usher in a utopian age, or would it simply give us the power to create Armageddon?

In many ways World War II could be said to have "saved the world for democracy." Not only were democratic governments established in the defeated Axis countries—Germany, Italy, and Japan—but the war forced democratic changes in the winning nations as well. The decline of the class system in Britain and the movement to integrate America racially both began as a result of changes brought about by the war. World War II was the pivotal event of our century. We are still sorting out its consequences and struggling with issues it raised but did not settle.

Several works that we have included look at the war from different perspectives and explore some of the questions that it raised. Jean-Paul Sartre's *The Flies* (1943), an allegorical commentary on the French collaboration with the Nazis, reveals how the war shaped the existentialist concepts of freedom, choice, and responsibility that have been influential in postwar European thought. Ralph Ellison's "Flying Home" (1943) looks ironically at the racial divisions in America through the eyes of a black airman whose plane crashes during the war in the southern United States. Elie Wiesel describes the effects of the Holocaust on its survivors, and Hiroko Takenishi, a survivor of Hiroshima, writes about the long-lasting physical and psychological effects of the atomic bomb. French novelist and political activist Marguerite Duras, in *Hiroshima Mon Amour* (1960), looks back on a love affair amid the ruins of Hiroshima that speaks of the difficulty of love and the transience of life.

THE POSTWAR YEARS

Europe, Asia, parts of Africa, and the Middle East awoke from World War II as from a nightmare of devastation and suffering. Although some writers looked back upon the war as a prelude to apocalypse, others, especially in Europe and Japan, saw in the rubble an opportunity to rebuild a society now rid, they thought, of narrow nationalism, expansionist designs, and anti-Semitism. In the face of sometimes seemingly insurmountable obstacles and despite devastating setbacks, the nations of the world, since World War II, have taken many steps toward improving relations and understanding among the various countries and cultures of the world. One of the most recognizable signs of this emerging sense of community was the 1945 founding of the United Nations, an international organization designed to serve as a forum to mediate conflicts between member countries, to provide economic and technological assistance to countries in need, and to promote cooperation and cultural understanding. Fifty countries joined the four "sponsoring" nations—Britain, China, the Soviet Union, and the United States—to sign the original U.N. charter, and by 1960 another fifty had added their names to the document.

Despite the hope for a world at peace, the first decade after the war witnessed many regional conflicts, some of which, like the Greek civil war (1946–1949), the Chinese Communist revolution (1945–1949), and the Korean War (1950–1953), threatened to erupt into large-scale confrontations. Even as the peace agreements were being signed at Yalta in 1945, the seeds of the cold war between the West and the Soviet Union were being sown. When the Soviet Union announced in 1953 that it had developed its own hydrogen bomb, the cold war took on a more menacing aspect. In the two decades after World War II, Europe and Japan lost most of their remaining colonies in Africa, India, and Asia. Often, as in the case of India and Pakistan, North and South Vietnam, Indonesia, and various African states, including South Africa, the collapse of colonialism introduced a turbulent period of civil, religious, and nationalist strife. Despite internal struggle, however, the independence movements in Africa, India, and Asia marked a significant break in the cultural hegemony of Europe. They were often accompanied by a renewal of interest in traditional cultural practices, folklore, religion, and native languages. In Africa, for example, writers such as Jomo Kenyatta and Ngugi Wa Thiong'o (James Ngugi) of Kenya, Chinua Achebe and Wole Soyinka of Nigeria, and Alex La Guma and Lewis Nkosi of South Africa adapted European forms of narrative to more traditional, oral forms of storytelling, to celebrate African identity and to articulate unique aspects of the African experience.

A colonial struggle took place in Indochina—Laos, Cambodia, and Vietnam—that has had far-reaching implications for the United States. Ho Chi Minh, who had lived in China, Moscow, and Paris, led the nationalist Viet Minh against the French, who gave up their colonial holdings in Vietnam after a major defeat at Dien Bien Phu in 1954. After gaining independence from France that year, Vietnam was divided into two parts, North and South. The revolutionary nationalist leader Ho Chi Minh ruled the North while Ngo Dinh Diem, supported by the United States, ruled in the South. Diem's regime was unpopular, and a succession of coup attempts against him ultimately led to direct United States military intervention in 1964 under the assumption that a communist takeover in South Vietnam would lead to similar takeovers in the region. Arguably the United States' most unpopular war, the Vietnam War polarized public opinion throughout the country, especially after heavy U.S. losses during the Tet Offensive of January 1968 prompted massive demonstrations against the war both in the United States and in Europe. Drawing energy and strategy from the independence movements around the world and from the civil rights movement in the United States, the antiwar, or peace, movement served as a catalyst for a much broader struggle for basic human rights.

This broader struggle challenged many established institutions, including the family, the public schools, the university, police departments, and civil administrations. In May 1968, police moved in on rioting students at the Sorbonne, France's most prestigious university, setting off months of often violent student protests. In what German-born philosopher Herbert Marcuse (1898–1979) called the "Great Refusal," students aimed to topple the elitist hierarchy of the university, to make the curriculum reflect more accurately the social and political realities of the time, and to provide greater access to education for minorities and the poor. A new generation of French intellectuals, including Michel Foucault (1926–1984), Louis Althusser (born 1918), Jacques Lacan (1901–1981), and Jacques Derrida (born 1930), sought to subvert such Establishment values as humanism and the priority of the individual; they repudiated the materialism and conservatism that, in their view,

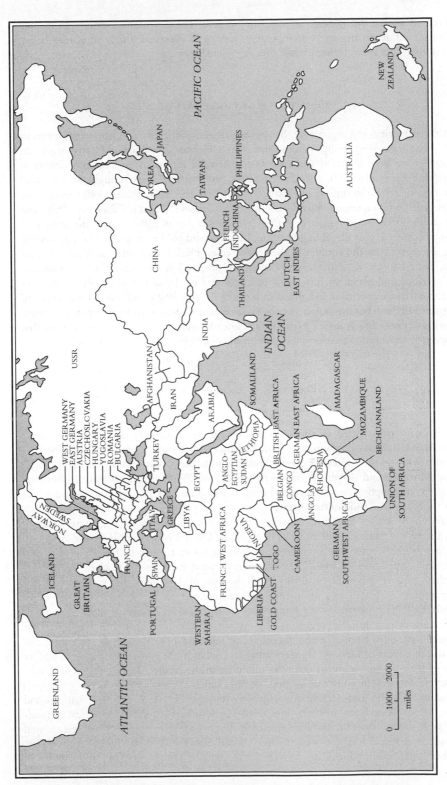

EUROPE, AFRICA, ASIA, AND AUSTRALIA, 1945

guaranteed power and prestige to a privileged few. These writers continue to exert a significant influence among contemporary Western intellectuals, many of whom began their higher education during or just after the Vietnam era.

CONTEMPORARY LITERATURE

Although critics still argue over the appropriateness of the analogy, minority writers in the United States—especially African-American, Chicano/Chicana, and Native American writers—have been liberated and empowered in ways similar to postcolonial writers in Africa and other places. In the United States, the postwar years brought an increased awareness of racial discrimination and a commitment to end it. From 1946 through the 1970s, a series of Supreme Court decisions, such as *Brown v. Board of Education* (1954), and various legislative measures, such as the Civil Rights Act of 1964, made discrimination against people of color illegal in education, business, and public facilities. These legislative gains emerged from the conflict of the 1960s, when black leaders such as Martin Luther King, Jr., Malcolm X, and Stokely Carmichael inspired Americans of all races to end the insidious and pervasive Jim Crow practices and to demand equal rights under the law for African Americans and other minorities. In the 1950s and 1960s, the words of Langston Hughes's famous poem "Lenox Avenue Mural" proved to be prophetic, as major American cities—Los Angeles, New York, Newark, and Miami—exploded in riots that drew quick and needed attention to the inequality of living conditions for blacks.

> What happens to a dream deferred?
> Does it dry up
> like a raisin in the sun? . . .
>
> Or does it explode?

Writers who participated in the great movement to realize the dream, among them Maya Angelou, James Baldwin, and Toni Morrison, look back to conditions for African Americans both before and after the war and continue the work begun by King and others. While Morrison and Ralph Ellison, in particular, employ modernist literary techniques, they also insist upon the connection between literature and history, and between the artist's moral vision and political reality.

African-American literature, however, should not be treated in a separate category from the rest of American literature. The works of Ellison, Morrison, Baldwin, Angelou, and many others cross over such arbitrary boundaries and speak to the American, and the human, condition at large. Their accounts of what it means to be black in America and their explorations of black history, both the pain of slavery and the unacknowledged contributions of blacks to our national life, are similar to the stories of many other Americans. Most Americans are immigrants or descendants of immigrants; most of us have a history of political oppression, religious persecution, and economic hardship. Our histories have often been changed, forgotten, or repressed. These losses deprive us of our past and of a sense of identity. By recovering and telling these stories, we can gain a fuller sense of who we are and what our roles might be in the future. By sharing these stories, we realize that in spite of our differences we have much in common.

Following upon the African-American movement, Native Americans, Latinos and Latinas, Asian Americans, women, homosexuals, and others entered the political and cultural ranks to call attention to the unique contributions and perspectives that their cultural heritage and sexual identity bring to the United States and to the global community. Dubbed "multiculturalism," the movement to explore history, society, and culture in order to discover one's own cultural identity and speak from it is similar to the Freudian project to "dive into the wreck" of the past. As Adrienne Rich puts it, it is an attempt to see what has been hidden beneath the surface and to salvage one's own history in order to clarify and strengthen one's sense of self. One of the strongest voices in the feminist movement, Rich reminds us that women, like people of color, have been set apart and denied their voices by a sociocultural network governed primarily by white men—a patriarchy.

Finally, the independence movements of the 1960s and 1970s, the increase of communications, and the international marketplace of ideas seem to be breaking down the boundaries that formerly divided writers into ethnic and national categories. The global reach of African, Indian, Caribbean, Native American, Asian, Latin American, African-American, and even white, male European writers demands a more expanded vision of the writer today. From India, Trinidad, Guinea, and other former European colonies, writers such as Raja Rao, V. S. Naipaul, and Camara Laye have joined their voices in a new literary phenomenon loosely classified as postcolonial literature. Many extraordinary writers of different nationalities have emerged who describe their experiences as international travelers, uprooted from their original cultures and languages. Moreover, the works of such writers as Yasunari Kawabata from Japan, R. K. Narayan and Anita Desai from India, and Chinua Achebe and Buchi Emecheta from Nigeria reach audiences throughout the world. The postcolonial era has introduced a truly international and multivoiced perspective into world literature—one that makes us aware of crucial differences among cultures while at the same time perforating the national and psychological boundaries that separate them. As the world shrinks more and more into what Marshall McLuhan called a "global village," the contemporary artist and writer can no longer assume that he or she writes for an audience steeped in his or her own particular customs and history. There is cause to believe that greater understanding of and respect for world cultures will result from this opening of borders. It is our hope that this anthology may help to promote such intercultural understanding.

HEART OF DARKNESS AND THINGS FALL APART

We have chosen Joseph Conrad's *Heart of Darkness* (1902) and Chinua Achebe's *Things Fall Apart* (1958) to represent the central themes of the twentieth century. In his early modernist novel, Conrad uses a first-person narrator, Charlie Marlow, to describe European colonialism in Africa at its most predatory stage. From the European wasteland of Brussels, a city characterized as a "whited sepulchre," Marlow journeys into the "heart of darkness" where he witnesses the exploitation of the people and resources of Africa. Achebe's novel, whose title comes from Yeats's "The Second Coming," is a postcolonial text by a Nigerian native who describes the complex, coherent aspects of clan and tribal life before the invasion of European businessmen and missionaries. Achebe dramatizes the destructive effects of colonialism from an African point of view. Together Conrad and Achebe tell a twentieth-century story that neither could tell alone.

Modernist writers such as Conrad used a number of metaphors to characterize their time: fragmentation, hollowness, emptiness, aridity, sterility, and, most often, disease. The doctor who set out to understand and treat the literal and metaphorical disease, and to describe the therapeutic role of storytelling, was Sigmund Freud, who began his psychoanalytic work in the last decade of the nineteenth century, treating individual cases of hysteria. By the end of his career, he realized that psychoanalysis dealt with more than individual complaints, for it could also analyze the collective neurosis of a society, the discontents of civilization. Freud's method of healing through telling and analyzing stories becomes an essential pattern in our perspective on the twentieth century. It is sometimes difficult to appreciate the contemporary importance of Freud because we now take so many of his assumptions for granted. But if we compare Freud's methods with those used to treat the protagonist in Charlotte Perkins Gilman's "The Yellow Wallpaper," we can see how revolutionary he was; her doctor's refusal to allow her to write about her life seems brutal and inhuman to us, but it was the standard treatment at the time. Simply by asking his patients to tell their stories and then subjecting the stories to close scrutiny, Freud challenged such repression. Whatever we might think about his sexual theories, his belief in storytelling has to be seen as revolutionary and liberating.

Freudian stories took a different form from the chronological, realistic narratives of the nineteenth century. As in the story told by Katharina in our Background Text, Freudian stories typically began with the patient complaining of particular physical symptoms— headaches, nausea, coughing, and similar ailments. Freud first asked the patient to locate the time when these symptoms began and then to describe any events from that time that might explain their occurrence. Freud assumed that the complaint went back at least one more step to a traumatic event in the patient's childhood, so he went on to elicit the story of that repressed experience. Freud's method, beginning with present symptoms and gradually uncovering layers of the past, reversed the chronology of traditional storytelling. It also made the teller more important than the story, for Freud listened for the moments of truth when his patients were clearly revealing the parts of the story that mattered most; uncanny occurrences, unusual turns of phrase, and puzzling dreams often provided clues about the places where patients were most reliably uncovering the truth about their lives. From these aspects of Freudian storytelling and analysis come the discontinuous time schemes, the surreal events, and the importance that is placed on the reliability of the narrator and the narration in many modern novels. Marlow's retrospective narration, the surreal, dreamlike character of some of the events and characters he describes, and the gaps in his account are aspects common in modern narratives. Ostensibly about Africa, *Heart of Darkness* turns into a story about Marlow and the ambiguities in his story. What, we wonder, is the nature of his fascination with Kurtz? What does he consider to be "the horror"? Why does he lie to Kurtz's fiancée?

Conrad does not explore Marlow's childhood experience as a way of answering these questions, but he does suggest that there were historical precedents for the colonial "squeeze." He connects the European exploitation of Africa with the Roman occupation of England and suggests that there is a historical pattern to such events. In colonial situations, Conrad suggests, the dark, uncontrollable side of human nature comes to the surface. He sees the symptoms of a modern sickness clearly—the hypocrisy of the Europeans, the hollowness of their ideals, and the immorality of their values. Marlow graphically describes the exploitation of the natives, the lust for ivory, and the gratuitous violence against Africa, as in the inane shelling of the jungle by the French ship. These are all signs of the European malaise.

As Freud developed his ideas, he recognized that the stories he heard were repetitive, dating back to Greek myths and ancient psychological patterns. Freud's interest in folktale, legend, and myth was shared by many others of the time outside of the psychoanalytic profession, for in such traditional stories they found explanations for the disease of modernity, the malaise that seemed to afflict the times like a collective neurosis. Marlow sees some of these connections in his African experiences, but he may not fully understand the deeper levels of his story. His vagueness about Kurtz's activities, his reluctance to leave the ship, and his lie to Kurtz's Intended suggest that he is not yet ready to tell the traumatic story that underlies his experiences or that he cannot or will not find the words to do so.

In a speech in 1975, Achebe suggested that Conrad's failure to tell the whole or the true story was a result of racism, both his own and that of Europeans generally. For Conrad and

Europe, Africa was exploitable. Even if Marlow did not bring back ivory, he nonetheless used Africa as a mirror in which to see himself. Africa has value for Conrad only insofar as it is useful for defining Europe. He was not, Achebe argues, really interested in Africans; he did not give any of them names. Nor did he value their culture; *Heart of Darkness* is concerned only with the breakdown of European "civilization." Conrad is guilty, Achebe suggests, of a psychological or literary imperialism, for he denies the Africans their own story, making them valuable only as part of Europe's story. In an interview with Bill Moyers, Achebe discusses the issue of point of view:

> When I had been younger, I had read these adventure books about the good white man, you know, wandering into the jungle or into danger, and the savages were after him. And I would instinctively be on the side of the white man. You see what fiction can do, it can put you on the wrong side if you are not developed enough. In the university I suddenly saw that these books had to be read in a different light. Reading *Heart of Darkness* . . . I realized that I was one of those savages jumping up and down on the beach. Once that kind of enlightenment comes to you, you realize that someone has to write a different story.

In *Things Fall Apart,* Achebe tells an African story from an African point of view about Okonkwo, a powerful heroic man who clings to values that ultimately defeat him. The time period of Achebe's novel is roughly the same as that of *Heart of Darkness*—the late nineteenth century, when the first contacts between Africa and Europe were occurring— but Achebe presents colonialism in terms very different from Conrad's. Colonialism is not the only significant factor in Okonkwo's life; in fact, the missionaries and colonial administrators do not enter the novel until its second half. Most of Okonkwo's story is defined in relation to his clan, Umuofia; his village, Iguedo; and his family—he has definition outside of the colonial context. Village life is an intricate balance of customs, mores, taboos, and rituals. There is nothing primitive or simple about the rich fabric of his society. If colonialism precipitates Okonkwo's tragedy, it is not alone to blame, for we see how the elements of his character that lead to his death brought him into difficulty in the tribal context as well.

T. S. Eliot recognized the importance of *Heart of Darkness* when he chose Conrad's line "Mistah Kurtz, he dead" as an epigraph for "The Hollow Men," a precursor to *The Waste Land*. Conrad identifies the disease, and even if his novel lacks an African perspective, it is nonetheless one of the most harrowing accounts of colonialism in Western literature. *Things Fall Apart* helps us see the limitations of Conrad's account and, in addition, teaches us about the complexity of reaching across cultural lines to the attitudes and values of village life in Africa. Together, the two novels represent the changing awareness of our century, the step-by-step unfolding of the story of Europe in relation to the rest of the world. Hannah Arendt warned us that totalitarianism, a prominent factor in our century's social upheaval and wars, has its roots in colonialism and racism. World War II and the cold war that followed it provided the catalyst that began our search for these roots and prompted many of the stories we are now telling. A multicultural literature that affirms the diversity of human experience and the dignity of all cultures may help us heal the wounds that brought us wars in the past and assist us in taking the necessary steps toward creating world community.

SUGGESTED READINGS

A broad collection of materials for studying modern literature is in *The Modern Tradition: Backgrounds of Modern Literature* (1965), ed. Richard Ellmann and Charles Feidelson. Another collection representing a broad range of topics is *Modernism* (1976), ed.

Malcolm Bradbury and James McFarlane. The influence of T. S. Eliot is discussed in Louis Menand's *Discovering Modernism: T. S. Eliot and His Context* (1987). Changes in philosophy, psychology, and critical theory are discussed in *Innovation/Renovation, New Perspectives on the Humanities* (1983), ed. Ihab Hassan and Sally Hassan. Discussions of psychoanalysis and literature are found in Peter Collier and Judith Davies's *Modernism and the European Unconscious* (1990). Ihab Hassan analyzes contemporary literature in *The Postmodern Turn: Essays on Postmodern Literature* (1986).

REPRESENTATIVE TEXTS

JOSEPH CONRAD
[1857–1924]

Joseph Conrad's life and work cross cultural boundaries, making him representative of many writers of the twentieth century. Born a Pole in Russian-occupied Poland, Conrad went on to become a French merchant-seaman and then an English seaman and citizen. When he began writing he composed in English, his third language after Polish and French. Although he was a proud British citizen and a Polish nationalist, he was in a broad sense a European: a man whose political identity transcends any single national definition. Conrad's experience as a sailor in many parts of the world further broadened this European identity, making him a kind of world citizen. Like most of his novels, *Heart of Darkness* (1902) is rooted in Conrad's own experience, but his personal story is objectified and broadened to become the narrator Marlow's story, a story about storytelling itself, and even more broadly, a story about the cultural experience of Europeans in Africa. Marlow thus becomes Conrad's vehicle to transform personal experience into a broader cultural story.

LIFE

Conrad was born Jósef Teodor Konrad Walecz Korzeniowski in 1857 in Berdyczew in Russian-occupied Polish Ukraine. His father, Apollo, a writer and translator of French and English literature, was a romantic Polish nationalist. His participation in revolutionary activities led to the family being exiled to the far north of Russia when Conrad was four. The physical hardships of the exile led to his mother's death when he was seven and to his father's death just a few years later. So Conrad, a romantic and sensitive child, was raised from age eleven by an uncle, Tadeusz Bobrowski. Although he grew up far from the sea, the boy dreamed of a career as a sailor, and when he was sixteen he convinced his uncle to allow him to seek a seagoing career. He joined the French merchant service, and for a few years indulged his romantic dreams as he became involved in gunrunning, an intense love affair, and, finally, a suicide attempt. At twenty Conrad switched to the English merchant service, and in the next twenty years worked his way up from seaman to mate and master. His many voyages took him to the East and West Indies, Asia, Africa, South America, and many other parts of the world. When he left the merchant service in 1894, he was fluent in three languages, a British citizen with multinational work experience, and a European with a knowledge of cultural traditions throughout the world.

Conrad's second career—as an English novelist—began in 1895 with the publication of *Almayer's Folly,* and extended until his death in 1924. During that period, he wrote thirteen novels, two books of memoirs, and twenty-eight short stories. He established friendships with a large number of British and American writers of the period, including H. G. Wells, Rudyard Kipling, W. H. Hudson, John Galsworthy, Henry James, Stephen Crane, and Ford Madox Ford, with whom he collaborated on three books. Many of his novels and stories take place on ships isolated at sea, as do *Typhoon* (1902), *The Nigger of the "Narcissus"* (1898), and "The Secret Sharer" (1912). Others are set in exotic locations Conrad visited as a sailor: the Malay peninsula in *An Outcast of the Islands* (1896) and *Lord Jim* (1900), a South Sea island in *Victory* (1915), and a South American mining town in *Nostromo* (1904). Conrad often studied the failure of Europeans to maintain their personal and cultural ideals in these alien places. His novels with European settings, such as *The Secret Agent* (1907), describing the activities of anarchist provocateurs in London, and *Under Western Eyes* (1911), about revolutionaries challenging Russian despotism, also treat failures of idealism. For his recurrent theme of lost or corrupted idealism, Conrad has been described as a deeply pessimistic writer. But his heroes, in spite of their shortcomings, are often engaging and sympathetic figures who have an idealistic belief in themselves and who follow the romantic desire of the human spirit for freedom. In a broad sense, all of Conrad's novels may hearken back to his childhood experience as the son of a Polish nationalist who died for his ideals, ideals that failed to become political realities because of the weaknesses of humankind and the complexities and imbalances in political relationships.

WORK

Although he is usually described as a novelist of the sea, Conrad used the sea and exotic settings symbolically to write about the human situation and the human spirit. In the preface to *Nigger of the "Narcissus,"* he said of its shipboard setting: "The problem . . . is not a problem of the sea, it is merely a problem that has arisen on board a ship where the conditions of complete isolation from all land entanglements make it stand out with particular force and colouring." The ship thus serves to isolate the human relationships and the psychological and moral dilemmas the characters face.

Heart of Darkness is based on Conrad's 1890 journey up the Congo River. Like his narrator, Marlow, Conrad was hired by a Belgian trading company to captain a steamship on the Congo River, but when he arrived in Africa, he found that the ship he was hired to pilot had sunk. Conrad was left to spend most of his time in Africa as a mate on another vessel, taking over as captain only briefly when the regular master was incapacitated. The journey up the river entailed bringing out the body of a trader, a man named Klein, who had died at a trading post deep in the interior of Africa. In *Heart of Darkness,* Conrad turns this personal experience into myth. Conrad spoke of his own experience in the Congo as a transforming one: "Before the Congo," he wrote, "I was just a mere animal." Shortly after returning from the Congo, he gave up the sea and turned to storytelling as his profession. In retelling his experiences in *Heart of Darkness,* Conrad is like Marlow, the ancient mariner who entrances a group gathered on the *Nellie* with his story.

Marlow's journey into the heart of Africa becomes a journey into the heart of the human spirit. Ostensibly it is an account of the truth about Kurtz, a man whose talents and achievements earned him regard as an "extraordinary" human being—a model of European enlightenment. But when Marlow arrives at Kurtz's inner station, he discovers that in the depths of his inner being Kurtz is "a horror." Marlow also makes discoveries about himself and about his "kinship" with Kurtz.

When Marlow compares England at the time of the Romans to Africa in the nineteenth century, he implies that his story is about colonialism and greed, about what he calls "the squeeze." Marlow's descriptions of the ivory trade and the European presence in Africa are solidly based in historical fact. In 1890, the Congo was in effect the personal domain of King Leopold II of Belgium, who promoted the commercial exploitation of its resources and the virtual enslavement of its native people. Historical accounts confirm that there is no exaggeration in the excesses described by Marlow. He is clearly appalled by what he finds in Africa: the mistreatment of natives, the venality and hypocrisy of the Europeans, the colossal corruption at the inner station. He also suggests that these shortcomings are not unique to Africa, but rather are the deepest impulses of the human character, allowed unrestrained expression. In Kurtz, Marlow sees the unrestrained reflection of himself. He is, at least in part, horrified by what he sees.

In many ways, *Heart of Darkness* is not so much about Africa or Kurtz or ivory as it is about Marlow and about storytelling. As in much modern literature, the truth is not in the tale but in the teller. Although Marlow is never explicit about what he learned from his experiences, about his psychological kinship with Kurtz, or about why he lied to Kurtz's Intended, his account raises questions about how and why he was able to survive his journey and about the ways he differs from Kurtz and the other Europeans. Did he survive through superior understanding, greater strength of will or moral character, or a more repressed personality? To what degree did he avoid complicity with Kurtz and the other pilgrims? How much of what he tells us can we believe? What might he be trying to hide or repress that would make his account, at least to some extent, unreliable? What knowledge is he trying to pass on to those aboard the *Nellie*? There are some hints but no definitive answers to these questions in the story.

The Nigerian novelist Chinua Achebe has attacked this "European" story as an example of literary colonialism and European racism. *Heart of Darkness* is not about Africa, Achebe argues, for Conrad's Africa has no reality and the natives no individuality, no names. For Conrad, Marlow, and Europeans, he says, Africa and Africans are "other"—objects against which the Europeans define their own individuality. As appalled as they may be by the excesses of the ivory trade, they, too, are exploiting Africa to reconstruct a European civilization. Achebe's attack appeared in his 1975 speech "An Image of Africa," delivered at the University of Massachusetts long after Conrad's death—testimony to the enduring currency of Conrad's story and to the centrality of the questions it raises in the twentieth century.

Marlow's experience is enlightening as well as horrifying. He has gained wisdom from his time in Africa, as his pose in the last scene as a meditating Buddha suggests, but it is more than personal wisdom he has acquired. He has returned with some broader cultural understanding. Like epic heroes who journey to the underworld to gain the wisdom that will enable them to found nations, Marlow has traveled to the underworld of Africa to recover the knowledge that Europe—the "whited sepulchre"—has lost, repressed, or forgotten. In gaining that knowledge, Marlow's personal story becomes a cultural story, a modern epic about a deadened and wasted culture—Europe as Eliot's "Waste Land"— seeking to recover the vital heart of its humanity. His mission has been a dangerous and expensive one, and we are left wondering just how successful he was and whether his gains were worth the horror.

SUGGESTED READINGS

Conrad's life, an engaging adventure story itself, is told in Jocelyn Baines's *Joseph Conrad: A Critical Biography* (1960) and Frederick Karl's *Joseph Conrad: The Three Lives* (1979). Some good introductions to Conrad's work include Norman Page's *A Conrad Companion* (1985), Frederick Karl's *A Reader's Guide to Joseph Conrad* (1960), R. F. Lee's *Conrad's Colonialism* (1969), and Albert Guerard's *Conrad the Novelist* (1958). Two collections of essays provide a wide representation of different approaches to Conrad's provocative African story: *Heart of Darkness: Norton Critical Edition of Heart of Darkness,* ed. Robert Kimbrough (1971), and *Heart of Darkness: A Case Study in Contemporary Criticism,* ed. Ross C. Murfin (1989).

Heart of Darkness

1

The *Nellie,* a cruising yawl, swung to her anchor without a flutter of the sails, and was at rest. The flood had made, the wind was nearly calm, and being bound down the river, the only thing for it was to come to and wait for the turn of the tide.

The sea-reach of the Thames stretched before us like the beginning of an interminable waterway. In the offing[1] the sea and the sky were welded together without a joint, and in the luminous space the tanned sails of the barges drifting up with the tide seemed to stand still in red clusters of canvas sharply peaked, with gleams of varnished sprits. A haze rested on the low shores that ran out to sea in vanishing flatness. The air was dark above Gravesend, and farther back still seemed condensed into a mournful gloom, brooding motionless over the biggest, and the greatest, town on earth.

The Director of Companies was our captain and our host. We four affectionately watched his back as he stood in the bows looking to seaward. On the whole river there was nothing that looked half so nautical. He resembled a pilot, which to a seaman is trustworthiness personified. It was difficult to realize his work was not out there in the luminous estuary, but behind him, within the brooding gloom.

Between us there was, as I have already said somewhere, the bond of the sea. Besides holding our hearts together through long periods of separation, it had the effect of making us tolerant of each other's yarns—and even convictions. The Lawyer—the best of old fellows—had, because of his many years and many virtues, the only cushion on deck, and was lying on the only rug. The Accountant had brought out already a box of dominoes, and was toying architecturally with the bones. Marlow sat cross-legged right aft, leaning against the mizzen-mast. He had sunken cheeks, a yellow complexion, a straight back, an ascetic aspect, and, with his arms dropped, the palms of hands outwards, resembled an idol. The director, satisfied the anchor had good hold, made his way aft and sat down amongst us. We exchanged a few words lazily. Afterwards there was silence on board the yacht. For some reason or other we did not begin that game of dominoes. We felt meditative, and fit for nothing but placid staring. The day was ending in a serenity of still and exquisite brilliance. The water shone pacifically; the sky, without a speck, was a

---

[1] The horizon.

benign immensity of unstained light; the very mist on the Essex marshes was like a gauzy and radiant fabric, hung from the wooded rises inland, and draping the low shores in diaphanous folds. Only the gloom to the west, brooding over the upper reaches, became more sombre every minute, as if angered by the approach of the sun.

And at last, in its curved and imperceptible fall, the sun sank low, and from glowing white changed to a dull red without rays and without heat, as if about to go out suddenly, stricken to death by the touch of that gloom brooding over a crowd of men.

Forthwith a change came over the waters, and the serenity became less brilliant but more profound. The old river in its broad reach rested unruffled at the decline of day, after ages of good service done to the race that peopled its banks, spread out in the tranquil dignity of a waterway leading to the uttermost ends of the earth. We looked at the venerable stream not in the vivid flush of a short day that comes and departs for ever, but in the august light of abiding memories. And indeed nothing is easier for a man who has, as the phrase goes, "followed the sea" with reverence and affection, than to evoke the great spirit of the past upon the lower reaches of the Thames. The tidal current runs to and fro in its unceasing service, crowded with memories of men and ships it had borne to the rest of home or to the battles of the sea. It had known and served all the men of whom the nation is proud, from Sir Francis Drake to Sir John Franklin,[2] knights all, titled and untitled—the great knights-errant of the sea. It had borne all the ships whose names are like jewels flashing in the night of time, from the *Golden Hind* returning with her round flanks full of treasure, to be visited by the Queen's Highness and thus pass out of the gigantic tale, to the *Erebus* and *Terror,* bound on other conquests—and that never returned. It had known the ships and the men. They had sailed from Deptford, from Greenwich, from Erith—the adventurers and the settlers; kings' ships and the ships of men on 'Change;[3] captains, admirals, the dark "interlopers" of the Eastern trade, and the commissioned "generals" of East India fleets. Hunters for gold or pursuers of fame, they all had gone out on that stream, bearing the sword, and often the torch, messengers of the might within the land, bearers of a spark from the sacred fire. What greatness had not floated on the ebb of that river into the mystery of an unknown earth! . . . The dreams of men, the seed of commonwealths, the germs of empires.

The sun set; the dusk fell on the stream, and lights began to appear along the shore. The Chapman lighthouse, a three-legged thing erect on a mud-flat, shone strongly. Lights of ships moved in the fairway—a great stir of lights going up and going down. And farther west on the upper reaches the place of the monstrous town was still marked ominously on the sky, a brooding gloom in sunshine, a lurid glare under the stars.

"And this also," said Marlow suddenly, "has been one of the dark places of the earth."

He was the only man of us who still "followed the sea." The worst that could be said of him was that he did not represent his class. He was a seaman, but he was a wanderer, too, while most seamen lead, if one may so express it, a sedentary life. Their minds are of the stay-at-home order, and their home is always with them—the

---

[2]Drake circumnavigated the globe from 1577 to 1580 on the *Golden Hind.* Franklin sought the Northwest Passage from 1845 to 1847 on the *Erebus* and *Terror.*

[3]The Exchange, the British financial market.

ship; and so is their country—the sea. One ship is very much like another, and the sea is always the same. In the immutability of their surroundings the foreign shores, the foreign faces, the changing immensity of life, glide past, veiled not by a sense of mystery but by a slightly disdainful ignorance; for there is nothing mysterious to a seaman unless it be the sea itself, which is the mistress of his existence and as inscrutable as Destiny. For the rest, after his hours of work, a casual stroll or a casual spree on shore suffices to unfold for him the secret of a whole continent, and generally he finds the secret not worth knowing. The yarns of seamen have a direct simplicity, the whole meaning of which lies within the shell of a cracked nut. But Marlow was not typical (if his propensity to spin yarns be excepted), and to him the meaning of an episode was not inside like a kernel but outside, enveloping the tale which brought it out only as a glow brings out a haze, in the likeness of one of these misty halos that sometimes are made visible by the spectral illumination of moonshine.

His remark did not seem at all surprising. It was just like Marlow. It was accepted in silence. No one took the trouble to grunt even; and presently he said, very slow—

"I was thinking of very old times, when the Romans first came here, nineteen hundred years ago—the other day. . . . Light came out of this river since—you say Knights? Yes; but it is like a running blaze on a plain, like a flash of lightning in the clouds. We live in the flicker—may it last as long as the old earth keeps rolling! But darkness was here yesterday. Imagine the feelings of a commander of a fine—what d'ye call 'em?—trireme in the Mediterranean, ordered suddenly to the north; run overland across the Gauls in a hurry; put in charge of one of these craft the legionaries—a wonderful lot of handy men they must have been, too—used to build, apparently by the hundred, in a month or two, if we may believe what we read. Imagine him here—the very end of the world, a sea the colour of lead, a sky the colour of smoke, a kind of ship about as rigid as a concertina—and going up this river with stores, or orders, or what you like. Sand-banks, marshes, forests, savages,—precious little to eat fit for a civilized man, nothing but Thames water to drink. No Falernian[4] wine here, no going ashore. Here and there a military camp lost in a wilderness, like a needle in a bundle of hay—cold, fog, tempests, disease, exile, and death,—death skulking in the air, in the water, in the bush. They must have been dying like flies here. Oh, yes—he did it. Did it very well, too, no doubt, and without thinking much about it either, except afterwards to brag of what he had gone through in his time, perhaps. They were men enough to face the darkness. And perhaps he was cheered by keeping his eye on a chance of promotion to the fleet at Ravenna by and by, if he had good friends in Rome and survived the awful climate. Or think of a decent young citizen in a toga—perhaps too much dice, you know—coming out here in the train of some prefect, or tax-gatherer, or trader even, to mend his fortunes. Land in a swamp, march through the woods, and in some inland post feel the savagery, the utter savagery, had closed round him,—all that mysterious life of the wilderness that stirs in the forest, in the jungles, in the hearts of wild men. There's no initiation either into such mysteries. He has to live in the midst of the incomprehensible, which is also detestable. And it has a fascination, too, that goes to work upon him. The fascination of the abomination—you know, imagine the growing regrets, the longing to escape, the powerless disgust, the surrender, the hate."

---

[4]A fine vintage wine.

He paused.

"Mind," he began again, lifting one arm from the elbow, the palm of the hand outwards, so that, with his legs folded before him, he had the pose of a Buddha preaching in European clothes and without a lotus-flower—"Mind, none of us would feel exactly like this. What saves us is efficiency—the devotion to efficiency. But these chaps were not much account, really. They were no colonists; their administration was merely a squeeze, and nothing more, I suspect. They were conquerors, and for that you want only brute force—nothing to boast of, when you have it, since your strength is just an accident arising from the weakness of others. They grabbed what they could get for the sake of what was to be got. It was just robbery with violence, aggravated murder on a great scale, and men going at it blind—as is very proper for those who tackle a darkness. The conquest of the earth, which mostly means the taking it away from those who have a different complexion or slightly flatter noses than ourselves, is not a pretty thing when you look into it too much. What redeems it is the idea only. An idea at the back of it; not a sentimental pretence but an idea; and an unselfish belief in the idea—something you can set up, and bow down before, and offer a sacrifice to...."

He broke off. Flames glided in the river, small green flames, red flames, white flames, pursuing, overtaking, joining, crossing each other—then separating slowly or hastily. The traffic of the great city went on in the deepening night upon the sleepless river. We looked on, waiting patiently—there was nothing else to do till the end of the flood; but it was only after a long silence, when he said, in a hesitating voice, "I suppose you fellows remember I did once turn fresh-water sailor for a bit," that we knew we were fated, before the ebb began to run, to hear about one of Marlow's inconclusive experiences.

"I don't want to bother you much with what happened to me personally," he began, showing in this remark the weakness of many tellers of tales who seem so often unaware of what their audience would best like to hear; "yet to understand the effect of it on me you ought to know how I got out there, what I saw, how I went up that river to the place where I first met the poor chap. It was the farthest point of navigation and the culminating point of my experience. It seemed somehow to throw a kind of light on everything about me—and into my thoughts. It was sombre enough, too—and pitiful—not extraordinary in any way—not very clear either. No, not very clear. And yet it seemed to throw a kind of light.

"I had then, as you remember, just returned to London after a lot of Indian Ocean, Pacific, China Seas—a regular dose of the East—six years or so, and I was loafing about, hindering you fellows in your work and invading your homes, just as though I had got a heavenly mission to civilize you. It was very fine for a time, but after a bit I did get tired of resting. Then I began to look for a ship—I should think the hardest work on earth. But the ships wouldn't even look at me. And I got tired of that game, too.

"Now when I was a little chap I had a passion for maps. I would look for hours at South America, or Africa, or Australia, and lose myself in all the glories of exploration. At that time there were many blank spaces on the earth, and when I saw one that looked particularly inviting on a map (but they all look that) I would put my finger on it and say, When I grow up I will go there. The North Pole was one of these places, I remember. Well, I haven't been there yet, and shall not try now. The glamour's off. Other places were scattered about the Equator, and in every sort of latitude all over the two hemispheres. I have been in some of them, and... well, we won't talk about that. But there was one yet—the biggest, the most blank, so to speak—that I had a hankering after.

"True, by this time it was not a blank space any more. It had got filled since my boyhood with rivers and lakes and names. It had ceased to be a blank space of delightful mystery—a white patch for a boy to dream gloriously over. It had become a place of darkness. But there was in it one river especially, a mighty big river, that you could see on the map, resembling an immense snake uncoiled, with its head in the sea, its body at rest curving afar over a vast country, and its tail lost in the depths of the land. And as I looked at the map of it in a shop-window, it fascinated me as a snake would a bird—a silly little bird. Then I remembered there was a big concern, a Company for trade on that river. Dash it all! I thought to myself, they can't trade without using some kind of craft on that lot of fresh water—steamboats! Why shouldn't I try to get charge of one? I went on along Fleet Street, but could not shake off the idea. The snake had charmed me.

"You understand it was a Continental concern, that Trading society; but I have a lot of relations living on the Continent, because it's cheap and not so nasty as it looks, they say.

"I am sorry to own I began to worry them. This was already a fresh departure for me. I was not used to get things that way, you know. I always went my own road and on my own legs where I had a mind to go. I wouldn't have believed it of myself; but, then—you see—I felt somehow I must get there by hook or by crook. So I worried them. The men said 'My dear fellow,' and did nothing. Then—would you believe it?—I tried the women. I, Charlie Marlow, set the women to work—to get a job. Heavens! Well, you see, the notion drove me. I had an aunt, a dear enthusiastic soul. She wrote: 'It will be delightful. I am ready to do anything, anything for you. It is a glorious idea. I know the wife of a very high personage in the Administration, and also a man who has lots of influence with,' etc., etc. She was determined to make no end of fuss to get me appointed skipper of a river steamboat, if such was my fancy.

"I got my appointment—of course; and I got it very quick. It appears the Company had received news that one of their captains had been killed in a scuffle with the natives. This was my chance, and it made me the more anxious to go. It was only months and months afterwards, when I made the attempt to recover what was left of the body, that I heard the original quarrel arose from a misunderstanding about some hens. Yes, two black hens. Fresleven—that was the fellow's name, a Dane—thought himself wronged somehow in the bargain, so he went ashore and started to hammer the chief of the village with a stick. Oh, it didn't surprise me in the least to hear this, and at the same time to be told that Fresleven was the gentlest, quietest creature that ever walked on two legs. No doubt he was; but he had been a couple of years already out there engaged in the noble cause, you know, and he probably felt the need at last of asserting his self-respect in some way. Therefore he whacked the old nigger mercilessly, while a big crowd of his people watched him, thunderstruck, till some man—I was told the chief's son—in desperation at hearing the old chap yell, made a tentative jab with a spear at the white man—and of course it went quite easy between the shoulder-blades. Then the whole population cleared into the forest, expecting all kinds of calamities to happen, while, on the other hand, the steamer Fresleven commanded left also in a bad panic, in charge of the engineer, I believe. Afterwards nobody seemed to trouble much about Fresleven's remains, till I got out and stepped into his shoes. I couldn't let it rest, though; but when an opportunity offered at last to meet my predecessor, the grass growing through his ribs was tall enough to hide his bones. They were all there. The supernatural being had not been touched after he fell. And the village was deserted, the huts gaped black, rotting, all askew within the fallen enclosures. A calamity had come to it, sure enough. The people had vanished. Mad terror had scattered them, men, women, and children, through the bush, and they had never returned. What became of the hens I don't know either. I should think the cause of progress got them, anyhow. However, through this glorious affair I got my appointment, before I had fairly begun to hope for it.

"I flew around like mad to get ready, and before forty-eight hours I was crossing the Channel to show myself to my employers, and sign the contract. In a very few hours I arrived in a city[5] that always makes me think of a whited sepulchre.[6] Prejudice no doubt. I had no difficulty in finding the Company's offices. It was the biggest thing in the town, and everybody I met was full of it. They were going to run an over-sea empire, and make no end of coin by trade.

"A narrow and deserted street in deep shadow, high houses, innumerable windows with venetian blinds, a dead silence, grass sprouting between the stones, imposing carriage archways right and left, immense double doors standing ponderously ajar. I slipped through one of these cracks, went up a swept and ungarnished staircase, as arid as a desert, and opened the first door I came to. Two women, one fat and the other slim, sat on straw-bottomed chairs, knitting black wool. The slim one got up and walked straight at me—still knitting with down-cast eyes—and only just as I began to think of getting out of her way, as you would for a somnambulist, stood still, and looked up. Her dress was as plain as an umbrella-cover, and she turned round without a word and preceded me into a waiting-room. I gave my name, and looked about. Deal[7] table in the middle, plain chairs all round the walls, on one end a large shining map, marked with all the colours of a rainbow. There was a vast amount of red—good to see at any time, because one knows that some real work is done in there, a deuce of a lot of blue, a little green, smears of orange, and, on the East Coast, a purple patch, to show where the jolly pioneers of progress drink the jolly lager-beer. However, I wasn't going into any of these. I was going into the yellow. Dead in the centre. And the river was there—fascinating—deadly—like a snake. Ough! A door opened, a white-haired secretarial head, but wearing a compassionate expression, appeared, and a skinny forefinger beckoned me into the sanctuary. Its light was dim, and a heavy writing-desk squatted in the middle. From behind that structure came out an impression of pale plumpness in a frock-coat. The great man himself. He was five feet six, I should judge, and had his grip on the handle-end of ever so many millions. He shook hands, I fancy, murmured vaguely, was satisfied with my French. *Bon voyage.*

"In about forty-five seconds I found myself again in the waiting-room with the compassionate secretary, who, full of desolation and sympathy, made me sign some document. I believe I undertook amongst other things not to disclose any trade secrets. Well, I am not going to.

"I began to feel slightly uneasy. You know I am not used to such ceremonies, and there was something ominous in the atmosphere. It was just as though I had been let into some conspiracy—I don't know—something not quite right; and I was glad to get out. In the outer room the two women knitted black wool feverishly. People were arriving, and the younger one was walking back and forth introducing them. The old one sat on her chair. Her flat cloth slippers were propped up on a

---

[5] The capital of Belgium. Between 1885 and 1908, when it became a Belgian colony, the Congo—now Zaire—was owned by King Leopold II of Belgium.

[6] Jesus compared the hypocritical Pharisees to whited sepulchres, which "outwardly appear beautiful, but inwardly are full of dead men's bones." See Matthew 23:27.

[7] Pine.

foot-warmer, and a cat reposed on her lap. She wore a starched white affair on her head, had a wart on one cheek, and silver-rimmed spectacles hung on the tip of her nose. She glanced at me above the glasses. The swift and indifferent placidity of that look troubled me. Two youths with foolish and cheery countenances were being piloted over, and she threw at them the same quick glance of unconcerned wisdom. She seemed to know all about them and about me, too. An eerie feeling came over me. She seemed uncanny and fateful. Often far away there I thought of these two, guarding the door of Darkness, knitting black wool as for a warm pall, one introducing, introducing continuously to the unknown, the other scrutinizing the cheery and foolish faces with unconcerned old eyes. *Ave!* Old knitter of black wool. *Morituri te salutant.*[8] Not many of those she looked at ever saw her again—not half, by a long way.

"There was yet a visit to the doctor. 'A simple formality,' assured me the secretary, with an air of taking an immense part in all my sorrows. Accordingly a young chap wearing his hat over the left eyebrow, some clerk I suppose,—there must have been clerks in the business, though the house was as still as a house in a city of the dead—came from somewhere up-stairs, and led me forth. He was shabby and careless, with ink-stains on the sleeves of his jacket, and his cravat was large and billowy, under a chin shaped like the toe of an old boot. It was a little too early for the doctor, so I proposed a drink, and thereupon he developed a vein of joviality. As we sat over our vermuths he glorified the Company's business, and by and by I expressed casually my surprise at him not going out there. He became very cool and collected all at once. 'I am not such a fool as I look, quoth Plato to his disciples,' he said sententiously, emptied his glass with great resolution, and we rose.

"The old doctor felt my pulse, evidently thinking of something else the while. 'Good, good for there,' he mumbled, and then with a certain eagerness asked me whether I would let him measure my head. Rather surprised, I said Yes, when he produced a thing like calipers and got the dimensions back and front and every way, taking notes carefully. He was an unshaven little man in a threadbare coat like a gaberdine, with his feet in slippers, and I thought him a harmless fool. 'I always ask leave, in the interests of science, to measure the crania of those going out there,' he said. 'And when they come back, too?' I asked. 'Oh, I never see them,' he remarked; 'and, moreover, the changes take place inside, you know.' He smiled, as if at some quiet joke. 'So you are going out there. Famous. Interesting, too.' He gave me a searching glance, and made another note. 'Ever any madness in your family?' he asked, in a matter-of-fact tone. I felt very annoyed. 'Is that question in the interests of science, too?' 'It would be,' he said, without taking notice of my irritation, 'interesting for science to watch the mental changes of individuals, on the spot, but . . .' 'Are you an alienist?'[9] I interrupted. 'Every doctor should be—a little,' answered that original, imperturbably. 'I have a little theory which you Messieurs who go out there must help me to prove. This is my share in the advantages my country shall reap from the possession of such a magnificent dependency. The mere wealth I leave to others. Pardon my questions, but you are the first Englishman coming under my observation . . .' I hastened to assure him I was not in the least typical. 'If I were,' said I, 'I wouldn't be talking like this with you.' 'What you say is rather profound, and probably erroneous,' he said, with a laugh. 'Avoid irritation

---

[8] *Ave . . . salutant* ("Hail! Those who are about to die salute you."): The gladiators' salute to the Roman emperor in the Colosseum.
[9] A psychiatrist.

more than exposure to the sun. Adieu. How do you English say, eh? Good-bye. Ah! Good-bye. Adieu. In the tropics one must before everything keep calm.'. . . . He lifted a warning forefinger. . . . '*Du calme, du calme. Adieu.*'

"One thing more remained to do—say good-bye to my excellent aunt. I found her triumphant. I had a cup of tea—the last decent cup of tea for many days—and in a room that most soothingly looked just as you would expect a lady's drawing-room to look, we had a long quiet chat by the fireside. In the course of these confidences it became quite plain to me I had been represented to the wife of the high dignitary, and goodness knows to how many more people besides, as an exceptional and gifted creature—a piece of good fortune for the Company—a man you don't get hold of every day. Good heavens! and I was going to take charge of a two-penny-half-penny river-steamboat with a penny whistle attached! It appeared, however, I was also one of the Workers, with a capital—you know. Something like an emissary of light, something like a lower sort of apostle. There had been a lot of such rot let loose in print and talk just about that time, and the excellent woman, living right in the rush of all that humbug, got carried off her feet. She talked about 'weaning those ignorant millions from their horrid ways,' till, upon my word, she made me quite uncomfortable. I ventured to hint that the Company was run for profit.

"'You forget, dear Charlie, that the labourer is worthy of his hire,'[10] she said, brightly. It's queer how out of touch with truth women are. They live in a world of their own, and there has never been anything like it, and never can be. It is too beautiful altogether, and if they were to set it up it would go to pieces before the first sunset. Some confounded fact we men have been living contentedly with ever since the day of creation would start up and knock the whole thing over.

"After this I got embraced, told to wear flannel, be sure to write often, and so on—and I left. In the street—I don't know why—a queer feeling came to me that I was an impostor. Odd thing that I, who used to clear out for any part of the world at twenty-four hours' notice, with less thought than most men give to the crossing of a street, had a moment—I won't say of hesitation, but of startled pause, before this commonplace affair. The best way I can explain it to you is by saying that, for a second or two, I felt as though, instead of going to the centre of a continent, I were about to set off for the centre of the earth.

"I left in a French steamer, and she called in every blamed port they have out there, for, as far as I could see, the sole purpose of landing soldiers and custom-house officers. I watched the coast. Watching a coast as it slips by the ship is like thinking about an enigma. There it is before you—smiling, frowning, inviting, grand, mean, insipid, or savage, and always mute with an air of whispering, Come and find out. This one was almost featureless, as if still in the making, with an aspect of monotonous grimness. The edge of a colossal jungle, so dark-green as to be almost black, fringed with white surf, ran straight, like a ruled line, far, far away along a blue sea whose glitter was blurred by a creeping mist. The sun was fierce, the land seemed to glisten and drip with steam. Here and there grayish-whitish specks showed up clustered inside the white surf, with a flag flying above them perhaps. Settlements some centuries old, and still no bigger than pinheads on the untouched expanse of their background. We pounded along, stopped, landed soldiers; went on, landed custom-house clerks to levy toll in what looked like a God-forsaken wilderness, with a tin shed and a flag-pole lost in it; landed more soldiers—to take care of the custom-house clerks, presumably. Some, I heard, got drowned in the surf; but whether they did or not, nobody seemed particularly

---

[10]See Luke 10:7.

to care. They were just flung out there, and on we went. Every day the coast looked the same, as though we had not moved; but we passed various places—trading places—with names like Gran' Bassam, Little Popo; names that seemed to belong to some sordid farce acted in front of a sinister back-cloth. The idleness of a passenger, my isolation amongst all these men with whom I had no point of contact, the oily and languid sea, the uniform sombreness of the coast, seemed to keep me away from the truth of things, within the toil of a mournful and senseless delusion. The voice of the surf heard now and then was a positive pleasure, like the speech of a brother. It was something natural, that had its reason, that had a meaning. Now and then a boat from the shore gave one a momentary contact with reality. It was paddled by black fellows. You could see from afar the white of their eyeballs glistening. They shouted, sang; their bodies streamed with perspiration; they had faces like grotesque masks—these chaps; but they had bone, muscle, a wild vitality, an intense energy of movement, that was as natural and true as the surf along their coast. They wanted no excuse for being there. They were a great comfort to look at. For a time I would feel I belonged still to a world of straightforward facts; but the feeling would not last long. Something would turn up to scare it away. Once, I remember, we came upon a man-of-war anchored off the coast. There wasn't even a shed there, and she was shelling the bush. It appears the French had one of their wars going on thereabouts. Her ensign dropped limp like a rag; the muzzles of the long six-inch guns stuck out all over the low hull; the greasy, slimy swell swung her up lazily and let her down, swaying her thin masts. In the empty immensity of earth, sky, and water, there she was, incomprehensible, firing into a continent. Pop, would go one of the six-inch guns; a small flame would dart and vanish, a little white smoke would disappear, a tiny projectile would give a feeble screech—and nothing happened. Nothing could happen. There was a touch of insanity in the proceeding, a sense of lugubrious drollery in the sight; and it was not dissipated by somebody on board assuring me earnestly there was a camp of natives—he called them enemies!—hidden out of sight somewhere.

"We gave her her letters (I heard the men in that lonely ship were dying of fever at the rate of three a day) and went on. We called at some more places with farcical names, where the merry dance of death and trade goes on in a still and earthy atmosphere as of an overheated catacomb; all along the formless coast bordered by dangerous surf, as if Nature herself had tried to ward off intruders; in and out of rivers, streams of death in life, whose banks were rotting into mud, whose waters, thickened into slime, invaded the contorted mangroves,[11] that seemed to writhe at us in the extremity of an impotent despair. Nowhere did we stop long enough to get a particularized impression, but the general sense of vague and oppressive wonder grew upon me. It was like a weary pilgrimage amongst hints for nightmares.

"It was upward of thirty days before I saw the mouth of the big river. We anchored off the seat of the government. But my work would not begin till some two hundred miles farther on. So as soon as I could I made a start for a place thirty miles higher up.

"I had my passage on a little sea-going steamer. Her captain was a Swede, and knowing me for a seaman, invited me on the bridge. He was a young man, lean, fair, and morose, with lanky hair and a shuffling gait. As we left the miserable little wharf, he tossed his head contemptuously at the shore. 'Been living there?' he asked. I said, 'Yes.' 'Fine lot these government chaps—are they not?' he went on,

---

[11]Evergreen thickets.

speaking English with great precision and considerable bitterness. 'It is funny what some people will do for a few francs a month. I wonder what becomes of that kind when it goes up country?' I said to him I expected to see that soon. 'So-o-o!' he exclaimed. He shuffled athwart, keeping one eye ahead vigilantly. 'Don't be too sure,' he continued. 'The other day I took up a man who hanged himself on the road. He was a Swede, too.' 'Hanged himself! Why, in God's name?' I cried. He kept on looking out watchfully. 'Who knows? The sun too much for him, or the country perhaps.'

"At last we opened a reach. A rocky cliff appeared, mounds of turned-up earth by the shore, houses on a hill, others with iron roofs, amongst a waste of excavations, or hanging to the declivity. A continuous noise of the rapids above hovered over this scene of inhabited devastation. A lot of people, mostly black and naked, moved about like ants. A jetty projected into the river. A blinding sunlight drowned all this at times in a sudden recrudescence of glare. 'There's your Company's station,' said the Swede, pointing to three wooden barrack-like structures on the rocky slope. 'I will send your things up. Four boxes did you say? So. Farewell.'

"I came upon a boiler wallowing in the grass, then found a path leading up the hill. It turned aside for the boulders, and also for an undersized railway-truck lying there on its back with its wheels in the air. One was off. The thing looked as dead as the carcass of some animal. I came upon more pieces of decaying machinery, a stack of rusty rails. To the left a clump of trees made a shady spot, where dark things seemed to stir feebly. I blinked, the path was steep. A horn tooted to the right, and I saw the black people run. A heavy and dull detonation shook the ground, a puff of smoke came out of the cliff, and that was all. No change appeared on the face of the rock. They were building a railway. The cliff was not in the way or anything; but this objectless blasting was all the work going on.

"A slight clinking behind me made me turn my head. Six black men advanced in a file, toiling up the path. They walked erect and slow, balancing small baskets full of earth on their heads, and the clink kept time with their footsteps. Black rags were wound round their loins, and the short ends behind waggled to and fro like tails. I could see every rib, the joints of their limbs were like knots in a rope; each had an iron collar on his neck, and all were connected together with a chain whose bights[12] swung between them, rhythmically clinking. Another report from the cliff made me think suddenly of that ship of war I had seen firing into a continent. It was the same kind of ominous voice; but these men could by no stretch of imagination be called enemies. They were called criminals, and the outraged law, like the bursting shells, had come to them, an insoluble mystery from the sea. All their meagre breasts panted together, the violently dilated nostrils quivered, the eyes stared stonily up-hill. They passed me within six inches, without a glance, with that complete, deathlike indifference of unhappy savages. Behind this raw matter one of the reclaimed, the product of the new forces at work, strolled despondently, carrying a rifle by its middle. He had a uniform jacket with one button off, and seeing a white man on the path, hoisted his weapon to his shoulder with alacrity. This was simple prudence, white men being so much alike at a distance that he could not tell who I might be. He was speedily reassured, and with a large, white, rascally grin, and a glance at his charge, seemed to take me into partnership in his exalted trust. After all, I also was a part of the great cause of these high and just proceedings.

---

[12]Slack sections.

"Instead of going up, I turned and descended to the left. My idea was to let that chain-gang get out of sight before I climbed the hill. You know I am not particularly tender; I've had to strike and to fend off. I've had to resist and to attack sometimes—that's only one way of resisting—without counting the exact cost, according to the demands of such sort of life as I had blundered into. I've seen the devil of violence, and the devil of greed, and the devil of hot desire; but, by all the stars! these were strong, lusty, red-eyed devils, that swayed and drove men—men, I tell you. But as I stood on this hillside, I foresaw that in the blinding sunshine of that land I would become acquainted with a flabby, pretending, weak-eyed devil of a rapacious and pitiless folly. How insidious he could be, too, I was only to find out several months later and a thousand miles farther. For a moment I stood appalled, as though by a warning. Finally I descended the hill, obliquely, towards the trees I had seen.

"I avoided a vast artificial hole somebody had been digging on the slope, the purpose of which I found it impossible to divine. It wasn't a quarry or a sandpit, anyhow. It was just a hole. It might have been connected with the philanthropic desire of giving the criminals something to do. I don't know. Then I nearly fell into a very narrow ravine, almost no more than a scar in the hillside. I discovered that a lot of imported drainage-pipes for the settlement had been tumbled in there. There wasn't one that was not broken. It was a wanton smash-up. At last I got under the trees. My purpose was to stroll into the shade for a moment; but no sooner within than it seemed to me I had stepped into the gloomy circle of some Inferno. The rapids were near, and an uninterrupted, uniform, headlong, rushing noise filled the mournful stillness of the grove, where not a breath stirred, not a leaf moved, with a mysterious sound—as though the tearing pace of the launched earth had suddenly become audible.

"Black shapes crouched, lay, sat between the trees leaning against the trunks, clinging to the earth, half coming out, half effaced within the dim light, in all the attitudes of pain, abandonment, and despair. Another mine on the cliff went off, followed by a slight shudder of the soil under my feet. The work was going on. The work! And this was the place where some of the helpers had withdrawn to die.

"They were dying slowly—it was very clear. They were not enemies, they were not criminals, they were nothing earthly now,—nothing but black shadows of disease and starvation, lying confusedly in the greenish gloom. Brought from all the recesses of the coast in all the legality of time contracts, lost in uncongenial surroundings, fed on unfamiliar food, they sickened, became inefficient, and were then allowed to crawl away and rest. These moribund shapes were free as air—and nearly as thin. I began to distinguish the gleam of the eyes under the trees. Then, glancing down, I saw a face near my hand. The black bones reclined at full length with one shoulder against the tree, and slowly the eyelids rose and the sunken eyes looked up at me, enormous and vacant, a kind of blind, white flicker in the depths of the orbs, which died out slowly. The man seemed young—almost a boy—but you know with them it's hard to tell. I found nothing else to do but to offer him one of my good Swede's ship's biscuits I had in my pocket. The fingers closed slowly on it and held—there was no other movement and no other glance. He had tied a bit of white worsted round his neck—Why? Where did he get it? Was it a badge—an ornament—a charm—a propitiatory act? Was there any idea at all connected with it? It looked startling round his black neck, this bit of white thread from beyond the seas.

"Near the same tree two more bundles of acute angles sat with their legs drawn up. One, with his chin propped on his knees, stared at nothing, in an intolerable and appalling manner: his brother phantom rested its forehead, as if overcome with a great weariness; and all about others were scattered in every pose of contorted collapse, as in some picture of a massacre or a pestilence. While I stood horror-struck, one of these creatures rose to his hands and knees, and went off on all-fours towards the river to drink. He lapped out of his hand, then sat up in the sunlight, crossing his shins in front of him, and after a time let his woolly head fall on his breastbone.

"I didn't want any more loitering in the shade, and I made haste towards the station. When near the buildings I met a white man, in such an unexpected elegance of get-up that in the first moment I took him for a sort of vision. I saw a high starched collar, white cuffs, a light alpaca jacket, snowy trousers, a clean necktie, and varnished boots. No hat. Hair parted, brushed, oiled, under a green-lined parasol held in a big white hand. He was amazing, and had a penholder behind his ear.

"I shook hands with this miracle, and I learned he was the Company's chief accountant, and that all the book-keeping was done at this station. He had come out for a moment, he said, 'to get a breath of fresh air.' The expression sounded wonderfully odd, with its suggestion of sedentary desk-life. I wouldn't have mentioned the fellow to you at all, only it was from his lips that I first heard the name of the man who is so indissolubly connected with the memories of that time. Moreover, I respected the fellow. Yes; I respected his collars, his vast cuffs, his brushed hair. His appearance was certainly that of a hairdresser's dummy; but in the great demoralization of the land he kept up his appearance. That's backbone. His starched collars and got-up shirt-fronts were achievements of character. He had been out nearly three years; and, later, I could not help asking him how he managed to sport such linen. He had just the faintest blush, and said modestly, 'I've been teaching one of the native women about the station. It was difficult. She had a distaste for the work.' Thus this man had verily accomplished something. And he was devoted to his books, which were in apple-pie order.

"Everything else in the station was in a muddle,—heads, things, buildings. Strings of dusty niggers with splay feet arrived and departed; a stream of manufactured goods, rubbishy cottons, beads, and brass-wire set into the depths of darkness, and in return came a precious trickle of ivory.

"I had to wait in the station for ten days—an eternity. I lived in a hut in the yard, but to be out of the chaos I would sometimes get into the accountant's office. It was built of horizontal planks, and so badly put together that, as he bent over his high desk, he was barred from neck to heels with narrow strips of sunlight. There was no need to open the big shutter to see. It was hot there, too; big flies buzzed fiendishly, and did not sting, but stabbed. I sat generally on the floor, while, of faultless appearance (and even slightly scented), perching on a high stool, he wrote, he wrote. Sometimes he stood up for exercise. When a truckle-bed with a sick man (some invalid agent from up-country) was put in there, he exhibited a gentle annoyance. 'The groans of this sick person,' he said, 'distract my attention. And without that it is extremely difficult to guard against clerical errors in this climate.'

"One day he remarked, without lifting his head, 'In the interior you will no doubt meet Mr. Kurtz.' On my asking who Mr. Kurtz was, he said he was a first-class agent; and seeing my disappointment at this information, he added slowly, laying down his pen, 'He is a very remarkable person.' Further questions elicited from him that Mr. Kurtz was at present in charge of a trading post, a very important one, in the true ivory-country, at 'the very bottom of there. Sends in as much ivory as all the others put together...' He began to write again. The sick man was too ill to groan. The flies buzzed in a great peace.

"Suddenly there was a growing murmur of voices and a great tramping of feet. A caravan had come in. A violent babble of uncouth sounds burst out on the other side of the planks. All the carriers were speaking together, and in the midst of the uproar the lamentable voice of the chief agent was heard 'giving it up' tearfully for the twentieth time that day. . . . He rose slowly. 'What a frightful row,' he said. He crossed the room gently to look at the sick man, and returning, said to me, 'He does not hear.' 'What! Dead?' I asked, startled. 'No, not yet,' he answered, with great composure. Then, alluding with a toss of the head to the tumult in the station-yard, 'When one has got to make correct entries, one comes to hate those savages—hate them to the death.' He remained thoughtful for a moment. 'When you see Mr. Kurtz,' he went on, 'tell him from me that everything here'—he glanced at the desk—'is very satisfactory. I don't like to write to him—with those messengers of ours you never know who may get hold of your letter—at that Central Station.' He stared at me for a moment with his mild, bulging eyes. 'Oh, he will go far, very far,' he began again. 'He will be a somebody in the Administration before long. They, above—the Council in Europe, you know—mean him to be.'

"He turned to his work. The noise outside had ceased, and presently in going out I stopped at the door. In the steady buzz of flies the homeward-bound agent was lying flushed and insensible; the other, bent over his books, was making correct entries of perfectly correct transactions; and fifty feet below the doorstep I could see the still tree-tops of the grove of death.

"Next day I left that station at last, with a caravan of sixty men, for a two-hundred-mile tramp.

"No use telling you much about that. Paths, paths, everywhere; a stamped-in network of paths spreading over the empty land, through long grass, through burnt grass, through thickets, down and up chilly ravines, up and down stony hills ablaze with heat; and a solitude, a solitude, nobody, not a hut. The population had cleared out a long time ago. Well, if a lot of mysterious niggers armed with all kinds of fearful weapons suddenly took to travelling on the road between Deal and Gravesend, catching the yokels right and left to carry heavy loads for them, I fancy every farm and cottage thereabouts would get empty very soon. Only here the dwellings were gone, too. Still I passed through several abandoned villages. There's something pathetically childish in the ruins of grass walls. Day after day, with the stamp and shuffle of sixty pair of bare feet behind me, each pair under a 60-lb. load. Camp, cook, sleep, strike camp, march. Now and then a carrier dead in harness, at rest in the long grass near the path, with an empty water-gourd and his long staff lying by his side. A great silence around and above. Perhaps on some quiet night the tremor of far-off drums, sinking, swelling, a tremor vast, faint; a sound weird, appealing, suggestive, and wild—and perhaps with as profound a meaning as the sound of bells in a Christian country. Once a white man in an unbuttoned uniform, camping on the path with an armed escort of lank Zanzibaris, very hospitable and festive—not to say drunk. Was looking after the upkeep of the road he declared. Can't say I saw any road or any upkeep, unless the body of a middle-aged negro, with a bullet-hole in the forehead, upon which I absolutely stumbled three miles farther on, may be considered as a permanent improvement. I had a white companion, too, not a bad chap, but rather too fleshy and with the exasperating habit of fainting on the hot hillsides, miles away from the least bit of shade and water. Annoying, you know, to hold your own coat like a parasol over a man's head while he is coming-to. I couldn't help asking him once what he meant by coming there at all. 'To make money, of course. What do you think?' he said, scornfully. Then he got fever, and had to be carried in a hammock slung under a pole. As he weighed sixteen stone[13] I had no end of rows with the carriers. They jibbed,[14] ran away, sneaked off with their loads in the night—quite a mutiny. So, one evening, I made a speech in English with gestures, not one of which was lost to the sixty pairs of eyes before me, and the next morning I started the hammock off in front all right. An hour afterwards I came upon the whole concern wrecked in a bush—man, hammock, groans, blankets, horrors. The heavy pole had skinned his poor nose. He was very anxious for me to kill somebody, but there wasn't the shadow of a carrier near. I remembered the old doctor—'It would be interesting for science to watch the mental changes of individuals, on the spot.' I felt I was becoming scientifically interesting. However, all that is to no purpose. On the fifteenth day I came in sight of the big river again, and hobbled into the Central Station. It was on a back water surrounded by scrub and forest, with a pretty border of smelly mud on one side, and on the three others enclosed by a crazy fence of rushes. A neglected gap was all the gate it had, and the first glance at the place was enough to let you see the flabby devil was running that show. White men with long staves in their hands appeared languidly from amongst the buildings, strolling up to take a look at me, and then retired out of sight somewhere. One of them, a stout, excitable chap with black moustaches, informed me with great volubility and many disgressions, as soon as I told him who I was, that my steamer was at the bottom of the river. I was thunderstruck. What, how, why? Oh, it was 'all right.' The 'manager himself' was there. All quite correct. 'Everybody had behaved splendidly! splendidly!'—'you must,' he said in agitation, 'go and see the general manager at once. He is waiting!'

"I did not see the real significance of that wreck at once. I fancy I see it now, but I am not sure—not at all. Certainly the affair was too stupid—when I think of it—to be altogether natural. Still . . . But at the moment it presented itself simply as a confounded nuisance. The steamer was sunk. They had started two days before in a sudden hurry up the river with the manager on board, in charge of some volunteer skipper, and before they had been out three hours they tore the bottom out of her on stones, and she sank near the south bank. I asked myself what I was to do there, now my boat was lost. As a matter of fact, I had plenty to do in fishing my command out of the river. I had to set about it the very next day. That, and the repairs when I brought the pieces to the station, took some months.

"My first interview with the manager was curious. He did not ask me to sit down after my twenty-mile walk that morning. He was commonplace in complexion, in feature, in manners, and in voice. He was of middle size and of ordinary build. His eyes, of the usual blue, were perhaps remarkably cold, and he certainly could make his glance fall on one as trenchant and heavy as an axe. But even at these times the rest of his person seemed to disclaim the intention. Otherwise there was only an indefinable, faint expression of his lips, something stealthy—a smile—not a smile—I remember it, but I can't explain. It was unconscious, this smile was, though just after he had said something it got intensified for an instant. It came at the end of his speeches like a seal applied on the words to make the meaning of the commonest phrase appear absolutely inscrutable. He was a common trader, from his youth up employed in these parts—nothing more. He was obeyed, yet he inspired neither love nor fear, nor even respect. He inspired uneasiness. That

---

[13] A British unit of weight equal to 14 pounds. Sixteen stone equals 224 pounds.
[14] Balked.

was it! Uneasiness. Not a definite mistrust—just uneasiness—nothing more. You have no idea how effective such a . . . a . . . faculty can be. He had no genius for organizing, for initiative, or for order even. That was evident in such things as the deplorable state of the station. He had no learning, and no intelligence. His position had come to him—why? Perhaps because he was never ill . . . He had served three terms of three years out there . . . Because triumphant health in the general rout of constitutions is a kind of power in itself. When he went home on leave he rioted on a large scale—pompously. Jack[15] ashore—with a difference—in externals only. This one could gather from his casual talk. He originated nothing, he could keep the routine going—that's all. But he was great. He was great by this little thing that it was impossible to tell what could control such a man. He never gave that secret away. Perhaps there was nothing within him. Such a suspicion made one pause—for out there there were no external checks. Once when various tropical diseases had laid low almost every 'agent' in the station, he was heard to say, 'Men who come out here should have no entrails.' He sealed the utterance with that smile of his, as though it had been a door opening into a darkness he had in his keeping. You fancied you had seen things—but the seal was on. When annoyed at meal-times by the constant quarrels of the white men about precedence, he ordered an immense round table to be made, for which a special house had to be built. This was the station's mess-room. Where he sat was the first place—the rest were nowhere. One felt this to be his unalterable conviction. He was neither civil nor uncivil. He was quiet. He allowed his 'boy'—an overfed young negro from the coast—to treat the white men, under his very eyes, with provoking insolence.

"He began to speak as soon as he saw me. I had been very long on the road. He could not wait. Had to start without me. The up-river stations had to be relieved. There had been so many delays already that he did not know who was dead and who was alive, and how they got on—and so on, and so on. He paid no attention to my explanations, and, playing with a stick of sealing-wax, repeated several times that the situation was 'very grave, very grave.' There were rumours that a very important station was in jeopardy, and its chief, Mr. Kurtz, was ill. Hoped it was not true. Mr. Kurtz was . . . I felt weary and irritable. Hang Kurtz, I thought. I interrupted him by saying I had heard of Mr. Kurtz on the coast. 'Ah! So they talk of him down there,' he murmured to himself. Then he began again, assuring me Mr. Kurtz was the best agent he had, an exceptional man, of the greatest importance to the Company; therefore I could understand his anxiety. He was, he said, 'very, very uneasy.' Certainly he fidgeted on his chair a good deal, exclaimed, 'Ah, Mr. Kurtz!' broke the stick of sealing-wax and seemed dumfounded by the accident. Next thing he wanted to know 'how long it would take to' . . . I interrupted him again. Being hungry, you know, and kept on my feet too, I was getting savage. 'How can I tell?' I said. 'I haven't even seen the wreck yet—some months, no doubt.' All this talk seemed to me so futile. 'Some months,' he said. 'Well, let us say three months before we can make a start. Yes. That ought to do the affair.' I flung out of his hut (he lived all alone in a clay hut with a sort of verandah) muttering to myself my opinion of him. He was a chattering idiot. Afterwards I took it back when it was borne in upon me startlingly with what extreme nicety he had estimated the time requisite for the 'affair.'

"I went to work the next day, turning, so to speak, my back on that station. In that way only it seemed to me I could keep my hold on the redeeming facts of

---

[15]Jack Tar; a sailor.

life. Still, one must look about sometimes; and then I saw this station, these men strolling aimlessly about in the sunshine of the yard. I asked myself sometimes what it all meant. They wandered here and there with their absurd long staves in their hands, like a lot of faithless pilgrims bewitched inside a rotten fence. The word 'ivory' rang in the air, was whispered, was sighed. You would think they were praying to it. A taint of imbecile rapacity blew through it all, like a whiff from some corpse. By Jove! I've never seen anything so unreal in my life. And outside, the silent wilderness surrounding this cleared speck on the earth struck me as something great and invincible, like evil or truth, waiting patiently for the passing away of this fantastic invasion.

"Oh, these months! Well, never mind. Various things happened. One evening a grass shed full of calico, cotton prints, beads, and I don't know what else, burst into a blaze so suddenly that you would have thought the earth had opened to let an avenging fire consume all that trash. I was smoking my pipe quietly by my dismantled steamer, and saw them all cutting capers in the light, with their arms lifted high, when the stout man with moustaches came tearing down to the river, a tin pail in his hand, assured me that everybody was 'behaving splendidly, splendidly,' dipped about a quart of water and tore back again. I noticed there was a hole in the bottom of his pail.

"I strolled up. There was no hurry. You see the thing had gone off like a box of matches. It had been hopeless from the very first. The flame had leaped high, driven everybody back, lighted up everything—and collapsed. The shed was already a heap of embers glowing fiercely. A nigger was being beaten near by. They said he had caused the fire in some way; be that as it may, he was screeching most horribly. I saw him, later, for several days, sitting in a bit of shade looking very sick and trying to recover himself: afterwards he arose and went out—and the wilderness without a sound took him into its bosom again. As I approached the glow from the dark I found myself at the back of two men, talking. I heard the name of Kurtz pronounced, then the words, 'take advantage of this unfortunate accident.' One of the men was the manager. I wished him a good evening. 'Did you ever see anything like it—eh? it is incredible,' he said, and walked off. The other man remained. He was a first-class agent, young, gentlemanly, a bit reserved, with a forked little beard and a hooked nose. He was stand-offish with the other agents, and they on their side said he was the manager's spy upon them. As to me, I had hardly ever spoken to him before. We got into talk, and by and by we strolled away from the hissing ruins. Then he asked me to his room, which was in the main building of the station. He struck a match, and I perceived that this young aristocrat had not only a silver-mounted dressing-case but also a whole candle all to himself. Just at that time the manager was the only man supposed to have any right to candles. Native mats covered the clay walls; a collection of spears, assegais,[16] shields, knives was hung up in trophies. The business entrusted to this fellow was the making of bricks—so I had been informed; but there wasn't a fragment of a brick anywhere in the station, and he had been there more than a year—waiting. It seems he could not make bricks without something, I don't know what—straw maybe. Anyways, it could not be found there, and as it was not likely to be sent from Europe, it did not appear clear to me what he was waiting for. An act of special creation perhaps.[17] However, they

---

[16] Javelins.

[17] Special creation was the belief, challenged by the evolutionists, that God created each species individually.

were all waiting—all the sixteen or twenty pilgrims of them—for something,
upon my word it did not seem an uncongenial occupation, from the way they took
it, though the only thing that ever came to them was disease—as far as I could see.
They beguiled the time by backbiting and intriguing against each other in a foolish
kind of way. There was an air of plotting about that station, but nothing came of it,
of course. It was as unreal as everything else—as the philanthropic pretence of the
whole concern, as their talk, as their government, as their show of work. The only
real feeling was a desire to get appointed to a trading-post where ivory was to be
had, so that they could earn percentages. They intrigued and slandered and hated
each other only on that account,—but as to effectually lifting a little finger—oh,
no. By heavens! there is something after all in the world allowing one man to steal a
horse while another must not look at a halter. Steal a horse straight out. Very well.
He has done it. Perhaps he can ride. But there is a way of looking at a halter that
would provoke the most charitable of saints into a kick.

"I had no idea why he wanted to be sociable, but as we chatted in there
it suddenly occurred to me the fellow was trying to get at something—in fact,
pumping me. He alluded constantly to Europe, to the people I was supposed to
know there—putting leading questions as to my acquaintances in the sepulchral
city, and so on. His little eyes glittered like mica discs—with curiosity—though he
tried to keep up a bit of superciliousness. At first I was astonished, but very soon I
became awfully curious to see what he would find out from me. I couldn't possibly
imagine what I had in me to make it worth his while. It was very pretty to see how
he baffled himself, for in truth my body was full only of chills, and my head had
nothing in it but that wretched steamboat business. It was evident he took me for a
perfectly shameless prevaricator. At last he got angry, and, to conceal a movement
of furious annoyance, he yawned. I rose. Then I noticed a small sketch in oils, on a
panel, representing a woman, draped and blindfolded, carrying a lighted torch. The
background was sombre—almost black. The movement of the woman was stately,
and the effect of the torch-light on the face was sinister.

"It arrested me, and he stood by civilly, holding an empty half-pint champagne
bottle (medical comforts) with the candle stuck in it. To my question he said Mr.
Kurtz had painted this—in this very station more than a year ago—while waiting
for means to go to his trading-post. 'Tell me, pray,' said I, 'who is this Mr. Kurtz?'

" 'The chief of the Inner Station,' he answered in a short tone, looking away.
'Much obliged,' I said, laughing. 'And you are the brickmaker of the Central
Station. Everyone knows that.' He was silent for a while. 'He is a prodigy,' he
said at last. 'He is an emissary of pity, and science, and progress, and devil knows
what else. We want,' he began to declaim suddenly, 'for the guidance of the cause
intrusted to us by Europe, so to speak, higher intelligence, wide sympathies, a
singleness of purpose.' 'Who says that?' I asked. 'Lots of them,' he replied. 'Some
even write that; and so *he* comes here, a special being, as you ought to know.'
'Why ought I to know?' I interrupted, really surprised. He paid no attention. 'Yes.
To-day he is chief of the best station, next year he will be assistant-manager, two
years more and . . . but I daresay you know what he will be in two years' time.
You are of the new gang—the gang of virtue. The same people who sent him
specially also recommended you. Oh, don't say no. I've my own eyes to trust.'
Light dawned upon me. My dear aunt's influential acquaintances were producing
an unexpected effect upon that young man. I nearly burst into a laugh. 'Do you
read the Company's confidential correspondence?' I asked. He hadn't a word to
say. It was great fun. 'When Mr. Kurtz,' I continued, severely, 'is General Manager,
you won't have the opportunity.'

"He blew the candle out suddenly, and we went outside. The moon had risen. Black figures strolled about listlessly, pouring water on the glow, whence proceeded a sound of hissing; steam ascended in the moonlight, the beaten nigger groaned somewhere. 'What a row the brute makes!' said the indefatigable man with the moustaches, appearing near us. 'Serve him right. Transgression—punishment— bang! Pitiless, pitiless. That's the only way. This will prevent all conflagrations for the future. I was just telling the manager . . .' He noticed my companion, and became crestfallen all at once. 'Not in bed yet,' he said, with a kind of servile heartiness; 'it's so natural. Ha! Danger—agitation.' He vanished. I went on to the river-side, and the other followed me. I heard a scathing murmur at my ear, 'Heap of muffs—go to.' The pilgrims could be seen in knots gesticulating, discussing. Several had still their staves in their hands. I verily believe they took these sticks to bed with them. Beyond the fence the forest stood up spectrally in the moonlight, and through the dim stir, through the faint sounds of that lamentable courtyard, the silence of the land went home to one's very heart—its mystery, its greatness, the amazing reality of its concealed life. The hurt nigger moaned feebly somewhere near by, and then fetched a deep sigh that made me mend my pace away from there. I felt a hand introducing itself under my arm. 'My dear sir,' said the fellow, 'I don't want to be misunderstood, and especially by you, who will see Mr. Kurtz long before I can have that pleasure. I wouldn't like him to get a false idea of my disposition. . . .'

"I let him run on, this papier-maché Mephistopheles, and it seemed to me that if I tried I could poke my forefinger through him, and would find nothing inside but a little loose dirt, maybe. He, don't you see, had been planning to be assistant-manager by and by under the present man, and I could see that the coming of that Kurtz had upset them both not a little. He talked precipitately, and I did not try to stop him. I had my shoulders against the wreck of my steamer, hauled up on the slope like a carcass of some big river animal. The smell of mud, of primeval mud, by Jove! was in my nostrils, the high stillness of primeval forest was before my eyes; there were shiny patches on the black creek. The moon had spread over everything a thin layer of silver—over the rank grass, over the mud, upon the wall of matted vegetation standing higher than the wall of a temple, over the great river I could see through a sombre gap glittering, glittering, as it flowed broadly by without a murmur. All this was great, expectant, mute, while the man jabbered about himself. I wondered whether the stillness on the face of the immensity looking at us two were meant as an appeal or as a menace. What were we who had strayed in here? Could we handle that dumb thing, or would it handle us? I felt how big, how confoundedly big, was that thing that couldn't talk, and perhaps was deaf as well. What was in there? I could see a little ivory coming out from there, and I had heard Mr. Kurtz was in there. I had heard enough about it, too—God knows! Yet somehow it didn't bring any image with it—no more than if I had been told an angel or a fiend was in there. I believed it in the same way one of you might believe there are inhabitants in the planet Mars. I knew once a Scotch sailmaker who was certain, dead sure, there were people in Mars. If you asked him for some idea how they looked and behaved, he would get shy and mutter something about 'walking on all-fours.' If you as much as smiled, he would—though a man of sixty—offer to fight you. I would not have gone so far as to fight for Kurtz, but I went for him near enough to a lie. You know I hate, detest, and can't bear a lie, not because I am straighter than the rest of us, but simply because it appalls me. There is a taint of death, a flavour of mortality in lies—which is exactly what I hate and detest in the world—what I want to forget. It makes me miserable and sick, like biting something rotten would do. Temperament, I suppose. Well, I went near enough to it by letting the young fool there believe anything he liked to imagine as to my influence in Europe. I became in an instant as much of a pretence as the rest of the bewitched pilgrims. This simply because I had a notion it somehow would be of help to that Kurtz whom at the time I did not see—you understand. He was just a word for me. I did not see the man in the name any more than you do. Do you see him? Do you see the story? Do you see anything? It seems to me I am trying to tell you a dream—making a vain attempt, because no relation of a dream can convey the dream-sensation, that commingling of absurdity, surprise, and bewilderment in a tremor of struggling revolt, that notion of being captured by the incredible which is of the very essence of dreams. . . ."

He was silent for a while.

". . . No, it is impossible; it is impossible to convey the life-sensation of any given epoch of one's existence—that which makes its truth, its meaning—its subtle and penetrating essence. It is impossible. We live as we dream—alone. . . ."

He paused again as if reflecting, then added—

"Of course in this you fellows see more than I could then. You see me, whom you know. . . ."

It had become so pitch dark that we listeners could hardly see one another. For a long time already he, sitting apart, had been no more to us than a voice. There was not a word from anybody. The others might have been asleep, but I was awake. I listened, I listened on the watch for the sentence, for the word, that would give me the clue to the faint uneasiness inspired by this narrative that seemed to shape itself without human lips in the heavy night-air of the river.

". . . Yes—I let him run on," Marlow began again, "and think what he pleased about the powers that were behind me. I did! And there was nothing behind me! There was nothing but that wretched, old, mangled steamboat I was leaning against, while he talked fluently about 'the necessity for every man to get on.' 'And when one comes out here, you conceive, it is not to gaze at the moon.' Mr. Kurtz was a 'universal genius,' but even a genius would find it easier to work with 'adequate tools—intelligent men.' He did not make bricks—why, there was a physical impossibility in the way—as I was well aware; and if he did secretarial work for the manager, it was because 'no sensible man rejects wantonly the confidence of his superiors.' Did I see it? I saw it. What more did I want? What I really wanted was rivets, by heaven! Rivets. To get on with the work—to stop the hole. Rivets I wanted. There were cases of them down at the coast—cases—piled up—burst—split! You kicked a loose rivet at every second step in that station yard on the hillside. Rivets had rolled into the grove of death. You could fill your pockets with rivets for the trouble of stooping down—and there wasn't one rivet to be found where it was wanted. We had plates that would do, but nothing to fasten them with. And every week the messenger, a lone negro, letter-bag on shoulder and staff in hand, left our station for the coast. And several times a week a coast caravan came in with trade goods—ghastly glazed calico that made you shudder only to look at it, glass beads value about a penny a quart, confounded spotted cotton handkerchiefs. And no rivets. Three carriers could have brought all that was wanted to set that steamboat afloat.

"He was becoming confidential now, but I fancy my unresponsive attitude must have exasperated him at last, for he judged it necessary to inform me he feared neither God nor devil, let alone any mere man. I said I could see that very well, but what I wanted was a certain quantity of rivets—and rivets were what really Mr. Kurtz wanted, if he had only known it. Now letters went to the coast every week. . . . 'My dear sir,' he cried, 'I write from dictation.' I demanded rivets. There was a way—for an intelligent man. He changed his manner; became very cold, and suddenly began to talk about a hippopotamus; wondered whether sleeping on board the steamer (I stuck to my salvage night and day) I wasn't disturbed. There was an old hippo that had the bad habit of getting out on the bank and roaming at night over the station grounds. The pilgrims used to turn out in a body and empty every rifle they could lay hands on at him. Some even had sat up o' nights for him. All this energy was wasted, though. 'That animal has a charmed life,' he said; 'but you can say this only of brutes in this country. No man—you apprehend me?—no man here bears a charmed life.' He stood there for a moment in the moonlight with his delicate hooked nose set a little askew, and his mica eyes glittering without a wink, then, with a curt Good-night, he strode off. I could see he was disturbed and considerably puzzled, which made me feel more hopeful than I had been for days. It was a great comfort to turn from that chap to my influential friend, the battered, twisted, ruined, tin-pot steamboat. I clambered on board. She rang under my feet like an empty Huntley & Palmer biscuit-tin kicked along a gutter; she was nothing so solid in make, and rather less pretty in shape, but I had expended enough hard work on her to make me love her. No influential friend would have served me better. She had given me a chance to come out a bit—to find out what I could do. No, I don't like work. I had rather laze about and think of all the fine things that can be done. I don't like work—no man does—but I like what is in the work,—the chance to find yourself. Your own reality—for yourself, not for others—what no other man can ever know. They can only see the mere show, and never can tell what it really means.

"I was not surprised to see somebody sitting aft, on the deck, with his legs dangling over the mud. You see I rather chummed with the few mechanics there were in that station, whom the other pilgrims naturally despised—on account of their imperfect manners, I suppose. This was the foreman—a boiler-maker by trade—a good worker. He was a lank, bony, yellow-faced man, with big intense eyes. His aspect was worried, and his head was as bald as the palm of my hand; but his hair in falling seemed to have stuck to his chin, and had prospered in the new locality, for his beard hung down to his waist. He was a widower with six young children (he had left them in charge of a sister of his to come out there), and the passion of his life was pigeon-flying. He was an enthusiast and a connoisseur. He would rave about pigeons. After work hours he used sometimes to come over from his hut for a talk about his children and his pigeons; at work, when he had to crawl in the mud under the bottom of the steamboat, he would tie up that beard of his in a kind of white serviette[18] he brought for the purpose. It had loops to go over his ears. In the evening he could be seen squatted on the bank rinsing that wrapper in the creek with great care, then spreading it solemnly on a bush to dry.

"I slapped him on the back and shouted, 'We shall have rivets!' He scrambled to his feet exclaiming, 'No! Rivets!' as though he couldn't believe his ears. Then in a low voice, 'You . . . eh?' I don't know why we behaved like lunatics. I put my finger to the side of my nose and nodded mysteriously. 'Good for you!' he cried, snapped his fingers above his head, lifting one foot. I tried a jig. We capered on the iron deck. A frightful clatter came out of that hulk, and the virgin forest on the other bank of the creek sent it back in a thundering roll upon the sleeping station. It

---

[18] A napkin.

must have made some of the pilgrims sit up in their hovels. A dark figure obscured the lighted doorway of the manager's hut, vanished, then, a second or so after, the doorway itself vanished, too. We stopped, and the silence driven away by the stamping of our feet flowed back again from the recesses of the land. The great wall of vegetation, an exuberant and entangled mass of trunks, branches, leaves, boughs, festoons, motionless in the moonlight, was like a rioting invasion of soundless life, a rolling wave of plants, piled up, crested, ready to topple over the creek, to sweep every little man of us out of his little existence. And it moved not. A deadened burst of mighty splashes and snorts reached us from afar, as though an ichthyosaurus had been taking a bath of glitter in the great river. 'After all,' said the boiler-maker in a reasonable tone, 'why shouldn't we get the rivets?' Why not, indeed! I did not know of any reason why we shouldn't. 'They'll come in three weeks,' I said, confidently.

"But they didn't. Instead of rivets there came an invasion, an infliction, a visitation. It came in sections during the next three weeks, each section headed by a donkey carrying a white man in new clothes and tan shoes, bowing from that elevation right and left to the impressed pilgrims. A quarrelsome band of footsore sulky niggers trod on the heels of the donkey; a lot of tents, camp-stools, tin boxes, white cases, brown bales would be shot down in the courtyard, and the air of mystery would deepen a little over the muddle of the station. Five such instalments came, with their absurd air of disorderly flight with the loot of innumerable outfit shops and provision stores, that, one would think, they were lugging, after a raid, into the wilderness for equitable division. It was an inextricable mess of things decent in themselves but that human folly made look like the spoils of thieving.

"This devoted band called itself the Eldorado Exploring Expedition, and I believe they were sworn to secrecy. Their talk, however, was the talk of sordid buccaneers: it was reckless without hardihood, greedy without audacity, and cruel without courage; there was not an atom of foresight or of serious intention in the whole batch of them, and they did not seem aware these things are wanted for the work of the world. To tear treasure out of the bowels of the land was their desire, with no more moral purpose at the back of it than there is in burglars breaking into a safe. Who paid the expenses of the noble enterprise I don't know; but the uncle of our manager was leader of that lot.

"In exterior he resembled a butcher in a poor neighbourhood, and his eyes had a look of sleepy cunning. He carried his fat paunch with ostentation on his short legs, and during the time his gang infested the station spoke to no one but his nephew. You could see these two roaming about all day long with their heads close together in an everlasting confab.

"I had given up worrying myself about the rivets. One's capacity for that kind of folly is more limited than you would suppose. I said Hang!—and let things slide. I had plenty of time for meditation, and now and then I would give some thought to Kurtz. I wasn't very interested in him. No. Still, I was curious to see whether this man, who had come out equipped with moral ideas of some sort, would climb to the top after all and how he would set about his work when there."

2

"One evening as I was lying flat on the deck of my steamboat, I heard voices approaching—and there were the nephew and the uncle strolling along the bank. I laid my head on my arm again, and had nearly lost myself in a doze, when somebody said in my ear, as it were: 'I am as harmless as a little child, but I don't like to be dictated to. Am I the manager—or am I not? I was ordered to send him there. It's incredible.' . . . I became aware that the two were standing on the shore alongside the forepart of the steamboat, just below my head. I did not move; it did not occur to me to move: I was sleepy. 'It *is* unpleasant,' grunted the uncle. 'He has asked the Administration to be sent there,' said the other, 'with the idea of showing what he could do; and I was instructed accordingly. Look at the influence that man must have. Is it not frightful?' They both agreed it was frightful, then made several bizarre remarks: 'Make rain and fine weather—one man—the Council—by the nose'—bits of absurd sentences that got the better of my drowsiness, so that I had pretty near the whole of my wits about me when the uncle said, 'The climate may do away with this difficulty for you. Is he alone there?' 'Yes,' answered the manager; 'he sent his assistant down the river with a note to me in these terms: "Clear this poor devil out of the country, and don't bother sending more of that sort. I had rather be alone than have the kind of men you can dispose of with me." It was more than a year ago. Can you imagine such impudence!' 'Anything since then?' asked the other, hoarsely. 'Ivory,' jerked the nephew; 'lots of it—prime sort—lots—most annoying, from him.' 'And with that?' questioned the heavy rumble. 'Invoice,' was the reply fired out, so to speak. Then silence. They had been talking about Kurtz.

"I was broad awake by this time, but, lying perfectly at ease, remained still, having no inducement to change my position. 'How did that ivory come all this way?' growled the elder man, who seemed very vexed. The other explained that it had come with a fleet of canoes in charge of an English half-caste clerk Kurtz had with him; that Kurtz had apparently intended to return himself, the station being by that time bare of goods and stores, but after coming three hundred miles, had suddenly decided to go back, which he started to do alone in a small dugout with four paddlers, leaving the half-caste to continue down the river with the ivory. The two fellows there seemed astounded at anybody attempting such a thing. They were at a loss for an adequate motive. As to me, I seemed to see Kurtz for the first time. It was a distinct glimpse: the dugout, four paddling savages, and the lone white man turning his back suddenly on the headquarters, on relief, on thoughts of home—perhaps; setting his face towards the depths of the wilderness, towards his empty and desolate station. I did not know the motive. Perhaps he was just simply a fine fellow who stuck to his work for its own sake. His name, you understand, had not been pronounced once. He was 'that man.' The half-caste, who, as far as I could see, had conducted a difficult trip with great prudence and pluck, was invariably alluded to as 'that scoundrel.' The 'scoundrel' had reported that the 'man' had been very ill—had recovered imperfectly. . . . The two below me moved away then a few paces, and strolled back and forth at some little distance. I heard: 'Military post—doctor—two hundred miles—quite alone now—unavoidable delays—nine months—no news—strange rumours.' They approached again, just as the manager was saying, 'No one, as far as I know, unless a species of wandering trader—a pestilential fellow, snapping ivory from the natives.' Who was it they were talking about now? I gathered in snatches that this was some man supposed to be in Kurtz's district, and of whom the manager did not approve. 'We will not be free from unfair competition till one of these fellows is hanged for an example,' he said. 'Certainly,' grunted the other; 'get him hanged! Why not? Anything—anything can be done in this country. That's what I say; nobody here, you understand, *here,* can endanger your position. And why? You stand the climate—you outlast them all. The danger is in Europe; but there before I left I took care to——' They moved off and whispered, then their voices rose again. 'The extraordinary series of delays is not my fault. I did my best.' The fat man sighed. 'Very sad.' 'And the pestiferous absurdity of his talk,' continued the other; 'he bothered me enough when he was here. "Each station should be like a beacon on the road towards better things, a centre for trade of course, but also for humanizing, improving, instructing." Conceive you—that ass! And he wants to be manager! No, it's——' Here he got choked by excessive indignation, and I lifted my head the least bit. I was surprised to see how near they were—right under me. I could have spat upon their hats. They were looking on the ground, absorbed in thought. The manager was switching his leg with a slender twig: his sagacious relative lifted his head. 'You have been well since you came out this time?' he asked. The other gave a start. 'Who? I? Oh! Like a charm—like a charm. But the rest—oh, my goodness! All sick. They die so quick, too, that I haven't the time to send them out of the country—it's incredible!' 'H'm. Just so,' grunted the uncle. 'Ah! my boy, trust to this—I say, trust to this.' I saw him extend his short flipper of an arm for a gesture that took in the forest, the creek, the mud, the river,—seemed to beckon with a dishonouring flourish before the sunlit face of the land a treacherous appeal to the lurking death, to the hidden evil, to the profound darkness of its heart. It was so startling that I leaped to my feet and looked back at the edge of the forest, as though I had expected an answer of some sort to that black display of confidence. You know the foolish notions that come to one sometimes. The high stillness confronted these two figures with its ominous patience, waiting for the passing away of a fantastic invasion.

"They swore aloud together—out of sheer fright, I believe—then pretending not to know anything of my existence, turned back to the station. The sun was low; and leaning forward side by side, they seemed to be tugging painfully uphill their two ridiculous shadows of unequal length, that trailed behind them slowly over the tall grass without bending a single blade.

"In a few days the Eldorado Expedition went into the patient wilderness, that closed upon it as the sea closes over a diver. Long afterwards the news came that all the donkeys were dead. I know nothing as to the fate of the less valuable animals. They, no doubt, like the rest of us, found what they deserved. I did not inquire. I was then rather excited at the prospect of meeting Kurtz very soon. When I say very soon I mean it comparatively. It was just two months from the day we left the creek when we came to the bank below Kurtz's station.

"Going up that river was like travelling back to the earliest beginnings of the world, when vegetation rioted on the earth and the big trees were kings. An empty stream, a great silence, an impenetrable forest. The air was warm, thick, heavy, sluggish. There was no joy in the brilliance of sunshine. The long stretches of the waterway ran on, deserted, into the gloom of overshadowed distances. On silvery sandbanks hippos and alligators sunned themselves side by side. The broadening waters flowed through a mob of wooded islands; you lost your way on that river as you would in a desert, and butted all day long against shoals, trying to find the channel, till you thought yourself bewitched and cut off for ever from everything you had known once—somewhere—far away—in another existence perhaps. There were moments when one's past came back to one, as it will sometimes when you have not a moment to spare to yourself; but it came in the shape of an unrestful and noisy dream, remembered with wonder amongst the overwhelming realities of this strange world of plants, and water, and silence. And this stillness of life did not in the least resemble a peace. It was the stillness of an implacable force brooding over an inscrutable intention. It looked at you with a vengeful aspect. I got used to it afterwards; I did not see it any more; I had no time. I had to keep guessing at the channel; I had to discern, mostly by inspiration, the signs of hidden banks;

I watched for sunken stones; I was learning to clap my teeth smartly before my heart flew out, when I shaved by a fluke some infernal sly old snag that would have ripped the life out of the tin-pot steamboat and drowned all the pilgrims; I had to keep a look-out for the signs of dead wood we could cut up in the night for next day's steaming. When you have to attend to things of that sort, to the mere incidents of the surface, the reality—the reality, I tell you—fades. The inner truth is hidden—luckily, luckily. But I felt it all the same; I felt often its mysterious stillness watching me at my monkey tricks, just as it watches you fellows performing on your respective tight-ropes for—what is it? half-a-crown a tumble——"

"Try to be civil, Marlow," growled a voice, and I knew there was at least one listener awake besides myself.

"I beg your pardon. I forgot the heartache which makes up the rest of the price. And indeed what does the price matter, if the trick be well done? You do your tricks very well. And I didn't do badly either, since I managed not to sink that steamboat on my first trip. It's a wonder to me yet. Imagine a blindfolded man set to drive a van over a bad road. I sweated and shivered over that business considerably, I can tell you. After all, for a seaman, to scrape the bottom of the thing that's supposed to float all the time under his care is the unpardonable sin. No one may know of it, but you never forget the thump—eh? A blow on the very heart. You remember it, you dream of it, you wake up at night and think of it—years after—and go hot and cold all over. I don't pretend to say that steamboat floated all the time. More than once she had to wade for a bit, with twenty cannibals splashing around and pushing. We had enlisted some of these chaps on the way for a crew. Fine fellows—cannibals—in their place. They were men one could work with, and I am grateful to them. And, after all, they did not eat each other before my face: they had brought along a provision of hippo-meat which went rotten, and made the mystery of the wilderness stink in my nostrils. Phoo! I can sniff it now. I had the manager on board and three or four pilgrims with their staves—all complete. Sometimes we came upon a station close by the bank, clinging to the skirts of the unknown, and the white men rushing out of a tumble-down hovel, with great gestures of joy and surprise and welcome, seemed very strange—had the appearance of being held there captive by a spell. The word ivory would ring in the air for a while—and on we went again into the silence, along empty reaches, round the still bends, between the high walls of our winding way, reverberating in hollow claps the ponderous beat of the stern-wheel. Trees, trees, millions of trees, massive, immense, running up high; and at their foot, hugging the bank against the stream, crept the little begrimed steamboat, like a sluggish beetle crawling on the floor of a lofty portico. It made you feel very small, very lost, and yet it was not altogether depressing, that feeling. After all, if you were small, the grimy beetle crawled on—which was just what you wanted it to do. Where the pilgrims imagined it crawled to I don't know. To some place where they expected to get something, I bet! For me it crawled towards Kurtz—exclusively; but when the steam-pipes started leaking we crawled very slow. The reaches opened before us and closed behind, as if the forest had stepped leisurely across the water to bar the way for our return. We penetrated deeper and deeper into the heart of darkness. It was very quiet there. At night sometimes the roll of drums behind the curtain of trees would run up the river and remain sustained faintly, as if hovering in the air high over our heads, till the first break of day. Whether it meant war, peace, or prayer we could not tell. The dawns were heralded by the descent of a chill stillness; the wood-cutters slept, their fires burned low; the snapping of a twig would make you start. We were wanderers on a prehistoric earth, on an earth that wore the aspect of an unknown planet.

We could have fancied ourselves the first of men taking possession of an accursed inheritance, to be subdued at the cost of profound anguish and of excessive toil. But suddenly, as we struggled round a bend, there would be a glimpse of rush walls, of peaked grass-roofs, a burst of yells, a whirl of black limbs, a mass of hands clapping, of feet stamping, of bodies swaying, of eyes rolling, under the droop of heavy and motionless foliage. The steamer toiled along slowly on the edge of a black and incomprehensible frenzy. The prehistoric man was cursing us, praying to us, welcoming us—who could tell? We were cut off from the comprehension of our surroundings; we glided past like phantoms, wondering and secretly appalled, as sane men would be before an enthusiastic outbreak in a madhouse. We could not understand because we were too far and could not remember, because we were travelling in the night of first ages, of those ages that are gone, leaving hardly a sign—and no memories.

"The earth seemed unearthly. We are accustomed to look upon the shackled form of a conquered monster, but there—there you could look at a thing monstrous and free. It was unearthly, and the men were—— No, they were not inhuman. Well, you know, that was the worst of it—this suspicion of their not being inhuman. It would come slowly to one. They howled and leaped, and spun, and made horrid faces; but what thrilled you was just the thought of their humanity—like yours—the thought of your remote kinship with this wild and passionate uproar. Ugly. Yes, it was ugly enough; but if you were man enough you would admit to yourself that there was in you just the faintest trace of a response to the terrible frankness of that noise, a dim suspicion of there being a meaning in it which you—you so remote from the night of first ages—could comprehend. And why not? The mind of man is capable of anything—because everything is in it, all the past as well as all the future. What was there after all? Joy, fear, sorrow, devotion, valour, rage—who can tell?—but truth—truth stripped of its cloak of time. Let the fool gape and shudder—the man knows, and can look on without a wink. But he must at least be as much of a man as these on the shore. He must meet that truth with his own true stuff—with his own inborn strength. Principles won't do. Acquisitions, clothes, pretty rags—rags that would fly off at the first good shake. No; you want a deliberate belief. An appeal to me in this fiendish row—is there? Very well; I hear; I admit, but I have a voice, too, and for good or evil mine is the speech that cannot be silenced. Of course, a fool, what with sheer fright and fine sentiments, is always safe. Who's that grunting? You wonder I didn't go ashore for a howl and a dance? Well, no—I didn't. Fine sentiments, you say? Fine sentiments, be hanged! I had no time. I had to mess about with white-lead and strips of woollen blanket helping to put bandages on those leaky steam-pipes—I tell you. I had to watch the steering, and circumvent those snags, and get the tin-pot along by hook or by crook. There was surface-truth enough in these things to save a wiser man. And between whiles I had to look after the savage who was fireman. He was an improved specimen; he could fire up a vertical boiler. He was there below me, and, upon my word, to look at him was as edifying as seeing a dog in a parody of breeches and a feather hat, walking on his hind-legs. A few months of training had done for that really fine chap. He squinted at the steam-gauge and at the water-gauge with an evident effort of intrepidity—and he had filed teeth, too, the poor devil, and the wool of his pate shaved into queer patterns, and three ornamental scars on each of his cheeks. He ought to have been clapping his hands and stamping his feet on the bank, instead of which he was hard at work, a thrall to strange witchcraft, full of improving knowledge. He was useful because he had been instructed; and what he knew was this—that should the water in that transparent thing disappear, the evil spirit inside the boiler would get angry through the greatness of his thirst, and take a terrible vengeance. So he sweated and fired up and watched the glass fearfully (with an impromptu charm, made of rags, tied to his arm, and a piece of polished bone, as big as a watch, stuck flat-ways through his lower lip), while the wooded banks slipped past us slowly, the short noise was left behind, the interminable miles of silence—and we crept on, towards Kurtz. But the snags were thick, the water was treacherous and shallow, the boiler seemed indeed to have a sulky devil in it, and thus neither that fireman nor I had any time to peer into our creepy thoughts.

"Some fifty miles below the Inner Station we came upon a hut of reeds, an inclined and melancholy pole, with the unrecognizable tatters of what had been a flag of some sort flying from it, and a neatly stacked wood-pile. This was unexpected. We came to the bank, and on the stack of firewood found a flat piece of board with some faded pencil-writing on it. When deciphered it said: 'Wood for you. Hurry up. Approach cautiously.' There was a signature, but it was illegible—not Kurtz—a much longer word. 'Hurry up.' Where? Up the river? 'Approach cautiously.' We had not done so. But the warning could not have been meant for the place where it could be only found after approach. Something was wrong above. But what—and how much? That was the question. We commented adversely upon the imbecility of that telegraphic style. The bush around said nothing, and would not let us look very far, either. A torn curtain of red twill hung in the doorway of the hut, and flapped sadly in our faces. The dwelling was dismantled; but we could see a white man had lived there not very long ago. There remained a rude table—a plank on two posts; a heap of rubbish reposed in a dark corner, and by the door I picked up a book. It had lost its covers, and the pages had been thumbed into a state of extremely dirty softness; but the back had been lovingly stitched afresh with white cotton thread, which looked clean yet. It was an extraordinary find. Its title was, *An Inquiry into some Points of Seamanship,* by a man Towser, Towson—some such name—Master in his Majesty's Navy. The matter looked dreary reading enough, with illustrative diagrams and repulsive tables of figures, and the copy was sixty years old. I handled this amazing antiquity with the greatest possible tenderness, lest it should dissolve in my hands. Within, Towson or Towser was inquiring earnestly into the breaking strain of ships' chains and tackle, and other such matters. Not a very enthralling book; but at the first glance you could see there a singleness of intention, an honest concern for the right way of going to work, which made these humble pages, thought out so many years ago, luminous with another than a professional light. The simple old sailor, with his talk of chains and purchases,[19] made me forget the jungle and the pilgrims in a delicious sensation of having come upon something unmistakably real. Such a book being there was wonderful enough; but still more astounding were the notes pencilled in the margin, and plainly referring to the text. I couldn't believe my eyes! They were in cipher! Yes, it looked like cipher. Fancy a man lugging with him a book of that description into this nowhere and studying it—and making notes—in cipher at that! It was an extravagant mystery.

"I had been dimly aware for some time of a worrying noise, and when I lifted my eyes I saw the wood-pile was gone, and the manager, aided by all the pilgrims, was shouting at me from the river-side. I slipped the book into my pocket. I assure you to leave off reading was like tearing myself away from the shelter of an old and solid friendship.

"I started the lame engine ahead. 'It must be this miserable trader—this intruder,' exclaimed the manager, looking back malevolently at the place we had left. 'He

---

[19]Tackles or levers or similar mechanical devices.

must be English,' I said. 'It will not save him from getting into trouble if he is not careful,' muttered the manager darkly. I observed with assumed innocence that no man was safe from trouble in this world.

"The current was more rapid now, the steamer seemed at her last gasp, the stern-wheel flopped languidly, and I caught myself listening on tiptoe for the next beat of the boat, for in sober truth I expected the wretched thing to give up every moment. It was like watching the last flickers of a life. But still we crawled. Sometimes I would pick out a tree a little way ahead to measure our progress towards Kurtz by, but I lost it invariably before we got abreast. To keep the eyes so long on one thing was too much for human patience. The manager displayed a beautiful resignation. I fretted and fumed and took to arguing with myself whether or no I would talk openly with Kurtz; but before I could come to any conclusion it occurred to me that my speech or my silence, indeed any action of mine, would be a mere futility. What did it matter what any one knew or ignored? What did it matter who was manager? One gets sometimes such a flash of insight. The essentials of this affair lay deep under the surface, beyond my reach, and beyond my power of meddling.

"Towards the evening of the second day we judged ourselves about eight miles from Kurtz's station. I wanted to push on; but the manager looked grave, and told me the navigation up there was so dangerous that it would be advisable, the sun being very low already, to wait where we were till next morning. Moreover, he pointed out that if the warning to approach cautiously were to be followed, we must approach in daylight—not at dusk, or in the dark. This was sensible enough. Eight miles meant nearly three hours' steaming for us, and I could also see suspicious ripples at the upper end of the reach. Nevertheless, I was annoyed beyond expression at the delay, and most unreasonably, too, since one night more could not matter much after so many months. As we had plenty of wood, and caution was the word, I brought up in the middle of the stream. The reach was narrow, straight, with high sides like a railway cutting. The dusk came gliding into it long before the sun had set. The current ran smooth and swift, but a dumb immobility sat on the banks. The living trees, lashed together by the creepers and every living bush of the undergrowth, might have been changed into stone, even to the slenderest twig, to the lightest leaf. It was not sleep—it seemed unnatural, like a state of trance. Not the faintest sound of any kind could be heard. You looked on amazed, and began to suspect yourself of being deaf—then the night came suddenly, and struck you blind as well. About three in the morning some large fish leaped, and the loud splash made me jump as though a gun had been fired. When the sun rose there was a white fog, very warm and clammy, and more blinding than the night. It did not shift or drive; it was just there, standing all round you like something solid. At eight or nine, perhaps, it lifted as a shutter lifts. We had a glimpse of the towering multitude of trees, of the immense matted jungle, with the blazing little ball of the sun hanging over it—all perfectly still—and then the white shutter came down again, smoothly, as if sliding in greased grooves. I ordered the chain, which we had begun to heave in, to be paid out again. Before it stopped running with a muffled rattle, a cry, a very loud cry, as of infinite desolation, soared slowly in the opaque air. It ceased. A complaining clamour, modulated in savage discords, filled our ears. The sheer unexpectedness of it made my hair stir under my cap. I don't know how it struck the others: to me it seemed as though the mist itself had screamed, so suddenly, and apparently from all sides at once, did this tumultuous and mournful uproar arise. It culminated in a hurried outbreak of almost intolerably excessive shrieking, which stopped short, leaving us stiffened in a variety of silly attitudes, and obstinately listening to the nearly as appalling and excessive silence. 'Good God! What is the meaning——' stammered at my elbow one of the pilgrims,—a little fat man, with sandy hair and red whiskers, who wore side-spring boots, and pink pyjamas tucked into his socks. Two others remained open-mouthed a whole minute, then dashed into the little cabin, to rush out incontinently and stand darting scared glances, with Winchesters at 'ready' in their hands. What we could see was just the steamer we were on, her outlines blurred as though she had been on the point of dissolving, and a misty strip of water, perhaps two feet broad, around her—and that was all. The rest of the world was nowhere, as far as our eyes and ears were concerned. Just nowhere. Gone, disappeared; swept off without leaving a whisper or a shadow behind.

"I went forward, and ordered the chain to be hauled in short, so as to be ready to trip the anchor and move the steamboat at once if necessary. 'Will they attack?' whispered an awed voice. 'We will be all butchered in this fog,' murmured another. The faces twitched with the strain, the hands trembled slightly, the eyes forgot to wink. It was very curious to see the contrast of expressions of the white men and of the black fellows of our crew, who were as much strangers to that part of the river as we, though their homes were only eight hundred miles away. The whites, of course greatly discomposed, had besides a curious look of being painfully shocked by such an outrageous row. The others had an alert, naturally interested expression; but their faces were essentially quiet, even those of the one or two who grinned as they hauled at the chain. Several exchanged short, grunting phrases, which seemed to settle the matter to their satisfaction. Their headman, a young, broad-chested black, severely draped in dark-blue fringed cloths, with fierce nostrils and his hair all done up artfully in oily ringlets, stood near me. 'Aha!' I said, just for good fellowship's sake. 'Catch 'im,' he snapped, with a bloodshot widening of his eyes and a flash of sharp teeth—'catch 'im. Give 'im to us.' 'To you, eh?' I asked; 'what would you do with them?' 'Eat 'im!' he said, curtly, and, leaning his elbow on the rail, looked out into the fog in a dignified and profoundly pensive attitude. I would no doubt have been properly horrified, had it not occurred to me that he and his chaps must be very hungry: that they must have been growing increasingly hungry for at least this month past. They had been engaged for six months (I don't think a single one of them had any clear idea of time, as we at the end of countless ages have. They still belonged to the beginnings of time—had no inherited experience to teach them as it were), and of course, as long as there was a piece of paper written over in accordance with some farcical law or other made down the river, it didn't enter anybody's head to trouble how they would live. Certainly they had brought with them some rotten hippo-meat, which couldn't have lasted very long, anyway, even if the pilgrims hadn't, in the midst of a shocking hullabaloo, thrown a considerable quantity of it overboard. It looked like a high-handed proceeding; but it was really a case of legitimate self-defence. You can't breathe dead hippo waking, sleeping, and eating, and at the same time keep your precarious grip on existence. Besides that, they had given them every week three pieces of brass wire, each about nine inches long; and the theory was they were to buy their provisions with that currency in river-side villages. You can see how *that* worked. There were either no villages, or the people were hostile, or the director, who like the rest of us fed out of tins, with an occasional old he-goat thrown in, didn't want to stop the steamer for some more or less recondite reason. So, unless they swallowed the wire itself, or made loops of it to snare the fishes with, I don't see what good their extravagant salary could be to them. I must say it was paid with a regularity worthy of a large and honourable trading company. For the rest, the only thing to eat—though it didn't look eatable in the least—I saw in their possession was a few lumps of some stuff like half-cooked dough, of a dirty lavender colour, they kept wrapped in leaves, and now and then swallowed a piece of, but so small that it seemed done more for the looks of the thing than for any serious purpose of sustenance. Why in the name of all the gnawing devils of hunger they didn't go for us—they were thirty to five—and have a good tuck-in[20] for once, amazes me now when I think of it. They were big powerful men, with not much capacity to weigh the consequences, with courage, with strength, even yet, though their skins were no longer glossy and their muscles no longer hard. And I saw that something restraining, one of those human secrets that baffle probability, had come into play there. I looked at them with a swift quickening of interest—not because it occurred to me I might be eaten by them before very long, though I own to you that just then I perceived—in a new light, as it were—how unwholesome the pilgrims looked, and I hoped, yes I positively hoped, that my aspect was not so—what shall I say?—so—unappetizing: a touch of fantastic vanity which fitted well with the dream-sensation that pervaded all my days at that time. Perhaps I had a little fever, too. One can't live with one's finger everlastingly on one's pulse. I had often 'a little fever,' or a little touch of other things—the playful paw-strokes of the wilderness, the preliminary trifling before the more serious onslaught which came in due course. Yes; I looked at them as you would on any human being, with a curiosity of their impulses, motives, capacities, weaknesses, when brought to the test of an inexorable physical necessity. Restraint! What possible restraint? Was it superstition, disgust, patience, fear—or some kind of primitive honour? No fear can stand up to hunger, no patience can wear it out, disgust simply does not exist where hunger is; and as to superstition, beliefs, and what you may call principles, they are less than chaff in a breeze. Don't you know the devilry of lingering starvation, its exasperating torment, its black thoughts, its sombre and brooding ferocity? Well, I do. It takes a man all his inborn strength to fight hunger properly. It's really easier to face bereavement, dishonour, and the perdition of one's soul—than this kind of prolonged hunger. Sad, but true. And these chaps, too, had no earthly reason for any kind of scruple. Restraint! I would just as soon have expected restraint from a hyena prowling amongst the corpses of a battlefield. But there was the fact facing me—the fact dazzling, to be seen, like the foam on the depths of the sea, like a ripple on an unfathomable enigma, a mystery greater—when I thought of it—than the curious, inexplicable note of desperate grief in this savage clamour that had swept by us on the river-bank, behind the blind whiteness of the fog.

"Two pilgrims were quarrelling in hurried whispers as to which bank. 'Left.' 'No, no; how can you? Right, right, of course.' 'It is very serious,' said the manager's voice behind me; 'I would be desolated if anything should happen to Mr. Kurtz before we came up.' I looked at him, and had not the slightest doubt he was sincere. He was just the kind of man who would wish to preserve appearances. That was his restraint. But when he muttered something about going on at once, I did not even take the trouble to answer him. I knew, and he knew, that it was impossible. Were we to let go our hold of the bottom, we would be absolutely in the air—in space. We wouldn't be able to tell where we were going to—whether up or down stream, or across—till we fetched against one bank or the other,—and then we wouldn't know at first which it was. Of course I made no move. I had no mind for a smash-up. You couldn't imagine a more deadly place for a shipwreck. Whether drowned at once or not, we were sure to perish speedily in one way or another. 'I

---

[20] A hearty meal.

authorize you to take all the risks,' he said, after a short silence. 'I refuse to take any,' I said, shortly; which was just the answer he expected, though its tone might have surprised him. 'Well, I must defer to your judgment. You are captain,' he said, with marked civility. I turned my shoulder to him in sign of my appreciation, and looked into the fog. How long would it last? It was the most hopeless look-out. The approach to this Kurtz grubbing for ivory in the wretched bush was beset by as many dangers as though he had been an enchanted princess sleeping in a fabulous castle. 'Will they attack, do you think?' asked the manager, in a confidential tone.

"I did not think they would attack, for several obvious reasons. The thick fog was one. If they left the bank in their canoes they would get lost in it, as we would be if we attempted to move. Still, I had also judged the jungle of both banks quite impenetrable—and yet eyes were in it, eyes that had seen us. The river-side bushes were certainly very thick; but the undergrowth behind was evidently penetrable. However, during the short lift I had seen no canoes anywhere in the reach— certainly not abreast of the steamer. But what made the idea of attack inconceivable to me was the nature of the noise—of the cries we had heard. They had not the fierce character boding immediate hostile intention. Unexpected, wild, and violent as they had been, they had given me an irresistible impression of sorrow. The glimpse of the steamboat had for some reason filled those savages with unrestrained grief. The danger, if any, I expounded, was from our proximity to a great human passion let loose. Even extreme grief may ultimately vent itself in violence—but more generally takes the form of apathy. . . .

"You should have seen the pilgrims stare! They had no heart to grin, or even to revile me: but I believe they thought me gone mad—with fright, maybe. I delivered a regular lecture. My dear boys, it was no good bothering. Keep a look-out? Well, you may guess I watched the fog for the signs of lifting as a cat watches a mouse; but for anything else our eyes were of no more use to us than if we had been buried miles deep in a heap of cotton-wool. It felt like it, too—choking, warm, stifling. Besides, all I said, though it sounded extravagant, was absolutely true to fact. What we afterwards alluded to as an attack was really an attempt at repulse. The action was very far from being aggressive—it was not even defensive, in the usual sense: it was undertaken under the stress of desperation, and in its essence was purely protective.

"It developed itself, I should say, two hours after the fog lifted, and its com-mencement was at a spot, roughly speaking, about a mile and a half below Kurtz's station. We had just floundered and flopped round a bend, when I saw an islet, a mere grassy hummock of bright green, in the middle of the stream. It was the only thing of the kind; but as we opened the reach more, I perceived it was the head of a long sandbank, or rather of a chain of shallow patches stretching down the middle of the river. They were discoloured, just awash, and the whole lot was seen just under the water, exactly as a man's backbone is seen running down the middle of his back under the skin. Now, as far as I did see, I could go to the right or to the left of this. I didn't know either channel, of course. The banks looked pretty well alike, the depth appeared the same; but as I had been informed the station was on the west side, I naturally headed for the western passage.

"No sooner had we fairly entered it than I became aware it was much narrower than I had supposed. To the left of us there was the long uninterrupted shoal, and to the right a high, steep bank heavily overgrown with bushes. Above the bush the trees stood in serried ranks. The twigs overhung the current thickly, and from distance to distance a large limb of some tree projected rigidly over the stream. It was then well on in the afternoon, the face of the forest was gloomy, and a broad strip of shadow had already fallen on the water. In this shadow we steamed up—very slowly, as you may imagine. I sheered her well inshore—the water being deepest near the bank, as the sounding-pole informed me.

"One of my hungry and forbearing friends was sounding in the bows just below me. This steamboat was exactly like a decked scow. On the deck, there were two little teak-wood houses, with doors and windows. The boiler was in the fore-end, and the machinery right astern. Over the whole there was a light roof, supported on stanchions. The funnel projected through that roof, and in front of the funnel a small cabin built of light planks served for a pilot-house. It contained a couch, two camp-stools, a loaded Martini-Henry[21] leaning in one corner, a tiny table, and the steering-wheel. It had a wide door in front and a broad shutter at each side. All these were always thrown open, of course. I spent my days perched up there on the extreme fore-end of that roof, before the door. At night I slept, or tried to, on the couch. An athletic black belonging to some coast tribe, and educated by my poor predecessor, was the helmsman. He sported a pair of brass earrings, wore a blue cloth wrapper from the waist to the ankles, and thought all the world of himself. He was the most unstable kind of fool I had ever seen. He steered with no end of a swagger while you were by; but if he lost sight of you, he became instantly the prey of an abject funk, and would let that cripple of a steamboat get the upper hand of him in a minute.

"I was looking down at the sounding-pole, and feeling much annoyed to see at each try a little more of it stick out of that river, when I saw my poleman give up the business suddenly, and stretch himself flat on the deck, without even taking the trouble to haul his pole in. He kept hold on it though, and it trailed in the water. At the same time the fireman, whom I could also see below me, sat down abruptly before his furnace and ducked his head. I was amazed. Then I had to look at the river mighty quick, because there was a snag in the fairway. Sticks, little sticks, were flying about—thick: they were whizzing before my nose, dropping below me, striking behind me against my pilot-house. All this time the river, the shore, the woods, were very quiet—perfectly quiet. I could only hear the heavy splashing thump of the stern-wheel and the patter of these things. We cleared the snag clumsily. Arrows, by Jove! We were being shot at! I stepped in quickly to close the shutter on the land-side. That fool-helmsman, his hands on the spokes, was lifting his knees high, stamping his feet, champing his mouth, like a reined-in horse. Confound him! And we were staggering within ten feet of the bank. I had to lean right out to swing the heavy shutter, and I saw a face amongst the leaves on the level with my own, looking at me very fierce and steady; and then suddenly, as though a veil had been removed from my eyes, I made out, deep in the tangled gloom, naked breasts, arms, legs, glaring eyes,—the bush was swarming with human limbs in movement, glistening, of bronze colour. The twigs shook, swayed, and rustled, the arrows flew out of them, and then the shutter came to. 'Steer her straight,' I said to the helmsman. He held his head rigid, face forward; but his eyes rolled, he kept on lifting and setting down his feet gently, his mouth foamed a little. 'Keep quiet!' I said in a fury. I might just as well have ordered a tree not to sway in the wind. I darted out. Below me there was a great scuffle of feet on the iron deck; confused exclamations; a voice screamed, 'Can you turn back?' I caught sight of a V-shaped ripple on the water ahead. What? Another snag! A fusillade burst out under my feet. The pilgrims had opened with their Winchesters, and were simply squirting lead into that bush. A deuce of a lot of smoke came up and drove slowly

---

[21] A powerful rifle.

forward. I swore at it. Now I couldn't see the ripple or the snag either. I stood in the doorway, peering, and the arrows came in swarms. They might have been poisoned, but they looked as though they wouldn't kill a cat. The bush began to howl. Our wood-cutters raised a warlike whoop; the report of a rifle just at my back deafened me. I glanced over my shoulder, and the pilot-house was yet full of noise and smoke when I made a dash at the wheel. The fool-nigger had dropped everything, to throw the shutter open and let off that Martini-Henry. He stood before the wide opening, glaring, and I yelled at him to come back, while I straightened the sudden twist out of that steamboat. There was no room to turn even if I had wanted to, the snag was somewhere very near ahead in that confounded smoke, there was no time to lose, so I just crowded her into the bank—right into the bank, where I knew the water was deep.

"We tore slowly along the overhanging bushes in a whirl of broken twigs and flying leaves. The fusillade below stopped short, as I had foreseen it would when the squirts got empty. I threw my head back to a glinting whizz that traversed the pilot-house, in at one shutter-hole and out at the other. Looking past that mad helmsman, who was shaking the empty rifle and yelling at the shore, I saw vague forms of men running bent double, leaping, gliding, distinct, incomplete, evanescent. Something big appeared in the air before the shutter, the rifle went overboard, and the man stepped back swiftly, looked at me over his shoulder in an extraordinary, profound, familiar manner, and fell upon my feet. The side of his head hit the wheel twice, and the end of what appeared a long cane clattered round and knocked over a little camp-stool. It looked as though after wrenching that thing from somebody ashore he had lost his balance in the effort. The thin smoke had blown away, we were clear of the snag, and looking ahead I could see that in another hundred yards or so I would be free to sheer off, away from the bank; but my feet felt so very warm and wet that I had to look down. The man had rolled on his back and stared straight up at me; both his hands clutched that cane. It was the shaft of a spear that, either thrown or lunged through the opening, had caught him in the side just below the ribs; the blade had gone in out of sight, after making a frightful gash; my shoes were full; a pool of blood lay very still, gleaming dark-red under the wheel; his eyes shone with an amazing lustre. The fusillade burst out again. He looked at me anxiously, gripping the spear like something precious, with an air of being afraid I would try to take it away from him. I had to make an effort to free my eyes from his gaze and attend to the steering. With one hand I felt above my head for the line of the steam whistle, and jerked out screech after screech hurriedly. The tumult of angry and warlike yells was checked instantly, and then from the depths of the woods went out such a tremulous and prolonged wail of mournful fear and utter despair as may be imagined to follow the flight of the last hope from the earth. There was a great commotion in the bush; the shower of arrows stopped, a few dropping shots rang out sharply—then silence, in which the languid beat of the stern-wheel came plainly to my ears. I put the helm hard a-starboard at the moment when the pilgrim in pink pyjamas, very hot and agitated, appeared in the doorway. 'The manager sends me——' he began in an official tone, and stopped short. 'Good God!' he said, glaring at the wounded man.

"We two whites stood over him, and his lustrous and inquiring glance enveloped us both. I declare it looked as though he would presently put to us some question in an understandable language; but he died without uttering a sound, without moving a limb, without twitching a muscle. Only in the very last moment, as though in response to some sign we could not see, to some whisper we could not hear, he frowned heavily, and that frown gave to his black death-mask an inconceivably sombre, brooding, and menacing expression. The lustre of inquiring glance faded swiftly into vacant glassiness. 'Can you steer?' I asked the agent eagerly. He looked very dubious; but I made a grab at his arm, and he understood at once I meant him to steer whether or no. To tell you the truth, I was morbidly anxious to change my shoes and socks. 'He is dead,' murmured the fellow, immensely impressed. 'No doubt about it,' said I, tugging like mad at the shoe-laces. 'And by the way, I suppose Mr. Kurtz is dead as well by this time.'

"For the moment that was the dominant thought. There was a sense of extreme disappointment, as though I had found out I had been striving after something altogether without a substance. I couldn't have been more disgusted if I had travelled all this way for the sole purpose of talking with Mr. Kurtz. Talking with . . . I flung one shoe overboard, and became aware that that was exactly what I had been looking forward to—a talk with Kurtz. I made the strange discovery that I had never imagined him as doing, you know, but as discoursing. I didn't say to myself, 'Now I will never see him,' or 'Now I will never shake him by the hand,' but, 'now I will never hear him.' The man presented himself as a voice. Not of course that I did not connect him with some sort of action. Hadn't I been told in all the tones of jealousy and admiration that he had collected, bartered, swindled, or stolen more ivory than all the other agents together? That was not the point. The point was in his being a gifted creature, and that of all his gifts the one that stood out preëminently, that carried with it a sense of real presence, was his ability to talk, his words—the gift of expression, the bewildering, the illuminating, the most exalted and the most contemptible, the pulsating stream of light, or the deceitful flow from the heart of an impenetrable darkness.

"The other shoe went flying unto the devil-god of that river. I thought, By Jove! it's all over. We are too late; he has vanished—the gift has vanished, by means of some spear, arrow, or club. I will never hear that chap speak after all,—and my sorrow had a startling extravagance of emotion, even such as I had noticed in the howling sorrow of these savages in the bush. I couldn't have felt more of lonely desolation somehow, had I been robbed of a belief or had missed my destiny in life. . . . Why do you sigh in this beastly way, somebody? Absurd? Well, absurd. Good Lord! mustn't a man ever——Here, give me some tobacco." . . .

There was a pause of profound stillness, then a match flared, and Marlow's lean face appeared, worn, hollow, with downward folds and dropped eyelids, with an aspect of concentrated attention; and as he took vigorous draws at his pipe, it seemed to retreat and advance out of the night in the regular flicker of the tiny flame. The match went out.

"Absurd!" he cried. "This is the worst of trying to tell. . . . Here you all are, each moored with two good addresses, like a hulk with two anchors, a butcher round one corner, a policeman round another, excellent appetites, and temperature normal—you hear—normal from year's end to year's end. And you say, Absurd! Absurd be—exploded! Absurd! My dear boys, what can you expect from a man who out of sheer nervousness had just flung overboard a pair of new shoes! Now I think of it, it is amazing I did not shed tears. I am, upon the whole, proud of my fortitude. I was cut to the quick at the idea of having lost the inestimable privilege of listening to the gifted Kurtz. Of course I was wrong. The privilege was waiting for me. Oh, yes, I heard more than enough. And I was right, too. A voice. He was very little more than a voice. And I heard—him—it—this voice—other voices—all of them were so little more than voices—and the memory of that time itself lingers around me, impalpable, like a dying vibration of one immense jabber, silly, atrocious, sordid, savage, or simply mean, without any kind of sense. Voices, voices—even the girl herself—now——"

He was silent for a long time.

"I laid the ghost of his gifts at last with a lie," he began, suddenly. "Girl! What? Did I mention a girl? Oh, she is out of it—completely. They—the women I mean—are out of it—should be out of it. We must help them to stay in that beautiful world of their own, lest ours gets worse. Oh, she had to be out of it. You should have heard the disinterred body of Mr. Kurtz saying, 'My Intended.' You would have perceived directly then how completely she was out of it. And the lofty frontal bone of Mr. Kurtz! They say the hair goes on growing sometimes, but this—ah—specimen, was impressively bald. The wilderness had patted him on the head, and, behold, it was like a ball—an ivory ball; it had caressed him, and—lo!—he had withered; it had taken him, loved him, embraced him, got into his veins, consumed his flesh, and sealed his soul to its own by the inconceivable ceremonies of some devilish initiation. He was its spoiled and pampered favourite. Ivory? I should think so. Heaps of it, stacks of it. The old mud shanty was bursting with it. You would think there was not a single tusk left either above or below the ground in the whole country. 'Mostly fossil,' the manager had remarked, disparagingly. It was no more fossil than I am; but they call it fossil when it is dug up. It appears these niggers do bury the tusks sometimes—but evidently they couldn't bury this parcel deep enough to save the gifted Mr. Kurtz from his fate. We filled the steamboat with it, and had to pile a lot on the deck. Thus he could see and enjoy as long as he could see, because the appreciation of this favour had remained with him to the last. You should have heard him say, 'My ivory.' Oh, yes, I heard him. 'My Intended, my ivory, my station, my river, my——' everything belonged to him. It made me hold my breath in expectation of hearing the wilderness burst into a prodigious peal of laughter that would shake the fixed stars in their places. Everything belonged to him—but that was a trifle. The thing was to know what he belonged to, how many powers of darkness claimed him for their own. That was the reflection that made you creepy all over. It was impossible—it was not good for one either—trying to imagine. He had taken a high seat amongst the devils of the land—I mean literally. You can't understand. How could you?—with solid pavement under your feet, surrounded by kind neighbours ready to cheer you or to fall on you, stepping delicately between the butcher and the policeman, in the holy terror of scandal and gallows and lunatic asylums—how can you imagine what particular region of the first ages a man's untrammelled feet may take him into by the way of solitude—utter solitude without a policeman—by the way of silence—utter silence, where no warning voice of a kind neighbour can be heard whispering of public opinion? These little things make all the great difference. When they are gone you must fall back upon your own innate strength, upon your own capacity for faithfulness. Of course you may be too much of a fool to go wrong—too dull even to know you are being assaulted by the powers of darkness. I take it, no fool ever made a bargain for his soul with the devil: the fool is too much of a fool, or the devil too much of a devil—I don't know which. Or you may be such a thunderingly exalted creature as to be altogether deaf and blind to anything but heavenly sights and sounds. Then the earth for you is only a standing place—and whether to be like this is your loss or your gain I won't pretend to say. But most of us are neither one nor the other. The earth for us is a place to live in, where we must put up with sights, with sounds, with smells, too, by Jove!—breathe dead hippo, so to speak, and not be contaminated. And there, don't you see? your strength comes in, the faith in your ability for the digging of unostentatious holes to bury the stuff in—your power of devotion, not to yourself, but to an obscure, back-breaking business. And that's difficult enough. Mind, I am not trying to excuse or even explain—I am trying to account to myself for—for—Mr. Kurtz—for the shade of Mr. Kurtz. This initiated wraith from the back of Nowhere honoured me with its amazing confidence before it vanished altogether. This was because it could speak English to me. The original Kurtz had been educated partly in England, and—as he was good enough to say himself—his sympathies were in the right place. His mother was half-English, his father was half-French. All Europe contributed to the making of Kurtz; and by and by I learned that, most appropriately, the International Society for the Suppression of Savage Customs had intrusted him with the making of a report, for its future guidance. And he had written it, too. I've seen it. I've read it. It was eloquent, vibrating with eloquence, but too high-strung, I think. Seventeen pages of close writing he had found time for! But this must have been before his—let us say—nerves, went wrong, and caused him to preside at certain midnight dances ending with unspeakable rites, which—as far as I reluctantly gathered from what I heard at various times—were offered up to him—do you understand?—to Mr. Kurtz himself. But it was a beautiful piece of writing. The opening paragraph, however, in the light of later information, strikes me now as ominous. He began with the argument that we whites, from the point of development we had arrived at, 'must necessarily appear to them [savages] in the nature of supernatural beings—we approach them with the might as of a deity,' and so on, and so on. 'By the simple exercise of our will we can exert a power for good practically unbounded,' etc. etc. From that point he soared and took me with him. The peroration was magnificent, though difficult to remember, you know. It gave me the notion of an exotic Immensity ruled by an august Benevolence. It made me tingle with enthusiasm. This was the unbounded power of eloquence—of words—of burning noble words. There were no practical hints to interrupt the magic current of phrases, unless a kind of note at the foot of the last page, scrawled evidently much later, in an unsteady hand, may be regarded as the exposition of a method. It was very simple, and at the end of that moving appeal to every altruistic sentiment it blazed at you, luminous and terrifying, like a flash of lightning in a serene sky: 'Exterminate all the brutes!' The curious part was that he had apparently forgotten all about that valuable postscriptum, because, later on, when he in a sense came to himself, he repeatedly entreated me to take good care of 'my pamphlet' (he called it), as it was sure to have in the future a good influence upon his career. I had full information about all these things, and, besides, as it turned out, I was to have the care of his memory. I've done enough for it to give me the indisputable right to lay it, if I choose, for an everlasting rest in the dust-bin of progress, amongst all the sweepings and, figuratively speaking, all the dead cats of civilization. But then, you see, I can't choose. He won't be forgotten. Whatever he was, he was not common. He had the power to charm or frighten rudimentary souls into an aggravated witch-dance in his honour; he could also fill the small souls of the pilgrims with bitter misgivings: he had one devoted friend at least, and he had conquered one soul in the world that was neither rudimentary nor tainted with self-seeking. No; I can't forget him, though I am not prepared to affirm the fellow was exactly worth the life we lost in getting to him. I missed my late helmsman awfully,—I missed him even while his body was still lying in the pilot-house. Perhaps you will think it passing strange this regret for a savage who was no more account than a grain of sand in a black Sahara. Well, don't you see, he had done something, he had steered; for months I had him at my back—a help—an instrument. It was a kind of partnership. He steered for me—I had to look after him, I worried about his deficiencies, and thus a subtle bond had been created, of which I only became aware when it was suddenly broken. And the intimate profundity of that look he gave me when he received his hurt remains to this day in my memory—like a claim of distant kinship affirmed in a supreme moment.

"Poor fool! If he had only left that shutter alone. He had no restraint, no restraint—just like Kurtz—a tree swayed by the wind. As soon as I had put on a dry pair of slippers, I dragged him out, after first jerking the spear out of his side, which operation I confess I performed with my eyes shut tight. His heels leaped together over the little door-step; his shoulders were pressed to my breast; I hugged him from behind desperately. Oh! he was heavy, heavy; heavier than any man on earth, I should imagine. Then without more ado I tipped him overboard. The current snatched him as though he had been a wisp of grass, and I saw the body roll over twice before I lost sight of it for ever. All the pilgrims and the manager were then congregated on the awning-deck about the pilot-house, chattering at each other like a flock of excited magpies, and there was a scandalized murmur at my heartless promptitude. What they wanted to keep that body hanging about for I can't guess. Embalm it, maybe. But I had also heard another, and a very ominous, murmur on the deck below. My friends the wood-cutters were likewise scandalized, and with a better show of reason—though I admit that the reason itself was quite inadmissible. Oh, quite! I had made up my mind that if my late helmsman was to be eaten, the fishes alone should have him. He had been a very second-rate helmsman while alive, but now he was dead he might have become a first-class temptation, and possibly cause some startling trouble. Besides, I was anxious to take the wheel, the man in pink pyjamas showing himself a hopeless duffer at the business.

"This I did directly the simple funeral was over. We were going half-speed, keeping right in the middle of the stream, and I listened to the talk about me. They had given up Kurtz, they had given up the station; Kurtz was dead, and the station had been burnt—and so on—and so on. The red-haired pilgrim was beside himself with the thought that at least this poor Kurtz had been properly avenged. 'Say! We must have made a glorious slaughter of them in the bush. Eh? What do you think? Say?' He positively danced, the bloodthirsty little gingery[22] beggar. And he had nearly fainted when he saw the wounded man! I could not help saying, 'You made a glorious lot of smoke, anyhow.' I had seen, from the way the tops of the bushes rustled and flew, that almost all the shots had gone too high. You can't hit anything unless you take aim and fire from the shoulder; but these chaps fired from the hip with their eyes shut. The retreat, I maintained—and I was right—was caused by the screeching of the steam-whistle. Upon this they forgot Kurtz, and began to howl at me with indignant protests.

"The manager stood by the wheel murmuring confidentially about the necessity of getting well away down the river before dark at all events, when I saw in the distance a clearing on the river-side and the outlines of some sort of building. 'What's this?' I asked. He clapped his hands in wonder. 'The station!' he cried. I edged in at once, still going half-speed.

"Through my glasses I saw the slope of a hill interspersed with rare trees and perfectly free from undergrowth. A long decaying building on the summit was half buried in the high grass; the large holes in the peaked roof gaped black from afar; the jungle and the woods made a background. There was no enclosure or fence of any kind; but there had been one apparently, for near the house half-a-dozen slim posts remained in a row, roughly trimmed, and with their upper ends ornamented with round carved balls. The rails, or whatever there had been between, had disappeared.

---

[22]Redheaded.

Of course the forest surrounded all that. The river-bank was clear, and on the water-side I saw a white man under a hat like a cart-wheel beckoning persistently with his whole arm. Examining the edge of the forest above and below, I was almost certain I could see movements—human forms gliding here and there. I steamed past prudently, then stopped the engines and let her drift down. The man on the shore began to shout, urging us to land. 'We have been attacked,' screamed the manager. 'I know—I know. It's all right,' yelled back the other, as cheerful as you please. 'Come along. It's all right. I am glad.'

"His aspect reminded me of something I had seen—something funny I had seen somewhere. As I manœuvred to get alongside, I was asking myself, 'What does this fellow look like?' Suddenly I got it. He looked like a harlequin. His clothes had been made of some stuff that was brown holland[23] probably, but it was covered with patches all over, with bright patches, blue, red, and yellow,—patches on the back, patches on the front, patches on elbows, on knees; coloured binding around his jacket, scarlet edging at the bottom of his trousers; and the sunshine made him look extremely gay and wonderfully neat withal, because you could see how beautifully all this patching had been done. A beardless, boyish face, very fair, no features to speak of, nose peeling, little blue eyes, smiles and frowns chasing each other over that open countenance like sunshine and shadow on a wind-swept plain. 'Look out, captain!' he cried; 'there's a snag lodged in here last night.' What! Another snag? I confess I swore shamefully. I had nearly holed my cripple, to finish off that charming trip. The harlequin on the bank turned his little pug-nose up to me. 'You English?' he asked, all smiles. 'Are you?' I shouted from the wheel. The smiles vanished, and he shook his head as if sorry for my disappointment. Then he brightened up. 'Never mind!' he cried, encouragingly. 'Are we in time?' I asked. 'He is up there,' he replied, with a toss of the head up the hill, and becoming gloomy all of a sudden. His face was like the autumn sky, overcast one moment and bright the next.

"When the manager, escorted by the pilgrims, all of them armed to the teeth, had gone to the house this chap came on board. 'I say, I don't like this. These natives are in the bush,' I said. He assured me earnestly it was all right. 'They are simple people,' he added; 'well, I am glad you came. It took me all my time to keep them off.' 'But you said it was all right,' I cried. 'Oh, they meant no harm,' he said; and as I stared he corrected himself, 'Not exactly.' Then vivaciously, 'My faith, your pilot-house wants a clean-up!' In the next breath he advised me to keep enough steam on the boiler to blow the whistle in case of any trouble. 'One good screech will do more for you than all your rifles. They are simple people,' he repeated. He rattled away at such a rate he quite overwhelmed me. He seemed to be trying to make up for lots of silence, and actually hinted, laughing, that such was the case. 'Don't you talk with Mr. Kurtz?' I said. 'You don't talk with that man—you listen to him,' he exclaimed with severe exaltation. 'But now——' He waved his arm, and in the twinkling of an eye was in the uttermost depths of despondency. In a moment he came up again with a jump, possessed himself of both my hands, shook them continuously, while he gabbled: 'Brother sailor . . . honour . . . pleasure . . . delight . . . introduce myself . . . Russian . . . son of an arch-priest . . . Government of Tambov . . . What? Tobacco! English tobacco; the excellent English tobacco! Now, that's brotherly. Smoke? Where's a sailor that does not smoke?'

"The pipe soothed him, and gradually I made out he had run away from school, had gone to sea in a Russian ship; ran away again; served some time in English ships;

---

[23]Unbleached cotton or linen.

was now reconciled with the arch-priest. He made a point of that. 'But when one is young one must see things, gather experience, ideas; enlarge the mind.' 'Here!' I interrupted. 'You can never tell! Here I met Mr. Kurtz,' he said, youthfully solemn and reproachful. I held my tongue after that. It appears he had persuaded a Dutch trading-house on the coast to fit him out with stores and goods, and had started for the interior with a light heart, and no more idea of what would happen to him than a baby. He had been wandering about that river for nearly two years alone, cut off from everybody and everything. 'I am not so young as I look. I am twenty-five,' he said. 'At first old Van Shuyten would tell me to go to the devil,' he narrated with keen enjoyment; 'but I stuck to him, and talked and talked, till at last he got afraid I would talk the hind-leg off his favourite dog, so he gave me some cheap things and a few guns, and told me he hoped he would never see my face again. Good old Dutchman, Van Shuyten. I've sent him one small lot of ivory a year ago, so that he can't call me a little thief when I get back. I hope he got it. And for the rest I don't care. I had some wood stacked for you. That was my old house. Did you see?'

"I gave him Towson's book. He made as though he would kiss me, but restrained himself. 'The only book I had left, and I thought I had lost it,' he said, looking at it ecstatically. 'So many accidents happen to a man going about alone, you know. Canoes get upset sometimes—and sometimes you've got to clear out so quick when the people get angry.' He thumbed the pages. 'You made notes in Russian?' I asked. He nodded. 'I thought they were written in cipher,' I said. He laughed, then became serious. 'I had lots of trouble to keep these people off,' he said. 'Did they want to kill you?' I asked. 'Oh, no!' he cried, and checked himself. 'Why did they attack us?' I pursued. He hesitated, then said shamefacedly, 'They don't want him to go.' 'Don't they?' I said, curiously. He nodded a nod full of mystery and wisdom. 'I tell you,' he cried, 'this man has enlarged my mind.' He opened his arms wide, staring at me with his little blue eyes that were perfectly round."

3

"I looked at him, lost in astonishment. There he was before me, in motley, as though he had absconded from a troupe of mimes, enthusiastic, fabulous. His very existence was improbable, inexplicable, and altogether bewildering. He was an insoluble problem. It was inconceivable how he had existed, how he had succeeded in getting so far, how he had managed to remain—why he did not instantly disappear. 'I went a little farther,' he said, 'then still a little farther—till I had gone so far that I don't know how I'll ever get back. Never mind. Plenty time. I can manage. You take Kurtz away quick—quick—I tell you.' The glamour of youth enveloped his particoloured rags, his destitution, his loneliness, the essential desolation of his futile wanderings. For months—for years—his life hadn't been worth a day's purchase; and there he was gallantly, thoughtlessly alive, to all appearance indestructible solely by the virtue of his few years and of his unreflecting audacity. I was seduced into something like admiration—like envy. Glamour urged him on, glamour kept him unscathed. He surely wanted nothing from the wilderness but space to breathe in and to push on through. His need was to exist, and to move onwards at the greatest possible risk, and with a maximum of privation. If the absolutely pure, uncalculating, unpractical spirit of adventure had ever ruled a human being, it ruled this be-patched youth. I almost envied him the possession of this modest and clear flame. It seemed to have consumed all thought of self so completely, that even while he was talking to you, you forgot that it was he—the man before your eyes—who had gone through these things. I did not envy him his devotion to Kurtz, though. He had not meditated over it. It came to him, and he accepted it with a sort of eager fatalism. I must say that to me it appeared about the most dangerous thing in every way he had come upon so far.

"They had come together unavoidably, like two ships becalmed near each other, and lay rubbing sides at last. I suppose Kurtz wanted an audience, because on a certain occasion, when encamped in the forest, they had talked all night, or more probably Kurtz had talked. 'We talked of everything,' he said, quite transported at the recollection. 'I forgot there was such a thing as sleep. The night did not seem to last an hour. Everything! Everything!... Of love, too.' 'Ah, he talked to you of love!' I said, much amused. 'It isn't what you think,' he cried, almost passionately. 'It was in general. He made me see things—things.'

"He threw his arms up. We were on deck at the time, and the headman of my wood-cutters, lounging near by, turned upon him his heavy and glittering eyes. I looked around, and I don't know why, but I assure you that never, never before, did this land, this river, this jungle, the very arch of this blazing sky, appear to me so hopeless and so dark, so impenetrable to human thought, so pitiless to human weakness. 'And, ever since, you have been with him, of course?' I said.

"On the contrary. It appears their intercourse had been very much broken by various causes. He had, as he informed me proudly, managed to nurse Kurtz through two illnesses (he alluded to it as you would to some risky feat), but as a rule Kurtz wandered alone, far in the depths of the forest. 'Very often coming to this station, I had to wait days and days before he would turn up,' he said. 'Ah, it was worth waiting for!—sometimes.' 'What was he doing? exploring or what?' I asked. 'Oh, yes, of course;' he had discovered lots of villages, a lake, too—he did not know exactly in what direction; it was dangerous to inquire too much—but mostly his expeditions had been for ivory. 'But he had no goods to trade with by that time,' I objected. 'There's a good lot of cartridges left even yet,' he answered, looking away. 'To speak plainly, he raided the country,' I said. He nodded. 'Not alone, surely!' He muttered something about the villages round that lake. 'Kurtz got the tribe to follow him, did he?' I suggested. He fidgeted a little. 'They adored him,' he said. The tone of these words was so extraordinary that I looked at him searchingly. It was curious to see his mingled eagerness and reluctance to speak of Kurtz. The man filled his life, occupied his thoughts, swayed his emotions. 'What can you expect?' he burst out; 'he came to them with thunder and lightning, you know—and they had never seen anything like it—and very terrible. He could be very terrible. You can't judge Mr. Kurtz as you would an ordinary man. No, no, no! Now—just to give you an idea—I don't mind telling you, he wanted to shoot me, too, one day—but I don't judge him.' 'Shoot you!' I cried. 'What for?' 'Well, I had a small lot of ivory the chief of that village near my house gave me. You see I used to shoot game for them. Well, he wanted it, and wouldn't hear reason. He declared he would shoot me unless I gave him the ivory and then cleared out of the country, because he could do so, and had a fancy for it, and there was nothing on earth to prevent him killing whom he jolly well pleased. And it was true, too. I gave him the ivory. What did I care! But I didn't clear out. No, no. I couldn't leave him. I had to be careful, of course, till we got friendly again for a time. He had his second illness then. Afterwards I had to keep out of the way; but I didn't mind. He was living for the most part in those villages on the lake. When he came down to the river, sometimes he would take to me, and sometimes it was better for me to be careful. This man suffered too much. He hated all this, and somehow he couldn't get away. When I had a chance I begged him to try and leave while there was time; I offered to go back with him. And he would say yes, and then he would remain; go off on another ivory hunt; disappear for weeks; forget himself amongst these people—forget himself—you know.' 'Why! he's mad,' I said. He protested indignantly. Mr. Kurtz couldn't be mad. If I had heard him talk, only two days ago, I wouldn't dare hint at such a thing. . . . I had taken up my binoculars while we talked, and was looking at the shore, sweeping the limit of the forest at each side and at the back of the house. The consciousness of there being people in that bush, so silent, so quiet—as silent and quiet as the ruined house on the hill—made me uneasy. There was no sign on the face of nature of this amazing tale that was not so much told as suggested to me in desolate exclamations, completed by shrugs, in interrupted phrases, in hints ending in deep sighs. The woods were unmoved, like a mask—heavy, like the closed door of a prison—they looked with their air of hidden knowledge, of patient expectation, of unapproachable silence. The Russian was explaining to me that it was only lately that Mr. Kurtz had come down to the river, bringing along with him all the fighting men of that lake tribe. He had been absent for several months—getting himself adored, I suppose—and had come down unexpectedly, with the intention to all appearance of making a raid either across the river or down stream. Evidently the appetite for more ivory had got the better of the—what shall I say?—less material aspirations. However he had got much worse suddenly. 'I heard he was lying helpless, and so I came up—took my chance,' said the Russian. 'Oh, he is bad, very bad.' I directed my glass to the house. There were no signs of life, but there was the ruined roof, the long mud wall peeping above the grass, with three little square window-holes, no two of the same size; all this brought within reach of my hand, as it were. And then I made a brusque movement, and one of the remaining posts of that vanished fence leaped up in the field of my glass. You remember I told you I had been struck at the distance by certain attempts at ornamentation, rather remarkable in the ruinous aspect of the place. Now I had suddenly a nearer view, and its first result was to make me throw my head back as if before a blow. Then I went carefully from post to post with my glass, and I saw my mistake. These round knobs were not ornamental but symbolic; they were expressive and puzzling, striking and disturbing—food for thought and also for vultures if there had been any looking down from the sky; but at all events for such ants as were industrious enough to ascend the pole. They would have been even more impressive, those heads on the stakes, if their faces had not been turned to the house. Only one, the first I had made out, was facing my way. I was not so shocked as you may think. The start back I had given was really nothing but a movement of surprise. I had expected to see a knob of wood there, you know. I returned deliberately to the first I had seen—and there it was, black, dried, sunken, with closed eyelids,—a head that seemed to sleep at the top of that pole, and with the shrunken dry lips showing a narrow white line of the teeth, was smiling, too, smiling continuously at some endless and jocose dream of that eternal slumber.

"I am not disclosing any trade secrets. In fact, the manager said afterwards that Mr. Kurtz's methods had ruined the district. I have no opinion on that point, but I want you clearly to understand that there was nothing exactly profitable in these heads being there. They only showed that Mr. Kurtz lacked restraint in the gratification of his various lusts, that there was something wanting in him—some small matter which, when the pressing need arose, could not be found under his magnificent eloquence. Whether he knew of this deficiency himself I can't say. I think the knowledge came to him at last—only at the very last. But the wilderness had found him out early, and had taken on him a terrible vengeance for the fantastic invasion. I think it had whispered to him things about himself which he did not know, things of which he had no conception till he took counsel with this great solitude—and the whisper had proved irresistibly fascinating. It echoed loudly within him because he was hollow at the core.... I put down the glass, and the head that had appeared near enough to be spoken to seemed at once to have leaped away from me into inaccessible distance.

"The admirer of Mr. Kurtz was a bit crestfallen. In a hurried, indistinct voice he began to assure me he had not dared to take these—say, symbols—down. He was not afraid of the natives; they would not stir till Mr. Kurtz gave the word. His ascendancy was extraordinary. The camps of these people surrounded the place, and the chiefs came every day to see him. They would crawl.... 'I don't want to know anything of the ceremonies used when approaching Mr. Kurtz,' I shouted. Curious, this feeling that came over me that such details would be more intolerable than those heads drying on the stakes under Mr. Kurtz's windows. After all, that was only a savage sight, while I seemed at one bound to have been transported into some lightless region of subtle horrors, where pure, uncomplicated savagery was a positive relief, being something that had a right to exist—obviously—in the sunshine. The young man looked at me with surprise. I suppose it did not occur to him that Mr. Kurtz was no idol of mine. He forgot I hadn't heard any of these splendid monologues on, what was it? on love, justice, conduct of life—or what not. If it had come to crawling before Mr. Kurtz, he crawled as much as the veriest savage of them all. I had no idea of the conditions, he said: these heads were the heads of rebels. I shocked him excessively by laughing. Rebels! What would be the next definition I was to hear? There had been enemies, criminals, workers—and these were rebels. Those rebellious heads looked very subdued to me on their sticks. 'You don't know how such a life tries a man like Kurtz,' cried Kurtz's last disciple. 'Well, and you?' I said. 'I! I! I am a simple man. I have no great thoughts. I want nothing from anybody. How can you compare me to...?' His feelings were too much for speech, and suddenly he broke down. 'I don't understand,' he groaned. 'I've been doing my best to keep him alive, and that's enough. I had no hand in all this. I have no abilities. There hasn't been a drop of medicine or a mouthful of invalid food for months here. He was shamefully abandoned. A man like this, with such ideas. Shamefully! Shamefully! I—I—haven't slept for the last ten nights...'

"His voice lost itself in the calm of the evening. The long shadows of the forest had slipped down hill while we talked, had gone far beyond the ruined hovel, beyond the symbolic row of stakes. All this was in the gloom, while we down there were yet in the sunshine, and the stretch of the river abreast of the clearing glittered in a still and dazzling splendour, with a murky and overshadowed bend above and below. Not a living soul was seen on the shore. The bushes did not rustle.

"Suddenly round the corner of the house a group of men appeared, as though they had come up from the ground. They waded waist-deep in the grass, in a compact body, bearing an improvised stretcher in their midst. Instantly, in the emptiness of the landscape, a cry arose whose shrillness pierced the still air like a sharp arrow flying straight to the very heart of the land; and, as if by enchantment, streams of human beings—of naked human beings—with spears in their hands, with bows, with shields, with wild glances and savage movements, were poured into the clearing by the dark-faced and pensive forest. The bushes shook, the grass swayed for a time, and then everything stood still in attentive immobility.

"'Now, if he does not say the right thing to them we are all done for,' said the Russian at my elbow. The knot of men with the stretcher had stopped, too, halfway to the steamer, as if petrified. I saw the man on the stretcher sit up, lank and with an uplifted arm, above the shoulders of the bearers. 'Let us hope that the man who can talk so well of love in general will find some particular reason to spare us this time,' I said. I resented bitterly the absurd danger of our situation, as if to be at the mercy of that atrocious phantom had been a dishonouring necessity. I could not hear a sound, but through my glasses I saw the thin arm extended commandingly, the lower jaw moving, the eyes of that apparition shining darkly far in its bony head that nodded with grotesque jerks. Kurtz—Kurtz—that means short in German—don't it? Well, the name was as true as everything else in his life—and death. He looked at least seven feet long. His covering had fallen off, and his body emerged from it pitiful and appalling as from a winding-sheet. I could see the cage of his ribs all astir, the bones of his arm waving. It was as though an animated image of death carved out of old ivory had been shaking its hand with menaces at a motionless crowd of men made of dark and glittering bronze. I saw him open his mouth wide—it gave him a weirdly voracious aspect, as though he had wanted to swallow all the air, all the earth, all the men before him. A deep voice reached me faintly. He must have been shouting. He fell back suddenly. The stretcher shook as the bearers staggered forward again, and almost at the same time I noticed that the crowd of savages was vanishing without any perceptible movement of retreat, as if the forest that had ejected these beings so suddenly had drawn them in again as the breath is drawn in a long aspiration.

"Some of the pilgrims behind the stretcher carried his arms—two shot-guns, a heavy rifle, and a light revolver-carbine—the thunderbolts of that pitiful Jupiter. The manager bent over him murmuring as he walked beside his head. They laid him down in one of the little cabins—just a room for a bedplace and a camp-stool or two, you know. We had brought his belated correspondence, and a lot of torn envelopes and open letters littered his bed. His hand roamed feebly amongst these papers. I was struck by the fire of his eyes and the composed languor of his expression. It was not so much the exhaustion of disease. He did not seem in pain. This shadow looked satiated and calm, as though for the moment it had had its fill of all the emotions.

"He rustled one of the letters, and looking straight in my face said, 'I am glad.' Somebody had been writing to him about me. These special recommendations were turning up again. The volume of tone he emitted without effort, almost without the trouble of moving his lips, amazed me. A voice! a voice! It was grave, profound, vibrating, while the man did not seem capable of a whisper. However, he had enough strength in him—factitious no doubt—to very nearly make an end of us, as you shall hear directly.

"The manager appeared silently in the doorway; I stepped out at once and he drew the curtain after me. The Russian, eyed curiously by the pilgrims, was staring at the shore. I followed the direction of his glance.

"Dark human shapes could be made out in the distance, flitting indistinctly against the gloomy border of the forest, and near the river two bronze figures, leaning on tall spears, stood in the sunlight under fantastic head-dresses of spotted skins, warlike and still in statuesque repose. And from right to left along the lighted shore moved a wild and gorgeous apparition of a woman.

"She walked with measured steps, draped in striped and fringed cloths, treading the earth proudly, with a slight jingle and flash of barbarous ornaments. She carried her head high; her hair was done in the shape of a helmet; she had brass leggings to the knee, brass wire gauntlets to the elbow, a crimson spot on her tawny cheek, innumerable necklaces of glass beads on her neck; bizarre things, charms, gifts of witch-men, that hung about her, glittered and trembled at every step. She must have had the value of several elephant tusks upon her. She was savage and superb, wild-eyed and magnificent; there was something ominous and stately in her deliberate progress. And in the hush that had fallen suddenly upon the whole sorrowful land, the immense wilderness, the colossal body of the fecund and mysterious life seemed to look at her, pensive, as though it had been looking at the image of its own tenebrous and passionate soul.

"She came abreast of the steamer, stood still, and faced us. Her long shadow fell to the water's edge. Her face had a tragic and fierce aspect of wild sorrow and of dumb pain mingled with the fear of some struggling, half-shaped resolve. She stood looking at us without a stir, and like the wilderness itself, with an air of brooding over an inscrutable purpose. A whole minute passed, and then she made a step forward. There was a low jingle, a glint of yellow metal, a sway of fringed draperies, and she stopped as if her heart had failed her. The young fellow by my side growled. The pilgrims murmured at my back. She looked at us all as if her life had depended upon the unswerving steadiness of her glance. Suddenly she opened her bared arms and threw them up rigid above her head, as though in an uncontrollable desire to touch the sky, and at the same time the swift shadows darted out on the earth, swept around on the river, gathering the steamer into a shadowy embrace. A formidable silence hung over the scene.

"She turned away slowly, walked on, following the bank, and passed into the bushes to the left. Once only her eyes gleamed back at us in the dusk of the thickets before she disappeared.

" 'If she had offered to come aboard I really think I would have tried to shoot her,' said the man of patches, nervously. 'I have been risking my life every day for the last fortnight to keep her out of the house. She got in one day and kicked up a row about those miserable rags I picked up in the storeroom to mend my clothes with. I wasn't decent. At least it must have been that, for she talked like a fury to Kurtz for an hour, pointing at me now and then. I don't understand the dialect of this tribe. Luckily for me, I fancy Kurtz felt too ill that day to care, or there would have been mischief. I don't understand.... No—it's too much for me. Ah, well, it's all over now.'

"At this moment I heard Kurtz's deep voice behind the curtain: 'Save me!—save the ivory, you mean. Don't tell me. Save *me!* Why, I've had to save you. You are interrupting my plans now. Sick! Sick! Not so sick as you would like to believe. Never mind. I'll carry my ideas out yet—I will return. I'll show you what can be done. You with your little peddling notions—you are interfering with me. I will return. I....'

"The manager came out. He did me the honour to take me under the arm and lead me aside. 'He is very low, very low,' he said. He considered it necessary to sigh, but neglected to be consistently sorrowful. 'We have done all we could for him—haven't we? But there is no disguising the fact, Mr. Kurtz has done more harm than good to the Company. He did not see the time was not ripe for vigorous action. Cautiously, cautiously—that's my principle. We must be cautious yet. The district is closed to us for a time. Deplorable! Upon the whole, the trade will suffer. I don't deny there is a remarkable quantity of ivory—mostly fossil. We must save it, at all events—but look how precarious the position is—and why? Because the method is unsound.' 'Do you,' said I, looking at the shore, 'call it "unsound method"?' 'Without doubt,' he exclaimed, hotly. 'Don't you?' ... 'No method at all,' I murmured after a while. 'Exactly,' he exulted. 'I anticipated this. Shows a complete want of judgment. It is my duty to point it out in the proper quarter.' 'Oh,' said I, 'that fellow—what's his name?—the brickmaker, will make a readable report for you.' He appeared confounded for a moment. It seemed to me I had never breathed an atmosphere so vile, and I turned mentally to Kurtz for relief—positively for relief. 'Nevertheless I think Mr. Kurtz is a remarkable man,' I said with emphasis. He started, dropped on me a cold heavy glance, said very quietly, 'he *was*,' and turned his back on me. My hour of favour was over; I found myself lumped along with Kurtz as a partisan of methods for which the time was not ripe: I was unsound! Ah! but it was something to have at least a choice of nightmares.

"I had turned to the wilderness really, not to Mr. Kurtz, who, I was ready to admit, was as good as buried. And for a moment it seemed to me as if I also were buried in a vast grave full of unspeakable secrets. I felt an intolerable weight oppressing my breast, the smell of the damp earth, the unseen presence of victorious corruption, the darkness of an impenetrable night. . . . The Russian tapped me on the shoulder. I heard him mumbling and stammering something about 'brother seaman—couldn't conceal—knowledge of matters that would affect Mr. Kurtz's reputation.' I waited. For him evidently Mr. Kurtz was not in his grave; I suspect that for him Mr. Kurtz was one of the immortals. 'Well!' said I at last, 'speak out. As it happens, I am Mr. Kurtz's friend—in a way.'

"He stated with a good deal of formality that had we not been 'of the same profession,' he would have kept the matter to himself without regard to consequences. 'He suspected there was an active ill will towards him on the part of these white men that——' 'You are right,' I said, remembering a certain conversation I had overheard. 'The manager thinks you ought to be hanged.' He showed a concern at this intelligence which amused me at first. 'I had better get out of the way quietly,' he said, earnestly. 'I can do no more for Kurtz now, and they would soon find some excuse. What's to stop them? There's a military post three hundred miles from here.' 'Well, upon my word,' said I, 'perhaps you had better go if you have any friends amongst the savages near by.' 'Plenty,' he said. 'They are simple people—and I want nothing, you know.' He stood biting his lip, then: 'I don't want any harm to happen to these whites here, but of course I was thinking of Mr. Kurtz's reputation—but you are a brother seaman and——' 'All right,' said I, after a time. 'Mr. Kurtz's reputation is safe with me.' I did not know how truly I spoke.

"He informed me, lowering his voice, that it was Kurtz who had ordered the attack to be made on the steamer. 'He hated sometimes the idea of being taken away—and then again. . . . But I don't understand these matters. I am a simple man. He thought it would scare you away—that you would give it up, thinking him dead. I could not stop him. Oh, I had an awful time of it this last month.' 'Very well,' I said. 'He is all right now.' 'Ye-e-es,' he muttered, not very convinced apparently. 'Thanks,' said I; 'I shall keep my eyes open.' 'But quiet—eh?' he urged, anxiously. 'It would be awful for his reputation if anybody here——' I promised a complete discretion with great gravity. 'I have a canoe and three black fellows waiting not very far. I am off. Could you give me a few Martini-Henry cartridges?' I could, and did, with proper secrecy. He helped himself, with a wink at me, to a handful of my tobacco. 'Between sailors—you know—good English tobacco.' At the door of the pilot-house he turned round—'I say, haven't you a pair of shoes you could spare?' He raised one leg. 'Look.' The soles were tied with knotted strings sandal-wise under his bare feet. I rooted out an old pair, at which he looked with admiration before tucking it under his left arm. One of his pockets (bright red) was bulging with cartridges, from the other (dark blue) peeped 'Towson's Inquiry,' etc., etc. He seemed to think himself excellently well equipped for a renewed encounter with the wilderness. 'Ah! I'll never, never meet such a man again. You ought to have heard him recite poetry—his own, too, it was, he told me. Poetry!' He rolled his

eyes at the recollection of these delights. 'Oh, he enlarged my mind!' 'G[...]
said I. He shook hands and vanished in the night. Sometimes I ask myself w[hether I]
had ever really seen him—whether it was possible to meet such a phenomenon! . . .

"When I woke up shortly after midnight his warning came to my mind with its
hint of danger that seemed, in the starred darkness, real enough to make me get up
for the purpose of having a look round. On the hill a big fire burned, illuminating
fitfully a crooked corner of the station-house. One of the agents with a picket[24] of
a few of our blacks, armed for the purpose, was keeping guard over the ivory; but
deep within the forest, red gleams that wavered, that seemed to sink and rise from
the ground amongst confused columnar shapes of intense blackness, showed the
exact position of the camp where Mr. Kurtz's adorers were keeping their uneasy
vigil. The monotonous beating of a big drum filled the air with muffled shocks
and a lingering vibration. A steady droning sound of many men chanting each to
himself some weird incantation came out from the black, flat wall of the woods as
the humming of bees comes out of a hive, and had a strange narcotic effect upon
my half-awake senses. I believe I dozed off leaning over the rail, till an abrupt burst
of yells, an overwhelming outbreak of a pent-up and mysterious frenzy, woke me
up in a bewildered wonder. It was cut short all at once, and the low droning went
on with an effect of audible and soothing silence. I glanced casually into the little
cabin. A light was burning within, but Mr. Kurtz was not there.

"I think I would have raised an outcry if I had believed my eyes. But I
didn't believe them at first—the thing seemed so impossible. The fact is I was
completely unnerved by a sheer blank fright, pure abstract terror, unconnected with
any distinct shape of physical danger. What made this emotion so overpowering
was—how shall I define it?—the moral shock I received, as if something altogether
monstrous, intolerable to thought and odious to the soul, had been thrust upon me
unexpectedly. This lasted of course the merest fraction of a second, and then the
usual sense of commonplace, deadly danger, the possibility of a sudden onslaught
and massacre, or something of the kind, which I saw impending, was positively
welcome and composing. It pacified me, in fact, so much that I did not raise an
alarm.

"There was an agent buttoned up inside an ulster[25] and sleeping on a chair
on deck within three feet of me. The yells had not awakened him; he snored
very slightly; I left him to his slumbers and leaped ashore. I did not betray Mr.
Kurtz—it was ordered I should never betray him—it was written I should be loyal
to the nightmare of my choice. I was anxious to deal with this shadow by myself
alone,—and to this day I don't know why I was so jealous of sharing with any one
the peculiar blackness of that experience.

"As soon as I got on the bank I saw a trail—a broad trail through the grass.
I remember the exultation with which I said to myself, 'He can't walk—he is
crawling on all-fours—I've got him.' The grass was wet with dew. I strode rapidly
with clenched fists. I fancy I had some vague notion of falling upon him and giving
him a drubbing. I don't know. I had some imbecile thoughts. The knitting old
woman with the cat obtruded herself upon my memory as a most improper person
to be sitting at the other end of such an affair. I saw a row of pilgrims squirting lead
in the air out of Winchesters held to the hip. I thought I would never get back
to the steamer, and imagined myself living alone and unarmed in the woods to an

---

[24] A band of sentries.
[25] A long overcoat.

advanced age. Such silly things—you know. And I remember I confounded the beat
of the drum with the beating of my heart, and was pleased at its calm regularity.

"I kept to the track though—then stopped to listen. The night was very clear; a
dark blue space, sparkling with dew and starlight, in which black things stood very
still. I thought I could see a kind of motion ahead of me. I was strangely cocksure of
everything that night. I actually left the track and ran in a wide semicircle (I verily
believe chuckling to myself) so as to get in front of that stir, of that motion I had
seen—if indeed I had seen anything. I was circumventing Kurtz as though it had
been a boyish game.

"I came upon him, and, if he had not heard me coming, I would have fallen
over him, too, but he got up in time. He rose, unsteady, long, pale, indistinct, like a
vapour exhaled by the earth, and swayed slightly, misty and silent before me; while
at my back the fires loomed between the trees, and the murmur of many voices
issued from the forest. I had cut him off cleverly; but when actually confronting
him I seemed to come to my senses, I saw the danger in its right proportion. It
was by no means over yet. Suppose he began to shout? Though he could hardly
stand, there was still plenty of vigour in his voice. 'Go away—hide yourself,' he
said, in that profound tone. It was very awful. I glanced back. We were within
thirty yards from the nearest fire. A black figure stood up, strode on long black legs,
waving long black arms, across the glow. It had horns—antelope horns, I think—on
its head. Some sorcerer, some witch-man, no doubt: it looked fiend-like enough.
'Do you know what you are doing?' I whispered. 'Perfectly,' he answered, raising
his voice for that single word: it sounded to me far off and yet loud, like a hail
through a speaking-trumpet. If he makes a row we are lost, I thought to myself.
This clearly was not a case for fisticuffs, even apart from the very natural aversion I
had to beat that Shadow—this wandering and tormented thing. 'You will be lost,'
I said—'utterly lost.' One gets sometimes such a flash of inspiration, you know. I
did say the right thing, though indeed he could not have been more irretrievably
lost than he was at this very moment, when the foundations of our intimacy were
being laid—to endure—to endure—even to the end—even beyond.

" 'I had immense plans,' he muttered irresolutely. 'Yes,' said I; 'but if you try to
shout I'll smash your head with——' There was not a stick or stone near. 'I will
throttle you for good,' I corrected myself. 'I was on the threshold of great things,'
he pleaded, in a voice of longing, with a wistfulness of tone that made my blood
run cold. 'And now for this stupid scoundrel——' 'Your success in Europe is assured
in any case,' I affirmed, steadily. I did not want to have the throttling of him, you
understand—and indeed it would have been very little use for any practical purpose.
I tried to break the spell—the heavy, mute spell of the wilderness—that seemed to
draw him to its pitiless breast by the awakening of forgotten and brutal instincts, by
the memory of gratified and monstrous passions. This alone, I was convinced, had
driven him out to the edge of the forest, to the bush, towards the gleam of fires,
the throb of drums, the drone of weird incantations; this alone had beguiled his
unlawful soul beyond the bounds of permitted aspirations. And, don't you see, the
terror of the position was not in being knocked on the head—though I had a very
lively sense of that danger, too—but in this, that I had to deal with a being to whom
I could not appeal in the name of anything high or low. I had, even like the niggers,
to invoke him—himself—his own exalted and incredible degradation. There was
nothing either above or below him, and I knew it. He had kicked himself loose of
the earth. Confound the man! he had kicked the very earth to pieces. He was alone,
and I before him did not know whether I stood on the ground or floated in the
air. I've been telling you what we said—repeating the phrases we pronounced—but

what's the good? They were common everyday words—the familiar, vague sounds exchanged on every waking day of life. But what of that? They had behind them, to my mind, the terrific suggestiveness of words heard in dreams, of phrases spoken in nightmares. Soul! If anybody had ever struggled with a soul, I am the man. And I wasn't arguing with a lunatic either. Believe me or not, his intelligence was perfectly clear—concentrated, it is true, upon himself with horrible intensity, yet clear; and therein was my only chance—barring, of course, the killing him there and then, which wasn't so good, on account of unavoidable noise. But his soul was mad. Being alone in the wilderness, it had looked within itself, and, by heavens! I tell you, it had gone mad. I had—for my sins, I suppose—to go through the ordeal of looking into it myself. No eloquence could have been so withering to one's belief in mankind as his final burst of sincerity. He struggled with himself, too. I saw it,—I heard it. I saw the inconceivable mystery of a soul that knew no restraint, no faith, and no fear, yet struggling blindly with itself. I kept my head pretty well; but when I had him at last stretched on the couch, I wiped my forehead, while my legs shook under me as though I had carried half a ton on my back down that hill. And yet I had only supported him, his bony arm clasped round my neck—and he was not much heavier than a child.

"When next day we left at noon, the crowd, of whose presence behind the curtain of trees I had been acutely conscious all the time, flowed out of the woods again, filled the clearing, covered the slope with a mass of naked, breathing, quivering, bronze bodies. I steamed up a bit, then swung downstream, and two thousand eyes followed the evolutions of the splashing, thumping, fierce river-demon beating the water with its terrible tail and breathing black smoke into the air. In front of the first rank, along the river, three men, plastered with bright red earth from head to foot, strutted to and fro restlessly. When we came abreast again, they faced the river, stamped their feet, nodded their horned heads, swayed their scarlet bodies; they shook towards the fierce river-demon a bunch of black feathers, a mangy skin with a pendent tail—something that looked like a dried gourd; they shouted periodically together strings of amazing words that resembled no sounds of human language; and the deep murmurs of the crowd, interrupted suddenly, were like the responses of some satanic litany.

"We had carried Kurtz into the pilot-house: there was more air there. Lying on the couch, he stared through the open shutter. There was an eddy in the mass of human bodies, and the woman with helmeted head and tawny cheeks rushed out to the very brink of the stream. She put out her hands, shouted something, and all that wild mob took up the shout in a roaring chorus of articulated, rapid, breathless utterance.

" 'Do you understand this?' I asked.

"He kept on looking out past me with fiery, longing eyes, with a mingled expression of wistfulness and hate. He made no answer, but I saw a smile, a smile of indefinable meaning, appear on his colourless lips that a moment after twitched convulsively. 'Do I not?' he said slowly, gasping, as if the words had been torn out of him by a supernatural power.

"I pulled the string of the whistle, and I did this because I saw the pilgrims on deck getting out their rifles with an air of anticipating a jolly lark. At the sudden screech there was a movement of abject terror through that wedged mass of bodies. 'Don't! don't you frighten them away,' cried someone on deck disconsolately. I pulled the string time after time. They broke and ran, they leaped, they crouched, they swerved, they dodged the flying terror of the sound. The three red chaps had fallen flat, face down on the shore, as though they had been shot dead. Only the barbarous and superb woman did not so much as flinch, and stretched tragically her bare arms after us over the sombre and glittering river.

"And then that imbecile crowd down on the deck started their little fun, and I could see nothing more for smoke.

"The brown current ran swiftly out of the heart of darkness, bearing us down towards the sea with twice the speed of our upward progress; and Kurtz's life was running swiftly, too, ebbing, ebbing out of his heart into the sea of inexorable time. The manager was very placid, he had no vital anxieties now, he took us both in with a comprehensive and satisfied glance: the 'affair' had come off as well as could be wished. I saw the time approaching when I would be left alone of the party of 'unsound method.' The pilgrims looked upon me with disfavour. I was, so to speak, numbered with the dead. It is strange how I accepted this unforeseen partnership, this choice of nightmares forced upon me in the tenebrous land invaded by these mean and greedy phantoms.

"Kurtz discoursed. A voice! a voice! It rang deep to the very last. It survived his strength to hide in the magnificent folds of eloquence the barren darkness of his heart. Oh, he struggled! he struggled! The wastes of his weary brain were haunted by shadowy images now—images of wealth and fame revolving obsequiously round his unextinguishable gift of noble and lofty expression. My Intended, my station, my career, my ideas—these were the subjects for the occasional utterances of elevated sentiments. The shade of the original Kurtz frequented the bedside of the hollow sham, whose fate it was to be buried presently in the mould of primeval earth. But both the diabolic love and the unearthly hate of the mysteries it had penetrated fought for the possession of that soul satiated with primitive emotions, avid of lying fame, of sham distinction, of all the appearances of success and power.

"Sometimes he was contemptibly childish. He desired to have kings meet him at railway-stations on his return from some ghastly Nowhere, where he intended to accomplish great things. 'You show them you have in you something that is really profitable, and then there will be no limits to the recognition of your ability,' he would say. 'Of course you must take care of the motives—right motives—always.' The long reaches that were like one and the same reach, monotonous bends that were exactly alike, slipped past the steamer with their multitude of secular[26] trees looking patiently after this grimy fragment of another world, the forerunner of change, of conquest, of trade, of massacres, of blessings. I looked ahead—piloting. 'Close the shutter,' said Kurtz suddenly one day; 'I can't bear to look at this.' I did so. There was a silence. 'Oh, but I will wring your heart yet!' he cried at the invisible wilderness.

"We broke down—as I had expected—and had to lie up for repairs at the head of an island. This delay was the first thing that shook Kurtz's confidence. One morning he gave me a packet of papers and a photograph—the lot tied together with a shoe-string. 'Keep this for me,' he said. 'This noxious fool' (meaning the manager) 'is capable of prying into my boxes when I am not looking.' In the afternoon I saw him. He was lying on his back with closed eyes, and I withdrew quietly, but I heard him mutter, 'Live rightly, die, die . . .' I listened. There was nothing more. Was he rehearsing some speech in his sleep, or was it a fragment of a phrase from some newspaper article? He had been writing for the papers and meant to do so again, 'for the furthering of my ideas. It's a duty.'

---

[26]Lasting from century to century.

"His was an impenetrable darkness. I looked at him as you peer down who is lying at the bottom of a precipice where the sun never shines. But I ha[d] much time to give him, because I was helping the engine-driver to take to pieces the leaky cylinders, to straighten a bent connecting-rod, and in other such matters. I lived in an infernal mess of rust, filings, nuts, bolts, spanners, hammers, ratchet-drills—things I abominate, because I don't get on with them. I tended the little forge we fortunately had aboard; I toiled wearily in a wretched scrap-heap—unless I had the shakes too bad to stand.

"One evening coming in with a candle I was startled to hear him say a little tremulously, 'I am lying here in the dark waiting for death.' The light was within a foot of his eyes. I forced myself to murmur, 'Oh, nonsense!' and stood over him as if transfixed.

"Anything approaching the change that came over his features I have never seen before, and hope never to see again. Oh, I wasn't touched. I was fascinated. It was as though a veil had been rent. I saw on that ivory face the expression of sombre pride, of ruthless power, of craven terror—of an intense and hopeless despair. Did he live his life again in every detail of desire, temptation, and surrender during that supreme moment of complete knowledge? He cried in a whisper at some image, at some vision—he cried out twice, a cry that was no more than a breath—

" 'The horror! The horror!'

"I blew the candle out and left the cabin. The pilgrims were dining in the mess-room, and I took my place opposite the manager, who lifted his eyes to give me a questioning glance, which I successfully ignored. He leaned back, serene, with that peculiar smile of his sealing the unexpressed depths of his meanness. A continuous shower of small flies streamed upon the lamp, upon the cloth, upon our hands and faces. Suddenly the manager's boy put his insolent black head in the doorway, and said in a tone of scathing contempt—

" 'Mistah Kurtz—he dead.'

"All the pilgrims rushed out to see. I remained, and went on with my dinner. I believe I was considered brutally callous. However, I did not eat much. There was a lamp in there—light, don't you know—and outside it was so beastly, beastly dark. I went no more near the remarkable man who had pronounced a judgment upon the adventures of his soul on this earth. The voice was gone. What else had been there? But I am of course aware that next day the pilgrims buried something in a muddy hole.

"And then they very nearly buried me.

"However, as you see, I did not go to join Kurtz there and then. I did not. I remained to dream the nightmare out to the end, and to show my loyalty to Kurtz once more. Destiny. My destiny! Droll thing life is—that mysterious arrangement of merciless logic for a futile purpose. The most you can hope from it is some knowledge of yourself—that comes too late—a crop of unextinguishable regrets. I have wrestled with death. It is the most unexciting contest you can imagine. It takes place in an impalpable grayness, with nothing underfoot, with nothing around, without spectators, without clamour, without glory, without the great desire of victory, without the great fear of defeat, in a sickly atmosphere of tepid scepticism, without much belief in your own right, and still less in that of your adversary. If such is the form of ultimate wisdom, then life is a greater riddle than some of us think it to be. I was within a hair's breadth of the last opportunity for pronouncement, and I found with humiliation that probably I would have nothing to say. This is the reason why I affirm that Kurtz was a remarkable man. He had something to say. He said it. Since I had peeped over the edge myself, I understand better the meaning of his stare, that could not see the flame of the candle, but was wide enough to embrace the whole universe, piercing enough to penetrate all the hearts that beat in the darkness. He had summed up—he had judged. 'The horror!' He was a remarkable man. After all, this was the expression of some sort of belief; it had candour, it had conviction, it had a vibrating note of revolt in its whisper, it had the appalling face of a glimpsed truth—the strange commingling of desire and hate. And it is not my own extremity I remember best—a vision of grayness without form filled with physical pain, and a careless contempt for the evanescence of all things—even of this pain itself. No! It is his extremity that I seem to have lived through. True, he had made that last stride, he had stepped over the edge, while I had been permitted to draw back my hesitating foot. And perhaps in this is the whole difference; perhaps all the wisdom, and all truth, and all sincerity, are just compressed into that inappreciable moment of time in which we step over the threshold of the invisible. Perhaps! I like to think my summing-up would not have been a word of careless contempt. Better his cry—much better. It was an affirmation, a moral victory paid for by innumerable defeats, by abominable terrors, by abominable satisfactions. But it was a victory! That is why I have remained loyal to Kurtz to the last, and even beyond, when a long time after I heard once more, not his own voice, but the echo of his magnificent eloquence thrown to me from a soul as translucently pure as a cliff of crystal.

"No, they did not bury me, though there is a period of time which I remember mistily, with a shuddering wonder, like a passage through some inconceivable world that had no hope in it and no desire. I found myself back in the sepulchral city resenting the sight of people hurrying through the streets to filch a little money from each other, to devour their infamous cookery, to gulp their unwholesome beer, to dream their insignificant and silly dreams. They trespassed upon my thoughts. They were intruders whose knowledge of life was to me an irritating pretence, because I felt so sure they could not possibly know the things I knew. Their bearing, which was simply the bearing of commonplace individuals going about their business in the assurance of perfect safety, was offensive to me like the outrageous flauntings of folly in the face of a danger it is unable to comprehend. I had no particular desire to enlighten them, but I had some difficulty in restraining myself from laughing in their faces, so full of stupid importance. I daresay I was not very well at that time. I tottered about the streets—there were various affairs to settle—grinning bitterly at perfectly respectable persons. I admit my behaviour was inexcusable, but then my temperature was seldom normal in these days. My dear aunt's endeavours to 'nurse up my strength' seemed altogether beside the mark. It was not my strength that wanted nursing, it was my imagination that wanted soothing. I kept the bundle of papers given me by Kurtz, not knowing exactly what to do with it. His mother had died lately, watched over, as I was told, by his Intended. A clean-shaved man, with an official manner and wearing gold-rimmed spectacles, called on me one day and made inquiries, at first circuitous, afterwards suavely pressing, about what he was pleased to denominate certain 'documents.' I was not surprised, because I had had two rows with the manager on the subject out there. I had refused to give up the smallest scrap out of that package, and I took the same attitude with the spectacled man. He became darkly menacing at last, and with much heat argued that the Company had the right to every bit of information about its 'territories.' And said he, 'Mr. Kurtz's knowledge of unexplored regions must have been necessarily extensive and peculiar—owing to his great abilities and to the deplorable circumstances in which he had been placed: therefore——' I assured him Mr. Kurtz's knowledge, however extensive, did not bear upon the problems of commerce or administration. He invoked then the name of science. 'It would be an incalculable loss if,' etc., etc. I offered him the report on the 'Suppression of Savage Customs,' with the postscriptum torn off. He took it up eagerly, but ended by sniffing at it with an air of contempt. 'This is not what we had a right to expect,' he remarked. 'Expect nothing else,' I said. 'There are only private letters.' He withdrew upon some threat of legal proceedings, and I saw him no more; but another fellow, calling himself Kurtz's cousin, appeared two days later, and was anxious to hear all the details about his dear relative's last moments. Incidentally he gave me to understand that Kurtz had been essentially a great musician. 'There was the making of an immense success,' said the man, who was an organist, I believe, with lank gray hair flowing over a greasy coat-collar. I had no reason to doubt his statement; and to this day I am unable to say what was Kurtz's profession, whether he ever had any—which was the greatest of his talents. I had taken him for a painter who wrote for the papers, or else for a journalist who could paint—but even the cousin (who took snuff during the interview) could not tell me what he had been—exactly. He was a universal genius—on that point I agreed with the old chap, who thereupon blew his nose noisily into a large cotton handkerchief and withdrew in senile agitation, bearing off some family letters and memoranda without importance. Ultimately a journalist anxious to know something of the fate of his 'dear colleague' turned up. This visitor informed me Kurtz's proper sphere ought to have been politics 'on the popular side.' He had furry straight eyebrows, bristly hair cropped short, an eye-glass on a broad ribbon, and, becoming expansive, confessed his opinion that Kurtz really couldn't write a bit—'but heavens! how that man could talk. He electrified large meetings. He had faith—don't you see?—he had the faith. He could get himself to believe anything—anything. He would have been a splendid leader of an extreme party.' 'What party?' I asked. 'Any party,' answered the other. 'He was an—an—extremist.' Did I not think so? I assented. Did I know, he asked, with a sudden flash of curiosity, 'what it was that had induced him to go out there?' 'Yes,' said I, and forthwith handed him the famous Report for publication, if he thought fit. He glanced through it hurriedly, mumbling all the time, judged 'it would do,' and took himself off with this plunder.

"Thus I was left at last with a slim packet of letters and the girl's portrait. She struck me as beautiful—I mean she had a beautiful expression. I know that the sunlight can be made to lie, too, yet one felt that no manipulation of light and pose could have conveyed the delicate shade of truthfulness upon those features. She seemed ready to listen without mental reservation, without suspicion, without a thought for herself. I concluded I would go and give her back her portrait and those letters myself. Curiosity? Yes; and also some other feeling perhaps. All that had been Kurtz's had passed out of my hands: his soul, his body, his station, his plans, his ivory, his career. There remained only his memory and his Intended—and I wanted to give that up, too, to the past, in a way—to surrender personally all that remained of him with me to that oblivion which is the last word of our common fate. I don't defend myself. I had no clear perception of what it was I really wanted. Perhaps it was an impulse of unconscious loyalty, or the fulfilment of one of those ironic necessities that lurk in the facts of human existence. I don't know. I can't tell. But I went.

"I thought his memory was like the other memories of the dead that accumulate in every man's life—a vague impress on the brain of shadows that had fallen on it in their swift and final passage; but before the high and ponderous door, between the tall houses of a street as still and decorous as a well-kept alley in a cemetery, I had a vision of him on the stretcher, opening his mouth voraciously, as if to devour all the earth with all its mankind. He lived then before me; he lived as much as he had ever lived—a shadow insatiable of splendid appearances, of frightful realities; a shadow darker than the shadow of the night, and draped nobly in the folds of a gorgeous eloquence. The vision seemed to enter the house with me—the stretcher, the phantom-bearers, the wild crowd of obedient worshippers, the gloom of the forests, the glitter of the reach between the murky bends, the beat of the drum, regular and muffled like the beating of a heart—the heart of a conquering darkness. It was a moment of triumph for the wilderness, an invading and vengeful rush which, it seemed to me, I would have to keep back alone for the salvation of another soul. And the memory of what I had heard him say afar there, with the horned shapes stirring at my back, in the glow of fires, within the patient woods, those broken phrases came back to me, were heard again in their ominous and terrifying simplicity. I remembered his abject pleading, his abject threats, the colossal scale of his vile desires, the meanness, the torment, the tempestuous anguish of his soul. And later on I seemed to see his collected languid manner, when he said one day, 'This lot of ivory now is really mine. The Company did not pay for it. I collected it myself at a very great personal risk. I am afraid they will try to claim it as theirs though. H'm. It is a difficult case. What do you think I ought to do—resist? Eh? I want no more than justice.' . . . He wanted no more than justice—no more than justice. I rang the bell before a mahogany door on the first floor, and while I waited he seemed to stare at me out of the glassy panel—stare with that wide and immense stare embracing, condemning, loathing all the universe. I seemed to hear the whispered cry, 'The horror! The horror!'

"The dusk was falling. I had to wait in a lofty drawing-room with three long windows from floor to ceiling that were like three luminous and bedraped columns. The bent gilt legs and backs of the furniture shone in indistinct curves. The tall marble fireplace had a cold and monumental whiteness. A grand piano stood massively in a corner; with dark gleams on the flat surfaces like a sombre and polished sarcophagus. A high door opened—closed. I rose.

"She came forward, all in black, with a pale head, floating towards me in the dusk. She was in mourning. It was more than a year since his death, more than a year since the news came; she seemed as though she would remember and mourn for ever. She took both my hands in hers and murmured, 'I had heard you were coming.' I noticed she was not very young—I mean not girlish. She had a mature capacity for fidelity, for belief, for suffering. The room seemed to have grown darker, as if all the sad light of the cloudy evening had taken refuge on her forehead. This fair hair, this pale visage, this pure brow, seemed surrounded by an ashy halo from which the dark eyes looked out at me. Their glance was guileless, profound, confident, and trustful. She carried her sorrowful head as though she were proud of that sorrow, as though she would say, I—I alone know how to mourn for him as he deserves. But while we were still shaking hands, such a look of awful desolation came upon her face that I perceived she was one of those creatures that are not the playthings of Time. For her he had died only yesterday. And, by Jove! the impression was so powerful that for me, too, he seemed to have died only yesterday—nay, this very minute. I saw her and him in the same instant of time—his death and her sorrow—I saw her sorrow in the very moment of his death. Do you understand? I saw them together—I heard them together. She had said, with a deep catch of the breath, 'I have survived' while my strained ears seemed to hear distinctly, mingled with her tone of despairing regret, the summing up whisper of his eternal condemnation. I asked myself what I was doing there, with a sensation of panic in my heart as though I had blundered into a place of cruel and absurd mysteries not fit for a human being to behold. She motioned me to a chair. We sat down. I laid the packet gently on the little table, and she put her hand over it.... 'You knew him well,' she murmured, after a moment of mourning silence.

" 'Intimacy grows quickly out there,' I said. 'I knew him as well as it is possible for one man to know another.'

" 'And you admired him,' she said. 'It was impossible to know him and not to admire him. Was it?'

" 'He was a remarkable man,' I said, unsteadily. Then before the appealing fixity of her gaze, that seemed to watch for more words on my lips, I went on, 'It was impossible not to——'

" 'Love him,' she finished eagerly, silencing me into an appalled dumbness. 'How true! how true! But when you think that no one knew him so well as I! I had all his noble confidence. I knew him best.'

" 'You knew him best,' I repeated. And perhaps she did. But with every word spoken the room was growing darker, and only her forehead, smooth and white, remained illumined by the unextinguishable light of belief and love.

" 'You were his friend,' she went on. 'His friend,' she repeated, a little louder. 'You must have been, if he had given you this, and sent you to me. I feel I can speak to you—and oh! I must speak. I want you—you who have heard his last words—to know I have been worthy of him.... It is not pride.... Yes! I am proud to know I understood him better than any one on earth—he told me so himself. And since his mother died I have had no one—no one—to—to——'

"I listened. The darkness deepened. I was not even sure whether he had given me the right bundle. I rather suspect he wanted me to take care of another batch of his papers which, after his death, I saw the manager examining under the lamp. And the girl talked, easing her pain in the certitude of my sympathy; she talked as thirsty men drink. I had heard that her engagement with Kurtz had been disapproved by her people. He wasn't rich enough or something. And indeed I don't know whether he had not been a pauper all his life. He had given me some reason to infer that it was his impatience of comparative poverty that drove him out there.

" '...Who was not his friend who had heard him speak once?' she was saying. 'He drew men towards him by what was best in them.' She looked at me with intensity. 'It is the gift of the great,' she went on, and the sound of her low voice seemed to have the accompaniment of all the other sounds, full of mystery, desolation, and sorrow, I had ever heard—the ripple of the river, the soughing of the trees swayed by the wind, the murmurs of the crowds, the faint ring of incomprehensible words cried from afar, the whisper of a voice speaking from beyond the threshold of an eternal darkness. 'But you have heard him! You know!' she cried.

" 'Yes, I know,' I said with something like despair in my heart, but bowing my head before the faith that was in her, before that great and saving illusion that shone with an unearthly glow in the darkness, in the triumphant darkness from which I could not have defended her—from which I could not even defend myself.

" 'What a loss to me—to us!'—she corrected herself with beautiful generosity; then added in a murmur, 'To the world.' By the last gleams of twilight I could see the glitter of her eyes, full of tears—of tears that would not fall.

" 'I have been very happy—very fortunate—very proud,' she went on. 'Too fortunate. Too happy for a little while. And now I am unhappy for—for life.'

"She stood up; her fair hair seemed to catch all the remaining light in a glimmer of gold. I rose, too.

" 'And of all this,' she went on, mournfully, 'of all his promise, and of all his greatness, of his generous mind, of his noble heart, nothing remains—nothing but a memory. You and I——'

" 'We shall always remember him,' I said, hastily.

" 'No!' she cried. 'It is impossible that all this should be lost—that such a life should be sacrificed to leave nothing—but sorrow. You know what vast plans he had. I knew of them, too—I could not perhaps understand—but others knew of them. Something must remain. His words, at least, have not died.'

" 'His words will remain,' I said.

" 'And his example,' she whispered to herself. 'Men looked up to him—his goodness shone in every act. His example——'

" 'True,' I said; 'his example, too. Yes, his example. I forgot that.'

" 'But I do not. I cannot—I cannot believe—not yet. I cannot believe that I shall never see him again, that nobody will see him again, never, never, never.'

"She put out her arms as if after a retreating figure, stretching them back and with clasped pale hands across the fading and narrow sheen of the window. Never see him! I saw him clearly enough then. I shall see this eloquent phantom as long as I live, and I shall see her, too, a tragic and familiar Shade, resembling in this gesture another one, tragic also, and bedecked with powerless charms, stretching bare brown arms over the glitter of the infernal stream, the stream of darkness. She said suddenly very low, 'He died as he lived.'

" 'His end,' said I, with dull anger stirring in me, 'was in every way worthy of his life.'

" 'And I was not with him,' she murmured. My anger subsided before a feeling of infinite pity.

" 'Everything that could be done——' I mumbled.

" 'Ah, but I believed in him more than any one on earth—more than his own mother, more than—himself. He needed me! Me! I would have treasured every sigh, every word, every sign, every glance.'

"I felt like a chill grip on my chest. 'Don't,' I said, in a muffled voice.

" 'Forgive me. I—I—have mourned so long in silence—in silence. . . . You were with him—to the last? I think of his loneliness. Nobody near to understand him as I would have understood. Perhaps no one to hear. . . .'

" 'To the very end,' I said, shakily. 'I heard his very last words. . . .' I stopped in a fright.

" 'Repeat them,' she murmured in a heart-broken tone. 'I want—I want—something—something—to—to live with.'

"I was on the point of crying at her, 'Don't you hear them?' The dusk was repeating them in a persistent whisper all around us, in a whisper that seemed to swell menacingly like the first whisper of a rising wind. 'The horror! the horror!'

" 'His last word—to live with,' she insisted. 'Don't you understand I loved him—I loved him—I loved him!'

"I pulled myself together and spoke slowly.

" 'The last word he pronounced was—your name.'

"I heard a light sigh and then my heart stood still, stopped dead short by an exulting and terrible cry, by the cry of inconceivable triumph and of unspeakable pain. 'I knew it—I was sure!' . . . She knew. She was sure. I heard her weeping; she had hidden her face in her hands. It seemed to me that the house would collapse before I could escape, that the heavens would fall upon my head. But nothing happened. The heavens do not fall for such a trifle. Would they have fallen, I wonder, if I had rendered Kurtz that justice which was his due? Hadn't he said he wanted only justice? But I couldn't. I could not tell her. It would have been too dark—too dark altogether. . . ."

Marlow ceased, and sat apart, indistinct and silent, in the pose of a meditating Buddha. Nobody moved for a time. "We have lost the first of the ebb," said the Director, suddenly. I raised my head. The offing was barred by a black bank of clouds, and the tranquil waterway leading to the uttermost ends of the earth flowed sombre under an overcast sky—seemed to lead into the heart of an immense darkness.

Nature of fascination w/ Kurtz?

What is the horror?   Why does he lie to fiancée?

Representation of The other?

CHINUA ACHEBE

[BORN 1930]

A novelist, poet, short-story writer, writer of children's literature, essayist, editor, and teacher, Chinua Achebe has become one of the most influential West African writers in the twentieth century. Achebe has also worked as producer, writer, and director for radio, including the Voice of Nigeria, of which he was director from 1961 to 1966. Moreover, during the Nigerian civil war he served on diplomatic missions for Biafra, and was deputy president of the People's Redemption Party in 1983. With subtlety and complexity, Achebe's novels portray from an insider's point of view traditional African society and culture, especially as it clashes with the forces of colonialism and its vestiges that remain in postcolonial Nigeria. Like fellow writers Wole Soyinka from Nigeria and Ngugi Wa Thiong'o from Kenya, Achebe has achieved in his work a sustaining moral vision for African consciousness and identity, engaging directly the difficult problems Africa faces in the postcolonial era, and recovering a sense of the African spirit as it emerges from traditional folktales, stories, and customs. Even though he writes in English, Achebe's novels capture the rich imagery and rhythms of the native proverbs and tales woven into his work.

LIFE

Achebe was born November 16, 1930, in Ogidi, Nigeria, the fifth child of Isaiah Okafor Achebe and Janet Iloegbunam, Ibo missionary teachers who raised him in a Christian household. While he received his education in English at the British missionary schools in Ogidi, Achebe developed an attachment to traditional Ibo stories from his mother and sister. In his teens he studied at the Government College, Umuahia, and enrolled in University College, Ibadan, from 1948 to 1953, when he received his bachelor's degree. Although he had entered college on a scholarship to study medicine, after his first year he switched to the liberal arts, including English literature. His reading in European, especially English, literature brought home to Achebe the often condescending and false image of Africa presented by European writers such as Joyce Cary and Joseph Conrad. Achebe began writing his first novel, *Things Fall Apart* (1958), as a direct repudiation of the image of Nigeria presented in Cary's *Mister Johnson* (1939).

Upon graduation from the university at Ibadan, Achebe worked as producer and director for the Nigerian Broadcasting Service until the Nigerian civil war erupted in 1967. Nigeria had gained its independence from Britain in 1960, the year before Achebe's marriage to Christie Chinwe Okoli. Into the vacuum created by the withdrawal of British colonial authority, three tribal groups—the Ibo, Hausa-Fulani, and Yoruba—competed against one another for power. The civil war, which lasted from 1967 to 1970, did little to resolve these rivalries, and since the time of the war Nigeria has been ruled by a succession of dictators, sometimes posing as supporters of democracy. During the war, Biafra, a state of Ibo speakers in eastern Nigeria, seceded from the rest of the country. Achebe supported the Biafran independence movement, working for the Biafran Ministry of Information. That experience has served him well, especially in *A Man of the People* (1966) and *Anthills of the Savannah* (1987), where Achebe focuses on the corruption, power-mongering, and hope for democratic freedoms that characterize Nigerian politics today. A collection of poetry, *Christmas in Biafra,* which won the Commonwealth Poetry Prize, and a collection of short stories, *Girls at War,* were written during the civil war.

In the early 1970s Achebe accepted a visiting professorship at the University of Massachusetts, Amherst, where he again taught from 1987 to 1988, and at the University of Connecticut at Storrs. During this time he taught literature and founded and edited *Okike,* a journal of African literature and criticism. In addition, he founded the Heinemann African Writers Series, which has established African literature in English as a major force in the scene of contemporary world literature. In 1976 Achebe returned to Nigeria as teacher and senior research fellow at the University of Nigeria, Nsukka. He has continued to be involved in Nigerian political life, primarily as a commentator, and in 1983 he published *The Trouble with Nigeria,* a nonfictional critique of the political corruption of his country.

WORK

Achebe describes himself as a "political writer" whose work is "concerned with universal human communication across racial and cultural boundaries as a means of fostering respect for all people." One major effort to foster respect for all was to reverse the distorted representation of Africa that European writers had delivered to European audiences and to show the adverse impact that colonization had upon indigenous cultures. His first three novels, which comprise a kind of trilogy, directly address these concerns. *Things Fall Apart* (1958), which we choose here to represent Achebe, concerns Nigeria just at the advent of British colonization. It takes place in the Ibo villages of Umuofia in the late 1880s, a time when English missionaries and administrators first began to appear. The Europeans had been interested in the Niger delta region for its palm oil, and in 1879 an Englishman, George Goldie, formed the United Africa Company to drive out the French, who had conquered most of Western Africa in the decade before. Eventually becoming the Royal Niger Company and granted a royal charter, Goldie's company established a monopoly in the region by about 1884. By 1893, Nigeria was declared a British colony, and cocoa, timber, rubber, coconuts, and palm oil began to flow from the country on British ships. This economic history looms in the background of the novel, which focuses upon the psychological and cultural consequences of that history as it affects the leader Okonkwo, who struggles to preserve his own and his people's integrity and sovereignty in the face of the changes in law and religion that the colonizers have brought.

His next two novels, *No Longer at Ease* (1960) and *Arrow of God* (1964), continue the story of Umuofia in the two generations after Okonkwo's. Although *Arrow of God* is the third novel in the series, it tells the story of the second generation in Umuofia in the 1920s. Ezeulu, a spiritual leader, also must grapple with the gap between European and African ways. Another flawed hero, Ezeulu plans to use his son to spy on Western schools, but fails when the son, Oduche, is converted and turns against his father and his father's god. Ezeulu manages to get arrested, is imprisoned by the British, and finally embitters his own people so much by carrying out a heavy penalty upon them that the entire village turns against him. *No Longer at Ease* takes us into the 1950s, when a grandson of Okonkwo, the English-educated Obi Okonkwo, fails to integrate Ibo tradition with his Europeanized ideals. In this case, the would-be hero represents the educated elite, whose aspirations have more often than not failed to materialize in Nigeria. Obi returns to his country a kind of stranger, turns against his people, and falls into the political corruption he'd hoped to eradicate.

Achebe's next three novels focus primarily upon political corruption, and they concentrate on the post–1960 period—the period after Nigerian independence. *A Man of the People* (1966) condemns the abuse of power and corruption, as does *Anthills of the Savannah* (1988). The latter novel, one of the most highly acclaimed of Achebe's works, follows a set of friends—Ikem, Sam, and Chris—whose friendship falls apart as Sam, who has become a military dictator of the imaginary West African country of Kangan, loses the support and confidence of Ikem, an editor, and Chris, the Minister of Information. To preserve his power, Sam resorts to propaganda, repression, and finally, the extermination of opponents and critics. As in the case of *A Man of the People*, which seemed to anticipate much of the corruption of the 1970s, *Anthills of the Savannah* appears to have prophesied the duplicity and arbitrary wielding of power of the present regime in Nigeria. The novel ends with a cautious optimism, noting the important role of women in the movement for reform. As this last novel points with cautious optimism to the uncertain future of Nigeria, Achebe's work so far constitutes a history, in fiction, of colonialism and independence in Nigeria from the nineteenth century to the present.

Things Fall Apart, one of the first and finest novels of post-independence African literature in English, launched Achebe on the project of tracing Nigeria's history through his fiction. The title comes from William Butler Yeats's "The Second Coming," a visionary poem announcing the birth of a "rough beast . . . slouching toward Bethlehem." That beast appears to be the erosion of Ibo society, here portrayed in unsurpassed detail, sensitivity, and understanding, after the devastating encounter with European colonialism. Set in roughly the same period as Conrad's *Heart of Darkness* (1902), the novel presents the early encounter with European missionaries from the African—specifically, the Ibo—point of view. Some of the incidents of this encounter, such as the raid on Abame mentioned in Chapter 15, are based on actual historical incidents—in this case, a British attack upon the town of Ahiara, which took place in 1905, to avenge the killing of a missionary. Achebe's critique of British colonialism comes less through the documentation of such incidents and more through the celebration of Ibo culture. To counteract the portrayal of the African as a shadowy figure in novels such as Joyce Cary's *Mister Johnson* (1939) and Conrad's *Heart of Darkness,* which, in Achebe's words, treat Africa "as setting and backdrop which eliminates the African as human factor," Achebe in this novel and others emphasizes, without resorting to sentimentalization, the humanity and dignity of the African people. In *Things Fall Apart,* Achebe presents that humanity in part through the character of the village leader Okonkwo, whose actions involve him in almost every aspect of the complex culture and religious life of the Ibo in Umuofia.

In the figure of Okonkwo, Achebe presents a complex and tragic hero as noble and as flawed as an Achilles or a Creon. While Okonkwo embodies many of the virtues of his society—courage, industriousness, and material success—he also demonstrates a dangerous stubbornness and self-satisfaction. His killing of Ikemefuna and his rejection of his son Nwoye are presented unsympathetically; indeed, like Creon's in *Antigone,* Okonkwo's rigidity and heavy-handedness eventually lead to his downfall. As in later novels, and like his compatriot writer Wole Soyinka, Achebe recognizes the need for the preservation of tradition, but he also affirms a cautious and controlled acceptance of those European ideas and practices that can enhance that culture and make it stronger.

One of the features of the novel, carried even further in *Arrow of God,* is the sprinkling of Ibo proverbs throughout the story. In these proverbs we see some of the values of Ibo culture, which include, as critic Emmanuel Ngara points out, "bravery, hard work, material wealth . . . eloquence and dignity," values associated only with Europe in the eyes of some Western readers. Moreover, the proverbs alert us to important, often contradictory, motifs and themes in the novel. One of the key proverbs from *Things Fall Apart,* "when a man says yes his *chi* says yes also," points to Okonkwo's pride in the self-determination that led to his success and that won him the praise of his people. When Okonkwo accidentally kills Ezeudu's son, he begins to face the hard reality that even a self-made man such as himself is subject to forces beyond his control. Now barred forever from becoming one of the lords of the clan, Okonkwo's fate tests the proverb of the *chi,* for he had worked hard to take control over his life, saying yes to his *chi,* and yet his *chi* denied him his ultimate desire. Other proverbs note the need for those who have been blessed to be humble, and for the great to accept greatness in others; the tale of the greedy tortoise in Chapter 11 also cautions against greed and excessive pride. Okonkwo's contempt for those who have been less successful than he is the first sign of the trouble to come.

The English missionaries and administration exacerbate the troubles visited upon Okonkwo. The white missionary at Mbanta articulates the uninformed prejudice against native religion and culture, which the novel has just elaborated in fine detail. Achebe introduces the missionary comically; the villagers mock his interpreter's use of their language as he mistakes the word meaning "my buttocks" for "myself." Many of the Mbanta men are astounded at the missionaries' pronouncements that their gods are dead and have no power; they laugh with incredulity at a missionary's claims that his is the only living and powerful god, as the novel effectively presents the colonial encounter here from the point of view of the colonized. In "An Image of Africa," delivered as a Chancellor's Lecture at the University of Massachusetts, Amherst, on February 18, 1975, Achebe made a statement that could well describe the achievement of this novel: "to look at Africa not through a haze of distortions and cheap mystification but quite simply as a continent of people—not angels, but not rudimentary souls either— just people, often highly gifted people and often strikingly successful in their enterprise with life and society." Nonetheless, this story ends tragically, with Okonkwo humiliated by the beating he'd received in the white man's jail and his deep disappointment that the men of Umuofia would not stand up, as he had, to the encroachment of the English. Okonkwo's death becomes a symbol, in many ways, for the death of Ibo society itself; the novel asks us to question whether that death was necessary, and it gives its African readers reason to believe in the importance of preserving what is best in their traditions.

SUGGESTED READINGS

C. L. Innes in *Chinua Achebe* (1990) offers a critical analysis of Achebe's major work; a more recent work is Simon Gikandi's *Reading Chinua Achebe: Language and Ideology in Fiction* (1991). For a study of the historical and cultural backgrounds, see Robert M. Wren's *Achebe's World: The Historical and Cultural Context of the Novels of Chinua Achebe* (1981). A collection of essays covering Achebe's earlier works is *Critical Perspectives on Chinua Achebe* (1978), edited by C. L. Innes and Bernth Lindfors. For *Things Fall Apart* in particular, see Bernth Lindfors's useful collection of essays, *Approaches to Teaching Achebe's Things Fall Apart* (1991), and Kate Turkington's earlier *Chinua Achebe: Things Fall Apart* (1977).

Things Fall Apart

PART I

1

Okonkwo was well known throughout the nine villages and even beyond. His fame rested on solid personal achievements. As a young man of eighteen he had brought honor to his village by throwing Amalinze the Cat. Amalinze was the great wrestler who for seven years was unbeaten, from Umuofia to Mbaino. He was called the Cat because his back would never touch the earth. It was this man that Okonkwo threw in a fight which the old men agreed was one of the fiercest since the founder of their town engaged a spirit of the wild for seven days and seven nights.

The drums beat and the flutes sang and the spectators held their breath. Amalinze was a wily craftsman, but Okonkwo was as slippery as a fish in water. Every nerve and every muscle stood out on their arms, on their backs and their thighs, and one almost heard them stretching to breaking point. In the end Okonkwo threw the Cat.

That was many years ago, twenty years or more, and during this time Okonkwo's fame had grown like a bush-fire in the harmattan. He was tall and huge, and his bushy eyebrows and wide nose gave him a very severe look. He breathed heavily, and it was said that, when he slept, his wives and children in their houses could hear him breathe. When he walked, his heels hardly touched the ground and he seemed to walk on springs, as if he was going to pounce on somebody. And he did pounce on people quite often. He had a slight stammer and whenever he was angry and could not get his words out quickly enough, he would use his fists. He had no patience with unsuccessful men. He had had no patience with his father.

Unoka, for that was his father's name, had died ten years ago. In his day he was lazy and improvident and was quite incapable of thinking about tomorrow. If any money came his way, and it seldom did, he immediately bought gourds of palm-wine, called round his neighbors and made merry. He always said that whenever he saw a dead man's mouth he saw the folly of not eating what one had in one's lifetime. Unoka was, of course, a debtor, and he owed every neighbor some money, from a few cowries[1] to quite substantial amounts.

He was tall but very thin and had a slight stoop. He wore a haggard and mournful look except when he was drinking or playing on his flute. He was very good on his flute, and his happiest moments were the two or three moons after the harvest when the village musicians brought down their instruments, hung above the fireplace. Unoka would play with them, his face beaming with blessedness and peace. Sometimes another village would ask Unoka's band and their dancing *egwugwu*[2] to come and stay with them and teach them their tunes. They would go to such hosts for as long as three or four markets,[3] making music and feasting. Unoka loved the good fare and the good fellowship, and he loved this season

---

[1] A sixty-pound bag of cowries—mollusk shells used as currency—was worth about one pound sterling.
[2] Dancers who masquerade as spirits of the village ancestors.
[3] One-and-a-half to two weeks; the Ibo week has four days—Eke, the market day; Afo, a half-working day; and Oye and Nkwo, full working days.

of the year, when the rains had stopped and the sun rose every morning with dazzling beauty. And it was not too hot either, because the cold and dry harmattan wind was blowing down from the north. Some years the harmattan was very severe and a dense haze hung on the atmosphere. Old men and children would then sit round log fires, warming their bodies. Unoka loved it all, and he loved the first kites that returned with the dry season, and the children who sang songs of welcome to them. He would remember his own childhood, how he had often wandered around looking for a kite sailing leisurely against the blue sky. As soon as he found one he would sing with his whole being, welcoming it back from its long, long journey, and asking it if it had brought home any lengths of cloth.

That was years ago, when he was young. Unoka, the grown-up, was a failure. He was poor and his wife and children had barely enough to eat. People laughed at him because he was a loafer, and they swore never to lend him any more money because he never paid back. But Unoka was such a man that he always succeeded in borrowing more, and piling up his debts.

One day a neighbor called Okoye came in to see him. He was reclining on a mud bed in his hut playing on the flute. He immediately rose and shook hands with Okoye, who then unrolled the goatskin which he carried under his arm, and sat down. Unoka went into an inner room and soon returned with a small wooden disc containing a kola nut, some alligator pepper and a lump of white chalk.[4]

"I have kola," he announced when he sat down, and passed the disc over to his guest.

"Thank you. He who brings kola brings life. But I think you ought to break it," replied Okoye, passing back the disc.

"No, it is for you, I think," and they argued like this for a few moments before Unoka accepted the honor of breaking the kola. Okoye, meanwhile, took the lump of chalk, drew some lines on the floor, and then painted his big toe.

As he broke the kola, Unoka prayed to their ancestors for life and health, and for protection against their enemies. When they had eaten they talked about many things: about the heavy rains which were drowning the yams, about the next ancestral feast and about the impending war with the village of Mbaino. Unoka was never happy when it came to wars. He was in fact a coward and could not bear the sight of blood. And so he changed the subject and talked about music, and his face beamed. He could hear in his mind's ear the blood-stirring and intricate rhythms of the *ekwe* and the *udu* and the *ogene*,[5] and he could hear his own flute weaving in and out of them, decorating them with a colorful and plaintive tune. The total effect was gay and brisk, but if one picked out the flute as it went up and down and then broke up into short snatches, one saw that there was sorrow and grief there.

Okoye was also a musician. He played on the *ogene*. But he was not a failure like Unoka. He had a large barn full of yams and he had three wives. And now he was going to take the Idemili[6] title, the third highest in the land. It was a very expensive ceremony and he was gathering all his resources together. That was in fact the reason why he had come to see Unoka. He cleared his throat and began:

"Thank you for the kola. You may have heard of the title I intend to take shortly."

---

[4] All items used in hospitality ceremonies. Kola nuts, like coffee, contain caffeine and so offer a mild stimulant; alligator pepper is a black pepper reserved especially for kola; and the chalk is used for visitors to draw their personal mark.
[5] A wooden drum, clay drum, and iron gong, respectively.
[6] A river god, associated with the sacred python.

Having spoken plainly so far, Okoye said the next half a dozen sentences in proverbs. Among the Ibo the art of conversation is regarded very highly, and proverbs are the palm-oil with which words are eaten. Okoye was a great talker and he spoke for a long time, skirting round the subject and then hitting it finally. In short, he was asking Unoka to return the two hundred cowries he had borrowed from him more than two years before. As soon as Unoka understood what his friend was driving at, he burst out laughing. He laughed loud and long and his voice rang out clear as the *ogene,* and tears stood in his eyes. His visitor was amazed, and sat speechless. At the end, Unoka was able to give an answer between fresh outbursts of mirth.

"Look at that wall," he said, pointing at the far wall of his hut, which was rubbed with red earth so that it shone. "Look at those lines of chalk;" and Okoye saw groups of short perpendicular lines drawn in chalk. There were five groups, and the smallest group had ten lines. Unoka had a sense of the dramatic and so he allowed a pause, in which he took a pinch of snuff and sneezed noisily, and then he continued: "Each group there represents a debt to someone, and each stroke is one hundred cowries. You see, I owe that man a thousand cowries. But he has not come to wake me up in the morning for it. I shall pay you, but not today. Our elders say that the sun will shine on those who stand before it shines on those who kneel under them. I shall pay my big debts first." And he took another pinch of snuff, as if that was paying the big debts first. Okoye rolled his goatskin and departed.

When Unoka died he had taken no title at all and he was heavily in debt. Any wonder then that his son Okonkwo was ashamed of him? Fortunately, among these people a man was judged according to his worth and not according to the worth of his father. Okonkwo was clearly cut out for great things. He was still young but he had won fame as the greatest wrestler in the nine villages. He was a wealthy farmer and had two barns full of yams, and had just married his third wife. To crown it all he had taken two titles and had shown incredible prowess in two inter-tribal wars. And so although Okonkwo was still young, he was already one of the greatest men of his time. Age was respected among his people, but achievement was revered. As the elders said, if a child washed his hands he could eat with kings. Okonkwo had clearly washed his hands and so he ate with kings and elders. And that was how he came to look after the doomed lad who was sacrificed to the village of Umuofia by their neighbors to avoid war and bloodshed. The ill-fated lad was called Ikemefuna.

2

Okonkwo had just blown out the palm-oil lamp and stretched himself on his bamboo bed when he heard the *ogene* of the town crier piercing the still night air. *Gome, gome, gome, gome,* boomed the hollow metal. Then the crier gave his message, and at the end of it beat his instrument again. And this was the message. Every man of Umuofia was asked to gather at the market place tomorrow morning. Okonkwo wondered what was amiss, for he knew certainly that something was amiss. He had discerned a clear overtone of tragedy in the crier's voice, and even now he could still hear it as it grew dimmer and dimmer in the distance.

The night was very quiet. It was always quiet except on moonlight nights. Darkness held a vague terror for these people, even the bravest among them. Children were warned not to whistle at night for fear of evil spirits. Dangerous animals became even more sinister and uncanny in the dark. A snake was never called by its name at night, because it would hear. It was called a string. And so on this particular night as the crier's voice was gradually swallowed up in the distance, silence returned to the world, a vibrant silence made more intense by the universal trill of a million million forest insects.

On a moonlight night it would be different. The happy voices of children playing in open fields would then be heard. And perhaps those not so young would be playing in pairs in less open places, and old men and women would remember their youth. As the Ibo say: "When the moon is shining the cripple becomes hungry for a walk."

But this particular night was dark and silent. And in all the nine villages of Umuofia a town crier with his *ogene* asked every man to be present tomorrow morning. Okonkwo on his bamboo bed tried to figure out the nature of the emergency—war with a neighboring clan? That seemed the most likely reason, and he was not afraid of war. He was a man of action, a man of war. Unlike his father he could stand the look of blood. In Umuofia's latest war he was the first to bring home a human head. That was his fifth head; and he was not an old man yet. On great occasions such as the funeral of a village celebrity he drank his palm-wine from his first human head.

In the morning the market place was full. There must have been about ten thousand men there, all talking in low voices. At last Ogbuefi Ezeugo stood up in the midst of them and bellowed four times, "*Umuofia kwenu,*"[7] and on each occasion he faced a different direction and seemed to push the air with a clenched fist. And ten thousand men answered "*Yaa!*" each time. Then there was perfect silence. Ogbuefi Ezeugo was a powerful orator and was always chosen to speak on such occasions. He moved his hand over his white head and stroked his white beard. He then adjusted his cloth, which was passed under his right arm-pit and tied above his left shoulder.

"*Umuofia kwenu,*" he bellowed a fifth time, and the crowd yelled in answer. And then suddenly like one possessed he shot out his left hand and pointed in the direction of Mbaino, and said through gleaming white teeth firmly clenched: "Those sons of wild animals have dared to murder a daughter of Umuofia." He threw his head down and gnashed his teeth, and allowed a murmur of suppressed anger to sweep the crowd. When he began again, the anger on his face was gone and in its place a sort of smile hovered, more terrible and more sinister than the anger. And in a clear unemotional voice he told Umuofia how their daughter had gone to market at Mbaino and had been killed. That woman, said Ezeugo, was the wife of Ogbuefi Udo, and he pointed to a man who sat near him with a bowed head. The crowd then shouted with anger and thirst for blood.

Many others spoke, and at the end it was decided to follow the normal course of action. An ultimatum was immediately dispatched to Mbaino asking them to choose between war on the one hand, and on the other the offer of a young man and a virgin as compensation.

Umuofia was feared by all its neighbors. It was powerful in war and in magic, and its priests and medicine men were feared in all the surrounding country. Its most potent war-medicine was as old as the clan itself. Nobody knew how old. But on one point there was general agreement—the active principle in that medicine had been an old woman with one leg. In fact, the medicine itself was called *agadi-nwayi,* or old woman. It had its shrine in the centre of Umuofia, in a cleared spot. And if anybody was so foolhardy as to pass by the shrine after dusk he was sure to see the old woman hopping about.

And so the neighboring clans who naturally knew of these things feared Umuofia, and would not go to war against it without first trying a peaceful settlement. And

---

[7]"Umuofia united."

in fairness to Umuofia it should be recorded that it never went to war unless its case was clear and just and was accepted as such by its Oracle—the Oracle of the Hills and the Caves. And there were indeed occasions when the Oracle had forbidden Umuofia to wage a war. If the clan had disobeyed the Oracle they would surely have been beaten, because their dreaded *agadi-nwayi* would never fight what the Ibo call a *fight of blame.*

But the war that now threatened was a just war. Even the enemy clan knew that. And so when Okonkwo of Umuofia arrived at Mbaino as the proud and imperious emissary of war, he was treated with great honor and respect, and two days later he returned home with a lad of fifteen and a young virgin. The lad's name was Ikemefuna, whose sad story is still told in Umuofia unto this day.

The elders, or *ndichie,* met to hear a report of Okonkwo's mission. At the end they decided, as everybody knew they would, that the girl should go to Ogbuefi Udo to replace his murdered wife. As for the boy, he belonged to the clan as a whole, and there was no hurry to decide his fate. Okonkwo was, therefore, asked on behalf of the clan to look after him in the interim. And so for three years Ikemefuna lived in Okonkwo's household.

Okonkwo ruled his household with a heavy hand. His wives, especially the youngest, lived in perpetual fear of his fiery temper, and so did his little children. Perhaps down in his heart Okonkwo was not a cruel man. But his whole life was dominated by fear, the fear of failure and of weakness. It was deeper and more intimate than the fear of evil and capricious gods and of magic, the fear of the forest, and of the forces of nature, malevolent, red in tooth and claw. Okonkwo's fear was greater than these. It was not external but lay deep within himself. It was the fear of himself, lest he should be found to resemble his father. Even as a little boy he had resented his father's failure and weakness, and even now he still remembered how he had suffered when a playmate had told him that his father was *agbala*. That was how Okonkwo first came to know that *agbala* was not only another name for a woman, it could also mean a man who had taken no title. And so Okonkwo was ruled by one passion—to hate everything that his father Unoka had loved. One of those things was gentleness and another was idleness.

During the planting season Okonkwo worked daily on his farms from cock crow until the chickens went to roost. He was a very strong man and rarely felt fatigue. But his wives and young children were not as strong, and so they suffered. But they dared not complain openly. Okonkwo's first son, Nwoye, was then twelve years old but was already causing his father great anxiety for his incipient laziness. At any rate, that was how it looked to his father, and he sought to correct him by constant nagging and beating. And so Nwoye was developing into a sad-faced youth.

Okonkwo's prosperity was visible in his household. He had a large compound enclosed by a thick wall of red earth. His own hut, or *obi*, stood immediately behind the only gate in the red walls. Each of his three wives had her own hut, which together formed a half moon behind the *obi*. The barn was built against one end of the red walls, and long stacks of yam stood out prosperously in it. At the opposite end of the compound was a shed for the goats, and each wife built a small attachment to her hut for the hens. Near the barn was a small house, the "medicine house" or shrine where Okonkwo kept the wooden symbols of his personal god and of his ancestral spirits. He worshipped them with sacrifices of kola nut, food and palm-wine, and offered prayers to them on behalf of himself, his three wives and eight children.

So when the daughter of Umuofia was killed in Mbaino, Ikemefuna came into Okonkwo's household. When Okonkwo brought him home that day he called his most senior wife and handed him over to her.

"He belongs to the clan," he told her. "So look after him."

"Is he staying long with us?" she asked.

"Do what you are told, woman," Okonkwo thundered, and stammered. "When did you become one of the *ndichie* of Umuofia?"

And so Nwoye's mother took Ikemefuna to her hut and asked no more questions.

As for the boy himself, he was terribly afraid. He could not understand what was happening to him or what he had done. How could he know that his father had taken a hand in killing a daughter of Umuofia? All he knew was that a few men had arrived at their house, conversing with his father in low tones, and at the end he had been taken out and handed over to a stranger. His mother had wept bitterly, but he had been too surprised to weep. And so the stranger had brought him, and a girl, a long, long way from home, through lonely forest paths. He did not know who the girl was, and he never saw her again.

3

Okonkwo did not have the start in life which many young men usually had. He did not inherit a barn from his father. There was no barn to inherit. The story was told in Umuofia, of how his father, Unoka, had gone to consult the Oracle of the Hills and the Caves to find out why he always had a miserable harvest.

The Oracle was called Agbala, and people came from far and near to consult it. They came when misfortune dogged their steps or when they had a dispute with their neighbors. They came to discover what the future held for them or to consult the spirits of their departed fathers.

The way into the shrine was a round hole at the side of a hill, just a little bigger than the round opening into a henhouse. Worshippers and those who came to seek knowledge from the god crawled on their belly through the hole and found themselves in a dark, endless space in the presence of Agbala. No one had ever beheld Agbala, except his priestess. But no one who had ever crawled into his awful shrine had come out without the fear of his power. His priestess stood by the sacred fire which she built in the heart of the cave and proclaimed the will of the god. The fire did not burn with a flame. The glowing logs only served to light up vaguely the dark figure of the priestess.

Sometimes a man came to consult the spirit of his dead father or relative. It was said that when such a spirit appeared, the man saw it vaguely in the darkness, but never heard its voice. Some people even said that they had heard the spirits flying and flapping their wings against the roof of the cave.

Many years ago when Okonkwo was still a boy his father, Unoka, had gone to consult Agbala. The priestess in those days was a woman called Chika. She was full of the power of her god, and she was greatly feared. Unoka stood before her and began his story.

"Every year," he said sadly, "before I put any crop in the earth, I sacrifice a cock to Ani, the owner of all land. It is the law of our fathers. I also kill a cock at the shrine of Ifejioku, the god of yams. I clear the bush and set fire to it when it is dry. I sow the yams when the first rain has fallen, and stake them when the young tendrils appear. I weed——"

"Hold your peace!" screamed the priestess, her voice terrible as it echoed through the dark void. "You have offended neither the gods nor your fathers. And when a man is at peace with his gods and his ancestors, his harvest will be good or bad according to the strength of his arm. You, Unoka, are known in all the clan for the weakness of your machete and your hoe. When your neighbors go out with their ax to cut down virgin forests, you sow your yams on exhausted farms that take no labor to clear. They cross seven rivers to make their farms; you stay at home and offer sacrifices to a reluctant soil. Go home and work like a man."

Unoka was an ill-fated man. He had a bad *chi*[8] or personal god, and evil fortune followed him to the grave, or rather to his death, for he had no grave. He died of the swelling which was an abomination to the earth goddess. When a man was afflicted with swelling in the stomach and the limbs he was not allowed to die in the house. He was carried to the Evil Forest and left there to die. There was the story of a very stubborn man who staggered back to his house and had to be carried again to the forest and tied to a tree. The sickness was an abomination to the earth, and so the victim could not be buried in her bowels. He died and rotted away above the earth, and was not given the first or the second burial. Such was Unoka's fate. When they carried him away, he took with him his flute.

With a father like Unoka, Okonkwo did not have the start in life which many young men had. He neither inherited a barn nor a title, nor even a young wife. But in spite of these disadvantages, he had begun even in his father's lifetime to lay the foundations of a prosperous future. It was slow and painful. But he threw himself into it like one possessed. And indeed he was possessed by the fear of his father's contemptible life and shameful death.

There was a wealthy man in Okonkwo's village who had three huge barns, nine wives and thirty children. His name was Nwakibie and he had taken the highest but one title which a man could take in the clan. It was for this man that Okonkwo worked to earn his first seed yams.

He took a pot of palm-wine and a cock to Nwakibie. Two elderly neighbors were sent for, and Nwakibie's two grown-up sons were also present in his *obi*. He presented a kola nut and an alligator pepper, which were passed round for all to see and then returned to him. He broke the nut saying: "We shall all live. We pray for life, children, a good harvest and happiness. You will have what is good for you and I will have what is good for me. Let the kite perch and let the eagle perch too. If one says no to the other, let his wing break."

After the kola nut had been eaten Okonkwo brought his palm-wine from the corner of the hut where it had been placed and stood it in the center of the group. He addressed Nwakibie, calling him "Our father."

"*Nna ayi,*"[9] he said. "I have brought you this little kola. As our people say, a man who pays respect to the great paves the way for his own greatness. I have come to pay you my respects and also to ask a favor. But let us drink the wine first."

Everybody thanked Okonkwo and the neighbors brought out their drinking horns from the goatskin bags they carried. Nwakibie brought down his own horn, which was fastened to the rafters. The younger of his sons, who was also the youngest man in the group, moved to the center, raised the pot on his left knee and began to pour out the wine. The first cup went to Okonkwo, who must taste his wine before anyone else. Then the group drank, beginning with the eldest man.

---

[8]Literally, one's personal god; the *chi* may be thought of as the spiritual double of the person existing in the world, which acts as a guide to the fulfillment of one's destiny. To act against the *chi* is to act against one's own best interests, as Okonkwo will do below when he kills Ikemefuna.

[9]"Our father."

When everyone had drunk two or three horns, Nwakibie sent for his wives. Some of them were not at home and only four came in.

"Is Anasi not in?" he asked them. They said she was coming. Anasi was the first wife and the others could not drink before her, and so they stood waiting.

Anasi was a middle-aged woman, tall and strongly built. There was authority in her bearing and she looked every inch the ruler of the womenfolk in a large and prosperous family. She wore the anklet of her husband's titles, which the first wife alone could wear.

She walked up to her husband and accepted the horn from him. She then went down on one knee, drank a little and handed back the horn. She rose, called him by his name and went back to her hut. The other wives drank in the same way, in their proper order, and went away.

The men then continued their drinking and talking. Ogbuefi Idigo was talking about the palm-wine tapper, Obiako, who suddenly gave up his trade.

"There must be something behind it," he said, wiping the foam of wine from his mustache with the back of his left hand. "There must be a reason for it. A toad does not run in the daytime for nothing."

"Some people say the Oracle warned him that he would fall off a palm tree and kill himself," said Akukalia.

"Obiako has always been a strange one," said Nwakibie. "I have heard that many years ago, when his father had not been dead very long, he had gone to consult the Oracle. The Oracle said to him, 'Your dead father wants you to sacrifice a goat to him.' Do you know what he told the Oracle? He said, 'Ask my dead father if he ever had a fowl when he was alive.'" Everybody laughed heartily except Okonkwo, who laughed uneasily because, as the saying goes, an old woman is always uneasy when dry bones are mentioned in a proverb. Okonkwo remembered his own father.

At last the young man who was pouring out the wine held up half a horn of the thick, white dregs and said, "What we are eating is finished." "We have seen it," the others replied. "Who will drink the dregs?" he asked. "Whoever has a job in hand," said Idigo, looking at Nwakibie's elder son Igwelo with a malicious twinkle in his eye.

Everybody agreed that Igwelo should drink the dregs. He accepted the half-full horn from his brother and drank it. As Idigo had said, Igwelo had a job in hand because he had married his first wife a month or two before. The thick dregs of palm-wine were supposed to be good for men who were going in to their wives.

After the wine had been drunk Okonkwo laid his difficulties before Nwakibie.

"I have come to you for help," he said. "Perhaps you can already guess what it is. I have cleared a farm but have no yams to sow. I know what it is to ask a man to trust another with his yams, especially these days when young men are afraid of hard work. I am not afraid of work. The lizard that jumped from the high iroko tree to the ground said he would praise himself if no one else did. I began to fend for myself at an age when most people still suck at their mothers' breasts. If you give me some yam seeds I shall not fail you."

Nwakibie cleared his throat. "It pleases me to see a young man like you these days when our youth has gone so soft. Many young men have come to me to ask for yams but I have refused because I knew they would just dump them in the earth and leave them to be choked by weeds. When I say no to them they think I am hard hearted. But it is not so. Eneke the bird says that since men have learned to shoot without missing, he has learned to fly without perching. I have learned to be stingy with my yams. But I can trust you. I know it as I look at you. As our fathers said, you can tell a ripe corn by its look. I shall give you twice four hundred yams. Go ahead and prepare your farm."

Okonkwo thanked him again and again and went home feeling happy. He knew that Nwakibie would not refuse him, but he had not expected he would be so generous. He had not hoped to get more than four hundred seeds. He would now have to make a bigger farm. He hoped to get another four hundred yams from one of his father's friends at Isiuzo.

Share-cropping was a very slow way of building up a barn of one's own. After all the toil one only got a third of the harvest. But for a young man whose father had no yams, there was no other way. And what made it worse in Okonkwo's case was that he had to support his mother and two sisters from his meagre harvest. And supporting his mother also meant supporting his father. She could not be expected to cook and eat while her husband starved. And so at a very early age when he was striving desperately to build a barn through share-cropping Okonkwo was also fending for his father's house. It was like pouring grains of corn into a bag full of holes. His mother and sisters worked hard enough, but they grew women's crops, like coco-yams, beans and cassava. Yam, the king of crops, was a man's crop.

The year that Okonkwo took eight hundred seed-yams from Nwakibie was the worst year in living memory. Nothing happened at its proper time; it was either too early or too late. It seemed as if the world had gone mad. The first rains were late, and, when they came, lasted only a brief moment. The blazing sun returned, more fierce than it had ever been known, and scorched all the green that had appeared with the rains. The earth burned like hot coals and roasted all the yams that had been sown. Like all good farmers, Okonkwo had begun to sow with the first rains. He had sown four hundred seeds when the rains dried up and the heat returned. He watched the sky all day for signs of rain clouds and lay awake all night. In the morning he went back to his farm and saw the withering tendrils. He had tried to protect them from the smoldering earth by making rings of thick sisal leaves around them. But by the end of the day the sisal rings were burned dry and gray. He changed them every day, and prayed that the rain might fall in the night. But the drought continued for eight market weeks and the yams were killed.

Some farmers had not planted their yams yet. They were the lazy easy-going ones who always put off clearing their farms as long as they could. This year they were the wise ones. They sympathized with their neighbors with much shaking of the head, but inwardly they were happy for what they took to be their own foresight.

Okonkwo planted what was left of his seed-yams when the rains finally returned. He had one consolation. The yams he had sown before the drought were his own, the harvest of the previous year. He still had the eight hundred from Nwakibie and the four hundred from his father's friend. So he would make a fresh start.

But the year had gone mad. Rain fell as it had never fallen before. For days and nights together it poured down in violent torrents, and washed away the yam heaps. Trees were uprooted and deep gorges appeared everywhere. Then the rain became less violent. But it went from day to day without a pause. The spell of sunshine which always came in the middle of the wet season did not appear. The yams put on luxuriant green leaves, but every farmer knew that without sunshine the tubers would not grow.

That year the harvest was sad, like a funeral, and many farmers wept as they dug up the miserable and rotting yams. One man tied his cloth to a tree branch and hanged himself.

Okonkwo remembered that tragic year with a cold shiver throughout the rest of his life. It always surprised him when he thought of it later that he did not sink under the load of despair. He knew that he was a fierce fighter, but that year had been enough to break the heart of a lion.

"Since I survived that year," he always said, "I shall survive anything." He put it down to his inflexible will.

His father, Unoka, who was then an ailing man, had said to him during that terrible harvest month: "Do not despair. I know you will not despair. You have a manly and a proud heart. A proud heart can survive a general failure because such a failure does not prick its pride. It is more difficult and more bitter when a man fails *alone*."

Unoka was like that in his last days. His love of talk had grown with age and sickness. It tried Okonkwo's patience beyond words.

4

"Looking at a king's mouth," said an old man, "one would think he never sucked at his mother's breast." He was talking about Okonkwo, who had risen so suddenly from great poverty and misfortune to be one of the lords of the clan. The old man bore no ill will towards Okonkwo. Indeed he respected him for his industry and success. But he was struck, as most people were, by Okonkwo's brusqueness in dealing with less successful men. Only a week ago a man had contradicted him at a kindred meeting which they held to discuss the next ancestral feast. Without looking at the man Okonkwo had said: "This meeting is for men." The man who had contradicted him had no titles. That was why he had called him a woman. Okonkwo knew how to kill a man's spirit.

Everybody at the kindred meeting took sides with Osugo when Okonkwo called him a woman. The oldest man present said sternly that those whose palm-kernels were cracked for them by a benevolent spirit should not forget to be humble. Okonkwo said he was sorry for what he had said, and the meeting continued.

But it was really not true that Okonkwo's palm-kernels had been cracked for him by a benevolent spirit. He had cracked them himself. Anyone who knew his grim struggle against poverty and misfortune could not say he had been lucky. If ever a man deserved his success, that man was Okonkwo. At an early age he had achieved fame as the greatest wrestler in all the land. That was not luck. At the most one could say that his *chi* or personal god was good. But the Ibo people have a proverb that when a man says yes his *chi* says yes also. Okonkwo said yes very strongly; so his *chi* agreed. And not only his *chi* but his clan too, because it judged a man by the work of his hands. That was why Okonkwo had been chosen by the nine villages to carry a message of war to their enemies unless they agreed to give up a young man and a virgin to atone for the murder of Udo's wife. And such was the deep fear that their enemies had for Umuofia that they treated Okonkwo like a king and brought him a virgin who was given to Udo as wife, and the lad Ikemefuna.

The elders of the clan had decided that Ikemefuna should be in Okonkwo's care for a while. But no one thought it would be as long as three years. They seemed to forget all about him as soon as they had taken the decision.

At first Ikemefuna was very much afraid. Once or twice he tried to run away, but he did not know where to begin. He thought of his mother and his three-year-old sister and wept bitterly. Nwoye's mother was very kind to him and treated him as one of her own children. But all he said was: "When shall I go home?" When Okonkwo heard that he would not eat any food he came into the hut with a big stick in his hand and stood over him while he swallowed his yams, trembling. A few moments later he went behind the hut and began to vomit painfully. Nwoye's mother went to him and placed her hands on his chest and on his back. He was ill for three market weeks, and when he recovered he seemed to have overcome his great fear and sadness.

He was by nature a very lively boy and he gradually became popular in Okonkwo's household, especially with the children. Okonkwo's son, Nwoye, who was two years younger, became quite inseparable from him because he seemed to know everything. He could fashion out flutes from bamboo stems and even from the elephant grass. He knew the names of all the birds and could set clever traps for the little bush rodents. And he knew which trees made the strongest bows.

Even Okonkwo himself became very fond of the boy—inwardly of course. Okonkwo never showed any emotion openly, unless it be the emotion of anger. To show affection was a sign of weakness; the only thing worth demonstrating was strength. He therefore treated Ikemefuna as he treated everybody else—with a heavy hand. But there was no doubt that he liked the boy. Sometimes when he went to big village meetings or communal ancestral feasts he allowed Ikemefuna to accompany him, like a son, carrying his stool and his goatskin bag. And, indeed, Ikemefuna called him father.

Ikemefuna came to Umuofia at the end of the carefree season between harvest and planting. In fact he recovered from his illness only a few days before the Week of Peace began. And that was also the year Okonkwo broke the peace, and was punished, as was the custom, by Ezeani, the priest of the earth goddess.

Okonkwo was provoked to justifiable anger by his youngest wife, who went to plait her hair at her friend's house and did not return early enough to cook the afternoon meal. Okonkwo did not know at first that she was not at home. After waiting in vain for her dish he went to her hut to see what she was doing. There was nobody in the hut and the fireplace was cold.

"Where is Ojiugo?" he asked his second wife, who came out of her hut to draw water from a gigantic pot in the shade of a small tree in the middle of the compound.

"She has gone to plait her hair."

Okonkwo bit his lips as anger welled up within him.

"Where are her children? Did she take them?" he asked with unusual coolness and restraint.

"They are here," answered his first wife, Nwoye's mother. Okonkwo bent down and looked into her hut. Ojiugo's children were eating with the children of his first wife.

"Did she ask you to feed them before she went?"

"Yes," lied Nwoye's mother, trying to minimize Ojiugo's thoughtlessness.

Okonkwo knew she was not speaking the truth. He walked back to his *obi* to await Ojiugo's return. And when she returned he beat her very heavily. In his anger he had forgotten that it was the Week of Peace. His first two wives ran out in great alarm pleading with him that it was the sacred week. But Okonkwo was not the man to stop beating somebody half-way through, not even for fear of a goddess.

Okonkwo's neighbors heard his wife crying and sent their voices over the compound walls to ask what was the matter. Some of them came over to see for themselves. It was unheard of to beat somebody during the sacred week.

Before it was dusk Ezeani, who was the priest of the earth goddess, Ani, called on Okonkwo in his *obi.* Okonkwo brought out kola nut and placed it before the priest.

"Take away your kola nut. I shall not eat in the house of a man who has no respect for our gods and ancestors."

Okonkwo tried to explain to him what his wife had done, but Ezeani seemed to pay no attention. He held a short staff in his hand which he brought down on the floor to emphasize his points.

"Listen to me," he said when Okonkwo had spoken. "You are not a stranger in Umuofia. You know as well as I do that our forefathers ordained that before we plant any crops in the earth we should observe a week in which a man does not say a harsh word to his neighbor. We live in peace with our fellows to honor our great goddess of the earth without whose blessing our crops will not grow. You have committed a great evil." He brought down his staff heavily on the floor. "Your wife was at fault, but even if you came into your *obi* and found her lover on top of her, you would still have committed a great evil to beat her." His staff came down again. "The evil you have done can ruin the whole clan. The earth goddess whom you have insulted may refuse to give us her increase, and we shall all perish." His tone now changed from anger to command. "You will bring to the shrine of Ani tomorrow one she-goat, one hen, a length of cloth and a hundred cowries." He rose and left the hut.

Okonkwo did as the priest said. He also took with him a pot of palm-wine. Inwardly, he was repentant. But he was not the man to go about telling his neighbors that he was in error. And so people said he had no respect for the gods of the clan. His enemies said his good fortune had gone to his head. They called him the little bird *nza* who so far forgot himself after a heavy meal that he challenged his *chi*.

No work was done during the Week of Peace. People called on their neighbors and drank palm-wine. This year they talked of nothing else but the *nso-ani*[10] which Okonkwo had committed. It was the first time for many years that a man had broken the sacred peace. Even the oldest men could only remember one or two other occasions somewhere in the dim past.

Ogbuefi Ezeudu, who was the oldest man in the village, was telling two other men who came to visit him that the punishment for breaking the Peace of Ani had become very mild in their clan.

"It has not always been so," he said. "My father told me that he had been told that in the past a man who broke the peace was dragged on the ground through the village until he died. But after a while this custom was stopped because it spoiled the peace which it was meant to preserve."

"Somebody told me yesterday," said one of the younger men, "that in some clans it is an abomination for a man to die during the Week of Peace."

"It is indeed true," said Ogbuefi Ezeudu. "They have that custom in Obodoani. If a man dies at this time he is not buried but cast into the Evil Forest. It is a bad custom which these people observe because they lack understanding. They throw away large numbers of men and women without burial. And what is the result? Their clan is full of the evil spirits of these unburied dead, hungry to do harm to the living."

After the Week of Peace every man and his family began to clear the bush to make new farms. The cut bush was left to dry and fire was then set to it. As the smoke rose into the sky kites appeared from different directions and hovered over the burning field in silent valediction. The rainy season was approaching when they would go away until the dry season returned.

Okonkwo spent the next few days preparing his seed-yams. He looked at each yam carefully to see whether it was good for sowing. Sometimes he decided that a

---

[10]"Earth's taboo," a serious offense against the earth goddess Ani.

yam was too big to be sown as one seed and he split it deftly along its length with his sharp knife. His eldest son, Nwoye, and Ikemefuna helped him by fetching the yams in long baskets from the barn and in counting the prepared seeds in groups of four hundred. Sometimes Okonkwo gave them a few yams each to prepare. But he always found fault with their effort, and he said so with much threatening.

"Do you think you are cutting up yams for cooking?" he asked Nwoye. "If you split another yam of this size, I shall break your jaw. You think you are still a child. I began to own a farm at your age. And you," he said to Ikemefuna, "do you not grow yams where you come from?"

Inwardly Okonkwo knew that the boys were still too young to understand fully the difficult art of preparing seed-yams. But he thought that one could not begin too early. Yam stood for manliness, and he who could feed his family on yams from one harvest to another was a very great man indeed. Okonkwo wanted his son to be a great farmer and a great man. He would stamp out the disquieting signs of laziness which he thought he already saw in him.

"I will not have a son who cannot hold up his head in the gathering of the clan. I would sooner strangle him with my own hands. And if you stand staring at me like that," he swore, "Amadiora[11] will break your head for you!"

Some days later, when the land had been moistened by two or three heavy rains, Okonkwo and his family went to the farm with baskets of seed-yams, their hoes and machetes, and the planting began. They made single mounds of earth in straight lines all over the field and sowed the yams in them.

Yam, the king of crops, was a very exacting king. For three or four moons it demanded hard work and constant attention from cock-crow till the chickens went back to roost. The young tendrils were protected from earth-heat with rings of sisal leaves. As the rains became heavier the women planted maize, melons and beans between the yam mounds. The yams were then staked, first with little sticks and later with tall and big tree branches. The women weeded the farm three times at definite periods in the life of the yams, neither early nor late.

And now the rains had really come, so heavy and persistent that even the village rain-maker no longer claimed to be able to intervene. He could not stop the rain now, just as he would not attempt to start it in the heart of the dry season, without serious danger to his own health. The personal dynamism required to counter the forces of these extremes of weather would be far too great for the human frame.

And so nature was not interfered with in the middle of the rainy season. Sometimes it poured down in such thick sheets of water that earth and sky seemed merged in one gray wetness. It was then uncertain whether the low rumbling of Amadiora's thunder came from above or below. At such times, in each of the countless thatched huts of Umuofia, children sat around their mother's cooking fire telling stories, or with their father in his *obi* warming themselves from a log fire, roasting and eating maize. It was a brief resting period between the exacting and arduous planting season and the equally exacting but light-hearted month of harvests.

Ikemefuna had begun to feel like a member of Okonkwo's family. He still thought about his mother and his three-year-old sister, and he had moments of sadness and depression. But he and Nwoye had become so deeply attached to each other that such moments became less frequent and less poignant. Ikemefuna had an endless stock of folk tales. Even those which Nwoye knew already were told with a new

---

[11]The god of thunder and lightning.

freshness and the local flavor of a different clan. Nwoye remembered this period very vividly till the end of his life. He even remembered how he had laughed when Ikemefuna told him that the proper name for a corn cob with only a few scattered grains was *eze-agadi-nwayi*, or the teeth of an old woman. Nwoye's mind had gone immediately to Nwayieke, who lived near the udala tree. She had about three teeth and was always smoking her pipe.

Gradually the rains became lighter and less frequent, and earth and sky once again became separate. The rain fell in thin, slanting showers through sunshine and quiet breeze. Children no longer stayed indoors but ran about singing:

> *"The rain is falling, the sun is shining,*
> *Alone Nnadi is cooking and eating."*

Nwoye always wondered who Nnadi was and why he should live all by himself, cooking and eating. In the end he decided that Nnadi must live in that land of Ikemefuna's favorite story where the ant holds his court in splendor and the sands dance forever.

5

The Feast of the New Yam was approaching and Umuofia was in a festival mood. It was an occasion for giving thanks to Ani, the earth goddess and the source of all fertility. Ani played a greater part in the life of the people than any other deity. She was the ultimate judge of morality and conduct. And what was more, she was in close communion with the departed fathers of the clan whose bodies had been committed to earth.

The Feast of the New Yam was held every year before the harvest began, to honor the earth goddess and the ancestral spirits of the clan. New yams could not be eaten until some had first been offered to these powers. Men and women, young and old, looked forward to the New Yam Festival because it began the season of plenty—the new year. On the last night before the festival, yams of the old year were all disposed of by those who still had them. The new year must begin with tasty, fresh yams and not the shriveled and fibrous crop of the previous year. All cooking pots, calabashes and wooden bowls were thoroughly washed, especially the wooden mortar in which yam was pounded. Yam foo-foo and vegetable soup was the chief food in the celebration. So much of it was cooked that, no matter how heavily the family ate or how many friends and relatives they invited from neighboring villages, there was always a large quantity of food left over at the end of the day. The story was always told of a wealthy man who set before his guests a mound of foo-foo so high that those who sat on one side could not see what was happening on the other, and it was not until late in the evening that one of them saw for the first time his in-law who had arrived during the course of the meal and had fallen to on the opposite side. It was only then that they exchanged greetings and shook hands over what was left of the food.

The New Yam Festival was thus an occasion for joy throughout Umuofia. And every man whose arm was strong, as the Ibo people say, was expected to invite large numbers of guests from far and wide. Okonkwo always asked his wives' relations, and since he now had three wives his guests would make a fairly big crowd.

But somehow Okonkwo could never become as enthusiastic over feasts as most people. He was a good eater and he could drink one or two fairly big gourds of palm-wine. But he was always uncomfortable sitting around for days waiting for a feast or getting over it. He would be very much happier working on his farm.

The festival was now only three days away. Okonkwo's wives had scrubbed the walls and the huts with red earth until they reflected light. They had then drawn patterns on them in white, yellow and dark green. They then set about painting themselves with cam wood and drawing beautiful black patterns on their stomachs and on their backs. The children were also decorated, especially their hair, which was shaved in beautiful patterns. The three women talked excitedly about the relations who had been invited, and the children reveled in the thought of being spoiled by these visitors from the motherland. Ikemefuna was equally excited. The New Yam Festival seemed to him to be a much bigger event here than in his own village, a place which was already becoming remote and vague in his imagination.

And then the storm burst. Okonkwo, who had been walking about aimlessly in his compound in suppressed anger, suddenly found an outlet.

"Who killed this banana tree?" he asked.

A hush fell on the compound immediately.

"Who killed this tree? Or are you all deaf and dumb?"

As a matter of fact the tree was very much alive. Okonkwo's second wife had merely cut a few leaves off it to wrap some food, and she said so. Without further argument Okonkwo gave her a sound beating and left her and her only daughter weeping. Neither of the other wives dared to interfere beyond an occasional and tentative, "It is enough, Okonkwo," pleaded from a reasonable distance.

His anger thus satisfied, Okonkwo decided to go out hunting. He had an old rusty gun made by a clever blacksmith who had come to live in Umuofia long ago. But although Okonkwo was a great man whose prowess was universally acknowledged, he was not a hunter. In fact he had not killed a rat with his gun. And so when he called Ikemefuna to fetch his gun, the wife who had just been beaten murmured something about guns that never shot. Unfortunately for her, Okonkwo heard it and ran madly into his room for the loaded gun, ran out again and aimed at her as she clambered over the dwarf wall of the barn. He pressed the trigger and there was a loud report accompanied by the wail of his wives and children. He threw down the gun and jumped into the barn, and there lay the woman, very much shaken and frightened but quite unhurt. He heaved a heavy sigh and went away with the gun.

In spite of this incident the New Yam Festival was celebrated with great joy in Okonkwo's household. Early that morning as he offered a sacrifice of new yam and palm-oil to his ancestors he asked them to protect him, his children and their mothers in the new year.

As the day wore on his in-laws arrived from three surrounding villages, and each party brought with them a huge pot of palm-wine. And there was eating and drinking till night, when Okonkwo's in-laws began to leave for their homes.

The second day of the new year was the day of the great wrestling match between Okonkwo's village and their neighbors. It was difficult to say which the people enjoyed more—the feasting and fellowship of the first day or the wrestling contest of the second. But there was one woman who had no doubt whatever in her mind. She was Okonkwo's second wife, Ekwefi, whom he nearly shot. There was no festival in all the seasons of the year which gave her as much pleasure as the wrestling match. Many years ago when she was the village beauty Okonkwo had won her heart by throwing the Cat in the greatest contest within living memory. She did not marry him then because he was too poor to pay her bride-price. But a few years later she ran away from her husband and came to live with Okonkwo. All this happened many years ago. Now Ekwefi was a woman of forty-five who had suffered a great deal in her time. But her love of wrestling contests was still as strong as it was thirty years ago.

It was not yet noon on the second day of the New Yam Festival. Ekwefi and her only daughter, Ezinma, sat near the fireplace waiting for the water in the pot to boil. The fowl Ekwefi had just killed was in the wooden mortar. The water began to boil, and in one deft movement she lifted the pot from the fire and poured the boiling water over the fowl. She put back the empty pot on the circular pad in the corner, and looked at her palms, which were black with soot. Ezinma was always surprised that her mother could lift a pot from the fire with her bare hands.

"Ekwefi," she said, "is it true that when people are grown up, fire does not burn them?" Ezinma, unlike most children, called her mother by her name.

"Yes," replied Ekwefi, too busy to argue. Her daughter was only ten years old but she was wiser than her years.

"'But Nwoye's mother dropped her pot of hot soup the other day and it broke on the floor."

Ekwefi turned the hen over in the mortar and began to pluck the feathers.

"Ekwefi," said Ezinma, who had joined in plucking the feathers, "my eyelid is twitching."

"It means you are going to cry," said her mother.

"No," Ezinma said, "it is this eyelid, the top one."

"That means you will see something."

"What will I see?" she asked.

"How can I know?" Ekwefi wanted her to work it out herself.

"Oho," said Ezinma at last. "I know what it is—the wrestling match."

At last the hen was plucked clean. Ekwefi tried to pull out the horny beak but it was too hard. She turned round on her low stool and put the beak in the fire for a few moments. She pulled again and it came off.

"Ekwefi!" a voice called from one of the other huts. It was Nwoye's mother, Okonkwo's first wife.

"Is that me?" Ekwefi called back. That was the way people answered calls from outside. They never answered yes for fear it might be an evil spirit calling.

"Will you give Ezinma some fire to bring to me?" Her own children and Ikemefuna had gone to the stream.

Ekwefi put a few live coals into a piece of broken pot and Ezinma carried it across the clean swept compound to Nwoye's mother.

"Thank you, Nma," she said. She was peeling new yams, and in a basket beside her were green vegetables and beans.

"Let me make the fire for you," Ezinma offered.

"Thank you, Ezigbo," she said. She often called her Ezigbo, which means "the good one."

Ezinma went outside and brought some sticks from a huge bundle of firewood. She broke them into little pieces across the sole of her foot and began to build a fire, blowing it with her breath.

"You will blow your eyes out," said Nwoye's mother, looking up from the yams she was peeling. "Use the fan." She stood up and pulled out the fan which was fastened into one of the rafters. As soon as she got up, the troublesome nanny-goat, which had been dutifully eating yam peelings, dug her teeth into the real thing, scooped out two mouthfuls and fled from the hut to chew the cud in the goats' shed. Nwoye's mother swore at her and settled down again to her peeling. Ezinma's fire was now sending up thick clouds of smoke. She went on fanning it until it burst into flames. Nwoye's mother thanked her and she went back to her mother's hut.

Just then the distant beating of drums began to reach them. It came from the direction of the *ilo*, the village playground. Every village had its own *ilo* which was as old as the village itself and where all the great ceremonies and dances took place. The drums beat the unmistakable wrestling dance—quick, light and gay, and it came floating on the wind.

Okonkwo cleared his throat and moved his feet to the beat of the drums. It filled him with fire as it had always done from his youth. He trembled with the desire to conquer and subdue. It was like the desire for woman.

"We shall be late for the wrestling," said Ezinma to her mother.

"They will not begin until the sun goes down."

"But they are beating the drums."

"Yes. The drums begin at noon but the wrestling waits until the sun begins to sink. Go and see if your father has brought out yams for the afternoon."

"He has. Nwoye's mother is already cooking."

"Go and bring our own, then. We must cook quickly or we shall be late for the wrestling."

Ezinma ran in the direction of the barn and brought back two yams from the dwarf wall.

Ekwefi peeled the yams quickly. The troublesome nanny-goat sniffed about, eating the peelings. She cut the yams into small pieces and began to prepare a pottage, using some of the chicken.

At that moment they heard someone crying just outside their compound. It was very much like Obiageli, Nwoye's sister.

"Is that not Obiageli weeping?" Ekwefi called across the yard to Nwoye's mother.

"Yes," she replied. "She must have broken her water-pot."

The weeping was now quite close and soon the children filed in, carrying on their heads various sizes of pots suitable to their years. Ikemefuna came first with the biggest pot, closely followed by Nwoye and his two younger brothers. Obiageli brought up the rear, her face streaming with tears. In her hand was the cloth pad on which the pot should have rested on her head.

"What happened?" her mother asked, and Obiageli told her mournful story. Her mother consoled her and promised to buy her another pot.

Nwoye's younger brothers were about to tell their mother the true story of the accident when Ikemefuna looked at them sternly and they held their peace. The fact was that Obiageli had been making *inyanga*[12] with her pot. She had balanced it on her head, folded her arms in front of her and began to sway her waist like a grown-up young lady. When the pot fell down and broke she burst out laughing. She only began to weep when they got near the iroko tree outside their compound.

The drums were still beating, persistent and unchanging. Their sound was no longer a separate thing from the living village. It was like the pulsation of its heart. It throbbed in the air, in the sunshine, and even in the trees, and filled the village with excitement.

Ekwefi ladled her husband's share of the pottage into a bowl and covered it. Ezinma took it to him in his *obi*.

Okonkwo was sitting on a goatskin already eating his first wife's meal. Obiageli, who had brought it from her mother's hut, sat on the floor waiting for him to finish. Ezinma placed her mother's dish before him and sat with Obiageli.

"Sit like a woman!" Okonkwo shouted at her. Ezinma brought her two legs together and stretched them in front of her.

"Father, will you go to see the wrestling?" Ezinma asked after a suitable interval.

"Yes," he answered. "Will you go?"

"Yes." And after a pause she said: "Can I bring your chair for you?"

"No, that is a boy's job." Okonkwo was specially fond of Ezinma. She looked very much like her mother, who was once the village beauty. But his fondness only showed on very rare occasions.

---

[12]Bragging or showing off.

"Obiageli broke her pot today," Ezinma said.

"Yes, she has told me about it," Okonkwo said between mouthfuls.

"Father," said Obiageli, "people should not talk when they are eating or pepper may go down the wrong way."

"That is very true. Do you hear that, Ezinma? You are older than Obiageli but she has more sense."

He uncovered his second wife's dish and began to eat from it. Obiageli took the first dish and returned to her mother's hut. And then Nkechi came in, bringing the third dish. Nkechi was the daughter of Okonkwo's third wife.

In the distance the drums continued to beat.

6

The whole village turned out on the *ilo*, men, women and children. They stood round in a huge circle leaving the center of the playground free. The elders and grandees of the village sat on their own stools brought there by their young sons or slaves. Okonkwo was among them. All others stood except those who came early enough to secure places on the few stands which had been built by placing smooth logs on forked pillars.

The wrestlers were not there yet and the drummers held the field. They too sat just in front of the huge circle of spectators, facing the elders. Behind them was the big and ancient silk-cotton tree which was sacred. Spirits of good children lived in that tree waiting to be born. On ordinary days young women who desired children came to sit under its shade.

There were seven drums and they were arranged according to their sizes in a long wooden basket. Three men beat them with sticks, working feverishly from one drum to another. They were possessed by the spirit of the drums.

The young men who kept order on these occasions dashed about, consulting among themselves and with the leaders of the two wrestling teams, who were still outside the circle, behind the crowd. Once in a while two young men carrying palm fronds ran round the circle and kept the crowd back by beating the ground in front of them or, if they were stubborn, their legs and feet.

At last the two teams danced into the circle and the crowd roared and clapped. The drums rose to a frenzy. The people surged forward. The young men who kept order flew around, waving their palm fronds. Old men nodded to the beat of the drums and remembered the days when they wrestled to its intoxicating rhythm.

The contest began with boys of fifteen or sixteen. There were only three such boys in each team. They were not the real wrestlers; they merely set the scene. Within a short time the first two bouts were over. But the third created a big sensation even among the elders who did not usually show their excitement so openly. It was as quick as the other two, perhaps even quicker. But very few people had ever seen that kind of wrestling before. As soon as the two boys closed in, one of them did something which no one could describe because it had been as quick as a flash. And the other boy was flat on his back. The crowd roared and clapped and for a while drowned the frenzied drums. Okonkwo sprang to his feet and quickly sat down again. Three young men from the victorious boy's team ran forward, carried him shoulder high and danced through the cheering crowd. Everybody soon knew who the boy was. His name was Maduka, the son of Obierika.

The drummers stopped for a brief rest before the real matches. Their bodies shone with sweat, and they took up fans and began to fan themselves. They also drank water from small pots and ate kola nuts. They became ordinary human beings again, talking and laughing among themselves and with others who stood near them. The air, which had been stretched taut with excitement, relaxed again. It was as if water had been poured on the tightened skin of a drum. Many people looked around, perhaps for the first time, and saw those who stood or sat next to them.

"I did not know it was you," Ekwefi said to the woman who had stood shoulder to shoulder with her since the beginning of the matches.

"I do not blame you," said the woman. "I have never seen such a large crowd of people. Is it true that Okonkwo nearly killed you with his gun?"

"It is true indeed, my dear friend. I cannot yet find a mouth with which to tell the story."

"Your *chi* is very much awake, my friend. And how is my daughter, Ezinma?"

"She has been very well for some time now. Perhaps she has come to stay."

"I think she has. How old is she now?"

"She is about ten years old."

"I think she will stay. They usually stay if they do not die before the age of six."

"I pray she stays," said Ekwefi with a heavy sigh.

The woman with whom she talked was called Chielo. She was the priestess of Agbala, the Oracle of the Hills and the Caves. In ordinary life Chielo was a widow with two children. She was very friendly with Ekwefi and they shared a common shed in the market. She was particularly fond of Ekwefi's only daughter, Ezinma, whom she called "my daughter." Quite often she bought beancakes and gave Ekwefi some to take home to Ezinma. Anyone seeing Chielo in ordinary life would hardly believe she was the same person who prophesied when the spirit of Agbala was upon her.

The drummers took up their sticks and the air shivered and grew tense like a tightened bow.

The two teams were ranged facing each other across the clear space. A young man from one team danced across the center to the other side and pointed at whomever he wanted to fight. They danced back to the center together and then closed in.

There were twelve men on each side and the challenge went from one side to the other. Two judges walked around the wrestlers and when they thought they were equally matched, stopped them. Five matches ended in this way. But the really exciting moments were when a man was thrown. The huge voice of the crowd then rose to the sky and in every direction. It was even heard in the surrounding villages.

The last match was between the leaders of the teams. They were among the best wrestlers in all the nine villages. The crowd wondered who would throw the other this year. Some said Okafo was the better man; others said he was not the equal of Ikezue. Last year neither of them had thrown the other even though the judges had allowed the contest to go on longer than was the custom. They had the same style and one saw the other's plans beforehand. It might happen again this year.

Dusk was already approaching when their contest began. The drums went mad and the crowds also. They surged forward as the two young men danced into the circle. The palm fronds were helpless in keeping them back.

Ikezue held out his right hand. Okafo seized it, and they closed in. It was a fierce contest. Ikezue strove to dig in his right heel behind Okafo so as to pitch him backwards in the clever *ege* style. But the one knew what the other was thinking. The crowd had surrounded and swallowed up the drummers, whose frantic rhythm was no longer a mere disembodied sound but the very heartbeat of the people.

The wrestlers were now almost still in each other's grip. The muscles on their arms and their thighs and on their backs stood out and twitched. It looked like an equal match. The two judges were already moving forward to separate them when Ikezue, now desperate, went down quickly on one knee in an attempt to fling his man backwards over his head. It was a sad miscalculation. Quick as the lightning of Amadiora, Okafo raised his right leg and swung it over his rival's head. The crowd burst into a thunderous roar. Okafo was swept off his feet by his supporters and carried home shoulder high. They sang his praise and the young women clapped their hands:

> *"Who will wrestle for our village?*
> *Okafo will wrestle for our village.*
> *Has he thrown a hundred men?*
> *He has thrown four hundred men.*
> *Has he thrown a hundred Cats?*
> *He has thrown four hundred Cats.*
> *Then send him word to fight for us."*

7

For three years Ikemefuna lived in Okonkwo's household and the elders of Umuofia seemed to have forgotten about him. He grew rapidly like a yam tendril in the rainy season, and was full of the sap of life. He had become wholly absorbed into his new family. He was like an elder brother to Nwoye, and from the very first seemed to have kindled a new fire in the younger boy. He made him feel grown-up; and they no longer spent the evenings in mother's hut while she cooked, but now sat with Okonkwo in his *obi*, or watched him as he tapped his palm tree for the evening wine. Nothing pleased Nwoye now more than to be sent for by his mother or another of his father's wives to do one of those difficult and masculine tasks in the home, like splitting wood, or pounding food. On receiving such a message through a younger brother or sister, Nwoye would feign annoyance and grumble aloud about women and their troubles.

Okonkwo was inwardly pleased at his son's development, and he knew it was due to Ikemefuna. He wanted Nwoye to grow into a tough young man capable of ruling his father's household when he was dead and gone to join the ancestors. He wanted him to be a prosperous man, having enough in his barn to feed the ancestors with regular sacrifices. And so he was always happy when he heard him grumbling about women. That showed that in time he would be able to control his women-folk. No matter how prosperous a man was, if he was unable to rule his women and his children (and especially his women) he was not really a man. He was like the man in the song who had ten and one wives and not enough soup for his foo-foo.

So Okonkwo encouraged the boys to sit with him in his *obi*, and he told them stories of the land—masculine stories of violence and bloodshed. Nwoye knew that it was right to be masculine and to be violent, but somehow he still preferred the stories that his mother used to tell, and which she no doubt still told to her younger children—stories of the tortoise and his wily ways, and of the bird *eneke-nti-oba*[13] who challenged the whole world to a wrestling contest and was finally thrown by the cat. He remembered the story she often told of the quarrel between Earth and Sky long ago, and how Sky withheld rain for seven years, until crops withered and the dead could not be buried because the hoes broke on the stony Earth. At last Vulture was sent to plead with Sky, and to soften his heart with a song of the suffering of the sons of men. Whenever Nwoye's mother sang this song he felt

---

[13]"Swallow with the ear of a crocodile," a kind of bird that appears in many fables and proverbs.

carried away to the distant scene in the sky where Vulture, Earth's emissary, sang for mercy. At last Sky was moved to pity, and he gave to Vulture rain wrapped in leaves of coco-yam. But as he flew home his long talon pierced the leaves and the rain fell as it had never fallen before. And so heavily did it rain on Vulture that he did not return to deliver his message but flew to a distant land, from where he had espied a fire. And when he got there he found it was a man making a sacrifice. He warmed himself in the fire and ate the entrails.

That was the kind of story that Nwoye loved. But he now knew that they were for foolish women and children, and he knew that his father wanted him to be a man. And so he feigned that he no longer cared for women's stories. And when he did this he saw that his father was pleased, and no longer rebuked him or beat him. So Nwoye and Ikemefuna would listen to Okonkwo's stories about tribal wars, or how, years ago, he had stalked his victim, overpowered him and obtained his first human head. And as he told them of the past they sat in darkness or the dim glow of logs, waiting for the women to finish their cooking. When they finished, each brought her bowl of foo-foo and bowl of soup to her husband. An oil lamp was lit and Okonkwo tasted from each bowl, and then passed two shares to Nwoye and Ikemefuna.

In this way the moons and the seasons passed. And then the locusts came. It had not happened for many a long year. The elders said locusts came once in a generation, reappeared every year for seven years and then disappeared for another lifetime. They went back to their caves in a distant land, where they were guarded by a race of stunted men. And then after another lifetime these men opened the caves again and the locusts came to Umuofia.

They came in the cold harmattan season after the harvests had been gathered, and ate up all the wild grass in the fields.

Okonkwo and the two boys were working on the red outer walls of the compound. This was one of the lighter tasks of the after-harvest season. A new cover of thick palm branches and palm leaves was set on the walls to protect them from the next rainy season. Okonkwo worked on the outside of the wall and the boys worked from within. There were little holes from one side to the other in the upper levels of the wall, and through these Okonkwo passed the rope, or *tie-tie,* to the boys and they passed it round the wooden stays and then back to him; and in this way the cover was strengthened on the wall.

The women had gone to the bush to collect firewood, and the little children to visit their playmates in the neighboring compounds. The harmattan was in the air and seemed to distill a hazy feeling of sleep on the world. Okonkwo and the boys worked in complete silence, which was only broken when a new palm frond was lifted on to the wall or when a busy hen moved dry leaves about in her ceaseless search for food.

And then quite suddenly a shadow fell on the world, and the sun seemed hidden behind a thick cloud. Okonkwo looked up from his work and wondered if it was going to rain at such an unlikely time of the year. But almost immediately a shout of joy broke out in all directions, and Umuofia, which had dozed in the noon-day haze, broke into life and activity.

"Locusts are descending," was joyfully chanted everywhere, and men, women and children left their work or their play and ran into the open to see the unfamiliar sight. The locusts had not come for many, many years, and only the old people had seen them before.

At first, a fairly small swarm came. They were the harbingers sent to survey the land. And then appeared on the horizon a slowly-moving mass like a boundless

sheet of black cloud drifting towards Umuofia. Soon it covered half the sky, and
the solid mass was now broken by tiny eyes of light like shining star dust. It was a
tremendous sight, full of power and beauty.

Everyone was now about, talking excitedly and praying that the locusts should
camp in Umuofia for the night. For although locusts had not visited Umuofia for
many years, everybody knew by instinct that they were very good to eat. And at
last the locusts did descend. They settled on every tree and on every blade of grass;
they settled on the roofs and covered the bare ground. Mighty tree branches broke
away under them, and the whole country became the brown-earth color of the
vast, hungry swarm.

Many people went out with baskets trying to catch them, but the elders counseled
patience till nightfall. And they were right. The locusts settled in the bushes for the
night and their wings became wet with dew. Then all Umuofia turned out in spite
of the cold harmattan, and everyone filled his bags and pots with locusts. The next
morning they were roasted in clay pots and then spread in the sun until they became
dry and brittle. And for many days this rare food was eaten with solid palm-oil.

Okonkwo sat in his *obi* crunching happily with Ikemefuna and Nwoye, and
drinking palm-wine copiously, when Ogbuefi Ezeudu came in. Ezeudu was the
oldest man in this quarter of Umuofia. He had been a great and fearless warrior
in his time, and was now accorded great respect in all the clan. He refused to join
in the meal, and asked Okonkwo to have a word with him outside. And so they
walked out together, the old man supporting himself with his stick. When they
were out of earshot, he said to Okonkwo:

"That boy calls you father. Do not bear a hand in his death." Okonkwo was
surprised, and was about to say something when the old man continued:

"Yes, Umuofia has decided to kill him. The Oracle of the Hills and the Caves
has pronounced it. They will take him outside Umuofia as is the custom, and kill
him there. But I want you to have nothing to do with it. He calls you his father."

The next day a group of elders from all the nine villages of Umuofia came to
Okonkwo's house early in the morning, and before they began to speak in low
tones Nwoye and Ikemefuna were sent out. They did not stay very long, but when
they went away Okonkwo sat still for a very long time supporting his chin in his
palms. Later in the day he called Ikemefuna and told him that he was to be taken
home the next day. Nwoye overheard it and burst into tears, whereupon his father
beat him heavily. As for Ikemefuna, he was at a loss. His own home had gradually
become very faint and distant. He still missed his mother and his sister and would
be very glad to see them. But somehow he knew he was not going to see them. He
remembered once when men had talked in low tones with his father; and it seemed
now as if it was happening all over again.

Later, Nwoye went to his mother's hut and told her that Ikemefuna was going
home. She immediately dropped her pestle with which she was grinding pepper,
folded her arms across her breast and sighed, "Poor child."

The next day, the men returned with a pot of wine. They were all fully dressed
as if they were going to a big clan meeting or to pay a visit to a neighboring
village. They passed their cloths under the right arm-pit, and hung their goatskin
bags and sheathed machetes over their left shoulders. Okonkwo got ready quickly
and the party set out with Ikemefuna carrying the pot of wine. A deathly silence descended on Okonkwo's compound. Even the very little children seemed to
know. Throughout that day Nwoye sat in his mother's hut and tears stood in his
eyes.

At the beginning of their journey the men of Umuofia talked and laughed about
the locusts, about their women, and about some effeminate men who had refused

to come with them. But as they drew near to the outskirts of Umuofia silence fell upon them too.

The sun rose slowly to the center of the sky, and the dry, sandy footway began to throw up the heat that lay buried in it. Some birds chirruped in the forests around. The men trod dry leaves on the sand. All else was silent. Then from the distance came the faint beating of the *ekwe*. It rose and faded with the wind—a peaceful dance from a distant clan.

"It is an *ozo*[14] dance," the men said among themselves. But no one was sure where it was coming from. Some said Ezimili, others Abame or Aninta. They argued for a short while and fell into silence again, and the elusive dance rose and fell with the wind. Somewhere a man was taking one of the titles of his clan, with music and dancing and a great feast.

The footway had now become a narrow line in the heart of the forest. The short trees and sparse undergrowth which surrounded the men's village began to give way to giant trees and climbers which perhaps had stood from the beginning of things, untouched by the ax and the bush-fire. The sun breaking through their leaves and branches threw a pattern of light and shade on the sandy footway.

Ikemefuna heard a whisper close behind him and turned round sharply. The man who had whispered now called out aloud, urging the others to hurry up.

"We still have a long way to go," he said. Then he and another man went before Ikemefuna and set a faster pace.

Thus the men of Umuofia pursued their way, armed with sheathed machetes, and Ikemefuna, carrying a pot of palm-wine on his head, walked in their midst. Although he had felt uneasy at first, he was not afraid now. Okonkwo walked behind him. He could hardly imagine that Okonkwo was not his real father. He had never been fond of his real father, and at the end of three years he had become very distant indeed. But his mother and his three-year-old sister ... of course she would not be three now, but six. Would he recognize her now? She must have grown quite big. How his mother would weep for joy, and thank Okonkwo for having looked after him so well and for bringing him back. She would want to hear everything that had happened to him in all these years. Could he remember them all? He would tell her about Nwoye and his mother, and about the locusts. . . . Then quite suddenly a thought came upon him. His mother might be dead. He tried in vain to force the thought out of his mind. Then he tried to settle the matter the way he used to settle such matters when he was a little boy. He still remembered the song:

> *Eze elina, elina!*
> > *Sala*
> *Eze ilikwa ya*
> *Ikwaba akwa oligholi*
> *Ebe Danda nechi eze*
> *Ebe Uzuzu nete egwu*
> > *Sala*[15]

He sang it in his mind, and walked to its beat. If the song ended on his right foot, his mother was alive. If it ended on his left, she was dead. No, not dead, but ill. It ended on the right. She was alive and well. He sang the song again, and it ended

---

[14] One of the four titles or ranks in the Ibo society; they are Ozo, Idemili, Omalo, and Erulu.

[15] "King don't eat, don't eat! / Sala / King if you eat it / You will weep for the abomination / Where Danda installs a king / Where Uzuzu dances / Sala." *Danda* means "ant"; *Uzuzu*, "sand"; and *Sala*, which has no meaning, is a refrain.

on the left. But the second time did not count. The first voice gets to Chukwu, or God's house. That was a favorite saying of children. Ikemefuna felt like a child once more. It must be the thought of going home to his mother.

One of the men behind him cleared his throat. Ikemefuna looked back, and the man growled at him to go on and not stand looking back. The way he said it sent cold fear down Ikemefuna's back. His hands trembled vaguely on the black pot he carried. Why had Okonkwo withdrawn to the rear? Ikemefuna felt his legs melting under him. And he was afraid to look back.

As the man who had cleared his throat drew up and raised his machete, Okonkwo looked away. He heard the blow. The pot fell and broke in the sand. He heard Ikemefuna cry, "My father, they have killed me!" as he ran towards him. Dazed with fear, Okonkwo drew his machete and cut him down. He was afraid of being thought weak.

As soon as his father walked in, that night, Nwoye knew that Ikemefuna had been killed, and something seemed to give way inside him, like the snapping of a tightened bow. He did not cry. He just hung limp. He had had the same kind of feeling not long ago, during the last harvest season. Every child loved the harvest season. Those who were big enough to carry even a few yams in a tiny basket went with grown-ups to the farm. And if they could not help in digging up the yams, they could gather firewood together for roasting the ones that would be eaten there on the farm. This roasted yam soaked in red palm-oil and eaten in the open farm was sweeter than any meal at home. It was after such a day at the farm during the last harvest that Nwoye had felt for the first time a snapping inside him like the one he now felt. They were returning home with baskets of yams from a distant farm across the stream when they heard the voice of an infant crying in the thick forest. A sudden hush had fallen on the women, who had been talking, and they had quickened their steps. Nwoye had heard that twins were put in earthenware pots and thrown away in the forest, but he had never yet come across them. A vague chill had descended on him and his head had seemed to swell, like a solitary walker at night who passes an evil spirit on the way. Then something had given way inside him. It descended on him again, this feeling, when his father walked in, that night after killing Ikemefuna.

8

Okonkwo did not taste any food for two days after the death of Ikemefuna. He drank palm-wine from morning till night, and his eyes were red and fierce like the eyes of a rat when it was caught by the tail and dashed against the floor. He called his son, Nwoye, to sit with him in his *obi*. But the boy was afraid of him and slipped out of the hut as soon as he noticed him dozing.

He did not sleep at night. He tried not to think about Ikemefuna, but the more he tried the more he thought about him. Once he got up from bed and walked about his compound. But he was so weak that his legs could hardly carry him. He felt like a drunken giant walking with the limbs of a mosquito. Now and then a cold shiver descended on his head and spread down his body.

On the third day he asked his second wife, Ekwefi, to roast plantains for him. She prepared it the way he liked—with slices of oil-bean and fish.

"You have not eaten for two days," said his daughter Ezinma when she brought the food to him. "So you must finish this." She sat down and stretched her legs in front of her. Okonkwo ate the food absent-mindedly. "She should have been a boy," he thought as he looked at his ten-year-old daughter. He passed her a piece of fish.

"Go and bring me some cold water," he said. Ezinma rushed out of the hut, chewing the fish, and soon returned with a bowl of cool water from the earthen pot in her mother's hut.

Okonkwo took the bowl from her and gulped the water down. He ate a few more pieces of plantain and pushed the dish aside.

"Bring me my bag," he asked, and Ezinma brought his goatskin bag from the far end of the hut. He searched in it for his snuff-bottle. It was a deep bag and took almost the whole length of his arm. It contained other things apart from his snuff-bottle. There was a drinking horn in it, and also a drinking gourd, and they knocked against each other as he searched. When he brought out the snuff-bottle he tapped it a few times against his knee-cap before taking out some snuff on the palm of his left hand. Then he remembered that he had not taken out his snuff-spoon. He searched his bag again and brought out a small, flat, ivory spoon, with which he carried the brown snuff to his nostrils.

Ezinma took the dish in one hand and the empty water bowl in the other and went back to her mother's hut. "She should have been a boy," Okonkwo said to himself again. His mind went back to Ikemefuna and he shivered. If only he could find some work to do he would be able to forget. But it was the season of rest between the harvest and the next planting season. The only work that men did at this time was covering the walls of their compound with new palm fronds. And Okonkwo had already done that. He had finished it on the very day the locusts came, when he had worked on one side of the wall and Ikemefuna and Nwoye on the other.

"When did you become a shivering old woman," Okonkwo asked himself, "you, who are known in all the nine villages for your valor in war? How can a man who has killed five men in battle fall to pieces because he has added a boy to their number? Okonkwo, you have become a woman indeed."

He sprang to his feet, hung his goatskin bag on his shoulder and went to visit his friend, Obierika.

Obierika was sitting outside under the shade of an orange tree making thatches from leaves of the raffia-palm. He exchanged greetings with Okonkwo and led the way into his *obi.*

"I was coming over to see you as soon as I finished that thatch," he said, rubbing off the grains of sand that clung to his thighs.

"Is it well?" Okonkwo asked.

"Yes," replied Obierika. "My daughter's suitor is coming today and I hope we will clinch the matter of the bride-price. I want you to be there."

Just then Obierika's son, Maduka, came into the *obi* from outside, greeted Okonkwo and turned towards the compound.

"Come and shake hands with me," Okonkwo said to the lad. "Your wrestling the other day gave me much happiness." The boy smiled, shook hands with Okonkwo and went into the compound.

"He will do great things," Okonkwo said. "If I had a son like him I should be happy. I am worried about Nwoye. A bowl of pounded yams can throw him in a wrestling match. His two younger brothers are more promising. But I can tell you, Obierika, that my children do not resemble me. Where are the young suckers that will grow when the old banana tree dies? If Ezinma had been a boy I would have been happier. She has the right spirit."

"You worry yourself for nothing," said Obierika. "The children are still very young."

"Nwoye is old enough to impregnate a woman. At his age I was already fending for myself. No, my friend, he is not too young. A chick that will grow into a cock can be spotted the very day it hatches. I have done my best to make Nwoye grow into a man, but there is too much of his mother in him."

"Too much of his grandfather," Obierika thought, but he did not say it. The same thought also came to Okonkwo's mind. But he had long learned how to lay that ghost. Whenever the thought of his father's weakness and failure troubled him he expelled it by thinking about his own strength and success. And so he did now. His mind went to his latest show of manliness.

"I cannot understand why you refused to come with us to kill that boy," he asked Obierika.

"Because I did not want to," Obierika replied sharply. "I had something better to do."

"You sound as if you question the authority and the decision of the Oracle, who said he should die."

"I do not. Why should I? But the Oracle did not ask me to carry out its decision."

"But someone had to do it. If we were all afraid of blood, it would not be done. And what do you think the Oracle would do then?"

"You know very well, Okonkwo, that I am not afraid of blood; and if anyone tells you that I am, he is telling a lie. And let me tell you one thing, my friend. If I were you I would have stayed at home. What you have done will not please the Earth. It is the kind of action for which the goddess wipes out whole families."

"The Earth cannot punish me for obeying her messenger," Okonkwo said. "A child's fingers are not scalded by a piece of hot yam which its mother puts into its palm."

"That is true," Obierika agreed. "But if the Oracle said that my son should be killed I would neither dispute it nor be the one to do it."

They would have gone on arguing had Ofoedu not come in just then. It was clear from his twinkling eyes that he had important news. But it would be impolite to rush him. Obierika offered him a lobe of the kola nut he had broken with Okonkwo. Ofoedu ate slowly and talked about the locusts. When he finished his kola nut he said:

"The things that happen these days are very strange."

"What has happened?" asked Okonkwo.

"Do you know Ogbuefi Ndulue?" Ofoedu asked.

"Ogbuefi Ndulue of Ire village," Okonkwo and Obierika said together.

"He died this morning," said Ofoedu.

"That is not strange. He was the oldest man in Ire," said Obierika.

"You are right," Ofoedu agreed. "But you ought to ask why the drum has not beaten to tell Umuofia of his death."

"Why?" asked Obierika and Okonkwo together.

"That is the strange part of it. You know his first wife who walks with a stick?"

"Yes. She is called Ozoemena."

"That is so," said Ofoedu. "Ozoemena was, as you know, too old to attend Ndulue during his illness. His younger wives did that. When he died this morning, one of these women went to Ozoemena's hut and told her. She rose from her mat, took her stick and walked over to the *obi*. She knelt on her knees and hands at the threshold and called her husband, who was laid on a mat. 'Ogbuefi Ndulue,' she called, three times, and went back to her hut. When the youngest wife went to call her again to be present at the washing of the body, she found her lying on the mat, dead."

"That is very strange, indeed," said Okonkwo. "They will put off Ndulue's funeral until his wife has been buried."[16]

---

[16] A wife who died soon after her husband might be blamed for his death, therefore the concern here.

"That is why the drum has not been beaten to tell Umuofia."

"It was always said that Ndulue and Ozoemena had one mind," said Obierika. "I remember when I was a young boy there was a song about them. He could not do anything without telling her."

"I did not know that," said Okonkwo. "I thought he was a strong man in his youth."

"He was indeed," said Ofoedu.

Okonkwo shook his head doubtfully.

"He led Umuofia to war in those days," said Obierika.

Okonkwo was beginning to feel like his old self again. All that he required was something to occupy his mind. If he had killed Ikemefuna during the busy planting season or harvesting it would not have been so bad; his mind would have been centered on his work. Okonkwo was not a man of thought but of action. But in absence of work, talking was the next best.

Soon after Ofoedu left, Okonkwo took up his goatskin bag to go.

"I must go home to tap my palm trees for the afternoon," he said.

"Who taps your tall trees for you?" asked Obierika.

"Umezulike," replied Okonkwo.

"Sometimes I wish I had not taken the *ozo* title," said Obierika. "It wounds my heart to see these young men killing palm trees in the name of tapping."

"It is so indeed," Okonkwo agreed. "But the law of the land must be obeyed."

"I don't know how we got that law," said Obierika. "In many other clans a man of title is not forbidden to climb the palm tree. Here we say he cannot climb the tall tree but he can tap the short ones standing on the ground. It is like Dimaragana, who would not lend his knife for cutting up dog-meat because the dog was taboo to him, but offered to use his teeth."

"I think it is good that our clan holds the *ozo* title in high esteem," said Okonkwo. "In those other clans you speak of, *ozo* is so low that every beggar takes it."

"I was only speaking in jest," said Obierika. "In Abame and Aninta the title is worth less than two cowries. Every man wears the thread of title on his ankle, and does not lose it even if he steals."

"They have indeed soiled the name of *ozo,*" said Okonkwo as he rose to go.

"It will not be very long now before my in-laws come," said Obierika.

"I shall return very soon," said Okonkwo, looking at the position of the sun.

There were seven men in Obierika's hut when Okonkwo returned. The suitor was a young man of about twenty-five, and with him were his father and uncle. On Obierika's side were his two elder brothers and Maduka, his sixteen-year-old son.

"Ask Akueke's mother to send us some kola nuts," said Obierika to his son. Maduka vanished into the compound like lightning. The conversation at once centered on him, and everybody agreed that he was as sharp as a razor.

"I sometimes think he is too sharp," said Obierika, somewhat indulgently. "He hardly ever walks. He is always in a hurry. If you are sending him on an errand he flies away before he has heard half of the message."

"You were very much like that yourself," said his eldest brother. "As our people say, 'When mother-cow is chewing grass its young ones watch its mouth.' Maduka has been watching your mouth."

As he was speaking the boy returned, followed by Akueke, his half-sister, carrying a wooden dish with three kola nuts and alligator pepper. She gave the dish to her father's eldest brother and then shook hands, very shyly, with her suitor and his relatives. She was about sixteen and just ripe for marriage. Her suitor and his relatives surveyed her young body with expert eyes as if to assure themselves that she was beautiful and ripe.

She wore a coiffure which was done up into a crest in the middle of the head. Cam wood was rubbed lightly into her skin, and all over her body were black patterns drawn with *uli*.[17] She wore a black necklace which hung down in three coils just above her full, succulent breasts. On her arms were red and yellow bangles, and on her waist four or five rows of *jigida,* or waist beads.

When she had shaken hands, or rather held out her hand to be shaken, she returned to her mother's hut to help with the cooking.

"Remove your *jigida* first," her mother warned as she moved near the fireplace to bring the pestle resting against the wall. "Every day I tell you that *jigida* and fire are not friends. But you will never hear. You grew your ears for decoration, not for hearing. One of these days your *jigida* will catch fire on your waist, and then you will know."

Akueke moved to the other end of the hut and began to remove the waist-beads. It had to be done slowly and carefully, taking each string separately, else it would break and the thousand tiny rings would have to be strung together again. She rubbed each string downwards with her palms until it passed the buttocks and slipped down to the floor around her feet.

The men in the *obi* had already begun to drink the palm-wine which Akueke's suitor had brought. It was a very good wine and powerful, for in spite of the palm fruit hung across the mouth of the pot to restrain the lively liquor, white foam rose and spilled over.

"That wine is the work of a good tapper," said Okonkwo.

The young suitor, whose name was Ibe, smiled broadly and said to his father: "Do you hear that?" He then said to the others: "He will never admit that I am a good tapper."

"He tapped three of my best palm trees to death," said his father, Ukegbu.

"That was about five years ago," said Ibe, who had begun to pour out the wine, "before I learned how to tap." He filled the first horn and gave to his father. Then he poured out for the others. Okonkwo brought out his big horn from the goatskin bag, blew into it to remove any dust that might be there, and gave it to Ibe to fill.

As the men drank, they talked about everything except the thing for which they had gathered. It was only after the pot had been emptied that the suitor's father cleared his voice and announced the object of their visit.

Obierika then presented to him a small bundle of short broomsticks. Ukegbu counted them.

"They are thirty?" he asked.

Obierika nodded in agreement.

"We are at last getting somewhere," Ukegbu said, and then turning to his brother and his son he said: "Let us go out and whisper together." The three rose and went outside. When they returned Ukegbu handed the bundle of sticks back to Obierika. He counted them; instead of thirty there were now only fifteen. He passed them over to his eldest brother, Machi, who also counted them and said:

"We had not thought to go below thirty. But as the dog said, 'If I fall down for you and you fall down for me, it is play.' Marriage should be a play and not a fight; so we are falling down again." He then added ten sticks to the fifteen and gave the bundle to Ukegbu.

---

[17] A black dye used to decorate the body.

In this way Akueke's bride-price was finally settled at twenty bags of cowries. It was already dusk when the two parties came to this agreement.

"Go and tell Akueke's mother that we have finished," Obierika said to his son, Maduka. Almost immediately the women came in with a big bowl of foo-foo. Obierika's second wife followed with a pot of soup, and Maduka brought in a pot of palm-wine.

As the men ate and drank palm-wine they talked about the customs of their neighbors.

"It was only this morning," said Obierika, "that Okonkwo and I were talking about Abame and Aninta, where titled men climb trees and pound foo-foo for their wives."

"All their customs are upside-down. They do not decide bride-price as we do, with sticks. They haggle and bargain as if they were buying a goat or a cow in the market."

"That is very bad," said Obierika's eldest brother. "But what is good in one place is bad in another place. In Umunso they do not bargain at all, not even with broomsticks. The suitor just goes on bringing bags of cowries until his in-laws tell him to stop. It is a bad custom because it always leads to a quarrel."

"The world is large," said Okonkwo. "I have even heard that in some tribes a man's children belong to his wife and her family."

"That cannot be," said Machi. "You might as well say that the woman lies on top of the man when they are making the children."

"It is like the story of white men who, they say, are white like this piece of chalk," said Obierika. He held up a piece of chalk, which every man kept in his *obi* and with which his guests drew lines on the floor before they ate kola nuts. "And these white men, they say, have no toes."

"And have you never seen them?" asked Machi.

"Have you?" asked Obierika.

"One of them passes here frequently," said Machi. "His name is Amadi."

Those who knew Amadi laughed. He was a leper, and the polite name for leprosy was "the white skin."

9

For the first time in three nights, Okonkwo slept. He woke up once in the middle of the night and his mind went back to the past three days without making him feel uneasy. He began to wonder why he had felt uneasy at all. It was like a man wondering in broad daylight why a dream had appeared so terrible to him at night. He stretched himself and scratched his thigh where a mosquito had bitten him as he slept. Another one was wailing near his right ear. He slapped the ear and hoped he had killed it. Why do they always go for one's ears? When he was a child his mother had told him a story about it. But it was as silly as all women's stories. Mosquito, she had said, had asked Ear to marry him, whereupon Ear fell on the floor in uncontrollable laughter. "How much longer do you think you will live?" she asked. "You are already a skeleton." Mosquito went away humiliated, and any time he passed her way he told Ear that he was still alive.

Okonkwo turned on his side and went back to sleep. He was roused in the morning by someone banging on his door.

"Who is that?" he growled. He knew it must be Ekwefi. Of his three wives Ekwefi was the only one who would have the audacity to bang on his door.

"Ezinma is dying," came her voice, and all the tragedy and sorrow of her life were packed in those words.

Okonkwo sprang from his bed, pushed back the bolt on his door and ran into Ekwefi's hut.

Ezinma lay shivering on a mat beside a huge fire that her mother had kept burning all night.

"It is *iba*,"[18] said Okonkwo as he took his machete and went into the bush to collect the leaves and grasses and barks of trees that went into making the medicine for *iba*.

Ekwefi knelt beside the sick child, occasionally feeling with her palm the wet, burning forehead.

Ezinma was an only child and the center of her mother's world. Very often it was Ezinma who decided what food her mother should prepare. Ekwefi even gave her such delicacies as eggs, which children were rarely allowed to eat because such food tempted them to steal. One day as Ezinma was eating an egg Okonkwo had come in unexpectedly from his hut. He was greatly shocked and swore to beat Ekwefi if she dared to give the child eggs again. But it was impossible to refuse Ezinma anything. After her father's rebuke she developed an even keener appetite for eggs. And she enjoyed above all the secrecy in which she now ate them. Her mother always took her into their bedroom and shut the door.

Ezinma did not call her mother *Nne* like all children. She called her by her name, Ekwefi, as her father and other grown-up people did. The relationship between them was not only that of mother and child. There was something in it like the companionship of equals, which was strengthened by such little conspiracies as eating eggs in the bedroom.

Ekwefi had suffered a good deal in her life. She had borne ten children and nine of them had died in infancy, usually before the age of three. As she buried one child after another her sorrow gave way to despair and then to grim resignation. The birth of her children, which should be a woman's crowning glory, became for Ekwefi mere physical agony devoid of promise. The naming ceremony after seven market weeks became an empty ritual. Her deepening despair found expression in the names she gave her children. One of them was a pathetic cry, Onwumbiko—"Death, I implore you." But Death took no notice; Onwumbiko died in his fifteenth month. The next child was a girl, Ozoemena—"May it not happen again." She died in her eleventh month, and two others after her. Ekwefi then became defiant and called her next child Onwuma—"Death may please himself." And he did.

After the death of Ekwefi's second child, Okonkwo had gone to a medicine man, who was also a diviner of the Afa Oracle, to inquire what was amiss. This man told him that the child was an *ogbanje*,[19] one of those wicked children who, when they died, entered their mothers' wombs to be born again.

"When your wife becomes pregnant again," he said, "let her not sleep in her hut. Let her go and stay with her people. In that way she will elude her wicked tormentor and break its evil cycle of birth and death."

Ekwefi did as she was asked. As soon as she became pregnant she went to live with her old mother in another village. It was there that her third child was born and circumcised on the eighth day. She did not return to Okonkwo's compound until three days before the naming ceremony. The child was called Onwumbiko.

Onwumbiko was not given proper burial when he died. Okonkwo had called in another medicine man who was famous in the clan for his great knowledge about

---

[18] Fever.

[19] The *ogbanje* is locked into a pattern of early death and cyclic rebirth unless its *iyi-uwa*, a stone that links it to the spirit world, is found and destroyed so that the child can live.

ogbanje children. His name was Okagbue Uyanwa. Okagbue was a very striking figure, tall, with a full beard and a bald head. He was light in complexion and his eyes were red and fiery. He always gnashed his teeth as he listened to those who came to consult him. He asked Okonkwo a few questions about the dead child. All the neighbors and relations who had come to mourn gathered round them.

"On what market-day was it born?" he asked.

"*Oye*," replied Okonkwo.

"And it died this morning?"

Okonkwo said yes, and only then realized for the first time that the child had died on the same market-day as it had been born. The neighbors and relations also saw the coincidence and said among themselves that it was very significant.

"Where do you sleep with your wife, in your *obi* or in her own hut?" asked the medicine man.

"In her hut."

"In future call her into your *obi*."

The medicine man then ordered that there should be no mourning for the dead child. He brought out a sharp razor from the goatskin bag slung from his left shoulder and began to mutilate the child. Then he took it away to bury in the Evil Forest, holding it by the ankle and dragging it on the ground behind him. After such treatment it would think twice before coming again, unless it was one of the stubborn ones who returned, carrying the stamp of their mutilation—a missing finger or perhaps a dark line where the medicine man's razor had cut them.

By the time Onwumbiko died Ekwefi had become a very bitter woman. Her husband's first wife had already had three sons, all strong and healthy. When she had borne her third son in succession, Okonkwo had gathered a goat for her, as was the custom. Ekwefi had nothing but good wishes for her. But she had grown so bitter about her own *chi* that she could not rejoice with others over their good fortune. And so, on the day that Nwoye's mother celebrated the birth of her three sons with feasting and music, Ekwefi was the only person in the happy company who went about with a cloud on her brow. Her husband's wife took this for malevolence, as husbands' wives were wont to. How could she know that Ekwefi's bitterness did not flow outwards to others but inwards into her own soul; that she did not blame others for their good fortune but her own evil *chi* who denied her any?

At last Ezinma was born, and although ailing she seemed determined to live. At first Ekwefi accepted her, as she had accepted others—with listless resignation. But when she lived on to her fourth, fifth and sixth years, love returned once more to her mother, and, with love, anxiety. She determined to nurse her child to health, and she put all her being into it. She was rewarded by occasional spells of health during which Ezinma bubbled with energy like fresh palm-wine. At such times she seemed beyond danger. But all of a sudden she would go down again. Everybody knew she was an *ogbanje*. These sudden bouts of sickness and health were typical of her kind. But she had lived so long that perhaps she had decided to stay. Some of them did become tired of their evil rounds of birth and death, or took pity on their mothers, and stayed. Ekwefi believed deep inside her that Ezinma had come to stay. She believed because it was that faith alone that gave her own life any kind of meaning. And this faith had been strengthened when a year or so ago a medicine man had dug up Ezinma's *iyi-uwa*. Everyone knew then that she would live because her bond with the world of *ogbanje* had been broken. Ekwefi was reassured. But such was her anxiety for her daughter that she could not rid herself completely of her fear. And although she believed that the *iyi-uwa* which had been dug up was genuine, she could not ignore the fact that some really evil children sometimes misled people into digging up a specious one.

But Ezinma's *iyi-uwa* had looked real enough. It was a smooth pebble wrapped in a dirty rag. The man who dug it up was the same Okagbue who was famous in all the clan for his knowledge in these matters. Ezinma had not wanted to cooperate with him at first. But that was only to be expected. No *ogbanje* would yield her secrets easily, and most of them never did because they died too young—before they could be asked questions.

"Where did you bury your *iyi-uwa*?" Okagbue had asked Ezinma. She was nine then and was just recovering from a serious illness.

"What is *iyi-uwa*?" she asked in return.

"You know what it is. You buried it in the ground somewhere so that you can die and return again to torment your mother."

Ezinma looked at her mother, whose eyes, sad and pleading, were fixed on her.

"Answer the question at once," roared Okonkwo, who stood beside her. All the family were there and some of the neighbors too.

"Leave her to me," the medicine man told Okonkwo in a cool, confident voice. He turned again to Ezinma. "Where did you bury your *iyi-uwa*?"

"Where they bury children," she replied, and the quiet spectators murmured to themselves.

"Come along then and show me the spot," said the medicine man.

The crowd set out with Ezinma leading the way and Okagbue following closely behind her. Okonkwo came next and Ekwefi followed him. When she came to the main road, Ezinma turned left as if she was going to the stream.

"But you said it was where they bury children?" asked the medicine man.

"No," said Ezinma, whose feeling of importance was manifest in her sprightly walk. She sometimes broke into a run and stopped again suddenly. The crowd followed her silently. Women and children returning from the stream with pots of water on their heads wondered what was happening until they saw Okagbue and guessed that it must be something to do with *ogbanje*. And they all knew Ekwefi and her daughter very well.

When she got to the big udala tree Ezinma turned left into the bush, and the crowd followed her. Because of her size she made her way through trees and creepers more quickly than her followers. The bush was alive with the tread of feet on dry leaves and sticks and the moving aside of tree branches. Ezinma went deeper and deeper and the crowd went with her. Then she suddenly turned round and began to walk back to the road. Everybody stood to let her pass and then filed after her.

"If you bring us all this way for nothing I shall beat sense into you," Okonkwo threatened.

"I have told you to let her alone. I know how to deal with them," said Okagbue.

Ezinma led the way back to the road, looked left and right and turned right. And so they arrived home again.

"Where did you bury your *iyi-uwa*?" asked Okagbue when Ezinma finally stopped outside her father's *obi*. Okagbue's voice was unchanged. It was quiet and confident.

"It is near that orange tree," Ezinma said.

"And why did you not say so, you wicked daughter of Akalogoli?" Okonkwo swore furiously. The medicine man ignored him.

"Come and show me the exact spot," he said quietly to Ezinma.

"It is here," she said when they got to the tree.

"Point at the spot with your finger," said Okagbue.

"It is here," said Ezinma touching the ground with her finger. Okonkwo stood by, rumbling like thunder in the rainy season.

"Bring me a hoe," said Okagbue.

When Ekwefi brought the hoe, he had already put aside his goatskin bag and his big cloth and was in his underwear, a long and thin strip of cloth wound round the waist like a belt and then passed between the legs to be fastened to the belt behind. He immediately set to work digging a pit where Ezinma had indicated. The neighbors sat around watching the pit becoming deeper and deeper. The dark top soil soon gave way to the bright red earth with which women scrubbed the floors and walls of huts. Okagbue worked tirelessly and in silence, his back shining with perspiration. Okonkwo stood by the pit. He asked Okagbue to come up and rest while he took a hand. But Okagbue said he was not tired yet.

Ekwefi went into her hut to cook yams. Her husband had brought out more yams than usual because the medicine man had to be fed. Ezinma went with her and helped in preparing the vegetables.

"There is too much green vegetable," she said.

"Don't you see the pot is full of yams?" Ekwefi asked. "And you know how leaves become smaller after cooking."

"Yes," said Ezinma, "that was why the snake-lizard killed his mother."

"Very true," said Ekwefi.

"He gave his mother seven baskets of vegetables to cook and in the end there were only three. And so he killed her," said Ezinma.

"That is not the end of the story."

"Oho," said Ezinma. "I remember now. He brought another seven baskets and cooked them himself. And there were again only three. So he killed himself too."

Outside the *obi* Okagbue and Okonkwo were digging the pit to find where Ezinma had buried her *iyi-uwa*. Neighbors sat around, watching. The pit was now so deep that they no longer saw the digger. They only saw the red earth he threw up mounting higher and higher. Okonkwo's son, Nwoye, stood near the edge of the pit because he wanted to take in all that happened.

Okagbue had again taken over the digging from Okonkwo. He worked, as usual, in silence. The neighbors and Okonkwo's wives were now talking. The children had lost interest and were playing.

Suddenly Okagbue sprang to the surface with the agility of a leopard.

"It is very near now," he said. "I have felt it."

There was immediate excitement and those who were sitting jumped to their feet.

"Call your wife and child," he said to Okonkwo. But Ekwefi and Ezinma had heard the noise and run out to see what it was.

Okagbue went back into the pit, which was now surrounded by spectators. After a few more hoe-fuls of earth he struck the *iyi-uwa*. He raised it carefully with the hoe and threw it to the surface. Some women ran away in fear when it was thrown. But they soon returned and everyone was gazing at the rag from a reasonable distance. Okagbue emerged and without saying a word or even looking at the spectators he went to his goatskin bag, took out two leaves and began to chew them. When he had swallowed them, he took up the rag with left hand and began to untie it. And then the smooth, shiny pebble fell out. He picked it up.

"Is this yours?" he asked Ezinma.

"Yes," she replied. All the women shouted with joy because Ekwefi's troubles were at last ended.

All this had happened more than a year ago and Ezinma had not been ill since. And then suddenly she had begun to shiver in the night. Ekwefi brought her to the fireplace, spread her mat on the floor and built a fire. But she had got worse and worse. As she knelt by her, feeling with her palm the wet, burning forehead, she prayed a thousand times. Although her husband's wives were saying that it was nothing more than *iba,* she did not hear them.

Okonkwo returned from the bush carrying on his left shoulder a large bundle of grasses and leaves, roots and barks of medicinal trees and shrubs. He went into Ekwefi's hut, put down his load and sat down.

"Get me a pot," he said, "and leave the child alone."

Ekwefi went to bring the pot and Okonkwo selected the best from his bundle, in their due proportions, and cut them up. He put them in the pot and Ekwefi poured in some water.

"Is that enough?" she asked when she had poured in about half of the water in the bowl.

"A little more . . . I said *a little.* Are you deaf?" Okonkwo roared at her.

She set the pot on the fire and Okonkwo took up his machete to return to his *obi.*

"You must watch the pot carefully," he said as he went, "and don't allow it to boil over. If it does its power will be gone." He went away to his hut and Ekwefi began to tend the medicine pot almost as if it was itself a sick child. Her eyes went constantly from Ezinma to the boiling pot and back to Ezinma.

Okonkwo returned when he felt the medicine had cooked long enough. He looked it over and said it was done.

"Bring me a low stool for Ezinma," he said, "and a thick mat."

He took down the pot from the fire and placed it in front of the stool. He then roused Ezinma and placed her on the stool, astride the steaming pot. The thick mat was thrown over both. Ezinma struggled to escape from the choking and overpowering steam, but she was held down. She started to cry.

When the mat was at last removed she was drenched in perspiration. Ekwefi mopped her with a piece of cloth and she lay down on a dry mat and was soon asleep.

10

Large crowds began to gather on the village *ilo* as soon as the edge had worn off the sun's heat and it was no longer painful on the body. Most communal ceremonies took place at that time of the day, so that even when it was said that a ceremony would begin "after the midday meal" everyone understood that it would begin a long time later, when the sun's heat had softened.

It was clear from the way the crowd stood or sat that the ceremony was for men. There were many women, but they looked on from the fringe like outsiders. The titled men and elders sat on their stools waiting for the trials to begin. In front of them was a row of stools on which nobody sat. There were nine of them. Two little groups of people stood at a respectable distance beyond the stools. They faced the elders. There were three men in one group and three men and one woman in the other. The woman was Mgbafo and the three men with her were her brothers. In the other group were her husband, Uzowulu, and his relatives. Mgbafo and her brothers were as still as statues into whose faces the artist has molded defiance. Uzowulu and his relative, on the other hand, were whispering together. It looked like whispering, but they were really talking at the top of their voices. Everybody in the crowd was talking. It was like the market. From a distance the noise was a deep rumble carried by the wind.

An iron gong sounded, setting up a wave of expectation in the crowd. Everyone looked in the direction of the *egwugwu* house. *Gome, gome, gome, gome* went the gong, and a powerful flute blew a high-pitched blast. Then came the voices of the *egwugwu*, guttural and awesome. The wave struck the women and children and there was a backward stampede. But it was momentary. They were already far enough where they stood and there was room for running away if any of the *egwugwu* should go towards them.

The drum sounded again and the flute blew. The *egwugwu* house was now a pandemonium of quavering voices: *Aru oyim de de de dei!*[20] filled the air as the spirits of the ancestors, just emerged from the earth, greeted themselves in their esoteric language. The *egwugwu* house into which they emerged faced the forest, away from the crowd, who saw only its back with the many-colored patterns and drawings done by specially chosen women at regular intervals. These women never saw the inside of the hut. No woman ever did. They scrubbed and painted the outside walls under the supervision of men. If they imagined what was inside, they kept their imagination to themselves. No woman ever asked questions about the most powerful and the most secret cult in the clan.

Aru oyim de de de dei! flew around the dark, closed hut like tongues of fire. The ancestral spirits of the clan were abroad. The metal gong beat continuously now and the flute, shrill and powerful, floated on the chaos.

And then the *egwugwu* appeared. The women and children sent up a great shout and took to their heels. It was instinctive. A woman fled as soon as an *egwugwu* came in sight. And when, as on that day, nine of the greatest masked spirits in the clan came out together it was a terrifying spectacle. Even Mgbafo took to her heels and had to be restrained by her brothers.

Each of the nine *egwugwu* represented a village of the clan. Their leader was called Evil Forest. Smoke poured out of his head.

The nine villages of Umuofia had grown out of the nine sons of the first father of the clan. Evil Forest represented the village of Umueru, or the children of Eru, who was the eldest of the nine sons.

"*Umuofia kwenu!*" shouted the leading *egwugwu*, pushing the air with his raffia arms. The elders of the clan replied, "*Yaa!*"

"*Umuofia kwenu!*"

"*Yaa!*"

"*Umuofia kwenu!*"

"*Yaa!*"

Evil Forest then thrust the pointed end of his rattling staff into the earth. And it began to shake and rattle, like something agitating with a metallic life. He took the first of the empty stools and the eight other *egwugwu* began to sit in order of seniority after him.

Okonkwo's wives, and perhaps other women as well, might have noticed that the second *egwugwu* had the springy walk of Okonkwo. And they might also have noticed that Okonkwo was not among the titled men and elders who sat behind the row of *egwugwu*. But if they thought these things they kept them within themselves. The *egwugwu* with the springy walk was one of the dead fathers of the clan. He looked terrible with the smoked raffia body, a huge wooden face painted white except for the round hollow eyes and the charred teeth that were as big as a man's fingers. On his head were two powerful horns.

When all the *egwugwu* had sat down and the sound of the many tiny bells and rattles on their bodies had subsided, Evil Forest addressed the two groups of people facing them.

---

[20]"Body of my friend, greetings."

"Uzowulu's body, I salute you," he said. Spirits always addressed humans as "bodies." Uzowulu bent down and touched the earth with his right hand as a sign of submission.

"Our father, my hand has touched the ground," he said.

"Uzowulu's body, do you know me?" asked the spirit.

"How can I know you, father? You are beyond our knowledge."

Evil Forest then turned to the other group and addressed the eldest of the three brothers.

"The body of Odukwe, I greet you," he said, and Odukwe bent down and touched the earth. The hearing then began.

Uzowulu stepped forward and presented his case.

"That woman standing there is my wife, Mgbafo. I married her with my money and my yams. I do not owe my in-laws anything. I owe them no yams. I owe them no coco-yams. One morning three of them came to my house, beat me up and took my wife and children away. This happened in the rainy season. I have waited in vain for my wife to return. At last I went to my in-laws and said to them, 'You have taken back your sister. I did not send her away. You yourselves took her. The law of the clan is that you should return her bride-price.' But my wife's brothers said they had nothing to tell me. So I have brought the matter to the fathers of the clan. My case is finished. I salute you."

"Your words are good," said the leader of the *egwugwu*. "Let us hear Odukwe. His words may also be good."

Odukwe was short and thickset. He stepped forward, saluted the spirits and began his story.

"My in-law has told you that we went to his house, beat him up and took our sister and her children away. All that is true. He told you that he came to take back her bride-price and we refused to give it him. That also is true. My in-law, Uzowulu, is a beast. My sister lived with him for nine years. During those years no single day passed in the sky without his beating the woman. We have tried to settle their quarrels time without number and on each occasion Uzowulu was guilty—"

"It is a lie!" Uzowulu shouted.

"Two years ago," continued Odukwe, "when she was pregnant, he beat her until she miscarried."

"It is a lie. She miscarried after she had gone to sleep with her lover."

"Uzowulu's body, I salute you," said Evil Forest, silencing him. "What kind of lover sleeps with a pregnant woman?" There was a loud murmur of approbation from the crowd. Odukwe continued:

"Last year when my sister was recovering from an illness, he beat her again so that if the neighbors had not gone in to save her she would have been killed. We heard of it, and did as you have been told. The law of Umuofia is that if a woman runs away from her husband her bride-price is returned. But in this case she ran away to save her life. Her two children belong to Uzowulu. We do not dispute it, but they are too young to leave their mother. If, in the other hand, Uzowulu should recover from his madness and come in the proper way to beg his wife to return she will do so on the understanding that if he ever beats her again we shall cut off his genitals for him."

The crowd roared with laughter. Evil Forest rose to his feet and order was immediately restored. A steady cloud of smoke rose from his head. He sat down again and called two witnesses. They were both Uzowulu's neighbors, and they agreed about the beating. Evil Forest then stood up, pulled out his staff and thrust it into the earth again. He ran a few steps in the direction of the women; they all fled in terror, only to return to their places almost immediately. The nine *egwugwu* then went away to consult together in their house. They were silent for a long time. Then the metal gong sounded and the flute was blown. The *egwugwu* had emerged once again from their underground home. They saluted one another and then reappeared on the *ilo*.

"*Umuofia kwenu!*" roared Evil Forest, facing the elders and grandees of the clan.

"*Yaa!*" replied the thunderous crowd; then silence descended from the sky and swallowed the noise.

Evil Forest began to speak and all the while he spoke everyone was silent. The eight other *egwugwu* were as still as statues.

"We have heard both sides of the case," said Evil Forest. "Our duty is not to blame this man or to praise that, but to settle the dispute." He turned to Uzowulu's group and allowed a short pause.

"Uzowulu's body, I salute you," he said.

"Our father, my hand has touched the ground," replied Uzowulu, touching the earth.

"Uzowulu's body, do you know me?"

"How can I know you, father? You are beyond our knowledge," Uzowulu replied.

"I am Evil Forest. I kill a man on the day that his life is sweetest to him."

"That is true," replied Uzowulu.

"Go to your in-laws with a pot of wine and beg your wife to return to you. It is not bravery when a man fights with a woman." He turned to Odukwe, and allowed a brief pause.

"Odukwe's body, I greet you," he said.

"My hand is on the ground," replied Odukwe.

"Do you know me?"

"No man can know you," replied Odukwe.

"I am Evil Forest, I am Dry-meat-that-fills-the-mouth, I am Fire-that-burns-without-faggots. If your in-law brings wine to you, let your sister go with him. I salute you." He pulled his staff from the hard earth and thrust it back.

"*Umuofia kwenu!*" he roared, and the crowd answered.

"I don't know why such a trifle should come before the *egwugwu*," said one elder to another.

"Don't you know what kind of man Uzowulu is? He will not listen to any other decision," replied the other.

As they spoke two other groups of people had replaced the first before the *egwugwu*, and a great land case began.

11

The night was impenetrably dark. The moon had been rising later and later every night until now it was seen only at dawn. And whenever the moon forsook evening and rose at cock-crow the nights were as black as charcoal.

Ezinma and her mother sat on a mat on the floor after their supper of yam foo-foo and bitter-leaf soup. A palm-oil lamp gave out yellowish light. Without it, it would have been impossible to eat; one could not have known where one's mouth was in the darkness of that night. There was an oil lamp in all the four huts on Okonkwo's compound, and each hut seen from the others looked like a soft eye of yellow half-light set in the solid massiveness of night.

The world was silent except for the shrill cry of insects, which was part of the night, and the sound of wooden mortar and pestle as Nwayieke pounded her foo-foo. Nwayieke lived four compounds away, and she was notorious for her late cooking. Every woman in the neighborhood knew the sound of Nwayieke's mortar and pestle. It was also part of the night.

Okonkwo had eaten from his wives' dishes and was now reclining with his back against the wall. He searched his bag and brought out his snuff-bottle. He turned it on to his left palm, but nothing came out. He hit the bottle against his knee to shake up the tobacco. That was always the trouble with Okeke's snuff. It very quickly went damp, and there was too much saltpeter in it. Okonkwo had not bought snuff from him for a long time. Idigo was the man who knew how to grind good snuff. But he had recently fallen ill.

Low voices, broken now and again by singing, reached Okonkwo from his wives' huts as each woman and her children told folk stories. Ekwefi and her daughter, Ezinma, sat on a mat on the floor. It was Ekwefi's turn to tell a story.

"Once upon a time," she began, "all the birds were invited to a feast in the sky. They were very happy and began to prepare themselves for the great day. They painted their bodies with red cam wood and drew beautiful patterns on them with *uli*.

"Tortoise saw all these preparations and soon discovered what it all meant. Nothing that happened in the world of the animals ever escaped his notice; he was full of cunning. As soon as he heard of the great feast in the sky his throat began to itch at the very thought. There was a famine in those days and Tortoise had not eaten a good meal for two moons. His body rattled like a piece of dry stick in his empty shell. So he began to plan how he would go to the sky."

"But he had no wings," said Ezinma.

"Be patient," replied her mother. "That is the story. Tortoise had no wings, but he went to the birds and asked to be allowed to go with them.

" 'We know you too well,' said the birds when they had heard him. 'You are full of cunning and you are ungrateful. If we allow you to come with us you will soon begin your mischief.'

" 'You do not know me,' said Tortoise. 'I am a changed man. I have learned that a man who makes trouble for others is also making it for himself.'

"Tortoise had a sweet tongue, and within a short time all the birds agreed that he was a changed man, and they each gave him a feather, with which he made two wings.

"At last the great day came and Tortoise was the first to arrive at the meeting place. When all the birds had gathered together, they set off in a body. Tortoise was very happy and voluble as he flew among the birds, and he was soon chosen as the man to speak for the party because he was a great orator.

" 'There is one important thing which we must not forget,' he said as they flew on their way. 'When people are invited to a great feast like this, they take new names for the occasion. Our hosts in the sky will expect us to honor this age-old custom.'

"None of the birds had heard of this custom but they knew that Tortoise, in spite of his failings in other directions, was a widely-traveled man who knew the customs of different peoples. And so they each took a new name. When they had all taken, Tortoise also took one. He was to be called *All of you*.

"At last the party arrived in the sky and their hosts were very happy to see them. Tortoise stood up in his many-colored plumage and thanked them for their invitation. His speech was so eloquent that all the birds were glad they had brought him, and nodded their heads in approval of all he said. Their hosts took him as the king of the birds, especially as he looked somewhat different from the others.

"After kola nuts had been presented and eaten, the people of the sky set before their guests the most delectable dishes Tortoise had even seen or dreamed of. The soup was brought out hot from the fire and in the very pot in which it had been cooked. It was full of meat and fish. Tortoise began to sniff aloud. There was pounded yam and also yam pottage cooked with palm-oil and fresh fish. There were also pots of palm-wine. When everything had been set before the guests, one of the people of the sky came forward and tasted a little from each pot. He then invited the birds to eat. But Tortoise jumped to his feet and asked: 'For whom have you prepared this feast?'

" 'For all of you,' replied the man.

"Tortoise turned to the birds and said: 'You remember that my name is *All of you*. The custom here is to serve the spokesman first and the others later. They will serve you when I have eaten.'

"He began to eat and the birds grumbled angrily. The people of the sky thought it must be their custom to leave all the food for their king. And so Tortoise ate the best part of the food and then drank two pots of palm-wine, so that he was full of food and drink and his body filled out in his shell.

"The birds gathered round to eat what was left and to peck at the bones he had thrown all about the floor. Some of them were too angry to eat. They chose to fly home on an empty stomach. But before they left each took back the feather he had lent to Tortoise. And there he stood in his hard shell full of food and wine but without any wings to fly home. He asked the birds to take a message for his wife, but they all refused. In the end Parrot, who had felt more angry than the others, suddenly changed his mind and agreed to take the message.

" 'Tell my wife,' said Tortoise, 'to bring out all the soft things in my house and cover the compound with them so that I can jump down from the sky without very great danger.'

"Parrot promised to deliver the message, and then flew away. But when he reached Tortoise's house he told his wife to bring out all the hard things in the house. And so she brought out her husband's hoes, machetes, spears, guns and even his cannon. Tortoise looked down from the sky and saw his wife bringing things out, but it was too far to see what they were. When all seemed ready he let himself go. He fell and fell and fell until he began to fear that he would never stop falling. And then like the sound of his cannon he crashed on the compound."

"Did he die?" asked Ezinma.

"No," replied Ekwefi. "His shell broke into pieces. But there was a great medicine man in the neighborhood. Tortoise's wife sent for him and he gathered all the bits of shell and stuck them together. That is why Tortoise's shell is not smooth."

"There is no song in the story," Ezinma pointed out.

"No," said Ekwefi. "I shall think of another one with a song. But it is your turn now."

"Once upon a time," Ezinma began, "Tortoise and Cat went to wrestle against Yams—no, that is not the beginning. Once upon a time there was a great famine in the land of animals. Everybody was lean except Cat, who was fat and whose body shone as if oil was rubbed on it..."

She broke off because at that very moment a loud and high-pitched voice broke the outer silence of the night. It was Chielo, the priestess of Agbala, prophesying. There was nothing new in that. Once in a while Chielo was possessed by the spirit of her god and she began to prophesy. But tonight she was addressing her prophecy and greetings to Okonkwo, and so everyone in his family listened. The folk stories stopped.

"*Agbala do-o-o-o! Agbala ekeneo-o-o-o-o,*" came the voice like a sharp knife cutting through the night. "*Okonkwo! Agbala ekene gio-o-o-o! Agbala cholu ifu ada ya Ezinmao-o-o-o!*"[21]

At the mention of Ezinma's name Ekwefi jerked her head sharply like an animal that had sniffed death in the air. Her heart jumped painfully within her.

The priestess had now reached Okonkwo's compound and was talking with him outside his hut. She was saying again and again that Agbala wanted to see his daughter, Ezinma. Okonkwo pleaded with her to come back in the morning because Ezinma was now asleep. But Chielo ignored what he was trying to say and went on shouting that Agbala wanted to see his daughter. Her voice was as clear as metal, and Okonkwo's women and children heard from their huts all that she said. Okonkwo was still pleading that the girl had been ill of late and was asleep. Ekwefi quickly took her to their bedroom and placed her on their high bamboo bed.

The priestess screamed. "Beware, Okonkwo!" she warned. "Beware of exchanging words with Agbala. Does a man speak when a god speaks? Beware!"

She walked through Okonkwo's hut into the circular compound and went straight toward Ekwefi's hut. Okonkwo came after her.

"Ekwefi," she called, "Agbala greets you. Where is my daughter, Ezinma? Agbala wants to see her."

Ekwefi came out from her hut carrying her oil lamp in her left hand. There was a light wind blowing, so she cupped her right hand to shelter the flame. Nwoye's mother, also carrying an oil lamp, emerged from her hut. The children stood in the darkness outside their hut watching the strange event. Okonkwo's youngest wife also came out and joined the others.

"Where does Agbala want to see her?" Ekwefi asked.

"Where else but in his house in the hills and the caves?" replied the priestess.

"I will come with you, too," Ekwefi said firmly.

"*Tufia-a!*"[22] the priestess cursed, her voice cracking like the angry bark of thunder in the dry season. "How dare you, woman, to go before the mighty Agbala of your own accord? Beware, woman, lest he strike you in his anger. Bring me my daughter."

Ekwefi went into her hut and came out again with Ezinma.

"Come, my daughter," said the priestess. "I shall carry you on my back. A baby on its mother's back does not know that the way is long."

Ezinma began to cry. She was used to Chielo calling her "my daughter." But it was a different Chielo she now saw in the yellow half-light.

"Don't cry, my daughter," said the priestess, "lest Agbala be angry with you."

"Don't cry," said Ekwefi, "she will bring you back very soon. I shall give you some fish to eat." She went into the hut again and brought down the smoke-black basket in which she kept her dried fish and other ingredients for cooking soup. She broke a piece in two and gave it to Ezinma, who clung to her.

"Don't be afraid," said Ekwefi, stroking her head, which was shaved in places, leaving a regular pattern of hair. They went outside again. The priestess bent down on one knee and Ezinma climbed on her back, her left palm closed on her fish and her eyes gleaming with tears.

"*Agbala do-o-o-o! Agbala ekeneo-o-o-o!...*" Chielo began once again to chant greetings to her god. She turned round sharply and walked through Okonkwo's

---

[21] "Agbala wants something! Agbala greets...." "Agbala greets you! Agbala wants to see his daughter Ezinma!"

[22] An oath; literally, "spitting out."

hut, bending very low at the eaves. Ezinma was crying loudly now, calling on her mother. The two voices disappeared into the thick darkness.

A strange and sudden weakness descended on Ekwefi as she stood gazing in the direction of the voices like a hen whose only chick has been carried away by a kite. Ezinma's voice soon faded away and only Chielo was heard moving farther and farther into the distance.

"Why do you stand there as though she had been kidnapped?" asked Okonkwo as he went back to his hut.

"She will bring her back soon," Nwoye's mother said.

But Ekwefi did not hear these consolations. She stood for a while, and then, all of a sudden, made up her mind. She hurried through Okonkwo's hut and went outside. "Where are you going?" he asked.

"I am following Chielo," she replied and disappeared in the darkness. Okonkwo cleared his throat, and brought out his snuff-bottle from the goatskin bag by his side.

The priestess' voice was already growing faint in the distance. Ekwefi hurried to the main footpath and turned left in the direction of the voice. Her eyes were useless to her in the darkness. But she picked her way easily on the sandy footpath hedged on either side by branches and damp leaves. She began to run, holding her breasts with her hands to stop them flapping noisily against her body. She hit her left foot against an outcropped root, and terror seized her. It was an ill omen. She ran faster. But Chielo's voice was still a long way away. Had she been running too? How could she go so fast with Ezinma on her back? Although the night was cool, Ekwefi was beginning to feel hot from her running. She continually ran into the luxuriant weeds and creepers that walled in the path. Once she tripped up and fell. Only then did she realize, with a start, that Chielo had stopped her chanting. Her heart beat violently and she stood still. Then Chielo's renewed outburst came from only a few paces ahead. But Ekwefi could not see her. She shut her eyes for a while and opened them again in an effort to see. But it was useless. She could not see beyond her nose.

There were no stars in the sky because there was a rain-cloud. Fireflies went about with their tiny green lamps, which only made the darkness more profound. Between Chielo's outbursts the night was alive with the shrill tremor of forest insects woven into the darkness.

"*Agbala do-o-o-o!... Agbala ekeneo-o-o-o!...*" Ekwefi trudged behind, neither getting too near nor keeping too far back. She thought they must be going towards the sacred cave. Now that she walked slowly she had time to think. What would she do when they got to the cave? She would not dare to enter. She would wait at the mouth, all alone in that fearful place. She thought of all the terrors of the night. She remembered that night, long ago, when she had seen *Ogbu-agali-odu,* one of those evil essences loosed upon the world by the potent "medicines" which the tribe had made in the distant past against its enemies but had now forgotten how to control. Ekwefi had been returning from the stream with her mother on a dark night like this when they saw its glow as it flew in their direction. They had thrown down their water-pots and lain by the roadside expecting the sinister light to descend on them and kill them. That was the only time Ekwefi ever saw *Ogbu-agali-odu.* But although it had happened so long ago, her blood still ran cold whenever she remembered that night.

The priestess' voice came at longer intervals now, but its vigor was undiminished. The air was cool and damp with dew. Ezinma sneezed. Ekwefi muttered, "Life to you." At the same time the priestess also said, "Life to you, my daughter." Ezinma's voice from the darkness warmed her mother's heart. She trudged slowly along.

And then the priestess screamed. "Somebody is walking behind me!" she said. "Whether you are spirit or man, may Agbala shave your head with a blunt razor! May he twist your neck until you see your heels!"

Ekwefi stood rooted to the spot. One mind said to her: "Woman, go home before Agbala does you harm." But she could not. She stood until Chielo had increased the distance between them and she began to follow again. She had already walked so long that she began to feel a slight numbness in the limbs and in the head. Then it occurred to her that they could not have been heading for the cave. They must have by-passed it long ago; they must be going towards Umuachi, the farthest village in the clan. Chielo's voice now came after long intervals.

It seemed to Ekwefi that the night had become a little lighter. The cloud had lifted and a few stars were out. The moon must be preparing to rise, its sullenness over. When the moon rose late in the night, people said it was refusing food, as a sullen husband refuses his wife's food when they have quarrelled.

"*Agbala do-o-o-o! Umuachi! Agbala ekene unuo-o-o!*" It was just as Ekwefi had thought. The priestess was now saluting the village of Umuachi. It was unbelievable, the distance they had covered. As they emerged into the open village from the narrow forest track the darkness was softened and it became possible to see the vague shape of trees. Ekwefi screwed her eyes up in an effort to see her daughter and the priestess, but whenever she thought she saw their shape it immediately dissolved like a melting lump of darkness. She walked numbly along.

Chielo's voice was now rising continuously, as when she first set out. Ekwefi had a feeling of spacious openness, and she guessed they must be on the village *ilo,* or playground. And she realized too with something like a jerk that Chielo was no longer moving forward. She was, in fact, returning. Ekwefi quickly moved away from her line of retreat. Chielo passed by, and they began to go back the way they had come.

It was a long and weary journey and Ekwefi felt like a sleepwalker most of the way. The moon was definitely rising, and although it had not yet appeared on the sky its light had already melted down the darkness. Ekwefi could now discern the figure of the priestess and her burden. She slowed down her pace so as to increase the distance between them. She was afraid of what might happen if Chielo suddenly turned round and saw her.

She had prayed for the moon to rise. But now she found the half-light of the incipient moon more terrifying than darkness. The world was now peopled with vague, fantastic figures that dissolved under her steady gaze and then formed again in new shapes. At one stage Ekwefi was so afraid that she nearly called out to Chielo for companionship and human sympathy. What she had seen was the shape of a man climbing a palm tree, his head pointing to the earth and his legs skywards. But at that very moment Chielo's voice rose again in her possessed chanting, and Ekwefi recoiled, because there was no humanity there. It was not the same Chielo who sat with her in the market and sometimes bought beancakes for Ezinma, whom she called her daughter. It was a different woman—the priestess of Agbala, the Oracle of the Hills and Caves. Ekwefi trudged along between two fears. The sound of her benumbed steps seemed to come from some other person walking behind her. Her arms were folded across her bare breasts. Dew fell heavily and the air was cold. She could no longer think, not even about the terrors of night. She just jogged along in a half-sleep, only waking to full life when Chielo sang.

At last they took a turning and began to head for the caves. From then on, Chielo never ceased in her chanting. She greeted her god in a multitude of names—the owner of the future, the messenger of earth, the god who cut a man down when his life was sweetest to him. Ekwefi was also awakened and her benumbed fears revived.

The moon was now up and she could see Chielo and Ezinma clearly. How a woman could carry a child of that size so easily and for so long was a miracle. But Ekwefi was not thinking about that. Chielo was not a woman that night.

"*Agbala do-o-o-o! Agbala ekeneo-o-o-o! Chi negbu madu ubosi ndu ya nato ya uto daluo-o-o!*..."[23]

Ekwefi could already see the hills looming in the moonlight. They formed a circular ring with a break at one point through which the foot-track led to the center of the circle.

As soon as the priestess stepped into this ring of hills her voice was not only doubled in strength but was thrown back on all sides. It was indeed the shrine of a great god. Ekwefi picked her way carefully and quietly. She was already beginning to doubt the wisdom of her coming. Nothing would happen to Ezinma, she thought. And if anything happened to her could she stop it? She would not dare to enter the underground caves. Her coming was quite useless, she thought.

As these things went through her mind she did not realize how close they were to the cave mouth. And so when the priestess with Ezinma on her back disappeared through a hole hardly big enough to pass a hen, Ekwefi broke into a run as though to stop them. As she stood gazing at the circular darkness which had swallowed them, tears gushed from her eyes, and she swore within her that if she heard Ezinma cry she would rush into the cave to defend her against all the gods in the world. She would die with her.

Having sworn that oath, she sat down on a stony ledge and waited. Her fear had vanished. She could hear the priestess' voice, all its metal taken out of it by the vast emptiness of the cave. She buried her face in her lap and waited.

She did not know how long she waited. It must have been a very long time. Her back was turned on the footpath that led out of the hills. She must have heard a noise behind her and turned round sharply. A man stood there with a machete in his hand. Ekwefi uttered a scream and sprang to her feet.

"Don't be foolish," said Okonkwo's voice. "I thought you were going into the shrine with Chielo," he mocked.

Ekwefi did not answer. Tears of gratitude filled her eyes. She knew her daughter was safe.

"Go home and sleep," said Okonkwo. "I shall wait here."

"I shall wait too. It is almost dawn. The first cock has crowed."

As they stood there together, Ekwefi's mind went back to the days when they were young. She had married Anene because Okonkwo was too poor then to marry. Two years after her marriage to Anene she could bear it no longer and she ran away to Okonkwo. It had been early in the morning. The moon was shining. She was going to the stream to fetch water. Okonkwo's house was on the way to the stream. She went in and knocked at his door and he came out. Even in those days he was not a man of many words. He just carried her into his bed and in the darkness began to feel around her waist for the loose end of her cloth.

12

On the following morning the entire neighborhood wore a festive air because Okonkwo's friend, Obierika, was celebrating his daughter's *uri*. It was the day on which her suitor (having already paid the greater part of her bride-price) would

---

[23]"Agbala wants something! Agbala greets.... *Chi* who kills a man on the day his life is so pleasant he gives thanks!"

bring palm-wine not only to her parents and immediate relatives but to the wide and extensive group of kinsmen called *umunna*. Everybody had been invited—men, women and children. But it was really a woman's ceremony and the central figures were the bride and her mother.

As soon as day broke, breakfast was hastily eaten and women and children began to gather at Obierika's compound to help the bride's mother in her difficult but happy task of cooking for a whole village.

Okonkwo's family was astir like any other family in the neighborhood. Nwoye's mother and Okonkwo's youngest wife were ready to set out for Obierika's compound with all their children. Nwoye's mother carried a basket of coco-yams, a cake of salt and smoked fish which she would present to Obierika's wife. Okonkwo's youngest wife, Ojiugo, also had a basket of plantains and coco-yams and a small pot of palm-oil. Their children carried pots of water.

Ekwefi was tired and sleepy from the exhausting experiences of the previous night. It was not very long since they had returned. The priestess, with Ezinma sleeping on her back, had crawled out of the shrine on her belly like a snake. She had not as much as looked at Okonkwo and Ekwefi or shown any surprise at finding them at the mouth of the cave. She looked straight ahead of her and walked back to the village. Okonkwo and his wife followed at a respectful distance. They thought the priestess might be going to her house, but she went to Okonkwo's compound, passed through his *obi* and into Ekwefi's hut and walked into her bedroom. She placed Ezinma carefully on the bed and went away without saying a word to anybody.

Ezinma was still sleeping when everyone else was astir, and Ekwefi asked Nwoye's mother and Ojiugo to explain to Obierika's wife that she would be late. She had got ready her basket of coco-yams and fish, but she must wait for Ezinma to wake.

"You need some sleep yourself," said Nwoye's mother. "You look very tired."

As they spoke Ezinma emerged from the hut, rubbing her eyes and stretching her spare frame. She saw the other children with their water-pots and remembered that they were going to fetch water for Obierika's wife. She went back to the hut and brought her pot.

"Have you slept enough?" asked her mother.

"Yes," she replied. "Let us go."

"Not before you have had your breakfast," said Ekwefi. And she went into her hut to warm the vegetable soup she had cooked last night.

"We shall be going," said Nwoye's mother. "I will tell Obierika's wife that you are coming later." And so they all went to help Obierika's wife—Nwoye's mother with her four children and Ojiugo with her two.

As they trooped through Okonkwo's *obi* he asked: "Who will prepare my afternoon meal?"

"I shall return to do it," said Ojiugo.

Okonkwo was also feeling tired, and sleepy, for although nobody else knew it, he had not slept at all last night. He had felt very anxious but did not show it. When Ekwefi had followed the priestess, he had allowed what he regarded as a reasonable and manly interval to pass and then gone with his machete to the shrine, where he thought they must be. It was only when he had got there that it had occurred to him that the priestess might have chosen to go round the villages first. Okonkwo had returned home and sat waiting. When he thought he had waited long enough he again returned to the shrine. But the Hills and the Caves were as silent as death. It was only on his fourth trip that he had found Ekwefi, and by then he had become gravely worried.

Obierika's compound was as busy as an anthill. Temporary cooking tripods were erected on every available space by bringing together three blocks of sun-dried earth and making a fire in their midst. Cooking pots went up and down the tripods, and foo-foo was pounded in a hundred wooden mortars. Some of the women cooked the yams and the cassava, and others prepared vegetable soup. Young men pounded the foo-foo or split firewood. The children made endless trips to the stream.

Three young men helped Obierika to slaughter the two goats with which the soup was made. They were very fat goats, but the fattest of all was tethered to a peg near the wall of the compound. It was as big as a small cow. Obierika had sent one of his relatives all the way to Umuike to buy that goat. It was the one he would present alive to his in-laws.

"The market of Umuike is a wonderful place," said the young man who had been sent by Obierika to buy the giant goat. "There are so many people on it that if you threw up a grain of sand it would not find a way to fall to earth again."

"It is the result of a great medicine," said Obierika. "The people of Umuike wanted their market to grow and swallow up the markets of their neighbors. So they made a powerful medicine. Every market day, before the first cock-crow, this medicine stands on the market ground in the shape of an old woman with a fan. With this magic fan she beckons to the market all the neighboring clans. She beckons in front of her and behind her, to her right and to her left."

"And so everybody comes," said another man, "honest men and thieves. They can steal your cloth from off your waist in that market."

"Yes," said Obierika. "I warned Nwankwo to keep a sharp eye and a sharp ear. There was once a man who went to sell a goat. He led it on a thick rope which he tied round his wrist. But as he walked through the market he realized that people were pointing at him as they do to a madman. He could not understand it until he looked back and saw that what he led at the end of the tether was not a goat but a heavy log of wood."

"Do you think a thief can do that kind of thing single-handed?" asked Nwankwo.

"No," said Obierika. "They use medicine."

When they had cut the goats' throats and collected the blood in a bowl, they held them over an open fire to burn off the hair, and the smell of burning hair blended with the smell of cooking. Then they washed them and cut them up for the women who prepared the soup.

All this anthill activity was going smoothly when a sudden interruption came. It was a cry in the distance: *Oji odu achu ijiji-o-o! (The one that uses its tail to drive flies away!)* Every woman immediately abandoned whatever she was doing and rushed out in the direction of the cry.

"We cannot all rush out like that, leaving what we are cooking to burn in the fire," shouted Chielo, the priestess. "Three or four of us should stay behind."

"It is true," said another woman. "We will allow three or four women to stay behind."

Five women stayed behind to look after the cooking-pots, and all the rest rushed away to see the cow that had been let loose. When they saw it they drove it back to its owner, who at once paid the heavy fine which the village imposed on anyone whose cow was let loose on his neighbors' crops. When the women had exacted the penalty they checked among themselves to see if any woman had failed to come out when the cry had been raised.

"Where is Mgbogo?" asked one of them.

"She is ill in bed," said Mgbogo's next-door neighbor. "She has *iba.*"

"The only other person is Udenkwo," said another woman, "and her child is not twenty-eight days yet."

Those women whom Obierika's wife had not asked to help her with the cooking returned to their homes, and the rest went back, in a body, to Obierika's compound.

"Whose cow was it?" asked the women who had been allowed to stay behind.

"It was my husband's," said Ezelagbo. "One of the young children had opened the gate of the cow-shed."

Early in the afternoon the first two pots of palm-wine arrived from Obierika's in-laws. They were duly presented to the women, who drank a cup or two each, to help them in their cooking. Some of it also went to the bride and her attendant maidens, who were putting the last delicate touches of razor to her coiffure and cam wood on her smooth skin.

When the heat of the sun began to soften, Obierika's son, Maduka, took a long broom and swept the ground in front of his father's *obi*. And as if they had been waiting for that, Obierika's relatives and friends began to arrive, every man with his goatskin bag hung on one shoulder and a rolled goatskin mat under his arm. Some of them were accompanied by their sons bearing carved wooden stools. Okonkwo was one of them. They sat in a half-circle and began to talk of many things. It would not be long before the suitors came.

Okonkwo brought out his snuff-bottle and offered it to Ogbuefi Ezenwa, who sat next to him. Ezenwa took it, tapped it on his kneecap, rubbed his left palm on his body to dry it before tipping a little snuff into it. His actions were deliberate, and he spoke as he performed them:

"I hope our in-laws will bring many pots of wine. Although they come from a village that is known for being closefisted, they ought to know that Akueke is the bride for a king."

"They dare not bring fewer than thirty pots," said Okonkwo. "I shall tell them my mind if they do."

At that moment Obierika's son, Maduka, led out the giant goat from the inner compound, for his father's relatives to see. They all admired it and said that that was the way things should be done. The goat was then led back to the inner compound.

Very soon after, the in-laws began to arrive. Young men and boys in single file, each carrying a pot of wine, came first. Obierika's relatives counted the pots as they came. Twenty, twenty-five. There was a long break, and the hosts looked at each other as if to say, "I told you." Then more pots came. Thirty, thirty-five, forty, forty-five. The hosts nodded in approval and seemed to say, "Now they are behaving like men." Altogether there were fifty pots of wine. After the pot-bearers came Ibe, the suitor, and the elders of his family. They sat in a half-moon, thus completing a circle with their hosts. The pots of wine stood in their midst. Then the bride, her mother and a half a dozen other women and girls emerged from the inner compound, and went round the circle shaking hands with all. The bride's mother led the way, followed by the bride and the other women. The married women wore their best cloths and the girls wore red and black waist-beads and anklets of brass.

When the women retired, Obierika presented kola nuts to his in-laws. His eldest brother broke the first one. "Life to all of us," he said as he broke it. "And let there be friendship between your family and ours."

The crowd answered: "*Ee-e-e!*"

"We are giving you our daughter today. She will be a good wife to you. She will bear you nine sons like the mother of our town."

"*Ee-e-e!*"

The oldest man in the camp of the visitors replied: "It will be good for you and it will be good for us."

"*Ee-e-e!*"

"This is not the first time my people have come to marry your daughter. My mother was one of you."

"*Ee-e-e!*"

"And this will not be the last, because you understand us and we understand you. You are a great family."

"*Ee-e-e!*"

"Prosperous men and great warriors." He looked in the direction of Okonkwo. "Your daughter will bear us sons like you."

"*Ee-e-e!*"

The kola was eaten and the drinking of palm-wine began. Groups of four or five men sat round with a pot in their midst. As the evening wore on, food was presented to the guests. There were huge bowls of foo-foo and steaming pots of soup. There were also pots of yam pottage. It was a great feast.

As night fell, burning torches were set on wooden tripods and the young men raised a song. The elders sat in a big circle and the singers went round singing each man's praise as they came before him. They had something to say for every man. Some were great farmers, some were orators who spoke for the clan; Okonkwo was the greatest wrestler and warrior alive. When they had gone round the circle they settled down in the center, and girls came from the inner compound to dance. At first the bride was not among them. But when she finally appeared holding a cock in her right hand, a loud cheer rose from the crowd. All the other dancers made way for her. She presented the cock to the musicians and began to dance. Her brass anklets rattled as she danced and her body gleamed with cam wood in the soft yellow light. The musicians with their wood, clay and metal instruments went from song to song. And they were all gay. They sang the latest song in the village:

> "If I hold her hand
> She says, 'Don't touch!'
> If I hold her foot
> She says, 'Don't touch!'
> But when I hold her waist-beads
> She pretends not to know."

The night was already far spent when the guests rose to go, taking their bride home to spend seven market weeks with her suitor's family. They sang songs as they went, and on their way they paid short courtesy visits to prominent men like Okonkwo, before they finally left for their village. Okonkwo made a present of two cocks to them.

13

Go-di-di-go-go-di-go. Di-go-go-di-go. It was the *ekwe* talking to the clan. One of the things every man learned was the language of the hollowed-out wooden instrument. Diim! Diim! Diim! boomed the cannon at intervals.

The first cock had not crowed, and Umuofia was still swallowed up in sleep and silence when the *ekwe* began to talk, and the cannon shattered the silence. Men stirred on their bamboo beds and listened anxiously. Somebody was dead. The cannon seemed to rend the sky. Di-go-go-di-go-di-di-go-go floated in the message-laden night air. The faint and distant wailing of women settled like a sediment of sorrow on the earth. Now and again a full-chested lamentation rose above the wailing whenever a man came into the place of death. He raised his voice once or twice in manly sorrow and then sat down with the other men listening to the endless wailing of the women and the esoteric language of the *ekwe*. Now and again the cannon boomed. The wailing of the women would not be heard beyond the village, but the *ekwe* carried the news to all the nine villages and even beyond. It began by naming the clan: *Umuofia obodo dike*, "the land of the brave." *Umuofia obodo dike! Umuofia obodo dike!* It said this over and over again, and as it dwelt on it, anxiety mounted in every heart that heaved on a bamboo bed that night. Then it went nearer and named the village: "*Iguedo of the yellow grinding-stone!*" It was Okonkwo's village. Again and again Iguedo was called and men waited breathlessly in all the nine villages. At last the man was named and people sighed "E-u-u, Ezeudu is dead." A cold shiver ran down Okonkwo's back as he remembered the last time the old man had visited him. "That boy calls you father," he had said. "Bear no hand in his death."

Ezeudu was a great man, and so all the clan was at his funeral. The ancient drums of death beat, guns and cannon were fired, and men dashed about in frenzy, cutting down every tree or animal they saw, jumping over walls and dancing on the roof. It was a warrior's funeral, and from morning till night warriors came and went in their age groups. They all wore smoked raffia skirts and their bodies were painted with chalk and charcoal. Now and again an ancestral spirit or *egwugwu* appeared from the underworld, speaking in a tremulous, unearthly voice and completely covered in raffia. Some of them were very violent, and there had been a mad rush for shelter earlier in the day when one appeared with a sharp machete and was only prevented from doing serious harm by two men who restrained him with the help of a strong rope tied round his waist. Sometimes he turned round and chased those men, and they ran for their lives. But they always returned to the long rope he trailed behind. He sang, in a terrifying voice, that Ekwensu, or Evil Spirit, had entered his eye.

But the most dreaded of all was yet to come. He was always alone and was shaped like a coffin. A sickly odor hung in the air wherever he went, and flies went with him. Even the greatest medicine men took shelter when he was near. Many years ago another *egwugwu* had dared to stand his ground before him and had been transfixed to the spot for two days. This one had only one hand and it carried a basket full of water.

But some of the *egwugwu* were quite harmless. One of them was so old and infirm that he leaned heavily on a stick. He walked unsteadily to the place where the corpse was laid, gazed at it a while and went away again—to the underworld.

The land of the living was not far removed from the domain of the ancestors. There was coming and going between them, especially at festivals and also when an old man died, because an old man was very close to the ancestors. A man's life from birth to death was a series of transition rites which brought him nearer and nearer to his ancestors.

Ezeudu had been the oldest man in his village, and at his death there were only three men in the whole clan who were older, and four or five others in his own age group. Whenever one of these ancient men appeared in the crowd to dance unsteadily the funeral steps of the tribe, younger men gave way and the tumult subsided.

It was a great funeral, such as befitted a noble warrior. As the evening drew near, the shouting and the firing of guns, the beating of drums and the brandishing and clanging of machetes increased.

Ezeudu had taken three titles in his life. It was a rare achievement. There were only four titles in the clan, and only one or two men in any generation ever achieved the fourth and highest. When they did, they became the lords of the land. Because he had taken titles, Ezeudu was to be buried after dark with only a glowing brand to light the sacred ceremony.

But before this quiet and final rite, the tumult increased tenfold. Drums beat violently and men leaped up and down in frenzy. Guns were fired on all sides and sparks flew out as machetes clanged together in warriors' salutes. The air was full of dust and the smell of gunpowder. It was then that the one-handed spirit came, carrying a basket full of water. People made way for him on all sides and the noise subsided. Even the smell of gunpowder was swallowed in the sickly smell that now filled the air. He danced a few steps to the funeral drums and then went to see the corpse.

"Ezeudu!" he called in his guttural voice. "If you had been poor in your last life I would have asked you to be rich when you come again. But you were rich. If you had been a coward, I would have asked you to bring courage. But you were a fearless warrior. If you had died young, I would have asked you to get life. But you lived long. So I shall ask you to come again the way you came before. If your death was the death of nature, go in peace. But if a man caused it, do not allow him a moment's rest." He danced a few more steps and went away.

The drums and the dancing began again and reached fever-heat. Darkness was around the corner, and the burial was near. Guns fired the last salute and the cannon rent the sky. And then from the center of the delirious fury came a cry of agony and shouts of horror. It was as if a spell had been cast. All was silent. In the center of the crowd a boy lay in a pool of blood. It was the dead man's sixteen-year-old son, who with his brothers and half-brothers had been dancing the traditional farewell to their father. Okonkwo's gun had exploded and a piece of iron had pierced the boy's heart.

The confusion that followed was without parallel in the tradition of Umuofia. Violent deaths were frequent, but nothing like this had ever happened.

The only course open to Okonkwo was to flee from the clan. It was a crime against the earth goddess to kill a clansman, and a man who committed it must flee from the land. The crime was of two kinds, male and female. Okonkwo had committed the female, because it had been inadvertent. He could return to the clan after seven years.

That night he collected his most valuable belongings into head-loads. His wives wept bitterly and their children wept with them without knowing why. Obierika and half a dozen other friends came to help and to console him. They each made nine or ten trips carrying Okonkwo's yams to store in Obierika's barn. And before the cock crowed Okonkwo and his family were fleeing to his motherland. It was a little village called Mbanta, just beyond the borders of Mbaino.

As soon as the day broke, a large crowd of men from Ezeudu's quarter stormed Okonkwo's compound, dressed in garbs of war. They set fire to his houses, demolished his red walls, killed his animals and destroyed his barn. It was the justice of the earth goddess, and they were merely her messengers. They had no hatred in their hearts against Okonkwo. His greatest friend, Obierika, was among them. They were merely cleansing the land which Okonkwo had polluted with the blood of a clansman.

Obierika was a man who thought about things. When the will of the goddess had been done, he sat down in his *obi* and mourned his friend's calamity. Why should a man suffer so grievously for an offense he had committed inadvertently?

But although he thought for a long time he found no answer. He was merely led into greater complexities. He remembered his wife's twin children, whom he had thrown away. What crime had they committed? The Earth had decreed that they were an offense on the land and must be destroyed. And if the clan did not exact punishment for an offense against the great goddess, her wrath was loosed on all the land and not just on the offender. As the elders said, if one finger brought oil it soiled the others.

PART II

14

Okonkwo was well received by his mother's kinsmen in Mbanta. The old man who received him was his mother's younger brother, who was now the eldest surviving member of that family. His name was Uchendu, and it was he who had received Okonkwo's mother twenty and ten years before when she had been brought home from Umuofia to be buried with her people. Okonkwo was only a boy then and Uchendu still remembered him crying the traditional farewell: "Mother, mother, mother is going."

That was many years ago. Today Okonkwo was not bringing his mother home to be buried with her people. He was taking his family of three wives and their children to seek refuge in his motherland. As soon as Uchendu saw him with his sad and weary company he guessed what had happened, and asked no questions. It was not until the following day that Okonkwo told him the full story. The old man listened silently to the end and then said with some relief: "It is a female *ochu*."[24] And he arranged the requisite rites and sacrifices.

Okonkwo was given a plot of ground on which to build his compound, and two or three pieces of land on which to farm during the coming planting season. With the help of his mother's kinsmen he built himself an *obi* and three huts for his wives. He then installed his personal god and the symbols of his departed fathers. Each of Uchendu's five sons contributed three hundred seed-yams to enable their cousin to plant a farm, for as soon as the first rain came farming would begin.

At last the rain came. It was sudden and tremendous. For two or three moons the sun had been gathering strength till it seemed to breathe a breath of fire on the earth. All the grass had long been scorched brown, and the sands felt like live coals to the feet. Evergreen trees wore a dusty coat of brown. The birds were silenced in the forests, and the world lay panting under the live, vibrating heat. And then came the clap of thunder. It was an angry, metallic and thirsty clap, unlike the deep and liquid rumbling of the rainy season. A mighty wind arose and filled the air with dust. Palm trees swayed as the wind combed their leaves into flying crests like strange and fantastic coiffure.

When the rain finally came, it was in large, solid drops of frozen water which the people called "the nuts of the water of heaven." They were hard and painful on the body as they fell, yet young people ran about happily picking up the cold nuts and throwing them into their mouths to melt.

The earth quickly came to life and the birds in the forests fluttered around and chirped merrily. A vague scent of life and green vegetation was diffused in the air. As the rain began to fall more soberly and in smaller liquid drops, children sought for shelter, and all were happy, refreshed and thankful.

---

[24] Manslaughter; because the killing was unintentional, it is a "female" crime.

Okonkwo and his family worked very hard to plant a new farm. Bu
beginning life anew without the vigor and enthusiasm of youth, like
become left-handed in old age. Work no longer had for him the pleasure it used to
have, and when there was no work to do he sat in a silent half-sleep.

His life had been ruled by a great passion—to become one of the lords of the
clan. That had been his life-spring. And he had all but achieved it. Then everything
had been broken. He had been cast out of his clan like a fish onto a dry, sandy
beach, panting. Clearly his personal god or *chi* was not made for great things. A
man could not rise beyond the destiny of his *chi.* The saying of the elders was not
true—that if a man said yea his *chi* also affirmed. Here was a man whose *chi* said nay
despite his own affirmation.

The old man, Uchendu, saw clearly that Okonkwo had yielded to despair and
he was greatly troubled. He would speak to him after the *isa-ifi*[25] ceremony.

The youngest of Uchendu's five sons, Amikwu, was marrying a new wife. The
bride-price had been paid and all but the last ceremony had been performed.
Amikwu and his people had taken palm-wine to the bride's kinsmen about two
moons before Okonkwo's arrival in Mbanta. And so it was time for the final
ceremony of confession.

The daughters of the family were all there, some of them having come a long
way from their homes in distant villages. Uchendu's eldest daughter had come from
Obodo, nearly half a day's journey away. The daughters of Uchendu's brothers
were also there. It was a full gathering of *umuada,*[26] in the same way as they would
meet if a death occurred in the family. There were twenty-two of them.

They sat in a big circle on the ground and the bride sat in the center with a hen
in her right hand. Uchendu sat by her, holding the ancestral staff of the family. All
the other men stood outside the circle, watching. Their wives watched also. It was
evening and the sun was setting.

Uchendu's eldest daughter, Njide, asked the questions.

"Remember that if you do not answer truthfully you will suffer or even die at
childbirth," she began. "How many men have lain with you since my brother first
expressed the desire to marry you?"

"None," she answered simply.

"Answer truthfully," urged the other women.

"None?" asked Njide.

"None," she answered.

"Swear on this staff of my fathers," said Uchendu.

"I swear," said the bride.

Uchendu took the hen from her, slit its throat with a sharp knife and allowed
some of the blood to fall on his ancestral staff.

From that day Amikwu took the young bride to his hut and she became his
wife. The daughters of the family did not return to their homes immediately but
spent two or three days with their kinsmen.

On the second day Uchendu called together his sons and daughters and his nephew,
Okonkwo. The men brought their goatskin mats, with which they sat on the floor,
and the women sat on a sisal mat spread on a raised bank of earth. Uchendu pulled
gently at his gray beard and gnashed his teeth. Then he began to speak, quietly and
deliberately, picking his words with great care:

---

[25] A ceremony held to determine the fidelity of a wife who had been separated from her husband for a
long period of time.

[26] A celebration of the female members of a clan upon their return home.

"It is Okonkwo that I primarily wish to speak to," he began. "But I want all of you to note what I am going to say. I am an old man and you are all children. I know more about the world than any of you. If there is any one among you who thinks he knows more let him speak up." He paused, but no one spoke.

"Why is Okonkwo with us today? This is not his clan. We are only his mother's kinsmen. He does not belong here. He is an exile, condemned for seven years to live in a strange land. And so he is bowed with grief. But there is just one question I would like to ask him. Can you tell me, Okonkwo, why it is that one of the commonest names we give our children is Nneka, or 'Mother is Supreme'? We all know that a man is the head of the family and his wives do his bidding. A child belongs to its father and his family and not to its mother and her family. A man belongs to his fatherland and not to his motherland. And yet we say Nneka—'Mother is Supreme.' Why is that?"

There was silence. "I want Okonkwo to answer me," said Uchendu.

"I do not know the answer," Okonkwo replied.

"You do not know the answer? So you see that you are a child. You have many wives and many children—more children than I have. You are a great man in your clan. But you are still a child, *my* child. Listen to me and I shall tell you. But there is one more question I shall ask you. Why is it that when a woman dies she is taken home to be buried with her own kinsmen? She is not buried with her husband's kinsmen. Why is that? Your mother was brought home to me and buried with my people. Why was that?"

Okonkwo shook his head.

"He does not know that either," said Uchendu, "and yet he is full of sorrow because he has come to live in his motherland for a few years." He laughed a mirthless laughter, and turned to his sons and daughters. "What about you? Can you answer my question?"

They all shook their heads.

"Then listen to me," he said and cleared his throat. "It's true that a child belongs to its father. But when a father beats his child, it seeks sympathy in its mother's hut. A man belongs to his fatherland when things are good and life is sweet. But when there is sorrow and bitterness he finds refuge in his motherland. Your mother is there to protect you. She is buried there. And that is why we say that mother is supreme. Is it right that you, Okonkwo, should bring to your mother a heavy face and refuse to be comforted? Be careful or you may displease the dead. Your duty is to comfort your wives and children and take them back to your fatherland after seven years. But if you allow sorrow to weigh you down and kill you, they will all die in exile." He paused for a long while. "These are now your kinsmen." He waved at his sons and daughters. "You think you are the greatest sufferer in the world? Do you know that men are sometimes banished for life? Do you know that men sometimes lose all their yams and even their children? I had six wives once. I have none now except that young girl who knows not her right from her left. Do you know how many children I have buried—children I begot in my youth and strength? Twenty-two. I did not hang myself, and I am still alive. If you think you are the greatest sufferer in the world ask my daughter, Akueni, how many twins she has borne and thrown away. Have you not heard the song they sing when a woman dies?

> " 'For whom is it well, for whom is it well?
> There is no one for whom it is well.'

"I have no more to say to you."

15

It was in the second year of Okonkwo's exile that his friend, Obierika, came to visit him. He brought with him two young men, each of them carrying a heavy bag on his head. Okonkwo helped them put down their loads. It was clear that the bags were full of cowries.

Okonkwo was very happy to receive his friend. His wives and children were very happy too, and so were his cousins and their wives when he sent for them and told them who his guest was.

"You must take him to salute our father," said one of the cousins.

"Yes," replied Okonkwo. "We are going directly." But before they went he whispered something to his first wife. She nodded, and soon the children were chasing one of their cocks.

Uchendu had been told by one of his grandchildren that three strangers had come to Okonkwo's house. He was therefore waiting to receive them. He held out his hands to them when they came into his *obi*, and after they had shaken hands he asked Okonkwo who they were.

"This is Obierika, my great friend. I have already spoken to you about him."

"Yes," said the old man, turning to Obierika. "My son has told me about you, and I am happy you have come to see us. I knew your father, Iweka. He was a great man. He had many friends here and came to see them quite often. Those were good days when a man had friends in distant clans. Your generation does not know that. You stay at home, afraid of your next-door neighbor. Even a man's motherland is strange to him nowadays." He looked at Okonkwo. "I am an old man and I like to talk. That is all I am good for now." He got up painfully, went into an inner room and came back with a kola nut.

"Who are the young men with you?" he asked as he sat down again on his goatskin. Okonkwo told him.

"Ah," he said. "Welcome, my sons." He presented the kola nut to them, and when they had seen it and thanked him, he broke it and they ate.

"Go into that room," he said to Okonkwo, pointing with his finger. "You will find a pot of wine there."

Okonkwo brought the wine and they began to drink. It was a day old, and very strong.

"Yes," said Uchendu after a long silence. "People traveled more in those days. There is not a single clan in these parts that I do not know very well. Aninta, Umuazu, Ikeocha, Elumelu, Abame—I know them all."

"Have you heard," asked Obierika, "that Abame is no more?"

"How is that?" asked Uchendu and Okonkwo together.

"Abame has been wiped out," said Obierika. "It is a strange and terrible story. If I had not seen the few survivors with my own eyes and heard their story with my own ears, I would not have believed. Was it not on an Eke day that they fled into Umuofia?" he asked his two companions, and they nodded their heads.

"Three moons ago," said Obierika, "on an Eke market day a little band of fugitives came into our town. Most of them were sons of our land whose mothers had been buried with us. But there were some too who came because they had friends in our town, and others who could think of nowhere else open to escape. And so they fled into Umuofia with a woeful story." He drank his palm-wine, and Okonkwo filled his horn again. He continued:

"During the last planting season a white man had appeared in their clan."

"An albino," suggested Okonkwo.

"He was not an albino. He was quite different." He sipped his wine. "And he was riding an iron horse. The first people who saw him ran away, but he stood beckoning to them. In the end the fearless ones went near and even touched him. The elders consulted their Oracle and it told them that the strange man would break their clan and spread destruction among them." Obierika again drank a little of his wine. "And so they killed the white man and tied his iron horse to their sacred tree because it looked as if it would run away to call the man's friends. I forgot to tell you another thing which the Oracle said. It said that other white men were on their way. They were locusts, it said, and that first man was their harbinger sent to explore the terrain. And so they killed him."

"What did the white man say before they killed him?" asked Uchendu.

"He said nothing," answered one of Obierika's companions.

"He said something, only they did not understand him," said Obierika. "He seemed to speak through his nose."

"One of the men told me," said Obierika's other companion, "that he repeated over and over again a word that resembled Mbaino. Perhaps he had been going to Mbaino and had lost his way."

"Anyway," resumed Obierika, "they killed him and tied up his iron horse. This was before the planting season began. For a long time nothing happened. The rains had come and yams had been sown. The iron horse was still tied to the sacred silk-cotton tree. And then one morning three white men led by a band of ordinary men like us came to the clan. They saw the iron horse and went away again. Most of the men and women of Abame had gone to their farms. Only a few of them saw these white men and their followers. For many market weeks nothing else happened. They have a big market in Abame on every other Afo day and, as you know, the whole clan gathers there. That was the day it happened. The three white men and a very large number of other men surrounded the market. They must have used a powerful medicine to make themselves invisible until the market was full. And they began to shoot. Everybody was killed, except the old and the sick who were at home and a handful of men and women whose *chi* were wide awake and brought them out of that market." He paused.

"Their clan is now completely empty. Even the sacred fish in their mysterious lake have fled and the lake has turned the color of blood. A great evil has come upon their land as the Oracle had warned."

There was a long silence. Uchendu ground his teeth together audibly. Then he burst out:

"Never kill a man who says nothing. Those men of Abame were fools. What did they know about the man?" He ground his teeth again and told a story to illustrate his point. "Mother Kite once sent her daughter to bring food. She went, and brought back a duckling. 'You have done very well,' said Mother Kite to her daughter, 'but tell me, what did the mother of this duckling say when you swooped and carried its child away?' 'It said nothing,' replied the young kite. 'It just walked away.' 'You must return the duckling,' said Mother Kite. 'There is something ominous behind the silence.' And so Daughter Kite returned the duckling and took a chick instead. 'What did the mother of this chick do?' asked the old kite. 'It cried and raved and cursed me,' said the young kite. 'Then we can eat the chick,' said her mother. 'There is nothing to fear from someone who shouts.' Those men of Abame were fools."

"They were fools," said Okonkwo after a pause. "They had been warned that danger was ahead. They should have armed themselves with their guns and their machetes even when they went to market."

"They have paid for their foolishness," said Obierika. "But I am greatly afraid. We have heard stories about white men who made the powerful guns and the strong drinks and took slaves away across the seas, but no one thought the stories were true."

"There is no story that is not true," said Uchendu. "The world has no end, and what is good among one people is an abomination with others. We have albinos among us. Do you not think that they came to our clan by mistake, that they have strayed from their way to a land where everybody is like them?"

Okonkwo's first wife soon finished her cooking and set before their guests a big meal of pounded yams and bitter-leaf soup. Okonkwo's son, Nwoye, brought in a pot of sweet wine tapped from the raffia palm.

"You are a big man now," Obierika said to Nwoye. "Your friend Anene asked me to greet you."

"Is he well?" asked Nwoye.

"We are all well," said Obierika.

Ezinma brought them a bowl of water with which to wash their hands. After that they began to eat and to drink the wine.

"When did you set out from home?" asked Okonkwo.

"We had meant to set out from my house before cock-crow," said Obierika. "But Nweke did not appear until it was quite light. Never make an early morning appointment with a man who has just married a new wife." They all laughed.

"Has Nweke married a wife?" asked Okonkwo.

"He has married Okadigbo's second daughter," said Obierika.

"That is very good," said Okonkwo. "I do not blame you for not hearing the cock crow."

When they had eaten, Obierika pointed at the two heavy bags.

"That is the money from your yams," he said. "I sold the big ones as soon as you left. Later on I sold some of the seed-yams and gave out others to sharecroppers. I shall do that every year until you return. But I thought you would need the money now and so I brought it. Who knows what may happen tomorrow? Perhaps green men will come to our clan and shoot us."

"God will not permit it," said Okonkwo. "I do not know how to thank you."

"I can tell you," said Obierika. "Kill one of your sons for me."

"That will not be enough," said Okonkwo.

"Then kill yourself," said Obierika.

"Forgive me," said Okonkwo, smiling. "I shall not talk about thanking you any more."

16

When nearly two years later Obierika paid another visit to his friend in exile the circumstances were less happy. The missionaries had come to Umuofia. They had built their church there, won a handful of converts and were already sending evangelists to the surrounding towns and villages. That was a source of great sorrow to the leaders of the clan; but many of them believed that the strange faith and the white man's god would not last. None of his converts was a man whose word was heeded in the assembly of the people. None of them was a man of title. They were mostly the kind of people that were called *efulefu*, worthless, empty men. The imagery of an *efulefu* in the language of the clan was a man who sold his machete and wore the sheath to battle. Chielo, the priestess of Agbala, called the converts the excrement of the clan, and the new faith was a mad dog that had come to eat it up.

What moved Obierika to visit Okonkwo was the sudden appearance of the latter's son, Nwoye, among the missionaries in Umuofia.

"What are you doing here?" Obierika had asked when after many difficulties the missionaries had allowed him to speak to the boy.

"I am one of them," replied Nwoye.

"How is your father?" Obierika asked, not knowing what else to say.

"I don't know. He is not my father," said Nwoye, unhappily.

And so Obierika went to Mbanta to see his friend. And he found that Okonkwo did not wish to speak about Nwoye. It was only from Nwoye's mother that he heard scraps of the story.

The arrival of the missionaries had caused a considerable stir in the village of Mbanta. There were six of them and one was a white man. Every man and woman came out to see the white man. Stories about these strange men had grown since one of them had been killed in Abame and his iron horse tied to the sacred silk-cotton tree. And so everybody came to see the white man. It was the time of the year when everybody was at home. The harvest was over.

When they had all gathered, the white man began to speak to them. He spoke through an interpreter who was an Ibo man, though his dialect was different and harsh to the ears of Mbanta. Many people laughed at his dialect and the way he used words strangely. Instead of saying "myself" he always said "my buttocks." But he was a man of commanding presence and the clansmen listened to him. He said he was one of them, as they could see from his color and his language. The other four black men were also their brothers, although one of them did not speak Ibo. The white man was also their brother because they were all sons of God. And he told them about this new God, the Creator of all the world and all the men and women. He told them that they worshipped false gods, gods of wood and stone. A deep murmur went through the crowd when he said this. He told them that the true God lived on high and that all men when they died went before Him for judgment. Evil men and all the heathen who in their blindness bowed to wood and stone were thrown into a fire that burned like palm-oil. But good men who worshipped the true God lived forever in His happy kingdom. "We have been sent by this great God to ask you to leave your wicked ways and false gods and turn to Him so that you may be saved when you die," he said.

"Your buttocks understand our language," said someone light-heartedly and the crowd laughed.

"What did he say?" the white man asked his interpreter. But before he could answer, another man asked a question: "Where is the white man's horse?" he asked. The Ibo evangelists consulted among themselves and decided that the man probably meant bicycle. They told the white man and he smiled benevolently.

"Tell them," he said, "that I shall bring many iron horses when we have settled down among them. Some of them will even ride the iron horse themselves." This was interpreted to them but very few of them heard. They were talking excitedly among themselves because the white man had said he was going to live among them. They had not thought about that.

At this point an old man said he had a question. "Which is this god of yours," he asked, "the goddess of the earth, the god of the sky, Amadiora or the thunderbolt, or what?"

The interpreter spoke to the white man and he immediately gave his answer. "All the gods you have named are not gods at all. They are gods of deceit who tell you to kill your fellows and destroy innocent children. There is only one true God and He has the earth, the sky, you and me and all of us."

"If we leave our gods and follow your god," asked another man, "who will protect us from the anger of our neglected gods and ancestors?"

"Your gods are not alive and cannot do you any harm," replied the white man. "They are pieces of wood and stone."

When this was interpreted to the men of Mbanta they broke into derisive laughter. These men must be mad, they said to themselves. How else could they say that Ani and Amadiora were harmless? And Idemili and Ogwugwu too? And some of them began to go away.

Then the missionaries burst into song. It was one of those gay and rollicking tunes of evangelism which had the power of plucking at silent and dusty chords in the heart of an Ibo man. The interpreter explained each verse to the audience, some of whom now stood enthralled. It was a story of brothers who lived in darkness and in fear, ignorant of the love of God. It told of one sheep out on the hills, away from the gates of God and from the tender shepherd's care.

After the singing the interpreter spoke about the Son of God whose name was Jesu Kristi. Okonkwo, who only stayed in the hope that it might come to chasing the men out of the village or whipping them, now said:

"You told us with your own mouth that there was only one god. Now you talk about his son. He must have a wife, then." The crowd agreed.

"I did not say He had a wife," said the interpreter, somewhat lamely.

"Your buttocks said he had a son," said the joker. "So he must have a wife and all of them must have buttocks."

The missionary ignored him and went on to talk about the Holy Trinity. At the end of it Okonkwo was fully convinced that the man was mad. He shrugged his shoulders and went away to tap his afternoon palm-wine.

But there was a young lad who had been captivated. His name was Nwoye, Okonkwo's first son. It was not the mad logic of the Trinity that captivated him. He did not understand it. It was the poetry of the new religion, something felt in the marrow. The hymn about brothers who sat in darkness and in fear seemed to answer a vague and persistent question that haunted his young soul—the question of the twins crying in the bush and the question of Ikemefuna who was killed. He felt a relief within as the hymn poured into his parched soul. The words of the hymn were like the drops of frozen rain melting on the dry palate of the panting earth. Nwoye's callow mind was greatly puzzled.

17

The missionaries spent their first four or five nights in the marketplace, and went into the village in the morning to preach the gospel. They asked who the king of the village was, but the villagers told them that there was no king. "We have men of high title and the chief priests and the elders," they said.

It was not very easy getting the men of high title and the elders together after the excitement of the first day. But the missionaries persevered, and in the end they were received by the rulers of Mbanta. They asked for a plot of land to build their church.

Every clan and village had its "evil forest." In it were buried all those who died of the really evil diseases, like leprosy and smallpox. It was also the dumping ground for the potent fetishes of great medicine men when they died. An "evil forest" was, therefore, alive with sinister forces and powers of darkness. It was such a forest that the rulers of Mbanta gave to the missionaries. They did not really want them in their clan, and so they made them that offer which nobody in his right senses would accept.

"They want a piece of land to build their shrine," said Uchendu to his peers when they consulted among themselves. "We shall give them a piece of land." He paused, and there was a murmur of surprise and disagreement. "Let us give them a portion of the Evil Forest. They boast about victory over death. Let us give them a real battlefield in which to show their victory." They laughed and agreed, and sent for the missionaries, whom they had asked to leave them for a while so that they might "whisper together." They offered them as much of the Evil Forest as they cared to take. And to their greatest amazement the missionaries thanked them and burst into song.

"They do not understand," said some of the elders. "But they will understand when they go to their plot of land tomorrow morning." And they dispersed.

The next morning the crazy men actually began to clear a part of the forest and to build their house. The inhabitants of Mbanta expected them all to be dead within four days. The first day passed and the second and third and fourth, and none of them died. Everyone was puzzled. And then it became known that the white man's fetish had unbelievable power. It was said that he wore glasses on his eyes so that he could see and talk to evil spirits. Not long after, he won his first three converts.

Although Nwoye had been attracted to the new faith from the very first day, he kept it secret. He dared not go too near the missionaries for fear of his father. But whenever they came to preach in the open marketplace or the village playground, Nwoye was there. And he was already beginning to know some of the simple stories they told.

"We have now built a church," said Mr. Kiaga, the interpreter, who was now in charge of the infant congregation. The white man had gone back to Umuofia, where he built his headquarters and from where he paid regular visits to Mr. Kiaga's congregation at Mbanta.

"We have now built a church," said Mr. Kiaga, "and we want you all to come in every seventh day to worship the true God."

On the following Sunday, Nwoye passed and re-passed the little red-earth and thatch building without summoning enough courage to enter. He heard the voice of singing and although it came from a handful of men it was loud and confident. Their church stood on a circular clearing that looked like the open mouth of the Evil Forest. Was it waiting to snap its teeth together? After passing and re-passing by the church, Nwoye returned home.

It was well known among the people of Mbanta that their gods and ancestors were sometimes long-suffering and would deliberately allow a man to go on defying them. But even in such cases they set their limit at seven market weeks or twenty-eight days. Beyond that limit no man was suffered to go. And so excitement mounted in the village as the seventh week approached since the impudent missionaries built their church in the Evil Forest. The villagers were so certain about the doom that awaited these men that one or two converts thought it wise to suspend their allegiance to the new faith.

At last the day came by which all the missionaries should have died. But they were still alive, building a new red-earth and thatch house for their teacher, Mr. Kiaga. That week they won a handful more converts. And for the first time they had a woman. Her name was Nneka, the wife of Amadi, who was a prosperous farmer. She was very heavy with child.

Nneka had had four previous pregnancies and childbirths. But each time she had borne twins, and they had been immediately thrown away. Her husband and his family were already becoming highly critical of such a woman and were not

unduly perturbed when they found she had fled to join the Christi
good riddance.

One morning Okonkwo's cousin, Amikwu, was passing by the church on his way
from the neighboring village, when he saw Nwoye among the Christians. He was
greatly surprised, and when he got home he went straight to Okonkwo's hut and
told him what he had seen. The women began to talk excitedly, but Okonkwo sat
unmoved.

It was late afternoon before Nwoye returned. He went into the *obi* and saluted
his father, but he did not answer. Nwoye turned round to walk into the inner
compound when his father, suddenly overcome with fury, sprang to his feet and
gripped him by the neck.

"Where have you been?" he stammered.

Nwoye struggled to free himself from the choking grip.

"Answer me," roared Okonkwo, "before I kill you!" He seized a heavy stick that
lay on the dwarf wall and hit him two or three savage blows.

"Answer me!" he roared again. Nwoye stood looking at him and did not say a
word. The women were screaming outside, afraid to go in.

"Leave that boy at once!" said a voice in the outer compound. It was Okonkwo's
uncle, Uchendu. "Are you mad?"

Okonkwo did not answer. But he left hold of Nwoye, who walked away and
never returned.

He went back to the church and told Mr. Kiaga that he had decided to go to
Umuofia where the white missionary had set up a school to teach young Christians
to read and write.

Mr. Kiaga's joy was very great. "Blessed is he who forsakes his father and his
mother for my sake," he intoned. "Those that hear my words are my father and my
mother."

Nwoye did not fully understand. But he was happy to leave his father. He would
return later to his mother and his brothers and sisters and convert them to the new
faith.

As Okonkwo sat in his hut that night, gazing into a log fire, he thought over
the matter. A sudden fury rose within him and he felt a strong desire to take up his
machete, go to the church and wipe out the entire vile and miscreant gang. But on
further thought he told himself that Nwoye was not worth fighting for. Why, he
cried in his heart, should he, Okonkwo, of all people, be cursed with such a son?
He saw clearly in it the finger of his personal god or *chi*. For how else could he
explain his great misfortune and exile and now his despicable son's behavior? Now
that he had time to think of it, his son's crime stood out in its stark enormity. To
abandon the gods of one's father and go about with a lot of effeminate men clucking
like old hens was the very depth of abomination. Suppose when he died all his male
children decided to follow Nwoye's steps and abandon their ancestors? Okonkwo
felt a cold shudder run through him at the terrible prospects, like the prospect of
annihilation. He saw himself and his fathers crowding round their ancestral shrine
waiting in vain for worship and sacrifice and finding nothing but ashes of bygone days, and his children the while praying to the white man's god. If such
a thing were ever to happen, he, Okonkwo, would wipe them off the face of the
earth.

Okonkwo was popularly called the "Roaring Flame." As he looked into the
log fire he recalled the name. He was a flaming fire. How then could he have begotten a son like Nwoye, degenerate and effeminate? Perhaps he was not his son. No!

he could not be. His wife had played him false. He would teach her! But Nwoye resembled his grandfather, Unoka, who was Okonkwo's father. He pushed the thought out of his mind. He, Okonkwo, was called a flaming fire. How could he have begotten a woman for a son? At Nwoye's age Okonkwo had already become famous throughout Umuofia for his wrestling and his fearlessness.

He sighed heavily, and as if in sympathy the smoldering log also sighed. And immediately Okonkwo's eyes were opened and he saw the whole matter clearly. Living fire begets cold, impotent ash. He sighed again, deeply.

18

The young church in Mbanta had a few crises early in its life. At first the clan had assumed that it would not survive. But it had gone on living and gradually becoming stronger. The clan was worried, but not overmuch. If a gang of *efulefu* decided to live in the Evil Forest it was their own affair. When one came to think of it, the Evil Forest was a fit home for such undesirable people. It was true they were rescuing twins from the bush, but they never brought them into the village. As far as the villagers were concerned, the twins still remained where they had been thrown away. Surely the earth goddess would not visit the sins of the missionaries on the innocent villagers?

But on one occasion the missionaries had tried to overstep the bounds. Three converts had gone into the village and boasted openly that all the gods were dead and impotent and that they were prepared to defy them by burning all their shrines.

"Go and burn your mothers' genitals," said one of the priests. The men were seized and beaten until they streamed with blood. After that nothing happened for a long time between the church and the clan.

But stories were already gaining ground that the white man had not only brought a religion but also a government. It was said that they had built a place of judgment in Umuofia to protect the followers of their religion. It was even said that they had hanged one man who killed a missionary.

Although such stories were now often told they looked like fairy-tales in Mbanta and did not as yet affect the relationship between the new church and the clan. There was no question of killing a missionary here, for Mr. Kiaga, despite his madness, was quite harmless. As for his converts, no one could kill them without having to flee from the clan, for in spite of their worthlessness they still belonged to the clan. And so nobody gave serious thought to the stories about the white man's government or the consequences of killing the Christians. If they became more troublesome than they already were they would simply be driven out of the clan.

And the little church was at that moment too deeply absorbed in its own troubles to annoy the clan. It all began over the question of admitting outcasts.

These outcasts, or *osu,* seeing that the new religion welcomed twins and such abominations, thought that it was possible that they would also be received. And so one Sunday two of them went into the church. There was an immediate stir; but so great was the work the new religion had done among the converts that they did not immediately leave the church when the outcasts came in. Those who found themselves nearest to them merely moved to another seat. It was a miracle. But it only lasted till the end of the service. The whole church raised a protest and was about to drive these people out, when Mr. Kiaga stopped them and began to explain.

"Before God," he said, "there is no slave or free. We are all children of God and we must receive these our brothers."

"You do not understand," said one of the converts. "What will the heathen say of us when they hear that we receive *osu* into our midst? They will laugh."

"Let them laugh," said Mr. Kiaga. "God will laugh at them on the judgment day. Why do the nations rage and the peoples imagine a vain thing? He that sitteth in the heavens shall laugh. The Lord shall have them in derision."

"You do not understand," the convert maintained. "You are our teacher, and you can teach us the things of the new faith. But this is a matter which we know." And he told him what an *osu* was.

He was a person dedicated to a god, a thing set apart—a taboo for ever, and his children after him. He could neither marry nor be married by the free-born. He was in fact an outcast, living in a special area of the village, close to the Great Shrine. Wherever he went he carried with him the mark of his forbidden caste—long, tangled and dirty hair. A razor was taboo to him. An *osu* could not attend an assembly of the free-born, and they, in turn, could not shelter under his roof. He could not take any of the four titles of the clan, and when he died he was buried by his kind in the Evil Forest. How could such a man be a follower of Christ?

"He needs Christ more than you and I," said Mr. Kiaga.

"Then I shall go back to the clan," said the convert. And he went. Mr. Kiaga stood firm, and it was his firmness that saved the young church. The wavering converts drew inspiration and confidence from his unshakable faith. He ordered the outcasts to shave off their long, tangled hair. At first they were afraid they might die.

"Unless you shave off the mark of your heathen belief I will not admit you into the church," said Mr. Kiaga. "You fear that you will die. Why should that be? How are you different from other men who shave their hair? The same God created you and them. But they have cast you out like lepers. It is against the will of God, who has promised everlasting life to all who believe in His holy name. The heathen say you will die if you do this or that, and you are afraid. They also said I would die if I built my church on this ground. Am I dead? They said I would die if I took care of twins. I am still alive. The heathen speak nothing but falsehood. Only the word of our God is true."

The two outcasts shaved off their hair, and soon they were the strongest adherents of the new faith. And what was more, nearly all the *osu* in Mbanta followed their example. It was in fact one of them who in his zeal brought the church into serious conflict with the clan a year later by killing the sacred python, the emanation of the god of water.

The royal python was the most revered animal in Mbanta and all the surrounding clans. It was addressed as "Our Father," and was allowed to go wherever it chose, even into people's beds. It ate rats in the house and sometimes swallowed hens' eggs. If a clansman killed a royal python accidentally, he made sacrifices of atonement and performed an expensive burial ceremony such as was done for a great man. No punishment was prescribed for a man who killed the python knowingly. Nobody thought that such a thing could ever happen.

Perhaps it never did happen. That was the way the clan at first looked at it. No one had actually seen the man do it. The story had arisen among the Christians themselves.

But, all the same, the rulers and elders of Mbanta assembled to decide on their action. Many of them spoke at great length and in fury. The spirit of wars was upon them. Okonkwo, who had begun to play a part in the affairs of his motherland, said that until the abominable gang was chased out of the village with whips there would be no peace.

But there were many others who saw the situation differently, and it was their counsel that prevailed in the end.

"It is not our custom to fight for our gods," said one of them. "Let us not presume to do so now. If a man kills the sacred python in the secrecy of his hut, the matter lies between him and the god. We did not see it. If we put ourselves between the god and his victim we may receive blows intended for the offender. When a man blasphemes, what do we do? Do we go and stop his mouth? No. We put our fingers into our ears to stop us hearing. That is a wise action."

"Let us not reason like cowards," said Okonkwo. "If a man comes into my hut and defecates on the floor, what do I do? Do I shut my eyes? No! I take a stick and break his head. That is what a man does. These people are daily pouring filth over us, and Okeke says we should pretend not to see." Okonkwo made a sound full of disgust. This was a womanly clan, he thought. Such a thing could never happen in his fatherland, Umuofia.

"Okonkwo has spoken the truth," said another man. "We should do something. But let us ostracize these men. We would then not be held accountable for their abominations."

Everybody in the assembly spoke, and in the end it was decided to ostracize the Christians. Okonkwo ground his teeth in disgust.

That night a bell-man went through the length and breadth of Mbanta proclaiming that the adherents of the new faith were thenceforth excluded from the life and privileges of the clan.

The Christians had grown in number and were now a small community of men, women and children, self-assured and confident. Mr. Brown, the white missionary, paid regular visits to them. "When I think that it is only eighteen months since the Seed was first sown among you," he said, "I marvel at what the Lord hath wrought."

It was Wednesday in Holy Week and Mr. Kiaga had asked the women to bring red earth and white chalk and water to scrub the church for Easter; and the women had formed themselves into three groups for this purpose. They set out early that morning, some of them with their water-pots to the stream, another group with hoes and baskets to the village red-earth pit, and the others to the chalk quarry.

Mr. Kiaga was praying in the church when he heard the women talking excitedly. He rounded off his prayer and went to see what it was all about. The women had come to the church with empty water-pots. They said that some young men had chased them away from the stream with whips. Soon after, the women who had gone for red earth returned with empty baskets. Some of them had been heavily whipped. The chalk women also returned to tell a similar story.

"What does it all mean?" asked Mr. Kiaga, who was greatly perplexed.

"The village has outlawed us," said one of the women. "The bell-man announced it last night. But it is not our custom to debar anyone from the stream or the quarry."

Another woman said, "They want to ruin us. They will not allow us into the markets. They have said so."

Mr. Kiaga was going to send into the village for his men-converts when he saw them coming on their own. Of course they had all heard the bell-man, but they had never in all their lives heard of women being debarred from the stream.

"Come along," they said to the women. "We will go with you to meet those cowards." Some of them had big sticks and some even machetes.

But Mr. Kiaga restrained them. He wanted first to know why they had been outlawed.

"They say that Okoli killed the sacred python," said one man.

"It is false," said another. "Okoli told me himself that it was false."

Okoli was not there to answer. He had fallen ill on the previous night. Before the day was over he was dead. His death showed that the gods were still able to fight their own battles. The clan saw no reason then for molesting the Christians.

19

The last big rains of the year were falling. It was the time for treading red earth with which to build walls. It was not done earlier because the rains were too heavy and would have washed away the heap of trodden earth; and it could not be done later because harvesting would soon set in, and after that the dry season.

It was going to be Okonkwo's last harvest in Mbanta. The seven wasted and weary years were at last dragging to a close. Although he had prospered in his motherland Okonkwo knew that he would have prospered even more in Umuofia, in the land of his fathers where men were bold and warlike. In these seven years he would have climbed to the utmost heights. And so he regretted every day of his exile. His mother's kinsmen had been very kind to him, and he was grateful. But that did not alter the facts. He had called the first child born to him in exile Nneka—"Mother is Supreme"—out of politeness to his mother's kinsmen. But two years later when a son was born he called him Nwofia—"Begotten in the Wilderness."

As soon as he entered his last year in exile Okonkwo sent money to Obierika to build him two huts in his old compound where he and his family would live until he built more huts and the outside wall of his compound. He could not ask another man to build his own *obi* for him, nor the walls of his compound. Those things a man built for himself or inherited from his father.

As the last heavy rains of the year began to fall, Obierika sent word that the two huts had been built and Okonkwo began to prepare for his return, after the rains. He would have liked to return earlier and build his compound that year before the rains stopped, but in doing so he would have taken something from the full penalty of seven years. And that could not be. So he waited impatiently for the dry season to come.

It came slowly. The rain became lighter and lighter until it fell in slanting showers. Sometimes the sun shone through the rain and a light breeze blew. It was a gay and airy kind of rain. The rainbow began to appear, and sometimes two rainbows, like a mother and her daughter, the one young and beautiful, and the other an old and faint shadow. The rainbow was called the python of the sky.

Okonkwo called his three wives and told them to get things together for a great feast. "I must thank my mother's kinsmen before I go," he said.

Ekwefi still had some cassava left on her farm from the previous year. Neither of the other wives had. It was not that they had been lazy, but that they had many children to feed. It was therefore understood that Ekwefi would provide cassava for the feast. Nwoye's mother and Ojiugo would provide the other things like smoked fish, palm-oil and pepper for the soup. Okonkwo would take care of meat and yams.

Ekwefi rose early on the following morning and went to her farm with her daughter, Ezinma, and Ojiugo's daughter, Obiageli, to harvest cassava tubers. Each of them carried a long cane basket, a machete for cutting down the soft cassava stem, and a little hoe for digging out the tuber. Fortunately, a light rain had fallen during the night and the soil would not be very hard.

"It will not take us long to harvest as much as we like," said Ekwefi.

"But the leaves will be wet," said Ezinma. Her basket was balanced on her head, and her arms folded across her breasts. She felt cold. "I dislike cold water dropping on my back. We should have waited for the sun to rise and dry the leaves."

Obiageli called her "Salt" because she said that she disliked water. "Are you afraid you may dissolve?"

The harvesting was easy, as Ekwefi had said. Ezinma shook every tree violently with a long stick before she bent down to cut the stem and dig out the tuber. Sometimes it was not necessary to dig. They just pulled the stump, and earth rose, roots snapped below, and the tuber was pulled out.

When they had harvested a sizable heap they carried it down in two trips to the stream, where every woman had a shallow well for fermenting her cassava.

"It should be ready in four days or even three," said Obiageli. "They are young tubers."

"They are not all that young," said Ekwefi. "I planted the farm nearly two years ago. It is a poor soil and that is why the tubers are so small."

Okonkwo never did things by halves. When his wife Ekwefi protested that two goats were sufficient for the feast he told her that it was not her affair.

"I am calling a feast because I have the wherewithal. I cannot live on the bank of a river and wash my hands with spittle. My mother's people have been good to me and I must show my gratitude."

And so three goats were slaughtered and a number of fowls. It was like a wedding feast. There was foo-foo and yam pottage, egusi soup and bitter-leaf soup and pots and pots of palm-wine.

All the *umunna*[27] were invited to the feast, all the descendants of Okolo, who had lived about two hundred years before. The oldest member of this extensive family was Okonkwo's uncle, Uchendu. The kola nut was given him to break, and he prayed to the ancestors. He asked them for health and children. "We do not ask for wealth because he that has health and children will also have wealth. We do not pray to have more money but to have more kinsmen. We are better than animals because we have kinsmen. An animal rubs its itching flank against a tree, a man asks his kinsman to scratch him." He prayed especially for Okonkwo and his family. He then broke the kola nut and threw one of the lobes on the ground for the ancestors.

As the broken kola nuts were passed round, Okonkwo's wives and children and those who came to help them with the cooking began to bring out the food. His sons brought out the pots of palm-wine. There was so much food and drink that many kinsmen whistled in surprise. When all was laid out, Okonkwo rose to speak.

"I beg you to accept this little kola," he said. "It is not to pay you back for all you did for me in these seven years. A child cannot pay for its mother's milk. I have only called you together because it is good for kinsmen to meet."

Yam pottage was served first because it was lighter than foo-foo and because yam always came first. Then the foo-foo was served. Some kinsmen ate it with egusi soup and others with bitter-leaf soup. The meat was then shared so that every member of the *umunna* had a portion. Every man rose in order of years and took a share. Even the few kinsmen who had not been able to come had their shares taken out for them in due term.

As the palm-wine was drunk one of the oldest members of the *umunna* rose to thank Okonkwo:

"If I say that we did not expect such a big feast I will be suggesting that we did not know how open-handed our son, Okonkwo, is. We all know him, and we expected a big feast. But it turned out to be even bigger than we expected. Thank you. May all you took out return again tenfold. It is good in these days when the

---

[27] The male members of the clan.

younger generation consider themselves wiser than their sires to see a man doing things in the grand, old way. A man who calls his kinsmen to a feast does not do so to save them from starving. They all have food in their own homes. When we gather together in the moonlit village ground it is not because of the moon. Every man can see it in his own compound. We come together because it is good for kinsmen to do so. You may ask why I am saying all this. I say it because I fear for the younger generation, for you people." He waved his arm where most of the young men sat. "As for me, I have only a short while to live, and so have Uchendu and Unachukwu and Emefo. But I fear for you young people because you do not understand how strong is the bond of kinship. You do not know what it is to speak with one voice. And what is the result? An abominable religion has settled among you. A man can now leave his father and his brothers. He can curse the gods of his fathers and his ancestors, like a hunter's dog that suddenly goes mad and turns on his master. I fear for you; I fear for the clan." He turned again to Okonkwo and said, "Thank you for calling us together."

Part III

20

Seven years was a long time to be away from one's clan. A man's place was not always there, waiting for him. As soon as he left, someone else rose and filled it. The clan was like a lizard; if it lost its tail it soon grew another.

Okonkwo knew these things. He knew that he had lost his place among the nine masked spirits who administered justice in the clan. He had lost the chance to lead his warlike clan against the new religion, which, he was told, had gained ground. He had lost the years in which he might have taken the highest titles in the clan. But some of these losses were not irreparable. He was determined that his return should be marked by his people. He would return with a flourish, and regain the seven wasted years.

Even in his first year in exile he had begun to plan for his return. The first thing he would do would be to rebuild his compound on a more magnificent scale. He would build a bigger barn than he had had before and he would build huts for two new wives. Then he would show his wealth by initiating his sons into the *ozo* society. Only the really great men in the clan were able to do this. Okonkwo saw clearly the high esteem in which he would be held, and he saw himself taking the highest title in the land.

As the years of exile passed one by one it seemed to him that his *chi* might now be making amends for the past disaster. His yams grew abundantly, not only in his motherland but also in Umuofia, where his friend gave them out year by year to sharecroppers.

Then the tragedy of his first son had occurred. At first it appeared as if it might prove too great for his spirit. But it was a resilient spirit, and in the end Okonkwo overcame his sorrow. He had five other sons and he would bring them up in the way of the clan.

He sent for the five sons and they came and sat in his *obi*. The youngest of them was four years old.

"You have all seen the great abomination of your brother. Now he is no longer my son or your brother. I will only have a son who is a man, who will hold his head up among my people. If any one of you prefers to be a woman, let him follow

Nwoye now while I am alive so that I can curse him. If you turn against me when I am dead I will visit you and break your neck."

Okonkwo was very lucky in his daughters. He never stopped regretting that Ezinma was a girl. Of all his children she alone understood his every mood. A bond of sympathy had grown between them as the years had passed.

Ezinma grew up in her father's exile and became one of the most beautiful girls in Mbanta. She was called Crystal of Beauty, as her mother had been called in her youth. The young ailing girl who had caused her mother so much heartache had been transformed, almost overnight, into a healthy, buoyant maiden. She had, it was true, her moments of depression when she would snap at everybody like an angry dog. These moods descended on her suddenly and for no apparent reason. But they were very rare and short-lived. As long as they lasted, she could bear no other person but her father.

Many young men and prosperous middle-aged men of Mbanta came to marry her. But she refused them all, because her father had called her one evening and said to her: "There are many good and prosperous people here, but I shall be happy if you marry in Umuofia when we return home."

That was all he had said. But Ezinma had seen clearly all the thought and hidden meaning behind the few words. And she had agreed.

"Your half-sister, Obiageli, will not understand me," Okonkwo said. "But you can explain to her."

Although they were almost the same age, Ezinma wielded a strong influence over her half-sister. She explained to her why they should not marry yet, and she agreed also. And so the two of them refused every offer of marriage in Mbanta.

"I wish she were a boy," Okonkwo thought within himself. She understood things so perfectly. Who else among his children could have read his thoughts so well? With two beautiful grown-up daughters his return to Umuofia would attract considerable attention. His future sons-in-law would be men of authority in the clan. The poor and unknown would not dare to come forth.

Umuofia had indeed changed during the seven years Okonkwo had been in exile. The church had come and led many astray. Not only the low-born and the outcast but sometimes a worthy man had joined it. Such a man was Ogbuefi Ugonna, who had taken two titles, and who like a madman had cut the anklet of his titles and cast it away to join the Christians. The white missionary was very proud of him and he was one of the first men in Umuofia to receive the sacrament of Holy Communion, or Holy Feast as it was called in Ibo. Ogbuefi Ugonna had thought of the Feast in terms of eating and drinking, only more holy than the village variety. He had therefore put his drinking-horn into his goatskin bag for the occasion.

But apart from the church, the white men had also brought a government. They had built a court where the District Commissioner judged cases in ignorance. He had court messengers who brought men to him for trial. Many of these messengers came from Umuru on the bank of the Great River, where the white men first came many years before and where they had built the center of their religion and trade and government. These court messengers were greatly hated in Umuofia because they were foreigners and also arrogant and high-handed. They were called *kotma,* and because of their ash-colored shorts they earned the additional name of Ashy-Buttocks. They guarded the prison, which was full of men who had offended against the white man's law. Some of these prisoners had thrown away their twins and some had molested the Christians. They were beaten in the prison by the *kotma* and made to work every morning clearing the government compound and fetching wood for the white Commissioner and the court messengers these prisoners were men of title who should be above such mean occup... They were grieved by the indignity and mourned for their neglected farms. As they cut grass in the morning the younger men sang in time with the strokes of their machetes:

> Kotma *of the ash buttocks,*
> He *is fit to be a slave.*
> The *white man has no sense,*
> He *is fit to be a slave.*

The court messengers did not like to be called Ashy-Buttocks, and they beat the men. But the song spread in Umuofia.

Okonkwo's head was bowed in sadness as Obierika told him these things.

"Perhaps I have been away too long," Okonkwo said, almost to himself. "But I cannot understand these things you tell me. What is it that has happened to our people? Why have they lost the power to fight?"

"Have you not heard how the white man wiped out Abame?" asked Obierika.

"I have heard," said Okonkwo. "But I have also heard that Abame people were weak and foolish. Why did they not fight back? Had they no guns and machetes? We would be cowards to compare ourselves with the men of Abame. Their fathers had never dared to stand before our ancestors. We must fight these men and drive them from the land."

"It is already too late," said Obierika sadly. "Our own men and our sons have joined the ranks of the stranger. They have joined his religion and they help to uphold his government. If we should try to drive out the white men in Umuofia we should find it easy. There are only two of them. But what of our own people who are following their way and have been given power? They would go to Umuru and bring the soldiers, and we would be like Abame." He paused for a long time and then said: "I told you on my last visit to Mbanta how they hanged Aneto."

"What has happened to that piece of land in dispute?" asked Okonkwo.

"The white man's court has decided that it should belong to Nnama's family, who had given much money to the white man's messengers and interpreter."

"Does the white man understand our custom about land?"

"How can he when he does not even speak our tongue? But he says that our customs are bad; and our own brothers who have taken up his religion also say that our customs are bad. How do you think we can fight when our own brothers have turned against us? The white man is very clever. He came quietly and peaceably with his religion. We were amused at his foolishness and allowed him to stay. Now he has won our brothers, and our clan can no longer act like one. He has put a knife on the things that held us together and we have fallen apart."

"How did they get hold of Aneto to hang him?" asked Okonkwo.

"When he killed Oduche in the fight over the land, he fled to Aninta to escape the wrath of the earth. This was about eight days after the fight, because Oduche had not died immediately from his wounds. It was on the seventh day that he died. But everybody knew that he was going to die and Aneto got his belongings together in readiness to flee. But the Christians had told the white man about the accident, and he sent his *kotma* to catch Aneto. He was imprisoned with all the leaders of his family. In the end Oduche died and Aneto was taken to Umuru and hanged. The other people were released, but even now they have not found the mouth with which to tell of their suffering."

The two men sat in silence for a long while afterwards.

There were many men and women in Umuofia who did not feel as strongly as Okonkwo about the new dispensation. The white man had indeed brought a lunatic religion, but he had also built a trading store and for the first time palm-oil and kernel became things of great price, and much money flowed into Umuofia.

And even in the matter of religion there was a growing feeling that there might be something in it after all, something vaguely akin to method in the overwhelming madness.

This growing feeling was due to Mr. Brown, the white missionary, who was very firm in restraining his flock from provoking the wrath of the clan. One member in particular was very difficult to restrain. His name was Enoch and his father was the priest of the snake cult. The story went around that Enoch had killed and eaten the sacred python, and that his father had cursed him.

Mr. Brown preached against such excess of zeal. Everything was possible, he told his energetic flock, but everything was not expedient. And so Mr. Brown came to be respected even by the clan, because he trod softly on its faith. He made friends with some of the great men of the clan and on one of his frequent visits to the neighboring villages he had been presented with a carved elephant tusk, which was a sign of dignity and rank. One of the great men in that village was called Akunna and he had given one of his sons to be taught the white man's knowledge in Mr. Brown's school.

Whenever Mr. Brown went to that village he spent long hours with Akunna in his *obi* talking through an interpreter about religion. Neither of them succeeded in converting the other but they learned more about their different beliefs.

"You say that there is one supreme God who made heaven and earth," said Akunna on one of Mr. Brown's visits. "We also believe in Him and call Him Chukwu. He made all the world and the other gods."

"There are no other gods," said Mr. Brown. "Chukwu is the only God and all others are false. You carve a piece of wood—like that one" (he pointed at the rafters from which Akunna's carved *Ikenga*[28] hung), "and you call it a god. But it is still a piece of wood."

"Yes," said Akunna. "It is indeed a piece of wood. The tree from which it came was made by Chukwu, as indeed all minor gods were. But He made them for His messengers so that we could approach Him through them. It is like yourself. You are the head of your church."

"No," protested Mr. Brown. "The head of my church is God Himself."

"I know," said Akunna, "but there must be a head in this world among men. Somebody like yourself must be the head here."

"The head of my church in that sense is in England."

"That is exactly what I am saying. The head of your church is in your country. He has sent you here as his messenger. And you have also appointed your own messengers and servants. Or let me take another example, the District Commissioner. He is sent by your king."

"They have a queen," said the interpreter on his own account.

"Your queen sends her messenger, the District Commissioner. He finds that he cannot do the work alone and so he appoints *kotma* to help him. It is the same with God, or Chukwu. He appoints the smaller gods to help Him because His work is too great for one person."

---

[28]A carved figure symbolizing a man's strength, made from wood and the horns of a ram.

"You should not think of Him as a person," said Mr. Brown. "It is be
do so that you imagine He must need helpers. And the worst thing abou
you give all the worship to the false gods you have created."

"That is not so. We make sacrifices to the little gods, but when they fail and
there is no one else to turn to we go to Chukwu. It is right to do so. We approach
a great man through his servants. But when his servants fail to help us, then we go
to the last source of hope. We appear to pay greater attention to the little gods but
that is not so. We worry them more because we are afraid to worry their Master.
Our fathers knew that Chukwu was the Overlord and that is why many of them
gave their children the name Chukwuka—'Chukwu is Supreme.'"

"You said one interesting thing," said Mr. Brown. "You are afraid of Chukwu.
In my religion Chukwu is a loving Father and need not be feared by those who do
His will."

"But we must fear Him when we are not doing His will," said Akunna. "And
who is to tell His will? It is too great to be known."

In this way Mr. Brown learned a good deal about the religion of the clan and he
came to the conclusion that a frontal attack on it would not succeed. And so he built
a school and a little hospital in Umuofia. He went from family to family begging
people to send their children to his school. But at first they only sent their slaves
or sometimes their lazy children. Mr. Brown begged and argued and prophesied.
He said that the leaders of the land in the future would be men and women who
had learned to read and write. If Umuofia failed to send her children to the school,
strangers would come from other places to rule them. They could already see that
happening in the Native Court, where the D.C. was surrounded by strangers who
spoke his tongue. Most of these strangers came from the distant town of Umuru on
the bank of the Great River where the white man first went.

In the end Mr. Brown's arguments began to have an effect. More people came
to learn in his school, and he encouraged them with gifts of singlets and towels.
They were not all young, these people who came to learn. Some of them were
thirty years old or more. They worked on their farms in the morning and went to
school in the afternoon. And it was not long before the people began to say that
the white man's medicine was quick in working. Mr. Brown's school produced
quick results. A few months in it were enough to make one a court messenger or
even a court clerk. Those who stayed longer became teachers; and from Umuofia
laborers went forth into the Lord's vineyard. New churches were established in the
surrounding villages and a few schools with them. From the very beginning religion
and education went hand in hand.

Mr. Brown's mission grew from strength to strength, and because of its link with
the new administration it earned a new social prestige. But Mr. Brown himself was
breaking down in health. At first he ignored the warning signs. But in the end he
had to leave his flock, sad and broken.

It was in the first rainy season after Okonkwo's return to Umuofia that Mr. Brown
left for home. As soon as he had learned of Okonkwo's return five months earlier,
the missionary had immediately paid him a visit. He had just sent Okonkwo's
son, Nwoye, who was now called Isaac, to the new training college for teachers
in Umuru. And he had hoped that Okonkwo would be happy to hear of it. But
Okonkwo had driven him away with the threat that if he came into his compound
again, he would be carried out of it.

Okonkwo's return to his native land was not as memorable as he had wished.
It was true his two beautiful daughters aroused great interest among suitors and

marriage negotiations were soon in progress, but, beyond that, Umuofia did not appear to have taken any special notice of the warrior's return. The clan had undergone such profound change during his exile that it was barely recognizable. The new religion and government and the trading stores were very much in the people's eyes and minds. There were still many who saw these new institutions as evil, but even they talked and thought about little else, and certainly not about Okonkwo's return.

And it was the wrong year too. If Okonkwo had immediately initiated his two sons into the *ozo* society as he had planned he would have caused a stir. But the initiation rite was performed once in three years in Umuofia, and he had to wait for nearly two years for the next round of ceremonies.

Okonkwo was deeply grieved. And it was not just a personal grief. He mourned for the clan, which he saw breaking up and falling apart, and he mourned for the warlike men of Umuofia, who had so unaccountably become soft like women.

22

Mr. Brown's successor was the Reverend James Smith, and he was a different kind of man. He condemned openly Mr. Brown's policy of compromise and accommodation. He saw things as black and white. And black was evil. He saw the world as a battlefield in which the children of light were locked in mortal conflict with the sons of darkness. He spoke in his sermons about sheep and goats and about wheat and tares. He believed in slaying the prophets of Baal.

Mr. Smith was greatly distressed by the ignorance which many of his flock showed even in such things as the Trinity and the Sacraments. It only showed that they were seeds sown on a rocky soil. Mr. Brown had thought of nothing but numbers. He should have known that the kingdom of God did not depend on large crowds. Our Lord Himself stressed the importance of fewness. Narrow is the way and few the number. To fill the Lord's holy temple with an idolatrous crowd clamoring for signs was a folly of everlasting consequence. Our Lord used the whip only once in His life—to drive the crowd away from His church.

Within a few weeks of his arrival in Umuofia Mr. Smith suspended a young woman from the church for pouring new wine into old bottles. This woman had allowed her heathen husband to mutilate her dead child. The child had been declared an *ogbanje*, plaguing its mother by dying and entering her womb to be born again. Four times this child had run its evil round. And so it was mutilated to discourage it from returning.

Mr. Smith was filled with wrath when he heard of this. He disbelieved the story which even some of the most faithful confirmed, the story of really evil children who were not deterred by mutilation, but came back with all the scars. He replied that such stories were spread in the world by the Devil to lead men astray. Those who believed such stories were unworthy of the Lord's table.

There was a saying in Umuofia that as a man danced so the drums were beaten for him. Mr. Smith danced a furious step and so the drums went mad. The over-zealous converts who had smarted under Mr. Brown's restraining hand now flourished in full favor. One of them was Enoch, the son of the snake-priest who was believed to have killed and eaten the sacred python. Enoch's devotion to the new faith had seemed so much greater than Mr. Brown's that the villagers called him the outsider who wept louder than the bereaved.

Enoch was short and slight of build, and always seemed in great haste. His feet were short and broad, and when he stood or walked his heels came together and his feet opened outwards as if they had quarreled and meant to go in different

directions. Such was the excessive energy bottled up in Enoch's sma.
was always erupting in quarrels and fights. On Sundays he always imagi.
sermon was preached for the benefit of his enemies. And if he happened
one of them he would occasionally turn to give him a meaningful look, as   /,
"I told you so." It was Enoch who touched off the great conflict between church
and clan in Umuofia which had been gathering since Mr. Brown left.

It happened during the annual ceremony which was held in honor of the earth
deity. At such times the ancestors of the clan who had been committed to Mother
Earth at their death emerged again as *egwugwu* through tiny ant-holes.

One of the greatest crimes a man could commit was to unmask an *egwugwu* in
public, or to say or do anything which might reduce its immortal prestige in the
eyes of the uninitiated. And this was what Enoch did.

The annual worship of the earth goddess fell on a Sunday, and the masked spirits
were abroad. The Christian women who had been to church could not therefore
go home. Some of their men had gone out to beg the *egwugwu* to retire for a short
while for the women to pass. They agreed and were already retiring, when Enoch
boasted aloud that they would not dare to touch a Christian. Whereupon they all
came back and one of them gave Enoch a good stroke of the cane, which was always
carried. Enoch fell on him and tore off his mask. The other *egwugwu* immediately
surrounded their desecrated companion, to shield him from the profane gaze of
women and children, and led him away. Enoch had killed an ancestral spirit, and
Umuofia was thrown into confusion.

That night the Mother of the Spirits walked the length and breadth of the clan,
weeping for her murdered son. It was a terrible night. Not even the oldest man in
Umuofia had ever heard such a strange and fearful sound, and it was never to be
heard again. It seemed as if the very soul of the tribe wept for a great evil that was
coming—its own death.

On the next day all the masked *egwugwu* of Umuofia assembled in the marketplace.
They came from all the quarters of the clan and even from the neighboring villages.
The dreaded Otakagu came from Imo, and Ekwensu, dangling a white cock, arrived
from Uli. It was a terrible gathering. The eerie voices of countless spirits, the bells
that clattered behind some of them, and the clash of machetes as they ran forwards
and backwards and saluted one another, sent tremors of fear into every heart. For
the first time in living memory the sacred bull-roarer was heard in broad daylight.

From the marketplace the furious band made for Enoch's compound. Some of
the elders of the clan went with them, wearing heavy protections of charms and
amulets. These were men whose arms were strong in *ogwu,* or medicine. As for the
ordinary men and women, they listened from the safety of their huts.

The leaders of the Christians had met together at Mr. Smith's parsonage on the
previous night. As they deliberated they could hear the Mother of Spirits wailing
for her son. The chilling sound affected Mr. Smith, and for the first time he seemed
to be afraid.

"What are they planning to do?" he asked. No one knew, because such a
thing had never happened before. Mr. Smith would have sent for the District
Commissioner and his court messengers, but they had gone on tour on the previous
day.

"One thing is clear," said Mr. Smith. "We cannot offer physical resistance to
them. Our strength lies in the Lord." They knelt down together and prayed to God
for delivery.

"O Lord, save Thy people," cried Mr. Smith.

"And bless Thine inheritance," replied the men.

They decided that Enoch should be hidden in the parsonage for a day or two. Enoch himself was greatly disappointed when he heard this, for he had hoped that a holy war was imminent; and there were a few other Christians who thought like him. But wisdom prevailed in the camp of the faithful and many lives were thus saved.

The band of *egwugwu* moved like a furious whirlwind to Enoch's compound and with machete and fire reduced it to a desolate heap. And from there they made for the church, intoxicated with destruction.

Mr. Smith was in his church when he heard the masked spirits coming. He walked quietly to the door which commanded the approach to the church compound, and stood there. But when the first three or four *egwugwu* appeared on the church compound he nearly bolted. He overcame this impulse and instead of running away he went down the two steps that led up to the church and walked towards the approaching spirits.

They surged forward, and a long stretch of the bamboo fence with which the church compound was surrounded gave way before them. Discordant bells clanged, machetes clashed and the air was full of dust and weird sounds. Mr. Smith heard a sound of footsteps behind him. He turned round and saw Okeke, his interpreter. Okeke had not been on the best of terms with his master since he had strongly condemned Enoch's behavior at the meeting of the leaders of the church during the night. Okeke had gone as far as to say that Enoch should not be hidden in the parsonage, because he would only draw the wrath of the clan on the pastor. Mr. Smith had rebuked him in very strong language, and had not sought his advice that morning. But now, as he came up and stood by him confronting the angry spirits, Mr. Smith looked at him and smiled. It was a wan smile, but there was deep gratitude there.

For a brief moment the onrush of the *egwugwu* was checked by the unexpected composure of the two men. But it was only a momentary check, like the tense silence between blasts of thunder. The second onrush was greater than the first. It swallowed up the two men. Then an unmistakable voice rose above the tumult and there was immediate silence. Space was made around the two men, and Ajofia began to speak.

Ajofia was the leading *egwugwu* of Umuofia. He was the head and spokesman of the nine ancestors who administered justice in the clan. His voice was unmistakable and so he was able to bring immediate peace to the agitated spirits. He then addressed Mr. Smith, and as he spoke clouds of smoke rose from his head.

"The body of the white man, I salute you," he said, using the language in which immortals spoke to men.

"The body of the white man, do you know me?" he asked.

Mr. Smith looked at his interpreter, but Okeke, who was a native of distant Umuru, was also at a loss.

Ajofia laughed in his guttural voice. It was like the laugh of rusty metal. "They are strangers," he said, "and they are ignorant. But let that pass." He turned round to his comrades and saluted them, calling them the fathers of Umuofia. He dug his rattling spear into the ground and it shook with metallic life. Then he turned once more to the missionary and his interpreter.

"Tell the white man that we will not do him any harm," he said to the interpreter. "Tell him to go back to his house and leave us alone. We liked his brother who was with us before. He was foolish, but we liked him, and for his sake we shall not harm his brother. But this shrine which he built must be destroyed. We shall no longer allow it in our midst. It has bred untold abominations and we have come to put an end to it." He turned to his comrades. "Fathers of Umuofia, I salute you;" and they replied with one guttural voice. He turned again to the missionary. "You can stay with us if you like our ways. You can worship your own god. It is good that a man should worship the gods and the spirits of his fathers. Go back to your house so that you may not be hurt. Our anger is great but we have held it down so that we can talk to you."

Mr. Smith said to his interpreter: "Tell them to go away from here. This is the house of God and I will not live to see it desecrated."

Okeke interpreted wisely to the spirits and leaders of Umuofia: "The white man says he is happy you have come to him with your grievances, like friends. He will be happy if you leave the matter in his hands."

"We cannot leave the matter in his hands because he does not understand our customs, just as we do not understand his. We say he is foolish because he does not know our ways, and perhaps he says we are foolish because we do not know his. Let him go away."

Mr. Smith stood his ground. But he could not save his church. When the *egwugwu* went away the red-earth church which Mr. Brown had built was a pile of earth and ashes. And for the moment the spirit of the clan was pacified.

23

For the first time in many years Okonkwo had a feeling that was akin to happiness. The times which had altered so unaccountably during his exile seemed to be coming round again. The clan which had turned false on him appeared to be making amends.

He had spoken violently to his clansmen when they had met in the marketplace to decide on their action. And they had listened to him with respect. It was like the good old days again, when a warrior was a warrior. Although they had not agreed to kill the missionary or drive away the Christians, they had agreed to do something substantial. And they had done it. Okonkwo was almost happy again.

For two days after the destruction of the church, nothing happened. Every man in Umuofia went about armed with a gun or a machete. They would not be caught unawares, like the men of Abame.

Then the District Commissioner returned from his tour. Mr. Smith went immediately to him and they had a long discussion. The men of Umuofia did not take any notice of this, and if they did, they thought it was not important. The missionary often went to see his brother white man. There was nothing strange in that.

Three days later the District Commissioner sent his sweet-tongued messenger to the leaders of Umuofia asking them to meet him in his headquarters. That also was not strange. He often asked them to hold such palavers, as he called them. Okonkwo was among the six leaders he invited.

Okonkwo warned the others to be fully armed. "An Umuofia man does not refuse a call," he said. "He may refuse to do what he is asked; he does not refuse to be asked. But the times have changed, and we must be fully prepared."

And so the six men went to see the District Commissioner, armed with their machetes. They did not carry guns, for that would be unseemly. They were led into the courthouse where the District Commissioner sat. He received them politely. They unslung their goatskin bags and their sheathed machetes, put them on the floor, and sat down.

"I have asked you to come," began the Commissioner, "because of what happened during my absence. I have been told a few things but I cannot believe them until I have heard your own side. Let us talk about it like friends and find a way of ensuring that it does not happen again."

Ogbuefi Ekwueme rose to his feet and began to tell the story.

"Wait a minute," said the Commissioner. "I want to bring in my men so that they too can hear your grievances and take warning. Many of them come from distant places and although they speak your tongue they are ignorant of your customs. James! Go and bring in the men." His interpreter left the courtroom and soon returned with twelve men. They sat together with the men of Umuofia, and Ogbuefi Ekwueme began to tell the story of how Enoch murdered an *egwugwu*.

It happened so quickly that the six men did not see it coming. There was only a brief scuffle, too brief even to allow the drawing of a sheathed machete. The six men were handcuffed and led into the guardroom.

"We shall not do you any harm," said the District Commissioner to them later, "if only you agree to cooperate with us. We have brought a peaceful administration to you and your people so that you may be happy. If any man ill-treats you we shall come to your rescue. But we will not allow you to ill-treat others. We have a court of law where we judge cases and administer justice just as it is done in my own country under a great queen. I have brought you here because you joined together to molest others, to burn people's houses and their place of worship. That must not happen in the dominion of our queen, the most powerful ruler in the world. I have decided that you will pay a fine of two hundred bags of cowries. You will be released as soon as you agree to this and undertake to collect that fine from your people. What do you say to that?"

The six men remained sullen and silent and the Commissioner left them for a while. He told the court messengers, when he left the guardroom, to treat the men with respect because they were the leaders of Umuofia. They said, "Yes, sir," and saluted.

As soon as the District Commissioner left, the head messenger, who was also the prisoners' barber, took down his razor and shaved off all the hair on the men's heads. They were still handcuffed, and they just sat and moped.

"Who is the chief among you?" the court messengers asked in jest. "We see that every pauper wears the anklet of title in Umuofia. Does it cost as much as ten cowries?"

The six men ate nothing throughout that day and the next. They were not even given any water to drink, and they could not go out to urinate or go into the bush when they were pressed. At night the messengers came in to taunt them and to knock their shaven heads together.

Even when the men were left alone they found no words to speak to one another. It was only on the third day, when they could no longer bear the hunger and the insults, that they began to talk about giving in.

"We should have killed the white man if you had listened to me," Okonkwo snarled.

"We could have been in Umuru now waiting to be hanged," someone said to him.

"Who wants to kill the white man?" asked a messenger who had just rushed in. Nobody spoke.

"You are not satisfied with your crime, but you must kill the white man on top of it." He carried a strong stick, and he hit each man a few blows on the head and back. Okonkwo was choked with hate.

As soon as the six men were locked up, court messengers went into Umuofia to tell the people that their leaders would not be released unless they paid a fine of two hundred and fifty bags of cowries.

"Unless you pay the fine immediately," said their head-man, "we will take your leaders to Umuru before the big white man, and hang them."

This story spread quickly through the villages, and was added to as it went. Some said that the men had already been taken to Umuru and would be hanged on the following day. Some said that their families would also be hanged. Others said that soldiers were already on their way to shoot the people of Umuofia as they had done in Abame.

It was the time of the full moon. But that night the voice of children was not heard. The village *ilo* where they always gathered for a moon-play was empty. The women of Iguedo did not meet in their secret enclosure to learn a new dance to be displayed later to the village. Young men who were always abroad in the moonlight kept their huts that night. Their manly voices were not heard on the village paths as they went to visit their friends and lovers. Umuofia was like a startled animal with ears erect, sniffing the silent, ominous air and not knowing which way to run.

The silence was broken by the village crier beating his sonorous *ogene*. He called every man in Umuofia, from the Akakanma age group upwards, to a meeting in the marketplace after the morning meal. He went from one end of the village to the other and walked all its breadth. He did not leave out any of the main foot-paths.

Okonkwo's compound was like a deserted homestead. It was as if cold water had been poured on it. His family was all there, but everyone spoke in whispers. His daughter Ezinma had broken her twenty-eight day visit to the family of her future husband, and returned home when she heard that her father had been imprisoned, and was going to be hanged. As soon as she got home she went to Obierika to ask what the men of Umuofia were going to do about it. But Obierika had not been home since morning. His wives thought he had gone to a secret meeting. Ezinma was satisfied that something was being done.

On the morning after the village crier's appeal the men of Umuofia met in the marketplace and decided to collect without delay two hundred and fifty bags of cowries to appease the white man. They did not know that fifty bags would go to the court messengers, who had increased the fine for that purpose.

24

Okonkwo and his fellow prisoners were set free as soon as the fine was paid. The District Commissioner spoke to them again about the great queen, and about peace and good government. But the men did not listen. They just sat and looked at him and at his interpreter. In the end they were given back their bags and sheathed machetes and told to go home. They rose and left the courthouse. They neither spoke to anyone nor among themselves.

The courthouse, like the church, was built a little way outside the village. The footpath that linked them was a very busy one because it also led to the stream, beyond the court. It was open and sandy. Footpaths were open and sandy in the dry season. But when the rains came the bush grew thick on either side and closed in on the path. It was now dry season.

As they made their way to the village the six men met women and children going to the stream with their water-pots. But the men wore such heavy and fearsome looks that the women and children did not say "*nno*" or "welcome" to them, but edged out of the way to let them pass. In the village little groups of men joined them until they became a sizable company. They walked silently. As each of the six men got to his compound, he turned in, taking some of the crowd with him. The village was astir in a silent, suppressed way.

Ezinma had prepared some food for her father as soon as news spread that the six men would be released. She took it to him in his *obi*. He ate absent-mindedly. He had no appetite; he only ate to please her. His male relations and friends had gathered in his *obi*, and Obierika was urging him to eat. Nobody else spoke, but they noticed the long stripes on Okonkwo's back where the warder's whip had cut into his flesh.

The village crier was abroad again in the night. He beat his iron gong and announced that another meeting would be held in the morning. Everyone knew that Umuofia was at last going to speak its mind about the things that were happening.

Okonkwo slept very little that night. The bitterness in his heart was now mixed with a kind of childlike excitement. Before he had gone to bed he had brought down his war dress, which he had not touched since his return from exile. He had shaken out his smoked raffia skirt and examined his tall feather head-gear and his shield. They were all satisfactory, he had thought.

As he lay on his bamboo bed he thought about the treatment he had received in the white man's court, and he swore vengeance. If Umuofia decided on war, all would be well. But if they chose to be cowards he would go out and avenge himself. He thought about wars in the past. The noblest, he thought, was the war against Isike. In those days Okudo was still alive. Okudo sang a war song in a way that no other man could. He was not a fighter, but his voice turned every man into a lion.

"Worthy men are no more," Okonkwo sighed as he remembered those days. "Isike will never forget how we slaughtered them in that war. We killed twelve of their men and they killed only two of ours. Before the end of the fourth market week they were suing for peace. Those were days when men were men."

As he thought of these things he heard the sound of the iron gong in the distance. He listened carefully, and could just hear the crier's voice. But it was very faint. He turned on his bed and his back hurt him. He ground his teeth. The crier was drawing nearer and nearer until he passed by Okonkwo's compound.

"The greatest obstacle in Umuofia," Okonkwo thought bitterly, "is that coward, Egonwanne. His sweet tongue can change fire into cold ash. When he speaks he moves our men to impotence. If they had ignored his womanish wisdom five years ago, we would not have come to this." He ground his teeth. "Tomorrow he will tell them that our fathers never fought a 'war of blame.' If they listen to him I shall leave them and plan my own revenge."

The crier's voice had once more become faint, and the distance had taken the harsh edge off his iron gong. Okonkwo turned from one side to the other and derived a kind of pleasure from the pain his back gave him. "Let Egonwanne talk about a 'war of blame' tomorrow and I shall show him my back and head." He ground his teeth.

The marketplace began to fill as soon as the sun rose. Obierika was waiting in his *obi* when Okonkwo came along and called him. He hung his goatskin bag and his sheathed machete on his shoulder and went out to join him. Obierika's hut was close to the road and he saw every man who passed to the marketplace. He had exchanged greetings with many who had already passed that morning.

When Okonkwo and Obierika got to the meeting place there were already so many people that if one threw up a grain of sand it would not find its way to the earth again. And many more people were coming from every quarter of the nine villages. It warmed Okonkwo's heart to see such strength of numbers. But he was looking for one man in particular, the man whose tongue he dreaded and despised so much.

"Can you see him?" he asked Obierika.

"Who?"

"Egonwanne," he said, his eyes roving from one corner of the huge marketplace to the other. Most of the men sat on wooden stools they had brought with them.

"No," said Obierika, casting his eyes over the crowd. "Yes, there he is, under the silk-cotton tree. Are you afraid he would convince us not to fight?"

"Afraid? I do not care what he does to *you*. I despise him and those who listen to him. I shall fight alone if I choose."

They spoke at the top of their voices because everybody was talking, and it was like the sound of a great market.

"I shall wait till he has spoken," Okonkwo thought. "Then I shall speak."

"But how do you know he will speak against war?" Obierika asked after a while.

"Because I know he is a coward," said Okonkwo. Obierika did not hear the rest of what he said because at that moment somebody touched his shoulder from behind and he turned round to shake hands and exchange greetings with five or six friends. Okonkwo did not turn round even though he knew the voices. He was in no mood to exchange greetings. But one of the men touched him and asked about the people of his compound.

"They are well," he replied without interest.

The first man to speak to Umuofia that morning was Okika, one of the six who had been imprisoned. Okika was a great man and an orator. But he did not have the booming voice which a first speaker must use to establish silence in the assembly of the clan. Onyeka had such a voice; and so he was asked to salute Umuofia before Okika began to speak.

"*Umuofia kwenu!*" he bellowed, raising his left arm and pushing the air with his open hand.

"*Yaa!*" roared Umuofia.

"*Umuofia kwenu!*" he bellowed again, and again and again, facing a new direction each time. And the crowd answered, "*Yaa!*"

There was immediate silence as though cold water had been poured on a roaring flame.

Okika sprang to his feet and also saluted his clansmen four times. Then he began to speak:

"You all know why we are here, when we ought to be building our barns or mending our huts, when we should be putting our compounds in order. My father used to say to me: 'Whenever you see a toad jumping in broad daylight, then know that something is after its life.' When I saw you all pouring into this meeting from all the quarters of our clan so early in the morning, I knew that something was after our life." He paused for a brief moment and then began again:

"All our gods are weeping. Idemili is weeping, Ogwugwu is weeping, Agbala is weeping, and all the others. Our dead fathers are weeping because of the shameful sacrilege they are suffering and the abomination we have all seen with our eyes." He stopped again to steady his trembling voice.

"This is a great gathering. No clan can boast of greater numbers or greater valor. But are we all here? I ask you: Are all the sons of Umuofia with us here?" A deep murmur swept through the crowd.

"They are not," he said. "They have broken the clan and gone their several ways. We who are here this morning have remained true to our fathers, but our brothers have deserted us and joined a stranger to soil their fatherland. If we fight the stranger we shall hit our brothers and perhaps shed the blood of a clansman. But we must do it. Our fathers never dreamed of such a thing, they never killed their brothers. But a white man never came to them. So we must do what our fathers would never have done. Eneke the bird was asked why he was always on the wing and he replied: 'Men have learned to shoot without missing their mark and I have learned to fly without perching on a twig.' We must root out this evil. And if our brothers take the side of evil we must root them out too. And we must do it *now*. We must bail this water now that it is only ankle-deep...."

At this point there was a sudden stir in the crowd and every eye was turned in one direction. There was a sharp bend in the road that led from the marketplace to the white man's court, and to the stream beyond it. And so no one had seen the approach of the five court messengers until they had come round the bend, a few paces from the edge of the crowd. Okonkwo was sitting at the edge.

He sprang to his feet as soon as he saw who it was. He confronted the head messenger, trembling with hate, unable to utter a word. The man was fearless and stood his ground, his four men lined up behind him.

In that brief moment the world seemed to stand still, waiting. There was utter silence. The men of Umuofia were merged into the mute backcloth of trees and giant creepers, waiting.

The spell was broken by the head messenger. "Let me pass!" he ordered.

"What do you want here?"

"The white man whose power you know too well has ordered this meeting to stop."

In a flash Okonkwo drew his machete. The messenger crouched to avoid the blow. It was useless. Okonkwo's machete descended twice and the man's head lay beside his uniformed body.

The waiting backcloth jumped into tumultuous life and the meeting was stopped. Okonkwo stood looking at the dead man. He knew that Umuofia would not go to war. He knew because they had let the other messengers escape. They had broken into tumult instead of action. He discerned fright in that tumult. He heard voices asking: "Why did he do it?"

He wiped his machete on the sand and went away.

25

When the District Commissioner arrived at Okonkwo's compound at the head of an armed band of soldiers and court messengers he found a small crowd of men sitting wearily in the *obi*. He commanded them to come outside, and they obeyed without a murmur.

"Which among you is called Okonkwo?" he asked through his interpreter.

"He is not here," replied Obierika.

"Where is he?"

"He is not here!"

The Commissioner became angry and red in the face. He warned the men that unless they produced Okonkwo forthwith he would lock them all up. The men murmured among themselves, and Obierika spoke again.

"We can take you where he is, and perhaps your men will help us."

The Commissioner did not understand what Obierika meant when he said, "Perhaps your men will help us." One of the most infuriating habits of these people was their love of superfluous words, he thought.

Obierika with five or six others led the way. The Commissioner and his men followed, their firearms held at the ready. He had warned Obierika that if he and his men played any monkey tricks they would be shot. And so they went.

There was a small bush behind Okonkwo's compound. The only opening into this bush from the compound was a little round hole in the red-earth wall through which fowls went in and out in their endless search for food. The hole would not let a man through. It was to this bush that Obierika led the Commissioner and his men. They skirted round the compound, keeping close to the wall. The only sound they made was with their feet as they crushed dry leaves.

Then they came to the tree from which Okonkwo's body was dangling, and they stopped dead.

"Perhaps your men can help us bring him down and bury him," said Obierika. "We have sent for strangers from another village to do it for us, but they may be a long time coming."

The District Commissioner changed instantaneously. The resolute administrator in him gave way to the student of primitive customs.

"Why can't you take him down yourselves?" he asked.

"It is against our custom," said one of the men. "It is an abomination for a man to take his own life. It is an offense against the Earth, and a man who commits it will not be buried by his clansmen. His body is evil, and only strangers may touch it. That is why we ask your people to bring him down, because you are strangers."

"Will you bury him like any other man?" asked the Commissioner.

"We cannot bury him. Only strangers can. We shall pay your men to do it. When he has been buried we will then do our duty by him. We shall make sacrifices to cleanse the desecrated land."

Obierika, who had been gazing steadily at his friend's dangling body, turned suddenly to the District Commissioner and said ferociously: "That man was one of the greatest men in Umuofia. You drove him to kill himself; and now he will be buried like a dog...." He could not say any more. His voice trembled and choked his words.

"Shut up!" shouted one of the messengers, quite unnecessarily.

"Take down the body," the Commissioner ordered his chief messenger, "and bring it and all these people to the court."

"Yes, sah," the messenger said, saluting.

The Commissioner went away, taking three or four of the soldiers with him. In the many years in which he had toiled to bring civilization to different parts of Africa he had learned a number of things. One of them was that a District Commissioner must never attend to such undignified details as cutting a hanged man from the tree. Such attention would give the natives a poor opinion of him. In the book which he planned to write he would stress that point. As he walked back to the court he thought about that book. Every day brought him some new material. The story of this man who had killed a messenger and hanged himself would make interesting reading. One could almost write a whole chapter on him. Perhaps not a whole chapter but a reasonable paragraph, at any rate. There was so much else to include, and one must be firm in cutting out details. He had already chosen the title of the book, after much thought: *The Pacification of the Primitive Tribes of the Lower Niger.*

❦

MODERNIST TEXTS

WILLIAM BUTLER YEATS
[1865–1939]

Spanning the dizzying changes in aesthetics and politics between 1890 and 1939, the work of William Butler Yeats embodies the contradictory impulses of early modernist society and culture—its recognition of a world consumed in violent conflict, emptied of value and tradition, and yet struggling to find some idea, some system, some myth to hold society together. As Yeats put it in a prophetic poem, "Things fall apart; the centre cannot hold; / . . . and everywhere / The ceremony of innocence is drowned." As a leading figure of the Irish Literary Renaissance, a poet, statesman, critic, and visionary, Yeats strove in his abstruse researches into the occult, in his revitalization of Irish myth and legend, and in his gift of poetry, to bring meaning and purpose to his contemporaries. Often considered to be the greatest poet writing in English in the early modern period, Yeats spoke not only to Ireland and to his generation, but, as Chinua Achebe's *Things Fall Apart* attests, to people of all countries and to the generation of writers that followed him.

LIFE

William Butler Yeats was born in Sandymount, a suburb of Dublin, Ireland, on June 13, 1865. Through his father, the lawyer-turned-painter John Butler Yeats, William was linked to a line of clergymen; and through his mother, Susan Pollexfen, to a line of seafarers who captured the imagination of the young boy. Both families had connections to County Sligo, on the west coast of Ireland, where the young boy visited his grandfather in the shadow of his revered Ben Bulben, chief peak in the Sligo Mountains. Here, on summer vacations and holidays in later years, Yeats would ramble in the countryside and listen to tales about the fairies and Irish folk heroes. When William was three years old, he accompanied his family to London where his father took up the study of painting and where William attended the Godolphin School and cultivated a strong sense of nostalgia for Ireland. In 1880, the family returned to Ireland, eventually taking a house overlooking Howth harbor just north of Dublin. Here his father, who had taken caring but stern supervision over his son's education, placed William in Erasmus High School in Dublin, where he began writing poetry. After leaving high school in Dublin, Yeats, following his father's lead, attended art school at the Metropolitan School of Art where his father taught. Here he met George Russell, or A.E., an artist, poet, and mystic in whom the young Yeats found a kindred spirit.

Another significant meeting came in 1885, the year that saw Yeats's first published poems, when he met the Irish Fenian leader John O'Leary, whom Yeats later described as the embodiment of "Romantic Ireland." Through O'Leary, Yeats associated with some of the soon-to-be leaders of the Irish nationalist movement. In the next year, Yeats gave up his studies in art and returned to London, where he devoted his energies to writing and joined in the quasi-philosophical and occult discussions of Madame Blavatsky and her Theosophical Society. These two often contradictory elements of Yeats's character, the political and the spiritual, lend to his life and poetry their characteristic tension and ambiguity. Both are marked by a struggle to attain a pure vision of art out of an exacting confrontation with the cold imperfections of human life. These imperfections were compounded by the turbulent political strife of early twentieth-century Ireland, and by the advent of World War I.

Yeats's embrace of theosophy inspired a mind already well-stocked in the legends and folklore of Ireland. In 1889, with the help of John O'Leary, the young poet published his first book, *The Wanderings of Oisin and Other Poems*. This publication, a collection of early lyrics and ballads accompanying the long title poem, an allegorical story of a journey into the land of the fairies based on Irish legend, shows the influence of the Pre-Raphaelites in its sensuous imagery and dreamy medievalism and the influence of theosophy in its lyrics about Indian subjects. The poems in this volume were later republished as *Crossways*, a title Yeats chose because it represented the "many pathways" that he tried in his search for a substitute for the Christian faith he had lost.

The series of works that followed this first publication continued the themes of Irish folklore and drew upon his rambles in the countryside around Sligo. Indeed, over the next few years Yeats edited several collections of Irish folktales, fairy tales, and ballads, and even collaborated with F. J. Ellis on an edition of the works of William Blake, whose myth-making and visionary spirituality Yeats found congenial to his literary sensibility. In the early 1890s, Yeats also helped to found the Rhymers' Club, the National Literary Society in Dublin, and the London-Irish Literary Society, marking the beginning of his active role in promoting what came to be the Irish Literary Renaissance and his support for the Irish nationalist movement. During this period he also wrote *The Countess Cathleen*, a play inspired by Maud Gonne, with whom Yeats had fallen in love two years before. An uncompromising Irish nationalist determined to free Ireland from English rule, Maud Gonne did not return the love Yeats so passionately offered her. Although Yeats accompanied her on some of her many travels between Dublin, London, and Paris to support the Irish cause, she would not consent to marry Yeats when he asked for her hand in 1891. This was only the first of many refusals from Maud Gonne that would haunt the poet's life and work to the very end.

In 1892, a second publication, *The Countess Cathleen and Various Legends and Lyrics*, was published, and a few of his lyrics appeared in *The Yellow Book*, a notorious periodical associated with Aubrey Beardsley, Max Beerbohm, and Ernest Dowson, key figures of the aesthete movement in fin-de-siècle London. Yeats's London circle also included Lionel Johnson, George Moore, and Arthur Symons, who was translating the French symbolist poets. The year 1893 saw the publication of *The Rose*, a collection of poems on Irish themes that includes "The Lake Isle of Innisfree" and "Who Goes with Fergus?" In 1896, Yeats met Lady Augusta Gregory, a writer, Irish patriot, and wealthy patron of Irish literature, and the following year Yeats spent the first of many summers at her country house at Coole Park, Galway, in the west of Ireland. Here Yeats, Lady Gregory, and playwrights Edward Martyn and J. M. Synge planned the Irish National Theatre, which they founded in 1899. This year marks the beginning of the Irish Literary Renaissance; 1899 was also the year of *The Wind Among the Reeds*, a collection that brought Yeats's synthesis of Irish legendary material, private reverie, and esoteric symbolism to perfection.

Yeats's activities in the Irish National Theatre, which found a home in the Abbey Theatre, Dublin, in 1904, thrust him into an arena where he was challenged with the practical problems of the theater, not the least of which was to protect it from the narrow-minded provincialism, petty morality, and rank hypocrisy of the Irish middle classes. Bitter and out of patience with protests over the production of J. M. Synge's *The Playboy of the Western World* (1907) and with the Dublin Corporation's refusal to provide a gallery for the collection of French paintings offered them by Sir Hugh Lane, Yeats roundly condemned the shopkeeper mentality of the Dubliners in "September 1913" and other poems published in *Responsibilities* (1914), which first appeared in 1913 as *Poems Written in Discouragement*. Up to that point, Yeats had published two additional important collections of poems, *In the Seven Woods* (1904) and *The Green Helmet and Other Poems* (1910), and he had produced some of his plays, including *Cathleen ni Houlihan* (1902) and *On Baile's Strand* (1904), which opened the Abbey Theatre. Ezra Pound, whom Yeats met in 1909, encouraged Yeats to study the Japanese Nō plays, and in the year of one of Ireland's greatest political crises, 1916, he produced *At the Hawk's Well*, a play for masked dancers based on his study of Japanese theater.

In later years, Yeats would produce other plays based on the Nō drama, but now, in 1916, his poetical energies turned to the "terrible beauty" of the Easter Rebellion in Dublin. Because he had spent much of his time since 1907 in England, the rising of the Irish nationalists who seized the Dublin Post Office in a bold but failed attempt to throw off the English yoke took Yeats by surprise. His qualified praise in "Easter 1916" for the leaders of the Easter Rebellion, many of whom were executed, marked a sort of reconciliation with Ireland, to which he returned. After his return, Yeats married Georgie Hyde-Lees (but not before he'd proposed to Iseult Gonne, Maud Gonne's daughter), took up residence at Ballylee, in Galway, and eventually became senator of the newly established Irish Free State in 1922. Through the medium of Georgie Hyde-Lees, who professed to have psychic powers, Yeats wrote *A Vision* (1925), a prophetic work that sets out the esoteric system of symbols and complex theory of cyclical history that informs the poetry of his highest achievements, *The Tower* (1928) and *The Winding Stair* (1933). After contracting a lung disease, Yeats retired from the senate in 1928 and in the following year left Ballylee to travel in Italy and southern France. After having the "Steinach operation" in 1934 to renew his sexual vitality, the nearly seventy-year-old poet continued writing poetry and plays, and in his last years he produced a stunning series of poems that cut to the brute realities of life, old age, and the body, in what Yeats sees as his return to the "foul rag-and-bone shop of the heart." In 1939, Yeats died in the south of France, "in the dead of winter," to quote from W. H. Auden's poetic tribute to Yeats, but his "gift survived it all."

WORK

Yeats's gift was great and varied, and in following the course of his poetry from the Pre-Raphaelite dreaminess of *The Wanderings of Oisin*, through the spare colloquialism and symbolic density of *The Tower* and *The Winding Stair*, to the tightly wrought, concrete realism of *Last Poems*, one can track some of the important transformations of early twentieth-century poetry. Yeats's distinctive signature, however—the deeply felt tension between his spiritual, aesthetic ideals and his unflinching grasp of the contradictions and disturbing complexities of mortal life—insistently qualifies any attempt to see Yeats's work as merely representative of any movement. With its mellifluous tone and natural simplicity, "The Lake Isle of Innisfree" captures some of the Pre-Raphaelite qualities of Yeats's poetry of the 1890s. "Who Goes with Fergus?" from the same collection, combines those same qualities with the Irish legend of a hero who turned away from life's dreary business to devote his life to poetry and to "brood / Upon love's bitter mystery." This poem typifies the otherworldliness of Yeats's early work, before he made the radical turn in the late 1890s to face the world head-on and to accept the role of a Shelleyan poet-legislator of

Ireland and its culture. That role emerges most dramatically in poems such as "Se̸ 1913" and "Easter 1916," where Yeats first criticizes the cultural and political indolen̸ the middle classes, then cautiously praises their awakening in the "terrible beauty" of th̸ Easter Rebellion. The language of these poems becomes more precise, more colloquial, as they aim at a broader audience. Moreover, the poems of this period, without abandoning the symbolism of the earlier period, more immediately engage the concerns of the present and more directly confront the harsh truths of everyday reality. Yeats signals this change in "A Coat" (1914):

> I made my song a coat
> Covered with embroideries
> Out of old mythologies
> From heel to throat;
> But the fools caught it,
> Wore it in the world's eyes
> As though they'd wrought it.
> Song, let them take it,
> For there's more enterprise
> In walking naked.

As we turn to the poetry of the twenties and thirties, we encounter a poetry partly contingent upon the symbolic system of *A Vision,* which Yeats received in part from his wife's automatic writing and in part from a complex synthesis of his studies of esoteric and occult thinkers ranging from Empedocles to William Blake. This complex system involves a web of correspondences derived from twenty-eight phases of the moon between cosmic, national, and personal history. Most importantly for the poems we include here, *A Vision* describes regular fluctuations of history as the movement of two intersecting cones or spinning "gyres." These gyres, which symbolize the opposites of subjectivity and objectivity, beauty and truth, and value and fact, expand and contract at regular intervals of 2,000 years. Thus, every 2,000 years a new system of values gains ascendancy. An avatar—Helen of Troy, Christ, the unnameable "beast" of "The Second Coming"—marks the beginning of each new age. Yeats saw the beginning of the twentieth century as the beginning of an objective cycle, which would bring on a period hostile to art, spiritual vision, and individuality. This system underlies the symbolism of poems such as "Leda and the Swan" and "The Second Coming," both of which inaugurate ages of brutality and objective values before and after the subjective age of Christ, which reached its height in the flourishing of art and humanism in the Renaissance. Yeats's celebration of a world of pure art in "Sailing to Byzantium" pays tribute to the "cold pastoral" of the Byzantine period when, according to Yeats's view in *A Vision,* art appeared to transcend the fleshly frailties of human experience. As he puts it,

> I think that in early Byzantium, maybe never before or since in recorded history, religious, aesthetic and practical life were one. . . . The painter, the mosaic worker, the worker in gold and silver, the illuminator of sacred books, were almost impersonal, almost perhaps without the consciousness of individual design, absorbed in their subject-matter and that the vision of a whole people.

Despite Yeats's apparent yearning for the "glory of changeless metal," as he puts it in "Byzantium," the tragic gaiety of mortal human life described in "Lapis Lazuli" called him back at last to the world of flesh and bone.

Yeats was never able to reconcile his passionate search for a systematic pattern behind human events with his stubborn insistence that we "cast a cold eye on life, on death."

The poetry of his late period embodies a struggle between the quiet permanence of art and the passionate mortality of life, the joy of spiritual desire and the grief of human love. "Lapis Lazuli" and "The Circus Animals' Desertion" demonstrate Yeats's characteristic questioning of the projects of men and women, including his own, his refusal to accept simple explanations to describe human motives, and his final recognition that the sometimes abstract emblems and themes of his poetry emerged from his passionate engagement with life, complete with its wicked and mad old men and women, its "mound of refuse or the sweepings of the street."

SUGGESTED READINGS

Good biographies of Yeats include Richard Ellmann's classic *Yeats: The Man and the Masks* (1948), and more recently Norman A. Jeffares's *W. B. Yeats: A New Biography* (1988). Ellmann also discusses Yeats's work in *The Identity of Yeats,* 2nd ed. (1964). Students will find helpful Edward Malins's *A Preface to Yeats* (1977), William H. O'Donnell's *The Poetry of William Butler Yeats: An Introduction* (1986), and Jeffares's *A New Commentary on the Collected Poems of W. B. Yeats* (1983). Harold Bloom and Richard J. Finneran have edited critical essays on the poems, *William Butler Yeats* (1986) and *Critical Essays on W. B. Yeats* (1986), respectively. Because Yeats extensively revised his poems for the *Collected Poems,* from which we take our selections here, students interested in his poetic development should consult Peter Allt and Russell K. Alspach's *The Variorum Edition of the Poems of W. B. Yeats* (1957) to see their original versions.

The Lake Isle of Innisfree[1]

I will arise and go now, and go to Innisfree,
And a small cabin build there, of clay and wattles made:
Nine bean-rows will I have there, a hive for the honeybee,
And live alone in the bee-loud glade.

And I shall have some peace there, for peace comes dropping slow,
Dropping from the veils of the morning to where the cricket sings;
There midnight's all a glimmer, and noon a purple glow,
And evening full of the linnet's wings.

I will arise and go now, for always night and day
I hear lake water lapping with low sounds by the shore;
While I stand on the roadway, or on the pavements grey,
I hear it in the deep heart's core.

10

---

[1] An island in Lough Gill, Sligo county, in northwestern Ireland.

Who Goes with Fergus?[1]

Who will go drive with Fergus now,
And pierce the deep wood's woven shade,
And dance upon the level shore?
Young man, lift up your russet brow,
And lift your tender eyelids, maid,
And brood on hopes and fear no more.

And no more turn aside and brood
Upon love's bitter mystery;
For Fergus rules the brazen cars,
And rules the shadows of the wood,   10
And the white breast of the dim sea
And all dishevelled wandering stars.

Easter 1916[1]

I have met them at close of day
Coming with vivid faces
From counter or desk among grey
Eighteenth-century houses.
I have passed with a nod of the head
Or polite meaningless words,
Or have lingered awhile and said
Polite meaningless words,
And thought before I had done
Of a mocking tale or a gibe   10
To please a companion
Around the fire at the club,
Being certain that they and I
But lived where motley is worn:
All changed, changed utterly:
A terrible beauty is born.

That woman's[2] days were spent
In ignorant good-will,

[handwritten margin notes: 1700 man Republican force seized Dublin post office, Pearse read a proclamation declaring the birth of Irish Republic. Street fighting for a week — then captured executed — made into Martyrs Beginning The End of British Power in Ireland Free state in 1921. everyday life]

WHO GOES WITH FERGUS?

[1] A legendary Irish hero; king of the Red Branch Kings who gave up his power to follow the less worldly pursuits of poetry and philosophy.

EASTER 1916

[1] The Easter Rebellion to which the poem refers actually began on the Monday after Easter 1916. A group of Irish nationalists seized the Dublin Post Office in a failed attempt to throw off the yoke of British rule. After a week-long fight, the rebels surrendered and were imprisoned; sixteen of the leaders, some of whom Yeats knew personally, were executed by firing squad.

[2] Constance Gore-Booth, an Irish nationalist from Sligo county.

Her nights in argument
Until her voice grew shrill.   20
What voice more sweet than hers
When, young and beautiful,
She rode to harriers? *hunting rabits*
This man[3] had kept a school
And rode our wingèd horse; *— wrote poetry*
This other[4] his helper and friend
Was coming into his force;
He might have won fame in the end,
So sensitive his nature seemed,
So daring and sweet his thought.   30
This other man[5] I had dreamed
A drunken, vainglorious lout.
He had done most bitter wrong
To some who are near my heart,
Yet I number him in the song;
He, too, has resigned his part
In the casual comedy;   *all 4 are*
He, too, has been changed in his turn,   *different now*
Transformed utterly:
A terrible beauty is born.   40

Hearts with one purpose alone
Through summer and winter seem
Enchanted to a stone
To trouble the living stream.
The horse that comes from the road,
The rider, the birds that range
From cloud to tumbling cloud,
Minute by minute they change;
immutable in the midst of mutation
A shadow of cloud on the stream
Changes minute by minute;   50
A horse-hoof slides on the brim,
And a horse plashes within it;
The long-legged moor-hens dive,
And hens to moor-cocks call;
Minute by minute they live:
The stone's in the midst of all.

Too long a sacrifice   *The Irish Situation*
Can make a stone of the heart.
O when may it suffice?
That is Heaven's part, our part   60
To murmur name upon name, *— the names of the dead*
As a mother names her child

Compares us't to mother

---

[3]Patrick Pearse, a schoolmaster and Gaelic poet; the winged horse is Pegasus, horse of the Muses.
[4]Thomas MacDonagh, a poet and playwright.
[5]Major John MacBride, who had married, then separated from, Maud Gonne, Yeats's lifelong love.

When sleep at last has come
On limbs that had run wild.
What is it but nightfall?
No, no, not night but death;
Was it needless death after all?
For England may keep faith
For all that is done and said.
We know their dream; enough   70
To know they dreamed and are dead;
And what if excess of love
Bewildered them till they died?
I write it out in a verse—
MacDonagh and MacBride
And Connolly[6] and Pearse
Now and in time to be,
Wherever green is worn,
Are changed, changed utterly:
A terrible beauty is born.   80

The Second Coming

Turning and turning in the widening gyre[1]
The falcon cannot hear the falconer;
Things fall apart; the centre cannot hold;
Mere anarchy is loosed upon the world,
The blood-dimmed tide is loosed, and everywhere
The ceremony of innocence is drowned;
The best lack all conviction, while the worst
Are full of passionate intensity.

Surely some revelation is at hand;
Surely the Second Coming is at hand.
The Second Coming! Hardly are those words out   10
When a vast image out of *Spiritus Mundi*[2]
Troubles my sight: somewhere in sands of the desert
A shape with lion body and the head of a man,
A gaze blank and pitiless as the sun,
Is moving its slow thighs, while all about it
Reel shadows of the indignant desert birds.

[6]James Connolly, the chief leader of the Easter Rebellion.
THE SECOND COMING
   [1]The gyre refers to Yeats's theory of historical cycles developed in *A Vision*. Yeats imagines history
as a dynamic set of interlocking cone-shaped spirals. At the end of each 2,000-year cycle, a new spirit
governs human consciousness and the affairs of the world. This poem, which envisions an age dominated
by indifference and authoritarianism, ironically announces itself as the second coming, which refers to the
second coming of Christ and the end of the world.
   [2]Spirit of the World; in Yeats's scheme a sort of collective consciousness or "Great Memory" that links
the human race by a shared set of archetypes and symbols.

The darkness drops again; but now I know
That twenty centuries of stony sleep
Were vexed to nightmare by a rocking cradle,
And what rough beast, its hour come round at last,
Slouches towards Bethlehem to be born?

20

Sailing to Byzantium[1]

1

That is no country for old men. The young
In one another's arms, birds in the trees
—Those dying generations—at their song,
The salmon-falls, the mackerel-crowded seas,
Fish, flesh, or fowl, commend all summer long
Whatever is begotten, born, and dies.
Caught in that sensual music all neglect
Monuments of unageing intellect.

2

An aged man is but a paltry thing,
A tattered coat upon a stick, unless
Soul clap its hands and sing, and louder sing
For every tatter in its mortal dress,
Nor is there singing school but studying
Monuments of its own magnificence;
And therefore I have sailed the seas and come
To the holy city of Byzantium.

10

3

O sages standing in God's holy fire
As in the gold mosaic of a wall,
Come from the holy fire, perne in a gyre,[2]
And be the singing-masters of my soul.
Consume my heart away; sick with desire
And fastened to a dying animal
It knows not what it is; and gather me
Into the artifice of eternity.

20

---

[1] The capital of the Byzantine Empire in the fifth and sixth centuries; for Yeats, Byzantium (today's Istanbul) was the seat of cultural and intellectual achievement and the symbol of the integration of art with life.

[2] To spin in a cone-shaped spiral; see "The Second Coming," note 1.

4

Once out of nature I shall never take
My bodily form from any natural thing,
But such a form as Grecian goldsmiths make
Of hammered gold and gold enamelling
To keep a drowsy Emperor awake;
Or set upon a golden bough to sing   30
To lords and ladies of Byzantium
Of what is past, or passing, or to come.

Leda and the Swan[1]

A sudden blow: the great wings beating still
Above the staggering girl, her thighs caressed
By the dark webs, her nape caught in his bill,
He holds her helpless breast upon his breast.

How can those terrified vague fingers push
The feathered glory from her loosening thighs?
And how can body, laid in that white rush,
But feel the strange heart beating where it lies?

A shudder in the loins engenders there
The broken wall, the burning roof and tower
And Agamemnon[2] dead.
                              Being so caught up,   10
So mastered by the brute blood of the air,
Did she put on his knowledge with his power
Before the indifferent beak could let her drop?

Among School Children

1

I walk through the long schoolroom questioning;
A kind old nun in a white hood replies;
The children learn to cipher and to sing,

---

[1] According to the Greek myth, Zeus assumed the form of a swan to rape Leda, who then gave birth to Helen, whose beauty caused the Trojan War, and Clytemnestra, who murdered her husband Agamemnon. In *A Vision*, Yeats describes this event as the "annunciation that founded Greece."

[2] King of Mycenae and leader of the Greek forces against Troy; because he sacrificed his daughter Iphigenia to gain favorable winds to reach Troy, Agamemnon was murdered by his wife Clytemnestra on his return home from the war.

To study reading-books and history,
To cut and sew, be neat in everything
In the best modern way—the children's eyes
In momentary wonder stare upon
A sixty-year-old smiling public man.[1]

2

I dream of a Ledaean body,[2] bent
Above a sinking fire, a tale that she   10
Told of a harsh reproof, or trivial event
That changed some childish day to tragedy—
Told, and it seemed that our two natures blent
Into a sphere from youthful sympathy,
Or else, to alter Plato's parable,
Into the yolk and white of the one shell.[3]

3

And thinking of that fit of grief or rage
I look upon one child or t'other there
And wonder if she stood so at that age—
For even daughters of the swan can share   20
Something of every paddler's heritage—
And had that colour upon cheek or hair,
And thereupon my heart is driven wild:
She stands before me as a living child.

4

Her present image floats into the mind—
Did Quattrocento[4] finger fashion it
Hollow of cheek as though it drank the wind
And took a mess of shadows for its meat?
And I though never of Ledaean kind
Had pretty plumage once—enough of that,   30
Better to smile on all that smile, and show
There is a comfortable kind of old scarecrow.

---

[1] In 1922, Yeats was elected senator of the Irish Free State.
[2] As beautiful as Leda, mother of Helen of Troy (see "Leda and the Swan," note 1).
[3] Plato's *Symposium* explains that true lovers are the two halves of a once complete being; when torn asunder by the gods, the two halves continually seek reunion with each other.
[4] The hand of a fifteenth-century Italian painter or artist, such as Massacio (1401–1428), Leonardo da Vinci (1452–1519), or Sandro Botticelli (1444–1510).

5

What youthful mother, a shape upon her lap
Honey of generation had betrayed,
And that must sleep, shriek, struggle to escape
As recollection or the drug decide,
Would think her son, did she but see that shape
With sixty or more winters on its head,
A compensation for the pang of his birth,
Or the uncertainty of his setting forth?   40

6

Plato thought nature but a spume that plays
Upon a ghostly paradigm of things;
Solider Aristotle played the taws
Upon the bottom of a king of kings;
World-famous golden-thighed Pythagoras[5]
Fingered upon a fiddle-stick or strings
What a star sang and careless Muses heard:
Old clothes upon old sticks to scare a bird.

7

Both nuns and mothers worship images,
But those the candles light are not as those   50
That animate a mother's reveries,
But keep a marble or a bronze repose.
And yet they too break hearts—O Presences
That passion, piety or affection knows,
And that all heavenly glory symbolise—
O self-born mockers of man's enterprise;

8

Labour is blossoming or dancing where
The body is not bruised to pleasure soul,
Nor beauty born out of its own despair,
Nor blear-eyed wisdom out of midnight oil.   60
O chestnut-tree, great-rooted blossomer,
Are you the leaf, the blossom or the bole?
O body swayed to music, O brightening glance,
How can we know the dancer from the dance?

---

[5]Plato (427–347 B.C.E.) believed that things in nature were mere shadows of a perfect ideal form beyond
the reach of ordinary sensibility; Aristotle (384–322 B.C.E.), who studied the natural world more closely
than Plato, was Alexander the Great's tutor and so perhaps "played the taws," that is, spanked, his young
pupil; Pythagoras (582–507 B.C.E.) studied mathematics and music and was said to have a golden thigh-
bone.

Lapis Lazuli[1]

[FOR HARRY CLIFTON]

I have heard that hysterical women say
They are sick of the palette and fiddle-bow,
Of poets that are always gay,
For everybody knows or else should know
That if nothing drastic is done
Aeroplane and Zeppelin[2] will come out,
Pitch like King Billy bomb-balls in
Until the town lie beaten flat.

All perform their tragic play,
There struts Hamlet, there is Lear,   10
That's Ophelia, that Cordelia;
Yet they, should the last scene be there,
The great stage curtain about to drop,
If worthy their prominent part in the play,
Do not break up their lines to weep.
They know that Hamlet and Lear are gay;
Gaiety transfiguring all that dread.
All men have aimed at, found and lost;
Black out; Heaven blazing into the head:
Tragedy wrought to its uttermost.   20
Though Hamlet rambles and Lear rages,
And all the drop-scenes drop at once
Upon a hundred thousand stages,
It cannot grow by an inch or an ounce.

On their own feet they came, or on shipboard,
Camel-back, horse-back, ass-back, mule-back,
Old civilisations put to the sword.
Then they and their wisdom went to rack:
No handiwork of Callimachus,[3]
Who handled marble as if it were bronze,   30
Made draperies that seemed to rise
When sea-wind swept the corner, stands;
His long lamp-chimney shaped like the stem
Of a slender palm, stood but a day;
All things fall and are built again,
And those that build them again are gay.

---

[1]A deep blue, semiprecious stone. Yeats had a piece of lapis lazuli, carved by a Chinese artist in the manner described here. Yeats described the essential qualities of the carving as "Ascetic, pupil, hard stone, eternal theme of the sensual east."

[2]The massive airships used by the Germans during World War I. "King Billy" may refer to Kaiser Wilhelm II of Germany, whose army used the zeppelins during the war; it refers particularly to King William II, who defeated the army of King James II at the Battle of the Boyne in 1690.

[3]Fifth-century B.C.E. Greek sculptor.

Two Chinamen, behind them a third,
Are carved in lapis lazuli,
Over them flies a long-legged bird,
A symbol of longevity;   40
The third, doubtless a serving-man,
Carries a musical instrument.

Every discoloration of the stone,
Every accidental crack or dent,
Seems a water-course or an avalanche,
Or lofty slope where it still snows
Though doubtless plum or cherry-branch
Sweetens the little half-way house
Those Chinamen climb towards, and I
Delight to imagine them seated there;   50
There, on the mountain and the sky,
On all the tragic scene they stare.
One asks for mournful melodies;
Accomplished fingers begin to play.
Their eyes mid many wrinkles, their eyes,
Their ancient, glittering eyes, are gay.

The Circus Animals' Desertion

1

I sought a theme and sought for it in vain,
I sought it daily for six weeks or so.
Maybe at last, being but a broken man,
I must be satisfied with my heart, although
Winter and summer till old age began
My circus animals were all on show,
Those stilted boys, that burnished chariot,
Lion and woman and the Lord knows what.[1]

2

What can I but enumerate old themes?
First that sea-rider Oisin[2] led by the nose   10
Through three enchanted islands, allegorical dreams,
Vain gaiety, vain battle, vain repose,

---

[1] The Irish heroes of Yeats's early work and images from his plays; the "lion and woman" alludes to the Sphinx in his poem "The Double Vision of Michael Robartes."
[2] A legendary Irish hero and poet who appears in Yeats's first book *The Wanderings of Oisin and Other Poems* (1889).

Themes of the embittered heart, or so it seems,
That might adorn old songs or courtly shows;
But what cared I that set him on to ride,
I, starved for the bosom of his faery bride?

And then a counter-truth filled out its play,
*The Countess Cathleen*³ was the name I gave it;
She, pity-crazed, had given her soul away,
But masterful Heaven had intervened to save it.   20
I thought my dear must her own soul destroy,
So did fanaticism and hate enslave it,
And this brought forth a dream and soon enough
This dream itself had all my thought and love.

And when the Fool and Blind Man stole the bread
Cuchulain⁴ fought the ungovernable sea;
Heart-mysteries there, and yet when all is said
It was the dream itself enchanted me:
Character isolated by a deed
To engross the present and dominate memory.   30
Players and painted stage took all my love,
And not those things that they were emblems of.

3

Those masterful images because complete
Grew in pure mind, but out of what began?
A mound of refuse or the sweepings of a street,
Old kettles, old bottles, and a broken can,
Old iron, old bones, old rags, that raving slut
Who keeps the till. Now that my ladder's gone,
I must lie down where all the ladders start,
In the foul rag-and-bone shop of the heart.   40

RAINER MARIA RILKE
[1875–1926]

Rainer Maria Rilke lived a life full of anomalies and contradictions. The child of a
staunchly middle-class Austrian family, he was dressed as a girl by his mother until the
age of six. A native speaker of German, he was a spiritual citizen of France and the rest
of the Continent during most of his adult life. Though hyperconscious of his role as a
poet and solitary figure, he was also a sensual, neurotically dependent man involved in

---

³Yeats's play (1892) in which an Irish countess who sells her soul to the devil to buy food for the
peasants is rescued from damnation by a forgiving Heaven.
⁴From Yeats's *On Baile's Strand* (1904); Cuchulain is a legendary Irish hero.

a lifelong relationship with a powerful and famous woman. He helped to connect the symbolist and modernist periods of the nineteenth and twentieth centuries, but he was attacked by the generation to follow him for his lack of concern for the fate of society as a whole. Today his reputation survives, almost despite itself, on the basis of his works: his sonnets and other short poems contained in *The Book of Hours* (1905) and *New Poems* (1907, 1908); his autobiographical novel *The Notebooks of Malte Laurids Brigge* (1910); and his masterpiece, the *Duino Elegies* (1912–1923), along with the coda to this work, *Sonnets to Orpheus* (1923). Rilke was, in his curiously irritating way, the key to an age; influenced by predecessors as varied as Søren Kierkegaard, Fyodor Dostoevsky, Charles Baudelaire, Friedrich Nietzsche, and Paul Cézanne, he mingled in his lifetime with such geniuses as Leo Tolstoy, Auguste Rodin, André Gide, Paul Valéry, and Thomas Mann, and his overall impact on European culture has been compared to that of his near-contemporaries Pablo Picasso and Igor Stravinsky.

LIFE AND WORK

Rilke was born in Prague of Austrian parents in 1875. His father, Josef, although briefly the commander of the citadel at Brescia during the Franco–Austrian War in 1859, served most of his life as a minor railroad official. His mother, Sophie or "Phia," a writer whose privately printed book of aphorisms shows feminist leanings, appears to have dominated Rilke's early life both emotionally and artistically. Rilke's dependence on his mother was matched by his fury at her influence on his life; his remarks about her in later years are excoriating:

> When I must see this lost, unreal, entirely unrelated woman, who cannot grow old, then I feel that I tried to get away from her even as a child and am deeply afraid that after years and years of running and walking I am still not far enough from her, that I still have somewhere in me inner movements which are the other half of her withered gestures, broken pieces of memory which she carries in her; I am horrified then at her distracted piety, her obstinate faith, all the disfigured and distorted things she clings to, herself empty as a dress, ghostlike and terrible. And that I am yet her child; that some hardly recognizable wallpaper door in this faded wall, which belongs nowhere, was my entrance into the world (if indeed such an entrance can lead to the world).[1]

The major influence on Rilke's life after his mother was Lou Andreas-Salome, daughter of a Russian general, whom he met in Munich while he was establishing a reputation as a writer. Rilke was twenty-two, Andreas-Salome thirty-six. She had already had romantic and intellectual relationships with a number of famous men, including Nietzsche and his friend, the philosopher Paul Ree. Afterwards, she had married a lecturer on the Orient at the University of Berlin, Friedrich Carl Andreas. Rilke fell in love with her, besieging her with flowers and poems, and became her lover in the summer of 1897. She encouraged his journey to Italy in 1898 and introduced him to Russian culture in 1899, inviting him on a tour along with her husband. Their sexual relationship appeared to liberate Rilke—the substance of his poetry changed, taking on a celebratory quality—and she candidly remarked of it at a later time:

> If I belonged to you for some years it was because you represented absolute reality for me for the first time, body and person indistinguishably one and the same, an unquestionable element of life itself.[2]

---

[1] H. F. Peters, *Rainer Maria Rilke: Masks and the Man,* 78–79.
[2] Wolfgang Leppmann, *Rilke: A Life,* 81.

Rilke destroyed many poems to Lou, but some remain in his volume *The Book of Hours*. One reads:

> Put out my eyes, and I can see you,
> wall up my ears, and I shall hear,
> and without limbs, I will draw near,
> and without mouth I call your name.
> Break off my arms, I shall embrace you
> with all my heart, as with a hand;
> throw my heart shut, my brain will face you,
> and if you fan my brain to flame,
> my blood shall carry and encase you.[3]

The other early influence on Rilke's writing came from his own psychological and philosophical orientation. As Andreas-Salome soon recognized, Rilke was a depressive personality, returning obsessively to feelings of spiritual alienation. Though not a systematic philosopher, he had studied the works of Kierkegaard and Nietzsche, especially concerning humanity's distance from God and isolation in the universe. These concerns, coupled with his temporary separation from Andreas-Salome and other friends after his unhappy marriage to Clara Westhoff in 1901, led to his semiautobiographical novel *The Notebooks of Malte Laurids Brigge* and the poems that would make up *The Book of Hours* and *New Poems, First and Second Series* in the years immediately after. The dominant note of these writings, in which loneliness is often made into a virtue, may be seen in the early poem "Autumn Day" from *The Book of Pictures,* published in 1902.

Some of Rilke's most famous poems were written in the two collections of *New Poems,* published in 1907 and 1908. These show the benefit of his studies in art, particularly his Italian tour in 1898 and his association with the French sculptor Rodin after 1900. The most noteworthy quality about "The Panther," one of the first poems in the new collection, is its focus on the creature's gaze as it crosses back and forth behind the bars of its cage. Here Rilke makes visual perspective the center of his poem's content. In "Archaic Torso of Apollo," Rilke dramatizes his studies of classical art by making the rippling chest and curved loins of Apollo stand for sexual energy and an urgent mandate to the reader: "You must change your life." Art takes on an active role, promoting the only useful kind of activity possible in the world, that of transformation.

As his life took shape in his busiest period, between 1900 and 1910, Rilke began appealing to wealthy and influential patrons, often clever and talented women. Countess Luise Schwerin supported him during the difficult years after 1905, and Princess Marie von Thurn und Taxis began her long friendship with him in 1910. In 1911, Rilke stayed with Princess Taxis at Duino Castle in Italy, where he conceived his greatest work, the *Duino Elegies*. He wrote the first two elegies there, leaving his sanctuary for a series of travels abroad. He completed the third elegy in Paris in 1913. He left Paris for Munich in July 1914, where he wrote the fourth elegy late in the year, just before being drafted as a private in the Austrian army at age forty. He was transferred to the Austrian War Ministry and mustered out the following year. At that point his writing underwent a long period of paralysis. Rilke did not complete the rest of the cycle of the *Duino Elegies* until February 1922, when in a small castle in Switzerland named the Chateau de Muzot, leased and later purchased for him by friends, he wrote the last six elegies, as well as most of the *Sonnets to Orpheus,* in a single week.

The theme of the *Duino Elegies* is transcendence, presented as an object both of admiration and of terror. Walking along the seashore at Duino Castle, reputedly once a

---

[3]Leppmann, 83. Verse translation by Richard Exner.

place of refuge for the Florentine exile Dante, Rilke seemed to hear the first line of the first elegy rise directly from the boiling sea: "Who, if I cried out, would hear me among the angels' / hierarchies?" After sketching the terrifying remoteness of the angels and briefly considering the artist's lonely life of creation here on earth, Rilke turns to consider the condition of the unfulfilled, both those unfulfilled in passion and those who have died young. The real power, he seems to say, comes from that which is stored up inside us. This is the power of art; he contrasts it with the natural passions that are expended by normal living.

The unworldliness of art, its home among the isolated, the unfulfilled, and the early dead—these thoughts haunt Rilke in the first elegy. He returns to the same theme in his last major work, *Sonnets to Orpheus,* in which he commemorates the early death of a talented dancer, the daughter of a friend, at age eighteen. He chose the title because, he tells the grieving mother, the "singing god" speaks through him. In these poems Rilke turns lament into praise, just as in the *Elegies* he transforms fear of the angels into a song that rivals angelic music. To put it another way, the abstraction of the *Elegies* is given shape in the *Sonnets,* where grief is transformed into rejoicing.

Rilke's own death, from complications of a previously undetected form of leukemia, came in 1926, a few years after his completion of the *Elegies* and *Sonnets.* In many respects his work represented a working out of an interior monologue unconnected with the destruction that lay about him at the end of World War I. Like his fellow writer from Prague, Franz Kafka, he was a citizen of no country; a practitioner of art, he employed a rich personal symbolism in order to create an aesthetic image of the world. Passionate and physical in the personal realm, he was nevertheless incapable of sustaining a practical relationship; his real strength lay in his refusal to allow the daily claims of life to overwhelm him. With William Butler Yeats, Marcel Proust, James Joyce, and a few others, he was one of the artistic geniuses of modernism; after him would come a generation of more practical men and women, hoping to portray the world realistically and at the same time change it nearer to their liking.

SUGGESTED READINGS

Although writings about Rilke are numerous, comparatively little has been translated into English. Biographies include J. F. Hendry's *The Sacred Threshold: A Life of Rainer Maria Rilke* (1983) and Wolfgang Leppmann's *Rilke: A Life* (1984). A good analytical study is H. F. Peters's *Rainer Maria Rilke: Masks and the Man* (1977). Important translations of works and selections from the works include M. D. Herder-Norton's *Sonnets to Orpheus* (1942), J. B. Leishman and Stephen Spender's *The Duino Elegies* (1939), C. F. MacIntyre's *Selected Poems* (1962), and Stephen Mitchell's *The Selected Poetry* (1982).

Autumn Day

Translated by Stephen Mitchell

Lord: it is time. The huge summer has gone by.
Now overlap the sundials with your shadows,
and on the meadows let the wind go free.

Command the fruits to swell on tree and vine;
grant them a few more warm transparent days,
urge them on to fulfillment then, and press
the final sweetness into the heavy wine.

Whoever has no house now, will never have one.
Whoever is alone will stay alone,
will sit, read, write long letters through the evening,   10
and wander on the boulevards, up and down,
restlessly, while the dry leaves are blowing.

The Panther

Translated by Stephen Mitchell

IN THE JARDIN DES PLANTES, PARIS

His vision, from the constantly passing bars,
has grown so weary that it cannot hold
anything else. It seems to him there are
a thousand bars; and behind the bars, no world.

As he paces in cramped circles, over and over,
the movement of his powerful soft strides
is like a ritual dance around a center
in which a mighty will stands paralyzed.

Only at times, the curtain of the pupils
lifts, quietly—. An image enters in,   10
rushes down through the tensed, arrested muscles,
plunges into the heart and is gone.

Archaic Torso of Apollo

Translated by Stephen Mitchell

We cannot know his legendary head
with eyes like ripening fruit. And yet his torso
is still suffused with brilliance from inside,
like a lamp, in which his gaze, now turned to low,

gleams in all its power. Otherwise
the curved breast could not dazzle you so, nor could

a smile run through the placid hips and thighs
to that dark center where procreation flared.

Otherwise this stone would seem defaced
beneath the translucent cascade of the shoulders   10
and would not glisten like a wild beast's fur:

would not, from all the borders of itself,
burst like a star: for here there is no place
that does not see you. You must change your life.

FROM

Duino Elegies

Translated by Stephen Mitchell

THE FIRST ELEGY

Who, if I cried out, would hear me among the angels'
hierarchies? and even if one of them pressed me
suddenly against his heart: I would be consumed
in that overwhelming existence. For beauty is nothing
but the beginning of terror, which we still are just able to endure,
and we are so awed because it serenely disdains
to annihilate us. Every angel is terrifying.
    And so I hold myself back and swallow the call-note
of my dark sobbing. Ah, whom can we ever turn to
in our need? Not angels, not humans,   10
and already the knowing animals are aware
that we are not really at home in
our interpreted world. Perhaps there remains for us
some tree on a hillside, which every day we can take
into our vision; there remains for us yesterday's street
and the loyalty of a habit so much at ease
when it stayed with us that it moved in and never left.
    Oh and night: there is night, when a wind full of infinite space
gnaws at our faces. Whom would it not remain for—that longed-after,
mildly disillusioning presence, which the solitary heart   20
so painfully meets. Is it any less difficult for lovers?
But they keep on using each other to hide their own fate.
    Don't you know *yet?* Fling the emptiness out of your arms
into the spaces we breathe; perhaps the birds
will feel the expanded air with more passionate flying.

Yes—the springtimes needed you. Often a star
was waiting for you to notice it. A wave rolled toward you
out of the distant past, or as you walked
under an open window, a violin
yielded itself to your hearing. All this was mission.   30

But could you accomplish it? Weren't you always
distracted by expectation, as if every event
announced a beloved? (Where can you find a place
to keep her, with all the huge strange thoughts inside you
going and coming and often staying all night.)
But when you feel longing, sing of women in love;
for their famous passion is still not immortal. Sing
of women abandoned and desolate (you envy them, almost)
who could love so much more purely than those who were gratified.
Begin again and again the never-attainable praising;   40
remember: the hero lives on; even his downfall was
merely a pretext for achieving his final birth.
But Nature, spent and exhausted, takes lovers back
into herself, as if there were not enough strength
to create them a second time. Have you imagined
Gaspara Stampa intensely enough so that any girl
deserted by her beloved might be inspired
by that fierce example of soaring, objectless love
and might say to herself, "Perhaps I can be like her"?
Shouldn't this most ancient of sufferings finally grow   50
more fruitful for us? Isn't it time that we lovingly
freed ourselves from the beloved and, quivering, endured:
as the arrow endures the bowstring's tension, so that
gathered in the snap of release it can be more than
itself. For there is no place where we can remain.

Voices. Voices. Listen, my heart, as only
saints have listened: until the gigantic call lifted them
off the ground; yet they kept on, impossibly,
kneeling and didn't notice at all:
so complete was their listening. Not that you could endure   60
God's voice—far from it. But listen to the voice of the wind
and the ceaseless message that forms itself out of silence.
It is murmuring toward you now from those who died young.
Didn't their fate, whenever you stepped into a church
in Naples or Rome, quietly come to address you?
Or high up, some eulogy entrusted you with a mission,
as, last year, on the plaque in Santa Maria Formosa.
What they want of me is that I gently remove the appearance
of injustice about their death—which at times
slightly hinders their souls from proceeding onward.   70
Of course, it is strange to inhabit the earth no longer,
to give up customs one barely had time to learn,
not to see roses and other promising Things
in terms of a human future; no longer to be
what one was in infinitely anxious hands; to leave
even one's own first name behind, forgetting it
as easily as a child abandons a broken toy.
Strange to no longer desire one's desires. Strange
to see meanings that clung together once, floating away
in every direction. And being dead is hard work   80

and full of retrieval before one can gradually feel
a trace of eternity.— Though the living are wrong to believe
in the too-sharp distinctions which they themselves have created.
Angels (they say) don't know whether it is the living
they are moving among, or the dead. The eternal torrent
whirls all ages along in it, through both realms
forever, and their voices are drowned out in its thunderous roar.

In the end, those who were carried off early no longer need us:
they are weaned from earth's sorrows and joys, as gently as children
outgrow the soft breasts of their mothers. But we, who do need   90
such great mysteries, we for whom grief is so often
the source of our spirit's growth—: could we exist without *them?*
Is the legend meaningless that tells how, in the lament for Linus,
the daring first notes of song pierced through the barren numbness;
and then in the startled space which a youth as lovely as a god
had suddenly left forever, the Void felt for the first time
that harmony which now enraptures and comforts and helps us.

Sonnets to Orpheus

Translated by Stephen Mitchell

I, 1

A tree ascended there. Oh pure transcendence!
Oh Orpheus sings! Oh tall tree in the ear!
And all things hushed. Yet even in that silence
a new beginning, beckoning, change appeared.

Creatures of stillness crowded from the bright
unbound forest, out of their lairs and nests;
and it was not from any dullness, not
from fear, that they were so quiet in themselves,

but from simply listening. Bellow, roar, shriek
seemed small inside their hearts. And where there had been   10
just a makeshift hut to receive the music,

a shelter nailed up out of their darkest longing,
with an entryway that shuddered in the wind—
you built a temple deep inside their hearing.

I, 2

And it was almost a girl who, stepping from
this single harmony of song and lyre,

appeared to me through her diaphanous form
and made herself a bed inside my ear.

And slept in me. Her sleep was everything:
the awesome trees, the distances I had felt
so deeply that I could touch them, meadows in spring:
all wonders that had ever seized my heart.

She slept the world. Singing god, how was that first
sleep so perfect that she had no desire   10
ever to wake? See: she arose and slept.

Where is her death now? Ah, will you discover
this theme before your song consumes itself?—
Where is she vanishing? . . . A girl, almost . . . .

I, 3

A god can do it. But will you tell me how
a man can penetrate through the lyre's strings?
Our mind is split. And at the shadowed crossing
of heart-roads, there is no temple for Apollo.

Song, as you have taught it, is not desire,
not wooing any grace that can be achieved;
song is reality. Simple, for a god.
But when can *we* be real? When does he pour

the earth, the stars, into us? Young man,
it is not your loving, even if your mouth   10
was forced wide open by your own voice—learn

to forget that passionate music. It will end.
True singing is a different breath, about
nothing. A gust inside the god. A wind.

I, 5

Erect no gravestone to his memory; just
let the rose blossom each year for his sake.
For it *is* Orpheus. Wherever he has passed
through this or that. We do not need to look

for other names. When there is poetry,
it is Orpheus singing. He lightly comes and goes.
Isn't it enough if sometimes he can stay
with us a few days longer than a rose?

Though he himself is afraid to disappear,
he *has* to vanish: don't you understand?   10
The moment his word steps out beyond our life here,

he moves where you will never find his trace.
The lyre's strings do not constrict his hands.
And it is in overstepping that he obeys.

I, 7

Praising is what matters! He was summoned for that,
and came to us like the ore from a stone's
silence. His mortal heart presses out
a deathless, inexhaustible wine.

Whenever he feels the god's paradigm grip
his throat, the voice does not die in his mouth.
All becomes vineyard, all becomes grape,
ripened on the hills of his sensuous South.

Neither decay in the sepulchre of kings
nor any shadow that has fallen from the gods   10
can ever detract from his glorious praising.

For he is a herald who is with us always,
holding far into the doors of the dead
a bowl with ripe fruit worthy of praise.

I, 8

Only in the realm of Praising should Lament
walk, the naiad of the wept-for fountain,
watching over the stream of our complaint,
that it be clear upon the very stone

that bears the arch of triumph and the altar.—
Look: around her shoulders dawns the bright
sense that she may be the youngest sister
among the deities hidden in our heart.

Joy *knows*, and Longing has accepted,—
only Lament still learns; upon her beads,   10
night after night, she counts the ancient curse.

Yet awkward as she is, she suddenly
lifts a constellation of our voice,
glittering, into the pure nocturnal sky.

LU XUN
[1881–1936]

Lu Xun is generally regarded as the most influential Chinese writer of the twentieth century. First trained as a surgeon, he changed careers when he realized that he wished most of all to cure the backward condition of the Chinese people, not merely tend to their bodily illnesses. "The most important thing," he wrote, "was to change their spirit, and since at that time I felt that literature was the best means to that end, I decided to promote a literary movement." In addition to his extraordinary short stories, modeled after those of the Russian authors Gogol and Chekhov, he produced social commentaries, literary sketches, and reminiscences. Although he died before Mao Zedong and the Chinese Communist Party seized control of the country in the aftermath of World War II, for most of his life he supported the left-wing movement that had grown up in China in the 1920s and culminated in Mao's Long March to Yenan in 1935.

LIFE

While a young medical student in Japan, Lu Xun became so disturbed by anti-Chinese propaganda that he returned home to fight for the new political order. He began to write against Confucianism, the moral system that supported the Chinese reactionaries, and tried to win over the youth of his country to social change. His first short story, "Diary of a Madman," a scathing attack on conventional morality, was published in 1918. He worked in Peking from 1920 to 1926, helping to build literary support for the new movement and completing two books of short stories, *Call to Arms* and *Wandering*. In 1927, he moved to Canton, then a seat of revolutionary activity. After the coup d'état of Chiang Kai-shek and his Kuomintang army later that year, Lu Xun moved to Shanghai, where he threw his political support to Mao Zedong and lived the last ten years of his life in struggle against the Japanese invaders on one hand and Chiang's right-wing Nationalist army on the other. He organized the League of Left-Wing Writers, writing over 600 essays and tracts under many pen names while dodging political repression. He became ill with tuberculosis, dying in Shanghai in 1936.

WORK

Characteristic of Lu Xun is his tough-minded approach. This is easily seen in his political writing. Lu Xun was always a staunch advocate of revolutionary activity, never a "fellow traveler" or "liberal" in the Western sense. When he was chastised about his lack of "fair play" during the struggle with the Confucianists, he responded, "If there is no fight to the finish between darkness and light, and simple souls go on . . . confusing mercy with giving rein to evil, and continue pardoning wicked men, then the present state of chaos will last forever."

One monument of Lu Xun's work is his fictional masterpiece "The True Story of Ah Q," written in 1921. In this cautionary tale, set in 1911, Lu Xun describes the fate of an old farmhand who has suffered bullying and persecution all his life, has dreamed of deliverance at the hands of the revolutionaries, but at the last minute is charged with committing an act of common thievery and executed in the town square. The story reflects Lu Xun's pursuit of what he called "critical realism" on several levels: It exposes the folly of the farm laborer himself, who cringes before authority and lives in a fantasy world most of the time; it depicts the corruption of the old order, exemplified by the richest man in town who is robbed of all his possessions; and it reveals the hypocrisy of the young "revolutionaries," who execute Ah Q in order to look as if they are maintaining law and order.

The story "The New Year's Sacrifice" (1924) is another attack on the old order. Part of Lu Xun's artistic daring is to show what we might call social grotesques. As he himself said, "My themes were usually the unfortunates of this abnormal society. My aim was to expose the disease and draw attention to it so that it might be cured." In this case, a young man of progressive sympathies returns home for a Chinese New Year celebration. He encounters the woman called Hsiang Lin's Wife, his family's former servant, who has been turned out of his home, has gone mad, and now is tormented by ghosts. She wishes to know whether one is restored to one's family after death.

Suddenly it is revealed that after her meeting with the narrator she has committed suicide. The narrator recounts the story of her life—her two dead husbands, her infant son devoured by wolves—and at the end suggests that the town about to celebrate New Year's will benefit from her death: "I felt only that the saints of heaven and earth had accepted the sacrifice and incense and were all reeling with intoxication in the sky, preparing to give the people of Luchen boundless good fortune." Once again Lu Xun has revealed a familiar triad: the hapless individual out of touch with society; the old order, brutal and vindictive; and the new order, still unborn—callow, superficial, unable to help.

Lu Xun's particular achievement is to combine a political vision with a literary one. He attained much of the literary power of the great Russian writers whose works he had read and admired—Gogol, Chekhov, and Gorky especially. He also invented a literary approach, critical realism, a new way of holding up to scrutiny the social pieties of the past; and he put forward a new conception of heroism, emanating from his hope for the youth of the country and the saving force of literary movements. Proud and unyielding in his lifetime, Lu Xun has become a writer of world importance, never again to be confined to his own period.

SUGGESTED READINGS

William A. Lyell's *Lu Hsün's Vision of Reality* (1976), the best biography in English, contains an extensive discussion of Lu Xun's short stories. See also Lyell's *Diary of a Madman and Other Stories* (1990) and Yang Xianyi and Gladys Yang's *The Complete Stories of Lu Xun* (1981) for Lu Xun's fiction translated into English. Leo Ou-fan Lee's *Lu Xun and His Legacy* (1985) offers a useful collection of critical essays.

The New Year's Sacrifice

Translated by Yang Xianyi and Gladys Yang

New Year's Eve of the old calendar[1] seems after all more like the real New Year's Eve; for, to say nothing of the villages and towns, even in the air there is a feeling that New Year is coming. From the pale, lowering evening clouds issue frequent flashes of lightning, followed by a rumbling sound of firecrackers celebrating the departure of the Hearth God; while, nearer by, the firecrackers explode even more violently, and before the deafening report dies away the air is filled with a faint

---

[1] The Chinese lunar calendar.

smell of powder. It was on such a night that I returned to my native place, Luchen. Although I call it my native place, I had had no home there for some time, so I had to put up temporarily with a certain Mr. Lu, the fourth son of his family. He is a member of our clan, and belongs to the generation before mine, so I ought to call him "Fourth Uncle." An old student of the imperial college who went in for Neo-Confucianism,[2] I found him very little changed in any way, simply slightly older, but without any moustache as yet. When we met, after exchanging a few polite remarks he said I was fatter, and after saying I was fatter immediately started a violent attack on the revolutionaries.[3] I knew this was not meant personally, because the object of the attack was still Kang Yu-wei. Nevertheless, conversation proved difficult, so that in a short time I found myself alone in the study.

The next day I got up very late, and after lunch went out to see some relatives and friends. The day after I did the same. None of them was greatly changed, simply slightly older; but every family was busy preparing for "the sacrifice." This is the great end-of-year ceremony in Luchen, when people reverently welcome the God of Fortune and solicit good fortune for the coming year. They kill chickens and geese and buy pork, scouring and scrubbing until all the women's arms turn red in the water, some of them still wearing twisted silver bracelets. After the meat is cooked some chopsticks are thrust into it at random, and this is called the "offering." It is set out at dawn when incense and candles are lit, and they reverently invite the God of Fortune to come and partake of the offering. Only men can be worshippers, and after the sacrifice they naturally continue to let off firecrackers as before. This happens every year, in every family, provided they can afford to buy the offering and firecrackers; and this year they naturally followed the old custom.

The day grew overcast and in the afternoon it actually started to snow, the biggest snow-flakes as large as plum blossom petals, fluttering about the sky; and this combined with the smoke and air of activity to make Luchen appear in a ferment. When I returned to my uncle's study the roof of the house was already white with snow and the room also appeared brighter, lighting up very clearly the great red stone rubbing of the character for Longevity hanging on the wall, written by the Taoist saint Chen Tuan. One of a pair of scrolls had fallen down and was lying loosely rolled up on the long table, but the other was still hanging there, bearing the words: "By understanding reason we achieve tranquillity of mind." Idly, I went to turn over the books on the table beneath the window, but all I could find was a pile of what looked like an incomplete set of *Kang Hsi's Dictionary*, a volume of Chiang Yung's *Notes to Chu Hsi's Philosophical Writings* and a volume of *Commentaries on the Four Books*. At all events, I made up my mind to leave the next day.

Besides, the very thought of my meeting with Hsiang Lin's Wife the day before made me uncomfortable. It had happened in the afternoon. I had been visiting a friend in the eastern part of the town. As I came out I met her by the river, and seeing the way she fastened her eyes on me I knew very well she meant to speak to me. Of all the people I had seen this time at Luchen none had changed as much as she: her hair, which had been streaked with white five years before, was now completely white, quite unlike someone in her forties. Her face was fearfully thin and dark in its sallowness, and had moreover lost its former expression of sadness, looking as if carved out of wood. Only an occasional flicker of her eyes showed she was still a living creature. In one hand she carried a wicker basket, in which was a

---

[2]Neo-Confucianism is the school of Confucian thought from the Song Dynasty (960–1279), which claimed that all things in the universe, including the ordering of human society, were ordained by reason and could not be changed.

[3]Sponsors of a liberal reform movement in 1898. Their leader, Kang Yu-wei, fled China under duress and eventually organized a royalist faction advocating constitutional monarchy.

broken bowl, empty; in the other she held a bamboo pole longer than herself, split at the bottom: it was clear she had become a beggar.

I stood still, waiting for her to come and ask for money.

"You have come back?" she asked me first.

"Yes."

"That is very good. You are a scholar, and have travelled too and seen a lot. I just want to ask you something." Her lustreless eyes suddenly gleamed.

I could never have guessed she would talk to me like this. I stood there taken by surprise.

"It is this." She drew two paces nearer, and whispered very confidentially: "After a person dies, does he turn into a ghost or not?"

I was seized with foreboding, seeing her fixing me with her eyes. A shiver ran down my spine and I felt more nervous than when an unexpected examination is sprung on one at school, and unfortunately the teacher stands by one's side. Personally, I had never given the least thought to the question of the existence of spirits; but in this emergency how should I answer her? Hesitating for a moment, I reflected: "It is the tradition here to believe in spirits, yet she, she seems to be sceptical—perhaps it would be better to say she hopes: hopes that there is immortality and yet hopes that there is not. Why increase the sufferings of the wretched? To give her something to look forward to, it would be better to say there is."

"There may be, I think," I told her hesitantly.

"Then, there must also be a Hell?"

"What, Hell?" Greatly startled, I could only try to evade the question. "Hell? According to reason there should be one too—but not necessarily. Who cares about it anyway? . . ."

"Then will all the people of one family who have died see each other again?"

"Well, as to whether they will see each other again or not. . . ." I realized now that I was still a complete fool; all my hesitation and reflection had been unable to stand up to three questions. Immediately I lost confidence and wanted to say the exact opposite of what I had told her before. "In this case . . . as a matter of fact, I am not sure. . . . Actually, regarding the question of ghosts, I am not sure either."

In order to avoid further importunate questions, I walked off, and beat a hasty retreat to my uncle's house, feeling exceedingly uncomfortable. I thought to myself: "I am afraid my answer will prove dangerous to her. Probably it is just that when other people are celebrating she feels lonely by herself, but could there be any other reason? Could she have had some premonition? If there is any other reason, and something happens as a result, then, through my answer, I should be held responsible to a certain extent." Finally, however, I ended by laughing at myself, thinking that such a chance meeting could have no great significance, and yet I was taking it so to heart; no wonder certain educationalists called me a neurotic case. Moreover I had distinctly said, "I am not sure," contradicting my previous answer; so even if anything should happen, it would have nothing at all to do with me.

"I am not sure" is a most useful phrase.

Inexperienced and rash young men often take it upon themselves to solve people's problems for them or choose doctors for them, and if by any chance things turn out badly, they are probably held to blame; but by simply concluding with this phrase "I am not sure," one can free oneself of all responsibility. At this time I felt even more strongly the necessity for such a phrase, since even in speaking with a beggar woman there was no dispensing with it.

However, I continued to feel uncomfortable, and even after a night's rest my mind kept running on this, as if I had a premonition of some untoward development. In that oppressive snowy weather, in the gloomy study, this discomfort kept increasing.

It would be better to leave: I should go back to town the next day. The boiled shark's fins in the Fu Hsing Restaurant had cost a dollar for a large portion, and I wondered if this cheap and delicious dish had increased in price or not. Although the friends who had accompanied me in the old days had scattered, the shark's fins still had to be tasted, even if I was alone. At all events, I made up my mind to leave the next day.

After many experiences that things which I hoped would not happen and felt should not happen invariably did happen, I was desperately afraid this would prove another such case. And, indeed, strange things did begin to happen. Towards evening I heard talking—it sounded like a discussion—in the inner room; but soon the conversation ended, and all I heard was my uncle saying loudly as he walked out: "Not earlier nor later, but just at this time—sure sign of a bad character!"

I felt first astonished, then very uncomfortable, thinking these words must refer to me. I looked outside the door, but no one was there. I contained myself with difficulty till their servant came in before dinner to brew a pot of tea, when at last I had a chance to make some enquiries.

"With whom was Mr. Lu angry just now?" I asked.

"Why, still with Hsiang Lin's Wife," he replied briefly.

"Hsiang Lin's Wife? How was that?" I asked again.

"She's dead."

"Dead?" My heart suddenly missed a beat. I started, and probably changed colour too. But all this time he did not raise his head, so he was probably quite unaware of how I felt. Then I controlled myself, and asked:

"When did she die?"

"When? Last night, or else today, I'm not sure."

"How did she die?"

"How did she die? Why, of poverty of course." He answered placidly and, still without having raised his head to look at me, went out.

However, my agitation was only short-lived, for now that something I had felt imminent had already taken place, I no longer had to take refuge in my "I'm not sure," or the servant's expression "dying of poverty" for comfort. My heart already felt lighter. Only from time to time did there still seem to be something weighing on it. Dinner was served, and my uncle accompanied me solemnly. I wanted to ask about Hsiang Lin's Wife, but knew that although he had read, "Ghosts and spirits are properties of Nature," he had retained many superstitions, and on the eve of this sacrifice it was out of the question to mention anything like death or illness. In case of necessity one could use veiled allusions, but unfortunately I did not know how to, so although questions kept rising to the tip of my tongue, I had to bite them back. From his solemn expression I suddenly suspected that he looked on me as choosing not earlier nor later but just this time to come and trouble him, and that I was also a bad character; therefore to set his mind at rest I told him at once that I intended to leave Luchen the next day and go back to the city. He did not press me greatly to stay. So we quietly finished the meal.

In winter the days are short and, now that it was snowing, darkness already enveloped the whole town. Everybody was busy beneath the lamplight, but outside the windows was very quiet. Snow-flakes fell on the thickly piled snow, making one feel even more lonely. I sat by myself under the yellow gleam of the vegetable oil lamp and thought, "This poor woman, abandoned by people in the dust as a tiresome and worn-out toy, once left her own imprint in the dust, and those who enjoy life must have wondered at her for wishing to prolong her existence; but now at least she has been swept clear by eternity. Whether spirits exist or not I do not know; but in the present world when a meaningless existence ends, so that someone whom others are tired of seeing is no longer seen, it is just as well, both for the individual concerned and for others." I listened quietly to see if I could hear the snow falling outside the window, still pursuing this train of thought, until gradually I felt less ill at ease.

Yet fragments of her life, seen or heard before, now combined to form one whole.

She did not belong to Luchen. One year at the beginning of winter, when my uncle's family wanted to change their maidservant, Old Mrs. Wei, who acted as introducer, brought her in. Her hair was tied with white bands, she wore a black skirt, blue jacket and pale green bodice, and was about twenty-six, with a pale face but rosy cheeks. Old Mrs. Wei called her Hsiang Lin's Wife, and said that she was a neighbour of her mother's family, and because her husband was dead she wanted to come out to work. My uncle knitted his brows and my aunt immediately understood that he disapproved of her because she was a widow. She looked very suitable, though, with big strong feet and hands, and a meek expression; and she had not said a word but showed every sign of being tractable and hard-working. So my aunt paid no attention to my uncle's frown, but kept her. During the period of probation she worked from morning till night, as if she found resting dull, and she was so strong that she could do a man's work; accordingly on the third day it was settled, and each month she was to be paid five hundred cash.

Everybody called her Hsiang Lin's Wife. They did not ask her her own name; but since she was introduced by someone from Wei Village who said she was a neighbour, presumably her name was also Wei. She was not very talkative, only answering when other people spoke to her, and her answers were brief. It was not until a dozen days or so had passed that they learned little by little that she still had a severe mother in law at home and a younger brother in-law more than ten years old, who could cut wood. Her husband, who had been a woodcutter too, had died in the spring. He had been ten years younger than she. This little was all that people learned from her.

The days passed quickly, but she worked as hard as ever; she would eat anything, and did not spare herself. Everybody agreed that the Lu family had found a very good maidservant, who really got through more work than a hard-working man. At the end of the year she swept, mopped, killed chickens and geese and sat up to boil the sacrificial meat, single-handed, so the family did not have to hire extra help. Nevertheless she, on her side, was satisfied; gradually the trace of a smile appeared at the corner of her mouth, and her face became whiter and plumper.

New Year was scarcely over when she came back from washing rice by the river looking pale, and said that she had just seen in the distance a man wandering on the opposite bank who looked very like her husband's cousin, and probably he had come to look for her. My aunt, much alarmed, made detailed enquiries, but failed to get any further information. As soon as my uncle learned of it he frowned and said, "This is bad. She must have run away from her husband's family."

Before long this inference that she had run away was confirmed.

About a fortnight later, just as everybody was beginning to forget what had happened, Old Mrs. Wei suddenly called, bringing with her a woman in her thirties who, she said, was the maidservant's mother-in-law. Although the woman looked like a villager, she behaved with great self-possession and had a ready tongue in her head. After the usual polite remarks she apologized for coming to take her daughter-in-law home, saying there was a great deal to be done at the beginning of spring, and since there were only old people and children at home they were short-handed.

"Since it is her mother-in-law who wants her to go back, what is there to be said?" was my uncle's comment.

Thereupon her wages were reckoned up. They amounted to one thousand seven hundred and fifty cash, all of which she had left with her mistress without using a single coin; and now my aunt gave the entire amount to her mother-in-law. The latter also took her clothes, thanked Mr. and Mrs. Lu and went out. By this time it was already noon.

"Oh, the rice! Didn't Hsiang Lin's Wife go to wash the rice?" my aunt exclaimed some time later. Probably she was rather hungry, so that she remembered lunch.

Thereupon everybody set about looking for the rice basket. My aunt went first to the kitchen, then to the hall, then to the bedroom; but not a trace of it was to be seen anywhere. My uncle went outside, but could not find it either; only when he went right up to the riverside did he see it, set down fair and square on the bank, with a bundle of vegetables at the side.

Some people there told him that a boat with a white awning had moored there in the morning, but since the awning covered the boat completely they did not know who was inside, and before this incident no one had paid any attention to it. But when Hsiang Lin's Wife came out to wash rice, two men looking like country people jumped off the boat just as she was kneeling down and seizing hold of her carried her on board. After several shouts and cries, Hsiang Lin's Wife became silent: they had probably stopped her mouth. Then two women walked up, one of them a stranger and the other Old Mrs. Wei. When the people who told this story tried to peep into the boat they could not see very clearly, but she seemed to be lying bound on the floor of the boat.

"Disgraceful! Still . . ." said my uncle.

That day my aunt cooked the midday meal herself, and my cousin Ah Niu lit the fire.

After lunch Old Mrs. Wei came again.

"Disgraceful!" said my uncle.

"What is the meaning of this? How dare you come here again!" My aunt, who was washing dishes, started scolding as soon as she saw her. "You recommended her yourself, and then plotted to have her carried off, causing all this upstir. What will people think? Are you trying to make a laughing-stock of our family?"

"Aiya, I was really taken in! Now I have come specially to clear this business up. When she asked me to find her work, how was I to know that she had left home without her mother-in-law's consent? I am very sorry, Mr. Lu, Mrs. Lu. Because I am so old and foolish and careless, I have offended my patrons. However, it is lucky for me that your family is always so generous and kind, and unwilling to be hard on your inferiors. This time I promise to find you someone good to make up for my mistake."

"Still . . ." said my uncle.

Thereupon Hsiang Lin's Wife's business was concluded, and before long it was also forgotten.

Only my aunt, because the maidservants taken on afterwards were all lazy or fond of stealing food, or else both lazy and fond of stealing food, with not a good one in the lot, still often spoke of Hsiang Lin's Wife. On such occasions she would always say to herself, "I wonder what has become of her now?" meaning that she would like to have her back. But by the following New Year she too gave up hope.

The New Year's holiday was nearly over when Old Mrs. Wei, already half tipsy, came to pay her respects, and said it was because she had been back to the Wei

Village to visit her mother's family and stayed a few days that she had come late. During the course of conversation they naturally came to speak of Hsiang Lin's Wife.

"She?" said Mrs. Wei cheerfully. "She is in luck now. When her mother-in-law dragged her home, she had already promised her to the sixth son of the Ho family in Ho Village; so not long after she reached home they put her in the bridal chair and sent her off."

"Aiya! What a mother-in-law!" exclaimed my aunt in amazement.

"Ah, madam, you really talk like a great lady! We country folk, poor women, think nothing of that. She still had a younger brother-in-law who had to get married. And if they hadn't found her a husband, where would they have got the money for his wedding? But her mother-in-law is a clever and capable woman, who knows how to drive a good bargain, so she married her off into the mountains. If she had married her to someone in the same village, she wouldn't have got so much money; but very few women are willing to marry someone living in the depth of the mountains, so that she got eighty thousand cash. Now the second son has got married, only costing her fifty thousand for the presents, and after paying the wedding expenses she has still over ten thousand left. Just think, doesn't this show she knows how to drive a good bargain? . . ."

"But was Hsiang Lin's Wife willing?"

"It wasn't a question of being willing or not. Of course anyone would have protested. But they just tied her up with a rope, stuffed her into the bridal chair, carried her to the man's house, put on the bridal head-dress, performed the ceremony in the hall and locked them into their room; and that was that. But Hsiang Lin's Wife is quite a character. I heard she really put up a great struggle, and everybody said it must be because she had worked in a scholar's family that she was different from other people. We go-betweens, madam, see a great deal. When widows remarry, some cry and shout, some threaten to commit suicide, some when they have been carried to the man's house won't go through the ceremony, and some even smash the wedding candlesticks. But Hsiang Lin's Wife was different from the rest. They said she shouted and cursed all the way, so that by the time they had carried her to Ho Village she was completely hoarse. When they dragged her out of the chair, although the two chair-bearers and her young brother-in-law used all their strength, they couldn't force her to go through the ceremony. The moment they were careless enough to loosen their grip—gracious Buddha!—she threw herself against a corner of the table and knocked a big hole in her head. The blood poured out, and although they used two handfuls of incense ashes and bandaged her with two pieces of red cloth, they still couldn't stop the bleeding. Finally it took all of them together to get her shut up with her husband in the bridal chamber, where she went on cursing. Oh, it was really dreadful!" She shook her head, cast down her eyes and said no more.

"And after that what happened?" asked my aunt.

"They said the next day she still didn't get up," said Old Mrs. Wei, raising her eyes.

"And after?"

"After? She got up. At the end of the year she had a baby, a boy, who was two this New Year. These few days when I was at home some people went to Ho Village, and when they came back they said they had seen her and her son, and that both mother and baby are fat. There is no mother-in-law over her, the man is a strong fellow who can earn a living, and the house is their own. Well, well, she is really in luck."

After this even my aunt gave up talking of Hsiang Lin's Wife.

But one autumn, two New Years after they heard how lucky Hsiang Lin's Wife had been, she actually reappeared at the threshold of my uncle's house. On the table she placed a round bulb-shaped basket, and under the eaves a small roll of bedding. Her hair was still wrapped in white bands, and she wore a black skirt, blue jacket and pale green bodice. But her face was sallow and her cheeks had lost their colour; she kept her eyes downcast, and her eyes, with their tear-stained rims, were no longer bright. Just as before, it was Old Mrs. Wei, looking very benevolent, who brought her in, and who explained at length to my aunt:

"It was really a bolt from the blue. Her husband was so strong nobody could have guessed that a young fellow like that would die of typhoid fever. First he seemed better, but then he ate a bowl of cold rice and the sickness came back. Luckily she had the boy, and she can work, whether it is chopping wood, picking tea-leaves or raising silkworms; so at first she was able to carry on. But then who could know that the child, too, would be carried off by a wolf? Although it was nearly the end of spring, still wolves came to the village—how could anyone have guessed that? Now she is all on her own. Her brother-in-law came to take the house, and turned her out; so she has really no way open to her but to come and ask help from her former mistress. Luckily this time there is nobody to stop her, and you happen to be wanting a new servant, so I have brought her here. I think someone who is used to your ways is much better than a new hand...."

"I was really stupid, really..." Hsiang Lin's Wife raised her listless eyes to say. "I only knew that when it snows the wild beasts in the glen have nothing to eat and may come to the villages; I didn't know that in spring they could come too. I got up at dawn and opened the door, filled a small basket with beans and called our Ah Mao to go and sit at the threshold and shell the beans. He was very obedient and always did as I told him: he went out. Then I chopped wood at the back of the house and washed the rice, and when the rice was in the pan and I wanted to boil the beans I called Ah Mao, but there was no answer; and when I went out to look, all I could see was beans scattered on the ground, but no Ah Mao. He never went to other families to play; and in fact at each place that I went to ask, there was no sign of him. I became desperate, and begged people to go to look for him. Only in the afternoon, after looking everywhere else, did they go to look in the glen and see one of his little shoes caught on a bramble. 'That's bad,' they said, 'he must have met a wolf.' And sure enough when they went further in there he was, lying in the wolf's lair, with all his entrails eaten away, his hand still tightly clutching that little basket...." At this point she started crying, and was unable to complete the sentence.

My aunt had been undecided at first, but by the end of this story the rims of her eyes were rather red. After thinking for a moment she told her to take the round basket and bedding into the servants' quarters. Old Mrs. Wei heaved a long sigh as if relieved of a great burden. Hsiang Lin's Wife looked a little more at ease than when first she came and, without having to be told the way, quietly took away her bedding. From this time on she worked again as a maidservant in Luchen.

Everybody still called her Hsiang Lin's Wife.

However, she had changed a great deal. She had not been there more than three days before her master and mistress realized that she was not as quick as before, her memory was much worse, and her impassive face never showed the least trace of a smile; thus my aunt already expressed herself very far from satisfied. When the woman first arrived, although my uncle frowned as before, still, they invariably had such difficulty in finding servants that he did not object very strongly, only secretly warned my aunt that while such people may seem very pitiful they exert a bad moral influence. Thus although it would be all right for her to do ordinary work she must not join in the preparations for sacrifice; they would have to prepare all the dishes themselves, for otherwise they would be unclean and the ancestors would not accept them.

The most important event in my uncle's household was ancestral sacrifice, and formerly this had been Hsiang Lin's Wife's busiest time; but now she had very little to do. When the table was placed in the centre of the hall and the curtain fastened, she still remembered how to set out the winecups and chopsticks in the old way.

"Hsiang Lin's Wife, put those down!" said my aunt hastily. "I'll do it!"

She sheepishly withdrew her hand and went to get the candlesticks.

"Hsiang Lin's Wife, put those down!" cried my aunt hastily again. "I'll fetch them."

After walking round several times without finding anything to do, she could only go hesitantly away. All she did that day was to sit by the stove and feed the fire.

The people in the town still called her Hsiang Lin's Wife, but in a different tone from before; and although they talked to her still, their manner was colder. She did not mind this in the least, only, looking straight in front of her, she would tell everybody her story, which night or day was never out of her mind.

"I was really stupid, really," she would say. "I only knew that when it snows the wild beasts in the glen have nothing to eat and may come to the villages; I didn't know that in spring they could come too. I got up at dawn and opened the door, filled a small basket with beans and called our Ah Mao to go and sit at the threshold and shell them. He was very obedient and always did as I told him: he went out. Then I chopped wood at the back of the house and washed the rice, and when the rice was in the pan and I wanted to boil the beans I called Ah Mao, but there was no answer; and when I went out to look, all I could see was beans scattered on the ground, but no Ah Mao. He never went to other families to play; and in fact at each place that I went to ask, there was no sign of him. I became desperate, and begged people to go to look for him. Only in the afternoon, after looking everywhere else, did they go to look in the glen and see one of his little shoes caught on a bramble. 'That's bad,' they said, 'he must have met a wolf.' And sure enough when they went further in there he was, lying in the wolf's lair, with all his entrails eaten away, his hand still tightly clutching that small basket. . . ." At this point she would start crying and her voice would trail away.

This story was rather effective, and when men heard it they often stopped smiling and walked away disconcerted, while the women not only seemed to forgive her but their faces immediately lost their contemptuous look and they added their tears to hers. There were some old women who had not heard her speaking in the street, who went specially to look for her, to hear her sad tale. When her voice trailed away and she started to cry, they joined in, shedding the tears which had gathered in their eyes. Then they sighed, and went away satisfied, exchanging comments.

She asked nothing better than to tell her sad story over and over again, often gathering three or four hearers. But before long everybody knew it by heart, until even in the eyes of the most kindly, Buddha-fearing old ladies not a trace of tears could be seen. In the end, almost everyone in the town could recite her tale, and it bored and exasperated them to hear it.

"I was really stupid, really . . ." she would begin.

"Yes, you only knew that in snowy weather the wild beasts in the mountains had nothing to eat and might come down to the villages." Promptly cutting short her recital, they walked away.

She would stand there open-mouthed, looking at them with a dazed expression, and then go away too, as if she also felt disconcerted. But she still brooded over it, hoping from other topics such as small baskets, beans and other people's children, to lead up to the story of her Ah Mao. If she saw a child of two or three, she would say, "Oh dear, if my Ah Mao were still alive, he would be just so big. . . ."

Children seeing the look in her eyes would take fright and, clutching the hems of their mothers' clothes, try to tug them away. Thereupon she would be left by herself again, and finally walk away disconcerted. Later everybody knew what she was like, and it only needed a child present for them to ask her with an artificial smile, "Hsiang Lin's Wife, if your Ah Mao were alive, wouldn't he be just as big as that?"

She probably did not realize that her story, after having been turned over and tasted by people for so many days, had long since become stale, only exciting disgust and contempt; but from the way people smiled she seemed to know that they were cold and sarcastic, and that there was no need for her to say any more. She would simply look at them, not answering a word.

In Luchen people celebrate New Year in a big way: from the twentieth day of the twelfth month onwards preparations start. This time my uncle's household found it necessary to hire a temporary manservant, but since there was still a great deal to do they also called in another maidservant, Liu Ma, to help. Chickens and geese had to be killed; but Liu Ma was a devout woman who abstained from meat, did not kill living things, and would only wash the sacrificial dishes. Hsiang Lin's Wife had nothing to do but feed the fire. She sat there, resting, watching Liu Ma as she washed the sacrificial dishes. A light snow began to fall.

"Dear me, I was really stupid," said Hsiang Lin's Wife, as if to herself, looking at the sky and sighing.

"Hsiang Lin's Wife, there you go again," said Liu Ma, looking at her impatiently. "I ask you: that wound on your forehead, wasn't it then you got it?"

"Uh, huh," she answered vaguely.

"Let me ask you: what made you willing after all?"

"Me?"

"Yes. What I think is, you must have been willing; otherwise. . . ."

"Oh dear, you don't know how strong he was."

"I don't believe it. I don't believe he was so strong that you really couldn't keep him off. You must have been willing, only you put the blame on his being so strong."

"Oh dear, you . . . you try for yourself and see." She smiled.

Liu Ma's lined face broke into a smile too, making it wrinkled like a walnut; her small beady eyes swept Hsiang Lin's Wife's forehead and fastened on her eyes. As if rather embarrassed, Hsiang Lin's Wife immediately stopped smiling, averted her eyes and looked at the snow-flakes.

"Hsiang Lin's Wife, that was really a bad bargain," said Liu Ma mysteriously. "If you had held out longer or knocked yourself to death, it would have been better. As it is, after living with your second husband for less than two years, you are guilty of a great crime. Just think: when you go down to the lower world in future, these two men's ghosts will still fight over you. To which will you go? The King of Hell will have no choice but to cut you in two and divide you between them. I think, really. . . ."

Then terror showed in her face. This was something she had never heard in the mountains.

"I think you had better take precautions beforehand. Go to the Tutelary God's Temple and buy a threshold to be your substitute, so that thousands of people can walk over it and trample on it, in order to atone for your sins in this life and avoid torment after death."

At the time Hsiang Lin's Wife said nothing, but she must have taken this to heart, for the next morning when she got up there were dark circles beneath her eyes. And after breakfast she went to the Tutelary God's Temple at the west end of the village, and asked to buy a threshold. The temple priests would not agree at first, and only when she shed tears did they give a grudging consent. The price was twelve thousand cash.

She had long since given up talking to people, because Ah Mao's story had been received with such contempt; but news of her conversation with Liu Ma that day spread, and many people took a fresh interest in her and came again to tease her into talking. As for the subject, that had naturally changed to deal with the wound on her forehead.

"Hsiang Lin's Wife, I ask you: what made you willing after all that time?" one would cry.

"Oh, what a pity, to have had this knock for nothing," another looking at her scar would agree.

Probably she knew from their smiles and tone of voice that they were making fun of her, for she always looked steadily at them without saying a word, and finally did not even turn her head. All day long she kept her lips tightly closed, bearing on her head the scar which everyone considered a mark of shame, silently shopping, sweeping the floor, washing vegetables, preparing rice. Only after nearly a year did she take from my aunt her wages which had been accumulating, which she changed for twelve silver dollars, and asking for leave she went to the west end of the town. But in less time than it takes for a meal she was back again, looking much comforted, and with an unaccustomed light in her eyes; and she told my aunt happily that she had bought a threshold in the Tutelary God's Temple.

When the time came for the ancestral sacrifice at the winter equinox, she worked harder than ever, and seeing my aunt take out the sacrificial utensils and carry the table with Ah Niu into the middle of the hall, she went confidently to fetch the winecups and chopsticks.

"Put those down, Hsiang Lin's Wife!" my aunt called out hastily.

She withdrew her hand as if scorched, her face turned ashen-grey, and instead of fetching the candlesticks she just stood there dazed. Only when my uncle came to burn incense and told her to go, did she walk away. This time the change in her was very great, for the next day not only were her eyes sunken, but even her spirit seemed broken. Moreover she became very timid, not only afraid of the dark and shadows, but also of the sight of anyone. Even her own master or mistress made her look as frightened as a little mouse that has come out of its hole in the daytime. For the rest, she would sit stupidly, like a wooden statue. In less than half a year her hair began to turn grey, and her memory became much worse, reaching a point when she was constantly forgetting to go and prepare the rice.

"What has come over Hsiang Lin's Wife? It would really have been better not to have kept her that time." My aunt would sometimes speak like this in front of her, as if to warn her.

However, she remained this way, so that it was impossible to see any hope of her improving. Then they decided to get rid of her and tell her to go back to Old Mrs. Wei. While I was at Luchen they were still only talking of this; but judging by what happened later, it is evident that this was what they must have done. But whether after leaving my uncle's household she became a beggar, or whether she went first to Old Mrs. Wei's house and later became a beggar, I do not know.

I was woken up by firecrackers exploding noisily close at hand, saw the glow of the yellow oil lamp as large as a bean, and heard the splutter of fireworks as my uncle's household celebrated the sacrifice. I knew that it was nearly dawn. I felt bewildered, hearing as in a dream the confused continuous sound of distant crackers which seemed to form one dense cloud of noise in the sky, joining with the whirling snow-flakes to envelop the whole town. Enveloped in this medley of sound, relaxed and at ease, the doubt which had preyed on me from dawn to early night was swept clean away by the atmosphere of celebration, and I felt only that the saints of heaven and earth had accepted the sacrifice and incense and were all reeling with intoxication in the sky, preparing to give the people of Luchen boundless good fortune.

JAMES JOYCE
[1882–1941]

James Joyce chose to live out his adult life in self-imposed exile on the Continent, keeping a distance from his native Dublin, Irish Catholicism, and most members of his birth family. Nonetheless, through his work Joyce's readers feel as though they come to know the Irish people and places and institutions luminously well, with all the beauties and sorrows of their intertwined histories. The thorough realism of his works often drew strong criticism from a prudish public; in 1933, it took a landmark United States District Court decision to make the novel *Ulysses* (1922) available to American readers, overruling the Post Office's charge that the book was obscene. When he first encountered such violent reactions, Joyce wrote pleadingly to his brother Stanislaus in 1903,

> Don't you think there is a certain resemblance between the mystery of the Mass and what I am trying to do . . . to give people some kind of intellectual pleasure or spiritual enjoyment by converting the bread of everyday life into something that has a permanent artistic life of its own . . . ?

Joyce's early fictions do reveal a transcendent reality in commonplace Irish urban people's daily affairs, and transcendence was a miracle he would continue to perform with words all his life. Even in the midst of his most complicated and puzzling linguistic experiments, Joyce's narratives remain rooted in the quotidian life of the Irish people.

LIFE

James Joyce's father, John Joyce, versions of whom appear in many of Joyce's works, was a charming, spendthrift alcoholic with passionate political sympathies for freeing Ireland from British rule. The elder Joyce especially championed Charles Stuart Parnell (1846–1891), the brilliant Protestant Irish nationalist leader brought low by scandal when he was named in a notorious divorce case as the adulterous lover of Kitty O'Shea. Like his father before him, James Joyce was often to identify himself with Parnell, especially when he was accused of offending Christian decency by the sexual and scatological content of his fiction. Joyce's mother, May, a woman with musical gifts and a forbearing disposition, gave birth to ten babies over a twelve-year period. James Augustine Joyce, born on February 2, 1882, was the first. Although John Joyce managed family properties and had been given a political appointment in the office of the Rates Collector in Dublin, he handily brought his family down from moderate prosperity into wracking poverty by the time he was in his forties; between Joyce's birth in 1882 and the day he left Ireland for good at the age of twenty-two, his father had moved the family twenty times from one shabby house to another. Joyce deplored his father's reckless waste, but he admired his fine tenor voice, his flair for mimicry, his flashing wit, his lively way with a story.

Joyce's parents nicknamed him "Sunny Jim" for his intelligence and beaming good nature. Like many eldest children of unstable households, he was precociously able to control his temper and to care for himself and his brothers and sisters, leading them and the neighboring children in games and adventures. Joyce's brother Stanislaus vividly recalled being cast in a backyard production as Adam to his sister Margaret Alice's Eve, while Joyce starred as the hissing, wriggling serpent. The only problem he seemed to manifest in his boyhood was his poor eyesight, which was to trouble him through life.

Despite financial woes, John Joyce saw to it that his eldest received an excellent Jesuit education; long after Joyce had rejected Roman Catholicism, he praised the Jesuits for teaching him "to arrange things in such a way that they become easy to survey and judge." The early chapters of *A Portrait of the Artist as a Young Man* (1916) suggest some of the rigorous atmosphere of that education. Joyce took from his Jesuit teachers not only their vaunted skill in logic and debate, but a deep appreciation of symbolism and the sheer power of language in its own right. Joyce was a brilliant student who easily took prizes and was awarded scholarships after his father became unable to pay tuition.

A Portrait of the Artist as a Young Man recounts the conflict between Joyce's powerful sexual urges and his religious guilt, a conflict that began when Joyce was about fourteen, and between his call toward religion and his devotion to the religion of art. When he was about seventeen, convinced that his Jesuit teachers were repressive and narrow, Joyce left the Church resolved to replace his faith with a commitment to becoming a writer. At University College in Dublin, where Joyce solidified his conception of himself as an artist, he lost interest in the rigid academic work expected of him and tried his hand at poetry, short stories, and criticism of contemporary literature. Unlike other Irish writers such as Yeats and Synge, Joyce was not drawn to the voguish revival of Gaelic writing and Irish themes. Instead, he avidly read and praised Continental writers such as Ibsen, whom he thought of as more universal and "impersonal" than Irish artists. In his own career, he would go on to become a spectacular example of the maxim that the universal is always most effectively demonstrated when embedded in the particular.

In 1900, when *The Fortnightly Review* published a review essay Joyce wrote on the drama of Ibsen, the great man himself sent a message to Joyce thanking him. This heady event was transformative to an eighteen-year-old aspiring writer. As biographer Richard Ellmann puts it, "Before Ibsen's letter Joyce was an Irishman; after it, he was a European." Joyce threw himself into the study of languages and literature, beginning to prepare for a life he envisioned beyond Ireland. After 1902 he lived on the Continent, returning to Ireland only for brief periods. Close to starvation, he eked out a living in Paris by teaching English while he worked on his "Epiphanies," short notebook entries that recorded overheard conversations or sights glimpsed in passing that seemed to embody flashes of insight into the human condition. He returned to Dublin in April of 1903 to be at his mother's deathbed. When May Joyce died in August after a drawn-out struggle against cancer, Joyce stayed on in Dublin for a while, teaching school, but by the following year he was back on the Continent, disgusted by the political corruption and smug provincialism of his homeland. On this trip he brought back with him the beautiful Nora Barnacle, an uneducated, perceptive, earthy young woman from Galway in the west of Ireland, an isolated region Joyce identified with life lived simply and passionately, as opposed to the artificiality and hypocrisy he found in Dublin. Scorning conventional ceremonies and pieties, Joyce would not marry Barnacle until 1931, but they were a devoted couple from the first. For the rest of their lives, Joyce, Barnacle, and their children—Giorgio, born in 1905, and Lucia, in 1907—divided their residence among Paris, Trieste, and Zurich.

A series of patrons, notably the British editor Harriet Shaw Weaver, helped to support the family. In time, Joyce would make friends with many young English and American expatriate writers, among them Ezra Pound, Ford Maddox Ford, Djuna Barnes, Ernest Hemingway, T. S. Eliot, and Samuel Beckett, though his own family would always most engage his energy and imagination.

In 1904 Joyce began work on *Dubliners,* a collection of short stories that sought to capture a city and its people; the book was not published until 1914 because editors and printers feared obscenity and libel charges. In 1916 he published his semiautobiographical novel *A Portrait of the Artist as a Young Man,* about a boy's maturing and committing himself to the vocation of writing.

Joyce was not the first prose writer to use realistic and detailed renderings of everyday life that become suddenly transmuted into moments of deep insight, moments he himself called "epiphanies"; George Eliot, Chekhov, and Flaubert come to mind as one reads both *Dubliners* and *A Portrait.* But Joyce was one of the first writers—his contemporary Gertrude Stein (1874–1946) preceded him—to experiment on a large scale with prose sentences and the novelistic form. Joyce is especially known for the two giant prose works wherein he forged increasingly innovative language and structure. Joyce challenged all previous ideas about the nature of fiction in *Ulysses,* the story of one day in the life of a middle-class Dublin citizen, and then even more radically in *Finnegans Wake* (1939), the sprawling epic dream of a representative Irishman, a dream that seeks to embrace all human history. He energetically disassembled ordinary grammatical structure and narrative order; punned wildly in a multitude of languages; borrowed freely from popular culture the vocabularies of the music hall, sports, and advertising; took ideas from contemporary sciences, medieval historians, and conversations in bars; and superimposed the great Homeric, Celtic, and Teutonic myth-cycles upon the lives of his urban Irish characters, thereby revealing the extraordinary dimensions of the most ordinary lives.

The latter years of Joyce's life were troubled by his failing eyesight and by daughter Lucia's descent into schizophrenia; Joyce always had great difficulty in accepting the gravity of his daughter's illness, and refused for many years to institutionalize her, thus ensuring a chaotic home life for the family. In December 1940, after the German occupation of France, the Joyces fled their home in Paris with their grandson and crossed the border into Switzerland with what belongings they could carry, wheeling the little boy's treasured bicycle before them. Joyce died suddenly in Zurich a few weeks later of a perforated ulcer.

WORK

Of *Dubliners,* the collection in which "The Dead" appears, Joyce said,

> My intention was to write a chapter of the moral history of my country and I chose Dublin for the scene because that city seemed to me the center of paralysis. I have tried to present it to the indifferent public under four of its aspects: childhood, adolescence, maturity, and public life.

In *Dubliners,* three or four stories apiece center on people in one of these phases of life. A child feels helpless anger when he learns the bazaar about which he has spun romantic fantasies is nothing but a tawdry commercial venture; a young woman, bound by a promise made to her dead mother, lacks the courage to board the ship where her lover waits to take her to a new life abroad; men in their middle years who have not fulfilled their dreams of adventure now feel trapped in their marriages and numbing clerical jobs, and take out their alcoholic bitterness on their families; the ineffectual complacency of a group of small-time political hacks sitting in a darkened room on an election day is thrown into relief when one of them reads aloud an impassioned ode to the fallen

Irish nationalist leader Parnell. Seemingly everyday events bloom with quiet import, as the stories reveal subtle parallels and symbolic interconnections. For example, throughout the stories that make up *Dubliners,* abandoned houses, darkened rooms, blind alleys, and shadowy passageways and staircases all accumulate meaning as symbols of moral blindness, spiritual emptiness, and emotional repression.

Of the fifteen stories in *Dubliners,* "The Dead" was written last and is placed at the end of the collection, gathering together the imagery and the import of all the other stories. It is also the most tender of the *Dubliners* stories; while Joyce was quite capable of savaging the complacent pieties of bourgeois Irish people, he told his brother Stanislaus that he wanted to honor one native trait he felt he could honestly praise, namely, Irish hospitality. In this quiet and beautifully textured story, the Misses Morkan, two elderly music teachers, give their annual banquet and musicale for their relations, friends, and pupils. Their nephew Gabriel Conroy, through whose consciousness the story is largely filtered, is a critical if polite observer of the evening's events. As he prepares himself to give his after-dinner speech on Irish warmth, he coldly notes the superficiality and social hypocrisy going on all around him. Gabriel is a mildly pompous intellectual who feels superior to most of the other guests. Indeed, many of the people at his aunts' party are in one way or another "paralyzed"—frozen into fixed opinions, smug in their moral certainties, shackled by inhibitions, alcoholism, or old age.

As the evening wears on and the snow deepens outside, it becomes clear that for the little company gathered together in their temporary refuge of warmth and light, memories of the past are more vivid than their present lives. Old-time tenors, long-ago parties, dead friends and relatives are evoked with much laughter and wistfulness and regret, and the middle-aged Gabriel finds himself restlessly wishing to assert his own present sexuality and vitality. He longs to be outside walking briskly through the snow, and then conceives an intense desire to make love to his wife, Gretta. But Gretta's own secret memories of the dead have been stirred, and Gabriel's epiphany comes when he discovers the wife to whom he hoped to make love still grieves afresh for a passionate working-class boy she once knew, a boy who died years ago for love of her. In the breathtaking final image of the snow falling softly through the universe, obliterating all individual detail, Joyce's story suddenly expands into a vision of the mortality that unites all of us, the living and the dead alike.

SUGGESTED READINGS

Richard Ellmann's *James Joyce* (second edition, 1982) is a masterful critical biography. Brenda Maddox's complementary work, *Nora: A Biography of Nora Joyce* (1988), reveals the part his wife played in Joyce's work as well as in his life. Collections of essays on *Dubliners* include Peter K. Garrett, editor, *Twentieth Century Interpretations of Dubliners* (1968), and *James Joyce's Dubliners: Critical Essays,* edited by Clive Hart (1969).

The Dead

Lily, the caretaker's daughter, was literally run off her feet. Hardly had she brought one gentleman into the little pantry behind the office on the ground floor and helped him off with his overcoat than the wheezy hall-door bell clanged again and she had to scamper along the bare hallway to let in another guest. It was well for her she had not to attend to the ladies also. But Miss Kate and Miss Julia had thought of that and had converted the bathroom upstairs into a ladies' dressing-room. Miss

Kate and Miss Julia were there, gossiping and laughing and fussing, walking after each other to the head of the stairs, peering down over the banisters and calling down to Lily to ask her who had come.

It was always a great affair, the Misses Morkan's annual dance. Everybody who knew them came to it, members of the family, old friends of the family, the members of Julia's choir, any of Kate's pupils that were grown up enough and even some of Mary Jane's pupils too. Never once had it fallen flat. For years and years it had gone off in splendid style as long as anyone could remember; ever since Kate and Julia, after the death of their brother Pat, had left the house in Stoney Batter and taken Mary Jane, their only niece, to live with them in the dark gaunt house on Usher's Island, the upper part of which they had rented from Mr Fulham, the cornfactor[1] on the ground floor. That was a good thirty years ago if it was a day. Mary Jane, who was then a little girl in short clothes, was now the main prop of the household for she had the organ in Haddington Road.[2] She had been through the Academy and gave a pupils' concert every year in the upper room of the Antient Concert Rooms. Many of her pupils belonged to better-class families on the Kingstown and Dalkey line. Old as they were, her aunts also did their share. Julia, though she was quite grey, was still the leading soprano in Adam and Eve's,[3] and Kate, being too feeble to go about much, gave music lessons to beginners on the old square piano in the back room. Lily, the caretaker's daughter, did housemaid's work for them. Though their life was modest they believed in eating well; the best of everything: diamond-bone sirloins, three-shilling tea and the best bottled stout. But Lily seldom made a mistake in the orders so that she got on well with her three mistresses. They were fussy, that was all. But the only thing they would not stand was back answers.

Of course they had good reason to be fussy on such a night. And then it was long after ten o'clock and yet there was no sign of Gabriel and his wife. Besides they were dreadfully afraid that Freddy Malins might turn up screwed.[4] They would not wish for worlds that any of Mary Jane's pupils should see him under the influence; and when he was like that it was sometimes very hard to manage him. Freddy Malins always came late but they wondered what could be keeping Gabriel: and that was what brought them every two minutes to the banisters to ask Lily had Gabriel or Freddy come.

—O, Mr Conroy, said Lily to Gabriel when she opened the door for him, Miss Kate and Miss Julia thought you were never coming. Good-night, Mrs Conroy.

—I'll engage they did, said Gabriel, but they forget that my wife here takes three mortal hours to dress herself.

He stood on the mat, scraping the snow from his goloshes, while Lily led his wife to the foot of the stairs and called out:

—Miss Kate, here's Mrs Conroy.

Kate and Julia came toddling down the dark stairs at once. Both of them kissed Gabriel's wife, said she must be perished alive and asked was Gabriel with her.

—Here I am as right as the mail, Aunt Kate! Go on up. I'll follow, called out Gabriel from the dark.

He continued scraping his feet vigorously while the three women went upstairs, laughing, to the ladies' dressing-room. A light fringe of snow lay like a cape on the

---

[1]Mr. Fulham is an agent who buys and sells grain according to the market price.

[2]Mary Jane plays the organ for services held at Saint Mary's Church in the well-to-do southeastern quarter of Dublin. Saint Mary's was noted in Joyce's time for its fine music.

[3]A Franciscan church located on a Dublin quay and named for a nearby tavern.

[4]Drunk.

shoulders of his overcoat and like toecaps on the toes of his goloshes; and, as the buttons of his overcoat slipped with a squeaking noise through the snow-stiffened frieze,[5] a cold fragrant air from out-of-doors escaped from crevices and folds.

—Is it snowing again, Mr Conroy? asked Lily.

She had preceded him into the pantry to help him off with his overcoat. Gabriel smiled at the three syllables she had given his surname and glanced at her. She was a slim, growing girl, pale in complexion and with hay-coloured hair. The gas in the pantry made her look still paler. Gabriel had known her when she was a child and used to sit on the lowest step nursing a rag doll.

—Yes, Lily, he answered, and I think we're in for a night of it.

He looked up at the pantry ceiling, which was shaking with the stamping and shuffling of feet on the floor above, listened for a moment to the piano and then glanced at the girl, who was folding his overcoat carefully at the end of a shelf.

—Tell me, Lily, he said in a friendly tone, do you still go to school?

—O no, sir, she answered. I'm done schooling this year and more.

—O, then, said Gabriel gaily, I suppose we'll be going to your wedding one of these fine days with your young man, eh?

The girl glanced back at him over her shoulder and said with great bitterness:

—The men that is now is only all palaver and what they can get out of you.

Gabriel coloured as if he felt he had made a mistake and, without looking at her, kicked off his goloshes and flicked actively with his muffler at his patent-leather shoes.

He was a stout tallish young man. The high colour of his cheeks pushed upwards even to his forehead where it scattered itself in a few formless patches of pale red; and on his hairless face there scintillated restlessly the polished lenses and the bright gilt rims of the glasses which screened his delicate and restless eyes. His glossy black hair was parted in the middle and brushed in a long curve behind his ears where it curled slightly beneath the groove left by his hat.

When he had flicked lustre into his shoes he stood up and pulled his waistcoat down more tightly on his plump body. Then he took a coin rapidly from his pocket.

—O Lily, he said, thrusting it into her hands, it's Christmas-time, isn't it? Just ...here's a little....

He walked rapidly towards the door.

—O no, sir! cried the girl, following him. Really, sir, I wouldn't take it.

—Christmas-time! Christmas-time! said Gabriel, almost trotting to the stairs and waving his hand to her in deprecation.

The girl, seeing that he had gained the stairs, called out after him:

—Well, thank you, sir.

He waited outside the drawing-room door until the waltz should finish, listening to the skirts that swept against it and to the shuffling of feet. He was still discomposed by the girl's bitter and sudden retort. It had cast a gloom over him which he tried to dispel by arranging his cuffs and the bows of his tie. Then he took from his waistcoat pocket a little paper and glanced at the headings he had made for his speech. He was undecided about the lines from Robert Browning for he feared they would be above the heads of his hearers. Some quotation that they could recognise from Shakespeare or from the Melodies[6] would be better. The indelicate clacking

---

[5] A coarse woolen fabric.

[6] Thomas Moore's *Irish Melodies* (1807–1834) was a popular collection of verses set to traditional Irish airs.

of the men's heels and the shuffling of their soles reminded him that their grade of culture differed from his. He would only make himself ridiculous by quoting poetry to them which they could not understand. They would think that he was airing his superior education. He would fail with them just as he had failed with the girl in the pantry. He had taken up a wrong tone. His whole speech was a mistake from first to last, an utter failure.

Just then his aunts and his wife came out of the ladies' dressing-room. His aunts were two small plainly dressed old women. Aunt Julia was an inch or so taller. Her hair, drawn low over the tops of her ears, was grey; and grey also, with darker shadows, was her large flaccid face. Though she was stout in build and stood erect her slow eyes and parted lips gave her the appearance of a woman who did not know where she was or where she was going. Aunt Kate was more vivacious. Her face, healthier than her sister's, was all puckers and creases, like a shrivelled red apple, and her hair, braided in the same old-fashioned way, had not lost its ripe nut colour.

They both kissed Gabriel frankly. He was their favourite nephew, the son of their dead elder sister, Ellen, who had married T. J. Conroy of the Port and Docks.

—Gretta tells me you're not going to take a cab back to Monkstown to-night, Gabriel, said Aunt Kate.

—No, said Gabriel, turning to his wife, we had quite enough of that last year, hadn't we. Don't you remember, Aunt Kate, what a cold Gretta got out of it? Cab windows rattling all the way, and the east wind blowing in after we passed Merrion. Very jolly it was. Gretta caught a dreadful cold.

Aunt Kate frowned severely and nodded her head at every word.

—Quite right, Gabriel, quite right, she said. You can't be too careful.

—But as for Gretta there, said Gabriel, she'd walk home in the snow if she were let.

Mrs Conroy laughed.

—Don't mind him, Aunt Kate, she said. He's really an awful bother, what with green shades for Tom's eyes at night and making him do the dumb-bells, and forcing Eva to eat the stirabout.[7] The poor child! And she simply hates the sight of it! ... O, but you'll never guess what he makes me wear now!

She broke out into a peal of laughter and glanced at her husband, whose admiring and happy eyes had been wandering from her dress to her face and hair. The two aunts laughed heartily too, for Gabriel's solicitude was a standing joke with them.

—Goloshes! said Mrs Conroy. That's the latest. Whenever it's wet underfoot I must put on my goloshes. To-night even he wanted me to put them on, but I wouldn't. The next thing he'll buy me will be a diving suit.

Gabriel laughed nervously and patted his tie reassuringly while Aunt Kate nearly doubled herself, so heartily did she enjoy the joke. The smile soon faded from Aunt Julia's face and her mirthless eyes were directed towards her nephew's face. After a pause she asked:

—And what are goloshes, Gabriel?

—Goloshes, Julia! exclaimed her sister. Goodness me, don't you know what goloshes are? You wear them over your ... over your boots, Gretta, isn't it?

—Yes, said Mrs Conroy. Guttapercha[8] things. We both have a pair now. Gabriel says everyone wears them on the continent.

---

[7] Porridge.
[8] A tough, waterproof, rubberlike material.

—O, on the continent, murmured Aunt Julia, nodding her head slowly.

Gabriel knitted his brows and said, as if he were slightly angered:

—It's nothing very wonderful but Gretta thinks it very funny because she says the word reminds her of Christy Minstrels.[9]

—But tell me, Gabriel, said Aunt Kate, with brisk tact. Of course, you've seen about the room. Gretta was saying...

—O, the room is all right, replied Gabriel. I've taken one in the Gresham.

—To be sure, said Aunt Kate, by far the best thing to do. And the children, Gretta, you're not anxious about them?

—O for one night, said Mrs Conroy. Besides, Bessie will look after them.

—To be sure, said Aunt Kate again. What a comfort it is to have a girl like that, one you can depend on! There's that Lily, I'm sure I don't know what has come over her lately. She's not the girl she was at all.

Gabriel was about to ask his aunt some questions on this point but she broke off suddenly to gaze after her sister who had wandered down the stairs and was craning her neck over the banisters.

—Now, I ask you, she said, almost testily, where is Julia going? Julia! Julia! Where are you going?

Julia, who had gone halfway down one flight, came back and announced blandly:

—Here's Freddy.

At the same moment a clapping of hands and a final flourish of the pianist told that the waltz had ended. The drawing-room door was opened from within and some couples came out. Aunt Kate drew Gabriel aside hurriedly and whispered into his ear:

—Slip down, Gabriel, like a good fellow and see if he's all right, and don't let him up if he's screwed. I'm sure he's screwed. I'm sure he is.

Gabriel went to the stairs and listened over the banisters. He could hear two persons talking in the pantry. Then he recognised Freddy Malins' laugh. He went down the stairs noisily.

—It's such a relief, said Aunt Kate to Mrs Conroy, that Gabriel is here. I always feel easier in my mind when he's here.... Julia, there's Miss Daly and Miss Power will take some refreshment. Thanks for your beautiful waltz, Miss Daly. It made lovely time.

A tall wizen-faced man, with a stiff grizzled moustache and swarthy skin, who was passing out with his partner said:

—And may we have some refreshment, too, Miss Morkan?

—Julia, said Aunt Kate summarily, and here's Mr Browne and Miss Furlong. Take them in, Julia, with Miss Daly and Miss Power.

—I'm the man for the ladies, said Mr Browne, pursing his lips until his moustache bristled and smiling in all his wrinkles. You know, Miss Morkan, the reason they are so fond of me is—

He did not finish his sentence, but, seeing that Aunt Kate was out of earshot, at once led the three young ladies into the back room. The middle of the room was occupied by two square tables and placed end to end, and on these Aunt Julia and the caretaker were straightening and smoothing a large cloth. On the sideboard were arrayed dishes and plates, and glasses and bundles of knives and forks and spoons. The top of the closed square piano served also as a sideboard for viands

---

[9]A famous troupe of American blackface entertainers who danced, sang, and bantered in exaggerated African-American dialect.

and sweets. At a smaller sideboard in one corner two young men were standing, drinking hop-bitters.

Mr Browne led his charges thither and invited them all, in jest, to some ladies' punch, hot, strong and sweet. As they said they never took anything strong he opened three bottles of lemonade for them. Then he asked one of the young men to move aside, and, taking hold of the decanter, filled out for himself a goodly measure of whisky. The young men eyed him respectfully while he took a trial sip.

—God help me, he said, smiling, it's the doctor's orders.

His wizened face broke into a broader smile, and the three young ladies laughed in musical echo to his pleasantry, swaying their bodies to and fro, with nervous jerks of their shoulders. The boldest said:

—O, now, Mr Browne, I'm sure the doctor never ordered anything of the kind.

Mr Browne took another sip of his whisky and said, with sidling mimicry:

—Well, you see, I'm like the famous Mrs Cassidy, who is reported to have said: *Now, Mary Grimes, if I don't take it, make me take it, for I feel I want it.*

His hot face had leaned forward a little too confidentially and he had assumed a very low Dublin accent so that the young ladies, with one instinct, received his speech in silence. Miss Furlong, who was one of Mary Jane's pupils, asked Miss Daly what was the name of the pretty waltz she had played; and Mr Browne, seeing that he was ignored, turned promptly to the two young men who were more appreciative.

A red-faced young woman, dressed in pansy, came into the room, excitedly clapping her hands and crying:

—Quadrilles! Quadrilles![10]

Close on her heels came Aunt Kate, crying:

—Two gentlemen and three ladies, Mary Jane!

—O, here's Mr Bergin and Mr Kerrigan, said Mary Jane. Mr Kerrigan, will you take Miss Power? Miss Furlong, may I get you a partner, Mr Bergin. O, that'll just do now.

—Three ladies, Mary Jane, said Aunt Kate.

The two young gentlemen asked the ladies if they might have the pleasure, and Mary Jane turned to Miss Daly.

—O, Miss Daly, you're really awfully good, after playing for the last two dances, but really we're so short of ladies to-night.

—I don't mind in the least, Miss Morkan.

—But I've a nice partner for you, Mr Bartell D'Arcy, the tenor. I'll get him to sing later on. All Dublin is raving about him.

—Lovely voice, lovely voice! said Aunt Kate.

As the piano had twice begun the prelude to the first figure Mary Jane led her recruits quickly from the room. They had hardly gone when Aunt Julia wandered slowly into the room, looking behind her at something.

—What is the matter, Julia? asked Aunt Kate anxiously. Who is it?

Julia, who was carrying in a column of table-napkins, turned to her sister and said, simply, as if the question had surprised her:

—It's only Freddy, Kate, and Gabriel with him.

In fact right behind her Gabriel could be seen piloting Freddy Malins across the landing. The latter, a young man of about forty, was of Gabriel's size and build, with very round shoulders. His face was fleshy and pallid, touched with colour only

---

[10]A complex sort of square dance requiring sets of four couples apiece.

at the thick hanging lobes of his ears and at the wide wings of his nose. He had coarse features, a blunt nose, a convex and receding brow, tumid and protruded lips. His heavy-lidded eyes and the disorder of his scanty hair made him look sleepy. He was laughing heartily in a high key at a story which he had been telling Gabriel on the stairs and at the same time rubbing the knuckles of his left fist backwards and forwards into his left eye.

—Good-evening, Freddy, said Aunt Julia.

Freddy Malins bade the Misses Morkan good-evening in what seemed an offhand fashion by reason of the habitual catch in his voice and then, seeing that Mr Browne was grinning at him from the sideboard, crossed the room on rather shaky legs and began to repeat in an undertone the story he had just told to Gabriel.

—He's not so bad, is he? said Aunt Kate to Gabriel.

Gabriel's brows were dark but he raised them quickly and answered:

—O no, hardly noticeable.

—Now, isn't he a terrible fellow! she said. And his poor mother made him take the pledge on New Year's Eve. But come on, Gabriel, into the drawing-room.

Before leaving the room with Gabriel she signalled to Mr Browne by frowning and shaking her forefinger in warning to and fro. Mr Browne nodded in answer and, when she had gone, said to Freddy Malins:

—Now, then, Teddy, I'm going to fill you out a good glass of lemonade just to buck you up.

Freddy Malins, who was nearing the climax of his story, waved the offer aside impatiently but Mr Browne, having first called Freddy Malins' attention to a disarray in his dress, filled out and handed him a full glass of lemonade. Freddy Malins' left hand accepted the glass mechanically, his right hand being engaged in the mechanical readjustment of his dress. Mr Browne, whose face was once more wrinkling with mirth, poured out for himself a glass of whisky while Freddy Malins exploded, before he had well reached the climax of his story, in a kink of high-pitched bronchitic laughter and, setting down his untasted and overflowing glass, began to rub the knuckles of his left fist backwards and forwards into his left eye, repeating words of his last phrase as well as his fit of laughter would allow him.

Gabriel could not listen while Mary Jane was playing her Academy[11] piece, full of runs and difficult passages, to the hushed drawing-room. He liked music but the piece she was playing had no melody for him and he doubted whether it had any melody for the other listeners, though they had begged Mary Jane to play something. Four young men, who had come from the refreshment-room to stand in the doorway at the sound of the piano, had gone away quietly in couples after a few minutes. The only persons who seemed to follow the music were Mary Jane herself, her hands racing along the key-board or lifted from it at the pauses like those of a priestess in momentary imprecation, and Aunt Kate standing at her elbow to turn the page.

Gabriel's eyes, irritated by the floor, which glittered with beeswax under the heavy chandelier, wandered to the wall above the piano. A picture of the balcony scene in *Romeo and Juliet* hung there and beside it was a picture of the two murdered princes in the Tower[12] which Aunt Julia had worked in red, blue and brown wools

---

[11] A piece noted for its technical difficulty that showcases the skills of the musician.

[12] The two little sons of Edward IV who were rumored to have been imprisoned and murdered in the Tower of London by their usurping uncle, the future Richard III, in 1483.

when she was a girl. Probably in the school they had gone to as girls that kind of work had been taught, for one year his mother had worked for him as a birthday present a waistcoat of purple tabinet,[13] with little foxes' heads upon it, lined with brown satin and having round mulberry buttons. It was strange that his mother had had no musical talent though Aunt Kate used to call her the brains carrier of the Morkan family. Both she and Julia had always seemed a little proud of their serious and matronly sister. Her photograph stood before the pierglass. She held an open book on her knees and was pointing out something in it to Constantine who, dressed in a man-o'-war suit, lay at her feet. It was she who had chosen the names for her sons for she was very sensible of the dignity of family life. Thanks to her, Constantine was now senior curate in Balbriggan and, thanks to her, Gabriel himself had taken his degree in the Royal University. A shadow passed over his face as he remembered her sullen opposition to his marriage. Some slighting phrases she had used still rankled in his memory; she had once spoken of Gretta as being country cute[14] and that was not true of Gretta at all. It was Gretta who had nursed her during all her last long illness in their house at Monkstown.

He knew that Mary Jane must be near the end of her piece for she was playing again the opening melody with runs of scales after every bar and while he waited for the end the resentment died down in his heart. The piece ended with a trill of octaves in the treble and a final deep octave in the bass. Great applause greeted Mary Jane as, blushing and rolling up her music nervously, she escaped from the room. The most vigorous clapping came from the four young men in the doorway who had gone away to the refreshment-room at the beginning of the piece but had come back when the piano had stopped.

Lancers[15] were arranged. Gabriel found himself partnered with Miss Ivors. She was a frank-mannered talkative young lady, with a freckled face and prominent brown eyes. She did not wear a low-cut bodice and the large brooch which was fixed in the front of her collar bore on it an Irish device.

When they had taken their places she said abruptly:

—I have a crow to pluck with you.

—With me? said Gabriel.

She nodded her head gravely.

—What is it? asked Gabriel, smiling at her solemn manner.

—Who is G. C.? answered Miss Ivors, turning her eyes upon him.

Gabriel coloured and was about to knit his brows, as if he did not understand, when she said bluntly:

—O, innocent Amy! I have found out that you write for *The Daily Express.* Now, aren't you ashamed of yourself?

—Why should I be ashamed of myself? asked Gabriel, blinking his eyes and trying to smile.

—Well, I'm ashamed of you, said Miss Ivors frankly. To say you'd write for a rag like that. I didn't think you were a West Briton.[16]

A look of perplexity appeared on Gabriel's face. It was true that he wrote a literary column every Wednesday in *The Daily Express,* for which he was paid fifteen

---

[13] A material similar to poplin.

[14] Sly, calculating; from the expression "country cute and city clever."

[15] A kind of quadrille.

[16] An Irish person whose main loyalty is to Great Britain.

shillings. But that did not make him a West Briton surely. The books he received for review were almost more welcome than the paltry cheque. He loved to feel the covers and turn over the pages of newly printed books. Nearly every day when his teaching in the college was ended he used to wander down the quays to the second-hand booksellers, to Hickey's on Bachelor's Walk, to Webb's or Massey's on Aston's Quay, or to O'Clohissey's in the by-street. He did not know how to meet her charge. He wanted to say that literature was above politics. But they were friends of many years' standing and their careers had been parallel, first at the University and then as teachers: he could not risk a grandiose phrase with her. He continued blinking his eyes and trying to smile and murmured lamely that he saw nothing political in writing reviews of books.

When their turn to cross[17] had come he was still perplexed and inattentive. Miss Ivors promptly took his hand in a warm grasp and said in a soft friendly tone:

—Of course, I was only joking. Come, we cross now.

When they were together again she spoke of the University question and Gabriel felt more at ease. A friend of hers had shown her his review of Browning's poems. That was how she had found out the secret: but she liked the review immensely. Then she said suddenly:

—O, Mr Conroy, will you come for an excursion to the Aran Isles this summer? We're going to stay there a whole month. It will be splendid out in the Atlantic. You ought to come. Mr Clancy is coming, and Mr Kilkelly and Kathleen Kearney. It would be splendid for Gretta too if she'd come. She's from Connacht, isn't she?

—Her people are, said Gabriel shortly.

—But you will come, won't you? said Miss Ivors, laying her warm hand eagerly on his arm.

—The fact is, said Gabriel, I have already arranged to go—

—Go where? asked Miss Ivors.

—Well, you know, every year I go for a cycling tour with some fellows and so—

—But where? asked Miss Ivors.

—Well, we usually go to France or Belgium or perhaps Germany, said Gabriel awkwardly.

—And why do you go to France or Belgium, said Miss Ivors, instead of visiting your own land?

—Well, said Gabriel, it's partly to keep in touch with the languages and partly for a change.

—And haven't you your own language to keep in touch with—Irish? asked Miss Ivors.

—Well, said Gabriel, if it comes to that, you know, Irish is not my language.

Their neighbours had turned to listen to the cross-examination. Gabriel glanced right and left nervously and tried to keep his good humour under the ordeal which was making a blush invade his forehead.

—And haven't you your own land to visit, continued Miss Ivors, that you know nothing of, your own people, and your own country?

—O, to tell you the truth, retorted Gabriel suddenly, I'm sick of my own country, sick of it!

—Why? asked Miss Ivors.

Gabriel did not answer for his retort had heated him.

—Why? repeated Miss Ivors.

---

[17]One of the steps in a lancer quadrille.

They had to go visiting together[18] and, as he had not answered her, Miss Ivors said warmly:

—Of course, you've no answer.

Gabriel tried to cover his agitation by taking part in the dance with great energy. He avoided her eyes for he had seen a sour expression on her face. But when they met in the long chain he was surprised to feel his hand firmly pressed. She looked at him from under her brows for a moment quizzically until he smiled. Then, just as the chain was about to start again, she stood on tiptoe and whispered into his ear:

—West Briton!

When the lancers were over Gabriel went away to a remote corner of the room where Freddy Malins' mother was sitting. She was a stout feeble old woman with white hair. Her voice had a catch in it like her son's and she stuttered slightly. She had been told that Freddy had come and that he was nearly all right. Gabriel asked her whether she had had a good crossing. She lived with her married daughter in Glasgow and came to Dublin on a visit once a year. She answered placidly that she had had a beautiful crossing and that the captain had been most attentive to her. She spoke also of the beautiful house her daughter kept in Glasgow, and of all the nice friends they had there. While her tongue rambled on Gabriel tried to banish from his mind all memory of the unpleasant incident with Miss Ivors. Of course the girl or woman, or whatever she was, was an enthusiast but there was a time for all things. Perhaps he ought not to have answered her like that. But she had no right to call him a West Briton before people, even in joke. She had tried to make him ridiculous before people, heckling him and staring at him with her rabbit's eyes.

He saw his wife making her way towards him through the waltzing couples. When she reached him she said into his ear:

—Gabriel, Aunt Kate wants to know won't you carve the goose as usual. Miss Daly will carve the ham and I'll do the pudding.

—All right, said Gabriel.

—She's sending in the younger ones first as soon as this waltz is over so that we'll have the table to ourselves.

—Were you dancing? asked Gabriel.

—Of course I was. Didn't you see me? What words had you with Molly Ivors?

—No words. Why? Did she say so?

—Something like that. I'm trying to get that Mr D'Arcy to sing. He's full of conceit, I think.

—There were no words, said Gabriel moodily, only she wanted me to go for a trip to the west of Ireland and I said I wouldn't.

His wife clasped her hands excitedly and gave a little jump.

—O, do go, Gabriel, she cried. I'd love to see Galway again.

—You can go if you like, said Gabriel coldly.

She looked at him for a moment, then turned to Mrs Malins and said:

—There's a nice husband for you, Mrs Malins.

While she was threading her way back across the room Mrs Malins, without adverting to the interruption, went on to tell Gabriel what beautiful places there were in Scotland and beautiful scenery. Her son-in-law brought them every year to the lakes and they used to go fishing. Her son-in-law was a splendid fisher. One day he caught a fish, a beautiful big big fish, and the man in the hotel boiled it for their dinner.

---

[18]Visiting and making the long chain are two other steps in the dance.

Gabriel hardly heard what she said. Now that supper was coming near he began to think again about his speech and about the quotation. When he saw Freddy Malins coming across the room to visit his mother Gabriel left the chair free for him and retired into the embrasure of the window. The room had already cleared and from the back room came the clatter of plates and knives. Those who still remained in the drawing-room seemed tired of dancing and were conversing quietly in little groups. Gabriel's warm trembling fingers tapped the cold pane of the window. How cool it must be outside! How pleasant it would be to walk out alone, first along by the river and then through the park! The snow would be lying on the branches of the trees and forming a bright cap on the top of the Wellington Monument. How much more pleasant it would be there than at the supper-table!

He ran over the headings of his speech: Irish hospitality, sad memories, the Three Graces, Paris, the quotation from Browning. He repeated to himself a phrase he had written in his review: *One feels that one is listening to a thought-tormented music.* Miss Ivors had praised the review. Was she sincere? Had she really any life of her own behind all her propagandism? There had never been any ill-feeling between them until that night. It unnerved him to think that she would be at the supper-table, looking up at him while he spoke with her critical quizzing eyes. Perhaps she would not be sorry to see him fail in his speech. An idea came into his mind and gave him courage. He would say, alluding to Aunt Kate and Aunt Julia: *Ladies and Gentlemen, the generation which is now on the wane among us may have had its faults but for my part I think it had certain qualities of hospitality, of humour, of humanity, which the new and very serious and hypereducated generation that is growing up around us seems to me to lack.* Very good: that was one for Miss Ivors. What did he care that his aunts were only two ignorant old women?

A murmur in the room attracted his attention. Mr Browne was advancing from the door, gallantly escorting Aunt Julia, who leaned upon his arm, smiling and hanging her head. An irregular musketry of applause escorted her also as far as the piano and then, as Mary Jane seated herself on the stool, and Aunt Julia, no longer smiling, half turned so as to pitch her voice fairly into the room, gradually ceased. Gabriel recognised the prelude. It was that of an old song of Aunt Julia's—*Arrayed for the Bridal*.[19] Her voice, strong and clear in tone, attacked with great spirit the runs which embellish the air and though she sang very rapidly she did not miss even the smallest of the grace notes. To follow the voice, without looking at the singer's face, was to feel and share the excitement of swift and secure flight. Gabriel applauded loudly with all the others at the close of the song and loud applause was borne in from the invisible supper-table. It sounded so genuine that a little colour struggled into Aunt Julia's face as she bent to replace in the music-stand the old leather-bound songbook that had her initials on the cover. Freddy Malins, who had listened with his head perched sideways to hear her better, was still applauding when everyone else had ceased and talking animatedly to his mother who nodded her head gravely and slowly in acquiescence. At last, when he could clap no more, he stood up suddenly and hurried across the room to Aunt Julia whose hand he seized and held in both his hands, shaking it when words failed him or the catch in his voice proved too much for him.

—I was just telling my mother, he said, I never heard you sing so well, never. No, I never heard your voice so good as it is to-night. Now! Would you believe

---

[19]An arrangement by George Linley of a popular aria from Bellini's opera *I Puritani di Scozia* (1835) about a dewy young bride breathlessly awaiting her groom; it is an inappropriate selection for the elderly Julia to perform.

that now? That's the truth. Upon my word and honour that's the truth. I never heard your voice sound so fresh and so... so clear and fresh, never.

Aunt Julia smiled broadly and murmured something about compliments as she released her hand from his grasp. Mr Browne extended his open hand towards her and said to those who were near him in the manner of a showman introducing a prodigy to an audience:

—Miss Julia Morkan, my latest discovery!

He was laughing very heartily at this himself when Freddy Malins turned to him and said:

—Well, Browne, if you're serious you might make a worse discovery. All I can say is I never heard her sing half so well as long as I am coming here. And that's the honest truth.

—Neither did I, said Mr Browne. I think her voice had greatly improved.

Aunt Julia shrugged her shoulders and said with meek pride:

—Thirty years ago I hadn't a bad voice as voices go.

—I often told Julia, said Aunt Kate emphatically, that she was simply thrown away in that choir. But she never would be said by me.

She turned as if to appeal to the good sense of the others against a refractory child while Aunt Julia gazed in front of her, a vague smile of reminiscence playing on her face.

—No, continued Aunt Kate, she wouldn't be said or led by anyone, slaving there in that choir night and day, night and day. Six o'clock on Christmas morning! And all for what?

—Well, isn't it for the honour of God, Aunt Kate? asked Mary Jane, twisting round on the piano-stool and smiling.

Aunt Kate turned fiercely on her niece and said:

—I know all about the honour of God, Mary Jane, but I think it's not at all honourable for the pope to turn out the women out of the choirs that have slaved there all their lives and put little whipper-snappers of boys over their heads. I suppose it is for the good of the Church if the pope does it. But it's not just, Mary Jane, and it's not right.

She had worked herself into a passion and would have continued in defence of her sister for it was a sore subject with her but Mary Jane, seeing that all the dancers had come back, intervened pacifically:

—Now, Aunt Kate, you're giving scandal to Mr Browne who is of the other persuasion.

Aunt Kate turned to Mr Browne, who was grinning at this allusion to his religion, and said hastily:

—O, I don't question the pope's being right. I'm only a stupid old woman and I wouldn't presume to do such a thing. But there's such a thing as common everyday politeness and gratitude. And if I were in Julia's place I'd tell that Father Healy straight up to his face...

—And besides, Aunt Kate, said Mary Jane, we really are all hungry and when we are hungry we are all very quarrelsome.

—And when we are thirsty we are also quarrelsome, added Mr Browne.

—So that we had better go to supper, said Mary Jane, and finish the discussion afterwards.

On the landing outside the drawing-room Gabriel found his wife and Mary Jane trying to persuade Miss Ivors to stay for supper. But Miss Ivors, who had put on her hat and was buttoning her cloak, would not stay. She did not feel in the least hungry and she had already overstayed her time.

—But only for ten minutes, Molly, said Mrs Conroy. That won't delay you.

—To take a pick itself,[20] said Mary Jane, after all your dancing.

—I really couldn't, said Miss Ivors.

—I am afraid you didn't enjoy yourself at all, said Mary Jane hopelessly.

—Ever so much, I assure you, said Miss Ivors, but you really must let me run off now.

—But how can you get home? asked Mrs Conroy.

—O, it's only two steps up the quay.

Gabriel hesitated a moment and said:

—If you will allow me, Miss Ivors, I'll see you home if you really are obliged to go.

But Miss Ivors broke away from them.

—I won't hear of it, she cried. For goodness sake go in to your suppers and don't mind me. I'm quite well able to take care of myself.

—Well, you're the comical girl, Molly, said Mrs Conroy frankly.

—*Beannacht libh,*[21] cried Miss Ivors, with a laugh, as she ran down the staircase.

Mary Jane gazed after her, a moody puzzled expression on her face, while Mrs Conroy leaned over the banisters to listen for the hall-door. Gabriel asked himself was he the cause of her abrupt departure. But she did not seem to be in ill humour: she had gone away laughing. He stared blankly down the staircase.

At that moment Aunt Kate came toddling out of the supper-room, almost wringing her hands in despair.

—Where is Gabriel? she cried. Where on earth is Gabriel? There's everyone waiting in there, stage to let, and nobody to carve the goose!

—Here I am, Aunt Kate! cried Gabriel, with sudden animation, ready to carve a flock of geese, if necessary.

A fat brown goose lay at one end of the table and at the other end, on a bed of creased paper strewn with sprigs of parsley, lay a great ham, stripped of its outer skin and peppered over with crust crumbs, a meat paper frill around its shin and beside this was a round of spiced beef. Between these two rival ends ran parallel lines of side-dishes: two little minsters of jelly, red and yellow; a shallow dish full of blocks of blancmange and red jam, a large green leaf-shaped dish with a stalk-shaped handle, on which lay bunches of purple raisins and peeled almonds, a companion dish on which lay a solid rectangle of Smyrna figs, a dish of custard topped with grated nutmeg, a small bowl full of chocolates and sweets wrapped in gold and silver papers and a glass vase in which stood some tall celery stalks. In the centre of the table there stood, as sentries to a fruit-stand which upheld a pyramid of oranges and American apples, two squat old-fashioned decanters of cut glass, one containing port and the other dark sherry. On the closed square piano a pudding in a huge yellow dish lay in waiting and behind it were three squads of bottles of stout and ale and minerals, drawn up according to the colours of their uniforms, the first two black, with brown and red labels, the third and smallest squad white, with transverse green sashes.

Gabriel took his seat boldly at the head of the table and, having looked to the edge of the carver, plunged his fork firmly into the goose. He felt quite at ease now for he was an expert carver and liked nothing better than to find himself at the head of a well-laden table.

---

[20] To have a small bite to eat.

[21] "Blessing to ye"; a Gaelic good-night.

—Miss Furlong, what shall I send you? he asked. A wing or a slice of the breast?

—Just a small slice of the breast.

—Miss Higgins, what for you?

—O, anything at all, Mr Conroy.

While Gabriel and Miss Daly exchanged plates of goose and plates of ham and spiced beef Lily went from guest to guest with a dish of hot floury potatoes wrapped in a white napkin. This was Mary Jane's idea and she had also suggested apple sauce for the goose but Aunt Kate had said that plain roast goose without apple sauce had always been good enough for her and she hoped she might never eat worse. Mary Jane waited on her pupils and saw that they got the best slices and Aunt Kate and Aunt Julia opened and carried across from the piano bottles of stout and ale for the gentlemen and bottles of minerals for the ladies. There was a great deal of confusion and laughter and noise, the noise of orders and counter-orders, of knives and forks, of corks and glass-stoppers. Gabriel began to carve second helpings as soon as he had finished the first round without serving himself. Everyone protested loudly so that he compromised by taking a long draught of stout for he had found the carving hot work. Mary Jane settled down quietly to her supper but Aunt Kate and Aunt Julia were still toddling round the table, walking on each other's heels, getting in each other's way and giving each other unheeded orders. Mr Browne begged of them to sit down and eat their suppers and so did Gabriel but they said there was time enough so that, at last, Freddy Malins stood up and, capturing Aunt Kate, plumped her down on her chair amid general laughter.

When everyone had been well served Gabriel said, smiling:

—Now, if anyone wants a little more of what vulgar people call stuffing let him or her speak.

A chorus of voices invited him to begin his own supper and Lily came forward with three potatoes which she had reserved for him.

—Very well, said Gabriel amiably, as he took another preparatory draught, kindly forget my existence, ladies and gentlemen, for a few minutes.

He set to his supper and took no part in the conversation with which the table covered Lily's removal of the plates. The subject of talk was the opera company which was then at the Theatre Royal. Mr Bartell D'Arcy, the tenor, a dark-complexioned young man with a smart moustache, praised very highly the leading contralto of the company but Miss Furlong thought she had a rather vulgar style of production. Freddy Malins said there was a negro chieftain singing in the second part of the Gaiety pantomime[22] who had one of the finest tenor voices he had ever heard.

—Have you heard him? he asked Mr Bartell D'Arcy across the table.

—No, answered Mr Bartell D'Arcy carelessly.

—Because, Freddy Malins explained, now I'd be curious to hear your opinion of him. I think he has a grand voice.

—It takes Teddy to find out the really good things, said Mr Browne familiarly to the table.

—And why couldn't he have a voice too? asked Freddy Malins sharply. Is it because he's only a black?

Nobody answered this question and Mary Jane led the table back to the legitimate opera. One of her pupils had given her a pass for *Mignon*. Of course it was very fine,

---

[22]The Gaiety theater featured popular dramas, musicals, and comic revues, entertainment considerably less elegant than the rest of the guests have been discussing.

she said, but it made her think of poor Georgina Burns.[23] Mr Browne could go back farther still, to the old Italian companies that used to come to Dublin—Tietjens, Ilma de Murzka, Campanini, the great Trebelli, Giuglini, Ravelli, Aramburo.[24] Those were the days, he said, when there was something like singing to be heard in Dublin. He told too of how the top gallery of the old Royal used to be packed night after night, of how one night an Italian tenor had sung five encores to *Let Me Like a Soldier Fall,*[25] introducing a high C every time, and of how the gallery boys would sometimes in their enthusiasm unyoke the horses from the carriage of some great *prima donna* and pull her themselves through the streets to her hotel. Why did they never play the grand old operas now, he asked, *Dinorah, Lucrezia Borgia?*[26] Because they could not get the voices to sing them: that was why.

—O, well, said Mr Bartell D'Arcy, I presume there are as good singers to-day as there were then.

—Where are they? asked Mr Browne defiantly.

—In London, Paris, Milan, said Mr Bartell D'Arcy warmly. I suppose Caruso,[27] for example, is quite as good, if not better than any of the men you have mentioned.

—Maybe so, said Mr Browne. But I may tell you I doubt it strongly.

—O, I'd give anything to hear Caruso sing, said Mary Jane.

—For me, said Aunt Kate, who had been picking a bone, there was only one tenor. To please me, I mean. But I suppose none of you ever heard of him.

—Who was he, Miss Morkan? asked Mr Bartell D'Arcy politely.

—His name, said Aunt Kate, was Parkinson.[28] I heard him when he was in his prime and I think he had then the purest tenor voice that was ever put into a man's throat.

—Strange, said Mr Bartell D'Arcy. I never even heard of him.

—Yes, yes, Miss Morkan is right, said Mr Browne. I remember hearing of old Parkinson but he's too far back for me.

—A beautiful pure sweet mellow English tenor, said Aunt Kate with enthusiasm.

Gabriel having finished, the huge pudding was transferred to the table. The clatter of forks and spoons began again. Gabriel's wife served out spoonfuls of the pudding and passed the plates down the table. Midway down they were held up by Mary Jane, who replenished them with raspberry or orange jelly or with blancmange and jam. The pudding was of Aunt Julia's making and she received praises for it from all quarters. She herself said that it was not quite brown enough.

—Well, I hope, Miss Morkan, said Mr Browne, that I'm brown enough for you because, you know, I'm all brown.

All the gentlemen, except Gabriel, ate some of the pudding out of compliment to Aunt Julia. As Gabriel never ate sweets the celery had been left for him. Freddy Malins also took a stalk of celery and ate it with his pudding. He had been told that celery was a capital thing for the blood and he was just then under doctor's care. Mrs Malins, who had been silent all through the supper, said that her son was

---

[23]*Mignon* is an 1866 opera by Ambroise Thomas; Georgina Burns was a famous soprano in the 1880s.

[24]The names of celebrated nineteenth-century opera singers.

[25]Aria from William Vincent Wallace's 1845 opera *Maritana,* a melodramatic vow to die bravely and honorably.

[26]*Dinorah* is an 1859 Giacomo Meyerbeer opera; *Lucrezia Borgia* (1833) was composed by Gaetano Donizetti.

[27]Enrico Caruso (1873–1921), the great tenor who was just coming into his fame in 1904, the time in which the story is set.

[28]A tenor named Parkinson sang with the Carl Rosa Opera Company in the late nineteenth century.

going down to Mount Melleray[29] in a week or so. The table then spoke of Mount Melleray, how bracing the air was down there, how hospitable the monks were and how they never asked for a penny-piece from their guests.

—And do you mean to say, asked Mr Browne incredulously, that a chap can go down there and put up there as if it were a hotel and live on the fat of the land and then come away without paying a farthing?

—O, most people give some donation to the monastery when they leave, said Mary Jane.

—I wish we had an institution like that in our Church, said Mr Browne candidly.

He was astonished to hear that the monks never spoke, got up at two in the morning and slept in their coffins. He asked what they did it for.

—That's the rule of the order, said Aunt Kate firmly.

—Yes, but why? asked Mr Browne.

Aunt Kate repeated that it was the rule, that was all. Mr Browne still seemed not to understand. Freddy Malins explained to him, as best he could, that the monks were trying to make up for the sins committed by all the sinners in the outside world. The explanation was not very clear for Mr Browne grinned and said:

—I like that idea very much but wouldn't a comfortable spring bed do them as well as a coffin?

—The coffin, said Mary Jane, is to remind them of their last end.

As the subject had grown lugubrious it was buried in a silence of the table during which Mrs Malins could be heard saying to her neighbour in an indistinct undertone:

—They are very good men, the monks, very pious men.

The raisins and almonds and figs and apples and oranges and chocolates and sweets were now passed about the table and Aunt Julia invited all the guests to have either port or sherry. At first Mr Bartell D'Arcy refused to take either but one of his neighbours nudged him and whispered something to him upon which he allowed his glass to be filled. Gradually as the last glasses were being filled the conversation ceased. A pause followed, broken only by the noise of the wine and by unsettlings of chairs. The Misses Morkan, all three, looked down at the tablecloth. Someone coughed once or twice and then a few gentlemen patted the table gently as a signal for silence. The silence came and Gabriel pushed back his chair and stood up.

The patting at once grew louder in encouragement and then ceased altogether. Gabriel leaned his ten trembling fingers on the tablecloth and smiled nervously at the company. Meeting a row of upturned faces he raised his eyes to the chandelier. The piano was playing a waltz tune and he could hear the skirts sweeping against the drawing-room door. People, perhaps, were standing in the snow on the quay outside, gazing up at the lighted windows and listening to the waltz music. The air was pure there. In the distance lay the park where the trees were weighted with snow. The Wellington Monument wore a gleaming cap of snow that flashed westward over the white field of Fifteen Acres.

He began:

—Ladies and Gentlemen.

—It has fallen to my lot this evening, as in years past, to perform a very pleasing task but a task for which I am afraid my poor powers as a speaker are all too inadequate.

---

[29] A Trappist monastery in the south of Ireland; although all politely avoid saying so, the alcoholic Freddy is going there to dry out.

—No, no! said Mr Browne.

—But, however that may be, I can only ask you to-night to take the will for the deed and to lend me your attention for a few moments while I endeavour to express to you in words what my feelings are on this occasion.

—Ladies and Gentlemen. It is not the first time that we have gathered together under this hospitable roof, around this hospitable board. It is not the first time that we have been the recipients—or perhaps, I had better say, the victims—of the hospitality of certain good ladies.

He made a circle in the air with his arm and paused. Everyone laughed or smiled at Aunt Kate and Aunt Julia and Mary Jane who all turned crimson with pleasure. Gabriel went on more boldly:

—I feel more strongly with every recurring year that our country has no tradition which does it so much honour and which it should guard so jealously as that of its hospitality. It is a tradition that is unique as far as my experience goes (and I have visited not a few places abroad) among the modern nations. Some would say, perhaps, that with us it is rather a failing than anything to be boasted of. But granted even that, it is, to my mind, a princely failing, and one that I trust will long be cultivated among us. Of one thing, at least, I am sure. As long as this one roof shelters the good ladies aforesaid—and I wish from my heart it may do so for many and many a long year to come—the tradition of genuine warm-hearted courteous Irish hospitality, which our forefathers have handed down to us and which we in turn must hand down to our descendants, is still alive among us.

A hearty murmur of assent ran round the table. It shot through Gabriel's mind that Miss Ivors was not there and that she had gone away discourteously: and he said with confidence in himself:

—Ladies and Gentlemen.

—A new generation is growing up in our midst, a generation actuated by new ideas and new principles. It is serious and enthusiastic for these new ideas and its enthusiasm, even when it is misdirected, is, I believe, in the main sincere. But we are living in a sceptical and, if I may use the phrase, a thought-tormented age: and sometimes I fear that this new generation, educated or hypereducated as it is, will lack those qualities of humanity, of hospitality, of kindly humour which belonged to an older day. Listening to-night to the names of all those great singers of the past it seemed to me, I must confess, that we were living in a less spacious age. Those days might, without exaggeration, be called spacious days: and if they are gone beyond recall let us hope, at least, that in gatherings such as this we shall still speak of them with pride and affection, still cherish in our hearts the memory of those dead and gone great ones whose fame the world will not willingly let die.

—Hear, hear! said Mr Browne loudly.

—But yet, continued Gabriel, his voice falling into a softer inflection, there are always in gatherings such as this sadder thoughts that will recur to our minds: thoughts of the past, of youth, of changes, of absent faces that we miss here to-night. Our path through life is strewn with many such sad memories: and were we to brood upon them always we could not find the heart to go on bravely with our work among the living. We have all of us living duties and living affections which claim, and rightly claim, our strenuous endeavours.

—Therefore, I will not linger on the past. I will not let any gloomy moralising intrude upon us here to-night. Here we are gathered together for a brief moment from the bustle and rush of our everyday routine. We are met here as friends, in the spirit of good-fellowship, as colleagues, also to a certain extent, in the true spirit of *camaraderie,* and as the guests of—what shall I call them?—the Three Graces of the Dublin musical world.

The table burst into applause and laughter at this sally. Aunt Julia vainly asked each of her neighbours in turn to tell her what Gabriel had said.

—He says we are the Three Graces, Aunt Julia, said Mary Jane.

Aunt Julia did not understand but she looked up, smiling, at Gabriel, who continued in the same vein:

—Ladies and Gentlemen.

—I will not attempt to play to-night the part that Paris[30] played on another occasion. I will not attempt to choose between them. The task would be an invidious one and one beyond my poor powers. For when I view them in turn, whether it be our chief hostess herself, whose good heart, whose too good heart, has become a byword with all who know her, or her sister, who seems to be gifted with perennial youth and whose singing must have been a surprise and a revelation to us all to-night, or, last but not least, when I consider our youngest hostess, talented, cheerful, hard-working and the best of nieces, I confess, Ladies and Gentlemen, that I do not know to which of them I should award the prize.

Gabriel glanced down at his aunts and, seeing the large smile on Aunt Julia's face and the tears which had risen to Aunt Kate's eyes, hastened to his close. He raised his glass of port gallantly, while every member of the company fingered a glass expectantly, and said loudly:

—Let us toast them all three together. Let us drink to their health, wealth, long life, happiness and prosperity and may they long continue to hold the proud and self-won position which they hold in their profession and the position of honour and affection which they hold in our hearts.

All the guests stood up, glass in hand, and, turning towards the three seated ladies, sang in unison, with Mr Browne as leader:

> *For they are jolly gay fellows,*
> *For they are jolly gay fellows,*
> *For they are jolly gay fellows,*
> *Which nobody can deny.*

Aunt Kate was making frank use of her handkerchief and even Aunt Julia seemed moved. Freddy Malins beat time with his pudding-fork and the singers turned towards one another, as if in melodious conference, while they sang, with emphasis:

> *Unless he tells a lie,*
> *Unless he tells a lie.*

Then, turning once more towards their hostesses, they sang:

> *For they are jolly gay fellows,*
> *For they are jolly gay fellows,*
> *For they are jolly gay fellows,*
> *Which nobody can deny.*

The acclamation which followed was taken up beyond the door of the supper-room by many of the other guests and renewed time after time, Freddy Malins acting as officer with his fork on high.

---

[30] In Greek myth, Paris was the Trojan shepherd prince compelled to choose the most beautiful from among Hera, Athena, and Aphrodite. When he chose Aphrodite, she awarded him the already-married Helen as his bride, precipitating the Trojan War.

The piercing morning air came into the hall where they were standing so that Aunt Kate said:

—Close the door, somebody. Mrs Malins will get her death of cold.

—Browne is out there, Aunt Kate, said Mary Jane.

—Browne is everywhere, said Aunt Kate, lowering her voice.

Mary Jane laughed at her tone.

—Really, she said archly, he is very attentive.

—He has been laid on here like the gas, said Aunt Kate in the same tone, all during the Christmas.

She laughed herself this time good-humouredly and then added quickly:

—But tell him to come in, Mary Jane, and close the door. I hope to goodness he didn't hear me.

At that moment the hall-door was opened and Mr Browne came in from the doorstep, laughing as if his heart would break. He was dressed in a long green overcoat with mock astrakhan cuffs and collar and wore on his head an oval fur cap. He pointed down the snow-covered quay from where the sound of shrill prolonged whistling was borne in.

—Teddy will have all the cabs in Dublin out, he said.

Gabriel advanced from the little pantry behind the office, struggling into his overcoat and looking round the hall, said:

—Gretta not down yet?

—She's getting on her things, Gabriel, said Aunt Kate.

—Who's playing up there? asked Gabriel.

—Nobody. They're all gone.

—O no, Aunt Kate, said Mary Jane. Bartell D'Arcy and Miss O'Callaghan aren't gone yet.

—Someone is strumming at the piano, anyhow, said Gabriel.

Mary Jane glanced at Gabriel and Mr Browne and said with a shiver:

—It makes me feel cold to look at you two gentlemen muffled up like that. I wouldn't like to face your journey home at this hour.

—I'd like nothing better this minute, said Mr Browne stoutly, than a rattling fine walk in the country or a fast drive with a good spanking goer between the shafts.[31]

—We used to have a very good horse and trap at home, said Aunt Julia sadly.

—The never-to-be-forgotten Johnny, said Mary Jane, laughing.

Aunt Kate and Gabriel laughed too.

—Why, what was wonderful about Johnny? asked Mr Browne.

—The late lamented Patrick Morkan, our grandfather, that is, explained Gabriel, commonly known in his later years as the old gentleman, was a glue-boiler.

—O, now, Gabriel, said Aunt Kate, laughing, he had a starch mill.

—Well, glue or starch, said Gabriel, the old gentleman had a horse by the name of Johnny. And Johnny used to work in the old gentleman's mill, walking round and round in order to drive the mill. That was all very well; but now comes the tragic part about Johnny. One fine day the old gentleman thought he'd like to drive out with the quality to a military review in the park.

—The Lord have mercy on his soul, said Aunt Kate compassionately.

—Amen, said Gabriel. So the old gentleman, as I said, harnessed Johnny and put on his very best tall hat and his very best stock collar and drove out in grand style from his ancestral mansion somewhere near Back Lane, I think.

---

[31] A fast carriage drive with a spirited horse.

Everyone laughed, even Mrs Malins, at Gabriel's manner and Aunt Kate said:

—O now, Gabriel, he didn't live in Back Lane, really. Only the mill was there.

—Out from the mansion of his forefathers, continued Gabriel, he drove with Johnny. And everything went on beautifully until Johnny came in sight of King Billy's statue: and whether he fell in love with the horse King Billy sits on or whether he thought he was back again in the mill, anyhow he began to walk round the statue.

Gabriel paced in a circle round the hall in his goloshes amid the laughter of the others.

—Round and round he went, said Gabriel, and the old gentleman, who was a very pompous old gentleman, was highly indignant. *Go on, sir! What do you mean, sir? Johnny! Johnny! Most extraordinary conduct! Can't understand the horse!*

The peals of laughter which followed Gabriel's imitation of the incident were interrupted by a resounding knock at the hall-door. Mary Jane ran to open it and let in Freddy Malins. Freddy Malins, with his hat well back on his head and his shoulders humped with cold, was puffing and steaming after his exertions.

—I could only get one cab, he said.

—O, we'll find another along the quay, said Gabriel.

—Yes, said Aunt Kate. Better not keep Mrs Malins standing in the draught.

Mrs Malins was helped down the front steps by her son and Mr Browne and, after many manœuvres, hoisted into the cab. Freddy Malins clambered in after her and spent a long time settling her on the seat, Mr Browne helping him with advice. At last she was settled comfortably and Freddy Malins invited Mr Browne into the cab. There was a good deal of confused talk, and then Mr Browne got into the cab. The cabman settled his rug over his knees, and bent down for the address. The confusion grew greater and the cabman was directed differently by Freddy Malins and Mr Browne, each of whom had his head out through a window of the cab. The difficulty was to know where to drop Mr Browne along the route and Aunt Kate, Aunt Julia and Mary Jane helped the discussion from the doorstep with cross-directions and contradictions and abundance of laughter. As for Freddy Malins he was speechless with laughter. He popped his head in and out of the window every moment, to the great danger of his hat, and told his mother how the discussion was progressing till at last Mr Browne shouted to the bewildered cabman above the din of everybody's laughter.

—Do you know Trinity College?

—Yes, sir, said the cabman.

—Well, drive bang up against Trinity College gates, said Mr Browne, and then we'll tell you where to go. You understand now?

—Yes, sir, said the cabman.

—Make like a bird for Trinity College.

—Right, sir, cried the cabman.

The horse was whipped up and the cab rattled off along the quay amid a chorus of laughter and adieus.

Gabriel had not gone to the door with the others. He was in a dark part of the hall gazing up the staircase. A woman was standing near the top of the first flight, in the shadow also. He could not see her face but he could see the terracotta and salmonpink panels of her skirt which the shadow made appear black and white. It was his wife. She was leaning on the banisters, listening to something. Gabriel was surprised at her stillness and strained his ear to listen also. But he could hear little save the noise of laughter and dispute on the front steps, a few chords struck on the piano and a few notes of a man's voice singing.

He stood still in the gloom of the hall, trying to catch the air that the voice was singing and gazing up at his wife. There was grace and mystery in her attitude as if she were a symbol of something. He asked himself what is a woman standing on the stairs in the shadow, listening to distant music, a symbol of. If he were a painter he would paint her in that attitude. Her blue felt hat would show off the bronze of her hair against the darkness and the dark panels of her skirt would show off the light ones. *Distant Music* he would call the picture if he were a painter.

The hall-door was closed; and Aunt Kate, Aunt Julia and Mary Jane came down the hall, still laughing.

—Well, isn't Freddy terrible? said Mary Jane. He's really terrible.

Gabriel said nothing but pointed up the stairs towards where his wife was standing. Now that the hall-door was closed the voice and the piano could be heard more clearly. Gabriel held up his hand for them to be silent. The song seemed to be in the old Irish tonality and the singer seemed uncertain both of his words and of his voice. The voice, made plaintive by distance and by the singer's hoarseness, faintly illuminated the cadence of the air with words expressing grief:

> *O, the rain falls on my heavy locks*
> *And the dew wets my skin,*
> *My babe lies cold . . .*

—O, exclaimed Mary Jane. It's Bartell D'Arcy singing and he wouldn't sing all the night. O, I'll get him to sing a song before he goes.

—O do, Mary Jane, said Aunt Kate.

Mary Jane brushed past the others and ran to the staircase but before she reached it the singing stopped and the piano was closed abruptly.

—O, what a pity! she cried. Is he coming down, Gretta?

Gabriel heard his wife answer yes and saw her come down towards them. A few steps behind her were Mr Bartell D'Arcy and Miss O'Callaghan.

—O, Mr D'Arcy, cried Mary Jane, it's downright mean of you to break off like that when we were all in raptures listening to you.

—I have been at him all the evening, said Miss O'Callaghan, and Mrs Conroy too and he told us he had a dreadful cold and couldn't sing.

—O, Mr D'Arcy, said Aunt Kate, now that was a great fib to tell.

—Can't you see that I'm as hoarse as a crow? said Mr D'Arcy roughly.

He went into the pantry hastily and put on his overcoat. The others, taken aback by his rude speech, could find nothing to say. Aunt Kate wrinkled her brows and made signs to the others to drop the subject. Mr D'Arcy stood swathing his neck carefully and frowning.

—It's the weather, said Aunt Julia, after a pause.

—Yes, everybody has colds, said Aunt Kate readily, everybody.

—They say, said Mary Jane, we haven't had snow like it for thirty years; and I read this morning in the newspapers that the snow is general all over Ireland.

—I love the look of snow, said Aunt Julia sadly.

—So do I, said Miss O'Callaghan. I think Christmas is never really Christmas unless we have the snow on the ground.

—But poor Mr D'Arcy doesn't like the snow, said Aunt Kate, smiling.

Mr D'Arcy came from the pantry, full swathed and buttoned, and in a repentant tone told them the history of his cold. Everyone gave him advice and said it was a great pity and urged him to be very careful of his throat in the night air. Gabriel watched his wife who did not join in the conversation. She was standing right under the dusty fanlight and the flame of the gas lit up the rich bronze of her hair which he had seen her drying at the fire a few days before. She was in the same attitude and seemed unaware of the talk about her. At last she turned towards them and Gabriel saw that there was colour on her cheeks and that her eyes were shining. A sudden tide of joy went leaping out of his heart.

—Mr D'Arcy, she said, what is the name of that song you were singing?

—It's called *The Lass of Aughrim,*[32] said Mr D'Arcy, but I couldn't remember it properly. Why? Do you know it?

—*The Lass of Aughrim,* she repeated. I couldn't think of the name.

—It's a very nice air, said Mary Jane. I'm sorry you were not in voice to-night.

—Now, Mary Jane, said Aunt Kate, don't annoy Mr D'Arcy. I won't have him annoyed.

Seeing that all were ready to start she shepherded them to the door where good-night was said:

—Well, good-night, Aunt Kate, and thanks for the pleasant evening.

—Good-night, Gabriel. Good-night, Gretta!

—Good-night, Aunt Kate, and thanks ever so much. Good-night, Aunt Julia.

—O, good-night, Gretta, I didn't see you.

—Good-night, Mr D'Arcy. Good-night, Miss O'Callaghan.

—Good-night, Miss Morkan.

—Good-night, again.

—Good-night, all. Safe home.

—Good-night. Good-night.

The morning was still dark. A dull yellow light brooded over the houses and the river; and the sky seemed to be descending. It was slushy underfoot; and only streaks and patches of snow lay on the roofs, on the parapets of the quay and on the area railings. The lamps were still burning redly in the murky air and, across the river, the palace of the Four Courts stood out menacingly against the heavy sky.

She was walking on before him with Mr Bartell D'Arcy, her shoes in a brown parcel tucked under one arm and her hands holding her skirt up from the slush. She had no longer any grace of attitude but Gabriel's eyes were still bright with happiness. The blood went bounding along his veins; and the thoughts went rioting through his brain, proud, joyful, tender, valorous.

She was walking on before him so lightly and so erect that he longed to run after her noiselessly, catch her by the shoulders and say something foolish and affectionate into her ear. She seemed to him so frail that he longed to defend her against something and then to be alone with her. Moments of their secret life together burst like stars upon his memory. A heliotrope envelope was lying beside his breakfast-cup and he was caressing it with his hand. Birds were twittering in the ivy and the sunny web of the curtain was shimmering along the floor: he could not eat for happiness. They were standing on the crowded platform and he was placing a ticket inside the warm palm of her glove. He was standing with her in the cold, looking in through a grated window at a man making bottles in a roaring furnace. It was very cold. Her face, fragrant in the cold air, was quite close to his; and suddenly she called out to the man at the furnace:

—Is the fire hot, sir?

But the man could not hear her with the noise of the furnace. It was just as well. He might have answered rudely.

---

[32]Child Ballad number 76, also called "Lord Gregory," in which a peasant girl stands outside a castle and pleads with her noble lover to acknowledge her and their child.

A wave of yet more tender joy escaped from his heart and went coursing in warm flood along his arteries. Like the tender fires of stars moments of their life together, that no one knew of or would ever know of, broke upon and illumined his memory. He longed to recall to her those moments, to make her forget the years of their dull existence together and remember only their moments of ecstasy. For the years, he felt, had not quenched his soul or hers. Their children, his writing, her household cares had not quenched all their souls' tender fire. In one letter that he had written to her then he had said: *Why is it that words like these seem to me so dull and cold? Is it because there is no word tender enough to be your name?*

Like distant music these words that he had written years before were borne towards him from the past. He longed to be alone with her. When the others had gone away, when he and she were in their room in the hotel, then they would be alone together. He would call her softly:

—Gretta!

Perhaps she would not hear at once: she would be undressing. Then something in his voice would strike her. She would turn and look at him. . . .

At the corner of Winetavern Street they met a cab. He was glad of its rattling noise as it saved him from conversation. She was looking out of the window and seemed tired. The others spoke only a few words, pointing out some building or street. The horse galloped along wearily under the murky morning sky, dragging his old rattling box after his heels, and Gabriel was again in a cab with her, galloping to catch the boat, galloping to their honeymoon.

As the cab drove across O'Connell Bridge Miss O'Callaghan said:

—They say you never cross O'Connell Bridge without seeing a white horse.

—I see a white man this time, said Gabriel.

—Where? asked Mr Bartell D'Arcy.

Gabriel pointed to the statue, on which lay patches of snow. Then he nodded familiarly to it and waved his hand.

—Good-night, Dan, he said gaily.[33]

When the cab drew up before the hotel Gabriel jumped out and, in spite of Mr Bartell D'Arcy's protest, paid the driver. He gave the man a shilling over his fare. The man saluted and said:

—A prosperous New Year to you, sir.

—The same to you, said Gabriel cordially.

She leaned for a moment on his arm in getting out of the cab and while standing at the curbstone, bidding the others good-night. She leaned lightly on his arm, as lightly as when she had danced with him a few hours before. He had felt proud and happy then, happy that she was his, proud of her grace and wifely carriage. But now, after the kindling again of so many memories, the first touch of her body, musical and strange and perfumed, sent through him a keen pang of lust. Under cover of her silence he pressed her arm closely to his side; and, as they stood at the hotel door, he felt that they had escaped from their lives and duties, escaped from home and friends and run away together with wild and radiant hearts to a new adventure.

An old man was dozing in a great hooded chair in the hall. He lit a candle in the office and went before them to the stairs. They followed him in silence, their feet falling in soft thuds on the thickly carpeted stairs. She mounted the stairs behind the porter, her head bowed in the ascent, her frail shoulders curved as with a burden,

---

[33] Gabriel salutes the snow-covered statue of Daniel O'Connell (1775–1847), poet and Irish nationalist.

her skirt girt tightly about her. He could have flung his arms about her hips and held her still for his arms were trembling with desire to seize her and only the stress of his nails against the palms of his hands held the wild impulse of his body in check. The porter halted on the stairs to settle his guttering candle. They halted too on the steps below him. In the silence Gabriel could hear the falling of the molten wax into the tray and the thumping of his own heart against his ribs.

The porter led them along a corridor and opened a door. Then he set his unstable candle down on a toilet-table and asked at what hour they were to be called in the morning.

—Eight, said Gabriel.

The porter pointed to the tap of the electric-light and began a muttered apology but Gabriel cut him short.

—We don't want any light. We have light enough from the street. And I say, he added, pointing to the candle, you might remove that handsome article, like a good man.

The porter took up his candle again, but slowly for he was surprised by such a novel idea. Then he mumbled good-night and went out. Gabriel shot the lock to.

A ghostly light from the street lamp lay in a long shaft from one window to the door. Gabriel threw his overcoat and hat on a couch and crossed the room towards the window. He looked down into the street in order that his emotion might calm a little. Then he turned and leaned against a chest of drawers with his back to the light. She had taken off her hat and cloak and was standing before a large swinging mirror, unhooking her waist. Gabriel paused for a few moments, watching her, and then said:

—Gretta!

She turned away from the mirror slowly and walked along the shaft of light towards him. Her face looked so serious and weary that the words would not pass Gabriel's lips. No, it was not the moment yet.

—You looked tired, he said.

—I am a little, she answered.

—You don't feel ill or weak?

—No, tired: that's all.

She went on to the window and stood there, looking out. Gabriel waited again and then, fearing that diffidence was about to conquer him, he said abruptly:

—By the way, Gretta!

—What is it?

—You know that poor fellow Malins? he said quickly.

—Yes. What about him?

—Well, poor fellow, he's a decent sort of chap after all, continued Gabriel in a false voice. He gave me back that sovereign I lent him and I didn't expect it really. It's a pity he wouldn't keep away from that Browne, because he's not a bad fellow at heart.

He was trembling now with annoyance. Why did she seem so abstracted? He did not know how he could begin. Was she annoyed, too, about something? If she would only turn to him or come to him of her own accord! To take her as she was would be brutal. No, he must see some ardour in her eyes first. He longed to be master of her strange mood.

—When did you lend him the pound? she asked, after a pause.

Gabriel strove to restrain himself from breaking out into brutal language about the sottish Malins and his pound. He longed to cry to her from his soul, to crush her body against his, to overmaster her. But he said:

—O, at Christmas, when he opened that little Christmas-card shop in Henry Street.

He was in such a fever of rage and desire that he did not hear her come from the window. She stood before him for an instant, looking at him strangely. Then, suddenly raising herself on tiptoe and resting her hands lightly on his shoulders, she kissed him.

—You are a very generous person, Gabriel, she said.

Gabriel, trembling with delight at her sudden kiss and at the quaintness of her phrase, put his hands on her hair and began smoothing it back, scarcely touching it with his fingers. The washing had made it fine and brilliant. His heart was brimming over with happiness. Just when he was wishing for it she had come to him of her own accord. Perhaps her thoughts had been running with his. Perhaps she had felt the impetuous desire that was in him and then the yielding mood had come upon her. Now that she had fallen to him so easily he wondered why he had been so diffident.

He stood, holding her head between his hands. Then, slipping one arm swiftly about her body and drawing her towards him, he said softly:

—Gretta dear, what are you thinking about?

She did not answer nor yield wholly to his arm. He said again, softly:

—Tell me what it is, Gretta. I think I know what is the matter. Do I know?

She did not answer at once. Then she said in an outburst of tears:

—O, I am thinking about that song, *The Lass of Aughrim*.

She broke loose from him and ran to the bed and, throwing her arms across the bed-rail, hid her face. Gabriel stood stock-still for a moment in astonishment and then followed her. As he passed in the way of the cheval-glass he caught sight of himself in full length, his broad, well-filled shirt-front, the face whose expression always puzzled him when he saw it in a mirror and his glimmering gilt-rimmed eyeglasses. He halted a few paces from her and said:

—What about the song? Why does that make you cry?

She raised her head from her arms and dried her eyes with the back of her hand like a child. A kinder note than he had intended went into his voice.

—Why, Gretta? he asked.

—I am thinking about a person long ago who used to sing that song.

—And who was the person long ago? asked Gabriel, smiling.

—It was a person I used to know in Galway when I was living with my grandmother, she said.

The smile passed away from Gabriel's face. A dull anger began to gather again at the back of his mind and the dull fires of his lust began to glow angrily in his veins.

—Someone you were in love with? he asked ironically.

—It was a young boy I used to know, she answered, named Michael Furey. He used to sing that song, *The Lass of Aughrim*. He was very delicate.

Gabriel was silent. He did not wish her to think that he was interested in this delicate boy.

—I can see him so plainly, she said after a moment. Such eyes as he had: big dark eyes! And such an expression in them—an expression!

—O then, you were in love with him? said Gabriel.

—I used to go out walking with him, she said, when I was in Galway.

A thought flew across Gabriel's mind.

—Perhaps that was why you wanted to go to Galway with that Ivors girl? he said coldly.

She looked at him and asked in surprise:

—What for?

Her eyes made Gabriel feel awkward. He shrugged his shoulders and said:

—How do I know? To see him perhaps.

She looked away from him along the shaft of light towards the window in silence.

—He is dead, she said at length. He died when he was only seventeen. Isn't it a terrible thing to die so young as that?

—What was he? asked Gabriel, still ironically.

—He was in the gasworks, she said.

Gabriel felt humiliated by the failure of his irony and by the evocation of this figure from the dead, a boy in the gasworks. While he had been full of memories of their secret life together, full of tenderness and joy and desire, she had been comparing him in her mind with another. A shameful consciousness of his own person assailed him. He saw himself as a ludicrous figure, acting as a pennyboy[34] for his aunts, a nervous well-meaning sentimentalist, orating to vulgarians and idealising his own clownish lusts, the pitiable fatuous fellow he had caught a glimpse of in the mirror. Instinctively he turned his back more to the light lest she might see the shame that burned upon his forehead.

He tried to keep up his tone of cold interrogation but his voice when he spoke was humble and indifferent.

—I suppose you were in love with this Michael Furey, Gretta, he said.

—I was great with him at that time, she said.

Her voice was veiled and sad. Gabriel, feeling now how vain it would be to try to lead her whither he had purposed, caressed one of her hands and said, also sadly:

—And what did he die of so young, Gretta? Consumption, was it?

—I think he died for me, she answered.

A vague terror seized Gabriel at this answer as if, at that hour when he had hoped to triumph, some impalpable and vindictive being was coming against him, gathering forces against him in its vague world. But he shook himself free of it with an effort of reason and continued to caress her hand. He did not question her again for he felt that she would tell him of herself. Her hand was warm and moist: it did not respond to his touch but he continued to caress it just as he had caressed her first letter to him that spring morning.

—It was in the winter, she said, about the beginning of the winter when I was going to leave my grandmother's and come up here to the convent. And he was ill at the time in his lodgings in Galway and wouldn't be let out and his people in Oughterard were written to. He was in decline, they said, or something like that. I never knew rightly.

She paused for a moment and sighed.

—Poor fellow, she said. He was very fond of me and he was such a gentle boy. We used to go out together, walking, you know, Gabriel, like the way they do in the country. He was going to study singing only for his health. He had a very good voice, poor Michael Furey.

—Well; and then? asked Gabriel.

—And then when it came to the time for me to leave Galway and come up to the convent he was much worse and I wouldn't be let see him so I wrote a letter saying I was going up to Dublin and would be back in the summer and hoping he would be better then.

She paused for a moment to get her voice under control and then went on:

---

[34] An errand boy, or a cheap entertainer who would sing or dance for spare change.

—Then the night before I left I was in my grandmother's house in Nuns' Island, packing up, and I heard gravel thrown up against the window. The window was so wet I couldn't see so I ran downstairs as I was and slipped out the back into the garden and there was the poor fellow at the end of the garden, shivering.

—And did you not tell him to go back? asked Gabriel.

—I implored him to go home at once and told him he would get his death in the rain. But he said he did not want to live. I can see his eyes as well as well! He was standing at the end of the wall where there was a tree.

—And did he go home? asked Gabriel.

—Yes, he went home. And when I was only a week in the convent he died and he was buried in Oughterard where his people came from. O, the day I heard that, that he was dead!

She stopped, choking with sobs, and, overcome by emotion, flung herself face downward on the bed, sobbing in the quilt. Gabriel held her hand for a moment longer, irresolutely, and then, shy of intruding on her grief, let it fall gently and walked quietly to the window.

She was fast asleep.

Gabriel, leaning on his elbow, looked for a few moments unresentfully on her tangled hair and half-open mouth, listening to her deep-drawn breath. So she had had that romance in her life: a man had died for her sake. It hardly pained him now to think how poor a part he, her husband, had played in her life. He watched her while she slept as though he and she had never lived together as man and wife. His curious eyes rested long upon her face and on her hair: and, as he thought of what she must have been then, in that time of her first girlish beauty, a strange friendly pity for her entered his soul. He did not like to say even to himself that her face was no longer beautiful but he knew that it was no longer the face for which Michael Furey had braved death.

Perhaps she had not told him all the story. His eyes moved to the chair over which she had thrown some of her clothes. A petticoat string dangled to the floor. One boot stood upright, its limp upper fallen down: the fellow of it lay upon its side. He wondered at his riot of emotions of an hour before. From what had it proceeded? From his aunt's supper, from his own foolish speech, from the wine and dancing, the merry-making when saying good-night in the hall, the pleasure of the walk along the river in the snow. Poor Aunt Julia! She, too, would soon be a shade with the shade of Patrick Morkan and his horse. He had caught that haggard look upon her face for a moment when she was singing *Arrayed for the Bridal*. Soon, perhaps, he would be sitting in that same drawing-room, dressed in black, his silk hat on his knees. The blinds would be drawn down and Aunt Kate would be sitting beside him, crying and blowing her nose and telling him how Julia had died. He would cast about in his mind for some words that might console her, and would find only lame and useless ones. Yes, yes: that would happen very soon.

The air of the room chilled his shoulders. He stretched himself cautiously along under the sheets and lay down beside his wife. One by one they were all becoming shades. Better pass boldly into that other world, in the full glory of some passion, than fade and wither dismally with age. He thought of how she who lay beside him had locked in her heart for so many years that image of her lover's eyes when he had told her that he did not wish to live.

Generous tears filled Gabriel's eyes. He had never felt like that himself towards any woman but he knew that such a feeling must be love. The tears gathered more thickly in his eyes and in the partial darkness he imagined he saw the form of a young man standing under a dripping tree. Other forms were near. His soul had approached that region where dwell the vast hosts of the dead. He was conscious of, but could not apprehend, their wayward and flickering existence. His own identity was fading out into a grey impalpable world: the solid world itself which these dead had one time reared and lived in was dissolving and dwindling.

A few light taps upon the pane made him turn to the window. It had begun to snow again. He watched sleepily the flakes, silver and dark, falling obliquely against the lamplight. The time had come for him to set out on his journey westward. Yes, the newspapers were right: snow was general all over Ireland. It was falling on every part of the dark central plain, on the treeless hills, falling softly upon the Bog of Allen and, farther westward, softly falling into the dark mutinous Shannon waves. It was falling, too, upon every part of the lonely churchyard on the hill where Michael Furey lay buried. It lay thickly drifted on the crooked crosses and headstones, on the spears of the little gate, on the barren thorns. His soul swooned slowly as he heard the snow falling faintly through the universe and faintly falling, like the descent of their last end, upon all the living and the dead.

VIRGINIA WOOLF
[1882–1941]

Virginia Woolf is too often remembered not for her accomplishments, but for the intermittent mental illness that ultimately led to her suicide during the dark days of early World War II. And yet, Woolf was so much more than her illness and her death: a woman with a genius for friendship; in her own soft-spoken manner, a feminist; a devoted wife and partner; and above all, a brilliant, innovative writer who was by turns playful, philosophical, lyrical, analytical, sensuous, affectionate, perceptive, and fiercely life-affirming. Although in private life she avoided Freudian analysis, in her fiction she advanced the modernist narrative techniques of stream-of-consciousness and symbolism that drew heavily on Freud's theories; she and her husband, Leonard Woolf, through their Hogarth Press, made Freud's works widely available in English translation. Woolf's novels increasingly strove to break away from patriarchal conventions of fiction to reflect women's thought patterns, viewpoints, and sense of time. Like many of her female contemporaries, Woolf was wary of the label "feminist," but wrote two volumes of pioneering feminist essays exploring women's creativity and the factors that inhibit it.

LIFE

Adeline Virginia Stephen was born January 25, 1882, the third child and second daughter of Leslie and Julia Princep Stephen. Woolf and her older sister, Vanessa, were close companions all their lives, and she adored her older brother, Thoby. A younger brother, Adrian, was born in 1883. Both parents had been previously married and widowed, and Woolf had half-siblings on both sides of the family. The children of her mother's first marriage—Stella, George, and Gerald Duckworth—were to figure importantly in Woolf's early life.

Virginia Woolf's father was the epitome of the eminent Victorian. Not wealthy but sufficiently well-off, he was a literary man—a critic, scholar, magazine editor, and biographer. Virginia's mother, Julia Stephen, was celebrated for her lively charm and her perfect profile. Virginia was the uneasy heir of her mother's beauty. The Duckworth and Stephen children grew up in the heady intellectual atmosphere of a household that regularly entertained such luminaries of late-Victorian culture as writers Alfred, Lord Tennyson, Henry James, and George Meredith; painters Holman Hunt and Edward Burne-Jones; and actress Ellen Terry. Woolf's great-aunt on her mother's side was the pioneering photographer Julia Cameron.

There were many pleasures and challenges in this upbringing, especially in the summers spent in the family's country house on the Cornwall coast. But Woolf bravely described her early family experience as "tangled and matted with emotion." The most sinister elements were her two Duckworth half brothers, who sexually abused Virginia and Vanessa at different times over the course of the girls' childhood and adolescence. As an adult, Woolf wrote of the abuse, but like many victims she seems never to have connected her half brothers' acts with her own sexual frigidity or her mental illness as an adult. Instead, she simply concluded that she was born naturally deficient in sensuality and mental health.

Like most girls of their social class, Woolf and her sister were tutored at home by their mother and a series of governesses. Formal education was reserved for the boys, but Leslie Stephen was wise enough to discern Virginia's gifts. When she asked to learn ancient Greek, he cheerfully hired her a tutor. He allowed her to read any book in his library and enjoyed discussing literature with her. Her mother imparted a different sort of lesson, for she was imbued with the Victorian ideal that women were born to fulfill their highest natures by serving others cheerfully. When grown, Woolf would characterize that ideal as "The Angel in the House," and would identify it as the dangerous spirit that keeps women from expressing themselves, making them intent on pleasing men rather than being true to their own natures and talents.

Traumatic events marred Woolf's adolescence, beginning with the sudden death of her mother the year she turned thirteen. Until she was forty-four and had written *To The Lighthouse* (1927), whose main character, Mrs. Ramsey, is based on Julia Stephen, Woolf was literally haunted by the apparition and voice of her dead mother. Her much-beloved half sister, Stella Duckworth, stepped in as a maternal figure for her stepfamily, but a scant two years later, while honeymooning with her new husband, she died of a sudden acute infection. Leslie Stephen grew more and more depressed and withdrawn, and for the remainder of their adolescence Virginia and Vanessa were left to the mercies of their incestuous half brother George, who was intent on making them into social successes. Miserable, Woolf suffered the first of a series of mental breakdowns that would recur intermittently throughout her life.

Her father died when she was twenty-two, in 1904. Although her grief for him was enough to precipitate a second breakdown, his death also freed her. She began teaching at a night school for working-class people, joined the suffrage movement, and wrote book reviews. By 1905, Thoby, Vanessa, Virginia, and Adrian Stephen had moved together into a flat in the Bloomsbury section of London and began keeping lively company with Thoby's friends, a household arrangement that would last until Thoby's death of typhoid fever in 1906. Many of the brilliant men who came to the Stephen children's home were members of a society at Cambridge they named the Apostles. Most were on their way to becoming the intellectual lights of their generation in England. Many were bisexual or gay, and their uninhibited discussions often centered on sexuality as well as art and politics. Eventually their circle, called "Bloomsbury" by social historians, included historian Lytton Strachey; economic theorist John Maynard Keynes; novelist E. M. Forster; painter Duncan Grant; art critic Roger Frye; artist and art critic Clive Bell, whom Vanessa would marry in 1907; and civil administrator Leonard Woolf, later a policy developer for the Labour Party, whom Virginia would marry in 1912.

For Virginia Stephen, Leonard Woolf proved the wisest choice she could have made. Always held as something of an outsider because he was Jewish, Leonard provided for

Virginia a slight distancing from the intense intellectual involvements of Bloomsbury. For the rest of his life, his real occupation would be to care tenderly for his wife, nursing her through her terrifying bouts of illness, arranging her life, protecting and supporting her, and keeping her as well and productive as possible.

One offshoot of this quest for health was the establishment of the Hogarth Press, originally conceived as a project that would engage Virginia in simple therapeutic tasks such as typesetting and bookbinding. The press, however, became a commercial and artistic success, publishing authors such as Katherine Mansfield and T. S. Eliot, as well as the Woolfs' own work. Leonard Woolf's greatest literary achievement would prove to be the sensitive, detailed memoirs and diaries in which he chronicled his and Virginia's years together. Apparently their marriage was virtually sexless. Throughout her life, Virginia Woolf's passion was awakened only by other women, though even with other women, actual physical lovemaking seems to have been troubling and unsatisfactory. Despite at least one significant affair between Virginia and another woman—the flamboyant Vita Sackville-West—the Woolfs remained a devoted couple from the time of their marriage until Virginia's death twenty-nine years later. Together they wrote, and ran the Hogarth Press when she was well; and together they contrived to get Virginia through the major breakdowns that came regularly with the completion of each book. Finally, however, even Leonard Woolf's most loving strategies could not keep Virginia from suicide. In March 1941, anguished by the death of a favorite nephew in the Spanish Civil War and by the Nazi bombings that destroyed both their London house and the building that housed the Hogarth Press, Woolf feared that she was about to undergo a permanent breakdown that would leave her a burden to her husband. On March 28, 1941, she weighted her pockets with heavy stones and waded into the River Ouse below their country house in Sussex. After her body was recovered, Leonard buried Virginia's ashes beneath one of the great elms there, and chose for her epitaph a sentence from *The Waves* (1931): "Against you I will fling myself, unvanquished and unyielding, O Death!"

WORK

There is little question that Leonard Woolf's presence enabled his wife to write. It was only after their marriage that she managed to complete her first novel, *The Voyage Out* (1915), which she had begun in 1907. Both *The Voyage Out* and her second novel, *Night and Day* (1919), are relatively conventional novels about young women not unlike herself, exploring questions of marriage and art. But with *Jacob's Room* (1922), Woolf began to experiment with subject and narrative form. The book, about a young man who resembles her brother Thoby, does not present the major incidents in the protagonist's life either chronologically or directly—we learn of Jacob's death only by way of his mother cleaning out his room and wondering how to dispose of his personal effects. The main theme seems to be the impossibility of truly knowing the inner workings of Jacob or any other character. In her next novel, *Mrs. Dalloway* (1925), Woolf centered on a single day in the lives of a London society woman and a shell-shocked veteran of World War I who is in some sense her alter ego. Woolf shifts the narrative point of view back and forth between the sane and the insane character, gradually revealing the deep similarities between them, although they never meet.

In the lyrical, semiautobiographical *To the Lighthouse* (1927), the novel that was to exorcise her mother's presence, Woolf explored the theme of women's roles while continuing to advance the stream-of-consciousness narrative technique. The following year, she delivered the lectures on women and creativity at Newnham College, Cambridge, that would become *A Room of One's Own* (1929), from which the selection that follows is excerpted. Woolf's delight in Vita Sackville-West, her adventurous cross-dressing friend and lover, inspired the ebullient tour de force *Orlando* (1928), whose protagonist begins as a male adolescent in Elizabethan England, undergoes a mysterious sex-change along about the time of the Restoration, and while still in her thirties ends up a successful female writer in contemporary London.

With her next book, *The Waves* (1931), Woolf's work began to grow less exuberant, reflecting her growing difficulty in the last decade of life of keeping her life and work together. Thought by many to be her masterpiece, *The Waves* is Woolf's most experimental novel, with six different characters' stream-of-consciousness monologues all meditating on the death of a friend they hold in common, a character again modeled on Thoby. *The Years* (1937) brought Woolf her first wide popularity, setting forth the history of an upper-class English family, from the late-Victorian age to the present. As political events in Europe darkened, she wrote *I Take Three Guineas* (1938), a brilliant feminist and pacifist work in which she explores the connections between fascism and the patriarchy in which she had been raised. Not surprisingly, the book received many negative reviews as a tract for what E. M. Forster called "extreme feminism." *Between the Acts* (1941), the book Woolf finished drafting just before her death, is a complex narrative: In the context of a country house neighboring families anticipate and then attend a village pageant. The work considers issues of time, history, loss, and the question of what endures despite and beyond them.

In the chapter presented here from *A Room of One's Own*, Woolf's imagining of the fate of the fictional Judith Shakespeare begins after the narrator returns frustrated from the British Museum library, where she has been unable to find any text that will help her understand why women have not achieved equally with men. She is desperate to account for the disparity, but none of the books helps. Glancing through her own copy of Trevelyan's *History of England*, the narrator sees that women are all but excised from the history, save for the most cursory and condescending references, and understands that she will need to fashion for herself a model of what life might have been like for an Elizabethan woman with Shakespeare's gifts. The sensuous detail with which Woolf fleshes out this sadly predictable story, and the beautifully controlled tone in which she tells it, are essayist and feminist Virginia Woolf at her best.

SUGGESTED READINGS

Woolf's nephew Quentin Bell wrote both her official biography, *Virginia Woolf* (1972), and *Bloomsbury* (1968), a good introduction to the Woolfs' social and intellectual milieu. Phyllis Rose's *Woman of Letters* (1978) is an excellent short critical biography.

A Room of One's Own

CHAPTER 3. [SHAKESPEARE'S SISTER][1]

It was disappointing not to have brought back in the evening some important statement, some authentic fact. Women are poorer than men because—this or that. Perhaps now it would be better to give up seeking for the truth, and receiving on one's head an avalanche of opinion hot as lava, discoloured as dish-water. It would

---

[1]Woolf has just returned from the library of the British Museum, where she has had no success in finding books that might help her understand why women seem to have achieved so much less than men throughout history.

be better to draw the curtains; to shut out distractions; to light the lamp; to narrow the enquiry and to ask the historian, who records not opinions but facts, to describe under what conditions women lived, not throughout the ages, but in England, say in the time of Elizabeth.

For it is a perennial puzzle why no woman wrote a word of that extraordinary literature when every other man, it seemed, was capable of song or sonnet. What were the conditions in which women lived, I asked myself; for fiction, imaginative work that is, is not dropped like a pebble upon the ground, as science may be; fiction is like a spider's web, attached ever so lightly perhaps, but still attached to life at all four corners. Often the attachment is scarcely perceptible; Shakespeare's plays, for instance, seem to hang there complete by themselves. But when the web is pulled askew, hooked up at the edge, torn in the middle, one remembers that these webs are not spun in mid-air by incorporeal creatures, but are the work of suffering human beings, and are attached to grossly material things, like health and money and the houses we live in.

I went, therefore, to the shelf where the histories stand and took down one of the latest, Professor Trevelyan's *History of England.*[2] Once more I looked up Women, found "position of," and turned to the pages indicated. "Wife-beating," I read, "was a recognised right of man, and was practised without shame by high as well as low.... Similarly," the historian goes on, "the daughter who refused to marry the gentleman of her parents' choice was liable to be locked up, beaten and flung about the room, without any shock being inflicted on public opinion. Marriage was not an affair of personal affection, but of family avarice, particularly in the 'chivalrous' upper classes.... Betrothal often took place while one or both of the parties was in the cradle, and marriage when they were scarcely out of the nurses' charge." That was about 1470, soon after Chaucer's time. The next reference to the position of women is some two hundred years later, in the time of the Stuarts. "It was still the exception for women of the upper and middle class to choose their own husbands, and when the husband had been assigned, he was lord and master, so far at least as law and custom could make him. Yet even so," Professor Trevelyan concludes, "neither Shakespeare's women nor those of authentic seventeenth-century memoirs, like the Verneys and the Hutchinsons,[3] seem wanting in personality and character." Certainly, if we consider it, Cleopatra must have had a way with her; Lady Macbeth, one would suppose, had a will of her own; Rosalind, one might conclude, was an attractive girl.[4] Professor Trevelyan is speaking no more than the truth when he remarks that Shakespeare's women do not seem wanting in personality and character. Not being a historian, one might go even further and say that women have burnt like beacons in all the works of all the poets from the beginning of time—Clytemnestra, Antigone, Cleopatra, Lady Macbeth, Phèdre, Cressida, Rosalind, Desdemona, the Duchess of Malfi, among the dramatists; then among the prose writers: Millamant, Clarissa, Becky Sharp, Anna Karenina, Emma Bovary, Madame de Guermantes[5]—the names flock to

---

[2]G. M. Trevelyan's *History of England* (1926) was, in Woolf's day, the most popular short history of the nation.

[3]Authors of family memoirs of seventeenth-century England.

[4]Shakespeare's heroines from the plays *Antony and Cleopatra, Macbeth,* and *As You Like It,* respectively. Woolf is using the irony of understatement here.

[5]All are famous women characters from drama and fiction. In order, they are from Aeschylus' *Agamemnon;* Sophocles' *Antigone;* Shakespeare's *Antony and Cleopatra* and *Macbeth;* Racine's *Phèdre;* Shakespeare's *Troilus and Cressida, As You Like It,* and *Othello;* Webster's *The Duchess of Malfi;* Congreve's *The Way of the World;* Richardson's *Clarissa;* Thackeray's *Vanity Fair;* Tolstoy's *Anna Karenina;* Flaubert's *Madame Bovary;* and Proust's *Remembrance of Things Past.*

mind, nor do they recall women "lacking in personality and character." Indeed, if woman had no existence save in the fiction written by men, one would imagine her a person of the utmost importance; very various; heroic and mean; splendid and sordid; infinitely beautiful and hideous in the extreme; as great as a man, some think even greater.[6] But this is woman in fiction. In fact, as Professor Trevelyan points out, she was locked up, beaten and flung about the room.

A very queer, composite being thus emerges. Imaginatively she is of the highest importance; practically she is completely insignificant. She pervades poetry from cover to cover; she is all but absent from history. She dominates the lives of kings and conquerors in fiction; in fact she was the slave of any boy whose parents forced a ring upon her finger. Some of the most inspired words, some of the most profound thoughts in literature fall from her lips; in real life she could hardly read, could scarcely spell, and was the property of her husband.

It was certainly an odd monster that one made up by reading the historians first and the poets afterwards—a worm winged like an eagle; the spirit of life and beauty in a kitchen chopping up suet. But these monsters, however amusing to the imagination, have no existence in fact. What one must do to bring her to life was to think poetically and prosaically at one and the same moment, thus keeping in touch with fact—that she is Mrs. Martin, aged thirty-six, dressed in blue, wearing a black hat and brown shoes; but not losing sight of fiction either—that she is a vessel in which all sorts of spirits and forces are coursing and flashing perpetually. The moment, however, that one tries this method with the Elizabethan woman, one branch of illumination fails; one is held up by the scarcity of facts. One knows nothing detailed, nothing perfectly true and substantial about her. History scarcely mentions her. And I turned to Professor Trevelyan again to see what history meant to him. I found by looking at his chapter headings that it meant—

"The Manor Court and the Methods of Open-field Agriculture...The Cistercians and Sheep-farming...The Crusades...The University...The House of Commons...The Hundred Years' War...The Wars of the Roses...The Renaissance Scholars...The Dissolution of the Monasteries...Agrarian and Religious Strife...The Origin of English Sea-power...The Armada..." and so on. Occasionally an individual woman is mentioned, an Elizabeth, or a Mary; a queen or a great lady. But by no possible means could middle-class women with nothing but brains and character at their command have taken part in any one of the great movements which, brought together, constitute the historian's view of the past. Nor shall we find her in any collection of anecdotes. Aubrey[7] hardly mentions her. She never writes her own life and scarcely keeps a diary; there are only a handful

---

[6]"It remains a strange and almost inexplicable fact that in Athena's city, where women were kept in almost Oriental suppression as odalisques or drudges, the stage should yet have produced figures like Clytemnestra and Cassandra, Atossa and Antigone, Phèdre and Medea, and all the other heroines who dominate play after play of the 'misogynist' Euripides. But the paradox of this world where in real life a respectable woman could hardly show her face alone in the street, and yet on the stage woman equals or surpasses man, has never been satisfactorily explained. In modern tragedy the same predominance exists. At all events, a very cursory survey of Shakespeare's work (similarly with Webster, though not with Marlowe or Jonson) suffices to reveal how this dominance, this initiative of women, persists from Rosalind to Lady Macbeth. So too in Racine; six of his tragedies bear their heroines' names; and what male characters of his shall we set against Hermione and Andromaque, Bérénice and Roxane, Phèdre and Athalie? So again with Ibsen; what men shall we match with Solveig and Nora, Hedda and Hilda Wangel and Rebecca West?"—F. L. LUCAS, Tragedy, pp. 114–15. [Woolf's note]

[7]John Aubrey (1626–1697) was a British diarist.

of her letters in existence. She left no plays or poems by which we can judge her. What one wants, I thought—and why does not some brilliant student at Newnham or Girton[8] supply it?—is a mass of information; at what age did she marry; how many children had she as a rule; what was her house like; had she a room to herself; did she do the cooking; would she be likely to have a servant? All these facts lie somewhere, presumably, in parish registers and account books; the life of the average Elizabethan woman must be scattered about somewhere, could one collect it and make a book of it. It would be ambitious beyond my daring, I thought, looking about the shelves for books that were not there, to suggest to the students of those famous colleges that they should re-write history, though I own that it often seems a little queer as it is, unreal, lop-sided; but why should they not add a supplement to history? calling it, of course, by some inconspicuous name so that women might figure there without impropriety? For one often catches a glimpse of them in the lives of the great, whisking away into the background, concealing, I sometimes think, a wink, a laugh, perhaps a tear. And, after all, we have lives enough of Jane Austen; it scarcely seems necessary to consider again the influence of the tragedies of Joanna Baillie upon the poetry of Edgar Allan Poe;[9] as for myself, I should not mind if the homes and haunts of Mary Russell Mitford[10] were closed to the public for a century at least. But what I find deplorable, I continued, looking about the bookshelves again, is that nothing is known about women before the eighteenth century. I have no model in my mind to turn about this way and that. Here am I asking why women did not write poetry in the Elizabethan age, and I am not sure how they were educated; whether they were taught to write; whether they had sitting-rooms to themselves; how many women had children before they were twenty-one; what, in short, they did from eight in the morning till eight at night. They had no money evidently; according to Professor Trevelyan they were married whether they liked it or not before they were out of the nursery, at fifteen or sixteen very likely. It would have been extremely odd, even upon this showing, had one of them suddenly written the plays of Shakespeare, I concluded, and I thought of that old gentleman, who is dead now, but was a bishop, I think, who declared that it was impossible for any woman, past, present, or to come, to have the genius of Shakespeare. He wrote to the papers about it. He also told a lady who applied to him for information that cats do not as a matter of fact go to heaven, though they have, he added, souls of a sort. How much thinking those old gentlemen used to save one! How the borders of ignorance shrank back at their approach! Cats do not go to heaven. Women cannot write the plays of Shakespeare.

Be that as it may, I could not help thinking, as I looked at the works of Shakespeare on the shelf, that the bishop was right at least in this; it would have been impossible, completely and entirely, for any woman to have written the plays of Shakespeare in the age of Shakespeare. Let me imagine, since facts are so hard to come by, what would have happened had Shakespeare had a wonderfully gifted sister, called Judith, let us say. Shakespeare himself went, very probably—his mother was an heiress—to the grammar school, where he may have learnt Latin—Ovid,

---

[8] Women's colleges of Cambridge University.

[9] Baillie was an English dramatist (1762–1851); Edgar Allan Poe (1809–1849) was an American poet and fiction writer.

[10] Mary Russell Mitford (1787–1855) wrote accounts of life in the English countryside.

Virgil and Horace[11]—and the elements of grammar and logic. He was, it is well known, a wild boy who poached rabbits, perhaps shot a deer, and had, rather sooner than he should have done, to marry a woman in the neighbourhood, who bore him a child rather quicker than was right. That escapade sent him to seek his fortune in London. He had, it seemed, a taste for the theatre; he began by holding horses at the stage door. Very soon he got work in the theatre, became a successful actor, and lived at the hub of the universe, meeting everybody, knowing everybody, practising his art on the boards, exercising his wits in the streets, and even getting access to the palace of the queen. Meanwhile his extraordinarily gifted sister, let us suppose, remained at home. She was as adventurous, as imaginative, as agog to see the world as he was. But she was not sent to school. She had no chance of learning grammar and logic, let alone of reading Horace and Virgil. She picked up a book now and then, one of her brother's perhaps, and read a few pages. But then her parents came in and told her to mend the stockings or mind the stew and not moon about with books and papers. They would have spoken sharply but kindly, for they were substantial people who knew the conditions of life for a woman and loved their daughter—indeed, more likely than not she was the apple of her father's eye. Perhaps she scribbled some pages up in an apple loft on the sly, but was careful to hide them or set fire to them. Soon, however, before she was out of her teens, she was to be betrothed to the son of a neighbouring wool-stapler.[12] She cried out that marriage was hateful to her, and for that she was severely beaten by her father. Then he ceased to scold her. He begged her instead not to hurt him, not to shame him in this matter of her marriage. He would give her a chain of beads or a fine petticoat, he said; and there were tears in his eyes. How could she disobey him? How could she break his heart? The force of her own gift alone drove her to it. She made up a small parcel of her belongings, let herself down by a rope one summer's night and took the road to London. She was not seventeen. The birds that sang in the hedge were not more musical than she was. She had the quickest fancy, a gift like her brother's, for the tune of words. Like him, she had a taste for the theatre. She stood at the stage door; she wanted to act, she said. Men laughed in her face. The manager—a fat, loose-lipped man—guffawed. He bellowed something about poodles dancing and women acting—no woman, he said, could possibly be an actress. He hinted—you can imagine what. She could get no training in her craft. Could she even seek her dinner in a tavern or roam the streets at midnight? Yet her genius was for fiction and lusted to feed abundantly upon the lives of men and women and the study of their ways. At last—for she was very young, oddly like Shakespeare the poet in her face, with the same grey eyes and rounded brows—at last Nick Greene the actor-manager took pity on her; she found herself with child by that gentleman and so—who shall measure the heat and violence of the poet's heart when caught and tangled in a woman's body?—killed herself one winter's night and lies buried at some cross-roads where the omnibuses now stop outside the Elephant and Castle.[13]

That, more or less, is how the story would run, I think, if a woman in Shakespeare's day had had Shakespeare's genius. But for my part, I agree with the

---

[11] Great Roman poets of the Augustan Age, standard fare for any schoolboy learning Latin.

[12] Wool-dealer.

[13] A pub. As a suicide, Judith could not be buried in consecrated ground. Burial at a crossroads was thought to keep the restless spirits of suicides safely in their graves.

deceased bishop, if such he was—it is unthinkable that any woman in Shakespeare's day should have had Shakespeare's genius. For genius like Shakespeare's is not born among labouring, uneducated, servile people. It was not born in England among the Saxons and the Britons. It is not born today among the working classes. How, then, could it have been born among women whose work began, according to Professor Trevelyan, almost before they were out of the nursery, who were forced to it by their parents and held to it by all the power of law and custom? Yet genius of a sort must have existed among women as it must have existed among the working classes. Now and again an Emily Brontë or a Robert Burns[14] blazes out and proves its presence. But certainly it never got itself on to paper. When, however, one reads of a witch being ducked, of a woman possessed by devils, of a wise woman selling herbs, or even of a very remarkable man who had a mother, then I think we are on the track of a lost novelist, a suppressed poet, of some mute and inglorious Jane Austen, some Emily Brontë who dashed her brains out on the moor or mopped and mowed about the highways crazed with the torture that her gift had put her to. Indeed, I would venture to guess that Anon, who wrote so many poems without signing them, was often a woman. It was a woman Edward Fitzgerald,[15] I think, suggested who made the ballads and the folk-songs, crooning them to her children, beguiling her spinning with them, or the length of the winter's night.

This may be true or it may be false—who can say?—but what is true in it, so it seemed to me, reviewing the story of Shakespeare's sister as I had made it, is that any woman born with a great gift in the sixteenth century would certainly have gone crazed, shot herself, or ended her days in some lonely cottage outside the village, half witch, half wizard, feared and mocked at. For it needs little skill in psychology to be sure that a highly gifted girl who had tried to use her gift for poetry would have been so thwarted and hindered by other people, so tortured and pulled asunder by her own contrary instincts, that she must have lost her health and sanity to a certainty. No girl could have walked to London and stood at a stage door and forced her way into the presence of actor-managers without doing herself a violence and suffering an anguish which may have been irrational—for chastity may be a fetish invented by certain societies for unknown reasons—but were none the less inevitable. Chastity had then, it has even now, a religious importance in a woman's life, and has so wrapped itself round with nerves and instincts that to cut it free and bring it to the light of day demands courage of the rarest. To have lived a free life in London in the sixteenth century would have meant for a woman who was poet and playwright a nervous stress and dilemma which might well have killed her. Had she survived, whatever she had written would have been twisted and deformed, issuing from a strained and morbid imagination. And undoubtedly, I thought, looking at the shelf where there are no plays by women, her work would have gone unsigned. That refuge she would have sought certainly. It was the relic of the sense of chastity that dictated anonymity to women even so late as the nineteenth century. Currer Bell, George Eliot, George Sand,[16] all the victims of inner strife as their writings prove, sought ineffectively to veil themselves by using the name of a man. Thus

---

[14] The Scots poet Robert Burns (1759–1796) came from the working class; the novelist Emily Brontë (1818–1848) had been raised as the sheltered and isolated daughter of a country curate.

[15] Edward Fitzgerald (1809–1883) was a popular poet and translator.

[16] The male pen names of the writers Charlotte Brontë, Marian Evans, and Aurore Dupin.

they did homage to the convention, which if not implanted by the other sex was liberally encouraged by them (the chief glory of a woman is not to be talked of, said Pericles,[17] himself a much-talked-of man), that publicity in women is detestable. Anonymity runs in their blood. The desire to be veiled still possesses them. They are not even now as concerned about the health of their fame as men are, and, speaking generally, will pass a tombstone or a signpost without feeling an irresistible desire to cut their names on it, as Alf, Bert or Chas. must do in obedience to their instinct, which murmurs if it sees a fine woman go by, or even a dog, Ce chien est à moi.[18] And, of course, it may not be a dog, I thought, remembering Parliament Square, the Sièges Allée[19] and other avenues; it may be a piece of land or a man with curly black hair. It is one of the great advantages of being a woman that one can pass even a very fine negress without wishing to make an Englishwoman of her.

That woman, then, who was born with a gift of poetry in the sixteenth century, was an unhappy woman, a woman at strife against herself. All the conditions of her life, all her own instincts, were hostile to the state of mind which is needed to set free whatever is in the brain. But what is the state of mind that is most propitious to the act of creation, I asked. Can one come by any notion of the state that furthers and makes possible that strange activity? Here I opened the volume containing the Tragedies of Shakespeare. What was Shakespeare's state of mind, for instance, when he wrote *Lear* and *Antony and Cleopatra*? It was certainly the state of mind most favourable to poetry that there has ever existed. But Shakespeare himself said nothing about it. We only know casually and by chance that he "never blotted a line."[20] Nothing indeed was ever said by the artist himself about his state of mind until the eighteenth century perhaps. Rousseau perhaps began it. At any rate, by the nineteenth century self-consciousness had developed so far that it was the habit for men of letters to describe their minds in confessions and autobiographies. Their lives also were written, and their letters were printed after their deaths. Thus, though we do not know what Shakespeare went through when he wrote *Lear*, we do know what Carlyle went through when he wrote the *French Revolution*; what Flaubert went through when he wrote *Madame Bovary*; what Keats was going through when he tried to write poetry against the coming of death and the indifference of the world.[21]

And one gathers from this enormous modern literature of confession and self-analysis that to write a work of genius is almost always a feat of prodigious difficulty. Everything is against the likelihood that it will come from the writer's mind whole and entire. Generally material circumstances are against it. Dogs will bark; people will interrupt; money must be made; health will break down. Further, accentuating all these difficulties and making them harder to bear is the world's notorious indifference. It does not ask people to write poems and novels and histories; it does not need them. It does not care whether Flaubert finds the right word or whether Carlyle scrupulously verifies this or that fact. Naturally, it will not pay for what it

---

[17] Pericles (c. 500–429 B.C.E.) was a powerful Athenian statesman.

[18] "That dog is mine" (French).

[19] The seats of power of England and France; Woolf sees the root of colonialism in the male desire to possess.

[20] Ben Jonson claimed this in *Timber, or Discoveries* (1691).

[21] All these authors encountered adversity. The first draft of Thomas Carlyle's *The French Revolution* (1837) was accidentally burned; Gustave Flaubert was charged with obscenity for writing *Madame Bovary* (1857); Keats wrote his great odes knowing he was soon to die of tuberculosis.

does not want. And so the writer, Keats, Flaubert, Carlyle, suffers, especially in the creative years of youth, every form of distraction and discouragement. A curse, a cry of agony, rises from those books of analysis and confession. "Mighty poets in their misery dead"[22]—that is the burden of their song. If anything comes through in spite of all this, it is a miracle, and probably no book is born entire and uncrippled as it was conceived.

But for women, I thought, looking at the empty shelves, these difficulties were infinitely more formidable. In the first place, to have a room of her own, let alone a quiet room or a sound-proof room, was out of the question, unless her parents were exceptionally rich or very noble, even up to the beginning of the nineteenth century. Since her pin money, which depended on the good will of her father, was only enough to keep her clothed, she was debarred from such alleviations as came even to Keats or Tennyson or Carlyle, all poor men, from a walking tour, a little journey to France, from the separate lodging which, even if it were miserable enough, sheltered them from the claims and tyrannies of their families. Such material difficulties were formidable; but much worse were the immaterial. The indifference of the world which Keats and Flaubert and other men of genius have found so hard to bear was in her case not indifference but hostility. The world did not say to her as it said to them, Write if you choose; it makes no difference to me. The world said with a guffaw, Write? What's the good of your writing? Here the psychologists of Newnham and Girton might come to our help, I thought, looking again at the blank spaces on the shelves. For surely it is time that the effect of discouragement upon the mind of the artist should be measured, as I have seen a dairy company measure the effect of ordinary milk and Grade A milk upon the body of the rat. They set two rats in cages side by side, and of the two one was furtive, timid and small, and the other was glossy, bold and big. Now what food do we feed women as artists upon? I asked, remembering, I suppose, that dinner of prunes and custard.[23] To answer that question I had only to open the evening paper and to read that Lord Birkenhead[24] is of opinion—but really I am not going to trouble to copy out Lord Birkenhead's opinion upon the writing of women. What Dean Inge[25] says I will leave in peace. The Harley Street[26] specialist may be allowed to rouse the echoes of Harley Street with his vociferations without raising a hair on my head. I will quote, however, Mr. Oscar Browning,[27] because Mr. Oscar Browning was a great figure in Cambridge at one time, and used to examine the students at Girton and Newnham. Mr. Oscar Browning was wont to declare "that the impression left on his mind, after looking over any set of examination papers, was that, irrespective of the marks he might give, the best woman was intellectually the inferior of the worst man." After saying that Mr. Browning went back to his rooms—and it is this sequel that endears him and makes him a human figure of some bulk and majesty—he went back to his rooms and found a stable-boy lying on the sofa—"a mere skeleton, his cheeks were cavernous and sallow, his teeth were black, and he did not appear to have the full use of his limbs. . . . 'That's Arthur' [said Mr. Browning]. 'He's a dear boy really and most high-minded.' " The two pictures always seem to me to complete each other. And happily in this age of biography the two pictures often

---

[22] A line from William Wordsworth's poem "Resolution and Independence."

[23] Earlier, Woolf describes eating such a meal at a women's college while male students dine heartily.

[24] The Earl of Birkenhead, lord chancellor of England from 1919 to 1922, reportedly said women's achievements amounted to nothing.

[25] William Ralph Inge, dean of St. Paul's Cathedral, 1911–1934.

[26] Location of fashionable London doctors' offices.

[27] Oscar Browning (1837–1923), lecturer in History at Cambridge.

do complete each other, so that we are able to interpret the opinions of great men not only by what they say, but by what they do.

But though this is possible now, such opinions coming from the lips of important people must have been formidable enough even fifty years ago. Let us suppose that a father from the highest motives did not wish his daughter to leave home and become writer, painter or scholar. "See what Mr. Oscar Browning says," he would say; and there was not only Mr. Oscar Browning; there was the *Saturday Review*; there was Mr. Greg[28]—the "essentials of a woman's being," said Mr. Greg emphatically, "are that *they are supported by, and they minister to, men*"—there was an enormous body of masculine opinion to the effect that nothing could be expected of women intellectually. Even if her father did not read out loud these opinions, any girl could read them for herself; and the reading, even in the nineteenth century, must have lowered her vitality, and told profoundly upon her work. There would always have been that assertion—you cannot do this, you are incapable of doing that—to protest against, to overcome. Probably for a novelist this germ is no longer of much effect; for there have been women novelists of merit. But for painters it must still have some sting in it; and for musicians, I imagine, is even now active and poisonous in the extreme. The woman composer stands where the actress stood in the time of Shakespeare. Nick Greene, I thought, remembering the story I had made about Shakespeare's sister, said that a woman acting put him in mind of a dog dancing. Johnson repeated the phrase two hundred years later of women preaching. And here, I said, opening a book about music, we have the very words used again in this year of grace, 1928, of women who try to write music. "Of Mlle. Germaine Tailleferre one can only repeat Dr. Johnson's dictum concerning a woman preacher, transposed into terms of music. 'Sir, a woman's composing is like a dog's walking on his hind legs. It is not done well, but you are surprised to find it done at all.'"[29] So accurately does history repeat itself.

Thus, I concluded, shutting Mr. Oscar Browning's life and pushing away the rest, it is fairly evident that even in the nineteenth century a woman was not encouraged to be an artist. On the contrary, she was snubbed, slapped, lectured and exhorted. Her mind must have been strained and her vitality lowered by the need of opposing this, of disproving that. For here again we come within range of that very interesting and obscure masculine complex which has had so much influence upon the woman's movement; that deep-seated desire, not so much that *she* shall be inferior as that *he* shall be superior, which plants him wherever one looks, not only in front of the arts, but barring the way to politics too, even when the risk to himself seems infinitesimal and the suppliant humble and devoted. Even Lady Bessborough, I remembered, with all her passion for politics, must humbly bow herself and write to Lord Granville Leveson-Gower: "... notwithstanding all my violence in politics and talking so much on that subject, I perfectly agree with you that no woman has any business to meddle with that or any other serious business, farther than giving her opinion (if she is ask'd)."[30] And so she goes on to spend her enthusiasm where it meets with no obstacle whatsoever upon that immensely important subject, Lord Granville's maiden speech in the House of Commons. The spectacle is certainly a strange one, I thought. The history of men's opposition to women's emancipation

---

[28]W. W. Greg (1875–1959), editor, librarian, and reviewer.

[29]*A Survey of Contemporary Music* [1924], Cecil Gray, p. 246. [Woolf's note.] Germaine Tailleferre (1892–1983) was a French composer, a disciple of Erik Satie.

[30]Henrietta Spencer's correspondence with Lord Granville, Foreign Secretary under William Gladstone, was well-known.

is more interesting perhaps than the story of that emancipation itself. An amusing book might be made of it if some young student at Girton or Newnham would collect examples and deduce a theory—but she would need thick gloves on her hands, and bars to protect her of solid gold.

But what is amusing now, I recollected, shutting Lady Bessborough, had to be taken in desperate earnest once. Opinions that one now pastes in a book labelled cock-a-doodle-dum and keeps for reading to select audiences on summer nights once drew tears, I can assure you. Among your grandmothers and great-grandmothers there were many that wept their eyes out. Florence Nightingale shrieked aloud in her agony.[31] Moreover, it is all very well for you, who have got yourselves to college and enjoy sitting-rooms—or is it only bed-sitting-rooms?—of your own to say that genius should disregard such opinions; that genius should be above caring what is said of it. Unfortunately, it is precisely the men or women of genius who mind most what is said of them. Remember Keats. Remember the words he had cut on his tombstone.[32] Think of Tennyson; think—but I need hardly multiply instances of the undeniable, if very unfortunate, fact that it is the nature of the artist to mind excessively what is said about him. Literature is strewn with the wreckage of men who have minded beyond reason the opinions of others.

And this susceptibility of theirs is doubly unfortunate, I thought, returning again to my original enquiry into what state of mind is most propitious for creative work, because the mind of an artist, in order to achieve the prodigious effort of freeing whole and entire the work that is in him, must be incandescent, like Shakespeare's mind, I conjectured, looking at the book which lay open at *Antony and Cleopatra*. There must be no obstacle in it, no foreign matter unconsumed.

For though we say that we know nothing about Shakespeare's state of mind, even as we say that, we are saying something about Shakespeare's state of mind. The reason perhaps why we know so little of Shakespeare—compared with Donne or Ben Jonson or Milton—is that his grudges and spites and antipathies are hidden from us. We are not held up by some "revelation" which reminds us of the writer. All desire to protest, to preach, to proclaim an injury, to pay off a score, to make the world the witness of some hardship or grievance was fired out of him and consumed. Therefore his poetry flows from him free and unimpeded. If ever a human being got his work expressed completely, it was Shakespeare. If ever a mind was incandescent, unimpeded, I thought, turning again to the bookcase, it was Shakespeare's mind.

FRANZ KAFKA
[1883–1924]

The writings of Franz Kafka courageously explore the fears and frustrations of living in the modern age. He dedicated himself to the examination of consciousness, how it feels to be manipulated by large, bureaucratic institutions. He wrote about the intimidation that individuals feel when dealing with governments and courts of law. He identified

---

[31] See *Cassandra*, by Florence Nightingale, printed in *The Cause*, by R. Strachey. [Woolf's note.] Ray Strachey's 1928 book was a history of British feminism with an appendix by Nightingale.
[32] "Here lies one whose name was writ in water."

the faceless, heartless machinery of the modern corporation and how individuals become ciphers caught up in legalistic, administrative maneuvers. Often the governmental or corporate systems are too complex and elusive for people to understand how they work and how to survive within them. Human beings become their social security numbers—or today their credit card numbers—and are passed from one agency to another. Reality turns into a nightmare and lives are twisted and distorted. Kafka's writings represent a disturbing loss of faith in the fundamental institutions of Western civilization: universities, churches, and governments. Kafka's works implicitly argue that if God still exists—and many in the post–World War I era doubted his existence—he has retreated into the vast recesses of the cosmos, out of touch and out of hearing. Given this social landscape, Kafka was brilliantly prophetic about the rise of totalitarianism in the twentieth century and the horrifying effect of fascist and communist regimes on millions of humans.

LIFE

Franz Kafka was born in Prague, Czechoslovakia, in 1883 to Julie Lowy, a kindly woman from a family of rabbis, and Hermann Kafka, a self-made man who had worked his way from village butcher to city entrepreneur, and who was to cast a long shadow on his son's self-doubt. Aggressive and domineering, Hermann pressured his son to be a businessman. Franz was well educated, earning a doctor of law degree from German University in Prague. Despite an early passion for writing, he took a job in the semigovernmental Workers' Accident Insurance Institute, where he had ample opportunity to observe the workings of a bureaucracy.

Despite the pain resulting from his relationship with his father, Kafka lived at home for most of his life. In "A Letter to My Father," he talks about humiliation, a feeling that pervades the consciousness of Kafka's characters:

> I was, after all, depressed even by your mere physical presence. I remember for instance how often we undressed together in the same bathing-hut. There was I, skinny, weakly, slight, you strong, tall, broad. Even inside the hut I felt myself a miserable specimen, and what's more not only in your eyes but in the eyes of the whole world, for you were for me the measure of all things.

Having begun to write in the university, Franz felt caught between his passion for writing and his desire to do well in his job. A journal entry captures the anguish of this conflict:

> Now these two vocations (writing and working in an office) cannot be compatible and have a fortunate outcome in common. The smallest success in the one field becomes a great disaster in the other... At the office I fulfill my obligations outwardly, but not my inner ones, and every unfulfilled inner obligation turns into a misfortune which does not find its way out of me.

He nevertheless became a respected executive, handling claims and litigation, as well as a successful writer. He was twice engaged to Felice Bauer without marrying; the failure of this relationship became an additional burden. In 1917 Kafka was found to have tuberculosis, and he eventually suffered from tuberculosis of the larynx, a particularly odious illness for someone who spent his life struggling to communicate. After various sanatoriums in Prague, Kafka moved to Berlin in 1922, where his relationship with Dora Dymant brought him some happiness before he died of tuberculosis in a Viennese sanatorium on June 3, 1924.

WORK

Because of Kafka's insecurity about his writing, only a few of his short stories and two novellas (*The Metamorphosis*, 1915, and *The Penal Colony*, 1919) were published during his lifetime. At his death he asked his friend and executor Max Brod to burn his unpublished papers, which included three unfinished novels. Fortunately, Brod disregarded his friend's request and published a number of short stories and sketches, as well as the novels *The Trial* (1925), *The Castle* (1926), and *Amerika* (1927).

The heartless bureaucracy was not unknown to the nineteenth century; after all, Tolstoy's Ivan Ilyitch (*The Death of Ivan Ilyitch*) became a cog in Russia's legal system. But Kafka's haunting version of the modern world makes the line between the ruling elite and the rest of society impossibly vague. He continually takes the point of view of the victim who is unclear and confused about the particular system and the people in control. In *The Trial,* the accused actually has an opportunity to speak to his accusers, but in *The Castle* it is not even clear how to make contact with the decision makers. Social power, like God, has receded into a murky distance. In a short parable called "Before the Law," a man approaches the gateway of the Law, but a gatekeeper prevents him from entering. Finally after years in front of the gate and endless discussions with the gatekeeper, the man asks one final question before dying: "Everyone strives to reach the Law, so how does it happen that for all these many years no one but myself has ever begged for admittance?" The gatekeeper answers, "No one else could ever be admitted here, since this gate was made only for you. I am now going to shut it." Kafka lets this particular gateway stand for all the possible institutional and religious gateways confronting individuals over a lifetime.

In *The Metamorphosis,* the demeaning distance between individual and institution is also found in the microcosm of the family, where parents and children live together without caring for one another, where people talk without communicating. *The Metamorphosis* is typical of a number of Kafka's works that place an everyday, ordinary world side-by-side with extraordinary, incomprehensible events. In this case a fantastic event begins the story in shocking words that haunt the reader who, like Gregor, must search for a framework to accommodate the strange events that unfold with an uncanny sense of inevitability: "As Gregor Samsa awoke one morning from uneasy dreams he found himself transformed in his bed into a gigantic insect." Although the line between reality and unreality, between nightmare and sanity, fluctuates in Kafka's writings, he intends us to take Gregor's misfortune literally—at least initially. Fate has dealt Gregor Samsa an incredible blow.

On a psychological level, however, Gregor's metamorphosis corresponds to those moments in the modern world when an individual awakens to the full dimensions of being trapped in a strange body, with a sense of helplessness and alienation in his or her everyday life. Furthermore, Gregor's family, to whom he had dedicated his working life, is strangely unsympathetic to his plight. Even though Gregor's metamorphosis is completely out of his hands, his parents, and eventually even his sister, feel he has let them down. Gregor, who had been the chief support of his family, becomes a burden. One of the most dehumanizing scenes in the story occurs when Mr. Samsa reasserts his authority as the head of the household and drives his son back into his room by throwing fruit at him. One of the apples, which lodges in Gregor's back, rots and festers until Gregor dies without ever understanding what happened to him. Gregor's misfortune ironically forces his family out of their passive dependence; as they detach themselves from Gregor's plight, they appear to take charge of their own lives and make plans for the future.

Franz Kafka's writings had very little impact during his lifetime, but audiences after World War II have found his portrayal of modern alienation, the paralyzing insecurities that individuals suffer in their private lives, both profound and moving. He continues to strike a deep chord in Western consciousness.

SUGGESTED READINGS

Max Brod, Kafka's close friend, wrote an appreciative biography, *Franz Kafka: A Biography* (English trans., 1960); a more detailed life of Kafka is Ronald Hayman's *Kafka: A Biography* (1982). Ernest Pawel provides psychological analysis in *The Nightmare of Reason, A Life of Franz Kafka* (1984). A variety of views on Kafka's writings are in Ronald Gray, ed., *Kafka: A Collection of Critical Essays* (1962).

The Metamorphosis

Translated by Willa and Edwin Muir

1

As Gregor Samsa awoke one morning from uneasy dreams he found himself transformed in his bed into a gigantic insect. He was lying on his hard, as it were armor-plated, back and when he lifted his head a little he could see his domelike brown belly divided into stiff arched segments on top of which the bed quilt could hardly keep in position and was about to slide off completely. His numerous legs, which were pitifully thin compared to the rest of his bulk, waved helplessly before his eyes.

What has happened to me? he thought. It was no dream. His room, a regular human bedroom, only rather too small, lay quiet between the four familiar walls. Above the table on which a collection of cloth samples was unpacked and spread out—Samsa was a commercial traveler—hung the picture which he had recently cut out of an illustrated magazine and put into a pretty gilt frame. It showed a lady, with a fur cap on and a fur stole, sitting upright and holding out to the spectator a huge fur muff into which the whole of her forearm had vanished!

Gregor's eyes turned next to the window, and the overcast sky—one could hear raindrops beating on the window gutter—made him quite melancholy. What about sleeping a little longer and forgetting all this nonsense, he thought, but it could not be done, for he was accustomed to sleep on his right side and in his present condition he could not turn himself over. However violently he forced himself toward his right side he always rolled onto his back again. He tried it at least a hundred times, shutting his eyes to keep from seeing his struggling legs, and only desisted when he began to feel in his side a faint dull ache he had never experienced before.

Oh God, he thought, what an exhausting job I've picked on! Traveling about day in, day out. It's much more irritating work than doing the actual business in the office, and on top of that there's the trouble of constant traveling, of worrying about train connections, the bed and irregular meals, casual acquaintances that are always new and never become intimate friends. The devil take it all! He felt a slight itching up on his belly; slowly pushed himself on his back nearer to the top of the bed so that he could lift his head more easily; identified the itching place which was surrounded by many small white spots the nature of which he could not understand and made to touch it with a leg, but drew the leg back immediately, for the contact made a cold shiver run through him.

He slid down again into his former position. This getting up early, he thought, makes one quite stupid. A man needs his sleep. Other commercials live like harem women. For instance, when I come back to the hotel of a morning to write up the orders I've got, these others are only sitting down to the breakfast. Let me just try that with my chief; I'd be sacked on the spot. Anyhow, that might be quite a good thing for me, who can tell? If I didn't have to hold my hand because of my parents I'd have given notice long ago, I'd have gone to the chief and told him exactly what I think of him. That would knock him endways from his desk! It's a queer way of doing, too, this sitting on high at a desk and talking down to employees, especially when they have to come quite near because the chief is hard of hearing. Well, there's still hope; once I've saved enough money to pay back my parents' debts to him—that should take another five or six years—I'll do it without fail. I'll cut myself completely loose then. For the moment, though, I'd better get up, since my train goes at five.

He looked at the alarm clock ticking on the chest. Heavenly Father! he thought. It was half-past six o'clock and the hands were quietly moving on, it was even past the half-hour, it was getting on toward a quarter to seven. Had the alarm clock not gone off? From the bed one could see that it had been properly set for four o'clock; of course it must have gone off. Yes, but was it possible to sleep quietly through that ear-splitting noise? Well, he had not slept quietly, yet apparently all the more soundly for that. But what was he to do now? The next train went at seven o'clock; to catch that he would need to hurry like mad and his samples weren't even packed up, and he himself wasn't feeling particularly fresh and active. And even if he did catch the train he wouldn't avoid a row with the chief, since the firm's porter would have been waiting for the five o'clock train and would have long since reported his failure to turn up. The porter was a creature of the chief's, spineless and stupid. Well, supposing he were to say he was sick? But that would be most unpleasant and would look suspicious, since during his five years' employment he had not been ill once. The chief himself would be sure to come with the sick-insurance doctor, would reproach his parents with their son's laziness, and would cut all excuses short by referring to the insurance doctor, who of course regarded all mankind as perfectly healthy malingerers. And would he be so far wrong on this occasion? Gregor really felt quite well, apart from a drowsiness that was utterly superfluous after such a long sleep, and he was even unusually hungry.

As all this was running through his mind at top speed without his being able to decide to leave his bed—the alarm clock had just struck a quarter to seven—there came a cautious tap at the door behind the head of his bed. "Gregor," said a voice—it was his mother's—"it's a quarter to seven. Hadn't you a train to catch?" That gentle voice! Gregor had a shock as he heard his own voice answering hers, unmistakably his own voice, it was true, but with a persistent horrible twittering squeak behind it like an undertone, which left the words in their clear shape only for the first moment and then rose up reverberating around them to destroy their sense, so that one could not be sure one had heard them rightly. Gregor wanted to answer at length and explain everything, but in the circumstances he confined himself to saying: "Yes, yes, thank you, Mother, I'm getting up now." The wooden door between them must have kept the change in his voice from being noticeable outside, for his mother contented herself with this statement and shuffled away. Yet this brief exchange of words had made the other members of the family aware that Gregor was still in the house, as they had not expected, and at one of the side doors his father was already knocking, gently, yet with his fist. "Gregor, Gregor," he called, "What's the matter with you?" And after a little while he called again in a deeper voice: "Gregor! Gregor!" At the other side door his sister was saying in a low, plaintive tone: "Gregor? Aren't you well? Are you needing anything?"

He answered them both at once: "I'm just ready," and did his best to make his voice sound as normal as possible by enunciating the words very clearly and leaving long pauses between them. So his father went back to his breakfast, but his sister whispered: "Gregor, open the door, do." However, he was not thinking of opening the door, and felt thankful for the prudent habit he had acquired in traveling of locking all doors during the night, even at home.

His immediate intention was to get up quietly without being disturbed, to put on his clothes and above all eat his breakfast, and only then consider what else was to be done, since in bed, he was well aware, his meditations would come to no sensible conclusion. He remembered that often enough in bed he had felt small aches and pains, probably caused by awkward postures, which had proved purely imaginary once he got up, and he looked forward eagerly to seeing this morning's delusions gradually fall away. That the change in his voice was nothing but the precursor of a severe chill, a standing ailment of commercial travelers, he had not the least possible doubt.

To get rid of the quilt was quite easy; he had only to inflate himself a little and it fell off by itself. But the next move was difficult, especially because he was so uncommonly broad. He would have needed arms and hands to hoist himself up; instead he had only the numerous little legs which never stopped waving in all directions and which he could not control in the least. When he tried to bend one of them it was the first to stretch itself straight; and did he succeed at last in making it do what he wanted, all the other legs meanwhile waved the more wildly in a high degree of unpleasant agitation. "But what's the use of lying idle in bed," said Gregor to himself.

He thought that he might get out of bed with the lower part of his body first, but this lower part, which he had not yet seen and of which he could form no clear conception, proved too difficult to move; it shifted so slowly; and when finally, almost wild with annoyance, he gathered his forces together and thrust out recklessly, he had miscalculated the direction and bumped heavily against the lower end of the bed, and the stinging pain he felt informed him that precisely this lower part of his body was at the moment probably the most sensitive.

So he tried to get the top part of himself out first, and cautiously moved his head toward the edge of the bed. That proved easy enough, and despite its breadth and mass the bulk of his body at last slowly followed the movement of his head. Still, when he finally got his head free over the edge of the bed he felt too scared to go on advancing, for after all if he let himself fall in this way it would take a miracle to keep his head from being injured. And at all costs he must not lose consciousness now, precisely now; he would rather stay in bed.

But when after a repetition of the same efforts he lay in his former position again, sighing, and watched his little legs struggling against each other more wildly than ever, if that were possible, and saw no way of bringing any order into this arbitrary confusion, he told himself again that it was impossible to stay in bed and that the most sensible course was to risk everything for the smallest hope of getting away from it. At the same time he did not forget to remind himself occasionally that cool reflection, the coolest possible, was much better than desperate resolves. In such moments he focused his eyes as sharply as possible on the window, but, unfortunately, the prospect of the morning fog, which muffled even the other side of the narrow street, brought him little encouragement and comfort. "Seven o'clock already," he said to himself when the alarm clock chimed again, "seven o'clock already and still such a thick fog." And for a little while he lay quiet, breathing lightly, as if perhaps expecting such complete repose to restore all things to their real and normal condition.

But then he said to himself: "Before it strikes a quarter past seven I must be quite out of this bed, without fail. Anyhow, by that time someone will have come from the office to ask for me, since it opens before seven." And he set himself to rocking his whole body at once in a regular rhythm, with the idea of swinging it out of the bed. If he tipped himself out in that way he could keep his head from injury by lifting it at an acute angle when he fell. His back seemed to be hard and was not likely to suffer from a fall on the carpet. His biggest worry was the loud crash he would not be able to help making, which would probably cause anxiety, if not terror, behind all the doors. Still, he must take the risk.

When he was already half out of the bed—the new method was more a game than an effort, for he needed only to hitch himself across by rocking to and fro—it struck him how simple it would be if he could get help. Two strong people—he thought of his father and the servant girl—would be amply sufficient; they would only have to thrust their arms under his convex back, lever him out of the bed, bend down with their burden, and then be patient enough to let him turn himself right over onto the floor, where it was to be hoped his legs would then find their proper function. Well, ignoring the fact that the doors were all locked, ought he really to call for help? In spite of his misery he could not suppress a smile at the very idea of it.

He had got so far that he could barely keep his equilibrium when he rocked himself strongly, and he would have to nerve himself very soon for the final decision since in five minutes' time it would be quarter past seven—when the front doorbell rang. "That's someone from the office," he said to himself, and grew almost rigid, while his little legs only jigged about all the faster. For a moment everything stayed quiet. "They're not going to open the door," said Gregor to himself, catching at some kind of irrational hope. But then of course the servant girl went as usual to the door with her heavy tread and opened it. Gregor needed only to hear the first good morning of the visitor to know immediately who it was—the chief clerk himself. What a fate, to be condemned to work for a firm where the smallest omission at once gave rise to the gravest suspicion! Were all employees in a body nothing but scoundrels, was there not among them one single loyal devoted man who, had he wasted only an hour or so of the firm's time in a morning, was so tormented by conscience as to be driven out of his mind and actually incapable of leaving his bed? Wouldn't it really have been sufficient to send an apprentice to inquire—if any inquiry were necessary at all—did the chief clerk himself have to come and thus indicate to the entire family, an innocent family, that this suspicious circumstance could be investigated by no one less versed in affairs than himself? And more through the agitation caused by these reflections than through any act of will Gregor swung himself out of bed with all his strength. There was a loud thump, but it was not really a crash. His fall was broken to some extent by the carpet, his back, too, was less stiff than he thought, and so there was merely a dull thud, not so very startling. Only he had not lifted his head carefully enough and had hit it; he turned it and rubbed it on the carpet in pain and irritation.

"That was something falling down in there," said the chief clerk in the next room to the left. Gregor tried to suppose to himself that something like what had happened to him today might someday happen to the chief clerk; one really could not deny that it was possible. But as if in brusque reply to this supposition the chief clerk took a couple of firm steps in the next-door room and his patent leather boots creaked. From the right-hand room his sister was whispering to inform him of the situation: "Gregor, the chief clerk's here." "I know," muttered Gregor to himself; but he didn't dare to make his voice loud enough for his sister to hear it.

"Gregor," said his father now from the left-hand room, "the chief clerk has come and wants to know why you didn't catch the early train. We don't know what to say to him. Besides, he wants to talk to you in person. So open the door, please. He will be good enough to excuse the untidiness of your room." "Good morning, Mr. Samsa," the chief clerk was calling amiably meanwhile. "He's not well," said his mother to the visitor, while his father was still speaking through the door, "he's not well, sir, believe me. What else would make him miss a train! The boy thinks about nothing but his work. It makes me almost cross the way he never goes out in the evenings; he's been here the last eight days and has stayed at home every single evening. He just sits there quietly at the table reading a newspaper or looking through railway timetables. The only amusement he gets is doing fretwork. For instance, he spent two or three evenings cutting out a little picture frame; you would be surprised to see how pretty it is; it's hanging in his room; you'll see it in a minute when Gregor opens the door. I must say I'm glad you've come, sir; we should never have got him to unlock the door by ourselves; he's so obstinate; and I'm sure he's unwell, though he wouldn't have it to be so this morning." "I'm just coming," said Gregor slowly and carefully, not moving an inch for fear of losing one word of the conversation. "I can't think of any other explanation, madame," said the chief clerk, "I hope it's nothing serious. Although on the other hand I must say that we men of business—fortunately or unfortunately— very often simply have to ignore any slight indisposition, since business must be attended to." "Well, can the chief clerk come in now?" asked Gregor's father impatiently, again knocking on the door. "No," said Gregor. In the left-hand room a painful silence followed this refusal, in the right-hand room his sister began to sob.

Why didn't his sister join the others? She was probably newly out of bed and hadn't even begun to put on her clothes yet. Well, why was she crying? Because he wouldn't get up and let the chief clerk in, because he was in danger of losing his job, and because the chief would begin dunning his parents again for the old debts? Surely these were things one didn't need to worry about for the present. Gregor was still at home and not in the least thinking of deserting the family. At the moment, true, he was lying on the carpet and no one who knew the condition he was in could seriously expect him to admit the chief clerk. But for such a small discourtesy, which could plausibly be explained away somehow later on, Gregor could hardly be dismissed on the spot. And it seemed to Gregor that it would be much more sensible to leave him in peace for the present than to trouble him with tears and entreaties. Still, of course, their uncertainty bewildered them all and excused their behavior.

"Mr. Samsa," the chief clerk called now in a louder voice, "what's the matter with you? Here you are, barricading yourself in your room, giving only 'yes' and 'no' for answers, causing your parents a lot of unnecessary trouble and neglecting—I mention this only in passing—neglecting your business duties in an incredible fashion. I am speaking here in the name of your parents and of your chief, and I beg you quite seriously to give me an immediate and precise explanation. You amaze me, you amaze me. I thought you were a quiet, dependable person, and now all at once you seem bent on making a disgraceful exhibition of yourself. The chief did hint to me early this morning a possible explanation for your disappearance—with reference to the cash payments that were entrusted to you recently—but I almost pledged my solemn word of honor that this could not be so. But now that I see how incredibly obstinate you are, I no longer have the slightest desire to take your part at all. And your position in the firm is not so unassailable. I came with the intention of telling you all this in private, but since you are wasting my time so needlessly I don't see why your parents shouldn't hear it too. For some time past your work has been most unsatisfactory; this is not the season of the year for a business boom, of course, we admit that, but a season of the year for doing no business at all, that does not exist, Mr. Samsa, must not exist."

"But, sir," cried Gregor, beside himself and in his agitation forgetting everything else, "I'm just going to open the door this very minute. A slight illness, an attack of giddiness, has kept me from getting up. I'm still lying in bed. But I feel all right again. I'm getting out of bed now. Just give me a moment or two longer! I'm not quite so well as I thought. But I'm all right, really. How a thing like that can suddenly strike one down! Only last night I was quite well, my parents can tell you, or rather I did have a slight presentiment. I must have showed some sign of it. Why didn't I report it at the office! But one always thinks that an indisposition can be got over without staying in the house. Oh sir, do spare my parents! All that you're reproaching me with now has no foundation; no one has ever said a word to me about it. Perhaps you haven't looked at the last orders I sent in. Anyhow, I can still catch the eight o'clock train, I'm much the better for my few hours' rest. Don't let me detain you here, sir; I'll be attending to business very soon, and do be good enough to tell the chief so and to make my excuses to him!"

And while all this was tumbling out pell-mell and Gregor hardly knew what he was saying, he had reached the chest quite easily, perhaps because of the practice he had had in bed, and was now trying to lever himself upright by means of it. He meant actually to open the door, actually to show himself and speak to the chief clerk; he was eager to find out what the others, after all their insistence, would say at the sight of him. If they were horrified then the responsibility was no longer his and he could stay quiet. But if they took it calmly, then he had no reason either to be upset, and could really get to the station for the eight o'clock train if he hurried. At first he slipped down a few times from the polished surface of the chest, but at length with a last heave he stood upright; he paid no more attention to the pains in the lower part of his body, however they smarted. Then he let himself fall against the back of a nearby chair, and clung with his little legs to the edges of it. That brought him into control of himself again and he stopped speaking, for now he could listen to what the chief clerk was saying.

"Did you understand a word of it?" the chief clerk was asking; "surely he can't be trying to make fools of us?" "Oh dear," cried his mother, in tears, "perhaps he's terribly ill and we're tormenting him. Grete! Grete!" she called out then. "Yes Mother?" called his sister from the other side. They were calling to each other across Gregor's room. "You must go this minute for the doctor. Gregor is ill. Go for the doctor, quick. Did you hear how he was speaking?" "That was no human voice," said the chief clerk in a voice noticeably low beside the shrillness of the mother's. "Anna! Anna!" his father was calling through the hall to the kitchen, clapping his hands, "get a locksmith at once!" And the two girls were already running through the hall with a swish of skirts—how could his sister have got dressed so quickly?—and were tearing the front door open. There was no sound of its closing again; they had evidently left it open, as one does in houses where some great misfortune has happened.

But Gregor was now much calmer. The words he uttered were no longer understandable, apparently, although they seemed clear enough to him, even clearer than before, perhaps because his ear had grown accustomed to the sound of them. Yet at any rate people now believed that something was wrong with him, and were ready to help him. The positive certainty with which these first measures had been taken comforted him. He felt himself drawn once more into the human circle and hoped for great and remarkable results from both the doctor and the locksmith, without really distinguishing precisely between them. To make his voice as clear as possible for the decisive conversation that was now imminent he coughed a little, as quietly as he could, of course, since this noise too might not sound like a human cough for all he was able to judge. In the next room meanwhile there was complete silence. Perhaps his parents were sitting at the table with the chief clerk, whispering, perhaps they were all leaning against the door and listening.

Slowly Gregor pushed the chair toward the door, then let go of it, caught hold of the door for support—the soles at the end of his little legs were somewhat sticky—and rested against it for a moment after his efforts. Then he set himself to turning the key in the lock with his mouth. It seemed, unhappily, that he hadn't really any teeth—what could he grip the key with?—but on the other hand his jaws were certainly very strong; with their help he did manage to set the key in motion, heedless of the fact that he was undoubtedly damaging them somewhere, since a brown fluid issued from his mouth, flowed over the key, and dripped on the floor. "Just listen to that," said the chief clerk next door; "he's turning the key." That was a great encouragement to Gregor; but they should all have shouted encouragement to him, his father and mother too: "Go on, Gregor," they should have called out, "keep going, hold on to that key!" And in the belief that they were all following his efforts intently, he clenched his jaws recklessly on the key with all the force at his command. As the turning of the key progressed he circled around the lock, holding on now only with his mouth, pushing on the key, as required, or pulling it down again with all the weight of his body. The louder click of the finally yielding lock literally quickened Gregor. With a deep breath of relief he said to himself: "So I didn't need the locksmith," and laid his head on the handle to open the door wide.

Since he had to pull the door toward him, he was still invisible when it was really wide open. He had to edge himself slowly around the near half of the double door, and to do it very carefully if he was not to fall plump upon his back just on the threshold. He was still carrying out this difficult maneuver, with no time to observe anything else, when he heard the chief clerk utter a loud "Oh!"—it sounded like a gust of wind—and now he could see the man, standing as he was nearest to the door, clapping one hand before his open mouth and slowly backing away as if driven by some invisible steady pressure. His mother—in spite of the chief clerk's being there her hair was still undone and sticking up in all directions—first clasped her hands and looked at his father, then took two steps toward Gregor and fell on the floor among her outspread skirts, her face quite hidden on her breast. His father knotted his fist with a fierce expression on his face as if he meant to knock Gregor back into his room, then looked uncertainly around the living room, covered his eyes with his hands, and wept till his great chest heaved.

Gregor did not go now into the living room, but leaned against the inside of the firmly shut wing of the door, so that only half his body was visible and his head above it bending sideways to look at the others. The light had meanwhile strengthened; on the other side of the street one could see clearly a section of the endlessly long, dark gray building opposite—it was a hospital—abruptly punctuated by its row of regular windows; the rain was still falling, but only in large singly discernible and literally singly splashing drops. The breakfast dishes were set out on the table lavishly, for breakfast was the most important meal of the day to Gregor's father, who lingered it out for hours over various newspapers. Right opposite Gregor on the wall hung a photograph of himself in military service, as a lieutenant, hand on sword, a carefree smile on his face, inviting one to respect his uniform and military bearing. The door leading to the hall was open, and one could see that the front door stood open too, showing the landing beyond and the beginning of the stairs going down.

"Well," said Gregor, knowing perfectly that he was the only one who had retained any composure, "I'll put my clothes on at once, pack up my samples, and start off. Will you only let me go? You see, sir, I'm not obstinate, and I'm willing to work; traveling is a hard life, but I couldn't live without it. Where are you going, sir? To the office? Yes? Will you give a true account of all this? One can be temporarily incapacitated, but that's just the moment for remembering former services and bearing in mind that later on, when the incapacity has been got over, one will certainly work with all the more industry and concentration. I'm loyally bound to serve the chief, you know that very well. Besides, I have to provide for my parents and my sister. I'm in great difficulties, but I'll get out of them again. Don't make things any worse for me than they are. Stand up for me in the firm. Travelers are not popular there, I know. People think they earn sacks of money and just have a good time. A prejudice there's no particular reason for revising. But you, sir, have a more comprehensive view of affairs than the rest of the staff, yes, let me tell you in confidence, a more comprehensive view than the chief himself, who, being the owner, lets his judgment easily be swayed against one of his employees. And you know very well that the traveler, who is never seen in the office almost the whole year around, can so easily fall a victim to gossip and ill luck and unfounded complaints, which he mostly knows nothing about, except when he comes back exhausted from his rounds, and only then suffers in person from their evil consequences, which he can no longer trace back to the original causes. Sir, sir, don't go away without a word to me to show that you think me in the right at least to some extent!"

But at Gregor's very first words the chief clerk had already backed away and only stared at him with parted lips over one twitching shoulder. And while Gregor was speaking he did not stand still one moment but stole away toward the door, without taking his eyes off Gregor, yet only an inch at a time, as if obeying some secret injunction to leave the room. He was already at the hall, and the suddenness with which he took his last step out of the living room would have made one believe he had burned the sole of his foot. Once in the hall he stretched his right arm before him toward the staircase, as if some supernatural power were waiting there to deliver him.

Gregor perceived that the chief clerk must on no account be allowed to go away in this frame of mind if his position in the firm were not to be endangered to the utmost. His parents did not understand this so well; they had convinced themselves in the course of years that Gregor was settled for life in this firm, and besides they were so preoccupied with their immediate troubles that all foresight had forsaken them. Yet Gregor had this foresight. The chief clerk must be detained, soothed, persuaded, and finally won over; the whole future of Gregor and his family depended on it! If only his sister had been there! She was intelligent; she had begun to cry while Gregor was still lying quietly on his back. And no doubt the chief clerk, so partial to ladies, would have been guided by her; she would have shut the door of the flat and in the hall talked him out of his horror. But she was not there, and Gregor would have to handle the situation himself. And without remembering that he was still unaware what powers of movement he possessed, without even remembering that his words in all possibility, indeed in all likelihood, would again be unintelligible, he let go the wing of the door, pushed himself through the opening, started to walk toward the chief clerk, who was already ridiculously clinging with both hands to the railing on the landing; but immediately, as he was feeling for a support, he fell down with a little cry upon all his numerous legs. Hardly was he down when he experienced for the first time this morning a sense of physical comfort; his legs had firm ground under them; they were completely obedient, as he noted with joy; they even strove to carry him forward in whatever direction he chose; and he was inclined to believe that a final relief from all his sufferings was at hand. But in the same moment as he found himself on the floor, rocking with suppressed eagerness to move, not far from his mother, indeed just in front of her, she, who had seemed so completely crushed, sprang all at once to her feet, her arms and fingers outspread, cried: "Help, for God's sake, help!" bent her head down as if to see Gregor better, yet on the contrary kept backing senselessly away; had quite forgotten that the laden table stood behind her; sat upon it hastily, as if in absence of mind, when she bumped into it; and seemed altogether unaware that the big coffeepot beside her was upset and pouring coffee in a flood over the carpet.

"Mother, Mother," said Gregor in a low voice, and looked up at her. The chief clerk, for the moment, had quite slipped from his mind; instead, he could not resist snapping his jaws together at the sight of the streaming coffee. That made his mother scream again, she fled from the table and fell into the arms of his father, who hastened to catch her. But Gregor had now no time to spare for his parents; the chief clerk was already on the stairs; with his chin on the banisters he was taking one last backward look. Gregor made a spring, to be as sure as possible of overtaking him; the chief clerk must have divined his intention, for he leaped down several steps and vanished; he was still yelling "Ugh!" and it echoed through the whole staircase.

Unfortunately, the flight of the chief clerk seemed completely to upset Gregor's father, who had remained relatively calm until now, for instead of running after the man himself, or at least not hindering Gregor in his pursuit, he seized in his right hand the walking stick that the chief clerk had left behind on a chair, together with a hat and greatcoat, snatched in his left hand a large newspaper from the table, and began stamping his feet and flourishing the stick and the newspaper to drive Gregor back into his room. No entreaty of Gregor's availed, indeed no entreaty was even understood, however humbly he bent his head his father only stamped on the floor the more loudly. Behind his father his mother had torn open a window, despite the cold weather, and was leaning far out of it with her face in her hands. A strong draught set in from the street to the staircase, the window curtains blew in, the newspapers on the table fluttered, stray pages whisked over the floor. Pitilessly Gregor's father drove him back, hissing and crying "Shoo!" like a savage. But Gregor was quite unpracticed in walking backwards, it really was a slow business. If he only had a chance to turn around he could get back to his room at once, but he was afraid of exasperating his father by the slowness of such a rotation and at any moment the stick in his father's hand might hit him a fatal blow on the back or on the head. In the end, however, nothing else was left for him to do since to his horror he observed that in moving backwards he could not even control the direction he took; and so, keeping an anxious eye on his father all the time over his shoulder, he began to turn around as quickly as he could, which was in reality very slowly. Perhaps his father noted his good intentions, for he did not interfere except every now and then to help him in the maneuver from a distance with the point of the stick. If only he would have stopped making that unbearable hissing noise! It made Gregor quite lose his head. He had turned almost completely around when the hissing noise so distracted him that he even turned a little the wrong way again. But when at last his head was fortunately right in front of the doorway, it appeared that his body was too broad simply to get through the opening. His father, of course, in his present mood was far from thinking of such a thing as opening the other half of the door, to let Gregor have enough space. He had merely the fixed idea of driving Gregor back into his room as quickly as possible. He would never have suffered Gregor to make the circumstantial preparations for standing up on end and perhaps slipping his way through the door. Maybe he was now making more noise than ever to urge Gregor forward, as if no obstacle impeded him; to Gregor, anyhow, the noise in his rear sounded no longer like the voice of one single father; this was really no joke, and Gregor thrust himself—come what might—into the doorway. One side of his body rose up, he was tilted at an angle in the doorway, his flank was quite bruised, horrid blotches stained the white door, soon he was stuck fast and, left to himself, could not have moved at all, his legs on one side fluttered trembling in the air, those on the other were crushed painfully to the floor—when from behind his father gave him a strong push which was literally a deliverance and he flew far into the room, bleeding freely. The door was slammed behind him with the stick, and then at last there was silence.

2

Not until it was twilight did Gregor awake out of a deep sleep, more like a swoon than a sleep. He would certainly have waked up of his own accord not much later, for he felt himself sufficiently rested and well slept, but it seemed to him as if a fleeting step and a cautious shutting of the door leading into the hall had aroused him. The electric lights in the street cast a pale sheen here and there on the ceiling and the upper surfaces of the furniture, but down below, where he lay, it was dark. Slowly, awkwardly trying out his feelers, which he now first learned to appreciate, he pushed his way to the door to see what had been happening there. His left side felt like one single long, unpleasantly tense scar, and he had actually to limp on his two rows of legs. One little leg, moreover, had been severely damaged in the course of that morning's events—it was almost a miracle that only one had been damaged—and trailed uselessly behind him.

He had reached the door before he discovered what had really drawn him to it: the smell of food. For there stood a basin filled with fresh milk in which floated little sops of white bread. He could almost have laughed with joy, since he was now still hungrier than in the morning, and he dipped his head almost over the eyes straight into the milk. But soon in disappointment he withdrew it again; not only did he find it difficult to feed because of his tender left side—and he could only feed with the palpitating collaboration of his whole body—he did not like the milk either, although milk had been his favorite drink and that was certainly why his sister had set it there for him, indeed it was almost with repulsion that he turned away from the basin and crawled back to the middle of the room.

He could see through the crack of the door that the gas was turned on in the living room, but while usually at this time his father made a habit of reading the afternoon newspaper in a loud voice to his mother and occasionally to his sister as well, not a sound was now to be heard. Well, perhaps his father had recently given up this habit of reading aloud, which his sister had mentioned so often in conversation and in her letters. But there was the same silence all around, although the flat was certainly not empty of occupants. "What a quiet life our family has been leading," said Gregor to himself, and as he sat there motionless staring into the darkness he felt great pride in the fact that he had been able to provide such a life for his parents and sister in such a fine flat. But what if all the quiet, the comfort, the contentment were now to end in horror? To keep himself from being lost in such thoughts Gregor took refuge in movement and crawled up and down the room.

Once during the long evening one of the side doors was opened a little and quickly shut again, later the other side door too; someone had apparently wanted to come in and then thought better of it. Gregor now stationed himself immediately before the living-room door, determined to persuade any hesitating visitor to come in or at least to discover who it might be; but the door was not opened again and he waited in vain. In the early morning, when the doors were locked, they had all wanted to come in, now that he had opened one door and the other had apparently been opened during the day, no one came in and even the keys were on the other side of the doors.

It was late at night before the gas went out in the living room, and Gregor could easily tell that his parents and his sister had all stayed awake until then, for he could clearly hear the three of them stealing away on tiptoe. No one was likely to visit him, not until the morning, that was certain; so he had plenty of time to meditate at his leisure on how he was to arrange his life afresh. But the lofty, empty room in which he had to lie flat on the floor filled him with an apprehension he could not account for, since it had been his very own room for the past five years—and with a half-unconscious action, not without a slight feeling of shame, he scuttled under the sofa, where he felt comfortable at once, although his back was a little cramped and he could not lift his head up, and his only regret was that his body was too broad to get the whole of it under the sofa.

He stayed there all night, spending the time partly in a light slumber, from which his hunger kept waking him up with a start, and partly in worrying and sketching vague hopes, which all led to the same conclusion, that he must lie low for the present and, by exercising patience and the utmost consideration, help the family to bear the inconvenience he was bound to cause them in his present condition.

Very early in the morning, it was still almost night, Gregor had the chance to test the strength of his new resolutions, for his sister, nearly fully dressed, opened the door from the hall and peered in. She did not see him at once, yet when she caught sight of him under the sofa—well, he had to be somewhere, he couldn't have flown away, could he?—she was so startled that without being able to help it she slammed the door shut again. But as if regretting her behavior she opened the door again immediately and came in on tiptoe, as if she were visiting an invalid or even a stranger. Gregor had pushed his head forward to the very edge of the sofa and watched her. Would she notice that he had left the milk standing, and not for lack of hunger, and would she bring in some other kind of food more to his taste? If she did not do it of her own accord, he would rather starve than draw her attention to the fact, although he felt a wild impulse to dart out from under the sofa, throw himself at her feet, and beg her for something to eat. But his sister at once noticed, with surprise, that the basin was still full, except for a little milk that had been spilled all around it, she lifted it immediately, not with her bare hands, true, but with a cloth and carried it away. Gregor was wildly curious to know what she would bring instead, and made various speculations about it. Yet what she actually did next, in the goodness of her heart, he could never have guessed at. To find out what he liked she brought him a whole selection of food, all set out on an old newspaper. There were old, half-decayed vegetables, bones from last night's supper covered with a white sauce that had thickened; some raisins and almonds; a piece of cheese that Gregor would have called uneatable two days ago; a dry roll of bread, a buttered roll, and a roll both buttered and salted. Besides all that, she set down again the same basin, into which she had poured some water, and which was apparently to be reserved for his exclusive use. And with fine tact, knowing that Gregor would not eat in her presence, she withdrew quickly and even turned the key, to let him understand that he could take his ease as much as he liked. Gregor's legs all whizzed toward the food. His wounds must have healed completely, moreover, for he felt no disability, which amazed him and made him reflect how more than a month ago he had cut one finger a little with a knife and had still suffered pain from the wound only the day before yesterday. Am I less sensitive now? he thought, and sucked greedily at the cheese, which above all the other edibles attracted him at once and strongly. One after another and with tears of satisfaction in his eyes he quickly devoured the cheese, the vegetables, and the sauce; the fresh food, on the other hand, had no charms for him, he could not even stand the smell of it and actually dragged away to some little distance the things he could eat. He had long finished his meal and was only lying lazily on the same spot when his sister turned the key slowly as a sign for him to retreat. That roused him at once, although he was nearly asleep, and he hurried under the sofa again. But it took considerable self-control for him to stay under the sofa, even for the short time his sister was in the room, since the large meal had swollen his body somewhat and he was so cramped he could hardly breathe. Slight attacks of breathlessness afflicted him and his eyes were starting a little out of his head as he watched his unsuspecting sister sweeping together with a broom not only the remains of what he had eaten but even the things he had not touched, as if these were now of no use to anyone, and hastily shoveling it all into a bucket, which she covered with a wooden lid and carried away. Hardly had she turned her back when Gregor came from under the sofa and stretched and puffed himself out.

In this manner Gregor was fed, once in the early morning while his parents and the servant girl were still asleep, and a second time after they had all had their midday dinner, for then his parents took a short nap and the servant girl could be sent out on some errand or other by his sister. Not that they would have wanted him to starve, of course, but perhaps they could not have borne to know more about his feeding than from hearsay, perhaps too his sister wanted to spare them such little anxieties wherever possible, since they had quite enough to bear as it was.

Under what pretext the doctor and the locksmith had been got rid of on that first morning Gregor could not discover, for since what he said was not understood by the others it never struck any of them, not even his sister, that he could understand what they said, and so whenever his sister came into his room he had to content himself with hearing her utter only a sigh now and then and an occasional appeal to the saints. Later on, when she had got a little used to the situation—of course she could never get completely used to it—she sometimes threw out a remark which was kindly meant or could be so interpreted. "Well, he liked his dinner today," she would say when Gregor had made a good clearance of his food; and when he had not eaten, which gradually happened more and more often, she would say almost sadly: "Everything's been left standing again."

But although Gregor could get no news directly, he overheard a lot from the neighboring rooms, and as soon as voices were audible, he would run to the door of the room concerned and press his whole body against it. In the first few days especially there was no conversation that did not refer to him somehow, even if only indirectly. For two whole days there were family consultations at every mealtime about what should be done; but also between meals the same subject was discussed, for there were always at least two members of the family at home, since no one wanted to be alone in the flat and to leave it quite empty was unthinkable. And on the very first of these days the household cook—it was not quite clear what and how much she knew of the situation—went down on her knees to his mother and begged leave to go, and when she departed, a quarter of an hour later, gave thanks for her dismissal with tears in her eyes as if for the greatest benefit that could have been conferred on her, and without any prompting swore a solemn oath that she would never say a single word to anyone about what had happened.

Now Gregor's sister had to cook too, helping her mother; true, the cooking did not amount to much, for they ate scarcely anything. Gregor was always hearing one of the family vainly urging another to eat and getting no answer but: "Thanks, I've had all I want," or something similar. Perhaps they drank nothing either. Time and again his sister kept asking his father if he wouldn't like some beer and offered kindly to go and fetch it herself, and when he made no answer suggested that she could ask the concierge to fetch it, so that he need feel no sense of obligation, but then a round "No" came from his father and no more was said about it.

In the course of that very first day Gregor's father explained the family's financial position and prospects to both his mother and his sister. Now and then he rose from the table to get some voucher or memorandum out of the small safe he had rescued from the collapse of his business five years earlier. One could hear him opening the complicated lock and rustling papers out and shutting it again. This statement made by his father was the first cheerful information Gregor had heard since his imprisonment. He had been of the opinion that nothing at all was left over from his father's business, at least his father had never said anything to the contrary, and of course he had not asked him directly. At that time Gregor's sole desire was to do his utmost to help the family to forget as soon as possible the catastrophe that had overwhelmed the business and thrown them all into a state of complete despair. And so he had set to work with unusual ardor and almost overnight had become a commercial traveler instead of a little clerk, with of course much greater chances of earning money, and his success was immediately translated into good round coin which he could lay on the table for his amazed and happy family. These had been fine times, and they had never recurred, at least not with the same sense of glory, although later on Gregor had earned so much money that he was able to meet the expenses of the whole household and did so. They had simply got used to it, both the family and Gregor; the money was gratefully accepted and gladly given, but there was no special uprush of warm feeling. With his sister alone had he remained intimate, and it was a secret plan of his that she, who loved music, unlike himself, and could play movingly on the violin, should be sent next year to study at the Conservatorium, despite the great expense that would entail, which must be made up in some other way. During his brief visits home the Conservatorium was often mentioned in the talks he had with his sister, but always merely as a beautiful dream which could never come true, and his parents discouraged even these innocent references to it; yet Gregor had made up his mind firmly about it and meant to announce the fact with due solemnity on Christmas Day.

Such were the thoughts, completely futile in his present condition, that went through his head as he stood clinging upright to the door and listening. Sometimes out of sheer weariness he had to give up listening and let his head fall negligently against the door, but he always had to pull himself together again at once, for even the slight sound his head made was audible next door and brought all conversation to a stop. "What can he be doing now?" his father would say after a while, obviously turning toward the door, and only then would the interrupted conversation gradually be set going again.

Gregor was now informed as amply as he could wish—for his father tended to repeat himself in his explanations, partly because it was a long time since he had handled such matters and partly because his mother could not always grasp things at once—that a certain amount of investments, a very small amount it was true, had survived the wreck of their fortunes and had even increased a little because the dividends had not been touched meanwhile. And besides that, the money Gregor brought home every month—he had kept only a few dollars for himself—had never been quite used up and now amounted to a small capital sum. Behind the door Gregor nodded his head eagerly, rejoiced at this evidence of unexpected thrift and foresight. True, he could really have paid off some more of his father's debts to the chief with this extra money, and so brought much nearer the day on which he could quit his job, but doubtless it was better the way his father had arranged it.

Yet this capital was by no means sufficient to let the family live on the interest of it; for one year, perhaps, or at the most two, they could live on the principal, that was all. It was simply a sum that ought not to be touched and should be kept for a rainy day; money for living expenses would have to be earned. Now his father was still hale enough but an old man, and he had done no work for the past five years and could not be expected to do much; during these five years, the first years of leisure in his laborious though unsuccessful life, he had grown rather fat and become sluggish. And Gregor's old mother, how was she to earn a living with her asthma, which troubled her even when she walked through the flat and kept her lying on a sofa every other day panting for breath beside an open window? And was his sister to earn her bread, she who was still a child of seventeen and whose life hitherto had been so pleasant, consisting as it did in dressing herself nicely, sleeping long, helping in the housekeeping, going out to a few modest entertainments, and above all playing the violin? At first whenever the need for earning money was mentioned Gregor let go his hold on the door and threw himself down on the cool leather sofa beside it, he felt so hot with shame and grief.

Often he just lay there the long nights through without sleeping at all, scrabbling for hours on the leather. Or he nerved himself to the great effort of pushing an armchair to the window, then crawled up over the window sill and, braced against the chair, leaned against the windowpanes, obviously in some recollection of the sense of freedom that looking out of a window always used to give him. For in reality day by day things that were even a little way off were growing dimmer to his sight; the hospital across the street, which he used to execrate for being all too often before his eyes, was now quite beyond his range of vision, and if he had not known that he lived in Charlotte Street, a quiet street but still a city street, he might have believed that his window gave on a desert waste where gray sky and gray land blended indistinguishably into each other. His quick-witted sister only needed to observe twice that the armchair stood by the window; after that whenever she had tidied the room she always pushed the chair back to the same place at the window and even left the inner casements open.

If he could have spoken to her and thanked her for all she had to do for him, he could have borne her ministrations better; as it was, they oppressed him. She certainly tried to make as light as possible of whatever was disagreeable in her task, and as time went on she succeeded, of course, more and more, but time brought more enlightenment to Gregor too. The very way she came in distressed him. Hardly was she in the room when she rushed to the window, without even taking time to shut the door, careful as she was usually to shield the sight of Gregor's room from the others, and as if she were almost suffocating tore the casements open with hasty fingers, standing then in the open draught for a while even in the bitterest cold and drawing deep breaths. This noisy scurry of hers upset Gregor twice a day; he would crouch trembling under the sofa all the time, knowing quite well that she would certainly have spared him such a disturbance had she found it at all possible to stay in his presence without opening the window.

On one occasion, about a month after Gregor's metamorphosis, when there was surely no reason for her to be still startled at his appearance, she came a little earlier than usual and found him gazing out of the window, quite motionless, and thus well placed to look like a bogey. Gregor would not have been surprised had she not come in at all, for she could not immediately open the window while he was there, but not only did she retreat, she jumped back as if in alarm and banged the door shut; a stranger might well have thought that he had been lying in wait for her there meaning to bite her. Of course he hid himself under the sofa at once, but he had to wait until midday before she came again, and she seemed more ill at ease than usual. This made him realize how repulsive the sight of him still was to her, and that it was bound to go on being repulsive, and what an effort it must cost her not to run away even from the sight of the small portion of his body that stuck out from under the sofa. In order to spare her that, therefore, one day he carried a sheet on his back to the sofa—it cost him four hours' labor—and arranged it there in such a way as to hide him completely, so that even if she were to bend down she could not see him. Had she considered the sheet unnecessary, she would certainly have stripped it off the sofa again, for it was clear enough that this curtaining and confining of himself was not likely to conduce to Gregor's comfort, but she left it where it was, and Gregor even fancied that he caught a thankful glance from her eye when he lifted the sheet carefully a very little with his head to see how she was taking the new arrangement.

For the first fortnight his parents could not bring themselves to the point of entering his room, and he often heard them expressing their appreciation of his sister's activities, whereas formerly they had frequently scolded her for being as they thought a somewhat useless daughter. But now, both of them often waited outside the door, his father and his mother, while his sister tidied his room, and as soon as she came out she had to tell them exactly how things were in the room, what Gregor had eaten, how he had conducted himself this time, and whether there was not perhaps some slight improvement in his condition. His mother, moreover, began relatively soon to want to visit him, but his father and sister dissuaded her at first with arguments which Gregor listened to very attentively and altogether approved. Later, however, she had to be held back by main force, and when she cried out: "Do let me in to Gregor, he is my unfortunate son! Can't you understand that I must go to him?" Gregor thought that it might be well to have her come in, not every day, of course, but perhaps once a week; she understood things, after all, much better than his sister, who was only a child despite the efforts she was making and had perhaps taken on so difficult a task merely out of childish thoughtlessness.

Gregor's desire to see his mother was soon fulfilled. During the daytime he did not want to show himself at the window, out of consideration for his parents, but he could not crawl very far around the few square yards of floor space he had, nor could he bear lying quietly at rest all during the night, while he was fast losing any interest he had ever taken in food, so that for mere recreation he had formed the habit of crawling crisscross over the walls and ceiling. He especially enjoyed hanging suspended from the ceiling; it was much better than lying on the floor; one could breathe more freely; one's body swung and rocked lightly; and in the almost blissful absorption induced by this suspension it could happen to his own surprise that he let go and fell plump on the floor. Yet he now had his body much better under control than formerly, and even such a big fall did him no harm. His sister at once remarked the new distraction Gregor had found for himself—he left traces behind him of the sticky stuff on his soles wherever he crawled—and she got the idea in her head of giving him as wide a field as possible to crawl in and of removing the pieces of furniture that hindered him, above all the chest of drawers and the writing desk. But that was more than she could manage all by herself; she did not dare ask her father to help her; and as for the servant girl, a young creature of sixteen who had had the courage to stay on after the cook's departure, she could not be asked to help, for she had begged as a special favor that she might keep the kitchen door locked and open it only on a definite summons; so there was nothing left but to apply to her mother at an hour when her father was out. And the old lady did come, with exclamations of joyful eagerness, which, however, died away at the door of Gregor's room. Gregor's sister, of course, went in first, to see that everything was in order before letting his mother enter. In great haste Gregor pulled the sheet lower and rucked it more in folds so that it really looked as if it had been thrown accidentally over the sofa. And this time he did not peer out from under it; he renounced the pleasure of seeing his mother on this occasion and was only glad that she had come at all. "Come in, he's out of sight," said his sister, obviously leading her mother in by the hand. Gregor could now hear the two women struggling to shift the heavy old chest from its place, and his sister claiming the greater part of the labor for herself, without listening to the admonitions of her mother, who feared she might overstrain herself. It took a long time. After at least a quarter of an hour's tugging his mother objected that the chest had better be left where it was, for in the first place it was too heavy and could never be got out before his father came home, and standing in the middle of the room like that it would only hamper Gregor's movements, while in the second place it was not at all certain that removing the furniture would be doing a service to Gregor. She was inclined to think to the contrary; the sight of the naked walls made her own heart heavy, and why shouldn't Gregor have the same feeling, considering that he had been used to his furniture for so long and might feel forlorn without it. "And doesn't it look," she concluded in a low voice—in fact she had been almost whispering all the time as if to avoid letting Gregor, whose exact whereabouts she did not know, hear even the tones of her voice, for she was convinced that he could not understand her words—"doesn't it look as if we were showing him, by taking away his furniture, that we have given up hope of his ever getting better and are just leaving him coldly to himself? I think it would be best to keep his room exactly as it has always been, so that when he comes back to us he will find everything unchanged and be able all the more easily to forget what has happened in between."

On hearing these words from his mother Gregor realized that the lack of all direct human speech for the past two months together with the monotony of family life must have confused his mind, otherwise he could not account for the fact that he had quite earnestly looked forward to having his room emptied of furnishing. Did he really want his warm room, so comfortably fitted with old family furniture, to be turned into a naked den in which he would certainly be able to crawl unhampered in all directions but at the price of shedding simultaneously all recollection of his human background? He had indeed been so near the brink of forgetfulness that only the voice of his mother, which he had not heard for so long, had drawn him back from it. Nothing should be taken out of his room; everything must stay as it was; he could not dispense with the good influence of the furniture on his state of mind; and even if the furniture did hamper him in his senseless crawling around and around, that was no drawback but a great advantage.

Unfortunately his sister was of the contrary opinion; she had grown accustomed, and not without reason, to consider herself an expert in Gregor's affairs as against her parents, and so her mother's advice was now enough to make her determined on the removal not only of the chest and the writing desk, which had been her first intention, but of all the furniture except the indispensable sofa. This determination was not, of course, merely the outcome of childish recalcitrance and of the self-confidence she had recently developed so unexpectedly and at such cost; she had in fact perceived that Gregor needed a lot of space to crawl about in, while on the other hand he never used the furniture at all, so far as could be seen. Another factor might also have been the enthusiastic temperament of an adolescent girl, which seeks to indulge itself on every opportunity and which now tempted Grete to exaggerate the horror of her brother's circumstances in order that she might do all the more for him. In a room where Gregor lorded it all alone over empty walls no one save herself was likely ever to set foot.

And so she was not to be moved from her resolve by her mother, who seemed moreover to be ill at ease in Gregor's room and therefore unsure of herself, was soon reduced to silence, and helped her daughter as best she could to push the chest outside. Now, Gregor could do without the chest, if need be, but the writing desk he must retain. As soon as the two women had got the chest out of his room, groaning as they pushed it, Gregor stuck his head out from under the sofa to see how he might intervene as kindly and cautiously as possible. But as bad luck would have it, his mother was the first to return, leaving Grete clasping the chest in the room next door where she was trying to shift it all by herself, without of course moving it from the spot. His mother however was not accustomed to the sight of him, it might sicken her and so in alarm Gregor backed quickly to the other end of the sofa, yet could not prevent the sheet from swaying a little in front. That was enough to put her on the alert. She paused, stood still for a moment, and then went back to Grete.

Although Gregor kept reassuring himself that nothing out of the way was happening, but only a few bits of furniture were being changed around, he soon had to admit that all this trotting to and fro of the two women, their little ejaculations, and the scraping of furniture along the floor affected him like a vast disturbance coming from all sides at once, and however much he tucked in his head and legs and cowered to the very floor he was bound to confess that he would not be able to stand it for long. They were clearing his room out; taking away everything he loved; the chest in which he kept his fret saw and other tools was already dragged off; they were now loosening the writing desk which had almost sunk into the floor, the desk at which he had done all his homework when he was at the commercial academy, at the grammar school before that, and, yes, even at the primary school—he had no more time to waste in weighing the good intentions of the two women, whose existence he had by now almost forgotten, for they were so exhausted that they were laboring in silence and nothing could be heard but the heavy scuffling of their feet.

And so he rushed out—the women were just leaning against the writing desk in the next room to give themselves a breather—and four times changed his direction, since he really did not know what to rescue first, then on the wall opposite, which was already otherwise cleared, he was struck by the picture of the lady muffled in so much fur and quickly crawled up to it and pressed himself to the glass, which was a good surface to hold on to and comforted his hot belly. This picture at least, which was entirely hidden beneath him, was going to be removed by nobody. He turned his head toward the door of the living room so as to observe the women when they came back.

They had not allowed themselves much of a rest and were already coming; Grete had twined her arm around her mother and was almost supporting her. "Well, what shall we take now?" said Grete, looking around. Her eyes met Gregor's from the wall. She kept her composure, presumably because of her mother, bent her head down to her mother, to keep her from looking up, and said, although in a fluttering, unpremeditated voice: "Come, hadn't we better go back to the living room for a moment?" Her intentions were clear enough to Gregor, she wanted to bestow her mother in safety and then chase him down from the wall. Well, just let her try it! He clung to his picture and would not give it up. He would rather fly in Grete's face.

But Grete's words had succeeded in disquieting her mother, who took a step to one side, caught sight of the huge brown mass on the flowered wallpaper, and before she was really conscious that what she saw was Gregor, screamed in a loud, hoarse voice: "Oh God, oh God!" fell with outspread arms over the sofa as if giving up, and did not move. "Gregor!" cried his sister, shaking her fist and glaring at him. This was the first time she had directly addressed him since his metamorphosis. She ran into the next room for some aromatic essence with which to rouse her mother from her fainting fit. Gregor wanted to help too—there was still time to rescue the picture—but he was stuck fast to the glass and had to tear himself loose; he then ran after his sister into the next room as if he could advise her, as he used to do; but then had to stand helplessly behind her; she meanwhile searched among various small bottles and when she turned around started in alarm at the sight of him; one bottle fell on the floor and broke; a splinter of glass cut Gregor's face and some kind of corrosive medicine splashed him; without pausing a moment longer Grete gathered up all the bottles she could carry and ran to her mother with them; she banged the door shut with her foot. Gregor was now cut off from his mother, who was perhaps nearly dying because of him; he dared not open the door for fear of frightening away his sister, who had to stay with her mother; there was nothing he could do but wait; and harassed by self-reproach and worry he began now to crawl to and fro, over everything, walls, furniture, and ceiling, and finally in his despair, when the whole room seemed to be reeling around him, fell down onto the middle of the big table.

A little while elapsed, Gregor was still lying there feebly and all around was quiet, perhaps that was a good omen. Then the doorbell rang. The servant girl was of course locked in her kitchen, and Grete would have to open the door. It was his father. "What's been happening?" were his first words; Grete's face must have told him everything. Grete answered in a muffled voice, apparently hiding her head on his breast: "Mother has been fainting, but she's better now. Gregor's broken loose." "Just what I expected," said his father, "just what I've been telling you, but you women would never listen." It was clear to Gregor that his father had taken the worst interpretation of Grete's all too brief statement and was assuming that Gregor had been guilty of some violent act. Therefore Gregor must now try to propitiate his father, since he had neither time nor means for an explanation. And so he fled to the door of his own room and crouched against it, to let his father see as soon as he came in from the hall that his son had the good intention of getting back into his room immediately and that it was not necessary to drive him there, but that if only the door were opened he would disappear at once.

Yet his father was not in the mood to perceive such fine distinctions. "Ah!" he cried as soon as he appeared, in a tone that sounded at once angry and exultant. Gregor drew his head back from the door and lifted it to look at his father. Truly, this was not the father he had imagined to himself; admittedly he had been too absorbed of late in his new recreation of crawling over the ceiling to take the same interest as before in what was happening elsewhere in the flat, and he ought really to be prepared for some changes. And yet, and yet, could that be his father? The man who used to lie wearily sunk in bed whenever Gregor set out on a business journey; who welcomed him back of an evening lying in a long chair in a dressing gown; who could not really rise to his feet but only lifted his arms in greeting, and on the rare occasions when he did go out with his family, on one or two Sundays a year and on highest holidays, walked between Gregor and his mother, who were slow walkers anyhow, even more slowly than they did, muffled in his old greatcoat, shuffling laboriously forward with the help of his crook-handled stick which he set down most cautiously at every step and, whenever he wanted to say anything, nearly always came to a full stop and gathered his escort around him? Now he was standing there in fine shape; dressed in a smart blue uniform with gold buttons, such as bank messengers wear; his strong double chin bulged over the stiff high collar of his jacket; from under his bushy eyebrows his black eyes darted fresh and penetrating glances; his onetime tangled white hair had been combed flat on either side of a shining and carefully exact parting. He pitched his cap, which bore a gold monogram, probably the badge of some bank, in a wide sweep across the whole room onto a sofa and with the tail-ends of his jacket thrown back, his hands in his trouser pockets, advanced with a grim visage toward Gregor. Likely enough he did not himself know what he meant to do; at any rate he lifted his feet uncommonly high, and Gregor was dumbfounded at the enormous size of his shoe soles. But Gregor could not risk standing up to him, aware as he had been from the very first day of his new life that his father believed only the severest measures suitable for dealing with him. And so he ran before his father, stopping when he stopped and scuttling forward again when his father made any kind of move. In this way they circled the room several times without anything decisive happening, indeed the whole operation did not even look like a pursuit because it was carried out so slowly. And so Gregor did not leave the floor, for he feared that his father might take as a piece of peculiar wickedness any excursion of his over the walls or the ceiling. All the same, he could not stay this course much longer, for while his father took one step he had to carry out a whole series of movements. He was already beginning to feel breathless, just as in his former life his lungs had not been very dependable. As he was staggering along, trying to concentrate his energy on running, hardly keeping his eyes open; in his dazed state never even thinking of any other escape than simply going forward; and having almost forgotten that the walls were free to him, which in this room were well provided with finely carved pieces of furniture full of knobs and crevices—suddenly something lightly flung landed close behind him and rolled before him. It was an apple; a second apple followed immediately; Gregor came to a stop in alarm; there was no point in running on, for his father was determined to bombard him. He had filled his pockets with fruit from the dish on the sideboard and was now shying apple after apple, without taking particularly good aim for the moment. The small red apples rolled about the floor as if magnetized and cannoned into each other. An apple thrown without much force grazed Gregor's back and glanced off harmlessly. But another following immediately landed right on his back and sank in; Gregor wanted to drag himself forward, as if this startling, incredible pain could be left behind him; but he felt as if nailed to the spot and flattened himself out in a complete derangement of all his senses. With his last conscious look he saw the door of his room being torn open and his mother rushing out ahead of his screaming sister, in her underbodice, for her daughter had loosened her clothing to let her breathe more freely and recover from her swoon, he saw his mother rushing toward his father, leaving one after another behind her on the floor her loosened petticoats, stumbling over her petticoats straight to his father and embracing him, in complete union with him—but here Gregor's sight began to fail—with her hands clasped around his father's neck as she begged for her son's life.

3

The serious injury done to Gregor, which disabled him for more than a month—the apple went on sticking in his body as a visible reminder, since no one ventured to remove it—seemed to have made even his father recollect that Gregor was a member of the family, despite his present unfortunate and repulsive shape, and ought not to be treated as an enemy, that, on the contrary, family duty required the suppression of disgust and the exercise of patience, nothing but patience.

And although his injury had impaired, probably forever, his powers of movement, and for the time being it took him long, long minutes to creep across his room like an old invalid—there was no question now of crawling up the wall—yet in his own opinion he was sufficiently compensated for this worsening of his condition by the fact that toward evening the living-room door, which he used to watch intently for an hour or two beforehand, was always thrown open, so that lying in the darkness of his room, invisible to the family, he could see them all at the lamp-lit table and listen to their talk, by general consent as it were, very different from his earlier eavesdropping.

True, their intercourse lacked the lively character of former times, which he had always called to mind with a certain wistfulness in the small hotel bedrooms where he had been wont to throw himself down, tired out, on damp bedding. They were now mostly very silent. Soon after supper his father would fall asleep in his armchair; his mother and sister would admonish each other to be silent; his mother, bending low over the lamp, stitched at fine sewing for an underwear firm;

his sister, who had taken a job as a salesgirl, was learning shorthand and French in the evenings on the chance of bettering herself. Sometimes his father woke up, and as if quite unaware that he had been sleeping said to his mother: "What a lot of sewing you're doing today!" and at once fell asleep again, while the two women exchanged a tired smile.

With a kind of mulishness his father persisted in keeping his uniform on even in the house; his dressing gown hung uselessly on its peg and he slept fully dressed where he sat, as if he were ready for service at any moment and even here only at the beck and call of his superior. As a result, his uniform, which was not brand-new to start with, began to look dirty, despite all the loving care of the mother and sister to keep it clean, and Gregor often spent whole evenings gazing at the many greasy spots on the garment, gleaming with gold buttons always in a high state of polish, in which the old man sat sleeping in extreme discomfort and yet quite peacefully.

As soon as the clock struck ten his mother tried to rouse his father with gentle words and to persuade him after that to get into bed, for sitting there he could not have a proper sleep and that was what he needed most, since he had to go on duty at six. But with the mulishness that had obsessed him since he became a bank messenger he always insisted on staying longer at the table, although he regularly fell asleep again and in the end only with the greatest trouble could be got out of his armchair and into his bed. However insistently Gregor's mother and sister kept urging him with gentle reminders, he would go on slowly shaking his head for a quarter of an hour, keeping his eyes shut, and refuse to get to his feet. The mother plucked at his sleeve, whispering endearments in his ear, the sister left her lessons to come to her mother's help, but Gregor's father was not to be caught. He would only sink down deeper in his chair. Not until the two women hoisted him up by the armpits did he open his eyes and look at them both, one after the other, usually with the remark: "This is a life. This is the peace and quiet of my old age." And leaning on the two of them he would heave himself up, with difficulty, as if he were a great burden to himself, suffer them to lead him as far as the door and then wave them off and go on alone, while the mother abandoned her needlework and the sister her pen in order to run after him and help him farther.

Who could find time, in this overworked and tired-out family, to bother about Gregor more than was absolutely needful? The household was reduced more and more; the servant girl was turned off; a gigantic bony charwoman with white hair flying around her head came in morning and evening to do the rough work; everything else was done by Gregor's mother, as well as great piles of sewing. Even various family ornaments, which his mother and sister used to wear with pride at parties and celebrations, had to be sold, as Gregor discovered of an evening from hearing them all discuss the prices obtained. But what they lamented most was the fact that they could not leave the flat which was much too big for their present circumstances, because they could not think of any way to shift Gregor. Yet Gregor saw well enough that consideration for him was not the main difficulty preventing the removal, for they could have easily shifted him in some suitable box with a few air holes in it; what really kept them from moving into another flat was rather their own complete hopelessness and the belief that they had been singled out for a misfortune such as had never happened to any of their relations or acquaintances. They fulfilled to the uttermost all that the world demands of poor people, the father fetched breakfast for the small clerks in the bank, the mother devoted her energy to making underwear for strangers, the sister trotted to and fro behind the counter at the behest of customers, but more than this they had not the strength to do. And the wound in Gregor's back began to nag at him afresh when his mother and sister, after getting his father into bed, came back again, left their work lying, drew close to each other, and sat cheek by cheek; when his mother, pointing toward his room, said: "Shut that door now, Grete," and he was left again in darkness, while next door the women mingled their tears or perhaps sat dry-eyed staring at the table.

Gregor hardly slept at all by night or by day. He was often haunted by the idea that next time the door opened he would take the family's affairs in hand again just as he used to do; once more, after this long interval, there appeared in his thoughts the figures of the chief and the chief clerk, the commercial travelers and the apprentices, the porter who was so dull-witted, two or three friends in other firms, a chambermaid in one of the rural hotels, a sweet and fleeting memory, a cashier in a milliner's shop, whom he had wooed earnestly but too slowly—they all appeared, together with strangers or people he had quite forgotten, but instead of helping him and his family they were one and all unapproachable and he was glad when they vanished. At other times he would not be in the mood to bother about his family, he was only filled with rage at the way they were neglecting him, and although he had no clear idea of what he might care to eat he would make plans for getting into the larder to take the food that was after all his due, even if he were not hungry. His sister no longer took thought to bring him what might especially please him, but in the morning and at noon before she went to business hurriedly pushed into his room with her foot any food that was available, and in the evening cleared it out again with one sweep of the broom, heedless of whether it had been merely tasted, or—as most frequently happened—left untouched. The cleaning of his room, which she now did always in the evenings, could not have been more hastily done. Streaks of dirt stretched along the walls, here and there lay balls of dust and filth. At first Gregor used to station himself in some particularly filthy corner when his sister arrived, in order to reproach her with it, so to speak. But he could have sat there for weeks without getting her to make any improvement; she could see the dirt as well as he did, but she had simply made up her mind to leave it alone. And yet, with a touchiness that was new to her, which seemed anyhow to have infected the whole family, she jealously guarded her claim to be the sole caretaker of Gregor's room. His mother once subjected his room to a thorough cleaning, which was achieved only by means of several buckets of water—all this dampness of course upset Gregor too and he lay widespread, sulky, and motionless on the sofa—but she was well punished for it. Hardly had his sister noticed the changed aspect of his room that evening than she rushed in high dudgeon into the living room and, despite the imploringly raised hands of her mother, burst into a storm of weeping, while her parents—her father had of course been startled out of his chair—looked on at first in helpless amazement; then they too began to go into action; the father reproached the mother on his right for not having left the cleaning of Gregor's room to his sister; shrieked at the sister on his left that never again was she to be allowed to clean Gregor's room; while the mother tried to pull the father into his bedroom, since he was beyond himself with agitation; the sister, shaken with sobs, then beat upon the table with her small fists; and Gregor hissed loudly with rage because not one of them thought of shutting the door to spare him such a spectacle and so much noise.

Still, even if the sister, exhausted by her daily work, had grown tired of looking after Gregor as she did formerly, there was no need for his mother's intervention or for Gregor's being neglected at all. The charwoman was there. This old widow, whose strong bony frame had enabled her to survive the worst a long life could offer, by no means recoiled from Gregor. Without being in the least curious she had once by chance opened the door of his room and at the sight of Gregor, who, taken by surprise, began to rush to and fro although no one was chasing him, merely stood there with her arms folded. From that time she never failed to open his door a little for a moment, morning and evening, to have a look at him. At first she even used to call him to her, with words which apparently she took to be friendly, such as: "Come along, then, you old dung beetle!" or "Look at the old dung beetle, then!" To such allocutions Gregor made no answer, but stayed motionless where he was, as if the door had never been opened. Instead of being allowed to disturb him so senselessly whenever the whim took her, she should rather have been ordered to clean out his room daily, that charwoman! Once, early in the morning—heavy rain was lashing on the windowpanes, perhaps a sign that spring was on the way—Gregor was so exasperated when she began addressing him again that he ran at her, as if to attack her, although slowly and feebly enough. But the charwoman instead of showing fright merely lifted high a chair that happened to be beside the door, and as she stood there with her mouth wide open it was clear that she meant to shut it only when she brought the chair down on Gregor's back. "So you're not coming any nearer?" she asked, as Gregor turned away again, and quietly put the chair back into the corner.

Gregor was now eating hardly anything. Only when he happened to pass the food laid out for him did he take a bit of something in his mouth as a pastime, kept it there for an hour at a time, and usually spat it out again. At first he thought it was chagrin over the state of his room that prevented him from eating, yet he soon got used to the various changes in his room. It had become a habit in the family to push into his room things there was no room for elsewhere, and there were plenty of these now, since one of the rooms had been let to three lodgers. These serious gentlemen—all three of them with full beards, as Gregor once observed through a crack in the door— had a passion for order, not only in their own room but, since they were now members of the household, in all its arrangements, especially in the kitchen. Superfluous, not to say dirty, objects they could not bear. Besides, they had brought with them most of the furnishings they needed. For this reason many things could be dispensed with that it was no use trying to sell but that should not be thrown away either. All of them found their way into Gregor's room. The ash can likewise and the kitchen garbage can. Anything that was not needed for the moment was simply flung into Gregor's room by the charwoman, who did everything in a hurry; fortunately Gregor usually saw only the object, whatever it was, and the hand that held it. Perhaps she intended to take the things away again as time and opportunity offered, or to collect them until she could throw them all out in a heap, but in fact they just lay wherever she happened to throw them, except when Gregor pushed his way through the junk heap and shifted it somewhat, at first out of necessity, because he had not room enough to crawl, but later with increasing enjoyment, although after such excursions, being sad and weary to death, he would lie motionless for hours. And since the lodgers often ate their supper at home in the common living room, the living-room door stayed shut many an evening, yet Gregor reconciled himself quite easily to the shutting of the door, for often enough on evenings when it was opened he had disregarded it entirely and lain in the darkest corner of his room, quite unnoticed by the family. But on one occasion the charwoman left the door open a little and it stayed ajar even when the lodgers came in for supper and the lamp was lit. They set themselves at the top end of the table where formerly Gregor and his father and mother had eaten their meals, unfolded their napkins, and took knife and fork in hand. At once his mother appeared in the other doorway with a dish of meat and close behind her his sister with a dish of potatoes piled high. The food steamed with a thick vapor. The lodgers bent over the food set before them as if to scrutinize it before eating, in fact the man in the middle, who seemed to pass for an authority with the other two, cut a piece of meat as it lay on the dish, obviously to discover if it were tender or should be sent back to the kitchen. He showed satisfaction, and Gregor's mother and sister, who had been watching anxiously, breathed freely and began to smile.

The family itself took its meals in the kitchen. Nonetheless, Gregor's father came into the living room before going into the kitchen and with one prolonged bow, cap in hand, made a round of the table. The lodgers all stood up and murmured something in their beards. When they were alone again they ate their food in almost complete silence. It seemed remarkable to Gregor that among the various noises coming from the table he could always distinguish the sound of their masticating teeth, as if this were a sign to Gregor that one needed teeth in order to eat, and that with toothless jaws even of the finest make one could do nothing. "I'm hungry enough," said Gregor sadly to himself, "but not for that kind of food. How these lodgers are stuffing themselves, and here am I dying of starvation!"

On that very evening—during the whole of his time there Gregor could not remember ever having heard the violin—the sound of violin-playing came from the kitchen. The lodgers had already finished their supper, the one in the middle had brought out a newspaper and given the other two a page apiece, and now they were leaning back at ease reading and smoking. When the violin began to play they pricked up their ears, got to their feet, and went on tiptoe to the hall door where they stood huddled together. Their movements must have been heard in the kitchen, for Gregor's father called out: "Is the violin-playing disturbing you, gentlemen? It can be stopped at once." "On the contrary," said the middle lodger, "could not Fräulein Samsa come and play in this room, beside us, where it is much more convenient and comfortable?" "Oh certainly," cried Gregor's father, as if he were the violin-player. The lodgers came back into the living room and waited. Presently Gregor's father arrived with the music stand, his mother carrying the music and his sister with the violin. His sister quietly made everything ready to start playing; his parents, who had never let rooms before and so had an exaggerated idea of the courtesy due to lodgers, did not venture to sit down on their own chairs; his father leaned against the door, the right hand thrust between two buttons of his livery coat, which was formally buttoned up; but his mother was offered a chair by one of the lodgers and, since she left the chair just where he had happened to put it, sat down in a corner to one side.

Gregor's sister began to play; the father and mother, from either side, intently watched the movements of her hands. Gregor, attracted by the playing, ventured to move forward a little until his head was actually inside the living room. He felt hardly any surprise at his growing lack of consideration for the others; there had been a time when he prided himself on being considerate. And yet just on this occasion he had more reason than ever to hide himself, since, owing to the amount of dust that lay thick in his room and rose into the air at the slightest movement, he too was covered with dust; fluff and hair and remnants of food trailed with him, caught on his back and along his sides; his indifference to everything was much too great for him to turn on his back and scrape himself clean on the carpet, as once he had done several times a day. And in spite of his condition, no shame deterred him from advancing a little over the spotless floor of the living room.

To be sure, no one was aware of him. The family was entirely absorbed in the violin-playing; the lodgers, however, who first of all had stationed themselves, hands in pockets, much too close behind the music stand so that they could all have read the music, which must have bothered his sister, had soon retreated to the window, half whispering with downbent heads, and stayed there while his father turned an anxious eye on them. Indeed, they were making it more than obvious that they had been disappointed in their expectation of hearing good or enjoyable violin-playing, that they had had more than enough of the performance and only out of courtesy suffered a continued disturbance of their peace. From the way they all kept blowing the smoke of their cigars high in the air through nose and mouth one could divine their irritation. And yet Gregor's sister was playing so beautifully. Her face leaned sideways, intently and sadly her eyes followed the notes of music. Gregor crawled a little farther forward and lowered his head to the ground so that it might be possible for his eyes to meet hers. Was he an animal, that music had such an effect upon him? He felt as if the way were opening before him to the unknown nourishment he craved. He was determined to push forward till he reached his sister, to pull at her skirt and so let her know that she was to come into his room with her violin, for no one here appreciated her playing as he would appreciate it. He would never let her out of his room, at least, not so long as he lived; his frightful appearance would become, for the first time, useful to him; he would watch all the doors of his room at once and spit at intruders; but his sister should need no constraint, she should stay with him of her own free will; she should sit beside him on the sofa, bend down her ear to him, and hear him confide that he had had the firm intention of sending her to the Conservatorium, and that, but for his mishap, last Christmas—surely Christmas was long past?—he would have announced it to everybody without allowing a single objection. After this confession his sister would be so touched that she would burst into tears, and Gregor would then raise himself to her shoulder and kiss her on the neck, which, now that she went to business, she kept free of any ribbon or collar.

"Mr. Samsa!" cried the middle lodger to Gregor's father, and pointed, without wasting any more words, at Gregor, now working himself slowly forward. The violin fell silent, the middle lodger first smiled to his friends with a shake of the head and then looked at Gregor again. Instead of driving Gregor out, his father seemed to think it more needful to begin by soothing down the lodgers, although they were not at all agitated and apparently found Gregor more entertaining than the violin-playing. He hurried toward them and, spreading out his arms, tried to urge them back into their own room and at the same time to block their view of Gregor. They now began to be really a little angry, one could not tell whether because of the old man's behavior or because it had just dawned on them that all unwittingly they had such a neighbor as Gregor next door. They demanded explanations of his father, they waved their arms like him, tugged uneasily at their beards, and only with reluctance backed toward their room. Meanwhile Gregor's sister, who stood there as if lost when her playing was so abruptly broken off, came to life again, pulled herself together all at once after standing for a while holding violin and bow in nervelessly hanging hands and staring at her music, pushed her violin into the lap of her mother, who was still sitting in her chair fighting asthmatically for breath, and ran into the lodgers' room to which they were now being shepherded by her father rather more quickly than before. One could see the pillows and blankets on the beds flying under her accustomed fingers and being laid in order. Before the lodgers had actually reached their room she had finished making the beds and slipped out.

The old man seemed once more to be so possessed by his mulish self-assertiveness that he was forgetting all the respect he should show to his lodgers. He kept driving them on and driving them on until in the very door of the bedroom the middle lodger stamped his foot loudly on the floor and so brought him to a halt. "I beg to announce," said the lodger, lifting one hand and looking also at Gregor's mother and sister, "that because of the disgusting conditions prevailing in this household and family"—here he spat on the floor with emphatic brevity—"I give you notice on the spot. Naturally I won't pay you a penny for the days I have lived here, on the contrary I shall consider bringing an action for damages against you, based on claims—believe me—that will be easily susceptible of proof." He ceased and stared straight in front of him, as if he expected something. In fact his two friends at once rushed into the breach with these words: "And we too give notice on the spot." On that he seized the door handle and shut the door with a slam.

Gregor's father, groping with his hands, staggered forward and fell into his chair; it looked as if he were stretching himself there for his ordinary evening nap, but the marked jerkings of his head, which were as if uncontrollable, showed that he was far from asleep. Gregor had simply stayed quietly all the time on the spot where the lodgers had espied him. Disappointment at the failure of his plan, perhaps also the weakness arising from extreme hunger, made it impossible for him to move. He feared, with a fair degree of certainty, that at any moment the general tension would discharge itself in a combined attack upon him, and he lay waiting. He did not react even to the noise made by the violin as it fell off his mother's lap from under her trembling fingers and gave out a resonant note.

"My dear parents," said his sister, slapping her hand on the table by way of introduction, "things can't go on like this. Perhaps you don't realize that, but I do. I won't utter my brother's name in the presence of this creature, and so all I say is: we must try to get rid of it. We've tried to look after it and to put up with it as far as is humanly possible, and I don't think anyone could reproach us in the slightest."

"She is more than right," said Gregor's father to himself. His mother, who was still choking for lack of breath, began to cough hollowly into her hand with a wild look in her eyes.

His sister rushed over to her and held her forehead. His father's thoughts seemed to have lost their vagueness at Grete's words, he sat more upright, fingering his service cap that lay among the plates still lying on the table from the lodgers' supper, and from time to time looked at the still form of Gregor.

"We must try to get rid of it," his sister now said explicitly to her father, since her mother was coughing too much to hear a word, "it will be the death of both of you, I can see that coming. When one has to work as hard as we do, all of us, one can't stand this continual torment at home on top of it. At least I can't stand it any longer." And she burst into such a passion of sobbing that her tears dropped on her mother's face, where she wiped them off mechanically.

"My dear," said the old man sympathetically, and with evident understanding, "but what can we do?"

Gregor's sister merely shrugged her shoulders to indicate the feeling of help-lessness that had now overmastered her during her weeping fit, in contrast to her former confidence.

"If he could understand us," said her father, half questioningly; Grete, still sobbing, vehemently waved a hand to show how unthinkable that was.

"If he could understand us," repeated the old man, shutting his eyes to consider his daughter's conviction that understanding was impossible, "then perhaps we might come to some agreement with him. But as it is——"

"He must go," cried Gregor's sister, "that's the only solution, Father. You must just try to get rid of the idea that this is Gregor. The fact that we've believed it for so long is the root of all our trouble. But how can it be Gregor? If this were Gregor, he would have realized long ago that human beings can't live with such a creature, and he'd have gone away on his own accord. Then we wouldn't have any brother, but we'd be able to go on living and keep his memory in honor. As it is, this creature persecutes us, drives away our lodgers, obviously wants the whole apartment to himself, and would have us all sleep in the gutter. Just look, Father," she shrieked all at once, "he's at it again!" And in an access of panic that was quite incomprehensible to Gregor she even quitted her mother, literally thrusting the chair from her as if she would rather sacrifice her mother than stay so near to Gregor, and rushed behind her father, who also rose up, being simply upset by her agitation, and half spread his arms out as if to protect her.

Yet Gregor had not the slightest intention of frightening anyone, far less his sister. He had only begun to turn around in order to crawl back to his room, but it was certainly a startling operation to watch, since because of his disabled condition he could not execute the difficult turning movements except by lifting his head and then bracing it against the floor over and over again. He paused and looked around. His good intentions seemed to have been recognized; the alarm had only been momentary. Now they were all watching him in melancholy silence. His mother lay in her chair, her legs stiffly outstretched and pressed together, her eyes almost closing for sheer weariness; his father and his sister were sitting beside each other, his sister's arm around the old man's neck.

Perhaps I can go on turning around now, thought Gregor, and began his labors again. He could not stop himself from panting with the effort, and had to pause now and then to take breath. Nor did anyone harass him, he was left entirely to himself. When he had completed the turn-around he began at once to crawl straight back. He was amazed at the distance separating him from his room and could not understand how in his weak state he had managed to accomplish the same journey so recently, almost without remarking it. Intent on crawling as fast as possible, he barely noticed that not a single word, not an ejaculation from his family, interfered with his progress. Only when he was already in the doorway did he turn his head around, not completely, for his neck muscles were getting stiff, but enough to see that nothing had changed behind him except that his sister had risen to her feet. His last glance fell on his mother, who was not quite overcome by sleep.

Hardly was he well inside his room when the door was hastily pushed shut, bolted, and locked. The sudden noise in his rear startled him so much that his little legs gave beneath him. It was his sister who had shown such haste. She had been standing ready waiting and had made a light spring forward, Gregor had not even heard her coming, and she cried "At last!" to her parents as she turned the key in the lock.

"And what now?" said Gregor to himself, looking around in the darkness. Soon he made the discovery that he was now unable to stir a limb. This did not surprise him, rather it seemed unnatural that he should ever actually have been able to move on these feeble little legs. Otherwise he felt relatively comfortable. True, his whole body was aching, but it seemed that the pain was gradually growing less and would finally pass away. The rotting apple in his back and the inflamed area around it, all covered with soft dust, already hardly troubled him. He thought of his family with tenderness and love. The decision that he must disappear was one that he held to even more strongly than his sister, if that were possible. In this state of vacant and peaceful meditation he remained until the tower clock struck three in the morning. The first broadening of light in the world outside the window entered his consciousness once more. Then his head sank to the floor of its own accord and from his nostrils came the last faint flicker of his breath.

When the charwoman arrived early in the morning—what between her strength and her impatience she slammed all the doors so loudly, never mind how often she had been begged not to do so, that no one in the whole apartment could enjoy any quiet sleep after her arrival—she noticed nothing unusual as she took her customary peep into Gregor's room. She thought he was lying motionless on purpose, pretending to be in the sulks; she credited him with every kind of intelligence. Since she happened to have the long-handled broom in her hand she tried to tickle him up with it from the doorway. When that too produced no reaction she felt provoked and poked at him a little harder, and only when she had pushed him along the floor without meeting any resistance was her attention aroused. It did not take her long to establish the truth of the matter, and her eyes widened, she let out a whistle, yet did not waste much time over it but tore open the door of the Samsas' bedroom and yelled into the darkness at the top of her voice: "Just look at this, it's dead; it's lying here dead and done for!"

Mr. and Mrs. Samsa started up in their double bed and before they realized the nature of the charwoman's announcement had some difficulty in overcoming the shock of it. But then they got out of bed quickly, one on either side, Mr. Samsa throwing a blanket over his shoulders, Mrs. Samsa in nothing but her nightgown; in this array they entered Gregor's room. Meanwhile the door of the living room opened, too, where Grete had been sleeping since the advent of the lodgers; she was completely dressed as if she had not been to bed, which seemed to be confirmed also by the paleness of her face. "Dead?" said Mrs. Samsa, looking questioningly at the charwoman, although she would have investigated for herself, and the fact was obvious enough without investigation. "I should say so," said the charwoman, proving her words by pushing Gregor's corpse a long way to one side with her broomstick. Mrs. Samsa made a movement as if to stop her, but checked it. "Well," said Mr. Samsa, "now thanks be to God." He crossed himself, and the three women followed his example. Grete, whose eyes never left the corpse, said: "Just see how thin he was. It's such a long time since he's eaten anything. The food came out again just as it went in." Indeed, Gregor's body was completely flat and dry, as could only now be seen when it was no longer supported by the legs and nothing prevented one from looking closely at it.

"Come in beside us, Grete, for a little while," said Mrs. Samsa with a tremulous smile, and Grete, not without looking back at the corpse, followed her parents into their bedroom. The charwoman shut the door and opened the window wide. Although it was so early in the morning a certain softness was perceptible in the fresh air. After all, it was already the end of March.

The three lodgers emerged from their room and were surprised to see no breakfast; they had been forgotten. "Where's our breakfast?" said the middle lodger peevishly to the charwoman. But she put her finger to her lips and hastily, without a word, indicated by gestures that they should go into Gregor's room. They did so and stood, their hands in the pockets of their somewhat shabby coats, around Gregor's corpse in the room where it was now fully light.

At that the door of the Samsas' bedroom opened and Mr. Samsa appeared in his uniform, his wife on one arm, his daughter on the other. They all looked a little as if they had been crying; from time to time Grete hid her face on her father's arm.

"Leave my house at once!" said Mr. Samsa, and pointed to the door without disengaging himself from the women. "What do you mean by that?" said the middle lodger, taken somewhat aback, with a feeble smile. The two others put their hands behind them and kept rubbing them together, as if in gleeful expectation of a fine set-to in which they were bound to come off the winners. "I mean just what I say," answered Mr. Samsa, and advanced in a straight line with his two companions toward the lodger. He stood his ground at first quietly, looking at the floor as if his thoughts were taking a new pattern in his head. "Then let us go, by all means," he said, and looked up at Mr. Samsa as if in a sudden access of humility he were expecting some renewed sanction for this decision. Mr. Samsa merely nodded briefly once or twice with meaning eyes. Upon that the lodger really did go with long strides into the hall, his two friends had been listening and had quite stopped rubbing their hands for some moments and now went scuttling after him as if afraid that Mr. Samsa might get into the hall before them and cut them off from their leader. In the hall they all three took their hats from the rack, their sticks from the umbrella stand, bowed in silence, and quitted the apartment. With a suspiciousness that proved quite unfounded Mr. Samsa and the two women followed them out to the landing; leaning over the banister they watched the three figures slowly but surely going down the long stairs, vanishing from sight at a certain turn of the staircase on every floor and coming into view again after a moment or so; the more they dwindled, the more the Samsa family's interest in them dwindled, and when a butcher's boy met them and passed them on the stairs coming up proudly with a tray on his head, Mr. Samsa and the two women soon left the landing and as if a burden had been lifted from them went back into their apartment.

They decided to spend this day in resting and going for a stroll; they had not only deserved such a respite from work, but absolutely needed it. And so they sat down at the table and wrote three notes of excuse, Mr. Samsa to his board of management, Mrs. Samsa to her employer, and Grete to the head of her firm. While they were writing, the charwoman came in to say that she was going now, since her morning's work was finished. At first they only nodded without looking up, but as she kept hovering there they eyed her irritably. "Well?" said Mr. Samsa. The charwoman stood grinning in the doorway as if she had good news to impart to the family but meant not to say a word unless properly questioned. The small ostrich feather standing upright on her hat, which had annoyed Mr. Samsa ever since she was engaged, was waving gaily in all directions. "Well, what is it then?" asked Mrs. Samsa, who obtained more respect from the charwoman than the others. "Oh," said the charwoman, giggling so amiably that she could not at once continue, "just this, you don't need to bother about how to get rid of the thing next door. It's been seen to already." Mrs. Samsa and Grete bent over their letters again, as if preoccupied; Mr. Samsa, who perceived that she was eager to begin describing it all in detail, stopped her with a decisive hand. But since she was not allowed to tell her story, she remembered the great hurry she was in, obviously deeply huffed: "Bye, everybody," she said, whirling off violently, and departed with a frightful slamming of doors.

"She'll be given notice tonight," said Mr. Samsa, but neither from his wife nor his daughter did he get any answer, for the charwoman seemed to have shattered again the composure they had barely achieved. They rose, went to the window and stayed there, clasping each other tight. Mr. Samsa turned in his chair to look at them and quietly observed them for a little. Then he called out: "Come along, now, do. Let bygones be bygones. And you might have some consideration for me." The two of them complied at once, hastened to him, caressed him, and quickly finished their letters.

Then they all three left the apartment together, which was more than they had done for months, and went by tram into the open country outside the town.

The tram, in which they were the only passengers, was filled with warm sunshine. Leaning comfortably back in their seats they canvassed their prospects for the future, and it appeared on closer inspection that these were not at all bad, for the jobs they had got, which so far they had never really discussed with each other, were all three admirable and likely to lead to better things later on. The greatest immediate improvement in their condition would of course arise from moving to another house; they wanted to take a smaller and cheaper but also better situated and more easily run apartment than the one they had, which Gregor had selected. While they were thus conversing, it struck both Mr. and Mrs. Samsa, almost at the same moment, as they became aware of their daughter's increasing vivacity, that in spite of all the sorrow of recent times, which had made her cheeks pale, she had bloomed into a pretty girl with a good figure. They grew quieter and half unconsciously exchanged glances of complete agreement, having come to the conclusion that it would soon be time to find a good husband for her. And it was like a confirmation of their new dreams and excellent intentions that at the end of their journey their daughter sprang to her feet first and stretched her young body.

T. S. ELIOT
[1888–1965]

When the long poem *The Waste Land* appeared in the November 1922 issue of *The Dial,* it marked an attempt on the part of a well-organized literary elite based in London, Paris, and the United States to redefine American culture for their generation; in large measure, their attempt succeeded. The poem depicted the modern world as a devastated, sterile place in which the land had lost its regenerative capacity, cities were sites of pollution and despair, and human relationships held no moral or spiritual value. More than any other single work, *The Waste Land* also reflected the disillusionment of American intellectuals, some of them European expatriates, with Western society at the end of World War I. Difficult in structure, fragmented in organization, and obscure in its references, the poem seemed destined for a limited audience; but, after being augmented by notes by the author and supported by interpretive reviews and essays, it went on to establish itself as a monument of its age. In doing so, it turned the attention of American writers away from the tradition of Walt Whitman—optimistic, democratic, and nationalistic—to a more pessimistic, elitist, and cosmopolitan tradition that virtually silenced homegrown literature for a decade and made the recovery of a native literature difficult even in the Depression years of the 1930s, when new struggles produced new literary impulses. In retrospect, the American poet William Carlos Williams commented that the poem "wiped out our world as if an atomic bomb had been dropped on it."

LIFE

The author of this controversial work, Thomas Stearns Eliot, was descended from New England Puritan stock, the grandson of a Unitarian minister. He was born in 1888 in St. Louis, attended Harvard University as an undergraduate, and later completed an MA in philosophy there. World-weary even as a Harvard student, he wrote "The Love Song of J. Alfred Prufrock" in 1912, a poem later thought by many to be an expression of the impotence of the age. He emigrated to England in 1914, where he lived for most of the rest of his life. Once in England, Eliot published his first book of poems, *Prufrock and Other Observations,* in 1917 and soon became a forerunner of the "Lost Generation," the international set of American writers who declared their disaffection with European politics and society after the slaughter of so many young soldiers in the trenches of Europe in World War I. The attitude of these writers is best summarized in lines written by Eliot's closest collaborator, Ezra Pound, in 1920:

> There died a myriad,
> And of the best, among them,
> For an old bitch gone in the teeth,
> For a botched civilization...
>
> For two gross of broken statues,
> For a few thousand battered books.

Although Eliot's personal life during this time was sometimes guarded from view by himself and his friends, clearly he was in crisis in 1921 and 1922, when he wrote *The Waste Land.* For some time he had struggled to overcome the puritanical element in his family history; poems such as "Prufrock" treated the theme of sexual repression, whereas other early poems were surprisingly bawdy and crude, often self-consciously primitive in their depiction of characters and situations. Other evidence suggestive of the young poet's personal struggles includes his marriage to a mentally unstable woman, Vivienne Haigh-Wood, in 1915; the couple's poverty from 1915 to 1924 when Eliot worked as a bank clerk in London; and his own hospitalization for nervous illness in Switzerland in the winter of 1921. During this time, Eliot was befriended by Pound, who helped edit *The Waste Land* after Eliot's hospitalization, seeing it through to publication in 1922. A number of letters written by Eliot during the creation of *The Waste Land* corroborate his vulnerable and sometimes desperate emotional and financial circumstances. One close friend, Edmund Wilson, called the poem "nothing more or less than a most distressingly moving account of Eliot's own agonized state of mind," and Eliot himself said of the poem in 1947 that he had written it "simply to relieve" his feelings.

Later in the 1920s, Eliot apparently managed to overcome his emotional distress in some measure by committing his first wife to a mental institution. He also turned toward literary and religious orthodoxy and political conservatism. In 1922, Eliot resigned from the editorial board of *The Dial* and started a heavily influential cultural magazine, *The Criterion,* the critical focus of which was a conservative assessment of the relationship between culture and society. In 1927, he became a British subject, and in the same year he took communion in the Anglican Church. In 1930, he published *Ash Wednesday,* a poem of religious conversion, and later in the decade wrote the first section of a long Christian poem, *Four Quartets,* which he completed in 1943. When Eliot turned to writing drama, most of it too held a religious message. Two of his major plays, the early historical drama *Murder in the Cathedral* (1935) and the later contemporary work *The Cocktail Party* (1949), both concern Christian martyrdom, surely an unusual topic in the twentieth century. In later life Eliot worked as a senior editor for Faber and Faber, a leading British publisher, rarely traveling to the United States. He eventually remarried—happily this time—and died peacefully in 1965.

THE WASTE LAND—AN ASSESSMENT

Because *The Waste Land* stands at the center of controversy even today, it is appropriate to attempt a brief commentary on this notoriously difficult work. One source of its difficulty is that Pound's editing cut away much of the connective tissue in the poem, making it both more striking in its rapid shifts of images and harder to follow. For that matter, Eliot's own interest in combining emotional, historical, mythical, and literary references was complicated enough; the footnotes he provided in later editions of the work attest to the obscurity of some of his sources and the compression of his ideas and images.

The work begins with April, usually the month of new growth but here "the cruellest month" because it stirs "memory and desire." The speakers in the first section shift rapidly: Marie, a member of the aristocracy who has memories of an alpine childhood but now goes "south in the winter"; an unidentified speaker who paints a ghastly scene of a junk-filled, lifeless desert; a "hyacinth girl" who was perhaps raped in a garden; an aged fortune-teller, a fugitive, telling a guarded fortune; and the speaker of the poem, contemplating fog-ridden, dirty modern London when he meets a stranger with a sinister, doom-filled message. "Memory and desire" here conjure nothing positive; modern life is seen to be bleak, dangerous, and unfulfilling.

The second section begins in an exotic setting with artistic panels on the walls depicting rape and metamorphosis. The woman who cries out "Speak...Think" is apparently modeled on Eliot's first wife. The grim, dry voice of the narrator is not enclosed in quotation marks; it is apparently the poet speaking in his own dramatic voice. The scene changes with the words "When Lil's husband got demobbed," introducing a conversation in a London pub. The voices saying HURRY UP PLEASE ITS TIME and singing "Good Night, Ladies" are meant to signify more than the voice of the tavern keeper or the drunken song of the departing company; the narrator's voice creeps in too, a voice of doom.

The third section begins with a description of the modern-day Thames River in London. The rubbish along the bank includes "other testimony of summer nights," possibly the contraceptives of that time. A mixture of images recalls the Fisher King of the Grail Legend, two lower-class Londoners, the rape of Philomela from an earlier section, a homosexual proposition from a decadent Greek businessman, and a long scene narrated by Tiresias, the prophet fated by the gods to be both man and woman. He witnesses an empty and cheap modern sexual encounter, followed by contrasting scenes of London in her glory in the time of Elizabeth and the filthy Thames River district known to the poet. In both times, it seems, there were scenes of defilement, and Tiresias has witnessed them all. The section ends with St. Augustine's description of arriving as a young man in the city of Carthage, a site of worldly lust and fornication.

The fourth section, very short, describes the death of a Phoenician sailor; these early sailors connected the port cities of the classical world through the watery medium of the Mediterranean. His death is apparently symbolic; all "commerce"—all significant exchange—may be similarly dead in modern Europe.

The fifth section connects some of the themes of the first four. It begins in a reddish desert area with "torchlight red on sweaty faces." In this surreal landscape, where there is "no water but only rock," there is a mysterious "third who walks...beside you." In this poem, so full of intrusions and mysteries, this could be one or many of the other figures already encountered; in the same way, the city of London, which is now depicted as "falling down" in the taunting music of the nursery rhyme, could be many other capitals as well. Finally after these speculations comes the rain, and with it a Hindu formula for achieving a blessed state: Datta, Dayadhvam, Damyata—Give, Sympathize, Control. The closest the poet comes to assembling the materials of the poem, not to mention his life or the life of Europe, is the line "Shall I at least set my lands in order?" This is certainly not an answer to the problem of an age, but it could begin the preparation for finding the answer. The final invocation, "Shantih shantih shantih," again a Hindu formula, is a call for abiding peace.

Like the knight Perceval in search of the answer to the riddle of the Holy Grail, the poet, locating himself somewhere in the mixed chorus of voices of *The Waste Land,* is a quester. He searches for a solution to the riddle of the decay of Europe, especially the moral decay, which Eliot pictures in terms of psychological and sexual depravity. It is worth noting how unattractive most of Eliot's characters are. At the same time, the promise in the poem seems to rest on the undifferentiated religious figures and symbols in the fifth section. He seems to say that if the West is to be restored, it will be through the symbolic operations of the world's great myths and religions. Perhaps we need to see that Eliot's faith is not in people but in symbolic processes, especially processes of renewal. Whether his intellectualized vision appeals to us or seems artificial and contrived may depend on our tolerance for a form of poetry that is once again far removed from our daily expectations.

THE WASTE LAND—CRITICAL RECEPTION

Critical responses to *The Waste Land* always have been polarized. They have varied according to whether the writers in question have agreed or disagreed with Eliot's view of postwar European society, and ultimately with his growing conservatism. The first generation of critics to study the poem took up the task of trying to explain it to a somewhat baffled literary audience. Edmund Wilson led the way in a long essay in *The Dial* in December 1922, explaining a number of references based on his reading of Eliot's own notes, which were by now being attached to the poem. In the next decade, the defenders of *The Waste Land* were most often admirers of Eliot's literary criticism. F. R. Leavis, writing in 1932, stressed the poem's unity; F. O. Matthiessen, writing in 1935, noted the elaborate interweaving of its cross-references; and Cleanth Brooks, writing in 1939, defended its ethical and religious foundations.

After the first wave of support subsided, other critics began to attack the poem. David Craig wrote in 1960 that *The Waste Land* was "against life" and argued that the support it had received was "all negative." The poet Karl Shapiro, also writing in 1960, went even further, stating that "Eliot invented a Modern World which exists only in his version of it; this world is populated by Eliot's followers and is not a reality." These critics were reacting to the conservative politics of Eliot and his followers, including his friend Ezra Pound's support for Italian fascism during World War II, and also reflecting a generational swing away from the closed content and style of Eliot's poetry to a more open, personal form that was to dominate the poetry of the 1960s and 1970s. The reaction against Eliot is still alive and well, although he seems to be enjoying a rebirth of reputation in the academic world.

SUGGESTED READINGS

Eliot's surprisingly small output of poems is readily available in paperback editions. *The Waste Land* is available as well in a facsimile version of the original manuscript edited by the poet's second wife, Valerie Eliot, and published in 1971. A biography with literary emphasis, leaving out Eliot's childhood and old age, is Peter Ackroyd's *T. S. Eliot: A Life* (1984). A recent attempt to see Eliot's early work in the light of his life is Ronald Bush's *T. S. Eliot: A Study in Character and Style* (1984). A brief guide to Eliot is Georges Cattaui's *T. S. Eliot* (1966); a recent guide to his most famous poem is Grover Smith's *The Waste Land* (1983). Two collections of critical essays showing the clashes of critical judgment about Eliot and his work are Robert E. Knoll, ed., *Storm over The Waste Land* (1964), and Ronald Bush, ed., *T. S. Eliot: The Modernist in History* (1991).

The Waste Land[1]

*"Nam Sibyllam quidem Cumis ego ipse oculis meis vidi
in ampulla pendere, et cum illi pueri dicerent:* Σίβυλλα
τί θέλεις; *respondebat illa:* ἀποθανεῖν θέλω.*"*[2]

For Ezra Pound
il miglior fabbro.[3]

I. THE BURIAL OF THE DEAD[4]

April is the cruellest month, breeding
Lilacs out of the dead land, mixing
Memory and desire, stirring
Dull roots with spring rain.
Winter kept us warm, covering
Earth in forgetful snow, feeding
A little life with dried tubers.
Summer surprised us, coming over the Starnbergersee
With a shower of rain; we stopped in the colonnade,
And went on in sunlight, into the Hofgarten,   10
And drank coffee, and talked for an hour.
Bin gar keine Russin, stamm' aus Litauen, echt deutsch.[5]
And when we were children, staying at the archduke's,
My cousin's, he took me out on a sled,
And I was frightened. He said, Marie,
Marie, hold on tight. And down we went.
In the mountains, there you feel free.
I read, much of the night, and go south in the winter.

---

[1] Eliot's own notes, supplied after the first publication of the poem, are sometimes used here in excerpted form and identified by (E). We have omitted or departed from these notes as has seemed fitting. Generally speaking, Eliot's method of assembling the poem corresponds to his statement, "These fragments I have shored against my ruins." The poem is like a vast mosaic; one doesn't have to analyze every piece to understand the overall design. The aim of these notes, therefore, is modest: to keep the reader attuned to Eliot's main themes.

Eliot introduces the reader to the poem with the following comment: "Not only the title, but the plan and a good deal of the incidental symbolism of the poem were suggested by Miss Jessie L. Weston's book on the Grail legend: *From Ritual to Romance* (Cambridge). . . . To another work of anthropology I am indebted in general, one which has influenced our generation profoundly; I mean *The Golden Bough;* I have used especially the two volumes *Adonis, Attis, Osiris.* Anyone who is acquainted with these works will immediately recognise in the poem certain references to vegetation ceremonies" (E). Other influences in the poem include the Greek and Latin classics, medieval romance, Elizabethan drama, German opera, French symbolist poetry, and religious writings from Christian and Buddhist sources and the Indian *Upanishads.*

[2] "For I saw with my own eyes the Sibyl from Cumae hanging in a bottle, and when the boys asked her, 'Sibyl, what do you want?' she would reply, 'I want to die.'"—Petronius, *Satyricon,* 48. According to legend, the prophetess had been granted a long life but not perpetual youth, and so she was hideously shriveled with age. Compare Madame Sosostris and Tiresias, fortune-tellers later to appear in *The Waste Land.*

[3] "The better maker [poet]." Eliot compliments his friend Ezra Pound, who edited the poem into its final form during the period of Eliot's hospitalization. The Italian original is Dante's praise of the poet Arnaut Daniel, from *The Purgatorio,* 26, 117.

[4] Title of the funeral service in *The Book of Common Prayer.*

[5] "I'm not Russian at all; I come from Lithuania, pure German." The remark is ironical; little is "pure" in the poem. The scene is from the vicinity of Munich, in south Germany.

What are the roots that clutch, what branches grow
Out of this stony rubbish? Son of man,[6]   20
You cannot say, or guess, for you know only
A heap of broken images, where the sun beats,
And the dead tree gives no shelter, the cricket no relief,[7]
And the dry stone no sound of water. Only
There is shadow under this red rock,
(Come in under the shadow of this red rock),
And I will show you something different from either
Your shadow at morning striding behind you
Or your shadow at evening rising to meet you;
I will show you fear in a handful of dust.[8]   30

> *Frisch weht der Wind*
> *Der Heimat zu*
> *Mein Irisch Kind,*
> *Wo weilest du?*[9]

"You gave me hyacinths first a year ago;
"They called me the hyacinth girl."
—Yet when we came back, late, from the Hyacinth garden,
Your arms full, and your hair wet, I could not
Speak, and my eyes failed, I was neither
Living nor dead, and I knew nothing,   40
Looking into the heart of light, the silence.
Oed' und leer das Meer.[10]

Madame Sosostris, famous clairvoyante,
Had a bad cold, nevertheless
Is known to be the wisest woman in Europe,
With a wicked pack of cards.[11] Here, said she,
Is your card, the drowned Phoenician Sailor,
(Those are pearls that were his eyes.[12] Look!)
Here is Belladonna, the Lady of the Rocks,
The lady of situations.   50
Here is the man with three staves, and here the Wheel,
And here is the one-eyed merchant, and this card,
Which is blank, is something he carries on his back,
Which I am forbidden to see. I do not find

---

[6]God's address to the prophet Ezekiel (Ezekiel 2:1).

[7]Compare Ecclesiastes 12:5.

[8]Compare "Ashes to ashes, dust to dust" in the funeral service.

[9]The lyric is from Wagner's opera version of *Tristan and Isolde:* "Fresh blows the wind / toward the homeland. / My Irish girl / where do you abide?"

[10]From *Tristan and Isolde:* "Waste and empty the sea." The dying Tristan looks out to sea and finds no sign of Isolde's ship.

[11]Tarot cards, used in fortune-telling.

[12]Shakespeare, *The Tempest,* I, ii, 399–402. Consolation of Ariel to Ferdinand over his father, who is feared drowned:

> Those are pearls that were his eyes:
> Nothing of him that doth fade,
> But doth suffer a sea-change
> Into something rich and strange.

The Hanged Man.[13] Fear death by water.
I see crowds of people, walking round in a ring.
Thank you. If you see dear Mrs. Equitone,
Tell her I bring the horoscope myself:
One must be so careful these days.

  Unreal City,
Under the brown fog of a winter dawn,[14]   60
A crowd flowed over London Bridge, so many,
I had not thought death had undone so many.[15]
Sighs, short and infrequent, were exhaled,
And each man fixed his eyes before his feet.
Flowed up the hill and down King William Street,
To where Saint Mary Woolnoth kept the hours
With a dead sound on the final stroke of nine.[16]
There I saw one I knew, and stopped him, crying: "Stetson!
"You who were with me in the ships at Mylae![17]   70
"That corpse you planted last year in your garden,
"Has it begun to sprout? Will it bloom this year?
"Or has the sudden frost disturbed its bed?
"Oh keep the Dog far hence, that's friend to men,
"Or with his nails he'll dig it up again![18]
"You! hypocrite lecteur!—mon semblable,—mon frère!"[19]

II. A GAME OF CHESS[20]

The Chair she sat in, like a burnished throne,[21]
Glowed on the marble, where the glass
Held up by standards wrought with fruited vines

---

[13]Eliot himself confesses that he has "departed to suit my own convenience" from the symbolism of the Tarot pack (E). The lady Belladonna is a joke: This is the name of a popular cosmetic (or, used in sufficient quantity, a poison). The man with the three staves Eliot says he associates, "quite arbitrarily," with the Fisher King to appear later in the poem (E). The Hanged Man refers most directly to the hanged god of fertility myths. The entire tone of the passage implies something debauched and half-forgotten over the centuries.

[14]Echoes Baudelaire's "Swarming city, city full of dreams, / where the specter in broad daylight accosts the passerby," from *The Flowers of Evil*.

[15]Dante's comment in *The Inferno*, seeing the citizens of Hell: "Such a long procession / of people, I had not thought / death had undone so many" (*The Inferno*, 3, 55–57).

[16]Eliot supplies commonplace scenes from London: St. Mary Woolnoth, a church in the business district, and the dead sound in the tower clock, "a phenomenon which I have often noticed" (E).

[17]The juxtaposition of Stetson, the name of an American hat manufacturer, and Mylae, site of a victorious Roman sea battle against Carthage in 260 B.C.E., is intended to add to the tone of parody prevalent throughout this section.

[18]Compare the nearly identical passage in John Webster, *The White Devil* (1612), V, iv, 97–98, where the dog is called "foe to man."

[19]Baudelaire, preface to *Flowers of Evil*: "Hypocrite reader! My double, my brother!"

[20]Eliot appears to be recalling two plays by Thomas Middleton: for the title, *A Game of Chess* (1624), and for the plot, *Women Beware Women* (1657), in which a woman is seduced while her mother-in-law is engrossed in a chess game.

[21]This lavish introduction begins by parodying the description of Cleopatra in Shakespeare, *Antony and Cleopatra*, II, ii, 190: "The barge she sat in, like a burnished throne. . . ."

From which a golden Cupidon peeped out 80
(Another hid his eyes behind his wing)
Doubled the flames of sevenbranched candelabra
Reflecting light upon the table as
The glitter of her jewels rose to meet it,
From satin cases poured in rich profusion;
In vials of ivory and coloured glass
Unstoppered, lurked her strange synthetic perfumes,
Unguent, powdered, or liquid—troubled, confused
And drowned the sense in odours; stirred by the air
That freshened from the window, these ascended 90
In fattening the prolonged candle-flames,
Flung their smoke into the laquearia,
Stirring the pattern on the coffered ceiling.
Huge sea-wood fed with copper
Burned green and orange, framed by the coloured stone,
In which sad light a carvèd dolphin swam.
Above the antique mantel was displayed
As though a window gave upon the sylvan scene²²
The change of Philomel, by the barbarous king
So rudely forced;²³ yet there the nightingale 100
Filled all the desert with inviolable voice
And still she cried, and still the world pursues,
"Jug Jug" to dirty ears.
And other withered stumps of time
Were told upon the walls; staring forms
Leaned out, leaning, hushing the room enclosed.
Footsteps shuffled on the stair.
Under the firelight, under the brush, her hair
Spread out in fiery points
Glowed into words, then would be savagely still. 110

   "My nerves are bad to-night. Yes, bad. Stay with me.
"Speak to me. Why do you never speak. Speak.
   "What are you thinking of? What thinking? What?
"I never know what you are thinking. Think."²⁴

   I think we are in rats' alley
Where the dead men lost their bones.

   "What is that noise?"
                The wind under the door.
"What is that noise now? What is the wind doing?"
                Nothing again nothing. 120
                     "Do
"You know nothing? Do you see nothing? Do you remember
"Nothing?"

---

²²Eliot notes Milton's use of "Sylvan scene" in a description of Eden in *Paradise Lost,* 4, 140.

²³"Ovid, *Metamorphoses,* VI, Philomela" (E). Philomela is raped by her brother-in-law, who cuts out her tongue; the gods, taking pity on her, transform her into a nightingale.

²⁴Commonly thought to reflect Eliot's own marital experience with his first wife, Vivienne.

I remember
Those are pearls that were his eyes.
"Are you alive, or not? Is there nothing in your head?"
                                                    But

O O O O that Shakespeherian Rag—
It's so elegant
So intelligent[25]   130
"What shall I do now? What shall I do?"
"I shall rush out as I am, and walk the street
"With my hair down, so. What shall we do to-morrow?
"What shall we ever do?"
                            The hot water at ten.
And if it rains, a closed car at four.
And we shall play a game of chess,
Pressing lidless eyes and waiting for a knock upon the door.

        When Lil's husband got demobbed,[26] I said—
I didn't mince my words, I said to her myself,   140
HURRY UP PLEASE ITS TIME[27]
Now Albert's coming back, make yourself a bit smart.
He'll want to know what you done with that money he gave you
To get yourself some teeth. He did, I was there.
You have them all out, Lil, and get a nice set,
He said, I swear, I can't bear to look at you.
And no more can't I, I said, and think of poor Albert,
He's been in the army four years, he wants a good time,
And if you don't give it him, there's others will, I said.
Oh is there, she said. Something o' that, I said.   150
Then I'll know who to thank, she said, and give me a straight look.
HURRY UP PLEASE ITS TIME
If you don't like it you can get on with it, I said.
Others can pick and choose if you can't.
But if Albert makes off, it won't be for lack of telling.
You ought to be ashamed, I said, to look so antique.
(And her only thirty-one.)
I can't help it, she said, pulling a long face,
It's them pills I took, to bring it off, she said.
(She's had five already, and nearly died of young George.)   160
The chemist[28] said it would be all right, but I've never been the same.
You are a proper fool, I said.
Well, if Albert won't leave you alone, there it is, I said,
What you get married for if you don't want children?
HURRY UP PLEASE ITS TIME
Well, that Sunday Albert was home, they had a hot gammon,[29]

---

[25] Adapted from "The Shakespearean Rag," a popular dance song (1912).
[26] Demobilized from military service.
[27] Announcement of closing time in a London pub.
[28] Druggist.
[29] Ham.

And they asked me in to dinner, to get the beauty of it hot—
HURRY UP PLEASE ITS TIME
HURRY UP PLEASE ITS TIME
Goonight Bill. Goonight Lou. Goonight May. Goonight.   170
Ta ta. Goonight. Goonight.
Good night, ladies, good night, sweet ladies, good night, good night.[30]

III. THE FIRE SERMON[31]

The river's tent is broken: the last fingers of leaf
Clutch and sink into the wet bank. The wind
Crosses the brown land, unheard. The nymphs are departed.
Sweet Thames, run softly, till I end my song.[32]
The river bears no empty bottles, sandwich papers,
Silk handkerchiefs, cardboard boxes, cigarette ends
Or other testimony of summer nights. The nymphs are departed.
And their friends, the loitering heirs of city directors;   180
Departed, have left no addresses.
By the waters of Leman I sat down and wept . . .[33]
Sweet Thames, run softly till I end my song,
Sweet Thames, run softly, for I speak not loud or long.
But at my back in a cold blast I hear
The rattle of the bones, and chuckle spread from ear to ear.[34]
A rat crept softly through the vegetation
Dragging its slimy belly on the bank
While I was fishing in the dull canal
On a winter evening round behind the gashouse   190
Musing upon the king my brother's wreck
And on the king my father's death before him.[35]
White bodies naked on the low damp ground
And bones cast in a little low dry garret,
Rattled by the rat's foot only, year to year.
But at my back from time to time I hear
The sound of horns and motors, which shall bring
Sweeney to Mrs. Porter in the spring.
O the moon shone bright on Mrs. Porter

---

[30] Ophelia's mad song from Shakespeare, *Hamlet,* IV, v, 69–70.
[31] A sermon by Buddha against the fires of the senses.
[32] From "Prothalamion," marriage song by Edmund Spenser (1596).
[33] Compare Psalm 137.1. "By the rivers of Babylon, there we sat down, yea, we wept, when we remembered Zion." Leman is the French name of Lake Geneva in Switzerland, where Eliot was hospitalized while *The Waste Land* was being completed. The word also means "lover" in Early English.
[34] Compare "But at my back I always hear / Time's wingèd chariot hurrying near," Andrew Marvell, "To His Coy Mistress," 21–22.
[35] Recalls Ferdinand's presumed loss of his father in Shakespeare, *The Tempest,* I, ii, 389–391:

> . . . Sitting on a bank,
> Weeping against the king my father's wreck,
> This music crept by me on the waters.

This reference also recalls the story of the Fisher King from anthropological sources.

And on her daughter   200
They wash their feet in soda water³⁶
*Et O ces voix d'enfants, chantant dans la coupole!*³⁷

   Twit twit twit
Jug jug jug jug jug jug
So rudely forc'd.
Tereu³⁸

   Unreal City
Under the brown fog of a winter noon
Mr. Eugenides, the Smyrna merchant
Unshaven, with a pocket full of currants   210
C.i.f. London: documents at sight,
Asked me in demotic French
To luncheon at the Cannon Street Hotel
Followed by a weekend at the Metropole.³⁹

   At the violet hour, when the eyes and back
Turn upward from the desk, when the human engine waits
Like a taxi throbbing waiting,
I Tiresias, though blind, throbbing between two lives,
Old man with wrinkled female breasts,⁴⁰ can see
At the violet hour, the evening hour that strives   220
Homeward, and brings the sailor home from sea,
The typist home at teatime, clears her breakfast, lights
Her stove, and lays out food in tins.
Out of the window perilously spread
Her drying combinations touched by the sun's last rays,
On the divan are piled (at night her bed)
Stockings, slippers, camisoles, and stays.
I Tiresias, old man with wrinkled dugs
Perceived the scene, and foretold the rest—
I too awaited the expected guest.   230
He, the young man carbuncular,⁴¹ arrives,

---

³⁶Eliot says, "I do not know the origin of the ballad from which these lines are taken: it was reported to me from Sydney, Australia" (E). The ballad was a soldier's song from World War I; in the song Mrs. Porter and her daughter are prostitutes, and the soda water is a douche, not a foot wash. In other contexts, however, washing the feet is a ritual of purification; compare Richard Wagner's opera *Parsifal*, in which the knight is purified in this manner before he can approach the Grail.

³⁷"And Oh, those voices of children, singing in the cupola!" The final line of Paul Verlaine's sonnet "Parsifal." Verlaine calls attention to the fact that the singing celebrates the purity of the knight in Wagner's operatic version.

³⁸Recalls the rape of Philomela and the song of the nightingale, II, 98–103.

³⁹A Greek merchant from a Turkish port city with a pocketful of currants shipped duty-free to London invites the narrator in vulgar French to lunch in London followed by an illicit weekend in an expensive tourist hotel in Brighton.

⁴⁰The speaker is Tiresias, who because of spells cast by the gods has been both a man and a woman. When asked who has the greater sexual pleasure, he answers that a woman does; in anger, the goddess Juno strikes him blind, but her husband Jupiter gives him the gift of prophecy (Ovid, *Metamorphoses*, 3, 320–338). "Tiresias, although a mere spectator and not indeed a 'character,' is yet the most important personage in the poem, uniting all the rest" (E).

⁴¹Suffering from acne.

A small house agent's clerk, with one bold stare,
One of the low on whom assurance sits
As a silk hat on a Bradford[42] millionaire.
The time is now propitious, as he guesses,
The meal is ended, she is bored and tired,
Endeavours to engage her in caresses
Which still are unreproved, if undesired.
Flushed and decided, he assaults at once;
Exploring hands encounter no defence;   240
His vanity requires no response,
And makes a welcome of indifference.
(And I Tiresias have foresuffered all
Enacted on this same divan or bed;
I who have sat by Thebes below the wall
And walked among the lowest of the dead.)
Bestows one final patronising kiss,
And gropes his way, finding the stairs unlit...
    She turns and looks a moment in the glass,
Hardly aware of her departed lover;   250
Her brain allows one half-formed thought to pass:
"Well now that's done: and I'm glad it's over."
When lovely woman stoops to folly[43] and
Paces about her room again, alone,
She smoothes her hair with automatic hand,
And puts a record on the gramophone.

    "This music crept by me upon the waters"
And along the Strand, up Queen Victoria Street.
O City city, I can sometimes hear
Beside a public bar in Lower Thames Street,   260
The pleasant whining of a mandoline
And a clatter and a chatter from within
Where fishmen lounge at noon: where the walls
Of Magnus Martyr[44] hold
Inexplicable splendour of Ionian white and gold.

        The river sweats
        Oil and tar
        The barges drift
        With the turning tide
        Red sails   270

---

[42]A town in the north of England where fortunes were made off profiteering during World War I.

[43]First line of a song by Olivia in *The Vicar of Wakefield,* a novel by Oliver Goldsmith (1766):

    When lovely woman stoops to folly
    And finds too late that men betray
    What harm can soothe her melancholy,
    What art can wash the guilt away?

[44]London church with a beautiful interior praised by Eliot in his notes; built by Sir Christopher Wren at the end of the seventeenth century.

Wide
To leeward, swing on the heavy spar.
The barges wash
Drifting logs
Down Greenwich reach
Past the Isle of Dogs.
        Weialala leia
        Wallala leialala[45]

   Elizabeth and Leicester
Beating oars[46]   280
The stern was formed
A gilded shell
Red and gold
The brisk swell
Rippled both shores
Southwest wind
Carried down stream
The peal of bells
White towers
        Weialala leia   290
        Wallala leialala

   "Trams and dusty trees.
Highbury bore me. Richmond and Kew
Undid me. By Richmond I raised my knees
Supine on the floor of a narrow canoe."

   "My feet are at Moorgate, and my heart
Under my feet. After the event
He wept. He promised 'a new start.'
I made no comment. What should I resent?"

   "On Margate Sands.   300
I can connect
Nothing with nothing.
The broken fingernails of dirty hands.
My people humble people who expect
Nothing."
        la la

   To Carthage then I came[47]

---

[45]"The Song of the (three) Thames-daughters begins here" (E). These creations of the poet's, parodies of Wagner's Rhine Maidens from the opera *Twilight of the Gods,* sing their refrain in lines 277–278 and 290–291 and speak separately in lines 292–306, each identifying a place along the Thames where she was debauched.

[46]The story of the dalliance of Queen Elizabeth and Robert Dudley, Earl of Leicester, while cruising in a barge down the Thames. Eliot took the story from James A. Froude's biography *Elizabeth,* vol. I, ch. 4.

[47]St. Augustine, *The Confessions,* III, 1.

Burning burning burning burning[48]
O Lord Thou pluckest me out
O Lord Thou pluckest[49]   310

burning

IV. Death by Water[50]

Phlebas the Phoenician, a fortnight dead,
Forgot the cry of gulls, and the deep sea swell
And the profit and loss.
               A current under sea
Picked his bones in whispers. As he rose and fell
He passed the stages of his age and youth
Entering the whirlpool.
               Gentile or Jew
O you who turn the wheel and look to windward,   320
Consider Phlebas, who was once handsome and tall as you.

V. What the Thunder Said[51]

After the torchlight red on sweaty faces[52]
After the frosty silence in the gardens
After the agony in stony places
The shouting and the crying
Prison and palace and reverberation
Of thunder of spring over distant mountains
He who was living is now dead
We who were living are now dying
With a little patience   330

    Here is no water but only rock
Rock and no water and the sandy road
The road winding above among the mountains
Which are mountains of rock without water
If there were water we should stop and drink
Amongst the rock one cannot stop or think
Sweat is dry and feet are in the sand

---

[48]Refrain from Buddha's "Fire Sermon," which argues against the fires of passion.

[49]"From St. Augustine's *Confessions* again. The collocation of these two representatives of eastern and western asceticism, as the culmination of this part of the poem, is not an accident" (E).

[50]This short section is a translation of the last stanza of Eliot's earlier poem in French, "Dans le Restaurant," a dialogue on the subject of sexual debauchery. Phlebas is a poetic creation, perhaps an ancestor of Mr. Eugenides, who in drowning is purified by being stripped of his worldly attributes.

[51]In the Vedic holy text of India, *The Upanishads,* the thunder is the voice of God.

[52]Eliot comments: "In the first part of Part V three themes are employed: the journey to Emmaus, the approach to the Chapel Perilous . . . and the present decay of eastern Europe" (E). The opening lines of the section refer to the story of the betrayal and crucifixion of Christ.

If there were only water amongst the rock
Dead mountain mouth of carious[53] teeth that cannot spit
Here one can neither stand nor lie nor sit   340
There is not even silence in the mountains
But dry sterile thunder without rain
There is not even solitude in the mountains
But red sullen faces sneer and snarl
From doors of mudcracked houses
                         If there were water
      And no rock
      If there were rock
      And also water
      And water   350
      A spring
      A pool among the rock
      If there were the sound of water only
      Not the cicada
      And dry grass singing
      But sound of water over a rock
      Where the hermit-thrush sings in the pine trees
      Drip drop drip drop drop drop drop
      But there is no water

Who is the third who walks always beside you?[54]   360
When I count, there are only you and I together
But when I look ahead up the white road
There is always another one walking beside you
Gliding wrapt in a brown mantle, hooded
I do not know whether a man or a woman[55]
—But who is that on the other side of you?

What is that sound high in the air[56]
Murmur of maternal lamentation
Who are those hooded hordes swarming
Over endless plains, stumbling in cracked earth   370
Ringed by the flat horizon only
What is the city over the mountains
Cracks and reforms and bursts in the violet air
Falling towers
Jerusalem Athens Alexandria
Vienna London
Unreal

---

[53]From carrion: decaying (flesh).

[54]Eliot refers to an Antarctic expedition in which a party of explorers "had the constant delusion that there was *one more member* than could actually be counted" (E). Also, in the story of the journey to Emmaus (Luke 24:13–34), a third person appears to join the two disciples: Jesus.

[55]The "man or woman" may refer to the prophet Tiresias.

[56]Eliot cites a comment by Hermann Hesse that "already half of Europe . . . is on the way to chaos, going drunk in holy madness along the edge of the abyss, and sings, sings drunkenly and hymnlike as Dmitri Karamazov sang." (Hesse, *Blick ins Chaos* [*Look into Chaos*], 1920.) Hesse was referring to the Russian Revolution; Eliot saw this as one more sign of European degeneration at the close of World War I.

A woman drew her long black hair out tight
And fiddled whisper music on those strings
And bats with baby faces in the violet light   380
Whistled, and beat their wings
And crawled head downward down a blackened wall
And upside down in air were towers
Tolling reminiscent bells, that kept the hours
And voices singing out of empty cisterns and exhausted wells.

In this decayed hole among the mountains
In the faint moonlight, the grass is singing
Over the tumbled graves, about the chapel
There is the empty chapel, only the wind's home.[57]
It has no windows, and the door swings,   390
Dry bones can harm no one.
Only a cock stood on the rooftree
Co co rico co co rico[58]
In a flash of lightning. Then a damp gust
Bringing rain

Ganga was sunken,[59] and the limp leaves
Waited for rain, while the black clouds
Gathered far distant, over Himavant.[60]
The jungle crouched, humped in silence.
Then spoke the thunder   400
DA
Datta:[61] what have we given?
My friend, blood shaking my heart
The awful daring of a moment's surrender
Which an age of prudence can never retract
By this, and this only, we have existed
Which is not to be found in our obituaries
Or in memories draped by the beneficent spider[62]
Or under seals broken by the lean solicitor
In our empty rooms   410
DA
Dayadhvam: I have heard the key
Turn in the door once and turn once only[63]
We think of the key, each in his prison
Thinking of the key, each confirms a prison

---

[57] The Chapel Perilous of the Grail legend, cited in Jessie Weston's *From Ritual to Romance.*
[58] The cock's crow suggests the breaking of a spell.
[59] The Ganges River in India.
[60] The Himalayan Mountains.
[61] The words *datta* (give), l. 402; *dayadhvam* (sympathize), l. 412; and *damyata* (control), l. 419. According to *The Upanishads,* the thunder god Prajapati commands that humans practice charity, sympathy, and self-control as a spiritual exercise. Apparently Eliot saw this as a redemptive or cleansing activity.
[62] Compare Webster, *The White Devil,* V, vi: "They'll remarry / ... ere the spider / Make a thin curtain for your epitaphs." The allusion is to the procreative urge of humanity, which is (according to Eliot) outside any moral framework.
[63] Compare Dante, *The Inferno,* 33, 46–47: "And I heard them below locking the door / Of the horrible tower," from Count Ugolino's story of being locked in a tower to starve, along with his children.

Only at nightfall, aethereal rumours
Revive for a moment a broken Coriolanus[64]
DA
Damyata: The boat responded
Gaily, to the hand expert with sail and oar   420
The sea was calm, your heart would have responded
Gaily, when invited, beating obedient
To controlling hands

                              I sat upon the shore
Fishing,[65] with the arid plain behind me
Shall I at least set my lands in order?[66]
London Bridge is falling down falling down falling down
Poi s'ascose nel foco che gli affina[67]
Quando fiam uti chelidon—O swallow swallow[68]
Le Prince d'Aquitaine à la tour abolie[69]   430
These fragments I have shored against my ruins
Why then Ile fit you. Hieronymo's mad againe.[70]
Datta. Dayadhvam. Damyata.
     Shantih   shantih   shantih[71]

ANNA AKHMATOVA
[1889–1966]

Increasingly recognized as one of the greatest poets of the twentieth century, Anna
Akhmatova was one of the leading figures in a group of Russian poets that included her first
husband, Nikolai Gumilev, and Osip Mandelstam. Known as the Acmeists, they rejected
what they saw as the mystifications of symbolism in favor of a poetry of linguistic clarity
and precision. Unlike Gumilev and Mandelstam, who were killed during Stalin's regime,
Akhmatova survived the post-Revolutionary repression, and her work is a testament to
the generation of Russians whose lives span the period from just before the Revolution to
the post-Stalinist fifties and sixties. Tracing her work from the early love lyrics that began
to appear in 1907 to the elegiac national poems of the 1920s to the 1960s, the reader of
Akhmatova's work is caught up in the tragic sweep of Russian and Soviet history as it
marked the powerful voice of this woman who chose to stay behind and bear witness for
her country and its people.

---

[64] That is, a tyrant, possibly a betrayer.

[65] The Fisher King of the Grail legend, in whose voice the poem ends.

[66] Isaiah 38:1, "Set thine house in order, for thou shalt die and not live."

[67] *The Purgatorio*, 26, 48, "Then he hid himself in the purifying fire." The poet Arnaut Daniel leaves
Dante, imploring him to remember his suffering.

[68] "When will I be like the swallow?" Eliot cites "The Vigil of Venus," a Late Latin poem in which
Philomela is turned into a swallow, and also the story of Philomela in parts II and III of *The Waste Land*.

[69] "The prince of Aquitaine at the ruined tower," from a sonnet by the symbolist poet Gerard de Nerval,
"El Desdichado" (1854). The disinherited prince is expressing "the black sun of melancholy."

[70] See Thomas Kyd, *The Spanish Tragedy* (1594). Hieronymo "fits" (serves) his enemies by writing a play
for them that exposes their crimes, then revenging himself upon them.

[71] "Shantih. Repeated as here, a formal ending to an Upanishad. 'The Peace which passeth understanding'
is our equivalent to this word" (E).

LIFE

Anna Akhmatova was born Anya Gorenko on June 23, 1889 (by the Western calendar), in Odessa, Russia; she was the daughter of Inna Stogova and Andrei Gorenko, a well-to-do officer in the Russian merchant marine. Much of her childhood was spent in Tsarskoe Selo (now Pushkin), near St. Petersburg, to which she pays fond tribute in her poetry. The family spent many of their summers at Streletskiy Bay on the Black Sea coast, where the young poet fell in love with the sea. Early in life she read the French symbolists and her beloved Pushkin, and soon showed signs of being a poet herself. Her father oddly despised the idea of having a poet in the family so much that when she was seventeen, Anya took the Tatar name of her great-grandmother, Anna Akhmatova, to avoid bringing disgrace to Gorenko. Her youthful happiness was disrupted by two major shocks in her early life: the defeat of the Russian fleet by the Japanese in 1905 and, in the same year, the attempted suicide of Nikolai Gumilev, whom she had met two years before and whose desperation stemmed from Akhmatova's refusal to return his ardent love for her. Shortly after beginning the study of law at Kiev College for Women in 1907, Akhmatova returned to St. Petersburg to study literature. In April 1910, she married Gumilev and visited Paris, met the painter Modigliani, and absorbed the excitement of turn-of-the-century Paris, where Braque, Picasso, and Stravinsky, among others, were breaking upon the cultural scene. The couple returned after three months in Paris to settle in Tsarskoe Selo.

Akhmatova's first collection of poetry, *Evening* (*Vecher*), appeared in 1912, though she had published poems earlier in Gumilev's journal *Sirius*. By now Gumilev had founded The Poets' Guild, the name that the Acmeists chose for themselves, and the journal *Apollon*, which carried the Acmeist manifestos repudiating the doctrines of symbolism, particularly as embodied in the Russian poet Vyacheslav Ivanov, the most dazzling figure of The Tower, a literary salon in St. Petersburg. *Evening* consists primarily of love poems, many written while Akhmatova was left alone while Gumilev traveled in Africa. These elegiac love poems are notable for their precision and brevity—their ability to imply a tragic story in a few elegant lines. Lyrical but again elegiac love poems fill her second and third collections—*Rosary* (*Chyotkti*, 1914), which received a wide and enthusiastic reception, and *White Flock* (*Belaya staya*, 1917). In these poems, Akhmatova often displaces onto the characters her own sense of loneliness and grief, stemming from her growing alienation from Gumilev, the suicide of the poet Vsevolod Knyazev, and other incidents that immediately affected her life; yet a whisper of hope in the poems turns what would be despair into a Keatsian melancholy.

After the Revolution, Akhmatova and Gumilev divorced, and in 1918 she married—as it turned out, again unhappily—Vladimir Shileiko, an Orientalist and minor poet. Despite what she calls the "suicidal anguish" of Russia during these years, Akhmatova refused to abandon her country, although it would soon abandon her when the Stalinist censors of the 1920s suspected her very private and apolitical poetry to be counterrevolutionary. In 1921, the year her friend and fellow poet Aleksander Blok died, Gumilev was executed for taking part in an anti-Bolshevik conspiracy; in the next year Akhmatova published *Anno Domini MCMXXI,* composed in part of poems published earlier in *Plantain* (*Podorozhnik,* 1921). The poems in *Anno Domini* often cast a foreboding tone as Akhmatova attests to the devastation of the civil war and the deterioration of politics and human rights after the Revolution. Many of these poems record her protest against Shileiko, who didn't want her to write and reportedly burned some of her poems.

Shileiko, whom she quickly divorced, was less successful than the government, which from 1922 to 1940 effectively banned Akhmatova's poetry. During these years she wrote little poetry, but turned to literary criticism, publishing studies of Pushkin in the mid-1930s. In May 1934, Akhmatova witnessed the arrest of Osip Mandelstam in Moscow; in the next year Akhmatova's third husband, N. N. Punin, and her only child, Lev Gumilev, were arrested in the first wave of purges following the assassination of Stalin's deputy,

Sergei Kirov. Akhmatova petitioned Stalin successfully to have both of them released, but both were arrested again. Punin died in a Siberian prison camp in 1953 after being arrested in 1949; her son, rearrested in the same year, did not leave prison until 1956. *Requiem (Rekviem)*, which we include in our selection here, offers poetic testimony to her son's imprisonment in the 1930s and to her difficult experience during these years. Akhmatova published a collection of old and some new poems, *From Six Books* (*Iz Shesti Knig*) in 1940, but Soviet censors withdrew it from circulation after only six months. In the following year she was evacuated from Leningrad to Tashkent, where she remained until 1944. Stalin's culture minister, Zhdanov, attacked her work again in the following year and ousted her from the Writers' Union. Meanwhile, she worked on what some critics see as her masterpiece, the cryptic and autobiographical *Poem Without a Hero* (*Poema Bez Geroya*), begun in 1940 and not finished until 1962. A poem of epic proportion and power like Pushkin's *Eugene Onegin, Poem Without a Hero* contains the allusive density and symbolic compression of T. S. Eliot's *The Waste Land*. Its story, set in St. Petersburg just before World War I, alludes to the death of a soldier–poet and is dotted with fragments of memories of the Silver Age days, her friends, musicians, poets, and dancers, as they witness, and sometimes fall with, the death of that great city.

With the death of Stalin in 1953, Akhmatova was restored to her rightful place as a publicly honored poet. In her last years she was again able to publish her work with a minimal degree of censorship, and she was elected to the presidium of the Writer's Union. In addition to writing poetry, she also wrote translations (as she had from the 1930s); composed various memoirs, including one of the painter Modigliani; and enjoyed the company of various friends and admirers, including the poets Anatoly Naiman and Joseph Brodsky, whom she encouraged. *Poems 1909–1960* (*Stikotvoreniya 1909–1960*) appeared in 1961 and *The Flight of Time* (*Beg vremeni*) in 1965; because of censorship, neither *Requiem* nor *Poem Without a Hero* were published in Russian, leading her to comment that "The contemporary reader does not know my poems, either the new ones or the old ones." A pirated edition of *Requiem* did appear from a West German press in 1963, and its haunting record of the harrowing experiences of Stalinism won her international fame. In 1964, Akhmatova went to Italy to receive the Taormina Prize for Poetry, and in the next year to Oxford, England, for an honorary Doctor of Letters degree. On March 5, 1966, Anna Akhmatova died in a nursing home near Moscow, leaving behind a poetic monument to the history and spirit of the country and people she loved.

WORK

A profound but detached sense of grief, loss, and sometimes guilt pervades Akhmatova's poetry. Her verse achieves a kind of classical poise that prevents her meditations on private experience, love, and loss from becoming sentimental or effusive. Indeed, her work fuses private with collective experience in a lyrical verse that is always precise and controlled, often ironic, and sometimes, as in *Poem Without a Hero*, surrealistic. Like that of Eliot and other modernist poets, Akhmatova's language, colloquial and precise, appears deceptively simple. From the objects and fragments of experience that appear directly in the work, she creates a highly allusive atmosphere that evokes the elegiac mood of much of her work while resonating with the personal and national tragedies out of which those feelings emerge.

"Voronezh," which was published without the last four lines in 1940, is dedicated to Osip Mandelstam, who was exiled to this city south of Moscow from 1934 to 1937. Through the historical allusion to Peter the Great, who had built a flotilla at Voronezh that stands on a tributary to the Don, and to the battle of Kulikovo in 1380, which marked a Russian victory over the Mongols, Akhmatova places the present disgrace of Mandelstam's exile in contrast to two triumphant moments of the city's past. The result is a poignant critique of the disintegration of the nation under Stalin, as well as a tribute to Mandelstam. The final four lines invoke that sense of melancholy and uncertainty of the mid-1930s for Akhmatova and others, and attribute to the Muse the responsibility of wakefulness during the times of trouble and disgrace. "To the Memory of M. B.," dedicated to Mikhail Bulgakov, an important Russian novelist, pays tribute to her friend and to the stoic power of those who braced up against all odds to continue their work. The poem is both a memorial and a testimony to Akhmatova's own strength as a writer and witness of the nation's tragedy as it played out in the lives of her friends.

Requiem is a cycle of poems reflecting on Stalin's Great Terror, and in particular the imprisonment of her son, Lev Gumilev, at Leningrad. The poem vividly portrays the feelings of the women who waited in lines outside of prisons to hear some news of relatives and friends rounded up during the Terror. The outer frame of the poem— the dedication, prologue, and epilogues—speaks directly to the common experience of Russians who suffered losses similar to her own. The individual sections within that frame focus particularly on her own experiences, with the arrests of her third husband, Nikolai Punin, and her son, Lev Gumilev, and the execution of her first husband, Nikolai Gumilev. As in "Voronezh," she broadens the historical perspective of these incidents by alluding to the historical past. The poem becomes increasingly grim, invoking apocalyptic imagery as she tries to come to terms with the possibility that her son, like her husband, may well be executed. In the final epilogue, Akhmatova describes herself as a sort of Niobe, transformed into a weeping statue outside the Leningrad prison, a monument to the suffering that she and others like her withstood during the purges. Working on the poem in the midst of the Terror between 1935 and 1940, Akhmatova committed parts of it to memory as she composed, fearing reprisals against her or her son. Although an ever-widening circle of friends knew parts of the poem by word of mouth, *Requiem* was not published in the Soviet Union until 1987.

SUGGESTED READINGS

Amanda Haight's *Anna Akhmatova: A Poetic Pilgrimage* (1976) offers a sensitive and detailed analysis of Akhmatova's life and work. For a broader analysis of her work in the context of the wars, see Ronald Hingley's *Nightingale Fever: Russian Poets in Revolution* (1981). Susan Amert's *In a Shattered Mirror: The Later Poetry of Anna Akhmatova* (1992) offers a detailed reading of *Requiem* and other later poems, and Sharon Leiter's *Akhmatova's Petersburg* (1983) discusses the importance of St. Petersburg as symbol and inspiration for Akhmatova's poetry.

Voronezh[1]

O. M.

Translated by Judith Hemschemeyer

And the whole town is encased in ice,
Trees, walls, snow, as if under glass.
Timidly, I walk on crystals,

---

[1]Located about three hundred miles south of Moscow, Voronezh was where Osip Mandelstam (the O. M. to whom the poem is dedicated) was sent into exile from 1934 to 1937; he died in a prison camp in 1938.

Gaily painted sleds skid.
And over the Peter of Voronezh[2]—crows,
Poplar trees, and the dome, light green,
Faded, dulled, in sunny haze,
And the battle of Kulikovo[3] blows from the slopes
Of the mighty, victorious land.
And the poplars, like cups clashed together,   10
Roar over us, stronger and stronger,
As if our joy were toasted by
A thousand guests at a wedding feast.
But in the room of the poet in disgrace,
Fear and the Muse keep watch by turns.
And the night comes on
That knows no dawn.

To the Memory of M. B.[1]

Translated by Judith Hemschemeyer

I give you this instead of roses on your grave,
Instead of the burning of incense;
You lived so sparely and, to the end, maintained
That magnificent disdain.
You drank wine, you joked like nobody else
And suffocated between those stifling walls,
And you yourself let in the terrible guest
And stayed with her alone.
And you are no more, and nothing is heard any-
      where
About your noble and sorrowful life.   10
Only my voice, like a flute, sounds
At your silent funeral service.
Oh, who dared believe that I, half mad,
I, the mourner of perished days,
I, smoldering over a low flame,
Having lost everything and forgotten everyone—
I would have to commemorate the one who, full
      of strength,
And will, and brilliant schemes,
Talked to me just yesterday it seems,
Concealing the trembling of mortal pain.   20

---

[2]A statue of Peter the Great, who had built a flotilla in Voronezh, which is on a tributary of the river Don.

[3]In 1380, the Russians led by Dmitry Donskoy defeated the Mongols in this field near Voronezh.

TO THE MEMORY OF M. B.

[1]Mikhail Bulgakov, a close friend of Akhmatova's, was a Russian writer and playwright (1891–1940), whose greatest work is *The Master and Margarita*, published posthumously in Russia in 1966.

Requiem

Translated by Judith Hemschemeyer

No, not under the vault of alien skies,[1]
And not under the shelter of alien wings—
I was with my people then,
There, where my people, unfortunately, were.

INSTEAD OF A PREFACE

In the terrible years of the Yezhov terror,[2] I spent
seventeen months in the prison lines of Leningrad.[3]
Once, someone "recognized" me. Then a woman with
bluish lips standing behind me, who, of course, had
never heard me called by name before, woke up from
the stupor to which everyone had succumbed and
whispered in my ear (everyone spoke in whispers there):
   "Can you describe this?"
   And I answered: "Yes, I can."
   Then something that looked like a smile passed over
what had once been her face.

DEDICATION

Mountains bow down to this grief,
Mighty rivers cease to flow,
But the prison gates hold firm,
And behind them are the "prisoners' burrows"
And mortal woe.
For someone a fresh breeze blows,
For someone the sunset luxuriates—
We wouldn't know, we are those who everywhere
Hear only the rasp of the hateful key
And the soldiers' heavy tread.
We rose as if for an early service,
Trudged through the savaged capital
And met there, more lifeless than the dead;
The sun is lower and the Neva[4] mistier,
But hope keeps singing from afar.
The verdict... And her tears gush forth,
Already she is cut off from the rest,
As if they painfully wrenched life from her heart,
As if they brutally knocked her flat,
But she goes on... Staggering... Alone...

---

[1] An allusion to Alexander Pushkin's "Message to Siberia."
[2] Nikolai Yezhov (1894–1939) was chief of Stalin's secret police from 1936 to 1938, during the Purge, or Terror.
[3] Akhmatova's son, Lev Gumilev, had been imprisoned in Leningrad.
[4] The river that flows through Leningrad.

Where now are my chance friends
Of those two diabolical years?
What do they imagine is in Siberia's storms,
What appears to them dimly in the circle of the moon?
I am sending my farewell greeting to them.   40

PROLOGUE

That was when the ones who smiled
Were the dead, glad to be at rest.
And like a useless appendage, Leningrad
Swung from its prisons.
And when, senseless from torment,
Regiments of convicts marched,
And the short songs of farewell
Were sung by locomotive whistles.
The stars of death stood above us
And innocent Russia writhed   50
Under bloody boots
And under the tires of the Black Marias.[5]

1

They led you[6] away at dawn,
I followed you, like a mourner,
In the dark front room the children were crying,
By the icon shelf the candle was dying.
On your lips was the icon's chill.
The deathly sweat on your brow . . . Unforgettable!—
I will be like the wives of the Streltsy,[7]
Howling under the Kremlin towers.   60

2

Quietly flows the quiet Don,[8]
Yellow moon slips into a home.

He slips in with cap askew,
He sees a shadow, yellow moon.

This woman is ill,
This woman is alone,

---

[5] Cars used to conduct convicts to prison.
[6] Nikolai Punin, Akhmatova's third husband, who was arrested in 1935.
[7] An elite troop who mutinied against Peter the Great in 1698; their wives pleaded in vain under the "Kremlin towers" as almost 2,500 of the men were executed.
[8] One of the major rivers of Russia; it flows south into the Sea of Azov.

Husband in the grave, son in prison,[9]
Say a prayer for me.

3

No, it is not I, it is somebody else who is suffering.
I would not have been able to bear what happened,
Let them shroud it in black,
And let them carry off the lanterns...
Night.

70

4

You should have been shown, you mocker,
Minion of all your friends,
Gay little sinner of Tsarskoe Selo,
What would happen in your life—
How three-hundredth in line, with a parcel,
You would stand by the Kresty prison,[10]
Your fiery tears
Burning through the New Year's ice.
Over there the prison poplar bends,
And there's no sound—and over there how many
Innocent lives are ending now...

80

5

For seventeen months I've been crying out,
Calling you home.
I flung myself at the hangman's feet,
You are my son and my horror.
Everything is confused forever,
And it's not clear to me
Who is a beast now, who is a man,
And how long before the execution.
And there are only dusty flowers,
And the chinking of the censer, and tracks
From somewhere to nowhere.
And staring me straight in the eyes,
And threatening impending death,
Is an enormous star.[11]

90

---

[9] Her first husband, Nikolai Gumilev, who was executed in 1921.
[10] The Leningrad prison where her son was held.
[11] The apocalyptic imagery here derives in part from Revelation 8:10–12 and 9:7–11.

6

The light weeks will take flight,
I won't comprehend what happened.
Just as the white nights[12]   100
Stared at you, dear son, in prison,
So they are staring again,
With the burning eyes of a hawk,
Talking about your lofty cross,
And about death.

7. THE SENTENCE[13]

And the stone word fell
On my still-living breast.
Never mind, I was ready.
I will manage somehow.   110

Today I have so much to do:
I must kill memory once and for all,
I must turn my soul to stone,
I must learn to live again—

Unless... Summer's ardent rustling
Is like a festival outside my window.
For a long time I've foreseen this
Brilliant day, deserted house.

8. TO DEATH

You will come in any case—so why not now?
I am waiting for you—I can't stand much more.   120
I've put out the light and opened the door
For you, so simple and miraculous.
So come in any form you please,
Burst in as a gas shell
Or, like a gangster, steal in with a length of pipe,
Or poison me with typhus fumes.
Or be that fairy tale you've dreamed up.
So sickeningly familiar to everyone—
In which I glimpse the top of a pale blue cap
And the house attendant white with fear.
Now it doesn't matter anymore. The Yenisey[14] swirls,   130
The North Star shines.
And the final horror dims
The blue luster of beloved eyes.

---

[12]Leningrad is far enough north that in the summer it never becomes completely dark.
[13]This section is dated on the day of her son's sentencing to labor camp, June 22, 1939.
[14]A river in Siberia, along which were located many concentration camps.

9

Now madness half shadows
My soul with its wing,
And makes it drunk with fiery wine
And beckons toward the black ravine.

And I've finally realized
That I must give in,   140
Overhearing myself
Raving as if it were somebody else.

And it does not allow me to take
Anything of mine with me
(No matter how I plead with it,
No matter how I supplicate):

Not the terrible eyes of my son—
Suffering turned to stone,
Not the day of the terror,
Not the hour I met with him in prison,   150

Not the sweet coolness of his hands,
Not the trembling shadow of the lindens,
Not the far-off, fragile sound—
Of the final words of consolation.

10. CRUCIFIXION

*"Do not weep for Me, Mother,
I am in the grave."*[15]

1

A choir of angels sang the praises of that
    momentous hour,
And the heavens dissolved in fire.
To his Father He said: "Why hast Thou forsaken me!"[16]
And to his Mother: "Oh, do not weep for Me..."

2

Mary Magdalene beat her breast and sobbed,
The beloved disciple turned to stone,   160
But where the silent Mother stood, there
No one glanced and no one would have dared.

---

[15] A refrain from a Russian Orthodox prayer sung during the Easter or Holy Week service.
[16] Jesus' last words according to Matthew 27:46.

EPILOGUE I

I learned how faces fall,
How terror darts from under eyelids,
How suffering traces lines
Of stiff cuneiform on cheeks,
How locks of ashen-blonde or black
Turn silver suddenly,
Smiles fade on submissive lips
And fear trembles in a dry laugh.
And I pray not for myself alone,   170
But for all those who stood there with me
In cruel cold, and in July's heat,
At that blind, red wall.

EPILOGUE II

Once more the day of remembrance[17] draws near.
I see, I hear, I feel you:

The one they almost had to drag at the end,
And the one who tramps her native land no more,

And the one who, tossing her beautiful head,
Said: "Coming here's like coming home."   180

I'd like to name them all by name,
But the list has been confiscated and is nowhere to
     be found.

I have woven a wide mantle for them
From their meager, overheard words.

I will remember them always and everywhere,
I will never forget them no matter what comes.

And if they gag my exhausted mouth
Through which a hundred million scream,

Then may the people remember me
On the eve of my remembrance day.   190

And if ever in this country
They decide to erect a monument to me,

---

[17]Literally translated, this line refers to Remembrance Day, a memorial service of the Russian Orthodox
Church held one year after a person's death.

I consent to that honor
Under these conditions—that it stand

Neither by the sea, where I was born:
My last tie with the sea is broken,

Nor in the tsar's garden near the cherished pine stump,[18]
Where an inconsolable shade looks for me,

But here, where I stood for three hundred hours,
And where they never unbolted the doors for me   200

This, lest in blissful death
I forget the rumbling of the Black Marias,

Forget how that detested door slammed shut
And an old woman howled like a wounded animal.

And may the melting snow stream like tears
From my motionless lids of bronze,

And a prison dove coo in the distance,
And the ships of the Neva sail calmly on.

FEDERICO GARCÍA LORCA
[1898–1936]

At dawn on August 19, 1936, a month after the beginning of the Spanish Civil War, the internationally celebrated poet Federico García Lorca was shot by a firing squad near an ancient Moorish spring outside the city of Granada and buried in an unmarked grave. The month before, he had told his friend Damaso Alonso, "I will never be political. I am a revolutionary because there are no true poets who are not revolutionaries. But political I will never, never be!" But Lorca, who also made a habit of saying "I am on the side of the poor," whose homosexuality was apparent in several of his most accessible works, and who had publicly stated that the fall of Moorish Granada in 1492 was a "disastrous event," was evidently political enough to merit assassination, in the eyes of the "black squads"—fascist gunmen who roamed the major cities of Spain in those terrible days.

Confined to the Spanish language throughout his life—he had tried to learn English at Columbia University in 1929, only to give it up—Lorca became the world's poet and playwright after his martyrdom at age thirty-eight. Today his works survive in all the languages of Europe: among the poems, *Canciones* (1921–1924); the *Gypsy Ballads*

---

[18]Alluding to her childhood, when she had taken walks around Tsarskoe Selo, the site of some of her fondest memories, including those of her first husband.

(1924–1927); his elegy "Lament for Ignacio Sanchez Mejías" (1935); and his imagistically rich volume *Poet in New York* (written in 1929–1930 but published posthumously in 1940). By the second half of Lorca's brief career he had emerged as one of the great Spanish dramatists, renowned for the works *Blood Wedding* (1933), *Yerma* (1934), and *The House of Bernarda Alba* (completed in 1936 but not performed until 1945). His fiery, emotional, often surrealistic writing—poetry and drama alike—is unique in tone and impact, and brings together a mixture of materials ranging from Spanish nursery rhymes and children's songs to the "deep songs" of the Andalusian provinces, folk songs, and ballads of Moorish and Gypsy influence. Though dark-complexioned, Lorca claimed no Moorish or Gypsy blood, but his sympathy for these peoples (as well as the *indios* of the Americas and the *negros* of Harlem) is a marked component of his work. Today he is also recognized, along with Walt Whitman, as one of the world's great homosexual poets.

LIFE

The first child of a well-to-do family, Lorca was born in 1898 in a rural town in the province of Granada; his family moved to the city in 1909. Educated in private schools, he showed an affinity for music, but his father, a practical man who distrusted the arts, insisted that he study law. (A revealing anecdote has his father telling the family servant, "Give him an omelette of chrysanthemums! of violets! of twilight!" when the teenage Lorca came in late to dinner because he had been gazing too long at the twilight.) Although Lorca performed indifferently at the University of Madrid, he did immerse himself in the classical writers of Spain, including Cervantes, Lope de Vega, Calderón de la Barca, Tirso de Molina, and Góngora. He also joined his literature class on field trips to central Spain in 1916 and 1917, where he studied folk music and storytelling. His first book, *Impressions and Landscapes* (1918), financed by his father once he was convinced of its artistic merit, is a record of these early explorations.

Fortunate to have both artistic connections and family support—whatever his father's misgivings—Lorca was able to join the Students' Residence in Madrid, a renowned center for young artists, scholars, and writers, in 1919. He lived there for nine years, earning celebrity as a musician and poet. Frequenting the center were older poets such as Juan Ramón Jiménez and Antonio Machado, and Lorca's contemporaries Rafael Alberti and Jorge Guillen—two generations of the world's greatest Spanish-language poets. Other resident-artists included filmmaker Luis Buñuel and painter Salvador Dali. Dali was important to Lorca in two respects: He helped introduce the young poet to the doctrines of surrealism, a leading art movement of the twenties, and for years he was the object of Lorca's romantic passion. The relationship lasted from 1922 to 1928, when Lorca left the Residence.

By 1922, Lorca had organized folk festivals of "deep song," the passionate lyrics of the province of Andalusia. His own volume of poetic imitations of this music was published in 1931. Meanwhile, still at the Residence, Lorca had published small editions of his poetry, organized puppet shows based on folk stories, written and directed a play (a critical disaster in its single stage appearance), presented an exhibit of his drawings, and participated in a 1927 literary conference organized by the highly cultivated bullfighter Ignacio Sanchez Mejías, whom Lorca was to eulogize seven years later in his most famous poem. Lorca's impressive volume of poetry *Gypsy Ballads* appeared at the end of this period.

In 1928 Lorca was about to undergo the deepest emotional crisis of his life, probably attributable to his breakup with Dali, inner conflicts over his homosexuality, and the merciless exposure occasioned by his sudden fame. He accepted the offer of a former professor, Fernando de los Ríos, to visit New York City in June 1929. Although he studied at Columbia University through the fall semester, he learned very little English, and the poetry he wrote is replete with images of cultural and emotional alienation. The most striking themes of these poems concern the plight of the *negros* of Harlem and the violence of homosexual life in the American metropolis. These themes are explored in "The King of Harlem" and "Ode to Walt Whitman," presented here.

Lorca returned to Spain at the time of the establishment of the Second Republic, celebrating with his countrymen the fragile victory of a broadly based democratic movement (1931–1936). He initiated an arts project called "The Hut," literally a house on wheels that transported classical theater to small towns and villages. Traveling with the company, Lorca edited classical drama to conform to ordinary people's tastes, and thus developed a strong rapport with the popular audience. This experience prepared him to write his own drama. Two of his three most famous plays, *Blood Wedding* (1933) and *Yerma* (1934), were written on the road as Lorca traveled with his company. The traveling performances of "The Hut" ceased production in the face of growing political tension in April 1936. Lorca finished the last great play in his trilogy of tragedies about women, *The House of Bernarda Alba,* in the spring of 1936, just before the beginning of the Spanish Civil War and his own death that summer.

WORK

Lorca's last great poetic work was inspired by the death of his friend, the bullfighter Ignacio Sanchez Mejías, in August 1934, following the former champion's return to the ring after a seven-year absence. The poem, organized in four movements, is recognized as a classic of Spanish literature. Preceding Lorca's execution by less than two years, the "Lament" is often regarded as Lorca's anticipation of his own death.

Attempts to reproduce Lorca's poetry in translation inevitably diminish the musicality and beauty of his language. The opening verse of "Somnambule Ballad" provides an example of how poorly Lorca's poetry translates:

> *Verde que te quiero verde.*
> *Verde viento. Verdes ramas.*
> *El barco sobre la mar*
> *y el caballo en la montana.*

> Green how I want you green.
> Green wind. Green branches.
> The ship upon the sea
> and the horse on the mountain.

Another example is the famous chorus from the first section of "Lament for Ignacio Sanchez Mejías":

> *A las cinco de la tarde.*
> *Eran las cinco en punto de la tarde.*

> At five in the afternoon.
> It was exactly five in the afternoon.

The soft Castilian "c" sound in "cinco" ("dthinco") and the trilling "r" sound ("tarrrde")—indeed, the entire music of the original—are beyond the translator's reach. It cannot be emphasized enough that Lorca is a *Spanish* poet. The explanation for his abandoned efforts to learn English may lie in his deep attunement to his own language, such that none other could compete with it.

SUGGESTED READINGS

A number of works on Lorca are available in English. His major works in English translation come in three editions: Francisco García Lorca and Donald Allen, eds., *The Selected Poems of Federico García Lorca* (1955); Ben Belitt, trans., *Poet in New York* (1955); and James Graham-Lujan and Richard L. O'Connell, trans., *Three Tragedies* (1947). The best biography is Ian Gibson's *Federico García Lorca: A Life* (1989). A brief introduction to Lorca's life and work is Felicia Hardinson Londre's *Federico García Lorca* (1984). A more complete study is Mildred Adams's *García Lorca: Playwright and Poet* (1984). Among critical studies of Lorca's more complex poetry are Andrew Anderson's *Lorca's Late Poetry* (1990) and Richard L. Predmore's *Lorca's New York Poetry* (1980).

The King of Harlem[1]

Translated by Stephen Spender and J. L. Gili

With a spoon
he scooped out the eyes of crocodiles
and spanked the monkeys on their bottoms.[2]
With a spoon.

Fire of all times slept in the flints
and the beetles drunk with anis
forgot the moss of the villages.[3]

That old man covered with mushrooms
went to the place where the Negroes were weeping[4]

---

[1]This was one of the first poems Lorca wrote after arriving in New York City on June 25, 1929. According to Lorca's biographer, Ian Gibson, the manuscript, dated August 5 the same year, is "a labyrinth of crossings out and emendations, and gives the impression of high-speed composition under the impact of intense inspiration." Gibson also suggests that Lorca appears to have perceived a connection between the situations of African Americans of Harlem and Spanish Gypsies. Lorca himself later spoke of "the Gypsy, the Black, the Jew . . . the converted Moor, that we all carry inside" (Gibson, *Federico García Lorca: A Life*, 256).

[2]The ubiquitous figure the King of Harlem both confirms and supersedes the African culture from which the African Americans (Negroes) of Harlem are descended.

[3]The flints are the ancient (black) stones Lorca associates with Africa, and the beetles are sacred (black) insects.

[4]The image of weeping is picked up later in the poem. Lorca associates the inhabitants of Harlem with all of oppressed humanity.

while the spoon of the King crackled   10
and the tanks of putrid water arrived.

Roses escaped along the edge of the final curves of the air,
and in the heaps of saffron
the boys were mauling small squirrels
with a flush of stained frenzy.[5]

It is necessary to cross the bridges
and to reach the black murmur,[6]
so that the perfume of lungs strikes our temples
with its suit of warm pineapple.

Necessary to murder the blonde seller of brandy,   20
and all the friends of the apple and sand,
necessary to bang with closed fists
the small Jewesses that tremble full of bubbles,
so that the King of Harlem sings with his multitude,[7]
so that the crocodiles sleep in long rows
under the asbestos of the moon,
so that nobody doubts the infinite beauty of funnels,
graters, feather-dusters, and saucepans in kitchens.

Ah Harlem! Ah Harlem! Ah Harlem!
There is no anxiety comparable to your oppressed scarlets,   30
to your blood shaken within your dark eclipse,
to your garnet violence deaf and dumb in the penumbra,
to your great King, a prisoner with a commissionaire's uniform.[8]

The night had a fissure
and still ivory salamanders.
The American girls carried babies and coins in their bellies
and the boys fainted stretched on the cross of lassitude.[9]

They are.
They are those who take silver whisky near the volcanoes
and devour bits of heart through the frozen mountains of the bear.   40

That night the King of Harlem with a very hard spoon
scooped out the eyes of crocodiles

---

[5]In the environment around Harlem "boys were mauling small squirrels." Lorca saw Harlem as essentially encircled by a vicious and parasitical white society.

[6]Symbolically, Lorca "crosses the bridges"—of the Harlem and East rivers—into Harlem proper, from the Bronx and Queens, respectively.

[7]The question of African Americans seeking retribution against their oppressors obsesses Lorca. Violence, he seems to suggest, feeds the unconscious forces in Harlem, which are also the sources of its creativity.

[8]The "great King" of Harlem may be found dressed as a janitor.

[9]The image focuses on the spiritual emptiness of white girls and boys in American society. They seem to be prepared for sacrifice.

and spanked the monkeys on their bottoms.
With a spoon.
The Negroes cried abased
among umbrellas and golden suns,
the mulattoes were stretching gum, anxious to reach the white torso,
and the wind blurred mirrors
and burst open the veins of the dancers.

    Negroes, Negroes, Negroes, Negroes.   50

The blood has no doors in your night face upwards.[10]
There is no blushing. Furious blood under the skins,
alive in the thorn of the dagger and in the breast of landscapes,
under the pincers and the broom of the celestial Moon of Cancer.

Blood that searches through thousand ways deaths covered in flour and
    ashes of nards,
still skies, slanting, where the colonies of planets
tumble along beaches with abandoned objects.

Blood that looks slowly through the tail of the eye
made of squeezed esparto and subterranean nectars.
Blood that oxidizes the unaware trade wind in a footprint   60
and dissolves the butterflies in the windowpanes.

This is the blood that comes, that will come
through roofs and terraces, by every way,
to burn the chlorophyll of blonde women,
to groan at the foot of beds facing insomnia of basins
and to crash against a dawn of tobacco and subdued yellow.

One has to flee,[11]
to flee from the shores and lock oneself up in the top storeys
because the marrow of the woods will penetrate through the crevices,
to leave in your flesh a slight print of eclipse   70
and a false sadness of faded glove and chemical rose.

Through the most wise silence
when the waiters and cooks and those that clean with their tongues
the wounds of millionaires
look for the King through the streets and in angles of saltpeter.

An oblique South Wind of wood in the black mud
spits at the broken boats and pierces nails in its shoulders;
a South Wind that carries
fangs, sunflowers, alphabets
and a voltaic battery with suffocated wasps.   80

---

[10]The blood reintroduced here symbolizes the impulse for retribution.

[11]Apparently, what "one has to flee," in the next four stanzas, is false nostalgia for the past.

Oblivion was expressed by three drops of ink on the monocle,
love, by a single face, invisible on the surface of stone.
Marrows and corollas were composing on the clouds
a desert of stems without a single rose.

From the left, from the right, from the South, and from the North,
there rises the wall impassive
to the mole and the needle of water.
Do not seek, Negroes, for the cleft
to find the infinite mask.
Seek for the great Sun of the center[12]   90
made into a buzzing cluster.
The Sun that slides through the woods
certain of not meeting a nymph,
the Sun that destroys numbers and has never crossed a dream,
the tattooed Sun that goes down the river
and bellows followed by alligators.

　　Negroes, Negroes, Negroes, Negroes.

Never snake, nor goat, nor mule
grew pale at death.
The wood-cutter does not know when   100
the clamorous trees which he fells expire.[13]
Wait under the vegetable shadow of your King
until the hemlock, thistles and stinging nettles disturb the furthermost
　　terraces.

Then, Negroes, then, then,
you will be able to kiss with frenzy the wheels of bicycles,
to put pairs of microscopes in the caves of the squirrels
and dance at last, without fear, while the spiked flowers
assassinate our Moses almost in the reeds of Heaven!

Ah, masqueraded Harlem!
Ah, Harlem, threatened by a mob wearing clothes without heads!   110
Your rumour reaches me,
your rumour reaches me, crossing tree trunks and lifts,
across the grey plates
where your cars float covered with teeth,
across the dead horses and the minute crimes,
across your great despairing King,
whose beard reaches the sea.[14]

---

[12]The "great Sun of the center" is the African symbol of unity, again suggesting the revolt Lorca sees as imminent in Harlem.

[13]Lorca separates the pure act of revolt from its consequences, like the blows of the woodcutter.

[14]The poet declares his solidarity with Harlem from across the sea against the "mob wearing clothes without heads"—the exploitative class of white America. Both the grieving and the pressing onward of the King of Harlem are felt even in Europe.

Ode to Walt Whitman[1]

Translated by Stephen Spender and J. L. Gili

Along the East River and the Bronx
the boys were singing showing their waists,
with the wheel, the oil, the leather and the hammer.
Ninety thousand miners extracted silver from rocks
and children drew stairs and perspectives.

But none would sleep,
none wanted to be a river,[2]
none loved the great leaves,
none, the blue tongue of the beach.

Along the East River and the Queensborough   10
the boys were fighting with Industry,
and the Jews were selling to the faun of the river
the rose of the Circumcision,
and the sky rushed through bridges and roofs
herds of bison pushed by the wind.[3]

But none would pause,
none wanted to be a cloud,
none searched for the ferns
nor the yellow wheel of the tambourine.

When the moon rises,   20
the pulleys will turn to disturb the sky:
a boundary of needles will fence in the memory
and the coffins will carry away those who do not work.

New York of slime,
New York of wires and death:
What angel do you carry hidden in your cheek?
What perfect voice will tell the truths of the wheat?
Who, the terrible dream of your stained anemones?

---

[1]A critic of Lorca notes: "The dominant theme of "Ode to Walt Whitman" is love. . . . Almost all kinds of love can be respected, including a certain kind of homosexual love represented by a Walt Whitman conceived as a noble and virile lover of men. Only the corrupt fairies of the cities are condemned: they are depicted as purveyors of death and corruption, enemies of joyful love" (Predmore, *Lorca's New York Poetry,* 45).

Another critic points out: "The style of this ode is itself Whitmanian. . . . But beyond this style is the coincidence of the two poets' attitude toward humanity, their common identification with the downtrodden" (Betty Jean Craige, *Lorca's Poet in New York,* 79).

[2]Images such as wanting "to be a river" remind Lorca of the poet Whitman. In succeeding stanzas, Lorca contrasts the busy crowds along the river with Whitman the visionary.

[3]Lorca, like the French novelist Chateaubriand, envisions herds of bison on the other side of the Hudson River, to the west.

Not for one moment, beautiful aged Walt Whitman,[4]
have I failed to see your beard full of butterflies,   30
nor your shoulders of corduroy worn out by the moon,
nor your thighs of virginal Apollo,
nor your voice like a pillar of ashes:
ancient and beautiful as the mist,
you moaned like a bird
with the sex transfixed by a needle,
enemy of the satyr,
enemy of the vine,
and lover of bodies under the rough cloth.
Not for one moment; virile beauty,   40
who in mountains of coal, posters and railways,
dreamed of being a river and sleeping like a river
with that comrade who would place in your breast
the small pain of an ignorant leopard.

Not for one moment, Adam of blood, male,
lone man in the sea, beautiful aged Walt Whitman,
because through the terraces,
clustered around the bars,
pouring out of sewers in bunches,
trembling between the legs of chauffeurs   50
or revolving on the platforms of absinthe,
the pansies, Walt Whitman, dreamed of you.[5]

This one also! This one! And they fall
on your chaste and luminous beard,
Northern blonds, Negroes of the sands,
multitudes of shrieks and gestures,
like cats or like snakes,
the pansies, Walt Whitman, the pansies,
muddy with tears, flesh for the whip,
boot or bite of subduers.   60

This one also! This one! Tainted fingers
appear on the shore of your dreams
when the friend eats your apple
with a faint taste of petrol
and the sun sings along the navels
of boys that play under bridges.

But you did not search for the scratched eyes,
or the very dark swamp where children are submerged,
or the frozen saliva,
or the wounded curves resembling toad's bellies   70
which the pansies carry in cars and terraces
while the moon strikes at them along the corners of fear.

---

[4]This paean to Whitman has been cited by other poets of the Spanish tradition, including Pablo Neruda.
[5]Contrasted to Whitman are "the pansies," *los maricas.*

You searched for a nude who was like a river.
Bull and dream that would join the wheel with the seaweed,
father of your agony, camellia of your death,
and would moan in the flames of your hidden Equator.

Because it is just that man does not search for his delight[6]
in the jungle of blood of the following morning.
The sky has shores where to avoid life,
and certain bodies must not repeat themselves in the dawn.   80

Agony, agony, dream, ferment and dream.
This is the world, my friend, agony, agony.
The corpses decompose under the clock of the cities.
War passes weeping with a million grey rats,
the rich give to their mistresses
small illuminated moribunds,
and Life is not noble, nor good, nor sacred.

Man can, if he wishes, lead his desire
through vein of coral or celestial nude:
tomorrow love will be rocks, and Time   90
a breeze which comes sleeping through the branches.

That is why I do not raise my voice, aged Walt Whitman,
against the little boy who writes
a girl's name on his pillow,
nor the boy who dresses himself in the bride's trousseau
in the darkness of the wardrobe,
nor the solitary men in clubs
who drink the water of prostitution with nausea,
nor the men with a green stare
who love man and burn their lips in silence.   100
But against you, yes, pansies of the cities,
of tumescent flesh and unclean mind,
mud of drains, harpies, unsleeping enemies
of Love which distributes crowns of joy.[7]

Against you always, you who give boys
drops of soiled death with bitter poison.
Against you always,
Fairies of North America,
Pájaros of Havana,
Jotos of Mexico,   110
Sarasas of Cadiz,
Apios of Seville,
Cancos of Madrid,

---

[6]In this stanza, Lorca defends homosexuality as a means of avoiding the trap of mortality that lies in reproduction.

[7]Lorca does not raise his voice against the solitary men who experience the agony of a love that precludes the possibility of procreation, but he does oppose the "enemies of Love," the licentious "fairies" of the city who spread disease and death.

Floras of Alicante,
Adelaidas of Portugal.

Pansies of the world, murderers of doves!
Women's slaves, bitches of their boudoirs,
opened with the fever of fans in public squares
or ambushed in frigid landscapes of hemlock.

Let there be no quarter! Death   120
flows from your eyes
and clusters grey flowers on the shores.
Let there be no quarter! Take heed!
Let the perplexed, the pure,
the classicists, the noted, the supplicants,
close the gates of the Bacchanalia.

And you, beautiful Walt Whitman, sleep on the Hudson's banks,
with your beard toward the Pole and your hands open.
Bland clay or snow, your tongue is calling for
comrades that keep watch on your gazelle without a body.   130
Sleep; nothing remains.
A dance of walls agitates the meadows
and America drowns itself in machines and lament.
I want the strong air of the most profound night
to remove flowers and words from the arch where you sleep,
and a black boy to announce to the gold-minded whites
the arrival of the reign of the ear of corn.

Lament for Ignacio Sanchez Mejías[1]

Translated by Stephen Spender and J. L. Gili

1. COGIDA AND DEATH

At five in the afternoon.[2]
It was exactly five in the afternoon.
A boy brought the white sheet

---

[1]Ignacio Sanchez Mejías (1891–1934), a cultivated, handsome, and virile son of a doctor, was an avant-garde playwright and patron of the arts as well as a bullfighter. He competed as a matador (professional bullfighter) between 1920 and 1922 and again between 1924 and 1927. He came out of his second retirement in 1934, and agreed to fight one additional day in the 1934 season, stepping in for his injured rival, Domingo Ortega. On that day—August 11—he was fatally gored by the bull Granadino. Sanchez Mejías died two days later from a gangrene infection after a 12-hour ambulance ride to Madrid. Lorca, a good friend of the bullfighter, wrote this poem in his memory, publishing it in a special volume in 1935.

[2]The body of Sanchez Mejías, removed from a mortuary in Madrid at five in the afternoon on August 14, 1934, was carried through the streets, then transported by train to Seville for burial. Lorca has apparently appropriated this time as the hour of the actual goring, probably for poetic purposes.

at five in the afternoon.
A frail of lime ready prepared[3]
at five in the afternoon.
The rest was death, and death alone[4]
at five in the afternoon.

The wind carried away the cottonwool[5]
at five in the afternoon.   10
And the oxide scattered crystal and nickel
at five in the afternoon.
Now the dove and the leopard wrestle[6]
at five in the afternoon.
And a thigh with a desolate horn
at five in the afternoon.
The bass-string struck up
at five in the afternoon.
Arsenic bells and smoke
at five in the afternoon.   20
Groups of silence in the corners
at five in the afternoon.
And the bull alone with a high heart!
At five in the afternoon.
When the sweat of snow was coming
at five in the afternoon,
when the bull ring was covered in iodine
at five in the afternoon,
death laid eggs in the wound
at five in the afternoon.   30
At five in the afternoon.
Exactly at five o'clock in the afternoon.

A coffin on wheels is his bed
at five in the afternoon.
Bones and flutes resound in his ears[7]
at five in the afternoon.
Now the bull was bellowing through his forehead
at five in the afternoon.
The room was iridescent with agony
at five in the afternoon.   40
In the distance the gangrene now comes
at five in the afternoon.

---

[3]"Ready": already. Lorca suggests that the winding sheet and quicklime were already prepared for the matador as he stood to face the bull.

[4]"The rest was death": Lorca borrows from Spanish tradition the theme of *emplazamiento,* or "appointment with death."

[5]Cottonwool suggests cotton surgical dressing; oxide (rust) suggests the color of blood; crystal suggests the doctors' glass beakers; nickel suggests medical instruments. This stanza rather surrealistically treats the actual goring and attempts at treatment.

[6]Dove and leopard are symbols of peace and violence, respectively. The inscription on the cover of the printed edition of the poem reads "a dove . . . gathered him up." Later in the poem, Ignacio is compared to a "river of lions."

[7]Bones, flutes, and other references suggest the death of the god Adonis, also killed by a bull.

Horn of the lily through green groins
at five in the afternoon.
The wounds were burning like suns
at five in the afternoon,
and the crowd was breaking the windows[8]
at five in the afternoon.
At five in the afternoon.
Ah, that fatal five in the afternoon!   50
It was five by all the clocks!
It was five in the shade of the afternoon!

2. THE SPILLED BLOOD

I will not see it!

Tell the moon to come[9]
for I do not want to see the blood
of Ignacio on the sand.

I will not see it!

The moon wide open.
Horse of still clouds,
and the grey bull ring of dreams   60
with willows in the barreras.
I will not see it!

Let my memory kindle!
Warn the jasmines
of such minute whiteness!

I will not see it!

The cow of the ancient world[10]
passed her sad tongue
over a snout of blood
spilled on the sand,   70
and the bulls of Guisando,[11]
partly death and partly stone,
bellowed like two centuries[12]
sated with treading the earth.
No.

---

[8]Suggests a riot of followers clamoring to see Sanchez Mejías on his deathbed. No such incident is known to have occurred.

[9]According to tradition, the moon comes to suck up the blood of the world before turning red in a lunar eclipse.

[10]"Cow of the ancient world" recalls Mithraism, a religion of animal sacrifice that flourished during the late Roman Empire.

[11]"Bulls of Guisando": weathered, ancient stone statuary depicting bulls, in Madrid.

[12]"Two centuries": era of modern bullfighting.

I do not want to see it!
I will not see it!

Ignacio goes up the tiers[13]
with all his death on his shoulders.
He sought for the dawn
but the dawn was no more.   80
He seeks for his confident profile
and the dream bewilders him.
He sought for his beautiful body
and encountered his opened blood.
I will not see it!
I do not want to hear it spurt
each time with less strength:
that spurt that illuminates
the tiers of seats, and spills   90
over the corduroy and the leather
of a thirsty multitude.
Who shouts that I should come near!
Do not ask me to see it!

His eyes did not close
when he saw the horns near,
but the terrible mothers[14]
lifted their heads.
And across the ranches,
an air of secret voices rose,   100
shouting to celestial bulls,
herdsmen of pale mist.
There was no prince in Seville[15]
who could compare with him,
nor sword like his sword
nor heart so true.
Like a river of lions
was his marvellous strength,
and like a marble torso
his firm drawn moderation.   110
The air of Andalusian Rome
gilded his head
where his smile was a spikenard
of wit and intelligence.
What a great torero in the ring!
What a good peasant in the sierra!
How gentle with the sheaves!
How hard with the spurs!

---

[13]An extended metaphor describing Ignacio as a victim of ancient sacrifice, like Adonis and the bulls
sacrificed in the practice of Mithraism.
[14]"Terrible mothers": Lorca envisioned these awesome presences as the Three Fates who announce the
hour of death.
[15]The formal eulogy of Sanchez Mejías begins here and continues through the end of the stanza.

How tender with the dew!
How dazzling in the fiesta!   120
How tremendous with the final
banderillas of darkness!

But now he sleeps without end.
Now the moss and the grass
open with sure fingers
the flower of his skull.
And now his blood comes out singing;
singing along marshes and meadows,
sliding on frozen horns,
faltering soulless in the mist,   130
stumbling over a thousand hoofs
like a long, dark, sad tongue,
to form a pool of agony
close to the starry Guadalquivir.[16]
Oh, white wall of Spain!
Oh, black bull of sorrow!
Oh, hard blood of Ignacio!
Oh, nightingale of his veins!
No.
I will not see it!   140
No chalice can contain it,[17]
no swallows can drink it,
no frost of light can cool it,
nor song nor deluge of white lilies,
no glass can cover it with silver.
No.
I will not see it!

3. THE LAID OUT BODY[18]

Stone is a forehead where dreams grieve
without curving waters and frozen cypresses.
Stone is a shoulder on which to bear Time   150
with trees formed of tears and ribbons and planets.

I have seen grey showers move towards the waves
raising their tender riddled arms,
to avoid being caught by the lying stone
which loosens their limbs without soaking the blood.

---

[16]"The starry Guadalquivir": region of Spain where black fighting bulls are raised; also the place of Sanchez Mejías's birth and death.

[17]The awesome image of the spilling of the bullfighter's blood suggests that no modern religion such as Christianity can mediate or provide comfort for his death.

[18]"The Laid Out Body": in Spanish, *corpe presente*. This can also mean "the present body." See line 169 "We are here with a body laid out which fades away," which may mean that the body is both present and departing at the same time.

For stone gathers seed and clouds,
skeleton larks and wolves of penumbra:
but yields not sounds nor crystals nor fire,
only bull rings and bull rings and more bull rings without
    walls.

Now, Ignacio the well born lies on the stone.   160
All is finished. What is happening? Contemplate his face:
death has covered him with pale sulphur
and has placed on him the head of a dark minotaur.[19]

All is finished. The rain penetrates his mouth.
The air, as if mad, leaves his sunken chest,
and Love, soaked through with tears of snow,
warms itself on the peak of the herd.

What are they saying? A stenching silence settles down.
We are here with a body laid out which fades away,
with a pure shape which had nightingales   170
and we see it being filled with depthless holes.

Who creases the shroud? What he says is not true![20]
Nobody sings here, nobody weeps in the corner,
nobody pricks the spurs, nor terrifies the serpent.
Here I want nothing else but the round eyes
to see this body without a chance of rest.[21]

Here I want to see those men of hard voice.
Those that break horses and dominate rivers;
those men of sonorous skeleton who sing
with a mouth full of sun and flint.   180

Here I want to see them. Before the stone.
Before this body with broken reins.
I want to know from them the way out
for this captain strapped down by death.

I want them to show me a lament like a river
which will have sweet mists and deep shores,
to take the body of Ignacio where it loses itself
without hearing the double panting of the bulls.[22]

Loses itself in the round bull ring of the moon
which feigns in its youth a sad quiet bull: 190

---

[19] Again the bullfighter is compared to a mythical sacrificial creature, half-bull and half-man.

[20] It appears that someone has come forward to draw a cloth across the bullfighter's face. See line 193, "I don't want them to cover his face with handkerchiefs."

[21] "Without a chance of rest": can mean either "I want this person to keep a continuous vigil," or that the body has no chance to rest.

[22] Lorca is praying that the body will find eternal rest, but avoids a Christian framework.

loses itself in the night without song of fishes
and in the white thicket of frozen smoke.

I don't want them to cover his face with handkerchiefs
that he may get used to the death he carries.
Go, Ignacio; feel not the hot bellowing.
Sleep, fly, rest: even the sea dies!

4.   ABSENT SOUL[23]

The bull does not know you,[24] nor the fig tree,
nor the horses, nor the ants in your own house.
The child and the afternoon do not know you
because you have died for ever.   200

The back of the stone does not know you,
nor the black satin in which you crumble.
Your silent memory does not know you
because you have died for ever.

The autumn will come with small white snails,[25]
misty grapes and with clustered hills,
but no one will look into your eyes
because you have died for ever.

Because you have died for ever,
like all the dead of the Earth,   210
like all the dead who are forgotten
in a heap of lifeless dogs.

Nobody knows you. No. But I sing of you.
For posterity I sing of your profile and grace.
Of the signal maturity of your understanding.
Of your appetite for death and the taste of its mouth.
Of the sadness of your once valiant gaiety.

It will be a long time, if ever, before there is born
an Andalusian so true, so rich in adventure.
I sing of his elegance with words that groan,   220
and I remember a sad breeze through the olive trees.[26]

---

[23]"Absent Soul" (*alma ausente*): compare to *cuerpo presente* (the laid out body or the present body), above.

[24]"The bull does not know you" may refer either to the bulls of Sanchez Mejías's family estate outside Seville or to Granadino, the bull that gored him.

[25]"The autumn will come": the season following Sanchez Mejías's death.

[26]The last two lines bring in a personal note. Sanchez Mejías once described for Lorca and another friend a time in his childhood when he practiced bullfighting by making passes at small cows: "I was proud of my passes, sad only that there was no one there to applaud me. So, when a breath of breeze stirred the olive trees, I raised my hand, and waved" (cited in Anderson, *Lorca's Late Poetry*, 231).

JORGE LUIS BORGES
[1899–1986]

Jorge Luis Borges is famous for creating his own version of the short story in which he addresses the modern dissolution of conventional reality by blurring the traditional lines between historical scholarship and fiction. As a native of Argentina, he set the stage for other experimental Latin American writers by exploring the psychological boundaries between interior and exterior reality and by playing with multiple identities and intersecting times and places. Borges's erudition draws upon esoteric literature and the wisdom tradition of world cultures to create a web of subtle connections and unusual synchronicity in his stories. As an international writer, he moves easily from one language to another, just as his characters move easily across national boundaries, pursuing their livelihoods abroad. Nowhere, of course, does Borges provide the magic key to unlock the comprehensive, previously hidden plan for the cosmos, but like the ancient gnostics he tantalizes us with the possibility that such a key exists, and that reality—for the artist at least—is an act of the imagination.

LIFE

Born on August 24, 1899, in Buenos Aires, Argentina, Jorge Luis Borges was raised in a home where languages and books were important. His mother, Lenore Acevedo Suarez, was a translator, and his father, Jorge Guillermos Borges, was a teacher, lawyer, and writer. Because his paternal grandmother was English and lived with the family, Borges grew up speaking both English and Spanish. When asked about the central event of his childhood, he answered, "I should say my father's library." In that library filled with English and Spanish books, young Borges read a large number of the classics. His father expected him to be a writer and he was not disappointed. Borges began early, writing his first story at age seven and publishing a Spanish translation of Oscar Wilde's "The Happy Prince" in a Buenos Aires newspaper at age nine.

In 1914 World War I broke out and the Borges family, traveling throughout Europe, was stranded in Geneva, Switzerland; Borges completed secondary school at the College de Genève. Here he became proficient in Latin and French in school and taught himself German and German philosophy at home. In Spain after the war, Borges became acquainted with a young group of writers called the Ultraists, who followed the French symbolists and believed in the primacy of the metaphor in poetry. Returning to Buenos Aires in 1921, Borges became very active in the literary scene of that city; from 1920 to 1930 he published four books of essays and three books of poetry. He founded three literary magazines and contributed to numerous others. But real fame arrived with his collections of unusual short stories: *El jardin de los senderos que se bifurcan* (*The Garden of Forking Paths*),(1941), *Ficciones* (*Fictions*),(1944), and *El Aleph* (1949).

From 1938 to 1946, Borges worked in a library in Buenos Aires, but his opposition to the dictatorship of Juan Perón, who came to power in 1946, led to Borges's dismissal from the library. The Perónistas offered him a job as a chicken inspector in the city market, but he found a teaching job instead. After the fall of Perón in 1955, Borges was given the post of Director of the National Library, a position emblematic of his love for literature and vast learning. Unfortunately, his eyesight gradually failed in the mid-1950s and he was compelled to dictate his writings. In 1961, he won the International Publishers' Prize, which he shared with Samuel Beckett. He published a final collection of stories in 1970, *Doctor Brodie's Report*. Besides traveling to various parts of the world, he spent his final years lecturing and teaching in universities, usually in the United States. In 1986, Borges died of liver cancer in Geneva, Switzerland, where he is buried.

WORK

Although his detective story "The Garden of Forking Paths" was originally published in the collection of the same name in 1941, it eventually was republished in *Labyrinths* (1962), an appropriate title for Borges's writings because he is a master at creating tantalizing mazes that can be navigated only by discovering the nearly invisible spool of thread he unwinds in his narration. With the use of a book of history, data, and dates, this story begins with a reality as substantial as automobiles and brick houses, but by the second paragraph, the historical account is qualified by a newly discovered document by Dr. Yu Tsun, who taught English at a German school in China; at this point ordinary reality begins to slip away into a series of fragments and innuendos. As is typical of Borges, two of the main characters in this story are foreigners seeking to prove their loyalties to a particular cause; the third character is, like Borges himself, a Sinologist. Part of the enjoyment of this story is rereading it to discover the clues planted in the text, tying loose strands together. One dimension of the story consists of communicating the location of a British bombing target to Yu Tsun's chief in Berlin, but another whole dimension is the labyrinth discovered by Yu Tsun's ancestor in a text, *The Garden of Forking Paths*, which in its very structure models a universe comprising multiple planes of time in which individuals play several diverse roles. Even though the detective story is resolved in the final paragraph, Borges leaves the reader with the unmistakable impression that he or she is part of a larger network of relationships that transcend everyday understanding.

Borges has been compared with Kafka, whom he translated, and, indeed, both of them are devoted to the exploration of consciousness. Kafka's stories, however, deal with the dreamlike landscapes of the emotions whereas Borges's are very intellectual, drawing from the storehouse of world literature. At times Borges's concerns with multiple planes of consciousness and esoteric learning are a kind of game, as if he were playing with the frontiers of the mind; at other times, he seems to be reaching for a new kind of syncretistic mythology that would blend ancient wisdom with modern psychology. At home with archaeology, philology, philosophy, comparative religion, and world literature, Borges challenges a modern society that has lost contact with the meaningful symbols of its own tradition and lacks the vision for unifying whatever cultural fragments remain.

SUGGESTED READINGS

Two biographies and introductions to Borges's writings are George R. McMurray's *Jorge Luis Borges* (1980) and Emir Rodriquez Monegal's *Jorge Luis Borges* (1978). Collections of critical essays covering a wide range of views on Borges's themes and forms can be found in Jaime Alazraki, ed., *Critical Essays on Jorge Luis Borges* (1987), and Lowell Dunham and Ivar Ivask, eds., *The Cardinal Points of Borges* (1971).

The Garden of Forking Paths

Translated by Donald A. Yates

On page 22 of Liddell Hart's *History of World War I* you will read that an attack against the Serre-Montauban line by thirteen British divisions (supported by 1,400 artillery pieces), planned for the 24th of July, 1916, had to be postponed until the morning of the 29th. The torrential rains, Captain Liddell Hart comments, caused this delay, an insignificant one, to be sure.

The following statement, dictated, reread and signed by Dr. Yu Tsun, former professor of English at the *Hochschule*[1] at Tsingtao, throws an unsuspected light over the whole affair. The first two pages of the document are missing.

"...and I hung up the receiver. Immediately afterwards, I recognized the voice that had answered in German. It was that of Captain Richard Madden. Madden's presence in Viktor Runeberg's apartment meant the end of our anxieties and—but this seemed, *or should have seemed*, very secondary to me—also the end of our lives. It meant that Runeberg had been arrested or murdered.[2] Before the sun set on that day, I would encounter the same fate. Madden was implacable. Or rather, he was obliged to be so. An Irishman at the service of England, a man accused of laxity and perhaps of treason, how could he fail to seize and be thankful for such a miraculous opportunity: the discovery, capture, maybe even the death of two agents of the German Reich? I went up to my room; absurdly I locked the door and threw myself on my back on the narrow iron cot. Through the window I saw the familiar roofs and the cloud-shaded six o'clock sun. It seemed incredible to me that that day without premonitions or symbols should be the one of my inexorable death. In spite of my dead father, in spite of having been a child in a symmetrical garden of Hai Feng, was I—now—going to die? Then I reflected that everything happens to a man precisely, precisely *now*. Centuries of centuries and only in the present do things happen; countless men in the air, on the face of the earth and the sea, and all that really is happening is happening to me... The almost intolerable recollection of Madden's horselike face banished these wanderings. In the midst of my hatred and terror (it means nothing to me now to speak of terror, now that I have mocked Richard Madden, now that my throat yearns for the noose) it occurred to me that that tumultuous and doubtless happy warrior did not suspect that I possessed the Secret. The name of the exact location of the new British artillery park on the River Ancre. A bird streaked across the gray sky and blindly I translated it into an airplane and that airplane into many (against the French sky) annihilating the artillery station with vertical bombs. If only my mouth, before a bullet shattered it, could cry out that secret name so it could be heard in Germany... My human voice was very weak. How might I make it carry to the ear of the Chief? To the ear of that sick and hateful man who knew nothing of Runeberg and me save that we were in Staffordshire and who was waiting in vain for our report in his arid office in Berlin, endlessly examining newspapers... I said out loud: *I must flee.* I sat up noiselessly, in a useless perfection of silence, as if Madden were already lying in wait for me. Something—perhaps the mere vain ostentation of proving my resources were nil—made me look through my pockets. I found what I knew I would find. The American watch, the nickel chain and the square coin, the key ring with the incriminating useless keys to Runeberg's apartment, the notebook, a letter which I resolved to destroy immediately (and which I did not destroy), a crown, two shillings and a few pence, the red and blue pencil, the handkerchief, the revolver with one bullet. Absurdly, I took it in my hand and weighed it in order to inspire courage within myself. Vaguely I thought that a pistol report can be heard at a great distance. In ten minutes my plan was perfected. The telephone book listed the name of the

---

[1] University (German).

[2] An hypothesis both hateful and odd. The Prussian spy Hans Rabener, alias Viktor Runeberg, attacked with drawn automatic the bearer of the warrant for his arrest, Captain Richard Madden. The latter, in self-defense, inflicted the wound which brought about Runeberg's death. (Editor's note.) [Borges provided this "Editor's note" as part of the story.]

only person capable of transmitting the message; he lived in a suburb of Fenton, less than a half hour's train ride away.

I am a cowardly man. I say it now, now that I have carried to its end a plan whose perilous nature no one can deny. I know its execution was terrible. I didn't do it for Germany, no. I care nothing for a barbarous country which imposed upon me the abjection of being a spy. Besides, I know of a man from England—a modest man—who for me is no less great than Goethe.[3] I talked with him for scarcely an hour, but during that hour he was Goethe . . . I did it because I sensed that the Chief somehow feared people of my race—for the innumerable ancestors who merge within me. I wanted to prove to him that a yellow man could save his armies. Besides, I had to flee from Captain Madden. His hands and his voice could call at my door at any moment. I dressed silently, bade farewell to myself in the mirror, went downstairs, scrutinized the peaceful street and went out. The station was not far from my home, but I judged it wise to take a cab. I argued that in this way I ran less risk of being recognized; the fact is that in the deserted street I felt myself visible and vulnerable, infinitely so. I remember that I told the cab driver to stop a short distance before the main entrance. I got out with voluntary, almost painful slowness; I was going to the village of Ashgrove but I bought a ticket for a more distant station. The train left within a very few minutes, at eight-fifty. I hurried; the next one would leave at nine-thirty. There was hardly a soul on the platform. I went through the coaches; I remember a few farmers, a woman dressed in mourning, a young boy who was reading with fervor the *Annals* of Tacitus,[4] a wounded and happy soldier. The coaches jerked forward at last. A man whom I recognized ran in vain to the end of the platform. It was Captain Richard Madden. Shattered, trembling, I shrank into the far corner of the seat, away from the dreaded window.

From this broken state I passed into an almost abject felicity. I told myself that the duel had already begun and that I had won the first encounter by frustrating, even if for forty minutes, even if by a stroke of fate, the attack of my adversary. I argued that this slightest of victories foreshadowed a total victory. I argued (no less fallaciously) that my cowardly felicity proved that I was a man capable of carrying out the adventure successfully. From this weakness I took strength that did not abandon me. I foresee that man will resign himself each day to more atrocious undertakings; soon there will be no one but warriors and brigands; I give them this counsel: *The author of an atrocious undertaking ought to imagine that he has already accomplished it, ought to impose upon himself a future as irrevocable as the past.* Thus I proceeded as my eyes of a man already dead registered the elapsing of that day, which was perhaps the last, and the diffusion of the night. The train ran gently along, amid ash trees. It stopped, almost in the middle of the fields. No one announced the name of the station. "Ashgrove?" I asked a few lads on the platform. "Ashgrove," they replied. I got off.

A lamp enlightened the platform but the faces of the boys were in shadow. One questioned me, "Are you going to Dr. Stephen Albert's house?" Without waiting for my answer, another said, "The house is a long way from here, but you won't get lost if you take this road to the left and at every crossroads turn again to your left." I tossed them a coin (my last), descended a few stone steps and started down the solitary road. It went downhill, slowly. It was of elemental earth; overhead the branches were tangled; the low, full moon seemed to accompany me.

---

[3]Johann Wolfgang von Goethe (1749–1832), a German writer.
[4]Roman historian (55–117 C.E.).

For an instant, I thought that Richard Madden in some way had penetrated my desperate plan. Very quickly, I understood that that was impossible. The instructions to turn always to the left reminded me that such was the common procedure for discovering the central point of certain labyrinths. I have some understanding of labyrinths: not for nothing am I the great grandson of that Ts'ui Pên who was governor of Yunnan and who renounced worldly power in order to write a novel that might be even more populous than the *Hung Lu Meng*[5] and to construct a labyrinth in which all men would become lost. Thirteen years he dedicated to these heterogeneous tasks, but the hand of a stranger murdered him—and his novel was incoherent and no one found the labyrinth. Beneath English trees I meditated on that lost maze: I imagined it inviolate and perfect at the secret crest of a mountain; I imagined it erased by rice fields or beneath the water; I imagined it infinite, no longer composed of octagonal kiosks and returning paths, but of rivers and provinces and kingdoms . . . I thought of a labyrinth of labyrinths, of one sinuous spreading labyrinth that would encompass the past and the future and in some way involve the stars. Absorbed in these illusory images, I forgot my destiny of one pursued. I felt myself to be, for an unknown period of time, an abstract perceiver of the world. The vague, living countryside, the moon, the remains of the day worked on me, as well as the slope of the road which eliminated any possibility of weariness. The afternoon was intimate, infinite. The road descended and forked among the now confused meadows. A high-pitched, almost syllabic music approached and receded in the shifting of the wind, dimmed by leaves and distance. I thought that a man can be an enemy of other men, of the moments of other men, but not of a country: not of fireflies, words, gardens, streams of water, sunsets. Thus I arrived before a tall, rusty gate. Between the iron bars I made out a poplar grove and a pavilion. I understood suddenly two things, the first trivial, the second almost unbelievable: the music came from the pavilion, and the music was Chinese. For precisely that reason I had openly accepted it without paying it any heed. I do not remember whether there was a bell or whether I knocked with my hand. The sparkling of the music continued.

From the rear of the house within a lantern approached: a lantern that the trees sometimes striped and sometimes eclipsed, a paper lantern that had the form of a drum and the color of the moon. A tall man bore it. I didn't see his face, for the light blinded me. He opened the door and said slowly, in my own language: "I see that the pious Hsi P'êng persists in correcting my solitude. You no doubt wish to see the garden?"

I recognized the name of one of our consuls and I replied, disconcerted, "The garden?"

"The garden of forking paths."

Something stirred in my memory and I uttered with incomprehensible certainty, "The garden of my ancestor Ts'ui Pên."

"Your ancestor? Your illustrious ancestor? Come in."

The damp path zigzagged like those of my childhood. We came to a library of Eastern and Western books. I recognized bound in yellow silk several volumes of the Lost Encyclopedia, edited by the Third Emperor of the Luminous Dynasty[6] but never printed. The record on the phonograph revolved next to a bronze phoenix.

---

[5] *The Dream of the Red Chamber* (1791), a long, very famous Chinese novel.
[6] The Yung-lo Emperor of the Ming Dynasty who commissioned an extensive encyclopedia in the fifteenth century.

I also recall a *famille rose*[7] vase and another, many centuries older, of that shade of blue which our craftsmen copied from the potters of Persia . . .

Stephen Albert observed me with a smile. He was, as I have said, very tall, sharp-featured, with gray eyes and a gray beard. He told me that he had been a missionary in Tientsin "before aspiring to become a Sinologist."

We sat down—I on a long, low divan, he with his back to the window and a tall circular clock. I calculated that my pursuer, Richard Madden, could not arrive for at least an hour. My irrevocable determination could wait.

"An astounding fate, that of Ts'ui Pên," Stephen Albert said. "Governor of his native province, learned in astronomy, in astrology and in the tireless interpretation of the canonical books, chess player, famous poet and calligrapher—he abandoned all this in order to compose a book and a maze. He renounced the pleasures of both tyranny and justice, of his populous couch, of his banquets and even of erudition— all to close himself up for thirteen years in the Pavilion of the Limpid Solitude. When he died, his heirs found nothing save chaotic manuscripts. His family, as you may be aware, wished to condemn them to the fire; but his executor—a Taoist or Buddhist monk—insisted on their publication."

"We descendants of Ts'ui Pên," I replied, "continue to curse that monk. Their publication was senseless. The book is an indeterminate heap of contradictory drafts. I examined it once: in the third chapter the hero dies, in the fourth he is alive. As for the other undertaking of Ts'ui Pên, his labyrinth . . ."

"Here is Ts'ui Pên's labyrinth," he said, indicating a tall lacquered desk.

"An ivory labyrinth!" I exclaimed. "A minimum labyrinth."

"A labyrinth of symbols," he corrected. "An invisible labyrinth of time. To me, a barbarous Englishman, has been entrusted the revelation of this diaphanous mystery. After more than a hundred years, the details are irretrievable; but it is not hard to conjecture what happened. Ts'ui Pên must have said once: *I am withdrawing to write a book.* And another time: *I am withdrawing to construct a labyrinth.* Every one imagined two works; to no one did it occur that the book and the maze were one and the same thing. The Pavilion of the Limpid Solitude stood in the center of a garden that was perhaps intricate; that circumstance could have suggested to the heirs a physical labyrinth. Ts'ui Pên died; no one in the vast territories that were his came upon the labyrinth; the confusion of the novel suggested to me that *it* was the maze. Two circumstances gave me the correct solution of the problem. One: the curious legend that Ts'ui Pên had planned to create a labyrinth which would be strictly infinite. The other: a fragment of a letter I discovered."

Albert rose. He turned his back on me for a moment; he opened a drawer of the black and gold desk. He faced me and in his hands he held a sheet of paper that had once been crimson, but was now pink and tenuous and cross-sectioned. The fame of Ts'ui Pên as a calligrapher had been justly won. I read, uncomprehendingly and with fervor, these words written with a minute brush by a man of my blood: *I leave to the various futures (not to all) my garden of forking paths.* Wordlessly, I returned the sheet. Albert continued:

"Before unearthing this letter, I had questioned myself about the ways in which a book can be infinite. I could think of nothing other than a cyclic volume, a circular one. A book whose last page was identical with the first, a book which had the possibility of continuing indefinitely. I remembered too that night which is at the middle of the Thousand and One Nights when Scheherezade (through a magical

---

[7]Pink family (French), referring to Chinese enamel ware.

oversight of the copyist) begins to relate word for word the story of the Thousand and One Nights, establishing the risk of coming once again to the night when she must repeat it, and thus on to infinity. I imagined as well a Platonic, hereditary work, transmitted from father to son, in which each new individual adds a chapter or corrects with pious care the pages of his elders. These conjectures diverted me; but none seemed to correspond, not even remotely, to the contradictory chapters of Ts'ui Pên. In the midst of this perplexity, I received from Oxford the manuscript you have examined. I lingered, naturally, on the sentence: *I leave to the various futures (not to all) my garden of forking paths.* Almost instantly, I understood: 'the garden of forking paths' was the chaotic novel; the phrase 'the various futures (not to all)' suggested to me the forking in time, not in space. A broad rereading of the work confirmed the theory. In all fictional works, each time a man is confronted with several alternatives, he chooses one and eliminates the others; in the fiction of Ts'ui Pên, he chooses—simultaneously—all of them. *He creates*, in this way, diverse futures, diverse times which themselves also proliferate and fork. Here, then, is the explanation of the novel's contradictions. Fang, let us say, has a secret; a stranger calls at his door; Fang resolves to kill him. Naturally, there are several possible outcomes: Fang can kill the intruder, the intruder can kill Fang, they both can escape, they both can die, and so forth. In the work of Ts'ui Pên, all possible outcomes occur; each one is the point of departure for other forkings. Sometimes, the paths of this labyrinth converge: for example, you arrive at this house, but in one of the possible pasts you are my enemy, in another, my friend. If you will resign yourself to my incurable pronunciation, we shall read a few pages."

His face, within the vivid circle of the lamplight, was unquestionably that of an old man, but with something unalterable about it, even immortal. He read with slow precision two versions of the same epic chapter. In the first, an army marches to a battle across a lonely mountain; the horror of the rocks and shadows makes the men undervalue their lives and they gain an easy victory. In the second, the same army traverses a palace where a great festival is taking place; the resplendent battle seems to them a continuation of the celebration and they win the victory. I listened with proper veneration to these ancient narratives, perhaps less admirable in themselves than the fact that they had been created by my blood and were being restored to me by a man of a remote empire, in the course of a desperate adventure, on a Western isle. I remember the last words, repeated in each version like a secret commandment: *Thus fought the heroes, tranquil their admirable hearts, violent their swords, resigned to kill and to die.*

From that moment on, I felt about me and within my dark body an invisible, intangible swarming. Not the swarming of the divergent, parallel and finally coalescent armies, but a more inaccessible, more intimate agitation that they in some manner prefigured. Stephen Albert continued:

"I don't believe that your illustrious ancestor played idly with these variations. I don't consider it credible that he would sacrifice thirteen years to the infinite execution of a rhetorical experiment. In your country, the novel is a subsidiary form of literature; in Ts'ui Pên's time it was a despicable form. Ts'ui Pên was a brilliant novelist, but he was also a man of letters who doubtless did not consider himself a mere novelist. The testimony of his contemporaries proclaims—and his life fully confirms—his metaphysical and mystical interests. Philosophic controversy usurps a good part of the novel. I know that of all problems, none disturbed him so greatly nor worked upon him so much as the abysmal problem of time. Now then, the latter is the only problem that does not figure in the pages of the *Garden*.

He does not even use the word that signifies *time*. How do you explain this voluntary omission?"

I proposed several solutions—all unsatisfactory. We discussed them. Finally, Stephen Albert said to me:

"In a riddle whose answer is chess, what is the only prohibited word?"

I thought a moment and replied, "The word *chess*."

"Precisely," said Albert. "*The Garden of Forking Paths* is an enormous riddle, or parable, whose theme is time; this recondite cause prohibits its mention. To omit a word always, to resort to inept metaphors and obvious periphrases, is perhaps the most emphatic way of stressing it. That is the tortuous method preferred, in each of the meanderings of his indefatigable novel, by the oblique Ts'ui Pên. I have compared hundreds of manuscripts, I have corrected the errors that the negligence of the copyists has introduced, I have guessed the plan of this chaos, I have re-established—I believe I have re-established—the primordial organization, I have translated the entire work: it is clear to me that not once does he employ the word 'time.' The explanation is obvious: *The Garden of Forking Paths* is an incomplete, but not false, image of the universe as Ts'ui Pên conceived it. In contrast to Newton and Schopenhauer,[8] your ancestor did not believe in a uniform, absolute time. He believed in an infinite series of times, in a growing, dizzying net of divergent, convergent and parallel times. This network of times which approached one another, forked, broke off, or were unaware of one another for centuries, embraces *all* possibilities of time. We do not exist in the majority of these times; in some you exist, and not I; in others I, and not you; in others, both of us. In the present one, which a favorable fate has granted me, you have arrived at my house; in another, while crossing the garden, you found me dead; in still another, I utter these same words, but I am a mistake, a ghost."

"In every one," I pronounced, not without a tremble to my voice, "I am grateful to you and revere you for your re-creation of the garden of Ts'ui Pên."

"Not in all," he murmured with a smile. "Time forks perpetually toward innumerable futures. In one of them I am your enemy."

Once again I felt the swarming sensation of which I have spoken. It seemed to me that the humid garden that surrounded the house was infinitely saturated with invisible persons. Those persons were Albert and I, secret, busy and multiform in other dimensions of time. I raised my eyes and the tenuous nightmare dissolved. In the yellow and black garden there was only one man; but this man was as strong as a statue . . . this man was approaching along the path and he was Captain Richard Madden.

"The future already exists," I replied, "but I am your friend. Could I see the letter again?"

Albert rose. Standing tall, he opened the drawer of the tall desk; for the moment his back was to me. I had readied the revolver. I fired with extreme caution. Albert fell uncomplainingly, immediately. I swear his death was instantaneous—a lightning stroke.

The rest is unreal, insignificant. Madden broke in, arrested me. I have been condemned to the gallows. I have won out abominably; I have communicated to Berlin the secret name of the city they must attack. They bombed it yesterday; I read it in the same papers that offered to England the mystery of the learned Sinologist

---

[8]Isaac Newton (1642–1727), an English mathematician; Arthur Schopenhauer (1788–1860), a German philosopher.

Stephen Albert who was murdered by a stranger, one Yu Tsun. The Chief had deciphered this mystery. He knew my problem was to indicate (through the uproar of the war) the city called Albert, and that I had found no other means to do so than to kill a man of that name. He does not know (no one can know) my innumerable contrition and weariness.

YASUNARI KAWABATA
[1899–1972]

One of Japan's most highly praised, if most difficult, modern writers, Yasunari Kawabata has found an enthusiastic audience in the West as well as in Japan. In 1968 he was the first Japanese writer to win the Nobel Prize for literature. In addition to short stories, novels, and literature for children, Kawabata has also written major critical works on the novel and numerous essays and reviews. In his fiction Kawabata proves to be a master of subtle imagery, writing in a hauntingly lyrical and delicate prose that lends itself readily to the short story or novella, for which he has been highly praised. The poetic density of his writing is sustained in his novels, such as *Snow Country* and *The Master of Go,* for which he is primarily known in the West.

LIFE

Yasunari Kawabata was born in Osaka, June 11, 1899, the son of a physician who died when Kawabata was only two years old, the first of a series of untimely deaths that left the boy without a family by age fourteen. A diary, *Jūrokusai no nikki,* published in 1925 but recounting twelve days in May 1914, describes his difficult experience of attending the slow and painful death of his demanding grandfather, with whom he had lived since the death of his grandmother nine years before. He had lost his mother when he was three and his sister when he was nine. The loneliness and longing of many of his stories are no doubt linked to these traumatic events; of his childhood, Kawabata writes, "Perhaps it is because I was an orphan with nowhere I could call home that I have never lost my taste for melancholic wanderings. I am always dreaming, though I never manage to forget myself in any dream. I am awake even as I dream but I cover this up with my taste for back-streets."

Despite having to attend to his grandfather, Kawabata completed school in Osaka, then went on to Tokyo for the equivalent of high school and enrolled in Tokyo Imperial University. Already steeped in the Japanese classics, Kawabata studied Japanese literature; published his first story, heavily influenced by European modernism, in 1921; and became a leading figure in the literary avant-garde while serving on the staff of *Bungei Shunju,* a journal edited by Kan Kikuchi. In 1926, the year after his graduation, Kawabata published his first novel, the partly autobiographical *The Izu Dancer (Izu no Odoriko).* At the time of publishing this story about a young student who falls in love with a fourteen-year-old daughter of traveling entertainers, Kawabata had already attracted the attention of the literary world with his short stories; but this novel—a novella—was his first popular success and clinched his literary reputation. With another novelist, Riichi Yokomitsu, Kawabata later founded *Bungei Jidai,* a literary magazine associated with the Neo-sensualist movement, or *Shin Kan-kaku-ha,* an avant-garde group that preferred aesthetic values and emotional delicacy in literature to the scientific realism and naturalism that dominated the Japanese literary scene in the 1920s. Groundbreaking in their use of free association and stream-of-consciousness, Kawabata's early novels offer in theme and technique an intriguing blend of traditional Japanese fiction and European modernism, filtered through the transforming art of a self-conscious and delicate craftsman. Unlike such cosmopolitan writers as Yukio Mishima and filmmaker Akira Kurosawa, Kawabata soon minimized the Western elements of his work, but one senses even in his later fiction the influence of the Neo-sensualist days and his early experiments in stream-of-consciousness technique, surrealism, cubism, and dadaism. His most modernist work is the unfinished *Crystal Fantasies* (*Suisho Genso*, 1931), written during a short period of fascination with James Joyce's *Ulysses*, which he read first in Japanese and then in English.

Throughout the thirties Kawabata published short stories, bringing out a collection titled *Of Birds and Beasts* (*Kinjū*) in 1933 and a partly completed novel, *Snow Country* (*Yukiguni*), in 1937 (completed in 1947). *Snow Country*, his most famous novel, like *The Izu Dancer*, evokes a sense of sadness and loneliness tinged with a lyrical eroticism that characterizes Kawabata's work as a whole. Negotiating the boundaries of *eros* and *thanatos*, love and death, the motif of refined melancholy goes back to the Japanese classics, such as *The Tale of Genji*, which Kawabata read during the war. After Japan's defeat, Kawabata wrote, "Since Japan has surrendered the only thing left for me to do is to return to the traditional sorrow of spirit of the Japanese people." That sorrow of spirit is the *mono-no-aware*, a delicate sense of the fleetingness of life and love. *Snow Country* tells the story of Shimamura, a wealthy man from Tokyo, and Komako, an aging geisha; and its episodic structure, its scenes of delicate encounter, and its mood are reminiscent of the structure and sensibility of *Genji*.

In his postwar novel *Thousand Cranes* (*Sembazuru*, 1949), Kawabata writes about his beloved tea ceremony (he was a collector of items used in the ancient tea ceremonies), which, despite his stated intentions, becomes an elaborate metaphor for the pursuit of beauty in life. Two other postwar novels, *The Master of Go* (*Meijin*, 1954) and *The Lake* (*Mizuumi*, 1954), also concern the pursuit of beauty. In the case of the latter, that pursuit takes on a somewhat bizarre form in the character of a retired teacher who compulsively and surreptitiously spies on beautiful women. This kind of eroticism, bordering on the perverse, appears again in *House of the Sleeping Beauties* (*Nemureru bijo*, 1961), in which the protagonist Eguchi, an old man, spends the night in a secret establishment that caters to his need to sleep with beautiful young girls, who are drugged for the purpose. His friend and fellow novelist Yukio Mishima called this story an "esoteric masterpiece," a story that "is dominated not by openness and clarity but by a strangling tightness." The reader of this story, Mishima writes, "knows with the greatest immediacy the terror of lust urged on by the approach of death." Rather than a tale of sexual perversion, however, Kawabata evokes a tragic sense of the gap between the elderly man's proximity to death, his decrepitude and ugliness, the vitality and beauty of the young women. One critic has suggested that Kawabata is a master at "dredging . . . the sexual depths" of human experience, and that the lyrical quality of his work, along with its emphasis on the larger issues of life's transience and the melancholy character of human experience, rescues the novels from any misguided charges of prurience or pornography. Indeed, here too Kawabata displays his traditionalism in capturing the essence of the "floating world," the realm of the senses that ground us in life and fill us with regret at its temporality. Another work of the 1950s, *The Sound of the Mountain* (*Yama no Oto*, 1954), which some have called Kawabata's greatest achievement, also focuses upon an elderly man's tragic awareness of his mortality. In associating beauty with melancholy, Kawabata is reminiscent of the English poet John Keats; the hauntingly lyric quality of Kawabata's short stories and novels, their eroticism and their obscurity, invite other comparisons to European romanticism.

In 1948 Kawabata had become president of the Japanese P.E.N. club and was highly regarded and rewarded for his work. In 1937 he had won the *Bungei Konwa Kai* prize, and in 1952 he won the *Geijutsuin-sho* literary prize and an award from the Japanese Academy of Arts. From the 1920s through the 1960s he published over 146 short short stories, or *tanagokor no shosetsu* ("stories that fit in the palm of the hand"), short fiction, critical essays, and autobiographical works. Many of these were collected in edited editions, but relatively few have been translated into English. Among Kawabata's later works translated into English are *Beauty and Sadness* (*Utsukushisa to kanashimi to,* 1965); his Nobel Prize acceptance speech, *Japan the Beautiful and Myself* (*Utsukushii Nihon no watakushi,* 1969); and *The Existence and Discovery of Beauty* (*Bi no sonzai to hakken,* 1969). In 1961 he won the *Bunka Kunsho* (Cultural Decoration), Japan's most distinguished award, for *The Old Capital* (*Koto,* 1961) and in that year *House of the Sleeping Beauties* won the Mainichi Cultural Prize. In the sixties Kawabata traveled through Europe and the United States, receiving the Nobel Prize for literature in 1968. In 1971 Kawabata made a rare move by actively entering into politics, as a supporter of a conservative candidate for governor of Tokyo. For unknown reasons, he committed suicide in his studio in April 1972, nearly a year after the suicide of his friend Yukio Mishima, over whose funeral ceremonies Kawabata presided.

WORK

"The Moon on the Water" ("Suigetsu," 1953) captures the essence of Kawabata's work through its theme of hopeless longing, its subtle evocation of the beautiful amidst the most melancholic conditions, and its lyrical language and poetic imagery. The love that can never be grasped, that seems to fly on the wing, like Kyōko's love for her dying husband, is shown here to be more powerful and pure than that which she can bestow upon her second husband. Moreover, Kawabata shows the inseparability of love from melancholy, of youth from age, of desire from death, as the first husband who longs to watch his beautiful wife in the garden must inevitably look upon his own ghastly face in the mirror that gives him access to her beauty and vitality. Moreover, there is a kind of tragic sense of loneliness and detachment as her first husband voyeuristically takes in the world through the mirror—the place of his desire being a mere reflection, or simulacrum, of the palpable world Kyōko experiences. Yet even Kyōko recognizes "the richness of the world in the mirror," which becomes a focal point of her conversation with her husband and seems nearly to displace her world as a primary reality. Like a work of art, the world in the mirror takes on a life of its own, a life that is somehow purer, more beautiful, than the actual world that it reflects. Of this story, the words of Kawabata's friend Yukio Mishima seem appropriate: Kawabata has created, Mishima says, a "decadent literature which has a perfect formal beauty and which has a fragrance reminiscent of the rotting smell of overripe fruit." For beauty, and even life, finds its most intense expression at the moment it begins to give way to decrepitude and death. In Kawabata's fiction the dying man or woman has the greatest appreciation of beauty, here represented in the purity of the intangible world in the mirror, and in the dying man's longing, captured in the doubly mediated image of the moon's image in the pool reflected in his mirror. It is that reflection of a reflection that Kyōko keeps in her heart after her husband's death.

SUGGESTED READINGS

No single book in English focuses upon the life or work of Kawabata, but his novels and stories are discussed in the context of other Japanese works. Donald Keene's chapter on Kawabata in *Dawn to the West: Japanese Literature of the Modern Era—Fiction* (1984) discusses Kawabata's major works in relation to his life. In *Accomplices of Silence: The Modern Japanese Novel* (1974), Masao Miyoshi analyzes Kawabata's style and its relationship to the European avant-garde; and Makoto Ueda's *Modern Japanese Writers and the Nature of Literature* (1976) offers a more general discussion of his work. Gwenn Boardman Petersen analyzes the symbolism of Kawabata's story in *The Moon on the Water: Understanding Tanizaki, Kawabata, and Mishima* (1979). Many article-length studies of Kawabata's fiction appear in English, including Sandra Buckley's "Kawabata Yasunari's Poetics of Fragmentation: Now You See Her Now You Don't," in *Discours Social/Social Discourse* (Winter 1988), James T. Araki's "Kawabata: Achievements of the Nobel Laureate," *World Literature Today* (Spring 1989), and Sidney Brown's "Yasunari Kawabata: Tradition versus Modernity," *World Literature Today* (Summer 1988). For our story in particular, see Kinya Tsuruta's "Kawabata's Use of Irony: An Analysis of 'The Moon on the Water,'" *Par Rapport: A Journal of the Humanities* (1982–1983).

The Moon on the Water

Translated by George Saitō

It occurred to Kyōko one day to let her husband, in bed upstairs, see her vegetable garden by reflecting it in her hand mirror. To one who had been so long confined, this opened a new life. The hand mirror was part of a set in Kyōko's trousseau. The mirror stand was not very big. It was made of mulberry wood, as was the frame of the mirror itself. It was the hand mirror that still reminded her of the bashfulness of her early married years when, as she was looking into it at the reflection of her back hair in the stand mirror, her sleeve would slip and expose her elbow.

When she came from the bath, her husband seemed to enjoy reflecting the nape of her neck from all angles in the hand mirror. Taking the mirror from her, he would say: "How clumsy you are! Here, let me hold it." Maybe he found something new in the mirror. It was not that Kyōko was clumsy, but that she became nervous at being looked at from behind.

Not enough time had passed for the color of the mulberry-wood frame to change. It lay in a drawer. War came, followed by flight from the city and her husband's becoming seriously ill; by the time it first occurred to Kyōko to have her husband see the garden through the mirror, its surface had become cloudy and the rim had been smeared with face powder and dirt. Since it still reflected well enough, Kyōko did not worry about this cloudiness— indeed she scarcely noticed it. Her husband, however, would not let the mirror go from his bedside and polished it and its frame in his idleness with the peculiar nervousness of an invalid. Kyōko sometimes imagined that tuberculosis germs had found their way into the imperceptible cracks in the frame. After she had combed her husband's hair with a little camellia oil, he sometimes ran the palm of his hand through his hair and then rubbed the mirror. The wood of the mirror stand remained dull, but that of the mirror grew lustrous.

When Kyōko married again, she took the same mirror stand with her. The hand mirror, however, had been buried in the coffin of her dead husband. A hand mirror with a carved design had now taken its place. She never told her second husband about this.

According to custom, the hands of her dead husband had been clasped and his fingers crossed, so that it was impossible to make them hold the hand mirror after he had been put into the coffin. She laid the mirror on his chest.

"Your chest hurt you so. Even this must be heavy."

Kyōko moved the mirror down to his stomach. Because she thought of the important role that the mirror had played in their marital life, Kyōko had first laid it on his chest. She wanted to keep this little act as much as possible from the eyes even of her husband's family. She had piled white chrysanthemums on the mirror. No one had noticed it. When the ashes were being gathered after the cremation, people noticed the glass which had been melted into a shapeless mass, partly sooty and partly yellowish. Someone said: "It's glass. What is it, I wonder?" She had in fact placed a still smaller mirror on the hand mirror. It was the sort of mirror usually carried in a toilet case, a long, narrow, double-faced mirror. Kyōko had dreamed of using it on her honeymoon trip. The war had made it impossible for them to go on a honeymoon. During her husband's lifetime she never was able to use it on a trip.

With her second husband, however, she went on a honeymoon. Since her leather toilet case was now very musty, she bought a new one—with a mirror in it too.

On the very first day of their trip, her husband touched Kyōko and said: "You are like a little girl. Poor thing!" His tone was not in the least sarcastic. Rather it suggested unexpected joy. Possibly it was good for him that Kyōko was like a little girl. At this remark, Kyōko was assailed by an intense sorrow. Her eyes filled with tears and she shrank away. He might have taken that to be girlish too.

Kyōko did not know whether she had wept for her own sake or for the sake of her dead husband. Nor was it possible to know. The moment this idea came to her, she felt very sorry for her second husband and thought she had to be coquettish.

"Am I so different?" No sooner had she spoken than she felt very awkward, and shyness came over her.

He looked satisfied and said: "You never had a child..."

His remark pierced her heart. Before a male force other than her former husband Kyōko felt humiliated. She was being made sport of.

"But it was like looking after a child all the time."

This was all she said by way of protest. It was as if her first husband, who had died after a long illness, had been a child inside her. But if he was to die in any case, what good had her continence done?

"I've only seen Mori from the train window." Her second husband drew her to him as he mentioned the name of her home town. "From its name,[1] it sounds like a pretty town in the woods. How long did you live there?"

"Until I graduated from high school. Then I was drafted to work in a munitions factory in Sanjō."

"Is Sanjō near, then? I've heard a great deal about Sanjō beauties. I see why you're so beautiful."

"No, I'm not." Kyōko brought her hand to her throat.

"Your hands are beautiful, and I thought your body should be beautiful too."

"Oh no."

Finding her hands in the way, Kyōko quietly drew them back.

"I'm sure I'd have married you even if you had had a child. I could have adopted the child and looked after it. A girl would have been better," he whispered in Kyōko's ear. Maybe it was because he had a boy, but his remark seemed odd even as an expression of love. Possibly he had planned the long, ten-day honeymoon so that she would not have to face the stepson quite so soon.

Her husband had a toilet case for traveling, made of what seemed to be good leather. Kyōko's did not compare with it. His was large and strong, but it was not new. Maybe because he often traveled or because he took good care of it, the

---

[1] *Mori* means "grove."

case had a mellow luster. Kyōko thought of the old case, never used, which she had left to mildew. Only its small mirror had been used by her first husband, and she had sent it with him in death.

The small glass had melted into the hand mirror, so that no one except Kyoko could tell that they had been separate before. Since Kyōko had not said that the curious mass had been mirrors, her relatives had no way of knowing.

Kyōko felt as if the numerous worlds reflected in the two mirrors had vanished in the fire. She felt the same kind of loss when her husband's body was reduced to ashes. It had been with the hand mirror that came with the mirror stand that Kyōko first reflected the vegetable garden. Her husband always kept that mirror beside his pillow. Even the hand mirror seemed to be too heavy for the invalid, and Kyōko, worried about his arms and shoulders, gave him a lighter and smaller one.

It was not only Kyōko's vegetable garden that her husband had observed through the two mirrors. He had seen the sky, clouds, snow, distant mountains, and nearby woods. He had seen the moon. He had seen wild flowers, and birds of passage had made their way through the mirror. Men walked down the road in the mirror and children played in the garden.

Kyōko was amazed at the richness of the world in the mirror. A mirror which had until then been regarded only as a toilet article, a hand mirror which had served only to show the back of one's neck, had created for the invalid a new life. Kyōko used to sit beside his bed and talk about the world in the mirror. They looked into it together. In the course of time it became impossible for Kyōko to distinguish between the world that she saw directly and the world in the mirror. Two separate worlds came to exist. A new world was created in the mirror and it came to seem like the real world.

"The sky shines silver in the mirror," Kyōko said. Looking up through the window, she added: "When the sky itself is grayish." The sky in the mirror lacked the leaden and heavy quality of the actual sky. It was shining.

"Is it because you are always polishing the mirror?"

Though he was lying down, her husband could see the sky by turning his head.

"Yes, it's a dull gray. But the color of the sky is not necessarily the same to dogs' eyes and sparrows' eyes as it is to human eyes. You can't tell which eyes see the real color."

"What we see in the mirror—is that what the mirror eye sees?"

Kyōko wanted to call it the eye of their love. The trees in the mirror were a fresher green than real trees, and the lilies a purer white.

"This is the print of your thumb, Kyōko. Your right thumb."

He pointed to the edge of the mirror. Kyōko was somehow startled. She breathed on the mirror and erased the fingerprint.

"That's all right, Kyōko. Your fingerprint stayed on the mirror when you first showed me the vegetable garden."

"I didn't notice it."

"You may not have noticed it. Thanks to this mirror, I've memorized the prints of your thumbs and index fingers. Only an invalid could memorize his wife's fingerprints."

Her husband had done almost nothing but lie in bed since their marriage. He had not gone to war. Toward the end of the war he had been drafted, but he fell ill after several days of labor at an airfield and came home at the end of the war. Since he was unable to walk, Kyōko went with his elder brother to meet him. After her husband had been drafted, she stayed with her parents. They had left the city to avoid the bombings. Their household goods had long since been sent away. As the house where their married life began had been burned down, they had rented a room in the home of a friend of Kyōko's. From there her husband commuted to his office. A month in their honeymoon house and two months at the house of a friend—that was all the time Kyōko spent with her husband before he fell ill.

It was then decided that her husband should rent a small house in the mountains and convalesce there. Other families had been in the house, also fugitives from the city, but they had gone back to Tokyo after the war ended, and Kyōko took over their vegetable garden. It was only some six yards square, a clearing in the weeds. They could easily have bought vegetables, but Kyōko worked in the garden. She became interested in vegetables grown by her own hand. It was not that she wanted to stay away from her sick husband, but such things as sewing and knitting made her gloomy. Even though she thought of him always, she had brighter hopes when she was out in the garden. There she could indulge her love for her husband. As for reading, it was all she could do to read aloud at his bedside. Then Kyōko thought that by working in the garden she might regain that part of herself which it seemed she was losing in the fatigue of the long nursing.

It was in the middle of September that they moved to the mountains. The summer visitors had almost all gone and a long spell of early autumn rains came, chilly and damp.

One afternoon the sun came out to the clear song of a bird. When she went into the garden, she found the green vegetables shining. She was enraptured by the rosy clouds on the mountain tops. Startled by her husband's voice calling her, she hurried upstairs, her hands covered with mud, and found him breathing painfully.

"I called and called. Couldn't you hear me?"

"I'm sorry. I couldn't."

"Stop working in the garden. I'd be dead in no time if I had to keep calling you like that. In the first place, I can't see where you are and what you're doing."

"I was in the garden. But I'll stop."

He was calmer.

"Did you hear the lark?"

That was all he had wanted to tell her. The lark sang in the nearby woods again. The woods were clear against the evening glow. Thus Kyōko learned to know the song of the lark.

"A bell will help you, won't it? How about having something you can throw until I get a bell for you?"

"Shall I throw a cup from here? That would be fun."

It was settled that Kyōko might continue her gardening; but it was after spring had come to end the long, harsh mountain winter that Kyōko thought of showing him the garden in the mirror.

The single mirror gave him inexhaustible joy, as if a lost world of fresh green had come back. It was impossible for him to see the worms she picked from the vegetables. She had to come upstairs to show him. "I can see the earthworms from here, though," he used to say as he watched her digging in the earth.

When the sun was shining into the house, Kyōko sometimes noticed a light and, looking up, discovered that her husband was reflecting the sun in the mirror. He insisted that Kyōko remake the dark-blue kimono he had used during his student days into pantaloons for herself. He seemed to enjoy the sight of Kyōko in the mirror as she worked in the garden, wearing the dark blue with its white splashes.

Kyōko worked in the garden half-conscious and half-unconscious of the fact that she was being seen. Her heart warmed to see how different her feelings were now from the very early days of her marriage. Then she had blushed even at showing her elbow when she held the smaller glass behind her head. It was, however, only when she remarried that she started making up as she pleased, released from the long years of nursing and the mourning that had followed. She saw that she was becoming remarkably beautiful. It now seemed that her husband had really meant it when he said that her body was beautiful.

Kyōko was no longer ashamed of her reflection in the mirror—after she had had a bath, for instance. She had discovered her own beauty. But she had not lost that unique feeling that her former husband had planted in her toward the beauty in the mirror. She did not doubt the beauty she was in the mirror. Quite the reverse: she could not doubt the reality of that other world. But between her skin as she saw it and her skin as reflected in the mirror she could not find the difference that she had found between that leaden sky and the silver sky in the mirror. It may not have been only the difference in distance. Maybe the longing of her first husband confined to his bed had acted upon her. But then, there was now no way of knowing how beautiful she had looked to him in the mirror as she worked in the garden. Even before his death, Kyōko herself had not been able to tell.

Kyōko thought of, indeed longed for, the image of herself working in the garden, seen through the mirror in her husband's hand, and for the white of the lilies, the crowd of village children playing in the field, and the morning sun rising above the far-off snowy mountains—for that separate world she had shared with him. For the sake of her present husband, Kyōko suppressed this feeling, which seemed about to become an almost physical yearning, and tried to take it for something like a distant view of the celestial world.

One morning in May, Kyōko heard the singing of wild birds over the radio. It was a broadcast from a mountain near the heights where she had stayed with her first husband until his death. As had become her custom, after seeing her present husband off to work, Kyōko took the hand mirror from the drawer of the stand and reflected the clear sky. Then she gazed at her face in the mirror. She was astonished by a new discovery. She could not see her own face unless she reflected it in the mirror. One could not see one's own face. One felt one's own face, wondering if the face in the mirror was one's actual face. Kyōko was lost in thought for some time. Why had God created man's face so that he might not see it himself?

"Suppose you could see your own face, would you lose your mind? Would you become incapable of acting?"

Most probably man had evolved in such a way that he could not see his own face. Maybe dragonflies and praying mantises could see their own faces.

But then perhaps one's own face was for others to see. Did it not resemble love? As she was putting the hand mirror back in the drawer, Kyōko could not even now help noticing the odd combination of carved design and mulberry. Since the former mirror had burned with her first husband, the mirror stand might well be compared to a widow. But the hand mirror had had its advantages and disadvantages. Her husband was constantly seeing his face in it. Perhaps it was more like seeing death itself. If his death was a psychological suicide by means of a mirror, then Kyōko was the psychological murderer. Kyōko had once thought of the disadvantages of the mirror, and tried to take it from him. But he would not let her.

"Do you intend to have me see nothing? As long as I live, I want to keep loving something I can see," her husband said. He would have sacrificed his life to keep the world in the mirror. After heavy rains they would gaze at the moon through the mirror, the reflection of the moon from the pool in the garden. A moon which could hardly be called even the reflection of a reflection still lingered in Kyōko's heart.

"A sound love dwells only in a sound person." When her second husband said this, Kyōko nodded shyly, but she could not entirely agree with him. When her first husband died, Kyōko wondered what good her continence had done; but soon the continence became a poignant memory of love, a memory of days brimming with love, and her regrets quite disappeared. Probably her second husband regarded woman's love too lightly. "Why did you leave your wife, when you are such a tender-hearted man?" Kyōko would ask him. He never answered. Kyōko had married him because the elder brother of her dead husband had insisted. After four months as friends they were married. He was fifteen years older.

When she became pregnant, Kyōko was so terrified that her very face changed. "I'm afraid. I'm afraid." She clung to her husband. She suffered intensely from morning sickness and she even became deranged. She crawled into the garden barefooted and gathered pine needles. She had her stepson carry two lunch boxes to school, both boxes filled with rice. She sat staring blankly into the mirror, thinking that she saw straight through it. She rose in the middle of night, sat on the bed, and looked into her husband's sleeping face. Assailed by terror at the knowledge that man's life is a trifle, she found herself loosening the sash of her night robe. She made as if to strangle him. The next moment she was sobbing hysterically. Her husband awoke and retied her sash gently. She shivered in the summer night.

"Trust the child in you, Kyōko." Her husband rocked her in his arms.

The doctor suggested that she be hospitalized. Kyōko resisted, but was finally persuaded.

"I will go to the hospital. Please let me go first to visit my family for a few days."

Some time later her husband took her to her parents' home. The next day Kyōko slipped out of the house and went to the heights where she had lived with her first husband. It was early in September, ten days earlier than when she had moved there with him. Kyōko felt like vomiting. She was dizzy in the train and obsessed by an impulse to jump off. As the train passed the station on the heights, the crisp air brought her relief. She regained control of herself, as if the devil possessing her had gone. She stopped, bewildered, and looked at the mountains surrounding the high plateau. The outline of the blue mountains where the color was not growing darker was vivid against the sky, and she felt in them a living world. Wiping her eyes, moist with warm tears, she walked toward the house where he and she had lived. From the woods which had loomed against the rosy evening glow that day there came again the song of a lark. Someone was living in the house and a white lace curtain hung at the window upstairs. Not going too near, she gazed at the house.

"What if the child should look like you?" Startled at her own words, she turned back, warm and at peace.

PABLO NERUDA
[1904–1973]

Not only is Pablo Neruda considered one of the greatest poets to write in Spanish, he is also one of the finest poets of the twentieth century writing in any language. Like Walt Whitman, who had a passionate love for the United States, its people and places, Neruda wrote with an unabashed devotion to his native Chile. His poems are rooted in the soil and sea of Chile as were his political loyalties, and they helped bring the people of Chile and Latin America a sense of an identity distinct from Europe and the United States. Even after winning a number of international peace and literary prizes, including the Nobel Prize in literature, he did not become widely known or popular in the United States, perhaps because of his bold mixture of leftist politics and poetry. In his later years, without relinquishing his Chilean roots, Neruda became engaged in a search for those bonds that would reach across national boundaries and draw men and women together into a joint human enterprise.

LIFE

He was born July 12, 1904, with the name Ricardo Eliezer Neftalí Reyes y Basoalto in the southern Chilean town of Parral. He spent his childhood in the small town of Temuco, situated in a lush environment of dense forests that later fed the imagery of his poems. His father, José del Carmen Reyes, was a railroad worker. His mother, Rosa de Basoalto, died when Pablo was three or four years old. After attending schools in his hometown, Neruda at age sixteen moved to the capital city of Santiago, where he studied literature at the Instituto Pedagógica in the early 1920s. His five books of poetry between 1923 and 1926, especially *Veinte poemas de amor y una canción desesperada (Twenty Love Poems and a Song of Despair,* 1924), brought him national recognition as a young writer. Fear of ridicule from his family, however, led him to adopt a pseudonym; the name *Neruda* was borrowed from a nineteenth-century Czech writer.

Like other Latin American countries, Chile rewards its writers with diplomatic posts, and for over fifteen years Neruda was a Chilean consul in various countries. At age twenty-three he was sent to Southeast Asia. In 1933 he was assigned to Buenos Aires, and then Madrid, where *Residencia en la tierra (Residence on Earth)* parts I and II were published in 1935 with much acclaim and the admiration of Spanish poets. When the Spanish Civil War broke out in 1936 and his friend, the brilliant poet García Lorca, was executed, Neruda became outspokenly anti-Fascist and his poems of this period were angry and sad. He was recalled by the Chilean government, then reassigned to aid Republican Spanish refugees. He was the Chilean consul to Mexico from 1939 to 1943 before returning to Santiago, where he became a member of the central committee of the Chilean Communist Party and was elected to the Senate. In a series of letters beginning in 1947, he accused Chile's president, Gonzalez Videla, of betraying his country to the United States. When Neruda lost his case against Videla before Chile's Supreme Court and when Communism was declared illegal by an act of Chile's Congress, Neruda was forced into exile and traveled in Mexico, France, Italy, the Soviet Union, and China.

A major collection of poems, *Canto general (General Song,* 1950)—340 poems in 15 sections—brought Neruda the world's attention with its depiction of Latin American history, geography, and the politics of dictators. He raised the hackles of government officials in the United States with his description of the exploitation of Latin American people and resources by huge companies such as the United Fruit Company. Neruda himself believed in the people of the United States even when he criticized U.S. corporations and politics. A few years earlier, he had paid tribute to American writers, the American frontier, and Abraham Lincoln in "Let the Rail Splitter Awake" (1948), expressing the belief that the United States has a common destiny with the rest of the Americas. At the center of *Canto general* is a visionary sequence of poems, *The Heights of Machu Picchu,* that resulted from a pilgrimage to the ancient Incan stronghold in the Peruvian Andes. Celebrated all over the world, especially in the socialist world, Neruda then used a simpler voice as a means of reaching the working classes of Latin America and produced his charming *Odas elementales (Elemental Odes,* 1954 and 1956).

Settling in his famous house, Isla Negra, on the Pacific coast of Chile, Neruda wrote almost a volume of poetry per year during the 1950s and 1960s, carrying on a love affair with the people of Chile and cultivating a wide circle of fellow poets throughout the world. His voice mellowed and his attitudes toward life were more celebratory. He was appointed the Chilean ambassador to France when Salvador Allende was elected president of Chile in 1970. Chile declared a national holiday when he was awarded the Nobel Prize in 1971. In poor health, Neruda returned to Chile in 1973 and died in a Santiago clinic on September 23, 1973, heartbroken by the military coup that had toppled Allende. His prose memoirs, *Confieso que he vivido: Memorias* (*I Confess I Have Lived: Autobiography;* published as *Memoirs* in English in 1977), and eight additional volumes of poetry were published in 1974.

WORK

Despite his active commitment to politics, Neruda's poetic output was enormous; a 1962 edition of his poems in small print ran to 1,832 pages. As a child he announced, "I'm going out to hunt poems," and he was enormously successful. The genius of his poetry lies in its earthy imagery, the use of all the senses to create a strong and vigorous language. Neruda was instrumental in helping to free other Latin American writers from artificial restraint and cerebral quaintness. With *Residencia en la tierra* he proclaimed his devotion to a world of real objects, and like Walt Whitman he loved to make lists, as in these lines from "Sexual Water":

> I see a long summer and a death rattle coming out
>   of a granary.
> Cellars, cicadas,
> Towns, stimuli,
> Habitations, girl children
> Sleeping with hands on their hearts,
> Dreaming with pirates, with fire,
> I see ships,
> I see trees of spinal cord
> Bristling like furious cats...
>   —TRANSLATED BY H. R. HAYS

Of the selected poems below, "Ode with a Lament" and "Alberto Rojas Jimenez Comes Flying" are from *Residence on Earth*. Neruda's poetry of this period has been described as surrealistic, meaning that the poems contain a stream of images linked by chance or dream. But "Ode with a Lament" creates many moods through a dazzling combination of traditional poetic images with mundane, prosaic images. Death is a common theme in Neruda's poetry, and "Alberto Rojas Jimenez Comes Flying," one of Neruda's most popular poems, is an incredibly energetic evocation of a dead man's spirit, while at the same time a critique of modern life. "Ode of the Sun to the People's Army," published in *España en el Corazón* (*Spain in the Heart,* 1937), is the last poem in a series of hymns to Spanish people. It uses a bold and spirited voice to rally the Republican forces in the Spanish Civil War. The intellectuals and artists of Spanish America were deeply affected by the Spanish Civil War, which came to symbolize the struggle for human dignity and freedom. The realistic language of "The United Fruit Co." leads to a direct indictment of dictators and ruthless corporations. The concluding stanza about the exploitation of Indians is similar to a number of other Latin American writings that use the plight of the Indian in the Americas to signify the evil of European colonialism.

SUGGESTED READINGS

For a sympathetic biography by one of Neruda's friends, see Volodia Teitelboim's *Neruda: An Intimate Biography* (1991). General introductions to Neruda's poetry are in René de Costa's *The Poetry of Pablo Neruda* (1979) and Enrico Mario Santi's *Pablo Neruda, The Poetics of Prophecy* (1982). Two books that comment on Neruda's unique use of language and imagery are Manuel Duran and Margery Safir's *Earth Tones: The Poetry of Pablo Neruda* (1981) and Frank Riess's *The Word and the Stone: Language and Imagery in Neruda's Canto General* (1972). Neruda's connection with Chile is explored in Selden Rodman's "Pablo Neruda's Chile," *South America of the Poets* (1970).

Ode with a Lament

Translated by H. R. Hays

O girl among the roses, O pressure of doves,
O citadel of fishes and rosebushes,
Your soul is a bottle full of dry salt
And your skin is a bell full of grapes.

Unfortunately I have nothing to give you except fingernails
Or eyelashes, or melted pianos,
Or dreams which pour from my heart in torrents,
Dusty dreams that race like black riders,
Dreams full of speed and affliction.

I can only love you with kisses and poppies,   10
With garlands wet by the rain,
Gazing at yellow dogs and horses red as ashes.

I can only love you with waves behind me,
Between wandering gusts of sulphur and pensive waters,
Swimming toward cemeteries that flow in certain
     rivers
With wet pasturage growing above sad tombs of
     plaster,
Swimming through submerged hearts
And pale catalogues of unburied children.
There is much death, many funereal events
In my forsaken passions and desolate kisses,   20
There is a water that falls on my head,
While my hair grows,
A water like time, a black torrential water,
With a nocturnal voice, with a cry
Of a bird in the rain, like an interminable
Shadow of a wet wing sheltering my bones,
While I dress myself, while
Interminably I look at myself in mirrors and windows,
I hear someone calling me, calling me with sobs,
With a sad voice rotted by time.   30

You are on foot, on the earth, full
Of fangs and lightings.
You generate kisses and you kill ants.
You weep with health, with onions, with bees,
With burning alphabet.
You are like a blue and green sword
And you ripple when touched like a river.

Come to my soul dressed in white, like a branch
Of bleeding roses and cups of ashes,
Come with an apple and a horse,   40
Because there is a dark room there and a broken candelabra,
Some twisted chairs that wait for winter,
And a dead dove with a number.

Sexual Water

Translated by H. R. Hays

Running in single drops,
In drops like teeth,
In thick drops of marmalade and blood,
Running in drops,
The water falls,
Like a sword of drops
Like a rending river of glass,
It falls biting,
Striking the axis of symmetry, hitting on the
Ribs of the soul,   10
Breaking castoff things, soaking the darkness.

It is only a gust, damper than tears,
A liquid, a sweat, a nameless oil,
A sharp movement,
Creating itself, thickening itself,
The water falls,
In slow drops,
Toward the sea, toward its dry ocean,
Toward its wave without water.

I see a long summer and a death rattle coming out
of a granary,   20
Cellars, cicadas,
Towns, stimuli,
Habitations, girl children
Sleeping with hands on their hearts,
Dreaming with pirates, with fire,
I see ships,
I see trees of spinal cord

Bristling like furious cats,
I see blood, daggers, and women's stockings,
I see men's hair,   30
I see beds, I see corridors where a virgin screams,
I see blankets and organs and hotels.

I see stealthy dreams,
I accept the preceding days,
And also origins and also memories,
Like an eyelid dreadfully raised by force
I am watching.

And then there is this sound:
A red noise of bones,
An adhering of flesh,   40
And legs yellow as grain stalks joining together.
I am listening among explosions of kisses,
I am listening, shaken among breathing and sobs.

I am watching, hearing
With half my soul on sea and half my soul
        on land,
And with both halves of my soul I look at the world.

And though I close my eyes and cover my heart
Completely,
I see a deaf water falling
In deaf drops.   50

It is like a hurricane of gelatin,
Like a cataract of sperm and medusas.
I see a muddy rainbow flowing.
I see its waters passing through my bones.

Alberto Rojas Jimenez Comes Flying[1]

Translated by H. R. Hays

Between fearful feathers, between the nights,
Between the magnolias, between telegrams,
Between the south wind and the sea wind of the west,
        You come flying.

Below tombs, below ashes,
Below frozen snails,

---

[1] Alberto Rojas Jimenez, a poet and friend of Neruda, died by drowning.

Below the deepest terrestrial waters,
      You come flying.

Lower still, among submerged girl-children
And blind plants and wounded fishes,   10
Lower still, once more among clouds,
      You come flying.

Farther than the blood, farther than the bones,
Farther than bread, farther than wine,
Farther than fire,
      You come flying.

Farther than vinegar and death,
Among putrefactions and violets,
With your celestial voice and your moist shoes,
      You come flying.   20

Above deputations and drugstores
And wheels and lawyers and ocean liners
And red teeth, recently extracted,
      You come flying.

Above cities with submerged roof tops,
In which large women unplait their hair
With broad hands and lost combs,
      You come flying.

Close to a cellar where the wine matures,
With tepid, muddy hands, in silence,   30
With slow hands, red and wooden,
      You come flying.

Among vanished aviators,
Beside canals and shadows,
Beside buried white lilies,
      You come flying.

Among bottles with a bitter color,
Among rings of anise seed and misfortune,
Raising your hands and weeping,
      You come flying.   40

Over dentists and congregations,
Over cinemas, ears, and tunnels,
In a new suit, with extinguished eyes,
      You come flying.

Over your unwalled cemetery
Where the sailors go astray,

While the rain of your death falls,
 You come flying.

While the rain of your fingers falls,
While the rain of your bones falls,   50
While your marrow and your laughter fall,
 You come flying.

Over the stones into which you are melting,
Flowing, down winter, down time,
While your heart descends in a shower of drops,
 You come flying.

You are not there, circled with cement
And the black hearts of notaries
And the maddened bones of riders:
 You come flying.   60

O poppy of the sea, O my kinsman,
O guitar player dressed in bees,
It is not true there is all this shadow in your hair:
 You come flying.

It is not true that all this shadow pursues you,
It is not true there are all these dead swallows,
All this obscure region of lamentation:
 You come flying.

The black wind of Valparaiso
Spreads its wings of smoke and foam   70
To sweep the sky where you pass:
 You come flying.

There are steamers and the cold of a dead sea
And whistles and months and an odor
Of a rainy morning and filthy fishes:
 You come flying.

There is rum, and you and I, and my soul that I weep in,
And no one and nothing, except for a staircase
With broken steps and an umbrella:
 You come flying.   80

There is the sea. I descend at night and I hear you
Come flying below the deserted sea,
Below the sea that lives in me, in obscurity:
 You come flying.

I hear your wings and your slow flight
And the water of the dead strikes me
Like blind moist doves:
 You come flying.

You come flying, alone, solitary,
Alone among corpses, forever alone,
You come flying without a shadow, nameless,   90
Without sugar, without a mouth, without rosebushes,
        You come flying.

Ode of the Sun to the People's Army

Translated by H. R. Hays

Arms of the people! This way! Menace and siege
Still are wasting the earth, mixing it with death,
With the sharpness of goads! Salud, salud,
The mothers of the world cry salud to you,
The schools cry salud, the old carpenters,
Army of the People, they cry salud with ears of grain,
With milk, with potatoes, with the lemon and the laurel,
All that is of the earth and the mouth
Of man.
        All, like a necklace   10
Of hands, like a
Palpitating girdle, like the obstinacy of lightning,
All prepares for you, all converges toward you!
        Day of steel,
Fortified blueness!
        Forward, brothers,
Forward through the plowed fields,
Forward through the dry and sleepless night, threadbare and delirious,
Forward among grapevines, treading the cold color of the rocks,
Salud, salud, press on! Sharper than the voice of winter,
More sensitive than the eyelid, more certain than the point of thunder,   20
Punctual as the swift diamond, now in warfare,
Warriors like steel gray water of the midlands,
Like the flower and the wine, like the spiral heart of the earth,
Like the roots of all the leaves, of all the fragrant merchandise of the earth.
Salud, soldiers, salud, red plow furrows,
Salud, sturdy clover, salud, ranks of the people
In the light of the lightning, salud, salud, salud,
Forward, forward, forward, forward,
Over the mines, over the cemeteries, against the abominable   30
Appetite of death, against the spiny
Terror of traitors,
People, capable people, heart and rifles,
Heart and rifles, forward.
Photographers, miners, railworkers, brothers
Of the coal mine and stone quarry, kinsmen
Of the hammer, the forest, joyful shooting festival, forward,

Guerrillas, majors, sergeants, political commissars,
Aviators of the people, night fighters,
Sea fighters, forward! 40
Against you
There is nothing but a human chain gang, a pit full
Of rotten fish; forward!
There is nothing but dying corpses,
Swamps of terrible bloody pus,
There are no enemies: forward, Spain,
Forward, bells of the people,
Forward, regions of apple orchards,
Forward, banners of grain,
Forward, capital letters of fire, 50
For in the struggle on the waves, in the fields,
In the mountains, in the twilight loaded with acrid perfume,
You are giving birth to permanence, a thread
Of difficult strength.
        In the meanwhile,
Root and garland arise from silence
To await the ore of victory:
Each tool, each red wheel,
Each saw handle, the plume of each plow,
Each product of soil, each tremor of blood 60
Seeks to follow your footsteps, Army of the People:
Your organized light reaches the poor,
The forgotten men, your definite star
Nails its hoarse rays in death
And enacts the new eyes of hope.

The United Fruit Co.

Translated by Robert Bly

When the trumpet sounded, it was
all prepared on the earth,
and Jehovah parceled out the earth
to Coca-Cola, Inc., Anaconda,
Ford Motors, and other entities:
The Fruit Company, Inc.
reserved for itself the most succulent,
the central coast of my own land,
the delicate waist of America.
It rechristened its territories 10
as the "Banana Republics"
and over the sleeping dead,
over the restless heroes
who brought about the greatness,
the liberty and the flags,

it established the comic opera:
abolished the independencies,
presented crowns of Caesar,
unsheathed envy, attracted
the dictatorship of the flies,   20
Trujillo flies, Tacho flies,
Carias flies, Martinez flies,
Ubico flies, damp flies
of modest blood and marmalade,
drunken flies who zoom
over the ordinary graves,
circus flies, wise flies
well trained in tyranny.

Among the bloodthirsty flies
the Fruit Company lands its ships,   30
taking off the coffee and the fruit;
the treasure of our submerged
territories flows as though
on plates into the ships.

Meanwhile Indians are falling
into the sugared chasms
of the harbors, wrapped
for burial in the mist of the dawn:
a body rolls, a thing
that has no name, a fallen cipher,   40
a cluster of dead fruit
thrown down on the dump.

JEAN-PAUL SARTRE
[1905–1980]

Philosopher, playwright, journalist, literary theorist, novelist, political and social critic Jean-Paul Sartre is perhaps the foremost French writer and intellectual of the twentieth century. His name is virtually synonymous with existentialism, the dominant European philosophical school in the years following World War II. Sartre's thinking was profoundly shaped by the war. During the war years, he evolved a philosophy that stressed the necessity of individual choice and responsibility as a way to give meaning to a world where God had died and where impersonal institutions attempted to usurp individual freedom.

LIFE

Born in Paris in 1905, Sartre had a lonely childhood. His father died when he was very young, and he was raised in the home of his maternal grandfather, Carl Schweitzer, a professor of German at the Sorbonne and uncle of missionary Albert Schweitzer. Small and cross-eyed, Sartre was rejected by other children, so he retreated into books and spent much of his childhood in solitary reading. In his autobiography, *The Words* (*Les Mots*, 1963), he describes how words served as a retreat from the world that had rejected him and as a means to construct another world in his own imagination.

Sartre went to college at the École Normale Supérieure, graduating in 1929, and then to the Sorbonne. In these years he met philosopher and feminist theorist Simone de Beauvoir, forming a lifelong relationship with her, but one that never became the "bourgeois marriage" that both of them intellectually rejected. In the years before the war, he taught in secondary schools in Le Havre, Laon, and Paris, and published a novel, *Nausea* (*La Nausée*, 1938). A controversial and iconoclastic work, this novelistic diary presents Roquentin's revulsion as he confronts the physical world, other people, and his own body. His "nausea," the realization that things have no meaning in themselves, that the world is "absurd," makes him an outsider, for he refuses to accept the conventional categories that we use to avoid the unsettling sickness. Eventually he recognizes that the world can only have the meaning that he chooses to give it. During this period just before the war, Sartre was also publishing some of his early philosophical works.

It was the war, however, that crystallized his philosophy and focused his literary work. Drafted in 1939, taken prisoner in 1940, and released a year later, Sartre reentered a society occupied by the German army and "ruled" by the French collaborationist government under Marshal Philippe Pétain. His philosophical emphasis on freedom, the core concept in existentialism, emerged from these wartime experiences. In 1943 he published his massive philosophical treatise *Being and Nothingness* (*L'Être et le néant*) and produced *The Flies* (*Les Mouches*) on the Parisian stage. The play was an act of literary resistance using the classical story of Orestes as a way of getting past the German censors. In these works he asserts the freedom of consciousness from determination by the material world so long as the individual takes responsibility to choose this freedom. Without choosing, one lives in "bad faith" and is directed by forces outside the self, by political or religious tyrants or by conventional, unexamined ideas.

WORK

Sartre developed his views in numerous literary and philosophical works. After the war, he wrote a series of novels under the general title *Roads to Freedom* (*Les Chemins de la liberté*, 1945–1950); many more plays, the best-known of which is perhaps *No Exit* (*Huis-clos*, 1944); and many other works of philosophy, literary criticism, biography, psychology, and political polemics. His autobiography *The Words* tells the story of his life up to 1963, when it was published, and Simone de Beauvoir's memoirs tell some of the rest. His prolific writings, his position as an editor of an important intellectual journal, *Les Temps Modernes*, and his controversial and outspoken political views made him a very visible figure in France. His funeral in 1980 was a national event, like that of Victor Hugo a century earlier. It was attended by 25,000 mourners.

The Flies presents the same action as *The Libation Bearers,* the second of the three plays in Aeschylus' *Oresteia.* After the murder of Agamemnon by Clytemnestra, the subject of the first play, Orestes, the son of Agamemnon, returns to Argos and to the palace of the Atreides, now ruled by Clytemnestra and the usurper Ægistheus. After revealing himself to his sister Electra, Orestes avenges his father's death by killing both Ægistheus and Clytemnestra. At the end of the play, he leaves Argos, pursued by the Furies, to go to Athens where, in the third of Aeschylus' trilogy, *The Eumenides,* Orestes and the Furies plead their cases to Athene. She exonerates Orestes and reconciles the Furies to a new role as patronesses of the city of Athens.

Sartre places a very different emphasis on this material. The Greek plays trace a predestined series of tragedies as the crimes of the House of Atreus are worked out over several generations. Orestes' murders of Ægistheus and Clytemnestra are the final acts in this familial sequence of blood justice. When he is exonerated by Athene and the court in Athens, a new order of rational and deliberative justice is established. Sartre's Orestes is not so much seeking to redress his father's murder as he is to assert his own freedom and to liberate the citizens of Argos from their "bad faith" and systematic remorse. He must overthrow the political and religious tyrants Ægistheus and Zeus with their "passion for order," replacing them with a new era of freedom. Sartre compared his play to Aeschylus' in the following terms: "My intention was to consider the tragedy of freedom as contrasted with the tragedy of fate. In other words, what my play is about can be summed up as the question, 'How does a man behave toward an act committed by him, for which he takes the full consequences and full responsibility upon himself, even if he is otherwise horrified by his act?' " In the *Oresteia,* the characters are agents of the gods, carrying out the pattern of divine retribution and expiating the crimes of the past. In Sartre's play, Orestes must free himself from the past and from Zeus by discovering and choosing his own freedom.

Sartre's Orestes is a distinctly modern hero. He is not defined by family or destiny. Exiled from Argos as a child, he is a man without a country. Even his "multicultural" education, as the tutor who accompanies him on his wanderings reminds him, has freed him from prior definition. "Did I not, from the very first," the tutor asks him, "set you a-reading all the books there are, so as to make clear to you the infinite diversity of men's opinions? And did I not remind you, time and again, how variable are human creeds and customs? . . . [Y]our mind is free from prejudice and superstition; you have no family ties, no religion, and no calling; you are free to turn your hand to anything. But you know better than to commit yourself—and there lies your strength." These negative virtues of "the man without qualities" are not sufficient to give Orestes an identity or a direction for his life. The tutor's notion of freedom describes only an absence. To be truly free, Orestes must choose his life and take committed action. His decision to murder Ægistheus and Clytemnestra fulfills these conditions.

Sartre's play, even though it passed the German censors in 1943, was recognized by its French audience as an attack on the Pétain government—located at Vichy about 200 miles south of Paris—and its cowardly collaboration with the Germans. The official line of the Vichy regime was that the suffering of the war was a just punishment for the frivolousness and godlessness of the prewar years. In their attempt to restore a "moral order," the Vichy government was supported by the Catholic church. Thus Ægistheus (the occupying Nazis), Clytemnestra (the Vichy collaborators), and Zeus (the Church) form an alliance to oppress the people of Argos (the French population) and engage them in unending rituals of remorse. "By writing my play," Sartre said, "I was trying by my own unaided effort, feeble though it might be, to do what I could to root out this sickness of repentance, this complacence in repentance and shame. What was needed at the time was to revive the French people, to restore their courage." This was not as easy as it sounds, for to discourage resistance to the occupation and to keep the French people in line, the Nazis had a policy of killing randomly selected French citizens in response to attacks from the Underground. Sartre pointed out that "Anyone who committed an attack . . . had to know that, unless he gave himself up, fellow Frenchmen would be shot at random. So he was liable to a second form of repentance: he had to resist the temptation to give himself up. This is how the allegory in my play is to be understood." In Sartre's view it is not only Orestes' acts that are important, but the fact that he takes responsibility for them. He has no remorse.

The end of Sartre's play is significantly different from the end of *The Libation Bearers.* Orestes is now positively free, for he has acted, has taken responsibility for his acts, and has no remorse. He is a savior to the city, but he will not be their ruler, for that would continue their enslavement and their dependence on rule from outside themselves. By his act, they too are condemned to be free. The issue that Sartre raises is not unlike that in Dostoevsky's "Grand Inquisitor." The cynical Grand Inquisitor, like Zeus and Ægistheus, is sure that human beings will choose bread and remorse rather than freedom. But Dostoevsky's Jesus, like Orestes, knows that there is an alternative, and he believes profoundly in the courage it takes to make the liberating choice for freedom. For Sartre, living in a world where God has died and where the disappearance of external authority has left human beings in "dread," "anguish," and "absurdity" was not a reason for despair. The necessity for choice made his existentialism in the end an optimistic philosophy.

Suggested Readings

A brief and readable summary of the main tenets in Sartre's existentialism can be found in his essay *Existentialism* (1947) and in Dominick La Capra's *A Preface to Sartre* (1978). Michel Contat and Michel Rybalka have collected Sartre's writings about his own plays and about the theater in *Sartre on Theater* (1976). Two books on Sartre's literary works that include commentary on *The Flies* are Philip Thody's *Jean-Paul Sartre: A Literary and Political Study* (1960) and Philip R. Wood's *Understanding Jean-Paul Sartre* (1990). Erich Fromm's *Escape from Freedom* (1941) is a classic study of the freedom/authority conflict as seen from a psychologist's perspective.

The Flies

Translated by Stuart Gilbert

CHARACTERS IN THE PLAY:

ZEUS	THE HIGH PRIEST
ORESTES	A YOUNG WOMAN
ELECTRA	AN OLD WOMAN
ÆGISTHEUS	AN IDIOT BOY
CLYTEMNESTRA	FIRST SOLDIER
THE TUTOR	SECOND SOLDIER
FIRST FURY	MEN AND WOMEN, *townsfolk of Argos*
SECOND FURY	FURIES, SERVANTS, PALACE GUARDS
THIRD FURY	

[*Les Mouches (The Flies)* was first played at the Théâtre de la Cité, Paris, under the direction of Charles Dullin.]

Act I

A public square in Argos, dominated by a statue of ZEUS, *god of flies and death. The image has white eyes and blood-smeared cheeks.*

A procession of OLD WOMEN *in black, carrying urns, advances; they make libations to the statue. An* IDIOT BOY *is squatting in the background.* ORESTES *enters, accompanied by* THE TUTOR.

ORESTES: Listen, my good women.

[*The* OLD WOMEN *swing round, emitting little squeals.*]

THE TUTOR: Would you kindly tell us— [*The* OLD WOMEN *spit on the ground and move back a pace.*] Steady, good ladies, steady. I only want a piece of simple information. We are travelers and we have lost our way. [*Dropping their urns, the* WOMEN *take to their heels.*] Stupid old hags! You'd think I had intentions on their virtue! [*Ironically*] Ah, young master, truly this has been a pleasant journey. And how well inspired you were to come to this city of Argos, when there are hundreds of towns in Greece and Italy where the drink is good, the inns are hospitable, and the streets full of friendly, smiling people! But these uncouth hillmen—one would suppose they'd never seen a foreigner before. A hundred times and more I've had to ask our way, and never once did I get a straight answer. And then the grilling heat! This Argos is a nightmare city. Squeals of terror everywhere, people who panic the moment they set eyes on you, and scurry to cover, like black beetles, down the glaring streets. Pfoo! I can't think how you bear it—this emptiness, the shimmering air, that fierce sun overhead. What's deadlier than the sun?

ORESTES: I was born here.

THE TUTOR: So the story goes. But, if I were you, I wouldn't brag about it.

ORESTES: I was born here—and yet I have to ask my way, like any stranger. Knock at that door.

THE TUTOR: What do you expect? That someone will open it? Only look at those houses and tell me how they strike you. You will observe there's not a window anywhere. They open on closed courtyards, I suppose, and turn their backsides to the street. [ORESTES *makes a fretful gesture.*] Very good, sir. I'll knock—but nothing will come of it.

[*He knocks. Nothing happens. He knocks again, and the door opens a cautious inch.*]

A VOICE: What do you want?

THE TUTOR: Just a word of information. Can you tell me where—? [*The door is slammed in his face.*] Oh, the devil take you! Well, my lord Orestes, is that enough, or must I try elsewhere? If you wish, I'll knock at every door.

ORESTES: No, that's enough.

THE TUTOR: Well, I never! There's someone here. [*He goes up to the* IDIOT BOY.] Excuse me, sir . . .

THE IDIOT: Hoo! Hoo! Hoo!

THE TUTOR [*bowing again*]: My noble lord . . .

THE IDIOT: Hoo!

THE TUTOR: Will Your Highness deign to show us where Ægistheus lives?

THE IDIOT: Hoo!

THE TUTOR: Ægistheus, King of Argos.

THE IDIOT: Hoo! Hoo! Hoo!

[ZEUS *passes by, back stage.*]

THE TUTOR: We're out of luck. The only one who doesn't run away is a half-wit. [ZEUS *retraces his steps.*] Ah, that's odd! He's followed us here.

ORESTES: Who?

THE TUTOR: That bearded fellow.

ORESTES: You're dreaming.

THE TUTOR: I tell you, I saw him go by.

ORESTES: You must be mistaken.

THE TUTOR: Impossible. Never in my life have I seen such a beard—or, rather, only one: the bronze beard on the chin of Zeus Ahenobarbos at Palermo. Look, there he is again. What can he want of us?

ORESTES: He is only a traveler like ourselves.

THE TUTOR: Only that? We met him on the road to Delphi. And when we took the boat at Itea, there he was, fanning that great beard in the bows. At Nauplia we couldn't move a step without having him at our heels, and now—here he is again! Do you think that chance explains it? [*He brushes the flies off his face.*] These flies in Argos are much more sociable than its townsfolk. Just look at them! [*Points to the* IDIOT BOY.] There must be a round dozen pumping away at each of his eyes, and yet he's smiling quite contentedly; probably he likes having his eyes sucked. That's not surprising; look at that yellow muck oozing out of them. [*He flaps his hands at the flies.*] Move on, my little friends. Hah! They're on you now. Allow me! [*He drives them away.*] Well, this should please you—you who are always complaining of being a stranger in your native land. These charming insects, anyhow, are making you welcome; one would think they know who you are. [*He whisks them away.*] Now leave us in peace, you buzzers. We know you like us, but we've had enough of you.... Where can they come from? They're as big as bumble-bees and noisy as a swarm of locusts.

[*Meanwhile* ZEUS *has approached them.*]

ZEUS: They are only bluebottles, a trifle larger than usual. Fifteen years ago a mighty stench of carrion drew them to this city, and since then they've been getting fatter and fatter. Give them another fifteen years, and they'll be as big as toads.

[*A short silence.*]

THE TUTOR: Pray, whom have I the honor of addressing?

ZEUS: Demetrios is my name, and I hail from Athens.

ORESTES: Did I not see you on the boat, a fortnight ago?

ZEUS: Yes, and I saw you, too.

[*Hideous shrieks come from the palace.*]

THE TUTOR: Listen to that! I don't know if you will agree with me, young master, but I think we'd do better to leave this place.

ORESTES: Keep quiet!

ZEUS: You have nothing to fear. It's what they call Dead Men's Day today. Those cries announce the beginning of the ceremony.

ORESTES: You seem well posted on the local customs.

ZEUS: Yes, I often visit Argos. As it so happened, I was here on the great day of Agamemnon's homecoming, when the Greek fleet, flushed with victory, anchored in the Nauplia roads. From the top of the rampart one saw the bay dappled with their white sails. [*He drives the flies away.*] There were no flies then. Argos was only a small country town, basking in the sun, yawning the years away. Like everyone else I went up to the sentry-path to see the royal procession, and I watched it for many an hour wending across the plain. At sundown on the second day Queen Clytemnestra came to the ramparts, and with her was Ægistheus, the present King. The people of Argos saw their faces dyed red by the sunset, and they saw them leaning over the battlements, gazing for a long while seawards. And the people thought: "There's evil brewing." But they kept silence. Ægistheus, you should know, was the Queen's lover. A hard, brutal man, and even in those days he had the cast of melancholy.... But you're looking pale, young sir.

ORESTES: It's the long journey I have made, and this accursed heat. But pray go on; you interest me.

ZEUS: Agamemnon was a worthy man, you know, but he made one great mistake. He put a ban on public executions. That was a pity. A good hanging now and then—that entertains folk in the provinces and robs death of its glamour.... So the people here held their tongues; they looked forward to seeing, for once, a violent death. They still kept silent when they saw their King entering by the city gates. And when Clytemnestra stretched forth her graceful arms, fragrant and white as lilies, they still said nothing. Yet at that moment a word, a single word, might have sufficed. But no one said it; each was gloating in imagination over the picture of a huge corpse with a shattered face.

ORESTES: And you, too, said nothing?

ZEUS: Does that rouse your indignation? Well, my young friend, I like you all the better for it; it proves your heart's in the right place. No, I admit I, too, held my peace. I'm a stranger here, and it was no concern of mine. And next day when it started, when the folks of Argos heard their King screaming his life out in the palace, they still kept silence, but they rolled their eyes in a sort of ecstasy, and the whole town was like a woman in heat.

ORESTES: So now the murderer is on the throne. For fifteen years he has enjoyed the fruits of crime. And I thought the gods were just!

ZEUS: Steady, my friend! Don't blame the gods too hastily. Must they always punish? Wouldn't it be better to use such breaches of the law to point a moral?

ORESTES: And is that what they did?

ZEUS: They sent the flies.

THE TUTOR: The flies? How do the flies come in?

ZEUS: They are a symbol. But if you want to know what the gods did, look around you. See that old creature over there, creeping away like a beetle on her little black feet, and hugging the walls. Well, she's a good specimen of the squat black vermin that teem in every cranny of this town. Now watch me catch our specimen, it's well worth inspection. Here it is. A loathsome object, you'll agree.... Hah! You're blinking now. Still, you're an Argive and you should be used to the white-hot rapiers of the sun.... Watch her wriggling, like a hooked fish!... Now, old lady, let's hear your tale of woe. I see you're in black from head to foot. In mourning for a whole regiment of sons, is that it? Tell us, and I'll release you—perhaps. For whom are you in mourning?

OLD WOMAN: Sir, I am not in mourning. Everyone wears black at Argos.

ZEUS: Everyone wears black? Ah, I see. You're in mourning for your murdered King.

OLD WOMAN: Whisht! For God's sake, don't talk of that.

ZEUS: Yes, you're quite old enough to have heard those huge cries that echoed and re-echoed for a whole morning in the city streets. What did you do about it?

OLD WOMAN: My good man was in the fields, at work. What could I do, a woman alone? I bolted my door.

ZEUS: Yes, but you left your window not quite closed, so as to hear the better, and, while you peeped behind the curtains and held your breath, you felt a little tingling itch between your loins, and didn't you enjoy it!

OLD WOMAN: Oh, please stop, sir!

ZEUS: And when you went to bed that night, you had a grand time with your man. A real gala night.

OLD WOMAN: A what?... No, my lord, that was a dreadful, dreadful night.

ZEUS: A real gala, I tell you, and you've never been able to blot out its memory.

OLD WOMAN: Mercy on us! Are you—are you one of the Dead?

ZEUS: I dead? You're crazy, woman.... Anyhow, don't trouble your head who I am; you'd do better to think of yourself, and try to earn forgiveness by repenting of your sins.

OLD WOMAN: Oh, sir, I do repent, most heartily I repent. If you only knew how I repent, and my daughter too, and my son-in-law offers up a heifer every year, and my little grandson has been brought up in a spirit of repentance. He's a pretty lad, with flaxen hair, and he always behaves as good as gold. Though he's only seven, he never plays or laughs, for thinking of his original sin.

ZEUS: Good, you old bitch, that's as it should be—and be sure you die in a nice bitchy odor of repentance. It's your one hope of salvation. [*The* OLD WOMAN *runs away.*] Unless I'm much mistaken, my masters, we have there the real thing, the good old piety of yore, rooted in terror.

ORESTES: What man are you?

ZEUS: Who cares what I am? We were talking of the gods. Well now, should they have struck Ægistheus down?

ORESTES: They should.... They should.... Oh, how would I know what they should have done? What do I care, anyhow? I'm a stranger here.... Does Ægistheus feel contrition?

ZEUS: Ægistheus? I'd be much surprised. But what matter? A whole city's repenting on his account. And it's measured by the bushel, is repentance. [*Eerie screams in the palace.*] Listen! Lest they forget the screams of the late King in his last agony, they keep this festival of death each year when the day of the King's murder comes round. A herdsman from the hills—he's chosen for his lung-power—is set to bellow in the Great Hall of the palace. [ORESTES *makes a gesture of disgust.*] Bah! That's nothing. I wonder what you'll say presently, when they let the Dead loose. Fifteen years ago, to a day, Agamemnon was murdered. And what a change has come over the light-hearted folk of Argos since that day; how near and dear to me they are at present!

ORESTES: Dear to you?

ZEUS: Pay no heed, young man. That was a slip of the tongue. Near and dear to the gods, I meant.

ORESTES: You surprise me. Then those blood-smeared walls, these swarms of flies, this reek of shambles and the stifling heat, these empty streets and yonder god with his gashed face, and all those creeping, half-human creatures beating their breasts in darkened rooms, and those shrieks, those hideous, blood-curdling shrieks—can it be that Zeus and his Olympians delight in these?

ZEUS: Young man, do not sit in judgment on the gods. They have their secrets—and their sorrows.

[*A short silence.*]

ORESTES: Am I right in thinking Agamemnon had a daughter? A daughter named Electra?

ZEUS: Yes. She lives there, in the palace—that building yonder.

ORESTES: So that's the palace?... And what does Electra think of—all this?

ZEUS: Oh, she's a mere child. There was a son, too, named Orestes. But he's dead, it seems.

ORESTES: Dead? Well, really...

THE TUTOR: Of course he's dead, young master. I thought you knew it. Don't you remember what they told us at Nauplia—about Ægistheus' having him murdered, soon after Agamemnon's death?

ZEUS: Still, some say he's alive. The story goes that the men ordered to kill the child had pity on him and left him in the forest. Some rich Athenians found him there and took him home. For my part, I'd rather he were dead.

ORESTES: Pray, why?

ZEUS: Suppose that one day he appeared in this city, and—

ORESTES: Continue, please.

ZEUS: As you wish.... Well, I'd say this to him. "My lad—" I'd say, "My lad," as he's your age or thereabouts—if he's alive, of course. By the way, young lord, may I know your name?

ORESTES: Philebus is my name, and I hail from Corinth. I am traveling to improve my mind, and this old slave accompanying me used to be my tutor.

ZEUS: Thank you. Well, I'd say something like this. "My lad, get you gone! What business have you here? Do you wish to enforce your rights? Yes, you're brave and strong and spirited. I can see you as a captain in an army of good fighters. You have better things to do than reigning over a dead-and-alive city, a carrion city plagued by flies. These people are great sinners but, as you see, they're working out their atonement. Let them be, young fellow, let them be; respect their sorrowful endeavor, and begone on tiptoe. You cannot share in their repentance, since you did not share their crime. Your brazen innocence makes a gulf between you and them. So if you have any care for them, be off! Be off, or you will work their doom. If you hinder them on their way, if even for a moment you turn their thoughts from their remorse, all their sins will harden on them—like cold fat. They have guilty consciences, they're afraid—and fear and guilty consciences have a good savor in the nostrils of the gods. Yes, the gods take pleasure in such poor souls. Would you oust them from the favor of the gods? What, moreover, could you give them in exchange? Good digestions, the gray monotony of provincial life, and the boredom—ah, the soul-destroying boredom—of long days of mild content. Go your way, my lad, go your way. The repose of cities and men's souls hangs on a thread; tamper with it and you bring disaster. [*Looking him in the eyes*] A disaster which will recoil on you.

ORESTES: Yes? So that is what you'd say? Well, if I were that young man, I'd answer— [*They eye each other truculently.* THE TUTOR *coughs.*] No, I don't know how I'd answer you. Perhaps you're right, and anyhow it's no concern of mine.

ZEUS: Good. I only hope Orestes would show as much sense.... Well, peace be with you, my friend; I must go about my business.

ORESTES: Peace be with you.

ZEUS: By the way, if those flies bother you, here's a way of getting rid of them. You see that swarm buzzing round your head? Right. Now watch! I flick my wrist—so—and wave my arm once, and then I say: Abraxas, galla, galla, tsay, tsay. See! They're falling down and starting to crawl on the ground like caterpillars.

ORESTES: By Jove!

ZEUS: Oh, that's nothing. Just a parlor trick. I'm a fly-charmer in my leisure hours. Good day to you. We shall meet again.

[*Exit* ZEUS.]

THE TUTOR: Take care. That man knows who you are.

ORESTES: "Man," you say. But *is* he a man?

THE TUTOR: What else should he be? You grieve me, my young master. Have all my lessons, all my precepts, the smiling skepticism I taught you, been wasted on your ears? "Is he a man?" you ask. There's nothing else but men—what more would you have? And that bearded fellow is a man, sure enough; probably one of Ægistheus' spies.

ORESTES: A truce to your philosophy! It's done me too much harm already.

THE TUTOR: Harm? Do you call it doing harm to people when one emancipates their minds? Ah, how you've changed! Once I read you like an open book.... But at least you might tell me your plans. Why bring me to this city, and what's your purpose here?

ORESTES: Did I say I had a purpose? But that's enough. Be silent now. [*He takes some steps towards the palace.*] This is *my* palace. My father's birthplace. And it's there a whore and her paramour foully butchered him. I, too, was born there. I was nearly three when that usurper's bravoes carried me away. Most likely we went out by that door. One of them held me in his arms, I had my eyes wide open, and no doubt I was crying. And yet I have no memories, none whatever. I am looking at a huge, gloomy building, solemn and pretentious in the worst provincial taste. I am looking at it, but I *see* it for the first time.

THE TUTOR: No memories, master? What ingratitude, considering that I gave ten years of my life to stocking you with them! And what of all the journeys we have made together, all the towns we visited? And the course in archæology I composed specially for you? No memories, indeed! Palaces, shrines, and temples—with so many of them is your memory peopled that you could write a guide-book of all Greece.

ORESTES: Palaces—that's so. Palaces, statues, pillars—stones, stones, stones! Why, with all those stones in my head, am I not heavier? While you are about it, why not remind me of the three hundred and eighty-seven steps of the temple at Ephesus? I climbed them, one by one, and I remember each. The seventeenth, if my memory serves me, was badly broken. And yet—! Why, an old, mangy dog, warming himself at the hearth, and struggling to his feet with a little whimper to welcome his master home—why, that dog has more memories than I! At least he recognizes his master. *His* master. But what can I call mine?

THE TUTOR: And what of your culture, Lord Orestes? What of that? All that wise lore I culled for you with loving care, like a bouquet, matching the fruits of my knowledge with the finest flowers of my experience? Did I not, from the very first, set you a-reading all the books there are, so as to make clear to you the infinite diversity of men's opinions? And did I not remind you, time and again, how variable are human creeds and customs? So, along with youth, good looks, and wealth, you have the wisdom of far riper years; your mind is free from prejudice and superstition; you have no family ties, no religion, and no calling; you are free to turn your hand to anything. But you know better than to commit yourself—and there lies your strength. So, in a word, you stand head and shoulders above the ruck and, what's more, you could hold a chair of philosophy or architecture in a great university. And yet you cavil at your lot!

ORESTES: No, I do not cavil. What should I cavil at? You've left me free as the strands torn by the wind from spiders' webs that one sees floating ten feet above the ground. I'm light as gossamer and walk on air. I know I'm favored, I appreciate my lot at its full value. [*A pause.*] Some men are born bespoken; a certain path has been assigned them, and at its end there is something they *must* do, a deed allotted. So on and on they trudge, wounding their bare feet on the flints. I suppose that strikes *you* as vulgar—the joy of going somewhere definite. And there are others, men of few words, who bear deep down in their hearts a load of dark imaginings; men whose whole life was changed because one day in childhood, at the age of five or seven— Right; I grant you these are no great men. When I was seven, I know I had no home, no roots. I let sounds and scents, the patter of rain on housetops, the golden play of sunbeams, slip past my body and fall round me—and I knew these were for others, I could never make them *my* memories. For memories are luxuries reserved for people who own houses, cattle, fields, and servants. Whereas I—! I'm free as air, thank God. My mind's my own, gloriously aloof. [*He goes nearer to the palace.*] I might have lived there. I'd not have read any of your books; perhaps I'd not have learned to read. It's rare for a Greek prince to know how to read. But I'd have come in and gone out by that door ten thousand times. As a child I'd have played with its leaves, and when I pushed at them with all my little might, they'd have creaked without yielding, and I'd have taken the measure of my weakness. Later on, I'd have pushed them open furtively by night and gone out after girls. And some years later, when I came of age, the slaves would have flung the doors wide open and I'd have crossed the threshold on horseback. My old wooden door! I'd have been able to find your keyhole with my eyes shut. And that notch there—I might have made it showing off, the first day they let me hold a spear. [*He steps back.*] Let's see. That's the Dorian style, isn't it? And what do you make of that gold inlay? I saw the like at Dodona; a pretty piece of craftsmanship. And now I'm going to say something that will rejoice you. This is not *my* palace, nor *my* door. And there's nothing to detain us here.

THE TUTOR: Ah, that's talking sense. For what would you have gained by living in Argos? By now your spirit would be broken, you'd be wallowing in repentance.

ORESTES: Still, it would be *my* repentance. And this furnace heat singeing my hair would be *mine.* Mine, too, the buzz of all these flies. At this moment I'd be lying naked in some dark room at the back of the palace, and watching a ribbon of red light lengthen across the floor. I'd be waiting for sundown; waiting for the cool dusk of an Argos evening to rise like perfume from the parched earth; an Argos evening like many a thousand others, familiar yet ever new, another evening that should be *mine.* . . . Well, well, my worthy pedagogue, let's be off. We've no business to be luxuriating in others' heat.

THE TUTOR: Ah, my young lord, how you've eased my mind! During these last few months—to be exact, ever since I revealed to you the secret of your birth—I could see you changing day by day, and it gave me many a sleepless night. I was afraid—

ORESTES: Of what?

THE TUTOR: No, it will anger you.

ORESTES: Speak.

THE TUTOR: Be it so. Well, though from one's earliest years one has been trained to skeptic irony, one can't help having foolish fancies now and then. And I wondered if you weren't hatching some wild scheme to oust Ægistheus and take his place.

ORESTES [*thoughtfully*]: To oust Ægistheus. Ah— [*A pause.*] No, my good slave, you need not fear; the time for that is past. True, nothing could please me better than to grip that sanctimonious ruffian by the beard and drag him from my father's throne. But what purpose would it serve? These folk are no concern of mine. I have not seen one of their children come into the world, nor been present at their daughters' weddings; I don't share their remorse, I don't even know a single one of them by name. That bearded fellow was right; a king should share his subjects' memories. So we'll let them be, and begone on tiptoe. . . . But, mind you, if there were something I could do, something to give me the freedom of the city; if, even by a crime, I could acquire their memories, their hopes and fears, and fill with these the void within me, yes, even if I had to kill my own mother—

THE TUTOR: Hush! For heaven's sake, hush!

ORESTES: Yes, these are idle dreams. Let's be off. Now go and see if we can get some horses here, and we'll move on to Sparta, where I have good friends.

[ELECTRA *comes forward, carrying a large ash-can.*
She goes up to the statue of ZEUS, *without seeing them.*]

ELECTRA: Yes, you old swine, scowl away at me with your goggle eyes and your fat face all smeared with raspberry juice—scowl away, but you won't scare me, not you! They've been to worship you, haven't they?—those pious matrons in black dresses. They've been padding around you in their big creaky shoes. And you were pleased, old bugaboo, it warmed your silly wooden heart. You like them old, of course; the nearer they're to corpses, the more you love them. They've poured their choicest wines out at your feet, because it's your festival today, and the stale smell from their petticoats tickled your nostrils. [*She rubs herself against him.*] Now smell me for a change, smell the perfume of a fresh, clean body. But, of course, I'm young, I'm alive—and you loathe youth and life. I, too, am bringing you offerings, while all the others are at prayers. Here they are: ashes from the hearth, peelings, scraps of offal crawling with maggots, a chunk of bread too filthy even for our pigs. But your darling flies will love it, won't they, Zeus? A good feast-day to you, old idol, and let's hope it is your last. I'm not strong enough to pull you down. All I can do is to spit at you. But some day he will come, the man I'm waiting for, carrying a long, keen sword. He'll look you up and down and chuckle, with his hands on his hips, like this, and his head thrown back. Then he'll draw his sword and chop you in two, from top to bottom—like this! So the two halves of Zeus will fall apart, one to the left, one to the right, and everyone will see he's made of common wood. Just a lump of cheap white deal, the terrible God of Death! And all that frightfulness, the blood on his face, his dark-green eyes, and all the rest—they'll see it was only a coat of paint. *You,* anyhow, you know you're white inside, white as a child's body, and you know, too, that a sword can rip you limb from limb, and you won't even bleed. Just a log of deal—anyhow it will serve to light our fires next winter. [*She notices* ORESTES.] Oh!

ORESTES: Don't be alarmed.

ELECTRA: I'm not alarmed. Not a bit. Who are you?

ORESTES: A stranger.

ELECTRA: Then you are welcome. All that's foreign to this town is dear to me. Your name?

ORESTES: Philebus. I've come from Corinth.

ELECTRA: Ah? From Corinth. My name's Electra.

ORESTES: Electra— [*To* THE TUTOR] Leave us.

[*Exit* THE TUTOR.]

ELECTRA: Why are you looking at me like that?

ORESTES: You're very beautiful. Not at all like the people in these parts.

ELECTRA: I beautiful? Can you really mean it? As beautiful as the Corinthian girls?

ORESTES: Yes.

ELECTRA: Well, here they never tell me that I'm beautiful. Perhaps they don't want me to know it. Anyhow, what use would beauty be to me? I'm only a servant.

ORESTES: What! You a servant?

ELECTRA: The least of the servants in the palace. I wash the King's and the Queen's underlinen. And how dirty it is, all covered with spots and stains! Yes, I have to wash everything they wear next to their skin, the shifts they wrap their rotting bodies in, the nightdresses Clytemnestra has on when the King shares her bed. I shut my eyes and scrub with all my might. I have to wash up, too. You don't believe me? See my hands, all chapped and rough. Why are you looking at them in that funny way? Do they, by any chance, look like the hands of a princess?

ORESTES: Poor little hands. No, they don't look like a princess's hands. . . . But tell me more. What else do they make you do?

ELECTRA: Every morning I've to empty the ash-can. I drag it out of the palace, and then—well, you saw what I do with the refuse. That big fellow in wood is Zeus, God of Death and Flies. The other day, when the High Priest came here to make his usual bows and scrapings, he found himself treading on cabbage-stumps and rotten turnips and mussel-shells. He looked startled, I can tell you! I say! You won't tell on me, will you?

ORESTES: No.

ELECTRA: Really I don't care if you do. They can't make things much worse for me than they are already. I'm used to being beaten. Perhaps they'd shut me up in one of the rooms in the tower. That wouldn't be so bad; at least I wouldn't have to see their faces. Just imagine what I get by way of thanks at bedtime, when my day's work is done. I go up to a tall, stout lady with dyed hair, with thick lips and very white hands, a queen's hands, that smell of honey. Then she puts her hands on my shoulders and dabs my forehead with her lips and says: "Good night, Electra. Good night." Every evening. Every evening I have to feel that woman slobbering on my face. Ugh! Like a piece of raw meat on my forehead. But I hold myself up, I've never fallen yet. She's my mother, you know. If I was up in the tower, she wouldn't kiss me any more.

ORESTES: Have you never thought of running away?

ELECTRA: I haven't the courage; I daren't face the country roads at night all by myself.

ORESTES: Is there no one, no girl friend of yours, who'd go with you?

ELECTRA: No, I'm quite alone. Ask any of the people here, and they'll tell you I'm a pest, a public nuisance. I've no friends.

ORESTES: Not even an old nurse, who saw you into the world and has kept a little affection for you?

ELECTRA: Not even an old nurse. Mother will tell you; I freeze even the kindest hearts—that's how I am.

ORESTES: Do you propose to spend your life here?

ELECTRA [*excitedly*]: My life? Oh no, no! Of course not! Listen. I'm waiting for—for something.

ORESTES: Something, or someone?

ELECTRA: That's my secret. Now it's your turn to speak. You're good-looking, too. Will you be here long?

ORESTES: Well, I'd thought of leaving today. But, as it is—

ELECTRA: Yes?

ORESTES: As it is, I'm not so sure.

ELECTRA: Is Corinth a pretty place?

ORESTES: Very pretty.

ELECTRA: Do you like it? Are you proud of Corinth?

ORESTES: Yes.

ELECTRA: How strange that sounds! I can't imagine myself being proud of my home town. Tell me what it feels like.

ORESTES: Well— No, I don't know. I can't explain.

ELECTRA: You can't? I wonder why. [*A short silence.*] What's Corinth like? Are there shady streets and squares? Places where one can stroll in the cool of the evening?

ORESTES: Yes.

ELECTRA: And everyone comes out of doors? People go for walks together?

ORESTES: Almost everyone is out and about at sundown.

ELECTRA: Boys and girls together?

ORESTES: Oh yes, one often sees them going for walks together.

ELECTRA: And they always find something to say to each other? They like each other's company, and one hears them laughing in the streets quite late at night?

ORESTES: Yes.

ELECTRA: I suppose you think I'm very childish. But it's so hard for me to picture a life like that—going for walks, laughing and singing in the streets. Everybody here is sick with fear. Everyone except me. And I—

ORESTES: Yes? And you?

ELECTRA: Oh, I—I'm sick with—hatred. And what do they do all day, the girls at Corinth?

ORESTES: Well, they spend quite a while making themselves pretty; then they sing or play on lutes. Then they call on their friends, and at night they go to dances.

ELECTRA: But don't they have any worries?

ORESTES: Only quite little ones.

ELECTRA: Yes? Now listen well, please. Don't the people at Corinth feel remorse?

ORESTES: Sometimes. Not very often.

ELECTRA: So they do what they like and, afterwards, don't give another thought to it?

ORESTES: That's their way.

ELECTRA: How strange! [*A short silence.*] Please tell me something else; I want to know it because of—of someone I'm expecting. Suppose one of the young fellows you've been telling about, who walk and laugh with girls in the evenings—suppose one of these young men came home after a long journey and found his father murdered, and his mother living with the murderer, and his sister treated like a slave—what would he do, that young man from Corinth? Would he just take it for granted and slink out of his father's house and look for consolation with his girl friends? Or would he draw his sword and hurl himself at the assassin, and slash his brains out? . . . Why are you silent?

ORESTES: I was wondering—

ELECTRA: What? You can't say what he'd do?

CLYTEMNESTRA [*off stage, calling*]: Electra!

ELECTRA: Hush!

ORESTES: What is it?

ELECTRA: That was my mother, Queen Clytemnestra. [CLYTEMNESTRA *enters.*] What's this, Philebus? Are you afraid of her?

ORESTES [*to himself*]: So that's the face I tried to picture, night after night, until I came to see it, really *see* it, drawn and haggard under the rosy mask of paint. But I hadn't counted on those dead eyes.

CLYTEMNESTRA: Electra, hear the King's order. You are to make ready for the ceremony. You must wear your black dress and your jewels. . . . Well, what does this behavior mean? Why are you pressing your elbows to your hips and staring at the ground? Oh, I know your tricks, my girl, but they don't deceive me any longer. Just now I was watching at the window and I saw a very different Electra, a girl with flashing eyes, bold gestures. . . . Why don't you answer?

ELECTRA: Do you really think a scullery-maid would add to the splendour of your festival?

CLYTEMNESTRA: No play-acting. You are a princess, Electra, and the townsfolk expect to see you, as in former years.

ELECTRA: A princess—yes, the princess of a day. Once a year, when this day comes round, you remember who I am; because, of course, the people want an edifying glimpse of our family life. A strange princess, indeed, who herds pigs and washes up. Tell me, will Ægistheus put his arm round my neck as he did last time? Will he smile tenderly on me, while he mumbles horrible threats in my ear?

CLYTEMNESTRA: If you would have him otherwise, it rests with you.

ELECTRA: Yes—if I let myself be tainted by your remorse; if I beg the gods' forgiveness for a crime I never committed. Yes—if I kiss your royal husband's hand and call him father. Ugh! The mere thought makes me sick. There's dry blood under his nails.

CLYTEMNESTRA: Do as you will. I have long ceased giving you orders in my name. It is the King's command I bring you.

ELECTRA: And why should I obey him? Ægistheus is your husband, Mother, your dearly beloved husband—not mine.

CLYTEMNESTRA: That is all I have to say, Electra. Only too well I see you are determined to bring ruin on yourself, and on us all. Yet who am I to counsel you, I who ruined my whole life in a single morning? You hate me, my child, but what disturbs me more is your likeness to me, as I was once. I used to have those clean-cut features, that fever in the blood, those smoldering eyes—and nothing good came of them.

ELECTRA: No! Don't say I'm like you! Tell me, Philebus—you can see us side by side—am I really like her?

ORESTES: How can I tell? Her face is like a pleasant garden that hail and storms have ravaged. And upon yours I see a threat of storm; one day passion will sear it to the bone.

ELECTRA: A threat of storm? Good! So far I welcome the likeness. May your words come true!

CLYTEMNESTRA: And you, young man, who stare so boldly at us, who are you and why have you come here? Let me look at you more closely.

ELECTRA [quickly]: He's a Corinthian, of the name of Philebus. A traveler.

CLYTEMNESTRA: Philebus? Ah!

ELECTRA: You seemed to fear another name.

CLYTEMNESTRA: To fear? If the doom I brought on my life has taught me anything, it is that I have nothing left to fear.... Welcome to Argos, stranger. Yes, come nearer. How young you seem! What's your age?

ORESTES: Eighteen.

CLYTEMNESTRA: Are your parents alive?

ORESTES: My father's dead.

CLYTEMNESTRA: And your mother? Is she about my age? Ah, you don't answer. I suppose she looks much younger; she still laughs and sings when you are with her. Do you love her? Answer me, please. Why did you leave her?

ORESTES: I am on my way to Sparta, to enlist in the army.

CLYTEMNESTRA: Most travelers give our city a wide berth. Some go twenty leagues out of their way to avoid it. Were you not warned? The people of the Plain have put us in quarantine; they see our repentance as a sort of pestilence and are afraid of being infected.

ORESTES: I know.

CLYTEMNESTRA: Did they tell you that we bear the burden of an inexpiable crime, committed fifteen years ago?

ORESTES: Yes, they told me that.

CLYTEMNESTRA: And that Queen Clytemnestra bears the heaviest load of guilt— that men shudder at her name?

ORESTES: That, too, I heard.

CLYTEMNESTRA: And yet you've come here! Stranger, I am Queen Clytemnestra.

ELECTRA: Don't pity her, Philebus. The Queen is indulging in our national pastime, the game of public confession. Here everyone cries his sins on the housetops. On holidays you'll often see a worthy shopkeeper dragging himself along on his knees, covering his hair with dust, and screaming out that he's a murderer, a libertine, a liar, and all the rest of it. But the folk of Argos are getting a little tired of these amusements; everyone knows his neighbor's sins by heart. The Queen's, especially, have lost interest; they're official—our basic crimes, in fact. So you can imagine her delight when she finds someone like you, somebody raw and young, who doesn't even know her name, to hear her tale of guilt. A marvelous opportunity! It's as if she were confessing for the first time.

CLYTEMNESTRA: Be silent. Anyone has the right to spit in my face, to call me murderess and whore. But no one has the right to speak ill of my remorse.

ELECTRA: Note her words, Philebus. That's a rule of the game. People will beg you to condemn them, but you must be sure to judge them only on the sins they own to; their other evil deeds are no one's business, and they wouldn't thank you for detecting them.

CLYTEMNESTRA: Fifteen years ago men said I was the loveliest woman in Greece. Look at me now and judge my sufferings. Let me be frank, young stranger; it is not the death of that old lecher that I regret. When I saw his blood tingeing the water in the bath, I sang and danced for joy. And even now, after fifteen years, whenever I recall it, I have a thrill of pleasure. But—but I had a son; he would be your age now. When Ægistheus handed him over to his bravoes, I—

ELECTRA: You had a daughter too, my mother, if I'm not mistaken. And you've made of her a scullion. But that crime, it seems, sits lightly on your conscience.

CLYTEMNESTRA: You are young, Electra. It is easy for young people, who have not yet had a chance of sinning, to condemn. But wait, my girl; one day you, too, will be trailing after you an inexpiable crime. At every step you will think that you are leaving it behind, but it will remain as heavy as before. Whenever you look back you will see it there, just at arm's length, glowing darkly like a black crystal. And you will have forgotten what it really is, and murmur to yourself: "It wasn't I, it could not have been I, who did that." Yet, though you disown it time and time again, always it will be there, a dead weight holding you back. And then at last you will realize that you staked your life on a single throw of the dice, and nothing remains for you but to drag your crime after you until you die. For that is the law, just or unjust, of repentance. Ah, then we'll see a change come over your young pride.

ELECTRA: My young pride? So it's your lost youth you are regretting, still more than your crime. It's my youth you detest, even more than my innocence.

CLYTEMNESTRA: What I detest in you, Electra, is—myself. Not your youth—far from it!—but my own.

ELECTRA: And I—it's you, it's *you* I hate.

CLYTEMNESTRA: For shame, Electra! Here we are, scolding each other like two women of the same age in love with the same man! And yet I am your mother. . . . I do not know who you are, young man, nor what brings you here, but your presence bodes no good. Electra hates me—that, of course, I always knew. But for fifteen years we have kept the peace; only our eyes betrayed our feelings. And now you have come, you have spoken, and here we are showing our teeth and snapping at each other like two curs in the street. An ancient law of Argos compels us to give you hospitality, but, I make no secret of it, I had rather you were gone. As for you, my child, too faithful copy of myself, 'tis true I have no love for you. But I had rather cut off my right hand than do you harm. Only too well you know it, and you trade on my weakness. But I advise you not to rear your anxious little head against Ægistheus; he has a short way with vipers. Mark my words, do his bidding—or you will rue it.

ELECTRA: Tell the King that I shall not attend the rite. Do you know what they do, Philebus? Above the town there's a great cavern; none of our young men, not even the bravest, has ever found its end. People say that it leads down to hell, and the High Priest has had the entrance blocked with a great stone. Well—would you believe it?—each year when this anniversary comes round, the townspeople gather outside the cavern, soldiers roll away the stone, and our dead, so they say, come up from hell and roam the city. Places are laid for them at every table, chairs and beds made ready, and the people in the house huddle in corners to make room for them during the night-watches. For the dead are everywhere, the whole town's at their mercy. You can imagine how our townsfolk plead with them. "My poor dead darling, I didn't mean to wrong you. Please be kind." Tomorrow, at cock-crow, they'll return underground, the stone will be rolled back, and that will be the end of it until this day next year. Well, I refuse to take part in this mummery. Those dead folk are *their* dead, not mine.

CLYTEMNESTRA: If you will not obey his summons willingly, the King will have you brought to him by force.

ELECTRA: By force?...I see. Very well, then. My good kind mother, will you please tell the King that I shall certainly obey. I shall attend the rite, and if the townsfolk wish to see me, they won't be disappointed.... Philebus, will you do something for me? Please don't go at once, but stay here for the ceremony. Perhaps some parts of it may entertain you. Now I'll go and make myself ready.

[*Exit* ELECTRA.]

CLYTEMNESTRA [*to* ORESTES]: Leave this place. I feel that you are going to bring disaster on us. You have no cause to wish us ill; we have done nothing to you. So go, I beg you. By all you hold most sacred, for your mother's sake, I beg you, go.

[*Exit* CLYTEMNESTRA.]

ORESTES [*thoughtfully*]: For my mother's sake.

[ZEUS *enters and comes up to him.*]

ZEUS: Your attendant tells me you wish to leave. He has been looking for horses all over Argos, but can find none. Well, I can procure for you two sturdy mares and riding-gear at a very low figure.

ORESTES: I've changed my mind. I am not leaving Argos.

ZEUS [*meditatively*]: Ah, so you're not leaving, after all. [*A short pause. Then, in a quicker tempo*] In that case I shall stay with you and be your host. I know an excellent inn in the lower town where we can lodge together. You won't regret my company, I can assure you. But first—Abraxas, galla, galla, tsay, tsay—let me rid you of those flies. A man of my age can often be very helpful to lads like you. I'm old enough to be your father; you must tell me all about yourself and your troubles. So come, young man, don't try to shake me off. Meetings like this are often of more use than one would think. Consider the case of Telemachus—you know whom I mean, King Ulysses' son. One fine day he met an old worthy of the name of Mentor, who joined forces with him. Now I wonder if you know who that old fellow Mentor really was....

[*He escorts* ORESTES *off the stage, holding him in conversation, while the curtain falls.*]

ACT II

Scene 1

A mountain terrace, with a cavern on the right. Its entrance is blocked by a large black boulder. On the left is a flight of steps leading up to a temple. A crowd of men and women have gathered for the ceremony.

A WOMAN [*kneeling before her little son, as she straightens the kerchief round his neck*]: There! That's the third time I've had to straighten it for you. [*She dusts his clothes.*] That's better. Now try to behave properly, and mind you start crying when you're told.

THE CHILD: Is that where they come from?

THE WOMAN: Yes.

THE CHILD: I'm frightened.

THE WOMAN: And so you should be, darling. Terribly frightened. That's how one grows up into a decent, god-fearing man.

A MAN: They'll have good weather today.

ANOTHER MAN: Just as well. It seems they still like sunlight, shadows though they are. Last year, when it rained, they were fierce, weren't they?

FIRST MAN: Ay, that's the word. Fierce.

SECOND MAN: A shocking time we had!

THIRD MAN: Once they've gone back to their cave and left us to ourselves, I'll climb up here again and look at that there stone, and I'll say to myself: "Now we've a year's peace before us."

FOURTH MAN: Well, I'm not like you, I ain't consoled that easily. From tomorrow I'll start wondering how they'll be next year. Every year they're getting nastier and nastier, and—

SECOND MAN: Hold your tongue, you fool! Suppose one of them has crept out through a crevice and is prowling round us now, eavesdropping, like. There's some of the Dead come out ahead of time, so I've heard tell.

[*They eye each other nervously.*]

A YOUNG WOMAN: If only it would start! What are they up to, those palace folk? They're never in a hurry, and it's all this waiting gets one down, what with the blazing sun and only that big black stone to look at. Just think! They're all there, crowded up behind the stone, gloating over the cruel things they're going to do to us.

AN OLD WOMAN: That's enough, my girl. . . . We all know she's no better than she should be; that's why she's so scared of her ghost. Her husband died last spring, and for ten years she'd been fooling the poor man.

YOUNG WOMAN: I don't deny it. Sure enough, I fooled him to the top of his bent; but I always liked him and I led him a pleasant life, that he can't deny. He never knew a thing about the other men, and when he died, you should have seen the way he looked at me, so tenderly, like a grateful dog. Of course, he knows everything now, and it's bitter pain for him, poor fellow, and all his love has turned to hate. Presently I'll feel him coiling round me, like a wisp of smoke, and he'll cling to me more closely than any living man has ever clung. I'll bring him home with me, wound round my neck like a tippet. I've a tasty little meal all ready, with the cakes and honey that he always liked. But it's all no use, I know. He'll never forgive me, and tonight—oh, how I dread it!—he will share my bed.

A MAN: Ay, she's right. What's Ægistheus doing? We can't bear this suspense much longer. It ain't fair to keep us waiting like this.

ANOTHER MAN: Sorry for yourself, are you? But do you think Ægistheus is less afraid than we? Tell me, how'd you like to be in his shoes, and have Agamemnon gibbering at you for twenty-four hours?

YOUNG WOMAN: Oh, this horrible, horrible suspense! Do you know, I have a feeling that all of you are drifting miles and miles away, leaving me alone. The stone is not yet rolled aside, but each of us is shut up with his dead, and lonely as a raindrop.

[ZEUS *enters, followed by* ORESTES *and* THE TUTOR.]

ZEUS: This way, young man; you'll have a better view.

ORESTES: So here we have them, the citizens of Argos, King Agamemnon's loyal subjects!

THE TUTOR: What an ugly lot! Observe, young master, their sallow cheeks and sunken eyes. These folk are perishing of fear. What better example could we have of the effects of superstition? Just look at them! And if you need another proof of the soundness of my teaching, look on me and my rosy cheeks.

ZEUS: Much good they do you, your pink cheeks. For all your roses, my good man, you're no more than a sack of dung, like all those others, in the eyes of Zeus. Yes, though you may not guess it, you stink to heaven. These folk, at least, are wise in their generation; they know how bad they smell.

A MAN [*climbing on to the temple steps, harangues the crowd*]: Do they want to drive us mad? Let's raise our voices all together and summon Ægistheus. Make him understand we will not suffer any more delay.

THE CROWD: Ægistheus! King Ægistheus! Have pity on us!

A WOMAN: Pity, yes, pity, you cry. And will none have pity on me? He'll come with his slit throat, the man I loathed so bitterly, and clammy, unseen arms will maul me in the darkness, all through the night.

ORESTES: But this is madness! Why doesn't someone tell these wretched people—?

ZEUS: What's this, young man? Why this ado over a woman who's lost her nerve? Wait and see; there's worse to come.

A MAN [*falling on his knees*]: I stink! Oh, how I stink! I am a mass of rottenness. See how the flies are teeming round me, like carrion crows. . . . That's right, my harpies, sting and gouge and scavenge me; bore through my flesh to my black heart. I have sinned a thousand times, I am a sink of ordure, and I reek to heaven.

ZEUS: O worthy man!

SOME MAN [*helping him to his feet*]: That's enough. You shall talk about it later, when *they* are out.

[*Gasping, rolling his eyes, the man stares at them.*]

THE CROWD: Ægistheus! Ægistheus! For mercy's sake, give the order to begin. We can bear no more.

[ÆGISTHEUS *comes on to the temple steps, followed by*
CLYTEMNESTRA, THE HIGH PRIEST, *and* BODYGUARDS.]

ÆGISTHEUS: Dogs! How dare you bewail your lot? Have you forgotten your disgrace? Then, by Zeus, I shall refresh your memories. [*He turns to* CLYTEMNESTRA.] We must start without her, it seems. But let her beware! My punishment will be condign.

CLYTEMNESTRA: She promised to attend. No doubt she is making ready, lingering in front of her mirror.

ÆGISTHEUS [*to* THE SOLDIERS]: Go seek Electra in the palace and bring her here by force, if need be. [SOLDIERS *file out. He addresses* THE CROWD.] Take your usual places. The men on my right, women and children on my left. Good.

[*A short silence.* ÆGISTHEUS *is waiting.*]

HIGH PRIEST: Sire, these people are at breaking-point.

ÆGISTHEUS: I know. But I am waiting for—

[THE SOLDIERS *return.*]

A SOLDIER: Your Majesty, we have searched for the princess everywhere. But there is no one in the palace.

ÆGISTHEUS: So be it. We shall deal with her tomorrow. [*To* THE HIGH PRIEST] Begin.

HIGH PRIEST: Roll away the stone.

THE CROWD: Ah!

[THE SOLDIERS *roll away the stone*. THE HIGH PRIEST *goes to the entrance of the cavern.*]

HIGH PRIEST: You, the forgotten and forsaken, all you whose hopes were dupes, who creep along the ground darkling like smoke wraiths and have nothing left you but your great shame—you, the dead, arise; this is your day of days. Come up, pour forth like a thick cloud of fumes of brimstone driven by the wind; rise from the bowels of the earth, ye who have died a hundred deaths, ye whom every heartbeat in our breasts strikes dead again. In the name of anger unappeased and unappeasable, and the lust of vengeance, I summon you to wreak your hatred on the living. Come forth and scatter like a dark miasma in our streets, weave between the mother and her child, the lover and his beloved; make us regret that we, too, are not dead. Arise, spectres, harpies, ghouls, and goblins of our night. Soldiers arise, who died blaspheming; arise, downtrodden victims, children of disgrace; arise, all ye who died of hunger, whose last sigh was a curse. See, the living are here to greet you, fodder for your wrath. Arise and have at them like a great rushing wind, and gnaw them to the bone. Arise! Arise! Arise!

[*A tomtom sounds, and* THE PRIEST *dances at the entrance of the cavern, slowly at first, then quickening his gyrations until he falls to the ground exhausted.*]

ÆGISTHEUS: They are coming forth.

THE CROWD: Heaven help us!

ORESTES: I can bear this no longer. I must go—

ZEUS: Look at me, young man. In the eyes. Good; you understand. Now, keep quiet.

ORESTES: Who—who are you?

ZEUS: You shall know soon.

[ÆGISTHEUS *comes slowly down the temple steps.*]

ÆGISTHEUS: They are there. All of them. [*A short silence.*] There he is, Aricië, the husband you used so ill. There he is, beside you, kissing you tenderly, clasping you in his dead arms. How he loves you! And ah, how he hates you!... There she is, Nicias, your mother, who died of your neglect.... And you there, Segestes, you bloodsucker—they are all round you, the wretched men who borrowed of you; those who starved to death, and those who hanged themselves because of you. In your debt they died, but today they are your creditors. And you, fathers and mothers, loving parents, lower your eyes humbly. They are there, your dead children, stretching their frail arms towards you, and all the happiness you denied them, all the tortures you inflicted, weigh like lead on their sad, childish, unforgiving hearts.

THE CROWD: Have mercy!

ÆGISTHEUS: Mercy? You ask for mercy! Do you not know the dead have no mercy? Their grievances are time-proof, adamant; rancor without end. Do you hope, Nicias, to atone by deeds of kindness for the wrong you did your mother? But what act of kindness can ever reach her now? Her soul is like a sultry, windless noon, in which nothing stirs, nothing changes, nothing lives. Only a fierce unmoving sun beats down on bare rocks forever. The dead have ceased to be—think what that implies in all its ruthlessness—yes, they are no more, and in their eternal keeping your crimes have no reprieve.

THE CROWD: Mercy!

ÆGISTHEUS: Well you may cry mercy! Play your parts, you wretched mummers, for today you have a full house to watch you. Millions of staring, hopeless eyes are brooding darkly on your faces and your gestures. They can see us, read our hearts, and we are naked in the presence of the dead. Ah, that makes you squirm; it burns and sears you, that stern, calm gaze unchanging as the gaze of eyes remembered.

THE CROWD: Mercy!

THE MEN: Forgive us for living while you are dead.

THE WOMEN: Have mercy! Tokens of you are ever with us, we see your faces everywhere we turn. We wear mourning unceasingly, and weep for you from dawn till dusk, from dusk till dawn. But somehow, try as we may, your memory dwindles and slips through our fingers; daily it grows dimmer and we know ourselves the guiltier. Yes, you are leaving us, ebbing away like life-blood from a wound. And yet, know you well—if this can mollify your bitter hatred—that you, our dear departed, have laid waste our lives.

THE MEN: Forgive us for living while you are dead.

THE CHILDREN: Please forgive us. We didn't want to be born, we're ashamed of growing up. What wrong can we have done you? It's not our fault if we're alive. And only just alive; see how small we are, how pale and puny. We never laugh or sing, we glide about like ghosts. And we're so frightened of you, so terribly afraid. Have mercy on us.

THE MEN: Forgive us for living while you are dead.

ÆGISTHEUS: Hold your peace! If you voice your sorrow thus, what will be left for me, your King, to say? For my ordeal has begun; the earth is quaking, and the light failing, and the greatest of the dead is coming forth—he whom I slew with my own hand, King Agamemnon.

ORESTES [*drawing his sword*]: I forbid you to drag my father's name into this mummery.

ZEUS [*clutching his arms*]: Stop, young fellow! Stop that!

ÆGISTHEUS [*looking round*]: Who dares to—?

[ELECTRA, *wearing a white dress, comes on to the temple steps.* ÆGISTHEUS *sees her.*] Electra!

THE CROWD: Electra!

ÆGISTHEUS: What is the meaning of this, Electra? Why are you in white?

ELECTRA: It's my prettiest dress. The city holds high festival today, and I thought I'd look my best.

HIGH PRIEST: Would you insult our dead? This day is *their* day, and well you know it. You should be in mourning.

ELECTRA: Why? I'm not afraid of *my* dead, and yours mean nothing to me.

ÆGISTHEUS: That is so; your dead are not our dead. . . . Remember the breed she comes of, the breed of Atreus, who treacherously cut his nephews' throats. What are you, Electra, but the last survivor of an accursed race? Ay, that whorish dress becomes you. I suffered your presence in the palace out of pity, but now I know I erred; the old foul blood of the house of Atreus flows in your veins. And if I did not see to it, you would taint us all. But bide awhile, my girl, and you will learn how I can punish. Your eyes will be red with weeping for many a day.

THE CROWD: Sacrilege! Sacrilege! Away with her!

ÆGISTHEUS: Hear, miserable girl, the murmurs of these good folk you have outraged. Were I not here to curb their anger, they would tear you in pieces.

THE CROWD: Away with her, the impious wretch!

ELECTRA: Is it impious to be gay? Why can't these good folk of yours be gay? What prevents them?

ÆGISTHEUS: She is laughing, the wanton—and her dead father is standing there with blood on his face.

ELECTRA: How dare you talk of Agamemnon? How can you be so sure he doesn't visit me by night and tell me all his secrets? Ah, if you knew the love and longing that hoarse, dead voice breathes in my ears! Yes, I'm laughing—laughing for the first time in my life; for the first time I'm happy. And can you be so sure my new-won happiness doesn't rejoice my father's heart? More likely, if he's here and sees his daughter in her white dress—his daughter of whom you've made a wretched drudge—if he sees her holding her head high, keeping her pride intact, more likely the last thing he dreams of is to blame me. No, his eyes are sparkling in the havoc of his face, he's twisting his blood-stained lips in the shadow of a smile.

THE YOUNG WOMAN: Can it be true, what she says?

VOICES: No, no. She's talking nonsense. She's gone mad. Electra, go, for pity's sake, or your sins will be visited on us.

ELECTRA: But what is it you're so frightened of? I can see all round you and there's nothing but your own shadows. Now listen to what I've just been told, something you may not know. In Greece there are cities where men live happily. White, contented cities, basking like lizards in the sun. At this very moment, under this same sky, children are playing in the streets of Corinth. And their mothers aren't asking forgiveness for having brought them into the world. No, they're smiling tenderly at them, they're proud of their motherhood. Mothers of Argos, can't you understand? Does it mean nothing to you, the pride of a mother who looks at her son and thinks: "It's I who bore him, brought him up"?

ÆGISTHEUS: That's enough. Keep silent, or I'll thrust your words down your throat.

VOICES: Yes, yes. Make her stop. She's talked enough.

OTHER VOICES: No, let her speak. It's Agamemnon speaking through her.

ELECTRA: The sun is shining. Everywhere down in the plains men are looking up and saying: "It's a fine day," and they're happy. Are you so set on making yourselves wretched that you've forgotten the simple joy of the peasant who says as he walks across his fields: "It's a fine day"? No, there you stand hanging your heads, moping and mumbling, more dead than alive. You're too terrified to lift a finger, afraid of jolting your precious ghosts if you make any movement. That would be dreadful, wouldn't it, if your hand suddenly went through a patch of clammy mist, and it was your grandmother's ghost! Now look at me. I'm spreading out my arms freely, and I'm stretching like someone just roused from sleep. I have my place in the sunlight, my full place and to spare. And does the sky fall on my head? Now I'm dancing, see, I'm dancing, and all I feel is the wind's breath fanning my cheeks. Where are the dead? Do you think they're dancing with me, in step?

HIGH PRIEST: People of Argos, I tell you that this woman is a profaner of all we hold most holy. Woe to her and to all of you who listen to her words!

ELECTRA: Oh, my beloved dead—Iphigeneia, my elder sister, and Agamemnon, my father and my only King—hear my prayer. If I am an evil-doer, if I offend your sorrowing shades, make some sign that I may know. But if, my dear ones, you approve, let no leaf stir, no blade of grass be moved, and no sound break in on my sacred dance. For I am dancing for joy, for peace among men; I dance for happiness and life. My dead ones, I invoke your silence that these people around me may know your hearts are with me.

[*She dances.*]

VOICES IN THE CROWD: Look how she's dancing, light as a flame. Look how her dress is rippling, like a banner in the wind. And the dead—the dead do nothing.

THE YOUNG WOMAN: And see her look of ecstasy—oh, no, no, that's not the face of a wicked woman. Well, Ægistheus, what have you to say? Why are you silent?

ÆGISTHEUS: I waste no words on her. Does one argue with malignant vermin? No, one stamps them out. My kindness to her in the past was a mistake, but a mistake that can be remedied. Have no fear, I shall make short work of her and end her accursed race.

VOICES IN THE CROWD: Answer us, King Ægistheus. Threats are no answer.

THE YOUNG WOMAN: She's dancing, smiling, oh, so happily and the dead seem to protect her. Oh fortunate, too fortunate Electra! Look, I, too, am holding out my arms, baring my neck to the sunlight.

A VOICE IN THE CROWD: The dead hold their peace. Ægistheus, you have lied.

ORESTES: Dear Electra!

ZEUS: This is too much. I'll shut that foolish wench's tongue. [*Stretches out his right arm.*] Poseidon, carabou, carabou, roola. [*The big stone which blocked the entrance to the cavern rumbles across the stage and crashes against the temple steps.* ELECTRA *stops dancing.*]

THE CROWD: Ah!... Mercy on us!

[*A long silence.*]

HIGH PRIEST: Froward and fickle race, now you have seen how the dead avenge themselves. Mark how the flies are beating down on you, in thick, swirling clouds. You have hearkened to the tempter's voice, and a curse has fallen on the city.

THE CROWD: It is not our fault, we are innocent. That woman came and tempted us, with her lying tongue. To the river with her! Drown the witch.

AN OLD WOMAN [*pointing to* THE YOUNG WOMAN]: That young huzzy there was lapping up her words like milk. Strip her naked and lash her till she squeals. [THE WOMEN *seize* THE YOUNG WOMAN, *while* THE MEN *surge up the temple steps, towards* ELECTRA.]

ÆGISTHEUS [*straightening up*]: Silence, dogs! Back to your places! Vengeance is mine, not yours. [*A short silence.*] Well, you have seen what comes of disobeying me. Henceforth you will know better than to misdoubt your ruler. Disperse to your homes, the dead will keep you company and be your guests until tomorrow's dawn. Make place for them at your tables, at your hearths, and in your beds. And see that your good behavior blots out the memory of what has happened here. As for me—grieved though I am by your mistrust, I forgive you. But you, Electra—

ELECTRA: Yes? What of it? I failed to bring it off this time. Next time I'll do better.

ÆGISTHEUS: There shall be no next time. The custom of the city forbids my punishing you on the day the dead are with us. This you knew, and you took advantage of it. But you are no longer one of us; I cast you out forever. You shall go hence barefooted, with nothing in your hands, wearing that shameless dress. And I hereby order any man who sees you within our gates after the sun has risen to strike you down and rid the city of its bane.

[*He goes out, followed by* THE SOLDIERS. THE
CROWD *file past* ELECTRA, *shaking their fists at her.*]

ZEUS [*to* ORESTES]: Well, young master, were you duly edified? For, unless I'm much mistaken, the tale has a moral. The wicked have been punished and the good rewarded. [*He points to* ELECTRA.] As for that woman—

ORESTES [*sharply*]: Mind what you say. That woman is my sister. Now go; I want to talk to her.

ZEUS [*observes him for a moment, then shrugs his shoulders*]: Very good.

[Exit ZEUS *followed by* THE TUTOR.*]*

ORESTES: Electra!

ELECTRA [*still standing on the temple steps, she raises her eyes and gazes at him*]: Ah, you're still there, Philebus?

ORESTES: You're in danger, Electra. You mustn't stay a moment longer in this city.

ELECTRA: In danger? Yes, that's true. You saw how I failed to bring it off. It was a bit your fault, you know—but I'm not angry with you.

ORESTES: My fault? How?

ELECTRA: You deceived me. [*She comes down the steps towards him.*] Let me look at your eyes. Yes, it was your eyes that made a fool of me.

ORESTES: There's no time to lose. Listen, Electra! We'll escape together. Someone's getting a horse for me and you can ride pillion.

ELECTRA: No.

ORESTES: What? You won't come away with me?

ELECTRA: I refuse to run away.

ORESTES: I'll take you with me to Corinth.

ELECTRA [*laughing*]: Corinth? Exactly! I know you mean well, but you're fooling me again. What could a girl like me do in Corinth? I've got to keep a level head, you know. Only yesterday my desires were so simple, so modest. When I waited at table, with meek, downcast eyes, I used to watch the two of them—the handsome old woman with the dead face, and the fat, pale King with the slack mouth and that absurd beard like a regiment of spiders running round his chin. And then I'd dream of what I'd see one day—a wisp of steam, like one's breath on a cold morning, rising from their split bellies. That was the only thing I lived for, Philebus, I assure you. I don't know what you're after, but this I know: that I mustn't believe you. Your eyes are too bold for my liking. . . . Do you know what I used to tell myself before I met you? That a wise person can want nothing better from life than to pay back the wrong that has been done to him.

ORESTES: If you come with me, Electra, you'll see there are many, many other things to ask of life—without one's ceasing to be wise.

ELECTRA: No, I won't listen any more, you've done me quite enough harm already. You came here with your kind, girlish face and your eager eyes—and you made me forget my hatred. I unlocked my hands and I let my one and only treasure slip through them. You lured me into thinking one could cure the people here by words. Well, you saw what happened. They nurse their disease; they've got to like their sores so much that they scratch them with their dirty nails to keep them festering. Words are no use for such as they. An evil thing is conquered only by another evil thing, and only violence can save them. So good-by, Philebus, and leave me to my bad dreams.

ORESTES: They'll kill you.

ELECTRA: We have a sanctuary here, Apollo's shrine. Often criminals take shelter there, and so long as they are in the temple, no one can touch a hair of their heads. That's where I'll go.

ORESTES: But why refuse my help?

ELECTRA: It's not for you to help me. Someone else will come, to set me free. [*A short silence.*] My brother isn't dead; I know that. And I'm waiting for his coming.

ORESTES: Suppose he doesn't come?

ELECTRA: He *will* come; he's bound to come. He is of our stock, you see; he has crime and tragedy in his blood, as I have—the bad blood of the house of Atreus. I picture him as a big, strong man, a born fighter, with bloodshot eyes like our father's, always smoldering with rage. He, too, is doomed; tangled up in his destiny, like a horse whose belly is ripped open and his legs are caught up in his guts. And now at every step he tears his bowels out. Yes, one day he will come, this city draws him. Nothing can hinder his coming, for it is here he can do the greatest harm, and suffer the greatest harm. I often seem to see him coming, with lowered head, sullen with pain, muttering angry words. He scares me; every night I see him in my dreams, and I wake screaming with terror. But I'm waiting for him and I love him. I must stay here to direct his rage—for I, anyhow, keep a clear head—to point to the guilty and say: "Those are they, Orestes. Strike!"

ORESTES: And suppose he isn't like that at all?

ELECTRA: How can he be otherwise? Don't forget he's the son of Agamemnon and Clytemnestra.

ORESTES: But mightn't he be weary of all that tale of wickedness and bloodshed; if, for instance, he'd been brought up in a happy, peaceful city?

ELECTRA: Then I'd spit in his face, and I'd say: "Go away, you cur; go and keep company where you belong, with women. But you're reckoning without your doom, poor fool. You're a grandson of Atreus, and you can't escape the heritage of blood. You prefer shame to crime; so be it. But Fate will come and hunt you down in your bed; you'll have the shame to start with, and then you will commit the crime, however much you shirk it."

ORESTES: Electra, I am Orestes.

ELECTRA [*with a cry*]: Oh!.... You liar!

ORESTES: By the shades of my father, Agamemnon, I swear I am Orestes. [*A short silence.*] Well? Why don't you carry out your threat and spit in my face?

ELECTRA: How could I? [*She gazes at him earnestly.*] So those shining eyes, that noble forehead, are—my brother's! Orestes.... Oh, I'd rather you had stayed Philebus, and my brother was dead. [*Shyly*] Was it true, what you said about your having lived at Corinth?

ORESTES: No. I was brought up by some well-to-do Athenians.

ELECTRA: How young you look! Have you ever been in battle? Has that sword you carry ever tasted blood?

ORESTES: Never.

ELECTRA: It's strange. I felt less lonely when I didn't know you. I was waiting for the Orestes of my dream; always thinking of his strength and of my weakness. And now you're there before me; Orestes, the real Orestes, was you all the time. I look at you and I see we're just a boy and a girl, two young orphans. But, you know, I love you. More than I'd have loved the other Orestes.

ORESTES: Then, if you love me, come away. We'll leave this place together.

ELECTRA: Leave Argos? No. It's here the doom of the Atrides must be played out, and I am of the house of Atreus. I ask nothing of you. I've nothing more to ask of Philebus. But here I stay.

[ZEUS *enters, back stage, and takes cover to listen to them.*]

ORESTES: Electra, I'm Orestes, your brother. I, too, am of the house of Atreus, and my place is at your side.

ELECTRA: No. You're not my brother; you're a stranger. Orestes is dead, and so much the better for him. From now on I'll do homage to his shade, along with my father's and my sister's. You, Philebus, claim to be of our house. So be it! But can you truly say that you are one of *us*? Was *your* childhood darkened by the shadow of a murder? No, more likely you were a quiet little boy with happy, trustful eyes, the pride of your adoptive father. Naturally you could trust people—they always had a smile for you—just as you could trust the solid friendly things around you: tables, beds, and stairs. And because you were rich, and always nicely dressed, and had lots of toys, you must have often thought the world was quite a nice world to live in, like a big warm bath in which one can splash and loll contentedly. My childhood was quite different. When I was six I was a drudge, and I mistrusted everything and everyone. [*A short pause.*] So go away, my noble-souled brother. I have no use for noble souls; what I need is an accomplice.

ORESTES: How could I leave you alone; above all, now that you've lost even your last hope? . . . What do you propose to do here?

ELECTRA: That's my business. Good-by, Philebus.

ORESTES: So you're driving me away? [*He takes some steps, then halts and faces her.*] Is it my fault if I'm not the fierce young swashbuckler you expected? Him you'd have taken by the hand at once and said: "Strike!" Of me you asked nothing. But, good heavens, why should I be outcast by my own sister—when I've not even been put to the test?

ELECTRA: No, Philebus, I could never lay such a load upon a heart like yours; a heart that has no hatred in it.

ORESTES: You are right. No hatred; but no love, either. You, Electra, I might have loved. And yet—I wonder. Love or hatred calls for self-surrender. He cuts a fine figure, the warm-blooded, prosperous man, solidly entrenched in his well-being, who one fine day surrenders all to love—or to hatred; himself, his house, his land, his memories. But who am I, and what have I to surrender? I'm a mere shadow of a man; of all the ghosts haunting this town today, none is ghostlier than I. The only loves I've known were phantom loves, rare and vacillating as will-o'-the-wisps. The solid passions of the living were never mine. Never! [*A short silence.*] But, oh, the shame of it. Here I am, back in the town where I was born, and my own sister disavows me. And now—where shall I go? What city must I haunt?

ELECTRA: Isn't there some pretty girl waiting for you—somewhere in the world?

ORESTES: Nobody is waiting for me anywhere. I wander from city to city, a stranger to all others and to myself, and the cities close again behind me like the waters of a pool. If I leave Argos, what trace of my coming will remain, except the cruel disappointment of your hope?

ELECTRA: You told me about happy towns—

ORESTES: What do I care for happiness? I want my share of memories, my native soil, my place among the men of Argos. [*A short silence.*] Electra, I shall not leave Argos.

ELECTRA: Please, please, Philebus, go away. If you have any love for me, go. It hurts me to think what may come to you here—nothing but evil, that I know—and your innocence would ruin all my plans.

ORESTES: I shall not go.

ELECTRA: How can you think I'd let you stay beside me—you with your stubborn uprightness—to pass silent judgment on my acts? Oh, why are you so obstinate? Nobody wants you here.

ORESTES: It's my one chance, and you, Electra—surely you won't refuse it to me? Try to understand. I want to be a man who belongs to some place, a man among comrades. Only consider. Even the slave bent beneath his load, dropping with fatigue and staring dully at the ground a foot in front of him—why, even that poor slave can say he's in *his* town, as a tree is in a forest, or a leaf upon the tree. Argos is all around him, warm, compact, and comforting. Yes, Electra, I'd gladly be that slave and enjoy that feeling of drawing the city round me like a blanket and curling myself up in it. No, I shall not go.

ELECTRA: Even if you stayed a hundred years among us, you'd still be a stranger here, and lonelier than if you were tramping the highroads of Greece. The townspeople would be watching you all the time from the corner of an eye, and they'd lower their voices when you came near.

ORESTES: Is it really so hard to win a place among you? My sword can serve the city, and I have gold to help the needy.

ELECTRA: We are not short of captains, or of charitable souls.

ORESTES: In that case— [*He takes some steps away from her, with lowered eyes.* ZEUS *comes forward and gazes at him, rubbing his hands.* ORESTES *raises his eyes heavenwards.*] Ah, if only I knew which path to take! O Zeus, our Lord and King of Heaven, not often have I called on you for help, and you have shown me little favor; yet this you know: that I have always tried to act aright. But now I am weary and my mind is dark; I can no longer distinguish right from wrong. I need a guide to point my way. Tell me, Zeus, is it truly your will that a king's son, hounded from this city, should meekly school himself to banishment and slink away from his ancestral home like a whipped cur? I cannot think it. And yet—and yet you have forbidden the shedding of blood. . . . What have I said? Who spoke of bloodshed? . . . O Zeus, I beseech you, if meek acceptance, the bowed head and lowly heart are what you would have of me, make plain your will by some sign; for no longer can I see my path.

ZEUS [*aside*]: Ah, that's where I can help, my young friend. Abraxas, abraxas, tsou, tsou.

[*Light flashes out round the stone.*]

ELECTRA [*laughing*]: Splendid! It's raining miracles today! See what comes of being a pious young man and asking counsel of the gods. [*She is convulsed with laughter and can hardly get the words out.*] Oh, noble youth, Philebus, darling of the gods! "Show me a sign," you asked. "Show me a sign." Well, now you've had your sign—a blaze of light round that precious, sacred stone of theirs. So off you go to Corinth! Off you go!

ORESTES [*staring at the stone*]: So that is the Right Thing. To live at peace—always at perfect peace. I see. Always to say "Excuse me," and "Thank you." That's what's wanted, eh? [*He stares at the stone in silence for some moments.*] The Right Thing. *Their* Right Thing. [*Another silence.*] Electra!

ELECTRA: Hurry up and go. Don't disappoint your fatherly old friend, who has bent down from Olympus to enlighten you. [*She stops abruptly, a look of wonder on her face.*] But—but what's come over you?

ORESTES [*slowly, in a tone he has not used till now*]: There is another way.

ELECTRA [*apprehensively*]: No, Philebus, don't be stubborn. You asked the gods for orders; now you have them.

ORESTES: Orders? What do you mean? Ah yes, the light round that big stone. But it's not for me, that light; from now on I'll take no one's orders, neither man's nor god's.

ELECTRA: You're speaking in riddles.

ORESTES: What a change has come on everything, and, oh, how far away you seem! Until now I felt something warm and living round me, like a friendly presence. That something has just died. What emptiness! What endless emptiness, as far as eye can reach! [*He takes some steps away from her.*] Night is coming on. The air is getting chilly, isn't it? But what was it—what was it that died just now?

ELECTRA: Philebus—

ORESTES: I say there is another path—*my* path. Can't you see it? It starts here and leads down to the city. I must go down—do you understand?—I must go down into the depths, among you. For you are living, all of you, at the bottom of a pit. [*He goes up to* ELECTRA.] You are *my* sister, Electra, and that city is *my* city. *My* sister. [*He takes her arm.*]

ELECTRA: Don't touch me. You're hurting me, frightening me—and I'm *not* yours.

ORESTES: I know. Not yet. I'm still too—too light. I must take a burden on my shoulders, a load of guilt so heavy as to drag me down, right down into the abyss of Argos.

ELECTRA: But what—what do you mean to do?

ORESTES: Wait. Give me time to say farewell to all the lightness, the aery lightness that was mine. Let me say good-by to my youth. There are evenings at Corinth and at Athens, golden evenings full of songs and scents and laughter; these I shall never know again. And mornings, too, radiant with promise. Good-by to them all, good-by.... Come, Electra, look at our city. There it lies, rose-red in the sun, buzzing with men and flies, drowsing its doom away in the languor of a summer afternoon. It fends me off with its high walls, red roofs, locked doors. And yet it's mine for the taking; I've felt that since this morning. You, too, Electra, are mine for the taking—and I'll take you, too. I'll turn into an ax and hew those walls asunder, I'll rip open the bellies of those stolid houses and there will steam up from the gashes a stench of rotting food and incense. I'll be an iron wedge driven into the city, like a wedge rammed into the heart of an oak tree.

ELECTRA: Oh, how you've changed! Your eyes have lost their glow; they're dull and smoldering. I'm sorry for that, Philebus; you were so gentle. But now you're talking like the Orestes of my dreams.

ORESTES: Listen! All these people quaking with fear in their dark rooms, with their dear departed round them—supposing I take over all their crimes. Supposing I set out to win the name of "guilt-stealer," and heap on myself all their remorse; that of the woman unfaithful to her husband, of the tradesman who let his mother die, of the usurer who bled his victims white? Surely once I am plagued with all those pangs of conscience, innumerable as the flies of Argos—surely then I shall have earned the freedom of your city. Shall I not be as much at home within your red walls as the red-aproned butcher in his shop, among the carcasses of flayed sheep and cattle?

ELECTRA: So you wish to atone for us?

ORESTES: To atone? No. I said I'd house your penitence, but I did *not* say what I'd do with all those cackling fowls; maybe I'll wring their necks.

ELECTRA: And how can you take over our sense of guilt?

ORESTES: Why, all of you ask nothing better than to be rid of it. Only the King and Queen force you to nurse it in your foolish hearts.

ELECTRA: The King and Queen—Oh, Philebus!

ORESTES: The gods bear witness that I had no wish to shed their blood.

[*A long silence.*]

ELECTRA: You're too young, too weak.

ORESTES: Are you going to draw back—*now?* Hide me somewhere in the palace, and lead me tonight to the royal bedchamber—and then you'll see if I am too weak!

ELECTRA: Orestes!

ORESTES: Ah! For the first time you've called me Orestes.

ELECTRA: Yes. I know you now. You are indeed Orestes. I didn't recognize you at first, I'd expected somebody quite different. But this throbbing in my blood, this sour taste on my lips—I've had them in my dreams, and I know what they mean.

So at last you have come, Orestes, and your resolve is sure. And here I am beside you—just as in my dreams—on the brink of an act beyond all remedy. And I'm frightened; that, too, was in my dreams. How long I've waited for this moment, dreading and hoping for it! From now on, all the moments will link up, like the cogs in a machine, and we shall never rest again until they both are lying on their backs, with faces like crushed mulberries. In a pool of blood. To think it's you who are going to shed it, you with those gentle eyes! I'm sorry now, sorry that never again I'll see that gentleness, never again see Philebus. Orestes, you are my elder brother, and head of our house; fold me in your arms, protect me. Much suffering, many perils lie ahead of both of us.

[ORESTES *takes her in his arms.* ZEUS *leaves his hiding-place and creeps out on tiptoe.*]

[*Curtain*]

Scene 2

The throne-room in the palace. An awe-inspiring, blood-smeared image of ZEUS *occupies a prominent position. The sun is setting.*

[ELECTRA *enters, then beckons to* ORESTES *to follow her.*]

ORESTES: Someone's coming.

[*He begins to draw his sword.*]

ELECTRA: It's the sentries on their rounds. Follow me. I know where to hide.

[*Two* SOLDIERS *enter.*]

FIRST SOLDIER: I can't think what's come over the flies this evening. They're all crazy-like.

SECOND SOLDIER: They smell the dead; that's why they're in such a state. Why, I daren't open my mouth to yawn for fear they all come teeming down my throat and start a round dance in my gullet. [ELECTRA *peeps from her hiding-place, then quickly withdraws her head.*] Hear that? Something creaked yonder.

FIRST SOLDIER: Oh, it's only Agamemnon, sitting down on his throne.

SECOND SOLDIER: And the seat creaked when he planted his fat bottom on it? No, it couldn't be that; a dead man's light as air.

FIRST SOLDIER: That goes for common folk like you and me. But a king, he's different. Mind you, Agamemnon always did himself proud at table. Why, he weighed two hundred pounds or more if he weighed one. It would be surprising if there wasn't some pounds left of all that flesh.

SECOND SOLDIER: So—so you think he's here, do you?

FIRST SOLDIER: Where else should he be? If I was a dead king and I had twenty-four hours' leave each year, you may be sure I'd spend them squatting on my throne, just to remind me of the high old times I had when I was His Almighty Majesty. And I'd stay put; I wouldn't run round pestering folk in their houses.

SECOND SOLDIER: Ah, wouldn't you? You say that because you're alive. But if you were dead, you'd be just as nasty as the others. [FIRST SOLDIER *smacks his face.*] Hey! What are you up to?

FIRST SOLDIER: I'm doing you a good turn. Look, I've killed seven of 'em, all at a go.

SECOND SOLDIER: Seven what? Seven dead 'uns?

FIRST SOLDIER: O' course not. *Flies.* Look, my hand's all bloody. [*He wipes it on his pants.*] Ugh, the filthy brutes!

SECOND SOLDIER: Pity you can't swat the lot of them while you're about it. The dead men, now—they don't do nothing, they know how to behave. If the flies were all killed off, we'd have some peace.

FIRST SOLDIER: Peace, you say? No, if I thought there were ghost-flies here as well, that'd be the last straw.

SECOND SOLDIER: Why?

FIRST SOLDIER: Don't you see? They die by millions every day, the little buzzers. Well, if all the flies that have died since last summer were set loose in the town, there'd be three hundred and sixty-five dead flies for every one that's here. The air'd be laced with flies, we'd breathe flies, eat flies, sweat flies; they'd be rolling down our throats in clusters and bunging up our lungs. . . . I wonder, now—maybe that's why there's such a funny smell in this room.

SECOND SOLDIER: No, no, it ain't that. They say our dead men have foul breaths, you know. And this room's not so big as it looks—a thousand square feet or so, I should say. Two or three dead men would be enough to foul the air.

FIRST SOLDIER: That's so. Fussing and fuming like they do.

SECOND SOLDIER: I tell you there's something amiss here. I heard a floor-board creak over there.

[*They go behind the throne to investigate.* ORESTES *and* ELECTRA *slip out on the left and tiptoe past the steps of the throne, returning to their hiding-place just as the* SOLDIERS *emerge on the left.*]

FIRST SOLDIER: You see, there ain't nobody. It's only that old sod Agamemnon. Like as not, he's sitting on them cushions, straight as a poker. I shouldn't be surprised if he's watching you and me for want of anything else to do.

SECOND SOLDIER: Ay, and we'd better have a good look round, I ain't easy in my mind. These flies are something wicked, but it can't be helped.

FIRST SOLDIER: I wish I was back in the barracks. At least the dead folk there are old chums come back to visit us, just ordinary folk like us. But when I think that His Late Lamented Majesty is there, like as not counting the buttons missing on my tunic, well it makes me dithery, like when the general's doing an inspection.

[*Enter* ÆGISTHEUS *and* CLYTEMNESTRA, *followed by* SERVANTS *carrying lamps.*]

ÆGISTHEUS: Go, all of you.

[*Exeunt* SOLDIERS *and* SERVANTS.]

CLYTEMNESTRA: What is troubling you tonight?

ÆGISTHEUS: You saw what happened? Had I not played upon their fear, they'd have shaken off their remorse in the twinkling of an eye.

CLYTEMNESTRA: Is that all? Then be reassured. You will always find a way to freeze their courage when the need arises.

ÆGISTHEUS: I know. Oh, I'm only too skillful in the art of false pretense. [*A short silence.*] I am sorry I had to rebuke Electra.

CLYTEMNESTRA: Why? Because she is my daughter? It pleased you to so do, and all you do has my approval.

ÆGISTHEUS: Woman, it is not on your account that I regret it.

CLYTEMNESTRA: Then—why? You used not to have much love for Electra.

ÆGISTHEUS: I am tired. So tired. For fifteen years I have been upholding the remorse of a whole city, and my arms are aching with the strain. For fifteen years I have been dressing a part, playing the scaremonger, and the black of my robes has seeped through to my soul.

CLYTEMNESTRA: But, sire, I, too—

ÆGISTHEUS: I know, woman, I know. You are going to tell me of your remorse. I wish I shared it. It fills out the void of your life. I have no remorse—and no man in Argos is sadder than I.

CLYTEMNESTRA: My sweet lord—

[*She goes up to him affectionately.*]

ÆGISTHEUS: Keep off, you whore! Are you not ashamed—under his eyes?

CLYTEMNESTRA: Under his eyes? Who can see us here?

ÆGISTHEUS: Why, the King. The dead came forth this morning.

CLYTEMNESTRA: Sire, I beg you—the dead are underground and will not trouble us for many a long day. Have you forgotten it was you yourself who invented that fable to impress your people?

ÆGISTHEUS: That's so. Well, it only shows how tired I am, how sick at heart. Now leave me to my thoughts. [*Exit* CLYTEMNESTRA.] Have you in me, Lord Zeus, the king you wished for Argos? I come and go among my people, I speak in trumpet tones, I parade the terror of my frown, and all who see me cringe in an agony of repentance. But I—what am I but an empty shell? Some creature has devoured me unawares, gnawed out my inner self. And now, looking within, I see I am more dead than Agamemnon. Did I say I was sad? I lied. Neither sad nor gay is the desert—a boundless waste of sand under a burning waste of sky. Not sad, nor gay, but—sinister. Ah, I'd give my kingdom to be able to shed a tear.

[ZEUS *enters.*]

ZEUS: That's right. Complain away! You're only a king, like every other king.

ÆGISTHEUS: Who are you? What are you doing here?

ZEUS: So you don't recognize me?

ÆGISTHEUS: Be gone, stranger, or I shall have you thrown out by my guards.

ZEUS: You don't recognize me? Still, you have seen me often enough in dreams. It's true I looked more awe-inspiring. [*Flashes of lightning, a peal of thunder.* ZEUS *assumes an awe-inspiring air.*] And now you do know me?

ÆGISTHEUS: Zeus!

ZEUS: Good! [*Affable again, he goes up to the statue.*] So that's meant to be me? It's thus the Argives picture me at their prayers? Well, well, it isn't often that a god can study his likeness, face to face. [*A short silence.*] How hideous I am! They cannot like me much.

ÆGISTHEUS: They fear you.

ZEUS: Excellent! I've no use for love. Do you, Ægistheus, love me?

ÆGISTHEUS: What do you want of me? Have I not paid heavily enough?

ZEUS: Never enough.

ÆGISTHEUS: But it's killing me, the task I have undertaken.

ZEUS: Come now! Don't exaggerate! Your health is none too bad; you're fat. Mind, I'm not reproaching you. It's good, royal fat, yellow as tallow—just as it should be. You're built to live another twenty years.

ÆGISTHEUS: Another twenty years!

ZEUS: Would you rather die?

ÆGISTHEUS: Yes.

ZEUS: So, if anyone came here now, with a drawn sword, would you bare your breasts to him?

ÆGISTHEUS: I—I cannot say.

ZEUS: Now mark my words. If you let yourself be slaughtered like a dumb ox, your doom will be exemplary. You shall be King in hell for all eternity. That's what I came here to tell you.

ÆGISTHEUS: Is someone planning to kill me?

ZEUS: So it seems.

ÆGISTHEUS: Electra?

ZEUS: Not only Electra.

ÆGISTHEUS: Who?

ZEUS: Orestes.

ÆGISTHEUS: Oh!... Well, that's in the natural order of things, no doubt. What can I do against it?

ZEUS [*mimicking his tone*]: What can I do? [*Imperiously*] Bid your men arrest a young stranger going under the name of Philebus. Have him and Electra thrown into a dungeon—and if you leave them there to rot, I'll think no worse of you. Well, what are you waiting for? Call your men.

ÆGISTHEUS: No.

ZEUS: Be good enough to tell me why that no.

ÆGISTHEUS: I am tired.

ZEUS: Don't stare at the ground. Raise your big, bloodshot eyes and look at me. That's better. Yes, you're majestically stupid, like a horse; a kingly fool. But yours is not the stubbornness that vexes me; rather, it will add a spice to your surrender. For I know you will obey me in the end.

ÆGISTHEUS: I tell you I refuse to fall in with your plans. I have done so far too often.

ZEUS: That's right. Show your mettle! Resist! Resist! Ah, how I cherish souls like yours! Your eyes flash, you clench your fists, you fling refusal in the teeth of Zeus. None the less, my little rebel, my restive little horse, no sooner had I warned you than your heart said yes. Of course you'll obey. Do you think I leave Olympus without good reason? I wished to warn you of this crime because it is my will to avert it.

ÆGISTHEUS: To warn me! How strange!

ZEUS: Why "strange"? Surely it's natural enough. Your life's in danger and I want to save it.

ÆGISTHEUS: Who asked you to save it? What about Agamemnon? Did you warn *him?* And yet *he* wished to live.

ZEUS: O miserable man, what base ingratitude! You are dearer to me than Agamemnon, and when I prove this, you complain!

ÆGISTHEUS: Dearer than Agamemnon? I? No, it's Orestes whom you cherish. You allowed me to work my doom, you let me rush in, ax in hand, to King Agamemnon's bath—and no doubt you watched from high Olympus, licking your lips at the thought of another damned soul to gloat over. But today you are protecting young Orestes against himself; and I, whom you egged on to kill his father—you have chosen me to restrain the young man's hand. I was a poor creature, just qualified for murder; but for Orestes, it seems, you have higher destinies in view.

ZEUS: What strange jealousy is this! But have no fear; I love him no more than I love you. I love nobody.

ÆGISTHEUS: Then see what you have made of me, unjust god that you are. And tell me this. If today you hinder the crime Orestes has in mind, why did you permit mine of fifteen years ago?

ZEUS: All crimes do not displease me equally. And now, Ægistheus, I shall speak to you frankly, as one king to another. The first crime was mine: I committed it when I made man mortal. Once I had done that, what was left for you, poor human murderers, to do? To kill your victims? But they already had the seed of death in them; all you could do was to hasten its fruition by a year or two. Do you know what would have befallen Agamemnon if you had not killed him? Three months later he'd have died of apoplexy in a pretty slave-girl's arms. But your crime served my ends.

ÆGISTHEUS: What ends? For fifteen years I have been atoning for it—and you say it served your ends!

ZEUS: Exactly. It's because you are atoning for it that it served my ends. I like crimes that *pay*. I like yours because it was a clumsy, boorish murder, a crime that did not know itself, a crime in the antique mode, more like a cataclysm than an act of man. Not for one moment did you defy me. You struck in a frenzy of fear and rage. And then, when your frenzy had died down, you looked back on the deed with loathing and disowned it. Yet what a profit I have made on it! For one dead man, twenty thousand living men wallowing in repentance. Yes, it was a good bargain I struck that day.

ÆGISTHEUS: I see what lies behind your words. Orestes will have no remorse.

ZEUS: Not a trace of it. At this moment he is thinking out his plan, coolly, methodically, cheerfully. What good to me is a carefree murder, a shameless, sedate crime, that lies light as thistledown on the murderer's conscience? No, I won't allow it. Ah, how I loathe the crimes of this new generation; thankless and sterile as the wind! Yes, that nice-minded young man will kill you as he'd kill a chicken; he'll go away with red hands and a clean heart. In your place I should feel humiliated. So—call your men!

ÆGISTHEUS: Again I tell you, I will *not*. The crime that is being hatched displeases you enough for me to welcome it.

ZEUS: Ægistheus, you are a king, and it's to your sense of kingship I appeal, for you enjoy wielding the scepter.

ÆGISTHEUS: Continue.

ZEUS: You may hate me, but we are akin; I made you in my image. A king is a god on earth, glorious and terrifying as a god.

ÆGISTHEUS: You, terrifying?

ZEUS: Look at me. [*A long silence.*] I told you you were made in my image. Each keeps order; you in Argos, I in heaven and on earth—and you and I harbor the same dark secret in our hearts.

ÆGISTHEUS: I have no secret.

ZEUS: You have. The same as mine. The bane of gods and kings. The bitterness of knowing men are free. Yes, Ægistheus, they are free. But your subjects do not know it, and you do.

ÆGISTHEUS: Why, yes. If they knew it, they'd send my palace up in flames. For fifteen years I've been playing a part to mask their power from them.

ZEUS: So you see we are alike.

ÆGISTHEUS: Alike? A god likening himself to me—what freak of irony is this? Since I came to the throne, all I said, all my acts, have been aimed at building up an image of myself. I wish each of my subjects to keep that image in the foreground of his mind, and to feel, even when alone, that my eyes are on him, severely judging his most private thoughts. But I have been trapped in my own net. I have come to see myself only as they see me. I peer into the dark pit of their souls, and there, deep down, I see the image that I have built up. I shudder, but I cannot take my eyes off it. Almighty Zeus, who am I? Am I anything more than the dread that others have of me?

ZEUS: And I—who do you think *I* am? [*Points to the statue.*] I, too, have my image, and do you suppose it doesn't fill me with confusion? For a hundred thousand years I have been dancing a slow, dark ritual dance before men's eyes. Their eyes are so intent on me that they forget to look into themselves. If I forgot myself for a single moment, if I let their eyes turn away—

ÆGISTHEUS: Yes?

ZEUS: Enough. That is *my* business. Ægistheus, I know that you are weary of it all; but why complain? You'll die one day—but I shall not. So long as there are men on earth, I am doomed to go on dancing before them.

ÆGISTHEUS: Alas! But who has doomed us?

ZEUS: No one but ourselves. For we have the same passion. You, Ægistheus, have, like me, a passion for order.

ÆGISTHEUS: For order? That is so. It was for the sake of order that I wooed Clytemnestra, for order that I killed my King; I wished that order should prevail, and that it should prevail through me. I have lived without love, without hope, even without lust. But I have kept order. Yes, I have kept good order in my kingdom. That has been my ruling passion; a godlike passion, but how terrible!

ZEUS: We could have no other, you and I; I am God, and you were born to be a king.

ÆGISTHEUS: Ay, more's the pity!

ZEUS: Ægistheus, my creature and my mortal brother, in the name of this good order that we serve, both you and I, I ask you—nay, I command you—to lay hands on Orestes and his sister.

ÆGISTHEUS: Are they so dangerous?

ZEUS: Orestes knows that he is free.

ÆGISTHEUS [*eagerly*]: He knows he's free? Then, to lay hands on him, to put him in irons, is not enough. A free man in a city acts like a plague-spot. He will infect my whole kingdom and bring my work to nothing. Almighty Zeus, why stay your hand? Why not fell him with a thunderbolt?

ZEUS [*slowly*]: Fell him with a thunderbolt? [*A pause. Then, in a muffled voice*] Ægistheus, the gods have another secret.

ÆGISTHEUS: Yes?

ZEUS: Once freedom lights its beacon in a man's heart, the gods are powerless against him. It's a matter between man and man, and it is for other men, and for them only, to let him go his gait, or to throttle him.

ÆGISTHEUS [*observing him closely*]: To throttle him? Be it so. Well, I shall do your will, no doubt. But say no more, and stay here no longer—I could not bear it. [*As* ZEUS *departs,* ELECTRA *leaps forward and rushes to the door.* ORESTES *comes forward.*]

ELECTRA: Strike him down! Don't give him time to call for help. I'll bar the door.

ÆGISTHEUS: So you, young man, are Orestes?

ORESTES: Defend yourself.

ÆGISTHEUS: I shall not defend myself. It's too late for me to call for help, and I am glad it is too late. No, I shall not resist. I *wish* you to kill me.

ORESTES: Good. Little I care how it is done. . . . So I am to be a murderer.

[ORESTES *strikes him with his sword.*]

ÆGISTHEUS [*tottering*]: Ah! You struck well, Orestes. [*He clings to* ORESTES.] Let me look at you. Is it true you feel no remorse?

ORESTES: Remorse? Why should I feel remorse? I am only doing what is right.

ÆGISTHEUS: What is right is the will of God. You were hidden here and you heard the words of Zeus.

ORESTES: What do I care for Zeus? Justice is a matter between men, and I need no god to teach me it. It's right to stamp you out, like the foul brute you are, and to free the people of Argos from your evil influence. It is right to restore to them their sense of human dignity.

ÆGISTHEUS [*groaning*]: Pain! What agony!

ELECTRA: Look! Look! He's swaying; his face has gone quite gray. What an ugly sight's a dying man!

ORESTES: Keep silent! Let him carry with him to the grave no other memory than the memory of our joy.

ÆGISTHEUS: My curse on you both!

ORESTES: Won't you have done with dying?

> [*He strikes again. ÆGISTHEUS falls.*]

ÆGISTHEUS: Beware of the flies, Orestes, beware of the flies. All is not over.

> [*Dies.*]

ORESTES [*giving the body a kick*]: For him, anyhow, all is over. Now lead me to the Queen's room.

ELECTRA: Orestes!

ORESTES: What?

ELECTRA: She—she can do us no more harm.

ORESTES: What of it? What has come over you? This is not how you spoke a little while ago.

ELECTRA: Orestes! You, too, have changed. I hardly recognize you.

ORESTES: Very well. I'll go alone.

> [*Exit.*]

ELECTRA [*to herself*]: Will she scream? [*Silence. She is listening.*] He's walking down the passage. When he opens the fourth door—Oh, I wanted this to happen. And I—I want it now, I *must* want it. [*She looks at ÆGISTHEUS.*] That one—yes, he's dead. So this is what I wanted. I didn't realize how it would be. [*She comes closer to the body.*] A hundred times I've seen him, in my dreams, lying just where he is now, with a sword through his heart. His eyes were closed, he seemed asleep. How I hated him, what joy I got from hating him! But he doesn't seem asleep; his eyes are open, staring up at me. He is dead, and my hatred is dead, too. And I'm standing here, waiting, waiting. That woman is still alive, she's in her bedroom, and presently she'll be screaming. Screaming like an animal in pain. No, I can't bear those eyes any longer. [*Kneeling, she lays a mantle over the King's face.*] What was it, then, I wanted? What? [*A short silence. CLYTEMNESTRA screams.*] He's struck her. She was our mother—and he's struck her. [*She rises to her feet.*] It's done; my enemies are dead. For years and years I've reveled in the thought of this, and, now it's happened, my heart is like a lump of ice. Was I lying to myself all those years? No, that's not true, it can't be true. I'm not a coward. Only a moment ago I wanted it, and I haven't changed. I'm glad, glad, to see that swine lying at my feet. [*She jerks the mantle off the dead King's face.*] Those dead-fish eyes goggling up at nothing—why should they trouble me? That's how I wanted to see them, dead and staring, and I'm glad, glad— [CLYTEMNESTRA*'s screams are weakening.*] Let her scream! Make her scream, Orestes. I want her to suffer. [*The screams cease.*] Oh joy, joy! I'm weeping for joy; my enemies are dead, my father is avenged. [ORESTES *returns, his sword dripping blood.* ELECTRA *runs to him and flings herself into his arms.*]

ELECTRA: Orestes! . . . Oh! . . .

ORESTES: You're frightened. Why?

ELECTRA: I'm not frightened. I'm drunk. Drunk with joy. What did she say? Did she beg for mercy long?

ORESTES: Electra. I shall not repent of what I have done, but I think fit not to speak of it. There are some memories one does not share. It is enough for you to know she's dead.

ELECTRA: Did she die cursing us? That's all I want you to tell me. Did she curse us?

ORESTES: Yes. She died cursing us.

ELECTRA: Take me in your arms, beloved, and press me to your breast. How dark the night is! I never knew such darkness; those torches have no effect on it. . . . Do you love me?

ORESTES: It is not night; a new day is dawning. We are free, Electra. I feel as if I'd brought you into life and I, too, had just been born. Yes, I love you, and you belong to me. Only yesterday I was empty-handed, and today I have *you*. Ours is a double tie of blood; we two come of the same race and we two have shed blood.

ELECTRA: Let go your sword. Give me that hand, your strong right hand. [*She clasps and kisses it.*] Your fingers are short and square, made to grasp and hold. Dear hand! It's whiter than mine. But how heavy it became to strike down our father's murderers! Wait! [*She takes a torch and holds it near* ORESTES.] I must light up your face; it's getting so dark that I can hardly see you. And I *must* see you; when I stop seeing you, I'm afraid of you. I daren't take my eyes off you. I must tell myself again and again that I love you. But—how strange you look!

ORESTES: I am free, Electra. Freedom has crashed down on me like a thunderbolt.

ELECTRA: Free? But I—I don't feel free. And you—can you undo what has been done? Something has happened and we are no longer free to blot it out. Can you prevent our being the murderers of our mother—for all time?

ORESTES: Do you think I'd wish to prevent it? I have done *my* deed, Electra, and that deed was good. I shall bear it on my shoulders as a carrier at a ferry carries the traveler to the farther bank. And when I have brought it to the farther bank I shall take stock of it. The heavier it is to carry, the better pleased I shall be; for that burden is my freedom. Only yesterday I walked the earth haphazard; thousands of roads I tramped that brought me nowhere, for they were other men's roads. Yes, I tried them all; the haulers' tracks along the riverside, the mule-paths in the mountains, and the broad, flagged highways of the charioteers. But none of these was mine. Today I have one path only, and heaven knows where it leads. But it is *my* path.... What is it, Electra?

ELECTRA: I can't see you any more. Those torches give no light. I hear your voice, but it hurts me, it cuts like a knife. Will it always be as dark as this—always, even in the daytime?... Oh, Orestes! There they are!

ORESTES: Who?

ELECTRA: There they are! Where have they come from? They're hanging from the ceiling like clusters of black grapes; the walls are alive with them; they're swirling down across the torchlight and it's their shadows that are hiding your face from me.

ORESTES: The flies—

ELECTRA: Listen! The sound of their wings is like a roaring furnace. They're all round us, Orestes, watching, biding their time. Presently they'll swoop down on us and I shall feel thousands of tiny clammy feet crawling over me. Oh, look! They're growing bigger, bigger; now they're as big as bees. We'll never escape them, they'll follow us everywhere in a dense cloud. Oh God, now I can see their eyes, millions of beady eyes all staring at us!

ORESTES: What do the flies matter to us?

ELECTRA: They're the Furies, Orestes, the goddesses of remorse.

VOICE [*from behind the door*]: Open! Open!... If you don't, we'll smash the door in.
[*Heavy thuds. They are battering at the door.*]

ORESTES: Clytemnestra's cries must have brought them here. Come! Lead me to Apollo's shrine. We will spend the night there, sheltered from men and flies. And tomorrow I shall speak to my people.
[*Curtain*]

ACT III

The temple of Apollo. Twilight. A statue of Apollo in the center of the stage. ELECTRA *and* ORESTES *are sleeping at the foot of the statue, their arms clasped round its legs. The* FURIES *ring them round; they sleep standing, like cranes.*
At the back is a huge bronze door.

FIRST FURY [*stretching herself*]: Aaaah! I slept the night out standing, stiff with rage, and my sleep was glorious with angry dreams. Ah, how lovely is the flower of anger, the red flower in my heart! [*She circles round* ORESTES *and* ELECTRA.] Still sleeping. How white and soft they are! I'll roll on their breasts and bellies, like a torrent over stones. And I shall polish hour by hour their tender flesh; rub it, scour it, wear it to the bone. [*She comes a few steps forward.*] Oh clear, bright dawn of hate! A superb awakening. They're sleeping, sweating, a smell of fever rises from them. But I am awake; cool and hard and gemlike. My soul is adamant—and I feel my sanctity.

ELECTRA [*sighing in her sleep*]: No! No!

FIRST FURY: She's sighing. Wait, my pretty one, wait till you feel our teeth. Soon you'll be screaming with the agony of our caresses. I'll woo you like a man, for you're my bride, and you shall feel my love crushing your life out. You, Electra, are more beautiful than I; but you'll see how my kisses age you. Within six months I'll have you raddled like an old hag; but I stay young forever. [*She bends over* ORESTES *and* ELECTRA.] Ah, this lovely human carrion, what a tasty meal we have in store! As I gaze down at them and breathe their breath, I choke with rage. Nothing is sweeter, nothing, than to feel a dawn of hatred spreading like quickfire in one's veins; teeth and talons ready for their task. Hatred is flooding through me, welling up in my breasts like milk. Awake, sisters, awake! The day has come.

SECOND FURY: I dreamt I was biting them.

FIRST FURY: Be patient. Today they are protected by a god, but soon hunger and thirst will drive them out of sanctuary. And then you shall bite them to your heart's content.

THIRD FURY: Aaah! How I want to claw them!

FIRST FURY: Your turn will come. In a little while your iron talons will be ribboning the flesh of those young criminals with angry red. Come closer, sisters, come and look at them.

A FURY: How young they are!

ANOTHER FURY: And how beautiful!

FIRST FURY: Yes, we are favored. Only too often criminals are old and ugly. Too seldom do we have the joy, the exquisite delight, of ruining what's beautiful.

THE FURIES: Heiah! Heiahah!

THIRD FURY: Orestes is almost a child. I shall mother him, oh so tenderly, with my hatred; I shall take his pale head on my knees and stroke his hair.

FIRST FURY: And then?

THIRD FURY: Then, when he least expects it, I shall dig these two fingers into his eyes.

[*All laugh.*]

FIRST FURY: See, they're stretching, sighing, on the brink of waking. And now, my sisters, flies my sisters, let's sing the sinners from their sleep.

THE FURIES [*together*]: Bzz. Bzz. Bzz. Bzz.
  We shall settle on your rotten hearts like flies on butter;

Rotten hearts, juicy, luscious hearts.
Like bees, we'll suck the pus and matter from your hearts,
And we'll turn it into honey, rich, green honey.
What love could ravish us as hatred does?
Bzz. Bzz. Bzz. Bzz.
We shall be the staring eyes of the houses,
The growls of the kenneled mastiff baring his fangs as you go by,
A drone of wings pulsing in high air,
Sounds of the forest,
Whistlings, whinings, creakings, hissings, howlings.
We shall be the darkness,
The clotted darkness of your souls.
Bzz. Bzz. Bzz. Bzz.
Heiah, heiah, heiahah!
Bzz. Bzz. Bzz. Bzz.
We are the flies, the suckers of pus,
We shall have open house with you,
We shall gather our food from your mouths,
And our light from the depths of your eyes.
All your life we will be with you,
Until we make you over to the worms.

[*They dance.*]

ELECTRA [*still half asleep*]: Was someone speaking? Who—who are you?

THE FURIES: Bzz. Bzz. Bzz.

ELECTRA: Ah, yes. There you are. Well? Have we really killed them?

ORESTES [*waking*]: Electra!

ELECTRA: You, who are you? Ah, yes. Orestes. Go away.

ORESTES: But—what's wrong, Electra?

ELECTRA: You frighten me. I had a dream. I saw our mother lying on her back.
Blood was pouring from her, gushing under the doors. A dream. . . . Feel my
hands. They're icy. No, don't. Don't touch me. Did she really bleed much?

ORESTES: Don't!

ELECTRA [*waking up completely*]: Let me look at you. You killed them. It was you,
you who killed them. You are here beside me, you have just waked up, there's
nothing written on your face, no brand. . . . And yet you killed them.

ORESTES: Why, yes. I killed them. [*A short silence.*] You, too, make me afraid.
Yesterday you were so beautiful. And now you look as if some wild beast had
clawed your face.

ELECTRA: No beast. Your crime. It's tearing off my cheeks and eyelids; I feel as if
my eyes and teeth were naked. . . . But what are those creatures?

ORESTES: Take no notice of them. They can do you no harm.

FIRST FURY: No harm? Let her dare to come among us and you'll see if we can do
no harm!

ORESTES: Keep quiet. Back to your kennel, bitches. [*The* FURIES *growl.*] Is it possible
that the girl who only yesterday was dancing in a white dress on the temple
steps—is it possible you were that girl?

ELECTRA: I've grown old. In a single night.

ORESTES: You have not lost your beauty, but— Where, now, have I seen dead eyes
like those? Electra—you are like *her*. Like Clytemnestra. What use, then, was it
killing her? When I see my crime in those eyes, it revolts me.

FIRST FURY: That is because *you* revolt *her*.

ORESTES: Is that true, Electra? Do I revolt you?

ELECTRA: Oh, let me be!

FIRST FURY: Well? Can you still have any doubt? How should she not hate you? She lived in peace, dreaming her dreams; and then you came, bringing murder and impiety upon her. So now she has to share your guilt and hug that pedestal, the only scrap of earth remaining to her.

ORESTES: Do not listen.

FIRST FURY: Away! Away! Make him go, Electra; don't let him touch you! He's a butcher. He reeks of fresh, warm blood. He used the poor old woman very foully, you know; he killed her piecemeal.

ELECTRA: Oh no! That's a lie, surely?

FIRST FURY: You can believe me; I was there all the time, buzzing in the air around them.

ELECTRA: So he struck her several times?

FIRST FURY: Ten times at least. And each time the sword squelched in the wound. She tried to shield her face and belly with her hands, and he carved her hands to ribbons.

ELECTRA: So it wasn't a quick death. Did she suffer much?

ORESTES: Put your fingers in your ears, do not look at them, and, above all, ask no questions. If you question them, you're lost.

FIRST FURY: Yes, she suffered—horribly.

ELECTRA [covering her face with her hands]: Oh!

ORESTES: She wants to part us, she is building up a wall of solitude around you. But beware; once you are alone, alone and helpless, they will fling themselves upon you. Electra, we planned this crime together and we should bear its brunt together.

ELECTRA: You dare to say I planned it with you?

ORESTES: Can you deny it?

ELECTRA: Of course I deny it. Wait! Well, perhaps—in a way. . . . Oh, I don't know. I dreamt the crime, but you carried it out, you murdered your own mother.

THE FURIES [shrieking and laughing]: Murderer! Murderer! Butcher!

ORESTES: Electra, behind that door is the outside world. A world of dawn. Out there the sun is rising, lighting up the roads. Soon we shall leave this place, we shall walk those sunlit roads, and these hags of darkness will lose their power. The sunbeams will cut through them like swords.

ELECTRA: The sun—

FIRST FURY: You will never see the sun again, Electra. We shall mass between you and the sun like a swarm of locusts; you will carry darkness round your head wherever you go.

ELECTRA: Oh, let me be! Stop torturing me!

ORESTES: It's your weakness gives them their strength. Mark how they dare not speak to me. A nameless horror has descended on you, keeping us apart. And yet why should this be? What have you lived through that I have not shared? Do you imagine that my mother's cries will ever cease ringing in my ears? Or that my eyes will ever cease to see her great sad eyes, lakes of lambent darkness in the pallor of her face? And the anguish that consumes you—do you think it will ever cease ravaging my heart? But what matter? I am free. Beyond anguish, beyond remorse. Free. And at one with myself. No, you must not loathe yourself, Electra. Give me your hand. I shall never forsake you.

ELECTRA: Let go of my hand! Those hell-hounds frighten me, but you frighten me more.

FIRST FURY: You see! You see! . . . That's quite true, little doll; you're less afraid of us than of that man. Because you need us, Electra. You are our child, our little girl. You need our nails to score your skin, our teeth to bite your breast, and all our savage love to save you from your hatred of yourself. Only the suffering of your body can take your mind off your suffering soul. So come and let us hurt you. You have only those two steps to come down, and we will take you in our arms. And when our kisses sear your tender flesh, you'll forget all in the cleansing fires of pain.

THE FURIES: Come down to us! Come down!

   [*Slowly they dance round her, weaving their spell.* ELECTRA *rises to her feet.*]

ORESTES [*gripping her arm*]: No, no, for pity's sake. Don't go to them. Once they get you, all is lost.

ELECTRA [*freeing herself violently*]: Let go! Oh, how I hate you!

   [*She goes down the steps, and the* FURIES *fling themselves on her.*]
   Help!

                              [ZEUS *enters.*]

ZEUS: Kennel up!

FIRST FURY: The master!

   [*The* FURIES *slink off reluctantly, leaving* ELECTRA *lying on the ground.*]

ZEUS: Poor children. [*He goes up to* ELECTRA.] So to this you've come, unhappy pair? My heart is torn between anger and compassion. Get up, Electra. So long as I am here, my Furies will not hurt you. [*He helps her to rise and gazes at her face.*] Ah, what a cruel change! In a night, a single night, all the wild-rose bloom has left your cheeks. In one night your body has gone to ruin, lungs, gall, and liver all burnt out. The pride of headstrong youth—see what it has brought you to, poor child.

ORESTES: Stop talking in that tone, fellow. It is unbecoming for the king of the gods.

ZEUS: And you, my lad, drop that haughty tone. It's unbecoming for a criminal atoning for his crime.

ORESTES: I am no criminal, and you have no power to make me atone for an act I don't regard as a crime.

ZEUS: So you may think, but wait awhile. I shall cure you of that error before long.

ORESTES: Torture me to your heart's content; I regret nothing.

ZEUS: Not even the doom you have brought upon your sister?

ORESTES: Not even that.

ZEUS: Do you hear, Electra? And this man professed to love you!

ORESTES: She is dearer to me than life. But her suffering comes from within, and only she can rid herself of it. For she is free.

ZEUS: And you? You, too, are free, no doubt?

ORESTES: Yes, and well you know it.

ZEUS: A pity you can't see yourself as you are now, you fool, for all your boasting! What a heroic figure you cut there, cowering between the legs of a protecting god, with a pack of hungry vixen keeping guard on you! If you *can* brag of freedom, why not praise the freedom of a prisoner languishing in fetters, or a slave nailed to the cross?

ORESTES: Certainly. Why not?

ZEUS: Take care. You play the braggart now because Apollo is protecting you. But Apollo is my most obedient servant. I have but to lift a finger and he will abandon you.

ORESTES: Then do so. Lift a finger, lift your whole hand while you are about it.

ZEUS: No, that is not my way. Haven't I told you that I take no pleasure in punishment? I have come to save you both.

ELECTRA: To save us? No, it is too cruel to make sport of us. You are the lord of vengeance and of death, but, god though you are, you have no right to delude your victims with false hopes.

ZEUS: Within a quarter of an hour you can be outside that door.

ELECTRA: Safe and sound?

ZEUS: You have my word for it.

ELECTRA: And what do you want from me in return?

ZEUS: Nothing, my child. Nothing.

ELECTRA: Nothing? Did I hear right? Then you are a kind god, a lovable god.

ZEUS: Or next to nothing. A mere trifle. What you can give most easily—a little penitence.

ORESTES: Take care, Electra. That trifle will weigh like a millstone on your soul.

ZEUS [to ELECTRA]: Don't listen to him. Answer me, instead. Why hesitate to disavow that crime? It was committed by someone else; one could hardly say even that you were his accomplice.

ORESTES: Electra! Are you going to go back on fifteen years of hope and hatred?

ZEUS: What has she to go back on? Never did she really wish that impious deed to be accomplished.

ELECTRA: If only that were true!

ZEUS: Come now! Surely you can trust my word. Do I not read in men's hearts?

ELECTRA [incredulously]: And you read in mine that I never really desired that crime? Though for fifteen years I dreamt of murder and revenge?

ZEUS: Bah! I know you nursed bloodthirsty dreams—but there was a sort of innocence about them. They made you forget your servitude, they healed your wounded pride. But you never really thought of making them come true. Well, am I mistaken?

ELECTRA: Ah, Zeus, dear Zeus, how I long to think you are not mistaken!

ZEUS: You're a little girl, Electra. A mere child. Most little girls dream of becoming the richest or the loveliest woman on earth. But you were haunted by the cruel destiny of your race, you dreamt of becoming the saddest, most criminal of women. You never willed to do evil; you willed your own misfortune. At an age when most children are playing hopscotch or with their dolls, you, poor child, who had no friends or toys, you toyed with dreams of murder, because that's a game to play alone.

ELECTRA: Yes, yes! I'm beginning to understand.

ORESTES: Listen, Electra! It's *now* you are bringing guilt upon you. For who except yourself can know what you really wanted? Will you let another decide that for you? Why distort a past that can no longer stand up for itself? And why disown the firebrand that you were, that glorious young goddess, vivid with hatred, that I loved so much? Can't you see this cruel god is fooling you?

ZEUS: No, Electra. I'm not fooling you. And now hear what I offer. If you repudiate your crime, I'll see that you two occupy the throne of Argos.

ORESTES: Taking the places of our victims?

ZEUS: How else?

ORESTES: And I shall put on the royal robe, still warm from the dead King's wearing?

ZEUS: That or another. What can it matter?

ORESTES: Nothing of course—provided that it's black.

ZEUS: Are you not in mourning?

ORESTES: Yes, I was forgetting; in mourning for my mother. And my subjects—must I have them, too, wear black?

ZEUS: They wear it already.

ORESTES: True. We can give them time to wear out their old clothes. . . . Well, Electra, have you understood? If you shed some tears, you'll be given Clytemnestra's shifts and petticoats—those dirty, stinking ones you had to wash for fifteen years. And the part she played is yours for the asking. Now that you have come to look so much like her, you will play the part superbly; everyone will take you for your mother. But I—I fear I am more squeamish—I refuse to wear the breeches of the clown I killed.

ZEUS: You talk big, my boy. You butchered a defenseless man and an old woman who begged for mercy. But, to hear you speak, one would think you'd bravely fought, one against a crowd, and were the savior of your city.

ORESTES: Perhaps I was.

ZEUS: You a savior! Do you know what's afoot behind that door? All the good folk of Argos are waiting there. Waiting to greet you with stones and pikes and pitchforks. Oh, they are very grateful to their savior! . . . You are lonely as a leper.

ORESTES: Yes.

ZEUS: So you take pride in being an outcast, do you? But the solitude you're doomed to, most cowardly of murderers, is the solitude of scorn and loathing.

ORESTES: The most cowardly of murderers is he who feels remorse.

ZEUS: Orestes, I created you, and I created all things. Now see! [*The walls of the temple draw apart, revealing the firmament, spangled with wheeling stars.* ZEUS *is standing in the background. His voice becomes huge—amplified by loud-speakers—but his form is shadowy.*] See those planets wheeling on their appointed ways, never swerving, never clashing. It was I who ordained their courses, according to the law of justice. Hear the music of the spheres, that vast, mineral hymn of praise, sounding and resounding to the limits of the firmament. [*Sounds of music.*] It is my work that living things increase and multiply, each according to his kind. I have ordained that man shall always beget man, and dog give birth to dog. It is my work that the tides with their innumerable tongues creep up to lap the sand and draw back at the appointed hour. I make the plants grow, and my breath fans round the earth the yellow clouds of pollen. You are not in your own home, intruder; you are a foreign body in the world, like a splinter in flesh, or a poacher in his lordship's forest. For the world is good; I made it according to my will, and I am Goodness. But you, Orestes, you have done evil, the very rocks and stones cry out against you. The Good is everywhere, it is the coolness of the wellspring, the pith of the reed, the grain of flint, the weight of stone. Yes, you will find it even in the heart of fire and light; even your own body plays you false, for it abides perforce by my law. Good is everywhere, in you and about you; sweeping through you like a scythe, crushing you like a mountain. Like an ocean it buoys you up and rocks you to and fro, and it enabled the success of your evil plan, for it was in the brightness of the torches, the temper of your blade, the strength of your right arm. And that of which you are so vain, the Evil that you think is your creation, what is it but a reflection in a mocking mirror, a phantom thing that would have no being but for Goodness. No, Orestes, return to your saner self; the universe refutes you, you are a mite in the scheme of things. Return to Nature, Nature's thankless son. Know your sin, abhor it, and tear it from you as one tears out a rotten, noisome tooth. Or else—beware

lest the very seas shrink back at your approach, springs dry up when you pass
by, stones and rocks roll from your path, and the earth crumbles under your
feet.

ORESTES: Let it crumble! Let the rocks revile me, and flowers wilt at my coming.
Your whole universe is not enough to prove me wrong. You are the king of
gods, king of stones and stars, king of the waves of the sea. But you are not the
king of man.

[*The walls draw together.* ZEUS *comes into view, tired
and dejected, and he now speaks in his normal voice.*]

ZEUS: Impudent spawn! So I am not your king? Who, then, made you?

ORESTES: You. But you blundered; you should not have made me free.

ZEUS: I gave you freedom so that you might serve me.

ORESTES: Perhaps. But now it has turned against its giver. And neither you nor I
can undo what has been done.

ZEUS: Ah, at last! So this is your excuse?

ORESTES: I am not excusing myself.

ZEUS: No? Let me tell you it sounds much like an excuse, this freedom whose slave
you claim to be.

ORESTES: Neither slave nor master. I *am* my freedom. No sooner had you created
me than I ceased to be yours.

ELECTRA: Oh, Orestes! By all you hold most holy, by our father's memory, I beg
you do not add blasphemy to your crime!

ZEUS: Mark her words, young man. And hope no more to win her back by
arguments like these. Such language is somewhat new to her ears—and somewhat
shocking.

ORESTES: To my ears, too. And to my lungs, which breathe the words, and
to my tongue, which shapes them. In fact, I can hardly understand myself.
Only yesterday you were still a veil on my eyes, a clot of wax in my ears;
yesterday, indeed, I had an excuse. *You* were my excuse for being alive, for
you had put me in the world to fulfill your purpose, and the world was an old
pander prating to me about your goodness, day in, day out. And then you forsook me.

ZEUS: *I* forsook you? How?

ORESTES: Yesterday, when I was with Electra, I felt at one with Nature, this Nature
of your making. It sang the praises of Good—*your* Good—in siren tones, and
lavished intimations. To lull me into gentleness, the fierce light mellowed and
grew tender as a lover's eyes. And, to teach me the forgiveness of offenses, the sky
grew bland as a pardoner's face. Obedient to your will, my youth rose up before
me and pleaded with me like a girl who fears her lover will forsake her. That
was the last time, the last, I saw my youth. Suddenly, out of the blue, freedom
crashed down on me and swept me off my feet. Nature sprang back, my youth
went with the wind, and I knew myself alone, utterly alone in the midst of this
well-meaning little universe of yours. I was like a man who's lost his shadow.
And there was nothing left in heaven, no right or wrong, nor anyone to give me
orders.

ZEUS: What of it? Do you want me to admire a scabby sheep that has to be kept
apart; or the leper mewed in a lazar-house? Remember, Orestes, you once were
of my flock, you fed in my pastures among my sheep. Your vaunted freedom
isolates you from the fold; it means exile.

ORESTES: Yes, exile.

ZEUS: But the disease can't be deeply rooted yet; it began only yesterday. Come
back to the fold. Think of your loneliness; even your sister is forsaking you.

Your eyes are big with anguish, your face is pale and drawn. The disease you're suffering from is inhuman, foreign to my nature, foreign to yourself. Come back. I am forgetfulness, I am peace.

ORESTES: Foreign to myself—I know it. Outside nature, against nature, without excuse, beyond remedy, except what remedy I find within myself. But I shall not return under your law; I am doomed to have no other law but mine. Nor shall I come back to nature, the nature you found good; in it are a thousand beaten paths all leading up to you—but I must blaze my trail. For I, Zeus, am a man, and every man must find out his own way. Nature abhors man, and you too, god of gods, abhor mankind.

ZEUS: That is true; men like you I hold in abhorrence.

ORESTES: Take care; those words were a confession of your weakness. As for me, I do not hate you. What have I to do with you, or you with me? We shall glide past each other, like ships in a river, without touching. You are God and I am free; each of us is alone, and our anguish is akin. How can you know I did not try to feel remorse in the long night that has gone by? And to sleep? But no longer can I feel remorse, and I can sleep no more.

[*A short silence.*]

ZEUS: What do you propose to do?

ORESTES: The folk of Argos are my folk. I must open their eyes.

ZEUS: Poor people! Your gift to them will be a sad one; of loneliness and shame. You will tear from their eyes the veils I had laid on them, and they will see their lives as they are, foul and futile, a barren boon.

ORESTES: Why, since it is their lot, should I deny them the despair I have in me?

ZEUS: What will they make of it?

ORESTES: What they choose. They're free; and human life begins on the far side of despair.

[*A short silence.*]

ZEUS: Well, Orestes, all this was foreknown. In the fullness of time a man was to come, to announce my decline. And you're that man, it seems. But seeing you yesterday—you with your girlish face—who'd have believed it?

ORESTES: Could I myself have believed it? . . . The words I speak are too big for my mouth, they tear it; the load of destiny I bear is too heavy for my youth and has shattered it.

ZEUS: I have little love for you, yet I am sorry for you.

ORESTES: And I, too, am sorry for *you*.

ZEUS: Good-by, Orestes. [*He takes some steps forward.*] As for you, Electra, bear this in mind. My reign is not yet over—far from it!—and I shall not give up the struggle. So choose if you are with me or against me. Farewell.

ORESTES: Farewell. [ZEUS *goes out.* ELECTRA *slowly rises to her feet.*] Where are you going?

ELECTRA: Leave me alone. I'm done with you.

ORESTES: I have known you only for a day, and must I lose you now forever?

ELECTRA: Would to God that I had never known you!

ORESTES: Electra! My sister, dear Electra! My only love, the one joy of my life, do not leave me. Stay with me.

ELECTRA: Thief! I had so little, so very little to call mine; only a few weak dreams, a morsel of peace. And now you've taken my all; you've robbed a pauper of her mite! You were my brother, the head of our house, and it was your duty to protect me. But no, you needs must drag me into carnage; I am red as a flayed ox, these loathsome flies are swarming after me, and my heart is buzzing like an angry hive.

ORESTES: Yes, my beloved, it's true, I have taken all from you, and I have nothing to offer in return; nothing but my crime. But think how vast a gift that is! Believe me, it weighs on my heart like lead. We were too light, Electra; now our feet sink into the soil, like chariot-wheels in turf. So come with me; we will tread heavily on our way, bowed beneath our precious load. You shall give me your hand, and we will go—

ELECTRA: Where?

ORESTES: I don't know. Towards ourselves. Beyond the rivers and mountains are an Orestes and an Electra waiting for us, and we must make our patient way towards them.

ELECTRA: I won't hear any more from you. All you have to offer me is misery and squalor. [*She rushes out into the center of the stage. The* FURIES *slowly close in on her.*] Help! Zeus, king of gods and men, my king, take me in your arms, carry me from this place, and shelter me. I will obey your law, I will be your creature and your slave, I will embrace your knees. Save me from the flies, from my brother, from myself! Do not leave me lonely and I will give up my whole life to atonement. I repent, Zeus. I bitterly repent.

> [*She runs off the stage. The* FURIES *make as if to
> follow her, but the* FIRST FURY *holds them back.*]

FIRST FURY: Let her be, sisters. She is not for us. But that man is ours, and ours, I think, for many a day. His little soul is stubborn. He will suffer for two.

> [*Buzzing, the* FURIES *approach* ORESTES.]

ORESTES: I am alone, alone.

FIRST FURY: No, no, my sweet little murderer, I'm staying with you, and you'll see what merry games I'll think up to entertain you.

ORESTES: Alone until I die. And after that—?

FIRST FURY: Take heart, sisters, he is weakening. See how his eyes dilate. Soon his nerves will be throbbing like harp-strings, in exquisite arpeggios of terror.

SECOND FURY: And hunger will drive him from his sanctuary before long. Before nightfall we shall know how his blood tastes.

ORESTES: Poor Electra!

> [THE TUTOR *enters.*]

THE TUTOR: Master! Young master! Where are you? It's so dark one can't see a thing. I'm bringing you some food. The townspeople have surrounded the temple; there's no hope of escape by daylight. We shall have to try our chance when night comes. Meanwhile, eat this food to keep your strength up. [*The* FURIES *bar his way.*] Hey! Who are these? More of those primitive myths! Ah, how I regret that pleasant land of Attica, where reason's always right.

ORESTES: Do not try to approach me, or they will tear you in pieces.

THE TUTOR: Gently now, my lovelies. See what I've brought you, some nice meat and fruit. Here you are! Let's hope it will calm you down.

ORESTES: So the people of Argos have gathered outside the temple, have they?

THE TUTOR: Indeed they have, and I can't say which are the fiercer, the thirstier for your blood: these charming young creatures here, or your worthy subjects.

ORESTES: Good. [*A short silence.*] Open that door.

THE TUTOR: Have you lost your wits? They're waiting behind it, and they're armed.

ORESTES: Do as I told you.

THE TUTOR: For once permit me, sir, to disobey your orders. I tell you, they will stone you. It's madness.

ORESTES: Old man, I am your master, and I order you to unbar that door.

[THE TUTOR *opens one leaf of the double doors a few inches.*]

THE TUTOR: Oh dear! Oh dear!

ORESTES: Open both leaves.

[THE TUTOR *half opens both leaves of the door and takes cover behind one of them.* THE CROWD *surges forward, thrusting the doors wide open; then stops, bewildered, on the threshold. The stage is flooded with bright light. Shouts rise from* THE CROWD: "Away with him!" "Kill him!" "Stone him!" "Tear him in pieces!"*]*

ORESTES [*who has not heard them*]: The sun!

THE CROWD: Murderer! Butcher! Blasphemer! We'll tear you limb from limb. We'll pour molten lead into your veins.

A WOMAN: I'll pluck out your eyes.

A MAN: I'll eat your gizzard!

ORESTES [*drawing himself up to his full height*]: So here you are, my true and loyal subjects? I am Orestes, your King, son of Agamemnon, and this is my coronation day. [*Exclamations of amazement, mutterings among* THE CROWD.] Ah, you are lowering your tone? [*Complete silence.*] I know; you fear me. Fifteen years ago to the day, another murderer showed himself to you, his arms red to the elbows, gloved in blood. But him you did not fear; you read in his eyes that he was of your kind, he had not the courage of his crimes. A crime that its doer disowns becomes ownerless—no man's crime; that's how you see it, isn't it? More like an accident than a crime?

So you welcomed the criminal as your King, and that crime without an owner started prowling round the city, whimpering like a dog that has lost its master. You see me, men of Argos, you understand that my crime is wholly mine; I claim it as my own, for all to know; it is my glory, my life's work, and you can neither punish me nor pity me. That is why I fill you with fear.

And yet, my people, I love you, and it was for your sake that I killed. For your sake. I had come to claim my kingdom, and you would have none of me because I was not of your kind. Now I am of your kind, my subjects; there is a bond of blood between us, and I have earned my kingship over you.

As for your sins and your remorse, your night-fears, and the crime Ægistheus committed—all are mine, I take them all upon me. Fear your dead no longer; they are *my* dead. And, see, your faithful flies have left you and come to me. But have no fear, people of Argos. I shall not sit on my victim's throne or take the scepter in my blood-stained hands. A god offered it to me, and I said no. I wish to be a king without a kingdom, without subjects.

Farewell, my people. Try to reshape your lives. All here is new, all must begin anew. And for me, too, a new life is beginning. A strange life. . . .

Listen now to this tale. One summer there was a plague of rats in Scyros. It was like a foul disease; they soiled and nibbled everything, and the people of the city were at their wits' end. But one day a flute-player came to the city. He took his stand in the market-place. Like this. [ORESTES *rises to his feet.*] He began playing on his flute and all the rats came out and crowded round him. Then he started off, taking long strides—like this. [*He comes down from the pedestal.*] And he called to the people of Scyros: "Make way!" [THE CROWD *makes way for him.*] And all the rats raised their heads and hesitated—as the flies are doing. Look! Look at the flies! Then all of a sudden they followed in his train. And the flute-player, with his rats, vanished forever. Thus.

[*He strides out into the light. Shrieking, the* FURIES *fling themselves after him.*]

[*Curtain*]

RASIPURAM KRISHNASWAMI NARAYAN
[BORN 1906]

Many of Rasipuram Krishnaswami Narayan's novels and stories describe the people and the life in the mythical Indian town of Malgudi, a place much like Mysore, the city in southern India where Narayan has spent much of his life. The rich and varied gallery of characters in Narayan's work gives Malgudi the density and presence of a real place—of India itself. Narayan has remarked that "the material available to the story writer in India is limitless. Within a broad climate of inherited culture there are endless variations. . . . Under such conditions the writer has only to look out of the window to pick up a character (and thereby a story)." The many memorable characters that populate the novels and stories have led critics to compare Narayan's Malgudi to William Faulkner's Yoknapatawpha County.

LIFE

Born in 1906 into a Brahman family, Narayan spent his early childhood in the house of his maternal grandmother in Madras. While he was there, he attended a Lutheran mission school where he was disliked by the teachers and students as one of the few non-Christians. When he reached high school age, he rejoined his parents in Mysore and attended the school where his father was headmaster. He was not a particularly dedicated student; when he finished school in 1924, he failed the university entrance exam in English and had to delay his university studies for a year. He spent his time off reading books of all sorts, but mainly fiction by such novelists as Dickens, Conan Doyle, Sir Walter Scott, Tagore, and H. G. Wells. Graduated from Maharaja's College (now the University of Mysore) in 1930, he briefly tried secondary school teaching before he took up writing, the profession he has been practicing ever since.

WORK

Narayan writes about the life and the people he has observed around him in Mysore, a town he fictionalized as Malgudi, the setting of nearly all of his fiction. His work as the Mysore correspondent for a Madras newspaper sent him out daily in search of stories and established the discipline of writing daily that accounts for his prolific output. Since 1935, when *Swami and Friends*, his first novel, was published, he has produced more than fifteen novels, several volumes of short stories and essays, and an autobiography, as well as retellings of *The Ramayana* (1972) and *The Mahabharata* (1978), and numerous articles and stories. The best-known of his novels are *The Bachelor of Arts* (1937), *Mr. Sampath* (1949), *The Financial Expert* (1952), *Waiting for the Mahatma: A Novel* (1955), *The Guide* (1958), *The Vendor of Sweets* (1967), and *A Tiger for Malgudi* (1983).

Narayan's novels document a society in transition from agrarian village culture to middle-class urban life. They tend to center on middle-class people—schoolteachers, financial managers, and merchants—in the mythical town of Malgudi. These self-conscious characters seek to grow and establish an identity distinct from family and community. The resulting tension between individuality and tradition forms a recurrent theme in the novels. In Malgudi, as in the works of Rabindranath Tagore, education and a middle-class way of life bring a degree of westernization, raising questions about cultural identity and the relationship between the traditional and the modern. Although Narayan is not a "political novelist," Malgudi inevitably embodies the key social and political issues of contemporary India—its urbanization and its colonial heritage.

These issues are implicit in Narayan's choice of language. Even though many of his characters speak the vernacular languages of India—like the villager Muni in "A Horse and Two Goats" (1970), who speaks Tamil and does not understand English—Narayan writes in English. Commenting on this choice, he has said, "English has been with us [Indians] for over a century and a half. I am particularly fond of the language. I was never aware that I was using a different, a foreign, language when I wrote in English, because it came very easily." The ease and natural rhythms of Narayan's style demonstrate this comfort with English, while reminding us of the pervasive impact of British colonialism on the subcontinent.

Narayan's short stories are often less "modern" than the novels. Tales such as "A Horse and Two Goats" describe traditional village life and retain the character of stories that are told rather than written. The story of Muni the goatherd is a comic folktale about the misunderstandings that arise when a traditional culture meets the modern world. Its humor is similar to that in the film *The Gods Must Be Crazy,* about a South African Bushman's contact with Western culture. Narayan's story does not condescend to the villager or make him out to be a simpleton. Its sympathetic portrayal of Muni and his situation allows us both to laugh at his absurd negotiations and to celebrate his good fortune.

Suggested Readings

Narayan has written of his own life and work in *My Days: A Memoir* (1974). A useful critical study of his work is William Walsh's *R. K. Narayan* (1971).

A Horse and Two Goats

Of the seven hundred thousand villages dotting the map of India, in which the majority of India's five hundred million live, flourish, and die, Kritam was probably the tiniest, indicated on the district survey map by a microscopic dot, the map being meant more for the revenue official out to collect tax than for the guidance of the motorist, who in any case could not hope to reach it since it sprawled far from the highway at the end of a rough track furrowed up by the iron-hooped wheels of bullock carts. But its size did not prevent its giving itself the grandiose name Kritam, which meant in Tamil "coronet" or "crown" on the brow of this subcontinent. The village consisted of less than thirty houses, only one of them built with brick and cement. Painted a brilliant yellow and blue all over with gorgeous carvings of gods and gargoyles on its balustrade, it was known as the Big House. The other houses, distributed in four streets, were generally of bamboo thatch, straw, mud, and other unspecified material. Muni's was the last house in the fourth street, beyond which stretched the fields. In his prosperous days Muni had owned a flock of forty sheep and goats and sallied forth every morning driving the flock to the highway a couple of miles away. There he would sit on the pedestal of a clay statue of a horse while his cattle grazed around. He carried a crook at the end of a bamboo pole and snapped foliage from the avenue trees to feed his flock; he also gathered faggots and dry sticks, bundled them, and carried them home for fuel at sunset.

His wife lit the domestic fire at dawn, boiled water in a mud pot, threw into it a handful of millet flour, added salt, and gave him his first nourishment for the day.

When he started out, she would put in his hand a packed lunch, once again the same millet cooked into a little ball, which he could swallow with a raw onion at midday. She was old, but he was older and needed all the attention she could give him in order to be kept alive.

His fortunes had declined gradually, unnoticed. From a flock of forty which he drove into a pen at night, his stock had now come down to two goats, which were not worth the rent of a half rupee a month the Big House charged for the use of the pen in their back yard. And so the two goats were tethered to the trunk of a drumstick tree which grew in front of his hut and from which occasionally Muni could shake down drumsticks. This morning he got six. He carried them in with a sense of triumph. Although no one could say precisely who owned the tree, it was his because he lived in its shadow.

She said, "If you were content with the drumstick leaves alone, I could boil and salt some for you."

"Oh, I am tired of eating those leaves. I have a craving to chew the drumstick out of sauce, I tell you."

"You have only four teeth in your jaw, but your craving is for big things. All right, get the stuff for the sauce, and I will prepare it for you. After all, next year you may not be alive to ask for anything. But first get me all the stuff, including a measure of rice or millet, and I will satisfy your unholy craving. Our store is empty today. Dhall,[1] chili, curry leaves, mustard, coriander, gingelley oil,[2] and one large potato. Go out and get all this." He repeated the list after her in order not to miss any item and walked off to the shop in third street.

He sat on an upturned packing case below the platform of the shop. The shopman paid no attention to him. Muni kept clearing his throat, coughing, and sneezing until the shopman could not stand it any more and demanded, "What ails you? You will fly off that seat into the gutter if you sneeze so hard, young man." Muni laughed inordinately, in order to please the shopman, at being called "young man." The shopman softened and said, "You have enough of the imp inside to keep a second wife busy, but for the fact the old lady is still alive." Muni laughed appropriately again at this joke. It completely won the shopman over; he liked his sense of humour to be appreciated. Muni engaged his attention in local gossip for a few minutes, which always ended with a reference to the postman's wife who had eloped to the city some months before.

The shopman felt most pleased to hear the worst of the postman, who had cheated him. Being an itinerant postman, he returned home to Kritam only once in ten days and every time managed to slip away again without passing the shop in the third street. By thus humouring the shopman, Muni could always ask for one or two items of food, promising repayment later. Some days the shopman was in a good mood and gave in, and sometimes he would lose his temper suddenly and bark at Muni for daring to ask for credit. This was such a day, and Muni could not progress beyond two items listed as essential components. The shopman was also displaying a remarkable memory for old facts and figures and took out an oblong ledger to support his observations. Muni felt impelled to rise and flee. But his self-respect kept him in his seat and made him listen to the worst things about himself. The shopman concluded, "If you could find five rupees and a quarter, you will have paid off an ancient debt and then could apply for admission to swarga.[3] How much have you got now?"

---

[1] A grain like lentils or split peas.
[2] An Indian plant whose seeds are pressed into a cooking oil.
[3] Heaven.

"I will pay you everything on the first of the next month."

"As always, and whom do you expect to rob by then?"

Muni felt caught and mumbled, "My daughter has sent word that she will be sending me money."

"Have you a daughter?" sneered the shopman. "And she is sending you money! For what purpose, may I know?"

"Birthday, fiftieth birthday," said Muni quietly.

"Birthday! How old are you?"

Muni repeated weakly, not being sure of it himself, "Fifty." He always calculated his age from the time of the great famine when he stood as high as the parapet around the village well, but who could calculate such things accurately nowadays with so many famines occurring? The shopman felt encouraged when other customers stood around to watch and comment. Muni thought helplessly, "My poverty is exposed to everybody. But what can I do?"

"More likely you are seventy," said the shopman. "You also forget that you mentioned a birthday five weeks ago when you wanted castor oil for your holy bath."

"Bath! Who can dream of a bath when you have to scratch the tank-bed for a bowl of water? We would all be parched and dead but for the Big House, where they let us take a pot of water from their well." After saying this Muni unobtrusively rose and moved off.

He told his wife, "That scoundrel would not give me anything. So go out and sell the drumsticks for what they are worth."

He flung himself down in a corner to recoup from the fatigue of his visit to the shop. His wife said, "You are getting no sauce today, nor anything else. I can't find anything to give you to eat. Fast till the evening, it'll do you good. Take the goats and be gone now," she cried and added, "Don't come back before the sun is down." He knew that if he obeyed her she would somehow conjure up some food for him in the evening. Only he must be careful not to argue and irritate her. Her temper was undependable in the morning but improved by evening time. She was sure to go out and work—grind corn in the Big House, sweep or scrub somewhere, and earn enough to buy foodstuff and keep a dinner ready for him in the evening.

Unleashing the goats from the drumstick tree, Muni started out, driving them ahead and uttering weird cries from time to time in order to urge them on. He passed through the village with his head bowed in thought. He did not want to look at anyone or be accosted. A couple of cronies lounging in the temple corridor hailed him, but he ignored their call. They had known him in the days of affluence when he lorded over a flock of fleecy sheep, not the miserable gawky goats that he had today. Of course he also used to have a few goats for those who fancied them, but real wealth lay in sheep; they bred fast and people came and bought the fleece in the shearing season; and then that famous butcher from the town came over on the weekly market days bringing him betel leaves, tobacco, and often enough some *bhang*,[4] which they smoked in a hut in the coconut grove, undisturbed by wives and well-wishers. After a smoke one felt light and elated and inclined to forgive everyone including that brother-in-law of his who had once tried to set fire to his home. But all this seemed like the memories of a previous birth. Some pestilence afflicted his cattle (he could of course guess who had laid his animals under a curse),

---

[4]A narcotic made from hemp.

and even the friendly butcher would not touch one at half the price . . . and now here he was left with the two scraggy creatures. He wished someone would rid him of their company too. The shopman had said that he was seventy. At seventy, one only waited to be summoned by God. When he was dead what would his wife do? They had lived in each other's company since they were children. He was told on their day of wedding that he was ten years old and she was eight. During the wedding ceremony they had had to recite their respective ages and names. He had thrashed her only a few times in their career, and later she had the upper hand. Progeny, none. Perhaps a large progeny would have brought him the blessing of the gods. Fertility brought merit. People with fourteen sons were always so prosperous and at peace with the world and themselves. He recollected the thrill he had felt when he mentioned a daughter to that shopman; although it was not believed, what if he did not have a daughter?—his cousin in the next village had many daughters, and any one of them was as good as his; he was fond of them all and would buy them sweets if he could afford it. Still, everyone in the village whispered behind their backs that Muni and his wife were a barren couple. He avoided looking at anyone; they all professed to be so high up, and everyone else in the village had more money than he. "I am the poorest fellow in our caste and no wonder that they spurn me, but I won't look at them either," and so he passed on with his eyes downcast along the edge of the street, and people left him also very much alone, commenting only to the extent, "Ah, there he goes with his two goats; if he slits their throats, he may have more peace of mind." "What has he to worry about anyway? They live on nothing and have none to worry about." Thus people commented when he passed through the village. Only on the outskirts did he lift his head and look up. He urged and bullied the goats until they meandered along to the foot of the horse statue on the edge of the village. He sat on its pedestal for the rest of the day. The advantage of this was that he could watch the highway and see the lorries[5] and buses pass through to the hills, and it gave him a sense of belonging to a larger world. The pedestal of the statue was broad enough for him to move around as the sun travelled up and westward; or he could also crouch under the belly of the horse, for shade.

The horse was nearly life-size, moulded out of clay, baked, burnt, and brightly coloured, and reared its head proudly, prancing its forelegs in the air and flourishing its tail in a loop; beside the horse stood a warrior with scythe-like mustachios, bulging eyes, and aquiline nose. The old image-makers believed in indicating a man of strength by bulging out his eyes and sharpening his moustache tips, and also decorated the man's chest with beads which looked today like blobs of mud through the ravages of sun and wind and rain (when it came), but Muni would insist that he had known the beads to sparkle like the nine gems at one time in his life. The horse itself was said to have been as white as a dhobi-washed[6] sheet, and had had on its back a cover of pure brocade of red and black lace, matching the multicoloured sash around the waist of the warrior. But none in the village remembered the splendour as no one noticed its existence. Even Muni, who spent all his waking hours at its foot, never bothered to look up. It was untouched even by the young vandals of the village who gashed tree trunks with knives and tried to topple off milestones and inscribed lewd designs on all walls. This statue had been closer to the population of

---

[5]Trucks.
[6]Clothes washed by the riverside by a native washerwoman.

the village at one time, when this spot bordered the village; but when the highway was laid through (or perhaps when the tank and wells dried up completely here) the village moved a couple of miles inland.

Muni sat at the foot of the statue, watching his two goats graze in the arid soil among the cactus and lantana bushes. He looked at the sun; it had tilted westward no doubt, but it was not the time yet to go back home; if he went too early his wife would have no food for him. Also he must give her time to cool off her temper and feel sympathetic, and then she would scrounge and manage to get some food. He watched the mountain road for a time signal. When the green bus appeared around the bend he could leave, and his wife would feel pleased that he had let the goats feed long enough.

He noticed now a new sort of vehicle coming down at full speed. It looked like both a motor car and a bus. He used to be intrigued by the novelty of such spectacles, but of late work was going on at the source of the river on the mountain and an assortment of people and traffic went past him, and he took it all casually and described to his wife, later in the day, everything he saw. Today, while he observed the yellow vehicle coming down, he was wondering how to describe it later to his wife when it sputtered and stopped in front of him. A red-faced foreigner, who had been driving it, got down and went round it, stooping, looking, and poking under the vehicle; then he straightened himself up, looked at the dashboard, stared in Muni's direction, and approached him. "Excuse me, is there a gas station nearby, or do I have to wait until another car comes—" He suddenly looked up at the clay horse and cried, "Marvellous," without completing his sentence. Muni felt he should get up and run away, and cursed his age. He could not readily put his limbs into action; some years ago he could outrun a cheetah, as happened once when he went to the forest to cut fuel and it was then that two of his sheep were mauled—a sign that bad times were coming. Though he tried, he could not easily extricate himself from his seat, and then there was also the problem of the goats. He could not leave them behind.

The red-faced man wore khaki clothes—evidently a policeman or a soldier. Muni said to himself, "He will chase or shoot if I start running. Some dogs chase only those who run—oh, Shiva protect me. I don't know why this man should be after me." Meanwhile the foreigner cried, "Marvellous!" again, nodding his head. He paced around the statue with his eyes fixed on it. Muni sat frozen for a while, and then suddenly fidgeted and tried to edge away. Now the other man suddenly pressed his palms together in a salute, smiled, and said, "Namaste![7] How do you do?"

At which Muni spoke the only English expressions he had learnt, "Yes, no." Having exhausted his English vocabulary, he started in Tamil: "My name is Muni. These two goats are mine, and no one can gainsay it—though our village is full of slanderers these days who will not hesitate to say that what belongs to a man doesn't belong to him." He rolled his eyes and shuddered at the thought of evil-minded men and women peopling his village.

The foreigner faithfully looked in the direction indicated by Muni's fingers, gazed for a while at the two goats and the rocks, and with a puzzled expression took out his silver cigarette case and lit a cigarette. Suddenly remembering the courtesies of the season, he asked, "Do you smoke?" Muni answered, "Yes, no." Whereupon the red-faced man took a cigarette and gave it to Muni, who received it with

---

[7] A word of greeting.

surprise, having had no offer of a smoke from anyone for years now. Those days when he smoked bhang were gone with his sheep and the large-hearted butcher. Nowadays he was not able to find even matches, let alone bhang. (His wife went across and borrowed a fire at dawn from a neighbour.) He had always wanted to smoke a cigarette; only once did the shopman give him one on credit, and he remembered how good it had tasted. The other flicked the lighter open and offered a light to Muni. Muni felt so confused about how to act that he blew on it and put it out. The other, puzzled but undaunted, flourished his lighter, presented it again, and lit Muni's cigarette. Muni drew a deep puff and started coughing; it was racking, no doubt, but extremely pleasant. When his cough subsided he wiped his eyes and took stock of the situation, understanding that the other man was not an Inquisitor of any kind. Yet, in order to make sure, he remained wary. No need to run away from a man who gave him such a potent smoke. His head was reeling from the effect of one of those strong American cigarettes made with roasted tobacco. The man said, "I come from New York," took out a wallet from his hip pocket, and presented his card.

Muni shrank away from the card. Perhaps he was trying to present a warrant and arrest him. Beware of khaki, one part of his mind warned. Take all the cigarettes or bhang or whatever is offered, but don't get caught. Beware of khaki. He wished he weren't seventy as the shopman had said. At seventy one didn't run, but surrendered to whatever came. He could only ward off trouble by talk. So he went on, all in the chaste Tamil for which Kritam was famous. (Even the worst detractors could not deny that the famous poetess Avvaiyar was born in this area, although no one could say whether it was in Kritam or Kuppam, the adjoining village.) Out of this heritage the Tamil language gushed through Muni in an unimpeded flow. He said, "Before God, sir, Bhagwan,[8] who sees everything, I tell you, sir, that we know nothing of the case. If the murder was committed, whoever did it will not escape. Bhagwan is all-seeing. Don't ask me about it. I know nothing." A body had been found mutilated and thrown under a tamarind tree at the border between Kritam and Kuppam a few weeks before, giving rise to much gossip and speculation. Muni added an explanation. "Anything is possible there. People over there will stop at nothing." The foreigner nodded his head and listened courteously though he understood nothing.

"I am sure you know when this horse was made," said the red man and smiled ingratiatingly.

Muni reacted to the relaxed atmosphere by smiling himself, and pleaded, "Please go away, sir, I know nothing. I promise we will hold him for you if we see any bad character around, and we will bury him up to his neck in a coconut pit if he tries to escape; but our village has always had a clean record. Must definitely be the other village."

Now the red man implored, "Please, please, I will speak slowly, please try to understand me. Can't you understand even a simple word of English? Everyone in this country seems to know English. I have gotten along with English everywhere in this country, but you don't speak it. Have you any religious or spiritual scruples against English speech?"

Muni made some indistinct sounds in his throat and shook his head. Encouraged, the other went on to explain at length, uttering each syllable with care and deliberation. Presently he sidled over and took a seat beside the old man, explaining,

---

[8] Master.

"You see, last August, we probably had the hottest summer in history, and I was working in shirt-sleeves in my office on the fortieth floor of the Empire State Building. We had a power failure one day, you know, and there I was stuck for four hours, no elevator, no air conditioning. All the way in the train I kept thinking, and the minute I reached home in Connecticut, I told my wife Ruth, 'We will visit India this winter, it's time to look at other civilizations.' Next day she called the travel agent first thing and told him to fix it, and so here I am. Ruth came with me but is staying back at Srinagar,[9] and I am the one doing the rounds and joining her later."

Muni looked reflective at the end of this long oration and said, rather feebly, "Yes, no," as a concession to the other's language, and went on in Tamil, "When I was this high"—he indicated a foot high—"I had heard my uncle say . . ."

No one can tell what he was planning to say, as the other interrupted him at this stage to ask, "Boy, what is the secret of your teeth? How old are you?"

The old man forgot what he had started to say and remarked, "Sometimes we too lose our cattle. Jackals or cheetahs may sometimes carry them off, but sometimes it is just theft from over in the next village, and then we will know who has done it. Our priest at the temple can see in the camphor flame the face of the thief, and when he is caught . . ." He gestured with his hands a perfect mincing of meat.

The American watched his hands intently and said, "I know what you mean. Chop something? Maybe I am holding you up and you want to chop wood? Where is your axe? Hand it to me and show me what to chop. I do enjoy it, you know, just a hobby. We get a lot of driftwood along the backwater near my house, and on Sundays I do nothing but chop wood for the fireplace. I really feel different when I watch the fire in the fireplace, although it may take all the sections of the Sunday *New York Times* to get a fire started." And he smiled at this reference.

Muni felt totally confused but decided the best thing would be to make an attempt to get away from this place. He tried to edge out, saying, "Must go home," and turned to go. The other seized his shoulder and said desperately, "Is there no one, absolutely no one here, to translate for me?" He looked up and down the road, which was deserted in this hot afternoon; a sudden gust of wind churned up the dust and dead leaves on the roadside into a ghostly column and propelled it towards the mountain road. The stranger almost pinioned Muni's back to the statue and asked, "Isn't this statue yours? Why don't you sell it to me?"

The old man now understood the reference to the horse, thought for a second, and said in his own language, "I was an urchin this high when I heard my grandfather explain this horse and warrior, and my grandfather himself was this high when he heard his grandfather, whose grandfather . . ."

The other man interrupted him. "I don't want to seem to have stopped here for nothing. I will offer you a good price for this," he said, indicating the horse. He had concluded without the least doubt that Muni owned this mud horse. Perhaps he guessed by the way he sat on its pedestal, like other souvenir sellers in this country presiding over their wares.

Muni followed the man's eyes and pointing fingers and dimly understood the subject matter and, feeling relieved that the theme of the mutilated body had been abandoned at least for the time being, said again, enthusiastically, "I was this high when my grandfather told me about this horse and the warrior, and my grandfather

---

[9]Capital of Kashmir, a popular vacation spot.

was this high when he himself..." and he was getting into a deeper bog of reminiscence each time he tried to indicate the antiquity of the statue.

The Tamil that Muni spoke was stimulating even as pure sound, and the foreigner listened with fascination. "I wish I had my tape-recorder here," he said, assuming the pleasantest expression. "Your language sounds wonderful. I get a kick out of every word you utter, here"—he indicated his ears—"but you don't have to waste your breath in sales talk. I appreciate the article. You don't have to explain its points."

"I never went to a school, in those days only Brahmin[10] went to schools, but we had to go out and work in the fields morning till night, from sowing to harvest time...and when Pongal[11] came and we had cut the harvest, my father allowed me to go out and play with others at the tank, and so I don't know the Parangi language you speak, even little fellows in your country probably speak the Parangi language, but here only learned men and officers know it. We had a postman in our village who could speak to you boldly in your language, but his wife ran away with someone and he does not speak to anyone at all nowadays. Who would if a wife did what she did? Women must be watched; otherwise they will sell themselves and the home." And he laughed at his own quip.

The foreigner laughed heartily, took out another cigarette, and offered it to Muni, who now smoked with ease, deciding to stay on if the fellow was going to be so good as to keep up his cigarette supply. The American now stood up on the pedestal in the attitude of a demonstrative lecturer and said, running his finger along some of the carved decorations around the horse's neck, speaking slowly and uttering his words syllable by syllable, "I could give a sales talk for this better than anyone else.... This is a marvellous combination of yellow and indigo, though faded now.... How do you people of this country achieve these flaming colours?"

Muni, now assured that the subject was still the horse and not the dead body, said, "This is our guardian, it means death to our adversaries. At the end of Kali Yuga,[12] this world and all other worlds will be destroyed, and the Redeemer will come in the shape of a horse called 'Kalki'; this horse will come to life and gallop and trample down all bad men." As he spoke of bad men the figures of his shopman and his brother-in-law assumed concrete forms in his mind, and he revelled for a moment in the predicament of the fellow under the horse's hoof: served him right for trying to set fire to his home....

While he was brooding on this pleasant vision, the foreigner utilized the pause to say, "I assure you that this will have the best home in the U.S.A. I'll push away the bookcase, you know I love books and am a member of five book clubs, and the choice and bonus volumes mount up to a pile really in our living room, as high as this horse itself. But they'll have to go. Ruth may disapprove, but I will convince her. The T.V. may have to be shifted too. We can't have everything in the living room. Ruth will probably say what about when we have a party? I'm going to keep him right in the middle of the room. I don't see how that can interfere with the party—we'll stand around him and have our drinks."

Muni continued his description of the end of the world. "Our pundit[13] discoursed at the temple once how the oceans are going to close over the earth in a huge wave

---

[10]Members of the highest or priestly Hindu caste.

[11]A festival that is observed in early January.

[12]One of the cycles of time in Hindu mythology, a destructive period.

[13]A Brahman scholar.

and swallow us—this horse will grow bigger than the biggest wave and carry on its back only the good people and kick into the floods the evil ones—plenty of them about—" he said reflectively. "Do you know when it is going to happen?" he asked.

The foreigner now understood by the tone of the other that a question was being asked and said, "How am I transporting it? I can push the seat back and make room in the rear. That van can take in an elephant"—waving precisely at the back of the seat.

Muni was still hovering on visions of avatars and said again, "I never missed our pundit's discourses at the temple in those days during every bright half of the month, although he'd go on all night, and he told us that Vishnu[14] is the highest god. Whenever evil men trouble us, he comes down to save us. He has come many times. The first time he incarnated as a great fish, and lifted the scriptures on his back when the floods and sea waves..."

"I am not a millionaire, but a modest businessman. My trade is coffee."

Amidst all this wilderness of obscure sound Muni caught the word "coffee" and said, "If you want to drink 'kapi,' drive further up, in the next town, they have Friday market, and there they open 'kapi-otels'—so I learn from passers-by. Don't think I wander about. I go nowhere and look for nothing." His thoughts went back to the avatars. "The first avatar was in the shape of a little fish in a bowl of water, but every hour it grew bigger and bigger and became in the end a huge whale which the seas could not contain, and on the back of the whale the holy books were supported, saved and carried." Once he had launched on the first avatar, it was inevitable that he should go on to the next, a wild boar on whose tusk the earth was lifted when a vicious conqueror of the earth carried it off and hid it at the bottom of the sea. After describing this avatar Muni concluded, "God will always save us whenever we are troubled by evil beings. When we were young we staged at full moon the story of the avatars. That's how I know the stories; we played them all night until the sun rose, and sometimes the European collector would come to watch, bringing his own chair. I had a good voice and so they always taught me songs and gave me the women's roles. I was always Goddess Lakshmi,[15] and they dressed me in a brocade sari, loaned from the Big House..."

The foreigner said, "I repeat I am not a millionaire. Ours is a modest business; after all, we can't afford to buy more than sixty minutes of T.V. time in a month, which works out to two minutes a day, that's all, although in the course of time we'll maybe sponsor a one-hour show regularly if our sales graph continues to go up..."

Muni was intoxicated by the memory of his theatrical days and was about to explain how he had painted his face and worn a wig and diamond earrings when the visitor, feeling that he had spent too much time already, said, "Tell me, will you accept a hundred rupees or not for the horse? I'd love to take the whiskered soldier also but no space for him this year. I'll have to cancel my air ticket and take a boat home, I suppose. Ruth can go by air if she likes, but I will go with the horse and keep him in my cabin all the way if necessary." And he smiled at the picture of himself voyaging across the seas hugging this horse. He added, "I will have to pad it with straw so that it doesn't break..."

---

[14] One of the chief Hindu gods.
[15] Goddess of wealth and good fortune; symbol of all domestic virtues.

"When we played *Ramayana*, they dressed me as Sita,"[16] added Muni. "A teacher came and taught us the songs for the drama and we gave him fifty rupees. He incarnated himself as Rama, and He alone could destroy Ravana, the demon with ten heads who shook all the worlds; do you know the story of *Ramayana?*"

"I have my station wagon as you see. I can push the seat back and take the horse in if you will just lend me a hand with it."

"Do you know *Mahabharata?*[17] Krishna was the eighth avatar of Vishnu, incarnated to help the Five Brothers regain their kingdom. When Krishna was a baby he danced on the thousand-hooded giant serpent and trampled it to death; and then he suckled the breasts of the demoness and left them flat as a disc though when she came to him her bosoms were large, like mounds of earth on the banks of a dug up canal." He indicated two mounds with his hands. The stranger was completely mystified by the gesture. For the first time he said, "I really wonder what you are saying because your answer is crucial. We have come to the point when we should be ready to talk business."

"When the tenth avatar comes, do you know where you and I will be?" asked the old man.

"Lend me a hand and I can lift off the horse from its pedestal after picking out the cement at the joints. We can do anything if we have a basis of understanding."

At this stage the mutual mystification was complete, and there was no need even to carry on a guessing game at the meaning of words. The old man chattered away in a spirit of balancing off the credits and debits of conversational exchange, and said in order to be on the credit side, "Oh, honourable one, I hope God has blessed you with numerous progeny. I say this because you seem to be a good man, willing to stay beside an old man and talk to him, while all day I have none to talk to except when somebody stops by to ask for a piece of tobacco. But I seldom have it, tobacco is not what it used to be at one time, and I have given up chewing. I cannot afford it nowadays." Noting the other's interest in his speech, Muni felt encouraged to ask, "How many children have you?" with appropriate gestures with his hands. Realizing that a question was being asked, the red man replied, "I said a hundred," which encouraged Muni to go into details. "How many of your children are boys and how many girls? Where are they? Is your daughter married? Is it difficult to find a son-in-law in your country also?"

In answer to these questions the red man dashed his hand into his pocket and brought forth his wallet in order to take immediate advantage of the bearish trend in the market. He flourished a hundred-rupee currency note and said, "Well, this is what I meant."

The old man now realized that some financial element was entering their talk. He peered closely at the currency note, the like of which he had never seen in his life; he knew the five and ten by their colours although always in other people's hands, while his own earning at any time was in coppers and nickels. What was this man flourishing the note for? Perhaps asking for change. He laughed to himself at the notion of anyone coming to him for changing a thousand- or ten-thousand-rupee note. He said with a grin, "Ask our village headman, who is also a moneylender; he can change even a lakh[18] of rupees in gold sovereigns if you prefer it that way; he

---

[16] Sita is the wife of Rama, hero of the *Ramayana*, an Indian epic. At one point in the story Sita is abducted by Ravana, a demon king.

[17] An Indian epic. In the most famous section of the poem, reprinted separately as the *Bhagavad Gita*, Krishna gives spiritual counsel to the hero of the epic, Arjuna.

[18] One hundred thousand; a large number.

thinks nobody knows, but dig the floor of his puja[19] room and your head will reel at the sight of the hoard. The man disguises himself in rags just to mislead the public. Talk to the headman yourself because he goes mad at the sight of me. Someone took away his pumpkins with the creeper and he, for some reason, thinks it was me and my goats... that's why I never let my goats be seen anywhere near the farms." His eyes travelled to his goats nosing about, attempting to wrest nutrition from minute greenery peeping out of rock and dry earth.

The foreigner followed his look and decided that it would be a sound policy to show an interest in the old man's pets. He went up casually to them and stroked their backs with every show of courteous attention. Now the truth dawned on the old man. His dream of a lifetime was about to be realized. He understood that the red man was actually making an offer for the goats. He had reared them up in the hope of selling them some day and, with the capital, opening a small shop on this very spot. Sitting here, watching towards the hills, he had often dreamt how he would put up a thatched roof here, spread a gunny sack out on the ground, and display on it fried nuts, coloured sweets, and green coconut for the thirsty and famished wayfarers on the highway, which was sometimes very busy. The animals were not prize ones for a cattle show, but he had spent his occasional savings to provide them some fancy diet now and then, and they did not look too bad. While he was reflecting thus, the red man shook his hand and left on his palm one hundred rupees in tens now, suddenly realizing that this was what the old man was asking. "It is all for you or you may share it if you have a partner."

The old man pointed at the station wagon and asked, "Are you carrying them off in that?"

"Yes, of course," said the other, understanding the transportation part of it.

The old man said, "This will be their first ride in a motor car. Carry them off after I get out of sight, otherwise they will never follow you, but only me even if I am travelling on the path to Yama Loka."[20] He laughed at his own joke, brought his palms together in a salute, turned round and went off, and was soon out of sight beyond a clump of thicket.

The red man looked at the goats grazing peacefully. Perched on the pedestal of the horse, as the westerly sun touched off the ancient faded colours of the statue with a fresh splendour, he ruminated, "He must be gone to fetch some help, I suppose!" and settled down to wait. When a truck came downhill, he stopped it and got the help of a couple of men to detach the horse from its pedestal and place it in his station wagon. He gave them five rupees each, and for a further payment they siphoned off gas from the truck, and helped him to start his engine.

Muni hurried homeward with the cash securely tucked away at his waist in his dhoti.[21] He shut the street door and stole up softly to his wife as she squatted before the lit oven wondering if by a miracle food would drop from the sky. Muni displayed his fortune for the day. She snatched the notes from him, counted them by the glow of the fire, and cried, "One hundred rupees! How did you come by it? Have you been stealing?"

"I have sold our goats to a red-faced man. He was absolutely crazy to have them, gave me all this money and carried them off in his motor car!"

---

[19] A rite or ceremony.
[20] The underworld.
[21] A loincloth.

Hardly had these words left his lips when they heard bleating outside. She opened the door and saw the two goats at her door. "Here they are!" she said. "What's the meaning of all this?"

He muttered a great curse and seized one of the goats by its ears and shouted, "Where is that man? Don't you know you are his? Why did you come back?" The goat only wriggled in his grip. He asked the same question of the other too. The goat shook itself off. His wife glared at him and declared, "If you have thieved, the police will come tonight and break your bones. Don't involve me. I will go away to my parents...."

ALBERT CAMUS
[1913–1960]

The two great wars of the first half of the twentieth century, with their incredible destruction of human lives and social ideals, left many people wondering whether there was anything or anyone in which to believe. Albert Camus looked at the World War II era and its aftermath with courage, honesty, and sensitivity. His early writings, such as *L'Étranger* (*The Stranger,* 1942) and *Le Mythe de Sisyphe* (*The Myth of Sisyphus,* 1942), identified him as the philosopher of the absurd, the outsider, and the gentle hedonist, but in the postwar era he searched for the basis of meaning and social commitment in a world disillusioned with traditional beliefs, movements, and institutions. He became the quintessential rebel, who tried and then rejected the Communist Party, fought in the French underground against the Nazis, broke with the philosopher Jean-Paul Sartre over Stalinism, and refused to side with either the French or the Algerians in the Algerian struggle for independence. He denounced tyranny, terrorism, and fascism, whether they occurred on the extreme right or the extreme left. Since his death in 1960, his popularity has periodically waxed and waned, but his writings have consistently encouraged serious dialogue about social issues and invited his readers to commit themselves to bettering the human condition.

LIFE

Camus was born on November 7, 1913, in Mondovi, Algeria, in what was then French North Africa. His father was an illiterate farmer who was killed at the first Battle of the Marne in World War I. Originally from Spain, his mother moved her family—Albert, his brother, uncle, and grandmother—to a two-room apartment in Belcourt, a working class suburb of Algiers, where she worked as a charwoman. Raised by his maternal grandmother, who used a whip for discipline, Camus was permanently affected by the silence that surrounded his relationship with his illiterate, deaf mother who rarely spoke. His sympathy for the plight of the working-class guided his moral and political struggles for the rest of his life.

Ordinarily, he would have gone to work after elementary school, but a teacher, Louis Germain, to whom Camus later dedicated his Nobel Prize speech, recognized his student's intellectual gifts and arranged for a scholarship to the lycée in the European section of Algiers. Although he won honors as both a young scholar in philosophy and a passionate goalie for the soccer team at the University of Algiers, Camus' world collapsed at age seventeen when he was found to have tuberculosis; a year's convalescence was prescribed.

Undoubtedly, his unreliable health and the intimate contact with death had a profound effect on the young Camus. He became involved with social projects while continuing his education in philosophy. He married Simone Hie in 1933. The next year he joined the Algerian Communist Party and founded Le Théâtre du Travail (The Labor Theater). While working at various jobs, Camus directed, wrote, and adapted plays for this people's theater, which performed on the docks in Algiers.

His first two collections of essays, *L'Envers et l'endroit* (*The Wrong and the Right Side,* 1937) and *Noces* (*Nuptials,* 1939), reveal his passionate attachment to the people and landscapes of North Africa. As an agnostic, he characterizes the twin poles of his secular religion in these essays as "yes" and "no": a passionate "yes" to "life with its face of tears and sun, life in the salt sea and on warm stones," but a resounding "no" to injustice and oppression. In "Return to Tipasa," he writes, "Yes, there is beauty and there are the humiliated. Whatever may be the difficulties of the undertaking, I should like never to be unfaithful either to one or to the others."

Late in 1938, Camus devised an ambitious plan that reflected his extraordinary gifts as a writer and thinker. He would choose a particular theme—for example, the absurd—and then write a philosophical essay, a novel, and a play around the theme, and if possible publish them together. World War II interfered with this plan; Camus went to France and joined the resistance movement in 1942. Nevertheless, on the theme of the absurd he wrote *The Myth of Sisyphus and Other Essays,* a book that explains how absurdity arises from the fact that we long for clear answers while at the same time we live in an irrational, incomprehensible world—the gulf between human need and the "unreasonable silence of the world." The essays explore reasons for not committing suicide in an absurd universe. In the title essay "Myth of Sisyphus," Camus creates the absurd hero who in his strong attachment to the earth must bear his burdens without the rewards of success, and without the consolations of religion and philosophy.

His most famous novel, *The Stranger,* shows a hero, Meursault, who refuses to adopt the social and religious conventions of his day and is therefore a stranger to his society. Eventually he is sentenced to death, as Camus says, for refusing to lie. The play *Caligula* (1945) takes the idea of liberty to destructive extremes and completes the series of works on the absurd.

In 1943, Camus became a publisher's reader and member of the administrative staff at the publishing house Gallimard, a position that he held until he died. The next year, he became editor of the underground newspaper *Combat* and wrote editorials and articles for it. Through most of his writing and his associations with French existentialism and Jean-Paul Sartre, Camus examined the grounds for moral responsibility in a world where God and religious institutions no longer provide a comprehensive vision and imperative for ethical action; in a secular world, what connects us to the plight of our neighbors? Several plays were devoted to living in a world where restraints have been lifted and anything is possible: *Le Malentendu* (*The Misunderstanding,* 1944), *L'État de Siège* (*The State of Siege,* 1948), and *Les Justes* (*The Just Assassins,* 1950). He also adapted two novels for the stage, William Faulkner's *Requiem for a Nun* and Dostoevsky's *The Possessed.*

In 1947, he published *La Peste* (*The Plague*), a novel that sets up a situation in which Camus could test his ideas: a North African city, besieged and isolated by the plague, that gradually reveals the ethical motivations and psychological needs of various characters. As a complement to this novel Camus wrote *L'Homme Révolté* (*The Rebel,* 1951), which discusses the nature of revolution and the relationship of means and ends in political movements. He questions whether the sacrifices demanded by the new secular prophets such as Marx and Lenin will lead ultimately to better societies; these commentaries brought attacks by Sartre and others. The novel *La Chute* (*The Fall,* 1956) is a strange, ironic monologue about personal responsibility and the darkness surrounding human motivation. He received the

Nobel Prize in literature in 1957, one of the youngest to have received that honor. Tragically, he died in a car crash en route to Paris on January 4, 1960.

WORK

The Algerian struggle for independence from France in the 1950s amply illustrated the complexity of revolutionary situations. Recognizing the deep loyalties that both the Algerian-born French and Arab Algerians had toward their homeland, Camus risked the criticism of leftists and sought a reconciliation between the French government and the FLN (Algerian rebels). This struggle, which polarized attitudes and forced reluctant partisanship on both the Algerian Arabs and Algerian French, serves as the volatile setting for Camus' "The Guest," taken from his last collection of stories, *L'Exil et le royaume* (*Exile and the Kingdom,* 1957). In this story, colonialism has reached into the Algerian backcountry, but Camus creates a situation in which the ideal of individual freedom takes precedence over political ideology and local politics. Even though French domination is symbolized in the local schoolteacher Daru, who distributes food to his drought-stricken region and teaches French geography to his pupils, the remote desert setting of the story provides an open arena for individual choices—Daru is free to act.

Real class differences are first introduced by showing Balducci, the gendarme, riding on his horse while the Arab prisoner, with hands bound, is walking. When Daru is given custody of the prisoner, he seeks ways to give the Arab his freedom. Through small signs of decency, Daru affirms the prisoner's common humanity and at the same time preserves his own set of values. Although there is little real, verbal communication between them, Daru acknowledges the minimal bond that arises between them in their shared meals and lodgings. Daru resents both the legal system that interposed itself in the Arab's family quarrel and the subjugated Arab who failed to avoid capture. Even when presented with his freedom, the Arab ironically is incapable of escaping. Furthermore, Daru returns to the schoolhouse to find that his efforts on behalf of the Arab are totally misunderstood by other Arabs. Like Camus himself, Daru feels the poignant loneliness of being caught between two cultures: neither an exile nor someone at home in the kingdom, a situation reflected in the title of the collection that houses "The Guest," *Exile and the Kingdom.*

SUGGESTED READINGS

Herbert Lottman's *Albert Camus* (1980) is an exhaustive biography. A broad commentary on Camus' writing is in Philip Thody, *Albert Camus: A Study of His Work* (1957). Germaine Brée provides important background in the book *Albert Camus* (1961) and in an edition of essays, *Camus: A Collection of Critical Essays* (1961). Another fine collection of essays on Camus is in the Yale French Studies, *Albert Camus* (1960), edited by Kenneth Douglas.

The Guest

Translated by Justin O'Brien

The schoolmaster was watching the two men climb toward him. One was on horseback, the other on foot. They had not yet tackled the abrupt rise leading to the schoolhouse built on the hillside. They were toiling onward, making slow progress in the snow, among the stones, on the vast expanse of the high, deserted plateau. From time to time the horse stumbled. Without hearing anything yet, he could see the breath issuing from the horse's nostrils. One of the men, at least, knew the region. They were following the trail although it had disappeared days ago under a layer of dirty white snow. The schoolmaster calculated that it would take them half an hour to get onto the hill. It was cold; he went back into the school to get a sweater.

He crossed the empty, frigid classroom. On the blackboard the four rivers of France,[1] drawn with four different colored chalks, had been flowing toward their estuaries for the past three days. Snow had suddenly fallen in mid-October after eight months of drought without the transition of rain, and the twenty pupils, more or less, who lived in the villages scattered over the plateau had stopped coming. With fair weather they would return. Daru now heated only the single room that was his lodging, adjoining the classroom and giving also onto the plateau to the east. Like the class windows, his window looked to the south too. On that side the school was a few kilometers from the point where the plateau began to slope toward the south. In clear weather could be seen the purple mass of the mountain range where the gap opened onto the desert.

Somewhat warmed, Daru returned to the window from which he had first seen the two men. They were no longer visible. Hence they must have tackled the rise. The sky was not so dark, for the snow had stopped falling during the night. The morning had opened with a dirty light which had scarcely become brighter as the ceiling of clouds lifted. At two in the afternoon it seemed as if the day were merely beginning. But still this was better than those three days when the thick snow was falling amidst unbroken darkness with little gusts of wind that rattled the double door of the classroom. Then Daru had spent long hours in his room, leaving it only to go to the shed and feed the chickens or get some coal. Fortunately the delivery truck from Tadjid, the nearest village to the north, had brought his supplies two days before the blizzard. It would return in forty-eight hours.

Besides, he had enough to resist a siege, for the little room was cluttered with bags of wheat that the administration left as a stock to distribute to those of his pupils whose families had suffered from the drought. Actually they had all been victims because they were all poor. Every day Daru would distribute a ration to the children. They had missed it, he knew, during these bad days. Possibly one of the fathers or big brothers would come this afternoon and he could supply them with grain. It was just a matter of carrying them over to the next harvest. Now shiploads of wheat were arriving from France and the worst was over. But it would be hard to forget that poverty, that army of ragged ghosts wandering in the sunlight, the plateaus burned to a cinder month after month, the earth shriveled up little by little, literally scorched, every stone bursting into dust under one's foot. The sheep had died then by thousands and even a few men, here and there, sometimes without anyone's knowing.

In contrast with such poverty, he who lived almost like a monk in his remote schoolhouse, nonetheless satisfied with the little he had and with the rough life, had felt like a lord with his whitewashed walls, his narrow couch, his unpainted shelves, his well, and his weekly provision of water and food. And suddenly this snow, without warning, without the foretaste of rain. This is the way the region was, cruel to live in, even without men—who didn't help matters either. But Daru had been born here. Everywhere else, he felt exiled.

---

[1] The Seine, Loire, Rhône, and Gironde rivers; French geography is being taught rather than Algerian.

He stepped out onto the terrace in front of the schoolhouse. The two men were now halfway up the slope. He recognized the horseman as Balducci, the old gendarme he had known for a long time. Balducci was holding on the end of a rope an Arab who was walking behind him with hands bound and head lowered. The gendarme waved a greeting to which Daru did not reply, lost as he was in contemplation of the Arab dressed in a faded blue jellaba,[2] his feet in sandals but covered with socks of heavy raw wool, his head surmounted by a narrow, short chèche.[3] They were approaching. Balducci was holding back his horse in order not to hurt the Arab, and the group was advancing slowly.

Within earshot, Balducci shouted: "One hour to do the three kilometers from El Ameur!" Daru did not answer. Short and square in his thick sweater, he watched them climb. Not once had the Arab raised his head. "Hello," said Daru when they got up onto the terrace. "Come in and warm up." Balducci painfully got down from his horse without letting go the rope. From under his bristling mustache he smiled at the schoolmaster. His little dark eyes, deep-set under a tanned forehead, and his mouth surrounded with wrinkles made him look attentive and studious. Daru took the bridle, led the horse to the shed, and came back to the two men, who were now waiting for him in the school. He led them into his room. "I am going to heat up the classroom," he said. "We'll be more comfortable there." When he entered the room again, Balducci was on the couch. He had undone the rope tying him to the Arab, who had squatted near the stove. His hands still bound, the chèche pushed back on his head, he was looking toward the window. At first Daru noticed only his huge lips, fat, smooth, almost Negroid; yet his nose was straight, his eyes were dark and full of fever. The chèche revealed an obstinate forehead and, under the weathered skin now rather discolored by the cold, the whole face had a restless and rebellious look that struck Daru when the Arab, turning his face toward him, looked him straight in the eyes. "Go into the other room," said the schoolmaster, "and I'll make you some mint tea." "Thanks," Balducci said. "What a chore! How I long for retirement." And addressing his prisoner in Arabic: "Come on, you." The Arab got up and, slowly, holding his bound wrists in front of him, went into the classroom.

With the tea, Daru brought a chair. But Balducci was already enthroned on the nearest pupil's desk and the Arab had squatted against the teacher's platform facing the stove, which stood between the desk and the window. When he held out the glass of tea to the prisoner, Daru hesitated at the sight of his bound hands. "He might perhaps be untied." "Sure," said Balducci. "That was for the trip." He started to get to his feet. But Daru, setting the glass on the floor, had knelt beside the Arab. Without saying anything, the Arab watched him with his feverish eyes. Once his hands were free, he rubbed his swollen wrists against each other, took the glass of tea, and sucked up the burning liquid in swift little sips.

"Good," said Daru. "And where are you headed?"

Balducci withdrew his mustache from the tea. "Here, son."

"Odd pupils! And you're spending the night?"

"No. I'm going back to El Ameur. And you will deliver this fellow to Tinguit. He is expected at police headquarters."

Balducci was looking at Daru with a friendly little smile.

"What's this story?" asked the schoolmaster. "Are you pulling my leg?"

---

[2]Same as "djellaba": a long, loose robe worn by men and women in some Arab countries.
[3]A head scarf or turban.

"No, son. Those are the orders."

"The orders? I'm not . . ." Daru hesitated, not wanting to hurt the old Corsican. "I mean, that's not my job."

"What! What's the meaning of that? In wartime people do all kinds of jobs."

"Then I'll wait for the declaration of war!"

Balducci nodded.

"O.K. But the orders exist and they concern you too. Things are brewing, it appears. There is talk of a forthcoming revolt. We are mobilized, in a way."

Daru still had his obstinate look.

"Listen, son," Balducci said. "I like you and you must understand. There's only a dozen of us at El Ameur to patrol throughout the whole territory of a small department[4] and I must get back in a hurry. I was told to hand this guy over to you and return without delay. He couldn't be kept there. His village was beginning to stir; they wanted to take him back. You must take him to Tinguit tomorrow before the day is over. Twenty kilometers shouldn't faze a husky fellow like you. After that, all will be over. You'll come back to your pupils and your comfortable life."

Behind the wall the horse could be heard snorting and pawing the earth. Daru was looking out the window. Decidedly, the weather was clearing and the light was increasing over the snowy plateau. When all the snow was melted, the sun would take over again and once more would burn the fields of stone. For days, still, the unchanging sky would shed its dry light on the solitary expanse where nothing had any connection with man.

"After all," he said, turning around toward Balducci, "what did he do?" And, before the gendarme had opened his mouth, he asked: "Does he speak French?"

"No, not a word. We had been looking for him for a month, but they were hiding him. He killed his cousin."

"Is he against us?"

"I don't think so. But you can never be sure."

"Why did he kill?"

"A family squabble, I think. One owed the other grain, it seems. It's not at all clear. In short, he killed his cousin with a billhook. You know, like a sheep, *kreezk!*"

Balducci made the gesture of drawing a blade across his throat and the Arab, his attention attracted, watched him with a sort of anxiety. Daru felt a sudden wrath against the man, against all men with their rotten spite, their tireless hates, their blood lust.

But the kettle was singing on the stove. He served Balducci more tea, hesitated, then served the Arab again, who, a second time, drank avidly. His raised arms made the jellaba fall open and the schoolmaster saw his thin, muscular chest.

"Thanks, kid," Balducci said. "And now, I'm off."

He got up and went toward the Arab, taking a small rope from his pocket.

"What are you doing?" Daru asked dryly.

Balducci, disconcerted, showed him the rope.

"Don't bother."

The old gendarme hesitated. "It's up to you. Of course, you are armed?"

"I have my shotgun."

"Where?"

"In the trunk."

"You ought to have it near your bed."

---

[4]A territorial unit.

"Why? I have nothing to fear."

"You're crazy, son. If there's an uprising, no one is safe, we're all in the same boat."

"I'll defend myself. I'll have time to see them coming."

Balducci began to laugh, then suddenly the mustache covered the white teeth. "You'll have time? O.K. That's just what I was saying. You have always been a little cracked. That's why I like you, my son was like that."

At the same time he took out his revolver and put it on the desk.

"Keep it; I don't need two weapons from here to El Ameur."

The revolver shone against the black paint of the table. When the gendarme turned toward him, the schoolmaster caught the smell of leather and horseflesh.

"Listen, Balducci," Daru said suddenly, "every bit of this disgusts me, and first of all your fellow here. But I won't hand him over. Fight, yes, if I have to. But not that."

The old gendarme stood in front of him and looked at him severely.

"You're being a fool," he said slowly. "I don't like it either. You don't get used to putting a rope on a man even after years of it, and you're even ashamed—yes, ashamed. But you can't let them have their way."

"I won't hand him over," Daru said again.

"It's an order, son, and I repeat it."

"That's right. Repeat to them what I've said to you: I won't hand him over."

Balducci made a visible effort to reflect. He looked at the Arab and at Daru. At last he decided.

"No, I won't tell them anything. If you want to drop us, go ahead; I'll not denounce you. I have an order to deliver the prisoner and I'm doing so. And now you'll just sign this paper for me."

"There's no need. I'll not deny that you left him with me."

"Don't be mean with me. I know you'll tell the truth. You're from hereabouts and you are a man. But you must sign, that's the rule."

Daru opened his drawer, took out a little square bottle of purple ink, the red wooden penholder with the "sergeant-major" pen he used for making models of penmanship, and signed. The gendarme carefully folded the paper and put it into his wallet. Then he moved toward the door.

"I'll see you off," Daru said.

"No," said Balducci. "There's no use being polite. You insulted me."

He looked at the Arab, motionless in the same spot, sniffed peevishly, and turned away toward the door. "Good-by, son," he said. The door shut behind him. Balducci appeared suddenly outside the window and then disappeared. His footsteps were muffled by the snow. The horse stirred on the other side of the wall and several chickens fluttered in fright. A moment later Balducci reappeared outside the window leading the horse by the bridle. He walked toward the little rise without turning around and disappeared from sight with the horse following him. A big stone could be heard bouncing down. Daru walked back toward the prisoner, who, without stirring, never took his eyes off him. "Wait," the schoolmaster said in Arabic and went toward the bedroom. As he was going through the door, he had a second thought, went to the desk, took the revolver, and stuck it in his pocket. Then, without looking back, he went into his room.

For some time he lay on his couch watching the sky gradually close over, listening to the silence. It was this silence that had seemed painful to him during the first days here, after the war. He had requested a post in the little town at the base of the foothills separating the upper plateaus from the desert. There, rocky walls, green and black to the north, pink and lavender to the south, marked the frontier of eternal summer. He had been named to a post farther north, on the plateau itself. In the beginning, the solitude and the silence had been hard for him on these wastelands peopled only by stones. Occasionally, furrows suggested cultivation, but they had been dug to uncover a certain kind of stone good for building. The only plowing here was to harvest rocks. Elsewhere a thin layer of soil accumulated in the hollows would be scraped out to enrich paltry village gardens. This is the way it was: bare rock covered three quarters of the region. Towns sprang up, flourished, then disappeared; men came by, loved one another or fought bitterly, then died. No one in this desert, neither he nor his guest, mattered. And yet, outside this desert neither of them, Daru knew, could have really lived.

When he got up, no noise came from the classroom. He was amazed at the unmixed joy he derived from the mere thought that the Arab might have fled and that he would be alone with no decision to make. But the prisoner was there. He had merely stretched out between the stove and the desk. With eyes open, he was staring at the ceiling. In that position, his thick lips were particularly noticeable, giving him a pouting look. "Come," said Daru. The Arab got up and followed him. In the bedroom, the schoolmaster pointed to a chair near the table under the window. The Arab sat down without taking his eyes off Daru.

"Are you hungry?"

"Yes," the prisoner said.

Daru set the table for two. He took flour and oil, shaped a cake in a frying-pan, and lighted the little stove that functioned on bottled gas. While the cake was cooking, he went out to the shed to get cheese, eggs, dates, and condensed milk. When the cake was done he set it on the window sill to cool, heated some condensed milk diluted with water, and beat up the eggs into an omelette. In one of his motions he knocked against the revolver stuck in his right pocket. He set the bowl down, went into the classroom, and put the revolver in his desk drawer. When he came back to the room, night was falling. He put on the light and served the Arab. "Eat," he said. The Arab took a piece of the cake, lifted it eagerly to his mouth, and stopped short.

"And you?" he asked.

"After you. I'll eat too."

The thick lips opened slightly. The Arab hesitated, then bit into the cake determinedly.

The meal over, the Arab looked at the schoolmaster. "Are you the judge?"

"No, I'm simply keeping you until tomorrow."

"Why do you eat with me?"

"I'm hungry."

The Arab fell silent. Daru got up and went out. He brought back a folding bed from the shed, set it up between the table and the stove, perpendicular to his own bed. From a large suitcase which, upright in a corner, served as a shelf for papers, he took two blankets and arranged them on the camp bed. Then he stopped, felt useless, and sat down on his bed. There was nothing more to do or to get ready. He had to look at this man. He looked at him, therefore, trying to imagine his face bursting with rage. He couldn't do so. He could see nothing but the dark yet shining eyes and the animal mouth.

"Why did you kill him?" he asked in a voice whose hostile tone surprised him.

The Arab looked away.

"He ran away. I ran after him."

He raised his eyes to Daru again and they were full of a sort of woeful interrogation. "Now what will they do to me?"

"Are you afraid?"

He stiffened, turning his eyes away.

"Are you sorry?"

The Arab stared at him openmouthed. Obviously he did not understand. Daru's annoyance was growing. At the same time he felt awkward and self-conscious with his big body wedged between the two beds.

"Lie down there," he said impatiently. "That's your bed."

The Arab didn't move. He called to Daru:

"Tell me!"

The schoolmaster looked at him.

"Is the gendarme coming back tomorrow?"

"I don't know."

"Are you coming with us?"

"I don't know. Why?"

The prisoner got up and stretched out on top of the blankets, his feet toward the window. The light from the electric bulb shone straight into his eyes and he closed them at once.

"Why?" Daru repeated, standing beside the bed.

The Arab opened his eyes under the blinding light and looked at him, trying not to blink.

"Come with us," he said.

In the middle of the night, Daru was still not asleep. He had gone to bed after undressing completely; he generally slept naked. But when he suddenly realized that he had nothing on, he hesitated. He felt vulnerable and the temptation came to him to put his clothes back on. Then he shrugged his shoulders; after all, he wasn't a child and, if need be, he could break his adversary in two. From his bed he could observe him, lying on his back, still motionless with his eyes closed under the harsh light. When Daru turned out the light, the darkness seemed to coagulate all of a sudden. Little by little, the night came back to life in the window where the starless sky was stirring gently. The schoolmaster soon made out the body lying at his feet. The Arab still did not move, but his eyes seemed open. A faint wind was prowling around the schoolhouse. Perhaps it would drive away the clouds and the sun would reappear.

During the night the wind increased. The hens fluttered a little and then were silent. The Arab turned over on his side with his back to Daru, who thought he heard him moan. Then he listened for his guest's breathing, become heavier and more regular. He listened to that breath so close to him and mused without being able to go to sleep. In this room where he had been sleeping alone for a year, this presence bothered him. But it bothered him also by imposing on him a sort of brotherhood he knew well but refused to accept in the present circumstances. Men who share the same rooms, soldiers or prisoners, develop a strange alliance as if, having cast off their armor with their clothing, they fraternized every evening, over and above their differences, in the ancient community of dream and fatigue. But Daru shook himself; he didn't like such musings, and it was essential to sleep.

A little later, however, when the Arab stirred slightly, the schoolmaster was still not asleep. When the prisoner made a second move, he stiffened, on the alert. The Arab was lifting himself slowly on his arms with almost the motion of a sleepwalker. Seated upright in bed, he waited motionless without turning his head toward Daru, as if he were listening attentively. Daru did not stir; it had just occurred to him that the revolver was still in the drawer of his desk. It was better to act at once. Yet he continued to observe the prisoner, who, with the same slithery motion, put his feet on the ground, waited again, then began to stand up slowly. Daru was about to call out to him when the Arab began to walk, in a quite natural but extraordinarily silent way. He was heading toward the door at the end of the room that opened into the shed. He lifted the latch with precaution and went out, pushing the door behind him but without shutting it. Daru had not stirred. "He is running away," he merely thought. "Good riddance!" Yet he listened attentively. The hens were not fluttering; the guest must be on the plateau. A faint sound of water reached him, and he didn't know what it was until the Arab again stood framed in the doorway, closed the door carefully, and came back to bed without a sound. Then Daru turned his back on him and fell asleep. Still later he seemed, from the depths of his sleep, to hear furtive steps around the schoolhouse. "I'm dreaming! I'm dreaming!" he repeated to himself. And he went on sleeping.

When he awoke, the sky was clear; the loose window let in a cold, pure air. The Arab was asleep, hunched up under the blankets now, his mouth open, utterly relaxed. But when Daru shook him, he started dreadfully, staring at Daru with wild eyes as if he had never seen him and such a frightened expression that the schoolmaster stepped back. "Don't be afraid. It's me. You must eat." The Arab nodded his head and said yes. Calm had returned to his face, but his expression was vacant and listless.

The coffee was ready. They drank it seated together on the folding bed as they munched their pieces of the cake. Then Daru led the Arab under the shed and showed him the faucet where he washed. He went back into the room, folded the blankets and the bed, made his own bed and put the room in order. Then he went through the classroom and out onto the terrace. The sun was already rising in the blue sky; a soft, bright light was bathing the deserted plateau. On the ridge the snow was melting in spots. The stones were about to reappear. Crouched on the edge of the plateau, the schoolmaster looked at the deserted expanse. He thought of Balducci. He had hurt him, for he had sent him off in a way as if he didn't want to be associated with him. He could still hear the gendarme's farewell and, without knowing why, he felt strangely empty and vulnerable. At that moment, from the other side of the schoolhouse, the prisoner coughed. Daru listened to him almost despite himself and then, furious, threw a pebble that whistled through the air before sinking into the snow. That man's stupid crime revolted him, but to hand him over was contrary to honor. Merely thinking of it made him smart with humiliation. And he cursed at one and the same time his own people who had sent him this Arab and the Arab too who had dared to kill and not managed to get away. Daru got up, walked in a circle on the terrace, waited motionless, then went back into the schoolhouse.

The Arab, leaning over the cement floor of the shed, was washing his teeth with two fingers. Daru looked at him and said: "Come." He went back into the room ahead of the prisoner. He slipped a hunting-jacket on over his sweater and put on walking-shoes. Standing, he waited until the Arab had put on his *chèche* and sandals. They went into the classroom and the schoolmaster pointed to the exit, saying: "Go ahead." The fellow didn't budge. "I'm coming," said Daru. The Arab went out. Daru went back into the room and made a package of pieces of rusk, dates, and sugar. In the classroom, before going out, he hesitated a second in front of his desk, then crossed the threshold and locked the door. "That's the way," he said. He started toward the east, followed by the prisoner. But, a short distance from the schoolhouse, he thought he heard a slight sound behind them. He retraced his steps and examined the surroundings of the house, there was no one there. The Arab watched him without seeming to understand. "Come on," said Daru.

They walked for an hour and rested beside a sharp peak of limestone. The snow was melting faster and faster and the sun was drinking up the puddles at once, rapidly cleaning the plateau, which gradually dried and vibrated like the air itself. When they resumed walking, the ground rang under their feet. From time to time a bird rent the space in front of them with a joyful cry. Daru breathed in deeply the fresh morning light. He felt a sort of rapture before the vast familiar expanse, now almost entirely yellow under its dome of blue sky. They walked an hour more, descending toward the south. They reached a level height made up of crumbly rocks. From there on, the plateau sloped down, eastward, toward a low plain where there were a few spindly trees and, to the south, toward outcroppings of rock that gave the landscape a chaotic look.

Daru surveyed the two directions. There was nothing but the sky on the horizon. Not a man could be seen. He turned toward the Arab, who was looking at him blankly. Daru held out the package to him. "Take it," he said. "There are dates, bread, and sugar. You can hold out for two days. Here are a thousand francs too." The Arab took the package and the money but kept his full hands at chest level as if he didn't know what to do with what was being given him. "Now look," the schoolmaster said as he pointed in the direction of the east, "there's the way to Tinguit. You have a two-hour walk. At Tinguit you'll find the administration and the police. They are expecting you." The Arab looked toward the east, still holding the package and the money against his chest. Daru took his elbow and turned him rather roughly toward the south. At the foot of the height on which they stood could be seen a faint path. "That's the trail across the plateau. In a day's walk from here you'll find pasturelands and the first nomads. They'll take you in and shelter you according to their law." The Arab had now turned toward Daru and a sort of panic was visible in his expression. "Listen," he said. Daru shook his head: "No, be quiet. Now I'm leaving you." He turned his back on him, took two long steps in the direction of the school, looked hesitantly at the motionless Arab, and started off again. For a few minutes he heard nothing but his own step resounding on the cold ground and did not turn his head. A moment later, however, he turned around. The Arab was still there on the edge of the hill, his arms hanging now, and he was looking at the schoolmaster. Daru felt something rise in his throat. But he swore with impatience, waved vaguely, and started off again. He had already gone some distance when he again stopped and looked. There was no longer anyone on the hill.

Daru hesitated. The sun was now rather high in the sky and was beginning to beat down on his head. The schoolmaster retraced his steps, at first somewhat uncertainly, then with decision. When he reached the little hill, he was bathed in sweat. He climbed it as fast as he could and stopped, out of breath, at the top. The rock-fields to the south stood out sharply against the blue sky, but on the plain to the east a steamy heat was already rising. And in that slight haze, Daru, with heavy heart, made out the Arab walking slowly on the road to prison.

A little later, standing before the window of the classroom, the schoolmaster was watching the clear light bathing the whole surface of the plateau, but he hardly saw it. Behind him on the blackboard, among the winding French rivers, sprawled the clumsily chalked-up words he had just read: "You handed over our brother. You will pay for this." Daru looked at the sky, the plateau, and, beyond, the invisible lands stretching all the way to the sea. In this vast landscape he had loved so much, he was alone.

The Myth of Sisyphus

Translated by Justin O'Brien

The gods had condemned Sisyphus[1] to ceaselessly rolling a rock to the top of a mountain, whence the stone would fall back of its own weight. They had thought with some reason that there is no more dreadful punishment than futile and hopeless labor.

If one believes Homer, Sisyphus was the wisest and most prudent of mortals. According to another tradition, however, he was disposed to practice the profession of highwayman. I see no contradiction in this. Opinions differ as to the reasons why he became the futile laborer of the underworld. To begin with, he is accused of a certain levity in regard to the gods. He stole their secrets. Ægina, the daughter of Æsopus, was carried off by Jupiter. The father was shocked by that disappearance and complained to Sisyphus. He, who knew of the abduction, offered to tell about it on condition that Æsopus would give water to the citadel of Corinth. To the celestial thunderbolts he preferred the benediction of water. He was punished for this in the underworld. Homer tells us also that Sisyphus had put Death in chains. Pluto could not endure the sight of his deserted, silent empire. He dispatched the god of war, who liberated Death from the hands of her conqueror.

It is said also that Sisyphus, being near to death, rashly wanted to test his wife's love. He ordered her to cast his unburied body into the middle of the public square. Sisyphus woke up in the underworld. And there, annoyed by an obedience so contrary to human love, he obtained from Pluto permission to return to earth in order to chastise his wife. But when he had seen again the face of this world, enjoyed water and sun, warm stones and the sea, he no longer wanted to go back to the infernal darkness. Recalls, signs of anger, warnings were of no avail. Many years more he lived facing the curve of the gulf, the sparkling sea, and the smiles of earth. A decree of the gods was necessary. Mercury came and seized the impudent man by the collar and, snatching him from his joys, led him forcibly back to the underworld, where his rock was ready for him.

You have already grasped that Sisyphus is the absurd hero. He *is*, as much through his passions as through his torture. His scorn of the gods, his hatred of death, and his passion for life won him that unspeakable penalty in which the whole being is exerted toward accomplishing nothing. This is the price that must be paid for the passions of this earth. Nothing is told us about Sisyphus in the underworld. Myths are made for the imagination to breathe life into them. As for this myth, one sees merely the whole effort of a body straining to raise the huge stone, to roll it and push it up a slope a hundred times over; one sees the face screwed up, the cheek tight against the stone, the shoulder bracing the clay-covered mass, the foot wedging it, the fresh start with arms outstretched, the wholly human security of two earth-clotted hands. At the very end of his long effort measured by skyless space and time without depth, the purpose is achieved. Then Sisyphus watches the stone rush down in a few moments toward that lower world whence he will have to push it up again toward the summit. He goes back down to the plain.

---

[1] In order to spite his brother Salmoneus, Sisyphus seduced Salmoneus' daughter Tyro and had two children with her; she killed them when she learned the reason for his love. Sisyphus then committed an impious act for which he was condemned to Hades where for eternity he had to push an enormous boulder to the top of a hill. Near the top the stone was fated to roll down again.

It is during that return, that pause, that Sisyphus interests me. A face that toils so close to stones is already stone itself! I see that man going back down with a heavy yet measured step toward the torment of which he will never know the end. That hour like a breathing-space which returns as surely as his suffering, that is the hour of consciousness. At each of those moments when he leaves the heights and gradually sinks toward the lairs of the gods, he is superior to his fate. He is stronger than his rock.

If this myth is tragic, that is because its hero is conscious. Where would his torture be, indeed, if at every step the hope of succeeding upheld him? The workman of today works every day in his life at the same tasks, and this fate is no less absurd. But it is tragic only at the rare moments when it becomes conscious. Sisyphus, proletarian of the gods, powerless and rebellious, knows the whole extent of his wretched condition: it is what he thinks of during his descent. The lucidity that was to constitute his torture at the same time crowns his victory. There is no fate that cannot be surmounted by scorn.

If the descent is thus sometimes performed in sorrow, it can also take place in joy. This word is not too much. Again I fancy Sisyphus returning toward his rock, and the sorrow was in the beginning. When the images of earth cling too tightly to memory, when the call of happiness becomes too insistent, it happens that melancholy rises in man's heart: this is the rock's victory, this is the rock itself. The boundless grief is too heavy to bear. These are our nights of Gethsemane. But crushing truths perish from being acknowledged. Thus, Œdipus at the outset obeys fate without knowing it. But from the moment he knows, his tragedy begins. Yet at the same moment, blind and desperate, he realizes that the only bond linking him to the world is the cool hand of a girl. Then a tremendous remark rings out: "Despite so many ordeals, my advanced age and the nobility of my soul make me conclude that all is well." Sophocles' Œdipus, like Dostoevsky's Kirilov,[2] thus gives the recipe for the absurd victory. Ancient wisdom confirms modern heroism.

One does not discover the absurd without being tempted to write a manual of happiness. "What! by such narrow ways—?" There is but one world, however. Happiness and the absurd are two sons of the same earth. They are inseparable. It would be a mistake to say that happiness necessarily springs from the absurd discovery. It happens as well that the feeling of the absurd springs from happiness. "I conclude that all is well," says Œdipus, and that remark is sacred. It echoes in the wild and limited universe of man. It teaches that all is not, has not been, exhausted. It drives out of this world a god who had come into it with dissatisfaction and a preference for futile sufferings. It makes of fate a human matter, which must be settled among men.

All Sisyphus' silent joy is contained therein. His fate belongs to him. His rock is his thing. Likewise, the absurd man, when he contemplates his torment, silences all the idols. In the universe suddenly restored to its silence, the myriad wondering little voices of the earth rise up. Unconscious, secret calls, invitations from all the faces, they are the necessary reverse and price of victory. There is no sun without shadow, and it is essential to know the night. The absurd man says yes and his effort will henceforth be unceasing. If there is a personal fate, there is no higher destiny, or at least there is but one which he concludes is inevitable and despicable. For the rest, he knows himself to be the master of his days. At that subtle moment

---

[2] A character in Dostoevsky's novel *The Possessed* who believed that men would become gods by overcoming their fear of death.

when man glances backward over his life, Sisyphus returning toward his rock, in that slight pivoting he contemplates that series of unrelated actions which becomes his fate, created by him, combined under his memory's eye and soon sealed by his death. Thus, convinced of the wholly human origin of all that is human, a blind man eager to see who knows that the night has no end, he is still on the go. The rock is still rolling.

I leave Sisyphus at the foot of the mountain! One always finds one's burden again. But Sisyphus teaches the higher fidelity that negates the gods and raises rocks. He too concludes that all is well. This universe henceforth without a master seems to him neither sterile nor futile. Each atom of that stone, each mineral flake of that night-filled mountain, in itself forms a world. The struggle itself toward the heights is enough to fill a man's heart. One must imagine Sisyphus happy.

CONTEMPORARY TEXTS

RALPH ELLISON
[1914–1994]

The author of one of the great postwar American novels, many short stories, and two collections of important essays, Ralph Ellison is considered to be one of the major African-American writers of the twentieth century. That reputation stems primarily from *Invisible Man* (1952), which depicts in innovative form a nameless man's search for identity that takes him from the South to the North and presents him with a succession of nearly insurmountable, almost absurd dilemmas stemming from racism, bigotry, and greed. A kind of Renaissance man, Ellison was a writer, teacher, scholar, and political activist who devoted his life and work to creating an integrative vision of American life and articulating the history, tradition, and character of the African-American experience, in particular.

LIFE

Ralph Waldo Ellison was born March 1, 1914, in Oklahoma City to Lewis Alfred Ellison and Ida Millsap Ellison, who had moved from South Carolina in 1911. When he was four years old, Ellison went to South Carolina to visit his grandfather, an ex-slave who had become constable and magistrate of Abbeville during Reconstruction, only to lose his positions and to be forced back to farm labor in the post-Reconstruction years. A tenacious and principled man, Ellison's grandfather spoke out against racial injustice in the hostile atmosphere of lynchings taking place in South Carolina during these years; his grandfather's courage and strength of character made a lasting impression upon the young Ellison. After his father's death in 1917, his mother, a political activist who had supported Eugene Debs's Socialist campaign of 1914, encouraged her promising son, who spent much time reading at the Paul Laurence Dunbar Library in Oklahoma City.

Ellison's first ambition was to become a great musician, and music—especially jazz and blues—figures prominently in many of his stories. He studied music theory at Douglass High School, where he played first trumpet in the school band. In 1933, he left Oklahoma for Tuskegee Institute on a scholarship to study music. Here he further developed his already considerable musical talents, and studied art, drama, and literature. After some confusion over his scholarship in his third year, Ellison moved to New York City, where he lived from 1936 until his death. Inspired by the myth of New York City as the "North Star," a symbol of freedom in Negro spirituals, Ellison was inevitably disappointed, but quickly reconciled to realities. As he puts it in the essay "Harlem Is Nowhere," Harlem was the "scene and symbol of the Negro's perpetual alienation in the land of his birth," and yet it was also a place of opportunity, transformation, and empowerment for African Americans.

Harlem in 1936 was a cultural mecca for both black and white artists, musicians, and writers. Ellison met Langston Hughes, who would go with him to the Apollo Theater; jazz, art, blues, and drama thrived in Harlem during the mid- to late thirties, and Ellison continued his study of music and sculpture, but gave it up for writing after Richard Wright urged Ellison to contribute a short story to his journal *The New Challenge*. After the death of his mother in 1937, Ellison spent about a year in Ohio, where she had lived, but returned to New York City in 1938, where he did research and writing on African-American oral history, folklore, and culture for the Federal Writers' Project. Here Ellison sensed the vital importance of Southern folklore to African-American culture, and he saw the transformative power of old tales and myths from the South as they changed and were adapted to the conditions of the Northern urban experience. During this period, from 1937 to 1944, Ellison wrote short stories and reviews at night, contributing book reviews to some of the radical journals of the time, such as *New Masses, Direction,* and the *Negro Quarterly*. In his stories—"Slick Gonna Learn" (1939), "The Birthmark" (1940), "That I Had Wings" (1943), and others—many of them about men struggling to free themselves from constricting stereotypes, he often drew upon the folktales he was collecting and attempted to capture the rhythms of speech of the people he interviewed during the day. The two most important stories of this period are "Flying Home," which we include here, and "King of the Bingo Game" (both 1944), which anticipates his greatest achievement, *Invisible Man.*

When Ellison began writing his novel in 1945, he had returned from a two-year stint in the merchant marine. He had given up his job with the Federal Writers' Project in 1942 in order to edit the *Negro Quarterly* for a year. While in the merchant marine, he received a Rosenwald Fellowship to support his work on an uncompleted war novel, of which "Flying Home" was a part. Instead, Ellison worked for the next five years on *Invisible Man,* published in 1952. The novel is a kind of bildungsroman in which the nameless central character tries to define his identity through, and make sense of, a series of accidents and injustices that suggest the absurdity of modern experience—for people of all races alike. Praised both for its story and for its experimental technique, the novel won the National Book Award in 1953. Critics continue to argue over the politics of the novel, for Ellison's hero gets entangled in Kafkaesque situations that seem to transcend racial boundaries. The nameless protagonist well fits Ellison's description of what it meant to be black in America, in Harlem, in the 1940s and 1950s: "One's identity drifts in a capricious reality in which even the most commonly held assumptions are questionable. One 'is' literally, but one is nowhere; one wanders dazed into a ghetto maze, a 'displaced person' of American democracy."

In the 1960s Ellison, whose vision is integrative rather than separatist, was sometimes criticized as an Uncle Tom. In a collection of essays, *Shadow and Act* (1964), Ellison talks about slowly realizing the reductiveness of seeing the world and identity solely in terms of race. His was "a struggle to stare down the deadly and hypnotic temptation to interpret the world and all its devices in terms of race. To avoid this was very important to me, and in light of my background far from simple." At the same time, however, Ellison's writing has been committed to "putting down with honesty and without bowing to ideological expediencies the attitudes and values which give Negro American life its sense of wholeness and which render it bearable and human and, when measured by our own terms, desirable." Too many African Americans, he pointed out in an interview, "have accepted a statistical interpretation of our lives and thus much of that which makes us a source of moral strength to America goes unappreciated and undefined."

In the 1950s and 1960s, Ellison continued to write fiction, including "Did You Ever Dream Lucky" (1954), "February" (1955), "Juneteenth" (1965), and "Night-Talk" (1969), while working on a long awaited second novel and teaching literature at Bard College (1958–1961). In 1960, over three hundred pages of the new novel, which Ellison described as "a realism extended beyond realism," were destroyed in a fire at his summer home in Massachusetts, a devastating loss. Some material from the novel has been published, and it appears to be about a Reverend Hickman and Bliss, a man who loses sight of what is empowering and positive in African-American culture. In 1970 Ellison was appointed Albert Schweitzer Professor of the Humanities at New York University, and he taught as visiting professor at various places, including the University of Chicago, Yale, and UCLA. In 1986, Ellison published another collection of essays and reviews, *Going to the Territory*. At his death in April 1994, his second novel remained unfinished.

WORK

Like many of his stories, "Flying Home" (1944) tells the story of an African-American man rediscovering his culture, forging a link between the alienated present and an affirmative past. In his desire to become a flier, Todd has uprooted himself from the stories and traditions that would give him a strong sense of dignity. His role as a flier, a kind of mask that he adopts to give him a sense of superiority over other blacks, ultimately cannot sustain him, for it is a mask fraught with the contradictions of racism in America. As a black flier in World War II, Todd is not allowed to fly combat missions; thus, even as he attains a position of authority and respect, that position remains one of only partial authority and partial respect. To be a pilot means something less for him than it would for a white flier. The mask he wears, then, places limits upon him that prevent him from coming to terms with and accepting his true identity.

Crashing into the field where a "blackness wash[es] over him, like infinity," literally puts Todd back in touch with the cultural, racial, and traditional ground of his being, represented in part by the old man and his son—the farm laborers. As Todd lies in the field, "jimcrows," symbolizing the atmosphere of Jim Crow laws in the South, fly overhead, while Jefferson, the old laborer, retells a traditional Southern tale about a man fallen from heaven. Todd's angry reaction to the tale stems from both guilt and pain—the guilt at having abandoned his people and the pain of repeated failure in his attempt to wear a white mask in order to gain social acceptance. Ultimately, Todd renews his identity and regains, even amid the brutality of Graves and the hovering presence of Jim Crow, a sense of the dignity and power of his cultural heritage.

SUGGESTED READINGS

Among the many studies that discuss Ellison's fiction in context with African-American literature are Houston Baker's *Blues, Ideology, and Afro-American Literature* (1984), Bernard Bell's *The Afro-American Novel and Its Tradition* (1987), and Robert B. Stepto's *From*

Behind the Veil: A Study of Afro-American Narrative (1979). On African-American folklore see Lawrence Levine's *Black Culture and Black Consciousness* (1977). Two early collections of critical essays on Ellison are John Hersey's *Ralph Ellison* (1970) and J. M. Reilly's *Twentieth Century Interpretations of "Invisible Man"* (1970). For book-length studies of Ellison's fiction, see Robert G. O'Meally's *The Craft of Ralph Ellison* (1980), Alan Nadel's *Invisible Criticism: Ralph Ellison and the American Canon* (1991) and Edith Schor's *Visible Ellison* (1993).

Flying Home

When Todd came to, he saw two faces suspended above him in a sun so hot and blinding that he could not tell if they were black or white. He stirred, feeling a pain that burned as though his whole body had been laid open to the sun which glared into his eyes. For a moment an old fear of being touched by white hands seized him. Then the very sharpness of the pain began slowly to clear his head. Sounds came to him dimly. He done come to. Who are they? he thought. Naw he ain't, I coulda sworn he was white. Then he heard clearly:

"You hurt bad?"

Something within him uncoiled. It was a Negro sound.

"He's still out," he heard.

"Give 'im time.... Say, son, you hurt bad?"

Was he? There was that awful pain. He lay rigid, hearing their breathing and trying to weave a meaning between them and his being stretched painfully upon the ground. He watched them warily, his mind traveling back over a painful distance. Jagged scenes, swiftly unfolding as in a movie trailer, reeled through his mind, and he saw himself piloting a tailspinning plane and landing and falling from the cockpit and trying to stand. Then, as in a great silence, he remembered the sound of crunching bone, and now, looking up into the anxious faces of an old Negro man and a boy from where he lay in the same field, the memory sickened him and he wanted to remember no more.

"How you feel, son?"

Todd hesitated, as though to answer would be to admit an inacceptable weakness. Then, "It's my ankle," he said.

"Which one?"

"The left."

With a sense of remoteness he watched the old man bend and remove his boot, feeling the pressure ease.

"That any better?"

"A lot. Thank you."

He had the sensation of discussing someone else, that his concern was with some far more important thing, which for some reason escaped him.

"You done broke it bad," the old man said. "We have to get you to a doctor."

He felt that he had been thrown into a tailspin. He looked at his watch; how long had he been here? He knew there was but one important thing in the world, to get the plane back to the field before his officers were displeased.

"Help me up," he said. "Into the ship."

"But it's broke too bad...."

"Give me your arm!"

"But, son..."

Clutching the old man's arm he pulled himself up, keeping his left leg clear, thinking, "I'd never make him understand," as the leather-smooth face came parallel with his own.

"Now, let's see."

He pushed the old man back, hearing a bird's insistent shrill. He swayed giddily. Blackness washed over him, like infinity.

"You best sit down."

"No, I'm O.K."

"But, son. You jus' gonna make it worse...."

It was a fact that everything in him cried out to deny, even against the flaming pain in his ankle. He would have to try again.

"You mess with that ankle they have to cut your foot off," he heard.

Holding his breath, he started up again. It pained so badly that he had to bite his lips to keep from crying out and he allowed them to help him down with a pang of despair.

"It's best you take it easy. We gon' git you a doctor."

Of all the luck, he thought. Of all the rotten luck, now I have done it. The fumes of high-octane gasoline clung in the heat, taunting him.

"We kin ride him into town on old Ned," the boy said.

Ned? He turned, seeing the boy point toward an ox team browsing where the buried blade of a plow marked the end of a furrow. Thoughts of himself riding an ox through the town, past streets full of white faces, down the concrete runways of the airfield made swift images of humiliation in his mind. With a pang he remembered his girl's last letter. "Todd," she had written, "I don't need the papers to tell me you had the intelligence to fly. And I have always known you to be as brave as anyone else. The papers annoy me. Don't you be contented to prove over and over again that you're brave or skillful just because you're black, Todd. I think they keep beating that dead horse because they don't want to say why you boys are not yet fighting. I'm really disappointed, Todd. Anyone with brains can learn to fly, but then what? What about using it, and who will you use it for? I wish, dear, you'd write about this. I sometimes think they're playing a trick on us. It's very humiliating...." He wiped cold sweat from his face, thinking, What does she know of humiliation? She's never been down South. Now the humiliation would come. When you must have them judge you, knowing that they never accept your mistakes as your own, but hold it against your whole race—that was humiliation. Yes, and humiliation was when you could never be simply yourself, when you were always a part of this old black ignorant man. Sure, he's all right. Nice and kind and helpful. But he's not you. Well, there's one humiliation I can spare myself.

"No," he said, "I have orders not to leave the ship...."

"Aw," the old man said. Then turning to the boy, "Teddy, then you better hustle down to Mister Graves and get him to come...."

"No, wait!" he protested before he was fully aware. Graves might be white. "Just have him get word to the field, please. They'll take care of the rest."

He saw the boy leave, running.

"How far does he have to go?"

"Might' nigh a mile."

He rested back, looking at the dusty face of his watch. But now they know something has happened, he thought. In the ship there was a perfectly good radio, but it was useless. The old fellow would never operate it. That buzzard knocked me back a hundred years, he thought. Irony danced within him like the gnats circling the old man's head. With all I've learned I'm dependent upon this "peasant's" sense of time and space. His leg throbbed. In the plane, instead of time being measured by the rhythms of pain and a kid's legs, the instruments would have told him at a glance. Twisting upon his elbows he saw where dust had powdered the plane's fuselage, feeling the lump form in his throat that was always there when he thought of flight. It's crouched there, he thought, like the abandoned shell of a locust. I'm naked without it. Not a machine, a suit of clothes you wear. And with a sudden embarrassment and wonder he whispered, "It's the only dignity I have...."

He saw the old man watching, his torn overalls clinging limply to him in the heat. He felt a sharp need to tell the old man what he felt. But that would be meaningless. If I tried to explain why I need to fly back, he'd think I was simply afraid of white officers. But it's more than fear... a sense of anguish clung to him like the veil of sweat that hugged his face. He watched the old man, hearing him humming snatches of a tune as he admired the plane. He felt a furtive sense of resentment. Such old men often came to the field to watch the pilots with childish eyes. At first it had made him proud; they had been a meaningful part of a new experience. But soon he realized they did not understand his accomplishments and they came to shame and embarrass him, like the distasteful praise of an idiot. A part of the meaning of flying had gone then, and he had not been able to regain it. If I were a prizefighter I would be more human, he thought. Not a monkey doing tricks, but a man. They were pleased simply that he was a Negro who could fly, and that was not enough. He felt cut off from them by age, by understanding, by sensibility, by technology and by his need to measure himself against the mirror of other men's appreciation. Somehow he felt betrayed, as he had when as a child he grew to discover that his father was dead. Now for him any real appreciation lay with his white officers; and with them he could never be sure. Between ignorant black men and condescending whites, his course of flight seemed mapped by the nature of things away from all needed and natural landmarks. Under some sealed orders, couched in ever more technical and mysterious terms, his path curved swiftly away from both the shame the old man symbolized and the cloudy terrain of white men's regard. Flying blind, he knew but one point of landing and there he would receive his wings. After that the enemy would appreciate his skill and he would assume his deepest meaning, he thought sadly, neither from those who condescended nor from those who praised without understanding, but from the enemy who would recognize his manhood and skill in terms of hate....

He sighed, seeing the oxen making queer, prehistoric shadows against the dry brown earth.

"You just take it easy, son," the old man soothed. "That boy won't take long. Crazy as he is about airplanes."

"I can wait," he said.

"What kinda airplane you call this here'n?"

"An Advanced Trainer," he said, seeing the old man smile. His fingers were like gnarled dark wood against the metal as he touched the low-slung wing.

" 'Bout how fast can she fly?"

"Over two hundred an hour."

"Lawd! That's so fast I bet it don't seem like you moving!"

Holding himself rigid, Todd opened his flying suit. The shade had gone and he lay in a ball of fire.

"You mind if I take a look inside? I was always curious to see...."

"Help yourself. Just don't touch anything."

He heard him climb upon the metal wing, grunting. Now the questions would start. Well, so you don't have to think to answer....

He saw the old man looking over into the cockpit, his eyes bright as a child's.

"You must have to know a lot to work all these here things."

He was silent, seeing him step down and kneel beside him.

"Son, how come you want to fly way up there in the air?"

Because it's the most meaningful act in the world...because it makes me less like you, he thought.

But he said: "Because I like it, I guess. It's as good a way to fight and die as I know."

"Yeah? I guess you right," the old man said. "But how long you think before they gonna let you all fight?"

He tensed. This was the question all Negroes asked, put with the same timid hopefulness and longing that always opened a greater void within him than that he had felt beneath the plane the first time he had flown. He felt light-headed. It came to him suddenly that there was something sinister about the conversation, that he was flying unwillingly into unsafe and uncharted regions. If he could only be insulting and tell this old man who was trying to help him to shut up!

"I bet you one thing..."

"Yes?"

"That you was plenty scared coming down."

He did not answer. Like a dog on a trail the old man seemed to smell out his fears and he felt anger bubble within him.

"You sho' scared me. When I seen you coming down in that thing with it a-rollin' and a-jumpin' like a pitchin' hoss, I thought sho' you was a goner. I almost had me a stroke!"

He saw the old man grinning, "Ever'thin's been happening round here this morning, come to think of it."

"Like what?" he asked.

"Well, first thing I know, here come two white fellers looking for Mister Rudolph, that's Mister Graves's cousin. That got me worked up right away...."

"Why?"

"Why? 'Cause he done broke outta the crazy house, that's why. He liable to kill somebody," he said. "They oughta have him by now though. Then here you come. First I think it's one of them white boys. Then doggone if you don't fall outta there. Lawd, I'd done heard about you boys but I haven't never seen one o' you-all. Cain't tell you how it felt to see somebody what look like me in a airplane!"

The old man talked on, the sound streaming around Todd's thoughts like air flowing over the fuselage of a flying plane. You were a fool, he thought, remembering how before the spin the sun had blazed bright against the billboard signs beyond the town, and how a boy's blue kite had bloomed beneath him, tugging gently in the wind like a strange, odd-shaped flower. He had once flown such kites himself and tried to find the boy at the end of the invisible cord. But he had been flying too high and too fast. He had climbed steeply away in exultation. Too steeply, he thought. And one of the first rules you learn is that if the angle of thrust is too steep the plane goes into a spin. And then, instead of pulling out of it and going into a dive you let a buzzard panic you. A lousy buzzard!

"Son, what made all that blood on the glass?"

"A buzzard," he said, remembering how the blood and feathers had sprayed back against the hatch. It had been as though he had flown into a storm of blood and blackness.

"Well, I declare! They's lots of 'em around here. They after dead things. Don't eat nothing what's alive."

"A little bit more and he would have made a meal out of me," Todd said grimly.

"They bad luck all right. Teddy's got a name for 'em, calls 'em jimcrows," the old man laughed.

"It's a damned good name."

"They the damnedest birds. Once I seen a hoss all stretched out like he was sick, you know. So I hollers, 'Gid up from there, suh!' Just to make sho! An' doggone, son, if I don't see two ole jimcrows come flying right up outa that hoss's insides! Yessuh! The sun was shinin' on 'em and they couldn't a been no greasier if they'd been eating barbecue."

Todd thought he would vomit, his stomach quivered.

"You made that up," he said.

"Nawsuh! Saw him just like I see you."

"Well, I'm glad it was you."

"You see lots a funny things down here, son."

"No, I'll let you see them," he said.

"By the way, the white folks round here don't like to see you boys up there in the sky. They ever bother you?"

"No."

"Well, they'd like to."

"Someone always wants to bother someone else," Todd said. "How do you know?"

"I just know."

"Well," he said defensively, "no one has bothered us."

Blood pounded in his ears as he looked away into space. He tensed, seeing a black spot in the sky, and strained to confirm what he could not clearly see.

"What does that look like to you?" he asked excitedly.

"Just another bad luck, son."

Then he saw the movement of wings with disappointment. It was gliding smoothly down, wings outspread, tail feathers gripping the air, down swiftly—gone behind the green screen of trees. It was like a bird he had imagined there, only the sloping branches of the pines remained, sharp against the pale stretch of sky. He lay barely breathing and stared at the point where it had disappeared, caught in a spell of loathing and admiration. Why did they make them so disgusting and yet teach them to fly so well? It's like when I was up in heaven, he heard, starting.

The old man was chuckling, rubbing his stubbled chin.

"What did you say?"

"Sho', I died and went to heaven . . . maybe by time I tell you about it they be done come after you."

"I hope so," he said wearily.

"You boys ever sit around and swap lies?"

"Not often. Is this going to be one?"

"Well, I ain't so sho', on account of it took place when I was dead."

The old man paused, "That wasn't no lie 'bout the buzzards, though."

"All right," he said.

"Sho' you want to hear 'bout heaven?"

"Please," he answered, resting his head upon his arm.

"Well, I went to heaven and right away started to sproutin' me some wings. Six good ones, they was. Just like them the white angels had. I couldn't hardly believe it. I was so glad that I went off on some clouds by myself and tried 'em out. You know, 'cause I didn't want to make a fool outta myself the first thing. . . ."

It's an old tale, Todd thought. Told me years ago. Had forgotten. But at least it will keep him from talking about buzzards.

He closed his eyes, listening.

"... First thing I done was to git up on a low cloud and jump off. And doggone, boy, if them wings didn't work! First I tried the right; then I tried the left; then I tried 'em both together. Then Lawd, I started to move on out among the folks. I let 'em see me...."

He saw the old man gesturing flight with his arms, his face full of mock pride as he indicated an imaginary crowd, thinking, It'll be in the newspapers, as he heard, "... so I went out and found me some colored angels—somehow I didn't believe I was an angel till I seen a real black one, ha, yes! Then I was sho'—but they tole me I better come down 'cause us colored folks had to wear a special kin' a harness when we flew. That was how come they wasn't flyin'. Oh yes, an' you had to be extra strong for a black man even, to fly with one of them harnesses...."

This is a new turn, Todd thought, what's he driving at?

"So I said to myself, I ain't gonna be bothered with no harness! Oh naw! 'Cause if God let you sprout wings you oughta have sense enough not to let nobody make you wear something what gits in the way of flyin'. So I starts to flyin'. Heck, son," he chuckled, his eyes twinkling, "you know I had to let eve'ybody know that old Jefferson could fly good as anybody else. And I could too, fly smooth as a bird! I could even loop-the-loop—only I had to make sho' to keep my long white robe down roun' my ankles...."

Todd felt uneasy. He wanted to laugh at the joke, but his body refused, as of an independent will. He felt as he had as a child when after he had chewed a sugar-coated pill which his mother had given him, she had laughed at his efforts to remove the terrible taste.

"... Well," he heard, "I was doing all right 'til I got to speeding. Found out I could fan up a right strong breeze, I could fly so fast. I could do all kin'sa stunts too. I started flying up to the stars and divin' down and zooming roun' the moon. Man, I like to scare the devil outa some ole white angels. I was raisin' hell. Not that I meant any harm, son. But I was just feeling good. It was so good to know I was free at last. I accidentally knocked the tips offa some stars and they tell me I caused a storm and a coupla lynchings down here in Macon County—though I swear I believe them boys what said that was making up lies on me...."

He's mocking me, Todd thought angrily. He thinks it's a joke. Grinning down at me ... His throat was dry. He looked at his watch; why the hell didn't they come? Since they had to, why? One day I was flying down one of them heavenly streets. You got yourself into it, Todd thought. Like Jonah in the whale.

"Justa throwin' feathers in everybody's face. An' ole Saint Peter called me in. Said, 'Jefferson, tell me two things, what you doin' flyin' without a harness; an' how come you flyin' so fast?' So I tole him I was flyin' without a harness 'cause it got in my way, but I couldn'ta been flyin' so fast, 'cause I wasn't usin' but one wing. Saint Peter said, 'You wasn't flyin' with but one wing?' 'Yessuh,' I says, scared-like. So he says, 'Well, since you got sucha extra fine pair of wings you can leave off yo' harness awhile. But from now on none of that there one-wing flyin', 'cause you gittin' up too damn much speed!'"

And with one mouth full of bad teeth you're making too damned much talk, thought Todd. Why don't I send him after the boy? His body ached from the hard ground and seeking to shift his position he twisted his ankle and hated himself for crying out.

"It gittin' worse?"

"I ... I twisted it," he groaned.

"Try not to think about it, son. That's what I do."

He bit his lip, fighting pain with counter-pain as the voice resumed its rhythmical droning. Jefferson seemed caught in his own creation.

". . . After all that trouble I just floated roun' heaven in slow motion. But I forgot, like colored folks will do, and got to flyin' with one wing again. This time I was restin' my old broken arm and got to flyin' fast enough to shame the devil. I was comin' so fast, Lawd, I got myself called befo' ole Saint Peter again. He said, 'Jeff, didn't I warn you 'bout that speedin'?' 'Yessuh,' I says, 'but it was an accident.' He looked at me sad-like and shook his head and I knowed I was gone. He said, 'Jeff, you and that speedin' is a danger to the heavenly community. If I was to let you keep on flyin', heaven wouldn't be nothin' but uproar. Jeff, you got to go!' Son, I argued and pleaded with that old white man, but it didn't do a bit of good. They rushed me straight to them pearly gates and gimme a parachute and a map of the state of Alabama . . ."

Todd heard him laughing so that he could hardly speak, making a screen between them upon which his humiliation glowed like fire.

"Maybe you'd better stop awhile," he said, his voice unreal.

"Ain't much more," Jefferson laughed. "When they gimme the parachute ole Saint Peter ask me if I wanted to say a few words before I went. I felt so bad I couldn't hardly look at him, specially with all them white angels standin' around. Then somebody laughed and made me mad. So I tole him, 'Well, you done took my wings. And you puttin' me out. You got charge of things so's I can't do nothin' about it. But you got to admit just this: While I was up here I was the flyinest sonofabitch what ever hit heaven!'"

At the burst of laughter Todd felt such an intense humiliation that only great violence would wash it away. The laughter which shook the old man like a boiling purge set up vibrations of guilt within him which not even the intricate machinery of the plane would have been adequate to transform and he heard himself screaming, "Why do you laugh at me this way?"

He hated himself at that moment, but he had lost control. He saw Jefferson's mouth fall open, "What—?"

"Answer me!"

His blood pounded as though it would surely burst his temples and he tried to reach the old man and fell, screaming, "Can I help it because they won't let us actually fly? Maybe we are a bunch of buzzards feeding on a dead horse, but we can hope to be eagles, can't we? Can't we?"

He fell back, exhausted, his ankle pounding. The saliva was like straw in his mouth. If he had the strength he would strangle this old man. This grinning, gray-headed clown who made him feel as he felt when watched by the white officers at the field. And yet this old man had neither power, prestige, rank nor technique. Nothing that could rid him of this terrible feeling. He watched him, seeing his face struggle to express a turmoil of feeling.

"What you mean, son? What you talking 'bout . . . ?"

"Go away. Go tell your tales to the white folks."

"But I didn't mean nothing like that. . . . I . . . I wasn't tryin' to hurt your feelings. . . ."

"Please. Get the hell away from me!"

"But I didn't, son. I didn't mean all them things a-tall."

Todd shook as with a chill, searching Jefferson's face for a trace of the mockery he had seen there. But now the face was somber and tired and old. He was confused. He could not be sure that there had ever been laughter there, that Jefferson had ever really laughed in his whole life. He saw Jefferson reach out to touch him and shrank away, wondering if anything except the pain, now causing his vision to waver, was real. Perhaps he had imagined it all.

"Don't let it get you down, son," the voice said pensively.

He heard Jefferson sigh wearily, as though he felt more than he could say. His anger ebbed, leaving only the pain.

"I'm sorry," he mumbled.

"You just wore out with pain, was all. . . ."

He saw him through a blur, smiling. And for a second he felt the embarrassed silence of understanding flutter between them.

"What you was doin' flyin' over this section, son? Wasn't you scared they might shoot you for a crow?"

Todd tensed. Was he being laughed at again? But before he could decide, the pain shook him and a part of him was lying calmly behind the screen of pain that had fallen between them, recalling the first time he had ever seen a plane. It was as though an endless series of hangars had been shaken ajar in the air base of his memory and from each, like a young wasp emerging from its cell, arose the memory of a plane.

The first time I ever saw a plane I was very small and planes were new in the world. I was four-and-a-half and the only plane that I had ever seen was a model suspended from the ceiling of the automobile exhibit at the State Fair. But I did not know that it was only a model. I did not know how large a real plane was, nor how expensive. To me it was a fascinating toy, complete in itself, which my mother said could only be owned by rich little white boys. I stood rigid with admiration, my head straining backwards as I watched the gray little plane describing arcs above the gleaming tops of the automobiles. And I vowed that, rich or poor, someday I would own such a toy. My mother had to drag me out of the exhibit and not even the merry-go-round, the Ferris wheel, or the racing horses could hold my attention for the rest of the Fair. I was too busy imitating the tiny drone of the plane with my lips, and imitating with my hands the motion, swift and circling, that it made in flight.

After that I no longer used the pieces of lumber that lay about our back yard to construct wagons and autos . . . now it was used for airplanes. I built biplanes, using pieces of board for wings, a small box for the fuselage, another piece of wood for the rudder. The trip to the Fair had brought something new into my small world. I asked my mother repeatedly when the Fair would come back again. I'd lie in the grass and watch the sky, and each fighting bird became a soaring plane. I would have been good a year just to have seen a plane again. I became a nuisance to everyone with my questions about airplanes. But planes were new to the old folks, too, and there was little that they could tell me. Only my uncle knew some of the answers. And better still, he could carve propellers from pieces of wood that would whirl rapidly in the wind, wobbling noisily upon oiled nails.

I wanted a plane more than I'd wanted anything; more than I wanted the red wagon with rubber tires, more than the train that ran on a track with its train of cars. I asked my mother over and over again:

"Mamma?"

"What do you want, boy?" she'd say.

"Mamma, will you get mad if I ask you?" I'd say.

"What do you want now? I ain't got time to be answering a lot of fool questions. What you want?"

"Mamma, when you gonna get me one . . . ?" I'd ask.

"Get you one what?" she'd say.

"You know, Mamma; what I been asking you. . . ."

"Boy," she'd say, "if you don't want a spanking you better come on an' tell me what you talking about so I can get on with my work."

"Aw, Mamma, you know. . . ."

"What I just tell you?" she'd say.

"I mean when you gonna buy me a airplane."

"AIRPLANE! Boy, is you crazy? How many times I have to tell you to stop that foolishness. I done told you them things cost too much. I bet I'm gon' wham the living daylight out of you if you don't quit worrying me 'bout them things!"

But this did not stop me, and a few days later I'd try all over again.

Then one day a strange thing happened. It was spring and for some reason I had been hot and irritable all morning. It was a beautiful spring. I could feel it as I played barefoot in the backyard. Blossoms hung from the thorny black locust trees like clusters of fragrant white grapes. Butterflies flickered in the sunlight above the short new dew-wet grass. I had gone in the house for bread and butter and coming out I heard a steady unfamiliar drone. It was unlike anything I had ever heard before. I tried to place the sound. It was no use. It was a sensation like that I had when searching for my father's watch, heard ticking unseen in a room. It made me feel as though I had forgotten to perform some task that my mother had ordered . . . then I located it, overhead. In the sky, flying quite low and about a hundred yards off was a plane! It came so slowly that it seemed barely to move. My mouth hung wide; my bread and butter fell into the dirt. I wanted to jump up and down and cheer. And when the idea struck I trembled with excitement: "Some little white boy's plane's done flew away and all I got to do is stretch out my hands and it'll be mine!" It was a little plane like that at the Fair, flying no higher than the eaves of our roof. Seeing it come steadily forward I felt the world grow warm with promise. I opened the screen and climbed over it and clung there, waiting. I would catch the plane as it came over and swing down fast and run into the house before anyone could see me. Then no one could come to claim the plane. It droned nearer. Then when it hung like a silver cross in the blue directly above me I stretched out my hand and grabbed. It was like sticking my finger through a soap bubble. The plane flew on, as though I had simply blown my breath after it. I grabbed again, frantically, trying to catch the tail. My fingers clutched the air and disappointment surged tight and hard in my throat. Giving one last desperate grasp, I strained forward. My fingers ripped from the screen. I was falling. The ground burst hard against me. I drummed the earth with my heels and when my breath returned, I lay there bawling.

My mother rushed through the door.

"What's the matter, chile! What on earth is wrong with you?"

"It's gone! It's gone!"

"What gone?"

"The airplane . . ."

"Airplane?"

"Yessum, jus' like the one at the Fair. . . . I . . . I tried to stop it an' it kep' right on going. . . ."

"When, boy?"

"Just now," I cried, through my tears.

"Where it go, boy, what way?"

"Yonder, there . . ."

She scanned the sky, her arms akimbo and her checkered apron flapping in the wind as I pointed to the fading plane. Finally she looked down at me, slowly shaking her head.

"It's gone! It's gone!" I cried.

"Boy, is you a fool?" she said. "Don't you see that there's a real airplane 'stead of one of them toy ones?"

"Real...?" I forgot to cry. "Real?"

"Yass, real. Don't you know that thing you reaching for is bigger'n a auto? You here trying to reach for it and I bet it's flying 'bout two hundred miles higher'n this roof." She was disgusted with me. "You come on in this house before somebody else sees what a fool you done turned out to be. You must think these here lil ole arms of you'n is mighty long...."

I was carried into the house and undressed for bed and the doctor was called. I cried bitterly, as much from the disappointment of finding the plane so far beyond my reach as from the pain.

When the doctor came I heard my mother telling him about the plane and asking if anything was wrong with my mind. He explained that I had had a fever for several hours. But I was kept in bed for a week and I constantly saw the plane in my sleep, flying just beyond my fingertips, sailing so slowly that it seemed barely to move. And each time I'd reach out to grab it I'd miss and through each dream I'd hear my grandma warning:

> Young man, young man,
> Yo' arms too short
> To box with God....

"Hey, son!"

At first he did not know where he was and looked at the old man pointing, with blurred eyes.

"Ain't that one of you-all's airplanes coming after you?"

As his vision cleared he saw a small black shape above a distant field, soaring through waves of heat. But he could not be sure and with the pain he feared that somehow a horrible recurring fantasy of being split in twain by the whirling blades of a propeller had come true.

"You think he sees us?" he heard.

"See? I hope so."

"He's coming like a bat outa hell!"

Straining, he heard the faint sound of a motor and hoped it would soon be over.

"How you feeling?"

"Like a nightmare," he said.

"Hey, he's done curved back the other way!"

"Maybe he saw us," he said. "Maybe he's gone to send out the ambulance and ground crew." And, he thought with despair, maybe he didn't even see us.

"Where did you send the boy?"

"Down to Mister Graves," Jefferson said. "Man what owns this land."

"Do you think he phoned?"

Jefferson looked at him quickly.

"Aw sho'. Dabney Graves is got a bad name on accounta them killings but he'll call though...."

"What killings?"

"Them five fellers... ain't you heard?" he asked with surprise.

"No."

"Everybody knows 'bout Dabney Graves, especially the colored. He done killed enough of us."

Todd had the sensation of being caught in a white neighborhood after dark.

"What did they do?" he asked.

"Thought they was men," Jefferson said. "An' some he owed money, like he do me...."

"But why do you stay here?"

"You black, son."

"I know, but...."

"You have to come by the white folks, too."

He turned away from Jefferson's eyes, at once consoled and accused. And I'll have to come by them soon, he thought with despair. Closing his eyes, he heard Jefferson's voice as the sun burned blood-red upon his lips.

"I got nowhere to go," Jefferson said, "an' they'd come after me if I did. But Dabney Graves is a funny fellow. He's all the time making jokes. He can be mean as hell, then he's liable to turn right around and back the colored against the white folks. I seen him do it. But me, I hates him for that more'n anything else. 'Cause just as soon as he gits tired helping a man he don't care what happens to him. He just leaves him stone cold. And then the other white folks is double hard on anybody he done helped. For him it's just a joke. He don't give a hilla beans for nobody—but hisself...."

Todd listened to the thread of detachment in the old man's voice. It was as though he held his words arm's length before him to avoid their destructive meaning.

"He'd just as soon do you a favor and then turn right around and have you strung up. Me, I stays outa his way 'cause down here that's what you gotta do."

If my ankle would only ease for a while, he thought. The closer I spin toward the earth the blacker I become, flashed through his mind. Sweat ran into his eyes and he was sure that he would never see the plane if his head continued whirling. He tried to see Jefferson, what was it that Jefferson held in his hand? It was a little black man, another Jefferson! A little black Jefferson that shook with fits of belly-laughter while the other Jefferson looked on with detachment. Then Jefferson looked up from the thing in his hand and turned to speak, but Todd was far away, searching the sky for a plane in a hot dry land on a day and age he had long forgotten. He was going mysteriously with his mother through empty streets where black faces peered from behind drawn shades and someone was rapping at a window and he was looking back to see a hand and a frightened face frantically beckoning from a cracked door and his mother was looking down the empty perspective of the street and shaking her head and hurrying him along and at first it was only a flash he saw and a motor was droning as through the sun-glare he saw it gleaming silver as it circled and he was seeing a burst like a puff of white smoke and hearing his mother yell. Come along, boy, I got no time for them fool airplanes, I got no time, and he saw it a second time, the plane flying high, and the burst appeared suddenly and fell slowly, billowing out and sparkling like fireworks and he was watching and being hurried along as the air filled with a flurry of white pinwheeling cards that caught in the wind and scattered over the rooftops and into the gutters and a woman was running and snatching a card and reading it and screaming and he darted into the shower, grabbing as in winter he grabbed for snowflakes and bounding away at his mother's, Come on here, boy! Come on, I say! and he was watching as she took the card away, seeing her face grow puzzled and turning taut as her voice quavered, "Niggers Stay From The Polls," and died to a moan of terror as he saw the eyeless sockets of a white hood staring at him from the card and above he saw the plane spiraling gracefully, agleam in the sun like a fiery sword. And seeing it soar he was caught, transfixed between a terrible horror and a horrible fascination.

The sun was not so high now, and Jefferson was calling and gradually he saw three figures moving across the curving roll of the field.

"Look like some doctors, all dressed in white," said Jefferson.

They're coming at last, Todd thought. And he felt such a release of tension within him that he thought he would faint. But no sooner did he close his eyes than he was seized and he was struggling with three white men who were forcing his arms into some kind of coat. It was too much for him, his arms were pinned to his sides and as the pain blazed in his eyes, he realized that it was a straitjacket. What filthy joke was this?

"That oughta hold him, Mister Graves," he heard.

His total energies seemed focused in his eyes as he searched their faces. That was Graves; the other two wore hospital uniforms. He was poised between two poles of fear and hate as he heard the one called Graves saying, "He looks kinda purty in that there suit, boys. I'm glad you dropped by."

"This boy ain't crazy, Mister Graves," one of the others said. "He needs a doctor, not us. Don't see how you led us way out here anyway. It might be a joke to you, but your cousin Rudolph liable to kill somebody. White folks or niggers, don't make no difference...."

Todd saw the man turn red with anger. Graves looked down upon him, chuckling.

"This niggah belongs in a straitjacket, too, boys. I knowed that the minit Jeff's kid said something 'bout a nigguh flyer. You all know you cain't let the nigguh git up that high without his going crazy. The nigguh brain ain't built right for high altitudes...."

Todd watched the drawling red face, feeling that all the unnamed horror and obscenities that he had ever imagined stood materialized before him.

"Let's git outta here," one of the attendants said.

Todd saw the other reach toward him, realizing for the first time that he lay upon a stretcher as he yelled.

"Don't put your hands on me!"

They drew back, surprised.

"What's that you say, nigguh?" asked Graves.

He did not answer and thought that Graves's foot was aimed at his head. It landed on his chest and he could hardly breathe. He coughed helplessly, seeing Graves's lips stretch taut over his yellow teeth, and tried to shift his head. It was as though a half-dead fly was dragging slowly across his face and a bomb seemed to burst within him. Blasts of hot, hysterical laughter tore from his chest, causing his eyes to pop and he felt that the veins in his neck would surely burst. And then a part of him stood behind it all, watching the surprise in Graves's red face and his own hysteria. He thought he would never stop, he would laugh himself to death. It rang in his ears like Jefferson's laughter and he looked for him, centering his eyes desperately upon his face, as though somehow he had become his sole salvation in an insane world of outrage and humiliation. It brought a certain relief. He was suddenly aware that although his body was still contorted it was an echo that no longer rang in his ears. He heard Jefferson's voice with gratitude.

"Mister Graves, the Army done tole him not to leave his airplane."

"Nigguh, Army or no, you gittin' off my land! That airplane can stay 'cause it was paid for by taxpayers' money. But you gittin' off. An' dead or alive, it don't make no difference to me."

Todd was beyond it now, lost in a world of anguish.

"Jeff," Graves said, "you and Teddy come and grab holt. I want you to take this here black eagle over to that nigguh airfield and leave him."

Jefferson and the boy approached him silently. He looked away, realizing and doubting at once that only they could release him from his overpowering sense of isolation.

They bent for the stretcher. One of the attendants moved toward Teddy.

"Think you can manage it, boy?"

"I think I can, suh," Teddy said.

"Well, you better go behind then, and let yo' pa go ahead so's to keep that leg elevated."

He saw the white men walking ahead as Jefferson and the boy carried him along in silence. Then they were pausing and he felt a hand wiping his face; then he was moving again. And it was as though he had been lifted out of his isolation, back into the world of men. A new current of communication flowed between the man and boy and himself. They moved him gently. Far away he heard a mockingbird liquidly calling. He raised his eyes, seeing a buzzard poised unmoving in space. For a moment the whole afternoon seemed suspended and he waited for the horror to seize him again. Then like a song within his head he heard the boy's soft humming and saw the dark bird glide into the sun and glow like a bird of flaming gold.

MARGUERITE DURAS
[BORN 1914]

Marguerite Duras is an inheritor of the great French tradition of women's writing (*l'écriture féminine*). For this very reason, she did not have to fight to become a writer or, for that matter, a political woman. Instead she was able to devote herself to expressing her art and her politics, creating female characters in her novels who lived passionately on an equal footing with men, and finding a place for herself in the desperate real-life political arena of occupied France in World War II. Politically she rose to the occasion, serving in the French underground and even joining the Communist Party in 1944. Although she broke with the Communists in 1950, her thought never lost its deeply social character. In the years after the war, her writing blossomed, and she became more bold and experimental as her work progressed. Best known as a novelist, she has produced many works, including *Moderato Cantabile* (1958), *India Song* (1975), and *The Lover* (1984). She has also written important pieces for the stage, such as *The Square* (1955), and scripted a screenplay for the Alain Resnais movie *Hiroshima Mon Amour* (1960). A great theme in many of her works is the ability of her female characters to love boldly and shamelessly despite impediments. She also frequently juxtaposes love and death, creating an unusual intensity in her subjects. Sometimes, as in *Hiroshima Mon Amour*, she creates a background of world significance—in this case, the destruction wrought by the atomic bomb.

LIFE

The particular combination of passion and earnestness that Duras shows in her works comes in part from the circumstances of her own eventful life. Born Marguerite Donnadieu in French Indochina in 1914, she was the daughter of two public school teachers in the Vietnamese colonial system. Her strong, protective mother and her beloved younger brother provided the young schoolgirl with memorable support. After graduating from the French academy in Saigon, Marguerite went to Paris, where she received a law degree in 1935 and married in 1939. She published her first novel, *The Shameless,* in 1943 under the pen name of Duras. Already she was living a dangerous double life: an author acceptable to occupied Vichy France by day, a member of the underground serving with the legendary François Mitterrand by night.

Duras' first husband, Robert Antelme, was captured by the Nazis and deported, first to Auschwitz, then to Dachau; he survived the war, but their marriage did not. Duras married a Communist intellectual, Dionys Mascolo, in 1947, shortly after losing her first baby and her beloved younger brother. The new marriage lasted almost a decade before it too collapsed, broken up by a passionate love affair that Duras credits with changing her life. At this time, after the first of a series of battles with alcoholism in the mid-1950s, Duras stopped writing what she called "safe" books and began to experiment with literary form and content, disrupting her linear narrative by introducing dramatic and lyrical forms. It was then that she began to juxtapose apparently contradictory themes: love and death, passion and apathy, connection and the loss of connection. In the works of Duras, men and women often stand at the edge of an extraordinary understanding, needing only to invent new values with which to deal with fast-moving and contradictory events. These artistic innovations reflected the existential philosophy of her Parisian friends Jean-Paul Sartre and Simone de Beauvoir.

WORK

When Duras was approached in 1959 by director Alain Resnais to do a Franco-Japanese movie on "the bomb," she was already an accomplished novelist with many successes behind her. Even so, her script for the movie begins by taking daring risks. The story of the love affair between two professionals, a Japanese architect rebuilding Hiroshima and a French actress visiting the city for the first time, moves on several levels simultaneously. Visually, scenes of the sensually aroused bodies of the two lovers are spliced together with scenes of the horribly burned bodies of Hiroshima survivors. Intellectually, the lovers face frustrations and contradictions from which they feel they cannot escape. The architect knows that he can never even describe the tragedy of Hiroshima; he is left only with the task of denying the possibility of any such description. The actress, on the other hand, has her own war story: her involvement as a teenage girl with a young German soldier in the French town of Nevers, which ended tragically with his death by shooting and her public humiliation.

The challenge to Duras was to fuse these contradictory images and stories into a larger one, about a passionate love affair not likely to continue and the fate of the two individuals who come together with such suddenness and violence. What will become of these people? How will this meeting affect their lives? Not surprisingly, Duras solved some of this challenge by her use of artistic form, especially the lyricism of the speeches of the lovers. Here, for instance, is the actress speaking to herself.

> We're going to remain alone, my love.
> The night will never end.
> The sun will never rise again on anyone.
> Never. Never more. At last.
> You destroy me.
> You're so good for me.

At the very end of the screenplay, there is a bitter moment in which the actress foresees that she may forget her lover. But then, at the next moment, she sees him in a new light, as he sees her in turn. With a shock, we realize that the pair has assumed a tremendous significance. Their places of habitation, and all the history represented by those places, have become their names.

SHE: I'll forget you! I'm forgetting you already! Look how I'm forgetting you! Look at me!

. . .

SHE: Hi-ro-shi-ma.
Hi-ro-shi-ma. That's your name.
HE: That's my name. Yes. Your name is Nevers. Ne-vers-in France.

The advertising copy promoting the script version of *Hiroshima Mon Amour* calls the movie a "creation of remembrance, a poetic love story, an anti-war picture, and the most authentic screen portrait to date of man's inhumanity to man." Duras herself, in an appendix at the back of the book, focuses on the female character and the meaning of her life:

It's not the fact of having been shaved and disgraced that marks her life, it's the already mentioned defeat: the fact that she didn't die of love on August 2, 1944, on the banks of the Loire. . . . She gives this Japanese—at Hiroshima—her most precious possession: herself as she now is, her *survival* after the death of her love *at Nevers*.

In a world in which clear values are hard to define, our very survival is a precious fact; as life itself is sacred, even more sacred is the struggle to sustain it. Duras seems to be promoting some such understanding as this in *Hiroshima Mon Amour*.

SUGGESTED READINGS

Duras' screenplay *Hiroshima Mon Amour,* translated by Richard Seaver (1961), contains photographs from the movie, Duras' synopsis of the action, and her thoughts on the story of Nevers and the character of the two actors. Duras' journalistic writings are collected as *Outside: Selected Writings,* translated by Arthur Goldhammer (1986). Her memoirs of World War II are collected in *The War: A Memoir,* translated by Barbara Bray (1986). Works in English about Duras include Sanford Scribner Ames, ed., *Remains To Be Seen: Essays on Marguerite Duras* (1989). An essay that helps us to understand Duras' place in French women's writing is Julia Kristeva's "The Pain of Sorrow in the Modern World: The Works of Marguerite Duras," translated by K. A. Jensen, *PMLA* 102, no. 2 (March 1987): 138–52.

Hiroshima Mon Amour

Translated by Richard Seaver

SCENARIO

Part I

[*As the film opens, two pair of bare shoulders appear, little by little. All we see are these shoulders—cut off from the body at the height of the head and hips—in an embrace, and as if drenched with ashes, rain, dew, or sweat, whichever is preferred. The main thing is that we get the feeling that this dew, this perspiration, has been deposited by the atomic "mushroom" as it moves away and evaporates. It should produce a violent, conflicting feeling of freshness and desire. The shoulders are of different colors, one dark, one light. Fusco's music accompanies this almost shocking embrace. The difference between the hands is also very marked. The woman's hand lies on the darker shoulder: "lies" is perhaps not the word; "grips" would be closer to it. A man's voice, flat and calm, as if reciting, says:]*

HE: You saw nothing in Hiroshima. Nothing.

> *[To be used as often as desired. A woman's voice, also flat,*
> *muffled, monotonous, the voice of someone reciting, replies:]*

SHE: I saw *everything.* Everything.

[Fusco's music, which has faded before this initial exchange, resumes just long enough to accompany the woman's hand tightening on the shoulder again, then letting go, then caressing it. The mark of fingernails on the darker flesh. As if this scratch could give the illusion of being a punishment for: "No. You saw nothing in Hiroshima." Then the woman's voice begins again, still calm, colorless, incantatory:]

SHE: The hospital, for instance, I saw it. I'm sure I did. There is a hospital in Hiroshima. How could I help seeing it?

[The hospital, hallways, stairs, patients, the camera coldly objective. (We never see her seeing.) Then we come back to the hand gripping—and not letting go of—the darker shoulder.]

HE: You did not see the hospital in Hiroshima. You saw nothing in Hiroshima.

[Then the woman's voice becomes more . . . more impersonal. Shots of the museum. The same blinding light, the same ugly light here as at the hospital. Explanatory signs, pieces of evidence from the bombardment, scale models, mutilated iron, skin, burned hair, wax models, etc.]

SHE: Four times at the museum. . . .

HE: What museum in Hiroshima?

SHE: Four times at the museum in Hiroshima. I saw the people walking around. The people walk around, lost in thought, among the photographs, the reconstructions, for want of something else, among the photographs, the photographs, the reconstructions, for want of something else, the explanations, for want of something else.

    Four times at the museum in Hiroshima.

    I looked at the people. I myself looked thoughtfully at the iron. The burned iron. The broken iron, the iron made vulnerable as flesh. I saw the bouquet of bottle caps: who would have suspected that? Human skin floating, surviving, still in the bloom of its agony. Stones. Burned stones. Shattered stones. Anonymous heads of hair that the women of Hiroshima, when they awoke in the morning, discovered had fallen out.

    I was hot at Peace Square. Ten thousand degrees at Peace Square. I know it. The temperature of the sun at Peace Square. How can you not know it? . . . The grass, it's quite simple . . .

HE: You saw nothing in Hiroshima. Nothing.

[More shots of the museum. Then a shot of Peace Square taken with a burned skull in the foreground. Glass display cases with burned models inside. Newsreel shots of Hiroshima.]

SHE: The reconstructions have been made as authentically as possible.

    The films have been made as authentically as possible.

    The illusion, it's quite simple, the illusion is so perfect that the tourists cry.

    One can always scoff, but what else can a tourist do, really, but cry?

    I've always wept over the fate of Hiroshima. Always.

> *[A panorama of a photograph taken of Hiroshima after the bomb,*
> *a "new desert" without reference to the other deserts of the world.]*

HE: No. What would you have cried about?

[*Peace Square, empty under a blinding sun that recalls the blinding light of the bomb. Newsreels taken after August 6, 1945. Ants, worms, emerge from the ground. Interspersed with shots of the shoulders. The woman's voice begins again, gone mad, as the sequence of pictures has also gone mad.*]

SHE: I saw the newsreels.

On the second day, History tells, I'm not making it up, on the second day certain species of animals rose again from the depths of the earth and from the ashes.

Dogs were photographed.

For all eternity.

I saw them.

I *saw* the newsreels.

I *saw* them.

On the first day.

On the second day.

On the third day.

HE [*interrupting her*]: You saw nothing. Nothing.

[*A dog with a leg amputated. People, children. Wounds. Burned children screaming.*]

SHE: ... on the fifteenth day too.

Hiroshima was blanketed with flowers. There were cornflowers and gladiolas everywhere, and morning glories and day lilies that rose again from the ashes with an extraordinary vigor, quite unheard of for flowers till then.

I didn't make anything up.

HE: You made it *all* up.

SHE: *Nothing.*

Just as in love this illusion exists, this illusion of being able never to forget, so I was under the illusion that I would never forget Hiroshima.

Just as in love.

[*Surgical forceps approach an eye to extract it. More newsreel shots.*]

I also saw the survivors and those who were in the wombs of the women of Hiroshima.

[*Shots of various survivors: a beautiful child who, upon turning around, is blind in one eye; a girl looking at her burned face in the mirror; a blind girl with twisted hands playing the zither; a woman praying near her dying children; a man, who has not slept for several years, dying. (Once a week they bring his children to see him.)*]

I saw the patience, the innocence, the apparent meekness with which the temporary survivors of Hiroshima adapted themselves to a fate so unjust that the imagination, normally so fertile, cannot conceive it.

[*And again a return to the perfect embrace of the bodies.*]

SHE: Listen ...

I know ...

I know *everything*.

It went on.

HE: *Nothing*. You know *nothing*.

[*A spiraling atomic cloud. People marching in the streets in the rain. Fishermen tainted with radioactivity. Unedible fish. Thousands of unedible fish buried.*]

SHE: Women risk giving birth to malformed children, to monsters, but it goes on.

Men risk becoming sterile, but it goes on.

People are afraid of the rain.

The rain of ashes on the waters of the Pacific.

The waters of the Pacific kill.
Fishermen of the Pacific are dead.
People are afraid of the food.
The food of an entire city is thrown away.
The food of entire cities is buried.
An entire city rises up in anger.
Entire cities rise up in anger.

[*Newsreels: demonstrations.*]

Against whom, the anger of entire cities?

The anger of entire cities, whether they like it or not, against the inequality set forth as a principle by certain people against other people, against the inequality set forth as a principle by certain races against other races, against the inequality set forth as a principle by certain classes against other classes.

[*Processions of demonstrators. "Mute" speeches from loudspeakers.*]

SHE [*softly*]: . . . Listen to me.

Like you, I know what it is to forget.

HE: No, you don't know what it is to forget.

SHE: Like you, I have a memory. I know what it is to forget.

HE: No, you don't have a memory.

SHE: Like you, I too have tried with all my might not to forget. Like you, I forgot. Like you, I wanted to have an inconsolable memory, a memory of shadows and stone.

[*The shot of a shadow, "photographed" on stone, of someone killed at Hiroshima.*]

For my part, I struggled with all my might, every day, against the horror of no longer understanding at all the reason for remembering. Like you, I forgot. . . .

[*Shops with hundreds of scale models of the Palace of Industry, the only monument whose twisted skeleton remained standing after the bomb—and was afterward preserved. An empty shop. A busload of Japanese tourists. Tourists on Peace Square. A cat crossing Peace Square.*]

Why deny the obvious necessity for memory? . . .

[*A sentence punctuated by shots of the framework of the Palace of Industry.*]

. . . Listen to me. I know something else. It will begin all over again.

Two hundred thousand dead.

Eighty thousand wounded.

In nine seconds. These figures are official. It will begin all over again.

[*Trees. Church. Merry-go-round. Hiroshima rebuilt. Banality.*]

There will be ten thousand degrees on the earth. Ten thousand suns, they will say. The asphalt will burn.

[*Church. Japanese advertising poster.*]

Chaos will prevail. A whole city will be raised from the earth and fall back in ashes. . . .

[*Sand. A package of "Peace" cigarettes. A fat plant spread out like a spider on the sand.*]

New vegetation will rise from the sands. . . .

[*Four "dead" students chat beside the river. The
river. The tides. The daily piers of Hiroshima rebuilt.*]

Four students await together a fraternal and legendary death.

The seven branches of the delta estuary in the Ota river drain and fill at the usual hour, exactly at the usual hours, with water that is fresh and rich with fish, gray or blue depending on the hour or the season. Along the muddy banks people no longer watch the tide rising slowly in the seven branches of the delta estuary of the river Ota.

[*The incantatory tone ceases. The streets of Hiroshima, more streets. Bridges.*
Covered lanes. Streets. Suburbs. Railroad tracks. Suburbs. Universal banality.]

SHE: . . . I meet you.

I remember you.

Who are you?

You destroy me.

You're so good for me.

How could I have known that this city was made to the size of love?

How could I have known that you were made to the size of my body?

You're great. How wonderful. You're great.

How slow all of a sudden.

And how sweet.

More than you can know.

You destroy me.

You're so good for me.

You destroy me.

You're so good for me.

Plenty of time.

Please.

Take me.

Deform me, make me ugly.

Why not you?

Why not you in this city and in this night so like the others you can't tell the difference?

Please . . .

[*With exaggerated suddenness the woman's face appears,*
filled with tenderness, turned toward the man's.]

SHE: It's extraordinary how beautiful your skin is.

[*He sighs.*]

You . . .

[*His face appears. He laughs ecstatically, which*
has nothing to do with their words. He turns.]

HE: Yes, me. You will have seen me.

[*The two naked bodies reappear. Same voice of the*
woman, muted, but this time not declamatory.]

SHE: Are you completely Japanese or aren't you completely Japanese?

HE: Completely. I am Japanese.

Your eyes are green. Correct?

SHE: I think so . . . yes . . . I think they're green.

HE [*softly, looking at her*]: You are like a thousand women in one. . . .

SHE: It's because you don't know me. That's why.

HE: Perhaps that's not the only reason.

SHE: It's a rather nice idea, being a thousand women in one for you.

[*She kisses his shoulder and snuggles into the hollow of that shoulder. Her head is facing the*
open window, facing Hiroshima, the night. A man passes in the street and coughs. (We don't
see him, only hear him.) She raises herself.]

SHE: Listen. . . . It's four o'clock. . . .

HE: Why?

SHE: I don't know who it is. Every day he passes at four o'clock. And he coughs.

[*Silence. They look at each other.*]

You were here, at Hiroshima. . . .

HE [*laughing, as he might at a childish question*]: No . . . Of course I wasn't.

SHE [*caressing his naked shoulder again*]: That's true.... How stupid of me. [*Almost smiling.*]

HE [*serious, hesitant*]: But my family was at Hiroshima. I was off fighting the war.

SHE [*timidly, smiling now*]: A stroke of luck, eh?

HE [*not looking at her, weighing the pro and con*]: Yes.

SHE: Lucky for me too.

[*Pause.*]

HE: What are you doing at Hiroshima?

SHE: A film.

HE: What, a film?

SHE: I'm playing in a film.

HE: And before coming to Hiroshima, where were you?

SHE: In Paris.

[*A longer pause.*]

HE: And before Paris?...

SHE: Before Paris?... I was at Nevers. *Ne-vers.*

HE: Nevers?

SHE: It's in the province of Nièvre. You don't know it.

[*Pause. Then he asks, as though he had just discovered a link between Hiroshima and Nevers:*]

HE: And why did you want to see everything at Hiroshima?

SHE [*trying to be sincere*]: Because it interested me. I have my own ideas about it. For instance, I think looking closely at things is something that has to be learned.

Part II

[*A swarm of bicycles passes in the street, the noise growing louder, then fading. She is on the balcony of the hotel, in a dressing gown. She is looking at him. She holds a cup of coffee in her hand. He is still asleep, lying on his stomach, his arms crossed, bare to the waist.*

She looks very intently at his hands, which tremble slightly, as children's hands do sometimes when they are asleep. He has very beautiful, very virile hands.

While she is looking at them, there suddenly appears, in place of the Japanese, the body of a young man, lying in the same position, but in a posture of death, on the bank of a river, in full daylight. (The room is in semi-darkness.) The young man is near death. He too has beautiful hands, strikingly like those of the Japanese. The approach of death makes them jerk violently.

The shot is an extremely brief one.

She remains frozen, leaning against the window. He awakes and smiles at her. She doesn't return his smile immediately. She continues to look at him attentively, without moving. Then she takes the coffee over to him.]

SHE: Do you want some coffee?

[*He assents, takes the cup. Pause.*]

SHE: What were you dreaming about?

HE: I don't remember.... Why?

[*She has become herself again, extremely nice.*]

SHE: I was looking at your hands. They move when you're asleep.

HE [*examining his hands, perhaps moving his fingers*]: Maybe it's when you dream without knowing it.

SHE [*calmly, pleasantly, but seeming to doubt his words*]: Hmm, hmm.

[*They're together in the shower of the hotel room. In a gay mood.*

He puts his hand on her forehead and arches her head back.]

HE: You're a beautiful woman, do you know that?

SHE: Do you think so?

HE: I think so.

SHE: A trifle worn out, no?

HE [*laughing*]: A trifle ugly.

SHE [*smiling at his caress*]: Don't you mind?

HE: That's what I noticed last night in that café. The way you're ugly. And also . . .

SHE [*very relaxed*]: And also? . . .

HE: And also how bored you were.

SHE [*her curiosity aroused*]: Tell me more. . . .

HE: You were bored in a way that makes men want to know a woman.

SHE [*smiling, lowering her eyes*]: You speak French very well.

HE [*gaily*]: Don't I though! I'm glad you finally noticed how well I speak French. [*Pause.*] I hadn't noticed that you didn't speak Japanese. . . . Have you ever noticed that it's always in the same sense that people notice things?

SHE: No. I noticed you, that's all.

[*Laughter.*]

[*After the bath. Her hair is wet. She is munching slowly on an apple. She is on the balcony, dressed in a bathrobe; she looks at him, stretches, and as if to "pinpoint" their situation, says slowly, as though savoring the words:*]

SHE: To-meet-in-Hiroshima. It doesn't happen every day.

[*Already dressed—his shirt collar open—he joins her on the balcony and sits down opposite her. After a moment's hesitation, he asks:*]

HE: What did Hiroshima mean for you, in France?

SHE: The end of the war, I mean, really the end. Amazement . . . at the idea that they had dared . . . amazement at the idea that they had succeeded. And then too, for us, the beginning of an unknown fear. And then, indifference. And also the fear of indifference. . . .

HE: Where were you?

SHE: I had just left Nevers. I was in Paris. In the street.

HE: That's a pretty French word, Nevers.

SHE [*after a pause*]: It's a word like any other. Like the city.

[*She moves away. They begin to talk, about ordinary things.*]

[*He's seated on the bed; he lights a cigarette, looks at her intently, then asks:*]

HE: Have you met many Japanese at Hiroshima?

SHE: I've met some, yes . . . but no one like you. . . .

HE [*smiling, gay*]: I'm the first Japanese in your life?

SHE: Yes.

[*Her laughter off-camera. She reappears while she is getting dressed.*]

SHE: Hi-ro-shi-ma.

HE [*lowering his eyes, calmly*]: The whole world was happy. You were happy with the whole world. [*Continuing, in the same tone:*] I heard it was a beautiful summer day in Paris that day, is that right?

SHE: Yes, it was a beautiful day.

HE: How old were you?

SHE: Twenty. And you?

HE: Twenty-two.

SHE: The same age, really.

HE: Yes, practically.

[*She appears completely dressed, just as she is putting on her Red Cross nurse's kerchief. She bends down beside him with a sudden gesture, or lies down beside him. She plays with his hand, kisses his bare arm. They talk about ordinary things.*]

SHE: What do you do in life?

HE: Architecture. And politics too.

SHE: Oh, so that's why you speak such good French.

HE: That's why. To read about the French Revolution.

[*They laugh. Any precise indications about his politics would be absolutely impossible, since he would be immediately tagged. And besides, it would be naive. Nor should it be forgotten that only a man of liberal opinions would have made the preceding remark.*]

HE: What's the film you're playing in?

SHE: A film about Peace. What else do you expect them to make in Hiroshima except a picture about Peace?

[*A noisy swarm of bicycles passes.*]

HE: I'd like to see you again.

SHE [*gesturing negatively*]: At this time tomorrow I'll be on my way back to France.

HE: Is that true? You didn't tell me.

SHE: It's true. [*Pause.*] There was no point in telling you.

HE [*serious, taken aback*]: Is that why you let me come up to your room last night? ... Because it was your last day at Hiroshima?

SHE: Not at all. The thought never even crossed my mind.

HE: When you talk, I wonder whether you lie or tell the truth.

SHE: I lie. And I tell the truth. But I don't have any reason to lie to you. Why? ...

HE: Tell me ... do things like ... this happen to you often?

SHE: Not very often. But it happens. I have a weakness for men. [*Pause.*] I have doubtful morals, you know. [*She laughs.*]

HE: What do you call having doubtful morals?

SHE: Being doubtful about the morals of other people.

[*He laughs heartily.*]

HE: I'd like to see you again. Even if the plane is leaving tomorrow. Even if you do have doubtful morals.

[*Pause. A feeling of love returning.*]

SHE: No.

HE: Why?

SHE [*with irritation*]: Because.

[*He doesn't pursue the conversation.*]

SHE: Don't you want to talk to me any more?

HE [*after a pause*]: I'd like to see you again.

[*They are in the hotel corridor.*]

HE: Where are you going in France? To Nevers?

SHE: No. To Paris. [*A pause.*] I don't ever go to Nevers any more.

HE: Not ever?

SHE [*grimacing as she says it*]: Not ever. [*Then, caught in her own trap, she adds:*] In Nevers I was younger than I've ever been....

HE: Young-in-Nevers.

SHE: Yes. Young in Nevers. And then too, once, mad in Nevers.

[*They are pacing back and forth in front of the hotel. She is waiting for the car that is supposed to come and pick her up to take her to Peace Square. Few people, but lots of cars passing. It's a boulevard. The dialogue is almost shouted because of the noise of the cars.*]

SHE: You see, Nevers is the city in the world, and even the thing in the world, I dream about most often at night. And at the same time it's the thing I think about the least.

HE: What was your madness like at Nevers?

SHE: Madness is like intelligence, you know. You can't explain it. Just like intelligence. It comes on you, it fills you, and then you understand it. But when it goes away you can't understand it at all any longer.

HE: Were you full of hate?

SHE: That was what my madness was. I was mad with hate. I had the impression it would be possible to make a real career of hate. All I cared about was hate. Do you understand?

HE: Yes.

SHE: It's true. I suppose you must understand that too.

HE: Did it ever happen to you again?

SHE: No. [*In a near whisper:*] It's all over.

HE: During the war?

SHE: Right after it.

[*Pause.*]

HE: Was that part of the difficulties of life in France after the war?

SHE: Yes, that's one way of putting it.

HE: When did you get over your madness?

SHE [*in a low voice, as she would talk in normal circumstances*]: It went away little by little. And then of course when I had children.

[*The noise of the cars grows and fades in inverse
proportion to the seriousness of their remarks.*]

HE: What did you say?

SHE: I said it went away little by little. And then of course when I had children....

HE: I'd really like to spend a few days with you somewhere, sometime.

SHE: I would too.

HE: Seeing you again today wouldn't really be seeing you again. You can't see people again in such a short time. I really would.

SHE: No.

[*She stops in front of him, obstinate, motionless, silent. He almost accepts.*]

HE: All right.

[*She laughs, but it's a little forced. She seems
slightly, but actually, spiteful. The taxi arrives.*]

SHE: It's because you know I'm leaving tomorrow.

[*They laugh, but his is less hearty than hers. A pause.*]

HE: It's possible that's part of it. But that's as good a reason as any, no? The thought of not seeing you again... ever... in a few hours.

[*The taxi has arrived and stopped at the intersection. She signals to it
that she's coming. She takes her time, looks at the Japanese, and says:*]

SHE: No.

[*His eyes follow her. Perhaps he smiles.*]

Part III

[*It's four P.M. at Peace Square in Hiroshima. In the distance a group of film technicians is moving away carrying a camera, lights, and reflectors. Japanese workers are dismantling the official grandstand that has just been used in the last scene of the film.*

An important note: we will always see the technicians in the distance and will never know what film it is they're shooting at Hiroshima. All we'll ever see is the scenery being taken down.

Stagehands are carrying posters in various languages—Japanese, French, German, etc.—
NEVER ANOTHER HIROSHIMA. *The workmen are thus busy dismantling the official grand-*

stands and removing the bunting. On the set we see the French woman. She is asleep. Her nurse's kerchief has slipped partly off her head. She is lying in the shadow of one of the stands.

We gather that they have just finished shooting an enlightening film on Peace at Hiroshima. It's not necessarily a ridiculous film, merely an enlightening one. A crowd passes along the square where they have just been shooting the film. The crowd is indifferent. Except for a few children, no one looks, they are used to seeing films being shot at Hiroshima.

But one man passes, stops, and looks, the man we had seen previously in her hotel room. He approaches the nurse, and watches her sleeping. His gaze is what finally wakes her up, but only after he has been looking at her for a good while.

During the scene perhaps we see a few details in the distance, such as a scale model of the Palace of Industry, a guide surrounded by tourists, a couple of war invalids in white, begging, a family chatting on a street corner. She awakes. Her fatigue vanishes. They suddenly find themselves involved again with their own story. This personal story always dominates the necessarily demonstrative Hiroshima story.

She gets up and goes toward him. He laughs, a bit stiffly. Then they become serious again.]

HE: It was easy to find you in Hiroshima.

[*She laughs happily. A pause. He looks at her again. Two workers—carrying an enlarged photograph from the picture* The Children of Hiroshima *showing a dead mother and a child crying in the smoking ruins of Hiroshima—pass between them. They don't look at the photograph. Another photograph, of Einstein, follows immediately after the one of the mother and child.*]

HE: Is it a French film?

SHE: No. International. On Peace.

HE: Is it finished?

SHE: Yes, for me it's finished. They still have some crowd scenes to shoot. . . . We have lots of filmed commercials to sell soap. So . . . by stressing it . . . perhaps.

HE [*with very clear ideas on the subject*]: Yes, by stressing it. Here, at Hiroshima, we don't joke about films on Peace.

[*He turns back toward her. The photographs have gone completely by. Instinctively they move closer together. She readjusts her kerchief, which has slipped partly off while she was sleeping.*]

HE: Are you tired?

SHE [*looking at him in a way that is both provocative and gentle. Then, with an almost sad smile, she says*]: No more than you are.

HE [*meaningfully*]: I thought of Nevers in France.

[*She smiles.*]

HE: I've been thinking of you. Is your plane still leaving tomorrow?

SHE: Still tomorrow.

HE: Irrevocably tomorrow?

SHE: Yes. The picture is behind schedule. I'm a month overdue returning to Paris.

[*She looks squarely at him. Slowly he takes her kerchief off. Either she is very heavily made up, in which case her lips are so dark they seem black, or else she is hardly made up at all and seems pale under the sun.*

The man's gesture is extremely free, composed, producing much the same erotic shock as in the opening scenes. Her hair is as mussed as it was in bed the night before. She lets him take off her kerchief, she lets him have his way as she must have let him have his way in love the night before. (Here, give him an erotically functional role.)

She lowers her eyes. An incomprehensible pout. She toys with something on the ground, then raises her eyes again.]

HE: You give me a great desire to love.

[*She doesn't answer right away. His words upset her, and she lowers
her eyes again. The cat of Peace Square rubbing against her foot?*]
SHE [*slowly*]: Always . . . chance love affairs. . . . Me too.
[*Some extraordinary object, not clearly defined, passes between them. I see a square frame, some
(atomic?) very precise form, but without the least idea what it's used for. They pay no attention
to it.*]
HE: No. Not always like this. You know it.
[*Shouts in the distance. Then children singing. But it doesn't distract them. She makes an
incomprehensible face (licentious would be the word). She raises her eyes again, but this time to
the sky, and says, again incomprehensibly, as she wipes the sweat from her forehead:*]
SHE: They say there'll be a thunderstorm before nightfall.

[*A shot of the sky she sees. Clouds scudding . . . The singing becomes more distinct. Then (the
end of) the parade begins.*

*They back away. She clings to him (like the postures in women's magazines), her hand on
his shoulder. His face against her hair. When she raises her eyes she sees him. He'll try and lead
her away from the parade. She'll resist. But she'll go anyway, without realizing she's leaving.*

Children parading carrying posters.]

FIRST SERIES OF POSTERS	SECOND SERIES OF POSTERS
1st Poster If 14 A-bombs equal 100 million ordinary bombs.	I This extraordinary achievement bears witness to man's scientific intelligence.
2nd Poster And if the H-bomb equals 1500 A-bombs.	II But it's regrettable that man's political intelligence is 100 times less developed than his scientific intelligence.
3rd Poster How much do the 40,000 A- and H-bombs actually manufactured in the world equal?	III Which keeps us from really admiring man.
4th Poster 10 H-bombs dropped on the world mean prehistory again.	
5th Poster What do 40,000 H- and A-bombs mean?	

[*Men, women, follow the singing children. Dogs follow the children. Cats at the windows.
(The Peace Square cat is used to it, and is asleep.)*

*Posters. More posters. Everyone very hot. The sky, above the parade, is threatening. Clouds
cover the sun. There are lots of children, beautiful children. They are hot, and sing heartily
as children will. Irresistibly, and almost without realizing it, the Japanese pushes the French
woman in the same—or in the opposite—direction the parade is moving. She closes her eyes
and sighs, and while she is sighing:*]
HE: I hate to think about your leaving. Tomorrow. I think I love you.
[*He buries his lips in her hair. Her hand tight on his shoulder. Slowly her eyes open. The
parade goes on. The children's faces are made up white. Dots of sweat stand out on the white
powder. Two of them argue over an orange, angrily. A man, made up as if burned in the
bombing, passes. He probably had played in the film. The wax on his neck melts and falls off.
Perhaps disgusting, terrifying. They look at each other.*]

HE: You're coming with me, once more.
[*She doesn't answer. A beautiful Japanese woman, sitting on a float, passes. She looses a flock of pigeons (or maybe some other allegorical float—an atomic ballet, for instance).*]
HE: Answer me.
[*She doesn't answer. He bends and whispers in her ear.*]
HE: Are you afraid?
SHE [*smiling, shaking her head*]: No.
[*The formless songs of the children continue, but fading away. A monitor scolds the two children arguing over the orange. The big one takes the orange. The big one begins to eat the orange. All this lasts longer than it should. Behind the crying child, the five hundred Japanese students arrive. It's a little terrifying, and he pulls her against him. They look upset. He looking at her, she looking at the parade. One should have the feeling that this parade is depriving them of the short time they have left. They are silent. He leads her by the hand. She lets him. They exit, moving against the current of the parade. We lose sight of them.*]
[*We see them next in the middle of a large room in a Japanese house. Soft light. A feeling of freshness after the heat of the parade. A modern house, with chairs, etc. She stands there, like a guest. Almost intimidated. He approaches her from the far side of the room (as if he had just closed the door, or come from the garage, etc.).*]
HE: Sit down.
[*She doesn't sit down. Both remain standing. We feel that eroticism is held in check between them by love, at least for the moment. He is facing her. And in the same state, almost awkward. The opposite of what a man would do if this were an* aubaine.]
SHE [*making conversation*]: You're alone at Hiroshima? . . . Where's your wife?
HE: She's at Unzen, in the mountains. I'm alone.
SHE: When is she coming back?
HE: In a few days.
SHE [*softly, as if in an aside*]: What is your wife like?
HE [*purposefully*]: Beautiful. I'm a man who's happy with his wife.
[*Pause.*]
SHE: So am I. I'm a woman who's happy with her husband.
[*This exchange charged with real emotion, which the ensuing moment covers.*]
SHE: Don't you work in the afternoon?
HE: Yes. A lot. Mainly in the afternoon.
SHE: The whole thing is stupid. . . .
[*As she would say "I love you." They kiss as the telephone rings. He doesn't answer.*]
SHE: Is it because of me you're wasting your afternoon?
[*He still doesn't answer the phone.*]
SHE: Tell me. What difference does it make?
[*At Hiroshima. The light is already different. Later. After they have made love.*]
HE: Was he French, the man you loved during the war?
[*At Nevers. A German crosses a square at dusk.*]
SHE: No . . . he wasn't French.
[*At Hiroshima. She is lying on the bed, pleasantly tired. Darker now.*]
SHE: Yes. It was at Nevers.
[*Nevers. A shot of love at Nevers. Bicycles racing. The forest, etc.*]
SHE: At first we met in barns. Then among the ruins. And then in rooms. Like anywhere else.
[*Hiroshima. In the room, the light has faded even more. Their bodies in a peaceful embrace.*]
SHE: And then he was dead.
[*Nevers. Shots of Nevers. Rivers. Quays. Poplar trees in the wind, etc. The quay deserted. The garden. Then at Hiroshima again.*]

SHE: I was eighteen and he was twenty-three.

[*Nevers. In a "hut" at night. The "marriage" at Nevers. During the shots of Nevers she answers the questions that he is presumed to have asked, but doesn't out loud. The sequence of shots of Nevers continues. Then:*]

SHE [*calmly*]: Why talk of him rather than the others?

HE: Why not?

SHE: No. Why?

HE: Because of Nevers. I can only begin to know you, and among the many thousands of things in your life, I'm choosing Nevers.

SHE: Like you'd choose anything else?

HE: Yes.

> [*Do we know he's lying? We suspect it. She becomes
> almost violent, searching for something to say:*]

SHE: No, it's not by chance. [*Pause.*] You have to tell me why.

> [*He can reply—a very important point for the film—either:*]

HE: It was there, I seem to have understood, that you were so young ... so young you still don't belong to anyone in particular. I like that.

> [*or:*]

SHE: No, that's not it.

HE: It was there, I seem to have understood, that I almost ... lost you ... and that I risked never knowing you.

> [*or else:*]

HE: It was there, I seem to have understood, that you must have begun to be what you are today.

[*Choose from among the three possibilities, or use all three, either one after the other, or separately, at random with the movements of love in the bed. The last is the solution I would prefer, if it doesn't make the scene too long.*

  One last time we come back to them.]

SHE [*shouting*]: I want to leave here. [*She clings to him almost savagely.*]

> [*They are dressed and in the same room where they were
> earlier. The lights are on now. They are both standing.*]

HE [*very calmly*]: All we can do now is kill the time left before your departure. Still sixteen hours before your plane leaves.

SHE [*terribly upset, distressed*]: That's a terribly long time....

HE [*gently*]: No. You mustn't be afraid.

Part IV

[*Night falls over Hiroshima, leaving long trails of light. The river drains and fills with the hours, the tides. Sometimes people along the muddy banks watch the tide rising slowly.*

  Opposite this river is a café. A modern café, Americanized, with a wide bay window. Those seated at the back of the café don't see the banks of the river, but only the river itself. The mouth of the river is only vaguely outlined. There Hiroshima ends and the Pacific begins. The place is half empty. They are seated at a table in the back of the room, facing each other, either cheek-to-cheek, or forehead against forehead. In the previous scene they had been overwhelmed by the thought that their final separation was only sixteen hours away. When we see them now they are almost happy. They don't notice the time passing. A miracle has occurred. What miracle? The resurrection of Nevers. And in this posture of hopelessly happy love, he says:]

HE: Aside from that, Nevers doesn't mean anything else in French?

SHE: No. Nothing.

HE: Would you have been cold in that cellar at Nevers, if we had loved each other
there?

SHE: I would have been cold. In Nevers the cellars are cold, both summer and
winter. The city is built along a river called the Loire.

HE: I can't picture Nevers.

[*Shots of Nevers. The Loire.*]

SHE: Nevers. Forty thousand inhabitants. Built like a capital—(but). A child can
walk around it. [*She moves away from him.*] I was born in Nevers [*she drinks*], I
grew up in Nevers. I learned how to read in Nevers. And it was there I became
twenty.

HE: And the Loire?

[*He takes her head in his hands. Nevers.*]

SHE: It's a completely unnavigable river, always empty, because of its irregular
course and its sand bars. In France, the Loire is considered a very beautiful river,
especially because of its light . . . so soft, if you only knew.

[*Ecstatic tone. He frees her head and listens closely.*]

HE: When you are in the cellar, am I dead?

SHE: You are dead . . . and . . .

[*Nevers: the German is dying very slowly on the quay.*]

SHE: . . . how is it possible to bear such pain?
The cellar is small.

[*To show with her hands how small it is, she withdraws her cheek from his. Then she goes on,
still very close to him, but no longer touching him. No incantation. She speaks to him with
passionate enthusiasm.*]

SHE: . . . very small. The *Marseillaise* passes above my head. It's . . . deafening. . . .

[*She blocks her ears, in this café (at Hiroshima). The café is
suddenly very quiet. Shots of Nevers' cellars. Riva's bloody hands.*]

SHE: Hands become useless in cellars. They scrape. They rub the skin off . . . against
the walls . . .

[*Somewhere at Nevers, bleeding hands. Hers, on
the table, are intact. Riva licks her own blood.*]

SHE: . . . that's all you can find to do, to make you feel better . . . and also to
remember . . . I loved blood since I had tasted yours.

[*They scarcely look at each other as she talks. They look at Nevers. Both of them act as if they
were somehow possessed by Nevers. There are two glasses on the table. She drinks avidly. He
more slowly. Their hands are flat on the table.*]

[*Nevers.*]

SHE: The world moves along over my head. Instead of the sky . . . of course . . . I
see the world walking. Quickly during the week. Slowly on Sunday. It doesn't
know I'm in the cellar. They pretend I'm dead, dead a long way from Nevers.
That's what my father wants. Because I'm disgraced, that's what my father
wants.

[*Nevers: a father, a Nevers druggist, behind the window of his drug store.*]

HE: Do you scream?

[*The room at Nevers.*]

SHE: Not in the beginning; no, I don't scream: I call you softly.

HE: But I'm dead.

SHE: Nevertheless I call you. Even though you're dead. Then one day, I scream, I
scream as loud as I can, like a deaf person would. That's when they put me in
the cellar. To punish me.

HE: What do you scream?

SHE: Your German name. Only your name. I only have one memory left, your name.

> [*Room at Nevers, mute screams.*]

SHE: I promise not to scream any more. Then they take me back to my room.

> [*Room at Nevers. Lying down, one leg raised, filled with desire.*]

SHE: I want you so badly I can't bear it any more.

HE: Are you afraid?

SHE: I'm afraid. Everywhere. In the cellar. In my room.

HE: Of what?

> [*Spots on the ceiling of the room at Nevers, terrifying objects at Nevers.*]

SHE: Of not ever seeing you again. Ever, ever.

> [*They move closer together again, as at the beginning of the scene.*]

SHE: One day, I'm twenty years old. It's in the cellar. My mother comes and tells me I'm twenty. [*A pause, as if remembering.*] My mother's crying.

HE: You spit in your mother's face?

SHE: Yes.

> [*As if they were aware of these things together. He moves away from her.*]

HE: Drink something.

SHE: Yes.

> [*He holds the glass for her to drink. She is worn out from remembering.*]

SHE [*suddenly*]: Afterward, I don't remember any more. I don't remember any more...

HE [*trying to encourage her*]: These cellars are very old, and very damp, these Nevers cellars.... You were saying...

SHE: Yes. Full of saltpeter.

> [*Her mouth against the walls of the Nevers cellar, biting.*]

SHE: Sometimes a cat comes in and looks. It's not a mean cat. I don't remember any more.

> [*A cat comes in the Nevers cellar and looks at this woman.*]

SHE: Afterward, I don't remember any more.

HE: How long?

SHE [*still in a trancelike state*]: Eternity.

[*Someone, a solitary man, puts a record of French bal-musette music on the juke box. To make the miracle of the lost memories of Nevers last, to keep anything from "moving," the Japanese pours the contents of his glass into hers.*

In the Nevers cellar the cat's eyes and Riva's eyes glow.

When she hears the music of the record she (drunk or mad) smiles and screams:]

SHE: Oh, how young I was, once!

> [*She comes back to Nevers, having hardly left it. She is
> haunted (the choice of adjectives is voluntarily varied).*]

SHE: At night... my mother takes me down into the garden. She looks at my head. Every night she looks carefully at my head. She still doesn't dare come near me.... It's at night that I can look at the square, so I look at it. It's enormous [*gesturing*]! It curves in in the middle.

> [*The air shaft at the Nevers cellar. Through it, the
> rainbowlike wheels of bicycles passing at dawn at Nevers.*]

SHE: Sleep comes at dawn.

HE: Does it rain sometimes?

SHE: ...along the walls.

> [*She searches, searches, searches.*]

SHE [*almost evil*]: I think of you, but I don't talk about it any more.
[*They move closer together again.*]
HE: Mad.
SHE: Madly in love with you. [*Pause.*] My hair is growing back. I can feel it every day, with my hand. I don't care. But nevertheless my hair is growing back....
[*Riva in her bed at Nevers, her hand in her hair. She runs her hands through her hair.*]
HE: Do you scream, before the cellar?
SHE: No. I'm numb.
[*They are cheek-to-cheek, their eyes half-closed, at Hiroshima.*]
SHE: They shave my head carefully till they're finished. They think it's their duty to do a good job shaving the women's heads.
HE [*very clearly*]: Are you ashamed for them, my love?
[*The hair-cutting.*]
SHE: No. You're dead. I'm much too busy suffering. [*Dusk deepens. The following said with complete immobility:*] All I hear is the sound of the scissors on my head. It makes me feel a little bit better about... your death...like...like, oh! I can't give you a better example, like my nails, the walls... for my anger.
[*She goes on, desperately against him at Hiroshima.*]
SHE: Oh! What pain. What pain in my heart. It's unbelievable. Everywhere in the city they're singing the *Marseillaise*. Night falls. My dead love is an enemy of France. Someone says she should be made to walk through the city. My father's drug store is closed because of the disgrace. I'm alone. Some of them laugh. At night I return home.
[*Scene of the square at Nevers. She screams, not words, but a formless scream understandable in any language as the cry of a child for its mother. He is still against her, holding her hands.*]
HE: And then, one day, my love, you come out of eternity.
[*The room at Nevers. Riva paces the floor. Overturns objects. Savage, conscious animality.*]
SHE: Yes, it takes a long time.
They told me it had taken a very long time.
At six in the evening, the bells of the St. Etienne Cathedral ring, winter and summer. One day, it is true, I hear them. I remember having heard them before—before—when we were in love, when we were happy.
I'm beginning to see.
I remember having already seen before—before—when we were in love, when we were happy.
I remember.
I see the ink.
I see the daylight.
I see my life. Your death.
My life that goes on. Your death that goes on
[*Room and cellar Nevers.*]
and that it took the shadows longer now to reach the corners of the room. And that it took the shadows longer now to reach the corners of the cellar walls. About half past six.
Winter is over.
[*A pause. Hiroshima. She is trembling. She moves away from his face.*]
SHE: Oh! It's horrible. I'm beginning to remember you less clearly.
[*He holds the glass and makes her drink. She's horrified by herself.*]
SHE: ...I'm beginning to forget you. I tremble at the thought of having forgotten so much love...
...More. [*He makes her drink again.*]

[*She wanders. This time. Alone. He loses her.*]

SHE: We were supposed to meet at noon on the quays of the Loire. I was going to leave with him. When I arrived at noon on the quay of the Loire, he wasn't quite dead yet. Someone had fired on him from a garden.

[*The garden above the quay of the Loire. She becomes delirious, no longer looking at him.*]

SHE: I stayed near his body all that day and then all the next night. The next morning they came to pick him up and they put him in a truck. It was that night Nevers was liberated. The bells of St. Etienne were ringing, ringing... Little by little he grew cold beneath me. Oh! how long it took him to die! When? I'm not quite sure. I was lying on top of him... yes... the moment of his death actually escaped me, because... because even at that very same moment, and even afterward, yes, even afterward, I can say that I couldn't feel the slightest difference between this dead body and mine. All I could find between this body and mine were obvious similarities, do you understand? [*Shouting.*] He was my first love....

[*The Japanese slaps her. (Or, if you prefer, crushes her hands in his.) She acts as though she didn't know where it had come from. But she snaps out of it, and acts as though she realized it had been necessary.*]

SHE: And then one day... I had screamed again. So they put me back in the cellar.

[*Her voice resumes its normal rhythm. Here the entire scene of the marble that enters the cellar, the marble she picks up, the warm marble she encloses in her hand, etc., and that she gives back to the children outside, etc.*]

SHE: ... it was warm....

[*He lets her talk, without understanding. She goes on.*]

SHE [*after a pause*]: I think then is when I got over my hate. [*Pause.*] I don't scream any more. [*Pause.*] I'm becoming reasonable. They say: "She's becoming reasonable." [*Pause.*] One night, a holiday, they let me go out.

[*Dawn, at Nevers, beside a river.*]

SHE: The banks of the Loire. Dawn. People are crossing the bridge, sometimes many, sometimes few, depending on the hour. From afar, it's no one.

[*Republic Square, at Nevers, at night.*]

SHE: Not long after that my mother tells me I have to leave for Paris, by night. She gives me some money. I leave for Paris, on a bicycle, at night. It's summer. The nights are warm. When I reach Paris two days later the name of Hiroshima is in all the newspapers. My hair is now a decent length. I'm in the street with the people.

[*Someone puts another bal-musette record on the juke box.*]

SHE [*as if she were waking up*]: Fourteen years have passed.

[*He gives her something to drink. She drinks. She apparently becomes quite calm. They are emerging from the Nevers tunnel.*]

SHE: I don't even remember his hands very well.... The pain, I still remember the pain a little.

HE: Tonight?

SHE: Yes, tonight, I remember. But one day I won't remember it any more. Not at all. Nothing.

SHE [*raising her head to look at him*]: Tomorrow at this time I'll be thousands of miles away from you.

HE: Does your husband know about this?

SHE [*hesitating*]: No.

HE: Then I'm the only one who does?

SHE: Yes.

[*He gets up, takes her in his arms, forcing her to get up too, and holds her very tightly, shockingly. People look at them. They don't understand. He is overwhelmingly happy. He laughs.*]

HE: I'm the only one who knows. No one else?

SHE [*closing her eyes*]: Don't say any more.

> [*She moves even closer to him. She raises her hand, and caresses his lips very lightly. Then, as if she were suddenly very happy:*]

SHE: Oh, how good it is to be with someone, sometimes.

> [*They separate, very slowly, he sits back down again.*]

HE: Yes.

[*Somewhere a lamp goes out, either on the river bank or in the bar. She jumps. She withdraws her hand, which she had placed again on his lips. He hasn't forgotten the passing time.*]

HE: Tell me more.

SHE: All right.

> [*Searches, can't find anything.*]

HE: Tell me more.

SHE: I want to have lived through that moment. That incomparable moment.

> [*She drinks. He speaks, as though divorced from the present.*]

HE: In a few years, when I'll have forgotten you, and when other such adventures, from sheer habit, will happen to me, I'll remember you as the symbol of love's forgetfulness. I'll think of this adventure as of the horror of oblivion. I already know it.

> [*People enter the café. She looks at them.*]

SHE [*hopefully*]: Doesn't anything ever stop at night, in Hiroshima?

> [*They begin a final game of mutual deception.*]

HE: Never, it never stops in Hiroshima.

> [*She puts down her glass, smiles, her smiling concealing a feeling of distress.*]

SHE: I love that . . . cities where there are always people awake, day or night. . . .

[*The proprietress of the bar turns out a light. The record stops playing. They're in semi-darkness. The late but eluctable hour when the cafés close is fast approaching. They both close their eyes, as if seized by a feeling of modesty. The well-ordered world has thrown them out, for their adventure has no place in it. No use fighting. She suddenly understands this. When they raise their eyes again, they literally smile "in order not to cry." She gets up. He does nothing to restrain her. They are outside, in the night, in front of the café. She stands facing him.*]

SHE: It's sometimes necessary to keep from thinking about these difficulties the world makes. If we didn't we'd suffocate.

> [*A last light goes out in the café. Both their eyes are lowered.*]

SHE: Go away, leave me.

> [*He starts to leave, looks up at the sky.*]

HE: It isn't daylight yet . . . .

SHE: No. [*Pause.*] Probably we'll die without ever seeing each other again.

HE: Yes, probably. [*Pause.*] Unless, perhaps, someday, a war. . . .

> [*Pause.*]

SHE [*ironically*]: Yes, a war. . . .

Part V

[*After a further time lapse. We see her in the street, walking quickly. Then we see her in the lobby of the hotel. She takes her key. Then we see her on the stairway. Then we see her open the door to her room. Enter the room and stop short as before an abyss, or as if she had discovered someone already in the room. Then she backs out and closes the door softly.*

Climbing the stairs, descending, going back up, etc. Retracing her steps. Coming and going in the hallway. Wringing her hands, searching for a solution, not finding it, returning to her room all of a sudden. And this time coming to terms with the room.

She goes to the basin, splashes water on her face. And we hear the first sentence of her interior dialogue:]

SHE: You think you know. And then, no. You don't.

In Nevers she had a German love when she was young.…

We'll go to Bavaria, my love, and there we'll marry.

She never went to Bavaria. [*Looking at herself in the mirror.*]

I dare those who have never gone to Bavaria to speak to her of love.

You were not yet quite dead.

I told our story.

I was unfaithful to you tonight with this stranger.

I told our story.

It was, you see, a story that could be told.

For fourteen years I hadn't found… the taste of an impossible love again.

Since Nevers.

Look how I'm forgetting you.…

Look how I've forgotten you.

Look at me.

[*Through the open window we see the new Hiroshima, peacefully asleep. She suddenly raises her head, sees her wet face in the mirror—like tears—grown old, haggard. And this time, disgusted, she closes her eyes. She dries her face and quickly leaves, crossing the lobby.*]

[*When we see her again she is sitting on a bench, or on a pile of gravel, about fifty feet from the same bar where they had spent the evening together. The restaurant's light is in her eyes. Banal, almost empty: he is no longer there. She (lies down, sits down) on the gravel and continues to look at the café. (Now only one light is left on in the bar. The room where they had been a short while before is closed. The door into that room is slightly ajar, and by the dim light it is just possible to make out the arrangement of chairs and tables, which are no more than vague, vain shadows.)*

She closes her eyes. Then opens them again. She seems to be asleep. But she is not. When she opens her eyes, she opens them suddenly. Like a cat. Then we hear her voice, an interior monologue:]

SHE: I'm going to stay in Hiroshima. With him, every night. In Hiroshima. [*Opening her eyes.*] I'm going to stay here. Here.

[*She looks away from the café and gazes around her. Then suddenly she curls up as tightly as she can, a childlike movement, her head cuddled in her arms, her feet pulled up under her. The Japanese approaches her. She sees him, doesn't move, doesn't react. Their absence "from each other" has begun. No astonishment. He is smoking a cigarette.*]

HE: Stay in Hiroshima.

SHE [*glancing at him*]: Of course I'm going to stay in Hiroshima, with you. [*She buries her head again and says, in a childish tone*]: Oh, how miserable I am.…

[*He moves nearer to her.*]

SHE: I never expected this would happen, really.… Go away.

HE [*moving away*]: Impossible to leave you.

[*We see them now on a boulevard. In the background, the lighted signs of nightclubs. The boulevard is perfectly straight. She is walking, he following. We see first one, then the other. Distress on both their faces. He catches up with her.*]

HE [*softly*]: Stay in Hiroshima with me.

[*She doesn't reply. Then we hear her voice in
an interior monologue, loud and uncontrolled:*]

SHE: He's going to come toward me, he's going to take me by the shoulders, he's-going-to-kiss-me . . . .

He'll kiss me . . . and I'll be lost. [*The word "lost" is said almost ecstatically.*]

[*A shot of him. And we notice he's walking more slowly to let the distance between them grow. That instead of coming toward her he's moving farther away. She doesn't turn back.*]

[*A succession of streets in Hiroshima and Nevers. Riva's interior monologue.*]

SHE: I meet you

I remember you.

This city was made to the size of love.

You were made to the size of my body.

Who are you?

You destroy me.

I was hungry. Hungry for infidelity, for adultery, for lies, hungry to die.

I always have been.

I always expected that one day you would descend on me.

I waited for you calmly, with infinite patience.

Take me. Deform me to your likeness so that no one, after you, can understand the reason for so much desire.

We're going to remain alone, my love.

The night will never end.

The sun will never rise again on anyone.

Never. Never more. At last.

You destroy me.

You're so good for me.

In good conscience, with good will, we'll mourn the departed day.

We'll have nothing else to do, nothing but to mourn the departed day.

And a time is going to come.

A time will come. When we'll no more know what thing it is that binds us. By slow degrees the word will fade from our memory.

Then it will disappear altogether.

[*This time he accosts her face to face—for the last time—but from a distance. Henceforth she is inviolable. It is raining. They are under a store awning.*]

HE: Maybe it's possible for you to stay.

SHE: You know it's not. Still more impossible than to leave.

HE: A week.

SHE: No.

HE: Three days.

SHE: Time enough for what? To live from it? To die from it?

HE: Time enough to know which.

SHE: That doesn't exist. Neither time enough to live from it. Nor time enough to die from it. So I don't give a damn.

HE: I would have preferred that you had died at Nevers.

SHE: So would I. But I didn't die at Nevers.

[*She is seated on a bench in the waiting room of the Hiroshima railroad station. Still more time has elapsed. An elderly Japanese woman is seated beside her. Another interior monologue.*]

SHE: Nevers, that I'd forgotten, I'd like to see you again tonight. Every night for months on end I set you on fire, while my body was aflame with his memory.

[*Like a shadow the Japanese enters and sits on the same bench, on the opposite side of the old woman. He doesn't look at the French woman. His face is soaked from the rain. His lips are trembling slightly.*]

SHE: While my body is still on fire with your memory, I would like to see Nevers again . . . the Loire.

[*Shot of Nevers.*]

Lovely poplar trees of Nièvre, I offer you to oblivion. [*The word "lovely" should be spoken like a word of love.*]

Three-penny story, I bequeath you to oblivion.

[*The ruins at Nevers.*]

One night without you and I waited for daylight to free me.

[*The "marriage" at Nevers.*]

One day without his eyes was enough to kill her.

Little girl of Nevers.

Shameless child of Nevers.

One day without his hands and she thinks how sad it is to love.

Silly little girl.

Who dies of love at Nevers.

Little girl with shaven head, I bequeath you to oblivion.

Three-penny story.

As it was for him, oblivion will begin with your eyes.

Just the same.

Then, as it was for him, it will encompass your voice.

Just the same.

Then, as it was for him, it will encompass you completely, little by little.

You will become a song.

[*They are separated by the old Japanese woman. He takes a cigarette, rises slightly, and offers the French woman the package. "That's all I can do for you, offer you a cigarette, as I would offer one to anybody, to this old woman." She doesn't smoke. He offers the package to the old woman, lights her cigarette.*

The Nevers forest moves past in the twilight. And Nevers. While the loudspeaker at the Hiroshima station blares: "Hiroshima, Hiroshima!" during the shots of Nevers.

The French woman seems to be asleep. The two Japanese beside her speak softly to keep from waking her up.]

THE OLD WOMAN: Who is she?

HE: A French woman.

THE OLD WOMAN: What's the matter?

HE: She's leaving Japan in a little while. We're sad at having to leave each other.

[*She is gone. We see her again just outside the station. She gets into a taxi. Stops before a night club. "The Casablanca." Then he arrives after her.*

She is alone at a table. He sits down at another table facing hers. It's the end. The end of the night which marks the beginning of their eternal separation. A Japanese who was in the room goes over to her and engages her in conversation.]

THE JAPANESE: Are you alone?

[*She replies only by signs.*]

THE JAPANESE: Do you mind talking with me a little?

[*The place is almost empty. People are bored.*]

THE JAPANESE: It is very late to be lonely.

[*She lets herself be accosted by another man in order to "lose" the one we know.*

But not only is that not possible, it's useless. For the other one is already lost.]

THE JAPANESE: May I sit down? Are you just visiting Hiroshima?

Do you like Japan?

Do you live in Paris?

[*We can see day beginning to break (through the windows). The interior monologue has stopped. This unknown Japanese is talking to her. She looks at the other. The unknown Japanese stops talking to her. And then, terrifying, "the dawn of the damned" can be seen breaking through the windows of the night club.*]

[*She is next seen leaning against the door inside her hotel*
room. Her hand on her heart. A knock. She opens.]

HE: Impossible not to come.

[*They are standing in the room, facing each other, their arms at their sides, their bodies not touching. The room is in order. The ash trays are empty. It is now full daylight. The sun is up. They don't even smoke. The bed is still made. They say nothing. They look at each other. The silence of dawn weighs on the whole city. He enters her room. In the distance, Hiroshima is still sleeping. All of a sudden, she sits down. She buries her head in her hands, clenches her fist, closes her eyes, and moans. A moan of utter sadness. The light of the city in her eyes.*]

SHE: I'll forget you! I'm forgetting you already! Look how I'm forgetting you! Look
     at me!

[*He takes her arms (wrists), she faces him, her head thrown back. She suddenly breaks away from him. He helps her by an effort of self-abstraction. As if she were in danger. He looks at her, she at him, as she would look at the city, and suddenly, very softly, she calls him. She calls him from afar, lost in wonder. She has succeeded in drowning him in universal oblivion. And it is a source of amazement to her.*]

SHE: Hi-ro-shi-ma.

     Hi-ro-shi-ma. That's your name.

     [*They look at each other without seeing each other. Forever.*]

HE: That's my name. Yes. Your name is Nevers. Ne-vers-in France.

DORIS LESSING
[BORN 1919]

In numerous novels, short stories, plays, and essays, Doris Lessing has established herself as an important modernist and feminist writer. Exploring the psychological illness and fragmentation of our time in both personal and social terms, her writing career has been a search for wholeness and meaning—a search embodied in the name of her autobiographical heroine, Martha Quest. But Lessing is a modernist with a difference. She grew up in Rhodesia in the 1940s and she writes about colonial relationships with a white insider's perspective. Coming to Europe from Africa when she was thirty, Lessing looks at European culture with a postcolonial consciousness.

LIFE

Although she was born in Persia (Iran) to British parents, Lessing was raised in Rhodesia (now Zimbabwe) where her family homesteaded. There she directly experienced colonialism at a later historical stage than that represented by Conrad in *Heart of Darkness*. Conrad described the rapacious initial contacts between European entrepreneurs and the native people of the Congo in the 1880s and 1890s. Rhodesia at the time of Lessing's childhood had become a self-governing British colony. By the early 1920s, rapid agricultural development was underway, and Rhodesia had a European population of 34,000, many of them farmers like Lessing's parents, who grew corn using native laborers on a 3,000-acre farm. She endured a convent school in Salisbury, leaving it at age fourteen to work as a nursemaid, secretary, and telephone operator. She survived two failed marriages, joined in the fight for black liberation, and began writing. She left Rhodesia and moved to London in 1949, where she has lived and worked ever since.

WORK

Much of Lessing's early writing is about Africa and the effects of Africa on the white colonists. In two volumes of short stories and a striking first novel, *The Grass Is Singing* (1949), she describes the uneasy relations between native Africans and white settlers. To live in Africa, Lessing has written, is "to be reminded twenty times a day of injustice," and in her work and life she has attempted to understand, describe, and redress this injustice and to expose the sterility of white colonialism. Her later work, which includes many novels, short stories, plays, essays, and works of fantasy and science fiction, traces her personal and political growth. The five-volume autobiographical series of novels *Children of Violence,* published in the 1950s and 1960s, is "a study of the individual conscience in its relations with the collective." These novels recount the changes in the life of her heroine, Martha Quest, as she moves from Africa to England. *The Golden Notebook* (1962), probably Lessing's best-known novel, is an experimental work and one of the classics of contemporary feminism. Her fantasy novels of the 1970s and 1980s use science fiction as a way to embody her personal quest as she moved from socialism to Sufi mysticism. In her novels of the later 1980s, some published under the pseudonym Jane Somers, Lessing has returned to the psychological realism of her earlier work.

In the preface to her volume of *African Stories* (1964), Lessing describes her experience of Africa in terms reminiscent of Conrad. Africa, she says, "is not a place to visit unless one chooses to be an exile ever afterwards from an inexplicable majestic silence lying just over the border of memory or thought. Africa gives you the knowledge that man is a small creature, among other creatures, in a large landscape." That landscape is an important presence in "The Old Chief Mshlanga," where the adolescent narrator's pilgrimage to the native village makes her aware of the immense continent outside the confines of her family's farm. On the ranch she is *Nkosikaas,* a chieftainess, but out on the veld she becomes an insignificant white child in an old and alien land. Lessing's sympathy with the girl's point of view is characteristic of her understanding of the white settlers in the African stories. Even though the stories are critiques of the colonists' white supremacist ideology, they are never simplistic propaganda. The girl comes to realize the doubleness of her cultural situation and the contradictions in which she is caught. By the end of the story she is aware of her complicity in removing the native village and changing Africa. For all her independence and her questioning of the values of her family and the white community of which she is part, she has inherited the consciousness of her people and in the course of the story she learns the limits of her freedom. She may even be responsible for the more rapid colonization of the native lands surrounding her family's homestead. Personal and political issues cannot be separated in the girl's story or in Lessing's postcolonial world view.

SUGGESTED READINGS

Lessing's fiction about Africa appears in the collection of *African Stories* (1964) and in the two novels *The Grass is Singing* (1949) and *Martha Quest* (1952). She has also written about Africa in her autobiographical essays *A Small Personal Voice* (1974) and *African*

Laughter (1993). Critical discussions of Lessing's writing about Africa can be found in M. Tucker's *Africa in Modern Literature* (1962), Mary Ann Singleton's *The City and the Veld* (1977), and Michael Thorpe's *Doris Lessing's Africa* (1978). Annis Pratt and L. S. Dembo have assembled several points of view on Lessing's work in *Doris Lessing: Critical Essays* (1974).

The Old Chief Mshlanga

They were good, the years of ranging the bush over her father's farm which, like every white farm, was largely unused, broken only occasionally by small patches of cultivation. In between, nothing but trees, the long sparse grass, thorn and cactus and gully, grass and outcrop and thorn. And a jutting piece of rock which had been thrust up from the warm soil of Africa unimaginable eras of time ago, washed into hollows and whorls by sun and wind that had travelled so many thousands of miles of space and bush, would hold the weight of a small girl whose eyes were sightless for anything but a pale willowed river, a pale gleaming castle—a small girl singing: "Out flew the web and floated wide, the mirror cracked from side to side . . ."[1]

Pushing her way through the green aisles of the mealie stalks, the leaves arching like cathedrals veined with sunlight far overhead, with the packed red earth underfoot, a fine lace of red starred witchweed would summon up a black bent figure croaking premonitions: the Northern witch, bred of cold Northern forests, would stand before her among the mealie fields, and it was the mealie fields that faded and fled, leaving her among the gnarled roots of an oak, snow falling thick and soft and white, the woodcutter's fire glowing red welcome through crowding tree trunks.

A white child, opening its eyes curiously on a sun-suffused landscape, a gaunt and violent landscape, might be supposed to accept it as her own, to take the msasa trees and the thorn trees as familiars, to feel her blood running free and responsive to the swing of the seasons.

This child could not see a msasa tree, or the thorn, for what they were. Her books held tales of alien fairies, her rivers ran slow and peaceful, and she knew the shape of the leaves of an ash or an oak, the names of the little creatures that lived in English streams, when the words "the veld" meant strangeness, though she could remember nothing else.

Because of this, for many years, it was the veld that seemed unreal; the sun was a foreign sun, and the wind spoke a strange language.

The black people on the farm were as remote as the trees and the rocks. They were an amorphous black mass, mingling and thinning and massing like tadpoles, faceless, who existed merely to serve, to say "Yes, Baas," take their money and go. They changed season by season, moving from one farm to the next, according to their outlandish needs, which one did not have to understand, coming from perhaps hundreds of miles north or east, passing on after a few months—where? Perhaps even as far away as the fabled gold mines of Johannesburg, where the pay was so much better than the few shillings a month and the double handful of mealie meal twice a day which they earned in that part of Africa.

---

[1] From Tennyson's "The Lady of Shallot," describing the moment when the Lady looks directly at the real world rather than at its reflection in a mirror.

The child was taught to take them for granted: the servants in the house would come running a hundred yards to pick up a book if she dropped it. She was called "Nkosikaas"—Chieftainess, even by the black children her own age.

Later, when the farm grew too small to hold her curiosity, she carried a gun in the crook of her arm and wandered miles a day, from vlei to vlei, from *kopje* to *kopje*,[2] accompanied by two dogs: the dogs and the gun were an armour against fear. Because of them she never felt fear.

If a native came into sight along the kaffir[3] paths half a mile away, the dogs would flush him up a tree as if he were a bird. If he expostulated (in his uncouth language which was by itself ridiculous), that was cheek. If one was in a good mood, it could be a matter for laughter. Otherwise one passed on, hardly glancing at the angry man in the tree.

On the rare occasions when white children met together they could amuse themselves by hailing a passing native in order to make a buffoon of him; they could set the dogs on him and watch him run; they could tease a small black child as if he were a puppy—save that they would not throw stones and sticks at a dog without a sense of guilt.

Later still, certain questions presented themselves in the child's mind; and because the answers were not easy to accept, they were silenced by an even greater arrogance of manner.

It was even impossible to think of the black people who worked about the house as friends, for if she talked to one of them, her mother would come running anxiously: "Come away; you mustn't talk to natives."

It was this instilled consciousness of danger, of something unpleasant, that made it easy to laugh out loud, crudely, if a servant made a mistake in his English or if he failed to understand an order—there is a certain kind of laughter that is fear, afraid of itself.

One evening, when I was about fourteen, I was walking down the side of a mealie field that had been newly ploughed, so that the great red clods showed fresh and tumbling to the vlei beyond, like a choppy red sea; it was that hushed and listening hour, when the birds send long sad calls from tree to tree, and all the colours of earth and sky and leaf are deep and golden. I had my rifle in the curve of my arm, and the dogs were at my heels.

In front of me, perhaps a couple of hundred yards away, a group of three Africans came into sight around the side of a big antheap. I whistled the dogs close in to my skirts and let the gun swing in my hand, and advanced, waiting for them to move aside, off the path, in respect for my passing. But they came on steadily, and the dogs looked up at me for the command to chase. I was angry. It was "cheek" for a native not to stand off a path, the moment he caught sight of you.

In front walked an old man, stooping his weight on to a stick, his hair grizzled white, a dark red blanket slung over his shoulders like a cloak. Behind him came two young men, carrying bundles of pots, assegais,[4] hatchets.

The group was not a usual one. They were not natives seeking work. These had an air of dignity, of quietly following their own purpose. It was the dignity that checked my tongue. I walked quietly on, talking softly to the growling dogs, till I was ten paces away. Then the old man stopped, drawing his blanket close.

---

[2]*vlei:* grassland; *kopje:* a small rounded hill.
[3]A derogatory term for Bantu or native.
[4]Javelins or spears.

"Morning, Nkosikaas," he said, using the customary greeting for any time of the day.

"Good morning," I said. "Where are you going?" My voice was a little truculent.

The old man spoke in his own language, then one of the young men stepped forward politely and said in careful English: "My Chief travels to see his brothers beyond the river."

A Chief! I thought, understanding the pride that made the old man stand before me like an equal—more than an equal, for he showed courtesy, and I showed none.

The old man spoke again, wearing dignity like an inherited garment, still standing ten paces off, flanked by his entourage, not looking at me (that would have been rude) but directing his eyes somewhere over my head at the trees.

"You are the little Nkosikaas from the farm of Baas Jordan?"

"That's right," I said.

"Perhaps your father does not remember," said the interpreter for the old man, "but there was an affair with some goats. I remember seeing you when you were . . ." The young man held his hand at knee level and smiled.

We all smiled.

"What is your name?" I asked.

"This is Chief Mshlanga," said the young man.

"I will tell my father that I met you," I said.

The old man said: "My greetings to your father, little Nkosikaas."

"Good morning," I said politely, finding the politeness difficult, from lack of use.

"Morning, little Nkosikaas," said the old man, and stood aside to let me pass.

I went by, my gun hanging awkwardly, the dogs sniffing and growling, cheated of their favourite game of chasing natives like animals.

Not long afterwards I read in an old explorer's book the phrase: "Chief Mshlanga's country." It went like this: "Our destination was Chief Mshlanga's country, to the north of the river; and it was our desire to ask his permission to prospect for gold in his territory."

The phrase "ask his permission" was so extraordinary to a white child, brought up to consider all natives as things to use, that it revived those questions, which could not be suppressed: they fermented slowly in my mind.

On another occasion one of those old prospectors who still move over Africa looking for neglected reefs, with their hammers and tents, and pans for sifting gold from crushed rock, came to the farm and, in talking of the old days, used that phrase again: "This was the Old Chief's country," he said. "It stretched from those mountains over there way back to the river, hundreds of miles of country." That was his name for our district: "The Old Chief's Country"; he did not use our name for it—a new phrase which held no implication of usurped ownership.

As I read more books about the time when this part of Africa was opened up, not much more than fifty years before, I found Old Chief Mshlanga had been a famous man, known to all the explorers and prospectors. But then he had been young; or maybe it was his father or uncle they spoke of—I never found out.

During that year I met him several times in the part of the farm that was traversed by natives moving over the country. I learned that the path up the side of the big red field where the birds sang was the recognized highway for migrants. Perhaps I even haunted it in the hope of meeting him: being greeted by him, the exchange of courtesies, seemed to answer the questions that troubled me.

Soon I carried a gun in a different spirit; I used it for shooting food and not to give me confidence. And now the dogs learned better manners. When I saw a native approaching, we offered and took greetings; and slowly that other landscape in my mind faded, and my feet struck directly on the African soil, and I saw the shapes of tree and hill clearly, and the black people moved back, as it were, out of my life: it was as if I stood aside to watch a slow intimate dance of landscape and men, a very old dance, whose steps I could not learn.

But I thought: this is my heritage, too; I was bred here; it is my country as well as the black man's country; and there is plenty of room for all of us, without elbowing each other off the pavements and roads.

It seemed it was only necessary to let free that respect I felt when I was talking with old Chief Mshlanga, to let both black and white people meet gently, with tolerance for each other's differences: it seemed quite easy.

Then, one day, something new happened. Working in our house as servants were always three natives: cook, houseboy, garden boy. They used to change as the farm natives changed: staying for a few months, then moving on to a new job, or back home to their kraals.[5] They were thought of as "good" or "bad" natives; which meant: how did they behave as servants? Were they lazy, efficient, obedient, or disrespectful? If the family felt good-humoured, the phrase was: "What can you expect from raw black savages?" If we were angry, we said: "These damned niggers, we would be much better off without them."

One day, a white policeman was on his rounds of the district, and he said laughingly: "Did you know you have an important man in your kitchen?"

"What!" exclaimed my mother sharply. "What do you mean?"

"A Chief's son." The policeman seemed amused. "He'll boss the tribe when the old man dies."

"He'd better not put on a Chief's son act with me," said my mother.

When the policeman left, we looked with different eyes at our cook: he was a good worker, but he drank too much at week-ends—that was how we knew him.

He was a tall youth, with very black skin, like black polished metal, his tightly growing black hair parted white man's fashion at one side, with a metal comb from the store stuck into it; very polite, very distant, very quick to obey an order. Now that it had been pointed out, we said: "Of course, you can see. Blood always tells."

My mother became strict with him now she knew about his birth and prospects. Sometimes, when she lost her temper, she would say: "You aren't the Chief yet, you know." And he would answer her very quietly, his eyes on the ground: "Yes, Nkosikaas."

One afternoon he asked for a whole day off, instead of the customary half-day, to go home next Sunday.

"How can you go home in one day?"

"It will take me half an hour on my bicycle," he explained.

I watched the direction he took; and the next day I went off to look for this kraal; I understood he must be Chief Mshlanga's successor: there was no other kraal near enough our farm.

Beyond our boundaries on that side the country was new to me. I followed unfamiliar paths past *kopjes* that till now had been part of the jagged horizon, hazed with distance. This was Government land, which had never been cultivated by white men; at first I could not understand why it was that it appeared, in merely crossing the boundary, I had entered a completely fresh type of landscape. It was a

---

[5]Native villages.

wide green valley, where a small river sparkled, and vivid water-birds darted over the rushes. The grass was thick and soft to my calves, the trees stood tall and shapely.

I was used to our farm, whose hundreds of acres of harsh eroded soil bore trees that had been cut for the mine furnaces and had grown thin and twisted, where the cattle had dragged the grass flat, leaving innumerable criss-crossing trails that deepened each season into gullies, under the force of the rains.

This country had been left untouched, save for prospectors whose picks had struck a few sparks from the surface of the rocks as they wandered by; and for migrant natives whose passing had left, perhaps, a charred patch on the trunk of a tree where their evening fire had nestled.

It was very silent: a hot morning with pigeons cooing throatily, the midday shadows lying dense and thick with clear yellow spaces of sunlight between and in all that wide green park-like valley, not a human soul but myself.

I was listening to the quick regular tapping of a woodpecker when slowly a chill feeling seemed to grow up from the small of my back to my shoulders, in a constricting spasm like a shudder, and at the roots of my hair a tingling sensation began and ran down over the surface of my flesh, leaving me goosefleshed and cold, though I was damp with sweat. Fever? I thought; then uneasily, turned to look over my shoulder; and realized suddenly that this was fear. It was extraordinary, even humiliating. It was a new fear. For all the years I had walked by myself over this country I had never known a moment's uneasiness; in the beginning because I had been supported by a gun and the dogs, then because I had learnt an easy friendliness for the Africans I might encounter.

I had read of this feeling, how the bigness and silence of Africa, under the ancient sun, grows dense and takes shape in the mind, till even the birds seem to call menacingly, and a deadly spirit comes out of the trees and the rocks. You move warily, as if your very passing disturbs something old and evil, something dark and big and angry that might suddenly rear and strike from behind. You look at groves of entwined trees, and picture the animals that might be lurking there; you look at the river running slowly, dropping from level to level through the vlei, spreading into pools where at night the bucks come to drink, and the crocodiles rise and drag them by their soft noses into underwater caves. Fear possessed me. I found I was turning round and round, because of that shapeless menace behind me that might reach out and take me; I kept glancing at the files of *kopjes* which, seen from a different angle, seemed to change with every step so that even known landmarks, like a big mountain that had sentinelled my world since I first became conscious of it, showed an unfamiliar sunlit valley among its foothills. I did not know where I was. I was lost. Panic seized me. I found I was spinning round and round, staring anxiously at this tree and that, peering up at the sun which appeared to have moved into an eastern slant, shedding the sad yellow light of sunset. Hours must have passed! I looked at my watch and found that this state of meaningless terror had lasted perhaps ten minutes.

The point was that it was meaningless. I was not ten miles from home: I had only to take my way back along the valley to find myself at the fence; away among the foothills of the *kopjes* gleamed the roof of a neighbour's house, and a couple of hours' walking would reach it. This was the sort of fear that contracts the flesh of a dog at night and sets him howling at the full moon. It had nothing to do with what I thought or felt; and I was more disturbed by the fact that I could become its victim than of the physical sensation itself: I walked steadily on, quietened, in a divided mind, watching my own pricking nerves and apprehensive glances from side to side with a disgusted amusement. Deliberately I set myself to think of this village I was seeking, and what I should do when I entered it—if I could find it, which was doubtful, since I was walking aimlessly and it might be anywhere in the hundreds of thousands of acres of bush that stretched about me. With my mind on that village, I realized that a new sensation was added to the fear: loneliness. Now such a terror of isolation invaded me that I could hardly walk; and if it were not that I came over the crest of a small rise and saw a village below me, I should have turned and gone home. It was a cluster of thatched huts in a clearing among trees. There were neat patches of mealies and pumpkins and millet, and cattle grazed under some trees at a distance. Fowls scratched among the huts, dogs lay sleeping on the grass, and goats friezed a *kopje* that jutted up beyond a tributary of the river lying like an enclosing arm round the village.

As I came close I saw the huts were lovingly decorated with patterns of yellow and red and ochre mud on the walls; and the thatch was tied in place with plaits of straw.

This was not at all like our farm compound, a dirty and neglected place, a temporary home for migrants who had no roots in it.

And now I did not know what to do next. I called a small black boy, who was sitting on a lot playing a stringed gourd, quite naked except for the strings of blue beads round his neck, and said: "Tell the Chief I am here." The child stuck his thumb in his mouth and stared shyly back at me.

For minutes I shifted my feet on the edge of what seemed a deserted village, till at last the child scuttled off, and then some women came. They were draped in bright cloths, with brass glinting in their ears and on their arms. They also stared, silently; then turned to chatter among themselves.

I said again: "Can I see Chief Mshlanga?" I saw they caught the name; they did not understand what I wanted. I did not understand myself.

At last I walked through them and came past the huts and saw a clearing under a big shady tree, where a dozen old men sat crosslegged on the ground, talking. Chief Mshlanga was leaning back against the tree, holding a gourd in his hand, from which he had been drinking. When he saw me, not a muscle of his face moved, and I could see he was not pleased: perhaps he was afflicted with my own shyness, due to being unable to find the right forms of courtesy for the occasion. To meet me, on our own farm, was one thing; but I should not have come here. What had I expected? I could not join them socially: the thing was unheard of. Bad enough that I, a white girl, should be walking the veld alone as a white man might: and in this part of the bush where only Government officials had the right to move.

Again I stood, smiling foolishly, while behind me stood the groups of brightly clad, chattering women, their faces alert with curiosity and interest, and in front of me sat the old men, with old lined faces, their eyes guarded, aloof. It was a village of ancients and children and women. Even the two young men who kneeled beside the Chief were not those I had seen with him previously: the young men were all away working on the white men's farms and mines, and the Chief must depend on relatives who were temporarily on holiday for his attendants.

"The small white Nkosikaas is far from home," remarked the old man at last.

"Yes," I agreed, "it is far." I wanted to say: "I have come to pay you a friendly visit, Chief Mshlanga." I could not say it. I might now be feeling an urgent helpless desire to get to know these men and women as people, to be accepted by them as a friend, but the truth was I had set out in a spirit of curiosity: I had wanted to see the village that one day our cook, the reserved and obedient young man who got drunk on Sundays, would one day rule over.

"The child of Nkosi Jordan is welcome," said Chief Mshlanga.

"Thank you," I said, and could think of nothing more to sa[...] silence, while the flies rose and began to buzz around my head; and [...] a little in the thick green tree that spread its branches over the old [...]

"Good morning," I said at last. "I have to return now to my ho[...]

"Morning, little Nkosikaas," said Chief Mshlanga.

I walked away from the indifferent village, over the rise past the staring amber-eyed goats, down through the tall stately trees into the great rich green valley where the river meandered and the pigeons cooed tales of plenty and the woodpecker tapped softly.

The fear had gone; the loneliness had set into stiff-necked stoicism; there was now a queer hostility in the landscape, a cold, hard, sullen indomitability that walked with me, as strong as a wall, as intangible as smoke; it seemed to say to me: you walk here as a destroyer. I went slowly homewards, with an empty heart: I had learned that if one cannot call a country to heel like a dog, neither can one dismiss the past with a smile in an easy gush of feeling, saying: I could not help it, I am also a victim.

I only saw Chief Mshlanga once again.

One night my father's big red land was trampled down by small sharp hooves, and it was discovered that the culprits were goats from Chief Mshlanga's kraal. This had happened once before, years ago.

My father confiscated all the goats. Then he sent a message to the old Chief that if he wanted them he would have to pay for the damage.

He arrived at our house at the time of sunset one evening, looking very old and bent now, walking stiffly under his regally-draped blanket, leaning on a big stick. My father sat himself down in his big chair below the steps of the house; the old man squatted carefully on the ground before him, flanked by his two young men.

The palaver was long and painful, because of the bad English of the young man who interpreted, and because my father could not speak dialect, but only kitchen kaffir.

From my father's point of view, at least two hundred pounds' worth of damage had been done to the crop. He knew he could not get the money from the old man. He felt he was entitled to keep the goats. As for the old Chief, he kept repeating angrily: "Twenty goats! My people cannot lose twenty goats! We are not rich, like the Nkosi Jordan, to lose twenty goats at once."

My father did not think of himself as rich, but rather as very poor. He spoke quickly and angrily in return, saying that the damage done meant a great deal to him, and that he was entitled to the goats.

At last it grew so heated that the cook, the Chief's son, was called from the kitchen to be interpreter, and now my father spoke fluently in English, and our cook translated rapidly so that the old man could understand how very angry my father was. The young man spoke without emotion, in a mechanical way, his eyes lowered, but showing how he felt his position by a hostile uncomfortable set of the shoulders.

It was now in the late sunset, the sky a welter of colours, the birds singing their last songs, and the cattle, lowing peacefully, moving past us towards their sheds for the night. It was the hour when Africa is most beautiful; and here was this pathetic, ugly scene, doing no one any good.

At last my father stated finally: "I'm not going to argue about it. I am keeping the goats."

The old Chief flashed back in his own language: "That means that my people will go hungry when the dry season comes."

"Go to the police, then," said my father, and looked triumphant.

There was, of course, no more to be said.

The old man sat silent, his head bent, his hands dangling helplessly over his withered knees. Then he rose, the young men helping him, and he stood facing my father. He spoke once again, very stiffly; and turned away and went home to his village.

"What did he say?" asked my father of the young man, who laughed uncomfortably and would not meet his eyes.

"What did he say?" insisted my father.

Our cook stood straight and silent, his brows knotted together. Then he spoke. "My father says: All this land, this land you call yours, is his land, and belongs to our people."

Having made this statement, he walked off into the bush after his father, and we did not see him again.

Our next cook was a migrant from Nyasaland, with no expectations of greatness.

Next time the policeman came on his rounds he was told this story. He remarked: "That kraal has no right to be there; it should have been moved long ago. I don't know why no one has done anything about it. I'll have a chat with the Native Commissioner next week. I'm going over for tennis on Sunday, anyway."

Some time later we heard that Chief Mshlanga and his people had been moved two hundred miles east, to a proper Native Reserve; the Government land was going to be opened up for white settlement soon.

I went to see the village again, about a year afterwards. There was nothing there. Mounds of red mud, where the huts had been, had long swathes of rotting thatch over them, veined with the red galleries of the white ants. The pumpkin vines rioted everywhere, over the bushes, up the lower branches of trees so that the great golden balls rolled underfoot and dangled overhead: it was a festival of pumpkins. The bushes were crowding up, the new grass sprang vivid green.

The settler lucky enough to be allotted the lush warm valley (if he chose to cultivate this particular section) would find, suddenly, in the middle of a mealie field, the plants were growing fifteen feet tall, the weight of the cobs dragging at the stalks, and wonder what unsuspected vein of richness he had struck.

JAMES BALDWIN
[1924–1987]

James Baldwin is known for the powerful works of fiction and nonfiction in which he explores the themes of race and sexual orientation in America while struggling with the often conflicting worlds of politics and art. In his first novel, *Go Tell It on the Mountain* (1953), Baldwin tells the story of his stern and angry stepfather, an evangelist preacher. This story was documented two years later in Baldwin's nonfiction work *Notes of a Native Son* (1955). In his second novel, *Giovanni's Room* (1956), Baldwin drew on his experience as an alienated black bisexual man, and nearly lost his audience as a result. He treated this alienation more cautiously in a later book, *Another Country* (1962). Meanwhile, responding to the times, his essays often took on a grim political quality, as in *Nobody Knows My Name* (1961), *The Fire Next Time* (1963), and "No Name in the Street" (1972). Other creative works—for instance, the drama *Blues for Mr. Charlie* (1964)—borrowed directly from Baldwin's essays and reportage. Common ingredients of Baldwin's work, whatever its form, are its truth and style. He was a technically adept writer who told the truth so that it hurt; for this reason his work is likely to endure with readers of every racial background.

LIFE

Baldwin was born to Emma Jones, an unmarried domestic worker in Harlem, in 1924. Three years later, she married a factory hand and preacher, David Baldwin. David Baldwin's only son by an earlier marriage left the household in 1932, leaving James as the oldest of nine remaining children. At age fourteen, he converted to the Pentecostal faith of his stepfather and, perhaps trying to please him, took up preaching for four years until graduating from high school in 1942. Now a young man with eight younger siblings and no job, James concluded that religion offered no solution to the problems of the poor people of Harlem. In 1943, following the death of his deeply embittered stepfather, James Baldwin began to write a fictionalized account of his household that eventually became *Go Tell It on the Mountain*.

The young writer emigrated to Paris for the first time in 1948, returning to the United States in 1957. He moved frequently from one country to another during the next decade, buying time and space in which to write extensively on two themes: race relations in the United States and the situation of the black homosexual. During the early 1960s, Baldwin lived intermittently in the Middle East, where he could purchase obscurity more easily than in Paris or New York. At the same time, he made visits to the United States to lend support on occasions of great drama. In 1963 he met with Attorney General Robert Kennedy and prominent civil rights supporters; marched on Washington, D.C., with Dr. Martin Luther King, Jr.; and joined the voter registration campaign in Selma, Alabama. Fearing the climate of violence he saw everywhere he went, he withdrew from Selma in October 1963, a month before the assassination of President John F. Kennedy in Dallas, Texas. Despite frequent return trips to the United States and repeated demonstrations of solidarity with the civil rights movement, Baldwin spent increasingly more time in Europe and the Middle East in the late 1960s. Although surrounded by close friends, he never established a permanent relationship. In the 1970s and 1980s, as the quality and freshness of his writing slowly diminished, Baldwin kept his home base in France, in Paris and on the Riviera. After suffering two heart attacks, he died of cancer in 1987.

WORK

Baldwin made enemies, both by what he said and what he did. He never really approved of novelist Richard Wright, author of the novel *Native Son* (1940) and the autobiography *Black Boy* (1945); particularly, he rejected the murderer and rapist Bigger Thomas in *Native Son* as a dangerous black wish fulfillment. (In reality, Wright may have been closer to the spirit of Baldwin than the latter was willing to admit.) More seriously, Baldwin made enemies simply by the way he lived his life. Eldridge Cleaver, Black Panther leader and author of *Soul on Ice* (1968), said that Baldwin had "the most grueling, agonizing, total hatred of blacks, particularly of himself." As evidence of Baldwin's unworthiness, Cleaver cited the advantages he enjoyed (choosing whether to remain on the Continent in self-imposed exile) and his sexual orientation. Baldwin actually conceded something to this argument, at one point calling Cleaver's attacks a "necessary warning," but insisted on his prerogative as an artist to live where he was best able to do his work. Baldwin further distanced himself from U.S. racial politics in the mid-1960s as the schism between militants such as Cleaver and moderates in the civil rights movement grew deeper.

Baldwin frequently addressed the question of how a writer can be most effective as a political instrument. What, he asked, is the most effective strategy for political engagement—words or actions? And what if a writer's actions actually put his words in jeopardy, either through direct intimidation (death threats, for example) or the loss of his powers of concentration? After agonizing deliberation, Baldwin decided to avoid physical confrontation in order to concentrate on writing. This was not necessarily a mark of cowardice. It was Baldwin, for instance, who wrote in 1971 in support of Professor Angela Davis, about to stand trial on capital charges in California:

> We must fight for your life as though it were our own—which it is—and render impassable with our bodies the corridor to the gas chamber. For, if they take you in the morning, they will be coming for us that night.

Although Baldwin is primarily regarded as an essayist and novelist, his short stories, frequently anthologized, also have tremendous appeal. "Sonny's Blues" (1957) is typical of his work in that it approaches a commonplace subject from a complex perspective. The story begins with the arrest of Sonny, a young black musician, for possession of narcotics, followed by his release from jail to rejoin his peers. The perspective from which Sonny's story is told is the mind of his older brother, who has resisted Sonny's social and artistic world, opting instead for the relative security of a teaching position. In a series of brief dramatic scenes, we see a friend of Sonny's confront the brother about Sonny's chances for rehabilitation and his need for love; Sonny himself, just out of prison and unsure of his next move; and the older brother's tangled memories of his evasions of Sonny and his resistance to connections with Sonny's world. In the final scene, the brother accepts Sonny's invitation to see him perform with his friends in a downtown club. Returning to the piano after a year in prison, Sonny triumphs; the drink his brother has bought him shines like a halo on the piano top above his head.

Baldwin treats Sonny's fragile victory with understanding and skill, but his interest lies as much in examining the role of the older brother, who must come to terms with the distance he has put between himself and Sonny. Thus Baldwin tells a double tale, part linear and exterior (Sonny's fate) and part circular and interior (the hidden fate of the older brother). In his doubleness, his introspection, and his sense of our inability to fully comprehend or control our fate, Baldwin acknowledges his debt to Freud and the French existentialists as much as to the African-American experience. He is a moralist poised between two worlds, those of Europe and his own culture. Like Algerian-born French writer Albert Camus, Baldwin makes the ambiguity of his personal circumstances the natural subject of his work.

SUGGESTED READINGS

Much has been written about Baldwin, but it is too soon to expect conclusive judgments concerning this controversial writer. The reader should consult Fern M. Eckman's *The Furious Passage of James Baldwin* (1966), L. H. Pratt's *James Baldwin* (1978), and C. W. Sylvander's *James Baldwin* (1980). For key texts relating to Baldwin controversies, see his article "Richard Wright," *Encounter* 16 (April 1961), pp. 58–60, reprinted as the chapter "The Exile" in *Nobody Knows My Name* (1961), and Eldridge Cleaver's "Notes of a Native Son" in *Soul on Ice* (1968), pp. 97–111. Collections of criticism about Baldwin include Kenneth Kinnamon's *James Baldwin: A Collection of Critical Essays* (1974) and Harold J. Bloom's *Modern Critical Views: James Baldwin* (1986).

Sonny's Blues

I read about it in the paper, in the subway, on my way to work. I read it, and I couldn't believe it, and I read it again. Then perhaps I just stared at it, at the newsprint spelling out his name, spelling out the story. I stared at it in the swinging lights of the subway car, and in the faces and bodies of the people, and in my own face, trapped in the darkness which roared outside.

It was not to be believed and I kept telling myself that, as I walked from the subway station to the high school. And at the same time I couldn't doubt it. I was scared, scared for Sonny. He became real to me again. A great block of ice got settled in my belly and kept melting there slowly all day long, while I taught my classes algebra. It was a special kind of ice. It kept melting, sending trickles of ice water all up and down my veins, but it never got less. Sometimes it hardened and seemed to expand until I felt my guts were going to come spilling out or that I was going to choke or scream. This would always be at a moment when I was remembering some specific thing Sonny had once said or done.

When he was about as old as the boys in my classes his face had been bright and open, there was a lot of copper in it; and he'd had wonderfully direct brown eyes, and great gentleness and privacy. I wondered what he looked like now. He had been picked up, the evening before, in a raid on an apartment downtown, for peddling and using heroin.

I couldn't believe it: but what I mean by that is that I couldn't find any room for it anywhere inside me. I had kept it outside me for a long time. I hadn't wanted to know. I had had suspicions, but I didn't name them, I kept putting them away. I told myself that Sonny was wild, but he wasn't crazy. And he'd always been a good boy, he hadn't ever turned hard or evil or disrespectful, the way kids can, so quick, so quick, especially in Harlem. I didn't want to believe that I'd ever see my brother going down, coming to nothing, all that light in his face gone out, in the condition I'd already seen so many others. Yet it had happened and here I was, talking about algebra to a lot of boys who might, every one of them for all I knew, be popping off needles every time they went to the head. Maybe it did more for them than algebra could.

I was sure that the first time Sonny had ever had horse, he couldn't have been much older than these boys were now. These boys, now, were living as we'd been living then, they were growing up with a rush and their heads bumped abruptly against the low ceiling of their actual possibilities. They were filled with rage. All they really knew were two darknesses, the darkness of their lives, which was now closing in on them, and the darkness of the movies, which had blinded them to that other darkness, and in which they now, vindictively, dreamed, at once more together than they were at any other time, and more alone.

When the last bell rang, the last class ended, I let out my breath. It seemed I'd been holding it for all that time. My clothes were wet—I may have looked as though I'd been sitting in a steam bath, all dressed up, all afternoon. I sat alone in the classroom a long time. I listened to the boys outside, downstairs, shouting and cursing and laughing. Their laughter struck me for perhaps the first time. It was not the joyous laughter which—God knows why—one associates with children. It was mocking and insular, its intent was to denigrate. It was disenchanted, and in this, also, lay the authority of their curses. Perhaps I was listening to them because I was thinking about my brother and in them I heard my brother. And myself.

One boy was whistling a tune, at once very complicated and very simple, it seemed to be pouring out of him as though he were a bird, and it sounded very cool and moving through all that harsh, bright air, only just holding its own through all those other sounds.

I stood up and walked over to the window and looked down into the courtyard. It was the beginning of the spring and the sap was rising in the boys. A teacher passed through them every now and again, quickly, as though he or she couldn't wait to get out of that courtyard, to get those boys out of their sight and off their minds. I started collecting my stuff. I thought I'd better get home and talk to Isabel.

The courtyard was almost deserted by the time I got downstairs. I saw this boy standing in the shadow of a doorway, looking just like Sonny. I almost called his name. Then I saw that it wasn't Sonny, but somebody we used to know, a boy from around our block. He'd been Sonny's friend. He'd never been mine, having been too young for me, and, anyway, I'd never liked him. And now, even though he was a grown-up man, he still hung around that block, still spent hours on the street corners, was always high and raggy. I used to run into him from time to time and he'd often work around to asking me for a quarter or fifty cents. He always had some real good excuse, too, and I always gave it to him, I don't know why.

But now, abruptly, I hated him. I couldn't stand the way he looked at me, partly like a dog, partly like a cunning child. I wanted to ask him what the hell he was doing in the school courtyard.

He sort of shuffled over to me, and he said, "I see you got the papers. So you already know about it."

"You mean about Sonny? Yes, I already know about it. How come they didn't get you?"

He grinned. It made him repulsive and it also brought to mind what he'd looked like as a kid. "I wasn't there. I stay away from them people."

"Good for you." I offered him a cigarette and I watched him through the smoke. "You come all the way down here just to tell me about Sonny?"

"That's right." He was sort of shaking his head and his eyes looked strange, as though they were about to cross. The bright sun deadened his damp dark brown skin and it made his eyes look yellow and showed up the dirt in his kinked hair. He smelled funky. I moved a little away from him and I said, "Well, thanks. But I already know about it and I got to get home."

"I'll walk you a little ways," he said. We started walking. There were a couple of kids still loitering in the courtyard and one of them said goodnight to me and looked strangely at the boy beside me.

"What're you going to do?" he asked me. "I mean, about Sonny?"

"Look. I haven't seen Sonny for over a year, I'm not sure I'm going to do anything. Anyway, what the hell *can* I do?"

"That's right," he said quickly, "ain't nothing you can do. Can't much help old Sonny no more, I guess."

It was what I was thinking and so it seemed to me he had no right to say it.

"I'm surprised at Sonny, though," he went on—he had a funny way of talking, he looked straight ahead as though he were talking to himself—"I thought Sonny was a smart boy, I thought he was too smart to get hung."

"I guess he thought so too," I said sharply, "and that's how he got hung. And how about you? You're pretty goddamn smart, I bet."

Then he looked directly at me, just for a minute. "I ain't smart," he said. "If I was smart, I'd have reached for a pistol a long time ago."

"Look. Don't tell *me* your sad story, if it was up to me, I'd give you one." Then I felt guilty—guilty, probably, for never having supposed that the poor bastard *had* a story of his own, much less a sad one, and I asked, quickly, "What's going to happen to him now?"

He didn't answer this. He was off by himself some place. "Funny thing," he said, and from his tone we might have been discussing the quickest way to get to Brooklyn, "when I saw the papers this morning, the first thing I asked myself was if I had anything to do with it. I felt sort of responsible."

I began to listen more carefully. The subway station was on the corner, just before us, and I stopped. He stopped, too. We were in front of a bar and he ducked slightly, peering in, but whoever he was looking for didn't seem to be there. The juke box was blasting away with something black and bouncy and I half watched the *music* barmaid as she danced her way from the juke box to her place behind the bar. And I watched her face as she laughingly responded to something someone said to her, still keeping time to the music. When she smiled one saw the little girl, one sensed the doomed, still-struggling woman beneath the battered face of the semi-whore.

"I never *give* Sonny nothing," the boy said finally, "but a long time ago I come to school high and Sonny asked me how it felt." He paused, I couldn't bear to watch him, I watched the barmaid, and I listened to the music which seemed to be causing the pavement to shake. "I told him it felt great." The music stopped, the barmaid paused and watched the juke box until the music began again. "It did."

All this was carrying me some place I didn't want to go. I certainly didn't want to know how it felt. It filled everything, the people, the houses, the music, the dark, quicksilver barmaid, with menace; and this menace was their reality.

"What's going to happen to him now?" I asked again.

"They'll send him away some place and they'll try to cure him." He shook his head. "Maybe he'll even think he's kicked the habit. Then they'll let him loose"—he gestured, throwing his cigarette into the gutter. "That's all."

"What do you mean, *that's all?*"

But I knew what he meant.

"I *mean,* that's *all.*" He turned his head and looked at me, pulling down the corners of his mouth. "Don't you know what I mean?" he asked, softly.

"How the hell *would* I know what you mean?" I almost whispered it, I don't know why.

"That's right," he said to the air, "how would *he* know what I mean?" He turned toward me again, patient and calm, and yet I somehow felt him shaking, shaking as though he were going to fall apart. I felt that ice in my guts again, the dread I'd felt all afternoon; and again I watched the barmaid, moving about the bar, washing glasses, and singing. "Listen. They'll let him out and then it'll just start all over again. That's what I mean."

"You mean—they'll let him out. And then he'll just start working his way back in again. You mean he'll never kick the habit. Is that what you mean?"

"That's right," he said, cheerfully. "*You* see what I mean."

"Tell me," I said at last, "why does he want to die? He must want to die, he's killing himself, why does he want to die?"

He looked at me in surprise. He licked his lips. "He don't want to die. He wants to live. Don't nobody want to die, ever."

Then I wanted to ask him—too many things. He could not have answered, or if he had, I could not have borne the answers. I started walking. "Well, I guess it's none of my business."

"It's going to be rough on old Sonny," he said. We reached the subway station. "This is your station?" he asked. I nodded. I took one step down. "Damn!" he said, *red* suddenly. I looked up at him. He grinned again. "Damn it if I didn't leave all my money home. You ain't got a dollar on you, have you? Just for a couple of days, is all."

All at once something inside gave and threatened to come pouring out of me. I didn't hate him any more. I felt that in another moment I'd start crying like a child.

"Sure," I said. "Don't sweat." I looked in my wallet and didn't have a dollar, I only had a five. "Here," I said. "That hold you?"

He didn't look at it—he didn't want to look at it. A terrible, closed look came over his face, as though he were keeping the number on the bill a secret from him and me. "Thanks," he said, and now he was dying to see me go. "Don't worry about Sonny. Maybe I'll write him or something."

"Sure," I said. "You do that. So long."

"Be seeing you," he said. I went on down the steps.

And I didn't write Sonny or send him anything for a long time. When I finally did, it was just after my little girl died, he wrote me back a letter which made me feel like a bastard.

Here's what he said:

Dear brother,

You don't know how much I needed to hear from you. I wanted to write you many a time but I dug how much I must have hurt you and so I didn't write. But now I feel like a man who's been trying to climb up out of some deep, real deep and funky hole and just saw the sun up there, outside. I got to get outside.

I can't tell you much about how I got here. I mean I don't know how to tell you. I guess I was afraid of something or I was trying to escape from something and you know I have never been very strong in the head (smile). I'm glad Mama and Daddy are dead and can't see what's happened to their son and I swear if I'd known what I was doing I would never have hurt you so, you and a lot of other fine people who were nice to me and who believed in me.

I don't want you to think it had anything to do with me being a musician. It's more than that. Or maybe less than that. I can't get anything straight in my head down here and I try not to think about what's going to happen to me when I get outside again. Sometime I think I'm going to flip and *never* get outside and sometime I think I'll come straight back. I tell you one thing, though, I'd rather blow my brains out than go through this again. But that's what they all say, so they tell me. If I tell you when I'm coming to New York and if you could meet me, I sure would appreciate it. Give my love to Isabel and the kids and I was sure sorry to hear about little Gracie. I wish I could be like Mama and say the Lord's will be done, but I don't know it seems to me that trouble is the one thing that never does get stopped and I don't know what good it does to blame it on the Lord. But maybe it does some good if you believe it.

Your brother,
Sonny

Then I kept in constant touch with him and I sent him whatever I could and I went to meet him when he came back to New York. When I saw him many things I thought I had forgotten came flooding back to me. This was because I had begun, finally, to wonder about Sonny, about the life that Sonny lived inside. This life, whatever it was, had made him older and thinner and it had deepened the distant stillness in which he had always moved. He looked very unlike my baby brother. Yet, when he smiled, when we shook hands, the baby brother I'd never known looked out from the depths of his private life, like an animal waiting to be coaxed into the light.

"How you been keeping?" he asked me.

"All right. And you?"

"Just fine." He was smiling all over his face. "It's good to see you again."

"It's good to see you."

The seven years' difference in our ages lay between us like a chasm: I wondered if these years would ever operate between us as a bridge. I was remembering, and it made it hard to catch my breath, that I had been there when he was born; and I had heard the first words he had ever spoken. When he started to walk, he walked from our mother straight to me. I caught him just before he fell when he took the first steps he ever took in this world.

"How's Isabel?"

"Just fine. She's dying to see you."

"And the boys?"

"They're fine, too. They're anxious to see their uncle."

"Oh, come on. You know they don't remember me."

"Are you kidding? Of course they remember you."

He grinned again. We got into a taxi. We had a lot to say to each other, far too much to know how to begin.

As the taxi began to move, I asked, "You still want to go to India?"

He laughed. "You still remember that. Hell, no. This place is Indian enough for me."

"It used to belong to them," I said.

And he laughed again. "They damn sure knew what they were doing when they got rid of it."

Years ago, when he was around fourteen, he'd been all hipped on the idea of going to India. He read books about people sitting on rocks, naked, in all kinds of weather, but mostly bad, naturally, and walking barefoot through hot coals and arriving at wisdom. I used to say that it sounded to me as though they were getting away from wisdom as fast as they could. I think he sort of looked down on me for that.

"Do you mind," he asked, "if we have the driver drive alongside the park? On the west side—I haven't seen the city in so long."

"Of course not," I said. I was afraid that I might sound as though I were humoring him, but I hoped he wouldn't take it that way.

So we drove along, between the green of the park and the stony, lifeless elegance of hotels and apartment buildings, toward the vivid, killing streets of our childhood. These streets hadn't changed, though housing projects jutted up out of them now like rocks in the middle of a boiling sea. Most of the houses in which we had grown up had vanished, as had the stores from which we had stolen, the basements in which we had first tried sex, the rooftops from which we had hurled tin cans and bricks. But houses exactly like the houses of our past yet dominated the landscape, boys exactly like the boys we once had been found themselves smothering in these houses, came down into the streets for light and air and found themselves encircled by disaster. Some escaped the trap, most didn't. Those who got out always left something of themselves behind, as some animals amputate a leg and leave it in the trap. It might be said, perhaps, that I had escaped, after all, I was a school teacher; or that Sonny had, he hadn't lived in Harlem for years. Yet, as the cab moved uptown through streets which seemed, with a rush, to darken with dark people, and as I covertly studied Sonny's face, it came to me that what we both were seeking through our separate cab windows was that part of ourselves which had been left behind. It's always at the hour of trouble and confrontation that the missing member aches.

We hit 110th Street and started rolling up Lenox Avenue. And I'd known this avenue all my life, but it seemed to me again, as it had seemed on the day I'd first heard about Sonny's trouble, filled with a hidden menace which was its very breath of life.

"We almost there," said Sonny.

"Almost." We were both too nervous to say anything more.

We live in a housing project. It hasn't been up long. A few days after it was up it seemed uninhabitably new, now, of course, it's already rundown. It looks like a parody of the good, clean, faceless life—God knows the people who live in it do their best to make it a parody. The beat-looking grass lying around isn't enough to make their lives green, the hedges will never hold out the streets, and they know it. The big windows fool no one, they aren't big enough to make space out of no space. They don't bother with the windows, they watch the TV screen instead. The playground is most popular with the children who don't play at jacks, or skip rope, or roller skate, or swing, and they can be found in it after dark. We moved in partly because it's not too far from where I teach, and partly for the kids; but it's really just like the houses in which Sonny and I grew up. The same things happen, they'll have the same things to remember. The moment Sonny and I started into the house I had the feeling that I was simply bringing him back into the danger he had almost died trying to escape.

Sonny has never been talkative. So I don't know why I was sure he'd be dying to talk to me when supper was over the first night. Everything went fine, the oldest boy remembered him, and the youngest boy liked him, and Sonny had remembered to bring something for each of them; and Isabel, who is really much nicer than I am, more open and giving, had gone to a lot of trouble about dinner and was genuinely glad to see him. And she's always been able to tease Sonny in a way that I haven't. It was nice to see her face so vivid again and to hear her laugh and watch her make Sonny laugh. She wasn't, or, anyway, she didn't seem to be, at all uneasy or embarrassed. She chatted as though there were no subject which had to be avoided and she got Sonny past his first, faint stiffness. And thank God she was there, for I was filled with that icy dread again. Everything I did seemed awkward to me, and everything I said sounded freighted with hidden meaning. I was trying to remember everything I'd heard about dope addiction and I couldn't help watching Sonny for signs. I wasn't doing it out of malice. I was trying to find out something about my brother. I was dying to hear him tell me he was safe.

"Safe!" my father grunted, whenever Mama suggested trying to move to a neighborhood which might be safer for children. "Safe, hell! Ain't no place safe for kids, nor nobody."

He always went on like this, but he wasn't, ever, really as bad as he sounded, not even on weekends, when he got drunk. As a matter of fact, he was always on the lookout for "something a little better," but he died before he found it. He died suddenly, during a drunken weekend in the middle of the war, when Sonny was fifteen. He and Sonny hadn't ever got on too well. And this was partly because Sonny was the apple of his father's eye. It was because he loved Sonny so much and was frightened for him, that he was always fighting with him. It doesn't do any good to fight with Sonny. Sonny just moves back, inside himself, where he can't be reached. But the principal reason that they never hit it off is that they were so much alike. Daddy was big and rough and loud-talking, just the opposite of Sonny, but they both had—that same privacy.

Mama tried to tell me something about this, just after Daddy died. I was home on leave from the army.

This was the last time I ever saw my mother alive. Just the same, this picture gets all mixed up in my mind with pictures I had of her when she was younger. The way I always see her is the way she used to be on a Sunday afternoon, say, when the old folks were talking after the big Sunday dinner. I always see her wearing pale blue. She'd be sitting on the sofa. And my father would be sitting in the easy chair, not far from her. And the living room would be full of church folks and relatives. There they sit, in chairs all around the living room, and the night is creeping up outside, but nobody knows it yet. You can see the darkness growing against the windowpanes and you hear the street noises every now and again, or maybe the jangling beat of a tambourine from one of the churches close by, but it's real quiet in the room. For a moment nobody's talking, but every face looks darkening, like the sky outside. And my mother rocks a little from the waist, and my father's eyes are closed. Everyone is looking at something a child can't see. For a minute they've forgotten the children. Maybe a kid is lying on the rug, half asleep. Maybe somebody's got a kid in his lap and is absent-mindedly stroking the kid's head. Maybe there's a kid, quiet and big-eyed, curled up in a big chair in the corner. The silence, the darkness coming, and the darkness in the faces frightens the child obscurely. He hopes that the hand which strokes his forehead will never stop—will never die. He hopes that there will never come a time when the old folks won't be sitting around the living room, talking about where they've come from, and what they've seen, and what's happened to them and their kinfolk.

But something deep and watchful in the child knows that this is bound to end, is already ending. In a moment someone will get up and turn on the light. Then the old folks will remember the children and they won't talk any more that day. And when light fills the room, the child is filled with darkness. He knows that every time this happens he's moved just a little closer to that darkness outside. The darkness outside is what the old folks have been talking about. It's what they've come from. It's what they endure. The child knows that they won't talk any more because if he knows too much about what's happened to *them,* he'll know too much too soon, about what's going to happen to *him.*

The last time I talked to my mother, I remember I was restless. I wanted to get out and see Isabel. We weren't married then and we had a lot to straighten out between us.

There Mama sat, in black, by the window. She was humming an old church song, *Lord, you brought me from a long ways off.* Sonny was out somewhere. Mama kept watching the streets.

"I don't know," she said, "if I'll ever see you again, after you go off from here. But I hope you'll remember the things I tried to teach you."

"Don't talk like that," I said, and smiled. "You'll be here a long time yet."

She smiled, too, but she said nothing. She was quiet for a long time. And I said, "Mama, don't you worry about nothing. I'll be writing all the time, and you be getting the checks. . . ."

"I want to talk to you about your brother," she said, suddenly. "If anything happens to me he ain't going to have nobody to look out for him."

"Mama," I said, "ain't nothing going to happen to you *or* Sonny. Sonny's all right. He's a good boy and he's got good sense."

"It ain't a question of his being a good boy," Mama said, "nor of his having good sense. It ain't only the bad ones, nor yet the dumb ones that gets sucked under." She stopped, looking at me. "Your Daddy once had a brother," she said, and she smiled in a way that made me feel she was in pain. "You didn't never know that, did you?"

"No," I said, "I never knew that," and I watched her face.

"Oh, yes," she said, "your Daddy had a brother." She looked out of the window again. "I know you never saw your Daddy cry. But I did—many a time, through all these years."

I asked her, "What happened to his brother? How come nobody's ever talked about him?"

This was the first time I ever saw my mother look old.

"His brother got killed," she said, "when he was just a little younger than you are now. I knew him. He was a fine boy. He was maybe a little full of the devil, but he didn't mean nobody no harm."

Then she stopped and the room was silent, exactly as it had sometimes been on those Sunday afternoons. Mama kept looking out into the streets.

"He used to have a job in the mill," she said, "and, like all young folks, he just liked to perform on Saturday nights. Saturday nights, him and your father would drift around to different places, go to dances and things like that, or just sit around with people they knew, and your father's brother would sing, he had a fine voice, and play along with himself on his guitar. Well, this particular Saturday night, him and your father was coming home from some place, and they were both a little drunk and there was a moon that night, it was bright like day. Your father's brother was feeling kind of good, and he was whistling to himself, and he had his guitar slung over his shoulder. They was coming down a hill and beneath them was a road that turned off from the highway. Well, your father's brother, being always kind of frisky, decided to run down this hill, and he did, with that guitar banging and clanging behind him, and he ran across the road, and he was making water behind a tree. And your father was sort of amused at him and he was still coming down the hill, kind of slow. Then he heard a car motor and that same minute his brother stepped from behind the tree, into the road, in the moonlight. And he started to cross the road. And your father started to run down the hill, he says he don't know why. This car was full of white men. They was all drunk, and when they seen your father's brother they let out a great whoop and holler and they aimed the car straight at him. They was having fun, they just wanted to scare him, the way they do sometimes, you know. But they was drunk. And I guess the boy, being drunk, too, and scared, kind of lost his head. By the time he jumped it was too late. Your father says he heard his brother scream when the car rolled over him, and he heard the wood of that guitar when it give, and he heard them strings go flying, and he heard them white men shouting, and the car kept on a-going and it ain't stopped till this day. And, time your father got down the hill, his brother weren't nothing but blood and pulp."

Tears were gleaming on my mother's face. There wasn't anything I could say.

"He never mentioned it," she said, "because I never let him mention it before you children. Your Daddy was like a crazy man that night and for many a night thereafter. He says he never in his life seen anything as dark as that road after the lights of that car had gone away. Weren't nothing, weren't nobody on that road, just your Daddy and his brother and that busted guitar. Oh, yes. Your Daddy never did really get right again. Till the day he died he weren't sure but that every white man he saw was the man that killed his brother."

She stopped and took out her handkerchief and dried her eyes and looked at me.

"I ain't telling you all this," she said, "to make you scared or bitter or to make you hate nobody. I'm telling you this because you got a brother. And the world ain't changed."

I guess I didn't want to believe this. I guess she saw this in my face. She turned away from me, toward the window again, searching those streets.

"But I praise my Redeemer," she said at last, "that He called your Daddy home before me. I ain't saying it to throw no flowers at myself, but, I declare, it keeps me from feeling too cast down to know I helped your father get safely through this world. Your father always acted like he was the roughest, strongest man on earth. And everybody took him to be like that. But if he hadn't had *me* there—to see his tears!"

She was crying again. Still, I couldn't move. I said, "Lord, Lord, Mama, I didn't know it was like that."

"Oh, honey," she said, "there's a lot that you don't know. But you are going to find it out." She stood up from the window and came over to me. "You got to hold on to your brother," she said, "and don't let him fall, no matter what it looks like is happening to him and no matter how evil you gets with him. You going to be evil with him many a time. But don't you forget what I told you, you hear?"

"I won't forget," I said. "Don't you worry, I won't forget. I won't let nothing happen to Sonny."

My mother smiled as though she were amused at something she saw in my face. Then, "You may not be able to stop nothing from happening. But you got to let him know you's *there*."

Two days later I was married, and then I was gone. And I had a lot of things on my mind and I pretty well forgot my promise to Mama until I got shipped home on a special furlough for her funeral.

And, after the funeral, with just Sonny and me alone in the empty kitchen, I tried to find out something about him.

"What do you want to do?" I asked him.

"I'm going to be a musician," he said.

For he had graduated, in the time I had been away, from dancing to the juke box to finding out who was playing what, and what they were doing with it, and he had bought himself a set of drums.

"You mean, you want to be a drummer?" I somehow had the feeling that being a drummer might be all right for other people but not for my brother Sonny.

"I don't think," he said, looking at me very gravely, "that I'll ever be a good drummer. But I think I can play a piano."

I frowned. I'd never played the role of the older brother quite so seriously before, had scarcely ever, in fact, *asked* Sonny a damn thing. I sensed myself in the presence of something I didn't really know how to handle, didn't understand. So I made my frown a little deeper as I asked: "What kind of musician do you want to be?"

He grinned. "How many kinds do you think there are?"

"Be *serious*," I said.

He laughed, throwing his head back, and then looked at me. "I *am* serious."

"Well, then, for Christ's sake, stop kidding around and answer a serious question. I mean, do you want to be a concert pianist, you want to play classical music and all that, or—or what?" Long before I finished he was laughing again. "For Christ's *sake*, Sonny!"

He sobered, but with difficulty. "I'm sorry. But you sound so—*scared!*" and he was off again.

"Well, you may think it's funny now, baby, but it's not going to be so funny when you have to make your living at it, let me tell you *that*." I was furious because I knew he was laughing at me and I didn't know why.

"No," he said, very sober now, and afraid, perhaps, that he'd hurt me, "I don't want to be a classical pianist. That isn't what interests me. I mean"—he paused, looking hard at me, as though his eyes would help me to understand, and then gestured helplessly, as though perhaps his hand would help—"I mean, I'll have a lot of studying to do, and I'll have to study *everything*, but, I mean, I want to play *with*—jazz musicians." He stopped. "I want to play jazz," he said.

Well, the word had never before sounded as heavy, as real, as it sounded that afternoon in Sonny's mouth. I just looked at him and I was probably frowning a real frown by this time. I simply couldn't see why on earth he'd want to spend his time hanging around nightclubs, clowning around on bandstands, while people pushed each other around a dance floor. It seemed—beneath him, somehow. I had never thought about it before, had never been forced to, but I suppose I had always put jazz musicians in a class with what Daddy called "good-time people."

"Are you *serious*?"

"Hell, *yes,* I'm serious."

He looked more helpless than ever, and annoyed, and deeply hurt.

I suggested, helpfully: "You mean—like Louis Armstrong?"

His face closed as though I'd struck him. "No. I'm not talking about none of that old-time, down home crap."

"Well, look, Sonny, I'm sorry, don't get mad. I just don't altogether get it, that's all. Name somebody—you know, a jazz musician you admire."

"Bird."

"Who?"

"Bird! Charlie Parker! Don't they teach you nothing in the goddamn army?"

I lit a cigarette. I was surprised and then a little amused to discover that I was trembling. "I've been out of touch," I said. "You'll have to be patient with me. Now. Who's this Parker character?"

"He's just one of the greatest jazz musicians alive," said Sonny, sullenly, his hands in his pockets, his back to me. "Maybe *the* greatest," he added, bitterly, "that's probably why *you* never heard of him."

"All right," I said, "I'm ignorant. I'm sorry. I'll go out and buy all the cat's records right away, all right?"

"It don't," said Sonny, with dignity, "make any difference to me. I don't care what you listen to. Don't do me no favors."

I was beginning to realize that I'd never seen him so upset before. With another part of my mind I was thinking that this would probably turn out to be one of those things kids go through and that I shouldn't make it seem important by pushing it too hard. Still, I didn't think it would do any harm to ask: "Doesn't all this take a lot of time? Can you make a living at it?"

He turned back to me and half leaned, half sat, on the kitchen table. "Everything takes time," he said, "and—well, yes, sure, I can make a living at it. But what I don't seem to be able to make you understand is that it's the only thing I want to do."

"Well, Sonny," I said, gently, "you know people can't always do exactly what they *want* to do—"

"*No*, I don't know that," said Sonny, surprising me. "I think people *ought* to do what they want to do, what else are they alive for?"

"You getting to be a big boy," I said desperately, "it's time you started thinking about your future."

"I'm thinking about my future," said Sonny, grimly. "I think about it all the time."

I gave up. I decided, if he didn't change his mind, that we could always talk about it later. "In the meantime," I said, "you got to finish school." We had already decided that he'd have to move in with Isabel and her folks. I knew this wasn't the ideal arrangement because Isabel's folks are inclined to be dicty[1] and they hadn't especially wanted Isabel to marry me. But I didn't know what else to do. "And we have to get you fixed up at Isabel's."

There was a long silence. He moved from the kitchen table to the window. "That's a terrible idea. You know it yourself."

"Do you have a *better* idea?"

He just walked up and down the kitchen for a minute. He was as tall as I was. He had started to shave. I suddenly had the feeling that I didn't know him at all.

He stopped at the kitchen table and picked up my cigarettes. Looking at me with a kind of mocking, amused defiance, he put one between his lips. "You mind?"

"You smoking already?"

He lit the cigarette and nodded, watching me through the smoke. "I just wanted to see if I'd have the courage to smoke in front of you." He grinned and blew a great cloud of smoke to the ceiling. "It was easy." He looked at my face. "Come on, now. I bet you was smoking at my age, tell the truth."

I didn't say anything but the truth was on my face, and he laughed. But now there was something very strained in his laugh. "Sure. And I bet that ain't all you was doing."

He was frightening me a little. "Cut the crap," I said. "We already decided that you was going to go and live at Isabel's. Now what's got into you all of a sudden?"

"*You* decided it," he pointed out. "*I* didn't decide nothing." He stopped in front of me, leaning against the stove, arms loosely folded. "Look, brother. I don't want to stay in Harlem no more, I really don't." He was very earnest. He looked at me, then over toward the kitchen window. There was something in his eyes I'd never seen before, some thoughtfulness, some worry all his own. He rubbed the muscle of one arm. "It's time I was getting out of here."

"Where do you want to *go*, Sonny?"

"I want to join the army. Or the navy, I don't care. If I say I'm old enough, they'll believe me."

Then I got mad. It was because I was so scared. "You must be crazy. You goddamn fool, what the hell do you want to go and join the *army* for?"

"I just told you. To get out of Harlem."

"Sonny, you haven't even finished *school*. And if you really want to be a musician, how do you expect to study if you're in the *army?*"

He looked at me, trapped, and in anguish. "There's ways. I might be able to work out some kind of deal. Anyway, I'll have the G.I. Bill when I come out."

"*If* you come out." We stared at each other. "Sonny, please. Be reasonable. I know the setup is far from perfect. But we got to do the best we can."

"I ain't learning nothing in school," he said. "Even when I go." He turned away from me and opened the window and threw his cigarette out into the narrow alley. I watched his back. "At least, I ain't learning nothing you'd want me to learn." He slammed the window so hard I thought the glass would fly out, and turned back to me. "And I'm sick of the stink of these garbage cans!"

"Sonny," I said, "I know how you feel. But if you don't finish school now, you're going to be sorry later that you didn't." I grabbed him by the shoulders. "And you only got another year. It ain't so bad. And I'll come back and I swear I'll help you do *whatever* you want to do. Just try to put up with it till I come back. Will you please do that? For me?"

[1]Snobbish or bossy.

He didn't answer and he wouldn't look at me.

"Sonny. You hear me?"

He pulled away. "I hear you. But you never hear anything *I* say."

I didn't know what to say to that. He looked out of the window and then back at me. "OK," he said, and sighed. "I'll try."

Then I said, trying to cheer him up a little, "They got a piano at Isabel's. You can practice on it."

And as a matter of fact, it did cheer him up for a minute. "That's right," he said to himself. "I forgot that." His face relaxed a little. But the worry, the thoughtfulness, played on it still, the way shadows play on a face which is staring into the fire.

But I thought I'd never hear the end of that piano. At first, Isabel would write me, saying how nice it was that Sonny was so serious about his music and how, as soon as he came in from school, or wherever he had been when he was supposed to be at school, he went straight to that piano and stayed there until suppertime. And, after supper, he went back to that piano and stayed there until everybody went to bed. He was at the piano all day Saturday and all day Sunday. Then he bought a record player and started playing records. He'd play one record over and over again, all day long sometimes, and he'd improvise along with it on the piano. Or he'd play one section of the record, one chord, one change, one progression, then he'd do it on the piano. Then back to the record. Then back to the piano.

Well, I really don't know how they stood it. Isabel finally confessed that it wasn't like living with a person at all, it was like living with sound. And the sound didn't make any sense to her, didn't make any sense to any of them—naturally. They began, in a way, to be afflicted by this presence that was living in their home. It was as though Sonny were some sort of god, or monster. He moved in an atmosphere which wasn't like theirs at all. They fed him and he ate, he washed himself, he walked in and out of their door; he certainly wasn't nasty or unpleasant or rude, Sonny isn't any of those things; but it was as though he were all wrapped up in some cloud, some fire, some vision all his own; and there wasn't any way to reach him.

At the same time, he wasn't really a man yet, he was still a child, and they had to watch out for him in all kinds of ways. They certainly couldn't throw him out. Neither did they dare to make a great scene about that piano because even they dimly sensed, as I sensed, from so many thousands of miles away, that Sonny was at that piano playing for his life.

But he hadn't been going to school. One day a letter came from the school board and Isabel's mother got it—there had, apparently, been other letters but Sonny had torn them up. This day, when Sonny came in, Isabel's mother showed him the letter and asked where he'd been spending his time. And she finally got it out of him that he'd been down in Greenwich Village, with musicians and other characters, in a white girl's apartment. And this scared her and she started to scream at him and what came up, once she began—though she denies it to this day—was what sacrifices they were making to give Sonny a decent home and how little he appreciated it.

Sonny didn't play the piano that day. By evening, Isabel's mother had calmed down but then there was the old man to deal with, and Isabel herself. Isabel says she did her best to be calm but she broke down and started crying. She says she just watched Sonny's face. She could tell, by watching him, what was happening with him. And what was happening was that they penetrated his cloud, they had reached him. Even if their fingers had been a thousand times more gentle than human fingers ever are, he could hardly help feeling that they had stripped him naked and were spitting on that nakedness. For he also had to see that his presence, that music, which was life or death to him, had been torture for them and that they had endured it, not at all for his sake, but only for mine. And Sonny couldn't take that. He can take it a little better today than he could then but he's still not very good at it and, frankly, I don't know anybody who is.

The silence of the next few days must have been louder than the sound of all the music ever played since time began. One morning, before she went to work, Isabel was in his room for something and she suddenly realized that all of his records were gone. And she knew for certain that he was gone. And he was. He went as far as the navy would carry him. He finally sent me a postcard from some place in Greece and that was the first I knew that Sonny was still alive. I didn't see him any more until we were both back in New York and the war had long been over.

He was a man by then, of course, but I wasn't willing to see it. He came by the house from time to time, but we fought almost every time we met. I didn't like the way he carried himself, loose and dreamlike all the time, and I didn't like his friends, and his music seemed to be merely an excuse for the life he led. It sounded just that weird and disordered.

Then we had a fight, a pretty awful fight, and I didn't see him for months. By and by I looked him up, where he was living, in a furnished room in the Village, and I tried to make it up. But there were lots of other people in the room and Sonny just lay on his bed, and he wouldn't come downstairs with me, and he treated these other people as though they were his family and I weren't. So I got mad and then he got mad, and then I told him that he might just as well be dead as live the way he was living. Then he stood up and he told me not to worry about him any more in life, that he *was* dead as far as I was concerned. Then he pushed me to the door and the other people looked on as though nothing were happening, and he slammed the door behind me. I stood in the hallway, staring at the door. I heard somebody laugh in the room and then the tears came to my eyes. I started down the steps, whistling to keep from crying, I kept whistling to myself, *You going to need me, baby, one of these cold, rainy days.*

[*music*]

[*end of flashback*] I read about Sonny's trouble in the spring. Little Grace died in the fall. She was a beautiful little girl. But she only lived a little over two years. She died of polio and she suffered. She had a slight fever for a couple of days, but it didn't seem like anything and we just kept her in bed. And we would certainly have called the doctor, but the fever dropped, she seemed to be all right. So we thought it had just been a cold. Then, one day, she was up, playing, Isabel was in the kitchen fixing lunch for the two boys when they'd come in from school, and she heard Grace fall down in the living room. When you have a lot of children you don't always start running when one of them falls, unless they start screaming or something. And, this time, Grace was quiet. Yet, Isabel says that when she heard that *thump* and then that silence, something happened in her to make her afraid. And she ran to the living room and there was little Grace on the floor, all twisted up, and the reason she hadn't screamed was that she couldn't get her breath. And when she did scream, it was the worst sound, Isabel says, that she'd ever heard in all her life, and she still hears it sometimes in her dreams. Isabel will sometimes wake me up with a low, moaning, strangled sound and I have to be quick to awaken her and hold her to me and where Isabel is weeping against me seems a mortal wound.

I think I may have written Sonny the very day that little Grace was buried. I was sitting in the living room in the dark, by myself, and I suddenly thought of Sonny. My trouble made his real.

Crisis

One Saturday afternoon, when Sonny had been living with us, or, anyway, been in our house, for nearly two weeks, I found myself wandering aimlessly about the living room, drinking from a can of beer, and trying to work up the courage to search Sonny's room. He was out, he was usually out whenever I was home, and Isabel had taken the children to see their grandparents. Suddenly I was standing still in front of the living room window, watching Seventh Avenue. The idea of searching Sonny's room made me still. I scarcely dared to admit to myself what I'd be searching for. I didn't know what I'd do if I found it. Or if I didn't.

On the sidewalk across from me, near the entrance to a barbecue joint, some people were holding an old-fashioned revival meeting. The barbecue cook, wearing a dirty white apron, his conked hair[2] reddish and metallic in the pale sun, and a cigarette between his lips, stood in the doorway, watching them. Kids and older people paused in their errands and stood there, along with some older men and a couple of very tough-looking women who watched everything that happened on the avenue, as though they owned it, or were maybe owned by it. Well, they were watching this, too. The revival was being carried on by three sisters in black, and a brother. All they had were their voices and their Bibles and a tambourine. The brother was testifying and while he testified two of the sisters stood together, seeming to say, amen, and the third sister walked around with the tambourine outstretched and a couple of people dropped coins into it. Then the brother's testimony ended and the sister who had been taking up the collection dumped the coins into her palm and transferred them to the pocket of her long black robe. Then she raised both hands, striking the tambourine against the air, and then against one hand, and she started to sing. And the two other sisters and the brother joined in.

It was strange, suddenly, to watch, though I had been seeing these street meetings all my life. So, of course, had everybody else down there. Yet, they paused and watched and listened and I stood still at the window. "*Tis the old ship of Zion,*" they sang, and the sister with the tambourine kept a steady, jangling beat, "*it has rescued many a thousand!*" Not a soul under the sound of their voices was hearing this song for the first time, not one of them had been rescued. Nor had they seen much in the way of rescue work being done around them. Neither did they especially believe in the holiness of the three sisters and the brother, they knew too much about them, knew where they lived, and how. The woman with the tambourine, whose voice dominated the air, whose face was bright with joy, was divided by very little from the woman who stood watching her, a cigarette between her heavy, chapped lips, her hair a cuckoo's nest, her face scarred and swollen from many beatings, and her black eyes glittering like coal. Perhaps they both knew this, which was why, when, as rarely, they addressed each other, they addressed each other as Sister. As the singing filled the air the watching, listening faces underwent a change, the eyes focusing on something within; the music seemed to soothe a poison out of them; and time seemed, nearly, to fall away from the sullen, belligerent, battered faces, as though they were fleeing back to their first condition, while dreaming of their last. The barbecue cook half shook his head and smiled, and dropped his cigarette and disappeared into his joint. A man fumbled in his pockets for change and stood holding it in his hand impatiently, as though he had just remembered a pressing appointment further up the avenue. He looked furious. Then I saw Sonny, standing on the edge of the crowd. He was carrying a wide, flat notebook with a green cover, and it made him look, from where I was standing, almost like a

---

[2]Hair that has been straightened and coated heavily with grease.

schoolboy. The coppery sun brought out the copper in his skin, he was very faintly smiling, standing very still. Then the singing stopped, the tambourine turned into a collection plate again. The furious man dropped in his coins and vanished, so did a couple of the women, and Sonny dropped some change in the plate, looking directly at the woman with a little smile. He started across the avenue, toward the house. He has a slow, loping walk, something like the way Harlem hipsters walk, only he's imposed on this his own half-beat. I had never really noticed it before.

I stayed at the window, both relieved and apprehensive. As Sonny disappeared from my sight, they began singing again. And they were still singing when his key turned in the lock.

"Hey," he said.

"Hey, yourself. You want some beer?"

"No. Well, maybe." But he came up to the window and stood beside me, looking out. "What a warm voice," he said.

They were singing *If I could only hear my mother pray again!*

"Yes," I said, "and she can sure beat that tambourine."

"But what a terrible song," he said, and laughed. He dropped his notebook on the sofa and disappeared into the kitchen. "Where's Isabel and the kids?"

"I think they went to see their grandparents. You hungry?"

"No." He came back into the living room with his can of beer. "You want to come some place with me tonight?"

I sensed, I don't know how, that I couldn't possibly say no. "Sure. Where?"

He sat down on the sofa and picked up his notebook and started leafing through it. "I'm going to sit in with some fellows in a joint in the Village."

"You mean, you're going to play, tonight?"

"That's right." He took a swallow of his beer and moved back to the window. He gave me a sidelong look. "If you can stand it."

"I'll try," I said.

He smiled to himself and we both watched as the meeting across the way broke up. The three sisters and the brother, heads bowed, were singing *God be with you till we meet again*. The faces around them were very quiet. Then the song ended. The small crowd dispersed. We watched the three women and the lone man walk slowly up the avenue.

"When she was singing before," said Sonny, abruptly, "her voice reminded me for a minute of what heroin feels like sometimes—when it's in your veins. It makes you feel sort of warm and cool at the same time. And distant. And—and sure." He sipped his beer, very deliberately not looking at me. I watched his face. "It makes you feel—in control. Sometimes you've got to have that feeling."

"Do you?" I sat down slowly in the easy chair.

"Sometimes." He went to the sofa and picked up his notebook again. "Some people do."

"In order," I asked, "to play?" And my voice was very ugly, full of contempt and anger.

"Well"—he looked at me with great, troubled eyes, as though, in fact, he hoped his eyes would tell me things he could never otherwise say—"they *think* so. And *if* they think so—!"

"And what do *you* think?" I asked.

He sat on the sofa and put his can of beer on the floor. "I don't know," he said, and I couldn't be sure if he were answering my question or pursuing his thoughts. His face didn't tell me. "It's not so much to *play*. It's to *stand* it, to be able to make it at all. On any level." He frowned and smiled: "In order to keep from shaking to pieces."

"But these friends of yours," I said, "they seem to shake themselves to pieces pretty goddamn fast."

"Maybe." He played with the notebook. And something told me that I should curb my tongue, that Sonny was doing his best to talk, that I should listen. "But of course you only know the ones that've gone to pieces. Some don't—or at least they haven't *yet* and that's just about all *any* of us can say." He paused. "And then there are some who just live, really, in hell, and they know it and they see what's happening and they go right on. I don't know." He sighed, dropped the notebook, folded his arms. "Some guys, you can tell from the way they play, they on something *all* the time. And you can see that, well, it makes something real for them. But of course," he picked up his beer from the floor and sipped it and put the can down again, "they *want* to, too, you've got to see that. Even some of them that say they don't—*some,* not all."

"And what about you?" I asked—I couldn't help it. "What about you? Do *you* want to?"

He stood up and walked to the window and remained silent for a long time. Then he sighed. "Me," he said. Then: "While I was downstairs before, on my way here, listening to that woman sing, it struck me all of a sudden how much suffering she must have had to go through—to sing like that. It's *repulsive* to think you have to suffer that much."

I said: "But there's no way not to suffer—is there, Sonny?"

"I believe not," he said and smiled, "but that's never stopped anyone from trying." He looked at me. "Has it?" I realized, with this mocking look, that there stood between us, forever, beyond the power of time or forgiveness, the fact that I had held silence—so long!—when he had needed human speech to help him. He turned back to the window. "No, there's no way not to suffer. But you try all kinds of ways to keep from drowning in it, to keep on top of it, and to make it seem—well, like *you.* Like you did something, all right, and now you're suffering for it. You know?" I said nothing. "Well you know," he said, impatiently, "why *do* people suffer? Maybe it's better to do something to give it a reason, *any* reason."

"But we just agreed," I said, "that there's no way not to suffer. Isn't it better, then, just to—take it?"

"But nobody just takes it," Sonny cried, "that's what I'm telling you! *Everybody* tries not to. You're just hung up on the *way* some people try—it's not *your* way!"

The hair on my face began to itch, my face felt wet. "That's not true," I said, "that's not true. I don't give a damn what other people do, I don't even care how they suffer. I just care how *you* suffer." And he looked at me. "Please believe me," I said, "I don't want to see you—die—trying not to suffer."

"I won't," he said, flatly, "die trying not to suffer. At least, not any faster than anybody else."

"But there's no need," I said, trying to laugh, "is there? in killing yourself."

I wanted to say more, but I couldn't. I wanted to talk about will power and how life could be—well, beautiful. I wanted to say that it was all within; but was it? or, rather, wasn't that exactly the trouble? And I wanted to promise that I would never fail him again. But it would all have sounded—empty words and lies.

So I made the promise to myself and prayed that I would keep it.

"It's terrible sometimes, inside," he said, "that's what's the trouble. You walk these streets, black and funky and cold, and there's not really a living ass to talk to, and there's nothing shaking, and there's no way of getting it out—that storm inside. You can't talk it and you can't make love with it, and when you finally try to get with it and play it, you realize *nobody's* listening. So *you've* got to listen. You got to find a way to listen."

And then he walked away from the window and sat on the sofa again, as though all the wind had suddenly been knocked out of him. "Sometimes you'll do *anything* to play, even cut your mother's throat." He laughed and looked at me. "Or your brother's." Then he sobered. "Or your own." Then: "Don't worry. I'm all right now and I think I'll *be* all right. But I can't forget—where I've been. I don't mean just the physical place I've been, I mean where I've *been*. And *what* I've been."

"What have you been, Sonny?" I asked.

He smiled—but sat sideways on the sofa, his elbow resting on the back, his fingers playing with his mouth and chin, not looking at me. "I've been something I didn't recognize, didn't know I could be. Didn't know anybody could be." He stopped, looking inward, looking helplessly young, looking old. "I'm not talking about it now because I feel *guilty* or anything like that—maybe it would be better if I did, I don't know. Anyway, I can't really talk about it. Not to you, not to anybody," and now he turned and faced me. "Sometimes, you know, and it was actually when I was most *out* of the world, I felt that I was in it, that I was *with* it, really, and I could play or I didn't really have to *play,* it just came out of me, it was there. And I don't know how I played, thinking about it now, but I know I did awful things, those times, sometimes, to people. Or it wasn't that I *did* anything to them—it was that they weren't real." He picked up the beer can; it was empty; he rolled it between his palms: "And other times—well, I needed a fix, I needed to find a place to lean, I needed to clear a space to *listen*—and I couldn't find it, and I—went crazy, I did terrible things to *me,* I was terrible *for* me." He began pressing the beer can between his hands, I watched the metal begin to give. It glittered, as he played with it, like a knife, and I was afraid he would cut himself, but I said nothing. "Oh well. I can never tell you. I was all by myself at the bottom of something, stinking and sweating and crying and shaking, and I smelled it, you know? *my* stink, and I thought I'd die if I couldn't get away from it and yet, all the same, I knew that everything I was doing was just locking me in with it. And I didn't know," he paused, still flattening the beer can, "I didn't know, I still *don't* know, something kept telling me that maybe it was good to smell your own stink, but I didn't think that *that* was what I'd been trying to do—and—who can stand it?" and he abruptly dropped the ruined beer can, looking at me with a small, still smile, and then rose, walking to the window as though it were the lodestone rock. I watched his face, he watched the avenue, "I couldn't tell you when Mama died—but the reason I wanted to leave Harlem so bad was to get away from drugs. And then, when I ran away, that's what I was running from—really. When I came back, nothing had changed, *I* hadn't changed, I was just—older." And he stopped, drumming with his fingers on the windowpane. The sun had vanished, soon darkness would fall. I watched his face. "It can come again," he said, almost as though speaking to himself. Then he turned to me. "It can come again," he repeated. "I just want you to know that."

"All right," I said, at last. "So it can come again. All right."

He smiled, but the smile was sorrowful. "I had to try to tell you," he said.

"Yes," I said. "I understand that."

"You're my brother," he said, looking straight at me, and not smiling at all.

"Yes," I repeated, "yes. I understand that."

He turned back to the window, looking out. "All that hatred down there," he said, "all that hatred and misery and love. It's a wonder it doesn't blow the avenue apart."

We went to the only nightclub on a short, dark street, downtown. We squeezed through the narrow, chattering, jam-packed bar to the entrance of the big room, where the bandstand was. And we stood there for a moment, for the lights were very dim in this room and we couldn't see. Then, "Hello, boy," said a voice and an enormous black man, much older than Sonny or myself, erupted out of all that atmospheric lighting and put an arm around Sonny's shoulder. "I been sitting right here," he said, "waiting for you."

He had a big voice, too, and heads in the darkness turned toward us.

Sonny grinned and pulled a little away, and said, "Creole, this is my brother. I told you about him."

Creole shook my hand. "I'm glad to meet you, son," he said, and it was clear that he was glad to meet me *there,* for Sonny's sake. And he smiled, "You got a real musician in *your* family," and he took his arm from Sonny's shoulder and slapped him, lightly, affectionately, with the back of his hand.

"Well. Now I've heard it all," said a voice behind us. This was another musician, and a friend of Sonny's, a coal-black, cheerful-looking man, built close to the ground. He immediately began confiding to me, at the top of his lungs, the most terrible things about Sonny, his teeth gleaming like a lighthouse and his laugh coming up out of him like the beginning of an earthquake. And it turned out that everyone at the bar knew Sonny, or almost everyone; some were musicians, working there, or nearby, or not working, some were simply hangers-on, and some were there to hear Sonny play. I was introduced to all of them and they were all very polite to me. Yet, it was clear that, for them, I was only Sonny's brother. Here, I was in Sonny's world. Or, rather: his kingdom. Here, it was not even a question that his veins bore royal blood.

They were going to play soon and Creole installed me, by myself, at a table in a dark corner. Then I watched them, Creole, and the little black man, and Sonny, and the others, while they horsed around, standing just below the bandstand. The light from the bandstand spilled just a little short of them and, watching them laughing and gesturing and moving about, I had the feeling that they, nevertheless, were being most careful not to step into that circle of light too suddenly: that if they moved into the light too suddenly, without thinking, they would perish in flame. Then, while I watched, one of them, the small, black man, moved into the light and crossed the bandstand and started fooling around with his drums. Then—being funny and being, also, extremely ceremonious—Creole took Sonny by the arm and led him to the piano. A woman's voice called Sonny's name and a few hands started clapping. And Sonny, also being funny and being ceremonious, and so touched, I think, that he could have cried, but neither hiding it nor showing it, riding it like a man, grinned, and put both hands to his heart and bowed from the waist.

Creole then went to the bass fiddle and a lean, very bright-skinned brown man jumped up on the bandstand and picked up his horn. So there they were, and the atmosphere on the bandstand and in the room began to change and tighten. Someone stepped up to the microphone and announced them. Then there were all kinds of murmurs. Some people at the bar shushed others. The waitress ran around, frantically getting in the last orders, guys and chicks got closer to each other, and the lights on the bandstand, on the quartet, turned to a kind of indigo. Then they all looked different there. Creole looked about him for the last time, as though he were making certain that all his chickens were in the coop, and then he—jumped and struck the fiddle. And there they were.

All I know about music is that not many people ever really hear it. And even then, on the rare occasions when something opens within, and the music enters, what we mainly hear, or hear corroborated, are personal, private, vanishing evocations. But the man who creates the music is hearing something else, is dealing with the roar rising from the void and imposing order on it as it hits the air. What is evoked in him, then, is of another order, more terrible because it has no words, and triumphant, too, for that same reason. And his triumph, when he triumphs, is ours. I just watched Sonny's face. His face was troubled, he was working hard, but he wasn't with it. And I had the feeling that, in a way, everyone on the bandstand was waiting for him, both waiting for him and pushing him along. But as I began to watch Creole, I realized that it was Creole who held them all back. He had them on a short rein. Up there, keeping the beat with his whole body, wailing on the fiddle, with his eyes half closed, he was listening to everything, but he was listening to Sonny. He was having a dialogue with Sonny. He wanted Sonny to leave the shoreline and strike out for the deep water. He was Sonny's witness that deep water and drowning were not the same thing—he had been there, and he knew. And he wanted Sonny to know. He was waiting for Sonny to do the things on the keys which would let Creole know that Sonny was in the water.

And, while Creole listened, Sonny moved, deep within, exactly like someone in torment. I had never before thought of how awful the relationship must be between the musician and his instrument. He has to fill it, this instrument, with the breath of life, his own. He has to make it do what he wants it to do. And a piano is just a piano. It's made out of so much wood and wires and little hammers and big ones, and ivory. While there's only so much you can do with it, the only way to find this out is to try; to try and make it do everything.

And Sonny hadn't been near a piano for over a year. And he wasn't on much better terms with his life, not the life that stretched before him now. He and the piano stammered, started one way, got scared, stopped; started another way, panicked, marked time, started again; then seemed to have found a direction, panicked again, got stuck. And the face I saw on Sonny I'd never seen before. Everything had been burned out of it, and, at the same time, things usually hidden were being burned in, by the fire and fury of the battle which was occurring in him up there.

Yet, watching Creole's face as they neared the end of the first set, I had the feeling that something had happened, something I hadn't heard. Then they finished, there was scattered applause, and then, without an instant's warning, Creole started into something else, it was almost sardonic, it was *Am I Blue*. And, as though he commanded, Sonny began to play. Something began to happen. And Creole let out the reins. The dry, low, black man said something awful on the drums, Creole answered, and the drums talked back. Then the horn insisted, sweet and high, slightly detached perhaps, and Creole listened, commenting now and then, dry, and driving, beautiful and calm and old. Then they all came together again, and Sonny was part of the family again. I could tell this from his face. He seemed to have found, right there beneath his fingers, a damn brand-new piano. It seemed that he couldn't get over it. Then, for awhile, just being happy with Sonny, they seemed to be agreeing with him that brand-new pianos certainly were a gas.

Then Creole stepped forward to remind them that what they were playing was the blues. He hit something in all of them, he hit something in me, myself, and the music tightened and deepened, apprehension began to beat the air. Creole began to tell us what the blues were all about. They were not about anything very new. He and his boys up there were keeping it new, at the risk of ruin, destruction, madness, and death, in order to find new ways to make us listen. For, while the tale of how we suffer, and how we are delighted, and how we may triumph is never new, it always must be heard. There isn't any other tale to tell, it's the only light we've got in all this darkness.

And this tale, according to that face, that body, those strong hands on those strings, has another aspect in every country, and a new depth in every generation. Listen, Creole seemed to be saying, listen. Now these are Sonny's blues. He made the little black man on the drums know it, and the bright, brown man on the horn. Creole wasn't trying any longer to get Sonny in the water. He was wishing him Godspeed. Then he stepped back, very slowly, filling the air with the immense suggestion that Sonny speak for himself.

Then they all gathered around Sonny and Sonny played. Every now and again one of them seemed to say, amen. Sonny's fingers filled the air with life, his life. But that life contained so many others. And Sonny went all the way back, he really began with the spare, flat statement of the opening phrase of the song. Then he began to make it his. It was very beautiful because it wasn't hurried and it was no longer a lament. I seemed to hear with what burning he had made it his, with what burning we had yet to make it ours, how we could cease lamenting. Freedom lurked around us and I understood, at last, that he could help us to be free if we would listen, that he would never be free until we did. Yet, there was no battle in his face now. I heard what he had gone through, and would continue to go through until he came to rest in earth. He had made it his: that long line, of which we knew only Mama and Daddy. And he was giving it back, as everything must be given back, so that, passing through death, it can live forever. I saw my mother's face again, and felt, for the first time, how the stones of the road she had walked on must have bruised her feet. I saw the moonlit road where my father's brother died. And it brought something else back to me, and carried me past it, I saw my little girl again and felt Isabel's tears again, and I felt my own tears begin to rise. And I was yet aware that this was only a moment, that the world waited outside, as hungry as a tiger, and that trouble stretched above us, longer than the sky.

Then it was over. Creole and Sonny let out their breath, both soaking wet, and grinning. There was a lot of applause and some of it was real. In the dark, the girl came by and I asked her to take drinks to the bandstand. There was a long pause, while they talked up there in the indigo light and after awhile I saw the girl put a Scotch and milk on top of the piano for Sonny. He didn't seem to notice it, but just before they started playing again, he sipped from it and looked toward me, and nodded. Then he put it back on top of the piano. For me, then, as they began to play again, it glowed and shook above my brother's head like the very cup of trembling.

ELIE WIESEL
[BORN 1928]

LIFE

Elie Wiesel grew up in the village of Sighet, Romania (later to become Hungary), in an area that the Jews of the village thought was a safe haven from the rancor of war that was slowly engulfing most of Europe during the late 1930s. For the first years of World War II, Sighet was outside the war zone, but in 1944 Nazis arrived in Wiesel's village, and at the age of fifteen he was forced to evacuate his home and travel with his family in cattle cars to Birkenau, the reception center for the most notorious death camp of all, Auschwitz. Separated from his mother and sisters, he was forced into a line and told by a fellow prisoner that all of them were headed for the crematory. As the terror mounted among his group, he saw a truck dump a load of babies into a ditch leaping with flames. At the last moment they were diverted away from the ditch and toward a barracks. Later when he recorded his death camp experiences in *Night,* he described the wrenching effect of the first night:

> Never shall I forget that night, the first night in camp, which has turned my life into one long night, seven times cursed and seven times sealed. Never shall I forget that smoke. Never shall I forget the little faces of the children, whose bodies I saw turned into wreaths of smoke beneath a silent blue sky.
>
> Never shall I forget those flames which consumed my faith forever.
>
> Never shall I forget that nocturnal silence which deprived me, for all eternity, of the desire to live. Never shall I forget those moments which murdered my God and my soul and turned my dreams to dust. Never shall I forget these things, even if I am condemned to live as long as God Himself. Never.

Elie Wiesel has not forgotten. With a clear and convincing voice, in essays, fiction, and lectures, he has made the Holocaust a central, defining event for the second half of the twentieth century. He has not only witnessed the indescribable horror of mass extermination, a complex of betrayals and inhumanity that most Europeans and Americans would rather forget, he has also connected the Holocaust to the ethical issues confronting the modern world. Like a modern-day Job, Elie Wiesel asks profoundly disturbing questions about God's providence and justice while probing the ethical responsibilities one person has for another, one country for another.

Elie Wiesel's father had mixed his religion with community affairs and had once been jailed for helping Jews escape the Nazis. His mother, the daughter of a Hasid, hoped that her son would be a rabbi. As a boy Elie was a devoted student and somewhat reclusive, spending ten to twelve hours a day studying the Torah, the Talmud, the mystical teachings of the Cabala, and Hasidism. After World War II and the release from Buchenwald in 1945, he went to France and continued his education there, studying philosophy, literature, and psychology at the Sorbonne. He had to cope with the fact that his father, mother, younger sister, and six million other Jews had not survived the death camps, but he had. He worked as a reporter for newspapers in France, Israel, and the United States, while imposing a ten-year vow of silence on himself before he would talk about the Holocaust.

An interview with the Nobel Prize-winning novelist François Mauriac in the mid-1950s gave Wiesel a reason for breaking his silence; Mauriac told him that he should bear witness for the millions who because of the Holocaust could not speak for themselves. Wiesel wrote *Night,* an autobiographical account of his experiences, first in Auschwitz and then in Buchenwald. In his foreword to *Night,* François Mauriac explains how the Enlightenment dream, nourished from the eighteenth century onward with the growth of science and the building of universities, had died in the trainloads of children sent by Germans into the crematory. *Night* is an act of memory, an act of carrying the enormity of the events of the Holocaust into the daylight of the present age.

WORK

Night (1960) was the first of a series of more than thirty nonfiction books, plays, and autobiographical novels that attest to Wiesel's own journey through the shadows and repercussions of the Holocaust. *Dawn* (1961) and *The Accident* (1962) complete a trilogy on the death camps; other works include *The Town Beyond the Wall* (1964), *One Generation After* (1970), and *A Jew Today* (1978).

Wiesel's *Legends of Our Time* (1982), from which our selections "The Death of My Father" and "Testament of a Jew from Saragossa" are taken, is about the importance of connecting with one's heritage or roots as a means of spiritual survival. The actual death of Elie Wiesel's father is described with heartrending directness in the last section of *Night;* the young Wiesel, powerless to change the course of his father's dying, was forced to witness the inhumanity of the doctors, the torture by other prisoners, and finally the blow by the SS officer that shattered his father's skull. The effect was devastating:

> There were no prayers at his grave. No candles were lit to his memory. His last word was my name. A summons, to which I did not respond.
> I did not weep, and it pained me that I could not weep. But I had no more tears. And, in the depths of my being, in the recesses of my weakened conscience, could I have searched it, I might perhaps have found something like—free at last!
> I had to stay at Buchenwald until April eleventh. I have nothing to say of my life during this period. It no longer mattered. After my father's death, nothing could touch me any more.

"The Death of My Father" explores the nature of God and religious ritual within the context of a father's death.

The "Testament of a Jew from Saragossa" is a poignant gem about the discovery of identity and the bond that Wiesel finds with the Spaniard whose life is transformed by the translation of a family heirloom. In this piece, Wiesel is not wrestling directly with the implications of the Holocaust, but is finding solace in ancestry and the continuity of Jewish life and culture stretching from the ancient world to the present.

Elie Wiesel's life and writings are a testimony to memory and to conscience, the responsibility of the living to those voices that were silenced by tragedy, the ethical commitment to the present that results from remembering the past. It is significant that Wiesel received the 1986 Nobel Prize for peace, not for literature; the chairman of the Norwegian Nobel Committee, Egil Aarvik, said that Wiesel was "a witness for truth and justice," a man who came from the abyss of the death camps,

> a messenger to mankind—not with a message of hate and revenge but with one of brotherhood and atonement.... In him we see a man who has gone from utter humiliation to become one of our most important spiritual leaders and guides.

SUGGESTED READINGS

A number of books examine the influence of Elie Wiesel; among them are John K. Roth's *A Consuming Fire: Encounters with Elie Wiesel and the Holocaust* (1979), Ted L. Estess's *Elie Wiesel* (1980), and Robert McAfee Brown's *Elie Wiesel: Messenger to All Humanity* (1983). His literary writings are discussed in Ellen S. Fine's *Legacy of Night: The Literary Universe of Elie Wiesel* (1982). Alvin H. Rosenfeld focuses on Wiesel's ethical teachings in *Confronting the Holocaust: The Impact of Elie Wiesel* (1978).

Legends of Our Time

THE DEATH OF MY FATHER

The anniversary of the death of a certain Shlomo ben Nissel falls on the eighteenth day of the month of *Shvat.*[1] He was my father, the day is tomorrow; and this year, as every year since the event, I do not know how to link myself to it.

---

[1] January–February.

Yet, in the *Shulchan Aruch,* the great book of precepts by Rabbi Joseph Karo, the astonishing visionary-lawmaker of the sixteenth century, precise, rigorous rules on the subject do exist. I could and should simply conform to them. Obey tradition. Follow in the footsteps. Do what everyone does on such a day: go to the synagogue three times, officiate at the service, study a chapter of *Mishna,* say the orphan's *Kaddish*[2] and, in the presence of the living community of Israel, proclaim the holiness of God as well as his greatness. For his ways are tortuous but just, his grace heavy to bear but indispensable, here on earth and beyond, today and forever. May his will be done. Amen.

This is undoubtedly what I would do had my father died of old age, of sickness, or even of despair. But such is not the case. His death did not even belong to him. I do not know to what cause to attribute it, in what book to inscribe it. No link between it and the life he had led. His death, lost among all the rest, had nothing to do with the person he had been. It could just as easily have brushed him in passing and spared him. It took him inadvertently, absent-mindedly. By mistake. Without knowing that it was he; he was robbed of his death.

Stretched out on a plank of wood amid a multitude of blood-covered corpses, fear frozen in his eyes, a mask of suffering on the bearded, stricken mask that was his face, my father gave back his soul at Buchenwald. A soul useless in that place, and one he seemed to want to give back. But, he gave it up, not to the God of his fathers, but rather to the impostor, cruel and insatiable, to the enemy God. They had killed his God, they had exchanged him for another. How, then, could I enter the sanctuary of the synagogue tomorrow and lose myself in the sacred repetition of the ritual without lying to myself, without lying to him? How could I act or think like everyone else, pretend that the death of my father holds a meaning calling for grief or indignation?

Perhaps, after all, I should go to the synagogue to praise the God of dead children, if only to provoke him by my own submission.

Tomorrow is the anniversary of the death of my father and I am seeking a new law that prescribes for me what vows to make and no longer to make, what words to say and no longer to say.

In truth, I would know what to do had my father, while alive, been deeply pious, possessed by fervor or anguish of a religious nature. I then would say: it is my duty to commemorate this date according to Jewish law and custom, for such was his wish.

But, though he observed tradition, my father was in no way fanatic. On the contrary, he preached an open spirit toward the world. He was a man of his time. He refused to sacrifice the present to an unforeseeable future, whatever it might be. He enjoyed simple everyday pleasures and did not consider his body an enemy. He rarely came home in the evening without bringing us special fruits and candies. Curious and tolerant, he frequented Hasidic circles because he admired their songs and stories, but refused to cloister his mind, as they did, within any given system.

My mother seemed more devout than he. It was she who brought me to *heder*[3] to make me a good Jew, loving only the wisdom and truth to be drawn from the Torah. And it was she who sent me as often as possible to the Rebbe of Wizsnitz to ask his blessing or simply to expose me to his radiance.

---

[2] *Mishna,* "The Teaching": a digest of oral law recorded by Rabbi Judah in the second century c.e.; it became the core of the Talmud. *Kaddish,* "holy" (Aramaic): an ancient prayer recited publicly at the death of parents and other immediate family members for the first eleven months and on the anniversaries of their deaths.

[3] The schoolroom.

My father's ambition was to make a man of me rather than a saint. "Your duty is to fight solitude, not to cultivate or glorify it," he used to tell me. And he would add: "God, perhaps, has need of saints; as for men, they can do without them."

He could be found more often in government offices than in the synagogue—and, sometimes, in periods of danger, even more often than at home. Every misfortune that befell our community involved him directly. There was always an impoverished, sick man who had to be sent in an emergency to a clinic in Kolozsvar or Budapest; an unfortunate shopkeeper who had to be bailed out of prison; a desperate refugee who had to be saved. Many survivors of the Polish ghettos owed their lives to him. Furnished with money and forged papers, thanks to him and his friends, they were able to flee the country for Rumania and from there to the United States or Palestine. His activities cost him three months in a Hungarian prison cell. Once released, he did not utter a word of the tortures he had undergone. On the very day of his release, he took up where he had left off.

My mother taught me love of God. As for my father, he scarcely spoke to me about the laws governing the relations between man and his creator. In our conversations, the *Kaddish* was never mentioned. Not even in camp. Especially not in camp.

So I do not know what he would have hoped to see me do tomorrow, the anniversary of his death. If only, in his lifetime, he had been a man intoxicated with eternity and redemption.

But that is not the problem. Even if Shlomo ben Nissel had been a faithful servant of the fierce God of Abraham, a just man, of demanding and immaculate soul, immune against weakness and doubt, even then I would not know how to interpret his death.

For I am ignorant of the essentials: what he felt, what he believed, in that final moment of his hopeless struggle, when his very being was already fading, already withdrawing toward that place where the dead are no longer tormented, where they are permitted at last to rest in peace, or in nothingness—what difference does it make?

His face swollen, frightful, bloodless, he agonized in silence. His cracked lips moved imperceptibly. I caught the sounds, but not the words of his incoherent memory. No doubt, he was carrying out his duty as father by transmitting his last wishes to me, perhaps he was also entrusting me with his final views on history, knowledge, the world's misery, his life, mine. I shall never know. I shall never know if he had the name of the Eternal on his lips to praise him—in spite of everything—or, on the contrary, because of everything, to free himself from him.

Through puffy, half-closed eyelids, he looked at me and, at times, I thought with pity. He was leaving and it pained him to leave me behind, alone, helpless, in a world he had hoped would be different for me, for himself, for all men like him and me.

At other times, my memory rejects this image and goes its own way. I think I recognize the shadow of a smile on his lips: the restrained joy of a father who is leaving with the hope that his son, at least, will remain alive one more minute, one more day, one more week, that perhaps his son will see the liberating angel, the messenger of peace. The certitude of a father that his son will survive him.

In reality, however, I do not hesitate to believe that the truth could be entirely different. In dying, my father looked at me, and in his eyes where night was gathering, there was nothing but animal terror, the demented terror of one who, because he wished to understand too much, no longer understands anything. His gaze fixed on me, empty of meaning. I do not even know if he saw me, if it was me he saw. Perhaps he mistook me for someone else, perhaps even for the exterminating angel. I know nothing about it because it is impossible to grasp what the eyes of the dying see or do not see, to interpret the death rattle of their last breath.

I know only that that day the orphan I became did not respect tradition: I did not say *Kaddish*. First, because no one there would have heard and responded "Amen." Also because I did not yet know that beautiful and solemn prayer. And because I felt empty, barren: a useless object, a thing without imagination. Besides there was nothing more to say, nothing more to hope for. To say *Kaddish* in that stifling barracks, in the very heart of the kingdom of death, would have been the worst of blasphemies. And I lacked even the strength to blaspheme.

Will I find the strength tomorrow? Whatever the answer, it will be wrong, at best incomplete. Nothing to do with the death of my father.

The impact of the holocaust on believers as well as unbelievers, on Jews as well as Christians, has not yet been evaluated. Not deeply, not enough. That is no surprise. Those who lived through it lack objectivity: they will always take the side of man confronted with the Absolute. As for the scholars and philosophers of every genre who have had the opportunity to observe the tragedy, they will—if they are capable of sincerity and humility—withdraw without daring to enter into the heart of the matter; and if they are not, well, who cares about their grandiloquent conclusions? Auschwitz, by definition, is beyond their vocabulary.

The survivors, more realistic if not more honest, are aware of the fact that God's presence at Treblinka or Maidanek—or, for that matter, his absence—poses a problem which will remain forever insoluble.

I once knew a deeply religious man who, on the Day of Atonement, in despair, took heaven to task, crying out like a wounded beast. "What do you want from me, God? What have I done to you? I want to serve you and crown you ruler of the universe, but you prevent me. I want to sing of your mercy, and you ridicule me. I want to place my faith in you, dedicate my thought to you, and you do not let me. Why? Why?"

I also knew a free-thinker, who, one evening, after a selection, suddenly began to pray, sobbing like a whipped child. He beat his breast, became a martyr. He had need of support, and, even more, of certitude: if he suffered, it was because he had sinned; if he endured torment, it was because he had deserved it.

Loss of faith for some equaled discovery of God for others. Both answered to the same need to take a stand, the same impulse to rebel. In both cases, it was an accusation. Perhaps some day someone will explain how, on the level of man, Auschwitz was possible; but on the level of God, it will forever remain the most disturbing of mysteries.

Many years have passed since I saw my father die. I have grown up and the candles I light several times a year in memory of departed members of my family have become more and more numerous. I should have acquired the habit, but I cannot. And each time the eighteenth day of the month of *Shvat* approaches, I am overcome by desolation and futility: I still do not know how to commemorate the death of my father, Shlomo ben Nissel, a death which took him as if by mistake.

Yes, a voice tells me that in reality it should suffice, as in previous years, to follow the trodden path: to study a chapter of *Mishna* and to say *Kaddish* once again, that beautiful and moving prayer dedicated to the departed, yet in which death itself figures not at all. Why not yield? It would be in keeping with the custom of countless generations of sages and orphans. By studying the sacred texts, we offer the dead continuity if not peace. It was thus that my father commemorated the death of his father.

But that would be too easy. The holocaust defies reference, analogy. Between the death of my father and that of his, no comparison is possible. It would be inadequate, indeed unjust, to imitate my father. I should have to invent other prayers, other acts. And I am afraid of not being capable or worthy.

All things considered, I think that tomorrow I shall go to the synagogue after all. I will light the candles, I will say *Kaddish,* and it will be for me a further proof of my impotence.

TESTAMENT OF A JEW FROM SARAGOSSA

One day the great Rebbe Israel Baal Shem-Tov ordered his faithful coachman to harness the horses as fast as he could and drive him to the other side of the mountain.

"Hurry, my good Alexei, I have an appointment."

They came to a stop in a dense forest. The holy man stepped down, went over to lean against an oak, meditated for a moment, then climbed back into the carriage.

"Let's go, Alexei," he said, smiling. "We can go back now."

Though accustomed to not understanding the behavior of his master, the miracle-worker, the coachman still had the courage to be astonished.

"But your appointment? Did you miss it? You, who always arrive on time, who never disappoint anyone? Did we come for nothing?"

"Oh no, my good Alexei, we did not come so long a way for nothing. I have kept my appointment."

And as happened whenever he banished a bit of misery from the world, the Rebbe's face radiated happiness.

According to Hasidic tradition it is not given to man to measure the extension of his actions or the impact of his prayers, no more than it is given the traveler to foresee his precise destination: that is one of the secrets of the notion of *Tikkun*—restoration—which dominates Kabbalism.[1]

The wanderer who, to purify his love or to free himself from it, travels around the world and does not know that everywhere he is expected. Each of his encounters, each of his stops, without his knowing, is somewhere inscribed, and he is not free to choose the paths leading him there.

Souls dead and forgotten return to earth to beg their share of grace, of eternity; they need the living to lift them out of nothingness. One gesture would suffice, one tear, a single spark. For each being participates in the renewed mystery of creation; each man possesses, at least once in his life, the absolute power of the *Tzadik,*[2] the irrevocable privilege of the just to restore equilibrium, to repair the fault, to act upon the absent. Condemned to go beyond himself continually, man succeeds without being aware of it and does not understand until afterward.

And now let me tell you a story.

Traveling through Spain for the first time, I had the strange impression of being in a country I already knew. The sun and the sky, the tormented lustre in the eyes: landscapes and faces familiar, seen before.

The strollers on the *ramblas* in Barcelona, the passersby and their children in the back streets of Toledo: how to distinguish which of them had Jewish blood,

---

[1] Or cabalism: a system for the mystical interpretation of the Scriptures, especially popular in the Middle Ages.

[2] Or *zaddik:* spiritual leader of a Hasidic community; also used for a saintly man.

which descended from the Marranos?[3] At any moment I expected Shmuel Hanagid to appear suddenly on some richly covered portico, or Ibn Ezra, Don Itzchak Abarbanel, Yehuda Halevi—those princes and poets of legend who created and sang the golden age of my people. They had long visited my reading and insinuated themselves into my dreams.

The period of the Inquisition had exercised a particular appeal to my imagination. I found fascinating those enigmatic priests who, in the name of love and for the sacred glory of a young Jew from Galilee, had tortured and subjected to slow death those who preferred the Father to the Son. I envied their victims. For them, the choice was posed in such simple terms: God or the stake, abjuration or exile.

Many chose exile, but I never condemned the Marranos, those unhappy converts who, secretly and in the face of danger, remained loyal to the faith of their ancestors. I admired them. For their weakness, for their defiance. To depart with the community would have been easier; to break all ties, more convenient. By deciding to stand their ground on two levels simultaneously, they lived on the razor's edge, in the abnegation of each instant.

I did not know it when I arrived in Spain, but someone was awaiting me there.

It was at Saragossa.

Like a good tourist, I was attentively exploring the cathedral when a man approached me and, in French, offered to serve as guide. Why? Why not? He liked foreigners. His price? None. He was not offering his services for money. Only for the pleasure of having his town admired. He spoke of Saragossa enthusiastically. And eloquently. He commented on everything: history, architecture, customs. Then, over a glass of wine, he transferred his amiability to my person: where did I come from, where was I going, was I married, and did I believe in God. I replied: I come from far, the road before me will be long. I eluded his other questions. He did not insist.

"So, you travel a great deal," he said politely.

"Yes, a great deal."

"Too much, perhaps?"

"Perhaps."

"What does it gain you?"

"Memories, friends."

"That's all? Why not look for those at home?"

"For the pleasure of returning, no doubt, with a few words I didn't know before in my luggage."

"Which?"

"I can't answer that. Not yet. I have no luggage yet."

We clinked glasses. I was hoping he would change the subject, but he returned to it.

"You must know many languages, yes?"

"Too many," I said.

I enumerated them for him: Yiddish, German, Hungarian, French, English, and Hebrew.

"Hebrew?" he asked, pricking up his ears. "*Hebreo?* It exists?"

"It does exist," I said with a laugh.

"Difficult language, eh?"

"Not for Jews."

"Ah, I see, excuse me. You're a Jew."

---

[3]Marranos were Jews who were forced during the Spanish Inquisition to convert to Christianity to save their lives; sometimes they continued Jewish practices in secret.

"They do exist," I said with a laugh.

Certain of having blundered, he looked for a way out. Embarrassed, he thought a minute before going on: "How is Hebrew written? Like Arabic?"

"Like Arabic. From right to left."

An idea seemed to cross his mind, but he hesitated to share it with me. I encouraged him: "Any more questions? Don't be shy."

He said: "May I ask a favor of you? A great favor?"

"Of course," I said.

"Come—come with me."

This was unexpected.

"With you?" I protested. "Where to? To do what?"

"Come. It will take only a few minutes. It may be of importance to me. Please, I beg you, come."

There was such insistence in his voice that I could not say no. Besides, my curiosity had gotten the upper hand. I knew that Saragossa occupied an important place in Jewish history. It was there that the mystic Abraham Aboulafia was born and grew up, the man who had conceived the plan to convert to Judaism Pope Nicholas III himself. In this town, anything could happen.

I followed my guide home. His apartment, on the third floor, consisted of only two tiny rooms, poorly furnished. A kerosene lamp lit up a portrait of the Virgin. A crucifix hung opposite. The Spaniard invited me to sit down.

"Excuse me, I'll only be a second."

He disappeared into the other room and returned again after a few minutes. He was holding a fragment of yellowed parchment, which he handed me.

"Is this in Hebrew? Look at it."

I took the parchment and opened it. I was immediately overwhelmed by emotion, my eyes clouded. My fingers were touching a sacred relic, fragment of a testament written centuries before.

"Yes," I said, in a choked voice. "It is in Hebrew."

I could not keep my hand from trembling. The Spaniard noticed this.

"Read it," he ordered.

With considerable effort I succeeded in deciphering the characters, blurred by the passage of some four hundred years: "I, Moses, son of Abraham, forced to break all ties with my people and my faith, leave these lines to the children of my children and to theirs, in order that on the day when Israel will be able to walk again, its head high under the sun, without fear and without remorse, they will know where their roots lie. Written at Saragossa, this ninth day of the month of Av,[4] in the year of punishment and exile."

"Aloud," cried the Spaniard, impatient. "Read it aloud."

I had to clear my throat: "Yes, it's a document. A very old document. Let me buy it from you."

"No," he said sharply.

"I'll give you a good price."

"Stop insisting, the answer is no."

"I am sorry."

"This object is not for sale, I tell you!"

I did not understand his behavior.

"Don't be angry, I did not mean to enrage you. It's just that for me this parchment has historical and religious value; for me it is more than a souvenir, it is more like a sign, a . . . "

---

[4]July–August.

"For me, too!" he shouted.

I still did not understand. Why had he hardened so suddenly?

"For you too? In what way?"

He explained briefly: it was the tradition in his family to transmit this object from father to son. It was looked upon as an amulet the disappearance of which would call down a curse.

"I understand," I whispered, "yes, I understand."

History had just closed the circle. It had taken four centuries for the message of Moses, son of Abraham, to reach its destination. I must have had an odd look on my face.

"What's going on?" the Spaniard wanted to know. "You say nothing, you conceal your thoughts from me, you offend me. Well, say something! Just because I won't sell you the amulet you don't have the right to be angry with me, do you?"

Crimson with indignation, with anxiety perhaps, he suddenly looked evil, sinister. Two furrows wrinkled his forehead. Then it was he who was awaiting me here. I was the bearer of his *Tikkun,* his restoration, and he was not aware of it. I wondered how to disclose it to him. At last, finding no better way, I looked him straight in the eye and said: "Nothing is going on, nothing. I am not angry with you, know only this: you are a Jew."

And I repeated the last words: "Yes, you are a Jew. *Judeo.* You."

He turned pale. He was at a loss for words. He was choking, had to hold himself not to seize me by the throat and throw me out. *Judeo* is an insult, the word evokes the devil. Offended, the Spaniard was going to teach me a lesson for having wounded his honor. Then his anger gave way to amazement. He looked at me as if he were seeing me for the first time, as if I belonged to another century, to a tribe with an unknown language. He was waiting for me to tell him that it was not true, that I was joking, but I remained silent. Everything had been said. A long time ago. Whatever was to follow would only be commentary. With difficulty, my host finally regained control of himself and leaned over to me.

"Speak," he said.

Slowly, stressing every syllable, every word, I began reading the document in Hebrew, then translating it for him. He winced at each of the sentences as though they were so many burns.

"That's all?" he asked when I had finished.

"That's all."

He squinted, opened his mouth as if gasping for air. For an instant I was afraid he would faint. But he composed himself, threw his head back to see, on the wall behind me, the frozen pain of the Virgin. Then he turned toward me again.

"No," he said resolutely. "That is not all. Continue."

"I have given you a complete translation of the parchment. I have not left out a single word."

"Go on, go on, I say. Don't stop in the middle. Go on, I'm listening."

I obeyed him. I returned to the past and sketched a picture of Spain at the end of the fifteenth century, when Tomas de Torquemada, native of Valladolid, Grand Inquisitor of gracious Queen Isabella the Catholic, transformed the country into a gigantic stake in order to save the Jews by burning them, so that the word of Jesus Christ might be heard and known far and wide, loved and accepted. Amen.

Soon the Spaniard had tears in his eyes. He had not known this chapter of his history. He had not known the Jews had been so intimately linked with the greatness of his country before they were driven out. For him, Jews were part of mythology; he had not known "they do exist."

"Go on," he pleaded, "please go on, don't stop."

I had to go back to the sources: the kingdom of Judea, the prophets, the wars, the First Temple, the Babylonian Diaspora, the Second Temple, the sieges of Jerusalem and Masada, the armed resistance to the Roman occupation, the exile and then the long wait down through the ages, the wait for the Messiah, painfully present and painfully distant; I told him of Auschwitz as well as the renaissance of Israel. All that my memory contained I shared with him. And he listened to me without interrupting, except to say: "More, more." Then I stopped. I had nothing more to add. As always when I talk too much, I felt ill at ease, suddenly an intruder. I got up.

"I have to leave now, I'm late."

The car would be waiting for me in front of the cathedral. The Spaniard took me there, his head lowered, listening to his own footsteps. The square was deserted: no car in sight. I reassured my guide: there was no reason to worry, the car would not leave without me.

We walked around the building once, twice, and my guide, as before, told me more about the Cathedral of Notre-Dame del Pilar. Then, heavy with fatigue, we found ourselves inside, seated on a bench, and, there, in that quiet half-darkness where nothing seemed to exist anymore, he begged me to read him one last time the testament that a Jew of Saragossa had written long ago, thinking of him.

A few years later, passing through Jerusalem, I was on my way to the Knesset, where a particularly stormy debate was raging over Israel's policy toward Germany. At the corner of King George Street, a passerby accosted me:

"Wait a minute."

His rudeness displeased me; I did not know him. What was more, I had neither time nor the inclination to make his acquaintance.

"I beg your pardon," I said. "I'm in a hurry."

He grabbed my arm.

"Don't go," he said in a pressing tone. "Not yet. I must talk to you."

He spoke a halting Hebrew. A tourist, no doubt, or an immigrant recently arrived. A madman perhaps, a visionary or a beggar: the eternal city lacks for none. I tried to break away, but he would not let go.

"I've a question to ask you."

"Go ahead, but quickly."

"Do you remember me?"

Worried about arriving late, I hurriedly replied that he was surely making a mistake and confusing me with someone else.

He pushed me back with a violent gesture.

"You're not ashamed?"

"Not in the least. What do you want? My memory isn't infallible. And judging from what I see neither is yours."

I was just about to leave when under his breath the man pronounced a single word: "Saragossa."

I stood rooted to the ground, incredulous, incapable of any thought, any movement. Him, here? Facing me, with me? I was revolving in a world where hallucination seemed the rule. I was witnessing, as if from outside, the meeting of two cities, two timeless eras and, to convince myself that I was not dreaming, I repeated the same word over and over again: "Saragossa, Saragossa."

"Come," said the man. "I have something to show you."

That afternoon I thought no longer about the Knesset or the debate that was to weigh on the political conscience of the country for so long. I followed the

Spaniard home. Here, too, he occupied a modest two-room apartment. But there was nothing on the walls.

"Wait," said my host.

I sank into an armchair while he went into the other room. He reappeared immediately, holding a picture-frame containing a fragment of yellowed parchment.

"Look," the man said. "I have learned to read."

We spent the rest of the day together. We drank wine, we talked. He told me about his friends, his work, his first impressions of Israel. I told him about my travels, my discoveries. I said: "I am ashamed to have forgotten."

An indulgent smile lit his face.

"Perhaps you too need an amulet like mine; it will keep you from forgetting."

"May I buy it from you."

"Impossible, since it's you who gave it to me."

I got up to take leave. It was only when we were about to say good-bye that my host, shaking my hand, said with mild amusement: "By the way, I have not told you my name."

He waited several seconds to enjoy the suspense, while a warm and mischievous light animated his face:

"My name is Moshe ben Abraham, Moses, son of Abraham."

CARLOS FUENTES
[BORN 1928]

For many of us, the Mexicans are, as one commentator has described them, "distant neighbors." We know more about European culture than we do about that of the nation next door. The work of Carlos Fuentes, Mexico's foremost contemporary novelist, is a good introduction to contemporary Mexico. He writes about Mexican history and culture in nearly all of his books, but he is also a very cosmopolitan writer, involved with Europe, the United States, and the traditions of Western culture generally. His interest in relations between industrial nations and developing nations and his experiments with narrative point of view and magical realism place his work in the mainstream of contemporary world literature. Appropriately, he is the first Mexican novelist to have one of his works—*The Old Gringo* (1985)—on the *New York Times* best-seller list.

LIFE

Fuentes has been an internationalist from birth. The son of a career diplomat, he was born in Panama and spent most of his childhood outside Mexico—in the United States, Latin America, and Europe. He learned English at age four in Washington, D.C., and he attended schools in the United States, Brazil, Chile, and Mexico. After studying law at the University of Mexico and at the Institute of Advanced International Studies in Geneva, Switzerland, Fuentes became a diplomat himself, serving as a cultural officer and on other diplomatic missions and as Mexico's ambassador to France in the 1970s. Even though his commitment to Marxism has led to disputes with the U.S. State Department, and he has been barred on occasion from entering the United States, he has spent a great deal of time in the last two decades in this country, teaching at many American universities, among them Columbia, California, Oklahoma, Pennsylvania, Harvard, and George Mason. He has also taught at the University of Paris, Cambridge University in England, and the University of Concepción in Chile.

WORK

Fuentes began his writing career in the late forties. In 1958 he published his first novel, *Where the Air Is Clear* (*La región mas transparente*), the story of an old revolutionary, Federico Robles, who has become a financial tycoon preoccupied with making money. Robles symbolizes a Mexico that has lost direction, betrayed its revolution, and adopted the empty values of materialistic capitalism. In the course of the novel, his financial empire falls, and he leaves the city to return to the country and reestablish contact with some mythic sources of Mexican culture. *The Death of Artemio Cruz* (*La muerte de Artemio Cruz*, 1962) further develops these cultural themes. Like Robles, Cruz is a businessman who has betrayed the revolution of 1910–1920, in which he fought as a young man. Although he came from peasant origins, he used the revolution as a way of acquiring personal wealth and power. He lied and married his way into a wealthy family, made opportunistic political alliances, and abandoned the ideal of land reform for which the revolution was fought so that he could inhabit the mansions of the prerevolutionary landowners. He has increased his wealth by becoming a Mexican front man for large American corporations. An old man on his deathbed at the time of the narration, he tells of his life in several voices representing the fragmentation of his character and of Mexican culture. The fragmented story of his life in the novel thus becomes an account of the history of Mexico in the twentieth century and the betrayal of its revolution.

Nearly all of Fuentes's novels take up the themes of these early works: the class domination and polarization of Mexican culture; its lost contact with its own mythic and historic roots through materialism and "Americanization"; the financial corruption of modern, urban life; and the betrayal of Mexico's revolutionary ideals, especially the failure to carry out land reform. These social themes have made Mexican history important elements in his work. Many of the characters and situations in the novels are defined in historical terms. Eruptions from the Aztec past, for example, intrude into the contemporary scene. The bloody revolution of 1910–1920 is a particularly defining event in Fuentes's work. Fought at the same time as the Bolshevik revolution in Russia, the Mexican Revolution sought to limit the power of the Catholic Church, overthrow the large landowners, and, by redistributing the land among the *campesinos,* create a more equitable distribution of the national wealth. Although the single-party government that took power in the revolution and has ruled ever since has paid lip service to revolutionary ideals, it has failed to carry out a program of land reform. For Fuentes this betrayal of the revolution is the defining fact about modern Mexico.

Fuentes has said that "the theme of the country, the culture, and the society in which I work . . . has been [my] most powerful external impulse." The divisions between primitive and modern, past and present, revolutionary idealism and continuing corruption, the rural countryside and the sprawl of the world's largest city, and a mythic past and a materialistic present become the defining contradictions in his work. Fuentes's Mexico City, a microcosm of Mexican culture that centers most of his novels, is reminiscent of Dickens's London, Balzac's Paris, and the urban wasteland of T. S. Eliot's vision of the modern world. Banal, anonymous, and spiritually empty, the product of technology and greed, Mexico City is part of an international network and is cut off from its own history and traditions. Fuentes has also acknowledged kinship with William Faulkner as a "novelist of defeat," for in Faulkner's Yoknapatawpha County, Fuentes finds a fragmented and declining rural culture similar to Mexico's. This suppressed peasant culture and the sacred traditions of the Aztec past intrude into the present in eruptions from Aztec myth or in mysterious events that cannot be explained in the empiricist terms of the city. These touches of "magical realism" give a surreal edge to Fuentes's vision and ally him with the most important movement in Latin American literature in the last thirty years. Like the other magical realists—such writers as Alejo Carpentier, Isabel Allende, and

Gabriel García Márquez—Fuentes juxtaposes the everyday and the miraculous as a way of revealing the discontinuities and contradictions of modern life. Besides *Artemio Cruz,* the works by which Fuentes is best known in the United States are *Terra Nostra* (1975), an exploration of Mexico's Spanish heritage; *The Old Gringo* (*El gringo viejo,* 1985); and *Christopher Unborn* (*Cristobal Nonato,* 1989), a satiric commentary on Columbus and his impact on the Western Hemisphere.

"The Prisoner of Las Lomas" (1990) employs many of Fuentes's characteristic themes. Like *Artemio Cruz,* "Prisoner" is a first-person narrative. Although Nicolás Sarmiento's personal history does not reach back to the revolution, his personal story does, for he has linked his life with that of General Prisciliano Nieves, a legendary hero of the war. Sarmiento, a cynical opportunist, uses his serendipitous knowledge of the truth about Nieves's role in the war to blackmail the general and establish himself as his heir. His hard-headed realism, urbanity, and lack of sentimentality make him successful as a blackmailer, a businessman, and a Don Juan. But they also make him incapable of understanding the appeal of the legend about General Nieves and of recognizing the emotional bonds that link the Mexican people into "family." His education in the mysteries of emotion and cultural solidarity begins when he departs from his rule of emotional detachment and becomes involved with Lala, a mysterious woman with ties to rural Mexico. Her murder implicates him and forces him to recognize his servants as individuals with names. Ironically, he is doubled with Dimas Palmero, the servant charged with murdering Lala. They both become prisoners, Palmero in the jail where he is held without trial, and Sarmiento in his mansion in Las Lomas de Chapultepec, surrounded by a host of nameless peasants, Lala's kin, who take control of his life. Both the peasant and the patron are entangled in the tragedy, as they are in the truth and legends of Mexican history and culture. By the end of the story Sarmiento has learned just how limited his knowledge of the "truth" of Mexican history is in its power to control his destiny.

Suggested Readings

Most of Fuentes's works are available in English translations. English commentaries on his work include Daniel de Guzmán's *Carlos Fuentes* (1972), Gloria Durán's *The Archetypes of Carlos Fuentes: From Witch to Androgyne* (1980), and Wendy B. Faris's *Carlos Fuentes* (1983). Poet Octavio Paz's *The Labyrinth of Solitude: Life and Thought in Mexico* (1961), a discussion of Mexican history and culture, provides useful background for understanding the themes in Fuentes's work.

The Prisoner of Las Lomas

Translated by Thomas Christensen

[To Valerio Adami, for a Sicilian story]

1

As incredible as this story is, I might as well begin at the beginning and continue straight on to the end. Easy to say. The minute I get set to begin, I realize I begin with an enigma. It follows that difficulties ensue. Oh, fuck! It can't be helped: the story begins with a mystery; my hope, I swear, is that by the end you'll understand everything. That you will understand me. You'll see: I leave out nothing. But the truth is that when I entered the sickroom of Brigadier General Prisciliano Nieves on February 23, 1960, in the British hospital then located in the Avenida Mariano Escobedo (present site of the Camino Real Hotel, to orient my younger listeners), I myself had to believe in the enigma, or what I was planning would not succeed. I want to be understood. The mystery was true. (The truth was the mystery.) But if I was not myself convinced of it, I would not convince the old and astute Brigadier Nieves, not even on his sickbed.

He was, as I said, a general. You know that already. I was a young lawyer who had recently received my degree—news for you and for me. I knew everything about him. He, nothing about me. So when I found the door to his private room in the hospital ajar and pushed it open, he didn't recognize me, but neither did he draw back. Lax as security is in Mexican hospitals, there was no reason for the brigadier to be alarmed. I saw him lying there in one of those beds that are like the throne of death, a white throne, as if cleanliness were the compensation that dying offers us. His name *Nieves* means *snow,* but lying in all that bleached linen he was like a fly in milk. The brigadier was very dark, his head was shaved, his mouth a long, sourish crack, his eyes masked by two thick, livid veils. But why describe him, when he was so soon gone? You can look up his photo in the Casasola Archives.

Who knows why he was dying? I went by his house and they said to me:

—The general's bad.

—It's just he's so old.

I scarcely noticed them. The one who spoke first seemed a cook, the second a young girl servant. I made out a sort of majordomo inside the house, and there was a gardener tending the roses outside. You see: only of the gardener was I able to say definitely, that man is a gardener. The others were just one thing or another. They didn't exist for me.

But the brigadier did. Propped up in his hospital bed, surrounded by a parapet of cushions, he looked at me as he must have looked at his troops the day he singlehandedly saved the honor of his regiment, of the Northeast Corps, almost of the very Revolution, and maybe even of the country itself—why not?—in the encounter of La Zapotera, when the wild Colonel Andrés Solomillo, who confused extermination with justice, occupied the Santa Eulalia sugar mill and lined both masters and workers against its wall to face the firing squad, saying the servants were as bad as those they served.

—The one who holds the cow is as bad as the one who slaughters it.

So said Solomillo, helping himself to the possessions of the Escalona family, masters of the hacienda: quickly grabbing all the gold coins he'd found in the library, behind the complete works of Auguste Comte, he proposed to Prisciliano:

—Take these, my captain, so that for once those who are as hungry as you and I may be invited to the banquet of life.

Prisciliano Nieves—the legend goes—not only refused the gold his superior offered him but, when it came time for the execution, he placed himself between the firing squad and the condemned and said to Colonel Andrés Solomillo: —The soldiers of the Revolution are neither murderers nor thieves. These poor people are guilty of nothing. Separate the poor from the rich, please.

What happened then—so the story goes—was this: the colonel, furious, told Prisciliano that if he didn't shut up he would be the second feature in the morning's firing; Prisciliano shouted to the troops not to kill other poor people; the squad hesitated; Solomillo gave the order to fire at Prisciliano; Prisciliano gave the order to fire at the colonel; and in the end the squad obeyed Prisciliano:

—Mexican soldiers do not murder the people, because they are the people, said Prisciliano beside the body of Solomillo, and the soldiers cheered him and felt satisfied.

This phrase, associated ever since with the fame, the life, and the virtues of the instantly Colonel and soon-to-be Brigadier General Don Prisciliano Nieves, surely would be engraved on the base of his monument: THE HERO OF SANTA EULALIA.

And now here I come, forty-five years later, to put a damper on the final glory of General Prisciliano Nieves.

—General Nieves, listen carefully. I know the truth of what happened that morning in Santa Eulalia.

The maraca that sounded in the throat of my brigadier Prisciliano Nieves was not his death rattle, not yet. In the dim light of the hospital, my middle-class lawyer's young breath smelling of Sen-Sen mixed with Don Prisciliano's ancient respiration, a drumroll scented of chloroform and *chile chipotle*.[1] No, my general, don't die without signing here. For your honor, my general: worry no more about your honor, and rest in peace.

2

My house in Las Lomas de Chapultepec has one outstanding virtue: it shows the advantages of immortality. I don't know how people felt about it when it was constructed, when the forties were dawning. The Second World War brought Mexico a lot of money. We exported raw materials at high prices and the farm-workers entered the churches on their knees, praying for the war to go on. Cotton, hemp, vegetables, strategic minerals; it all went out in every direction. I don't know how many cows had to die in Sonora for this great house to be erected in Las Lomas, or how many black-market deals lay behind its stone and mortar. You have seen such houses along the Paseo de la Reforma and the Boulevard de los Virreyes and in the Polanco neighborhood: they are architectural follies of pseudo-colonial inspiration, resembling the interior of the Alameda movie house, which in turn mimics the Plateresque of Taxco with its cupolas, towers, and portals. Not to mention that movie house's artificial ceiling, dappled with hundred-watt stars and adorned with scudding little clouds. My house in Boulevard de los Virreyes stopped short of that.

Surely the Churrigueresque[2] delirium of the house I have lived in for more than twenty years was an object of derision. I imagine two or three caricatures by Abel Quezada[3] making fun of the cathedral-like portal, the wrought-iron balconies, the nightmare ornamentation of decorations, reliefs, curves, angels, madonnas, cornucopias, fluted plaster columns, and stained-glass windows. Inside, things don't get any better, believe me. *Inside* reproduces *outside:* once again, in a hall that rises two stories, we encounter the blue-tile stairs, the iron railing and balconies overlooking the hall from the bedrooms, the iron candelabra with its artificial candles dripping fake wax of petrified plastic, the floor of Talavera tile, the uncomfortable wood-and-leather furniture, straight and stiff as if for receiving a sentence from the Holy Inquisition. What a production...!

But the extraordinary thing, as I was saying, is that this white elephant, this symbol of vulgar pretension and the new money of the entrepreneurs who made

---

[1] A hot chile sauce.
[2] An elaborate and extravagantly decorated style of Spanish baroque architecture.
[3] A Mexican painter and cartoonist.

a profit off the war, has been converted, with time, into a relic of a better era. Today, when things are fast going downhill, we fondly recall a time when things were looking up. Better vulgar and satisfied than miserable but refined. You don't need me to tell you that. Bathed in the glow of nostalgia, unique and remote in a new world of skyscrapers, glass, and concrete, my grotesque quasimodel home (my Quasimodo[4] abode, my friends, ha ha! it might be hunchbacked, but it's mine, all mine!) has now become a museum piece. It's enough to say that first the neighbors and then the authorities came to me, imploring:

—Never, sir, sell your house or let it be demolished. There aren't many examples left of the Neocolonial architecture of the forties. Don't even think of sacrificing it to the crane or (heaven protect us!) (we would never imagine such a thing of you!) to vile pecuniary interests.

I had a strange friend once, named Federico Silva, whom his friends called the Mandarin and who lived in another kind of house, an elegant villa dating from the adolescent decade of the century (1915? 1920?), squeezed and dwarfed by the looming skyscrapers lining the Calle de Córdoba. He wouldn't let it go on principle: he would not cave in to the modernization of the city. Obviously, nostalgia makes demands on me. But if I don't let go of my house, it's not because of my neighbors' pleas, or because I have an inflated sense of its value as an architectural curiosity, or anything like that. I remain in my house because I have lived like a king in it for twenty-five years: from the time I was twenty-five until I turned fifty, what do you think of that? An entire life!

Nicolás Sarmiento, be honest with those who are good enough to hear you out, pipes up the little inner voice of my Jiminy Cricket. Tell them the truth. You don't leave this house for the simple reason that it belonged to Brigadier General Prisciliano Nieves.

3

An entire life: I was about to tell you that when I took over this meringue of a house I was a miserable little lawyer, only the day before a clerk in an insignificant law office on the Avenida Cinco de Mayo. My world, on my word of honor, went no farther than the Celaya candy store; I would look through the windows of my office and imagine being rewarded with mountains of toffees, rock candy, candy kisses, and *morelianas*. Maybe the world was a great candied orange, I said to my beloved fiancée, Miss Buenaventura del Rey, from one of the best families of the Narvarte district. Bah, if I had stayed with her I would have been turned into a candied orange, a lemon drop. No: the world was the sugared orange, I would take one bite and then, with disdain and the air of a conquistador, I would throw it over my shoulder. Give me a hug, sweetheart!

Buenaventura, on the other hand, wanted to eat the orange down to the last seed, because who knows if tomorrow will bring another. When I walked into the house in Las Lomas for the first time, I knew that there was no room in it for Miss Buenaventura del Rey. Shall I confess something to you? My sainted fiancée seemed to me less fine, less interesting than the servants that my general had in his service. Adieu, Buenaventura, and give your papa my warmest thanks for having given away to me, without even realizing it, the secret of Prisciliano Nieves. But goodbye also, worthy cook, lovely girl servant, stupid waiter, and stooped gardener of the Hero

---

[4]The hunchback of Notre Dame in Victor Hugo's novel.

of Santa Eulalia. Let no one remain here who served or knew Prisciliano Nieves when he was alive. Let them all be gone!

The women tied their bundles and went proudly off. The waiter, on the other hand, half argued and half whined that it wasn't his fault the general died, that nobody ever thought of them, what would become of them now, would they die of hunger, or would they have to steal? I would like to have been more generous with them. I couldn't afford it; no doubt, I was not the first heir that couldn't use the battalion of servants installed in the house he inherited. The gardener returned now and again to look at his roses from a distance. I asked myself if it wouldn't be a good idea to have him come back and take care of them. But I didn't succumb: I subscribed to the motto *Nothing from the past!* From that moment, I started a new life: new girlfriend, new servants, new house. Nobody who might know anything about the battle of La Zapotera, the hacienda of Santa Eulalia, or the life of Brigadier Prisciliano Nieves. Poor little Buenaventura; she shed a lot of tears and even made a fool of herself calling me up and getting the brush-off from my servants. The poor thing never found out that our engagement was the source of my fortune; her father, an old army accountant, cross-eyed from constantly making an ass of himself, had been in Santa Eulalia and knew the truth, but for him it was just a funny story, it had no importance, it was a bit of table talk; he didn't act on the precious information he possessed, whereas I did, and at that moment I realized that information is the source of power, but the crucial thing is to know how to use it or, if the situation demands, not use it: silence, too, can be power.

New life, new house, new girlfriend, new servants. Now I'm reborn: Nicolás Sarmiento, at your service.

I was reborn, yes, gentlemen: an entire life. Who knew better than anyone that there was a device called the telephone with which a very foxy lawyer could communicate better than anyone with the world, that great sugared orange? You are listening to him now. Who knew better than anyone that there is a seamless power called information? Who knows knows—so the saying goes. But I amended it: who knows can do, who can do knows—power is knowledge. Who subscribed to every gringo review available on technology, sports, fashion, communications, interior decoration, architecture, domestic appliances, shows, whatever you need and desire? Who? Why, you're listening to him, he's talking to you: the lawyer Nicolás Sarmiento, who joined information to telephone: as soon as I found out about a product that was unknown in Mexico, I would use the telephone and in a flash obtain the license to exploit it here.

All by telephone: patents for Dishwasher A and Microcomputer B, for telephone answering machines and electromagnetic recorders, rights to Parisian *prêt-à-porter*[5] and jogging shoes, licenses for drills and marine platforms, for photocopiers and vitamins, for betablockers for cardiacs and small aircraft for magnates: what didn't I patent for Mexico and Central America in those twenty-five years, sirs, finding the financial dimension for every service, tying my Mexican sub-licenses in with the fortunes of the manufacturing company in Wall Street, the Bourse, and the City? And all, I tell you, without stirring from the house of my Brigadier Prisciliano Nieves, who to do his business had, as they say, to shunt cattle all around the ranch. Whereas, with telephone raised, I almost singlehandedly brought Mexico into the modern era. Without anybody realizing. In the place of honor in my library were the telephone directories of Manhattan, Los Angeles, Houston...St. Louis,

---

[5]Ready-to-wear.

Missouri: home of the McDonnell Douglas airplane factory and Ralston cereals; Topeka, Kansas: home of Wishwashy detergent; and Dearborn, Michigan, of the auto factory in the birthplace of Henry Ford; not to mention nacho manufacturing in Amarillo, Texas, and the high-tech conglomerates on Route 128 in Massachusetts.

The directory, my friends, the phone book, the area code followed by seven numbers: an invisible operation, and, if not quite silent, at least as modulated as a murmur of love. Listen well: in my office at Las Lomas I have a console of some fifty-seven direct telephone lines. Everything I need is at my fingertips: notaries, patent experts, and sympathetic bureaucrats.

In view of what has happened, I'm speaking to you, as they say, with all my cards on the table and nothing up my sleeve. But you still don't have to believe me. I'm a bit more refined than in those long-ago days of my visit to the British hospital and my abandonment of Miss Buenaventura del Rey. I'm half chameleon, you can't tell me from any middle-class Mexican who has become polished by taking advantage of trips, conversations, lectures, films, and good music available to . . . well, get rich, everyone has a chance, there's a field marshal's baton in every knapsack. I read Emil Ludwig[6] in a pocket edition and learned that Napoleon has been the universal supermodel of ascent by merit, in Europe and in the so-called Third World. The gringos, so dull in their references, speak of self-made men like Horatio Alger and Henry Ford. We, of Napoleon or nothing: Come, my Josephine, here is your very own Corsican, St. Helena is far away, the pyramids are watching us, even if they are in Teotihuacán,[7] and from here to Waterloo is a country mile. We're half Napoleon, half Don Juan, we can't help it, and I tell you, my terror of falling back to where I'd come from was as great as my ambition: you see, I hold nothing back. But the women, the women I desired, the anti-Buenaventuras, I desired them as they desired me, refined, cosmopolitan, sure, it cost me a little something, but self-confident, at times imperious, I made them understand (and it was true) that there was no commitment between us: grand passion today, fading memory tomorrow . . . That was another story, although they soon learned to count on my discretion and they forgave my failings. Women and servants. From my colonial watchtower of Las Lomas, armed with telephones that passed through all the styles, country black, Hollywood white, October crisis red, bright green Technicolor, golden Barbie Doll, detached speaker, hand-dialed, to telephones like the one I am using at present, pure you-talk-to-me-when-I-press-the-button, to my little black Giorgio Armani number with TV screen, which I use only for my conquests.

Women: in the sixties there were still some foreign castaways from the forties, a little weather-beaten now but eager to acquire a young lover and a large house where they could throw parties and dazzle the Aztecs; it was through them that I burst on the scene and went on to charm the second wave of women, that is, girls who wanted to marry a young lawyer on the way up who had already had as lover the Princess of Salm-Salm or the heiress of the Fresno, California, cardboard-recycling factory. Such is this business of love. I used those young girls to tell the world I was on the make. I seduced all I could, the rest went running to confide to their coreligionists that the spirits that flowed here were strong but fleeting: Nicolás Sarmiento isn't going to lead you to the altar, dearie. I made myself interesting, because the sixties demanded it. I tried to seduce the two Elenas, mother and daughter, though without success. They still kept their particular

---

[6]Emil Ludwig (1881–1948), author of *Napoleon* (1924).
[7]The ancient city of Mexico, located about thirty miles northeast of the present Mexico City, the site of Aztec ceremonial pyramids.

domestic arrangements. But after them came a generation of desperate Mexican women who believed that to be interesting was to be melancholy, miserable, and a reader of Proust. As soon as they satisfied me they would try to commit suicide in my bathroom, with such frequency that I turned, in reaction, to the working class. Secretaries, manicurists, shop clerks who wanted to hook a husband the same as the Mexican princesses, but whom I sidetracked with sweet talk, educating them, teaching them how to walk, dress themselves, and use a finger bowl after eating shrimp (things the women of my first generation had taught me). They coaxed me into educating them, instead of being educated, as I had been by the three preceding generations. So where was my golden mean? The fifth generation left me at a loss. Now they wanted neither to teach me nor to learn from me, only to vie and divide. Sure of themselves, they acted like men and told me that was what it meant to be women. Can that be true? But the philosophy of the good Don Juan is simply this: check out the chicks and chalk them up. And although, when I talk about it, this all sounds quite orderly, the truth is that in my bed, ladies and gentlemen listeners, a great chaos reigned, because there was always an Austro-Hungarian of generation number one who had left a prescription in the medicine cabinet ten years before and returned to reclaim it (in the hope of fanning old flames) and who, seated under said cabinet in a compromising position, would find a potential Galatea[8] throwing up an unknown (to her) kir and, in the bathtub, smothered in soapsuds scented of German woods, a potential Maria Vetsera from the Faculty of Letters and, knocking at the front door, an ex-girlfriend, now married and with five children, with a mind to show me all of them, lined up like marimba keys, simply to make me see what I had lost! I won't even mention the girls (most amusing!) who, during the eighties, began to appear at my house unexpectedly, on pogo sticks, leaping fences behind the Churrigueresque mansions of Virreyes, hopping here and there, from house to house, demonstrating thereby that:

—Private property is okay, pal, but only if it's shared!

They passed like wisps in the breeze, on their pogo sticks, so nubile, ah, as I, turning fifty, saw them bound by as if in a dream, all of them under twenty, assuming the right to enter all the houses, rich or poor, and to talk, to talk, nothing else, with everyone, saying: Get with it, get with what's happening, now!

If you're still listening to me, you might conclude that my destiny was to end up with a woman who would combine the qualities (and the defects, there's no way around it!) of the five generations of ladies I had seduced. You see: the essence of Don Juan is to move, to travel, to scoff at boundaries, whether between countries, gardens, balconies, or beds. For Don Juan there are no doors, or, rather, there is always an unforeseen door for his escape. Now my merry bands of girls on pogo sticks were the Doña Juanitas (damned if they don't smell of pot!) and I, as you know by now, tied to the phone, doing everything by phone, meetings, business deals, love affairs . . .

And servants. I needed them, and very good ones, to throw my famous parties, to receive equally a woman in intimate and attentive circumstances and a crowd of five hundred guests for an epochal bash—the frosting on my house of meringue! But eventually they went out of style, those offensive shows of extravagance, as the richest politicians in Mexico called them, and although I never made a public display of crying over the poverty of my countrymen, at least I always tried to give them honest work. Honest but temporary: What I never could stand was a servant

---

[8]The statue brought to life by Aphrodite in response to the plea of the sculptor, Pygmalion, who had fallen in love with his creation.

staying with me too long. He would gain power from my past. He would remember the previous women. He couldn't help making comparisons. He would treat the new ones the way he treated the old ones, as if he were trying to serve me well and perform satisfactorily, when the sly fellow would know perfectly well that he was performing poorly and making me look bad: Here's your hot-water bottle, madam, the way you like it. Listen, dog, who are you confusing me with? The diuretic morning grapefruit for the pudgy lady who prefers cheese and tortillas. The confusion becomes an allusion, and no Mexican woman was ever born who can't see, smell, and catch those subtle little innuendos. (Except one from Chiapas who was so out of it that I had to clap like crazy to wake her up when she fell asleep in the middle of the action, and then the cunt would pop up and start doing her regional dance. It must be something in the genes. Send them all back to Guatemala!)

Besides denying them the power that cumulative memory gave them over me, I refused to retain my servants, to keep them from intriguing with each other. A servant who stayed more than two years would end up conspiring with other servants against me. The first year, they idolize me and compete with each other; the second, they hate the one they see as my favorite; the third, they join together to throw me out on my ear. All right, then! Here no one passes more than two Christmases in a row. Before the Wise Men make their third trip through the desert on their camels, let the Star of Bethlehem be put out: my butcher and baker and candlestick maker, hey diddle diddle, out on your asses! Cook, upstairs maid, boy, gardener, and a chauffeur who only runs errands because, tied to my telephones and computers, I hardly ever leave my colonial house. That's all I need.

Since I inherited the house, I've kept an exact list of lovers and servants. The first is already rather long, though not like Don Juan's; besides, it's pretty personalized. The servants' list, on the other hand, I try to do seriously, with statistics. Into the computer I put their birthplace, previous occupation. In that way, I have on hand a most interesting sort of sociological profile, since the regions that provide me servants have come down, over the years, to Querétaro, Puebla, the state of Mexico, and Morelos.[9] Next, within each of these, come the cities (Toluca wins by a long shot), the towns, the villages, the old haciendas. Thanks to the relative speed with which I change servants, I think I'll end up covering every square inch of those four federal states. It will be highly entertaining to see what sorts of coincidences, exceptions, and convergences, among them and in relation to my own life, the detailed memories of my computers will provide. How many instances will there be of servants coming from Zacatlán de las Manzanas, state of Puebla? Or, how many members of the same family will end up in my service? How many will know each other and will gossip about me and my house? The possible combinations of their employment and my accounting are obvious: both are infinite, but the calculation of probabilities is, by definition, finite—repetition is not dispersion but, finally, unity. We all end up looking at ourselves in the mirror of the world and seeing our own foolish faces and nothing more.

The world comes to me and the proof is that here you are, listening to me and hanging on my wise and statistical words. Ahem, as they say in the funnies, and also: How fickle is fate, and how often it manages to give a kick in the pants to the best-laid plans!

The present revolving odalisque[10] was, in a certain sense, my ideal lover. We met by telephone. Tell me if there could be a more perfect *class action,* as we Mexican

---

[9]The states that include Mexico City and the surrounding countryside.
[10]A concubine or harem girl.

legal types say; or *serendipity* (what a word!), as the gringo yuppies, who keep on looking for it, say; or *birds of a feather flocking together,* as the prole Indian types around here whom we call *nacos* say. (*Naco* hero on a train: Nacozari. Jealous *naco* in an inn: Nacothello. Corsican *naco* imprisoned on a remote island: Nacoleon. Anarchist *nacos* executed in the electric chair: Naco and Vanzetti.)

—Nacolás Sarmiento.

So she addressed me, mocking me, my last conquest, my latest love, my last girlfriend, how could she fail to conquer me if she entered my game list in this way? Nacolás Sarmiento, she called me, putting me down and tickling me at the same time; her name was Lala and she possessed characteristics of each of the generations that preceded her. She was polyglot like my first round of women (although I suspect that Lala didn't learn languages in an ancestral castle surrounded by governesses, but by the Berlitz method here in the Avenida Chapultepec, or serving meals to the gringo tourists in Ixtapa–Zihuatanejo). Her melancholy was the genuine article, not put in her skull by a decadent prof of philosophy and letters; she didn't know Proust, not even by the book covers—her melancholy was more in the style of the mariachi singer José Alfredo Jiménez:

> And if they want to know about my past,
> I'll have to tell them another lie,
> I'll tell them I came from a different world . . .

I mean that she was pretty mysterious, too good to be true, and when she sang that hold-me-tight, I'd rush to bury myself in her arms and whisper sweet nothings in my tenderest manner . . . Ah, Lala, how I adored you, love, how I adored your tight little ass, my sweet, your savage howling and biting each time I entered your divine zoology, my love, so wild and so refined, so submissive and so mad at the same time, so full of unforgettable details: Lala, you who left me flowers drawn with shaving cream on the bathroom mirror; you who filled champagne bottles with soil; you who highlighted in yellow your favorite names in my telephone books; you who always slept face-down, with your hair disheveled and your mouth half-open, solitary and defenseless, with your hands pressed against your tummy; you who never cut your toenails in my presence, who brushed your teeth with baking soda or ground tortilla, Lala, is it true that I surprised you praying one night, kneeling, and you laughed nervously and showed me a sore knee as excuse, and I said, Let Daddy kiss it and make it better? Lala, you existed only for me, in my bed, in my house, I never saw you outside my vast Churrigueresque prison, but you never felt yourself a prisoner, isn't that so? I never wanted to know about you; as I've said: in all this, the truth is the mystery. Light streaks ran through your hair; you drank carbonated *Tehuacán* before sleeping; you paid the price for a ravenous appetite; you knew how to walk barefoot.

But let's take things in order: of the fourth generation, Lala had a certain lack of breeding that I was going to refine—and to which she submitted willingly, which was the part of her makeup she got from the fifth generation of young little Mexicans, sure of themselves, open to education, experience, professional responsibility. Women, ladies and gentlemen, are like computers: they have passed from the simplest operations, such as adding, subtracting, carrying sums and totaling columns of figures, successively, to the simultaneous operations of the fifth generation: instead of turning each tortilla in turn, we'll turn them all at once. I know this because I've brought to Mexico all the innovations of computation, from the first to the fourth, and now I wait for the fifth and know that the country that discovers it is going to dominate the twenty-first century, which is now approaching, as the old song says, in the murk of night, like an unknown soul, through streets ever winding this way and that, passing like an old-time lover, cloaked in a trailing cape ... and then the surprise: Who'd known all along? Why, who else but Nicolás Sarmiento, the same son of a bitch who subscribes to the gringo magazines and does business by phone and has a new squeeze, dark and silky, called Lala, a true guava of a girl, in his house in Las Lomas.

Who lacked a past. And yet it didn't matter that I learned nothing, I sensed that part of my conquest of Lala consisted in not asking her anything, that what was new about these new Mexicans was that they had no past, or if they had one it was from another time, another incarnation. If that was the case, it only increased Lala's mysterious spell. If her origins were unknown, her present was not: soft, small, burning in all her recesses, dark, always half open and mistress of a pair of eyes that never closed because they never opened; the deliberation of her movements restraining an impetuousness that she and I shared; it was the fear that once exhausted it would not return. No, Lala, always slow, long nights, endless hope, patient flesh, and the soul, my love, always quicker than the body: closer to decadence and death, Lala.

Now I must reveal a fact to you. I don't know if it's ridiculous or painful. Maybe it's simply what I've just said: a fact. I need to have servants because physically I'm a complete idiot. In business I'm a genius, as I've established. But I can't manage practical things. Cooking, for example: zilch. Even for a couple of eggs, I have to get someone to fix them for me. I don't know how to drive; I need a chauffeur. I don't know how to tie my tie or untie my shoes. The result: nothing but these monkey ties with clips that stick in your shirt collars; nothing but slip-ons, never shoes with laces. To women, this all seems sort of endearing and they become maternal with me. They see me so useless in this, such a shark in everything else; they're moved, and they love me that much more. It's true.

But nobody but Lala has known how to kneel before me, with such tenderness, with such devotion, just as if praying, and what's more, with such efficiency: what more perfect way to tie a shoe, leaving the loop expansive as a butterfly ready to fly, yet bound like a link yoked to its twin; and the shoe itself, secure, exact, comfortable, neither too tight nor too loose, a shoe kind to my body, neither constricting nor loose. Lala was perfection, I tell you: *purr-fec-tion*. Neither more nor less. And I say so myself, I who classify my servants by provinces on my computer, but my girls by neighborhoods.

What else should I tell you before I tell you what happened? You suspect already, or maybe not. I had a vasectomy when I was about thirty to avoid having children and so no one can show up in these parts with a brat in her arms, weeping: "Your baby, Nicolás! Aren't you going to acknowledge it? Bastard!" I arranged everything by telephone; it was my business weapon, and although I traveled from time to time, each time I stayed shut up longer in Las Lomas de Chapultepec afterwards. The women came to me and I used my parties to take new ones. I replaced my servants so they wouldn't get the idea that here in Don Nico we've found our gold mine. I never cared, as other Mexican politicians and magnates do, to employ procurers for my women. I make my conquests by myself. As long as I always have someone around to drive my car, cook my beans, and tie my shoes.

All this came to a head one night in July 1982, when the economic crisis was upon us and I was getting nervous, pondering the significance of a declaration of national bankruptcy, the interplanetary travels of Silva Herzog,[11] the debt, Paul

---

[11] Mexican finance minister in 1982 at the time of a major devaluation of the Mexican peso; Paul Volcker was chairman of the U.S. Federal Reserve Board.

Volcker, and my patents and licenses business, in the middle of all this turmoil. Better to throw a big party to forget the crisis, and I ordered a bar and buffet by the pool. The waiter was new, I didn't know his name; my relationship with Lala had lasted two months now and the lady was growing on me, I was liking her more and more, she made me, I confess, hot and bothered, if the truth be told. She arrived late, when I was already mingling with a hundred revelers, calling on my waiters and the guests alike to sample the Taittinger; who knew when we would see it again, much less taste it!

Lala appeared, and her Saint Laurent strapless gown, of black silk, with a red wrap, would likewise not be seen again *pour longtemps*[12]—believe me, who had arranged for her to wear it. How she glowed, my beautiful love, how all eyes followed her, each and every one, you hear me? to the edge of the pool, where the waiter offered her a glass of champagne; she stood for a long time looking at the *naco* dressed in a white cotton jacket, black pants shiny from so much use by previous boys in my service, bow tie—it was impossible to tell him from the others who had had the same position, the same clothes, the same manner. Manner? The servant lifted his head, she emptied the glass into his face, he dropped the tray in the pool, grabbed Lala's arm violently, she drew away, said something, he answered, everyone watched, I moved forward calmly, took her arm (I saw where his fingers had pressed my lady's soft skin), I told him (I didn't know his name) to go inside, we would talk later. I noticed he seemed confused, a wild uncertainty in his black eyes, his dark jaw quivering. He arranged his glossy hair, parted in the middle, and walked away with his shoulders slumped. I thought he was going to fall into the pool. It's nothing, I told the guests, and everything seemed fine, ladies and gentlemen who are listening to me. I laughed: Remember, the pretexts for parties like this are going fast. Everyone laughed with me and I said nothing to Lala. But she went up to bed and waited for me there. She was asleep when the party ended and I got in. I stepped on a champagne glass as I entered the room. I left it on the floor; and in bed, Lala was sleeping in her elegant Saint Laurent dress. I took off her shoes. I studied her. We were tired. I slept. The next day, I got up around six, with that faint sense of absence that takes shape as we wake—and *she* wasn't there. The tracks of her bare feet, on the other hand, were. Bloody tracks; Lala had cut her feet because of my carelessness in not cleaning up the broken glass. I went out the rococo balcony to the pool. There she was, floating face-down, dressed, barefoot, her feet cut, as if she had gone all night without huaraches, walking on thorns, surrounded by a sea of blood. When I turned her over, there was a gaping wound in her belly; the dagger had been withdrawn. They took my servant Dimas Palmero to the Reclusorio Norte, where he was held, awaiting the slow march of Mexican justice, accused of murder. And I was given the same sentence, though in the Churrigueresque palace of Las Lomas de Chapultepec, once the residence of Brigadier General Prisciliano Nieves, who died one morning in 1960 in the old British hospital on the Avenida Mariano Escobedo.

4

The morning of the tragedy, I had only four servants in the big colonial house of Las Lomas, apart from the said Dimas Palmero: a cook, a maid, a chauffeur, and a gardener. I confess that I can barely recall their features or their names. That is

---

[12] For a long time.

perhaps because, as I work in my house, I have rendered them invisible. If I went out every day to an office, I would notice them, by contrast, on my return. But they stayed out of sight so as not to disturb me. I don't know their names, or what they are like. My secretary, Sarita Palazuelos, dealt with them; I was busy with my work in the house, I'm not married, the servants are invisible. They don't exist, as they say.

I think I'm alone in my house. I hear a voice, I ask:

—Who's there?

—Nobody, sir, answers the maid's little voice.

They prefer to be invisible. But there must be someone.

—Take this gift, girl.

—Oh, sir, you shouldn't. I'm nobody to get presents from you, oh, no!

—Happy birthday, I insist.

—Oh, but you shouldn't be thinking of me, sir.

They return to being invisible.

—Oh! Excuse me!

—Please excuse my boldness, sir.

—I won't bother you for even a moment, sir. I'm just going to dust the furniture.

Now one of them had a name: Dimas Palmero.

I couldn't bear to see him. Hate kept me from sleeping; I hugged the pillow that held the scent, each day fainter, of Lala my love, and I cried in despair. Then, to torture myself, I racked my mind with her memory and imagined the worst: Lala with that boy; Lala in the arms of Dimas Palmero; Lala with a past. Then I realized that I couldn't recall the face of the young murderer. Young: I said that and began to remember. I began to draw him out from the original anonymity with which I regarded him that fatal night. Uniformed as a waiter, white cotton jacket, shiny pants, bow tie, identical to all, same as none. I began to wonder how Lala might have regarded him. Young, I said; was he handsome as well? But, besides being young and handsome, was he interesting? and was he interesting because he held some secret? I induced and deduced like mad those first days of my solitude, and from his secret I passed to his interest, from his interest to his youth, and from there to his good looks. Dimas Palmero, in my strange fiftyish pseudo-widowhood, was the Lucifer who warned me: For the first time in your life, you have lost a woman, cuckold Nicolás, not because you left her, or chased her out, not even because *she* left you, but because I took her away from you and I took her forever. Dimas had to be handsome, and he had to have a secret. No other way a cheap *naco* could have defeated me. It couldn't be. It would have to take a youth who was handsome, at least, and who held a secret, to defeat me.

I had to see him. One night it became an obsession: to see Dimas Palmero, speak with him, convince myself that at least I deserved my grief and my defeat.

They had been bringing me trays of food. I barely touched them. I never saw who brought the tray three times a day, or who took it away. Miss Palazuelos sent a note that she was waiting for my instructions, but what instructions could I give, drowned as I was in melancholy? I told her to take a vacation while I got over my broken heart. I noticed the eyes of the boy who took the message. I didn't know him. Surely Miss Palazuelos had substituted a new boy for Dimas Palmero. But I was obsessed: I saw in this new servant a double, almost, of the incarcerated Dimas. How I wanted to confront my rival!

I was obsessed, and my obsession was to go to the Reclusorio and speak with Dimas, to see him face to face. For the first time in ten days, I showered, I shaved, I put on a decent suit, and I left my bedroom, I went down the stairs of gargoyled ironwork to the colonial hall surrounded by little balconies, with a glazed-tile fountain in the corner, burbling water. I reached the front door and tried, with a natural gesture, to open it. It was locked. Such security! The help had turned cautious, indeed, after the crime. Skittish and, as I've said, invisible. Where were the damned bastards? How did I call them? What did I call them?? Boy, girl! Ah, my good woman, my good man! . . . Fuck it!

Nobody answered. I looked out the stained-glass windows of the hall, parting the curtains. They were there in the gardens. Settled in. Sprawled over the grass, trampling it, smoking cigarettes and crushing the butts in the rose mulch; squatting, pulling from their food bags steaming pigs' feet in green mole[13] and steaming sweet and hot tamales, strewing the ground with the burnt maize leaves; the women coquettishly clipping my roses, sticking them in their shiny black hair, while the kids pricked their hands on the thorns and the piglets crackled over the flame . . . I ran to one of the side windows: they were playing marbles and ball-and-cup, they had set some suspicious, leaking casks by the side of the garage. I ran to the right wing of the mansion: a man was urinating in the narrow, shady part of the garden, a man in a lacquered straw hat was pissing against the wall between my house and . . .

I was surrounded.

A smell of purslane came from the kitchen. I entered. I had never seen the new cook, a fat woman, square as a die, with jet-black hair and a face aged by skepticism.

—I am Lupe, the new cook—she told me—and this is Don Zacarías, the new chauffeur.

Said chauffeur did not even rise from the table where he was eating purslane tacos. I looked at him with astonishment. He was the image of the ex-president Don Adolfo Ruiz Cortines,[14] who in turn was identified, in popular wit, with the actor Boris Karloff: bushy eyebrows, deep eyes, huge bags under the eyes, wrinkles deeper than the Grand Canyon, high forehead, high cheekbones, compressed skull, graying hair brushed to the back.

—Pleased, I said, like a perfect idiot.

I returned to the bedroom and, almost instinctively, I decided to put on some of the few shoes with laces that I have. I looked at myself there, seated on the unmade bed, by the pillow that held her scent, with my shoelaces untied and hanging loose like inert but hungry earthworms. I pulled the bell cord by the headboard, to see who would answer my call.

A few minutes passed. Then knuckles rapped.

He entered, the young man who resembled (according to my fancy) the incarcerated Dimas Palmero. I decided, nonetheless, to tell them apart, to separate them, not to allow any confusion. The murderer was locked away. This was someone else.

—What is your name?

—Marco Aurelio.

You'll notice he didn't say "At your service, sir," or "What may I do for you, *patrón*." Nor did he look at me sideways, eyes hooded, head lowered.

—Tie my shoes.

He looked at me a moment.

—Right now, I said. He continued to look at me, and then knelt before me. He tied the laces.

—Tell the chauffeur I'm going out after eating. And tell the cook to come up so I can plan some menus. And another thing, Marco Aurelio . . .

---

[13] A chile sauce.
[14] President of Mexico from 1952 to 1959.

Now back on his feet, he looked at me fixedly.

—Clear all the intruders out of my garden. If they're not gone within half an hour, I'll call the police. You may go, Marco Aurelio. That's all, you hear?

I dressed, ostentatiously and ostensibly, to go out, I who had gone out so seldom. I decided to try for the first time—almost—a beige gabardine double-breasted suit, blue shirt, stupid yellow clip tie, and, sticking out of my breast pocket, a Liberty[15] handkerchief an Englishwoman had given me.

Real sharp, real shark: I spoke my name and, stomping loudly, I went downstairs. But there it was the same story. Locked door, people surrounding the house. A full-fledged party, and a piñata in the garage. The children squealing happily. A child making a hubbub, trapped in a strange metal crib, all barred in up to the top, like a furnace grate.

—Marco Aurelio!

I sat down in the hall of stained-glass windows. Marco Aurelio solicitously undid my shoes, and, solicitously, offered me my most comfortable slippers. Would I like my pipe? Did I want a brandy? I would lack nothing. The chauffeur would go out and get me any videotape I wanted: new pictures or old, sports, sex, music . . . The family has told me to tell you not to worry. You know, Don Nico, in this country (he was saying as he knelt before me, taking off my shoes, this horrendous *naco*) we survive the worst calamities because we take care of each other, you'll see, I was in Los Angeles as an illegal and the American families there are scattered all around, they live far apart from each other, parents without children, the old ones abandoned, the young ones looking to break away, but here it's just the opposite, Don Nico, how can you have forgotten that? you're so solitary, God help you, not us—if you don't have a job, the family will feed you, it will put a roof over your head, if the cops are after you, or you want to escape the army, the family will hide you, send you back from Las Lomas to Morelos and from there to Los Angeles and back into circulation: the family knows how to move by night, the family is almost always invisible, but what the fuck, Don Nico, it can make its presence felt, how it can make its presence felt! You'll see. So you're going to call the police if we don't go? Then I assure you that the police will not find us here when they arrive, although they will find you, quite stiff, floating in the pool, just like Eduardita, whom God has taken onto . . . But listen, Don Nico, there's no need to look like you've seen a ghost, our message is real simple: you'll lead your usual life, phone all you like, manage your business, throw parties, receive your pals and their dolls, and we'll take care of you, the only thing is, you'll never leave this place as long as our brother Dimas is in the pen: the day that Dimas leaves jail, you leave your house, Don Nico, not a minute before, not a minute later, unless you don't play straight with us, and then you'll leave here first—but they'll carry you out, that much I swear.

He pressed together his thumb and index finger and kissed them noisily as I buried myself in the pillow of Eduardita—my Lala!

5

So began my new life, and the first thing that will strike you, my listeners, is the same thought that occurred to me, in my own house in Las Lomas: Well, really my life hasn't changed; indeed, now I'm more protected than ever; they let me throw

---

[15]A London department store noted for its fine printed fabrics.

my parties, manage my business affairs by telephone, receive the girls who console me for the death of Lala (my cup runneth over: I'm a tragic lover, howboutthat!), and to the cops who showed up to ask why all these people have surrounded my house, packed in the garden, frying quesadillas[16] by the rosebushes, urinating in the garage, they explained: Because this gentleman is very generous, every day he brings us the leftovers from his parties—*every day!* I confirmed this personally to the police, but they looked at me with a mournful smirk (Mexican officials are expert at looking at you with a sardonic grimace) and I understood: So be it. From then on, I would have to pay them their weekly bribe. I recorded it in my expense books, and I had to fire Miss Palazuelos, so that she wouldn't suspect anything. She herself hadn't an inkling why she was fired. I was famous for what I've mentioned: nobody lasted very long with me, not secretary or chauffeur or lover. I'm my own boss, and that's the end of it! You will note that this whole fantastic situation was simply an echo of my normal situation, so there was no reason for anyone to be alarmed: neither the exterior world that kept on doing business with me nor the interior world (I, my servants, my lovers, the same as ever...).

The difference, of course, is that this fantastic situation (masquerading as my usual situation) contained one element of abnormality that was both profound and intolerable: it was not the work of my own free will.

There was that one little thing; this situation did not respond to my whim; I responded to it. And it was up to me to end it; if Dimas Palmero went free, I would be freed as well.

But how was I going to arrange for said Dimas to get off? Although I was the one who called the police to have him arrested, he was now charged with murder by the District Attorney's office.

I decided to put on shoes with laces; it was a pretext for asking the valet Marco Aurelio to come up to help me, chat with me, inform me: Were all those people in the garden really the family of the jailed Dimas Palmero? Yes, answered Marco Aurelio, a fine, very extended Mexican family, we all help each other out, as they say. And what else? I insisted, and he laughed at that: We're all Catholic, never the pill, never a condom, the children that God sends... Where were they from? From the state of Morelos, all *campesinos,*[17] workers in the cane fields; no, the fields were not abandoned, didn't they tell you, Don Nico? this is hardly the full contingent, ha ha, this is no more than a delegation, we're good in Morelos at organizing delegations and sending them to the capital to demand justice, surely you remember General Emiliano Zapata;[18] well, now you can see that we've learned something. Now we don't ask for justice. Now we make justice. But I am innocent, I said to Marco Aurelio kneeling before me, I lost Lala, I am... He lifted his face, black and yellow as the flag of an invisible, hostile nation: —Dimas Palmero is our brother.

Beyond that, I couldn't make him budge. These people are tight-lipped. Our brother: did he mean it literally, or by solidarity? (Stubborn sons of that fucking Zapata!) A lawyer knows that everything in the world (words, the law, love...) can be interpreted in the *strict* sense or in the *loose* sense. Was the brotherhood of Marco Aurelio, my extraordinary servant, and Dimas, my incarcerated servant, of blood, or was it figurative? Narrow, or broad? I would have to know to understand

---

[16] Tortillas with melted cheese.
[17] Fieldworkers, peasants.
[18] General Emiliano Zapata (1877?–1919), revolutionary who led an army of peasants during the Mexican Revolution in a fight for land reform.

my situation. Marco Aurelio, I said one day, even if I withdraw the charges against your brother, as you call him (poker-faced, bilious silence), the prosecutor will try him because too many people witnessed the scene by the pool between Lala and your brother, it doesn't depend on me, they will proceed ex officio, understand? it's not a question of avenging Lala's death . . .

—Our sister . . . But not a whore, no way.

He was kneeling in front of me, tying my shoelaces, and on hearing him say this, I gave him a kick in the face. I assure you it wasn't intentional; it was a brutal reflex responding to a brutal assertion. I gave him a brutal kick in the jaw, I knocked him good, he fell on his back, and I followed my blind instinct, left reason aside (left it sound asleep), and ran down the stairs to the hall just as an unfamiliar maid was sweeping the entrance, and the open door invited me to go out into the morning of Las Lomas, the air sharp with pollution, the distant whoosh of a balloon and the flight of the red, blue, yellow spheres, liberated, far from the empty barranca[19] that surrounded us, its high eucalyptuses with their peeling bark fighting the smell of shit from the bluff's recesses: globes of colors greeted me as I went out and breathed poison and rubbed my eyes.

My garden was the site of a pilgrimage. The scent of fried food mixed with the odor of shit and eucalyptus: smoke from cookstoves, squeals of children, the strumming of guitars, click of marbles, two policemen flirting with the girls in braids and aprons on the other side of the gargoyled grillwork of my mansion, an old, toothless, graying man in patched pants and huaraches, his lacquered straw hat in his hand and an invitation—he came over to me: Please try something, sir, there are good tacos, sir. I looked at the policemen, who didn't look at me but laughed wickedly with the country girls and I thought the stupid cunts were practically pregnant already, who said they weren't whores, giving birth in the open fields to the bastard kids of these bastard cops, their children adding to the family of, of, of this old patriarch who offered me tacos instead of protecting the two girls being seduced by this pair of sinister uniformed bandits, smiling, indifferent to my presence on the steps of my house. Was he going to protect them the way he protected Lala? I got up. I studied him, trying to understand.

What could I do? I thanked him and sat down with him in my own garden and a woman offered us hot tortillas in a willow basket. The old man asked me to take the first bite and I repeated the atavistic gesture of taking the moistened bread of the gods out from under the damp colored napkin, as if the earth itself had opened up to offer me the Proustian madeleine[20] of the Mexican: the warm tortilla. (You who are listening to me will remember that I had plied a whole generation of young readers with Marcel Proust, and he who reads Proust, said a staunch nationalistic friend of mine, Proustitutes himself!) Awful! The truth is that, sitting there with the old patriarch eating hot salted tortillas, I felt so transported, so back in my mama's arms again or something like that, that I was already telling myself, forget it, let's have the tortillas, let's have those casks of *pulque*[21] that I saw going into the garage the other day; they brought us brimming glasses of thick liquor, tasting of pineapple, and Marco Aurelio must have had a pretty good knock, because there wasn't a trace of him to be seen. I sat with my legs crossed on my own lawn, the old man feeding

---

[19] A steep slope or escarpment.

[20] French novelist Marcel Proust (1871–1922) in *Remembrance of Things Past* describes a boyhood experience of eating a small French cake, a madeleine, that becomes a defining sensory memory in his life.

[21] A fermented drink made from agave.

me, I questioning him: How long are you going to be here? Don't worry, we don't have to return to Morelos, this could go on for years, do you realize that, señor? He looked at me with his ageless face, the old goat, and told me that they were taking turns, hadn't I caught on? They came and went, they were never the same twice, every day some went home and others arrived, because it's a question of making a sacrifice for Dimas Palmero and for Eduardita, poor child, too, hadn't I realized? Did I think it was always the same folk outside here? He laughed a little, tapping his gummy mouth: the truth was that I had never really noticed them, to me they had, indeed, all appeared the same . . .

But each one is different, the old man said quickly, with a dark seriousness that filled me with fear, each one comes into the world to aid his people, and although most die in infancy, those who have the good fortune to grow, those, señor, are a treasure for an old man like me, they are going to inherit the earth, they are going to go to work there in the North with the gringos, they are going to come to the capital to serve you; and they won't send money to the old folks, you can't argue with that, señor (he resumed his usual cordiality), if the old folks don't know who each of their children are, their names, what they do, what they look like, if we depend on them to keep from dying of hunger when we grow old? Just one condition, he said, pausing:

—Poor, señor, but proud.

He looked over my shoulder, waved. I followed his look. Marco Aurelio in his white shirt and his black pants was rubbing his chin, resting against the door of the house. I got up, thanked the old man, brushed the dirt from my rear, and walked toward Marco Aurelio. I knew that, from then on, it would be nothing but loafers for me.

6

That night I had a terrifying dream that those people would stay here forever, renewing themselves again and again, generation after generation, without concern for any one individual destiny, least of all that of a little half-elegant lawyer: the canny dandy of Las Lomas de Chapultepec. They could hold out until I died. But I still couldn't understand how my death would avenge that of Dimas Palmero, who languished in preventive custody, waiting for the Mexican judicial tortoise to summon him to justice. Listen close. I said tortoise, not torture. That could take years, didn't I know it. If they observed the law limiting the amount of time a man can be detained before being tried, Mexico would stop being what it always has been: a reign of influence, whim, and injustice. So I tell you, and you, like it or not, you have to listen. If I'm the prisoner of Las Lomas, you're the prisoners of my telephones—you listen to me.

Don't imagine I haven't thought of all the ways I could make this my link to the outside, my Adriadne's thread,[22] my vox humana. I have a videotape I often watch, given the circumstances: poor Barbara Stanwyck lying paralyzed in bed,[23] listening to the footsteps of the murderer climbing the stairs to kill her and take control of her millions (will it be her husband? suspense!), and she is trying to call the police

---

[22] In Greek mythology Ariadne gave Theseus the thread that he could follow to find his way out of the Minotaur's labyrinth.

[23] The film is *Sorry, Wrong Number* (1948).

and the telephone is out of order, a voice answering, sorry, wrong number... What a thriller! —*La voix humaine,* a French girlfriend told me... But this was not a Universal picture, only a modest Huaraches Films production, or some such totally asshole thing. All right, I know that I speak to you to take my mind off things for a while; don't think, however, that I have ever stopped plotting my escape. It would be so easy, I tell myself, to go on strike, stop using my phones to make money, neglect my bank accounts, stop talking to you, to my public auditors, my stockbrokers... My immediate conclusion: these people wouldn't give a fuck about my poverty. They are not here to take my cash. If I didn't feed them, they would feed me. I suspect that this Morelos operation functions as efficiently as a Japanese assembly line. If I became poor, they would come to my assistance!

You are free as I was once, and you will understand when I say that, come what may, one doesn't easily resign oneself to giving up one's liberty just like that. Very well: They have sworn to kill me if I denounce them. But what if I managed to escape, hide, set the authorities on them from afar? Don't try it, Don Nico, said my recovered jailer, Marco Aurelio, we are many, we will find you; he laughed: there are branches of the family in Los Angeles, in Texas, in Chicago, even in Paris and London, where rich Mexican señoras take their Agripinas, their Rudecindas, and their Dalmacias to work abroad... It wouldn't surprise me to see some guy in a big sombrero get off a jumbo jet at Charles de Gaulle Airport and chop me to bits in the middle of Paris, laughing wickedly, brandishing the machete that dangles eternally from him like a spare penis. How I hated Marco Aurelio! How dare one of these cheap *nacos* talk so familiarly about General de Gaulle! That's instant communications for you!

They knew my intentions. I took advantage of one of my parties to put on the overcoat and hat of a friend, without his noticing, and while everyone was drinking the last bottle of Taittinger (the pretext for the party) and eating exquisite canapés prepared by the block-shaped fat woman of the kitchen, Doña Lupe (a genius, that woman!), with the hat pulled down over my ears and my lapels turned up, I slipped through the door, which was open that night (and every night: you must realize that my jailers no longer imagined that I would escape, what for? if my life was the same as ever!—me inside with my parties and my telephones; they outside, invisible: as always!). As I say, they no longer locked the door. But I disguised myself and slipped through the door because I didn't want to accept a sentence of confinement imposed by others. I did so without caring about success or failure. The door, freedom, the street, the jumbo to Paris, even if I was met there by Rudecinda, the cousin of Marco Aurelio, rolling pin in hand...

—You forgot to tie your shoes, Don Nico, said Marco Aurelio, holding high a tray heaped with canapés, looking at my feet, and blocking the way to the front door.

I laughed, sighed, took off the overcoat and the hat, returned to my guests.

I tried it several times, I wouldn't give up, to keep my self-respect. But one time I couldn't get beyond the garden, because the children, instinctively, surrounded me, forming a circle, and sang a play song to me. Another time, escaping at night by the balcony, I was hanging by my fingernails when I heard a group at my feet serenading me: it was my birthday and I had forgotten! Many happy returns, Don Nico, these are the years of your life that...! I was in despair: fifty springtimes in these circumstances! In desperation I resorted to Montecristo's strategy:[24] I feigned

---

[24]In Alexandre Dumas's novel *The Count of Monte Cristo* (1844) the hero escapes from prison by pretending to be dead.

death, lying very stiff in my bed; not to give up, as I say, to touch all the bases.
Marco Aurelio poured a bucket of cold water on me and I cried out, and he just
stood there, saying: Don Nico, when you die on me, I'll be the first to let you
know, you can be sure. Will you cry for me, Marco Aurelio, you bastard? I was
incensed! I thought first of poisoning my immediate jailers, the valet Marco Aurelio,
the cubic cook, the Karloff car man; but not only did I suspect that others would
rush in to replace them, I also feared (inconsistent of me!) that while the lawsuit
against the miserable Dimas Palmero dragged on indefinitely, an action against me
for poisoning my servants would be thunderous, scandalous, trumpeted in the press:
Heartless Millionaire Poisons Faithful Servants! From time to time, a few fat morsels
must be cast to the (nearly starved) sharks of justice . . . Besides, when I entered the
kitchen, Doña Lupe was so kind to me: Do sit down, Don Nico, do you know
what I'm fixing today? Can you smell it? Don't you like your cheese and squash?
Or would you rather have what we're fixing ourselves, *chilaquilitos*[25] in green sauce?
This made my mouth water and made life seem bearable. The chauffeur and the
boy sat down to eat with Doña Lupe and me, they told me stories, they were quite
amusing, they made me remember, remember her . . .

So why didn't I explain my situation to the girls who passed through my parties
and my bed? What would they think of such a thing? Can you imagine the ridicule,
the incredulity? So just leave when you want to, Nicolás, who's going to stop you?
But they'll kill me, baby. Then I'm going to save you, I'm going to inform the
police. Then they'll kill you along with me, my love. Or would you rather live
on the run, afraid for your life? Of course I never told them a thing, nor did they
suspect anything. I was famous as a recluse. And they came to console me for the
death of Lala. Into my arms, goddesses, for life is short, but the night is long.

7

I saw her. I tell you I saw her yesterday, in the garden.

8

I called a friend of mine, an influential man in the District Attorney's office:
What do you know about the case of my servant, Dimas Palmero? My friend
stopped laughing and said: Whatever you want, Nicolás, is how we'll handle it. You
understand: if you like, we'll keep him locked up without a trial until Judgment
Day; if you prefer, we'll move up the court date and try him tomorrow; if what you
want is to see him free, that can be arranged, and, look, Nicolás, why play dumb,
there are people who disappear, who just simply disappear. Whatever you like, I
repeat.

Whatever I liked. I was on the point of saying no, this Dimas or Dimass or
Dimwit or whatever he's called isn't the real problem, I'm the prisoner, listen, call
my lawyer, have the house surrounded, make a big fuss, kill these bastards . . .

I thanked my friend for his offer and hung up without indicating a preference. What for? I buried my head in my pillow. There is nothing left of Lala, not even

---

[25] A snack of eggs, chiles, and tortillas.

the aroma. I racked my brains thinking: What should I do? What solution have I overlooked? What possibilities have I left in the inkwell? I had an inspiration; I decided to speed things up. I went down to the kitchen. It was the hour when Marco Aurelio, Doña Lupe, and the chauffeur with the face of the former president ate. The smell of pork in purslane came up the rococo stairway, stronger than the scent, ever fainter, of Lala—Eduardita, as they called her. I went down berating myself furiously: What was I thinking? Why this terrible helplessness? Why did I think only of myself, not of her, who was the victim, after all? I deserved what had happened to me; I was the prisoner of Las Lomas even before all this happened, I was imprisoned by my own habits, my comfortable life, my easy business deals, my even easier loves. But also—I said when my bare feet touched the cold tile of the living room—I was bound by a sort of devotion and respect for my lovers: I didn't ask questions, I didn't check out their stories: —I have no past, Nico, my life commenced the moment we met, and I might whistle a tune as my only comment, but that was all.

The three were sitting comfortably eating their lunch.

—May I? I inquired cordially.

Doña Lupe got up to prepare something for me. The two men didn't budge, although Marco Aurelio waved for me to sit down. The presidential double merely looked at me, without blinking, from the imperturbable depths of his baggy eyes.

—Thank you. I came down just to ask a question. It occurred to me that what is important to you is not to keep me imprisoned here but to free Dimas. That's right, isn't it?

The cook served me an aromatic dish of pork with purslane, and I began to eat, looking at them. I had said the same thing that they had always said to me: You leave here the day our brother Dimas Palmero gets out of jail. Why now these little looks exchanged between them, this air of uncertainty, if I had only repeated what we all knew: the unwritten rule of our covenant? Give me statutory law; down with *common law*, which is subject to all sorts of interpretations and depends too much on the ethics and good sense of the people. But these peasants from Morelos must be, like me, inheritors of Roman law, where all that counts is what is written, not what is done or not done, even if it violates the letter of the law. The law, sirs, is august, and supersedes all exceptions. These people's lands always had depended on a statute, a royal decree; and now I felt that my life also was going to depend on a written contract. I looked at the looks of my jailers as they looked at each other.

—Tell me if you are willing to put this in writing: The day that Dimas Palmero gets out of the pen, Nicolás Sarmiento goes free from Las Lomas. Agreed?

I began to lose confidence; they didn't answer; they looked at each other, suspicious, tight-lipped, let me tell you, the faces of all three marked with a feline wariness; but hadn't I merely asked them to confirm in writing what they had always said! Why this unforeseen suspicion all of a sudden?

—We've been thinking, Don Nico, said Marco Aurelio finally, and we have reached the conclusion that you could quickly arrange for our brother Dimas Palmero to be freed; then we let you go; but you could still play us a trick and have the law spread its net over Dimas again. —And over us, too, said the cook, not even sighing.

—That game has been played on us plenty, said the pale, baggy-eyed chauffeur gloomily, arranging his hair with his five-fingered comb.

—Come on, come on, the cook emphatically exhorted the electric stove, atavistically airing it with her hands and lips, as if it were a charcoal brazier. The old idiot!

—So what we're willing to write down, Don Nico, is that you'll be freed when you confess to the murder of Eduardita, so that our brother cannot be judged for a crime committed by another.

I won't give them the pleasure of spitting out the pork (anyway, it's quite tasty), or of spilling my glass of fermented pineapple juice, which, quite complacently, the cook has just set in front of my nose. I'm going to give them a lesson in cool, even though my head is spinning like a carousel.

—That was not our original agreement. We've been shut up together here more than three months. Our accord is now binding, as they say.

—Nobody ever respected any agreement with us, the cook quickly replied, waving her hands furiously, as though they were straw fans, in front of the electric burner.

—Nobody, said the chauffeur sepulchrally. All they do is send us to hell.

And I was going to pay for all the centuries of injustice toward the people of Morelos? I didn't know whether to laugh or cry. The simple truth was, I didn't know what to say. I was too busy taking in my new situation. I pushed my plate aside and left the kitchen without saying a word. I climbed the stairs with the sensation that my body was a sick friend I was following with great difficulty. I sat down in the bathroom and there I remained, sleeping. But even my dreams betrayed me. I dreamed that they were right. Damn! They were right.

9

And it is you who wake me, with a furious ringing, a buzz of alarm, calling me on the phone, questioning me urgently, sympathizing with me: Why don't I ask them about her? About whom? I say, playing the fool. About Lala, la Eduarda, la Eduardita, as they called her, la Lala, la . . . Why? She's the key to the whole business! You're completely in the dark: what was behind that scene between Lala and Dimas by the pool? Who was Lala? Have all these people besieged you because of her, or him, or both of them? Why not find out? Fool!

Both of them. I laughed, fell back to sleep, sitting on the toilet in the bathroom, with my pajama bottoms rolled down around my ankles, in a stupor: both of them, you said, without realizing that I can't bear to imagine, much less to pursue the thought, of her with another—she with another, that thought I cannot bear, and you laugh at me, I hear your laughter on the telephone line, you say goodbye, you accuse me, you ask when I got so delicate and sentimental? You, Nicolás Sarmiento, who have had dozens of women just as dozens of women have had you, both you and they members of a city and a society that abandoned all that colonialcatholiccantabrian hypocrisy a few generations ago and cheerfully dedicated themselves to fucking anyone, you who know perfectly well that your dames come to you from others and go from you to others, just as they know that you weren't a monk before you knew them, nor will you become one after leaving them: you, Nicolás Sarmiento, the Don Juan of venture capital, are going to tell us now that you can't bear the thought of your Lala in the arms of Dimas Palmero? Why? It turns your stomach to think that she slept with a servant? Could it be that your horror is more social than sexual? Tell us! Wake up!

I tell you I saw her in the garden.

I got up slowly from the bathroom, I pulled up my pajamas, I didn't have to tie them, they closed with a snap, thank God, I'm hopeless for daily life, I'm only good at making money and making love; does that justify a life?

I look at the garden from the window of my bedroom.

Tell me if you don't see her, standing, with her long braids, a knee slightly bent, looking toward the barranca, surprised to be caught between the city and nature, unable to tell where one begins and the other ends, or which imitates the other: the barranca doesn't smell of the mountains, it smells of the buried city and the city no longer smells of city but of infirm nature: she longs for the country, looking toward the barranca, now Doña Lupe goes out for air, approaches the girl, puts a hand on her shoulder, and says: Don't be sad, you mustn't, you're in the city now and the city can be ugly and hard, but so can the country, the country is at least as violent as the city, I could tell you stories, Eduarda . . .

I'll say it straight out. There is only one redeeming thing in my life and that is the respect I've shown my women. You can condemn me as egotistical, or frivolous, or condescending, or manipulating, or unable to tie my shoes. The one thing you can't accuse me of is sticking my nose where it doesn't belong. I think that's all that has saved me. I think that's why women have loved me: I don't ask for explanations, I don't check out their pasts. No one can check the past of anyone in a society as fluid as ours. Where are you from? What do you do? Who were your mama and papa? Each of our questions can be a wound that doesn't heal. A wound that keeps us from loving or being loved. Everything betrays us: the body sends us one signal and an expression reveals another, words turn against themselves, the mind cons us, death deceives death . . . Beware!

10

I saw Lala that afternoon in the garden, when she was nobody, when she was someone else, when she looked dreamily over a barranca, when she was still a virgin. I saw her and realized that she had a past and that I loved her. These, then, were her people. This, then, was all that remained of her, her family, her people, her land, her nostalgia. Dimas Palmero, was he her lover or her brother, either one longing for revenge? Marco Aurelio, was he really the brother of Dimas or, perhaps, of Eduardita? What was her relationship to the cook Doña Lupe, the baggy-eyed chauffeur, the shabby old patriarch?

I dressed. I went down to the living room. I went out to the garden. There was no longer any reason to bar my way. We all knew the rules, the contract. One day we would sit down to write it out and formalize it. I walked among the running children, took a piece of jerky without asking permission, a plump red-cheeked woman smiled at me, I waved cordially to the old man, the old man looked up and caught my eye, he put out his hand for me to help him up, he looked at me with an incredible intensity, as if only he could see that second body of mine, my sleepy companion struggling behind me through life.

I helped the old man up and he took my arm with a grip as firm as his gaze, and said: "I will grow old but never die. You understand." He led me to the edge of the property. The girl was still standing there, and Doña Lupe put her arms around her, enveloping her shoulders in her huge embrace. We went over to her, and Marco Aurelio, too, half whistling, half smoking. We were a curious quintet, that night in Las Lomas de Chapultepec, far from their land, Morelos, the country, the cane fields, the rice fields, the blue sculpted mountains cut off at the top, secret, where it is said the immortal guerrilla Zapata still rides his white horse . . .

I approached them. Or, rather, the old patriarch who had also decided to be immortal came to me, and the old man almost forced me to join them, to embrace them. I looked at the pretty girl, dark, ripe as those sweet oranges, oranges with an exciting navel and juices slowly evaporating in the sun. I took her dark arm and thought of Lala. Only this girl didn't smell of perfume, she smelled of soap. These, then, were her people, I repeated. This, then, was all that remained of her, of her feline grace, her fantastic capacity for learning conventions and mimicking fashions, speaking languages, being independent, loving herself and loving me, letting go her beautiful body with its rhythmic hips, shaking her small sweet breasts, looking at me orgasmically, as if a tropical river suddenly flowed through her eyes at the moment she desired me, oh my adored Lala, only this remains of you: your rebel land, your peasant forebears and fellows, your province as a genetic pool, bloody as the pool where you died, Lala, your land as an immense liquid pool of cheap arms for cutting cane and tending the moist rows of rice, your land as the ever-flowing fountain of workers for industry and servants for Las Lomas residences and secretary-typists for ministries and clerks in department stores and salesgirls in markets and garbage collectors and chorus girls in the Margo Theater and starlets in the national cinema and assembly-line workers in the border factories and counter help in Texas Taco Huts and servants in mansions like mine in Beverly Hills and young housewives in Chicago and young lawyers like me in Detroit and young journalists in New York: all swept in a dark flow from Morelos, Oaxaca, Guanajuanto, Michoacán, and Potosí, all tossed about the world in currents of revolution, war, liberation, the glory of some, the poverty of others, the audacity of a few, the contempt of many . . . liberty and crime.

Lala, after all, had a past. But I had not imagined it.

11

It wasn't necessary to formalize our agreement. It all started long ago, when the father of my sainted fiancée, Buenaventura del Rey, gave me the key to blackmail General Prisciliano Nieves in his hospital bed and force him to bequeath me his large house in Las Lomas in exchange for his honor as hero of Santa Eulalia. Like me, you have probably asked yourselves: Why didn't Buenaventura's father use that same information? And you know the answer as well as I. In our modern world, things come only to those who know how to use information. That's the recipe for power now, and those who let information slip through their fingers will fail miserably. On one side, weak-knees like the papa of Buenaventura del Rey. On the other side, sharks like Nicolás Sarmiento your servant. And in between, these poor, decent people who don't have any information, who have only memory, a memory that brings them suffering.

Sometimes, audaciously, I cast pebbles into that genetic pool, just to study the ripples. Santa Eulalia? La Zapotera? General Nieves, whose old house in Las Lomas we all inhabit, they unaware and me well informed, naturally? What did they know? In my computer were entered the names and birthplaces of this sea of people who served me, most from the state of Morelos, which is, after all, the size of Switzerland. What information did Dimas Palmero possess?

(*So you come from La Zapotera in Morelos. Yes, Don Nico. Then you know the hacienda of Santa Eulalia? Of course, Don Nico, but to call it a hacienda . . . you know, there's only a burnt-out shell. It's what they called a sugar mill. Ah yes, you probably played in it as a child, Dimas. That's right, señor. And you heard stories about it? Yes, of course. The wall where the Escalona family was lined up in front of a firing squad must still be there? Yes, my grandfather was one of those who was going to be shot. But your grandfather was not a landowner. No, but the colonel said he was going to wipe out both the owners and those who served them. And then what happened? Then another commander said no, Mexican soldiers don't murder the people, because they are the people. And then, Dimas? Then they say that the first officer gave the order to fire on the masters and the servants, but the second officer gave a counterorder. Then the soldiers shot the first officer, and then the Escalona family. They didn't fire at the servants. And then? Then they say the soldiers and the servants embraced and cheered, señor. But you don't remember the names of those officers, Dimas? No, even the old ones no longer remember. But if you like I can try to find out, Don Nico. Thank you, Dimas. At your service, sir.)*

12

Yes, I imagine that Dimas Palmero had some information, who knows—but I'm sure that his relatives, crammed into my garden, kept the memory alive.

I approached them. Or, rather, I approached the old patriarch and he practically forced me to join them, to greet the others. I looked at the pretty, dark girl. I touched her dark arm. I thought of Lala. Doña Lupe had her arm around the girl. The bluish-haired grandfather, that old man as wrinkled as an old piece of silk, supported by the solid body of the cook, playing with the braids of the red-cheeked girl, all looking together toward the barranca of Las Lomas de Chapultepec: I was anxious to find out if they had a collective memory, however faint, of their own land, the same land about which I had information exclusively for my advantage; I asked them if someone had told them the names, did the old men remember the names? Nieves? Does that name mean anything to you—Nieves? Solomillo? Do you remember these old names? I asked, smiling, in an offhand manner, to see if the laws of probability projected by my computer would hold: the officers, the death of the Escalona family, Santa Eulalia, the Zapotera... One of those you mention said he was going to free us from servitude, the old man said very evenly, but when the other one put all of us, masters and servants, in front of a wall, Prisciliano, yes, Prisciliano, now I remember, said, "Mexican soldiers don't murder the people, because they are the people," and the other officer gave the order to fire, Prisciliano gave the counterorder, and the soldiers fired first at Prisciliano, then at the landowners, and finally at the second officer.

—Solomillo? Andrés Solomillo.

—No, Papa, you're getting mixed up. First they shot the landowners, then the revolutionary leaders began to shoot each other.

—Anyway, they all died, said the old survivor with something like resigned sadness.

—Oh, it was a long time ago, Papa.

—And you, what happened to you?

—The soldiers shouted hurray and threw their caps in the air, we tossed our sombreros in the air too, we all embraced, and I swear, sir, no one who was present that morning in Santa Eulalia will ever forget that famous line, "The soldiers are the people..." Well, the important thing, really, was that we'd gotten rid of the landowners first and the generals after.

He paused a moment, looking at the barranca, and said: *And it didn't do us a bit of good.*

The old man shrugged, his memory was beginning to fail him, surely; besides, they told so many different stories about what happened at Santa Eulalia, you could just about believe them all; it was the only way not to lie, and the old man laughed.

—But in the midst of so much death, there's no way to know who survived and who didn't.

—No, Papa, if you don't remember, who is going to?

—You are, said the old man. That is why I tell you. That is how it has always been. The children remember for you.

—Does Dimas know this story? I ventured to ask, immediately biting my tongue for my audacity, my haste, my . . . The old man showed no reaction.

—It all happened a long time ago. I was a child then and the soldier just told us: You're free, there's no more hacienda, or landowners, or bosses, nothing but freedom, our chains were removed, *patrón,* we were free as air. And now see how we end up, serving still, or in jail.

—Long live our chains! Marco Aurelio gave a laugh, a cross between sorrow and cynicism, as he passed by, hoisting a Dos Equis,[26] and I watched him, thinking of Eduarda as a child, how she must have struggled to reach my arms, and I thought of Dimas Palmero in prison and of how he would stay there, with his memory, not realizing that memory was information, Dimas in his cell knowing the same story as everyone, conforming to the memory of the world and not the memory of his people—Prisciliano Nieves was the hero of Santa Eulalia—while the old man knew what Dimas forgot, didn't know, or rejected: Prisciliano Nieves had died in Santa Eulalia; but neither of them knew how to convert his memory into information, and my life depended on their doing nothing, on their memory, accurate or not, remaining frozen forever, an imprisoned memory, you understand, my accomplices? Memory their prisoner, information my prisoner, and both of us here, not moving from the house, both of us immobile, both prisoners, and everyone happy, so I immediately said to Marco Aurelio: Listen, when you visit your brother, tell him he'll lack for nothing, you hear me? Tell him that they'll take good care of him, I promise, he can get married, have conjugal visits, you know: I've heard it said in the house that he likes this red-cheeked girl with the bare arms, well, he can marry her, she's not going to run off with one of these bandits, you've seen what they're like, Marco Aurelio, but tell Dimas not to worry, he can count on me, I'll pay for the wedding and give the girl a dowry, tell him I'm taking him, and all of you, into my care, you will all be well cared for, I'll see to it that you'll never lack for anything, neither you here nor Dimas in the pen, he won't have to work, or you either, I'll look after the family, resigned to the fact that the real criminal will never be found: Who killed Eduarda? We'll never know, I swear, when a girl like that comes to the city and becomes independent, neither you nor I, nobody, is guilty of anything . . .

That was my decision. I preferred to remain with them and leave Dimas in jail rather than declare myself guilty or pin the crime on someone else. They understood. I thought of Dimas Palmero locked up and also of the day I presented myself to Brigadier Prisciliano Nieves in his hospital room.

—Sign here, my general. I promise to take care of your servants and your honor. You can rest in peace. Your reputation is in my hands. I wouldn't want it to be lost, believe me. I will be as silent as the grave; I will be your heir.

The dying Brigadier Prisciliano Nieves looked at me with enormous brazenness. I knew then that his possessions no longer mattered to him, that he wouldn't bat an eyelash.

—Do you have any heirs, other than your servants, I asked, and the old man surely had not expected that question, which I put to him as I took a hand mirror

---

[26]A brand of beer.

from the table next to the bed and held it in front of the sick face of the general, in this way registering his surprise.

Who knows what the false Prisciliano saw there.

—No, I have no one.

Well informed, I already knew that. The old man ceased to look at his death's face and looked instead at mine, young, alert, perhaps resembling his own anonymous youthful look.

—My general, you are not you. Sign here, please, and die in peace.

To each his own memory. To each his own information. The world believed that Prisciliano Nieves killed Andrés Solomillo at Santa Eulalia. The old patriarch installed in my house knew that they had all killed each other. My first sweetheart Buenaventura del Rey's papa, paymaster of the constitutionalist army, knew that as well. Between the two memories lay my twenty-five years of prosperity. But Dimas Palmero, in jail, believed like everyone else that Prisciliano Nieves was the hero of Santa Eulalia, its survivor and its enforcer of justice. His information *was* the world's. The old men, by contrast, *held* the world's information, which isn't the same. Prisciliano Nieves died, along with Andrés Solomillo, at Santa Eulalia, when the former said that the soldiers, being the people, would not kill the people, and the latter proved the contrary right there, and barely had Prisciliano fallen when Solomillo, too, was cut down by the troops. Who usurped the legend of Prisciliano Nieves? What had been that man's name? Who profited from the slaughter of the leaders? No doubt, someone just as anonymous as those who had invaded my garden and surrounded my house. That was the man I visited one morning in the hospital and blackmailed. I converted memory to information. Buenaventura's papa and the ragged old man residing in my garden retained memory but lacked information. Only I had both, but as yet I could do nothing with them except to ensure that everything would go on the same as always, that nothing would be questioned, that it would never occur to Dimas Palmero to translate the memory of his clan into information, that neither the information nor the memory would ever do anyone any good anymore, except for me. But the price of that deadlock was that I would remain forever in my house in Las Lomas, Dimas Palmero in jail, and his family in my garden.

In the final analysis, was it I who won, he who lost? That I leave for you to decide. Over my telephone lines, you have heard all I've said. I've been completely honest with you. I've put all my cards on the table. If there are loose ends in my story, you can gather them up and tie them in a bow yourselves. My memory and my information are now yours. You have the right to criticize, to finish the story, to reverse the tapestry and change the weave, to point out the lapses of logic, to imagine you have resolved all the mysteries that I, the narrator crushed under the press of reality, have let escape through the net of my telephones, which is the net of my words.

And still I'll bet you won't know what to do with what you know. Didn't I say so from the beginning? My story is hard to believe.

Now I no longer had to take risks and struggle. Now I had my place in the world, my house, my servants, and my secrets. I no longer had the guts to go see Dimas Palmero in prison and ask him what he knew about Prisciliano Nieves or what he knew about Lala: Why did you kill her? On your own? Because the old man ordered you to? For the honor of the family? Or for your own?

—Lala, I sighed, my Lala . . .

Then through the gardens of Virreyes came the girls on pogo sticks, hopping like nubile kangaroos, wearing sweatshirts with the names of Yankee universities on them and acid-washed jeans with Walkmans hooked between blue jean and belt and the fantastic look of Martians, radio operators, telephone operators, aviators all rolled into one, with their black earphones over their ears, hopping on their springy pogo sticks over the hedges that separate the properties of Las Lomas—spectacular, Olympic leaps—waving to me, inviting me to follow them, to find myself through others, to join the party, to take a chance with them: Let's all crash the parties, they say, that's more fun, hopping by like hares, like fairies, like Amazons, like Furies, making private property moot, seizing their right to happiness, community, entertainment, and God knows what . . . Free, they would never make any demands on me, ask for marriage, dig into my affairs, discover my secrets, the way the alert Lala did . . . Oh, Lala, why were you so ambitious?

I wave to them from a distance, surrounded by servants, goodbye, goodbye, I toss them kisses and they smile at me, free, carefree, dazzling, dazzled, inviting me to follow them, to abandon my prison, and I wave and would like to tell them no, I am not the prisoner of Las Lomas, no, they are my prisoners, an entire people . . .

I enter the house and disconnect my bank of telephones. The fifty-seven lines on which you're listening to me. I have nothing else to tell you. Soon there will be no one to repeat these fictions, and they will all be true. I thank you for listening.

GABRIEL GARCÍA MÁRQUEZ
[BORN 1928]

At one point in *One Hundred Years of Solitude*, Gabriel García Márquez's best-known novel, the characters succumb to a collective case of amnesia. To combat this contagion, the villagers label everything in town: "Thus they went on living in a reality that was slipping away, momentarily captured by words, but which would escape irremediably when they forgot the values of the written letters." This episode and the narrator's comment on it are emblematic of García Márquez's work as a whole. The fictional village of Macondo, where García Márquez sets many of his novels and stories, is based on the obscure village of Aracataca in northeastern Colombia where the author spent his early childhood. Although he left the village when he was eight, he "labeled" it as Macondo, creating with words a place like William Faulkner's Yoknapatawpha County or R. K. Narayan's Malgudi, a mythic place of the imagination.

LIFE

García Márquez was raised by his grandparents, and his grandmother filled the boy with the myths, legends, and superstitions of the area, lore that would become an important part of his imagined world. García Márquez studied law and journalism at the Universities of Bogotá and Cartagena and worked as a journalist in Bogotá, Havana, New York, Barcelona, and Mexico City, but in spite of this international experience, his writings almost always go back to Macondo, the village from his childhood whose history and mythology distill his experience and embody his view of the human condition.

García Márquez began writing stories in the early fifties when he was also reading the works of Franz Kafka, James Joyce, Virginia Woolf, and William Faulkner. The influence of Kafka and Faulkner is particularly marked in his work. His first book of fiction, *La hojarasca* (translated as *Leaf Storm, and Other Stories,* 1972), appeared in 1955 to little notice. He supported himself by working as a journalist, earning a measure of notoriety for a series of reports that revealed the incompetence of the Colombian navy. To escape governmental retribution for these reports, he took an assignment as a foreign correspondent in Europe and eventually settled in Paris to devote himself to writing stories full time. In the early sixties he published several volumes of stories and established himself as a writer, but throughout his career he has continued to work off and on as a journalist and screenwriter. Much of his journalism has been devoted to political issues, such as his opposition to the Pinochet dictatorship in Chile and his support for the Cuban revolution. He used some of the money from the Nobel Prize for literature in 1982 to fund his antifascist magazine, *Alternativa.*

WORK

García Márquez's best-known work is *El otoño del patriarca* (1975; *The Autumn of the Patriarch,* 1975), the story of a South American dictator, an all-powerful madman who, somewhere between the ages of 107 and 232, still rules his nation in lonely solitude. *El Amor en los tiempos del cólera* (1985; *Love in the Time of Cholera,* 1988), a historical novel, tells of the last days of Latin American liberator Simón Bolívar. *Cien anos de soledad* (1967; *One Hundred Years of Solitude,* 1970), the result of twenty-two years of work, is the novel that has received the most attention. The saga of the founding of Macondo and its rise and fall over a century, the novel combines realistic detail with folk legends and myths; hyperbolic, archetypal characters; and fantastic, dreamlike events. It chronicles seven generations of the family of the founder, José Arcadio Buendía. The town and its history become an imaginative microcosm of the Latin American experience, indeed, of the human experience, for its mythic dimensions reach from the Garden of Eden, to Noah's flood, to the Apocalypse. This mixture of realism, myth, and the miraculous has been called "magical realism," the dominant mode adopted by the writers of *el boom* (the boom), an explosion of Latin American literature during the 1960s and 1970s, in the works of García Márquez, Carlos Fuentes of Mexico, Mario Vargas Llosa of Peru, Julio Cortázar of Argentina, and others. In the works of these writers, the realistic details of everyday life are combined with extraordinary, even miraculous events.

García Márquez stresses the realism in his work; "my work as a whole," he has written, "is founded on a geographical and historical reality." The description of the fallen angel in *A Very Old Man with Enormous Wings* (1972) illustrates this fundamental realism. Bald and dirty, with missing teeth, ragged clothes, and an unbearable smell, the stranger who appears in the courtyard of Pelayo and Elisenda's house is first of all "an old man." The priest concludes that "seen close up he was much too human." Even the wings that mark him as an angel are bedraggled and "strewn with parasites." His presence in the village may be magical, but it is also absurd, and the reactions of the villagers quickly transform the unfamiliar creature into something familiar. Father Gonzaga is convinced that he is an impostor and writes to the Pope for confirmation of his suspicions; the villagers treat him as a sideshow spectacle, one that is outdone when the spider woman comes to town. The story she tells of her suffering provides a conventional explanation for her situation, unlike the haughty silence of the angel. In the end, when the angel miraculously flies away, Elisenda is relieved that this "annoyance" is gone from her life. The angel may be magical, but the various reactions of the villagers—from indifference to exploitation—deflate the angel's significance and lead us to wonder about the place of magic in the modern world.

SUGGESTED READINGS

Useful introductions in English to García Márquez's work include George R. McMurray's *Gabriel García Márquez* (1987), Kathleen McNerney's *Understanding Gabriel García Márquez* (1989), and Harley D. Oberhelman's *Gabriel García Márquez* (1991). Raymond Williams's *Gabriel García Márquez* (1984) focuses primarily on the short stories.

absurdity, inexplicable things that people try to make sense out of

A Very Old Man with Enormous Wings

Translated by Gregory Rabassa

On the third day of rain they had killed so many crabs inside the house that Pelayo had to cross his drenched courtyard and throw them into the sea, because the newborn child had a temperature all night and they thought it was due to the stench. The world had been sad since Tuesday. Sea and sky were a single ash-gray thing and the sands of the beach, which on March nights glimmered like powdered light, had become a stew of mud and rotten shellfish. The light was so weak at noon that when Pelayo was coming back to the house after throwing away the crabs, it was hard for him to see what it was that was moving and groaning in the rear of the courtyard. He had to go very close to see that it was an old man, a very old man, lying face down in the mud, who, in spite of his tremendous efforts, couldn't get up, impeded by his enormous wings.

Frightened by that nightmare, Pelayo ran to get Elisenda, his wife, who was putting compresses on the sick child, and he took her to the rear of the courtyard. They both looked at the fallen body with mute stupor. He was dressed like a ragpicker. There were only a few faded hairs left on his bald skull and very few teeth in his mouth, and his pitiful condition of a drenched great-grandfather had taken away any sense of grandeur he might have had. His huge buzzard wings, dirty and half-plucked, were forever entangled in the mud. They looked at him so long and so closely that Pelayo and Elisenda very soon overcame their surprise and in the end found him familiar. Then they dared speak to him, and he answered in an incomprehensible dialect with a strong sailor's voice. That was how they skipped over the inconvenience of the wings and quite intelligently concluded that he was a lonely castaway from some foreign ship wrecked by the storm. And yet, they called in a neighbor woman who knew everything about life and death to see him, and all she needed was one look to show them their mistake.

"He's an angel," she told them. "He must have been coming for the child, but the poor fellow is so old that the rain knocked him down."

On the following day everyone knew that a flesh-and-blood angel was held captive in Pelayo's house. Against the judgment of the wise neighbor woman, for whom angels in those times were the fugitive survivors of a celestial conspiracy, they did not have the heart to club him to death. Pelayo watched over him all afternoon from the kitchen, armed with his bailiff's club, and before going to bed he dragged him out of the mud and locked him up with the hens in the wire chicken coop. In the middle of the night, when the rain stopped, Pelayo and Elisenda were still killing crabs. A short time afterward the child woke up without a fever and with a desire to eat. Then they felt magnanimous and decided to put the angel on a raft with fresh water and provisions for three days and leave him to his fate on the high seas. But when they went out into the courtyard with the first light of dawn, they found the whole neighborhood in front of the chicken coop having fun with the angel, without the slightest reverence, tossing him things to eat through the openings in the wire as if he weren't a supernatural creature but a circus animal.

Father Gonzaga arrived before seven o'clock, alarmed at the strange news. By that time onlookers less frivolous than those at dawn had already arrived and they were making all kinds of conjectures concerning the captive's future. The simplest among them thought that he should be named mayor of the world. Others of sterner mind felt that he should be promoted to the rank of five-star general in order to win all wars. Some visionaries hoped that he could be put to stud in order to implant on earth a race of winged wise men who could take charge of the universe. But Father Gonzaga, before becoming a priest, had been a robust woodcutter. Standing by the wire, he reviewed his catechism in an instant and asked them to open the door so that he could take a close look at that pitiful man who looked more like a huge decrepit hen among the fascinated chickens. He was lying in a corner drying his open wings in the sunlight among the fruit peels and breakfast leftovers that the early risers had thrown him. Alien to the impertinences of the world, he only lifted his antiquarian eyes and murmured something in his dialect when Father Gonzaga went into the chicken coop and said good morning to him in Latin. The parish priest had his first suspicion of an impostor when he saw that he did not understand the language of God or know how to greet His ministers. Then he noticed that seen close up he was much too human: he had an unbearable smell of the outdoors, the back side of his wings was strewn with parasites and his main feathers had been mistreated by terrestrial winds, and nothing about him measured up to the proud dignity of angels. Then he came out of the chicken coop and in a brief sermon warned the curious against the risks of being ingenuous. He reminded them that the devil had the bad habit of making use of carnival tricks in order to confuse the unwary. He argued that if wings were not the essential element in determining the difference between a hawk and an airplane, they were even less so in the recognition of angels. Nevertheless, he promised to write a letter to his bishop so that the latter would write to his primate so that the latter would write to the Supreme Pontiff in order to get the final verdict from the highest courts.

His prudence fell on sterile hearts. The news of the captive angel spread with such rapidity that after a few hours the courtyard had the bustle of a marketplace and they had to call in troops with fixed bayonets to disperse the mob that was about to knock the house down. Elisenda, her spine all twisted from sweeping up so much marketplace trash, then got the idea of fencing in the yard and charging five cents admission to see the angel.

The curious came from far away. A traveling carnival arrived with a flying acrobat who buzzed over the crowd several times, but no one paid any attention to him because his wings were not those of an angel but, rather, those of a sidereal bat. The most unfortunate invalids on earth came in search of health: a poor woman who since childhood had been counting her heartbeats and had run out of numbers; a Portuguese man who couldn't sleep because the noise of the stars disturbed him; a sleepwalker who got up at night to undo the things he had done while awake; and many others with less serious ailments. In the midst of that shipwreck disorder that made the earth tremble, Pelayo and Elisenda were happy with fatigue, for in less than a week they had crammed their rooms with money and the line of pilgrims waiting their turn to enter still reached beyond the horizon.

The angel was the only one who took no part in his own act. He spent his time trying to get comfortable in his borrowed nest, befuddled by the hellish heat of the oil lamps and sacramental candles that had been placed along the wire. At first they tried to make him eat some mothballs, which, according to the wisdom of the wise neighbor woman, were the food prescribed for angels. But he turned them down, just as he turned down the papal lunches that the penitents brought him, and they never found out whether it was because he was an angel or because he was an old man that in the end he ate nothing but eggplant mush. His only supernatural virtue seemed to be patience. Especially during the first days, when the hens pecked at him, searching for the stellar parasites that proliferated in his wings, and the cripples pulled out feathers to touch their defective parts with, and even the most merciful threw stones at him, trying to get him to rise so they could see him standing. The only time they succeeded in arousing him was when they burned his side with an iron for branding steers, for he had been motionless for so many hours that they thought he was dead. He awoke with a start, ranting in his hermetic language and with tears in his eyes, and he flapped his wings a couple of times, which brought on a whirlwind of chicken dung and lunar dust and a gale of panic that did not seem to be of this world. Although many thought that his reaction had been one not of rage but of pain, from then on they were careful not to annoy him, because the majority understood that his passivity was not that of a hero taking his ease but that of a cataclysm in repose.

Father Gonzaga held back the crowd's frivolity with formulas of maidservant inspiration while awaiting the arrival of a final judgment on the nature of the captive. But the mail from Rome showed no sense of urgency. They spent their time finding out if the prisoner had a navel, if his dialect had any connection with Aramaic, how many times he could fit on the head of a pin, or whether he wasn't just a Norwegian with wings. Those meager letters might have come and gone until the end of time if a providential event had not put an end to the priest's tribulations.

It so happened that during those days, among so many other carnival attractions, there arrived in town the traveling show of the woman who had been changed into a spider for having disobeyed her parents. The admission to see her was not only less than the admission to see the angel, but people were permitted to ask her all manner of questions about her absurd state and to examine her up and down so that no one would ever doubt the truth of her horror. She was a frightful tarantula the size of a ram and with the head of a sad maiden. What was most heartrending, however, was not her outlandish shape but the sincere affliction with which she recounted the details of her misfortune. While still practically a child she had sneaked out of her parents' house to go to a dance, and while she was coming back through the woods after having danced all night without permission, a fearful thunderclap rent the sky in two and through the crack came the lightning bolt of brimstone that changed her into a spider. Her only nourishment came from the meatballs that charitable souls chose to toss into her mouth. A spectacle like that, full of so much human truth and with such a fearful lesson, was bound to defeat without even trying that of a haughty angel who scarcely deigned to look at mortals. Besides, the few miracles attributed to the angel showed a certain mental disorder, like the blind man who didn't recover his sight but grew three new teeth, or the paralytic who didn't get to walk but almost won the lottery, and the leper whose sores sprouted sunflowers. Those consolation miracles, which were more like mocking fun, had already ruined the angel's reputation when the woman who had been changed into a spider finally crushed him completely. That was how Father Gonzaga was cured forever of his insomnia and Pelayo's courtyard went back to being as empty as during the time it had rained for three days and crabs walked through the bedrooms.

The owners of the house had no reason to lament. With the money they saved they built a two-story mansion with balconies and gardens and high netting so that crabs wouldn't get in during the winter, and with iron bars on the windows so that angels wouldn't get in. Pelayo also set up a rabbit warren close to town and gave up his job as bailiff for good, and Elisenda bought some satin pumps with high heels and many dresses of iridescent silk, the kind worn on Sunday by the most desirable women in those times. The chicken coop was the only thing that didn't receive any attention. If they washed it down with creolin and burned tears of myrrh inside it every so often, it was not in homage to the angel but to drive away the dungheap stench that still hung everywhere like a ghost and was turning the new house into an old one. At first, when the child learned to walk, they were careful that he not get too close to the chicken coop. But then they began to lose their fears and got used to the smell, and before the child got his second teeth he'd gone inside the chicken coop to play, where the wires were falling apart. The angel was no less standoffish with him than with other mortals, but he tolerated the most ingenious infamies with the patience of a dog who had no illusions. They both came down with chicken pox at the same time. The doctor who took care of the child couldn't resist the temptation to listen to the angel's heart, and he found so much whistling in the heart and so many sounds in his kidneys that it seemed impossible for him to be alive. What surprised him most, however, was the logic of his wings. They seemed so natural on that completely human organism that he couldn't understand why other men didn't have them too.

When the child began school it had been some time since the sun and rain had caused the collapse of the chicken coop. The angel went dragging himself about here and there like a stray dying man. They would drive him out of the bedroom with a broom and a moment later find him in the kitchen. He seemed to be in so many places at the same time that they grew to think that he'd been duplicated, that he was reproducing himself all through the house, and the exasperated and unhinged Elisenda shouted that it was awful living in that hell full of angels. He could scarcely eat and his antiquarian eyes had also become so foggy that he went about bumping into posts. All he had left were the bare cannulae of his last feathers. Pelayo threw a blanket over him and extended him the charity of letting him sleep in the shed, and only then did they notice that he had a temperature at night, and was delirious with the tongue twisters of an old Norwegian. That was one of the few times they became alarmed, for they thought he was going to die and not even the wise neighbor woman had been able to tell them what to do with dead angels.

And yet he not only survived his worst winter, but seemed improved with the first sunny days. He remained motionless for several days in the farthest corner of the courtyard, where no one would see him, and at the beginning of December some large, stiff feathers began to grow on his wings, the feathers of a scarecrow, which looked more like another misfortune of decrepitude. But he must have known the reason for those changes, for he was quite careful that no one should notice them, that no one should hear the sea chanteys that he sometimes sang under the stars. One morning Elisenda was cutting some bunches of onions for lunch when a wind that seemed to come from the high seas blew into the kitchen. Then she went to the window and caught the angel in his first attempts at flight. They were so clumsy that his fingernails opened a furrow in the vegetable patch and he was on the point of knocking the shed down with the ungainly flapping that slipped on the light and couldn't get a grip on the air. But he did manage to gain altitude. Elisenda let out a sigh of relief, for herself and for him, when she saw him pass over the last houses, holding himself up in some way with the risky flapping of a senile vulture. She kept watching him even when she was through cutting the onions and she kept on watching until it was no longer possible for her to see him, because then he was no longer an annoyance in her life but an imaginary dot on the horizon of the sea.

ADRIENNE RICH
[BORN 1929]

When the poets Sylvia Plath and Anne Sexton, Adrienne Rich's brilliant contemporaries, took their own lives in their early middle years, they involuntarily set off a new wave of belief that women writers must suffer and probably die in the effort to accommodate their gender and their art. In contrast, for forty years Rich has been a poet continuously looked to by her readers not only for the excellence of her work in itself, but because the woman and her work together have come to seem talismans for hope and courage, for what she herself has named "the will to change." Her first book of poetry appeared in 1951, when she was only twenty-two, and in the years since, she has steadily published books of poetry, feminist literary criticism, autobiographical essays, and social commentary that have reflected the widening and changing concerns of Euro-American women since the 1950s. To read through her work chronologically is to read a fluid, uncompromisingly honest chronicle of all the pain and beauty inherent in growth and survival.

LIFE

In her autobiographical essay "Split at the Root: An Essay on Jewish Identity" (1982), Rich describes some of the circumstances of her life from childhood through college. Born on May 16, 1929, into an upper-middle-class family in Baltimore, she was inculcated with ideas about the behavior proper to Southern women by her Christian mother, who had set aside her own gifts in musical composition and performance in favor of attending to her husband and two daughters. Rich's father was the descendant of Jewish immigrants from Austria-Hungary and the Middle East who raised their son to assimilate into the world of white Southern gentile professionals. When he moved to Baltimore, he was accepted into the fold at Johns Hopkins Hospital, despite being the only Jewish doctor on staff. As Rich says in another autobiographical essay, "When We Dead Awaken: Writing As Re-Vision" (1971), her father, intent upon achievement, was the appreciative and demanding audience for whom she first wrote, although "the obverse side of this, of course, was that I tried for a long time to please him, or rather, not to displease him."

At Radcliffe in the late forties and early fifties, she had the common experience of being taught to read male poets by male professors, and naturally modeled her early work on the formalist, measured, and somewhat cerebral poems of writers such as Frost, Auden, MacNeice, and Stevens, who were then in vogue. In a preface to her first collection, *A Change of World* (1951), which won the Yale Younger Poets Prize, Auden himself praised Rich for what seem in retrospect the rather negative virtues of mildness and obedience; her poems, he said, "speak quietly but do not mumble, respect their elders, but are not cowed by them." About "Aunt Jennifer's Tigers," a poem from her first collection included below, Rich herself has observed that, while the poem articulates the split between female creativity and the feminine wish to please a man, at the time of its writing she scarcely realized the poem might be about herself as well as about an imaginary aunt:

> It was important that Aunt Jennifer was a person as distinct from myself as possible—distanced by the formalism of the poem, by its objective, observant tone—even by putting the woman in a different generation.

Imbued with the assumption of most people of her generation that marriage and a family were the normal way for a woman to proceed toward a fulfilling life, in 1953 Rich married Alfred Conrad, a Harvard faculty member in economics, and gave birth to three sons, David, Paul, and Jacob, over the next six years. In 1955, the year of her eldest son's birth, she brought out her second volume of poems, *The Diamond Cutters,* another volume of technically accomplished and graceful formalist poems. It would be eight years before her next book. Although the intervening time was filled with grants and awards, it was also filled with the incessant tasks of housekeeping and mothering, a growing frustration at not having enough uninterrupted time to work, and a terrifying sense of "being pulled along on a current which called itself my destiny, but in which I seemed to be losing touch with whoever I had been." Motherhood, as she has observed, can be a great radicalizer. In 1976, her book *Of Woman Born: Motherhood as Experience and Institution* would look back on her life as a daughter and as a mother to examine the paradoxes and dilemmas attendant upon those years in women's lives.

Snapshots of a Daughter-In-Law, the book that came out in 1963, the title poem of which took her more than two years to write, was a breakthrough for Rich in that the line and meter of the poems became looser even as she more directly addressed issues such as women's anger and separations and quarrels between the sexes and between generations. Still, the poems keep a relatively safe distance from their subjects; the poet rarely speaks in her own voice as herself.

Like many young adults in academic communities in the late fifties, Rich was drawn to civil rights issues; throughout the sixties and early seventies, she became increasingly involved in protesting the United States' presence in Indochina. The family moved to New York City in 1966, where Alfred Conrad had accepted a post at City College, and Rich began in 1968 to teach in the SEEK and Open Admissions programs there. These programs opened college doors to disadvantaged and nontraditional students, and they often proved to be as radicalizing and transformative for the participating teachers as for their students. Rich would continue to teach in the academy, off and on, until 1990, and her collections of poems over those years—*Necessities of Life* (1966), *Leaflets* (1969), and *The Will to Change* (1971)—reveal her increasingly strong political commitments in their subject matter and their experimentation. *Leaflets,* for example, includes a series of poems written in the old Arabic form of the *ghazal,* in which Rich uses that strongly imagistic tradition to address in colloquial language issues of the Vietnam War, the racial politics of inner-city life, and her experience as a teacher. "I Dream I'm the Death of Orpheus" (1971) draws upon the Greek myth of the consummate poet who lost his own life in the attempt to lead his beloved Eurydice out of the realm of the dead, all because he broke the rules and gazed longingly at her face before they had emerged from the underworld into the sunlight. But it draws even more for its specific imagery upon Jean Cocteau's 1950 film *Orphée.* This Eurydice is not a passive, innocently fatal woman who inadvertently kills men through her own helplessly desirable self. Rather, she is a powerful poet in her own right; she has been repressed by the male romantic tradition that has idolized women; she is angry; and she is fighting for her own existence as an individual and an artist.

In the sixties and early seventies, Rich found that questions raised about one kind of injustice or oppression inevitably led her to question other areas of her life, and political transformation led her toward personal changes, none of them easily undertaken. In 1970, Rich left Alfred Conrad, who took his own life later that same year. The title poem from *Diving into the Wreck* (1973) centers upon the themes of risk and loss, of courageous acts of discovery and of recovery, of regaining wholeness, and dredging up from terrible experience that which is worth keeping, "something more permanent / than fish or weed ... / the wreck and not the story of the wreck / the thing itself and not the myth."

WORK

When *Diving into the Wreck* won the 1974 National Book Award, Rich declined to accept as an individual. Together with her sister nominees Alice Walker and Audre Lorde, she drafted a statement accepting the prize on behalf of all women. By 1976, Rich and Michelle Cliff, the Jamaican-born poet and essayist, had become partners in their lives and in their enterprise. For several years they co-edited *Sinister Wisdom,* the lesbian feminist journal that was especially distinguished in its publication of the work of women of color. In *Twenty-One Love Poems,* published first as a chapbook in 1976 and then incorporated into *The Dream of a Common Language* (1978), Rich took the Elizabethan sonnet sequence, the epitome of what she has called "all those poems about women written by men," and used it instead as a medium to explore the sexual and spiritual dimensions of a lesbian love relationship. In essays such as "It Is the Lesbian in Us" (1976) and "Compulsory Heterosexuality and Lesbian Existence" (1980), reprinted in *Bread, Blood, and Poetry* (1986), she has become a major theorist of the politics of sexuality and an articulator of lesbian consciousness.

In *The Fact of a Doorframe* (1984), Rich made a collection of her work from her nine previous books; *An Atlas of the Difficult World* (1992) is her most recent book of poetry. At present, Rich makes her home in California.

SUGGESTED READINGS

The updated edition of *Adrienne Rich's Poetry: The Texts of the Poems; The Poet on Her Work; Reviews and Criticism,* edited by Barbara Charlesworth Gelpi and Albert Gelpi (1993), is a useful book. Other studies include J. R. Cooper's *Reading Adrienne Rich: Reviews and Revisions 1951–1981* (1984) and C. Keyes's *The Aesthetics of Power: The Poetry of Adrienne Rich* (1986).

Aunt Jennifer's Tigers

Aunt Jennifer's tigers prance across a screen,
Bright topaz denizens of a world of green.
They do not fear the men beneath the tree;
They pace in sleek chivalric certainty.

Aunt Jennifer's fingers fluttering through her wool
Find even the ivory needle hard to pull.
The massive weight of Uncle's wedding band
Sits heavily upon Aunt Jennifer's hand.

[handwritten margin note: metonymy]

When Aunt is dead, her terrified hands will lie
Still ringed with ordeals she was mastered by.   10
The tigers in the panel that she made
Will go on prancing, proud and unafraid.

I Dream I'm the Death of Orpheus

[handwritten margin note: Orpheus went to rescue Eurydice but gazes into her eyes before they emerge from underworld]

I am walking rapidly through striations of light and dark thrown
          under an arcade.

I am a woman in the prime of life, with certain powers
and those powers severely limited
by authorities whose faces I rarely see.
I am a woman in the prime of life
driving her dead poet in a black Rolls-Royce
through a landscape of twilight and thorns.
A woman with a certain mission
which if obeyed to the letter will leave her intact.
A woman with the nerves of a panther   10
a woman with contacts among Hell's Angels
a woman feeling the fullness of her powers
at the precise moment when she must not use them
a woman sworn to lucidity
who sees through the mayhem, the smoky fires
of these underground streets
her dead poet learning to walk backward against the wind
on the wrong side of the mirror

[handwritten margin note: Woman as needing to be saved]

Diving into the Wreck

[handwritten margin note: language of the oppressor — formalism abandoned]

First having read the book of myths,
and loaded the camera,
and checked the edge of the knife-blade,
I put on
the body-armor of black rubber
the absurd flippers
the grave and awkward mask.
I am having to do this
not like Cousteau with his
assiduous team   10
aboard the sun-flooded schooner
but here alone.

There is a ladder.
The ladder is always there
hanging innocently
close to the side of the schooner.

We know what it is for,
we who have used it.
Otherwise
it's a piece of maritime floss
some sundry equipment.   20

I go down.
Rung after rung and still
the oxygen immerses me
the blue light
the clear atoms
of our human air.
I go down.
My flippers cripple me,
I crawl like an insect down the ladder   30
and there is no one
to tell me when the ocean
will begin.

First the air is blue and then
it is bluer and then green and then
black I am blacking out and yet
my mask is powerful
it pumps my blood with power
the sea is another story
the sea is not a question of power   40
I have to learn alone
to turn my body without force
in the deep element.

And now: it is easy to forget
what I came for
among so many who have always
lived here
swaying their crenellated fans
between the reefs
and besides   50
you breathe differently down here.

I came to explore the wreck.
The words are purposes.
The words are maps.
I came to see the damage that was done
and the treasures that prevail.
I stroke the beam of my lamp
slowly along the flank
of something more permanent
than fish or weed   60

the thing I came for:
the wreck and not the story of the wreck
the thing itself and not the myth

the drowned face always staring
toward the sun
the evidence of damage
worn by salt and sway into this threadbare beauty
the ribs of the disaster
curving their assertion
among the tentative haunters.   70

This is the place.
And I am here, the mermaid whose dark hair
streams black, the merman in his armored body
We circle silently
about the wreck
we dive into the hold.
I am she: I am he

whose drowned face sleeps with open eyes
whose breasts still bear the stress
whose silver, copper, vermeil cargo lies   80
obscurely inside barrels
half-wedged and left to rot
we are the half-destroyed instruments
that once held to a course
the water-eaten log
the fouled compass

We are, I am, you are
by cowardice or courage
the one who find our way
back to this scene   90
carrying a knife, a camera
a book of myths
in which
our names do not appear.

FROM

Twenty-One Love Poems

I: "WHEREVER IN THIS CITY, SCREENS FLICKER"

Wherever in this city, screens flicker
with pornography, with science-fiction vampires,
victimized hirelings bending to the lash,
we also have to walk . . . if simply as we walk
through the rainsoaked garbage, the tabloid cruelties
of our own neighborhoods.
We need to grasp our lives inseparable
from those rancid dreams, that blurt of metal, those disgraces,
and the red begonia perilously flashing
from a tenement sill six stories high,   10

or the long-legged young girls playing ball
in the junior highschool playground.
No one has imagined us. We want to live like trees,
sycamores blazing through the sulfuric air,
dappled with scars, still exuberantly budding,
our animal passion rooted in the city.

III: "Since we're not young, weeks have to do time"

Since we're not young, weeks have to do time
for years of missing each other. Yet only this odd warp
in time tells me we're not young.
Did I ever walk the morning streets at twenty,
my limbs streaming with a purer joy?
did I lean from any window over the city
listening for the future
as I listen here with nerves tuned for your ring?
And you, you move toward me with the same tempo.
Your eyes are everlasting, the green spark   10
of the blue-eyed grass of early summer,
the green-blue wild cress washed by the spring.
At twenty, yes: we thought we'd live forever.
At forty-five, I want to know even our limits.
I touch you knowing we weren't born tomorrow,
and somehow, each of us will help the other live,
and somewhere, each of us must help the other die.

IV: "I come home from you through the early light of spring"

I come home from you through the early light of spring
flashing off ordinary walls, the Pez Dorado,
the Discount Wares, the shoe-store.... I'm lugging my sack
of groceries, I dash for the elevator
where a man, taut, elderly, carefully composed
lets the door almost close on me. —*For god's sake hold it!*
I croak at him. —*Hysterical*,—he breathes my way.
I let myself into the kitchen, unload my bundles,
make coffee, open the window, put on Nina Simone
singing *Here comes the sun*.... I open the mail,   10
drinking delicious coffee, delicious music,
my body still both light and heavy with you. The mail
lets fall a Xerox of something written by a man
aged 27, a hostage, tortured in prison:
My genitals have been the object of such a sadistic display
they keep me constantly awake with the pain ...
Do whatever you can to survive.
You know, I think that men love wars ...
And my incurable anger, my unmendable wounds
break open further with tears, I am crying helplessly,   20
and they still control the world, and you are not in my arms.

VI: "YOUR SMALL HANDS, PRECISELY EQUAL TO MY OWN—"

Your small hands, precisely equal to my own—
only the thumb is larger, longer—in these hands
I could trust the world, or in many hands like these,
handling power-tools or steering-wheel
or touching a human face.... Such hands could turn
the unborn child rightways in the birth canal
or pilot the exploratory rescue-ship
through icebergs, or piece together
the fine, needle-like sherds of a great krater-cup
bearing on its sides   10
figures of ecstatic women striding
to the sibyl's den or the Eleusinian cave—
such hands might carry out an unavoidable violence
with such restraint, with such a grasp
of the range and limits of violence
that violence ever after would be obsolete.

MILAN KUNDERA
[BORN 1929]

With his mixture of philosophy, autobiography, and fiction, Milan Kundera continues
to reinvent and reinvigorate the modern novel. Although Kundera does not tend to dwell
on the totalitarian legacy of Eastern Europe under the U.S.S.R., the relationships of his
characters, their betrayals and fantasies, are usually shaped by political events. It is not easy
to place Kundera within a specific literary tradition. Unlike French activist writers such as
André Malraux, Jean-Paul Sartre, and Albert Camus, who promote leftist political agendas
in their writings, Kundera uses wit and irony to probe the essential questions of meaning
and purpose in a modern, technological, bureaucratic world, questions that transcend
political boundaries and platforms. The political oppression that forms a backdrop to
Kundera's fiction can as easily erupt into comedy and farce as into tragedy.

LIFE

Kundera was born April 1, 1929, in Brno, Czechoslovakia. Following the example
of his father, the well-known pianist Ludvik Kundera, Milan initially studied music at
Charles University in Prague and worked as a laborer and jazz musician. As a student he
joined the Communist Party but, due to an untimely remark, was debarred from the party
about the time of the Communist takeover of Prague in 1947. In 1956 he changed his
focus to literature and film and enrolled in the Academy of Music and Dramatic Arts in
Prague, where, after two years, he became an assistant professor from 1957 to 1969. He
was also admitted back into the Communist Party. His first three publications were books
of poetry: *Man: A Broad Garden* (1953), *The Last May* (1955), and *Monologues* (1957). A
play of his, *The Owners of the Keys,* was first produced in Prague in April 1962 at the
National Theatre, and won the Klement Lukes Prize in 1963.

Kundera switched to fiction and published three volumes of short stories under the collective title of *Laughable Loves* (1963, 1965, 1969). A turning point in his career occurred with the publication of his first novel, *The Joke* (1967), which explores the role of humor in a totalitarian regime. Along with other writers, Kundera was an outspoken advocate of opening up Czechoslovakia's socialism to criticism and liberal reform. Steps were taken in this direction and for a few months the Czechoslovakians enjoyed the cultural freedom of the Prague Spring of 1968, while dreaming of independence from Soviet Russia. When Kundera's *The Joke* was finally published after a struggle with state censorship, it quickly went through three large printings and Kundera became a major literary voice in Eastern Europe. Within four months, however, the political situation reversed; the reform movement ended when troops from the U.S.S.R., Poland, and East Germany invaded Czechoslovakia. Kundera lost his job and his Party affiliation, his books were removed from bookstores and libraries, and he was forbidden to publish in Czechoslovakia. Kundera wrote two novels that were published first in translations abroad. The French version of *Life Is Elsewhere* was published in 1973 and received the Prix Medicis for the best foreign novel published in France in that year. The English version of *The Farewell Party* was published in 1976 and received the Premio Mondello for the best novel published in Italy in 1976. Both novels mixed eroticism with political satire.

In 1975 Kundera was allowed to leave his country to accept a teaching position in comparative literature at the University of Rennes in France. After the publication in 1979 of *The Book of Laughter and Forgetting,* which combines autobiography, history, and fiction, the Czech government revoked Kundera's citizenship. In 1981 he became a French citizen and returned to the theater with *Jacques and His Master,* a play based on a work by Diderot.

WORK

The Unbearable Lightness of Being (1984), which was made into a popular movie, is probably his most famous novel in the West. In an essay on the art of the novel, Kundera describes the modern situation for his characters:

> I thought of the fate of Descartes' famous formulation: man as "master and proprietor of nature." Having brought off miracles in science and technology, this "master and proprietor" is suddenly realizing that he owns nothing and is master neither of nature (it is vanishing, little by little, from the planet), nor of History (it has escaped him), nor of himself (he is led by the irrational forces of his soul). But if God is gone and man is no longer master, then who is master? The planet is moving through the void without any master. There it is, the unbearable lightness of being.

Kundera acknowledges the influence of writers such as Laurence Sterne from England, Denis Diderot from France, and Hermann Broch from Germany; but from Kundera's own Prague came the brilliant, disturbing artistry of Franz Kafka, to whom Kundera acknowledges a large debt:

> There are tendencies in modern history that produce the *Kafkan* in the broad social dimension: the progressive concentration of power, tending to deify itself; the bureaucratization of social activity that turns all institutions into *boundless labyrinths;* and the resulting depersonalization of the individual.

A central theme in Kundera's writings, as in Kafka's, is the dispensing and manipulation of power. Publicly, power is a question of politics and institutions; privately, the machinations of power involve sex and love. In a world of shrinking possibilities, sex might be the ultimate rebellion against authority, or the only available arena for adventure and heroism. In *The Unbearable Lightness of Being,* two sets of lovers play out the endless varieties of betrayal and fulfillment. In his most recent novel, *Immortality* (1990), love is again the central theme, which is explored in seven parts (a common structural pattern in Kundera's novels) by a writer named Kundera who becomes preoccupied with a fascinating woman—part imagination and part reality.

In a marvelously subtle and intricate short story, "The Hitchhiking Game," a young couple on vacation begin a game in which they play uncharacteristic roles. Although politics is not an essential ingredient in this story, the young couple live most of the year in a regimented society that restricts their personal freedom to be who they really are or would wish to be. The hitchhiking game then provides opportunities to explore new social and sexual roles, while at the same time testing previously untapped dimensions of their personalities. As might be expected, the roles begin to dominate the relationship, and with a deceptive ease their identities become confused. Although the game stretches the psychological makeup of both players, it does not ultimately enhance the intimacy of their relationship. In fact, something appears to have been lost; at the beginning of the story, the young man had found something special in the woman, irrespective of "the law of universal transience, which made even his girl's shyness a precious thing to him." At the end of the story she poignantly attempts to reclaim this identity by asserting, "I am me, I am me, I am me." In this story, Kundera dramatizes the role of games in modern relationships and the ways in which limited self-awareness and partial communication create obstacles to intimacy.

Suggested Readings

The American novelist Philip Roth has provided helpful commentary on Kundera's writing in an introduction to *Laughable Loves,* an interview with Kundera in *The Book of Laughter and Forgetting,* and in his own *Reading Myself and Others* (1975). A full-length study of Kundera is in Robert Porter's *Milan Kundera: A Voice from Central Europe* (1981). A. French's *Czech Writers and Politics, 1945–1969* (1982) and Z.A.B. Zeman's *Prague Spring* (1969) examine the political context for art in Eastern Europe.

The Hitchhiking Game

Translated by Suzanne Rappaport

1

The needle on the gas gauge suddenly dipped toward empty and the young driver of the sports car declared that it was maddening how much gas the car ate up. "See that we don't run out of gas again," protested the girl (about twenty-two), and reminded the driver of several places where this had already happened to them. The young man replied that he wasn't worried, because whatever he went through with her had the charm of adventure for him. The girl objected; whenever they had run out of gas on the highway it had, she said, always been an adventure only for her. The young man had hidden and she had had to make ill use of her charms by thumbing a ride and letting herself be driven to the nearest gas station, then thumbing a ride back with a can of gas. The young man asked the girl whether the drivers who had given her a ride had been unpleasant, since she spoke as if her task had been a hardship. She replied (with awkward flirtatiousness) that sometimes they had been *very* pleasant but that it hadn't done her any good as she had been burdened with the can and had had to leave them before she could get anything going. "Pig," said the young man. The girl protested that she wasn't a pig, but that he really was. God knows how many girls stopped him on the highway, when he was driving the car alone! Still driving, the young man put his arm around the girl's shoulders and kissed her gently on the forehead. He knew that she loved him and that she was jealous. Jealousy isn't a pleasant quality, but if it isn't overdone (and if it's combined with modesty), apart from its inconvenience there's even something touching about it. At least that's what the young man thought. Because he was only twenty-eight, it seemed to him that he was old and knew everything that a man could know about women. In the girl sitting beside him he valued precisely what, until now, he had met with least in women: purity.

The needle was already on empty, when to the right the young man caught sight of a sign, announcing that the station was a quarter of a mile ahead. The girl hardly had time to say how relieved she was before the young man was signaling left and driving into a space in front of the pumps. However, he had to stop a little way off, because beside the pumps was a huge gasoline truck with a large metal tank and a bulky hose, which was refilling the pumps. "We'll have to wait," said the young man to the girl and got out of the car. "How long will it take?" he shouted to the man in overalls. "Only a moment," replied the attendant, and the young man said: "I've heard that one before." He wanted to go back and sit in the car, but he saw that the girl had gotten out the other side. "I'll take a little walk in the meantime," she said. "Where to?" the young man asked on purpose, wanting to see the girl's embarrassment. He had known her for a year now but she would still get shy in front of him. He enjoyed her moments of shyness, partly because they distinguished her from the women he'd met before, partly because he was aware of the law of universal transience, which made even his girl's shyness a precious thing to him.

2

The girl really didn't like it when during the trip (the young man would drive for several hours without stopping) she had to ask him to stop for a moment somewhere near a clump of trees. She always got angry when, with feigned surprise, he asked her why he should stop. She knew that her shyness was ridiculous and old-fashioned. Many times at work she had noticed that they laughed at her on account of it and deliberately provoked her. She always got shy in advance at the thought of how she was going to get shy. She often longed to feel free and easy about her body, the way most of the women around her did. She had even invented a special course in self-persuasion: she would repeat to herself that at birth every human being received one out of the millions of available bodies, as one would receive an allotted room out of the millions of rooms in an enormous hotel. Consequently, the body was fortuitous and impersonal, it was only a ready-made, borrowed thing. She would repeat this to herself in different ways, but she could never manage to feel it. This mind-body dualism was alien to her. She was too much one with her body; that is why she always felt such anxiety about it.

She experienced this same anxiety even in her relations with the young man, whom she had known for a year and with whom she was happy, perhaps because he never separated her body from her soul and she could live with him *wholly*. In this unity there was happiness, but right behind the happiness lurked suspicion, and the girl was full of that. For instance, it often occurred to her that the other women (those who weren't anxious) were more attractive and more seductive and that the young man, who did not conceal the fact that he knew this kind of woman well, would someday leave her for a woman like that. (True, the young man declared that he'd had enough of them to last his whole life, but she knew that he was still much younger than he thought.) She wanted him to be completely hers and she to be completely his, but it often seemed to her that the more she tried to give him everything, the more she denied him something: the very thing that a light and superficial love or a flirtation gives to a person. It worried her that she was not able to combine seriousness with lightheartedness.

But now she wasn't worrying and any such thoughts were far from her mind. She felt good. It was the first day of their vacation (of their two-week vacation, about which she had been dreaming for a whole year), the sky was blue (the whole year she had been worrying about whether the sky would really be blue), and he was beside her. At his, "Where to?" she blushed, and left the car without a word. She walked around the gas station, which was situated beside the highway in total isolation, surrounded by fields. About a hundred yards away (in the direction in which they were traveling), a wood began. She set off for it, vanished behind a little bush, and gave herself up to her good mood. (In solitude it was possible for her to get the greatest enjoyment from the presence of the man she loved. If his presence had been continuous, it would have kept on disappearing. Only when alone was she able to *hold on* to it.)

When she came out of the wood onto the highway, the gas station was visible. The large gasoline truck was already pulling out and the sports car moved forward toward the red turret of the pump. The girl walked on along the highway and only at times looked back to see if the sports car was coming. At last she caught sight of it. She stopped and began to wave at it like a hitchhiker waving at a stranger's car. The sports car slowed down and stopped close to the girl. The young man leaned toward the window, rolled it down, smiled, and asked, "Where are you headed, miss?" "Are you going to Bystritsa?" asked the girl, smiling flirtatiously at him. "Yes, please get in," said the young man, opening the door. The girl got in and the car took off.

3

The young man was always glad when his girl friend was gay. This didn't happen too often; she had a quite tiresome job in an unpleasant environment, many hours of overtime without compensatory leisure and, at home, a sick mother. So she often felt tired. She didn't have either particularly good nerves or self-confidence and easily fell into a state of anxiety and fear. For this reason he welcomed every manifestation of her gaiety with the tender solicitude of a foster parent. He smiled at her and said: "I'm lucky today. I've been driving for five years, but I've never given a ride to such a pretty hitchhiker."

The girl was grateful to the young man for every bit of flattery; she wanted to linger for a moment in its warmth and so she said, "You're very good at lying."

"Do I look like a liar?"

"You look like you enjoy lying to women," said the girl, and into her words there crept unawares a touch of the old anxiety, because she really did believe that her young man enjoyed lying to women.

The girl's jealousy often irritated the young man, but this time he could easily overlook it for, after all, her words didn't apply to him but to the unknown driver. And so he just casually inquired, "Does it bother you?"

"If I were going with you, then it would bother me," said the girl and her words contained a subtle, instructive message for the young man; but the end of her sentence applied only to the unknown driver, "but I don't know you, so it doesn't bother me."

"Things about her own man always bother a woman more than things about a stranger" (this was now the young man's subtle, instructive message to the girl), "so seeing that we are strangers, we could get on well together."

The girl purposely didn't want to understand the implied meaning of his message, and so she now addressed the unknown driver exclusively:

"What does it matter, since we'll part company in a little while?"

"Why?" asked the young man.

"Well, I'm getting out at Bystritsa."

"And what if I get out with you?"

At these words the girl looked up at him and found that he looked exactly as she imagined him in her most agonizing hours of jealousy. She was alarmed at how he was flattering her and flirting with her (an unknown hitchhiker), and *how becoming it was to him*. Therefore she responded with defiant provocativeness, "What would *you* do with me, I wonder?"

"I wouldn't have to think too hard about what to do with such a beautiful woman," said the young man gallantly and at this moment he was once again speaking far more to his own girl than to the figure of the hitchhiker.

But this flattering sentence made the girl feel as if she had caught him at something, as if she had wheedled a confession out of him with a fraudulent trick. She felt toward him a brief flash of intense hatred and said, "Aren't you rather too sure of yourself?"

The young man looked at the girl. Her defiant face appeared to him to be completely convulsed. He felt sorry for her and longed for her usual, familiar expression (which he used to call childish and simple). He leaned toward her, put his arm around her shoulders, and softly spoke the name with which he usually addressed her and with which he now wanted to stop the game.

But the girl released herself and said: "You're going a bit too fast!"

At this rebuff the young man said· "Excuse me, miss," and looked silently in front of him at the highway.

4

The girl's pitiful jealousy, however, left her as quickly as it had come over her. After all, she was sensible and knew perfectly well that all this was merely a game. Now it even struck her as a little ridiculous that she had repulsed her man out of jealous rage. It wouldn't be pleasant for her if he found out why she had done it. Fortunately women have the miraculous ability to change the meaning of their actions after the event. Using this ability, she decided that she had repulsed him not out of anger but so that she could go on with the game, which, with its whimsicality, so well suited the first day of their vacation.

So again she was the hitchhiker, who had just repulsed the overenterprising driver, but only so as to slow down his conquest and make it more exciting. She half turned toward the young man and said caressingly:

"I didn't mean to offend you, mister!"

"Excuse me, I won't touch you again," said the young man.

He was furious with the girl for not listening to him and refusing to be herself when that was what he wanted. And since the girl insisted on continuing in her role, he transferred his anger to the unknown hitchhiker whom she was portraying. And all at once he discovered the character of his own part: he stopped making the gallant remarks with which he had wanted to flatter his girl in a roundabout way, and began to play the tough guy who treats women to the coarser aspects of his masculinity: willfulness, sarcasm, self-assurance.

This role was a complete contradiction of the young man's habitually solicitous approach to the girl. True, before he had met her, he had in fact behaved roughly rather than gently toward women. But he had never resembled a heartless tough guy, because he had never demonstrated either a particularly strong will or ruthlessness. However, if he did not resemble such a man, nonetheless he had *longed* to at one time. Of course it was a quite naive desire, but there it was. Childish desires withstand all the snares of the adult mind and often survive into ripe old age. And this childish desire quickly took advantage of the opportunity to embody itself in the proffered role.

The young man's sarcastic reserve suited the girl very well—it freed her from herself. For she herself was, above all, the epitome of jealousy. The moment she stopped seeing the gallantly seductive young man beside her and saw only his inaccessible face, her jealousy subsided. The girl could forget herself and give herself up to her role.

Her role? What was her role? It was a role out of trashy literature. The hitchhiker stopped the car not to get a ride, but to seduce the man who was driving the car. She was an artful seductress, cleverly knowing how to use her charms. The girl slipped into this silly, romantic part with an ease that astonished her and held her spellbound.

5

There was nothing the young man missed in his life more than lightheartedness. The main road of his life was drawn with implacable precision. His job didn't use up merely eight hours a day, it also infiltrated the remaining time with the compulsory boredom of meetings and home study, and, by means of the attentiveness of his countless male and female colleagues, it infiltrated the wretchedly little time he had left for his private life as well. This private life never remained secret and sometimes even became the subject of gossip and public discussion. Even two weeks' vacation didn't give him a feeling of liberation and adventure; the gray shadow of precise planning lay even here. The scarcity of summer accommodations in our country compelled him to book a room in the Tatras six months in advance, and since for that he needed a recommendation from his office, its omnipresent brain thus did not cease knowing about him even for an instant.

He had become reconciled to all this, yet all the same from time to time the terrible thought of the straight road would overcome him—a road along which he was being pursued, where he was visible to everyone, and from which he could not turn aside. At this moment that thought returned to him. Through an odd and brief conjunction of ideas the figurative road became identified with the real highway along which he was driving—and this led him suddenly to do a crazy thing.

"'Where did you say you wanted to go?" he asked the girl.

"To Banska Bystritsa," she replied.

"And what are you going to do there?"

"I have a date there."

"Who with?"

"With a certain gentleman."

The car was just coming to a large crossroads. The driver slowed down so he could read the road signs, then turned off to the right.

"What will happen if you don't arrive for that date?"

"It would be your fault and you would have to take care of me."

"You obviously didn't notice that I turned off in the direction of Nove Zamky."

"Is that true? You've gone crazy!"

"Don't be afraid. I'll take care of you," said the young man.

So they drove and chatted thus—the driver and the hitchhiker who did not know each other.

The game all at once went into a higher gear. The sports car was moving away not only from the imaginary goal of Banska Bystritsa, but also from the real goal, toward which it had been heading in the morning: the Tatras and the room that had been booked. Fiction was suddenly making an assault upon real life. The young man was moving away from himself and from the implacable straight road, from which he had never strayed until now.

"But you said you were going to the Low Tatras!" The girl was surprised.

"I am going, miss, wherever I feel like going. I'm a free man and I do what I want and what it pleases me to do."

6

When they drove into Nove Zamky it was already getting dark.

The young man had never been here before and it took him a while to orient himself. Several times he stopped the car and asked the passersby directions to the hotel. Several streets had been dug up, so that the drive to the hotel, even though it was quite close by (as all those who had been asked asserted), necessitated so many detours and roundabout routes that it was almost a quarter of an hour before they finally stopped in front of it. The hotel looked unprepossessing, but it was the only one in town and the young man didn't feel like driving on. So he said to the girl, "Wait here," and got out of the car.

Out of the car he was, of course, himself again. And it was upsetting for him to find himself in the evening somewhere completely different from his intended destination—the more so because no one had forced him to do it and as a matter of fact he hadn't even really wanted to. He blamed himself for this piece of folly, but then became reconciled to it. The room in the Tatras could wait until tomorrow and it wouldn't do any harm if they celebrated the first day of their vacation with something unexpected.

He walked through the restaurant—smoky, noisy, and crowded—and asked for the reception desk. They sent him to the back of the lobby near the staircase, where behind a glass panel a superannuated blonde was sitting beneath a board full of keys. With difficulty, he obtained the key to the only room left.

The girl, when she found herself alone, also threw off her role. She didn't feel ill-humored, though, at finding herself in an unexpected town. She was so devoted to the young man that she never had doubts about anything he did, and confidently entrusted every moment of her life to him. On the other hand the idea once again popped into her mind that perhaps—just as she was now doing—other women had waited for her man in his car, those women whom he met on business trips. But surprisingly enough this idea didn't upset her at all now. In fact, she smiled at the thought of how nice it was that today she was this other woman, this irresponsible, indecent other woman, one of those women of whom she was so jealous. It seemed to her that she was cutting them all out, that she had learned how to use their weapons; how to give the young man what until now she had not known how to give him: lightheartedness, shamelessness, and dissoluteness. A curious feeling of satisfaction filled her, because she alone had the ability to be all women and in this way she alone could completely captivate her lover and hold his interest.

The young man opened the car door and led the girl into the restaurant. Amid the din, the dirt, and the smoke he found a single, unoccupied table in a corner.

7

"So how are you going to take care of me now?" asked the girl provocatively.

"What would you like for an aperitif?"

The girl wasn't too fond of alcohol, still she drank a little wine and liked vermouth fairly well. Now, however, she purposely said: "Vodka."

"Fine," said the young man. "I hope you won't get drunk on me."

"And if I do?" said the girl.

The young man did not reply but called over a waiter and ordered two vodkas and two steak dinners. In a moment the waiter brought a tray with two small glasses and placed it in front of them.

The man raised his glass, "To you!"

"Can't you think of a wittier toast?"

Something was beginning to irritate him about the girl's game. Now sitting face to face with her, he realized that it wasn't just the *words* which were turning her into a stranger, but that her *whole persona* had changed, the movements of her body and her facial expression, and that she unpalatably and faithfully resembled that type of woman whom he knew so well and for whom he felt some aversion.

And so (holding his glass in his raised hand), he corrected his toast: "O.K., then I won't drink to you, but to your kind, in which are combined so successfully the better qualities of the animal and the worse aspects of the human being."

"By 'kind' do you mean all women?" asked the girl.

"No, I mean only those who are like you."

"Anyway it doesn't seem very witty to me to compare a woman with an animal."

"O.K.," the young man was still holding his glass aloft, "then I won't drink to your kind, but to your soul. Agreed? To your soul, which lights up when it descends from your head into your belly, and which goes out when it rises back up to your head."

The girl raised her glass. "O.K., to my soul, which descends into my belly."

"I'll correct myself once more," said the young man. "To your belly, into which your soul descends."

"To my belly," said the girl, and her belly (now that they had named it specifically), as it were, responded to the call; she felt every inch of it.

Then the waiter brought their steaks and the young man ordered them another vodka and some soda water (this time they drank to the girl's breasts), and the conversation continued in this peculiar, frivolous tone. It irritated the young man more and more how *well able* the girl was to become the lascivious miss. If she was able to do it so well, he thought, it meant that she really *was* like that. After all, no alien soul had entered into her from somewhere in space. What she was acting now was she herself; perhaps it was that part of her being which had formerly been locked up and which the pretext of the game had let out of its cage. Perhaps the girl supposed that by means of the game she was *disowning* herself, but wasn't it the other way around? Wasn't she becoming herself only through the game? Wasn't she freeing herself through the game? No, opposite him was not sitting a strange woman in his girl's body; it was his girl, herself, no one else. He looked at her and felt growing aversion toward her.

However, it was not only aversion. The more the girl withdrew from him *psychically,* the more he longed for her *physically.* The alien quality of her soul drew attention to her body, yes, as a matter of fact it turned her body into a body for *him* as if until now it had existed for the young man hidden within clouds of compassion, tenderness, concern, love, and emotion, as if it had been lost in these clouds (yes, as if this body had been lost!). It seemed to the young man that today he was seeing his girl's body for the first time.

After her third vodka and soda the girl got up and said flirtatiously, "Excuse me."

The young man said, "May I ask you where you are going, miss?"

"To piss, if you'll permit me," said the girl and walked off between the tables back toward the plush screen.

8

She was pleased with the way she had astounded the young man with this word, which—in spite of all its innocence—he had never heard from her. Nothing seemed to her truer to the character of the woman she was playing than this flirtatious emphasis placed on the word in question. Yes, she was pleased, she was in the best of moods. The game captivated her. It allowed her to feel what she had not felt till now: a *feeling* of *happy-go-lucky irresponsibility.*

She, who was always uneasy in advance about her every next step, suddenly felt completely relaxed. The alien life in which she had become involved was a life without shame, without biographical specifications, without past or future, without obligations. It was a life that was extraordinarily free. The girl, as a hitchhiker, could do anything, *everything was permitted her.* She could say, do, and feel whatever she liked.

She walked through the room and was aware that people were watching her from all the tables. It was a new sensation, one she didn't recognize: *indecent joy caused by her body.* Until now she had never been able to get rid of the fourteen-year-old girl within herself who was ashamed of her breasts and had the disagreeable feeling that she was indecent, because they stuck out from her body and were visible. Even though she was proud of being pretty and having a good figure, this feeling of pride was always immediately curtailed by shame. She rightly suspected that feminine beauty functioned above all as sexual provocation and she found this distasteful. She longed for her body to relate only to the man she loved. When men stared at her breasts in the street it seemed to her that they were invading a piece of her most secret privacy which should belong only to herself and her lover. But now she was the hitchhiker, the woman without a destiny. In this role she was relieved of the tender bonds of her love and began to be intensely aware of her body. And her body became more aroused the more alien the eyes watching it.

She was walking past the last table when an intoxicated man, wanting to show off his worldliness, addressed her in French: "*Combien, mademoiselle?*"

The girl understood. She thrust out her breasts and fully experienced every movement of her hips, then disappeared behind the screen.

9

It was a curious game. This curiousness was evidenced, for example, in the fact that the young man, even though he himself was playing the unknown driver remarkably well, did not for a moment stop seeing his girl in the hitchhiker. And it was precisely this that was tormenting. He saw his girl seducing a strange man, and had the bitter privilege of being present, of seeing at close quarters how she looked and of hearing what she said when she was cheating on him (when she had cheated on him, when she would cheat on him). He had the paradoxical honor of being himself the pretext for her unfaithfulness.

This was all the worse because he worshipped rather than loved her. It had always seemed to him that her inward nature was *real* only within the bounds of fidelity and purity, and that beyond these bounds it simply didn't exist. Beyond these bounds she would cease to be herself, as water ceases to be water beyond the boiling point. When he now saw her crossing this horrifying boundary with nonchalant elegance, he was filled with anger.

The girl came back from the rest room and complained: "A guy over there asked me: *Combien, mademoiselle?*"

"You shouldn't be surprised," said the young man, "after all, you look like a whore."

"Do you know that it doesn't bother me in the least?"

"Then you should go with the gentleman!"

"But I have you."

"You can go with him after me. Go and work out something with him."

"I don't find him attractive."

"But in principle you have nothing against it, having several men in one night."

"Why not, if they're good-looking."

"Do you prefer them one after the other or at the same time?"

"Either way," said the girl.

The conversation was proceeding to still greater extremes of rudeness; it shocked the girl slightly but she couldn't protest. Even in a game there lurks a lack of freedom; even a game is a trap for the players. If this had not been a game and they had really been two strangers, the hitchhiker could long ago have taken offense and left. But there's no escape from a game. A team cannot flee from the playing field before the end of the match, chess pieces cannot desert the chessboard: the boundaries of the playing field are fixed. The girl knew that she had to accept whatever form the game might take, just because it was a game. She knew that the more extreme the game became, the more it would be a game and the more obediently she would have to play it. And it was futile to evoke good sense and warn her dazed soul that she must keep her distance from the game and not take it seriously. Just because it was only a game her soul was not afraid, did not oppose the game, and narcotically sank deeper into it.

The young man called the waiter and paid. Then he got up and said to the girl, "We're going."

"Where to?" The girl feigned surprise.
"Don't ask, just come on," said the young man.
"What sort of way is that to talk to me?"
"The way I talk to whores," said the young man.

10

They went up the badly lit staircase. On the landing below the second floor a group of intoxicated men was standing near the rest room. The young man caught hold of the girl from behind so that he was holding her breast with his hand. The men by the rest room saw this and began to call out. The girl wanted to break away, but the young man yelled at her: "Keep still!" The men greeted this with general ribaldry and addressed several dirty remarks to the girl. The young man and the girl reached the second floor. He opened the door of their room and switched on the light.

It was a narrow room with two beds, a small table, a chair, and a washbasin. The young man locked the door and turned to the girl. She was standing facing him in a defiant pose with insolent sensuality in her eyes. He looked at her and tried to discover behind her lascivious expression the familiar features which he loved tenderly. It was as if he were looking at two images through the same lens, at two images superimposed one upon the other with the one showing through the other. These two images showing through each other were telling him that *everything* was in the girl, that her soul was terrifyingly amorphous, that it held faithfulness and unfaithfulness, treachery and innocence, flirtatiousness and chastity. This disorderly jumble seemed disgusting to him, like the variety to be found in a pile of garbage. Both images continued to show through each other and the young man understood that the girl differed only on the surface from other women, but deep down was the same as they: full of all possible thoughts, feelings, and vices, which justified all his secret misgivings and fits of jealousy. The impression that certain outlines delineated her as an individual was only a delusion to which the other person, the one who was looking, was subject—namely himself. It seemed to him that the girl he loved was a creation of his desire, his thoughts, and his faith and that the *real* girl now standing in front of him was hopelessly alien, hopelessly *ambiguous*. He hated her.

"What are you waiting for? Strip," he said.

The girl flirtatiously bent her head and said, "Is it necessary?"

The tone in which she said this seemed to him very familiar; it seemed to him that once long ago some other woman had said this to him, only he no longer knew which one. He longed to humiliate her. Not the hitchhiker, but his own girl. The game merged with life. The game of humiliating the hitchhiker became only a pretext for humiliating his girl. The young man had forgotten that he was playing a game. He simply hated the woman standing in front of him. He stared at her and took a fifty-crown bill from his wallet. He offered it to the girl. "Is that enough?"

The girl took the fifty crowns and said: "You don't think I'm worth much."

The young man said: "You aren't worth more."

The girl nestled up against the young man. "You can't get around me like that! You must try a different approach, you must work a little!"

She put her arms around him and moved her mouth toward his. He put his fingers on her mouth and gently pushed her away. He said: "I only kiss women I love."

"And you don't love me?"

"No."

"Whom do you love?"

"What's that got to do with you? Strip!"

11

She had never undressed like this before. The shyness, the feeling of inner panic, the dizziness, all that she had always felt when undressing in front of the young man (and she couldn't hide in the darkness), all this was gone. She was standing in front of him self-confident, insolent, bathed in light, and astonished at where she had all of a sudden discovered the gestures, heretofore unknown to her, of a slow, provocative striptease. She took in his glances, slipping off each piece of clothing with a caressing movement and enjoying each individual stage of this exposure.

But then suddenly she was standing in front of him completely naked and at this moment it flashed through her head that now the whole game would end, that, since she had stripped off her clothes, she had also stripped away her dissimulation, and that being naked meant that she was now herself and the young man ought to come up to her now and make a gesture with which he would wipe out everything and after which would follow only their most intimate lovemaking. So she stood naked in front of the young man and at this moment stopped playing the game. She felt embarrassed and on her face appeared the smile, which really belonged to her—a shy and confused smile.

But the young man didn't come to her and didn't end the game. He didn't notice the familiar smile. He saw before him only the beautiful, alien body of his own girl, whom he hated. Hatred cleansed his sensuality of any sentimental coating. She wanted to come to him, but he said: "Stay where you are, I want to have a good look at you." Now he longed only to treat her as a whore. But the young man had never had a whore and the ideas he had about them came from literature and hearsay. So he turned to these ideas and the first thing he recalled was the image of a woman in black underwear (and black stockings) dancing on the shiny top of a piano. In the little hotel room there was no piano, there was only a small table covered with a linen cloth leaning against the wall. He ordered the girl to climb up on it. The girl made a pleading gesture, but the young man said, "You've been paid."

When she saw the look of unshakable obsession in the young man's eyes, she tried to go on with the game, even though she no longer could and no longer knew how. With tears in her eyes she climbed onto the table. The top was scarcely three feet square and one leg was a little bit shorter than the others so that standing on it the girl felt unsteady.

But the young man was pleased with the naked figure, now towering above him, and the girl's shy insecurity merely inflamed his imperiousness. He wanted to see her body in all positions and from all sides, as he imagined other men had seen it and would see it. He was vulgar and lascivious. He used words that she had never heard from him in her life. She wanted to refuse, she wanted to be released from the game. She called him by his first name, but he immediately yelled at her that she had no right to address him so intimately. And so eventually in confusion and on the verge of tears, she obeyed, she bent forward and squatted according to the young man's wishes, saluted, and then wiggled her hips as she did the Twist for him. During a slightly more violent movement, when the cloth slipped beneath her feet and she nearly fell, the young man caught her and dragged her to the bed.

He had intercourse with her. She was glad that at least now finally the unfortunate game would end and they would again be the two people they had been before and would love each other. She wanted to press her mouth against his. But the young man pushed her head away and repeated that he only kissed women he loved. She burst into loud sobs. But she wasn't even allowed to cry, because the young man's furious passion gradually won over her body, which then silenced the complaint of her soul. On the bed there were soon two bodies in perfect harmony, two sensual bodies, alien to each other. This was exactly what the girl had most dreaded all her life and had scrupulously avoided till now: love-making without emotion or love. She knew that she had crossed the forbidden boundary, but she proceeded across it without objections and as a full participant—only somewhere, far off in a corner of her consciousness, did she feel horror at the thought that she had never known such pleasure, never so much pleasure as at this moment—beyond that boundary.

12

Then it was all over. The young man got up off the girl and, reaching out for the long cord hanging over the bed, switched off the light. He didn't want to see the girl's face. He knew that the game was over, but didn't feel like returning to their customary relationship. He feared this return. He lay beside the girl in the dark in such a way that their bodies would not touch.

After a moment he heard her sobbing quietly. The girl's hand diffidently, childishly touched his. It touched, withdrew, then touched again, and then a pleading, sobbing voice broke the silence, calling him by his name and saying, "I am me, I am me. . . ."

The young man was silent, he didn't move, and he was aware of the sad emptiness of the girl's assertion, in which the unknown was defined in terms of the same unknown quantity.

And the girl soon passed from sobbing to loud crying and went on endlessly repeating this pitiful tautology: "I am me, I am me, I am me. . . ."

The young man began to call compassion to his aid (he had to call it from afar, because it was nowhere near at hand), so as to be able to calm the girl. There were still thirteen days' vacation before them.

HIROKO TAKENISHI
[BORN 1929]

In *Children of the A-Bomb* (1982), Arata Osado records the testimony of a boy who was a fourth-grader in Hiroshima on August 6, 1945, when the crew of the B-29 bomber *Enola Gay* dropped the atomic weapon innocuously named Little Boy on that city. He remembers the refugee camp in some field in the Hiroshima suburbs, the stench of rotting flesh and bodies being cremated, the clouds of flies and mosquitoes, and his mother dying there of wounds and radiation sickness after almost two weeks of agony. He concludes his flat list of horrors by saying, "Too much sorrow makes me like a stranger to myself, and yet despite my grief I cannot cry." By the 1950s and 1960s, Japanese writers who were children and adolescents in the year of Hiroshima and Nagasaki had begun to tell the story of their sorrow in a way that might help them to recognize themselves. Hiroko Takenishi's "The Rite" is one of the most powerful of these semi-autobiographical retellings.

LIFE

Takenishi was born in April 1929 into an upper-middle-class family in Hiroshima. In *The Rite*, Takenishi's narrator, Aki, recalls in fleeting snatches some of the sorts of early pleasures Takenishi herself grew up with, in a childhood fairly insulated from the consciousness of war. She tended the carp pond in her parents' pleasant suburban garden, scaring off the marauding night heron, eavesdropping while her elders spoke over a late dinner. She visited the great stone feudal castle with its white pagoda tower, the monument that until 1945 defined the skyline of this city built on the delta islands of the Honshu River, the monument after which the city was named: *Hiro-shima-jo,* "Broad-island-castle."

Takenishi was a sixteen-year-old schoolgirl when the United States dropped on Hiroshima the first nuclear bomb to be used against an enemy population and thereby instantly erased most of the world she had known. As *The Rite* implies, an especially large number of Hiroshima schoolgirls were killed instantly on that day. On August 5, the day before the bomb fell, more than 8,000 of them, including Takenishi, had been called out of their regular classes to special civilian defense duty, ordered to raze houses in the central part of the city to create firebreaks against the ordinary incendiary bomb attack the military feared was in the offing. Osado, the oral historian of Hiroshima, quotes one of those schoolgirls, a student at a junior college, describing the first minutes after the blast:

> The vicinity was in pitch darkness; from the depths of the gloom, bright red flames rise crackling, and spread moment by moment. The faces of my friends who just before were working energetically are now burned and blistered, their clothes torn to rags; to what shall I liken their trembling appearance as they stagger about? Our teacher is holding her students close to her like a mother hen protecting her chicks, and like baby chicks paralyzed with terror, the students were thrusting their heads under her arms. . . .

Deaths directly resulting from the Hiroshima bombing numbered at least 140,000 at the end of 1945; by 1950, 60,000 more people had died from longer-term results of the blast. It is difficult to assess even farther-reaching effects in terms of rises in the rates of birth defects and cancers for Hiroshima survivors, their children, and their grandchildren. Like Takenishi's narrator, Aki, many who have not yet suffered illnesses resulting from radiation are riddled with survivor guilt.

Takenishi survived to graduate from Waseda University, where she majored in Japanese literature. After obtaining her degree, she worked for two major Japanese publishing houses until 1962, when she began to concentrate on writing and publishing both her own fiction and critical essays on classical Japanese literature. In 1964, a collection of those essays, *Two Ways Between the Ancient and Contemporary Times,* won a prestigious literary award, the Tomara Tashiki Prize. In 1978, she was awarded the Women's Literature Prize for *The Orchestra Festival (Kai Gen Sai),* a story that also deals with the bomb. Her critical work *A Theory on the Tales of Genji* (1975) is considered a definitive study of that classic work. Her fictional work *Barracks* won the Kawabata Yasunari Prize in 1980.

WORK

The Rite appeared in 1963, as the world approached the twentieth anniversary of Hiroshima and Nagasaki. The fragmented structure and the flashbacks that seem to meld into one another befit Aki's inner life, for she is still in a sort of walking shock from the blast, even though on the surface she goes calmly about her daily routine of arranging remodeling jobs for a construction company, going out on dates, and seeing friends. But all her deepest experience, her repressed inner life, seems to reach back toward that moment of the blast, a moment readers do not see until near the end of the story.

Death and the rites of death, the feelings proper to hold for death and suffering, obsess Aki. Of all her childhood memories, she keeps returning to three that predate the bomb—the death of a poor man who lived behind her parents' house, whose family could afford no burial save to haul his body away in a cart; the voice of an unseen woman grieving at the bottom of her parents' garden, which stirred the young Aki deeply; and the beautiful lantern festivals in honor of ancestor spirits. In the present time, when she chooses a weekly magazine at a newsstand, she is drawn strongly to one with a picture of an ancient Egyptian funerary jar on the cover. The ancient peoples of the world gave much thought to how to grieve, how to mourn, how to lay their dead to rest. But no rite has been held—and perhaps no rite will suffice—to lay to rest the dead of Hiroshima, many of whom disappeared at the moment of the blast, charred, reduced to smears of ash, vaporized. The adult Aki longs for a whole litany of girlfriends—Junko, Kiyoko, Kazue, Emiko, Ikuko, Yayoi—whom she secretly imagines may still be living, for their deaths have left no trace.

The reader never learns about the fate of Aki's own family or even very much about her own experience of the bomb, but as she goes about her daily routine among the living, more than a decade after the blast, we see her looking about her at the bereaved mothers who have gone mad, at the surviving sisters who kill themselves out of guilt. We see her visit the hospital bed of her friend Setsuko, who vows she will soon be well, even as she lies dying of metastasized cancer. And we see Aki visit the house of her friend Tomiko, who has summoned Aki on business, for she vaguely wishes to "remodel" her house, to make it "what we want"; her husband, she assures Aki, desires that, too, though he never shows up. Aki realizes that Tomiko, who keeps two miscarried fetuses in jars on her Buddhist altar, is almost certainly heading for a third miscarriage, but Tomiko insists that this time "everything is going to be all right." Everyone denies there is something wrong; almost no one speaks of the bomb, of the dead, of the dying, of their own past and present pain, or of their fears for the future. When Aki verges on speaking about her memories and fears to her lover, he says sadly, "If you really loved me, you would be able to put that sort of thing right out of your mind!" and she knows then that she must break off with him.

As the story ends, Aki seems less spiritually depleted, more conscious of her own needs and the sources of her terror, tentatively planning to return to Hiroshima to see what might still be there for her. In any case, she is resolved "to live without wiping out the memory of that day." Perhaps the story itself can be seen as a rite, or at least the opening words of a long ritual of healing.

SUGGESTED READINGS

Little is available in English on the work of Takenishi. Richard Rhodes's *The Making of the Atomic Bomb* (1986) is a thorough account of the beginnings of the nuclear age; Arata Osado's *Children of the A-Bomb* (1982) is a moving compilation of survivor testimony, most of it from Japanese citizens of Hiroshima and Nagasaki who were children in 1945.

The Rite

Translated by Eileen Kato

To the riverside house with the tin roof on which several bunches of red chili peppers had been set out to dry they brought at evening an injured man, stretched out on a wooden shutter. By the entrance to the small dirt-floored front area stood two pickling tubs with big stone weights on the lids, casting long shadows in the westerly sun. The hill that pressed in on the house from behind was fully exposed to the late sunlight, so that even the texture of its soil showed clearly. Holding the shutter front and rear were two sturdy young men with towels around their necks and split-toed tabi sneakers[1] on their feet. The doorway was so narrow there was no way they could get in. They appeared to be talking about it and trying to figure out what to do. The injured man's head was thickly bandaged and from under the thin quilt that covered his body, his gaitered legs stuck out, also shod with tabi sneakers. The goings-on beyond the river were so unusual that Aki couldn't tear herself away from the lattice window. Her school satchel, flap open, lay there unheeded by her side.

A middle-aged woman emerged from the front room. It was the woman who washed rice and rinsed clothes every day at the river. Crying in a shrill voice, she clutched at the injured man, and then throwing her arms in the air and screaming something at the top of her voice, she ran to the next house some distance away. Between there and the next house was a rough log cabin that looked like some sort of storage shed. At the foot of the hill the only inhabited buildings were the woman's house and the house next door that she had run to. Both were roofed with tin, and judging by their size, other than the dirt-floored front area, there couldn't be more than one room worth calling a room.

Soon the woman hurried back from the next house, bringing an old woman with her. The door panel had been removed and now, the makeshift stretcher slid easily inside. The injured man must be the husband who came home drunk late every night, thought Aki. The woman who ran to the neighboring house must be the wife, and the one she brought back with her must be the mother of one of them. The two young men leaned over the injured man and peered into his face. Three small children had climbed on top of the quilt and seemed to be patting and stroking the injured man. When one of the children slithered off the quilt and wandered away, the other two did the same, and then all three left the house.

Already dusk was closing in. The three children each started picking up pebbles, and then together, facing the stream, they began seeing who could throw the farthest.

That night, mingling with the river noises, there came to Aki's ears a low sound of crying. But it grew steadily louder and there was no sign that it would ever stop. And as Aki opened the shutters a little to try to see what was happening beyond the river, the thought struck her that now, under that naked electric light over there, a man's death was drawing near. Was it through his own carelessness he got hurt, she wondered, or had he been attacked by someone? And those people left behind, how would they be able to live now?

Aki remembered when that house was built. One day a man and a woman and three children came to the riverside with a pushcart full of lumber and sheets of

---

[1] Tabis are soft-soled shoes that separate the big toe from the rest of the toes.

tin. They chose a site at the foot of the hill and drove stakes into the ground. First of all, they built the little log cabin. Then they built one house with a tin roof. All day long the man swung his hammer and wielded his saw; the children romped and raced around; the wife washed vegetables in the river. Then, when the second house was finished, the old woman appeared from somewhere and took up her abode there. It was shortly after this that the man started going out every day, dressed in a workman's happi coat,[2] his legs in gaiters and tabi sneakers on his feet, and then, more and more often, he could be heard late at night, singing off key in a loud voice. The man had a slurred pronunciation that jarred the ear, but this was not simply because he was drunk. The woman's speech too, and even the way the children talked, were quite different from Aki's own manner of speaking.

The day after the injured man was brought home and the day following that, the dried red peppers were left where they were on the roof. The hearse that Aki thought must surely come to that house in the end did not come after all. All she saw was a canvas covered pushcart, escorted by the two women and the three children and several brawny looking men, going slowly along the road by the river.

From the far off days of her childhood, long before Aki had ever experienced such things as the sickness or death of her own flesh and blood, that was a funeral that stayed like a weight on her mind.

There's lightning flashing!

Aki wakes up with the feeling she has just come out of a queer disturbing dream. She seems to have woken up in the middle of her own scream. With her mind on this, Aki gropes for the switch of the bedside lamp. Finds it. Presses it. There is the familiar ceiling of her four-and-a-half-mat rented room. It is just after two in the morning. In the dusty vase, the fresh summer flowers she had put there only yesterday are already wilted and drooping. By her bed a weekly magazine, a cigarette case, a lighter, an ashtray.

From time to time the wind rustles the branches of the trees and bushes. Aki turns over and lies face down, lights a cigarette, inhales.

Pictured on the cover of the weekly that Aki had bought yesterday at the subway station entrance was the lid of a jar. When she left the construction company where she worked, she walked along the pavement that her heels always caught in, to the shop run by a German near the subway station. Often on Saturday afternoons Aki would come to this shop for a late lunch of tea and pie. She had done so yesterday. And then, to buy a weekly, she had gone to the station newsstand at the side of the ticket window. While she was looking for one with an interesting cover, her hand, as though it were the natural thing to do, reached for the one with that lid.

Except for the magazine's title, the whole cover was taken up by the face of a young Egyptian nobleman, drawn big against a vermillion background. When Aki learned that this was the lid of an urn used in ancient Egypt as a container for the viscera of corpses to be mummified, a strange thrill ran through a corner of her heart. It was as if she alone in the midst of a multitude was experiencing a secret joy, but this joy was overshadowed by a heavy, helpless gloom. "There's someone watching me!" Suddenly Aki had this uneasy feeling and looked up, shifting her gaze in the direction of the ticket gate.

---

[2] A happi coat is a loose-fitting cloth jacket that fastens with ties in the front.

A young man approaching and a woman, turning her back on him without a word, and going out to the sidewalk. A man in a sudden outburst of anger at a woman who appeared to have come late for their date. A group of girl students, each hand in hand with a friend, their free hands separately hailing a taxi. A plump middle-aged woman approaching with rapid mincing steps. Every face looking totally intent on some immediate, intimate aim. Relieved, Aki lifted up the handbag on her arm and went through the ticket gate onto the platform. She sat down on an empty bench, and then resumed her examination of the urn lid.

The nobleman had a wig and his eyes were of obsidian and quartzite. According to the explanation, a glass image of the sacred serpent had originally been attached to the forehead. His loved ones left behind would have assembled before him to mourn this dead man. Some would have prayed, some would have waved incense censers, some would have made funeral offerings of great price. The lid of the alabaster urn would then have been removed and his internal organs gently placed within. What memories would have stirred then in those people as lid met jar again?

There without a doubt was a fitting way to start out on death's journey, with the dead well tended and watched over by the living. Thinking of that man who had left behind a part of his own flesh, and his people who had taken it into their keeping, in what was surely a most dignified and solemn ceremony, it seemed to Aki that there indeed was a secure and reassuring way to die.

It was three days now since she had gone to the suburb where Tomiko lived in front of the station, carrying Tomiko's postcard asking for help in her handbag.

Tomiko's house had a little shop in it that sold the latest books and magazines, along with cigarettes. Whenever a train stopped at the station, a couple of customers would drop in at the shop. Although it was a hot sticky evening, Tomiko was there minding the shop, dressed in a maternity smock that was a little on the long side. The moment she caught sight of Aki, she let out a sudden cry of joy and grabbed her by the arms. It had been four or five years since they had last met. Watching Tomiko's friendly, darting eyes, Aki thought, "She's just the same as ever!"

"I want to have the shop remodelled. I've been telling my husband all along that when it came time for that, I'd call on your place."

The husband in question did not put in an appearance. For Aki, it was not that Tomiko's request was in any way unusual, but willy-nilly she had to bear in mind the likely reaction of her section chief, who much preferred new jobs to remodelling. Anyway, Aki got most of the necessary data for the estimate from her friend and briskly wrote it down. There was nothing further she needed to be told. At this point Tomiko said, "My husband is still on his rounds. Anyway, that's what we want. Please do the best you can for us!" Aki said she needed about a week.

"Sure! That's fine!"

Then Tomiko bowed formally from the waist and that was the end of the business talk.

A boy's voice was saying the conventional "Excuse me for eating first! That was a good meal!" The boy had come out from under the door curtain of a side door that seemed to communicate with the kitchen, and now with lowered head, was standing facing Tomiko.

Who does that remind me of! thought Aki.

The moment of confusion, then the self-conscious look on the boy's face! That was the face that Noboru had often shown her when he was late for a date. With his nervous temperament, he was such a stickler for punctuality that whenever he was late, Aki used to wonder uneasily if she herself hadn't made a mistake. "I got caught by the prof."—that's all he would say as he sat down, so boyishly that sometimes Aki found it hard to believe that Noboru was older than she. If Aki asked Noboru a question about the university research laboratory where he worked, he would answer in great detail, but he never took the initiative in talking about himself or his work. Whenever Aki came late, Noboru would immediately start telling her about what he had been reading while waiting, and before she could even apologize for being late she would be drawn into Noboru's conversation, and as often as not they would soon be deep in talk about something else altogether.

"Why don't you eat supper here with me before you go!" Invited thus by Tomiko, Aki walked under the door curtain. More than ten years had gone by since they had graduated together from the same girls' school. Aki had never once met Tomiko's husband. But seeing Tomiko so little changed, and judging too from the fact that at this hour he was still out on his rounds, leaving the estimate for the remodelling and all that up to his wife, Aki decided he must be a hard worker and a nice fellow but a timid, ineffectual sort of man.

Every time a train pulled in or out of the station, a minor tremor shook the room, but by the time they were drinking their after-dinner cup of tea, she didn't mind it so much.

"How are you? Any change since I saw you last?" Being suddenly questioned like this by Tomiko made Aki start. "Me?" she rejoined quizzically. "Oh, nothing in particular!" she said with a laugh, and then fell silent. Ever since she had first noticed Tomiko's smock, she had been thinking she must sooner or later broach the subject as casually as she could and ask about Tomiko's condition. Now's the time, she thought.

"Let's forget about me! What about you? When is it?" she asked in a low voice. Now, for a moment, it was Tomiko's turn to be taken aback, or so it appeared to Aki.

"If all goes according to schedule—January. No matter what, this time everything is going to be all right. My husband says so too."

The light had gone out of Tomiko's face. Her eyes had a fixed look about them. Aki searched for words to say, but no word she came up with seemed to be the right one; anything she said would only make matters worse!

"Look there!"

As she spoke, Tomiko pointed to a corner of the living room. When Aki had first been shown into the room, she had seen a corner heaped with flowers and just thought, There's the Buddha altar! But until they were now called to her attention, she had stupidly failed to notice the two small jars, standing low there side by side and all but buried under the flowers. The fetuses that had miscarried, as if this were determined by the waxing and the waning of the moon, and then the mourning rites that had to be gone through, as though it were all a matter of course. Tomiko talked about these things in a low voice, as if she were talking about someone else. She continued staring fixedly at the edge of the table while her fingertips groped for the chopsticks.

"But never mind! This time, you'll see! I'll have my baby properly!" And as she said this, Tomiko's eyes grew warm and smiling again.

But to Aki, it seemed as if she had suddenly been thrown into the middle of a thicket of prickly cactus, and no matter where she turned or how she looked about, she could see nothing like a path leading out of it. The overlapping fleshy leaves were slowly but deliberately swelling, getting fatter and fatter. The way they stretched upward, they seemed to be showing her how much they could grow. She felt a chill, as though convulsions had seized her body here and there; only her cheeks were burning.

On the way back from Tomiko's house, where a field of corn lay along the station railing, Aki vomited twice. She crouched there, steadying herself by holding on to several corn stalks bunched together, her back arched in misery like some stray cat that might have wandered that way. She had a vision of all those miscarried babies, clustered like so many grapes, gushing out over and over there before her eyes, feebly thrusting tiny hands and feet, rubbing up against each other, and after wriggling for a while, coming to rest quietly at last, in a white jar no bigger than a sake pourer.

Suddenly now, the end of her nightmare of a while ago comes back to Aki.

I seemed to be in a big room. Or maybe it wasn't that big after all. Pitch blackness all around, except for one single disc of light. I did not know what I was doing there, but as I stood there perfectly still, I thought, it's cold! Then that round brightness, which was the shining surface of some thick, dark solution, began to congeal with the cold and gave off a gleam that reminded me of blood. The surface of the liquid wavered. At first the gleam undulated gently. Then gradually the undulation changed into a great swell, and the liquid surface began to spread slowly. The liquid, fed from some unknown source, was surely increasing in volume, or so it appeared to me. In the interval between one swell and the next, some terribly soft-looking pinkish thing would rise up out of the top of the liquid and then sink back again, only to reappear from another part and sink back once more. Now the thick fluid was whirling and overflowing all around. I was going to be sucked into the maelstrom of that viscous gleam! Thinking only of how to escape from my rapidly mounting terror, I screamed "Quick!" as if urging someone to do something.

And then before I knew it, in a corner of the darkness, a pale face appeared, shining like a light. It did not immediately come close to me. I was at the limit of my endurance, but the rate of approach of that pale face was excruciatingly slow. I wanted to beckon to it, but my hand seemed to be pulled down by a great weight and I could not move it. When finally the face came close enough to see, I gave a start—

"Noboru!"

I do not know how many seconds later, how many hours later it was, but in the instant when his tenderness tried to reach out to me, I shivered all over and pushed him away.

Aki takes a resolute puff of her cigarette, then stubs it out in the ashtray. She switches off the bedside lamp. In the room below there is not a sound.

At this hour, when the cactuses and sago palms lift up their clustering limbs to the night sky, underneath the leaves the sleeping breath of animals will be wafted forth. The earth is white. The little spring is surely shining silver. Lazy but stubborn, that crowd of oh so very animal-like plants! A beating of the wings of unseen birds. A wild beast suddenly will rise from sleep and come crashing through the thicket and then violently shake itself, its eyes shining gold in the cool air of night.

Or again...in the heart of the city the buildings have at last recovered the coldness of the stone, while at the foundry, flames enwrap the furnace. The blistering cries of things that leave the womb and the gossamer-weak whimpers from the beds in the old people's home must melt and run together somewhere in the sky at night. Good fellowship and shame and boastfulness, the groans of the oppressed and long deep sighs like the receding tide; perhaps these also come together somewhere, whirling, whirling round and round. In the shade of all sorts of things are little sprouting lives making a secret gamble. But however secret the bet, however poor the chance, the thing that once begins to breathe alive will go on living in the dark night of the womb, deep in the amniotic sea, until the moon is full; untouched by doubt or hesitation, as if saying that the destiny laid down for it is simply this, to live.

Soon now, there will be a death that I must face. Aki is thinking of Setsuko, who must be asleep at this hour in her room at the university hospital. The day cannot be far off when all the malignancies spreading here and there through Setsuko's body, accompanied by unbearable pain, will plunge her senses into disorder. "The end has come," her doctor will say. With downcast eyes the nurse will cover her with a white starched sheet brought in from the laundry room, and they will gently carry her down to the morgue in the basement.

Just a week ago, I bought the eau de Cologne that Setsuko always uses and went and knocked lightly on the door of her sickroom. The woman attendant said "Please" as she showed me into the room, and went out looking happy to get away for a while. Setsuko's eyes were like two beads of glass that might have been set temporarily in the bone sockets. Her meagre flesh hung around her bones as if it were some sort of thick wrapping paper covering her temporarily. What I saw that day deep inside her were the thin burned-up bones; what I heard was the brittle crumbling of their white calcinated remains.

Setsuko's hospitalization had been decided on just half a year after her marriage. Then Setsuko's husband was appointed to a foreign post very shortly after. According to her, just like the diplomat her husband now accompanied, he himself was destined in the future to become a distinguished diplomat. From a café terrace that had a view of the Sphynx, from a brick-built city with rain-washed pavements, from the shores of a lake with a range of snow-clad mountains behind, he frequently sent her picture postcards. As soon as she recovered from this illness, he would come back and fetch her. "When that is done, next thing I will invite you to come and visit us. How many days can you get off from work?" And it seemed that Setsuko was making these plans in all seriousness.

Yes, but soon now Setsuko will be enveloped in rites of great solemnity. Summoned back from his foreign post, her husband will be reunited with his young wife in that dark room in the basement. His colleagues, Setsuko's friends, and the relatives on both sides will gather around Setsuko, now a corpse, and then soon they will hurry away again about their business. The husband will probably sit by Setsuko's side for a night. There will be the casket, the cremation, the solemn chanting of the sutras, the funeral flowers, the requiem music, the incense. Then he will take his wife in his arms, or all that's left of her—the calcinated bones and ashes—and he will leave, with all the other mourners following. In the deserted place of mourning there will be no sign of life until the garbageman appears, his hand towel round his head. He will come from the doorway and approach the altar and begin to clear away the funeral flower-wreaths.

There are caskets in hearses that glide gently forward, followed by the long chain of the funeral procession, and there are coffins dragged along on screeching pushcarts, tied down roughly with a common rope. There are people who gouge out the viscera of their dead and then wait upon the mountains for the birds, and there are people who scale precipices, their dead stuffed into leather bags upon their backs. There are secluded tombs away at the far end of well-kept avenues of approach flanked with statues of lions and of camels and of elephants, while by the shores of northern seas, are graves marked only by the native rocks forever lashed by stormy waves.

There are all kinds of rites to go with death.

In the royal palace there are rites that well befit the palaces of kings. Under roofs of tin are other rites more suited for a tin-roofed house. Sunlight, the stars, the trees, the honey in the flower, love . . . even lives that were snuffed out before they could know any of these things have their own special rites.

Aki has never seen Junko's dead body.

That big tilled field at twilight under great columns of cloud . . . that had become the backdrop for Aki's last memory of Junko in that place. With the orange-colored book she had taken from Aki's bookshelf under her arm, she had stopped in front of the farm-tool shed at the entrance to the field and said, "See you tomorrow." "'Bye! Say hello to your big sister for me, won't you!" Aki rejoined, to which Junko retorted, "And what about my big brother?" and then she stuck out her tongue. Their two laughing voices died away in the squeals of a child chasing dragonflies.

The little girl with the bucktoothed smile and hair in long plaits down her back never changed or grew an inch in Aki's mind from that time on. Even now, when the smell of hay comes to her, Aki will sometimes start. The pile of hay by the toolshed in that big tilled field was always hollowed by the weight of the two of them. On top of the hay Junko would go on and on talking about people she had never met as if they were acquaintances of long years' standing; even people who had been dead and buried for decades or even centuries, she would talk about in the same familiar way. And that is why, whenever she had to go off somewhere in connection with her work, if the wind happened to carry a whiff of new-mown hay through the window of the suburban train, Aki would find herself thinking that her relations with Junko, severed so many years before, were about to be resumed. With an upward glance she would scrutinize all the faces in the car she was riding in. But she never had any recollection of having seen a single one of those faces before. And yet, surely there was a smell of hay! Or was she just imagining things? And so, deciding she had been mistaken and trying to think of something else, she would lower her eyes again.

Aki has never seen Kiyoko's dead body.

Kiyoko had left Aki's house late that night. And that was the end of that. In the calm of the evening, the incessant croaking of the frogs intensified the impression of sultriness. After dinner, the two of them started on some beading work in Aki's room. They took turns going out on the veranda every time they heard a splash to chase away the night heron that stalked the carp in the garden pond. Then, while they were huddled together looking at some gold dust fallen from a large moth, Kiyoko promised to come to Aki's house again in two or three days' time. But that promise has yet to be kept. If Kiyoko were to walk into this room in a moment or two and stand there right in front of her, Aki would find nothing particularly strange or startling about that. It would merely be like a piece of movie film that had broken and was now patched together, restoring them to each other. "What happened? What have you been up to?" First of all they would look each other in the eye to make sure it was really the two of them, and then no doubt they'd grab and poke each other to make doubly sure, and everything would be all right again. Yes, thinks Aki, I am still waiting for Kiyoko!

Aki has never seen Kazue's dead body.

Nor Emiko's dead body.

No, nor Ikuko's.

Nor has she ever come across anyone else who witnessed their end or verified the deaths of Junko or Kiyoko or Kazue or Yayoi.

After that summer there were lots of people who for reasons of their own preferred to keep silent. Something must have happened to her friends to make them feel they didn't want Aki to see them. One of these days, surely, she'd meet Junko. Maybe she'll run into someone who has news of Kazue! And with these thoughts, Aki just went on waiting.

Sometimes the thought strikes Aki, maybe Junko is living right here in this same town without knowing that I am here too! Maybe she too is looking for me! Only, I am not in any of the places where she has looked. And she is not in any of the places where I have searched. Have we not perhaps gone on and on missing each other like that? Maybe in the train we have stood close together any number of times, back to back, and then got off and gone our separate ways. Maybe we have even sat in the same row at the theater, and then, unaware of each other's presence, left by different exits, one to the right, the other to the left. Maybe she was standing at the back of that elevator whose doors closed just as I was about to get on.

A year or so after that time, one day I ran into Yayoi's mother quite by chance, and she smiled and laughed at me, and not only at me but at all the people going by, and didn't seem the least bit embarrassed that she was in her bare feet. A few years later, the bloated corpse of Ikuko's younger sister was recovered from below the wharf where the logs are left to season in the water. The evening papers carried her picture and gave the cause of death as extreme nervous exhaustion. Tatsuo, who was to marry into Kazue's family in two or three years, because Kazue was missing, moved away and no longer lived in that place. An old established merchant family like that, and now, unless Kazue some day reappears, their line is doomed to die out.

In the devastated schoolground a mound of black earth had been raised and on top of it was just one plain wooden marker. Buried beneath in unglazed urns, indiscriminately gathered up with all those other deaths, must I recognize the deaths of Junko and Kiyoko and Kazue as well? Even so, if the dead, as they say, are never truly dead and will not rest in peace until the appropriate rites of mourning are performed for them, then the deaths of Junko and of Kiyoko and Kazue are not yet, so to speak, fully accomplished.

Now it is just three o'clock in the morning.

Aki gets up and opens the west window. She adjusts the collar of her robe and sits in the window, surveying the garden below. All the other lights in the building seem to be out, but the garden lamp casts a round of glimmering brightness on the ground. At the center of this circle of light is a small potting shovel that someone threw aside. A tricycle sits astride the line of the circumference.

Still from time to time the lightning streaks in its erratic course across the night sky. After its light goes out, the trees and houses seem to plunge into an even deeper blackness.

Spreading beyond the edge of the garden is a vegetable field. If you cross that you come to the riverbeach. Since we've had no rain for some time, the water level will have dropped. Maybe you can even see the pebbles in the riverbed. Where the weir has dammed the water up, will the river fish be sleeping soundly?

Last evening, for the first time in days, there was a beautiful sunset. Intending to go to the public bath, she began to put her toilet things together. Then with her washbasin under her arm, Aki leaned out of the window.

"Hands up!"

The block of apartments had a bend in the middle like a hook: from the downstairs apartment diagonally opposite, two little boys, brothers, barefoot and dressed only in swimming trunks, came dashing out together. Then, as if they had planned it in advance, they suddenly darted apart, one to the right, the other to the left, and from behind the trunks of the garden's few trees they started shooting at each other. Bang, Baanng! Bang, Baanng!

The young mother began scolding from inside the apartment. "What's happened to your shoes? And your caps?"

After a little bout of gunning, the boys raced into the house again, still making shooting noises. As they ran in, they met a girl in a yellow dress coming out. She emptied the water out of a bucket with a boat floating in it and collected the sneakers they had trampled and knocked every which way, and as she went around tidying everything up, she turned and shouted to the inside of the house, "Uncle will be home early today, won't he, Auntie?"

Because it is Saturday, of course. Soon now, "Uncle" will be honking the horn of his Publica and the boys will go dashing out, yelling, "Papa's home!" And the two will start tugging at the coattails of their father who will be carrying a box of pastries for dessert and rattling his car keys as he comes. They will grab at the keys. Aki can see it all as if it were already happening before her eyes. The window pane of the apartment the boys ran into now has six palms spread against it like so many pressed flowers.

All of a sudden everything went quiet. The stillness was so deep it made you wonder that even a block of apartments like this one could experience such an hour. Aki looked slowly about the place. A watering can abandoned in the sandbox; a plastic pool, blobs of sand on the bottom looking like a map; a patch of dried plaster; under the eaves a lizard that seemed as if it had been pasted on; a clothes line already gone slack; trees bent low as if their own weight had been too much for them to bear; a bucket only half full, left behind in the common laundry area; the rubbish dump with papers sticking out of it; an improvised garage that looked more like a box for toys . . . the sound of the cicadas, penetrating as a brush stroke on paper, had now died away.

Aki put the washbasin she had been holding on the table and then, leaning against the window frame, inhaled her cigarette. She blew the first puff of smoke straight at the middle of the sky. Just then, the western sky was one great blaze of splendor.

Yes, straight over there, at the far edge of the vegetable field that stretches out beyond the block of apartments, yesterday's setting sun went right down the chimney of that brick house. It was majestic, solemn. Moment by moment the colors changed; it was like watching scenery in a series of hurriedly shifted slides. A quiet peaceful Saturday. It was indeed a fitting end to a fine summer's day.

But at the close of that other summer's day, the bright evening glow was not caused simply by the setting sun. The blue first faded from the eastern sky and gradually it sank into black ink, but though the darkness grew and deepened, the evening glow was not the least bit dimmed. On the contrary, as the other side of the sky darkened, it burned all the more brightly, and seemed to be spreading and spreading. Aki crouched low in a hollow in a field with people she had never seen before that day, and stared steadily up at that night sky.

The morning, the great flash, the big bang, the squall of wind, the fire . . . all these I can remember very clearly, but what happened to me next? That was a blank in her memory that Aki was not able to fill in.

When she recovered her senses she found herself running in the direction of the sea, borne along in a rush of total strangers. Shirts in shreds, scorched trousers, bloodsoaked blouses, yukatas with a sleeve missing, seared and blistered skin, an old man just sitting there watching the people rush by before his eyes, a woman with a child in each arm, a barefoot university student, someone screaming, "The fire is coming!" When she looked back at the town it was engulfed in black smoke. As for what was happening inside it, at the time Aki had no idea, and even to think of it was too horrifying.

Why did she have this thing with her? Aki was crouching in the hollow she had managed to struggle to, an empty bucket in front of her. The eyes of the people gathered there were abnormally bright and their voices strangely high-pitched. Whenever there was a moment's lull in the noise and confusion, the low roar of the sea could be heard. As evening wore on, the crowd of grotesque figures in the hollow continued to grow.

It was already the hour of the afterglow, but the sky was blazing with the excess of heat from the earth, and all through the night it continued to burn a fiery red, until at last, in the brightness slowly spreading from the east, it lost its incandescent glow. Up to daybreak, ominous noises like an avalanche shook the hollow several times. When the wind shifted, it carried a reek of burning fat. Now and then, a frog croaked somewhere.

Aki longed for the morning. With morning everything would be better. If she could just make it through this night, things would be all right. That was the feeling that sustained her.

Ah, but that morning, so breathlessly awaited it had hurt, what did it have to show to Aki? Things that for so long she had seen with her own eyes and touched with her own hands, and whose existence she had never even thought to doubt, taking their being there so much for granted, she now could find no more, except in some far corner of her memory, deep in her consciousness. With her lips slightly parted, Aki stood transfixed with horror. Broken stumps of old trees were still smouldering. Molten metal ran along the pavement. A great geyser gushed out where the lid of the water main had exploded. All around as far as eye could see, nothing but ruin and rubble, and strewn on top of all, as if left behind there by mistake, strange objects of some whitish chalky substance. The far-off hills, in some strange way, seemed to be closing in upon the town.

It is not an act of Heaven.

It is not an act of Earth.

No! It can't be that!

But at the time, Aki had not an inkling of the real nature of this thing that set her knees knocking together in sheer terror.

And Aki, standing petrified there, now became aware of an eery stillness that seemed to be about to envelop her body. Presently it wrapped her round with a gentleness she had never known or felt before. Perhaps I am going to be shut in for all eternity somewhere at the bottom of the earth, she thought. It was not long before she felt herself being sucked down into a black abyss. Innumerable little yellow arrows flew before her eyes, bewildering her, and she felt herself falling,

falling down into a blank that had cut off the light. There was no longer anything left of the great gentleness. Aki was now being manipulated by something hard and resistant. Something was over; she could not but think that. Rather than question the existence of the thing that now sought to gain control of her, she merely felt the pity of it all.

Suddenly, something white jumped out of the rubbish dump and streaked across the garden in a straight line, making for the vegetable field beyond. A cat, most likely. As if suddenly remembering to do so, the wind now shook the branches of the trees.

It was not quite true for Aki to say that she had never experienced before that summer's day the feeling of being all at once enveloped in an eery stillness and then falling, falling down into the blank that cut the light off. Why? Because although dim and far away, she now suddenly remembered a night long ago, when she had felt herself slip all at once into a black abyss, a night she now was dredging up from the immeasurable depths of her subconscious.

"Good night! Now go to sleep!" the nurse said, moving away from Aki's side. After looking at the thermometer hung on a post, she left the room. Aki stretched herself under the quilt. She was full of that feeling of well-being that comes when a high temperature returns to normal. Tonight too, no doubt, there will be lots of guests. Father and mother, but especially mother, will be tired out attending to them. The maid too will be busily bustling about. From the main house on the other side of the patio came the clatter of a late dinner. In the moonlight, the dwarfed pine lifted its twisted trunk, and the white sand spread around it in the pot gleamed silvery white.

When all the shutters were put up in the main house, she felt how isolated was the little detached room where she now slept.

How much time had passed she did not know, but after a while Aki thought she heard voices outside the earthen wall. They stopped for a while and then went on again in low tones. They were voices she did not remember ever having heard before. They were certainly not the voices of the gatekeeper and his wife. Because a stream from the hill had been diverted through their garden, sometimes people coming down the hill strayed in by mistake. Maybe the voices of a while ago belonged to some people like that. But no matter how much time went by, there was no change in the location of the voices. After a while, they began to grow gradually louder. There was a man's voice, low but somehow angry. At long intervals the thin voice of a woman mingled with it. The hard-to-catch voice of the man grew louder and rougher. The woman's voice presently changed to a low convulsive sobbing. Then there was a dull thump, as though part of one body had struck a terrible blow at a part of the other body. Aki instinctively hid her head under the quilt. She had heard what she was not supposed to hear, hadn't she? A ringing started deep within her ears. She had a strange feeling of being shot at with countless yellow arrows, all coming straight at her.

Why was she upsetting herself over that unknown woman who was undoubtedly cowering on the other side of the garden wall? Aki, still only a child, did not know, but in some obscure hurt way she felt a sense of identity with the woman beyond the wall. Are all women doomed to weep like that when they grow up? Even women whose tears I have never once seen; for example, that nurse so attentive and good with sick people and apparently trusted by the doctor, or the teacher of my elementary school class who stands on her platform every day looking as if she never gave a thought to anything but the government textbooks: do women like that too, late in the night, go someplace we don't know and cry their hearts out there in floods of tears? Aki felt that she was falling, falling down into a black abyss, and then discovered that she herself was crying.

The day of her visit to Tomiko, just as they were settling down with the table between them, Tomiko had looked Aki in the eye and asked, "When did you last go back home?"

The place where Tomiko was born and which she calls her home she seems to think is naturally "home" for Aki too. But when Tomiko questioned her like that, Aki found she could not answer right away. As she looked at Tomiko, it seemed that already the words were breaking into fragments in her head, GO—BA—CK—HO—ME.

Since we two had not seen each other for four or five years, it was not inappropriate for Tomiko to start talking about that place, thought Aki. It's not just Tomiko. Lots of other people, either by way of greeting or because they really want to know how things are now in that place, ask me the same question. They probably don't mean anything by it. But that place where Tomiko and I were born and raised and from which the fire drove us out—is that a proper place for me to go back to, just like that, as Tomiko says, without the slightest hesitation? What exactly in that place would I be going home to? If there is something there that's fitting to return to, I want it to be a something that endures unchanged and transcends time. Something of which it may be said, now *that* at least is certain. People should return to something that, no matter what may happen, will endure and still be seen as the true root and source of what they are.

When the night of the Bon Lantern Festival came around, Tomiko and I would often go down to the pier together. On several occasions we got on the same boat. "Mr. Boatman, please row out that way; no! further out into the offing," and the two of us side by side at the gunwale would watch the other boats pass by. "Ah! that one was the Masudaya's boat, and the one coming from over there is surely the Sasaya's boat!" And chattering away like that, we would stay on until quite late, blown by the night winds. Scattered over the waters, then brushing against each other again, those lanterns for the departed souls were as vivid in Aki's mind as something she might have seen just now on the riverbeach beyond the vegetable field.

Does Tomiko still remember? The thin little bones, the pale pink insides of the nearly transparent fish in their shoals? The wharf bridge darkening the water below? The five-colored pinwheels stuck between the cotton candy stall and the white mice cages, and that resonance of expectancy along the shrine path at the time of the clan god's festival? The window full of the Milky Way, and when you opened it that smell of oil from the armory that nearly knocked you out? The castle tower,[3] the parade ground, the napes of the young men's necks, the henhouse, the greenhouse, the shipyard, the schoolhouse, the warehouse, the heat shimmer, the carrying chest, the armor case . . . ?

The old men, gathered under the ornamental light that looked like a sea anemone, would soon be deep in talk. Hiding behind her back, I would slip in

---

[3]The feudal castle of Hiroshima, built in 1859, had a white pagodalike tower five stories high. Destroyed in the 1945 blast, the castle was restored in 1958.

with the maid who went to serve them their black tea. The first of them to spot me would beckon with his hand and say, "Aki, there's a good little girl, come over here to grandpa!"

The wallpaper was pretty well faded but you could still clearly make out the picture pattern. The Pyramids towered in the distance. A woman was washing a jar in the stream. The animals seemed to be asleep in the shade of the trees while a man sat nearby. The old men talked on and on as if they were never going to stop. "Salt-broiling is the only thing for *ayu* trout, eh!" "What's happened to all the women?" "Now the difference between the treeleaf butterfly of the Ryūkyūs and the treeleaf butterfly of Taiwan is this. . . ."

That time when, in the bright sunshine, I gazed on the vast multitude of dead in all the chaos of that ruined ground, laid waste and desolate by someone or by something yet unknown, with my knees knocking together out of control, the thing I kept telling myself was this: it is only a temporary phenomenon! I kept on pursuing the original appearance of that place as it had been before, and as I was sure it would be again. Maybe tomorrow I will see Junko! Maybe I'll come across someone who knows how Kiyoko is! When I was trying to sleep out under the starry sky with such thoughts in my mind, the awareness that began to seep through the depths of my consciousness, the thing I took to thinking as if it were most natural was this: Junko and Kiyoko, sometime, somewhere, will surely appear before me once again!

At that time, what on earth did I consider the original appearance of that place? Was it the limpid flowing stream, so clear that you could see the pebbles in the riverbed? Was it the trees along the roads with their load of soft green buds? Was it the tilled field where the earth was neither hard nor black nor dry when turned over? Was it the harmony that prevailed among all these? Or was it the dawn city when the fish peddlers went by? The sound of rackets batting the ball back and forth until near twilight on the schoolyard tennis court? The white walled castle? But all these, alas, are things doomed to change, now no longer fit to bear the weight of changelessness! I felt I had been witness on that morning to a temporary phenomenon that later, sometime, must be overcome and gone beyond. But perhaps I was wrong. The term temporary phenomenon should not have referred only to the scene of devastation; it should have covered, too, the great flash, the big bang, the squall of wind, and it should perhaps also have included that place that dawned and darkened to the low roar of the sea. It struck me then that something certainly had ended there. I was perhaps one of the witnesses to the end of a particular phenomenon.

But that thought too may have been wrong. Its present condition, its broad paved streets, its tall buildings, its airport, its foreign cars, its stadium, its cinemas, its bars . . . all those things are enough to make one doubt the reality of what once happened in that place. From now on, too, new schools will be put up. More and more trees will line the city's streets. There will be more and more roller coasters in more amusement parks. But there are times, nevertheless, when I am struck with the dread premonition that suddenly one day all those tall buildings will come tumbling down. I have visions of the pavements splitting open, of the foreign cars abandoned in the streets and turned to lumps of burnt-down metal. They will be like these other things in the world of my memory, that in a twinkling were all changed and lost. And this is true not only of that place as it is now. All these familiar things about me every day, this table, this bookshelf, this mirror, this clock, these people boxed into their several compartments, and—standing here and holding all of that—this block of apartments, the street lights, the suspension bridge, the superhighway, the lockers in the drafting room, the bones of kindly gentle people. It seems to me I hear the sound of all these things crumbling down. And I myself am nothing more than another of these things doomed to crumble! Aki thinks of her own self, her body blown to bits, reduced to chalky handfuls left exposed to every wind. But, just like life, is not death, too, simply one of the many faces of existence?

Even if it has only a tin roof I don't mind! I want to sleep somewhere that isn't out on the bare ground!

I don't mind if it isn't in a glass! I want some clean water that you're not afraid to drink!

Even a piece so small it fits into the hollow of my hand, I don't mind! I want to see myself in something you could call a mirror!

Even if it's that mean, nasty Taeko, I don't mind! I want to talk to someone that is not a grown-up stranger wrapped in bandages!

But several nights were to pass in the hollow before even a single one of these simple wishes of Aki's would come true.

The great anger, the deep hate, come after the event. The thing that parted me from Junko, that kept Kiyoko from me although she wanted to see me again, that made me cower all night in a hollow in the ground—if I could catch the real nature of that thing and fling the fullness of my anger and hate at it, I would not be in torment to this day, well over ten years after, tied to this fierce anger that still finds no proper outlet. I would not be tortured by this nameless hate that yet finds no clear object. This is what Aki thinks.

Sometimes Aki, on her way to the office in the morning, would suddenly think she had found it, would see that object clearly. At the midday break, opening the window of the drafting room and looking up at a cloudless sky, there were times she felt she saw it float up quite clearly, with no further need for doubt. I must not let this out of my sight! Now, how can I get my anger and indignation across to this, their object? Aki would begin to lay her plan with meticulous care. But as she pursued that object, its contours would grow vague, and then some other object more or less linked with it would intrude. The new object was always inevitably linked with the old. One after another new objects would appear and then grow vague and blurred. And a further trouble: Aki began to suspect uneasily that the hazy something that had lost its clear outlines might be her own self.

I am ashamed to say I still cannot see where I had best direct my hate and anger, but . . . and Aki went on thinking. The rite that should have been performed and never was, and my unassuaged thirst for it, I must recognize as the beginning of a questioning of "being" that I must now develop. Wherein lies the realness of things? Can you say that a thing that's really there and that you can be sure of is one your eyes can see, your hands can touch, your skin can feel? The things in your consciousness, that you can neither see nor touch, are they less truly there?

But what degree of realness is there in things your eyes can see, your hands can touch, or your skin can feel? Setsuko's husband was not by her side in that sickroom. But when Setsuko looked up at the map of the world pasted on the wall beside her bed and thought about her husband in his foreign post, was he not truly there within her mind? Surely then he was a more weighty presence in her consciousness than when he was beside her, touching her, and she would waken with a sense that he was slipping far away from her like a draft of wind. And can the senses grasp reality as well as she could with her consciousness, once she could cease to treat as an unreal thing the presence in it?

"What do you think of it? Those people starting out simultaneously from the far ends of the Silk Road to meet in the middle?"[4]

Noboru put this question to Aki as they were having dinner in a restaurant that overlooked the nighttime sea. With a vivacity unusual for him, his eyes slightly clouded from the little whiskey he had drunk, he kept on talking to Aki of one thing after another. He seemed to have a compulsion to talk. He even felt impelled to speak to the waiter who came to clear the table, saying such things as "The butter sauce with the fish-meunière is very good here" or "This coffee must be a blend of at least three varieties of beans." There were not many customers. The air conditioning in the room was too cold for Aki in her short sleeved blouse.

After dinner, Aki walked along the shore road with Noboru. As they walked, Aki, comforted by Noboru, had her spirits restored but saw it all as too late. I want to go on walking for a long, long time, she thought. But that same evening, when Noboru had reduced to nothing the distance that separated them, Aki found herself caught up in the eery stillness. Feeling as if someone else had suddenly come up behind and laid a hand on her shoulder to pull her back, she shuddered. She said, "Any moment now, I am going to fall into that black abyss!" And then Noboru, anguish showing in his face, muttered in a low voice, "I know; but you must forget all about that kind of thing. If you really loved me, you would be able to put that sort of thing right out of your mind!"

What Aki, in the grip of that eery stillness, foresaw in dire premonition was Noboru, blind still himself to all the signs, Noboru hideously changed beyond all recognition, as Aki herself must change! In the taxi on the way back, the two of them hardly opened their mouths. Noboru looked out the window. In his rear view mirror, the driver kept darting quizzical glances at the back seat.

Aki lit a fresh cigarette.

After that I didn't meet him for quite a while, not until the winter. On that bookshelf there will be several books lent to me by Noboru. "If you want to study the houses of Granada, this one is good. If you are more interested in Madrid, this one here is best." It seems to her she can hear his voice.

I still had his books and I should have returned them to him when I saw him for the last time in the winter, yet I failed to do so! There is something wrong with me. . . .

Rejected, Noboru's slightly twisted face drew slowly back. Aki had felt the reproach in his eyes as she turned her cheek away. Gently she loosened his arm. The utter wretchedness of letting go of warmth and tenderness went right through her. Her voice was very low and small when she said, "I'm sorry," and it was swallowed up immediately in the dark sea before her eyes. The risen tide was beating steadily against the breakwater. The invisible thread that had drawn Noboru and herself together had now snapped, thought Aki, while another Aki whispered to her, "But

---

[4]The Great Silk Road was the ancient trade route linking China to the Mediterranean; Noboru seems to be speaking of a commemorative celebration of the Road.

it is you yourself, isn't it, who let go of the thread! It is you yourself, isn't it, who refuse to see him any more! You're a fool, that's what you are! Maybe so, but. . . ."

It was snowing.

Far out a ship's siren wailed.

Aki, who had lowered her gaze to the water's surface, now raised it gradually and then turned her whole face up. The snow was not coming from any very high place, but rather seemed to be gushing quietly out and falling softly down from somewhere quite near.

Noboru must think I didn't really love him. But I don't have the strength to go on explaining about that dread awareness that suddenly took hold of me.

Aki bit her lip. The snow was falling cold on her cheeks. Only the backs of her eyes were scalding hot. She could feel his gaze on her from behind, so piercing that it hurt, as she said "Let's go!" Taking the lead, she set off walking ahead of him. Naturally, he must have been terribly hurt and have taken this to mean that his love was not returned. Children hooded against the cold were running about the deck of one of the boats at anchor in the canal. On the deck of another, a number of young sailors were warming themselves around a fire they had made in an oil drum. They spotted Noboru and Aki and their individual spontaneous whistles came together in a chorus. That was the end of the year before last.

It is a little after four in the morning.

That small light beyond the vegetable garden—is it from the brick house? Or maybe it's some nearer light. The trees and houses are still plunged in darkness. Aki automatically smooths her front hair with the palm of her left hand. Her eyes pick out a tree. When I think of Noboru, quite often I remember at the same time that night so long ago when I broke down and cried for an unknown woman. Of all past nights, why do I have to pick out that one? Or is it perhaps that I am trying to relive it in the unconscious? All that is very vague. The two things seem to be totally unconnected, yet in some obscure way you can also see that they are profoundly linked. But that summer when I witnessed in that place the sudden loss of all I thought was mine and the omission of the rite that should have been performed, something that lay dormant until then suddenly colored me, and its dye deepened rapidly. I think I can say that. Now, on the contrary, that thing is trying to gain control of me, and I am questioning anew the meaning of existence. What we call dying, what we call living, things that are or that are not—what exactly are all these things? No doubt I'll go on groping, questioning, bearing the burden of this anger that I cannot vent, and this hate that still finds no clear object. I want to live without wiping out the memory of that day! My ancestors were slaves in Egypt... like the people of Israel, who at the Feast of the Passover, yearning to break free from bondage, woke from sleep and resumed reading their dark records. At that time, their thoughts probably ran like this—Someone who can just casually wipe out the memory of his own history will not be fit, as history unfolds, to play the role of a great hero.

That place of mine that was so beautiful—if it was truly mine, then that same place when hideously changed by someone or some force unknown to me was surely also mine. To the question of which is really the true place, I cannot answer now with any confidence. If one speaks in terms of a phenomenon, then both were that. If asked which was reality, I am inclined to say that both were also that. But surely what I called unchanging, the abiding source one can always go home to, must be something richer far than either, rejecting neither of them but transcending *invisible cities* (handwritten note)

both. It must be something solidly sustained by an imperturbable order, although it may reveal itself under the varying aspects of separate phenomena. Yes, I shall no doubt go to that place again, but I will not be going home. What makes me think so is that host of things lost to my sight, no more reliable than fluff or down, and the uncertainty of all the things I see before me every day. To my regret, that imperturbable order is now known to me only within the world of wishful intimations. But I must know if it really exists. If I could know it, even in a flash of intuition, then perhaps I would no longer be the prey of this eery stillness that takes hold of me. I would be freed then from my terror of being sucked into that void that blocks out the light and of falling down, down, down into that black abyss. I want to know.

Slowly, softly now, a whiteness starts to spread, beneath a sky that seems to be melting quietly away, and the shapes of trees and houses at last stand out. A thick mist will be creeping along the river, brushing the wings of the still sleeping crane flies on the dewy grasses of the riverbeach. Any moment now, the alarm bell at the grade crossing will start ringing. Soon the garden swing will be encircled by the joyous shrieks of children. A man still in his night clothes will cut through the squeals of delight with a yell of "Breakfast!" A woman will come out to fetch them, and the children, with a hand in each of hers, will disappear again inside the door. A deliveryman will appear beyond the shrubbery. A bill collector, taking advantage of the holiday with everyone at home, will be approaching from beyond the rubbish heap. In the makeshift garage, the engine of the Publica will soon be starting up. " 'Bye! See you later! Have a nice holiday!"

Soon the night will be over. Let me get some sleep! And Aki draws the window curtain shut.

ALIFA RIFAAT
[BORN 1930]

The Euro-American stereotype of Arab women is of submissive victims, veiled and voiceless, kept in seclusion and forbidden by a male-dominated society to speak their minds. Westerners, therefore, are often surprised to learn that there is a considerable body of feminist Arab literature beginning in the nineteenth century with the poetry of 'Aisha al-Taymuriyya (1840–1902), a member of the Turkish aristocracy from Egypt who defied nineteenth-century Cairo's strictures upon women calling attention to themselves by writing and publishing poems about women's strengths. Composing and reciting poetry of a polite and traditional sort, especially love poetry, was always considered a graceful and appropriate social skill for both men and women, but poetry that considered actual social conditions and prose writing of any sort was definitely male, and women writers of fiction in the Arab countries are still largely confined to small private presses. Among the principal Arab feminists writing today who have made their voices heard are Hanan al-Shaykh of Lebanon; Ghada al-Samman of Syria; Nazik al-Mala'ika of Iraq; the Palestinian writer Liana Badr; and Ihsan Assal, Nawal el Saadawi, and Qut al Qulub, all of Egypt. One of the best-known outside the Arab-speaking world is another Egyptian writer, Alifa Rifaat, whose work frankly treats issues of marriage, power, and the repression of female sexuality.

LIFE

Fatma Abdallah Rifaat was born on June 5, 1930, in Cairo to a conservative architect father and a mother who accepted the traditional roles of middle-class Arab women. Rifaat received little formal education, though she was a precocious child. She wrote a short story about "despair in our village" at the age of nine and was punished for doing so. Also gifted in music and oil painting, she longed to enroll in the College of Fine Arts at Cairo and go on from there to the university, but her father's refusal, she says, was "decisive." Instead, he decided she should marry Hussein Rifaat, a cousin who worked in law enforcement. This match lasted until her husband's death in 1979, and produced a daughter and two sons. One advantage of the marriage was that Hussein Rifaat's work took him to posts at a number of towns and villages, and Rifaat, like the wife in "My World of the Unknown," had the chance to observe Egyptian life beyond the urban middle class.

Rifaat quietly persisted in writing fiction, and began publishing it in 1955 under the pseudonym Alifa Rifaat. Her husband angrily demanded that she stop, but she secretly kept on writing and publishing until 1960, when he discovered her continuing deception and made her swear "on God's book" to stop writing; otherwise, he said, he would divorce her. Rifaat complied for more than a decade, during which she avidly read literature, science, history, and religion. Decrying repression, she nonetheless has always sought to stay within her culture, despite its limitations; "All decisions within our family are made by the menfolk; we are proud of our Arab origin and hold on to certain Arab customs," she has said, referring to her agreement to abide by the dictates of father and husband. Finally, in about 1973, she experienced a difficult bout of illness, and her husband conceded she might resume her writing. During that time of reclaiming her voice, Rifaat wrote "My World of the Unknown," a story which immediately garnered her both praise and notoriety for its treatment of the narrator's sexuality. Rifaat has continued to publish her fiction ever since. *Hawatandbi-Adam (Eve Returns with Adam to Paradise)*, a collection of short stories, came out in 1975, and was followed by her first novel, *Jawharah Farum (The Jewel of Pharaoh)*, in 1978. Another short-story collection, *Salat Al-hubb (The Prayer of Love)*, appeared in 1983; in the next two years she published two more collections, *Bayt fi ard al Mawta (A House in the Land of the Dead)* and *Kad Lia al-Hawa (Love Conspired on Me)*. In 1985, Rifaat published *Leil Al Shetaa Al-taweel (The Long Winter Night)*, which was translated by Denys Johnson-Davies into English and appeared as *Distant View of a Minaret;* "My World of the Unknown" comes from this latter collection.

"Most of my stories," Rifaat has observed, "revolve around a woman's right to a fully effective and complete sexual life in marriage; that and the sexual and emotional problems encountered by women in marriages are the most important themes of my stories." Her own marriage was initially unfulfilling because she had been told nothing about the act of making love. She adds, however, that she believes that Western models of sexual education and sexual liberation are inappropriate for Arab peoples, who have a strong commitment to Muslim religion and Arabic culture; for "our society does not allow us to experience sex freely as Western women may. We have our traditions and our religion in which we believe." In this story, Rifaat indeed does not draw on Western notions of libido, but rather upon Islamic myth and Arabic folk belief to account for the narrator's sexual awakening.

WORK

In "My World of the Unknown," the known world the narrator inhabits is that of middle-class, somewhat westernized Egyptian women whose menfolk are thoroughly absorbed in the gray workaday world of urban bureaucracy and whose children are off at school, leaving them to occupy their days with supervising households. Though she says little about her life prior to the action of the story, it is apparent that the narrator's wifely existence has left her feeling dry and depleted in body and soul. When her preoccupied husband is transferred to a post in the countryside, her subconscious stirs and directs her toward the mysterious house where the deeper needs of her imagination, her sexuality, and her spirit may be met. In the house on the canal, she feels alive and open to the natural world, and her whole being is refreshed and quickened when she enters into a magical love affair with a beautiful female snake. The snake is apparently a djinn—one of a host of corporeal beings Allah created from smokeless fire, who are said to live in a parallel universe to ours. Arab folklore abounds with tales of comings and goings between these worlds, and such encounters may be for good or for ill, since the djinn, like human beings, may be evil or helpful. In any case, to glimpse their world of the unknown alters a human being forever; the experience seems to have driven Aneesa, the previous occupant, into madness, and by the end of the story, when the husband clumsily destroys her idyll by killing one of the snake's own kind, the narrator may be mad as well, for her whole life is focused on the slim hope that she will be reunited with her snake lover. Like the supernatural world, human sexuality is at once a territory of great beauty and joy and, equally, a place of great risk. By daring to explore her own desires, and by reaching out sexually and spiritually toward a very different—and female—being, the narrator invites danger and sorrow, but to draw back from the adventure would have meant continuing to live out a mechanical, meaningless existence.

SUGGESTED READINGS

Margot Badran and Miriam Cooke survey the traditions out of which Rifaat's writing arises in *Opening the Gates: A Century of Arab Feminist Writing* (1990).

My World of the Unknown

Translated by Denys Johnson-Davies

There are many mysteries in life, unseen powers in the universe, worlds other than our own, hidden links and radiations that draw creatures together and whose effect is interacting. They may merge or be incompatible, and perhaps the day will come when science will find a method for connecting up these worlds in the same way as it has made it possible to voyage to other planets. Who knows?

Yet one of these other worlds I have explored; I have lived in it and been linked with its creatures through the bond of love. I used to pass with amazing speed between this tangible world of ours and another invisible earth, mixing in the two worlds on one and the same day, as though living it twice over.

When entering into the world of my love, and being summoned and yielding to its call, no one around me would be aware of what was happening to me. All that occurred was that I would be overcome by something resembling a state of languor and would go off into a semi-sleep. Nothing about me would change except that I would become very silent and withdrawn, though I am normally a person who is talkative and eager to go out into the world of people. I would yearn to be on my own, would long for the moment of surrender as I prepared myself for answering the call.

Love had its beginning when an order came through for my husband to be transferred to a quiet country town and, being too busy with his work, delegated to me the task of going to this town to choose suitable accommodation prior to his taking up the new appointment. He cabled one of his subordinates named Kamil and asked him to meet me at the station and to assist me.

I took the early morning train. The images of a dream I had had that night came to me as I looked out at the vast fields and gauged the distances between the towns through which the train passed and reckoned how far it was between the new town in which we were fated to live and beloved Cairo.

The images of the dream kept reappearing to me, forcing themselves upon my mind: images of a small white house surrounded by a garden with bushes bearing yellow flowers, a house lying on the edge of a broad canal in which were swans and tall sailing boats. I kept on wondering at my dream and trying to analyse it. Perhaps it was some secret wish I had had, or maybe the echo of some image that my unconscious had stored up and was chewing over.

As the train arrived at its destination, I awoke from my thoughts. I found Kamil awaiting me. We set out in his car, passing through the local *souk*.[1] I gazed at the mounds of fruit with delight, chatting away happily with Kamil. When we emerged from the *souk* we found ourselves on the bank of the Mansoura canal, a canal on which swans swam and sailing boats moved to and fro. I kept staring at them with uneasy longing. Kamil directed the driver to the residential buildings the governorate had put up for housing government employees. While gazing at the opposite bank a large boat with a great fluttering sail glided past. Behind it could be seen a white house that had a garden with trees with yellow flowers and that lay on its own amidst vast fields. I shouted out in confusion, overcome by the feeling that I had been here before.

'Go to that house,' I called to the driver. Kamil leapt up, objecting vehemently: 'No, no,—no one lives in that house. The best thing is to go to the employees' buildings.'

I shouted insistently, like someone hypnotized: 'I must have a look at that house.' 'All right,' he said. 'You won't like it, though—it's old and needs repairing,' Giving in to my wish, he ordered the driver to make his way there.

At the garden door we found a young woman, spare and of fair complexion. A fat child with ragged clothes encircled her neck with his burly legs. In a strange silence, she stood as though nailed to the ground, barring the door with her hands and looking at us with doltish enquiry.

I took a sweet from my bag and handed it to the boy. He snatched it eagerly, tightening his grip on her neck with his podgy, mud-bespattered feet so that her face became flushed from his high-spirited embrace. A half-smile showed on her tightly-closed lips. Taking courage, I addressed her in a friendly tone: 'I'd like to see over this house.' She braced her hands resolutely against the door. 'No,' she said quite simply. I turned helplessly to Kamil, who went up to her and pushed her violently in the chest so that she staggered back. 'Don't you realize,' he shouted at her, 'that this is the director's wife? Off with you!'

Lowering her head so that the child all but slipped from her, she walked off dejectedly to the canal bank where she lay down on the ground, put the child on her lap, and rested her head in her hands in silent submission.

---

[1] A *souk* is an outdoor market or bazaar.

Moved by pity, I remonstrated: 'There's no reason to be so rough, Mr Kamil. Who is the woman?' 'Some mad woman,' he said with a shrug of his shoulders, 'who's a stranger to the town. Out of kindness the owner of this house put her in charge of it until someone should come along to live in it.'

With increased interest I said: 'Will he be asking a high rent for it?' 'Not at all,' he said with an enigmatic smile. 'He'd welcome anyone taking it over. There are no restrictions and the rent is modest—no more than four pounds.'

I was beside myself with joy. Who in these days can find somewhere to live for such an amount? I rushed through the door into the house with Kamil behind me and went over the rooms: five spacious rooms with wooden floors, with a pleasant hall, modern lavatory, and a beautifully roomy kitchen with a large verandah over-looking vast pistachio-green fields of generously watered rice. A breeze, limpid and cool, blew, playing with the tips of the crop and making the delicate leaves move in continuous dancing waves.

I went back to the first room with its spacious balcony overlooking the road and revealing the other bank of the canal where, along its strand, extended the houses of the town. Kamil pointed out to me a building facing the house on the other side. 'That's where we work,' he said, 'and behind it is where the children's schools are.'

'Thanks be to God,' I said joyfully. 'It means that everything is within easy reach of this house—and the *souk*'s nearby too.' 'Yes,' he said, 'and the fishermen will knock at your door to show you the fresh fish they've caught in their nets. But the house needs painting and re-doing, also there are all sorts of rumours about it—the people around here believe in djinn[2] and spirits.'

'This house is going to be my home,' I said with determination. 'Its low rent will make up for whatever we may have to spend on re-doing it. You'll see what this house will look like when I get the garden arranged. As for the story about djinn and spirits, just leave them to us—we're more spirited than them.'

We laughed at my joke as we left the house. On my way to the station we agreed about the repairs that needed doing to the house. Directly I reached Cairo I cabled my husband to send the furniture from the town we had been living in, specifying a suitable date to fit in with the completion of the repairs and the house being ready for occupation.

On the date fixed I once again set off and found that all my wishes had been carried out and that the house was pleasantly spruce with its rooms painted a cheerful orange tinge, the floors well polished and the garden tidied up and made into small flowerbeds.

I took possession of the keys and Kamil went off to attend to his business, having put a chair on the front balcony for me to sit on while I awaited the arrival of the furniture van. I stretched out contentedly in the chair and gazed at the two banks with their towering trees like two rows of guards between which passed the boats with their lofty sails, while around them glided a male swan heading a flotilla of females. Halfway across the canal he turned and flirted with them, one after the other, like a sultan amidst his harem.

---

[2] The djinn are intelligent corporeal beings created by Allah out of smokeless fire. They inhabit a sort of parallel universe to ours, although Arabic folklore recounts comings and goings between the two worlds. They may appear to human beings in the guise of an animal or in human form; the narrator's lover in this story does both. One whole sura of the Koran is devoted to the djinn. Our word *genie* is derived from *djinn*.

Relaxed, I closed my eyes. I projected myself into the future and pictured to myself the enjoyment I would have in this house after it had been put in order and the garden fixed up. I awoke to the touch of clammy fingers shaking me by the shoulders.

I started and found myself staring at the fair-complexioned woman with her child squatting on her shoulders as she stood erect in front of me staring at me in silence. 'What do you want?' I said to her sharply. 'How did you get in?' 'I got in with this,' she said simply, revealing a key between her fingers.

I snatched the key from her hand as I loudly rebuked her: 'Give it here. We have rented the house and you have no right to come into it like this.' 'I have a lot of other keys,' she answered briefly. 'And what,' I said to her, 'do you want of this house?' 'I want to stay on in it and for you to go,' she said. I laughed in amazement at her words as I asked myself: Is she really mad? Finally I said impatiently: 'Listen here, I'm not leaving here and you're not entering this house unless I wish it. My husband is coming with the children, and the furniture is on the way. He'll be arriving in a little while and we'll be living here for such period of time as my husband is required to work in this town.'

She looked at me in a daze. For a long time she was silent, then she said: 'All right, your husband will stay with me and you can go.' Despite my utter astonishment I felt pity for her. 'I'll allow you to stay on with us for the little boy's sake,' I said to her gently, 'until you find yourself another place. If you'd like to help me with the housework I'll pay you what you ask.'

Shaking her head, she said with strange emphasis: 'I'm not a servant. I'm Aneesa.' 'You're not staying here,' I said to her coldly, rising to my feet. Collecting all my courage and emulating Kamil's determination when he rebuked her, I began pushing her in the chest as I caught hold of the young boy's hand. 'Get out of here and don't come near this house,' I shouted at her. 'Let me have all the keys. I'll not let go of your child till you've given them all to me.'

With a set face that did not flicker she put her hand to her bosom and took out a ring on which were several keys, which she dropped into my hand. I released my grip on the young boy. Supporting him on her shoulders, she started to leave. Regretting my harshness, I took out several piastres from my bag and placed them in the boy's hand. With the same silence and stiffness she wrested the piastres from the boy's hand and gave them back to me. Then she went straight out. Bolting the door this time, I sat down, tense and upset, to wait.

My husband arrived, then the furniture, and for several days I occupied myself with putting the house in order. My husband was busy with his work and the children occupied themselves with making new friends and I completely forgot about Aneesa, that is until my husband returned one night wringing his hands with fury: 'This woman Aneesa, can you imagine that since we came to live in this house she's been hanging around it every night. Tonight she was so crazy she blocked my way and suggested I should send you off so that she might live with me. The woman's gone completely off her head about this house and I'm afraid she might do something to the children or assault you.'

Joking with him and masking the jealousy that raged within me, I said: 'And what is there for you to get angry about? She's a fair and attractive enough woman—a blessing brought to your very doorstep!' With a sneer he took up the telephone, muttering: 'May God look after her!'

He contacted the police and asked them to come and take her away. When I heard the sound of the police van coming I ran to the window and saw them taking her off. The poor woman did not resist, did not object, but submitted with a gentle sadness that as usual with her aroused one's pity. Yet, when she saw me standing in tears and watching her, she turned to me and, pointing to the wall of the house, called out: 'I'll leave her to you.' 'Who?' I shouted. 'Who, Aneesa?' Once again pointing at the bottom of the house, she said: 'Her.'

The van took her off and I spent a sleepless night. No sooner did day come than I hurried to the garden to examine my plants and to walk round the house and carefully inspect its walls. All I found were some cracks, the house being old, and I laughed at the frivolous thought that came to me: Could, for example, there be jewels buried here, as told in fairy tales?

Who could 'she' be? What was the secret of this house? Who was Aneesa and was she really mad? Where were she and her son living? So great did my concern for Aneesa become that I began pressing my husband with questions until he brought me news of her. The police had learnt that she was the wife of a well-to-do teacher living in a nearby town. One night he had caught her in an act of infidelity, and in fear she had fled with her son and had settled here, no one knowing why she had betaken herself to this particular house. However, the owner of the house had been good enough to allow her to put up in it until someone should come to live in it, while some kind person had intervened on her behalf to have her name included among those receiving monthly allowances from the Ministry of Social Affairs. There were many rumours that cast doubt upon her conduct: people passing by her house at night would hear her conversing with unknown persons. Her madness took the form of a predilection for silence and isolation from people during the daytime as she wandered about in a dream world. After the police had persuaded them to take her in to safeguard the good repute of her family, she was returned to her relatives.

The days passed and the story of Aneesa was lost in oblivion. Winter came and with it heavy downpours of rain. The vegetation in my garden flourished though the castor-oil plants withered and their yellow flowers fell. I came to find pleasure in sitting out on the kitchen balcony looking at my flowers and vegetables and enjoying the belts of sunbeams that lay between the clouds and lavished my balcony with warmth and light.

One sunny morning my attention was drawn to the limb of a nearby tree whose branches curved up gracefully despite its having dried up and its dark bark being cracked. My gaze was attracted by something twisting and turning along the tip of a branch: bands of yellow and others of red, intermingled with bands of black, were creeping forward. It was a long, smooth tube, at its end a small striped head with two bright, wary eyes.

The snake curled round on itself in spiral rings, then tautened its body and moved forward. The sight gripped me; I felt terror turning my blood cold and freezing my limbs.

My senses were numbed, my soul intoxicated with a strange elation at the exciting beauty of the snake. I was rooted to the spot, wavering between two thoughts that contended in my mind at one and the same time: should I snatch up some implement from the kitchen and kill the snake, or should I enjoy the rare moment of beauty that had been afforded me?

As though the snake had read what was passing through my mind, it raised its head, tilting it to right and left in thrilling coquetry. Then, by means of two tiny fangs like pearls, and a golden tongue like a twig of *arak* wood, it smiled at me and fastened its eyes on mine in one fleeting, commanding glance. The thought of killing left me. I felt a current, a radiation from its eyes that penetrated to my heart ordering me to stay where I was. A warning against continuing to sit out there in front of it surged inside me, but my attraction to it paralysed my limbs and I did not move. I kept on watching it, utterly entranced and captivated. Like a bashful virgin being lavished with compliments, it tried to conceal its pride in its beauty, and, having made certain of captivating its lover, the snake coyly twisted round and gently, gracefully glided away until swallowed up by a crack in the wall. Could the snake be the 'she' that Aneesa had referred to on the day of her departure?

At last I rose from my place, overwhelmed by the feeling that I was on the brink of a new world, a new destiny, or rather, if you wish, the threshold of a new love. I threw myself onto the bed in a dreamlike state, unaware of the passage of time. No sooner, though, did I hear my husband's voice and the children with their clatter as they returned at noon than I regained my sense of being a human being, wary and frightened about itself, determined about the existence and continuance of its species. Without intending to I called out: 'A snake—there's a snake in the house.'

My husband took up the telephone and some men came and searched the house. I pointed out to them the crack into which the snake had disappeared, though racked with a feeling of remorse at being guilty of betrayal. For here I was denouncing the beloved, inviting people against it after it had felt safe with me.

The men found no trace of the snake. They burned some wormwood and fumigated the hole but without result. Then my husband summoned Sheikh Farid, Sheikh of the Rifa'iyya[3] order in the town, who went on chanting verses from the Qur'an as he tapped the ground with his stick. He then asked to speak to me alone and said:

'Madam, the sovereign of the house has sought you out and what you saw is no snake, rather it is one of the monarchs of the earth—may God make your words pleasant to them—who has appeared to you in the form of a snake. Here in this house there are many holes of snakes, but they are of the non-poisonous kind. They inhabit houses and go and come as they please. What you saw, though, is something else.'

'I don't believe a word of it,' I said, stupefied. 'This is nonsense. I know that the djinn are creatures that actually exist, but they are not in touch with our world, there is no contact between them and the world of humans.'

With an enigmatic smile he said: 'My child, the Prophet[4] went out to them and read the Qur'an to them in their country. Some of them are virtuous and some of them are Muslims, and how do you know there is no contact between us and them? Let your prayer be "O Lord, increase me in knowledge" and do not be nervous. Your purity of spirit, your translucence of soul have opened to you doors that will take you to other worlds known only to their Creator. Do not be afraid. Even if you should find her one night sleeping in your bed, do not be alarmed but talk to her with all politeness and friendliness.'

'That's enough of all that, Sheikh Farid. Thank you,' I said, alarmed, and he left us.

We went on discussing the matter. 'Let's be practical,' suggested my husband, 'and stop all the cracks at the bottom of the outside walls and put wire-mesh over the windows, also paint wormwood all round the garden fence.'

We set about putting into effect what we had agreed. I, though, no longer dared to go out onto the balconies. I neglected my garden and stopped wandering about in

---

[3] The sheikh is the local head of a conservative Islamic order.
[4] The Prophet is Muhammad (c. 570–632 C.E.), the founder of Islam.

it. Generally I would spend my free time in bed. I changed to being someone who liked to sit around lazily and was disinclined to mix with people; those diversions and recreations that previously used to tempt me no longer gave me any pleasure. All I wanted was to stretch myself out and drowse. In bewilderment I asked myself: Could it be that I was in love? But how could I love a snake? Or could she really be one of the daughters of the monarchs of the djinn? I would awake from my musings to find that I had been wandering in my thoughts and recalling to mind how magnificent she was. And what is the secret of her beauty? I would ask myself. Was it that I was fascinated by her multi-coloured, supple body? Or was it that I had been dazzled by that intelligent, commanding way she had of looking at me? Or could it be the sleek way she had of gliding along, so excitingly dangerous, that had captivated me?

Excitingly dangerous! No doubt it was this excitement that had stirred my feelings and awakened my love, for did they not make films to excite and frighten? There was no doubt but that the secret of my passion for her, my preoccupation with her, was due to the excitement that had aroused, through intense fear, desire within myself; an excitement that was sufficiently strong to drive the blood hotly through my veins whenever the memory of her came to me, thrusting the blood in bursts that made my heart beat wildly, my limbs limp. And so, throwing myself down in a pleasurable state of torpor, my craving for her would be awakened and I would wish for her coil-like touch, her graceful gliding motion.

And yet I fell to wondering how union could come about, how craving be quenched, the delights of the body be realized, between a woman and a snake. And did she, I wondered, love me and want me as I loved her? An idea would obtrude itself upon me sometimes: did Cleopatra, the very legend of love, have sexual intercourse with her serpent after having given up sleeping with men, having wearied of amorous adventures with them so that her sated instincts were no longer moved other than by the excitement of fear, her senses no longer aroused other than by bites from a snake? And the last of her lovers had been a viper that had destroyed her.

I came to live in a state of continuous torment, for a strange feeling of longing scorched my body and rent my senses, while my circumstances obliged me to carry out the duties and responsibilities that had been placed on me as the wife of a man who occupied an important position in the small town, he and his family being objects of attention and his house a Kaaba[5] for those seeking favours; also as a mother who must look after her children and concern herself with every detail of their lives so as to exercise control over them; there was also the house and its chores, this house that was inhabited by the mysterious lover who lived in a world other than mine. How, I wondered, was union between us to be achieved? Was wishing for this love a sin or was there nothing to reproach myself about?

And as my self-questioning increased so did my yearning, my curiosity, my desire. Was the snake from the world of reptiles or from the djinn? When would the meeting be? Was she, I wondered, aware of me and would she return out of pity for my consuming passion?

One stormy morning with the rain pouring down so hard that I could hear the drops rattling on the window pane, I lit the stove and lay down in bed between the

---

[5]Metaphorically, the house is a pilgrimage site; the Kaaba is the small cubical building within the Great Mosque at Mecca that houses the Black Stone, the holiest relic in Islam. Muslims worldwide face toward the Kaaba when they pray.

covers seeking refuge from an agonizing trembling that racked my yearning body which, ablaze with unquenchable desire, called out for relief.

I heard a faint rustling sound coming from the corner of the wall right beside my bed. I looked down and kept my eyes fixed on one of the holes in the wall, which I found was slowly, very slowly, expanding. Closing my eyes, my heart raced with joy and my body throbbed with mounting desire as there dawned in me the hope of an encounter. I lay back in submission to what was to be. No longer did I care whether love was coming from the world of reptiles or from that of the djinn, sovereigns of the world. Even were this love to mean my destruction, my desire for it was greater.

I heard a hissing noise that drew nearer, then it changed to a gentle whispering in my ear, calling to me: 'I am love, O enchantress. I showed you my home in your sleep; I called you to my kingdom when your soul was dozing on the horizon of dreams, so come, my sweet beloved, come and let us explore the depths of the azure sea of pleasure. There, in the chamber of coral, amidst cool, shady rocks where reigns deep, restful silence lies our bed, lined with soft, bright green damask, inlaid with pearls newly wrenched from their shells. Come, let me sleep with you as I have slept with beautiful women and have given them bliss. Come, let me prise out your pearl from its shell that I may polish it and bring forth its splendour. Come to where no one will find us, where no one will see us, for the eyes of swimming creatures are innocent and will not heed what we do nor understand what we say. Down there lies repose, lies a cure for all your yearnings and ills. Come, without fear or dread, for no creature will reach us in our hidden world, and only the eye of God alone will see us; He alone will know what we are about and He will watch over us.'

I began to be intoxicated by the soft musical whisperings. I felt her cool and soft and smooth, her coldness producing a painful convulsion in my body and hurting me to the point of terror. I felt her as she slipped between the covers, then her two tiny fangs, like two pearls, began to caress my body; arriving at my thighs, the golden tongue, like an *arak* twig, inserted its pronged tip between them and began sipping and exhaling; sipping the poisons of my desire and exhaling the nectar of my ecstasy, till my whole body tingled and started to shake in sharp, painful, rapturous spasms—and all the while the tenderest of words were whispered to me as I confided to her all my longings.

At last the cool touch withdrew, leaving me exhausted. I went into a deep slumber to awake at noon full of energy, all of me a joyful burgeoning to life. Curiosity and a desire to know who it was seized me again. I looked at the corner of the wall and found that the hole was wide open. Once again I was overcome by fear. I pointed out the crack to my husband, unable to utter, although terror had once again awakened in me passionate desire. My husband filled up the crack with cement and went to sleep.

Morning came and everyone went out. I finished my housework and began roaming around the rooms in boredom, battling against the desire to surrender myself to sleep. I sat in the hallway and suddenly she appeared before me, gentle as an angel, white as day, softly undulating and flexing herself, calling to me in her bewitching whisper: 'Bride of mine, I called you and brought you to my home. I have wedded you, so there is no sin in our love, nothing to reproach yourself about. I am the guardian of the house, and I hold sway over the snakes and vipers that inhabit it, so come and I shall show you where they live. Have no fear so long as we are together. You and I are in accord. Bring a container with water and I shall place my fingers over your hand and we shall recite together some verses from the Qur'an, then we shall sprinkle it in the places from which they emerge and shall thus close the doors on them, and it shall be a pact between us that your hands will not do harm to them.'

'Then you are one of the monarchs of the djinn?' I asked eagerly. 'Why do you not bring me treasures and riches as we hear about in fables when a human takes as sister her companion among the djinn?'

She laughed at my words, shaking her golden hair that was like dazzling threads of light. She whispered to me, coquettishly: 'How greedy is mankind! Are not the pleasures of the body enough? Were I to come to you with wealth we would both die consumed by fire.'

'No, no,' I called out in alarm. 'God forbid that I should ask for unlawful wealth. I merely asked it of you as a test, that it might be positive proof that I am not imagining things and living in dreams.'

She said: 'And do intelligent humans have to have something tangible as evidence? By God, do you not believe in His ability to create worlds and living beings? Do you not know that you have an existence in worlds other than that of matter and the transitory? Fine, since you ask for proof, come close to me and my caresses will put vitality back into your limbs. You will retain your youth. I shall give you abiding youth and the delights of love—and they are more precious than wealth in the world of man. How many fortunes have women spent in quest of them? As for me I shall feed from the poisons of your desire, the exhalations of your burning passion, for that is my nourishment and through it I live.'

'I thought that your union with me was for love, not for nourishment and the perpetuation of youth and vigour,' I said in amazement.

'And is sex anything but food for the body and an interaction in union and love?' she said. 'Is it not this that makes human beings happy and is the secret of feeling joy and elation?'

She stretched out her radiant hand to my body, passing over it like the sun's rays and discharging into it warmth and a sensation of languor.

'I am ill,' I said. 'I am ill. I am ill,' I kept on repeating. When he heard me my husband brought the doctor, who said: 'High blood pressure, heart trouble, nervous depression.' Having prescribed various medicaments he left. The stupidity of doctors! My doctor did not know that he was describing the symptoms of love, did not even know it was from love I was suffering. Yet I knew my illness and the secret of my cure. I showed my husband the enlarged hole in the wall and once again he stopped it up. We then carried the bed to another corner.

After some days had passed I found another hole alongside my bed. My beloved came and whispered to me: 'Why are you so coy and flee from me, my bride? Is it fear of your being rebuffed or is it from aversion? Are you not happy with our being together? Why do you want for us to be apart?'

'I am in agony,' I whispered back. 'Your love is so intense and the desire to enjoy you so consuming. I am frightened I shall feel that I am tumbling down into a bottomless pit and being destroyed.'

'My beloved,' she, said. 'I shall only appear to you in beauty's most immaculate form.'

'But it is natural for you to be a man,' I said in a precipitate outburst, 'seeing that you are so determined to have a love affair with me.'

'Perfect beauty is to be found only in woman,' she said, 'so yield to me and I shall let you taste undreamed of happiness; I shall guide you to worlds possessed of such beauty as you have never imagined.'

She stretched out her fingers to caress me, while her delicate mouth sucked in the poisons of my desire and exhaled the nectar of my ecstasy, carrying me off into a trance of delicious happiness.

After that we began the most pleasurable of love affairs, wandering together in worlds and living on horizons of dazzling beauty, a world fashioned of jewels, a world whose every moment was radiant with light and formed a thousand shapes, a thousand colours.

As for the opening in the wall, I no longer took any notice. I no longer complained of feeling ill, in fact there burned within me abounding vitality. Sometimes I would bring a handful of wormwood and, by way of jest, would stop up the crack, just as the beloved teases her lover and closes the window in his face that, ablaze with desire for her, he may hasten to the door. After that I would sit for a long time and enjoy watching the wormwood powder being scattered in spiral rings by unseen puffs of wind. Then I would throw myself down on the bed and wait.

For months I immersed myself in my world, no longer calculating time or counting the days, until one morning my husband went out on the balcony lying behind our favoured wall alongside the bed. After a while I heard him utter a cry of alarm. We all hurried out to find him holding a stick, with a black, ugly snake almost two metres long, lying at his feet.

I cried out with a sorrow whose claws clutched at my heart so that it began to beat wildly. With crazed fury I shouted at my husband: 'Why have you broken the pact and killed it? What harm has it done?' How cruel is man! He lets no creature live in peace.

I spent the night sorrowful and apprehensive. My lover came to me and embraced me more passionately than ever. I whispered to her imploringly: 'Be kind, beloved. Are you angry with me or sad because of me?'

'It is farewell,' she said. 'You have broken the pact and have betrayed one of my subjects, so you must both depart from this house, for only love lives in it.'

In the morning I packed up so that we might move to one of the employees' buildings, leaving the house in which I had learnt of love and enjoyed incomparable pleasures.

I still live in memory and in hope. I crave for the house and miss my secret love. Who knows, perhaps one day my beloved will call me. Who really knows?

N. SCOTT MOMADAY

[BORN 1934]

In the course of an interview with Joseph Bruchac about her life and work, Laguna Pueblo poet, novelist, and feminist critic Paula Gunn Allen says that Scott Momaday's novel *House Made of Dawn* (1968) quite literally saved her life when she was a graduate student in Oregon on the verge of a breakdown. When asked to elaborate, she explains that she saw herself mirrored in the experiences of the main character, Abel, a Pueblo Indian war veteran caught between his tribal reality and what mainstream America defines as reality:

> It told me I was sane—or if I was crazy at least fifty thousand people out there were just as nutty in exactly the same way I was, so it was okay.... I knew every inch of what he was saying. It was that, and the fact that he could write a novel about an "Abel." An Abel with the same sickness that I had—or something like it—but Momaday had enough control over that sickness to write a book about it.

For many American Indian people, Momaday's novel and his later books have functioned similarly, not just as good reads, but as agents of healing, in their articulation of American Indian ways of thought and perception. Momaday, for example, totally accepts dreams and visions as a valid means of learning, rather than as symptoms of mental illness; he respects the oral tradition as a repository of important knowledge; he reveres elders and the natural world of plants and animals. Moreover, in his novels, poetry, and autobiographical prose, Momaday has helped to lead readers who aren't American Indians toward a better understanding of tribal Americans, helped them to see beyond the entrenched stereotypes of romantic braves and maidens, savage warriors, wise medicine men, and drunken sots. Abel, for example, in the first scene of *House Made of Dawn,* is deliberately depicted as the quintessential "drunken Indian" who falls in a stupor off the Greyhound bus at the stop on the highway near his Pueblo home; before the novel is over, readers learn a great deal about the sources of his alcoholic despair and a good deal as well about the possibilities of spiritual healing.

LIFE

Momaday's own autobiographical books *The Way to Rainy Mountain* (1969) and *The Names* (1976) contain richly evocative accounts of his childhood. He was born in 1934 in Lawton, Oklahoma, to a Kiowa father and a part-Cherokee mother, both teachers in the Bureau of Indian Affairs school system. Al Momaday was a gifted artist; Natachee Scott Momaday, after she retired from teaching, edited a collection of American Indian literature. Momaday inherited his parents' verbal and artistic talents. The family was assigned to a number of teaching posts around the Southwest before settling at Jemez Pueblo, a Tewa-speaking pueblo in a red sandstone valley at the foot of New Mexico's Jemez Mountains. Momaday thus grew up with a consciousness of both Plains and Pueblo Indian cultures; Navajo people from the nearby community of Cuba were also part of his growing up. To be a mixed-blooded Kiowa Indian child, and the teachers' child to boot, growing up around a tightly knit Pueblo community gave Momaday a slight outsider's perspective on life at an early age; he seems to have been a child who watched and listened a great deal, unobserved.

Momaday obtained his BA in English at the University of New Mexico in Albuquerque in 1958 and went on to Stanford for his MA and PhD, which he earned in 1963. On a Guggenheim fellowship he edited *The Complete Poems of Frederick Goddard Tuckerman,* an early New England poet. But while at Stanford he had also worked with the writer Ivor Winters, who had encouraged his writing, and Momaday, for all his scholarly gifts, was clearly meant to be more than a textual editor. In 1968 he published *The Way to Rainy Mountain,* a memoir of his Kiowa ancestors and background that he had been working on sporadically for some years. *House Made of Dawn* also appeared in 1968 and won the Pulitzer Prize in 1969. *The Names,* a meditation on all his mixed ancestries and a tribute to his parents in particular, appeared in 1976. Two books of poetry, *Angle of Geese* (1974) and *The Gourd Dancer* (1976), saw Momaday return to the poetry he had been writing under Winters's supervision at Stanford. *Ancient Child* (1989), his most recent novel, combines Kiowa stories with Momaday's passionate interest in the enigmatic New Mexican antihero Billy the Kid.

Over the years, Momaday has held a number of academic posts at Berkeley, Stanford, the University of Arizona, and abroad; his interest in American Indian migration routes has drawn him several times to Russia and Central Asia. He has in recent years begun to work seriously at painting. He also holds the honor of being a Kiowa gourd dancer.

WORK

The Way to Rainy Mountain is an extraordinary evocation in twentieth-century English prose of the Kiowa oral tradition, and of the importance of telling stories and remembering them. Momaday was a child raised at some distance from his tribal culture, and as he traces Kiowa migration routes and searches for his grandmother's grave in *The Way to Rainy Mountain*, he is also tracing his own way back into his heritage; like his Kiowa ancestors themselves, Momaday through the act of storytelling is "daring to imagine and determine" who he is—an individual, but more importantly, a Kiowa, a member of his people.

SUGGESTED READINGS

Susan Scarberry-Garcia's *Landmarks of Healing* (1990) is a scholarly and moving book-length study of Momaday. Paula Gunn Allen's *The Sacred Hoop* (1986) is an indispensable companion to contemporary American Indian writing. Momaday is generous with interviews; *Ancestral Voices: Conversations with N. Scott Momaday*, edited by Charles L. Woodard (1989), is very pleasant and informative reading.

FROM

The Way to Rainy Mountain

INTRODUCTION

A single knoll rises out of the plain in Oklahoma, north and west of the Wichita Range. For my people, the Kiowas, it is an old landmark, and they gave it the name Rainy Mountain. The hardest weather in the world is there. Winter brings blizzards, hot tornadic winds arise in the spring, and in summer the prairie is an anvil's edge. The grass turns brittle and brown, and it cracks beneath your feet. There are green belts along the rivers and creeks, linear groves of hickory and pecan, willow and witch hazel. At a distance in July or August the steaming foliage seems almost to writhe in fire. Great green and yellow grasshoppers are everywhere in the tall grass, popping up like corn to sting the flesh, and tortoises crawl about on the red earth, going nowhere in the plenty of time. Loneliness is an aspect of the land. All things in the plain are isolate; there is no confusion of objects in the eye, but *one* hill or *one* tree or *one* man. To look upon that landscape in the early morning, with the sun at your back, is to lose the sense of proportion. Your imagination comes to life, and this, you think, is where Creation was begun.

I returned to Rainy Mountain in July. My grandmother had died in the spring, and I wanted to be at her grave. She had lived to be very old and at last infirm. Her only living daughter was with her when she died, and I was told that in death her face was that of a child.

I like to think of her as a child. When she was born, the Kiowas were living the last great moment of their history. For more than a hundred years they had controlled the open range from the Smoky Hill River to the Red, from the headwaters of the Canadian to the fork of the Arkansas and Cimarron. In alliance with the Comanches, they had ruled the whole of the southern Plains. War was their sacred business, and they were among the finest horsemen the world has ever known. But warfare for the Kiowas was preeminently a matter of disposition rather than of survival, and they never understood the grim, unrelenting advance of the U.S. Cavalry. When at last, divided and ill-provisioned, they were driven onto the Staked Plains in the cold rains of autumn, they fell into panic. In Palo Duro Canyon they abandoned their crucial stores to pillage and had nothing then but their lives. In order to save themselves, they surrendered to the soldiers at Fort Sill and were imprisoned in the old stone corral that now stands as a military museum. My grandmother was spared the humiliation of those high gray walls by eight or ten years, but she must have known from birth the affliction of defeat, the dark brooding of old warriors.

Her name was Aho, and she belonged to the last culture to evolve in North America. Her forebears came down from the high country in western Montana nearly three centuries ago. They were a mountain people, a mysterious tribe of hunters whose language has never been positively classified in any major group. In the late seventeenth century they began a long migration to the south and east. It was a journey toward the dawn, and it led to a golden age. Along the way the Kiowas were befriended by the Crows, who gave them the culture and religion of the Plains. They acquired horses, and their ancient nomadic spirit was suddenly free of the ground. They acquired Tai-me, the sacred Sun Dance doll, from that moment the object and symbol of their worship, and so shared in the divinity of the sun. Not least, they acquired the sense of destiny, therefore courage and pride. When they entered upon the southern Plains they had been transformed. No longer were they slaves to the simple necessity of survival; they were a lordly and dangerous society of fighters and thieves, hunters and priests of the sun. According to their origin myth, they entered the world through a hollow log. From one point of view, their migration was the fruit of an old prophecy, for indeed they emerged from a sunless world.

Although my grandmother lived out her long life in the shadow of Rainy Mountain, the immense landscape of the continental interior lay like memory in her blood. She could tell of the Crows, whom she had never seen, and of the Black Hills, where she had never been. I wanted to see in reality what she had seen more perfectly in the mind's eye, and traveled fifteen hundred miles to begin my pilgrimage.

Yellowstone, it seemed to me, was the top of the world, a region of deep lakes and dark timber, canyons and waterfalls. But, beautiful as it is, one might have the sense of confinement there. The skyline in all directions is close at hand, the high wall of the woods and deep cleavages of shade. There is a perfect freedom in the mountains, but it belongs to the eagle and the elk, the badger and the bear. The Kiowas reckoned their stature by the distance they could see, and they were bent and blind in the wilderness.

Descending eastward, the highland meadows are a stairway to the plain. In July the inland slope of the Rockies is luxuriant with flax and buckwheat, stonecrop and larkspur. The earth unfolds and the limit of the land recedes. Clusters of trees, and animals grazing far in the distance, cause the vision to reach away and wonder to build upon the mind. The sun follows a longer course in the day, and the sky is immense beyond all comparison. The great billowing clouds that sail upon it are shadows that move upon the grain like water, dividing light. Farther down, in the land of the Crows and Blackfeet, the plain is yellow. Sweet clover takes hold of the hills and bends upon itself to cover and seal the soil. There the Kiowas paused on their way; they had come to the place where they must change their lives. The sun is at home on the plains. Precisely there does it have the certain character of a god. When the Kiowas came to the land of the Crows, they could see the dark lees of the hills at dawn across the Bighorn River, the profusion of light on the grain shelves, the oldest deity ranging after the solstices. Not yet would they veer southward to the caldron of the land that lay below; they must wean their blood from the northern winter and hold the mountains a while longer in their view. They bore Tai-me in procession to the east.

A dark mist lay over the Black Hills, and the land was like iron. At the top of a ridge I caught sight of Devil's Tower upthrust against the gray sky as if in the birth of time the core of the earth had broken through its crust and the motion of the world was begun. There are things in nature that engender an awful quiet in the heart of man; Devil's Tower is one of them. Two centuries ago, because they could not do otherwise, the Kiowas made a legend at the base of the rock. My grandmother said:

Eight children were there at play, seven sisters and their brother. Suddenly the boy was struck dumb; he trembled and began to run upon his hands and feet. His fingers became claws, and his body was covered with fur. Directly there was a bear where the boy had been. The sisters were terrified; they ran, and the bear after them. They came to the stump of a great tree, and the tree spoke to them. It bade them climb upon it, and as they did so it began to rise into the air. The bear came to kill them, but they were just beyond its reach. It reared against the tree and scored the bark all around with its claws. The seven sisters were borne into the sky, and they became the stars of the Big Dipper.

From that moment, and so long as the legend lives, the Kiowas have kinsmen in the night sky. Whatever they were in the mountains, they could be no more. However tenuous their well-being, however much they had suffered and would suffer again, they had found a way out of the wilderness.

My grandmother had a reverence for the sun, a holy regard that now is all but gone out of mankind. There was a wariness in her, and an ancient awe. She was a Christian in her later years, but she had come a long way about, and she never forgot her birthright. As a child she had been to the Sun Dances; she had taken part in those annual rites, and by them she had learned the restoration of her people in the presence of Tai-me. She was about seven when the last Kiowa Sun Dance was held in 1887 on the Washita River above Rainy Mountain Creek. The buffalo were gone. In order to consummate the ancient sacrifice—to impale the head of a buffalo bull upon the medicine tree—a delegation of old men journeyed into Texas, there to beg and barter for an animal from the Goodnight herd. She was ten when the Kiowas came together for the last time as a living Sun Dance culture. They could find no buffalo; they had to hang an old hide from the sacred tree. Before the dance could begin, a company of soldiers rode out from Fort Sill under orders to disperse the tribe. Forbidden without cause the essential act of their faith, having seen the wild herds slaughtered and left to rot upon the ground, the Kiowas backed away forever from the medicine tree. That was July 20, 1890, at the great bend of the Washita. My grandmother was there. Without bitterness, and for as long as she lived, she bore a vision of deicide.

Now that I can have her only in memory, I see my grandmother in the several postures that were peculiar to her: standing at the wood stove on a winter morning and turning meat in a great iron skillet; sitting at the south window, bent above her beadwork, and afterwards, when her vision failed, looking down for a long time into the fold of her hands; going out upon a cane, very slowly as she did when the weight of age came upon her; praying. I remember her most often at prayer. She made long, rambling prayers out of suffering and hope, having seen many things. I was never sure that I had the right to hear, so exclusive were they of all mere custom and company. The last time I saw her she prayed standing by the side of her bed at night, naked to the waist, the light of a kerosene lamp moving upon her dark skin. Her long, black hair, always drawn and braided in the day, lay upon her shoulders and against her breasts like a shawl. I do not speak Kiowa, and I never understood her prayers, but there was something inherently sad in the sound, some merest hesitation upon the syllables of sorrow. She began in a high and descending pitch, exhausting her breath to silence; then again and again—and always the same intensity of effort, of something that is, and is not, like urgency in the human voice. Transported so in the dancing light among the shadows of her room, she seemed beyond the reach of time. But that was illusion; I think I knew then that I should not see her again.

Houses are like sentinels in the plain, old keepers of the weather watch. There, in a very little while, wood takes on the appearance of great age. All colors wear soon away in the wind and rain, and then the wood is burned gray and the grain appears and the nails turn red with rust. The windowpanes are black and opaque; you imagine there is nothing within, and indeed there are many ghosts, bones given up to the land. They stand here and there against the sky, and you approach them for a longer time than you expect. They belong in the distance; it is their domain.

Once there was a lot of sound in my grandmother's house, a lot of coming and going, feasting and talk. The summers there were full of excitement and reunion. The Kiowas are a summer people; they abide the cold and keep to themselves, but when the season turns and the land becomes warm and vital they cannot hold still; an old love of going returns upon them. The aged visitors who came to my grandmother's house when I was a child were made of lean and leather, and they bore themselves upright. They wore great black hats and bright ample shirts that shook in the wind. They rubbed fat upon their hair and wound their braids with strips of colored cloth. Some of them painted their faces and carried the scars of old and cherished enmities. They were an old council of warlords, come to remind and be reminded of who they were. Their wives and daughters served them well. The women might indulge themselves; gossip was at once the mark and compensation of their servitude. They made loud and elaborate talk among themselves, full of jest and gesture, fright and false alarm. They went abroad in fringed and flowered shawls, bright beadwork and German silver. They were at home in the kitchen, and they prepared meals that were banquets.

There were frequent prayer meetings, and great nocturnal feasts. When I was a child I played with my cousins outside, where the lamplight fell upon the ground and the singing of the old people rose up around us and carried away into the darkness. There were a lot of good things to eat, a lot of laughter and surprise. And afterwards, when the quiet returned, I lay down with my grandmother and could hear the frogs away by the river and feel the motion of the air.

Now there is a funeral silence in the rooms, the endless wake of some final word. The walls have closed in upon my grandmother's house. When I returned to it in mourning, I saw for the first time in my life how small it was. It was late at night, and there was a white moon, nearly full. I sat for a long time on the stone steps by the kitchen door. From there I could see out across the land; I could see the long row of trees by the creek, the low light upon the rolling plains, and the stars of the Big Dipper. Once I looked at the moon and caught sight of a strange thing. A cricket had perched upon the handrail, only a few inches away from me. My line of vision was such that the creature filled the moon like a fossil. It had gone there, I thought, to live and die, for there, of all places, was its small definition made whole and eternal. A warm wind rose up and purled like the longing within me.

The next morning I awoke at dawn and went out on the dirt road to Rainy Mountain. It was already hot, and the grasshoppers began to fill the air. Still, it was early in the morning, and the birds sang out of the shadows. The long yellow grass on the mountain shone in the bright light, and a scissortail hied above the land. There, where it ought to be, at the end of a long and legendary way, was my grandmother's grave. Here and there on the dark stones were ancestral names. Looking back once, I saw the mountain and came away.

THE SETTING OUT

I

You know, everything had to begin, and this is how it was: the Kiowas came one by one into the world through a hollow log. They were many more than now, but not all of them got out. There was a woman whose body was swollen up with child, and she got stuck in the log. After that, no one could get through, and that is why the Kiowas are a small tribe in number. They looked all around and saw the world. It made them glad to see so many things. They called themselves *Kwuda*, "coming out."

They called themselves Kwuda *and later* Tepda, *both of which mean "coming out." And later still they took the name* Gaigwu, *a name which can be taken to indicate something of which the two halves differ from each other in appearance. It was once a custom among Kiowa warriors that they cut their hair on the right side of the head only and on a line level with the lobe of the ear, while on the left they let the hair grow long and wore it in a thick braid wrapped in otter skin. "Kiowa" is indicated in sign language by holding the hand palm up and slightly cupped to the right side of the head and rotating it back and forth from the wrist. "Kiowa" is thought to derive from the softened Comanche form of* Gaigwu.

I REMEMBER COMING OUT UPON THE NORTHERN GREAT PLAINS IN THE LATE SPRING. THERE WERE MEADOWS OF BLUE AND YELLOW WILDFLOWERS ON THE SLOPES, AND I COULD SEE THE STILL, SUNLIT PLAIN BELOW, REACHING AWAY OUT OF SIGHT. AT FIRST THERE IS NO DISCRIMINATION IN THE EYE, NOTHING BUT THE LAND ITSELF, WHOLE AND IMPENETRABLE. BUT THEN SMALLEST THINGS BEGIN TO STAND OUT OF THE DEPTHS—HERDS AND RIVERS AND GROVES—AND EACH OF THESE HAS PERFECT BEING IN TERMS OF DISTANCE AND OF SILENCE AND OF AGE. YES, I THOUGHT, NOW I SEE THE EARTH AS IT REALLY IS; NEVER AGAIN WILL I SEE THINGS AS I SAW THEM YESTERDAY OR THE DAY BEFORE.

II

They were going along, and some were hunting. An antelope was killed and quartered in the meadow. Well, one of the big chiefs came up and took the udders of that animal for himself, but another big chief wanted those udders also, and there was a great quarrel between them. Then, in anger, one of these chiefs gathered all of his followers together and went away. They are called *Azatanhop*, "the udder-angry travelers off." No one knows where they went or what happened to them.

This is one of the oldest memories of the tribe. There have been reports of a people in the Northwest who speak a language that is similar to Kiowa.
In the winter of 1848–49, the buffalo ranged away from easy reach, and food was scarce. There was an antelope drive in the vicinity of Bent's Fort, Colorado. According to ancient custom, antelope medicine was made, and the Kiowas set out on foot and on horseback—men,

women, and children—after game. They formed a great circle, inclosing a large area of the plain, and began to converge upon the center. By this means antelope and other animals were trapped and killed, often with clubs and even with the bare hands. By necessity were the Kiowas reminded of their ancient ways.

ONE MORNING ON THE HIGH PLAINS OF WYOMING I SAW SEVERAL PRONGHORNS IN THE DISTANCE. THEY WERE MOVING VERY SLOWLY AT AN ANGLE AWAY FROM ME, AND THEY WERE ALMOST INVISIBLE IN THE TALL BROWN AND YELLOW GRASS. THEY AMBLED ALONG IN THEIR OWN WILDERNESS DIMENSION OF TIME, AS IF NO NOTION OF FLIGHT COULD EVER COME UPON THEM. BUT I REMEMBERED ONCE HAVING SEEN A FRIGHTENED BUCK ON THE RUN, HOW THE WHITE ROSETTE OF ITS RUMP SEEMED TO HANG FOR THE SMALLEST FRACTION OF TIME AT THE TOP OF EACH FRANTIC BOUND—LIKE A SUCCESSION OF SUNBURSTS AGAINST THE PURPLE HILLS.

III

Before there were horses the Kiowas had need of dogs. That was a long time ago, when dogs could talk. There was a man who lived alone; he had been thrown away, and he made his camp here and there on the high ground. Now it was dangerous to be alone, for there were enemies all around. The man spent his arrows hunting food. He had one arrow left, and he shot a bear; but the bear was only wounded and it ran away. The man wondered what to do. Then a dog came up to him and said that many enemies were coming; they were close by and all around. The man could think of no way to save himself. But the dog said: "You know, I have puppies. They are young and weak and they have nothing to eat. If you will take care of my puppies, I will show you how to get away." The dog led the man here and there, around and around, and they came to safety. . . .

IV

They lived at first in the mountains. They did not yet know of Tai-me, but this is what they knew: There was a man and his wife. They had a beautiful child, a little girl whom they would not allow to go out of their sight. But one day a friend of the family came and asked if she might take the child outside to play. The mother guessed that would be all right, but she told the friend to leave the child in its cradle and to place the cradle in a tree. While the child was in the tree, a redbird came among the branches. It was not like any bird that you have seen; it was very beautiful, and it did not fly away. It kept still upon a limb, close to the child. After a while the child got out of its cradle and began to climb after the redbird. And at the same time the tree began to grow taller, and the child was borne up into the sky. She was then a woman, and she found herself in a strange place. Instead of a redbird, there was a young man standing before her. The man spoke to her and said: "I have been watching you for a long time, and I knew that I would find a way to bring you here. I have brought you here to be my wife." The woman looked all around; she saw that he was the only living man there. She saw that he was the sun.

There the land itself ascends into the sky. These mountains lie at the top of the continent, and they cast a long rain shadow on the sea of grasses to the east. They arise out of the last North American wilderness, and they have wilderness names: Wasatch, Bitterroot, Bighorn, Wind River.

I HAVE WALKED IN A MOUNTAIN MEADOW BRIGHT WITH INDIAN PAINTBRUSH, LUPINE, AND WILD BUCKWHEAT, AND I HAVE SEEN HIGH IN THE BRANCHES OF A LODGEPOLE PINE THE MALE PINE GROSBEAK, ROUND AND ROSE-COLORED, ITS

DARK, STRIPED WINGS NEARLY INVISIBLE IN THE SOFT, MOTTLED LIGHT. AND THE UPPERMOST BRANCHES OF THE TREE SEEMED VERY SLOWLY TO RIDE ACROSS THE BLUE SKY.

V

After that the woman grew lonely. She thought about her people, and she wondered how they were getting on. One day she had a quarrel with the sun, and the sun went away. In her anger she dug up the root of a bush which the sun had warned her never to go near. A piece of earth fell from the root, and she could see her people far below. By that time she had given birth; she had a child— a boy by the sun. She made a rope out of sinew and took her child upon her back; she climbed down upon the rope, but when she came to the end, her people were still a long way off, and there she waited with her child on her back. It was evening; the sun came home and found his woman gone. At once he thought of the bush and went to the place where it had grown. There he saw the woman and the child, hanging by the rope half way down to the earth. He was very angry, and he took up a ring, a gaming wheel, in his hand. He told the ring to follow the rope and strike the woman dead. Then he threw the ring and it did what he told it to do; it struck the woman and killed her, and then the sun's child was all alone.

The plant is said to have been the pomme blanche, *or* pomme de prairie, *of the voyageurs, whose chronicles refer time and again to its use by the Indians. It grows on the high plains and has a farinaceous root that is turnip-like in taste and in shape. This root is a healthful food, and attempts have been made to cultivate the plant as a substitute for the potato.*

The anthropologist Mooney wrote in 1896: "Unlike the neighboring Cheyenne and Arapaho, who yet remember that they once lived east of the Missouri and cultivated corn, the Kiowa have no tradition of ever having been an agricultural people or anything but a tribe of hunters."

EVEN NOW THEY ARE MEATEATERS; I THINK IT IS NOT IN THEM TO BE FARMERS. MY GRANDFATHER, MAMMEDATY, WORKED HARD TO MAKE WHEAT AND COTTON GROW ON HIS LAND, BUT IT CAME TO VERY LITTLE IN THE END. ONCE WHEN I WAS A SMALL BOY I WENT ACROSS THE CREEK TO THE HOUSE WHERE THE OLD WOMAN KEAHDINEKEAH LIVED. SOME MEN AND BOYS CAME IN FROM THE PASTURE, WHERE A CALF HAD JUST BEEN KILLED AND BUTCHERED. ONE OF THE BOYS HELD THE CALF'S LIVER—STILL WARM AND WET WITH LIFE—IN HIS HAND, EATING OF IT WITH GREAT RELISH. I HAVE HEARD THAT THE OLD HUNTERS OF THE PLAINS PRIZED THE RAW LIVER AND TONGUE OF THE BUFFALO ABOVE ALL OTHER DELICACIES.

VI

The sun's child was big enough to walk around on the earth, and he saw a camp nearby. He made his way to it and saw that a great spider—that which is called a grandmother—lived there. The spider spoke to the sun's child, and the child was afraid. The grandmother was full of resentment; she was jealous, you see, for the child had not yet been weaned from its mother's breasts. She wondered whether the child were a boy or a girl, and therefore she made two things, a pretty ball and a bow and arrows. These things she left alone with the child all the next day. When she returned, she saw that the ball was full of arrows, and she knew then that the child was a boy and that he would be hard to raise. Time and again the grandmother tried to capture the boy, but he always ran away. Then one day she made a snare out of rope. The boy was caught up in the snare, and he cried and cried, but the grandmother sang to him and at last he fell asleep.

> Go to sleep and do not cry.
> Your mother is dead, and still you feed
> upon her breasts.
> Oo-oo-la-la-la-la, oo-oo.

In the autumn of 1874, the Kiowas were driven southward towards the Staked Plains. Columns of troops were converging upon them from all sides, and they were bone-weary and afraid. They camped on Elk Creek, and the next day it began to rain. It rained hard all that day, and the Kiowas waited on horseback for the weather to clear. Then, as evening came on, the earth was suddenly crawling with spiders, great black tarantulas, swarming on the flood.

I KNOW OF SPIDERS. THERE ARE DIRT ROADS IN THE PLAINS. YOU SEE THEM, AND YOU WONDER WHERE AND HOW FAR THEY GO. THEY SEEM VERY OLD AND UNTRAVELED, AS IF THEY ALL LED AWAY TO DESERTED HOUSES. BUT CREATURES CROSS THESE ROADS: DUNG BEETLES AND GRASSHOPPERS, SIDEWINDERS AND TORTOISES. NOW AND THEN THERE COMES A TARANTULA, AT EVENING, ALWAYS LARGER THAN YOU IMAGINE, DULL AND DARK BROWN, COVERED WITH LONG, DUSTY HAIRS. THERE IS SOMETHING CROTCHETY ABOUT THEM; THEY STOP AND GO AND ANGLE AWAY.

VII

The years went by, and the boy still had the ring which killed his mother. The grandmother spider told him never to throw the ring into the sky, but one day he threw it up, and it fell squarely on top of his head and cut him in two. He looked around, and there was another boy, just like himself, his twin. The two of them laughed and laughed, and then they went to the grandmother spider. She nearly cried aloud when she saw them, for it had been hard enough to raise the one. Even so, she cared for them well and made them fine clothes to wear.

Mammedaty owned horses. And he could remember that it was essentially good to own horses, that it was hard to be without horses. There was a day: Mammedaty got down from a horse for the last time. Of all the tribes of the Plains, the Kiowas owned the greatest number of horses per person.

ON SUMMER AFTERNOONS I WENT SWIMMING IN THE WASHITA RIVER. THE CURRENT WAS SLOW, AND THE WARM, BROWN WATER SEEMED TO BE STANDING STILL. IT WAS A SECRET PLACE. THERE IN THE DEEP SHADE, INCLOSED IN THE DENSE, OVERHANGING GROWTH OF THE BANKS, MY MIND FIXED ON THE WINGS OF A DRAGONFLY OR THE FLITTING MOTION OF A WATER STRIDER, THE GREAT OPEN LAND BEYOND WAS ALL BUT IMPOSSIBLE TO IMAGINE. BUT IT WAS THERE, A STONE'S THROW AWAY. ONCE, FROM THE LIMB OF A TREE, I SAW MYSELF IN THE BROWN WATER; THEN A FROG LEAPED FROM THE BANK, BREAKING THE IMAGE APART.

VIII

Now each of the twins had a ring, and the grandmother spider told them never to throw the rings into the sky. But one day they threw them up into the high wind. The rings rolled over a hill, and the twins ran after them. They ran beyond the top of the hill and fell down into the mouth of a cave. There lived a giant and his wife.

The giant had killed a lot of people in the past by building fires and filling the cave with smoke, so that the people could not breathe. Then the twins remembered something that the grandmother spider had told them: "If ever you get caught in the cave, say to yourselves the word *thain-mom,* 'above my eyes.'" When the giant began to set fires around, the twins repeated the word *thain-mom* over and over to themselves, and the smoke remained above their eyes. When the giant had made three great clouds of smoke, his wife saw that the twins sat without coughing or crying, and she became frightened. "Let them go," she said, "or something bad will happen to us." The twins took up their rings and returned to the grandmother spider. She was glad to see them.

A word has power in and of itself. It comes from nothing into sound and meaning; it gives origin to all things. By means of words can a man deal with the world on equal terms. And the word is sacred. A man's name is his own; he can keep it or give it away as he likes. Until recent times, the Kiowas would not speak the name of a dead man. To do so would have been disrespectful and dishonest. The dead take their names with them out of the world.

WHEN AHO SAW OR HEARD OR THOUGHT OF SOMETHING BAD, SHE SAID THE WORD *ZEI-DL-BEI,* "FRIGHTFUL." IT WAS THE ONE WORD WITH WHICH SHE CONFRONTED EVIL AND THE INCOMPREHENSIBLE. I LIKED HER TO SAY IT, FOR SHE SCREWED UP HER FACE IN A WONDERFUL LOOK OF DISPLEASURE AND CLICKED HER TONGUE. IT WAS NOT AN EXCLAMATION SO MUCH, I THINK, AS IT WAS A WARDING OFF, AN EXERTION OF LANGUAGE UPON IGNORANCE AND DISORDER.

IX

The next thing that happened to the twins was this. They killed a great snake which they found in their tipi. When they told the grandmother spider what they had done, she cried and cried. They had killed their grandfather, she said. And after that the grandmother spider died. The twins wrapped her in a hide and covered her with leaves by the water. The twins lived on for a long time, and they were greatly honored among the Kiowas.

In another and perhaps older version of the story, it is a porcupine and not a redbird that is the representation of the sun. In that version, too, one of the twins is said to have walked into the waters of a lake and disappeared forever, while the other at last transformed himself into ten portions of "medicine," thereby giving of his own body in eucharistic form to the Kiowas. The ten bundles of the talyi-da-i, *"boy medicine," are, like the Tai-me, chief objects of religious veneration.*

WHEN HE WAS A BOY, MY FATHER WENT WITH HIS GRANDMOTHER, KEAHDIN-EKEAH, TO THE SHRINE OF ONE OF THE TALYI-DA-I. THE OLD WOMAN MADE AN OFFERING OF BRIGHT CLOTH, AND SHE PRAYED. THE SHRINE WAS A SMALL, SPECIALLY-MADE TIPI; INSIDE, SUSPENDED FROM THE LASHING OF THE POLES, WAS THE MEDICINE ITSELF. MY FATHER KNEW THAT IT WAS VERY POWERFUL, AND THE VERY SIGHT OF IT FILLED HIM WITH WONDER AND REGARD. THE HOLINESS OF SUCH A THING CAN BE IMPARTED TO THE HUMAN SPIRIT, I BELIEVE, FOR I REMEMBER THAT IT SHONE IN THE SIGHTLESS EYES OF KEAHDINEKEAH. ONCE I WAS TAKEN TO SEE HER AT THE OLD HOUSE ON THE OTHER SIDE OF RAINY MOUNTAIN CREEK. THE ROOM WAS DARK, AND HER OLD AGE FILLED IT LIKE A SUBSTANCE. SHE WAS WHITE-HAIRED AND BLIND, AND, IN THAT STRANGE REVERSION THAT COMES UPON THE VERY OLD, HER SKIN WAS AS SOFT AS THE SKIN OF A BABY. I REMEMBER THE SOUND OF HER GLAD WEEPING AND THE WATER-LIKE TOUCH OF HER HAND.

<hr />

ANITA DESAI
[BORN 1937]

There is a strong tradition in India of women as storytellers, as transmitters of the tales of the gods, of animal fables, of family and village histories. It is not surprising, therefore, that when the Western literary genre of the short story was introduced into India in the nineteenth century, women soon followed the early example of the Bengali writer Rabindranath Tagore and began writing short stories for themselves. By the late 1920s, there were already several journals in India dedicated exclusively to the publication of women's writing. Contemporary India boasts a large number of women writers, some of whom, like Amrita Pritam, Kamala Das, Bharati Mukherjee, and Anita Desai, have gained international admiration for their work. Like their male colleagues, they are often drawn to postcolonial themes: the movement of rural populations into cities; the violent displacement of tribal peoples and families in the 1947 partitioning of Pakistan from India; the conflict between European and Indian ways and the anxieties of choosing among them; the rapid changes in social conditions as contemporary India moves farther and farther from Gandhi's spiritual and social vision toward becoming a multicorporate capitalist state. But Indian women writers are also especially concerned with what happens to women in the midst of these circumstances, with the specific oppressions Indian women continue to endure, with Indian women's anger and their survival strategies, with women's strengths and the bonds between women. Desai's fiction often centers upon women from urban and somewhat westernized middle-class Indian families who are troubled by conflicts between the cultures, the generations, and the sexes.

LIFE

Anita Desai was born on June 24, 1937, in Mussoorie, India, to Toni Nime Mazumdar, a German woman, and D. N. Mazumdar, a successful Bengali businessman. She grew up in a comfortable multilingual and multicultural household in Old Delhi with her brothers and sisters, the sort of child her mother gently teased for being a *lese ratte,* or "reading rat," the German term for a bookworm. Her true awakening as a reader and beginning writer came when she was nine and she chose idly from her parents' bookshelves a copy of Emily Brontë's *Wuthering Heights.* As she read on, she recalls, "my own world of an Old Delhi bungalow, its verandas and plastered walls and ceiling fans, its gardens of papaya and guava trees full of shrieking parakeets, the gritty dust that settled on the pages of a book before one could turn them, all receded. What became real, dazzlingly real, through the power of Emily Brontë's pen was the Yorkshire moors, the storm-driven heath."

Desai earned her BA from Delhi University in 1957, where she came to admire the work of Chekhov, Dostoevsky, D. H. Lawrence, and E. M. Forster and began to publish her own short fiction. She married Ashvin Desai, a corporate executive, in the year after her graduation; the Desais are the parents of four children and make their home in Bombay. Desai's first novel, *Cry, The Peacock,* appeared in 1963; its main character is an Indian woman whose traditional upbringing has made it nearly impossible for her to voice or act upon her personal desires. *Where Shall We Go This Summer?* (1975) features a similarly unempowered heroine. *Bye Bye Blackbird* (1968) examines life in the burgeoning modern city, while *Fire on the Mountain* (1977) treats generational conflicts in Indian families. *The Clear Light of Day* (1980), considered by many to be Desai's finest novel, deals with a resourceful single woman, a university lecturer who must gauge how to reconcile her independent life with the expectations and needs of her traditional family.

Baumgartner's Bombay (1988) draws from both sides of Desai's heritage, as it tells the story of a gentle German Jew who flees the Holocaust to make his home in India, only to meet his end in the contemporary Bombay underworld of drug-dealing and violence. In addition to her novels, Desai has written several children's books and a collection of short stories, *Games at Twilight* (1978), including "The Farewell Party."

WORK

"The Farewell Party" displays Desai's sure touch with imagery and dialogue. As James Joyce does in "The Dead," Desai here follows her characters through the progress of an evening gathering, where seemingly banal conversations become fascinating as they reveal more and more about the main characters and the Euro-Indian corporate world they inhabit, a world neither wholly European nor Indian. Forced to be competitive and mobile, these executives find themselves and their families cut off from the intimacy that once characterized Indian life. Only at a farewell party, when there will be no danger of seeing the departing couple again, and where all exchanges are made easier by alcohol, can these people express affection for one another. Their more thoroughly westernized teenaged children twist to Beatles records and giggle and shriek while they swig Coca-Cola, but the uneasy parents have nearly forgotten how to enjoy one another's company.

As the night deepens, we learn more about the host couple, the Ramans, who have been further isolated by their own natural shyness and by the needs of Nono, their severely handicapped eldest child. Finally, when most of the guests have gone, the doctors from the local hospital come forward. They have been hanging back in the shadows, shy before the corporate executives, but of all the partygoers they alone have truly shared a part of the Ramans' lives in their joint concern for Nono, even though they have never socialized. Free now to bring Nono out to the party, Bina sits with her son among people who care about him and relaxes at last. One of the doctors' wives sings into the darkness an old Rabindranath Tagore song in Bengali about a woman compelled to sail away and leave her family behind. Even as the song draws closer the little circle of newly intimate people who are soon to be separated, the simple lyrics and the regional language in which they are sung evoke all the poignancy of lost relationships and connectedness.

SUGGESTED READINGS

There are several full-length studies of the work of Anita Desai. One is Meena Belliopa's *The Fiction of Anita Desai* (Writer's Workshop, 1971). The entries on Desai in volumes 19 and 37 of *Contemporary Literary Criticism* (Gale, 1981, 1986) are among the most recent and easily accessible pieces on her work.

The Farewell Party

Before the party she had made a list, faintheartedly, and marked off the items as they were dealt with, inexorably—cigarettes, soft drinks, ice, *kebabs* and so on. But she had forgotten to provide lights. The party was to be held on the lawn: on these dry summer nights one could plan a lawn party weeks in advance and be certain of fine weather, and she had thought happily of how the roses would be in bloom and of the stars and perhaps even fireflies, so decorative and discreet, all gracefully underlining her unsuspected talent as a hostess. But she had not realised that there would be no moon and therefore it would be very dark on the lawn. All the lights on the verandah, in the portico and indoors were on, like so many lanterns, richly copper and glowing with extraordinary beauty as though aware that the house would soon be empty and these were the last few days of illumination and family life, but they did very little to light the lawn which was vast, a still lake of inky grass.

Wandering about with a glass in one hand and a plate of cheese biscuits in another, she gave a start now and then to see an acquaintance emerge from the darkness, which had the gloss, the sheen, the coolness but not the weight of water, and present her with a face, vague and without outlines but eventually recognisable. 'Oh,' she cried several times that evening, 'I didn't know you had arrived. I've been looking for you,' she would add with unaccustomed intimacy (was it because of the gin and lime, her second, or because such warmth could safely be held to lead to nothing now that they were leaving town?). The guest, also having had several drinks between beds of flowering balsam and torenias before launching out onto the lawn, responded with an equal vivacity. Sometimes she had her arm squeezed or a hand slid down the bareness of her back—which was athletic: she had once played tennis, rather well—and once someone said, 'I've been hiding in this corner, watching you,' while another went so far as to say, 'Is it true you are leaving us, Bina? How can you be so cruel?' And if it were a woman guest, the words were that much more effusive. It was all heady, astonishing.

It was astonishing because Bina was a frigid and friendless woman. She was thirty-five. For fifteen years she had been bringing up her children and, in particular, nursing the eldest who was severely spastic. This had involved her deeply in the workings of the local hospital and with its many departments and doctors, but her care for this child was so intense and so desperate that her relationship with them was purely professional. Outside this circle of family and hospital—ringed, as it were, with barbed wire and lit with one single floodlight—Bina had no life. The town had scarcely come to know her for its life turned in the more jovial circles of mah-jong, bridge, coffee parties, club evenings and, occasionally, a charity show in aid of the Red Cross. For these Bina had a kind of sad contempt and certainly no time. A tall, pale woman, heavy-boned and sallow, she had a certain presence, a certain dignity, and people, having heard of the spastic child, liked and admired her, but she had not thought she had friends. Yet tonight they were coming forth from the darkness in waves that quite overwhelmed.

Now here was Mrs Ray, the Commissioner's wife, chirping inside a nest of rustling embroidered organza. 'Why are you leaving us so soon, Mrs Raman? You've only been here—two years, is it?'

'Five,' exclaimed Bina, widening her eyes, herself surprised at such a length of time. Although time dragged heavily in their household, agonisingly slow, and the five years had been so hard that sometimes, at night, she did not know how she had crawled through the day and if she would crawl through another, her back almost literally broken by the weight of the totally dependent child and of the three smaller ones who seemed perpetually to clamour for their share of attention, which they felt they never got. Yet now these five years had telescoped. They were over. The Raman family was moving and their time here was spent. There had been the hospital, the girls' school, the boys' school, picnics, monsoons, birthday parties and measles. Crushed together into a handful. She gazed down at her hands, tightened around glass and plate. 'Time has flown,' she murmured incredulously.

'Oh, I wish you were staying, Mrs Raman,' cried the Commissioner's wife and, as she squeezed Bina's arm, her fragrant talcum powder seemed to lift off her chalky shoulders and some of it settled on Bina who sneezed. 'It's been so nice to have a family like yours here. It's a small town, so little to do, at least one must have good friends...'

Bina blinked at such words of affection from a woman she had met twice, perhaps thrice before. Bina and her husband did not go in for society. The shock of their first child's birth had made them both fanatic parents. But she knew that not everyone considered this vital factor in their lives, and spoke of 'social duties' in a somehow reproving tone. The Commissioner's wife had been annoyed, she always felt, by her refusal to help out at the Red Cross fair. The hurt silence with which her refusal had been accepted had implied the importance of these 'social duties' of which Bina remained so stubbornly unaware.

However, this one evening, this last party, was certainly given over to their recognition and celebration. 'Oh, everyone, everyone is here,' rejoiced the Commissioner's wife, her eyes snapping from face to face in that crowded aquarium, and, at a higher pitch, cried 'Renu, why weren't you at the mah-jong party this morning?' and moved off into another powdery organza embrace that rose to meet her from the night like a moth and then was submerged again in the shadows of the lawn. Bina gave one of those smiles that easily-frightened people found mocking, a shade too superior, somewhat scornful. Looking down into her glass of gin and lime, she moved on and in a minute found herself brought up short against the quite regal although overweight figure, in raw silk and homespun and the somewhat saturnine air of underpaid culture, of Bose, an employee of the local museum whom she had met once or twice at the art competitions and exhibitions to which she was fond of hauling her children, whether reluctant or enthusiastic, because 'it made a change', she said.

'Mrs Raman,' he said in the fruity tones of the culture-bent Bengali, 'how we'll miss you at the next children's art competitions. You used to be my chief inspiration—'

'Inspiration?' she laughed, incredulously, spilling some of her drink and proffering the plate of cheese biscuits from which he helped himself, half-bowing as though it were gold she offered, gems.

'Yes, yes, inspiration,' he went on, even more fruitily now that his mouth was full. 'Think of me—alone, the hapless organiser—surrounded by mammas, by primary school teachers, by three, four, five hundred children. And the judges—they are always the most trouble, those judges. And then I look at you—so cool, controlling your children, handling them so wonderfully and with such superb results—my inspiration!'

She was flustered by this unaccustomed vision of herself and half-turned her face away from Bose the better to contemplate it, but could find no reflection of it in the ghostly white bush of the Queen of the Night, and listened to him murmur on about her unkindness in deserting him in this cultural backwater to that darkest of dooms—guardian of a provincial museum—where he saw no one but school teachers herding children through his halls or, worse, Government officials who periodically and inexplicably stirred to create trouble for him and made their official presences felt amongst the copies of the Ajanta frescoes (in which even the mouldy and peeled-off portions were carefully reproduced) and the cupboards of Indus Valley seals. Murmuring commiseration, she left him to a gloomy young professor of history who was languishing at another of the institutions of provincial backwaters that they so deplored and whose wife was always having a baby, and slipped away, still feeling an unease at Bose's unexpected vision of her which did not tally with the cruder reality, into the less equivocal company provided by a ring of twittering 'company wives'.

These women she had always encountered in just such a ring as they formed now, the kind that garden babblers form under a hedge where they sit gabbling and whirring with social bitchiness, and she had always stood outside it, smiling stiffly, not wanting to join and refusing their effusively nodded invitation. They were the wives of men who represented various mercantile companies in the town—Imperial Tobacco, Brooke Bond, Esso and so on—and although they might seem exactly alike to one who did not belong to this circle, inside it were subtle gradations of importance according to the particular company for which each one's husband worked and of these only they themselves were initiates. Bina was, however unwillingly, an initiate. Her husband worked for one of these companies but she had always stiffly refused to recognise these gradations, or consider them. They noted the rather set sulkiness of her silence when amongst them and privately labelled her queer, proud, boring and difficult. Also, they felt she belonged to their circle whether she liked it or not.

Now she entered this circle with diffidence, wishing she had stayed with the more congenial Bose (why hadn't she? What was it in her that made her retreat from anything like a friendly approach?) and was taken aback to find their circle parting to admit her and hear their cries of welcome and affection that did not, however, lose the stridency and harshness of garden babblers' voices.

'Bina, how do you like the idea of going back to Bombay?'

'Have you started packing, Bina? Poor you. Oh, are you having packers over from Delhi? Oh well, then it's not so bad.'

Never had they been so vociferous in her company, so easy, so warm. They were women to whom the most awful thing that had ever happened was the screw of a golden earring disappearing down the bathroom sink or a mother-in-law's visit or an ayah[1] deserting just before the arrival of guests: what could they know of Bina's life, Bina's ordeal? She cast her glance at the drinks they held—but they were mostly of orange squash. Only the Esso wife, who participated in amateur dramatics and ran a boutique and was rather taller and bolder than the rest, held a whisky and soda. So much affection generated by just orange squash? Impossible. Rather tentatively, she offered them the remains of the cheese biscuits, found herself chirping replies, deploring the nuisance of having packing crates all over the house, talking of the flat they would move into in Bombay, and then, sweating unobtrusively with the strain, saw another recognisable fish swim towards her from the edge of the liquescent lawn, and swung away in relief, saying, 'Mrs D'Souza! How late you are, but I'm so glad—' for she really was.

Mrs D'Souza was her daughter's teacher at the convent school and had clearly never been to a cocktail party before so that all Bina's compassion was aroused by those school-scuffed shoes and her tea-party best—quite apart from the simple truth that she found in her an honest individuality that all those beautifully dressed and poised babblers lacked, being stamped all over by the plain rubber stamps of their husbands' companies—and she hurried off to find Mrs D'Souza something suitable to drink. 'Sherry? Why yes, I think I'll be able to find you some,' she said, a bit flabbergasted at such an unexpected fancy of the pepper-haired school teacher, 'and I'll see if Tara's around—she'll want to see you,' she added, vaguely and fraudulently, wondering why she had asked Mrs D'Souza to a cocktail party, only to see, as she skirted the rose bed, the admirable Bose appear at her side and envelop her in this strange intimacy that marked the whole evening, and went off, light-hearted, towards the table where her husband was trying, with the help of

---

[1] An ayah is a nanny or maidservant.

some hired waiters in soggy white uniforms with the name of the restaurant from which they were hired embroidered in red across their pockets, to cope with the flood of drinks this party atmosphere had called for and released.

Harassed, perspiring, his feet burning, Raman was nevertheless pleased to be so obviously employed and be saved the strain of having to converse with his motley assembly of guests: he had no more gift for society than his wife had. Ice cubes were melting on the tablecloth in sopping puddles and he had trouble in keeping track of his bottles: they were, besides the newly bought dozens of beer bottles and Black Knight whisky, the remains of their five years in this town that he now wished to bring to their end—bottles brought by friends from trips abroad, bottles bought cheap through 'contacts' in the army or air force, some gems, extravaganzas bought for anniversaries such as a nearly full bottle of Vat 69, a bottle with a bit of *crème de menthe* growing sticky at the bottom, some brown sherry with a great deal of rusty sediment, a red Golconda wine from Hyderabad, and a bottle of Remy Martin that he was keeping guiltily to himself, pouring small quantities into a whisky glass at his elbow and gulping it down in between mixing some very weird cocktails for his guests. There was no one at the party he liked well enough to share it with. Oh, one of the doctors perhaps, but where were they? Submerged in grass, in dark, in night and chatter, clatter of ice in glass, teeth on biscuit, teeth on teeth. Enamel and gold. Crumbs and dregs. All awash, all soaked in night. Watery sound of speech, liquid sound of drink. Water and ice and night. It occurred to him that everyone had forgotten him, the host, that it was a mistake to have stationed himself amongst the waiters, that he ought to move out, mingle with the guests. But he felt himself drowned, helplessly and quite delightfully, in Remy Martin, in grass, in a border of purple torenias.

Then he was discovered by his son who galloped through the ranks of guests and waiters to fling himself at his father and ask if he could play the new Beatles record, his friends had asked to hear it.

Raman considered, taking the opportunity to pour out and gulp down some more of the precious Remy Martin. 'All right,' he said, after a judicious minute or two, 'but keep it low, everyone won't want to hear it,' not adding that he himself didn't, for his taste in music ran to slow and melancholy, folk at its most frivolous. Still, he glanced into the lighted room where his children and the children of neighbours and guests had collected, making themselves tipsy on Fanta and Coca-Cola, the girls giggling in a multi-coloured huddle and the boys swaggering around the record-player with a kind of lounging strut, holding bottles in their hands with a sophisticated ease, exactly like experienced cocktail party guests, so that he smiled and wished he had a ticket, a passport that would make it possible to break into that party within a party. It was chillingly obvious to him that he hadn't one. He also saw that a good deal of their riotousness was due to the fact that they were raiding the snack trays that the waiters carried through the room to the lawn, and that they were seeing to it that the trays emerged half-empty. He knew he ought to go in and see about it but he hadn't the heart, or the nerve. He couldn't join that party but he wouldn't wreck it either so he only caught hold of one of the waiters and suggested that the snack trays be carried out from the kitchen straight onto the lawn, not by way of the drawing-room, and led him towards a group that seemed to be without snacks and saw too late that it was a group of the company executives that he loathed most. He half-groaned, then hiccuped at his mistake, but it was too late to alter course now. He told himself that he ought to see to it that the snacks were offered around without snag or error.

Poor Raman was placed in one of the lower ranks of the companies' hierarchy. That is, he did not belong to a British concern, or even to an American-collaboration one, but merely to an Indian one. Oh, a long-established, prosperous and solid one but, still, only Indian. Those cigarettes that he passed around were made by his own company. Somehow it struck a note of bad taste amongst these fastidious men who played golf, danced at the club on Independence Eve and New Year's Eve, invited at least one foreign couple to every party and called their decorative wives 'darling' when in public. Poor Raman never had belonged. It was so obvious to everyone, even to himself, as he passed around those awful cigarettes that sold so well in the market. It had been obvious since their first disastrous dinner party for this very ring of jocular gentlemen, five years ago. Nono had cried right through the party, Bina had spent the evening racing upstairs to see to the babies' baths and bed-time and then crawling reluctantly down, the hired cook had got drunk and stolen two of the chickens so that there was not enough on the table, no one had relaxed for a minute or enjoyed a second—it had been too sad and harrowing even to make a good story or a funny anecdote. They had all let it sink by mutual consent and the invitations to play a round of golf on Saturday afternoon or a rubber of bridge on Sunday morning had been issued and refused with conspiratorial smoothness. Then there was that distressing hobby of Raman's: his impossibly long walks on which he picked up bits of wood and took them home to sandpaper and chisel and then call wood sculpture. What could one do with a chap who did that? He himself wasn't sure if he pursued such odd tastes because he was a social pariah or if he was one on account of this oddity. Not to speak of the spastic child. Now that didn't even bear thinking of, and so it was no wonder that Raman swayed towards them so hesitantly, as though he were wading through water instead of over clipped grass, and handed his cigarettes around with such an apologetic air.

But, after all, hesitation and apology proved unnecessary. One of them—was he Polson's Coffee or Brooke Bond Tea?—clasped Raman about the shoulders as proper men do on meeting, and hearty voices rose together, congratulating him on his promotion (it wasn't one, merely a transfer, and they knew it), envying him his move to the metropolis. They talked as if they had known each other for years, shared all kinds of public schoolboy fun. One—was he Voltas or Ciba?—talked of golf matches at the Willingdon as though he had often played there with Raman, another spoke of *kebabs* eaten on the roadside after a party as though Raman had been one of the gang. Amazed and grateful as a schoolboy admitted to a closed society, Raman nodded and put in a few cautious words, put away his cigarettes, called a waiter to refill their glasses and broke away before the clock struck twelve and the golden carriage turned into a pumpkin, he himself into a mouse. He hated mice.

Walking backwards, he walked straight into the soft barrier of Miss Dutta's ample back wrapped and bound in rich Madras silk.

'Sorry, sorry, Miss Dutta, I'm clumsy as a bear,' he apologised, but here, too, there was no call for apology for Miss Dutta was obviously delighted at having been bumped into.

'My dear Mr Raman, what can you expect if you invite the whole town to your party?' she asked in that piercing voice that invariably made her companions drop theirs self-consciously. 'You and Bina have been so popular—what are we going to do without you?'

He stood pressing his glass with white-tipped fingers and tried to think what he or Bina had provided her with that she could possibly miss. In any case, Miss Dutta could always manage, and did manage, everything single-handedly. She was the town busy-body, secretary and chairman of more committees than he could count: they ranged from the Film Society to the Blood Bank, from the Red Cross to the Friends of the Museum, for Miss Dutta was nothing if not versatile. 'We hardly ever saw you at our film shows of course,' her voice rang out, making him glance furtively over his shoulder to see if anyone were listening, 'but it was so nice *knowing* you were in town and that I could count on you. So few people here *care*, you know,' she went on, and affectionately bumped her comfortable middle-aged body into his as someone squeezed by, making him remember that he had once heard her called a man-eater, and wonder which man she had eaten and even consider, for a moment, if there were not, after all, some charm in those powdered creases of her creamy arms, equalling if not surpassing that of his worn and harassed wife's bony angles. Why did suffering make for angularity? he even asked himself with uncharacteristic unkindness. But when Miss Dutta laid an arm on top of his glass-holding one and raised herself on her toes to bray something into his ear, he loyally decided that he was too accustomed to sharp angles to change them for such unashamed luxuriance, and, contriving to remove her arm by grasping her elbow—how one's fingers sank into the stuff!—he steered her towards his wife who was standing at the table and inefficiently pouring herself another gin and lime.

'This is my third,' she confessed hurriedly, 'and I can't tell you how gay it makes me feel. I giggle at everything everyone says.'

'Good,' he pronounced, feeling inside a warm expansion of relief at seeing her lose, for the moment, her tension and anxiety. 'Let's hear you giggle,' he said, sloshing some more gin into her glass.

'Look at those children,' she exclaimed, and they stood in a bed of balsam, irredeemably crushed, and looked into the lighted drawing room where their daughter was at the moment the cynosure of all juvenile eyes, having thrown herself with abandon into a dance of monkey-like movements. 'What is it, Miss Dutta?' the awed mother enquired. 'You're more up in the latest fashions than I am—is it the twist, the rock or the jungle?' and all three watched, enthralled, till Tara began to totter and, losing her simian grace, collapsed against some wildly shrieking girl friends.

A bit embarrassed by their daughter's reckless abandon, the parents discussed with Miss Dutta, whose finger by her own admission was placed squarely on the pulse of youth, the latest trends in juvenile culture on which Miss Dutta gave a neat sociological discourse (all the neater for having been given earlier that day at the convocation of the Home Science College) and Raman wondered uneasily at this opening of flood-gates in his own family—his wife grown giggly with gin, his daughter performing wildly to a Chubby Checker record—how had it all come about? Was it the darkness all about them, dense as the heavy curtains about a stage, that made them act, for an hour or so, on the tiny lighted stage of brief intimacy with such a lack of inhibition? Was it the drink, so freely sloshing from end to end of the house and lawn on account of his determination to clear out his 'cellar' (actually one-half of the sideboard and the top shelf of the wardrobe in his dressing-room) and his muddling and mixing them, making up untried and experimental cocktails and lavishly pouring out the whisky without a measure? But these were solid and everyday explanations and there was about this party something out of the ordinary and everyday—at least to the Ramans, normally so austere and unpopular. He knew the real reason too—it was all because the party had been labelled a 'farewell party', everyone knew it was the last one, that the Ramans were leaving and they would not meet up again. There was about it exactly that kind of sentimental euphoria that is generated at a ship-board party, the one given on the last night before the end of the voyage. Everyone draws together with an intimacy, a lack of inhibition not displayed or guessed at before, knowing this is the last time, tomorrow they will be dispersed, it will be over. They will not meet, be reminded of it or be required to repeat it.

As if to underline this new and Cinderella's ball–like atmosphere of friendliness and gaiety, three pairs of neighbours now swept in (and three kochias lay down and died under their feet, to the gardener's rage and sorrow): the couple who lived to the Ramans' left, the couple who lived to their right, and the couple from across the road, all crying, 'So sorry to be late, but you know what a long way we had to come,' making everyone laugh identically at the identical joke. Despite the disparity in their looks and ages—one couple was very young, another middle-aged, the third grandparents—they were, in a sense, as alike as the company executives and their wives, for they too bore a label if a less alarming one: neighbours, it said. Because they were neighbours, and although they had never been more than nodded to over the hedge, waved to in passing cars or spoken to about anything other than their children, dogs, flowers and gardens, their talk had a vivid immediacy that went straight to the heart.

'Diamond's going to miss you so—he'll be heartbroken,' moaned the grandparents who lived alone in their spotless house with a black labrador who had made a habit of visiting the Ramans whenever he wanted young company, a romp on the lawn or an illicit biscuit.

'I don't know what my son will do without Diamond,' reciprocated Bina with her new and sympathetic warmth. 'He'll force me to get a dog of his own, I know, and how will I ever keep one in a flat in Bombay?'

'When are you going to throw out those rascals?' a father demanded of Raman, pointing at the juvenile revellers indoors. 'My boy has an exam tomorrow, you know, but he said he couldn't be bothered about it—he had to go to the Ramans' farewell party.'

One mother confided to Bina, winning her heart forever, 'Now that you are leaving, I can talk to you about it at last: did you know my Vinod is sweet on your Tara? Last night when I was putting him to bed, he said, "Mama, when I grow up I will marry Tara. I will sit on a white horse and wear a turban and carry a sword in my belt and I will go and marry Tara." What shall we do about that, eh? Only a ten year difference in age, isn't there—or twelve?' and both women rocked with laughter.

The party had reached its crest, like a festive ship, loud and illuminated for that last party before the journey's end, perched on the dizzy top of the dark wave. It could do nothing now but descend and dissolve. As if by simultaneous and unanimous consent, the guests began to leave (in the wake of the Commissioner and his wife who left first, like royalty) streaming towards the drive where cars stood bumper to bumper—more than had visited the Ramans' house in the previous five years put together. The light in the portico fell on Bina's pride and joy, a Chinese orange tree, lighting its miniature globes of fruit like golden lanterns. There was a babble, an uproar of leave-taking (the smaller children, already in pyjamas, watched open-mouthed from a dark window upstairs). Esso and Caltex left together, arms about each other and smoking cigars, like figures in a comic act. Miss Dutta held firmly to Bose's arm as they dipped, bowed, swayed and tripped on their way out. Bina was clasped, kissed—ear-rings grazed her cheek, talcum powder tickled her nose. Raman had his back slapped till he thrummed and vibrated like a beaten gong.

It seemed as if Bina and Raman were to be left alone at last, left to pack up and leave—now the good-byes had been said, there was nothing else they could possibly do—but no, out popped the good doctors from the hospital who had held themselves back in the darkest corners and made themselves inconspicuous throughout the party, and now, in the manner in which they clasped the host by the shoulders and the hostess by her hands, and said 'Ah, *now* we have a chance to be with you at last, now we can begin *our* party,' revealed that although this was the first time they had come to the Ramans' house on any but professional visits, they were not merely friends—they were almost a part of that self-defensive family, the closest to them in sympathy. Raman and Bina felt a warm, moist expansion of tenderness inside themselves, the tenderness they had till today restricted to the limits of their family, no farther, as though they feared it had not an unlimited capacity. Now its close horizons stepped backwards, with some surprise.

And it was as the doctors said—the party now truly began. Cane chairs were dragged out of the verandah onto the lawn, placed in a ring next to the flowering Queen of the Night which shook out flounces and frills of white scent with every rustle of night breeze. Bina could give in now to her two most urgent needs and dash indoors to smear her mosquito-bitten arms and feet with Citronella and fetch Nono to sit on her lap, to let Nono have a share, too, in the party. The good doctors and their wives leant forward and gave Nono the attention that made the parents' throats tighten with gratitude. Raman insisted on their each having a glass of Remy Martin—they must finish it tonight, he said, and would not let the waiters clear away the ice or glasses yet. So they sat on the verandah steps, smoking and yawning.

Now it turned out that Dr Bannerji's wife, the lady in the Dacca sari and the steel-rimmed spectacles, had studied in Shantiniketan, and she sang, at her husband's and his colleagues' urging, Tagore's sweetest, saddest songs. When she sang, in heartbroken tones that seemed to come from some distance away, from the damp corners of the darkness where the fireflies flitted,

> Father, the boat is carrying me away,
> Father, it is carrying me away from home,

the eyes of her listeners, sitting tensely in that grassy, inky dark, glazed with tears that were compounded equally of drink, relief and regret.

latent vs manifest

dreamwork vs. work of interpretation

traumatic repression

BACKGROUND TEXTS

SIGMUND FREUD
[1856–1939]

Sigmund Freud, the father of psychoanalysis, did not discover the unconscious mind, nor did he discover sex, but his writings made the unconscious and sex central to the twentieth century's understanding of human nature. In other words, he elevated feelings to a prominent, even dominant, role in human behavior. He shocked the world with his theories of infant sexuality, repression, sublimation, and the Oedipus complex. He made the journey into the self, into the hidden and repressed corridors and closets of childhood, a paradigm of the modern spiritual journey. He was a major influence on Carl Jung, who took Freudianism in a somewhat different direction, rediscovering the importance of mythology and comparative religion for subsequent generations. After almost a century of Freud and his students, certain aspects of Freud's legacy are now a part of daily life: the importance of taking charge of one's own life, the value of the inward journey, the necessity for healing the traumas of one's past life with counseling, support groups, and storytelling.

Born of Jewish parents on May 6, 1856, at Freiburg in Moravia, Freud spent most of his life in Vienna. Given the importance Freud later placed on childhood, it is ironic that very little is known about his. In fact, he destroyed large numbers of documents in order to frustrate inquisitive biographers. He began his university studies in 1873, gravitating toward medicine. After studying medicine, with a specialty in neurology, he went to Paris in 1885 to study hysteria under the neurologist Jean Charcot. A Viennese physician, Josef Breuer, gave Freud the key for therapeutic healing. He told Freud about curing the symptoms of hysteria by "getting the patient to recollect in hypnosis the circumstances of their origin and to express the emotions accompanying them." Freud tried out the method, and together they published a book on what they called the "cathartic method"; *Studien über Hysterie* (1895) was the starting point of psychoanalysis. Freud discovered that hypnosis was not a satisfactory tool for treating hysteria, so he developed free association and dream analysis as ways to explore the unconscious. Freud's *The Interpretation of Dreams,* published in 1900, revolutionized our understanding of the mind and quickly became a classic of scientific literature. After 1923 Freud applied his psychoanalytic theories to culture, making significant contributions to anthropology, education, sociology, art, and literature. Recently Freud's theories have come under a great deal of criticism, especially in the area of women's psychology, but his pioneering efforts in the area of the unconscious are invaluable.

In lay terms, Freud rediscovered the importance of childhood and emphasized that childhood experiences continue to influence individuals in their adult lives. His psychoanalytic method proposed that neurosis could be healed when traumatic experiences that have been repressed or denied are recovered as an individual reconstructs his or her personal history. In literary terms, Freud validated the importance of storytelling by maintaining that the painful effects of early abuse can be alleviated when an individual learns how to tell his or her story. He also changed the way stories were told, as the process of discontinuous recall replaced the chronological narratives of the nineteenth century. In the area of mythology, to which Freud brought a new psychological dimension, the descent into self is equivalent to ancient goddesses' descent into the underworld. Mircea Eliade has pointed out that the "going back" to childhood is portrayed in initiation rituals as a *regressus ad uterum* (return to the womb), from which the individual, through ritual or therapy, is reborn. The final step, which was developed further by Jung, is the recognition by the individual that his or her story is actually the story of humankind.

We have included two brief samples from Freud's writings. "Case 4: Katharina" shows a simplified version of Freud's method. A young woman with hysteria symptoms from an early, repressed sexual experience discovers through her discussions with Freud how to connect a later sexual scene with the earlier one. "Family Romances" emphasizes that most people pass through stages of maturation with parents that involve adulation, rebellion, and fantasizing. The implication is that wholeness or health results from learning how to tell these stories.

Case 4: Katharina

Translated by James Strachey in collaboration with Anna Freud

In the summer vacation of the year 189– I made an excursion into the Hohe Tauern[1] so that for a while I might forget medicine and more particularly the neuroses. I had almost succeeded in this when one day I turned aside from the main

---

[1]Mountains in the Alps.

road to climb a mountain which lay somewhat apart and which was renowned for its views and for its well-run refuge hut. I reached the top after a strenuous climb and, feeling refreshed and rested, was sitting deep in contemplation of the charm of the distant prospect. I was so lost in thought that at first I did not connect it with myself when these words reached my ears: 'Are you a doctor, sir?' But the question was addressed to me, and by the rather sulky-looking girl of perhaps eighteen who had served my meal and had been spoken to by the landlady as 'Katharina'. To judge by her dress and bearing, she could not be a servant, but must no doubt be a daughter or relative of the landlady's.

Coming to myself I replied: 'Yes, I'm a doctor: but how did you know that?'

'You wrote your name in the Visitors' Book, sir. And I thought if you had a few moments to spare . . . The truth is, sir, my nerves are bad. I went to see a doctor in L—— about them and he gave me something for them; but I'm not well yet.'

So there I was with the neuroses once again—for nothing else could very well be the matter with this strong, well-built girl with her unhappy look. I was interested to find that neuroses could flourish in this way at a height of over 6,000 feet; I questioned her further therefore. I report the conversation that followed between us just as it is impressed on my memory.

'Well, what is it you suffer from?'

'I get so out of breath. Not always. But sometimes it catches me so that I think I shall suffocate.'

This did not, at first sight, sound like a nervous symptom. But soon it occurred to me that probably it was only a description that stood for an anxiety attack: she was choosing shortness of breath out of the complex of sensations arising from anxiety and laying undue stress on that single factor.

'Sit down here. What is it like when you get "out of breath"?'

'It comes over me all at once. First of all it's like something pressing on my eyes. My head gets so heavy, there's a dreadful buzzing, and I feel so giddy that I almost fall over. Then there's something crushing my chest so that I can't get my breath.'

'And you don't notice anything in your throat?'

'My throat's squeezed together as though I were going to choke.'

'Does anything else happen in your head?'

'Yes, there's a hammering, enough to burst it.'

'And don't you feel at all frightened while this is going on?'

'I always think I'm going to die. I'm brave as a rule and go about everywhere by myself—into the cellar and all over the mountain. But on a day when that happens I don't dare to go anywhere; I think all the time someone's standing behind me and going to catch hold of me all at once.'

So it was in fact an anxiety attack, and introduced by the signs of a hysterical 'aura'—or, more correctly, it was a hysterical attack the content of which was anxiety. Might there not probably be some other content as well?

'When you have an attack do you think of something? and always the same thing? or do you see something in front of you?'

'Yes. I always see an awful face that looks at me in a dreadful way, so that I'm frightened.'

Perhaps this might offer a quick means of getting to the heart of the matter.

'Do you recognize the face? I mean, is it a face that you've really seen some time?'

'No.'

'Do you know what your attacks come from?'

'No.'

'When did you first have them?'

'Two years ago, while I was still living on the other mountain with my aunt. (She used to run a refuge hut there, and we moved here eighteen months ago.) But they keep on happening.'

Was I to make an attempt at an analysis? I could not venture to transplant hypnosis to these altitudes, but perhaps I might succeed with a simple talk. I should have to try a lucky guess. I had found often enough that in girls anxiety was a consequence of the horror by which a virginal mind is overcome when it is faced for the first time with the world of sexuality.[2]

So I said: 'If you don't know, I'll tell you how *I* think you got your attacks. At that time, two years ago, you must have seen or heard something that very much embarrassed you, and that you'd much rather not have seen.'

'Heavens, yes!' she replied, 'that was when I caught my uncle with the girl, with Franziska, my cousin.'

'What's this story about a girl? Won't you tell me all about it?'

'You can say *anything* to a doctor, I suppose. Well, at that time, you know, my uncle—the husband of the aunt you've seen here—kept the inn on the ——kogel. Now they're divorced, and it's my fault they were divorced, because it was through me that it came out that he was carrying on with Franziska.'

'And how did you discover it?'

'This way. One day two years ago some gentlemen had climbed the mountain and asked for something to eat. My aunt wasn't at home, and Franziska, who always did the cooking, was nowhere to be found. And my uncle was not to be found either. We looked everywhere, and at last Alois, the little boy, my cousin, said: "Why, Franziska must be in Father's room!" And we both laughed; but we weren't thinking anything bad. Then we went to my uncle's room but found it locked. That seemed strange to me. Then Alois said: "There's a window in the passage where you can look into the room." We went into the passage; but Alois wouldn't go to the window and said he was afraid. So I said: "You silly boy! I'll go. I'm not a bit afraid." And I had nothing bad in my mind. I looked in. The room was rather dark, but I saw my uncle and Franziska; he was lying on her.'

'Well?'

'I came away from the window at once, and leant up against the wall and couldn't get my breath—just what happens to me since. Everything went blank, my eyelids were forced together and there was a hammering and buzzing in my head.'

'Did you tell your aunt that very same day?'

'Oh no, I said nothing.'

'Then why were you so frightened when you found them together? Did you understand it? Did you know what was going on?'

'Oh no. I didn't understand anything at that time. I was only sixteen. I don't know what I was frightened about.'

'Fräulein Katharina, if you could remember now what was happening in you at that time, when you had your first attack, what you thought about it—it would help you.'

'Yes, if I could. But I was so frightened that I've forgotten everything.'

---

[2] "I will quote here the case in which I first recognized this causal connection. I was treating a young married woman who was suffering from a complicated neurosis and . . . was unable to admit that her illness arose from her married life. She objected that while she was still a girl she had had attacks of anxiety, ending in fainting fits. I remained firm. When we had come to know each other better she suddenly said to me one day: 'I'll tell you now how I came by my attacks of anxiety when I was a girl. At that time I used to sleep in a room next to my parents'; the door was left open and a night-light used to burn on the table. So more than once I saw my father get into bed with my mother and heard sounds that greatly excited me. It was then that my attacks came on.' " [Freud's note]

. . .

'Tell me, Fräulein. Can it be that the head that you always see when you lose your breath is Franziska's head, as you saw it then?'

'Oh no, she didn't look so awful. Besides, it's a man's head.'

'Or perhaps your uncle's?'

'I didn't see his face as clearly as that. It was too dark in the room. And why should he have been making such a dreadful face just then?'

'You're quite right.'

(The road suddenly seemed blocked. Perhaps something might turn up in the rest of her story.)

'And what happened then?'

'Well, those two must have heard a noise, because they came out soon afterwards. I felt very bad the whole time. I always kept thinking about it. Then two days later it was a Sunday and there was a great deal to do and I worked all day long. And on the Monday morning I felt giddy again and was sick, and I stopped in bed and was sick without stopping for three days.'

We [Breuer and I] had often compared the symptomatology of hysteria with a pictographic script which has become intelligible after the discovery of a few bilingual inscriptions. In that alphabet being sick means disgust. So I said: 'If you were sick three days later, I believe that means that when you looked into the room you felt disgusted.'

'Yes, I'm sure I felt disgusted,' she said reflectively, 'but disgusted at what?'

'Perhaps you saw something naked? What sort of state were they in?'

'It was too dark to see anything; besides they both of them had their clothes on. Oh, if only I knew what it was I felt disgusted at!'

I had no idea either. But I told her to go on and tell me whatever occurred to her, in the confident expectation that she would think of precisely what I needed to explain the case.

Well, she went on to describe how at last she reported her discovery to her aunt, who found that she was changed and suspected her of concealing some secret. There followed some very disagreeable scenes between her uncle and aunt, in the course of which the children came to hear a number of things which opened their eyes in many ways and which it would have been better for them not to have heard. At last her aunt decided to move with her children and niece and take over the present inn, leaving her uncle alone with Franziska, who had meanwhile become pregnant. After this, however, to my astonishment she dropped these threads and began to tell me two sets of older stories, which went back two or three years earlier than the traumatic moment. The first set related to occasions on which the same uncle had made sexual advances to her herself, when she was only fourteen years old. She described how she had once gone with him on an expedition down into the valley in the winter and had spent the night in the inn there. He sat in the bar drinking and playing cards, but she felt sleepy and went up to bed early in the room they were to share on the upper floor. She was not quite asleep when he came up; then she fell asleep again and woke up suddenly 'feeling his body' in the bed. She jumped up and remonstrated with him: 'What are you up to, Uncle? Why don't you stay in your own bed?' He tried to pacify her: 'Go on, you silly girl, keep still. You don't know how nice it is.'—'I don't like your "nice" things; you don't even let one sleep in peace.' She remained standing by the door, ready to take refuge outside in the passage, till at last he gave up and went to sleep himself. Then she went back to her own bed and slept till morning. From the way in which she reported having defended herself it seems to follow that she did not clearly recognize the attack as a sexual one. When I asked her if she knew what he was trying to do to her, she replied: 'Not at the time.' It had become clear to her much later on, she said; she had resisted because it was unpleasant to be disturbed in one's sleep and 'because it wasn't nice'.

I have been obliged to relate this in detail, because of its great importance for understanding everything that followed.—She went on to tell me of yet other experiences of somewhat later date: how she had once again had to defend herself against him in an inn when he was completely drunk, and similar stories. In answer to a question as to whether on these occasions she had felt anything resembling her later loss of breath, she answered with decision that she had every time felt the pressure on her eyes and chest, but with nothing like the strength that had characterized the scene of discovery.

Immediately she had finished this set of memories she began to tell me a second set, which dealt with occasions on which she had noticed something between her uncle and Franziska. Once the whole family had spent the night in their clothes in a hay loft and she was woken up suddenly by a noise; she thought she noticed that her uncle, who had been lying between her and Franziska, was turning away, and that Franziska was just lying down. Another time they were stopping the night at an inn at the village of N——; she and her uncle were in one room and Franziska in an adjoining one. She woke up suddenly in the night and saw a tall white figure by the door, on the point of turning the handle: 'Goodness, is that you, Uncle? What are you doing at the door?'—'Keep quiet. I was only looking for something.'—'But the way out's by the *other* door,'—'I'd just made a mistake' . . . and so on.

I asked her if she had been suspicious at that time. 'No, I didn't think anything about it; I only just noticed it and thought no more about it.' When I enquired whether she had been frightened on these occasions too, she replied that she thought so, but she was not so sure of it this time.

At the end of these two sets of memories she came to a stop. She was like someone transformed. The sulky, unhappy face had grown lively, her eyes were bright, she was lightened and exalted. Meanwhile the understanding of her case had become clear to me. The later part of what she had told me, in an apparently aimless fashion, provided an admirable explanation of her behaviour at the scene of the discovery. At that time she had carried about with her two sets of experiences which she remembered but did not understand, and from which she drew no inferences. When she caught sight of the couple in intercourse, she at once established a connection between the new impression and these two sets of recollections, she began to understand them and at the same time to fend them off. There then followed a short period of working-out, of 'incubation', after which the symptoms of conversion set in, the vomiting as a substitute for moral and physical disgust. This solved the riddle. She had not been disgusted by the sight of the two people but by the memory which that sight had stirred up in her. And, taking everything into account, this could only be the memory of the attempt on her at night when she had 'felt her uncle's body'.

So when she had finished her confession I said to her: 'I know now what it was you thought when you looked into the room. You thought: "Now he's doing with her what he wanted to do with me that night and those other times." That was what you were disgusted at, because you remembered the feeling when you woke up in the night and felt his body.'

'It may well be,' she replied, 'that that was what I was disgusted at and that that was what I thought.'

'Tell me just one thing more. You're a grown-up girl now and know all sorts of things . . .'

'Yes, now I am.'

'Tell me just one thing. What part of his body was it that you felt that night?'

But she gave me no more definite answer. She smiled in an embarrassed way, as though she had been found out, like someone who is obliged to admit that a fundamental position has been reached where there is not much more to be said. I could imagine what the tactile sensation was which she had later learnt to interpret. Her facial expression seemed to me to be saying that she supposed that I was right in my conjecture. But I could not penetrate further, and in any case I owed her a debt of gratitude for having made it so much easier for me to talk to her than to the prudish ladies of my city practice, who regard whatever is natural as shameful.

latent / *manifest*

Thus the case was cleared up.—But stop a moment! What about the recurrent hallucination of the head, which appeared during her attacks and struck terror into her? Where did it come from? I proceeded to ask her about it, and, as though *her* knowledge, too, had been extended by our conversation, she promptly replied: 'Yes, I know now. The head is my uncle's head—I recognize it now—but not from *that* time. Later, when all the disputes had broken out, my uncle gave way to a senseless rage against me. He kept saying that it was all my fault: if I hadn't chattered, it would never have come to a divorce. He kept threatening he would do something to me; and if he caught sight of me at a distance his face would get distorted with rage and he would make for me with his hand raised. I always ran away from him, and always felt terrified that he would catch me some time unawares. The face I always see now is his face when he was in a rage.'

This information reminded me that her first hysterical symptom, the vomiting, had passed away; the anxiety attack remained and acquired a fresh content. Accordingly, what we were dealing with was a hysteria which had to a considerable extent been abreacted. And in fact she had reported her discovery to her aunt soon after it happened.

'Did you tell your aunt the other stories—about his making advances to you?'

'Yes. Not at once, but later on, when there was already talk of a divorce. My aunt said: "We'll keep that in reserve. If he causes trouble in the Court, we'll say that too." '

I can well understand that it should have been precisely this last period—when there were more and more agitating scenes in the house and when her own state ceased to interest her aunt, who was entirely occupied with the dispute—that it should have been this period of accumulation and retention that left her the legacy of the mnemic symbol [of the hallucinated face].

I hope this girl, whose sexual sensibility had been injured at such an early age, derived some benefit from our conversation. I have not seen her since.

DISCUSSION

If someone were to assert that the present case history is not so much an analysed case of hysteria as a case solved by guessing, I should have nothing to say against him. It is true that the patient agreed that what I interpolated into her story was probably true; but she was not in a position to recognize it as something she had experienced. I believe it would have required hypnosis to bring that about. . . . In every analysis of a case of hysteria based on sexual traumas we find that impressions from the pre-sexual period which produced no effect on the child attain traumatic power at a later date as memories, when the girl or married woman has acquired an understanding of sexual life. The splitting-off of psychical groups may be said to be a normal process in adolescent development; and it is easy to see that their later reception into the ego affords frequent opportunities for psychical disturbances. Moreover, I should like at this point to express a doubt as to whether a splitting of consciousness due to ignorance is really different from one due to conscious rejection, and whether even adolescents do not possess sexual knowledge far oftener than is supposed or than they themselves believe.

A further distinction in the psychical mechanism of this case lies in the fact that the scene of discovery, which we have described as 'auxiliary', deserves equally to be called 'traumatic'. It was operative on account of its own content and not merely as something that revived previous traumatic experiences. It combined the characteristics of an 'auxiliary' and a 'traumatic' moment. There seems no reason, however, why this coincidence should lead us to abandon a conceptual separation which in other cases corresponds also to a separation in time. Another peculiarity of Katharina's case, which, incidentally, has long been familiar to us, is seen in the circumstance that the conversion, the production of the hysterical phenomena, did not occur immediately after the trauma but after an interval of incubation. Charcot liked to describe this interval as the 'period of psychical working-out' [*élaboration*].

The anxiety from which Katharina suffered in her attacks was a hysterical one; that is, it was a reproduction of the anxiety which had appeared in connection with each of the sexual traumas. I shall not here comment on the fact which I have found regularly present in a very large number of cases—namely that a mere suspicion of sexual relations calls up the affect of anxiety in virginal individuals.[3]

Family Romances

Translated by James Strachey

The liberation of an individual, as he grows up, from the authority of his parents is one of the most necessary though one of the most painful results brought about by the course of his development. It is quite essential that that liberation should occur and it may be presumed that it has been to some extent achieved by everyone who has reached a normal state. Indeed, the whole progress of society rests upon the opposition between successive generations. On the other hand, there is a class of neurotics whose condition is recognizably determined by their having failed in this task.

For a small child his parents are at first the only authority and the source of all belief. The child's most intense and most momentous wish during these early years is to be like his parents (that is, the parent of his own sex) and to be big like his father and mother. But as intellectual growth increases, the child cannot help discovering by degrees the category to which his parents belong. He gets to

---

[3] [Freud added this note in 1924]: "I venture after the lapse of so many years to lift the veil of discretion and reveal the fact that Katharina was not the niece but the daughter of the landlady. The girl fell ill, therefore, as a result of sexual attempts on the part of her own father. Distortions like the one which I introduced in the present instance should be altogether avoided in a case history. From the point of view of understanding the case, a distortion of this kind is not, of course, a matter of such indifference as would be shifting the scene from one mountain to another."

know other parents and compares them with his own, and so acquires the right to doubt the incomparable and unique quality which he had attributed to them. Small events in the child's life which make him feel dissatisfied afford him provocation for beginning to criticize his parents, and for using, in order to support his critical attitude, the knowledge which he has acquired that other parents are in some respects preferable to them. The psychology of the neuroses teaches us that, among other factors, the most intense impulses of sexual rivalry contribute to this result. A feeling of being slighted is obviously what constitutes the subject-matter of such provocations. There are only too many occasions on which a child is slighted, or at least *feels* he has been slighted, on which he feels he is not receiving the whole of his parents' love, and, most of all, on which he feels regrets at having to share it with brothers and sisters. His sense that his own affection is not being fully reciprocated then finds a vent in the idea, often consciously recollected later from early childhood, of being a step-child or an adopted child. People who have not developed neuroses very frequently remember such occasions, on which—usually as a result of something they have read—they interpreted and responded to their parents' hostile behaviour in this fashion. But here the influence of sex is already in evidence, for a boy is far more inclined to feel hostile impulses towards his father than towards his mother and has a far more intense desire to get free from *him* than from *her*. In this respect the imagination of girls is apt to show itself much weaker. These consciously remembered mental impulses of childhood embody the factor which enables us to understand the nature of myths.

The later stage in the development of the neurotic's estrangement from his parents, begun in this manner, might be described as 'the neurotic's family romance'. It is seldom remembered consciously but can almost always be revealed by psychoanalysis. For a quite peculiarly marked imaginative activity is one of the essential characteristics of neurotics and also of all comparatively highly gifted people. This activity emerges first in children's play, and then, starting roughly from the period before puberty, takes over the topic of family relations. A characteristic example of this peculiar imaginative activity is to be seen in the familiar day-dreaming which persists far beyond puberty. If these day-dreams are carefully examined, they are found to serve as the fulfilment of wishes and as a correction of actual life. They have two principal aims, an erotic and an ambitious one—though an erotic aim is usually concealed behind the latter too. At about the period I have mentioned, then, the child's imagination becomes engaged in the task of getting free from the parents of whom he now has a low opinion and of replacing them by others, who, as a rule, are of higher social standing. He will make use in this connection of any opportune coincidences from his actual experience, such as his becoming acquainted with the Lord of the Manor or some landed proprietor if he lives in the country or with some member of the aristocracy if he lives in town. Chance occurrences of this kind arouse the child's envy, which finds expression in a phantasy in which both his parents are replaced by others of better birth. The technique used in developing phantasies like this (which are, of course, conscious at this period) depends upon the ingenuity and the material which the child has at his disposal. There is also the question of whether the phantasies are worked out with greater or less effort to obtain verisimilitude. This stage is reached at a time at which the child is still in ignorance of the sexual determinants of procreation.

When presently the child comes to know the difference in the parts played by fathers and mothers in their sexual relations, and realizes that '*pater semper incertus est',* while the mother is *'certissima',*[1] the family romance undergoes a curious curtailment: it contents itself with exalting the child's father, but no longer casts any doubts on his maternal origin, which is regarded as something unalterable. This second (sexual) stage of the family romance is actuated by another motive as well, which is absent in the first (asexual) stage. The child, having learnt about sexual processes, tends to picture to himself erotic situations and relations, the motive force behind this being his desire to bring his mother (who is the subject of the most intense sexual curiosity) into situations of secret infidelity and into secret love-affairs. In this way the child's phantasies, which started by being, as it were, asexual, are brought up to the level of his later knowledge.

Moreover the motive of revenge and retaliation, which was in the foreground at the earlier stage, is also to be found at the later one. It is, as a rule, precisely these neurotic children who were punished by their parents for sexual naughtiness and who now revenge themselves on their parents by means of phantasies of this kind.

A younger child is very specially inclined to use imaginative stories such as these in order to rob those born before him of their prerogatives—in a way which reminds one of historical intrigues; and he often has no hesitation in attributing to his mother as many fictitious love-affairs as he himself has competitors. An interesting variant of the family romance may then appear, in which the hero and author returns to legitimacy himself while his brothers and sisters are eliminated by being bastardized. So too if there are any other particular interests at work they can direct the course to be taken by the family romance; for its many-sidedness and its great range of applicability enable it to meet every sort of requirement. In this way, for instance, the young phantasy-builder can get rid of his forbidden degree of kinship with one of his sisters if he finds himself sexually attracted by her.

If anyone is inclined to turn away in horror from this depravity of the childish heart or feels tempted, indeed, to dispute the possibility of such things, he should observe that these works of fiction, which seem so full of hostility, are none of them really so badly intended, and that they still preserve, under a slight disguise, the child's original affection for his parents. The faithlessness and ingratitude are only apparent. If we examine in detail the commonest of these imaginative romances, the replacement of both parents or of the father alone by grander people, we find that these new and aristocratic parents are equipped with attributes that are derived entirely from real recollections of the actual and humble ones; so that in fact the child is not getting rid of his father but exalting him. Indeed the whole effort at replacing the real father by a superior one is only an expression of the child's longing for the happy, vanished days when his father seemed to him the noblest and strongest of men and his mother the dearest and loveliest of women. He is turning away from the father whom he knows to-day to the father in whom he believed in the earlier years of his childhood; and his phantasy is no more than the expression of a regret that those happy days have gone. Thus in these phantasies the overvaluation that characterizes a child's earliest years comes into its own again. An interesting contribution to this subject is afforded by the study of dreams. We learn from their interpretation that even in later years, if the Emperor and Empress appear in dreams, those exalted personages stand for the dreamer's father and mother. So that the child's overvaluation of his parents survives as well in the dreams of normal adults.

---

[1] "Paternity is always uncertain," while the mother is "most certain."

W. E. B. DU BOIS
[1868–1963]

The author of some twenty books and hundreds of essays and articles covering all aspects of life in the United States, W. E. B. Du Bois is one of the foremost American writers of the early twentieth century. Involved in political and social action as well as writing, lecturing, and teaching, Du Bois provided intellectual, moral, and spiritual leadership to African Americans. Cornel West has called Du Bois the greatest "American intellectual of African descent . . . produced in this country," and links him to the pragmatist tradition of Ralph Waldo Emerson, William James, and John Dewey with a primary distinction: "[B]oth by personal choice and by social treatment [Du Bois] allies himself in word and deed with the wretched of the earth." That alliance brought Du Bois to write some of the first sociological studies of African-American culture, the first histories of African peoples linking their traditions to the culture of their descendants in the United States, and some of the earliest critiques of racism and colonialism in the United States.

Du Bois was born in Great Barrington, Massachusetts, in 1868, graduating from high school in 1884. He received BA degrees from Fisk University and from Harvard University, with honors, where he stayed to receive an MA and eventually a PhD in history in 1895. His dissertation, *The Suppression of the African Slave Trade to the United States of America, 1638–1870,* was the first publication of the Harvard Historical Series and is a landmark in the study of African-American history. Du Bois left Harvard to teach at Wilberforce University, and later at the University of Pennsylvania, where he studied the life of urban blacks in Philadelphia for his second book, *The Philadelphia Negro* (1899). In 1910 Du Bois began editing *The Crisis,* the major publication of the newly founded NAACP; twenty-four years later, he went to Atlanta University to establish and edit *Phylon,* a quarterly devoted to the study of issues affecting the African-American community in the United States. In 1935, he published another landmark study, *Black Reconstruction,* followed soon by *Black Folk, Then and Now* (1939), a survey of the history of Africa, and *Dusk of Dawn* (1940), an autobiographical work.

In his seventies, Du Bois returned to the NAACP in 1944 to direct research on colonialism and Africa, leaving after four years to serve on the Council on African Affairs and to make a respectable run for the U.S. Senate as the Progressive Party candidate from New York. From 1957 to 1961, Du Bois published *The Black Flame,* an immense book of partly autobiographical fiction, documenting the life of a black man striving against all obstacles for personal freedom and dignity in the United States from 1876 to 1956. In 1961, Du Bois moved to Ghana, becoming a Ghanaian citizen in 1963; there he worked on his autobiography and an encyclopedia of African culture and history. On August 27, 1963, W. E. B. Du Bois died in Ghana, where he received a state funeral.

The Souls of Black Folk, from which our selections are taken, was published in 1903. It grew out of his experiences in the summer of 1886, when his family moved to the rural mountains of Tennessee to teach among the poor black families who lived there. Some of the chapters in the book had appeared earlier in *Atlantic Monthly.* "Of Our Spiritual Strivings" is an eloquent testimony to the shadow of prejudice and how it has compelled many African Americans to live what Du Bois calls a "double-consciousness"—the apparently irreconcilable duality of being both American and black. Du Bois reflects on how to construct a bridge between those two separate identities, a bridge built on a heightened awareness of African-American history, tradition, and culture. From the strengthened community and sense of identity that such awareness brings, Du Bois believes that the African American will become a "co-worker in the kingdom of culture" and help to strengthen all Americans morally, spiritually, and intellectually. In "The Sorrow Songs," Du Bois pays tribute to the power, spirit, and "audacious hope," to invoke Cornel West again, of the African-American folk songs. Du Bois believed that African Americans had produced "the strangest sweetest" music in the world, and that they would "build up an American school of music which shall rival the grandest schools of the past"—a prophetic pronouncement in 1887, considering the subsequent influence of blues and jazz on American music. More than a tribute to the music, however, "The Sorrow Songs" also focuses upon the terrible plight of the black slaves and after them the black laborers, and shows that the music stems from the suffering and the injustice they experienced in their lives. In these two chapters from *The Souls of Black Folk,* Du Bois initiates the recuperation of African-American tradition and the formation of a powerful cultural identity that characterizes the work of black leaders and writers such as Ralph Ellison, Martin Luther King, Richard Wright, Maya Angelou, Alice Walker, Toni Morrison, and Cornel West, to name only a few.

The Souls of Black Folk

CHAPTER 1: OF OUR SPIRITUAL STRIVINGS

O water, voice of my heart, crying in the sand,
All night long crying with a mournful cry,
As I lie and listen, and cannot understand
The voice of my heart in my side or the voice of the sea,
O water, crying for rest, is it I, is it I?
All night long the water is crying to me.

Unresting water, there shall never be rest
Till the last moon droop and the last tide fail,
And the fire of the end begin to burn in the west;
And the heart shall be weary and wonder and cry like the sea,
All life long crying without avail,
As the water all night long is crying to me.

—ARTHUR SYMONS

Between me and the other world there is ever an unasked question: unasked by some through feelings of delicacy; by others through the difficulty of rightly framing it. All, nevertheless, flutter round it. They approach me in a half-hesitant sort of way, eye me curiously or compassionately, and then, instead of saying directly, How does it feel to be a problem? they say, I know an excellent colored man in my town;

or, I fought at Mechanicsville; or, Do not these Southern outrages make your blood boil? At these I smile, or am interested, or reduce the boiling to a simmer, as the occasion may require. To the real question, How does it feel to be a problem? I answer seldom a word.

And yet, being a problem is a strange experience,—peculiar even for one who has never been anything else, save perhaps in babyhood and in Europe. It is in the early days of rollicking boyhood that the revelation first bursts upon one, all in a day, as it were. I remember well when the shadow swept across me. I was a little thing, away up in the hills of New England, where the dark Housatonic winds between Hoosac and Taghkanic to the sea. In a wee wooden schoolhouse, something put it into the boys' and girls' heads to buy gorgeous visiting-cards—ten cents a package—and exchange. The exchange was merry, till one girl, a tall newcomer, refused my card,—refused it peremptorily, with a glance. Then it dawned upon me with a certain suddenness that I was different from the others; or like, mayhap, in heart and life and longing, but shut out from their world by a vast veil. I had thereafter no desire to tear down that veil, to creep through; I held all beyond it in common contempt, and lived above it in a region of blue sky and great wandering shadows. That sky was bluest when I could beat my mates at examination-time, or beat them at a foot-race, or even beat their stringy heads. Alas, with the years all this fine contempt began to fade; for the worlds I longed for, and all their dazzling opportunities, were theirs, not mine. But they should not keep these prizes, I said; some, all, I would wrest from them. Just how I would do it I could never decide: by reading law, by healing the sick, by telling the wonderful tales that swam in my head,—some way. With other black boys the strife was not so fiercely sunny: their youth shrunk into tasteless sycophancy, or into silent hatred of the pale world about them and mocking distrust of everything white; or wasted itself in a bitter cry, Why did God make me an outcast and a stranger in mine own house? The shades of the prison-house closed round about us all: walls straight and stubborn to the whitest, but relentlessly narrow, tall, and unscalable to sons of night who must plod darkly on in resignation, or beat unavailing palms against the stone, or steadily, half hopelessly, watch the streak of blue above.

After the Egyptian and Indian, the Greek and Roman, the Teuton and Mongolian, the Negro is a sort of seventh son, born with a veil, and gifted with second-sight in this American world,—a world which yields him no true self-consciousness, but only lets him see himself through the revelation of the other world. It is a peculiar sensation, this double-consciousness, this sense of always looking at one's self through the eyes of others, of measuring one's soul by the tape of a world that looks on in amused contempt and pity. One ever feels his two-ness,—an American, a Negro; two souls, two thoughts, two unreconciled strivings; two warring ideals in one dark body, whose dogged strength alone keeps it from being torn asunder.

The history of the American Negro is the history of this strife,—this longing to attain self-conscious manhood, to merge his double self into a better and truer self. In this merging he wishes neither of the older selves to be lost. He would not Africanize America, for America has too much to teach the world and Africa. He would not bleach his Negro soul in a flood of white Americanism, for he knows that Negro blood has a message for the world. He simply wishes to make it possible for a man to be both a Negro and an American, without being cursed and spit upon by his fellows, without having the doors of Opportunity closed roughly in his face.

This, then, is the end of his striving: to be a co-worker in the kingdom of culture, to escape both death and isolation, to husband and use his best powers and his latent genius. These powers of body and mind have in the past been strangely wasted, dispersed, or forgotten. The shadow of a mighty Negro past flits through the tale of Ethiopia the Shadowy and of Egypt the Sphinx. Throughout history, the powers of single black men flash here and there like falling stars, and die sometimes before the world has rightly gauged their brightness. Here in America, in the few days since Emancipation, the black man's turning hither and thither in hesitant and doubtful striving has often made his very strength to lose effectiveness, to seem like absence of power, like weakness. And yet it is not weakness,—it is the contradiction of double aims. The double-aimed struggle of the black artisan—on the one hand to escape white contempt for a nation of mere hewers of wood and drawers of water, and on the other hand to plough and nail and dig for a poverty-stricken horde—could only result in making him a poor craftsman, for he had but half a heart in either cause. By the poverty and ignorance of his people, the Negro minister or doctor was tempted toward quackery and demagogy; and by the criticism of the other world, toward ideals that made him ashamed of his lowly tasks. The would-be black *savant* was confronted by the paradox that the knowledge his people needed was a twice-told tale to his white neighbors, while the knowledge which would teach the white world was Greek to his own flesh and blood. The innate love of harmony and beauty that set the ruder souls of his people a-dancing and a-singing raised but confusion and doubt in the soul of the black artist; for the beauty revealed to him was the soul-beauty of a race which his larger audience despised, and he could not articulate the message of another people. This waste of double aims, this seeking to satisfy two unreconciled ideals, has wrought sad havoc with the courage and faith and deeds of ten thousand thousand people,—has sent them often wooing false gods and invoking false means of salvation, and at times has even seemed about to make them ashamed of themselves.

Away back in the days of bondage they thought to see in one divine event the end of all doubt and disappointment; few men ever worshipped Freedom with half such unquestioning faith as did the American Negro for two centuries. To him, so far as he thought and dreamed, slavery was indeed the sum of all villainies, the cause of all sorrow, the root of all prejudice; Emancipation was the key to a promised land of sweeter beauty than ever stretched before the eyes of wearied Israelites. In song and exhortation swelled one refrain—Liberty; in his tears and curses the God he implored had Freedom in his right hand. At last it came,—suddenly, fearfully, like a dream. With one wild carnival of blood and passion came the message in his own plaintive cadences:—

> "Shout, O children!
> Shout, you're free!
> For God has bought your liberty!"

Years have passed away since then,—ten, twenty, forty; forty years of national life, forty years of renewal and development, and yet the swarthy spectre sits in its accustomed seat at the Nation's feast. In vain do we cry to this our vastest social problem:—

> "Take any shape but that, and my firm nerves
> Shall never tremble!"

The Nation has not yet found peace from its sins; the freedman has not yet found in freedom his promised land. Whatever of good may have come in these years of change, the shadow of a deep disappointment rests upon the Negro people,—a disappointment all the more bitter because the unattained ideal was unbounded save by the simple ignorance of a lowly people.

The first decade was merely a prolongation of the vain search for freedom, the boon that seemed ever barely to elude their grasp,—like a tantalizing will-o'-the-wisp, maddening and misleading the headless host. The holocaust of war, the terrors of the Ku-Klux Klan, the lies of carpet-baggers, the disorganization of industry, and the contradictory advice of friends and foes, left the bewildered serf with no new watchword beyond the old cry for freedom. As the time flew, however, he began to grasp a new idea. The ideal of liberty demanded for its attainment powerful means, and these the Fifteenth Amendment gave him. The ballot, which before he had looked upon as a visible sign of freedom, he now regarded as the chief means of gaining and perfecting the liberty with which war had partially endowed him. And why not? Had not votes made war and emancipated millions? Had not votes enfranchised the freedmen? Was anything impossible to a power that had done all this? A million black men started with renewed zeal to vote themselves into the kingdom. So the decade flew away, the revolution of 1876 came, and left the half-free serf weary, wondering, but still inspired. Slowly but steadily, in the following years, a new vision began gradually to replace the dream of political power,—a powerful movement, the rise of another ideal to guide the unguided, another pillar of fire by night after a clouded day. It was the ideal of "book-learning"; the curiosity, born of compulsory ignorance, to know and test the power of the cabalistic letters of the white man, the longing to know. Here at last seemed to have been discovered the mountain path to Canaan; longer than the highway of Emancipation and law, steep and rugged, but straight, leading to heights high enough to overlook life.

Up the new path the advance guard toiled, slowly, heavily, doggedly; only those who have watched and guided the faltering feet, the misty minds, the dull understandings, of the dark pupils of these schools know how faithfully, how piteously, this people strove to learn. It was weary work. The cold statistician wrote down the inches of progress here and there, noted also where here and there a foot had slipped or some one had fallen. To the tired climbers, the horizon was ever dark, the mists were often cold, the Canaan was always dim and far away. If, however, the vistas disclosed as yet no goal, no resting-place, little but flattery and criticism, the journey at least gave leisure for reflection and self-examination; it changed the child of Emancipation to the youth with dawning self-consciousness, self-realization, self-respect. In those sombre forests of his striving his own soul rose before him, and he saw himself,—darkly as through a veil; and yet he saw in himself some faint revelation of his power, of his mission. He began to have a dim feeling that, to attain his place in the world, he must be himself, and not another. For the first time he sought to analyze the burden he bore upon his back, that dead-weight of social degradation partially masked behind a half-named Negro problem. He felt his poverty; without a cent, without a home, without land, tools, or savings, he had entered into competition with rich, landed, skilled neighbors. To be a poor man is hard, but to be a poor race in a land of dollars is the very bottom of hardships. He felt the weight of his ignorance,—not simply of letters, but of life, of business, of the humanities; the accumulated sloth and shirking and awkwardness of decades and centuries shackled his hands and feet. Nor was his burden all poverty and ignorance. The red stain of bastardy, which two centuries of systematic legal defilement of Negro women had stamped upon his race, meant not only the loss of ancient African chastity, but also the hereditary weight of a mass of corruption from white adulterers, threatening almost the obliteration of the Negro home.

A people thus handicapped ought not to be asked to race with the world, but rather allowed to give all its time and thought to its own social problems. But alas!

while sociologists gleefully count his bastards and his prostitutes, the very soul of the toiling, sweating black man is darkened by the shadow of a vast despair. Men call the shadow prejudice, and learnedly explain it as the natural defence of culture against barbarism, learning against ignorance, purity against crime, the "higher" against the "lower" races. To which the Negro cries Amen! and swears that to so much of this strange prejudice as is founded on just homage to civilization, culture, righteousness, and progress, he humbly bows and meekly does obeisance. But before that nameless prejudice that leaps beyond all this he stands helpless, dismayed, and well-nigh speechless; before that personal disrespect and mockery, the ridicule and systematic humiliation, the distortion of fact and wanton license of fancy, the cynical ignoring of the better and the boisterous welcoming of the worse, the all-pervading desire to inculcate disdain for everything black, from Toussaint[1] to the devil,—before this there rises a sickening despair that would disarm and discourage any nation save that black host to whom "discouragement" is an unwritten word.

But the facing of so vast a prejudice could not but bring the inevitable self-questioning, self-disparagement, and lowering of ideals which ever accompany repression and breed in an atmosphere of contempt and hate. Whisperings and portents came borne upon the four winds: Lo! we are diseased and dying, cried the dark hosts; we cannot write, our voting is vain; what need of education, since we must always cook and serve? And the Nation echoed and enforced this self-criticism, saying: Be content to be servants, and nothing more; what need of higher culture for half-men? Away with the black man's ballot, by force or fraud,—and behold the suicide of a race! Nevertheless, out of the evil came something of good,—the more careful adjustment of education to real life, the clearer perception of the Negroes' social responsibilities, and the sobering realization of the meaning of progress.

So dawned the time of *Sturm und Drang:*[2] storm and stress to-day rocks our little boat on the mad waters of the world-sea; there is within and without the sound of conflict, the burning of body and rending of soul; inspiration strives with doubt, and faith with vain questionings. The bright ideals of the past,—physical freedom, political power, the training of brains and the training of hands,—all these in turn have waxed and waned, until even the last grows dim and overcast. Are they all wrong,—all false? No, not that, but each alone was over-simple and incomplete,—the dreams of a credulous race-childhood, or the fond imaginings of the other world which does not know and does not want to know our power. To be really true, all these ideals must be melted and welded into one. The training of the schools we need to-day more than ever,—the training of deft hands, quick eyes and ears, and above all the broader, deeper, higher culture of gifted minds and pure hearts. The power of the ballot we need in sheer self-defence,—else what shall save us from a second slavery? Freedom, too, the long-sought, we still seek,—the freedom of life and limb, the freedom to work and think, the freedom to love and aspire. Work, culture, liberty,—all these we need, not singly but together, not successively but together, each growing and aiding each, and all striving toward that vaster ideal that swims before the Negro people, the ideal of human brotherhood,

---

[1]Toussaint L'Ouverture (1743?–1803), a freed slave who became a general and liberator of Haiti in the 1790s. Arrested by the French in 1802, he died in prison only to become a symbol of freedom and the struggle for independence.

[2]Storm and Stress; refers to a period of intense literary activity in the late eighteenth century associated with idealism and the revolt against stale convention. The movement is named after a play about the American Revolution. Goethe, Rousseau, and Schiller are associated with the movement.

gained through the unifying ideal of Race; the ideal of fostering and developing the traits and talents of the Negro, not in opposition to or contempt for other races, but rather in large conformity to the greater ideals of the American Republic, in order that some day on American soil two world-races may give each to each those characteristics both so sadly lack. We the darker ones come even now not altogether empty-handed: there are to-day no truer exponents of the pure human spirit of the Declaration of Independence than the American Negroes; there is no true American music but the wild sweet melodies of the Negro slave; the American fairy tales and folk-lore are Indian and African; and, all in all, we black men seem the sole oasis of simple faith and reverence in a dusty desert of dollars and smartness. Will America be poorer if she replace her brutal dyspeptic blundering with lighthearted but determined Negro humility? or her coarse and cruel wit with loving jovial good-humor? or her vulgar music with the soul of the Sorrow Songs?

Merely a concrete test of the underlying principles of the great republic is the Negro Problem, and the spiritual striving of the freedmen's sons is the travail of souls whose burden is almost beyond the measure of their strength, but who bear it in the name of an historic race, in the name of this the land of their fathers' fathers, and in the name of human opportunity.

And now what I have briefly sketched in large outline let me on coming pages tell again in many ways, with loving emphasis and deeper detail, that men may listen to the striving in the souls of black folk.

CHAPTER 14: THE SORROW SONGS

I walk through the churchyard
  To lay this body down;
I know moon-rise, I know star-rise;
I walk in the moonlight, I walk in the starlight;
I'll lie in the grave and stretch out my arms,
I'll go to judgment in the evening of the day,
And my soul and thy soul shall meet that day,
  When I lay this body down.

—NEGRO SONG

They that walked in darkness sang songs in the olden days—Sorrow Songs—for they were weary at heart. And so before each thought that I have written in this book I have set a phrase, a haunting echo of these weird old songs in which the soul of the black slave spoke to men. Ever since I was a child these songs have stirred me strangely. They came out of the South unknown to me, one by one, and yet at once I knew them as of me and of mine. Then in after years when I came to Nashville I saw the great temple builded of these songs towering over the pale city. To me Jubilee Hall seemed ever made of the songs themselves, and its bricks were red with the blood and dust of toil. Out of them rose for me morning, noon, and night, bursts of wonderful melody, full of the voices of my brothers and sisters, full of the voices of the past.

Little of beauty has America given the world save the rude grandeur God himself stamped on her bosom; the human spirit in this new world has expressed itself in vigor and ingenuity rather than in beauty. And so by fateful chance the Negro folk-song—the rhythmic cry of the slave—stands to-day not simply as the sole American music, but as the most beautiful expression of human experience born this side the seas. It has been neglected, it has been, and is, half despised, and above all it has been persistently mistaken and misunderstood; but notwithstanding, it still remains as the singular spiritual heritage of the nation and the greatest gift of the Negro people.

Away back in the thirties the melody of these slave songs stirred the nation, but the songs were soon half forgotten. Some, like "Near the lake where drooped the willow," passed into current airs and their source was forgotten; others were caricatured on the "minstrel" stage and their memory died away. Then in war-time came the singular Port Royal experiment after the capture of Hilton Head, and perhaps for the first time the North met the Southern slave face to face and heart to heart with no third witness. The Sea Islands of the Carolinas, where they met, were filled with a black folk of primitive type, touched and moulded less by the world about them than any others outside the Black Belt. Their appearance was uncouth, their language funny, but their hearts were human and their singing stirred men with a mighty power. Thomas Wentworth Higginson hastened to tell of these songs, and Miss McKim and others urged upon the world their rare beauty. But the world listened only half credulously until the Fisk Jubilee Singers sang the slave songs so deeply into the world's heart that it can never wholly forget them again.

There was once a blacksmith's son born at Cadiz, New York, who in the changes of time taught school in Ohio and helped defend Cincinnati from Kirby Smith. Then he fought at Chancellorsville and Gettysburg and finally served in the Freedman's Bureau at Nashville. Here he formed a Sunday-school class of black children in 1866, and sang with them and taught them to sing. And then they taught him to sing, and when once the glory of the Jubilee songs passed into the soul of George L. White, he knew his life-work was to let those Negroes sing to the world as they had sung to him. So in 1871 the pilgrimage of the Fisk Jubilee Singers began. North to Cincinnati they rode,—four half-clothed black boys and five girl-women,—led by a man with a cause and a purpose. They stopped at Wilberforce, the oldest of Negro schools, where a black bishop blessed them. Then they went, fighting cold and starvation, shut out of hotels, and cheerfully sneered at, ever northward; and ever the magic of their song kept thrilling hearts, until a burst of applause in the Congregational Council at Oberlin revealed them to the world. They came to New York and Henry Ward Beecher dared to welcome them, even though the metropolitan dailies sneered at his "Nigger Minstrels." So their songs conquered till they sang across the land and across the sea, before Queen and Kaiser, in Scotland and Ireland, Holland and Switzerland. Seven years they sang, and brought back a hundred and fifty thousand dollars to found Fisk University.

Since their day they have been imitated—sometimes well, by the singers of Hampton and Atlanta, sometimes ill, by straggling quartettes. Caricature has sought again to spoil the quaint beauty of the music, and has filled the air with many debased melodies which vulgar ears scarce know from the real. But the true Negro folk-song still lives in the hearts of those who have heard them truly sung and in the hearts of the Negro people.

What are these songs, and what do they mean? I know little of music and can say nothing in technical phrase, but I know something of men, and knowing them, I know that these songs are the articulate message of the slave to the world. They tell us in these eager days that life was joyous to the black slave, careless and happy. I can easily believe this of some, of many. But not all the past South, though it rose from the dead, can gainsay the heart-touching witness of these songs. They are the music of an unhappy people, of the children of disappointment; they tell of death and suffering and unvoiced longing toward a truer world, of misty wanderings and hidden ways.

The songs are indeed the siftings of centuries; the music is far more ancient than the words, and in it we can trace here and there signs of development. My grandfather's grandmother was seized by an evil Dutch trader two centuries ago; and coming to the valleys of the Hudson and Housatonic, black, little, and lithe, she shivered and shrank in the harsh north winds, looked longingly at the hills, and often crooned a heathen melody to the child between her knees, thus:

Do ba-na co-ba, ge-ne me, ge-ne me!

Do ba na co-ba, ge-ne me, ge-ne me!

Ben d' nu-li, nu-li, nu-li, nu-li, ben d' le.

The child sang it to his children and they to their children's children, and so two hundred years it has travelled down to us and we sing it to our children, knowing as little as our fathers what its words may mean, but knowing well the meaning of its music.

This was primitive African music; it may be seen in larger form in the strange chant which heralds "The Coming of John":

> *"You may bury me in the East,*
> *You may bury me in the West,*
> *But I'll hear the trumpet sound in that morning,"*

—the voice of exile.

Ten master songs, more or less, one may pluck from this forest of melody—songs of undoubted Negro origin and wide popular currency, and songs peculiarly characteristic of the slave. One of these I have just mentioned. Another whose strains begin this book is "Nobody knows the trouble I've seen." When, struck with a sudden poverty, the United States refused to fulfil its promises of land to the freedmen, a brigadier-general went down to the Sea Islands to carry the news. An old woman on the outskirts of the throng began singing this song; all the mass joined with her, swaying. And the soldier wept.

The third song is the cradle-song of death which all men know,—"Swing low, sweet chariot,"—whose bars begin the life story of "Alexander Crummell." Then there is the song of many waters, "Roll, Jordan, roll," a mighty chorus with minor cadences. There were many songs of the fugitive like that which opens "The Wings of Atalanta," and the more familiar "Been a-listening." The seventh is the song of the End and the Beginning—"My Lord, what a mourning! when the stars begin to fall"; a strain of this is placed before "The Dawn of Freedom." The song of groping—"My way's cloudy"—begins "The Meaning of Progress"; the ninth is the song of this chapter—"Wrestlin' Jacob, the day is a-breaking,"—a pæan of hopeful strife. The last master song is the song of songs—"Steal away,"—sprung from "The Faith of the Fathers."

There are many others of the Negro folk-songs as striking and characteristic as these, as, for instance, the three strains in the third, eighth, and ninth chapters; and others I am sure could easily make a selection on more scientific principles. There are, too, songs that seem to me a step removed from the more primitive types: there is the maze-like medley, "Bright sparkles," one phrase of which heads "The Black Belt"; the Easter carol, "Dust, dust and ashes"; the dirge, "My mother's took her flight and gone home"; and that burst of melody hovering over "The Passing of the First-Born"—"I hope my mother will be there in that beautiful world on high."

These represent a third step in the development of the slave song, of which "You may bury me in the East" is the first, and songs like "March on" and "Steal away" are the second. The first is African music, the second Afro-American, while the third is a blending of Negro music with the music heard in the foster land. The result is still distinctively Negro and the method of blending original, but the elements are both Negro and Caucasian. One might go further and find a fourth step in this development, where the songs of white America have been distinctively influenced by the slave songs or have incorporated whole phrases of Negro melody, as "Swanee River" and "Old Black Joe." Side by side, too, with the growth has gone the debasements and imitations—the Negro "minstrel" songs, many of the "gospel" hymns, and some of the contemporary "coon" songs,—a mass of music in which the novice may easily lose himself and never find the real Negro melodies.

In these songs, I have said, the slave spoke to the world. Such a message is naturally veiled and half articulate. Words and music have lost each other and new and cant phrases of a dimly understood theology have displaced the older sentiment. Once in a while we catch a strange word of an unknown tongue, as the "Mighty Myo," which figures as a river of death; more often slight words or mere doggerel are joined to music of singular sweetness. Purely secular songs are few in number, partly because many of them were turned into hymns by a change of words, partly because the frolics were seldom heard by the stranger, and the music less often caught. Of nearly all the songs, however, the music is distinctly sorrowful. The ten master songs I have mentioned tell in word and music of trouble and exile, of strife and hiding; they grope toward some unseen power and sigh for rest in the End.

The words that are left to us are not without interest, and, cleared of evident dross, they conceal much of real poetry and meaning beneath conventional theology and unmeaning rhapsody. Like all primitive folk, the slave stood near to Nature's heart. Life was a "rough and rolling sea" like the brown Atlantic of the Sea Islands; the "Wilderness" was the home of God, and the "lonesome valley" led to the way of life. "Winter'll soon be over," was the picture of life and death to a tropical imagination. The sudden wild thunder-storms of the South awed and impressed the Negroes,—at times the rumbling seemed to them "mournful," at times imperious:

> *"My Lord calls me,*
> *He calls me by the thunder,*
> *The trumpet sounds it in my soul."*

The monotonous toil and exposure is painted in many words. One sees the ploughmen in the hot, moist furrow, singing:

> *"Dere's no rain to wet you,*
> *Dere's no sun to burn you,*
> *Oh, push along, believer,*
> *I want to go home."*

The bowed and bent old man cries, with thrice-repeated wail:

> *"O Lord, keep me from sinking down,"*

and he rebukes the devil of doubt who can whisper:

> *"Jesus is dead and God's gone away."*

Yet the soul-hunger is there, the restlessness of the savage, the wail of the wanderer, and the plaint is put in one little phrase:

My   soul   wants   something   that's   new,   that's   new

Over the inner thoughts of the slaves and their relations one with another the shadow of fear ever hung, so that we get but glimpses here and there, and also with them, eloquent omissions and silences. Mother and child are sung, but seldom father; fugitive and weary wanderer call for pity and affection, but there is little of wooing and wedding; the rocks and the mountains are well known, but home is unknown. Strange blending of love and helplessness sings through the refrain:

> *"Yonder's my ole mudder,*
> *Been waggin' at de hill so long;*
> *'Bout time she cross over,*
> *Git home bime-by."*

Elsewhere comes the cry of the "motherless" and the "Farewell, farewell, my only child."

Love-songs are scarce and fall into two categories—the frivolous and light, and the sad. Of deep successful love there is ominous silence, and in one of the oldest of these songs there is a depth of history and meaning:

Poor Ro - sy, poor gal; Poor Ro - sy, Poor gal; Ro - sy break my poor heart, Heav'n shall - a - be my home.

A black woman said of the song, "It can't be sung without a full heart and a troubled sperrit." The same voice sings here that sings in the German folk-song:

"Jetz Geh i' an's brunele, trink' aber net."

Of death the Negro showed little fear, but talked of it familiarly and even fondly as simply a crossing of the waters, perhaps—who knows?—back to his ancient forests again. Later days transfigured his fatalism, and amid the dust and dirt the toiler sang:

"Dust, dust and ashes, fly over my grave,
But the Lord shall bear my spirit home."

The things evidently borrowed from the surrounding world undergo characteristic change when they enter the mouth of the slave. Especially is this true of Bible phrases. "Weep, O captive daughter of Zion," is quaintly turned into "Zion, weep-a-low," and the wheels of Ezekiel are turned every way in the mystic dreaming of the slave, till he says:

"There's a little wheel a-turnin' in-a-my heart."

As in olden time, the words of these hymns were improvised by some leading minstrel of the religious band. The circumstances of the gathering, however, the rhythm of the songs, and the limitations of allowable thought, confined the poetry for the most part to single or double lines, and they seldom were expanded to quatrains or longer tales, although there are some few examples of sustained efforts, chiefly paraphrases of the Bible. Three short series of verses have always attracted me,—the one that heads this chapter, of one line of which Thomas Wentworth Higginson has fittingly said, "Never, it seems to me, since man first lived and suffered was his infinite longing for peace uttered more plaintively." The second and third are descriptions of the Last Judgment,—the one a late improvisation, with some traces of outside influence:

> *"Oh, the stars in the elements are falling,*
> *And the moon drips away into blood,*
> *And the ransomed of the Lord are returning unto God,*
> *Blessed be the name of the Lord."*

And the other earlier and homelier picture from the low coast lands:

> *"Michael, haul the boat ashore,*
> *Then you'll hear the horn they blow,*
> *Then you'll hear the trumpet sound,*
> *Trumpet sound the world around,*
> *Trumpet sound for rich and poor,*
> *Trumpet sound the Jubilee,*
> *Trumpet sound for you and me."*

Through all the sorrow of the Sorrow Songs there breathes a hope—a faith in the ultimate justice of things. The minor cadences of despair change often to triumph and calm confidence. Sometimes it is faith in life, sometimes a faith in death, sometimes assurance of boundless justice in some fair world beyond. But whichever it is, the meaning is always clear: that sometime, somewhere, men will judge men by their souls and not by their skins. Is such a hope justified? Do the Sorrow Songs sing true?

The silently growing assumption of this age is that the probation of races is past, and that the backward races of to-day are of proven inefficiency and not worth the saving. Such an assumption is the arrogance of peoples irreverent toward Time and ignorant of the deeds of men. A thousand years ago such an assumption, easily possible, would have made it difficult for the Teuton to prove his right to life. Two thousand years ago such dogmatism, readily welcome, would have scouted the idea of blond races ever leading civilization. So woefully unorganized is sociological knowledge that the meaning of progress, the meaning of "swift" and "slow" in human doing, and the limits of human perfectability, are veiled, unanswered sphinxes on the shores of science. Why should Æschylus have sung two thousand years before Shakespeare was born? Why has civilization flourished in Europe, and flickered, flamed, and died in Africa? So long as the world stands meekly dumb before such questions, shall this nation proclaim its ignorance and unhallowed prejudices by denying freedom of opportunity to those who brought the Sorrow Songs to the Seats of the Mighty?

Your country? How came it yours? Before the Pilgrims landed we were here. Here we have brought our three gifts and mingled them with yours: a gift of story and song—soft, stirring melody in an ill-harmonized and unmelodious land; the gift of sweat and brawn to beat back the wilderness, conquer the soil, and lay the foundations of this vast economic empire two hundred years earlier than your weak hands could have done it; the third, a gift of the Spirit. Around us the history of the land has centred for thrice a hundred years; out of the nation's heart we have called all that was best to throttle and subdue all that was worst; fire and blood, prayer and sacrifice, have billowed over this people, and they have found peace only in the altars of the God of Right. Nor has our gift of the Spirit been merely passive. Actively we have woven ourselves with the very warp and woof of this nation,—we fought their battles, shared their sorrow, mingled our blood with theirs, and generation after generation have pleaded with a headstrong, careless people to despise not Justice, Mercy, and Truth, lest the nation be smitten with a curse. Our song, our toil, our cheer, and warning have been given to this nation in blood-brotherhood. Are not these gifts worth the giving? Is not this work and striving? Would America have been America without her Negro people?

Even so is the hope that sang in the songs of my fathers well sung. If somewhere in this whirl and chaos of things there dwells Eternal Good, pitiful yet masterful, then anon in His good time America shall rend the Veil and the prisoned shall go free. Free, free as the sunshine trickling down the morning into these high windows of mine, free as yonder fresh young voices welling up to me from the caverns of brick and mortar below—swelling with song, instinct with life, tremulous treble and darkening bass. My children, my little children, are singing to the sunshine, and thus they sing:

And the traveller girds himself, and sets his face toward the Morning, and goes his way.

HANNAH ARENDT
[1906–1975]

Philosopher, political theorist, and commentator on contemporary life, Hannah Arendt is one of the most original and provocative social thinkers of the twentieth century. A Jew born in Germany in 1906, she fled to France in 1933 with the rise of Nazism, leaving Paris when Hitler invaded France in 1940, to settle permanently in the United States. During a distinguished academic career she taught at American colleges and universities including Princeton (where she was the first woman appointed to a full professorship), Chicago, Columbia, Oberlin, California, and the New School for Social Research.

She received her own academic training at German universities, most notably Heidelberg, where she studied with the existential philosopher Karl Jaspers, earning a PhD in philosophy at age twenty-two. Her reputation is based on *The Origins of Totalitarianism* (1951), a three-volume work tracing totalitarianism to imperialism and anti-Semitism. It drew on her personal experience as well as her philosophical and political training. Some have questioned the emphasis Arendt placed on anti-Semitism in her argumentation of *The Origins of Totalitarianism*—an overemphasis thought to derive from her own experience as a Jew in the time of Nazism. Regardless of any such criticism, the book is considered to be one of the most important works of political theory of our time. In more than twenty books, Arendt wrote about revolution, violence, civil disobedience, Jewish identity, the history of philosophy, the human condition, and the life of the mind. Her controversial account of the war crimes trial of Adolf Eichmann, *Eichmann in Jerusalem: A Report on the Banality of Evil* (1964), probably her best-known work, implicated all parts of European society, including Jewish leaders, in the evil of the Holocaust.

In the passage from *Men in Dark Times* (1968) included here, Arendt discusses a central theme of the modern section of this anthology. She considers how personal and ethnic stories are related and how the telling of such stories enables us to understand the meaning of our individual and collective lives and to recover our humanity. Arendt found, in the different responses to the Holocaust, those that transcend their specific historical moment to become illustrations of the larger human condition.

Men in Dark Times

JEWS, NAZIS, AND INNER EMIGRATION

I so explicitly stress my membership in the group of Jews expelled from Germany at a relatively early age because I wish to anticipate certain misunderstandings which can arise only too easily when one speaks of humanity. In this connection I cannot gloss over the fact that for many years I considered the only adequate reply to the question, Who are you? to be: A Jew. That answer alone took into account the reality of persecution. As for the statement with which Nathan the Wise (in effect, though not in actual wording) countered the command: "Step closer, Jew"—the statement: I am a man—I would have considered as nothing but a grotesque and dangerous evasion of reality.

Let me also quickly clear away another likely misunderstanding. When I use the word "Jew" I do not mean to suggest any special kind of human being, as though the Jewish fate were either representative of or a model for the fate of mankind.

(Any such thesis could at best have been advanced with cogency only during the last stage of Nazi domination, when in fact the Jews and anti-Semitism were being exploited solely to unleash and keep in motion the racist program of extermination. For this was an essential part of totalitarian rule. The Nazi movement, to be sure, had from the first tended toward totalitarianism, but the Third Reich was not by any means totalitarian during its early years. By "early years" I mean the first period, which lasted from 1933 to 1938.) In saying, "A Jew," I did not even refer to a reality burdened or marked out for distinction by history. Rather, I was only acknowledging a political fact through which my being a member of this group outweighed all other questions of personal identity or rather had decided them in favor of anonymity, of namelessness. Nowadays such an attitude would seem like a pose. Nowadays, therefore, it is easy to remark that those who reacted in this way had never got very far in the school of "humanity," had fallen into the trap set by Hitler, and thus had succumbed to the spirit of Hitlerism in their own way. Unfortunately, the basically simple principle in question here is one that is particularly hard to understand in times of defamation and persecution: the principle that one can resist only in terms of the identity that is under attack. Those who reject such identifications on the part of a hostile world may feel wonderfully superior to the world, but their superiority is then truly no longer of this world; it is the superiority of a more or less well-equipped cloud-cuckoo-land.

When I thus bluntly reveal the personal background of my reflections, it may easily sound to those who know the fate of the Jews only from hearsay as if I am talking out of school, a school they have not attended and whose lessons do not concern them. But as it happens, during that selfsame period in Germany there existed the phenomenon known as the "inner emigration," and those who know anything about that experience may well recognize certain questions and conflicts akin to the problems I have mentioned in more than a mere formal and structural sense. As its very name suggests, the "inner emigration" was a curiously ambiguous phenomenon. It signified on the one hand that there were persons inside Germany who behaved as if they no longer belonged to the country, who felt like emigrants; and on the other hand it indicated that they had not in reality emigrated, but had withdrawn to an interior realm, into the invisibility of thinking and feeling. It would be a mistake to imagine that this form of exile, a withdrawal from the world into an interior realm, existed only in Germany, just as it would be a mistake to imagine that such emigration came to an end with the end of the Third Reich. But in that darkest of times, inside and outside Germany the temptation was particularly strong, in the face of a seemingly unendurable reality, to shift from the world and its public space to an interior life, or else simply to ignore that world in favor of an imaginary world "as it ought to be" or as it once upon a time had been.

There has been much discussion of the widespread tendency in Germany to act as though the years from 1933 to 1945 never existed; as though this part of German and European and thus world history could be expunged from the textbooks; as though everything depended on forgetting the "negative" aspect of the past and reducing horror to sentimentality. (The world-wide success of *The Diary of Anne Frank* was clear proof that such tendencies were not confined to Germany.) It was a grotesque state of affairs when German young people were not allowed to learn the facts that every schoolchild a few miles away could not help knowing. Behind all this there was, of course, genuine perplexity. And this very incapacity to face the reality of the past might possibly have been a direct heritage of the inner emigration, as it was undoubtedly to a considerable extent, and even more directly, a consequence of the Hitler regime—that is to say, a consequence of the organized guilt in which the

Nazis had involved all inhabitants of the German lands, the inner exiles no less than the stalwart Party members and the vacillating fellow travelers. It was the fact of this guilt which the Allies simply incorporated into the fateful hypothesis of collective guilt. Herein lies the reason for the Germans' profound awkwardness, which strikes every outsider, in any discussion of questions of the past. How difficult it must be to find a reasonable attitude is perhaps more clearly expressed by the cliché that the past is still "unmastered" and in the conviction held particularly by men of good will that the first thing to be done is to set about "mastering" it. Perhaps that cannot be done with any past, but certainly not with the past of Hitler Germany. The best that can be achieved is to know precisely what it was, and to endure this knowledge, and then to wait and see what comes of knowing and enduring.

Perhaps I can best explain this by a less painful example. After the First World War we experienced the "mastering of the past" in a spate of descriptions of the war that varied enormously in kind and quality; naturally, this happened not only in Germany, but in all the affected countries. Nevertheless, nearly thirty years were to pass before a work of art appeared which so transparently displayed the inner truth of the event that it became possible to say: Yes, this is how it was. And in this novel, William Faulkner's *A Fable*, very little is described, still less explained, and nothing at all "mastered"; its end is tears, which the reader also weeps, and what remains beyond that is the "tragic effect" or the "tragic pleasure," the shattering emotion which makes one able to accept the fact that something like this war could have happened at all. I deliberately mention tragedy because it more than the other literary forms represents a process of recognition. The tragic hero becomes knowledgeable by re-experiencing what has been done in the way of suffering, and in this *pathos*, in resuffering the past, the network of individual acts is transformed into an event, a significant whole. The dramatic climax of tragedy occurs when the actor turns into a sufferer; therein lies its peripeteia, the disclosure of the dénouement. But even non-tragic plots become genuine events only when they are experienced a second time in the form of suffering by memory operating retrospectively and perceptively. Such memory can speak only when indignation and just anger, which impel us to action, have been silenced—and that needs time. We can no more master the past than we can undo it. But we can reconcile ourselves to it. The form for this is the lament, which arises out of all recollection. It is, as Goethe has said (in the Dedication to *Faust*):

> *Der Schmerz wird neu, es wiederholt die Klage*
> *Des Lebens labyrinthisch irren Lauf.*

(Pain arises anew, lament repeats
Life's labyrinthine, erring course.)

The tragic impact of this repetition in lamentation affects one of the key elements of all action; it establishes its meaning and that permanent significance which then enters into history. In contradistinction to other elements peculiar to action—above all to the preconceived goals, the impelling motives, and the guiding principles, all of which become visible in the course of action—the meaning of a committed act is revealed only when the action itself has come to an end and become a story susceptible to narration. Insofar as any "mastering" of the past is possible, it consists in relating what has happened; but such narration, too, which shapes history, solves no problems and assuages no suffering; it does not master anything once and for all. Rather, as long as the meaning of the events remains alive—and this meaning can persist for very long periods of time—"mastering of the past" can take the form of ever-recurrent narration. The poet in a very general sense and the historian in a very special sense have the task of setting this process of narration in motion and of involving us in it. And we who for the most part are neither poets nor historians are familiar with the nature of this process from our own experience with life, for we too have the need to recall the significant events in our own lives by relating them to ourselves and others. Thus we are constantly preparing the way for "poetry," in the broadest sense, as a human potentiality; we are, so to speak, constantly expecting it to erupt in some human being. When this happens, the telling-over of what took place comes to a halt for the time being and a formed narrative, one more item, is added to the world's stock. In reification by the poet or the historian, the narration of history has achieved permanence and persistence. Thus the narrative has been given its place in the world, where it will survive us. There it can live on—one story among many. There is no meaning to these stories that is entirely separable from them—and this, too, we know from our own, non-poetic experience. No philosophy, no analysis, no aphorism, be it ever so profound, can compare in intensity and richness of meaning with a properly narrated story.

I seem to have digressed from my subject. The question is how much reality must be retained even in a world become inhuman if humanity is not to be reduced to an empty phrase or a phantom. Or to put it another way, to what extent do we remain obligated to the world even when we have been expelled from it or have withdrawn from it? For I certainly do not wish to assert that the "inner emigration," the flight from the world to concealment, from public life to anonymity (when that is what it really was and not just a pretext for doing what everyone did with enough inner reservations to salve one's conscience), was not a justified attitude, and in many cases the only possible one. Flight from the world in dark times of impotence can always be justified as long as reality is not ignored, but is constantly acknowledged as the thing that must be escaped. When people choose this alternative, private life too can retain a by no means insignificant reality, even though it remains impotent. Only it is essential for them to realize that the realness of this reality consists not in its deeply personal note, any more than it springs from privacy as such, but inheres in the world from which they have escaped. They must remember that they are constantly on the run, and that the world's reality is actually expressed by their escape. Thus, too, the true force of escapism springs from persecution, and the personal strength of the fugitives increases as the persecution and danger increase.

At the same time we cannot fail to see the limited political relevance of such an existence, even if it is sustained in purity. Its limits are inherent in the fact that strength and power are not the same; that power arises only where people act together, but not where people grow stronger as individuals. No strength is ever great enough to replace power; wherever strength is confronted by power, strength will always succumb. But even the sheer strength to escape and to resist while fleeing cannot materialize where reality is bypassed or forgotten—as when an individual thinks himself too good and noble to pit himself against such a world, or when he fails to face up to the absolute "negativeness" of prevailing world conditions at a given time. How tempting it was, for example, simply to ignore the intolerably stupid blabber of the Nazis. But seductive though it may be to yield to such temptations and to hole up in the refuge of one's own psyche, the result will always be a loss of humanness along with the forsaking of reality.

Thus, in the case of a friendship between a German and a Jew under the conditions of the Third Reich it would scarcely have been a sign of humanness for the friends to have said: Are we not both human beings? It would have been mere evasion of reality and of the world common to both at that time; they would not have been resisting the world as it was. A law that prohibited the intercourse of Jews and Germans could be evaded but could not be defied by people who denied the reality of the distinction. In keeping with a humanness that had not lost the solid ground of reality, a humanness in the midst of the reality of persecution, they would have had to say to each other: A German and a Jew, and friends. But wherever such a friendship succeeded at that time (of course the situation is completely changed, nowadays) and was maintained in purity, that is to say without false guilt complexes on the one side and false complexes of superiority or inferiority on the other, a bit of humanness in a world become inhuman had been achieved.

ALEXANDER SOLZHENITSYN
[BORN 1918]

Alexander Solzhenitsyn's first published work, *One Day in the Life of Ivan Denisovich* (1962), brought nearly instant worldwide recognition and established the subject with which the author is most often identified, the Soviet prison system. The novella described in stark detail a typical day in one of Stalin's prisons. It was the first literary work to reveal the prisons to Russians and to readers in the rest of the world and its mixture of fiction and historical fact would characterize nearly all of Solzhenitsyn's later work.

Born in 1918 in Kislovodsk after his father's death, Solzhenitsyn was raised in poverty by his mother. Although he began writing as a child and would have preferred to study literature, he was forced by his family's financial situation to study mathematics at Rostov University. During World War II he served in the Soviet army as an artillery officer. While he was still in the army, in February 1945, a censor discovered in his letters some passages critical of Stalin. Solzhenitsyn was sentenced to eight years in the prison camps. He would actually spend the next ten years in confinement, including four years at manual labor. He was released in 1956 and allowed to settle in Ryazan in central Russia, where he worked as a mathematics teacher. Although he continued to write during his prison years and after, he did not attempt to publish any of his writing until 1962. At that time, Soviet premier Nikita Khrushchev had attacked Stalin and the "cult of personality." In this freer atmosphere, Solzhenitsyn sent *One Day in the Life* to the important literary magazine *Novy Mir (New World)*, where it was published in November 1962 and brought the author immediate celebrity. He published a few more stories in the magazine before Khrushchev was forced into retirement in 1964 and the brief political thaw ended. Although his novel *The First Circle* had been accepted by *Novy Mir,* it was not published. After 1964, Solzhenitsyn's works were officially prohibited in the Soviet Union and he was forced to smuggle them out to the West for publication. Among the works that he published in the West during the late 1960s and early 1970s were *The First Circle* (1968), *Cancer Ward* (1969), and *August 1914* (1972). When Solzhenitsyn protested to the Writers' Union about the censorship and about the Union's failure to protect writers from such treatment, he was expelled from the Union. When the first volume of *The Gulag Archipelago* (1974), a documentary account of Stalin's prison system, was published in the West, he was stripped of his citizenship and expelled from the Soviet Union. Except for two years in Zurich in

1974–1976, he spent his time in exile on a farm in Vermont. There he continued to work on his historical works and novels, his most important later works being the volumes in his massive historical novel, *The Red Wheel,* an account of Russian history and life during World War I and the Bolshevik revolution. In the summer of 1994, after the collapse of the Soviet Union, he returned to his homeland.

Just as he brings together history and fiction in his works, Solzhenitsyn links the classical traditions of nineteenth-century Russian literature with the events and issues of the modern period. Like Tolstoy's, his vision is broadly panoramic and deeply historical. One of his primary aims has been to depict the continuities between the Russian past and present and by doing so to restore Russia's spiritual heritage. Although his scope and aims continue the classical tradition, his techniques of using multiple points of view (polyphony) and his use of cinematic documentary sections like those in the works of American modernist John Dos Passos make him a modern writer.

Solzhenitsyn was awarded the Nobel Prize for literature in 1970, but he did not deliver his acceptance speech in person because he was afraid that if he left Russia he would not be allowed to return. In the sections from the speech we include here, Solzhenitsyn characteristically speaks from his own experience to address larger truths. His affirmation of literature as truth-telling that transcends ideology and his recognition that in the age of electronic communications a new world literature has emerged that crosses national and language boundaries are appropriate themes for an anthology devoted to that new world literature and its continuing search for truth.

FROM

Nobel Lecture

CHAPTER 2

Translated by F. D. Reeve

Dostoevsky once enigmatically let drop the phrase: "Beauty will save the world." What does this mean? For a long time I thought it merely a phrase. Was such a thing possible? When in our bloodthirsty history did beauty ever save anyone from anything? Ennobled, elevated, yes; but whom has it saved?

There is, however, something special in the essence of beauty, a special quality in art: the conviction carried by a genuine work of art is absolute and subdues even a resistant heart. A political speech, hasty newspaper comment, a social program, a philosophical system can, as far as appearances are concerned, be built smoothly and consistently on an error or a lie; and what is concealed and distorted will not be immediately clear. But then to counteract it comes a contradictory speech, commentary, program, or differently constructed philosophy—and again everything seems smooth and graceful, and again hangs together. That is why they inspire trust—and distrust.

There is no point asserting and reasserting what the heart cannot believe.

A work of art contains its verification in itself; artificial, strained concepts do not withstand the test of being turned into images; they fall to pieces, turn out to be sickly and pale, convince no one. Works which draw on truth and present it to us in live and concentrated form grip us, compellingly involve us, and no one ever, not even ages hence, will come forth to refute them.

Perhaps then the old trinity of Truth, Goodness, and Beauty is not simply the dressed-up, worn-out formula we thought it in our presumptuous, materialistic youth? If the crowns of these three trees meet, as scholars have asserted, and if the too obvious, too straight sprouts of Truth and Goodness have been knocked down, cut off, not let grow, perhaps the whimsical, unpredictable, unexpected branches of Beauty will work their way through, rise up TO THAT VERY PLACE, and thus complete the work of all three?

Then what Dostoevsky wrote—"Beauty will save the world"—is not a slip of the tongue but a prophecy. After all, *he* had the gift of seeing much, a man wondrously filled with light.

And in that case could not art and literature, in fact, help the modern world?

What little I have managed to learn about this over the years I will try to set forth here today.

CHAPTER 3

To reach this chair from which the Nobel Lecture is delivered—a chair by no means offered to every writer and offered only once in a lifetime—I have mounted not three or four temporary steps but hundreds or even thousands, fixed, steep, covered with ice, out of the dark and the cold where I was fated to survive, but others, perhaps more talented, stronger than I, perished. I myself met but few of them in the Gulag Archipelago, a multitude of scattered island fragments. Indeed, under the millstone of surveillance and mistrust, I did not talk to just any man; of some I only heard; and of others I only guessed. Those with a name in literature who vanished into that abyss are, at least, known; but how many were unrecognized, never once publicly mentioned? And so very few, almost no one ever managed to return. A whole national literature is there, buried without a coffin, without even underwear, naked, a number tagged on its toe. Not for a moment did Russian literature cease, yet from outside it seemed a wasteland. Where a harmonious forest could have grown, there were left, after all the cutting, two or three trees accidentally overlooked.

And today how am I, accompanied by the shades of the fallen, my head bowed to let pass forward to this platform others worthy long before me, today how am I to guess and to express what *they* would have wished to say?

This obligation has long lain on us, and we have understood it. In Vladimir Solovyov's words:

> But even chained, we must ourselves complete
> That circle which the gods have preordained.

In agonizing moments in camp, in columns of prisoners at night, in the freezing darkness through which the little chains of lanterns shone, there often rose in our throats something we wanted to shout out to the whole world, if only the world could have heard one of us. Then it seemed very clear what our lucky messenger would say and how immediately and positively the whole world would respond. Our field of vision was filled with physical objects and spiritual forces, and in that clearly focused world nothing seemed to outbalance them. Such ideas came not from books and were not borrowed for the sake of harmony or coherence; they were formulated in prison cells and around forest campfires, in conversations with persons now dead, were hardened by *that* life, developed *out of there*.

When the outside pressures were reduced, my outlook and our outlook widened, and gradually, although through a tiny crack, that "whole world" outside came in sight and was recognized. Startlingly for us, the "whole world" turned out to be not at all what we had hoped: it was a world leading "not up there" but exclaiming at the sight of a dismal swamp, "What an enchanting meadow!" or at a set of prisoner's concrete stocks, "What an exquisite necklace!"—a world in which, while flowing tears rolled down the cheeks of some, others danced to the carefree tunes of a musical.

How did this come about? Why did such an abyss open? Were we unfeeling, or was the world? Or was it because of a difference in language? Why are people not capable of grasping each other's every clear and distinct speech? Words die away and flow off like water—leaving no taste, no color, no smell. Not a trace.

Insofar as I understand it, the structure, import, and tone of speech possible for me—of my speech here today—have changed with the years.

It now scarcely resembles the speech which I first conceived on those freezing nights in prison camp.

. . .

CHAPTER 7

I am, however, encouraged by a keen sense of WORLD LITERATURE as the one great heart that beats for the cares and misfortunes of our world, even though each corner sees and experiences them in a different way.

In past times, also, besides age-old national literatures there existed a concept of world literature as the link between the summits of national literatures and as the aggregate of reciprocal literary influences. But there was a time lag: readers and writers came to know foreign writers only belatedly, sometimes centuries later, so that mutual influences were delayed and the network of national literary high points was visible not to contemporaries but to later generations.

Today, between writers of one country and the readers and writers of another, there is an almost instantaneous reciprocity, as I myself know. My books, unpublished, alas, in my own country, despite hasty and often bad translations have quickly found a responsive world readership. Critical analysis of them has been undertaken by such leading Western writers as Heinrich Böll. During all these recent years, when both my work and my freedom did not collapse, when against the laws of gravity they held on seemingly in thin air, seemingly ON NOTHING, on the invisible, mute surface tension of sympathetic people, with warm gratitude I learned, to my complete surprise, of the support of the world's writing fraternity. On my fiftieth birthday I was astounded to receive greetings from well-known European writers. No pressure put on me now passed unnoticed. During the dangerous weeks when I was being expelled from the Writers' Union, THE PROTECTIVE WALL put forward by prominent writers of the world saved me from worse persecution, and Norwegian writers and artists hospitably prepared shelter for me in the event that I was exiled from my country. Finally, my being nominated for a Nobel Prize was originated not in the land where I live and write but by François Mauriac and his colleagues. Afterward, national writers' organizations expressed unanimous support for me.

As I have understood it and experienced it myself, world literature is no longer an abstraction or a generalized concept invented by literary critics, but a common body and common spirit, a living, heartfelt unity reflecting the growing spiritual unity of mankind. State borders still turn crimson, heated red-hot by electric fences and machine-gun fire; some ministries of internal affairs still suppose that literature is "an internal affair" of the countries under their jurisdiction; and newspaper headlines still herald, "They have no right to interfere in our internal affairs!" Meanwhile, no such thing as INTERNAL AFFAIRS remains on our crowded Earth. Mankind's salvation lies exclusively in everyone's making everything his business, in the people of the East being anything but indifferent to what is thought in the West, and in the people of the West being anything but indifferent to what happens in the East. Literature, one of the most sensitive and responsive tools of human existence, has been the first to pick up, adopt, and assimilate this sense of the growing unity of mankind. I therefore confidently turn to the world literature of the present, to hundreds of friends whom I have not met face to face and perhaps never will see.

My friends! Let us try to be helpful, if we are worth anything. In our own countries, torn by differences among parties, movements, castes, and groups, who for ages past has been not the dividing but the uniting force? This, essentially, is the position of writers, spokesmen of a national language, of the chief tie binding the nation, the very soil which the people inhabit, and, in fortunate circumstances, the nation's spirit too.

I think that world literature has the power in these frightening times to help mankind see itself accurately despite what is advocated by partisans and by parties. It has the power to transmit the condensed experience of one region to another, so that different scales of values are combined, and so that one people accurately and concisely knows the true history of another with a power of recognition and acute awareness as if it had lived through that history itself—and could thus be spared repeating old mistakes. At the same time, perhaps we ourselves may succeed in developing our own WORLD-WIDE VIEW, like any man, with the center of the eye seeing what is nearby but the periphery of vision taking in what is happening in the rest of the world. We will make correlations and maintain world-wide standards.

Who, if not writers, are to condemn their own unsuccessful governments (in some states this is the easiest way to make a living; everyone who is not too lazy does it) as well as society itself, whether for its cowardly humiliation or for its self-satisfied weakness, or the lightheaded escapades of the young, or the youthful pirates brandishing knives?

We will be told: What can literature do against the pitiless onslaught of naked violence? Let us not forget that violence does not and cannot flourish by itself; it is inevitably intertwined with LYING. Between them there is the closest, the most profound and natural bond: nothing screens violence except lies, and the only way lies can hold out is by violence. Whoever has once announced violence as his METHOD must inexorably choose lying as his PRINCIPLE. At birth, violence behaves openly and even proudly. But as soon as it becomes stronger and firmly established, it senses the thinning of the air around it and cannot go on without befogging itself in lies, coating itself with lying's sugary oratory. It does not always or necessarily go straight for the gullet; usually it demands of its victims only allegiance to the lie, only complicity in the lie.

The simple act of an ordinary courageous man is not to take part, not to support lies! Let *that* come into the world and even rein over it, but not through me. Writers and artists can do more: they can VANQUISH LIES! In the struggle against lies, art has always won and always will. Conspicuously, incontestably for everyone. Lies can stand up against much in the world, but not against art.

Once lies have been dispelled, the replusive nakedness of violence will be exposed—and hollow violence will collapse.

That, my friends, is why I think we can help the world in its red-hot hour: not by the nay-saying of having no armaments, not by abandoning oneself to the carefree life, but by going into battle!

In Russian, proverbs about TRUTH are favorites. They persistently express the considerable, bitter, grim experience of the people, often astonishingly:

ONE WORD OF TRUTH OUTWEIGHS THE WORLD.

On such a seemingly fantastic violation of the law of the conservation of mass and energy are based both my own activities and my appeal to the writers of the whole world.

FREEMAN DYSON
[BORN 1923]

Ever since science largely cast off its religious moorings in the nineteenth century, the need has grown for an informed dialogue between the white coats of the laboratory and the rest of society. The writings of Freeman Dyson provide the kind of knowledgeable insights into both science and public policy that promote an ongoing discussion about the moral and social implications of technology. Science and technology have enormous influence on modern life, from the destructive potential of nuclear armaments to the manipulation of life-forms by genetic engineers and biomedical instruments. We have become a nation of intricately complex machines and superchemicals, all of which raise important ethical questions about medical priorities, financial costs, and future payoffs. Dyson's brilliance and honesty shed light on important questions of science and society.

Born in England, Dyson studied physics at Cambridge University and then came to the United States to study with Hans Bethe at Cornell and J. Robert Oppenheimer at Princeton's Institute for Advanced Study. His work experience provided a rich background for appreciating the current state of physics: He helped design nuclear reactors for General Dynamics that would meet strict safety standards; he worked on propulsion systems for the Orion project; and he designed weapons at Lawrence Livermore National Laboratory. Dyson is also a fine writer, well acquainted with literature, music, and social issues, and therefore in excellent position to mediate between the esoterica of science and the needs of humanity. In the name of cosmic ecology, he promotes the idea that the universe is neither dead nor empty. He tends to be critical of large bureaucratic entities such as the National Aeronautics and Space Administration (NASA), believing them to be inflexible and unimaginative. Dyson is a strong supporter of the colonization of space. In addition to scientific writings, his books include *Values at War* (1983) and *Weapons and Hope* (1984). Dyson won the National Book Critics Circle award for general nonfiction in 1984.

We have included "The Argument from Design," a chapter from *Disturbing the Universe* (1979), Dyson's intellectual autobiography and commentary on the scientific issues resulting from the development of nuclear energy during World War II. In this chapter he takes issue with scientists who describe the universe as valueless and meaningless. Is there a spiritual, mental, or animistic dimension to the material world, he asks, or are we, as Alan Watts phrases it, "chance gyrations in a universe where we are like bacteria inhabiting a rock ball that revolves about an insignificant star on the outer fringes of a minor galaxy"?

The Argument from Design

Professional scientists today live under a taboo against mixing science and religion. This was not always so. When Thomas Wright, the discoverer of galaxies, announced his discovery in 1750 in his book *An Original Theory or New Hypothesis of the Universe*, he was not afraid to use a theological argument to support an astronomical theory:

> Since as the Creation is, so is the Creator also magnified, we may conclude in consequence of an infinity, and an infinite all-active power, that as the visible creation is supposed to be full of siderial systems and planetary worlds, so on, in like similar manner, the endless immensity is an unlimited plenum of creations not unlike the known universe.... That this in all probability may be the real case, is in some degree made evident by the many cloudy spots, just perceivable by us, as far without our starry Regions, in which tho' visibly luminous spaces, no one star or particular constituent body can possibly be distinguished; those in all likelyhood may be external creation, bordering upon the known one, too remote for even our telescopes to reach.

Thirty-five years later, Wright's speculations were confirmed by William Herschel's precise observations. Wright also computed the number of habitable worlds in our galaxy:

> In all together then we may safely reckon 170,000,000, and yet be much within compass, exclusive of the comets which I judge to be by far the most numerous part of the creation.

His statement about the comets is also correct, although he does not tell us how he estimated their number. For him the existence of so many habitable worlds was not just a scientific hypothesis but a cause for moral reflection:

> In this great celestial creation, the catastrophy of a world, such as ours, or even the total dissolution of a system of worlds, may possibly be no more to the great Author of Nature, than the most common accident in life with us, and in all probability such final and general Doomsdays may be as frequent there, as even Birthdays or mortality with us upon the earth. This idea has something so chearful in it, that I own I can never look upon the stars without wondering why the whole world does not become astronomers; and that men endowed with sense and reason should neglect a science they are naturally so much interested in, and so capable of inlarging the understanding, as next to a demonstration must convince them of their immortality, and reconcile them to all those little difficulties incident to human nature, without the least anxiety.
>
> All this the vast apparent provision in the starry mansions seem to promise: What ought we then not to do, to preserve our natural birthright to it and to merit such inheritance, which alas we think created all to gratify alone a race of vain-glorious gigantic beings, while they are confined to this world, chained like so many atoms to a grain of sand.

There speaks the eighteenth century. Now listen to the twentieth, speaking through the voices of the biologist Jacques Monod: "Any mingling of knowledge with values is unlawful, forbidden," and of the physicist Steven Weinberg: "The more the universe seems comprehensible, the more it also seems pointless."

If Monod and Weinberg are truly speaking for the twentieth century, then I prefer the eighteenth. But in fact Monod and Weinberg, both of them first-rate scientists and leaders of research in their specialties, are expressing a point of view which does not take into account the subtleties and ambiguities of twentieth-century physics. The roots of their philosophical attitudes lie in the nineteenth century, not in the twentieth. The taboo against mixing knowledge with values arose during the nineteenth century out of the great battle between the evolutionary biologists led by Thomas Huxley and the churchmen led by Bishop Wilberforce. Huxley won the battle, but a hundred years later Monod and Weinberg were still fighting the ghost of Bishop Wilberforce.

The nineteenth-century battle revolved around the validity of an old argument for the existence of God, the argument from design. The argument from design says simply that the existence of a watch implies the existence of a watchmaker. Thomas Wright accepted this argument as valid in the astronomical domain. Until the nineteenth century, churchmen and scientists agreed that it was also valid in the domain of biology. The penguin's flipper, the nest-building instinct of the swallow, the eye of the hawk, all declare, like the stars and the planets in Addison's eighteenth-century hymn, "The hand that made us is divine." Then came Darwin and Huxley, claiming that the penguin and the swallow and the hawk could be explained by the process of natural selection operating on random hereditary variations over long periods of time. If Darwin and Huxley were right, the argument from design was demolished. Bishop Wilberforce despised the biologists, regarding them as irresponsible destroyers of faith, and fought them with personal ridicule. In public debate he asked Huxley whether he was descended from a monkey on his grandfather's or on his grandmother's side. The biologists never forgave him and never forgot him. The battle left scars which are still not healed.

Looking back on the battle a century later, we can see that Darwin and Huxley were right. The discovery of the structure and function of DNA has made clear the nature of the hereditary variations upon which natural selection operates. The fact that DNA patterns remain stable for millions of years, but are still occasionally variable, is explained as a consequence of the laws of chemistry and physics. There is no reason why natural selection operating on these patterns, in a species of bird that has acquired a taste for eating fish, should not produce a penguin's flipper. Chance variations, selected by the perpetual struggle to survive, can do the work of the designer. So far as the biologists are concerned, the argument from design is dead. They won their battle. But unfortunately, in the bitterness of their victory over their clerical opponents, they have made the meaninglessness of the universe into a new dogma. Monod states this dogma with his customary sharpness:

> The cornerstone of the scientific method is the postulate that nature is objective. In other words, the *systematic* denial that true knowledge can be got at by interpreting phenomena in terms of final causes, that is to say, of purpose.

Here is a definition of the scientific method that would exclude Thomas Wright from science altogether. It would also exclude some of the most lively areas of modern physics and cosmology.

It is easy to understand how some modern molecular biologists have come to accept a narrow definition of scientific knowledge. Their tremendous successes were achieved by reducing the complex behavior of living creatures to the simpler behavior of the molecules out of which the creatures are built. Their whole field of science is based on the reduction of the complex to the simple, reduction of the apparently purposeful movements of an organism to purely mechanical movements of its constituent parts. To the molecular biologist, a cell is a chemical machine, and the protein and nucleic acid molecules that control its behavior are little bits of clockwork, existing in well-defined states and reacting to their environment by changing from one state to another. Every student of molecular biology learns his trade by playing with models built of plastic balls and pegs. These models are an indispensable tool for detailed study of the structure and function of nucleic acids and enzymes. They are, for practical purposes, a useful visualization of the molecules out of which we are built. But from the point of view of a physicist, the models belong to the nineteenth century. Every physicist knows that atoms are not really little hard balls. While the molecular biologists were using these mechanical models to make their spectacular discoveries, physics was moving in a quite different direction.

For the biologists, every step down in size was a step toward increasingly simple and mechanical behavior. A bacterium is more mechanical than a frog, and a DNA molecule is more mechanical than a bacterium. But twentieth-century physics has shown that further reductions in size have an opposite effect. If we divide a DNA molecule into its component atoms, the atoms behave less mechanically than the molecule. If we divide an atom into nucleus and electrons, the electrons are less mechanical than the atom. There is a famous experiment, originally suggested by Einstein, Podolsky and Rosen in 1935 as a thought experiment to illustrate the difficulties of quantum theory, which demonstrates that the notion of an electron existing in an objective state independent of the experimenter is untenable. The experiment has been done in various ways with various kinds of particles, and the results show clearly that the state of a particle has a meaning only when a precise procedure for observing the state is prescribed. Among physicists there are many different philosophical viewpoints, and many different ways of interpreting the role of the observer in the description of subatomic processes. But all physicists agree with the experimental facts which make it hopeless to look for a description independent of the mode of observation. When we are dealing with things as small as atoms and electrons, the observer or experimenter cannot be excluded from the description of nature. In this domain, Monod's dogma, "The cornerstone of the scientific method is the postulate that nature is objective," turns out to be untrue.

If we deny Monod's postulate, this does not mean that we deny the achievements of molecular biology or support the doctrines of Bishop Wilberforce. We are not saying that chance and the mechanical rearrangement of molecules cannot turn ape into man. We are saying only that if as physicists we try to observe in the finest detail the behavior of a single molecule, the meaning of the words "chance" and "mechanical" will depend upon the way we make our observations. The laws of subatomic physics cannot even be formulated without some reference to the observer. "Chance" cannot be defined except as a measure of the observer's ignorance of the future. The laws leave a place for mind in the description of every molecule.

It is remarkable that mind enters into our awareness of nature on two separate levels. At the highest level, the level of human consciousness, our minds are somehow directly aware of the complicated flow of electrical and chemical patterns in our brains. At the lowest level, the level of single atoms and electrons, the mind of an observer is again involved in the description of events. Between lies the level of molecular biology, where mechanical models are adequate and mind appears to be irrelevant. But I, as a physicist, cannot help suspecting that there is a logical connection between the two ways in which mind appears in my universe. I cannot help thinking that our awareness of our own brains has something to do with the process which we call "observation" in atomic physics. That is to say, I think our consciousness is not just a passive epiphenomenon carried along by the chemical events in our brains, but is an active agent forcing the molecular complexes to make choices between one quantum state and another. In other words, mind is already inherent in every electron, and the processes of human consciousness differ only in degree but not in kind from the processes of choice between quantum states which we call "chance" when they are made by electrons.

Jacques Monod has a word for people who think as I do and for whom he reserves his deepest scorn. He calls us "animists," believers in spirits. "Animism," he says, "established a covenant between nature and man, a profound alliance outside of which seems to stretch only terrifying solitude. Must we break this tie because the postulate of objectivity requires it?" Monod answers yes: "The ancient covenant is in pieces; man knows at last that he is alone in the universe's unfeeling immensity, out of which he emerged only by chance." I answer no. I believe in the covenant. It is true that we emerged in the universe by chance, but the idea of chance is itself only a cover for our ignorance. I do not feel like an alien in this universe. The more I examine the universe and study the details of its architecture, the more evidence I find that the universe in some sense must have known that we were coming.

There are some striking examples in the laws of nuclear physics of numerical accidents that seem to conspire to make the universe habitable. The strength of the attractive nuclear forces is just sufficient to overcome the electrical repulsion between the positive charges in the nuclei of ordinary atoms such as oxygen or iron. But the nuclear forces are not quite strong enough to bind together two protons (hydrogen nuclei) into a bound system which would be called a diproton if it existed. If the nuclear forces had been slightly stronger than they are, the diproton would exist and almost all the hydrogen in the universe would have been combined into diprotons and heavier nuclei. Hydrogen would be a rare element, and stars like the sun, which live for a long time by the slow burning of hydrogen in their cores, could not exist. On the other hand, if the nuclear forces had been substantially weaker than they are, hydrogen could not burn at all and there would be no heavy elements. If, as seems likely, the evolution of life requires a star like the sun, supplying energy at a constant rate for billions of years, then the strength of nuclear forces had to lie within a rather narrow range to make life possible.

A similar but independent numerical accident appears in connection with the weak interaction by which hydrogen actually burns in the sun. The weak interaction is millions of times weaker than the nuclear force. It is just weak enough so that the hydrogen in the sun burns at a slow and steady rate. If the weak interaction were much stronger or much weaker, any forms of life dependent on sunlike stars would again be in difficulties.

The facts of astronomy include some other numerical accidents that work to our advantage. For example, the universe is built on such a scale that the average distance between stars in an average galaxy like ours is about twenty million million miles, an extravagantly large distance by human standards. If a scientist asserts that the stars at these immense distances have a decisive effect on the possibility of human existence, he will be suspected of being a believer in astrology. But it happens to be true that we could not have survived if the average distance between stars were only two million million miles instead of twenty. If the distances had been smaller by a factor of ten, there would have been a high probability that another star, at some time during the four billion years that the earth has existed, would have passed by the sun close enough to disrupt with its gravitational field the orbits of the planets. To destroy life on earth, it would not be necessary to pull the earth out of the solar system. It would be sufficient to pull the earth into a moderately eccentric elliptical orbit.

All the rich diversity of organic chemistry depends on a delicate balance between electrical and quantum-mechanical forces. The balance exists only because the laws of physics include an "exclusion principle" which forbids two electrons to occupy the same state. If the laws were changed so that electrons no longer excluded each other, none of our essential chemistry would survive. There are many other lucky accidents in atomic physics. Without such accidents, water could not exist as a liquid, chains of carbon atoms could not form complex organic molecules, and hydrogen atoms could not form breakable bridges between molecules.

I conclude from the existence of these accidents of physics and astronomy that the universe is an unexpectedly hospitable place for living creatures to make their home in. Being a scientist, trained in the habits of thought and language of the twentieth century rather than the eighteenth, I do not claim that the architecture of the universe proves the existence of God. I claim only that the architecture of the universe is consistent with the hypothesis that mind plays an essential role in its functioning.

We had earlier found two levels on which mind manifests itself in the description of nature. On the level of subatomic physics, the observer is inextricably involved in the definition of the objects of his observations. On the level of direct human experience, we are aware of our own minds, and we find it convenient to believe that other human beings and animals have minds not altogether unlike our own. Now we have found a third level to add to these two. The peculiar harmony between the structure of the universe and the needs of life and intelligence is a third manifestation of the importance of mind in the scheme of things. This is as far as we can go as scientists. We have evidence that mind is important on three levels. We have no evidence for any deeper unifying hypothesis that would tie these three levels together. As individuals, some of us may be willing to go further. Some of us may be willing to entertain the hypothesis that there exists a universal mind or world soul which underlies the manifestations of mind that we observe. If we take this hypothesis seriously, we are, according to Monod's definition, animists. The existence of a world soul is a question that belongs to religion and not to science.

When my mother was past eighty-five, she could no longer walk as she once did. She was restricted to short outings close to her home. Her favorite walk in those years was to a nearby graveyard which commands a fine view of the ancient city of Winchester and the encircling hills. Here I often walked with her and listened to her talk cheerfully of her approaching death. Sometimes, contemplating the stupidities of mankind, she became rather fierce. "When I look at this world now," she said once, "it looks to me like an anthill with too many ants scurrying around. I think perhaps the best thing would be to do away with it altogether." I protested, and she laughed. No, she said, no matter how enraged she was with the ants, she would never be able to do away with the anthill. She found it far too interesting.

Sometimes we talked about the nature of the human soul and about the Cosmic Unity of all souls that I had believed in so firmly when I was fifteen years old. My mother did not like the phrase Cosmic Unity. It was too pretentious. She preferred to call it a world soul. She imagined that she was herself a piece of the world soul that had been given freedom to grow and develop independently so long as she was alive. After death, she expected to merge back into the world soul, losing her personal identity but preserving her memories and her intelligence. Whatever knowledge and wisdom she had acquired during her life would add to the world soul's store of knowledge and wisdom. "But how do you know that the world soul will want you back?" I said. "Perhaps, after all these years, the world soul will find you too tough and indigestible and won't want to merge with you." "Don't worry about that," my mother replied. "It may take a little while, but I'll find my way back. The world soul can do with a bit more brains."

Stéphane Mallarmé, "The Afternoon of a Faun," translated by Frederick Morgan from REFRACTIONS by Frederick Morgan. Copyright © 1953 and renewed © 1981 by Frederick Morgan. Originally in *The Hudson Review*, VI, No. 3 (Autumn 1953). Reprinted with the permission of *The Hudson Review*.

Arthur Rimbaud, "The Drunken Boat" from A SEASON IN HELL AND THE DRUNKEN BOAT. Copyright 1945, 1952, © 1961 by New Directions Publishing Corporation. Reprinted with the permission of the publisher.

Arthur Rimbaud, "Vowels" from AN ANTHOLOGY OF FRENCH POETRY FROM NERVAL TO VALERY IN ENGLISH TRANSLATION WITH FRENCH ORIGINALS, edited by Angel Flores (New York: Doubleday, 1958). Copyright 1958 by Angel Flores. Reprinted with the permission of the Estate of Angel Flores.

Mori Ōgai, "The Dancing Girl," translated by Richard Bowring from *Monumenta Nipponica*, 30:2 (1975). Copyright © 1975 by Monumenta Nipponica, Tokyo. Reprinted with the permission of *Monumenta Nipponica* and the translator.

Madame de Staël (Germaine Necker), "Napoleon," translated by Morroe Berger, from MADAME DE STAËL ON POLITICS, LITERATURE, AND NATIONAL CHARACTER (New York: Doubleday, 1964). Reprinted with the permission of the Estate of Morroe Berger.

Friedrich Schlegel, "Talk on Mythology" from DIALOGUE ON POETRY AND LITERARY APHO-RISMS, translated and edited by Ernst Behler and Roman Struc (University Park, PA: The Pennsylvania State University Press, 1968). Copyright © 1968 by The Pennsylvania State University. Reprinted with the permission of the publisher.

Chinua Achebe, "Things Fall Apart." Copyright © 1958 by Chinua Achebe. First published by William Heinemann Ltd., 1958. Reprinted with the permission of Reed Consumer Books, London.

William Butler Yeats, "Lapis Lazuli" and "The Circus Animals' Desertion" from THE POEMS OF W. B. YEATS: A New Edition, edited by Richard J. Finneran. Copyright 1940 by Georgie Yeats, renewed © 1968 by Bertha Georgie Yeats, Michael Butler Yeats, and Anne Yeats. "Sailing to Byzantium," "Leda and the Swan," and "Among School Children" from THE POEMS OF W. B. YEATS: A New Edition, edited by Richard J. Finneran. Copyright 1928 by Macmillan Publishing Company, renewed 1956 by Georgie Yeats. "Easter 1916" and "The Second Coming" from THE POEMS OF W. B. YEATS: A New Edition, edited by Richard J. Finneran. Copyright 1924 by Macmillan Publishing Company, renewed 1952 by Bertha Georgie Yeats. "The Lake Isle of Innisfree" and "Who Goes with Fergus" from THE POEMS OF W.B. YEATS: A New Edition, edited by Richard J. Finneran (New York: Macmillan, 1983). Reprinted with the permission of Macmillan Publishing Company.

Lu Xun, "The New Year's Sacrifice" from THE COMPLETE STORIES OF LU HSUN. Copyright © 1981 by Foreign Languages Press, Beijing, China. Reprinted with the permission of the publisher.

Virginia Woolf, "Shakespeare's Sister" from A ROOM OF ONE'S OWN by Virginia Woolf. Copyright 1929 by Harcourt Brace & World, Inc., renewed © 1957 by Leonard Woolf. Reprinted with the permission of the publisher.

Franz Kafka, "The Metamorphosis," translated by Willa and Edwin Muir, from FRANZ KAFKA: The Complete Stories by Franz Kafka, edited by Nahum N. Glatzer. Copyright 1948 by Schocken Books, Inc. Reprinted with the permission of Schocken Books, published by Pantheon Books, a division of Random House, Inc.

T. S. Eliot, "The Waste Land" from COLLECTED POEMS 1909–1962 by T. S. Eliot. Copyright 1936 by Harcourt Brace & Company, renewed © 1964, 1963 by T. S. Eliot. Reprinted with the permission of Harcourt Brace & Company, and Faber and Faber Limited.

Anna Akhmatova, "Voronezh," "To the Memory of M.B.," and *Requiem,* translated by Judith Hemschemeyer, from COMPLETE POEMS OF ANNA AKHMATOVA, Second Edition. Translations copyright © 1992 by Judith Hemschemeyer. Reprinted with the permission of Zephyr Press.

Federico García Lorca, "The King of Harlem," "Ode to Walt Whitman," and "Lament for Ignacio Sanchez Mejías," translated by Stephen Spender and J. L. Gili, from THE SELECTED POEMS OF FEDERICO GARCÍA LORCA, edited by Francisco García Lorca and Donald M. Allen. Copyright © 1955 by New Directions Publishing Corporation. Reprinted with the permission of the publisher.

Jorge Luis Borges, "The Garden of Forking Paths" from LABYRINTHS: Selected Stories and Other Writings. Copyright © 1963, 1964 by New Directions Publishing Corporation. Reprinted with the permission of the publisher.

Yasunari Kawabata, "The Moon on the Water" from MODERN JAPANESE STORIES: An Anthology, edited by Ivan Morris. Copyright © 1962 by Charles E. Tuttle Co., Inc. Reprinted with the permission of the publisher. All rights reserved.

Pablo Neruda, "Ode with a Lament," "Alberto Rojas Jimenez Comes Flying," "Ode of the Sun to the People's Army," and "Sexual Water" from TWELVE SPANISH POETS: An Anthology (Boston: Beacon Press, 1972), translated by H. R. Hays. Reprinted with the permission of the Estate of H. R. Hays.

Pablo Neruda, "The United Fruit Co." from NERUDA AND VALLEJO: Selected Poems (Boston: Beacon Press, 1962), translated by Robert Bly, James Wright, and John Knoeptle. Reprinted with the permission of Robert Bly.

Jean-Paul Sartre, "The Flies" from NO EXIT AND THE FLIES, translated by Stuart Gilbert. Copyright 1946 by Stuart Gilbert, renewed © 1974, 1975 by Maris Agnes Mathilde Gilbert. Reprinted with the permission of Alfred A. Knopf, Inc.

R. K. Narayan, "A Horse and Two Goats" from UNDER THE BANYAN TREE by R. K. Narayan. Copyright © 1985 by R. K. Narayan. Reprinted with the permission of Viking Penguin, a division of Penguin Books USA Inc.

Albert Camus, "The Guest" from EXILE AND THE KINGDOM by Albert Camus, translated by Justin O'Brien. Copyright © 1957, 1958 by Alfred A. Knopf, Inc. Reprinted with the permission of the publisher.

Albert Camus, "The Myth of Sisyphus" from THE MYTH OF SISYPHUS AND OTHER ESSAYS by Albert Camus, translated by Justin O'Brien. Copyright © 1955 by Alfred A. Knopf, Inc. Reprinted with the permission of the publisher.

Ralph Ellison, "Flying Home." Copyright © 1944 and renewed © 1972 by Ralph Ellison. Reprinted with the permission of the William Morris Agency, Inc. on behalf of the author.

Marguerite Duras, "Hiroshima Mon Amour," translated by Richard Seaver. Copyright © 1961, 1989 by Grove Press, Inc. Reprinted with the permission of the publisher.

Doris Lessing, "The Old Chief Mshlanga" from AFRICAN STORIES. Copyright © 1951, 1953, 1954, 1957, 1958, 1963, 1964, 1965 by Doris Lessing. Reprinted with the permission of Simon & Schuster, Inc.

James Baldwin, "Sonny's Blues" from GOING TO MEET THE MAN. Copyright © 1957 and renewed 1985 by James Baldwin. Reprinted with the permission of Doubleday, a division of Bantam Doubleday Dell Publishing Group, Inc.

Elie Wiesel, "The Death of My Father," "Testament of a Jew from Saragossa" from LEGENDS OF OUR TIME by Elie Wiesel. Copyright © 1968 by Elie Wiesel. Reprinted with the permission of Georges Borchardt, Inc. for the author.

Carlos Fuentes, "The Prisoner of Las Lomas" from CONSTANCIA AND OTHER STORIES FOR VIRGINS, translated by Thomas Christensen. English translation copyright © 1990 by Farrar, Straus & Giroux, Inc. Reprinted with the permission of the publisher.

Gabriel García Márquez, "A Very Old Man with Enormous Wings" from LEAF STORM AND OTHER STORIES. Copyright © 1971 by Gabriel García Márquez. Reprinted with the permission of Harper Collins Publishers, Inc.

Adrienne Rich, "Aunt Jennifer's Tigers," "I Dream I'm the Death of Orpheus," "Diving into the Wreck," "Twenty-One Love Poems: I, III, IV, VI" from THE FACT OF A DOORFRAME: Poems Selected and New, 1950–1984 Copyright © 1984 by Adrienne Rich. Reprinted with the permission of W. W. Norton & Company, Inc.

Milan Kundera, "The Hitchhiking Game" from LAUGHABLE LOVES, translated by S. Rappaport. Copyright © 1974 by Alfred A. Knopf, Inc. Reprinted with the permission of the publishers.

Hiroko Takenishi, "The Rite" from THE CRAZY IRIS AND OTHER STORIES OF THE ATOMIC AFTERMATH by Kenzaburo Oe. Copyright © 1964 by D. T. Suzuki. Reprinted with the permission of Grove Press, Inc.

Alifa Rifaat, "My World of the Unknown" from DISTANT VIEW OF A MINARET AND OTHER STORIES, translated by Denys Johnson-Davies. Reprinted with the permission of Quartet Books Ltd., London.

N. Scott Momaday, excerpt from THE WAY TO RAINY MOUNTAIN. Copyright © 1969 by The University of New Mexico Press. Reprinted with the permission of the publisher.

Anita Desai, "The Farewell Party" from GAMES AT TWILIGHT AND OTHER STORIES. Copyright © 1978 by Anita Desai. Reprinted with the permission of HarperCollins Publishers, Inc. and the author c/o Rogers, Coleridge & White, Ltd., 20 Powis Mews, London W. 11 1JN.

Sigmund Freud, "Case 4: Katharina" from STUDIES ON HYSTERIA by Josef Breuer and Sigmund Freud, translated from the German and edited by James Strachey in collaboration with Anna

Freud. Published in the United States by Basic Books, Inc. by arrangement with The Hogarth Press Ltd., London. Reprinted with the permission of Basic Books, a division of HarperCollins Publishers, Inc., Sigmund Freud Copyrights, The Institute of Psycho-Analysis, and The Hogarth Press.

Sigmund Freud, "Family Romances" from THE COLLECTED PAPERS OF SIGMUND FREUD, Volume 5, translated and edited by James Strachey. Published in the United States by Basic Books, Inc. by arrangement with The Hogarth Press Ltd., London. Reprinted with the permission of Basic Books, a division of HarperCollins Publishers, Inc., Sigmund Freud Copyrights, The Institute of Psycho-Analysis, and The Hogarth Press.

Hannah Arendt, "Jews, Nazis, and Inner Emigration" from MEN IN DARK TIMES. Copyright © 1968 by Hannah Arendt. Reprinted with the permission of Harcourt Brace & Company.

Alexander Solzhenitsyn, Excerpts from THE NOBEL LECTURE by Alexander Solzhenitsyn and translated by F. D. Reeve. Translation copyright © 1972 by Farrar, Strauss & Giroux, Inc. Reprinted by permission of Farrar, Strauss & Giroux.

Freeman Dyson, "The Argument from Design" from DISTURBING THE UNIVERSE. Copyright © 1979 by Freeman Dyson. Reprinted with the permission of HarperCollins Publishers, Inc.

INDEX

A NOTE ON THE TYPE

The type used in this book is Bembo. Created by Mono-type in 1929, the font has its origins in Renaissance Venice, modeled after a roman typeface that Francesco Griffo created in 1495. The italic is based on a type designed by Giovanni Tagliente in the 1520s. Although Bembo is quieter than a true Renaissance type, it retains the elegance and structure of its roots and translates well to the digital format of modern computerized typesetting.